Student Writers on Active Reading and Writing about Literature

P9-EMH-009

There are those experiences when I write something late at night and wake up the next morning and go back to what I have written and see it all differently (usually all wrong), but that experience is always so odd and strangely energizing. I really enjoy going back to my drafts (most of them) — to play, distort, delete, add — and that silent energy tells me this writing world is a place I belong in.   **Alicia Abood**

Reading literature gives me an opportunity to escape the scientific textbooks and journal articles that usually fill my desk. Reading for me has almost always been for pleasure. On the other hand, writing has always felt like work. As one who likes to talk, I assumed that putting my voice on paper would be easy. It isn't. I find myself revising sentences several times to achieve an effective style and tone. I especially enjoy attempting to write in the style of classic writers: I learn a lot about their style and can even feel myself escaping into their voices.   **Julian Hinson**

I'm writing in my head constantly. Sometimes the words appear in print or in cursive on the chalkboard of my mind, but the act of writing is what matters. Writing is not something I can stop. I'm constantly writing in my head, with a pen and paper, by computer, or scribbling in the dirt with my fingers.   **Kristina Martinez**

Approaching Literature

Writing + Reading + Thinking

Approaching Literature

Writing + Reading + Thinking

Second Edition

Peter Schakel
Hope College

Jack Ridl
Hope College

Bedford/St. Martin's   Boston ◆ New York

For Bedford/St. Martin's

Executive Editor: Stephen A. Scipione
Developmental Editor: Genevieve Hamilton Day
Senior Production Editor: Bridget Leahy
Senior Production Supervisor: Nancy Myers
Marketing Manager: Adrienne Petsick
Editorial Assistant: Melissa Cook
Copyeditor: Mary Lou Wilshaw-Watts
Text Design: Glenna Collett and Sandra Rigney
Cover Design: Kim Cevoli
Cover Art: = by Jacek Szydlowski
Composition: TexTech International
Printing and Binding: Quebecor World Taunton

President: Joan E. Feinberg
Editorial Director: Denise B. Wydra
Editor in Chief: Karen S. Henry
Director of Marketing: Karen Melton Soeltz
Director of Editing, Design, and Production: Marcia Cohen
Managing Editor: Elizabeth M. Schaaf

Library of Congress Control Number: 2007934305

Copyright © 2008 by Bedford/St. Martin's

All rights reserved. No part of this book may be reproduced, stored in a retrieval system, or transmitted in any form or by any means, electronic, mechanical, photocopying, recording, or otherwise, except as may be expressly permitted by the applicable copyright statutes or in writing by the Publisher.

Manufactured in the United States of America.

1   2   3   4   5   6   12   11   10   09   08

For information, write: Bedford/St. Martin's, 75 Arlington Street, Boston, MA 02116 (617-399-4000)

ISBN-10: 0-312-45283-7   ISBN-10: 0-312-48697-9 (high school edition)
ISBN-13: 978-0-312-45283-4   ISBN-13: 978-0-312-48697-6

Acknowledgments

Ai, "Why Can't I Leave You?" from *Vice: New and Selected Poems* by Ai. Copyright © 1999 by Ai. Used by permission of W.W. Norton & Company, Inc.

Anna Akhmatova, "The Song of the Last Meeting" from *Complete Poems of Anna Akhmatova*, translated by Judith Hemschemeyer, edited and introduced by Roberta Reeder. Copyright © 1989, 1992, 1997 by Judith Hemschemeyer. Reprinted by permission of Zephyr Press, www.zephyrpress.org.

Sherman Alexie, "The Joy of Reading and Writing: Superman and Me," first published in *The Most Wonderful Books*, edited by Michael Dorris and Emilie Buchwald. Copyright © 1997 by Sherman Alexie. Reprinted with permission of Nancy Stauffer Associates. "The Lone Ranger and Tonto Fistfight in Heaven," "Somebody Kept Saying Powwow," "This Is What It Means to Say Phoenix, Arizona" from *The Lone Ranger and Tonto Fistfight in Heaven* by Sherman Alexie. Copyright © 1993 and 2005 by Sherman Alexie. Used by permission of Grove/Atlantic, Inc.

Acknowledgments and copyrights are continued at the back of the book on pages 1628–1636, which constitute an extension of the copyright page. It is a violation of the law to reproduce these selections by any means whatsoever without the written permission of the copyright holder.

Preface for Instructors

Our intention in *Approaching Literature: Writing + Reading + Thinking* was to create a fresh, inviting, accessible introduction to fiction, poetry, and drama for all students, whatever their previous exposure to literature. We hope it will contribute to a richly dynamic reading experience for students while in class, and demonstrate why and how reading is a personally important part of their lives.

To the best of our abilities, and without making the book unwieldy, we have tried to have the contents reflect the extraordinary diversity of contemporary literature. We doubt our students are the only ones who have asked for such representation — a choice of literature that speaks to their wide interests, varied cultures, and unique circumstances. But as long-time teachers who grew up with and have been sustained by the traditional canon, we also want students to be introduced to important writers and works of the past, so they may come to see how timeless great literature can be, and affirm its enduring value. (The emotions of the narrator in James Joyce's "Araby" still resonate with students, even if their own experiences of young love are more like what the spunky narrator of Katherine Min's "Courting a Monk" relates.) Throughout, therefore, *Approaching Literature* mingles, juxtaposes, and connects diverse authors and works from the twentieth and twenty-first centuries with works from the traditional canon, often using the one to access the other.

In keeping with our inclusive approach to literary works, we teach reading and writing as processes. The reading process we emphasize expands the notion of what a work is "about," because reading, we believe, should open up a literary work itself as well as the experiences it can create in the reader, not close them down. That is, we want students to understand that any literary work concerns itself with a multiplicity of things, not a single topic, theme, or view that readers must identify through some seemingly mysterious and esoteric method. This book's approach both affirms students' own experiences and cultural backgrounds and enlarges their ways of perceiving and understanding. By savoring the lines of Julia Alvarez's poem "How I Learned to Sweep," by discerning — and deciding — what she learned in learning, by comparing her "lesson" with similar lessons from their own lives, students are empowered to see that reading literature involves an exploration of *all* that can be discovered in a work, and that such exploration can start from wherever they are, whatever their background.

Throughout the text, we show how active reading can lead directly to student writing. We introduce writing sequentially, starting with observations that students write in the margins of books as they read and progressing by sensible, gradual steps to notes, journal writing, short critical papers, and longer research papers. The comments that students scribble in the margins of David Henry Hwang's *As the Crow Flies* may culminate in a paper that compares the ghosts in that short contemporary play with the spirit that haunts Shakespeare's *Hamlet*. Moreover, we emphasize that each strategy and form of writing, while valuable in itself, is part of an overall repertoire of skills that apply in many other reading-writing situations beyond a literature course.

In brief: we have tried to make *Approaching Literature* as fresh in its selections and as accessible and inclusive in its pedagogy as possible. The general principles outlined above guided us in all of our work developing this book. That will become clearer in a more detailed look at how these principles have influenced and shaped specific elements of the first edition as well as the second edition of our text.

Features of *Approaching Literature*

A Common Ground for Exploring Contemporary and Classic Literature

Lucille Clifton has said, "In this polyglot we call America, literature *has* to include all voices. Nothing else makes sense." This anthology, of course, does not include all voices (what anthology could?) but it does include, juxtapose, and connect an uncommon number of fresh, contemporary works with some of the most frequently taught texts from the traditional canon. It uses current voices to help students recognize the relevance of older works, and older works to see the depth and significance of newer works.

Chapter 4, for example, includes three stories dealing with cars, one from the 1990s, one from the 1980s, and one from the 1960s, giving the students a way to see how some human experiences tend to remain consistent even though the particulars change with the passing of time. Observing in Dagoberto Gilb's short, humorous story "Love in L.A." how structure carries along the narrative, recognizing ways the author brings distinctive characters to life, and noticing both what an author emphasizes and leaves out prepares students for reading two stories with confrontational characters and situations that are a bit more demanding, Louise Erdrich's "The Red Convertible" and Joyce Carol Oates's "Where Are You Going, Where Have You Been?" Similarly, pairing two city poems — Garrett Kaoru Hongo's "Yellow Light" and Jonathan Swift's "A Description of the Morning" — provides an opening for students to compare differences in form, imagery, and attitude in a poem from eighteenth-century England and one from twentieth-century California.

A Student-Friendly Approach to Literature

We need hardly tell you that students enter Introduction to Literature or Literature for Composition courses with varied levels of education and experience. *Approaching Literature* attempts to bridge those levels by addressing students in a way that does not presuppose prior knowledge of or experience with literature. We present information compactly and concisely, in step-by-step fashion, avoiding overly technical vocabulary. Each chapter treating the literary elements begins with a short, engaging story, poem, or play that sets an inviting tone for the chapter and provides illustrations for discussing the topic at hand. Such brief works as "The House on Mango Street," "We Real Cool," and *The New New* may provide students with lasting and valuable memories of what a story, poem, or play can be and what effect they can have.

We pause frequently to summarize and remind (for example, every chapter ends with boxed checklists that serve as memory refreshers and quick references). We include pictures of the students whose papers we reprint, along with their comments about writing those papers, in the expectation that your students will discover that their concerns are shared and their experiences reflected in the book. Finally, we think you will find the pages of *Approaching Literature* to be more reader friendly—more open and less crowded—than those of other textbooks and anthologies. Such design should make for a more pleasurable reading experience (and may even encourage your students to annotate right in the margins of the book).

A Focus on Active Reading

Right from the start, *Approaching Literature* invites students to become active readers. Our discussion of the reading process in Chapter 1 is built around a personal essay by Sherman Alexie and a story by Julia Alvarez, both of which testify to how reading "saved their lives." Seeing how these writers participate fully with a work, connecting with it intellectually, emotionally, and imaginatively, reveals reading as a vital part of one's life and serves as an inspiration and a model for students' own active reading. Throughout the book, "Approaching the Reading" prompts that follow stories, poems, and plays give students ways to reflect on and apply the techniques of reading they learn. By placing emphasis on what literary techniques and elements *do* and what readers do *with* them, we try to help students engage more deeply with literature and realize how enjoyable and meaningful stories, poems, and plays can be.

An Emphasis on Critical Thinking

A central aim of this book is to foster habits and skills of critical thinking. By critical thinking, we mean two things: a set of skills for examining information, and a developed ability to use those skills to guide one's responses. Critical thinking contrasts with passively taking in information and confining the reasons for remembering it only to comprehension. It is not just possessing a set of skills; it always involves using those skills in active, practical ways.

Accordingly, Chapter 1 stresses how students can develop habits of mind to engage fully with the texts they read — not simply to track what is going on in texts, but to enter them imaginatively, to ask questions of them, and to resist settling for trite or simple answers. Chapter 2 helps students see themselves as makers of knowledge, as they read with pens or pencils in hand, participate in discussions, analyze questions and topics, and construct argumentative theses and papers. Subsequent chapters on the elements of fiction, poetry, and drama discuss how to connect with literary texts, how to understand them on a deeper level than merely comprehending what is going on, how to analyze, interrogate, and value them — critical skills reinforced throughout the book by the reading prompts and writing assignments.

Developing critical thinking skills and the disposition to use them is a never-completed, life-long endeavor, and as students work with the texts and activities in *Approaching Literature*, they will not only come to understand, appreciate, and enjoy reading and literature more, but they will also improve their abilities to think clearly, incisively, and dare we say wisely — not just about literature, but about all areas of their lives.

Practical Explanation of the Writing Process

Chapters 2, 8, 17, 25, and 29 lead students in a unified, cumulative, step-by-step way through the writing process. We begin with how to find possibilities to write about and how to shape these into successful topics by using critical thinking skills. We go on to show how to turn the organization and development of ideas into convincing, well-supported arguments. The book provides four complete student papers, with explanations by the student writers of how they carried out the assignments. Our aim is to offer the students who use the book models to follow that will give them confidence that they can do the work described in the chapters. The book provides, in addition, sample marginal annotations, journal entries, and exam answers to clarify the different forms of writing.

Clear, Sensible Guidance on Using Sources and Research

Chapter 28 provides practical instruction on how to approach and read the academic and critical essay, a genre in itself that is unfamiliar to many students, and which students may be asked to use as sources in their own writing. The chapter includes a provocative critical essay on a story that students like: Susan Farrell's article "Fight vs. Flight: A Re-evaluation of Dee in Alice Walker's 'Everyday Use'" uses sources to build an argument for a more sympathetic view of Dee (Wangero) than many readers are inclined to give her. As a reading, the essay challenges students to think critically, as they reconsider the story from a different perspective, and to decide which approach to it seems more appropriate and helpful. As a model of writing, it features marginal annotations that show students what to look for in a critical essay, in particular rhetorical strategies that they can use in their own writing.

Chapter 29 guides students step by step through the literary research process, from finding material, to reading it, evaluating it, incorporating it effectively, citing it accurately, and avoiding plagiarism. It is particularly attentive to twenty-first-century research challenges and includes clear, specific coverage of the benefits and pitfalls involved in using electronic resources. It offers thorough, detailed, easy-to-use information about parenthetical citations and bibliography form and an annotated sample paper that provides a clear, helpful model for handling various situations students may encounter and that is introduced by a first-person account of how the writer moved from conception to completion.

New to the Second Edition

Our overarching goal in the second edition has been to make the book even more accessible and inclusive than the first edition. The choice of new literary works and the additions to our pedagogy reflect these dual concerns.

72 New Selections

We have selected 18 new stories, 48 new poems, and 6 new plays for this edition, many of them by authors who did not appear in the first edition (12 fiction writers, 22 poets, and 4 playwrights). Some of the new writers and works are from the established canon, while others are writers just emerging on the literary scene. The new works include:

- fiction by Melissa Bank, Edward P. Jones, David Means, George Saunders, and Zadie Smith
- contemporary poetry by Laure-Anne Bosselaar, Ana Castillo, Lucia Perillo, Carl Phillips, Mary Ruefle, and Patricia Jabbeth Wesley, among many others
- the recent Pulitzer Prize-winning play *Topdog/Underdog* by Suzi Lori Parks
- a dozen new canonical selections from writers such as John Donne, James Joyce, William Shakespeare, Sophocles, and John Steinbeck

An Introduction to Graphic Fiction

We have added graphic fiction to this edition along with what we think is an unusually thoughtful, detailed introduction to reading and responding to it. The works are integrated into chapters in the fiction section to show that writers of graphic fiction rely on the same literary elements other fiction writers use, such as plot, characters, setting, point of view, style, and tone. The terminology and techniques specific to graphic fiction are defined and discussed as well. The form is represented by two writers who are among the most popular of those currently working in the form, Lynda Barry and Bill Willingham.

Casebooks for Exploring Different Approaches to Literature

Because critical thinking and writing require sustained attention, we have prepared three casebooks, each of which introduces a different way to study literature in depth. In the fiction section we look at an author in depth, presenting three stories by Sherman Alexie, along with his own comments on, and some critical responses to, his fiction. In the poetry section we demonstrate a thematic approach, with a cluster of works that show poets being inspired by the quotidian, transforming mundane events into illuminating art. In the drama section we present materials for studying an individual literary work in depth, with reviews, interviews, and criticism focusing on August Wilson's *Fences*.

Thematic "Connections" Assignments

We sought in the first edition to help students make connections between literary works. Noticing relationships and making comparisons are important habits and skills to develop, crucial to active reading and critical thinking. In the second edition, new "Writing about Connections" assignments in each chapter (you can see them in the table of contents) prompt students to explore thematic connections between contemporary and classic works. The pairings in these assignments provide fresh entry points into enduring older works while suggesting intriguing ways to approach current writing that may be less familiar — as, for example, pairing Edward P. Jones' "Bad Neighbors" with Nathaniel Hawthorne's "Young Goodman Brown," Vievee Francis' "Private Smith's Primer" with Wilfred Owen's "Dulce et Decorum Est," and August Wilson's *Fences* with William Shakespeare's *Hamlet*.

More — and Even More Accessible — Writing Instruction

We have added several features in this edition that supplement the first edition's discussions and illustrations of the writing process:

- **"Tips on Writing" checklists**   These lists complement the "Checklists for Reading" in each of the elements chapters, providing practical suggestions on how to deal with the special demands and problems involved in writing effectively about each literary element.
- **Expanded focus on literary research**   The writing prompts at the end of each elements chapter now include research assignments, and

Chapter 29, on writing literary research papers, now features more help for students in finding, evaluating, and incorporating sources.

- **Guidance on researching contemporary literature** This edition includes a special section on locating sources for contemporary authors and a new cluster modeling how the research process may be different when dealing with contemporary figures.

Additional Electronic and Print Resources for Teaching and Learning

Approaching Literature is fully integrated with its companion Web site and with the *LiterActive* CD-ROM, using a variety of new media to expand the world of literature for students. Marginal icons throughout the book direct students to relevant, informative, and stimulating resources, including:

The Companion Web Site at bedfordstmartins.com/approachinglit

The companion website features resources that are useful, plentiful — and completely free and open to students. They include:

- **LitLinks** These are annotated links to carefully chosen Web sites intended to supplement the book's coverage of individual authors. The links provide biographical, critical, and cultural information for every fiction writer and playwright and many of the poets.
- **LitQuiz Online Quizzes** The online quizzes, which are provided for each story and play, can be used for self-study because they provide with immediate feedback for students. Instructors can use them to monitor student progress, as the results are collated automatically and available online.
- **The VirtuaLit Interactive Literature Tutorials** For fiction, poetry, and drama, students are guided step by step as they explore the literary elements, critical perspectives, and cultural contexts of eleven featured works, helping them to become engaged readers.

LiterActive CD-ROM, ISBN: 0-312-48451-8

An innovative CD-ROM, LiterActive, is packed with hundreds of images, contextual documents, audio and video clips, activities for exploring literature, and help for doing research and documenting sources.

- **VirtuaLit Interactive Tutorials** also available on the companion Web site)
- **A Multimedia & Document Library** provides hundreds of images, audio clips, and contextual documents supporting forty-three authors, enriching students' experience and comprehension of literature.

- **A Research and Documentation Guide**   gives students concrete advice for working with sources — how to find, evaluate, summarize, interpret, and document them. The inclusion of easy-to-score exercises as well as advice for avoiding plagiarism help students evaluate and improve their research and documentation practices.

The Instructor's Manual

We wrote *Resources for Teaching* APPROACHING LITERATURE to be a comprehensive, practical guide to the selections in the book and to using the textbook in Literature and Literature for Composition courses. For each work in the elements chapters and the anthologies we provide:

- **Entry Points**   For all stories, poems, and plays except those in the casebooks, the instructor's manual offers suggestions for ways to enter the work in a classroom: ways to get at the key questions and issues a text raises, and ways to introduce a work successfully in class. Often having a successful class turns on having a few good questions or topics for discussion; other questions or topics can then flow out of those as the class proceeds. They are a healthy reminder, for instructor and students alike, that there are many ways of opening up a work, many ways of entering it besides the usual "What does it mean?" or "What is it about?"
- **Starters**   Beginnings are difficult, whether in writing or opening a class or discussion. The instructor's manual suggests ideas for opening discussion for each selection contained in the elements chapters. These may be a "watch for this as you read" type assignment to give students the previous class, or an activity to focus their attention as they arrive at class. All are ones that we have used, and they're offered in part to stimulate your thinking and help you come up with better ideas yourself.
- **Provocative Pairings**   Each selection is paired with at least one similar or contrasting work to which it is related in subject matter, theme, technique, or form.
- **Teaching Tips**   The instructor's manual contains a host of practical ideas for designing active-learning assignments and for engaging students in the classroom.

Literary Reprints

Additional works of literature from any of Bedford/St. Martin's literary reprint series are available at a special price with *Approaching Literature*, including volumes from the Bedford Cultural Editions, the Bedford Shakespeare Series, Case Studies in Contemporary Criticism, and Case Studies in Critical Controversy. (To view a complete list of titles, visit the Bedford/St.Martin's web site (bedfordstmartins.com) and click through "English" and "Literature and Linguistics" to reach "Literary Reprints.")

Video and DVD Library

Selected videos and DVDs of plays and stories included in the text are available from Bedford/St. Martin's video library to qualified adopters. Please contact your Bedford/St. Martin's sales representative for more information.

Acknowledgments

We want to express again our appreciation to many colleagues at Hope College for their generous assistance and encouragement as we worked on the earlier edition of *Approaching Literature*: Ion Agheana, Miguel De La Torre, Natalie Dykstra, Curtis Gruenler, Stephen Hemenway, Charles Huttar, Rhoda Janzen, Marla Lunderberg, Jesus Montaño, William Pannapacker, William Reynolds, Heather Sellers, and Jennifer Young. We want to thank especially John Cox, David Klooster, and Carla Vissers, who provided valuable assistance on this edition as well as the earlier one, and Elizabeth Trembley for her help in selecting and discussing graphic fiction for this edition and for allowing us to use ideas and insights from her work-in-progress on reading graphic fiction. Jane Currie, a reference librarian at the Van Wylen Library, once again read parts of the chapter on literary research and provided helpful guidance. And Myra Kohsel, office manager for the English department, again assisted us in her usual capable, cheerful, and efficient way.

We are grateful also to our students at Hope College, from whom we learn as they learn, and especially to Alicia Abood, Dan Carter, Kortney DeVito, Julian Hinson, Kristina Martinez, and Annie Otto for allowing us to include their writing in the book.

We appreciate also the help given by colleagues elsewhere on the first edition, especially Sue Beebe, Southwest Texas State University; Daniel Cano, Santa Monica College; Emily Dial-Driver, Rogers State University; Tamara Kuzmenkov, Tacoma Community College; Laurie F. Leach, Hawaii Pacific University; Refugio Romo, Northwest Vista College; Tracy L. Schaelen, Southwestern College; William E. Sheidley, Colorado State University–Pueblo; James G. Van Belle, Edmonds Community College; and Sallie Wolf, Arapahoe Community College. And we express special thanks for those who provided help in shaping the new edition, especially Marilyn Boutwell, Long Island University, Brooklyn Campus; Janice Carello, SUNY Brockport; Dr. Keith Coplin, Colby Community College; Terence A. Dalrymple, Angelo State University; Robert T. Davis, University of West Florida; James Flavin, Shawnee State University; Sharon G. Levy, Northampton Community College; Mary E. Galvin, Palm Beach Community College; Donald Gilzinger Jr, Suffolk Community College; Peter Goldstein, Juniata College; Eunice Hargett, Broward Community College; Robin Havenick, Linn Benton Community College; Steve Kaufman, Minneapolis Community and Technical College; Erica Lara, Southwest Texas Junior College; Jeremy Saint Larance, West Liberty State

College; Cara McClintock-Walsh, Northampton Community College; Janice Mckay, SUNY College at Brockport; Jennifer Nader, Bergen Community College; Bill Nedrow, Triton College; Gregory M. Neubauer, West Liberty State College; Darlene Pagán, Pacific University; Melanie Fahlman Reid, Capilano College; Michelle Salman, Pima Community College; Nicole Staub, West Liberty State College; David Thomson, Henderson State University; Catherine Vedder, Kentucky State University; Sheri Weinstein, Kingsborough Community College, City University of New York; and Shari Weiss, San Francisco State University.

Finally, we want to thank those at Bedford/St. Martin's who made this book possible and worked hard on it. We are grateful to Charles Christensen and Joan Feinberg for their support of the project and their vision for what the book should be, and to Steve Scipione for his help in developing the book and his excellent advice on contents, style, and other aspects of both editions. And we are grateful to those who helped develop the current edition: to Denise Wydra and Karen Henry for their editorial insights; to Bridget Leahy for guiding the book expertly through the production process and for her patience and understanding as she dealt with our questions and requests; to Mary Lou Wilshaw-Watts for her attentive and knowledgable copyediting; to Sandy Schechter for her careful and alert work on permissions; and to Melissa Cook for her work on developing the companion Web site and her helpfulness to us in a variety of ways. Finally, we want to express again our gratitude to Genevieve Hamilton Day for her outstanding work as editor of both editions of *Approaching Literature*. Through her intelligence, creativity, attentiveness to detail, good sense, and hard work, Genevieve has contributed more to both editions than we could ever describe. We are deeply indebted to her.

And daily we are profoundly grateful for the support of our wives, Karen Schakel and Julie Ridl.

Brief Contents

Contents

PART 2   Approaching FICTION   53

3 Reading Fiction

4 Plot and Character

5   Point of View and Theme

PART **3**   **Approaching POETRY**   **539**

11 Reading Poetry
Realizing the Richness in Poems   **541**

12 Words and Images
Seizing on Sense and Sight   **546**

13 Voice, Tone, and Sound

14 Form and Type

15 Figurative Language

    Wondering What This Has to Do with That   **631**

16 Rhythm and Meter

17   Writing about Poetry

18   The Ordinary in Poetry – A Theme in Depth

19 A Collection of Poems

23 Theaters and Their Influence

Imagining the Impact of Stage and Space   **964**

24 Dramatic Types and Their Effects

25 Writing about Drama

29 Writing a Literary Research Paper

Incorporating the Larger Conversation   **1468**

Using This Book

- Terms that are **boldface** in the text are defined in the Glossary of Literary Terms at the end of the book.
- The dates provided for stories indicated their earliest publication; dates for poems give the first publication in a book; dates for plays are for their initial performance. For some poems, when publication was delayed, the probable date of composition is given as well, in *Italics*.
- A rule (———) indicates a space break (in a story) or a stanza break (in a poem) that falls at the bottom or top of a page and otherwise might be undetectable.
- For untitled poems, the first line is often used as a convenient form of reference, though it should not be thought of as a title and thus does not follow the capitalization rules for titles.

Approaching Literature

Writing + Reading + Thinking

Approaching LITERATURE

Overleaf: The novelist, essayist, poet, and children's book author Julia Alvarez was photo-graphed in her home in Vermont, where she has lived and worked since 1988. Alvarez teaches creative writing and is currently the writer-in-residence at Middlebury College. Alvarez and her husband divide their time between their home in Vermont and a cooperative coffee farm — a sustainable farm–literacy center called Alta Gracia — in the Dominican Republic, where Alvarez was raised. When asked why she writes in so many different genres, she says, "I blame my life. Something happens which sends me in a new direction . . . and the telling requires a different form, rhythm, voice." (See p. 1518 for a short biography.)
Reprinted by permission of Cameron Davidson.

I read because it takes me out of myself, it enlarges me. Reading is a transformative activity. **Kathleen Norris**

Reading Literature
Taking Part in a Process

Why read? Why write? Why take the time and effort a story, poem, or play requires when we have movies, televisions, and DVDs? The answer this book assumes is that we need to, we all need to. Writing and reading fill a human need to express, communicate, and experience connection and communion in ways that are of deep personal value. To be ourselves in the fullest sense, we need to enter the worlds and experiences of other selves, and reading is one of the best ways to do this.

READING TO CONNECT WITH OTHERS Although writing and reading may seem at first like individual acts, they are by their nature shared and communal: We write so that others will read, and we read what others have written. Writing and reading are sources of ideas, challenges, and meaning as well as invitations to understanding, empathy, sympathy, judgment, and compassion. They enable us to connect with others, to enter the thoughts, feelings, and experiences of those both similar to and different from ourselves. Writing and reading fill a deep need, assisting us in our endless growth toward being fully human and fully humane.

READING TO LIVE For some people, reading forms a central part of their lives. It is so vital to them that a day without some time for reading seems empty or incomplete — much as a pianist wants to spend time at the piano every day and a jogger is frustrated if she or he can't get in a daily run. And just as a musician or runner can become devoted to music and running, so can anyone get hooked on reading.

ENTRY POINTS The following essay was written by Sherman Alexie, who grew up on the Spokane Indian Reservation in Wellpinit, Washington,

3

where — surprisingly, he says — he found that first reading and then writing became essential to his very being. As you read it, pay attention to the way Alexie began reading — not at all a passive taking in, but an active engagement with the work before him. Notice also what goes on as you read the essay, how it requires you also to actively involve yourself in the process.

Sherman Alexie b. 1966

Superman and Me   [1997]

I learned to read with a *Superman* comic book. Simple enough, I suppose. I cannot recall which particular *Superman* comic book I read, nor can I remember which villain he fought in that issue. I cannot remember the plot, nor the means by which I obtained the comic book. What I can remember is this: I was three years old, a Spokane Indian boy living with his family on the Spokane Indian Reservation in eastern Washington state. We were poor by most standards, but one of my parents usually managed to find some minimum-wage job or another, which made us middle class by reservation standards. I had a brother and three sisters. We lived on a combination of irregular paychecks, hope, fear, and government-surplus food.

My father, who is one of the few Indians who went to Catholic school on purpose, was an avid reader of westerns, spy thrillers, murder mysteries, gangster epics, basketball-player biographies, and anything else he could find. He bought his books by the pound at Dutch's Pawn Shop, Goodwill, Salvation Army, and Value Village. When he had extra money, he bought new novels at supermarkets, convenience stores, and hospital gift shops. Our house was filled with books. They were stacked in crazy piles in the bathroom, bedrooms, and living room. In a fit of unemployment-inspired creative energy, my father built a set of bookshelves and soon filled them with a random assortment of books about the Kennedy assassination, Watergate, the Vietnam War, and the entire twenty-three-book series of the Apache westerns. My father loved books, and since I loved my father with an aching devotion, I decided to love books as well.

I can remember picking up my father's books before I could read. The words themselves were mostly foreign, but I still remember the exact moment when I first understood, with a sudden clarity, the purpose of a paragraph. I didn't have the vocabulary to say "paragraph," but I realized that a paragraph was a fence that held words. The words inside a paragraph worked together for a common purpose. They had some specific reason for being inside the same fence. This knowledge delighted me. I began to think of everything in terms of paragraphs. Our reservation was a small paragraph within the United States. My family's house was a paragraph, distinct from the other paragraphs of the LeBrets to the north, the Fords to our south, and the Tribal School to the west. Inside our house, each family member existed as a separate paragraph, but still had genetics and common experiences to link us. Now, using this logic, I can see my changed family as an essay of seven paragraphs: mother, father, older brother, the deceased sister, my younger twin sisters, and our adopted little brother.

At the same time I was seeing the world in paragraphs, I also picked up that *Superman* comic book. Each panel, complete with picture, dialogue, and narrative, was a three-dimensional paragraph. In one panel, Superman breaks through a door. His suit is red, blue, and yellow. The brown door shatters into many pieces. I look at the narrative above the picture. I cannot read the words, but I assume it tells me that Superman is breaking down the door. Aloud, I pretend to read the words and say "Superman is breaking down the door." Words, dialogue, also float out of Superman's mouth. Because he is breaking down the door, I assume he says, "I am breaking down the door." Once again, I pretend to read the words and say aloud, "I am breaking down the door." In this way, I learned to read.

This might be an interesting story all by itself. A little Indian boy teaches 5 himself to read at an early age and advances quickly. He reads *Grapes of Wrath* in kindergarten when other children are struggling through Dick and Jane. If he'd been anything but an Indian boy living on the reservation, he might have been called a prodigy. But he is an Indian boy living on the reservation, and is simply an oddity. He grows into a man who often speaks of his childhood in the third-person, as if it will somehow dull the pain and make him sound more modest about his talents.

A smart Indian is a dangerous person, widely feared and ridiculed by Indians and non-Indians alike. I fought with my classmates on a daily basis. They wanted me to stay quiet when the non-Indian teacher asked for answers, for volunteers, for help. We were Indian children who were expected to be stupid. Most lived up to those expectations inside the classroom, but subverted them on the outside. They struggled with basic reading in school, but could remember how to sing a few dozen powwow songs. They were monosyllabic in front of their non-Indian teachers, but could tell complicated stories and jokes at the dinner table. They submissively ducked their heads when confronted by a non-Indian adult, but would slug it out with the Indian bully who was ten years older. As Indian children, we were expected to fail in the non-Indian world. Those who failed were ceremonially accepted by other Indians and appropriately pitied by non-Indians.

I refused to fail. I was smart. I was arrogant. I was lucky. I read books late into the night, until I could barely keep my eyes open. I read books at recess, then during lunch, and in the few minutes left after I had finished my classroom assignments. I read books in the car when my family traveled to powwows or basketball games. In shopping malls, I ran to the bookstores and read bits and pieces of as many books as I could. I read the books my father brought home from the pawnshops and secondhand stores. I read the books I borrowed from the library. I read the backs of cereal boxes. I read the newspaper. I read the bulletins posted on the walls of the school, the clinic, the tribal offices, the post office. I read junk mail. I read auto-repair manuals. I read magazines. I read anything that had words and paragraphs. I read with equal parts joy and desperation. I loved those books, but I also knew that love had only one purpose. I was trying to save my life.

Despite all the books I read, I am still surprised I became a writer. I was going to be a pediatrician. These days, I write novels, short stories, and poems. I visit schools and teach creative writing to Indian kids. In all my years in the reservation school system, I was never taught how to write poetry, short stories, or novels. I was certainly never taught that Indians wrote poetry, short stories, and novels. Writing was something beyond Indians. I cannot recall a single time that a guest teacher visited the reservation. There must have been visiting teachers. Who were they? Where are they now? Do they exist? I visit the schools as often as possible. The Indian kids crowd the classroom. Many are writing their own poems, short stories, and novels. They have read my books. They have read many other books. They look at me with bright eyes and arrogant wonder. They are trying to save their lives. Then there are the sullen and already defeated Indian kids who sit in the back rows and ignore me with theatrical precision. The pages of their notebooks are empty. They carry neither pencil nor pen. They stare out the window. They refuse and resist. "Books," I say to them. "Books," I say. I throw my weight against their locked doors. The door holds. I am smart. I am arrogant. I am lucky. I am trying to save our lives.

APPROACHING THE READING

1. This chapter opens by giving some reasons people need to read. Which of those reasons do you think apply to Alexie? Why does he need to read?
2. List some things in Alexie's life that made love of reading difficult to sustain, that worked against his learning and growth. Think briefly about your own life. Do you love to read, the way Alexie does? If not, are there factors that work against reading, that make it difficult to do or love?
3. Think about what is involved in the process of reading. How do ideas, feelings, and descriptions get from Alexie's heart and mind to your heart and mind? In what sense are you essential for the communication process to be complete?

THE VALUE OF READING   Alexie says he read to save his life. He doesn't mean surviving physically, of course. Rather, he realized that his mind and heart and imagination required regular nourishment, which he found could come from books. Without this nourishment, parts of himself, parts essential to his very identity that make him who he really is, would weaken and perhaps eventually starve. You may be just like him, someone who loves to read and reads to live. Or you may not be at that point yet, or may have lost your love of reading, or may never have enjoyed literature. In that case, we hope this course and this book will lead you to the real value of making reading and writing a vital part of your life, and perhaps even change your life. We hope that you will give reading a new chance, will put into reading the attentiveness and receptivity it requires and deserves. If it doesn't *save* your life, at least it certainly will *enrich* it.

PERSONAL ESSAYS   "Superman and Me" is a personal essay. An *essay* is a brief discussion, usually in prose, of a limited topic or idea; a *personal* essay deals with a particular part of the author's life and experience. An essay is not a story. It is *expository writing* (an explanation and discussion of ideas), not *imaginative writing* (at least partially "made up"). Most of this textbook concerns creative writing — fiction (made-up stories), poetry, and drama, and all of the examples included in the book are considered works of literature.

WORKS OF LITERATURE   In his essay, Alexie says that he is a writer of "novels, short stories, and poems"; he also has written screenplays for two award-winning films, *Smoke Signals* and *The Business of Fancydancing*. Alexie's works are considered works of literature because their lasting value is based on their artistic quality and the way they portray and reflect on issues important to human experience. Alexie's writing explores personal identity, ethnicity, alienation, and love.

Many of the other works selected for inclusion in this book examine such issues as well. They ask readers to notice and reflect on *borders* that divide and connect people, on the *diversity of voices* we hear when we are willing to listen, and on the way many people are treated as *outsiders*. Reading such works can be personally rewarding, deepen your understanding of others, and expand the borders of your own world.

THE NATURE OF READING

WHAT IS READING?   If reading is so important, it only makes sense to look more closely at it. What *is* reading? What goes on when you read? How does a person "read well"? One view appears in the movie *Driving Miss Daisy*. Reading is easy, Daisy Werthan tells Hoke, her chauffeur. "If you know your letters, then you can read." She draws a *B* and an *R* in the dust and then sends him off to find a tombstone marked *BAUER*.

Reading used to be thought of that way — as just taking in the letters and combinations of letters on the page. The meaning was "there" in the marks on paper, waiting to be extracted. And because each reader was looking at the same marks, it was assumed that the meaning would be the same for everyone.

That is not, however, either an adequate or an accurate view of this human activity called reading. We are not mechanical decoders like a radio set receiving signals and emitting sounds. Nevertheless, this idea is still common and sometimes misleads students in a literature class. What actually happens when we read?

AUTHOR, TEXT, AND READER   Most reading specialists agree that reading is a sense-*making* activity. It involves an encounter between an author, a text, and a reader in a cultural context. The writer puts ideas, details, and emotions into words (a *text*). The reader takes in the writer's words, processes them mentally, relates them to knowledge and information she or he already possesses, and constructs out of them pictures, feelings, and meanings. The writer depends on the reader to complete the communication process, to lift the inert marks off the page and fill them with life and meaning.

PERSONAL INTERACTION   Understanding writing and reading as an interactive process — a three-way transaction between author, text, and reader — makes it clear that what is written does not convey the same thing to every reader. Your engagement with a writer's words is an individual act; it depends on your mind and your personality. Each reader gains an understanding of the words in relation to her or his knowledge and experience, to the specific context and cultural situation, and even to the stage of life in which she or he is reading.

COMPLETING WHAT THE AUTHOR STARTED   Take, for example, a writer who provides a detailed description of an Indian reservation in the mountains of eastern Washington. The pictures you form in your mind are a key part of the meaning of such a text. The mental pictures are not there on the page; what the writer started is not completed until you interact with the text, form mental images related to the written words, and respond to them with your senses and emotions.

If you have seen reservations in Washington or elsewhere, those experiences will help form sharp, precise mental pictures as you read the text and bring its meaning to life. Your mental pictures will be richer and more precise than ones formed by someone who has never been on a reservation or knows about them only from watching Western movies.

But your response as a reader is not confined to just the precision of the mental pictures (or, for more complex material, the ideas) formed. If you have been to Washington, for example, you also recall emotions associated with traveling in the mountains and being with certain companions. Those emotions also influence the understanding you construct; they become part of the meaning of what is being read, of what makes the reading itself meaningful.

ACTIVE READING

A SENSE-MAKING ACTIVITY   As we read, we constantly relate what we see on the page to our own knowledge and experiences. We grasp ideas, imagine details, and feel emotions as we process words to things stored in our memories; we bring our prior knowledge, attitudes, and assumptions to bear as we take in what the author wrote. Reading as a sense-making activity is inevitably personal and individual. That doesn't mean, of course, that a text means anything a reader says it means. "It is going to snow" cannot mean "An elephant is doing math," no matter what a particular reader asserts. There *is* a text; there *are* words and sentences on the page that we must look at, take in, and respond to. But *we* fill the words with meaning — personal meaning. Thus, readers in Michigan may read "It is going to snow" differently from the ways readers in Hawaii read the same sentence, just as an elephant trainer in India may read "An elephant is doing math" differently from the way a literature professor in Michigan reads the same sentence.

ENGAGING WITH TEXTS   The stories, poems, and plays in this book are not objects, not just writing on the page, but potential works that need to be *completed in the reader's mind.* There can be a text (the words of the writer, written or spoken) without a reader (we "read" a spoken text just as we do a written one), but there can't be a living literary work (a story, poem, or play) without a reader (or listener) to complete what the writer began. Texts are similar to musical scores: The notes on paper are only potential music until a musician brings them to life by performing them. So too the reader "performs" a story, poem, or play by bringing it to life in her or his mind through the method of active reading.

RESPONDING INDIVIDUALLY   *Meaning,* then, is the result of an interaction between a piece of writing and an individual reader. Since no two people have the same personality and the same experiences, the story, poem, or play they actualize out of the same text, though perhaps similar, will not be identical. The rooms filled with books that you see in your mind's eye as you read "Superman and Me" may be similar to those someone else imagines, but they won't be the same, and we shouldn't gloss over the difference by saying that it is only what they have in common that really matters. Thus, also, although you as a reader can reread the same text, you cannot experience the work in the same way a second time. Your second reading is different because you know from the beginning what is ahead, so you see things differently: It is a new story (or poem or play). If a good bit of time passes between the readings, you also are a different person, bringing new knowledge, experiences, and maturity to the process. The text does not change, but as you the reader change and the context changes, the experience of the story, poem, or play changes.

RESPONDING HOLISTICALLY   Your whole being — intellect, imagination, emotions, values — can be and should be involved in the reading process. As we read, we select from our memories definitions and pictures that make sense of the words and phrases we encounter; we anticipate what may be ahead; we revise our earlier anticipations in light of what we find later; we make judgments about what is said and done, and sometimes need to revise those judgments and come to a different conclusion. Reading is not a spectator sport — we do not observe passively from the sidelines. To be a good reader, you need to participate, to be actively involved at every moment, with every word.

RESPONDING ATTENTIVELY   All reading is not the same. Active reading of a chemistry book takes different skills from those used in actively reading a novel; reading an Internet site actively is different from actively reading a newspaper. Reading literature actively requires you to pay attention to the way things are written as well as to what is said, and to the techniques a writer uses to develop a work. Such attentiveness doesn't happen automatically — we all, at some point, have to learn how to pay attention and to judge what is worth attending to. Active reading of literary texts entails imagining characters, forming mental images, visualizing locations and series of actions, and listening for sounds and rhythms. This book is designed to help you do these things. Its chapters introduce features and techniques that will enrich your reading experience and develop your skills at "literary observation." It describes specific strategies for reading fiction, poetry, and drama, and it introduces strategies for writing about each of them.

ASKING QUESTIONS   Active reading also involves asking questions, wondering "why? why? why?" It includes talking with other readers, talking back to the author or text, underlining words and phrases, jotting notes in the margins, and perhaps writing an outline or drawing a map inside the back cover. (More is said about these active reading strategies in Chapter 2.)

By now it should be clear that Hoke in *Driving Miss Daisy* isn't really reading. He identifies the first and last letters of a word, but he lacks the skills and the background for interacting dynamically with that word. *Bauer* means nothing to him; he hadn't known the Bauers, and their name provokes no cluster of memories and emotions as it does for Miss Daisy, clusters of associations that are crucial to the construction of meaning that constitutes real reading. Active reading is a complicated skill, but an exciting one. We hope this book encourages you to want to get better and better at it and helps you find greater and greater pleasure and enrichment from your reading.

ENTRY POINTS   Here is a story about the importance reading and writing came to have in the life of a young woman whose family emigrated from the Dominican Republic to New York City. The point is similar to that in "Superman and Me," but notice the difference in form. As an essay, "Superman and Me" explains and discusses personal experiences and their effect on the author. "Daughter of Invention" brings a personal experience to life, telling it as a story, through characters and a sequence of events. As you

☑ CHECKLIST on Active Reading

❏ Read attentively and alertly — don't put off reading until the last thing at night when it's hard to concentrate.

❏ Adjust to the kind of material you are reading — when reading a chemistry textbook, your mind must be principally involved in studying the material, while literary works in addition to demanding your intellect also require the involvement of your emotions and imagination.

❏ Respond to literature with your whole being — empathize with characters and situations, and let yourself feel a rich complex of emotions when the work calls for it.

❏ Use a pen or pencil — mark up the text if you own and plan to keep the book; take notes if you don't. Jotting things down helps you to concentrate and to remember.

❏ Interrogate the text — ask questions as you read, such as why some things are omitted, why other things are included, why a certain approach or technique is used, and what difference looking at things from another perspective would make.

read, practice the kinds of active reading skills we've just discussed — paying close attention to everything in the text, imagining, visualizing, listening, asking questions, noticing what's left out, filling gaps, underlining words and phrases you might want to look at again, and jotting notes in the margins.

Julia Alvarez b. 1950
Daughter of Invention   [1988]

She wanted to invent something, my mother. There was a period after we arrived in this country, until five or so years later, when my mother was inventing. They were never pressing, global needs she was addressing with her pencil and pad. She would have said that was for men to do, rockets and engines that ran on gasoline and turned the wheels of the world. She was just fussing with little house things, don't mind her.

She always invented at night, after settling her house down. On his side of the bed my father would be conked out for an hour already, his Spanish newspaper draped over his chest, his glasses, propped up on his bedside table, looking out eerily at the darkened room like a disembodied guard. But in her lighted corner, like some devoted scholar burning the midnight oil, my mother was inventing, sheets pulled to her lap, pillows propped up behind her, her reading glasses riding the bridge of her nose like a schoolmarm's. On her lap lay one of those innumerable pads of paper my father always brought home from his office, compliments of some pharmaceutical company, advertising tranquilizers or antibiotics or skin cream; in her other hand, my mother held a pencil that looked like a pen with a little cylinder of lead inside. She would work on a sketch of something familiar, but drawn at such close range so she could attach a special nozzle or handier handle, the thing looked peculiar. Once, I mistook the spiral of a corkscrew for a nautilus shell, but it could just as well have been a galaxy forming.

It was the only time all day we'd catch her sitting down, for she herself was living proof of the *perpetuum mobile* machine so many inventors had sought over the ages. My sisters and I would seek her out now when she seemed to have a moment to talk to us: We were having trouble at school or we wanted her to persuade my father to give us permission to go into the city or to a shopping mall or a movie — in broad daylight! My mother would wave us out of her room. "The problem with you girls . . ." I can tell you right now what the problem always boiled down to: We wanted to become Americans and my father — and my mother, at first — would have none of it.

"You girls are going to drive me crazy!" She always threatened if we kept nagging. "When I end up in Bellevue,° you'll be safely sorry!"

She spoke in English when she argued with us, even though, in a matter of   5 months, her daughters were the fluent ones. Her English was much better than my father's, but it was still a mishmash of mixed-up idioms and sayings that showed she was "green behind the ears," as she called it.

If my sisters and I tried to get her to talk in Spanish, she'd snap, "When in Rome, do unto the Romans . . ."

I had become the spokesman for my sisters, and I would stand my ground in that bedroom. "We're not going to that school anymore, Mami!"

"You have to." Her eyes would widen with worry. "In this country, it is against the law not to go to school. You want us to get thrown out?"

"You want us to get killed? Those kids were throwing stones today!"

"Sticks and stones don't break bones . . ." she chanted. I could tell, though,   10 by the look on her face, it was as if one of those stones the kids had aimed at us had hit her. But she always pretended we were at fault. "What did you do to provoke them? It takes two to tangle, you know."

"Thanks, thanks a lot, Mom!" I'd storm out of that room and into mine. I never called her *Mom* except when I wanted her to feel how much she had failed us in this country. She was a good enough Mami, fussing and scolding and giving advice, but a terrible girlfriend parent, a real failure of a Mom.

Back she'd go to her pencil and pad, scribbling and tsking and tearing off paper, finally giving up, and taking up her *New York Times*. Some nights, though,

---

Bellevue: Bellevue Psychiatric Hospital, a division of Bellevue Hospital Center in New York City.

she'd get a good idea, and she'd rush into my room, a flushed look on her face, her tablet of paper in her hand, a cursory knock on the door she'd just thrown open: "Do I have something to show you, Cukita!"

This was my time to myself, after I'd finished my homework, while my sisters were still downstairs watching TV in the basement. Hunched over my small desk, the overhead light turned off, my lamp shining poignantly on my paper, the rest of the room in warm, soft, uncreated darkness, I wrote my secret poems in my new language.

"You're going to ruin your eyes!" My mother would storm into my room, turning on the overly bright overhead light, scaring off whatever shy passion I had just begun coaxing out of a labyrinth of feelings with the blue thread of my writing.

"Oh Mami!" I'd cry out, my eyes blinking up at her. "I'm writing."   15

"Ay, Cukita." That was her communal pet name for whoever was in her favor. "Cukita, when I make a million, I'll buy you your very own typewriter." (I'd been nagging my mother for one just like the one father had bought her to do his order forms at home.) "Gravy on the turkey" was what she called it when someone was buttering her up. She'd butter and pour. "I'll hire you your very own typist."

Down she'd plop on my bed and hold out her pad to me. "Take a guess, Cukita?" I'd study her rough sketch a moment: soap sprayed from the nozzle head of a shower when you turned the knob a certain way? Coffee with creamer already mixed in? Time-released water capsules for your plants when you were away? A key chain with a timer that would go off when your parking meter was about to expire? (The ticking would help you find your keys easily if you mislaid them.) The famous one, famous only in hindsight, was the stick person dragging a square by a rope — a suitcase with wheels? "Oh, of course," we'd humor her. "What every household needs: a shower like a car wash, keys ticking like a bomb, luggage on a leash!" By now, as you can see, it'd become something of a family joke, our Thomas Edison Mami, our Benjamin Franklin Mom.

Her face would fall. "Come on now! Use your head." One more wrong guess, and she'd tell me, pressing with her pencil point the different highlights of this incredible new wonder. "Remember that time we took the car to Bear Mountain, and we re-ah-lized that we had forgotten to pack an opener with our pick-a-nick?" (We kept correcting her, but she insisted this is how it should be said.) "When we were ready to eat we didn't have any way to open the refreshments cans?" (This before fliptop lids, which she claimed had crossed her mind.) "You know what this is now?" A shake of my head. "Is a car bumper, but see this part is a removable can opener. So simple and yet so necessary, no?"

"Yeah, Mami. You should patent it." I'd shrug. She'd tear off the scratch paper and fold it, carefully, corner to corner, as if she were going to save it. But then, she'd toss it in the wastebasket on her way out of the room and give a little laugh like a disclaimer. "It's half of one or two dozen of another . . ."

I suppose none of her daughters was very encouraging. We resented her   20 spending time on those dumb inventions. Here, we were trying to fit in America among Americans; we needed help figuring out who we were, why these Irish kids whose grandparents were micks two generations ago, why they were calling us spics. Why had we come to the country in the first place? Important, crucial, final things, you see, and here was our own mother, who didn't have a second to help us puzzle any of this out, inventing gadgets to make life easier for American moms. Why, it seemed as if she were arming our own enemy against us!

One time, she did have a moment of triumph. Every night, she liked to read *The New York Times* in bed before turning off her light, to see what the Americans were up to. One night, she let out a yelp to wake up my father beside her, bolt upright, reaching for his glasses which, in his haste, he knocked across the room. *"Que pasa? Que pasa?"* What is wrong? There was terror in his voice, fear she'd seen in his eyes in the Dominican Republic before we left. We were being watched there; he was being followed; he and mother had often exchanged those looks. They could not talk, of course, though they must have whispered to each other in fear at night in the dark bed. Now in America, he was safe, a success even; his Centro Medico in Brooklyn was thronged with the sick and the homesick. But in dreams, he went back to those awful days and long nights, and my mother's screams confirmed his secret fear: We had not gotten away after all; they had come for us at last.

"Ay, Papi, I'm sorry. Go back to sleep, Cukito. It's nothing, nothing really." My mother held up the *Times* for him to squint at the small print, back page headline, one hand tapping all over the top of the bedside table for his glasses, the other rubbing his eyes to wakefulness.

"Remember, remember how I showed you that suitcase with little wheels so we would not have to carry those heavy bags when we traveled? Someone stole my idea and made a million!" She shook the paper in his face. She shook the paper in all our faces that night. "See! See! This man was no *bobo*! He didn't put all his pokers on a back burner. I kept telling you, one of these days my ship would pass me by in the night!" She wagged her finger at my sisters and my father and me, laughing all the while, one of those eerie laughs crazy people in movies laugh. We had congregated in her room to hear the good news she'd been yelling down the stairs, and now we eyed her and each other. I suppose we were all thinking the same thing: Wouldn't it be weird and sad if Mami did end up in Bellevue as she'd always threatened she might?

"Ya, ya! Enough!" She waved us out of her room at last. "There is no use trying to drink spilt milk, that's for sure."

It was the suitcase rollers that stopped my mother's hand; she had weather 25 vaned a minor brainstorm. She would have to start taking herself seriously. That blocked the free play of her ingenuity. Besides, she had also begun working at my father's office, and at night, she was too tired and busy filling in columns with how much money they had made that day to be fooling with gadgets!

She did take up her pencil and pad one last time to help me out. In ninth grade, I was chosen by my English teacher, Sister Mary Joseph, to deliver the teacher's day address at the school assembly. Back in the Dominican Republic, I was a terrible student. No one could ever get me to sit down to a book. But in

New York, I needed to settle somewhere, and the natives were unfriendly, the country inhospitable, so I took root in the language. By high school, the nuns were reading my stories and compositions out loud to my classmates as examples of imagination at work.

This time my imagination jammed. At first I didn't want and then I couldn't seem to write that speech. I suppose I should have thought of it as a "great honor," as my father called it. But I was mortified. I still had a pronounced lilt to my accent, and I did not like to speak in public, subjecting myself to my classmates' ridicule. Recently, they had begun to warm toward my sisters and me, and it took no great figuring to see that to deliver a eulogy for a convent full of crazy, old overweight nuns was no way to endear myself to the members of my class.

But I didn't know how to get out of it. Week after week, I'd sit down, hoping to polish off some quick, noncommittal little speech. I couldn't get anything down.

The weekend before our Monday morning assembly I went into a panic. My mother would just have to call in and say I was in the hospital, in a coma. I was in the Dominican Republic. Yeah, that was it! Recently, my father had been talking about going back home to live.

My mother tried to calm me down. "Just remember how Mister Lincoln 30 couldn't think of anything to say at the Gettysburg, but then, Bang! 'Four score and once upon a time ago,'" she began reciting. Her version of history was half invention and half truths and whatever else she needed to prove a point. "Something is going to come if you just relax. You'll see, like the Americans say, 'Necessity is the daughter of invention.' I'll help you."

All weekend, she kept coming into my room with help. "Please, Mami, just leave me alone, please," I pleaded with her. But I'd get rid of the goose only to have to contend with the gander. My father kept poking his head in the door just to see if I had "fulfilled my obligations," a phrase he'd used when we were a little younger, and he'd check to see whether we had gone to the bathroom before a car trip. Several times that weekend around the supper table, he'd recite his valedictorian speech from when he graduated from high school. He'd give me pointers on delivery, on the great orators and their tricks. (Humbleness and praise and falling silent with great emotion were his favorites.)

My mother sat across the table, the only one who seemed to be listening to him. My sisters and I were forgetting a lot of our Spanish, and my father's formal, florid diction was even harder to understand. But my mother smiled softly to herself, and turned the Lazy Susan at the center of the table around and around as if it were the prime mover, the first gear of attention.

That Sunday evening, I was reading some poetry to get myself inspired: Whitman in an old book with an engraved cover my father had picked up in a thrift shop next to his office a few weeks back. "I celebrate myself and sing myself . . . ." "He most honors my style who learns under it to destroy the teacher." The poet's words shocked and thrilled me. I had gotten used to the nuns, a literature of appropriate sentiments, poems with a message, expurgated texts. But here was a flesh and blood man, belching and laughing and sweating in poems. "Who touches this book touches a man."

That night, at last, I started to write, recklessly, three, five pages, looking up once only to see my father passing by the hall on tiptoe. When I was done, I read over my words, and my eyes filled. I finally sounded like myself in English!

As soon as I had finished that first draft, I called my mother to my room. She   35 listened attentively, as she had to my father's speech, and in the end, her eyes were glistening too. Her face was soft and warm and proud. "That is a beautiful, beautiful speech, Cukita. I want for your father to hear it before he goes to sleep. Then I will type it for you, all right?"

Down the hall we went, the two of us, faces flushed with accomplishment. Into the master bedroom where my father was propped up on his pillows, still awake, reading the Dominican papers, already days old. He had become interested in his country's fate again. The dictatorship had been toppled. The interim government was going to hold the first free elections in thirty years. There was still some question in his mind whether or not we might want to move back. History was in the making, freedom and hope were in the air again! But my mother had gotten used to the life here. She did not want to go back to the old country where she was only a wife and a mother (and a failed one at that, since she had never had the required son). She did not come straight out and disagree with my father's plans. Instead, she fussed with him about reading the papers in bed, soiling those sheets with those poorly printed, foreign tabloids. "*The Times* is not that bad!" she'd claim if my father tried to humor her by saying they shared the same dirty habit.

The minute my father saw my mother and me, filing in, he put his paper down, and his face brightened as if at long last his wife had delivered a son, and that was the news we were bringing him. His teeth were already grinning from the glass of water next to his bedside lamp, so he lisped when he said, "Eh-speech, eh-speech!"

"It is so beautiful, Papi," my mother previewed him, turning the sound off on his TV. She sat down at the foot of the bed. I stood before both of them, blocking their view of the soldiers in helicopters landing amid silenced gun reports and explosions. A few weeks ago it had been the shores of the Dominican Republic. Now it was the jungles of Southeast Asia they were saving. My mother gave me the nod to begin reading.

I didn't need much encouragement. I put my nose to the fire, as my mother would have said, and read from start to finish without looking up. When I was done, I was a little embarrassed at my pride in my own words. I pretended to quibble with a phrase or two I was sure I'd be talked out of changing. I looked questioningly to my mother. Her face was radiant. She turned to share her pride with my father.

But the expression on his face shocked us both. His toothless mouth had   40 collapsed into a dark zero. His eyes glared at me, then shifted to my mother, accusingly. In barely audible Spanish, as if secret microphones or informers were all about, he whispered, "You will permit her to read *that*?"

My mother's eyebrows shot up, her mouth fell open. In the old country, any whisper of a challenge to authority could bring the secret police in their black V.W.'s. But this was America. People could say what they thought. "What is wrong with her speech?" my mother questioned him.

"What ees wrrrong with her eh-speech?" My father wagged his head at her. His anger was always more frightening in his broken English. As if he had mutilated the language in his fury — and now there was nothing to stand between us and his raw, dumb anger. "What is wrong? I will tell you what is wrong. It shows no gratitude. It is boastful. 'I celebrate myself'? 'The best student learns to destroy the teacher'?" He mocked my plagiarized words. "That is insubordinate. It is improper. It is disrespecting of her teachers —" In his anger he had forgotten his fear of lurking spies: Each wrong he voiced was a decibel higher than the last outrage. Finally, he was yelling at me, "As your father, I forbid you to say that eh-speech!"

My mother leapt to her feet, a sign always that she was about to make a speech or deliver an ultimatum. She was a small woman, and she spoke all her pronouncements standing up, either for more protection or as a carry-over from her girlhood in convent schools where one asked for, and literally took, the floor in order to speak. She stood by my side, shoulder to shoulder; we looked down at my father. "That is no tone of voice, Eduardo —" she began.

By now, my father was truly furious. I suppose it was bad enough I was rebelling, but here was my mother joining forces with me. Soon he would be surrounded by a house full of independent American women. He too leapt from his bed, throwing off his covers. The Spanish newspapers flew across the room. He snatched my speech out of my hands, held it before my panicked eyes, a vengeful, mad look in his own, and then once, twice, three, four, countless times, he tore my prize into shreds.

"Are you crazy?" My mother lunged at him. "Have you gone mad? That is her speech for tomorrow you have torn up!"   45

"Have *you* gone mad?" He shook her away. "You were going to let her read that . . . that insult to her teachers?"

"Insult to her teachers!" My mother's face had crumpled up like a piece of paper. On it was written a love note to my father. Ever since they had come to this country, their life together was a constant war. "This is America, Papi, America!" she reminded him now. "You are not in a savage country any more!"

I was on my knees, weeping wildly, collecting all the little pieces of my speech, hoping that I could put it back together before the assembly tomorrow morning. But not even a sibyl could have made sense of all those scattered pieces of paper. All hope was lost. "He broke it, he broke it," I moaned as I picked up a handful of pieces.

Probably, if I had thought a moment about it, I would not have done what I did next. I would have realized my father had lost brothers and comrades to the dictator Trujillo.° For the rest of his life, he would be haunted by blood in the

---

Trujillo: Rafael Leónidas Trujillo Molina (1891–1961) was dictator of the Dominican Republic (1930–1961).

streets and late night disappearances. Even after he had been in the states for years, he jumped if a black Volkswagen passed him on the street. He feared anyone in uniform: the meter maid giving out parking tickets, a museum guard approaching to tell him not to touch his favorite Goya at the Metropolitan.

I took a handful of the scraps I had gathered, stood up, and hurled them in his face. "Chapita!"° I said in a low, ugly whisper. "You're just another Chapita!" 50

It took my father only a moment to register the hated nickname of our dictator, and he was after me. Down the halls we raced, but I was quicker than he and made it to my room just in time to lock the door as my father threw his weight against it. He called down curses on my head, ordered me on his authority as my father to open that door this very instant! He throttled that doorknob, but all to no avail. My mother's love of gadgets saved my hide that night. She had hired a locksmith to install good locks on all the bedroom doors after our house had been broken into while we were away the previous summer. In case burglars broke in again, and we were in the house, they'd have a second round of locks to contend with before they got to us.

"Eduardo," she tried to calm him down. "Don't you ruin my new locks."

He finally did calm down, his anger spent. I heard their footsteps retreating down the hall. I heard their door close, the clicking of their lock. Then, muffled voices, my mother's peaking in anger, in persuasion, my father's deep murmurs of explanation and of self-defense. At last, the house fell silent, before I heard, far off, the gun blasts and explosions, the serious, self-important voices of newscasters reporting their TV war.

A little while later, there was a quiet knock at my door, followed by a tentative attempt at the doorknob. "Cukita?" my mother whispered. "Open up, Cukita."

"Go away," I wailed, but we both knew I was glad she was there, and I needed only a moment's protest to save face before opening that door. 55

What we ended up doing that night was putting together a speech at the last moment. Two brief pages of stale compliments and the polite commonplaces on teachers, wrought by necessity without much invention by mother for daughter late into the night in the basement on the pad of paper and with the same pencil she had once used for her own inventions, for I was too upset to compose the speech myself. After it was drafted, she typed it up while I stood by, correcting her misnomers and mis-sayings.

She was so very proud of herself when I came home the next day with the success story of the assembly. The nuns had been flattered, the audience had stood up and given "our devoted teachers a standing ovation," what my mother had suggested they do at the end of my speech.

She clapped her hands together as I recreated the moment for her. "I stole that from your father's speech, remember? Remember how he put that in at the end?" She quoted him in Spanish, then translated for me into English.

That night, I watched him from the upstairs hall window where I'd retreated the minute I heard his car pull up in front of our house. Slowly, my father came

---

Chapita: "Chapita" (Spanish for *bottlecap*) was Trujillo's childhood nickname (one that he hated).

up the driveway, a grim expression on his face as he grappled with a large, heavy cardboard box. At the front door, he set the package down carefully and patted all his pockets for his house keys—precisely why my mother had invented her ticking key chain. I heard the snapping open of the locks downstairs. Heard as he struggled to maneuver the box through the narrow doorway. Then, he called my name several times. But I would not answer him.

"My daughter, your father, he love you very much," he explained from the 60 bottom of the stairs. "He just want to protect you." Finally, my mother came up and pleaded with me to go down and reconcile with him. "Your father did not mean to harm. You must pardon him. Always it is better to let bygones be forgotten, no?"

I guess she was right. Downstairs, I found him setting up a brand new electric typewriter on the kitchen table. It was even better than the one I'd been begging to get like my mother's. My father had outdone himself with all the extra features: a plastic carrying case with my initials, in decals, below the handle, a brace to lift the paper upright while I typed, an erase cartridge, an automatic margin tab, a plastic hood like a toaster cover to keep the dust away. Not even my mother, I think, could have invented such a machine!

But her inventing days were over just as mine were starting up with my schoolwide success. That's why I've always thought of that speech my mother wrote for me as her last invention rather than the suitcase rollers everyone else in the family remembers. It was as if she had passed on to me her pencil and pad and said, "Okay, Cukita, here's the buck. You give it a shot."

APPROACHING THE READING

1. "Daughter of Invention" divides into two parts. The first third provides background: about the family relocating to New York, about the mother's inventions, about the difficulties the sisters face in adjusting to a new country and a different culture. The rest of the story, beginning at "She did take up her pencil and pad one last time to help me out," deals with the speech the speaker must deliver at the school assembly. *Invention* in the first part refers primarily to what the mother dreams up; in the second part, it refers mostly to the speech they are making up, or inventing. In both parts, could *invention* have a wider application? Are the characters engaged in other forms of invention as they adjust to a new place and culture?

2. Reflect on things you engaged with as you read the text actively. What questions did you raise? At what points did you feel concern, anticipating possible difficulty for the characters? (Think about how you would experience those points differently on a second reading.) What parts did you enjoy most? Why? Which parts were you able to imagine most vividly, perhaps drawing on past experiences? Which ones left your visualizings less sharp and distinct?

3. Make a list of tensions and conflicts among the family members: the mother and father, the daughters and the parents, the sisters and their mother, the

speaker and her mother, the speaker and her father. Reflect on those tensions and conflicts. Which ones would exist regardless of whether the family had moved to the United States? Which ones are created or heightened by their relocation?

4. Why does writing become so important to the speaker? Was she writing to save her life? In what ways is reading also important, and how does it relate to her writing? If you have not read anything by Walt Whitman before, read some of the parts of his long poem *Song of Myself* (included in this book on p. 875) — that's an element of active reading, too. What is it in Whitman that the speaker finds so inspiring? Why would Whitman be so influential in her particular life situation?

5. The speaker, like Sherman Alexie, reads (and writes) to save her life. Reflect on similarities between what reading and writing mean to both of them. Consider also ways in which their situations are different, making the ways that reading and writing save them different as well.

6. List some gaps in the story. Be ready to discuss why you think things were left out and whether the gaps are unimportant or become a part of the total meaning of the story.

7. Reflect on the last two paragraphs. Why does her father give the speaker the gift that he does? What is he saying through it? What do the final paragraphs suggest about the continuing importance of writing in his daughter's life?

*R*eading makes me want to write, and writing makes me want to read. And both reading and writing make it a joy to be a part of the great human adventure we call life.

Katherine Patterson

Writing in Response to Literature

CHAPTER **2**

Entering the Conversation

Responding to literature is like participating in a great, ongoing conversation — perhaps like posting messages in the most gigantic chatroom the world has ever known because it has postings from the distant past as well as the present and all times in between. Some portions of this conversation are personal and some are public, and they cover an endlessly wide range of subjects. Included are conversations between authors and existing literary works, held directly or indirectly (see **allusion**, p. 235); conversations between a work and its readers; conversations between readers and other readers; conversations held orally, in writing, or through other media and art forms. This chapter offers specific suggestions for ways an active reader — the kind described in Chapter 1 — can take part in some of these conversations.

ENTRY POINTS Throughout this chapter, we draw illustrations from a very short story by Alice Walker. Read it and reflect on it before you move on.

Alice Walker b. 1944

The Flowers

[1973]

It seemed to Myop as she skipped lightly from hen house to pigpen to smokehouse that the days had never been as beautiful as these. The air held a keenness that made her nose twitch. The harvesting of the corn and cotton, peanuts and squash, made each day a golden surprise that caused excited little tremors to run up her jaws.

Myop carried a short, knobby stick. She struck out at random at chickens she liked, and worked out the beat of a song on the fence around the pigpen. She felt light and good in the warm sun. She was ten, and nothing existed for her but her song, the stick clutched in her dark brown hand, and the tat-de-ta-ta-ta of accompaniment.

Turning her back on the rusty boards of her family's sharecropper cabin, Myop walked along the fence till it ran into the stream made by the spring. Around the spring, where the family got drinking water, silver ferns and wild-flowers grew. Along the shallow banks pigs rooted. Myop watched the tiny white bubbles disrupt the thin black scale of soil and the water that silently rose and slid away down the stream.

She had explored the woods behind the house many times. Often, in late autumn, her mother took her to gather nuts among the fallen leaves. Today she made her own path, bouncing this way and that way, vaguely keeping an eye out for snakes. She found, in addition to various common but pretty ferns and leaves, an armful of strange blue flowers with velvety ridges and a sweetsuds bush full of the brown, fragrant buds.

By twelve o'clock, her arms laden with sprigs of her findings, she was a mile 5 or more from home. She had often been as far before, but the strangeness of the land made it not as pleasant as her usual haunts. It seemed gloomy in the little cove in which she found herself. The air was damp, the silence close and deep.

Myop began to circle back to the house, back to the peacefulness of the morning. It was then she stepped smack into his eyes. Her heel became lodged in the broken ridge between brow and nose, and she reached down quickly, un-afraid, to free herself. It was only when she saw his naked grin that she gave a little yelp of surprise.

He had been a tall man. From feet to neck covered a long space. His head lay beside him. When she pushed back the leaves and layers of earth and debris Myop saw that he'd had large white teeth, all of them cracked or broken, long fingers, and very big bones. All his clothes had rotted away except some threads of blue denim from his overalls. The buckles of the overalls had turned green.

Myop gazed around the spot with interest. Very near where she'd stepped into the head was a wild pink rose. As she picked it to add to her bundle she no-ticed a raised mound, a ring, around the rose's root. It was the rotted remains of a noose, a bit of shredding plowline, now blending benignly into the soil. Around an overhanging limb of a great spreading oak clung another piece. Frayed, rotted, bleached, and frazzled — barely there — but spinning restlessly in the breeze. Myop laid down her flowers.

And the summer was over.

WRITING IN THE MARGINS

Chapter 1 describes reading as an interactive process: The text speaks to the reader, and the reader responds to the text. Reading should never be a one-way "lecture," the reader merely taking in the work passively. You, as an active reader, can talk back to the work, agreeing with it, interrogating it, connecting with it, challenging it. One way of doing that is to read with a pencil in hand, jotting down your side of the conversation.

MARKING UP THE BOOK   If you own the book you are reading, you can jot notes in and around the text itself. If you don't own the book you're reading, have paper available, maybe as a bookmark, and use it for keeping notes.

- **Mark Up the Text**   Underline sentences or phrases that you really like or that strike you as especially important. But don't underline or highlight *everything* — then nothing stands out. Circle words you find particularly noteworthy.
- **Flag Key Sentences in the Text**   Put a star, a question mark, or an exclamation point, especially during a first reading, next to passages you might want to return to later to figure out a difficulty or to ponder in light of later events.
- **Talk Back to the Text**   Write comments in the margins as you move through a work: "What does this mean?" "Big point!" "Stupid idea!" "Tone shifts."
- **Jot Comments on the Text**   Enter into dialogue with the work — raising questions, disagreeing with what is said, noting things that remind you of other works by the same writer or by a different writer or that connect you to something important, jotting down possibilities for papers.
- **Write Notes about the Text**   Write out definitions and explanations of words and details you had to look up.

This form of "engaged reading," writing in a book, is an ancient and honored tradition. Reading the marginal notes (or *marginalia*) that people of all ages wrote in their books can be interesting and informative.

MAKING THE BOOK YOURS   Personally annotating a book is a way to make the book "yours." It now contains your ideas and inquiries as well as the author's. Try it in this book. You might find it interesting to revisit this book years from now, to reread stories, poems, and plays you liked especially, and to look again at the notes you wrote about them. You may wonder who that person was who wrote those notes; you might reacquaint yourself with who you were then; or you might discover how much you have added to your experience with literature since then.

To illustrate what we mean (not to prescribe how it should be done), here is some writing in the margins of "The Flowers" done by one of our students, Kortney DeVito (pictured at left). She later uses these notes to write a journal entry on the story (see p. 27), which she could use as the starting point for a paper.

Alice Walker

The Flowers

interesting name

It seemed to (Myop) as she skipped lightly from hen house to pigpen to smokehouse that the days had never been as beautiful as these. The air held a keenness that made her nose twitch. <u>The harvesting of the corn and cotton, peanuts and squash, made</u> *Great imagery!* <u>each day a golden surprise that caused excited little tremors to run up her jaws.</u>

Myop carried a short, knobby stick. She struck out at random at chickens she liked, and worked out the beat of a song on the fence around the pigpen. She felt light and good in the warm sun.
I can nearly She was ten, and nothing existed for her but her song, the stick
hear her sing. clutched in her dark brown hand, and the <u>tat-de-ta-ta-ta of accompaniment.</u>

Turning her back on the rusty boards of her family's sharecropper cabin, Myop walked along the fence till it ran into the
I adore this stream made by the spring. Around the spring, where the family
description. got drinking water, silver ferns and wildflowers grew. Along the shallow banks pigs rooted. <u>Myop watched the tiny white bubbles</u>
Does Myop <u>disrupt the thin black scale of soil and the water that silently rose</u>
see the <u>and slid away down the stream.</u>
stream the She had explored the woods behind the house many times.
same way as Often, in late autumn, her mother took her to gather nuts among
the narrator? the fallen leaves. Today she made (her own path,) bouncing this way and that way, vaguely keeping an eye out for snakes. She
growing older, found, in addition to various common but pretty ferns and leaves,
independent an armful of strange blue flowers with velvety ridges and a sweet-suds bush full of the brown, fragrant buds.

By twelve o'clock, her arms laden with sprigs of her find- 5 ings, she was a mile or more from home. She had often been as

far before, but the strangeness of the land made it not as pleasant as her usual haunts. It seemed gloomy in the little cove in
which she found herself. The air was damp, the silence close
and deep.

*Uh-oh, fore-
shadowing—
sounds creepy.*

Myop began to circle back to the house, back to the peacefulness of the morning. It was then she stepped smack into his eyes.
Her heel became lodged in the broken ridge between brow and
nose, and she reached down quickly, unafraid, to free herself. It
was only when she saw his naked grin that she gave a little yelp
of surprise.

Yuck!

He had been a tall man. From feet to neck covered a long space.
His head lay beside him. When she pushed back the leaves and layers of earth and debris Myop saw that he'd had large white teeth,
all of them cracked or broken, long fingers, and very big bones. All
his clothes had rotted away except some threads of blue denim
from his overalls. The buckles of the overalls had turned green.

Past tense!

*He had been
there for a
while.*

Myop gazed around the spot with interest. Very near where
she'd stepped into the head was a wild pink rose. As she picked
it to add to her bundle she noticed a raised mound, a ring, around
the rose's root. It was the rotted remains of a noose, a bit of
shredding plowline, now blending benignly into the soil. Around
an overhanging limb of a great spreading oak clung another piece.
Frayed, rotted, bleached, and frazzled—barely there—but spinning restlessly in the breeze. Myop laid down her flowers.

*Most 10-year-
olds would
have run away!*

Gross!!!

And the summer was over.

*For the dead man or her
childhood and innocence?*

JOURNAL WRITING

Journal writing enables you to go beyond the brief notes you jot in the
margins of a book to longer responses in which you develop your reactions,
insights, and ideas in greater detail. A journal is a good place to store information, quotations, related ideas, personal anecdotes, tangential insights—
anything that might be connected to what you are studying or that can be
extended from or associated with it.

JOURNALING FOR YOURSELF   Think of a journal as something you write
primarily for yourself—something halfway between a diary and a class notebook. It's not intimate or confessional as diaries often are, nor is it as

objective, remote, and impersonal as the notebook. A journal can contain personal reactions to literature and give practice in applying skills of analysis and interpretation. Not wholly private, it is not wholly public either. You can keep track of characters' names; notes on specific elements; lines you want to remember; unusual uses of form, diction, or sounds; things you were drawn to or put off by. You could regard your journal as an extension of the notes you take in class, reorganizing the notes, perhaps, and clarifying and expanding them (which can be a great help for reviewing later). A journal also provides a place where you can express ideas or emotions stimulated by what you read or by conversations with other people.

JOURNALING FOR CLASS   In some courses, journals are assigned as part of the writing. A benefit (or intention) of this is to illustrate the value of keeping a journal so that students may decide to continue them after the course is over. Instructors who include journals in their courses do so because journals allow for immediate, reactive, personal, and flexible responses to reading. Often the writing itself emerges from a deeply intimate connection of the self with a literary work. We tap into the part of ourselves that seeks to respond, record, and retain things that feel meaningful to us. Many storywriters and poets keep notebooks or journals of impressions, reactions, names, and lists of words and phrases, not just from what they read but from what they experience daily.

Writing a journal as a class assignment changes its nature to some degree, especially if the journal is handed in and read by the teacher. A personal journal is usually private; an assigned journal is not. Assigned journals differ also in that some of the writing in them may be directed; that is, the teacher could ask you to focus on a specific topic in a given entry ("Identify and record examples of nature imagery in 'The Flowers' and discuss its effect in the story"). Teachers do not necessarily want specific answers or interpretations. Rather, they are looking for clear evidence that you have read the works carefully; that you have made a thoughtful effort to engage with the material and to respond sensibly and sensitively to its emotional, aesthetic, and intellectual dimensions; and that your comments are clear and specific. They are looking for evidence of your mind at work as you read.

METHODS   A journal can be kept in a notebook; some people divide it into two columns or use the left- and right-hand pages differently — one side for notes or information, the other side for reactions, reflections, and observations. Or it can be kept in a computer file or series of files — that's helpful for cutting and pasting notes from your journal into a paper later and for doing searches of related items. If you put entries in separate files, develop a good labeling system so you can find entries easily. If you put multiple entries in the same file, be sure to include searchable identifying tags introducing entries.

GETTING STARTED   If a journal is assigned for your course or if keeping a journal simply appeals to you, buy a notebook or a memory stick for your computer and begin entering responses to literary works, to chapters of this book, or to discussions and assignments connected with this course. The suggestions for writing at the ends of chapters may stimulate some ideas; your teacher will bring up some; you will think of others yourself. Try to be specific and precise (include brief quotations and page numbers), and date each entry. Keeping journals can help you trace your own development and growth in taste, judgment, and attitudes. As mentioned before, it can be surprising, interesting, and helpful one day to look back at them.

Here is a page from Kortney's journal on "The Flowers." Notice the places where she carries over ideas from her marginal notations and elaborates on or changes them.

Alice Walker, "The Flowers"

Why the need for a story such as this? Why combine such a beautiful beginning with such a hauntingly grotesque ending? It conveys that throughout life there is death — not just of others but of ourselves. Not one person can stay in one season of his/her life forever. Each season of our lives teaches something special, but at the same time each season becomes obsolete and passes away.

Myop was going through the season known as childhood at the beginning of the story. She thought there was nothing but beauty in the world; each day was a "golden surprise." When she encountered the head of the decaying man, she began to realize the harsh reality that life can possess. It was almost as if she was Eve eating from the Tree of Knowledge in the Garden of Eden — she began to see the horrible truths life is capable of delivering — not just death, but the evil of death by lynching. At the end of the story Myop "laid down her flowers." A question is: where and for whom? Some may say it was to the man whose life was cut short. I believe Myop laid the flowers down for her childhood — the innocence she once possessed was now dead to her.

> ## ➤ TIPS for Effective Journal Writing
>
> ➤ **Choose the right format**   Decide what format (such as notebook, note cards, or computer files) will be most effective, most readily available to you, and most convenient — that is, one that you will actually use and keep up.
>
> *(continued)*

> ➤ **Don't put it off** Jot notes and reactions directly after reading, while your thoughts are fresh. Later, add your further reflections to what you wrote first.

> ➤ **Be honest** Express your genuine responses and opinions, not what you think a teacher wants you to say or think. Jot down quotations or page references that support your responses and opinions.

> ➤ **Make quotations apparent** Including quotations helps you remember favorite passages and key points and saves you from needing to go back to the work to find them. Be careful to make clear what is quoted and what is summarized or paraphrased (you don't want a paraphrase to appear as if it's a direct quote or vice versa).

> ➤ **Include page references** Check to be sure you include titles and page numbers so you can find the passages you wrote about or quoted. This too can save you valuable time later.

DISCUSSING LITERATURE

Talking to someone is another way of responding to literature. We do that with most things that interest us. After a good concert or game or movie, we want to talk about it with somebody — to compare notes, share enthusiasms, relive favorite moments, ask questions about things we found puzzling or confusing. The same is true about literature. Most people who enjoy reading like to talk about books. Sometimes they form reading groups: Members get together to spend an evening discussing works they've read. Literature classes often try to replicate that situation by having classes small enough to be conducted mainly by discussion or by breaking large lecture classes into discussion groups.

PREPARING To participate effectively in a discussion requires preparation. That's true for discussing other things as well. It's more fun to talk about baseball or movies with someone who watches closely, knows some background, and thinks before speaking. For a discussion group or class to work, it is essential that all members do the reading before the group or class meets. For a literature class, that means having the work in your mind, fresh and at the forefront — not as a vague memory of which the class will remind you. This requires reading works more than once before class.

Being prepared for discussion also requires thinking about the reading. The kind of active reading described in Chapter 1 and the marginal annotations illustrated in the first part of this chapter are good preparation. Writing down questions you might raise in class or points you might make also is good preparation, especially for those who are reserved and don't find it easy to join in. Even if you feel hesitant, are usually quiet, or lack confidence, try to add to the conversation by reading from your notations. It's the conjoining of a democracy of ideas and perspectives — each of them equal, all of them needed to form a whole — that makes a discussion interesting and valuable. Each member should feel welcome to take part.

PARTICIPATING   Engaging in a discussion does not require thoroughly thought-out statements or authoritative positions, but it does require honesty, alertness, a questioning attitude, and a willingness to stick one's neck out at least a little way. You can play a valuable role by sharing your enthusiasm for something, asking someone to elaborate on what she or he said, adding evidence for an idea someone else proposed, agreeing with someone, disagreeing, and so forth. Attentive, respectful listening, showing obvious interest in what is being said, or nodding your head in agreement are all valuable to a group. On the other hand, talking too often or too long or too assertively dampens others' enthusiasm and sense of community. Quality, not quantity, is important — along with genuineness, thoughtfulness, and timeliness.

TAKING NOTES   Some students are confused about how to take notes during a discussion class. It seems easier to take notes on a lecture — things usually proceed in an orderly way, the professor does all the talking, and what she or he says is surely accurate and worth writing down. In a discussion, it's hard to tell whose ideas are "right" and therefore what to write down. It is important, however, that you take notes to have a record of the vital topics and ideas discussed. Here's a suggestion: Organize your notes for the discussion by writing down the *questions* taken up in class. Remembering the questions raised is often as important as the answers given. Then, jot down interesting ideas, with the names of the people who offered them. Having the names attached helps you remember the point and helps you evaluate it later.

USING DISCUSSION BOARDS   In some classes, discussion is carried out partially or entirely by means of Web-based discussion boards. For people who express themselves better through a keyboard than through speaking, online discussions offer real advantages: You may hear insights from them that they never would offer in class. Online discussions also enable everyone to participate, something the size of a class might make impossible in the classroom. The principles of online participation are the same as in class: Ask questions, answer questions other people have posted, write comments expressing what you would have said about the works and authors in class. But there's a difference: Tone is difficult to control online, so you may hurt or offend others without intending to; and since you don't see the other person's face, you may not be as careful about what you say online.

Here are some guidelines for participating in online discussions.

- **Be attentive** Just as you should listen carefully to what others say in a class discussion, you should read carefully what others have written on a topic before you post your comments. The host usually retains the right to change the subject.
- **Be articulate** The rules of grammar, punctuation, and spelling still apply to Web posts. If your writing is sloppy, what you say won't be taken as seriously, even if it deserves to be.
- **Be courteous** Think before you post. Don't flame people. Be polite and reasonable. Never write anything obscene or libelous.
- **Be careful** Remember that anything published on the Web with your name can follow you for the rest of your life, especially if the discussion board has open access to anyone surfing the Net. Once the Send button is pressed, your comment is public knowledge, now and possibly forever.

Getting the most from a discussion and growing as a reader requires follow-up as well as advance preparation. After class, reread the works discussed in class as well as your class notes. Usually you will find much more in them than you did before class, and the approaches and methods used in class will be imprinted much more deeply in your memory.

➤ TIPS for Participating in Class Discussions

➤ **Prepare** Read the assignment more than once, attentively, and after you finish, reflect on it; plant the work in your memory, so you can look up at your classmates, not down at the text, except to cite a specific passage.

➤ **Write out** Write out in advance questions you can ask in class and some things you can point out about the work that might be overlooked.

➤ **Speak up** If you tend to be reluctant about participating, push yourself to speak up early in the class session: Be ready to ask a question or offer a reaction to the assigned reading, and do it before someone else says what you planned to. Talk to your instructor about what you're comfortable with and what makes you uncomfortable.

➤ **Don't dominate** Just as some people hesitate to talk in class, others at times talk more than is useful. Try to notice if you're talking too much, lots more than anyone else. Give other people a chance to participate, and even try to draw others into the conversation (perhaps by posing a question to other students).

> ➤ **Jot down** Take notes, writing down questions that are raised in discussion and in your own mind by what is said, along with brief phrases that will remind you of the most helpful comments made about them.

WRITING ESSAY EXAMINATION ANSWERS

Teachers often include essay questions on examinations to see how well students can think through a problem. The question and the answer become a sort of conversation between you and your teacher. Think of it as an opportunity for talking to your teacher one-on-one, of having your teacher's undivided attention for what you want to get across. The object is not just to find out *what* you know but also what you can *do with* what you know — synthesize it, apply it, see it in relation to other things, and respond to its challenges. Here are a few tips for writing essay answers.

Read the Question Carefully

Read the question several times and make sure you understand what it asks you to do. It is crucial to understand what the question is focusing on. Look for two things: a *subject* (the work, or character, or kind of images, or whatever it asks you to write about), and an *approach* (what it asks you to *do with* that subject, such as explain, compare, contrast, compare and contrast, or discuss).

Explain [APPROACH] what the final sentence [SUBJECT] of "The Flowers" indicates about the long-term effect of this experience on Myop [SUBJECT].

Compare and contrast [APPROACH] Myop's experience in "The Flowers" with that of the speaker as a young boy in Countee Cullen's "Incident" [SUBJECT].

If you need clarification of the subject or approach, ask your teacher for it rather than risk going at the essay incorrectly. If it's an open-book exam (one in which you are allowed to use your book in class), double-check about whether and how you may use notes or the marginalia you've jotted in your book.

Organize Your Thoughts

After reading the question, you probably will want to plunge right in since time is limited and you feel under pressure. But most students use their time more effectively if they pause briefly to plan and organize before beginning to write. Reflect on how the approach relates to the material (why was that approach selected for exploring this subject?), and think about what details you need to support what you want to say about the subject. Your answer should be more than just a list of comparisons and contrasts; the list should add up to something, make a point. Jot that point down as your "thesis" and make sure that you state it clearly in your answer — at the beginning, the end, or both. Sketch an outline of points that will clarify what you mean and will support and illustrate its validity.

Start Writing

The most efficient way to get moving is to state your central point in the first sentence of the answer. As you do, repeat words from the question to indicate that you are answering it directly, meeting it head-on. Keep your outline in mind but don't stick to it slavishly. An exciting part of writing is that in the process of thinking and searching, you make discoveries and get insights and ideas you didn't expect when you began. These often take off in new directions and may even be opposite to what you originally intended to say. When you're writing a paper, you can revise it to incorporate such discoveries in a unified way. But there's no time to revise essay exam answers. So, do you ignore the new insight and stick to the outline, or include it? We think it's better to include it, but you should explain that you're changing directions ("That's the way it looked to me at first, but as I examine the work more closely I see something different in it"). Don't leave the teacher thinking you don't realize that what you are saying now doesn't fit with the way you started.

Divide Your Answer into Paragraphs

Start a new paragraph when you move to a new subpoint. This makes the answer clearer and easier for your teacher to read and follow. And whatever you do, don't write so fast that your handwriting becomes illegible — the best ideas in the world are useless if your teacher can't read them.

Proofread Your Answer

Try to leave yourself a couple of minutes to read through your answer. Be sure you have offered support (explanations, details, quotations) for each subpoint. Check spelling and grammar.

The best way to learn how to write better essay answers is to look at examples of ineffective and effective ones. The second of these answers (the effective one) is by Annie Otto. In the first one, we rewrote Annie's answer to make it less effective.

LESS EFFECTIVE EXAMPLE   (30 minutes) Explain the difference in effect if Alice Walker's story had been titled "The Corpse" instead of "The Flowers."

Titles have a large influence on a reader. When one reads a title, one expects to read about things that relate to it. When I first saw "The Flowers" I thought of feelings and ideas. I imagined sunshine, fields, joy, beauty. As I started reading Alice Walker's short story, I got everything I expected.

The opening is too broad — not closely related to the topic.

If Alice Walker's story had been titled "The Corpse," I would not have been so surprised when Myop ran into the corpse, but as it was, I was shocked. When Myop first started picking the flowers, I expected her to skip back to her family's cabin to put them in a jar for display. I had no idea that they would be used for mourning a man's death.

Doesn't respond directly to the topic.

Myop is ten years old. She feels the sun shining warm rays down to her and she has her very own song to sing. She feels as though she needs to go for a walk and pick wild flowers. Walker includes specific pictures of sunshine, fields, joy, beauty, and a peaceful scene. Then Myop steps into the rotten corpse of a man who was hanged long ago. Whatever my expectations were for Myop, they were not for her to push the debris around to uncover the face of the corpse. Nor did I think that she would "gaze around the spot with interest." Why? Why would a little girl be interested in that?

Not outlined as clearly as it should be.

The cove that Myop found the corpse in gave me a cold feeling, an uncomfortable feeling. When Myop picked that wild pink rose that grew in the center of the rotted noose and added it to her bundle of flowers to lay down by the remains, she paid her respects to the man that used to be. That day she lost her childish innocence.

Includes specific details, but they're not connected to "effect."

The title of a piece of literature prepares readers for specific images. When the story twists so rapidly on us, it is quite unexpected. "The Flowers" ended entirely opposite of what I anticipated.

Never actually addresses the assigned topic.

MORE EFFECTIVE EXAMPLE   (30 minutes) Explain the difference in effect if Alice Walker's story had been titled "The Corpse" instead of "The Flowers."

The main difference in effect when "The Corpse" is substituted for "The Flowers" in Walker's story is that it wipes out the surprising twist built into the plot construction, and lessens the sense of horror the reader experiences.

Clear statement of central point in the opening sentence; repeats words from the topic.

Focuses well on "effect."

The title "The Flowers" puts an initial expectation into the reader's mind. Walker tells us of a little girl, Myop, skipping around her yard and enjoying the warm sun's rays. She goes for a walk to pick wild flowers. There is so much life in the story and the descriptions pull the reader into the scene. Walker includes specific pictures of sunshine, fields, joy, beauty, and harmony as seen through the eyes of a child.

Clear, logical outline throughout.

As I continued to read, I noticed words like "haunts" and "gloomy." I wondered why the author had added some darkness to the story. Myop wanted to turn back to the "peacefulness of the morning," which to me, meant that there was a whisper of unrest.

Good example of "effect."

Then there came a scream of surprise, shock and horror. That scream was not from the ten-year-old, Myop. It was from me, the twenty-year-old reader. Myop had stepped into the rotten corpse of a man who was hanged long ago. The shock effect was huge, in-

Good use of specific supporting details.

tensified by the contrast between the beauty of nature (the flowers) and the ugliness of a decayed body. I suppose that I tend to react extremely when I get startled as I did when reading this story. I expected that Myop would react similarly and run home screaming, not that she would "gaze around the spot with interest." Why? Why would a little girl be interested in that?

The realization of a person's death is a difficult thing for a child to handle, and death by lynching is an action full of hate. When Myop picked that wild pink rose that grew in the center of the rotted noose and added it to her bundle of flowers to lay down by the remains, she paid her respects to the man that used to be. That day she lost her childish innocence.

Clear contrast to actual title; wraps up discussion nicely.

If the story had been titled "The Corpse," I would have expected a corpse to appear and would not have been so surprised at what Myop found. As it was, I was shocked, and that shock intensified the horror I felt not only at Myop's finding a corpse, but also at the horrible way the man had met his end.

WRITING SHORT PAPERS

Think of writing papers on literature as an opportunity rather than as an obligation. Like essay exam answers, papers give you a chance to communicate directly with your teacher, to have your teacher's undivided attention for what you want to get across. They also give you the opportunity to think through a topic carefully, develop an idea or position about it, and express it for others to hear. Because papers on stories, poems, and plays handle topics and supporting material differently, specific suggestions for writing papers on each genre, and sample papers for each genre, are given at the end of Parts 2, 3, and 4. In this chapter we offer suggestions that apply to literature papers of all kinds.

Getting Started

Before getting into the writing process, we should pause to touch on that sticky difficulty, getting started. It's not uncommon for someone to spend as much time trying to get going as doing the actual writing. The key to getting started is to *start*. Don't wait to be "in the right mood." Start writing, and more often than not you will find yourself getting caught up in your subject. Also, don't start by spending hours trying to come up with a wonderful introduction. The first paragraph you write is likely to be discarded anyhow.

CENTRAL IDEA To get going, you might read the work again so its words fill your mind. Do some more underlining and annotating as you read. Then, make yourself put words on paper or on your computer screen. Try starting with a bald, direct statement of an idea you can explore: "This paper will explain the point of view in 'The Flowers' and show how the powerful final sentence depends for its effect on the point of view." Such a

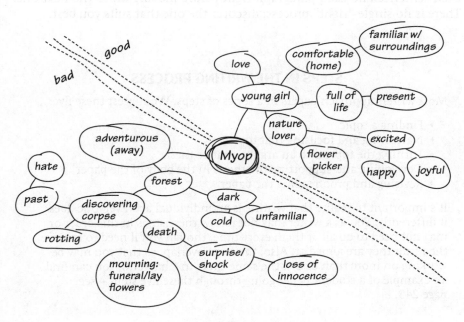

Annie Otto's clustering for "The Flowers"

sentence makes it clear to you what you need to do. When you get to the end of the paper, you can sharpen the thesis, in style and in the point it makes, and then develop an introduction that leads into it. That's right — do the introduction last. You will know better what will lead a reader into your paper after you've written the paper. In some cases, the last paragraph you write, the one you planned as the conclusion, becomes a good introduction.

FREEWRITING AND CLUSTERING   If ideas don't start coming at first, try *freewriting* — writing anything that comes to mind about the topic for five minutes, in any order, without stopping, editing, or changing anything. Or try *clustering*: Write down your main point and circle it. Then write points related to the topic in a ring around the main point, circle them, and use lines to connect them to the first circle. For each circle in the ring, write any ideas, examples, facts, and details you think of and use lines to connect them to the points with which they are associated. On page 35 you can see some clustering that Annie Otto did to pull together her thinking about "The Flowers." For some writers, clustering is useful in grasping relationships among the various parts of a topic and clarifying what materials are available or needed for developing subtopics.

FIND WHAT'S RIGHT FOR YOU   Some people find that it works best to write a first draft rapidly, getting their ideas down without worrying about neatness, grammar, or spelling. Others need to work more slowly, getting each sentence and each paragraph right before moving on to the next one. There is no single "right" process; discover the one that suits you best.

STEPS IN THE WRITING PROCESS

Most writers approach papers in a series of steps. We suggest these five:

- Finding a topic
- Narrowing and focusing that topic
- Turning the topic into an argumentative thesis
- Developing and supporting the thesis in the body of the paper
- Revising and proofreading the paper

It's important to realize that writing is an individual act: Everyone does it differently. You as a writer may not follow these steps in this order or may not need to do all of them every time, though you'll need to achieve the result they are aimed at. Also, the steps overlap, so that you may be working on more than one at the same time. In Chapter 8, you can find an example of a student paper going through these five steps — see page 243.

Finding a Topic

Before choosing a topic for your paper, be sure you are clear about what is expected of you. Double-check the assignment and clear up any uncertainties about the expected length, form, subject matter, approach, format, and deadline.

TEACHER'S CHOICE   Your teacher may give you a topic or a list of topics to choose from. You may feel that this limits your options, but it can also save you from the sometimes difficult and time-consuming task of coming up with a workable and interesting subject yourself. If you are given a topic, read the assignment carefully several times to make sure you understand the terms being used and what idea the topic is getting at. And keep in mind that although you are being given a topic, you still need to find a thesis that develops a central idea about the topic (see p. 39).

YOUR CHOICE   If you can choose your own topic, you have more freedom but also more work to do. Your marginal jottings and journal entries often are good places to start. Look through them for works that engaged you — ones that intrigued you, or puzzled you, or opened up new perceptions, insights, or ideas. Topics that struggle with a problem, suggest ambiguous resolutions, or explore a conflict often work well. And, of course, you should check the topics suggested at the end of the elements chapters and in the chapters on writing about fiction, poetry, and drama in this book. One of those might turn out to be right for you.

GETTING INTO THE WORK   If you are given or choose an unfamiliar work to write about, use marginal writing and a journal entry to help you get into it. Look for an unusual technique or approach in the work, the most important or most intriguing issue in it, or a question or difficulty you struggled with while you read. If you write about something that you struggled with or that intrigued you, you are likely to interest your readers in it as well. Look for connections, patterns, focuses, questions, or problems. Begin asking *why*: Why is the speaker's tone this way? Why did the character make that decision? Why does the work end this way? Why was that word used to describe this character? Consider alternatives: Ask how the work's effect would change if it had used a different speaker or different metaphors, been arranged in a different order, or been written in third person instead of first.

Narrowing the Topic

The process we just described generates ideas, which could lead you to an interesting subject area to work with. But it's important to remember that a key aspect of planning a paper involves narrowing and focusing that broad subject area to a clearly defined topic that you can explore in detail within the assigned length. Too large a topic for the length ("Gender and Sexuality in the Novels of Alice Walker" for a five-page paper) will prove ineffective; it will skim rather than cover. Too limited a topic ("Lynching in Alice Walker's 'The Flowers'") can leave you without enough to say to fill the needed pages.

A DISPUTABLE ISSUE   The topic also needs to focus on a disputable issue. Literary papers are *argumentative* papers in the sense of developing and presenting a reasoned argument in support of a position about which someone could disagree (for example, "The effectiveness of Walker's 'The Flowers' depends mostly on its use of archetypal motifs, particularly of a journey and the seasons"). Your tasks are to state your central idea in the first paragraph and then to present a series of paragraphs that explain the idea further and support it with reasons, explanations, and illustrations.

If you don't focus on a disputable issue, you may end up with an *illustrative* paper instead of an argumentative one ("Alice Walker's 'The Flowers' employs two archetypal motifs, that of a journey and that of the seasons"). Illustrative papers start with statements of fact (or summaries) in the first paragraph. Readers may learn from them, but there's nothing to disagree with (except whether the statements reflect the story accurately). The rest of an illustrative paper continues with statements of fact that expand and illustrate further the statements made in the first paragraph. But they do not argue for a central idea or try to convince readers of the writer's point of view.

A LIMITED FOCUS   In narrowing your topic to an argumentative issue, it's helpful to focus on questions. Phrase your topic initially as a question: "Could the detail Walker uses to describe the route Myop takes and the distance she travels that day, and the many references to the seasons, especially in the last line, be a key to the story?" The paper then provides your answer. (Later you will need to convert the question into a statement; your final thesis should not be phrased as a question.) Think of controversies in the text, things about which different readers will have different views. But be sure the controversy isn't too broad to handle in the space allotted. You may need to concentrate on one aspect of the issue or make just one point instead of covering everything about it. Limiting the topic in this way enables you to go into depth and achieve some fresh insights about a small slice of the topic. Attempting to touch on everything at a surface level makes both the paper and you come across as shallow or superficial. Or perhaps the complete point you want to make in a paper involves two or three steps or aspects, which together would take too long to develop. You might summarize all of the steps in the introduction or second paragraph and then say that, because of space limitations, you are dealing thoroughly with only one of the steps.

Framing an Argumentative Thesis

Once you've narrowed the topic, you need to sharpen what you want to say about that topic. Readers can read a poem or story for themselves. They can follow the outline and pick out images. But what they can't know in any other way are *your* explanations, interpretations, observations, perceptions, and connections. That's what you need to get across, in as clear, inviting, and accessible a way as possible. The central point you want to make should be stated in a thesis, a proposition put forward for consideration and placed, usually, at or near the end of the first paragraph.

TOPIC VERSUS THESIS   It's important to notice the difference between a topic and a thesis. A *topic* just names a subject area: "Point of view in 'The Flowers.'" It merely states a fact. A *thesis* adds a *comment* about the subject and turns it into something disputable: "The third-person, limited omniscient point of view is crucial to the effectiveness of the ending of 'The Flowers.'" A thesis states an idea that readers could disagree with or reject. Your job is to convince them that your point is worth accepting.

WORKING THESIS   As you think about your topic and what to say about it, you might start by framing a working thesis, a statement of the main argument you think you will make in the paper. The student who wrote the thesis sentence in the previous paragraph might have started with "'The Flowers' would have been very different if told from Myop's point of view" as a working thesis. The working thesis often changes or develops as you write — that's natural. But beginning with a tentative argument, even one you know is not your final version, helps to organize the rest of the paper.

When you finish the first draft of your paper, reexamine the working thesis. Ask yourself if the arguments developed in the paper match the central point expressed in the thesis. If they don't, revise the thesis (if you're satisfied with the arguments) or revise the paragraphs (if you want to stay with the original thesis).

Developing and Supporting the Thesis as an Effective Argument

Developing an argumentative paper begins with analysis of the thesis to determine what parts of it need to be explained and supported. A thesis such as "The third-person, limited omniscient point of view is crucial to the effectiveness of the ending of 'The Flowers'" implies a series of steps that will develop the argument. You will need to demonstrate that "The Flowers" is presented from a third-person, limited omniscient point of view; you will need to argue that this point of view is appropriate and crucial to the effectiveness of the story; and you will need to show that point of view is particularly important in setting up the story's conclusion. Here you have a potential outline for the body of the paper, a three-part or three-paragraph development. Analyzing the thesis carefully often yields an outline for the paper as well as an understanding of its central argument.

EXPLANATIONS AND EXAMPLES   Having determined those steps, you need to develop and support each point in two ways: (1) by your explanations and (2) by details and quotations from the story. The two need to go together. Details and quotations by themselves do not prove anything. Your explanations are needed to indicate what is important about them and to tie them in to the whole fabric you are weaving in the paper. Likewise, explanations without details and quotations are not specific enough and do not anchor themselves to the work. The key to a successful paper lies in its development and support of its ideas: explaining ideas so readers understand them readily and supporting ideas with details and quotations so readers have confidence that the points are well grounded and worth considering.

TOPIC SENTENCES   The way you start the paragraphs in the body of an argumentative paper is very important. Just as the thesis of your paper must state an idea, not just a fact, so should the first sentence of each paragraph. The opening sentence of a paragraph in an argumentative paper is a mini-thesis: It states the idea developed in that paragraph. If a paragraph starts with a statement of fact rather than with a statement of idea, the rest of the paragraph likely consists of summary and more factual statements, neither of which explores an idea or develops an argument. Many writers begin paragraphs with a short topic sentence stating the idea succinctly, followed by a sentence explaining the idea more fully, before they go on to support and illustrate it.

OUTLINE   It is often helpful to have an outline—a plan, an advance sketch of the argumentative steps the paper will take the reader through. Some students write out a detailed, formal outline, one with roman numerals, letters, and arabic numerals as headings. Others jot down a list of subtopics. Still others have a plan clear in their heads and don't write it down. People work in different ways, so find what works best for you. For some, thinking ahead before beginning to write is essential for the essay to have a focus and direction from the start. Others begin by brainstorming or freewriting. For them, it's the writing that gets them thinking. If you have found an outlining system useful in other courses, you might also use it here.

Revising and Proofreading

Once you finish a draft of the paper, the next steps are to revise and then proofread it. Notice that these are separate steps. Revising doesn't mean correcting spelling and grammar errors: That's proofreading, the final step. Revising comes first. The word *revision* derives from the Latin words for *look* and *again*: Revising means examining closely what you've written, thinking through it again, and trying to find ways to improve its content, organization, and expression.

LOOKING AGAIN   Look again at the order of the paragraphs: Are they in the most effective order? Do they build from one to the next? Would it be more effective to rearrange them? Pay attention to transitions between paragraphs: Are the connections clear and easy to follow? Examine the way ideas are explained and developed: Have you said enough to make your points convincing? Have you supplied enough details and examples to show that your points are well grounded in the work? Listen to the sentences: Is there variety in their length and structure? Do they read easily, with graceful, appealing rhythms? (Reading the paper aloud is a helpful way to test its style.)

GAINING SOME DISTANCE   It's hard to get a fresh look right after you finish writing. You are usually still too close to it to come up with different ways of explaining, arranging, or expressing. Revision often works best if you can lay your paper aside for a day or two or even more before thinking about changes. It also may help to have someone else read the paper, to check if ideas and organization are clear and adequately supported. You may have done this in a composition class; it often helps in a literature class, too. But choose this person wisely. Some friends worry about offending you. Give your reader clear direction about the kind of feedback you need.

REVISING   For most people, revision is crucial to effective writing: Making your paper the best possible usually requires several drafts. You may be able to write one draft and get a C or even a B, but the writing simply won't be as good as it would be if you revised, and you won't learn as much about writing. Granted, you may not always have time to revise an essay several times, but you should always do at least one revision, and try to allow time for more. An old cliché says that good writing requires perspiration, not inspiration. That's trite, yes, but most of the time it's true.

SELECTING A TITLE   Your paper also needs a title. Make sure you create a *title* (indicating the subject of or an idea about the paper — for instance, "Point of View in Alice Walker's 'The Flowers'"), not a heading (as, for example, "Point of View"). Don't use the title of the work as the label for your paper: "The Flowers" is Walker's title; it can't be yours. Your own title at the top of the paper should not be put in quotation marks (see the sample paper on p. 247).

CHECKING FOR ERRORS   After revising your paper, proofread and edit it carefully to check for errors in spelling and grammar, for inconsistencies, and for any awkward expressions. If you do your paper on a computer, use its programs to check spelling and grammar. There's no excuse for simple typos when spending a few minutes on spell-checking would catch them.

A computer check, of course, doesn't free you from the need to read closely as well. The computer can tell you that it doesn't recognize *thier* and ask if you intended to write *their;* but it won't notice if you wrote *their* when you should have used *there*. Again, distance (coming back after a couple of days) can be helpful because you may have become so familiar with your essay that it is hard to see what should be different. Some writers proofread by starting at the end and reading backwards as a way of looking at the words instead of getting caught up in the meaning. Again, having another person read your essay is sometimes useful — if she or he is a good speller and an attentive reader.

Even if you revise and proofread initially on a computer screen, we recommend at least one revision (and the final proofreading and editing) be done from a printed copy. It is helpful to see the sentences and paragraphs the way they will look on paper in the finished product.

MAKING LITERARY PAPERS EFFECTIVE

In addition to the five central steps in the writing process, here are five suggested guidelines for making papers effective:

- Adapt to your audience
- Use the literary present
- Incorporate quotations gracefully
- Bring in outside sources judiciously, if needed
- Format properly

Don't begin thinking about these guidelines only *after* the five steps in the writing process. They ought to be in your mind as you are conceptualizing the paper and developing its arguments.

Adapting to Your Audience

WRITE FOR READERS   All writers need to be aware of the audience they are addressing. Readers differ in age, reading ability, levels of understanding, background, interest in the subject, and so on. An effective writer takes those differences into account in planning and developing what she or he writes. A paper for a literature course should include a larger audience than your teacher alone. In practice, only your teacher may read it, but ideally other people would read it too. And that is how your teacher will read your paper, as if she or he is part of this larger audience. In some classes, students read each other's papers to learn from each other, to help each other, and to create a sense that they are writing for an audience larger than one.

WHAT TO ASSUME   When you write a paper for a literature course, address the same group you talk to in class. Visualize your fellow students as well as your teacher as readers. These are smart, thoughtful people who have begun to think about the work and are curious to know more about it. Assume that your audience has read the stories, poems, or plays you are writing about. Thus you don't need to retell or summarize the work. That's important. Take for granted that your audience knows the plot or subject matter, but assume that readers could benefit from help in understanding the work more fully or in seeing all the implications you can see. Think of your paper as part of the continuing conversation described at the beginning of this chapter, helping interested readers by talking clearly about things they would like to think more about.

Using the "Literary Present"

USE PRESENT-TENSE VERBS   When describing, discussing, or introducing specific passages or events from works of literature, use the present tense, even if the work was written in ancient times and even if the work itself uses the past tense. This is referred to as the *literary present* — that is, action within a literary work continues to happen even if the telling about it looks back at it from a later point. Thus, if you are writing about Myop's character in Alice Walker's "The Flowers" (p. 21), the story says "She *was* ten, and nothing *existed* for her but her song," but you should say, "Myop *is* a ten-year-old whose happy songs *demonstrate* the innocent, carefree life she *leads* before encountering the skeleton." It may seem confusing at times or occasionally to defy logic, but always use present tense when writing about characters and events from literary works. Use past tense, however, to relate historical fact, as, for example, "Alice Walker first *published* 'The Flowers' in 1973."

MAKE VERBS CONSISTENT   Also, always use present tense when introducing quotes. Instead of writing, "The narrator in 'The Flowers' *noted* that 'Myop carried a short, knobby stick' as she *walked* through the barnyard," write, "The narrator in 'The Flowers' *points* out that 'Myop carried a short, knobby stick' as she *walks* through the barnyard." In some cases changing the tense of the verbs in a quotation to match those in the rest of your sentence (using square brackets to indicate the alternation) will make it read more smoothly: "The narrator in 'The Flowers' *points* out that 'Myop [*carries*] a short, knobby stick' as she *walks* through the barnyard." Better still, in a case like this one, you might decide to quote only the nouns, not the verb — if it's the nouns that you want to emphasize here: "The narrator in 'The Flowers' *tells* us that Myop *carries* 'a short, knobby stick' as she *walks* through the barnyard."

Handling Quotations

A literary paper almost always includes at least some quotations from the work or works being discussed. Quotations connect your explanations and interpretations directly to the work(s) and show that they are firmly based. Be careful that the phrases or sentences you quote convey what they mean in their context. The way words are selected for quotation must never distort the way they are used in the original text.

DON'T OVERDO IT   How often you should quote requires good judgment based on specific situations. If you find your paragraphs using an alternating pattern — quotation, explanatory sentence, quotation, explanatory sentence — you're probably overdoing quotations. Keep most quotations brief. Pick out the most telling phrases and weave them into your sentence structures rather than quoting long, stand-alone blocks of text. Remember, a reader goes to your paper to learn your approach, your explanations, and your ideas. The work can be read elsewhere, but your ideas can't be.

LEAD INTO QUOTATIONS SMOOTHLY   To ensure the smooth incorporation of quotes into your writing, introduce them by indicating who you are quoting or where the quote comes from. Don't just insert a quotation after the end of your sentence:

> The crucial detail for Myop's growing up is discovering that the man whose skeleton she finds had been lynched. "It was the rotted remains of a noose."

Instead, lead into the quotation and incorporate it into your sentence:

> The crucial detail for Myop's growing up was discovering that the man whose skeleton she finds had been lynched. The narrator tells us that the ring Myop finds around a rose's root "was the rotted remains of a noose."

As a rule, avoid beginning a sentence with a quotation: Begin sentences with your own words. Doing so helps ensure that the reader understands how the quotation supports your argument.

Also, avoid referring to a quotation as one in your writing. Phrases such as "the following quotation shows" are awkward and not an informative introduction to the quoted material.

MAKE QUOTATIONS FIT GRAMMATICALLY   Beyond indicating who you are quoting or where a quotation comes from, also make sure that (1) the quote fits into your sentence grammatically — not "Esperanza's key realization occurs when *she* 'knew *I* had to have a house. A real house,'" but "Esperanza's key insight occurs when she realizes she 'had to have a house. A real house'" — and (2) the reader can easily understand all references within the quotation (pronouns, especially) — not "The narrator says '*she* struck out at random at chickens she liked,'" but "The narrator says *Myop* 'struck out at random at chickens she liked.'"

AVOID CONCLUDING WITH A QUOTATION   Avoid ending paragraphs with quotations: Literally, you should have the last word. When a paragraph ends in a quotation, it may suggest to the reader that you are relying too heavily on your cited source to make your case *for* you. Quotations should not *make* your primary points in an essay; instead, they should *support* or *illustrate* claims that you have already made in your own words. At the very least, close the paragraph by reiterating what is said in the quotation. Even if you are relying heavily on sources, have the final say in a paragraph yourself.

IDENTIFY QUOTATIONS PROPERLY   You need to make clear where any quoted lines or phrases can be found. For papers on literature, MLA (Modern Language Association) style is generally used for citations. (For a summary of MLA guidelines, see pp. 1496–1509.) If you're writing on one poem, story, or play from this book, it should be acceptable to put line or page numbers in parentheses at the end of the quotation. (See the sample papers on pp. 248, 687, 1020, and 1512.) Note that the parenthesis goes outside the quotation marks (it is not a part of the quotation), and a period or comma, if needed, goes after the parenthesis (so it doesn't float unattached between sentences), except for block quotations. If you are discussing a work that's not in this book, include a footnote or bibliographic entry to inform the reader where the work can be found.

Passages from a story or play usually are cited by page numbers (except William Shakespeare's plays, which typically are cited by act, scene, and line numbers). But passages in poetry usually are referred to by line numbers, with page numbers given to indicate the location of the whole poem. If you include several works in the paper, you may need a shortened title as well as a line or page number in the parenthetical references to make the source clear. (For a more complete discussion of proper citation style, see Chapter 29.)

Formatting the Paper

TYPING AND PRINTING   Papers should be typed (word processed) double-spaced, with one-inch margins all around, and printed in a 12-point font on good quality 8½" × 11" white paper. Use a paper clip to hold pages together, unless your instructor asks that they be stapled. Use Tab to indent the first line of each paragraph one-half inch.

INDENTIFICATION AND TITLE   MLA style does not require a title page. Instead, at the top of the first page, against the left margin, on separate lines, place your name, your instructor's name, the course title, and the date. Then, center your title. (See page 247 for a sample first page.) If your instructor requires a title page, ask for guidelines on formatting it.

PAGINATION   Place the page number (in arabic numerals) preceded by your last name in the upper right-hand corner of each page, one-half inch below the top edge (see the sample paper on pp. 1512–16).

WRITING RESEARCH PAPERS

Using Outside Sources

Should you do library or Internet research on the work or author? That depends on what your teacher wants for a particular assignment (not, by the way, on length — short papers as well as long can involve research; long as well as short can be done without using outside sources). For some subjects, teachers may encourage you to see what you come up with on your own and may therefore ask you to refrain from reading interpretations by others. In other situations, teachers may have different objectives in mind and require such reading. When the assignment doesn't specify whether you may or should read critics, it's best to ask about it. If the answer is yes, it changes the nature of the paper to some extent; you should go to Part 5 (pp. 1453–1516) for help on doing literary research and writing research papers. However, we will include a couple of preliminary points about research here.

READ THE WORK FIRST   Some students think it's a good idea to read studies of a literary work before reading the work itself, to help them know what to look for. However, doing this robs you of discovering your own reactions uninfluenced by others. Before reading any critical studies of a literary work, read the work itself at least twice and form your own ideas about it, and raise your own questions — questions that continue to puzzle you and about which you feel a need for some hints from others. If you read about a work before reading the work itself, your understanding is shaped by someone else's perceptions rather than by your own experience.

GIVE CREDIT WHERE IT'S DUE   A key issue in all academic work involves giving proper credit for anything taken from another source. If you do consult any books other than your course textbook and dictionaries, you must enclose within quotation marks words quoted directly from the source. You must also supply the location in which you found the passage. Even if you do not quote directly from an outside source, you must acknowledge in notes or a bibliography any sources you have consulted. (MLA style guidelines for citing sources can be found on pp. 1496–1509.) In fact, you should acknowledge *any* external assistance, like discussing the assigned poem with your former high school teacher or another student who is especially knowledgeable about the topic. Failure to do so, and thus presenting the ideas or work of others — intentionally or unintentionally — as if they were your own, is *plagiarism*, a very serious academic offense. (See pp. 1494–96.)

Ten Guidelines for Handling Quotations

The section above provides guidance for incorporating quotations into your writing smoothly and coherently. Handling quotations well also requires proper punctuation and formatting. Read the guidelines below carefully and return to them as you work on your first couple of papers. Try to fix them in your mind firmly so you get them right automatically, without needing to think about them.

1. In some cases it is most effective to introduce a quotation formally, with your sentence coming to a full stop, followed by a colon.

> The most powerful statement in "Superman and Me" comes when the speaker explains why he read everything he could get his hands on: "I was trying to save my life."

2. Often, however, you can use a less formal construction, blending the quotation smoothly and effectively into your sentence.

> Sherman Alexie describes his father as "an avid reader of westerns" and of many other types of popular writing.

Commas are needed with the quotation marks only if the same words would require commas even if they were not a quotation.

3. Place quotation marks outside commas and periods (." or ,") but inside semicolons and colons ("; or ":). U.S. punctuation conventions never put the period or comma outside quotation marks.

4. Always use double quotation marks ("), except for a quotation within a quotation, which is indicated by single marks ('). However, if an entire quotation consists of dialogue by one speaker and is so introduced, it is not necessary to use the extra single quotation marks.

5. Treat longer passages (more than three lines of poetry or more than four lines of a prose passage) as block quotations, set off from the rest of the text by starting a new line and indenting the passage one inch — sometimes more for poetry — from the left margin. (See the sample papers on pp. 248 and 687.) Block quotations should be double spaced. Treating a passage as a block quotation is the same as putting quotation marks around it. Use quotation marks around an indented passage only if it has quotation marks around it in the source. If, however, the entire quotation consists of dialogue by one speaker and is so introduced, quotation marks are not necessary.

6. The end punctuation of a quotation may be (often should be) dropped and replaced by punctuation appropriate to your sentence; thus, a period ending a quotation may be replaced with a comma if your sentence goes on (thus you should never have a .", or ,". in a paper) or it can be omitted if a parenthetical citation follows: " **(source)**. Note that the period or comma is placed *after* a parenthetical citation (as at the end of the previous

sentence), not before it. The parenthesis should not be left unattached between two sentences.

7. In all other respects, quotations must be precisely accurate, including original spelling, capitalization, and punctuation. The initial letter of a line of poetry must be capitalized if it is capitalized in the original, even if the quotation is not indented. Always double-check quotations to be sure you have everything down correctly. If you need to insert a word into a quotation (if, for example, the part you are quoting needs a verb) or if you need to change a pronoun to a noun for clarity, place the inserted word not in parentheses but in square brackets: **[ ]**.

8. In some cases, you will want to omit words or punctuation marks to shorten quotations and to make them fit your sentence construction more effectively. Ellipsis points (three periods with a space before and after each: . . .) must be used whenever you omit something from *within* a quotation. Ellipsis points are not used at the beginning or end of a quotation if what is quoted coincides with the beginning or end of the original sentence or if it is obvious that what is quoted is not a complete sentence in the original. If the passage being quoted has ellipsis points in it, square brackets should be placed around your ellipsis to clarify that yours have been added: [. . .].

9. Four dots (a period plus the three ellipsis dots) are needed if you omit (1) the last part of a quoted sentence; (2) the first part of the following sentence; (3) a whole sentence or more; or (4) a whole paragraph or more. If a sentence ends with a question mark or an exclamation point in the original, that punctuation is used instead of the fourth period. What precedes and follows four dots should be grammatically complete sentences, either as quoted or as connected to the text surrounding it.

10. You need not (even should not) start a new paragraph after a quotation. With rare exception, follow each quotation with an explanation of the point being illustrated, tying it into the rest of the paper.

Guidelines for Handling Titles

1. Titles of books or long poems (the names of any long work published independently, with its name on the title page) and the names of plays, movies, and TV shows are underlined or italicized (underlining is a mark editors use to tell typesetters "this should be italicized"). The *MLA Handbook* recommends that underlining be used for student papers. Titles of books, TV shows, movies, or plays are not placed within quotation marks.

2. Titles of short works (poems, short stories, essays), ones that name a part of a book rather than the whole, are placed within quotation marks:

"The Flowers" is found in Alice Walker's book In Love & Trouble: Stories of Black Women.

TIPS for Writing a Successful Short Paper

Characteristics of a successful short paper:

> **Significant topic** A successful paper grows out of asking a probing question; it focuses on a specific problem and explores it in some depth.

> **Appropriate approach** It develops an *idea*, or an *angle*, about the problem, selecting an insightful approach to it.

> **Solid preparation** It shows evidence of careful, perceptive reading and clear critical thinking.

> **Strong development** It avoids broad generalizations and plot summary but provides precise, pointed explanations and uses details and brief quotations as support and expansion of the idea or interpretation.

> **Good writing** It is unified and organized coherently and is written in clear, polished prose with correct grammar, spelling, and punctuation.

Quotation marks are also used around chapter titles in a book or titles of individual episodes of a TV series:

The final episode of <u>Baywatch</u> in 2001 was entitled "Rescue Me."

The authoritative guidebook to matters of style and punctuation is *The Chicago Manual of Style*, 15th edition (Chicago: University of Chicago Press, 2003). Or you can consult the *MLA Handbook for Writers of Research Papers*, 6th edition (New York: Modern Language Association of America, 2003), or a college writing handbook such as Andrea A. Lunsford's *The St. Martin's Handbook*, 6th edition (Boston: Bedford/St. Martin's, 2008).

WRITING PAPERS IN OTHER FORMATS

Papers can be developed in ways other than the standard explanation, analysis, or compare and contrast formats. Sometimes developing a paper as a letter — writing to a friend, to the author, to the narrator in the work, as an answer to a question from a former English teacher, or as a reply to a hostile critic — can stimulate ideas. The letter form supplies a context and an audience you can write to. If you're looking for a way to present both sides of an issue strongly or want to be more imaginative, try developing a paper as a dialogue or a debate in which you imagine the characters participating, expressing their voices as well as developing the ideas and positions you want to convey.

Alternative forms require the same preliminary steps as a conventional paper. You should review the ideas discussed in the preceding section on "Writing Short Papers": selecting and narrowing a topic, identifying a central point and framing a thesis, outlining the subpoints you will cover, and perhaps using freewriting or clustering to generate ideas. For a mock letter, the outline will be much like that for a conventional essay; for a dialogue or debate, an outline will likely become a plan for what the characters are like, what their opinions are, and what they will talk about. Realize, too, that adapting to your audience is just as important when using an alternative form.

If you have not worked before with an unconventional format, keep in mind that doing this type of paper can take just as much, or even more, time and effort as a traditional form. But this time and work may yield outstanding results if using such a format enables you to get into the material at a more thoughtful level or to present your ideas more clearly or in a more attractive and inviting manner. Before using such a format, however, check with your teacher to make sure it is acceptable. Sometimes practice in using a conventional approach is part of what a teacher wants students to gain in a particular assignment.

COMPOSING IN OTHER ART FORMS

Not all communication relies on words. Some people are better at conversing nonverbally. One way of responding to literature as an art form is through another art form: through dance, a visual art, dramatics, film, or music.

There is a long tradition of original artistic responses. Choreographing a dance, creating music or artwork, making a film, or designing a set are ways of responding to a literary work. Many poets, from all ages, have written responses or replies to other poems, as, for example, the way Sir Walter Ralegh responded to Christopher Marlowe's "The Passionate Shepherd to His Love" (1599; see p. 822) by writing "The Nymph's Reply to the Shepherd" (1600; see p. 843). Many artists have created paintings or sculptures to depict characters or scenes from literature: from classical myths and legends, Dante's *Divine Comedy*, and John Milton's *Paradise Lost*, to mention only a few famous examples. The poet and artist William Blake did watercolor paintings and engravings of scenes from the works of many authors, including Virgil, Dante, Chaucer, and Milton; see, for example, the National Gallery of Victoria Web site's page on Blake, at ngv.vic.gov.au/blake/sections.html. For an example of how many artists do such illustrations, in a variety of styles, go to the *Paradise Lost Illustrated* Web site at pitt.edu/~ulin/Paradise/.

Countless poets have written poems in response to paintings or sculpture. Two are included in this book: W. H. Auden's "Musée des Beaux Arts" (1940), written as a response to a painting by Pieter Breughel the Elder,

Landscape with the Fall of Icarus (see p. 737); and Cathy Song's "Girl Powdering Her Neck" (1983), responding to a painting by Kitagawa Utamaro (see p. 855). Composers have often responded to literature through music. You may have heard the music Felix Mendelssohn wrote in response to Shakespeare's *A Midsummer Night's Dream* (heard it perhaps without realizing it in the 1999 film version of the play directed by Michael Hoffman) or seen the musical *Cats* by Andrew Lloyd Webber, which was inspired by T. S. Eliot's *Old Possum's Book of Practical Cats* (1939). If you have talent in another art, you might try responding to a story, poem, or play through your art — if that is acceptable to your teacher. Be sure to ask first.

An alternative to creating original art as a nonverbal response to literature is connecting existing works into what seem to you meaningful pairs or groups. You might be reminded of some music that seems a perfect complement to the first several paragraphs of "The Flowers," for example, or of a photograph or painting that evokes the mood of a poem you come across later in this book. Or you might gather a variety of pictures into a collage that provides a visual representation of the content and complexity of a story, poem, or play. As you do, you may find that a nonverbal response can be expressive in ways and to degrees that a written response is unable to be.

Approaching FICTION

Overleaf: The author James Baldwin in a relaxed portrait of a writer at work, photographed in his New York apartment in 1963. Not yet forty years old when this photograph was taken, Baldwin was already established as a major literary presence with the publication of his semiautographical first novel, Go Tell It on the Mountain *(1953), the essay collection* Notes of a Native Son *(1955), and his second novel,* Giovanni's Room *(1956), among other works. Baldwin's work explores what it meant to be an African American in the twentieth century, and he was a lifelong and fierce defender of racial justice and equality. The responsibility of the writer, Baldwin told an interviewer, "is to excavate the experience of the people who produced him." (See p. 1520 for a short biography.)*

Copyright © Bettmann/Corbis.

Literary works do not endure as objects but as presences. When you read anything worth remembering, you liberate a human voice; you release into the world again a companion spirit.

Louise Glück

Reading Fiction

CHAPTER 3

Responding to the Real World of Stories

What are your own stories? What books and movies do you love? What television shows do you follow? The stories that you own, that you love, may incline toward realism, or science fiction, or romance—each of us is different, with individual tastes. But almost all of us are drawn toward stories of some sort. What is it about stories that draws you into their world, that makes you not want to put the book down or miss the show, or want to rent the DVD a third and fourth time? We know that what we are reading or watching is not factual: These are made-up characters doing imaginary things.

Yet we become deeply invested in their lives: We begin to think about the characters as if they are real, and we care about what happens to them. Why do we begin to sympathize deeply with a grieving mother or delight in the achievements of a college sophomore, neither of whom actually exists? The answer to these questions must start with the impressive power of imagination—with the way our imaginations respond to the imaginative creations of excellent writers. In the chapters to come, we look closely at such imaginative creations and at the way we use our own imaginations to enter, enjoy, and appreciate them.

WHAT IS FICTION?

STORY   Before we start that closer look, we need to clarify what it is we're talking about. *Story*, considered broadly, is any account of a related series of events in sequential order, usually chronological order (the order in which they happened). Stories did not start out as something to be read: Long before people read stories or watched them being acted out in plays, they listened to stories being told or sung. From the time ancient peoples gathered around fires in the evening for warmth and safety, they told stories to each other. And although we no longer need campfires for warmth and protection, the storytelling tradition of "stories around the campfire" continues wherever people gather for companionship. Generation after generation of children around the world have said to parents, "Tell me a story."

Story, in this broad sense, includes events that are true or made up — an account of the invading of Normandy in World War II, the planning for the prom during your junior year in high school, or the landing of three-headed cyborgs in an Iowa cornfield. The account can be narrated (told by a storyteller) or dramatized (acted out in drama). It can be told in prose or verse. Chapters 4 to 7 deal only with narrated stories, only with stories in prose, and only with stories that are fictional.

FICTION   Fiction refers to narrated stories that are drawn from the imagination or are an imaginative reworking of actual experiences. Incidents and details in a work of fiction can originate in fact, history, or everyday life, but the characters and events as a whole are primarily invented, or altered, in the author's imagination. Imaginative fiction (like movies) varies widely in types, from fast-paced adventures that focus on action to stories that examine characters and ideas in depth; they can be told at great length (**novels** or **epics**) or more briefly (**novellas** or **short stories**).

SHORT STORIES   The works of fiction included in this book are **short stories, relatively brief fictional narratives in prose that often focus on the essential aspects of a character (instead of showing character development over time, the way a novel can) and on a single event or episode — often a life-changing circumstance. They are characterized by careful, deliberate craftsmanship (in handling of plot, characterization, and point of view).

The short stories included in this book explore the complexities of life and people; they lead us to interact imaginatively with significant human issues; they offer us an opportunity to expand our understanding of ourselves, others, and the multiple cultures we find ourselves living with and within. They are widely respected by other writers, scholars, and general readers for the way they handle the techniques of fiction (ones discussed in Chapters 4 to 7) and for their insights into people, their values, their experiences, and their cultures.

WHY READ FICTION?

ENTERING OTHER LIVES   What is the value of reading such stories? Most important, perhaps, is the way they can take us outside of ourselves and through our imaginations enable us to enter other lives, other selves, other places and cultures, other feelings and experiences. All of us live limited lives. We want to see more, expand our range of experiences, meet people whose lives are different from our own. That's why many people like to travel, and why many students want to go away to college. A story enables us, without leaving our chairs, to escape our boundaries and broaden our understanding and vision. Think again of Sherman Alexie (see p. 4) and what reading stories did to "save his life."

ENLARGEMENT OF BEING   Author and literary critic C. S. Lewis explained the appeal of story this way: "We seek an enlargement of our being. We want to be more than ourselves. . . . We want to see with other eyes, to imagine with other imaginations, to feel with other hearts, as well as with our own" (*An Experiment in Criticism* [Cambridge University Press, 1961], p. 137). Fiction can do that. A story can mirror our own world, take us to a world that is not part of our daily experience, or create a world entirely new to us. To read fiction is to enter a place where you both disappear and find yourself — a place where, when you put the book down and look up, you feel even more yourself than you did before reading.

THE TRUTH OF FICTION   You have likely heard someone say, "Fiction? I don't read fiction. I want to read what's true." Fiction is not fact. It may contain facts, but it is still fiction. A literary scholar and a historian who were on a panel together were asked the difference between the two disciplines. The historian spoke about how important it was to get the facts correct in his work. The literary scholar then replied, "Yes. You deal with facts. I deal with truth." What was the literary scholar implying? Not that the historian wasn't searching for the truth within the facts, but that fiction is the embodiment of truth, at times factual truth, but always — if it is a fine work of fiction — the kind of truth that exists within, around, or beyond fact. This is a different kind of truth, the kind of truth that needs story to contain it, the truth of what it is like to live the facts, the kind of truth that exists and comes to life through what the writer "makes up." It is the truth of Captain Ahab's obsession with a white whale, Jane Eyre's dreams, Sherman Alexie's Superman. We need this truth. We need our stories.

ACTIVE READING: Fiction

The more you read, and the more widely you read, the more confident you will become in your ability to follow a story and understand the characters in it. The purpose of Chapters 4 to 7 is to help you become a more skilled reader of fiction — more alert to the richness of a work of fiction, to the fascinating variety of good things it has to offer. Most of the things covered in those chapters, however, should not concern you the first time you read a short story or novel. Here are some suggestions for the first time you go through a story with an active imagination.

- *Give the work a fair chance.* Writers generally try to catch a reader's interest immediately, but some short stories and novels start slowly. Don't quit reading after a few paragraphs or pages. Give yourself enough time to get involved in the action and characters.

- *Keep going.* Even if some things aren't completely clear, later events probably will clarify them.

- *Watch for what's happening.* As in movies, some stories are filled with action and excitement. Others, often ones that deal with inner struggles, move more deliberately and with less external action.

- *Watch for who it is happening to.* Pay attention to the characters—their appearances, personalities, values, attitudes, struggles, weaknesses, strengths, and so forth.

- *Watch for "why"—why does what happens happen?* What happens that leads to the situations and actions? What causes the action? What motivates the characters?

REREADING: Fiction

Experiencing a story fully requires reading it more than once. The first time through, you primarily concentrate on what's going on. The second and third times through, you begin paying attention to other things—to easily overlooked details and nuances concerning plot and character, and to the way the piece is written, the subtlety of techniques the author used.

You probably already do this with movies and music you love. Good movies, ones you really like, you watch twice, or many times, and you listen to favorite CDs over and over. We enjoy experiencing again the things we liked at first, of course; but our follow-up experience is different, richer, because we notice what we didn't notice before. It's the same for reading. Once you get into it, you'll enjoy rereading books or stories for the same reasons you like watching films or listening to music again. Here are some suggestions for rereading.

- *Slow down.* Let yourself absorb the flavor and style; roll the sentences and rhythms around on your tongue; reread paragraphs that aren't fully clear or that you find especially well written and enjoyable; go back to earlier parts to check on details that tie in with later ones.

- *Pay attention to the title.* Often it's significant and revealing, though its significance may not be evident during the first reading. In such cases, as you reread, it's worth reflecting on possible ways the title links to the actions and characters.

- *Look up things that aren't familiar.* Check unfamiliar words in a dictionary. The context often clarifies new words, but in other cases it doesn't, and you can miss something. Do some research on people from history, other literature, or historical events mentioned in the story. Look at a map when real places are used.

- *Pay attention to the first sentence and the first paragraph, especially for short stories.* Authors often embed within them a lot of important indicators about tone, style, setting, and subject. For the same reasons, pay close attention to the last paragraph and last sentence.

- *Pay attention to things that do not seem needed.* What appears insignificant may actually be a subtlety. Reflecting on its part in the whole can open up a deeper understanding of the characters or events.

P lot grows out of character. . . . Characters should not, conversely, serve as pawns for some plot.

Anne Lamott

CHAPTER 4

Plot and Character
Watching What Happens, to Whom

Probably the first thing you notice as you read a story is what happens, to whom. Plot and characters: These are the foundation stones of fiction. As such, they're worth a closer look. We connect with those probably because they're so basic to life: We care about people (family, friends, the famous and influential) and about what goes on in their lives. In literature, we meet not with actual people and events but imaginative constructs; as readers of literature, beyond our fascination with what happens to whom, we should be interested in the way they are constructed and brought to life. This chapter focuses on the skills and techniques we should be alert to in the development of plots and characters in fiction.

READING FOR PLOT

STORY AND PLOT   The first thing to consider in reading fiction is plot. **Plot**, in a literary sense, is the way events are selected and arranged in narrative work to present them most effectively to the reader. Comparing *plot* with *story* can help clarify that. *Story*, as we used the word in Chapter 3, "Reading Fiction," is a straightforward account of everything that happens, in the order it happens. Story provides the materials (the events, the characters, the outcome) from which a plot is constructed.

PLOT AS STRUCTURE   As a story is converted to a plot, some things are left out (ones that aren't essential for the effect and emphasis desired), things are sometimes rearranged (the story may start in the middle or at the end instead of at the beginning), and causal connections between key events are brought out. The interest in plot is not just in what happens but in why it happens and in the implications or results of what happens: What does it all "mean"? What does it "say" to us? Another way to put it is that plot provides the **structure** of a story, that is, the arrangement of material in it, the ordering of its parts, the design used to draw out and convey its significance.

ENTRY POINTS   Pay attention to plot in the following short story about an unexpected encounter between a young man and a young woman on a street in Los Angeles. In addition to what's going on in it, consider what details the author includes, how they are arranged, and how they relate to each other and work together to convey a unified effect.

Dagoberto Gilb   b. 1950

Love in L.A.   [1993]

Jake slouched in a clot of near motionless traffic, in the peculiar gray of concrete, smog, and early morning beneath the overpass of the Hollywood Freeway on Alvarado Street. He didn't really mind because he knew how much worse it could be trying to make a left onto the onramp. He certainly didn't do that every day of his life, and he'd assure anyone who'd ask that he never would either. A steady occupation had its advantages and he couldn't deny thinking about that too. He needed an FM radio in something better than this '58 Buick he drove. It would have crushed velvet interior with electric controls for the L.A. summer, a nice warm heater and defroster for the winter drives at the beach, a cruise control for those longer trips, mellow speakers front and rear of course, windows that hum closed, snuffing out that nasty exterior noise of freeways. The fact was that he'd probably have to change his whole style. Exotic colognes, plush, dark nightclubs, maitais and daquiris, necklaced ladies in satin gowns, misty and sexy like in a tequila ad. Jake could imagine lots of possibilities when he let himself, but none that ended up with him pressed onto a stalled freeway.

Jake was thinking about this freedom of his so much that when he glimpsed its green light he just went ahead and stared bye bye to the steadily employed. When he turned his head the same direction his windshield faced, it was maybe one second too late. He pounced the brake pedal and steered the front wheels away from the tiny brakelights but the smack was unavoidable. Just one second sooner and it would only have been close. One second more and he'd be crawling up the Toyota's trunk. As it was, it seemed like only a harmless smack, much less solid than the one against his back bumper.

Jake considered driving past the Toyota but was afraid the traffic ahead would make it too difficult. As he pulled up against the curb a few carlengths ahead, it occurred to him that the traffic might have helped him get away too. He slammed the car door twice to make sure it was closed fully and to give himself another second more, then toured front and rear of his Buick for damage on or near the bumpers. Not an impressionable scratch even in the chrome. He perked up. Though the car's beauty was secondary to its ability to start and move, the body and paint were clean except for a few minor dings. This stood out as one of his few clearcut accomplishments over the years.

Before he spoke to the driver of the Toyota, whose looks he could see might present him with an added complication, he signaled to the driver of the car that hit him, still in his car and stopped behind the Toyota, and waved his hands and shook his head to let the man know there was no problem as far as he was concerned. The driver waved back and started his engine.

"It didn't even scratch my paint," Jake told her in that way of his. "So how 5 you doin? Any damage to the car? I'm kinda hoping so, just so it takes a little more time and we can talk some. Or else you can give me your phone number now and I won't have to lay my regular b.s. on you to get it later."

He took her smile as a good sign and relaxed. He inhaled her scent like it was clean air and straightened out his less than new but not unhip clothes.

"You've got Florida plates. You look like you must be Cuban."

"My parents are from Venezuela."

"My name's Jake." He held out his hand.

"Mariana." 10

They shook hands like she'd never done it before in her life.

"I really am sorry about hitting you like that." He sounded genuine. He fondled the wide dimple near the cracked taillight. "It's amazing how easy it is to put a dent in these new cars. They're so soft they might replace waterbeds soon." Jake was confused about how to proceed with this. So much seemed so unlikely, but there was always possibility. "So maybe we should go out to breakfast somewhere and talk it over."

"I don't eat breakfast."

"Some coffee then."

"Thanks, but I really can't." 15

"You're not married, are you? Not that that would matter that much to me. I'm an openminded kinda guy."

She was smiling. "I have to get to work."

"That sounds boring."

"I better get your driver's license," she said.

Jake nodded, disappointed. "One little problem," he said. "I didn't bring it. I 20 just forgot it this morning. I'm a musician," he exaggerated greatly, "and, well, I dunno, I left my wallet in the pants I was wearing last night. If you have some paper and a pen I'll give you my address and all that."

He followed her to the glove compartment side of her car.

"What if we don't report it to the insurance companies? I'll just get it fixed for you."

"I don't think my dad would let me do that."

"Your dad? It's not your car?"

"He bought it for me. And I live at home."   25

"Right." She was slipping away from him. He went back around to the back of her new Toyota and looked over the damage again. There was the trunk lid, the bumper, a rear panel, a taillight.

"You do have insurance?" she asked, suspicious, as she came around the back of the car.

"Oh yeah," he lied.

"I guess you better write the name of that down too."

He made up a last name and address and wrote down the name of an insur- 30 ance company an old girlfriend once belonged to. He considered giving a real phone number but went against that idea and made one up.

"I act too," he lied to enhance the effect more. "Been in a couple of movies." She smiled like a fan.

"So how about your phone number?" He was rebounding maturely. She gave it to him.

"Mariana, you are beautiful," he said in his most sincere voice.   35

"Call me," she said timidly.

Jake beamed. "We'll see you, Mariana," he said holding out his hand. Her hand felt so warm and soft he felt like he'd been kissed.

Back in his car he took a moment or two to feel both proud and sad about his performance. Then he watched the rear view mirror as Mariana pulled up behind him. She was writing down the license plate numbers on his Buick, ones that he'd taken off a junk because the ones that belonged to his had expired so long ago. He turned the ignition key and revved the big engine and clicked into drive. His sense of freedom swelled as he drove into the now moving street traffic, though he couldn't stop the thought about that FM stereo radio and crushed velvet interior and the new car smell that would even make it better.

APPROACHING THE READING

1. Try sketching out the story, what happens in the order it happens. Then think about what is left out, and what added or emphasized, in plotting the story. Is what Jake was thinking about important to the basic story? If not, why is it included as part of the plot? Are the exact words Jake and Mariana use necessary to the story? Why are they included in the plot?

2. Reflect on the organization of the plot: Why does it start where it does? Why does it linger on certain sections and go into great detail? Why does it stop where it does and not follow through to the outcomes of what happens here?

3. What significance or implications seem to grow out of the decisions about what to include, what not to include, and how to organize? What's the "point" of it all?

Aristotle, in one of the earliest works on imaginative writing, said a plot must have a beginning, a middle, and an end. Those terms have been used as the basis for the way readers talk about plot ever since. *Beginning*, *middle*, and *end*, and other terminology such as *suspense* and *conflict*, grew out of analyses of drama, which focus on action and suspense. These terms were transferred successfully to the novel, also centered on action, and to the early short story. However, they are less applicable to some modern fiction, especially short stories, which focus often on inner struggles without much physical action or external conflict. In the following pages, we use the traditional terms but also note their limitations.

Beginning

WHAT IS INCLUDED   A plot usually starts at a point that relates directly and significantly to the series of events being recorded: "Love in L.A." starts with Jake in his car caught in a traffic jam. Earlier events in his day are not included: what time he got up, whether he had breakfast, where he is going. These details may be important in Jake's larger life, but because they are not relevant to his encounter with Mariana, they do not concern readers. For fiction writers, decisions about what to leave out are as important as decisions about what to include.

HOW IT IS ARRANGED   Equally important is the arrangement of the events that follow the opening. "Love in L.A." is told in *chronological order*, the order in which the events occur. But that's not always the case for works of fiction. Sometimes the first events in the related sequence, though necessary to the story, are not the best place to start. The most interesting or exciting or important events occur later. Readers become more quickly and deeply involved when the plot starts at an engaging point well into the story and fills in the background events later as needed.

STARTING IN THE MIDDLE   In fact, for thousands of years this has been a common way for storytellers to proceed — the Latin phrase **in medias res** (meaning "into the middle of things") is used to describe it. The background events are usually filled in through a **flashback** (in which events prior to the beginning of a story or play are presented as an inserted narrative or a scene, perhaps with a character remembering earlier times) or through **exposition** (a nondramatized explanation, often a speech by a character or the narrator, explaining things that occurred before the initial action of a story or play). "Love in L.A." could have begun in the middle, with Jake's car bumping Mariana's, and then gone back to explain what Jake was daydreaming about instead of paying attention to his driving; and if Gilb had wanted to emphasize the accident instead of Jake's character, that probably would have been a better way to start.

Middle – Conflict

Of course a story must have a middle — something has to come between the beginning and the end. But what goes into a middle? Can't a writer just lay out what happens the way it happens? Of course, but often that is not the best way to hold a reader's interest. Remember, plot involves the arrangement of the action whereby the story builds on the beginning and leads to the ending — that requires particular techniques for increasing intensity and holding the reader's interest.

At the heart of that pattern of action usually is some kind of **conflict**, some struggle or confrontation between opposing characters or a character and opposing forces. Usually, at least one side of the struggle involves the main character.

Identifying a conflict is a helpful way to "get into" a story, when you want to look at the story's complexity more closely and discuss why the conflict is one worth thinking about. The range of possible opposing forces is large, but ordinarily they fall into three broad categories.

PHYSICAL CONFLICT   One basic kind of conflict occurs as a physical struggle or confrontation between a character or group of characters and another character or group of characters: the showdown between a sheriff's posse and a gang of outlaws in an old Western, for example, or a fistfight between two rivals at a high school prom (or the punch with which Derek knocks out Terence in "Bad Neighbors," p. 164). Physical conflict can also involve humans struggling against nature: a group of sailors, perhaps led by a courageous captain, attempting to survive a fierce storm. "Love in L.A." has no physical conflict, but it's easy to imagine how the events could have turned into a road-rage story with physical conflict at its center.

SOCIAL CONFLICT   A further type of conflict involves differences regarding personal or societal relationships or values. This is a common motif in modern fiction. Examples could include a teenager challenging her or his parents, the differing gender outlooks a man and a woman might bring to the same situation, or an activist confronting a social injustice. Part of the conflict in "Love in L.A." is the way Jake's lifestyle runs counter to social norms: Society expects drivers to have insurance and accept responsibility for any damage they cause to other people's property; it requires people to carry their driver's licenses and have accurate license plates on their cars. The story gives you as reader the options of identifying with Jake and enjoying the way he flouts social expectations, or dismissing him as irresponsible, or perhaps feeling caught between accepting Jake's laid-back charm and rejecting what he does as illegal and immoral.

INTERNAL OR PSYCHOLOGICAL CONFLICT   Another variety of conflict deals with struggles within a character, as she or he wrestles with competing moral claims or a difficult decision. This has always been a central issue for literature. Numerous stories in this book show characters engaged in such inner struggles: Jig in "Hills Like White Elephants" (p. 136), the title character in "Young Goodman Brown" (p. 374), Farogh in "Departures" (p. 484), and Sammy in "A & P" (p. 529).

Inner conflicts often appear at crucial moments in a person's life: facing the moment of death like the grandmother does in "A Good Man Is Hard to Find" (p. 455); an identity crisis when an event forces a person to a new or deeper sense of self-knowledge or self-awareness, often a moment of maturation like Myop's in "The Flowers" (p. 21); a belief crisis when something causes a person to reexamine the foundation of what she or he puts faith or trust in, as in "Young Goodman Brown" (p. 374); a values crisis when something forces a person to decide how to make a moral or ethical decision, such as Sammy's in "A&P" (p. 529), or sometimes to decide whether to adhere to standards she or he has held to — or should have adhered to — in the past.

Equally important is a lack of inner conflict: One of the most revealing things about Jake in "Love in L.A." is his lack of internal struggle, despite doing some things that would trouble most readers' consciences at least somewhat.

Middle – Structural Techniques

Having identified the key conflicts, you should go on to look at techniques and structures used in developing the middle part of a story. We will discuss five of them.

SUSPENSE   To hold readers' interest, the middle of a plot often creates some degree of **suspense**, some uncertainty and concern about how things will turn out, who did what, what the effects on the characters or events will be, or when disaster will fall or rescue will occur. The word *suspense* might be too strong for "Love in L.A." (as it is for much modern fiction), but we are curious, at least, to find out if Jake can get away with all that he's trying to.

FORESHADOWING   The beginning and middle of a story often contain **foreshadowings**, anticipations of things that will happen later. For example, when the mother in "Daughter of Invention" (p. 11) says " 'When I make a million, I'll buy you your very own typewriter.' (I'd been nagging my mother for one just like the one father had bought her to do his order forms at home)," it foreshadows the ending where her father gives her "a brand new electric typewriter . . . even better than the one I'd been begging to get like my mother's" (pp. 13, 19).

REPETITION   **Repetitions** are also often included to draw our attention to especially important aspects of the story. The repeated references to the mother's inventions in "Daughter of Invention," from the title on, set up the key invention later, when mother and daughter together invent a speech to replace the one the father tore up. Similarly, the repetition of "that FM stereo radio and crushed velvet interior" in "Love in L.A." (p. 61) signals what is most important in Jake's value system, and the repeated references to death in Flannery O'Connor's "A Good Man Is Hard to Find" (p. 455) foreshadow events at the end of the story.

CLIMAX   The middle of a plot holds its readers' attention by becoming more complex and more intense (sometimes referred to as **rising action** or **complication**), until it reaches a crisis of some sort, the **climax**, the thing the suspense builds toward. This terminology grew out of action-based plots, where the most intense moment is the peak of the physical conflict. The climax of a sci-fi action movie might come when, just before the gelatin-coated cyborg sends an earth-freezing probe into the center of the planet, the kung-fu master heroine shoots a laser into the monster's ultra-sensitive fifth eye and saves the world. In a story focusing on inner conflict, by contrast, the climax might be a moment of inner realization — the point at which the main character realizes that gambling is destroying his family and decides to go into rehab, which turns his life around.

Picking out a climax is not the same as understanding a work of fiction, nor is it a definite feature all readers identify in the same way. There can be differences of opinion about what a story's climax is or even about whether a given story has one. If "Love in L.A." has a climax, it might well come in the next-to-last paragraph when Jake seems not only to have avoided responsibility for the accident but also to have won Mariana's interest in him: "Her hand felt so warm and soft he felt like he'd been kissed" (p. 63).

EPIPHANY   One particular type of climax is called an **epiphany**, a moment when a character experiences a sudden moment of illumination or revelation, especially as the result of perceiving a commonplace object in a new way or through a new context. Esperanza in "The House on Mango Street" might be said to experience an epiphany when the nun points to her third-floor apartment and says "You live *there*?" (p. 99). Suddenly she realizes how other people regard her house, what the house says about her and her family, how much she needs to have "a real house" to improve her sense of self-worth and identity.

Middle – Gaps

A literary work can't (and shouldn't) include everything that happens during the series of events it is relating — reading or hearing everything would get pretty boring. But what things are omitted? Whatever is not significant to the action typically is left out. For example, if characters are ordinary people, they need to eat or get some sleep, but except where these activities contribute to the overall story, they are omitted. Since lots of unimportant things are left out, you usually can assume that anything that *is* included is significant. You can be confident that almost everything in the work is there for a reason—every detail, maybe even every word. Excellent authors are very careful and deliberate in selecting what to include, presenting only those things that contribute something to the overall effect of the story.

INEVITABLE GAPS   Because an author can't include everything, stories inevitably leave *gaps*, that is, places where things are omitted or not filled in. As active readers, we need to use our imaginations to fill any significant gaps, supplying information or explanations the story doesn't spell out. But some gaps are insignificant and appear only to avoid cluttering the story with irrelevant detail. For example, we aren't told the circumstances under which the family in "Daughter of Invention" (p. 11) left the Dominican Republic. Even though we may wonder about why or how they went, and though it could be significant, it is not important to what this story is focusing on.

INTENTIONAL GAPS   Authors often create gaps intentionally (sometimes withholding information in early parts of a story that will be supplied later) as a way of getting readers actively involved. Mystery and detective stories always create gaps (who did it? why?) as part of the structure. Part of the enjoyment of reading stories is reaching with our imaginations for what is omitted, seeking to supply missing details or connecting links, anticipating what may be ahead, and revising our earlier anticipations in light of what we find out later. In a milder way, as we read about the mother's ideas in "Daughter of Invention," we begin anticipating that this emphasis on inventions is leading to something. We begin wondering what, maybe trying to guess: Will she manage to come up with a crazily sane possibility that makes the family rich? In the end, we find that we are partly right. There is a last important invention, but inventing a speech is nothing that we could have predicted.

UNINTENTIONAL GAPS   In some cases gaps are unintentional (for example, not including women in a story, or relegating them to minor roles). But such gaps are significant nonetheless. What the author does *not* think about is part of her or his idea framework, as much as what she or he consciously does think about. Paying attention not just to what is there but also to what is not there requires alert, active involvement in a *process*. Reading this way is demanding, but the rewards are well worth the effort.

Ending

A SENSE OF WHOLENESS   A story must end, of course—it can't go on forever. But it also can't just stop. The difference between just stopping and an effective ending is that the latter gives a sense of wholeness and leaves you satisfied, or satisfyingly unsatisfied, as a reader or listener. One of the big differences between fiction and real life is that life carries on after reaching a "big event," while the series of events in a fictional plot reaches a terminal point, the conflicts around which it was shaped are resolved (or shown to be unresolvable), and the story ends.

DÉNOUEMENT   The French term **dénouement** is often used in discussing the ending of a story. It literally means "unknotting," the untying of the threads that are tangled and knotted, the solution of the mysteries, the explanation of the secrets and misunderstandings. An ending, in addition to unknotting tangles, often ties up the loose ends, leaving us with a sense of finality or a momentary stay against ordinary chaos. That doesn't mean that everything turns out happily — some stories have unresolved, unhappy endings. But it does mean that the questions and problems we have been involved with, if not solved or even resolved, at least are adequately accounted for. We know all that we need to know to comprehend and reflect on the story as a whole.

A FEELING OF FINALITY   The last paragraph of "Love in L.A," for example, has a feeling of finality — the lives of Jake and Mariana do not end, but nothing that follows is relevant to the story of their encounter under the Alvarado Street overpass (though an active reader will imagine Mariana's pained and disappointed reaction, and her father's furious reaction, when they find out that all the information Jake gave her was false — and that may form an important part of how we feel about Jake's actions). Jake and Mariana have a personal encounter that could have touched Jake and made a difference in his life, but the last sentence shows that it didn't. The end takes us back to the beginning and the daydreams he prefers over reality.

READING FOR CHARACTER

When you read a story, you may first be interested in the events of the plot. Important as the events are, however, they cannot be separated from the people involved in the events who carry out the actions. **Characters**, the created persons who appear or are referred to in narratives and dramas (and at times in poems), are in many cases the aspect that is of greatest appeal and interest in the work. Literature offers us the opportunity to learn about, and even imaginatively to enter, the lives of people we would otherwise never get close to, at least not close enough for us to understand their lives and situations to such a significant extent and to sympathize, even empathize, with them.

When we meet such people in literature, we want to know what they are like, what makes them tick, how they deal with the situations and relationships they encounter. **Characterization** refers to the methods and techniques an author uses to represent people and to enable us to know and relate to them. As we read a work of fiction, we understand characters more fully and accurately if we pay attention to the means by which we attain our knowledge, to the kind of techniques through which they are brought to life in the story.

Techniques of Characterization

Here are some of the most important means of characterization to pay attention to. They can appear individually or in a variety of combinations.

TELLING   In the most direct way of characterization, we are simply told what the characters are like, all at once as they are first introduced or bit by bit as they reappear in the story. That is the case for some aspects of Connie's character in "Where Are You Going, Where Have You Been?," especially aspects that would be difficult, or would take a lot of space, to demonstrate: "Everything about her had two sides to it, one for home and one for anywhere that was not home" (p. 82). Even the narrator's choice of words can be a way of telling something about a character: The use of *slouched* and *lied* in the opening sentence for example, gives us direct insight into Jake's character in "Love in L.A."

SHOWING   What a character is like can come out through the character's actions, which may be presented without interpretive comment, leaving the reader to conclude what a character is like from what she or he does. What Jake does in response to hitting Mariana's car shows the kind of person he is; words the narrator selects may suggest some reservations about Jake as a person, but the narrator does not explicitly evaluate his behavior. In many cases, showing is combined with telling, often with differing weights of emphasis. Only telling what a character is like is often less effective than showing what the character is like through her or his actions, or through a combination of telling and showing.

SAYING   What a character is like can be brought out by having other characters say things about her or him. It's important, however, to keep in mind that how we take what the characters say depends, of course, on how those characters relate to the main characters: What is said may need to be taken with a grain of salt because of a bias for or against the character. A great deal can also be revealed about a character by what she or he says — **dialogue** (conversation between characters) is an important characterization technique. Thus we gain valuable insights into Jake as a person when he says "You're not married, are you? Not that that would matter that much to me. I'm an openminded kinda guy" and "I left my wallet in the pants I was wearing last night" and "[I've] been in a couple of movies" (pp. 62, 63).

ENTERING A CHARACTER'S MIND   What a character is like can be revealed through her or his thoughts and feelings. The author takes us into a character's mind using techniques such as a partially or wholly omniscient narrator (the way the narrator shows us what goes on in Jake's mind through his daydreams, his thoughts, and things he observes), stream of consciousness, or interior monologue (see pp. 61–63).

NAMING   In some cases, the names an author gives to characters reveal aspects of what they are like. Henry Fielding, one of the first English novelists, names one of his characters Squire Allworthy to reveal how admirable he is in every respect. In other cases, Fielding uses an **allusion** (see p. 235) to the Bible in naming a character: Parson Abraham Adams, for example, is a man of great faith (like the biblical Abraham), but is also a person as innocent and trusting as the Adam of Genesis 2–3. In many cases, however, names are simply names, and yet they invariably somehow sound right (think of David Copperfield or Huckleberry Finn).

MOTIVATION   After you know what the characters are like, you will want to know why they do the things they do, why they make the kinds of decisions and choices they do. This important aspect of characterization is **motivation**, the reasons, explanations, or justifications behind a character's behavior. Motivation in fiction usually grows out of a sense of what a character deeply wants or desires, and how that leads the character to react in a specific situation.

CONSISTENCY   A great deal is revealed about characters also by the *way* they handle situations — especially difficult, problematic, or tragic situations or relationships. For characters to be plausible, they must be consistent in the way they deal with circumstances. If they respond to a situation one way at one time and differently at another, there should be clear reasons for the difference (their inconsistency must be understandable and believable).

Types of Characterization

Our understanding and appreciation of characters in a story are enhanced when we are alert to the varying degrees of a character's complexity and importance. Here are some of the ways those varying degrees are indicated.

ROUND/FLAT   The novelist E. M. Forster used the terms *flat* and *round* to illustrate differences in complexity. **Round characters** are complex and sometimes even challenging to understand. We are offered many sides and facets of their lives and personalities, leading us sometimes to need to reconcile what seem to be incompatible ideas or behaviors. Round characters often are **dynamic**, shown as changing and growing because of what happens to them. But they also can be **static**, not shown as changing, though they may be described in such rich detail that we have a clear sense of how they would, or will, change, even though we don't see it happening. We are shown enough about Connie in "Where Are You Going, Where Have You Been?" (p. 81) for her character to be rounded out; the story shows her changing, at least in the sense of having to confront a totally new area of experience.

Flat characters are generally developed less fully than round, or dynamic, characters. Usually they are static and are represented through only one or two main features or aspects. Unlike round characters, they often can be summed up in a sentence or two. If these one or two traits are developed in considerable detail, the characters may be very interesting and enjoyable to read about. But we can't come to know them as thoroughly and in as much depth as characters who are depicted with more complexity or developed more fully and shown to be changing and growing throughout the story. Jake and Mariana in "Love in L.A." are flat characters — a thoroughgoing cad and a rather gullible innocent. That's all they need to be and all that could be expected in such a short short story.

MAJOR/MINOR   Most major characters in a story or play are round characters, while minor characters are usually flat. Minor characters are at times **stock characters**, stereotypes easily recognized by readers or audiences from their frequent uses, such as the absent-minded professor, the evil stepmother, the nerdy computer geek, or the smart but quiet detective or police sergeant. Use of flat characters is not necessarily "bad writing." Some excellent fiction writers create central characters who are flat but are described in such rich detail that they come to life fully and in an enjoyable way. There isn't time in most short stories to develop more than one character in a rounded way, perhaps not even one. Even in a novel or play, the reader might find it too much to handle if every character were rounded out fully.

PROTAGONIST/ANTAGONIST   The terms *protagonist* and *antagonist* are often used to define relationships between characters. The **protagonist** is the central character in a work (the older term **hero** seems less useful because the central character doesn't have to be "heroic"). The **antagonist** is the character, force, or collected forces opposed to the protagonist that give rise to the central conflict of the work — the rival, opponent, or enemy of the protagonist (the older term *villain* works less well because the antagonist isn't always evil and isn't always a person). In the stories included in this chapter, Connie is the protagonist of "Where Are You Going, Where Have You Been?"; Arnold Friend is the antagonist. Henry is the protagonist of "The Red Convertible"; white society and the world outside the reservation are the antagonists.

www

Further explore plot and characters, including interactive exercises, with VirtuaLit Fiction at bedfordstmartins.com/approachinglit.

☑ **CHECKLIST on Reading for Plot and Character**

❑ Notice the structuring of plot:
  - the handling of beginning, middle, and ending
  - its use of action, background, development, climax, and conclusion
  - its use of gaps, flashbacks, suspense, foreshadowing, and repetition

❑ Look for conflicts — physical, social, internal — and use them as a way to get into the story and to explore its complexity.

❑ Be attentive to the methods of characterization: by noticing what we are told and shown, listening to what a character says and what other characters say about her or him, entering a character's mind, and considering the way she or he is named.

❑ Consider how fully characters are developed: whether they are round or flat, whether they change or stay pretty much the same.

FURTHER READING

Below are two stories for further reading, both about young persons encountering situations new to them that change their lives. As you read and then think back on them, apply to them what you have learned in this chapter about plot and character.

ENTRY POINTS   The first is a story about two brothers, Lyman and Henry, and a car that comes to epitomize their love for each other. It was written by Louise Erdrich, who grew up near the Turtle Mountain Reservation and is a member of the Turtle Mountain Band of Chippewa. Many of the place names in the story can be found on maps of North and South Dakota. Pay attention to its handling of plot — which details the author includes, how these details are arranged, and how they relate to each other and work together to convey a unified effect. Note the story's handling of characters — what they are like and how you come to know them.

Louise Erdrich   b. 1954

The Red Convertible   [1984]

I was the first one to drive a convertible on my reservation. And of course it was red, a red Olds. I owned that car along with my brother Henry Junior. We owned it together until his boots filled with water on a windy night and he bought out my share. Now Henry owns the whole car, and his younger brother Lyman (that's myself), Lyman walks everywhere he goes.

How did I earn enough money to buy my share in the first place? My one talent was I could always make money. I had a touch for it, unusual in a Chippewa. From the first I was different that way, and everyone recognized it. I was the only kid they let in the American Legion Hall to shine shoes, for example, and one Christmas I sold spiritual bouquets for the mission door to door. The nuns let me keep a percentage. Once I started, it seemed the more money I made the easier the money came. Everyone encouraged it. When I was fifteen I got a job washing dishes at the Joliet Café, and that was where my first big break happened.

It wasn't long before I was promoted to busing tables, and then the short-order cook quit and I was hired to take her place. No sooner than you know it I was managing the Joliet. The rest is history. I went on managing. I soon became part owner, and of course there was no stopping me then. It wasn't long before the whole thing was mine.

After I'd owned the Joliet for one year, it blew over in the worst tornado ever seen around here. The whole operation was smashed to bits. A total loss. The fryalator was up in a tree, the grill torn in half like it was paper. I was only sixteen. I had it all in my mother's name, and I lost it quick, but before I lost it I had every one of my relatives, and their relatives, to dinner, and I also bought that red Olds I mentioned, along with Henry.

The first time we saw it! I'll tell you when we first saw it. We had gotten a   5
ride up to Winnipeg, and both of us had money. Don't ask me why, because we never mentioned a car or anything, we just had all our money. Mine was cash, a big bankroll from the Joliet's insurance. Henry had two checks — a week's extra pay for being laid off, and his regular check from the Jewel Bearing Plant.

We were walking down Portage anyway, seeing the sights, when we saw it. There it was, parked, large as life. Really as *if* it was alive. I thought of the word *repose*, because the car wasn't simply stopped, parked, or whatever. That car reposed, calm and gleaming, a FOR SALE sign in its left front window. Then, before we had thought it over at all, the car belonged to us and our pockets were empty. We had just enough money for gas back home.

We went places in that car, me and Henry. We took off driving all one whole summer. We started off toward the Little Knife River and Mandaree in Fort Berthold and then we found ourselves down in Wakpala somehow, and then suddenly we were over in Montana on the Rocky Boy, and yet the summer was not even half over. Some people hang on to details when they travel, but we didn't let them bother us and just lived our everyday lives here to there.

I do remember this one place with willows. I remember I laid under those trees and it was comfortable. So comfortable. The branches bent down all around me like a tent or a stable. And quiet, it was quiet, even though there was a powwow close enough so I could see it going on. The air was not too still, not too windy either. When the dust rises up and hangs in the air around the dancers like that, I feel good. Henry was asleep with his arms thrown wide. Later on, he woke up and we started driving again. We were somewhere in Montana, or maybe on the Blood Reserve — it could have been anywhere. Anyway it was where we met the girl.

All her hair was in buns around her ears, that's the first thing I noticed about her. She was posed alongside the road with her arm out, so we stopped. That girl was short, so short her lumber shirt looked comical on her, like a nightgown. She had jeans on and fancy moccasins and she carried a little suitcase.

"Hop on in," says Henry. So she climbs in between us.   10

"We'll take you home," I says. "Where do you live?"

"Chicken," she says.

"Where the hell's that?" I ask her.

"Alaska."

"Okay," says Henry, and we drive.   15

We got up there and never wanted to leave. The sun doesn't truly set there in summer, and the night is more a soft dusk. You might doze off, sometimes, but before you know it you're up again, like an animal in nature. You never feel like you have to sleep hard or put away the world. And things would grow up there. One day just dirt or moss, the next day flowers and long grass. The girl's name was Susy. Her family really took to us. They fed us and put us up. We had our own tent to live in by their house, and the kids would be in and out of there all day and night. They couldn't get over me and Henry being brothers, we looked so different. We told them we knew we had the same mother, anyway.

One night Susy came in to visit us. We sat around in the tent talking of this and that. The season was changing. It was getting darker by that time, and the cold was even getting just a little mean. I told her it was time for us to go. She stood up on a chair.

"You never seen my hair," Susy said.

That was true. She was standing on a chair, but still, when she unclipped her buns the hair reached all the way to the ground. Our eyes opened. You couldn't tell how much hair she had when it was rolled up so neatly. Then my brother Henry did something funny. He went up to the chair and said, "Jump on my shoulders." So she did that, and her hair reached down past his waist, and he started twirling, this way and that, so her hair was flung out from side to side.

"I always wondered what it was like to have long pretty hair," Henry says.   20 Well we laughed. It was a funny sight, the way he did it. The next morning we got up and took leave of those people.

On to greener pastures, as they say. It was down through Spokane and across Idaho then Montana and very soon we were racing the weather right along under the Canadian border through Columbus, Des Lacs, and then we were in Bottineau County and soon home. We'd made most of the trip, that summer, without putting up the car hood at all. We got home just in time, it turned out, for the army to remember Henry had signed up to join it.

I don't wonder that the army was so glad to get my brother that they turned him into a Marine. He was built like a brick outhouse anyway. We liked to tease him that they really wanted him for his Indian nose. He had a nose big and sharp as a hatchet, like the nose on Red Tomahawk, the Indian who killed Sitting Bull, whose profile is on signs all along the North Dakota highways. Henry went off to training camp, came home once during Christmas, then the next thing you know we got an overseas letter from him. It was 1970, and he said he was stationed up in the northern hill country. Whereabouts I did not know. He wasn't such a hot letter writer, and only got off two before the enemy caught him. I could never keep it straight, which direction those good Vietnam soldiers were from.

I wrote him back several times, even though I didn't know if those letters would get through. I kept him informed all about the car. Most of the time I had it up on blocks in the yard or half taken apart, because that long trip did a hard job on it under the hood.

I always had good luck with numbers, and never worried about the draft myself. I never even had to think about what my number was.° But Henry was never lucky in the same way as me. It was at least three years before Henry came home. By then I guess the whole war was solved in the government's mind, but for him it would keep on going. In those years I'd put his car into almost perfect shape. I always thought of it as his car while he was gone, even though when he left he said, "Now it's yours," and threw me his key.

"Thanks for the extra key," I'd said. "I'll put it up in your drawer just in case   25
I need it." He laughed.

When he came home, though, Henry was very different, and I'll say this: the change was no good. You could hardly expect him to change for the better, I know. But he was quiet, so quiet, and never comfortable sitting still anywhere but always up and moving around. I thought back to times we'd sat still for whole afternoons, never moving a muscle, just shifting our weight along the ground, talking to whoever sat with us, watching things. He'd always had a joke, then, too, and now you couldn't get him to laugh, or when he did it was more the sound of a man choking, a sound that stopped up the throats of other people around him. They got to leaving him alone most of the time, and I didn't blame them. It was a fact: Henry was jumpy and mean.

I'd bought a color TV set for my mom and the rest of us while Henry was away. Money still came very easy. I was sorry I'd ever bought it though, because of Henry. I was also sorry I'd bought color, because with black-and-white the pictures seem older and farther away. But what are you going to do? He sat in

---

what my number was: A lottery system based on birthdays was used for the military draft from 1970 until 1973. Capsules containing the 365 days of the year were prepared and the days listed in the order drawn. Men like Henry, with birthdays drawn early (approximately the upper third), were certain to be called up for service, while those whose birthdays came in the bottom third (like Lyman) were likely not to be needed. In 1973, the draft ended and the United States converted to an all-volunteer military.

front of it, watching it, and that was the only time he was completely still. But it was the kind of stillness that you see in a rabbit when it freezes and before it will bolt. He was not easy. He sat in his chair gripping the armrests with all his might, as if the chair itself was moving at a high speed and if he let go at all he would rocket forward and maybe crash right through the set.

Once I was in the room watching TV with Henry and I heard his teeth click at something. I looked over, and he'd bitten through his lip. Blood was going down his chin. I tell you right then I wanted to smash that tube to pieces. I went over to it but Henry must have known what I was up to. He rushed from his chair and shoved me out of the way, against the wall. I told myself he didn't know what he was doing.

My mom came in, turned the set off real quiet, and told us she had made something for supper. So we went and sat down. There was still blood going down Henry's chin, but he didn't notice it and no one said anything, even though every time he took a bite of his bread his blood fell onto it until he was eating his own blood mixed in with the food.

While Henry was not around we talked about what was going to happen to 30 him. There were no Indian doctors on the reservation, and my mom couldn't come around to trusting the old man, Moses Pillager, because he courted her long ago and was jealous of her husbands. He might take revenge through her son. We were afraid that if we brought Henry to a regular hospital they would keep him.

"They don't fix them in those places," Mom said; "they just give them drugs."

"We wouldn't get him there in the first place," I agreed, "so let's just forget about it."

Then I thought about the car.

Henry had not even looked at the car since he'd gotten home, though like I said, it was in tip-top condition and ready to drive. I thought the car might bring the old Henry back somehow. So I bided my time and waited for my chance to interest him in the vehicle.

One night Henry was off somewhere. I took myself a hammer. I went out to 35 that car and I did a number on its underside. Whacked it up. Bent the tail pipe double. Ripped the muffler loose. By the time I was done with the car it looked worse than any typical Indian car that has been driven all its life on reservation roads, which they always say are like government promises — full of holes. It just about hurt me, I'll tell you that! I threw dirt in the carburetor and I ripped all the electric tape off the seats. I made it look just as beat up as I could. Then I sat back and waited for Henry to find it.

Still, it took him over a month. That was all right, because it was just getting warm enough, not melting, but warm enough to work outside.

"Lyman," he says, walking in one day, "that red car looks like shit."

"Well it's old," I says. "You got to expect that."

"No way!" says Henry. "That car's a classic! But you went and ran the piss right out of it, Lyman, and you know it don't deserve that. I kept that car in

A-one shape. You don't remember. You're too young. But when I left, that car was running like a watch. Now I don't even know if I can get it to start again, let alone get it anywhere near its old condition."

"Well you try," I said, like I was getting mad, "but I say it's a piece of junk."   40

Then I walked out before he could realize I knew he'd strung together more than six words at once.

After that I thought he'd freeze himself to death working on that car. He was out there all day, and at night he rigged up a little lamp, ran a cord out the window, and had himself some light to see by while he worked. He was better than he had been before, but that's still not saying much. It was easier for him to do the things the rest of us did. He ate more slowly and didn't jump up and down during the meal to get this or that or look out the window. I put my hand in the back of the TV set, I admit, and fiddled around with it good, so that it was almost impossible now to get a clear picture. He didn't look at it very often anyway. He was always out with that car or going off to get parts for it. By the time it was really melting outside, he had it fixed.

I had been feeling down in the dumps about Henry around this time. We had always been together before. Henry and Lyman. But he was such a loner now that I didn't know how to take it. So I jumped at the chance one day when Henry seemed friendly. It's not that he smiled or anything. He just said, "Let's take that old shitbox for a spin." Just the way he said it made me think he could be coming around.

We went out to the car. It was spring. The sun was shining very bright. My only sister, Bonita, who was just eleven years old, came out and made us stand together for a picture. Henry leaned his elbow on the red car's windshield, and he took his other arm and put it over my shoulder, very carefully, as though it was heavy for him to lift and he didn't want to bring the weight down all at once.

"Smile," Bonita said, and he did.   45

That picture. I never look at it anymore. A few months ago, I don't know why, I got his picture out and tacked it on the wall. I felt good about Henry at the time, close to him. I felt good having his picture on the wall, until one night when I was looking at television. I was a little drunk and stoned. I looked up at the wall and Henry was staring at me. I don't know what it was, but his smile had changed, or maybe it was gone. All I know is I couldn't stay in the same room with that picture. I was shaking. I got up, closed the door, and went into the kitchen. A little later my friend Ray came over and we both went back into that room. We put the picture in a brown bag, folded the bag over and over tightly, then put it way back in a closet.

I still see that picture now, as if it tugs at me, whenever I pass that closet door. The picture is very clear in my mind. It was so sunny that day Henry had to squint against the glare. Or maybe the camera Bonita held flashed like a mirror, blinding him, before she snapped the picture. My face is right out in the sun, big and round. But he might have drawn back, because the shadows on his face are deep as holes. There are two shadows curved like little hooks around the ends of his smile, as if to frame it and try to keep it there — that one, first smile that looked like it might have hurt his face. He has his field jacket on and the worn-in clothes he'd come back in and kept wearing ever since. After Bonita took the picture, she went into the house and we got into the car. There was a full cooler in the trunk. We started off, east, toward Pembina and the Red River because Henry said he wanted to see the high water.

The trip over there was beautiful. When everything starts changing, drying up, clearing off, you feel like your whole life is starting. Henry felt it, too. The top was down and the car hummed like a top. He'd really put it back in shape, even the tape on the seats was very carefully put down and glued back in layers. It's not that he smiled again or even joked, but his face looked to me as if it was clear, more peaceful. It looked as though he wasn't thinking of anything in par-ticular except the bare fields and windbreaks and houses we were passing.

The river was high and full of winter trash when we got there. The sun was still out, but it was colder by the river. There were still little clumps of dirty snow here and there on the banks. The water hadn't gone over the banks yet, but it would, you could tell. It was just at its limit, hard swollen, glossy like an old gray scar. We made ourselves a fire, and we sat down and watched the current go. As I watched it I felt something squeezing inside me and tightening and trying to let go all at the same time. I knew I was not just feeling it myself; I knew I was feel-ing what Henry was going through at that moment. Except that I couldn't stand it, the closing and opening. I jumped to my feet. I took Henry by the shoulders and I started shaking him. "Wake up," I says, "wake up, wake up, wake up!" I didn't know what had come over me. I sat down beside him again.

His face was totally white and hard. Then it broke, like stones break all of a   50 sudden when water boils up inside them.

"I know it," he says. "I know it. I can't help it. It's no use."

We start talking. He said he knew what I'd done with the car. It was obvious it had been whacked out of shape and not just neglected. He said he wanted to give the car to me for good now, it was no use. He said he'd fixed it just to give it back and I should take it.

"No way," I says. "I don't want it."

"That's okay," he says, "you take it."

"I don't want it, though," I says back to him, and then to emphasize, just to   55 emphasize, you understand, I touch his shoulder. He slaps my hand off.

"Take that car," he says.

"No," I say. "Make me," I say, and then he grabs my jacket and rips the arm loose. That jacket is a class act, suede with tags and zippers. I push Henry back-wards, off the log. He jumps up and bowls me over. We go down in a clinch and come up swinging hard, for all we're worth, with our fists. He socks my jaw so hard I feel like it swings loose. Then I'm at his rib cage and land a good one under his chin so his head snaps back. He's dazzled. He looks at me and I look at him and then his eyes are full of tears and blood and at first I think he's crying. But no, he's laughing. "Ha! Ha!" he says. "Ha! Ha! Take good care of it."

"Okay," I says. "Okay, no problem. Ha! Ha!"

I can't help it, and I start laughing, too. My face feels fat and strange, and after a while I get a beer from the cooler in the trunk, and when I hand it to Henry he takes his shirt and wipes my germs off. "Hoof-and-mouth disease," he says. For some reason this cracks me up, and so we're really laughing for a while, and then we drink all the rest of the beers one by one and throw them in the river and see how far, how fast, the current takes them before they fill up and sink.

"You want to go on back?" I ask after a while. "Maybe we could snag a 60 couple nice Kashpaw girls."

He says nothing. But I can tell his mood is turning again.

"They're all crazy, the girls up here, every damn one of them."

"You're crazy too," I say, to jolly him up. "Crazy Lamartine boys!"

He looks as though he will take this wrong at first. His face twists, then clears, and he jumps up on his feet. "That's right!" he says. "Crazier 'n hell. Crazy Indians!"

I think it's the old Henry again. He throws off his jacket and starts springing 65 his legs up from the knees like a fancy dancer.° He's down doing something between a grass dance and a bunny hop, no kind of dance I ever saw before, but neither has anyone else on all this green growing earth. He's wild. He wants to pitch whoopee! He's up and at me and all over. All this time I'm laughing so hard, so hard my belly is getting tied up in a knot.

"Got to cool me off!" he shouts all of a sudden. Then he runs over to the river and jumps in.

There's boards and other things in the current. It's so high. No sound comes from the river after the splash he makes, so I run right over. I look around. It's getting dark. I see he's halfway across the water already, and I know he didn't swim there but the current took him. It's far. I hear his voice, though, very clearly across it.

"My boots are filling," he says.

He says this in a normal voice, like he just noticed and he doesn't know what to think of it. Then he's gone. A branch comes by. Another branch. And I go in.

By the time I get out of the river, off the snag I pulled myself onto, the sun is 70 down. I walk back to the car, turn on the high beams, and drive it up the bank. I put it in first gear and then I take my foot off the clutch. I get out, close the door, and watch it plow softly into the water. The headlights reach in as they go down, searching, still lighted even after the water swirls over the back end. I wait. The wires short out. It is all finally dark. And then there is only the water, the sound of it going and running and going and running and running.

---

fancy dancer: A person performing (often in contests) a style of Native American dance based on traditional and grass dances but done in brilliant costumes, at rapid speeds, with fancy footwork, acrobatic steps, and varied body movements.

APPROACHING THE READING

1. Outline the plot of the story. Then comment on the way it starts, the way it builds in the middle (what kinds of conflicts appear, how the material is arranged), and the way it ends. What effects are achieved through the way plot is organized and developed?

2. Think about what is left out and what is added or emphasized in plotting the story. What gaps are left in the story? How do they force you to become actively involved as a reader? What does the inclusion of the episodes about their travels — the place under the willows where they rested, and their taking Susy home to Alaska — contribute to the story? What would be lost if those details were not there?

   > Research this author in depth with cultural documents and multimedia resources on *LiterActive*.

3. Describe what the main characters are like and how we come to know them (telling? showing? saying? entering their minds? by their names?). Are they dynamic characters or static ones? To what extent does what we know about Henry depend on what we know about Lyman, and what difference does that make?

4. Why does Henry walk into the river? Does he intend to drown, or is it accidental? In what ways does he change in the story, and what things cause him to change? Why does Lyman roll the car into the river?

ENTRY POINTS   Here is another story about cars and young people, but in a very different style and tone (more like a psychological thriller). It was written by Joyce Carol Oates, whose work has extensively explored the nature of violence in America. It too is a carefully constructed story with interesting characters. Be alert to what is included, the way it is arranged, what is left out, what the characters are like, and the ways in which they are developed.

Joyce Carol Oates b. 1938

Where Are You Going, Where Have You Been?   [1966]

For Bob Dylan

Her name was Connie. She was fifteen and she had a quick, nervous giggling habit of craning her neck to glance into mirrors or checking other people's faces to make sure her own was all right. Her mother, who noticed everything and knew everything and who hadn't much reason any longer to look at her own face, always scolded Connie about it. "Stop gawking at yourself. Who are you? You think you're so pretty?" she would say. Connie would raise her eyebrows at these familiar old complaints and look right through her mother, into a shadowy vision of herself as she was right at that moment: she knew she was pretty and that was everything. Her mother had been pretty once too, if you could believe those old snapshots in the album, but now her looks were gone and that was why she was always after Connie.

"Why don't you keep your room clean like your sister? How've you got your hair fixed — what the hell stinks? Hair spray? You don't see your sister using that junk."

Her sister June was twenty-four and still lived at home. She was a secretary in the high school Connie attended, and if that wasn't bad enough — with her in the same building — she was so plain and chunky and steady that Connie had to hear her praised all the time by her mother and her mother's sisters. June did this, June did that, she saved money and helped clean the house and cooked and Connie couldn't do a thing, her mind was all filled with trashy daydreams. Their father was away at work most of the time and when he came home he wanted supper and he read the newspaper at supper and after supper he went to bed. He didn't bother talking much to them, but around his bent head Connie's mother kept picking at her until Connie wished her mother was dead and she herself was dead and it was all over. "She makes me want to throw up sometimes," she complained to her friends. She had a high, breathless, amused voice that made everything she said sound a little forced, whether it was sincere or not.

There was one good thing: June went places with girl friends of hers, girls who were just as plain and steady as she, and so when Connie wanted to do that her mother had no objections. The father of Connie's best girl friend drove the girls the three miles to town and left them at a shopping plaza so they could walk through the stores or go to a movie, and when he came to pick them up again at eleven he never bothered to ask what they had done.

They must have been familiar sights, walking around the shopping plaza in 5 their shorts and flat ballerina slippers that always scuffed the sidewalk, with charm bracelets jingling on their thin wrists; they would lean together to whisper and laugh secretly if someone passed who amused or interested them. Connie had long dark blond hair that drew anyone's eye to it, and she wore part of it pulled up on her head and puffed out and the rest of it she let fall down her back. She wore a pullover jersey blouse that looked one way when she was at home and another way when she was away from home. Everything about her had two sides to it, one for home and one for anywhere that was not home: her walk, which could be childlike and bobbing, or languid enough to make anyone think she was hearing music in her head; her mouth, which was pale and smirking most of the time, but bright and pink on these evenings out; her laugh, which was cynical and drawling at home — "Ha, ha, very funny" — but high-pitched and nervous anywhere else, like the jingling of the charms on her bracelet.

Sometimes they did go shopping or to a movie, but sometimes they went across the highway, ducking fast across the busy road, to a drive-in restaurant where older kids hung out. The restaurant was shaped like a big bottle, though squatter than a real bottle, and on its cap was a revolving figure of a grinning boy holding a hamburger aloft. One night in midsummer they ran across, breathless with daring, and right away someone leaned out a car window and invited them over, but it was just a boy from high school they didn't like. It made them feel good to be able to ignore him. They went up through the maze of parked and cruising cars to the bright-lit, fly-infested restaurant, their faces pleased and expectant as if they were entering a sacred building that loomed up out of the night to give them what haven and blessing they yearned for. They sat at the counter and crossed their legs at the ankles, their thin shoulders rigid with excitement, and listened to the music that made everything so good: the music was always in the background, like music at a church service; it was something to depend upon.

A boy named Eddie came in to talk with them. He sat backwards on his stool, turning himself jerkily around in semicircles and then stopping and turning back again, and after a while he asked Connie if she would like something to eat. She said she would and so she tapped her friend's arm on her way out — her friend pulled her face up into a brave, droll look — and Connie said she would meet her at eleven, across the way. "I just hate to leave her like that," Connie said earnestly, but the boy said that she wouldn't be alone for long. So they went out to his car, and on the way Connie couldn't help but let her eyes wander over the windshields and faces all around her, her face gleaming with a joy that had nothing to do with Eddie or even this place; it might have been the music. She drew her shoulders up and sucked in her breath with the pure pleasure of being alive, and just at that moment she happened to glance at a face just a few feet from hers. It was a boy with shaggy black hair, in a convertible jalopy painted gold. He stared at her and then his lips widened into a grin. Connie slit her eyes at him and turned away, but she couldn't help glancing back and there he was, still watching her. He wagged a finger and laughed and said, "Gonna get you, baby," and Connie turned away again without Eddie noticing anything.

She spent three hours with him, at the restaurant where they ate hamburgers and drank Cokes in wax cups that were always sweating, and then down an alley a mile or so away, and when he left her off at five to eleven only the movie house was still open at the plaza. Her girl friend was there, talking with a boy. When Connie came up, the two girls smiled at each other and Connie said, "How was the movie?" and the girl said, "*You* should know." They rode off with the girl's father, sleepy and pleased, and Connie couldn't help but look back at the darkened shopping plaza with its big empty parking lot and its signs that were faded and ghostly now, and over at the drive-in restaurant where cars were still circling tirelessly. She couldn't hear the music at this distance.

Next morning June asked her how the movie was and Connie said, "So-so."

She and that girl and occasionally another girl went out several times 10 a week, and the rest of the time Connie spent around the house — it was summer vacation — getting in her mother's way and thinking, dreaming about the boys she met. But all the boys fell back and dissolved into a single face that was not even a face but an idea, a feeling, mixed up with the urgent insistent pounding of the music and the humid night of July. Connie's mother kept dragging her back to the daylight by finding things for her to do or saying suddenly, "What's this about the Pettinger girl?"

And Connie would say nervously, "Oh, her. That dope." She always drew thick clear lines between herself and such girls, and her mother was simple and kind enough to believe it. Her mother was so simple, Connie thought, that it was maybe cruel to fool her so much. Her mother went scuffling around the house in old bedroom slippers and complained over the telephone to one sister about the other, then the other called up and the two of them complained about the third one. If June's name was mentioned her mother's tone was approving, and if Connie's name was mentioned it was disapproving. This did not really mean she disliked Connie, and actually Connie thought that her mother preferred her to June just because she was prettier, but the two of them kept up a pretense of exasperation, a sense that they were tugging and struggling over something of little value to either of them. Sometimes, over coffee, they were almost friends, but something would come up — some vexation that was like a fly buzzing suddenly around their heads — and their faces went hard with contempt.

One Sunday Connie got up at eleven — none of them bothered with church — and washed her hair so that it could dry all day long in the sun. Her parents and sister were going to a barbecue at an aunt's house and Connie said no, she wasn't interested, rolling her eyes to let her mother know just what she thought of it. "Stay home alone then," her mother said sharply. Connie sat out back in a lawn chair and watched them drive away, her father quiet and bald, hunched around so that he could back the car out, her mother with a look that was still angry and not at all softened through the windshield, and in the back seat poor old June, all dressed up as if she didn't know what a barbecue was, with all the running yelling kids and the flies. Connie sat with her eyes closed in the sun, dreaming and dazed with the warmth about her as if this were a kind of love, the caresses of love, and her mind slipped over onto thoughts of the boy she had been with the night before and how nice he had been, how sweet it always was, not the way someone like June would suppose but sweet, gentle, the way it was in movies and promised in songs; and when she opened her eyes she hardly knew where she was, the back yard ran off into weeds and a fence-like line of trees and behind it the sky was perfectly blue and still. The asbestos "ranch house" that was now three years old startled her — it looked small. She shook her head as if to get awake.

It was too hot. She went inside the house and turned on the radio to drown out the quiet. She sat on the edge of her bed, barefoot, and listened for an hour and a half to a program called XYZ Sunday Jamboree, record after record of hard, fast, shrieking songs she sang along with, interspersed by exclamations from "Bobby King": "An' look here, you girls at Napoleon's — Son and Charley want you to pay real close attention to this song coming up!"

And Connie paid close attention herself, bathed in a glow of slow-pulsed joy that seemed to rise mysteriously out of the music itself and lay languidly about the airless little room, breathed in and breathed out with each gentle rise and fall of her chest.

After a while she heard a car coming up the drive. She sat up at once, 15
startled, because it couldn't be her father so soon. The gravel kept crunching all
the way in from the road — the driveway was long — and Connie ran to the window. It was a car she didn't know. It was an open jalopy, painted a bright gold
that caught the sunlight opaquely. Her heart began to pound and her fingers
snatched at her hair, checking it, and she whispered, "Christ, Christ," wondering how bad she looked. The car came to a stop at the side door and the horn
sounded four short taps, as if this were a signal Connie knew.

She went into the kitchen and approached the door slowly, then hung out
the screen door, her bare toes curling down off the step. There were two boys in
the car and now she recognized the driver: he had shaggy, shabby black hair that
looked crazy as a wig and he was grinning at her.

"I ain't late, am I?" he said.

"Who the hell do you think you are?" Connie said.

"Toldja I'd be out, didn't I?"

"I don't even know who you are." 20

She spoke sullenly, careful to show no interest or pleasure, and he spoke in a
fast, bright monotone. Connie looked past him to the other boy, taking her
time. He had fair brown hair, with a lock that fell onto his forehead. His side-
burns gave him a fierce, embarrassed look, but so far he hadn't even bothered to
glance at her. Both boys wore sunglasses. The driver's glasses were metallic and
mirrored everything in miniature.

"You wanta come for a ride?" he said.

Connie smirked and let her hair fall loose over one shoulder.

"Don'tcha like my car? New paint job," he said. "Hey."

"What?" 25

"You're cute."

She pretended to fidget, chasing flies away from the door.

"Don'tcha believe me, or what?" he said.

"Look, I don't even know who you are," Connie said in disgust.

"Hey, Ellie's got a radio, see. Mine broke down." He lifted his friend's arm 30
and showed her the little transistor radio the boy was holding, and now Connie
began to hear the music. It was the same program that was playing inside the
house.

"Bobby King?" she said.

"I listen to him all the time. I think he's great."

"He's kind of great," Connie said reluctantly.

"Listen, that guy's *great*. He knows where the action is."

Connie blushed a little, because the glasses made it impossible for her to see 35
just what this boy was looking at. She couldn't decide if she liked him or if he
was just a jerk, and so she dawdled in the doorway and wouldn't come down or
go back inside. She said, "What's all that stuff painted on your car?"

"Can'tcha read it?" He opened the door very carefully, as if he were afraid it
might fall off. He slid out just as carefully, planting his feet firmly on the
ground, the tiny metallic world in his glasses slowing down like gelatine hardening, and in the midst of it Connie's bright green blouse. "This here is my name,

to begin with," he said. ARNOLD FRIEND was written in tarlike black letters on the side, with a drawing of a round, grinning face that reminded Connie of a pumpkin, except it wore sunglasses. "I wanta introduce myself, I'm Arnold Friend and that's my real name and I'm gonna be your friend, honey, and inside the car's Ellie Oscar, he's kinda shy." Ellie brought his transistor radio up to his shoulder and balanced it there. "Now, these numbers are a secret code, honey," Arnold Friend explained. He read off the numbers 33, 19, 17 and raised his eyebrows at her to see what she thought of that, but she didn't think much of it. The left rear fender had been smashed and around it was written, on the gleaming gold background: DONE BY CRAZY WOMAN DRIVER. Connie had to laugh at that. Arnold Friend was pleased at her laughter and looked up at her. "Around the other side's a lot more — you wanta come and seem them?"

"No."

"Why not?"

"Why should I?"

"Don'tcha wanta see what's on the car? Don'tcha wanta go for a ride?"   40

"I don't know."

"Why not?"

"I got things to do."

"Like what?"

"Things."   45

He laughed as if she had said something funny. He slapped his thighs. He was standing in a strange way, leaning back against the car as if he were balancing himself. He wasn't tall, only an inch or so taller than she would be if she came down to him. Connie liked the way he was dressed, which was the way all of them dressed: tight faded jeans stuffed into black, scuffed boots, a belt that pulled his waist in and showed how lean he was, and a white pullover shirt that was a little soiled and showed the hard small muscles of his arms and shoulders. He looked as if he probably did hard work, lifting and carrying things. Even his neck looked muscular. And his face was a familiar face, somehow: the jaw and chin and cheeks slightly darkened because he hadn't shaved for a day or two, and the nose long and hawklike, sniffing as if she were a treat he was going to gobble up and it was all a joke.

"Connie, you ain't telling the truth. This is your day set aside for a ride with me and you know it," he said, still laughing. The way he straightened and recovered from his fit of laughing showed that it had been all fake.

"How do you know what my name is?" she said suspiciously.

"It's Connie."

"Maybe and maybe not."   50

"I know my Connie," he said, wagging his finger. Now she remembered him even better, back at the restaurant, and her cheeks warmed at the thought of how she had sucked in her breath just at the moment she passed him — how she must have looked to him. And he had remembered her. "Ellie and I come out here especially for you," he said. "Ellie can sit in back. How about it?"

"Where?"

"Where what?"

"Where're we going?"

He looked at her. He took off the sunglasses and she saw how pale the skin 55
around his eyes was, like holes that were not in shadow but instead in light. His
eyes were like chips of broken glass that catch the light in an amiable way. He
smiled. It was as if the idea of going for a ride somewhere, to someplace, was a
new idea to him.

"Just for a ride, Connie sweetheart."

"I never said my name was Connie," she said.

"But I know what it is. I know your name and all about you, lots of things,"
Arnold Friend said. He had not moved yet but stood still leaning back against the
side of his jalopy. "I took a special interest in you, such a pretty girl, and found
out all about you—like I know your parents and sister are gone somewheres and
I know where and how long they're going to be gone, and I know who you were
with last night, and your best girl friend's name is Betty. Right?"

He spoke in a simple lilting voice, exactly as if he were reciting the words to
a song. His smile assured her that everything was fine. In the car Ellie turned up
the volume on his radio and did not bother to look around at them.

"Ellie can sit in the back seat," Arnold Friend said. He indicated his friend 60
with a casual jerk of his chin, as if Ellie did not count and she should not bother
with him.

"How'd you find out all that stuff?" Connie said.

"Listen: Betty Schultz and Tony Fitch and Jimmy Pettinger and Nancy Pettinger," he said in a chant. "Raymond Stanley and Bob Hutter—"

"Do you know all those kids?"

"I know everybody."

"Look, you're kidding. You're not from around here."   65

"Sure."

"But—how come we never saw you before?"

"Sure you saw me before," he said. He looked down at his boots, as if he
were a little offended. "You just don't remember."

"I guess I'd remember you," Connie said.

"Yeah?" He looked up at this, beaming. He was pleased. He began to mark 70
time with the music from Ellie's radio, tapping his fists lightly together. Connie
looked away from his smile to the car, which was painted so bright it almost
hurt her eyes to look at it. She looked at that name, ARNOLD FRIEND. And up at the
front fender was an expression that was familiar—MAN THE FLYING SAUCERS. It was
an expression kids had used the year before but didn't use this year. She looked
at it for a while as if the words meant something to her that she did not yet
know.

"What're you thinking about? Huh?" Arnold Friend demanded. "Not worried about your hair blowing around in the car, are you?"

"No."

"Think I maybe can't drive good?"

"How do I know?"

"You're a hard girl to handle. How come?" he said. "Don't you know I'm 75
your friend? Didn't you see me put my sign in the air when you walked by?"

"What sign?"

"My sign." And he drew an X in the air, leaning out toward her. They were maybe ten feet apart. After his hand fell back to his side the X was still in the air, almost visible. Connie let the screen door close and stood perfectly still inside it, listening to the music from her radio and the boy's blend together. She stared at Arnold Friend. He stood there so stiffly relaxed, pretending to be relaxed, with one hand idly on the door handle as if he were keeping himself up that way and had no intention of ever moving again. She recognized most things about him, the tight jeans that showed his thighs and buttocks and the greasy leather boots and the tight shirt, and even that slippery friendly smile of his, that sleepy dreamy smile that all the boys used to get across ideas they didn't want to put into words. She recognized all this and also the singsong way he talked, slightly mocking, kidding, but serious and a little melancholy, and she recognized the way he tapped one fist against the other in homage to the perpetual music behind him. But all these things did not come together.

She said suddenly, "Hey, how old are you?"

His smile faded. She could see then that he wasn't a kid, he was much older — thirty, maybe more. At this knowledge her heart began to pound faster.

"That's a crazy thing to ask. Can'tcha see I'm your own age?" 80

"Like hell you are."

"Or maybe a coupla years older. I'm eighteen."

"Eighteen?" she said doubtfully.

He grinned to reassure her and lines appeared at the corners of his mouth. His teeth were big and white. He grinned so broadly his eyes became slits and she saw how thick the lashes were, thick and black as if painted with a black tarlike material. Then, abruptly, he seemed to become embarrassed and looked over his shoulder at Ellie. "*Him*, he's crazy," he said. "Ain't he a riot? He's a nut, a real character." Ellie was still listening to the music. His sunglasses told nothing about what he was thinking. He wore a bright orange shirt unbuttoned halfway to show his chest, which was a pale, bluish chest and not muscular like Arnold Friend's. His shirt collar was turned up all around and the very tips of the collar pointed out past his chin as if they were protecting him. He was pressing the transistor radio up against his ear and sat there in a kind of daze, right in the sun.

"He's kinda strange," Connie said. 85

"Hey, she says you're kinda strange! Kinda strange!" Arnold Friend cried. He pounded on the car to get Ellie's attention. Ellie turned for the first time and Connie saw with shock that he wasn't a kid either — he had a fair, hairless face, cheeks reddened slightly as if the veins grew too close to the surface of his skin, the face of a forty-year-old baby. Connie felt a wave of dizziness rise in her at this sight and she stared at him as if waiting for something to change the shock of the moment, make it all right again. Ellie's lips kept shaping words, mumbling along with the words blasting in his ear.

"Maybe you two better go away," Connie said faintly.

"What? How come?" Arnold Friend cried. "We come out here to take you for a ride. It's Sunday." He had the voice of the man on the radio now. It was the same voice, Connie thought. "Don'tcha know it's Sunday all day? And honey, no matter who you were with last night, today you're with Arnold Friend and don't you forget it! Maybe you better step out here," he said, and this last was in a different voice. It was a little flatter, as if the heat was finally getting to him.

"No. I got things to do."

"Hey."

"You two better leave."

"We ain't leaving until you come with us."

"Like hell I am —"

"Connie, don't fool around with me. I mean — I mean, don't fool *around*," he said, shaking his head. He laughed incredulously. He placed his sunglasses on top of his head, carefully, as if he were indeed wearing a wig, and brought the stems down behind his ears. Connie stared at him, another wave of dizziness and fear rising in her so that for a moment he wasn't even in focus but was just a blur standing there against his gold car, and she had the idea that he had driven up the driveway all right but had come from nowhere before that and belonged nowhere and that everything about him and even about the music that was so familiar to her was only half real.

"If my father comes and sees you —"

"He ain't coming. He's at a barbecue."

"How do you know that?"

"Aunt Tillie's. Right now they're — uh — they're drinking. Sitting around," he said vaguely, squinting as if he were staring all the way to town and over to Aunt Tillie's back yard. Then the vision seemed to get clear and he nodded energetically. "Yeah. Sitting around. There's your sister in a blue dress, huh? And high heels, the poor sad bitch — nothing like you, sweetheart! And your mother's helping some fat woman with the corn, they're cleaning the corn — husking the corn —"

"What fat woman?" Connie cried.

"How do I know what fat woman, I don't know every goddamn fat woman in the world!" Arnold Friend laughed.

"Oh, that's Mrs. Hornsby. . . . Who invited her?" Connie said. She felt a little lightheaded. Her breath was coming quickly.

"She's too fat. I don't like them fat. I like them the way you are, honey," he said, smiling sleepily at her. They stared at each other for a while through the screen door. He said softly, "Now, what you're going to do is this: you're going to come out that door. You're going to sit up front with me and Ellie's going to sit in the back, the hell with Ellie, right? This isn't Ellie's date. You're my date. I'm your lover, honey."

"What? You're crazy —"

"Yes, I'm your lover. You don't know what that is but you will," he said. "I know that too. I know all about you. But look: it's real nice and you couldn't ask for nobody better than me, or more polite. I always keep my word. I'll tell you how it is, I'm always nice at first, the first time. I'll hold you so tight you won't think you have to try to get away or pretend anything because you'll know you can't. And I'll come inside you where it's all secret and you'll give in to me and you'll love me—"

"Shut up! You're crazy!" Connie said. She backed away from the door. She   105
put her hands up against her ears as if she'd heard something terrible, something not meant for her. "People don't talk like that, you're crazy," she muttered. Her heart was almost too big now for her chest and its pumping made sweat break out all over her. She looked out to see Arnold Friend pause and then take a step toward the porch, lurching. He almost fell. But, like a clever drunken man, he managed to catch his balance. He wobbled in his high boots and grabbed hold of one of the porch posts.

"Honey?" he said. "You still listening?"

"Get the hell out of here!"

"Be nice, honey. Listen."

"I'm going to call the police—"

He wobbled again and out of the side of his mouth came a fast spat curse,   110
an aside not meant for her to hear. But even this "Christ!" sounded forced. Then he began to smile again. She watched this smile come, awkward as if he were smiling from inside a mask. His whole face was a mask, she thought wildly, tanned down to his throat but then running out as if he had plastered makeup on his face but had forgotten about his throat.

"Honey—? Listen, here's how it is. I always tell the truth and I promise you this: I ain't coming in that house after you."

"You better not! I'm going to call the police if you—if you don't—"

"Honey," he said, talking right through her voice, "honey, I'm not coming in there but you are coming out here. You know why?"

She was panting. The kitchen looked like a place she had never seen before, some room she had run inside but that wasn't good enough, wasn't going to help her. The kitchen window had never had a curtain, after three years, and there were dishes in the sink for her to do—probably—and if you ran your hand across the table you'd probably feel something sticky there.

"You listening, honey? Hey?"   115

"—going to call the police—"

"Soon as you touch the phone I don't need to keep my promise and can come inside. You won't want that."

She rushed forward and tried to lock the door. Her fingers were shaking. "But why lock it," Arnold Friend said gently, talking right into her face. "It's just a screen door. It's just nothing." One of his boots was at a strange angle, as if his foot wasn't in it. It pointed out to the left, bent at the ankle. "I mean, anybody can break through a screen door and glass and wood and iron or anything else if he needs to, anybody at all, and specially Arnold Friend. If the place got lit up with a fire, honey, you'd come runnin' out into my arms, right into my arms an' safe at home—like you knew I was your lover and'd stopped fooling around." Part of those words were spoken with a slight rhythmic lilt, and Connie somehow recognized them—the echo of a song from last year, about a girl rushing into her boy friend's arms and coming home again—

Connie stood barefoot on the linoleum floor, staring at him. "What do you
want?" she whispered.

"I want you," he said.   120

"What?"

"Seen you that night and thought, that's the one, yes sir. I never needed to
look anymore."

"But my father's coming back. He's coming to get me. I had to wash my hair
first —" She spoke in a dry, rapid voice, hardly raising it for him to hear.

"No, your daddy is not coming and yes, you had to wash your hair and you
washed it for me. It's nice and shining and all for me. I thank you sweetheart,"
he said with a mock bow, but again he almost lost his balance. He had to bend
and adjust his boots. Evidently his feet did not go all the way down; the boots
must have been stuffed with something so that he would seem taller. Connie
stared out at him and behind him at Ellie in the car, who seemed to be looking
off toward Connie's right, into nothing. This Ellie said, pulling the words out of
the air one after another as if he were just discovering them, "You want me to
pull out the phone?"

"Shut your mouth and keep it shut," Arnold Friend said, his face red from   125
bending over or maybe from embarrassment because Connie had seen his boots.
"This ain't none of your business."

"What — what are you doing? What do you want?" Connie said. "If I call the
police they'll get you, they'll arrest you —"

"Promise was not to come in unless you touch that phone, and I'll keep that
promise," he said. He resumed his erect position and tried to force his shoulders
back. He sounded like a hero in a movie, declaring something important. But he
spoke too loudly and it was as if he were speaking to someone behind Connie. "I
ain't made plans for coming in that house where I don't belong but just for you
to come out to me, the way you should. Don't you know who I am?"

"You're crazy," she whispered. She backed away from the door but did not
want to go into another part of the house, as if this would give him permission
to come through the door. "What do you . . . you're crazy, you. . . ."

"Huh? What're you saying, honey?"

Her eyes darted everywhere in the kitchen. She could not remember what it   130
was, this room.

"This is how it is, honey: you come out and we'll drive away, have a nice
ride. But if you don't come out we're gonna wait till your people come home and
then they're all going to get it."

"You want that telephone pulled out?" Ellie said. He held the radio away
from his ear and grimaced, as if without the radio the air was too much for him.

"I toldja shut up, Ellie," Arnold Friend said, "you're deaf, get a hearing aid,
right? Fix yourself up. This little girl's no trouble and's gonna be nice to me, so
Ellie keep to yourself, this ain't your date — right? Don't hem in on me, don't
hog, don't crush, don't bird dog, don't trail me," he said in a rapid, meaningless
voice, as if he were running through all the expressions he'd learned but was no
longer sure which of them was in style, then rushing on to new ones, making

them up with his eyes closed. "Don't crawl under my fence, don't squeeze in my chipmunk hole, don't sniff my glue, suck my popsicle, keep your own greasy fingers on yourself!" He shaded his eyes and peered in at Connie, who was backed against the kitchen table. "Don't mind him, honey, he's just a creep. He's a dope. Right? I'm the boy for you and like I said, you come out here nice like a lady and give me your hand, and nobody else gets hurt, I mean, your nice old bald-headed daddy and your mummy and your sister in her high heels. Because listen: why bring them in this?"

"Leave me alone," Connie whispered.

"Hey, you know that old woman down the road, the one with the chickens   135
and stuff—you know her?"

"She's dead!"

"Dead? What? You know her?" Arnold Friend said.

"She's dead—"

"Don't you like her?"

"She's dead—she's—she isn't here any more—"   140

"But don't you like her, I mean, you got something against her? Some grudge or something?" Then his voice dipped as if he were conscious of a rudeness. He touched the sunglasses perched up on top of his head as if to make sure they were still there. "Now, you be a good girl."

"What are you going to do?"

"Just two things, or maybe three," Arnold Friend said. "But I promise it won't last long and you'll like me the way you get to like people you're close to. You will. It's all over for you here, so come on out. You don't want your people in any trouble, do you?"

She turned and bumped against a chair or something, hurting her leg, but she ran into the back room and picked up the telephone. Something roared in her ear, a tiny roaring, and she was so sick with fear that she could do nothing but listen to it—the telephone was clammy and very heavy and her fingers groped down to the dial but were too weak to touch it. She began to scream into the phone, into the roaring. She cried out, she cried for her mother, she felt her breath start jerking back and forth in her lungs as if it were something Arnold Friend was stabbing her with again and again with no tenderness. A noisy sorrowful wailing rose all about her and she was locked inside it the way she was locked inside this house.

After a while she could hear again. She was sitting on the floor with her wet   145
back against the wall.

Arnold Friend was saying from the door, "That's a good girl. Put the phone back."

She kicked the phone away from her.

"No, honey. Pick it up. Put it back right."

She picked it up and put it back. The dial tone stopped.

"That's a good girl. Now, you come outside."   150

She was hollow with what had been fear but what was now just an emptiness. All that screaming had blasted it out of her. She sat, one leg cramped under her, and deep inside her brain was something like a pinpoint of light that kept going and would not let her relax. She thought, I'm not going to see my mother again. She thought, I'm not going to sleep in my bed again. Her bright green blouse was all wet.

Arnold Friend said, in a gentle-loud voice that was like a stage voice, "The place where you came from ain't there any more, and where you had in mind to go is cancelled out. This place you are now — inside your daddy's house — is nothing but a cardboard box I can knock down any time. You know that and always did know it. You hear me?"

She thought, I have got to think. I have got to know what to do.

"We'll go out to a nice field, out in the country here where it smells so nice and it's sunny," Arnold Friend said. "I'll have my arms tight around you so you won't need to try to get away and I'll show you what love is like, what it does. The hell with this house! It looks solid all right," he said. He ran a fingernail down the screen and the noise did not make Connie shiver, as it would have the day before. "Now, put your hand on your heart, honey. Feel that? That feels solid too but we know better. Be nice to me, be sweet like you can because what else is there for a girl like you but to be sweet and pretty and give in? — and get away before her people come back?"

She felt her pounding heart. Her hand seemed to enclose it. She thought for   155
the first time in her life that it was nothing that was hers, that belonged to her, but just a pounding, living thing inside this body that wasn't really hers either.

"You don't want them to get hurt," Arnold Friend went on. "Now, get up, honey. Get up all by yourself."

She stood.

"Now, turn this way. That's right. Come over here to me. — Ellie, put that away, didn't I tell you? You dope. You miserable creepy dope," Arnold Friend said. His words were not angry but only part of an incantation. The incantation was kindly. "Now, come out through the kitchen to me, honey, and let's see a smile, try it, you're a brave, sweet little girl and now they're eating corn and hot dogs cooked to bursting over an outdoor fire, and they don't know one thing about you and never did and honey, you're better than them because not a one of them would have done this for you."

Connie felt the linoleum under her feet; it was cool. She brushed her hair back out of her eyes. Arnold Friend let go of the post tentatively and opened his arms for her, his elbows pointing in toward each other and his wrists limp, to show that this was an embarrassed embrace and a little mocking, he didn't want to make her self-conscious.

She put out her hand against the screen. She watched herself push the door   160
slowly open as if she were back safe somewhere in the other doorway, watching this body and this head of long hair moving out into the sunlight where Arnold Friend waited.

"My sweet little blue-eyed girl," he said in a half-sung sigh that had nothing to do with her brown eyes but was taken up just the same by the vast sunlit reaches of the land behind him and on all sides of him — so much land that Connie had never seen before and did not recognize except to know that she was going to it.

APPROACHING THE READING

1. Look closely at the way the story begins — at the first sentence and the first paragraph, for example — and think about what effect they have on you.

2. Pick out the steps in the story's development — outline the plot development. Why do you think the story includes the paragraphs about June, about trips to the mall, about evenings with Eddie and other friends? The plot changes direction with the seemingly harmless phrase "One Sunday Connie got up at eleven" (p. 84). Notice the way the encounter with Arnold Friend is organized to make it build in intensity and suspense.

3. Oates says the story grew out of reading about an actual serial rapist and murderer in Arizona. The story ends with Connie going out the door to join Arnold Friend. What do you assume would have happened next, if the story hadn't ended there? Why do you think the author chose not to continue the story further? In what ways might stopping there indicate what is of greatest interest or importance for the story and what is not of central interest or importance?

4. Describe the main characters and comment on the techniques and approaches through which we come to know them. Are they round or flat? Are they static or dynamic? Consider characters' names and how they contribute to the story.

5. The story is dedicated to singer and composer Bob Dylan. References to music appear frequently in the story. Consider what these references say and what they contribute to effect and theme. If you aren't familiar with Bob Dylan's music, listen to some and do some research on him. Is his music the kind that "made everything so good" for Connie? Does the Dylan reference relate to the story, or is it simply an honorific dedication?

6. Suggest two or three different ways the title could relate to the story.

RESPONDING THROUGH Writing

WRITING ABOUT PLOT AND CHARACTER

Journal Entries

1. Experiment with the basic principles of plot construction by writing a plot analysis of a TV show or a movie: its beginning, its handling of gaps, its use of flashbacks, its rising action or development (look for conflict, suspense, foreshadowing, and repetitions), and its ending. Write a journal entry summarizing the result and discussing whether, how, and why basic aspects of plot are the same everywhere.

2. Choose a crucial event from your past. In a journal entry, outline it as a plot. Consider what you need to include and what you can leave out, what

order would be most effective for presenting it, and so on. Add a few sentences pointing out the techniques you bring in and discussing what you learn about plot construction.

3. Write an analysis of characterization techniques in a TV show or a movie: Look for how telling, showing, what a character says and what other characters say about her or him, conveying a character's thoughts, and the way she or he is named are used to reveal character. Consider which characters are round and which are flat. Write a journal entry summarizing the result and discussing whether, how, and why basic aspects of characterization are similar across different genres.

Research the authors in this chapter with LitLinks, or take a quiz on the stories with LitQuiz, at bedfordstmartins.com/ approachinglit.

Literary Analysis Papers

4. Write a paper on the importance and handling of gaps in the plotting of Louise Erdrich's "The Red Convertible" (p. 73).

5. Write a paper examining relation of plot construction to title in James Baldwin's "Sonny's Blues" (p. 309), James Joyce's "Araby" (p. 393), or Toni Morrison's "Recitatif" (p. 431).

6. Write a paper discussing characterization techniques in Monica Ali's "Dinner with Dr. Azad" (p. 292), Katherine Anne Porter's "The Jilting of Granny Weatherall" (p. 478), or Salman Rushdie's "The Prophet's Hair" (p. 490).

Comparison-Contrast Papers

7. Write a paper comparing and contrasting Arnold Friend in Joyce Carol Oates's "Where Are You Going, Where Have You Been?" (p. 81) and the Misfit in Flannery O'Connor's "A Good Man Is Hard to Find" (p. 455).

8. Write a paper comparing the inside view of the Vietnam War presented by the plot of Tim O'Brien's "The Things They Carried" (p. 150) with the outside view found in "The Red Convertible" (p. 73). (You could focus on the handling of gaps in both stories.)

▶ TIPS for Writing about Plot and Character

➤ **Explain techniques** In writing about plot, be sure to *explain* the selection and arrangement of events; don't just summarize what happens in the story.

➤ **Limit your scope** In writing about plot, focus on an aspect — or perhaps two or three — that are unique or particularly significant; don't try to deal with everything covered in this chapter.

(continued)

➤ **Start with conflicts** As you select a topic related to plot, look for the key conflict or conflicts in the story then at how its structure makes it or them stand out. Notice if the story includes an epiphany; if so, notice how it is set up. That can often turn into a valuable topic.

➤ **Focus on methods** In writing about character, it's usually best to focus on methods of characterization: Show how aspects of the character are brought out, don't just describe what the character is like. Watch especially for juxtapositions: comparisons and contrasts between characters in addition to the specific techniques covered in this chapter. Juxtapositions often provide a useful way to get into and organize a paper.

➤ **Connect to theme** Plot and character are of most interest as they relate to and bring out theme in the story; try to connect your discussion of plot or character to the overall effect of the story.

WRITING ABOUT CONNECTIONS

One of the most important skills for you to develop is how to make connections between the great variety of things you are learning, things that may even appear at first to be unrelated — between things dealt with early in a course and those that come later, for example, and between what you have learned in one course or discipline and what you have covered in others. Making connections is crucial also for literature. Throughout this book, this skill is emphasized by the way it pairs elements in its chapters, often in unusual combinations, to bring out the connections between them and between all the elements used in writing.

It's important for readers to make connections between different works that they read. Doing so can enhance the reading experience and reveal valuable insights. The connections can be between similar (or contrasting) plots and characters or other techniques, and they can be thematic. To give you practice and encouragement in making connections, each chapter includes some prompts for "Writing about Connections." The pairings suggested are for works of the same genre, though equally appropriate pairings could be made across genres. We have selected connections, often between contemporary works and earlier works from the literary canon, that we hope you will find thought-provoking and challenging. Here are three such suggestions, which are intended to provide you a model for coming up with others on your own.

1. "Love and the City": Realizing Relationships in Dagoberto Gilb's "Love in L.A." (p. 61) and Raymond Carver's "What We Talk about When We Talk about Love" (p. 337)
2. "My Brother's Keeper": Supporting Siblings in Louise Erdrich's "The Red Convertible" (p. 73) and James Baldwin's "Sonny's Blues" (p. 309)

3. "Good Men Are Hard to Find": Encounters with Evil in Joyce Carol Oates's "Where Are You Going, Where Have You Been?" (p. 81) and Flannery O'Connor's "A Good Man Is Hard to Find" (p. 455)

WRITING RESEARCH PAPERS

1. In the United States and many other societies, cars carry a lot of cultural importance. Research the role cars play in American culture and write a paper on the significance of cars in Dagoberto Gilb's "Love in L.A." (p. 61), Louise Erdrich's "The Red Convertible" (p. 73), Joyce Carol Oates's "Where Are You Going, Where Have You Been?" (p. 81), and your own experience. Consider what types of cars carry various meanings for different cultures. How do cars embody distinctions, and at times conflicts, between cultures? Consider ironies you find in this "car culture."

2. Henry's experiences on leaving the reservation to enter basic training and then on going to Vietnam for active service are not covered in Louise Erdrich's "The Red Convertible" (p. 73) because of the point of view. But they remain very much a part of the story. Do research on what Native Americans often encounter when they leave the reservation and about what military action in Vietnam was like. Then write a paper describing what Henry's experiences probably were like and why he had changed the way he did when he returned.

COMPOSING IN OTHER ART FORMS

1. Respond to the references to Bob Dylan and to music in Joyce Carol Oates's "Where Are You Going, Where Have You Been?" (p. 81) by preparing a sound track to accompany the story.

2. Draw or paint a series of portraits of several characters from Sandra Cisneros's "The House on Mango Street" (p. 99), Joyce Carol Oates's "Where Are You Going, Where Have You Been?" (p. 81), or another story of your choice.

Properly speaking, the theme is what is left, like a resonance, in the reader's mind.

R. V. Cassill

CHAPTER **5** **Point of View and Theme**

Being Alert to Angles, Open to Insights

This book is about *reading* literature, specifically reading in the interactive manner described in Chapters 1 and 2. But reading literature differs from most other reading: It is often more like listening to someone, more like hearing a voice, than what we usually think of as reading. You've probably heard the phrase "seeing with the mind's eye"; you can also hear with the mind's ear. Responding fully to literature requires training the ear so you can enjoy and benefit from hearing many voices from a variety of places and cultures. This chapter focuses on *voice* in stories, particularly as it is affected by the perspective from which the story is told, and on the way stories give voice to a central idea or *theme*.

ENTRY POINTS   Using your "mind's ear," listen to the following story as if it were being spoken directly to you. It is the first in a series of forty-six connected stories, or a *collective story*, told by a young girl, Esperanza Cordero, growing up in a Latino section of Chicago and seeking both to escape that world and to find herself.

98

Sandra Cisneros b. 1954

The House on Mango Street [1983]

We didn't always live on Mango Street. Before that we lived on Loomis on the third floor, and before that we lived on Keeler. Before Keeler it was Paulina, and before that I can't remember. But what I remember most is moving a lot. Each time it seemed there'd be one more of us. By the time we got to Mango Street we were six — Mama, Papa, Carlos, Kiki, my sister Nenny, and me.

The house on Mango Street is ours, and we don't have to pay rent to anybody, or share the yard with the people downstairs, or be careful not to make too much noise, and there isn't a landlord banging on the ceiling with a broom. But even so, it's not the house we'd thought we'd get.

We had to leave the flat on Loomis quick. The water pipes broke and the landlord wouldn't fix them because the house was too old. We had to leave fast. We were using the washroom next door and carrying water over in empty milk gallons. That's why Mama and Papa looked for a house, and that's why we moved into the house on Mango Street, far away, on the other side of town.

They always told us that one day we would move into a house, a real house that would be ours for always so we wouldn't have to move each year. And our house would have running water and pipes that worked. And inside it would have real stairs, not hallway stairs, but stairs inside like the houses on TV. And we'd have a basement and at least three washrooms so when we took a bath we wouldn't have to tell everybody. Our house would be white with trees around it, a great big yard, and grass growing without a fence. This was the house Papa talked about when he held a lottery ticket and this was the house Mama dreamed up in the stories she told us before we went to bed.

But the house on Mango Street is not the way they told it at all. It's small 5 and red with tight steps in front and windows so small you'd think they were holding their breath. Bricks are crumbling in places, and the front door is so swollen you have to push hard to get in. There is no front yard, only four little elms the city planted by the curb. Out back is a small garage for the car we don't own yet and a small yard that looks smaller between the two buildings on either side. There are stairs in our house, but they're ordinary hallway stairs, and the house has only one washroom. Everybody has to share a bedroom — Mama and Papa, Carlos and Kiki, me and Nenny.

Once when we were living on Loomis, a nun from my school passed by and saw me playing out front. The laundromat downstairs had been boarded up because it had been robbed two days before and the owner had painted on the wood YES WE'RE OPEN so as not to lose business.

Where do you live? she asked.

There, I said pointing up to the third floor.

You live *there*?

There. I had to look to where she pointed — the third floor, the paint peel- 10 ing, wooden bars Papa had nailed on the windows so we wouldn't fall out. You live *there?* The way she said it made me feel like nothing. *There.* I lived *there.* I nodded.

I knew then I had to have a house. A real house. One I could point to. But this isn't it. The house on Mango Street isn't it. For the time being, Mama says. Temporary, says Papa. But I know how those things go.

APPROACHING THE READING

1. Describe the voice you hear in "The House on Mango Street." How old do you imagine the speaker is? What makes you think that? What else can you tell about her from the way she sounds as you listen to her?

Research this author in depth with cultural documents and multimedia resources on LiterActive.

2. What is the effect of having the voice and perspective be that of Esperanza? How do you think the story would differ if told by Esperanza's mother? Her father? One of her brothers?

3. Considering the story as a whole, what central point comes through as you listen to what Esperanza says?

READING FOR NARRATOR

As you read a work of fiction, one of the first things to listen for is who is telling, or narrating, the story. "The House on Mango Street" has a **first-person narrator**: the story is told by a character speaking in the first person, referring to herself as "I." (Occasionally, but rarely, a first-person narrator uses "we" instead of "I," to suggest that the story is being told by a group rather than an individual.) The *I* in any story, however, should *not* be assumed to be the author: The **narrator** in a story always is a *narrative construct*, an imagined speaker created by the writer.

True, many details about Esperanza's life parallel the author's: Cisneros was born in Chicago; was part of a large family (six brothers, no sisters); moved often during her childhood between Chicago and Mexico, where her father was born; and shared Esperanza's sense of dislocation and a lack of permanence. However, Cisneros was not writing an autobiographical essay, the way Sherman Alexie did in "Superman and Me" (p. 4). She clearly drew upon her own experiences as she wrote, but she used her imagination to alter the facts of her own life and to invent new ones. She constructed a character as the narrator, one who takes part in, as well as relates, the story. The story's power depends on hearing it from a child's perspective. We, as readers older than Esperanza is, can see implications in her story that she is not aware of yet, about poverty, class distinctions, housing patterns, and the power of landlords.

A first-person narrator who seems to speak directly for the author is often referred to as a **persona**: the "character" projected by the author, the *I* of a narrative poem or novel, or the speaker whose voice is heard in a lyric poem. Even if a first-person narrator seems to speak directly for the author or is given the author's name, the speaker created by the words of the story is not identical to the real-life author who writes the words.

"Love in L.A." (p. 61) and "Where Are You Going, Where Have You Been?" (p. 81) have **third-person narrators**. That is, both stories are told by anonymous outside observers who do not refer to themselves using the pronouns *I* or *we*. A third-person narrator can come as close to expressing the voice of the author directly as a first-person narrator does. But here, too, it is wise to keep in mind that any narrator is an imaginative construct, fashioned by the author as a vehicle for telling the story.

READING FOR POINT OF VIEW

The way a story is narrated is part of its **point of view**, the approach used in presenting the events of the story. To describe and discuss point of view effectively requires giving attention to the *person* telling the story and the *perspective* from which it is told.

PERSON   Consideration of point of view starts with listening to who is telling the story: Does it use a first-person narrator or a third-person narrator? Is the narrator given a name, or is the narrator an unnamed, unidentified voice relating what happens from outside the events? You cannot always identify a specific person as the narrator, but you usually can discern the narrator's relation to the action. Does the narrator participate in the action as a major or minor character, or does she or he observe the action, looking on from the outside?

PERSPECTIVE: INSIDE OR OUTSIDE   Understanding point of view continues with paying attention to the *perspective* from which the story is told. The narrator inevitably relates the story from a certain vantage point. To get the most from a story, it is important to determine what that vantage point is. Think of it in terms of camera angle in cinema: The camera can pull back and let you see everything, showing the scene from the outside, or it can seem to enter the mind of a particular character and show you only what that character sees and the way she or he sees it. The film can show us one side of the events by staying focused on one character or group of characters, or it can show two or more sides of the events by switching from one group of characters to another. Thus, a cops-and-robbers film shown from the perspective of the robbers looks very different from one presented from the perspective of the cops. And some films take advantage of that by moving back and forth between the two. Point of view matters — a lot.

The same is true in fiction. You can be told everything from both outside and inside the characters and events so that you know all that happens and the reasons why. Or you can hear everything from the outside but nothing from the inside, so you have to deduce the why (the characters' motivations) for yourself. Or you can hear about what only one character experiences and know only as much about the events as she or he knows. Or you can be told things from different perspectives as the story progresses, sometimes switching back and forth. (This happens more often in longer works such as novels; with some exceptions, short stories don't have enough room for a lot of switching.)

Each of these options has its own rewards and makes its own demands on the reader. Thus, for example, when a story is presented from the perspective of one character, as an active reader you should consider what that story would sound like from the perspective of other characters. Doing so gives you a deeper understanding of the character through whose consciousness you are hearing about the events as well as, in many cases, of the events themselves.

PERSPECTIVE: TIME   In fiction, the perspective of time also needs your consideration. Unlike film, which usually shows events as they are occurring, narrative necessarily relates events after they happened (a narrative in present tense would need to use the techniques of a play-by-play announcer at a sports event — but even here the announcer is describing not what *is* happening but what just did happen). As you read actively, therefore, you need to ask if the narrator is looking back to past events. If so, are they recent events or from the distant past? Can you tell how long ago? Does it matter how much time has passed? Does the narrator tell things differently now from the way she or he saw them earlier?

First-Person Narration

A first-person point of view is easily recognized by the narrator's use of *I* or *we* in telling the story. First-person narration is necessarily limited because an "I" or "we" cannot have omniscient awareness of events. First-person narrators can only tell about what they experience, observe, or are told. They cannot look into other characters' minds or feelings, and they may not understand fully the implications of what they see, hear, or experience.

Esperanza, the first-person narrator of "The House on Mango Street," for example, knows what the family's dream house would be like, and she knows their present house falls far short of their dreams. But she doesn't understand, until the day the nun sees her playing out front, what the house they live in says about their social situation, and she doesn't realize the kind of economic realities her family is up against.

In many cases, a first-person narrator is very knowledgeable about what has happened and why, often because the events happen either to the narrator or in the narrator's presence. But for just that reason, because the narrator is closely involved, the narrator's knowledge and understanding inevitably are limited. The narrator knows what happened to her- or himself or to some other characters, but may not know all that is happening to others related to the events. The narrator may not understand now, or did not understand then, why things happened as they did. She or he may not understand things about her- or himself. Often the narrator is looking back at things that happened much earlier, which she or he did not understand fully at the time but comes to grasp more fully later.

NAÏVE NARRATOR   Two specific variations on first-person perspectives should be noted. First is the use of a **naïve narrator**, a narrator too young or too inexperienced to understand fully the implications of what she or he is talking about. In such cases, active reading is even more important than usual, as the reader — who understands more than the narrator — must fill in implications the narrator cannot grasp. Such is the case in "The House on Mango Street": Much of the power of the latter comes from our ability to understand the reasons behind Esperanza's pains and disappointments, even though she is not fully aware of them.

RELIABLE NARRATOR   The other variation involves the use of a narrator who is not completely trustworthy. If the narrator tells her or his story accurately and honestly (as far as we can tell), the story has a **reliable narrator**: We can believe or rely on what she or he says, as we can in such examples as Katherine Min's "Courting a Monk" (p. 219), Judith Ortiz Cofer's "American History" (p. 346), and James Joyce's "Araby" (p. 393).

UNRELIABLE NARRATOR   But in some cases, we may suspect that a narrator is not telling the whole truth or is distorting some things, perhaps deliberately to make them look better or unintentionally because they are too painful to face. The narrator may not have the mental capacity to provide a coherent account of events, or she or he may have prejudices (against a race or class, or against a particular individual in the story) that the reader perceives even though the narrator is unaware of them. In all these cases, the narrator is **unreliable**: We can't trust everything she or he says. Here active reading is essential because you must try to determine what you can take straightforwardly and where you need to raise questions and make allowances for or corrections in what you are being told.

Third-Person Omniscient

In describing and discussing third-person point of view, you always need to include both a person and a perspective. It's not enough to say a story uses a third-person point of view. You need to add the *perspective* from which the third-person narrative is being presented, such as omniscient, objective, or limited.

When a story is told by an external narrator who seems to know everything about some events, both the present and the past, and is able to see into the minds and hearts of more than one character, the point of view is referred to as third-person *omniscient* (that is, "having unlimited knowledge"). At times, such a narrator describes what happens or what characters are like from outside, either objectively or by conveying opinions about them. At other points, the narrator may relate things from within the perspective of one character, or tell what that character or other characters are thinking or feeling or experiencing.

It's important to keep in mind that omniscient point of view doesn't mean the narrator has to tell the reader everything about a sequence of events or a set of characters; no story can tell everything. However, not disclosing everything doesn't mean the narrator is therefore limited. And the fact that the narrator *can* see into every character doesn't mean she or he *will* do so. A narrator will usually reveal the thoughts or feelings of a few characters, but not of all. That, too, doesn't mean the narrator has limited access to knowledge but rather that the narrator voluntarily limits what she or he relates.

Thus, Zora Neale Hurston's "Sweat" (p. 384) is told by an anonymous third-person narrator primarily from Delia Jones's perspective. It's her story. But occasionally the perspective shifts to the men sitting in front of the village store and occasionally to Sykes, the husband who abuses Delia. Many events are described objectively, but often we are told by the narrator what Delia is thinking or feeling ("A great terror took hold of her," p. 384). Other times, however, the narrator tells us what her husband is feeling ("A little awed by this new Delia," p. 386) or experiencing ("Inside, Sykes heard nothing until he knocked a pot lid off the stove while trying to reach the match safe in the dark," p. 392). Such access to the consciousness of more than one character is a clear indicator of an omniscient point of view.

Third-Person Objective

A third-person objective point of view differs in a crucial way from that of third-person omniscient. The narrator does not look into the mind of any of the characters or explain why any of the characters do what they do. The narrator describes events only from the outside, leaving it to the reader to draw conclusions from the details and dialogue provided. The invisible narrator in Ernest Hemingway's "Hills Like White Elephants" (p. 136), for example, simply describes where two characters are and what they do, and relates what they say to each other, never looking into their thoughts or commenting on or explaining what is going on between them. However, and this is often misunderstood, for a story to be narrated objectively does not necessarily mean that the story is objective. The way the man in "Hills Like White Elephants" pressures Jig and seems insensitive to her feelings may give grounds for concluding that the story is more sympathetic to Jig than to the man.

Third-Person Limited

When a story is told by a narrator who seems to know everything about some parts of the story, or everything that happens to or affects one character or a few characters, but does not know about other important things, the point of view is third-person *limited* (that is, "having limited omniscience"). Like an omniscient narrator, a narrator with limited omniscience sometimes describes what happens or reveals what characters are like from the outside and other times relates things from the perspective of a particular character or tells what that character is thinking or feeling or experiencing. The difference between a narrator with limited omniscience and an omniscient narrator is that the former seems not to have access to the consciousness of all characters, while the latter does.

Jhumpa Lahiri's "A Temporary Matter" (p. 398), for example, is told by a narrator who seems totally knowledgeable about the lives of Shoba and Shukumar except what Shoba is thinking and feeling. The narrator frequently relates facts objectively: "Six months ago, in September, Shukumar was at an academic conference in Baltimore when Shoba went into labor, three weeks before her due date" (p. 399) or "But nothing was pushing Shukumar" (p. 400). But most of the time the story is told from Shukumar's perspective; we know what he is thinking, feeling, and experiencing. But the narrator does not seem to have similar access to Shoba's thoughts and plans. Indeed, the story depends for its effect on that limitation.

Center of Consciousness

A widely used variant on the third-person limited point of view is a **center of consciousness** approach. In it, the narrator relates the story in the third person but does so by centering attention on one character. We are told things that character is conscious of, what she or he does, sees, thinks, remembers, feels, and experiences. The character may be the central character or a minor character, but only that character's perceptions, thoughts, and feelings are shown, and what others do or say is usually shown only through her or his perspective. The author may give some third-person description or background information, but it will be a limited amount.

Ana Menéndez's "Her Mother's House" (p. 419) uses a center of consciousness approach. Most of the story centers on Lisette. It follows where she goes and shows scenes through her eyes or memory. The story includes dialogue, but only what Lisette hears or participates in. The narrator occasionally states a fact objectively: "She was born in Miami, two years after the revolution" (p. 419), for example, and "Lisette married a round-faced boy whose parents were from Varadero" (p. 420), but most of the story relates what Lisette is conscious of, what she sees, hears, thinks, feels, and experiences ("The thick warm air curled through the open window. . . . It was the first time she had been alone in years and the new quiet seemed something she could touch," p. 419).

Interior Monologue

A technique sometimes used in presenting center of consciousness is **interior monologue**. A *monologue* in drama is an extended, uninterrupted speech by a single speaker; an *interior monologue* is such a speech occurring within a character's mind. It is the representation of unspoken mental activity as if directly overheard by the reader without being selected and organized by a narrator. It can be thoughts, impressions, and memories presented in an associative, disjointed, nonlogical way as they flow through a person's mind. Or it can be a more logical, grammatical flow of thoughts and memories moving through a person's mind, as if being spoken to an external listener (the way we rehearse in our minds what we plan to say to someone later, but digress along the way, following things we are reminded of before getting back to the topic at hand).

In Tillie Olsen's "I Stand Here Ironing," for example, the narrator, while doing her ironing, runs through her mind what she would like to say, but probably never will, to the school counselor or social worker who asks her to come in to talk about her daughter, who the counselor feels is in need of help: "You think because I am her mother I have a key, or that in some way you could use me as a key? She has lived for nineteen years. There is all that life that has happened outside of me, beyond me" (p. 467). This whole story is an interior monologue. A story or novel, however, can be presented partly through interior monologue or stream of consciousness and partly through an omniscient or objective perspective.

Stream of Consciousness

A story, or parts of a story, can be told by conveying the continuous flow of whatever passes through the mind (consciousness) of a character. This includes sense perceptions as well as thoughts, memories, and feelings — the total sense of awareness and the mental and emotional response to it. This approach is referred to as **stream of consciousness**. It must not be confused with the approach described above: A *center of consciousness* story can use a *stream of consciousness* approach, but it doesn't need to. A true stream of consciousness style is used infrequently and is characterized by a distinctive style. Usually, to capture the fact that much mental activity is nonverbal, stream of consciousness does not use ordinary punctuation or complete sentences (after all, we don't always think in complete sentences), is associative rather than logical, and seems disjointed and haphazard. It is an unstructured, even at times chaotic, flow of random sense perceptions, mental pictures, sounds, thoughts, and details — an attempt to represent prerational mental activity before the mind orders it into a coherent form or shape.

Realizing that an author has selected these seemingly random thoughts and perceptions, an active reader must make connections between them and find a meaning the character is usually unaware of. Here, for example, is a stream of consciousness passage from James Joyce's novel *Ulysses* (1922), as the main character Leopold Bloom strolls through Dublin, with his mind absorbing impressions and connecting them to random thoughts and memories:

> Pineapple rock, lemon platt, butter scotch. A sugar-sticky girl shoveling scoopfuls of creams for a christian brother. Some school great. Bad for their tummies. Lozenge and comfit manufacturer to His Majesty the King. God. Save. Our. Sitting on his throne, sucking red jujubes white.

READING FOR THEME

Along with listening for what happens to whom and who tells the story from what perspective, active readers listen for what the story as a whole says, what it is about in the sense of "what it all adds up to." Many people refer to what it all adds up to as the **theme**: the central idea or concept conveyed by a literary work. The *all* in "what it all adds up to" is important — theme must take everything into account, all the different techniques used in telling the story (everything discussed in Chapters 4 to 7), and all the things that happen to all the characters.

STATING A THEME   A statement on theme should be expressed in two parts: a *subject* and a *predicate* (something about the subject). The subject of "The House on Mango Street" could be said to be a poor immigrant family's search for adequate housing; a statement of the theme might be that a poor immigrant family's search for adequate housing reveals that the effect of inadequate housing goes beyond discomfort and inconvenience to undermining the occupants' sense of respect and self-worth.

LIMITS OF THEME   Theme can never encompass the work as a whole; it is always less than the work and is never an adequate substitute for the work. Because theme is an artificial abstraction from the work, it has the risk of diminishing reading from a holistic experience, which involves the emotions and imagination as well as the intellect, to an intellectual one only. A good reader does not read simply for theme. Articulating a theme is one of the many ways of responding to a work, but it is not the only or necessarily the most important one.

VALIDITY OF THEME   Theme is always at least somewhat subjective. Works rarely have a single "right" theme that all readers find and express in the same way. Each of us may find different themes in a rich work of literature, and we may express them in different ways, but that does not mean that every interpretation is equally valid. If someone says the theme of "The House on Mango Street" is the importance of mothers in holding families

www

Further explore point of view and theme, including interactive exercises, with VirtuaLit Fiction at bedfordstmartins.com/ approachinglit.

together through difficult circumstances, there would be good reason to object that such an interpretation is not grounded in the story, that it is more an effort to extract a lesson from the story than to draw together what it all adds up to.

Statements of theme must grow out of details in the story, not out of ideas, experiences, or values we bring to the story. Stating a theme should not be thought of as finding a moral or lesson in the work; there may be a lesson, but often a literary work is more interested in depicting human behavior than in judging it or drawing lessons from it. We do not need to agree with characters' beliefs or approve of their actions to enjoy and appreciate the work in which they appear.

☑ CHECKLIST for Reading about Point of View and Theme

❑ Notice who is telling the story (the narrator) and the point-of-view (the perspective, or vantage, from which the story is told):

- *First-person:* a partially knowing *I* or *we*, sometimes reliable, sometimes naïve or unreliable
- *Third-person omniscient:* an all-knowing, often anonymous, reporter
- *Third-person objective:* a reporter of words and actions, not thoughts or motives
- *Third-person limited:* a partially knowing observer or participant (often using a center of consciousness — seeing a story through the consciousness of a particular character — and occasionally interior monologue — direct presentation of a character's thoughts and memories, without intervention by a narrator)
- *Stream of consciousness:* the seemingly unstructured perceptions, images, and reflections flowing through a mind

❑ Think about a story's theme, the central idea or concept conveyed in the story — what it all adds up to. Be sure the theme you come up with is firmly grounded in the story and that you have specific details to support the theme's presence and importance.

FURTHER READING

ENTRY POINTS   The following story takes us back to the 1960s, when African Americans began turning back to Africa in their search for roots and identity, when Afro hairdos, African-influenced clothing, and adoption of African names to connect with one's heritage were new and startling (especially in the old world of the rural South). As you read it, pay attention to the voice you hear and to the handling of point of view and perspective. Think about the extent to which the way the story "works," the way it achieves its effects, depends on the voice and personality of the narrator.

Alice Walker   b. 1944

Everyday Use   [1973]

for your grandmama

I will wait for her in the yard that Maggie and I made so clean and wavy yesterday afternoon. A yard like this is more comfortable than most people know. It is not just a yard. It is like an extended living room. When the hard clay is swept clean as a floor and the fine sand around the edges lined with tiny, irregular grooves, anyone can come and sit and look up into the elm tree and wait for the breezes that never come inside the house.

Maggie will be nervous until after her sister goes: she will stand hopelessly in corners, homely and ashamed of the burn scars down her arms and legs, eyeing her sister with a mixture of envy and awe. She thinks her sister has held life always in the palm of one hand, that "no" is a word the world never learned to say to her.

You've no doubt seen those TV shows where the child who has "made it" is confronted, as a surprise, by her own mother and father, tottering in weakly from backstage. (A pleasant surprise, of course: What would they do if parent and child came on the show only to curse out and insult each other?) On TV mother and child embrace and smile into each other's faces. Sometimes the mother and father weep, the child wraps them in her arms and leans across the table to tell how she would not have made it without their help. I have seen these programs.

Sometimes I dream a dream in which Dee and I are suddenly brought together on a TV program of this sort. Out of a dark and soft-seated limousine I am ushered into a bright room filled with many people. There I meet a smiling, gray, sporty man like Johnny Carson° who shakes my hand and tells me what a

---

Johnny Carson: (1925–2005) U.S. comedian and host of *The Tonight Show Starring Johnny Carson* from 1962 to 1992.

fine girl I have. Then we are on the stage and Dee is embracing me with tears in her eyes. She pins on my dress a large orchid, even though she has told me once that she thinks orchids are tacky flowers.

In real life I am a large, big-boned woman with rough, man-working hands. 5 In the winter I wear flannel nightgowns to bed and overalls during the day. I can kill and clean a hog as mercilessly as a man. My fat keeps me hot in zero weather. I can work outside all day, breaking ice to get water for washing; I can eat pork liver cooked over the open fire minutes after it comes steaming from the hog. One winter I knocked a bull calf straight in the brain between the eyes with a sledge hammer and had the meat hung up to chill before nightfall. But of course all this does not show on television. I am the way my daughter would want me to be: a hundred pounds lighter, my skin like an uncooked barley pancake. My hair glistens in the hot bright lights. Johnny Carson has much to do to keep up with my quick and witty tongue.

But that is a mistake. I know even before I wake up. Who ever knew a Johnson with a quick tongue? Who can even imagine me looking a strange white man in the eye? It seems to me I have talked to them always with one foot raised in flight, with my head turned in whichever way is farthest from them. Dee, though. She would always look anyone in the eye. Hesitation was no part of her nature.

"How do I look, Mama?" Maggie says, showing just enough of her thin body enveloped in pink skirt and red blouse for me to know she's there, almost hidden by the door.

"Come out into the yard," I say.

Have you ever seen a lame animal, perhaps a dog run over by some careless person rich enough to own a car, sidle up to someone who is ignorant enough to be kind to him? That is the way my Maggie walks. She has been like this, chin on chest, eyes on ground, feet in shuffle, ever since the fire that burned the other house to the ground.

Dee is lighter than Maggie, with nicer hair and a fuller figure. She's a 10 woman now, though sometimes I forget. How long ago was it that the other house burned? Ten, twelve years? Sometimes I can still hear the flames and feel Maggie's arms sticking to me, her hair smoking and her dress falling off her in little black papery flakes. Her eyes seemed stretched open, blazed open by the flames reflected in them. And Dee. I see her standing off under the sweet gum tree she used to dig gum out of; a look of concentration on her face as she watched the last dingy gray board of the house fall in toward the red-hot brick chimney. Why don't you do a dance around the ashes? I'd wanted to ask her. She had hated the house that much.

I used to think she hated Maggie, too. But that was before we raised the money, the church and me, to send her to Augusta to school. She used to read to us without pity; forcing words, lies, other folks' habits, whole lives upon us two, sitting trapped and ignorant underneath her voice. She washed us in a river of make-believe, burned us with a lot of knowledge we didn't necessarily need to know. Pressed us to her with the serious way she read, to shove us away at just the moment, like dimwits, we seemed about to understand.

Dee wanted nice things. A yellow organdy dress to wear to her graduation from high school; black pumps to match a green suit she'd made from an old suit somebody gave me. She was determined to stare down any disaster in her efforts. Her eyelids would not flicker for minutes at a time. Often I fought off the temptation to shake her. At sixteen she had a style of her own: and knew what style was.

I never had an education myself. After second grade the school was closed down. Don't ask me why: in 1927 colored asked fewer questions than they do now. Sometimes Maggie reads to me. She stumbles along good-naturedly but can't see well. She knows she is not bright. Like good looks and money, quickness passed her by. She will marry John Thomas (who has mossy teeth in an earnest face) and then I'll be free to sit here and I guess just sing church songs to myself. Although I never was a good singer. Never could carry a tune. I was always better at a man's job. I used to love to milk till I was hooked in the side in '49. Cows are soothing and slow and don't bother you, unless you try to milk them the wrong way.

I have deliberately turned my back on the house. It is three rooms, just like the one that burned, except the roof is tin; they don't make shingle roofs any more. There are no real windows, just some holes cut in the sides, like the portholes in a ship, but not round and not square, with rawhide holding the shutters up on the outside. This house is in a pasture, too, like the other one. No doubt when Dee sees it she will want to tear it down. She wrote me once that no matter where we "choose" to live, she will manage to come see us. But she will never bring her friends. Maggie and I thought about this and Maggie asked me, "Mama, when did Dee ever *have* any friends?"

She had a few. Furtive boys in pink shirts hanging about on washday after 15 school. Nervous girls who never laughed. Impressed with her they worshiped the well-turned phrase, the cute shape, the scalding humor that erupted like bubbles in lye. She read to them.

When she was courting Jimmy T she didn't have much time to pay to us, but turned all her faultfinding power on him. He *flew* to marry a cheap city girl from a family of ignorant flashy people. She hardly had time to recompose herself.

When she comes I will meet — but there they are!

Maggie attempts to make a dash for the house, in her shuffling way, but I stay her with my hand. "Come back here," I say. And she stops and tries to dig a well in the sand with her toe.

It is hard to see them clearly through the strong sun. But even the first glimpse of leg out of the car tells me it is Dee. Her feet were always neat-looking, as if God himself had shaped them with a certain style. From the other side of the car comes a short, stocky man. Hair is all over his head a foot long and hanging from his chin like a kinky mule tail. I hear Maggie suck in her breath.

"Uhnnnh," is what it sounds like. Like when you see the wriggling end of a snake just in front of your foot on the road. "Uhnnnh."

Dee next. A dress down to the ground, in this hot weather. A dress so loud it 20 hurts my eyes. There are yellows and oranges enough to throw back the light of the sun. I feel my whole face warming from the heat waves it throws out. Ear-rings gold, too, and hanging down to her shoulders. Bracelets dangling and making noises when she moves her arm up to shake the folds of the dress out of her armpits. The dress is loose and flows, and as she walks closer, I like it. I hear Maggie go "Uhnnnh" again. It is her sister's hair. It stands straight up like the wool on a sheep. It is black as night and around the edges are two long pigtails that rope about like small lizards disappearing behind her ears.

"Wa-su-zo-Tean-o!" she says, coming on in that gliding way the dress makes her move. The short stocky fellow with the hair to his navel is all grin-ning and he follows up with "Asalamalakim, my mother and sister!" He moves to hug Maggie but she falls back, right up against the back of my chair. I feel her trembling there and when I look up I see the perspiration falling off her chin.

"Don't get up," says Dee. Since I am stout it takes something of a push. You can see me trying to move a second or two before I make it. She turns, showing white heels through her sandals, and goes back to the car. Out she peeks next with a Polaroid. She stoops down quickly and lines up picture after picture of me sitting there in front of the house with Maggie cowering behind me. She never takes a shot without making sure the house is included. When a cow comes nib-bling around the edge of the yard she snaps it and me and Maggie *and* the house. Then she puts the Polaroid in the back seat of the car, and comes up and kisses me on the forehead.

Meanwhile Asalamalakim is going through motions with Maggie's hand. Maggie's hand is as limp as a fish, and probably as cold, despite the sweat, and she keeps trying to pull it back. It looks like Asalamalakim wants to shake hands but wants to do it fancy. Or maybe he don't know how people shake hands. Any-how, he soon gives up on Maggie.

"Well," I say. "Dee."

"No, Mama," she says. "Not 'Dee,' Wangero Leewanika Kemanjo!" 25

"What happened to 'Dee'?" I wanted to know.

"She's dead," Wangero said. "I couldn't bear it any longer, being named after the people who oppress me."

"You know as well as me you was named after your aunt Dicie," I said. Dicie is my sister. She named Dee. We called her "Big Dee" after Dee was born.

"But who was *she* named after?" asked Wangero.

"I guess after Grandma Dee," I said. 30

"And who was she named after?" asked Wangero.

"Her mother," I said, and saw Wangero was getting tired. "That's about as far back as I can trace it," I said. Though, in fact, I probably could have carried it back beyond the Civil War through the branches.

"Well," said Asalamalakim, "there you are."

"Uhnnnh," I heard Maggie say.

"There I was not," I said, "before 'Dicie' cropped up in our family, so why 35 should I try to trace it that far back?"

He just stood there grinning, looking down on me like somebody inspecting a Model A car. Every once in a while he and Wangero sent eye signals over my head.

"How do you pronounce this name?" I asked.

"You don't have to call me by it if you don't want to," said Wangero.

"Why shouldn't I?" I asked. "If that's what you want us to call you, we'll call you."

"I know it might sound awkward at first," said Wangero. 40

"I'll get used to it," I said. "Ream it out again."

Well, soon we got the name out of the way. Asalamalakim had a name twice as long and three times as hard. After I tripped over it two or three times he told me to just call him Hakim-a-barber. I wanted to ask him was he a barber, but I didn't really think he was, so I didn't ask.

"You must belong to those beef-cattle peoples down the road," I said. They said "Asalamalakim" when they met you, too, but they didn't shake hands. Always too busy: feeding the cattle, fixing the fences, putting up salt-lick shelters, throwing down hay. When the white folks poisoned some of the herd the men stayed up all night with rifles in their hands. I walked a mile and a half just to see the sight.

Hakim-a-barber said, "I accept some of their doctrines, but farming and raising cattle is not my style." (They didn't tell me, and I didn't ask, whether Wangero (Dee) had really gone and married him.)

We sat down to eat and right away he said he didn't eat collards and pork 45 was unclean. Wangero, though, went on through the chitlins and corn bread, the greens and everything else. She talked a blue streak over the sweet potatoes. Everything delighted her. Even the fact that we still used the benches her daddy made for the table when we couldn't afford to buy chairs.

"Oh, Mama!" she cried. Then turned to Hakim-a-barber. "I never knew how lovely these benches are. You can feel the rump prints," she said, running her hands underneath her and along the bench. Then she gave a sigh and her hand closed over Grandma Dee's butter dish. "That's it!" she said. "I knew there was something I wanted to ask you if I could have." She jumped up from the table and went over in the corner where the churn stood, the milk in it clabber by now. She looked at the churn and looked at it.

"This churn top is what I need," she said. "Didn't Uncle Buddy whittle it out of a tree you all used to have?"

"Yes," I said.

"Uh huh," she said happily. "And I want the dasher, too."

"Uncle Buddy whittle that, too?" asked the barber. 50

Dee (Wangero) looked up at me.

"Aunt Dee's first husband whittled the dash," said Maggie so low you almost couldn't hear her. "His name was Henry, but they called him Stash."

"Maggie's brain is like an elephant's," Wangero said, laughing. "I can use the churn top as a centerpiece for the alcove table," she said, sliding a plate over the churn, "and I'll think of something artistic to do with the dasher."

When she finished wrapping the dasher the handle stuck out. I took it for a moment in my hands. You didn't even have to look close to see where hands pushing the dasher up and down to make butter had left a kind of sink in the wood. In fact, there were a lot of small sinks; you could see where thumbs and fingers had sunk into the wood. It was beautiful light yellow wood, from a tree that grew in the yard where Big Dee and Stash had lived.

After dinner Dee (Wangero) went to the trunk at the foot of my bed and 55 started rifling through it. Maggie hung back in the kitchen over the dishpan. Out came Wangero with two quilts. They had been pieced by Grandma Dee and then Big Dee and me had hung them on the quilt frames on the front porch and quilted them. One was in the Lone Star pattern. The other was Walk Around the Mountain. In both of them were scraps of dresses Grandma Dee had worn fifty and more years ago. Bits and pieces of Grandpa Jarrell's Paisley shirts. And one teeny faded blue piece, about the size of a penny matchbox, that was from Great Grandpa Ezra's uniform that he wore in the Civil War.

"Mama," Wangero said sweet as a bird. "Can I have these old quilts?"

I heard something fall in the kitchen, and a minute later the kitchen door slammed.

"Why don't you take one or two of the others?" I asked. "These old things was just done by me and Big Dee from some tops your grandma pieced before she died."

"No," said Wangero. "I don't want those. They are stitched around the borders by machine."

"That'll make them last better," I said. 60

"That's not the point," said Wangero. "These are all pieces of dresses Grandma used to wear. She did all this stitching by hand. Imagine!" She held the quilts securely in her arms, stroking them.

"Some of the pieces, like those lavender ones, come from old clothes her mother handed down to her," I said, moving up to touch the quilts. Dee (Wangero) moved back just enough so that I couldn't reach the quilts. They already belonged to her.

"Imagine!" she breathed again, clutching them closely to her bosom.

"The truth is," I said, "I promised to give them quilts to Maggie, for when she marries John Thomas."

She gasped like a bee had stung her. 65

"Maggie can't appreciate these quilts!" she said. "She'd probably be backward enough to put them to everyday use."

"I reckon she would," I said. "God knows I been saving 'em for long enough with nobody using 'em. I hope she will!" I didn't want to bring up how I had offered Dee (Wangero) a quilt when she went away to college. Then she had told me they were old-fashioned, out of style.

"But they're *priceless*!" she was saying now, furiously; for she has a temper. "Maggie would put them on the bed and in five years they'd be in rags. Less than that!"

"She can always make some more," I said. "Maggie knows how to quilt."

Dee (Wangero) looked at me with hatred. "You just will not understand. 70 The point is these quilts, *these* quilts!"

"Well," I said, stumped. "What would *you* do with them?"

"Hang them," she said. As if that was the only thing you *could* do with quilts.

Maggie by now was standing in the door. I could almost hear the sound her feet made as they scraped over each other.

"She can have them, Mama," she said, like somebody used to never winning anything, or having anything reserved for her. "I can 'member Grandma Dee without the quilts."

I looked at her hard. She had filled her bottom lip with checkerberry snuff 75 and it gave her face a kind of dopey, hangdog look. It was Grandma Dee and Big Dee who taught her how to quilt herself. She stood there with her scarred hands hidden in the folds of her skirt. She looked at her sister with something like fear but she wasn't mad at her. This was Maggie's portion. This was the way she knew God to work.

When I looked at her like that something hit me in the top of my head and ran down to the soles of my feet. Just like when I'm in church and the spirit of God touches me and I get happy and shout. I did something I never had done before: hugged Maggie to me, then dragged her on into the room, snatched the quilts out of Miss Wangero's hands and dumped them into Maggie's lap. Maggie just sat there on my bed with her mouth open.

"Take one or two of the others," I said to Dee.

But she turned without a word and went out to Hakim-a-barber.

"You just don't understand," she said, as Maggie and I came out to the car.

"What don't I understand?" I wanted to know. 80

"Your heritage," she said. And then she turned to Maggie, kissed her, and said, "You ought to try to make something of yourself, too, Maggie. It's really a new day for us. But from the way you and Mama still live you'd never know it."

She put on some sunglasses that hid everything above the tip of her nose and her chin.

Maggie smiled; maybe at the sunglasses. But a real smile, not scared. After we watched the car dust settle I asked Maggie to bring me a dip of snuff. And then the two of us sat there just enjoying, until it was time to go in the house and go to bed.

APPROACHING THE READING

1. Describe the voice you hear in "Everyday Use." What can you tell about the narrator from the way she sounds as you listen to her? What kind of personality comes through what she says and the way she says it?

2. Identify the point of view used in the story. What is the particular effect of having the narrator address the reader as *you*? In what ways does the effect of story depend on its voice and perspective?
3. Explain the theme of the story, as you see it. What central point comes through, considering the story as a whole? Point to particular parts of the story that support what you say.
4. Look carefully at the final paragraph of the story. Does it fit well with what you said about voice and theme? Is it an effective and satisfying ending? If so, how and why? If you find it unsatisfying, explain why.

ENTRY POINTS   The following story, unlike the other two in this chapter, takes place in an expensive house in a fashionable neighborhood. It appears calm and cozy from the outside, but the situation inside turns murky both for its human inhabitants and the pet goldfish. After you read the story and become acquainted with the characters and conflicts developed in it, reread it closely considering the point of view from which it is told and watching for themes that emerge in it.

David Means   b. 1961

The Secret Goldfish   [2004]

He had a weird growth along his dorsal fin, and that gape-mouth grimace you see in older fish. Way too big for his tank, too, having outgrown the standard goldfish age limit. Which is what? About one month? He was six years old — outlandishly old for a fish. One afternoon, Teddy, as he was called then, now just Ted, took notice of the condition of Fish's tank: a wedge of sunlight plunged through the window of his bedroom and struck the water's surface, disappearing. The water was so clotted it had become a solid mass, a putty within which Fish was presumably swimming, or dead. Most likely dead. Where's Fish? Where's Fish? Teddy yelled to his mom. She came into his room, caught sight of the tank, and gave a small yelp. Once again, a fish had been neglected.

Everyone knows the story. The kids beg and plead: Please, please get us a fish (or a dog), we'll feed it, we will, honest, we'll take care of it and you won't have to do a single thing. We'll clean the tank walls with the brush and make sure the filter charcoal is replaced regularly and refill the water when it evaporates. Please, please, we can handle it, we're old enough now, we are, it'll be so much fun, it will, so much fun. But in the end they don't. They dump too much food in no matter how often they're told to be careful, to use just a pinch, and even after they've read biblical-sounding fables about the fish who ate too much and grew too large for its bowl, shattering the sides, they watch gleefully while he consumes like mad, unable to stop. It's fun to watch him eat, to witness the physical manifestation of a fact: the level of Fish's hunger is permanently set to high. In the metaphysics of the fish universe, gluttony is not a sin. The delicate wafers of food fall lightly onto the water, linger on the surface tension, and are broken apart on infinitely eager lips. She overfeeds, too (on the days when she's pretty sure the kids haven't fed him). Her shaking mechanics are sloppy. The light flakes become moist, collude, collect their inertia, and all too often fall out of the can in a large clump. Really, she hasn't neglected the poor fish. "Neglect" seems a word too heavy with submerged intent. Something was bound to slip to the side amid the chaos of the domestic arena. But Fish has sustained himself in terrible conditions. He is the king of all goldfish survivors.

Her own childhood goldfish — named Fred — ended his days in Grayling Pond, a hole near her house in northern Michigan, dug out by the state D.N.R.° on a pond-production grant. (Why the Great Lakes state needed more ponds is anyone's guess.) Garnished with a wide band of lily pads, the water a pale yellow, speckled with skeeter-bug ripples, the pond was close to becoming a marsh. Hope you survive, Fred, her father had said as he slopped the fish out of the pail and into the pond. She did not forget the sight of her beloved fish as he slipped from the lip of the bucket and rode the glassine tube of water into the pond. The rest of the summer she imagined his orange form — brilliantly bright and fluorescent against the glimmer of water — in a kind of slow-motion replay. Dumbest animals on earth, she remembered her father adding. Nothing dumber than a carp. Except maybe a catfish, or your goddam mother.

Not long after that afternoon at Grayling Pond, her father left the house in a fit of rage. Gone for good, her mother said. Thank Christ. Then, a few months later, he was killed in a freak accident, crushed between hunks of ice and the hull of a container ship in Duluth. Superior's slush ice was temperamental that winter, chewing up the coastline, damaging bulkheads. Her father had signed on as one of the men who went down with poles and gave furtive pokes and prods, in the tradition of those Michigan rivermen who had once dislodged logjams with their peaveys and pike poles, standing atop the timber in their spiked boots, sparring with magnificent forces. Accounts varied, but the basic story was that the ice shifted, some kind of crevasse formed, and he slipped in. Then the lake gave a heave and his legs were crushed, clamped in the jaw of God's stupid justice. As she liked to imagine it, he had just enough time to piece together a little prayer asking for forgiveness for being a failure of a father ("Dear Heavenly Father, forgive me for my huge failings as a father to my dear daughter and even more for my gaping failure as a husband to my wife") and for dumping Fred ("and for getting rid of that fish my daughter loved more than me"), and then to watch as the pale winter sun slipped quickly away while the other men urged him to remain calm and told him that he'd be fine and they'd have him out in a minute or so, while knowing for certain that they wouldn't.

D.N.R.: Department of Natural Resources.

Long after her father was gone, she imagined Fred lurking in the lower ⁵
reaches of Grayling Pond, in the coolest pockets, trying to conserve his energy.
Sometimes, when she was cleaning upstairs and dusting Teddy's room, she
would pause in the deep, warm, silent heart of a suburban afternoon and watch
Fish as he dangled asleep, wide-eyed, unmoving, just fluffing his fins softly on
occasion. One time she even tried it herself, standing still, suspended in the
dense fluid of an unending array of demanding tasks — cleaning, cooking, washing, grocery shopping, snack-getting — while outside the birds chirped and the
traffic hissed past on the parkway.

The marriage had fallen apart abruptly. Her husband — who worked in the
city as a corporate banker and left the house each morning at dawn with the
Times, still wrapped in its bright-blue delivery bag, tucked beneath his arm — had
betrayed his vows. One evening, he'd arrived home from work with what seemed
to be a new face: his teeth were abnormally white. He'd had them bleached in
the city. (In retrospect, she saw that his bright teeth were the first hint of his infidelity.) He had found a dentist on Park Avenue. Soon he was coming home late
on some nights and not at all on others, under the vague pretense of work obligations. In Japan, he explained, people sleep overnight in town as a sign of their
dedication to business; they rent cubicles just wide enough for a body, like
coffins, he said, and for days when he did not return she thought of those small
compartments and she chose to believe him. (Of course I know about the Japanese, she had said, emphatically.) Then one night she found him in the bathroom with a bar of soap, rubbing it gently against his wedding ring. It's too tight,
he said. I'm just trying to loosen it. When others were perplexed by the fact that
she had not deduced his infidelity, picked up on the clues, during those fall
months, she felt compelled (though she never did) to describe the marriage in
all of its long complexity — fifteen years — starting with the honeymoon in Spain:
the parador in Chinchón, outside Madrid, that had once been a monastery,
standing naked with him at the balcony door in the dusky night air listening
to the sounds of the village and the splash of the pool. She had given up her
career for the relationship, for the family. She had given up plenty in order to
stay home for Teddy's and Annie's formative years, to make sure those brain
synapses formed correctly, to be assured that the right connections were fused.
(Because studies had made it clear that a kid's success depends on the first few
years. It was important to develop the fine motor skills, to have the appropriate
hand play, not to mention critical reasoning skills, before the age of four!) So,
yes, she guessed the whole decision to give herself over to the domestic job had
been an act of free will, but now it felt as though the act itself had been carried
out in the conditions of betrayal that would eventually unfold before her.

Fish had come into the family fold in a plastic Baggie of water, bulging dan-
gerously, knotted at the top, with a mate, Sammy, who would end up a floater
two days later. Pet Universe had given free goldfish to all the kids on a preschool
field trip. In less than a year, Fish had grown too big for his starter bowl and

begun to tighten his spiralled laps, restricted in his movements by his gathering bulk and the glass walls of the bowl. Then he graduated to a classic five-gallon bowl, where, in the course of the next few years, he grew, until one afternoon, still deep in what seemed to be a stable domestic situation, with the kids off at school, she went out to Pet Universe and found a large tank and some water-prep drops and a filter unit, one that sat on the rim and produced a sleek, fountainlike curl of water, and some turquoise gravel and a small figurine to keep the fish company: a cartoonish pirate galleon — a combination of Mark Twain riverboat and man-of-war — with an exaggerated bow and an orange plastic paddle wheel that spun around in the tank's currents until it gobbed up and stuck. The figurine, which was meant to please the eyes of children, had that confused mix of design that put commercial viability ahead of the truth. Teddy and Annie hated it. Ultimately, the figure served one purpose. It rearranged the conceptual space of the tank and gave the illusion that Fish now had something to do, something to work around, during his languorous afternoon laps, and she found herself going in to watch him, giving deep philosophical consideration to his actions: Did Fish remember that he had passed that way before? Was he aware of his eternal hell, caught in the tank's glass grip? Or did he feel wondrously free, swimming — for all he knew — in Lake Superior, an abundant, wide field of water, with some glass obstructions here and there? Was he basically free of wants, needs, and everything else? Did he wonder at the food miraculously appearing atop the surface tension, food to be approached with parted lips?

One evening, after observing Fish, when she was at the sink looking out the window at the yard, she saw her husband there, along the south side, holding his phone to his ear and lifting his free hand up and down from his waist in a slight flapping gesture that she knew indicated that he was emotionally agitated.

Shortly after that, the tank began to murk up. Through the dim months of January and February, the filter clotted, the flow stopped, and stringy green silk grew on the lip of the waterfall. The murk thickened. In the center of the darkness, Fish swam in random patterns and became a sad, hopeless entity curled into his plight. He was no longer fooled by his short-term memory into thinking that he was eternally free. Nor was he bored by the repetitive nature of his laps, going around the stupid ship figurine, sinking down into the gravel, picking — typical bottom-feeder — for scraps. Instead, he was lost in the eternal roar of an isotropic universe, flinging himself wildly within the expanding big bang of tank murk. On occasion, he found his way to the light and rubbed his eye against the glass, peering out in a judgmental way. But no one was there to see him. No one seemed available to witness these outward glances. Until the day when Teddy, now just Ted, noticed and said, Mom, Mom, the tank, and she went and cleaned it, but only after she had knocked her knuckle a few times on the glass and seen that he was alive, consumed in the dark but moving and seemingly healthy. Then she felt awe at the fact that life was sustainable even under the most abhorrent conditions. She felt a fleeting connection between this awe and the possibility that God exists. But then she reminded herself that it was only Fish. Just frickin' Fish, she thought. Here I am so weepy and sad, trying to make sense of my horrible situation, that something like this will give me hope. Of course, she was probably also thinking back to that afternoon, watching her father sluice Fred down into the warm waters of the shallow pond in Michigan. Her memory of it was profoundly clear. The vision of the fish itself — pristine and orange — travelling through the water as it spilled from the bucket was exact and perfect.

She set to work scooping out the water with an old Tupperware bowl, replac-   10
ing it in increments so the chlorine would evaporate, driving to Pet Universe to get another cotton filter, some water-clarifying drops, and a pound sack of activated charcoal nuggets. She disassembled the pump mechanism — a small magnet attached to a ring of plastic that hovered, embraced by a larger magnet. Somehow the larger magnet cooperated with the magnet on the plastic device and used physical laws of some sort to suck the water up and through the filter, where it cascaded over the wide lip and twisted as it approached the surface. It seemed to her as her fingers cleaned the device that it was not only a thing of great simplicity and beauty but also something much deeper, a tool meant to sustain Fish's life and, in turn, his place in the family. The afternoon was clear, blue-skied, wintry bright — and out the kitchen window she saw the uncut lawn, dark straw brown, matted down in van Gogh swirls, frosted with cold. Past the lawn, the woods, through which she could see the cars moving on the parkway, stood stark and brittle in the direct implications of the winter light. It was a fine scene, embarrassingly suburban, but certainly fine. Back upstairs, she saw Fish swimming jauntily in his new conditions and she was pretty sure that he was delighted, moving with swift strokes from one end of the tank to the other, skirting the figurine professionally, wagging his back fin — what was that called? was it the caudal fin? — fashionably, like a cabaret dancer working her fan. A beautiful tail, unfurling in a windswept motion in the clearing water. When she leaned down for a closer look, it became apparent that the fin was much, much larger than it seemed when it was in action and twining in on itself. When Fish paused, it swayed open beautifully — a fine, healthy, wide carp tail. Along his sides, he had the usual scars of an abused fish, a wound or two, a missing scale, a new, smaller growth of some kind down near his anal fin. But otherwise he seemed big, brutally healthy, still blinking off the shock of the sudden glare.

Then the tank fell back into its murk, got worse, stank up, and became, well, completely, utterly, fantastically murky. Here one might note tangentially: if, as Aristotle claims, poetry is something of graver import than history — partly because of the naturalness of its statements — then Fish was more important than any domestic history, because Fish was poetic, in that he had succumbed to the darkness that had formed around him, and yet he was unwilling to die — or, rather, he *did not* die. He kept himself alive. He kept at it. Somehow he gathered enough oxygen from the water — perhaps by staying directly under the trickle that made its way over the lip of the filter. Of course, by nature he was a bottom-feeder, a mud-fish, accustomed to slime and algae and to an environment that, for other fish, would be insufferable. No trout could sustain itself in these conditions. Not even close. A good brookie would've gone belly up long ago. A brookie would want cool pockets of a fast-moving stream, sweet riffles, bubbling swirls, to live a good life. But Fish stood in his cave of slime, graver than the history of the household into which his glass enclave had been placed: Dad packing his suitcases, folding and refolding his trousers and taking his ties off the electric tie rack and carefully folding them inside sheets of tissue, and then taking his shoes and putting each pair, highly glossed oxfords (he was one of the few to make regular use of the shoeshine stand at Grand Central), into cotton drawstring sacks, and then emptying his top dresser drawer, taking his cufflinks, his old wallets, and a few other items. All of this stuff, the history of the house, the legal papers signed and sealed and the attendant separation agreement and, of course, the divorce that left her the house — all this historical material was transpiring outside the gist of Fish. He could chart his course and touch each corner of the tank and still not know shit. But he understood something. That much was clear. The world is a mucky mess. It gets clotted up, submerged in its own gunk. End of story.

He brushed softly against the beard of algae that hung from the filter device, worked his way over to the figurine, leaned his flank against her side, and felt the shift of temperature as night fell — Teddy liked to sleep with the window cracked a bit — and the oxygen content increased slightly as the water cooled. During the day, the sun cranked through the window, the tank grew warm, and he didn't move at all, unless someone came into the room and knocked on the tank or the floor, and then he jerked forward slightly before quickly settling down. A few times the downstairs door slammed hard enough to jolt him awake. Or there was a smashing sound from the kitchen. Or voices. "What in the world should we do?" "I would most certainly like this to be amicable, for the sake of the kids." Or a shoe striking the wall in the adjacent master bedroom. At times he felt a kinship with the figurine, as if another carp were there alongside him, waiting, hovering. Other times he felt a slight kinship with the sides of the tank, which touched his gill flaps when he went in search of light. God, if only he knew that he, Fish, was at the very center of the domestic arena, holding court with his own desire to live. He might have died happily right there! But he was not a symbolic fish. He seemed to have no desire to stand as the tragic hero in this drama.

Sent out, told to stay out, the kids were playing together down in the yard so that, inside, the two central figures, Dad and Mom, might have one final talk. The kids were standing by the playhouse — which itself was falling to decrepitude, dark-gray smears of mildew growing on its fake logs — pretending to be a mom and a dad themselves, although they were a bit too old and self-conscious for playacting. Perhaps they were old enough to know that they were faking it on two levels, regressing to a secondary level of playacting they'd pretty much rejected but playing Mom and Dad anyway, Teddy saying, I'm gonna call my lawyer if you don't settle with me, and Annie responding, in her high sweet voice, I knew you'd lawyer up on me, I just knew it, and then both kids giggling in that secretive, all-knowing way they have. Overhead, the tree branches were fuzzed with the first buds of spring, but it was still a bit cold, and words hovered in vapor from their mouths and darkness was falling fast over the trees, and beyond the trees the commuter traffic hissed unnoticed.

If you were heading south on the Merritt Parkway on the afternoon of April 3rd, and you happened to look to your right through the trees after Exit 35, you might've seen them, back beyond the old stone piles, the farm fences that no longer held significance except maybe as a reminder of the Robert Frost poem about good fences and good neighbors and all of that: two kids leaning against an old playhouse while the house behind them appeared cozy, warm, and, clearly, expensive. A fleeting tableau without much meaning to the commuting folk aside from the formulaic economics of the matter: near the parkway = reduced value, but an expensive area + buffer of stone walls + old trees + trendiness of area = more value.

There is something romantic and heartening about seeing those homes 15 through the trees from the vantage of the parkway — those safe, confided Connecticut lives. Inside the house, the secret goldfish is going about his deeply moving predicament, holding his life close to the gills, subdued by the dark but unwilling to relinquish his cellular activities, the Krebs cycle still spinning its carbohydrate breakdown. The secret goldfish draws close to the center of the cosmos. In the black hole of familial carelessness, he awaits the graceful moment when the mother, spurred on by Teddy, will give yet another soft shriek. She'll lean close to the glass and put her eye there to search for Fish. Fish will be there, of course, hiding in the core of the murk near the figurine, playing possum, so that she will, when she sees him, feel the pitiful sinking in her gut — remembering the preschool field trip to Pet Universe — and a sorrow so deep it will send her to her knees to weep. She'll think of the sad little pet funeral she hoped to perform when Fish died (when Fish's sidekick died, Dad flushed him away): a small but deeply meaningful moment in the back yard, with the trowel, digging a shoebox-size hole, putting the fish in, performing a small rite ("Dear Lord, dear Heavenly Father, dear Fish God, God of Fish, in Fish's name we gather here to put our dear fish to rest"), and then placing atop the burial mound a big rock painted with the word "FISH." It would be a moment designed to teach the children the ways of loss, and the soft intricacies of seeing something that was once alive now dead, and to clarify that sharp defining difference, to smooth it over a bit, so that they will remember the moment and know, later, recalling it, that she was a good mother, the kind who would hold pet funerals.

But Fish is alive. His big old carp gills clutch and lick every tiny trace of oxygen from the froth of depravity in the inexplicably determinate manner that only animals have. He will have nothing to do with this household. And later that evening, once Dad is gone, they'll hold a small party to celebrate his resurrection, because they had assumed — as was natural in these circumstances — that he was dead, or near enough death to be called dead, having near-death visions, as the dead are wont: that small pinpoint of light at the end of the tunnel and visions of an existence as a fish in some other ethery world, a better world for a fish, with fresh clear water bursting with oxygen and other carp large and small in communal bliss and just enough muck and mud for good pickings. After the celebration, before bedtime, they'll cover the top of the clean tank in plastic wrap and, working together, moving slowly with the unison of pallbearers, being careful not to slosh the water, carry it down the stairs to the family room, where with a soft patter of congratulatory applause they'll present Fish with a new home, right next to the television set.

APPROACHING THE READING

1. Describe the way the plot is structured — notice how what we are told is arranged, the way the story progresses, and the way it uses parallels and contrasts. Point out specific passages that illustrate and support what you say.
2. Consider the point of view in the story and how it helps develop the story's structure. Pick out specific illustrative passages and be ready to talk about how they clarify what the point of view is and how they contribute to the development of the story.
3. Explain the theme or themes of the story, what it "all adds up to." Again, pick out specific illustrative passages so you can show how what you say is grounded firmly in the story.
4. In this story, like in "Everyday Use," the reader is addressed directly as "you" (para. 14). In what ways does the direct address in this story differ from that of the previous one? What, do you think, is the reason for or value of this paragraph and its use of direct address?

APPROACHING GRAPHIC FICTION

Graphic storytelling has a long history in many parts of the world, a history which has led it to be regarded in those places as a serious literary form. But in the United States, until the 1980s, it was pretty much relegated to comic books and the comics sections of newspapers and was usually thought of as writing meant for kids, and the drawings were taken simply as illustrations of what the words were saying. In the past few decades, however, graphic writing for adults has emerged in the United States, and it has begun to be respected by the literary community. Indeed, many people now see graphic literature as an important, or even defining, part of reading and literacy in the twenty-first century because, in an age of increased visual literacy, of the way it requires a person simultaneously to read words and to read images.

Older adults, accustomed to following lines of words from left to right then down a page, may find it difficult to read a form that requires shifting from one image to another while taking in both words and visual components. However, a generation that has grown up with television, computers, and video games is readily able to engage with and respond to graphic literature.

For that group, graphic literature is an accessible window through which to view our world and to imagine others.

For a close look at graphic fiction, it is wise to start with attention to some vocabulary and methods. Basic to graphic literature are "panels," the series of individual units containing drawings and words that make up the work. Panels can fill a whole page, or several panels can be presented on the same page. Sometimes they are surrounded by a border, which frames them on the page or separates the various panels. Borders are part of the art and help channel the effect on the reader: a border tends to turn the reader into an outside observer, and can create a sense of confinement or restriction. The space between panels is called a "gutter." Sometimes panels do not have borders, but "bleed" out to the edge of the page or into other panels on the same page. A panel without a border can suggest the reader is being invited in and can increase the reader's involvement; it can give a sense of openness or escape.

Active reading is crucial to fully enjoying and appreciating graphic literature. This kind of reading can be compared to watching a film: in watching a film, you must listen to the sounds and absorb the images simultaneously, integrating the two into a single experience. Similarly, in reading graphic literature, you must read the words of the text and read the images simultaneously, as a unified experience: in the hands of the finest graphic fiction artists, the written words and the drawings are interdependent, forming a seamless whole. They need to happen together. With a bit of practice, reading this way can become as natural as watching and listening to a film at the same time.

Active reading is necessary also because of the fragmentary nature of graphic literature: some words of text here, a cropped image there. The reader must be able to fill out and connect the fragments in order to understand and experience the story. And active reading is needed in order to follow the passage of time. Graphic literature presents time through the use of space: time passes as we read words, one following another, and simultaneously we see action happening in the visual images. Arrangement on the page leads to a sense of movement in time, as our eyes move sequentially from frame to frame, or are guided from one part of a large frame to another. A series of small panels seems to move rapidly; a larger panel slows down our reading and the passage of time.

Through active reading we imagine sounds — we listen with our eyes. The style, size, and color of the lettering affects what we "hear" in terms of volume and emotional tone. Large or bold lettering indicates loudness, while small letters suggest soft speech. Wavy letters may indicate a voice expressing uneasiness or fear, while a rough style of lettering may convey a harsh attitude or cruelty. In some cases words are incorporated directly into the frame; in other cases words are enclosed in balloons that connect them to their speakers. Active reading is required in interpreting the visual aspects of the balloons and the order in which the balloons are to be read.

In addition to these techniques, graphic fiction makes use of the elements of fiction described in chapters 4–7 of this book, and responding to these elements also requires active reading. Just like other fiction, the plots of graphic fiction involve beginnings, middles, endings, conflicts, foreshadowings, repetitions, gaps, and a sense of wholeness. Depiction of character in graphic fiction includes the same telling, showing, saying, and so forth as in other fiction, but it also requires that the reader be attentive to visual features: facial expressions, gestures, poses, clothes, shading, and lighting, for example. Theme, symbol, style, tone, and irony can be employed to good effect in graphic fiction just as in other fiction.

Point of view in graphic fiction starts with who is telling the story (first person or third person) and that person's relation to the story, as in traditional fiction. But in graphic fiction the panel affects viewpoint, establishing perimeters and perspective. The artist can have us look down from above in a detached way, for example, or up from below, which tends to make the reader feel smaller and at times feel fear. Notice how similar this is to film: the artist, in choosing these frame angles, is like the director of a film. When we watch a movie, we know if we are looking through a person's eyes or not; it's the same with graphic fiction.

Setting in a graphic story involves location and time, as in any other story, but it offers visual images to supplement the imagined ones of conventional fiction. The handling of setting varies with the nature and purpose of the writing: the background can be very detailed, or sketched out in broad strokes. Often an "establishing shot" is used — lots of detail about the place, with the character very small then zoomed in on in later panels (here too the terminology used in discussing graphic fiction is carried over from the film world). It can be helpful to remind yourself when reading graphic fiction that, as with any visual art, the form of the drawings could take a multiplicity of alternatives. The artist has chosen a particular way of presenting the visual — for a purpose, for an effect, as something you should "read."

Reading has become a word that we apply to almost everything. We read faces and places and moods, for example. Graphic fiction extends the idea of reading to include both the written and the visual. You are being asked to attend to both simultaneously, using your ability to realize implications, nuances, and subtleties in the language and in the visual art. To get the fullest experience from such a work, you must "read" the pictures and the words and understand that "graphic" applies to both the visual and the written.

ENTRY POINTS   The following graphic story deals with some of the same issues as the previous two short stories — relating to others, growing up, dealing with problems caused by other people. As you read it, try to take in the pictures and the words together, to experience them as interdependent and seamless. Pay attention to point of view, which is important to the effect of this story, and to the theme or themes developed in it.

Lynda Barry b. 1956
Today's Demon: Magic   [2002]

Used courtesy of Darhansoff, Verrill, Feldman Literary Agents.

"DO YOU BELIEVE IN MAGIC?" IT WAS A SONG ON THE RADIO THAT PLAYED THE SUMMER I DECIDED TO MOVE MY BEDROOM INTO THE BASEMENT.

I'LL MEETCHA TOMORROW SORTA LATE AT NIGHT

I WAS GROWING MY HAIR OUT AND IT WAS IN AN IN-BETWEEN STAGE THAT DIDN'T MAKE SENSE TO ANYBODY. I'D WANTED LONG HAIR ALL MY LIFE. I WAS WILLING TO LOOK INSANE WHILE I WAITED FOR IT.

DO YOU BELIEVE LIKE I BELIEVE

100

THERE WERE BIG CHANGES GOING ON IN MY HOUSE. GRANDMA MOVED OUT, AND BOTH MY PARENTS WERE "SECRETLY" SEEING OTHER PEOPLE. THEY WERE NEVER AROUND.

HALT! GET OUT OF MY WAY.

NO ONE SAID YOU COULD MOVE TO THE BASEMENT.

BUG OFF.

MAKE ME.

I WAS LEFT TO WATCH MY TWO YOUNGER BROTHERS AND KEEP HOUSE. I WAS SUPPOSED TO STAY AT HOME ALL DAY, EVERY DAY, THE SUMMER THAT SONG PLAYED ON THE RADIO.

WE'RE HUNGRY, MAN! YOU GOTTA MAKE US FOOD, MAN!

CHICKEN POT PIES, OVEN AT 350°.

WE'RE SICK OF CHICKEN POT PIE, MAN!

I'M NOT.

101

MY BROTHERS COULD GO WHEREVER THEY WANTED BUT I WAS NEVER ALLOWED TO LEAVE. NOT THAT I HAD ANY PLACE TO GO. I WAS AT AN IN-BETWEEN STAGE IN FRIENDSHIPS.

102

MY BEST FRIEND, EV, LIVED RIGHT ACROSS THE STREET. SHE WAS AN EXTREMELY KIND AND FUNNY PERSON. WE WERE ALWAYS TOGETHER. SHE WAS TWO YEARS YOUNGER THAN ME BUT IT NEVER MATTERED UNTIL I TURNED 13.

ONCE I TURNED 13 AND STARTED JUNIOR HIGH AND REALIZED HOW WEIRD AND LAME I REALLY WAS, THERE WAS NO WAY I COULD HAVE AN 11-YEAR OLD BEST FRIEND.

I NEVER TALKED TO EV ABOUT IT. I NEVER EXPLAINED WHAT WAS GOING ON. I JUST AVOIDED HER AND HOPED SHE WOULD FORGET ABOUT ME. I DID THIS 31 YEARS AGO BUT MY STOMACH STILL KNOTS UP WHEN I THINK OF IT.

SERIOUSLY! HOW COME YOU GOTTA BE SO COLD-BLOODED TO EV, MAN? EV'S NICE.

SHUT UP!

THINK YOU'RE TOO GOOD FOR HER, DONTCHA?

EV'S THE NICEST FRIEND OF YOUR LIFE!

SHUT! UP!

103

IT WASN'T ONLY THAT SHE WAS YOUNGER. SOMETHING HAD HAPPENED INSIDE OF ME. I DIDN'T HAVE A NAME FOR IT. MAYBE IT WAS THE THING THAT HITS WHEN YOU STOP BELIEVING IN MAGIC.

SHE ASKED ME WHY YOU DON'T PLAY WITH HER NO MORE.

PLAY? I DON'T PLAY WITH ANYBODY IF YOU DON'T KNOW IT.

YEAH, WELL I SAID IT WAS BECAUSE YOU TURNED INTO A STUCK UP HOG

ONE DAY YOU JUST NOTICE SOMETHING IS GONE. POSSIBILITY IS GONE. IT'S SO GONE THAT EVERYONE A-ROUND YOU SEEMS LIKE AN IDIOT OR A LIAR. THERE IS A MOOD THAT SETS IN.

GET OUT!

EVERYONE JUST GET AWAY FROM ME!!

104

THE BASEMENT WAS THE PERFECT PLACE FOR IT. I COULD BE ALONE WITH THE RADIO THERE. MUSIC WAS BECOMING SO IMPORTANT. WHAT IS IT ABOUT A SONG PLAYING IN A DARK ROOM?

HELLO IT'S ME...

WHY ARE SOME SONGS SO PERFECT IN A WAY THAT NEVER HAPPENS AGAIN IN OUR LIVES? WHAT IS IT A-BOUT MUSIC AND BEING OLDER THAN 12 BUT YOUNGER THAN 20?

I'VE THOUGHT ABOUT US FOR A LONG LONG TIME

105

DID THE SAME THING HAP-
PEN TO EV? I DON'T KNOW
BECAUSE BY THE TIME SHE
TURNED 13, WE WERE GHOSTS
TO EACH OTHER. I NEVER
KNEW HER SONGS AND SHE
NEVER KNEW MINE.

FIND
IT?

YEAH.
THIS IS EV.

THIS IS EV AND
ME IN A
PHOTO BOOTH.

I REMEMBER CLIMBING ONTO
THE ROOF OF THE SCHOOL
WITH HER ONCE, LONG BEFORE
MY PARENTS WERE DIVORCED,
LONG BEFORE HER FATHER
LOST HIS JOB. I REMEMBER
LAYING DOWN FLAT SO THE
COPS WOULDN'T SEE US AND
TALKING ABOUT
INFINITY.

I KNOW NUMBERS CAN GO
ON FOREVER. I KNOW EV IS
IN HER 40'S NOW. I KNOW
ABOUT THE DIFFERENCE BE-
TWEEN THE BASEMENT AND
THE ROOF OF THE SCHOOL.
WHAT'S INFINITY MINUS 13?
MINUS 11?

WHAT'S INFINITY MINUS ALL
THE SONGS IN THE WORLD?
THE ONES YOU LISTENED TO,
THE ONES SHE LISTENED TO,
THE ONES YOU SANG TOGE-
THER THAT DAY. DO YOU BELIEVE
IN MAGIC? YES OR NO?

♪ DOWN THE WAY WHERE THE NIGHTS ARE GAY ♪
AND THE SUN SHINES DAILY ON THE MOUNTAIN
TOP-

ON THE ROOF OF THE SCHOOL, "FOREVER, BEST FRIENDS FOREVER," SEEMED SO OBVIOUS. WHAT FORCE IN THE UNIVERSE COULD EVER BREAK US UP? WE KNEW NOTHING ABOUT NEGATIVE NUMBERS.

THIS IS EV. THIS IS EV AND ME IN A PHOTO BOOTH IN A WOOLWORTH'S A THOUSAND YEARS AGO. EV, IF YOU'RE READING THIS, HELLO, IT'S ME.

108

APPROACHING THE READING

1. Words of the first-person narrator appear in every panel. How would you describe the narrator and the narrator's voice? In what ways do the drawings contribute to or affect your description? Is there a seamless unity between the verbal and the visual in this story? Explain your answer.

2. Some panels also have words in balloons that function like dialogue in a written story. How do these words relate to what the narrator says? In what sense are they integral to the story?

3. In the sixteenth panel (page 130), the narrator uses "you" instead of "I." Why do you think the author made that switch? What is the effect of it?

4. Compare this narrator's voice to that of the first-person narrators of "The House on Mango Street" (p. 99) and "The Wonder Spot" (p. 332). What are the similarities and differences? Do the graphics influence the ways you compare? In what ways does your imagination affect your interpretation of the nongraphic stories?

5. What would you say is the primary theme of this story? In what ways do the drawings support your conclusion? Is the theme more readily discernable in the graphic story? Why or why not?

RESPONDING THROUGH Writing

WRITING ABOUT POINT OF VIEW AND THEME

Journal Entries

1. As a way of getting hold of point of view in fiction, pay attention to point of view in several TV shows or movies. Notice the perspective from which each is presented: Does it stick to one character or group of characters, or does it switch back and forth between two (or more) characters or groups of characters? Watch the use of the camera as an "eye": From what perspective does it let you see what's happening — only from "outside" and at a distance? Does it ever show you just what a character is seeing? Write a journal entry summarizing what you observe and discussing how what you observed might apply to or clarify point of view in fiction.

www Research the authors in this chapter with LitLinks, or take a quiz on the stories with LitQuiz, at bedfordstmartins.com/approachinglit.

2. In your journal, rewrite part of a story from a different perspective, as, for example, Sandra Cisneros's "The House on Mango Street" (p. 99) or John Updike's "A & P" (p. 529) from the perspective of the narrator's mother.

3. In your journal, rewrite part of a story using a different point of view — Sandra Cisneros's "The House on Mango Street" (p. 99) or John Updike's "A & P" (p. 529) as a third-person narrative instead of first-person, for example.

Literary Analysis Papers

4. Write a paper in which you examine how the handling of point of view and time contribute to theme in Lynda Barry's "Today's Demon: Magic" (p. 126).

5. Discussions of point of view usually center on the question of how appropriate and effective the point of view is in terms of the best way to present the action and characters and to develop the story's theme. Write a paper discussing the appropriateness and effectiveness, to presentation and theme, of the point of view in one of the following stories:

   • first-person unreliable in Toni Morrison's "Recitatif" (p. 431)
   • first-person reliable in John Updike's "A & P" (p. 529)
   • third-person omniscient in Zora Neale Hurston's "Sweat" (p. 384)
   • third-person limited in Leslie Marmon Silko's "The Man to Send Rain Clouds" (p. 505)
   • third-person limited and center of consciousness in Jhumpa Lahiri's "A Temporary Matter" (p. 398)
   • third-person limited and stream of consciousness in Katherine Anne Porter's "The Jilting of Granny Weatherall" (p. 478)
   • interior monologue in Tillie Olsen's "I Stand Here Ironing" (p. 467)

6. Write a paper discussing the title "Everyday Use" as it applies to Dee (Wangero) and to her mother and sister. Consider what Dee means by saying "You just don't understand" (p. 115). What does Dee not understand?

Comparison-Contrast Papers

7. Stories about "outsiders" look different depending on the point of view from which they are told. Does a character feel, or is she or he made to feel, like an outsider? Does one character look at another as an outsider? Compare and contrast both perspectives in a story dealing with an outsider — either Esperanza in Sandra Cisneros's "The House on Mango Street" (p. 99), or Henry in Louise Erdrich's "The Red Convertible" (p. 73), Arnold in Joyce Carol Oates's "Where Are You Going, Where Have You Been?" (p. 81), Nazneen and/or Chanu in Monica Ali's "Dinner with Dr. Azad" (p. 292), the narrator in Ralph Ellison's "Battle Royal" (p. 352), or Cody in George Saunders's "The End of FIRPO in the World" (p. 501).

8. Write a paper that compares and contrasts the handling of parent-child conflict in two of the following stories: Alice Walker's "Everyday Use" (p. 109), Judith Ortiz Cofer's "American History" (p. 346), or Tillie Olsen's "I Stand Here Ironing" (p. 467).

> ### ➤ TIPS for Writing about Point of View and Theme
>
> ➤ **Point out point of view** Almost every paper about a work of fiction should identify its point of view, usually through a passing reference.
>
> ➤ **Analyze if unusual** Point of view should be a central focus in a paper only if it is unusual or complex or crucial to the way the story works.
>
> ➤ **Be thorough** When a paper focuses on point of view, clarify both the person and the perspective precisely, using quotations to illustrate and support what you say. Then explain, with supporting evidence, what is important about how they are handled in the story.
>
> ➤ **Refer to theme regularly** Because theme is what a story "all adds up to," most papers discussing a story should at least mention its theme and explain how other elements relate to or bring out that theme.
>
> ➤ **Explore complex themes in depth** When a story is particularly complex or unusual, a paper can be an in-depth exploration of the story's meaning and implications. Be sure that you do more than summarize what the story is about or restate what is obvious in it.

WRITING ABOUT CONNECTIONS

Points of view and themes, by the way they work a story, connect us with the complexities, both joyful and disappointing, of our own and others' lives.

Such connections often yield even richer and more nuanced experiences and insights when stories are paired with each other, especially when two stories from different cultures or different time periods are brought together. Here are just a few examples to consider:

1. "Staring Out Front Windows": Seeking Escape in Sandra Cisneros's "The House on Mango Street" (p. 99) and James Joyce's "Araby" (p. 393)
2. "Can You Come Home Again?": The Difficulty of Returning in Alice Walker's "Everyday Use" (p. 109) and Monica Ali's "Dinner with Dr. Azad" (p. 292)
3. "Tales of Entrapment": Lives Lacking Fulfillment in David Means's "The Secret Goldfish" (p. 116) and John Steinbeck's "The Chrysanthemums" (p. 513)

WRITING RESEARCH PAPERS

1. Conduct research into the cultural meaning of houses — of owning one's own place, of the type of house one owns and its location. In what ways does the house one lives in affect one's self and life, have power, and lead to acceptance or conflict or rejection? Write a paper on this topic, focusing on Sandra Cisneros's "The House on Mango Street" (p. 99) and Alice Walker's "Everyday Use" (p. 109) as starting points.
2. Read Judith Ortiz Cofer's "American History" (p. 346) and do some research on Ortiz Cofer, reading interviews with her, her memoir "Silent Dancing" (in her book by the same name), and scholarly articles about her work. Write a paper on how her personal experiences helped shape the narrator, point of view, and theme of "American History."

COMPOSING IN OTHER ART FORMS

1. As a way of responding to a story through use of another art, make a collage of materials cut from magazines or newspapers and add appropriate captions. Think about using bits from both visual and written materials, juxtaposing images and language from hard and soft news, advertising, comics and cartoons, headlines, TV listings, and anywhere else you can find relevant material. For example, you could illustrate a story that works with contrasting perspectives, though it's told from one point of view — as, for example, Yiyun Li's "Persimmons" (p. 411) or Toni Morrison's "Recitatif" (p. 431).
2. Do some exploring into the importance of quilts as cultural artifacts. In what ways are they important beyond providing warmth? What do they reveal about the people who make them and the society that values them? Write a paper applying what you find to Alice Walker's "Everyday Use" (p. 109), showing how a deeper knowledge of quilts adds more meaning to the story.

The place of birth itself becomes a metaphor for the things we must all leave behind; the assimilation of a new culture is the coming into maturity by accepting the terms necessary for survival.

Judith Ortiz Cofer

Setting and Symbol CHAPTER 6
Meeting Meaning in Places and Objects

Of the memories we look back on, those involving places often carry particularly important emotional weight. We may have special memories of grandmother's house or a good friend's apartment; a street corner or a park down the street; a gymnasium or playground across town; or a theme park in Florida — or even nightmarish memories of an abandoned house in the country, a cemetery, or a back alley. Reflect for a moment on some significant places in your own life.

Place (or setting) is very important in stories as well, as the area and context in which the characters live and where the events occur. Place may just be the key locale of a story, or it may convey a symbolic meaning, taking on an expanding significance beyond that of just the location of the action. This chapter explores setting and symbol to help you realize more fully what these two contribute to a story and how they sometimes interrelate.

READING FOR SETTING

ENTRY POINTS   The **setting** of a story, poem, or play is its overall context — where, when, and in what circumstances the action occurs. In the following story, setting plays an important role. Two characters, a young woman named Jig and her male companion, are waiting for a train. As you read about them, listen for a major conflict in their relationship and what their discussion of it reveals about their characters. Focus also on where they are (the country, the part of the country, the specific building and its surroundings) and on how the place is described. Look for connections between where they are and what they are talking about.

Ernest Hemingway   1899–1961

Hills Like White Elephants   [1927]

The hills across the valley of the Ebro were long and white. On this side there was no shade and no trees and the station was between two lines of rails in the sun. Close against the side of the station there was the warm shadow of the building and a curtain, made of strings of bamboo beads, hung across the open door into the bar, to keep out flies. The American and the girl with him sat at a table in the shade, outside the building. It was very hot and the express from Barcelona would come in forty minutes. It stopped at this junction for two minutes and went on to Madrid.

"What should we drink?" the girl asked. She had taken off her hat and put it on the table.

"It's pretty hot," the man said.

"Let's drink beer."

"Dos cervezas,"° the man said into the curtain.   5

"Big ones?" a woman asked from the doorway.

"Yes. Two big ones."

The woman brought two glasses of beer and two felt pads. She put the felt pads and the beer glasses on the table and looked at the man and the girl. The girl was looking off at the line of hills. They were white in the sun and the country was brown and dry.

"They look like white elephants," she said.

"I've never seen one," the man drank his beer.   10

"No, you wouldn't have."

"I might have," the man said. "Just because you say I wouldn't have doesn't prove anything."

The girl looked at the bead curtain. "They've painted something on it," she said. "What does it say?"

"Anis del Toro. It's a drink."

"Could we try it?"   15

The man called "Listen" through the curtain. The woman came out from the bar.

"Four reales."

"We want two Anis del Toro."

"With water?"

"Do you want it with water?"   20

"I don't know," the girl said. "Is it good with water?"

"It's all right."

"You want them with water?" asked the woman.

"Yes, with water."

"It tastes like licorice," the girl said and put the glass down.   25

Dos cervezas: Two beers (Spanish).

"That's the way with everything."

"Yes," said the girl. "Everything tastes of licorice. Especially all the things you've waited so long for, like absinthe."

"Oh, cut it out."

"You started it," the girl said. "I was being amused. I was having a fine time."

"Well, let's try and have a fine time." 30

"All right. I was trying. I said the mountains looked like white elephants. Wasn't that bright?"

"That was bright."

"I wanted to try this new drink. That's all we do, isn't it — look at things and try new drinks?"

"I guess so."

The girl looked across at the hills. 35

"They're lovely hills," she said. "They don't really look like white elephants. I just meant the coloring of their skin through the trees."

"Should we have another drink?"

"All right."

The warm wind blew the bead curtain against the table.

"The beer's nice and cool," the man said. 40

"It's lovely," the girl said.

"It's really an awfully simple operation, Jig," the man said. "It's not really an operation at all."

The girl looked at the ground the table legs rested on.

"I know you wouldn't mind it, Jig. It's really not anything. It's just to let the air in."

The girl did not say anything. 45

"I'll go with you and I'll stay with you all the time. They just let the air in and then it's all perfectly natural."

"Then what will we do afterward?"

"We'll be fine afterward. Just like we were before."

"What makes you think so?"

"That's the only thing that bothers us. It's the only thing that's made us un- 50 happy."

The girl looked at the bead curtain, put her hand out and took hold of two of the strings of beads.

"And you think then we'll be all right and be happy."

"I know we will. You don't have to be afraid. I've known lots of people that have done it."

"So have I," said the girl. "And afterward they were all so happy."

"Well," the man said, "if you don't want to you don't have to. I wouldn't 55 have you do it if you didn't want to. But I know it's perfectly simple."

"And you really want to?"

"I think it's the best thing to do. But I don't want you to do it if you don't really want to."

"And if I do it you'll be happy and things will be like they were and you'll love me?"

"I love you now. You know I love you."

"I know. But if I do it, then it will be nice again if I say things are like white elephants, and you'll like it?"

"I'll love it. I love it now but I just can't think about it. You know how I get when I worry."

"If I do it you won't ever worry?"

"I won't worry about that because it's perfectly simple."

"Then I'll do it. Because I don't care about me."

"What do you mean?"

"I don't care about me."

"Well, I care about you."

"Oh, yes. But I don't care about me. And I'll do it and then everything will be fine."

"I don't want you to do it if you feel that way."

The girl stood up and walked to the end of the station. Across, on the other side, were fields of grain and trees along the banks of the Ebro. Far away, beyond the river, were mountains. The shadow of a cloud moved across the field of grain and she saw the river through the trees.

"And we could have all this," she said. "And we could have everything and every day we make it more impossible."

"What did you say?"

"I said we could have everything."

"We can have everything."

"No, we can't."

"We can have the whole world."

"No, we can't."

"We can go everywhere."

"No, we can't. It isn't ours any more."

"It's ours."

"No, it isn't. And once they take it away, you never get it back."

"But they haven't taken it away."

"We'll wait and see."

"Come on back in the shade," he said. "You mustn't feel that way."

"I don't feel any way," the girl said. "I just know things."

"I don't want you to do anything that you don't want to do—"

"Nor that isn't good for me," she said. "I know. Could we have another beer?"

"All right. But you've got to realize—"

"I realize," the girl said. "Can't we maybe stop talking?"

They sat down at the table and the girl looked across at the hills on the dry side of the valley and the man looked at her and at the table.

"You've got to realize," he said, "that I don't want you to do it if you don't want to. I'm perfectly willing to go through with it if it means anything to you."

"Doesn't it mean anything to you? We could get along."

"Of course it does. But I don't want anybody but you. I don't want any one else. And I know it's perfectly simple."

"Yes, you know it's perfectly simple."

"It's all right for you to say that, but I do know it."   95

"Would you do something for me now?"

"I'd do anything for you."

"Would you please please please please please please please stop talking?"

He did not say anything but looked at the bags against the wall of the station. There were labels on them from all the hotels where they had spent nights.

"But I don't want you to," he said, "I don't care anything about it."   100

"I'll scream," the girl said.

The woman came out through the curtains with two glasses of beer and put them down on the damp felt pads. "The train comes in five minutes," she said.

"What did she say?" asked the girl.

"That the train is coming in five minutes."

The girl smiled brightly at the woman, to thank her.   105

"I'd better take the bags over to the other side of the station," the man said. She smiled at him.

"All right. Then come back and we'll finish the beer."

He picked up the two heavy bags and carried them around the station to the other tracks. He looked up the tracks but could not see the train. Coming back, he walked through the barroom, where people waiting for the train were drinking. He drank an Anis at the bar and looked at the people. They were all waiting reasonably for the train. He went out through the bead curtain. She was sitting at the table and smiled at him.

"Do you feel better?" he asked.

"I feel fine," she said. "There's nothing wrong with me. I feel fine."   110

APPROACHING THE READING

1. Think first about what you saw as you read the story. References to Barcelona, Madrid, and the Ebro broadly identify the place where the scene happens as Spain. You might look at a map to identify where these places are and find a book with pictures of that area so you can visualize the scene more precisely. How does it affect you to have the story occur in Europe? How might the effect differ if it had occurred in the United States?

2. Think about the immediate location—a train junction out in the middle of nowhere. What is the effect of the rural train junction? How would it be different if the American and Jig were in a big train station in Madrid? Sitting in a coffee shop in Paris, or New York, or a small town in the United States?

3. White elephants are mentioned in the title and several times in the story. Jig says she is referring to elephants that are white. Could there be more to the

words than that? Look them up in a dictionary. Might the words have a symbolic significance?

4. Consider possible connections between white elephants and the conflict, or conflicts, between the main characters. What do you think is the operation the man is urging on Jig? What details from the story support your answer? Is the operation their only conflict?

5. "We'll be fine afterward. Just like we were before," the American says to Jig (para. 48). This line opens an enormous gap — their future — for you to fill in. Where do you think they would go if the story continued? What would happen? How does ending where it does indicate what is important in the story? How do you respond to Jig's concluding lines?

Setting as Place

INDICATING PLACE   Basic to a story's context is place, or locale — the physical environment. We need to know the locale in a broad sense: Where does the action take place? What country? What city or region of that country? We also need to know the locale in a specific, narrower sense: What kind of place — downtown, suburban neighborhood, rural area, or highway? What specific street, house, farm, or junction? Physical setting — whether an apartment, a factory, a train station, or a prision camp — can be presented through vibrant, specific details, or it can be sketched broadly with a few, quick strokes. The setting of "Hills Like White Elephants" is indicated in the first paragraph: the broad setting — eastern Spain, about a third of the way from Barcelona to Madrid — and the specific setting — a hot day at a rural train station, a junction where two lines meet in the middle of nowhere.

SIGNIFICANCE OF PLACE   The description of a setting often evokes its significance, what it conveys and suggests. Reflect, for example, on the significance of the principal setting in "The Red Convertible" (p. 73) being a reservation. Ask yourself how the story would be different if Lyman and Henry lived in Chicago. Think about the locale of "Hills Like White Elephants," how by creating a sense of isolation, the story focuses our attention on the two people and their problem. There are other people in the bar, but we see no one else except the waitress — the other people are just there, like the chairs and tables.

The location includes only a railway junction: No town or city is indicated, which increases the sense of isolation. There is no community to support or affect them in what they face or decide (especially in what Jig faces and must decide) — just two individuals, making an individual decision as if it affects no one but themselves (at least that's how the man views it). Using a train station as locale also creates a sense of transience — no roots, no home, no ties. And placing the story at a junction suggests that the characters are facing a decision about the direction in which they should go.

Setting as Time

Setting also includes the time in which the events occur, time in all its dimensions: the century, the year, the season, the day, the hour, maybe even the exact second. In some cases, a specific time is not indicated: The events are universal and could as well have occurred a minute or a millennium ago. Often, however, a specific or approximate time is either assumed (the time seems the same as when the story was written or published) or indicated — perhaps by giving a date in the story, by mentioning historical events that were going on at the time of the story, or by describing the way people talk, act, or dress. In those cases, the specific time may be significant, and knowing something about that time period may help you understand what is going on or the significance of what occurs.

HISTORICAL EVENTS   Assessing the significance of a specific time may require asking questions and then doing some investigating — in an encyclopedia, or on the Internet, or through more specialized books, depending on the time period involved and the way the story uses its setting.

Consider, for example, "Hills Like White Elephants." The action is probably contemporaneous with when it was written, in the mid-1920s. To decide if that time setting is significant to the story, ask what was going on at that time, what was significant or noteworthy. You might check a time line of world or European historical events. You'll notice that the story takes place less than ten years after the end of World War I (1914–1918).

To gain the full impact of the story's setting in time, you might need to do some reading about the war and its aftermath (an encyclopedia entry on the war probably would suffice). The war caused immense loss of life, physical suffering, and psychological and emotional damage from trench warfare and use of nerve gas. It is estimated that 8.5 million military personnel died (a high percentage of a whole generation's young men), along with 10 million civilians. Although the corresponding numbers in World War II were much greater, at the time the number of deaths and amount of devastation were unprecedented. It was called the Great War with good reason.

SOCIAL MILIEU   Your investigation will need to include the social environment of the era, especially the social changes that took place during and after the war. Understanding the background of "Hills Like White Elephants" might require using an encyclopedia, books, or Internet articles to learn about what was going on. The war shattered the optimistic outlook held by much of the population in Western Europe and the United States. After the war ended, many people reacted by deciding to enjoy life fully in the present, since the war showed that life can end so quickly, and by rejecting older values (including prevailing sexual mores) and traditional roles (especially for women). The war led to changes in gender roles: With young men away in the military, young women had to work in factories instead of in homes, schools, or offices.

The war also led to changes in family and community life. Having seen large cities and other countries, young people found it difficult to return to the sheltered, conservative communities in which they grew up. Many of them wanted to travel and to live in more cosmopolitan locations. A large number of writers, artists, and socialites — Ernest Hemingway among them — moved from the United States to Europe, which they considered more sophisticated. The American man in "Hills Like White Elephants" seems to be one of them, and to reflect the sense of restlessness and desire to see new places and have new experiences. "That's all we do, isn't it," Jig says, "look at things and try new drinks?" (para. 33).

Setting as Cultural Context

SOCIAL CIRCUMSTANCES   Setting also involves the social circumstances of the time and place. Here too, active reading may require some research. Beyond the historical events at the time, try to find what attitudes people held about what was going on. What social and political problems were people facing? How were people below the poverty line treated, and what were the attitudes of the economically secure? What kinds of social change were occurring?

Such social and cultural contexts are closely related to the kind of historical events we discussed above — actually, all aspects of setting are interrelated and inseparable. So, for example, to understand "The Red Convertible" fully it helps to know something about the Vietnam War and attitudes toward it. Notice also how it involves transplanting a young Native American from his familiar, traditional culture to a strikingly different military culture and then to a strange foreign culture.

CULTURAL TRANSPLANTATION   Like "The Red Convertible," "Hills Like White Elephants" involves cultural transplantation: an American writer, Ernest Hemingway, living in Paris, writing in English (thus mainly for an American audience), about an American traveling in Spain (a conservative, predominantly Catholic country) with a companion (to whom he does not seem to be married) from an unspecified country. The fact that he is called "the American" suggests that Jig is not American; she apparently is not from Spain since she cannot converse with the waitress (we are supposed to assume the man is talking to the waitress in Spanish, even though his words and hers are written in English). Such details economically and efficiently convey a mixture of cultures and values, as well as a cosmopolitan outlook.

The Effects of Setting

Setting, thus, provides a "world" for the story to take place in, a location and a background for the events. But as you pay even closer attention to setting, you'll see that it usually does more. Again, you need to ask questions, especially about further implications of when and where the events happen. Ask yourself what setting reveals about characters. What is suggested by where a person lives (the kind of house and furniture) or the place in which we encounter her or him (a bar, a gym, a library, a woods)? Does setting help clarify what she or he is like? Think, for example, about Connie in "Where Are You Going, Where Have You Been?" (p. 81). The amount of time she spends at the shopping mall and the drive-in restaurant reveals aspects of her character.

Setting and Atmosphere

Ask yourself also how the setting affects the way you feel about the characters and events. Setting can be important in evoking **atmosphere** — that is, the mood or emotional aura that surrounds and permeates a literary work. Part of the effect in the **Gothic** story "A Rose for Emily" (p. 362) is created by the eerie atmosphere of the house in which Miss Emily secludes herself for much of her life. In other stories the emotional aura may be less dramatic, but it is always there and affects how you respond to the work as a whole.

As you consider setting in a story, watch for connections to other aspects, such as characters, conflicts, or actions. If handled well, setting adds to or reinforces meanings, ideas, or impressions in a work. Think, for example, about the effect of the setting in "Hills Like White Elephants." The isolated train station reflects the isolation of the two characters; the barren aridity Jig sees on one side of the station and the fertile growth on the other echo the social conflict between her and the American as well as the internal conflict within her.

READING FOR SYMBOLS

Works of literature not only help us see things in fresh and meaningful ways, they also can lead us to see deeply *into* and *beyond* things through the use of symbols. A **symbol** is something that represents both itself and an abstract quality beyond itself. In literature, a symbol is usually an object, although it is sometimes a character or an action. Every day you encounter symbols. You send a rose to someone you love. A rose is an object, something that can be touched and smelled. But of course you hope that the recipient will recognize it as more than just an object, will know it suggests the depth of your love, concern, and support, and therefore will respond to its *symbolic* implications.

Note that *implications* in the previous sentence is plural. Symbols usually convey a cluster of possible meanings; they are rich, suggestive, and evocative. Knowledgeable readers do not reduce them to a single, definite meaning: The verb *suggests* may be safer to use than the verb *symbolizes* because it conveys better a sense of a symbol's openness, inclusivity, and plurality.

A symbol's characteristics usually relate closely to the abstractions it represents: A rose is a symbol of love because it is beautiful, because it is the reproductive organ of a plant, and because its red color — the color of blood or a blush — has long been connected to passion. In contrast, a *sign* is an object that conveys an abstract meaning but does so through an arbitrary relationship: By common agreement, a red octagonal sign means "stop," but a white triangular sign could just as well mean "stop."

Recognizing Symbols

Even though almost anything can take on symbolic significance, not every object, character, or act in a literary work should be labeled a symbol. Symbols draw their power from standing out, and they don't stand out if we call everything a symbol. A prudent way to proceed is to assume that objects, characters, and actions are just themselves and are not meant to be taken as symbols *unless* a further sense of meaning forces itself on us. If you miss something others regard as a symbol, don't worry. Symbols add to a work's meaning, but a work usually doesn't depend on your recognizing them. It's better to miss a symbolic meaning than to impose one and reduce a work to a string of abstractions.

PROMINENCE OR WEIGHTINESS   How, then, do you recognize a symbol? The key signal is *prominence*: Objects that are mentioned repeatedly, described in detail, or appear in noticeable or strategic positions (at the beginning or end, in the title, at a crucial moment, in the climactic lines) may point toward a meaning beyond themselves. The red convertible in Louise Erdrich's story (p. 73) certainly meets all these criteria. Signals, however, are not always structural. Another signal can be a sense of *weightiness* or *significance*: Sometimes you may notice that an image, character, or action differs from others, that it is beginning to embody an idea related to an area of major concern in the work. In such a case, it might be a symbol.

IMAGE COMES FIRST   Be careful, however, not to undermine the use of concrete details by dismissing their crucial part in the work because you see them as symbols. Their literal role always comes first. A symbol is first an image, and its representation of an actual thing plays a key role in a work even if it also becomes a symbol. The quilts in "Everyday Use" (p. 109) come to symbolize the Johnson family's culture and heritage, but first and foremost they are actual quilts. At the end of the story, the narrator gives Maggie coverings she can put on a bed, not some abstract "heritage" (though the bed coverings carry that sense of heritage with them). To separate the symbolic meaning from the literal diminishes the richness of both. The warmth of the Johnsons' heritage comes alive in the warmth provided by the quilts.

Be careful also not to turn an abstraction into a symbol. A rose can be a symbol of love, but love (an abstraction) can never be a symbol of something else. And be sure that the symbolic meaning seems plausible: Its connection to the image, character, or action must seem likely and convincing within the context of the story. To claim that the red convertible is a symbol of Lyman's Marxist leanings (since red was associated with communism during the Cold War) seems totally far-fetched and implausible.

PRIVATE SYMBOLS   Symbols appear in several overlapping varieties. Think of some things you keep — a toy, a hat, a photo, a souvenir — that for you carry personal meanings although for others suggest nothing more than what they are. These *private symbols* are objects that hold a special meaning for you because of certain experiences or people. Since it is difficult, if not impossible, to convey their meaning to another person, private symbols ordinarily are not used in literary works. Several types of symbols, however, are important for literature.

Literary Symbols

A *literary symbol* is an object, character, or action that is part of the literal story in a literary work — it can be seen, touched, smelled, heard, tasted, encountered, or experienced by people in the work — *and* suggests abstract meanings beyond itself. The red convertible is a real object in Erdrich's story: Lyman and Henry buy a car, fix it up, and drive around in it. But beyond being an object the brothers own, the car also represents their friendship and the bond they share. It suggests carefreeness, spontaneity, and freedom (think of the difference if the car was a tan minivan); perhaps it even reflects Henry's life and soul. When Lyman rolls the car into the river, the red convertible becomes part of a symbolic act. He isn't just getting rid of the car; he is giving it to Henry, evidence of his love for and close connection with his brother.

The red convertible is a literary symbol because it derives its meanings from the context of the literary work itself. Red convertibles have a certain cultural status in society — they're sexy. But they do not carry the particular symbolic meanings that are relied on in Erdrich's story. The car in "The Red Convertible" develops its meanings from its specific associations with Lyman and Henry and their situation. It is a "story-specific" symbol, one that receives its significance from the work and may not have the same significance outside of that work. If you see a red convertible on the street, it may remind you of this story and its symbolic significance in the story, but it won't suggest the same significance for someone who hasn't read the story.

Conventional and Traditional Symbols

In contrast to literary symbols are conventional and traditional symbols, which have significance outside literary works and can carry that significance into a work. *Conventional symbols* are objects like a national flag, a dove, a Star of David; they are objects that can be seen and touched, but they also ripple with associations and meanings particular groups have consciously agreed to assign to them. *Traditional symbols* are objects that over years or even centuries have had certain meanings become attached to them in a culture, or in many cultures. The rose, to use that example again, an object that is beautiful and fragile, has by tradition, in many cultures, become a symbol of love, but the cultures did not deliberately decide to attach that significance to the rose.

WHITE ELEPHANTS AS IMAGE   Conventional and traditional symbols bring into a literary work the clusters of meaning they already possess outside the work. For us to respond to them according to usual expectations depends on our having, or our learning about, the shared background and experiences they depend on. No white elephants appear in the setting of Hemingway's story: They are the imaginative half of a simile. The title itself should make us begin asking in what ways hills are like white elephants. We should start with the physical, with the hills as images: In the story, Jig is looking at the line of hills, white in the sun, and says "They look like white elephants" (para. 9). She surely is talking about physical appearance: The hills are rounded and lumpy (not with sharp peaks and points), so they look sort of, a little bit, like the bodies of elephants. Jig says later, "They don't really look like white elephants. I just meant the coloring of their skin through the trees" (para. 36), but by then most readers probably have a visual image of their shape as well.

PROMINENCE OF WHITE ELEPHANTS   If that was the only time the phrase was used in the story, it would simply be a part of the description of the setting. But it is repeated three times, as well as being the title phrase. Dwelling on it this way suggests there is more to it than an imaginative description of setting. And if Jig had said only that the hills are like elephants, the phrase probably wouldn't get beyond the physical. But she says they are like *white* elephants. That takes us further, probably requiring us to explore what white elephants are. The *Oxford English Dictionary* gives the following definitions for *white elephant* (all current when Hemingway was writing):

> a. A rare albino variety of elephant which is highly venerated in some Asian countries. b. *fig.* A burdensome or costly possession (from the story that the kings of Siam were accustomed to make a present of one of these animals to courtiers who had rendered themselves obnoxious, in order to ruin the recipient by the cost of its maintenance). Also, an object, scheme, etc., considered to be without use or value.

White elephants have taken on traditional symbolic significance in Eastern cultures and, to some extent, Western societies. Some of that traditional symbolic significance is carried into "Hills Like White Elephants" through the repeated references to, and resulting prominence of, white elephants in the story.

SIGNIFICANCE OF WHITE ELEPHANTS   The story implies that Jig, unlike the man, has seen white elephants:

> "They look like white elephants," she said.
> "I've never seen one," the man drank his beer.
> "No, you wouldn't have." (paras. 9–11)

If she has, she probably knows that they are both rare and venerated and (figuratively) a burdensome or useless possession. Their conversation goes from "all the things you've waited so long for" to "white elephants" to the operation: the "simple operation" that is "not really an operation at all." It's left to the reader to decide what the operation is. One possibility is an abortion (see if that fits the way they talk about it). In that case, her use of *white elephant* suggests an ambiguity—whether she intends the application or not—between pregnancy and new life as, on the one hand, a highly valued treasure and, on the other, a burden or an object without value. In addition, the story implies that, if Jig stays pregnant, the man may soon think of her as a burdensome and unwanted possession.

Archetypal Symbols

A special type of traditional symbol is an *archetypal symbol*. **Archetypes** are original models or patterns from which later things are made: The first automobile that was constructed is the archetype of all later models. *Literary archetypes* are symbols, character types, and plot lines that trace back to original models or patterns, especially in early myths, folktales, fairy tales, and religious writings. They are used again and again in literature until they come to carry a wide, nearly universal significance and thus touch most readers at a very deep emotional level.

TRADITIONAL ARCHETYPES   Here is a list of some archetypal symbols—a small sampling of all those that could be listed—to illustrate what you can look for:

- A *meal* or *feast* as a symbol of harmony and union
- A *garden* as a type of paradise
- The *country* as a place of natural beauty, freedom, or innocence, in contrast to a *city* as a place of artificiality and corruption or of order and community
- A *forest* as natural beauty or as a scary place where one can be lost
- A *spring* or *fountain* as a symbol of purity and fertility
- The *sea* as a source of life or as a symbol of danger, leading to death
- A *desert* or *wilderness* as a symbol of barrenness, emptiness
- A *river* as boundary between worlds, thus as death; sometimes as fertility and source of life

• Cycles of nature — the *phases of the day* (dawn, noon, sunset, and night) and the *seasons* (spring, summer, autumn, and winter) — suggesting the cycles of human life (birth and youth, adulthood, old age, and death)

TRADITIONAL TYPES AND MOTIFS   Character types can also take on symbolic significance. Among archetypal characters used through the centuries are the hero, the villain, the witch, the wanderer, the benevolent ruler, the tyrant, the trickster, the siren, the angel, the keeper of wisdom. And narrative motifs can carry archetypal significance. Examples used throughout literature and now rich with symbolic implications include creation stories, salvation stories, and tales of temptation.

TRADITION OF THE JOURNEY   Among the most frequently used symbolic motifs, especially in longer stories and poems, is the archetype of the *journey*, which throughout the centuries has suggested growth or achievement or maturing, especially through experience and education. Because, in that sense, all of us are on a journey, stories, poems, and plays involving journeys are often especially meaningful and include some of the world's best-known literary works such as the *Odyssey, Gulliver's Travels,* and *Huckleberry Finn.* The car as a symbol in "The Red Convertible" suggests that Lyman and Henry are on such a journey of growth and experience, with Henry's experiences in Vietnam, though implied rather than described, forming a crucial part of his journey. The railway brings a similar significance into "Hills Like White Elephants," as the wanderings across Europe undertaken by Jig and the American (their luggage is covered with labels "from all the hotels where they had spent nights") echo the directionless journey or wandering that is shaping their lives.

READING FOR ALLEGORY

Closely related to symbol is **allegory**: a form or manner, usually narrative, in which objects, persons, and actions are themselves in a story on the literal level, but also are equated in a sustained and obvious way with meanings that lie outside the story, usually designated by names or characteristics. Those meanings, in allegory, often seem or are of more importance to the work than the literal story. The qualification *sustained* points to the allegory's key difference from symbolism: In a work using allegory, many (or all) details carry a related abstract meaning, not just prominent or repeated details.

EXAMPLES OF ALLEGORY   A classic example of allegory is John Bunyan's *Pilgrim's Progress* (1678), an allegorical dream vision in which a character named Christian undertakes a journey through the wilderness of this world, passing through such places as the Slough (swamp) of Despair and a carnival called Vanity Fair on his way to the Celestial City (heaven). Each character, place, and action in the narrative has an equivalent meaning in the Christian journey of faith and salvation. George Orwell's *Animal Farm* (1944) is an example of a satiric political allegory, with the farmer, various animals, and their actions representing aspects of a workers' revolution, the establishment of a Communist state, and its corruption as the new leaders take on the same tyrannical attitudes the original owners had.

A CAUTION ABOUT READING ALLEGORICALLY   Be careful not to impose an allegorical way of reading (looking for representational meaning everywhere) on works that are not allegorical. This happens especially when readers are taught to search for "deeper meanings" in literary works and to ask, for almost every character, object, and event, "What does it stand for?" That may appear to be active reading, but it's not. Active readers wisely refrain from trying to find meanings hidden below the surface. Rather, they seek to engage actively with what is right there on the surface. It is vitally important to get to know characters, actions, and objects as themselves, to understand them as thoroughly as possible — which in some cases includes their representational significance but in most cases does not.

www

Further explore setting and symbol, including interactive exercises, with VirtuaLit Fiction at bedfordstmartins.com/approachinglit.

Symbols are powerful, among the most evocative experiences for a reader. If read undiscerningly, they can turn a literary work into a hunt for "hidden meaning." But when read with thoughtful common sense, they add a rich, suggestive aura and depth to a work, and help us realize that meanings are not hidden but embodied and revealed, suggested, or evoked.

☑ CHECKLIST on Reading for Setting and Symbol

❏ Be attentive to setting in a literary work:
  - setting in terms of place, in its broad sense and in its sense of narrower, individual places
  - setting in time
  - setting as historical, social, and cultural context

❏ Be aware of different effects setting can have in a work — revealing character, conveying atmosphere, reinforcing meaning, serving as a symbol or occasionally almost as a character.

❏ Be able to explain the difference between an image or action or character that is only itself and one used as a symbol (an image or action or character that also embodies an idea).

(*continued*)

❏ Know the formal devices commonly used for indicating that an image, action, or character may be a symbol: repetition, description, prominent placement (title, beginning, ending, climactic scene), or a sense of weightiness or significance beyond the literal function in the work. Be able to use those signals to perceive when a work is using symbols.

❏ Be alert to different kinds of symbols (private, literary, conventional, traditional, and archetypal) and the various ways they affect works.

❏ Be able to recognize allegory (a sustained equating of objects, persons, or actions in a story with a pattern of abstract meaning outside the story, which is often more important than the literal story), and be able to differentiate that from symbol.

❏ Be comfortable with allowing details to be details.

FURTHER READING

ENTRY POINTS   Setting and symbol figure significantly in the following story, about a platoon of soldiers on patrol during the Vietnam War. Through the things they carried with them, we come to know a lot about them, and about war. The setting in a broad sense is Vietnam. Watch for particular local settings and their effect on the story. The story is packed with objects that are just images in the story, but watch for some that seem to be more than images and carry symbolic importance.

Tim O'Brien b. 1946

The Things They Carried   [1986]

First Lieutenant Jimmy Cross carried letters from a girl named Martha, a junior at Mount Sebastian College in New Jersey. They were not love letters, but Lieutenant Cross was hoping, so he kept them folded in plastic at the bottom of his rucksack. In the late afternoon, after a day's march, he would dig his fox-hole, wash his hands under a canteen, unwrap the letters, hold them with the tips of his fingers, and spend the last hour of light pretending. He would imagine romantic camping trips into the White Mountains in New Hampshire. He would sometimes taste the envelope flaps, knowing her tongue had been there. More than anything, he wanted Martha to love him as he loved her, but the letters were mostly chatty, elusive on the matter of love. She was a virgin, he was almost sure. She was an English major at Mount Sebastian, and she wrote beau-tifully about her professors and roommates and midterm exams, about her re-spect for Chaucer and her great affection for Virginia Woolf. She often quoted lines of poetry; she never mentioned the war, except to say, Jimmy, take care of yourself. The letters weighed 10 ounces. They were signed Love, Martha, but Lieutenant Cross understood that Love was only a way of signing and did not mean what he sometimes pretended it meant. At dusk, he would carefully return the letters to his rucksack. Slowly, a bit distracted, he would get up and move among his men, checking the perimeter, then at full dark he would return to his hole and watch the night and wonder if Martha was a virgin.

The things they carried were largely determined by necessity. Among the necessities or near-necessities were P-38 can openers, pocket knives, heat tabs, wristwatches, dog tags, mosquito repellent, chewing gum, candy, cigarettes, salt tablets, packets of Kool-Aid, lighters, matches, sewing kits, Military Payment Certificates, C rations, and two or three canteens of water. Together, these items weighed between 15 and 20 pounds, depending upon a man's habits or rate of metabolism. Henry Dobbins, who was a big man, carried extra rations; he was especially fond of canned peaches in heavy syrup over pound cake. Dave Jensen, who practiced field hygiene, carried a toothbrush, dental floss, and several hotel-sized bars of soap he'd stolen on R&R° in Sydney, Australia. Ted Lavender, who was scared, carried tranquilizers until he was shot in the head outside the village of Than Khe in mid-April. By necessity, and because it was SOP,° they all carried steel helmets that weighed 5 pounds including the liner and camouflage cover. They carried the standard fatigue jackets and trousers. Very few carried underwear. On their feet they carried jungle boots — 2.1 pounds — and Dave Jensen carried three pairs of socks and a can of Dr. Scholl's foot powder as a precaution against trench foot. Until he was shot, Ted Lavender carried six or seven ounces of premium dope, which for him was a necessity. Mitchell Sanders, the RTO,° carried condoms. Norman Bowker carried a diary. Rat Kiley carried comic books. Kiowa, a devout Baptist, carried an illustrated New Testament that had been presented to him by his father, who taught Sunday school in Oklahoma City, Oklahoma. As a hedge against bad times, however, Kiowa also carried his grandmother's distrust of the white man, his grandfather's old hunting hatchet. Necessity dictated. Because the land was mined and booby-trapped, it was SOP for each man to carry a steel-centered, nylon-covered flak jacket, which weighed 6.7 pounds, but which on hot days seemed much heavier. Because you could die so quickly, each man carried at least one large compress bandage, usually in the helmet band for easy access. Because the nights were cold, and because the monsoons were wet, each carried a green plastic poncho that could be used as a raincoat or groundsheet or makeshift tent. With its quilted liner, the poncho weighed almost two pounds, but it was worth every ounce. In April, for instance, when Ted Lavender was shot, they used his poncho to wrap him up, then to carry him across the paddy, then to lift him into the chopper that took him away.

———————

R&R: Rest and recreation; a brief getaway from active service.   **SOP:** Standard operating procedure.   **RTO:** Radio and telephone operator.

They were called legs or grunts.

To carry something was to hump it, as when Lieutenant Jimmy Cross humped his love for Martha up the hills and through the swamps. In its intransitive form, to hump meant to walk, or to march, but it implied burdens far beyond the intransitive.

Almost everyone humped photographs. In his wallet, Lieutenant Cross carried two photographs of Martha. The first was a Kodacolor snapshot signed Love, though he knew better. She stood against a brick wall. Her eyes were gray and neutral, her lips slightly open as she stared straight-on at the camera. At night, sometimes, Lieutenant Cross wondered who had taken the picture, because he knew she had boyfriends, because he loved her so much, and because he could see the shadow of the picture-taker spreading out against the brick wall. The second photograph had been clipped from the 1968 Mount Sebastian yearbook. It was an action shot — women's volleyball — and Martha was bent horizontal to the floor, reaching, the palms of her hands in sharp focus, the tongue taut, the expression frank and competitive. There was no visible sweat. She wore white gym shorts. Her legs, he thought, were almost certainly the legs of a virgin, dry and without hair, the left knee cocked and carrying her entire weight, which was just over one hundred pounds. Lieutenant Cross remembered touching that left knee. A dark theater, he remembered, and the movie was *Bonnie and Clyde*, and Martha wore a tweed skirt, and during the final scene, when he touched her knee, she turned and looked at him in a sad, sober way that made him pull his hand back, but he would always remember the feel of the tweed skirt and the knee beneath it and the sound of the gunfire that killed Bonnie and Clyde, how embarrassing it was, how slow and oppressive. He remembered kissing her good night at the dorm door. Right then, he thought, he should've done something brave. He should've carried her up the stairs to her room and tied her to the bed and touched that left knee all night long. He should've risked it. Whenever he looked at the photographs, he thought of new things he should've done.

What they carried was partly a function of rank, partly of field specialty.

As a first lieutenant and platoon leader, Jimmy Cross carried a compass, maps, code books, binoculars, and a .45-caliber pistol that weighed 2.9 pounds fully loaded. He carried a strobe light and the responsibility for the lives of his men.

As an RTO, Mitchell Sanders carried the PRC-25 radio, a killer, 26 pounds with its battery.

As a medic, Rat Kiley carried a canvas satchel filled with morphine and plasma and malaria tablets and surgical tape and comic books and all the things a medic must carry, including M&M's° for especially bad wounds, for a total weight of nearly 20 pounds.

As a big man, therefore a machine gunner, Henry Dobbins carried the M-60, which weighed 23 pounds unloaded, but which was almost always

5

10

M&M's: Medical supplies.

loaded. In addition, Dobbins carried between 10 and 15 pounds of ammunition draped in belts across his chest and shoulders.

As PFCs or Spec 4s, most of them were common grunts and carried the standard M-16 gas-operated assault rifle. The weapon weighed 7.5 pounds unloaded, 8.2 pounds with its full 20-round magazine. Depending on numerous factors, such as topography and psychology, the riflemen carried anywhere from 12 to 20 magazines, usually in cloth bandoliers, adding on another 8.4 pounds at minimum, 14 pounds at maximum. When it was available, they also carried M-16 maintenance gear—rods and steel brushes and swabs and tubes of LSA oil—all of which weighed about a pound. Among the grunts, some carried the M-79 grenade launcher, 5.9 pounds unloaded, a reasonably light weapon except for the ammunition, which was heavy. A single round weighed 10 ounces. The typical load was 25 rounds. But Ted Lavender, who was scared, carried 34 rounds when he was shot and killed outside Than Khe, and he went down under an exceptional burden, more than 20 pounds of ammunition, plus the flak jacket and helmet and rations and water and toilet paper and tranquilizers and all the rest, plus the unweighed fear. He was dead weight. There was no twitching or flopping. Kiowa, who saw it happen, said it was like watching a rock fall, or a big sandbag or something—just boom, then down—not like the movies where the dead guy rolls around and does fancy spins and goes ass over teakettle—not like that, Kiowa said, the poor bastard just flat-fuck fell. Boom. Down. Nothing else. It was a bright morning in mid-April. Lieutenant Cross felt the pain. He blamed himself. They stripped off Lavender's canteens and ammo, all the heavy things, and Rat Kiley said the obvious, the guy's dead, and Mitchell Sanders used his radio to report one U.S. KIA° and to request a chopper. Then they wrapped Lavender in his poncho. They carried him out to a dry paddy, established security, and sat smoking the dead man's dope until the chopper came. Lieutenant Cross kept to himself. He pictured Martha's smooth young face, thinking he loved her more than anything, more than his men, and now Ted Lavender was dead because he loved her so much and could not stop thinking about her. When the dustoff arrived, they carried Lavender aboard. Afterward they burned Than Khe. They marched until dusk, then dug their holes, and that night Kiowa kept explaining how you had to be there, how fast it was, how the poor guy just dropped like so much concrete. Boom-down, he said. Like cement.

In addition to the three standard weapons—the M-60, M-16, and M-79—they carried whatever presented itself, or whatever seemed appropriate as a means of killing or staying alive. They carried catch-as-catch-can. At various times, in various situations, they carried M-14s and CAR-15s and Swedish Ks and grease guns and captured AK-47s and Chi-Coms and RPGs and Simonov carbines and black market Uzis and .38-caliber Smith & Wesson handguns and 66 mm LAWs and shotguns and silencers and blackjacks and bayonets and C-4 plastic explosives. Lee Strunk carried a slingshot; a weapon of last resort, he called it. Mitchell Sanders carried brass knuckles. Kiowa carried his grandfather's

---

KIA: Killed in action.

feathered hatchet. Every third or fourth man carried a Claymore antipersonnel mine — 3.5 pounds with its firing device. They all carried fragmentation grenades — 14 ounces each. They all carried at least one M-18 colored smoke grenade — 24 ounces. Some carried CS or tear gas grenades. Some carried white phosphorus grenades. They carried all they could bear, and then some, including a silent awe for the terrible power of the things they carried.

In the first week of April, before Lavender died, Lieutenant Jimmy Cross received a good-luck charm from Martha. It was a simple pebble, an ounce at most. Smooth to the touch, it was a milky white color with flecks of orange and violet, oval-shaped, like a miniature egg. In the accompanying letter, Martha wrote that she had found the pebble on the Jersey shoreline, precisely where the land touched water at high tide, where things came together but also separated. It was this separate-but-together quality, she wrote, that had inspired her to pick up the pebble and to carry it in her breast pocket for several days, where it seemed weightless, and then to send it through the mail, by air, as a token of her truest feelings for him. Lieutenant Cross found this romantic. But he wondered what her truest feelings were, exactly, and what she meant by separate-but-together. He wondered how the tides and waves had come into play on that afternoon along the Jersey shoreline when Martha saw the pebble and bent down to rescue it from geology. He imagined bare feet. Martha was a poet, with the poet's sensibilities, and her feet would be brown and bare, the toenails unpainted, the eyes chilly and somber like the ocean in March, and though it was painful, he wondered who had been with her that afternoon. He imagined a pair of shadows moving along the strip of sand where things came together but also separated. It was phantom jealousy, he knew, but he couldn't help himself. He loved her so much. On the march, through the hot days of early April, he carried the pebble in his mouth, turning it with his tongue, tasting sea salt and moisture. His mind wandered. He had difficulty keeping his attention on the war. On occasion he would yell at his men to spread out the column, to keep their eyes open, but then he would slip away into daydreams, just pretending, walking barefoot along the Jersey shore, with Martha, carrying nothing. He would feel himself rising. Sun and waves and gentle winds, all love and lightness.

What they carried varied by mission.

When a mission took them to the mountains, they carried mosquito netting, machetes, canvas tarps, and extra bug juice.

If a mission seemed especially hazardous, or if it involved a place they knew to be bad, they carried everything they could. In certain heavily mined AOs,° where the land was dense with Toe Poppers and Bouncing Betties, they took turns humping a 28-pound mine detector. With its headphones and big sensing plate, the equipment was a stress on the lower back and shoulders, awkward to handle, often useless because of the shrapnel in the earth, but they carried it anyway, partly for safety, partly for the illusion of safety.

AOs: Areas of operations.

On ambush, or other night missions, they carried peculiar little odds and ends. Kiowa always took along his New Testament and a pair of moccasins for silence. Dave Jensen carried night-sight vitamins high in carotene. Lee Strunk carried his slingshot; ammo, he claimed, would never be a problem. Rat Kiley carried brandy and M&M's candy. Until he was shot, Ted Lavender carried the starlight scope, which weighed 6.3 pounds with its aluminum carrying case. Henry Dobbins carried his girlfriend's pantyhose wrapped around his neck as a comforter. They all carried ghosts. When dark came, they would move out single file across the meadows and paddies to their ambush coordinates, where they would quietly set up the Claymores and lie down and spend the night waiting.

Other missions were more complicated and required special equipment. In mid-April, it was their mission to search out and destroy the elaborate tunnel complexes in the Than Khe area south of Chu Lai. To blow the tunnels, they carried one-pound blocks of pentrite high explosives, four blocks to a man, 68 pounds in all. They carried wiring, detonators, and battery-powered clackers. Dave Jensen carried earplugs. Most often, before blowing the tunnels, they were ordered by higher command to search them, which was considered bad news, but by and large they just shrugged and carried out orders. Because he was a big man, Henry Dobbins was excused from tunnel duty. The others would draw numbers. Before Lavender died there were 17 men in the platoon, and whoever drew the number 17 would strip off his gear and crawl in headfirst with a flashlight and Lieutenant Cross's .45-caliber pistol. The rest of them would fan out as security. They would sit down or kneel, not facing the hole, listening to the ground beneath them, imagining cobwebs and ghosts, whatever was down there—the tunnel walls squeezing in—how the flashlight seemed impossibly heavy in the hand and how it was tunnel vision in the very strictest sense, compression in all ways, even time, and how you had to wiggle in—ass and elbows—a swallowed-up feeling—and how you found yourself worrying about odd things: Will your flashlight go dead? Do rats carry rabies? If you screamed, how far would the sound carry? Would your buddies hear it? Would they have the courage to drag you out? In some respects, though not many, the waiting was worse than the tunnel itself. Imagination was a killer.

On April 16, when Lee Strunk drew the number 17, he laughed and muttered something and went down quickly. The morning was hot and very still. Not good, Kiowa said. He looked at the tunnel opening, then out across a dry paddy toward the village of Than Khe. Nothing moved. No clouds or birds or people. As they waited, the men smoked and drank Kool-Aid, not talking much, feeling sympathy for Lee Strunk but also feeling the luck of the draw. You win some, you lose some, said Mitchell Sanders, and sometimes you settle for a rain check. It was a tired line and no one laughed.

Henry Dobbins ate a tropical chocolate bar. Ted Lavender popped a tranquil- 20 izer and went off to pee.

After five minutes, Lieutenant Jimmy Cross moved to the tunnel, leaned down, and examined the darkness. Trouble, he thought—a cave-in maybe. And then suddenly, without willing it, he was thinking about Martha. The stresses and fractures, the quick collapse, the two of them buried alive under all that weight. Dense, crushing love. Kneeling, watching the hole, he tried to concentrate on Lee Strunk and the war, all the dangers, but his love was too much for him, he felt paralyzed, he wanted to sleep inside her lungs and breathe her blood and be smothered. He wanted her to be a virgin and not a virgin, all at once. He wanted to know her. Intimate secrets: Why poetry? Why so sad? Why that grayness in her eyes? Why so alone? Not lonely, just alone — riding her bike across campus or sitting off by herself in the cafeteria — even dancing, she danced alone — and it was the aloneness that filled him with love. He remembered telling her that one evening. How she nodded and looked away. And how, later, when he kissed her, she received the kiss without returning it, her eyes wide open, not afraid, not a virgin's eyes, just flat and uninvolved.

Lieutenant Cross gazed at the tunnel. But he was not there. He was buried with Martha under the white sand at the Jersey shore. They were pressed together, and the pebble in his mouth was her tongue. He was smiling. Vaguely, he was aware of how quiet the day was, the sullen paddies, yet he could not bring himself to worry about matters of security. He was beyond that. He was just a kid at war, in love. He was twenty-four years old. He couldn't help it.

A few moments later Lee Strunk crawled out of the tunnel. He came up grinning, filthy but alive. Lieutenant Cross nodded and closed his eyes while the others clapped Strunk on the back and made jokes about rising from the dead.

Worms, Rat Kiley said. Right out of the grave. Fuckin' zombie.

The men laughed. They all felt great relief.   25

Spook city, said Mitchell Sanders.

Lee Strunk made a funny ghost sound, a kind of moaning, yet very happy, and right then, when Strunk made that high happy moaning sound, when he went *Ahhooooo*, right then Ted Lavender was shot in the head on his way back from peeing. He lay with his mouth open. The teeth were broken. There was a swollen black bruise under his left eye. The cheekbone was gone. Oh shit, Rat Kiley said, the guy's dead. The guy's dead, he kept saying, which seemed profound — the guy's dead. I mean really.

The things they carried were determined to some extent by superstition. Lieutenant Cross carried his good-luck pebble. Dave Jensen carried a rabbit's foot. Norman Bowker, otherwise a very gentle person, carried a thumb that had been presented to him as a gift by Mitchell Sanders. The thumb was dark brown, rubbery to the touch, and weighed four ounces at most. It had been cut from a VC corpse, a boy of fifteen or sixteen. They'd found him at the bottom of an irrigation ditch, badly burned, flies in his mouth and eyes. The boy wore black shorts and sandals. At the time of his death he had been carrying a pouch of rice, a rifle, and three magazines of ammunition.

You want my opinion, Mitchell Sanders said, there's a definite moral here.

He put his hand on the dead boy's wrist. He was quiet for a time, as if count-   30
ing a pulse, then he patted the stomach, almost affectionately, and used Kiowa's hunting hatchet to remove the thumb.

Henry Dobbins asked what the moral was.

Moral?

You know. *Moral.*

Sanders wrapped the thumb in toilet paper and handed it across to Norman Bowker. There was no blood. Smiling, he kicked the boy's head, watched the flies scatter, and said, It's like with that old TV show — Paladin. Have gun, will travel.

Henry Dobbins thought about it.

Yeah, well, he finally said. I don't see no moral.

There it *is*, man.

Fuck off.

They carried USO° stationery and pencils and pens. They carried Sterno, safety pins, trip flares, signal flares, spools of wire, razor blades, chewing tobacco, liberated joss sticks and statuettes of the smiling Buddha, candles, grease pencils, *The Stars and Stripes*, fingernail clippers, Psy Ops° leaflets, bush hats, bolos, and much more. Twice a week, when the resupply choppers came in, they carried hot chow in green mermite cans and large canvas bags filled with iced beer and soda pop. They carried plastic water containers, each with a two-gallon capacity. Mitchell Sanders carried a set of starched tiger fatigues for special occasions. Henry Dobbins carried Black Flag insecticide. Dave Jensen carried empty sandbags that could be filled at night for added protection. Lee Strunk carried tanning lotion. Some things they carried in common. Taking turns, they carried the big PRC-77 scrambler radio, which weighed 30 pounds with its battery. They shared the weight of memory. They took up what others could no longer bear. Often, they carried each other, the wounded or weak. They carried infections. They carried chess sets, basketballs, Vietnamese-English dictionaries, insignia of rank, Bronze Stars and Purple Hearts, plastic cards imprinted with the Code of Conduct. They carried diseases, among them malaria and dysentery. They carried lice and ringworm and leeches and paddy algae and various rots and molds. They carried the land itself — Vietnam, the place, the soil — a powdery orange-red dust that covered their boots and fatigues and faces. They carried the sky. The whole atmosphere, they carried it, the humidity, the monsoons, the stink of fungus and decay, all of it, they carried gravity. They moved like mules. By daylight they took sniper fire, at night they were mortared, but it was not battle, it was just the endless march, village to village, without purpose, nothing won or lost. They marched for the sake of the march. They plodded along slowly, dumbly, leaning forward against the heat, unthinking, all blood and bone, simple grunts, soldiering with their legs, toiling up the hills and down into the paddies and across the rivers and up again and down, just humping, one step and then the next and then another, but no volition, no will, because it was automatic, it was anatomy, and the war was entirely a matter of posture and carriage, the hump was everything, a kind of inertia, a kind of emptiness, a dullness of desire and intellect and conscience and hope and human

35

USO: United Service Organization.   Psy Ops: Psychological operations.

sensibility. Their principles were in their feet. Their calculations were biological. They had no sense of strategy or mission. They searched the villages without knowing what to look for, not caring, kicking over jars of rice, frisking children and old men, blowing tunnels, sometimes setting fires and sometimes not, then forming up and moving on to the next village, then other villages, where it would always be the same. They carried their own lives. The pressures were enormous. In the heat of early afternoon, they would remove their helmets and flak jackets, walking bare, which was dangerous but which helped ease the strain. They would often discard things along the route of march. Purely for comfort, they would throw away rations, blow their Claymores and grenades, no matter because by nightfall the resupply choppers would arrive with more of the same, then a day or two later still more, fresh watermelons and crates of ammunition and sunglasses and woolen sweaters—the resources were stunning—sparklers for the Fourth of July, colored eggs for Easter—it was the great American war chest—the fruits of science, the smokestacks, the canneries, the arsenals at Hartford, the Minnesota forests, the machine shops, the vast fields of corn and wheat—they carried like freight trains; they carried it on their backs and shoulders—and for all the ambiguities of Vietnam, all the mysteries and unknowns, there was at least the single abiding certainty that they would never be at a loss for things to carry.

After the chopper took Lavender away, Lieutenant Jimmy Cross led his men 40 into the village of Than Khe. They burned everything. They shot chickens and dogs, they trashed the village well, they called in artillery and watched the wreckage, then they marched for several hours through the hot afternoon, and then at dusk, while Kiowa explained how Lavender died, Lieutenant Cross found himself trembling.

He tried not to cry. With his entrenching tool, which weighed five pounds, he began digging a hole in the earth.

He felt shame. He hated himself. He had loved Martha more than his men, and as a consequence Lavender was now dead, and this was something he would have to carry like a stone in his stomach for the rest of the war.

All he could do was dig. He used his entrenching tool like an ax, slashing, feeling both love and hate, and then later, when it was full dark, he sat at the bottom of his foxhole and wept. It went on for a long while. In part, he was grieving for Ted Lavender, but mostly it was for Martha, and for himself, because she belonged to another world, which was not quite real, and because she was a junior at Mount Sebastian College in New Jersey, a poet and a virgin and uninvolved, and because he realized she did not love him and never would.

Like cement, Kiowa whispered in the dark. I swear to God—boom, down. Not a word.

I've heard this, said Norman Bowker.   45

A pisser, you know? Still zipping himself up. Zapped while zipping.

All right, fine. That's enough.

Yeah, but you had to see it, the guy just —

I *heard*, man. Cement. So why not shut the fuck *up*?

Kiowa shook his head sadly and glanced over at the hole where Lieutenant 50
Jimmy Cross sat watching the night. The air was thick and wet. A warm dense
fog had settled over the paddies and there was the stillness that precedes rain.

After a time Kiowa sighed.

One thing for sure, he said. The lieutenant's in some deep hurt. I mean that
crying jag — the way he was carrying on — it wasn't fake or anything, it was real
heavy-duty hurt. The man cares.

Sure, Norman Bowker said.

Say what you want, the man does care.

We all got problems.   55

Not Lavender.

No, I guess not, Bowker said. Do me a favor, though.

Shut up?

That's a smart Indian. Shut up.

Shrugging, Kiowa pulled off his boots. He wanted to say more, just to 60
lighten up his sleep, but instead he opened his New Testament and arranged it
beneath his head as a pillow. The fog made things seem hollow and unattached.
He tried not to think about Ted Lavender, but then he was thinking how fast it
was, no drama, down and dead, and how it was hard to feel anything except surprise. It seemed unchristian. He wished he could find some great sadness, or
even anger, but the emotion wasn't there and he couldn't make it happen.
Mostly he felt pleased to be alive. He liked the smell of the New Testament under
his cheek, the leather and ink and paper and glue, whatever the chemicals were.
He liked hearing the sounds of night. Even his fatigue, it felt fine, the stiff
muscles and the prickly awareness of his own body, a floating feeling. He enjoyed not being dead. Lying there, Kiowa admired Lieutenant Jimmy Cross's capacity for grief. He wanted to share the man's pain, he wanted to care as Jimmy
Cross cared. And yet when he closed his eyes, all he could think was Boom-
down, and all he could feel was the pleasure of having his boots off and the fog
curling in around him and the damp soil and the Bible smells and the plush
comfort of night.

After a moment Norman Bowker sat up in the dark.

What the hell, he said. You want to talk, *talk*. Tell it to me.

Forget it.

No, man, go on. One thing I hate, it's a silent Indian.

For the most part they carried themselves with poise, a kind of dignity. Now 65
and then, however, there were times of panic, when they squealed or wanted to
squeal but couldn't, when they twitched and made moaning sounds and covered
their heads and said Dear Jesus and flopped around on the earth and fired their
weapons blindly and cringed and sobbed and begged for the noise to stop and
went wild and made stupid promises to themselves and to God and to their
mothers and fathers, hoping not to die. In different ways, it happened to all of

them. Afterward, when the firing ended, they would blink and peek up. They would touch their bodies, feeling shame, then quickly hiding it. They would force themselves to stand. As if in slow motion, frame by frame, the world would take on the old logic — absolute silence, then the wind, then sunlight, then voices. It was the burden of being alive. Awkwardly, the men would reassemble themselves, first in private, then in groups, becoming soldiers again. They would repair the leaks in their eyes. They would check for casualties, call in dustoffs, light cigarettes, try to smile, clear their throats and spit and begin cleaning their weapons. After a time someone would shake his head and say, No lie, I almost shit my pants, and someone else would laugh, which meant it was bad, yes, but the guy had obviously not shit his pants, it wasn't that bad, and in any case nobody would ever do such a thing and then go ahead and talk about it. They would squint into the dense, oppressive sunlight. For a few moments, perhaps, they would fall silent, lighting a joint and tracking its passage from man to man, inhaling, holding in the humiliation. Scary stuff, one of them might say. But then someone else would grin or flick his eyebrows and say, Roger-dodger, almost cut me a new asshole, *almost*.

There were numerous such poses. Some carried themselves with a sort of wistful resignation, others with pride or stiff soldierly discipline or good humor or macho zeal. They were afraid of dying but they were even more afraid to show it.

They found jokes to tell.

They used a hard vocabulary to contain the terrible softness. *Greased* they'd say. *Offed, lit up, zapped while zipping*. It wasn't cruelty, just stage presence. They were actors. When someone died, it wasn't quite dying, because in a curious way it seemed scripted, and because they had their lines mostly memorized, irony mixed with tragedy, and because they called it by other names, as if to encyst and destroy the reality of death itself. They kicked corpses. They cut off thumbs. They talked grunt lingo. They told stories about Ted Lavender's supply of tranquilizers, how the poor guy didn't feel a thing, how incredibly tranquil he was.

There's a moral here, said Mitchell Sanders.

They were waiting for Lavender's chopper, smoking the dead man's dope.   70

The moral's pretty obvious, Sanders said, and winked. Stay away from drugs. No joke, they'll ruin your day every time.

Cute, said Henry Dobbins.

Mind blower, get it? Talk about wiggy. Nothing left, just blood and brains.

They made themselves laugh.

There it is, they'd say. Over and over — there it is, my friend, there it is — as if   75 the repetition itself were an act of poise, a balance between crazy and almost crazy, knowing without going, there it is, which meant be cool, let it ride, because Oh yeah, man, you can't change what can't be changed, there it is, there it absolutely and positively and fucking well *is*.

They were tough.

They carried all the emotional baggage of men who might die. Grief, terror, love, longing — these were intangibles, but the intangibles had their own mass and specific gravity, they had tangible weight. They carried shameful memories. They carried the common secret of cowardice barely restrained, the instinct to run or freeze or hide, and in many respects this was the heaviest burden of all, for it could never be put down, it required perfect balance and perfect posture. They carried their reputations. They carried the soldier's greatest fear, which was the fear of blushing. Men killed, and died, because they were embarrassed not to. It was what had brought them to the war in the first place, nothing positive, no dreams of glory or honor, just to avoid the blush of dishonor. They died so as not to die of embarrassment. They crawled into tunnels and walked point and advanced under fire. Each morning, despite the unknowns, they made their legs move. They endured. They kept humping. They did not submit to the obvious alternative, which was simply to close the eyes and fall. So easy, really. Go limp and tumble to the ground and let the muscles unwind and not speak and not budge until your buddies picked you up and lifted you into the chopper that would roar and dip its nose and carry you off to the world. A mere matter of falling, yet no one ever fell. It was not courage, exactly; the object was not valor. Rather, they were too frightened to be cowards.

By and large they carried these things inside, maintaining the masks of composure. They sneered at sick call. They spoke bitterly about guys who had found release by shooting off their own toes or fingers. Pussies, they'd say. Candyasses. It was fierce, mocking talk, with only a trace of envy or awe, but even so the image played itself out behind their eyes.

They imagined the muzzle against flesh. So easy: squeeze the trigger and blow away a toe. They imagined it. They imagined the quick, sweet pain, then the evacuation to Japan, then a hospital with warm beds and cute geisha nurses.

And they dreamed of freedom birds.   80

At night, on guard, staring into the dark, they were carried away by jumbo jets. They felt the rush of takeoff. *Gone!* they yelled. And then velocity — wings and engines — a smiling stewardess — but it was more than a plane, it was a real bird, a big sleek silver bird with feathers and talons and high screeching. They were flying. The weights fell off; there was nothing to bear. They laughed and held on tight, feeling the cold slap of wind and altitude, soaring, thinking *It's over, I'm gone!* — they were naked, they were light and free — it was all lightness, bright and fast and buoyant, light as light, a helium buzz in the brain, a giddy bubbling in the lungs as they were taken up over the clouds and the war, beyond duty, beyond gravity and mortification and global entanglements — *Sin loi!*° they yelled. *I'm sorry, motherfuckers, but I'm out of it, I'm goofed, I'm on a space cruise, I'm gone!* — and it was a restful, unencumbered sensation, just riding the light waves, sailing that big silver freedom bird over the mountains and oceans, over America, over the farms and great sleeping cities and cemeteries and highways and the golden arches of McDonald's, it was flight, a kind of fleeing, a kind of falling, falling higher and higher, spinning off the edge of the earth and beyond the sun and through the vast, silent vacuum where there were no burdens

---

Sin loi: Vietnamese for "sorry."

and where everything weighed exactly nothing — *Gone!* they screamed. *I'm sorry but I'm gone!* — and so at night, not quite dreaming, they gave themselves over to lightness, they were carried, they were purely borne.

On the morning after Ted Lavender died, First Lieutenant Jimmy Cross crouched at the bottom of his foxhole and burned Martha's letters. Then he burned the two photographs. There was a steady rain falling, which made it difficult, but he used heat tabs and Sterno to build a small fire, screening it with his body, holding the photographs over the tight blue flame with the tips of his fingers.

He realized it was only a gesture. Stupid, he thought. Sentimental, too, but mostly just stupid.

Lavender was dead. You couldn't burn the blame.

Besides, the letters were in his head. And even now, without photographs,   85
Lieutenant Cross could see Martha playing volleyball in her white gym shorts and yellow T-shirt. He could see her moving in the rain.

When the fire died out, Lieutenant Cross pulled his poncho over his shoulders and ate breakfast from a can.

There was no great mystery, he decided.

In those burned letters Martha had never mentioned the war, except to say, Jimmy, take care of yourself. She wasn't involved. She signed the letters Love, but it wasn't love, and all the fine lines and technicalities did not matter. Virginity was no longer an issue. He hated her. Yes, he did. He hated her. Love, too, but it was a hard, hating kind of love.

The morning came up wet and blurry. Everything seemed part of everything else, the fog and Martha and the deepening rain.

He was a soldier, after all.   90

Half smiling, Lieutenant Jimmy Cross took out his maps. He shook his head hard, as if to clear it, then bent forward and began planning the day's march. In ten minutes, or maybe twenty, he would rouse the men and they would pack up and head west, where the maps showed the country to be green and inviting. They would do what they had always done. The rain might add some weight, but otherwise it would be one more day layered upon all the other days.

He was realistic about it. There was that new hardness in his stomach. He loved her but he hated her.

No more fantasies, he told himself.

Henceforth, when he thought about Martha, it would be only to think that she belonged elsewhere. He would shut down the daydreams. This was not Mount Sebastian, it was another world, where there were no pretty poems or mid-term exams, a place where men died because of carelessness and gross stupidity. Kiowa was right. Boom-down, and you were dead, never partly dead.

Briefly, in the rain, Lieutenant Cross saw Martha's gray eyes gazing back   95
at him.

He understood.

It was very sad, he thought. The things men carried inside. The things men did or felt they had to do.

He almost nodded at her, but didn't.

Instead he went back to his maps. He was now determined to perform his duties firmly and without negligence. It wouldn't help Lavender, he knew that, but from this point on he would comport himself as an officer. He would dispose of his good-luck pebble. Swallow it, maybe, or use Lee Strunk's slingshot, or just drop it along the trail. On the march he would impose strict field discipline. He would be careful to send out flank security, to prevent straggling or bunching up, to keep his troops moving at the proper pace and at the proper interval. He would insist on clean weapons. He would confiscate the remainder of Lavender's dope. Later in the day, perhaps, he would call the men together and speak to them plainly. He would accept the blame for what had happened to Ted Lavender. He would be a man about it. He would look them in the eyes, keeping his chin level, and he would issue the new SOPs in a calm, impersonal tone of voice, a lieutenant's voice, leaving no room for argument or discussion. Commencing immediately, he'd tell them, they would no longer abandon equipment along the route of march. They would police up their acts. They would get their shit together, and keep it together, and maintain it neatly and in good working order.

He would not tolerate laxity. He would show strength, distancing himself.   100

Among the men there would be grumbling, of course, and maybe worse, because their days would seem longer and their loads heavier, but Lieutenant Jimmy Cross reminded himself that his obligation was not to be loved but to lead. He would dispense with love; it was not now a factor. And if anyone quarreled or complained, he would simply tighten his lips and arrange his shoulders in the correct command posture. He might give a curt little nod. Or he might not. He might just shrug and say, Carry on, then they would saddle up and form into a column and move out toward the villages west of Than Khe.

APPROACHING THE READING

1. The setting for the story is Vietnam during the Vietnam War. If you are not familiar with this conflict, do some research on it. Perhaps you know people in your family or a friend's family who were in the war. Talk to them about their experience, especially what it was like living in that terrain.

2. What role does the setting itself play in the story? Think about how an environment affects us. How does this setting/environment affect those in the story? In what ways do you think the characters would appear to be different in a different environment? In what ways does this setting force them to struggle to maintain their identities? In what ways does the setting press them to change?

3. Consider the setting of the jungle itself. What makes it appropriate for this story even if it weren't the actual setting? Do you think it could also be a symbol? In what ways? Today we often use the term *rain forest* instead of jungle. What differences do you think that change in terminology makes? Is anything gained or lost?

4. Note the things that each man carries. Do you find yourself considering them, or some of them, as symbols? If so, which ones? If you think they are symbols, what meanings ripple out from each thing?

5. The story talks about how the soldiers changed the words they used: "They used a hard vocabulary to contain the terrible softness" (para. 68). In what ways do you think the setting had an impact on why they did this?

ENTRY POINTS   Setting is also important in the next story. Its action takes place in Washington, DC, mostly in a specific block of a neighborhood in which the population had changed from white to African American and by the end of the story has changed again, this time to a new generation of African Americans and then to regentrifying whites. As you read, think about the importance of place and location (people are even associated with their house numbers) and about how changes in place and location can have a significant impact. Notice also the use of style for characterizing the new residents, the way they drop their g's and use potentially offensive language. The story ends in the very recent past, but its events cover a number of years. Notice how the story starts before the central event ("the fracas") and repeatedly flips back or ahead. As you read the story a second time, consider the effect of its handling of time and ask yourself if any objects or actions rise to the level of symbolic significance.

Edward P. Jones b. 1951

Bad Neighbors   [2006]

Even before the fracas with Terence Stagg, people all along both sides of the 1400 block of 8th Street, N.W., could see the Benningtons for what they really were. First, the family moved in not on Saturday or on a weekday, but on Sunday, which was still the Lord's Day even though church for many was now only a place to visit for a wedding, or a funeral. Perhaps Easter or Christmas. And those watching that Sunday, from behind discreetly parted, brocaded curtains and on porches rarely used except to go back and forth into homes, had to wonder why the Bennington family even bothered to bring along most of their furniture. They had a collection of junk that included a stained queen-size mattress, a dining room table with three legs, a mirror with a large missing piece in one corner, and a refrigerator dented on two sides. One neighbor, his second cup of morning coffee in hand, joked to his wife that the Bennington refrigerator probably wouldn't work without a big block of ice in it to cool things. During the move-in, the half-dressed little Benningtons occupied themselves running to and from the two medium-size moving trucks, taking in clothes that had busted out of the cardboard boxes during the trip from whatever countrified shack they had left. Over the next two weeks or so, it became clear that the house at 1406 8th, with its three bedrooms, would be containing at least twelve people, though that number was always fluid, so neighbors on both sides of the street would never get a proper accounting, and they would never know who was related to whom.

They came in the middle of October, the Benningtons, bringing children — a bunch of five or so, from a two-year-old to a girl on the verge of being a teenager. Children who sometimes played outside on Friday and Saturday nights until at least nine thirty. And they were loud children, loud in a neighborhood where most of the children were now in their teens and did no more harm than play their portable radios too loudly as they washed their parents' cars. And the Benningtons came with a few men who sat on the porch on a legless couch with a cheap bedspread, drinking from containers in paper bags. Grace Bennington appeared to be the matriarch; she could have been fifty, but with her broad weight and gray hair, it was difficult for anyone to be certain. On a good day, her 8th Street neighbors might have been able to say forty or forty-five, but on a bad day, and the Benningtons seemed to have not a few bad days, seventy-five would not have been an unfair number. Only one thing was certain — she, in face and body, had known hard work. She moved about on stubby legs, favoring the outsides of her feet as she walked, so that all her shoes had soles run down on those sides. The soles of her shoes on the inside were almost as new as the day she brought them out of the store. There was a man — always bringing groceries — far older than Grace, tallish, a less flashy dresser than most of the men in the rest of the family; he came and went, always in the uniform of a man who worked in the railroad yards. A woman who could have been a bit younger than Grace was rarely seen, and when she was, the children would be holding her hand as they took her for a walk. She wore coats and sweaters even on the warmest day, and that fall and winter saw many good days. She might have been beautiful, but no one could tell because she was always wearing sunglasses and a scarf pulled around to cover most of her face. Then there was Amanda, no more than seventeen. Amanda in her tight blue jeans. The oldest male the neighbors saw most often was Derek, a man in his early twenties, a well-built and too often shirtless loudmouth, who seemed to go off, maybe to some job, whenever he could get his nineteen-year-old Ford to run, the kind of car most of the men in the neighborhood had owned on their way up to where they were now. There were two or three men in that family, but they also came and went. Only Derek was constant.

It was the quietness of Neil Bennington that caused Sharon Palmer — who had noticed in his demeanor even across 8th Street in those first weeks after the clan moved in — to introduce herself to him at his locker in the hall at Cardozo High School. He was in the tenth grade, small for his age and somewhat awkward, unlike his brother Derek. Sharon Palmer, who lived at 1409 directly across 8th from the Benningtons, was to witness the fracas between Derek and Terence Stagg, and seeing the fight, which was actually far less than that, she would begin to think her father and most of their neighbors might not be so wrong about most of those Benningtons. By then she would have had her third date with Terence, and he would have kissed her five times, twice surprising her as he thrust his tongue into her mouth. She mistook what she felt at that moment for blossoming love.

A senior, Sharon had, in the eleventh grade, become aware of her effect on boys — almost all of them (Terence Stagg, whom she had long had eyes and heart for, was a week or so from paying her any attention). And Sharon, coming rather late to an awareness of her womanhood, had begun to take some delight in seeing boys wither as they stood close enough to smell the mystery that had nothing to do with perfume and look into her twinkling brown eyes she had inherited from a grandmother who had seen only the morning, afternoon, and evening of a cotton field.

Neil was bent over into his locker, and when she said Hello, he rose slowly   5 as though he knew all too well the accidents that came with quick movements. He seemed more befuddled than taken with her femaleness after she told him who she was, and the innocence of him made her wish that just this once she could turn down all that mystery that transformed boys into fools. He squinted and blinked, and with each blink he appeared to get closer to knowing just who she was. And as the brief conversation went on, it occurred to her that he was very much like one of her younger brothers — Neil and the brother had the forever look of true believers who had to start every morning learning all over again that the Easter bunny and Santa Claus did not exist.

That day of the first conversation, she saw him walking alone down 11th Street after school and she separated from her friends to go with him the rest of the way home. She thought Neil, like her brother, was adorable, a word she had started using just after the New Year. Her father, Hamilton Palmer, saw them turn the corner from P and thought nothing about it. As the morning and afternoon supervisor at the main post office at North Capitol Street, he was home most days by three thirty. He was watering plants on his porch, and Neil said good-bye to his daughter and Hamilton opened the little gate on the porch that had been installed ages ago when his children and the puppy were too small to know all the ways the world beyond the gate could hurt them.

It was three weeks later, more than a month after the Benningtons moved in, that Sharon's father Hamilton began to think something might be amiss. Thanksgiving had come and gone, and people all over Washington were complaining that it just didn't feel like Christmas weather. Who could think of Christmas with people still in their fall sweaters and trees threatening to bud again? Neil and Sharon turned the corner again, this time accompanied by three other students who lived farther down 8th. Before the four left Sharon in front of her house, Hamilton's daughter touched Neil's shoulder, and the boy smiled. It was not the touch so much as the smile that bothered him. He had been thinking that his Sharon and Terence Stagg might be a good match some time down the line when they had finished their education. Hamilton noticed for the first time that Derek was watching everything from across the street. He could not tell for certain, but he thought he saw Derek Bennington smirking.

Two days later the Prevosts up the street at 1404 had their place burgled, with a television being the most expensive thing taken. No one said anything, but the neighbors knew it had to be Derek. The next week the Thorntons at 1414 had their car stolen. The car was only a Chevy. Five years old, but that was not the point, said Bill Forsythe at 1408 next door to the Benningtons. His wife, Prudence, had complained about what a noisy heap the Thornton car was and the neighborhood was well rid of it. A man's property is a man's property, Bill said, even if it's one skate with three wheels. After the car was taken, someone called the police and they came out and spoke for some fifteen minutes to the Benningtons in their house. No one knew what went down, as the police came out and left without talking to any of the neighbors. Derek walked out soon afterward and stood on his porch, smoking a cigarette. He was alone for a good while, and then his mother Grace came and said something that made him put out the cigarette in the ashtray. She continued talking to him, and for every second she was speaking, he was nodding his head slightly.

More than a month before the January fracas between Derek and Terence Stagg, Sharon Palmer returned to Neil a book she had borrowed from him. It was a Saturday afternoon, and she went up the steps to the Bennington home at 1406 and saw that the screen door was shut but that the main door was open. There was no one she could see from the threshold and she called "Hello" and "Neil," and then, with no answer after moments, she knocked on the wood of the screen door. The radio and the television were playing. She did not want to think it, but she felt it said something about them, maybe not Neil but all the rest of them. She waited about two minutes and after she again called for Neil, she opened the screen and stepped into the house, saying "Hello, hello, hello" all the way. On the couch the woman in the sunglasses was watching her, and when Sharon asked for Neil, the woman said nothing. There were two small children on either side of her and they were watching a black-and-white television. Sharon immediately thought about the Prevosts' television, but she did not know if it had been color or black-and-white.

"I knocked, but I got no answer," Sharon said. "Is Neil here? I brought his   10 book back." The woman tilted her head to the side as though to better consider what she had heard. "Is he here?" The children were silent and their eyes were big as though Sharon was a creature they had not seen before. Sharon told the woman again that she was looking for Neil. It would be better, Sharon thought, if I could see her eyes. Finally, the woman moved her face toward the next room. "Thank you."

The dining room was crowded with boxes, the state it must have been in since the first day they moved in. The dining table's missing leg had been replaced with one that had yet to be painted the color of the rest of the table.

"Hello, Neil? Neil?" She stepped into the kitchen, and she was not prepared for what she saw. It was immaculate, the kind of room her mother would be happy with. "Hello?" The floor was clean, the counters were clean, the stove was clean, the tiny table and its three chairs were clean. "Hello?" She turned and looked about the room with great curiosity. When she turned back, Derek was standing at the open screen door to the backyard, watching her.

"You lost?"

"No, I'm sorry. I knocked but no one answered."

"The May maid swayed away to pray in the day's hay," Derek said, not smil- 15
ing "Thas why you got no answer."

"I just came to return Neil's book. Is he here?"

Derek shouted twice for Neil. "Well, you can just leave it on the table, lady
from across the street."

"He said I could borrow another. A book of Irish stories the library doesn't
seem to have."

He shouted for Neil again, and as she listened to his voice thunder through
the house, she noticed the small bookcase beside the refrigerator. Four shelves,
each a little more than two feet across. He saw her looking at it. "Just leave it on
the table. That readin fool'll get it."

"I can come back for it another time." She set the book on the table.   20

"Which one was it?" He was wearing an undershirt, and it hung on him in
a way that did not threaten the way those shirts seemed to on other men. The
bare muscular arms were simply bare muscular arms, not possible weapons. It
was a small moment in the kitchen, but she was to think of those arms years
later as she stood naked and looked down at the bare arms of her husband as the
red light of the expensive German clock shone down on him. A night-light.

"A book of stories—Mary Lavin's *Tales from Bective Bridge*. My teacher
shared two with me and I'm hooked."

"Hooked is good cept with junk, ask any junkie," Derek said, and he looked
across at the bookcase. "The almighty reader might have it upstairs or in some
box somewhere. His shit is all over the fuckin place." Shit, fuckin, she thought.
Shit, fuckin. In a few quiet, swift steps, he was at the table. He took up the book
and looked at the spine and wrinkled his face. "Hooked, hooked," he said. The
same kind of steps took him to the bookcase. He knelt, peered for a moment,
and put the book between two green books on the second shelf up from the bottom "L is for Lavin," Derek said and found the book. "M is for Mary." He looked
at it front and back. "I know one thing for sure: He loves this woman's work so
you bet not lose it. I think the almighty reader is part Irish and don't know it
yet." In two more steps he was before her, and she took the book and promised
to return it just as it was. There was nothing untoward in his face, the lust, the
hunger, the way it was in all the boys except Neil, boys with pimples, and boys
without. There was no smile from him and he did not look into her eyes, the
twinkling and the brown. He turned and went to the refrigerator and opened it.
"You know," he said, his back to her, his head bent to look in, and the light of
the refrigerator pouring out over him, "you shouldn't be afraid of wearin blue."
He took out a beer and closed the icebox with great care. "Forget the red. You
wear too much red." He did not turn around but found on the counter beside
the icebox an opener for the beer.

"What?"

Neil came in, and Derek pointed to him. "Where you been, boy?" Derek 25
said. "Your girlfriend been waitin. You the worse fuckin boyfriend in the world."

"She ain't my girlfriend," Neil said and raised his hand Hello to Sharon.

"I gave your girlfriend one of Lavin's books, man."

"I told you she's not my girlfriend, Dee."

"Whatever, man." He still had not turned around and he drank from the beer as he walked to the back door. "You should tell your girlfriend that red doesn't suit her. She ain't believe me so maybe if it comes from her boyfriend." He went out the screen door, and Neil walked her back to the front of the house.

Three neighbors saw Sharon Palmer leave the Bennington house that day — her father Hamilton from his upstairs bedroom, Terence Stagg next door to the home of Sharon and Hamilton Palmer, and Prudence Forsythe next to the Benningtons. This was a little more than a month before that January thing between Terence and Derek. Terence was standing at his living room window and watched Sharon walk down the Bennington steps with a book in her hand. Neil Bennington was a wisp of a boy, not worth noticing to a young man like Terence. But Terence had seen Derek about, and like most of the men on 8th Street he didn't think much of him; men like Derek had never seen the inside of Howard University, where Terence was in his second year, and they never would. As Sharon waited for the few passing cars going up and down 8th, she lowered her head in a most engaging way, lowered it only for a second, as if to consider something, and Terence could see how Sharon had filled out. Filled out in her pink sweater and her blue jeans not trampy tight, but tight enough to let a man know if he should bother or not. She had filled out since the last time he had really taken a look at her, and that was a time he could not remember.

Terence was at her door that evening, asking a beaming Hamilton Palmer, who had also gone to Howard, how he was doing these warm days and then asking the father if he might talk a bit with his daughter this evening. He and Sharon stepped out onto the porch and Terence invited her to a movie and a meal on Friday night. She had had two dates before — and one of those had been with a young man who was brother to her cousin's husband. Sharon was not one to keep a diary, but if she had been, the meeting of a few minutes with Terence would have taken up at least two pages.

Terence stepped back into her house and called good-bye to Hamilton Palmer, who came out of the kitchen with Sharon's mother. The parents said they hadn't seen much of him lately and then wanted to know how his studies were going and Terence told them they were going very well and that he was hitting his stride. He was, in fact, going with a fellow Howard student, but Howard students not D.C. natives were taught from day one never to venture into Washington neighborhoods except where they could find a better class of people, meaning white people for the most part, and so that Newark girl would never know about 8th Street. That girl at Howard was so clingy, with her Terence this and her Terence that. And as he had watched Sharon earlier come across 8th, he remembered something his father Lane had recently told him: You are young and the world is your oyster. You shuck it, don't let it shuck you. What oyster would Derek ever shuck? Well, fine, Hamilton said about Terence hitting his stride, and Hamilton came across the living room with his hand extended. And he added that Terence was way ahead of the game, because Lord knows he didn't hit his own stride until he was a junior at least, isn't that right, honey? And his wife just smiled.

Sharon, ecstatic, did not get to Mary Lavin's *Tales from Bective Bridge* that evening as she had planned. She could think of nothing else but an evening with Terence. She tried sleeping, but found it was no use and so got up from bed and sat in the dark at her window, which, like the one in her parents' bedroom, faced 8th Street. She would be at the window three nights before Christmas, near about midnight, when she saw Neil Bennington, carrying a small package that was bright even in the dark, dash across the street to her house, take the steps two at a time, and then dash back across the street to his place, his hands now apparently empty. It would be a rare cold night for that December, and she was tempted not to go downstairs. But she did. She opened the main door to find a small gift-wrapped package on the threshold between the door and the storm door. It had her name on it. With anxious fingers, just inside the living room, she tore open the shiny wrapping and found in a velvet-covered box a figure of brown wood, nearly perfectly carved, a figure of a little girl no more than an inch and a half, in a dress that came down to her feet. She had on a bonnet. When Sharon held the figure to the light of the lamp on a table in the living room, the girl's nose told her unmistakably that the figure was of a black girl. The child seemed somehow recognizable, but for years she was never able to recall where she had seen it. One of the girl's arms was extended somewhat, and there was a bracelet on it. Through the bracelet ran a gold-like chain; that the chain was shining told it might be gold, that it was from a boy of no means from across the street told her that it might not be.

She was disappointed because she did not want Neil to think that there could ever be anything between them, and such a thing, with such intricacy, with a compellingly quiet beauty, told her that was what he was thinking. But she did not want to hurt his feelings by returning the gift. Adorable people should not be hurt. She thought for a day and decided to give him a book, and she chose a small paperback edition of Ann Petry's *The Street*. She came up to him as he stood at his locker at school, his head cocked to the side as if he was trying to decide what was needed for the final period of the day. Terence was picking her up after school. Neil Bennington seemed genuinely surprised. "I didn't get you anything," he said, blushing and blinking. "This is straight-up embarrassin."

"That doesn't matter," Sharon said. "It's the season for giving. What are neighbors for?"   35

"I'll get you somethin, I promise," he said, biting his lip.

"If you do, I'll think you'll be trying to reciprocate, and you'll hurt my feelings."

"All right," Neil said. "All right, but I won't forget this. Ever."

In more than three years after that day, on her way to becoming a nurse, she would attend a party at the home of one of her Georgetown University professors. Her husband would not be able to be with her that night, but that was the way it had become. She would spend a good part of the evening near a corner with a glass of ginger ale; none of the food would appeal to her. Just as she was about to excuse herself and leave, a white woman of some seventy years would come up to her.

"I have been admiring that wondrous thing you're wearing," the white 40 woman said. "Even from across the room, you can see how unique it is." She looked closer. "The carver must have used up all his eyesight making it. You have exquisite taste." The woman smiled, not at Sharon but at the Christmas gift that she would only recently have unearthed from a trunk in her parents' basement.

"It's not much. Someone gave it to me. It isn't very much."

"It is much in that other way," the woman said. "I know a place down on F Street that would give you five hundred dollars for it. . . . Please. May I?" and the woman raised a tentative hand, and Sharon nodded and the woman took up the little girl in the bonnet and rested it between her fingers and then looked fully into Sharon's eyes. "If the carver lost his sight, he may well have thought it was well worth it." That evening, for the first time, Sharon would notice the initials down in one of the folds of the girl's dress. No, she said to herself, I would not sell it. I don't even know if the carver is living anymore.

It was actually Amanda Bennington who first got into it with Terence Stagg, which led to something that ultimately allowed the whole neighborhood to see the Benningtons for what they were. She and her brother Derek had come from the Safeway late on a Saturday morning in mid-January. They parked in front of the Staggs' house, across the street at 1407. Derek took bags of groceries into their house while Amanda looked to be tidying up the car.

Sharon Palmer was watching from her bedroom next door to the Staggs'. Nothing had really been spoken, but it might as well have been said that she and Terence Stagg were a couple. Neighbors all said what a nice couple they made; she and Terence had driven up in his father's Cadillac one evening the week before and she saw Neil watching from his porch. She waved and he waved back. They were not walking home as much as they had been, but they still shared books. Derek came out and stood beside Neil as Terence walked Sharon into her house.

Terence, that Saturday morning, was heading out his door when he saw 45 Amanda fussing around in the trunk of Derek's Ford, which was parked in the same spot his father, Lane Stagg, had been parking his Cadillacs in since even before Terence knew what good things life had in store for him. It may as well be said that his father owned that dot of public real estate. Before his family had awakened, Lane had gone out on an errand that morning, purring quietly away about seven thirty in that new tan Cadillac that had less than three thousand miles on it.

"Hey, you," Terence said to Amanda and came down the steps to the sidewalk, too upset to even take full notice of her behind as she bent over and puttered in the trunk. He was to excel in anatomy and dermatology when he got to Howard's medical school, but genetics and neurology would nearly cost him his future. Amanda took her head out of the trunk, holding jumper cables, and looked Terence up and down. "Hey! You know you parked in my father's space?" Then, watching Amanda toss the cables back in the trunk and try to clean the dirt from her hands with a Kleenex she pulled from her back pocket, he pointed to the space her car was in and said: "Hey, do you know that you are parked in my father's space?" Since the first month at Howard as a freshman, he had stopped referring to Lane as "my daddy" when talking to a third party.

"Hay for horses, not for people. Go down Hecht's and get em cheaper," Amanda said. Words of a child of eight or nine, and they upset Terence even more. "It's a free country, man," Amanda said. "We all got a right to park where we wanna park." She pulled another bunched-up Kleenex from the back pocket of her jeans and tried to wipe her hands with it. She was dark and pretty, and in another universe Terence would have been able to appreciate that. "And be-sides" — she turned and pointed with the hand with the Kleenex across the street — "somebody's got my brother's regular spot." The Forsythes at 1408 next door to the Benningtons were already fed up with them and showed it by park-ing in front of their house as often as they could, though the Benningtons had never complained. That Saturday, the Forsythes had company from out of town and the visitors' Trans Am was where Derek's Ford would have gone, on a spot covered in oil that was forever leaking from his car. "We had stuff to take and it whatn't no use parkin way down at the corner. Maybe that Trans Am'll move be-fore your daddy gets back."

"I don't care about that," Terence said. "You're just going to have to move that thing somewhere else."

Her mother Grace had been trying to teach her to control her temper, but Amanda knew there were days and then there were days. "First off," Amanda said, "I ain't movin shit. Second off, it ain't no thing. It's a classic. Third off, you better get out my damn face. This a free country, man. You ain't no fuckin parkin police." She closed the trunk with both hands to make the loudest sound she could manage.

"I would expect something like this from trash like you."   50

She flicked the Kleenex at him and he dodged it. "Since it's that way, you the biggest trash around here." She had seen him about many times, and in another universe before that moment she would have liked him to come across the street and knock at her door and invite her to the Broadway on 7th Street for a movie and a hamburger and soda afterward. She had also seen Terence's well-dressed mother, Helen Stagg, quite often as well, had studied the woman as she came out of her house and looked up and down 8th Street as if waiting for the world to tell her that it was once again worthy of having her. She loved her own mother, in all her dowdiness, more than any human being, but she knew Grace would never be Helen Stagg. "If I'm trash, you trash."

"Typical," Terence said. "Real damn typical."

"Whas up here?" Derek came across the street, his keys in his hand.

"Derek, this guy say we gotta move the car cause his father's got the spot."

"Ain't nobody own no parkin spot, neighbor. This a free country, neighbor,"   55 Derek said, the keys jingling with his arm at his side.

"I'm not your neighbor."

"Oh, oh, it's like that, huh?" Derek said, turning around twice and raising his arms in faux surrender. "You one of those, huh? All right." Amanda had stayed in the street behind the car but Derek had continued on up to the sidewalk. "All right, big shot. Les just clear the way, cause I don't want no trouble. Nobody want any trouble." He stepped back into the gutter. "All I can say is we got a right to be there, as much right as your daddy and that Cadillac of his with that punk-ass color." He looked at Amanda. "You done?"

"Yeah, I'm cool."

"Well, les go," and they waited to cross as two cars passed going up 8th Street.

"I told you to move that damn thing," Terence said. His knuckles tapped the 60 top of the trunk. "You people should learn to wash your ears out." Terence spat on the car.

Derek turned. "Just leave that somebitch alone, Derek," Amanda said. "He ain't worth it."

Grace Bennington came out of her house and yelled at Derek to come on in. Neil stood beside her and he held the hand of a girl of seven or eight. "Wipe that shit off," Derek said of the spit, a slow-moving blob on the black paint heading down toward the fender. The car didn't always run, but he kept it clean.

Derek counted all the way to ten and Terence said, "Tell your funky mother to wipe it off."

"Even you, even poor you," Derek said calmly, "should know the law against sayin somethin like that. Man oh man oh man . . ."

It took but one hit to the lower part of the jaw to send Terence to the 65 ground. He had seen the fist coming, but because he had not been in very many fights in his life, it took him far too long to realize the fist was coming for him. Grace and Amanda screamed. The Bryants at 1401 and the Prevosts at 1404 came out, as did the Forsythes and their company who had the Trans Am, all of them still digesting their breakfast. Sharon Palmer had watched with growing concern from her bedroom window. She had not been able to hear all that was said by the three, but, on the path to love, she had admired the way Terence seemed to be standing up to Derek. By the time she got downstairs and out to the sidewalk, Amanda and Grace were comforting Terence, and only seconds after he awoke and saw the women, he told them to get the fuck away from him. Neil was holding his little sister by the hand to keep her from going into the street to be with their mother, and Derek was already back across the street and on the legless couch, watching the group around Terence and smoking a cigarette and waiting for the police to show up.

Lane Stagg was more disturbed about what had happened to his son than if it had been a mere fight between young men of equal age and status, and his Terence had simply lost after doing his best. No doubt, Lane Stagg knew, men like Derek Bennington had never learned to fight fair. Terence, after the trip from the hospital, was out of it for a day and a half, but his father did not need to hear from his son that he had been jumped before he could properly defend himself. Terence suffered no permanent damage, and he would recover and become the first person anyone in the neighborhood knew to become a doctor. "Let them crackers," Lane Stagg said at the graduation dinner after his second drink, "write that up in their immigration brochures about how descendants of slaves aren't any good and so all you hardworking immigrants just come on over."

The police came out that Saturday, but because they didn't like doing paperwork and because no white person had been hurt, Derek was not arrested. That would not be the case with the white man in Arlington who owned the Bennington home.

That Saturday evening, after the hospital visit, Lane, working on his second drink, broached the idea again of buying the house the Benningtons were renting from the white man. He sat in his living room with his wife perched on the arm of his easy chair, and across from him, on the couch, were Hamilton Palmer, Arthur Atwell, and Bill and Prudence Forsythe. Just after the third sip of that drink, Lane Stagg started in on how the neighborhood was changing for the worse. And Hamilton, already seeing the Staggs as future in-laws, agreed. He was not drinking. And neither was Bill Forsythe. Prudence had quietly come upon Bill two weeks before looking out their bedroom window at Amanda Bennington collecting toys from her front yard. Prudence watched him for more than five minutes before going to see what had captured him. Bill had a drink in his hand and Amanda was wearing the tight blue jeans she would have on the day of the fracas and it was not even one thirty. "Nice day," Bill said to his wife, already drifting toward happy land and so unable to compose something better. "I'm fucking tired of you getting ideas," Prudence said. "I'm fucking tired of you and your ideas." "Honey," Bill said, "keep your voice down. The neighbors, honey. The neighbors." Meaning not the Benningtons on one side, but Arthur and Beatrice Atwell on the other side. She took the drink from Bill, and Prudence did it in such a way that the ice cubes did not clink against the sides of the glass.

Lane Stagg, pained about his Terence, was as eloquent that evening as he would be at the last meeting of the neighbors years later. He said that though the prior neighbors in the Bennington house had not been in the same league as those sitting now in his living room, the good neighbors of 8th Street could live with them. But he had to admit that the building had really not housed the proper sort of folk in years. "What," he asked, "does that white man across the river in Arlington care about our neighborhood?" He had been the captain of his debating team in high school when the schools had such things. He would have made a good lawyer, everyone said. But the son of a coal and ice man rose only so far. His wife, whose father and mother were lawyers, married him anyway.

It was not a long meeting, but before it ended, they agreed that they would 70 raise the money to buy the house from the white man who lived across the Potomac River in Arlington. The white man and his family had been the last whites to live in that neighborhood. "Come on over to Arlington," his white former neighbors kept saying, "the blacks are all off in *that* neighborhood so you hardly ever see them." The white man and his wife had a son, deep into puberty, and the son was growing ever partial to blondes, which 8th Street didn't grow any-more.

So the good neighbors of 8th Street decided to raise the money and buy the house and rent it to more agreeable people. "Let's drink to that," Lane said and stood up. About then Sharon Palmer came down from upstairs where she had been comforting Terence. The medicine had finally overcome him and he had fallen asleep. "Thank you, sweet Sharon, thank you, thank you," Lane said and he sat his drink on the table beside his chair and put his arms around her. "It was the least I could do," she said. "It was the very least."

After everyone had left, and his wife had gone to bed, Lane sat beside his son's bed. He had enjoyed that house for a long time, and it saddened him, be-yond the effects of the liquor, to think that he would not see his grandchildren enjoy it. He loved Washington, and as he sat and watched Terence sleep, he feared he would have to leave. He was hearing good things about Prince George County, but that place, abutting the even more redneck areas of the Maryland suburbs, was not home like D.C. He had heard, too, that the police there were brutes, straight out of the worst Southern town, but he had come a long way since the boyhood days of helping his father deliver coal and ice throughout Washington. Dirty nigger coal man and his dirty nigger coal son, children had called them. And that was in the colored neighborhoods of maids and shoe shiners and janitors and cooks and elevator operators. But he was a thousand lives from that now, even though he wasn't anybody's lawyer. With his reputa-tion as a GS 15 at the Labor Department and a wife high up in the D.C. school system and a bigger Maryland house and a son on the way to being a doctor, the police in Prince George would know just what sort he was.

The good neighbors were helped by one major thing—the white man and his wife across the Potomac who owned the Bennington house had been think-ing for some time about moving to Florida. Their son, who had no interest in real estate in Washington, was now off to a great start nevertheless—he owned two used car lots, one in Arlington and the other in Alexandria. He had a lovely wife and two children in Great Falls, and he had a mistress in both cities where the car lots were. Of the three blond women, only one had been born blond.

Lane Stagg, Hamilton Palmer, Arthur Atwell, and Prudence Forsythe met with the white man on the highway in Arlington named for Robert E. Lee, in a restaurant that had been segregated less than two years before. They offered him $31,000 for the Bennington house. The white man whistled at the figure. Arthur Atwell was silent, as usual. He was semi-retired and liked to think he had more money than he really did have; his widow, Beatrice, was to discover that when he died not long after that meeting. The white man, Nicholas Riccocelli, whistled again, this time even louder, because the $31,000 sounded good—he really had no idea how much the house was worth. For several moments, he studied a cheap print of a Dutch windmill on the wall beside the table and thought about how many days on a Florida beach $31,000 would provide. That plus the money from some other property and his investments in his son's businesses.

Riccocelli said give him a week to think it over, and he called Lane Stagg in 75
four days and said they had a deal. The white man had never had any trouble
with the Benningtons and so felt he owed it to them to tell them himself, formally, that they would have to move. He came late one Saturday afternoon in
early February, and when Derek told him his mother wasn't home, Riccocelli
wanted to know if she would be gone long.

"If there's something important," Derek said, "you can tell me." And when
the white man told him that they would have to be gone in two months, Derek
turned from his spot in the middle of the living room to look at Amanda and Neil
standing in the doorway to the dining room. "Can you believe this shit?" Then to
Riccocelli, he asked, "Why? Ain't we always paid rent on time? Ain't we?"

"Yes, but the new owners would like to start anew."

"Who are they?" Derek said. "You tell em we good tenants and everything'll
be all right."

"I'm afraid," the white man said, "that will not work. The new owners wish
to go in another direction altogether."

"Who the fuck are these people? What kinda direction you talkin about?" 80
Derek came two steps closer to the man.

"Why . . . why . . ." and Riccocelli seemed unable to complete the sentence
because he had thought their neighbors would have somehow let the Benningtons know. "Why your neighbors around you." The man sensed something bad
about to happen and backed toward the front door. Where, he wondered, was
the mother? She had always seemed so sensible.

"Get the fuck out!" Derek said and grabbed the man by his coat collar. The
man opened the door and Derek pushed him out. "You sorry motherfucker!"
The woman who always wore sunglasses, seated between two children, began to
cry, and the children, following her, began crying as well.

"Derek, leave him alone," Amanda said. "Leave him be."

Out on the porch, Derek still had Riccocelli by the collar. He pulled him
down the stairs. "Derek!" Amanda shouted. "Please!"

"Don't hurt me, Mr. Bennington." The ride over from Arlington had been 85
pleasant enough. Riccocelli was a small man, and his eyes only came about thirteen inches above the dashboard, but he enjoyed driving. There had been gentle
and light snow most of the way from Arlington, and a few times he saw lightning across the sky. Snow and lightning, and then the thunder. How could a day
go wrong that quickly? He would miss the snow in Florida, he had thought all
the way across Key Bridge. Now, as the two men stumbled and fell their way
down the steps to the sidewalk, there was rain, also gentle, but the sky was quiet.
"You mustn't molest me, Mr. Bennington." Riccocelli had parked behind
Derek's Ford, and Derek pushed and half carried him to the car and slammed
him against it. "You come back and you dead meat."

After the man was gone, Derek went up and down both sides of the street,
shouting to the neighbors to come out and confront him. "Don't be punks!" he
shouted. As he neared the middle of the other side of 8th, Grace came around
the corner, and she and Amanda and Neil, who had been standing in the yard,

went to him. "We got babies in that house, man! It's winter, for Godsakes!" Sharon opened her door and came out on the porch, but she was the only neighbor to do so. "We got sweet innocent babies in that house, man! What can yall be thinkin?" They were able to calm him but before they could get him across the street, the police came.

Arthur Atwell died of a heart attack not long after the Benningtons moved at the end of February, two days before Derek got out of D.C. Jail. Arthur's widow, Beatrice, found that despite all Arthur had said, there was not much money, and she had to back out of the Bennington house deal. She moved to Claridge Towers on M Street, into an apartment with a bathroom where she could hide when the thunder and lightning came. Everyone was sad to see her leave because she had been a better neighbor than most. Those still in on the Bennington house deal did manage to buy the house, but the good neighbors rarely found their sort of people to rent the place to.

Sharon Palmer Stagg's car had been in the shop two days when she finished her shift at Georgetown University Hospital one Saturday night in March. It was too late for a bus, and she thought she would have a better chance for a cab at Wisconsin Avenue and so she made her way out of the hospital grounds to P Street. She was not yet a nurse, but did have a part-time job as a nurse's assistant at the hospital, where she often volunteered on her days off. Just before 36th Street that night, she saw a small group of young men coming toward her, loud, singing a song too garbled for her to understand. She was used to such crowds — Georgetown University students, many with bogus identification cards they used to buy drinks at the bars along Wisconsin Avenue and M Street.

She had been married for nine months. Terence Stagg was in medical school at Howard. His maternal grandparents, the attorneys, had been killed in a car accident by a drunken driver who was himself an attorney, and they had left their only grandchild more money than was good for him. Terence and his wife lived more than well in a part of upper Northwest Washington where the Benningtons could only serve and never live.

Just before Sharon reached 35th Street, the group of young men came under 90 a streetlight and she could see that two of them were white and the third was black. The black one, six or so feet from her, said to the white ones, "I spy with my little eye something good to eat," and the three spread out and blocked her from passing. "I always have these fantasies about nurses and sponge baths," the black one said. She was wearing a white uniform and that had told them all they needed to know. They came to within three feet of her and one of the white ones held his arms out to Sharon, while the other two surrounded her. She did not hear the car door behind her open and close.

The black one touched her cheek and then her breasts with both hands and one of the white students did the same, and both young men breathed sour beer into her face. Sharon pulled away, and the two looked at each other and giggled. The third student gave a rah-rah cry and came up and slapped her behind twice.

As the black student inhaled deeply for another blast into her face, something punched him in the side of the face and the black student fell hard against a car and passed out. "Hey! Hey!" the white student who had had his hands on Sharon said to the puncher. "Whatcha do to our Rufus?" The puncher pulled Sharon back behind him and she saw that it was a face from a long time ago, and her knees buckled to see it. He may well have been a ghost because she had not seen him in that long a time. "They spoil the best nights we have," Derek said to her.

The white student who had not touched her pulled out a knife, the blade more than three inches. Derek reached into his own pocket, but before his hand came out, the white student had stabbed him in his left side, through his leather jacket, through his shirt, into the vicinity of his heart, and Sharon screamed as Derek first faltered and then pulled himself up. In a second his switchblade was out and the blade tore through the student's jacket and into his arm, and the student ran out into P Street and down toward his university. "I wanted to keep this clean," Derek said. "But white trash won't let me."

"Hey! Hey!" the second white student said as he sobered up. "We didn't mean anything." He raised his arms high. "See, see . . ."

"Oh, you fucks always mean somethin," Derek said, holding his knife to the man's cheek and flicking it once to open a wound in the cheek, less than two inches from his nostrils. The man crumpled, both hands to his face. His black friend was still out, and the man with the arm wound was shouting as he ran that they were all being killed by niggers. Derek sheathed his knife and returned it to his pocket and then pulled Sharon down the street to his car.

Within moments he had driven them down P, slowly, across Wisconsin and   95
to a spot before the P Street Bridge, where he stopped. He turned on the light and inspected his side. "Shit!" he said. "Bad but maybe not fatal. Damn!"

"Let me help you," Sharon said.

He started the car up, and after looking in the sideview mirror he continued on down P Street, again slowly. Two patrol cars sped past them, and she watched him watching them go away in the rearview mirror. "Dead or alive, the black dude won't matter," he said to the mirror, joining the traffic moving around Dupont Circle. "But them white dudes are princes and the world gon pay for that." He became part of the flow going up Connecticut Avenue. "And it happened in Georgetown. They'll make sure somebody pays for that. But they were drunk and so describin might be a problem. Real drunk." He seemed unaware that she was there. "Thas why I never went to college, Derek. Black people gotta leave all their common sense at the front door. College is the business of miseducatin. Like them people would ever open the door anyway." She feared he might pass out, and in the near darkness of the car, she was comforted by the fact that she could not see blood creeping around to the right side from the left. Two more police cars passed them, screaming. "They gonna pull that one patrol car they have in Southeast and the only one they got in Northeast and bring em over here to join the dozens they keep in Georgetown. You watch, Derek," he said to the mirror. "You just watch."

"Derek," she said. "Stop and let me help you."

They had crossed Calvert, they had crossed Woodley, and he looked at her for the first time since they entered the car. "I lied," he said. "I lied. Red wasn't a bad color. It was way good anough for you. Any color you put on is a good color, didn't you know that? You make the world. It ain't never been the other way around. You first, then the world follows." They were nearing Porter. Two blocks from the University of the District of Columbia he stopped, not far from her condominium building, which had one of the few doormen in Washington. "You can walk the rest of the way home," he said. "All the bad thas gonna happen to you done already happened."

She moved his jacket aside and saw where the blood had darkened his blue 100 shirt, and when she touched him, the blood covered her hand and began to drip. "Come with me and let me help you." And as she said this, her mind ticked off the actual number of years when she had last seen him. Three days later she would have the time down to weeks. She took a handkerchief and Kleenex from her pocketbook and pressed them gently to his side. "It's bad, but manageable, I think. We need to get you help, though."

He took her hand and placed it in her lap. "Let me be," he said. "You best get home. You best go home to the man you married to."

"Come in. You helped me, so let me help you."

"You should tell that glorious husband of yours that a wife should be protected, that he shouldn't be sleepin while you have to come home through the jungle of some white neighborhood. Tell him thas not what bein married should be about."

She took the bloody handkerchief and Kleenex and returned them to her pocketbook. She did not now want to go home. She wanted to stay and go wherever he was going to recover. She snapped the pocketbook shut. Her father had walked her down the aisle, beaming all the way at the coming together of his two favorite families. The church had been packed and Terence had stood at the end of the aisle, waiting, standing as straight as he could after a night of drinking and pals and two strippers. . . .

"You best go home." "Please," she said. "Let me stay." He reached across her 105 and opened the door. "And one last thing," he said. "Neil been at me for the longest time to have me tell you it was never him. He was always afraid that you went about thinkin he was stuck on you, and he always wanted me to set the record straight. Now the record is straight." How long can the hear carry it around? How long? The answer came to her in a whisper.

She got out and shut the door, and he continued on up Connecticut Avenue, his back red lights, throbbing and brightly vital, soon merging with all the rest of the lights of the Washington night. Her BMW was in the shop. The man had promised that it would be ready by the end of the week. Terence's Mercedes had never seen a bad day.

———————

As soon as she locked the door to the condominium, she heard the hum of the new refrigerator, and then the icemaker clicked on, and ice tumbled into the bucket, as if to welcome her home. The fan over the stove was going and she turned it off, along with the light over the stove, the two switches side by side. In the living room she noticed the blood on her uniform; if the doorman had seen it, he did not say. In the half darkness, the spots seemed fresh, almost alive in some eerie way, as if they had just that second come from Derek's wound. Bleeding. Bleedin. She had emerged unscathed. The overhead fan of grand, golden wood in the living room was going, slowly, and she considered for the longest whether to switch it off. In the end she chose to stop the spinning. Her family had moved away from 8th Street when she was in college. And so had the Forsythes and the Spoonhours and the Prevosts and all the people she had known as she grew into womanhood. We are the future, her father-in-law Lane Stagg had proclaimed at a final dinner party at the Sheraton Hotel for the good neighbors. Who was left there now? Bad neighbors, her father had called those who came after them. Bad neighbors. Before the whites came back and planted their flags in the new world. The motor on the fish tank hummed right along; the light over the tank was on and she turned that off. The expensive tropical fish swam on even without the light. The stereo, which had cost the equivalent of seven of her paychecks, was not playing but the power light was on and she pushed the button to put the whole console to rest. She placed one finger against the fish tank, and all the fish in their colorful finery ignored it. Her father had risen at that hotel dinner and given the first toast, his hand trembling and his voice breaking at every fifth word. And he was followed by Lane Stagg, who was as eloquent as ever.

Terence was sleeping peacefully, one foot sticking out of the covers, the exquisite German clock's dull red numbers shining down on him from the bedside table with the reassurance of a child's night-light. Her father hated such clocks, the digital ones that told the time right out; he believed, as he had tried to teach Sharon and her brother, that children should learn to tell time the way he had learned, with the big hand and the little hand moving around a circle of numbers. Possibly a second hand, but that was not needed to know what time of day it was. She stood in the doorway and watched Terence and the clock, and for all the time she was there he did not stir. A burglar could come in, she thought, and he would never know it. She could stab him to death and end his world and he would never know it. She could smother him. The whole world could end and he would not know that either. The insurance they paid on all that they owned — not including the cars and their own lives, which had separate policies — came to $273.57 month. It is worth it, the white insurance man had said as he dotted the final *i*, "because you will sleep better at night knowing you are protected." Knowing. Knowin.

She got out of her clothes in the bathroom, took off everything she had on, even her underwear, and found that the blood had seeped through all the way to her skin. She held her uniform up before her. She stared at her name tag and found it hard to connect herself with the name and the uniform and the naked person they belonged to. Am I really who they say I am? The blood reminded her of someone that had a name but the name escaped her. Bleeding. Bleedin. None of Derek's people had ever used the g on their *ing* words; one of the first things she herself had been taught early in life was never to lose the g. The g is there for a reason, they had told her. It separates you from all the rest of them, those who do not know any better. Sharon did not shower. Another Sharon in another time might have been unsettled by him appearing from nowhere, by the thought that he had been following her. But the idea that he had been there, out there in weather of whatever sort, out there in the dark offering no sign and no sound, out there for months and perhaps years of her life, seemed to give her something to measure her life by. But she did not know how to do that. After she turned out the bathroom light, she stood in the dark for a long time. In their bedroom she decided against putting on underwear and so got into bed the way she came into the world. Terence stirred, pulled his foot back under the covers, but beyond that, he did nothing. Almost imperceptibly, the rightmost red number on the fine German clock went from two to three.

APPROACHING THE READING

1. Try listing the events of the story in chronological order. Where does the "fracas" fit in? Why is it important enough to be mentioned in the first sentence? Consider the effect of returning to past events and anticipating events in the future. For example, how does this lead you to make connections between events that you might not otherwise make?

2. Reflect on the effect of emphasizing a specific neighborhood and particular houses. How would the story be different if it used setting in a less definite way? "Everyday Use" (p. 109) and "The House on Mango Street" (p. 99) explore how houses relate to people's identities and economic security. Does that become a factor here too? If you think so, be ready to explain in what ways. If you think not, be prepared to explain why.

3. Consider the title. Does it refer straightforwardly to the Benningtons? If so, be ready to discuss the nuances and complications that involves: According to whom are they "bad neighbors"? By objective criteria? If not, by what standards? Partly by the way they talk — dropping their g's and purposefully using what for many would be offensive language? Or is the title ironic? If so, be prepared to explain what is ironic about it. Could it refer to others instead of, or as well as, the Benningtons? Again, be able to explain how, and be ready to discuss the nuances and complications that creates.

4. Derek may be the most complex and interesting character in the story. What do the "good neighbors" think of him? Locate specific places where their impressions come through. Point out some details that could call those impressions into question.

5. The story focuses mostly on Sharon (examine how the point of view directs attention toward her). What is she like? What do the decisions she makes

show about her? What do the last three paragraphs convey about her, her life, and what happens throughout the story? Take setting into account in these paragraphs: Where is she living and what does that indicate?

6. Two objects receive repeated attention in the story—the carved figure Sharon receives as a Christmas gift and the fine German clock in Sharon and Terence's bedroom. Do you think that either suggests abstract implications (serves as a symbol) or that both do? If so, be ready to explain what those implications are and to point out specific passages in the text that support what you say. Are there other objects or actions that might be considered symbols? Which ones? How are they symbolic?

ENTRY POINTS   The following story is part of a series of books involving characters from old legends and fairy tales—like Snow White or the Big Bad Wolf—explaining "what really happened" or what happened before or after the familiar stories. The fairy tale characters were driven out of their magical homelands by the armies of an evil warlord known as The Adversary, and they were forced into exile. Eventually they reached our mundane world and formed a secret community, Fabletown, in a corner of New York City, where they waited for an opportunity to reclaim their lost homelands. "The Christmas Pies" is one of a group of stories that recount earlier events, at least a century before the founding of Fabletown. As you read it, pay attention to the significance of setting (and the way it is portrayed graphically) and to the use of symbols, particularly archetypal characters, motifs, and symbols.

Bill Willingham   b. 1956

The Christmas Pies   [2006]

Bill Willingham. From *Fables: 1001 Nights of Snowfall.* © 2006 Bill Willingham & DC Comics. All Rights Reserved. Used with Permission of DC Comics.

IT CAME TO PASS THAT THE ARMIES OF THE ADVERSARY OCCUPIED THE SPRAWLING FORESTED VALLEY RULED BY KING NOBLE, THE LION.

ACCORDING TO THEIR STANDARD PRACTICE, THE INVADERS LET NOBLE CONTINUE TO RULE THE NEW IMPERIAL DISTRICT, AS LONG AS HE KEPT HIS SUBJECTS PACIFIED, AND SENT REGULAR TITHES OF TAXES AND FOODSTUFFS TO THE DISTANT EMPEROR.

REYNARD HAS BEEN ACTING UP AGAIN.

WHEN IS HE *NOT?*

THE GOBLIN SOLDIERS WERE MORE INTERESTED IN SECURING THE FOREST'S MAGIC GATEWAY TO THE MUNDANE SANCTUARY WORLD. THEY ARRESTED ANYONE ATTEMPTING TO FLEE THROUGH IT.

PLEASE LET US GO!

WE'LL PAY YOU *ANYTHING* WE HAVE!

WE'RE TAKING THAT ANYWAY.

EVERY KINGDOM HAS ITS VILLAINS AND THIS ONE WAS NO EXCEPTION.

REYNARD WAS A THIEF, LIAR, TRICKSTER AND GENERAL CONTRARIAN OF CONSIDERABLE RENOWN.

NOW IT HAPPENED ONE WINTER'S EVENING THAT THE CLEVER REYNARD PAID A VISIT TO THE GOBLIN ENCAMPMENT.

I'M HERE TO SPEAK TO YOUR KAIDAN.

THAT'S WHAT YOU *GREENIES* CALL A SERGEANT, ISN'T IT?

GREETINGS, GRUBEL KAIDAN.

WHAT IS WORTH INTERRUPTING MY *DINNER*, FOX?

I'M HERE TO MAKE YOU A HERO OF THE EMPIRE.

AFTER WE'RE DONE, THEY'LL PROMOTE YOU TO *CAPTAIN* AT LEAST, OR MAYBE EVEN MAKE A *GENERAL* OF YOU.

AND NO DOUBT POST YOU TO A BETTER PLACE THAN *THIS* FRIGID BACKWOODS DISTRICT.

MAKE *SENSE*, BEAST.

HOW WOULD IT BE IF I ARRANGED FOR YOU TO CAPTURE *EVERY* REBEL MALCONTENT, ALL IN ONE NIGHT?

185

DID YOU KNOW THAT CHRISTMAS IS NIGH, AND THERE ARE STILL BEASTS IN THIS LAND WHO PLAN TO *CELEBRATE* IT?

THEY'D BEST NOT!

CHRISTMAS IS NO LONGER NUMBERED AMONG THE EMPEROR'S SIX HUNDRED AND TWELVE APPROVED WINTER CELEBRATIONS.

AND YET THOSE *BLACKGUARDS* INTEND TO PROCEED, IN BOLD DEFIANCE OF YOUR VERY REASONABLE SEASONAL EDICTS.

NAME THESE SCOUNDRELS, SO I MAY ARREST AND CHASTISE THEM.

AH, BUT THEY'RE CUNNING BEASTS--FLEET OF FOOT AND QUICK TO SCATTER. ATTEMPT TO APPROACH THEM AND THEY MIGHT FLY TO THE FOUR WINDS.

BUT DON'T WORRY, HONORABLE GRUBEL. I'VE NO LOVE FOR THESE BRIGANDS AND HAVE A PLAN WHEREBY YOU WILL *SURELY* CAPTURE THE LOT.

AND THEREBY COVER YOURSELF IN GLORY, IN THE EYES OF YOUR SUPERIORS.

SPEAK ON. I'M INTERESTED.

DID YOU EVER HEAR OF THE LOCAL FOLK-LEGEND INVOLVING THE MIRACLE OF THE CHRISTMAS PIES?

186

FOLLOWING REYNARD'S PLAN, GRUBEL KAIDAN CAUSED THE VILLAGERS TO BAKE UP A HOST OF TASTY PIES.

TELL YOUR TROOPS TO STOP *NIBBLING* AT THEM, KAIDAN, OR WE WON'T HAVE ANY LEFT FOR OUR SCHEME.

THEY WERE FILLED WITH EVERY DELICACY THE VALLEY HAD TO OFFER--ROASTED FOWL, SPICED LAMB AND KIDNEY PUDDING.

WHAT NOW?

WE PLACE THEM HERE IN THE CLEARING AND LEAVE, LETTING THE FALLING SNOW CONCEAL OUR TRACKS.

AND CUSTARD CREAM AND EVERY MANNER OF FRUIT THAT WAS EVER PULLED, PLUCKED OR PICKED.

WE JUST LEAVE?

YES, AND IN THE MORNING BAKE UP EVEN *MORE* PIES FOR TOMORROW NIGHT.

OH LOOK, BROTHERS! FOR HERE WE FIND DELECTABLE PIES OF EVERY VARIETY!

IN TRUTH, I BELIEVE IT IS THE MIRACLE OF THE LEGEND!

187

EACH OF THREE NIGHTS, GRUBEL KAIDAN AND HIS GOBLIN TROOPS PLACED GOODLY PIES IN THE FOREST CLEARING.

SO FAR, ALL I'VE DONE IS *FEED* EVERY CREATURE IN THE FOREST, AT GREAT EXPENSE TO THE EMPEROR! WHEN DO WE MAKE *ARRESTS?*

TONIGHT, IN FACT, YOUR SURLINESS.

THE FIRST NIGHT, THEY WERE FAR TOO WARY TO BE EASILY CAPTURED. THE SECOND NIGHT SOMEWHAT LESS SO.

BUT BY THE THIRD NIGHT THEY FINALLY TRUSTED THAT THIS *IS* INDEED THE FABLED SEVEN NIGHTS OF FREE CHRISTMAS PIES.

TONIGHT THEY WILL RECEIVE THEIR FOURTH SERVING OF MIRACLE PIES, AND WHILE THEY FEAST, YOU AND YOUR TROOPS WILL BE ON HAND TO SCOOP THEM UP.

AND JUST TO MAKE SURE THEY CAN'T GET AWAY, *THESE* PIES WILL BE BAKED WITH STONES AS THEIR ONLY FILLING.

WITH BELLIES FULL OF ROCKS, THEY'LL BE TOO LETHARGIC TO ESCAPE EVEN THE *SLOWEST* OF YOUR TROOPS.

THAT'S TRULY A *MARVELOUS* PLAN!

YOU'RE A CREDIT TO THE EMPIRE, REYNARD!

I LIVE TO SERVE.

APPROACHING THE READING

1. Consider the handling and effect of setting in the story, both location and time, indicated through words and drawings. Notice the initial paradisal fairyland background and the way it changes in later panels. Notice also the summerlike appearance of panel two and the fallen leaves in panel three, indicating the passing of time since the occupation, and the wintry background from the fourth panel on. Reflect on how the indications of location and the passage of time affect your reading of the story.

2. Pay attention to the way the words of the third-person narrator float at the top of—and sometimes even extend outside of—some panels and the way the words of characters (dialogue) appear in balloons. Consider how both ways relate to the passing of time. Is there a difference in effect? Explain.

3. Focus on the character traits and motivation of Reynard. Be ready to discuss how his character follows and plays off traditional depictions of him, and what motivates him to carry out the scheme he thinks up.

4. Consider also techniques contributing to characterization generally in the story—what characters say and do, what is said about them, and what motivates them, of course, but also the graphic images (appearance, facial expressions, body language).

5. Look for words or graphic images in the story that might function as symbols and for characters, motifs, or symbols that might have archetypal overtones. For any that you select, be ready to explain why you selected them and what symbolic or archetypal effects they create.

6. Notice the graphic techniques used in the story, especially the handling of panels. Be ready to talk about the unique design of page 184, with an inset box and the use of a tree branch to divide the second panel from the third; about the way different sizes of panels affect the passage of time; about the effects of the full-page panels and the way the sequence of speeches is conveyed.

7. After reading Chapter 7, reread this story and consider the way style, tone, and irony are used in it. Try talking about their use in graphics as well as in the text.

RESPONDING THROUGH Writing

WRITING ABOUT SETTING AND SYMBOL

Journal Entries

1. Focus on the way settings are handled in two or three TV shows or movies. Pay attention to what was discussed in this chapter: setting as place broadly and specifically, setting in time, setting in social and cultural context. Consider uses and effects of setting: for atmosphere, characterization, symbol, and meaning. Then write a journal entry discussing ways that what you found can enhance your grasp of setting in literature.

www
Research the authors in this chapter with LitLinks, or take a quiz on the stories with LitQuiz, at bedfordstmartins.com/approachinglit.

2. After carefully reading "The Things They Carried" (p. 150) find ways to deepen your visual sense of what it was like for these characters. Find a book of photographs on the Vietnam War and/or watch films such as *Platoon*; *Good Morning, Vietnam*; or *Apocalypse Now*. Write a journal entry in which you describe how these visual texts affect your experience of the story. Does it make a significant difference? Think about why it does or does not in light of the power of literary description.

3. Write a journal entry discussing the use of archetypal characters, motifs, symbols, and their effects in "The Christmas Pies" (p. 183).

Literary Analysis Papers

4. Write a paper discussing the importance of setting in Toni Cade Bambara's "The Lesson" (p. 212), John Updike's "A & P" (p. 529), or Isabel Allende's "And of Clay Are We Created" (p. 302).

5. Write a paper discussing the relationship between setting, symbol, and character in Ralph Ellison's "Battle Royal" (p. 352), Ana Menéndez's "Her Mother's House" (p. 419), John Steinbeck's "The Chrysanthemums" (p. 513), or another story of your choice.

6. Write a paper on the literal and symbolic uses of music in Joyce Carol Oates's "Where Are You Going, Where Have You Been?" (p. 81) or James Baldwin's "Sonny's Blues" (p. 309).

Comparison-Contrast Papers

7. Compare and contrast the use and significance of setting in Edward P. Jones's "Bad Neighbors" (p. 164) and James Baldwin's "Sonny's Blues" (p. 309) or Judith Ortiz Cofer's "American History" (p. 346).

8. Compare and contrast the use of darkness as a symbol in James Baldwin's "Sonny's Blues" (p. 309) and Ralph Ellison's "Battle Royal" (p. 352).

▶ **TIPS for Writing about Setting and Symbol**

➤ **Include setting when it's important** Setting ordinarily is brought into a paper only if it stands out or has special significance. Discuss its effect in the story precisely and specifically.

➤ **Cover setting completely** When writing about setting, be sure to cover place in whatever dimension is important (a room, a building, a city, a country, another planet or world) and to treat time and social milieu, when relevant.

> ➤ **Show, don't just say, it's a symbol** When you write about a symbol, be sure to explain the features that justify calling it so (as we do, for example, on pp. 145 and 146–47); don't assume your reader will agree automatically that the item is symbolic.

> ➤ **Look for meanings, not *a* meaning** Remember that usually a rich symbol does not have one definite meaning that you must find, but rather it is the focal point of a central aspect in the story.

> ➤ **Avoid using *symbolize*** In discussing symbols, it is preferable to use a verb like *suggests* or *conveys*, rather than *symbolizes* or *means*.

WRITING ABOUT CONNECTIONS

Setting and symbol are all about connections. We connect with people by being in the same place and time as they are, and symbols by their nature connect an image with an abstract quality closely associated with it. Thus, any paper you write on setting or symbol will inevitably deal with connections. Along with those connections are thematic connections between stories with similar (or contrasting) settings and symbols. These often can lead to interesting and illuminating papers. Here are a few possibilities:

1. "Secrets of the Heart": Keeping Hope Alive in Ernest Hemingway's "Hills Like White Elephants" (p. 136) and David Means's "The Secret Goldfish" (p. 116)
2. "Dying a Good Death": Struggles over What Matters in Tim O'Brien's "The Things They Carried" (p. 150) and Yiyun Li's "Persimmons" (p. 411)
3. "'A Good Man Is Hard to Find'": Nature versus Nurture in Edward P. Jones's "Bad Neighbors" (p. 164) and Nathaniel Hawthorne's "Young Goodman Brown" (p. 374)

WRITING RESEARCH PAPERS

1. Find and read several stories about the war in Vietnam by authors other than Tim O'Brien, and do research on the climate and topography of the country. Write a research paper exploring the way O'Brien and two or three other writers depict the setting and use it in a meaningful way in their stories.
2. Do some research into Yoknapatawpha County, the county in Mississippi in which most of William Faulkner's stories take place. Using "A Rose for Emily" (p. 362) and perhaps other stories by Faulkner, write a paper exploring how his imaginary locale becomes as real and meaningful as an actual one as a setting for his stories.

COMPOSING IN OTHER ART FORMS

1. Pick out background music that you think is appropriate in evoking the atmosphere of a particular setting for one of the stories in Chapters 4 to 7 or another story of your choice. Write a journal entry or a short paper explaining your choices.
2. Draw or paint the setting(s) in Sandra Cisneros's "The House on Mango Street" (p. 99), Ernest Hemingway's "Hills Like White Elephants" (p. 136), William Faulkner's "A Rose for Emily" (p. 362), or another story of your choice. You could do a single picture showing the main setting for the story or two or three that depict different settings, or you could illustrate different aspects of the main setting or the way it might look from various angles.

I like short sentences. They are forceful and can get you out of big trouble.

Annie Dillard

Style, Tone, and Irony

CHAPTER **7**

Attending to Expression and Attitude

The way things are said, their style and tone, matters—a lot. The way things are phrased and expressed can affect the meaning words convey (some people can talk their way out of anything, right?), and the tone of voice can decidedly alter the message. "Nice shirt!" can mean you love it or you hate it, depending on whether you say it enthusiastically about a friend's birthday present or mutter it bitterly about a ragged T-shirt with an offensive slogan on the back.

The same is true for a work of fiction. A work's style is important because it is interesting and enjoyable to read a distinctive style of writing, and because style helps shape tone, the "tone of voice" that affects how we take what is being said—whether what the narrator and characters say should be taken straightforwardly, or with a grain of salt, or the opposite way from which it is stated. This chapter focuses on some of the key elements that contribute to style and tone—and on the specific tone of irony—to help you be more alert to subtleties of fine writing as you listen to a work of literature.

ENTRY POINTS   As you read the following short story the first time, you'll probably focus more on what's happening and why than on the way it's said. Most readers listen more intently for style on a second reading. So read it a second time, paying close attention to the way things are phrased and expressed—to word choice, for example (listening for the sounds of words as well as determining their meaning), and to the way sentences are constructed. Think about whether the style seems to you appropriate and effective in conveying what happens to the central character and the feelings she experiences on hearing that her husband has died.

Kate Chopin   1851–1904

The Story of an Hour   [1894]

Knowing that Mrs. Mallard was afflicted with a heart trouble, great care was taken to break to her as gently as possible the news of her husband's death.

It was her sister Josephine who told her, in broken sentences; veiled hints that revealed in half concealing. Her husband's friend Richards was there, too, near her. It was he who had been in the newspaper office when intelligence of the railroad disaster was received, with Brently Mallard's name leading the list of "killed." He had only taken the time to assure himself of its truth by a second telegram, and had hastened to forestall any less careful, less tender friend in bearing the sad message.

She did not hear the story as many women have heard the same, with a paralyzed inability to accept its significance. She wept at once, with sudden, wild abandonment, in her sister's arms. When the storm of grief had spent itself she went away to her room alone. She would have no one follow her.

There stood, facing the open window, a comfortable, roomy armchair. Into this she sank, pressed down by a physical exhaustion that haunted her body and seemed to reach into her soul.

She could see in the open square before her house the tops of trees that were 5 all aquiver with the new spring life. The delicious breath of rain was in the air. In the street below a peddler was crying his wares. The notes of a distant song which some one was singing reached her faintly, and countless sparrows were twittering in the eaves.

There were patches of blue sky showing here and there through the clouds that had met and piled one above the other in the west facing her window.

She sat with her head thrown back upon the cushion of the chair, quite motionless, except when a sob came up into her throat and shook her, as a child who has cried itself to sleep continues to sob in its dreams.

She was young, with a fair, calm face, whose lines bespoke repression and even a certain strength. But now there was a dull stare in her eyes, whose gaze was fixed away off yonder on one of those patches of blue sky. It was not a glance of reflection, but rather indicated a suspension of intelligent thought.

There was something coming to her and she was waiting for it, fearfully. What was it? She did not know; it was too subtle and elusive to name. But she felt it, creeping out of the sky, reaching toward her through the sounds, the scents, the color that filled the air.

Now her bosom rose and fell tumultuously. She was beginning to recognize 10 this thing that was approaching to possess her, and she was striving to beat it back with her will—as powerless as her two white slender hands would have been.

When she abandoned herself a little whispered word escaped her slightly parted lips. She said it over and over under her breath: "free, free, free!" The vacant stare and the look of terror that had followed it went from her eyes. They stayed keen and bright. Her pulses beat fast, and the coursing blood warmed and relaxed every inch of her body.

She did not stop to ask if it were or were not a monstrous joy that held her. A clear and exalted perception enabled her to dismiss the suggestion as trivial.

She knew that she would weep again when she saw the kind, tender hands folded in death; the face that had never looked save with love upon her, fixed and gray and dead. But she saw beyond that bitter moment a long procession of years to come that would belong to her absolutely. And she opened and spread her arms out to them in welcome.

There would be no one to live for her during those coming years; she would live for herself. There would be no powerful will bending hers in that blind persistence with which men and women believe they have a right to impose a private will upon a fellow-creature. A kind intention or a cruel intention made the act seem no less a crime as she looked upon it in that brief moment of illumination.

And yet she had loved him—sometimes. Often she had not. What did it 15 matter! What could love, the unsolved mystery, count for in face of this possession of self-assertion which she suddenly recognized as the strongest impulse of her being!

"Free! Body and soul free!" she kept whispering.

Josephine was kneeling before the closed door with her lips to the keyhole, imploring for admission. "Louise, open the door! I beg; open the door—you will make yourself ill. What are you doing, Louise? For heaven's sake open the door."

"Go away. I am not making myself ill." No; she was drinking in a very elixir of life through that open window.

Her fancy was running riot along those days ahead of her. Spring days, and summer days, and all sorts of days that would be her own. She breathed a quick prayer that life might be long. It was only yesterday she had thought with a shudder that life might be long.

She arose at length and opened the door to her sister's importunities. There 20 was a feverish triumph in her eyes, and she carried herself unwittingly like a goddess of Victory. She clasped her sister's waist, and together they descended the stairs. Richards stood waiting for them at the bottom.

Some one was opening the front door with a latchkey. It was Brently Mallard who entered, a little travel-stained, composedly carrying his grip-sack and umbrella. He had been far from the scene of accident, and did not even know there had been one. He stood amazed at Josephine's piercing cry; at Richards' quick motion to screen him from the view of his wife.

But Richards was too late.

When the doctors came they said she had died of heart disease—of joy that kills.

APPROACHING THE READING

1. Consider the word choice as an aspect of style. Chopin's language may sound a bit formal. Even in the 1890s, words such as *afflicted, intelligence, forestall, bespoke,* and *fancy,* although part of an educated person's vocabulary, were seldom used in everyday speech. Did you hear other words that struck you as distinctly formal? What would be the effect on the depiction of Mrs. Mallard's situation if the style were less formal?

2. Look also at sentence constructions in the story. Do they tend to be long or short? Are they mostly formal and "written" or casual and conversational? Do they read rapidly or more slowly and deliberately? Does the handling of sentences seem appropriate to the events and the characters involved in them?

www
Explore this author and story in depth, including images and cultural documents, with VirtuaLit Fiction at bedfordstmartins .com/approachinglit.

3. Think about comparisons used in the story: for example, of grief to a storm (para. 3) and the treatment of exhaustion as a spiritual emanation that presses Mrs. Mallard down, haunts her body, and reaches into her soul (para. 4). List several other examples. What do you think such comparisons add to the story? What would be changed or lost if the comparisons were omitted and the points stated only in straightforward terms?

4. Consider the handling of the two single-sentence paragraphs at the end. Ask yourself how the effect would be different if the two sentences were combined into a single paragraph. What is the advantage of the very short next-to-last paragraph?

The most striking thing about style in "The Story of an Hour" is its formality of word choice and sentence construction. The subject announced in the first sentence, "her husband's death," is one that must be treated seriously, of course. A formal style seems entirely appropriate — for the narrator to refer to her as Mrs. Mallard rather than as Louise maintains a sense of dignity and respect.

STYLE AFFECTS RESPONSE   The formal, dignified style helps channel a reader's response as the story develops. It is surprising to learn that the fearful "something" that overcomes her is a sudden realization of release and freedom. If the unexpectedness of Mrs. Mallard's line "free, free, free!" would cause readers to laugh or even smile, the effect of the story would be destroyed. But the style guards against that possibility by suggesting that her response to her husband's death, as well as the death itself, must be taken very seriously.

STYLE AND TONE   The specific, detailed language of the style is important also as it affects the tone of the story. Our sympathy for Mrs. Mallard is aroused in the first two paragraphs, with the sudden death of her husband. It continues in the following paragraphs, as she seems devastated by the news. Then comes the twist: She isn't devastated, she's elated. The story risks losing our sympathy at that point, if it seems she didn't care about him. But through its handling of details the story seeks to shift our feelings to a different ground, not sympathy for her as a widow but empathy for her as a woman.

RESPONDING ACTIVELY   The story goes on to say that, kind and loving though her husband had been toward her, his personality dominated their relationship, and she felt trapped. Instead of looking forward to her future, she dreaded what lay ahead. Our sympathy, thus, can turn to happiness for her when she spreads out her arms to welcome the "long procession of years to come that would belong to her absolutely." Only readers who respond to the tone actively, as it changes along the way, receive the full effect of the surprise ending: the sadness and regret that she didn't get to enjoy the new life of which she had a brief glimpse.

READING FOR STYLE – EFFECTIVENESS OF EXPRESSION

In everyday speech, *style* is used in at least two important ways, as "that's a stylish suit" (it's attentive to the elements that are contemporary, "in," attractive, effective) and "that's their style of doing things" (their distinctive way or approach). Both uses apply when discussing literature, and they usually are closely related.

DEFINITION OF STYLE   **Style**, when applied to writing, is the manner in which a writer uses words, constructs sentences, incorporates nonliteral expressions, and handles rhythm, timing, and tone, all resulting in the effectiveness and individuality of a writer's work. The "Approaching the Reading" questions after "The Story of an Hour" are meant to direct your attention to some of the issues involved in style. In the pages that follow, we explore two aspects of style: style as effectiveness of expression and style as individuality of expression.

ATTENDING TO STYLE   If your teacher asks you to discuss the style of a work, she or he wants you to describe how or explain why the words, sentences, and imaginative comparisons are effective in terms of what is being created: Is it done "with style," that is, with proper care and in ways appropriate to the content and purpose of the work? Such a question requires that you listen actively and attentively for at least three features: words, sentences, and imaginative comparisons.

APPROPRIATENESS OF STYLE   Effectiveness always depends on appropriateness to a specific context. In expository writing, that means the appropriateness of the style to the writing's purpose: a formal style for a business letter or a research paper, an informal style for a personal letter or an essay describing your first day at college. In fiction, the style in the narrative passages must be appropriate to the narrator, and in dialogue it must fit the characters and the contexts in which they appear. A work of fiction usually has multiple styles, one for the narrative portions and different styles for the thoughts or words of different characters.

Word Choice

Central to style is an author's diction. **Diction** specifically means word choice, but in a broader sense it can refer to the overall character of language used in writing or speech and include *vocabulary* (choice of words) and *syntax* (arrangement of words, their ordering, grouping, and placement within phrases, clauses, and sentences). We discuss vocabulary here and syntax a few pages later.

TYPES OF DICTION   A writer can employ any of several types of diction, and the kind that predominates defines one aspect of a work's style. The words selected by a published author, or by you as a student writer, affect the way the work articulates the subject as well as the sound, rhythm, and feel of the writing. We already pointed to the formal diction in "The Story of an Hour," which seems to fit the strong, reserved character of Mrs. Mallard and the tight, careful plotting that sets up the surprise ending. Here are some other types of diction, though such a list can never be complete and exhaustive.

- *Simple words:* "When Miss Emily Grierson died, our whole town went to her funeral" (William Faulkner, "A Rose for Emily," p. 362) — except for the names, all the words are everyday words, as is the language the narrator uses for objective description: "She was sick for a long time. When we saw her again, her hair was cut short, making her look like a girl" (p. 365). The diction in the first sentence of "Everyday Use" is similar: "I will wait for her in the yard that Maggie and I made so clean and wavy yesterday afternoon" (p. 109).

- *Complex words:* "But garages and cotton gins had *encroached* and *obliterated* even the *august* names of that neighborhood" ("A Rose for Emily," p. 362). To convey an attitude toward something carefully and precisely, Faulkner uses words derived from French or Latin, rather than simpler Anglo equivalents: New people and modern ways don't *edge in*, they *encroach* (trespass) where they don't belong; they don't just *wipe away* the *worthy* names, they *obliterate* (destroy violently) names that were *august* (awe-inspiring, deserving reverence and respect). Here is more such diction from later in the story: "With the crayon face of her father *musing profoundly* above the bier and the ladies *sibilant* and *macabre*" (p. 368).

- *Concrete words:* "She had *jeans* on and fancy *moccasins* and she carried a little *suitcase*" ("The Red Convertible," p. 75). Lyman's words describing Susy fit his usual emphasis on the down-to-earth when describing how things are. He relates the facts, rarely trying to provide abstract theories or explanations. Similarly, "the *hard clay* is *swept* clean as a *floor* and the *fine sand* around the *edges* lined with *tiny, irregular grooves*" ("Everyday Use," p. 109).

- *Abstract words:* "You just don't understand . . . your *heritage* . . . make *something* of yourself . . . *a new day*" ("Everyday Use," p. 115). Dee's vague, empty parting words of advice help bring out the irony that it is she, not her mother or sister, who needs deeper understanding. Likewise, "on the rare *occasions* when *something* opens within, and the music enters, what we mainly hear, or hear corroborated, are *personal*, *private*, vanishing *evocations*" (James Baldwin, "Sonny's Blues," p. 330).

- *Colloquialisms* (informal, conversational expressions): "*Don'tcha* know it's Sunday all day?" ("Where Are You Going, Where Have You Been?" p. 89). The slurred syllables are characteristic of speech, not written prose; the casual way Arnold Friend expresses himself helps us know more of what his character is like. Two other examples are "I'm an openminded *kinda* guy" ("Love in L.A.," p. 62), and "I *ain't learning nothing* in school" ("Sonny's Blues," p. 321).

- *Slang:* "A sweet broad soft-looking *can*" (John Updike, "A & P," p. 529). Most of us wouldn't use the word *can* in a school paper, but it fits perfectly the breezy "with it" personality Sammy wants to project. Another example is the narrator's use of a slang term for heroin in "Sonny's Blues": "the first time Sonny had ever had *horse*" (p. 309).

- *Dignified, sophisticated terminology:* "A week later the mayor wrote her himself, offering to call or to send his car for her, and received in reply a note on paper of an archaic shape, in a thin, flowing calligraphy in faded ink, to the effect that she no longer went out at all" ("A Rose for Emily," p. 363)—the words convey the polite, formal, old-fashioned way the mayor and Miss Emily treat each other in what is a very delicate situation.

- *Technical terms:* "The milk in it *clabber* [thickly curdled and sour] by now" ("Everyday Use," p. 113)—the word is precise and informs us that the churn whose top Dee takes away as a keepsake is one still being used in the household. Also, "behind *jalousies* [a window, shade, or door of horizontal slats of glass, wood, or metal that can be adjusted for regulating air or light] closed upon the sun of Sunday afternoon" ("A Rose for Emily," p. 366).

APPROPRIATENESS OF DICTION   As you read and reread a story, pause to notice the kinds of words, or the level of diction, being used and think about how word choice contributes to the work's effectiveness. Listen to the language of the character or the narrator. To be effective, the choice of words — like style generally — must be well suited to its purpose (formal, educated diction for an analytic paper; slangy, conversational diction for an e-mail message to a friend) and its context (diction in narrative passages appropriate to the narrator, and in dialogue fitting the characters and the situations in which they appear).

DICTION AND CHARACTERIZATION   In many cases, diction becomes a part of characterization. In "The Red Convertible," for example, Lyman uses a lot of clichés — "The rest is history," "large as life," "But what are you going to do?" — and misuses them: "On to greener pastures, as they say." His choice of words sometimes is imprecise, as when he says that Susy "was *posed* alongside the road" or that ripping up the car "*just about* hurt me, I'll tell you." His handling of words, as he tells his story, shows that he is not polished and reveals at times how little he understands about such things as war and government: "By then I guess the whole war was *solved* in the government's mind."

Sentence Structure

SYNTAX   Equally important to creating an effective style is **syntax**, the way phrases and sentences are put together. Writers can work with long sentences or short ones. They can structure and craft them tightly, using subordinate clauses and forcing one to read to the end of the sentence to grasp the meaning:

> All I know about music is that not many people ever really hear it. And even then, on the rare occasions when something opens within, and the music enters, what we mainly hear, or hear corroborated, are personal, private, vanishing evocations. ("Sonny's Blues," p. 330)

Or they can structure them loosely, using cumulative clauses, adding on phrases connected by commas or *and* or *but*:

> Connie sat with her eyes closed in the sun, dreaming and dazed with the warmth about her as if this were a kind of love, the caresses of love, and her mind slipped over onto thoughts of the boy she had been with the night before and how nice he had been, how sweet it always was, not the way someone like June would suppose but sweet, gentle, the way it was in movies and promised in songs. ("Where Are You Going, Where Have You Been?" p. 84)

Writers can create a narrator or characters who use grammatically correct sentences or ones who treat grammar in a more casual, conversational manner.

APPROPRIATENESS   Here too appropriateness is the key, suitability to the speaker and the occasion. Using incomplete sentences would hardly ever be effective in a scholarly article but might work well in a memoir; long, elegant, carefully shaped sentences would likely seem out of character for a streetwise gang leader but might be exactly right for a pompous clergyman. As with word choice, the sentences used in the narrative parts of a story must suit the narrator, and those used in dialogue must be appropriate for the characters and the contexts using them. Lyman's sentences as he narrates "The Red Convertible" (p. 73), for example — mostly short and simple, or when long, made up of short phrases strung together — fit his character well.

LISTENING TO SENTENCES   Paying attention to differences in language and sentence structure helps you develop your ear, leading to greater appreciation and understanding of a work of literature and a more rewarding reading experience. What do you hear in the following passages, the opening paragraphs of two stories included later in this book?

> Young Goodman Brown came forth, at sunset, into the street of Salem village, but put his head back, after crossing the threshold, to exchange a parting kiss with his young wife. And Faith, as the wife was aptly named, thrust her own pretty head into the street, letting the wind play with the pink ribbons of her cap, while she called to Goodman Brown. (Nathaniel Hawthorne, "Young Goodman Brown," p. 374)

> In walks these three girls in nothing but bathing suits. I'm in the third checkout slot, with my back to the door, so I don't see them until they're over by the bread. The one that caught my eye first was the one in the plaid green two-piece. She was a chunky kid, with a good tan and a sweet broad soft-looking can with those two crescents of white just under it, where the sun never seems to hit, at the top of the backs of her legs. I stood there with my hand on a box of HiHo crackers trying to remember if I rang it up or not. I ring it up again and the customer starts giving me hell. ("A & P," p. 529)

The diction of "Young Goodman Brown" — simple, clear, and constrained — and the precise, grammatically correct sentences suit the narrator's somber tone. The style is fitting for a story about a community that upholds rigid social and moral codes, or appears to uphold them, regardless of the internal conflict they engender in some citizens' hearts.

The diction and sentence structures of the second passage would feel terribly wrong if used for a story about Goodman Brown, but they suit Sammy, the first-person narrator of "A & P," perfectly. The style itself, the way Sammy tells his story, does a great deal to embody and express his character — the almost affectedly breezy, off-handed, "with-it" manner of "in walks," "two-piece," "can," and "giving me hell." The sentences are grammatical, yet structured in a loose, conversational way — quite a contrast to the terse, formal phrasings of "Young Goodman Brown."

Rhythm

DESCRIBING PROSE RHYTHMS   An important ingredient of prose style is **rhythm**, the pattern of flow and movement created by the choice of words and the arrangement of phrases and sentences. There is no set of precise labels to describe rhythm, so we are forced to borrow language from other arts, such as music. Thus we say that the rhythm of a piece of prose is, for example, fast, slow, syncopated, disjointed, smooth, halting, graceful, rough, or deliberate.

FACTORS AFFECTING RHYTHM   Prose rhythm is affected particularly by the length and composition of sentences (everything said in the preceding section on sentence structures has an effect on rhythm), the use of pauses (punctuation) within the sentences, the use of repetitions, and the ease or difficulty in pronouncing the combinations of word sounds in the sentences. Long sentences with little punctuation might have a smooth and flowing rhythm, but the rhythm also could be almost breathless or fast or slow depending on how quickly or slowly the words can be spoken. Short sentences, or longer ones broken by punctuation into short phrases, may have a rough or choppy rhythm. If such sentences use a lot of short, single-syllable words, the rhythm may have a fast, even staccato-type rhythm.

Listen for a smooth, graceful, almost wavelike rhythm in the following sentence from the opening paragraph of "Sonny's Blues":

> I stared at it in the swinging lights of the subway car, and in the faces and bodies of the people, and in my own face, trapped in the darkness which roared outside. (p. 309)

Compare that with the faster, edgy, staccato rhythm of this sentence from "Where Are You Going, Where Have You Been?":

> Her mother, who noticed everything and knew everything and who hadn't much reason any longer to look at her own face, always scolded Connie about it. (p. 81)

Actually, the possibilities for different types of prose rhythm are endless. The best approach as an active reader is to listen closely to the flow of the words, phrases, and sentences and describe as best you can the way they sound and feel as you read them aloud.

Imaginative Use of Language

FIGURES OF SPEECH   Another factor contributing to style is the inclusion of comparisons, of nonliteral, or imaginative, expressions. The technical term for such usage is **figure of speech** — by definition, an unusual use of language that often associates or compares dissimilar things. In "The Story of an Hour" (p. 196), grief is compared to a storm in paragraph three, and the treatment of exhaustion, in paragraph four, is described as a spiritual emanation that presses Mrs. Mallard down, haunts her body, and reaches into her soul.

RECOGNIZING FIGURES   Figures of speech are discussed in more detail in Part 3, "Approaching Poetry," because they are so central to understanding poems (see Chapter 15). But they also can be very significant in stories and plays, and recognizing expressions that are not to be taken literally can greatly enrich your reading. The title of "Hills Like White Elephants" contains a figure of speech — a surprising, imaginative comparison. And Lyman, in "The Red Convertible," uses figurative comparisons to convey more clearly the extremely difficult emotions and actions he needs to describe near the end of the story: "His face was totally white and hard. Then it broke, *like stones break all of a sudden when water boils up inside them*" (p. 79) and "I can tell his mood is *turning* again" (p. 80).

READING FOR STYLE – INDIVIDUALITY OF EXPRESSION

INDIVIDUAL MANNER   Another aspect of style is the way styles differ. The way one person develops a characteristic manner or approach ("that's his style of doing things") can be differentiated from another's. *Style* in this sense refers to the unique, individual manner in which almost anything can be carried out: singing, dancing, composing music, playing an instrument, making any visual art, designing buildings or bridges or clothes, walking, talking, playing a sport, wearing a hat, or relating to other people. A person who does something a lot develops a distinctive way of doing it, readily identifiable as hers or his by an attentive and knowledgeable audience. Someone who knows art can recognize a painting as one done by Picasso because of distinctive characteristics in its style. Someone well versed in jazz can identify a piece by Miles Davis because of unique features of its style.

DISTINCTIVE WRITING   The same is true of writers: Most authors have their own distinctive style recognizable by readers familiar with their work. Although creative writers must adjust their diction, sentence structures, and imaginative comparisons to fit the particular characters and situations of each story, some characteristic attributes still show through. Preferences in word choice or sentence and paragraph construction, ways of shaping phrases, uses of adjectives or adverbs, attention to certain types of details, or combinations of sounds can be constant in the background in spite of adaptations to specific characters or contexts in the foreground.

FAULKNER'S STYLE   A reader familiar with the works of William Faulkner would immediately identify the following sentence from "A Rose for Emily" as his from its style (as well as the reference to Colonel Sartoris, who appears in other stories by Faulkner):

> Alive, Miss Emily had been a tradition, a duty, and a care; a sort of hereditary obligation upon the town, dating from that day in 1894 when Colonel Sartoris, the mayor—he who fathered the edict that no Negro woman should appear on the streets without an apron—remitted her taxes, the dispensation dating from the death of her father on into perpetuity (p. 363).

The recognizable features include the educated, exact diction; the long, languid sentences; phrases interrupting and words piled on to add even more precision, to get a point or feeling or image exactly right. Even though the narrator has his own sense of consciousness, Faulkner's personal style is there as well—it can't help but be, for these are the structures and rhythms in which Faulkner thought, imagined, talked, and wrote.

You will find the same characteristics, even more intensely, in the opening sentence of Faulkner's novel *Absalom, Absalom!* (1936):

> From a little after two o'clock until almost sundown of the long still hot weary dead September afternoon they sat in what Miss Coldfield still called the office because her father had called it that—a dim hot airless room with the blinds all closed and fastened for forty-three summers because when she was a girl someone had believed that light and moving air carried heat and that dark was always cooler, and which (as the sun shone fuller and fuller on that side of the house) became latticed with yellow slashes full of dust motes which Quentin thought of as being flecks of the dead old dried paint blown inward from the scaling blinds as wind might have blown them.

HEMINGWAY'S STYLE   Contrast Faulkner's style with that of Ernest Hemingway, as in the opening paragraph of "Hills Like White Elephants":

> The hills across the valley of the Ebro were long and white. On this side there was no shade and no trees and the station was between two lines of rails in the sun. Close against the side of the station there was the warm shadow of the building and a curtain, made of strings of bamboo beads, hung across the open door into the bar, to keep out flies. The American and the girl with him sat at a table in the shade, outside the building. It was very hot and the express from Barcelona would come in forty minutes. It stopped at this junction for two minutes and went on to Madrid. (p. 136)

This passage is typical Hemingway, with its ordinary, largely concrete, diction and its mostly short, concise, simple but tightly knit sentences, or cumulative longer sentences made up of short phrases connected by *and* or just a comma.

Notice these stylistic features again in another work, the opening paragraphs of his story "Soldier's Home" (1925):

> Krebs went to the war from a Methodist college in Kansas. There is a picture which shows him among his fraternity brothers, all of them wearing exactly the same height and style collar. He enlisted in the Marines in 1917 and did not return to the United States until the second division returned from the Rhine in the summer of 1919.
>
> There is a picture which shows him on the Rhine with two German girls and another corporal. Krebs and the corporal look too big for their uniforms. The German girls are not beautiful. The Rhine does not show in the picture.
>
> By the time Krebs returned to his home town in Oklahoma the greeting of heroes was over. He came back much too late. The men from the town who had been drafted had all been welcomed elaborately on their return. There had been a great deal of hysteria. Now the reaction had set in. People seemed to think it was rather ridiculous for Krebs to be getting back so late, years after the war was over.

Hemingway's style seems at first glance easy to copy, and many people have tried, but they quickly found out that it, like any distinctive style, is difficult to imitate because its roots lie deep within the whole personality and imagination of its originator.

Giving attention to the appropriateness of word choice, sentence structures, and imaginative expression can help you recognize and appreciate individuality of expression. This is another important component of active reading—making the effort to notice the *way* things are said rather than just passively taking in *what* is said. The more you read, and read carefully, the more you will appreciate the effectiveness of style and be able to differentiate one author's unique style from those of other authors.

READING FOR TONE

When you listen to a story, it's important to pay attention to its **tone**, the "tone of voice" it projects, the attitude or "stance" it takes toward the characters and actions. Tone is a significant aspect of style, and of communication generally: It can add to, modify, or even invert the meaning of the words expressed. If someone says "Please close the door behind you," it makes a big difference if the words are spoken as a simple reminder or as an angry demand. Either way, the tone adds a lot that the words themselves don't say: In the former case, tone conveys respect, acceptance, and confidence; in the latter, rebuke, rejection, separation. Tone in a literary work similarly gets in, around, and behind the words to indicate the attitude the work takes toward the characters, setting, subject, or issues, or the attitude a character evinces toward an issue, situation, setting, or another character.

TONE IN PROSE WRITING   When we talk, our own tone is conveyed by the inflections in our voice. For a writer, spoken inflections, obviously, are not available, so tone must usually be indicated through style: word choice, ways of phrasing, and kinds of comparisons all can convey an attitude toward what is being described or discussed. Recall the way "The Story of an Hour" describes the beauty of the spring day and then compares Mrs. Mallard's sense of release and freedom to a living thing, "creeping out of the sky, reaching toward her through the sounds, the scents, the color that filled the air" and forcing itself on her (p. 196). The nature of the comparison, words such as "possess her" and "striving to beat it back," and her powerlessness to stop the approach of "this thing" create momentarily an ominous and threatening tone. That turns to relief when Mrs. Mallard accepts it willingly, and the fact that she has had this sense of freedom and release thrust on her unsought evokes sympathy for her, even though we might generally be unsympathetic toward a wife who feels relief at her spouse's death.

Examples of Tone in Several Stories

A story can convey a wide variety of attitudes toward characters and events. A predominant and important attitude is that of irony, so important, in fact, that it is discussed later in a section of its own. The best way to distinguish various kinds of tone is to look at some stories, taken from Chapters 4 to 6, as specific examples.

"Where Are You Going, Where Have You Been?"   The story "Where Are You Going, Where Have You Been?" (p. 81) opens with a *comic* tone, expressing amusement at Connie's self-centeredness ("She was fifteen and she had a quick, nervous giggling habit of craning her neck to glance into mirrors") and poking fun at the romantic attitudes she has absorbed from movies and popular music: "And Connie paid close attention herself, bathed in a glow of slow-pulsed joy that seemed to rise mysteriously out of the music itself." But the tone gradually turns to *horror* ("She could see then that he wasn't a kid, he was much older — thirty, maybe more. At this knowledge her heart began to pound faster") and *sadness* ("She thought, I'm not going to see my mother again. She thought, I'm not going to sleep in my bed again") at what is happening.

"The House on Mango Street"   The overall tone conveyed in "The House on Mango Street" (p. 99) is *sympathy* with Esperanza and her family through its use of details about the kind of housing they put up with: "the third floor, the paint peeling, wooden bars Papa had nailed on the windows so we wouldn't fall out." But through comments on why the housing was the way it was ("The water pipes broke and the landlord wouldn't fix them because the house was too old") and the nun's disbelief that Esperanza lived where she did ("You live *there*?"), it also conveys a tone of subdued *anger at* or *frustration with* the social system that makes it impossible, or extremely difficult at least, for some families and groups to live in areas with adequate housing and living conditions.

"Hills Like White Elephants"   The tone of "Hills Like White Elephants" (p. 136) seems at first *objective* and *dispassionate*. But a good deal is going on through tones used by the characters — readers need to decide, for every line in the dialogue, what tone is being used. Jig's tones vary considerably. When the man says he's never seen a white elephant and Jig replies, "No, you wouldn't have," the tone seems *scornful*, a put-down. When the man says he's known lots of people who have had the operation and Jig replies, "And afterward they were all so happy," the tone seems *ironic* (she means the opposite of what she is saying). When she says, "And if I do it you'll be happy and things will be like they were and you'll love me?" her tone seems *hopeful*, even full of longing. And when she says, "Then I'll do it. Because I don't care about me," the tone seems *serious*, even *resignedly sad*.

That variety of tones shapes an attitude toward her: Although the narrator is objective, the story can strike us as being sympathetic toward her, and unsympathetic toward the man, partly because of the serious, *badgering* tone behind much of what he says, which treats her like an object to be manipulated ("I wouldn't have you do it if you didn't want to. But I know it's perfectly simple" and "I think it's the best thing to do. But I don't want you to do it if you don't really want to"), and because of his obvious attitude of concern only for himself ("That's the only thing that bothers us [me?]. It's the only thing that's made us [me?] unhappy").

The tone you hear in a literary work, then, can be serious, sober, solemn, playful, excited, impassioned, and a host of other possibilities as well as mixtures of them. As the examples above indicate, a work can have a single tone, but more often the tone is mixed, with two or more tones juxtaposed, or mingled, or played off each other. And tone, especially when it is complex, cannot always be easy to determine. When Jig in "Hills Like White Elephants" says "Everything tastes of licorice. Especially all the things you've waited so long for" (p. 137), the tone is difficult to assess: Is it wistful? Angry? Bitter? Wondering about tone, in a situation like that, is part of the richness and reward of being an active reader. Tone rarely can be summed up in a word or two. It needs to be described and discussed in a way that does justice to its full complexity.

READING FOR IRONY

One of the more complex tones is **irony**, a way of expression in which the writer or speaker creates a discrepancy or incongruity between what is (reality) and what seems to be (appearance). Dealing with irony requires active reading because the words don't mean what they literally say. Therefore the reader has to be active in recognizing and processing the difference between what is said and what is meant. Irony appears in a variety of forms. The sections that follow describe the most important types of irony and indicate what to listen for to discern each type.

Verbal Irony

In **verbal irony**, what is said is the opposite of what is meant ("Beautiful day!" when the weather is miserable). The name *Arnold Friend*, in "Where Are You Going, Where Have You Been?" (p. 81), is an example, for Arnold is anything but a friend to Connie. You need to recognize the incongruity between the name and the person. Verbal irony requires listening for signals that what is said is not to be taken in a straightforward way — exaggerated and contradictory word choice, for example, or the sheer absurdity of what is said (it can't be straightforwardly true), or the cutting tone in which a word or phrase seems intended to be spoken.

A specific form of verbal irony, **sarcasm**, is an especially direct, harsh, and cutting form ("Oh, no, these eggs are fine. I *prefer* them black and fused to the plate"). The narrator's put-down of Sonny's friend, in "Sonny's Blues," "And how about you? You're pretty goddamn smart, I bet" (p. 311), is sarcastic. If we miss such signals, we risk misreading the work.

Dramatic Irony

Dramatic irony arises when a character says or does something that the reader or audience realizes has a meaning opposite to what the character intends. To detect dramatic irony, watch for occasions when characters don't realize the full implications of what they are saying or of what happens to them, and when you see more about it than they do.

Dramatic irony is a prominent feature of Greek tragedies. The plays are retellings of stories that were familiar to the audience, so when a character makes a decision that will eventually lead to a tragic end that she or he does not expect, the audience realizes implications in the words spoken that the character does not. Thus when Creon, in Sophocles' *Antigone*, says to his son, "You'll never marry her, not while she's alive" (p. 1133), he has no idea what the results of his words will be. But the audience, already knowing the outcome, watches with horror as Creon, disregarding every warning, pushes forward on a course that will end with his son "marrying" Antigone in death.

Similarly, the last line of "The Story of an Hour" (p. 196) depends on dramatic irony: We know that Mrs. Mallard wasn't killed by joy at seeing her husband alive and well, but died from shock and disappointment instead. Also, be alert for the possibility of dramatic irony when a work of fiction uses an unreliable narrator, in cases where you are aware of more than the narrator is or the characters are.

Situational Irony

In **situational irony**, a result or situation turns out very differently from what was expected or hoped for. To notice situational irony, look for reversals — when something turns around from what it used to be, or what was expected, or what was desired. In many cases, such a reversal has ironic implications.

In "Everyday Use," for example, as Dee insists on being given the quilts her grandmother made, Mama recalls how she had "offered Dee (Wangero) a quilt when she went away to college. Then she had told me they were old-fashioned, out of style" (p. 114). Irony arises out of the changed situation, a change in Dee's attitude toward her heritage. And it's ironic when Dee accuses Mama of not appreciating her heritage when the situation has made clear that it's Dee who lacks such understanding.

www

Further explore style, tone, and irony, including interactive exercises, with VirtuaLit Fiction at bedfordstmartins.com/approachinglit.

Unlike dramatic irony, in situational irony the reader does not necessarily know more than the characters and may be as surprised by what happens as the characters are. That is the case with the unexpected double situational ironies in "The Story of an Hour" (p. 196). First, the "something" coming toward Mrs. Mallard, for which she waits fearfully, is not the sense of overwhelming loss and grief we expect her to feel; her reaction to the situation turns out to be the opposite. Second, the few moments in which Mrs. Mallard does experience a desire for life and an expectation of happiness end up being the result of a clerical error and, instead of the wonderful future she glimpsed, lead to her death.

☑ CHECKLIST on Reading for Style, Tone, and Irony

❏ Be especially attentive to style: word selection, sentence construction, sentence rhythms, choice of nonliteral expressions, and handling of timing and tone.

❏ Consider the effectiveness (appropriateness) of the narrative style and the style used in characters' dialogue and thoughts, and, when applicable, how style differs in various parts of a story.

❏ Develop your ability to discern individuality of style — how one author's style differs from that of other authors, and how each author possesses a unique, individual manner of writing.

❏ Listen for tone, the attitude toward the subject implied in a literary work, the "tone of voice" that indicates how what is said should be taken — seriously, ironically, sympathetically, condescendingly. Does the tone convey humor, affection, anger, frustration, horror, grief, concern, scorn, bitterness (to name only a few possibilities)?

(continued)

❑ Be alert for irony, an expression involving a discrepancy between appearance and reality, between what is said and what is intended. Identify the kind of irony being employed:

- *Verbal irony:* A discrepancy between what is said and intended; saying the opposite of what is actually meant.
- *Dramatic irony:* A discrepancy between what a reader or audience knows and what is known by a speaker or character; usually the reader or audience knows more than the speaker or character, or recognizes implications the speaker or character is not aware of.
- *Situational irony:* A discrepancy between what is expected or what should be and what actually occurs; in it, a result or situation turns out very differently from what was anticipated or hoped for.

FURTHER READING

ENTRY POINTS   The following story is about a young African American girl growing up in Harlem, whose horizons are expanded in several ways through a visit to FAO Schwarz, one of the most famous (and expensive) toy stores in the world. Even on first reading, you'll notice that it depends heavily on its style and tone. As you reread it, listen for the way style helps create the voice. Pay attention to the diction, sentence length, sentence constructions (some of them nongrammatical), and rhythm. Listen for the tone, or actually the complex mixture of tones — the attitude of the speaker toward Miss Moore and toward the world at large, and the attitude of the story toward the speaker. And watch for ironies.

Toni Cade Bambara 1939–1995

The Lesson   [1972]

Back in the days when everyone was old and stupid or young and foolish and me and Sugar were the only ones just right, this lady moved on our block with nappy hair and proper speech and no makeup. And quite naturally we laughed at her, laughed the way we did at the junk man who went about his business like he was some big-time president and his sorry-ass horse his secretary. And we kinda hated her too, hated the way we did the winos who cluttered up our parks and pissed on our handball walls and stank up our hallways and stairs so you couldn't halfway play hide-and-seek without a goddamn gas mask. Miss Moore was her name. The only woman on the block with no first name. And she was black as hell, cept for her feet, which were fish-white and spooky. And she was always planning these boring-ass things for us to do, us being my cousin, mostly, who lived on the block cause we all moved North the same time and to the same apartment then spread out gradual to breathe. And our parents would yank our heads into some kinda shape and crisp up our clothes so we'd be presentable for travel with Miss Moore, who always looked like she was going to church, though she never did. Which is just one of the things the grownups talked about when they talked behind her back like a dog. But when she came calling with some sachet she'd sewed up or some gingerbread she'd made or some book, why then they'd all be too embarrassed to turn her down and we'd get handed over all spruced up. She'd been to college and said it was only right that she should take responsibility for the young ones' education, and she not even related by marriage or blood. So they'd go for it. Specially Aunt Gretchen. She was the main gofer in the family. You got some ole dumb shit foolishness you want somebody to go for, you send for Aunt Gretchen. She been screwed into the go-along for so long, it's a blood-deep natural thing with her. Which is how she got saddled with me and Sugar and Junior in the first place while our mothers were in a la-de-da apartment up the block having a good ole time.

So this one day Miss Moore rounds us all up at the mailbox and it's puredee hot and she's knockin herself out about arithmetic. And school suppose to let up in summer I heard, but she don't never let up. And the starch in my pinafore scratching the shit outta me and I'm really hating this nappy-head bitch and her goddamn college degree. I'd much rather go to the pool or to the show where it's cool. So me and Sugar leaning on the mailbox being surly, which is a Miss Moore word. And Flyboy checking out what everybody brought for lunch. And Fat Butt already wasting his peanut-butter-and-jelly sandwich like the pig he is. And Junebug punchin on Q.T.'s arm for potato chips. And Rosie Giraffe shifting from one hip to the other waiting for somebody to step on her foot or ask her if she from Georgia so she can kick ass, preferably Mercedes'. And Miss Moore asking us do we know what money is, like we a bunch of retards. I mean real money, she say, like it's only poker chips or monopoly papers we lay on the grocer. So right away I'm tired of this and say so. And would much rather snatch Sugar and go to the Sunset and terrorize the West Indian kids and take their hair ribbons and their money too. And Miss Moore files that remark away for next week's lesson on brotherhood, I can tell. And finally I say we oughta get to the subway cause it's cooler and besides we might meet some cute boys. Sugar done swiped her mama's lipstick, so we ready.

So we heading down the street and she's boring us silly about what things cost and what our parents make and how much goes for rent and how money ain't divided up right in this country. And then she gets to the part about we all poor and live in the slums, which I don't feature. And I'm ready to speak on that, but she steps out in the street and hails two cabs just like that. Then she hustles half the crew in with her and hands me a five-dollar bill and tells me to calculate 10 percent tip for the driver. And we're off. Me and Sugar and Junebug and Flyboy hangin out the window and hollering to everybody, putting lipstick on each other cause Flyboy a faggot anyway, and making farts with our sweaty armpits. But I'm mostly trying to figure how to spend this money. But they all fascinated with the meter ticking and Junebug starts laying bets as to how much it'll read when Flyboy can't hold his breath no more. Then Sugar lays bets as to how much it'll be when we get there. So I'm stuck. Don't nobody want to go for my plan, which is to jump out at the next light and run off to the first bar-b-que we can find. Then the driver tells us to get the hell out cause we there already. And the meter reads eighty-five cents. And I'm stalling to figure out the tip and Sugar say give him a dime. And I decide he don't need it bad as I do, so later for him. But then he tries to take off with Junebug foot still in the door so we talk about his mama something ferocious. Then we check out that we on Fifth Avenue and everybody dressed up in stockings. One lady in a fur coat, hot as it is. White folks crazy.

"This is the place," Miss Moore say, presenting it to us in the voice she uses at the museum. "Let's look in the windows before we go in."

"Can we steal?" Sugar asks very serious like she's getting the ground rules 5 squared away before she plays. "I beg your pardon," say Miss Moore, and we fall out. So she leads us around the windows of the toy store and me and Sugar screamin, "This is mine, that's mine, I gotta have that, that was made for me, I was born for that," till Big Butt drowns us out.

"Hey, I'm goin to buy that there."

"That there? You don't even know what it is, stupid."

"I do so," he say punchin on Rosie Giraffe. "It's a microscope."

"Whatcha gonna do with a microscope, fool?"

"Look at things."   10

"Like what, Ronald?" ask Miss Moore. And Big Butt ain't got the first notion. So here go Miss Moore gabbing about the thousands of bacteria in a drop of water and the somethinorother in a speck of blood and the million and one living things in the air around us is invisible to the naked eye. And what she say that for? Junebug go to town on that "naked" and we rolling. Then Miss Moore ask what it cost. So we all jam into the window smudgin it up and the price tag say $300. So then she ask how long'd take for Big Butt and Junebug to save up their allowances. "Too long," I say. "Yeh," adds Sugar, "outgrown it by that time." And Miss Moore say no, you never outgrow learning instruments. "Why, even medical students and interns and," blah, blah, blah. And we ready to choke Big Butt for bringing it up in the first damn place.

"This here costs four hundred eighty dollars," say Rosie Giraffe. So we pile up all over her to see what she pointin out. My eyes tell me it's a chunk of glass cracked with something heavy, and different-color inks dripped into the splits, then the whole thing put into a oven or something. But for $480 it don't make sense.

"That's a paperweight made of semi-precious stones fused together under tremendous pressure," she explains slowly, with her hands doing the mining and all the factory work.

"So what's a paperweight?" asks Rosie Giraffe.

"To weigh paper with, dumbbell," say Flyboy, the wise man from the East.   15

"Not exactly," say Miss Moore, which is what she say when you warm or way off too. "It's to weigh paper down so it won't scatter and make your desk untidy." So right away me and Sugar curtsy to each other and then to Mercedes who is more the tidy type.

"We don't keep paper on top of the desk in my class," say Junebug, figuring Miss Moore crazy or lyin one.

"At home, then," she say. "Don't you have a calendar and a pencil case and a blotter and a letter-opener on your desk at home where you do your home-work?" And she know damn well what our homes look like cause she nosys around in them every chance she gets.

"I don't even have a desk," say Junebug. "Do we?"

"No. And I don't get no homework neither," say Big Butt.   20

"And I don't even have a home," say Flyboy like he do at school to keep the white folks off his back and sorry for him. Send this poor kid to camp posters, is his specialty.

"I do," says Mercedes. "I have a box of stationery on my desk and a picture of my cat. My godmother bought the stationery and the desk. There's a big rose on each sheet and the envelopes smell like roses."

"Who wants to know about your smelly-ass stationery," say Rosie Giraffe fore I can get my two cents in.

"It's important to have a work area all your own so that . . ."

"Will you look at this sailboat, please," say Flyboy, cuttin her off and   25
pointin to the thing like it was his. So once again we tumble all over each other to gaze at this magnificent thing in the toy store which is just big enough to maybe sail two kittens across the pond if you strap them to the posts tight. We all start reciting the price tag like we in assembly. "Handcrafted sailboat of fiber-glass at one thousand one hundred ninety-five dollars."

"Unbelievable," I hear myself say and am really stunned. I read it again for myself just in case the group recitation put me in a trance. Same thing. For some reason this pisses me off. We look at Miss Moore and she lookin at us, waiting for I dunno what.

"Who'd pay all that when you can buy a sailboat set for a quarter at Pop's, a tube of glue for a dime, and a ball of string for eight cents? It must have a motor and a whole lot else besides," I say. "My sailboat cost me about fifty cents."

"But will it take water?" say Mercedes with her smart ass.

"Took mine to Alley Pond Park once," say Flyboy. "String broke. Lost it. Pity."

"Sailed mine in Central Park and it keeled over and sank. Had to ask my   30
father for another dollar."

"And you got the strap," laugh Big Butt. "The jerk didn't even have a string on it. My old man wailed on his behind."

Little Q.T. was staring hard at the sailboat and you could see he wanted it bad. But he too little and somebody'd just take it from him. So what the hell. "This boat for kids, Miss Moore?"

"Parents silly to buy something like that just to get all broke up," say Rosie Giraffe.

"That much money it should last forever," I figure.

"My father'd buy it for me if I wanted it."   35

"Your father, my ass," say Rosie Giraffe getting a chance to finally push Mercedes.

"Must be rich people shop here," say Q.T.

"You are a very bright boy," say Flyboy. "What was your first clue?" And he rap him on the head with the back of his knuckles, since Q.T. the only one he could get away with. Though Q.T. liable to come up behind you years later and get his licks in when you half expect it.

"What I want to know is," I says to Miss Moore though I never talk to her, I wouldn't give the bitch that satisfaction, "is how much a real boat costs? I figure a thousand'd get you a yacht any day."

"Why don't you check that out," she says, "and report back to the group?"   40
Which really pains my ass. If you gonna mess up a perfectly good swim day least you could do is have some answers. "Let's go in," she say like she got something up her sleeve. Only she don't lead the way. So me and Sugar turn the corner to where the entrance is, but when we get there I kinda hang back. Not that I'm scared, what's there to be afraid of, just a toy store. But I feel funny, shame. But what I got to be shamed about? Got as much right to go in as anybody. But somehow I can't seem to get hold of the door, so I step away for Sugar to lead. But she hangs back too. And I look at her and she looks at me and this is ridicu-lous. I mean, damn, I have never ever been shy about doing nothing or going nowhere. But then Mercedes steps up and then Rosie Giraffe and Big Butt crowd in behind and shove, and next thing we all stuffed into the doorway with only Mercedes squeezing past us, smoothing out her jumper and walking right down the aisle. Then the rest of us tumble in like a glued-together jigsaw done all wrong. And people lookin at us. And it's like the time me and Sugar crashed into the Catholic church on a dare. But once we got in there and everything so hushed and holy and the candles and the bowin and the handkerchiefs on all the drooping heads, I just couldn't go through with the plan. Which was for me to run up to the altar and do a tap dance while Sugar played the nose flute and messed around in the holy water. And Sugar kept givin me the elbow. Then later teased me so bad I tied her up in the shower and turned it on and locked her in. And she'd be there till this day if Aunt Gretchen hadn't finally figured I was lyin about the boarder takin a shower.

Same thing in the store. We all walkin on tiptoe and hardly touchin the games and puzzles and things. And I watched Miss Moore who is steady watchin us like she waitin for a sign. Like Mama Drewery watches the sky and sniffs the air and takes note of just how much slant is in the bird formation. Then me and Sugar bump smack into each other, so busy gazing at the toys, 'specially the sail-boat. But we don't laugh and go into our fat-lady bump-stomach routine. We just stare at that price tag. Then Sugar run a finger over the whole boat. And I'm jealous and want to hit her. Maybe not her, but I sure want to punch somebody in the mouth.

"Watcha bring us here for, Miss Moore?"

"You sound angry, Sylvia. Are you mad about something?" Givin me one of them grins like she tellin a grown-up joke that never turns out to be funny. And she's lookin very closely at me like maybe she plannin to do my portrait from memory. I'm mad, but I won't give her that satisfaction. So I slouch around the store bein very bored and say, "Let's go."

Me and Sugar at the back of the train watchin the tracks whizzin by large then small then gettin gobbled up in the dark. I'm thinkin about this tricky toy I saw in the store. A clown that somersaults on a bar then does chin-ups just cause you yank lightly at his leg. Cost $35. I could see me askin my mother for a $35 birthday clown. "You wanna who that costs what?" she'd say, cocking her head to the side to get a better view of the hole in my head. Thirty-five dollars could buy new bunk beds for Junior and Gretchen's boy. Thirty-five dollars and the whole household could go visit Granddaddy Nelson in the country. Thirty-five dollars would pay for the rent and the piano bill too. Who are these people that spend that much for performing clowns and $1,000 for toy sailboats? What kinda work they do and how they live and how come we ain't in on it? Where we are is who we are, Miss Moore always pointin out. But it don't necessarily have to be that way, she always adds then waits for somebody to say that poor people have to wake up and demand their share of the pie and don't none of us know what kind of pie she talkin about in the first damn place. But she ain't so smart cause I still got her four dollars from the taxi and she sure ain't gettin it. Messin up my day with this shit. Sugar nudges me in my pocket and winks.

Miss Moore lines us up in front of the mailbox where we started from, seem   45
like years ago, and I got a headache for thinkin so hard. And we lean all over each other so we can hold up under the draggy-ass lecture she always finishes us off with at the end before we thank her for borin us to tears. But she just looks at us like she readin tea leaves. Finally she say, "Well, what did you think of F.A.O. Schwarz?"

Rosie Giraffe mumbles, "White folks crazy."

"I'd like to go there again when I get my birthday money," says Mercedes, and we shove her out the pack so she has to lean on the mailbox by herself.

"I'd like a shower. Tiring day," say Flyboy.

Then Sugar surprises me by sayin, "You know, Miss Moore, I don't think all of us here put together eat in a year what that sailboat costs." And Miss Moore lights up like somebody goosed her. "And?" she say, urging Sugar on. Only I'm standin on her foot so she don't continue.

"Imagine for a minute what kind of society it is in which some people can   50
spend on a toy what it would cost to feed a family of six or seven. What do you think?"

"I think," say Sugar pushing me off her feet like she never done before, cause I whip her ass in a minute, "that this is not much of a democracy if you ask me. Equal chance to pursue happiness means an equal crack at the dough, don't it?" Miss Moore is besides herself and I am disgusted with Sugar's treachery. So I stand on her foot one more time to see if she'll shove me. She shuts up, and Miss Moore looks at me, sorrowfully I'm thinkin. And somethin weird is goin on, I can feel it in my chest.

"Anybody else learn anything today?" lookin dead at me. I walk away and Sugar has to run to catch up and don't even seem to notice when I shrug her arm off my shoulder.

"Well, we got four dollars anyway," she says.

"Uh hunh."

"We could go to Hascombs and get half a chocolate layer and then go to the 55 Sunset and still have plenty money for potato chips and ice-cream sodas."

"Uh hunh."

"Race you to Hascombs," she say.

We start down the block and she gets ahead which is O.K. by me cause I'm goin to the West End and then over to the Drive to think this day through. She can run if she want to and even run faster. But ain't nobody gonna beat me at nuthin.

APPROACHING THE READING

1. Describe the style in "The Lesson." Consider the word choices, sentence structures, rhythm. How does the story establish the voice you listen to? What is Sylvia, the narrator of the story, like? Try sketching her character. In what ways does the style in and of itself help develop Sylvia's character?

2. Consider how the style reveals and helps create tone. Be ready to discuss the attitude Sylvia shows toward Miss Moore, the other kids, white people, the world in general. How did you feel about her in your first reading of the story? Did your feelings about her change or become more complex on rereading the story or as you thought back over it?

3. Is there evidence that Sylvia changes? If so, in what ways? Point out specific things that both cause and indicate a change (including stylistic ones, if any).

4. In what ways is the point of view important to the effect of the story? How would the story change if it had a different point of view? How would you describe the story's attitude toward Sylvia? How does it come through, given the use of the first-person point of view?

5. What lessons do the kids learn that day? Are they the ones Miss Moore intended them to learn? Why do you think so, or not? Does she have a teaching plan? It seems clear that Sugar is affected by what she experiences. Is Sylvia similarly affected, or does she resist it all? What sort of person would you predict she would turn out to be at your age, if the story followed her life further?

ENTRY POINTS   Here is another story about personal growth, narrated by a character named Gina who doesn't seem to want to learn more about herself. In it, too, style is important. The narrator says that words were not her father's medium, but they were hers: "I pursued words. English words. . . . It was important to get it right, every word, every nuance." As you reread it, focus on word choice, sentence constructions, and rhythms, as you did for the previous story, and see if you think Gina got it right. Also pay close attention to tone, watching particularly for uses of irony.

Katherine Min b. 1959
Courting a Monk   [1996]

When I first saw my husband he was sitting cross-legged under a tree on the quad, his hair as short as peach fuzz, large blue eyes staring upward, the smile on his face so wide and undirected as to seem moronic. I went flying by him every minute or two, guarding man-to-man, or chasing down a pass, and out of the corner of my eye I would see him watching and smiling. What I noticed about him most was his tremendous capacity for stillness. His hands were like still-life objects resting on his knees; his posture was impeccable. He looked so rooted there, like some cheerful, exotic mushroom, that I began to feel awkward in my exertion. Sweat funneled into the valley of my back, cooling and sticking when I stopped, hands on knees, to regain my breath. I tried to stop my gape-mouthed panting, refashioned my ponytail, and wiped my hands on the soft front of my sweatpants.

He was still there two plays later when my team was down by one. Sully stole a pass and flipped to Graham. Graham threw me a long bomb that sailed wide and I leapt for it, sailing with the Frisbee for a moment in a parallel line — floating, flying, reaching — before coming down whap! against the ground. I groaned. I'd taken a tree root in the solar plexus. The wind was knocked out of me. I lay there, the taste of dry leaves in my mouth.

"Sorry, Gina. Lousy pass," Graham said, coming over. "You O.K.?"

"Fine," I gasped, fingering my ribs. "Just let me sit out for a while."

I sat down in the leaves, breathing carefully as I watched them play. The day 5 was growing dark and the Frisbee was hard to see. Everyone was tired and played in a sloppy rhythm of errant throws and dropped passes.

Beside me on the grass crept the guy from under the tree. I had forgotten about him. He crouched shyly next to me, leaves cracking under his feet, and, when I looked up, he whispered, "You were magnificent," and walked away smiling.

I spotted him the next day in the vegetarian dining hall. I was passing through with my plate of veal cordon bleu when I saw him sitting by himself next to the window. He took a pair of wooden chopsticks out of the breast pocket of his shirt and poked halfheartedly at his tofu and wilted mung beans. I sat down across from him and demanded his life story.

It turned out he wanted to be a monk. Not the Chaucerian kind, bald-pated and stout, with a hooded robe, ribald humor, and penchant for wine. Something even more baffling — a Buddhist. He had just returned from a semester in Nepal, studying in a monastery in the Himalayas. His hair was coming back in in soft spikes across his head and he had a watchful manner — not cautious but receptive, waiting.

He was from King of Prussia, off the Philadelphia Main Line, and this made me mistrust the depth of his beliefs. I have discovered that a fascination for the East is often a prelude to a pass, a romantic overture set in motion by an "I think Oriental girls are so beautiful," and a viselike grip on the upper thigh. But Micah was different. He understood I was not impressed by his belief, and he did not aim to impress.

"My father was raised Buddhist," I told him. "But he's a scientist now."   10

"Oh," said Micah. "So, he's not spiritual."

"Spirit's insubstantial," I said. "He doesn't hold with intangibility."

"Well, you can't hold atoms in your hand," Micah pointed out.

"Ah," I said, smiling, "but you can count them."

––––––––––––––

I told Micah my father was a man of science, and this was true. He was a   15
man, also, of silence. Unlike Micah, whose reticence seemed calming, so undisturbed, like a pool of light on still water, my father's silence was like the lid on a pot, sealing off some steaming, inner pressure.

Words were not my father's medium. "Language," my father liked to say, "is an imprecise instrument." (For though he said little, when he hit upon a phrase he liked, he said it many times.) He was fond of Greek letters and numerals set together in intricate equations, symbolizing a certain physical law or experimental hypothesis. He filled yellow legal pads in a strong, vertical hand, writing these beauties down in black, indelible felt-tip pen. I think it was a source of tremendous irritation to him that he could not communicate with other people in so ordered a fashion, that he could not simply draw an equals sign after something he'd said, have them solve for x or y.

That my father's English was not fluent was only part of it. He was not a garrulous man, even in Korean, among visiting relatives, or alone with my mother. And with me, his only child — who could speak neither of his preferred languages, Korean or science — my father had conspicuously little to say. "Pick up this mess," he would tell me, returning from work in the evening. "Homework finished?" he would inquire, raising an eyebrow over his rice bowl as I excused myself to go watch television.

He limited himself to the imperative mood, the realm of injunction and command; the kinds of statement that required no answer, that left no opening for discussion or rejoinder. These communications were my father's verbal equivalent to his neat numerical equations. They were hermetically sealed.

When I went away to college, my father's parting words constituted one of the longest speeches I'd heard him make. Surrounded by station wagons packed with suitcases, crates of books, and study lamps, amid the excited chattering and calling out of students, among the adults with their nervous, parental surveillance of the scene, my father leaned awkwardly forward with his hands in his pockets, looking at me intently. He said, "Study hard. Go to bed early. Do not goof off. And do not let the American boys take advantages."

This was the same campus my father had set foot on twenty years before, 20 when he was a young veteran of the Korean War, with fifty dollars in his pocket and about that many words of English. Stories of his college years constituted family legend and, growing up, I had heard them so often they were as vivid and dreamlike as my own memories. My father in the dorm bathroom over Christmas, vainly trying to hard-boil an egg in a sock by running it under hot water; his triumph in the physics lab where his ability with the new language did not impede him, and where his maturity and keen scientific mind garnered him highest marks and the top physics prize in his senior year—these were events I felt I'd witnessed, like some obscure, envious ghost.

In the shadow of my father's achievements then, on the same campus where he had first bowed his head to a microscope, lost in a chalk-dust mathematical dream, I pursued words. English words. I committed myself to expertise. I studied Shakespeare and Eliot, Hardy and Conrad, Joyce and Lawrence and Hemingway and Fitzgerald. It was important to get it right, every word, every nuance, to fill in my father's immigrant silences, the gaps he had left for me.

Other gaps he'd left. Staying up late and studying little, I did things my father would have been too shocked to merely disapprove. As for American boys, I heeded my father's advice and did not let them take advantage. Instead I took advantage of them, of their proximity, their good looks, and the amiable way they would fall into bed with you if you gave them the slightest encouragement. I liked the way they moved in proud possession of their bodies, the rough feel of their unshaven cheeks, their shoulders and smooth, hairless chests, the curve of their backs like burnished wood. I liked the way I could look up at them, or down, feeling their shuddering climax like a distant earthquake; I could make it happen, moving in undulant circles from above or below, watching them, holding them, making them happy. I collected boys like baubles, like objects not particularly valued, which you stash away in the back of some drawer. It was the pleasant interchangeability of their bodies I liked. They were all white boys.

Micah refused to have sex with me. It became a matter of intellectual disagreement between us. "Sex saps the will," he said.

"Not necessarily," I argued. "Just reroutes it."

"There are higher forms of union," he said.   25

"Not with your clothes off," I replied.

"Gina," he said, looking at me with kindness, a concern that made me flush with anger. "What need do you have that sex must fill?"

"Fuck you, Micah," I said. "Be a monk, not a psychologist."

He laughed. His laughter was always a surprise to me, like a small disturbance to the universe. I wanted to seduce him, this was true. I considered Micah
the only real challenge among an easy field. But more than seduction, I wanted
to rattle him, to get under that sense of peace, that inward contentment. No one
my age, I reasoned, had the right to such self-possession.

We went for walks in the bird sanctuary, rustling along the paths slowly, 30
discussing Emily Dickinson or maple-syrup-making, but always I brought the
subject around.

"What a waste of a life," I said once. "Such indulgence. All that monkly devotion and quest for inner peace. Big deal. It's selfish. Not only is it selfish, it's a
cop-out. An escape from this world and its messes."

Micah listened, a narrow smile on his lips, shaking his head regretfully.
"You're so wonderfully passionate, Gina, so alive and in the world. I can't make
you see. Maybe it is a cop-out, as you say, but Buddhism makes no distinction
between the world outside or the world within the monastery. And historically,
monks have been in the middle of political protest and persecution. Look at
Tibet."

"I was thinking about, ahem, something more basic," I said.

Micah laughed. "Of course," he said. "You don't seem to understand, Gina,
Buddhism is all about the renunciation of desire."

I sniffed. "What's wrong with desire? Without desire, you might as well not 35
be alive."

The truth was that I was fascinated by this idea, the renunciation of desire.
My life was fueled by longing, by vast and clamorous desires; a striving toward
things I did not have and, perhaps, had no hope of having. I could vaguely imagine an end, some point past desiring, of satiety, but I could not fathom the laying down of desire, walking away in full appetite.

"The desire to renounce desire," I said now, "is still desire, isn't it?"

Micah sunk his hands into his pockets and smiled. "It's not," he said, walking ahead of me. "It's a conscious choice."

We came to a pond, sun-dappled in a clearing, bordered by white birch and
maples with the bright leaves of mid-autumn. A fluttering of leaves blew from
the trees, landing on the water as gently as if they'd been placed. The color of the
pond was a deep canvas green; glints of light snapped like sparks above the surface. There was the lyric coo of a mourning dove, the chitter-chitter of late-
season insects. Micah's capacity for appreciation was vast. Whether this had
anything to do with Buddhism, I didn't know, but watching him stand on the
edge of the pond, his head thrown back, his eyes eagerly taking in the light, I felt
his peace and also his sense of wonder. He stood motionless for a long time.

I pulled at ferns, weaved their narrow leaves in irregular samplers, braided 40
tendrils together, while Micah sat on a large rock and, taking his chopsticks
from his breast pocket, began to tap them lightly against one another in a
solemn rhythm.

"Every morning in the monastery," he said, "we woke to the prayer drum. Four o'clock and the sky would be dark and you'd hear the hollow wooden sound — plock, plock, plock — summoning you to meditation." He smiled dreamily. The chopsticks made a somewhat less effectual sound, a sort of ta ta ta. I imagined sunrise across a Himalayan valley — the wisps of pink-tinged cloud on a cold spring morning, the austerity of a monk's chamber.

Micah had his eyes closed, face to the sun. He continued to tap the chopsticks together slowly. He looked singular and new, sitting on that rock, like an advance scout for some new tribe, with his crest of hair and calm, and the attentiveness of his body to his surroundings.

I think it was then I fell in love with him, or, it was in that moment that my longing for him became so great that it was no longer a matter of simple gratification. I needed his response. I understood what desire was then, the disturbance of a perfect moment in anticipation of another.

"Wake-up call," I said. I peeled off my turtleneck and sweater in one clever motion and tossed them at Micah's feet. Micah opened his eyes. I pulled my pants off and my underwear and stood naked. "Plock, plock, who's there?"

Micah did not turn away. He looked at me, his chopsticks poised in the air. 45 He raised one toward me and held it, as though he were an artist with a paintbrush raised for a proportion, or a conductor ready to lead an orchestra. He held the chopstick suspended in the space between us, and it was as though I couldn't move for as long as he held it. His eyes were fathomless blue. My nipples constricted with the cold. Around us leaves fell in shimmering lights to the water, making a soft rustling sound like the rub of stiff fabric. He brought his hand down and I was released. I turned and leapt into the water.

A few nights later I bought a bottle of cheap wine and goaded Micah into drinking it with me. We started out on the steps of the library after it had closed for the night, taking sloppy swigs from a brown paper bag. The lights of the Holyoke range blinked in the distance, across the velvet black of the freshman quad. From there we wandered the campus, sprawling on the tennis courts, bracing a stiff wind from the terrace of the science center, sedately rolling down Memorial Hill like a pair of tumbleweeds.

"J'a know what a koan is?" he asked me, when we were perched at the top of the bleachers behind home plate. We unsteadily contemplated the steep drop off the back side.

"You mean like ice cream?" I said.

"No, a ko-an. In Buddhism."

"Nope."   50

"It's a question that has no answer, sort of like a riddle. You know, like 'What is the sound of one hand clapping?' Or 'What was your face before you were born?'"

" 'What was my face before it was born?' That makes no sense."

"Exactly. You're supposed to contemplate the koan until you achieve a greater awareness."

"Of what?"

"Of life, of meaning."

"Oh, O.K.," I said. "I've got it." I was facing backwards, the bag with the bottle in both my hands. "How 'bout, 'What's the sound of one cheek farting?'"

He laughed for a long time, then retched off the side of the bleachers. I got him home and put him to bed; his forehead was feverish, his eyes glassy with sickness.

"Sorry," I said. "I'm a bad influence." I kissed him. His lips were hot and slack.

"Don't mind," he murmured, half-asleep.

The next night we slept in the same bed together for the first time. He kept his underwear on and his hands pressed firmly to his sides, like Gandhi° among his young virgins. I was determined to make it difficult for him. I kept brushing my naked body against him, draping a leg across his waist, stroking his narrow chest with my fingertips. He wiggled and pushed away, feigning sleep. When I woke in the morning, he was gone and the *Ode to Joy* was blasting from my stereo.

Graham said he missed me. We'd slept together a few times before I met Micah, enjoying the warm, healthful feeling we got from running or playing Ultimate, taking a quick sauna, and falling into bed. He was good-looking, dark and broad, with sinewy arms and a tight chest. He made love to a woman like he was lifting Nautilus, all grim purpose and timing. It was hard to believe that had ever been appealing. I told him I was seeing someone else.

"Not the guy with the crew cut?" he said. "The one who looks like a baby seal?"

I shrugged.

Graham looked at me skeptically. "He doesn't seem like your type," he said.

"No," I agreed. "But at least he's not yours."

Meanwhile I stepped up my attack. I asked endless questions about Buddhist teaching. Micah talked about *dukkha*; the four noble truths; the five aggregates of attachment; the noble eightfold path to enlightenment. I listened dutifully, willing to acknowledge that it all sounded nice, that the goal of perfect awareness and peace seemed worth attaining. While he talked, I stretched my feet out until my toes touched his thigh; I slid my hand along his back; or leaned way over so he could see down my loose, barely-buttoned blouse.

"Too bad you aren't Tantric°," I said. I'd been doing research.

Micah scoffed. "Hollywood Buddhism," he said. "Heavy breathing and theatrics."

Gandhi: Mahatma Gandhi (1869–1948), leader of the independence movement in India, is reputed to have slept next to naked virgins as a way of testing his vow of *brahmacharya*, or total chastity in thought and deed.   **Tantric:** A variant in several Indian religions that reveres the body as a temple, instead of rejecting it, and includes sexual rituals as one of its ways to seek ultimate reality.

"They believe in physical desire," I said. "They have sex."

"Buddha believes in physical desire," Micah said. "It's impermanent, that's all. Something to get beyond." 70

"To get beyond it," I said petulantly, "you have to do it."

Micah sighed. "Gina," he said, "you are beautiful, but I can't. There are a lot of guys who will."

"A lot of them do."

He smiled a bit sadly. "Well, then . . ."

I leaned down to undo his shoelaces. I tied them together in double knots. 75 "But I want you," I said.

My parents lived thirty miles from campus and my mother frequently asked me to come home for dinner. I went only once that year, and that was with Micah. My parents were not the kind of people who enjoyed the company of strangers. They were insular people who did not like to socialize much or go out — or anyway, my father was that way, and my mother accommodated herself to his preferences.

My mother had set the table in the dining room with blue linen. There were crystal wine glasses and silver utensils in floral patterns. She had made some dry baked chicken with overcooked peas and carrots — the meal she reserved for when Americans came to dinner. When it came to Korean cooking, my mother was a master. She made fabulous marinated short ribs and sautéed transparent bean noodles with vegetables and beef, pork dumplings and batter-fried shrimp, and cucumber and turnip kimchis which she made herself and fermented in brown earthenware jars. But American cuisine eluded her; it bored her. I think she thought it was meant to be tasteless.

"Just make Korean," I had urged her on the phone. "He'll like that."

My mother was skeptical. "Too spicy," she said. "I know what Americans like."

"Not the chicken dish," I pleaded. "He's a vegetarian." 80

"We'll see," said my mother, conceding nothing.

Micah stared down at his plate. My mother smiled serenely. Micah nodded. He ate a forkful of vegetables, took a bite of bread. His Adam's apple seemed to be doing a lot of work. My father, too, was busy chewing, his Adam's apple moving up and down his throat like the ratchets of a tire jack. No one had said a thing since my father had uncorked the Chardonnay and read to us the description from his well-creased paperback edition of *The New York Times Guide to Wine*.

The sound of silverware scraping on ceramic plates seemed amplified. I was aware of my own prolonged chewing. My father cleared his throat. My mother looked at him expectantly. He coughed.

"Micah studied Buddhism in Nepal," I offered into the silence.

"Oh!" my mother exclaimed. She giggled. 85

My father kept eating. He swallowed exaggeratedly and looked up. "That so?" he said, sounding almost interested.

Micah nodded. "I was only there four months," he said. "Gina tells me you were brought up Buddhist."

My father grunted. "Well, of course," he said, "in Korea in those days, our families were all Buddhist. I do not consider myself a Buddhist now."

Micah and I exchanged a look.

"It's become quite fashionable, I understand," my father went on. "With you American college kids. Buddhism has become fad."   90

I saw Micah wince.

"I think it is wonderful, Hi Joon," my mother interceded, "for Americans to learn about Asian religion and philosophy. I was a philosophy major in college, Micah. I studied Whitehead, American pragmatism."

My father leaned back in his chair and watched, frowning, while my mother and Micah talked. It was like he was trying to analyze Micah, not as a psychiatrist analyzes — my father held a dim view of psychology — but as a chemist would, breaking him down to his basic elements, the simple chemical formula that would define his makeup.

Micah was talking about the aggregates of matter, sensation, perception, mental formations, and consciousness that comprise being in Buddhist teaching. "It's a different sense of self than in Christian religions," he explained, looking at my mother.

"Nonsense," my father interrupted. "There is no self in Buddhist doctrine. . . ."   95

My mother and I watched helplessly as they launched into discussion. I was surprised that my father seemed to know so much about it, and by how much he was carrying forth. I was surprised also by Micah's deference. He seemed to have lost all his sureness, the walls of his conviction. He kept nodding and conceding to my father certain points that he had rigorously defended to me before. "I guess I don't know as much about it," he said more than once, and "Yes, I see what you mean" several times, with a sickening air of humility.

I turned from my father's glinting, pitiless intelligence, to Micah's respectfulness, his timid manner, and felt a rising irritation I could not place, anger at my father's belligerence, at Micah's backing down, at my own strange motives for having brought them together. Had I really expected them to get along? And yet, my father was concentrating on Micah with such an intensity — almost as though he were a rival — in a way in which he never focused on me.

When the dialogue lapsed, and after we had consumed as much of the food as we deemed polite, my mother took the dishes away and brought in a bowl of rice with kimchi for my father. Micah's eyes lit up. "May I have some of that, too, Mrs. Kim?"

My mother looked doubtful. "Too spicy," she said.

"Oh, I love spicy food," Micah assured her. My mother went to get him a bowl.   100

"You can use chopsticks?" my mother said, as Micah began eating with them.

"Mom, it's no big deal," I said.

My father looked up from his bowl. Together, my parents watched while Micah ate a large piece of cabbage kimchi.

"Hah!" my father said, suddenly smiling. "Gina doesn't like kimchi," he said. He looked at me. "Gina," he said. "This boy more Korean than you."

"Doesn't take much," I said.   105

My father ignored me. "Gina always want to be American," he told Micah. "Since she was little girl, she want blue eyes, yellow hair." He stabbed a chopstick toward Micah's face. "Like yours."

"If I had hair," said Micah, grinning, rubbing a hand across his head.

My father stared into his bowl. "She doesn't want to be Korean girl. She thinks she can be 100 percent American, but she cannot. She has Korean blood — 100 percent. Doesn't matter where you grow up — blood is most important. What is in the blood." He gave Micah a severe look. "You think you can become Buddhist. Same way. But it is not in your blood. You cannot know real Buddha's teaching. You should study Bible."

"God, Dad!" I said. "You sound like a Nazi!"

"Gina!" my mother warned.   110

"You're embarrassing me," I said. "Being rude to my guest. Discussing me as if I wasn't here. You can say what you want, Dad, I'm American whether you like it or not. Blood's got nothing to do with it. It's what's up here." I tapped my finger to my temple.

"It's not Nazi," my father said. "Is fact! What you have here," he pointed to his forehead, "is all from blood, from genetics. You got from me!"

"Heaven help me," I said.

"Gina!" my mother implored.

"Mr. Kim—" Micah began.   115

"You just like American girl in one thing," my father shouted. "You have no respect for father. In Korea, daughters do not talk back to their parents, is big shame!"

"In Korea, girls are supposed to be submissive doormats for fathers to wipe their feet on!" I shouted back.

"What do you know about Korea? You went there only once when you were six years old."

"It's in my blood," I said. I stood up. "I'm not going to stay here for this. Come on, Micah."

Micah looked at me uncertainly, then turned to my father.   120

My father was eating again, slowly levering rice to his mouth with his chopsticks. He paused. "She was always this way," he said, seeming to address the table. "So angry. Even as a little girl."

"Mr. Kim," Micah said, "Um, thank you very much. We're . . . I think we're heading out now."

My father chewed ruminatively. "I should never have left Korea," he said quietly, with utter conviction.

"Gina," my mother said. "Sit down. Hi Joon, please!"

"Micah," I said. "You coming?"   125

We left my father alone at the dining-room table.

"I should have sent you to live with Auntie Soo!" he called after me.

My mother followed us out to the driveway with a Tupperware container of chicken Micah hadn't eaten.

———————

On the way home we stopped for ice cream. Koans, I told Micah. "What is the sound of Swiss chocolate almond melting?" I asked him. "What was the vanilla before it was born?"

Inside the ice-cream parlor the light was too strong, a ticking fluorescence   130 bleaching everything bone-white. Micah leaned down to survey the cardboard barrels of ice cream in their plastic cases. He looked shrunken, subdued. He ordered a scoop of mint chocolate chip and one of black cherry on a sugar cone and ate it with the long, regretful licks of a child who'd spent the last nickel of his allowance. There was a ruefulness to his movements, a sense of apology. He had lost his monklike stillness and seemed suddenly adrift.

The cold of the ice cream gave me a headache, all the blood vessels in my temples seemed strung out and tight. I shivered and the cold was like fury, spreading through me with the chill.

Micah rubbed my back.

"You're hard on your father," he said. "He's not a bad guy."

"Forget it," I said. "Let's go."

We walked from the dorm parking lot in silence. There were lights going on   135 across the quad and music spilling from the windows out into the cool air. What few stars there were seemed too distant to wage a constant light.

Back in my room, I put on the Rolling Stones at full blast. Mick Jagger's voice was taunting and cruel. I turned out the lights and lit a red candle.

"O.K., this is going to stop," I said. I felt myself trembling. I pushed Micah back on the bed. I was furious. He had ruined it for me, the lightness, the skimming quality of my life. It had seemed easy, with the boys, the glib words and feelings, the simple heat and surface pleasures. It was like the sensation of flying, leaping for the Frisbee and sailing through the air. For a moment you lose a feeling for gravity, for the consciousness of your own skin or species. For a moment you are free.

I started to dance, fast, swinging and swaying in front of the bed. I closed my eyes and twirled wildly, bouncing off the walls like a pinball, stumbling on my own stockings. I danced so hard the stereo skipped, Jagger forced to stutter in throaty monosyllables, gulping repetitions. I whirled and circled, threw my head from side to side until I could feel the baffled blood, brought my hair up off my neck and held it with both hands.

Micah watched me dance. His body made an inverted-S upon my bed, his head propped by the pillar of his own arm. The expression on his face was the same as he'd had talking with my father, that look of deference, of fawn-eyed yielding. But I could see there was something hidden.

With white-knuckled fingers, I undid the buttons of my sweater and ripped   140 my shirt lifting it off my head. I danced out of my skirt and underthings, kicking them into the corner, danced until the song was over, until I was soaked with sweat and burning — and then I jumped him.

It was like the taste of food after a day's starvation — unexpectedly strong and substantial. Micah responded to my fury, met it with his own mysterious passion; it was like a brawl, a fight, with something at stake that neither of us wanted to lose. Afterward we sat up in bed and listened to *Ode to Joy* while Micah, who had a surplus supply of chopsticks lying around the room, did his Leonard Bernstein impersonation. Later, we went out for a late-night snack to All-Star Dairy and Micah admitted to me that he was in love.

————————

My father refused to attend the wedding. He liked Micah, but he did not want me to marry a Caucasian. It became a joke I would tell people. Korean custom, I said, to give the bride away four months before the ceremony.

Micah became a high-school biology teacher. I am an associate dean of students at the local college. We have two children. When Micah tells the story of our courtship, he tells it with great self-deprecation and humor. He makes it sound as though he were crazy to ever consider becoming a monk. "Think of it," he tells our kids. "Your dad."

Lately I've taken to reading books about Buddhism. Siddhartha Gotama° was thirty-five years old when he sat under the Bodhi-tree on the bank of the river Neranjara and gained Enlightenment. Sometimes, when I see my husband looking at me across the breakfast table, or walking toward me from the other side of a room, I catch a look of distress on his face, a blinking confusion, as though he cannot remember who I am. I have happened on him a few times, on a Sunday when he has disappeared from the house, sitting on a bench with the newspaper in his lap staring across the town common, so immersed in his thoughts that he is not roused by my calling of his name.

I remember the first time I saw him, that tremendous stillness he carried, 145 the contentment in his face. I remember how he looked on the rocks by that pond, like a pioneer in a new land, and I wonder if he regrets, as I do, the loss of his implausible faith. Does he miss the sound of the prayer drum, the call to an inner life without the configuration of desire? I think of my father, running a sock under heated water thousands of miles from home, as yet unaware of the daughter he will raise with the same hopeful, determined, and ultimately futile, effort. I remember the way I used to play around with koans, and I wonder, "What is the sound of a life not lived?"

———————

Siddhartha Gotama: Born in India some 2500 years ago, he is whom Theravada Buddhists generally are referring to when they speak of "the Buddha."

APPROACHING THE READING

1. Pick out words — make a list — that characterize or describe the narrator's tone. Study the list and reflect on why you think these are appropriate for the attitude of the narrator and for the themes in the story. Are any of the words ironic when applied to the narrator and the story? If so, in what ways? Are the ironies appropriate, fitting?

2. Notice how Katherine Min varies her sentence structures. Look, for example, at the second paragraph. Reflect on the effect of this style. What might you say to someone to help her or him realize that style creates an impact on the reader? Find other examples where style creates an impact.

3. Recall the types of irony. Where do you see them at play in the story? What particular cultural ironies does the story bring out? Are there moments of irony that the characters themselves are unaware of?

4. Where and how does Min change the tone in the story? Think about the ways characters speak, the shifts in tone from one paragraph or section to another, sentence structure, word choice, intensity of verbs, and descriptions.

RESPONDING THROUGH Writing

WRITING ABOUT STYLE, TONE, AND IRONY

Journal Entries

1. In the course of a day, listen and watch for the word *style* in regard to anything — music, clothes, sports. Pay attention to radio, TV, advertisements, what you say, what you overhear other people saying, and so forth. Write a journal entry describing several styles you discover and discussing how ways the word is used elsewhere can help clarify its uses in literature.

www
Research the authors in this chapter with LitLinks, or take a quiz on the stories with LitQuiz, at bedfordstmartins.com/approachinglit.

2. Analyze a recording star in terms of style. Think not only about the music itself but also about everything else that goes into the making of the image, the style. Write a journal entry summarizing your conclusions and commenting on how this exercise can help clarify what style is and what style in writing means.

3. In your journal, list examples of irony that you notice during a day. Discuss how and why verbal irony in particular was used and how it affected the people at whom it was directed.

Literary Analysis Papers

4. Choose a paragraph from one of the stories in this chapter and rewrite it in the style of a different author. Then write a short paper explaining why you chose the authors you did and in what ways the changes in style changed the nature and effect of the story as a whole.

5. Write a paper analyzing the relation of style, tone, and theme in David Means's "The Secret Goldfish" (p. 116), Jamaica Kincaid's "Girl" (p. 397), George Saunders's "The End of FIRPO in the World" (p. 501), or Zadie Smith's "The Girl with Bangs" (p. 508).

6. Write a paper discussing the importance of irony in Katherine Min's "Courting a Monk" (p. 219), Yiyun Li's "Persimmons" (p. 411), Flannery

O'Connor's "A Good Man Is Hard to Find" (p. 455), George Saunders's "The End of FIRPO in the world" (p. 501).

Comparison-Contrast Papers

7. Write a paper exploring how Katherine Min's use of comparisons and contrasts in "Courting a Monk" (between Gina and her father, for example, Micah and Gina's father, and Gina and Micah) contribute to its richness of tone and theme.

8. Write a paper in which you compare and contrast style, tone, and theme in Ernest Hemingway's "Hills Like White Elephants" (p. 136) and Melissa Bank's "The Wonder Spot" (p. 332).

> ## ➤ TIPS for Writing about Style, Tone, and Irony
>
> ➤ **Including style** Prose style is one of the most challenging and rewarding topics to write about, requiring close, careful analysis and precise, detailed explanations. Include it in a paper only when the style is unusual or important, perhaps bringing it up in passing or treating it in one paragraph, as an aspect contributing to a broader analysis of the story. Be sure to discuss its effect in the story and its connections to other elements.
>
> ➤ **Centering on style** In some cases, when style is unusually complex or distinctive, it can be the subject of an entire paper. In that case, three or four stylistic features become the outline of the paper.
>
> ➤ **Concentrating on tone** Tone can be the central topic of a paper if it is a crucial element in achieving the effect of a story or novel. The outline for such an analysis could include two or three aspects or techniques used to create tone(s) or two or three points about how tone alters or shifts in significant ways in the work.
>
> ➤ **Pointing out irony** When irony plays an important role in a story, it is essential at least to point it out in a paper and explain its role in creating the story's effect.
>
> ➤ **Focusing on irony** If irony plays a major part in a story's approach and effect, analyzing the techniques through which it is established or the way it shapes meaning can form the topic for a whole paper. Be sure to ground your discussion in specific details and examples.

WRITING ABOUT CONNECTIONS

Style, tone, and irony are used by writers not only for the story itself but also to connect with readers, to help shape the effect a story has on people as they read it. To focus on the way style, tone, and/or irony are handled in a story, and the ways they contribute to the story's theme, can be an interesting and valuable paper topic. Style, tone, and/or irony can also contribute to a discussion of connections between two stories. The results can be especially revealing when the stories come from different eras or cultures. Here are a few possibilities:

1. "Time for a Change": Kate Chopin's "The Story of an Hour" (p. 196) and Jhumpa Lahiri's "A Temporary Matter" (p. 398)
2. "Learning Out of School": Personal Maturity in Toni Cade Bambara's "The Lesson" (p. 212) and John Updike's "A & P" (p. 529)
3. "'Gather Ye Rosebuds'": Looking for Love in Katherine Min's "Courting a Monk" (p. 219) and William Faulkner's "A Rose for Emily" (p. 362)

WRITING RESEARCH PAPERS

1. A full understanding of and appreciation for Katherine Min's "Courting a Monk" (p. 219) requires some knowledge of Buddhism. Research Buddhism and write a research paper in which you clarify and illuminate parts of the text that could benefit from such explanation and explicate the reversal of roles at the end of the story.
2. Many members of ethnic minorities in the United States live in hope of achieving the American dream. Do some research into that concept—what it means, how it arose, how realistic its attainment has been and can be. Write a research paper using what you learn as you compare and contrast ways that theme is embodied (and the tone in which it is handled) in Katherine Min's "Courting a Monk" (p. 219) and James Baldwin's "Sonny's Blues" (p. 309).

COMPOSING IN OTHER ART FORMS

1. Ernest Hemingway's style has been compared to that of the cubist painters. As a way of responding to fiction through use of another art, do some research on cubism and read another story or two by Hemingway, in addition to "Hills Like White Elephants" (p. 136). Then pair up some passages from Hemingway with some cubist art and prepare a class presentation in which you explain how the artworks are helpful in grasping his writing style.
2. Sylvia in Toni Cade Bambara's "The Lesson" (p. 212) comes through as a dynamic and fairly unforgettable character. Bring out the vitality and richness of her personality by preparing and delivering parts of what she says as a dramatic reading. Select several passages from the story that can be read aloud in about 6 to 7 minutes and that are particularly effective in capturing her character and relate to each other well (you may need to add some transitions to tie the passages together smoothly).

When you write you invite a reader to look in through a
window on everything.

William Stafford

Writing about Fiction

CHAPTER **8**

Applying What You've Learned

Writing papers about fiction is a well-established way of taking part in the ongoing conversation about literature described in Chapter 2. There's a natural progression from asking a friend or classmate about what happened in a story (Did the narrator really seal up Fortunato behind a masonry wall in the cellar? Did I get that right?) to discussing the story in class (What sort of person could do that, could have that attitude toward revenge?) to writing a paper on the disturbed personality of the narrator in "The Cask of Amontillado" (p. 472).

Chapters 4 to 7 helped equip you to read fiction actively and confidently. At the same time, they were preparing you to write about fiction effectively and with assurance. These chapters provided ways to "enter" a short story or novel and be able not only to understand all that is involved within a piece of fiction but also to talk and write about what makes it work, how its effects are achieved. The section on "Writing Short Papers" in Chapter 2 (pp. 34–46) provided you with general guidance for writing any literary paper. This chapter builds on that chapter by offering suggestions particularly applicable to writing about stories.

TOPICS

Topics for papers about fiction can be grouped into three categories: those focusing on what goes on *inside* the story (literary analysis), those

233

focusing on what *surrounds* the story (comparison-contrast), and those focusing on what infuses but also goes *beyond* the story (social and cultural criticism).

Writing a Literary Analysis Paper about Fiction

You can write a paper about what goes on inside the story, doing a literary analysis of it. *Analysis* is the process of separating something complex into its various elements as a way of studying its nature, determining its essential features, and examining their relationships to each other.

TECHNICAL ANALYSIS   One way of writing about a story is to focus on one or more of the technical elements used in creating it — for example, point of view, plot structure, characters and characterization, setting, symbols, style, tone, and irony. Another way is to focus on its theme, looking at how ideas, feelings, insights, issues, and implications relate to each other. Or you can focus on how technique and theme relate to each other to constitute an effective whole.

SEPARATE AND INTEGRATED   Literary analysis is not "tearing a story apart." Thinking of it that way is reductive and often diminishes our experience. Instead, analysis is somewhat like isolating a particular musician and discussing her or his role in a group's performance. Analysis draws our attention to aspects of a story we may have overlooked and leads us to reflect further on them. It involves not just separating a story into its constituent features but also examining the features themselves. Each feature is complex and can itself be explored and studied as a way of clarifying its contributions to the whole. Chapters 4 to 7 separated the elements of fiction, as indicated by chapter titles, and then examined those parts closely within the chapters. A literary analysis paper applies such a procedure to a particular work.

DON'T COVER EVERYTHING   A thorough analysis of all techniques in a story of typical length is likely to take fifteen to twenty pages or more — longer than freshman composition and introduction to literature papers are usually expected to be. Trying to cover all aspects in fewer pages, however, is likely to result in thin, superficial, shallow coverage. Usually, therefore, in a literary analysis of a story you should select one or two features to analyze in detail, making only brief comments on other aspects if needed. You might do a character analysis, or an analysis of structure, or an analysis of prose style, but not all three.

TAKE ON A CHALLENGE   In selecting a feature for analysis, avoid the easy and obvious. Instead, look for what is fresh, unusual, subtle, or particularly thought provoking about the story or what it does best. Or you might focus on what is most difficult to understand or accept or on what raises questions or problems. What you choose to write on does not have to be what is most central in or important to the story—very strong and interesting papers often focus on the handling of a small detail that has considerable significance or on a minor character who makes a major difference, such as the importance of Red Sammy in "A Good Man Is Hard to Find" (p. 455). Look for something that you find interesting to think and write about. When you do, there's a good chance someone else will find your piece interesting to read.

THEMATIC ANALYSIS   Alternatively, you can do a thematic analysis, that is, separate the thematic elements of a story and show how they relate to each other—how each character, or each scene, or each imaginative comparison and symbol contributes to the development of a theme. Thematic analysis works best for stories that use rich and complex thematic development, as, for example, a paper on the theme of suffering in James Baldwin's "Sonny's Blues" (p. 309).

PAY ATTENTION TO GAPS   Either a technical or a thematic analysis can involve not just what is in the story but also what is left out. Such omissions can be strategic gaps that force a reader to be actively involved in filling out the story or the inadvertent neglect or overlooking of things that reveal biases or incomplete understanding. Analyzing gaps of either type can make excellent topics for papers: the enormity of the gaps in "The Red Convertible" (p. 73), for example.

ANALYSIS OF INFLUENCES   Literary analysis papers also can explore how an author builds on or expands an earlier work. Or they can examine the way the artistry and ideas in one work are illuminated by details in another work, whether earlier or later, even if the author didn't consciously intend to make the connections you find. More narrowly, a paper can study the *influences* on an author: the effect or impact a writer, work, or group of writers has on another writer or work. To build an argument that a writer read other authors or works, had them in mind while writing, and was affected by them takes careful, thorough research and precise argumentation.

ANALYSIS OF ALLUSIONS   Literary analysis papers also can examine literary allusions. An **allusion** is a brief reference to a literary or an artistic work or to a historical figure, event, or object. The allusion is usually intended to place an author's work within, or alongside, the whole other context of the work that is evoked by the reference. Allusions to Walt Whitman's *Leaves of Grass* in Julia Alvarez's "Daughter of Invention" (p. 11), for example, carries into Alvarez's story the entire context of Whitman's themes of freedom, individualism, and self-reliance. Pointing out allusions and discussing what they add to a story often leads to a good topic for a paper.

> ➤ **TIPS for Writing Literary Analysis Papers**
>
> ➤ **Examine the text closely** Read with your intellect, imagination, and feelings fully engaged (at least once aloud), paying attention to every word, sentence, image, figure of speech, and literary technique.
>
> ➤ **Narrow your scope** Limit yourself to one or two elements, or one section of the story; don't try to cover too much.
>
> ➤ **Provide ample illustrations** Back up your analysis with specific examples (including quotations). This grounds and substantiates your conclusions.
>
> ➤ **Avoid summary** Retelling what happens is not leterary analysis. Your emphasis needs to be on clarification and explanation of *how* and *why* the writing works.

Many of the "Approaching the Reading" questions and topics following stories in Chapters 4 to 7 lead to topics for analytical papers. Also, many of the suggestions for writing at the end of these same chapters involve technical literary analyses. Here are some other possibilities.

1. The interconnectedness of plot, point of view, and theme in Yiyun Li's "Persimmons" (p. 411) or Haruki Murakami's "Birthday Girl" (p. 445).
2. The handling of time in Kate Chopin's "The Story of an Hour" (p. 196), Helena María Viramontes's "The Moths" (p. 534), William Faulkner's "A Rose for Emily" (p. 362), or another story of your choice. Try focusing on the way short stories frequently include an unusual moment in which time moves in a different way—faster or slower than usual—or stops briefly, forcing a character to a point of crisis or a crucial decision.
3. The effect of mixing fantasy with techniques of realism in Helena María Viramontes's "The Moths" (p. 534) or Gabriel García Márquez's "A Very Old Man with Enormous Wings" (p. 369).
4. The character of the narrator in Zadie Smith's "The Girl with Bangs" (p. 508).
5. Character, symbol, and theme in John Steinbeck's "The Chrysanthemums" (p. 513).
6. The relevance of the title in Toni Morrison's "Recitatif" (p. 731).

Writing a Comparison-Contrast Paper about Fiction

You can write a paper about the literary context surrounding a story, about its relations to other literary works. Connecting a story with another story, a novel, a poem, a play, or another author usually involves the rhetorical strategy of comparison and/or contrast. To *compare* things is to point out similarities between or among them; to *contrast* things is to focus on their differences. Note, however, that sometimes when *compare* is used alone, it is intended to mean "call attention to both similarities *and* differences." Be sure you're clear about how the word is meant if it's used in an assignment.

SELECT A COMPARABLE TOPIC   A paper comparing and/or contrasting two or more literary works can focus on any aspect of them: their subjects, plot events, characters, themes, points of view, settings, symbols, or styles. For such a paper to be effective, however, the works must have a good deal in common or share one especially important feature: Perhaps the stories are set in the same city or contain characters who fought in Vietnam or who live in the same decade. A character wearing a chartreuse dress in each story is not probably significant enough to build a compare/contrast paper around. These same principles apply to a contrast paper: If two things are totally different, with nothing in common, there's little value in pointing out the differences.

BE SURE IT'S SIGNIFICANT   The similarities and differences should be something significant, something that really matters. Use the "So what?" principle many writing teachers suggest. Suppose both stories have a scene in the Empire State Building: So what? Does that make connecting them meaningful? Louise Erdrich's story "The Red Convertible" (p. 73) and Linda Hogan's poem "The History of Red" (p. 799) have a title word in common, but comparing and contrasting them probably would not be profitable. But comparing and contrasting the way a first-person plural point of view is used in William Faulkner's "A Rose for Emily" (p. 362) with the way it is used in Yiyun Li's "Persimmons" (p. 411) could prove helpful and illuminating.

ORGANIZE IT EFFECTIVELY   A paper comparing and contrasting two works could use the first half to discuss one work and the second half to bring out similar points about the second. Two difficulties with that structure are keeping your reader interested in the first half, before the actual comparisons begin, and making sure the two halves are unified, so your paper doesn't end up coming across as two separate minipapers on the same topic. A safer alternative is to outline the points of similarity and difference you want to cover and then discuss first the one work and then the other for each point. It is not necessary to give equal space to comparing and to contrasting. In some cases, it makes sense to treat similarities in more detail; in other cases, treating differences in more detail creates a stronger paper. Nor is it essential to give equal time to both works. One might be sketched out and the other treated in detail.

Comparison and/or contrast can be used, of course, within a story as well as between stories. One could write a paper, for example, comparing and contrasting Lyman and Henry in Louise Erdrich's "The Red Convertible" (p. 73) or Roberta and Twyla in Toni Morrison's "Recitatif" (p. 431), or contrasting the way Sylvia in Toni Cade Bambara's "The Lesson" (p. 212) acts and talks while outside and inside the toy store, using this as the basis for discussing the lesson she learns.

DEVELOP A THESIS   What is important is making sure your points, of whatever length, thoroughly and precisely develop and support your thesis (see pp. 39–40). And it's important that the thesis bring out a point about the significance of the comparisons and contrasts. "The effect of the first-person plural point of view in William Faulkner's 'A Rose for Emily' is both similar to and different from its effect in Yiyun Li's 'Persimmons'" is not an effective thesis. A more promising thesis is, "Although the first-person plural point of view is used in both William Faulkner's 'A Rose for Emily' and Yiyun Li's 'Persimmons' to convey the opinions of the whole community, a contrasting degree of perceptiveness in the members of those communities creates widely differing effects and themes in the two stories."

> ## ▶ TIPS for Writing Comparison-Contrast Papers
>
> ➤ **Watch for meaningful pairings** As you read, watch for things that pair up: a plot, scene, character, setting, or symbol that reminds you of another in a significant way. And always be alert for comparisons that come from unlikely pairings.
>
> ➤ **Outline similarities and differences** Make lists, then group related items and select two or three topics to focus on.
>
> ➤ **Spell out comparisons and contrasts** Don't just describe the things you are comparing and contrasting; explain why you think there is a connection and why you think it has significance.
>
> ➤ **Don't retell what happens in the stories** Your paper should point out and discuss similarities and differences regarding specific aspects within the story or between stories, not just summarize how things differ in the plot.

Here are some topic suggestions, but the possibilities are almost endless. Picking out your own pairings and things to focus on is a valuable part of the discovery process.

1. A comparison-contrast of the characters and characterization of Sonny and his brother in James Baldwin's "Sonny's Blues" (p. 309).
2. A comparison and contrast of how two stories about brothers, Louise Erdrich's "The Red Convertible" (p. 73) and James Baldwin's "Sonny's Blues" (p. 309), use setting and symbol to bring out the differences between the characters.
3. A comparison and contrast of the marital relationships in Monica Ali's "Dinner with Dr. Azad" (p. 292) and Jhumpa Lahiri's "A Temporary Matter" (p. 398).
4. A comparison and contrast of the effects of memory in Ana Menéndez's "Her Mother's House" (p. 419) and Toni Morrison's "Recitatif" (p. 431).

5. Comparing and contrasting what love means in two or more of the following: Monica Ali's "Dinner with Dr. Azad" (p. 292), Melissa Bank's "The Wonder Spot" (p. 332), Raymond Carver's "What We Talk about When We Talk about Love" (p. 337), Tillie Olsen's "I Stand Here Ironing" (p. 467), and Katherine Anne Porter's "The Jilting of Granny Weatherall" (p. 478).
6. A comparison and contrast of the use of the first-person plural point of view in William Faulkner's "A Rose for Emily" (p. 362) and Yiyun Li's "Persimmons" (p. 411).

Writing Social or Cultural Criticism about Fiction

In addition to literary analysis topics and comparison-contrast topics, papers can examine a story's relation to the cultural and social context that infuses it but that also connects the story to real-world issues all of us confront. Such topics involve the use of *cultural criticism*.

In general, cultural criticism is not usually focused on analysis of technique or connections to other literature or art forms. It is concerned instead with what a story conveys about social attitudes and relations generally and, more specifically, with issues regarding such things as social background, sex, class, ethnicity, power, and privilege. Authors write works of fiction at a specific time, surrounded by specific circumstances and attitudes. Even if the story does not refer directly to events or attitudes contemporary to the writing, those events and attitudes influence the writer and the story, consciously or unconsciously, whether she or he accepts and reflects prevailing attitudes or ignores, rejects, or challenges them.

THINK IN CULTURAL TERMS   Cultural critics direct our attention to such issues and clarify the relationship between the author and story and the cultural context in which they exist. Stories are generally set in a specific time (perhaps the same as that in which they are written, but often not), with specific circumstances imagined in the background, whether the story develops that background in detail or not. Cultural critics concentrate on the way a work embodies a cultural context, how the events, ideas, or attitudes in a story are influenced by the economic conditions, political situations, or social conventions that existed when it was written. But they also explore the way a work is a part of a culture and can influence, and perhaps change, the economic conditions, political situations, or social conventions of its time or later times.

MAKE CULTURAL CONNECTIONS   Cultural criticism can, but doesn't have to, use the comparison/contrast method. You could, for example, write a paper comparing and/or contrasting social or cultural details in a story to those in a poem or a play or to the real-world conditions existing today. Cultural critics, however, do not limit themselves to literary works of the type included in this book. For them, such works are no more important or privileged than any other cultural artifact. They study popular culture from all times alongside what is considered classic literature or art, believing that popular culture reveals as much about a society as "high culture." If you take this approach, you might write a paper comparing what is going on in a classic story or novel with what is going on in a comic strip, Hollywood movie, television show, or popular work of "genre fiction" (a mystery or romance, for example).

INCORPORATE ANOTHER THEORETICAL APPROACH Cultural criticism can also extend to particular approaches that are concerned with social attitudes and influences, such as feminist criticism and Marxist criticism, which are described in more detail in the appendix on theoretical approaches to literature (see p. 1584). Both are concerned with social power, particularly the indirect, unobvious, often ignored or unconscious kinds of power that underlie most societies — the patriarchal structures that have traditionally given men power over women and the ideologies used by the upper classes to maintain power over the lower classes. Feminist and Marxist critics focus on who has power and how they use it, and who doesn't have power and how they suffer as a result. Both provide helpful ways to open up literary texts, to see more in them, and, as a result, to gain fresh understandings of society and culture as well as of the work.

Some of the writing suggestions in Chapters 4 to 7 involve cultural issues, and some of the "Approaching the Reading" questions following stories in Chapters 4 to 7 can lead to topics for cultural criticism papers. Here are some additional possibilities for topics, though you shouldn't limit yourself to them. Looking for cultural issues and framing questions that can be explored further is an important part of the learning process.

> ## ▶ TIPS for Writing Social and Cultural Criticism
>
> ➤ **Read expansively** Look beyond structure, characters, and literary techniques and consider issues raised (intentionally or not) in and by the text.
>
> ➤ **Plan on doing research** Social or cultural criticism usually involves information beyond what is found in the text or in common knowledge; it often deals with background information you'll find only by further investigation.
>
> ➤ **Connections are crucial** Social and cultural criticism usually involves making connections of various kinds: between issues within and outside the text, for example or between a text and historical/cultural events contemporary with it or between a text and a theoretical text.
>
> ➤ **Make a point** Simply describing cultural connections is not enough. A paper has to apply such connections, by exploring their relevance and implications, and cohere them into a significant thesis.

1. Women and work in Zora Neale Hurston's "Sweat" (p. 384), Tillie Olsen's "I Stand Here Ironing" (p. 467), and Katherine Anne Porter's "The Jilting of Granny Weatherall" (p. 478).
2. Struggles with questions of personal/ethnic identity and cultural borders in Louise Erdrich's "The Red Convertible" (p. 73), Alice Walker's "Everyday Use" (p. 109), Katherine Min's "Courting a Monk" (p. 219), James Baldwin's "Sonny's Blues" (p. 309), and/or Judith Ortiz Cofer's "American History" (p. 346).
3. The effect houses have on the people who live in them. Start by doing some reading on the social and economic implications of adequate housing; then apply what you find to two or more of the following: Sandra Cisneros's "The House on Mango Street" (p. 99), Alice Walker's "Everyday Use" (p. 109), Edward P. Jones's "Bad Neighbors" (p. 164), Monica Ali's "Dinner with Dr. Azad" (p. 292), Judith Ortiz Cofer's "American History" (p. 346), Zora Neale Hurston's "Sweat" (p. 384), and Ana Menéndez's "Her Mother's House" (p. 419).
4. Racial stereotypes and racial tensions in Toni Morrison's "Recitatif" (p. 431).
5. John Updike's "A & P" (p. 529) examined from a feminist approach.
6. The weight, in various senses, of everything U.S. military personnel in Vietnam carried, in Tim O'Brien's "The Things They Carried" (p. 150).

DEVELOPMENT

Once you've picked out a technique or question or problem or issue, you need to decide what to do with it, how to focus and develop it. The section "Writing Short Papers" in Chapter 2 (pp. 34–46) applies equally to papers on fiction, poetry, and drama. At this point it would be helpful to read or review the first four of the "Steps in the Writing Process" (p. 35). Here we comment briefly on developing an argument specifically for a paper on fiction.

DEVELOP AN IDEA   You must do more than just summarize or describe the story—that's seldom interesting or valuable for you or your reader. You need to develop a central idea of some originality, interest, and significance. In an argumentative paper, the central idea must be disputable, one about which there can be disagreement. Your job is to persuade readers that your views are sound and convincing. One way to bring out the argumentative nature of your topic is to mention and reply to other ways of looking at the issue, thus explaining why your way of approaching the matter is stronger than other ways.

ASK QUESTIONS   A good strategy in reaching a disputable central idea is to begin asking questions about the technique or problem or issue. What is distinctive or unique or striking about the way the technique is handled? In what ways is that technique particularly important to the story? How does the technique relate to the theme? How is the problem or issue embodied in the plot, characters, or setting? Is the problem or issue embedded in a symbol? What are some broader implications of the problem or issue? What is controversial, or puzzling, or difficult about what the text seems to say about the issues raised in it?

EXPLAIN AND ILLUSTRATE YOUR ANSWERS   It is often helpful to phrase your central idea as a question and then to use each of the paper's body paragraphs to develop a point answering part of the question. Develop each paragraph by elaborating the point, by supplying details and quotations to illustrate, support, and confirm the point, and by explaining how the illustration relates to the point being developed. Illustration and explanation need to go together. Details and quotations by themselves do not prove anything. Your explanations are needed to indicate what is important about the details and to tie them in to the whole fabric you are weaving in the paper. Likewise, explanations without details and quotations are not specific enough and are not anchored to the work. The key to a successful paper lies in its development and support of its ideas: explaining ideas so readers can understand them readily and supporting them with details and quotations so readers have confidence that the points are well grounded and worth considering.

START PARAGRAPHS WITH IDEA SENTENCES   The way you start the paragraphs in the body of an argumentative paper is very important. Just as the thesis of your paper must state an idea, not just a fact, so should the first sentence of each paragraph. The opening sentence of a paragraph in an argumentative paper is a mini-thesis: It should state briefly the point or idea to be developed in that paragraph. If a paragraph starts with a statement of fact rather than with a statement of idea, the rest of the paragraph is likely to consist of summary and more factual statements and not explore an idea or develop an argument. The second sentence of the paragraph should expand on the point or idea stated briefly in the topic sentence, bringing out its significance and implications. The rest of the paragraph must develop and support the point or idea.

ORGANIZE TOPICALLY   In supporting points in a paper about fiction, you can't talk about every paragraph in the story or novel, the way you can go line by line through a short poem. A solid paper is specific and goes into detail without summarizing the plot. One way to guard against too much summary is not using the plot as the outline for your paper. It's often better to organize the paper instead by topics or ideas, a series of techniques, or a series of points about your central idea.

FOCUS ON KEY PASSAGES   Another way to be specific and detailed without summarizing is to focus on key passages. As we listen to and look at a story, we take the whole work into consideration as we seek to grasp its essence. In doing so, we usually find that a particular section—a sentence, a few sentences, a paragraph, a particular scene — seems to shed light on all the other parts of the story. Teacher-critic Benjamin De Mott calls such sections *key passages*. They are not something writers insert deliberately into a story as clues to readers but are simply parts of the story that appear particularly meaningful to an individual reader and to that reader's interpretation of the story. So, instead of trying to discuss every part of a story, try focusing on a key passage in depth, or perhaps two or three key passages, and use it or them to represent, connect with, and illuminate what is occurring in the work as a whole.

INCLUDE QUOTATIONS   Some of the supporting illustrations in any literary paper must be quotations. You may be tempted to quote at length from a short story or novel to support a point or illustrate style or technique. At times, long quotations are unavoidable, but as a rule keep quotations short. Look in the long passage you want to quote for a key sentence or phrase or word and quote that instead of the whole passage. Often a carefully phrased introduction provides the context and reduces the need for a long quotation.

For guidance on fitting quotations into your paragraphs and sentences, review the section on handling quotations (pp. 44–45) and the "Ten Guidelines for Handling Quotations" (pp. 47–48). If your paper uses quotations only from stories included in this book, you do not need to add a bibliography page. Your teacher will take for granted that page numbers refer to this book (if you quote from more than one story, you may need to include the author's name with the page number — see p. 1497). When you include quotations from other sources or from stories you find in another book, you will need to include a bibliography page (see pp. 1499–1509).

REVISE, REVISE, REVISE   When you've completed a draft of your paper, read or review the fifth step in the writing process, "Revising and Proofreading" (pp. 40–42), the guidelines "Making Literary Papers Effective" (p. 42), and the "Ten Guidelines for Handling Quotations" (pp. 47–48) from Chapter 2. Remember, titles of short stories are placed within quotation marks; titles of novels or collections of short stories are underlined or italicized:

> One of Alice Walker's stories is "The Flowers." It was published in her short story collection *In Love and Trouble: Stories of Black Women*.

A STUDENT WRITER AT WORK: ALICIA ABOOD ON THE WRITING PROCESS

Students in one of our introduction to literature classes were asked to write an analytical paper on Dagoberto Gilb's "Love in L.A." (p. 61). (If you don't remember the story, go back and reread it now.) The assignment was, "Write a two- to three-page paper analyzing the effectiveness of point of view, setting, or style in 'Love in L.A.'" We are going to follow one of our students, Alicia

Abood, through the writing process in completing that assignment, using her own words as she retraces her steps.

On Finding a Topic

"I read 'Love in L.A.' for the first time while sitting in an airport terminal, waiting for my flight to board. At first, I read the piece silently to myself, and the second time I whispered it aloud. I refused to hold a pen in my hand so that I wouldn't be tempted to mark it up right away. I just read. I was immediately enticed by the sounds of the words in relation to what was happening in the story. I found it intriguing that the language was rather sparse and delicate but still rich and full of texture — full of color and emotion. Considering the short length of the story, I was surprised by how much I could see and hear.

"After the initial reading, I put the story back into my backpack, and left it alone for a while. When I reread the piece two days later, I marked it up. I read it three times in a row — each time marking it up in different areas — noticing things that I hadn't noticed before. Several ideas for paper topics circulated in my head: how the title 'Love in L.A.' related to the plot and the language; the stance Gilb took on the theme of love and relationships; elements of plot and/or elements of time in the story. I took a quick glance over the notes that I had made, and put the piece away again.

"When I brought the piece out after a week or so, I noticed that I was most captivated by particular elements of the diction in the piece: the verbs were strong and fulfilling, the similes were surprising and vibrant. At the end of the story, I made the comment that 'every single word feels like it needs to be here.' I felt compelled to write about the language."

On Narrowing and Focusing the Topic

"Having decided to focus on the effect of diction in Gilb's story, I went through a debate about how I wanted to present this issue in a paper. I was a little stuck on whether to confront one element like the use of verbs, or to confront a few elements like simile and imagery. I decided that the use of sound, verbs, and similes were the most captivating aspects of Gilb's story, but I was also curious about the dialogue. To maintain the focus and length of the paper, I had to cut out the discussion of dialogue completely.

"In terms of outline, I didn't do much. I made a very rough, skeleton-like outline as to how I would set up the paper but I 'outline' best through making lists. I made a list of the verbs that jumped out to me while reading the piece.

glimpsed	smack	fondled	clicked
stared	crawling	beamed	swelled
pounced	inhale	revved	

I wrote down the similes that I particularly enjoyed and silently dialogued to myself how these similes were effective to me personally and to the overall unity of the story."

On Turning the Topic into an Argumentative Thesis

"When beginning to physically put the piece into essay form, I spent too much time on the introduction. I always do that. It is evident that my starting introductions were weak, loose, and removed from the gut of the story. After a little frustration, I made myself just move on from the introduction and begin discussing the language—the sounds, verbs, and similes. For some odd reason I always have to have some sort of introduction *there* in my paper before I want to begin writing the rest. Even if it is weak, I want it there. It is an unfortunate habit to have, I suppose.

"I drafted a working thesis: Gilb's language in 'Love in L.A.' is particularly strong in its use of sound, similes, and active verbs. But I realized that, although it covered the topics I wanted to discuss, it didn't go anywhere, didn't have an argumentative slant. So I revised it to this: Gilb's handling of language—especially the sounds, the similes, and the verbs—lets us enter these characters' lives and the nature of love in L.A. That version gave me both an outline and an idea to develop as I discussed each technique and the various examples."

On Developing and Supporting the Thesis

"I really enjoyed writing this piece. I think part of my enjoyment stems from the amount of time that I spent reading the story in different settings, without doing much to it at all. I read it within the noisiness of the airport and a coffeehouse, but also within the confines of a library. There were lines, verbs, and similes that I really liked but had to leave out for the sake of space. Even though I had read the piece many times before I went to put down my thoughts on paper, I kept rereading it while in the essay writing process. I was often tempted to put another verb in, but I had to force myself to leave it alone. The practice of reading while writing did really help me to keep writing. Whenever I felt stuck, I'd just read the story again, and be reminded of a thought I wanted to add or a line I wanted to discuss. This story and writing project again reminded me that the catalyst behind writing an essay is reading the literature over and over again. Doing this kept me on my toes. Kept my thoughts going, moving, digressing, and returning.

"My initial plan was, because the story is short, to follow the order of events in the story and relate them to my three techniques. I liked the idea of tracing the plot through the paper. But I found that my first draft got too long, as I summarized too much of what was going on instead of focusing on language. And I found that my topic sentences were following the plot instead of focusing on my ideas. Here are the opening sentences of each paragraph in the body of that draft:

> The immediate attention to language from the start of the story places the reader in the backseat of Jake's car as he drives to work.

> The language within the second paragraph shifts slightly in tone when Jake hits the vehicle in front of him.
>
> When Jake discovers that the passenger inside of the Toyota he has hit is an attractive young woman, he doesn't hold back from displaying a persistent interest in her.
>
> In the final paragraphs of the story Jake's character is further unveiled when he lies to Mariana by giving her the false impression that he is an actor.
>
> Gilb effectively creates vivid verbs through the remainder of the story.

When I revised that draft, I combined some paragraphs, cut a lot of plot summary, and wrote topic sentences that named the technique discussed in that paragraph followed by a sentence that expands upon the topic and gives more detail about it. That kept me focused on my ideas and explanations of Gilb's ability to use language in exciting ways, instead of on following the plot. The new topic sentences were:

> The importance of sound in the diction of the story is evident from the first sentence.
>
> In addition to its sounds, language is important in a series of similes used to describe Jake and Mariana.
>
> Along with sound and similes, the importance of language in the story comes out in its use of vivid verbs.

Within each paragraph I concentrated on giving several examples of the technique, explaining what about them was so striking that they were good illustrations of the technique and attempting to convince readers that they were effective in the story and contributed to the development of the rather ironic "love" theme in the story. I tried to keep examples short and specific so they didn't take too much space and so I would keep myself focused on explaining and arguing, not just illustrating."

On Revising and Proofreading the Paper

"My first revisions were, as I described above, reorganizing the paper from following the plot to focusing on techniques and reshaping the thesis and topic sentences. I also did a lot of rearranging, to bring out the steps in my thinking more clearly, and a lot of cutting, to make the style more concise. Here is an example of the way I revised one paragraph (boldface for additions, strike-throughs for deletions):

> **In addition to the sounds of the language, the use of similes is an important technique in the story. Gilb uses a series of similes to describe the growing connection between Jake and Mariana (another kind**

of love developing in L.A.). When Jake discovers that the passenger inside of the Toyota he has hit is an attractive young woman, **for example,** he **can't help feeling** ~~doesn't hold back from displaying a persistent~~ interest in her~~.~~**:** ~~To convey her impact on Jake, Gilb uses a simile:~~ "He inhaled her scent like it was clean air and straightened out his less than new but not unhip clothes." This comparison **to** ~~captures the attraction Jake feels toward this woman, Mariana. The refreshing image of~~ "clean air~~"~~ comes through powerfully ~~in this section of the story~~ because in previous paragraphs~~,~~ the highway traffic and Jake's unventilated car create~~s~~ a **stuffy** ~~tight~~ and claustrophobic feel. **Later, as they introduce themselves to each other,** ~~As the story continues, Gilb continues to use similes to more fully describe the impact that Mariana made on Jake's character. To describe the first time Jake and Mariana come into physical contact, Gilb writes~~ "They shook hands like she'd never done it before in her life." An apparent separation is created in this line, **contrasting** ~~as it causes the reader to think of~~ Jake's experienced and sly attitude **with** ~~next to~~ Mariana's young, naïve, and timid character.

"My final step was to proofread for slips in spelling, grammar, and punctuation (I tend to write fast and not pay much attention to agreement and apostrophes in the first draft). Also, at that point I inserted page numbers to go with the quoted words and phrases. If the story had been longer, I would have put them in as I wrote, but for this story it was easy to find them by going back. Because I used only one story, one that was included in our textbook, I didn't need to add a bibliography page."

SAMPLE PAPER

Alicia Abood
Professors Ridl and Schakel
English 105-04
October 8, 2007

Clips of Language:
The Effect of Diction in Dagoberto Gilb's "Love in L.A."

Short stories often use words to capture a small glimpse of time. That is certainly the case in Dagoberto Gilb's "Love in L.A." Gilb invites his readers into a snippet of time cut out of what feels like a cinematic slide show. His carefully crafted diction helps to establish his characters and his sense of place and entices the reader to linger on words and taste each sentence. Vivid images and catchy similes are rhythmically blended into

Thesis sentence.   each paragraph. Close attention to Gilb's diction will demonstrate that it is his handling of language--especially the sounds of the words, the use of similes, and the choice of strong verbs--that lets us enter a few moments in two characters' lives and offers us a glimpse into the nature of love in L.A.

Topic sentence, expansion of topic sentence.   The first way language becomes important in the story is through its handling of sound. Gilb chooses words carefully to make their sounds fit and reinforce their meaning and seem enjoyable for the reader. The importance of sound is evident from the first sentence: "Jake slouched in a clot of near motionless traffic" (61). The sounds of "slouched" and "clot" evoke the still, thick, and anguished moods that recur throughout the plot. Jake is "slouched" in traffic; moreover, he is "slouched" in and stuck with the terms of his lifestyle. He is vying for more before he even begins his day. As the opening paragraph continues, the speaker informs the audience that Jake is longing to upgrade from his '59 Buick to something newer and more stylish:

Block quotation (ellipses used to shorten it).
> It would have crushed velvet interior with electric controls for the L.A. summer, a nice warm heater and defroster . . . , a cruise control . . . , mellow speakers front and rear of course, [and] windows that hum closed. (61)

The luxuries he dreams of for his vehicle extend to qualities he desires for his lifestyle. The very sounds of "crushed velvet interior," "cruise control," and "mellow speakers" convey notions of a free and easygoing daily regiment. He feels too mellow, in fact, and doesn't notice the car ahead until

Verb tenses changed to the literary present.   it's too late. Trying to avoid a crash, he "pounce[s] the brake pedal and steer[s] the front wheels away from the tiny brakelights but the smack [is] unavoidable" (61). The sound of "pounce" conveys an urgency that "steps on" would lack. The sound of "smack" echoes the actual impact of Jake's vehicle on the Toyota in front of him, and the way it jolts Jake back to reality. A few lines later, "smack" is repeated (61), emphasizing that the damage has been done and cannot be avoided. Jake's dreams, and the sounds of the words that describe them, suggest that one aspect of love in L.A. is a love of freedom and a good life.

Transition and topic sentence.   In addition to the sounds of the language, the use of similes is an important technique in the story. Gilb uses a series of similes to describe the growing connection between Jake and Mariana (another kind of love developing in L.A.). These similes, coming as they do through Jake's consciousness and showing his perspective, may indicate more about her impact on him than his on her. When Jake discovers that the passenger inside of the Toyota he has hit is an attractive young woman, for example,

Quotation introduced formally with a colon.   he can't help feeling interest in her: "He inhale[s] her scent like it was clean air and straighten[s] out his less than new but not unhip clothes"

(62). This comparison to clean air comes through powerfully because in previous paragraphs the highway traffic and Jake's unventilated car create a stuffy and claustrophobic feel. Later, as they introduce themselves to each other, "They [shake] hands like she'd never done it before in her life" (62). An apparent separation is created in this line, contrasting Jake's experienced and sly attitude with Mariana's young, naïve, and timid character. Similes continue in the final paragraphs when Jake gives Mariana the false impression that he is an actor, "[b]een in a couple of movies," and she "smile[s] like a fan" (63). The simile causes us to question whether she is falling for his lies, or whether Jake is just imagining that she is. When Jake says goodbye to Mariana, he initiates another handshake: "Her hand felt so warm and soft he felt like he'd been kissed" (63). Once again, this moment enforces the heightened sense of happiness that Jake feels when around Mariana. Similes throughout the story give a romantic aura to this snippet of time in which we see Jake and Mariana together.

Quotation integrated into sentence with a comma.

Quotation blended fully into sentence.

Along with sound and similes, the importance of language in the story comes out in its handling of verbs. Gilb chooses vivid, active verbs that bring out aspects of the characters and that energize the story for the reader. After Jake realizes that the scratch in the chrome of his own vehicle is hardly noticeable, for example, he "perk[s] up" (62). The word "perk" conveys a lifted and elevated spirit. The fact that Jake is most concerned with the appearance of his vehicle implies a certain self-centeredness. After apologizing for hitting her car, Jake "fondle[s]" the "wide dimple near the cracked taillight" (62). The use of the word "fondle" emphasizes the sensual and evocative (and again self-centered) emotions that Jake feels toward Mariana. In the final paragraph, his self-absorption is reiterated: "Back in his car he took a moment or two to feel both proud and sad about his performance" (63). (I know "performance" is not a verb, but he *was* performing.) Describing Jake's actions in terms of the way he performs further indicates that Jake is completely conscious of putting on a façade for Mariana in order to amplify his persona. When he notices that Mariana is writing down his license number and remembers that the plate is one he removed from a junkyard, it fuses the wavering, unsteadiness of Jake's lifestyle from the beginning and ending of the story. After he turns the ignition key, he revs the big engine and his sense of freedom swells as he drives away from the scene. The use of the verbs "revved" and "swelled" fill the ongoing sense of elation and accomplishment within Jake. He had pulled it off.

Development through elaboration, illustration, and explanation.

Gilb's language, particularly his use of sounds, similes, and verbs, carries the reader through the moments described in "Love in L.A." It starts with Jake dreaming about his need for an FM radio and ends, a few minutes later, as Jake drives back into the "now moving" traffic (63), with his

Conclusion, tying back to the introduction.

mind back to thinking about the FM radio for his car. Love in L.A., at least as this story portrays it, isn't deep and genuine but consists of a brief, hurried moment in a self-centered life. Gilb's writing resonates like a poem, as he steers his audience through the traffic and the minds of his characters. His poetic prose effectively weaves his audience in and out of a small yet significant slice of time.

I don't want to write books that provide [entertainment and a form of escape]. I want books that challenge, anger, and possibly offend.

Sherman Alexie

Sherman Alexie— An Author in Depth

CHAPTER 9

"I've always had crazy dreams"

Sherman Alexie was born in 1966 in Wellpinit, a tiny town on the 150,000-acre Spokane Indian Reservation in eastern Washington, about fifty miles northeast of Spokane. His father is Coeur d'Alene Indian and his mother is Spokane Indian. When he was six months old, he was diagnosed with hydrocephalus, an abnormal buildup of fluid creating too much pressure on the brain, and underwent surgery. It was expected that he would not survive or, if he survived, that he would be left mentally retarded. But he did survive, without retardation, though he suffered seizures and uncontrollable bed-wetting well into childhood.

Alexie learned to read by age three, and his love of reading as he grew up created barriers between him and his peers: He describes himself as a geek during his school years. His parents decided to have him attend high school in nearby Reardan, where he could receive a better education than he could on the reservation. He was the only Native American in the school. Throughout his time there, he was an excellent student and a star basketball player. He attended Gonzaga University in Spokane for two years, then Washington State University in Pullman, from which he graduated in 1991. He

Sherman Alexie
Reprinted by permission of Rob Casey.© Rob Casey.

A still from Sherman Alexie's movie Smoke Signals, *with Adam Beach (left) as Victor Joseph and Evan Adams as Thomas Builds-the-Fire.*
© Miramax Films/Jill Sabella/Everett Collection. Reprinted by permission.

started out as a premed student, but a human anatomy class on the one hand and a poetry workshop on the other changed his direction. He discovered he loved writing, and was good at it, and didn't love human anatomy. Writing soon became the center of his life.

His early efforts as a poet were supported by a Washington State Arts Commission Poetry Fellowship in 1991 and a National Endowment for the Arts Poetry Fellowship in 1992. He wrote prolifically and found success immediately, publishing two poetry collections — *The Business of Fancydancing* (1992) and *I Would Steal Horses* (1993). His first collection of short stories, *The Lone Ranger and Tonto Fistfight in Heaven* (1993), was equally successful, receiving a PEN/Hemingway Award and the Great Lakes Colleges Association Award for best first book of fiction, and a Lila Wallace-Reader's Digest Writers' Award. His first novel, *Reservation Blues* (1995), won the Before Columbus Foundation's American Book Award and the Murray Morgan Prize, and he was named one of Granta's Best of Young American Novelists. His second novel, *Indian Killer* (1996), was selected as one of *People*'s Best of Pages and a *New York Times* Notable Book. In June 1999, Alexie was featured in the *New Yorker*'s Summer Fiction Edition, "20 Writers for the 21st Century."

In 1997 he began work on a screenplay based on "This Is What It Means to Say Phoenix, Arizona," a short story from *The Lone Ranger and Tonto Fistfight in Heaven*. Written in collaboration with Chris Eyre, a Cheyenne/

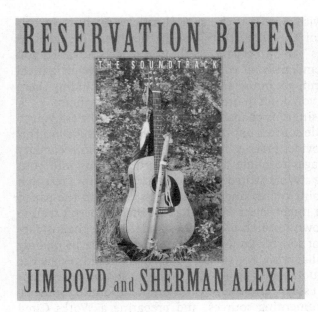

Cover of the Jim Boyd
(music) and Sherman
Alexie (words) collaboration
Reservation Blues.
Reprinted by permission of Jim
Boyd.

Arapaho Indian who also directed, the film was produced by Shadow Catcher Entertainment as *Smoke Signals*. Released at the Sundance Film Festival in January 1998, it won two awards, the Audience Award and the Filmmakers Trophy, and was subsequently distributed by Miramax Films. *Smoke Signals* was the first Indian-produced, Indian-directed, Indian-written feature film ever distributed in the United States. It received a Christopher Award, presented to the creators of artistic works "which affirm the highest values of the human spirit." Alexie was also nominated for the Independent Feature Project/West 1999 Independent Spirit Award for Best First Screenplay.

Alexie wrote another screenplay, *The Business of Fancydancing*, which he directed and produced in 2002 as a low-budget, independent film production filmed on digital video, thus freeing him from the artistic constraints imposed by commercial filmmakers. His most recent books are a collection of poetry, *Dangerous Astronomy* (2005); a novel, *Flight* (2007); and a young adult novel, *The Absolutely True Diary of a Part-Time Indian* (2007).

Alexie does occasional reading and stand-up performances with musician Jim Boyd, a Colville Indian. They recorded an album, *Reservation Blues*, made up of songs from Alexie's novel by that name. Alexie made his debut as a stand-up comedian at the Foolproof Northwest Comedy Festival in Seattle in April 1999 and was the featured performer at the Vancouver International Comedy Festival's opening night gala in July 1999. Alexie continues making public appearances as an author and writing in several genres from his home in Seattle, where he lives with his wife and two sons.

There are three ways of using the material in this chapter for writing assignments. The first is to write a paper on one or more of the stories without reading the interviews with Alexie or the critical articles on him. In this case, you would think of the three stories as if they were included in the "Collection of Stories" and do a paper without outside sources. If you choose this option, remember that if you do read the interviews or critical essays, or any part of them, you must acknowledge that by including them in a bibliography, even if you don't quote from them or refer to them.

In a second way of using this chapter, your instructor might ask you to write a paper using outside sources but limit you to what is included in this chapter. Such a paper provides practice incorporating ideas from secondary materials, selecting passages to quote and blending quotations into your writing, and constructing a Works Cited page. But it isn't actually a research paper since you aren't going out to find the materials to use in the paper. The reasons an instructor might select this option are that it doesn't require as much time as a full-blown research project does and it allows the instructor to evaluate your use of sources knowledgeably, since you are using only sources she or he is familiar with. For such a paper, you should review the guidelines for handling quotations (pp. 47–48); and you should read Chapter 28, "Reading Critical Essays" and the sections on incorporating sources, avoiding plagiarism, documenting sources, and preparing a Works Cited page in Chapter 29 (pp. 1491–1509).

A third way to use this chapter is as a starting point for an actual research paper. That is, after reading the stories and essays in this chapter, you would begin searching — perhaps only in the library or perhaps also using electronic sources, as your instructor prefers — to locate additional sources. You might read more primary works by Alexie; you surely will be expected to read and use additional biographical or critical works about his thoughts and works. For such a project, in addition to reviewing the guidelines for handling quotations (pp. 47–48) and reading Chapter 28, "Reading Critical Essays," you should read all of Chapter 29, "Writing a Literary Research Paper."

This Is What It Means to Say Phoenix, Arizona   [1993]

Just after Victor lost his job at the BIA, he also found out that his father had died of a heart attack in Phoenix, Arizona. Victor hadn't seen his father in a few years, only talked to him on the telephone once or twice, but there still was a genetic pain, which was soon to be pain as real and immediate as a broken bone.

Victor didn't have any money. Who does have money on a reservation, except the cigarette and fireworks salespeople? His father had a savings account waiting to be claimed, but Victor needed to find a way to get to Phoenix. Victor's mother was just as poor as he was, and the rest of his family didn't have any use at all for him. So Victor called the Tribal Council.

"Listen," Victor said. "My father just died. I need some money to get to Phoenix to make arrangements."

"Now, Victor," the council said. "You know we're having a difficult time financially."

"But I thought the council had special funds set aside for stuff like this."

"Now, Victor, we do have some money available for the proper return of tribal members' bodies. But I don't think we have enough to bring your father all the way back from Phoenix."

"Well," Victor said. "It ain't going to cost all that much. He had to be cremated. Things were kind of ugly. He died of a heart attack in his trailer and nobody found him for a week. It was really hot, too. You get the picture."

"Now, Victor, we're sorry for your loss and the circumstances. But we can really only afford to give you one hundred dollars."

"That's not even enough for a plane ticket."

"Well, you might consider driving down to Phoenix."

"I don't have a car. Besides, I was going to drive my father's pickup back up here."

"Now, Victor," the council said. "We're sure there is somebody who could drive you to Phoenix. Or is there somebody who could lend you the rest of the money?"

"You know there ain't nobody around with that kind of money."

"Well, we're sorry, Victor, but that's the best we can do."

Victor accepted the Tribal Council's offer. What else could he do? So he signed the proper papers, picked up his check, and walked over to the Trading Post to cash it.

While Victor stood in line, he watched Thomas Builds-the-Fire standing near the magazine rack, talking to himself. Like he always did. Thomas was a storyteller that nobody wanted to listen to. That's like being a dentist in a town where everybody has false teeth.

Victor and Thomas Builds-the-Fire were the same age, had grown up and played in the dirt together. Ever since Victor could remember, it was Thomas who always had something to say.

Once, when they were seven years old, when Victor's father still lived with the family, Thomas closed his eyes and told Victor this story: "Your father's heart is weak. He is afraid of his own family. He is afraid of you. Late at night he sits in the dark. Watches the television until there's nothing but that white noise. Sometimes he feels like he wants to buy a motorcycle and ride away. He wants to run and hide. He doesn't want to be found."

Thomas Builds-the-Fire had known that Victor's father was going to leave, knew it before anyone. Now Victor stood in the Trading Post with a one-hundred-dollar check in his hand, wondering if Thomas knew that Victor's father was dead, if he knew what was going to happen next.

Just then Thomas looked at Victor, smiled, and walked over to him.

"Victor, I'm sorry about your father," Thomas said.

"How did you know about it?" Victor asked.

"I heard it on the wind. I heard it from the birds. I felt it in the sunlight. Also, your mother was just in here crying."

"Oh," Victor said and looked around the Trading Post. All the other Indians stared, surprised that Victor was even talking to Thomas. Nobody talked to Thomas anymore because he told the same damn stories over and over again. Victor was embarrassed, but he thought that Thomas might be able to help him. Victor felt a sudden need for tradition.

"I can lend you the money you need," Thomas said suddenly. "But you have to take me with you." 25

"I can't take your money," Victor said. "I mean, I haven't hardly talked to you in years. We're not really friends anymore."

"I didn't say we were friends. I said you had to take me with you."

"Let me think about it."

Victor went home with his one hundred dollars and sat at the kitchen table. He held his head in his hands and thought about Thomas Builds-the-Fire, remembered little details, tears and scars, the bicycle they shared for a summer, so many stories.

Thomas Builds-the-Fire sat on the bicycle, waited in Victor's yard. He was 30 ten years old and skinny. His hair was dirty because it was the Fourth of July.

"Victor," Thomas yelled. "Hurry up. We're going to miss the fireworks."

After a few minutes, Victor ran out of his house, jumped the porch railing, and landed gracefully on the sidewalk.

"And the judges award him a 9.95, the highest score of the summer," Thomas said, clapped, laughed.

"That was perfect, cousin," Victor said. "And it's my turn to ride the bike."

Thomas gave up the bike and they headed for the fairgrounds. It was nearly 35 dark and the fireworks were about to start.

"You know," Thomas said. "It's strange how us Indians celebrate the Fourth of July. It ain't like it was *our* independence everybody was fighting for."

"You think about things too much," Victor said. "It's just supposed to be fun. Maybe Junior will be there."

"Which Junior? Everybody on this reservation is named Junior."

And they both laughed.

The fireworks were small, hardly more than a few bottle rockets and a foun- 40 tain. But it was enough for two Indian boys. Years later, they would need much more.

Afterwards, sitting in the dark, fighting off mosquitoes, Victor turned to Thomas Builds-the-Fire.

"Hey," Victor said. "Tell me a story."

Thomas closed his eyes and told this story: "There were these two Indian boys who wanted to be warriors. But it was too late to be warriors in the old way. All the horses were gone. So the two Indian boys stole a car and drove to the city. They parked the stolen car in front of the police station and then hitchhiked back home to the reservation. When they got back, all their friends cheered and their parents' eyes shone with pride. *You were very brave*, everybody said to the two Indian boys. *Very brave*."

"Ya-hey," Victor said. "That's a good one. I wish I could be a warrior."

"Me too," Thomas said.

They went home together in the dark, Thomas on the bike now, Victor on foot. They walked through shadows and light from streetlamps.

"We've come a long ways," Thomas said. "We have outdoor lighting."

"All I need is the stars," Victor said. "And besides, you still think about things too much."

They separated then, each headed for home, both laughing all the way.

Victor sat at his kitchen table. He counted his one hundred dollars again and again. He knew he needed more to make it to Phoenix and back. He knew he needed Thomas Builds-the-Fire. So he put his money in his wallet and opened the front door to find Thomas on the porch.

"Ya-hey, Victor," Thomas said. "I knew you'd call me."

Thomas walked into the living room and sat down on Victor's favorite chair.

"I've got some money saved up," Thomas said. "It's enough to get us down there, but you have to get us back."

"I've got this hundred dollars," Victor said. "And my dad had a savings account I'm going to claim."

"How much in your dad's account?"

"Enough. A few hundred."

"Sounds good. When we leaving?"

When they were fifteen and had long since stopped being friends, Victor and Thomas got into a fistfight. That is, Victor was really drunk and beat Thomas up for no reason at all. All the other Indian boys stood around and watched it happen. Junior was there and so were Lester, Seymour, and a lot of others. The beating might have gone on until Thomas was dead if Norma Many Horses hadn't come along and stopped it.

"Hey, you boys," Norma yelled and jumped out of her car. "Leave him alone."

If it had been someone else, even another man, the Indian boys would've just ignored the warnings. But Norma was a warrior. She was powerful. She could have picked up any two of the boys and smashed their skulls together. But worse than that, she would have dragged them all over to some tipi and made them listen to some elder tell a dusty old story.

The Indian boys scattered, and Norma walked over to Thomas and picked him up.

"Hey, little man, are you okay?" she asked.

Thomas gave her a thumbs up.

"Why they always picking on you?"

Thomas shook his head, closed his eyes, but no stories came to him, no words or music. He just wanted to go home, to lie in his bed and let his dreams tell his stories for him.

———

Thomas Builds-the-Fire and Victor sat next to each other in the airplane, coach section. A tiny white woman had the window seat. She was busy twisting her body into pretzels. She was flexible.

"I have to ask," Thomas said, and Victor closed his eyes in embarrassment.

"Don't," Victor said.

"Excuse me, miss," Thomas asked. "Are you a gymnast or something?"

"There's no something about it," she said. "I was first alternate on the 1980   70
Olympic team."

"Really?" Thomas asked.

"Really."

"I mean, you used to be a world-class athlete?" Thomas asked.

"My husband still thinks I am."

Thomas Builds-the-Fire smiled. She was a mental gymnast, too. She pulled   75
her leg straight up against her body so that she could've kissed her kneecap.

"I wish I could do that," Thomas said.

Victor was ready to jump out of the plane. Thomas, that crazy Indian story-teller with ratty old braids and broken teeth, was flirting with a beautiful Olympic gymnast. Nobody back home on the reservation would ever believe it.

"Well," the gymnast said. "It's easy. Try it."

Thomas grabbed at his leg and tried to pull it up into the same position as the gymnast. He couldn't even come close, which made Victor and the gymnast laugh.

"Hey," she asked. "You two are Indian, right?"   80

"Full-blood," Victor said.

"Not me," Thomas said. "I'm half magician on my mother's side and half clown on my father's."

They all laughed.

"What are your names?" she asked.

"Victor and Thomas."   85

"Mine is Cathy. Pleased to meet you all."

The three of them talked for the duration of the flight. Cathy the gymnast complained about the government, how they screwed the 1980 Olympic team by boycotting.

"Sounds like you all got a lot in common with Indians," Thomas said.

Nobody laughed.

After the plane landed in Phoenix and they had all found their way to the   90
terminal, Cathy the gymnast smiled and waved good-bye.

"She was really nice," Thomas said.

"Yeah, but everybody talks to everybody on airplanes," Victor said. "It's too bad we can't always be that way."

"You always used to tell me I think too much," Thomas said. "Now it sounds like you do."

"Maybe I caught it from you."

"Yeah."   95

Thomas and Victor rode in a taxi to the trailer where Victor's father died.

"Listen," Victor said as they stopped in front of the trailer. "I never told you I was sorry for beating you up that time."

"Oh, it was nothing. We were just kids and you were drunk."

"Yeah, but I'm still sorry."

"That's all right."   100

Victor paid for the taxi and the two of them stood in the hot Phoenix summer. They could smell the trailer.

"This ain't going to be nice," Victor said. "You don't have to go in."

"You're going to need help."

Victor walked to the front door and opened it. The stink rolled out and made them both gag. Victor's father had lain in that trailer for a week in hundred-degree temperatures before anyone found him. And the only reason anyone found him was because of the smell. They needed dental records to identify him. That's exactly what the coroner said. They needed dental records.

"Oh, man," Victor said. "I don't know if I can do this."   105

"Well, then don't."

"But there might be something valuable in there."

"I thought his money was in the bank."

"It is. I was talking about pictures and letters and stuff like that."

"Oh," Thomas said as he held his breath and followed Victor into the trailer.   110

When Victor was twelve, he stepped into an underground wasp nest. His foot was caught in the hole, and no matter how hard he struggled, Victor couldn't pull free. He might have died there, stung a thousand times, if Thomas Builds-the-Fire had not come by.

"Run," Thomas yelled and pulled Victor's foot from the hole. They ran then, hard as they ever had, faster than Billy Mills,° faster than Jim Thorpe,° faster than the wasps could fly.

Victor and Thomas ran until they couldn't breathe, ran until it was cold and dark outside, ran until they were lost and it took hours to find their way home. All the way back, Victor counted his stings.

"Seven," Victor said. "My lucky number."

Victor didn't find much to keep in the trailer. Only a photo album and a   115
stereo. Everything else had that smell stuck in it or was useless anyway.

"I guess this is all," Victor said. "It ain't much."

"Better than nothing," Thomas said.

"Yeah, and I do have the pickup."

Billy Mills: An Oglala Sioux from Pine Ridge, South Dakota, Mills (b. 1938) won the 10,000-meter race at the 1964 summer Olympic games in Tokyo, Japan, and went on to set several other records in distance running.   **Jim Thorpe:** Of mixed descent but raised as a Sac and Fox, Thorpe (1888–1953) won the decathlon and the pentathlon at the 1912 summer Olympics in Stockholm, Sweden, and went on to play professional baseball, football, and basketball. In 1950 he was named by the Associated Press the greatest athlete of the first half of the twentieth century, and in 1999 he ranked third on the Associated Press list of athletes of the century.

"Yeah," Thomas said. "It's in good shape."

"Dad was good about that stuff."   120

"Yeah, I remember your dad."

"Really?" Victor asked. "What do you remember?"

Thomas Builds-the-Fire closed his eyes and told this story: "I remember when I had this dream that told me to go to Spokane, to stand by the Falls in the middle of the city and wait for a sign. I knew I had to go there but I didn't have a car. Didn't have a license. I was only thirteen. So I walked all the way, took me all day, and I finally made it to the Falls. I stood there for an hour waiting. Then your dad came walking up. *What the hell are you doing here?* he asked me. I said, *Waiting for a vision.* Then your father said, *All you're going to get here is mugged.* So he drove me over to Denny's, bought me dinner, and then drove me home to the reservation. For a long time I was mad because I thought my dreams had lied to me. But they didn't. Your dad was my vision. *Take care of each other* is what my dreams were saying. *Take care of each other.*"

Victor was quiet for a long time. He searched his mind for memories of his father, found the good ones, found a few bad ones, added it all up, and smiled.

"My father never told me about finding you in Spokane," Victor said.   125

"He said he wouldn't tell anybody. Didn't want me to get in trouble. But he said I had to watch out for you as part of the deal."

"Really?"

"Really. Your father said you would need the help. He was right."

"That's why you came down here with me, isn't it?" Victor asked.

"I came because of your father."   130

Victor and Thomas climbed into the pickup, drove over to the bank, and claimed the three hundred dollars in the savings account.

Thomas Builds-the-Fire could fly.

Once, he jumped off the roof of the tribal school and flapped his arms like a crazy eagle. And he flew. For a second, he hovered, suspended above all the other Indian boys who were too smart or too scared to jump.

"He's flying," Junior yelled, and Seymour was busy looking for the trick wires or mirrors. But it was real. As real as the dirt when Thomas lost altitude and crashed to the ground.

He broke his arm in two places.   135

"He broke his wing," Victor chanted, and the other Indian boys joined in, made it a tribal song.

"He broke his wing, he broke his wing, he broke his wing," all the Indian boys chanted as they ran off, flapping their wings, wishing they could fly, too. They hated Thomas for his courage, his brief moment as a bird. Everybody has dreams about flying. Thomas flew.

One of his dreams came true for just a second, just enough to make it real.

Victor's father, his ashes, fit in one wooden box with enough left over to fill a cardboard box.

"He always was a big man," Thomas said.   140

Victor carried part of his father and Thomas carried the rest out to the pickup. They set him down carefully behind the seats, put a cowboy hat on the wooden box and a Dodgers cap on the cardboard box. That's the way it was supposed to be.

"Ready to head back home," Victor asked.

"It's going to be a long drive."

"Yeah, take a couple days, maybe."

"We can take turns," Thomas said.   145

"Okay," Victor said, but they didn't take turns. Victor drove for sixteen hours straight north, made it halfway up Nevada toward home before he finally pulled over.

"Hey, Thomas," Victor said. "You got to drive for a while."

"Okay."

Thomas Builds-the-Fire slid behind the wheel and started off down the road. All through Nevada, Thomas and Victor had been amazed at the lack of animal life, at the absence of water, of movement.

"Where is everything?" Victor had asked more than once.   150

Now when Thomas was finally driving they saw the first animal, maybe the only animal in Nevada. It was a long-eared jackrabbit.

"Look," Victor yelled. "It's alive."

Thomas and Victor were busy congratulating themselves on their discovery when the jackrabbit darted out into the road and under the wheels of the pickup.

"Stop the goddamn car," Victor yelled, and Thomas did stop, backed the pickup off the dead jackrabbit.

"Oh, man, he's dead," Victor said as he looked at the squashed animal.   155

"Really dead."

"The only thing alive in this whole state and we just killed it."

"I don't know," Thomas said. "I think it was suicide."

Victor looked around the desert, sniffed the air, felt the emptiness and loneliness, and nodded his head.

"Yeah," Victor said. "It had to be suicide."   160

"I can't believe this," Thomas said. "You drive for a thousand miles and there ain't even any bugs smashed on the windshield. I drive for ten seconds and kill the only living thing in Nevada."

"Yeah," Victor said. "Maybe I should drive."

"Maybe you should."

Thomas Builds-the-Fire walked through the corridors of the tribal school by himself. Nobody wanted to be anywhere near him because of all those stories. Story after story.

Thomas closed his eyes and this story came to him: "We are all given one   165
thing by which our lives are measured, one determination. Mine are the stories which can change or not change the world. It doesn't matter which as long as I continue to tell the stories. My father, he died on Okinawa in World War II, died fighting for this country, which had tried to kill him for years. My mother, she

died giving birth to me, died while I was still inside her. She pushed me out into the world with her last breath. I have no brothers or sisters. I have only my stories which came to me before I even had the words to speak. I learned a thousand stories before I took my first thousand steps. They are all I have. It's all I can do."

Thomas Builds-the-Fire told his stories to all those who would stop and listen. He kept telling them long after people had stopped listening.

Victor and Thomas made it back to the reservation just as the sun was rising. It was the beginning of a new day on earth, but the same old shit on the reservation.

"Good morning," Thomas said.

"Good morning."

The tribe was waking up, ready for work, eating breakfast, reading the news- 170 paper, just like everybody else does. Willene LeBret was out in her garden wearing a bathrobe. She waved when Thomas and Victor drove by.

"Crazy Indians made it," she said to herself and went back to her roses.

Victor stopped the pickup in front of Thomas Builds-the-Fire's HUD house. They both yawned, stretched a little, shook dust from their bodies.

"I'm tired," Victor said.

"Of everything," Thomas added.

They both searched for words to end the journey. Victor needed to thank 175 Thomas for his help, for the money, and make the promise to pay it all back.

"Don't worry about the money," Thomas said. "It don't make any difference anyhow."

"Probably not, enit?"

"Nope."

Victor knew that Thomas would remain the crazy storyteller who talked to dogs and cars, who listened to the wind and pine trees. Victor knew that he couldn't really be friends with Thomas, even after all that had happened. It was cruel but it was real. As real as the ashes, as Victor's father, sitting behind the seats.

"I know how it is," Thomas said. "I know you ain't going to treat me any 180 better than you did before. I know your friends would give you too much shit about it."

Victor was ashamed of himself. Whatever happened to the tribal ties, the sense of community? The only real thing he shared with anybody was a bottle and broken dreams. He owed Thomas something, anything.

"Listen," Victor said and handed Thomas the cardboard box which contained half of his father. "I want you to have this."

Thomas took the ashes and smiled, closed his eyes, and told this story: "I'm going to travel to Spokane Falls one last time and toss these ashes into the water. And your father will rise like a salmon, leap over the bridge, over me, and find his way home. It will be beautiful. His teeth will shine like silver, like a rainbow. He will rise, Victor, he will rise."

Victor smiled.

"I was planning on doing the same thing with my half," Victor said. "But I 185 didn't imagine my father looking anything like a salmon. I thought it'd be like cleaning the attic or something. Like letting things go after they've stopped having any use."

"Nothing stops, cousin," Thomas said. "Nothing stops."

Thomas Builds-the-Fire got out of the pickup and walked up his driveway. Victor started the pickup and began the drive home.

"Wait," Thomas yelled suddenly from his porch. "I just got to ask one favor."

Victor stopped the pickup, leaned out the window, and shouted back. "What do you want?"

"Just one time when I'm telling a story somewhere, why don't you stop and 190 listen?" Thomas asked.

"Just once?"

"Just once."

Victor waved his arms to let Thomas know that the deal was good. It was a fair trade, and that was all Victor had ever wanted from his whole life. So Victor drove his father's pickup toward home while Thomas went into his house, closed the door behind him, and heard a new story come to him in the silence afterwards.

The Lone Ranger and Tonto Fistfight in Heaven   [1993]

Too hot to sleep so I walked down to the Third Avenue 7-11 for a Creamsicle and the company of a graveyard-shift cashier. I know that game. I worked graveyard for a Seattle 7-11 and got robbed once too often. The last time the bastard locked me in the cooler. He even took my money and basketball shoes.

The graveyard-shift worker in the Third Avenue 7-11 looked like they all do. Acne scars and a bad haircut, work pants that showed off his white socks, and those cheap black shoes that have no support. My arches still ache from my year at the Seattle 7-11.

"Hello," he asked when I walked into his store. "How you doing?"

I gave him a half-wave as I headed back to the freezer. He looked me over so he could describe me to the police later. I knew the look. One of my old girl-friends said I started to look at her that way, too. She left me not long after that. No, I left her and don't blame her for anything. That's how it happened. When one person starts to look at another like a criminal, then the love is over. It's logical.

"I don't trust you," she said to me. "You get too angry."   5

She was white and I lived with her in Seattle. Some nights we fought so bad that I would just get in my car and drive all night, only stop to fill up on gas. In fact, I worked the graveyard shift to spend as much time away from her as possible. But I learned all about Seattle that way, driving its back ways and dirty alleys.

Sometimes, though, I would forget where I was and get lost. I'd drive for hours, searching for something familiar. Seems like I'd spent my whole life that way, looking for anything I recognized. Once, I ended up in a nice residential neighborhood and somebody must have been worried because the police showed up and pulled me over.

"What are you doing out here?" the police officer asked me, as he looked over my license and registration.

"I'm lost."

"Well, where are you supposed to be?" he asked me, and I knew there were   10
plenty of places I wanted to be, but none where I was supposed to be.

"I got in a fight with my girlfriend," I said. "I was just driving around, blowing off steam, you know?"

"Well, you should be more careful where you drive," the officer said. "You're making people nervous. You don't fit the profile of the neighborhood."

I wanted to tell him that I didn't really fit the profile of the country but I knew it would just get me into trouble.

"Can I help you?" the 7-11 clerk asked me loudly, searching for some response that would reassure him that I wasn't an armed robber. He knew this dark skin and long, black hair of mine was dangerous. I had potential.

"Just getting a Creamsicle," I said after a long interval. It was a sick twist to   15
pull on the guy, but it was late and I was bored. I grabbed my Creamsicle and walked back to the counter slowly, scanned the aisles for effect. I wanted to whistle low and menacingly but I never learned to whistle.

"Pretty hot out tonight?" he asked, that old rhetorical weather bullshit question designed to put us both at ease.

"Hot enough to make you go crazy," I said and smiled. He swallowed hard like a white man does in those situations. I looked him over. Same old green, red, and white 7-11 jacket and thick glasses. But he wasn't ugly, just misplaced and marked by loneliness. If he wasn't working there that night, he'd be at home alone, flipping through channels and wishing he could afford HBO or Showtime.

"Will this be all?" he asked me, in that company effort to make me do some impulse shopping. Like adding a clause onto a treaty. *We'll take Washington and Oregon and you get six pine trees and a brand-new Chrysler Cordoba.* I knew how to make and break promises.

"No," I said and paused. "Give me a Cherry Slushie, too."

"What size?" he asked, relieved.   20

"Large," I said, and he turned his back to me to make the drink. He realized his mistake but it was too late. He stiffened, ready for the gunshot or the blow behind the ear. When it didn't come, he turned back to me.

"I'm sorry," he said. "What size did you say?"

"Small," I said and changed the story.

"But I thought you said large."

"If you knew I wanted a large, then why did you ask me again?" I asked him 25
and laughed. He looked at me, couldn't decide if I was giving him serious shit or
just goofing. There was something about him I liked, even if it was three in the
morning and he was white.

"Hey," I said. "Forget the Slushie. What I want to know is if you know all
the words to the theme from 'The Brady Bunch'?"

He looked at me, confused at first, then laughed.

"Shit," he said. "I was hoping you weren't crazy. You were scaring me."

"Well, I'm going to get crazy if you don't know the words."

He laughed loudly then, told me to take the Creamsicle for free. He was the 30
graveyard-shift manager and those little demonstrations of power tickled him.
All seventy-five cents of it. I knew how much everything cost.

"Thanks," I said to him and walked out the door. I took my time walking
home, let the heat of the night melt the Creamsicle all over my hand. At three in
the morning I could act just as young as I wanted to act. There was no one
around to ask me to grow up.

In Seattle, I broke lamps. She and I would argue and I'd break a lamp, just
pick it up and throw it down. At first she'd buy replacement lamps, expensive
and beautiful. But after a while she'd buy lamps from Goodwill or garage sales.
Then she just gave up the idea entirely and we'd argue in the dark.

"You're just like your brother," she'd yell. "Drunk all the time and stupid."

"My brother don't drink that much."

She and I never tried to hurt each other physically. I did love her, after all, 35
and she loved me. But those arguments were just as damaging as a fist. Words
can be like that, you know? Whenever I get into arguments now, I remember her
and I also remember Muhammad Ali. He knew the power of his fists but, more
importantly, he knew the power of his words, too. Even though he only had an
IQ of 80 or so, Ali was a genius. And she was a genius, too. She knew exactly
what to say to cause me the most pain.

But don't get me wrong. I walked through that relationship with an execu-
tioner's hood. Or more appropriately, with war paint and sharp arrows. She was
a kindergarten teacher and I continually insulted her for that.

"Hey, schoolmarm," I asked. "Did your kids teach you anything new today?"

And I always had crazy dreams. I always have had them, but it seemed they
became nightmares more often in Seattle.

In one dream, she was a missionary's wife and I was a minor war chief. We
fell in love and tried to keep it secret. But the missionary caught us fucking in
the barn and shot me. As I lay dying, my tribe learned of the shooting and attacked the whites all across the reservation. I died and my soul drifted above the
reservation.

Disembodied, I could see everything that was happening. Whites killing In- 40
dians and Indians killing whites. At first it was small, just my tribe and the few

whites who lived there. But my dream grew, intensified. Other tribes arrived on horseback to continue the slaughter of whites, and the United States Cavalry rode into battle.

The most vivid image of that dream stays with me. Three mounted soldiers played polo with a dead Indian woman's head. When I first dreamed it, I thought it was just a product of my anger and imagination. But since then, I've read similar accounts of that kind of evil in the old West. Even more terrifying, though, is the fact that those kinds of brutal things are happening today in places like El Salvador.

All I know for sure, though, is that I woke from that dream in terror, packed up all my possessions, and left Seattle in the middle of the night.

"I love you," she said as I left her. "And don't ever come back."

I drove through the night, over the Cascades, down into the plains of central Washington, and back home to the Spokane Indian Reservation.

When I finished the Creamsicle that the 7-11 clerk gave me, I held the 45 wooden stick up into the air and shouted out very loudly. A couple lights flashed on in windows and a police car cruised by me a few minutes later. I waved to the men in blue and they waved back accidentally. When I got home it was still too hot to sleep so I picked up a week-old newspaper from the floor and read.

There was another civil war, another terrorist bomb exploded, and one more plane crashed and all aboard were presumed dead. The crime rate was rising in every city with populations larger than 100,000, and a farmer in Iowa shot his banker after foreclosure on his 1,000 acres.

A kid from Spokane won the local spelling bee by spelling the word *rhinoceros*.

When I got back to the reservation, my family wasn't surprised to see me. They'd been expecting me back since the day I left for Seattle. There's an old Indian poet who said that Indians can reside in the city, but they can never live there. That's as close to truth as any of us can get.

Mostly I watched television. For weeks I flipped through channels, searched for answers in the game shows and soap operas. My mother would circle the want ads in red and hand the paper to me.

"What are you going to do with the rest of your life?" she asked.   50

"Don't know," I said, and normally, for almost any other Indian in the country, that would have been a perfectly fine answer. But I was special, a former college student, a smart kid. I was one of those Indians who was supposed to make it, to rise above the rest of the reservation like a fucking eagle or something. I was the new kind of warrior.

For a few months I didn't even look at the want ads my mother circled, just left the newspaper where she had set it down. After a while, though, I got tired of television and started to play basketball again. I'd been a good player in high school, nearly great, and almost played at the college I attended for a couple years. But I'd been too out of shape from drinking and sadness to ever be good again. Still, I liked the way the ball felt in my hands and the way my feet felt inside my shoes.

At first I just shot baskets by myself. It was selfish, and I also wanted to learn the game again before I played against anybody else. Since I had been good before and embarrassed fellow tribal members, I knew they would want to take revenge on me. Forget about the cowboys versus Indians business. The most intense competition on any reservation is Indians versus Indians.

But on the night I was ready to play for real, there was this white guy at the gym, playing with all the Indians.

"Who is that?" I asked Jimmy Seyler.   55

"He's the new BIA chief's kid."

"Can he play?"

"Oh, yeah."

And he could play. He played Indian ball, fast and loose, better than all the Indians there.

"How long's he been playing here?" I asked.   60

"Long enough."

I stretched my muscles, and everybody watched me. All these Indians watched one of their old and dusty heroes. Even though I had played most of my ball at the white high school I went to, I was still all Indian, you know? I was Indian when it counted, and this BIA kid needed to be beaten by an Indian, any Indian.

I jumped into the game and played well for a little while. It felt good. I hit a few shots, grabbed a rebound or two, played enough defense to keep the other team honest. Then that white kid took over the game. He was too good. Later, he'd play college ball back East and would nearly make the Knicks team a couple years on. But we didn't know any of that would happen. We just knew he was better that day and every other day.

The next morning I woke up tired and hungry, so I grabbed the want ads, found a job I wanted, and drove to Spokane to get it. I've been working at the high school exchange program ever since, typing and answering phones. Sometimes I wonder if the people on the other end of the line know that I'm Indian and if their voices would change if they did know.

One day I picked up the phone and it was her, calling from Seattle.   65

"I got your number from your mom," she said. "I'm glad you're working."

"Yeah, nothing like a regular paycheck."

"Are you drinking?"

"No, I've been on the wagon for almost a year."

"Good."   70

The connection was good. I could hear her breathing in the spaces between our words. How do you talk to the real person whose ghost has haunted you? How do you tell the difference between the two?

"Listen," I said. "I'm sorry for everything."

"Me, too."

"What's going to happen to us?" I asked her and wished I had the answer for myself.

"I don't know," she said. "I want to change the world."   75

These days, living alone in Spokane, I wish I lived closer to the river, to the falls where ghosts of salmon jump. I wish I could sleep. I put down my paper or book and turn off all the lights, lie quietly in the dark. It may take hours, even years, for me to sleep again. There's nothing surprising or disappointing in that.

I know how all my dreams end anyway.

Somebody Kept Saying Powwow   [1993]

I knew Norma before she ever met her husband-to-be, James Many Horses. I knew her back when there was good fry bread to be eaten at the powwow, before the old women died and took their recipes with them. That's how it's going. Sometimes it feels like our tribe is dying a piece of bread at a time. But Norma, she was always trying to save it, she was a cultural lifeguard, watching out for those of us that were so close to drowning.

She was really young, too, not all that much older than me, but everybody called her grandmother anyway, as a sign of respect.

"Hey, grandmother," I said when she walked by me as I sat at another terrible fry bread stand.

"Hi, Junior," she said and walked over to me. She shook my hand, loosely, like Indians do, using only her fingers. Not like those tight grips that white people use to prove something. She touched my hand like she was glad to see me, not like she wanted to break bones.

"Are you dancing this year?" I asked.   5

"Of course. Haven't you been down to the dance hall?"

"Not yet."

"Well, you should go watch the dancing. It's important."

We talked for a while longer, told some stories, and then she went on about her powwow agenda. Everybody wanted to talk to Norma, to share some time with her. I just liked to sit with her, put my reservation antennas up and adjust my reception. Didn't you know that Indians are born with two antennas that rise up and field emotional signals? Norma always said that Indians are the most sensitive people on the planet. For that matter, Indians are more sensitive than animals, too. We don't just watch things happen. Watching automatically makes the watcher part of the happening. That's what Norma taught me.

"Everything matters," she said. "Even the little things."   10

But it was more than just some bullshit Native religion, some fodder for the crystal-happy. Norma lived her life like we should all do. She didn't drink or smoke. But she could spend a night in the Powwow Tavern and dance hard. She could dance Indian and white. And that's a mean feat, since the two methods of dancing are mutually exclusive. I've seen Indians who are champion fancy-dancers trip all over themselves when Paula Abdul is on the jukebox in the bar. And I've seen Indians who could do all this MTV Club dancing, electric slides and shit, all over the place and then look like a white person stumbling through the sawdust of a powwow.

One night I was in the Powwow Tavern and Norma asked me to dance. I'd never danced with her before, hadn't really danced much at all, Indian or white.

"Move your ass," she said. "This ain't Browning, Montana. It's Las Vegas."

So I moved my ass, shook my skinny brown butt until the whole bar was laughing, which was good. Even if I was the one being laughed at. And Norma and I laughed all night long and danced together all night long. Most nights, before James Many Horses showed up, Norma would dance with everybody, not choosing any favorites. She was a diplomat. But she only danced with me that night. Believe me, it was an honor. After the bar closed, she even drove me home since everybody else was headed to parties and I wanted to go to sleep.

"Hey," she said on the way home. "You can't dance very good but you got 15
the heart of a dancer."

"Heart of the dancer," I said. "And feet like the buffalo."

And we laughed.

She dropped me at home, gave me a good night hug, and then drove on to her own HUD house. I went into my house and dreamed about her. Not like you think. I dreamed her a hundred years ago, riding bareback down on Little Falls Flats. Her hair was unbraided and she was yelling something to me as she rode closer to where I stood. I couldn't understand what she was saying, though. But it was a dream and I listen to my dreams.

"I dreamed about you the other night," I said to Norma the next time I saw her. I told her about the dream.

"I don't know what that means," she said. "I hope it's nothing bad." 20

"Maybe it just means I have a crush on you."

"No way," she said and laughed. "I've seen you hanging around with that Nadine Moses woman. You must have been dreaming about her."

"Nadine don't know how to ride a horse," I said.

"Who said anything about horses?" Norma said, and we both laughed for a good long time.

Norma could ride horses like she did live one hundred years ago. She was a 25
rodeo queen, but not one of those rhinestone women. She was a roper, a breaker of wild ponies. She wrestled steers down to the ground and did that goofy old three-legged knot dance. Norma just wasn't quite as fast as some of the other Indian cowboys, though. I think, in the end, she was just having a good time. She'd hang with the cowboys and they'd sing songs for her, 49er songs that echoed beyond the evening's last campfire.

Norma, I want to marry you
Norma, I want to make you mine
And we'll go dancing, dancing, dancing

until the sun starts to shine.
Way yah hi yo, Way yah hi yo!

Some nights Norma took an Indian cowboy or a cowboy Indian back to her
tipi. And that was good. Some people would have you believe it's wrong, but it
was two people sharing some body medicine. It wasn't like Norma was out snag-
ging for men all the time. Most nights she just went home alone and sang herself to sleep.

Some people said that Norma took a woman home with her once in a while,
too. Years ago, homosexuals were given special status within the tribe. They had
powerful medicine. I think it's even more true today, even though our tribe has
assimilated into homophobia. I mean, a person has to have magic to assert their
identity without regard to all the bullshit, right?

Anyhow, or as we say around here, anyhoo, Norma held on to her status
within the tribe despite all the rumors, the stories, the lies and jealous gossip.
Even after she married that James Many Horses, who told so many jokes that he
even made other Indians get tired of his joking.

The funny thing is that I always thought Norma would end up marrying
Victor since she was so good at saving people and Victor needed more saving
than most anybody besides Lester FallsApart. But she and Victor never got along,
much. Victor was kind of a bully in his younger days, and I don't think Norma
ever forgave him. I doubt Victor ever forgave himself for it. I think he said *I'm
sorry* more than any other human being alive.

I remember once when Norma and I were sitting in the Powwow Tavern and 30
Victor walked in, drunker than drunk.

"Where's the powwow?" Victor yelled.

"You're in the Powwow," somebody yelled back.

"No, I don't mean this goddamn bar. I mean, where's the powwow?"

"In your pants," somebody else yelled and we all laughed.

Victor staggered up to our table. 35

"Junior," he asked. "Where's the powwow?"

"There ain't no powwow going on," I said.

"Well," Victor said. "Somebody out in the parking lot kept saying powwow.
And you know I love a good goddamn powwow."

"We all love a good powwow," Norma said.

Victor smiled a drunk smile at her, one of those smiles only possible through 40
intoxication. The lips fall at odd angles, the left side of the face is slightly paralyzed, and skin shines with alcohol sweat. Nothing remotely approaching beauty.

"I'm going to go find the goddamn powwow," Victor said then and staggered out the door. He's on the wagon now but he used to get so drunk.

"Good luck," Norma said. That's one of the strangest things about the tribal
ties that still exists. A sober Indian has infinite patience with a drunk Indian,
even most of the Indians who have completely quit drinking. There ain't many
who do stay sober. Most spend time in Alcoholics Anonymous meetings, and

everybody gets to know the routines and use them on all occasions, not just at
A.A. meetings.

"Hi, my name is Junior," I usually say when I walk into a bar or party where
Indians have congregated.

"Hi, Junior," all the others shout in an ironic unison.

A few of the really smart-asses about the whole A.A. thing carry around 45
little medals indicating how long they've been continuously drunk.

"Hi, my name is Lester FallsApart, and I've been drunk for twenty-seven
straight years."

Norma didn't much go for that kind of humor, though. She laughed when
it was funny but she didn't start anything up. Norma, she knew all about Indian
belly laughter, the kind of laughter that made Indians squeeze their eyes up so
tight they looked Chinese. Maybe that's where those rumors about crossing the
Bering Bridge started. Maybe some of us Indians just laughed our way over to
China 25,000 years ago and jumpstarted that civilization. But whenever I started
in on my crazy theories, Norma would put her finger to my lips really gently.

"Junior," she would say with gentleness and patience. "Shut the fuck up."

Norma always was a genius with words. She used to write stories for the
tribal newspaper. She was even their sports reporter for a while. I still got the
news clipping of a story she wrote about the basketball game I won back in high
school. In fact, I keep it tucked in my wallet and if I get drunk enough, I'll pull it
out and read from it aloud, like it was a goddamn poem or something. But the
way Norma wrote, I guess it was something close to a poem:

Junior's Jumpshot Just Enough for Redskin Win

With three seconds left on the clock last Saturday night and the
Springdale Chargers in possession of the ball, it looked like even the
Wellpinit Redskins might have to call in the United States Cavalry to help
them win the first game of this just-a-baby basketball season.

But Junior Polatkin tipi-creeped the Chargers by stealing the inbounds
pass and then stealing the game away when he hit a three-thousand-foot
jumper at the buzzer.

"I doubt we'll be filing any charges against Junior for theft," Tribal
Chief of Police David WalksAlong said. "This was certainly a case of self-
defense."

People were gossiping all around the rez about Junior's true identity.

"I think he was Crazy Horse for just a second," said an anonymous and
maybe-just-a-little-crazy-themselves source.

This reporter thinks Junior happened to be a little lucky so his new Indian name will be Lucky Shot. Still, luck or not, Junior has earned a couple
points more on the Warrior Scale.

Whenever I pull that clipping out with Norma around, she always threatens 50
to tear it up. But she never does. She's proud of it, I can tell. I'd be proud, too. I
mean, I'm proud I won that game. It was the only game we won that year. In

fact, it was the only game the Wellpinit Redskins won in three years. It wasn't like we had bad teams. We always had two or three of the best players in the league, but winning wasn't always as important as getting drunk after the game for some and for going to the winter powwows for others. Some games, we'd only have five players.

I always wished we could have suited Norma up. She was taller than all of us and a better player than most of us. I don't really remember her playing in high school, but people say she could have played college ball if she would've gone to college. Same old story. But the reservation people who say things like that have never been off the reservation.

"What's it like out there?" Norma asked me when I came back from college, from the city, from cable television and delivered pizza.

"It's like a bad dream you never wake up from," I said, and it's true. Sometimes I still feel like half of me is lost in the city, with its foot wedged into a steam grate or something. Stuck in one of those revolving doors, going round and round while all the white people are laughing. Standing completely still on an escalator that will not move, but I didn't have the courage to climb the stairs by myself. Stuck in an elevator between floors with a white woman who keeps wanting to touch my hair.

There are some things that Indians would've never invented if given the chance.

"But the city gave you a son," Norma said, and that was true enough. Some-   55
times, though, it felt like half a son because the city had him during the week and every other weekend. The reservation only got him for six days a month. Visitation rights. That's how the court defined them. Visitation rights.

"Do you ever want kids?" I asked Norma.

"Yeah, of course," she said. "I want a dozen. I want my own tribe."

"You're kidding."

"Kind of. Don't know if I want to raise kids in this world. It's getting uglier by the second. And not just on the reservation."

"I know what you mean," I said. "You see where two people got shot in the   60
bus station in Spokane last week? In Spokane! It's getting to be like New York City."

"New York City enough."

Norma was the kind of person who made you honest. She was so completely honest herself that you couldn't help it. Pretty soon I'd be telling her all my secrets, the bad and good.

"What's the worst thing you ever did?" she asked me.

"Probably that time I watched Victor beat the shit out of Thomas Builds-the-Fire."

"I remember that. I'm the one who broke it up. But you were just a kid.   65
Must be something worse than that."

I thought about it awhile, but it didn't take me long to figure out what the worst thing I ever did was.

It was at a basketball game when I was in college. I was with a bunch of guys from my dormitory, all white guys, and we were drunk, really drunk. The other team had this player who just got out of prison. I mean, this guy was about twenty-eight and had a tough life. Grew up in inner-city Los Angeles and finally made it out, made it to college and was playing and studying hard. If you think about it, he and I had a whole lot in common. Much more in common than I had with those white boys I was drunk with.

Anyway, when that player comes out, I don't even remember his name or maybe I don't want to remember it, we all start chanting at him. Really awful shit. Hateful. We all had these big cards we made to look like those GET OUT OF JAIL FREE cards in Monopoly. One guy was running around in a black-and-white convict shirt with a fake ball-and-chain. It was a really bad scene. The local newspaper had a big write-up. We even made it into a *People* Magazine article. It was about that player and how much he'd gone through and how he still had to fight so much ignorance and hate. When they asked him how it felt during that game where we all went crazy, he said, *It hurt.*

After I told Norma that story, she was quiet for a long time. A long time.

"If I drank," she said, "I would be getting drunk right about now because of that one." 70

"I've gotten drunk on it a few times."

"And if it still bothers you this much now," Norma said, "then think how bad that guy feels about it."

"I think about him all the time."

After I told Norma that story, she treated me differently for about a year. She wasn't mean or distant. Just different. But I understood. People can do things completely against their nature, completely. It's like some tiny earthquake comes roaring through your body and soul, and it's the only earthquake you'll ever feel. But it damages so much, cracks the foundations of your life forever.

So I just figured Norma wouldn't ever forgive me. She was like that. She was 75 probably the most compassionate person on the reservation but she was also the most passionate. Then one day in the Trading Post she walked up to me and smiled.

"Pete Rose," she said.

"What?" I asked, completely confused.

"Pete Rose," she repeated.

"What?" I asked again, even more confused.

"That's your new Indian name," she said. "Pete Rose." 80

"Why?"

"Because you two got a whole lot in common."

"How?"

"Listen," Norma said. "Pete Rose played major league baseball in four different decades, has more hits than anybody in history. Hell, think about it. Going back to Little League and high school and all that, he's probably been smacking the ball around forever. Noah probably pitched him a few on the Ark. But after all that, all that greatness, he's only remembered for the bad stuff."

"Gambling," I said.   85

"That ain't right," she said.

"Not at all."

After that, Norma treated me the same as she did before she found out what I did in college. She made me try to find that basketball player, but I didn't have any luck. What would I have told him if I did find him? Would I just tell him that I was Pete Rose? Would he have understood that?

Then, on one strange, strange day when a plane had to emergency land on the reservation highway, and the cooler in the Trading Post broke down and they were giving away ice cream because it would've been wasted, and a bear fell asleep on the roof of the Catholic church, Norma ran up to me, nearly breathless.

"Pete Rose," she said. "They just voted to keep you out of the Hall of Fame.   90 I'm sorry. But I still love you."

"Yeah, I know, Norma. I love you, too."

Tomson Highway

Interview with Sherman Alexie   [1997]

Tomson Highway: *When did you start writing?*

Sherman Alexie: I started writing because I kept fainting in human anatomy class and needed a career change. The only class that fit where the human anatomy class had been was a poetry writing workshop. I always liked poetry. I'd never heard of, or nobody'd ever showed me, a book written by a First Nations person, ever. I got into the class, and my professor, Alex Kwo, gave me an anthology of contemporary Native American poetry called *Songs from This Earth on Turtle's Back*. I opened it up and — oh my gosh — I saw my life in poems and stories for the very first time.

T.H.: *Who were some of the writers in the book?*

S.A.: Linda Hogan, Simon Ortiz, Joy Harjo, James Welch, Adrian Louis. There were poems about reservation life: fry bread, bannock, 49's, fried baloney, government food, and terrible housing. But there was also joy and happiness.

There's a line by a Paiute poet named Adrian Louis that says, "Oh, Uncle Adrian, I'm in the reservation of my mind." I thought, "Oh my God, somebody understands me!" At that moment I realized, "I can do this!" That's when I started writing — in 1989.

T.H.: *The poetry that you would have studied in American Studies, for instance, the poetry of Wallace Stevens or e. e. cummings or Emily Dickinson never influenced you at all?*

S.A.: Of course it did. I loved that stuff. I still love it. Walt Whitman and Emily Dickinson are two of my favorites. Wallace Stevens leaves me kind of dry, but the other poets, they're still a primary influence. I always tell people my literary influences are Stephen King, John Steinbeck, my mother, my grandfather, and the Brady Bunch.

T.H.: *Then you moved on to short stories.*

S.A.: I'd written a couple of them in college. After my first book of poems, *The Business of Fancydancing*, was published by Hanging Loose Press in Brooklyn, New York, I got a great *New York Times* book review. The review called me "one of the major lyric voices of our time." I was a twenty-five-year-old Spokane Indian guy working as a secretary at a high school exchange program in Spokane, Washington, when my poetry editor faxed that review to me. I pulled it out of the fax machine beside my desk and read, "one of the major lyric voices of our time." I thought, "Great! Where do I go from here!?" After that, the agents started calling *me*.

T.H.: *Where did that book of poetry come from?*

S.A.: It was my first semester poetry manuscript. Part of the assignment was to submit to literary magazines. The one I liked in the Washington State library was *Hanging Loose* magazine. I liked that it started the same year I was born. The magazine, the press, and I are the same age. Over the next year and a half they kept taking poems of mine to publish. Then they asked if I had a manuscript. I said, "Yes!" and sent it in.

It was a *thousand* copies. I figured I'd sell a hundred and fifty to my family. My mom would buy a hundred herself and that would be about it. But, it took off. I never expected it. Sometimes I think it would have been nicer if it had not been as big, because my career has been a rocket ride. There's a lot of pressure.

Åse Nygren

A World of Story-Smoke: A Conversation with Sherman Alexie   [2005]

Åse Nygren: What are some of the inspirations and motivations behind your writing? Are they autobiographical, political, or historical?

Sherman Alexie: Like we were saying just before we turned the tape on, people in Scandinavia don't really know about Indian writers or know that there even are Indian writers. I didn't know either. Even though I was growing up on a reservation, and going to reservation schools, I had never really been shown Indian literature before. So it wasn't even a possibility growing up. I loved reading but I hadn't thought of a career as a writer. I hadn't thought about books as a career in any form. I took a class in creative writing because I couldn't handle human anatomy lab and it was the only class that fit my schedule. This was the first time anyone had shown me contemporary poetry. The most contemporary poem I had read before was "The Waste Land." I had no idea you could write about NOW. I read Allen Ginsberg's "Howl" for the first time. Even Langston

Hughes felt new to me. And I fell in love with it immediately. Over night, I knew I was going to be a writer.

ÅN: Were there any Indian writers on the reading list for the poetry class you took?

SA: The poetry teacher gave me a book called *Songs from This Earth on Turtle's Back*, an anthology on Native literature by Joseph Bruchac. Before I read that book I had no idea that you could write about Indian life with powwows, ceremonies, broken down cars, cheap motels; all this stuff that was my life as I was growing up on the reservation. I remember in particular one line by Adrian Louis, a Pauite poet: "Adrian, I'm in the reservation of my mind!" It captured for me the way I felt about myself, at least then. It was nothing I'd ever had before. I thought to myself: I want to write like this! So that's where it began. The beginning was accidental. But I got very serious about it quickly. I went through the college library looking at poetry journals trying to figure out what was going on in the world, trying to catch up, essentially, for a lifetime of not reading.

ÅN: Did you read all different kinds of poetry, or did you focus on works by American Indians?

SA: Any poetry. Anything and everything. I pulled books off the shelves randomly because I liked the title, or the cover, or the author photo. I read hundreds of poems over a year or so to catch up. As I sat there in the poetry stacks in the library a whole new world opened to me. Before, I had always thought that I was a freak in the way I saw and felt about the world. As I started reading the works of all these poets I realized that I, at least, wasn't the only freak! [Laughs] I think we belong to a lot of tribes; culturally, ethnically, and racially. I'm a poet and this is the world in which I belong.

ÅN: So your ambitions and motivations weren't political to begin with?

SA: No. My writing was very personal and autobiographical. I was simply finding out who I was and who I wanted to be. As I started writing I became more political, much because of people's reactions to me. I was writing against so many ideas of what I was supposed to be writing. So even though much of my early work deals with alcohol and alcoholism because of personal experiences, I got a lot of criticism because alcoholism is such a loaded topic for Indians. People thought I was writing about stereotypes, but more than anything I was writing about my own life. As an Indian, you don't have the luxury of being called an autobiographical writer often. You end up writing for the whole race. At the beginning of my career I was twenty-one years old, and I didn't have any defense against that. So I became political because people viewed me politically. I got political to fight people's ideas about me. It is only in the last few years that my politics has found a way into my work that feels natural. Part of the reason is because you grow older. The way I think about it is that I used to spend more time looking inside myself, looking internally. Now I look at more of the world and a wider range of people. . . .

ÅN: One important concern among American Indian writers has been the question of how one deals with a painful past, such as the one shared by the Indian peoples of the United States, without falling into the trap of victimization. How important is this issue for you when you write your fiction?

SA: I write autobiographically, so when you talk about surviving pain and trauma and getting out of it — I did, I have! But the people I know have not. So what do I do in my literature? Do I portray the Indian world as I see it? And I do see it as doomed, and that you have to get lucky to escape that. Should I write the literature of hope no matter how I feel? No! I'm not hopeful. So how do you avoid victimization? We can't. We are victims. . . .

ÅN: I find the concept of "collective trauma" particularly useful concerning the suffering that many of your characters are experiencing. Many of them suffer from not only personal losses and grievances — absent fathers, poverty, unemployment, alcoholism, etc. — but also from a cultural loss and a collective trauma, which include experiences of racism and stereotyping. Their losses and grievances affect their behavior and their lives on many levels. In my view, your fiction explores how such trauma both damages and creates community and identity alike. Both identity and community are, of course, condemned to ongoing dysfunction. Do you think that suffering is part of what constitutes Indianness? Perhaps in a somewhat comparable way by which we have come to associate African American identity with slavery, or Jewish identity with the Holocaust? If so, how does this relation differ from, e.g., the relation between African Americans and suffering, or Jews and suffering?

SA: Yes! The phrase I've also used is "blood memory." I think the strongest parallel in my mind has always been the Jewish people and the Holocaust. Certainly, their oppression has been constant for 1900 years longer, but the fact is that you cannot separate our identity from our pain. At some point it becomes primarily our identity. The whole idea of authenticity — "How Indian are you?" — is the most direct result of the fact that we don't know what an American Indian identity is. There is no measure anymore. There is no way of knowing, except perhaps through our pain. And so, we're lost. We're always wandering. . . .

ÅN: Although the subject matters in your texts are morally and ethically engaging, the same texts are often ironic, satiric, and full of humor. I read your ironic and satiric rethinking, even defamiliarization, of a painful past, in alignment with writer Art Spiegelmann and filmmaker Roberto Benigni. Spiegelmann's two books in cartoon form, entitled *Maus: A Survivor's Tale I* and *II*, and Benigni's film *Life Is Beautiful* both deal with the Jewish Holocaust in the comic mode, and have, consequently, shocked readers/viewers out of any lingering sense of familiarity with the historic events described. Would you like your books to have a similar effect on your readers? What are some of the gains? Dangers?

SA: Well, I'm a big fan of graphic novels. I like their immediacy. Automatically when you look at a graphic novel, or when you look at a cartoon, there is always an ironical, satirical edge and an underlying humor. So yes, I aim to be funny, and I aim for my humor to be very political. But I think more along the lines of political stand-up comedians like Richard Pryor and Lenny Bruce than I do about other writers.

ÅN: What might be some of the gains and dangers?

SA: Dangers? Playing to the audience. Reacting completely to the audience rather than generating it from yourself, so that you're reflexive and you're performing rather than dealing with something on an emotional level. I think I have a tendency in my work to lapse into performance mode. Rather than something out of my heart, it ends up being something on the surface designed for effect. One of the great things is that through that immediacy of performance and humor you can reach people who otherwise might not be listening. I think being funny breaks down barriers between people. I can get up in front of any crowd, and if I make them laugh first I can say almost anything to them. . . .

ÅN: Are you ever afraid that the comical element will subvert attention from the gravitas of your writing?

SA: Yes, it happens all the time. People assume that you're not being serious because you're being funny. By and large I figure that people who say those sort of things aren't funny. And being funny is just how I am. I can't just stop . . . [Laughs]. But it's also a personal defense, of course. When I don't want to talk about something, or when I'm uncomfortable. It's not all good, humor, but it's always serious.

Joseph L. Coulombe

The Approximate Size of His Favorite Humor: Sherman Alexie's Comic Connections and Disconnections in *The Lone Ranger and Tonto Fistfight in Heaven*   [2002]

In this essay I will argue that Alexie's humor is central to a constructive social and moral purpose evident throughout his fiction but particularly in his collection of short stories, *The Lone Ranger and Tonto Fistfight in Heaven*. He uses humor—or his characters use humor—to reveal injustice, protect self-esteem, heal wounds, and create bonds. The function of humor changes from scene to scene, shifting to serve these myriad goals. In *Indi'n Humor* Kenneth Lincoln explains the many different roles of humor within Indian communities. He describes "the contrary powers of Indian humor" as "[t]he powers to heal and to hurt, to bond and to exorcize, to renew and to purge" (5). Like the legendary Trickster figure, humor in Indian communities embodies shifting meanings and serves conflicting ends. However, rather than a sign of his "hip" irreverence for all things Indian, Alexie's sophisticated use of humor unsettles conventional ways of thinking and compels reevaluation and growth, which ultimately allows Indian characters to connect to their heritage in novel ways and forces non-Indian readers to reconsider simplistic generalizations.

In his best work to date, *The Lone Ranger and Tonto Fistfight in Heaven*, humor allows his characters to display strengths and hide weaknesses, to expose prejudices and avoid realities, and to create bonds and construct barricades. These "contrary powers" often coexist simultaneously, requiring the characters and readers to position and then reposition themselves within shifting personal and cultural contexts. Alexie's cross-cultural humor alternately engages readers — creating positive connections between individuals of diverse backgrounds — and disrupts communities (both Indian and white), erecting barriers that make constructive communication difficult. Here lies its principal challenge for readers. Alexie's shifting treatment of humor serves as a means of connection as well as an instrument of separation. However, it is precisely this complexity and plasticity that allow him to negotiate successfully the differences between Indian communities and mainstream American society, while simultaneously instigating crucial dialogue about social and moral issues especially important to Indian communities. . . .

I contend that Alexie's brand of humor, more than others perhaps, is "that trickster at the heart of the Native American imagination." As such, it embodies the potential for facilitating mutual understanding and respect between diverse peoples. By exploding expectations and compelling dialogue, humor teaches self-knowledge and social awareness, much like Trickster. Alexie's use of humor encourages readers to think anew by creating a space of shared inquiry and reciprocal empathy. . . . Alexie's humor . . . provides an emotional and intellectual meeting ground for his readers to reconsider reductive stereotypes and expectations. . . . Alexie challenges readers of diverse backgrounds to join together to reevaluate past and present ideologies. Humor generates a freely occupied space in which readers can begin sorting through the myriad connections and disconnections that face us all today. Stephen Evans, in an evaluation of Alexie's refashioning of stereotypes (particularly that of the "drunken Indian"), correctly notes how satire compels "the collaborative making of meaning between Alexie and his readers" (54). Readers are not passive receptacles; they engage, question, resist, learn, and grow during the reading process. They join Alexie . . . to hash out interpretations of the past, responses to the present, and prospects for the future. This delicate alliance between author and audience — facilitated in large part by humor — promises to be more effective than purely logical, historical, or traditional efforts to promote understanding. With its shifting layers and elaborate surprises, Alexie's humor disrupts readers' complacency and necessitates analysis, clarification, and, ultimately, identification.

Works Cited

Alexie, Sherman. *The Lone Ranger and Tonto Fistfight in Heaven*. New York: Harper Perennial, 1993.

Evans, Stephen F. "'Open Containers': Sherman Alexie's Drunken Indians." *American Indian Quarterly* 25.1 (Winter 2001): 46–72.

Lincoln, Kenneth. *Indi'n Humor: Bicultural Play in Native America*. New York: Oxford UP, 1993.

Jerome DeNuccio

Slow Dancing with Skeletons:
Sherman Alexie's *The Lone Ranger*
and Tonto Fistfight in Heaven   [2002]

The Spokane Indian characters in Sherman Alexie's short story collection *The Lone Ranger and Tonto Fistfight in Heaven* wage daily battle against small humiliations and perennial hurts. Situated on a reservation where the Department of Housing and Urban Development (HUD) houses, the Bureau of Indian Affairs (BIA) trucks, and commodity foods continually mirror paternalism and dependency, and where "tribal ties" and a cohesive "sense of community" (74) have waned, Alexie's characters confront the dilemma of how to be "real Indians," of how to find "their true names, their adult names" (20), of how to find a warrior dignity and courage when it is "too late to be warriors in the old way" (63), of how to ameliorate what Adrian C. Louis has termed "the ghost-pain of history" (35) — that haunting sense of personal and cultural loss that generates a paralyzing sense of ineffectuality. They struggle to cope with passivity, cynicism, and despair to find healing for the pain that turns into self-pity and the anger that turns into self-loathing.

One of Alexie's characters, Thomas Builds-the-Fire, a Spokane storyteller, articulates a useful image for understanding the distress and anguish these characters experience: *"There are things you should learn,"* he tells Victor and Junior, two young Spokanes who either narrate or are featured in eighteen of the collection's twenty-two stories. "Your past is a skeleton walking one step behind you, and your future is a skeleton walking one step in front of you." Indians, thus, are always *"trapped in the now."* But the skeletons are "not necessarily evil, unless you let them be." Because "these skeletons are made of memories, dreams, and voices," and because they are "wrapped up in the now," it becomes imperative to "keep moving, keep walking, in step with your skeletons." To stop or slow down, to "slow dance" with one's skeletons, risks being caught "in the in-between, between touching and becoming," the immediately felt and the potentially experienced. Such a situation severs the necessary relation between the structure of experience that at any one moment has shaped each life and the structure of ongoing time to which that life must continuously adapt and in which it develops. Keeping in step is not easy, however, for "your skeletons will talk to you, tell you to sit down and take a rest, . . . make you promises, tell you all the things you want to hear." They can "dress up" as seductive women, as a best friend offering a drink, as parents offering gifts. But, "no matter what they do," Thomas warns, "keep walking, keep moving" (21–22).

Thomas's image of the skeletons suggests that Indian subjectivity is dislogic, an interplay of perspectives and points of view that Bakhtin describes as "a plurality of unmerged consciousness" (Bakhtin, *Art and Answerability* 26). The self is positioned in a social space replete with memories, dreams, and voices that invite attention and response, that must be accommodated and negotiated if the self as an individual and a tribal subject is to emerge. Such negotiation, although paramount, is never easy. Memories, dreams, and voices form a dense network of social significations. They bear traces, are mediated by social relations and cultural dynamics, are inflected by family, friends, lovers, traditions, mass media, history. The term *Indian* names a subject position traversed by competing claims, saturated by multiple insinuations, the confusion or mastering force of which can induce a capitulation that Thomas identifies as failing to keep "in step with your skeletons." Such capitulation forecloses choice, and the result is often self-sabotage. Commenting on what appears to a white state trooper as an unmotivated suicide by a successful tribal member, Junior notes that "when we look in the mirror, see the history of our tribe in our eyes, taste failure in the tap water, and shake with old tears, we understand completely" (178). To "keep moving, keep walking, in step with your skeletons," then, suggests the necessity of listening to *and answering* the multiple voices that clamor for attention, a process of accommodation *and negotiation* that resists totalization and keeps the self "unconsummated" and "yet-to-be" (Bakhtin, *Art and Answerability* 13), moving always toward "becoming" rather than trapped "between touching and becoming," moving so that some coherent story of the self can be discovered. Thomas's image of the skeletons resonates throughout the collection's twenty-two stories, precisely because so many characters have fallen out of step and, thus, are suspended, passively and destructively, in a seemingly incoherent present.

Appropriately enough, the collection's opening story, "Every Little Hurricane," displays the provenance of those elements that problematize Indian subjectivity. Significantly, Alexie sets the story at a New Year's Eve party ushering in 1976, the bicentennial year. Nine-year-old Victor, whose parents are hosting the party, awakens to what he thinks is a hurricane but is really a metaphor Alexie uses to represent Victor's experience of the intensifying anger and painful memories, unleashed by alcohol, that circulate among the Indian partygoers. Victor's father, for instance, remembers his father being spit on at a Spokane bus stop; his mother remembers being involuntarily sterilized by an Indian Health Service (IHS) doctor after Victor's birth; his uncles Adolph and Arnold fight savagely because each reminds the other of childhood poverty so great that they hid crackers in their bedroom so they wouldn't have to go to bed hungry. Lying in his basement bedroom, Victor thinks he sees the ceiling lower "with the weight of each Indian's pain, until it was just inches from [his] nose" (8). As the adults' drunken rage fills the house, it blends with and feeds Victor's own nightmare fears of drowning in the rain, of alcoholic "fluids swallowing him," for at the age of five he had witnessed at a powwow an Indian man drown after passing out and falling "facedown into the water collected in a tire track." "Even at five," the narrator notes, "Victor understood what that meant, how it defined nearly everything" (7). Seeking the comfort of physical connection, he lies between his unconscious parents, and, putting a hand on each of their stomachs, feels "enough hunger in both, enough movement, enough geography and history, enough of everything to destroy the reservations" (10–11). As this image suggests, the confluence of past currents of suffering meet in Victor.

Given the intensity of the pain that presses upon Indian subjectivity, it is not surprising that the adults and their children get caught "in the in-between, between touching and becoming." The now of felt experience becomes ceaseless repetition of what has been. Without a viable counterbalance of Spokane culture — a point Alexie implies by setting his opening story on the eve of America's bicentennial festivities — the self appears finalized, unmodifiable because personal history appears consumed by the totalizing narrative of History. There is no sense of particularity, of difference that prevents the self from being absorbed into the larger culture's dominant narrative, no way to position the self so that its story unfolds within, not into, ongoing time, no "outsidedness" (Bakhtin, *Speech Genres* 7) where the choice to keep moving in step with one's skeletons keeps the impinging or "touching" now provisionally open to "becoming." . . .

Alexie's Indian characters are caught, as Bakhtin puts it, in the "framework of *other people's* words" about them, a framework that can "finalize and deaden" the self. But Alexie also demonstrates that in his characters "there is always something that only [they themselves] can reveal, in a free act of self-consciousness and discourse, something that does not submit to an externalizing second-hand definition" (Bakhtin, *Problems* 59, 58). And Alexie again uses the Spokane storyteller Thomas Builds-the-Fire to explain this resistant something.

> We are all given one thing by which our lives are measured, one determination. Mine are the stories which can change or not change the world. It doesn't matter which as long as I continue to tell the stories. . . . They are all I have. It's all I can do. (72–73)

Thomas's "one determination" posits subjectivity as both determined and particular, given, and its own measure of value. There is a personal narrative that unfolds within the larger culture's master narrative, which situates an individual subjectivity within the cultural topography and keeps it in step with the skeletons of past and future. For Thomas, only recognizing and choosing to follow that "one determination" matters. Thomas himself is widely ignored by his tribe, yet he tells his stories, stories that he does not author but that come to him from the culturally specific ground to which he is connected and which his storytelling articulates. What Thomas transmits, then, is the persistence and adaptability of Spokane signifying practices. . . .

Stories, then, teach survival. They *re*-member, bridging the rupture created by "what we have lost" (143), reconnecting time to aspect, past and present to progressive and perfective. Talking stories yields something "aboriginal and recognizable," something, as Thomas says, "by which our lives are measured." In the story "Family Portrait," Junior, contemplating his hands, is led to an acute realization of cultural loss:

> Years ago, the hands might have held the spear that held the salmon that held the dream of the tribe. Years ago, the hands might have touched

the hands of the dark-skinned men who touched medicine and the magic of ordinary gods. (196)

He then recalls a story his father told about "the first television he ever saw." It had "just one channel and all it showed was a woman sitting on top of the same television. Over and over until it hurt your eyes and head" (197). That image, persistently reflexive, depicts the kind of storytelling Alexie himself enacts: an unsparing examination of what is gone and what remains. That, Junior declares, is "how we find our history." And repossess it, too, for although such story-telling must, of necessity, measure "heartbreak" and "fear," it also becomes the means "by which we measure the beginning of all our lives," the means "by which we measure all our stories, until we understand that one story" — the offi-cial historiography — "can never be all" (197). Like the television that continu-ously frames the image it continuously represents, broadcasting in the present its backward gaze, Alexie's storytelling links "now" with "then," Indian lives with "five hundred years of convenient lies" (150), repeatedly, for though "it hurt[s] your eyes and head," it speaks survival.

Works Cited

Alexie, Sherman. *The Lone Ranger and Tonto Fistfight in Heaven*. New York: HarperCollins, 1994.

Bakhtin, Mikhail. *Art and Answerability: Early Philosophical Essays*. Eds. Michael Holquist and Vadim Liapunov. Trans. Vadim Liapunov. Austin: U of Texas P, 1990.

——. *Problems of Dostoevsky's Poetics*. Ed. and trans. Caryl Emerson. Min-neapolis: U of Minnesota P, 1984.

——. *Speech Genres and Other Late Essays*. Eds. Caryl Emerson and Michael Holquist. Trans. Vern W. McGee. Austin: U of Texas P, 1986.

Louis, Adrian C. *Skins*. New York: Crown, 1995.

James Cox

Muting White Noise: The Subversion of Popular Culture Narratives of Conquest in Sherman Alexie's Fiction [1997]

"Partisan writers have chronicled the story of conquest, and political stran-glers see to it that the public is kept blinded to actual conditions."
— *Cogewea* in Cogewea: The Half-Blood,
by Mourning Dove (Hum-Ishu-Ma)

Scholars from many academic disciplines have considered in detail the his-tory of European and Euro-American (mis)representation of Native American peoples. In *Savagism and Civilization* (1953), American literature professor Roy

Harvey Pearce considered the misrepresentations the result of the culturally sanctioned European belief in a binary of civilized and savage, of god-fearing and godless. Historian Robert Berkhofer Jr. entitles his study of misrepresentation *The White Man's Indian* (1978), and in *God Is Red* (1994), lawyer, political activist, and Native American studies professor Vine Deloria Jr. calls the stereotypical images "The Indians of the American Imagination." Native American novelists are also interested in this history of misrepresentation defined by written and visual ethnocentric narratives that tell a story of the European conquest of North America. These authors and their characters are involved in a narrative construction or reconstruction of a Native American-identified self that counters a racist historical context and the conquest narratives that are often sustained by the ubiquitous white man's Indian. Whether in brief critique, as in Louise Erdrich's, Louis Owens's, and James Welch's novels, or in full-scale revision and subversion, as in Sherman Alexie's work, Native American authors write new narratives of self-representation that critically question and often radically revise and subvert the dominant culture's conquest narratives and mass-produced misrepresentations of Native Americans. . . .

In *The Lone Ranger and Tonto Fistfight in Heaven*, Sherman Alexie's critical response to popular culture differs from Owens's, Erdrich's, and Welch's; rather than exclusively offering critiques of the conquest narratives the dominant culture produces and consumes, he illustrates the damage these narratives engender in his Native American characters, then rewrites or revises and subverts them. The radio and television program *The Lone Ranger* is a conquest narrative in that the American Indian, Tonto, is present only to serve the white hero/master, the Lone Ranger.[1] In Alexie's eight-word revision, Tonto refuses to be the loyal companion, a twentieth-century incarnation of the noble savage, literally a white man's (the Lone Ranger's) Indian. Tonto engages the Lone Ranger in a fistfight, and thereby refuses to occupy the subordinate social space defined and assigned to him by the Lone Ranger, the iconographic Western hero and the representative of the dominant culture. The subversive title is a guide to the short stories that follow. Alexie's characters are engaged in the same metaphorical fistfight as the titular Tonto: they struggle for self-definition and self-representation against the oppressive technological narratives that define Native Americans as a conquered people, as decontextualized, romanticized, subservient Tontos, and Native America as a conquered landscape.

A white noise infiltrates the fictionalized Spokane Reservation in several stories in Alexie's collection. White noise is the static on a television after a station plays "The Star-Spangled Banner," then ends its broadcasting day. Alexie uses the static to signify a broad historical context in which European and Euro-American culture has attempted to assimilate and destroy the Spokane. The white noise is, literally, the oppressive noise of white mass-produced culture, the loud demand to abandon all that is Indian and conform to the dictates of the invader's cultural belief system or be destroyed. As the source of the white noise, television is an instrument of late-twentieth-century colonialism. In

Alexie's fiction, conquest narratives disseminated by the technological tools of the dominant culture, such as television, have a pervasive, destructive influence on Native America. Cumulative references to television's destructive presence on Alexie's fictionalized reservation indicate this Euro-American technology is an iconographic evil against which the Spokane must struggle.[2]

Alexie composes "All I Wanted to Do Was Dance" of several narrative threads in the life of the primary character, Victor. In the episode that begins the story, Victor drinks at a bar and dances with Indian women as his "compensation, his confession, largest sin, and penance" for having fallen in love with a white woman who left him (83). After Victor shouts, "I started World War I . . . I shot Lincoln," Alexie writes, "He was underwater drunk, staring up at the faces of his past. He recognized Neil Armstrong and Christopher Columbus, his mother and father, James Dean, Sal Mineo, Natalie Wood" (84). Victor's desperate shout to be acknowledged is an attempt to inscribe himself into a history the dominant culture privileges, a history of great wars and great white men. In the catalog of the "faces of his past," Victor's image of his parents is trapped between a Euro-American and European cultural hero and the actors who play heroes of white middle-class rebellion in Nicholas Ray's 1955 film *Rebel Without a Cause*. He searches for an identity in a past confused and distorted by historical and popular culture narratives from which he has been excluded. . . .

Confused, distracted, and literally colonized by the omnipresent white noise permeating the reservation, Alexie's characters ignore Thomas Builds-the-Fire, the Spokane's best storyteller. Alexie introduces Thomas in *The Business of Fancy-dancing* in "Special Delivery," in which Thomas explains his friend Simon's definition of truth: "If there's a tree in the distance and you run to get there, run across the grass with all your heart, and you make it and touch the tree, press your face against the bark, then it's all true. But if you stumble and fall, lose your way, move to the city and buy a VCR and watch cowboy movies all the time, then nothing is true" (47). While truth cannot emerge from Hollywood's Westerns, Thomas's imagination produces truths when his ideas manifest as powerful images to other characters. In "Special Delivery," he commits a crime for which he is on trial in "The Trial of Thomas Builds-the-Fire" in *The Lone Ranger and Tonto Fistfight in Heaven*. A BIA agent explains Thomas is dangerous because of "[a] storytelling fetish accompanied by an extreme need to tell the truth" (93), and Alexie adds, "Thomas was in the holding cell because he had once held the reservation postmaster hostage for eight hours with the *idea* of a gun and had also threatened to make significant changes in the tribal vision" (93; emphasis mine). Thomas's ideas are powerful enough to hold people captive, to make them listen, and with a receptive audience, he threatens a reservation power structure defined by a tribal vision that readers know has been distorted and corrupted by dominant media culture.

At his trial, Thomas decides "to represent himself," an act with a specific legal meaning, but one that also suggests Thomas will construct an image of himself and tell his own story as a defense (95). He refuses to have his narrative diffused through another medium; Thomas, like the Tonto of the title, will fight to speak for himself. As part of his self-representation, Thomas inserts himself as a character in Spokane tribal history. In the first story, he is a horse in a Spokane herd that Colonel Wright of the U.S. Army slaughtered in 1858.[3] Thomas writes his own escape into the story: "They could not break me. Some may have wanted to kill me for my arrogance, but others respected my anger, my refusal to admit defeat. I lived that day, even escaped Colonel Wright, and galloped into other histories" (98). Thomas establishes himself as a transhistorical and mythological figure who creates victories for his tribe out of defeats. He writes a narrative of survival that subverts any narratives about a "vanishing race" and repopulates the landscape with Native Americans.

In his second story, Thomas speaks of himself as Qualchan, the son of an Upper Yakima chief who fought against the U.S. Army. Thomas does not revise this historical event because the "point" of the story, which the judge demands, is, "The City of Spokane is now building a golf course named after me, Qualchan, located in the valley where I was hanged" (99).[4] Qualchan transcends time and his physical death to voice his grievances against the abuse of his name; Thomas invokes Spokane tribal history to protest how Euro-American culture commercializes and consumes Native America. In "The Only Traffic Signal on the Reservation Doesn't Flash Red Anymore," Victor says, "Indians need heroes to help them learn how to survive" (49). Thomas creates the hero that Victor says the Spokane need. After this story, "[t]he courtroom burst into motion and emotion" (99); Thomas's story successfully elicits activity from people numbed by past and present defeat and popular culture narratives that assume the defeat was absolute.

The judge, who sentences Thomas to "two concurrent life terms in the Walla Walla State Penitentiary," is the representative of the dominant culture, and his judicial decision implies his investment in the image of Native America as presented in the conventional Lone Ranger narrative (102). But the newspaper clipping that reports the end of the trial notes Thomas was "transported away from this story and into the next" (103). Thomas is the physical manifestation of a living Spokane history, and his transhistorical, mythological identity makes imprisonment impossible. Alexie suggests Thomas is present in the margins or between the lines of the other stories, though the characters do not see him. Thomas's active storytelling benefits the tribe by offering an alternative to Euro-American popular culture's definitions of what it means to be Native American. As a mythological figure, Thomas exists beyond the boundaries of the visual and written ethnocentric stories of European conquest; he cannot be commercialized and commodified. In addition, Thomas is a more powerful hero than the Lone Ranger, whose actions are restricted by the static generic constraints of his narrative.

In "The Only Traffic Signal on the Reservation Doesn't Flash Red Anymore," Victor explains the significance of Tonto's uprising in the title of Alexie's short story collection. He says, "It's the small things that hurt the most. The white waitress who wouldn't take an order, Tonto, the Washington Redskins" (49). The story of Tonto's rebellion, briefly encapsulated in the title, is Alexie's revision and subversion of the legend of the Lone Ranger and, concomitantly, an attempt at Indian self-representation and an effort to alleviate the hurt of characters like Victor. Thomas Builds-the-Fire, like Alexie, is a storyteller who subverts the image of Tonto constructed by the dominant culture. Thomas revisits and enlivens Spokane history in his search for answers to what being Native American in the twentieth century means; he does not seek answers in the popular culture propaganda that, like an omnipresent white noise, silences all other narratives. In his essay "White Men Can't Drum," Alexie writes, "What does it mean to be a man? What does it mean to be Indian? What does it mean to be an Indian man? I press the mute button on the remote control so that everyone can hear the answer" (31). Thomas, who mutes the white noise that infects the reservation in order to speak his stories, is the source of this answer in *The Lone Ranger and Tonto Fistfight in Heaven.* . . .

The difference between subverting popular culture narratives and revising Spokane tribal history is that a larger, non-Spokane audience has access to the source of his popular culture allusions. Alexie exploits this accessibility. With a superficial foundation constructed around a fanciful cultural ideal, mass-produced reductive narratives of white culture, such as the small-town middle-class story depicted in *Leave It to Beaver*, are vulnerable to mockery and subversion. In addition, the dominant culture distributes self-defining narratives in a large public arena with technology that disconnects the authors from the stories, thereby relinquishing control of audience interpretation. By intervening in a media the dominant culture privileges, Alexie claims an authoritative place from which to speak. Once he occupies an authoritative space, his narrative subversions enliven the voices the dominant culture's stories of conquest silence and exposes the absurd incongruities between the European and Euro-American narratives and what Cogewea in Mourning Dove's novel calls "actual conditions."

The cumulative effect of Alexie's attention to the practice of storytelling is to privilege the narrative power to create perception and, therefore, a culturally sanctioned version of reality. European and Euro-American writers had presented their uncontested version of history for hundreds of years. As Louis Owens states in *Other Destinies: Understanding the American Indian Novel*, "Native cultures — their voices systematically silenced — had no part in the ongoing discourse that evolved over several centuries to define the utterance 'Indian' in the language of the invaders" (*Other* 7). Alexie revises the narratives from the perspective of the invaded, and the cultural conflict becomes a battle of stories, or, more precisely, a battle between storytellers. By telling the same stories over and over again, Euro-Americans make the stories one-dimensional, static, and vulnerable to parodic revision. Alexie exploits this weakness by intervening in the narratives, exposing their destructive cultural biases and ideologies, and re-visioning them to tell new tales of Native American resistance.

Notes

[1]See Terrace, *The Complete Encyclopedia of Television Programs: 1947–1979*, 575–76. *The Lone Ranger* ran for 221 episodes between September 15, 1949, and September 4, 1965. An additional 26 episodes of an animated version ran between September 10, 1966, and September 6, 1969. A radio program of *The Lone Ranger* preceded the television and subsequent cinematic incarnations.

[2]In her article "Reservation Home Movies: Sherman Alexie's Poetry," Jennifer Gillan discusses how Alexie, in his poetry and several short stories from *The Lone Ranger and Tonto Fistfight in Heaven*, confronts and attempts to resist the dominant culture's technology and the ubiquitous, destructive images disseminated by that technology.

[3]Robert H. Ruby and John A. Brown have written two histories of the Spokane, *The Spokane Indians: Children of the Sun* and *Half-Sun on the Columbia: A Biography of Chief Moses*. For their account of the massacre of the Spokane's horses, see *The Spokane Indians*, 136–37. Alexie includes *The Spokane Indians: Children of the Sun* on the "Acknowledgments" page of *Reservation Blues*.

[4]For an account of Qualchan's hanging, see Ruby and Brown, *The Spokane Indians: Children of the Sun*, 139–40.

Works Cited

Alexie, Sherman. *The Business of Fancydancing*. Brooklyn, NY: Hanging Loose, 1992.

——. *The Lone Ranger and Tonto Fistfight in Heaven*. New York: Harper, 1994.

——. "White Men Can't Drum." *New York Times Magazine* 4 Oct. 1992: 30–31.

Berkhofer, Robert F., Jr. *The White Man's Indian: Images of the American Indian from Columbus to the Present*. New York: Vintage, 1978.

Deloria, Vine, Jr. *God Is Red: A Native View of Religion*. 1972. Golden, CO: Fulcrum, 1994.

Erdrich, Louise. *Love Medicine*. New and Expanded Edition. New York: Harper, 1993.

Gillan, Jennifer. "Reservation Home Movies: Sherman Alexie's Poetry." *American Literature* 68 (1996): 91–110.

Owens, Louis. *Bone Game: A Novel*. Norman: U of Oklahoma P, 1994.

——. *Other Destinies: Understanding the American Indian Novel*. Norman: U of Oklahoma P, 1992.

Pearce, Roy Harvey. *Savagism and Civilization: A Study of the Indian and the American Mind*. Berkeley: U of California P, 1988. (1967).

Ruby, Robert H., and John A. Brown. *Half-Sun on the Columbia: A Biography of Chief Moses*. Norman: U of Oklahoma P, 1965.

——. *The Spokane Indians: Children of the Sun*. Norman: U of Oklahoma P, 1970.

Terrace, Vincent. *The Complete Encyclopedia of Television Programs: 1947–1979*. Volume 1, A–L. New York: AS Barnes, 1979.

Welch, James. *Winter in the Blood*. New York: Penguin, 1974.

RESPONDING THROUGH Writing

Here are some suggestions for writing on Sherman Alexie, but for a chapter like this one, you should not limit yourself to these topics. An important purpose behind it is learning how to find good topics on your own.

PAPERS USING NO OUTSIDE SOURCES

Literary Analysis Papers

1. Write an analytical paper discussing the narrators, and the effect of their use, in "This Is What It Means to Say Phoenix, Arizona" (p. 254) and "The Lone Ranger and Tonto Fistfight in Heaven" (p. 263).
2. Write a paper on the complexity of love and trust in "The Lone Ranger and Tonto Fistfight in Heaven" (p. 263) and "Somebody Kept Saying Powwow" (p. 268).

Comparison-Contrast Papers

3. Write a paper comparing and contrasting Thomas and Victor in "This Is What It Means to Say Phoenix, Arizona" (p. 254) and explaining what Sherman Alexie is bringing out by juxtaposing them in the story.
4. Write a paper comparing and contrasting the narrative techniques and their effects in "This Is What It Means to Say Phoenix, Arizona" (p. 254) and "The Lone Ranger and Tonto Fistfight in Heaven" (p. 263).

Cultural Studies Papers

5. Write a paper analyzing the thematic use of allusions to aspects of mainstream popular culture in "The Lone Ranger and Tonto Fistfight in Heaven" (p. 263).
6. Write a paper on the theme of "outsiders" in "This Is What It Means to Say Phoenix, Arizona" (p. 254), "The Lone Ranger and Tonto Fistfight in Heaven" (p. 263), and "Somebody Kept Saying Powwow" (p. 268).

PAPERS USING LIMITED OUTSIDE SOURCES

Literary Analysis Papers

1. Joseph L. Coulombe says that "[r]eaders are not passive receptacles; they engage, question, resist, learn, and grow during the reading process" (p. 279). Write a paper discussing techniques Sherman Alexie uses to engage readers in his fiction and examining the effects of such reader engagement.

2. Write a paper on the importance of memories, dreams, and voices (DeNuccio, p. 280) in "This Is What It Means to Say Phoenix, Arizona" (p. 254), "The Lone Ranger and Tonto Fistfight in Heaven" (p. 263), and "Somebody Kept Saying Powwow" (p. 268).

Comparison-Contrast Papers

3. Write a paper comparing and contrasting the types of humor and its uses and effects in "This Is What It Means to Say Phoenix, Arizona" (p. 254) and "The Lone Ranger and Tonto Fistfight in Heaven" (p. 263).

4. In "Superman and Me" (p. 4), Sherman Alexie says he read "to save [his] life." Write a paper comparing and contrasting what Alexie *says* there, in a nonfiction essay, and in the interview with Åse Nygren, with what he *does* in "This Is What It Means to Say Phoenix, Arizona" (p. 254), "The Lone Ranger and Tonto Fistfight in Heaven" (p. 263), and "Somebody Kept Saying Powwow" (p. 268). In the fiction, is he also *writing* to save his life?

Cultural Studies Papers

5. Write a paper that examines "This Is What It Means to Say Phoenix, Arizona" (p. 254), "The Lone Ranger and Tonto Fistfight in Heaven" (p. 263), and "Somebody Kept Saying Powwow" (p. 268) as tales of Native American resistance (Cox, p. 283).

6. In his interview with Åse Nygren, Sherman Alexie says Native Americans are "lost." "We're always wandering" (p. 275). Write a paper that explores a motif of wandering in "This Is What It Means to Say Phoenix, Arizona" (p. 254), "The Lone Ranger and Tonto Fistfight in Heaven" (p. 263), and "Somebody Kept Saying Powwow" (p. 268).

PAPERS INVOLVING FURTHER RESEARCH

Literary Analysis Paper

1. Write a research paper on the archetypal Trickster figure in Native American mythology and literature, focusing particularly on how it is adapted and used in selected works by Sherman Alexie.

2. Write a research paper on a recurring symbol (such as salmon, dancing, 7-11 stores, or many others) in Sherman Alexie's works, both fiction and poetry, and its effect or importance in his thinking or writing.

Comparison-Contrast Papers

3. Write a paper comparing and contrasting how action, characters, and details are handled in "This Is What It Means to Say Phoenix, Arizona" (p. 254) and the movie or screenplay of *Smoke Signals*. You might, for example, focus on what such a comparison shows about differences between writing fiction and screenwriting.

4. Do research on the depiction of Native Americans in popular culture (especially in films, some before 1960 and some after), and use what you find to write a paper in which you compare and contrast those stereotypes with how Sherman Alexie depicts his characters.

Cultural Studies Papers

5. Write a paper on Sherman Alexie's use of baseball and basketball in his writings, focusing on the importance of sports in mainstream culture and Native American culture. Doing so will require reading some of his poetry and more of his fiction and reading literary critics who have worked on this topic.
6. Write a paper on the importance of story in Sherman Alexie's thought and works. Doing so will require reading some of his poetry and more of his fiction and reading literary critics who have explored this topic.

10 A Collection of Stories

Investigating a Variety of Vistas

Monica Ali b. 1967

Dinner with Dr. Azad [2003]

Nazneen waved at the tattoo lady. The tattoo lady was always there when Nazneen looked out across the dead grass and broken paving stones to the block opposite. Most of the flats that closed three sides of a square had net curtains and the life behind was all shapes and shadows. But the tattoo lady had no curtains. Morning and afternoon she sat with her big thighs spilling over the sides of her chair, tipping forward to drop ash in a bowl, tipping back to slug from her can. She drank now, and tossed the can out of the window.

It was the middle of the day. Nazneen had finished the housework. Soon she would start preparing the evening meal, but for a while she would let the time pass. It was hot and the sun fell flat on the metal window frames and glared off the glass. A red and gold sari hung out of a top-floor flat in Rosemead block. A baby's bib and miniature dungarees lower down. The sign screwed to the brickwork was in stiff English capitals and the curlicues beneath were Bengali. NO DUMPING. NO PARKING. NO BALL GAMES. Two old men in white panjabi-pyjama and skullcaps walked along the path, slowly, as if they did not want to go where they were going. A thin brown dog sniffed along to the middle of

WWW

Research the authors in this collection with LitLinks, or take a quiz on the stories with LitQuiz, at bedfordstmartins.com/approachinglit.

the grass and defecated. The breeze on Nazneen's face was thick with the smell from the overflowing communal bins.

Six months now since she'd been sent away to London. Every morning before she opened her eyes she thought, *if I were the wishing type, I know what I would wish.* And then she opened her eyes and saw Chanu's puffy face on the pillow next to her, his lips parted indignantly even as he slept. She saw the pink dressing table with the curly-sided mirror, and the monstrous black wardrobe that claimed most of the room. Was it cheating? To think, *I know what I would wish?* Was it not the same as making the wish? If she knew what the wish would be, then somewhere in her heart she had already made it.

The tattoo lady waved back at Nazneen. She scratched her arms, her shoulders, the accessible portions of her buttocks. She yawned and lit a cigarette. At least two-thirds of the flesh on show was covered in ink. Nazneen had never been close enough (never closer than this, never further) to decipher the designs. Chanu said the tattoo lady was Hell's Angel, which upset Nazneen. She thought the tattoos might be flowers, or birds. They were ugly and they made the tattoo lady more ugly than was necessary, but the tattoo lady clearly did not care. Every time Nazneen saw her she wore the same look of boredom and detachment. Such a state was sought by the sadhus° who walked in rags through the Muslim villages, indifferent to the kindness of strangers, the unkind sun.

Nazneen thought sometimes of going downstairs, crossing the yard and 5 climbing the Rosemead stairwell to the fourth floor. She might have to knock on a few doors before the tattoo lady answered. She would take something, an offering of samosas° or bhajis,° and the tattoo lady would smile and Nazneen would smile and perhaps they would sit together by the window and let the time pass more easily. She thought of it but she would not go. Strangers would answer if she knocked on the wrong door. The tattoo lady might be angry at an unwanted interruption. It was clear she did not like to leave her chair. And even if she wasn't angry, what would be the point? Nazneen could say two things in English: sorry and thank you. She could spend another day alone. It was only another day.

She should be getting on with the evening meal. The lamb curry was prepared. She had made it last night with tomatoes and new potatoes. There was chicken saved in the freezer from the last time Dr. Azad had been invited but had cancelled at the last minute. There was still the dhal° to make, and the vegetable dishes, the spices to grind, the rice to wash, and the sauce to prepare for the fish that Chanu would bring this evening. She would rinse the glasses and rub them with newspaper to make them shine. The tablecloth had some spots to be scrubbed out. What if it went wrong? The rice might stick. She might over-salt the dhal. Chanu might forget the fish.

---

sadhus: Hindu ascetics, or monks, dedicated to achieving *moksha* (liberation) through meditation and contemplation of God.   **samosas:** Fried triangular-shaped pastries stuffed with potato, onion, and peas and sometimes minced meat or fish.   **bhajis:** Vegetables dipped in batter and deep fried.   **dhal:** A traditional dish of lentils with spices.

It was only dinner. One dinner. One guest.

She left the window open. Standing on the sofa to reach, she picked up the Holy Qur'an from the high shelf that Chanu, under duress, had specially built. She made her intention as fervently as possible, seeking refuge from Satan with fists clenched and fingernails digging into her palms. Then she selected a page at random and began to read.

> To God belongs all that the heavens and the earth contain. We exhort you, as We have exhorted those to whom the Book was given before you, to fear God. If you deny Him, know that to God belongs all that the heavens and earth contain. God is self-sufficient and worthy of praise.

The words calmed her stomach and she was pleased. Even Dr. Azad was nothing as to God. To God belongs all that the heavens and the earth contain. She said it over a few times, aloud. She was composed. Nothing could bother her. Only God, if he chose to. Chanu might flap about and squawk because Dr. Azad was coming for dinner. Let him flap. To God belongs all that the heavens and the earth contain. How would it sound in Arabic? More lovely even than in Bengali she supposed, for those were the actual Words of God.

She closed the book and looked around the room to check it was tidy 10 enough. Chanu's books and papers were stacked beneath the table. They would have to be moved or Dr. Azad would not be able to get his feet in. The rugs which she had held out of the window earlier and beaten with a wooden spoon needed to be put down again. There were three rugs: red and orange, green and purple, brown and blue. The carpet was yellow with a green leaf design. One hundred per cent nylon and, Chanu said, very hard-wearing. The sofa and chairs were the color of dried cow dung, which was a practical color. They had little sheaths of plastic on the headrests to protect them from Chanu's hair oil. There was a lot of furniture, more than Nazneen had seen in one room before. Even if you took all the furniture in the compound back home, from every auntie and uncle's ghar,° it would not match up to this one room. There was a low table with a glass center and orange plastic legs, three little wooden tables that stacked together, the big table they used for the evening meal, a bookcase, a corner cupboard, a rack for newspapers, a trolley° filled with files and folders, the sofa and armchairs, two footstools, six dining chairs and a showcase. The walls were papered in yellow with brown squares and circles lining neatly up and down. Nobody in Gouripur had anything like it. It made her proud. Her father was the second wealthiest man in the village and he never had anything like it. He had made a good marriage for her. There were plates on the wall attached by hooks and wires, which were not for eating from but only for display. Some were rimmed in gold paint. "Gold leaf," Chanu called it. His certificates were framed and mixed with the plates. She had everything here. All these beautiful things.

---

ghar: House.   trolley: Cart.

She put the Qur'an back in its place. Next to it lay the most Holy Book wrapped inside a cloth covering: the Qur'an in Arabic. She touched her fingers to the cloth.

Nazneen stared at the glass showcase stuffed with pottery animals, china figures, and plastic fruits. Each one had to be dusted. She wondered how the dust got in and where it came from. All of it belonged to God. She wondered what He wanted with clay tigers, trinkets, and dust.

And then, because she had let her mind drift and become uncentered again, she began to recite in her head from the Holy Qur'an one of the suras° she had learned in school. She did not know what the words meant but the rhythm of them soothed her.

"She is an unspoilt girl. From the village."

She had got up one night to fetch a glass of water. It was one week since they   15
married. She had gone to bed and he was still up, talking on the telephone as she stood outside the door.

"No," said Chanu. "I would not say so. Not beautiful, but not so ugly either. The face is broad, big forehead. Eyes are a bit too close together."

Nazneen put her hand up to her head. It was true. The forehead was large. But she had never thought of her eyes being too close.

"Not tall. Not short. Around five foot two. Hips are a bit narrow but wide enough, I think, to carry children. All things considered, I am satisfied. Perhaps when she gets older she'll grow a beard on her chin but now she is only eighteen. And a blind uncle is better than no uncle. I waited too long to get a wife."

Narrow hips! You could wish for such a fault, Nazneen said to herself, thinking of the rolls of fat that hung low from Chanu's stomach. It would be possible to tuck all your hundred pens and pencils under those rolls and keep them safe and tight. You could stuff a book or two up there as well. If your spindle legs could take the weight.

"What's more, she is a good worker. Cleaning and cooking and all that. The   20
only complaint I could make is she can't put my files in order, because she has no English. I don't complain though. As I say, a girl from the village: totally un-spoilt."

Chanu went on talking but Nazneen crept away, back to bed. A blind uncle is better than no uncle. Her husband had a proverb for everything. Any wife is better than no wife. Something is better than nothing. What had she imagined? That he was in love with her? That he was grateful because she, young and grace-ful, had accepted him? That in sacrificing herself to him, she was owed some-thing? Yes. Yes. She realized in a stinging rush she had imagined all these things. Such a foolish girl. Such high notions. What self-regard.

What she missed most was people. Not any people in particular but just people. If she put her ear to the wall she could hear sounds. The television on.

---

suras: The sections, or "chapters," of the Koran.

Coughing. Sometimes the lavatory flushing. Someone upstairs scraping a chair. A shouting match below. Everyone in their boxes, counting their possessions. In all her eighteen years, she could scarcely remember a moment that she had spent alone. Until she married. And came to London to sit day after day in this large box with the furniture to dust, and the muffled sound of private lives sealed away above, below, and around her.

Dr. Azad was a small, precise man who, contrary to the Bengali custom, spoke at a level only one-quarter of a decibel above a whisper. Anyone who wished to hear what he was saying was obliged to lean in towards him, so that all evening Chanu gave the appearance of hanging on his every word.

"Come," said Dr. Azad, when Nazneen was hovering behind the table ready to serve, "Come and sit down with us."

"My wife is very shy." Chanu smiled and motioned with his head for her to   25
be seated.

"This week I saw two of our young men in a very sorry state," said the doctor. "I told them straight, this is your choice: stop drinking alcohol now, or by Eid° your liver will be finished. Ten years ago this would be unthinkable. Two in one week! But now our children are copying what they see here, going to the pub, to nightclubs. Or drinking at home in their bedrooms where their parents think they are perfectly safe. The problem is our community is not properly educated about these things." Dr. Azad drank a glass of water down in one long draught and poured himself another. "I always drink two glasses before starting the meal." He drank the second glass. "Good. Now I will not overeat."

"Eat! Eat!" said Chanu. "Water is good for cleansing the system, but food is also essential." He scooped up lamb and rice with his fingers and chewed. He put too much in his mouth at once, and he made sloppy noises as he ate. When he could speak again, he said, "I agree with you. Our community is not educated about this, and much else besides. But for my part, I don't plan to risk these things happening to my children. We will go back before they get spoiled."

"This is another disease that afflicts us," said the doctor. "I call it Going Home Syndrome. Do you know what that means?" He addressed himself to Nazneen.

She felt a heat on the back of her neck and formed words that did not leave her mouth.

"It is natural," said Chanu. "These people are basically peasants and they   30
miss the land. The pull of the land is stronger even than the pull of blood."

"And when they have saved enough they will get on an airplane and go?"

"They don't ever really leave home. Their bodies are here, but their hearts are back there. And anyway, look how they live: just recreating the villages here."

Eid: Abbreviation for *Eid ul-Fitr* (or *Eid al-Fitr*), the Islamic holiday that marks the end of Ramadan, the month of fasting that celebrates Allah's revelation of the Qur'an to Muhammad.

"But they will never save enough to go back." Dr. Azad helped himself to vegetables. His shirt was spotless white, and his collar and tie so high under his chin that he seemed to be missing a neck. Nazneen saw an oily yellow stain on her husband's shirt where he had dripped food.

Dr. Azad continued, "Every year they think, just one more year. But whatever they save, it's never enough."

"We would not need very much," said Nazneen. Both men looked at her. She 35 spoke to her plate. "I mean, we could live very cheaply." The back of her neck burned.

Chanu filled the silence with his laugh. "My wife is just settling in here." He coughed and shuffled in his chair. "The thing is, with the promotion coming up, things are beginning to go well for me now. If I just get the promotion confirmed then many things are possible."

"I used to think all the time of going back," said Dr. Azad. He spoke so quietly that Nazneen was forced to look directly at him, because to catch all the words she had to follow his lips. "Every year I thought, 'Maybe this year.' And I'd go for a visit, buy some more land, see relatives and friends and make up my mind to return for good. But something would always happen. A flood, a tornado that just missed the building, a power cut, some mind-numbing piece of petty bureaucracy, bribes to be paid out to get anything done. And I'd think, 'Well, maybe not this year.' And now, I don't know. I just don't know."

Chanu cleared his throat. "Of course, it's not been announced yet. Other people have applied. But after my years of service . . . Do you know, in six years I have not been late on one single day! And only three sick days, even with the ulcer. Some of my colleagues are very unhealthy, always going off sick with this or that. It's not something I could bring to Mr. Dalloway's attention. Even so, I feel he ought to be aware of it."

"I wish you luck," said Dr. Azad.

"Then there's the academic perspective. Within months I will be a fully 40 fledged academic, with two degrees. One from a British University. Bachelor of Arts degree. With honors."

"I'm sure you have a good chance."

"Did Mr. Dalloway tell you that?"

"Who's that?"

"Mr. Dalloway."

The doctor shrugged his neat shoulders. 45

"My superior. Mr. Dalloway. He told you I have a good chance?"

"No."

"He said I didn't have a good chance?"

"He didn't say anything at all. I don't know the gentleman in question."

"He's one of your patients. His secretary made an appointment for him to 50 see you about his shoulder sprain. He's a squash player. Very active man. Average build, I'd say. Red hair. Wears contact lenses — perhaps you test his eyes as well."

"It's possible he's a patient. There are several thousand on the list for my practice."

"What I should have told you straight away — he has a harelip. Well, it's been put right, reconstructive surgery and all that, but you can always tell. That should put you on to him."

The guest remained quiet. Nazneen heard Chanu suppress a belch. She wanted to go to him and stroke his forehead. She wanted to get up from the table and walk out of the door and never see him again.

"He might be a patient. I do not know him." It was nearly a whisper.

"No," said Chanu. "I see." 55

"But I wish you luck."

"I am forty years old," said Chanu. He spoke quietly like the doctor, with none of his assurance. "I have been in this country for sixteen years. Nearly half my life." He gave a dry-throated gargle. "When I came I was a young man. I had ambitions. Big dreams. When I got off the airplane, I had my degree certificate in my suitcase and a few pounds in my pocket. I thought there would be a red carpet laid out for me. I was going to join the Civil Service and become Private Secretary to the Prime Minister." As he told his story, his voice grew. It filled the room. "That was my plan. And then I found things were a bit different. These people here didn't know the difference between me, who stepped off an airplane with a degree certificate, and the peasants who jumped off the boat possessing only the lice on their heads. What can you do?" He rolled a ball of rice and meat in his fingers and teased it around his plate.

"I did this and that. Whatever I could. So much hard work, so little reward. More or less it is true to say, I have been chasing wild buffaloes and eating my own rice. You know that saying? All the begging letters from home I burned. And I made two promises to myself. I will be a success, come what may. That's promise number one. Number two, I will go back home. When I am a success. And I will honor these promises." Chanu, who had grown taller and taller in his chair, sank back down.

"Very good, very good," said Dr. Azad. He checked his watch.

"The begging letters still come," said Chanu. "From old servants, from the 60 children of servants. Even from my own family, although they are not in need. All they can think of is money. They think there is gold lying about in the streets here and I am just hoarding it all in my palace. But I did not come here for money. Was I starving in Dhaka? I was not. Do they inquire about my diplomas?" He gestured to the wall, where his various framed certificates were displayed. "They do not. What is more..." He cleared his throat, although it was already clear. Dr. Azad looked at Nazneen and, without meaning to, she returned his gaze so that she was caught in a complicity of looks, given and returned, which said something about her husband that she ought not to be saying.

Chanu talked on. Dr. Azad finished the food on his plate while Chanu's food grew cold. Nazneen picked at the cauliflower curry. The doctor declined with a waggle of the head either a further helping or any dessert. He sat with his hands folded on the table while Chanu, his oration at an end, ate noisily and quickly. Twice more he checked his watch.

At half past nine Dr. Azad said, "Well, Chanu. I thank you and your wife for a most pleasant evening and a delicious meal."

Chanu protested that it was still early. The doctor was adamant. "I always retire at ten-thirty and I always read for half an hour in bed before that."

"We intellectuals must stick together," said Chanu, and he walked with his guest to the door.

"If you take my advice, one intellectual to another, you will eat more slowly,   65
chew more thoroughly and take only a small portion of meat. Otherwise, I'll see you back at the clinic again with another ulcer."

"Just think," said Chanu, "if I did not have the ulcer in the first place, then we would not have met and we would not have had this dinner together."

"Just think," said the doctor. He waved stiffly and disappeared behind the door.

The television was on. Chanu liked to keep it glowing in the evenings, like a fire in the corner of the room. Sometimes he went over and stirred it by pressing the buttons so that the light flared and changed colors. Mostly he ignored it. Nazneen held a pile of the last dirty dishes to take to the kitchen, but the screen held her. A man in a very tight suit (so tight that it made his private parts stand out on display) and a woman in a skirt that did not even cover her bottom gripped each other as an invisible force hurtled them across an oval arena. The people in the audience clapped their hands together and then stopped. By some magic they all stopped at exactly the same time. The couple broke apart. They fled from each other and no sooner had they fled than they sought each other out. Every move they made was urgent, intense, a declaration. The woman raised one leg and rested her boot (Nazneen saw the thin blade for the first time) on the other thigh, making a triangular flag of her legs, and spun around until she would surely fall but didn't. She did not slow down. She stopped dead, and flung her arms above her head with a look so triumphant that you knew she had conquered everything: her body, the laws of nature, and the heart of the tight-suited man who slid over on his knees, vowing to lay down his life for her.

"What is this called?" said Nazneen.

Chanu glanced at the screen. "Ice skating," he said, in English.   70

"Ice e-skating," said Nazneen.

"Ice skating," said Chanu.

"Ice e-skating."

"No, no. No *e*. Ice skating. Try it again."

Nazneen hesitated.   75

"Go on!"

"Ice es-skating," she said, with deliberation.

Chanu smiled. "Don't worry about it. It's a common problem for Bengalis. Two consonants together causes a difficulty. I have conquered this issue after a long time. But you are unlikely to need these words in any case."

"I would like to learn some English," said Nazneen.

Chanu puffed his cheeks and spat the air out in a *fuff*. "It will come. Don't 80 worry about it. Where's the need anyway?" He looked at his book and Nazneen watched the screen.

"He thinks he will get the promotion because he goes to the *pub* with the boss. He is so stupid he doesn't even realize there is any other way of getting promotion." Chanu was supposed to be studying. His books were open on the table. Every so often he looked in one, or turned a page. Mostly, he talked. *Pub, pub, pub.* Nazneen turned the word over in her mind. Another drop of English that she knew. There were other English words that Chanu sprinkled into his conversation, other things she could say to the tattoo lady. At this moment she could not think of any.

"This Wilkie—I told you about him—he has one or maybe two O levels.° Every lunchtime he goes to the *pub* and he comes back half an hour late. Today I saw him sitting in Mr. Dalloway's office using the phone with his feet up on the desk. The jackfruit° is still on the tree but already he is oiling his moustache. No way is he going to get promoted."

Nazneen stared at the television. There was a close-up of the woman. She had sparkly bits around her eyes like tiny sequins glued to her face. Her hair was scraped back and tied on top of her head with plastic flowers. Her chest pumped up and down as if her heart would shoot out and she smiled pure, gold joy. She must be terrified, thought Nazneen, because such things cannot be held, and must be lost.

"No," said Chanu. "I don't have anything to fear from Wilkie. I have a degree from Dhaka University in English Literature. Can Wilkie quote from Chaucer or Dickens or Hardy?"

Nazneen, who feared her husband would begin one of his long quotations, 85 stacked a final plate and went to the kitchen. He liked to quote in English and then give her a translation, phrase by phrase. And when it was translated it usually meant no more to her than it did in English, so that she did not know what to reply or even if a reply was required.

She washed the dishes and rinsed them and Chanu came and leaned against the ill-fitting cupboards and talked some more. "You see," he said, a frequent opener although often she did not see, "it is the white underclass, like Wilkie, who are most afraid of people like me. To him, and people like him, we are the only thing standing in the way of them sliding totally to the bottom of the pile. As long as we are below them, then they are above something. If they see us rise then they are resentful because we have left our proper place. That is why you get the phenomenon of *National Front*.° They can play on those fears to create

---

has . . . O levels: That is, has only passing scores in one or two areas of the O (Ordinary) level examinations taken by sixteen year olds, and no A levels, the Advanced level examinations taken by eighteen year olds as a prerequisite for university-level study.   jackfruit: The largest of tree-borne fruits, filled with bulbs of yellow, banana-flavored paste around a large seed, growing on handsome, stately trees, which may reach a height of seventy feet in the tropics. *National Front:* A white nationalist organization founded in Britain in 1967 to oppose immigration and multiculturalist policies.

racial tensions, and give these people a superiority complex. The middle classes are more secure, and therefore more relaxed." He drummed his fingers against the Formica.

Nazneen took a tea towel and dried the plates. She wondered if the ice e-skating woman went home and washed and wiped. It was difficult to imagine. But there were no servants here. She would have to manage by herself.

Chanu ploughed on. "Wilkie is not exactly underclass. He has a job, so technically I would say no, he is not. But that is the mindset. This is what I am studying in the subsection on *Race, Ethnicity, and Identity*. It is part of the sociology module. Of course, when I have my Open University° degree then nobody can question my credentials. Although Dhaka University is one of the best in the world, these people here are by and large ignorant and know nothing of the Brontës or Thackeray."

Nazneen began to put things away. She needed to get in the cupboard that Chanu blocked with his body. He didn't move although she waited in front of him. Eventually she left the pans on the cooker to be put away in the morning.

90

After a minute or two in the dark, when her eyes had adjusted and the snoring began, Nazneen turned on her side and looked at her husband. She scrutinized his face, round as a ball, the blunt-cut thinning hair on top, and the dense eyebrows. His mouth was open and she began to regulate her breathing so that she inhaled as he did. When she got it wrong she could smell his breath. She looked at him for a long time. It was not a handsome face. In the month before her marriage, when she looked at his face in the photograph, she thought it ugly. Now she saw that it was not handsome, but it was kind. His mouth, always on duty, always moving, was full-lipped and generous, without a hint of cruelty. His eyes, small and beleaguered beneath those thick brows, were anxious or far away, or both. Now that they were closed she could see the way the skin puckered up across the lids and drooped down to meet the creases at the corners. He shifted in his sleep and moved onto his stomach with his arms down by his side and his face squashed against the pillow.

Nazneen got out of bed and crossed the hall. She caught hold of the bead curtain that partitioned the kitchen from the narrow hallway, to stop it tinkling, and went to the fridge. She got out the Tupperware containers of rice and fish and chicken and took a spoon from the drawer. As she ate, standing beside the sink, she looked out at the moon which hung above the dark flats checkered with lights. It was large and white and untroubled. She tried to imagine what it would be like to fall in love. She looked down into the courtyard. Two boys exchanged mock punches, feinting left and right. Cigarettes burned in their mouths. She opened the window and leaned into the breeze. Across the way the tattoo lady raised a can to her lips.

Open University: Britain's largest university for part-time, distance-learning higher education, open to all students eighteen years of age and older.

Isabel Allende   Chile, b. 1942

And of Clay Are We Created   [1984]

Translated by Margaret Sayers Peden

They discovered the girl's head protruding from the mudpit, eyes wide open, calling soundlessly. She had a First Communion name, Azucena. Lily. In that vast cemetery where the odor of death was already attracting vultures from far away, and where the weeping of orphans and wails of the injured filled the air, the little girl obstinately clinging to life became the symbol of the tragedy. The television cameras transmitted so often the unbearable image of the head budding like a black squash from the clay that there was no one who did not recognize her and know her name. And every time we saw her on the screen, right behind her was Rolf Carlé, who had gone there on assignment, never suspecting that he would find a fragment of his past, lost thirty years before.

First a subterranean sob rocked the cotton fields, curling them like waves of foam. Geologists had set up their seismographs weeks before and knew that the mountain had awakened again. For some time they had predicted that the heat of the eruption could detach the eternal ice from the slopes of the volcano, but no one heeded their warnings; they sounded like the tales of frightened old women. The towns in the valley went about their daily life, deaf to the moaning of the earth, until that fateful Wednesday night in November when a prolonged roar announced the end of the world, and walls of snow broke loose, rolling in an avalanche of clay, stones, and water that descended on the villages and buried them beneath unfathomable meters of telluric vomit. As soon as the survivors emerged from the paralysis of that first awful terror, they could see that houses, plazas, churches, white cotton plantations, dark coffee forests, cattle pastures — all had disappeared. Much later, after soldiers and volunteers had arrived to rescue the living and try to assess the magnitude of the cataclysm, it was calculated that beneath the mud lay more than twenty thousand human beings and an indefinite number of animals putrefying in a viscous soup. Forests and rivers had also been swept away, and there was nothing to be seen but an immense desert of mire.

When the station called before dawn, Rolf Carlé and I were together. I crawled out of bed, dazed with sleep, and went to prepare coffee while he hurriedly dressed. He stuffed his gear in the green canvas backpack he always carried, and we said goodbye, as we had so many times before. I had no presentiments. I sat in the kitchen, sipping my coffee and planning the long hours without him, sure that he would be back the next day.

He was one of the first to reach the scene, because while other reporters were fighting their way to the edges of that morass in jeeps, bicycles, or on foot, each getting there however he could, Rolf Carlé had the advantage of the television helicopter, which flew him over the avalanche. We watched on our screens the footage captured by his assistant's camera, in which he was up to his knees in muck, a microphone in his hand, in the midst of a bedlam of lost children, wounded survivors, corpses, and devastation. The story came to us in his calm voice. For years he had been a familiar figure in newscasts, reporting live at the scene of battles and catastrophes with awesome tenacity. Nothing could stop him, and I was always amazed at his equanimity in the face of danger and suffering; it seemed as if nothing could shake his fortitude or deter his curiosity. Fear seemed never to touch him, although he had confessed to me that he was not a courageous man, far from it. I believe that the lens of the camera had a strange effect on him; it was as if it transported him to a different time from which he could watch events without actually participating in them. When I knew him better, I came to realize that this fictive distance seemed to protect him from his own emotions.

Rolf Carlé was in on the story of Azucena from the beginning. He filmed the volunteers who discovered her, and the first persons who tried to reach her; his camera zoomed in on the girl, her dark face, her large desolate eyes, the plastered-down tangle of her hair. The mud was like quicksand around her, and anyone attempting to reach her was in danger of sinking. They threw a rope to her that she made no effort to grasp until they shouted to her to catch it; then she pulled a hand from the mire and tried to move, but immediately sank a little deeper. Rolf threw down his knapsack and the rest of his equipment and waded into the quagmire, commenting for his assistant's microphone that it was cold and that one could begin to smell the stench of corpses.

"What's your name?" he asked the girl, and she told him her flower name. "Don't move, Azucena," Rolf Carlé directed, and kept talking to her, without a thought for what he was saying, just to distract her, while slowly he worked his way forward in mud up to his waist. The air around him seemed as murky as the mud.

It was impossible to reach her from the approach he was attempting, so he retreated and circled around where there seemed to be firmer footing. When finally he was close enough, he took the rope and tied it beneath her arms, so they could pull her out. He smiled at her with that smile that crinkles his eyes and makes him look like a little boy; he told her that everything was fine, that he was here with her now, that soon they would have her out. He signaled the others to pull, but as soon as the cord tensed, the girl screamed. They tried again, and her shoulders and arms appeared, but they could move her no farther; she was trapped. Someone suggested that her legs might be caught in the collapsed walls of her house, but she said it was not just rubble, that she was also held by the bodies of her brothers and sisters clinging to her legs.

"Don't worry, we'll get you out of here," Rolf promised. Despite the quality of the transmission, I could hear his voice break, and I loved him more than ever. Azucena looked at him, but said nothing.

During those first hours Rolf Carlé exhausted all the resources of his ingenuity to rescue her. He struggled with poles and ropes, but every tug was an intolerable torture for the imprisoned girl. It occurred to him to use one of the poles as a lever but got no result and had to abandon the idea. He talked a couple of soldiers into working with him for a while, but they had to leave because so many other victims were calling for help. The girl could not move, she barely could breathe, but she did not seem desperate, as if an ancestral resignation allowed her to accept her fate. The reporter, on the other hand, was determined to snatch her from death. Someone brought him a tire, which he placed beneath her arms like a life buoy, and then laid a plank near the hole to hold his weight and allow him to stay closer to her. As it was impossible to remove the rubble blindly, he tried once or twice to dive toward her feet, but emerged frustrated, covered with mud, and spitting gravel. He concluded that he would have to have a pump to drain the water, and radioed a request for one, but received in return a message that there was no available transport and it could not be sent until the next morning.

"We can't wait that long!" Rolf Carlé shouted, but in the pandemonium no 10 one stopped to commiserate. Many more hours would go by before he accepted that time had stagnated and reality had been irreparably distorted.

A military doctor came to examine the girl, and observed that her heart was functioning well and that if she did not get too cold she could survive the night.

"Hang on, Azucena, we'll have the pump tomorrow," Rolf Carlé tried to console her.

"Don't leave me alone," she begged.

"No, of course I won't leave you."

Someone brought him coffee, and he helped the girl drink it, sip by sip. The 15 warm liquid revived her and she began telling him about her small life, about her family and her school, about how things were in that little bit of world before the volcano had erupted. She was thirteen, and she had never been outside her village. Rolf Carlé, buoyed by a premature optimism, was convinced that everything would end well: the pump would arrive, they would drain the water, move the rubble, and Azucena would be transported by helicopter to a hospital where she would recover rapidly and where he could visit her and bring her gifts. He thought, She's already too old for dolls, and I don't know what would please her; maybe a dress. I don't know much about women, he concluded, amused, reflecting that although he had known many women in his lifetime, none had taught him these details. To pass the hours he began to tell Azucena about his travels and adventures as a newshound, and when he exhausted his memory, he called upon imagination, inventing things he thought might entertain her. From time to time she dozed, but he kept talking in the darkness, to assure her that he was still there and to overcome the menace of uncertainty.

That was a long night.

Many miles away, I watched Rolf Carlé and the girl on a television screen. I could not bear the wait at home, so I went to National Television, where I often spent entire nights with Rolf editing programs. There, I was near his world, and I could at least get a feeling of what he lived through during those three decisive days. I called all the important people in the city, senators, commanders of the armed forces, the North American ambassador, and the president of National

Petroleum, begging them for a pump to remove the silt, but obtained only vague promises. I began to ask for urgent help on radio and television, to see if there wasn't *someone* who could help us. Between calls I would run to the newsroom to monitor the satellite transmissions that periodically brought new details of the catastrophe. While reporters selected scenes with most impact for the news report, I searched for footage that featured Azucena's mudpit. The screen reduced the disaster to a single plane and accentuated the tremendous distance that separated me from Rolf Carlé; nonetheless, I was there with him. The child's every suffering hurt me as it did him; I felt his frustration, his impotence. Faced with the impossibility of communicating with him, the fantastic idea came to me that if I tried, I could reach him by force of mind and in that way give him encouragement. I concentrated until I was dizzy—a frenzied and futile activity. At times I would be overcome with compassion and burst out crying; at other times, I was so drained I felt as if I were staring through a telescope at the light of a star dead for a million years.

I watched that hell on the first morning broadcast, cadavers of people and animals awash in the current of new rivers formed overnight from the melted snow. Above the mud rose the tops of trees and the bell towers of a church where several people had taken refuge and were patiently awaiting rescue teams. Hundreds of soldiers and volunteers from the Civil Defense were clawing through rubble searching for survivors, while long rows of ragged specters awaited their turn for a cup of hot broth. Radio networks announced that their phones were jammed with calls from families offering shelter to orphaned children. Drinking water was in scarce supply, along with gasoline and food. Doctors, resigned to amputating arms and legs without anesthesia, pled that at least they be sent serum and painkillers and antibiotics; most of the roads, however, were impassable, and worse were the bureaucratic obstacles that stood in the way. To top it all, the clay contaminated by decomposing bodies threatened the living with an outbreak of epidemics.

Azucena was shivering inside the tire that held her above the surface. Immobility and tension had greatly weakened her, but she was conscious and could still be heard when a microphone was held out to her. Her tone was humble, as if apologizing for all the fuss. Rolf Carlé had a growth of beard, and dark circles beneath his eyes; he looked near exhaustion. Even from that enormous distance I could sense the quality of his weariness, so different from the fatigue of other adventures. He had completely forgotten the camera; he could not look at the girl through a lens any longer. The pictures we were receiving were not his assistant's but those of other reporters who had appropriated Azucena, bestowing on her the pathetic responsibility of embodying the horror of what had happened in that place. With the first light Rolf tried again to dislodge the obstacles that held the girl in her tomb, but he had only his hands to work with; he did not dare use a tool for fear of injuring her. He fed Azucena a cup of the cornmeal mush and bananas the Army was distributing, but she immediately vomited it up. A doctor stated that she had a fever, but added that there was little he could do: antibiotics were being reserved for cases of gangrene. A priest also passed by and blessed her, hanging a medal of the Virgin around her neck. By evening a gentle, persistent drizzle began to fall.

"The sky is weeping," Azucena murmured, and she, too, began to cry.   20

"Don't be afraid," Rolf begged "You have to keep your strength up and be calm. Everything will be fine. I'm with you, and I'll get you out somehow."

Reporters returned to photograph Azucena and ask her the same questions, which she no longer tried to answer. In the meanwhile, more television and movie teams arrived with spools of cable, tapes, film, videos, precision lenses, recorders, sound consoles, lights, reflecting screens, auxiliary motors, cartons of supplies, electricians, sound technicians, and cameramen: Azucena's face was beamed to millions of screens around the world. And all the while Rolf Carlé kept pleading for a pump. The improved technical facilities bore results, and National Television began receiving sharper pictures and clearer sound; the distance seemed suddenly compressed, and I had the horrible sensation that Azucena and Rolf were by my side, separated from me by impenetrable glass. I was able to follow events hour by hour; I knew everything my love did to wrest the girl from her prison and help her endure her suffering; I overheard fragments of what they said to one another and could guess the rest; I was present when she taught Rolf to pray, and when he distracted her with the stories I had told him in a thousand and one nights beneath the white mosquito netting of our bed.

When darkness came on the second day, Rolf tried to sing Azucena to sleep with old Austrian folk songs he had learned from his mother, but she was far beyond sleep. They spent most of the night talking, each in a stupor of exhaustion and hunger, and shaking with cold. That night, imperceptibly, the unyielding floodgates that had contained Rolf Carlé's past for so many years began to open, and the torrent of all that had lain hidden in the deepest and most secret layers of memory poured out, leveling before it the obstacles that had blocked his consciousness for so long. He could not tell it all to Azucena; she perhaps did not know there was a world beyond the sea or time previous to her own; she was not capable of imagining Europe in the years of the war. So he could not tell her of defeat, nor of the afternoon the Russians had led them to the concentration camp to bury prisoners dead from starvation. Why should he describe to her how the naked bodies piled like a mountain of firewood resembled fragile china? How could he tell this dying child about ovens and gallows? Nor did he mention the night that he had seen his mother naked, shod in stiletto-heeled red boots, sobbing with humiliation. There was much he did not tell, but in those hours he relived for the first time all the things his mind had tried to erase. Azucena had surrendered her fear to him and so, without wishing it, had obliged Rolf to confront his own. There, beside that hellhole of mud, it was impossible for Rolf to flee from himself any longer, and the visceral terror he had lived as a boy suddenly invaded him. He reverted to the years when he was the age of Azucena, and younger, and, like her, found himself trapped in a pit without escape, buried in life, his head barely above ground; he saw before his eyes the boots and legs of his father, who had removed his belt and was whipping it in the air with the never-forgotten hiss of a viper coiled to strike. Sorrow flooded through him, intact and precise, as if it had lain always in his mind, waiting. He was once again in the armoire where his father locked him to punish him for imagined misbehavior, there where for eternal hours he had crouched with his eyes closed, not to see the darkness, with his hands over his ears, to shut out the beating of his heart, trembling, huddled like a cornered animal. Wandering in the mist of his memories he found his sister Katharina, a sweet, retarded child who spent her life hiding, with the hope that her father would forget the disgrace of her having been born. With Katharina, Rolf crawled beneath the dining room table, and with her hid there under the long white tablecloth, two children forever embraced, alert to footsteps and voices. Katharina's scent melded with his own sweat, with aromas of cooking, garlic, soup, freshly baked bread, and the unexpected odor of putrescent clay. His sister's hand in his, her frightened breathing, her silk hair against his cheek, the candid gaze of her eyes. Katharina . . . Katharina materialized before him, floating on the air like a flag, clothed in the white tablecloth, now a winding sheet, and at last he could weep for her death and for the guilt of having abandoned her. He understood then that all his exploits as a reporter, the feats that had won him such recognition and fame, were merely an attempt to keep his most ancient fears at bay, a stratagem for taking refuge behind a lens to test whether reality was more tolerable from that perspective. He took excessive risks as an exercise of courage, training by day to conquer the monsters that tormented him by night. But he had come face to face with the moment of truth; he could not continue to escape his past. He *was* Azucena; he was buried in the clayey mud; his terror was not the distant emotion of an almost forgotten childhood, it was a claw sunk in his throat. In the flush of his tears he saw his mother, dressed in black and clutching her imitation-crocodile pocketbook to her bosom, just as he had last seen her on the dock when she had come to put him on the boat to South America. She had not come to dry his tears, but to tell him to pick up a shovel: the war was over and now they must bury the dead.

"Don't cry. I don't hurt anymore. I'm fine," Azucena said when dawn came.

"I'm not crying for you," Rolf Carlé smiled. "I'm crying for myself. I hurt all   25 over."

The third day in the valley of the cataclysm began with a pale light filtering through storm clouds. The President of the Republic visited the area in his tailored safari jacket to confirm that this was the worst catastrophe of the century; the country was in mourning; sister nations had offered aid; he had ordered a state of siege; the Armed Forces would be merciless, anyone caught stealing or committing other offenses would be shot on sight. He added that it was impossible to remove all the corpses or count the thousands who had disappeared; the entire valley would be declared holy ground, and bishops would come to celebrate a solemn mass for the souls of the victims. He went to the Army field tents to offer relief in the form of vague promises to crowds of the rescued, then to the improvised hospital to offer a word of encouragement to doctors and nurses worn down from so many hours of tribulations. Then he asked to be taken to see Azucena, the little girl the whole world had seen. He waved to her with a limp statesman's hand, and microphones recorded his emotional voice and paternal tone as he told her that her courage had served as an example to the nation. Rolf Carlé interrupted to ask for a pump, and the President assured him that he personally would attend to the matter. I caught a glimpse of Rolf for a few seconds kneeling beside the mudpit. On the evening news broadcast, he was still in the same position; and I, glued to the screen like a fortuneteller to her crystal ball, could tell that something fundamental had changed in him. I knew somehow that during the night his defenses had crumbled and he had given in to grief; finally he was vulnerable. The girl had touched a part of him that he himself had no access to, a part he had never shared with me. Rolf had wanted to console her, but it was Azucena who had given him consolation.

I recognized the precise moment at which Rolf gave up the fight and surrendered to the torture of watching the girl die. I was with them, three days and two nights, spying on them from the other side of life. I was there when she told him that in all her thirteen years no boy had ever loved her and that it was a pity to leave this world without knowing love. Rolf assured her that he loved her more than he could ever love anyone, more than he loved his mother, more than his sister, more than all the women who had slept in his arms, more than he loved me, his life companion, who would have given anything to be trapped in that well in her place, who would have exchanged her life for Azucena's, and I watched as he leaned down to kiss her poor forehead, consumed by a sweet, sad emotion he could not name. I felt how in that instant both were saved from despair, how they were freed from the clay, how they rose above the vultures and helicopters, how together they flew above the vast swamp of corruption and laments. How, finally, they were able to accept death. Rolf Carlé prayed in silence that she would die quickly, because such pain cannot be borne.

By then I had obtained a pump and was in touch with a general who had agreed to ship it the next morning on a military cargo plane. But on the night of that third day, beneath the unblinking focus of quartz lamps and the lens of a hundred cameras, Azucena gave up, her eyes locked with those of the friend who had sustained her to the end. Rolf Carlé removed the life buoy, closed her eyelids, held her to his chest for a few moments, and then let her go. She sank slowly, a flower in the mud.

You are back with me, but you are not the same man. I often accompany you to the station and we watch the videos of Azucena again; you study them intently, looking for something you could have done to save her, something you did not think of in time. Or maybe you study them to see yourself as if in a mirror, naked. Your cameras lie forgotten in a closet; you do not write or sing; you sit long hours before the window, staring at the mountains. Beside you, I wait for you to complete the voyage into yourself, for the old wounds to heal. I know that when you return from your nightmares, we shall again walk hand in hand, as before.

James Baldwin   1924–1987

Sonny's Blues   [1957]

I read about it in the paper, in the subway, on my way to work. I read it, and I couldn't believe it, and I read it again. Then perhaps I just stared at it, at the newsprint spelling out his name, spelling out the story. I stared at it in the swinging lights of the subway car, and in the faces and bodies of the people, and in my own face, trapped in the darkness which roared outside.

It was not to be believed and I kept telling myself that, as I walked from the subway station to the high school. And at the same time I couldn't doubt it. I was scared, scared for Sonny. He became real to me again. A great block of ice got settled in my belly and kept melting there slowly all day long, while I taught my classes algebra. It was a special kind of ice. It kept melting, sending trickles of ice water all up and down my veins, but it never got less. Sometimes it hardened and seemed to expand until I felt my guts were going to come spilling out or that I was going to choke or scream. This would always be at a moment when I was remembering some specific thing Sonny had once said or done.

When he was about as old as the boys in my classes his face had been bright and open, there was a lot of copper in it; and he'd had wonderfully direct brown eyes, and great gentleness and privacy. I wondered what he looked like now. He had been picked up, the evening before, in a raid on an apartment downtown, for peddling and using heroin.

I couldn't believe it: but what I mean by that is that I couldn't find any room for it anywhere inside me. I had kept it outside me for a long time. I hadn't wanted to know. I had had suspicions, but I didn't name them, I kept putting them away. I told myself that Sonny was wild, but he wasn't crazy. And he'd always been a good boy, he hadn't ever turned hard or evil or disrespectful, the way kids can, so quick, so quick, especially in Harlem. I didn't want to believe that I'd ever see my brother going down, coming to nothing, all that light in his face gone out, in the condition I'd already seen so many others. Yet it had happened and here I was, talking about algebra to a lot of boys who might, every one of them for all I knew, be popping off needles every time they went to the head. Maybe it did more for them than algebra could.

I was sure that the first time Sonny had ever had horse, he couldn't have 5 been much older than these boys were now. These boys, now, were living as we'd been living then, they were growing up with a rush and their heads bumped abruptly against the low ceiling of their actual possibilities. They were filled with rage. All they really knew were two darknesses, the darkness of their lives, which was now closing in on them, and the darkness of the movies, which had blinded them to that other darkness, and in which they now, vindictively, dreamed, at once more together than they were at any other time, and more alone.

When the last bell rang, the last class ended, I let out my breath. It seemed I'd been holding it for all that time. My clothes were wet — I may have looked as though I'd been sitting in a steam bath, all dressed up, all afternoon. I sat alone in the classroom a long time. I listened to the boys outside, downstairs, shouting and cursing and laughing. Their laughter struck me for perhaps the first time. It was not the joyous laughter which — God knows why — one associates with children. It was mocking and insular, its intent to denigrate. It was disenchanted, and in this, also, lay the authority of their curses. Perhaps I was listening to them because I was thinking about my brother and in them I heard my brother. And myself.

One boy was whistling a tune, at once very complicated and very simple, it seemed to be pouring out of him as though he were a bird, and it sounded very cool and moving through all that harsh, bright air, only just holding its own through all those other sounds.

I stood up and walked over to the window and looked down into the courtyard. It was the beginning of the spring and the sap was rising in the boys. A teacher passed through them every now and again, quickly, as though he or she couldn't wait to get out of that courtyard, to get those boys out of their sight and off their minds. I started collecting my stuff. I thought I'd better get home and talk to Isabel.

The courtyard was almost deserted by the time I got downstairs. I saw this boy standing in the shadow of a doorway, looking just like Sonny. I almost called his name. Then I saw that it wasn't Sonny, but somebody we used to know, a boy from around our block. He'd been Sonny's friend. He'd never been mine, having been too young for me, and, anyway, I'd never liked him. And now, even though he was a grown-up man, he still hung around that block, still spent hours on the street corners, was always high and raggy. I used to run into him from time to time and he'd often work around to asking me for a quarter or fifty cents. He always had some real good excuse, too, and I always gave it to him, I don't know why.

But now, abruptly, I hated him. I couldn't stand the way he looked at me, 10 partly like a dog, partly like a cunning child. I wanted to ask him what the hell he was doing in the school courtyard.

He sort of shuffled over to me, and he said, "I see you got the papers. So you already know about it."

"You mean about Sonny? Yes, I already know about it. How come they didn't get you?"

He grinned. It made him repulsive and it also brought to mind what he'd looked like as a kid. "I wasn't there. I stay away from them people."

"Good for you." I offered him a cigarette and I watched him through the smoke. "You come all the way down here just to tell me about Sonny?"

"That's right." He was sort of shaking his head and his eyes looked strange, 15 as though they were about to cross. The bright sun deadened his damp dark brown skin and it made his eyes look yellow and showed up the dirt in his kinked hair. He smelled funky. I moved a little away from him and I said, "Well, thanks. But I already know about it and I got to get home."

"I'll walk you a little ways," he said. We started walking. There were a couple of kids still loitering in the courtyard and one of them said goodnight to me and looked strangely at the boy beside me.

"What're you going to do?" he asked me. "I mean, about Sonny?"

"Look. I haven't seen Sonny for over a year, I'm not sure I'm going to do anything. Anyway, what the hell *can* I do?"

"That's right," he said quickly, "ain't nothing you can do. Can't much help old Sonny no more, I guess."

It was what I was thinking and so it seemed to me he had no right to say it.   20

"I'm surprised at Sonny, though," he went on — he had a funny way of talking, he looked straight ahead as though he were talking to himself — "I thought Sonny was a smart boy, I thought he was too smart to get hung."

"I guess he thought so too," I said sharply, "and that's how he got hung. And how about you? You're pretty goddamn smart, I bet."

Then he looked directly at me, just for a minute. "I ain't smart," he said. "If I was smart, I'd have reached for a pistol a long time ago."

"Look. Don't tell *me* your sad story, if it was up to me, I'd give you one." Then I felt guilty — guilty, probably, for never having supposed that the poor bastard *had* a story of his own, much less a sad one, and I asked, quickly, "What's going to happen to him now?"

He didn't answer this. He was off by himself some place. "Funny thing," he   25 said, and from his tone we might have been discussing the quickest way to get to Brooklyn, "when I saw the papers this morning, the first thing I asked myself was if I had anything to do with it. I felt sort of responsible."

I began to listen more carefully. The subway station was on the corner, just before us, and I stopped. He stopped, too. We were in front of a bar and he ducked lightly, peering in, but whoever he was looking for didn't seem to be there. The juke box was blasting away with something black and bouncy and I half watched the barmaid as she danced her way from the juke box to her place behind the bar. And I watched her face as she laughingly responded to something someone said to her, still keeping time to the music. When she smiled one saw the little girl, one sensed the doomed, still-struggling woman beneath the battered face of the semi-whore.

"I never *give* Sonny nothing," the boy said finally, "but a long time ago I come to school high and Sonny asked me how it felt." He paused, I couldn't bear to watch him, I watched the barmaid, and I listened to the music which seemed to be causing the pavement to shake. "I told him it felt great." The music stopped, the barmaid paused and watched the juke box until the music began again. "It did."

All this was carrying me some place I didn't want to go. I certainly didn't want to know how it felt. It filled everything, the people, the houses, the music, the dark, quicksilver barmaid, with menace; and this menace was their reality.

"What's going to happen to him now?" I asked again.

"They'll send him away some place and they'll try to cure him." He shook   30 his head. "Maybe he'll even think he's kicked the habit. Then they'll let him loose" — he gestured, throwing his cigarette into the gutter. "That's all."

"What do you mean, that's *all*?"

But I knew what he meant.

"I *mean*, that's *all*." He turned his head and looked at me, pulling down the corners of his mouth. "Don't you know what I mean?" he asked, softly.

"How the hell *would* I know what you mean?" I almost whispered it, I don't know why.

"That's right," he said to the air, "how would *he* know what I mean?" He turned toward me again, patient and calm, and yet I somehow felt him shaking, shaking as though he were going to fall apart. I felt that ice in my guts again, the dread I'd felt all afternoon; and again I watched the barmaid, moving about the bar, washing glasses, and singing. "Listen. They'll let him out and then it'll just start all over again. That's what I mean."

"You mean — they'll let him out. And then he'll just start working his way back in again. You mean he'll never kick the habit. Is that what you mean?"

"That's right," he said, cheerfully. "*You* see what I mean."

"Tell me," I said at last, "why does he want to die? He must want to die, he's killing himself, why does he want to die?"

He looked at me in surprise. He licked his lips. "He don't want to die. He wants to live. Don't nobody want to die, ever."

Then I wanted to ask him — too many things. He could not have answered, or if he had, I could not have borne the answers. I started walking. "Well, I guess it's none of my business."

"It's going to be rough on old Sonny," he said. We reached the subway station. "This is your station?" he asked. I nodded. I took one step down. "Damn!" he said, suddenly. I looked up at him. He grinned again. "Damn it if I didn't leave all my money home. You ain't got a dollar on you, have you? Just for a couple of days, is all."

All at once something inside gave and threatened to come pouring out of me. I didn't hate him any more. I felt that in another moment I'd start crying like a child.

"Sure," I said. "Don't sweat." I looked in my wallet and didn't have a dollar, I only had a five. "Here," I said. "That hold you?"

He didn't look at it — he didn't want to look at it. A terrible closed look came over his face, as though he were keeping the number on the bill a secret from him and me. "Thanks," he said, and now he was dying to see me go. "Don't worry about Sonny. Maybe I'll write him or something."

"Sure," I said. "You do that. So long."

"Be seeing you," he said. I went on down the steps.

And I didn't write Sonny or send him anything for a long time. When I finally did, it was just after my little girl died, he wrote me back a letter which made me feel like a bastard.

Here's what he said:

Dear brother,

You don't know how much I needed to hear from you. I wanted to write you many a time but I dug how much I must have hurt you and so I didn't write. But now I feel like a man who's been trying to climb up out of some deep, real deep and funky hole and just saw the sun up there, outside. I got to get outside.

I can't tell you much about how I got here. I mean I don't know how to tell you. I guess I was afraid of something or I was trying to escape from something and you know I have never been very strong in the head (smile). I'm glad Mama and Daddy are dead and can't see what's happened to their son and I swear if I'd known what I was doing I would never have hurt you so, you and a lot of other fine people who were nice to me and who believed in me.

I don't want you to think it had anything to do with me being a musician. It's more than that. Or maybe less than that. I can't get anything straight in my head down here and I try not to think about what's going to happen to me when I get outside again. Sometime I think I'm going to flip and *never* get outside and sometime I think I'll come straight back. I tell you one thing, though, I'd rather blow my brains out than go through this again. But that's what they all say, so they tell me. If I tell you when I'm coming to New York and if you could meet me, I sure would appreciate it. Give my love to Isabel and the kids and I was sure sorry to hear about little Gracie. I wish I could be like Mama and say the Lord's will be done, but I don't know it seems to me that trouble is the one thing that never does get stopped and I don't know what good it does to blame it on the Lord. But maybe it does some good if you believe it.

> Your brother,
> Sonny

Then I kept in constant touch with him and I sent him whatever I could and I went to meet him when he came back to New York. When I saw him many things I thought I had forgotten came flooding back to me. This was because I had begun, finally, to wonder about Sonny, about the life that Sonny lived inside. This life, whatever it was, had made him older and thinner and it had deepened the distant stillness in which he had always moved. He looked very unlike my baby brother. Yet, when he smiled, when we shook hands, the baby brother I'd never known looked out from the depths of his private life, like an animal waiting to be coaxed into the light.

"How you been keeping?" he asked me.   50

"All right. And you?"

"Just fine." He was smiling all over his face. "It's good to see you again."

"It's good to see you."

The seven years' difference in our ages lay between us like a chasm: I wondered if these years would ever operate between us as a bridge. I was remembering, and it made it hard to catch my breath, that I had been there when he was born; and I had heard the first words he had ever spoken. When he started to walk, he walked from our mother straight to me. I caught him just before he fell when he took the first steps he ever took in this world.

"How's Isabel?"   55

"Just fine. She's dying to see you."

"And the boys?"

"They're fine, too. They're anxious to see their uncle."

"Oh, come on. You know they don't remember me."

"Are you kidding? Of course they remember you."

He grinned again. We got into a taxi. We had a lot to say to each other, far too much to know how to begin.

As the taxi began to move, I asked, "You still want to go to India?"

He laughed. "You still remember that. Hell, no. This place is Indian enough for me."

"It used to belong to them," I said.

And he laughed again. "They damn sure knew what they were doing when they got rid of it."

Years ago, when he was around fourteen, he'd been all hipped on the idea of going to India. He read books about people sitting on rocks, naked, in all kinds of weather, but mostly bad, naturally, and walking barefoot through hot coals and arriving at wisdom. I used to say that it sounded to me as though they were getting away from wisdom as fast as they could. I think he sort of looked down on me for that.

"Do you mind," he asked, "if we have the driver drive alongside the park? On the west side—I haven't seen the city in so long."

"Of course not," I said. I was afraid that I might sound as though I were humoring him, but I hoped he wouldn't take it that way.

So we drove along, between the green of the park and the stony, lifeless elegance of hotels and apartment buildings, toward the vivid, killing streets of our childhood. These streets hadn't changed, though housing projects jutted up out of them now like rocks in the middle of a boiling sea. Most of the houses in which we had grown up had vanished, as had the stores from which we had stolen, the basements in which we had first tried sex, the rooftops from which we had hurled tin cans and bricks. But houses exactly like the houses of our past yet dominated the landscape, boys exactly like the boys we once had been found themselves smothering in these houses, came down into the streets for light and air and found themselves encircled by disaster. Some escaped the trap, most didn't. Those who got out always left something of themselves behind, as some animals amputate a leg and leave it in the trap. It might be said, perhaps, that I had escaped, after all, I was a school teacher; or that Sonny had, he hadn't lived in Harlem for years. Yet, as the cab moved uptown through streets which seemed, with a rush, to darken with dark people, and as I covertly studied Sonny's face, it came to me that what we both were seeking through our separate cab windows was that part of ourselves which had been left behind. It's always at the hour of trouble and confrontation that the missing member aches.

We hit 110th Street and started rolling up Lenox Avenue. And I'd known this avenue all my life, but it seemed to me again, as it had seemed on the day I'd first heard about Sonny's trouble, filled with a hidden menace which was its very breath of life.

"We almost there," said Sonny.

"Almost." We were both too nervous to say anything more.

We live in a housing project. It hasn't been up long. A few days after it was up it seemed uninhabitably new, now, of course, it's already rundown. It looks like a parody of the good, clean, faceless life — God knows the people who live in it do their best to make it a parody. The beat-looking grass lying around isn't enough to make their lives green, the hedges will never hold out the streets, and they know it. The big windows fool no one, they aren't big enough to make space out of no space. They don't bother with the windows, they watch the TV screen instead. The playground is most popular with the children who don't play at jacks, or skip rope, or roller skate, or swing, and they can be found in it after dark. We moved in partly because it's not too far from where I teach, and partly for the kids; but it's really just like the houses in which Sonny and I grew up. The same things happen, they'll have the same things to remember. The moment Sonny and I started into the house I had the feeling that I was simply bringing him back into the danger he had almost died trying to escape.

Sonny has never been talkative. So I don't know why I was sure he'd be dying to talk to me when supper was over the first night. Everything went fine, the oldest boy remembered him, and the youngest boy liked him, and Sonny had remembered to bring something for each of them; and Isabel, who is really much nicer than I am, more open and giving, had gone to a lot of trouble about dinner and was genuinely glad to see him. And she's always been able to tease Sonny in a way that I haven't. It was nice to see her face so vivid again and to hear her laugh and watch her make Sonny laugh. She wasn't, or, anyway, she didn't seem to be, at all uneasy or embarrassed. She chatted as though there were no subject which had to be avoided and she got Sonny past his first, faint stiffness. And thank God she was there, for I was filled with that icy dread again. Everything I did seemed awkward to me, and everything I said sounded freighted with hidden meaning. I was trying to remember everything I'd heard about dope addiction and I couldn't help watching Sonny for signs. I wasn't doing it out of malice. I was trying to find out something about my brother. I was dying to hear him tell me he was safe.

"Safe!" my father grunted, whenever Mama suggested trying to move to a 75 neighborhood which might be safer for children. "Safe, hell! Ain't no place safe for kids, nor nobody."

He always went on like this, but he wasn't, ever, really as bad as he sounded, not even on weekends, when he got drunk. As a matter of fact, he was always on the lookout for "something a little better," but he died before he found it. He died suddenly, during a drunken weekend in the middle of the war, when Sonny was fifteen. He and Sonny hadn't ever got on too well. And this was partly because Sonny was the apple of his father's eye. It was because he loved Sonny so much and was frightened for him, that he was always fighting with him. It doesn't do any good to fight with Sonny. Sonny just moves back, inside himself, where he can't be reached. But the principal reason that they never hit it off is that they were so much alike. Daddy was big and rough and loud-talking, just the opposite of Sonny, but they both had — that same privacy.

Mama tried to tell me something about this, just after Daddy died. I was home on leave from the army.

This was the last time I ever saw my mother alive. Just the same, this picture gets all mixed up in my mind with pictures I had of her when she was younger. The way I always see her is the way she used to be on a Sunday afternoon, say, when the old folks were talking after the big Sunday dinner. I always see her wearing pale blue. She'd be sitting on the sofa. And my father would be sitting in the easy chair, not far from her. And the living room would be full of church folks and relatives. There they sit, in chairs all around the living room, and the night is creeping up outside, but nobody knows it yet. You can see the darkness growing against the windowpanes and you hear the street noises every now and again, or maybe the jangling beat of a tambourine from one of the churches close by, but it's real quiet in the room. For a moment nobody's talking, but every face looks darkening, like the sky outside. And my mother rocks a little from the waist, and my father's eyes are closed. Everyone is looking at something a child can't see. For a minute they've forgotten the children. Maybe a kid is lying on the rug, half asleep. Maybe somebody's got a kid in his lap and is absent-mindedly stroking the kid's head. Maybe there's a kid, quiet and big-eyed, curled up in a big chair in the corner. The silence, the darkness coming, and the darkness in the faces frightens the child obscurely. He hopes that the hand which strokes his forehead will never stop — will never die. He hopes that there will never come a time when the old folks won't be sitting around the living room, talking about where they've come from, and what they've seen, and what's happened to them and their kinfolk.

But something deep and watchful in the child knows that this is bound to end, is already ending. In a moment someone will get up and turn on the light. Then the old folks will remember the children and they won't talk any more that day. And when light fills the room, the child is filled with darkness. He knows that everytime this happens he's moved just a little closer to that darkness outside. The darkness outside is what the old folks have been talking about. It's what they've come from. It's what they endure. The child knows that they won't talk any more because if he knows too much about what's happened to *them*, he'll know too much too soon, about what's going to happen to *him*.

The last time I talked to my mother, I remember I was restless. I wanted to 80 get out and see Isabel. We weren't married then and we had a lot to straighten out between us.

There Mama sat, in black, by the window. She was humming an old church song, *Lord, you brought me from a long ways off.* Sonny was out somewhere. Mama kept watching the streets.

"I don't know," she said, "if I'll ever see you again, after you go off from here. But I hope you'll remember the things I tried to teach you."

"Don't talk like that," I said, and smiled. "You'll be here a long time yet."

She smiled, too, but she said nothing. She was quiet for a long time. And I said, "Mama, don't you worry about nothing. I'll be writing all the time, and you be getting the checks. . . ."

"I want to talk to you about your brother," she said, suddenly. "If anything 85 happens to me he ain't going to have nobody to look out for him."

"Mama," I said, "ain't nothing going to happen to you *or* Sonny. Sonny's all right. He's a good boy and he's got good sense."

"It ain't a question of his being a good boy," Mama said, "nor of his having good sense. It ain't only the bad ones, nor yet the dumb ones that gets sucked under." She stopped, looking at me. "Your Daddy once had a brother," she said, and she smiled in a way that made me feel she was in pain. "You didn't never know that, did you?"

"No," I said, "I never knew that," and I watched her face.

"Oh, yes," she said, "your Daddy had a brother." She looked out of the window again. "I know you never saw your Daddy cry. But *I* did — many a time, through all these years."

I asked her, "What happened to his brother? How come nobody's ever 90 talked about him?"

This was the first time I ever saw my mother look old.

"His brother got killed," she said, "when he was just a little younger than you are now. I knew him. He was a fine boy. He was maybe a little full of the devil, but he didn't mean nobody no harm."

Then she stopped and the room was silent, exactly as it had sometimes been on those Sunday afternoons. Mama kept looking out into the streets.

"He used to have a job in the mill," she said, "and, like all young folks, he just liked to perform on Saturday nights. Saturday nights, him and your father would drift around to different places, go to dances and things like that, or just sit around with people they knew, and your father's brother would sing, he had a fine voice, and play along with himself on his guitar. Well, this particular Saturday night, him and your father was coming home from some place, and they were both a little drunk and there was a moon that night, it was bright like day. Your father's brother was feeling kind of good, and he was whistling to himself, and he had his guitar slung over his shoulder. They was coming down a hill and beneath them was a road that turned off from the highway. Well, your father's brother, being always kind of frisky, decided to run down this hill, and he did, with that guitar banging and clanging behind him, and he ran across the road, and he was making water behind a tree. And your father was sort of amused at him and he was still coming down the hill, kind of slow. Then he heard a car motor and that same minute his brother stepped from behind the tree, into the road, in the moonlight. And he started to cross the road. And your father started to run down the hill, he says he don't know why. This car was full of white men. They was all drunk, and when they seen your father's brother they let out a great whoop and holler and they aimed the car straight at him. They was having fun, they just wanted to scare him, the way they do sometimes, you know. But they was drunk. And I guess the boy, being drunk, too, and scared, kind of lost his head. By the time he jumped it was too late. Your father says he heard his brother scream when the car rolled over him, and he heard the wood of that guitar when it give, and he heard them strings go flying, and he heard them white men shouting, and the car kept on a-going and it ain't stopped till this day. And, time your father got down the hill, his brother weren't nothing but blood and pulp."

Tears were gleaming on my mother's face. There wasn't anything I could say.   95

"He never mentioned it," she said, "because I never let him mention it before you children. Your Daddy was like a crazy man that night and for many a night thereafter. He says he never in his life seen anything as dark as that road after the lights of that car had gone away. Weren't nothing, weren't nobody on that road, just your Daddy and his brother and that busted guitar. Oh, yes. Your Daddy never did really get right again. Till the day he died he weren't sure but that every white man he saw was the man that killed his brother."

She stopped and took out her handkerchief and dried her eyes and looked at me.

"I ain't telling you all this," she said, "to make you scared or bitter or to make you hate nobody. I'm telling you this because you got a brother. And the world ain't changed."

I guess I didn't want to believe this. I guess she saw this in my face. She turned away from me, toward the window again, searching those streets.

"But I praise my Redeemer," she said at last, "that He called your Daddy   100 home before me. I ain't saying it to throw no flowers at myself, but, I declare, it keeps me from feeling too cast down to know I helped your father get safely through this world. Your father always acted like he was the roughest, strongest man on earth. And everybody took him to be like that. But if he hadn't had *me* there—to see his tears!"

She was crying again. Still, I couldn't move. I said, "Lord, Lord, Mama, I didn't know it was like that."

"Oh, honey," she said, "there's a lot that you don't know. But you are going to find it out." She stood up from the window and came over to me. "You got to hold on to your brother," she said, "and don't let him fall, no matter what it looks like is happening to him and no matter how evil you gets with him. You going to be evil with him many a time. But don't you forget what I told you, you hear?"

"I won't forget," I said. "Don't you worry, I won't forget. I won't let nothing happen to Sonny."

My mother smiled as though she were amused at something she saw in my face. Then, "You may not be able to stop nothing from happening. But you got to let him know you's *there*."

Two days later I was married, and then I was gone. And I had a lot of things   105 on my mind and I pretty well forgot my promise to Mama until I got shipped home on a special furlough for her funeral.

And, after the funeral, with just Sonny and me alone in the empty kitchen, I tried to find out something about him.

"What do you want to do?" I asked him.

"I'm going to be a musician," he said.

For he had graduated, in the time I had been away, from dancing to the juke box to finding out who was playing what, and what they were doing with it, and he had bought himself a set of drums.

"You mean, you want to be a drummer?" I somehow had the feeling that 110 being a drummer might be all right for other people but not for my brother Sonny.

"I don't think," he said, looking at me very gravely, "that I'll ever be a good drummer. But I think I can play a piano."

I frowned. I'd never played the role of the older brother quite so seriously before, had scarcely ever, in fact, *asked* Sonny a damn thing. I sensed myself in the presence of something I didn't really know how to handle, didn't understand. So I made my frown a little deeper as I asked: "What kind of musician do you want to be?"

He grinned. "How many kinds do you think there are?"

"Be *serious*," I said.

He laughed, throwing his head back, and then looked at me. "I *am* serious." 115

"Well, then, for Christ's sake, stop kidding around and answer a serious question. I mean, do you want to be a concert pianist, you want to play classical music and all that, or — or what?" Long before I finished he was laughing again. "For Christ's *sake*, Sonny!"

He sobered, but with difficulty. "I'm sorry. But you sound so — *scared*!" and he was off again.

"Well, you may think it's funny now, baby, but it's not going to be so funny when you have to make your living at it, let me tell you *that*. I was furious because I knew he was laughing at me and I didn't know why.

"No," he said, very sober now, and afraid, perhaps, that he'd hurt me, "I don't want to be a classical pianist. That isn't what interests me. I mean" — he paused, looking hard at me, as though his eyes would help me to understand, and then gestured helplessly, as though perhaps his hand would help — "I mean, I'll have a lot of studying to do, and I'll have to study *everything*, but, I mean, I want to play *with* — jazz musicians." He stopped. "I want to play jazz," he said.

Well, the word had never before sounded as heavy, as real, as it sounded 120 that afternoon in Sonny's mouth. I just looked at him and I was probably frowning a real frown by this time. I simply couldn't see why on earth he'd want to spend his time hanging around nightclubs, clowning around on bandstands, while people pushed each other around a dance floor. It seemed — beneath him, somehow. I had never thought about it before, had never been forced to, but I suppose I had always put jazz musicians in a class with what Daddy called "good-time people."

"Are you *serious*?"

"Hell, *yes*, I'm serious."

He looked more helpless than ever, and annoyed, and deeply hurt.

I suggested, helpfully: "You mean — like Louis Armstrong?"

His face closed as though I'd struck him. "No. I'm not talking about none of 125 that old-time, down home crap."

"Well, look, Sonny, I'm sorry, don't get mad. I just don't altogether get it, that's all. Name somebody — you know, a jazz musician you admire."

"Bird."

"Who?"

"Bird! Charlie Parker!° Don't they teach you nothing in the goddamn army?"

I lit a cigarette. I was surprised and then a little amused to discover that I 130 was trembling. "I've been out of touch," I said. "You'll have to be patient with me. Now. Who's this Parker character?"

"He's just one of the greatest jazz musicians alive," said Sonny, sullenly, his hands in his pockets, his back to me. "Maybe *the* greatest," he added, bitterly, "that's probably why you never heard of him."

"All right," I said, "I'm ignorant. I'm sorry. I'll go out and buy all the cat's records right away, all right?"

"It don't," said Sonny, with dignity, "make any difference to me. I don't care what you listen to. Don't do me no favors."

I was beginning to realize that I'd never seen him so upset before. With another part of my mind I was thinking that this would probably turn out to be one of those things kids go through and that I shouldn't make it seem important by pushing it too hard. Still, I didn't think it would do any harm to ask: "Doesn't all this take a lot of time? Can you make a living at it?"

He turned back to me and half leaned, half sat, on the kitchen table. "Every- 135 thing takes time," he said, "and — well, yes, sure, I can make a living at it. But what I don't seem to be able to make you understand is that it's the only thing I want to do."

"Well, Sonny," I said, gently, "you know people can't always do exactly what they *want* to do —"

"*No*, I don't know that," said Sonny, surprising me. "I think people *ought* to do what they want to do, what else are they alive for?"

"You getting to be a big boy," I said desperately, "it's time you started thinking about your future."

"I'm thinking about my future," said Sonny, grimly. "I think about it all the time."

I gave up. I decided, if he didn't change his mind, that we could always talk 140 about it later. "In the meantime," I said, "you got to finish school." We had already decided that he'd have to move in with Isabel and her folks. I knew this wasn't the ideal arrangement because Isabel's folks are inclined to be dicty and they hadn't especially wanted Isabel to marry me. But I didn't know what else to do. "And we have to get you fixed up at Isabel's."

There was a long silence. He moved from the kitchen table to the window. "That's a terrible idea. You know it yourself."

"Do you have a *better* idea?"

Charlie Parker: Parker (1920–1955), saxophonist and composer, is widely regarded as one of the greatest jazz musicians. His original nickname "Yardbird" (of disputed origin) was later shortened to "Bird."

He just walked up and down the kitchen for a minute. He was as tall as I was. He had started to shave. I suddenly had the feeling that I didn't know him at all.

He stopped at the kitchen table and picked up my cigarettes. Looking at me with a kind of mocking, amused defiance, he put one between his lips. "You mind?"

"You smoking already?"   145

He lit the cigarette and nodded, watching me through the smoke. "I just wanted to see if I'd have the courage to smoke in front of you." He grinned and blew a great cloud of smoke to the ceiling. "It was easy." He looked at my face. "Come on, now. I bet you was smoking at my age, tell the truth."

I didn't say anything but the truth was on my face, and he laughed. But now there was something very strained in his laugh. "Sure. And I bet that ain't all you was doing."

He was frightening me a little. "Cut the crap," I said. "We already decided that you was going to go and live at Isabel's. Now what's got into you all of a sudden?"

"*You* decided it," he pointed out. "*I* didn't decide nothing." He stopped in front of me, leaning against the stove, arms loosely folded. "Look, brother. I don't want to stay in Harlem no more, I really don't." He was very earnest. He looked at me, then over toward the kitchen window. There was something in his eyes I'd never seen before, some thoughtfulness, some worry all his own. He rubbed the muscle of one arm. "It's time I was getting out of here."

"Where do you want to *go*, Sonny?"   150

"I want to join the army. Or the navy, I don't care. If I say I'm old enough, they'll believe me."

Then I got mad. It was because I was so scared. "You must be crazy. You god-damn fool, what the hell do you want to go and join the *army* for?"

"I just told you. To get out of Harlem."

"Sonny, you haven't even finished *school*. And if you really want to be a musician, how do you expect to study if you're in the *army*?"

He looked at me, trapped, and in anguish. "There's ways. I might be able to   155 work out some kind of deal. Anyway, I'll have the G.I. Bill when I come out."

"*If* you come out." We stared at each other. "Sonny, please. Be reasonable. I know the setup is far from perfect. But we got to do the best we can."

"I ain't learning nothing in school," he said. "Even when I go." He turned away from me and opened the window and threw his cigarette out into the narrow alley. I watched his back. "At least, I ain't learning nothing you'd want me to learn." He slammed the window so hard I thought the glass would fly out, and turned back to me. "And I'm sick of the stink of these garbage cans!"

"Sonny," I said, "I know how you feel. But if you don't finish school now, you're going to be sorry later that you didn't." I grabbed him by the shoulders. "And you only got another year. It ain't so bad. And I'll come back and I swear I'll help you do *whatever* you want to do. Just try to put up with it till I come back. Will you please do that? For me?"

He didn't answer and he wouldn't look at me.

"Sonny. You hear me?"

He pulled away. "I hear you. But you never hear anything *I* say."

I didn't know what to say to that. He looked out of the window and then back at me. "OK," he said, and sighed. "I'll try."

Then I said, trying to cheer him up a little, "They got a piano at Isabel's. You can practice on it."

And as a matter of fact, it did cheer him up for a minute. "That's right," he said to himself. "I forgot that." His face relaxed a little. But the worry, the thoughtfulness, played on it still, the way shadows play on a face which is staring into the fire.

But I thought I'd never hear the end of that piano. At first, Isabel would write me, saying how nice it was that Sonny was so serious about his music and how, as soon as he came in from school, or wherever he had been when he was supposed to be at school, he went straight to that piano and stayed there until suppertime. And, after supper, he went back to that piano and stayed there until everybody went to bed. He was at the piano all day Saturday and all day Sunday. Then he bought a record player and started playing records. He'd play one record over and over again, all day long sometimes, and he'd improvise along with it on the piano. Or he'd play one section of the record, one chord, one change, one progression, then he'd do it on the piano. Then back to the record. Then back to the piano.

Well, I really don't know how they stood it. Isabel finally confessed that it wasn't like living with a person at all, it was like living with sound. And the sound didn't make any sense to her, didn't make any sense to any of them — naturally. They began, in a way, to be afflicted by this presence that was living in their home. It was as though Sonny were some sort of god, or monster. He moved in an atmosphere which wasn't like theirs at all. They fed him and he ate, he washed himself, he walked in and out of their door; he certainly wasn't nasty or unpleasant or rude, Sonny isn't any of those things; but it was as though he were all wrapped up in some cloud, some fire, some vision all his own; and there wasn't any way to reach him.

At the same time, he wasn't really a man yet, he was still a child, and they had to watch out for him in all kinds of ways. They certainly couldn't throw him out. Neither did they dare to make a great scene about that piano because even they dimly sensed, as I sensed, from so many thousands of miles away, that Sonny was at that piano playing for his life.

But he hadn't been going to school. One day a letter came from the school board and Isabel's mother got it — there had, apparently, been other letters but Sonny had torn them up. This day, when Sonny came in, Isabel's mother showed him the letter and asked where he'd been spending his time. And she finally got it out of him that he'd been down in Greenwich Village, with musicians and other characters, in a white girl's apartment. And this scared her and she started to scream at him and what came up, once she began — though she denies it to this day — was what sacrifices they were making to give Sonny a decent home and how little he appreciated it.

Sonny didn't play the piano that day. By evening, Isabel's mother had calmed down but then there was the old man to deal with, and Isabel herself. Isabel says she did her best to be calm but she broke down and started crying. She says she just watched Sonny's face. She could tell, by watching him, what was happening with him. And what was happening was that they penetrated his cloud, they had reached him. Even if their fingers had been a thousand times more gentle than human fingers ever are, he could hardly help feeling that they had stripped him naked and were spitting on that nakedness. For he also had to see that his presence, that music, which was life or death to him, had been torture for them and that they had endured it, not at all for his sake, but only for mine. And Sonny couldn't take that. He can take it a little better today than he could then but he's still not very good at it and, frankly, I don't know anybody who is.

The silence of the next few days must have been louder than the sound of all   170
the music ever played since time began. One morning, before she went to work, Isabel was in his room for something and she suddenly realized that all of his records were gone. And she knew for certain that he was gone. And he was. He went as far as the navy would carry him. He finally sent me a postcard from some place in Greece and that was the first I knew that Sonny was still alive. I didn't see him any more until we were both back in New York and the war had long been over.

He was a man by then, of course, but I wasn't willing to see it. He came by the house from time to time, but we fought almost every time we met. I didn't like the way he carried himself, loose and dreamlike all the time, and I didn't like his friends, and his music seemed to be merely an excuse for the life he led. It sounded just that weird and disordered.

Then we had a fight, a pretty awful fight, and I didn't see him for months. By and by I looked him up, where he was living, in a furnished room in the Village, and I tried to make it up. But there were lots of people in the room and Sonny just lay on his bed, and he wouldn't come downstairs with me, and he treated these other people as though they were his family and I weren't. So I got mad and then he got mad, and then I told him that he might just as well be dead as live the way he was living. Then he stood up and he told me not to worry about him any more in life, that he *was* dead as far as I was concerned. Then he pushed me to the door and the other people looked on as though nothing were happening, and he slammed the door behind me. I stood in the hallway, staring at the door. I heard somebody laugh in the room and then the tears came to my eyes. I started down the steps, whistling to keep from crying, I kept whistling to myself, *You going to need me, baby, one of these cold, rainy days.*

I read about Sonny's trouble in the spring. Little Grace died in the fall. She was a beautiful little girl. But she only lived a little over two years. She died of polio and she suffered. She had a slight fever for a couple of days, but it didn't seem like anything and we just kept her in bed. And we would certainly have called the doctor, but the fever dropped, she seemed to be all right. So we thought it had just been a cold. Then, one day, she was up, playing, Isabel was in the kitchen fixing lunch for the two boys when they'd come in from school, and she heard Grace fall down in the living room. When you have a lot of children you don't always start running when one of them falls, unless they start screaming or something. And, this time, Grace was quiet. Yet, Isabel says that when she heard that *thump* and then that silence, something happened in her to make her afraid. And she ran to the living room and there was little Grace on the floor, all twisted up, and the reason she hadn't screamed was that she couldn't get her breath. And when she did scream, it was the worst sound, Isabel says, that she'd ever heard in all her life, and she still hears it sometimes in her dreams. Isabel will sometimes wake me up with a low, moaning, strangled sound and I have to be quick to awaken her and hold her to me and where Isabel is weeping against me seems a mortal wound.

I think I may have written Sonny the very day that little Grace was buried. I was sitting in the living room in the dark, by myself, and I suddenly thought of Sonny. My trouble made his real.

One Saturday afternoon, when Sonny had been living with us, or, anyway, been in our house, for nearly two weeks, I found myself wandering aimlessly about the living room, drinking from a can of beer, and trying to work up the courage to search Sonny's room. He was out, he was usually out whenever I was home, and Isabel had taken the children to see their grandparents. Suddenly I was standing still in front of the living room window, watching Seventh Avenue. The idea of searching Sonny's room made me still. I scarcely dared to admit to myself what I'd be searching for. I didn't know what I'd do if I found it. Or if I didn't.

On the sidewalk across from me, near the entrance to a barbecue joint, some people were holding an old-fashioned revival meeting. The barbecue cook, wearing a dirty white apron, his conked hair reddish and metallic in the pale sun, and a cigarette between his lips, stood in the doorway, watching them. Kids and older people paused in their errands and stood there, along with some older men and a couple of very tough-looking women who watched everything that happened on the avenue, as though they owned it, or were maybe owned by it. Well, they were watching this, too. The revival was being carried on by three sisters in black, and a brother. All they had were their voices and their Bibles and a tambourine. The brother was testifying and while he testified two of the sisters stood together, seeming to say, amen, and the third sister walked around with the tambourine outstretched and a couple of people dropped coins into it. Then the brother's testimony ended and the sister who had been taking up the collection dumped the coins into her palm and transferred them to the pocket of her long black robe. Then she raised both hands, striking the tambourine against the air, and then against one hand, and she started to sing. And the two other sisters and the brother joined in.

It was strange, suddenly, to watch, though I had been seeing these street meetings all my life. So, of course, had everybody else down there. Yet, they

175

paused and watched and listened and I stood still at the window. *"Tis the old ship of Zion,"* they sang, and the sister with the tambourine kept a steady, jangling beat, *"it has rescued many a thousand!"* Not a soul under the sound of their voices was hearing this song for the first time, not one of them had been rescued. Nor had they seen much in the way of rescue work being done around them. Neither did they especially believe in the holiness of the three sisters and the brother, they knew too much about them, knew where they lived, and how. The woman with the tambourine, whose voice dominated the air, whose face was bright with joy, was divided by very little from the woman who stood watching her, a cigarette between her heavy, chapped lips, her hair a cuckoo's nest, her face scarred and swollen from many beatings, and her black eyes glittering like coal. Perhaps they both knew this, which was why, when, as rarely, they addressed each other, they addressed each other as Sister. As the singing filled the air the watching, listening faces underwent a change, the eyes focusing on something within; the music seemed to soothe a poison out of them; and time seemed, nearly, to fall away from the sullen, belligerent, battered faces, as though they were fleeing back to their first condition, while dreaming of their last. The barbecue cook half shook his head and smiled, and dropped his cigarette and disappeared into his joint. A man fumbled in his pockets for change and stood holding it in his hand impatiently, as though he had just remembered a pressing appointment further up the avenue. He looked furious. Then I saw Sonny, standing on the edge of the crowd. He was carrying a wide, flat notebook with a green cover, and it made him look, from where I was standing, almost like a schoolboy. The coppery sun brought out the copper in his skin, he was very faintly smiling, standing very still. Then the singing stopped, the tambourine turned into a collection plate again. The furious man dropped in his coins and vanished, so did a couple of the women, and Sonny dropped some change in the plate, looking directly at the woman with a little smile. He started across the avenue, toward the house. He has a slow, loping walk something like the way Harlem hipsters walk, only he's imposed on this his own half-beat. I had never really noticed it before.

    I stayed at the window, both relieved and apprehensive. As Sonny disappeared from my sight, they began singing again. And they were still singing when his key turned in the lock.

    "Hey," he said.

    "Hey, yourself. You want some beer?"   180

    "No. Well, maybe." But he came up to the window and stood beside me, looking out. "What a warm voice," he said.

    They were singing *If I could only hear my mother pray again!*

    "Yes," I said, "and she can sure beat that tambourine."

    "But what a terrible song," he said, and laughed. He dropped his notebook on the sofa and disappeared into the kitchen. "Where's Isabel and the kids?"

    "I think they went to see their grandparents. You hungry?"   185

    "No." He came back into the living room with his can of beer. "You want to come some place with me tonight?"

    I sensed, I don't know how, that I couldn't possibly say no. "Sure. Where?"

He sat down on the sofa and picked up his notebook and started leafing through it. "I'm going to sit in with some fellows in a joint in the Village."

"You mean, you're going to play, tonight?"

"That's right." He took a swallow of his beer and moved back to the window. 190 He gave me a sidelong look. "If you can stand it."

"I'll try," I said.

He smiled to himself and we both watched as the meeting across the way broke up. The three sisters and the brother, heads bowed, were singing *God be with you till we meet again*. The faces around them were very quiet. Then the song ended. The small crowd dispersed. We watched the three women and the lone man walk slowly up the avenue.

"When she was singing before," said Sonny, abruptly, "her voice reminded me for a minute of what heroin feels like sometimes — when it's in your veins. It makes you feel sort of warm and cool at the same time. And distant. And — and sure." He sipped his beer, very deliberately not looking at me. I watched his face. "It makes you feel — in control. Sometimes you've got to have that feeling."

"Do you?" I sat down slowly in the easy chair.

"Sometimes." He went to the sofa and picked up his notebook again. "Some 195 people do."

"In order," I asked, "to play?" And my voice was very ugly, full of contempt and anger.

"Well" — he looked at me with great, troubled eyes, as though, in fact, he hoped his eyes would tell me things he could never otherwise say — "they *think* so. And *if* they think so — !"

"And what do *you* think?" I asked.

He sat on the sofa and put his can of beer on the floor. "I don't know," he said, and I couldn't be sure if he were answering my question or pursuing his thoughts. His face didn't tell me. "It's not so much to *play*. It's to *stand* it, to be able to make it at all. On any level." He frowned and smiled: "In order to keep from shaking to pieces."

"But these friends of yours," I said, "they seem to shake themselves to pieces 200 pretty goddamn fast."

"Maybe." He played with the notebook. And something told me that I should curb my tongue, that Sonny was doing his best to talk, that I should listen. "But of course you only know the ones that've gone to pieces. Some don't — or at least they haven't *yet* and that's just about all *any* of us can say." He paused. "And then there are some who just live, really, in hell, and they know it and they see what's happening and they go right on. I don't know." He sighed, dropped the notebook, folded his arms. "Some guys, you can tell from the way they play, they on something *all* the time. And you can see that, well, it makes something real for them. But of course," he picked up his beer from the floor and sipped it and put the can down again, "they want to, too, you've got to see that. Even some of them that say they don't — *some*, not all."

"And what about you?" I asked — I couldn't help it. "What about you? Do *you* want to?"

He stood up and walked to the window and remained silent for a long time. Then he sighed. "Me," he said. Then: "While I was downstairs before, on my way here, listening to that woman sing, it struck me all of a sudden how much suffering she must have had to go through — to sing like that. It's *repulsive* to think you have to suffer that much."

I said: "But there's no way not to suffer — is there, Sonny?"

"I believe not," he said and smiled, "but that's never stopped anyone from 205 trying." He looked at me. "Has it?" I realized, with this mocking look, that there stood between us, forever, beyond the power of time or forgiveness, the fact that I had held silence — so long! — when he had needed human speech to help him. He turned back to the window. "No, there's no way not to suffer. But you try all kinds of ways to keep from drowning in it, to keep on top of it, and to make it seem — well, like *you*. Like you did something, all right, and now you're suffering for it. You know?" I said nothing. "Well you know," he said, impatiently, "why *do* people suffer? Maybe it's better to do something to give it a reason, *any* reason."

"But we just agreed," I said, "that there's no way not to suffer. Isn't it better, then, just to — take it?"

"But nobody just takes it," Sonny cried, "that's what I'm telling you! *Everybody* tries not to. You're just hung up on the *way* some people try — it's not *your* way!"

The hair on my face began to itch, my face felt wet. "That's not true," I said, "that's not true. I don't give a damn what other people do, I don't even care how they suffer. I just care how *you* suffer." And he looked at me. "Please believe me," I said, "I don't want to see you — die — trying not to suffer."

"I won't," he said, flatly, "die trying not to suffer. At least, not any faster than anybody else."

"But there's no need," I said, trying to laugh, "is there? in killing yourself." 210

I wanted to say more, but I couldn't. I wanted to talk about will power and how life could be — well, beautiful. I wanted to say that it was all within; but was it? or, rather, wasn't that exactly the trouble? And I wanted to promise that I would never fail him again. But it would all have sounded — empty words and lies.

So I made the promise to myself and prayed that I would keep it.

"It's terrible sometimes, inside," he said, "that's what's the trouble. You walk these streets, black and funky and cold, and there's not really a living ass to talk to, and there's nothing shaking, and there's no way of getting it out — that storm inside. You can't talk it and you can't make love with it, and when you finally try to get with it and play it, you realize *nobody's* listening. So *you've* got to listen. You got to find a way to listen."

And then he walked away from the window and sat on the sofa again, as though all the wind had suddenly been knocked out of him. "Sometimes you'll do *anything* to play, even cut your mother's throat." He laughed and looked at me. "Or your brother's." Then he sobered. "Or your own." Then: "Don't worry. I'm all right now and I think I'll *be* all right. But I can't forget — where I've been. I don't mean just the physical place I've been, I mean where I've *been*. And *what* I've been."

"What have you been, Sonny?" I asked.   215

He smiled — but sat sideways on the sofa, his elbow resting on the back his fingers playing with his mouth and chin, not looking at me. "I've been something I didn't recognize, didn't know I could be. Didn't know anybody could be." He stopped, looking inward, looking helplessly young, looking old. "I'm not talking about it now because I feel *guilty* or anything like that — maybe it would be better if I did, I don't know. Anyway, I can't really talk about it. Not to you, not to anybody," and now he turned and faced me. "Sometimes, you know, and it was actually when I was most *out* of the world, I felt that I was in it, that I was *with* it, really, and I could play or I didn't really have to *play*, it just came out of me, it was there. And I don't know how I played, thinking about it now, but I know I did awful things, those times, sometimes, to people. Or it wasn't that I *did* anything to them — it was that they weren't real." He picked up the beer can; it was empty; he rolled it between his palms: "And other times — well, I needed a fix, I needed to find a place to lean, I needed to clear a space to *listen* — and I couldn't find it, and I — went crazy, I did terrible things to *me*, I was terrible *for* me." He began pressing the beer can between his hands, I watched the metal begin to give. It glittered, as he played with it, like a knife, and I was afraid he would cut himself, but I said nothing. "Oh well. I can never tell you. I was all by myself at the bottom of something, stinking and sweating and crying and shaking, and I smelled it, you know? *my* stink, and I thought I'd die if I couldn't get away from it and yet, all the same, I knew that everything I was doing was just locking me in with it. And I didn't know," he paused, still flattening the beer can, "I didn't know, I still *don't* know, something kept telling me that maybe it was good to smell your own stink, but I didn't think that *that* was what I'd been trying to do — and — who can stand it?" and he abruptly dropped the ruined beer can, looking at me with a small, still smile, and then rose, walking to the window as though it were the lodestone rock. I watched his face, he watched the avenue. "I couldn't tell you when Mama died — but the reason I wanted to leave Harlem so bad was to get away from drugs. And then, when I ran away, that's what I was running from — really. When I came back, nothing had changed, *I* hadn't changed, I was just — older." And he stopped, drumming with his fingers on the windowpane. The sun had vanished, soon darkness would fall. I watched his face. "It can come again," he said, almost as though speaking to himself. Then he turned to me. "It can come again," he repeated. "I just want you to know that."

"All right," I said, at last. "So it can come again. All right."

He smiled, but the smile was sorrowful. "I had to try to tell you," he said.

"Yes," I said. "I understand that."

"You're my brother," he said, looking straight at me, and not smiling at all.   220

"Yes," I repeated, "yes. I understand that."

He turned back to the window, looking out. "All that hatred down there," he said, "all that hatred and misery and love. It's a wonder it doesn't blow the avenue apart."

We went to the only nightclub on a short, dark street, downtown. We squeezed through the narrow, chattering, jam-packed bar to the entrance of the big room, where the bandstand was. And we stood there for a moment, for the lights were very dim in this room and we couldn't see. Then, "Hello, boy," said a voice and an enormous black man, much older than Sonny or myself, erupted out of all that atmospheric lighting and put an arm around Sonny's shoulder. "I been sitting right here," he said, "waiting for you."

He had a big voice, too, and heads in the darkness turned toward us.

Sonny grinned and pulled a little away, and said, "Creole, this is my brother. I told you about him."   225

Creole shook my hand. "I'm glad to meet you, son," he said, and it was clear that he was glad to meet me *there*, for Sonny's sake. And he smiled, "You got a real musician in *your* family," and he took his arm from Sonny's shoulder and slapped him, lightly, affectionately, with the back of his hand.

"Well. Now I've heard it all," said a voice behind us. This was another musician, and a friend of Sonny's, a coal-black cheerful-looking man, built close to the ground. He immediately began confiding to me, at the top of his lungs, the most terrible things about Sonny, his teeth gleaming like a lighthouse and his laugh coming up out of him like the beginning of an earthquake. And it turned out that everyone at the bar knew Sonny, or almost everyone; some were musicians, working there, or nearby, or not working, some were simply hangers-on, and some were there to hear Sonny play. I was introduced to all of them and they were all very polite to me. Yet, it was clear that, for them, I was only Sonny's brother. Here, I was in Sonny's world. Or, rather: his kingdom. Here, it was not even a question that his veins bore royal blood.

They were going to play soon and Creole installed me, by myself, at a table in a dark corner. Then I watched them, Creole, and the little black man, and Sonny, and the others, while they horsed around, standing just below the bandstand. The light from the bandstand spilled just a little short of them and, watching them laughing and gesturing and moving about, I had the feeling that they, nevertheless, were being most careful not to step into that circle of light too suddenly: that if they moved into the light too suddenly, without thinking, they would perish in flame. Then, while I watched, one of them, the small, black man, moved into the light and crossed the bandstand and started fooling around with his drums. Then — being funny and being, also, extremely ceremonious — Creole took Sonny by the arm and led him to the piano. A woman's voice called Sonny's name and a few hands started clapping. And Sonny, also being funny and being ceremonious, and so touched, I think, that he could have cried, but neither hiding it nor showing it, riding it like a man, grinned, and put both hands to his heart and bowed from the waist.

Creole then went to the bass fiddle and a lean, very bright-skinned brown man jumped up on the bandstand and picked up his horn. So there they were, and the atmosphere on the bandstand and in the room began to change and tighten. Someone stepped up to the microphone and announced them. Then there were all kinds of murmurs. Some people at the bar shushed others. The waitress ran around, frantically getting in the last orders, guys and chicks got closer to each other, and the lights on the bandstand, on the quartet, turned to a kind of indigo. Then they all looked different there. Creole looked about him for the last time, as though he were making certain that all his chickens were in the coop, and then he — jumped and struck the fiddle. And there they were.

All I know about music is that not many people ever really hear it. And even then, on the rare occasions when something opens within, and the music enters, what we mainly hear, or hear corroborated, are personal, private, vanishing evocations. But the man who creates the music is hearing something else, is dealing with the roar rising from the void and imposing order on it as it hits the air. What is evoked in him, then, is of another order, more terrible because it has no words, and triumphant, too, for that same reason. And his triumph, when he triumphs, is ours. I just watched Sonny's face. His face was troubled, he was working hard, but he wasn't with it. And I had the feeling that, in a way, everyone on the bandstand was waiting for him, both waiting for him and pushing him along. But as I began to watch Creole, I realized that it was Creole who held them all back. He had them on a short rein. Up there, keeping the beat with his whole body, wailing on the fiddle, with his eyes half closed, he was listening to everything, but he was listening to Sonny. He was having a dialogue with Sonny. He wanted Sonny to leave the shoreline and strike out for the deep water. He was Sonny's witness that deep water and drowning were not the same thing — he had been there, and he knew. And he wanted Sonny to know. He was waiting for Sonny to do the things on the keys which would let Creole know that Sonny was in the water.

And, while Creole listened, Sonny moved, deep within, exactly like someone in torment. I had never before thought of how awful the relationship must be between the musician and his instrument. He has to fill it, this instrument, with the breath of life, his own. He has to make it do what he wants it to do. And a piano is just a piano. It's made out of so much wood and wires and little hammers and big ones, and ivory. While there's only so much you can do with it, the only way to find this out is to try; to try and make it do everything.

And Sonny hadn't been near a piano for over a year. And he wasn't on much better terms with his life, not the life that stretched before him now. He and the piano stammered, started one way, got scared, stopped; started another way, panicked, marked time, started again; then seemed to have found a direction, panicked again, got stuck. And the face I saw on Sonny I'd never seen before. Everything had been burned out of it, and, at the same time, things usually hidden were being burned in, by the fire and fury of the battle which was occurring in him up there.

Yet, watching Creole's face as they neared the end of the first set, I had the feeling that something had happened, something I hadn't heard. Then they finished, there was scattered applause, and then, without an instant's warning, Creole started into something else, it was almost sardonic, it was *Am I Blue.* And, as though he commanded, Sonny began to play. Something began to hap-

230

pen. And Creole let out the reins. The dry, low, black man said something awful on the drums, Creole answered, and the drums talked back. Then the horn insisted, sweet and high, slightly detached perhaps, and Creole listened, commenting now and then, dry, and driving, beautiful and calm and old. Then they all came together again, and Sonny was part of the family again. I could tell this from his face. He seemed to have found, right there beneath his fingers, a damn brand-new piano. It seemed that he couldn't get over it. Then, for awhile, just being happy with Sonny, they seemed to be agreeing with him that brand-new pianos certainly were a gas.

Then Creole stepped forward to remind them that what they were playing was the blues. He hit something in all of them, he hit something in me, myself, and the music tightened and deepened, apprehension began to beat the air. Creole began to tell us what the blues were all about. They were not about anything very new. He and his boys up there were keeping it new, at the risk of ruin, destruction, madness, and death, in order to find new ways to make us listen. For, while the tale of how we suffer, and how we are delighted, and how we may triumph is never new, it always must be heard. There isn't any other tale to tell, it's the only light we've got in all this darkness.

And this tale, according to that face, that body, those strong hands on those strings, has another aspect in every country, and a new depth in every generation. Listen, Creole seemed to be saying, listen. Now these are Sonny's blues. He made the little black man on the drums know it, and the bright, brown man on the horn. Creole wasn't trying any longer to get Sonny in the water. He was wishing him Godspeed. Then he stepped back, very slowly, filling the air with the immense suggestion that Sonny speak for himself.

Then they all gathered around Sonny and Sonny played. Every now and again one of them seemed to say, amen. Sonny's fingers filled the air with life, his life. But that life contained so many others. And Sonny went all the way back, he really began with the spare, flat statement of the opening phrase of the song. Then he began to make it his. It was very beautiful because it wasn't hurried and it was no longer a lament. I seemed to hear with what burning he had made it his, with what burning we had yet to make it ours, how we could cease lamenting. Freedom lurked around us and I understood, at last, that he could help us to be free if we would listen, that he would never be free until we did. Yet, there was no battle in his face now. I heard what he had gone through, and would continue to go through until he came to rest in earth. He had made it his: that long line, of which we knew only Mama and Daddy. And he was giving it back, as everything must be given back, so that, passing through death, it can live forever. I saw my mother's face again, and felt, for the first time, how the stones of the road she had walked on must have bruised her feet. I saw the moonlit road where my father's brother died. And it brought something else back to me, and carried me past it. I saw my little girl again and felt Isabel's tears again, and I felt my own tears begin to rise. And I was yet aware that this was only a moment, that the world waited outside, as hungry as a tiger, and that trouble stretched above us, longer than the sky.

Then it was over. Creole and Sonny let out their breath, both soaking wet, and grinning. There was a lot of applause and some of it was real. In the dark, the girl came by and I asked her to take drinks to the bandstand. There was a long pause, while they talked up there in the indigo light and after awhile I saw the girl put a Scotch and milk on top of the piano for Sonny. He didn't seem to notice it, but just before they started playing again, he sipped from it and looked toward me, and nodded. Then he put it back on top of the piano. For me, then, as they began to play again, it glowed and shook above my brother's head like the very cup of trembling.

Melissa Bank b. 1960

The Wonder Spot   [2000]

Seth talks me into going to a party in Brooklyn. He says that we can just drop by. I tell him that a party in Brooklyn is a commitment. It takes effort. It's like a wedding: You can't just drop by.

"We can just drop by," he says again, in a tone that says, *We can do anything we want.*

This will be our first party as a couple.

He says, "It'll be fun."

My boyfriend is a decade younger than I am; he is full of hope.   5

We drive to Brooklyn in his old Mustang convertible, with the top down. Because of the wind and because I'm on the side of Seth's bad ear, we can't really talk — or I can't. But he tells me that we're going to Williamsburg, the section of Brooklyn that's been called the New Downtown. After the party we can walk around and have dinner at a restaurant his friend Bob is about to open there. Bob has offered to let us try everything on the menu-to-be if we'll help him name the restaurant; the finalists are The Shiny Diner, Bob's, and The Wonder Spot. "Start thinking," Seth says, and I do.

Across the bridge and into the land of Brooklyn, we go under overpasses and down streets so dark and deserted you know they're used only to get lost on. I get this pang for Manhattan, where I am never farther than a block from a bodega, never more than a raised arm from a cab. But then we turn a corner and — lights! people! action — we park.

Walking to the party, I tell Seth about the Williamsburg I've already been to, the one in Virginia. I expect him to have heard of it — he's from Canada and knows more about the U.S. than I do — but he hasn't. I tell him that I was five or six at the time, and I didn't understand the concept of historical reenactment. I thought that we'd just found a place where women in bonnets churned butter and men in breeches shoed horses. I tell him the real drama of the trip: I lost the dollar my father had given me for the gift shop.

"What period do they reenact?" Seth says, teasing.

"You know," I say, "colonial times."   10

"When was that exactly?"

"Sometime before 1910," I say.

I'm having such a good time that I forget about the party until we're on the elevator up. I say, "Maybe we should have a code for 'I want to go.'"

He starts to make a joke but sees that I'm serious and squeezes my hand three times. I okay the code.

The elevator door opens right into the loft. I was counting on those extra few seconds of hallway before facing the party, the party we are now part of and in, a party with people talking and laughing and having a party time. I think, *I am a solid, trying to do a liquid's job.*

I am only a third joking when I squeeze Seth's hand three times. He squeezes back four, and before I can ask what four means, our hostess is upon us. She is tall and slinky, with ultra-short hair and a gold dot in one of her perfect nostrils; I feel every pound of my weight, every year of my age, until Seth tells her, "This is my girlfriend, Meg."

I'm not sure I've ever had a boyfriend who introduced me as his girlfriend. I smile up at this ghosty-pale sweetie-pie man o' mine.

As soon as our hostess slinks off to greet her next arrivals, I say, "What does four mean?"

"It means, 'I love you, too,'" he says.

I want to be happy to hear these words — it's the first time we've squeezed them — but I feel so close to him at this moment, I say the truth, which is, "I feel old."

He puts his coat around my shoulders and says, "Is that better?" and I realize that I've spoken into his bad ear.

I nod, and we move deeper into the party. He introduces me as his girlfriend to each of the friends we pass, all of whom seem happy to meet me, and I think, *I am his girlfriend, Meg; I am girlfriend; I am Meg, girlfriend of Seth.*

I'm fine, even super-fine, until he goes to get a glass of wine for me. Now I look around, trying to pretend, as I always do at parties, that I could be talking to a fellow partygoer if I wanted to, but at the moment I am just too captivated by my own fascinating observations of the crowd.

The women are young, young, young, liquidy and sweet-looking; they are batter, and I am the sponge cake they don't know they'll become. I stand here, a lone loaf, stuck to the pan.

It is at this moment that I see Vincent — only from behind, but I know it's him. Vincent is my ex-boyfriend, or X[7], if you count all the times we broke up and got back together.

I've told Seth almost nothing about my ex-boyfriends. Now he'll meet the one who told me my head was too big for my body.

When Seth returns with my wine, he says, "Still cold?" and he rubs my shoulders and arms and back warm. "Better?" he says.

I do feel better, and I say so.

A small crowd gathers around us — the drummer in Seth's band, and his entourage — girlfriend, brother, and girlfriend of brother. They try to talk to me, and I try to talk back. One of the girlfriends, I'm not sure whose, works in public radio. Since I'm a public-radio lover, I can keep this conversation going, program to program, until she asks me what I do.

I say, "I'm a weaver," and both girlfriends look at me like they're not sure 30 they've heard correctly.

"I weave," I say, and this leads to an almost post-nuclear silence, the usual effect.

But the one who works in public radio says, "Do you like weaving?"

"Except for the stress," I say. She laughs, and we are insta-friends.

Then we girlfriends return to them boyfriends. I plant myself beside Seth like a fire hydrant, my back to where I imagine Vincent to be.

But he's not; he's right across the room, his arm slung like a belt around the 35 hips of a girl who I can tell right away is a model. She has the long, straight hair I used to wish for and sky-high thighs you can see through her mesh stockings.

Just like the bad old days, Vincent doesn't seem to recognize me. Then he gives me a look of mock shock.

I inadvertently squeeze Seth's hand, and he smiles without looking at me, like we have a secret language, and I wish we did.

I watch Vincent steer his girlfriend toward us.

He's grown his hair long and now sports a weird beard and mustache, Lucifer-style. Plus, he's wearing a shirt with huge pointy collars jutting out like fangs over his jacket.

When he reaches us, I say, "Happy Halloween." 40

"Hello, Meg," he says, Dr. Droll.

I say, "Seth, this is —"

Vincent interrupts and introduces himself as "Enzo."

"Enzo?" I say.

He doesn't answer, and I remember his New Jersey friends calling him Vin- 45 nie, and his firm correction: "Vincent."

He pulls his model front and center and says, "This is Amanda."

"I'm Meg," I say to her. Then I get to say, "This is my boyfriend, Seth."

"Hi." She is both chirpy and cool, an ice chick. "We know each other," she says about the man I've just introduced as my boyfriend, and she kisses him — just his cheek, but so far back that her pouty mouth appears to be traveling neck- or ear-ward.

I stare at her, even while I am telling myself not to. I fall under the spell not of her eyes but her eyebrows, which are perfectly arched and skinny and make me aware of my own thick and feral pair; mine are a forest and hers are a trail.

When I blink myself out of my trance, Vincent is saying, "Whenever anyone 50 would say, 'Small world,' Meg used to say, 'Actually, it's medium-sized.'"

I say, "I was about eleven when I knew Vincent."

Then, like the hostess my mother taught me to be, I say, "Vincent is a musician, too."

"I used to be," he says and names the best-known of the bands he played in, though I happen to know it was only for about fifteen minutes. Then he asks Seth, "Who do you play with?"

I can tell Vincent's impressed by Seth's band and doesn't want to be; he fast talks about starting up a start-up — an on-line recording studio, a real-time distribution outlet, a virtual record label — he goes on and on, Vincent style, grandiose and impossible to understand.

I say, "Basically, you do everything but teach kindergarten?"   55

Vincent says, "There is an educational component."

Seth comes off as gentle, even meek, but I know he's intolerant of talk like this. He squeezes my hand three times.

"Oh, shoot," I say, looking a my wrist for a watch I'm not wearing, "we have to go," and I love the sound of *we*, and I love that it's Seth who wants to go and I love that we are going.

Vincent says they're headed to another party themselves. He kisses both my cheeks — what now must be the signature Enzo kiss — and he looks at me as though he cares deeply for me, a look I never got when we were together, a look that Seth notices, and I think, *Phew*: Seth will think another man loved me; he will think I am the lovable kind of woman, the kind a man better love right or somebody else will.

Vincent says, "You look great, Meg," and I think of saying, *Whereas you look* 60
a little strange, but I just say, "See you, Vinnie."

A few more pleasantries and we're in the elevator.

As soon as the elevator doors close, I say, "Good thing she was just a model." I am giddy just to be out. "I think that would've been really hard if she were a supermodel."

Seth looks at me, not sure what I mean.

Out on the street, I say, "How do you know her, by the way?" and instantly regret how deliberately offhanded I sound.

"I don't really know her," he says. "She came up to me after a show a few 65
weeks ago."

I think, *Came* up *to you or* on *to you?* but I give myself the open, amused look of a bystander eager to hear more about one of life's funny little coincidences.

"She asked me if I would help her celebrate her half-birthday," he says, and his tone tells me I would be crazy to think he'd ever be attracted to her.

Unfortunately, now I am crazy, and I have to stop myself from saying a tone-deaf and tone-dumb, *So you're saying you didn't eat her half-birthday cake?*

Suddenly I feel like I'm Mary Poppins floating with an umbrella and a spoonful of sugar into the city of sexual menace, population a million Amandas with ultra-short and long straight hair and pouty mouths and thighs you can see through mesh stockings.

From there I go straight to *This will never work. He has models coming on to* 70
him after his show. He'll be forty-nine when you're turning sixty. He is young and hip and you don't even know the hip word for hip anymore. You belong at home in bed with a book.

I remind myself that this is what I always say and what I always do. As soon as I'm in a relationship, I promote fear from clerk to president, even though all it can do is sweep up, turn off the lights, and lock the door.

I am so deep in my own argument that I almost don't hear Seth say, "Meg."

He stops me on the pavement, and turns me toward him. His face practically glows white; he is a ghost of the ghost he usually looks like.

He says, "When did you go out with him?"

"So long ago," I say, "he had a different name."   75

"Beelzebub?" he says. Then: "Sorry."

I tell him that I hadn't seen Vincent for ten-plus years—he was still in purgatory when I knew him.

"But it was hard for you to see him with somebody else, tonight?"

"No," I say, a little surprised.

He nods, not quite believing. "But the thing you said about her being a   80 model?"

"Models are always hard," I say. "And it was hard to see her necking with your cheek."

After I've said this, I want to say that I don't usually use the word "neck" as a verb, it's a fifties word, my mother's word, but he is shaking his head and I can see he is not thinking about how old I sound or look or am.

"Obviously he still has a thing for you," Seth says, and shakes his head again and swallows a couple of times, like he's trying to get rid of a bad taste in his mouth. "The way he looked at you."

My *phew* gives me an Indian burn of shame. "That look was for Amanda's benefit," I say, and I know it's true. For a second, I am an older sister to my younger self. "And if she brings it up later," I say, "he'll tell her she's crazy."

"Very nice," Seth says, and his voice tells me that he doesn't want to hear   85 any more about Vincent and Amanda, he doesn't care about them, and that he's wishing he didn't care so much about me.

It scares me. But then I get this big feeling, simple but exalted: *He's like me, just with different details.*

His eyes are closed, and I think maybe he's picturing me with Vincent or other men he assumes I've slept with or loved. Maybe he's telling himself that he's too tall or doesn't hear well enough. Usually, he pulls me in for the hug, but now I do it. I pull him in and we stay like this, his chin on my head, my face on his chest.

I find myself thinking of Amanda at another party with Vincent, and feeling sorry for her. It occurs to me that if I were as beautiful as she is, every passing half-birthday would be harder to celebrate. But mostly I am just glad I am not her and glad we are not them, and glad just to be out here on the curb, breathing the sweet air of Williamsburg and postcolonial freedom.

We are quiet for a while, walking. I begin to see where we are now. We pass the Miss Williamsburg Diner. Little bookstores I could spend my life in. We pass a gallery with black-light art hung above a reflecting pool.

Then we're standing in a parking lot, outside of what Seth tells me is Bob's   90 restaurant. I'm saying that living in Manhattan gives you a real appreciation of parking lots, when Seth takes something out of his pocket and puts it in my hand. It's a dollar. "For the gift shop," he says. "Don't lose it now."

With my dollar hand, I squeeze Seth's about thirty-seven times, telling him everything I feel.

He says, "What does that mean?"

I say, " 'I'm hungry.' "

What I feel is, *Right now I am having the life I want, here outside The Shiny Diner, Bob's, or The Wonder Spot, with my dollar to spend and dinner to come.* We will try everything on the menu. Then we will drive through Brooklyn and cross the bridge with the Manhattan skyline in front of us, which looks new to me every time I see it, and we will drive right into it. We'll find a parking space a few blocks from my apartment on Tenth Street, and we'll pick up milk and tomorrow's paper. We will undress and get into bed.

Raymond Carver   1938–1988

What We Talk about When We Talk about Love   [1981]

My friend Mel McGinnis was talking. Mel McGinnis is a cardiologist, and sometimes that gives him the right.

The four of us were sitting around his kitchen table drinking gin. Sunlight filled the kitchen from the big window behind the sink. There were Mel and me and his second wife, Teresa — Terri, we called her — and my wife, Laura. We lived in Albuquerque then. But we were all from somewhere else.

There was an ice bucket on the table. The gin and the tonic water kept going around, and we somehow got on the subject of love. Mel thought real love was nothing less than spiritual love. He said he'd spent five years in a seminary before quitting to go to medical school. He said he still looked back on those years in the seminary as the most important years in his life.

Terri said the man she lived with before she lived with Mel loved her so much he tried to kill her. Then Terri said, "He beat me up one night. He dragged me around the living room by my ankles. He kept saying, 'I love you, I love you, you bitch.' He went on dragging me around the living room. My head kept knocking on things." Terri looked around the table. "What do you do with love like that?"

She was a bone-thin woman with a pretty face, dark eyes, and brown hair ₅ that hung down her back. She liked necklaces made of turquoise, and long pendant earrings.

"My God, don't be silly. That's not love, and you know it," Mel said. "I don't know what you'd call it, but I sure know you wouldn't call it love."

"Say what you want to, but I know it was," Terri said. "It may sound crazy to you, but it's true just the same. People are different, Mel. Sure, sometimes he may have acted crazy. Okay. But he loved me. In his own way maybe, but he loved me. There was love there, Mel. Don't say there wasn't."

Mel let out his breath. He held his glass and turned to Laura and me. "The man threatened to kill me," Mel said. He finished his drink and reached for the gin bottle. "Terri's a romantic. Terri's of the kick-me-so-I'll-know-you-love-me school. Terri, hon, don't look that way." Mel reached across the table and touched Terri's cheek with his fingers. He grinned at her.

"Now he wants to make up," Terri said.

"Make up what?" Mel said. "What is there to make up? I know what I know. 10 That's all."

"How'd we get started on this subject, anyway?" Terri said. She raised her glass and drank from it. "Mel always has love on his mind," she said. "Don't you, honey?" She smiled, and I thought that was the last of it.

"I just wouldn't call Ed's behavior love. That's all I'm saying, honey," Mel said. "What about you guys?" Mel said to Laura and me. "Does that sound like love to you?"

"I'm the wrong person to ask," I said. "I didn't even know the man. I've only heard his name mentioned in passing. I wouldn't know. You'd have to know the particulars. But I think what you're saying is that love is an absolute."

Mel said, "The kind of love I'm talking about is. The kind of love I'm talking about, you don't try to kill people."

Laura said, "I don't know anything about Ed, or anything about the situa- 15 tion. But who can judge anyone else's situation?"

I touched the back of Laura's hand. She gave me a quick smile. I picked up Laura's hand. It was warm, the nails polished, perfectly manicured. I encircled the broad wrist with my fingers, and I held her.

"When I left, he drank rat poison," Terri said. She clasped her arms with her hands. "They took him to the hospital in Santa Fe. That's where we lived then, about ten miles out. They saved his life. But his gums went crazy from it. I mean they pulled away from his teeth. After that, his teeth stood out like fangs. My God," Terri said. She waited a minute, then let go of her arms and picked up her glass.

"What people won't do!" Laura said.

"He's out of the action now," Mel said. "He's dead."

Mel handed me the saucer of limes. I took a section, squeezed it over my 20 drink, and stirred the ice cubes with my finger.

"It gets worse," Terri said. "He shot himself in the mouth. But he bungled that too. Poor Ed," she said. Terri shook her head.

"Poor Ed nothing," Mel said. "He was dangerous."

Mel was forty-five years old. He was tall and rangy with curly soft hair. His face and arms were brown from the tennis he played. When he was sober, his gestures, all his movements, were precise, very careful.

"He did love me though, Mel. Grant me that," Terri said. "That's all I'm ask-ing. He didn't love me the way you love me. I'm not saying that. But he loved me. You can grant me that, can't you?"

"What do you mean, he bungled it?" I said. 25

Laura leaned forward with her glass. She put her elbows on the table and held her glass in both hands. She glanced from Mel to Terri and waited with a look of bewilderment on her open face, as if amazed that such things happened to people you were friendly with.

"How'd he bungle it when he killed himself?" I said.

"I'll tell you what happened," Mel said. "He took this twenty-two pistol he'd bought to threaten Terri and me with. Oh, I'm serious, the man was always threatening. You should have seen the way we lived in those days. Like fugitives. I even bought a gun myself. Can you believe it? A guy like me? But I did. I bought one for self-defense and carried it in the glove compartment. Sometimes I'd have to leave the apartment in the middle of the night. To go to the hospital, you know? Terri and I weren't married then, and my first wife had the house and kids, the dog, everything, and Terri and I were living in this apartment here. Sometimes, as I say, I'd get a call in the middle of the night and have to go in to the hospital at two or three in the morning. It'd be dark out there in the parking lot, and I'd break into a sweat before I could even get to my car. I never knew if he was going to come up out of the shrubbery or from behind a car and start shooting. I mean, the man was crazy. He was capable of wiring a bomb, anything. He used to call my service at all hours and say he needed to talk to the doctor, and when I'd return the call, he'd say, 'Son of a bitch, your days are numbered.' Little things like that. It was scary, I'm telling you."

"I still feel sorry for him," Terri said.

"It sounds like a nightmare," Laura said. "But what exactly happened after 30 he shot himself?"

Laura is a legal secretary. We'd met in a professional capacity. Before we knew it, it was a courtship. She's thirty-five, three years younger than I am. In addition to being in love, we like each other and enjoy one another's company. She's easy to be with.

"What happened?" Laura said.

Mel said, "He shot himself in the mouth in his room. Someone heard the shot and told the manager. They came in with a passkey, saw what had happened, and called an ambulance. I happened to be there when they brought him in, alive but past recall. The man lived for three days. His head swelled up to twice the size of a normal head. I'd never seen anything like it, and I hope I never do again. Terri wanted to go in and sit with him when she found out about it. We had a fight over it. I didn't think she should see him like that. I didn't think she should see him, and I still don't."

"Who won the fight?" Laura said.

"I was in the room with him when he died," Terri said. "He never came out 35 of it. But I sat with him. He didn't have anyone else."

"He was dangerous," Mel said. "If you call that love, you can have it."

"It was love," Terri said. "Sure, it's abnormal in most people's eyes. But he was willing to die for it. He did die for it."

"I sure as hell wouldn't call it love," Mel said. "I mean, no one knows what he did it for. I've seen a lot of suicides, and I couldn't say anyone ever knew what they did it for."

Mel put his hands behind his neck and tilted his chair back. "I'm not interested in that kind of love," he said. "If that's love, you can have it."

Terri said, "We were afraid. Mel even made a will out and wrote to his 40 brother in California who used to be a Green Beret. Mel told him who to look for if something happened to him."

Terri drank from her glass. She said, "But Mel's right—we lived like fugitives. We were afraid. Mel was, weren't you, honey? I even called the police at one point, but they were no help. They said they couldn't do anything until Ed actually did something. Isn't that a laugh?" Terri said.

She poured the last of the gin into her glass and waggled the bottle. Mel got up from the table and went to the cupboard. He took down another bottle.

"Well, Nick and I know what love is," Laura said. "For us, I mean," Laura said. She bumped my knee with her knee. "You're supposed to say something now," Laura said, and turned her smile on me.

For an answer, I took Laura's hand and raised it to my lips. I made a big production out of kissing her hand. Everyone was amused.

"We're lucky," I said.   45

"You guys," Terri said. "Stop that now. You're making me sick. You're still on the honeymoon, for God's sake. You're still gaga, for crying out loud. Just wait. How long have you been together now? How long has it been? A year? Longer than a year?"

"Going on a year and a half," Laura said, flushed and smiling.

"Oh, now," Terri said. "Wait awhile."

She held her drink and gazed at Laura.

"I'm only kidding," Terri said.   50

Mel opened the gin and went around the table with the bottle.

"Here, you guys," he said. "Let's have a toast. I want to propose a toast. A toast to love. To true love," Mel said.

We touched glasses.

"To love," we said.

Outside in the backyard, one of the dogs began to bark. The leaves of 55
the aspen that leaned past the window ticked against the glass. The afternoon sun was like a presence in this room, the spacious light of ease and generosity. We could have been anywhere, somewhere enchanted. We raised our glasses again and grinned at each other like children who had agreed on something forbidden.

"I'll tell you what real love is," Mel said. "I mean, I'll give you a good example. And then you can draw your own conclusions." He poured more gin into his glass. He added an ice cube and a sliver of lime. We waited and sipped our drinks. Laura and I touched knees again. I put a hand on her warm thigh and left it there.

"What do any of us really know about love?" Mel said. "It seems to me we're just beginners at love. We say we love each other and we do, I don't doubt it. I love Terri and Terri loves me, and you guys love each other too. You know the kind of love I'm talking about now. Physical love, that impulse that drives you to someone special, as well as love of the other person's being, his or her essence, as it were. Carnal love and, well, call it sentimental love, the day-to-day caring about the other person. But sometimes I have a hard time accounting for the fact that I must have loved my first wife too. But I did, I know I did. So I suppose I am like Terri in that regard. Terri and Ed." He thought about it and then he went on. "There was a time when I thought I loved my first wife more than life itself. But now I hate her guts. I do. How do you explain that? What happened to that love? What happened to it, is what I'd like to know. I wish someone could tell me. Then there's Ed. Okay, we're back to Ed. He loves Terri so much he tries to kill her and he winds up killing himself." Mel stopped talking and swallowed from his glass. "You guys have been together eighteen months and you love each other. It shows all over you. You glow with it. But you both loved other people before you met each other. You've both been married before, just like us. And you probably loved other people before that too, even. Terri and I have been together five years, been married for four. And the terrible thing, the terrible thing is, but the good thing too, the saving grace, you might say, is that if something happened to one of us — excuse me for saying this — but if something happened to one of us tomorrow, I think the other one, the other person, would grieve for a while, you know, but then the surviving party would go out and love again, have someone else soon enough. All this, all of this love we're talking about, it would just be a memory. Maybe not even a memory. Am I wrong? Am I way off base? Because I want you to set me straight if you think I'm wrong. I want to know. I mean, I don't know anything, and I'm the first one to admit it."

"Mel, for God's sake," Terri said. She reached out and took hold of his wrist. "Are you getting drunk? Honey? Are you drunk?"

"Honey, I'm just talking," Mel said. "All right? I don't have to be drunk to say what I think. I mean, we're all just talking, right?" Mel said. He fixed his eyes on her.

"Sweetie, I'm not criticizing," Terri said.   60

She picked up her glass.

"I'm not on call today," Mel said. "Let me remind you of that. I am not on call," he said.

"Mel, we love you," Laura said.

Mel looked at Laura. He looked at her as if he could not place her, as if she was not the woman she was.

"Love you too, Laura," Mel said. "And you, Nick, love you too. You know   65 something?" Mel said. "You guys are our pals," Mel said.

He picked up his glass.

Mel said, "I was going to tell you about something. I mean, I was going to prove a point. You see, this happened a few months ago, but it's still going on right now, and it ought to make us feel ashamed when we talk like we know what we're talking about when we talk about love."

"Come on now," Terri said. "Don't talk like you're drunk if you're not drunk."

"Just shut up for once in your life," Mel said very quietly. "Will you do me a favor and do that for a minute? So as I was saying, there's this old couple who had this car wreck out on the interstate. A kid hit them and they were all torn to shit and nobody was giving them much chance to pull through."

Terri looked at us and then back at Mel. She seemed anxious, or maybe 70 that's too strong a word.

Mel was handing the bottle around the table.

"I was on call that night," Mel said. "It was May or maybe it was June. Terri and I had just sat down to dinner when the hospital called. There'd been this thing out on the interstate. Drunk kid, teenager, plowed his dad's pickup into this camper with this old couple in it. They were up in their mid-seventies, that couple. The kid — eighteen, nineteen, something — he was DOA. Taken the steering wheel through his sternum. The old couple, they were alive, you understand. I mean, just barely. But they had everything. Multiple fractures, internal injuries, hemorrhaging, contusions, lacerations, the works, and they each of them had themselves concussions. They were in a bad way, believe me. And, of course, their age was two strikes against them. I'd say she was worse off than he was. Ruptured spleen along with everything else. Both kneecaps broken. But they'd been wearing their seatbelts and, God knows, that's what saved them for the time being."

"Folks, this is an advertisement for the National Safety Council," Terri said. "This is your spokesman, Dr. Melvin R. McGinnis, talking." Terri laughed. "Mel," she said, "sometimes you're just too much. But I love you, hon," she said.

"Honey, I love you," Mel said.

He leaned across the table. Terri met him halfway. They kissed.   75

"Terri's right," Mel said as he settled himself again. "Get those seatbelts on. But seriously, they were in some shape, those oldsters. By the time I got down there, the kid was dead, as I said. He was off in a corner, laid out on a gurney. I took one look at the old couple and told the ER nurse to get me a neurologist and an orthopedic man and a couple of surgeons down there right way."

He drank from his glass. "I'll try to keep this short," he said. "So we took the two of them up to the OR and worked like fuck on them most of the night. They had these incredible reserves, those two. You see that once in a while. So we did everything that could be done, and toward morning we're giving them a fifty-fifty chance, maybe less than that for her. So here they are, still alive the next morning. So, okay, we move them into the ICU, which is where they both kept plugging away at it for two weeks, hitting it better and better on all the scopes. So we transfer them out to their own room."

Mel stopped talking. "Here," he said, "let's drink this cheapo gin the hell up. Then we're going to dinner, right? Terri and I know a new place. That's where we'll go, to this new place we know about. But we're not going until we finish up this cut-rate, lousy gin."

Terri said, "We haven't actually eaten there yet. But it looks good. From the outside, you know."

"I like food," Mel said. "If I had it to do all over again, I'd be a chef, you 80 know? Right, Terri?" Mel said.

He laughed. He fingered the ice in his glass.

"Terri knows," he said. "Terri can tell you. But let me say this. If I could come back again in a different life, a different time and all, you know what? I'd like to come back as a knight. You were pretty safe wearing all that armor. It was all right being a knight until gunpowder and muskets and pistols came along."

"Mel would like to ride a horse and carry a lance," Terri said.

"Carry a woman's scarf with you everywhere," Laura said.

"Or just a woman," Mel said.   85

"Shame on you," Laura said.

Terri said, "Suppose you came back as a serf. The serfs didn't have it so good in those days," Terri said.

"The serfs never had it good," Mel said. "But I guess even the knights were vessels to someone. Isn't that the way it worked? But then everyone is always a vessel to someone. Isn't that right? Terri? But what I liked about knights, besides their ladies, was that they had that suit of armor, you know, and they couldn't get hurt very easy. No cars in those days, you know? No drunk teenagers to tear into your ass.

"Vassals," Terri said.

"What?" Mel said.   90

"Vassals," Terri said. "They were called vassals, not vessels."

"Vassals, vessels," Mel said, "what the fuck's the difference? You knew what I meant anyway. All right," Mel said. "So I'm not educated. I learned my stuff. I'm a heart surgeon, sure, but I'm just a mechanic. I go in and I fuck around and I fix things. Shit," Mel said.

"Modesty doesn't become you," Terri said.

"He's just a humble sawbones," I said. "But sometimes they suffocated in all that armor, Mel. They'd even have heart attacks if it got too hot and they were too tired and worn out. I read somewhere that they'd fall off their horses and not be able to get up because they were too tired to stand with all that armor on them. They got trampled by their own horses sometimes."

"That's terrible," Mel said. "That's a terrible thing, Nicky. I guess they'd just 95
lay there and wait until somebody came along and made a shish kebab out of them."

"Some other vessel," Terri said.

"That's right," Mel said. "Some vassal would come along and spear the bastard in the name of love. Or whatever the fuck it was they fought over in those days."

"Same things we fight over these days," Terri said.

Laura said, "Nothing's changed."

The color was still high in Laura's cheeks. Her eyes were bright. She brought 100
her glass to her lips.

Mel poured himself another drink. He looked at the label closely as if studying a long row of numbers. Then he slowly put the bottle down on the table and slowly reached for the tonic water.

———————

"What about the old couple?" Laura said. "You didn't finish that story you started."

Laura was having a hard time lighting her cigarette. Her matches kept going out.

The sunshine inside the room was different now, changing, getting thinner. But the leaves outside the window were still shimmering, and I stared at the pattern they made on the panes and on the Formica counter. They weren't the same patterns, of course.

"What about the old couple?" I said.   105

"Older but wiser," Terri said.

Mel stared at her.

Terri said, "Go on with your story, hon. I was only kidding. Then what happened?"

"Terri, sometimes," Mel said.

"Please, Mel," Terri said. "Don't always be so serious, sweetie. Can't you   110
take a joke?"

"Where's the joke?" Mel said.

He held his glass and gazed steadily at his wife.

"What happened?" Laura said.

Mel fastened his eyes on Laura. He said, "Laura, if I didn't have Terri and if I didn't love her so much, and if Nick wasn't my best friend, I'd fall in love with you. I'd carry you off, honey," he said.

"Tell your story," Terri said. "Then we'll go to that new place, okay?"   115

"Okay," Mel said. "Where was I?" he said. He stared at the table and then he began again.

"I dropped in to see each of them every day, sometimes twice a day if I was up doing other calls anyway. Casts and bandages, head to foot, the both of them. You know, you've seen it in the movies. That's just the way they looked, just like in the movies. Little eye-holes and nose holes and mouth-holes. And she had to have her legs slung up on top of it. Well, the husband was very depressed for the longest while. Even after he found out that his wife was going to pull through, he was still very depressed. Not about the accident, though. I mean, the accident was one thing, but it wasn't everything. I'd get up to his mouth-hole, you know, and he'd say no, it wasn't the accident exactly but it was because he couldn't see her through his eye-holes. He said that was what was making him feel so bad. Can you imagine? I'm telling you, the man's heart was breaking because he couldn't turn his goddamn head and *see* his goddamn wife."

Mel looked around the table and shook his head at what he was going to say.

"I mean, it was killing the old fart just because he couldn't *look* at the fucking woman."

We all looked at Mel.   120

"Do you see what I'm saying?" he said.

Maybe we were a little drunk by then. I know it was hard keeping things in focus. The light was draining out of the room, going back through the window where it had come from. Yet nobody made a move to get up from the table to turn on the overhead light.

"Listen," Mel said. "Let's finish this fucking gin. There's about enough left here for one shooter all around. Then let's go eat. Let's go to the new place."

"He's depressed," Terri said. "Mel, why don't you take a pill?"

Mel shook his head. "I've taken everything there is." 125

"We all need a pill now and then," I said.

"Some people are born needing them," Terri said.

She was using her finger to rub at something on the table. Then she stopped rubbing.

"I think I want to call my kids," Mel said. "Is that all right with everybody? I'll call my kids," he said.

Terri said, "What if Marjorie answers the phone? You guys, you've heard us 130 on the subject of Marjorie? Honey, you know you don't want to talk to Marjorie. It'll make you feel even worse."

"I don't want to talk to Marjorie," Mel said. "But I want to talk to my kids."

"There isn't a day goes by that Mel doesn't say he wishes she'd get married again. Or else die," Terri said. "For one thing," Terri said, "she's bankrupting us. Mel says it's just to spite him that she won't get married again. She has a boyfriend who lives with her and the kids, so Mel is supporting the boyfriend too."

"She's allergic to bees," Mel said. "If I'm not praying she'll get married again, I'm praying she'll get herself stung to death by a swarm of fucking bees."

"Shame on you," Laura said.

"Bzzzzzzz," Mel said, turning his fingers into bees and buzzing them at 135 Terri's throat. Then he let his hands drop all the way to his sides.

"She's vicious," Mel said. "Sometimes I think I'll go up there dressed like a beekeeper. You know, that hat that's like a helmet with the plate that comes down over your face, the big gloves, and the padded coat? I'll knock on the door and let loose a hive of bees in the house. But first I'd make sure the kids were out, of course."

He crossed one leg over the other. It seemed to take him a lot of time to do it. Then he put both feet on the floor and leaned forward, elbows on the table, his chin cupped in his hands.

"Maybe I won't call the kids, after all. Maybe it isn't such a hot idea. Maybe we'll just go eat. How does that sound?"

"Sounds fine to me," I said. "Eat or not eat. Or keep drinking. I could head right on out into the sunset."

"What does that mean, honey?" Laura said. 140

"It just means what I said," I said. "It means I could just keep going. That's all it means."

"I could eat something myself," Laura said. "I don't think I've ever been so hungry in my life. Is there something to nibble on?"

"I'll put out some cheese and crackers," Terri said.

But Terri just sat there. She did not get up to get anything.

Mel turned his glass over. He spilled it out on the table. 145

"Gin's gone," Mel said.

Terri said, "Now what?"

I could hear my heart beating. I could hear everyone's heart. I could hear the human noise we sat there making, not one of us moving, not even when the room went dark.

Judith Ortiz Cofer   b. 1952

American History   [1993]

I once read in a *Ripley's Believe It or Not* column that Paterson, New Jersey, is the place where the Straight and Narrow (streets) intersect. The Puerto Rican tenement known as El Building was one block up from Straight. It was, in fact, the corner of Straight and Market; not "at" the corner, but *the* corner. At almost any hour of the day, El Building was like a monstrous jukebox, blasting out *salsas* from open windows as the residents, mostly new immigrants just up from the island, tried to drown out whatever they were currently enduring with loud music. But the day President Kennedy was shot, there was a profound silence in El Building, even the abusive tongues of viragoes,° the cursing of the unemployed, and the screeching of small children had been somehow muted. President Kennedy was a saint to these people. In fact, soon his photograph would be hung alongside the Sacred Heart and over the spiritist altars that many women kept in their apartments. He would become part of the hierarchy of martyrs they prayed to for favors that only one who had died for a cause would understand.

On the day that President Kennedy was shot, my ninth grade class had been out in the fenced playground of Public School Number 13. We had been given "free" exercise time and had been ordered by our P.E. teacher, Mr. DePalma, to "keep moving." That meant that the girls should jump rope and the boys toss basketballs through a hoop at the far end of the yard. He in the meantime would "keep an eye" on us from just inside the building.

It was a cold gray day in Paterson. The kind that warns of early snow. I was miserable, since I had forgotten my gloves and my knuckles were turning red and raw from the jump rope. I was also taking a lot of abuse from the black girls for not turning the rope hard and fast enough for them.

"Hey, Skinny Bones, pump it, girl. Ain't you got no energy today?" Gail, the biggest of the black girls who had the other end of the rope yelled, "Didn't you eat your rice and beans and pork chops for breakfast today?"

The other girls picked up the "pork chop" and made it into a refrain: "pork   5 chop, pork chop, did you eat your pork chop?" They entered the double ropes in pairs and exited without tripping or missing a beat. I felt a burning on my

---

viragoes: Loud, bossy, and quarrelsome women.

cheeks, and then my glasses fogged up so that I could not manage to coordinate the jump rope with Gail. The chill was doing to me what it always did, entering my bones, making me cry, humiliating me. I hated the city, especially in winter. I hated Public School Number 13. I hated my skinny flat-chested body, and I envied the black girls who could jump rope so fast that their legs became a blur. They always seemed to be warm while I froze.

There was only one source of beauty and light for me that school year. The only thing I had anticipated at the start of the semester. That was seeing Eugene. In August, Eugene and his family had moved into the only house on the block that had a yard and trees. I could see his place from my window in El Building. In fact, if I sat on the fire escape I was literally suspended above Eugene's backyard. It was my favorite spot to read my library books in the summer. Until that August the house had been occupied by an old Jewish couple. Over the years I had become part of their family, without their knowing it, of course. I had a view of their kitchen and their backyard, and though I could not hear what they said, I knew when they were arguing, when one of them was sick, and many other things. I knew all this by watching them at mealtimes. I could see their kitchen table, the sink, and the stove. During good times, he sat at the table and read his newspapers while she fixed the meals. If they argued, he would leave and the old woman would sit and stare at nothing for a long time. When one of them was sick, the other would come and get things from the kitchen and carry them out on a tray. The old man had died in June. The last week of school I had not seen him at the table at all. Then one day I saw that there was a crowd in the kitchen. The old woman had finally emerged from the house on the arm of a stocky middle-aged woman whom I had seen there a few times before, maybe her daughter. Then a man had carried out suitcases. The house had stood empty for weeks. I had had to resist the temptation to climb down into the yard and water the flowers the old lady had taken such good care of.

By the time Eugene's family moved in, the yard was a tangled mass of weeds. The father had spent several days mowing, and when he finished, I didn't see the red, yellow, and purple clusters that meant flowers to me from where I sat. I didn't see this family sit down at the kitchen table together. It was just the mother, a red-headed tall woman who wore a white uniform — a nurse's, I guessed it was; the father was gone before I got up in the morning and was never there at dinner time. I only saw him on weekends when they sometimes sat on lawn chairs under the oak tree, each hidden behind a section of the newspaper; and there was Eugene. He was tall and blond, and he wore glasses. I liked him right away because he sat at the kitchen table and read books for hours. That summer, before we had even spoken one word to each other, I kept him company on my fire escape.

Once school started I looked for him in all my classes, but P.S. 13 was a huge, overpopulated place and it took me days and many discreet questions to discover that Eugene was in honors classes for all his subjects; classes that were not open to me because English was not my first language, though I was a straight A student. After much maneuvering I managed "to run into him" in the hallway where his locker was — on the other side of the building from mine — and in study hall at the library, where he first seemed to notice me but did not speak; and finally, on the way home after school one day when I decided to approach him directly, though my stomach was doing somersaults.

I was ready for rejection, snobbery, the worst. But when I came up to him, practically panting in my nervousness, and blurted out: "You're Eugene. Right?" He smiled, pushed his glasses up on his nose, and nodded. I saw then that he was blushing deeply. Eugene liked me, but he was shy. I did most of the talking that day. He nodded and smiled a lot. In the weeks that followed, we walked home together. He would linger at the corner of El Building for a few minutes then walk down to his two-story house. It was not until Eugene moved into that house that I noticed that El Building blocked most of the sun and that the only spot that got a little sunlight during the day was the tiny square of earth the old woman had planted with flowers.

I did not tell Eugene that I could see inside his kitchen from my bedroom. I   10
felt dishonest, but I liked my secret sharing of his evenings, especially now that I knew what he was reading, since we chose our books together at the school library.

One day my mother came into my room as I was sitting on the windowsill staring out. In her abrupt way she said: "Elena, you are acting 'moony.'" *Enamorada* was what she really said — that is, like a girl stupidly infatuated. Since I had turned fourteen and started menstruating my mother had been more vigilant than ever. She acted as if I was going to go crazy or explode or something if she didn't watch me and nag me all the time about being a señorita now. She kept talking about virtue, morality, and other subjects that did not interest me in the least. My mother was unhappy in Paterson, but my father had a good job at the blue jeans factory in Passaic, and soon, he kept assuring us, we would be moving to our own house there. Every Sunday we drove out to the suburbs of Paterson, Clifton, and Passaic, out to where people mowed grass on Sundays in the summer and where children made snowmen in the winter from pure white snow, not like the gray slush of Paterson, which seemed to fall from the sky in that hue. I had learned to listen to my parents' dreams, which were spoken in Spanish, as fairy tales, like the stories about life in the island paradise of Puerto Rico before I was born. I had been to the Island once as a little girl, to grandmother's funeral, and all I remembered was wailing women in black, my mother becoming hysterical and being given a pill that made her sleep two days, and me feeling lost in a crowd of strangers all claiming to be my aunts, uncles, and cousins. I had actually been glad to return to the city. We had not been back there since then, though my parents talked constantly about buying a house on the beach someday, retiring on the island — that was a common topic among the residents of El Building. As for me, I was going to go to college and become a teacher.

But after meeting Eugene I began to think of the present more than of the future. What I wanted now was to enter that house I had watched for so many years. I wanted to see the other rooms where the old people had lived and where the boy I liked spent his time. Most of all, I wanted to sit at the kitchen table with Eugene like two adults, like the old man and his wife had done, maybe drink some coffee and talk about books. I had started reading *Gone with the Wind*. I was enthralled by it, with the daring and the passion of the beautiful girl living in a mansion, and with her devoted parents and the slaves who did everything for them. I didn't believe such a world had ever really existed, and I wanted to ask Eugene some questions, since he and his parents, he had told me, had come up from Georgia, the same place where the novel was set. His father worked for a company that had transferred him to Paterson. His mother was very unhappy, Eugene said, in his beautiful voice that rose and fell over words in a strange, lilting way. The kids at school called him the Hick and made fun of the way he talked. I knew I was his only friend so far, and I liked that, though I felt sad for him sometimes. Skinny Bones and the Hick, was what they called us at school when we were seen together.

The day Mr. DePalma came out into the cold and asked us to line up in front of him was the day that President Kennedy was shot. Mr. DePalma, a short, muscular man with slicked-down black hair, was the science teacher, P.E. coach, and disciplinarian at P.S. 13. He was the teacher to whose homeroom you got assigned if you were a troublemaker, and the man called out to break up playground fights, and to escort violently angry teenagers to the office. And Mr. DePalma was the man who called your parents in for "a conference."

That day, he stood in front of two rows of mostly black and Puerto Rican kids, brittle from their efforts to "keep moving" on a November day that was turning bitter cold. Mr. DePalma, to our complete shock, was crying. Not just silent adult tears, but really sobbing. There were a few titters from the back of the line where I stood, shivering.

"Listen," Mr. DePalma raised his arms over his head as if he were about to   15 conduct an orchestra. His voice broke, and he covered his face with his hands. His barrel chest was heaving. Someone giggled behind me.

"Listen," he repeated, "something awful has happened." A strange gurgling came from his throat, and he turned around and spit on the cement behind him.

"Gross," someone said, and there was a lot of laughter.

"The president is dead, you idiots. I should have known that wouldn't mean anything to a bunch of losers like you kids. Go home." He was shrieking now. No one moved for a minute or two, but then a big girl let out a "yeah!" and ran to get her books piled up with the others against the brick wall of the school building. The others followed in a mad scramble to get to their things before somebody caught on. It was still an hour to the dismissal bell.

A little scared, I headed for El Building. There was an eerie feeling on the streets. I looked into Mario's drugstore, a favorite hangout for the high school crowd, but there were only a couple of old Jewish men at the soda bar, talking with the short order cook in tones that sounded almost angry, but they were keeping their voices low. Even the traffic on one of the busiest intersections in Paterson — Straight Street and Park Avenue — seemed to be moving slower. There were no horns blasting that day. At El Building, the usual little group of unemployed men were not hanging out on the front stoop, making it difficult for women to enter the front door. No music spilled out from open doors in the hallway. When I walked into our apartment, I found my mother sitting in front of the grainy picture of the television set.

She looked up at me with a tear-streaked face and just said: "Dios, mío," 20 turning back to the set as if it were pulling at her eyes. I went into my room.

Though I wanted to feel the right thing about President Kennedy's death, I could not fight the feeling of elation that stirred in my chest. Today was the day I was to visit Eugene in his house. He had asked me to come over after school to study for an American history test with him. We had also planned to walk to the public library together. I looked down into his yard. The oak tree was bare of leaves, and the ground looked gray with ice. The light through the large kitchen window of his house told me that El Building blocked the sun to such an extent that they had to turn lights on in the middle of the day. I felt ashamed about it. But the white kitchen table with the lamp hanging just above it looked cozy and inviting. I would soon sit there, across from Eugene, and I would tell him about my perch just above his house. Maybe I would.

In the next thirty minutes I changed clothes, put on a little pink lipstick, and got my books together. Then I went in to tell my mother that I was going to a friend's house to study. I did not expect her reaction.

"You are going out *today*?" The way she said "today" sounded as if a storm warning had been issued. It was said in utter disbelief. Before I could answer, she came toward me and held my elbows as I clutched my books.

"*Hija*, the president has been killed. We must show respect. He was a great man. Come to church with me tonight."

She tried to embrace me, but my books were in the way. My first impulse 25 was to comfort her, she seemed so distraught, but I had to meet Eugene in fifteen minutes.

"I have a test to study for, Mama. I will be home by eight."

"You are forgetting who you are, *Niña*. I have seen you staring down at that boy's house. You are heading for humiliation and pain." My mother said this in Spanish and in a resigned tone that surprised me, as if she had no intention of stopping me from "heading for humiliation and pain." I started for the door. She sat in front of the TV, holding a white handkerchief to her face.

I walked out to the street and around the chain-link fence that separated El Building from Eugene's house. The yard was neatly edged around the little walk that led to the door. It always amazed me how Paterson, the inner core of the city, had no apparent logic to its architecture. Small, neat, single residences like this one could be found right next to huge, dilapidated apartment buildings like El Building. My guess was that the little houses had been there first, then the immigrants had come in droves, and the monstrosities had been raised for them — the Italians, the Irish, the Jews, and now us, the Puerto Ricans, and the blacks.

The door was painted a deep green: *verde,* the color of hope. I had heard my mother say it: *Verde-Esperanza.*

I knocked softly. A few suspenseful moments later the door opened just a crack. The red, swollen face of a woman appeared. She had a halo of red hair floating over a delicate ivory face — the face of a doll — with freckles on the nose. Her smudged eye makeup made her look unreal to me, like a mannequin seen through a warped store window.

"What do you want?" Her voice was tiny and sweet-sounding, like a little 30 girl's, but her tone was not friendly.

"I'm Eugene's friend. He asked me over. To study." I thrust out my books, a silly gesture that embarrassed me almost immediately.

"You live there?" She pointed up to El Building, which looked particularly ugly, like a gray prison with its many dirty windows and rusty fire escapes. The woman had stepped halfway out, and I could see that she wore a white nurse's uniform with "St. Joseph's Hospital" on the name tag.

"Yes. I do."

She looked intently at me for a couple of heartbeats, then said as if to herself, "I don't know how you people do it." Then directly to me: "Listen. Honey. Eugene doesn't want to study with you. He is a smart boy. Doesn't need help. You understand me. I am truly sorry if he told you you could come over. He cannot study with you. It's nothing personal. You understand? We won't be in this place much longer, no need for him to get close to people — it'll just make it harder for him later. Run back home now."

I couldn't move. I just stood there in shock at hearing these things said to 35 me in such a honey-drenched voice. I had never heard an accent like hers except for Eugene's softer version. It was as if she were singing me a little song.

"What's wrong? Didn't you hear what I said?" She seemed very angry, and I finally snapped out of my trance. I turned away from the green door and heard her close it gently.

Our apartment was empty when I got home. My mother was in someone else's kitchen, seeking the solace she needed. Father would come in from his late shift at midnight. I would hear them talking softly in the kitchen for hours that night. They would not discuss their dreams for the future, or life in Puerto Rico, as they often did; that night they would talk sadly about the young widow and her two children, as if they were family. For the next few days, we would observe *luto* in our apartment; that is, we would practice restraint and silence — no loud music or laughter. Some of the women of El Building would wear black for weeks.

That night, I lay in my bed, trying to feel the right thing for our dead president. But the tears that came up from a deep source inside me were strictly for me. When my mother came to the door, I pretended to be sleeping. Sometime during the night, I saw from my bed the streetlight come on. It had a pink halo around it. I went to my window and pressed my face to the cool glass. Looking up at the light I could see the white snow falling like a lace veil over its face. I did not look down to see it turning gray as it touched the ground below.

Ralph Ellison   1914–1994

Battle Royal   [1952]

It goes a long way back, some twenty years. All my life I had been looking for something, and everywhere I turned someone tried to tell me what it was. I accepted their answers too, though they were often in contradiction and even self-contradictory. I was naïve. I was looking for myself and asking everyone except myself questions which I, and only I, could answer. It took me a long time and much painful boomeranging of my expectations to achieve a realization everyone else appears to have been born with: That I am nobody but myself. But first I had to discover that I am an invisible man!

And yet I am no freak of nature, nor of history. I was in the cards, other things having been equal (or unequal) eighty-five years ago. I am not ashamed of my grandparents for having been slaves. I am only ashamed of myself for having at one time been ashamed. About eighty-five years ago they were told that they were free, united with others of our country in everything pertaining to the common good, and, in everything social, separate like the fingers of the hand. And they believed it. They exulted in it. They stayed in their place, worked hard, and brought up my father to do the same. But my grandfather is the one. He was an odd old guy, my grandfather, and I am told I take after him. It was he who caused the trouble. On his deathbed he called my father to him and said, "Son, after I'm gone I want you to keep up the good fight. I never told you, but our life is a war and I have been a traitor all my born days, a spy in the enemy's country ever since I give up my gun back in the Reconstruction. Live with your head in the lion's mouth. I want you to overcome 'em with yeses, undermine 'em with grins, agree 'em to death and destruction, let 'em swoller you till they vomit or bust wide open." They thought the old man had gone out of his mind. He had been the meekest of men. The younger children were rushed from the room, the shades drawn and the flame of the lamp turned so low that it sputtered on the wick like the old man's breathing. "Learn it to the younguns," he whispered fiercely; then he died.

But my folks were more alarmed over his last words than over his dying. It was as though he had not died at all, his words caused so much anxiety. I was warned emphatically to forget what he had said and, indeed, this is the first time it has been mentioned outside the family circle. It had a tremendous effect upon me, however. I could never be sure of what he meant. Grandfather had been a quiet old man who never made any trouble, yet on his deathbed he had called himself a traitor and a spy, and he had spoken of his meekness as a dangerous activity. It became a constant puzzle which lay unanswered in the back of my mind. And whenever things went well for me I remembered my grandfather and felt guilty and uncomfortable. It was as though I was carrying out his advice in spite of myself. And to make it worse, everyone loved me for it. I was praised by the most lily-white men of the town. I was considered an example of desirable conduct—just as my grandfather had been. And what puzzled me was that the old man had defined it as *treachery*. When I was praised for my conduct I felt a guilt that in some way I was doing something that was really against the wishes of the white folks, that if they had understood they would have desired me to act just the opposite, that I should have been sulky and mean, and that that really would have been what they wanted, even though they were fooled and thought they wanted me to act as I did. It made me afraid that some day they would look upon me as a traitor and I would be lost. Still I was more afraid to act any other way because they didn't like that at all. The old man's words were like a curse. On my graduation day I delivered an oration in which I showed that humility was the secret, indeed, the very essence of progress. (Not that I believed this — how could I, remembering my grandfather? — I only believed that it worked.) It was a great success. Everyone praised me and I was invited to give the speech at a gathering of the town's leading white citizens. It was a triumph for our whole community.

It was in the main ballroom of the leading hotel. When I got there I discovered that it was on the occasion of a smoker, and I was told that since I was to be there anyway I might as well take part in the battle royal to be fought by some of my schoolmates as part of the entertainment. The battle royal came first.

All of the town's big shots were there in their tuxedoes, wolfing down the 5 buffet foods, drinking beer and whiskey and smoking black cigars. It was a large room with a high ceiling. Chairs were arranged in neat rows around three sides of a portable boxing ring. The fourth side was clear, revealing a gleaming space of polished floor. I had some misgivings over the battle royal, by the way. Not from a distaste for fighting, but because I didn't care too much for the other fellows who were to take part. They were tough guys who seemed to have no grandfather's curse worrying their minds. No one could mistake their toughness. And besides, I suspected that fighting a battle royal might detract from the dignity of my speech. In those pre-invisible days I visualized myself as a potential Booker T. Washington. But the other fellows didn't care too much for me either, and there were nine of them. I felt superior to them in my way, and I didn't like the manner in which we were all crowded together into the servants' elevator. Nor did they like my being there. In fact, as the warmly lighted floors flashed past the elevator we had words over the fact that I, by taking part in the fight, had knocked one of their friends out of a night's work.

We were led out of the elevator through a rococo hall into an anteroom and told to get into our fighting togs. Each of us was issued a pair of boxing gloves and ushered out into the big mirrored hall, which we entered looking cautiously about us and whispering, lest we might accidentally be heard above the noise of the room. It was foggy with cigar smoke. And already the whiskey was taking effect. I was shocked to see some of the most important men of the town quite tipsy. They were all there — bankers, lawyers, judges, doctors, fire chiefs, teachers, merchants. Even one of the more fashionable pastors. Something we could not see was going on up front. A clarinet was vibrating sensuously and the men were standing up and moving eagerly forward. We were a small tight group, clustered together, our bare upper bodies touching and shining with anticipatory sweat;

while up front the big shots were becoming increasingly excited over something we still could not see. Suddenly I heard the school superintendent, who had told me to come, yell, "Bring up the shines, gentlemen! Bring up the little shines!"

We were rushed up to the front of the ballroom, where it smelled even more strongly of tobacco and whiskey. Then we were pushed into place. I almost wet my pants. A sea of faces, some hostile, some amused, ringed around us, and in the center, facing us, stood a magnificent blonde—stark naked. There was dead silence. I felt a blast of cold air chill me. I tried to back away, but they were behind me and around me. Some of the boys stood with lowered heads, trembling. I felt a wave of irrational guilt and fear. My teeth chattered, my skin turned to goose flesh, my knees knocked. Yet I was strongly attracted and looked in spite of myself. Had the price of looking been blindness, I would have looked. The hair was yellow like that of a circus kewpie doll, the face heavily powdered and rouged, as though to form an abstract mask, the eyes hollow and smeared a cool blue, the color of a baboon's butt. I felt a desire to spit upon her as my eyes brushed slowly over her body. Her breasts were firm and round as the domes of East Indian temples, and I stood so close as to see the fine skin texture and beads of pearly perspiration glistening like dew around the pink and erected buds of her nipples. I wanted at one and the same time to run from the room, to sink through the floor, or go to her and cover her from my eyes and the eyes of the others with my body; to feel the soft thighs, to caress her and destroy her, to love her and murder her, to hide from her, and yet to stroke where below the small American flag tattooed upon her belly her thighs formed a capital V. I had a notion that of all in the room she saw only me with her impersonal eyes.

And then she began to dance, a slow sensuous movement; the smoke of a hundred cigars clinging to her like the thinnest of veils. She seemed like a fair bird-girl girdled in veils calling to me from the angry surface of some gray and threatening sea. I was transported. Then I became aware of the clarinet playing and the big shots yelling at us. Some threatened us if we looked and others if we did not. On my right I saw one boy faint. And now a man grabbed a silver pitcher from a table and stepped close as he dashed ice water upon him and stood him up and forced two of us to support him as his head hung and moans issued from his thick bluish lips. Another boy began to plead to go home. He was the largest of the group, wearing dark red fighting trunks much too small to conceal the erection which projected from him as though in answer to the insinuating low-registered moaning of the clarinet. He tried to hide himself with his boxing gloves.

And all the while the blonde continued dancing, smiling faintly at the big shots who watched her with fascination, and faintly smiling at our fear. I noticed a certain merchant who followed her hungrily, his lips loose and drooling. He was a large man who wore diamond studs in a shirtfront which swelled with the ample paunch underneath, and each time the blonde swayed her undulating hips he ran his hand through the thin hair of his bald head and, with his arms upheld, his posture clumsy like that of an intoxicated panda, wound his belly in a slow and obscene grind. This creature was completely hypnotized. The music had quickened. As the dancer flung herself about with a detached expression on her face, the men began reaching out to touch her. I could see their beefy fingers sink into the soft flesh. Some of the others tried to stop them and she began to move around the floor in graceful circles, as they gave chase, slipping and sliding over the polished floor. It was mad. Chairs went crashing, drinks were spilt, as they ran laughing and howling after her. They caught her just as she reached a door, raised her from the floor, and tossed her as college boys are tossed at a hazing, and above her red, fixed-smiling lips I saw the terror and disgust in her eyes, almost like my own terror and that which I saw in some of the other boys. As I watched, they tossed her twice and her soft breasts seemed to flatten against the air and her legs flung wildly as she spun. Some of the more sober ones helped her to escape. And I started off the floor, heading for the anteroom with the rest of the boys.

Some were still crying and in hysteria. But as we tried to leave we were 10 stopped and ordered to get into the ring. There was nothing to do but what we were told. All ten of us climbed under the ropes and allowed ourselves to be blindfolded with broad bands of white cloth. One of the men seemed to feel a bit sympathetic and tried to cheer us up as we stood with our backs against the ropes. Some of us tried to grin. "See that boy over there?" one of the men said. "I want you to run across at the bell and give it to him right in the belly. If you don't get him, I'm going to get you. I don't like his looks." Each of us was told the same. The blindfolds were put on. Yet even then I had been going over my speech. In my mind each word was as bright as flame. I felt the cloth pressed into place, and frowned so that it would be loosened when I relaxed.

But now I felt a sudden fit of blind terror. I was unused to darkness. It was as though I had suddenly found myself in a dark room filled with poisonous cottonmouths. I could hear the bleary voices yelling insistently for the battle royal to begin.

"Get going in there!"

"Let me at that big nigger!"

I strained to pick up the school superintendent's voice, as though to squeeze some security out of that slightly more familiar sound.

"Let me at those black sonsabitches!" someone yelled.   15

"No, Jackson, no!" another voice yelled. "Here, somebody, help me hold Jack."

"I want to get at that ginger-colored nigger. Tear him limb from limb," the first voice yelled.

I stood against the ropes trembling. For in those days I was what they called ginger-colored, and he sounded as though he might crunch me between his teeth like a crisp ginger cookie.

Quite a struggle was going on. Chairs were being kicked about and I could hear voices grunting as with a terrific effort. I wanted to see, to see more desperately than ever before. But the blindfold was tight as a thick skin-puckering scab and when I raised my gloved hands to push the layers of white aside a voice yelled, "Oh, no you don't, black bastard! Leave that alone!"

"Ring the bell before Jackson kills him a coon!" someone boomed in the 20 sudden silence. And I heard the bell clang and the sound of the feet scuffling forward.

A glove smacked against my head. I pivoted, striking out stiffly as someone went past, and felt the jar ripple along the length of my arm to my shoulder. Then it seemed as though all nine of the boys had turned upon me at once. Blows pounded me from all sides while I struck out as best I could. So many blows landed upon me that I wondered if I were not the only blindfolded fighter in the ring, or if the man called Jackson hadn't succeeded in getting me after all.

Blindfolded, I could no longer control my motions. I had no dignity. I stumbled about like a baby or a drunken man. The smoke had become thicker and with each new blow it seemed to sear and further restrict my lungs. My saliva became like hot bitter glue. A glove connected with my head, filling my mouth with warm blood. It was everywhere. I could not tell if the moisture I felt upon my body was sweat or blood. A blow landed hard against the nape of my neck. I felt myself going over, my head hitting the floor. Streaks of blue light filled the black world behind the blindfold. I lay prone, pretending that I was knocked out, but felt myself seized by hands and yanked to my feet. "Get going, black boy! Mix it up!" My arms were like lead, my head smarting from blows. I managed to feel my way to the ropes and held on, trying to catch my breath. A glove landed in my mid-section and I went over again, feeling as though the smoke had become a knife jabbed into my guts. Pushed this way and that by the legs milling around me, I finally pulled erect and discovered that I could see the black, sweat-washed forms weaving in the smoky-blue atmosphere like drunken dancers weaving to the rapid drum-like thuds of blows.

Everyone fought hysterically. It was complete anarchy. Everybody fought everybody else. No group fought together for long. Two, three, four, fought one, then turned to fight each other, were themselves attacked. Blows landed below the belt and in the kidney, with the gloves open as well as closed, and with my eye partly opened now there was not so much terror. I moved carefully, avoiding blows, although not too many to attract attention, fighting from group to group. The boys groped about like blind, cautious crabs crouching to protect their mid-sections, their heads pulled in short against their shoulders, their arms stretched nervously before them, with their fists testing the smoke-filled air like the knobbed feelers of hyper-sensitive snails. In one corner I glimpsed a boy violently punching the air and heard him scream in pain as he smashed his hand against a ring post. For a second I saw him bent over holding his hand, then going down as a blow caught his unprotected head. I played one group against the other, slipping in and throwing a punch then stepping out of range while pushing the others into the melee to take the blows blindly aimed at me. The smoke was agonizing and there were no rounds, no bells at three minute intervals to relieve our exhaustion. The room spun round me, a swirl of lights, smoke, sweating bodies surrounded by tense white faces. I bled from both nose and mouth, the blood spattering upon my chest.

The men kept yelling, "Slug him, black boy! Knock his guts out!"

"Uppercut him! Kill him! Kill that big boy!"   25

Taking a fake fall, I saw a boy going down heavily beside me as though we were felled by a single blow, saw a sneaker-clad foot shoot into his groin as the two who had knocked him down stumbled upon him. I rolled out of range, feeling a twinge of nausea.

The harder we fought the more threatening the men became. And yet, I had begun to worry about my speech again. How would it go? Would they recognize my ability? What would they give me?

I was fighting automatically when suddenly I noticed that one after another of the boys was leaving the ring. I was surprised, filled with panic, as though I had been left alone with an unknown danger. Then I understood. The boys had arranged it among themselves. It was the custom for the two men left in the ring to slug it out for the winner's prize. I discovered this too late. When the bell sounded two men in tuxedoes leaped into the ring and removed the blindfold. I found myself facing Tatlock, the biggest of the gang. I felt sick at my stomach. Hardly had the bell stopped ringing in my ears than it clanged again and I saw him moving swiftly toward me. Thinking of nothing else to do I hit him smash on the nose. He kept coming, bringing the rank sharp violence of stale sweat. His face was a black blank of a face, only his eyes alive—with hate of me and aglow with a feverish terror from what had happened to us all. I became anxious. I wanted to deliver my speech and he came at me as though he meant to beat it out of me. I smashed him again and again, taking his blows as they came. Then on a sudden impulse I struck him lightly and as we clinched, I whispered, "Fake like I knocked you out, you can have the prize."

"I'll break your behind," he whispered hoarsely.

"For *them?*"   30

"For *me*, sonofabitch!"

They were yelling for us to break it up and Tatlock spun me half around with a blow, and as a joggled camera sweeps in a reeling scene, I saw the howling red faces crouching tense beneath the cloud of blue-gray smoke. For a moment the world wavered, unraveled, flowed, then my head cleared and Tatlock bounced before me. That fluttering shadow before my eyes was his jabbing left hand. Then falling forward, my head against his damp shoulder, I whispered,

"I'll make it five dollars more."

"Go to hell!"

But his muscles relaxed a trifle beneath my pressure and I breathed, "Seven?"   35

"Give it to your ma," he said, ripping me beneath the heart.

And while I still held him I butted him and moved away. I felt myself bombarded with punches. I fought back with hopeless desperation. I wanted to deliver my speech more than anything else in the world, because I felt that only these men could judge truly my ability, and now this stupid clown was ruining my chances. I began fighting carefully now, moving in to punch him and out again with my greater speed. A lucky blow to his chin and I had him going too—until I heard a loud voice yell, "I got my money on the big boy."

Hearing this, I almost dropped my guard. I was confused: Should I try to win against the voice out there? Would not this go against my speech, and was not this a moment for humility, for nonresistance? A blow to my head as I danced about sent my right eye popping like a jack-in-the-box and settled my dilemma. The room went red as I fell. It was a dream fall, my body languid and fastidious as to where to land, until the floor became impatient and smashed up to meet me. A moment later I came to. An hypnotic voice said FIVE emphatically. And I lay there, hazily watching a dark red spot of my own blood shaping itself into a butterfly, glistening and soaking into the soiled gray world of the canvas.

When the voice drawled TEN I was lifted up and dragged to a chair. I sat dazed. My eye pained and swelled with each throb of my pounding heart and I wondered if now I would be allowed to speak. I was wringing wet, my mouth still bleeding. We were grouped along the wall now. The other boys ignored me as they congratulated Tatlock and speculated as to how much they would be paid. One boy whimpered over his smashed hand. Looking up front, I saw attendants in white jackets rolling the portable ring away and placing a small square rug in the vacant space surrounded by chairs. Perhaps, I thought, I will stand on the rug to deliver my speech.

Then the M.C. called to us, "Come on up here boys and get your money."   40

We ran forward to where the men laughed and talked in their chairs, waiting. Everyone seemed friendly now.

"There it is on the rug," the man said. I saw the rug covered with coins of all dimensions and a few crumpled bills. But what excited me, scattered here and there, were the gold pieces.

"Boys, it's all yours," the man said. "You get all you grab."

"That's right, Sambo," a blond man said, winking at me confidentially.

I trembled with excitement, forgetting my pain. I would get the gold and the   45 bills, I thought. I would use both hands. I would throw my body against the boys nearest me to block them from the gold.

"Get down around the rug now," the man commanded, "and don't anyone touch it until I give the signal."

"This ought to be good," I heard.

As told, we got around the square rug on our knees. Slowly the man raised his freckled hand as we followed it upward with our eyes.

I heard, "These niggers look like they're about to pray!"

Then, "Ready," the man said. "Go!"   50

I lunged for a yellow coin lying on the blue design of the carpet, touching it and sending a surprised shriek to join those rising around me. I tried frantically to remove my hand but could not let go. A hot, violent force tore through my body, shaking me like a wet rat. The rug was electrified. The hair bristled up on my head as I shook myself free. My muscles jumped, my nerves jangled, writhed. But I saw that this was not stopping the other boys. Laughing in fear and embarrassment, some were holding back and scooping up the coins knocked off by the painful contortions of the others. The men roared above us as we struggled.

"Pick it up, goddamnit, pick it up!" someone called like a bass-voiced parrot. "Go on, get it!"

I crawled rapidly around the floor, picking up the coins, trying to avoid the coppers and to get greenbacks and the gold. Ignoring the shock by laughing, as I brushed the coins off quickly, I discovered that I could contain the electricity—a contradiction, but it works. Then the men began to push us onto the rug. Laughing embarrassedly, we struggled out of their hands and kept after the coins. We were all wet and slippery and hard to hold. Suddenly I saw a boy lifted into the air, glistening with sweat like a circus seal, and dropped, his wet back landing flush upon the charged rug, heard him yell and saw him literally dance upon his back, his elbows beating a frenzied tattoo upon the floor, his muscles twitching like the flesh of a horse stung by many flies. When he finally rolled off, his face was gray and no one stopped him when he ran from the floor amid booming laughter.

"Get the money," the M.C. called. "That's good hard American cash!"

And we snatched and grabbed, snatched and grabbed. I was careful not to 55 come too close to the rug now, and when I felt the hot whiskey breath descend upon me like a cloud of foul air I reached out and grabbed the leg of a chair. It was occupied and I held on desperately.

"Leggo, nigger! Leggo!"

The huge face wavered down to mine as he tried to push me free. But my body was slippery and he was too drunk. It was Mr. Colcord, who owned a chain of movie houses and "entertainment palaces." Each time he grabbed me I slipped out of his hands. It became a real struggle. I feared the rug more than I did the drunk, so I held on, surprising myself for a moment by trying to topple *him* upon the rug. It was such an enormous idea that I found myself actually carrying it out. I tried not to be obvious, yet when I grabbed his leg, trying to tumble him out of the chair, he raised up roaring with laughter, and, looking at me with soberness dead in the eye, kicked me viciously in the chest. The chair leg flew out of my hand and I felt myself going and rolled. It was as though I had rolled through a bed of hot coals. It seemed a whole century would pass before I would roll free, a century in which I was seared through the deepest levels of my body to the fearful breath within me and the breath seared and heated to the point of explosion. It'll all be over in a flash, I thought as I rolled clear. It'll all be over in a flash.

But not yet, the men on the other side were waiting, red faces swollen as though from apoplexy as they bent forward in their chairs. Seeing their fingers coming toward me I rolled away as a fumbled football rolls off the receiver's fingertips, back into the coals. That time I luckily sent the rug sliding out of place and heard the coins ringing against the floor and the boys scuffling to pick them up and the M.C. calling, "All right, boys, that's all. Go get dressed and get your money."

I was limp as a dish rag. My back felt as though it had been beaten with wires.

When we had dressed the M.C. came in and gave us each five dollars, except 60 Tatlock, who got ten for being last in the ring. Then he told us to leave. I was not to get a chance to deliver my speech, I thought. I was going out into the dim alley in despair when I was stopped and told to go back. I returned to the ballroom, where the men were pushing back their chairs and gathering in groups to talk.

The M.C. knocked on a table for quiet. "Gentlemen," he said, "we almost forgot an important part of the program. A most serious part, gentlemen. This boy was brought here to deliver a speech which he made at his graduation yesterday . . ."

"Bravo!"

"I'm told that he is the smartest boy we've got out there in Greenwood. I'm told that he knows more big words than a pocket-sized dictionary."

Much applause and laughter.

"So now, gentlemen, I want you to give him your attention." 65

There was still laughter as I faced them, my mouth dry, my eye throbbing. I began slowly, but evidently my throat was tense, because they began shouting, "Louder! Louder!"

"We of the younger generation extol the wisdom of that great leader and educator," I shouted, "who first spoke these flaming words of wisdom: 'A ship lost at sea for many days suddenly sighted a friendly vessel. From the mast of the unfortunate vessel was seen a signal: "Water, water; we die of thirst!" The answer from the friendly vessel came back: "Cast down your bucket where you are." The captain of the distressed vessel, at last heeding the injunction, cast down his bucket, and it came up full of fresh sparkling water from the mouth of the Amazon River.' And like him I say, and in his words, 'To those of my race who depend upon bettering their condition in a foreign land, or who underestimate the importance of cultivating friendly relations with the Southern white man, who is his next-door neighbor, I would say: "Cast down your bucket where you are" — cast it down in making friends in every manly way of the people of all races by whom we are surrounded . . .'"

I spoke automatically and with such fervor that I did not realize that the men were still talking and laughing until my dry mouth, filling up with blood from the cut, almost strangled me. I coughed, wanting to stop and go to one of the tall brass, sand-filled spittoons to relieve myself, but a few of the men, especially the superintendent, were listening and I was afraid. So I gulped it down, blood, saliva and all, and continued. (What powers of endurance I had during those days! What enthusiasm! What a belief in the rightness of things!) I spoke even louder in spite of the pain. But still they talked and still they laughed, as though deaf with cotton in dirty ears. So I spoke with greater emotional emphasis. I closed my ears and swallowed blood until I was nauseated. The speech seemed a hundred times as long as before, but I could not leave out a single word. All had to be said, each memorized nuance considered, rendered. Nor was that all. Whenever I uttered a word of three or more syllables a group of voices would yell for me to repeat it. I used the phrase "social responsibility" and they yelled:

"What's that word you say, boy?"

"Social responsibility," I said.   70

"What?"

"Social . . ."

"Louder."

". . . responsibility."

"More!"   75

"Respon—"

"Repeat!"

"—sibility."

The room filled with the uproar of laughter until, no doubt distracted by having to gulp down my blood, I made a mistake and yelled a phrase I had often seen denounced in newspaper editorials, heard debated in private.

"Social . . ."   80

"What?" they yelled.

". . . equality—"

The laughter hung smokelike in the sudden stillness. I opened my eyes, puzzled. Sounds of displeasure filled the room. The M.C. rushed forward. They shouted hostile phrases at me. But I did not understand.

A small dry mustached man in the front row blared out, "Say that slowly, son!"

"What, sir?"

"What you just said!"   85

"Social responsibility, sir," I said.

"You weren't being smart, were you, boy?" he said, not unkindly.

"No, sir!"

"You sure that about 'equality' was a mistake?"   90

"Oh, yes, sir," I said. "I was swallowing blood."

"Well, you had better speak more slowly so we can understand. We mean to do right by you, but you've got to know your place at all times. All right, now, go on with your speech."

I was afraid. I wanted to leave but I wanted also to speak and I was afraid they'd snatch me down.

"Thank you, sir," I said, beginning where I had left off, and having them ignore me as before.

Yet when I finished there was a thunderous applause. I was surprised to see 95 the superintendent come forth with a package wrapped in white tissue paper, and, gesturing for quiet, address the men.

"Gentlemen, you see that I did not overpraise this boy. He makes a good speech and some day he'll lead his people in the proper paths. And I don't have to tell you that that is important in these days and times. This is a good, smart boy, and so to encourage him in the right direction, in the name of the Board of Education I wish to present him a prize in the form of this . . ."

He paused, removing the tissue paper and revealing a gleaming calfskin brief case.

". . . in the form of this first-class article from Shad Whitmore's shop."

"Boy," he said, addressing me, "take this prize and keep it well. Consider it a badge of office. Prize it. Keep developing as you are and some day it will be filled with important papers that will help shape the destiny of your people."

I was so moved that I could hardly express my thanks. A rope of bloody   100
saliva forming a shape like an undiscovered continent drooled upon the leather and I wiped it quickly away. I felt an importance that I had never dreamed.

"Open it and see what's inside," I was told.

My fingers a-tremble, I complied, smelling the fresh leather and finding an official-looking document inside. It was a scholarship to the state college for Negroes. My eyes filled with tears and I ran awkwardly off the floor.

I was overjoyed; I did not even mind when I discovered that the gold pieces I had scrambled for were brass pocket tokens advertising a certain make of automobile.

When I reached home everyone was excited. Next day the neighbors came to congratulate me. I even felt safe from grandfather, whose deathbed curse usually spoiled my triumphs. I stood beneath his photograph with my brief case in hand and smiled triumphantly into his stolid black peasant's face. It was a face that fascinated me. The eyes seemed to follow everywhere I went.

That night I dreamed I was at a circus with him and that he refused to laugh   105
at the clowns no matter what they did. Then later he told me to open my brief case and read what was inside and I did, finding an official envelope stamped with the state seal; and inside the envelope I found another and another, endlessly, and I thought I would fall of weariness. "Them's years," he said. "Now open that one." And I did and in it I found an engraved document containing a short message in letters of gold. "Read it," my grandfather said. "Out loud!"

"To Whom It May Concern," I intoned. "Keep This Nigger-Boy Running."

I awoke with the old man's laughter ringing in my ears.

Research Ralph Ellison in depth with cultural documents and multimedia resources on *LiterActive*.

(It was a dream I was to remember and dream again for many years after. But at that time I had no insight into its meaning. First I had to attend college.)

William Faulkner   1897–1962

A Rose for Emily   [1931]

I

When Miss Emily Grierson died, our whole town went to her funeral: the men through a sort of respectful affection for a fallen monument, the women mostly out of curiosity to see the inside of her house, which no one save an old manservant — a combined gardener and cook — had seen in at least ten years.

It was a big, squarish frame house that had once been white, decorated with cupolas and spires and scrolled balconies in the heavily lightsome style of the seventies, set on what had once been our most select street. But garages and cotton gins had encroached and obliterated even the august names of that neighborhood; only Miss Emily's house was left, lifting its stubborn and coquettish decay above the cotton wagons and the gasoline pumps — an eyesore among eyesores. And now Miss Emily had gone to join the representatives of those august names where they lay in the cedar-bemused cemetery among the ranked and anonymous graves of Union and Confederate soldiers who fell at the battle of Jefferson.

Alive, Miss Emily had been a tradition, a duty, and a care; a sort of hereditary obligation upon the town, dating from that day in 1894 when Colonel Sartoris, the mayor — he who fathered the edict that no Negro woman should appear on the streets without an apron — remitted her taxes, the dispensation dating from the death of her father on into perpetuity. Not that Miss Emily would have accepted charity. Colonel Sartoris invented an involved tale to the effect that Miss Emily's father had loaned money to the town, which the town, as a matter of business, preferred this way of repaying. Only a man of Colonel Sartoris' generation and thought could have invented it, and only a woman could have believed it.

When the next generation, with its more modern ideas, became mayors and aldermen, this arrangement created some little dissatisfaction. On the first of the year they mailed her a tax notice. February came, and there was no reply. They wrote her a formal letter, asking her to call at the sheriff's office at her convenience. A week later the mayor wrote her himself, offering to call or to send his car for her, and received in reply a note on paper of an archaic shape, in a thin, flowing calligraphy in faded ink, to the effect that she no longer went out at all. The tax notice was also enclosed, without comment.

They called a special meeting of the Board of Aldermen. A deputation waited 5 upon her, knocked at the door through which no visitor had passed since she ceased giving china-painting lessons eight or ten years earlier. They were admitted by the old Negro into a dim hall from which a stairway mounted into still more shadow. It smelled of dust and disuse — a close, dank smell. The Negro led them into the parlor. It was furnished in heavy, leather-covered furniture. When the Negro opened the blinds of one window, they could see that the leather was cracked; and when they sat down, a faint dust rose sluggishly about their thighs, spinning with slow motes in the single sun-ray. On a tarnished gilt easel before the fireplace stood a crayon portrait of Miss Emily's father.

They rose when she entered — a small, fat woman in black, with a thin gold chain descending to her waist and vanishing into her belt, leaning on an ebony cane with a tarnished gold head. Her skeleton was small and spare; perhaps that was why what would have been merely plumpness in another was obesity in her. She looked bloated, like a body long submerged in motionless water, and of that pallid hue. Her eyes, lost in the fatty ridges of her face, looked like two small pieces of coal pressed into a lump of dough as they moved from one face to another while the visitors stated their errand.

She did not ask them to sit. She just stood in the door and listened quietly until the spokesman came to a stumbling halt. Then they could hear the invisible watch ticking at the end of the gold chain.

Her voice was dry and cold. "I have no taxes in Jefferson. Colonel Sartoris explained it to me. Perhaps one of you can gain access to the city records and satisfy yourselves."

"But we have. We are the city authorities, Miss Emily. Didn't you get a notice from the sheriff, signed by him?"

"I received a paper, yes," Miss Emily said. "Perhaps he considers himself the 10 sheriff . . . I have no taxes in Jefferson."

"But there is nothing on the books to show that, you see. We must go by the—"

"See Colonel Sartoris. I have no taxes in Jefferson."

"But, Miss Emily—"

"See Colonel Sartoris." (Colonel Sartoris had been dead almost ten years.) "I have no taxes in Jefferson. Tobe!" The Negro appeared. "Show these gentlemen out."

II

So she vanquished them, horse and foot, just as she had vanquished their 15 fathers thirty years before about the smell. That was two years after her father's death and a short time after her sweetheart—the one we believed would marry her—had deserted her. After her father's death she went out very little; after her sweetheart went away, people hardly saw her at all. A few of the ladies had the temerity to call, but were not received, and the only sign of life about the place was the Negro man—a young man then—going in and out with a market basket.

"Just as if a man—any man—could keep a kitchen properly," the ladies said; so they were not surprised when the smell developed. It was another link between the gross, teeming world and the high and mighty Griersons.

A neighbor, a woman, complained to the mayor, Judge Stevens, eighty years old.

"But what will you have me do about it, madam?" he said.

"Why, send her word to stop it," the woman said. "Isn't there a law?"

"I'm sure that won't be necessary," Judge Stevens said. "It's probably just a 20 snake or a rat that nigger of hers killed in the yard. I'll speak to him about it."

The next day he received two more complaints, one from a man who came in diffident deprecation. "We really must do something about it, Judge. I'd be the last one in the world to bother Miss Emily, but we've got to do something." That night the Board of Aldermen met—three graybeards and one younger man, a member of the rising generation.

"It's simple enough," he said. "Send her word to have her place cleaned up. Give her a certain time to do it in, and if she don't . . ."

"Dammit, sir," Judge Stevens said, "will you accuse a lady to her face of smelling bad?"

So the next night, after midnight, four men crossed Miss Emily's lawn and slunk about the house like burglars, sniffing along the base of the brickwork and at the cellar openings while one of them performed a regular sowing motion with his hand out of a sack slung from his shoulder. They broke open the cellar door and sprinkled lime there, and in all the outbuildings. As they recrossed the lawn, a window that had been dark was lighted and Miss Emily sat in it, the light behind her, and her upright torso motionless as that of an idol. They crept quietly across the lawn and into the shadow of the locusts that lined the street. After a week or two the smell went away.

That was when people had begun to feel really sorry for her. People in our 25 town, remembering how old lady Wyatt, her great-aunt, had gone completely crazy at last, believed that the Griersons held themselves a little too high for what they really were. None of the young men were quite good enough for Miss Emily and such. We had long thought of them as a tableau,° Miss Emily a slender figure in white in the background, her father a spraddled silhouette in the foreground, his back to her and clutching a horsewhip, the two of them framed by the back-flung front door. So when she got to be thirty and was still single, we were not pleased exactly, but vindicated; even with insanity in the family she wouldn't have turned down all of her chances if they had really materialized.

When her father died, it got about that the house was all that was left to her; and in a way, people were glad. At last they could pity Miss Emily. Being left alone, and a pauper, she had become humanized. Now she too would know the old thrill and the old despair of a penny more or less.

The day after his death all the ladies prepared to call at the house and offer condolence and aid, as is our custom. Miss Emily met them at the door, dressed as usual and with no trace of grief on her face. She told them that her father was not dead. She did that for three days, with the ministers calling on her, and the doctors, trying to persuade her to let them dispose of the body. Just as they were about to resort to law and force, she broke down, and they buried her father quickly.

We did not say she was crazy then. We believed she had to do that. We remembered all the young men her father had driven away, and we knew that with nothing left, she would have to cling to that which had robbed her, as people will.

III

She was sick for a long time. When we saw her again, her hair was cut short, making her look like a girl, with a vague resemblance to those angels in colored church windows — sort of tragic and serene.

The town had just let the contracts for paving the sidewalks, and in the 30 summer after her father's death they began the work. The construction company came with niggers and mules and machinery, and a foreman named Homer Barron, a Yankee — a big, dark, ready man, with a big voice and eyes lighter than

---

tableau: short for *tableau vivant* (French), "living painting"; a depiction of a scene or picture by a person or group in costume, posing silently without moving.

his face. The little boys would follow in groups to hear him cuss the niggers, and the niggers singing in time to the rise and fall of picks. Pretty soon he knew everybody in town. Whenever you heard a lot of laughing anywhere about the square, Homer Barron would be in the center of the group. Presently we began to see him and Miss Emily on Sunday afternoons driving in the yellow-wheeled buggy and the matched team of bays from the livery stable.

At first we were glad that Miss Emily would have an interest, because the ladies all said, "Of course a Grierson would not think seriously of a Northerner, a day laborer." But there were still others, older people, who said that even grief could not cause a real lady to forget *noblesse oblige*° — without calling it *noblesse oblige*. They just said, "Poor Emily. Her kinsfolk should come to her." She had some kin in Alabama; but years ago her father had fallen out with them over the estate of old lady Wyatt, the crazy woman, and there was no communication between the two families. They had not even been represented at the funeral.

And as soon as the old people said, "Poor Emily," the whispering began. "Do you suppose it's really so?" they said to one another. "Of course it is. What else could . . ." This behind their hands; rustling of craned silk and satin behind jalousies closed upon the sun of Sunday afternoon as the thin, swift clop-clop-clop of the matched team passed: "Poor Emily."

She carried her head high enough — even when we believed that she was fallen. It was as if she demanded more than ever the recognition of her dignity as the last Grierson; as if it had wanted that touch of earthiness to reaffirm her imperviousness. Like when she bought the rat poison, the arsenic. That was over a year after they had begun to say "Poor Emily," and while the two female cousins were visiting her.

"I want some poison," she said to the druggist. She was over thirty then, still a slight woman, though thinner than usual, with cold, haughty black eyes in a face the flesh of which was strained across the temples and about the eye-sockets as you imagine a lighthouse-keeper's face ought to look. "I want some poison," she said.

"Yes, Miss Emily. What kind? For rats and such? I'd recom —"   35

"I want the best you have. I don't care what kind."

The druggist named several. "They'll kill anything up to an elephant. But what you want is —"

"Arsenic," Miss Emily said. "Is that a good one?"

"Is . . . arsenic? Yes, ma'am. But what you want —"

"I want arsenic."   40

The druggist looked down at her. She looked back at him, erect, her face like a strained flag. "Why, of course," the druggist said. "If that's what you want. But the law requires you to tell what you are going to use it for."

Miss Emily just stared at him, her head tilted back in order to look him eye for eye, until he looked away and went and got the arsenic and wrapped it up.

---

noblesse oblige: "Nobility obligates" (French); the inferred obligation of people of high rank or social position to behave nobly, generously, and kindly toward others.

The Negro delivery boy brought her the package; the druggist didn't come back. When she opened the package at home there was written on the box, under the skull and bones: "For rats."

IV

So the next day we all said, "She will kill herself"; and we said it would be the best thing. When she had first begun to be seen with Homer Barron, we had said, "She will marry him." Then we said, "She will persuade him yet," because Homer himself had remarked—he liked men, and it was known that he drank with the younger men in the Elks' Club—that he was not a marrying man. Later we said, "Poor Emily" behind the jalousies as they passed on Sunday afternoon in the glittering buggy, Miss Emily with her head high and Homer Barron with his hat cocked and a cigar in his teeth, reins and whip in a yellow glove.

Then some of the ladies began to say that it was a disgrace to the town and a bad example to the young people. The men did not want to interfere, but at last the ladies forced the Baptist minister—Miss Emily's people were Episcopal—to call upon her. He would never divulge what happened during that interview, but he refused to go back again. The next Sunday they again drove about the streets, and the following day the minister's wife wrote to Miss Emily's relations in Alabama.

So she had blood-kin under her roof again and we sat back to watch develop-   45 ments. At first nothing happened. Then we were sure that they were to be married. We learned that Miss Emily had been to the jeweler's and ordered a man's toilet set in silver, with the letters H. B. on each piece. Two days later we learned that she had bought a complete outfit of men's clothing, including a nightshirt, and we said, "They are married." We were really glad. We were glad because the two female cousins were even more Grierson than Miss Emily had ever been.

So we were not surprised when Homer Barron—the streets had been finished some time since—was gone. We were a little disappointed that there was not a public blowing-off, but we believed that he had gone on to prepare for Miss Emily's coming, or to give her a chance to get rid of the cousins. (By that time it was a cabal, and we were all Miss Emily's allies to help circumvent the cousins.) Sure enough, after another week they departed. And, as we had expected all along, within three days Homer Barron was back in town. A neighbor saw the Negro man admit him at the kitchen door at dusk one evening.

And that was the last we saw of Homer Barron. And of Miss Emily for some time. The Negro man went in and out with the market basket, but the front door remained closed. Now and then we would see her at a window for a moment, as the men did that night when they sprinkled the lime, but for almost six months she did not appear on the streets. Then we knew that this was to be expected too; as if that quality of her father which had thwarted her woman's life so many times had been too virulent and too furious to die.

When we next saw Miss Emily, she had grown fat and her hair was turning gray. During the next few years it grew grayer and grayer until it attained an even pepper-and-salt iron-gray, when it ceased turning. Up to the day of her death at seventy-four it was still that vigorous iron-gray, like the hair of an active man.

From that time on her front door remained closed, save for a period of six or seven years, when she was about forty, during which she gave lessons in china-painting. She fitted up a studio in one of the downstairs rooms, where the daughters and granddaughters of Colonel Sartoris' contemporaries were sent to her with the same regularity and in the same spirit that they were sent to church on Sundays with a twenty-five-cent piece for the collection plate. Meanwhile her taxes had been remitted.

Then the newer generation became the backbone and the spirit of the town,   50 and the painting pupils grew up and fell away and did not send their children to her with boxes of color and tedious brushes and pictures cut from the ladies' magazines. The front door closed upon the last one and remained closed for good. When the town got free postal delivery, Miss Emily alone refused to let them fasten the metal numbers above her door and attach a mailbox to it. She would not listen to them.

Daily, monthly, yearly we watched the Negro grow grayer and more stooped, going in and out with the market basket. Each December we sent her a tax notice, which would be returned by the post office a week later, unclaimed. Now and then we would see her in one of the downstairs windows — she had evidently shut up the top floor of the house — like the carven torso of an idol in a niche, looking or not looking at us, we could never tell which. Thus she passed from generation to generation — dear, inescapable, impervious, tranquil, and perverse.

And so she died. Fell ill in the house filled with dust and shadows, with only a doddering Negro man to wait on her. We did not even know she was sick; we had long since given up trying to get any information from the Negro. He talked to no one, probably not even to her, for his voice had grown harsh and rusty, as if from disuse.

She died in one of the downstairs rooms, in a heavy walnut bed with a curtain, her gray head propped on a pillow yellow and moldy with age and lack of sunlight.

V

The Negro met the first of the ladies at the front door and let them in, with their hushed, sibilant voices and their quick, curious glances, and then he disappeared. He walked right through the house and out the back and was not seen again.

The two female cousins came at once. They held the funeral on the second   55 day, with the town coming to look at Miss Emily beneath a mass of bought flowers, with the crayon face of her father musing profoundly above the bier and the ladies sibilant and macabre; and the very old men — some in their brushed Confederate uniforms — on the porch and the lawn, talking of Miss Emily as if she had been a contemporary of theirs, believing that they had danced with her and courted her perhaps, confusing time with its mathematical progression, as the old do, to whom all the past is not a diminishing road but, instead, a huge meadow which no winter ever quite touches, divided from them now by the narrow bottle-neck of the most recent decade of years.

Already we knew that there was one room in that region above stairs which no one had seen in forty years, and which would have to be forced. They waited until Miss Emily was decently in the ground before they opened it.

The violence of breaking down the door seemed to fill this room with pervading dust. A thin, acrid pall as of the tomb seemed to lie everywhere upon this room decked and furnished as for a bridal: upon the valance curtains of faded rose color, upon the rose-shaded lights, upon the dressing table, upon the delicate array of crystal and the man's toilet things backed with tarnished silver, silver so tarnished that the monogram was obscured. Among them lay a collar and tie, as if they had just been removed, which, lifted, left upon the surface a pale crescent in the dust. Upon a chair hung the suit, carefully folded; beneath it the two mute shoes and the discarded socks.

Research William Faulkner in depth with cultural documents and multimedia resources on *Literactive*.

The man himself lay in the bed.

For a long while we just stood there, looking down at the profound and fleshless grin. The body had apparently once lain in the attitude of an embrace, but now the long sleep that outlasts love, that conquers even the grimace of love, had cuckolded him. What was left of him, rotted beneath what was left of the nightshirt, had become inextricable from the bed in which he lay; and upon him and upon the pillow beside him lay that even coating of the patient and biding dust.

Then we noticed that in the second pillow was the indentation of a head. 60 One of us lifted something from it, and leaning forward, that faint and invisible dust dry and acrid in the nostrils, we saw a long strand of iron-gray hair.

Gabriel García Márquez   Colombia, b. 1928

A Very Old Man with Enormous Wings   [1955]
A Tale for Children

Translated by Gregory Rabassa

On the third day of rain they had killed so many crabs inside the house that Pelayo had to cross his drenched courtyard and throw them into the sea, because the newborn child had a temperature all night and they thought it was due to the stench. The world had been sad since Tuesday. Sea and sky were a single ash-gray thing and the sands of the beach, which on March nights glimmered like powdered light, had become a stew of mud and rotten shellfish. The light was so weak at noon that when Pelayo was coming back to the house after throwing away the crabs, it was hard for him to see what it was that was moving and groaning in the rear of the courtyard. He had to go very close to see that it was an old man, a very old man, lying face down in the mud, who, in spite of his tremendous efforts, couldn't get up, impeded by his enormous wings.

Frightened by that nightmare, Pelayo ran to get Elisenda, his wife, who was putting compresses on the sick child, and he took her to the rear of the courtyard. They both looked at the fallen body with mute stupor. He was dressed like a ragpicker. There were only a few faded hairs left on his bald skull and very few teeth in his mouth, and his pitiful condition of a drenched great-grandfather had taken away any sense of grandeur he might have had. His huge buzzard wings, dirty and half-plucked, were forever entangled in the mud. They looked at him so long and so closely that Pelayo and Elisenda very soon overcame their surprise and in the end found him familiar. Then they dared speak to him, and he answered in an incomprehensible dialect with a strong sailor's voice. That was how they skipped over the inconvenience of the wings and quite intelligently concluded that he was a lonely castaway from some foreign ship wrecked by the storm. And yet, they called in a neighbor woman who knew everything about life and death to see him, and all she needed was one look to show them their mistake.

"He's an angel," she told them. "He must have been coming for the child, but the poor fellow is so old that the rain knocked him down."

On the following day everyone knew that a flesh-and-blood angel was held captive in Pelayo's house. Against the judgment of the wise neighbor woman, for whom angels in those times were the fugitive survivors of a celestial conspiracy, they did not have the heart to club him to death. Pelayo watched over him all afternoon from the kitchen, armed with his bailiff's club, and before going to bed he dragged him out of the mud and locked him up with the hens in the wire chicken coop. In the middle of the night, when the rain stopped, Pelayo and Elisenda were still killing crabs. A short time afterward the child woke up without a fever and with a desire to eat. Then they felt magnanimous and decided to put the angel on a raft with fresh water and provisions for three days and leave him to his fate on the high seas. But when they went out into the courtyard with the first light of dawn, they found the whole neighborhood in front of the chicken coop having fun with the angel, without the slightest reverence, tossing him things to eat through the openings in the wire as if he weren't a supernatural creature but a circus animal.

Father Gonzaga arrived before seven o'clock, alarmed at the strange news. 5 By that time onlookers less frivolous than those at dawn had already arrived and they were making all kinds of conjectures concerning the captive's future. The simplest among them thought that he should be named mayor of the world. Others of sterner mind felt that he should be promoted to the rank of five-star general in order to win all wars. Some visionaries hoped that he could be put to stud in order to implant on earth a race of winged wise men who could take charge of the universe. But Father Gonzaga, before becoming a priest, had been a robust woodcutter. Standing by the wire, he reviewed his catechism in an instant and asked them to open the door so that he could take a close look at that pitiful man who looked more like a huge decrepit hen among the fascinated chickens. He was lying in a corner drying his open wings in the sunlight among the fruit peels and breakfast leftovers that the early risers had thrown him. Alien to the impertinences of the world, he only lifted his antiquarian eyes and murmured something in his dialect when Father Gonzaga went into the chicken coop and said good morning to him in Latin. The parish priest had his first suspicion of an imposter when he saw that he did not understand the language of God or know how to greet His ministers. Then he noticed that seen close up he was much too human: he had an unbearable smell of the outdoors, the back side of his wings was strewn with parasites and his main feathers had been mistreated by terrestrial winds, and nothing about him measured up to the proud dignity of angels. Then he came out of the chicken coop and in a brief sermon warned the curious against the risks of being ingenuous. He reminded them that the devil had the bad habit of making use of carnival tricks in order to confuse the unwary. He argued that if wings were not the essential element in determining the difference between a hawk and an airplane, they were even less so in the recognition of angels. Nevertheless, he promised to write a letter to his bishop so that the latter would write to his primate so that the latter would write to the Supreme Pontiff in order to get the final verdict from the highest courts.

His prudence fell on sterile hearts. The news of the captive angel spread with such rapidity that after a few hours the courtyard had the bustle of a marketplace and they had to call in troops with fixed bayonets to disperse the mob that was about to knock the house down. Elisenda, her spine all twisted from sweeping up so much marketplace trash, then got the idea of fencing in the yard and charging five cents admission to see the angel.

The curious came from far away. A traveling carnival arrived with a flying acrobat who buzzed over the crowd several times, but no one paid any attention to him because his wings were not those of an angel but, rather, those of a sidereal° bat. The most unfortunate invalids on earth came in search of health: a poor woman who since childhood had been counting her heartbeats and had run out of numbers; a Portuguese man who couldn't sleep because the noise of the stars disturbed him; a sleepwalker who got up at night to undo the things he had done while awake; and many others with less serious ailments. In the midst of that shipwreck disorder that made the earth tremble, Pelayo and Elisenda were happy with fatigue, for in less than a week they had crammed their rooms with money and the line of pilgrims waiting their turn to enter still reached beyond the horizon.

The angel was the only one who took no part in his own act. He spent his time trying to get comfortable in his borrowed nest, befuddled by the hellish heat of the oil lamps and sacramental candles that had been placed along the wire. At first they tried to make him eat some mothballs, which, according to the wisdom of the wise neighbor woman, were the food prescribed for angels. But he turned them down, just as he turned down the papal lunches that the penitents

---

sidereal: Coming from the stars.

brought him, and they never found out whether it was because he was an angel or because he was an old man that in the end he ate nothing but eggplant mush. His only supernatural virtue seemed to be patience. Especially during the first days, when the hens pecked at him, searching for the stellar parasites that proliferated in his wings, and the cripples pulled out feathers to touch their defective parts with, and even the most merciful threw stones at him, trying to get him to rise so they could see him standing. The only time they succeeded in arousing him was when they burned his side with an iron for branding steers, for he had been motionless for so many hours that they thought he was dead. He awoke with a start, ranting in his hermetic language and with tears in his eyes, and he flapped his wings a couple of times, which brought on a whirlwind of chicken dung and lunar dust and a gale of panic that did not seem to be of this world. Although many thought that his reaction had been one not of rage but of pain, from then on they were careful not to annoy him, because the majority understood that his passivity was not that of a hero taking his ease but that of a cataclysm in repose.

Father Gonzaga held back the crowd's frivolity with formulas of maidservant inspiration while awaiting the arrival of a final judgment on the nature of the captive. But the mail from Rome showed no sense of urgency. They spent their time finding out if the prisoner had a navel, if his dialect had any connection with Aramaic, how many times he could fit on the head of a pin, or whether he wasn't just a Norwegian with wings. Those meager letters might have come and gone until the end of time if a providential event had not put an end to the priest's tribulations.

It so happened that during those days, among so many other carnival attractions, there arrived in town the traveling show of the woman who had been changed into a spider for having disobeyed her parents. The admission to see her was not only less than the admission to see the angel, but people were permitted to ask her all manner of questions about her absurd state and to examine her up and down so that no one would ever doubt the truth of her horror. She was a frightful tarantula the size of a ram and with the head of a sad maiden. What was most heartrending, however, was not her outlandish shape but the sincere affliction with which she recounted the details of her misfortune. While still practically a child she had sneaked out of her parents' house to go to a dance, and while she was coming back through the woods after having danced all night without permission, a fearful thunderclap rent the sky in two and through the crack came the lightning bolt of brimstone that changed her into a spider. Her only nourishment came from the meatballs that charitable souls chose to toss into her mouth. A spectacle like that, full of so much human truth and with such a fearful lesson, was bound to defeat without even trying that of a haughty angel who scarcely deigned to look at mortals. Besides, the few miracles attributed to the angel showed a certain mental disorder, like the blind man who didn't recover his sight but grew three new teeth, or the paralytic who didn't get to walk but almost won the lottery, and the leper whose sores sprouted sunflowers. Those consolation miracles, which were more like mocking fun, had already ruined the angel's reputation when the woman who had been changed into a spider finally crushed him completely. That was how Father Gonzaga was cured forever of his insomnia and Pelayo's courtyard went back to being as empty as during the time it had rained for three days and crabs walked through the bedrooms.

The owners of the house had no reason to lament. With the money they saved they built a two-story mansion with balconies and gardens and high netting so that crabs wouldn't get in during the winter, and with iron bars on the windows so that angels wouldn't get in. Pelayo also set up a rabbit warren close to town and gave up his job as bailiff for good, and Elisenda bought some satin pumps with high heels and many dresses of iridescent silk, the kind worn on Sunday by the most desirable women in those times. The chicken coop was the only thing that didn't receive any attention. If they washed it down with creolin and burned tears of myrrh inside it every so often, it was not in homage to the angel but to drive away the dungheap stench that still hung everywhere like a ghost and was turning the new house into an old one. At first, when the child learned to walk, they were careful that he not get too close to the chicken coop. But then they began to lose their fears and got used to the smell, and before the child got his second teeth he'd gone inside the chicken coop to play, where the wires were falling apart. The angel was no less standoffish with him than with other mortals, but he tolerated the most ingenious infamies with the patience of a dog who had no illusions. They both came down with chicken pox at the same time. The doctor who took care of the child couldn't resist the temptation to listen to the angel's heart, and he found so much whistling in the heart and so many sounds in his kidneys that it seemed impossible for him to be alive. What surprised him most, however, was the logic of his wings. They seemed so natural on that completely human organism that he couldn't understand why other men didn't have them too.

When the child began school it had been some time since the sun and rain had caused the collapse of the chicken coop. The angel went dragging himself about here and there like a stray dying man. They would drive him out of the bedroom with a broom and a moment later find him in the kitchen. He seemed to be in so many places at the same time that they grew to think that he'd been duplicated, that he was reproducing himself all through the house, and the exasperated and unhinged Elisenda shouted that it was awful living in that hell full of angels. He could scarcely eat and his antiquarian eyes had also become so foggy that he went about bumping into posts. All he had left were the bare cannulae° of his last feathers. Pelayo threw a blanket over him and extended him the charity of letting him sleep in the shed, and only then did they notice that he had a temperature at night, and was delirious with the tongue twisters of an old Norwegian. That was one of the few times they became alarmed, for they thought he was going to die and not even the wise neighbor woman had been able to tell them what to do with dead angels.

---

cannulae: The tubelike quills by which feathers are attached to a body.

And yet he not only survived his worst winter, but seemed improved with the first sunny days. He remained motionless for several days in the farthest corner of the courtyard, where no one would see him, and at the beginning of December some large, stiff feathers began to grow on his wings, the feathers of a scarecrow, which looked more like another misfortune of decrepitude. But he must have known the reason for those changes, for he was quite careful that no one should notice them, that no one should hear the sea chanteys that he sometimes sang under the stars. One morning Elisenda was cutting some bunches of onions for lunch when a wind that seemed to come from the high seas blew into the kitchen. Then she went to the window and caught the angel in his first attempts at flight. They were so clumsy that his fingernails opened a furrow in the vegetable patch and he was on the point of knocking the shed down with the ungainly flapping that slipped on the light and couldn't get a grip on the air. But he did manage to gain altitude. Elisenda let out a sigh of relief, for herself and for him, when she saw him pass over the last houses, holding himself up in some way with the risky flapping of a senile vulture. She kept watching him even when she was through cutting the onions and she kept on watching until it was no longer possible for her to see him, because then he was no longer an annoyance in her life but an imaginary dot on the horizon of the sea.

Nathaniel Hawthorne   1804–1864
Young Goodman Brown   [1835]

Young Goodman° Brown came forth, at sunset, into the street of Salem village,° but put his head back, after crossing the threshold, to exchange a parting kiss with his young wife. And Faith, as the wife was aptly named, thrust her own pretty head into the street, letting the wind play with the pink ribbons of her cap, while she called to Goodman Brown.

"Dearest heart," whispered she, softly and rather sadly, when her lips were close to his ear, "pr'y thee, put off your journey until sunrise, and sleep in your own bed to-night. A lone woman is troubled with such dreams and such thoughts, that she's afeard of herself, sometimes. Pray, tarry with me this night, dear husband, of all nights in the year!"

"My love and my Faith," replied young Goodman Brown, "of all nights in the year, this one night must I tarry away from thee. My journey, as thou callest it, forth and back again, must needs be done 'twixt now and sunrise. What, my sweet, pretty wife, dost thou doubt me already, and we but three months married!"

"Then, God bless you!" said Faith, with the pink ribbons, "and may you find all well when you come back."

Goodman: A man of ordinary status who was head of a household.   Salem village: Village in the Massachusetts Bay Colony.

"Amen!" cried Goodman Brown. "Say thy prayers, dear Faith, and go to bed 5
at dusk, and no harm will come to thee."

So they parted; and the young man pursued his way, until, being about to
turn the corner by the meeting-house, he looked back, and saw the head of Faith
still peeping after him, with a melancholy air, in spite of her pink ribbons.

"Poor little Faith!" thought he, for his heart smote him. "What a wretch am
I, to leave her on such an errand! She talks of dreams, too. Methought, as she
spoke, there was trouble in her face, as if a dream had warned her what work is
to be done to-night. But, no, no! 'twould kill her to think it. Well; she's a blessed
angel on earth; and after this one night, I'll cling to her skirts and follow her to
Heaven."

With this excellent resolve for the future, Goodman Brown felt himself justified in making more haste on his present evil purpose. He had taken a dreary
road, darkened by all the gloomiest trees of the forest, which barely stood aside
to let the narrow path creep through, and closed immediately behind. It was all
as lonely as could be; and there is this peculiarity in such a solitude, that the
traveller knows not who may be concealed by the innumerable trunks and the
thick boughs overhead; so that, with lonely footsteps, he may yet be passing
through an unseen multitude.

"There may be a devilish Indian behind every tree," said Goodman Brown,
to himself; and he glanced fearfully behind him, as he added, "What if the devil
himself should be at my very elbow!"

His head being turned back, he passed a crook of the road, and looking for- 10
ward again, beheld the figure of a man, in grave and decent attire, seated at the
foot of an old tree. He arose, at Goodman Brown's approach, and walked onward, side by side with him.

"You are late, Goodman Brown," said he. "The clock of the Old South was
striking as I came through Boston; and that is full fifteen minutes agone."°

"Faith kept me back awhile," replied the young man, with a tremor in his
voice, caused by the sudden appearance of his companion, though not wholly
unexpected.

It was now deep dusk in the forest, and deepest in that part of it where these
two were journeying. As nearly as could be discerned, the second traveller was
about fifty years old, apparently in the same rank of life as Goodman Brown,
and bearing a considerable resemblance to him, though perhaps more in expression than features. Still, they might have been taken for father and son. And yet,
though the elder person was as simply clad as the younger, and as simple in
manner too, he had an indescribable air of one who knew the world, and would
not have felt abashed at the governor's dinnertable, or in King William's court,°
were it possible that his affairs should call him thither. But the only thing about
him, that could be fixed upon as remarkable, was his staff, which bore the like-

---

full fifteen minutes agone: This mysterious figure apparently traveled the sixteen miles from
Old South Church in Boston to woods outside Salem in a quarter of an hour.   **King William's
court:** William III was king of England from 1689 to 1702, ruling jointly with his wife Mary II
until her death in 1694.

ness of a great black snake, so curiously wrought, that it might almost be seen to twist and wriggle itself, like a living serpent. This, of course, must have been an ocular deception, assisted by the uncertain light.

"Come, Goodman Brown!" cried his fellow-traveller, "this is a dull pace for the beginning of a journey. Take my staff, if you are so soon weary."

"Friend," said the other, exchanging his slow pace for a full stop, "having kept covenant by meeting thee here, it is my purpose now to return whence I came. I have scruples, touching the matter thou wot'st° of."   15

"Sayest thou so?" replied he of the serpent, smiling apart. "Let us walk on, nevertheless, reasoning as we go, and if I convince thee not, thou shalt turn back. We are but a little way in the forest, yet."

"Too far, too far!" exclaimed the goodman, unconsciously resuming his walk. "My father never went into the woods on such an errand, nor his father before him. We have been a race of honest men and good Christians, since the days of the martyrs.° And shall I be the first of the name of Brown, that ever took this path, and kept—"

"Such company, thou wouldst say," observed the elder person, interpreting his pause. "Well said, Goodman Brown! I have been as well acquainted with your family as with ever a one among the Puritans; and that's no trifle to say. I helped your grandfather, the constable, when he lashed the Quaker woman so smartly through the streets of Salem. And it was I that brought your father a pitch-pine knot, kindled at my own hearth, to set fire to an Indian village, in King Philip's war.° They were my good friends, both; and many a pleasant walk have we had along this path, and returned merrily after midnight. I would fain be friends with you, for their sake."

"If it be as thou sayest," replied Goodman Brown, "I marvel they never spoke of these matters. Or, verily, I marvel not, seeing that the least rumor of the sort would have driven them from New-England. We are a people of prayer, and good works, to boot, and abide no such wickedness."

"Wickedness or not," said the traveller with the twisted staff, "I have a very   20
general acquaintance here in New-England. The deacons of many a church have drunk the communion wine with me; the selectmen, of divers towns, make me their chairman; and a majority of the Great and General Court° are firm supporters of my interest. The governor and I, too—but these are state-secrets."

"Can this be so!" cried Goodman Brown, with a stare of amazement at his undisturbed companion. "Howbeit, I have nothing to do with the governor and council; they have their own ways, and are no rule for a simple husbandman,° like me. But, were I to go on with thee, how should I meet the eye of that good

---

wot'st: Know.   days of the martyrs: Period in England during the rule of a Catholic monarch, Mary I (1553–1558), when Protestants were persecuted and many ancestors of the New England Pilgrims lost their lives for their religious faith.   King Philip's war: A bitter conflict (1675–1676) between the colonists and several New England tribes led by Metacomet, chief of the Wampanoag Indians, who was called King Philip by the colonists.   Great and General Court: Colonial legislature.   husbandman: Farmer.

old man, our minister, at Salem village? Oh, his voice would make me tremble, both Sabbath-day and lecture-day!"°

Thus far, the elder traveller had listened with due gravity, but now burst into a fit of irrepressible mirth, shaking himself so violently, that his snake-like staff actually seemed to wriggle in sympathy.

"Ha! ha! ha!" shouted he, again and again; then composing himself, "Well, go on, Goodman Brown, go on; but pr'y thee, don't kill me with laughing!"

"Well, then, to end the matter at once," said Goodman Brown, considerably nettled, "there is my wife, Faith. It would break her dear little heart; and I'd rather break my own!"

"Nay, if that be the case," answered the other, "e'en go thy ways, Goodman 25 Brown. I would not, for twenty old women like the one hobbling before us, that Faith should come to any harm."

As he spoke, he pointed his staff at a female figure on the path, in whom Goodman Brown recognized a very pious and exemplary dame, who had taught him his catechism, in youth, and was still his moral and spiritual adviser, jointly with the minister and Deacon Gookin.

"A marvel, truly, that Goody° Cloyse should be so far in the wilderness, at night-fall!" said he. "But, with your leave, friend, I shall take a cut through the woods, until we have left this Christian woman behind. Being a stranger to you, she might ask whom I was consorting with, and whither I was going."

"Be it so," said his fellow-traveller. "Betake you to the woods, and let me keep the path."

Accordingly, the young man turned aside, but took care to watch his companion, who advanced softly along the road, until he had come within a staff's length of the old dame. She, meanwhile, was making the best of her way, with singular speed for so aged a woman, and mumbling some indistinct words, a prayer, doubtless, as she went. The traveller put forth his staff, and touched her withered neck with what seemed the serpent's tail.

"The devil!" screamed the pious old lady.   30

"Then Goody Cloyse knows her old friend?" observed the traveller, confronting her, and leaning on his writhing stick.

"Ah, forsooth, and is it your worship, indeed?" cried the good dame. "Yea, truly is it, and in the very image of my old gossip,° Goodman Brown, the grandfather of the silly fellow that now is. But—would your worship believe it?—my broomstick hath strangely disappeared, stolen, as I suspect, by that unhanged witch, Goody Cory, and that, too, when I was all anointed with the juice of smallage and cinque-foil and wolf's-bane—"°

---

lecture-day: A weekday church service with a sermon.   **Goody:** Short for Goodwife, a married woman of ordinary status (cf. "goodman"). Goody Cloyse and Goody Cory, along with Martha Carrier, were sentenced to death at the Salem witchcraft trials of 1692, at which Hawthorne's great-grandfather was a judge.   **gossip:** Godfather or godmother, sponsor at a baptism.   **smallage . . . bane:** "Smallage" is wild celery or water parsley; "cinque-foil" is a type of rose; "wolf's-bane" is aconite or monkshood. All are ingredients in a witch's brew.

"Mingled with fine wheat and the fat of a new-born babe," said the shape of old Goodman Brown.

"Ah, your worship knows the receipt," cried the old lady, cackling aloud. "So, as I was saying, being all ready for the meeting, and no horse to ride on, I made up my mind to foot it; for they tell me, there is a nice young man to be taken into communion to-night. But now your good worship will lend me your arm, and we shall be there in a twinkling."

"That can hardly be," answered her friend. "I may not spare you my arm,   35 Goody Cloyse, but here is my staff, if you will."

So saying, he threw it down at her feet, where, perhaps, it assumed life, being one of the rods which its owner had formerly lent to the Egyptian Magi.° Of this fact, however, Goodman Brown could not take cognizance. He had cast up his eyes in astonishment, and looking down again, beheld neither Goody Cloyse nor the serpentine staff, but his fellow-traveller alone, who waited for him as calmly as if nothing had happened.

"That old woman taught me my catechism!" said the young man; and there was a world of meaning in this simple comment.

They continued to walk onward, while the elder traveller exhorted his companion to make good speed and persevere in the path, discoursing so aptly, that his arguments seemed rather to spring up in the bosom of his auditor, than to be suggested by himself. As they went, he plucked a branch of maple, to serve for a walking-stick, and began to strip it of the twigs and little boughs, which were wet with evening dew. The moment his fingers touched them, they became strangely withered and dried up, as with a week's sunshine. Thus the pair proceeded, at a good free pace, until suddenly, in a gloomy hollow of the road, Goodman Brown sat himself down on the stump of a tree, and refused to go any farther.

"Friend," said he, stubbornly, "my mind is made up. Not another step will I budge on this errand. What if a wretched old woman do choose to go to the devil, when I thought she was going to Heaven! Is that any reason why I should quit my dear Faith, and go after her?"

"You will think better of this, by-and-by," said his acquaintance, compos-   40 edly. "Sit here and rest yourself awhile; and when you feel like moving again, there is my staff to help you along."

Without more words, he threw his companion the maple stick, and was as speedily out of sight, as if he had vanished into the deepening gloom. The young man sat a few moments, by the road-side, applauding himself greatly, and thinking with how clear a conscience he should meet the minister, in his morning-walk, nor shrink from the eye of good old Deacon Gookin. And what calm sleep would be his, that very night, which was to have been spent so wickedly, but purely and sweetly now, in the arms of Faith! Amidst these pleasant and praise-worthy meditations, Goodman Brown heard the tramp of horses along the road,

---

Egyptian Magi: Egyptian magicians who were able, like Aaron in the biblical account, to turn rods into serpents. See Exodus 7:11–12.

and deemed it advisable to conceal himself within the verge of the forest, conscious of the guilty purpose that had brought him thither, though now so happily turned from it.

On came the hoof-tramps and the voices of the riders, two grave old voices, conversing soberly as they drew near. These mingled sounds appeared to pass along the road, within a few yards of the young man's hiding-place; but owing, doubtless, to the depth of the gloom, at that particular spot, neither the travellers nor their steeds were visible. Though their figures brushed the small boughs by the way-side, it could not be seen that they intercepted, even for a moment, the faint gleam from the strip of bright sky, athwart which they must have passed. Goodman Brown alternately crouched and stood on tip-toe, pulling aside the branches, and thrusting forth his head as far as he durst, without discerning so much as a shadow. It vexed him the more, because he could have sworn, were such a thing possible, that he recognized the voices of the minister and Deacon Gookin, jogging along quietly, as they were wont to do, when bound to some ordination or ecclesiastical council. While yet within hearing, one of the riders stopped to pluck a switch.

"Of the two, reverend Sir," said the voice like the deacon's, "I had rather miss an ordination-dinner than to-night's meeting. They tell me that some of our community are to be here from Falmouth and beyond, and others from Connecticut and Rhode-Island; besides several of the Indian powows,° who, after their fashion, know almost as much deviltry as the best of us. Moreover, there is a goodly young woman to be taken into communion."

"Mighty well, Deacon Gookin!" replied the solemn old tones of the minister. "Spur up, or we shall be late. Nothing can be done, you know, until I get on the ground."

The hoofs clattered again, and the voices, talking so strangely in the empty 45 air, passed on through the forest, where no church had ever been gathered, nor solitary Christian prayed. Whither, then, could these holy men be journeying, so deep into the heathen wilderness? Young Goodman Brown caught hold of a tree, for support, being ready to sink down on the ground, faint and overburthened with the heavy sickness of his heart. He looked up to the sky, doubting whether there really was a Heaven above him. Yet, there was the blue arch, and the stars brightening in it.

"With Heaven above, and Faith below, I will yet stand firm against the devil!" cried Goodman Brown.

While he still gazed upward, into the deep arch of the firmament, and had lifted his hands to pray, a cloud, though no wind was stirring, hurried across the zenith, and hid the brightening stars. The blue sky was still visible, except directly overhead, where this black mass of cloud was sweeping swiftly northward. Aloft in the air, as if from the depths of the cloud, came a confused and doubtful sound of voices. Once, the listener fancied that he could distinguish the accents of town's-people of his own, men and women, both pious and ungodly, many of

---

powows: Medicine men.

whom he had met at the communion-table, and had seen others rioting at the tavern. The next moment, so indistinct were the sounds, he doubted whether he had heard aught but the murmur of the old forest, whispering without a wind. Then came a stronger swell of those familiar tones, heard daily in the sunshine, at Salem village, but never, until now, from a cloud of night. There was one voice, of a young woman, uttering lamentations, yet with an uncertain sorrow, and entreating for some favor, which, perhaps, it would grieve her to obtain. And all the unseen multitude, both saints and sinners, seemed to encourage her onward.

"Faith!" shouted Goodman Brown, in a voice of agony and desperation; and the echoes of the forest mocked him, crying— "Faith! Faith!" as if bewildered wretches were seeking her, all through the wilderness.

The cry of grief, rage, and terror, was yet piercing the night, when the un-happy husband held his breath for a response. There was a scream, drowned im-mediately in a louder murmur of voices, fading into far-off laughter, as the dark cloud swept away, leaving the clear and silent sky above Goodman Brown. But something fluttered lightly down through the air, and caught on the branch of a tree. The young man seized it, and beheld a pink ribbon.

"My Faith is gone!" cried he, after one stupefied moment. "There is no good on earth; and sin is but a name. Come, devil! for to thee is this world given." 50

And maddened with despair, so that he laughed loud and long, did Good-man Brown grasp his staff and set forth again, at such a rate, that he seemed to fly along the forest-path, rather than to walk or run. The road grew wilder and drearier, and more faintly traced, and vanished at length, leaving him in the heart of the dark wilderness, still rushing onward, with the instinct that guides mortal man to evil. The whole forest was peopled with frightful sounds; the creaking of the trees, the howling of wild beasts, and the yell of Indians; while, sometimes, the wind tolled like a distant church-bell, and sometimes gave a broad roar around the traveller, as if all Nature were laughing him to scorn. But he was himself the chief horror of the scene, and shrank not from its other horrors.

"Ha! ha! ha!" roared Goodman Brown, when the wind laughed at him. "Let us hear which will laugh loudest! Think not to frighten me with your deviltry! Come witch, come wizard, come Indian powow, come devil himself! and here comes Goodman Brown. You may as well fear him as he fear you!"

In truth, all through the haunted forest, there could be nothing more frightful than the figure of Goodman Brown. On he flew, among the black pines, brandishing his staff with frenzied gestures, now giving vent to an inspi-ration of horrid blasphemy, and now shouting forth such laughter, as set all the echoes of the forest laughing like demons around him. The fiend in his own shape is less hideous, than when he rages in the breast of man. Thus sped the de-moniac on his course, until, quivering among the trees, he saw a red light before him, as when the felled trunks and branches of a clearing have been set on fire, and throw up their lurid blaze against the sky, at the hour of midnight. He paused, in a lull of the tempest that had driven him onward, and heard the swell of what seemed a hymn, rolling solemnly from a distance, with the weight of many voices. He knew the tune; it was a familiar one in the choir of the village meetinghouse. The verse died heavily away, and was lengthened by a chorus, not of human voices, but of all the sounds of the benighted wilderness, pealing in awful harmony together. Goodman Brown cried out; and his cry was lost to his own ear, by its unison with the cry of the desert.

In the interval of silence, he stole forward, until the light glared full upon his eyes. At one extremity of an open space, hemmed in by the dark wall of the forest, arose a rock, bearing some rude, natural resemblance either to an altar or a pulpit, and surrounded by four blazing pines, their tops aflame, their stems untouched, like candles at an evening meeting. The mass of foliage, that had overgrown the summit of the rock, was all on fire, blazing high into the night, and fitfully illuminating the whole field. Each pendent twig and leafy festoon was in a blaze. As the red light arose and fell, a numerous congregation alternately shone forth, then disappeared in shadow, and again grew, as it were, out of the darkness, peopling the heart of the solitary woods at once.

"A grave and dark-clad company!" quoth Goodman Brown.   55

In truth, they were such. Among them, quivering to-and-fro, between gloom and splendor, appeared faces that would be seen, next day, at the council-board of the province, and others which, Sabbath after Sabbath, looked devoutly heavenward, and benignantly over the crowded pews, from the holiest pulpits in the land. Some affirm, that the lady of the governor was there. At least, there were high dames well known to her, and wives of honored husbands, and widows, a great multitude, and ancient maidens, all of excellent repute, and fair young girls, who trembled, lest their mothers should espy them. Either the sudden gleams of light, flashing over the obscure field, bedazzled Goodman Brown, or he recognized a score of the church-members of Salem village, famous for their especial sanctity. Good old Deacon Gookin had arrived, and waited at the skirts of that venerable saint, his revered pastor. But, irreverently consorting with these grave, reputable, and pious people, these elders of the church, these chaste dames and dewy virgins, there were men of dissolute lives and women of spotted fame, wretches given over to all mean and filthy vice, and suspected even of horrid crimes. It was strange to see, that the good shrank not from the wicked, nor were the sinners abashed by the saints. Scattered, also, among their pale-faced enemies, were the Indian priests, or powows, who had often scared their native forest with more hideous incantations than any known to English witchcraft.

"But, where is Faith?" thought Goodman Brown; and, as hope came into his heart, he trembled.

Another verse of the hymn arose, a slow and mournful strain, such as the pious love, but joined to words which expressed all that our nature can conceive of sin, and darkly hinted at far more. Unfathomable to mere mortals is the lore of fiends. Verse after verse was sung, and still the chorus of the desert swelled between, like the deepest tone of a mighty organ. And, with the final peal of that dreadful anthem, there came a sound, as if the roaring wind, the rushing streams, the howling beasts, and every other voice of the unconverted wilderness, were mingling and according with the voice of guilty man, in homage to the prince of all. The four blazing pines threw up a loftier flame, and obscurely discovered shapes and visages of horror on the smoke-wreaths, above the impious assembly. At the same moment, the fire on the rock shot redly forth, and formed a glowing arch above its base, where now appeared a figure. With reverence be it spoken, the figure bore no slight similitude, both in garb and manner, to some grave divine of the New-England churches.

"Bring forth the converts!" cried a voice, that echoed through the field and rolled into the forest.

At the word, Goodman Brown stept forth from the shadow of the trees, and 60 approached the congregation, with whom he felt a loathful brotherhood, by the sympathy of all that was wicked in his heart. He could have well nigh sworn, that the shape of his own dead father beckoned him to advance, looking downward from a smoke-wreath, while a woman, with dim features of despair, threw out her hand to warn him back. Was it his mother? But he had no power to retreat one step, nor to resist, even in thought, when the minister and good old Deacon Gookin seized his arms, and led him to the blazing rock. Thither came also the slender form of a veiled female, led between Goody Cloyse, that pious teacher of the catechism, and Martha Carrier, who had received the devil's promise to be queen of hell. A rampant hag was she! And there stood the proselytes, beneath the canopy of fire.

"Welcome, my children," said the dark figure, "to the communion of your race! Ye have found, thus young, your nature and your destiny. My children, look behind you!"

They turned; and flashing forth, as it were, in a sheet of flame, the fiend-worshippers were seen; the smile of welcome gleamed darkly on every visage.

"There," resumed the sable form, "are all whom ye have reverenced from youth. Ye deemed them holier than yourselves, and shrank from your own sin, contrasting it with their lives of righteousness, and prayerful aspirations heavenward. Yet, here are they all, in my worshipping assembly! This night it shall be granted you to know their secret deeds; how hoary-bearded elders of the church have whispered wanton words to the young maids of their households; how many a woman, eager for widow's weeds, has given her husband a drink at bedtime, and let him sleep his last sleep in her bosom; how beardless youths have made haste to inherit their fathers' wealth; and how fair damsels—blush not, sweet ones!—have dug little graves in the garden, and bidden me, the sole guest, to an infant's funeral. By the sympathy of your human hearts for sin, ye shall scent out all the places—whether in church, bed-chamber, street, field, or forest—where crime has been committed, and shall exult to behold the whole earth one stain of guilt, one mighty bloodspot. Far more than this! It shall be yours to penetrate, in every bosom, the deep mystery of sin, the fountain of all wicked arts, and which inexhaustibly supplies more evil impulses than human power—than my power, at its utmost!—can make manifest in deeds. And now, my children, look upon each other."

They did so; and, by the blaze of the hell-kindled torches, the wretched man beheld his Faith, and the wife her husband, trembling before that unhallowed altar.

"Lo! there ye stand, my children," said the figure, in a deep and solemn 65 tone, almost sad, with its despairing awfulness, as if his once angelic nature could yet mourn for our miserable race. "Depending upon one another's hearts, ye had still hoped, that virtue were not all a dream. Now are ye undeceived! Evil is the nature of mankind. Evil must be your only happiness. Welcome, again, my children, to the communion of your race!"

"Welcome!" repeated the fiend-worshippers, in one cry of despair and triumph.

And there they stood, the only pair, as it seemed, who were yet hesitating on the verge of wickedness, in this dark world. A basin was hollowed, naturally, in the rock. Did it contain water, reddened by the lurid light? or was it blood? or, perchance, a liquid flame? Herein did the Shape of Evil dip his hand, and prepare to lay the mark of baptism upon their foreheads, that they might be partakers of the mystery of sin, more conscious of the secret guilt of others, both in deed and thought, than they could now be of their own. The husband cast one look at his pale wife, and Faith at him. What polluted wretches would the next glance shew them to each other, shuddering alike at what they disclosed and what they saw!

"Faith! Faith!" cried the husband. "Look up to Heaven, and resist the Wicked One!"

Whether Faith obeyed, he knew not. Hardly had he spoken, when he found himself amid calm night and solitude, listening to a roar of the wind, which died heavily away through the forest. He staggered against the rock and felt it chill and damp, while a hanging twig, that had been all on fire, besprinkled his cheek with the coldest dew.

The next morning, young Goodman Brown came slowly into the street of 70 Salem village, staring around him like a bewildered man. The good old minister was taking a walk along the grave-yard, to get an appetite for breakfast and meditate his sermon, and bestowed a blessing, as he passed, on Goodman Brown. He shrank from the venerable saint, as if to avoid an anathema.° Old Deacon Gookin was at domestic worship, and the holy words of his prayer were heard through the open window. "What God doth the wizard pray to?" quoth Goodman Brown. Goody Cloyse, that excellent old Christian, stood in the early sunshine, at her own lattice, catechising a little girl, who had brought her a pint of morning's milk. Goodman Brown snatched away the child, as from the grasp of the fiend himself. Turning the corner by the meeting-house, he spied the head of Faith, with the pink ribbons, gazing anxiously forth, and bursting into such joy at sight of him, that she skipt along the street, and almost kissed her husband before the whole village. But, Goodman Brown looked sternly and sadly into her face, and passed on without a greeting.

---

anathema: A thing accursed or consigned to damnation by an official decree of the church.

Had Goodman Brown fallen asleep in the forest, and only dreamed a wild dream of a witch-meeting?

Be it so, if you will. But, alas! it was a dream of evil omen for young Goodman Brown. A stern, a sad, a darkly meditative, a distrustful, if not a desperate man, did he become, from the night of that fearful dream. On the Sabbath-day, when the congregation were singing a holy psalm, he could not listen, because an anthem of sin rushed loudly upon his ear, and drowned all the blessed strain. When the minister spoke from the pulpit, with power and fervid eloquence, and, with his hand on the open Bible, of the sacred truths of our religion, and of saint-like lives and triumphant deaths, and of future bliss or misery unutterable, then did Goodman Brown turn pale, dreading, lest the roof should thunder down upon the gray blasphemer and his hearers. Often, awakening suddenly at midnight, he shrank from the bosom of Faith, and at morning or eventide, when the family knelt down at prayer, he scowled, and muttered to himself, and gazed sternly at his wife, and turned away. And when he had lived long, and was borne to his grave, a hoary corpse, followed by Faith, an aged woman, and children and grandchildren, a goodly procession, besides neighbors, not a few, they carved no hopeful verse upon his tomb-stone; for his dying hour was gloom.

www

Explore Nathaniel Hawthorne and "Young Goodman Brown" in depth, including images and cultural documents, with VirtuaLit Fiction at bedfordstmartins.com/approachinglit.

Zora Neale Hurston   1891–1960

Sweat   [1926]

It was eleven o'clock of a Spring night in Florida. It was Sunday. Any other night, Delia Jones would have been in bed for two hours by this time. But she was a washwoman, and Monday morning meant a great deal to her. So she collected the soiled clothes on Saturday when she returned the clean things. Sunday night after church, she sorted them and put the white things to soak. It saved her almost a half day's start. A great hamper in the bedroom held the clothes that she brought home. It was so much neater than a number of bundles lying around.

She squatted on the kitchen floor beside the great pile of clothes, sorting them into small heaps according to color, and humming a song in a mournful key, but wondering through it all where Sykes, her husband, had gone with her horse and buckboard.

Just then something long, round, limp and black fell upon her shoulders and slithered to the floor beside her. A great terror took hold of her. It softened her knees and dried her mouth so that it was a full minute before she could cry out or move. Then she saw that it was the big bull whip her husband liked to carry when he drove.

She lifted her eyes to the door and saw him standing there bent over with laughter at her fright. She screamed at him.

"Sykes, what you throw dat whip on me like dat? You know it would skeer   5
me — looks just like a snake, an' you knows how skeered Ah is of snakes."

"Course Ah knowed it! That's how come Ah done it." He slapped his leg with his hand and almost rolled on the ground in his mirth. "If you such a big fool dat you got to have a fit over a earth worm or a string, Ah don't keer how bad Ah skeer you."

"You aint got no business doing it. Gawd knows it's a sin. Some day Ah'm gointuh drop dead from some of yo' foolishness. 'Nother thing, where you been wid mah rig? Ah feeds dat pony. He aint fuh you to be drivin' wid no bull whip."

"You sho is one aggravatin' nigger woman!" he declared and stepped into the room. She resumed her work and did not answer him at once. "Ah done tole you time and again to keep them white folks' clothes outa dis house."

He picked up the whip and glared down at her. Delia went on with her work. She went out into the yard and returned with a galvanized tub and sat it on the washbench. She saw that Sykes had kicked all of the clothes together again, and now stood in her way truculently, his whole manner hoping, *praying*, for an argument. But she walked calmly around him and commenced to re-sort the things.

"Next time, Ah'm gointer kick 'em outdoors," he threatened as he struck a   10
match along the leg of his corduroy breeches.

Delia never looked up from her work, and her thin, stooped shoulders sagged further.

"Ah aint for no fuss t'night, Sykes. Ah just come from taking sacrament at the church house."

He snorted scornfully. "Yeah, you just come from de church house on a Sunday night, but heah you is gone to work on them clothes. You ain't nothing but a hypocrite. One of them amen-corner Christians — sing, whoop, and shout, then come home and wash white folks clothes on the Sabbath."

He stepped roughly upon the whitest pile of things, kicking them helter-skelter as he crossed the room. His wife gave a little scream of dismay, and quickly gathered them together again.

"Sykes, you quit grindin' dirt into these clothes! How can Ah git through by   15
Sat'day if Ah don't start on Sunday?"

"Ah don't keer if you never git through. Anyhow, Ah done promised Gawd and a couple of other men, Ah aint gointer have it in mah house. Don't gimme no lip neither, else Ah'll throw 'em out and put mah fist up side yo' head to boot."

Delia's habitual meekness seemed to slip from her shoulders like a blown scarf. She was on her feet; her poor little body, her bare knuckly hands bravely defying the strapping hulk before her.

"Looka heah, Sykes, you done gone too fur. Ah been married to you fur fifteen years, and Ah been takin' in washin' fur fifteen years. Sweat, sweat, sweat! Work and sweat, cry and sweat, pray and sweat!"

"What's that got to do with me?" he asked brutally.

"What's it got to do with you, Sykes? Mah tub of suds is filled yo' belly with 20
vittles more times than yo' hands is filled it. Mah sweat is done paid for this
house and Ah reckon Ah kin keep on sweatin' in it."

She seized the iron skillet from the stove and struck a defensive pose, which
act surprised him greatly, coming from her. It cowed him and he did not strike
her as he usually did.

"Naw you won't," she panted, "that ole snaggle-toothed black woman you
runnin' with aint comin' heah to pile up on *mah* sweat and blood. You aint paid
for nothin' on this place, and Ah'm gointer stay right heah till Ah'm toted out
foot foremost."

"Well, you better quit gittin' me riled up, else they'll be totin' you out
sooner than you expect. Ah'm so tired of you Ah don't know whut to do. Gawd!
how Ah hates skinny wimmen!"

A little awed by this new Delia, he sidled out of the door and slammed the
back gate after him. He did not say where he had gone, but she knew too well.
She knew very well that he would not return until nearly daybreak also. Her
work over, she went on to bed but not to sleep at once. Things had come to a
pretty pass!

She lay awake, gazing upon the debris that cluttered their matrimonial trail. 25
Not an image left standing along the way. Anything like flowers had long ago
been drowned in the salty stream that had been pressed from her heart. Her
tears, her sweat, her blood. She had brought love to the union and he had
brought a longing after the flesh. Two months after the wedding, he had given
her the first brutal beating. She had the memory of his numerous trips to Orlando with all of his wages when he had returned to her penniless, even before
the first year had passed. She was young and soft then, but now she thought of
her knotty, muscled limbs, her harsh knuckly hands, and drew herself up into
an unhappy little ball in the middle of the big feather bed. Too late now to hope
for love, even if it were not Bertha it would be someone else. This case differed
from the others only in that she was bolder than the others. Too late for everything except her little home. She had built it for her old days, and planted one by
one the trees and flowers there. It was lovely to her, lovely.

Somehow, before sleep came, she found herself saying aloud: "Oh well,
whatever goes over the Devil's back, is got to come under his belly. Sometime or
ruther, Sykes, like everybody else, is gointer reap his sowing." After that she was
able to build a spiritual earthworks against her husband. His shells could no
longer reach her. *Amen.* She went to sleep and slept until he announced his presence in bed by kicking her feet and rudely snatching the cover away.

"Gimme some kivah heah, an' git yo' damn foots over on yo' own side! Ah
oughter mash you in yo' mouf fuh drawing dat skillet on me."

Delia went clear to the rail without answering him. A triumphant indiffer-
ence to all that he was or did.

The week was as full of work for Delia as all other weeks, and Saturday
found her behind her little pony, collecting and delivering clothes.

It was a hot, hot day near the end of July. The village men on Joe Clarke's 30 porch even chewed cane listlessly. They did not hurl the cane-knots as usual. They let them dribble over the edge of the porch. Even conversation had collapsed under the heat.

"Heah come Delia Jones," Jim Merchant said, as the shaggy pony came 'round the bend of the road toward them. The rusty buckboard was heaped with baskets of crisp, clean laundry.

"Yep," Joe Lindsay agreed. "Hot or col', rain or shine, jes ez reg'lar ez de weeks roll roun' Delia carries 'em an' fetches 'em on Sat'day."

"She better if she wanter eat," said Moss. "Sykes Jones aint wuth de shot an' powder hit would tek tuh kill 'em. Not to *huh* he aint."

"He sho' aint," Walter Thomas chimed in. "It's too bad, too, cause she wuz a right pritty li'l trick when he got huh. Ah'd uh mah'ied huh mahseff if he hadnter beat me to it."

Delia nodded briefly at the men as she drove past. 35

"Too much knockin' will ruin *any* 'oman. He done beat huh 'nough tuh kill three women, let 'lone change they looks," said Elijah Moseley. "How Sykes kin stommuck dat big black greasy Mogul he's layin' roun' wid, gits me. Ah swear dat eight-rock couldn't kiss a sardine can Ah done thowed out de back do' 'way las' yeah."

"Aw, she's fat, thass how come. He's allus been crazy 'bout fat women," put in Merchant. "He'd a' been tied up wid one long time ago if he could a' found one tuh have him. Did Ah tell yuh 'bout him come sidlin' roun' *mah* wife— bringin' her a basket uh pee-cans outa his yard fuh a present? Yessir, mah wife! She tol' him tuh take 'em right straight back home, cause Delia works so hard ovah dat washtub she reckon everything on de place taste lak sweat an' soap- suds. Ah jus' wisht Ah'd a' caught 'im 'roun' dere! Ah'd a' made his hips ketch on fiah down dat shell road."

"Ah know he done it, too. Ah sees 'im grinnin' at every 'oman dat passes," Walter Thomas said. "But even so, he useter eat some mighty big hunks uh humble pie tuh git dat lil' 'oman he got. She wuz ez pritty ez a speckled pup! Dat wuz fifteen yeahs ago. He useter be so skeered uh losin' huh, she could make him do some parts of a husband's duty. Dey never wuz de same in de mind."

"There oughter be a law about him," said Lindsay. "He aint fit tuh carry guts tuh a bear."

Clarke spoke for the first time. "Taint no law on earth dat kin make a man 40 be decent if it aint in 'im. There's plenty men dat takes a wife lak dey do a joint uh sugar-cane. It's round, juicy an' sweet when dey gits it. But dey squeeze an' grind, squeeze an' grind an' wring tell dey wring every drop uh pleasure dat's in 'em out. When dey's satisfied dat dey is wrung dry, dey treats 'em jes lak dey do a cane-chew. Dey thows 'em away. Dey knows whut dey is doin' while dey is at it, an' hates theirselves fuh it but they keeps on hangin' after huh tell she's empty. Den dey hates huh fuh bein' a cane-chew an' in de way."

"We oughter take Sykes an' dat stray 'oman uh his'n down in Lake Howell swamp an' lay on de rawhide till they cain't say 'Lawd a' mussy.' He allus wuz uh ovahbearin' niggah, but since dat white 'oman from up north done teached 'im how to run a automobile, he done got too biggety to live — an' we oughter kill 'im," Old Man Anderson advised.

A grunt of approval went around the porch. But the heat was melting their civic virtue and Elijah Moseley began to bait Joe Clarke.

"Come on, Joe, git a melon outa dere an' slice it up for yo' customers. We'se all sufferin' wid de heat. De bear's done got *me*!"

"Thass right, Joe, a watermelon is jes' whut Ah needs tuh cure de eppizudicks." Walter Thomas joined forces with Moseley. "Come on dere, Joe. We all is steady customers an' you aint set us up in a long time. Ah chooses dat long, bowlegged Floridy favorite."

"A god, an' be dough. You all gimme twenty cents and slice away," Clarke 45 retorted. "Ah needs a col' slice m'self. Heah, everybody chip in. Ah'll lend y'all mah meat knife."

The money was quickly subscribed and the huge melon brought forth. At that moment, Sykes and Bertha arrived. A determined silence fell on the porch and the melon was put away again.

Merchant snapped down the blade of his jack-knife and moved toward the store door.

"Come on in, Joe, an' gimme a slab uh sow belly an' uh pound uh coffee — almost fuhgot 'twas Sat'day. Got to git on home." Most of the men left also.

Just then Delia drove past on her way home, as Sykes was ordering magnificently for Bertha. It pleased him for Delia to see.

"Git whutsoever yo' heart desires, Honey. Wait a minute, Joe. Give huh two 50 bottles uh strawberry soda-water, uh quart uh parched ground-peas, an a block uh chewin' gum."

With all this they left the store, with Sykes reminding Bertha that this was his town and she could have it if she wanted it.

The men returned soon after they left, and held their watermelon feast.

"Where did Sykes Jones git dat 'oman from nohow?" Lindsay asked.

"Ovah Apopka. Guess dey musta been cleanin' out de town when she lef'. She don't look lak a thing but a hunk uh liver wid hair on it."

"Well, she sho' kin squall," Dave Carter contributed. "When she gits ready 55 tuh laff, she jes' opens huh mouf an' latches it back tuh de las' notch. No ole grandpa alligator down in Lake Bell aint got nothin' on huh."

Bertha had been in town three months now. Sykes was still paying her room rent at Della Lewis' — the only house in town that would have taken her in. Sykes took her frequently to Winter Park to "stomps." He still assured her that he was the swellest man in the state.

"Sho' you kin have dat lil' ole house soon's Ah kin git dat 'oman outa dere. Everything b'longs tuh me an' you sho' kin have it. Ah sho' 'bominates uh skinny 'oman. Lawdy, you sho' is got one portly shape on you! You kin git *anything* you wants. Dis is *mah* town an' you sho' kin have it."

Delia's work-worn knees crawled over the earth in Gethsemane° and up the rocks of Calvary many, many times during these months. She avoided the villagers and meeting places in her efforts to be blind and deaf. But Bertha nullified this to a degree, by coming to Delia's house to call Sykes out to her at the gate.

Delia and Sykes fought all the time now with no peaceful interludes. They slept and ate in silence. Two or three times Delia had attempted a timid friendliness, but she was repulsed each time. It was plain that the breaches must remain agape.

The sun had burned July to August. The heat streamed down like a million 60
hot arrows, smiting all things living upon the earth. Grass withered, leaves browned, snakes went blind in shedding and men and dogs went mad. Dog days!

Delia came home one day and found Sykes there before her. She wondered, but started to go on into the house without speaking, even though he was standing in the kitchen door and she must either stoop under his arm or ask him to move. He made no room for her. She noticed a soap box beside the steps, but paid no particular attention to it, knowing that he must have brought it there. As she was stooping to pass under his outstretched arm, he suddenly pushed her backward, laughingly.

"Look in de box dere Delia, Ah done brung yuh somethin'!"

She nearly fell upon the box in her stumbling, and when she saw what it held, she all but fainted outright.

"Sykes! Sykes, mah Gawd! You take dat rattlesnake 'way from heah! You *gottuh*. Oh, Jesus, have mussy!"

"Ah aint gut tuh do nuthin' uh de kin' — fact is Ah aint got tuh do nothin' 65
but die. Taint no use uh you puttin' on airs makin' out lak you skeered uh dat snake — he's gointer stay right heah tell he die. He wouldn't bite me cause Ah knows how tuh handle 'im. Nohow he wouldn't risk breakin' out his fangs 'gin yo' skinny laigs."

"Naw, now Sykes, don't keep dat thing 'roun' heah tuh skeer me tuh death. You knows Ah'm even feared uh earth worms. Thass de biggest snake Ah evah did see. Kill 'im Sykes, please."

"Doan ast me tuh do nothin' fuh yuh. Goin' 'roun' tryin' tuh be so damn astorperious. Naw, Ah aint gonna kill it. Ah think uh damn sight mo' uh him dan you! Dat's a nice snake an' anybody doan lak 'im kin jes' hit de grit."

The village soon heard that Sykes had the snake, and came to see and ask questions.

"How de hen-fire did you ketch dat six-foot rattler, Sykes?" Thomas asked.

Gethsemane: The garden in which Jesus agonized and prayed (Matthew 26:36–46) before being taken prisoner and crucified on a hill called Calvary (Luke 23:33).

"He's full uh frogs so he caint hardly move, thass how Ah eased up on 'm. 70
But Ah'm a snake charmer an' knows how tuh handle 'em. Shux, dat aint
nothin'. Ah could ketch one eve'y day if Ah so wanted tuh."

"Whut he needs is a heavy hick'ry club leaned real heavy on his head. Dat's
de bes 'way tuh charm a rattlesnake."

"Naw, Walt, y'all jes' don't understand dese diamon' backs lak Ah do," said
Sykes in a superior tone of voice.

The village agreed with Walter, but the snake stayed on. His box remained
by the kitchen door with its screen wire covering. Two or three days later it had
digested its meal of frogs and literally came to life. It rattled at every movement
in the kitchen or the yard. One day as Delia came down the kitchen steps she
saw his chalky-white fangs curved like scimitars hung in the wire meshes. This
time she did not run away with averted eyes as usual. She stood for a long time
in the doorway in a red fury that grew bloodier for every second that she regarded the creature that was her torment.

That night she broached the subject as soon as Sykes sat down to the table.

"Sykes, Ah wants you tuh take dat snake 'way fum heah. You done starved 75
me an' Ah put up widcher, you done beat me an Ah took dat, but you done kilt
all mah insides bringin' dat varmint heah."

Sykes poured out a saucer full of coffee and drank it deliberately before he
answered her.

"A whole lot Ah keer 'bout how you feels inside uh out. Dat snake aint goin'
no damn wheah till Ah gits ready fuh 'im tuh go. So fur as beatin' is concerned,
yuh aint took near all dat you gointer take ef yuh stay 'roun' *me*."

Delia pushed back her plate and got up from the table. "Ah hates you,
Sykes," she said calmly. "Ah hates you tuh de same degree dat Ah useter love yuh.
Ah done took an' took till mah belly is full up tuh mah neck. Dat's de reason Ah
got mah letter fum de church an' moved mah membership tuh Woodbridge — so
Ah don't haftuh take no sacrament wid yuh. Ah don't wantuh see yuh 'roun' me
a-tall. Lay 'roun' wid dat 'oman all yuh wants tuh, but gwan 'way fum me an'
mah house. Ah hates yuh lak uh suck-egg dog."

Sykes almost let the huge wad of corn bread and collard greens he was
chewing fall out of his mouth in amazement. He had a hard time whipping himself up to the proper fury to try to answer Delia.

"Well, Ah'm glad you does hate me. Ah'm sho' tiahed uh you hangin' ontuh 80
me. Ah don't want yuh. Look at yuh stringey ole neck! Yo' rawbony laigs an'
arms is enough tuh cut uh man tuh death. You looks jes' lak de devvul's doll-
baby tuh *me*. You cain't hate me no worse dan Ah hates you. Ah been hatin' *you*
fuh years."

"Yo' ole black hide don't look lak nothin' tuh me, but uh passel uh wrinkled
up rubber, wid yo' big ole yeahs flappin' on each side lak uh paih uh buzzard
wings. Don't think Ah'm gointuh be run 'way fum mah house neither. Ah'm
goin' tuh de white folks bout *you*, mah young man, de very nex' time you lay yo'
han's on me. Mah cup is done run ovah." Delia said this with no signs of fear

and Sykes departed from the house, threatening her, but made not the slightest move to carry out any of them.

That night he did not return at all, and the next day being Sunday, Delia was glad that she did not have to quarrel before she hitched up her pony and drove the four miles to Woodbridge.

She stayed to the night service — "love feast" — which was very warm and full of spirit. In the emotional winds her domestic trials were borne far and wide so that she sang as she drove homeward,

> Jurden water, black an' col'
> Chills de body, not de soul
> An' Ah wantah cross Jurden in uh calm time.

She came from the barn to the kitchen door and stopped.

"Whut's de mattah, ol' satan, you aint kickin' up yo' racket?" She addressed   85
the snake's box. Complete silence. She went on into the house with a new hope in its birth struggles. Perhaps her threat to go to the white folks had frightened Sykes! Perhaps he was sorry! Fifteen years of misery and suppression had brought Delia to the place where she would hope *anything* that looked towards a way over or through her wall of inhibitions.

She felt in the match safe behind the stove at once for a match. There was only one there.

"Dat niggah wouldn't fetch nothin' heah tuh save his rotten neck, but he kin run thew whut Ah brings quick enough. Now he done toted off nigh on tuh haff uh box uh matches. He done had dat 'oman heah in mah house, too."

Nobody but a woman could tell how she knew this even before she struck the match. But she did and it put her into a new fury.

Presently she brought in the tubs to put the white things to soak. This time she decided she need not bring the hamper out of the bedroom; she would go in there and do the sorting. She picked up the pot-bellied lamp and went in. The room was small and the hamper stood hard by the foot of the white iron bed. She could sit and reach through the bedposts — resting as she worked.

"Ah wantah cross Jurden in uh calm time." She was singing again. The   90
mood of the "love feast" had returned. She threw back the lid of the basket almost gaily. Then, moved by both horror and terror, she sprung back toward the door. *There lay the snake in the basket!* He moved sluggishly at first, but even as she turned round and round, jumped up and down in an insanity of fear, he began to stir vigorously. She saw him pouring his awful beauty from the basket upon the bed, then she seized the lamp and ran as fast as she could to the kitchen. The wind from the open door blew out the light and the darkness added to her terror. She sped to the darkness of the yard, slamming the door after her before she thought to set down the lamp. She did not feel safe even on the ground, so she climbed up in the hay barn.

There for an hour or more she lay sprawled upon the hay a gibbering wreck.

Finally she grew quiet, and after that, coherent thought. With this, stalked through her a cold, bloody rage. Hours of this. A period of introspection, a space of retrospection, then a mixture of both. Out of this an awful calm.

"Well, Ah done de bes' Ah could. If things aint right, Gawd knows taint mah fault."

She went to sleep — a twitchy sleep — and woke up to a faint gray sky. There was a loud hollow sound below. She peered out. Sykes was at the wood-pile, demolishing a wire-covered box.

He hurried to the kitchen door, but hung outside there some minutes before 95
he entered, and stood some minutes more inside before he closed it after him.

The gray in the sky was spreading. Delia descended without fear now, and crouched beneath the low bedroom window. The drawn shade shut out the dawn, shut in the night. But the thin walls held back no sound.

"Dat ol' scratch is woke up now!" She mused at the tremendous whirr inside, which every woodsman knows, is one of the sound illusions. The rattler is a ventriloquist. His whirr sounds to the right, to the left, straight ahead, behind, close under foot — everywhere but where it is. Woe to him who guesses wrong unless he is prepared to hold up his end of the argument! Sometimes he strikes without rattling at all.

Inside, Sykes heard nothing until he knocked a pot lid off the stove while trying to reach the match safe in the dark. He had emptied his pockets at Bertha's.

The snake seemed to wake up under the stove and Sykes made a quick leap into the bedroom. In spite of the gin he had had, his head was clearing now.

"Mah Gawd!" he chattered, "ef Ah could on'y strack uh light!"   100

The rattling ceased for a moment as he stood paralyzed. He waited. It seemed that the snake waited also.

"Oh fuh de light! Ah thought he'd be too sick" — Sykes was muttering to himself when the whirr began again, closer, right underfoot this time. Long before this, Sykes' ability to think had been flattened down to primitive instinct and he leaped — onto the bed.

Outside Delia heard a cry that might have come from a maddened chimpanzee, a stricken gorilla. All the terror, all the horror, all the rage that man possibly could express, without a recognizable human sound.

A tremendous stir inside there, another series of animal screams, the intermittent whirr of the reptile. The shade torn violently down from the window, letting in the red dawn, a huge brown hand seizing the window stick, great dull blows upon the wooden floor punctuating the gibberish of sound long after the rattle of the snake had abruptly subsided. All this Delia could see and hear from her place beneath the window, and it made her ill. She crept over to the four-o'clocks and stretched herself on the cool earth to recover.

She lay there. "Delia, Delia!" She could hear Sykes calling in a most despair- 105
ing tone as one who expected no answer. The sun crept on up, and he called. Delia could not move — her legs were gone flabby. She never moved, he called, and the sun kept rising.

"Mah Gawd!" she heard him moan. "Mah Gawd fum Heben!" She heard him stumbling about and got up from her flower-bed. The sun was growing warm. As she approached the door she heard him call out hopefully, "Delia, is dat you Ah heah?"

She saw him on his hands and knees as soon as she reached the door. He crept an inch or two toward her — all that he was able, and she saw his horribly swollen neck and his one open eye shining with hope. A surge of pity too strong to support bore her away from that eye that must, could not, fail to see the tubs. He would see the lamp. Orlando with its doctors was too far. She could scarcely reach the Chinaberry tree, where she waited in the growing heat while inside she knew the cold river was creeping up and up to extinguish that eye which must know by now that she knew.

James Joyce 1882–1941

Araby   [1914]

North Richmond Street, being blind, was a quiet street except at the hour when the Christian Brothers' School set the boys free. An uninhabited house of two storeys stood at the blind end, detached from its neighbors in a square ground. The other houses of the street, conscious of decent lives within them, gazed at one another with brown imperturbable faces.

The former tenant of our house, a priest, had died in the back drawing-room. Air, musty from having been long enclosed, hung in all the rooms, and the waste room behind the kitchen was littered with old useless papers. Among these I found a few paper-covered books, the pages of which were curled and damp: *The Abbot*, by Walter Scott, *The Devout Communicant*, and *The Memoirs of Vidocq*. I liked the last best because its leaves were yellow. The wild garden behind the house contained a central apple-tree and a few straggling bushes under one of which I found the late tenant's rusty bicycle-pump. He had been a very charitable priest; in his will he had left all his money to institutions and the furniture of his house to his sister.

When the short days of winter came dusk fell before we had well eaten our dinners. When we met in the street the houses had grown somber. The space of sky above us was the color of ever-changing violet and towards it the lamps of the street lifted their feeble lanterns. The cold air stung us and we played till our bodies glowed. Our shouts echoed in the silent street. The career of our play brought us through the dark muddy lanes behind the houses where we ran the gauntlet of the rough tribes from the cottages, to the back doors of the dark dripping gardens where odors arose from the ashpits, to the dark odorous stables where a coachman smoothed and combed the horse or shook music from the buckled harness. When we returned to the street light from the kitchen windows had filled the areas. If my uncle was seen turning the corner we hid in the shadow until we had seen him safely housed. Or if Mangan's sister came out on the doorstep to call her brother in to his tea we watched her from our shadow peer up and down the street. We waited to see whether she would remain or go in and, if she remained, we left our shadow and walked up to Mangan's steps resignedly. She was waiting for us, her figure defined by the light from the half-opened door. Her brother always teased her before he obeyed and I stood by the railings looking at her. Her dress swung as she moved her body and the soft rope of her hair tossed from side to side.

Every morning I lay on the floor in the front parlor watching her door. The blind was pulled down to within an inch of the sash so that I could not be seen. When she came out on the doorstep my heart leaped. I ran to the hall, seized my books, and followed her. I kept her brown figure always in my eye and, when we came near the point at which our ways diverged, I quickened my pace and passed her. This happened morning after morning. I had never spoken to her, except for a few casual words, and yet her name was like a summons to all my foolish blood.

Her image accompanied me even in places the most hostile to romance. On   5 Saturday evenings when my aunt went marketing I had to go to carry some of the parcels. We walked through the flaring streets, jostled by drunken men and bargaining women, amid the curses of laborers, the shrill litanies of shop-boys who stood on guard by the barrel of pigs' cheeks, the nasal chanting of street-singers, who sang a *come-all-you* about O'Donovan Rossa, or a ballad about the troubles in our native land. These noises converged in a single sensation of life for me: I imagined that I bore my chalice safely through a throng of foes. Her name sprang to my lips at moments in strange prayers and praises which I myself did not understand. My eyes were often full of tears (I could not tell why) and at times a flood from my heart seemed to pour itself out into my bosom. I thought little of the future. I did not know whether I would ever speak to her or not or, if I spoke to her, how I could tell her of my confused adoration. But my body was like a harp and her words and gestures were like fingers running upon the wires.

One evening I went into the back drawing-room in which the priest had died. It was a dark rainy evening and there was no sound in the house. Through one of the broken panes I heard the rain impinge upon the earth, the fine incessant needles of water playing in the sodden beds. Some distant lamp or lighted window gleamed below me. I was thankful that I could see so little. All my senses seemed to desire to veil themselves and, feeling that I was about to slip from them, I pressed the palms of my hands together until they trembled, murmuring: "O love! O love!" many times.

At last she spoke to me. When she addressed the first words to me I was so confused that I did not know what to answer. She asked me was I going to *Araby*. I forgot whether I answered yes or no. It would be a splendid bazaar, she said she would love to go.

"And why can't you?" I asked.

While she spoke she turned a silver bracelet round and round her wrist. She could not go, she said, because there would be a retreat that week in her convent. Her brother and two other boys were fighting for their caps and I was alone at the railings. She held one of the spikes, bowing her head towards me. The light from the lamp opposite our door caught the white curve of her neck, lit up her hair that rested there and, falling, lit up the hand upon the railing. It fell over one side of her dress and caught the white border of a petticoat, just visible as she stood at ease.

"It's well for you," she said.

"If I go," I said, "I will bring you something."

What innumerable follies laid waste my waking and sleeping thoughts after that evening! I wished to annihilate the tedious intervening days. I chafed against the work of school. At night in my bedroom and by day in the classroom her image came between me and the page I strove to read. The syllables of the word *Araby* were called to me through the silence in which my soul luxuriated and cast an Eastern enchantment over me. I asked for leave to go to the bazaar on Saturday night. My aunt was surprised and hoped it was not some Freemason affair. I answered few questions in class. I watched my master's face pass from amiability to sternness; he hoped I was not beginning to idle. I could not call my wandering thoughts together. I had hardly any patience with the serious work of life which, now that it stood between me and my desire, seemed to me child's play, ugly monotonous child's play.

On Saturday morning I reminded my uncle that I wished to go to the bazaar in the evening. He was fussing at the hallstand, looking for the hat-brush, and answered me curtly:

"Yes, boy, I know."

As he was in the hall I could not go into the front parlor and lie at the window. I left the house in bad humor and walked slowly towards the school. The air was pitilessly raw and already my heart misgave me.

When I came home to dinner my uncle had not yet been home. Still it was early. I sat staring at the clock for some time and, when its ticking began to irritate me, I left the room. I mounted the staircase and gained the upper part of the house. The high cold empty gloomy rooms liberated me and I went from room to room singing. From the front window I saw my companions playing below in the street. Their cries reached me weakened and indistinct and, leaning my forehead against the cool glass, I looked over at the dark house where she lived. I may have stood there for an hour, seeing nothing but the brown-clad figure cast by my imagination, touched discreetly by the lamplight at the curved neck, at the hand upon the railings and at the border below the dress.

When I came downstairs again I found Mrs. Mercer sitting at the fire. She was an old garrulous woman, a pawnbroker's widow, who collected used stamps for some pious purpose. I had to endure the gossip of the tea-table. The meal was prolonged beyond an hour and still my uncle did not come. Mrs. Mercer stood up to go: she was sorry she couldn't wait any longer, but it was after eight o'clock and she did not like to be out late, as the night air was bad for her. When she had gone I began to walk up and down the room, clenching my fists. My aunt said:

"I'm afraid you may put off your bazaar for this night of Our Lord."

At nine o'clock I heard my uncle's latchkey in the halldoor. I heard him talking to himself and heard the hallstand rocking when it had received the weight of his overcoat. I could interpret these signs. When he was midway through his dinner I asked him to give me the money to go to the bazaar. He had forgotten.

"The people are in bed and after their first sleep now," he said.   20

I did not smile. My aunt said to him energetically:

"Can't you give him the money and let him go? You've kept him late enough as it is."

My uncle said he was very sorry he had forgotten. He said he believed in the old saying: "All work and no play makes Jack a dull boy." He asked me where I was going and, when I had told him a second time he asked me did I know *The Arab's Farewell to his Steed*. When I left the kitchen he was about to recite the opening lines of the piece to my aunt.

I held a florin tightly in my hand as I strode down Buckingham Street towards the station. The sight of the streets thronged with buyers and glaring with gas recalled to me the purpose of my journey. I took my seat in a third-class carriage of a deserted train. After an intolerable delay the train moved out of the station slowly. It crept onward among ruinous houses and over the twinkling river. At Westland Row Station a crowd of people pressed to the carriage doors; but the porters moved them back, saying that it was a special train for the bazaar. I remained alone in the bare carriage. In a few minutes the train drew up beside an improvised wooden platform. I passed out on to the road and saw by the lighted dial of a clock that it was ten minutes to ten. In front of me was a large building which displayed the magical name.

I could not find any sixpenny entrance and, fearing that the bazaar would be   25 closed, I passed in quickly through a turnstile, handing a shilling to a weary-looking man. I found myself in a big hall girdled at half its height by a gallery. Nearly all the stalls were closed and the greater part of the hall was in darkness. I recognized a silence like that which pervades a church after a service. I walked into the center of the bazaar timidly. A few people were gathered about the stalls which were still open. Before a curtain, over which the words *Café Chantant* were written in colored lamps, two men were counting money on a salver. I listened to the fall of the coins.

Remembering with difficulty why I had come I went over to one of the stalls and examined porcelain vases and flowered tea-sets. At the door of the stall a young lady was talking and laughing with two young gentlemen. I remarked their English accents and listened vaguely to their conversation.

"O, I never said such a thing!"

"O, but you did!"

"O, but I didn't!"

"Didn't she say that?"   30

"Yes. I heard her."

"O, there's a . . . fib!"

Observing me the young lady came over and asked me did I wish to buy anything. The tone of her voice was not encouraging; she seemed to have spoken to me out of a sense of duty. I looked humbly at the great jars that stood like eastern guards at either side of the dark entrance to the stall and murmured:

"No, thank you."

The young lady changed the position of one of the vases and went back to 35 the two young men. They began to talk of the same subject. Once or twice the young lady glanced at me over her shoulder.

I lingered before her stall, though I knew my stay was useless, to make my interest in her wares seem the more real. Then I turned away slowly and walked down the middle of the bazaar. I allowed the two pennies to fall against the sixpence in my pocket. I heard a voice call from one end of the gallery that the light was out. The upper part of the hall was now completely dark.

Gazing up into the darkness I saw myself as a creature driven and derided by vanity; and my eyes burned with anguish and anger.

Jamaica Kincaid   b. 1949

Girl   [1978]

Wash the white clothes on Monday and put them on the stone heap; wash the color clothes on Tuesday and put them on the clothesline to dry; don't walk barehead in the hot sun; cook pumpkin fritters in very hot sweet oil; soak your little cloths right after you take them off; when buying cotton to make yourself a nice blouse, be sure that it doesn't have gum on it, because that way it won't hold up well after a wash; soak salt fish overnight before you cook it; is it true that you sing benna° in Sunday school?; always eat your food in such a way that it won't turn someone else's stomach; on Sundays try to walk like a lady and not like the slut you are so bent on becoming; don't sing benna in Sunday school; you mustn't speak to wharf-rat boys, not even to give directions; don't eat fruits on the street — flies will follow you; *but I don't sing benna on Sundays at all and never in Sunday school*; this is how to sew on a button; this is how to make a buttonhole for the button you have just sewed on; this is how to hem a dress when you see the hem coming down and so to prevent yourself from looking like the slut I know you are so bent on becoming; this is how you iron your father's khaki shirt so that it doesn't have a crease; this is how you iron your father's khaki pants so that they don't have a crease; this is how you grow okra — far from the house, because okra tree harbors red ants; when you are growing dasheen,° make sure it gets plenty of water or else it makes your throat itch when you are eating it; this is how you sweep a corner; this is how you sweep a whole house; this is how you sweep a yard; this is how you smile to someone you

---

benna: Calypso music.   **dasheen:** Caribbean herb.

don't like too much; this is how you smile to someone you don't like at all; this is how you smile to someone you like completely; this is how you set a table for tea; this is how you set a table for dinner; this is how you set a table for dinner with an important guest; this is how you set a table for lunch; this is how you set a table for breakfast; this is how to behave in the presence of men who don't know you very well, and this way they won't recognize immediately the slut I have warned you against becoming; be sure to wash every day, even if it is with your own spit; don't squat down to play marbles — you are not a boy, you know; don't pick people's flowers — you might catch something; don't throw stones at blackbirds, because it might not be a blackbird at all; this is how to make a bread pudding; this is how to make doukona;° this is how to make pepper pot; this is how to make a good medicine for a cold; this is how to make a good medicine to throw away a child before it even becomes a child; this is how to catch a fish; this is how to throw back a fish you don't like, and that way something bad won't fall on you; this is how to bully a man; this is how a man bullies you; this is how to love a man, and if this doesn't work there are other ways, and if they don't work don't feel too bad about giving up; this is how to spit up in the air if you feel like it, and this is how to move quick so that it doesn't fall on you; this is how to make ends meet; always squeeze bread to make sure it's fresh; *but what if the baker won't let me feel the bread?*; you mean to say that after all you are really going to be the kind of woman who the baker won't let near the bread?

www Explore Jamaica Kincaid and "Girl" in depth, including images and cultural documents, with VirtuaLit Fiction at bedfordstmartins.com/ approachinglit.

---

doukona: A spicy Caribbean pudding.

Jhumpa Lahiri b. 1967
A Temporary Matter   [1999]

The notice informed them that it was a temporary matter: for five days their electricity would be cut off for one hour, beginning at eight P.M. A line had gone down in the last snowstorm, and the repairmen were going to take advantage of the milder evenings to set it right. The work would affect only the houses on the quiet tree-lined street, within walking distance of a row of brick-faced stores and a trolley stop, where Shoba and Shukumar had lived for three years.

"It's good of them to warn us," Shoba conceded after reading the notice aloud, more for her own benefit than Shukumar's. She let the strap of her leather satchel, plump with files, slip from her shoulders, and left it in the hallway as she walked into the kitchen. She wore a navy blue poplin raincoat over gray sweatpants and white sneakers, looking, at thirty-three, like the type of woman she'd once claimed she would never resemble.

She'd come from the gym. Her cranberry lipstick was visible only on the outer reaches of her mouth, and her eyeliner had left charcoal patches beneath her lower lashes. She used to look this way sometimes, Shukumar thought, on mornings after a party or a night at a bar, when she'd been too lazy to wash her face, too eager to collapse into his arms. She dropped a sheaf of mail on the table without a glance. Her eyes were still fixed on the notice in her other hand. "But they should do this sort of thing during the day."

"When I'm here, you mean," Shukumar said. He put a glass lid on a pot of lamb, adjusting it so only the slightest bit of steam could escape. Since January he'd been working at home, trying to complete the final chapters of his dissertation on agrarian revolts in India. "When do the repairs start?"

"It says March nineteenth. Is today the nineteenth?" Shoba walked over to   5
the framed corkboard that hung on the wall by the fridge, bare except for a calendar of William Morris° wallpaper patterns. She looked at it as if for the first time, studying the wallpaper pattern carefully on the top half before allowing her eyes to fall to the numbered grid on the bottom. A friend had sent the calendar in the mail as a Christmas gift, even though Shoba and Shukumar hadn't celebrated Christmas that year.

"Today then," Shoba announced. "You have a dentist appointment next Friday, by the way."

He ran his tongue over the tops of his teeth; he'd forgotten to brush them that morning. It wasn't the first time. He hadn't left the house at all that day, or the day before. The more Shoba stayed out, the more she began putting in extra hours at work and taking on additional projects, the more he wanted to stay in, not even leaving to get the mail, or to buy fruit or wine at the stores by the trolley stop.

Six months ago, in September, Shukumar was at an academic conference in Baltimore when Shoba went into labor, three weeks before her due date. He hadn't wanted to go to the conference, but she had insisted; it was important to make contacts, and he would be entering the job market next year. She told him that she had his number at the hotel, and a copy of his schedule and flight numbers, and she had arranged with her friend Gillian for a ride to the hospital in the event of an emergency. When the cab pulled away that morning for the airport, Shoba stood waving good-bye in her robe, with one arm resting on the mound of her belly as if it were a perfectly natural part of her body.

Each time he thought of that moment, the last moment he saw Shoba pregnant, it was the cab he remembered most, a station wagon, painted red with blue lettering. It was cavernous compared to their own car. Although Shukumar was six feet tall, with hands too big ever to rest comfortably in the pockets of his jeans, he felt dwarfed in the back seat. As the cab sped down Beacon Street, he imagined a day when he and Shoba might need to buy a station wagon of their

---

William Morris: English artist, writer, socialist, and activist (1834–1896), one of the principal founders of the British arts and crafts movement and well known as a designer of wallpaper and patterned fabrics.

own, to cart their children back and forth from music lessons and dentist appointments. He imagined himself gripping the wheel, as Shoba turned around to hand the children juice boxes. Once, these images of parenthood had troubled Shukumar, adding to his anxiety that he was still a student at thirty-five. But that early autumn morning, the trees still heavy with bronze leaves, he welcomed the image for the first time.

A member of the staff had found him somehow among the identical con-   10 vention rooms and handed him a stiff square of stationery. It was only a telephone number, but Shukumar knew it was the hospital. When he returned to Boston it was over. The baby had been born dead. Shoba was lying on a bed, asleep, in a private room so small there was barely enough space to stand beside her, in a wing of the hospital they hadn't been to on the tour for expectant parents. Her placenta had weakened and she'd had a cesarean, though not quickly enough. The doctor explained that these things happen. He smiled in the kindest way it was possible to smile at people known only professionally. Shoba would be back on her feet in a few weeks. There was nothing to indicate that she would not be able to have children in the future.

These days Shoba was always gone by the time Shukumar woke up. He would open his eyes and see the long black hairs she shed on her pillow and think of her, dressed, sipping her third cup of coffee already, in her office downtown, where she searched for typographical errors in textbooks and marked them, in a code she had once explained to him, with an assortment of colored pencils. She would do the same for his dissertation, she promised, when it was ready. He envied her the specificity of her task, so unlike the elusive nature of his. He was a mediocre student who had a facility for absorbing details without curiosity. Until September he had been diligent if not dedicated, summarizing chapters, outlining arguments on pads of yellow lined paper. But now he would lie in their bed until he grew bored, gazing at his side of the closet which Shoba always left partly open, at the row of the tweed jackets and corduroy trousers he would not have to choose from to teach his classes that semester. After the baby died it was too late to withdraw from his teaching duties. But his adviser had arranged things so that he had the spring semester to himself. Shukumar was in his sixth year of graduate school. "That and the summer should give you a good push," his adviser had said. "You should be able to wrap things up by next September."

But nothing was pushing Shukumar. Instead he thought of how he and Shoba had become experts at avoiding each other in their three-bedroom house, spending as much time on separate floors as possible. He thought of how he no longer looked forward to weekends, when she sat for hours on the sofa with her colored pencils and her files, so that he feared that putting on a record in his own house might be rude. He thought of how long it had been since she looked into his eyes and smiled, or whispered his name on those rare occasions they still reached for each other's bodies before sleeping.

In the beginning he had believed that it would pass, that he and Shoba would get through it all somehow. She was only thirty-three. She was strong, on her feet again. But it wasn't a consolation. It was often nearly lunchtime when Shukumar would finally pull himself out of bed and head downstairs to the coffeepot, pouring out the extra bit Shoba left for him, along with an empty mug, on the countertop.

Shukumar gathered onion skins in his hands and let them drop into the garbage pail, on top of the ribbons of fat he'd trimmed from the lamb. He ran the water in the sink, soaking the knife and the cutting board, and rubbed a lemon half along his fingertips to get rid of the garlic smell, a trick he'd learned from Shoba. It was seven-thirty. Through the window he saw the sky, like soft black pitch. Uneven banks of snow still lined the sidewalks, though it was warm enough for people to walk about without hats or gloves. Nearly three feet had fallen in the last storm, so that for a week people had to walk single file, in narrow trenches. For a week that was Shukumar's excuse for not leaving the house. But now the trenches were widening, and water drained steadily into grates in the pavement.

"The lamb won't be done by eight," Shukumar said. "We may have to eat in   15
the dark."

"We can light candles," Shoba suggested. She unclipped her hair, coiled neatly at her nape during the days, and pried the sneakers from her feet without untying them. "I'm going to shower before the lights go," she said, heading for the staircase. "I'll be down."

Shukumar moved her satchel and her sneakers to the side of the fridge. She wasn't this way before. She used to put her coat on a hanger, her sneakers in the closet, and she paid bills as soon as they came. But now she treated the house as if it were a hotel. The fact that the yellow chintz armchair in the living room clashed with the blue-and-maroon Turkish carpet no longer bothered her. On the enclosed porch at the back of the house, a crisp white bag still sat on the wicker chaise, filled with lace she had once planned to turn into curtains.

While Shoba showered, Shukumar went into the downstairs bathroom and found a new toothbrush in its box beneath the sink. The cheap, stiff bristles hurt his gums, and he spit some blood into the basin. The spare brush was one of many stored in a metal basket. Shoba had bought them once when they were on sale, in the event that a visitor decided, at the last minute, to spend the night.

It was typical of her. She was the type to prepare for surprises, good and bad. If she found a skirt or a purse she liked she bought two. She kept the bonuses from her job in a separate bank account in her name. It hadn't bothered him. His own mother had fallen to pieces when his father died, abandoning the house he grew up in and moving back to Calcutta, leaving Shukumar to settle it all. He liked that Shoba was different. It astonished him, her capacity to think ahead. When she used to do the shopping, the pantry was always stocked with extra bottles of olive and corn oil, depending on whether they were cooking Italian or Indian. There were endless boxes of pasta in all shapes and colors, zippered sacks of basmati rice, whole sides of lambs and goats from the Muslim butchers at Haymarket, chopped up and frozen in endless plastic bags. Every other Saturday they wound through the maze of stalls Shukumar eventually knew by heart. He watched in disbelief as she bought more food, trailing behind her with canvas bags as she pushed through the crowd, arguing under the morning sun with boys too young to shave but already missing teeth, who twisted up brown paper bags of artichokes, plums, gingerroot, and yams, and dropped them on their scales, and tossed them to Shoba one by one. She didn't mind being jostled, even when she was pregnant. She was tall, and broad-shouldered, with hips that her obstetrician assured her were made for childbearing. During the drive back home, as the car curved along the Charles, they invariably marveled at how much food they'd bought.

It never went to waste. When friends dropped by, Shoba would throw to- 20 gether meals that appeared to have taken half a day to prepare, from things she had frozen and bottled, not cheap things in tins but peppers she had marinated herself with rosemary, and chutneys that she cooked on Sundays, stirring boiling pots of tomatoes and prunes. Her labeled mason jars lined the shelves of the kitchen, in endless sealed pyramids, enough, they'd agreed, to last for their grandchildren to taste. They'd eaten it all by now. Shukumar had been going through their supplies steadily, preparing meals for the two of them, measuring out cupfuls of rice, defrosting bags of meat day after day. He combed through her cookbooks every afternoon, following her penciled instructions to use two teaspoons of ground coriander seeds instead of one, or red lentils instead of yellow. Each of the recipes was dated, telling the first time they had eaten the dish together. April 2, cauliflower with fennel. January 14, chicken with almonds and sultanas.° He had no memory of eating those meals, and yet there they were, recorded in her neat proofreader's hand. Shukumar enjoyed cooking now. It was the one thing that made him feel productive. If it weren't for him, he knew, Shoba would eat a bowl of cereal for her dinner.

Tonight, with no lights, they would have to eat together. For months now they'd served themselves from the stove, and he'd taken his plate into his study, letting the meal grow cold on his desk before shoving it into his mouth without pause, while Shoba took her plate to the living room and watched game shows, or proofread files with her arsenal of colored pencils at hand.

At some point in the evening she visited him. When he heard her approach he would put away his novel and begin typing sentences. She would rest her hands on his shoulders and stare with him into the blue glow of the computer screen. "Don't work too hard," she would say after a minute or two, and head off to bed. It was the one time in the day she sought him out, and yet he'd come to dread it. He knew it was something she forced herself to do. She would look around the walls of the room, which they had decorated together last summer with a border of marching ducks and rabbits playing trumpets and drums. By the end of August there was a cherry crib under the window, a white changing table with mint-green knobs, and a rocking chair with checkered cushions. Shukumar had disassembled it all before bringing Shoba back from

---

sultanas: Raisins.

the hospital, scraping off the rabbits and ducks with a spatula. For some reason the room did not haunt him the way it haunted Shoba. In January, when he stopped working at his carrel in the library, he set up his desk there deliberately, partly because the room soothed him, and partly because it was a place Shoba avoided.

Shukumar returned to the kitchen and began to open drawers. He tried to locate a candle among the scissors, the eggbeaters and whisks, the mortar and pestle she'd bought in a bazaar in Calcutta, and used to pound garlic cloves and cardamom pods, back when she used to cook. He found a flashlight, but no batteries, and a half-empty box of birthday candles. Shoba had thrown him a surprise birthday party last May. One hundred and twenty people had crammed into the house — all the friends and the friends of friends they now systematically avoided. Bottles of vinho verde° had nested in a bed of ice in the bathtub. Shoba was in her fifth month, drinking ginger ale from a martini glass. She had made a vanilla cream cake with custard and spun sugar. All night she kept Shukumar's long fingers linked with hers as they walked among the guests at the party.

Since September their only guest had been Shoba's mother. She came from Arizona and stayed with them for two months after Shoba returned from the hospital. She cooked dinner every night, drove herself to the supermarket, washed their clothes, put them away. She was a religious woman. She set up a small shrine, a framed picture of a lavender-faced goddess and a plate of marigold petals, on the bedside table in the guest room, and prayed twice a day for healthy grandchildren in the future. She was polite to Shukumar without being friendly. She folded his sweaters with an expertise she had learned from her job in a department store. She replaced a missing button on his winter coat and knit him a beige and brown scarf, presenting it to him without the least bit of ceremony, as if he had only dropped it and hadn't noticed. She never talked to him about Shoba; once, when he mentioned the baby's death, she looked up from her knitting, and said, "But you weren't even there."

It struck him as odd that there were no real candles in the house. That   25 Shoba hadn't prepared for such an ordinary emergency. He looked now for something to put the birthday candles in and settled on the soil of a potted ivy that normally sat on the windowsill over the sink. Even though the plant was inches from the tap, the soil was so dry that he had to water it first before the candles would stand straight. He pushed aside the things on the kitchen table, the pile of mail, the unread library books. He remembered their first meals there, when they were so thrilled to be married, to be living together in the same house at last, that they would just reach for each other foolishly, more eager to make love than to eat. He put down two embroidered place mats, a wedding gift from an uncle in Lucknow, and set out the plates and wineglasses they usually saved for guests. He put the ivy in the middle, the white-edged, star-shaped

---

vinho verde: A light, fresh, slightly sparkling wine from northern Portugal.

leaves girded by ten little candles. He switched on the digital clock radio and tuned it to a jazz station.

"What's all this?" Shoba said when she came downstairs. Her hair was wrapped in a thick white towel. She undid the towel and draped it over a chair, allowing her hair, damp and dark, to fall across her back. As she walked absently toward the stove she took out a few tangles with her fingers. She wore a clean pair of sweatpants, a T-shirt, an old flannel robe. Her stomach was flat again, her waist narrow before the flare of her hips, the belt of the robe tied in a floppy knot.

It was nearly eight. Shukumar put the rice on the table and the lentils from the night before into the microwave oven, punching the numbers on the timer.

"You made *rogan josh*," Shoba observed, looking through the glass lid at the bright paprika stew.

Shukumar took out a piece of lamb, pinching it quickly between his fingers so as not to scald himself. He prodded a larger piece with a serving spoon to make sure the meat slipped easily from the bone. "It's ready," he announced.

The microwave had just beeped when the lights went out, and the music   30 disappeared.

"Perfect timing," Shoba said.

"All I could find were birthday candles." He lit up the ivy, keeping the rest of the candles and a book of matches by his plate.

"It doesn't matter," she said, running a finger along the stem of her wine-glass. "It looks lovely."

In the dimness, he knew how she sat, a bit forward in her chair, ankles crossed against the lowest rung, left elbow on the table. During his search for the candles, Shukumar had found a bottle of wine in a crate he had thought was empty. He clamped the bottle between his knees while he turned in the corkscrew. He worried about spilling, and so he picked up the glasses and held them close to his lap while he filled them. They served themselves, stirring the rice with their forks, squinting as they extracted bay leaves and cloves from the stew. Every few minutes Shukumar lit a few more birthday candles and drove them into the soil of the pot.

"It's like India," Shoba said, watching him tend his makeshift candelabra.   35 "Sometimes the current disappears for hours at a stretch. I once had to attend an entire rice ceremony in the dark. The baby just cried and cried. It must have been so hot."

Their baby had never cried, Shukumar considered. Their baby would never have a rice ceremony, even though Shoba had already made the guest list, and decided on which of her three brothers she was going to ask to feed the child its first taste of solid food, at six months if it was a boy, seven if it was a girl.

"Are you hot?" he asked her. He pushed the blazing ivy pot to the other end of the table, closer to the piles of books and mail, making it even more difficult for them to see each other. He was suddenly irritated that he couldn't go upstairs and sit in front of the computer.

"No. It's delicious," she said, tapping her plate with her fork. "It really is."

He refilled the wine in her glass. She thanked him.

They weren't like this before. Now he had to struggle to say something that interested her, something that made her look up from her plate, or from her proofreading files. Eventually he gave up trying to amuse her. He learned not to mind the silences.

"I remember during power failures at my grandmother's house, we all had to say something," Shoba continued. He could barely see her face, but from her tone he knew her eyes were narrowed, as if trying to focus on a distant object. It was a habit of hers.

"Like what?"

"I don't know. A little poem. A joke. A fact about the world. For some reason my relatives always wanted me to tell them the names of my friends in America. I don't know why the information was so interesting to them. The last time I saw my aunt she asked after four girls I went to elementary school with in Tucson. I barely remember them now."

Shukumar hadn't spent as much time in India as Shoba had. His parents, who settled in New Hampshire, used to go back without him. The first time he'd gone as an infant he'd nearly died of amoebic dysentery. His father, a nervous type, was afraid to take him again, in case something were to happen, and left him with his aunt and uncle in Concord. As a teenager he preferred sailing camp or scooping ice cream during the summers to going to Calcutta. It wasn't until after his father died, in his last year of college, that the country began to interest him, and he studied its history from course books as if it were any other subject. He wished now that he had his own childhood story of India.

"Let's do that," she said suddenly.

"Do what?"

"Say something to each other in the dark."

"Like what? I don't know any jokes."

"No, no jokes." She thought for a minute. "How about telling each other something we've never told before."

"I used to play this game in high school," Shukumar recalled. "When I got drunk."

"You're thinking of truth or dare. This is different. Okay, I'll start." She took a sip of wine. "The first time I was alone in your apartment, I looked in your address book to see if you'd written me in. I think we'd known each other two weeks."

"Where was I?"

"You went to answer the telephone in the other room. It was your mother, and I figured it would be a long call. I wanted to know if you'd promoted me from the margins of your newspaper."

"Had I?"

"No. But I didn't give up on you. Now it's your turn."

He couldn't think of anything, but Shoba was waiting for him to speak. She hadn't appeared so determined in months. What was there left to say to her? He thought back to their first meeting, four years earlier at a lecture hall in

Cambridge, where a group of Bengali poets were giving a recital. They'd ended up side by side, on folding wooden chairs. Shukumar was soon bored; he was unable to decipher the literary diction, and couldn't join the rest of the audience as they sighed and nodded solemnly after certain phrases. Peering at the newspaper folded in his lap, he studied the temperatures of cities around the world. Ninety-one degrees in Singapore yesterday, fifty-one in Stockholm. When he turned his head to the left, he saw a woman next to him making a grocery list on the back of a folder, and was startled to find that she was beautiful.

"Okay," he said, remembering. "The first time we went out to dinner, to the Portuguese place, I forgot to tip the waiter. I went back the next morning, found out his name, left money with the manager."

"You went all the way back to Somerville just to tip a waiter?"

"I took a cab."

"Why did you forget to tip the waiter?"   60

The birthday candles had burned out, but he pictured her face clearly in the dark, the wide tilting eyes, the full grape-toned lips, the fall at age two from her high chair still visible as a comma on her chin. Each day, Shukumar noticed, her beauty, which had once overwhelmed him, seemed to fade. The cosmetics that had seemed superfluous were necessary now, not to improve her but to define her somehow.

"By the end of the meal I had a funny feeling that I might marry you," he said, admitting it to himself as well as to her for the first time. "It must have distracted me."

The next night Shoba came home earlier than usual. There was lamb left over from the evening before, and Shukumar heated it up so that they were able to eat by seven. He'd gone out that day, through the melting snow, and bought a packet of taper candles from the corner store, and batteries to fit the flashlight. He had the candles ready on the countertop, standing in brass holders shaped like lotuses, but they ate under the glow of the copper-shaded ceiling lamp that hung over the table.

When they had finished eating, Shukumar was surprised to see that Shoba was stacking her plate on top of his, and then carrying them over to the sink. He had assumed she would retreat to the living room, behind her barricade of files.

"Don't worry about the dishes," he said, taking them from her hands.   65

"It seems silly not to," she replied, pouring a drop of detergent onto a sponge. "It's nearly eight o'clock."

His heart quickened. All day Shukumar had looked forward to the lights going out. He thought about what Shoba had said the night before, about looking in his address book. It felt good to remember her as she was then, how bold yet nervous she'd been when they first met, how hopeful. They stood side by side at the sink, their reflections fitting together in the frame of the window. It made him shy, the way he felt the first time they stood together in a mirror. He couldn't recall the last time they'd been photographed. They had stopped attending parties, went nowhere together. The film in his camera still contained pictures of Shoba, in the yard, when she was pregnant.

After finishing the dishes, they leaned against the counter, drying their hands on either end of a towel. At eight o'clock the house went black. Shukumar lit the wicks of the candles, impressed by their long, steady flames.

"Let's sit outside," Shoba said. "I think it's warm still."

They each took a candle and sat down on the steps. It seemed strange to be 70 sitting outside with patches of snow still on the ground. But everyone was out of their houses tonight, the air fresh enough to make people restless. Screen doors opened and closed. A small parade of neighbors passed by with flashlights.

"We're going to the bookstore to browse," a silver-haired man called out. He was walking with his wife, a thin woman in a windbreaker, and holding a dog on a leash. They were the Bradfords, and they had tucked a sympathy card into Shoba and Shukumar's mailbox back in September. "I hear they've got their power."

"They'd better," Shukumar said. "Or you'll be browsing in the dark."

The woman laughed, slipping her arm through the crook of her husband's elbow. "Want to join us?"

"No thanks," Shoba and Shukumar called out together. It surprised Shukumar that his words matched hers.

He wondered what Shoba would tell him in the dark. The worst possibilities 75 had already run through his head. That she'd had an affair. That she didn't respect him for being thirty-five and still a student. That she blamed him for being in Baltimore the way her mother did. But he knew those things weren't true. She'd been faithful, as had he. She believed in him. It was she who had insisted he go to Baltimore. What didn't they know about each other? He knew she curled her fingers tightly when she slept, that her body twitched during bad dreams. He knew it was honeydew she favored over cantaloupe. He knew that when they returned from the hospital the first thing she did when she walked into the house was pick out objects of theirs and toss them into a pile in the hallway: books from the shelves, plants from the windowsills, paintings from walls, photos from tables, pots and pans that hung from the hooks over the stove. Shukumar had stepped out of her way, watching as she moved methodically from room to room. When she was satisfied, she stood there staring at the pile she'd made, her lips drawn back in such distaste that Shukumar had thought she would spit. Then she'd started to cry.

He began to feel cold as he sat there on the steps. He felt that he needed her to talk first, in order to reciprocate.

"That time when your mother came to visit us," she said finally. "When I said one night that I had to stay late at work. I went out with Gillian and had a martini."

He looked at her profile, the slender nose, the slightly masculine set of her jaw. He remembered that night well; eating with his mother, tired from teaching two classes back to back, wishing Shoba were there to say more of the right things because he came up with only the wrong ones. It had been twelve years since his father had died, and his mother had come to spend two weeks with him and Shoba, so they could honor his father's memory together. Each night his mother cooked something his father had liked, but she was too upset to eat the dishes herself, and her eyes would well up as Shoba stroked her hand. "It's so touching," Shoba had said to him at the time. Now he pictured Shoba with Gillian, in a bar with striped velvet sofas, the one they used to go to after the movies, making sure she got her extra olive, asking Gillian for a cigarette. He imagined her complaining, and Gillian sympathizing about visits from in-laws. It was Gillian who had driven Shoba to the hospital.

"Your turn," she said, stopping his thoughts.

At the end of their street Shukumar heard sounds of a drill and the electri- 80 cians shouting over it. He looked at the darkened facades of the houses lining the street. Candles glowed in the windows of one. In spite of the warmth, smoke rose from the chimney.

"I cheated on my Oriental Civilization exam in college," he said. "It was my last semester, my last set of exams. My father had died a few months before. I could see the blue book of the guy next to me. He was an American guy, a maniac. He knew Urdu and Sanskrit. I couldn't remember if the verse we had to identify was an example of a *ghazal*° or not. I looked at his answer and copied it down."

It had happened over fifteen years ago. He felt relief now, having told her.

She turned to him, looking not at his face, but at his shoes — old moccasins he wore as if they were slippers, the leather at the back permanently flattened. He wondered if it bothered her, what he'd said. She took his hand and pressed it. "You didn't have to tell me why you did it," she said, moving closer to him.

They sat together until nine o'clock, when the lights came on. They heard some people across the street clapping from their porch, and televisions being turned on. The Bradfords walked back down the street, eating ice-cream cones and waving. Shoba and Shukumar waved back. Then they stood up, his hand still in hers, and went inside.

Somehow, without saying anything, it had turned into this. Into an ex- 85 change of confessions — the little ways they'd hurt or disappointed each other, and themselves. The following day Shukumar thought for hours about what to say to her. He was torn between admitting that he once ripped out a photo of a woman in one of the fashion magazines she used to subscribe to and carried it in his books for a week, or saying that he really hadn't lost the sweater-vest she bought him for their third wedding anniversary but had exchanged it for cash at Filene's, and that he had gotten drunk alone in the middle of the day at a hotel bar. For their first anniversary, Shoba had cooked a ten-course dinner just for him. The vest depressed him. "My wife gave me a sweater-vest for our anniversary," he complained to the bartender, his head heavy with cognac. "What do you expect?" the bartender had replied. "You're married."

As for the picture of the woman, he didn't know why he'd ripped it out. She wasn't as pretty as Shoba. She wore a white sequined dress, and had a sullen face and lean, mannish legs. Her bare arms were raised, her fists around her head, as if she were about to punch herself in the ears. It was an advertisement for stock-

---

ghazal: A Middle Eastern and South Asian lyric form consisting of five to twelve couplets sharing the same rhyme.

ings. Shoba had been pregnant at the time, her stomach suddenly immense, to the point where Shukumar no longer wanted to touch her. The first time he saw the picture he was lying in bed next to her, watching her as she read. When he noticed the magazine in the recycling pile he found the woman and tore out the page as carefully as he could. For about a week he allowed himself a glimpse each day. He felt an intense desire for the woman, but it was a desire that turned to disgust after a minute or two. It was the closest he'd come to infidelity.

He told Shoba about the sweater on the third night, the picture on the fourth. She said nothing as he spoke, expressed no protest or reproach. She simply listened, and then she took his hand, pressing it as she had before. On the third night, she told him that once after a lecture they'd attended, she let him speak to the chair of his department without telling him that he had a dab of pâté on his chin. She'd been irritated with him for some reason, and so she'd let him go on and on, about securing his fellowship for the following semester, without putting a finger to her own chin as a signal. The fourth night, she said that she never liked the one poem he'd ever published in his life, in a literary magazine in Utah. He'd written the poem after meeting Shoba. She added that she found the poem sentimental.

Something happened when the house was dark. They were able to talk to each other again. The third night after supper they'd sat together on the sofa, and once it was dark he began kissing her awkwardly on her forehead and her face, and though it was dark he closed his eyes, and knew that she did, too. The fourth night they walked carefully upstairs, to bed, feeling together for the final step with their feet before the landing, and making love with a desperation they had forgotten. She wept without sound, and whispered his name, and traced his eyebrows with her finger in the dark. As he made love to her he wondered what he would say to her the next night, and what she would say, the thought of it exciting him. "Hold me," he said, "hold me in your arms." By the time the lights came back on downstairs, they'd fallen asleep.

The morning of the fifth night Shukumar found another notice from the electric company in the mailbox. The line had been repaired ahead of schedule, it said. He was disappointed. He had planned on making shrimp *malai* for Shoba, but when he arrived at the store he didn't feel like cooking anymore. It wasn't the same, he thought, knowing that the lights wouldn't go out. In the store the shrimp looked gray and thin. The coconut milk tin was dusty and overpriced. Still, he bought them, along with a beeswax candle and two bottles of wine.

She came home at seven-thirty. "I suppose this is the end of our game," he 90 said when he saw her reading the notice.

She looked at him. "You can still light candles if you want." She hadn't been to the gym tonight. She wore a suit beneath the raincoat. Her makeup had been retouched recently.

When she went upstairs to change, Shukumar poured himself some wine and put on a record, a Thelonius Monk album he knew she liked.

When she came downstairs they ate together. She didn't thank him or compliment him. They simply ate in a darkened room, in the glow of a beeswax candle. They had survived a difficult time. They finished off the shrimp. They finished off the first bottle of wine and moved on to the second. They sat together until the candle had nearly burned away. She shifted in her chair, and Shukumar thought that she was about to say something. But instead she blew out the candle, stood up, turned on the light switch, and sat down again.

"Shouldn't we keep the lights off?" Shukumar asked.

She set her plate aside and clasped her hands on the table. "I want you to see   95
my face when I tell you this," she said gently.

His heart began to pound. The day she told him she was pregnant, she had used the very same words, saying them in the same gentle way, turning off the basketball game he'd been watching on television. He hadn't been prepared then. Now he was.

Only he didn't want her to be pregnant again. He didn't want to have to pretend to be happy.

"I've been looking for an apartment and I've found one," she said, narrowing her eyes on something, it seemed, behind his left shoulder. It was nobody's fault, she continued. They'd been through enough. She needed some time alone. She had money saved up for a security deposit. The apartment was on Beacon Hill, so she could walk to work. She had signed the lease that night before coming home.

She wouldn't look at him, but he stared at her. It was obvious that she'd rehearsed the lines. All this time she'd been looking for an apartment, testing the water pressure, asking a Realtor if heat and hot water were included in the rent. It sickened Shukumar, knowing that she had spent these past evenings preparing for a life without him. He was relieved and yet he was sickened. This was what she'd been trying to tell him for the past four evenings. This was the point of her game.

Now it was his turn to speak. There was something he'd sworn he would   100
never tell her, and for six months he had done his best to block it from his mind. Before the ultrasound she had asked the doctor not to tell her the sex of their child, and Shukumar had agreed. She had wanted it to be a surprise.

Later, those few times they talked about what had happened, she said at least they'd been spared that knowledge. In a way she almost took pride in her decision, for it enabled her to seek refuge in a mystery. He knew that she assumed it was a mystery for him, too. He'd arrived too late from Baltimore — when it was all over and she was lying on the hospital bed. But he hadn't. He'd arrived early enough to see their baby, and to hold him before they cremated him. At first he had recoiled at the suggestion, but the doctor said holding the baby might help him with the process of grieving. Shoba was asleep. The baby had been cleaned off, his bulbous lids shut tight to the world.

"Our baby was a boy," he said. "His skin was more red than brown. He had black hair on his head. He weighed almost five pounds. His fingers were curled shut, just like yours in the night."

Shoba looked at him now, her face contorted with sorrow. He had cheated on a college exam, ripped a picture of a woman out of a magazine. He had returned a sweater and got drunk in the middle of the day instead. These were the things he had told her. He had held his son, who had known life only within her, against his chest in a darkened room in an unknown wing of the hospital. He had held him until a nurse knocked and took him away, and he promised himself that day that he would never tell Shoba, because he still loved her then, and it was the one thing in her life that she had wanted to be a surprise.

Shukumar stood up and stacked his plate on top of hers. He carried the plates to the sink, but instead of running the tap he looked out the window. Outside the evening was still warm, and the Bradfords were walking arm in arm. As he watched the couple the room went dark, and he spun around. Shoba had turned the lights off. She came back to the table and sat down, and after a moment Shukumar joined her. They wept together, for the things they now knew.

Yiyun Li   b. 1972

Persimmons   [2005]

April comes and April goes, and May, and June, all passing by without shedding a drop of rain. The sky has been a blue desert since spring. The sun rises every morning, a bright white disc growing larger and hotter each day. Cicadas drawl halfheartedly in the trees. The reservoir outside the village has shrunken into a bathtub for the boys, peeing at one another in the waist-deep water. Two girls, four or five, stand by the main road, their bare arms waving like desperate wings of baby birds as they chant to the motionless air, "Come the east wind. Come the west wind. Come the east-west-north-south wind and cool my armpits."

Now that July has only to move its hind foot out the door in a matter of days, we have started to wish, instead of rain, that no rain will fall and the drought will last till the end of the harvest season. Peasants as we are, and worrying about the grainless autumn as we are, the drought has, to our surprise, brought a languid satisfaction to our lives. Every day, from morning till evening, we sit under the old pagoda tree, smoking our pipes and moving our bodies only when the tree's shade threatens to leave us to the full spotlight of the sunshine. Our women are scratching their heads to come up with decent meals for us at home. The rice from last year will be running out soon, and before that, our women's hair will be thinning from too much scratching until they will all go bald, but this, like all the minor tragedies in the world, has stopped bothering us. We sit and smoke until our daily bags of tobacco leaves run out. We stuff grass roots and half-dead leaves into the bags, and when they run out, we smoke dust.

"Heaven's punishment, this drought." Someone, one of us, finally speaks after a long period of silent smoking.

"Yes, too many deaths."

"In that case, Heaven will never be happy again. People always die."   5

"And we'll never get a drop of rain."

"Suits me well. I'm tired of farming anyway."

"Yeah, right. Heaven comes to spank you, and you hurry up to bare your butts and say, Come and scratch me, I've got an itch here."

"It's called optimism, better than crying and begging for pardon."

"A soft persimmon is what you are. I would just grab His pants and spank   10
Him back."

"Whoa, a hero we've got here."

"Why not?"

"Because we were born soft persimmons. See any hero coming out of a persimmon?"

"Lao Da."

"Lao Da? They popped his brain like a watermelon."   15

Lao Da was one of us. He should have been sitting here with us, smoking and waiting for his turn to speak out a line or two, to agree, or to contradict. When night falls, he would, like all of us, walk home and dote on his son, dripping drops of rice wine from his chopsticks to the boy's mouth. Lao Da would have never bragged about being a hero, a man like him, who knew his place between the sky and the earth. But the thing is, Lao Da was executed before this drought began. On New Year's Eve, he went into the county seat and shot seventeen people, fourteen men and three women, in seventeen different houses, sixteen of them dead on the spot, and the seventeenth lived only to see half a day of the new year.

"If you were born a soft persimmon, you'd better stay one" — someone says the comforting old wisdom.

"Persimmons are not born soft."

"But they are valued for their softness."

"Their ripeness."   20

"What then if we stay soft and ripened?"

"Heaven will squeeze us until He gets tired of squeezing."

"He may even start to like us because we are so much fun for Him."

"We'll just have our skins left by then."

"Better than having no skins."   25

"Better than having a bullet pop your brain."

"Better than having no son to inherit your name."

Silent for a moment, we all relish the fact that we are alive, with boys to carry on our family names. Last year at this time, Lao Da's son was one of the boys, five years old, running behind older boys like all small kids do, picking up the cicadas that the older boys shot down with their sling guns, adding dry twigs and dead leaves to the fire that was lit up to roast the bodies, waiting for his share of a burned cicada or two.

"Lao Da's son died a bad one."

"As if there is a good way to die!"   30

"Those seventeen, weren't theirs good? Fast and painless."

"But in the city, they said those seventeen all died badly."

"Mercilessly murdered — wasn't that how they put it in the newspapers?"

"But that's true. They were murdered."

"True, but in the city, they wouldn't say the boy died badly. They didn't even 35
mention Lao Da's son."

"Of course they wouldn't. Who would want to hear about a murderer's son?
A dead son, not to mention."

"Even if they had written about him, what could they have said?"

"Drowned in a swimming accident, that's what was written in his death
certificate."

"An accident happens every day, they would say."

"The boy's death wasn't worth a story."   40

The seventeen men and women's stories, however, were read aloud to us at
Lao Da's trial, their enlarged pictures looking down at us from the top of the
stage of a theater, a makeshift courthouse to contain the audience. We no
longer remember their names, but some of the faces, a woman in heavy makeup
who looked like a girl we were all obsessed with when we were young, a man
with a sinister mole just below his left eye, another man with a pair of caterpillar-
like eyebrows, these faces have stuck with us ever since. So have a few of the
stories. A man who had been ice-swimming for twenty years and had never been
ill for one day of his adult life. A mother of a teenage girl who had died earlier
that year from leukemia. An official and his young secretary, who, as we heard
from rumors, had been having an affair, but in the read-aloud stories, they were
both the dear husband and wife to their spouses. The stories went on, and after a
while we dozed off. What was the point of telling these dead people's stories to
us? Lao Da had no chance of getting away. He turned himself in to the police,
knowing he would get a death sentence. Why not spare those relatives the embarrassment of wailing in the court? Besides, no story was read aloud about Lao
Da. He was an atrocious criminal was all that was said about him.

"Think about it: Lao Da was the only one who died a good death."

"A worthy one."

"Got enough companions for the trip to the next world."

"Got us into trouble, too."   45

"It wasn't his mistake. Heaven would've found another reason to squeeze us."

"True. Lao Da was just an excuse."

"Maybe — I have been thinking — maybe Heaven is angry not because of Lao
Da, but for him?"

"How?"

"I heard from my grandpa, who heard from his grandpa, that there was this 50
woman who was beheaded as a murderer, and for three years after her execution, not a drop of rain fell on the area."

"I heard that from my grandpa, too. Heaven was avenging the woman."

"But she was wronged. She did not kill her husband."

"True."

Lao Da was not wronged. You killed seventeen people and you had to pay with your life. Even Lao Da nodded in agreement when the judge read the sentence. He bowed to the judge and then to the guards when he was escorted off the stage. "I'm leaving one step earlier," he said. "Will be waiting for you on the other side." The guards, the judge, and the officials on and off the stage, they all tried to turn their eyes away from Lao Da, but he was persistent in his farewell. "Come over soon. Don't let me wait for too long," he said. We never expected Lao Da to have such a sense of humor. We grinned at him and he grinned back, but for a short moment only, as the judge waved for two more guards to push him to the backstage before he had time to give out too many invitations.

"Lao Da was a man."   55

"Spanked Heaven."

"But who's got the upper hand now?"

"It means nothing to Lao Da now. He had his moment."

"But it matters to us. We are punished for those who were wronged by death."

"Who?"   60

"Those seventeen."

"Not the wife of the cuckold, I hope."

"Certainly not. She deserved it."

"That woman was smaller than a toenail of Lao Da's wife."

"That woman was cheaper than a fart of Lao Da's wife."   65

"True."

"Good woman Lao Da had as a wife."

"Worthy of his life."

We nod, and all think about Lao Da's wife, secretly comparing her with our own women. Lao Da's wife worked like a man in the field and behaved like a woman at home. She was plump, and healthy, and never made a sound when Lao Da beat her for good or bad reasons, or for no reason at all. Our wives are not as perfect. If they are not too thin they are too fat. If they are diligent, they do not leave us alone, nagging us for our laziness. They scream when beaten; even worse, sometimes they fight back.

"That good woman deserved better luck."   70

"She deserved another son."

"But her tubes were tied."

"The poor woman would've lived if not for the Birth Control Office."

"A group of pests they are, aren't they?"

The Birth Control Office had been after Lao Da and his wife when they had   75
not reported to the office after their firstborn. *One child per family*, they brushed in big red words on Lao Da's house. *Only pigs and dogs give birth to more than one child*, they wrote. But Lao Da and his woman never gave up. They played hide-and-seek with the Birth Control Office, hiding in different relatives' places when the woman's belly was growing big. After three daughters and a big debt for the fines, they finally had a son. The day the boy turned a hundred days old, Lao Da killed a goat and two suckling pigs for a banquet; afterward, the wife was sent to the clinic to have her tubes triumphantly tied.

"What's the point of living if she could not bear another son for Lao Da? What's the use of a hen if it doesn't lay eggs?"

"True."

"But that woman, she was something."

"Wasn't she?"

We exchange looks of awe, all knowing that our own women would never   80 have had the courage to do what Lao Da's wife did. Our women would have screamed and begged when we faced no other choices but divorcing them for a fertile belly, but Lao Da's wife, she never acted like an ordinary woman. When we, along with Lao Da, dived into the reservoir to look for the body of Lao Da's son, she drank all the pesticide she could lay her hands on, six bottles in a row, and lay down in bed. Six bottles of pesticide with that strength could cut her into pieces, but she did not make a single sound, her jaws clenched, waiting for death.

"An extraordinary woman."

"Maybe Heaven is angry on her behalf."

"She was not wronged by anybody."

"But her soul was let down."

"By whom?"   85

"Lao Da."

"Lao Da avenged her, and their son."

"Was it what she wanted?"

"What did she want?"

"Listen, she was making room for a new wife, so Lao Da could have more   90 sons. She didn't poison herself just to make Lao Da lose his mind and carry out some stupid plan to shoot seventeen people. Think about it. Lao Da got everything wrong."

"Her death could have borne more fruits."

"That's true. Now she died for nothing."

"And Lao Da, too."

"And those seventeen."

"And the three daughters, orphaned for nothing."   95

We shake our heads, thinking about the three girls, their screaming and crying piercing our eardrums when the county officials grabbed their arms and pushed them into the jeep. They were sent to different orphanages in three counties, bad seeds of a cold-blooded killer. Lao Da should have listened to us and drowned them right after they were born, sparing them their troubles of living in pain.

"Lao Da could have done better."

"Reckless man."

We could have made a wiser choice than Lao Da. We would have let the dead be buried and gone on living, finding a new wife to bear a new son, working, our backs bent, to feed the wife and the children. There would be the pain, naturally, of waking up to the humiliation of being a soft persimmon, but humiliation does not kill a man. Nothing beats clinging to this life. Death ferries us nowhere.

"One man's mistake can capsize a whole ship of people."   100

"True."

"Death of a son is far from the biggest tragedy."

"Death of anybody shouldn't be an excuse to lose one's mind."

"But Lao Da had the right to seek justice for his boy."

"Justice? What kind of justice is there for us?"   105

"If one kills, one has to pay with his life. Nothing's wrong with the old rule. The man who killed Lao Da's son should have been punished."

"He was punished all right. The first one Lao Da shot that night, wasn't he?"

"Two shots in the brain. Two shots in the heart."

"In front of his woman."

"Well done it was."   110

"Couldn't be better."

"When I heard the news, I felt I had just downed a full pot of sorghum wine."

"It beats the best wine out there."

"See, that's what justice is."

"True. One can never run away from justice's palm."   115

"You just have to wait for the time."

"Heaven sees, doesn't He?"

"But if He does see, why are we punished? What kind of justice is this?"

"I've told you: there is no justice for us persimmons."

"If you kill one person, you are a murderer. If you kill a lot, you are a hero."   120

"Lao Da killed seventeen."

"Not quite enough."

"If you've made a point, you are a hero. If you've failed to make a point, you are nothing."

"What's the point to make?"

"There should be an order for everyone to follow."   125

"A dreamer is what you are, asking for the impossible."

"We all asked for that at the riot, but it didn't get us anywhere."

"That was because we gave up."

"Bullshit. What's the point fighting for a dead boy?"

"True."   130

"What's the point risking our lives for a nonexistent order?"

"True."

We all nod, eager to shoo away the tiny doubt that circles us like a persistent fly. Of course, we did what we could—after the boy was found in the water, we marched together with his little body to the county seat, asking for justice. Hoes and spades and axes and our fists and throats we all brought with us, but when the government sent the troop of armed police in our direction, we decided to go back home. Violence will not solve your problem, we said to Lao Da. Go to the court and sue the man; follow what the law says, we told Lao Da.

"Maybe we shouldn't have put the seed in Lao Da's mind to sue the man."

"Had I been him, I would have done the same."   135

"The same what? Going around the city and asking justice for his son's death? His son was drowned in a swimming accident—black words on a white page in his death certificate."

"The other boys told a different story."

"Why would the court want to listen to the story?"

We sit and smoke and wait for someone to answer the question. A group of boys are returning to the village from the reservoir, all dripping wet. Lao Da's boy would never have been drowned if there had been a drought last year. We don't worry about our sons this year, even the youngest ones, who cannot swim well. But last year was a different story. Last year's reservoir was deep enough to kill Lao Da's son.

"But don't you think the officials made some mistakes too? What if they 140
gave Lao Da some money to shut him up?"

"What if they put that man in jail, even for a month or two?"

"Isn't that a smart idea? Or pretend to put the man in jail?"

"Yes, just tell Lao Da the man got his punishment."

"At least treat Lao Da a little better."

"Would have saved themselves."   145

"But how could they have known? They thought Lao Da was a soft persimmon."

"Squeezed him enough for fun."

"Squeezed a murderer out of it."

"Lao Da was the last one you would think to snap like that."

"Amazing how much one could take and then all of a sudden he broke."   150

"True."

"But back to my point, what's the good losing one's mind over a dead son and a dead wife?"

"Easier said than done."

"True. How many times did we tell him to stop pursuing the case?"

"Sometimes a man sets his mind on an idea, and he becomes a hunting dog,   155
only seeing one thing."

"And now we are punished for his stupidity."

We shake our heads, sorry for Lao Da, more so for ourselves. Lao Da should have listened to us. Instead, he was writing down the names and addresses of those officials who had treated him like a dog. How long he had been preparing for the killing we do not know. He had the patience to wait for half a year until New Year's Eve, the best time to carry out a massive murder, when all the people were staying home for the year-end banquet.

"At least we have to give Lao Da the credit for carrying out his plan thoroughly."

"He had a brain when it came to revenge."

"And those seventeen dead souls. Think about how shocked they were when 160
they saw Lao Da that night."

"I hope they had time to regret what they had done to Lao Da."

"I hope their families begged Lao Da for them as Lao Da had begged them for his boy."

"You'd never know what could come from a soft persimmon."

"I hope they were taught a lesson."

"They're dead."   165

"Then someone else was taught the lesson."

"Quiet! Be careful in case someone from the county hears you."

"So hot they won't be here."

"The reservoir is not deep enough for them now."

"The reservoir is really the cause of all these bad things. Think about the 170
labors we put into the reservoir."

We nod and sigh. A few years ago, we put all our free time into building the reservoir, hoping to end our days of relying on Heaven's mood for the rain. The reservoir soon became an entertaining site for the county officials. On summer afternoons, they came in jeeps, swimming in our water, fishing our fish. The man was one of the judges — but what indeed was his line of work we never got to know, as we call everybody working in the county court "judge." That judge and his companions came, all drunk before they went into the water. Something Lao Da's son said, a joke maybe, or just a nickname he gave to the judge, made him angry. He picked up Lao Da's son and threw him into the deeper water of the reservoir. A big splash the other boys remembered. They cried, begged, but the judges all said it would teach the little bastard a lesson. The boys sent the fastest one among them to run for help. Lao Da's son was found later that night, his eyelids, lips, fingers, toes, and penis all eaten into bad shapes by the feasting fish.

"Remember, Lao Da was one of those who really pushed for the reservoir."

"He worked his back bent for it."

"The poor man didn't know what he was sweating for."

"None of us knows." 175

"At least we don't have to sweat this summer."

"Of course, you don't sweat waiting for death."

"Death? No, not that bad."

"Not that bad? Let me ask you — what will we feed our women and kids in the winter?"

"Whatever is left from the autumn." 180

"Nothing will be left."

"Then feed them our cows and horses."

"Then what?"

"Then we'll all go to the county and become beggars."

"It's illegal to beg." 185

"I don't care."

"If you want to do something illegal, why be a beggar and be spat at by everybody? I would go to the county and request to be fed."

"How?"

"With my fist and my axe."

"Don't talk big. We were there once with our fists and our axes." 190

"But that was for the dead boy. This time it'll be for our own sons."

"Do you think it'll work?"

"You have to try."

"Nonsense. If it works, it would have worked last time. Lao Da wouldn't have had to kill and we wouldn't have to be punished."

Nobody talks. The sun has slowly hauled itself to the southwest sky. The ci- 195
cadas stop their chanting, but before we have time to enjoy the silence, they pick
up the old tune again. Some of us draw and puff imaginary smokes from our
pipes that are no longer lit; others pick up dry twigs from the ground, sketching
in the dust fat clouds, heavy with rain.

Ana Menéndez   b. 1970

Her Mother's House   [2001]

The road to her mother's house crossed a wooden bridge into a field of
sugarcane that bent green and wide to the horizon before it narrowed into a
path flanked on both sides by proud stands of royal palms. It was a late afternoon in summer and the men were coming in from the fields, hauling their machetes behind them. They stepped aside with their backs against the palms to let
her pass and then stood waiting for the dust to settle, their hats flopping softly
in the breeze. Lisette watched the men in the mirror until they retook the road
and then her eyes were on the green fields ahead of her, the blue hills that
dipped over the edge of sky. The thick warm air curled through the open window
and the uneven road bumped her along in a seamless and predictable rhythm.
She hummed a tune she had heard last night in the hotel and then she was
silent, listening to the palm wind, the road beneath the wheels. It was the first
time she had been alone in years and the new quiet seemed something she could
touch, an opening in her chest that was as real as her childhood faith.

She was born in Miami, two years after the revolution. Her parents had met
waiting in line at the Freedom Tower and married just two months later. He was
a young student from Oriente, who'd come fleeing Batista. She was from a
wealthy landowning family outside Varadero, who'd come fleeing Castro. For
years, Lisette thought Batista Castro° was one man, the all-powerful tyrant of
the Caribbean, the bearded mulatto who shot poor workers in the fields and
stole her mother's house with all her photographs in it.

That house. Always in the air, behind every reproach. Her mother half mad
with longing. And that winter morning when Lisette thought she began to know
her mother. Twelve years old. Reading alone in her room, she heard the sobbing
before she saw that her mother had crawled in on her knees, a long end of toilet
paper in her hands.

Batista, Castro: Fulgencio Batista y Zaldívar (1901–1973) was the authoritarian leader of
Cuba from 1933–1959. Fidel Alejandro Castro Ruz (b. 1926) led the 1959 revolution that over-
threw Batista and since then has been prime minister and, later, president of Cuba.

"Look at this, feel how soft this is," she cried, holding out the paper to Lisette. "In Cuba today the little children have to use whatever scraps of paper they can find in the trash, bits of newspaper, cardboard. Oh, feel how soft this is."

Her mother had let her body drop to the floor and she lay there for a long 5 time, shredding the paper into smaller and smaller pieces. Lisette sat at the edge of her bed, watching and waiting for her father to come in the room and gently lift her mother. She had turned to Lisette, her eyes open wide.

"When the soldiers came for the house, I walked straight, not turning once to look at the stained-glass windows," she cried softly now. "Not even the white columns that climbed to the second floor."

And the iron railing on the balcony where the rattan furniture was laid out for company, the clink of glasses. Lisette began to remember all of it too.

Lisette married a round-faced boy whose parents were from Varadero, a short drive from her mother's hometown. They each needed someone to agree with. After everything, she still kept the photo that made it into the society pages, Lisette smooth-faced and skinny in the billowy dress, Erminio's arm wrapped tight around her waist, as if already he worried she was a wisp of smoke, a thin memory of herself.

She was a new reporter, covering city hall and trying to find a world within the small concerns of small towns, the wider life in berms and set-asides. He was a young lawyer who hated the law and preferred to make poems out of her stories. Every Sunday, he recited his creations in a deep sleepy voice:

The

Sweetwater city council

today

approved pre-

liminary plans for new

shopping center on

the

corner

of

Eighth Street and

107th Avenue.

The first months, he waited for her to wake. He poured her the orange juice 10 and the coffee and read her his newspaper poems. Some mornings, when the night's images had vanished, she would kiss him. And they would return to the bedroom and he would whisper her breath back to her.

Later, she began to linger in bed alone, waiting for him to go. Even after they stopped talking, he'd leave a poem by the toast. Paint a heart. Some mornings she could still smell him in the kitchen and her heart would turn.

At lunch she would take a sandwich and sit alone by the bay, imagining the stories in each ripple of water, each cloud that had the strength to push across the sky.

One Christmas Eve she sat apart from Erminio as she had for months and watched him with the women. He said something and they giggled, clapping their hands together like little girls playing at tea. How they loved him, his long frame and freckled skin. They sat in a circle around the pool, under the lights her father had strung from the second-floor balcony to the roof of the gazebo. It was one of those clear December nights that Lisette still loved about Miami, everything clean. One of her cousins produced a guitar and began to sing a bolero, a soft and sad contemplation behind the notes. The applause was slow. Her cousin's father took the guitar away. "Playing sad songs on Christmas, what kind of musician are you?" and he began to strum out an old danzón.° Erminio stood and walked to where she was. He sat next to her, took her hand. He squeezed it. She looked at the pool, at the ripples of light.

"It makes me afraid," he said. "How much I need you."

Lisette moved her head with the music.   15

"It's true," he said. He squeezed her hand. She looked at him and he squeezed harder.

"You're hurting me," she said. "What's the matter with you?" She stood. The music stopped and the others looked up. Erminio sat staring down at the ground, his shoulders bent a little toward his chest. His right hand shook. "Can't you leave me alone for one minute?" Lisette whispered at him. "One minute."

It was terrible the way he kept believing that history would reignite the now. He really thought they could be like they were. Not just them. Everything. Everybody. It made Lisette want to scream. The past wasn't something you could play again like an old song.

Erminio got up and walked to the far end of the yard, falling away from the gazebo lights. Fine, go, she said. And already Lisette was regretting the night.

There were moments that seemed, in their first rush of happiness, strong 20 enough to outrun the inevitable. The night in Isla Mujeres, the wet breeze and the call of fishermen. They had lain skin to skin, remembering, Lisette watching the reflected water draw patterns on the wall. Later, when he went down to phone his parents in Miami, she had wrapped herself in the blanket and slipped away to the terrace off the hallway to smoke a cigarette. She saw him return to their room. She watched him shut the door. She waited until the door flung open again and she saw Erminio pause in the hallway, his face gray. He turned toward the next room, as if listening. He passed his hand over his face and then made a sudden run for the stairs. She stepped out and called after him. He looked up and saw her. He ran back and swept her in the air. She cried. She wanted so badly to love him.

And then Lisette was in the back roads of Cuba thinking it had been so long since she'd been alone.

---

danzón: Very popular traditional Cuban dance music.

The green fields turned yellow and then brown. Lisette had set out from Havana in the early morning, but now the day was stiffening, the light falling in heavy sheets that made the loose gravel shimmer in the distance. She had been driving for more than five hours and the feeling began to creep on her that she had made a wrong turn somewhere.

But she drove on, the road desolate except for the royal palms that were so much like the stories she remembered. Her mother had shut her eyes when Lisette told her she was going to Cuba. It was a simple reporting trip, a stroke of luck. She wasn't going to explain to her mother things she could barely explain to herself. How every story needed a beginning. How her past had come to seem like a blank page, waiting for the truth to darken it.

Her mother had frowned. What kind of paper sends a young woman to Cuba alone, with the rafters churning more and more chaos. She had bent in closer and looked Lisette in the eyes. After a moment she had leaned back and put her hands in her lap. She wouldn't find the answers to her failures there, if that's what she thought. The remark had cut into Lisette. But she pretended not to understand. Maybe her mother could give her a map to the old house? Cuba's changed, it's not the Cuba I was born in, her mother had said. And then finally, It's a mistake for you to go now. The now was deliberate. And Lisette recognized it as part of the sentence her mother left unsaid: Now that you're divorced. Her mother had taken it hardest. Her family weren't failures. In the end, Lisette promised to go without the map or her mother's blessing. She knew the house was outside Varadero, near Cárdenas. She would find it on her own.

At the airport, her mother had parked and walked her to the terminal. Her face was puffy. 25

"So you're going."

Lisette nodded. Her mother hugged her and took her hand. She pressed a note.

In Havana, Lisette had worn her mother's map smooth, like tissue paper. The names had changed, but the streets remained. The Malecón still faced toward Miami even after all these years. On every old street, the billboards insisted on the revolution. "We defend the right to happiness" and "The revolution is eternal." Lisette thought back to her marriage. The reassurances built upon their own disintegration. The more they said I Love You, the more they knew it was an empty incantation. Still, she thought she had been right to come. The people had been kind. The police hadn't followed. In the mornings, when everything was fresh and new, she had thought that they had something here that her parents' generation had lost in exile. The feeling evaporated by the end of the day, replaced by a watery feeling that she would never understand herself, much less this country that seemed intent on killing itself slowly. And before she fell asleep each night, despair took her again.

The road curved and the fields were green again and the blue hills were visible to the south. A man approached on horseback, growing in relation to the hills with every step. She pulled to the side of the road and examined her mother's map. On the lower right-hand side, her mother had painted a large box and labeled it simply, M. Lisette looked outside at the expanse of palms and orange trees. Her mother and her cryptics. She was probably afraid Lisette would be stopped with an incriminating document. Lisette got out of the car and sat on the bumper to wait for the man. The afternoon was hot, but the air smelled of oranges as if it were dawn. Now and then a weak breeze moved through and made a sound in the grass. The man got closer, filling up more and more of the sky, until he was upon her and Lisette sat waving her soft map like a small flag.

The man took off his hat and nodded, as if unsure he would be understood. 30 It had happened to her in Havana and Lisette had been vaguely hurt that no one recognized her as Cuban.

"Buenas tardes,"° Lisette said, exaggerating the contours of the words so the man would have no doubt she was one of them.

He smiled. "¿En qué la puedo ayudar?"°

Lisette showed him the map and pointed at the road that was supposed to lead to her mother's house. She pointed to the block in the right-hand corner, where the road branched to the right. She looked up.

"Militar," the man said and shrugged as if something struck him as silly. The notion of a military base in the middle of the campo?° Her mother's precautions?

He took the map and studied it. Then he turned it upside down and nodded, 35 smiling, to point where she was. If she continued this way past the small cane refinery and turned right on the first main road, she would pass the military installation on her right. Then if she took the first left, she should get to where she wanted to go. No photos at the military installation. He handed the map back. They'll take your camera.

Thank you, she said. "Gracias."

The man put his hat back on and watched her for a moment before returning to the road.

The military base looked deserted, but as she got closer, Lisette noticed one soldier standing in the middle of the road. She slowed. He was very young and held his rifle carelessly. She gripped the wheel as she came up beside him. Suddenly, he took a step out of the way. Lisette heard herself take a breath. The boy knocked his feet together and saluted. Lisette stared for a moment, then smiled. She thought of waving and decided instead to nod as she passed the boy. Surrounded now by the wet green of the countryside, Lisette doubted anyone had either the inclination or the money to follow anyone else. It was as if the whole country had agreed to stop caring. Only Miami still cared. And that made Lisette feel an unexpected pang for her parents. She took a left at the road the old man had told her to and began to rehearse what she would say to the people living there now. Apologies, of course: I can go away if you want. I only needed to see my mother's old room. Upstairs, near the back, the one with a balcony with an iron railing and a view of the rose garden.

"**Buenas tardes**": "Good afternoon" (Spanish).   "**¿En qué la puedo ayudar?**": "What can I help with?"   **campo**: Countryside.

If they let her, Lisette would take pictures for her father. Show him the lost space from where his wife had emerged, naked except for her stories. The first years of their marriage, all her mother did was talk about her lost plantation. Her father told Lisette how she used to lie in bed giving him imaginary tours of the house. The graceful stairway laced with gardenias in the summer, the marble fireplace her father had installed on a whim after visiting the States, the long white-shuttered windows that looked out over the gardens, the mar pacíficos,° the royal palms. Your grandfather was the only one who could grow roses in Cuba. People came from as far as Oriente to see them.

Lisette turned onto the first opening in the field, a bumpy road of loose sand   40 and stone. The men stepped aside to let her pass. The landscape was green and flat but for the hills. She came to the end of the road where it disappeared into a field of sugarcane. And in the next minute, Lisette was pressing her tongue to the roof of her mouth, determined not to cry, not now, not over something so stupid as the colors of afternoon. She got out and stood for a moment wondering if it wasn't too late to drive to Varadero. Get a room on the beach, come back in the morning.

She looked at the sky. It had cleared and the air seemed cooler by the cane. She got in the car and sat for a while. She was hungry and tired, not herself. She turned the car around and drove slowly back the way she'd come. When she came upon the field men, she drove beside them for a while until they got off the road to let her pass. But she stopped the car and rolled down the window. She didn't give them a chance to address her in English.

"Buenas tardes," she said.

The men looked at one another, then nodded.

She asked if they knew of the old Aruna house.

"Aruna?"   45

The men discussed it. The man she had addressed laid down his machete and came to her window. "Santo's granddaughter?"

Lisette thought for a moment and then motioned to him to get closer as she stepped out of the car. She nodded. "Mabella's daughter."

The man's eyes narrowed before he turned to face the others.

"Oye, la hija de° Mabi."

When he turned back to her, he was smiling. He took her hands. "I knew it,   50 I knew it when I saw you, the same eyes."

"Lisidro Padron," he said, holding out his hand. "El carpintero.° Your mother has told you about me probably?"

The other men crowded around her before she could disappoint Lisidro. Questions. Where were they? How were they? Any sisters? Are the old Arunas still alive? Lisette shook her head to the last one. Died in Venezuela a few years after the revolution. The man bent his head. He motioned back to his friends. "I'll take you to the house."

---

mar pacíficos: Peaceful sea.   la hija de: The daughter of.   El carpintero: The carpenter.

He paused and looked at Lisette, deciding something. "El viejo° Matún and his wife are living there." Lisette shook her head like a question. "You don't know Matún and Alicia? They worked for your grandparents all their lives, since they were children almost. Matún was the only man who could grow roses in Cuba." Lisette raised her head and looked at Lisidro. After a moment she said, "Yes, of course, the roses."

Twice in the walk to the house, she tried to ask Lisidro something, a question about the winds this time of year, where the road emptied. But he walked on without turning, as if he hadn't heard her or thought her poorly bred for disturbing the silence this way. Their footsteps loosened the top thin layer of dirt on the road and sent up clouds of red-brown dust behind them. The royal palms had thinned and in between them, by the edge of the road, pink flowers grew, their petals curled under where they were beginning to brown. The air was still, the thin white clouds high in the sky, and Lisette thought again how much she often preferred the journey to the destination. Even when she was a girl and they made the long drives to visit her father's parents in Tampa, she had reveled in the passing trucks, the outposts of life, the burger joints, and the dried-fruit stands, most of them gone now, the road long since widened. But those early mornings with the stars still out, she used to sit in the back and wish they would never get there, that their whole life could become this car trip. She felt it now, comfortable in her stride behind Lisidro, accustomed to the silence, not caring anymore where the road ended.

Lisidro stopped suddenly ahead of her. He turned back and waved his arm 55
for her to hurry. He stood in front of a little iron gate painted white. He shouted into a tangle of trees and plants. Lisette came up beside him. A slender stone path led from the gate into the garden. Out of the foliage, as Lisette stood watching, came a short woman, bent over, her head covered in a black shawl. She came up to the gate, resting a brown hand on the latch, and looked into Lisette's eyes.

"La nieta de° Aruna," Lisidro said. "Lisette, this is Alicia. She and Matún have been here. Have been taking care of things."

Alicia watched Lisette. Her eyes were dark brown, almost black. As Lisette watched, the woman's eyes filled with tears.

"Yes, I see the resemblance," she said.

Alicia's eyes shifted down and a tear fell slowly along her nose. Lisette put her hand over the woman's hand, like rough paper and dry as the road. Alicia turned to Lisidro and back again. She removed her hand from under Lisette's abruptly and wiped the corners of her eyes with the shawl.

"You are here to take the house."   60

The hardness of the woman's words startled Lisette. She looked from Lisidro to Alicia and brought her arms to her chest.

El viejo: The old.   **La nieta de:** The niece of.

"I swear to you it's not that at all," Lisette said. "Never."

Lisidro put a hand on her shoulder and motioned with the other to go through the gate.

"La Señorita Aruna has no such intentions. She only wants to see the house. And then she'll leave."

Lisette nodded and looked back to Alicia, whose hand had come to rest on   65 the latch again.

"The resemblance. It's quite striking," Alicia said. "Igualita."°

Lisidro had to give her a small shove to get them through the gate.

When they came to the garden, the first thing Lisette saw was a rooster and then the dry dusty ground that it pecked and then a speckle of sunlight like a pebble and beyond it, above it, in a weak shadow, the house.

The house, the idea of her mother's house there in the shadow, is a present thought in this retelling, the way she described it to herself much later. Back then, standing next to Lisidro and Alicia, Lisette saw that it was a house, but it could not be the house she had come all this way to see. This was a house with small windows carved high on the uneven walls. A flat, pitted roof of red tile. A single front door, wooden and cracked. An iron latch that hung open. A house with small windows. Uneven walls. Red tiles. Iron latches. The house of some- one else's imaginings, a different story. Beyond the house stood the blue hills and Cuba green and unknown, the way the first Spaniards must have seen it be- fore they brought their straight rows of cane, tamed the wild green with double stands of palms.

Lisette saw the way Lisidro bent his head toward this house, this little   70 dream. His lips moved, wordless. Alicia took her hand. And then Lisette was sit- ting at a wood table inside a small kitchen. A kerosene stove, a bucket of oil, a yellowed basin filled with water, a refrigerator covered in silver tape, black at the edges. Lisidro kept moving his lips at Lisette. She blinked. Was that her laughter? Inside it was dark; the contrast with the outdoors made her eyes hurt. She tried to look at Alicia, her polished coconut face.

Then a small door from the back of the kitchen opened and in it stood a man, naked to the waist. He carried a black bucket of dimpled fruit. When he saw the stranger at the table, he put the bucket down. Lisidro moved his lips. The man threw his arms in the air. He picked Lisette out of the chair and hugged her.

He went back to the fruit and put the bucket on the table. He picked out two pieces and laid them on a sheet of newspaper. Lisette stared at the fruit. The man finally took one in his hand and split the skin with his fingernail. The fruit smelled like roses. Lisette hesitated. The others watched her. She bit, the taste gritty and sweet, nothing like the sticky red paste that was the only thing she had known of guava in Miami. She swallowed and looked up at the man. His lips moved. And the air came rushing back.

Igualita: Exactly the same.

"Your mother tell you about the guava° trees here?" he said, and Lisette hearing for the first time. "Biggest fruit in all of Cuba."

Matún sat down at the last chair and pulled it up close to Lisette.

"Oye, you okay?'   75

He turned to his wife.

"Oye, Alicia, tráele un baso de agua."°

"No, no," Lisette said. "I don't need water. I'm okay."

"You're red. This heat."

"I'm okay. Thank you.   80

Lisette swallowed. Matún shook a guava at her slowly.

"Tu mamá," he began. Then shook his head. "I can't believe you're here. I always used to tell my wife, it's only a matter of time before Santo's people show up again. Ay. What a wonderful thing, eh?"

He stood and walked back to a small room. Alicia and Lisidro stayed behind at the table. Lisette closed her eyes to shut out the truth that sat with its arms crossed in front of her. And what of it! she wanted to shout. So she lied for years. So she lied! If only Lisette could get up now and return to the hotel in Havana, the men dancing on the Malecón, back to the Cuba she could talk about later, the simple stories of the rafters, the plain facts of their sadness.

"Are you comfortable?" Alicia asked.

Lisette opened her eyes and nodded. "Sí, gracias."   85

Matún returned with a small wooden picture frame. He handed it to Lisette. A little girl in pigtails sitting in that very kitchen, all the furniture the same, a bucket of guava in front of her.

"Tu mamá," Matún said. He shook his head, smiling.

"Your grandparents loved this house," Alicia said.

"We've tried to keep it up for them," Matún said. "Of course" — he waved his hands — "old age gets us all!" He laughed.

"Speaking of viejos° —"   90

Lisidro stopped him. "Los viejos murieron en° Venezuela."

"Ah. So sorry about your grandparents." Matún wiped his hands over his chest. "Now, you see, that makes me very sad to hear. They loved this house." Matún folded his hands. He was lost for a few seconds in contemplation. Lisidro cleared his throat. Were they waiting for Lisette to speak? She was afraid she might shout if she tried.

Matún sighed. "Of course, we didn't live here then. We lived out back." He pointed toward the window, past the empty yard. "It was a small house, ours was, nothing like this. I finally had to tear it down to build the chicken coop. You saw the roosters? Prize-winning. Back when they gave out prizes." Matún laughed again.

---

guava: Shrub or small tree bearing round to pear-shaped fruit, approximately 2–4 inches in diameter, with a thin delicate rind, pale green to yellow or pink to red at maturity; a creamy white or orange-salmon flesh, juicy, acid, subacid, or sweet in flavor; and a strong, sweet, musky aroma. **tráele un baso de agua:** Bring her a glass of water. **viejos:** The old people. **Los viejos murieron en:** The old people died in.

They were silent.

"Yes, your grandparents were very good people. There was never any prob- 95
lem because of" — he paused and rubbed his skin — "you know. Not with them.
They'd make coffee here and holler out the back for us to come and sit with
them. They had no problems that way." Alicia looked at him and then at her
hands, folded on the table.

Lisette handed Matún the photograph.

"Same with us," Matún said, taking back the frame. "We'd make coffee,
we'd call them over, we'd all sit together. We had no problems either. In some
ways, it was better then." He looked at Lisidro and stopped. "We're just here taking care of the house. If you ever wanted to return —"

Lisette shook her head. "First time," she began. "What I mean is, if this is
my first time here, how could I return?"

She looked around the table and thought to smile. Finally, Alicia laughed
and they all joined in. Alicia took Lisette by the hand.

"Come, I'll show you the rest."   100

Lisette paused. She could see from where she sat that the rest was another
small room with a chair and beyond that a room that she guessed to be where
Matún and Alicia slept.

"No, gracias." Lisette pulled her hand out of Alicia's and patted her shoulder. "Later — I'll see it for the next time."

"You can't come all this way and not see the house!" Matún shouted.

"It's okay," Alicia said, looking at Lisette. "She's tired."

"Yes, I'm enough tired from the trip."   105

"Nonsense!"

Matún took her by the hand.

"One minute only."

Lisette stood and nodded. She let her hand relax in Matún's.

The narrow hallway that ran from the kitchen connected a small sitting 110
room to two back rooms, each painted green.

"Your mother slept here," Matún said with a flourish of his arm.

A lace curtain covered the top half of the window, darkening the room. A
wooden dresser was pushed up against the corner, its knobs worn black and
shiny. The narrow bed was straight and tidy under the window.

Matún followed her gaze and nodded.

"Everything here was hers."

The others walked out and Lisette stood for a moment at the door. She 115
walked into the room, half hearing Matún, not seeing the small rug, the low
double bed, the flowered curtain strung across one corner.

She turned and walked out, following a crack in the floorboards. Lisidro and
Alicia sat in two rocking chairs. A broom leaned against the door.

"My mother —" Lisette began, then stopped. She turned toward the door.
When she turned back, she could feel the heat in her cheeks.

"My husband would have been so pleased to see this," she said. "It's too
bad." She folded her hands and said more to herself, "My husband, Erminio."

She let his name hang in the air. Alicia and Lisidro looked at one another, but no one spoke. Lisette breathed in and smiled. She took Matún's hands and kissed him on both cheeks.

"Gracias," she said. "I must go. I have much work."   120

Matún kissed her. Then he put his hands behind his back and turned his head to look out the small window as he spoke.

"You know. The government has been very helpful to us. Yes, very generous with us. They gave us this land when your grandparents left. Every Sunday, me and the wife drive the scooter to Havana and sell guavas and mangoes. We are not poor; we are doing very well," he said. "Thanks to our government and the grace of God."

Alicia pulled her shawl closer. The silence of the countryside was like a weight. Lisette looked from Alicia to Matún. He was nodding to himself. "Thanks to the grace of God."

Lisette reached into her purse as if she were looking for her map. Then she took Matún's hands. She pressed the bill.

"Un regalito,"° she whispered.   125

His eyes never changed expression until he closed them and bowed ever so slightly. Gratitude and reproach, the small space between knowing and forgetting.

———

Lisette walked through the hallways, dragging one piece of furniture after another. She didn't know what she was doing. She needed to do something. And so she moved the armchair into the family room, the bar stools out to the pool. She stood and remembered the lights her father had strung all those years ago, that Christmas when the women loved Erminio. The gazebo was shabby now, a vein of mold running down one column. The lawn had grown over the flowers. It was as if the house had declined in sympathy with her father. In the last days of his illness, the Coral Gables code-enforcement board had sent them a complaint about the tall grass. Lisette had run two red lights in her anger. At city hall, she had ranted about the rights of man until a security guard escorted her out. She had regretted it and written a letter of apology later, a very proper repentance. She was an editor at the paper now, had her own office overlooking the bay. She was a little in love with a German psychologist who loved her back. In the evenings they had long conversations about the will and happiness. On Sundays, they had some people from his practice for lunch and she put out her good crystal and the leather-bound Rilke.°

When, alone with him, the people gone home, she would complain of despair, her sick parents, he would hold her face and tenderly ask, "Why do you not kill yourself?"

———

Un regalito: A present.   **Rilke:** Rainer Maria Rilke (1875–1926), famous twentieth-century German poet.

It was an old joke with them. And Lisette always laughed. Logotherapy, he called it the first time. And she'd understood loco therapy. There is meaning in this, he insisted. And he waved his arms, meaning everything. Yes, she'd said, it's all loco.

Lisette stopped at the door to her old room. She walked to the closet. From   130
the top shelf she pulled down a box and sat on the bed. It was the kind of box young women keep and she hadn't opened it since her last weeks in college. A graduation program sat on the top, yellowed and brittle and almost twenty years old. Bits of the foil that condoms came wrapped in. A dried corsage from her junior prom. A translucent pink cocktail stirrer whose origins had long ago disappeared into her memory. Below, near the bottom, a pink diary with a lock and a stack of photographs tight in a rubber band. Lisette winced. Had this been her life?

She sifted through the letters, names she'd forgotten, dates and places. She stopped, reached to her chest for her glasses. Love letters. Letters from friends. One note on linen paper which she opened, the paper crackling back into the present.

> L.:
> So happy you've finally decided to write that novel. I think the Cuban experience is a great idea for a book. You have to promise me one thing: You have to make fun of them. There's no other way to write this. Send what you have.
>   Love you. Miss you. Can't wait to see you.
>   A.

The letter was typed, as if the sender wanted to remove the last trace of himself. She couldn't remember receiving it. Who was A.? Had she ever thought of writing a novel? She remembered writers she'd known in college, students, a man who had followed her for days. Was it the editor who had told her she had Great Potential? A lover? A prankster? Her ex-husband?

Had she written the note herself? She sat at her old bed and tried to reach back into the years. She met herself going the other way. Promising she would never write, never publish, never be a special section in the bookstore. Better to write about berms and set-asides, last night's vote in a small room of microphones and lights.

She took a pencil from the box. She read the letter again and folded it in half. She stared for a moment at her hand. And then she began to write:

> Beautiful Coral Gables home, five bedrooms, three baths, vaulted ceilings in the dining room. Balcony with wrought-iron railings overlooking large pool. Entrance flanked by royal palms.

She paused and added, The house of your dreams.

Outside by the gazebo, she slipped the letter into her pocket. She stood still   135
to hear a peacock send its melancholy wail through the yard. A car passed the

house slowly, its engine low and hungry. Tomorrow she would air the house out and the next day she would call the realtor, tell her she was in a hurry. She walked up the creaking wood steps and sat on the railing, looking out over the fraying yard. Her parents had thrown a party here after she'd returned from Cuba, all of them healthy and young, the orange trees in blossom, her cousin's daughters splashing in the pool. She'd looked up at the house, the palms framed against the sky.

What was it like? What was the house like? The children's laughter like punctuation marks.

Only her mother was silent. She sat across from her, her hands in her lap. Lisette followed her gaze. The day was bright, shimmering above the water. Lisette spoke slowly. It was too bad, she began, that the soldier had taken her camera. There was so much to see. The road to the house that crossed a wooden bridge into a field of sugarcane. The narrow path flanked on both sides by royal palms. It was a late afternoon in summer and the men were coming in from the fields, their hats flopping softly in the breeze.

But the house. What about the house?

Lisette paused, making a circle with her arms. She looked at her mother. Watched her hands turn in her lap.

"Everything was the same," Lisette said after a moment. "The stairway, the balconies. Even the marble fireplace. Somehow, it all made it through the revolution."   140

She faced her mother. Held her chin in her hands.

"And the long white-shuttered windows that looked over the rose garden still let in the very brightest sunshine."

The children had stopped by the edge of the pool to listen. One by one they moved away to resume their game. Her father let his gaze fall. Lisette's mother looked up. She stood and Lisette watched her go. Her cousin came out with the guitar. The chatter of the afternoon resumed. Someone passed by and patted her on the head.

Lisette closed her eyes. The guitar played a slow bolero and Lisette remembered Erminio, his Sunday poems; she saw him again against the light, pouring her morning coffee. He had wrapped his arms around her tight, held her steady against the day.

Toni Morrison b. 1931

Recitatif   [1983]

My mother danced all night and Roberta's was sick. That's why we were taken to St. Bonny's. People want to put their arms around you when you tell them you were in a shelter, but it really wasn't bad. No big long room with one hundred beds like Bellevue. There were four to a room, and when Roberta and me came, there was a shortage of state kids, so we were the only ones assigned to 406 and could go from bed to bed if we wanted to. And we wanted to, too. We changed beds every night and for the whole four months we were there we never picked one out as our own permanent bed.

It didn't start out that way. The minute I walked in and the Big Bozo introduced us, I got sick to my stomach. It was one thing to be taken out of your own bed early in the morning — it was something else to be stuck in a strange place with a girl from a whole other race. And Mary, that's my mother, she was right. Every now and then she would stop dancing long enough to tell me something important and one of the things she said was that they never washed their hair and they smelled funny. Roberta sure did. Smell funny, I mean. So when the Big Bozo (nobody ever called her Mrs. Itkin, just like nobody ever said St. Bonaventure) — when she said, "Twyla, this is Roberta. Roberta, this is Twyla. Make each other welcome." I said, "My mother won't like you putting me in here."

"Good," said Bozo. "Maybe then she'll come and take you home."

How's that for mean? If Roberta had laughed I would have killed her, but she didn't. She just walked over to the window and stood with her back to us.

"Turn around," said the Bozo. "Don't be rude. Now Twyla. Roberta. When   5 you hear a loud buzzer, that's the call for dinner. Come down to the first floor. Any fights and no movie." And then, just to make sure we knew what we would be missing, *"The Wizard of Oz."*

Roberta must have thought I meant that my mother would be mad about my being put in the shelter. Not about rooming with her, because as soon as Bozo left she came over to me and said, "Is your mother sick too?"

"No," I said. "She just likes to dance all night."

"Oh," she nodded her head and I liked the way she understood things so fast. So for the moment it didn't matter that we looked like salt and pepper standing there and that's what the other kids called us sometimes. We were eight years old and got F's all the time. Me because I couldn't remember what I read or what the teacher said. And Roberta because she couldn't read at all and didn't even listen to the teacher. She wasn't good at anything except jacks, at which she was a killer: pow scoop pow scoop pow scoop.

We didn't like each other all that much at first, but nobody else wanted to play with us because we weren't real orphans with beautiful dead parents in the sky. We were dumped. Even the New York City Puerto Ricans and the upstate Indians ignored us. All kinds of kids were in there, black ones, white ones, even two Koreans. The food was good, though. At least I thought so. Roberta hated it and left whole pieces of things on her plate: Spam, Salisbury steak — even jello with fruit cocktail in it, and she didn't care if I ate what she wouldn't. Mary's idea of supper was popcorn and a can of Yoo-Hoo. Hot mashed potatoes and two weenies was like Thanksgiving for me.

It really wasn't bad, St. Bonny's. The big girls on the second floor pushed us   10 around now and then. But that was all. They wore lipstick and eyebrow pencil and wobbled their knees while they watched TV. Fifteen, sixteen, even, some of them were. They were put-out girls, scared runaways most of them. Poor little girls who fought their uncles off but looked tough to us, and mean. God did they look mean. The staff tried to keep them separate from the younger children, but sometimes they caught us watching them in the orchard where they played radios and danced with each other. They'd light out after us and pull our hair or twist our arms. We were scared of them, Roberta and me, but neither of us wanted the other one to know it. So we got a good list of dirty names we could shout back when we ran from them through the orchard. I used to dream a lot and almost always the orchard was there. Two acres, four maybe, of these little apple trees. Hundreds of them. Empty and crooked like beggar women when I first came to St. Bonny's but fat with flowers when I left. I don't know why I dreamt about that orchard so much. Nothing really happened there. Nothing all that important, I mean. Just the big girls dancing and playing the radio. Roberta and me watching. Maggie fell down there once. The kitchen woman with legs like parentheses. And the big girls laughed at her. We should have helped her up, I know, but we were scared of those girls with lipstick and eyebrow pencil. Maggie couldn't talk. The kids said she had her tongue cut out, but I think she was just born that way: mute. She was old and sandy-colored and she worked in the kitchen. I don't know if she was nice or not. I just remember her legs like parentheses and how she rocked when she walked. She worked from early in the morning till two o'clock, and if she was late, if she had too much cleaning and didn't get out till two-fifteen or so, she'd cut through the orchard so she wouldn't miss her bus and have to wait another hour. She wore this really stupid little hat — a kid's hat with ear flaps — and she wasn't much taller than we were. A really awful little hat. Even for a mute, it was dumb — dressing like a kid and never saying anything at all.

"But what about if somebody tries to kill her?" I used to wonder about that. "Or what if she wants to cry? Can she cry?"

"Sure," Roberta said. "But just tears. No sounds come out."

"She can't scream?"

"Nope. Nothing."

"Can she hear?"

"I guess."

"Let's call her," I said. And we did.

"Dummy! Dummy!" She never turned her head.

"Bow legs! Bow legs!" Nothing. She just rocked on, the chin straps of her baby-boy hat swaying from side to side. I think we were wrong. I think she could hear and didn't let on. And it shames me even now to think there was somebody in there after all who heard us call her those names and couldn't tell on us.

We got along all right, Roberta and me. Changed beds every night, got F's in civics and communication skills and gym. The Bozo was disappointed in us, she said. Out of 130 of us state cases, 90 were under twelve. Almost all were real orphans with beautiful dead parents in the sky. We were the only ones dumped and the only ones with F's in three classes including gym. So we got along — what with her leaving whole pieces of things on her plate and being nice about not asking questions.

I think it was the day before Maggie fell down that we found out our mothers were coming to visit us on the same Sunday. We had been at the shelter twenty-eight days (Roberta twenty-eight and a half) and this was their first visit with us. Our mothers would come at ten o'clock in time for chapel, then lunch with us in the teachers' lounge. I thought if my dancing mother met her sick mother it might be good for her. And Roberta thought her sick mother would get a big bang out of a dancing one. We got excited about it and curled each other's hair. After breakfast we sat on the bed watching the road from the window. Roberta's socks were still wet. She washed them the night before and put them on the radiator to dry. They hadn't, but she put them on anyway because their tops were so pretty—scalloped in pink. Each of us had a purple construction-paper basket that we had made in craft class. Mine had a yellow crayon rabbit on it. Roberta's had eggs with wiggly lines of color. Inside were cellophane grass and just the jelly beans because I'd eaten the two marshmallow eggs they gave us. The Big Bozo came herself to get us. Smiling she told us we looked very nice and to come downstairs. We were so surprised by the smile we'd never seen before, neither of us moved.

"Don't you want to see your mommies?"

I stood up first and spilled the jelly beans all over the floor. Bozo's smile disappeared while we scrambled to get the candy up off the floor and put it back in the grass.

She escorted us downstairs to the first floor, where the other girls were lining up to file into the chapel. A bunch of grown-ups stood to one side. Viewers mostly. The old biddies who wanted servants and the fags who wanted company looking for children they might want to adopt. Once in a while a grandmother. Almost never anybody young or anybody whose face wouldn't scare you in the night. Because if any of the real orphans had young relatives they wouldn't be real orphans. I saw Mary right away. She had on those green slacks I hated and hated even more now because didn't she know we were going to chapel? And that fur jacket with the pocket linings so ripped she had to pull to get her hands out of them. But her face was pretty—like always, and she smiled and waved like she was the little girl looking for her mother—not me.

I walked slowly, trying not to drop the jelly beans and hoping the paper handle would hold. I had to use my last Chiclet because by the time I finished cutting everything out, all the Elmer's was gone. I am left-handed and the scissors never worked for me. It didn't matter, though; I might just as well have chewed the gum. Mary dropped to her knees and grabbed me, mashing the basket, the jelly beans, and the grass into her ratty fur jacket.

"Twyla, baby. Twyla, baby!"

I could have killed her. Already I heard the big girls in the orchard the next time saying, "Twyyyyyla, baby!" But I couldn't stay mad at Mary while she was smiling and hugging me and smelling of Lady Esther dusting powder. I wanted to stay buried in her fur all day.

To tell the truth I forgot about Roberta. Mary and I got in line for the traipse into chapel and I was feeling proud because she looked so beautiful even in those ugly green slacks that made her behind stick out. A pretty mother on earth is better than a beautiful dead one in the sky even if she did leave you all alone to go dancing.

I felt a tap on my shoulder, turned, and saw Roberta smiling. I smiled back, but not too much lest somebody think this visit was the biggest thing that ever happened in my life. Then Roberta said, "Mother, I want you to meet my room-mate, Twyla. And that's Twyla's mother."

I looked up it seemed for miles. She was big. Bigger than any man and on her chest was the biggest cross I'd ever seen. I swear it was six inches long each way. And in the crook of her arm was the biggest Bible ever made.

Mary, simple-minded as ever, grinned and tried to yank her hand out of the pocket with the raggedy lining — to shake hands, I guess. Roberta's mother looked down at me and then looked down at Mary too. She didn't say anything, just grabbed Roberta with her Bible-free hand and stepped out of line, walking quickly to the rear of it. Mary was still grinning because she's not too swift when it comes to what's really going on. Then this light bulb goes off in her head and she says "That bitch!" really loud and us almost in the chapel now. Organ music whining; the Bonny Angels singing sweetly. Everybody in the world turned around to look. And Mary would have kept it up — kept calling names if I hadn't squeezed her hand as hard as I could. That helped a little, but she still twitched and crossed and uncrossed her legs all through service. Even groaned a couple of times. Why did I think she would come there and act right? Slacks. No hat like the grandmothers and viewers, and groaning all the while. When we stood for hymns she kept her mouth shut. Wouldn't even look at the words on the page. She actually reached in her purse for a mirror to check her lipstick. All I could think of was that she really needed to be killed. The sermon lasted a year, and I knew the real orphans were looking smug again.

We were supposed to have lunch in the teachers' lounge, but Mary didn't bring anything, so we picked fur and cellophane grass off the mashed jelly beans and ate them. I could have killed her. I sneaked a look at Roberta. Her mother had brought chicken legs and ham sandwiches and oranges and a whole box of chocolate-covered grahams. Roberta drank milk from a thermos while her mother read the Bible to her.

Things are not right. The wrong food is always with the wrong people. Maybe that's why I got into waitress work later — to match up the right people with the right food. Roberta just let those chicken legs sit there, but she did bring a stack of grahams up to me later when the visit was over. I think she was sorry that her mother would not shake my mother's hand. And I liked that and I liked the fact that she didn't say a word about Mary groaning all the way through the service and not bringing any lunch.

Roberta left in May when the apple trees were heavy and white. On her last day we went to the orchard to watch the big girls smoke and dance by the radio. It didn't matter that they said, "Twyyyyyla, baby." We sat on the ground and breathed. Lady Esther. Apple blossoms. I still go soft when I smell one or the other. Roberta was going home. The big cross and the big Bible was coming to get her and she seemed sort of glad and sort of not. I thought I would die in that room of four beds without her and I knew Bozo had plans to move some other dumped kid in there with me. Roberta promised to write every day, which was really sweet of her because she couldn't read a lick so how could she write anybody. I would have drawn pictures and sent them to her but she never gave me her address. Little by little she faded. Her wet socks with the pink scalloped tops and her big serious-looking eyes — that's all I could catch when I tried to bring her to mind.

I was working behind the counter at the Howard Johnson's on the Thruway 35 just before the Kingston exit. Not a bad job. Kind of a long ride from Newburgh, but okay once I got there. Mine was the second night shift — eleven to seven. Very light until a Greyhound checked in for breakfast around six-thirty. At that hour the sun was all the way clear of the hills behind the restaurant. The place looked better at night — more like shelter — but I loved it when the sun broke in, even if it did show all the cracks in the vinyl and the speckled floor looked dirty no matter what the mop boy did.

It was August and a bus crowd was just unloading. They would stand around a long while: going to the john, and looking at gifts and junk-for-sale machines, reluctant to sit down so soon. Even to eat. I was trying to fill the coffee pots and get them all situated on the electric burners when I saw her. She was sitting in a booth smoking a cigarette with two guys smothered in head and facial hair. Her own hair was so big and wild I could hardly see her face. But the eyes. I would know them anywhere. She had on a powder-blue halter and shorts outfit and earrings the size of bracelets. Talk about lipstick and eyebrow pencil. She made the big girls look like nuns. I couldn't get off the counter until seven o'clock, but I kept watching the booth in case they got up to leave before that. My replacement was on time for a change, so I counted and stacked my receipts as fast as I could and signed off. I walked over to the booth, smiling and wondering if she would remember me. Or even if she wanted to remember me. Maybe she didn't want to be reminded of St. Bonny's or to have anybody know she was ever there. I know I never talked about it to anybody.

I put my hands in my apron pockets and leaned against the back of the booth facing them.

"Roberta? Roberta Fisk?"

She looked up. "Yeah?"

"Twyla."

She squinted for a second and then said, "Wow." 40

"Remember me?"

"Sure. Hey. Wow."

"It's been a while," I said, and gave a smile to the two hairy guys.

"Yeah. Wow. You work here?" 45

"Yeah," I said. "I live in Newburgh."

"Newburgh? No kidding?" She laughed then a private laugh that included the guys but only the guys, and they laughed with her. What could I do but laugh too and wonder why I was standing there with my knees showing out from under that uniform. Without looking I could see the blue and white triangle on my head, my hair shapeless in a net, my ankles thick in white oxfords. Nothing could have been less sheer than my stockings. There was this silence that came down right after I laughed. A silence it was her turn to fill up. With introductions, maybe, to her boyfriends or an invitation to sit down and have a Coke. Instead she lit a cigarette off the one she'd just finished and said, "We're on our way to the Coast. He's got an appointment with Hendrix." She gestured casually toward the boy next to her.

"Hendrix? Fantastic," I said. "Really fantastic. What's she doing now?"

Roberta coughed on her cigarette and the two guys rolled their eyes up at the ceiling.

"Hendrix. Jimi Hendrix, asshole. He's only the biggest—Oh, wow. Forget it." 50

I was dismissed without anyone saying goodbye, so I thought I would do it for her.

"How's your mother?" I asked. Her grin cracked her whole face. She swallowed. "Fine," she said. "How's yours?"

"Pretty as a picture," I said and turned away. The backs of my knees were damp. Howard Johnson's really was a dump in the sunlight.

James is as comfortable as a house slipper. He liked my cooking and I liked his big loud family. They have lived in Newburgh all of their lives and talk about it the way people do who have always known a home. His grandmother is a porch swing older than his father and when they talk about streets and avenues and buildings they call them names they no longer have. They still call the A & P Rico's because it stands on property once a mom and pop store owned by Mr. Rico. And they call the new community college Town Hall because it once was. My mother-in-law puts up jelly and cucumbers and buys butter wrapped in cloth from a dairy. James and his father talk about fishing and baseball and I can see them all together on the Hudson in a raggedy skiff. Half the population of Newburgh is on welfare now, but to my husband's family it was still some upstate paradise of a time long past. A time of ice houses and vegetable wagons, coal furnaces and children weeding gardens. When our son was born my mother-in-law gave me the crib blanket that had been hers.

But the town they remembered had changed. Something quick was in the 55 air. Magnificent old houses, so ruined they had become shelter for squatters and rent risks, were bought and renovated. Smart IBM people moved out of their suburbs back into the city and put shutters up and herb gardens in their backyards. A brochure came in the mail announcing the opening of a Food Emporium. Gourmet food it said—and listed items the rich IBM crowd would want. It was located in a new mall at the edge of town and I drove out to shop there one day—just to see. It was late in June. After the tulips were gone and the Queen Elizabeth roses were open everywhere. I trailed my cart along the aisle tossing in smoked oysters and Robert's sauce and things I knew would sit in my cupboard for years. Only when I found some Klondike ice cream bars did I feel less guilty about spending James's fireman's salary so foolishly. My father-in-law ate them with the same gusto little Joseph did.

Waiting in the check-out line I heard a voice say, "Twyla!"

The classical music piped over the aisles had affected me and the woman leaning toward me was dressed to kill. Diamonds on her hand, a smart white summer dress. "I'm Mrs. Benson," I said.

"Ho. Ho. The Big Bozo," she sang.

For a split second I didn't know what she was talking about. She had a bunch of asparagus and two cartons of fancy water.

"Roberta!"

"Right."

"For heaven's sake. Roberta."

"You look great," she said.

"So do you. Where are you? Here? In Newburgh?"

"Yes. Over in Annandale."

I was opening my mouth to say more when the cashier called my attention to her empty counter.

"Meet you outside." Roberta pointed her finger and went into the express line.

I placed the groceries and kept myself from glancing around to check Roberta's progress. I remembered Howard Johnson's and looking for a chance to speak only to be greeted with a stingy "wow." But she was waiting for me and her huge hair was sleek now, smooth around a small, nicely shaped head. Shoes, dress, everything lovely and summery and rich. I was dying to know what happened to her, how she got from Jimi Hendrix to Annandale, a neighborhood full of doctors and IBM executives. Easy, I thought. Everything is so easy for them. They think they own the world.

"How long," I asked her. "How long have you been here?"

"A year. I got married to a man who lives here. And you, you're married too, right? Benson, you said."

"Yeah. James Benson."

"And is he nice?"

"Oh, is he nice?"

"Well, is he?" Roberta's eyes were steady as though she really meant the question and wanted an answer.

"He's wonderful, Roberta. Wonderful."

"So you're happy."

"Very."

"That's good," she said and nodded her head. "I always hoped you'd be happy. Any kids? I know you have kids."

"One. A boy. How about you?"

"Four."

"Four?"

She laughed. "Step kids. He's a widower."

"Oh."

"Got a minute? Let's have a coffee."

I thought about the Klondikes melting and the inconvenience of going all the way to my car and putting the bags in the trunk. Served me right for buying all that stuff I didn't need. Roberta was ahead of me.

"Put them in my car. It's right here."
And then I saw the dark blue limousine.
"You married a Chinaman?"
"No," she laughed. "He's the driver."
"Oh, my. If the Big Bozo could see you now."   90

We both giggled. Really giggled. Suddenly, in just a pulse beat, twenty years disappeared and all of it came rushing back. The big girls (whom we called gar girls—Roberta's misheard word for the evil stone faces described in a civics class) there dancing in the orchard, the ploppy mashed potatoes, the double weenies, the Spam with pineapple. We went into the coffee shop holding on to one another and I tried to think why we were glad to see each other this time and not before. Once, twelve years ago, we passed like strangers. A black girl and a white girl meeting in a Howard Johnson's on the road and having nothing to say. One in a blue and white triangle waitress hat—the other on her way to see Hendrix. Now we were behaving like sisters separated for much too long. Those four short months were nothing in time. Maybe it was the thing itself. Just being there, together. Two little girls who knew what nobody else in the world knew—how not to ask questions. How to believe what had to be believed. There was politeness in that reluctance and generosity as well. Is your mother sick too? No, she dances all night. Oh—and an understanding nod.

We sat in a booth by the window and fell into recollection like veterans.
"Did you ever learn to read?"
"Watch." She picked up the menu. "Special of the day. Cream of corn soup. Entrées. Two dots and a wriggly line. Quiche. Chef salad, scallops . . ."
I was laughing and applauding when the waitress came up.   95
"Remember the Easter baskets?"
"And how we tried to *introduce* them?"
"Your mother with that cross like two telephone poles."
"And yours with those tight slacks."
We laughed so loudly heads turned and made the laughter harder to suppress. 100
"What happened to the Jimi Hendrix date?"
Roberta made a blow-out sound with her lips.
"When he died I thought about you."
"Oh, you heard about him finally?"
"Finally. Come on, I was a small-town country waitress."   105
"And I was a small-town country dropout. God, were we wild. I still don't know how I got out of there alive."
"But you did."
"I did. I really did. Now I'm Mrs. Kenneth Norton."
"Sounds like a mouthful."
"It is."   110
"Servants and all?"
Roberta held up two fingers.
"Ow! What does he do?"
"Computers and stuff. What do I know?"

"I don't remember a hell of a lot from those days, but Lord, St. Bonny's is as   115
clear as daylight. Remember Maggie? The day she fell down and those gar girls
laughed at her?"

Roberta looked up from her salad and stared at me. "Maggie didn't fall," she
said.

"Yes, she did. You remember."

"No, Twyla. They knocked her down. Those girls pushed her down and tore
her clothes. In the orchard."

"I don't—that's not what happened."

"Sure it is. In the orchard. Remember how scared we were?"   120

"Wait a minute. I don't remember any of that."

"And Bozo was fired."

"You're crazy. She was there when I left. You left before me."

"I went back. You weren't there when they fired Bozo."

"What?"   125

"Twice. Once for a year when I was about ten, another for two months
when I was fourteen. That's when I ran away."

"You ran away from St. Bonny's?"

"I had to. What do you want? Me dancing in that orchard?"

"Are you sure about Maggie?"

"Of course I'm sure. You've blocked it, Twyla. It happened. Those girls had   130
behavior problems, you know."

"Didn't they, though. But why can't I remember the Maggie thing?"

"Believe me. It happened. And we were there."

"Who did you room with when you went back?" I asked her as if I would
know her. The Maggie thing was troubling me.

"Creeps. They tickled themselves in the night."

My ears were itching and I wanted to go home suddenly. This was all very well   135
but she couldn't just comb her hair, wash her face and pretend everything was
hunky-dory. After the Howard Johnson's snub. And no apology. Nothing.

"Were you on dope or what that time at Howard Johnson's?" I tried to make
my voice sound friendlier than I felt.

"Maybe, a little. I never did drugs much. Why?"

"I don't know; you acted sort of like you didn't want to know me then."

"Oh, Twyla, you know how it was in those days: black—white. You know
how everything was."

But I didn't know. I thought it was just the opposite. Busloads of blacks and   140
whites came into Howard Johnson's together. They roamed together then: students, musicians, lovers, protesters. You got to see everything at Howard Johnson's and blacks were very friendly with whites in those days. But sitting there
with nothing on my plate but two hard tomato wedges wondering about the
melting Klondikes it seemed childish remembering the slight. We went to her
car, and with the help of the driver, got my stuff into my station wagon.

"We'll keep in touch this time," she said.

"Sure," I said. "Sure. Give me a call."

"I will," she said, and then just as I was sliding behind the wheel, she leaned into the window. "By the way. Your mother. Did she ever stop dancing?"

I shook my head. "No. Never."

Roberta nodded.   145

"And yours? Did she ever get well?"

She smiled a tiny sad smile. "No. She never did. Look, call me, okay?"

"Okay," I said, but I knew I wouldn't. Roberta had messed up my past some-how with that business about Maggie. I wouldn't forget a thing like that. Would I?

Strife came to us that fall. At least that's what the paper called it. Strife. Racial strife. The word made me think of a bird—a big shrieking bird out of 1,000,000,000 B.C. Flapping its wings and cawing. Its eye with no lid always bearing down on you. All day it screeched and at night it slept on the rooftops. It woke you in the morning and from the *Today* show to the eleven o'clock news it kept you an awful company. I couldn't figure it out from one day to the next. I knew I was supposed to feel something strong, but I didn't know what, and James wasn't any help. Joseph was on the list of kids to be transferred from the junior high school to another one at some far-out-of-the-way place and I thought it was a good thing until I heard it was a bad thing. I mean I didn't know. All the schools seemed dumps to me, and the fact that one was nicer looking didn't hold much weight. But the papers were full of it and then the kids began to get jumpy. In August, mind you. Schools weren't even open yet. I thought Joseph might be frightened to go over there, but he didn't seem scared so I forgot about it, until I found myself driving along Hudson Street out there by the school they were trying to integrate and saw a line of women marching. And who do you suppose was in line, big as life, holding a sign in front of her bigger than her mother's cross? MOTHERS HAVE RIGHTS TOO! —it said.

I drove on, and then changed my mind. I circled the block, slowed down,   150 and honked my horn.

Roberta looked over and when she saw me she waved. I didn't wave back, but I didn't move either. She handed her sign to another woman and came over to where I was parked.

"Hi."

"What are you doing?"

"Picketing. What's it look like?"

"What for?"   155

"What do you mean, 'What for?' They want to take my kids and send them out of the neighborhood. They don't want to go."

"So what if they go to another school? My boy's being bussed too, and I don't mind. Why should you?"

"It's not about us, Twyla. Me and you. It's about our kids."

"What's more *us* than that?"

"Well, it is a free country."   160

"Not yet, but it will be."

"What the hell does that mean? I'm not doing anything to you."

"You really think that?"

"I know it."

"I wonder what made me think you were different."   165

"I wonder what made me think you were different."

"Look at them," I said. "Just look. Who do they think they are? Swarming all over the place like they own it. And now they think they can decide where my child goes to school. Look at them, Roberta. They're Bozos."

Roberta turned around and looked at the women. Almost all of them were standing still now, waiting. Some were even edging toward us. Roberta looked at me out of some refrigerator behind her eyes. "No, they're not. They're just mothers."

"And what am I? Swiss cheese?"

"I used to curl your hair."   170

"I hated your hands in my hair."

The women were moving. Our faces looked mean to them of course and they looked as though they could not wait to throw themselves in front of a police car, or better yet, into my car and drag me away by my ankles. Now they surrounded my car and gently, gently began to rock it. I swayed back and forth like a sideways yo-yo. Automatically I reached for Roberta, like the old days in the orchard when they saw us watching them and we had to get out of there, and if one of us fell the other pulled her up and if one of us was caught the other stayed to kick and scratch, and neither would leave the other behind. My arm shot out of the car window but no receiving hand was there. Roberta was look-ing at me sway from side to side in the car and her face was still. My purse slid from the car seat down under the dashboard. The four policemen who had been drinking Tab in their car finally got the message and strolled over, forcing their way through the women. Quietly, firmly they spoke. "Okay, ladies. Back in line or off the streets."

Some of them went away willingly; others had to be urged away from the car doors and the hood. Roberta didn't move. She was looking steadily at me. I was fumbling to turn on the ignition, which wouldn't catch because the gearshift was still in drive. The seats of the car were a mess because the swaying had thrown my grocery coupons all over it and my purse was sprawled on the floor.

"Maybe I am different now, Twyla. But you're not. You're the same little state kid who kicked a poor old black lady when she was down on the ground. You kicked a black lady and you have the nerve to call me a bigot."

The coupons were everywhere and the guts of my purse were bunched under   175
the dashboard. What was she saying? Black? Maggie wasn't black.

"She wasn't black," I said.

"Like hell she wasn't, and you kicked her. We both did. You kicked a black lady who couldn't even scream."

"Liar!"

"You're the liar! Why don't you just go on home and leave us alone, huh?"

She turned away and I skidded away from the curb.   180

The next morning I went into the garage and cut the side out of the carton our portable TV had come in. It wasn't nearly big enough, but after a while I had

a decent sign: red spray-painted letters on a white background — AND SO DO CHIL-
DREN****. I meant just to go down to the school and tack it up somewhere so
those cows on the picket line across the street could see it, but when I got there,
some ten or so others had already assembled — protesting the cows across the
street. Police permits and everything. I got in line and we strutted in time on our
side while Roberta's group strutted on theirs. That first day we were all dignified,
pretending the other side didn't exist. The second day there was name calling
and finger gestures. But that was about all. People changed signs from time to
time, but Roberta never did and neither did I. Actually my sign didn't make
sense without Roberta's. "And so do children what?" one of the women on my
side asked me. Have rights, I said, as though it was obvious.

Roberta didn't acknowledge my presence in any way and I got to thinking
maybe she didn't know I was there. I began to pace myself in the line, jostling
people one minute and lagging behind the next, so Roberta and I could reach the
end of our respective lines at the same time and there would be a moment in our
turn when we would face each other. Still, I couldn't tell whether she saw me
and knew my sign was for her. The next day I went early before we were scheduled to assemble. I waited until she got there before I exposed my new creation.
As soon as she hoisted her MOTHERS HAVE RIGHTS TOO I began to wave my new one,
which said, HOW WOULD YOU KNOW? I know she saw that one, but I had gotten
addicted now. My signs got crazier each day, and the women on my side decided
that I was a kook. They couldn't make heads or tails out of my brilliant screaming posters.

I brought a painted sign in queenly red with huge black letters that said, IS
YOUR MOTHER WELL? Roberta took her lunch break and didn't come back for the
rest of the day or any day after. Two days later I stopped going too and couldn't
have been missed because nobody understood my signs anyway.

It was a nasty six weeks. Classes were suspended and Joseph didn't go to
anybody's school until October. The children — everybody's children — soon got
bored with that extended vacation they thought was going to be so great. They
looked at TV until their eyes flattened. I spent a couple of mornings tutoring my
son, as the other mothers said we should. Twice I opened a text from last year
that he had never turned in. Twice he yawned in my face. Other mothers organized living room sessions so the kids would keep up. None of the kids could
concentrate so they drifted back to *The Price Is Right* and *The Brady Bunch*.
When the school finally opened there were fights once or twice and some sirens
roared through the streets every once in a while. There were a lot of photographers from Albany. And just when ABC was about to send up a news crew, the
kids settled down like nothing in the world had happened. Joseph hung my HOW
WOULD YOU KNOW? sign in his bedroom. I don't know what became of AND SO DO
CHILDREN****. I think my father-in-law cleaned some fish on it. He was always
puttering around in our garage. Each of his five children lived in Newburgh and
he acted as though he had five extra homes.

I couldn't help looking for Roberta when Joseph graduated from high 185
school, but I didn't see her. It didn't trouble me much what she had said to me
in the car. I mean the kicking part. I know I didn't do that, I couldn't do that.

But I was puzzled by her telling me Maggie was black. When I thought about it I actually couldn't be certain. She wasn't pitch-black, I knew, or I would have remembered that. What I remember was the kiddie hat, and the semicircle legs. I tried to reassure myself about the race thing for a long time until it dawned on me that the truth was already there, and Roberta knew it. I didn't kick her; I didn't join in with the gar girls and kick that lady, but I sure did want to. We watched and never tried to help her and never called for help. Maggie was my dancing mother. Deaf, I thought, and dumb. Nobody inside. Nobody who would hear you if you cried in the night. Nobody who could tell you anything important that you could use. Rocking, dancing, swaying as she walked. And when the gar girls pushed her down, and started roughhousing, I knew she wouldn't scream, couldn't — just like me — and I was glad about that.

We decided not to have a tree, because Christmas would be at my mother-in-law's house, so why have a tree at both places? Joseph was at SUNY New Paltz and we had to economize, we said. But at the last minute, I changed my mind. Nothing could be that bad. So I rushed around town looking for a tree, something small but wide. By the time I found a place, it was snowing and very late. I dawdled like it was the most important purchase in the world and the tree man was fed up with me. Finally I chose one and had it tied onto the trunk of the car. I drove away slowly because the sand trucks were not out yet and the streets could be murder at the beginning of a snowfall. Downtown the streets were wide and rather empty except for a cluster of people coming out of the Newburgh Hotel. The one hotel in town that wasn't built out of cardboard and Plexiglas. A party, probably. The men huddled in the snow were dressed in tails and the women had on furs. Shiny things glittered from underneath their coats. It made me tired to look at them. Tired, tired, tired. On the next corner was a small diner with loops and loops of paper bells in the window. I stopped the car and went in. Just for a cup of coffee and twenty minutes of peace before I went home and tried to finish everything before Christmas Eve.

"Twyla?"

There she was. In a silvery evening gown and dark fur coat. A man and another woman were with her, the man fumbling for change to put in the cigarette machine. The woman was humming and tapping on the counter with her fingernails. They all looked a little bit drunk.

"Well. It's you."

"How are you?"   190

I shrugged. "Pretty good. Frazzled. Christmas and all."

"Regular?" called the woman from the counter.

"Fine," Roberta called back and then, "Wait for me in the car."

She slipped into the booth beside me. "I have to tell you something, Twyla. I made up my mind if I ever saw you again, I'd tell you."

"I'd just as soon not hear anything, Roberta. It doesn't matter now,   195 anyway."

"No," she said. "Not about that."

"Don't be long," said the woman. She carried two regulars to go and the man peeled his cigarette pack as they left.

"It's about St. Bonny's and Maggie."

"Oh, please."

"Listen to me. I really did think she was black. I didn't make that up. I really 200 thought so. But now I can't be sure. I just remember her as old, so old. And because she couldn't talk—well, you know, I thought she was crazy. She'd been brought up in an institution like my mother was and like I thought I would be too. And you were right. We didn't kick her. It was the gar girls. Only them. But, well, I wanted to. I really wanted them to hurt her. I said we did it, too. You and me, but that's not true. And I don't want you to carry that around. It was just that I wanted to do it so bad that day—wanting to is doing it."

Her eyes were watery from the drinks she'd had, I guess. I know it's that way with me. One glass of wine and I start bawling over the littlest thing.

"We were kids, Roberta."

"Yeah. Yeah. I know, just kids."

"Eight."

"Eight."   205

"And lonely."

"Scared, too."

She wiped her cheeks with the heel of her hand and smiled. "Well, that's all I wanted to say."

I nodded and couldn't think of any way to fill the silence that went from the diner past the paper bells on out into the snow. It was heavy now. I thought I'd better wait for the sand trucks before starting home.

"Thanks, Roberta."   210

"Sure."

"Did I tell you? My mother, she never did stop dancing."

"Yes. You told me. And mine, she never got well." Roberta lifted her hands from the tabletop and covered her face with her palms. When she took them away she really was crying. "Oh shit, Twyla. Shit, shit, shit. What the hell happened to Maggie?"

Haruki Murakami   Japan, b. 1949

Birthday Girl   [2004]

Translated by Jay Rubin

She waited on tables as usual that day, her twentieth birthday. She always worked on Fridays, but if things had gone according to plan that particular Friday, she would have had the night off. The other part-time girl had agreed to switch shifts with her as a matter of course: being screamed at by an angry chef while lugging pumpkin gnocchi and seafood fritto misto to customers' tables was no way to spend one's twentieth birthday. But the other girl had aggravated a cold and gone to bed with unstoppable diarrhea and a fever of 104, so she ended up working after all on short notice.

She found herself trying to comfort the sick girl, who had called to apologize. "Don't worry about it," she said. "I wasn't going to do anything special anyway, even if it is my twentieth birthday."°

And in fact she was not all that disappointed. One reason was the terrible argument she had had a few days earlier with the boyfriend who was supposed to be with her that night. They had been going together since high school. The argument had started from nothing much but it had taken an unexpected turn for the worse until it became a long and bitter shouting match — one bad enough, she was pretty sure, to have snapped their long-standing ties once and for all. Something inside her had turned rock-hard and died. He had not called her since the blowup, and she was not about to call him.

Her workplace was one of the better-known Italian restaurants in the tony Roppongi district of Tokyo. It had been in business since the late sixties, and while its cuisine was hardly cutting edge, its high reputation was fully justified. It had many repeat customers and they were never disappointed. The dining room had a calm, relaxed atmosphere without a hint of pushiness. Rather than a young crowd, the restaurant drew an older clientele that included some famous stage people and writers.

The two full-time waiters worked six days a week. She and the other part-time waitress were students who took turns working three days each. In addition there was one floor manager and, at the register, a skinny middle-aged woman who supposedly had been there since the restaurant opened — literally sitting in the one place, it seemed, like some gloomy old character from *Little Dorrit*.° She had exactly two functions: to accept payment from the customers and to answer the phone. She spoke only when necessary and always wore the same black dress. There was something cold and hard about her: if you set her afloat on the nighttime sea, she would probably sink any boat that happened to ram her.

The floor manager was perhaps in his late forties. Tall and broad-shouldered, his build suggested that he had been a sportsman in his youth, but excess flesh was now beginning to accumulate on his belly and chin. His short, stiff hair was thinning at the crown, and a special aging bachelor smell clung to him — like newsprint that had been stored in a drawer with cough drops. She had a bachelor uncle who smelled like that.

The manager always wore a black suit, white shirt, and bow tie — not a clip-on bow tie, but the real thing, tied by hand. It was a point of pride for him that he could tie it perfectly without looking in the mirror. He performed his duties adroitly day after day. They consisted of checking the arrival and departure of guests, keeping abreast of the reservation schedule, knowing the names of regular customers, greeting them with a smile, lending a respectful ear to any com-

---

twentieth birthday: In Japan, the "coming of age" year, the beginning of adulthood. *Little Dorrit:* Satiric novel by Charles Dickens (1812–1870), published serially from 1885–1857.

plaints that might arise, giving expert advice on wines, and overseeing the work
of the waiters and waitresses. It was also his special task to deliver dinner to the
room of the restaurant's owner.

———————

"The owner had his own room on the sixth floor of the same building where
the restaurant was," she said. "An apartment, or office or something."

Somehow she and I had gotten on to the subject of our twentieth birthdays — what sort of day it had been for each of us. Most people remember the
day they turned twenty. Hers had happened more than ten years earlier.

"He never, ever showed his face in the restaurant, though. The only one who   10
saw him was the manager. It was strictly *his* job to deliver the owner's dinner to
him. None of the other employees knew what he looked like."

"So basically, the owner was getting home delivery from his own restaurant."

"Right," she said. "Every night at eight, the manager had to bring dinner to
the owner's room. It was the restaurant's busiest time, so having the manager
disappear just then was always a problem for us, but there was no way around it
because that was the way it had always been done. They'd load the dinner onto
one of those carts that hotels use for room service, the manager would push it
into the elevator wearing a respectful look on his face, and fifteen minutes later
he'd come back empty-handed. Then, an hour later, he'd go up again and bring
down the cart with empty plates and glasses. Every day, like clockwork. I thought
it was really weird the first time I saw it happen. It was like some kind of religious ritual, you know? But after a while I got used to it, and never gave it a second thought."

The owner always had chicken. The recipe and the vegetable sides were a
little different every day, but the main dish was always chicken. A young chef
once told her that he had tried sending up the same exact roast chicken every
day for a week just to see what would happen, but there was never any complaint. A chef wants to try different ways of preparing things, of course, and
each new chef would challenge himself with every technique for chicken that he
could think of. They'd make elegant sauces, they'd try chickens from different
suppliers, but none of their efforts had any effect: they might just as well have
been throwing pebbles into an empty cave. In the end, every one of them gave up
and sent the owner some run-of-the-mill chicken dish every day. That's all that
was ever asked of them.

Work started as usual on her twentieth birthday, November 17. It had been
raining on and off since the afternoon, and pouring since early evening. At five
o'clock the manager gathered the employees together to explain the day's spe-
cials. Servers were required to memorize them word for word and not use crib
sheets: veal Milanese, pasta topped with sardines and cabbage, chestnut mousse.
Sometimes the manager would play the role of a customer and test them with
questions. Then came the employees' meal: waiters in *this* restaurant were not
going to have growling stomachs as they took their customers' orders!

The restaurant opened its doors at six o'clock, but guests were slow to arrive 15 because of the downpour, and several reservations were simply canceled. Women didn't want their dresses ruined by the rain. The manager walked around tight-lipped, and the waiters killed time polishing the salt and pepper shakers or chatting with the chef about cooking. She surveyed the dining room with its single couple at table and listened to the harpsichord music flowing discreetly from ceiling speakers. A deep smell of late autumn rain worked its way into the restaurant.

It was after seven thirty when the manager started feeling sick. He stumbled over to a chair and sat there for a while pressing his stomach, as if he had just been shot. A greasy sweat clung to his forehead. "I think I'd better go to the hospital," he muttered. For him to be taken ill was a most unusual occurrence: he had never missed a day since he started working in the restaurant over ten years earlier. It was another point of pride for him that he had never been out with illness or injury, but his painful grimace made it clear that he was in very bad shape.

She stepped outside with an umbrella and hailed a cab. One of the waiters held the manager steady and climbed into the car with him to take him to a nearby hospital. Before ducking into the cab, the manager said to her hoarsely, "I want you to take a dinner up to room 604 at eight o'clock. All you have to do is ring the bell, say 'Your dinner is here,' and leave it."

"That's room 604, right?" she said.

"At eight o'clock," he repeated. "On the dot." He grimaced again, climbed in, and the taxi took him away.

The rain showed no signs of letting up after the manager had left, and cus- 20 tomers arrived at long intervals. No more than one or two tables were occupied at a time, so if the manager and one waiter had to be absent, this was a good time for it to happen. Things could get so busy that it was not unusual even for the full staff to have trouble coping.

When the owner's meal was ready at eight o'clock, she pushed the room service cart into the elevator and rode up to the sixth floor. It was the standard meal for him: a half bottle of red wine with the cork loosened, a thermal pot of coffee, a chicken entree with steamed vegetables, rolls and butter. The heavy aroma of cooked chicken quickly filled the little elevator. It mingled with the smell of the rain. Water droplets dotted the elevator floor, suggesting that someone with a wet umbrella had recently been aboard.

She pushed the cart down the corridor, bringing it to a stop in front of the door marked "604." She double-checked her memory: 604. That was it. She cleared her throat and pressed the doorbell.

There was no answer. She stood there for a good twenty seconds. Just as she was thinking of pressing the bell again, the door opened inward and a skinny old man appeared. He was shorter than she was, by some four or five inches. He had on a dark suit and a necktie. Against his white shirt, the tie stood out distinctly, its brownish yellow coloring like withered leaves. He made a very clean impression, his clothes perfectly pressed, his white hair smoothed down: he looked as though he were about to go out for the night to some sort of gathering. The deep wrinkles that creased his brow made her think of ravines in an aerial photograph.

"Your dinner, sir," she said in a husky voice, then quietly cleared her throat again. Her voice grew husky whenever she was tense.

"Dinner?"   25

"Yes, sir. The manager suddenly took sick. I had to take his place today. Your meal, sir."

"Oh, I see," the old man said, almost as if talking to himself, his hand still perched on the doorknob. "Took sick, eh? You don't say."

"His stomach started to hurt him all of a sudden. He went to the hospital. He thinks he might have appendicitis."

"Oh, that's not good," the old man said, running his fingers along the wrinkles of his forehead. "Not good at all."

She cleared her throat again. "Shall I bring your meal in, sir?" she asked.   30

"Ah yes, of course," the old man said. "Yes, of course, if you wish. That's fine with me."

If I wish? she thought. What a strange way to put it. What am I supposed to wish?

The old man opened the door the rest of the way, and she wheeled the cart inside. The floor had short gray carpeting with no area for removing shoes. The first room was a large study, as though the apartment was more a workplace than a residence. The window looked out on the nearby Tokyo Tower, its steel skeleton outlined in lights. A large desk stood by the window, and beside the desk was a compact sofa and love seat. The old man pointed to the plastic laminate coffee table in front of the sofa. She arranged his meal on the table: white napkin and silverware, coffeepot and cup, wine and wineglass, bread and butter, and the plate of chicken and vegetables.

"If you would be kind enough to set the dishes in the hall as usual, sir, I'll come to get them in an hour."

Her words seemed to snap him out of an appreciative contemplation of his   35
dinner. "Oh yes, of course. I'll put them in the hall. On the cart. In an hour. If you wish."

Yes, she replied inwardly, for the moment that is exactly what I wish. "Is there anything else I can do for you, sir?"

"No, I don't think so," he said after a moment's consideration. He was wearing black shoes polished to a high sheen. They were small and chic. He's a stylish dresser, she thought. And he stands very straight for his age.

"Well, then, sir, I'll be getting back to work."

"No, wait just a moment," he said.

"Sir?"   40

"Do you think it might be possible for you to give me five minutes of your time, miss? I have something I'd like to say to you."

He was so polite in his request that it made her blush. "I . . . think it should be all right," she said "I mean, if it really is just five minutes." He was her employer, after all. He was paying her by the hour. It was not a question of her giving or his taking her time. And this old man did not look like a person who would do anything bad to her.

"By the way, how old are you?" the old man asked, standing by the table with arms folded and looking directly into her eyes.

"I'm twenty now," she said.

"Twenty *now*," he repeated, narrowing his eyes as if peering through some kind of crack. "Twenty *now*. As of when?" 45

"Well, I just turned twenty," she said. After a moment's hesitation, she added, "Today is my birthday, sir."

"I *see*," he said, rubbing his chin as if this explained a great deal for him. "Today, is it? Today is your twentieth birthday?"

She nodded.

"Your life in this world began exactly twenty years ago today."

"Yes, sir," she said, "that is true." 50

"I see, I see," he said. "That's wonderful. Well, then, happy birthday."

"Thank you very much," she said, and then it dawned on her that this was the very first time all day that anyone had wished her a happy birthday. Of course, if her parents had called from Oita, she might find a message from them on her answering machine when she got home from work.

"Well, well, this is certainly a cause for celebration," he said. "How about a little toast? We can drink this red wine."

"Thank you, sir, but I couldn't, I'm working now."

"Oh, what's the harm in a little sip? No one's going to blame you if I say it's 55 all right. Just a token drink to celebrate."

The old man slid the cork from the bottle and dribbled a little wine into his glass for her. Then he took an ordinary drinking glass from a glass-doored cabinet and poured some wine for himself.

"Happy birthday," he said. "May you live a rich and fruitful life, and may there be nothing to cast dark shadows on it."

They clinked glasses.

May there be nothing to cast dark shadows on it: she silently repeated his remark to herself. Why had he chosen such unusual words for her birthday toast?

"Your twentieth birthday comes only once in a lifetime, miss. It's an irre- 60 placeable day."

"Yes, sir, I know," she said, taking one cautious sip of wine.

"And here, on your special day, you have taken the trouble to deliver my dinner to me like a kindhearted fairy."

"Just doing my job, sir."

"But still," the old man said with a few quick shakes of the head. "But still, lovely young miss."

The old man sat down in the leather chair by his desk and motioned her to 65 the sofa. She lowered herself gingerly onto the edge of the seat, with the wineglass still in her hand. Knees aligned, she tugged at her skirt, clearing her throat again. She saw raindrops tracing lines down the windowpane. The room was strangely quiet.

"Today just happens to be your twentieth birthday, and on top of that you have brought me this wonderful warm meal," the old man said as if reconfirming the situation. Then he set his glass on the desktop with a little thump. "This has to be some kind of special convergence, don't you think?"

Not quite convinced, she managed a nod.

"Which is why," he said, touching the knot of his withered-leaf-colored necktie, "I feel it is important for me to give you a birthday present. A special birthday calls for a special commemorative gift."

Flustered, she shook her head and said, "No, please, sir, don't give it a second thought. All I did was bring your meal the way they ordered me to."

The old man raised both hands, palms toward her. "No, miss, don't *you* give   70 it a second thought. The kind of 'present' I have in mind is not something tangible, not something with a price tag. To put it simply" — he placed his hands on the desk and took one long, slow breath — "what I would like to do for a lovely young fairy such as you is to grant a wish you might have, to make your wish come true. Anything. Anything at all that you wish for — assuming that you *do* have such a wish."

"A wish?" she asked, her throat dry.

"Something you would like to have happen, miss. If you have a wish — one wish, I'll make it come true. That is the kind of birthday present I can give you. But you had better think about it very carefully because I can grant you only one." He raised a finger. "Just one. You can't change your mind afterward and take it back."

She was at a loss for words. One wish? Whipped by the wind, raindrops tapped unevenly at the windowpane. As long as she remained silent, the old man looked into her eyes, saying nothing. Time marked its irregular pulse in her ears.

"I have to wish for something, and it will be granted?"

Instead of answering her question, the old man — hands still side by side on   75 the desk — just smiled. He did it in the most natural and amiable way.

"Do you *have* a wish, miss — or not?" he asked gently.

"This really did happen," she said, looking straight at me. "I'm not making it up."

"Of course not," I said. She was not the sort of person to invent some goofy story out of thin air. "So did you make a wish?"

She went on looking at me for a while, then released a tiny sigh. "Don't get me wrong," she said. "I wasn't taking him one hundred percent seriously myself. I mean, at twenty you're not exactly living in a fairy-tale world anymore. If this was his idea of a joke, though, I had to hand it to him for coming up with it on the spot. He was a dapper old fellow with a twinkle in his eye, so I decided to play along with him. It *was* my twentieth birthday, after all: I figured I ought to have *something* not-so-ordinary happen to me that day. It wasn't a question of believing or not believing."

I nodded without saying anything.

"You can understand how I felt, I'm sure. My twentieth birthday was coming to an end without anything special happening, nobody wishing me a happy birthday, and all I'm doing is carrying tortellini with anchovy sauce to people's tables."

I nodded again. "Don't worry," I said. "I understand."

"So I made a wish."

The old man kept his gaze fixed on her, saying nothing, hands still on the desk. Also on the desk were several thick folders that might have been account books, plus writing implements, a calendar, and a lamp with a green shade. Lying among them, his small hands looked like another set of desktop furnishings. The rain continued to beat against the window, the lights of Tokyo Tower filtering through the shattered drops.

The wrinkles on the old man's forehead deepened slightly. "That is your wish?"

"Yes," she said. "That is my wish."

"A bit unusual for a girl your age," he said. "I was expecting something different."

"If it's no good, I'll wish for something else," she said, clearing her throat. "I don't mind. I'll think of something else."

"No, no," the old man said, raising his hands and waving them like flags. "There's nothing wrong with it, not at all. It's just a little surprising, miss. Don't you have something else? Like, say, you want to be prettier, or smarter, or rich: you're OK with not wishing for something like that—something an ordinary girl would ask for?"

She took some moments to search for the right words. The old man just waited, saying nothing, his hands at rest together on the desk again.

"Of course I'd like to be prettier or smarter or rich. But I really can't imagine what would happen to me if any of those things came true. They might be more than I could handle. I still don't really know what life is all about. I don't know how it *works*."

"I see," the old man said, intertwining his fingers and separating them again. "I see."

"So, is my wish OK?"

"Of course," he said. "Of course. It's no trouble at all for me."

The old man suddenly fixed his eyes on a spot in the air. The wrinkles of his forehead deepened: they might have been the wrinkles of his brain itself as it concentrated on his thoughts. He seemed to be staring at something—perhaps all-but-invisible bits of down—floating in the air. He opened his arms wide, lifted himself slightly from his chair, and whipped his palms together with a dry smack. Settling in the chair again, he slowly ran his fingertips along the wrinkles of his brow as if to soften them, and then turned to her with a gentle smile.

"That did it," he said. "Your wish has been granted."

"Already?"

"Yes, it was no trouble at all. Your wish has been granted, lovely miss. Happy birthday. You may go back to work now. Don't worry, I'll put the cart in the hall."

She took the elevator down to the restaurant. Empty-handed now, she felt almost disturbingly light, as though she were walking on some kind of mysterious fluff.

"Are you OK? You look spaced out," the younger waiter said to her.   100

She gave him an ambiguous smile and shook her head. "Oh, really? No, I'm fine."

"Tell me about the owner. What's he like?"

"I dunno, I didn't get a very good look at him," she said, cutting the conversation short.

An hour later she went to bring the cart down. It was out in the hall, utensils in place. She lifted the lid to find the chicken and vegetables gone. The wine bottle and coffeepot were empty. The door to room 604 stood there, closed and expressionless. She stared at it for a time, feeling it might open at any moment, but it did not open. She brought the cart down in the elevator and wheeled it in to the dishwasher. The chef looked blankly at the plate: empty as always.

"I never saw the owner again," she said. "Not once. The manager turned out   105 to have just an ordinary stomachache and went back to delivering the owner's meal again himself the next day. I quit the job after New Year's, and I've never been back to the place. I don't know, I just felt it was better not to go near there, kind of like a premonition."

She toyed with a paper coaster, thinking her own thoughts. "Sometimes I get the feeling that everything that happened to me on my twentieth birthday was some kind of illusion. It's as though something happened to make me think that things happened that never really happened at all. But I know for sure that they *did* happen. I can still bring back vivid images of every piece of furniture and every knickknack in room 604. What happened to me in there really happened, and it had an important meaning for me, too."

The two of us kept silent, drinking our drinks and thinking our separate thoughts.

"Do you mind if I ask you one thing?" I asked. "Or, more precisely, *two* things."

"Go right ahead," she said. "I imagine you're going to ask me what I wished for that time. That's the first thing you want to know."

"But it looks as though you don't want to talk about that."   110

"Does it?"

I nodded.

She put the coaster down and narrowed her eyes as if staring at something in the distance. "You're not supposed to tell anybody what you wished for, you know."

"I won't try to drag it out of you," I said. "I *would* like to know whether or not it came true, though. And also — whatever the wish itself might have been — whether or not you later came to regret what it was you chose to wish for. Were you ever sorry you didn't wish for something else?"

"The answer to the first question is yes and also no. I still have a lot of living left to do, probably. I haven't seen how things are going to work out to the end." 115

"So it was a wish that takes time to come true?"

"You could say that. Time is going to play an important role."

"Like in cooking certain dishes."

She nodded.

I thought about that for a moment, but the only thing that came to mind 120 was the image of a gigantic pie cooking slowly in an oven at low heat.

"And the answer to my second question?"

"What was that again?"

"Whether you ever regretted your choice of what to wish for."

A moment of silence followed. The eyes she turned on me seemed to lack any depth. The desiccated shadow of a smile flickered at the corners of her mouth, suggesting a kind of hushed sense of resignation.

"I'm married now," she said. "To a CPA three years older than me. And I 125 have two children, a boy and a girl. We have an Irish setter. I drive an Audi, and I play tennis with my girlfriends twice a week. That's the life I'm living now."

"Sounds pretty good to me," I said.

"Even if the Audi's bumper has two dents?"

"Hey, bumpers are *made* for denting."

"That would make a great bumper sticker," she said. "'Bumpers are for denting.'"

I looked at her mouth when she said that. 130

"What I'm trying to tell you is this," she said more softly, scratching an earlobe. It was a beautifully shaped earlobe. "No matter what they wish for, no matter how far they go, people can never be anything but themselves. That's all."

"There's another good bumper sticker," I said. "'No matter how far they go, people can never be anything but themselves.'"

She laughed aloud, with a real show of pleasure, and the shadow was gone.

She rested her elbow on the bar and looked at me. "Tell me," she said. "What would you have wished for if you had been in my position?"

"On the night of my twentieth birthday, you mean?" 135

"Uh-huh."

I took some time to think about that, but I couldn't come up with a single wish.

"I can't think of anything," I confessed. "I'm too far away now from my twentieth birthday."

"You really can't think of anything?"

I nodded.

"Not one thing?"

"Not one thing."

She looked into my eyes again — straight in — and said, "That's because you've already *made* your wish."

140

"But you had better think about it very carefully, my lovely young fairy, because I can grant you only one." In the darkness somewhere, an old man wearing a withered-leaf-colored tie raises a finger. "Just one. You can't change your mind afterward and take it back."

Flannery O'Connor 1925–1964
A Good Man Is Hard to Find   [1955]

The grandmother didn't want to go to Florida. She wanted to visit some of her connections in east Tennessee and she was seizing at every chance to change Bailey's mind. Bailey was the son she lived with, her only boy. He was sitting on the edge of his chair at the table, bent over the orange sports section of the *Journal*. "Now look here, Bailey," she said, "see here, read this," and she stood with one hand on her thin hip and the other rattling the newspaper at his bald head. "Here this fellow that calls himself The Misfit is aloose from the Federal Pen and headed toward Florida and you read here what it says he did to these people. Just you read it. I wouldn't take my children in any direction with a criminal like that aloose in it. I couldn't answer to my conscience if I did."

Bailey didn't look up from his reading so she wheeled around then and faced the children's mother, a young woman in slacks, whose face was as broad and innocent as a cabbage and was tied around with a green head-kerchief that had two points on the top like rabbit's ears. She was sitting on the sofa, feeding the baby his apricots out of a jar. "The children have been to Florida before," the old lady said. "You all ought to take them somewhere else for a change so they would see different parts of the world and be broad. They never have been to east Tennessee."

The children's mother didn't seem to hear her but the eight-year-old boy, John Wesley, a stocky child with glasses, said, "If you don't want to go to Florida, why dontcha stay at home?" He and the little girl, June Star, were reading the funny papers on the floor.

"She wouldn't stay at home to be queen for a day,°" June Star said without raising her yellow head.

Queen for a day: Alluding to the American radio (1945–1957) and television (1956–1964, 1969–1970) show on which several women experiencing difficult circumstances competed, by telling their stories winsomely, to be treated like royalty for a day.

"Yes and what would you do if this fellow, The Misfit, caught you?" the   5
grandmother asked.

"I'd smack his face," John Wesley said.

"She wouldn't stay at home for a million bucks," June Star said. "Afraid
she'd miss something. She has to go everywhere we go."

"All right, Miss," the grandmother said. "Just remember that the next time
you want me to curl your hair."

June Star said her hair was naturally curly.

The next morning the grandmother was the first one in the car, ready to go.   10
She had her big black valise that looked like the head of a hippopotamus in one
corner, and underneath it she was hiding a basket with Pitty Sing, the cat, in it.
She didn't intend for the cat to be left alone in the house for three days because
he would miss her too much and she was afraid he might brush against one of
the gas burners and accidentally asphyxiate himself. Her son, Bailey, didn't like
to arrive at a motel with a cat.

She sat in the middle of the back seat with John Wesley and June Star on either side of her. Bailey and the children's mother and the baby sat in front and
they left Atlanta at eight forty-five with the mileage on the car at 55890. The
grandmother wrote this down because she thought it would be interesting to say
how many miles they had been when they got back. It took them twenty minutes to reach the outskirts of the city.

The old lady settled herself comfortably, removing her white cotton gloves
and putting them up with her purse on the shelf in front of the back window.
The children's mother still had on slacks and still had her head tied up in a green
kerchief, but the grandmother had on a navy blue straw sailor hat with a bunch
of white violets on the brim and a navy blue dress with a small white dot in the
print. Her collars and cuffs were white organdy trimmed with lace and at her
neckline she had pinned a purple spray of cloth violets containing a sachet. In
case of an accident, anyone seeing her dead on the highway would know at once
that she was a lady.

She said she thought it was going to be a good day for driving, neither too
hot nor too cold, and she cautioned Bailey that the speed limit was fifty-five
miles an hour and that the patrolmen hid themselves behind billboards and
small clumps of trees and sped out after you before you had a chance to slow
down. She pointed out interesting details of the scenery: Stone Mountain; the
blue granite that in some places came up to both sides of the highway; the brilliant red clay banks slightly streaked with purple; and the various crops that
made rows of green lace-work on the ground. The trees were full of silver-white
sunlight and the meanest of them sparkled. The children were reading comic
magazines and their mother had gone back to sleep.

"Let's go through Georgia fast so we won't have to look at it much," John
Wesley said.

"If I were a little boy," said the grandmother, "I wouldn't talk about my na-   15
tive state that way. Tennessee has the mountains and Georgia has the hills."

"Tennessee is just a hillbilly dumping ground," John Wesley said, "and
Georgia is a lousy state too."

"You said it," June Star said.

"In my time," said the grandmother, folding her thin veined fingers, "children were more respectful of their native states and their parents and everything else. People did right then. Oh look at the cute little pickaninny!" she said and pointed to a Negro child standing in the door of a shack. "Wouldn't that make a picture, now?" she asked and they all turned and looked at the little Negro out of the back window. He waved.

"He didn't have any britches on," June Star said.

"He probably didn't have any," the grandmother explained. "Little niggers 20
in the country don't have things like we do. If I could paint, I'd paint that picture," she said.

The children exchanged comic books.

The grandmother offered to hold the baby and the children's mother passed him over the front seat to her. She set him on her knee and bounced him and told him about the things they were passing. She rolled her eyes and screwed up her mouth and stuck her leathery thin face into his smooth bland one. Occasionally he gave her a faraway smile. They passed a large cotton field with five or six graves fenced in the middle of it, like a small island. "Look at the graveyard!" the grandmother said, pointing it out. "That was the old family burying ground. That belonged to the plantation."

"Where's the plantation?" John Wesley asked.

"Gone With the Wind,"° said the grandmother. "Ha. Ha."

When the children finished all the comic books they had brought, they 25
opened the lunch and ate it. The grandmother ate a peanut butter sandwich and an olive and would not let the children throw the box and the paper napkins out the window. When there was nothing else to do they played a game by choosing a cloud and making the other two guess what shape it suggested. John Wesley took one the shape of a cow and June Star guessed a cow and John Wesley said, no, an automobile, and June Star said he didn't play fair, and they began to slap each other over the grandmother.

The grandmother said she would tell them a story if they would keep quiet. When she told a story, she rolled her eyes and waved her head and was very dramatic. She said once when she was a maiden lady she had been courted by a Mr. Edgar Atkins Teagarden from Jasper, Georgia. She said he was a very good-looking man and a gentleman and that he brought her a watermelon every Saturday afternoon with his initials cut in it, E. A. T. Well, one Saturday, she said, Mr. Teagarden brought the watermelon and there was nobody at home and he left it on the front porch and returned in his buggy to Jasper, but she never got the watermelon, she said, because a nigger boy ate it when he saw the initials, E. A. T.! This story tickled John Wesley's funny bone and he giggled and giggled but June Star didn't think it was any good. She said she wouldn't marry a man that just brought her a watermelon on Saturday. The grandmother said she would

---

Gone With the Wind: The title of the best-selling 1936 novel by Margaret Mitchell dealing with the period of the American Civil War and the Reconstruction, made into an Academy Award–winning film in 1939.

have done well to marry Mr. Teagarden because he was a gentleman and had bought Coca-Cola stock when it first came out and that he had died only a few years ago, a very wealthy man.

They stopped at The Tower for barbecued sandwiches. The Tower was a part stucco and part wood filling station and dance hall set in a clearing outside of Timothy. A fat man named Red Sammy Butts ran it and there were signs stuck here and there on the building and for miles up and down the highway saying, TRY RED SAMMY'S FAMOUS BARBECUE. NONE LIKE FAMOUS RED SAMMY'S! RED SAM! THE FAT BOY WITH THE HAPPY LAUGH. A VETERAN! RED SAMMY'S YOUR MAN!

Red Sammy was lying on the bare ground outside The Tower with his head under a truck while a gray monkey about a foot high, chained to a small chinaberry tree, chattered nearby. The monkey sprang back into the tree and got on the highest limb as soon as he saw the children jump out of the car and run toward him.

Inside, The Tower was a long dark room with a counter at one end and tables at the other and dancing space in the middle. They all sat down at a board table next to the nickelodeon and Red Sam's wife, a tall burnt-brown woman with hair and eyes lighter than her skin, came and took their order. The children's mother put a dime in the machine and played "The Tennessee Waltz," and the grandmother said that tune always made her want to dance. She asked Bailey if he would like to dance but he only glared at her. He didn't have a naturally sunny disposition like she did and trips made him nervous. The grandmother's brown eyes were very bright. She swayed her head from side to side and pretended she was dancing in her chair. June Star said play something she could tap to so the children's mother put in another dime and played a fast number and June Star stepped out onto the dance floor and did her tap routine.

"Ain't she cute?" Red Sam's wife said, leaning over the counter. "Would you 30 like to come be my little girl?"

"No I certainly wouldn't," June Star said. "I wouldn't live in a broken-down place like this for a million bucks!" and she ran back to the table.

"Ain't she cute?" the woman repeated, stretching her mouth politely.

"Aren't you ashamed?" hissed the grandmother.

Red Sam came in and told his wife to quit lounging on the counter and hurry up with these people's order. His khaki trousers reached just to his hip bones and his stomach hung over them like a sack of meal swaying under his shirt. He came over and sat down at a table nearby and let out a combination sigh and yodel. "You can't win," he said. "You can't win," and he wiped his sweating red face off with a gray handkerchief. "These days you don't know who to trust," he said. "Ain't that the truth?"

"People are certainly not nice like they used to be," said the grandmother.   35

"Two fellers come in here last week," Red Sammy said, "driving a Chrysler. It was a old beat-up car but it was a good one and these boys looked all right to me. Said they worked at the mill and you know I let them fellers charge the gas they bought? Now why did I do that?"

"Because you're a good man!" the grandmother said at once.

"Yes'm, I suppose so," Red Sam said as if he were struck with this answer.

His wife brought the orders, carrying the five plates all at once without a tray, two in each hand and one balanced on her arm. "It isn't a soul in this green world of God's that you can trust," she said. "And I don't count nobody out of that, not nobody," she repeated, looking at Red Sammy.

"Did you read about that criminal, The Misfit, that's escaped?" asked the grandmother. 40

"I wouldn't be a bit surprised if he didn't attact this place right here," said the woman. "If he hears about it being here, I wouldn't be none surprised to see him. If he hears it's two cent in the cash register, I wouldn't be a tall surprised if he . . ."

"That'll do," Red Sam said. "Go bring these people their Co'-Colas," and the woman went off to get the rest of the order.

"A good man is hard to find," Red Sammy said. "Everything is getting terrible. I remember the day you could go off and leave your screen door unlatched. Not no more."

He and the grandmother discussed better times. The old lady said that in her opinion Europe was entirely to blame for the way things were now. She said the way Europe acted you would think we were made of money and Red Sam said it was no use talking about it, she was exactly right. The children ran outside into the white sunlight and looked at the monkey in the lacy chinaberry tree. He was busy catching fleas on himself and biting each one carefully between his teeth as if it were a delicacy.

They drove off again into the hot afternoon. The grandmother took cat naps 45 and woke up every few minutes with her own snoring. Outside of Toombsboro she woke up and recalled an old plantation that she had visited in this neighborhood once when she was a young lady. She said the house had six white columns across the front and that there was an avenue of oaks leading up to it and two little wooden trellis arbors on either side in front where you sat down with your suitor after a stroll in the garden. She recalled exactly which road to turn off to get to it. She knew that Bailey would not be willing to lose any time looking at an old house, but the more she talked about it, the more she wanted to see it once again and find out if the little twin arbors were still standing. "There was a secret panel in this house," she said craftily, not telling the truth but wishing that she were, "and the story went that all the family silver was hidden in it when Sherman came through° but it was never found . . ."

"Hey!" John Wesley said. "Let's go see it! We'll find it! We'll poke all the woodwork and find it! Who lives there? Where do you turn off at? Hey Pop, can't we turn off there?"

"We never have seen a house with a secret panel!" June Star shrieked. "Let's go to the house with the secret panel! Hey Pop, can't we go see the house with the secret panel!"

Sherman came through: In November and December 1864, General William Tecumseh Sherman marched with over 60,000 Union soldiers from Atlanta to the Atlantic coast, pillaging and burning towns and farms along the way.

"It's not far from here, I know," the grandmother said. "It wouldn't take over twenty minutes."

Bailey was looking straight ahead. His jaw was as rigid as a horseshoe. "No," he said.

The children began to yell and scream that they wanted to see the house 50 with the secret panel. John Wesley kicked the back of the front seat and June Star hung over her mother's shoulder and whined desperately into her ear that they never had any fun even on their vacation, that they could never do what THEY wanted to do. The baby began to scream and John Wesley kicked the back of the seat so hard that his father could feel the blows in his kidney.

"All right!" he shouted and drew the car to a stop at the side of the road. "Will you all shut up? Will you all just shut up for one second? If you don't shut up, we won't go anywhere."

"It would be very educational for them," the grandmother murmured.

"All right," Bailey said, "but get this: this is the only time we're going to stop for anything like this. This is the one and only time."

"The dirt road that you have to turn down is about a mile back," the grandmother directed. "I marked it when we passed."

"A dirt road," Bailey groaned.   55

After they had turned around and were headed toward the dirt road, the grandmother recalled other points about the house, the beautiful glass over the front doorway and the candle-lamp in the hall. John Wesley said that the secret panel was probably in the fireplace.

"You can't go inside this house," Bailey said. "You don't know who lives there."

"While you all talk to the people in front, I'll run around behind and get in a window," John Wesley suggested.

"We'll all stay in the car," his mother said.

They turned onto the dirt road and the car raced roughly along in a swirl of 60 pink dust. The grandmother recalled the times when there were no paved roads and thirty miles was a day's journey. The dirt road was hilly and there were sudden washes in it and sharp curves on dangerous embankments. All at once they would be on a hill, looking down over the blue tops of trees for miles around, then the next minute, they would be in a red depression with the dust-coated trees looking down on them.

"This place had better turn up in a minute," Bailey said, "or I'm going to turn around."

The road looked as if no one had traveled on it in months.

"It's not much farther," the grandmother said and just as she said it, a horrible thought came to her. The thought was so embarrassing that she turned red in the face and her eyes dilated and her feet jumped up, upsetting her valise in the corner. The instant the valise moved, the newspaper top she had over the basket under it rose with a snarl and Pitty Sing, the cat, sprang onto Bailey's shoulder.

The children were thrown to the floor and their mother, clutching the baby, was thrown out the door onto the ground; the old lady was thrown into the front seat. The car turned over once and landed right-side-up in a gulch off the side of the road. Bailey remained in the driver's seat with the cat — gray-striped with a broad white face and an orange nose — clinging to his neck like a caterpillar.

As soon as the children saw they could move their arms and legs, they scrambled out of the car, shouting, "We've had an ACCIDENT!" The grandmother was curled up under the dashboard, hoping she was injured so that Bailey's wrath would not come down on her all at once. The horrible thought she had had before the accident was that the house she had remembered so vividly was not in Georgia but in Tennessee.

Bailey removed the cat from his neck with both hands and flung it out the window against the side of a pine tree. Then he got out of the car and started looking for the children's mother. She was sitting against the side of the red gutted ditch, holding the screaming baby, but she only had a cut down her face and a broken shoulder. "We've had an ACCIDENT!" the children screamed in a frenzy of delight.

"But nobody's killed," June Star said with disappointment as the grandmother limped out of the car, her hat still pinned to her head but the broken front brim standing up at a jaunty angle and the violet spray hanging off the side. They all sat down in the ditch, except the children, to recover from the shock. They were all shaking.

"Maybe a car will come along," said the children's mother hoarsely.

"I believe I have injured an organ," said the grandmother, pressing her side, but no one answered her. Bailey's teeth were clattering. He had on a yellow sport shirt with bright blue parrots designed in it and his face was as yellow as the shirt. The grandmother decided that she would not mention that the house was in Tennessee.

The road was about ten feet above and they could see only the tops of the trees on the other side of it. Behind the ditch they were sitting in there were more woods, tall and dark and deep. In a few minutes they saw a car some distance away on top of a hill, coming slowly as if the occupants were watching them. The grandmother stood up and waved both arms dramatically to attract their attention. The car continued to come on slowly, disappeared around a bend and appeared again, moving even slower, on top of the hill they had gone over. It was a big black battered hearse-like automobile. There were three men in it.

It came to a stop just over them and for some minutes, the driver looked down with a steady expressionless gaze to where they were sitting, and didn't speak. Then he turned his head and muttered something to the other two and they got out. One was a fat boy in black trousers and a red sweat shirt with a silver stallion embossed on the front of it. He moved around on the right side of them and stood staring, his mouth partly open in a kind of loose grin. The other had on khaki pants and a blue striped coat and a gray hat pulled down very low, hiding most of his face. He came around slowly on the left side. Neither spoke.

The driver got out of the car and stood by the side of it, looking down at them. He was an older man than the other two. His hair was just beginning to gray and he wore silver-rimmed spectacles that gave him a scholarly look. He had a long creased face and didn't have on any shirt or undershirt. He had on blue jeans that were too tight for him and was holding a black hat and a gun. The two boys also had guns.

"We've had an ACCIDENT!" the children screamed.

The grandmother had the peculiar feeling that the bespectacled man was someone she knew. His face was as familiar to her as if she had known him all her life but she could not recall who he was. He moved away from the car and began to come down the embankment, placing his feet carefully so that he wouldn't slip. He had on tan and white shoes and no socks, and his ankles were red and thin. "Good afternoon," he said. "I see you all had you a little spill."

"We turned over twice!" said the grandmother.   75

"Oncet," he corrected. "We seen it happen. Try their car and see will it run, Hiram," he said quietly to the boy with the gray hat.

"What you got that gun for?" John Wesley asked. "Whatcha gonna do with that gun?"

"Lady," the man said to the children's mother, "would you mind calling them children to sit down by you? Children make me nervous. I want all you all to sit down right together there where you're at."

"What are you telling US what to do for?" June Star asked.

Behind them the line of woods gaped like a dark open mouth. "Come here,"   80
said their mother.

"Look here now," Bailey began suddenly, "we're in a predicament! We're in . . ."

The grandmother shrieked. She scrambled to her feet and stood staring. "You're The Misfit!" she said. "I recognized you at once!"

"Yes'm," the man said, smiling slightly as if he were pleased in spite of himself to be known, "but it would have been better for all of you, lady, if you hadn't of reckernized me."

Bailey turned his head sharply and said something to his mother that shocked even the children. The old lady began to cry and The Misfit reddened.

"Lady," he said, "don't you get upset. Sometimes a man says things he don't   85
mean. I don't reckon he meant to talk to you thataway."

"You wouldn't shoot a lady, would you?" the grandmother said and removed a clean handkerchief from her cuff and began to slap at her eyes with it.

The Misfit pointed the toe of his shoe into the ground and made a little hole and then covered it up again. "I would hate to have to," he said.

"Listen," the grandmother almost screamed, "I know you're a good man. You don't look a bit like you have common blood. I know you must come from nice people!"

"Yes mam," he said, "finest people in the world." When he smiled he showed a row of strong white teeth. "God never made a finer woman than my mother and my daddy's heart was pure gold," he said. The boy with the red sweat shirt had come around behind them and was standing with his gun at his hip.

The Misfit squatted down on the ground. "Watch them children, Bobby Lee," he said. "You know they make me nervous." He looked at the six of them huddled together in front of him and he seemed to be embarrassed as if he couldn't think of anything to say. "Ain't a cloud in the sky," he remarked, looking up at it. "Don't see no sun but don't see no cloud neither."

"Yes, it's a beautiful day," said the grandmother. "Listen," she said, "you shouldn't call yourself The Misfit because I know you're a good man at heart. I can just look at you and tell." 90

"Hush!" Bailey yelled. "Hush! Everybody shut up and let me handle this!" He was squatting in the position of a runner about to sprint forward but he didn't move.

"I pre-chate that, lady," The Misfit said and drew a little circle in the ground with the butt of his gun.

"It'll take a half a hour to fix this here car," Hiram called, looking over the raised hood of it.

"Well, first you and Bobby Lee get him and that little boy to step over yonder with you," The Misfit said, pointing to Bailey and John Wesley. "The boys want to ast you something," he said to Bailey. "Would you mind stepping back in them woods there with them?"

"Listen," Bailey began, "we're in a terrible predicament! Nobody realizes what this is," and his voice cracked. His eyes were as blue and intense as the parrots in his shirt and he remained perfectly still. 95

The grandmother reached up to adjust her hat brim as if she were going to the woods with him but it came off in her hand. She stood staring at it and after a second she let it fall on the ground. Hiram pulled Bailey up by the arm as if he were assisting an old man. John Wesley caught hold of his father's hand and Bobby Lee followed. They went off toward the woods and just as they reached the dark edge, Bailey turned and supporting himself against a gray naked pine trunk, he shouted, "I'll be back in a minute, Mamma, wait on me!"

"Come back this instant!" his mother shrilled but they all disappeared into the woods.

"Bailey Boy!" the grandmother called in a tragic voice but she found she was looking at The Misfit squatting on the ground in front of her. "I just know you're a good man," she said desperately. "You're not a bit common!"

"Nome, I ain't a good man," The Misfit said after a second as if he had considered her statement carefully, "but I ain't the worst in the world neither. My daddy said I was a different breed of dog from my brothers and sisters. 'You know,' Daddy said, 'it's some that can live their whole life out without asking about it and it's others has to know why it is, and this boy is one of the latters. He's going to be into everything!'" He put on his black hat and looked up suddenly and then away deep into the woods as if he were embarrassed again. "I'm sorry I don't have on a shirt before you ladies," he said, hunching his shoulders slightly. "We buried our clothes that we had on when we escaped and we're just making do until we can get better. We borrowed these from some folks we met," he explained.

"That's perfectly all right," the grandmother said. "Maybe Bailey has an extra shirt in his suitcase." 100

"I'll look and see terreclty," The Misfit said.

"Where are they taking him?" the children's mother screamed.

"Daddy was a card himself," The Misfit said. "You couldn't put anything over on him. He never got in trouble with the Authorities though. Just had the knack of handling them."

"You could be honest too if you'd only try," said the grandmother. "Think how wonderful it would be to settle down and live a comfortable life and not have to think about somebody chasing you all the time."

The Misfit kept scratching in the ground with the butt of his gun as if 105 he were thinking about it. "Yes'm, somebody is always after you," he murmured.

The grandmother noticed how thin his shoulder blades were just behind his hat because she was standing up looking down on him. "Do you ever pray?" she asked.

He shook his head. All she saw was the black hat wiggle between his shoulder blades. "Nome," he said.

There was a pistol shot from the woods, followed closely by another. Then silence. The old lady's head jerked around. She could hear the wind move through the tree tops like a long satisfied insuck of breath. "Bailey Boy!" she called.

"I was a gospel singer for a while," The Misfit said. "I been most everything. Been in the arm service, both land and sea, at home and abroad, been twict married, been an undertaker, been with the railroads, plowed Mother Earth, been in a tornado, seen a man burnt alive oncet," and he looked up at the children's mother and the little girl who were sitting close together, their faces white and their eyes glassy; "I even seen a woman flogged," he said.

"Pray, pray," the grandmother began, "pray, pray . . ." 110

"I never was a bad boy that I remember of," The Misfit said in an almost dreamy voice, "but somewheres along the line I done something wrong and got sent to the penitentiary. I was buried alive," and he looked up and held her attention to him by a steady stare.

"That's when you should have started to pray," she said. "What did you do to get sent to the penitentiary that first time?"

"Turn to the right, it was a wall," The Misfit said, looking up again at the cloudless sky. "Turn to the left, it was a wall. Look up it was a ceiling, look down it was a floor. I forget what I done, lady. I set there and set there, trying to remember what it was I done and I ain't recalled it to this day. Oncet in a while, I would think it was coming to me, but it never come."

"Maybe they put you in by mistake," the old lady said vaguely.

"Nome," he said. "It wasn't no mistake. They had the papers on me." 115

"You must have stolen something," she said.

The Misfit sneered slightly. "Nobody had nothing I wanted," he said. "It was a head-doctor at the penitentiary said what I had done was kill my daddy but I known that for a lie. My daddy died in nineteen ought nineteen of the epidemic flu° and I never had a thing to do with it. He was buried in the Mount Hopewell Baptist churchyard and you can go there and see for yourself."

"If you would pray," the old lady said, "Jesus would help you."

"That's right," The Misfit said.

"Well then, why don't you pray?" she asked trembling with delight suddenly.   120

"I don't want no hep," he said. "I'm doing all right by myself."

Bobby Lee and Hiram came ambling back from the woods. Bobby Lee was dragging a yellow shirt with bright blue parrots in it.

"Thow me that shirt, Bobby Lee," The Misfit said. The shirt came flying at him and landed on his shoulder and he put it on. The grandmother couldn't name what the shirt reminded her of. "No, lady," The Misfit said while he was buttoning it up, "I found out the crime don't matter. You can do one thing or you can do another, kill a man or take a tire off his car, because sooner or later you're going to forget what it was you done and just be punished for it."

The children's mother had begun to make heaving noises as if she couldn't get her breath. "Lady," he asked, "would you and that little girl like to step off yonder with Bobby Lee and Hiram and join your husband?"

"Yes, thank you," the mother said faintly. Her left arm dangled helplessly   125 and she was holding the baby, who had gone to sleep, in the other. "Hep that lady up, Hiram," The Misfit said as she struggled to climb out of the ditch, "and Bobby Lee, you hold onto that little girl's hand."

"I don't want to hold hands with him," June Star said. "He reminds me of a pig."

The fat boy blushed and laughed and caught her by the arm and pulled her off into the woods after Hiram and her mother.

Alone with The Misfit, the grandmother found that she had lost her voice. There was not a cloud in the sky nor any sun. There was nothing around her but woods. She wanted to tell him that he must pray. She opened and closed her mouth several times before anything came out. Finally she found herself saying, "Jesus. Jesus," meaning, Jesus will help you, but the way she was saying it, it sounded as if she might be cursing.

"Yes'm," The Misfit said as if he agreed. "Jesus thown everything off balance. It was the same case with Him as with me except He hadn't committed any crime and they could prove I had committed one because they had the papers on me. Of course," he said, "they never shown me my papers. That's why I sign myself now. I said long ago, you get you a signature and sign everything you do and keep a copy of it. Then you'll know what you done and you can hold up the crime to the punishment and see do they match and in the end you'll have something to prove you ain't been treated right. I call myself The Misfit," he said, "because I can't make what all I done wrong fit what all I gone through in punishment."

---

epidemic flu: An influenza epidemic in 1918–1919 killed twenty to forty million people worldwide.

There was a piercing scream from the woods, followed closely by a pistol re-   130
port. "Does it seem right to you, lady, that one is punished a heap and another
ain't punished at all?"

"Jesus!" the old lady cried. "You've got good blood! I know you wouldn't
shoot a lady! I know you come from nice people! Pray! Jesus, you ought not to
shoot a lady. I'll give you all the money I've got!"

"Lady," The Misfit said, looking beyond her far into the woods, "there never
was a body that give the undertaker a tip."

There were two more pistol reports and the grandmother raised her head
like a parched old turkey hen crying for water and called, "Bailey Boy, Bailey
Boy!" as if her heart would break.

"Jesus was the only One that ever raised the dead," The Misfit continued,
"and He shouldn't have done it. He thrown everything off balance. If He did
what He said, then it's nothing for you to do but throw away everything and follow Him, and if He didn't, then it's nothing for you to do but enjoy the few minutes you got left the best way you can — by killing somebody or burning down his
house or doing some other meanness to him. No pleasure but meanness," he
said and his voice had become almost a snarl.

"Maybe He didn't raise the dead," the old lady mumbled, not knowing what   135
she was saying and feeling so dizzy that she sank down in the ditch with her legs
twisted under her.

"I wasn't there so I can't say He didn't," The Misfit said. "I wisht I had of
been there," he said, hitting the ground with his fist. "It ain't right I wasn't there
because if I had of been there I would of known. Listen lady," he said in a high
voice, "if I had of been there I would of known and I wouldn't be like I am now."
His voice seemed about to crack and the grandmother's head cleared for an instant. She saw the man's face twisted close to her own as if he were going to cry
and she murmured, "Why you're one of my babies. You're one of my own children!" She reached out and touched him on the shoulder. The Misfit sprang
back as if a snake had bitten him and shot her three times through the chest.
Then he put his gun down on the ground and took off
his glasses and began to clean them.

Hiram and Bobby Lee returned from the woods and
stood over the ditch, looking down at the grandmother
who half sat and half lay in a puddle of blood with her
legs crossed under her like a child's and her face smiling
up at the cloudless sky.

Research Flannery
O'Connor in depth with
cultural documents and
multimedia resources on
LiterActive.

Without his glasses, The Misfit's eyes were red-rimmed and pale and
defenseless-looking. "Take her off and thow her where you thown the others,"
he said, picking up the cat that was rubbing itself against his leg.

"She was a talker, wasn't she?" Bobby Lee said, sliding down the ditch with
a yodel.

"She would of been a good woman," The Misfit said, "if it had been some-   140
body there to shoot her every minute of her life."

"Some fun!" Bobby Lee said.

"Shut up, Bobby Lee," The Misfit said. "It's no real pleasure in life."

Tillie Olsen   (1913–2007)

I Stand Here Ironing   [1961]

I stand here ironing, and what you asked me moves tormented back and forth with the iron.

"I wish you would manage the time to come in and talk with me about your daughter. I'm sure you can help me understand her. She's a youngster who needs help and whom I'm deeply interested in helping."

"Who needs help." . . . Even if I came, what good would it do? You think because I am her mother I have a key, or that in some way you could use me as a key? She has lived for nineteen years. There is all that life that has happened outside of me, beyond me.

And when is there time to remember, to sift, to weigh, to estimate, to total? I will start and there will be an interruption and I will have to gather it all together again. Or I will become engulfed with all I did or did not do, with what should have been and what cannot be helped.

She was a beautiful baby. The first and only one of our five that was beautiful at birth. You do not guess how new and uneasy her tenancy in her now-loveliness. You did not know her all those years she was thought homely, or see her poring over her baby pictures, making me tell her over and over how beautiful she had been — and would be, I would tell her — and was now, to the seeing eye. But the seeing eyes were few or nonexistent. Including mine.

I nursed her. They feel that's important nowadays. I nursed all the children, but with her, with all the fierce rigidity of first motherhood, I did like the books then said. Though her cries battered me to trembling and my breasts ached with swollenness, I waited till the clock decreed.

Why do I put that first? I do not even know if it matters, or if it explains anything.

She was a beautiful baby. She blew shining bubbles of sound. She loved motion, loved light, loved color and music and textures. She would lie on the floor in her blue overalls patting the surface so hard in ecstasy her hands and feet would blur. She was a miracle to me, but when she was eight months old I had to leave her daytimes with the woman downstairs to whom she was no miracle at all, for I worked or looked for work and for Emily's father, who "could no longer endure" (he wrote in his good-bye note) "sharing want with us."

I was nineteen. It was the pre-relief, pre-WPA world of the depression. I would start running as soon as I got off the streetcar, running up the stairs, the place smelling sour, and awake or asleep to startle awake, when she saw me she would break into a clogged weeping that could not be comforted, a weeping I can hear yet.

After a while I found a job hashing at night so I could be with her days, and it was better. But it came to where I had to bring her to his family and leave her.

It took a long time to raise the money for her fare back. Then she got chicken pox and I had to wait longer. When she finally came, I hardly knew her, walking quick and nervous like her father, looking like her father, thin, and dressed in a shoddy red that yellowed her skin and glared at the pockmarks. All the baby loveliness gone.

She was two. Old enough for nursery school they said, and I did not know then what I know now — the fatigue of the long day, and the lacerations of group life in the kinds of nurseries that are only parking places for children.

Except that it would have made no difference if I had known. It was the only place there was. It was the only way we could be together, the only way I could hold a job.

And even without knowing, I knew. I knew the teacher that was evil because all these years it has curdled into my memory, the little boy hunched in the corner, her rasp, "why aren't you outside, because Alvin hits you? that's no reason, go out, scaredy." I knew Emily hated it even if she did not clutch and implore "don't go Mommy" like the other children, mornings.

She always had a reason why we should stay home. Momma, you look sick. 15 Momma, I feel sick. Momma, the teachers aren't there today, they're sick. Momma, we can't go, there was a fire there last night. Momma, it's a holiday today, no school, they told me.

But never a direct protest, never rebellion. I think of our others in their three-, four-year-oldness — the explosions, the tempers, the denunciations, the demands — and I feel suddenly ill. I put the iron down. What in me demanded that goodness in her? And what was the cost to her of such goodness?

The old man living in the back once said in his gentle way: "You should smile at Emily more when you look at her." What *was* in my face when I looked at her? I loved her. There were all the acts of love.

It was only with the others I remembered what he said, and it was the face of joy, and not of care or tightness or worry I turned to them — too late for Emily. She does not smile easily, let alone almost always as her brothers and sisters do. Her face is closed and sombre, but when she wants, how fluid. You must have seen it in her pantomimes, you spoke of her rare gift for comedy on the stage that rouses a laughter out of the audience so dear they applaud and applaud and do not want to let her go.

Where does it come from, that comedy? There was none of it in her when she came back to me that second time, after I had had to send her away again. She had a new daddy now to learn to love, and I think perhaps it was a better time.

Except when we left her alone nights, telling ourselves she was old enough. 20 "Can't you go some other time, Mommy, like tomorrow?" she would ask. "Will it be just a little while you'll be gone? Do you promise?"

The time we came back, the front door open, the clock on the floor in the hall. She rigid awake. "It wasn't just a little while. I didn't cry. Three times I called you, just three times, and then I ran downstairs to open the door so you could come faster. The clock talked loud. I threw it away, it scared me what it talked."

She said the clock talked loud again that night I went to the hospital to have Susan. She was delirious with the fever that comes before red measles, but she was fully conscious all the week I was gone and the week after we were home when she could not come near the new baby or me.

She did not get well. She stayed skeleton thin, not wanting to eat, and night after night she had nightmares. She would call for me, and I would rouse from exhaustion to sleepily call back: "You're all right, darling, go to sleep, it's just a dream," and if she still called, in a sterner voice, "now go to sleep, Emily, there's nothing to hurt you." Twice, only twice, when I had to get up for Susan anyhow, I went in to sit with her.

Now when it is too late (as if she would let me hold and comfort her like I   25 do the others) I get up and go to her at once at her moan or restless stirring. "Are you awake, Emily? Can I get you something?" And the answer is always the same: "No, I'm all right, go back to sleep, Mother."

They persuaded me at the clinic to send her away to a convalescent home in the country where "she can have the kind of food and care you can't manage for her, and you'll be free to concentrate on the new baby." They still send children to that place. I see pictures on the society page of sleek young women planning affairs to raise money for it, or dancing at the affairs, or decorating Easter eggs or filling Christmas stockings for the children.

They never have a picture of the children so I do not know if the girls still wear those gigantic red bows and the ravaged looks on the every other Sunday when parents can come to visit "unless otherwise notified" — as we were notified the first six weeks.

Oh it is a handsome place, green lawns and tall trees and fluted flower beds. High up on the balconies of each cottage the children stand, the girls in their red bows and white dresses, the boys in white suits and giant red ties. The parents stand below shrieking up to be heard and the children shriek down to be heard, and between them the invisible wall "Not To Be Contaminated by Parental Germs or Physical Affection."

There was a tiny girl who always stood hand in hand with Emily. Her parents never came. One visit she was gone. "They moved her to Rose Cottage" Emily shouted in explanation. "They don't like you to love anybody here."

She wrote once a week, the labored writing of a seven-year-old. "I am fine.   30 How is the baby. If I write my leter nicly I will have a star. Love." There never was a star. We wrote every other day, letters she could never hold or keep but only hear read — once. "We simply do not have room for children to keep any personal possessions," they patiently explained when we pieced one Sunday's shrieking together to plead how much it would mean to Emily, who loved so to keep things, to be allowed to keep her letters and cards.

Each visit she looked frailer. "She isn't eating," they told us.

(They had runny eggs for breakfast or mush with lumps, Emily said later, I'd hold it in my mouth and not swallow. Nothing ever tasted good, just when they had chicken.)

It took us eight months to get her released home, and only the fact that she gained back so little of her seven lost pounds convinced the social worker.

I used to try to hold and love her after she came back, but her body would stay stiff, and after a while she'd push away. She ate little. Food sickened her, and I think much of life too. Oh she had physical lightness and brightness, twinkling by on skates, bouncing like a ball up and down up and down over the jump rope, skimming over the hill; but these were momentary.

She fretted about her appearance, thin and dark and foreign-looking at a   35
time when every little girl was supposed to look or thought she should look a chubby blonde replica of Shirley Temple. The doorbell sometimes rang for her, but no one seemed to come and play in the house or be a best friend. Maybe because we moved so much.

There was a boy she loved painfully through two school semesters. Months later she told me how she had taken pennies from my purse to buy him candy. "Licorice was his favorite and I brought him some every day, but he still liked Jennifer better'n me. Why, Mommy?" The kind of question for which there is no answer.

School was a worry to her. She was not glib or quick in a world where glibness and quickness were easily confused with ability to learn. To her overworked and exasperated teachers she was an overconscientious "slow learner" who kept trying to catch up and was absent entirely too often.

I let her be absent, though sometimes the illness was imaginary. How different from my now-strictness about attendance with the others. I wasn't working. We had a new baby, I was home anyhow. Sometimes, after Susan grew old enough, I would keep her home from school, too, to have them all together.

Mostly Emily had asthma, and her breathing, harsh and labored, would fill the house with a curiously tranquil sound. I would bring the two old dresser mirrors and her boxes of collections to her bed. She would select beads and single earrings, bottle tops and shells, dried flowers and pebbles, old postcards and scraps, all sorts of oddments; then she and Susan would play Kingdom, setting up landscapes and furniture, peopling them with action.

Those were the only times of peaceful companionship between her and   40
Susan. I have edged away from it, that poisonous feeling between them, that terrible balancing of hurts and needs I had to do between the two, and did so badly, those earlier years.

Oh there are conflicts between the others too, each one human, needing, demanding, hurting, taking — but only between Emily and Susan, no, Emily toward Susan that corroding resentment. It seems so obvious on the surface, yet it is not obvious. Susan, the second child, Susan, golden- and curly-haired and chubby, quick and articulate and assured, everything in appearance and manner Emily was not; Susan, not able to resist Emily's precious things, losing or sometimes clumsily breaking them; Susan telling jokes and riddles to company for applause while Emily sat silent (to say to me later: that was *my* riddle, Mother, I told it to Susan); Susan, who for all the five years' difference in age was just a year behind Emily in developing physically.

I am glad for that slow physical development that widened the difference between her and her contemporaries, though she suffered over it. She was too vulnerable for that terrible world of youthful competition, of preening and parading, of constant measuring of yourself against every other, of envy, "If I had that copper hair," "If I had that skin. . . ." She tormented herself enough about not looking like the others, there was enough of the unsureness, the having to be conscious of words before you speak, the constant caring—what are they thinking of me? without having it all magnified by the merciless physical drives.

Ronnie is calling. He is wet and I change him. It is rare there is such a cry now. That time of motherhood is almost behind me when the ear is not one's own but must always be racked and listening for the child cry, the child call. We sit for a while and I hold him, looking out over the city spread in charcoal with its soft aisles of light. "Shoogily," he breathes and curls closer. I carry him back to bed, asleep. Shoogily. A funny word, a family word, inherited from Emily, invented by her to say: comfort.

In this and other ways she leaves her seal, I say aloud. And startle at my saying it. What do I mean? What did I start to gather together, to try and make coherent? I was at the terrible, growing years. War years. I do not remember them well. I was working, there were four smaller ones now, there was not time for her. She had to help be a mother, and housekeeper, and shopper. She had to set her seal. Mornings of crisis and near hysteria trying to get lunches packed, hair combed, coats and shoes found, everyone to school or Child Care on time, the baby ready for transportation. And always the paper scribbled on by a smaller one, the book looked at by Susan then mislaid, the homework not done. Running out to that huge school where she was one, she was lost, she was a drop; suffering over the unpreparedness, stammering and unsure in her classes.

There was so little time left at night after the kids were bedded down. She 45 would struggle over books, always eating (it was in those years she developed her enormous appetite that is legendary in our family) and I would be ironing, or preparing food for the next day, or writing V-mail to Bill, or tending the baby. Sometimes, to make me laugh, or out of her despair, she would imitate happenings or types at school.

I think I said once: "Why don't you do something like this in the school amateur show?" One morning she phoned me at work, hardly understandable through the weeping: "Mother, I did it. I won, I won; they gave me first prize; they clapped and clapped and wouldn't let me go."

Now suddenly she was Somebody, and as imprisoned in her difference as she had been in anonymity.

She began to be asked to perform at other high schools, even in colleges, then at city and statewide affairs. The first one we went to, I only recognized her that first moment when thin, shy, she almost drowned herself into the curtains. Then: Was this Emily? The control, the command, the convulsing and deadly clowning, the spell, then the roaring, stamping audience, unwilling to let this rare and precious laughter out of their lives.

Afterwards: You ought to do something about her with a gift like that—but without money or knowing how, what does one do? We have left it all to her, and the gift has as often eddied inside, clogged and clotted, as been used and growing.

She is coming. She runs up the stairs two at a time with her light graceful 50 step, and I know she is happy tonight. Whatever it was that occasioned your call did not happen today.

"Aren't you ever going to finish the ironing, Mother? Whistler painted his mother in a rocker. I'd have to paint mine standing over an ironing board." This is one of her communicative nights and she tells me everything and nothing as she fixes herself a plate of food out of the icebox.

She is so lovely. Why did you want me to come in at all? Why were you concerned? She will find her way.

She starts up the stairs to bed. "Don't get me up with the rest in the morning." "But I thought you were having midterms." "Oh, those," she comes back in, kisses me, and says quite lightly, "in a couple of years when we'll all be atom-dead they won't matter a bit."

She has said it before. She *believes* it. But because I have been dredging the past, and all that compounds a human being is so heavy and meaningful in me, I cannot endure it tonight.

I will never total it all. I will never come in to say: She was a child sel- 55 dom smiled at. Her father left me before she was a year old. I had to work her first six years when there was work, or I sent her home and to his relatives. There were years she had care she hated. She was dark and thin and foreign-looking in a world where the prestige went to blondeness and curly hair and dimples, she was slow where glibness was prized. She was a child of anxious, not proud, love. We were poor and could not afford for her the soil of easy growth. I was a young mother, I was a distracted mother. There were the other children pushing up, demanding. Her younger sister seemed all that she was not. There were years she did not want me to touch her. She kept too much in herself, her life was such she had to keep too much in herself. My wisdom came too late. She has much to her and probably nothing will come of it. She is a child of her age, of depression, of war, of fear.

Let her be. So all that is in her will not bloom — but in how many does it? There is still enough left to live by. Only help her to know — help make it so there is cause for her to know — that she is more than this dress on the ironing board, helpless before the iron.

Edgar Allan Poe   1809–1849

The Cask of Amontillado   [1846]

The thousand injuries of Fortunato I had borne as I best could; but when he ventured upon insult, I vowed revenge. You, who so well know the nature of my soul, will not suppose, however, that I gave utterance to a threat. *At length* I would be avenged; this was a point definitively settled — but the very definitiveness with which it was resolved precluded the idea of risk. I must not only punish, but punish with impunity. A wrong is unredressed when retribution overtakes its redresser. It is equally unredressed when the avenger fails to make himself felt as such to him who has done the wrong.

It must be understood that neither by word nor deed had I given Fortunato cause to doubt my good will. I continued, as was my wont, to smile in his face, and he did not perceive that my smile *now* was at the thought of his immolation.

He had a weak point — this Fortunato — although in other regards he was a man to be respected and even feared. He prided himself on his connoisseurship in wine. Few Italians have the true virtuoso spirit. For the most part their enthusiasm is adopted to suit the time and opportunity — to practice imposture upon the British and Austrian *millionaires*. In painting and gemmary Fortunato, like his countrymen, was a quack — but in the matter of old wines he was sincere. In this respect I did not differ from him materially; I was skilful in the Italian vintages myself, and bought largely whenever I could.

It was about dusk, one evening during the supreme madness of the carnival season, that I encountered my friend. He accosted me with excessive warmth, for he had been drinking much. The man wore motley. He had on a tight-fitting parti-striped dress, and his head was surmounted by the conical cap and bells. I was so pleased to see him that I thought I should never have done wringing his hand.

I said to him — "My dear Fortunato, you are luckily met. How remarkably   5 well you are looking to-day! But I have received a pipe° of what passes for Amontillado, and I have my doubts."

"How?" said he. "Amontillado? A pipe? Impossible! And in the middle of the carnival!"

"I have my doubts," I replied; "and I was silly enough to pay the full Amontillado price without consulting you in the matter. You were not to be found, and I was fearful of losing a bargain."

"Amontillado!"

"I have my doubts."

"Amontillado!"   10

"And I must satisfy them."

"Amontillado!"

"As you are engaged, I am on my way to Luchesi. If any one has a critical turn, it is he. He will tell me —"

"Luchesi cannot tell Amontillado from Sherry."

"And yet some fools will have it that his taste is a match for your own."   15

"Come, let us go."

"Whither?"

"To your vaults."

"My friend, no; I will not impose upon your good nature. I perceive you have an engagement. Luchesi —"

---

pipe: A large keg or cask.

"I have no engagement; — come." 20

"My friend, no. It is not the engagement, but the severe cold with which I perceive you are afflicted. The vaults are insufferably damp. They are encrusted with nitre."

"Let us go, nevertheless. The cold is merely nothing. Amontillado! You have been imposed upon. And as for Luchesi, he cannot distinguish Sherry from Amontillado."

Thus speaking, Fortunato possessed himself of my arm. Putting on a mask of black silk, and drawing a *roquelaire*° closely about my person, I suffered him to hurry me to my palazzo.

There were no attendants at home; they had absconded to make merry in honor of the time. I had told them that I should not return until the morning, and had given them explicit orders not to stir from the house. These orders were sufficient, I well knew, to insure their immediate disappearance, one and all, as soon as my back was turned.

I took from their sconces two flambeaux, and giving one to Fortunato, 25 bowed him through several suites of rooms to the archway that led into the vaults. I passed down a long and winding staircase, requesting him to be cautious as he followed. We came at length to the foot of the descent, and stood together on the damp ground of the catacombs of the Montresors.

The gait of my friend was unsteady, and the bells upon his cap jingled as he strode.

"The pipe," said he.

"It is farther on," said I; "but observe the white web-work which gleams from these cavern walls."

He turned towards me, and looked into my eyes with two filmy orbs that distilled the rheum of intoxication.

"Nitre?" he asked, at length. 30

"Nitre," I replied. "How long have you had that cough?"

"Ugh! ugh! ugh! — ugh! ugh! ugh! — ugh! ugh! ugh! — ugh! ugh! ugh! — ugh! ugh! ugh!"

My poor friend found it impossible to reply for many minutes.

"It is nothing," he said, at last.

"Come," I said, with decision, "we will go back; your health is precious. You 35 are rich, respected, admired, beloved; you are happy, as once I was. You are a man to be missed. For me it is no matter. We will go back; you will be ill, and I cannot be responsible. Besides, there is Luchesi —"

"Enough," he said; "the cough is a mere nothing; it will not kill me. I shall not die of a cough."

"True — true," I replied; "and, indeed, I had no intention of alarming you unnecessarily — but you should use all proper caution. A draught of this Medoc will defend us from the damps."

---

roquelaire: A short cloak.

Here I knocked off the neck of a bottle which I drew from a long row of its fellows that lay upon the mould.

"Drink," I said, presenting him the wine.

He raised it to his lips with a leer. He paused and nodded to me familiarly, 40 while his bells jingled.

"I drink," he said, "to the buried that repose around us."

"And I to your long life."

He again took my arm, and we proceeded.

"These vaults," he said, "are extensive."

"The Montresors," I replied, "were a great and numerous family." 45

"I forget your arms."

"A huge human foot d'or,° in a field azure; the foot crushes a serpent rampant whose fangs are imbedded in the heel."

"And the motto?"

"Nemo me impune lacessit."°

"Good!" he said. 50

The wine sparkled in his eyes and the bells jingled. My own fancy grew warm with the Medoc. We had passed through walls of piled bones, with casks and puncheons intermingling, into the inmost recesses of the catacombs. I paused again, and this time I made bold to seize Fortunato by an arm above the elbow.

"The nitre!" I said; "see, it increases. It hangs like moss upon the vaults. We are below the river's bed. The drops of moisture trickle among the bones. Come, we will go back ere it is too late. Your cough—"

"It is nothing," he said; "let us go on. But first, another draught of the Medoc."

I broke and reached him a flaçon of De Grâve. He emptied it at a breath. His eyes flashed with a fierce light. He laughed and threw the bottle upwards with a gesticulation I did not understand.

I looked at him in surprise. He repeated the movement—a grotesque one. 55

"You do not comprehend?" he said.

"Not I," I replied.

"Then you are not of the brotherhood."

"How?"

"You are not of the masons." 60

"Yes, yes," I said, "yes, yes."

"You? Impossible! A mason?"

"A mason," I replied.

"A sign," he said.

"It is this," I answered, producing a trowel from beneath the folds of my 65 *roquelaire.*

"You jest," he exclaimed, recoiling a few paces. "But let us proceed to the Amontillado."

---

d'or: Of gold.   ***Nemo me impune lacessit:*** No one provokes me with impunity (Latin; the motto of the Order of the Thistle in Scotland and the national motto of Scotland).

"Be it so," I said, replacing the tool beneath the cloak, and again offering him my arm. He leaned upon it heavily. We continued our route in search of the Amontillado. We passed through a range of low arches, descended, passed on, and descending again, arrived at a deep crypt, in which the foulness of the air caused our flambeaux rather to glow than flame.

At the most remote end of the crypt there appeared another less spacious. Its walls had been lined with human remains, piled to the vault overhead, in the fashion of the great catacombs of Paris. Three sides of this interior crypt were still ornamented in this manner. From the fourth the bones had been thrown down, and lay promiscuously upon the earth, forming at one point a mound of some size. Within the wall thus exposed by the displacing of the bones, we perceived a still interior recess, in depth about four feet, in width three, in height six or seven. It seemed to have been constructed for no especial use within itself, but formed merely the interval between two of the colossal supports of the roof of the catacombs, and was backed by one of their circumscribing walls of solid granite.

It was in vain that Fortunato, uplifting his dull torch, endeavored to pry into the depth of the recess. Its termination the feeble light did not enable us to see.

"Proceed," I said; "herein is the Amontillado. As for Luchesi —"   70

"He is an ignoramus," interrupted my friend, as he stepped unsteadily forward, while I followed immediately at his heels. In an instant he had reached the extremity of the niche, and finding his progress arrested by the rock, stood stupidly bewildered. A moment more and I had fettered him to the granite. In its surface were two iron staples, distant from each other about two feet, horizontally. From one of these depended a short chain, from the other a padlock. Throwing the links about his waist, it was but the work of a few seconds to secure it. He was too much astounded to resist. Withdrawing the key I stepped back from the recess.

"Pass your hand," I said, "over the wall; you cannot help feeling the nitre. Indeed it is *very* damp. Once more let me *implore* you to return. No? Then I must positively leave you. But I must first render you all the little attentions in my power."

"The Amontillado!" ejaculated my friend, not yet recovered from his astonishment.

"True," I replied; "the Amontillado."

As I said these words I busied myself among the pile of bones of which I have   75
before spoken. Throwing them aside, I soon uncovered a quantity of building stone and mortar. With these materials and with the aid of my trowel, I began vigorously to wall up the entrance of the niche.

I had scarcely laid the first tier of the masonry when I discovered that the intoxication of Fortunato had in a great measure worn off. The earliest indication I had of this was a low moaning cry from the depth of the recess. It was *not* the cry of a drunken man. There was then a long and obstinate silence. I laid the second tier, and the third, and the fourth; and then I heard the furious vibrations of the chain. The noise lasted for several minutes, during which, that I might hearken to it with the more satisfaction, I ceased my labors and sat down upon the bones. When at last the clanking subsided, I resumed the trowel, and finished without interruption the fifth, the sixth, and the seventh tier. The wall was now nearly upon a level with my breast. I again paused, and holding the flambeaux over the mason-work, threw a few feeble rays upon the figure within.

A succession of loud and shrill screams, bursting suddenly from the throat of the chained form, seemed to thrust me violently back. For a brief moment I hesitated — I trembled. Unsheathing my rapier, I began to grope with it about the recess: but the thought of an instant reassured me. I placed my hand upon the solid fabric of the catacombs, and felt satisfied. I reapproached the wall. I replied to the yells of him who clamored. I re-echoed — I aided — I surpassed them in volume and in strength. I did this, and the clamorer grew still.

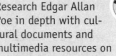

Research Edgar Allan Poe in depth with cultural documents and multimedia resources on *LiterActive*.

It was now midnight, and my task was drawing to a close. I had completed the eighth, the ninth, and the tenth tier. I had finished a portion of the last and the eleventh; there remained but a single stone to be fitted and plastered in. I struggled with its weight; I placed it partially in its destined position. But now there came from out the niche a low laugh that erected the hairs upon my head. It was succeeded by a sad voice, which I had difficulty in recognizing as that of the noble Fortunato. The voice said —

"Ha! ha! ha! — he! he! — a very good joke indeed — an excellent jest. We will have many a rich laugh about it at the palazzo — he! he! he! — over our wine — he! he! he!"

"The Amontillado!" I said.   80

"He! he! he! — he! he! he! — yes, the Amontillado. But is it not getting late? Will not they be awaiting us at the palazzo, the Lady Fortunato and the rest? Let us be gone."

"Yes," I said, "let us be gone."

"For the love of God, Montresor!"

"Yes," I said, "for the love of God!"

But to these words I hearkened in vain for a reply. I grew impatient. I called   85
aloud —

"Fortunato!"

No answer. I called again —

"Fortunato!"

No answer still. I thrust a torch through the remaining aperture and let it fall within. There came forth in return only a jingling of the bells. My heart grew sick — on account of the dampness of the catacombs. I hastened to make an end of my labor. I forced the last stone into its position; I plastered it up. Against the new masonry I re-erected the old rampart of bones. For the half of a century no mortal has disturbed them. *In páce requiescat!*°

In páce requiescat!: May he rest in peace!

Katherine Anne Porter   1890–1980

The Jilting of Granny Weatherall   [1929]

She flicked her wrist neatly out of Doctor Harry's pudgy careful fingers and pulled the sheet up to her chin. The brat ought to be in knee breeches. Doctoring around the country with spectacles on his nose! "Get along now, take your schoolbooks and go. There's nothing wrong with me."

Doctor Harry spread a warm paw like a cushion on her forehead where the forked green vein danced and made her eyelids twitch. "Now, now, be a good girl, and we'll have you up in no time."

"That's no way to speak to a woman nearly eighty years old just because she's down. I'd have you respect your elders, young man."

"Well, Missy, excuse me." Doctor Harry patted her cheek. "But I've got to warn you, haven't I? You're a marvel, but you must be careful or you're going to be good and sorry."

"Don't tell me what I'm going to be. I'm on my feet now, morally speaking.   5 It's Cornelia. I had to go to bed to get rid of her."

Her bones felt loose, and floated around in her skin, and Doctor Harry floated like a balloon around the foot of the bed. He floated and pulled down his waistcoat and swung his glasses on a cord. "Well, stay where you are, it certainly can't hurt you."

"Get along and doctor your sick," said Granny Weatherall. "Leave a well woman alone. I'll call for you when I want you. . . . Where were you forty years ago when I pulled through milk-leg and double pneumonia? You weren't even born. Don't let Cornelia lead you on," she shouted, because Doctor Harry appeared to float up to the ceiling and out. "I pay my own bills, and I don't throw my money away on nonsense!"

She meant to wave good-by, but it was too much trouble. Her eyes closed of themselves, it was like a dark curtain drawn around the bed. The pillow rose and floated under her, pleasant as a hammock in a light wind. She listened to the leaves rustling outside the window. No, somebody was swishing newspapers: no, Cornelia and Doctor Harry were whispering together. She leaped broad awake, thinking they whispered in her ear.

"She was never like this, *never* like this!" "Well, what can we expect?" "Yes, eighty years old. . . ."

Well, and what if she was? She still had ears. It was like Cornelia to whisper   10 around doors. She always kept things secret in such a public way. She was always being tactful and kind. Cornelia was dutiful; that was the trouble with her. Dutiful and good: "So good and dutiful," said Granny, "that I'd like to spank her." She saw herself spanking Cornelia and making a fine job of it.

"What'd you say, Mother?"

Granny felt her face tying up in hard knots.

"Can't a body think, I'd like to know?"

"I thought you might want something."

"I do. I want a lot of things. First off, go away and don't whisper."   15

She lay and drowsed, hoping in her sleep that the children would keep out and let her rest a minute. It had been a long day. Not that she was tired. It was always pleasant to snatch a minute now and then. There was always so much to be done, let me see: tomorrow.

Tomorrow was far away and there was nothing to trouble about. Things were finished somehow when the time came; thank God there was always a little margin over for peace: then a person could spread out the plan of life and tuck in the edges orderly. It was good to have everything clean and folded away, with the hair brushes and tonic bottles sitting straight on the white embroidered linen: the day started without fuss and the pantry shelves laid out with rows of jelly glasses and brown jugs and white stone-china jars with blue whirligigs and words painted on them: coffee, tea, sugar, ginger, cinnamon, allspice: and the bronze clock with the lion on top nicely dusted off. The dust that lion could collect in twenty-four hours! The box in the attic with all those letters tied up, well, she'd have to go through that tomorrow. All those letters — George's letters and John's letters and her letters to them both — lying around for the children to find afterwards made her uneasy. Yes, that would be tomorrow's business. No use to let them know how silly she had been once.

While she was rummaging around she found death in her mind and it felt clammy and unfamiliar. She had spent so much time preparing for death there was no need for bringing it up again. Let it take care of itself now. When she was sixty she had felt very old, finished, and went around making farewell trips to see her children and grandchildren, with a secret in her mind: This is the very last of your mother, children! Then she made her will and came down with a long fever. That was all just a notion like a lot of other things, but it was lucky too, for she had once for all got over the idea of dying for a long time. Now she couldn't be worried. She hoped she had better sense now. Her father had lived to be one hundred and two years old and had drunk a noggin of strong hot toddy on his last birthday. He told the reporters it was his daily habit, and he owed his long life to that. He had made quite a scandal and was very pleased about it. She believed she'd just plague Cornelia a little.

"Cornelia! Cornelia!" No footsteps, but a sudden hand on her cheek. "Bless you, where have you been?"

"Here, Mother."   20

"Well, Cornelia, I want a noggin of hot toddy."

"Are you cold, darling?"

"I'm chilly, Cornelia. Lying in bed stops the circulation. I must have told you that a thousand times."

Well, she could just hear Cornelia telling her husband that Mother was getting a little childish and they'd have to humor her. The thing that most annoyed her was that Cornelia thought she was deaf, dumb, and blind. Little hasty glances and tiny gestures tossed around her and over her head saying, "Don't cross her, let her have her way, she's eighty years old," and she sitting there as if she lived in a thin glass cage. Sometimes Granny almost made up her mind to pack up and move back to her own house where nobody could remind her every minute that she was old. Wait, wait, Cornelia, till your own children whisper behind your back!

In her day she had kept a better house and had got more work done. She wasn't too old yet for Lydia to be driving eighty miles for advice when one of the children jumped the track, and Jimmy still dropped in and talked things over: "Now, Mammy, you've a good business head, I want to know what you think of this?..." Old. Cornelia couldn't change the furniture around without asking. Little things, little things! They had been so sweet when they were little. Granny wished the old days were back again with the children young and everything to be done over. It had been a hard pull, but not too much for her. When she thought of all the food she had cooked, and all the clothes she had cut and sewed, and all the gardens she had made — well, the children showed it. There they were, made out of her, and they couldn't get away from that. Sometimes she wanted to see John again and point to them and say, Well, I didn't do so badly, did I? But that would have to wait. That was for tomorrow. She used to think of him as a man, but now all the children were older than their father, and he would be a child beside her if she saw him now. It seemed strange and there was something wrong in the idea. Why, he couldn't possibly recognize her. She had fenced in a hundred acres once, digging the post holes herself and clamping the wires with just a negro boy to help. That changed a woman. John would be looking for a young woman with the peaked Spanish comb in her hair and the painted fan. Digging post holes changed a woman. Riding country roads in the winter when women had their babies was another thing: sitting up nights with sick horses and sick negroes and sick children and hardly ever losing one. John, I hardly ever lost one of them! John would see that in a minute, that would be something he could understand, she wouldn't have to explain anything!

It made her feel like rolling up her sleeves and putting the whole place to rights again. No matter if Cornelia was determined to be everywhere at once, there were a great many things left undone on this place. She would start tomorrow and do them. It was good to be strong enough for everything, even if all you made melted and changed and slipped under your hands, so that by the time you finished you almost forgot what you were working for. What was it I set out to do? she asked herself intently, but she could not remember. A fog rose over the valley, she saw it marching across the creek swallowing the trees and moving up the hill like an army of ghosts. Soon it would be at the near edge of the orchard, and then it was time to go in and light the lamps. Come in, children, don't stay out in the night air.

Lighting the lamps had been beautiful. The children huddled up to her and breathed like little calves waiting at the bars in the twilight. Their eyes followed the match and watched the flame rise and settle in a blue curve, then they moved away from her. The lamp was lit, they didn't have to be scared and hang on to mother any more. Never, never, never more. God, for all my life I thank Thee. Without Thee, my God, I could never have done it. Hail, Mary, full of grace.

I want you to pick all the fruit this year and see that nothing is wasted. There's always someone who can use it. Don't let good things rot for want of using. You waste life when you waste good food. Don't let things get lost. It's bitter to lose things. Now, don't let me get to thinking, not when I am tired and taking a little nap before supper. . . .

The pillow rose about her shoulders and pressed against her heart and the memory was being squeezed out of it: oh, push down the pillow, somebody: it would smother her if she tried to hold it. Such a fresh breeze blowing and such a green day with no threats in it. But he had not come, just the same. What does a woman do when she has put on the white veil and set out the white cake for a man and he doesn't come? She tried to remember. No, I swear he never harmed me but in that. He never harmed me but in that . . . and what if he did? There was the day, the day, but a whirl of dark smoke rose and covered it, crept up and over into the bright field where everything was planted so carefully in orderly rows. That was hell, she knew hell when she saw it. For sixty years she had prayed against remembering him and against losing her soul in the deep pit of hell, and now the two things were mingled in one and the thought of him was a smoky cloud from hell that moved and crept in her head when she had just got rid of Doctor Harry and was trying to rest a minute. Wounded vanity, Ellen, said a sharp voice in the top of her mind. Don't let your wounded vanity get the upper hand of you. Plenty of girls get jilted. You were jilted, weren't you? Then stand up to it. Her eyelids wavered and let in streamers of blue-gray light like tissue paper over her eyes. She must get up and pull the shades down or she'd never sleep. She was in bed again and the shades were not down. How could that happen? Better turn over, hide from the light, sleeping in the light gave you nightmares. "Mother, how do you feel now?" and a stinging wetness on her forehead. But I don't like having my face washed in cold water!

Hapsy? George? Lydia? Jimmy? No, Cornelia, and her features were swollen and full of little puddles. "They're coming, darling, they'll all be here soon." Go wash your face, child, you look funny.

Instead of obeying, Cornelia knelt down and put her head on the pillow. She seemed to be talking but there was no sound. "Well, are you tongue-tied? Whose birthday is it? Are you going to give a party?"

Cornelia's mouth moved urgently in strange shapes. "Don't do that, you bother me, daughter."

"Oh, no, Mother. Oh, no. . . ."

Nonsense. It was strange about children. They disputed your every word. "No what, Cornelia?"

"Here's Doctor Harry."

"I won't see that boy again. He just left five minutes ago."

"That was this morning, Mother. It's night now. Here's the nurse."

"This is Doctor Harry, Mrs. Weatherall. I never saw you look so young and happy!"

"Ah, I'll never be young again—but I'd be happy if they'd let me lie in peace and get rested."

She thought she spoke up loudly, but no one answered. A warm weight on 40
her forehead, a warm bracelet on her wrist, and a breeze went on whispering,
trying to tell her something. A shuffle of leaves in the everlasting hand of God,
He blew on them and they danced and rattled. "Mother, don't mind, we're
going to give you a little hypodermic." "Look here, daughter, how do ants get in
this bed? I saw sugar ants yesterday." Did you send for Hapsy too?

It was Hapsy she really wanted. She had to go a long way back through
a great many rooms to find Hapsy standing with a baby on her arm. She seemed
to herself to be Hapsy also, and the baby on Hapsy's arm was Hapsy and himself
and herself, all at once, and there was no surprise in the meeting. Then Hapsy
melted from within and turned flimsy as gray gauze and the baby was a gauzy
shadow, and Hapsy came up close and said, "I thought you'd never come," and
looked at her very searchingly and said, "You haven't changed a bit!" They
leaned forward to kiss, when Cornelia began whispering from a long way off,
"Oh, is there anything you want to tell me? Is there anything I can do for you?"

Yes, she had changed her mind after sixty years and she would like to see
George. I want you to find George. Find him and be sure to tell him I forgot him.
I want him to know I had my husband just the same and my children and my
house like any other woman. A good house too and a good husband that I loved
and fine children out of him. Better than I hoped for even. Tell him I was given
back everything he took away and more. Oh, no, oh, God, no, there was something else besides the house and the man and the children. Oh, surely they were
not all? What was it? Something not given back. . . . Her breath crowded down
under her ribs and grew into a monstrous frightening shape with cutting edges;
it bored up into her head, and the agony was unbelievable: Yes, John, get the
Doctor now, no more talk, my time has come.

When this one was born it should be the last. The last. It should have been
born first, for it was the one she had truly wanted. Everything came in good
time. Nothing left out, left over. She was strong, in three days she would be as
well as ever. Better. A woman needed milk in her to have her full health.

"Mother, do you hear me?"

"I've been telling you —"   45

"Mother, Father Connolly's here."

"I went to Holy Communion only last week. Tell him I'm not so sinful as all
that."

"Father just wants to speak to you."

He could speak as much as he pleased. It was like him to drop in and inquire
about her soul as if it were a teething baby, and then stay on for a cup of tea and
a round of cards and gossip. He always had a funny story of some sort, usually
about an Irishman who made his little mistakes and confessed them, and the
point lay in some absurd thing he would blurt out in the confessional showing
his struggles between native piety and original sin. Granny felt easy about her
soul. Cornelia, where are your manners? Give Father Connolly a chair. She had
her secret comfortable understanding with a few favorite saints who cleared a
straight road to God for her. All as surely signed and sealed as the papers for the

new Forty Acres. Forever . . . heirs and assigns forever. Since the day the wedding cake was not cut, but thrown out and wasted. The whole bottom dropped out of the world, and there she was blind and sweating with nothing under her feet and the walls falling away. His hand had caught her under the breast, she had not fallen, there was the freshly polished floor with the green rug on it, just as before. He had cursed like a sailor's parrot and said, "I'll kill him for you." Don't lay a hand on him, for my sake leave something to God. "Now, Ellen, you must believe what I tell you. . . ."

So there was nothing, nothing to worry about any more, except sometimes   50
in the night one of the children screamed in a nightmare, and they both hustled out shaking and hunting for the matches and calling, "There, wait a minute, here we are!" John, get the doctor now, Hapsy's time has come. But there was Hapsy standing by the bed in a white cap. "Cornelia, tell Hapsy to take off her cap. I can't see her plain."

Her eyes opened very wide and the room stood out like a picture she had seen somewhere. Dark colors with the shadows rising towards the ceiling in long angles. The tall black dresser gleamed with nothing on it but John's picture, enlarged from a little one, with John's eyes very black when they should have been blue. You never saw him, so how do you know how he looked? But the man insisted the copy was perfect, it was very rich and handsome. For a picture, yes, but it's not my husband. The table by the bed had a linen cover and a candle and a crucifix. The light was blue from Cornelia's silk lampshades. No sort of light at all, just frippery. You had to live forty years with kerosene lamps to appreciate honest electricity. She felt very strong and she saw Doctor Harry with a rosy nimbus around him.

"You look like a saint, Doctor Harry, and I vow that's as near as you'll ever come to it."

"She's saying something."

"I heard you, Cornelia. What's all this carrying-on?"

"Father Connolly's saying—"   55

Cornelia's voice staggered and bumped like a cart in a bad road. It rounded corners and turned back again and arrived nowhere. Granny stepped up in the cart very lightly and reached for the reins, but a man sat beside her and she knew him by his hands, driving the cart. She did not look in his face, for she knew without seeing, but looked instead down the road where the trees leaned over and bowed to each other and a thousand birds were singing a Mass. She felt like singing too, but she put her hand in the bosom of her dress and pulled out a rosary, and Father Connolly murmured Latin in a very solemn voice and tickled her feet. My God, will you stop that nonsense? I'm a married woman. What if he did run away and leave me to face the priest by myself? I found another a whole world better. I wouldn't have exchanged my husband for anybody except St. Michael himself, and you may tell him that for me with a thank you in the bargain.

Light flashed on her closed eyelids, and a deep roaring shook her. Cornelia, is that lightning? I hear thunder. There's going to be a storm. Close all the windows. Call the children in. . . . "Mother, here we are, all of us." "Is that you, Hapsy?" "Oh, no, I'm Lydia. We drove as fast as we could." Their faces drifted above her, drifted away. The rosary fell out of her hands and Lydia put it back. Jimmy tried to help, their hands fumbled together, and Granny closed two fingers around Jimmy's thumb. Beads wouldn't do, it must be something alive. She was so amazed her thoughts ran round and round. So, my dear Lord, this is my death and I wasn't even thinking about it. My children have come to see me die. But I can't, it's not time. Oh, I always hated surprises. I wanted to give Cornelia the amethyst set — Cornelia, you're to have the amethyst set, but Hapsy's to wear it when she wants, and, Doctor Harry, do shut up. Nobody sent for you. Oh, my dear Lord, do wait a minute. I meant to do something about the Forty Acres, Jimmy doesn't need it and Lydia will later on, with that worthless husband of hers. I meant to finish the altar cloth and send six bottles of wine to Sister Borgia for her dyspepsia. I want to send six bottles of wine to Sister Borgia, Father Connolly, now don't let me forget.

Cornelia's voice made short turns and tilted over and crashed. "Oh, Mother, oh, Mother, oh, Mother. . . ."

"I'm not going, Cornelia. I'm taken by surprise. I can't go."

You'll see Hapsy again. What about her? "I thought you'd never come." 60 Granny made a long journey outward, looking for Hapsy. What if I don't find her? What then? Her heart sank down and down, there was no bottom to death, she couldn't come to the end of it. The blue light from Cornelia's lampshade drew into a tiny point in the center of her brain, it flickered and winked like an eye, quietly it fluttered and dwindled. Granny lay curled down within herself, amazed and watchful, staring at the point of light that was herself; her body was now only a deeper mass of shadow in an endless darkness and this darkness would curl around the light and swallow it up. God, give a sign!

For the second time there was no sign. Again no bridegroom and the priest in the house. She could not remember any other sorrow because this grief wiped them all away. Oh, no, there's nothing more cruel than this — I'll never forgive it. She stretched herself with a deep breath and blew out the light.

Nahid Rachlin b. 1946

Departures   [1992]

I have no choice, I have to let him go, Farogh thought, as she went about making last-minute preparations for a farewell lunch for her son. But how can I really accept his going to a war that has killed and maimed hundreds of young men? Seventeen years of attachment, of interdependency, could be severed in an instant. Teheran was not the same. On every street at least one family had lost someone to the war. War was like a wild, blood-thirsty animal, merciless in its killing. Black flags indicating mourning hung on so many of the doors of houses. A fountain of red water, to symbolize blood, stood on Martyrdom Square, a few blocks away.

She spread a cloth on the living room rug and set plates and silverware on it. Then she put several bouquets of flowers she had picked from the courtyard on different spots of the cloth. The room was spacious with a high ceiling and two long, rectangular windows overlooking the courtyard. But the room, the whole house, had an empty, forlorn feel to it already, now that Ahmad was going away and might not come back to it for weeks, if ever. I must not let my thoughts get so carried away.

She went into the adjacent room and began to change. She took her blue dress with green floral designs on it out of the trunk in the corner of the room and put it on. Then she pulled her hair back with a tortoise-shell barrette. I should go and wake up Hassan, she thought. It is almost noon, but then he came home late from the rug shop last night. Let him sleep. He is no solace to me anyway. For the first time in years she thought of her old job, working as a pharmacist's assistant, and felt a pang of sadness that she had given it up. She used to like helping out the customers or talking with the other employees, two nice men, about drugs, world affairs. But Hassan had started to complain, "The house is a mess, we never have a proper meal." And then when she became pregnant with Ahmad he insisted, "You can't go to work like that, it makes me ashamed. I'm the man . . ." Maybe I had given in to him too easily, she thought regretfully. And now at my age, it would be hard to find employment. Jobs are scarce for women anyway.

Her eyes went to Ahmad's photograph in a silver frame on the mantle. Something about his eyes caught her attention. They reminded her of someone . . . Karim. They had the same eyes, dark and dreamy. What would her life have been like if she had married Karim instead of Hassan? Over the expanse of years, she could vividly see Karim — thin, tall, sensitive looking. She remembered meeting him one summer when both of their families had rented cottages in Darband. They had begun to talk by the stream that ran in front of the cottages. Then they would meet secretly behind the hill and walk together through cherry and quince orchards, holding hands, kissing. They had continued meeting for a while when they returned to the city. They would go to an afternoon movie in a far off neighborhood or to a distant park or a restaurant where no one would recognize them. A year later he left for America to study. He wrote letters to her in code but after a while they slowed down and then she did not hear from him again. Before he left he gave her a silver bracelet with a garnet stone on it. For years she had worn the bracelet. Then the stone fell off and got lost and the silver became dented and finally broke. Now she wore a row of thin, gold bracelets that Ahmad had given to her last year for her fortieth birthday. In the photograph Ahmad was standing in a boat on a lake with a pole in his hands. Curls of hair hung over his forehead. Farogh remembered sitting with Karim in a rowboat at dusk in Darband far away from where they were staying. His face was lit with lights reflected from cottages around the lake. Karim could have been Ahmad's father just as easily as Hassan, if judged by physical appearance. Did

Ahmad really look that much like Karim or was that just how she recalled it? She wished she had a photograph of Karim, wished she could catch a glimpse of his face. She was only sixteen years old when Hassan's mother and sister came over to her parents' house to request that she marry her son. She had seen Hassan around the neighborhood—a fat, indolent looking man, fifteen years older than herself. She had tried to resist, but her parents had given her little choice. It suddenly seemed that Hassan had kept her in captivity all these years.

A few relatives had come over for lunch, to say goodbye to Ahmad—Hassan's mother and sister, her own nephews, nieces and cousins. The meal she had spent days preparing was lavish and colorful. Large platters were filled with a variety of rices and stews and salads she had garnished with fresh mint and tarragon leaves. The lacy tablecloth one of her daughters had knitted herself and sent to her went well with the silver utensils with floral designs embossed on them. The air was filled with the aroma of turmeric, saffron, dried lemon, pepper. Conversation, laughter, the clatter of dishes, created a lively chorus. Everyone was wearing their good clothes. Her nieces had shiny shoes on and wore ribbons in their hair. It was as if no one were aware that the country was torn by war. An alley cat with long, yellow hair found its way into the room. It stood by the cloth and mewed for food. Farogh put some meat and sauce in a platter and placed it before the cat. A sudden breeze outside made the wind chimes hanging on a hook on the door jangle.

Hassan was talking with others in a haughty manner, interrupting them with remarks like, "Let me explain," "I know what you're trying to say." He talked about life after death as if no one had ever heard of it—finding oneself in heaven: a vast garden redolent with fruit, flowers, streams flowing everywhere, angels with pink and blue wings flying in the air ready to be of service, some of them singing beautiful songs. Ahmad was lucky to be given the chance to fight in the war, he said. If he himself were a young man he would be eager to do so. She felt her cheeks flushing with anger. Didn't he see the danger hanging over Ahmad?

They were fussing over Ahmad now. Hassan's mother added food to his plate and said, "You won't get anything this good for a long time." Hassan kept leaning over and squeezing his arm affectionately. Ahmad's cousins glanced at him with adoring eyes—particularly Soosan, a pretty, fourteen-year-old girl, who had a crush on him. And Mohsen, a year younger than he and going to the same high school, always looked up to him as if he were an older brother. Then why aren't they as deeply upset as I am? She felt really apart from everyone. Then she thought, I have never been like all the others around me.

When she and her three sisters were growing up, she was the one, and the only one among them, who said, "Mother, why can't I go to the university?"

"University? How does that help you with diapering a baby?"

"Mother, why do some people die young?"

"How do I know, am I God?"

And then she was the only one who had resisted marrying the man selected for her. She had grown to like him (she even loved him at moments) but a part of her remained unconnected to him, to the life in this alley. Ahmad was her strongest bond . . . What good would it do to start an argument — Ahmad had to go no matter what.

Ahmad seemed strangely calm after weeks of turmoil and vacillation. At first he had tried to get himself exempted by pretending he could not hear in one ear but that had not worked. They had said, "You have one good ear . . ." Finally he was reconciled to going.

Ahmad's aunt, a gaunt looking woman, said, "Farogh, don't think so much, your hair is going to fall out."

"Yes, like my sister, one day her hair fell off in patches. She was very   15 thoughtful too," Hassan's mother said. She was not wearing her artificial teeth and her mouth was sunken. She ate and spoke with difficulty.

Farogh tried to smile but she could not stop her thoughts jumping away from the scene. Her mind went to those days of growing up, the daily changes coming on herself and her sisters, bodily changes (when one of her breasts started budding while the other lagged behind), her sister Mehri growing taller and prettier, her oldest sister Narghes getting married, her face radiant behind the gauzy veil, sequins shining in her hair and dress. Her own first awareness that looking at a boy made her feel different. Then her mind drifted to those cool, fragrant orchards, the winding, hilly roads where she and Karim had taken walks and talked — two heedless adolescents. One evening she was wearing a pale blue dress with short ruffled sleeves, which she had a tailor make for her. Her hair, wavy and black, thicker than now, hung loose over her shoulders. She had been feeling very carefree. The other person, the person I was then, was so much more real than the one I am now. Hassan's creation, she thought.

The next day Farogh watched Ahmad polish his boots and put them on. He was already wearing his army clothes. He looked determined, even proud. Was that an act? As a boy he had been timid. He would stand and watch other boys in rough play without ever participating, she remembered. He was introspective, unlike his father. She went over to him and gave him several handkerchiefs on which she had embroidered his name. He put them in his already packed suitcase.

Hassan came into the room and the three of them waited for the honking of the army truck which was supposed to pick Ahmad up. Then the honking came. Ahmad shut his suitcase and picked it up and they all went outside. By the door Ahmad kissed each of them quickly.

"Write soon, will you?" she said.

"Of course," Ahmad said. But he seemed distracted, with a faraway look   20 about him. He walked rapidly toward the truck which had parked on the avenue running perpendicular to the small alley.

Farogh turned to Hassan and for the first time she could see his composure was broken. But then he quickly looked away from her, shutting her out. She had flashes of herself alone in the house with Hassan, the two of them eating together and then going to bed and she had a sudden, aching wish that it were Hassan rather than Ahmad who was leaving, whose life was at risk.

After Ahmad's departure, she continued to feel the pain of that other departure, when Karim had left the country, for a bigger, freer world. He had said he would come back and apply what he had learned there, but of course he had not. He had written her a few letters from America the first year he was there, then they stopped abruptly. She had an impulse to write to him, to make some connection with him. She still had his address in an old address book. He was in the same place, his mother had said to her once in passing as they met in a line buying food. His mother had added, "He got married to an American girl, a mistake." She had not elaborated but now the remark made Farogh think: maybe he too looks back at those days. She took out a sheet of paper from a stationery box and began to write a letter to him. She hesitated. I am a married woman. But then, she thought, I need someone.

". . . It's difficult for me to write this letter, it has been so many years . . . Still, I remember all the walks we took together. I saw my son going to the army a few days ago and it was like that day I saw you leaving. You were the same age then as Ahmad is now. I hope you'll write back if you get this . . ."

After she sealed the letter she stood and studied herself in the mirror as if she had not looked at her reflection for a long time. Her face was round, her features delicate. She was on the plump side. That and the roundness of her face made her look young for her age. She was attractive in a healthy, robust way. Odd, she thought, I've been living in hell since Ahmad left. It made her feel that she was not quite connected to her body.

She went out to mail the letter. She passed the burnt-out, boarded-up tea 25 house, the sooty, grimy facade of an old hotel, but more than anything she was keenly aware of the black flags on the doors and the sound of prayers for the dead coming out from Noori Mosque. She paused by Jaafari's house. One of their sons had been wounded in the war and flown to Teheran to be treated at a hospital. Should I go in and ask about their son, she wondered. But the door was locked and there was a silence about it that was forbidding. She walked on, passing the house where the opium addict lived with his mother.

As she dropped the letter into the post office mailbox and heard the quiet thud of its hitting the bottom, a surge of happiness came over her, thinking of the letter traveling so far away — in a truck to the airport and then on the plane and from the plane in a truck again and finally landing at the address where Karim lived. Would his face light up at seeing her name or would he just be surprised?

Three weeks later she found a letter in the hallway which the mailman must have dropped in. It was an air-letter from America, she immediately noticed. She was startled by the sight. She realized she had not really expected an answer and so quickly. She opened it, her hand shaky. It was very brief, only a few lines.

". . . I'm coming home for a five-day visit — that's all that my schedule will permit. From Sept. 1–5. Can you come to my mother's house and see me? . . ." It was cool, detached. "That's all my schedule will permit," he had said. He had not asked to see her privately. She put the letter in a box, and put the box at the bottom of the trunk in the basement.

But as the date he had mentioned approached, she felt an urge to drop in at his mother's house and see him. Now she was grateful that Hassan stayed at his shop so late at night and slept most of the day, making him oblivious of the changes in her mood, swinging back and forth. On September first, as soon as she woke up, she thought of Karim. This is the first day of his arrival. I should wait a day or two before going over, she thought.

On the afternoon of September third, as soon as Hassan left for work she 30 began to get ready to go over to Zeinab's house. She wondered what she should wear. Something that would not draw attention to itself, she decided. She put on an inconspicuous brown dress and her dark blue *chador.*°

She was hesitant again when she reached the house but she forced herself to knock. Zeinab opened the door to her.

"Oh, Farogh Joon, how are you, how nice to see you."

"I have a favor to ask," Farogh said, feeling nervous. "If I could borrow a coupon for sugar."

"Of course. I owe you so many coupons, I'll be happy to help you out. By the way my son is here. He comes every year at this time, stays only a few days."

"Every year . . ." she said inaudibly. How odd, all these years he has come back 35 here to this street a few blocks from my house and I had no idea. She had a sharp sense of having been betrayed. Then she thought, that's absurd . . .

"Have you had any word from Ahmad?"

"A couple of letters."

"Who is there?" Farogh heard a male voice. It was undeniably Karim's.

"It's Farogh," Zeinab said. "We're coming in." Then she turned to her, "Come and sit down for a while, I just had the samovar set up for tea."

Farogh followed Zeinab into the courtyard. A man, Karim, was sitting there 40 on the rug in the shade of a plum tree, glancing at a book. He rose as she and Zeinab approached. "I don't know if I would have recognized you after so many years," he said.

She could not bring herself to say anything. He was so unfamiliar. He was older of course, with patches of gray showing in his hair, and there were lines on his face, but that was not what made him different. His eyes were not so much dreamy as wary now. And there was something stiff and alien in his manner and tone.

"Sit down, I'll bring up some cups," Zeinab said.

He sat down again and Farogh sat next to him on the rug, staring awkwardly at the yellow butterflies flitting in the parched bushes by the small, algae-covered pool.

"What have you been doing with yourself?" he asked.

"What does a wife and mother do?" she said formally, catching his tone. 45 "Do you have any children?"

---

chador: Full-length outer garment, thrown over the head and held shut in front, worn in public by Muslim women, especially in Iran.

"No, not yet," he said. "I've been so busy with work. I've been teaching at UCLA."

The foreign word made her even more uncomfortable. "Do you write books?"

He chuckled. "I read them more than write them."

The samovar was hissing, giving out sparks, which hung in the air for an instant and then faded. Zeinab came up the kitchen stairs, carrying a tray containing cups and sugar. She sat down and began to pour tea for everyone. They started to drink slowly, quietly for a moment.

"I wish Karim would come and live here," Zeinab said, looking at her son 50 and then at her. "He's past the age of being drafted."

He patted his mother on the back, in a patronizing way, it seemed to Farogh. His movements were controlled as if he had practiced them and he knew precisely what effect they would have on others. So then, was it intentional that his gaze on her was at once detached and scrutinizing, reflecting a certain skepticism that made her feel diminished? Time has really played tricks, changed everything, him, myself. She looked at him, still hoping to reach the person he had been and to then see a reflection of herself, the way she was at fifteen, but none of it came. "I should be going, I have a lot of errands to do before dark."

"Here is a coupon," Zeinab said, putting a piece of paper in her hand.

Farogh put it in her purse and got up. "I hope you have a good visit," she said to Karim.

He and his mother got up also and followed her to the outside door. At the door he said to her cryptically, "We were children . . ." Then he turned around and went inside.

"Come back again soon," Zeinab said and then went inside also.   55

The sun was about to set as Farogh walked back. A kite had gotten caught in the branches of a tree and children had collected around it, shaking it, trying to get the kite free. She had a mental picture of Ahmad when he was a child and would go up to the roof of their house to fly his kites—he had bought one, lantern-shaped and lit from the inside, from a fancy store in another neighborhood. She thought of other stages of his growing up too, of when his voice had started to become streaky and bristles of hair to grow on his face. How is he going to have changed when he comes back, when I see him next?

She watched the busy street, taking in as much of it as she could, as if it were a mirage that might slip away from her at any moment.

Salman Rushdie   India, b. 1947

The Prophet's Hair   [1994]

Early in the year 19—, when Srinagar was under the spell of a winter so fierce it could crack men's bones as if they were glass, a young man upon whose cold-pinked skin there lay, like a frost, the unmistakable sheen of wealth was to be seen entering the most wretched and disreputable part of the city, where the houses of wood and corrugated iron seemed perpetually on the verge of losing their balance, and asking in low, grave tones where he might go to engage the services of a dependably professional burglar. The young man's name was Atta, and the rogues in that part of town directed him gleefully into ever darker and less public alleys, until in a yard wet with the blood of a slaughtered chicken he was set upon by two men whose faces he never saw, robbed of the substantial bank-roll which he had insanely brought on his solitary excursion, and beaten within an inch of his life.

Night fell. His body was carried by anonymous hands to the edge of the lake, whence it was transported by shikara across the water and deposited, torn and bleeding, on the deserted embankment of the canal which led to the gardens of Shalimar. At dawn the next morning a flower-vendor was rowing his boat through water to which the cold of the night had given the cloudy consistency of wild honey when he saw the prone form of young Atta, who was just beginning to stir and moan, and on whose now deathly pale skin the sheen of wealth could still be made out dimly beneath an actual layer of frost.

The flower-vendor moored his craft and by stooping over the mouth of the injured man was able to learn the poor fellow's address, which was mumbled through lips that could scarcely move; whereupon, hoping for a large tip, the hawker rowed Atta home to a large house on the shores of the lake, where a beautiful but inexplicably bruised young woman and her distraught, but equally handsome mother, neither of whom, it was clear from their eyes, had slept a wink from worrying, screamed at the sight of their Atta—who was the elder brother of the beautiful young woman—lying motionless amidst the funereally stunted winter blooms of the hopeful florist.

The flower-vendor was indeed paid off handsomely, not least to ensure his silence, and plays no further part in our story. Atta himself, suffering terribly from exposure as well as a broken skull, entered a coma which caused the city's finest doctors to shrug helplessly. It was therefore all the more remarkable that on the very next evening the most wretched and disreputable part of the city received a second unexpected visitor. This was Huma, the sister of the unfortunate young man, and her question was the same as her brother's, and asked in the same low, grave tones:

"Where may I hire a thief?"   5

The story of the rich idiot who had come looking for a burglar was already common knowledge in those insalubrious gullies, but this time the young woman added: "I should say that I am carrying no money, nor am I wearing any jewelry items. My father has disowned me and will pay no ransom if I am kidnapped; and a letter has been lodged with the Deputy Commissioner of Police, my uncle, to be opened in the event of my not being safe at home by morning. In that letter he will find full details of my journey here, and he will move Heaven and Earth to punish my assailants."

Her exceptional beauty, which was visible even through the enormous welts and bruises disfiguring her arms and forehead, coupled with the oddity of her inquiries, had attracted a sizable group of curious onlookers, and because her little speech seemed to them to cover just about everything, no one attempted to injure her in any way, although there were some raucous comments to the effect that it was pretty peculiar for someone who was trying to hire a crook to invoke the protection of a high-up policeman uncle.

She was directed into ever darker and less public alleys until finally in a gully as dark as ink an old woman with eyes which stared so piercingly that Huma instantly understood she was blind motioned her through a doorway from which darkness seemed to be pouring like smoke. Clenching her fists, angrily ordering her heart to behave normally, Huma followed the old woman into the gloom-wrapped house.

The faintest conceivable rivulet of candlelight trickled through the darkness; following this unreliable yellow thread (because she could no longer see the old lady), Huma received a sudden sharp blow to the shins and cried out involuntarily, after which she at once bit her lip, angry at having revealed her mounting terror to whoever or whatever waited before her, shrouded in blackness.

She had, in fact, collided with a low table on which a single candle burned and 10 beyond which a mountainous figure could be made out, sitting cross-legged on the floor. "Sit, sit," said a man's calm, deep voice, and her legs, needing no more flowery invitation, buckled beneath her at the terse command. Clutching her left hand in her right, she forced her voice to respond evenly:

"And you, sir, will be the thief I have been requesting?"

Shifting its weight very slightly, the shadow-mountain informed Huma that all criminal activity originating in this zone was well organized and also centrally controlled, so that all requests for what might be termed freelance work had to be channelled through this room.

He demanded comprehensive details of the crime to be committed, including a precise inventory of items to be acquired, also a clear statement of all financial inducements being offered with no gratuities excluded, plus, for filing purposes only, a summary of the motives for the application.

At this, Huma, as though remembering something, stiffened both in body and resolve and replied loudly that her motives were entirely a matter for herself; that she would discuss details with no one but the thief himself; but that the rewards she proposed could only be described as "lavish."

"All I am willing to disclose to you, sir, since it appears that I am on the 15 premises of some sort of employment agency, is that in return for such lavish rewards I must have the most desperate criminal at your disposal, a man for whom life holds no terrors, not even the fear of God.

"The worst of fellows, I tell you — nothing less will do!"

———————

At this a paraffin storm-lantern was lighted, and Huma saw facing her a grey-haired giant down whose left cheek ran the most sinister of scars, a cicatrice° in the shape of the letter *sín* in the Nastaliq script. She was gripped by the insupportably nostalgic notion that the bogeyman of her childhood nursery had risen up to confront her, because her ayah° had always forestalled any incipient acts of disobedience by threatening Huma and Atta: "You don't watch out and I'll send that one to steal you away—that Sheikh Sín, the Thief of Thieves!"

Here, grey-haired but unquestionably scarred, was the notorious criminal himself—and was she out of her mind, were her ears playing tricks, or had he truly just announced that, given the stated circumstances, he himself was the only man for the job?

Struggling hard against the newborn goblins of nostalgia, Huma warned the fearsome volunteer that only a matter of extreme urgency and peril would have brought her unescorted into these ferocious streets.

"Because we can afford no last-minute backings-out," she continued, "I am   20 determined to tell you everything, keeping back no secrets whatsoever. If, after hearing me out, you are still prepared to proceed, then we shall do everything in our power to assist you, and to make you rich."

The old thief shrugged, nodded, spat. Huma began her story.

Six days ago, everything in the household of her father, the wealthy money-lender Hashim, had been as it always was. At breakfast her mother had spooned khichri° lovingly on to the moneylender's plate; the conversation had been filled with those expressions of courtesy and solicitude on which the family prided itself.

Hashim was fond of pointing out that while he was not a godly man he set great store by "living honorably in the world." In that spacious lakeside resi-dence, all outsiders were greeted with the same formality and respect, even those unfortunates who came to negotiate for small fragments of Hashim's large for-tune, and of whom he naturally asked an interest rate of over seventy percent, partly, as he told his khichri-spooning wife, "to teach these people the value of money; let them only learn that, and they will be cured of this fever of bor-rowing borrowing all the time—so you see that if my plans succeed, I shall put myself out of business!"

In their children, Atta and Huma, the moneylender and his wife had suc-cessfully sought to inculcate the virtues of thrift, plain dealing and a healthy in-dependence of spirit. On this, too, Hashim was fond of congratulating himself.

Breakfast ended; the family members wished one another a fulfilling day.   25 Within a few hours, however, the glassy contentment of that household, of that

---

cicatrice: The scar of a healed wound.   **ayah:** A native maid or nursemaid in India. **khichri:** An Indian dish made from rice, lentils, onion, tomato, and spices.

life of porcelain delicacy and alabaster sensibilities, was to be shattered beyond all hope of repair.

The moneylender summoned his personal shikara° and was on the point of stepping into it when, attracted by a glint of silver, he noticed a small vial floating between the boat and his private quay. On an impulse, he scooped it out of the glutinous water.

It was a cylinder of tinted glass cased in exquisitely wrought silver, and Hashim saw within its walls a silver pendant bearing a single strand of human hair.

Closing his fist around this unique discovery, he muttered to the boatman that he'd changed his plans, and hurried to his sanctum, where, behind closed doors, he feasted his eyes on his find.

There can be no doubt that Hashim the moneylender knew from the first that he was in possession of the famous relic of the Prophet Muhammad, that revered hair whose theft from its shrine at Hazratbal mosque the previous morning had created an unprecedented hue and cry in the valley.

The thieves — no doubt alarmed by the pandemonium, by the procession 30 through the streets of endless ululating crocodiles of lamentation, by the riots, the political ramifications and by the massive police search which was commanded and carried out by men whose entire careers now hung upon the finding of this lost hair — had evidently panicked and hurled the vial into the gelatine bosom of the lake.

Having found it by a stroke of great good fortune, Hashim's duty as a citizen was clear: the hair must be restored to its shrine, and the state to equanimity and peace.

But the moneylender had a different notion.

All around him in his study was the evidence of his collector's mania. There were enormous glass cases full of impaled butterflies from Gulmarg, three dozen scale models in various metals of the legendary cannon Zamzama, innumerable swords, a Naga spear, ninety-four terracotta camels of the sort sold on railway station platforms, many samovars, and a whole zoology of tiny sandalwood animals, which had originally been carved to serve as children's bathtime toys.

"And after all," Hashim told himself, "the Prophet would have disapproved mightily of this relic-worship. He abhorred the idea of being deified! So, by keeping this hair from its distracted devotees, I perform — do I not? — a finer service than I would by returning it! Naturally, I don't want it for its religious value . . . I'm a man of the world, of this world. I see it purely as a secular object of great rarity and blinding beauty. In short, it's the silver vial I desire, more than the hair.

"They say there are American millionaires who purchase stolen art master- 35 pieces and hide them away — they would know how I feel. I must, must have it!"

---

shikara: A type of covered wooden boat used in India.

Every collector must share his treasures with one other human being, and Hashim summoned — and told — his only son Atta, who was deeply perturbed but, having been sworn to secrecy, only spilled the beans when the troubles became too terrible to bear.

The youth excused himself and left his father alone in the crowded solitude of his collections. Hashim was sitting erect in a hard, straight-backed chair, gazing intently at the beautiful vial.

It was well known that the moneylender never ate lunch, so it was not until evening that a servant entered the sanctum to summon his master to the dining-table. He found Hashim as Atta had left him. The same, and not the same — for now the moneylender looked swollen, distended. His eyes bulged even more than they always had, they were red-rimmed, and his knuckles were white.

He seemed to be on the point of bursting! As though, under the influence of the misappropriated relic, he had filled up with some spectral fluid which might at any moment ooze uncontrollably from his every bodily opening.

He had to be helped to the table, and then the explosion did indeed take 40 place.

Seemingly careless of the effect of his words on the carefully constructed and fragile constitution of the family's life, Hashim began to gush, to spume long streams of awful truths. In horrified silence, his children heard their father turn upon his wife, and reveal to her that for many years their marriage had been the worst of his afflictions. "An end to politeness!" he thundered. "An end to hypocrisy."

Next, and in the same spirit, he revealed to his family the existence of a mistress; he informed them also of his regular visits to paid women. He told his wife that, far from being the principal beneficiary of his will, she would receive no more than the eighth portion which was her due under Islamic law. Then he turned upon his children, screaming at Atta for his lack of academic ability — "A dope! I have been cursed with a dope!" — and accusing his daughter of lasciviousness, because she went around the city barefaced, which was unseemly for any good Muslim girl to do. She should, he commanded, enter purdah° forthwith.

Hashim left the table without having eaten and fell into the deep sleep of a man who has got many things off his chest, leaving his children stunned, in tears, and the dinner going cold on the sideboard under the gaze of an anticipatory bearer.

At five o'clock the next morning the moneylender forced his family to rise, wash, and say their prayers. From then on, he began to pray five times daily for the first time in his life, and his wife and children were obliged to do likewise.

---

purdah: The practice by women of covering their bodies in public, often with a burqa (a loose full-length robe, usually with veiled eyeholes, worn by Muslim women, especially in South Asia).

Before breakfast, Huma saw the servants, under her father's direction, con- 45
structing a great heap of books in the garden and setting fire to it. The only volume
left untouched was the Qur'an, which Hashim wrapped in a silken cloth and
placed on a table in the hall. He ordered each member of his family to read passages
from this book for at least two hours per day. Visits to the cinema were forbidden.
And if Atta invited male friends to the house, Huma was to retire to her room.

By now, the family had entered a state of shock and dismay; but there was
worse to come.

That afternoon, a trembling debtor arrived at the house to confess his inability to pay the latest installment of interest owed, and made the mistake of reminding Hashim, in somewhat blustering fashion, of the Qur'an's strictures
against usury. The moneylender flew into a rage and attacked the fellow with
one of his large collection of bullwhips.

By mischance, later the same day a second defaulter came to plead for time,
and was seen fleeing Hashim's study with a great gash in his arm, because
Huma's father had called him a thief of other men's money and had tried to cut
off the wretch's right hand with one of the thirty-eight kukri knives hanging on
the study walls.

These breaches of the family's unwritten laws of decorum alarmed Atta and
Huma, and when, that evening, their mother attempted to calm Hashim down,
he struck her on the face with an open hand. Atta leapt to his mother's defense
and he, too, was sent flying.

"From now on," Hashim bellowed, "there's going to be some discipline 50
around here!"

The moneylender's wife began a fit of hysterics which continued throughout
that night and the following day, and which so provoked her husband that he
threatened her with divorce, at which she fled to her room, locked the door, and
subsided into a raga of sniffling. Huma now lost her composure, challenged her
father openly, and announced (with that same independence of spirit which he
had encouraged in her) that she would wear no cloth over her face; apart from
anything else, it was bad for the eyes.

On hearing this, her father disowned her on the spot and gave her one week
in which to pack her bags and go.

By the fourth day, the fear in the air of the house had become so thick that
it was difficult to walk around. Atta told his shock-numbed sister: "We are descending to gutter-level—but I know what must be done."

That afternoon, Hashim left home accompanied by two hired thugs to
extract the unpaid dues from his two insolvent clients. Atta went immediately
to his father's study. Being the son and heir, he possessed his own key to the
moneylender's safe. This he now used, and removing the little vial from its
hiding-place, he slipped it into his trouser pocket and re-locked the safe door.

Now he told Huma the secret of what his father had fished out of Lake Dal, 55
and exclaimed: "Maybe I'm crazy—maybe the awful things that are happening
have made me cracked—but I am convinced there will be no peace in our house
until this hair is out of it."

His sister at once agreed that the hair must be returned, and Atta set off in a
hired shikara to Hazratbal mosque. Only when the boat had delivered him into
the throng of the distraught faithful which was swirling around the desecrated
shrine did Atta discover that the relic was no longer in his pocket. There was
only a hole, which his mother, usually so attentive to household matters, must
have overlooked under the stress of recent events.

Atta's initial surge of chagrin was quickly replaced by a feeling of profound
relief.

"Suppose," he imagined, "that I had already announced to the mullahs that
the hair was on my person! They would never have believed me now—and this
mob would have lynched me! At any rate, it has gone, and that's a load off my
mind." Feeling more contented than he had for days, the young man returned
home.

Here he found his sister bruised and weeping in the hall; upstairs, in her
bedroom, his mother wailed like a brand-new widow. He begged Huma to tell
him what had happened, and when she replied that their father, returning from
his brutal business trip, had once again noticed a glint of silver between boat
and quay, had once again scooped up the errant relic, and was consequently in a
rage to end all rages, having beaten the truth out of her—then Atta buried his
face in his hands and sobbed out his opinion, which was that the hair was perse-
cuting them, and had come back to finish the job.

It was Huma's turn to think of a way out of their troubles.   60

While her arms turned black and blue and great stains spread across her
forehead, she hugged her brother and whispered to him that she was determined
to get rid of the hair *at all costs*—she repeated this last phrase several times.

"The hair," she then declared, "was stolen from the mosque; so it can be
stolen from this house. But it must be a genuine robbery, carried out by a bona-
fide thief, not by one of us who are under the hair's thrall—by a thief so desperate that he fears neither capture nor curses."

Unfortunately, she added, the theft would be ten times harder to pull off
now that their father, knowing that there had already been one attempt on the
relic, was certainly on his guard.

"Can you do it?"

Huma, in a room lit by candle and storm-lantern, ended her account with 65
one further question: "What assurances can you give that the job holds no terrors for you still?"

The criminal, spitting, stated that he was not in the habit of providing references, as a cook might, or a gardener, but he was not alarmed so easily, certainly

not by any children's djinni° of a curse. Huma had to be content with this boast, and proceeded to describe the details of the proposed burglary.

"Since my brother's failure to return the hair to the mosque, my father has taken to sleeping with his precious treasure under his pillow. However, he sleeps alone, and very energetically; only enter his room without waking him, and he will certainly have tossed and turned quite enough to make the theft a simple matter. When you have the vial, come to my room," and here she handed Sheikh Sín a plan of her home, "and I will hand over all the jewelery owned by my mother and myself. You will find . . . it is worth . . . that is, you will be able to get a fortune for it . . ."

It was evident that her self-control was weakening and that she was on the point of physical collapse.

"Tonight," she burst out finally. "You must come tonight!"

No sooner had she left the room than the old criminal's body was 70 convulsed by a fit of coughing: he spat blood into an old vanaspati° can. The great Sheikh, the "Thief of Thieves," had become a sick man, and every day the time drew nearer when some young pretender to his power would stick a dagger in his stomach. A lifelong addiction to gambling had left him almost as poor as he had been when, decades ago, he had started out in this line of work as a mere pickpocket's apprentice; so in the extraordinary commission he had accepted from the moneylender's daughter he saw his opportunity of amassing enough wealth at a stroke to leave the valley for ever, and acquire the luxury of a respectable death which would leave his stomach intact.

As for the Prophet's hair, well, neither he nor his blind wife had ever had much to say for prophets—that was one thing they had in common with the moneylender's thunderstruck clan.

It would not do, however, to reveal the nature of this, his last crime, to his four sons. To his consternation, they had all grown up to be hopelessly devout men, who even spoke of making the pilgrimage to Mecca some day. "Absurd!" their father would laugh at them. "Just tell me how you will go?" For, with a parent's absolutist love, he had made sure they were all provided with a lifelong source of high income by crippling them at birth, so that, as they dragged themselves around the city, they earned excellent money in the begging business.

The children, then, could look after themselves.

He and his wife would be off soon with the jewel-boxes of the moneylender's women. It was a timely chance indeed that had brought the beautiful bruised girl into his corner of the town.

That night, the large house on the shore of the lake lay blindly waiting, with 75 silence lapping at its walls. A burglar's night: clouds in the sky and mists on the

---

djinni: Genie or jinn; in Muslim legend, a spirit that can assume human or animal form and exercise supernatural influence over people.   vanaspati: Vegetable cooking oil.

winter water. Hashim the moneylender was asleep, the only member of his family to whom sleep had come that night. In another room, his son Atta lay deep in the coils of his coma with a blood-clot forming on his brain, watched over by a mother who had let down her long greying hair to show her grief, a mother who placed warm compresses on his head with gestures redolent of impotence. In a third bedroom Huma waited, fully dressed, amidst the jewel-heavy caskets of her desperation.

At last a bulbul° sang softly from the garden below her window and, creeping downstairs, she opened a door to the bird, on whose face there was a scar in the shape of the Nastaliq letter *sín*.

Noiselessly, the bird flew up the stairs behind her. At the head of the staircase they parted, moving in opposite directions along the corridor of their conspiracy without a glance at one another.

Entering the moneylender's room with professional ease, the burglar, Sín, discovered that Huma's predictions had been wholly accurate. Hashim lay sprawled diagonally across his bed, the pillow untenanted by his head, the prize easily accessible. Step by padded step, Sín moved towards the goal.

It was at this point that, in the bedroom next door, young Atta sat bolt upright in his bed, giving his mother a great fright, and without any warning — prompted by goodness knows what pressure of the blood-clot upon his brain — began screaming at the top of his voice:

"Thief! Thief! Thief!"

80

It seems probable that his poor mind had been dwelling, in these last moments, upon his own father; but it is impossible to be certain, because having uttered these three emphatic words the young man fell back upon his pillow and died.

At once his mother set up a screeching and a wailing and a keening and a howling so earsplittingly intense that they completed the work which Atta's cry had begun — that is, her laments penetrated the walls of her husband's bedroom and brought Hashim wide awake.

Sheikh Sín was just deciding whether to dive beneath the bed or brain the moneylender good and proper when Hashim grabbed the tiger-striped swordstick which always stood propped up in a corner beside his bed, and rushed from the room without so much as noticing the burglar who stood on the opposite side of the bed in the darkness. Sín stooped quickly and removed the vial containing the Prophet's hair from its hiding-place.

Meanwhile Hashim had erupted into the corridor, having unsheathed the sword inside his cane. In his right hand he held the weapon and was waving it about dementedly. His left hand was shaking the stick. A shadow came rushing towards him through the midnight darkness of the passageway and, in his

---

bulbul: A type of songbird found in Africa and tropical Asia.

somnolent anger, the moneylender thrust his sword fatally through its heart. Turning up the light, he found that he had murdered his daughter, and under the dire influence of this accident he was so overwhelmed by remorse that he turned the sword upon himself, fell upon it and so extinguished his life. His wife, the sole surviving member of the family, was driven mad by the general carnage and had to be committed to an asylum for the insane by her brother, the city's Deputy Commissioner of Police.

Sheikh Sín had quickly understood that the plan had gone awry.   85

Abandoning the dream of the jewel-boxes when he was but a few yards from its fulfilment, he climbed out of Hashim's window and made his escape during the appalling events described above. Reaching home before dawn, he woke his wife and confessed his failure. It would be necessary, he whispered, for him to vanish for a while. Her blind eyes never opened until he had gone.

The noise in the Hashim household had roused their servants and even managed to awaken the night-watchman, who had been fast asleep as usual on his charpoy by the street-gate. They alerted the police, and the Deputy Commissioner himself was informed. When he heard of Huma's death, the mournful officer opened and read the sealed letter which his niece had given him, and instantly led a large detachment of armed men into the light-repellent gullies of the most wretched and disreputable part of the city.

The tongue of a malicious cat-burglar named Huma's fellow-conspirator; the finger of an ambitious bank-robber pointed at the house in which he lay concealed; and although Sín managed to crawl through a hatch in the attic and attempt a roof-top escape, a bullet from the Deputy Commissioner's own rifle penetrated his stomach and brought him crashing messily to the ground at the feet of Huma's enraged uncle.

From the dead thief's pocket rolled a vial of tinted glass, cased in filigree silver.

The recovery of the Prophet's hair was announced at once on All-India   90 Radio. One month later, the valley's holiest men assembled at the Hazratbal mosque and formally authenticated the relic. It sits to this day in a closely guarded vault by the shores of the loveliest of lakes in the heart of the valley which was once closer than any other place on earth to Paradise.

But before our story can properly be concluded, it is necessary to record that when the four sons of the dead Sheikh awoke on the morning of his death, having unwittingly spent a few minutes under the same roof as the famous hair, they found that a miracle had occurred, that they were all sound of limb and strong of wind, as whole as they might have been if their father had not thought to smash their legs in the first hours of their lives. They were, all four of them, very properly furious, because the miracle had reduced their earning powers by 75 percent, at the most conservative estimate; so they were ruined men.

Only the Sheikh's widow had some reason for feeling grateful, because although her husband was dead she had regained her sight, so that it was possible for her to spend her last days gazing once more upon the beauties of the valley of Kashmir.

George Saunders b. 1958
The End of FIRPO in the World   [1998]

The boy on the bike flew by the chink's house, and the squatty-body's house, and the house where the dead guy had rotted for five days, remembering that the chink had once called him nasty, the squatty-body had once called the cops when he'd hit her cat with a lug nut on a string, the chick in the dead guy's house had once asked if he, Cody, ever brushed his teeth. Someday when he'd completed the invention of his special miniaturizing ray he would shrink their houses and flush them down the shitter while in tiny voices all three begged for some sophisticated mercy, but he would only say, Sophisticated? When were you ever sophisticated to me? And from the toilet bowl they would say, Well, yes, you're right, we were pretty mean, flush us down, we deserve it; but no, at the last minute he would pluck them out and place them in his lunchbox so he could send them on secret missions such as putting hideous boogers of assassination in Lester Finn's thermos if Lester Finn ever again asked him in Civics why his rear smelled like hot cotton with additional crap cling-ons.

It was a beautiful sunny day and the aerobics class at the Rec had let out and cars were streaming out of the parking lot with sun glinting off their hoods, and he rode along on the sidewalk, racing the cars as they passed.

Here was the low-hanging willow where you had to duck down, here was the place with the tilty sidewalk square that served as a ramp when you jerked hard on the handlebars, which he did, and the crowd went wild, and the announcers in the booth above the willow shook their heads, saying, Wow, he takes that jump like there's no tomorrow while them other racers fret about it like some kind of tiny crying babies!

Were the Dalmeyers home?

Their gray car was still in the driveway.   5

He would need to make another lap.

Yesterday he had picked up a bright-red goalie pad and all three Dalmeyers had screamed at him, Not that pad Cody you dick, we never use those pads in the driveway because they get scuffed, you rectum, those are only for ice, were you born a rectal shitbrain or did you take special rectal shitbrain lessons, in rectal shitbrain lessons did they teach you how to ruin everybody's things?

Well yes, he had ruined a few Dalmeyer things in his life, he had yes pounded a railroad spike in a good new volleyball, he had yes secretly scraped a ski with a nail, he had yes given the Dalmeyer dog Rudy a cut on its leg with a shovel, but that had been an accident, he'd thrown the shovel at a rosebush and stupid Rudy had walked in front of it.

And the Dalmeyers had snatched away the goalie pad and paraded around the driveway making the nosehole sound, and when he tried to laugh to show he was a good sport he made the nosehole sound for real, and they totally cracked up, and Zane Dalmeyer said why didn't he take his trademark nosehole sound on Broadway so thousands could crap their pants laughing? And Eric Dalmeyer said hey if only he had like fifty different-sized noseholes that each made a different sound then he could play songs. And they laughed so hard at the idea of him playing songs on Broadway on his fifty different-sized noseholes that they fell to the driveway thrashing their idiotic Dalmeyer limbs, even Ginnie, the baby Dalmeyer, and ha ha ha that had been a laugh, that had been so funny he had almost gone around one two three four and smashed their cranial cavities with his off-brand gym shoes, which was another puzzling dilemmoid, because why did he have Arroes when every single Dalmeyer, even Ginnie, had the Nikes with the lights in the heel that lit up?

Fewer cars were coming by now from the Rec. The ones that did were going 10 faster, and he no longer tried to race them.

Well, it would be revenge, sweet revenge, when he stuck the lozenge stolen from wood shop up the Dalmeyers' water hose, and the next time they turned the hose on it exploded, and all the Dalmeyers, even Dad Dalmeyer, stood around in their nice tan pants puzzling over it like them guys on *Nova*. And the Dalmeyers were so stupid they would conclude that it had been a miracle, and would call some guys from a science lab to confirm the miracle, and one of the lab guys would flip the wooden lozenge into the air and say to Dad Dalmeyer, You know what, a very clever Einstein lives in your neighborhood and I suggest that in the future you lock this hose up, because in all probability this guy cannot be stopped. And he, Cody, would give the lab guy a wink, and later, as they were getting into the lab van, the lab guy would say, Look, why not come live with us in the experimental space above our lab and help us discover some amazing compounds with the same science brain that apparently thought up this brilliant lozenge, because, frankly, when we lab guys were your age, no way, this lozenge concept was totally beyond us, we were just playing with baby toys and doing baby math, but you, you're really something scientifically special.

And when the Dalmeyers came for a lab tour with a school group they would approach him with their big confident underwater watches and say wow oh boy had they ever missed the boat in terms of him, sorry, they were so very sorry, what was this beaker for, how did this burner work, was it really true that he had built a whole entire *T. rex* from scratch and energized it by taming the miraculous power of cosmic thunder? And down in the basement the *T. rex* would rear up its ugly head and want to have a Dalmeyer snack, but using his special system of codes, pounding on a heat pipe a different number of times for each alphabet letter, he would tell the *T. rex*, No no no, don't eat a single Dalmeyer, although why not lift Eric Dalmeyer up just for the fun of it on the tip of your tremendous green snout and give him a lesson in what kind of power those crushing jaws would have if he, Cody, pounded out on the heat pipe Kill Kill Kill.

Pedaling wildly now, he passed into the strange and dangerous zone of three consecutive Monte Vistas, and inside of each lived an old wop in a dago tee, and sometimes in the creepy trees there were menacing gorillas he took potshots at from bike-back, but not today, he was too busy with revenge to think about monkeys, and then he was out, into the light, coasting into a happier zone of forthright and elephantine Bueno Verdes that sat very honestly with the big open eyes that were their second-story windows, and in his mind as he passed he said hello HELLO to the two elephants and they in turn said to him in kind Dumbo voices hey Cody HEY CODY.

The block was shaped something like South America, and as he took the tight turn that was Cape Horn he looked across The Field to his small yellow house, which was neither Monte Vista nor Bueno Verde, but predated the sub-division and smelled like cat pee and hamburger blood and had recently been christened by Mom's boyfriend Daryl, that dick, The House of FIRPO, FIRPO being the word Daryl used to describe anything he, Cody, did that was bad or dorky. Sometimes Mom and Daryl tried to pretend FIRPO was a lovey-dovey term by tousling his hair when they said it, but other times they gave him a poke or pinch and sometimes when they thought he couldn't hear they whispered very darkly and meanly to each other *FIRP attack in progress* and he would go to his room and make the nosehole sound in his closet, after which they would come in and fine him a quarter for each nosehole sound they thought they had heard him make, which was often many, many more than he had actually really made.

Sometimes at night in his room Mom babied him by stroking his big wide head and saying he didn't have to pay all the quarters he owed for making the nosehole sound, but other times she said if he didn't knock it off and lose a few pounds how was he ever going to get a date in junior high, because who wanted to date a big chubby nosehole snorter, and then he couldn't help it, it made him nervous to think of junior high, and he made the nosehole sound and she said, Very funny I hope you're amusing your own self because you're not amusing my ass one bit.

The Dalmeyer house now came into sight.

The Dalmeyer car was gone.

It was Go Time.

The decisive butt-kicking he was about to give the Dalmeyer hose would constitute the end of FIRPO in the world, and all, including Ma, would have to bow down before him, saying, Wow wow wow, do we ever stand corrected in terms of you, how could someone FIRPO hatch and execute such a daring manly plan?

The crowd was on its feet now, screaming his name, and he passed the 20
chink's house again, here was the driveway down which he must turn to cross
the street to the Dalmeyers', but then oh crap he was going too fast and missed
it, and the announcers in the booth above the willow gasped in pleasure at his
sudden decisive decision to swerve across the newly sodded lawn of the squatty-
body's house. His bike made a trough in the sod and went *humpf* over the curb,
and as the white car struck him the boy and the bike flew together in a high
comic arc across the street and struck the oak on the opposite side with such
violence that the bike wrapped around the tree and the boy flew back into the
street.

Arghh arghh Daryl will be pissed and say Cody why are you bleeding like a
stuck pig you little shit. There was something red wrong with his Arroes. At Pay-
less when they bought the Arroes, Mom said, If you squirm once more you're
gonna be facedown on this carpet with my hand whacking your big fat ass.
Daryl will say, I buy you a good bike and what do you do, you ruin it. Ma will
come up with a dish towel and start swiping at the blood and Daryl will say,
Don't ruin that dish towel, he made his bed let him sleep in it, I'll hose him off
in the yard, a little shivering won't kill him, he did the crime let him do the
time. Or Mom might throw a fit like the night he slipped and fell in the school
play, and Ms. Phillips said, Tell your mother, Cody, how you came to slip and fall
during the school play so that everyone in the auditorium was looking at you instead of Julia who was at that time speaking her most important line.

And Mom said: Cody are you deaf?

And Ms. Phillips said: He slipped because when I told him stay out of that
mopped spot did he do it? No, he did not, he walked right through it on purpose
and then down he went.

Which is exactly what he does at home, Mom said. Sometimes I think he's
wired wrong.

And Ms. Phillips said, Well, today, Cody, you learned a valuable lesson, which 25
is if someone tells you don't do something, don't do it, because maybe that someone knows something you don't from having lived a longer time than you.

And Daryl said, Or maybe he liked falling on his butt in front of all his
friends.

Now a white-haired stickman with no shirt was bending over him, so
skinny, touch touch touching him all over, like looking to see if he was wearing
a bulletproof vest, doing some very nervous mouthbreathing, with a silver cross
hanging down, and around his nipples were sprigs of white hair.

Oh boy, oh God, said the stickman. Say something, pal, can you talk?

And he tried to talk but nothing came, and tried to move but nothing
moved.

Oh God, said the stickman, don't go, pal, please say something, stay here 30
with me now, we'll get through this.

What crazy teeth. What a stickman. The stickman's hands flipped around
like nervous old-lady hands in movies where the river is rising and the men are
away. What a Holy Roller. What a FIRPO. A Holy Roller FIRPO stickman with
hairy nips and plus his breath smelled like coffee.

Listen, God loves you, said the stickman. You're going, okay, I see you're going, but look, please don't go without knowing you are beautiful and loved. Okay? Do you hear me? You are good, do you know that? God loves you. God loves you. He sent His son to die for you.

Oh the freaking FIRPO, why couldn't he just shut up? If the stickman thought he, Cody, was good, he must be FIRPO because he, Cody, wasn't good, he was FIRPO, Mom had said so and Daryl had said so and even Mr. Dean in Science had told him to stop lying the time he tried to tell about seeing the falling star. The announcers in the booth above the willow began weeping as he sat on Mom's lap and said he was very sorry for having been such a FIRPO son and Mom said, Oh thank you, thank you, Cody, for finally admitting it, that makes it nice, and her smile was so sweet he closed his eyes and felt a certain urge to sort of shake things out and oh Christ dance.

You are beautiful, beautiful, the stickman kept saying, long after the boy had stopped thrashing, God loves you, you are beautiful in His sight.

Leslie Marmon Silko b. 1948
The Man to Send Rain Clouds   [1981]

They found him under a big cottonwood tree. His Levi jacket and pants were faded light blue so that he had been easy to find. The big cottonwood tree stood apart from a small grove of winterbare cottonwoods which grew in the wide, sandy arroyo. He had been dead for a day or more, and the sheep had wandered and scattered up and down the arroyo. Leon and his brother-in-law, Ken, gathered the sheep and left them in the pen at the sheep camp before they returned to the cottonwood tree. Leon waited under the tree while Ken drove the truck through the deep sand to the edge of the arroyo. He squinted up at the sun and unzipped his jacket — it sure was hot for this time of year. But high and northwest the blue mountains were still in snow. Ken came sliding down the low, crumbling bank about fifty yards down, and he was bringing the red blanket.

Before they wrapped the old man, Leon took a piece of string out of his pocket and tied a small gray feather in the old man's long white hair. Ken gave him the paint. Across the brown wrinkled forehead he drew a streak of white and along the high cheekbones he drew a strip of blue paint. He paused and watched Ken throw pinches of corn meal and pollen into the wind that fluttered the small gray feather. Then Leon painted with yellow under the old man's broad nose, and finally, when he had painted green across the chin, he smiled.

"Send us rain clouds, Grandfather." They laid the bundle in the back of the pickup and covered it with a heavy tarp before they started back to the pueblo.

They turned off the highway onto the sandy pueblo road. Not long after they passed the store and post office they saw Father Paul's car coming toward them. When he recognized their faces he slowed his car and waved for them to stop. The young priest rolled down the car window.

"Did you find old Teofilo?" he asked loudly.

5

Leon stopped the truck. "Good morning, Father. We were just out to the sheep camp. Everything is O.K. now."

"Thank God for that. Teofilo is a very old man. You really shouldn't allow him to stay at the sheep camp alone."

"No, he won't do that any more now."

"Well, I'm glad you understand. I hope I'll be seeing you at Mass this week — we missed you last Sunday. See if you can get old Teofilo to come with you." The priest smiled and waved at them as they drove away.

Louise and Teresa were waiting. The table was set for lunch, and the coffee   10 was boiling on the black iron stove. Leon looked at Louise and then at Teresa.

"We found him under a cottonwood tree in the big arroyo near sheep camp. I guess he sat down to rest in the shade and never got up again." Leon walked toward the old man's bed. The red plaid shawl had been shaken and spread carefully over the bed, and a new brown flannel shirt and pair of stiff new Levi's were arranged neatly beside the pillow. Louise held the screen door open while Leon and Ken carried in the red blanket. He looked small and shriveled, and after they dressed him in the new shirt and pants he seemed more shrunken.

It was noontime now because the church bells rang the Angelus. They ate the beans with hot bread, and nobody said anything until after Teresa poured the coffee.

Ken stood up and put on his jacket. "I'll see about the gravediggers. Only the top layer of soil is frozen. I think it can be ready before dark."

Leon nodded his head and finished his coffee. After Ken had been gone for a while, the neighbors and clanspeople came quietly to embrace Teofilo's family and to leave food on the table because the gravediggers would come to eat when they were finished.

The sky in the west was full of pale yellow light. Louise stood outside with   15 her hands in the pockets of Leon's green army jacket that was too big for her. The funeral was over, and the old men had taken their candles and medicine bags and were gone. She waited until the body was laid into the pickup before she said anything to Leon. She touched his arm, and he noticed that her hands were still dusty from the corn meal that she had sprinkled around the old man. When she spoke, Leon could not hear her.

"What did you say? I didn't hear you."

"I said that I had been thinking about something."

"About what?"

"About the priest sprinkling holy water for Grandpa. So he won't be thirsty."

Leon stared at the new moccasins that Teofilo had made for the ceremonial   20 dances in the summer. They were nearly hidden by the red blanket. It was getting colder, and the wind pushed gray dust down the narrow pueblo road. The sun was approaching the long mesa where it disappeared during the winter. Louise stood there shivering and watching his face. Then he zipped up his jacket and opened the truck door. "I'll see if he's there."

Ken stopped the pickup at the church, and Leon got out; and then Ken drove down the hill to the graveyard where people were waiting. Leon knocked at the old carved door with its symbols of the Lamb. While he waited he looked up at the twin bells from the king of Spain with the last sunlight pouring around them in their tower.

The priest opened the door and smiled when he saw who it was. "Come in! What brings you here this evening?"

The priest walked toward the kitchen, and Leon stood with his cap in his hand, playing with the earflaps and examining the living room — the brown sofa, the green armchair, and the brass lamp that hung down from the ceiling by links of chain. The priest dragged a chair out of the kitchen and offered it to Leon.

"No thank you, Father. I only came to ask you if you would bring your holy water to the graveyard."

The priest turned away from Leon and looked out the window at the patio   25 full of shadows and the dining-room windows of the nuns' cloister across the patio. The curtains were heavy, and the light from within faintly penetrated; it was impossible to see the nuns inside eating supper. "Why didn't you tell me he was dead? I could have brought the Last Rites anyway."

Leon smiled. "It wasn't necessary, Father."

The priest stared down at his scuffed brown loafers and the worn hem of his cassock. "For a Christian burial it was necessary."

His voice was distant, and Leon thought that his blue eyes looked tired.

"It's O.K. Father, we just want him to have plenty of water."

The priest sank down into the green chair and picked up a glossy missionary   30 magazine. He turned the colored pages full of lepers and pagans without looking at them.

"You know I can't do that, Leon. There should have been the Last Rites and a funeral Mass at the very least."

Leon put on his green cap and pulled the flaps down over his ears. "It's getting late, Father. I've got to go."

When Leon opened the door Father Paul stood up and said, "Wait." He left the room and came back wearing a long brown overcoat. He followed Leon out the door and across the dim churchyard to the adobe steps in front of the church. They both stooped to fit through the low adobe entrance. And when they started down the hill to the graveyard only half of the sun was visible above the mesa.

The priest approached the grave slowly, wondering how they had managed to dig into the frozen ground; and then he remembered that this was New Mexico, and saw the pile of cold loose sand beside the hole. The people stood close to each other with little clouds of steam puffing from their faces. The priest looked at them and saw a pile of jackets, gloves, and scarves in the yellow, dry tumbleweeds that grew in the graveyard. He looked at the red blanket, not sure that Teofilo was so small, wondering if it wasn't some perverse Indian trick — something they did in March to ensure a good harvest — wondering if maybe old Teofilo was actually at sheep camp corraling the sheep for the night. But there he was, facing into a cold dry wind and squinting at the last sunlight, ready to bury a red wool blanket while the faces of his parishioners were in shadow with the last warmth of the sun on their backs.

His fingers were stiff, and it took him a long time to twist the lid off the holy   35
water. Drops of water fell on the red blanket and soaked into dark icy spots. He sprinkled the grave and the water disappeared almost before it touched the dim, cold sand; it reminded him of something — he tried to remember what it was, because he thought if he could remember he might understand this. He sprinkled more water; he shook the container until it was empty, and the water fell through the light from sundown like August rain that fell while the sun was still shining, almost evaporating before it touched the wilted squash flowers.

The wind pulled at the priest's brown Franciscan robe and swirled away the corn meal and pollen that had been sprinkled on the blanket. They lowered the bundle into the ground, and they didn't bother to untie the stiff pieces of new rope that were tied around the ends of the blanket. The sun was gone, and over on the highway the eastbound lane was full of headlights. The priest walked away slowly. Leon watched him climb the hill, and when he had disappeared within the tall, thick walls, Leon turned to look up at the high blue mountains in the deep snow that reflected a faint red light from the west. He felt good because it was finished, and he was happy about the sprinkling of the holy water; now the old man could send them big thunderclouds for sure.

Zadie Smith   b. 1975

The Girl with Bangs   [2001]

I fell in love with a girl once. Some time ago, now. She had bangs. I was twenty years old at the time and prey to the usual rag-bag of foolish ideas. I believed, for example, that one might meet some sweet kid and like them a lot — maybe even marry them — while all the time allowing that kid to sleep with other kids, and that this could be done with no fuss at all, just a chuck under the chin, and no tears. I believed the majority of people to be bores, however you cut them; that the mark of their dullness was easy to spot (clothes, hair) and impossible to avoid, running right through them like a watermark. I had made mental notes, too, on other empty notions — the death of certain things (socialism, certain types of music, old people), the future of others (film, footwear, poetry) — but no one need be bored with those now. The only significant bit of nonsense I carried around in those days, the only one that came from the gut, if you like, was this feeling that a girl with soft black bangs falling into eyes the color of a

Perrier bottle must be good news. Look at her palming the bangs away from her face, pressing them back along her hairline, only to have them fall forward again! I found this combination to be good, *intrinsically* good in both form and content, the same way you think of cherries (life is a bowl of; she was a real sweet) until the very center of one becomes lodged in your windpipe. I believed Charlotte Greaves and her bangs to be good news. But Charlotte was emphatically bad news, requiring only eight months to take me entirely apart; the kind of clinically efficient dismembering you see when a bright child gets his hand on some toy he assembled in the first place. I'd never dated a girl before, and she was bad news the way boys can never be, because with boys it's always possible to draw up a list of pros and cons, and see the matter rationally, from either side. But you could make a list of cons on Charlotte stretching to Azerbaijan, and "her bangs" sitting solitary in the pros column would outweigh all objections. Boys are just boys after all, but sometimes girls *really seem to be* the turn of a pale wrist, or the sudden jut of a hip, or a clutch of very dark hair falling across a freckled forehead. I'm not saying that's what they really are. I'm just saying sometimes it seems that way, and that those details (a thigh mole, a full face flush, a scar the precise shape and size of a cashew nut) are so many hooks waiting to land you. In this case, it was those bangs, plush and dramatic; curtains opening on to a face one would queue up to see. All women have a backstage, of course, of course. Labyrinthine, many-roomed, no doubt, no doubt. But you come to see the show, that's all I'm saying.

I first set eyes on Charlotte when she was seeing a Belgian who lived across the hall from me in college. I'd see her first thing, shuffling around the communal bathroom looking a mess — undone, always, in every sense — with her T-shirt tucked in her knickers, a fag hanging out of her mouth, some kind of toothpaste or maybe mouthwash residue by her lips, and those bangs in her eyes. It was hard to understand why this Belgian, Maurice, had chosen to date her. He had this great accent, Maurice, *elaborately* French, like you couldn't *be* more French, and a jaw line that seemed in fashion at the time, and you could tick all the boxes vis-à-vis personal charms; Maurice was an impressive kind of a guy. Charlotte was the kind of woman who has only two bras, both of them gray. But after a while, if you paid attention, you came to realize that she had a look about her like she just got out of a bed, no matter what time of day you collided with her (she had a stalk of a walk, never looked where she was going, so you had no choice) and this tendency, if put under the heading "Qualities That Girls Sometimes Have," was a kind of poor relation of "Bedroom Eyes" or "Looks Like She's Thinking About Sex All the Time" — and it worked. She seemed always to be stumbling away from someone else, toward you. A limping figure smiling widely, arms outstretched, dressed in rags, a smoldering city as backdrop. I had watched too many films, possibly. But still: a bundle of precious things thrown at you from a third-floor European window, wrapped loosely in a blanket, chosen frantically and at random by the well-meaning owner, slung haphazardly from a burning building; launched at you; it could hurt, this bundle; but look! You have caught it! A little chipped, but otherwise fine. Look what you have saved! (You understand me, I know. This is how it feels. What is the purpose of metaphor, anyway, if not to describe women?)

Now, it came to pass that this Maurice was offered a well-paid TV job in Thailand as a newscaster, and he agonized, and weighed Charlotte in one hand and the money in the other and found he could not leave without the promise that she would wait for him. This promise she gave him, but he was still gone, and gone is gone, and that's where I came in. Not immediately — I am no thief — but by degrees; studying near her in the library, watching her hair make reading difficult. Sitting next to her at lunch watching the bangs go hither, and, I suppose, thither, as people swished by with their food trays. Befriending her friends and then her; making as many nice noises about Maurice as I could. I became a boy for the duration. I stood under the window with my open arms. I did all the old boy tricks. These tricks are not as difficult as some boys will have you believe, but they are indeed slow, and work only by a very gradual process of accumulation. You have sad moments when you wonder if there will ever be an end to it. But then, usually without warning, the hard work pays off. With Charlotte it went like this: she came by for a herbal tea one day, and I rolled a joint and then another and soon enough she was lying across my lap, spineless as a mollusk, and I had my fingers in those bangs — teasing them, as the hairdressers say — and we had begun.

Most of the time we spent together was in her room. At the beginning of an affair you've no need to be outside. And it was like a filthy cocoon, her room, ankle deep in rubbish; it was the kind of room that took you in and held you close. With no clocks and my watch lost and buried, we passed time by the degeneration of things; the rotting of fruit, the accumulation of bacteria, the rising-tideline of cigarettes in the vase we used to put them out. It was a quarter past this apple. The third Saturday in the month of that stain. These things were unpleasant and tiresome. And she was no intellectual; any book I gave her she treated like a kid treats a Christmas present — fascination for a day and then the quick pall of boredom; by the end of the week it was flung across the room and submerged; weeks later when we made love I'd find the spine of the novel sticking into the small of my back, paper cuts on my toes. There was no bed to speak of. There was just a bit of the floor that was marginally clearer than the rest of it. (But wait! Here she comes, falling in an impossible arc, and here I am by careful design in just the right spot, under the window, and here she is, landing and nothing is broken, and I cannot believe my luck. You understand me. Every time I looked at the bangs, the bad stuff went away.)

Again: I know it doesn't sound great, but let's not forget the bangs. Let 5 us not forget that after a stand-up row, a real screaming match, she could look at me from underneath the distinct hairs, separated by sweat, and I had no more resistance. *Yes, you can leave the overturned plant pot where it is. Yes,*

Rousseau° is an idiot if you say so. So this is what it's like being a boy. The cobbled street, the hopeful arms hugging air. There is nothing you won't do.

Charlotte's exams were coming up. I begged her to look through her reading list once more, and plan some strategic line of attack, but she wanted to do it her way. Her way meant reading the same two books—Rousseau's *Social Contract* and Plato's *Republic* (her paper was to be on people, and the way they organize their lives, or the way they did, or the way they should, I don't remember; it had a technical title, I don't remember that either)—again and again, in the study room that sat in a quiet corner of the college. The study room was meant to be for everyone but since Charlotte had moved in, all others had gradually moved out. I recall one German graduate who stood his ground for a month or so, who cleared his throat regularly and pointedly picked up things that she had dropped—but she got to him, finally. Charlotte's papers all over the floor, Charlotte's old lunches on every table, Charlotte's clothes and my clothes (now indistinguishable) thrown over every chair. People would come up to me in the bar and say, "Look, Charlotte did X. Could you please, for the love of God, stop Charlotte doing X, *please?*" and I would try, but Charlotte's bangs kept Charlotte in the world of Charlotte and she barely heard me. And now, please, before we go any further: tell me. Tell me if you've ever stood under a window and caught an unworthy bundle of chintz. Gold plating that came off with one rub; faked signatures, worthless trinkets. Have you? Maybe the bait was different—not bangs, but deep pockets either side of the smile or unusually vivid eye pigmentation. Or some other bodily attribute (hair, skin, curves) that recalled in you some natural phenomenon (wheat, sea, cream). Same difference. So, have you? Have you ever been out with a girl like this?

Some time after Charlotte's exams, after the 2.2 that had been stalking her for so long finally pounced, there was a knock on the door. *My* door—I recall now that we were in my room that morning. I hauled on a dressing-gown and went to answer it. It was Maurice, tanned and dressed like one of the Beatles when they went to see the Maharashi; a white suit with a Nehru collar, his own bangs and tousled hair, slightly long at the back. He looked terrific. He said, "Someone in ze bar says you might have an idea where Charlotte is. I need to see 'er—it is very urgent. Have you seen 'er?" I had seen her. She was in my bed, about five feet from where Maurice stood, but obscured by a partition wall. "No . . ." I said. "No, not this morning. She'll probably be in the hall for breakfast though, she usually is. So, Maurice! When did you get back?" He said, "All zat must come later. I 'ave to find Charlotte. I sink I am going to marry 'er." And I thought, *Christ, which bad movie am I in?*

Rousseau: Jean-Jacques Rousseau (1712–1778, born in Geneva) was a philosopher whose political ideas influenced the French Revolution and the growth of nationalism.

I got Charlotte up, shook her, poured her into some clothes, and told her to run around the back of the college and get to the dining hall before Maurice. I saw her in my head, the moment the door closed — no great feat of imagination, I had seen her run before; like a naturally uncoordinated animal (a panda?) that somebody has just shot — I saw her dashing incompetently past the ancient walls, catching herself on ivy, tripping up steps, and finally falling through the swing doors, looking wildly round the dining hall like those movie time-travellers who know not in which period they have just landed. But still she managed it, apparently she got there in time, though as the whole world now knows, Maurice took one look at her strands matted against her forehead, running in line with the ridge-ways of sleep left by the pillows, and said, "You're sleeping with her?" (Or maybe, "You're sleeping with *her*?" — I don't know; this is all reported speech) and Charlotte, who, like a lot of low-maintenance women, cannot tell a lie, said "Er . . . yes. Yes" and then made that signal of feminine relief; bottom lip out, air blown upward; bangs all of a flutter.

Later that afternoon, Maurice came back round to my room, looking all the more noble, and seemingly determined to have a calm man-to-man "you see, I have returned to marry her / I will not stand in your way" type of chat, which was very reasonable and English of him. I let him have it alone. I nodded when it seemed appropriate; sometimes I lifted my hands in protest but soon let them fall again. You can't fight it when you've been replaced; a simple side-step and here is some old/new Belgian guy standing in the cobbled street with his face upturned, and his arms wide open, judging the angles. I thought of this girl he wanted back, who had taken me apart piece by piece, causing me nothing but trouble, with her bangs and her antisocial behavior. I was all (un)done, I realized. I sort of marvelled at the devotion he felt for her. From a thousand miles away, with a smoldering city as a backdrop, I watched him beg me to leave them both alone; tears in his eyes, the works. I agreed it was the best thing, all round. I had the impression that here was a girl who would be thrown from person to person over years, and each would think they had saved her by some miracle when in actual fact she was in no danger at all. Never. Not even for a second.

He said, "Let us go, zen, and tell 'er the decision we 'ave come to," and I said 10 yes, let's, but when we got to Charlotte's room, someone else was putting his fingers through her curls. Charlotte was always one of those people for whom sex is available at all times — it just happens to her, quickly, and with a minimum of conversation. This guy was some other guy that she'd been sleeping with on the days when she wasn't with me. It had been going on for four months. This all came out later, naturally.

Would you believe he married her anyway? And not only that, he married her after she'd shaved her head that afternoon just to spite us. All of us — even the other guy no one had seen before. Maurice took a bald English woman with a strange lopsided walk and a temper like a gorgon back to Thailand and married her despite friends' complaints and the voluble protest of Aneepa Kapoor, who was the woman he read the news with. The anchorwoman, who had that Hitchcock style: hair tied back tight in a bun, a spiky nose, and a vicious red mouth. The kind of woman who doesn't need catching. "Maurice," she said, "you *owe* me. You can't just throw four months away like it wasn't worth a bloody thing!" He emailed me about it. He admitted that he'd been stringing Aneepa along for a while, and she'd been expecting something at the end of it. For in the real world, or so it seems to me, it is almost always women and not men who are waiting under windows, and they are almost always disappointed. In this matter, Charlotte was unusual.

John Steinbeck   1902–1968

The Chrysanthemums   [1937]

The high grey-flannel fog of winter closed off the Salinas Valley from the sky and from all the rest of the world. On every side it sat like a lid on the mountains and made of the great valley a closed pot. On the broad, level land floor the gang plows bit deep and left the black earth shining like metal where the shares had cut. On the foothill ranches across the Salinas River, the yellow stubble fields seemed to be bathed in pale cold sunshine, but there was no sunshine in the valley now in December. The thick willow scrub along the river flamed with sharp and positive yellow leaves.

It was a time of quiet and of waiting. The air was cold and tender. A light wind blew up from the southwest so that the farmers were mildly hopeful of a good rain before long; but fog and rain do not go together.

Across the river, on Henry Allen's foothill ranch there was little work to be done, for the hay was cut and stored and the orchards were plowed up to receive the rain deeply when it should come. The cattle on the higher slopes were becoming shaggy and rough-coated.

Elisa Allen, working in her flower garden, looked down across the yard and saw Henry, her husband, talking to two men in business suits. The three of them stood by the tractor shed, each man with one foot on the side of the little Fordson. They smoked cigarettes and studied the machine as they talked.

Elisa watched them for a moment and then went back to her work. She was   5 thirty-five. Her face was lean and strong and her eyes were as clear as water. Her figure looked blocked and heavy in her gardening costume, a man's black hat pulled low down over her eyes, clod-hopper shoes, a figured print dress almost completely covered by a big corduroy apron with four big pockets to hold the snips, the trowel and scratcher, the seeds and the knife she worked with. She wore heavy leather gloves to protect her hands while she worked.

She was cutting down the old year's chrysanthemum stalks with a pair of short and powerful scissors. She looked down toward the men by the tractor shed now and then. Her face was eager and mature and handsome; even her work with the scissors was over-eager, over-powerful. The chrysanthemum stems seemed too small and easy for her energy.

She brushed a cloud of hair out of her eyes with the back of her glove, and left a smudge of earth on her cheek in doing it. Behind her stood the neat white farm house with red geraniums close-banked around it as high as the windows. It was a hard-swept looking little house, with hard-polished windows, and a clean mud-mat on the front steps.

Elisa cast another glance toward the tractor shed. The strangers were getting into their Ford coupe. She took off a glove and put her strong fingers down into the forest of new green chrysanthemum sprouts that were growing around the old roots. She spread the leaves and looked down among the close-growing stems. No aphids were there, no sowbugs or snails or cutworms. Her terrier fingers destroyed such pests before they could get started.

Elisa started at the sound of her husband's voice. He had come near quietly, and he leaned over the wire fence that protected her flower garden from cattle and dogs and chickens.

"At it again," he said. "You've got a strong new crop coming."   10

Elisa straightened her back and pulled on the gardening glove again. "Yes. They'll be strong this coming year." In her tone and on her face there was a little smugness.

"You've got a gift with things," Henry observed. "Some of those yellow chrysanthemums you had this year were ten inches across. I wish you'd work out in the orchard and raise some apples that big."

Her eyes sharpened. "Maybe I could do it, too. I've a gift with things, all right. My mother had it. She could stick anything in the ground and make it grow. She said it was having planters' hands that knew how to do it."

"Well, it sure works with flowers," he said.

"Henry, who were those men you were talking to?"   15

"Why, sure, that's what I came to tell you. They were from the Western Meat Company. I sold those thirty head of three-year-old steers. Got nearly my own price, too."

"Good," she said. "Good for you."

"And I thought," he continued, "I thought how it's Saturday afternoon, and we might go into Salinas for dinner at a restaurant, and then to a picture show — to celebrate, you see."

"Good," she repeated. "Oh, yes. That will be good."

Henry put on his joking tone. "There's fights tonight. How'd you like to go 20 to the fights?"

"Oh, no," she said breathlessly. "No, I wouldn't like fights."

"Just fooling, Elisa. We'll go to a movie. Let's see. It's two now. I'm going to take Scotty and bring down those steers from the hill. It'll take us maybe two hours. We'll go in town about five and have dinner at the Cominos Hotel. Like that?"

"Of course I'll like it. It's good to eat away from home."

"All right, then. I'll go get up a couple of horses."

She said, "I'll have plenty of time to transplant some of these sets, I 25 guess."

She heard her husband calling Scotty down by the barn. And a little later she saw the two men ride up the pale yellow hillside in search of the steers.

There was a little square sandy bed kept for rooting the chrysanthemums. With her trowel she turned the soil over and over, and smoothed it and patted it firm. Then she dug ten parallel trenches to receive the sets. Back at the chrysanthemum bed she pulled out the little crisp shoots, trimmed off the leaves of each one with her scissors and laid it on a small orderly pile.

A squeak of wheels and plod of hoofs came from the road. Elisa looked up. The country road ran along the dense bank of willows and cottonwoods that bordered the river, and up this road came a curious vehicle, curiously drawn. It was an old spring-wagon, with a round canvas top on it like the cover of a prairie schooner. It was drawn by an old bay horse and a little grey-and-white burro. A big stubble-bearded man sat between the cover flaps and drove the crawling team. Underneath the wagon, between the hind wheels, a lean and rangy mongrel dog walked sedately. Words were painted on the canvas, in clumsy, crooked letters. "Pots, pans, knives, sisors, lawn mores, Fixed." Two rows of articles, and the triumphantly definitive "Fixed" below. The black paint had run down in little sharp points beneath each letter.

Elisa, squatting on the ground, watched to see the crazy, loose-jointed wagon pass by. But it didn't pass. It turned into the farm road in front of her house, crooked old wheels skirling and squeaking. The rangy dog darted from between the wheels and ran ahead. Instantly the two ranch shepherds flew out at him. Then all three stopped, and with stiff and quivering tails, with taut straight legs, with ambassadorial dignity, they slowly circled, sniffing daintily. The caravan pulled up to Elisa's wire fence and stopped. Now the newcomer dog, feeling out-numbered, lowered his tail and retired under the wagon with raised hackles and bared teeth.

The man on the wagon seat called out, "That's a bad dog in a fight when he 30 gets started."

Elisa laughed. "I see he is. How soon does he generally get started?"

The man caught up her laughter and echoed it heartily. "Sometimes not for weeks and weeks," he said. He climbed stiffly down, over the wheel. The horse and the donkey drooped like unwatered flowers.

Elisa saw that he was a very big man. Although his hair and beard were greying, he did not look old. His worn black suit was wrinkled and spotted with grease. The laughter had disappeared from his face and eyes the moment his laughing voice ceased. His eyes were dark, and they were full of the brooding that gets in the eyes of teamsters and of sailors. The calloused hands he rested on the wire fence were cracked, and every crack was a black line. He took off his battered hat.

"I'm off my general road, ma'am," he said. "Does this dirt road cut over across the river to the Los Angeles highway?"

Elisa stood up and shoved the thick scissors in her apron pocket. "Well, yes, 35
it does, but it winds around and then fords the river. I don't think your team
could pull through the sand."

He replied with some asperity, "It might surprise you what them beasts can
pull through."

"When they get started?" she asked.

He smiled for a second. "Yes. When they get started."

"Well," said Elisa, "I think you'll save time if you go back to the Salinas road
and pick up the highway there."

He drew a big finger down the chicken wire and made it sing. "I ain't in any 40
hurry, ma'am. I go from Seattle to San Diego and back every year. Takes all my
time. About six months each way. I aim to follow nice weather."

Elisa took off her gloves and stuffed them in the apron pocket with the scissors. She touched the under edge of her man's hat, searching for fugitive hairs.
"That sounds like a nice kind of a way to live," she said.

He leaned confidentially over the fence. "Maybe you noticed the writing on
my wagon. I mend pots and sharpen knives and scissors. You got any of them
things to do?"

"Oh, no," she said quickly. "Nothing like that." Her eyes hardened with resistance.

"Scissors is the worst thing," he explained. "Most people just ruin scissors
trying to sharpen 'em, but I know how. I got a special tool. It's a little bobbit
kind of thing, and patented. But it sure does the trick."

"No. My scissors are all sharp."   45

"All right, then. Take a pot," he continued earnestly, "a bent pot, or a pot
with a hole. I can make it like new so you don't have to buy no new ones. That's
a saving for you."

"No," she said shortly. "I tell you I have nothing like that for you to do."

His face fell to an exaggerated sadness. His voice took on a whining under-
tone. "I ain't had a thing to do today. Maybe I won't have no supper tonight. You
see I'm off my regular road. I know folks on the highway clear from Seattle to
San Diego. They save their things for me to sharpen up because they know I do it
so good and save them money."

"I'm sorry," Elisa said irritably. "I haven't anything for you to do."

His eyes left her face and fell to searching the ground. They roamed about 50
until they came to the chrysanthemum bed where she had been working.
"What's them plants, ma'am?"

The irritation and resistance melted from Elisa's face. "Oh, those are chrysanthemums, giant whites and yellows. I raise them every year, bigger than anybody around here."

"Kind of a long-stemmed flower? Looks like a quick puff of colored smoke?"
he asked.

"That's it. What a nice way to describe them."

"They smell kind of nasty till you get used to them," he said.

"Its a good bitter smell," she retorted, "not nasty at all."   55

He changed his tone quickly. "I like the smell myself."

"I had ten-inch blooms this year," she said.

The man leaned farther over the fence. "Look. I know a lady down the road a piece, has got the nicest garden you ever seen. Got nearly every kind of flower but no chrysantheums. Last time I was mending a copper-bottom washtub for her (that's a hard job but I do it good), she said to me, 'If you ever run acrost some nice chrysantheums I wish you'd try to get me a few seeds.' That's what she told me."

Elisa's eyes grew alert and eager. "She couldn't have known much about chrysanthemums. You *can* raise them from seed, but it's much easier to root the little sprouts you see here."

"Oh," he said. "I s'pose I can't take none to her, then."   60

"Why yes you can," Elisa cried. "I can put some in damp sand, and you can carry them right along with you. They'll take root in the pot if you keep them damp. And then she can transplant them."

"She'd sure like to have some, ma'am. You say they're nice ones?"

"Beautiful," she said. "Oh, beautiful." Her eyes shone. She tore off the battered hat and shook out her dark pretty hair. "I'll put them in a flower pot, and you can take them right with you. Come into the yard."

While the man came through the picket gate Elisa ran excitedly along the geranium-bordered path to the back of the house. And she returned carrying a big red flower pot. The gloves were forgotten now. She kneeled on the ground by the starting bed and dug up the sandy soil with her fingers and scooped it into the bright new flower pot. Then she picked up the little pile of shoots she had prepared. With her strong fingers she pressed them into the sand and tamped around them with her knuckles. The man stood over her. "I'll tell you what to do," she said. "You remember so you can tell the lady."

"Yes, I'll try to remember."   65

"Well, look. These will take root in about a month. Then she must set them out, about a foot apart in good rich earth like this, see?" She lifted a handful of dark soil for him to look at. "They'll grow fast and tall. Now remember this: In July tell her to cut them down, about eight inches from the ground."

"Before they bloom?" he asked.

"Yes, before they bloom." Her face was tight with eagerness. "They'll grow right up again. About the last of September the buds will start."

She stopped and seemed perplexed. "It's the budding that takes the most care," she said hesitantly. "I don't know how to tell you." She looked deep into his eyes, searchingly. Her mouth opened a little, and she seemed to be listening. "I'll try to tell you," she said "Did you ever hear of planting hands?"

"Can't say I have, ma'am."   70

"Well, I can only tell you what it feels like. It's when you're picking off the buds you don't want. Everything goes right down into your fingertips. You watch your fingers work. They do it themselves. You can feel how it is. They pick and pick the buds. They never make a mistake. They're with the plant. Do you see? Your fingers and the plant. You can feel that, right up your arm. They know.

They never make a mistake. You can feel it. When you're like that you can't do anything wrong. Do you see that? Can you understand that?"

She was kneeling on the ground looking up at him. Her breast swelled passionately.

The man's eyes narrowed. He looked away self-consciously. "Maybe I know," he said. "Sometimes in the night in the wagon there —"

Elisa's voice grew husky. She broke in on him, "I've never lived as you do, but I know what you mean. When the night is dark — why, the stars are sharp-pointed, and there's quiet. Why, you rise up and up! Every pointed star gets driven into your body. It's like that. Hot and sharp and — lovely."

Kneeling there, her hand went out toward his legs in the greasy black 75 trousers. Her hesitant fingers almost touched the cloth. Then her hand dropped to the ground. She crouched low like a fawning dog.

He said, "It's nice, just like you say. Only when you don't have no dinner, it ain't."

She stood up then, very straight, and her face was ashamed. She held the flower pot out to him and placed it gently in his arms. "Here. Put it in your wagon, on the seat, where you can watch it. Maybe I can find something for you to do."

At the back of the house she dug in the can pile and found two old and battered aluminum saucepans. She carried them back and gave them to him. "Here, maybe you can fix these."

His manner changed. He became professional. "Good as new I can fix them." At the back of his wagon he set a little anvil, and out of an oily tool box dug a small machine hammer. Elisa came through the gate to watch him while he pounded out the dents in the kettles. His mouth grew sure and knowing. At a difficult part of the work he sucked his under-lip.

"You sleep right in the wagon?" Elisa asked.   80

"Right in the wagon, ma'am. Rain or shine I'm dry as a cow in there."

"It must be nice," she said. "It must be very nice. I wish women could do such things."

"It ain't the right kind of a life for a woman."

Her upper lip raised a little, showing her teeth. "How do you know? How can you tell?" she said.

"I don't know, ma'am," he protested. "Of course I don't know. Now here's 85 your kettles, done. You don't have to buy no new ones."

"How much?"

"Oh, fifty cents'll do. I keep my prices down and my work good. That's why I have all them satisfied customers up and down the highway."

Elisa brought him a fifty-cent piece from the house and dropped it in his hand. "You might be surprised to have a rival some time. I can sharpen scissors, too. And I can beat the dents out of little pots. I could show you what a woman might do."

He put his hammer back in the oily box and shoved the little anvil out of sight. "It would be a lonely life for a woman, ma'am, and a scarey life, too, with animals creeping under the wagon all night." He climbed over the singletree, steadying himself with a hand on the burro's white rump. He settled himself in the seat, picked up the lines. "Thank you kindly, ma'am," he said. "I'll do like you told me; I'll go back and catch the Salinas road."

"Mind," she called, "if you're long in getting there, keep the sand damp."   90

"Sand, ma'am? . . . Sand? Oh, sure. You mean around the chrysantheums. Sure I will." He clucked his tongue. The beasts leaned luxuriously into their collars. The mongrel dog took his place between the back wheels. The wagon turned and crawled out the entrance road and back the way it had come, along the river.

Elisa stood in front of her wire fence watching the slow progress of the caravan. Her shoulders were straight, her head thrown back, her eyes half-closed, so that the scene came vaguely into them. Her lips moved silently, forming the words "Good-bye—good-bye." Then she whispered, "That's a bright direction. There's a glowing there." The sound of her whisper startled her. She shook herself free and looked about to see whether anyone had been listening. Only the dogs had heard. They lifted their heads toward her from their sleeping in the dust, and then stretched out their chins and settled asleep again. Elisa turned and ran hurriedly into the house.

In the kitchen she reached behind the stove and felt the water tank. It was full of hot water from the noonday cooking. In the bathroom she tore off her soiled clothes and flung them into the corner. And then she scrubbed herself with a little block of pumice, legs and thighs, loins and chest and arms, until her skin was scratched and red. When she had dried herself she stood in front of a mirror in her bedroom and looked at her body. She tightened her stomach and threw out her chest. She turned and looked over her shoulder at her back.

After a while she began to dress, slowly. She put on her newest underclothing and her nicest stockings and the dress which was the symbol of her prettiness. She worked carefully on her hair, penciled her eyebrows and rouged her lips.

Before she was finished she heard the little thunder of hoofs and the shouts   95 of Henry and his helper as they drove the red steers into the corral. She heard the gate bang shut and set herself for Henry's arrival.

His step sounded on the porch. He entered the house calling, "Elisa, where are you?"

"In my room, dressing. I'm not ready. There's hot water for your bath. Hurry up. It's getting late."

When she heard him splashing in the tub, Elisa laid his dark suit on the bed, and shirt and socks and tie beside it. She stood his polished shoes on the floor beside the bed. Then she went to the porch and sat primly and stiffly down. She looked toward the river road where the willow-line was still yellow with frosted leaves so that under the high grey fog they seemed a thin band of sunshine. This was the only color in the grey afternoon. She sat unmoving for a long time. Her eyes blinked rarely.

Henry came banging out of the door, shoving his tie inside his vest as he came. Elisa stiffened and her face grew tight. Henry stopped short and looked at her. "Why—why, Elisa. You look so nice!"

"Nice? You think I look nice? What do you mean by 'nice'?" 100

Henry blundered on. "I don't know. I mean you look different, strong and happy."

"I am strong? Yes, strong. What do you mean 'strong'?"

He looked bewildered. "You're playing some kind of game," he said helplessly. "It's a kind of a play. You look strong enough to break a calf over your knee, happy enough to eat it like a watermelon."

For a second she lost her rigidity. "Henry! Don't talk like that. You didn't know what you said." She grew complete again. "I'm strong," she boasted. "I never knew before how strong."

Henry looked down toward the tractor shed, and when he brought his eyes 105 back to her, they were his own again. "I'll get out the car. You can put on your coat while I'm starting."

Elisa went into the house. She heard him drive to the gate and idle down his motor, and then she took a long time to put on her hat. She pulled it here and pressed it there. When Henry turned the motor off she slipped into her coat and went out.

The little roadster bounced along on the dirt road by the river, raising the birds and driving the rabbits into the brush. Two cranes flapped heavily over the willow-line and dropped into the river-bed.

Far ahead on the road Elisa saw a dark speck. She knew.

She tried not to look as they passed it, but her eyes would not obey. She whispered to herself sadly, "He might have thrown them off the road. That wouldn't have been much trouble, not very much. But he kept the pot," she explained. "He had to keep the pot. That's why he couldn't get them off the road."

The roadster turned a bend and she saw the caravan ahead. She swung full 110 around toward her husband so she could not see the little covered wagon and the mismatched team as the car passed them.

In a moment it was over. The thing was done. She did not look back.

She said loudly, to be heard above the motor, "It will be good, tonight, a good dinner."

"Now you're changed again," Henry complained. He took one hand from the wheel and patted her knee. "I ought to take you in to dinner oftener. It would be good for both of us. We get so heavy out on the ranch."

"Henry," she asked, "could we have wine at dinner?"

"Sure we could. Say! That will be fine." 115

She was silent for a while; then she said, "Henry, at those prize fights, do the men hurt each other very much?"

"Sometimes a little, not often. Why?"

"Well, I've read how they break noses, and blood runs down their chests. I've read how the fighting gloves get heavy and soggy with blood."

He looked around at her. "What's the matter, Elisa? I didn't know you read things like that." He brought the car to a stop, then turned to the right over the Salinas River bridge.

"Do any women ever go to the fights?" she asked. 120

"Oh, sure, some. What's the matter, Elisa? Do you want to go? I don't think you'd like it, but I'll take you if you really want to go."

She relaxed limply in the seat. "Oh, no. No. I don't want to go. I'm sure I don't." Her face was turned away from him. "It will be enough if we can have wine. It will be plenty." She turned up her coat collar so he could not see that she was crying weakly — like an old woman.

Amy Tan   b. 1952

Two Kinds   [1989]

My mother believed you could be anything you wanted to be in America. You could open a restaurant. You could work for the government and get good retirement. You could buy a house with almost no money down. You could become rich. You could become instantly famous.

"Of course you can be prodigy, too," my mother told me when I was nine. "You can be best anything. What does Auntie Lindo know? Her daughter, she is only best tricky."

America was where all my mother's hopes lay. She had come here in 1949 after losing everything in China: her mother and father, her family home, her first husband, and two daughters, twin baby girls. But she never looked back with regret. There were so many ways for things to get better.

We didn't immediately pick the right kind of prodigy. At first my mother thought I could be a Chinese Shirley Temple. We'd watch Shirley's old movies on TV as though they were training films. My mother would poke my arm and say, *"Ni kan"* — You watch. And I would see Shirley tapping her feet, or singing a sailor song, or pursing her lips into a very round O while saying, "Oh my goodness."

"*Ni kan,*" said my mother as Shirley's eyes flooded with tears. "You already 5 know how. Don't need talent for crying!"

Soon after my mother got this idea about Shirley Temple, she took me to a beauty training school in the Mission district and put me in the hands of a student who could barely hold the scissors without shaking. Instead of getting big fat curls, I emerged with an uneven mass of crinkly black fuzz. My mother dragged me off to the bathroom and tried to wet down my hair.

"You look like Negro Chinese," she lamented, as if I had done this on purpose.

The instructor of the beauty training school had to lop off these soggy clumps to make my hair even again. "Peter Pan is very popular these days," the instructor assured my mother. I now had hair the length of a boy's, with straight-across bangs that hung at a slant two inches above my eyebrows. I liked the haircut and it made me actually look forward to my future fame.

In fact, in the beginning, I was just as excited as my mother, maybe even more so. I pictured this prodigy part of me as many different images, trying each one on for size. I was a dainty ballerina girl standing by the curtains, waiting to hear the right music that would send me floating on my tiptoes. I was like the Christ child lifted out of the straw manger, crying with holy indignity. I was Cinderella stepping from her pumpkin carriage with sparkly cartoon music filling the air.

In all of my imaginings, I was filled with a sense that I would soon become 10
perfect. My mother and father would adore me. I would be beyond reproach. I would never feel the need to sulk for anything.

But sometimes the prodigy in me became impatient. "If you don't hurry up and get me out of here, I'm disappearing for good," it warned. "And then you'll always be nothing."

Every night after dinner, my mother and I would sit at the Formica kitchen table. She would present new tests, taking her examples from stories of amazing children she had read in *Ripley's Believe It or Not*, or *Good Housekeeping*, *Reader's Digest*, and a dozen other magazines she kept in a pile in our bathroom. My mother got these magazines from people whose houses she cleaned. And since she cleaned many houses each week, we had a great assortment. She would look through them all, searching for stories about remarkable children.

The first night she brought out a story about a three-year-old boy who knew the capitals of all the states and even most of the European countries. A teacher was quoted as saying the little boy could also pronounce the names of the foreign cities correctly.

"What's the capital of Finland?" my mother asked me, looking at the magazine story.

All I knew was the capital of California, because Sacramento was the name 15
of the street we lived on in Chinatown. "Nairobi!" I guessed, saying the most foreign word I could think of. She checked to see if that was possibly one way to pronounce "Helsinki" before showing me the answer.

The tests got harder — multiplying numbers in my head, finding the queen of hearts in a deck of cards, trying to stand on my head without using my hands, predicting the daily temperatures in Los Angeles, New York, and London.

One night I had to look at a page from the Bible for three minutes and then report everything I could remember. "Now Jehoshaphat had riches and honor in abundance and . . . that's all I remember, Ma," I said.

And after seeing my mother's disappointed face once again, something inside of me began to die. I hated the tests, the raised hopes and failed expectations. Before going to bed that night, I looked in the mirror above the bathroom sink and when I saw only my face staring back — and that it would always be this ordinary face — I began to cry. Such a sad, ugly girl! I made high-pitched noises like a crazed animal, trying to scratch out the face in the mirror.

And then I saw what seemed to be the prodigy side of me — because I had never seen that face before. I looked at my reflection, blinking so I could see more clearly. The girl staring back at me was angry, powerful. This girl and I were the same. I had new thoughts, willful thoughts, or rather thoughts filled with lots of won'ts. I won't let her change me, I promised myself. I won't be what I'm not.

So now on nights when my mother presented her tests, I performed list- 20
lessly, my head propped on one arm. I pretended to be bored. And I was. I got so bored I started counting the bellows of the foghorns out on the bay while my mother drilled me in other areas. The sound was comforting and reminded me of the cow jumping over the moon. And the next day, I played a game with myself, seeing if my mother would give up on me before eight bellows. After a while I usually counted only one, maybe two bellows at most. At last she was beginning to give up hope.

Two or three months had gone by without any mention of my being a prodigy again. And then one day my mother was watching *The Ed Sullivan Show* on TV. The TV was old and the sound kept shorting out. Every time my mother got halfway up from the sofa to adjust the set, the sound would go back on and Ed would be talking. As soon as she sat down, Ed would go silent again. She got up, the TV broke into loud piano music. She sat down. Silence. Up and down, back and forth, quiet and loud. It was like a stiff embraceless dance between her and the TV set. Finally she stood by the set with her hand on the sound dial.

She seemed entranced by the music, a little frenzied piano piece with this mesmerizing quality, sort of quick passages and then teasing lilting ones before it returned to the quick playful parts.

"*Ni kan,*" my mother said, calling me over with hurried hand gestures, "Look here."

I could see why my mother was fascinated by the music. It was being pounded out by a little Chinese girl, about nine years old, with a Peter Pan haircut. The girl had the sauciness of a Shirley Temple. She was proudly modest like a proper Chinese child. And she also did this fancy sweep of a curtsy, so that the fluffy skirt of her white dress cascaded slowly to the floor like the petals of a large carnation.

In spite of these warning signs, I wasn't worried. Our family had no piano 25
and we couldn't afford to buy one, let alone reams of sheet music and piano lessons. So I could be generous in my comments when my mother bad-mouthed the little girl on TV.

"Play note right, but doesn't sound good! No singing sound," complained my mother.

"What are you picking on her for?" I said carelessly. "She's pretty good. Maybe she's not the best, but she's trying hard." I knew almost immediately I would be sorry I said that.

"Just like you," she said. "Not the best. Because you not trying." She gave a little huff as she let go of the sound dial and sat down on the sofa.

The little Chinese girl sat down also to play an encore of "Anitra's Dance" by Grieg. I remember the song, because later on I had to learn how to play it.

Three days after watching *The Ed Sullivan Show,* my mother told me what 30 my schedule would be for piano lessons and piano practice. She had talked to Mr. Chong, who lived on the first floor of our apartment building. Mr. Chong was a retired piano teacher and my mother had traded housecleaning services for weekly lessons and a piano for me to practice on every day, two hours a day, from four until six.

When my mother told me this, I felt as though I had been sent to hell. I whined and then kicked my foot a little when I couldn't stand it anymore.

"Why don't you like me the way I am? I'm *not* a genius! I can't play the piano. And even if I could, I wouldn't go on TV if you paid me a million dollars!" I cried.

My mother slapped me. "Who ask you be genius?" she shouted. "Only ask you be your best. For you sake. You think I want you be genius? Hnnh! What for! Who ask you!"

"So ungrateful," I heard her mutter in Chinese. "If she had as much talent as she has temper, she would be famous now."

Mr. Chong, whom I secretly nicknamed Old Chong, was very strange, al- 35 ways tapping his fingers to the silent music of an invisible orchestra. He looked ancient in my eyes. He had lost most of the hair on top of his head and he wore thick glasses and had eyes that always looked tired and sleepy. But he must have been younger than I thought, since he lived with his mother and was not yet married.

I met Old Lady Chong once and that was enough. She had this peculiar smell like a baby that had done something in its pants. And her fingers felt like a dead person's, like an old peach I once found in the back of the refrigerator; the skin just slid off the meat when I picked it up.

I soon found out why Old Chong had retired from teaching piano. He was deaf. "Like Beethoven!" he shouted to me. "We're both listening only in our head!" And he would start to conduct his frantic silent sonatas.

Our lessons went like this. He would open the book and point to different things, explaining their purpose: "Key! Treble! Bass! No sharps or flats! So this is C major! Listen now and play after me!"

And then he would play the C scale a few times, a simple chord, and then, as if inspired by an old, unreachable itch, he gradually added more notes and running trills and a pounding bass until the music was really something quite grand.

I would play after him, the simple scale, the simple chord, and then I just 40 played some nonsense that sounded like a cat running up and down on top of garbage cans. Old Chong smiled and applauded and then said, "Very good! But now you must learn to keep time!"

So that's how I discovered that Old Chong's eyes were too slow to keep up with the wrong notes I was playing. He went through the motions in half-time. To help me keep rhythm, he stood behind me, pushing down on my right shoulder for every beat. He balanced pennies on top of my wrists so I would keep them still as I slowly played scales and arpeggios. He had me curve my hand around an apple and keep that shape when playing chords. He marched stiffly to show me how to make each finger dance up and down, staccato like an obedient little soldier.

He taught me all these things, and that was how I also learned I could be lazy and get away with mistakes, lots of mistakes. If I hit the wrong notes because I hadn't practiced enough, I never corrected myself. I just kept playing in rhythm. And Old Chong kept conducting his own private reverie.

So maybe I never really gave myself a fair chance. I did pick up the basics pretty quickly, and I might have become a good pianist at that young age. But I was so determined not to try, not to be anybody different that I learned to play only the most ear-splitting preludes, the most discordant hymns.

Over the next year, I practiced like this, dutifully in my own way. And then one day I heard my mother and her friend Lindo Jong both talking in a loud bragging tone of voice so others could hear. It was after church, and I was leaning against the brick wall wearing a dress with stiff white petticoats. Auntie Lindo's daughter, Waverly, who was about my age, was standing farther down the wall about five feet away. We had grown up together and shared all the closeness of two sisters squabbling over crayons and dolls. In other words, for the most part, we hated each other. I thought she was snotty. Waverly Jong had gained a certain amount of fame as "Chinatown's Littlest Chinese Chess Champion."

"She bring home too many trophy," lamented Auntie Lindo that Sunday. 45 "All day she play chess. All day I have no time do nothing but dust off her winnings." She threw a scolding look at Waverly, who pretended not to see her.

"You lucky you don't have this problem," said Auntie Lindo with a sigh to my mother.

And my mother squared her shoulders and bragged: "Our problem worser than yours. If we ask Jing-mei wash dish, she hear nothing but music. It's like you can't stop this natural talent."

And right then, I was determined to put a stop to her foolish pride.

A few weeks later, Old Chong and my mother conspired to have me play in a talent show which would be held in the church hall. By then, my parents had saved up enough to buy me a secondhand piano, a black Wurlitzer spinet with a scarred bench. It was the showpiece of our living room.

For the talent show, I was to play a piece called "Pleading Child" from Schu- 50 mann's *Scenes from Childhood*. It was a simple, moody piece that sounded more difficult than it was. I was supposed to memorize the whole thing, playing the repeat parts twice to make the piece sound longer. But I dawdled over it, playing a few bars and then cheating, looking up to see what notes followed. I never really listened to what I was playing. I daydreamed about being somewhere else, about being someone else.

The part I liked to practice best was the fancy curtsy: right foot out, touch the rose on the carpet with a pointed foot, sweep to the side, left leg bends, look up and smile.

My parents invited all the couples from the Joy Luck Club to witness my debut. Auntie Lindo and Uncle Tin were there. Waverly and her two older brothers had also come. The first two rows were filled with children both younger and older than I was. The littlest ones got to go first. They recited simple nursery rhymes, squawked out tunes on miniature violins, twirled Hula Hoops, pranced in pink ballet tutus, and when they bowed or curtsied, the audience would sigh in unison, "Awww," and then clap enthusiastically.

When my turn came, I was very confident. I remember my childish excitement. It was as if I knew, without a doubt, that the prodigy side of me really did exist. I had no fear whatsoever, no nervousness. I remember thinking to myself, This is it! This is it! I looked out over the audience, at my mother's blank face, my father's yawn, Auntie Lindo's stiff-lipped smile, Waverly's sulky expression. I had on a white dress layered with sheets of lace, and a pink bow in my Peter Pan haircut. As I sat down I envisioned people jumping to their feet and Ed Sullivan rushing up to introduce me to everyone on TV.

And I started to play. It was so beautiful. I was so caught up in how lovely I looked that at first I didn't worry how I would sound. So it was a surprise to me when I hit the first wrong note and I realized something didn't sound quite right. And then I hit another and another followed that. A chill started at the top of my head and began to trickle down. Yet I couldn't stop playing, as though my hands were bewitched. I kept thinking my fingers would adjust themselves back, like a train switching to the right track. I played this strange jumble through two repeats, the sour notes staying with me all the way to the end.

When I stood up, I discovered my legs were shaking. Maybe I had just been 55 nervous and the audience, like Old Chong, had seen me go through the right motions and had not heard anything wrong at all. I swept my right foot out, went down on my knee, looked up and smiled. The room was quiet, except for Old Chong, who was beaming and shouting, "Bravo! Bravo! Well done!" But then I saw my mother's face, her stricken face. The audience clapped weakly, and as I walked back to my chair, with my whole face quivering as I tried not to cry, I heard a little boy whisper loudly to his mother, "That was awful," and the mother whispered back, "Well, she certainly tried."

And now I realized how many people were in the audience, the whole world it seemed. I was aware of eyes burning into my back. I felt the shame of my mother and father as they sat stiffly throughout the rest of the show.

We could have escaped during intermission. Pride and some strange sense of honor must have anchored my parents to their chairs. And so we watched it all: the eighteen-year-old boy with a fake mustache who did a magic show and juggled flaming hoops while riding a unicycle. The breasted girl with white makeup who sang from *Madama Butterfly* and got honorable mention. And the eleven-year-old boy who won first prize playing a tricky violin song that sounded like a busy bee.

After the show, the Hsus, the Jongs, and the St. Clairs from the Joy Luck Club came up to my mother and father.

"Lots of talented kids," Auntie Lindo said vaguely, smiling broadly.

"That was somethin' else," said my father, and I wondered if he was referring 60
to me in a humorous way, or whether he even remembered what I had done.

Waverly looked at me and shrugged her shoulders. "You aren't a genius like
me," she said matter-of-factly. And if I hadn't felt so bad, I would have pulled
her braids and punched her stomach.

But my mother's expression was what devastated me: a quiet, blank look
that said she had lost everything. I felt the same way, and it seemed as if everybody were now coming up, like gawkers at the scene of an accident, to see what
parts were actually missing. When we got on the bus to go home, my father was
humming the busy-bee tune and my mother was silent. I kept thinking she
wanted to wait until we got home before shouting at me. But when my father
unlocked the door to our apartment, my mother walked in and then went to the
back, into the bedroom. No accusations. No blame. And in a way, I felt disappointed. I had been waiting for her to start shouting, so I could shout back and
cry and blame her for all my misery.

I assumed my talent-show fiasco meant I never had to play the piano again.
But two days later, after school, my mother came out of the kitchen and saw me
watching TV.

"Four clock," she reminded me as if it were any other day. I was stunned, as
though she were asking me to go through the talent-show torture again. I
wedged myself more tightly in front of the TV.

"Turn off TV," she called from the kitchen five minutes later. 65

I didn't budge. And then I decided. I didn't have to do what my mother said
anymore. I wasn't her slave. This wasn't China. I had listened to her before and
look what happened. She was the stupid one.

She came out from the kitchen and stood in the arched entryway of the living room. "Four clock," she said once again, louder.

"I'm not going to play anymore," I said nonchalantly. "Why should I? I'm
not a genius."

She walked over and stood in front of the TV. I saw her chest was heaving up
and down in an angry way.

"No!" I said, and I now felt stronger, as if my true self had finally emerged. 70
So this was what had been inside me all along.

"No! I won't!" I screamed.

She yanked me by the arm, pulled me off the floor, snapped off the TV. She
was frighteningly strong, half pulling, half carrying me toward the piano as I
kicked the throw rugs under my feet. She lifted me up and onto the hard bench.
I was sobbing by now, looking at her bitterly. Her chest was heaving even more
and her mouth was open, smiling crazily as if she were pleased I was crying.

"You want me to be someone that I'm not!" I sobbed. "I'll never be the kind
of daughter you want me to be!"

"Only two kinds of daughters," she shouted in Chinese. "Those who are
obedient and those who follow their own mind! Only one kind of daughter can
live in this house. Obedient daughter!"

"Then I wish I wasn't your daughter. I wish you weren't my mother," I 75
shouted. As I said these things I got scared. It felt like worms and toads and slimy
things crawling out of my chest, but it also felt good, as if this awful side of me
had surfaced, at last.

"Too late change this," said my mother shrilly.

And I could sense her anger rising to its breaking point. I wanted to see it
spill over. And that's when I remembered the babies she had lost in China, the
ones we never talked about. "Then I wish I'd never been born!" I shouted. "I
wish I were dead! Like them."

It was as if I had said the magic words. Alakazam! — and her face went blank,
her mouth closed, her arms went slack, and she backed out of the room, stunned,
as if she were blowing away like a small brown leaf, thin, brittle, lifeless.

It was not the only disappointment my mother felt in me. In the years that
followed, I failed her so many times, each time asserting my own will, my right
to fall short of expectations. I didn't get straight As. I didn't become class president. I didn't get into Stanford. I dropped out of college.

For unlike my mother, I did not believe I could be anything I wanted to be. I 80
could only be me.

And for all those years, we never talked about the disaster at the recital or my
terrible accusations afterward at the piano bench. All that remained unchecked,
like a betrayal that was now unspeakable. So I never found a way to ask her why
she had hoped for something so large that failure was inevitable.

And even worse, I never asked her what frightened me the most: Why had
she given up hope?

For after our struggle at the piano, she never mentioned my playing again.
The lessons stopped. The lid to the piano was closed, shutting out the dust, my
misery, and her dreams.

So she surprised me. A few years ago, she offered to give me the piano, for
my thirtieth birthday. I had not played in all those years. I saw the offer as a sign
of forgiveness, a tremendous burden removed.

"Are you sure?" I asked shyly. "I mean, won't you and Dad miss it?" 85

"No, this your piano," she said firmly. "Always your piano. You only one
can play."

"Well, I probably can't play anymore," I said. "It's been years."

"You pick up fast," said my mother, as if she knew this was certain. "You
have natural talent. You could been genius if you want to."

"No I couldn't."

"You just not trying," said my mother. And she was neither angry nor sad. 90
She said it as if to announce a fact that could never be disproved. "Take it," she
said.

But I didn't at first. It was enough that she had offered it to me. And after
that, every time I saw it in my parents' living room, standing in front of the bay
windows, it made me feel proud, as if it were a shiny trophy I had won back.

Last week I sent a tuner over to my parents' apartment and had the piano reconditioned, for purely sentimental reasons. My mother had died a few months before and I had been getting things in order for my father, a little bit at a time. I put the jewelry in special silk pouches. The sweaters she had knitted in yellow, pink, bright orange — all the colors I hated — I put those in moth-proof boxes. I found some old Chinese silk dresses, the kind with little slits up the sides. I rubbed the old silk against my skin, then wrapped them in tissue and decided to take them home with me.

After I had the piano tuned, I opened the lid and touched the keys. It sounded even richer than I remembered. Really, it was a very good piano. Inside the bench were the same exercise notes with handwritten scales, the same secondhand music books with their covers held together with yellow tape.

> Research Amy Tan in depth with cultural documents and multimedia resources on *LiterActive*.

I opened up the Schumann book to the dark little piece I had played at the recital. It was on the left-hand side of the page, "Pleading Child." It looked more difficult than I remembered. I played a few bars, surprised at how easily the notes came back to me.

And for the first time, or so it seemed, I noticed the piece on the right-hand 95 side. It was called "Perfectly Contented." I tried to play this one as well. It had a lighter melody but the same flowing rhythm and turned out to be quite easy. "Pleading Child" was shorter but slower; "Perfectly Contented" was longer, but faster. And after I played them both a few times, I realized they were two halves of the same song.

John Updike   b. 1932

A & P°   [1961]

In walks these three girls in nothing but bathing suits. I'm in the third checkout slot, with my back to the door, so I don't see them until they're over by the bread. The one that caught my eye first was the one in the plaid green two-piece. She was a chunky kid, with a good tan and a sweet broad soft-looking can with those two crescents of white just under it, where the sun never seems to hit, at the top of the backs of her legs. I stood there with my hand on a box of HiHo crackers trying to remember if I rang it up or not. I ring it up again and the customer starts giving me hell. She's one of these cash-register-watchers, a witch about fifty with rouge on her cheekbones and no eyebrows, and I know it made her day to trip me up. She'd been watching cash registers for fifty years and probably never seen a mistake before.

A & P: Grocery stores operated by the Great Atlantic & Pacific Tea Company, which was founded in New York City in 1859 and is currently headquartered in Montvale, New Jersey.

By the time I got her feathers smoothed and her goodies into a bag—she gives me a little snort in passing, if she'd been born at the right time they would have burned her over in Salem—by the time I get her on her way the girls had circled around the bread and were coming back, without a pushcart, back my way along the counters, in the aisle between the checkouts and the Special bins. They didn't even have shoes on. There was this chunky one, with the two-piece—it was bright green and the seams on the bra were still sharp and her belly was still pretty pale so I guessed she just got it (the suit)—there was this one, with one of those chubby berry-faces, the lips all bunched together under her nose, this one, and a tall one, with black hair that hadn't quite frizzed right, and one of these sunburns right across under the eyes, and a chin that was too long—you know, the kind of girl other girls think is very "striking" and "attractive" but never quite makes it, as they very well know, which is why they like her so much—and then the third one, that wasn't quite so tall. She was the queen. She kind of led them, the other two peeking around and making their shoulders round. She didn't look around, not this queen, she just walked straight on slowly, on these long white prima-donna legs. She came down a little hard on her heels, as if she didn't walk in her bare feet that much, putting down her heels and then letting the weight move along to her toes as if she was testing the floor with every step, putting a little deliberate extra action into it. You never know for sure how girls' minds work (do you really think it's a mind in there or just a little buzz like a bee in a glass jar?) but you got the idea she had talked the other two into coming in here with her, and now she was showing them how to do it, walk slow and hold yourself straight.

She had on a kind of dirty-pink—beige maybe, I don't know—bathing suit with a little nubble all over it and, what got me, the straps were down. They were off her shoulders looped loose around the cool tops of her arms, and I guess as a result the suit had slipped a little on her, so all around the top of the cloth there was this shining rim. If it hadn't been there you wouldn't have known there could have been anything whiter than those shoulders. With the straps pushed off, there was nothing between the top of the suit and the top of her head except just *her*, this clean bare plane of the top of her chest down from the shoulder bones like a dented sheet of metal tilted in the light. I mean, it was more than pretty.

She had sort of oaky hair that the sun and salt had bleached, done up in a bun that was unravelling, and a kind of prim face. Walking into the A & P with your straps down, I suppose it's the only kind of face you *can* have. She held her head so high her neck, coming up out of those white shoulders, looked kind of stretched, but I didn't mind. The longer her neck was, the more of her there was.

She must have felt in the corner of her eye me and over my shoulder Stoke- 5 sie in the second slot watching, but she didn't tip. Not this queen. She kept her eyes moving across the racks, and stopped, and turned so slow it made my stomach rub the inside of my apron, and buzzed to the other two, who kind of huddled against her for relief, and then they all three of them went up the cat-and-dog-food-breakfast-cereal-macaroni-rice-raisins-seasonings-spreads-spaghetti-soft-drinks-crackers-and-cookies aisle. From the third slot I look straight up this aisle to the meat counter, and I watched them all the way. The fat one with the tan sort of fumbled with the cookies, but on second thought she put the package back. The sheep pushing their carts down the aisle — the girls were walking against the usual traffic (not that we have one-way signs or anything) — were pretty hilarious. You could see them, when Queenie's white shoulders dawned on them, kind of jerk, or hop, or hiccup, but their eyes snapped back to their own baskets and on they pushed. I bet you could set off dynamite in an A & P and the people would by and large keep reaching and checking oatmeal off their lists and muttering "Let me see, there was a third thing, began with A, asparagus, no, ah, yes, applesauce!" or whatever it is they do mutter. But there was no doubt, this jiggled them. A few houseslaves in pin curlers even looked around after pushing their carts past to make sure what they had seen was correct.

You know, it's one thing to have a girl in a bathing suit down on the beach, where what with the glare nobody can look at each other much anyway, and another thing in the cool of the A & P, under the fluorescent lights, against all those stacked packages, with her feet paddling along naked over our checkerboard green-and-cream rubber-tile floor.

"Oh Daddy," Stokesie said beside me. "I feel so faint."

"Darling," I said. "Hold me tight." Stokesie's married, with two babies chalked up on his fuselage already, but as far as I can tell that's the only difference. He's twenty-two, and I was nineteen this April.

"Is it done?" he asks, the responsible married man finding his voice. I forgot to say he thinks he's going to be manager some sunny day, maybe in 1990 when it's called the Great Alexandrov and Petrooshki Tea Company or something.

What he meant was, our town is five miles from a beach, with a big summer 10 colony out on the Point, but we're right in the middle of town, and the women generally put on a shirt or shorts or something before they get out of the car into the street. And anyway these are usually women with six children and varicose veins mapping their legs and nobody, including them, could care less. As I say, we're right in the middle of town, and if you stand at our front doors you can see two banks and the Congregational church and the newspaper store and three real-estate offices and about twenty-seven old freeloaders tearing up Central Street because the sewer broke again. It's not as if we're on the Cape; we're north of Boston and there's people in this town haven't seen the ocean for twenty years.

The girls had reached the meat counter and were asking McMahon something. He pointed, they pointed, and they shuffled out of sight behind a pyramid of Diet Delight peaches. All that was left for us to see was old McMahon patting his mouth and looking after them sizing up their joints. Poor kids, I began to feel sorry for them, they couldn't help it.

Now here comes the sad part of the story, at least my family says it's sad, but I don't think it's so sad myself. The store's pretty empty, it being Thursday afternoon, so there was nothing much to do except lean on the register and wait for the girls to show up again. The whole store was like a pinball machine and I didn't know which tunnel they'd come out of. After a while they come around out of the far aisle, around the light bulbs, records at discount of the Caribbean Six or Tony Martin Sings or some such gunk you wonder they waste the wax on, sixpacks of candy bars, and plastic toys done up in cellophane that fall apart when a kid looks at them anyway. Around they come, Queenie still leading the way, and holding a little gray jar in her hand. Slots Three through Seven are un-manned and I could see her wondering between Stokes and me, but Stokesie with his usual luck draws an old party in baggy gray pants who stumbles up with four giant cans of pineapple juice (what do these bums *do* with all that pine-apple juice? I've often asked myself) so the girls come to me. Queenie puts down the jar and I take it into my fingers icy cold. Kingfish Fancy Herring Snacks in Pure Sour Cream: 49¢. Now her hands are empty, not a ring or a bracelet, bare as God made them, and I wonder where the money's coming from. Still with that prim look she lifts a folded dollar bill out of the hollow at the center of her nubbled pink top. The jar went heavy in my hand. Really, I thought that was so cute.

Then everybody's luck begins to run out. Lengel comes in from haggling with a truck full of cabbages on the lot and is about to scuttle into that door marked MANAGER behind which he hides all day when the girls touch his eye. Lengel's pretty dreary, teaches Sunday school and the rest, but he doesn't miss that much. He comes over and says, "Girls, this isn't the beach."

Queenie blushes, though maybe it's just a brush of sunburn I was noticing for the first time, now that she was so close. "My mother asked me to pick up a jar of herring snacks." Her voice kind of startled me, the way voices do when you see the people first, coming out so flat and dumb yet kind of tony, too, the way it ticked over "pick up" and "snacks." All of a sudden I slid right down her voice into her living room. Her father and the other men were standing around in ice-cream coats and bow ties and the women were in sandals picking up herring snacks on toothpicks off a big glass plate and they were all holding drinks the color of water with olives and sprigs of mint in them. When my parents have somebody over they get lemonade and if it's a real racy affair Schlitz in tall glasses with "They'll Do It Every Time" cartoons stencilled on.

"That's all right," Lengel said. "But this isn't the beach." His repeating this 15 struck me as funny, as if it had just occurred to him, and he had been thinking all these years the A & P was a great big dune and he was the head lifeguard. He didn't like my smiling — as I say he doesn't miss much — but he concentrates on giving the girls that sad Sunday-school-superintendent stare.

Queenie's blush is no sunburn now, and the plump one in plaid, that I liked better from the back — a really sweet can — pipes up, "We weren't doing any shopping. We just came in for the one thing."

"That makes no difference," Lengel tells her, and I could see from the way his eyes went that he hadn't noticed she was wearing a two-piece before. "We want you decently dressed when you come in here."

"We *are* decent," Queenie says suddenly, her lower lip pushing, getting sore now that she remembers her place, a place from which the crowd that runs the A & P must look pretty crummy. Fancy Herring Snacks flashed in her very blue eyes.

"Girls, I don't want to argue with you. After this come in here with your shoulders covered. It's our policy." He turns his back. That's policy for you. Policy is what the kingpins want. What the others want is juvenile delinquency.

All this while, the customers had been showing up with their carts but, you know, sheep, seeing a scene, they had all bunched up on Stokesie, who shook open a paper bag as gently as peeling a peach, not wanting to miss a word. I could feel in the silence everybody getting nervous, most of all Lengel, who asks me, "Sammy, have you rung up their purchase?" 20

I thought and said "No" but it wasn't about that I was thinking. I go through the punches, 4, 9, GROC, TOT—it's more complicated than you think, and after you do it often enough, it begins to make a little song, that you hear words to, in my case "Hello (*bing*) there, you (*gung*) hap-py *pee*-pul (*splat*)!"—the *splat* being the drawer flying out. I uncrease the bill, tenderly as you may imagine, it just having come from between the two smoothest scoops of vanilla I had ever known were there, and pass a half and a penny into her narrow pink palm, and nestle the herrings in a bag and twist its neck and hand it over, all the time thinking.

The girls, and who'd blame them, are in a hurry to get out, so I say "I quit" to Lengel quick enough for them to hear, hoping they'll stop and watch me, their unsuspected hero. They keep right on going, into the electric eye; the door flies open and they flicker across the lot to their car, Queenie and Plaid and Big Tall Goony-Goony (not that as raw material she was so bad), leaving me with Lengel and a kink in his eyebrow.

"Did you say something, Sammy?"

"I said I quit."

"I thought you did." 25

"You didn't have to embarrass them."

"It was they who were embarrassing us."

I started to say something that came out "Fiddle-de-doo." It's a saying of my grandmother's, and I know she would have been pleased.

"I don't think you know what you're saying," Lengel said.

"I know you don't," I said. "But I do." I pull the bow at the back of my apron 30 and start shrugging it off my shoulders. A couple customers that had been heading for my slot begin to knock against each other, like scared pigs in a chute.

Lengel sighs and begins to look very patient and old and gray. He's been a friend of my parents for years. "Sammy, you don't want to do this to your Mom and Dad," he tells me. It's true, I don't. But it seems to me that once you begin a gesture it's fatal not to go through with it. I fold the apron, "Sammy" stitched in red on the pocket, and put it on the counter, and drop the bow tie on top of it. The bow tie is theirs, if you've ever wondered. "You'll feel this for the rest of your life," Lengel says, and I know that's true, too, but remembering how he made that pretty girl blush makes me so scrunchy inside I punch the No Sale tab and the machine whirs "pee-pul" and the drawer splats out. One advantage to this scene taking place in summer, I can follow this up with a clean exit, there's no fumbling around getting your coat and galoshes, I just saunter into the electric eye in my white shirt that my mother ironed the night before, and the door heaves itself open, and outside the sunshine is skating around on the asphalt.

I look around for my girls, but they're gone, of course. There wasn't anybody but some young married screaming with her children about some candy they didn't get by the door of a powder-blue Falcon station wagon. Looking back in the big windows, over the bags of peat moss and aluminum lawn furniture stacked on the pavement, I could see Lengel in my place in the slot, checking the sheep through. His face was dark gray and his back stiff, as if he'd just had an injection of iron, and my stomach kind of fell as I felt how hard the world was going to be to me hereafter.

Research John Updike in depth with cultural documents and multimedia resources on *LiterActive*.

Helena María Viramontes b. 1954

The Moths [1985]

I was fourteen years old when Abuelita requested my help. And it seemed only fair. Abuelita° had pulled me through the rages of scarlet fever by placing, removing and replacing potato slices on the temples of my forehead; she had seen me through several whippings, an arm broken by a dare jump off Tío Enrique's toolshed, puberty, and my first lie. Really, I told Amá, it was only fair.

Not that I was her favorite granddaughter or anything special. I wasn't even pretty or nice like my older sisters and I just couldn't do the girl things they could do. My hands were too big to handle the fineries of crocheting or embroidery and I always pricked my fingers or knotted my colored threads time and time again while my sisters laughed and called me bull hands with their cute waterlike voices. So I began keeping a piece of jagged brick in my sock to bash my sisters or anyone who called me bull hands. Once, while we all sat in the bedroom, I hit Teresa on the forehead, right above her eyebrow and she ran to Amá with her mouth open, her hand over her eye while blood seeped between her fingers. I was used to the whippings by then.

I wasn't respectful either. I even went so far as to doubt the power of Abuelita's slices, the slices she said absorbed my fever. "You're still alive, aren't you?" Abuelita snapped back, her pasty gray eye beaming at me and burning holes in my suspicions. Regretful that I had let secret questions drop out of my mouth, I couldn't look into her eyes. My hands began to fan out, grow like a

---

Abuelita: Grandmother.

liar's nose until they hung by my side like low weights. Abuelita made a balm out of dried moth wings and Vicks and rubbed my hands, shaped them back to size and it was the strangest feeling. Like bones melting. Like sun shining through the darkness of your eyelids. I didn't mind helping Abuelita after that, so Amá would always send me over to her.

In the early afternoon Amá would push her hair back, hand me my sweater and shoes, and tell me to go to Mama Luna's. This was to avoid another fight and another whipping, I knew. I would deliver one last direct shot on Marisela's arm and jump out of our house, the slam of the screen door burying her cries of anger, and I'd gladly go help Abuelita plant her wild lilies or jasmine or heliotrope or cilantro or hierbabuena in red Hills Brothers coffee cans. Abuelita would wait for me at the top step of her porch holding a hammer and nail and empty coffee cans. And although we hardly spoke, hardly looked at each other as we worked over root transplants, I always felt her gray eye on me. It made me feel, in a strange sort of way, safe and guarded and not alone. Like God was supposed to make you feel.

On Abuelita's porch, I would puncture holes in the bottom of the coffee 5 cans with a nail and a precise hit of a hammer. This completed, my job was to fill them with red clay mud from beneath her rose bushes, packing it softly, then making a perfect hole, four fingers round, to nest a sprouting avocado pit, or the spidery sweet potatoes that Abuelita rooted in mayonnaise jars with toothpicks and daily water, or prickly chayotes that produced vines that twisted and wound all over her porch pillars, crawling to the roof, up and over the roof, and down the other side, making her small brick house look like it was cradled within the vines that grew pear-shaped squashes ready for the pick, ready to be steamed with onions and cheese and butter. The roots would burst out of the rusted coffee cans and search for a place to connect. I would then feed the seedlings with water.

But this was a different kind of help, Amá said, because Abuelita was dying. Looking into her gray eye, then into her brown one, the doctor said it was just a matter of days. And so it seemed only fair that these hands she had melted and formed found use in rubbing her caving body with alcohol and marihuana, rubbing her arms and legs, turning her face to the window so that she could watch the Bird of Paradise blooming or smell the scent of clove in the air. I toweled her face frequently and held her hand for hours. Her gray wiry hair hung over the mattress. Since I could remember, she'd kept her long hair in braids. Her mouth was vacant and when she slept, her eyelids never closed all the way. Up close, you could see her gray eye beaming out the window, staring hard as if to remember everything. I never kissed her. I left the window open when I went to the market.

Across the street from Jay's Market there was a chapel. I never knew its denomination, but I went in just the same to search for candles. I sat down on one of the pews because there were none. After I cleaned my fingernails, I looked up at the high ceiling. I had forgotten the vastness of these places, the coolness of the marble pillars and the frozen statues with blank eyes. I was alone. I knew why I had never returned.

That was one of Apá's biggest complaints. He would pound his hands on the table, rocking the sugar dish or spilling a cup of coffee and scream that if I didn't go to mass every Sunday to save my goddamn sinning soul, then I had no reason to go out of the house, period. Punto final. He would grab my arm and dig his nails into me to make sure I understood the importance of catechism. Did he make himself clear? Then he strategically directed his anger at Amá for her lousy ways of bringing up daughters, being disrespectful and unbelieving, and my older sisters would pull me aside and tell me if I didn't get to mass right this minute, they were all going to kick the holy shit out of me. Why am I so selfish? Can't you see what it's doing to Amá, you idiot? So I would wash my feet and stuff them in my black Easter shoes that shone with Vaseline, grab a missal and veil, and wave good-bye to Amá.

I would walk slowly down Lorena to First to Evergreen, counting the cracks on the cement. On Evergreen I would turn left and walk to Abuelita's. I liked her porch because it was shielded by the vines of the chayotes and I could get a good look at the people and car traffic on Evergreen without them knowing. I would jump up the porch steps, knock on the screen door as I wiped my feet and call Abuelita? mi Abuelita? As I opened the door and stuck my head in, I would catch the gagging scent of toasting chile on the placa.° When I entered the sala,° she would greet me from the kitchen, wringing her hands in her apron. I'd sit at the corner of the table to keep from being in her way. The chiles made my eyes water. Am I crying? No, Mama Luna, I'm sure not crying. I don't like going to mass, but my eyes watered anyway, the tears dropping on the tablecloth like candle wax. Abuelita lifted the burnt chiles from the fire and sprinkled water on them until the skins began to separate. Placing them in front of me, she turned to check the menudo.° I peeled the skins off and put the flimsy, limp looking green and yellow chiles in the molcajete° and began to crush and crush and twist and crush the heart out of the tomato, the clove of garlic, the stupid chiles that made me cry, crushed them until they turned into liquid under my bull hand. With a wooden spoon, I scraped hard to destroy the guilt, and my tears were gone. I put the bowl of chile next to a vase filled with freshly cut roses. Abuelita touched my hand and pointed to the bowl of menudo that steamed in front of me. I spooned some chile into the menudo and rolled a corn tortilla thin with the palms of my hands. As I ate, a fine Sunday breeze entered the kitchen and a rose petal calmly feathered down to the table.

I left the chapel without blessing myself and walked to Jay's. Most of the time Jay didn't have much of anything. The tomatoes were always soft and the cans of Campbell soups had rusted spots on them. There was dust on the tops of cereal boxes. I picked up what I needed: rubbing alcohol, five cans of chicken broth, a big bottle of Pine Sol. At first Jay got mad because I thought I had forgotten the money. But it was there all the time, in my back pocket.   10

placa: Plate.   sala: Living room.   menudo: Traditional Mexican soup made with tripe.
molcajete: Stone bowl for grinding spices and chiles with a pestle (tejolote).

When I returned from the market, I heard Amá crying in Abuelita's kitchen. She looked up at me with puffy eyes. I placed the bags of groceries on the table and began putting the cans of soup away. Amá sobbed quietly. I never kissed her. After a while, I patted her on the back for comfort. Finally: "¿Y mi Amá?"° she asked in a whisper, then choked again and cried into her apron.

Abuelita fell off the bed twice yesterday, I said, knowing that I shouldn't have said it and wondering why I wanted to say it because it only made Amá cry harder. I guess I became angry and just so tired of the quarrels and beatings and unanswered prayers and my hands just there hanging helplessly by my side. Amá looked at me again, confused, angry, and her eyes were filled with sorrow. I went outside and sat on the porch swing and watched the people pass. I sat there until she left. I dozed off repeating the words to myself like rosary prayers: when do you stop giving when do you start giving when do you . . . and when my hands fell from my lap, I awoke to catch them. The sun was setting, an orange glow, and I knew Abuelita was hungry.

There comes a time when the sun is defiant. Just about the time when moods change, inevitable seasons of a day, transitions from one color to another, that hour or minute or second when the sun is finally defeated, finally sinks into the realization that it cannot with all its power to heal or burn, exist forever, there comes an illumination where the sun and earth meet, a final burst of burning red orange fury reminding us that although endings are inevitable, they are necessary for rebirths, and when that time came, just when I switched on the light in the kitchen to open Abuelita's can of soup, it was probably then that she died.

The room smelled of Pine Sol and vomit and Abuelita had defecated the remains of her cancerous stomach. She had turned to the window and tried to speak, but her mouth remained open and speechless. I heard you, Abuelita, I said, stroking her cheek, I heard you. I opened the windows of the house and let the soup simmer and overboil on the stove. I turned the stove off and poured the soup down the sink. From the cabinet I got a tin basin, filled it with lukewarm water and carried it carefully to the room. I went to the linen closet and took out some modest bleached white towels. With the sacredness of a priest preparing his vestments, I unfolded the towels one by one on my shoulders. I removed the sheets and blankets from her bed and peeled off her thick flannel nightgown. I toweled her puzzled face, stretching out the wrinkles, removing the coils of her neck, toweled her shoulders and breasts. Then I changed the water. I returned to towel the creases of her stretch-marked stomach, her sporadic vaginal hairs, and her sagging thighs. I removed the lint from between her toes and noticed a mapped birthmark on the fold of her buttock. The scars on her back which were as thin as the life lines on the palms of her hands made me realize how little I really knew of Abuelita. I covered her with a thin blanket and went into the bathroom. I washed my hands, and turned on the tub faucets and watched the water

---

"¿Y mi Amá?": "And my Mama?"

pour into the tub with vitality and steam. When it was full, I turned off the water and undressed. Then, I went to get Abuelita.

She was not as heavy as I thought and when I carried her in my arms, her   15 body fell into a V, and yet my legs were tired, shaky, and I felt as if the distance between the bedroom and bathroom was miles and years away. Amá, where are you?

I stepped into the bathtub one leg first, then the other. I bent my knees slowly to descend into the water slowly so I wouldn't scald her skin. There, there, Abuelita, I said, cradling her, smoothing her as we descended, I heard you. Her hair fell back and spread across the water like eagle's wings. The water in the tub overflowed and poured onto the tile of the floor. Then the moths came. Small, gray ones that came from her soul and out through her mouth fluttering to light, circling the single dull light bulb of the bathroom. Dying is lonely and I wanted to go to where the moths were, stay with her and plant chayotes whose vines would crawl up her fingers and into the clouds; I wanted to rest my head on her chest with her stroking my hair, telling me about the moths that lay within the soul and slowly eat the spirit up; I wanted to return to the waters of the womb with her so that we would never be alone again. I wanted. I wanted my Amá. I removed a few strands of hair from Abuelita's face and held her small light head within the hollow of my neck. The bathroom was filled with moths, and for the first time in a long time I cried, rocking us, crying for her, for me, for Amá, the sobs emerging from the depths of anguish, the misery of feeling half born, sobbing until finally the sobs rippled into circles and circles of sadness and relief. There, there, I said to Abuelita, rocking us gently, there, there.

Approaching POETRY

Overleaf: *The celebrated poet Marianne Moore, photographed in 1953 in Brooklyn, New York, by the well-known photojournalist Esther Bubley. A Gaston Lachaise bust sculpture of Moore from 1921 can be seen in the background. Moore was recognized early on for her talents as a writer, and she earned the support of many major American figures including T. S. Eliot, William Carlos Williams, and Elizabeth Bishop. Her* Collected Poems *won the 1951 Pulitzer Prize for Poetry along with the National Book Award. Moore is known for her use of imagery of the natural world in her poems and has written that poetry "is the art of creating imaginary gardens with real toads." (See p. 827 for her poem "Poetry" and p. 1551 for a short biography.)* Reprinted by permission of Jean B. Bubley.

> oetry is a conversation with the world; poetry is a conversation
> with the words on the page in which you allow those words to
> speak back to you; and poetry is a conversation with yourself.
> Naomi Shihab Nye

Reading Poetry
Realizing the Richness in Poems

CHAPTER 11

Why would a person feel suddenly compelled to write a poem? After the events of September 11, 2001, thousands of poems were written, sent, stored away, stuck in a wallet or purse, pasted in a scrapbook. Students took time out from their usual classroom studies and wrote poems. Parents sent their poems to their children away at school or gone from the nest. Poems expressed by "nonpoets" showed up on Web sites and subway walls, in newsletters, within in-house publications, during school announcements, and in memos, letters, and e-mails. People from every walk of life wrote and expressed their reactions, what they were feeling. Very few if any of us who are not fiction writers or playwrights decide one day to sit down and write a novel or a play. And yet time and time again, people who do not consider themselves poets write poems. Why do people write poetry? What does that show about them? About us? And what does that suggest about the nature and value of poetry—about what poetry is and what poetry does?

WHAT IS POETRY?

We can usually tell someone what a novel, a play, or an essay is, but a poem can be baffling to explain. It can't be defined as writing that has meter: A lot of poetry is nonmetrical. It's not confined to writing that rhymes, for many poems do not use rhyme. Though most poetry is written in lines, prose poems don't have line divisions. Much poetry uses figurative language and is intense and emotional—but the same is true for powerful prose. Whatever characteristics one tries to apply are never typical of all poetry or exclusive to poetry alone. So, what is this thing we call poetry?

Those who we'd think ought to know usually offer personal responses: E. E. Cummings said that poetry is "dancing on your own grave." Ezra Pound purportedly said it is "what poets write." Emily Dickinson described poetry by its effect: "If I read a book [and] it makes my whole body so cold no fire ever can warm me, I know THAT is poetry. If I feel physically as if the top of my head were taken off, I know THAT is poetry. These are the only ways I know it. Is there any other way?"

What Does Poetry Do?

POETRY SAYS "AH-H-H"   Maybe a better way to approach the question "What is poetry?" is to ask "What does poetry do?" Poetry comes from some deep impulse that needs expression; it arises when no other form of expression is sufficient under the circumstances. The poem comes from a sense of urgency; it feels it must be "let out," shared, given, offered up. Lucille Clifton once said, "Poetry began when somebody walked off a savanna or out of a cave and looked up at the sky with wonder and said, 'Ah-h-h!' *That* was the first poem. The urge toward 'Ah-h-h' is very human, it's in everybody." Every day, each of us feels that impulse, and we go "Ah-h-h!" or "Wow!" or "Oh no!" or simply sigh.

POETRY CROSSES BOUNDARIES   Poetry often crosses, or even eliminates, boundaries. We are all citizens in the culture of joy, pain, anger, love, fear, despair, hope. Every one of us carries the emotions of every other one of us. Our situations and stories and conflicts may differ, but the news from the heart comes to each of us. And though we can't claim "I know just how you feel," we can say with confidence, "I, too, have known that feeling."

POETRY GIVES VOICE   And poetry gives voice. For many of us in our day-to-day lives, voices come at us — from the news media, sales pitches, movies, and general information overload. It often seems our voices are not heard. Poetry offers a chance to speak, and speak from the deepest part of our selves: We feel liberated and in touch with our selves. The words are our words, the rhythms are our rhythms, the clumsiness and sophistication of phrasings are ours, the sounds, the tones, even the attempts to be artful are ours.

POETRY IS PART OF OUR LIVES   Former Poet Laureate Rita Dove has stated, "[I want] to help people see that poetry is not something above them or somehow distant; it's part of their very lives. I would like to remind people that we *have* an interior life — even if we don't talk about it because it's not expedient, because it's not cool, because it's potentially embarrassing — and without that interior life, we are shells, we are nothing." Is that also why, under a sense of urgency, many feel the impulse to express themselves in poetry? Do they suddenly experience that connection to their inner lives? Do thoughts and feelings rise up and ask, even demand, to be expressed, and expressed in their own voice?

WHY READ POETRY?

EFFECTS OF POETRY   Poetry gives the poet a voice, but why do others read poetry? People read poetry to hear that what they themselves are moved by and want to express is something others do too. They read poetry to relish an artist's craftsmanship; to experience the beauty of the words and sounds and pictures through which a poem expresses emotions and ideas or tells a story; to feel life with greater intensity and to open themselves to wider and more inclusive experiences; to feel connected to many things that they are pulled away from, things they cherish and need in their lives. People read poetry to recover what they have lost or to hold on to what they have, to be challenged, to be shaken, to be comforted.

TYPES OF POETRY   Traditionally poetry has been classified in three major types: *narrative*, poems that follow a sequence of events; *dramatic*, plays written in verse or shorter poems that use techniques from drama, such as dialogue; and *lyric*, usually shorter poems characterized by imagination, melody, and intensity of feelings, all combined to create a unified effect. Other less central types include poetry of ideas (verse essays), satiric poetry, and light verse. A number of the poems in this book tell stories. Many of the rest are lyric poems or combine narrative with lyric. **Lyric** poetry focuses on an event, experience, idea, reaction, or feeling that has impressed the poet deeply, and renders it in such sharp, concrete detail, with such an imaginative approach and a musical use of language, that readers often feel that the experience, and the poem, are actually their own.

One of the principles in choosing poems for this book was to provide examples of many different poetic styles, approaches, and types. Some poems and some kinds of poetry you will like better than others, but we hope that you give them all a chance and remain open to the variety of cultures and experiences they embody.

ACTIVE READING: Poetry

The essence of poetry is elusive. There is no one way to pin it down. Although that may be intimidating, it is also part of the appeal, part of the seductiveness of poetry. We enter the world of a poem, every poem, not really knowing what to expect. And whenever we enter something new — whether an unfamiliar city, or a new job, or a new relationship — we tend to feel uncertain. We have to look around. We have to be attentive. Here are some suggestions for reading poetry with an active imagination.

- *Look and listen.* Be attentive to everything in and about the poem. Start with its shape, the way the poem appears on the page. Listen to its sounds — the way it sounds when it's read aloud, the rhythms, the word sounds, and the combinations of sounds. Look for what it helps you see — the mental pictures called up by some of the words.

- *Watch the words.* After noting shape and sounds, start paying attention to what the words say — not what the whole poem means, but what the words say. Don't be overly eager to figure out what a poem "means," especially some deep, "hidden" meaning. When you walk through a wood, you don't keep saying, "What does that tree mean?" or "What does that stone mean?" You accept them for what they are. So it should be with poetry: Look at the words, listen for what they say, and understand them as best you can. And if at first you don't understand all that much, don't worry — there are many things in a poem that you can experience even before you "understand" it.

- *Read straight through.* Go straight through a poem the first time you read it. If you wonder about a word or want to savor a line, stop only briefly. Then keep going. Get a feel for the poem without worrying about what you don't know or understand.

- *Interact with the work.* Reading a poem differs from reading a newspaper or an e-mail message or a textbook. You usually read those to glean some information or ideas. Many poems, of course, also contain information and ideas. But they can do other things: They can lead us to feel intensely, to experience deeply, to perceive freshly, to extend our understanding of experiences different from our own, and to affirm our own ideas, feelings, and experiences.

- *Take in what is happening.* Consider what the speaker or primary character in the poem is experiencing, dealing with, going through, or feeling, much like you would with a character in a work of fiction or drama.

REREADING: Poetry

Rereading is just as important for poetry as for fiction, perhaps more so. Reread until you've internalized parts of the poem. Focus on something different each time you go back. If you're open to the poem, it will give and give. Here are some suggestions for rereading.

- *Slow down.* You have to slow down to read a poem. You can't speed-read a poem any more than you can speed-listen to your favorite recordings. So slow down and listen: Listen for, and to, the poem.

- *Read aloud.* Many poems are meant to be heard. Their sounds and rhythms need to be read aloud. In poet Robert Pinsky's phrase, you should "say the poem" so the poem comes out from within you as you vocalize the poem and feel the words, phrases, and rhythms in your mouth, the way you did as a kid when you kept saying certain words over and over just because they felt good. Hide if you are worried that someone will laugh at you.

- *Hear the "music."* Poems work with what is often called the musicality of language, by blending the sounds and rhythms of words and word connections. It's not unlike a song lyric together with its music, but in this case the poem is aspiring to music through the sounds and rhythms of language.

- *Focus on what catches your attention.* You might be drawn to a particular image, how it alters your usual perception of something. Maybe you like the sounds of the language or the way the rhythm shifts or remains regular in every line. Maybe the poem is funny or poignant or both. You don't have to have a masterful grasp of the whole poem to notice things within it or wonder about it or begin talking about it. Paying passionate attention to what is actually in a poem is a wise way to start.

- *Follow the sentences.* The sentences in the poem may be broken up into lines, but they are still sentences. Get their sense correct. If the order of words in a sentence is inverted, it's important to pay attention to cues that identify what is subject and what is object. If a poet uses incomplete sentences, "fragments," try to figure out the purpose behind them. After working out where sentences start and stop, focus on the lines: Begin noticing what the line divisions and line breaks add to the experience of the sentence.

- *Ask questions.* You can, of course, ask what a poem means, but you don't need to start with that question. Try instead asking questions such as, What is going on in this poem? What is this poem doing? Why am I drawn to that phrase or line? What is the poem connecting me with or challenging me about? How is the poem shifting my usual way of perceiving things and leading me to reconsider the ways I've thought and felt?

The imagery of one line exudes a sparkling fountain of energy
that fills your spirit.

Jimmy Santiago Baca

CHAPTER **12** **Words and Images**
Seizing on Sense and Sight

Perhaps you are hesitant about your ability to understand a poem, or
even have the feeling that a poem is in some code you have to break or that
only the poet or your teacher can comprehend it. Or perhaps you think that
poetry can "just mean anything." With prose, we usually gain understanding by reading whole units of focused meaning (sentences and paragraphs).
But poems are often not written that way, and maybe that's a reason why we
feel poems are difficult to grasp. Poems ask you to look both at and within
lines and sentences, to focus your attention on particular words and particular images in them.

POETS RELY ON WORDS   To comprehend a poem, then, requires attention to its words. That's obvious enough. How can you read without looking
at the words? But when you read poetry, you not only have to look at words
but also need to pay closer attention than you usually would. **Diction**, the
choice and arrangement of words, is an important aspect of style, whether
in prose (see p. 200) or poetry. And, like fiction, but more so, you need not
only to look for the "meaning" of words with your mind but also to respond
to many words with your senses. This chapter's aim is to enable you to enjoy
and appreciate poetry more fully by enjoying and appreciating words and
images more fully.

POETS LOVE WORDS   Like most writers, poets love words — their look,
their sounds, their textures, the associations clustered around them, what
they evoke, their power. Poets roll words around on their tongues and
in their minds, experimenting with different combinations, playing with

them, listening to the results. They care about their meanings, and the uses and abuses of those meanings. They look for ways to put their feelings or ideas into exactly the right words, ones with the right sounds and textures and meanings. So, even though this chapter focuses on words — on their denotations and connotations and the images many of them create — in one sense all the chapters in this book are about the precise and imaginative use of words.

POETS USE WORDS   Poets work with words in three ways: to report ("It was a moonless night"), to describe ("It was so dark we couldn't see the tree right outside our window"), and to provide a new or fresh way of perceiving ("It was so dark outside the window that it made us feel as if the night were anonymous"). All three are found in the opening lines of Robert Hayden's "Those Winter Sundays" (p. 548). The speaker reports: "Sundays too my father got up early." He describes: "cracked hands that ached / from labor in the weekday weather." And he gives us a fresh way of perceiving: "hear the cold splintering, breaking." Watching for those uses as you continue reading poetry can help you be alert to and responsive to the denotations and connotations words convey.

READING FOR DENOTATION

WHAT WORDS MEAN   In focusing attention on words, it's important to realize that words have two dimensions, denotation and connotation. **Denotation** refers to what words mean, to their dictionary definitions. It may seem obvious that, in reading, we need to pay attention to what the words mean; but sometimes it takes effort, and at times you will probably need to use different dictionaries. In other kinds of reading, the context may convey adequately the general meaning of an unfamiliar word, but in reading poetry, approximate meanings aren't enough. And sometimes in poetry the secondary, less familiar meanings of a word may be as important as, or more important than, the first meaning.

CURRENT MEANINGS   It is usually easier to understand the denotations of words in poems written in your own time and from your own culture. Because they are connected to something you are familiar with, you can count on having a vocabulary pretty much in common with that of the poet. But even in these cases, it may help to check in a dictionary for any key words you're not certain about.

EARLIER MEANINGS   Denotations pose a bigger problem when you read poems from the past or from a culture different from your own. You already know you need to look up unfamiliar words. Much trickier are words that look familiar but seem unusual in the context of the poem. In some cases, often in poems written several centuries ago, word meanings have changed or previous meanings are no longer used. A desk dictionary may indicate such changes, but a better resource is the *Oxford English Dictionary*, often called the *OED*. It is a historical dictionary found in most libraries and on-line through many libraries. It gives you what words meant in earlier times as well as now, and it shows, through illustrative quotes, when each meaning was in use and, if it is no longer current, when that usage ceased.

Consider the following lines from Shakespeare's *Julius Caesar*, where Portia asks Brutus what has been bothering him.

> Is Brutus sick? And is it physical
> To walk unbraced and suck up the humors
> Of the dank morning? (2.1.262)

Both *physical* and *humor* are familiar words, but none of our current uses seems to fit these lines. Looking in an ordinary desk dictionary won't help, but using the *OED* does. If you look up *physical*, under definition 5b, you find, "Beneficial to health; curative, remedial" (if this seems odd, think of the word *physician*). The line from *Julius Caesar* is quoted as an illustration of this definition. If you look up *humor* (it appears under the British spelling *humour*), the first entry fits — "Moisture; damp exhalation; vapour." The last example cited for this usage is from 1697 — this is the latest example of this usage that has been found in print. By then that meaning may already have disappeared from spoken language, or it may have lingered in speech a bit longer; in any case, it died out completely around 1700, so present-day dictionaries do not bother to include it (not even as an "archaic" usage).

ENTRY POINTS   The denotations of words in the following poem probably seem straightforward and clear, even from your first reading. But spend some time looking up words that you're unfamiliar with or that look important and perhaps might mean more than the context conveys (perhaps the words *banked*, *chronic*, *austere*, and *offices*; and what about *blueblack*?). Remember too that denotation involves not just the meaning of individual words but the meaning of words combined with other words: Think about the meaning of "chronic angers" and "love's austere and lonely offices."

Robert Hayden   1913–1980

Those Winter Sundays   [1962]

Sundays too my father got up early
and put his clothes on in the blueblack cold,

then with cracked hands that ached
from labor in the weekday weather made
banked fires blaze. No one ever thanked him.   5

I'd wake and hear the cold splintering, breaking.
When the rooms were warm, he'd call,
and slowly I would rise and dress,
fearing the chronic angers of that house,

Speaking indifferently to him,   10
who had driven out the cold
and polished my good shoes as well.
What did I know, what did I know
of love's austere and lonely offices?

APPROACHING THE READING

1. In addition to "important" words such as *banked, chronic, austere, offices,* and *blueblack,* pay attention to easily overlooked "little" words such as *those* in the title and *too* in line 1. Why do they matter? Discuss their effect and impact.
2. What is suggested in line 9 by the phrase "chronic angers of that house"? Why did the son speak "indifferently" to his father? What does word choice indicate about relationships in the family?
3. What do you make of the last five words of the poem? Why do you think they are effective or ineffective as the ending of this poem?
4. What is the effect of the repetition in line 13? How is what the speaker now knows different from what he thought as a child?

One could readily argue that the success of this poem in all its elements and effects is the result of Hayden's accomplished use of diction. Notice the beautifully muted combinations of words, each of which reveals a profound intelligence quietly coming to life-changing realizations throughout the poem: "Sundays too" rather than "Even on Sunday"; "The blueblack cold" — the words and order mysteriously convey both how the cold felt to the father and how the son came to recognize the depth and continuity of the father's responsibility; "banked" starts the fifth line and rhymes with "thanked" later in the line, gently emphasizing the contrast between duty fulfilled and a lack of gratitude. "Chronic angers" (l. 9) is striking in combining a technical word, *chronic,* with a prosaic one, *angers.* The result leads us to realize and imagine the atmosphere the speaker grew up within. And the unusual combination of the word *love* with *austere, lonely,* and *offices* provokes us to reflect on and reconsider what real love is.

READING FOR CONNOTATION

WHAT WORDS IMPLY   Of course, words are more than their dictionary definitions. Words also have **connotations**, the shared or communal implications and associations they carry in addition to their dictionary meanings. Two words may have almost the same denotation but very different connotations; the associations a reader connects with them could make one suitable and the other unsuitable in a certain situation. For example, in "Those Winter Sundays," "working in the weekday weather" means almost the same thing, denotatively, as "labor in the weekday weather." But Hayden uses *labor* in line 4 probably because its connotations suggest work of a harder and more fatiguing kind than *working* does, and that's what Hayden wants to say about his father.

COMPLEXITY OF CONNOTATION   Connotations are often shaped by cultures and sets of belief, and to feel what "most readers" feel requires being able to share their context. For example, denotatively, the word *mother* means "a woman who has borne a child"; for many people, *mother* connotes tenderness, support, caring. For those whose mothers abused them, however, the word *mother* would not have the "common" connotation, and it could be difficult for such readers to respond to it imaginatively. Also, the word can be used as a denigrating term, as in "you mother." Today's society is so diverse that a common effect in language is less usual than it was in the past. It's very important to recognize that connotation is complex and problematic, and at the same time that it is crucial in determining how any of us as readers experience a poem.

ENTRY POINTS   Most poets search for the word that has exactly the right meaning, sound, and feeling, and then depend on you as reader to weigh denotations and connotations carefully. The words in the following poem seem very carefully chosen. As you read it, pay particular attention to the words — to what the denotations of familiar and unfamiliar words and the connotations of simple, ordinary words contribute to the poem's meaning and effect.

Gwendolyn Brooks   1917–2000

The Bean Eaters   [1960]

They eat beans mostly, this old yellow pair.
Dinner is a casual affair.
Plain chipware on a plain and creaking wood,
Tin flatware.

Two who are Mostly Good. 5
Two who have lived their day,
But keep on putting on their clothes
And putting things away.

And remembering . . .
Remembering, with twinklings and twinges, 10
As they lean over the beans in their rented back room that is full of beads
    and receipts and dolls and cloths, tobacco crumbs, vases and fringes.

APPROACHING THE READING

1. Look up any words whose denotations are not clear to you.
2. What words are particularly important for their connotations?
3. Brooks chose the words she did for both denotations and connotations. Consider why they are appropriate for this couple, their daily lives, the setting, and their circumstances. How do Brooks's words reveal the speaker and poet's empathy?
4. Pick out some uses of diction that seem particularly striking or important and explain why you feel that they are.

Research this author in depth with cultural documents and multimedia resources on *LiterActive*.

The denotations of words in "The Bean Eaters" are likely clear to you. You might look up *flatware* (utensils, such as knives, forks, and spoons) or *chipware* (though you are not likely to find it in a dictionary; it appears to be a term Brooks coined for beat-up china). You can probably figure out most of the words, including *chipware*, from the context. More important to this poem, however, are the words' connotations.

WORDS CARRY ASSOCIATIONS   What beans are, denotatively, is not the crucial thing; what they suggest and what we associate them with is. The feeling or association generated by a word depends to some extent on the background and experiences of the readers. Brooks probably expects that readers will associate beans with being inexpensive and ordinary. Given those connotations, it seems safe to conclude that this couple's eating beans *mostly* suggests that they are poor. *Yellow* may factually, denotatively, describe the color of their skin, but equally important are the feelings of age, health, and fragility that many people associate with the word *yellow*. The facts of what chipware and tin flatware are do not solely create their effect as words in the poem; the way we perceive them as inexpensive, utilitarian products does.

Denotatively, "rented back room" simply states that the room the couple lives in is not in the front of the building and is owned by someone else. But the connotations are meaningful. Back rooms are cheaper (and less desirable) than front rooms. Presumably, Brooks's couple is renting a room because they cannot afford to own a house, and a back room because they cannot afford even to rent a front room.

WORDS CONVEY FEELINGS   Finally, the things listed in the last line are more important to the couple — and to us — for the feelings they evoke than for what they are in and of themselves. This old pair lives more in the past than in the present, and memories cluster with "twinklings and twinges" around the objects that fill the room. Perhaps you have more — or other — connotations for the words in the poem. Bring them into the reading of it and discuss how they differ from those we present here. Also, think about what part your background plays in your response to the poem. (Be aware, however, that connotations are different from the "personal associations" a word or image carries for a particular individual because of an experience connected with it — "sailboats always make me think of people who own them and how they got the money to buy them" — though such personal associations do contribute to the way connotations affect us.)

READING FOR IMAGES

Our earliest knowledge of the world comes through the senses. Babies become acquainted with objects by looking at them, touching them, putting them in their mouths; everything to them is wonderfully sensate and interesting. As poet W. S. Merwin has said, "A child picks up a fallen leaf and doesn't say, what is it good for? To the child, a leaf is what it is, full of color." The senses remain crucial sources of knowledge for us as adults as well, but as we get older, we become accustomed to the things we encounter and cease to find amazement in ordinary things. One of the beauties of poetry is that it reconnects us to the world of our senses and thus to a world of wonder.

MENTAL IMAGES   As child or adult, we experience the things around us through mental representations or "mental images." An image is formed in the mind as we look at a tree or hear a band play. Light rays fall on the retina or sound waves on the ear drum, sending messages to the brain that constructs them into images — mental representations — of sight or sound. Because of the way imagination works, images also are formed in the mind by reading the words "enormous oak tree" or "the percussion section of the Rockford High School marching band."

LITERARY IMAGES   In literature, an **image** is a word or group of words that evokes a mental representation of an object or action that can be known by one or more of the senses. An image is a specific detail in a story, poem, or play that triggers in our minds an impression of a sight, sound, touch, taste, or smell. Poetry relies heavily on images. To comprehend and *experience* what is going on in poems and therefore to enjoy reading them, being attentive to images is vital.

ENTRY POINTS   Focus on verbal images in the following poem, which describes the sights and sounds of night at a lakeshore cottage and is full of sensory detail. Let yourself enter the scene fully, and notice how your imagination converts words to mental images you see in your mind's eye.

Maxine Kumin b. 1925

The Sound of Night   [1961]

And now the dark comes on, all full of chitter noise.
Birds huggermugger crowd the trees,
the air thick with their vesper cries,
and bats, snub seven-pointed kites,
skitter across the lake, swing out,   5
squeak, chirp, dip, and skim on skates
of air, and the fat frogs wake and prink
wide-lipped, noisy as ducks, drunk
on the boozy black, gloating chink-chunk.

And now on the narrow beach we defend ourselves from dark.   10
The cooking done, we build our firework
bright and hot and less for outlook
than for magic, and lie in our blankets
while night nickers around us. Crickets
chorus hallelujahs; paws, quiet   15
and quick as raindrops, play on the stones
expertly soft, run past and are gone;
fish pulse in the lake; the frogs hoarsen.

Now every voice of the hour — the known, the supposed, the strange,
the mindless, the witted, the never seen —   20
sing, thrum, impinge, and rearrange
endlessly; and debarred from sleep we wait
for the birds, importantly silent,
for the crease of first eye-licking light,
for the sun, lost long ago and sweet.   25
By the lake, locked black away and tight,
we lie, day creatures, overhearing night.

APPROACHING THE READING

1. This poet clearly loves to explore the possibilities of language. Pick out examples of unusual uses of language and consider if they are effective. Look up words that aren't familiar. Why does each seem the right word for the place it's used?
2. Kumin seems especially to like verbs. Notice examples of active, energetic verbs. Consider why they are effective in creating mental images.
3. Pick out words and phrases that create mental images of the way things look, sound, and feel.

The diction of this poem aims to bring to life a scene for readers to recall or create in their imaginations. Its emphasis is not on an intellectual meaning or an abstract idea, but on evoking not only what you see at the lake but especially what you hear. Because nouns are not as effective in describing sounds, the poem emphasizes verbs, such as "skitter," "squeak, chirp, dip, and skim," and "prink" in the first stanza. Look for other examples in stanzas two and three. Notice also that the verbs are present tense, giving the scene immediacy, a perpetual quality. This is not a scene from the past, which is over and gone, but a scene that continues to go on, in fact (somewhere, for someone) as well as in the memory of the speaker, and now in you the reader. Memories come to life through images. Realizing this gives us a solid sense of the remarkable power of images, of imagistic language.

ENTRY POINTS   The power of concrete detail is at the heart of William Carlos Williams's short and much-discussed poem, "The Red Wheelbarrow." Pay attention to the mental picture the words of the poem evoke for you, and reflect on whether that picture is what the poem is about or whether it is only the starting point for something more abstract.

William Carlos Williams   1883–1963

The Red Wheelbarrow   [1923]

so much depends
upon

a red wheel
barrow

glazed with rain   5
water

beside the white
chickens.

APPROACHING THE READING

1. Pick out words in the poem that help create sensory impressions in your mind (its images). Approximately what percentage of the words is imagistic?
2. Try sketching the scene on paper or visualizing it clearly in your mind. Consider what it would look like as a still-life painting in an art gallery. Even though this poem is highly visual, why might a sketch or painting fail to "capture" the poem?
3. What do you think is the "so much" that "depends" (l. 1)? Why does it "depend"?

Some readers distrust or overlook the literal effects of Williams's images and search for "deeper meanings." The opening line of "The Red Wheelbarrow" seems to invite digging for deeper meaning — if "so much depends" on the objects mentioned, we had better figure out what they *really* mean. But the line more likely asserts the importance of images as themselves: So much depends on sensuously experiencing and respecting and realizing the value of things as themselves, on *really* using our senses, on experiencing the world with our senses alert and sensitive. As you did in answering "Approaching the Reading" question 2, imagine the scene Williams describes as a still-life painting. Still lifes celebrate concrete detail, and that's a good place to start with much poetry as well.

LETTING IMAGES FORM IN THE MIND   We call these sense-centered words "images," but in a way they are only potential images; they are the means for calling up sights, sounds, smells, tastes, and tactile sensations in each reader's mind. If you have spent your summers at a lake cottage, images of that location probably come to your mind as you read Kumin's "The Sound of Night." If you've never spent a night on a lakeshore, your mental images probably are influenced by pictures of such scenes or by movies or TV shows with such a setting. The important thing for you as a reader is to let such images form in your mind as you read, and to encourage them by giving them time to form. The clearer the images in your mind are, the more fully you will enjoy the poem.

WWW
Further explore words and images, including interactive exercises, with VirtuaLit Poetry at bedfordstmartins.com/ approachinglit.

VISUALIZING SPECIFIC DETAILS   Writers help by supplying specific details and precise images that use concrete language rather than abstract language (see p. 201). If you hear, "Think of a dog," you may visualize a spaniel, poodle, mutt, or whatever you choose. *Dog* is general. You make up the particular dog. However, if you hear, "Don't imagine a golden retriever," such is the power of images that, even though you're told not to, you can't help visualizing a fairly large dog with a thick golden coat and feathering on its neck, legs, and tail (provided that you know what a golden retriever looks like).

TRUSTING THE LITERAL   Some people are convinced that all poetry is indirect and symbolic—even a "code." They think that reading poetry means finding hidden meanings, as if poets think of meanings and then hide them. These readers often distrust or even overlook the literal and search instead for "deeper meanings." But an image is, first and foremost, simply itself. Poems do use symbols, and much of what was said about symbols in fiction (pp. 143–48) applies as well to poetry: A symbol is initially "an image that is exactly what it is." True, an image may suggest further meanings, but it doesn't "turn into" something else. It is always itself. And it always retains its literal meaning. Because imagery is so rich a part of poetry, one starting point in reading poems is to look at—and trust—the literal, to realize, appreciate, and enjoy the images for what they are and for what they do.

FURTHER READING

ENTRY POINTS   A culture is deeply imbedded in its language. You learned about your own culture partly through its words. To begin to learn about a different culture, a key step is to learn its language. Words are important to your individual identity as well: To some extent, you are the kind of words you use.

Because language is so important to all of us, it's not surprising that poets often write poems that talk about language. In the following poem, look for what it says about words, and for the way it uses words and sounds to consider the effect of language on culture and relationships between different ethnic groups.

☑ CHECKLIST on Reading for Words and Images

❑ Pay careful attention to denotations—the pertinent dictionary definitions of words in a poem.

❑ Use a desk dictionary and specialized dictionaries (such as the *Oxford English Dictionary*) for finding useful and sometimes surprising denotations.

❑ Be open to the connotations of words in poetry—the overtones or associations that become connected with a word through repeated uses.

❑ Respond with your senses, intellect, and emotions to images (words representing sensory experience or objects that can be known by one or more of the senses) and to sense images (mental representations of sensory experience) in a poem.

Allison Joseph b. 1967

On Being Told I Don't Speak Like a Black Person [1999]

Emphasize the "h," you hignorant ass,
was what my mother was told
when colonial-minded teachers
slapped her open palm with a ruler
in that Jamaican schoolroom.   5
Trained in England, they tried
to force their pupils to speak
like Eliza Doolittle° after
her transformation, fancying themselves
British as Henry Higgins,°   10
despite dark, sun-ripened skin.
Mother never lost her accent,
though, the music of her voice
charming everyone, an infectious lilt
I can imitate, not duplicate.   15
No one in the States told her
to eliminate the accent,
my high school friends adoring
the way her voice would lift
when she called me to the phone —   20
A-ll-i-son, it's friend Cathy.
Why don't you sound like her,
they'd ask. I didn't sound
like anyone or anything,
no grating New Yorker nasality,   25
no fastidious British mannerisms
like the ones my father affected
when he wanted to sell someone
something. And I didn't sound
like a Black American,   30
college acquaintances observed,
sure they knew what a black person
was supposed to sound like.
Was I supposed to sound lazy,
dropping syllables here and there   35
not finishing words but

8–10. Eliza Doolittle . . . Henry Higgins: Flower-girl with a strong Cockney (working-class) accent in George Bernard Shaw's play *Pygmalion* and the musical based on it, *My Fair Lady*. Henry Higgins, a linguistics professor, takes on the challenge of teaching her how to speak (and act and dress) like a proper British lady.

slurring their final letters
so each sentence joined
the next, sliding past the listener?
Were certain words off limits,   40
too erudite for someone whose skin
came with a natural tan?
I asked them what they meant
and they stuttered, blushed,
said *you know, Black English,*   45
applying a term from that
semester's text. *Does everyone
in your family speak alike,*
I'd ask, and they'd say *don't
take this the wrong way,*   50
nothing personal.

Now I realize there's nothing
more personal than speech,
that I don't have to defend
how I speak, how any person,   55
black, white, chooses to speak.
Let us speak. Let us talk
with the sounds of our mothers
and fathers still reverberating
in our minds, wherever our mothers   60
or fathers come from:
Arkansas, Belize, Alabama,
Brazil, Aruba, Arizona.
Let us simply speak
to one another,   65
listen and prize the inflections,
never assuming how any person will sound
until his mouth opens, until her
mouth opens, greetings welcome
in any language.   70

APPROACHING THE READING

1. Most of the language of the poem is straightforward. Look up any words you aren't familiar with. Pick out a few phrases you like, with especially effective or interesting diction, and be prepared to explain why.
2. The speaker mentions that her acquaintances seemed sure they knew what a black person is supposed to sound like. What does she mean by that? Reflect on the cultural assumptions that lie behind such certainty.

3. The speaker says in lines 52–55 that "there's nothing / more personal than speech, / that I don't have to defend / how I speak." Think about your own speech. In what ways is it yours? When do you feel you have to defend your speech or even abandon or change or modify it?

ENTRY POINTS   Forming images in your imagination is easiest with poems from familiar settings such as from our own neighborhood or culture. It becomes more challenging with poems from places or cultures or climates we are less familiar with — but such poems provide opportunities to expand our range of knowledge and imaginative experience.

The author of the following poem was born in Minnesota and was living there when this poem was written. But its action could occur anyplace that has winter weather. If you live in such a location, your imagination can readily form images out of your own experiences. If you do not and have never lived in an area that has a lot of snow, you will need to project such images from television or movies and try to imagine what driving on a snowy night would be like.

Robert Bly   b. 1926

Driving to Town Late to Mail a Letter   [1962]

It is a cold and snowy night. The main street is deserted.
The only things moving are swirls of snow.
As I lift the mailbox door, I feel its cold iron.
There is a privacy I love in this snowy night.
Driving around, I will waste more time.   5

APPROACHING THE READING

1. In this poem, notice how spare the language and images are. Think about why that is appropriate to the feeling that the poem creates and evokes.
2. The last line suddenly shifts our attention. Clearly something has happened to the speaker that has led him to say this line. It can be argued that something about the images he has experienced led to this pronouncement. Think about the images and articulate how and why they have affected him as they have.
3. Do you think the images the words create enable you to experience something close to what the speaker felt? Why or why not?

4. Bly said that when he graduated from Harvard he was left with only a half-dozen words that were still his. What do you make of that statement? Have you ever felt that way? Is there evidence of his concern in the choice of words for this poem?

ENTRY POINTS   The setting of the next poem is London, but it could have been any large city in the early 1700s. The opportunity here is to imagine the sights and sounds of a city three hundred years ago. Doing so requires dealing with some words that are unfamiliar today, but the images the poem creates are as vivid now as they were then.

Jonathan Swift 1667–1745

A Description of the Morning   [1709]

Now hardly° here and there a hackney-coach°	*barely; coach for hire*
Appearing, showed the ruddy morn's approach.	
Now Betty from her master's bed had flown,	
And softly stole to discompose her own;	
The slip-shod 'prentice° from his master's door	5
Had pared the dirt and sprinkled round the floor.	
Now Moll had whirled her mop with dext'rous airs,	
Prepared to scrub the entry and the stairs.	
The youth with broomy stumps° began to trace	*worn broom*
The kennel-edge,° where wheels had worn the place.	*gutter* 10
The small-coal man° was heard with cadence deep,	*coal vendor*
Till drowned in shriller notes of chimney-sweep:	
Duns° at his lordship's gate began to meet;	*debt collectors*
And brickdust Moll° had screamed through half the street	
The turnkey° now his flock° returning sees,	*jailer; (inmates)* 15
Duly let out a-nights to steal for fees:°	
The watchful bailiffs take their silent stands,	
And schoolboys lag with satchels in their hands.	

---

5. slip-shod 'prentice: Slovenly, careless apprentice.   **14. brickdust Moll:** Woman selling powdered brick.   **16. Fees:** Payments for food and better treatment.

APPROACHING THE READING

1. Consider what it is about the words and images in this poem that create such a strikingly atmospheric experience. How would you describe the feeling? What does the language evoke in you?
2. Though the diction is not contemporary, what it describes and evokes could be seen as relevant today in its harsh realism. Reflect on how the language,

dated as much of it is, creates such a realistic experience, perhaps one that you recognize in your own life.

3. Note how many senses are appealed to in the poem. Think about what the cumulative effect of them is both in creating the scenes and on you as reader.

4. When you read the title, what did you expect the poem would deal with? In what ways did the poem fulfill or contradict your expectations?

5. Consider what the sounds of particular words add to the experience in and of the poem.

6. Which of the poem's words that are no longer in popular use do you wish still were? Which would you like to add to your vocabulary? Why?

ENTRY POINTS   The following poem is packed with specific images that, combined, create a larger image — of a Los Angeles neighborhood, with the sights and sounds and smells of an evening in early fall just as the moon emerges, casting a yellow glow over the entire scene. The details will trigger sharp images if you are familiar with the foods, shops, games, plants, and architecture in the poem. The images will be less crisp if you aren't, but the overall effect of the poem is still very evocative.

Garrett Kaoru Hongo b. 1951

Yellow Light   [1982]

One arm hooked around the frayed strap
of a tar-black patent-leather purse,
the other cradling something for dinner:
fresh bunches of spinach from a J-Town *yaoya*,°
sides of a split Spanish mackerel from Alviso's,   5
maybe a loaf of Langendorf;° she steps
off the hissing bus at Olympic and Fig,
begins the three-block climb up the hill,
passing gangs of schoolboys playing war,
Japs against Japs, Chicanas chalking sidewalks   10
with the holy double-yoked crosses of hopscotch,
and the Korean grocer's wife out for a stroll
around this neighborhood of Hawaiian apartments
just starting to steam with cooking

---

4. **J-Town *yaoya*:** A vegetable shop or stand in Japan-Town.   6. **a loaf of Langendorf:** Bread from a well-known California bakery.

and the anger of young couples coming home   15
from work, yelling at kids, flicking on
TV sets for the Wednesday Night Fights.

If it were May, hydrangeas and jacaranda
flowers in the streetside trees would be
blooming through the smog of late spring.   20
Wisteria in Masuda's front yard would be
shaking out the long tresses of its purple hair.
Maybe mosquitoes, moths, a few orange butterflies
settling on the lattice of monkey flowers
tangled in chain-link fences by the trash.   25

But this is October, and Los Angeles
seethes like a billboard under twilight.
From used-car lots and the movie houses uptown,
long silver sticks of light probe the sky.
From the Miracle Mile, whole freeways away,   30
a brilliant fluorescence breaks out
and makes war with the dim squares
of yellow kitchen light winking on
in all the side streets of the Barrio.

She climbs up the two flights of flagstone   35
stairs to 201-B, the spikes of her high heels
clicking like kitchen knives on a cutting board,
props the groceries against the door,
fishes through memo pads, a compact,
empty packs of chewing gum, and finds her keys.   40

The moon then, cruising from behind
a screen of eucalyptus across the street,
covers everything, everything in sight,
in a heavy light like yellow onions.

APPROACHING THE READING

1. Look up any words that you don't recognize or aren't sure of.
2. As an exercise on imagery, circle nouns and underline verbs that evoke sensory impressions — sights, sounds, smells, tastes, touch. Notice how much of the language in the poem is devoted to the senses.
3. In contrast to Swift's "A Description of the Morning," vegetation is important in this poem. If you aren't familiar with *hydrangea*, *jacaranda*, *wisteria*, *monkey flowers*, and *eucalyptus*, looking them up will help sharpen the images for you. How does the presence or absence of such images convey a different portrait of a city in the two poems?

4. Draw a square box around words the poem uses to make images sharper or clearer for the reader — for example, adjectives that make nouns more specific ("the *frayed* strap / of a *tar-black, patent-leather* purse"), or comparisons that make images easier to imagine ("clicking *like* kitchen knives on a cutting board").
5. What is the point or theme of the poem? What does it all add up to?

When discussing or writing about literature, the word **imagery** is used in two ways: (1) It can mean all language in a literary work collectively that refers to a sensory experience or to objects that can be known by one or more of the senses in a poem — "The rich imagery in the first stanza of 'Those Winter Sundays' establishes a strong empathy with the father," for example. (2) It can mean a related pattern of imaginative comparisons and allusions running through an entire literary work or a portion of one — for example, "The use of Nazi imagery to convey the speaker's ambivalence about her father makes Sylvia Plath's 'Daddy' (p. 840) one of the most unsettling and controversial poems of the twentieth century."

ENTRY POINTS   Much of the imagery in "Yellow Light" is of nature and sounds in an October night. Here is another autumn poem full of nature imagery — an elderly man reflects on the crop of apples he has just finished picking and on his life, which is nearing its end. As you read it, pay special attention to its use of connotations and to the way its words create images appealing to various senses.

Robert Frost   1874–1963

After Apple-Picking   [1914]

My long two-pointed ladder's sticking through a tree
Toward heaven still,
And there's a barrel that I didn't fill
Beside it, and there may be two or three
Apples I didn't pick upon some bough.   5
But I am done with apple-picking now.
Essence of winter sleep is on the night,
The scent of apples: I am drowsing off.
I cannot rub the strangeness from my sight
I got from looking through a pane of glass   10
I skimmed this morning from the drinking trough
And held against the world of hoary grass.

It melted, and I let it fall and break.
But I was well
Upon my way to sleep before it fell,   15
And I could tell
What form my dreaming was about to take.
Magnified apples appear and disappear,
Stem end and blossom end,
And every fleck of russet showing clear.   20
My instep arch not only keeps the ache,
It keeps the pressure of a ladder-round.
I feel the ladder sway as the boughs bend.
And I keep hearing from the cellar bin
The rumbling sound   25
Of load on load of apples coming in.
For I have had too much
Of apple-picking: I am overtired
Of the great harvest I myself desired.
There were ten thousand thousand fruit to touch,   30
Cherish in hand, lift down, and not let fall.
For all
That struck the earth,
No matter if not bruised or spiked with stubble,
Went surely to the cider-apple heap   35
As of no worth.
One can see what will trouble
This sleep of mine, whatever sleep it is.
Were he not gone,
The woodchuck could say whether it's like his   40
Long sleep, as I describe its coming on,
Or just some human sleep.

APPROACHING THE READING

1. In this poem, descriptive images convey what the speaker experienced at a particular time of year. Notice how they do this. What things has the speaker experienced that have occupied him so totally that they even fill his dreams?

2. Look for images invoking various senses. What do they contribute to the poem? What do you make of the contrast between the richly sensuous detail and the speaker's matter-of-fact tone?

Research this author in depth with cultural documents and multimedia resources on *LiterActive*.

3. Consider word choice in the poem. How does the diction help give us a sense of what the speaker is like?

Notice the words "Toward heaven" (l. 2). How would the poem be affected if the line read "toward the sky" instead?

4. Review the discussion of archetypes in Chapter 6 (pp. 147–48). Do some of the images in this poem also function as archetypes? If you think they do, point out examples and explain their effect in the poem. How do they contribute to what the poem adds up to?

ENTRY POINTS Nature also is important in the following poem, but the focus is on a relationship involving vulnerable, hurting individuals: the strong friendship of two young girls—one who is blind, the other who misses her father. Consider how denotations, connotations, and images are important in it.

Anita Endrezze b. 1952

The Girl Who Loved the Sky   [1992]

Outside the second grade room,
the jacaranda tree blossomed
into purple lanterns, the papery petals
drifted, darkening the windows.
Inside, the room smelled like glue.   5
The desks were made of yellowed wood,
the tops littered with eraser rubbings,
rulers, and big fat pencils.
Colored chalk meant special days.
The walls were covered with precise   10
bright tulips and charts with shiny stars
by certain names. There, I learned
how to make butter by shaking a jar
until the pale cream clotted
into one sweet mass. There, I learned   15
that numbers were fractious beasts
with dens like dim zeros. And there,
I met a blind girl who thought the sky
tasted like cold metal when it rained
and whose eyes were always covered   20
with the bruised petals of her lids.

She loved the formless sky, defined
only by sounds, or the cool umbrellas
of clouds. On hot, still days

we listened to the sky falling   25
like chalk dust. We heard the noon
whistle of the pig-mash factory,
smelled the sourness of home-bound men.

I had no father; she had no eyes;
we were best friends. The other girls   30
drew shaky hopscotch squares
on the dusty asphalt, talked about
pajama parties, weekend cookouts,
and parents who bought sleek-finned cars.
Alone, we sat in the canvas swings,   35
our shoes digging into the sand, then pushing,
until we flew high over their heads,
our hands streaked with red rust
from the chains that kept us safe.

I was born blind, she said, an act of nature.   40
Sure, I thought, like birds born
without wings, trees without roots.
I didn't understand. The day she moved
I saw the world clearly: the sky
backed away from me like a departing father.   45
I sat under the jacaranda, catching
the petals in my palm, enclosing them
until my fist was another lantern
hiding a small and bitter flame.

APPROACHING THE READING

1. Notice the rich sensory texture of this poem. Find examples of words that evoke each of the five senses — sight, hearing, smell, taste, and touch. Why is sensory imagery so important to this poem?
2. If you have never seen a jacaranda tree or its blossoms, look at pictures of them in an encyclopedia or plant book or online. How do those pictures help sharpen the way you visualize lines 1–4, 20–21, and 46–49?
3. We get to know the speaker and her friend partly through the poem's images, through the kinds of things they notice and experience. Describe what both girls are like, grounding your response in the poem's details.
4. Discuss the nature of the girls' friendship. What makes it solid, touching, vulnerable? How do certain images help convey it?
5. Reread the final stanza of the poem on the effect of the experience on the narrator. Explain how images help get her points across. How fully did the speaker understand the experience then? What indication is there that the poet, in looking back, has a different understanding of it now?

RESPONDING THROUGH Writing

WRITING ABOUT WORDS AND IMAGES

Journal Entries

www

Research the authors in this chapter with LitLinks at bedfordstmartins.com/ approachinglit.

1. As an exercise on language, write in your journal lists of words that you notice during an entire day: unfamiliar words, moving words, words that sound beautiful, words that look good, and so on. At the end of the day and a few days later, look back over the list and run through the words using your memory and imagination. Jot some notes about experiences, feelings, and associations some of the words bring back to you: It may give you a new sense of the power and importance words have.

2. Choose a nonpoetic text — a letter, an advertisement, a magazine article, or an editorial, for example — and look closely at its handling of language. Discuss in your journal how the denotations and connotations of the words are or are not manipulated.

3. Images — visual and verbal — are enormously important for the advertising industry. In your journal, list some examples of how advertisers use words and pictures to imprint images in your mind and to stimulate your imagination, to get you to notice and remember their products. Write some reflections on some ways advertisers use the same techniques as poets, though with a different purpose in mind.

Literary Analysis Papers

4. Write a paper that examines the diction in Garrett Kaoru Hongo's "Yellow Light" (p. 561), especially how its mixing of ordinary, everyday words with evocatively lush language creates a portrait that changes our usual perceptions of the world of the city.

5. Write a paper discussing the imagery of Garrett Kaoru Hongo's "Yellow Light" (p. 561) or another poem by thinking of it in terms of cinematography. See the poem as film. Note where in the poem you would use crucial camera angles, shots, close-ups, pans, and so forth. Help your reader see the poem as a film. Explain why you decided to film it as you did.

6. Write a paper on the use of imagery in capturing and conveying the atmosphere of a season: autumn, for example, in John Keats's "To Autumn" (p. 645), or the harvest season (June) in Gary Soto's "The Elements of San Joaquin" (p. 858), or spring in William Carlos Williams's "Spring and All" (p. 880).

Comparison-Contrast Papers

7. Write a paper comparing and contrasting what two or more poems about words say about language (perhaps including the cultural implications of

language) and the diction they use to communicate it. Some poems you might consider are Kimiko Hahn's "Mother's Mother" (p. 792), Allison Joseph's "On Being Told I Don't Speak Like a Black Person" (p. 557), Gary Miranda's "Love Poem" (p. 668), and Alberto Ríos's "Nani" (p. 847).

8. Write a paper comparing and contrasting the expressions of love in Elizabeth Barrett Browning's "How do I love thee? Let me count the ways" (p. 751) and Gary Miranda's "Love Poem" (p. 668). Consider the extent to which each relies on images and how the effect of each differs.

> ## TIPS for Writing about Words and Images

> **Read words attentively** Assume that every word a poet chooses is used deliberately, and pay careful attention to each one. Of course you can't write about all the words, even in a short poem, so it's a good idea to focus on diction that is unusual, unexpected, striking, or especially significant.

> **Use a dictionary** Make ample use of a good dictionary when you're writing about diction or imagery. Pay attention to etymologies as well as various definitions. Remember that a poet may want you to use more than one definition for a word, that doing so will add even more to the poem.

> **Look for patterns** As you study a poem, watch for patterns, connections, or relationships among the words and images. Also, notice how poetic images sometimes change our usual ways of perceiving things. These often can result in insightful paper topics.

> **Avoid the general** Don't just give lists of images or tell your reader what she or he already knows, like "The image of the stabbing was violent" or "the 'splintering cold' helps a reader feel how cold it was in the room" (you might instead focus on how "splintering" changes our usual way of thinking about coldness).

> **Relate to effect or theme** Whenever you write about words and images, as the topic of an entire paper or as passing comments within a larger topic, your comments need to be used to help clarify the way words or images contribute to the overall effect or theme of the poem.

WRITING ABOUT CONNECTIONS

Words and images are the key vehicles through which writers connect with readers, through which they convey their meaning. Examining a poet's choices and handling of diction and imagery in a poem can be an effective paper topic. Another way to deal with words and images in a paper is to look for thematic connections between two poems that use similar or contrasting diction and/or imagery, especially a contemporary poem and a poem from an earlier period. Here are a few examples of such topic possibilities.

1. "Autumn Leaves": The Changing Seasons of Life in Robert Frost's "After Apple-Picking" (p. 563) and Joseph Awad's "Autumnal" (p. 739)
2. "Seeing the City": The Contrasting Perspectives of Jonathan Swift's "A Description of the Morning" (p. 560) and Cheryl Savageau's "Bones — A City Poem" (p. 852)
3. "Impermanence's Permanence": Anita Endrezze's "The Girl Who Loved the Sky" (p. 565) and Edmund Spenser's "One day I wrote her name upon the strand" (p. 861)

WRITING RESEARCH PAPERS

1. Research the way the British taught the English language in their colonies, and reflect on what might have been the effects and consequences of doing so. In what ways do your research findings compare and contrast with the issues raised by today's controversies over bilingual education? Also look into Ebonics, or "black English." Use what you find to illuminate Allison Joseph's "On Being Told I Don't Speak Like a Black Person" (p. 557), especially what the poem suggests about the teaching or learning of language.
2. Select a poem of political protest, such as Ana Doina's "The Extinct Homeland — A Conversation with Czeslaw Milosz" (p. 771), Carolyn Forché's "The Colonel" (p. 783), or Sonia Sanchez's "An Anthem" (p. 851). Research the historical and social/political/economic backgrounds of the poem. Write a paper showing how awareness of this contextual knowledge helps clarify the meaning and impact of the poem and how the poem's use of diction and images reflects the background, helping to present the situation in a powerful way.

COMPOSING IN OTHER ART FORMS

1. Create a set of drawings representing or illustrating Anita Endrezze's "The Girl Who Loved the Sky" (p. 565), Angelina Weld Grimké's "A Winter Twilight" (p. 638), E. E. Cummings's "in Just-" (p. 765), or another poem of your choice.
2. Write a poem consisting mostly of images. Do your best not to convey any ideas or feelings outright. Try to embody the experience entirely in images, the way Maxine Kumin does in "The Sound of Night" (p. 553).

Poetic speech is a way of sounding in order to hear that voice. And once you hear it, everything else is like dishwater.

CHAPTER 13 Voice, Tone, and Sound

Hearing How Sense Is Said

We said in Chapter 3 that stories did not originate as something to be read: People listened to stories being told long before they read them. The same is true of poems. Even today, when poems are written down, most poems are not meant only to be read; they are also meant to be heard. In fiction and narrative poetry, you listen with your mind's ear to a storyteller, a first- or third-person narrator. In nonnarrative poetry, you hear the imagined voice of a **speaker**, of someone "speaking" the poem, either the poet directly or a character who expresses views or feelings the poet may or may not share. This chapter aims to develop your ability to listen for the voice of the speaker (or narrator), or the voice of the poem, and to help you hear the sounds and rhythms that create the musicality of poetry and are an important part of that voice.

READING FOR VOICE

In a first-person poem, a key question to ask is whether the *I* speaking in the poem is a voice very similar to that of the author or is a character different from the author. Just as you should not assume that the *I* in a story is identical to the author, you shouldn't automatically assume that the *I* in a poem is the author. Thomas Hardy, for example, wrote a poem in which the *I* is a dead man; Gerald Stern wrote a poem in which the *I* is a dead dog.

ENTRY POINTS   Pay attention to the speaker in the following poem as he recalls his father and expresses his love for what is now lost. Watch for indications of what the *I* is like—character traits and attitudes. And listen for indications of whether the voice you hear represents that of the author or of a character separate and different from the author.

Li-Young Lee   b. 1957

Eating Alone   [1986]

I've pulled the last of the year's young onions.
The garden is bare now. The ground is cold,
brown and old. What is left of the day flames
in the maples at the corner of my
eye. I turn, a cardinal vanishes.   5
By the cellar door, I wash the onions,
then drink from the icy metal spigot.

Once, years back, I walked beside my father
among the windfall pears. I can't recall
our words. We may have strolled in silence. But   10
I still see him bend that way—left hand braced
on knee, creaky—to lift and hold to my
eye a rotten pear. In it, a hornet
spun crazily, glazed in slow, glistening juice.

It was my father I saw this morning   15
waving to me from the trees. I almost
called to him, until I came close enough
to see the shovel, leaning where I had
left it, in the flickering, deep green shade.

White rice steaming, almost done. Sweet green peas   20
fried in onions. Shrimp braised in sesame
oil and garlic. And my own loneliness.
What more could I, a young man, want.

APPROACHING THE READING

1. Focus on the *I* who speaks the poem. Does anything suggest that the *I* is different from, or distanced from, the author of the poem?
2. Describe the voice you hear as you listen to the poem. What personal qualities and attributes come through what is said?

3. How does the last stanza of the poem relate to the previous three stanzas? What is the meaning of the last line?
4. How does the title affect your sense of the voice of the poem?
5. In what ways does hearing the poem's voice enrich your experience of the poem? What would be lost if you did not hear the voice?

In the text of "Eating Alone," there seems to be no reason for thinking the *I* is significantly different from the author, and biographical information about the author (including the biographical sketch on p. 1546) confirms basic similarities between the speaker and the poem. The voice we hear appears to be Li-Young Lee's voice. Or, perhaps we should say, his voice as a poet in this poem.

VOICE AS AUTHORIAL PRESENCE   What we're really considering when we talk about **voice** is authorial presence not as a biographical personality but as the sense conveyed by a poem of an intelligence and moral sensibility that has invented, arranged, and expressed the elements and ideas in a particular manner. For a poem in which the *I* is close to the poet, the *I* supplies the voice we listen to; for a poem in which the *I* is different from the poet, to consider the poet's presence we need to listen for the voice of the poem, which is likely to be somewhat different from the speaker's voice.

CONVEYING VOICE DIRECTLY   From the beginning of "Eating Alone," the person speaking seems low-keyed, matter-of-fact, unemotional. He is very observant, someone who notices the appearance of the now-barren earth, the brilliant sunset shining through the leaves of a maple tree, the flight of a cardinal. Clearly this person is in touch with his surroundings. The voice in the second stanza sounds soft, sensitive, perhaps pensive, as he recalls a particular moment, years ago, with his father, who seems no longer to be living. The moment was memorable not for what they said to each other but for the particular way his father bent over to pick up a rotting pear and showed him a hornet circling drunkenly in its hollowed-out center. From his father, it seems, the speaker learned the attentiveness to nature demonstrated in the first stanza.

CONVEYING VOICE INDIRECTLY   The third stanza makes clear that the speaker is not in fact unemotional: He felt a great deal of emotion when he thought he saw his father, but then realized what he saw was actually a shovel in flickering light. But the voice we hear restrains that deep emotion, understates it, which may end up making it sound all the stronger. The understated emotion is carried over to the final stanza, in the details of an excellent meal, fit for a festive, shared occasion, in contrast to the speaker's "loneliness."

COMPLEXITY OF VOICE   The word *loneliness* and the final line raise key questions about voice, questions of the kind that each reader must think through for herself or himself. What kind of voice says the words "my own loneliness"? Is it a depressing, isolated loneliness brought on by his feeling lost without his father? Is it accepted loneliness, in which he misses his father's physical presence but is consoled by a sense of the father's continuing presence because of his memories? Or could it be a mixture of the two, or something else?

Similarly, what kind of voice says the last line, "What more could I, a young man, want"? Is the voice heavy with irony? (There's a lot more I could want, starting with having my father back!) Does it express the genuine consolations that are found in good food and the flood of memories associated with the food and with other experiences? The title brings those questions about the voice into focus: Is eating alone a sad, solitary activity for the speaker? Does he actually feel lonely as he eats alone? When do being alone and not being lonely coincide? When do they not?

It is important when working with a poem to allow for complexity of emotion. Our feelings are always "mixed," meaning complex, even contradictory. A poem—an effective, honest poem—is never emotionally simplistic.

GROUNDING VOICE IN SPECIFIC DETAILS   Notice, too, that in the previous paragraphs, whenever the voice is described we support the description with specific details from the poem itself. Nothing is stated and then followed up by an ungrounded impression or a phrase such as "that's how it feels to me." Each description is linked to a concrete passage, part of the poem.

ENTRY POINTS   As you read the following poem about a father-son relationship rather different from that in "Eating Alone," watch for any indications that the *I* speaking in the poem does not represent the author's voice. Notice character traits of the speaker and be able to describe what the speaker is like as a person.

Charles Bukowski   1920–1994

my old man   [1977]

16 years old
during the depression
I'd come home drunk
and all my clothing—
shorts, shirts, stockings—   5
suitcase, and pages of
short stories

would be thrown out on the
front lawn and about the
street.   10

my mother would be
waiting behind a tree:
"Henry, Henry, don't
go in . . . he'll
kill you, he's read   15
your stories . . ."

"I can whip his
ass . . ."

"Henry, please take
this . . . and   20
find yourself a room."

but it worried him
that I might not
finish high school
so I'd be back   25
again.

one evening he walked in
with the pages of
one of my short stories
(which I had never submitted   30
to him)
and he said, "this is
a great short story."
I said, "o.k.,"
and he handed it to me   35
and I read it.
it was a story about
a rich man
who had a fight with
his wife and had   40
gone out into the night
for a cup of coffee
and had observed
the waitress and the spoons
and forks and the   45
salt and pepper shakers
and the neon sign
in the window
and then had gone back
to his stable   50

to see and touch his
favorite horse
who then
kicked him in the head
and killed him.   55

somehow
the story held
meaning for him
though
when I had written it   60
I had no idea
of what I was
writing about.

so I told him,
"o.k., old man, you can   65
have it."
and he took it
and walked out
and closed the door.
I guess that's   70
as close
as we ever got.

APPROACHING THE READING

1. Describe the voice you hear in the poem. Is it the voice of the poet directly, of a character expressing views or feelings the poet shares, or of a character distinct from the poet?
2. How would you characterize the father and the son? Do you sympathize with either? Why or why not?
3. Why do you think the father likes the story?
4. Why do you think Henry wrote the story? He says he had no idea of what he was writing about.
5. Why do you think the poet included the story? How does it fit the voice of the poem?

   This is a first-person poem, and the fact that the *I* is a writer can make it seem that the voice in this poem, like that in "Eating Alone," is pretty much the same as the author's. But the mother calls the speaker (narrator, actually, since this is a poem telling a story) "Henry," which suggests that the *I* may be a character different from the author. In that case, we need to listen for the voice of the poem behind Henry's words and attitudes.

VOICE AND POINT OF VIEW   In this poem, thinking in terms of point of view (see p. 101) helps. We hear everything from Henry's perspective. What happens and what is said would sound quite different from the father's vantage point. Perhaps we can hear the voice of the poem — its authorial presence, the intelligence and moral sensibility that has invented, arranged, and expressed the elements and ideas — if we listen for both perspectives and consider whether the poem might be indicating some degree of disapproval of the son's attitude. If so, that could affect how we think about several key issues in the poem.

> Some books use the term **persona** for the first-person narrator through whom an author speaks or the speaker whose voice is heard in a lyric poem. They assume that one can never hear the author directly in a written work, even when he or she uses *I*, that the author always, inevitably talks through a mask the way actors did in Greek plays (which is where the term *persona* came from). This book does not make that assumption, though it stresses that an *I* should never automatically be equated with the author.

READING A DRAMATIC MONOLOGUE

One poetic form in which the *I* is not the author is the **dramatic monologue**. In dramatic monologues, there is only one speaker, a character overheard in a dramatic moment, usually addressing another character or characters who do not speak. The speaker's words reveal what is going on in the scene and bring out significant aspects of what the speaker is like. You can, therefore, figure out who is speaking, to whom, and on what occasion, and the substance and tone of what she or he is saying. See, for example, Robert Browning's "My Last Duchess" (p. 595). (If the character is speaking to her- or himself, the poem is using interior monologue — see p. 106; that is probably the case in T. S. Eliot's "The Love Song of J. Alfred Prufrock" — p. 776.)

READING FOR TONE

When you are hearing a voice, an important aspect of what you are hearing is its tone. **Tone** was defined in Chapter 7 (p. 207) as the attitude or "stance" toward the subject and toward the reader or audience implied in a work. As we said there, tone can be, for example, serious, playful, exaggerated, understated, poignant, distanced, formal, informal, ironic, blunt, or something other than these.

Tone is as important in poems as it is in stories. Poems can have a single tone, but usually the tone is not singular and straightforward; it cannot be summed up in a word or two. More often two or more tones mix and play off or with each other. In "my old man" (p. 573), for example, one needs to consider Henry's tone—his attitude toward his father and perhaps toward life in general—and the tone of the poem toward Henry.

ENTRY POINTS   Here is another poem about a son's memories of his father. Listen carefully for its voice and tone. Pay attention to the diction, connotations, and images. Does the father-son relationship seem closer to that of "Eating Alone" or that of "my old man"?

Theodore Roethke   1908–1963

My Papa's Waltz   [1948]

The whiskey on your breath
Could make a small boy dizzy;
But I hung on like death:
Such waltzing was not easy.

We romped until the pans   5
Slid from the kitchen shelf;
My mother's countenance
Could not unfrown itself.

The hand that held my wrist
Was battered on one knuckle;   10
At every step you missed
My right ear scraped a buckle.

You beat time on my head
With a palm caked hard by dirt,
Then waltzed me off to bed   15
Still clinging to your shirt.

APPROACHING THE READING

1. Consider the voice in the poem. Is the *I* a character narrating the episode or the voice of the poet?
2. Unlike "Eating Alone" (p. 571) and "my old man" (p. 573), which address the reader, this poem addresses *you*, the father. How does that affect the voice of the poem?
3. Be ready to discuss the age of the speaker whose voice we hear—his age now and at the time of the

www

Explore this author and poem in depth, including images and cultural documents, with VirtuaLit Poetry at bedfordstmartins .com/approachinglit.

event—and what you think he felt then and feels now. What difference does it make to the way we hear the voice whether the father is living or has died?

4. Discuss the effect of the word *papa* on the tone of the poem. Substitute *daddy* or *father* or *old man*. What happens?

5. Discuss the effect of the word *waltz* on the tone of the poem. Substitute *romps* or *craziness*. What happens?

A DARK TONE?   "My Papa's Waltz" affects readers in different ways. For some the poem describes a troubled relationship or dysfunctional home. The word *whiskey* suggests for them that the father has a drinking problem; the mother's disapproval suggests that the father and mother have a difficult relationship. *Battered* indicates that the father abuses his son and perhaps his wife. The simile "I hung on like death" in line 3 suggests a home in which fear pervades the atmosphere. For these readers, the poem has a dark tone, perhaps a tragic one, as a little boy—too young to be aware of what he's doing—puts up with his father's frightening romps because he is forced to physically and desperately tries to gain his father's love and approval.

OR A JOYFUL TONE?   Other readers discern a different tone in the poem. For them words such as *waltz* and *romped* convey a lighter tone—a waltz is a graceful, flowing, lyrical dance that suggests joy and celebration (though, of course, the poet could be using the word ironically). The father described is a physical laborer (his hands are battered and caked with dirt) who has a couple of drinks with his buddies after work on a Friday. Feeling good, he frolics with his son, more wildly than he probably should, creating disorder in the kitchen, and more roughly than he should, thus scraping the boy's ear and tapping on his head enthusiastically. The romp is scary for the small boy ("dizzy," "like death," "clinging")—but excitingly scary. For these readers, the poem describes a speaker looking back at his childhood, recalling a happy memory, a memory that evinces his father's affection (people generally waltz with people they love) and his own positive response to his father (one can cling out of love as well as fear).

COMPLEXITY OF TONE   Assessing tone is a central part of the total interpretation of a literary work. As in all interpretation, it's not simple or straightforward. Every aspect of the work can come to bear on tone. It's important always to be alert for indicators of tone in a poem. Some are the same as in fiction—word choice, ways of phrasing, repetitions, understatement, overstatement, a particular figure of speech. Others—such as the handling of sounds and rhythm—are more particular to poetry. And as "My Papa's Waltz" makes clear, tone is not an objective detail on which all readers must agree. Readers can read tones differently, and discussions about tone often form a vital part of conversations about literature, with each side pointing to aspects that lead them to respond to the work the way they do.

READING FOR IRONY

As you read a poem, always be alert for signals that what is said is not to be taken in a literal way: word choice, the sheer absurdity of what is said, the way a thought is phrased, the sounds and rhythms in which it is expressed. Recognition of irony is crucial to reading well. But it's not just identifying irony that's important. Active reading of a poem, like active reading of other literature, involves the whole person — intellect, senses, emotions, ideas, and values. Responding to any kind of tone is crucial to enjoying a poem fully and meaningfully.

ENTRY POINTS   Irony is as important in poetry as it is in stories. Review the discussion of irony in Chapter 7 (pp. 209–12), especially — for poetry — the sections on verbal irony and sarcasm. Then try out your ear for irony as you read the following poem. Pay attention especially to word choice, exaggerations, and incongruities.

Marge Piercy b. 1936

Barbie Doll   [1973]

This girlchild was born as usual
and presented dolls that did pee-pee
and miniature GE stoves and irons
and wee lipsticks the color of cherry candy.
Then in the magic of puberty, a classmate said: 5
You have a great big nose and fat legs.

She was healthy, tested intelligent,
possessed strong arms and back,
abundant sexual drive and manual dexterity.
She went to and fro apologizing.   10
Everyone saw a fat nose on thick legs.

She was advised to play coy,
exhorted to come on hearty,
exercise, diet, smile and wheedle.
Her good nature wore out   15
like a fan belt.
So she cut off her nose and her legs
and offered them up.

In the casket displayed on satin she lay
with the undertaker's cosmetics painted on,   20
a turned-up putty nose,
dressed in a pink and white nightie.

Doesn't she look pretty? everyone said.
Consummation at last.
To every woman a happy ending. 25

APPROACHING THE READING

1. What effect on tone do words such as *girlchild*, *pee-pee*, *wee*, and *cherry candy* have? How did they strike you the first time you read them?
2. What do you think the speaker means by the "magic" of puberty in line 5? How does the wording of line 6 connect with it? What tone do you think the two lines convey?
3. At what point in the poem did you realize this poem critiques prevailing social attitudes?
4. Point out several examples of irony in the poem.

THE VOICE   This poem is narrated by an unidentified, third-person observer, not the poet in first person and not a character involved in the action. The voice may well be that of the poet, but it has a heavily ironic tone. In such cases, of course, it is important to distinguish between the voice of the speaker (who seems to say the events have a happy ending) and the voice of the poem (which means the opposite).

THE IRONIES   The title and opening lines can seem straightforward initially, with words such as "girlchild" and "did pee-pee" creating a childlike simplicity. However, a deeper seriousness begins to emerge in line 6: "You have a great big nose and fat legs." The middle stanzas develop the contrast between what this young woman was and the Barbie Doll and supermodel expectations society imposes on women. Phrasings such as "went to and fro apologizing" (l. 10) and "a fat nose on thick legs" (l. 11) and the comparison "wore out / like a fan belt" (ll. 15–16) are signals that the voice is not to be heard as straightforward. Line 17 is certainly not straightforward: "So she cut off her nose and her legs" is the speaker's ironic way of saying that, unable to cope with what she perceived as society's expectations, she committed suicide.

THE EFFECTS   The ironies intensify in the final paragraph. In her coffin, thanks to the undertakers' skills, she looks like a Barbie doll and everyone now, when she can't hear them, says how pretty she looks. The poem's voice continues to intensify as the final lines convey the author's sentiments: "Consummation at last" (l. 24) is highly ironic in that her consummation — completion, fulfillment, perfection — is found only after death. The most common use of *consummation* — the completion of a marriage by sexual intercourse — makes the irony even stronger since she did not feel sexually attractive when she was living, and perhaps did not seem so to young men, with their society-shaped expectations. In the final line — "To every woman a happy ending" — the ironic voice turns sarcastic.

The rest of this chapter, along with the chapters that follow, goes on to discuss specific techniques and elements poets draw from when they compose a poem. As we focus on sounds, metaphors, rhythm, and form, however, it is important that you continue to listen for, and to, the voices in poems. Listen to the variety of voices, from different times, different experiences, and different backgrounds. Listen for and to the variety of things they give voice to in their poems. *Hear* the poems and *hear* what the poems are saying.

READING FOR SOUND

Fine writers have "good ears." They attend to sounds of words as well as combinations of sounds, listening for the way sound and rhythm work together to create the poem's "music," all of which contribute to the voice of a

 TIPS for Reading Poems Aloud

Because of the importance of voice and sounds, it can be helpful to read poems aloud at least once, if not several times, and to listen to someone else read them. Attending to the sounds and rhythms will bring out aspects of the poem that you otherwise might overlook. Here are some suggestions for reading aloud:

➤ **Don't rush** Reading too fast distorts the rhythms and blurs the words and sounds.

➤ **Pay attention to punctuation** Take a full stop at a period or semicolon and a brief pause at a comma, both within lines and at the ends of lines.

➤ **Pause for line endings** Even when the end of a line has no punctuation, lengthen the last sound with level pitch to signal the movement to a new line.

➤ **Read with expression** Your voice needs to convey what the sentences are saying, which means you need to understand the content and tone.

➤ **Read to communicate** Even if you are reading to yourself, pretend that you have an audience and that you are trying hard to help them receive and appreciate the poem fully.

Reading aloud might feel uncomfortable at first, but soon you may find yourself enjoying what can happen when you do. It can also influence your silent reading, making you more attentive to your mental voice.

poem. Rhythm is treated later in the book, in Chapter 16. Here we focus on the effects of repeating or contrasting syllable sounds, vowel sounds, and consonant sounds. To gain the full experience of effective writing, a reader needs to hear not only the words but also the repetitions, connections, contrasts, and combinations of vowels, consonants, and syllables that form the words.

ENTRY POINTS   The following poem is about an African American driver being stopped by a police officer. Listen for the sounds made by the words and phrases — repetitions of words, parallel constructions, felicitous phrasings, echoes of vowel and consonant sounds, and rhyming words as well as the sound of the speaker's voice. Think about the ways that the sounds help convey the meaning.

Sekou Sundiata   b. 1948–2007

Blink Your Eyes   [1995]

Remembering Sterling A. Brown°

I was on my way to see my woman
but the Law said I was on my way
thru a red light red light red light
and if you saw my woman
you could understand,   5
I was just being a man
It wasn't about no light
it was about my ride
and if you saw my ride
you could dig that too, you dig?   10
Sunroof stereo radio black leather
bucket seats sit low you know,
the body's cool, but the tires are worn.
Ride when the hard time come, ride
when they're gone, in other words   15
the light was green.

I could wake up in the morning
without a warning
and my world could change:

Sterling A. Brown: Brown (1901–1989) was an African American poet and a longtime professor at Howard University. See his poem "Riverbank Blues" (p. 750) and biographical sketch (p. 1523).

blink your eyes.   20
All depends, all depends on the skin,
all depends on the skin you're living in.

Up to the window comes the Law
with his hand on his gun
what's up? what's happening?   25
I said I guess
that's when I really broke the law.
He said *a routine, step out the car*
a routine, assume the position.
Put your hands up in the air   30
you know the routine, like you just don't care.
License and registration.
Deep was the night and the light
from the North Star on the car door, déjà vu
we've been through this before,   35
why did you stop me?
Somebody had to stop you.
I watch the news, you always lose.
You're unreliable, that's undeniable.
This is serious, you could be dangerous.   40

I could wake up in the morning
without a warning
and my world could change:
blink your eyes.
All depends, all depends on the skin,   45
all depends on the skin you're living in.

New York City, they got laws
Can't no bruthas drive outdoors,
in certain neighborhoods, on particular streets
near and around certain types of people.   50
They got laws.
All depends, all depends on the skin,
all depends on the skin you're living in.

APPROACHING THE READING

1. As you listen to the *I* in this poem, does it seem like you are hearing the
   voice of the author directly, a character speaking for the author, or a character different from the author?
2. Is there an overall tone in the poem, or do different types of tone appear in
   different parts? Or would you say that both are true? What would you say is
   the tone of the repeated phrase "all depends on the skin you're living in"?

3. Read the first stanza of the poem aloud. Pay close attention to the sounds of the syllables, words, and phrases in those lines (not sounds they describe, but the sounds you hear as you say them aloud). Find examples of repeated consonant sounds and vowel sounds, of words repeated rhythmically, of words that rhyme. Reflect on the "feel" and tone the sounds create.

A significant portion of the effect of "Blink Your Eyes" arises from the sounds — the rhymes, the repetitions, the echoes of vowels and consonants that create an aura and reinforce the poem's ironies.

The poem describes an experience of racial profiling: Encountering such racism has the potential to change one's world in the blink of an eye. Even though the speaker voices the poem as an event in his past, he is still able to remember the innocence of his excited anticipation of driving to see his lover. We can feel that throughout the poem's opening section with its vivid picture of how "cool" his car was, as conveyed by the images, and how hip he was, as conveyed by the sounds and rhythms of the words he uses.

Then he is accused of running a red light and everything changes. He realizes there are two different worlds with two different ways of enforcing the law, that it "all depends on the skin you're living in." The subject turns more serious after line 23, but the use of rhyme, the repetition of phrases, and the echoes of vowels and consonants continue, creating a spirit of positive defiance in the face of injustice.

Close examination of techniques of sound can become technical and abstract, and risks making you want to back away. Yet, only by looking closely can we see exactly how the effects we appreciate are created. We ask you to focus on just four important types of sound technique — alliteration, assonance, repetition, and rhyme — with examples from "Blink Your Eyes" to illustrate them.

Alliteration

One kind of sound, **alliteration**, is the repetition of identical consonant sounds in words relatively near one another (in the same line or adjacent lines usually). Alliteration is most common at the beginnings of words or syllables, especially the beginnings of stressed syllables ("*green* as *grass*"), though it sometimes can occur within words and syllables as well ("*golden baggage*"). But in every case the sound must be stressed sufficiently that it is heard clearly. Throughout this chapter, the pronunciation is what matters, not the letters. "*Call* the *kid* in the *center*" does alliterate, but "Call" and "center" do not. Notice the alliterative *s*, *r*, *b*, and *l* sounds in these lines:

Sunroof stereo radio black leather
bucket seats sit low you know.

Alliteration usually sounds appealing, as it does in these lines. It also calls attention to words, giving them greater emphasis, linking words together to get us to connect their meanings, and making phrases more memorable.

A variant on alliteration is **consonance**, the use of words whose consonant sounds are the same but whose vowels are different. In perfect examples, all the consonants are alike: *live, love; chitter, chatter; reader, rider*; or, in Romeo's words, "I'll *look* to *like*, if *looking liking* move" (*Romeo and Juliet* 1.4.98). The more usual examples of consonance are words in which the consonants following the main vowels are identical: *dive, love; swatter, chitter; sound, bond.* Line 5 of "Blink Your Eyes" (p. 582) employs consonance: "you *could* understand"; likewise, lines 7–8: "It wasn't about no light / it was about my ride."

Thus, alliteration is the repetition of *initial* consonant sounds; consonance is the repetition of *final* consonant sounds.

Assonance

Another kind of sound, **assonance**, is the repetition of identical vowel sounds in words whose consonants differ. It too can be initial, within a line or perhaps adjacent lines ("*under* the *umbrella*"), though internal is more usual ("*tree* by *leaf*," "*tree* and *treat*"). Its strongest effect is a subtle musical quality that often reinforces the tone of a poem, adds gradations to its feel, and contributes to levels of meaning by making connections and adding emphasis. Listen for the assonance in lines 14–16 from "Blink Your Eyes." Then reread them, thinking about its effects.

Ride when the hard time come, ride
when they're gone, in other words
the light was green.

Repetition

Repetition is the reuse of a word, group of words, line, or lines later in the same poem, but close enough so readers remember the earlier use. They may hear the later use as an echo or as a contrast created by a shift in intensity or implication, depending on the context. The lines "All depends, all depends on the skin, / all depends on the skin you're living in" repeat "all depends" and "all depends on the skin" for rhythmic effect and to build up to the climactic key phrase "on the skin you're living in." These two lines are repeated three times in the poem, intensifying their emphasis. Because these lines occur at the end of a stanza (or section), they could be called a **refrain**.

Rhyme

You are probably familiar with rhyme. Rhyme, often thought of, wrongly, as a defining characteristic of poetry, is, in fact, only one of many kinds of sound that can appear in a poem. Many poems do not rhyme. **Rhyme** is the repetition of the final vowel sound and all following consonant sounds in two or more words that have differing consonant sounds preceding the vowel, as in the words *air* and *care* in lines 30–31 from "Blink Your Eyes":

> Put your hands up in the air
> you know the routine, like you just don't care.

Rhyme leads to various effects. In the lines above, the rhymes become a bitter comic device, used to ridicule the officer who has stopped and racially profiled the speaker. In other situations, rhyme emphasizes important words; it creates a connection or a bonding; it tightens the organization and strengthens unity; it contains meaning; it provides a sense of completion, or termination, to lines, stanzas, and whole poems; and it pleases the ear through its musicality and expectation or surprise. If well written — and well read — rhyme does not distract us from the poem itself but blends with everything else in the poem. When reading a poem aloud, make sure to say the rhyming words in a way that enables a listener to hear the rhymes as echoes of sound, without letting them "steal the show."

Rhyme is described according to several categories: exact or approximate, end or internal, single or double.

EXACT OR APPROXIMATE The definition given above is for **exact rhyme**, in which the vowel and the consonant sounds following the vowel are the same: b*right* and n*ight*, *art* and he*art*, "I watch the *news*, you always *lose*."

Approximate rhyme, or **slant rhyme**, is a form of rhyme in which words contain similar sounds but do not rhyme perfectly (usually involving assonance or, more frequently, consonance): d*eep* and f*eet*; rhyme and writhe; g*ate* and m*at*; a*ll* and sto*le*, wi*ll*, or ha*le*.

END OR INTERNAL **End rhyme** involves rhyming words that occur at the ends of lines, such as *air* and *care*:

> Put your hands up in the air
> you know the routine, like you just don't care.

In **internal rhyme**, two or more words within a line, or within lines near each other, rhyme with each other, or words within lines rhyme with words at the ends:

> I watch the news, you always lose.
> You're unreliable, that's undeniable.

SINGLE OR DOUBLE   **Single rhyme** involves only the final, stressed syllable in rhyming words: *west* and *vest*, *away* and *today*.

> All depends, all depends on the *skin*,
> all depends on the *skin* you're living *in*.

In **double rhyme** the accented, rhyming syllable is followed by one or more identical, unstressed syllables: *thrilling* and *killing*, *marry* and *tarry*, *unreliable* and *undeniable*.

> I could wake up in the *morning*
> without a *warning*.

Unless specified otherwise, *rhyme* used alone means exact, end, single rhyme.

> Single rhyme used to be called **masculine rhyme** (because it was considered "strong" and "forceful"), and double rhyme was called **feminine rhyme** (because it was regarded as "weaker" than single rhyme). These labels generally are no longer used because of their sexist overtones.

The pattern of end rhymes in a poem or stanza, that is, its recurring sequence, is called its **rhyme scheme**. The pattern is usually described by assigning a letter to each word sound, the same word sounds having the same letter. For poems in stanzas, the pattern is usually the same for each stanza. In that case, you need to mark the rhyme scheme only once. Thus the rhyme scheme of Samuel Hazo's "For Fawzi in Jerusalem" (p. 795) is *abcba*.

SOUNDS SUGGESTING MEANING   There has long been debate among students of language about the suggestive quality of sounds themselves. Attempts have been made to associate individual vowel and consonant sounds with specific feelings or meanings: high vowels ($\bar{e}$, $\breve{i}$,), for example, with excitement (*scream*, *giddy*); low vowels (*ou*, *oo*) with power or gloominess; the nasal consonants (*m, n, ng*) with warm, positive associations (*mother*); *sn* with usually unpleasant things (*snake*, *sneer*); and *st* with strong, stable, energetic things. Those attempts have been countered with claims that meanings are being read into the sounds, rather than the sounds shaping meaning. In either case, something meaningful and interesting is being created or elicited by sound.

ONOMATOPOEIA   Beyond the notion that vowels and consonants can be associated with a feeling or meaning is the concept of **onomatopoeia**, words whose pronunciation suggests their meaning. Samuel Johnson, in the eighteenth century, described it this way: "Every language has some words framed to exhibit the noises which they express, as *thump, rattle, growl, hiss*." Onomatopoeia, at its best, involves not just individual words but entire passages that carry their meaning in their sounds. Listen to these lines from "The Princess" by Alfred, Lord Tennyson: "The moan of doves in immemorial elms, / And murmuring of innumerable bees." Reread Maxine Kumin's "The Sound of Night" (p. 553) and notice her effective use of onomatopoetic language such as "chitter noise," "huggermugger crowd," "skitter across," and "squeak, chirp, dip, and skim."

SOUNDS FITTING MEANING   The important thing to notice is that sounds in a poem do generally seem to fit the meanings being expressed. Alexander Pope illustrated that point in his poem "An Essay on Criticism" (1711) by suggesting differences in the sounds of the words used to describe a gentle breeze and a fierce storm: "Soft is the strain when Zephyr gently blows" and "The hoarse, rough verse shou'd like the Torrent roar." For an active reader of poetry, therefore, listening attentively to the sounds of words and syllables is a step toward understanding the meaning those words are creating.

www
Further explore voice, tone, and sound, including interactive exercises, with VirtuaLit Poetry at bedfordstmartins.com/ approachinglit.

☑ CHECKLIST on Reading for Voice, Tone, and Sound

❑ Listen for the voice of the speaker, if the speaker and poet are almost the same, or for the voice of the speaker and the voice of the poem if they are different. In either case, listen for the intelligence and sensibility that has invented, arranged, and expressed the elements and ideas in a particular manner.

❑ Listen for the tone: the tone of voice or attitude toward the subject or situation in the poem (playful, serious, ironic, cheerful, pessimistic, sorrowful, and so forth).

❑ Listen for irony: an expression involving a discrepancy or incongruity between appearance and reality, between what is said and what is intended. In poetry, verbal irony (saying what is nearly opposite of what is meant) is used most often, though situational irony (things turning out not as hoped or expected) is frequent as well.

❑ Listen for and respond to patterns of sound, such as alliteration (repetition of initial consonant sounds), consonance (repetition of all consonant sounds or of final consonant sounds), assonance (repetition of identical vowel sounds), rhyme (repetition of the accented vowel sound of a word and all succeeding sounds), onomatopoeia (words whose pronunciation suggests their meaning), and repetitions (of words, phrases, or lines).

FURTHER READING

ENTRY POINTS   Poetry provides many people—published and unpublished authors—a way to "give voice to" things they are not able to express, or to express adequately, any other way. As you read the poems below, in addition to paying attention to voice and sounds, listen for and keep in mind what the poet is giving voice to. In the following two poems, former soldiers wrestle with their feelings about World War I and the Vietnam War.

Wilfred Owen   1893–1918
Dulce et Decorum Est   [1920]

Bent double, like old beggars under sacks,
Knock-kneed, coughing like hags, we cursed through sludge,
Till on the haunting flares we turned our backs
And towards our distant rest began to trudge.
Men marched asleep. Many had lost their boots   5
But limped on, blood-shod. All went lame; all blind;
Drunk with fatigue; deaf even to the hoots
Of tired, outstripped Five-Nines° that dropped behind.

Gas! GAS! Quick, boys!—An ecstasy of fumbling,
Fitting the clumsy helmets just in time;   10
But someone still was yelling out and stumbling
And flound'ring like a man in fire or lime . . .
Dim, through the misty panes° and thick green light,
As under a green sea, I saw him drowning.

In all my dreams, before my helpless sight,   15
He plunges at me, guttering, choking, drowning.

If in some smothering dreams you too could pace
Behind the wagon that we flung him in,
And watch the white eyes writhing in his face,
His hanging face, like a devil's sick of sin;   20
If you could hear, at every jolt, the blood
Come gargling from the froth-corrupted lungs,
Obscene as cancer, bitter as the cud
Of vile, incurable sores on innocent tongues,—
My friend, you would not tell with such high zest   25
To children ardent for some desperate glory,

---

8. Five-Nines: 5.9-inch caliber shells.   **13. misty panes:** Of a gas mask.

The old Lie: Dulce et decorum est
Pro patria mori.°

———————————

27–28. Dulce . . . mori: It is sweet and fitting / to die for one's country (Horace, *Odes* 3.12.13).

APPROACHING THE READING

1. Summarize what the speaker is describing and reflecting on in the poem, what he is "giving voice to." If you are uncertain about any sections or lines, ask questions about them.

2. Describe the speaker/voice of the poem. The poem looks back at the incident it describes. (From how much later, do you think? Does it matter?) What difference does it make to have it told from a later point? How do you think the distance in time has affected the speaker?

3. Consider the speaker's use of second person beginning in line 17. On the original draft of the poem, a dedication "To Jessie Pope" is scratched out and replaced with "To a certain Poetess." Jessie Pope published patriotic poems in a popular London newspaper during World War I. Neither dedication was included in published versions of "Dulce et Decorum Est." How does knowledge of the dedication affect your reading of the poem? Should "you" and "My friend" be limited to Jessie Pope?

4. Pick out uses of alliteration, assonance, and rhyme. What do such sound techniques contribute to the effect of the poem? Specifically, what tone is achieved by rhyming "glory" with the Latin word for "to die"?

Research this author in depth with cultural documents and multimedia resources on LiterActive.

Yusef Komunyakaa b. 1947

Facing It   [1988]

My black face fades,
hiding inside the black granite.
I said I wouldn't,
dammit: No tears.
I'm stone. I'm flesh.   5
My clouded reflection eyes me
like a bird of prey, the profile of night
slanted against morning. I turn
this way — the stone lets me go.
I turn that way — I'm inside   10
the Vietnam Veterans Memorial

again, depending on the light
to make a difference.
I go down the 58,022 names,
half-expecting to find   15
my own in letters like smoke.
I touch the name Andrew Johnson;
I see the booby trap's white flash.
Names shimmer on a woman's blouse
but when she walks away   20
the names stay on the wall.
Brushstrokes flash, a red bird's
wings cutting across my stare.
The sky. A plane in the sky.
A white vet's image floats   25
closer to me, then his pale eyes
look through mine. I'm a window.
He's lost his right arm
inside the stone. In the black mirror
a woman's trying to erase names: 30
No, she's brushing a boy's hair.

APPROACHING THE READING

1. Characterize the speaker of the voice you hear in the poem. What can you
   tell about the speaker's experiences and feelings?
2. How does the title fit the poem and the speaker? How does the last line fit?
3. Discuss the tone of the poem and point to specific details or techniques that
   help shape it.
4. If you have not visited the Vietnam Veterans Memorial in Washington,
   D.C., look at pictures of it and read about it (you can do both on the Web or
   in books). Talk to someone who has seen it, if you can. Reflect on how all
   this helps you visualize and experience the poem more fully.
5. Pick out examples of sound techniques such as alliteration, assonance,
   rhyme. What do such sound techniques contribute to the effect of the poem?

ENTRY POINTS   Part of what many poems, like the two above, give voice
to is the way that our feelings about things are varied and complicated, not
simple and straightforward. The tone in a poem, as a result, often changes and
is usually complex. That is the case in the following two poems. One is about a
departure (leaving the church); the other is about a nondeparture (the benefits of not going abroad). On the surface, both could be viewed as lighter than
the two previous poems, but there is complexity below that surface, leading us
to ask in what way and how seriously we ought to take what each is saying.

Richard Garcia b. 1941

Why I Left the Church   [1993]

Maybe it was
because the only time
I hit a baseball
it smashed the neon cross
on the church across   5
the street. Even
twenty-five years later
when I saw Father Harris
I would wonder
if he knew it was me.   10
Maybe it was the demon-stoked
rotisseries of purgatory
where we would roast
hundreds of years
for the smallest of sins.   15
Or was it the day
I wore my space helmet
to catechism? Clear plastic
with a red-and-white
inflatable rim.   20
Sister Mary Bernadette
pointed toward the door
and said, "Out! Come back
when you're ready."
I rose from my chair   25
and kept rising
toward the ceiling
while the children
screamed and Sister
kept crossing herself.   30
The last she saw of me
was my shoes disappearing
through cracked plaster.
I rose into the sky and beyond.
It is a good thing   35
I am wearing my helmet,
I thought as I floated
and turned in the blackness
and brightness of outer space,
my body cold on one side and hot   40
on the other. It would

have been very quiet
if my blood had not been
rumbling in my ears so loud.
I remember thinking,   45
Maybe I will come back
when I'm ready.
But I won't tell
the other children
what it was like.   50
I'll have to make something up.

APPROACHING THE READING

1. Listen carefully to the voice of the poem. How would you describe it? Do you think the speaker is the same as the poet? Why are you sure? Why are you not sure?
2. The speaker is looking back at things that happened earlier in his life. How would you describe the speaker's feeling toward himself as the kid in the poem?
3. The speaker offers several possibilities for why he left the church. Why do you think he left? Why doesn't he give a straightforward explanation?
4. Describe the tone or tones within the poem. What is it that justifies calling the poem complex in tone?
5. The poem's poignancy and humor are inseparable. Think about why that is realistic and why it is an effectively appropriate fusion for this poem.

Billy Collins   b. 1941

Consolation   [1995]

How agreeable it is not to be touring Italy this summer,
wandering her cities and ascending her torrid hill towns.
How much better to cruise these local, familiar streets,
fully grasping the meaning of every road sign and billboard
and all the sudden hand gestures of my compatriots.   5

There are no abbeys here, no crumbling frescoes or famous
domes and there is no need to memorize a succession
of kings or tour the dripping corners of a dungeon.
No need to stand around a sarcophagus, see Napoleon's
little bed on Elba, or view the bones of a saint under glass.   10

How much better to command the simple precinct of home
than be dwarfed by pillar, arch, and basilica.

Why hide my head in phrase books and wrinkled maps?
Why feed scenery into a hungry, one-eyed camera
eager to eat the world one monument at a time?   15

Instead of slouching in a café ignorant of the word for ice,
I will head down to the coffee shop and the waitress
known as Dot. I will slide into the flow of the morning
paper, all language barriers down,
rivers of idiom running freely, eggs over easy on the way.   20

And after breakfast, I will not have to find someone
willing to photograph me with my arm around the owner.
I will not puzzle over the bill or record in a journal
what I had to eat and how the sun came in the window.
It is enough to climb back into the car   25

as if it were the great car of English itself
and sounding my loud vernacular horn, speed off
down a road that will never lead to Rome, not even Bologna.

APPROACHING THE READING

1. Pay attention to the details in the poem, to the way they set up a "here vs. there" contrast. In what ways does it seem agreeable not to be in Italy "this summer"? In what ways does it seem being in Italy might in fact be agreeable?
2. Describe the voice in the poem. Do you think the speaker is the same as the poet? Why or why not?
3. Consider the title. Is there consolation here? If so, what kind of consolation is it?
4. Think about tone in the poem. What is complex about it? Is there irony in the poem? If so, describe how it works.
5. The poem is partly about language (find several examples in the first four stanzas). Look closely at the final four lines, especially the analogy in lines 26–27: "as if it were the great car of English itself / and sounding my loud vernacular horn." What is the point being made in these lines? Describe their tone or tones.

ENTRY POINTS   The following poem is based on events that occurred in the life of Alfonso II, Duke of Ferrara in sixteenth-century northern Italy. The speaker is the duke. He is giving a guest a personal guided tour of his palace and pauses to show him a portrait of his previous wife painted by a fictitious but supposedly famous painter, Frà (that is, "brother," or monk) Pandolf. Ferrara's first wife, Lucrezia, died in 1561 at age seventeen after three years of marriage. We overhear what he says about the painting and about her. From that we are left to determine what he is like, what she was like, who the guest is, and why the duke says what he does.

Robert Browning   1812–1889

My Last Duchess   [1842]

Ferrara

That's my last Duchess painted on the wall,
Looking as if she were alive. I call
That piece a wonder, now: Frà Pandolf's hands
Worked busily a day, and there she stands.
Will't please you sit and look at her? I said   5
"Frà Pandolf" by design, for never read
Strangers like you that pictured countenance,
The depth and passion of its earnest glance,
But to myself they turned (since none puts by
The curtain I have drawn for you, but I)   10
And seemed as they would ask me, if they durst,
How such a glance came there; so, not the first
Are you to turn and ask thus. Sir, 'twas not
Her husband's presence only, called that spot
Of joy into the Duchess' cheek: perhaps   15
Frà Pandolf chanced to say "Her mantle laps
Over my lady's wrist too much," or "Paint
Must never hope to reproduce the faint
Half-flush that dies along her throat": such stuff
Was courtesy, she thought, and cause enough   20
For calling up that spot of joy. She had
A heart—how shall I say?—too soon made glad,
Too easily impressed; she liked whate'er
She looked on, and her looks went everywhere.
Sir, 'twas all one! My favour at her breast,   25
The dropping of the daylight in the West,
The bough of cherries some officious fool
Broke in the orchard for her, the white mule
She rode with round the terrace—all and each
Would draw from her alike the approving speech,   30
Or blush, at least. She thanked men,—good! but thanked
Somehow—I know not how—as if she ranked
My gift of a nine-hundred-year-old name

With anybody's gift. Who'd stoop to blame
This sort of trifling? Even had you skill   35
In speech — (which I have not) — to make your will
Quite clear to such an one, and say, "Just this
Or that in you disgusts me; here you miss,
Or there exceed the mark" — and if she let
Herself be lessoned so, nor plainly set   40
Her wits to yours, forsooth, and made excuse,
— E'en then would be some stooping; and I choose
Never to stoop. Oh sir, she smiled, no doubt,
Whene'er I passed her; but who passed without
Much the same smile? This grew; I gave commands;   45
Then all smiles stopped together. There she stands
As if alive. Will't please you rise? We'll meet
The company below, then. I repeat,
The Count your master's known munificence
Is ample warrant that no just pretence   50
Of mine for dowry will be disallowed;
Though his fair daughter's self, as I avowed
At starting, is my object. Nay, we'll go
Together down, sir. Notice Neptune, though,
Taming a sea-horse, thought a rarity,   55
Which Claus of Innsbruck° cast in bronze for me!

---

56. **Claus of Innsbruck:** A fictional sculptor.

APPROACHING THE READING

1. In a dramatic monologue, you listen to the voice of a character speaking in a setting and situation. What are they like in this poem? Who is the duke talking to in the poem? Try thinking in terms of "a person who . . ." Some dramatic movement and action takes place. Summarize what's going on.

2. The point of a dramatic monologue is that the speaker's voice and what it says reveal his or her character. What sort of person is the duke? Point out the details that lead you to your conclusions about him.

3. What the duke says also reveals all that we can know about the duchess. What sort of person was she? What happened to her?

Research this author in depth with cultural documents and multimedia resources on *LiterActive.*

4. Consider tone in the poem. What is the duke's attitude toward the duchess? What is the poem's attitude toward the duke?

5. This is a good poem for reviewing the techniques of sound. Look for examples of alliteration and assonance; think about what they contribute to

the effect of the poem. The poem is written in couplets, two consecutive lines of poetry with the same end rhyme, though the rhyme is not so obvious because of the use of run-on lines (see p. 656). What does the rhyme add to the poem? How would its effect be different if it did not rhyme or if the rhyme was more obvious?

RESPONDING THROUGH Writing

WRITING ABOUT VOICE, TONE, AND SOUND

Journal Entries

1. Reflect on the variety of voices we hear during an average day. Often we're bombarded with voices: from radios or TVs, at home, on the street, on a bus, in class. The list could go on and on. To some we give close attention; others we pretty much ignore. In your journal, write a list of voices you notice during a morning or even an hour. Note which ones you pay attention to and which you don't. Of the ones you do pay attention to, reflect on what matters about the quality of each voice — whether it's interesting, engaging, honest, pleasant, appealing, and so on.

   > **www**
   > Research the authors in this chapter with LitLinks at bedfordstmartins.com/ approachinglit.

2. The same techniques for word sounds discussed in this chapter are also very important in the world of advertising. As you read or hear advertisements during a day or a few hours, keep track of techniques you notice (alliteration, assonance, repetition, rhyme, and so forth). Jot notes describing the effects the techniques achieve.

3. Take a poem and change some of the diction (words) to alter the tone. Write a journal entry describing what you did and why the effect of the poem now is different.

Literary Analysis Papers

4. Write a paper on the voice and tone, or shifts in them, in Robert Hayden's "Those Winter Sundays" (p. 548), Elizabeth Bishop's "In the Waiting Room" (p. 742), Agha Shahid Ali's "I Dream It Is Afternoon When I Return to Delhi" (p. 734), Eavan Boland's "The Pomegranate" (p. 748), Gary Soto's "The Elements of San Joaquin" (p. 734), or another poem of your choice.

5. Write a paper discussing techniques of sound and their effect in Robert Browning's "My Last Duchess" (p. 595), Leslie Marmon Silko's "Prayer to the Pacific" (p. 614), Samuel Taylor Coleridge's "Kubla Khan" (p. 761), Samuel Hazo's "For Fawzi in Jerusalem" (p. 795), Alberto Ríos's "Nani" (p. 847), or another poem of your choice.

6. Write a paper discussing the character of the speaker in T. S. Eliot's "The Love Song of J. Alfred Prufrock" (p. 776). The poem is usually regarded as a dramatic monologue, but readers differ on whether it uses interior monologue. If you think it does, show how that contributes to characterization and the effect of the poem.

Comparison-Contrast Papers

7. Write a paper on Wilfred Owen's "Dulce et Decorum Est" (p. 589) and Richard Lovelace's "To Lucasta, Going to the Wars" (p. 817), exploring what you discover about similarities and differences in what they say about war and in how they express their ideas through voice, tone, and sound.
8. Write a paper in which you compare and contrast the way William Blake's "The Chimney Sweeper" (p. 744) and Ana Castillo's "I Heard the Cries of Two Hundred Children" (p. 753) deal with the exploitation or neglect of children, comparing and contrasting how each uses voice, tone, and sound to convey a similar message to audiences from different eras.

> ### ➤ TIPS for Writing about Voice, Tone, and Sound
>
> ➤ **Hear the poem** Poems often are meant to be heard. As part of your preparation for writing, read the poem aloud several times, listening for its voice, tone, and sound dimensions; then listen while someone else reads it aloud to you.
>
> ➤ **Focus on tone** Tone can be an interesting topic especially when the tone is unusual or complex or one that changes or shifts in intensity as you move through the poem.
>
> ➤ **Sounds' effects** The use of sounds (alliteration, assonance, repetition, rhyme) can be a challenging paper topic, especially for poems that make prominent use of such devices — but even their absence can be worth attention as a topic or subtopic in a paper. In addition to describing what devices are used, your paper should consider how they are used, to what degree, and in what contexts and discuss in what ways they are appropriate for what the poem is dealing with.
>
> ➤ **Illustrations and explanations** A paper on voice, tone, or sound must include quotations that illustrate the relevant points you are making. You also will want to explain how the effects of voice, tone, or sound are achieved, what goes into creating those effects.
>
> ➤ **Relationship to effect or theme** A crucial part in any paper on voice, tone, or sound must be a discussion of how that element contributes to the effect, theme, or significance of the poem.

WRITING ABOUT CONNECTIONS

Although this chapter focuses particularly on poems' use of voice, tone, and sound, those aspects can also be useful in exploring poems thematically. Interesting paper topics that lead to fresh insights can result from making connections between poems, especially ones from different eras. Here are a few possibilities:

1. "All the Comforts of Home": Contrasting Spirits of Adventure in Billy Collins's "Consolation" (p. 593) and Alfred, Lord Tennyson's "Ulysses" (p. 864)
2. "Arms and the Man": War without Glory in Wilfred Owen's "Dulce et Decorum Est" (p. 589) and Vievee Francis's "Private Smith's Primer" (p. 784)
3. "Dancing with the Dark": Movement and Memory in Theodore Roethke's "My Papa's Waltz" (p. 577) and Cornelius Eady's "My Mother, If She Had Won Free Dance Lessons" (p. 775)

WRITING RESEARCH PAPERS

1. Research racial profiling and, if possible, talk to people who have experienced it. Write a paper discussing Sekou Sundiata's "Blink Your Eyes" (p. 582) in light of what you discover.
2. Conduct interviews with at least two war veterans. Listen to the way they talk about their experiences as well as to what they say. Write a paper discussing similarities and/or differences between their ways of "voicing" their experiences and that in Wilfred Owen's "Dulce et Decorum Est" (p. 589) or Yosef Komunyakaa's "Facing It" (p. 590).

COMPOSING IN OTHER ART FORMS

1. Compose a piece of music that evokes the tones of Maxine Kumin's "The Sound of Night" (p. 553), Samuel Hazo's "For Fawzi in Jerusalem" (p. 795), Gary Miranda's "Love Poem" (p. 668), or another poem of your choice.
2. If you're not interested in composing music, pick out a piece of music that captures the tones of one of the poems mentioned in question 5 on page 597 or of another poem of your choice. Write a journal entry explaining why you chose it.

That's something which is not always recognized, the freeing effect of a lot of traditional techniques. Richard Wilbur

CHAPTER **14** **Form and Type**
Delighting in Design

Think of the effect when a well-designed Internet site appears on the screen — how it catches your eye, grabs your attention, and makes you want to explore the site further. We notice such effective uses of shape or layout every day all around us. The same quality, the immediate impression made by form, is true also of poetry: The impact of visual design, along with internal design, is often part of its appeal. The word *form* is used for "design" in both internal and external construction. **Form** can refer to external structure, the way the poem looks on the page — which may relate to the type of poem it is (to its "genre") and to what the poem is dealing with. It can refer also to the inner structure that arranges, organizes, or connects the various elements in a work. Every poem has form, in both senses. This chapter helps you see poems more distinctly and completely by discussing the role of form and of poetic types, as well as what form may mean, embody, express, or reveal in a given poem.

In some cases, poets start out with an external form in mind and work to blend the words of the poem with this form. It may be an "inherited" form related to or demanded by the type, or "genre," of poem the poet wants to write — perhaps a haiku or a sonnet or a villanelle. In other cases, instead of starting with a form in mind, poets begin with an image, feeling, experience, or idea, or with a few words or lines. The writing itself leads to or creates the form, both the inner arrangement and the external shape. The form, therefore, is a result of working with the other elements of poetry.

READING FOR LINES

Perhaps the most obvious aspect of the external shape of a poem involves its division into **lines**. Most poems are written in lines, and each line normally focuses our attention and holds something of significance to the whole poem. Lines offer additional opportunities for effect. In prose, the layout on the page is controlled by margins. Poets, however, control the beginnings and ends of lines — positions that can confer added attention, anticipation, and emphasis. Each line also creates a rhythm, what Ezra Pound called "the musical phrase."

Lines can interplay with sentences, becoming units of rhythm discovered or decided on within a sentence. Lineation invites you to read line by line, feeling the musicality with each; but you also need to read "past" the lines to follow the meaning of the sentences. This superimposing of lines on sentences also directs our attention to words that might get passed over. Watch for this in the following poem.

Gwendolyn Brooks   1917–2000

We Real Cool   [1960]

The Pool Players.
Seven at the Golden Shovel.

We real cool. We
Left school. We

Lurk late. We
Strike straight. We

Sing sin. We   5
Thin gin. We

Jazz June. We
Die soon.

APPROACHING THE READING

1. Read the poem aloud, pausing at the end of each line by emphasizing the *We*. Don't let your voice drop, since the sentence continues in the next line.
2. What is the effect of dividing the sentences into two lines?
3. What is the effect of starting each new sentence at the end of each line?

Research this author in depth with cultural documents and multimedia resources on *LiterActive*.

4. Notice the cumulative effect of the various things the pool players at the Golden Shovel boast about doing. What poetic devices are used to unify and build the intensity of the lines?
5. What is the effect of having a deliberate rhyme scheme (see p. 587), even a typical end rhyme format? How is it affected by the addition of the repeated *We* at the line's end?
6. Notice the last line, lacking the *We* and the third beat. What effect does this create?

The unusual line breaks create anticipation and a jazzlike rhythm; they place emphasis on both the subjects and predicates of the sentences; and they lead to the isolated and unsettling last line. Test the effect of the poem's line breaks and the importance of its form by reading it this way:

We real cool.
We left school.

We lurk late.
We strike straight.

We sing sin.
We thin gin.

We jazz June.
We die soon.

The words are the same, but it is not the same poem. Changing the form of a poem gives it a different effect and makes it a different work. Form is integral to poetry, as it is to all art.

Part of the pleasure for us as readers is that we can respond to the rhythms of lines, can notice and feel how certain words get emphasized by their position in the line, can appreciate the interplay between line and sentence, and can recognize and experience the role of each line in the life of a poem. Notice and feel the rhythms and emphases in the lines as they are used in varying ways throughout the rest of this chapter.

Not all poems are separated into lines: **Prose poems** are a notable exception. The prose poem works with all the elements of poetry except line. It is often written in common paragraph form. It is a hybrid form, drawing together some of the best aspects of both prose and poetry, creating new possibilities out of the challenges presented by the way it fuses the two forms. For examples of prose poems, see Carolyn Forché's "The Colonel" (p. 783), Vievee Francis's "Private Smith's Primer" (p. 784), and A. Van Jordan's "From" (p. 806).

READING FOR STANZAS

Another thing you may notice as you look at certain poems is the presence of stanzas. A **stanza** is a grouping of poetic lines into a section, set off by a space, either according to a given form — each section having the same number of lines and the same arrangement of line lengths, meter, and rhyme — or according to shifts in thought, moment, setting, effect, voice, time, and so on, creating units comparable to paragraphs in prose. The word *stanza* derives from the Italian word for "room," so one could say that stanzas are "rooms" into which some poems are divided. In some poems, all the "rooms" look alike; in other poems, they differ from each other.

INVENTED STANZA FORMS   Stanza shapes can be *invented*, that is, individually created, unique to a particular poem. The poet may plan out such a stanza form before beginning to write or may create it in the process of writing. Look again at "We Real Cool" (p. 601). Probably no other poem in existence has stanzas just like these. Perhaps the first stanza found its own form, without conscious attention to it; perhaps Brooks initially wrote

We real cool.
We left school.

and then realized the powerful effect of ending the lines with *We*. If so, at that point Brooks began consciously thinking about the form and making the other stanzas fit the form she had "found" for the first one.

INHERITED STANZA FORMS   Many stanza patterns, however, are not invented but *inherited*: handed down through the centuries, from one generation of poets to another, often with a prescribed meter and sometimes a set rhyme scheme. The most frequently used inherited stanza forms, in the past and today, are four-line stanzas called **quatrains**. One variety of quatrain, the **ballad stanza**, has a long history, used in traditional ballads for many centuries. The ballad stanza is a simple but easily adaptable form — four-line stanzas rhyming *abcb* with eight syllables in the first and third lines, six in the second and fourth. Perhaps it is easier to visualize in diagram form (each square equals one syllable):

Look for that structure in the following poem (in some of its lines you will find an extra syllable — that's typical of the form).

Countee Cullen 1903–1946

Incident [1925]

for Eric Walrond°

Once riding in old Baltimore,
    Heart-filled, head-filled with glee,
I saw a Baltimorean
    Keep looking straight at me.

Now I was eight and very small,   5
    And he was no whit bigger,
And so I smiled, but he poked out
    His tongue, and called me, "Nigger."

I saw the whole of Baltimore
    From May until December;   10
Of all the things that happened there
    That's all that I remember.

Eric Walrond: Walrond (1898–1966) was a writer and activist in the New York literary community from the early 1920s.

APPROACHING THE READING

1. Notice that each stanza is made up of one sentence. What is the effect of the spaces after lines 4 and 8 that divide the poem into three stanzas? How would the poem read differently if it were a single unit of twelve lines, without stanza breaks? Explain.

2. Each sentence is divided into four lines. On the one hand, we need to read past the lines and grasp the meaning of the sentence as a whole. But we also should give attention to the lines as units. What is the effect of the division into lines? What is lost when you read straight through without such divisions?

Traditionally, ballad stanzas were used for narrative poems, often tragic stories with a melancholy tone. Cullen's use of the form seems appropriate: Like the early folk ballads, it tells a sad story, with a distinctly melancholy tone. A great deal of the poem's emotional power is generated by its form. The stanzas divide the incident into three distinct segments, each building to a climax. The lines help control the rhythm, leading us to pause after each line and focus on each statement individually, letting its point sink in. And the words at the end of the second and fourth lines in each stanza receive strong emphasis, from their position in the stanzas and from the rhyme. The poem opens with an "old world" sense of decorum conveying the child's natural excitement, void of any apprehension. Then comes the "incident" and we move to the speaker's later realization: that no matter how much positive experience he accumulates, it is the impact of cruelty that is remembered. The word *incident* usually carries a connotation of inconsequence. The irony of Cullen's title is certainly bitter.

> Other stanza forms are used less frequently. Some well-known inherited examples are described in the Glossary (pp. 1609–27). Look, for example, at **Chaucerian stanza**, **ottava rima**, **Spenserian stanza**, and **terza rima**.

INHERITED POETIC TYPES   In addition to inheriting stanza patterns, poems can inherit patterns for the entire poem. The poet may plan from the beginning to use an inherited form, perhaps setting out to write a poem in a preset pattern such as a sestina or a sonnet. The poet may feel the traditional form is most appropriate for the subject. Or the poet may want to participate in a centuries-old poetic tradition, to refresh an inherited form, to embody meaning within the form, or to meet the challenge of working within the form's requirements. The opportunities offered by a prescribed form can lead a writer's imagination to come up with something it likely would not have without the "pressure" of the form.

Or the poet may think about an inherited form while writing — may start with a subject or images but no particular form in mind, and then discover that an effective way the poem can develop is as a sonnet, as a sestina, as couplets, or as a variation on a particular form. In such cases, the poet discovers that the material "needs" or perhaps even "demands" that form, or the poet may realize that the form may be the perfect "fit" for that poem.

READING SONNETS

Some inherited forms have become well known as types of poems significant in their own right. The one you are likely to encounter most often is the **sonnet**. These fourteen-line poems originally were lyrical love poems, but they came to be used also for meditations on death and nature. Poets now use the sonnet form for all subjects. In English, they are usually written in lines of ten syllables each, the odd ones unstressed (traditionally indicated by ˘) and the even ones stressed (´) — more on this can be found in Chapter 16 (pp. 659–62) and the appendix on scansion (p. 1574). You could visualize a typical sonnet as a grid of 140 squares in fourteen lines and ten columns. The poet must fit one syllable into each square, with those in the even-numbered columns usually being stressed, those in the odd-numbered columns unstressed, and the final syllables fitting a given rhyme scheme. Sonnets in English typically fall into two types, differentiated by the structure of their development and their rhyme schemes.

English (or Shakespearean) Sonnet

The **English sonnet** is formed of three quatrains (four-line units, typically rhyming *abab cdcd efef*) and a couplet (two rhyming lines), as in the following diagram:

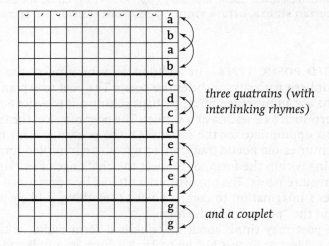

Usually the subject is introduced in the first quatrain, expanded or restated in different terms in the second, and expanded further or restated again in the third; the couplet adds a logical, pithy conclusion or a surprising twist.

ENTRY POINTS   See, for example, this sonnet by William Shakespeare. Shakespeare is known today as one of the great playwrights of all time; but in the 1590s he also wrote a good deal of lyric poetry, including 154 sonnets, all in the form that now bears his name.

William Shakespeare   1564–1616

That time of year thou mayst in me behold   [1609]

That time of year thou mayst in me behold
When yellow leaves, or none, or few, do hang
Upon those boughs which shake against the cold,

Bare ruined choirs,° where late° the sweet birds sang.   *choirstalls; lately*
In me thou seest the twilight of such day   5
As after sunset fadeth in the west,
Which by and by black night doth take away,
Death's second self, that seals up all in rest.
In me thou seest the glowing of such fire
That on the ashes of his youth doth lie,   10
As the deathbed whereon it must expire,
Consumed with that which it was nourished by.
       This thou perceiv'st, which makes thy love more strong,
       To love that well which thou must leave ere long.

APPROACHING THE READING

1. Outline the poem by summarizing the ideas developed in the quatrains and explain how they relate to
   each other.
2. Explain the relationship between lines 1–12 and the
   concluding couplet.
3. Consider how the subject matter of the poem seems appropriate to the traditional uses of the sonnet form.

> Research this author
> in depth with cultural
> documents and multimedia
> resources on *LiterActive*.

   In this case, the three quatrains express essentially the same idea — that
the speaker is getting older, approaching death — but they use different archetypal symbols (see pp. 147–48) to convey it: The first four lines describe
old age in terms of late autumn, with few leaves left on the branches; lines
5–8 describe the approach of death in terms of twilight, with darkness —
which closely resembles death — approaching; and lines 9–12 compare the
speaker's stage in life to a bed of coals, what is left of a fire that earlier had
burned brightly, consuming the firewood that nourished it. The pithy conclusion in lines 13–14 clarifies that the "thou" is not us, the readers, but
someone who cares about the speaker and who loves him not less as he
grows older and less "lovely" but more because it is clear that they do not
have all that much time left together.

   ENTRY POINTS   Here is another sonnet in Shakespearean form, written
in response to a summer of antiblack violence in several cities, particularly
Chicago. McKay said later that the poem did not refer directly to blacks and
whites.

Claude McKay   1890–1948

If we must die   [1919]

If we must die, let it not be like hogs
Hunted and penned in an inglorious spot,
While round us bark the mad and hungry dogs,
Making their mock at our accursed lot.
If we must die, O let us nobly die,   5
So that our precious blood may not be shed
In vain; then even the monsters we defy
Shall be constrained to honor us though dead!
O kinsmen! we must meet the common foe!
Though far outnumbered let us show us brave,   10
And for their thousand blows deal one deathblow!
What though before us lies the open grave?
Like men we'll face the murderous, cowardly pack,
Pressed to the wall, dying, but fighting back!

APPROACHING THE READING

1. Outline the movement of the poem's inspiring challenge to the speaker's comrades, quatrain by quatrain, as we did with the Shakespeare sonnet above. Note the way sentences are used to structure the four sections of the poem.
2. Consider the appropriateness of using a traditional sonnet for the poem's subject. Why is it effective to use a prescribed form for such an emotional situation?
3. Imagine the poem without meter, rhyme, and these specific line breaks. In what ways does its actual form contribute to its effect? What things might it lose if it were written in a freer form?
4. What ironies are suggested by having an African American voice speak within this most Anglo of poetic forms?

Whether intended or not, much of this poem's power comes from the juxtaposition of the passionate voice expressing intense feeling with this most traditional and exact of poetic forms. One can ask if the form adds to and amplifies what is being said, if it is a way to reveal the speaker's ability to balance passion and reason, or if the form depicts a confining of the speaker, something the voice is being constrained by, something the voice wants to break down. Notice how the intensity of feeling alters the traditional form: The third quatrain does not repeat or expand the subject of the first two quatrains; instead, it makes explicit what was implied in the "If we must die" quatrains — we must fight back aggressively, even if it means dying in the attempt. The closing couplet is not a pithy summary or surprising twist, but a trumpetlike call to action. Perhaps the intensity of feelings being expressed in the poem forced this African American writer to break from the traditional pattern handed down from sonneteers in the past.

Italian (or Petrarchan) Sonnet

The **Italian sonnet** is composed of an **octave** (an eight-line unit), rhyming *abbaabba*, and a **sestet** (a six-line unit), often rhyming *cdecde* or *cd-cdcd*, though variations are frequent.

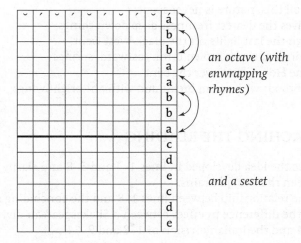

an octave (with
enwrapping
rhymes)

and a sestet

The octave usually develops an idea or question or problem; then the poem pauses or "turns," and the sestet completes the idea, answers the question, or resolves the difficulty. See, for example, Gary Miranda's "Love Poem" (p. 668) and the following poem.

ENTRY POINTS   Gerard Manley Hopkins is recognized as one of the most important poets in English, admired both for his theories concerning rhythm (what he called "Sprung Rhythm") and for his religious poetry. He was a member of the Church of England until 1866, when he converted to Roman Catholicism. In 1877, he was ordained a Catholic priest. Almost all of the poetry he wrote after becoming a Catholic was, though seldom dogmatic, deeply religious in nature. The octet of "God's Grandeur" declares that the beauty of the world is a reflection of God's glory and expresses profound concern that humankind has not respected and taken adequate care of that world. The sestet then affirms that, despite such neglect, God continues to love and nurture it.

Gerard Manley Hopkins   1844–1889

God's Grandeur   [*1877*; 1918]

The world is charged with the grandeur of God.
   It will flame out, like shining from shook foil;°   *shaken gold foil*
   It gathers to a greatness, like the ooze of oil°   *from olives*
Crushed. Why do men then now not reck° his rod?°   *recognize; discipline*
Generations have trod, have trod, have trod;   5
   And all is seared with trade; bleared, smeared with toil;
   And wears man's smudge and shares man's smell: the soil
Is bare now, nor can foot feel, being shod.

And, for° all this, nature is never spent;   *despite*
   There lives the dearest freshness deep down things;   10
And though the last lights off the black West went
   Oh, morning, at the brown brink eastward, springs —
Because the Holy Ghost over the bent
   World broods with warm breast and with ah! bright wings.

APPROACHING THE READING

1. Summarize the idea developed in lines 1–4 and 5–8 and clarify the connection between the two quatrains.
2. Explain the relationship between lines 1–8 and the concluding sestet.
3. Consider the difference in effect between a Shakespearean division of 1–12 and 13–14 and the Italian division of 1–8 and 9–14.

The opening quatrain affirms that the natural world, in its great beauty, is filled with — loaded to capacity with — God's glory. It should be unmissable — it should flash in our eyes the way sunlight shines off a piece of gold foil; it collects around us the way olive oil emerges as olives are crushed. Yet, people ignore God by neglecting their responsibility to the world God created. The second quatrain images that neglect: For generations people have focused on trade, industry, and self-advancement. That they are out of touch with nature is signaled by shoes: No longer do we feel the soil and thus care about its condition.

    The sestet is set off by a space, as if the speaker pauses to draw a big breath and then give vent to an outburst of praise and affirmation: No matter what human beings do to the earth, they will never eliminate God from it. Even if they destroy all human life, put out the "last lights," and leave the planet in darkness, God's presence will be there still, arising as the light of a new day. The poem concludes by comparing God's constant, caring presence to a mother bird brooding over her newborn chicks, but with the bright wings of an angel.

The tight, orderly traditional form of the sonnet seems fitting for a poem conveying a sense of orderliness — that God has a plan for the world itself that humans should not violate. The rhythms and sounds are intensified by their confinement in a compressed space: The energy of the poem seems to burst out as the reader opens the poem.

ENTRY POINTS   Here is another example of a sonnet in Italian form. This sonnet also celebrates beauty in the world, but beauty of a more specific kind. The poem is a paean of appreciation for the appearance and demeanor of a man who, while standing on a street in Harlem, arrests the attention of the speaker. Consider how the sonnet form in this poem compares to Hopkins's "God's Grandeur" in evoking power and intensity.

Helene Johnson   1907–1995

Sonnet to a Negro in Harlem   [1927]

You are disdainful and magnificent —
Your perfect body and your pompous gait,
Your dark eyes flashing solemnly with hate,
Small wonder that you are incompetent
To imitate those whom you so despise —   5
Your shoulders towering high above the throng,
Your head thrown back in rich, barbaric song,
Palm trees and mangoes stretched before your eyes.
Let others toil and sweat for labor's sake
And wring from grasping hands their meed° of gold.   reward 10
Why urge ahead your supercilious feet?
Scorn will efface each footprint that you make.
I love your laughter arrogant and bold.
You are too splendid for this city street.

APPROACHING THE READING

1. Notice the way the subject is adapted to the structure, with its turn after the octave. Summarize what is said in lines 1–8, in 9–12, and then in 13–14. In what ways are the form and its handling appropriate and effective?
2. In this sonnet, sentences do not coincide with the quatrains — the poem seems to be playing off against the form as well as adopting it. What makes that appropriate and effective for the content?

3. Like McKay in "If we must die" (p. 608), Johnson employs a form from the white literary tradition. What ironies do you see in that? It could be said she is claiming the form for her race as well as her purposes. Does anything in the poem support saying that?

This poem is as much about the speaker and cultural perceptions as it is about the person it is written to. Notice how the speaker shifts what the culture usually judges negatively, revealing its embodiment as "magnificent." The speaker celebrates the man's attitude and, by implication, criticizes the cultural mores as well as what causes the man's behavior. The easy "either/or" of what is proper and improper is shown to be both false and oppressive.

> There are many other inherited types of poem. Some of the well-known examples are described in the Glossary (pp. 1609–27). Look, for example, at **haiku**, **sestina**, and **villanelle**.

READING BLANK VERSE AND COUPLETS

There are also inherited patterns for nonstanzaic verse. These specify line lengths and sometimes sequences of rhyme, but not any specific separation into similar groupings of lines.

BLANK VERSE   The best known among these patterns is **blank verse** (unrhymed iambic pentameter — see pp. 660 and 662), the most widely used verse form of English poetry. Shakespeare's plays, Milton's *Paradise Lost* and *Paradise Regained*, Wordsworth's *Prelude*, and countless other long poems were composed in blank verse. Here are the inspiring closing lines from Alfred, Lord Tennyson's poem "Ulysses" (p. 864), in which the old adventurer Ulysses (Odysseus) seeks to inspire his aging comrades to leave the safety and comfort of their homes and join him in another, perhaps final, adventure, sailing westward through the Strait of Gibraltar and into the unknown sea:

Though much is taken, much abides; and though
We are not now that strength which in old days
Moved earth and heaven, that which we are, we are —
One equal temper of heroic hearts,
Made weak by time and fate, but strong in will
To strive, to seek, to find, and not to yield.

Iambic is often considered the "natural" meter of English. One of the most common and oldest explanations for the use and impact of the iambic foot is that it echoes the natural beat of the human heart. When we talk or write in English, we often fall into loose iambics that can be divided into groups about ten syllables long. Many say that is the primary reason it is so widely used.

COUPLETS Another important inherited form, **couplets** (two lines rhyming), can be grouped into stanzas (as in A. E. Housman's "To an Athlete Dying Young" — p. 802), but more often they are strung out in extended, nonstanzaic passages. They provide a simple pattern, like blank verse, but because of the rhyme, the effect is different. Other poems in couplets include Robert Browning's "My Last Duchess" (p. 595), Gwendolyn Brooks's "We Real Cool" (p. 601), and Angelina Weld Grimké's "A Winter Twilight" (p. 638).

In seventeenth- and eighteenth-century England, the **heroic couplet** (couplets in iambic pentameter with a full stop, usually, at the end of the second line) was widely used for short and long poems. See, for example, Anne Bradstreet's "To My Dear and Loving Husband" (p. 749) and Jonathan Swift's "A Description of the Morning" (p. 560). Couplets also are used as parts of other forms, as, for example, the concluding lines of the English sonnet.

READING FREE VERSE

Many modern and contemporary poets do not use inherited or preplanned forms, preferring to work without a blueprint for a poem's form. They allow the entire poem to "find" its own shape. The poem may emerge from the poet's imagination and skillful intuition in the form that it needs, or the form may develop in the process of writing and revising. In either case, the poet's attention is focused primarily on other things — on images, sounds, rhythms — and the poet allows the form to develop, either consciously shaping it as it is discovered or letting it result from attention to line, line break, rhythm, and so forth.

Such poems traditionally have been called **free verse** because they are free of predetermined metrical and stanzaic patterns. The term *free verse* is misleading, however, if it is interpreted to mean "anything goes," that form and the other elements don't matter. Some books use the term **open form** to try to avoid such misunderstanding. Either term is usually acceptable. Just remember that no matter how "free" a poem appears, it *does have form.* Every poem does.

Unlike metrical or stanzaic poetry, free verse does not rely on organized structural repetition (like those of meter, rhyme, stanza, or identical syllable counts) to achieve form and coherence. Instead, it relies on connected images and sounds, parallelism in phrasing, and handlings of lines, spaces, rhythms, indentations, gaps, and timing. For the beginning poet, writing in open form may look easier than writing in inherited forms. However, each approach requires an ability to work with the elements of poetry. Each is challenging when one is aware of the complexities of writing any poem well. Each is easy only if done carelessly.

ENTRY POINTS   In the following poem, the speaker stands at the shore of the Pacific and offers thanks to the ocean for carrying her people to this land and for continuing to provide them with the gift of rain. Obviously, the poem is not written in traditional Anglo-European meter and stanza patterns; however, it is certainly influenced by tradition and an understanding of form. Reflect on how its form contributes to the effect of what it is saying.

Leslie Marmon Silko b. 1948

Prayer to the Pacific   [1981]

I traveled to the ocean
            distant
                        from my southwest land of sandrock
                        to the moving blue water
                        Big as the myth of origin.   5

Pale
pale water in the yellow-white light of
                  sun   floating west
                              to China
                        where ocean herself was born.   10
Clouds that blow across the sand are wet.

Squat in the wet sand and speak to the Ocean:
            I return to you   turquoise   the red coral you sent us,
                        sister spirit of Earth.
Four round stones in my pocket   I carry back the ocean   15
                  to suck and to taste.

Thirty thousand years ago
                  Indians came riding across the ocean
                  carried by giant sea turtles.

Waves were high that day   20
                  great sea turtles waded   slowly out
                              from the gray sundown sea.

Grandfather Turtle rolled in the sand   four times
                  and disappeared

                                swimming into the sun.   25

And so   from that time
                   immemorial,
                                as the old people say,
rain clouds drift from the west
                                gift from the ocean.   30

Green leaves in the wind
Wet earth on my feet
                swallowing raindrops
                        clear from China.

APPROACHING THE READING

1. Examine the form of the poem carefully, focusing on its visual appearance.
   Consider how the structure affects your reading of the poem, how the lines'
   placement creates a kind of choreography of movement for your eyes. How
   is this structure essential to the timing, energy, and rhythm within the
   poem?
2. Follow the way sentences run through several lines. Discuss what the juxtaposition of lines with sentences adds to the effect of the poem.
3. Why does the speaker go to the seashore to offer a prayer to the Pacific? In
   what ways is the form appropriate to the speaker and to the prayer being
   offered?

A striking formal feature of this poem is the attractiveness of its layout
on the page. To look at the poem is like observing a work of visual art, with
its clear attention to composition, design, and proportion. There is a kinetic
sense to Silko's poem, the way the lines move through our eyes and into our
actual physical nature. As we follow the movement of the lines, we can feel
in our bodies the energy, oceanic rhythm, and "flow" of the poem.

Along with such visual appeal, the poem's division into lines and its
arrangement on the page indicate how it should be read — which lines go together, where pauses amplify its impact, what particular words should be
emphasized. The poem describes the speaker's journey to the seaside to offer
a prayer to the ocean — by dropping four round stones into its waters. It is a
prayer of gratitude for the gift in the past of the ocean carrying the speaker's
ancestors to these shores on giant turtles and for the gift in the present of
carrying clouds with much-needed rain across the waters to the land the
speaker inhabits.

The use of open, seemingly organic, form to evoke a trust in the natural
world feels appropriate to the Native American stories it recounts, certainly
more appropriate than to use an inherited verse form from another culture,
such as those discussed earlier in this chapter.

READING FOR INTERNAL FORM

In addition to shape, or external form, a poem also has an *internal form*, the inner arrangement or organization of its parts and content. The variety of techniques and arrangements used by poets is extensive; we list here some of the most important ones.

Parallelism

This key organizing technique is used in conjunction with other ways of handling inner form. **Parallelism** can be considered in two ways: (1) When elements of equal weight within phrases, sentences, or paragraphs are expressed in a similar grammatical order and structure. It can appear within a line or pair of lines: "And he was always quietly arrayed, / And he was always human when he talked" — Edwin Arlington Robinson's "Richard Cory" (p. 640); or, more noticeably, it can appear as a series of parallel items, as in Langston Hughes's "Harlem" (p. 634). (2) When two consecutive lines in open form are related by the second line's repeating, expanding on, or contrasting with the idea of the first, as, for example, in the poetry of Walt Whitman (p. 875).

Juxtaposition

This important organizational technique is also used in conjunction with other ways of handling inner form. **Juxtaposition** is the placement of things (often very different things) side by side or close together for comparison or contrast or to create something new from the union, without necessarily making them grammatically parallel. See, for example, how Victor Hernandez Cruz's "Problems with Hurricanes" (p. 764) juxtaposes the seriousness of an honorable death during a hurricane (drowning or being hurled by the wind against a mountain) with the ludicrous danger of dying dishonorably from being smashed by a mango, banana, or plantain.

Looking for juxtapositions can be an effective and interesting starting point in trying to "get hold" of a poem (or story or play). Juxtaposition is not always present, but it often is, and often with an ironic twist. Juxtaposition usually has the effect of placing you between paired items, so that you must work through the oppositions, perhaps reconciling them, perhaps being left with an inherent tension or reaching to the wonderful strangeness of what is created.

Narrative

One of the most basic approaches to structure is **narrative**, a poet recounting an event as a sequence of actions and details, as in Jimmy Santiago Baca's "Family Ties" (p. 739), Heather McHugh's "What He Thought"

(p. 820), and or Robert Morgan's "Mountain Bride" (p. 828). There are also *long* narrative poems, stories cast in poetic form, from Homer on down to the present.

Logical Pattern

Materials can be arranged in a logical pattern of development. This could be in the form of a logical argument, like the three-part attempt at persuasion in Andrew Marvell's "To His Coy Mistress" (p. 823), or of logical explanation, like the "wonderings" in Cornelius Eady's "My Mother, If She Had Won Free Dance Lessons" (p. 775), or of raising a problem and offering a solution or a response, as in John Milton's "When I consider how my light is spent" (p. 825).

Question-Answer

Poems can raise a question (explicitly or implicitly) and work toward an answer (which also can be stated or implied). Emily Dickinson's "I'm Nobody! Who are you?" (p. 670) raises a deep, perennial question and explores it playfully, but seriously. Langston Hughes's "Harlem" (p. 634) is a series of questions with an implied answer phrased as a final question, and the title of Ai's "Why Can't I Leave You?" (p. 733) raises a question that the rest of the poem seeks to answer.

Meditative Movement

Some poems are arranged as meditations, often moving from a reflection on a physical place or object or a scene to personal or spiritual perceptions, as in James Wright's "A Blessing" (p. 619) or Lucille Clifton's "at the cemetery, walnut grove plantation, south carolina, 1989" (p. 664).

Association

Poems can be arranged through association, moving from word or image or idea or other element to another word, image, idea, or other element connected to it on the basis of free associations, as in Jayne Cortez's "Into This Time" (p. 762), Linda Hogan's "The History of Red" (p. 799), and Mary Ruefle's "Naked Ladies" (p. 849).

Lists (or Catalogs) and Litanies

Lists and litanies may be the most common use of form (we all construct them). Poets employ them by laying out a series of details, often referred to as a catalog. Lists can create range, rhythm, intensity, and texture. For a poem structured as a litany, a ceremonial form of prayer using a series of invocations and repeated responses, see Joy Harjo's "She Had Some Horses" (p. 620). Catalogs also can structure parts of a poem, as in the last line of Gwendolyn Brooks's "The Bean Eaters" (p. 550).

www

Further explore form and type, including interactive exercises, with VirtuaLit Poetry at bedfordstmartins.com/ approachinglit.

Poetic Types That Impose Structure

A number of traditional types of poetry, such as **epic**, **ballad**, **epigram**, song, and hymn, carry with them expectations of what the poem should include and sometimes how it should be organized. An epic, for example, must open *in medias res* (see p. 64) and include such features as a formal statement of theme; an invocation to a deity; catalogs of warriors, ships, and armies; and a journey to the underworld.

Combinations of the Above

Almost any of the structures described above can be used with another or others to create fresh and interesting combinations. See what combinations you can find in, for example, Nikki Giovanni's "Nikka-Rosa" (p. 785) and Heather McHugh's "What He Thought" (p. 820).

☑ CHECKLIST on Reading for Form and Type

❑ Notice the role form plays in a poem and the effect it has on your experience of reading the poem.

❑ Watch for the handlings of lines and consider the various ways they affect a poem's appearance, rhythm, and emphasis, and the way they interact with sentences.

❑ Be aware of both a poem's external form (the way the poem looks on the page) and its inner form (the artistic design or structure that arranges, organizes, or connects the various elements).

❑ For poems in stanzas, consider the effectiveness and appropriateness of the form selected for the poem. If the poet introduces a variation in the form once established, consider what the changes convey in meaning, tone, and effect.

❑ Watch for inherited forms (such as the English sonnet, the Italian sonnet, ballad stanza, couplets, and blank verse) and consider the kind of creativity and imaginativeness that writing such poetry entails.

❑ Watch for poetry written as free verse (lacking such repeated features as rhyme, meter, or stanza, but using unity of pattern, such as visual structures, parallelism, or rhythm) and consider the kind of creativity and craft that writing such poetry requires.

FURTHER READING

ENTRY POINTS   Consider form in the following poems, asking such questions as: How would you describe the structuring of the poem? Is it an inherited or invented structure? In what ways is the form appropriate for the poem? In what ways does the form itself carry, add to, or intensify the meaning or effect of the poem? In what ways is the form aesthetically satisfying?

The first two poems have a common subject, horses, but are very different in form, content, and effect.

James Wright   1927–1980

A Blessing   [1963]

Just off the highway to Rochester, Minnesota,
Twilight bounds softly forth on the grass.
And the eyes of those two Indian ponies
Darken with kindness.
They have come gladly out of the willows   5
To welcome my friend and me.
We step over the barbed wire into the pasture
Where they have been grazing all day, alone.
They ripple tensely, they can hardly contain their happiness
That we have come.   10
They bow shyly as wet swans. They love each other.
There is no loneliness like theirs.
At home once more,
They begin munching the young tufts of spring in the darkness.
I would like to hold the slenderer one in my arms,   15
For she has walked over to me
And nuzzled my left hand.
She is black and white,
Her mane falls wild on her forehead,
And the light breeze moves me to caress her long ear   20
That is delicate as the skin over a girl's wrist.
Suddenly I realize
That if I stepped out of my body I would break
Into blossom.

APPROACHING THE READING

1. The form of the poem relies on lineation. Consider the effects of the longer and shorter lines and of the variation between longer and shorter.

2. What techniques of inner arrangement do you find in the poem? Do you feel any are particularly effective? Why?
3. What mood is evoked by the images throughout the poem?
4. Why do you think the speaker refers to this experience as a blessing? What are the denotations and connotations of *blessing*? Do any of them fit this poem?
5. Explain what is suggested by the last three lines.

Joy Harjo b. 1951

She Had Some Horses   [1983]

She had some horses.

She had horses who were bodies of sand.
She had horses who were maps drawn of blood.
She had horses who were skins of ocean water.
She had horses who were the blue air of sky.   5
She had horses who were fur and teeth.
She had horses who were clay and would break.
She had horses who were splintered red cliff.

She had some horses.

She had horses with long, pointed breasts.   10
She had horses with full, brown thighs.
She had horses who laughed too much.
She had horses who threw rocks at glass houses.
She had horses who licked razor blades.

She had some horses.   15

She had horses who danced in their mothers' arms.
She had horses who thought they were the sun and their
bodies shone and burned like stars.
She had horses who waltzed nightly on the moon.
She had horses who were much too shy, and kept quiet   20
in stalls of their own making.

She had some horses.

She had horses who liked Creek Stomp Dance songs.
She had horses who cried in their beer.
She had horses who spit at male queens who made   25
them afraid of themselves.
She had horses who said they weren't afraid.

She had horses who lied.
She had horses who told the truth, who were stripped
bare of their tongues. 30

She had some horses.

She had horses who called themselves, "horse."
She had horses who called themselves, "spirit," and kept
their voices secret and to themselves.
She had horses who had no names. 35
She had horses who had books of names.

She had some horses.

She had horses who whispered in the dark, who were afraid to speak.
She had horses who screamed out of fear of the silence, who
carried knives to protect themselves from ghosts. 40
She had horses who waited for destruction.
She had horses who waited for resurrection.

She had some horses.

She had horses who got down on their knees for any saviour.
She had horses who thought their high price had saved them. 45
She had horses who tried to save her, who climbed in her
bed at night and prayed as they raped her.

She had some horses.

She had some horses she loved.
She had some horses she hated. 50

These were the same horses.

APPROACHING THE READING

1. This poem is in one of the oldest of forms, the litany. Read it aloud, feeling the rhythms of its lines and inner arrangement. Consider what the rhythm and repetition of litany contribute to the impact, effect, and power of the poem.
2. Describe how the external form struck you when you first saw it. Was it inviting? Why or why not?
3. The poem uses other techniques for inner arrangement along with the list or litany. Pick out at least three.
4. What do you make of the last three lines?
5. Harjo has said that she has been asked the most about this poem and has the least to say about it. Speculate on why you think each is the case.

ENTRY POINTS   Here are two poems about nature and ways it relates or speaks to human life. Both poems are in stanzas, but of very different types. As you read, think about whether the form is appropriate for the poem; ways the form carries, adds to, or intensifies meaning; ways the form is aesthetically satisfying; and ways the form affects your reading.

William Butler Yeats 1865–1939

The Lake Isle of Innisfree   [1892]

I will arise and go now, and go to Innisfree,
And a small cabin build there, of clay and wattles made:
Nine bean-rows will I have there, a hive for the honey-bee,
And live alone in the bee-loud glade.

And I shall have some peace there, for peace comes dropping slow,   5
Dropping from the veils of the morning to where the cricket sings;
There midnight's all a glimmer, and noon a purple glow,
And evening full of the linnet's wings.

I will arise and go now, for always night and day
I hear lake water lapping with low sounds by the shore;   10
While I stand on the roadway, or on the pavements grey,
I hear it in the deep heart's core.

APPROACHING THE READING

1. Describe the stanza form of the poem. *Stanza* is derived from the Italian word for *room*. In what ways do the stanzas fulfill the idea of different "rooms" in the poem?
2. Notice that each stanza is a single sentence, with phrases arranged within the sentence to create a lyrical musicality. Read the poem again, paying attention to the phrasing and how it makes you feel. What makes this use of phrasing especially appropriate for the poem's subject?
3. The poem is rich with sounds. Read the poem aloud, listening for them, and point out a number of the techniques you notice. What do they create in the poem and in what ways are they appropriate? Notice, too, how Yeats uses words that create sounds in keeping with the images. Pick out some and describe their effect.
4. Describe the speaker. What is the speaker feeling? What does the speaker want? Think about the last line. What do you think the speaker means by, "I hear it in the deep heart's core"? Notice that it says "the deep heart's core" not "the heart's deep core." What for you is the difference?

Robert Herrick   1591–1674

To Daffodils   [1648]

Fair daffodils, we weep to see
   You haste away so soon;
As yet the early-rising sun
   Has not attained his noon.
      Stay, stay,   5
    Until the hasting day
       Has run
   But to the evensong;
And, having prayed together, we
    Will go with you along.   10

We have short time to stay, as you,
   We have as short a spring;
As quick a growth to meet decay,
   As you, or anything.
      We die,   15
   As your hours do, and dry
      Away,
    Like to the summer's rain;
Or as the pearls of morning's dew,
    Ne'er to be found again.   20

APPROACHING THE READING

1. In this poem, like the Yeats poem before it, the speaker seems deeply affected by an experience with nature, but affected in different ways. In this poem, looking at the daffodils makes the speaker reflect on life. Describe the nature of those reflections as the speaker expresses them to the daffodils.

2. This poem may appear to be written in a traditional, inherited form, but it isn't. It's a form Herrick created. One wonders if he thought of it prior to writing the poem or if he began to write, noticed a pattern, and followed it. Think about the effect of that form. Does it attract your attention and appear aesthetically pleasing on the page? Do you think its form makes it more appealing to read than it would be in four-line stanzas, like those of Yeats's poem? Why or why not?

3. What is the effect of having lines of varying lengths, with varying degrees of indentation? Consider the lines that have only two words or a two-syllable word in them. What impact does that use of form create? In what ways does this use of such a short line reveal what the speaker is experiencing? Do you think the effect would be different if these lines and all the others were aligned at the left margin? If so, how or why?

4. Consider the value of having the two stanzas be identical in form. Does that affect the way the stanzas relate to each other? If so, explain how.

5. Does this poem seem more dated than the Yeats poem? If so, what aspects seem particularly dated? What aspects seem as relevant today as they were in 1648?

ENTRY POINTS   The following two poems are about grandparents and grandchildren, thus about generational separation, or even distance. In form they are very different: One is written in almost prose-like lines, the other is in a set, complicated, repetitive pattern. As you read and reflect on the two poems, think about the appropriateness of each form to its subject, how each form contributes to meaning, ways the form is aesthetically satisfying, and ways the form affects the way you read the poem.

David Mura   b. 1952

Grandfather-in-Law   [1989]

It's nothing really, and really, it could have been worse, and of course,
        he's now several years dead,
and his widow, well, if oftentimes she's somewhat distracted, overly
        cautious when we visit —
after all, Boston isn't New York — she seems, for some reason, enormously
        proud that there's now a writer in the family,
and periodically, sends me clippings about the poet laureate, Thoreau,
        Anne Sexton's daughter, Lowell, New England literary lore —
in which I fit, if I fit at all, simply because I write in English — as if
        color of skin didn't matter anymore.   5
Still, years ago, during my first visit to Boston, when we were all
        asleep,
he, who used to require that my wife memorize lines of Longfellow or Poe
        and recite them on the phone,
so that, every time he called, she ran outdoors and had to be coaxed back,
        sometimes with threats, to talk to Pops
(though she remembers too his sly imitations of Lincoln, ice cream at
        Brighams, burgers and fries, all the usual grandfatherly treats),
he, who for some reason was prejudiced against Albanians — where
        on earth did he find them I wondered —   10
who, in the thirties, would vanish to New York, catch a show, buy a suit,
        while up north,
the gas and water bills pounded the front door (his spendthrift ways
        startled me with my grandfather's resemblance),

who for over forty years came down each morning, "How's the old goat?"
    with a tie only his wife could knot circling his neck,
he slipped into my wife's room — we were unmarried at the time —
    and whispered so softly she thought
he almost believed she was really asleep, and was saying this like a wish
    or spell, some bohunk miscalculated Boston sense of duty: 15
"Don't make a mistake with your life, Susie. Don't make a
    mistake . . ."
Well. The thing that gets me now, despite the dangling rantings I've let
    go, is that, at least at that time,
he was right: There was, inside me, some pressing, raw unpeeled persis-
    tence, some libidinous desire for dominance
that, in the scribbled first drafts of my life, seemed to mark me as wastrel
    and rageful, bound to be unfaithful,
to destroy, in some powerful, nuclear need, fissioned both by child-
    hood and racism, whatever came near —   20
And I can't help but feel, forgiving him now, that if she had listened, if
    she had been awake,
if this flourishing solace, this muscled-for-happiness, shared by us
    now, had never awakened,
he would have become for me a symbol of my rage and self-destruction,
    another raw, never healing wound,
and not this silenced grandfatherly presence, a crank and scoundrel, red-
    necked Yankee who created the delicate seed of my wife, my child.

APPROACHING THE READING

1. The most notable formal feature of the poem is the use of long, prose-like lines. What effect do they create — in terms of the speaker, the overall situation, the tone, your role as reader?
2. Give some attention to the interplay of lines and sentences. What is the effect of the long, rambling sentences — on character, on tone, on rhythm?
3. Consider the inner arrangement of the poem. How does it bring out the conflicts between generations and its resolution? How does the idea of forgiveness in line 21 fit in?

Elizabeth Bishop   1911–1979

Sestina   [1965]

September rain falls on the house.
In the failing light, the old grandmother
sits in the kitchen with the child

beside the Little Marvel Stove,
reading the jokes from the almanac,   5
laughing and talking to hide her tears.

She thinks that her equinoctial tears
and the rain that beats on the roof of the house
were both foretold by the almanac,
but only known to a grandmother.   10
The iron kettle sings on the stove.
She cuts some bread and says to the child,

It's time for tea now; but the child
is watching the teakettle's small hard tears
dance like mad on the hot black stove,   15
the way the rain must dance on the house.
Tidying up, the old grandmother
hangs up the clever almanac

on its string. Birdlike, the almanac
hovers half open above the child,   20
hovers above the old grandmother
and her teacup full of dark brown tears.
She shivers and says she thinks the house
feels chilly, and puts more wood in the stove.

It was to be, says the Marvel Stove.   25
I know what I know, says the almanac.
With crayons the child draws a rigid house
and a winding pathway. Then the child
puts in a man with buttons like tears
and shows it proudly to the grandmother.   30

But secretly, while the grandmother
busies herself about the stove,
the little moons fall down like tears
from between the pages of the almanac
into the flower bed the child   35
has carefully placed in the front of the house.

Time to plant tears, says the almanac.
The grandmother sings to the marvellous stove
and the child draws another inscrutable house.

APPROACHING THE READING

1. Summarize what the poem is about, what's going on in it. What gives
   the poem a kind of folktale or children's story or fable feel? What do you

make of the juxtaposition of that feeling with the "adultness" of the subject material?

2. Look up *sestina* in the glossary (p. 1623) and go through the poem, checking how it meets the specifications of the form. Consider the choice of repeated words and the effects created by repetition. In what ways does the repetition affect your reading?

3. In what ways does the sestina form add to the feel, the impact, of the poem? How does the form fit the subject? How does the form take part in creating the atmosphere of the poem?

4. Think about the speaker and the way the speaker uses language and syntax. How would you characterize the poem's tone?

5. A nineteenth-century poet, the Comte de Gramont, described the sestina as "a reverie in which the same ideas, the same objects, occur to the mind in a succession of different aspects, which nonetheless resemble one another, fluid and changing shape like the clouds in the sky." Bishop's sestina has often been praised as one of the finest sestinas ever written. In light of Gramont's description, why do you think it has received that commendation?

RESPONDING THROUGH Writing

WRITING ABOUT FORM AND TYPE

Journal Entries

1. Choose a poem and change the way it is divided into lines. Then write in your journal about what you discovered from these changes.

2. Be on the lookout for **found poetry**, that is, prose found in newspapers, magazines, advertisements, textbooks, or elsewhere in everyday life that contains elements of poetry, such as meter, effective rhythm, phrasings that can be divided into lines, imaginative uses of language and sound, and so on. Collect several examples for your journal, dividing them carefully into poetic lines. Comment briefly on what this revealed to you about choices poets make about line divisions and about their effect.

> **www**
>
> Research the authors in this chapter with *LitLinks* at bedfordstmartins.com/approachinglit.

3. In your journal, describe and discuss briefly the inner arrangements of the following poems: Laure-Anne Bosselaar's "Bench in Aix-en-Provence" (p. 696), Donald Hall's "Names of Horses" (p. 793), Richard Lovelace's "To Lucasta, Going to the Wars" (p. 817), Cheryl Savageau's "Bones — A City Poem" (p. 852), Charles Simic's "Classical Ballroom Dances" (p. 855), and Mark Strand's "Eating Poetry" (p. 862).

Literary Analysis Papers

4. For one of the following poems, write a paper describing its form and discussing the effectiveness and appropriateness of its distinctive handling of lines: Charles Bukowski's "my old man" (p. 573), Rosemary Catacalos's "David Talamántez on the Last Day of Second Grade" (p. 757), Allen Ginsberg's "A Supermarket in California" (p. 784), Dwight Okita's "In Response to Executive Order 9066" (p. 832), or Wendy Rose's "Loo-Wit" (p. 848).

5. The form of Peter Blue Cloud's "Rattle" (p. 745), with different things going on in parallel columns, makes unusual demands of a reader. Write a paper discussing what is going on in the poem and how form contributes to its effectiveness.

6. Write a paper explicating a sonnet with emphasis on the way its structure fits and brings out its subject and theme. Use a traditional sonnet such as John Milton's "When I consider how my light is spent" (p. 825) or Edmund Spenser's "One day I wrote her name upon the strand" (p. 861), or use a sonnet that seems surprising to see in that form, such as Gary Miranda's "Love Poem" (p. 668) or Vijay Seshadri's "The Refugee" (p. 853).

Comparison-Contrast Papers

7. Write a paper on two or more poems that focus on what poetry is and does, as for example Heather McHugh's "What He Thought" (p. 820), Marianne Moore's "Poetry" (p. 827), and Mark Strand's "Eating Poetry" (p. 862). Compare and contrast their ideas and the way form and type contribute to what the poems say and do.

8. Write a paper comparing the free verse form used in two of the following poems and discussing for each how the invented form fits and accentuates the poem's subject and theme: Lucille Clifton's "at the cemetery, walnut grove plantation, south carolina, 1989" (p. 664), Gerald Barrax's "Dara" (p. 741), Tina Chang's "Origin & Ash" (p. 758), Cornelius Eady's "My Mother, If She Had Won Free Dance Lessons" (p. 775), Linda Hogan's "The History of Red" (p. 799), Jane Kenyon's "From Room to Room" (p. 809), or Mary Ruefle's "Naked Ladies" (p. 849).

> ## ▶ TIPS for Writing about Form and Type
>
> ➤ **Look for the unusual** When a poem's form is quite unusual, or when it contributes in a significant way to the effect or meaning, it can make a revealing topic for a paper. Handling it successfully requires describing the form in detail and explaining carefully how and why it creates the effects it does. But even when you are writing about other elements in a poem, it can be helpful to include a brief description of

the poem's form or type (for example, mentioning that it's in blank verse or a variation on Italian sonnet or free verse).

➤ **Look for juxtapositions** Even when writing about other elements, it is wise to watch for juxtapositions. They can highlight the importance of particular images or the speaker's vision or point of view, or how a poem takes a common way of seeing and turns it into a fresh way. They can be an important structural feature, often emphasizing how things that ordinarily are not associated with one another create a dynamic experience when placed together. A single juxtaposition can sometimes make an entire poem cohere.

➤ **Consider what to cover** A paper dealing with form doesn't have to cover all aspects. Good papers can result from focusing on one aspect, such as handling of line breaks, line lengths, meter, stanza structures, collage, or shape.

➤ **Consider form in free verse** Form can lead to a perceptive paper (or part of a topic) on free-verse poetry, especially when the form is unusual. Such a paper must go beyond describing the form and include discussion of the form's appropriateness, its effects, its possible meaningfulness, and the ways it embodies the artistry of the poem as a whole.

➤ **Consider the effect of using a traditional type** For poems written in traditional types (such as sonnet, sestina, or villanelle), you might discuss why the choice of type is fitting and why it is effective. This can make for a whole paper or a segment of a broader one.

WRITING ABOUT CONNECTIONS

Obviously connections occur between poems using the same inherited form, and several of the topics above involve looking at how two or more poets handle sonnets and sestinas. One can also find connections between free-verse poems through formal strategies or techniques. In addition to formal connections, thematic connections can be found between poems in the same form and across forms, between poets writing in the same century or different centuries. Here are a few topic possibilities:

1. "Amazing Grace": Being Blessed from Within and from Without in James Wright's "A Blessing" (p. 619) and Galway Kinnell's "Saint Francis and the Sow" (p. 809)
2. " 'Which thou must leave ere long' ": Confronting Separation in Elizabeth Bishop's "Sestina" (p. 625) and William Shakespeare's "That time of year thou mayst in me behold" (p. 606)
3. "The Solace of Solitude": Place and Peace in W. B. Yeats's "The Lake Isle of Innisfree" (p. 622) and Lorine Niedecker's "My Life by Water" (p. 831)

WRITING RESEARCH PAPERS

1. Research the significance of turtles (especially Grandfather Turtle) in Native American legends and use what you find to illuminate the Father Turtle story in Leslie Marmon Silko's "Prayer to the Pacific" (p. 614).
2. Research the history, use, and development of the **villanelle** as a form, and write a paper in which you discuss how a villanelle "works" (how it affects and appeals to poets and to readers), illustrating it with examples from at least two villanelles, perhaps the ones in this book — Dylan Thomas's "Do not go gentle into that good night" (p. 866) and John Yau's "Chinese Villanelle" (p. 883) — or others that you find.

COMPOSING IN OTHER ART FORMS

1. A good way to learn about how a sonnet works is to try writing one (English or Italian). Use contemporary diction, the language you speak. Remember, you are "inheriting" the *form* from the past, not the past's language. Then write a short description of what trying it was like.
2. Try writing a free-verse poem working with an important event in your personal life. Take advantage of what you have learned about line, line breaks, and form to add to the impact of your poem. Then write a paragraph about why you decided to do what you did with each of those elements.

*M*etaphor has interested me more as a way of knowledge, a way of grasping something. I like to . . . use the metaphor as a way to discover something about the nature of reality.

Charles Simic

Figurative Language

CHAPTER **15**

Wondering What This Has to Do with That

When Romeo says, "But, soft, what light through yonder window breaks? / It is the east, and Juliet is the sun," the hearer or reader of Shakespeare's *Romeo and Juliet* knows perfectly well that Romeo doesn't think Juliet actually is the sun. He may be lovesick, but he's not loony. The ability almost all of us have to process language lets us understand, almost instantaneously, that Romeo is comparing Juliet to, or identifying her with, the sun. Romeo is making imaginative, not logical, sense. He is using a **figure of speech** or **figurative language**, that is, a shift from standard or customary usage of words to achieve a special effect or particular meaning. He is trying to pack lots of meaning into a few words: that Juliet's beauty dazzles like the sun, that Juliet is the center of his life the way the sun is the center of our solar system. An important part of comprehending poetry is being able to recognize when language is to be taken "figuratively" instead of at face value, and what its figurativeness conveys.

From the dozens of specific types of figurative language available to writers, you need to know and recognize only about half a dozen. It helps to be able to call them by name. Some people grimace when they are asked to learn the particular vocabulary of poetry. But think about it. When you are talking about a sound system, you might use the terms *bass* or *amplifier*. If you can assume that your listener understands these terms, you don't need to take the time to explain them. Similarly, attaching names to figures helps in getting to know them and provides a useful, shared shorthand when talking

631

about a poem. Knowing the terms makes it easier to communicate. Equally or even more important than using the correct label is being able to describe what the figure's role is and how it functions in the poem and in your reading. That is the focus in this chapter.

READING FOR SIMILE

To help someone understand something—how you felt on the first day of the new school year, for example—you might use a *comparison*: "When I walked into my first class, my mind seemed as blank as the paper in my notebook." Writers of fiction, poetry, and drama often use comparisons that are unexpected and imaginative (thus, figurative).

Figurative comparisons occur when we discover that two things we thought were entirely dissimilar actually have attributes in common or when the comparison leads us to a new way of perceiving or considering something. The comparison stretches our ideas about perception and about experiences of the things compared ("I've never thought about or seen it that way before"). The following lines may do this for you.

Julie Moulds b. 1962
From "Wedding Iva"   [1995]

When he held her
she became
white and armless
like a goddess
or a bowling pin.

At first you may see a similarity in a rather conventional way: the comparison to a goddess. However, when you look more closely, you realize that the woman feels "armless" like a goddess. You may wonder to yourself, how is she being held? Our assumption that being compared to a goddess is positive is brought into tension. Then comes the surprise of the last line which shifts the comparison to a startlingly dissimilar object, a bowling pin. You may now see the embrace, the comparison to a goddess, and the way the woman feels in an uncommon way that challenges your common perceptions.

FIGURES STRETCH OUR IMAGINATIONS   Reread Anita Endrezze's poem "The Girl Who Loved the Sky" (p. 565). Endrezze uses comparisons to get across how a blind girl experiences the world, especially how she conceives the sky she cannot see: "I met a blind girl who thought the sky / tasted like cold metal when it rained." What is the taste of cold metal? Is its taste different in the rain? How can the sky have taste at all? The blind girl uses her imagination to grasp what the sky is like since she can't see it. Endrezze helps us experience that imaginative process by giving us language that stretches our imaginations to a point where our rational minds can't grasp or put into logical terms what the words are expressing. And yet we intuitively understand it.

FIGURES IN EVERYDAY LANGUAGE   Actually, figurative language isn't limited to literary writers. All of us use it all the time: "I worked like a dog," "tough as nails." In fact, much of language by its very nature is figurative. Almost all of the words we use, except ones that identify concrete objects or actions such as *cup* or *kick*, involve figures. Often the figures go unnoticed. You are reading this section to comprehend it. *Comprehend*, in that context, is figurative: Its root is the Latin word *hendere*, "to grasp or hold with the thumb." That physical action has been extended imaginatively to include "grasping" or "taking hold of" an idea or concept.

We don't notice or react to most of the figures we use in everyday language because they have become either too familiar or stale. Some originally inventive figures (a river bed, a table leg) have been absorbed into the language to such an extent that, though they still are figures, we seldom think of them as figurative. And yet even these, when you look again at them as figures, may surprise you.

DIRECT, SURPRISING COMPARISONS   Surprising comparisons, using direct, explicit signal words such as *like*, *as*, *than*, or *similar to*, are called **similes** (from the Latin word for "similar"). Direct comparisons are usually the easiest figures to notice because they carry the signal word with them. But only surprising, unexpected comparisons are similes. The comparison discussed above from Anita Endrezze's "The Girl Who Loved the Sky" was a simile. So is this, a few lines further: "On hot, still days / we listened to the sky falling / like chalk dust." The comparison is definitely surprising: It takes very keen hearing to catch the sound of chalk dust falling; one would have to be even more alert to hear the sound of the sky falling. Similes appear again later in the poem:

> I was born blind, she said, an act of nature.
> Sure, I thought, like birds born
> without wings, trees without roots.

Here the speaker's comparisons bring out her anger at her friend's fate, but also her failure to understand that her friend, though she cannot see physically, is not rendered helpless the way a bird without wings would be. And,

The day she moved
I saw the world clearly: the sky
backed away from me like a departing father.

The simile connects two great losses in the speaker's world — her father's absence and her friend's departure — and those losses, at this point anyhow, come to define the way she views her world.

NONFIGURATIVE COMPARISONS   On the other hand, Endrezze's line "the room smells like glue" is not a simile: It is not surprising and not imaginative (the room smells the way glue smells or smells of glue because glue is used in the room). Comparisons between similar things (squid tastes like chicken; his eyes are like his father's) are straightforward analogies, not similes and not figurative.

ENTRY POINTS   The following poem uses a series of six comparisons to suggest the effect of having the attainment of one's hopes and aspirations delayed indefinitely. Watch for them as you read and notice how the sixth is different from the first five.

Langston Hughes   1902–1967

Harlem   [1951]

What happens to a dream deferred?

Does it dry up
like a raisin in the sun?
Or fester like a sore —
And then run?
Does it stink like rotten meat?   5
Or crust and sugar over —
like a syrupy sweet?

Maybe it just sags
like a heavy load.   10

Or does it explode?

APPROACHING THE READING

1. Explain why each of the comparisons is effective and meaningful.
2. How is the comparison in the final line different from the other five? How does that difference increase its power as well as the impact of the whole poem?

3. The poem refers to any dreams, but especially to the "American dream." If you are not familiar with the term, look it up. Relate it to the title of the poem and consider the bitter ironies that reading evokes.

Research this author in depth with cultural documents and multimedia resources on *LiterActive*.

In response to the question raised in the opening line, Hughes's poem poses further questions, suggesting a number of possible answers. These follow-up questions rely on similes to intensify their points. Read the lines without the similes and notice what happens: "What happens to a dream deferred? Does it dry up or fester? Does it stink, or crust and sugar over? Maybe it just sags." The points make sense. Dreams can dry up if their fulfillment keeps getting put off and the dreamer loses hope of ever achieving or receiving what she or he dreams about. But the points by themselves lack emotional impact; they aren't memorable.

Much of the poem's power derives from the comparisons, the way they amplify the points, their appropriateness and the variety of applications they invite. For example, a dream deferred can be compared to a raisin drying up in the sun because as a once-juicy raisin dries up it shrivels, becomes smaller and smaller, and looks withered and unappealing. Try doing the same for the other comparisons.

READING FOR METAPHOR

"All the world is like a stage." "All the world is a stage." Sense the difference? The former is a simile; the latter is a **metaphor**, a figure of speech in which two things usually thought to be dissimilar are treated as if they were the same, the same because they have characteristics in common. The word *metaphor* is derived from the Greek *metaphora*, "carry (*phor*) across (*meta*)." In a metaphor, characteristics of one thing are "carried across" to another, from the thing used to illustrate ("stage") to the subject being illustrated ("world").

NOT "LIKE" BUT "THE SAME AS"   Metaphors are basic to poetry and are widely used in fiction and drama as well. Shakespeare's character Jaques asserts, "All the world's a stage," in the comedy *As You Like It*. Without even thinking about it, we may treat this as a comparison ("the world is *like* a stage," with people playing roles, making entrances and exits, and so on). The line, however, does not say that the world is *like* a stage, but that it *is* a stage. Common sense and logic, of course, claim that the world is not part of a theater. But the figure says it is. Here metaphor opens our minds to see what they may not have seen before. A metaphor can break down a barrier and carry us into a world in which, through our imaginations, we discover transformations and uncommon relationships, sometimes even new "realities" and ways of experiencing.

NOT EXPLICIT BUT IMPLIED   Metaphors are easiest to recognize when the comparison is explicit, when *is* or *are* or some other linking word is present, as in "All the world is a stage." More difficult to recognize and explain are **implied metaphors**, in which the *to be* verb is omitted and the comparison may be implied, or "buried," rather than stated directly. "A car thief is a dirty dog" is direct metaphor. "Some dirty dog stole my car" contains an implied metaphor: The key term ("car thief") is implied, and you must supply it to complete the equation involved. Look again at "Harlem." Notice how it relies on a shift from similes in lines 2–10 to the implied metaphor of line 11: *"Or does it explode?"* The reader must supply the object that describes the ultimate effect of having dreams deferred: the possibility of frustration exploding into riot? defeat? revolution? despair? The fact that the poem doesn't use the word it refers to but has the reader think of it makes the conclusion more interactive and its impact all the stronger.

EMOTIVE AS WELL AS INFORMATIVE   In "The Girl Who Loved the Sky" (p. 565), Endrezze uses both explicit and implied metaphors. "I learned / that numbers were fractious beasts" is an explicit metaphor: Math is equated with a beast that lives in a den, something wild, threatening, and hard to manage. The comparison conveys her feelings vividly. "The bruised petals of her lids" is implied, or buried, metaphor: The blind girl's eyelids apparently are dark, and this line compares them, even equates them, to the purple petals of the jacaranda tree outside the classroom. Similarly, the final lines of the poem also use metaphor: "until my fist was another lantern / hiding a small and bitter flame." Her fist is not a lantern, but the figure equates it with one; and her fist, like her heart, holds not a literal flame but petals and memories that remind her how the world takes from her those she loves, leaving her lonely and angry.

ENTRY POINTS   Read the following poem in which the speaker reflects on a southern African city at night and expresses his affection for it, despite its many problems. The poem is filled with figurative language, especially similes and implied metaphors. Watch for the way the figures pack the poem with meaning, beyond what literal equivalents could convey.

Dennis Brutus b. 1924

Nightsong: City   [1963]

Sleep well, my love, sleep well:
the harbour lights glaze over restless docks,
police cars cockroach through the tunnel streets;

from the shanties creaking iron-sheets
violence like a bug-infested rag is tossed   5
and fear is immanent as sound in the wind-swung bell;

the long day's anger pants from sand and rocks;
but for this breathing night at least,
my land, my love, sleep well.

APPROACHING THE READING

1. The poem starts off as if it were a love poem addressed to a person. At what point do you realize that line one is figurative and the "love" it refers to is the city the speaker calls home? What leads you to that realization?
2. In line 3, the author uses a noun (*cockroach*) as a verb and turns it into a vivid metaphor. Explain how it works figuratively and why you think it is effective.
3. Line 4 takes us to a shantytown and helps us see houses with sheet-metal walls and roofs and hear the sounds as they creak in the wind. The following two lines use similes to convey the violence and fear that pervade the area. Explain the comparisons and discuss their effectiveness.
4. Pick out the metaphors in lines 7 and 8 and, after reading the next section, the personification in line 9, and explain what each contributes to the poem.

The poem starts out with "Sleep well, my love." The title might suggest that a city is the setting for a night song to someone. It might be only after reading it a second time or looking back from the end of the poem that you realize that "my love" is the city the speaker loves. Saying that a city can sleep compares it to, or identifies it with, a living creature—an animal (metaphor) or a human being (see the next section on personification). The latter seems to fit best: The words of the first line sound like ones the speaker would offer at night to someone cherished. It may come as a surprise that the words are spoken to a city, but of course that shows how much he cares about it.

In this poem, the figurative comparisons add distinctness and vivid immediacy to the appearance of the city at night (harbor lights make the docks look shiny, the way a glaze does when applied to pottery or china; police cars dart around between rows of high-rise buildings with the quickness and agility of cockroaches). And they intensify the emotional impact of the descriptions of life in the city: violence pervades the shantytowns the way bugs infest a rag, fear is as present through the city as the sound of a bell, and the anger that fills the days "pants" everywhere like a fierce animal. But for the moment, the speaker wants to forget all that. For this one living, "breathing" night, he hopes his beloved city rests quietly and sleeps well.

READING FOR PERSONIFICATION

Personification is a figure of speech in which something nonhuman is given attributes of a person or is treated as if it has human characteristics or takes human actions. Sometimes abstract qualities are treated as if they are human. In Patricia Goedicke's lines, "Speak to me, Trouble, / Tell me how to move" (p. 787), for example, trouble does not have a voice; it is treated as if it is human. In other cases, concrete things are given human characteristics: in the phrase "a brilliant fluorescence breaks out / and makes war with the dim squares / of yellow kitchen light," from "Yellow Light" (p. 561), "fluorescence" is being given, briefly, the human attribute of warring. And in "the sky / backed away from me like a departing father," from "The Girl Who Loved the Sky" (p. 565), the sky is made human for a moment, able to walk away from the speaker the way her father did.

Personification is sometimes defined incorrectly as treating something not living in terms of just being alive rather than specifically being human. For example, in Shakespeare's *Romeo and Juliet*, Juliet, fearful of being drugged and buried in a vault, expresses fear of the tomb's "foul mouth [that] no healthsome air breathes in" (4.3.34). "Mouth" here is metaphor, not personification, since animals as well as humans have mouths and breathe through them.

A particular type of personification is **apostrophe**, that is, addressing someone not present or something ordinarily not spoken to as if present or capable of understanding, as when Macbeth says "Time, thou anticipatest my dread exploits" (4.1.144). Dennis Brutus uses apostrophe as well when his speaker in "Nightsong: City" talks to the city as if it could hear and understand.

ENTRY POINTS   Watch in the following poem for places where a nonliving thing is spoken of as if living. Then decide which of these exemplify personification and consider what such personifications contribute to the effect of the poem.

Angelina Weld Grimké 1880–1958

A Winter Twilight   [1923]

A silence slipping around like death,
Yet chased by a whisper, a sigh, a breath;
One group of trees, lean, naked and cold,

Inking their crest 'gainst a sky green-gold;
One path that knows where the corn flowers were;   5
Lonely, apart, unyielding, one fir;
And over it softly leaning down,
One star that I loved ere the fields went brown.

APPROACHING THE READING

1. What examples do you find of nonliving things treated as if alive? Point out ones that are personification — where the living attributes apply only to humans — and ones that are metaphors — where the connection could also apply to animals.
2. Consider the effect of personifications in the poem. What do they contribute that a comparison to something nonhuman wouldn't?

You may have heard someone speak of how a painting "brings a scene to life." That could be said of "A Winter Twilight" as well. The poem creates a picture, almost a verbal landscape painting. And, as with a painting, it slows everything to a stop, arrests this one moment, suspending it in time so that we can truly experience it. In our lives actual life experiences go by so fast that we can't experience them fully. We need the arts to give us the chance to stop and really take in what otherwise goes by and is lost.

This poet wants not only to see the scene — she wants to bring alive its feeling and aura. She does so through metaphors and personifications comparing landscape features to living things. That this is a quiet scene is evoked by the way silence "slips around" in it, as an animal or a person would, and the way it is "chased by a whisper." For the trees to be "naked" treats them as living beings, as persons really since that word generally is applied only to humans. Similarly, the path comes alive through personification (since it "knows" where the corn flowers are), as does the "lonely" fir tree (a word usually reserved for a human conscious reaction to feeling cut off from what matters).

A winter scene can seem dead and lifeless, and the poem is acutely aware of death, mentioning it in the opening line; but that very awareness heightens the way the figures of speech bring out the life present even in a "barren" landscape. The poem closes with a sense of the intimacy of life and death: The star is given the living attribute of "leaning down," but this is a star the speaker loved (past tense — does she or he no longer love it?) before the fields "went brown" (died? lost their appeal and desirability?).

READING FOR METONYMY AND SYNECDOCHE

SUBSTITUTING SOMETHING CLOSELY ASSOCIATED   Another figure of speech that, like metaphor, talks about one thing in terms of another is

metonymy, a figure of speech in which the name of one thing is substituted for that of something closely associated with it. Like similes and metaphors, metonymies are used every day. When you hear a news reporter say, "The White House announced today...," you've encountered a metonymy: "White House" invites you to visualize a familiar image closely associated with the president that substitutes for the staff members who issued the announcement. When the speaker in "The Girl Who Loved the Sky" (p. 565) says her friend "had no eyes," she does not mean that the girl's eye sockets were empty; she substitutes "eyes" for what is closely associated with eyes, "sight," because the word *eyes* is more concrete and vivid than the abstract word *sight*.

SUBSTITUTING A PART FOR THE WHOLE   A subset of metonymy is **synecdoche**, a special kind of metonymy in which a part of a thing is substituted for the whole of which it is a part. When someone says to you, "Give me a hand," she or he actually wants help not just from your hands but also from the rest of you. Likewise, the familiar phrases "many mouths to feed" or "let's count noses" use synecdoche. When the two girls in "The Girl Who Loved the Sky" (p. 565) are swinging and flying (note the metaphor—riding in a swing is something like flying) high over the other girls' heads, "heads" is synecdoche, a part substituted for the whole because it is the highest part of their bodies.

THE IMPORTANCE OF LITTLE THINGS   Recognizing metonymies and synecdoches helps you appreciate the way little things can have greater importance than they seem to at first. Robert Frost said, "If I must be classified as a poet, I might be called a Synecdochist, for I prefer the synecdoche in poetry," that figure of speech in which "a little thing touches a larger thing." Instead of starting with huge, complex themes and issues, Frost often uses local, everyday experiences as subjects, trusting our minds will be led to "a larger thing." Read his poem "Mending Wall" (p. 700) and think about how it embodies Frost's idea.

ENTRY POINTS   Look in the following poem for examples of nonliteral expression, figures of various sorts, including metonymy and synecdoche. Consider how the figures work (what is compared to what or what is substituted for what), and why the use of figures is effective and contributes to the poem's overall effect.

Edwin Arlington Robinson 1869–1935

Richard Cory   [1897]

Whenever Richard Cory went down town,
We people on the pavement looked at him:

He was a gentleman from sole to crown,
Clean favored, and imperially slim.

And he was always quietly arrayed,   5
And he was always human when he talked;
But still he fluttered pulses when he said,
"Good-morning," and he glittered when he walked.

And he was rich—yes, richer than a king—
And admirably schooled in every grace: 10
In fine, we thought that he was everything
To make us wish that we were in his place.

So on we worked, and waited for the light,
And went without the meat, and cursed the bread;
And Richard Cory, one calm summer night,   15
Went home and put a bullet through his head.

APPROACHING THE READING

1. Pick out examples of metonymy and synecdoche and explain how they work
   (what is being substituted for what). What do they contribute to the effect
   of the poem?
2. Describe the speaker. What is the effect of using *we* for the speaker instead
   of *I*? Could one say that "We people on the pavement" is a kind of synecdoche? Explain.
3. Pick out examples of other figures of speech and explain how they work and
   what they bring to the poem. Also point out examples of irony (see p. 579).
   Consider how both figures and irony bring out the "point" of the poem.

Robinson's poem seems a good example of Frost's point about being a
synecdochist: The poem has lots of little things that touch larger things.
One person speaks the poem but uses the pronoun *we*, thus attempting to
suggest that what he felt was true for the whole population of the town.
The poem focuses on "little" details—the way Richard Cory dresses, walks,
and talks (even the way he says so little a thing as "Good-morning" makes
hearts beat faster). The townspeople long for any little thing to improve
their lives, "light" substituting for "better days" because they see only dark
despair around them and get by on almost nothing ("bread" substituted for
"bare essentials") because they can't afford anything more ("meat" substituted for luxuries of any sort).

Meanwhile Richard Cory, whose life seems so large, who seems to have
so much, in an example of situational irony, ends his life with a little thing,
a bullet through the head. Robinson could have told the story without figures of speech, but the use of synecdoches especially, with their emphasis on

Here are three other figures of speech that you will frequently encounter:

- **Paradox:** A figure of speech in which a statement initially seeming self-contradictory or absurd turns out to make good sense when seen in another light. In Shakespeare's *Much Ado about Nothing*, for example, when the Friar says to Hero, "Come, lady, die to live" (4.1.252), he is using paradox. By pretending to die, she may regain the reputation she has lost through false slander. A subset of paradox is **oxymoron**, a self-contradictory combination of words or phrases, such as "O brawling love! O loving hate! . . . Feather of lead, bright smoke, cold fire, sick health!" in Shakespeare's *Romeo and Juliet* (1.1).
- **Hyperbole:** Exaggeration, or overstatement; a figure of speech in which something is stated more strongly than is warranted. Hyperbole is often used to make a point emphatically, as when Hamlet protests that he loved Ophelia much more than her brother did: "Forty thousand brothers / Could not with all their quantity of love / Make up my sum" (p. 1250).
- **Understatement:** A figure of speech that expresses something in an unexpectedly restrained way. Paradoxically, to deemphasize through understatement can be a way of emphasizing, of making people react with "there must be more to it than that." When Mercutio in *Romeo and Juliet*, after being stabbed by Tybalt, calls his wound "a scratch, a scratch" (3.1.92), he is understating, for the wound is serious. He calls for a doctor in the next line and dies a few minutes later.

parts and small aspects, seems perfect for a poem that contrasts having a lot and having very little.

TWO OTHER OBSERVATIONS ABOUT FIGURES

No sharp lines divide figures of speech from one another. Read the following poem about a driver coming upon a deer that an earlier driver had struck and killed. Watch for the way it relies on images and figures for its effect, and for the way some figures could be labeled and explained in different ways.

William Stafford 1914–1995

Traveling through the Dark   [1962]

Traveling through the dark I found a deer
dead on the edge of the Wilson River road.
It is usually best to roll them into the canyon:
that road is narrow; to swerve might make more dead.

By glow of the tail-light I stumbled back of the car 5
and stood by the heap, a doe, a recent killing;
she had stiffened already, almost cold.
I dragged her off; she was large in the belly.

My fingers touching her side brought me the reason —
her side was warm; her fawn lay there waiting, 10
alive, still, never to be born.
Beside that mountain road I hesitated.

The car aimed ahead its lowered parking lights;
under the hood purred the steady engine.
I stood in the glare of the warm exhaust turning red; 15
around our group I could hear the wilderness listen.

I thought hard for us all — my only swerving —
then pushed her over the edge into the river.

APPROACHING THE READING

1. Pick out several figures of speech, identify them, and explain how they work. Which ones could be labeled as more than one type of figure? Explain why or how.
2. Consider why images seem appropriate in the first twelve lines and figures in the last six.
3. The figures supply a large part of the poetic impact of the poem. However, there are other poetic aspects that come through the use of alliteration and assonance, along with some slant rhyme (see pp. 584–86). Mark examples of such sound techniques. Think about how they cooperate with the figurative language to develop the theme of the poem.

The first twelve lines of the poem are narrative, describing what happened. They rely on images, without any figures. Lines 13–18 reflect on the experience and use a good deal of figurative language, such as bringing the car to life by having it purr like a harmless cat (though ironically it was a similar car that killed the deer) and making the wilderness not just a living thing but one that listens and presumably understands. And the word *swerve*, which is used in a literal sense in line 4, comes back in a figurative sense in line 17 as the speaker momentarily avoids doing what he must before proceeding to do it.

ALTERNATIVE WAYS OF EXPLAINING FIGURES The poem illustrates two important characteristics of figurative language. First, a figure often fits into more than one category. "I could hear the wilderness listen," for example, stands either as metonymy ("wilderness" being substituted for the creatures and the natural habitat in it) or as personification ("wilderness" given humanlike ability to understand, not just hear). In this and most cases, applying labels to figures is a means to an end: It alerts you to their presence, helps you talk and write about them, and helps clarify the nature of the imaginative action you experience as you read them.

WWW
Further explore figurative language, including interactive exercises, with VirtuaLit Poetry at bedfordstmartins.com/approachinglit.

POEMS ARE NOT FIGURES   In addition to being aware that figures overlap with each other, keep in mind that figures of speech occur *within* poems, not *as* poems. Some people attempt to treat entire poems as figures of speech. After reading "Traveling through the Dark," they may say, "On the surface it's about a man finding a deer on the road, but what it's *really* about is our journey through life and the difficult decisions we face along the way." They substitute an abstract "meaning" for the concrete images of the poem. The poem is *really* about a deer on the road, though it may *also* (as opposed to *really*) be about life's journey. This book discusses images before figures because of the importance of grounding the experience in images and of letting the action or description be first and always itself.

✓ CHECKLIST on Reading for Figurative Language

❑ Notice any figurative language and the way it works imaginatively, especially these five types:

- Simile: the expression of a direct similarity, using words such as *like*, *as*, or *than*, between two things usually regarded as dissimilar
- Metaphor: treating two things usually thought to be dissimilar as if they are the same and have characteristics in common
- Personification: treating something nonhuman as if it has human characteristics or takes human actions
- Metonymy: substituting the name of one thing for that of something closely associated with it
- Synecdoche: substituting a part of something for the whole of it

❑ Consider how the choice of a figure affects the concept being developed.

FURTHER READING

ENTRY POINTS   The following four poems, like "Traveling through the Dark," explore aspects and implications of nature. Read each, and then reread the group, looking for imaginative uses of language. Pick out figures of speech and be ready to explain what is figurative about them and how they contribute to the effect of the poem.

The first two offer fresh, unusual, and striking ways of experiencing and reflecting on autumn and a snowstorm. The second two connect snow and winter to the death of a person. This is a familiar, archetypal association (see p. 147), but these poems use it in uncommon and very different ways.

John Keats   1795–1821

To Autumn   [1820]

I

Season of mists and mellow fruitfulness,
   Close bosom-friend of the maturing sun;
Conspiring with him how to load and bless
   With fruit the vines that round the thatch-eves run;
To bend with apples the mossed cottage-trees,   5
   And fill all fruit with ripeness to the core;
      To swell the gourd, and plump the hazel shells
With a sweet kernel; to set budding more,
   And still more, later flowers for the bees,
   Until they think warm days will never cease,   10
      For Summer has o'er-brimmed their clammy cells.

II

Who hath not seen thee oft amid thy store?
   Sometimes whoever seeks abroad may find
Thee sitting careless on a granary floor,
   Thy hair soft-lifted by the winnowing wind;   15
Or on a half-reaped furrow sound asleep,
   Drowsed with the fume of poppies, while thy hook°   *scythe*
      Spares the next swath and all its twinèd flowers:
And sometimes like a gleaner thou dost keep
   Steady thy laden head across a brook;   20
   Or by a cider-press, with patient look,
      Thou watchest the last oozings hours by hours.

III

Where are the songs of Spring? Aye, where are they?
   Think not of them, thou hast thy music too, —
While barrèd clouds bloom the soft-dying day,   25
   And touch the stubble-plains with rosy hue;

Then in a wailful choir the small gnats mourn
    Among the river sallows,° borne aloft   *willows*
    Or sinking as the light wind lives or dies;
And full-grown lambs loud bleat from hilly bourn;°   *region*   30
    Hedge-crickets sing; and now with treble soft
    The red-breast whistles from a garden-croft;
    And gathering swallows twitter in the skies.

APPROACHING THE READING

1. As the title and line 12 make clear, the poem is addressed to "Autumn," thus making personification and apostrophe central to the poem's impact. Are there other examples of personification as well?

2. John Keats's use of images is stunningly sensuous. Notice how many senses are evoked in the poem. Reflect on why they are especially appropriate for the subject.

Research this author in depth with cultural documents and multimedia resources on LiterActive.

3. Find places where figurative language is used to create or enhance the poem's imagery and sensuousness, and be ready to explain how the effects are created.

4. There is something palpably "autumnal" about this poem. What is it about the images and figures that lead to this feeling?

5. Seasons can in some cases carry archetypal significance (see p. 147). Do you think autumn does so in this poem? Is that part of what makes it profoundly autumnal? Some readers would say that the poem is talking about more than just the seasons. Be ready to explain and support why you agree or disagree.

Mary Oliver b. 1935

First Snow   [1983]

The snow
began here
this morning and all day
continued, its white
rhetoric everywhere   5
calling us back to *why, how,*
whence such beauty and *what*
the meaning; such
an oracular fever! flowing
past windows, an energy it seemed   10

would never ebb, never settle
less than lovely! and only now,
deep into night,
it has finally ended.
The silence   15
is immense,
and the heavens still hold
a million candles; nowhere
the familiar things:
stars, the moon,   20
the darkness we expect
and nightly turn from. Trees
glitter like castles
of ribbons, the broad fields
smolder with light, a passing   25
creekbed lies
heaped with shining hills;
and though the questions
that have assailed us all day
remain — not a single   30
answer has been found —
walking out now
into the silence and the light
under the trees,
and through the fields,   35
feels like one.

APPROACHING THE READING

1. The poem begins with a narrative account of the snow falling all day, using several figures that invite readers to reflect and wonder. For a couple of them, you may need to look up words ("white *rhetoric*," "*oracular* fever"); be ready to explain them, as well as the use of *flowing* and *ebb*.

2. About halfway through, the figures turn visual. Pick out several examples and be able to explain their imaginative actions. What is the effect of that change? How do the images and figures in the first half relate to those in the second half?

3. Think back to the discussion of the meaningful use of form. How has Mary Oliver used form to carry the feeling and meaning?

4. What do you think the speaker implies by saying that walking out into the snowfall feels like an "answer"?

Judith Ortiz Cofer   b. 1952

Cold as Heaven   [1995]

Before there is a breeze again
before the cooling days of Lent, she may be gone.
My grandmother asks me to tell her
again about the snow.
We sit on her white bed   5
in this white room, while outside
the Caribbean sun winds up the world
like an old alarm clock. I tell her
about the enveloping blizzard I lived through
that made everything and everyone the same;   10
how we lost ourselves in drifts so tall
we fell through our own footprints;
how wrapped like mummies in layers of wool
that almost immobilized us, we could only
take hesitant steps like toddlers   15
toward food, warmth, shelter.
I talk winter real for her,
as she would once conjure for me to dream
at sweltering siesta time,
cool stone castles in lands far north.   20
Her eyes wander to the window,
to the teeming scene of children
pouring out of a yellow bus, then to the bottle
dripping minutes through a tube
into her veins. When her eyes return to me,   25
I can see she's waiting to hear more
about the purifying nature of ice,
how snow makes way for a body,
how you can make yourself an angel
by just lying down and waving your arms   30
as you do when you say
good-bye.

APPROACHING THE READING

1. Consider weather in the poem. How does literal weather fit in the poem? In
   what ways is weather metaphorical? Why are both essential for the poem to
   have the deepest impact?
2. Pick out uses of simile, metaphor, metonymy, and synecdoche. What do
   they add to the poem's meaning and effect?

3. Discuss the relationship between the granddaughter and grandmother. How would you describe the tone (attitude of the speaker toward her grandmother's death and toward herself)? Point out figures that express what both are feeling.
4. Explain the implications of the simile in the poem's title. Consider the contrasts between cold and heat. What does snow convey in the poem? What does the speaker mean in line 17 by saying, "I talk winter real for her"?

Geoffrey Hill b. 1932

In Memory of Jane Fraser   [1959]

When snow like sheep lay in the fold
And winds went begging at each door,
And the far hills were blue with cold,
And a cold shroud lay on the moor,

She kept the siege. And every day   5
We watched her brooding over death
Like a strong bird above its prey.
The room filled with the kettle's breath.

Damp curtains glued against the pane
Sealed time away. Her body froze   10
As if to freeze us all, and chain
Creation to a stunned repose.

She died before the world could stir.
In March the ice unloosed the brook
And water ruffled the sun's hair.   15
Dead cones upon the alder shook.

APPROACHING THE READING

1. This poem relies heavily on figurative language. Each line except the last contains at least one use of simile, metaphor, or personification. Pick out as many of them as you can and identify each type of figure used. Be ready to explain how they work imaginatively and what different effects they create.
2. What contributes to the atmosphere of chill, of coldness, in the poem? What effect does that atmosphere have?
3. The poem is written in stanzas made up of quatrains. In what ways does this formal presentation affect your reading? What makes this way of structuring the poem fitting for the subject?

4. What role do you think rhyme plays in the poem? What other forms of sound do you notice that are especially meaningful for this poem? What is their effect?
5. The last line, unlike the others, does not use simile, metaphor, or personification. What is the effect of making this line different? Does it use another type of figure, or does it rely just on images? What is meaningful and resonant about the line: How does it "work"?

ENTRY POINTS   The following poem, like the previous two, deals with mortality, but in this case with a young girl learning about death as she watches a television news program. Thus, in a sense, it is a poem about losing one's innocence, about growing up and learning that the adult world is sometimes threatening. As you reread the poem, watch for ways that the images and figures of speech incorporate and convey what the speaker is learning.

Julia Alvarez   b. 1950

How I Learned to Sweep   [1996]

My mother never taught me sweeping.
One afternoon she found me watching
t.v. She eyed the dusty floor
boldly, and put a broom before
me, and said she'd like to be able   5
to eat her dinner off that table,
and nodded at my feet, then left.
I knew right off what she expected
and went at it. I stepped and swept;
the t.v. blared the news; I kept   10
my mind on what I had to do,
until in minutes, I was through.
Her floor was as immaculate
as a just-washed dinner plate.
I waited for her to return   15
and turned to watch the President,
live from the White House, talk of war:
in the Far East our soldiers were
landing in their helicopters
into jungles their propellers   20
swept like weeds seen underwater
while perplexing shots were fired

from those beautiful green gardens
into which these dragonflies
filled with little men descended.   25
I got up and swept again
as they fell out of the sky.
I swept all the harder when
I watched a dozen of them die —
as if their dust fell through the screen   30
upon the floor I had just cleaned.
She came back and turned the dial;
the screen went dark. *That's beautiful*,
she said, and ran her clean hand through
my hair, and on, over the window-   35
sill, coffee table, rocker, desk, ·
and held it up — I held my breath —
That's beautiful, she said, impressed,
she hadn't found a speck of death.

APPROACHING THE READING

1. Explain what is going on in lines 1–14, 15–25, and 26–39, and how the three
   sections relate to each other. Pick out similes, metaphors, and metonymies
   that clarify each section. How does the occasional use of rhyme contribute
   to the poem?
2. Is the title itself a metonymy? What is the mother teaching the speaker?
   What is the speaker learning?
3. Look again at the last line. One expects to read "speck of dust," or "dirt." In
   what ways is the substitution of "death" meaningful?

RESPONDING THROUGH Writing

WRITING ABOUT FIGURATIVE LANGUAGE

Journal Entries

www

Research the authors
in this chapter with LitLinks
at bedfordstmartins.com/
approachinglit.

1. Look for similes as you read your favorite magazine,
   look at advertisements in magazines or on billboards, or watch commercials on TV. List several
   examples in your journal and comment on why use
   of similes makes for effective advertising.
2. As a journal entry, finish this line: "Waiting for you is like _____ ."
   Come up with three different similes, each having the effect of "stretching
   your reader's perception." Try to push each one further than the one before.
   For example:

like waiting for summer
like listening to a scratched CD
like Thursday

Then, choose a subject and write several different figures for it. For example:

Love is like _____.

Love is _____.

Love _____.

Write a paragraph in which you discuss the varied effects the different figures create.

3. Watch and/or listen to several comedians. Write a journal entry discussing their uses of paradox, overstatement, and understatement.

Literary Analysis Papers

4. Select a poem with striking use of figures, such as Geoffrey Hill's elegy "In Memory of Jane Fraser" (p. 649), Claude McKay's sonnet "America" (p. 821), or Andrew Marvell's love poem "To His Coy Mistress" (p. 823). Write a paper in which you discuss what the poem's figures suggest, what they help you realize, and how they affect your perceptions.

5. Go back to one of the poems in chapters 12–14 that relies heavily on figurative language, such as Robert Hayden's "Those Winter Sundays" (p. 548) or William Shakespeare's "That time of year thou mayst in me behold" (p. 606). Write a paper discussing the effect of figurative language in the poem.

6. Write a paper discussing the use of figures and archetypes in A. E. Housman's "To an Athlete Dying Young" (p. 802). Consider how the poem's ideas relate to the present-day emphasis on superstar athletes and athletics.

Comparison-Contrast Papers

7. Write a paper comparing and contrasting two poems about the death of a child — Michael S. Harper's "Nightmare Begins Responsibility" (p. 794) and Ben Jonson's "On My First Son" (p. 806) — including the differences in their choice and handling of figurative language.

8. Write a paper comparing and contrasting what Margaret Atwood in "True Stories" (p. 736) and Li-Young Lee in "Visions and Interpretations" (p. 813) say about seeking or knowing the truth, focusing particularly on the way they use figures of speech to explore the subject.

WRITING ABOUT CONNECTIONS

Figures of speech by their nature make connections, and many of the topics suggested above involve discussions of the surprising but meaningful comparisons,

> **TIPS for Writing about Figurative Language**

> **Main topic or subtopic** As with most elements of poetry, you can concentrate on figurative language as the main subject of a paper or include it as a subtopic in a paper that concentrates on other aspects of the poem.

> **How it works and what it achieves** When writing about figurative language, you should both explain how the figure works (what is compared to what or equated with what or substituted for what) and discuss the effect, role, or meaning the imaginative language contributes to the poem.

> **Focusing on altered perceptions** Figurative language often alters the ways we perceive things. For example, it may lead readers to see an image in a fresh, unusual, even challenging way. Explaining in detail how that occurs can turn into an engaging topic for a paper or a section of a paper.

> **Focusing on figurative patterns** A discussion of the imagery of a poem or group of poems, in the sense of "a related pattern of imaginative comparisons and allusions running through an entire literary work or a portion of one" (see above, p. 563), can be an illuminating topic for a paper.

> **Using correct labels** For a paper dealing specifically with figurative language, it is wise to use the traditional terminology (simile, metaphor, implied metaphor, personification, metonymy, synecdoche, and paradox) and to use it precisely.

equations, and substitutions that establish such imaginative connections. The same kind of imaginative thinking can be used in noticing surprising but meaningful thematic connections between poems and turning them into interesting paper topics. Here are a few possibilities to illustrate:

1. "Innocence and Experience": Confrontations with Evil in Julia Alvarez's "How I Learned to Sweep" (p. 650) and William Blake's "The Chimney Sweeper" (p. 744)
2. "A Joyful Melancholy": Nature and Beauty in Mary Oliver's "First Snow" (p. 646) and William Wordsworth's "I wandered lonely as a cloud" (p. 713)
3. "Knowing Deep the Seasons": Antitheses of Life in John Keats's "To Autumn" (p. 645) and William Carlos Williams's "Spring and All" (p. 880)

WRITING RESEARCH PAPERS

1. Research the history of lynching in the United States and use what you find to illuminate Thylias Moss's "The Lynching" (p. 829) and the second section

of Toi Derricotte's "A Note on My Son's Face" (p. 768), particularly the figures of speech both poets employ.

2. Conduct research into the problem of spouse or partner abuse and into poems related to the subject, such as Louise Erdrich's "A Love Medicine" (p. 780), Jo Carson's "I Cannot Remember All the Times" (available online), and poems in Mary Marecek's book *Breaking Free from Partner Abuse: Voices of Battered Women Caught in the Cycle of Domestic Violence* (1993) or another similar book. Write a paper on how poetry has been and can be used as a way of dealing with the problem or communicating to others about the problem.

COMPOSING IN OTHER ART FORMS

1. Come up with a screenplay for William Stafford's "Traveling through the Dark" (p. 642). Include camera shots for each moment, explain why you chose each shot, and include a discussion of how you would convey the figurative language.

2. Find or compose music for one or more of the poems in this chapter and write a paragraph explaining why you think the music is an appropriate "score" for the poem.

There's poetry in the language I speak. There's poetry, therefore, in my culture, and in this place.

Sekou Sundiata

Rhythm and Meter   CHAPTER 16
Feeling the Beat, the Flux, and the Flow

Our lives are rich with rhythms: the regular rhythms of sunrise and sunset, the change of seasons, the waves on the shore, the beats of our heart, even the routines in our lives — holidays, trash days, final exam week, income tax time. Life also has irregular rhythms that are, paradoxically, rhythmical: the syncopations of the city, the stutter step of a basketball player, the anxious cadence of our speech under stress and uncertainty, people dropping by, and the infamous pop quiz. We need rhythms and live by them, regardless of whether we are aware of them. The same can be said of poetry: Every poem has rhythm, and experiencing a poem fully requires being attentive to its rhythms. This chapter focuses on the ways rhythms, regular and irregular, contribute to a poem's impact and meanings and on ways to help you hear and feel these rhythms more accurately and more intensely.

READING FOR RHYTHM

All careful writing has **rhythm**, the patterned "movement" created by words and their arrangement. Poetry in particular emphasizes it. Rhythm is somewhat difficult to describe. Because no set of precise descriptive labels is available, we turn to metaphorical language. We say that rhythm is, for example, fast, slow, syncopated, disjointed, smooth, halting, graceful, rough, deliberate, frenzied, or a mixture of any of these. The rhythms in a poem are affected by the way the poet handles various features.

Line Length

Short lines can have one effect, long lines another, though the effect varies from poem to poem. Usually short lines create a faster rhythm and longer lines a slower rhythm, but that's not always the case. Compare the rapid rhythms in the short lines of "my old man" (p. 573) with the slower ones of "In the Waiting Room" (p. 742), and the fairly rapid long lines of "Grandfather-in-Law" (p. 624) with the slower ones of "God's Grandeur" (p. 610).

Phrasings

The combinations of short and longer groups of words into phrases affect a poem's rhythm, especially the speed of reading and the regularity or irregularity of movement across and down the page. See, for example, how phrasings contribute to Leslie Marmon Silko's "Prayer to the Pacific" (p. 614).

Line Endings

Lines without end punctuation are said to "run on" into the next line (**run-on lines**; also called **enjambment**), which tends toward a faster, smoother pace from line to line. Lines with end punctuation, especially periods and semicolons (**end-stopped lines**), often slow down. Notice the difference in rhythm between lines 1–2 (end-stopped) and lines 3–4 (run-on) of the third stanza of "Richard Cory" (p. 640):

> And he was rich — yes, richer than a king —
> And admirably schooled in every grace:
> In fine, we thought that he was everything
> To make us wish that we were in his place.

Lines broken at unexpected or irregular places create a jolt and break up the rhythmic flow; line breaks at expected or "natural" places create a gentle shift carrying the rhythm along smoothly.

Pauses

Pauses (or lack of them) within lines can affect their pace and smoothness. A **pause**, called a **caesura** and usually indicated by punctuation, tends to break up the flow of a line, slow it down a bit, perhaps make it "jagged" or "halting." Lack of pauses can propel a line and make it either flowing and graceful or hurried, even frenetic. Compare the first three lines, broken by pauses, with the unbroken last line of the final stanza of "Richard Cory":

> So on we worked, and waited for the light,
> And went without the meat, and cursed the bread;

And Richard Cory, one calm summer night,
Went home and put a bullet through his head. (p. 641)

How would placing a comma after "home" in the last line change the effect?

Spaces

Leaving gaps within, at the beginning or end of, or between lines can slow up the movement, even stop it altogether, or indicate which words to group together; crowding things together can speed up a rhythm. (Note the various uses of spacing in "Buffalo Bill 's" on p. 657.)

Word Choice and Combinations of Sounds

Words that are easy to say together can create a steady, smooth, harmonious pace in a line; those hard to say can make it "jagged" or "harsh" or "tired" or simply slow and deliberate. Notice the difference between the way sounds slide into each other and are easy to say in the five-word line "Clean favored, and imperially slim," from the first stanza in "Richard Cory," and the way the nine words in the last line, "Went home and put a bullet through his head," force us to enunciate each separately and distinctly. The sounds don't flow together but come from different parts of the mouth, which takes longer to get them out.

It is important to realize that different rhythms may be appropriate for the same experience. For example, a frantic or a calm rhythm may be appropriate for a poem about a traffic accident, depending on what the poet wants you to experience.

ENTRY POINTS   The following poem celebrates a hero of the old American West. As you read it, notice the effects of line lengths, line endings, pauses within lines (or lack of them), spaces, word choices, and combinations of sounds.

E. E. Cummings   1894–1962

Buffalo Bill 's   [1923]

Buffalo Bill 's
defunct
          who used to
          ride a watersmooth-silver
                                        stallion   5
and break onetwothreefourfive pigeonsjustlikethat
                                        Jesus

> he was a handsome man
>   and what i want to know is
> how do you like your blueeyed boy   10
> Mister Death

APPROACHING THE READING

Research this author in depth with cultural documents and multimedia resources on *LiterActive*.

1. Try reading the poem aloud, respecting line divisions by pausing briefly at the ends of lines (but without letting your voice drop the way it does at the end of a sentence) and reading "onetwothreefourfive" as nearly like one word as possible. Listen for how all this affects pace and rhythm.

2. Then read for meaning. What is the effect on meaning to put individual words on separate lines, to break lines and situate words at unexpected places, and to jam several words together? Write a brief statement of your interpretation of the poem's theme.

To help focus on the effect of gaps, spaces, line divisions, and line groupings, listen to the poem the way it could have been written — in six lines, using conventional punctuation, and a fairly regular beat:

> Buffalo Bill's defunct, who used to ride
> A water-smooth silver stallion and break
> One, two, three, four, five pigeons, just like that.
> Jesus, he was a handsome man.
> And what I want to know is,
> How do you like your blue-eyed boy, Mister Death?

Notice how Cummings's form of the poem creates a rhythm entirely different from this version written in six conventional lines. The rhythm definitely affects the meaning.

- A line break invites you to pause briefly after "Buffalo Bill 's," to linger on the name and give it emphasis as well as creating a moment of anticipation. Without the line break, the emphasis would fall on "defunct," instead of each line receiving emphasis.
- The pause in the middle of the infinitive "to ride" shifts meaning from "used to *ride*" to "who *used to*," which reinforces the meaning of "defunct" (used to, but does so no more). This break simultaneously sets up anticipation and emphasizes the loss.
- Emphasis falls next on "a watersmooth-silver" and on "stallion," a single-word line emphatic in both rhythm and meaning.

- Jamming the words "onetwothreefourfive" and "pigeonsjustlikethat" together creates a quick staccato rhythm that echoes the rapid firing of a revolver.
- The rhythm slows with "Jesus" set off in a line of its own far to the right: Its position far to the right requires a pause, not unlike the exhaled sigh one expresses when saying "Jesus" in this manner, but so does the extra space between it and the next line of text.
- The next three phrases also are slower and more reflective. Their similarity in length (six, seven, and eight syllables) creates a rhythmical similarity that makes the short, abrupt last line surprising in rhythm as well as in meaning and tone.

After saying all this about rhythmic strategies in "Buffalo Bill 's," it is important to emphasize that rhythm is not fixed. Your involvement as a reader is crucial. How long a word is to be "held," how much stress is to be put on a syllable, how short a short line is and how long a long line is, and how much pause there is in a pause are effects you create or decide on.

READING FOR METER

As part of their rhythm, poems can have a regular "beat." You're already familiar with beat: When you listen to certain types of music, you are probably struck by or react to the beat. You may say or hear someone else say, "I love the beat of that song."

STRESSED AND UNSTRESSED SYLLABLES   A beat in poetry arises from the contrast of emphasized (stressed or accented) and muted (unstressed or unaccented) syllables. Poetry with a steady beat, or measured pulse, is said to have **meter**, a regularized beat created by a repeating pattern of accents, syllables, or both. The most widely used type of meter in English (called *accentual-syllabic*) takes into account both the number of stresses and the number of syllables per line. If you're unsure about syllables and accents for a particular word, check a dictionary: It divides words into syllables and indicates where the stress is put.

The process of picking out a poem's meter by marking stressed and unstressed syllables is called **scansion**. For a fuller and more technical discussion of meter and scansion, see the appendix on scansion (pp. 1574–83).

POETIC FEET   The basis of accentual-syllabic meter is the repetition of metrical "feet." A **foot** is a two- or three-syllable metrical unit made up (usually) of one stressed and one or two unstressed syllables. As these combinations of stressed plus unstressed syllables (*da DA*, or *da da DA*) are repeated, a regular pattern or beat (*da DA da DA da DA*, or *da da DA da da DA*) becomes established in your ear; you unconsciously expect to continue to hear it, and you notice variations from the "norm."

IAMBIC METER   There are terms, or names, for these feet. The *da DA* feet, called **iambs**, create iambic meter. Listen for it in this line:

i AM bic ME ter GOES like THIS.

Now listen for it in the opening lines of Claude McKay's sonnet "America" (p. 821):

AlTHOUGH she FEEDS me BREAD of BITterNESS,
And SINKS inTO my THROAT her TIger's TOOTH,
STEALing my BREATH of LIFE, i WILL conFESS
i LOVE this CULtured HELL that TESTS my YOUTH!

Iambic is by far the most frequently used foot. The other feet are often used for variation in mostly iambic poems, though sometimes they are found as the dominant foot in an entire poem.

TROCHAIC METER   The inversion of the iambic foot is the **trochee** (*DA da*), which forms a trochaic meter (again, listen for it):

TRO chees PUT the AC cent FIRST.

In the third line quoted above from "America," "STEALing" is a trochaic foot, used as a **substitution** (a different kind of foot put in place of the one normally demanded by the meter). Substitutions add variety, emphasize the dominant foot by contrasting with it, and often coincide with a switch in meaning. Here the substitution makes "stealing" more emphatic and foregrounds its meaning.

Listen for trochaic feet in this stanza from the introduction to William Blake's (mostly cheerful) *Songs of Innocence*:

PIPing DOWN the VALleys WILD,
PIPing SONGS of PLEASant GLEE,
ON a CLOUD i SAW a CHILD,
AND he LAUGHing SAID to ME:

"PIPE a SONG aBOUT a LAMB."
SO i PIPED with MERry CHEER.

Stresses are never equally strong; that is one way of attaining rhythmic variety even in lines that are metrically regular. Thus, in the third line, CLOUD and CHILD get more stress than ON and SAW. Some syllables (AND in the fourth line, SO in line 6) are given a light stress mainly because we expect, from the pattern established, that they *should* be stressed (likewise the "into" in the McKay passage above). You may have noticed that these lines have four stressed syllables but only three unstressed syllables; the fourth trochee in each line is incomplete, lacking its unstressed syllable, which is replaced by a mandatory pause: All the lines are end-stopped. This is another way to do something unusual with, and add variety to, a metrical poem.

ANAPESTIC AND DACTYLIC METERS   Two other feet add an unstressed syllable to the feet described above: an **anapest** adds one to an iamb (*da da DA*), and a **dactyl** adds one to a trochee (*DA da da*). Whole poems in these meters are unusual; they are typically used for substitutions in predominantly iambic or trochaic poems. Here, however, are the final lines from a poem mostly in anapestic meter, also by William Blake, "The Chimney Sweeper" (p. 744), which appeared in his more pessimistic *Songs of Experience*. The poem describes the awful lives of small boys forced to climb up chimneys and clean out the soot. The lilting anapests create a sharply ironic contrast with the content, as Tom receives comfort from a dream about heaven he had the night before:

> Though the MORNing was COLD, Tom was HAPpy and WARM;
> So if ALL do their DUty, they NEED not fear HARM.

SPONDEE   One other important foot, the **spondee**, has two stressed syllables (*DA DA*), with no unstressed syllables, as in GOOD NIGHT and RAGE, RAGE in these lines from a poem by Dylan Thomas pleading to his father not to accept death passively and quietly (p. 866):

> Do NOT go GENtle INto THAT GOOD NIGHT.
> RAGE, RAGE aGAINST the DYing OF the LIGHT.

Many other feet have been given names, but knowing these five (iamb, trochee, anapest, dactyl, spondee) will enable you to describe the basic meter and variations from it in most poems — and describing them will help you hear them more clearly.

LINE LENGTHS   The other thing to notice in poems in traditional meters involves the length of the lines. Line lengths are measured by the number of feet in each line and are labeled with names derived from Greek roots; for example,

> **monometer** = a line with one foot
> **dimeter** = a line with two feet
> **trimeter** = a line with three feet

tetrameter = a line with four feet

pentameter = a line with five feet

hexameter = a line with six feet (and so on)

The line we used above ("iAMbic MEter GOES like THIS") is *iambic tetrameter*. The description identifies the predominant foot (here, iamb) and the predominant line length (four feet) in a poem — that is, the ones used the majority of the time.

ENTRY POINTS   The following poem by a late-nineteenth-century African American poet expresses the conflict experienced for persons of color forced to conform to societal expectations of behavior and attitude. Try picking out the meter in the poem by noting the syllables stressed in each line.

Paul Laurence Dunbar   1872–1906

We Wear the Mask   [1896]

We wear the mask that grins and lies,
It hides our cheeks and shades our eyes, —
This debt we pay to human guile;
With torn and bleeding hearts we smile,
And mouth with myriad subtleties.   5

Why should the world be over-wise,
In counting all our tears and sighs?
Nay, let them only see us, while
　　We wear the mask.

We smile, but, O great Christ, our cries   10
To thee from tortured souls arise.
We sing, but oh the clay is vile
Beneath our feet, and long the mile;
But let the world dream otherwise,
　　We wear the mask!   15

APPROACHING THE READING

1. Hearing a regular beat in the first few lines should be fairly easy: All the words have one syllable, and important words alternate with less important ones. Label the predominant meter and the predominant line length.

Do you find any variations (substitutions) from the predominant feet? If so, point them out.

2. Label the metrical feet and length of lines 9 and 15. What is the effect of changing from the longer lines to which our ears have become accustomed to a shorter line?

3. Notice the interplay between rhythmic devices and meter. The meter provides a very regular beat, but pauses and variance in line endings break up the rhythm and keep the beat from dominating the poem. Point out examples, especially from lines 8–15.

4. In what sense could writing a poem on this topic in a traditional meter be thought of as an example of wearing a mask?

In this poem, the meter stands out; it is almost glaringly regular. Here and there a spondee may be substituted for one of the predominant iambs, depending on where a reader decides to place particular emphasis. "We" might well be stressed equally with the verb following it in lines 1, 9, 10, 12, and 15, in order to emphasize the *people* who are forced to present a false image to others while hiding their authentic self: "WE WEAR," "WE SMILE," "WE SING." A poem that calls attention to the mask also lifts it off, enabling us to realize that it is a mask, that it is a lie (line 1), and, ironically, that it is a form of resistance at the same time it is a mark of servitude.

One could even ask, in that regard, if the use of meter in Dunbar's poem serves also as a mask. In the late nineteenth century, meter was still expected in poetry. Only a few poets, such as Walt Whitman, wrote nonmetrical poems, and Whitman was regarded warily as a radical. An African American poet had to use meter to have her or his work be read widely and not be dismissed as unskilled. But it must have created some tension to write in the cadences of white educated society instead of the cadences and rhythms sung by workers in the fields or when they gathered in the evenings. So Dunbar wrote in meter, probably to have his verse accepted but also perhaps because its strict, almost excessive regularity might suggest that the metrical form is a mask, a lie, a form not freely chosen but forced on him.

What does paying attention to meter gain you? It can help you hear more clearly a central rhythmic feature in a metrical poem, its regular beat and the irregular alterations in that beat. Poems written in meter usually have a dominant foot, that is, one used the majority of the time. Once you get accustomed to the meter, your ear becomes attuned to that foot, begins to expect it, and notices when a different foot is substituted and alters the "sameness." Such substitution is an important means of controlling emphasis as well as adding variety.

www

Further explore rhythm and meter, including interactive exercises, with VirtuaLit Poetry at bedfordstmartins.com/approachinglit.

> ☑ **CHECKLIST on Reading for Rhythm and Meter**
>
> ❑ Listen for and respond to the rhythms of poems.
>
> ❑ Note formal structures that affect rhythm (such as line length, line endings, pauses, word choice, combinations of sound).
>
> ❑ Listen for the difference between poems with metrical (written in meter with a regular beat, such as "Richard Cory" — p. 640) and nonmetrical verse (such as "Cold as Heaven" — p. 648).
>
> ❑ Listen for the recurring beat in metrical poems and be able to identify the most important traditional metrical feet: iamb (*da DA*), trochee (*DA da*), anapest (*da da DA*), dactyl (*DA da da*), and spondee (*DA DA*).

FURTHER READING

ENTRY POINTS   Here are two poems about remembrance — one about whether people are remembered after their deaths for what they have been and done, the other about the desire to go home again and the difficulty of doing so. The first reflects on a visit to a southern plantation and on what the tour guide points out (and doesn't point out). In the second, the speaker returns to the urban scene she once wanted to get away from, with the hope that by going there she will get in touch with a part of her identity. Listen for rhythm in both — how the handling of lines, line endings and groupings, combinations of words and sounds and pauses all lead you to speed up, slow down, pause, and adjust your timing.

Lucille Clifton   b. 1936

at the cemetery, walnut grove plantation, south carolina, 1989   [1991]

among the rocks
at walnut grove
your silence drumming
in my bones,
tell me your names.   5

nobody mentioned slaves
and yet the curious tools
shine with your fingerprints.
nobody mentioned slaves

but somebody did this work   10
who had no guide, no stone,
who moulders under rock.

tell me your names,
tell me your bashful names
and i will testify.   15

the inventory lists ten slaves
but only men were recognized.

among the rocks
at walnut grove
some of these honored dead   20
were dark
some of these dark
were slaves
some of these slaves
were women   25
some of them did this
honored work.
tell me your names
foremothers, brothers,
tell me your dishonored names.   30
here lies
here lies
here lies
here lies
hear   35

APPROACHING THE READING

1. This begins as a poem of address: The speaker addresses the dead slaves. Consider whether the rhythms of the poem fit or enhance the addressing. Why is this way of writing on this subject effective?
2. Select groups of two or three lines anywhere in the poem and mark the stressed syllables (see the appendix on scansion [pp. 1574–83] for the traditional method of doing so). Is there a regular beat all the time, or some of the time, or never? If there is a regular beat at all, comment on how it contributes to the rhythm and effect of the poem.
3. Describe the rhythm of the last five lines. Is the list effective? What is the effect of the serious pun as the last line?
4. "[T]ell me your names," the speaker says, "and i will testify" (ll. 13, 15). What does "testify" denote and connote here? In what sense is the poem itself a testimony? In what sense does it have the rhythms of testimony? Can the speaker testify even though she receives no response to her request in line 13?

Lorna Dee Cervantes b. 1954

Freeway 280   [1981]

Las casitas° near the gray cannery,   *little houses*
nestled amid wild abrazos° of climbing roses   *hugs*
and man-high red geraniums
are gone now. The freeway conceals it
all beneath a raised scar.   5

But under the fake windsounds of the open lanes,
in the abandoned lots below, new grasses sprout,
wild mustard remembers, old gardens
come back stronger than they were,
trees have been left standing in their yards.   10
Albaricoqueros, cerezos, nogales° . . .   *apricot, cherry, walnut trees*
Viejitas° come here with paper bags to gather greens.   *old women*
Espinaca, verdolagas, yerbabuena° . . .   *spinach, purslane, mint*

I scramble over the wire fence
that would have kept me out.   15
Once, I wanted out, wanted the rigid lanes
to take me to a place without sun,
without the smell of tomatoes burning
on swing shift in the greasy summer air.

Maybe it's here   20
en los campos extraños de esta ciudad°   *in the strange fields of this city*
where I'll find it, that part of me
mown under
like a corpse
or a loose seed.   25

APPROACHING THE READING

1. The poem starts with description of a scene, juxtaposing the way it was before, as the speaker looks back, and the way it is now. Listen to the rhythms
   in the first two sections of the poem. How do they fit the subject and tone?
   Why does the speaker use Spanish words part of the time? In what ways do
   they fit the subject and tone? The rhythm?
2. Listen to the rhythm of each line in stanzas 3 and 4, as well as the rhythm of
   the whole poem. The speaker says that in the past she "wanted out" (l. 16).
   Why? What is the speaker's attitude now? What was it before? How does
   the rhythm fit and reinforce what she is saying?

3. Where does this poem have meter? Be ready to talk about how the meter interacts with, or becomes a part of, the rhythm, and how the meter shapes or contributes to intensity, emphasis, meaning, and implications.
4. Consider the comparisons to a corpse or a loose seed in the short closing lines. Why does the speaker see the comparison differently now? How does the rhythm of the three short concluding lines fit the poem?
5. How does the title fit the poem? Why that as title?

ENTRY POINTS   The following poem, like the previous one, is about a road. It too is a memory poem, as the speaker thinks back on a decision, a turning point she or he will long remember and reflect on. Unlike the previous two poems, this one is metrical throughout. Read the poem, emphasizing the meter. Then reread it, concentrating on words and expression, feeling the meter as you would a bass guitar behind a rhythm guitar. Think about how meter contributes in significant ways to the poem's rhythm.

Robert Frost   1874–1963

The Road Not Taken   [1916]

Two roads diverged in a yellow wood,
And sorry I could not travel both
And be one traveler, long I stood
And looked down one as far as I could
To where it bent in the undergrowth;   5

Then took the other, as just as fair,
And having perhaps the better claim,
Because it was grassy and wanted wear;
Though as for that, the passing there
Had worn them really about the same,   10

And both that morning equally lay
In leaves no step had trodden black.
Oh, I kept the first for another day!
Yet knowing how way leads on to way,
I doubted if I should ever come back.   15

I shall be telling this with a sigh
Somewhere ages and ages hence:
Two roads diverged in a wood, and I—
I took the one less traveled by,
And that has made all the difference.   20

APPROACHING THE READING

1. This poem is often read as a poem about not conforming to the majority, taking the road that most do NOT take. However, Robert Frost was hesitant about advocating that reading. What other reading or readings could you give to the poem? Think about a choice you made in your life and what you found yourself thinking about it afterwards.

2. Robert Frost called himself a "Synecdochist," because he preferred poetry in which "a little thing touches a larger thing" (see p. 640 for the quote and pp. 639–40 for **synecdoche**). What does this suggest about the choice the speaker made and about the poem as a whole? What does it suggest about details in the poem? Consider the little word *by* in line 19. What different ways can you read that line based on the meanings of the word?

Research this author in depth with cultural documents and multimedia resources on *LiterActive*.

3. Robert Frost commented that his poems often say one thing in order to mean another. Where do you see possible instances of that in this poem? For example, what do you make of the word *sigh* (l. 16)? Think about some of its connotations.

4. Mark the stressed and unstressed syllables in the poem and try dividing them into poetic feet. What foot is predominant? Label it and the line length. Note instances that vary from the predominant foot and consider how such variations affect the way you read the poem.

5. Describe the poem's rhythm and point out techniques that shape the rhythm. Be ready to comment on how meter contributes to the overall rhythm.

6. Why would a poet as intelligent and crafty as Robert Frost end this famous poem with a cliché, with something so trite?

ENTRY POINTS   The following poem, like the three previous ones, is a memory poem, or at least culminates as a memory poem. Unlike the others, it is a love poem, albeit an unusual one since it approaches its subject indirectly. Notice rhythms, as you read and reread it: The poem talks about rhythm ("slow motion," music, dancing) as well as employs it. Reflect on how the poem's rhythm fits with and contributes to its meaning and effect.

Gary Miranda   b. 1938

Love Poem   [1978]

A kind of slant: the way a ball will glance
off the end of a bat when you swing for the fence

and miss — that is, if you could watch that once,
up close and in slow motion; or the chance
meanings, not even remotely intended, that dance   5
at the edge of words, like sparks. Bats bounce
just so off the edges of the dark at a moment's
notice, as swallows do off sunlight. Slants

like these have something to do with why *angle*
is one of my favorite words, whenever it chances   10
to be a verb; and with why the music I single
out tonight — eighteenth-century dances —
made me think just now of you untangling
blueberries, carefully, from their dense branches.

APPROACHING THE READING

1. Miranda brings together a group of things that one would not expect to go together, let alone in a love poem: a foul ball when the batter swings for a homerun, the music of eighteenth-century dances, untangling blueberry branches, his love of the word "angle" when used as a verb, bats and swallows, dense branches. What do you make of this combination, and what do you think these things have to do with love?
2. Notice as you read how the rhythms of the lines fit what the poem is saying. Think about how you would describe that.
3. Look for where there is a regular beat (a metrical beat) and where you find that breaking down or becoming more of a syncopated rhythm. Consider whether or not you think that this is appropriate, effective for what the poem is working with.
4. Notice that the poem is in sonnet form and uses rhyme. Be ready to discuss the rhymes, the rhyme scheme, and the handling of sonnet form. Can you think of reasons why these are appropriate for a contemporary love poem?
5. How would you describe the speaker and the speaker's attitude toward love?

ENTRY POINTS   The following four poems extend the theme of identity touched on in the last two poems. Decide which of them is/are written in meter and which is/are nonmetrical. Watch for how their handling of rhythm, metrical or nonmetrical, contributes to the effect and meaning of each poem.

A. K. Ramanujan   1929–1993
Self-Portrait   [1966]

I resemble everyone
but myself, and sometimes see
in shop-windows,
    despite the well-known laws
    of optics,   5
the portrait of a stranger,
date unknown,
often signed in a corner
by my father.

Emily Dickinson   1830–1886
I'm Nobody! Who are you?   [c. 1861; 1891]

I'm Nobody! Who are you?
Are you — Nobody — Too?
Then there's a pair of us?
Don't tell! they'd advertise — you know!

How dreary — to be — Somebody!   5
How public — like a Frog —
To tell one's name — the livelong June —
To an admiring Bog!

Sylvia Plath   1932–1963
Metaphors   [1960]

Research this author
in depth with cultural
documents and multimedia
resources on *LiterActive*.

I'm a riddle in nine syllables,
An elephant, a ponderous house,
A melon strolling on two tendrils.
O red fruit, ivory, fine timbers!
This loaf's big with its yeasty rising.   5
Money's new-minted in this fat purse.
I'm a means, a stage, a cow in calf.
I've eaten a bag of green apples,
Boarded the train there's no getting off.

Georgia Douglas Johnson   1880–1966

Wishes   [1927]

I'm tired of pacing the petty round of the ring of the thing I know —
I want to stand on the daylight's edge and see where the sunsets go.

I want to sail on a swallow's tail and peep through the sky's blue glass.
I want to see if the dreams in me shall perish or come to pass.

I want to look through the moon's pale crook and gaze on the
    moon-man's face.   5
I want to keep all the tears I weep and sail to some unknown place.

APPROACHING THE READING

1. Read each poem aloud. Listen for a regular beat or look for a regular pattern; if you find one, mark syllables in several lines to help decide if the poem is metrical.
2. If the lines are metrical, label the metrical form and listen for how the meter interacts with and becomes a part of the rhythm. Consider how the meter shapes or contributes to intensity, emphasis, meaning, and implications.
3. If the lines are not metrical, consider how the rhythm seems appropriate to and helps develop the subject, tone, and theme.
4. For each poem, write a brief statement of theme and a brief explanation of how rhythm contributes to the way the poem works.

RESPONDING THROUGH Writing

WRITING ABOUT RHYTHM AND METER

Journal Entries

1. Review the discussion of prose rhythms in Chapter 7 (p. 204). Then read a poem written in long, prose-like lines, such as David Mura's "Grandfather-in-Law" (p. 624), Allen Ginsberg's "A Supermarket in California" (p. 784), and Etheridge Knight's "Hard Rock Returns to Prison from the Hospital for the Criminal Insane" (p. 810). In your journal, discuss ways rhythms in prose and rhythms in poetry are similar and different (and are created in similar and different ways).
2. Fill in the following sentence: I got up this morning and _____, then I _____, and then I _____. Now

break it into rhythmic units, writing each unit as a line of poetry. Try dividing it in other places. In your journal, discuss how rhythm and emphasis change as a result of different breaks, and reflect on the kinds of aesthetic decisions a writer has to make about where to divide lines.

www

Research the authors in this chapter with LitLinks at bedfordstmartins.com/approachinglit.

3. Nursery rhymes and children's poetry are often written in meter. Choose two or three examples, write a few lines of each in your journal, mark the stressed syllables, and label the metric foot and line length. Then perhaps write a paper examining the handling of meter in a nursery rhyme or children's poem — or more than one of them — and discussing why meter is an effective technique in verse for children.

Literary Analysis Papers

4. Write a paper on the effect of sound and rhythm on the characterization of the speaker and the development of theme in T. S. Eliot's "The Love Song of J. Alfred Prufrock" (p. 776).
5. Rhythm is important in poems that are about or draw upon music. Write a paper discussing the relation of rhythm to what is being said in one of the following poems, or one not in this book: Sterling A. Brown's "Riverbank Blues" (p. 750), Jayne Cortez's "Into This Time" (p. 762), Sonia Sanchez's "An Anthem" (p. 851), or Al Young's "A Dance for Ma Rainey" (p. 885).
6. Write a paper discussing the interaction of meter and rhythm in Wilfred Owen's "Dulce et Decorum Est" (p. 589), Samuel Taylor Coleridge's "Kubla Khan" (p. 761), Andrew Marvell's "To His Coy Mistress" (p. 823), Dudley Randall's "Ballad of Birmingham" (p. 843), or Dylan Thomas's "Do not go gentle into that good night" (p. 866).

Comparison-Contrast Papers

7. Write a paper comparing and contrasting what Lawson Fusao Inada's "Plucking Out a Rhythm" (p. 803) and Quincy Troupe's "Poem from the Root Doctor of Rock n Roll" (p. 867) say about rhythm and the way they use rhythm as an integral part of what the poems explore and express.
8. Rhythm is important in poems about dance, often to theme as well as technique. Write a paper comparing and contrasting the presence of rhythm in two or more of the following poems: Theodore Roethke's "My Papa's Waltz" (p. 577), Cornelius Eady's "My Mother, If She Had Won Free Dance Lessons" (p. 775), Charles Simic's "Classic Ballroom Dances" (p. 855), Al Young's "A Dance for Ma Rainey" (p. 885).

WRITING ABOUT CONNECTIONS

There is a tendency to think in terms of relating metrical poems to other metrical poems and nonmetrical poems to nonmetrical ones, but that overlooks

> ## ➤ TIPS for Writing about Rhythm and Meter

> ➤ **Deciding about rhythm and meter** If rhythm and meter are integral to the discussion of your topic, it is essential to include them, even as a subtopic. Be sure to use specific examples (including quotations) and thorough explanations. Otherwise, making them a part of your paper is seldom crucial in the way it might be for diction, tone, or figurative language. However, finding a way to refer to them could enrich your paper and add more sophistication to it.

> ➤ **Focusing on rhythm** When working with a poem's rhythm as the main subject of a paper, it is important to make sure that you choose a poem or poems in which the rhythm plays a key role, is distinctive, carries meaning and/or feeling, creates an impact, or is handled in an otherwise especially subtle or distinctive way. Such a paper will need to include a careful analysis of the techniques used to achieve the poem's rhythmic effects and of the way they contribute to its theme or significance.

> ➤ **Focusing on appropriateness** An interesting approach to a paper about rhythm can be one in which you examine how the rhythm of a poem is appropriate for the speaker or the speaker's tone and voice in dealing with the poem's subject or some combination thereof.

> ➤ **Focusing on form and rhythm in free verse** For free verse, writing about the relationship between form and rhythm, especially how form often results from decisions about rhythm, can be a fruitful topic for a paper or a subtopic in a paper focusing on other aspects of the poem.

> ➤ **Focusing on meter** For an example of how to write a paper focused on meter and its effect on rhythm, see the appendix on scansion (pp. 1574–83). Working with such a topic turns out best when an author uses meter in especially meaningful, integrated, or unusual ways. A metrical poem that is almost entirely regular and predictable won't give you much to talk about unless there is particular significance, accomplishment, or irony in its regularity.

other significant linkages. Valuable thematic connections can occur from pairing two poems that have similar subjects but that handle rhythm quite differently. Here are some possibilities:

1. "Remembering the Unremembered": The Language of Preservation in Lucille Clifton's "at the cemetery, walnut grove plantation, south carolina, 1989" (p. 664) and Thomas Gray's "Elegy Written in a Country Churchyard" (p. 788)
2. "On the Road Again": The Search for Self in Lorna Dee Cervantes's "Freeway 280" (p. 666) and Alfred, Lord Tennyson's "Ulysses" (p. 864)
3. "Grief beyond Grief": Dealing with Death in Ben Jonson's "On My First Son" (p. 806) and Michael S. Harper's "Nightmare Begins Responsibility" (p. 794)

WRITING RESEARCH PAPERS

1. Do research on Saint Francis of Assisi and use what you find in explicating Galway Kinnell's "Saint Francis and the Sow" (p. 809), including in your discussion the appropriateness of its use of images, rhythm, and form.
2. Write a paper on William Blake's critique of the social and/or economic situation in early nineteenth-century England, especially the neglect and exploitation of children. Do research on the topic and read several poems by Blake that deal with the subject, including one in this book ("The Chimney Sweeper," p. 744, from Blake's *Songs of Innocence*) and others from Blake's *Songs of Experience*, such as "Holy Thursday," "The Chimney Sweeper," and "London." Consider as part of your analysis the appropriateness of Blake's use of form, meter, rhythm, and rhyme in developing his themes.

COMPOSING IN OTHER ART FORMS

1. Try your hand at choreographing a poem or at creating a rhythmic accompaniment to a poem.
2. Abstract expressionism in the visual arts often reveals feeling and energy. Pick a poem and create an abstract drawing, painting, sculpture, or collage that evokes what you think the poem is trying to express.

Writing about Poetry

Applying What You've Learned

We write about poetry for the same reasons we write about fiction — to participate in an ongoing conversation about things that interest, provoke, excite, or puzzle us about the literary works we read. After asking a friend or classmate about the meaning of a line (What's the point behind Marge Piercy's "Barbie Doll" cutting off her nose and legs and "offer[ing] them up"?) and participating in class discussion of the poem (What does it show about attitudes toward women that she was "advised to play coy, / exhorted to come on hearty, / exercise, diet, smile and wheedle"? Would men be told things like that?), you might decide to write a paper on "Marge Piercy's Critique of Social Attitudes toward Women in 'Barbie Doll.'"

Chapters 11–16 helped prepare you to read poetry with increasing sensitivity, alertness, and confidence, and also prepared you to write about poetry. Each chapter provided ways to move into a poem and to enlarge your experience of the variety of things happening in it: in subject matter, formal elements, the range of effects, and the techniques through which the effects are achieved. The section on short papers in Chapter 2 (pp. 34–46) provided you with general guidance for essays on literature. Also notice that some of the suggestions in Chapter 8 on writing about fiction can be carried over to your writing about poetry. This chapter examines what is different about poetry and the particular challenges it poses.

TOPICS

The difference starts with preparation. To write effectively about a particular poem, it's wise to live with it for a while. Even though a poem is usually a shorter piece to read than a story, you should plan to spend a similar amount of time exploring a poem as you would a short story. If possible, spread the time you spend with it over at least a week. Read the poem two or three times a day, sometimes aloud, sometimes — if you can arrange it — listening to someone else read it. Each time you read the poem, focus on a different aspect — one time on the speaker and voice, another on images, another on rhythm, and so on. Photocopy the poem and mark it up; jot notes that you can come back to later. By doing this, the poem becomes part of you (you'll probably even be able to recite parts or all of it from memory).

Papers about poetry, like those about fiction, can focus on what goes on *inside* the work (literary analysis), what *surrounds* the work (comparison-contrast), and what goes *beyond* the work (social and cultural criticism). But in each case, papers on poetry take a slightly different slant from that taken toward fiction.

Writing a Literary Analysis Paper about Poetry

You can do a literary analysis of a poem, writing about what goes on inside it. The process is similar to the way you analyze a story (read or review pp. 234–35). It involves separating out the elements of a poem as a way of studying its nature and the relationships of its central features to each other, the way figurative language relates to tone and theme, for example.

ANALYZE AND INTEGRATE   A literary analysis of a poem might focus on one of the technical features covered in Chapters 11–16 — diction, imagery, sounds, figures, rhythm, meter — clarifying how the technique is used and relating that feature to the effect, or theme, of the poem. Thus, you might examine the use of figurative language in attempting to convey the effect of seeing a human body land on a sidewalk in Gerry LaFemina's "The Sound a Body Makes" (p. 812). Integrating the feature with the poem as a whole is crucial. Your analysis should not isolate a feature from the rest of the work; instead, looking closely at one aspect should be a way toward seeing the entire poem more clearly and fully.

SELECT SOMETHING INTERESTING   Select for your analysis a feature, or two or three features, that are striking, unusual, complex, or subtle, are difficult to understand or accept, or raise questions or problems. The subject doesn't have to be a major or central aspect — a minor feature, like the handling of lines and space in Carl Phillips's "To the Tune of a Small, Repeatable, and Passing Kindness" (p. 838) could result in a good paper. Look for something that you will find interesting to think and write about.

MAKE A POINT   Be careful to avoid just summarizing the poem by restating what it's about in different words. Your paper needs to make a point about the feature and its relation to the whole poem — it needs to have a thesis (see p. 39). And be sure that your point is not one that is obvious to someone on first or even second reading of the poem. That's another reason why it's important to live with the poem before you begin to write about it. Its subtleties and complexities can then sink into your mind and you can write from a more thoughtful understanding of it.

EXPLICATING A POEM   A literary analysis of a short poem often takes the form of **explication**. Explication involves looking closely at the work, opening it up line by line, clarifying how diction, images, figurative language, symbols, sounds, rhythm, form, and allusions contribute toward shaping the poem's meaning and effect. An insightful close reading helps the reader understand and enjoy a poem more completely.

Explication focuses especially on ambiguities, complexities, gaps, what's left unsaid, and interrelationships within a text. It requires being very attentive to specific words and phrases, considering their effects (perhaps considering why the effects of alternate expressions would be different), discussing the impact and meaning of ambiguities and subtleties, and explaining how these elements work together (as they will in an effective poem) toward a particular purpose or theme. For poems up to twenty or thirty lines, you may be able to explicate the entire poem in a four- or five-page paper; for longer poems, you may need to write a longer paper or explicate only a key passage (see pp. 242–43) and relate it to the whole poem.

ORGANIZING LINE BY LINE   One way of organizing an explication paper is to go through the poem from beginning to end, line by line (or by groups of lines), clarifying how techniques and features in the lines create their meaning or effect. In using a line-by-line approach, be careful not to slide into just restating what the poem is about in different words. Make sure you have a unifying principle in your paper, for example, following a technique (such as the use of images or of a certain kind of images or of related figures of speech) through the poem. Doing this avoids having the paper lapse into being merely a series of disconnected paragraphs.

Paragraphs should build on each other to develop the central point (thesis) of the paper. Thus, the way you handle topic sentences (the first sentence of each paragraph, setting up the topic, or main point, of that paragraph) and transitions between paragraphs is important in achieving a unified paper.

ORGANIZING TOPICALLY   Alternatively, an explication paper can be organized topically. That is, one paragraph might discuss the poem's use of images, another its use of figures, and others its tone, use of sound techniques, and rhythm. Each paragraph should include examples from different parts of the poem, chosen so that somewhere in the paper nearly every line is discussed (though not necessarily in the order they appear in the poem). Each paragraph needs to explain how the element it covers contributes to building the total effect of the poem.

This approach is less likely to slide into summarizing what the poem is about than the line-by-line approach, but it requires decisions about what features should be chosen for the different paragraphs and about which lines or phrases should be used for illustrations at various points, to make sure all parts of the poem receive attention. Here, too, unity is important: Without a unifying principle, this approach also can result in disconnected mini-essays. Building each paragraph on the one before and using effective topic sentences and transitions are important.

 TIPS for Writing Literary Analysis Papers

➤ **Examine the text closely** Read (at least once aloud) with your intellect, imagination, and feelings fully engaged, paying attention to every word, sentence, image, figure of speech, and literary technique.

➤ **Narrow your scope** Limit yourself to two or three elements if necessary in discussing a short poem and to selected sections of a long poem. Don't try to cover too much.

➤ **Provide ample illustrations** Back up your analysis with specific examples (including quotations). This grounds and substantiates your conclusions.

➤ **Avoid summary** Summarizing is not literary analysis. Your emphasis needs to be on clarification and explanation of *how* and *why* the writing works.

Some of the "Approaching the Reading" questions and topics following poems in Chapters 11–16 make good topics for analytical or explication papers. Also, many of the suggestions for writing at the end of each chapter involve literary analyses and could be turned into explication topics. Here are some sample topics, out of hundreds of possibilities using poems from this book alone:

1. An analysis of the denotations and connotations of "red" in the vision of history in Linda Hogan's "The History of Red" (p. 799).
2. An analysis of the interaction of form and feeling in Li-Young Lee's "Visions and Interpretations" (p. 813).
3. An analysis of the use of an unconventional form to convey theme in Vievee Francis's "Private Smith's Primer" (p. 784) and/or A. Van Jordan's "From" (p. 806).

4. An explication focused on the role of personification and metaphor in Emily Dickinson's "Because I could not stop for Death" (p. 770).
5. An examination of the way figurative language is used to capture the plight of oppressed children in Ana Castillo's "I Heard the Cries of Two Hundred Children" (p. 753).
6. An explication dealing with diction and meaning in Michael S. Harper's "Nightmare Begins Responsibility" (p. 794).

Writing a Comparison-Contrast Paper about Poetry

A second approach to writing a poetry paper is to work with the literary context surrounding a poem and its connections to other literary works. Poems, like stories, are surrounded by other poems, as well as by stories, novels, and plays, all of which form a meaningful interactive network. A poem can relate to other works in that network by similarities and differences between them, and a literary paper can compare and/or contrast a poem with another poem, a novel, a story, or a play (read or review the pointers about comparison/contrast on pp. 236–38). Possibilities for topics are almost endless. Picking out your own pairings and things to focus on can be enjoyable and can lead you to see things you otherwise might not realize.

SELECTING A TOPIC   A comparison/contrast paper can discuss any aspects of the works, but the works must have a good deal in common or share one especially important feature. If two things are totally different, with nothing in common, there's little value in pointing out the differences. A paper comparing and contrasting Reza Baraheni's "Autumn in Tehran" (p. 890) and Nikki Giovanni's "Nikka-Rosa" (p. 785) would have little value because the two have almost nothing in common. And the similarities and differences should be something of significance, something that really matters. Both "Autumn in Tehran" and Joseph Awad's "Autumnal" (p. 739) use imagery of autumn and are written by poets of Middle Eastern origin. So what? Does that make connecting them meaningful?

MAKE A SIGNIFICANT POINT   It's important that your discussion of the similarities and differences makes a point worth considering. Simply noticing and presenting the similarities and differences seldom, if ever, results in an effective paper. Your paper should have an argumentative thesis that unifies the discussion and brings out its significance. You might, for example, consider comparing and contrasting Joseph Awad's "Autumnal" (p. 739) and William Shakespeare's "That time of year thou mayst in me behold" (p. 606). A paper with a thesis sentence stating that "Autumnal" and "That time of year" have interesting similarities in technique and meaning is off to a good start. Much better is something like, "Although 'Autumnal' and 'That time of year' are similar in their use of archetypal symbols to affirm their devotion to a loved one, Awad's poem goes a step beyond

Shakespeare's in the significant way it leads the reader to explore the meaning of life."

NOTICE ALLUSIONS   Literary works relate to each other also through the use of **allusions**, brief references to a literary or an artistic work or to a historical figure, event, or object intended usually to place one's work within, or alongside, the whole other context of the work, figure, event, or object that is evoked by the reference and thus create comparisons and contrasts between them. Allusions are among the ways works talk to each other, part of the great literary conversation we've mentioned a number of times. It is exciting to notice such communication between literary works and to write about it; the more literature you read, the more such conversations you will notice.

WRITING ABOUT ALLUSIONS   T. S. Eliot, for example, was keenly aware of working within the whole Western literary tradition and packed his poems with allusions to other works. Writing a paper on the use of literary and biblical allusions in T. S. Eliot's "The Love Song of J. Alfred Prufrock" (p. 776) would be challenging but also exciting and rewarding. Poems that draw on ancient myths or retell them are also interesting to study. Writing a paper on a poem that retells a classical myth, examining how the poem compares to the original story — what it retains, what it changes, how it adjusts the emphasis — can prove interesting and informative, as, for example, W. H. Auden's handling of the Icarus myth in "Musée des Beaux Arts" (p. 737) and Eavan Boland's use of the myth of Demeter and Persephone in "The Pomegranate" (p. 748).

CONSIDERING LITERARY TRADITIONS   A significant part of the literary relationships of some poems is their sharing of traditional literary forms, ones used again and again by earlier poets, perhaps for hundreds of years. By writing in such a form, a poet enters the "world" of the sonnet or the blues, the chant, the villanelle, or whatever form is chosen and makes her or his contribution to that ongoing tradition, using the form in ways that are similar to and different from previous uses. Poets often find it meaningful and exciting to feel that, by writing in a traditional form, they are facing the same challenges and feeling the same satisfactions that such writers as William Shakespeare, Bashō, Langston Hughes, and many other great writers have before them. You could choose to write a paper about a poet's handling of a traditional form, as, for example, the use and adaptation of a traditional sonnet form in Gary Miranda's "Love Poem" (p. 668) or Vijay Seshadri's "The Refugee" (p. 853), comparing and contrasting it to its traditional handling and considering the appropriateness of the form to the content and the effect of the way the form is handled.

FOCUS ON A SIGNIFICANT ISSUE   Keep in mind that just demonstrating that a poem adheres to the conventions of its type is seldom interesting or

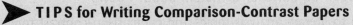

> ### ➤ TIPS for Writing Comparison-Contrast Papers
>
> ➤ **Watch for meaningful pairings** As you read, watch for things that pair up: subject matter, theme, imagery, form, type, technique in one poem that reminds you of another poem in a significant way. Always be alert for comparisons that come from unlikely pairings.
>
> ➤ **Outline similarities and differences** Make lists, then group related items and select two or three topics to focus on.
>
> ➤ **Spell out comparisons and contrasts** Don't just describe the things you are comparing and contrasting; explain why you think there is a connection and why you think it has significance.
>
> ➤ **Don't summarize what happens in the poems** Your paper should point out and discuss similarities and differences regarding specific aspects within the poems, not just offer summaries of what they say.

valuable. Your paper will be effective and helpful when you write about how an author employs a traditional form in a new or unusual or subtle or particularly meaningful way. To point out both what is traditional and what is unexpected and to evaluate the effectiveness of the innovations can result in an enjoyable and enlightening paper.

The "Responding through Writing" sections at the end of Chapters 12–16 include suggestions for comparison-contrast topics. Here are some additional possibilities, though, of course, there are countless options:

1. Compare and contrast tone, technique, and theme in Lucille Clifton's "at the cemetery, walnut grove plantation, south carolina, 1989" (p. 664) and Thomas Gray's "Elegy Written in a Country Churchyard" (p. 788).
2. Compare and contrast the handling of the loss of innocence or "coming of age" theme in Elizabeth Bishop's "In the Waiting Room" (p. 742) and Julia Alvarez's "How I Learned to Sweep" (p. 650).
3. Compare and contrast the theme of searching for truth in Margaret Atwood's "True Stories" (p. 736) and Li-Young Lee's "Visions and Interpretations" (p. 813).
4. Compare and contrast the reaction to enduring warfare by the Israeli poet Yehuda Amichai ("Wildpeace," p. 890) and the Palestinian American poet Naomi Shihab Nye ("The Small Vases from Hebron," p. 708).
5. Analyze how Dudley Randall's "Ballad of Birmingham" (p. 843) follows and adapts the ballad tradition, bringing in "Sir Patrick Spens" (p. 735) as an example of the traditional ballad.
6. Compare and contrast two poems about fathers, Seamus Heaney's "Digging" (p. 797) and Stanley Kunitz's "Father and Son" (p. 811).

Writing Social or Cultural Criticism about Poetry

In addition to literary analysis topics and comparison-contrast topics, papers on poetry can focus on its relation to its cultural and social context and to the real-world issues it deals with. Poetry, like fiction, responds well to cultural criticism (review the discussion of cultural approaches to fiction, pp. 239–41).

IN NARRATIVE POETRY   Narrative poetry lends itself to the same critical approach as fiction. Stories, whether in fiction or narrative poetry, often show characters acting within a cultural situation. Thus, a paper might discuss and evaluate the implications of what they do and say — the exploitation of young boys in William Blake's "The Chimney Sweeper" (p. 744) or of adults in Robert Pinsky's "Shirt" (p. 839), for example.

IN LYRIC POETRY   Applying cultural criticism to lyric poetry requires a different approach. Lyric poems tend not to depict an action but to express, explore, or reflect on a reaction, dwelling on a particular moment, idea, situation, feeling, or event, as in the speaker's reflections on the exploitation of slaves in Lucille Clifton's "at the cemetery, walnut grove plantation, south carolina, 1989" (p. 664). A paper on a lyric poem, instead of examining how a character acts, is likely to focus on the poet's or speaker's or poem's response to a cultural issue or situation — as a critique of, an answer to, a relating to, or a reply or reaction to it. Thus, a cultural criticism paper might explore the ideas of homeland and exile in Ana Doina's "The Extinct Homeland — A Conversation with Czeslaw Milosz" (p. 771).

A THESIS IS ESSENTIAL   Just as for all paper topics, a cultural criticism paper needs to make a point. Simply describing a social or cultural attitude or context will not be especially interesting or useful. You need a thesis that unifies your paper and states the position or hypothesis it is advancing.

Topics for papers dealing with social and cultural criticism can range widely. Many of the "Approaching the Reading" questions following poems in Chapters 12–16 can lead to papers on cultural and social topics. Here are some additional possibilities, though the list could go on and on:

1. The critique of teachers and education in Rosemary Catacalos's "David Talamántez on the Last Day of Second Grade" (p. 757).
2. Cultural misunderstandings and tensions in Samuel Hazo's "For Fawzi in Jerusalem" (p. 795) or Dwight Okita's "In Response to Executive Order 9066" (p. 832).
3. A comparison and contrast of the tensions faced by young people attempting to find a place in U.S. society in Sandra Castillo's poem "Exile" (p. 754) and Julia Alvarez's short story "Daughter of Invention" (p. 11).

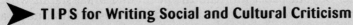

> **TIPS for Writing Social and Cultural Criticism**

> ➤ **Read expansively** Look beyond structure, characters, and literary techniques and consider issues raised (intentionally or not) in and by the text.

> ➤ **Plan on doing research** Social or cultural criticism usually involves information beyond what is found in the text or in common knowledge; it often deals with background information you'll find only by further investigation.

> ➤ **Connections are crucial** Social and cultural criticism usually involves making connections of various kinds: between issues within and outside the text, for example, or between a text and historical/cultural events contemporary with it or between a text and a theoretical text.

> ➤ **Make a point** Simply describing cultural connections is not enough. A paper has to apply such connections, by exploring their relevance and implications, and cohere in a significant thesis.

4. The repression of women as explored in Taslima Nasrin's "Things Cheaply Had" (p. 900) and Dahlia Ravikovitch's "Clockwork Doll" (p. 901).
5. The critique of country in Claude McKay's "If we must die" (p. 608) and "America" (p. 821).
6. The relation of language to cultural separation and acceptance, in such poems as Allison Joseph's "On Being Told I Don't Speak Like a Black Person" (p. 557), Rosemary Catacalos's "David Talamántez on the Last Day of Second Grade" (p. 757), or Alberto Ríos's "Nani" (p. 847). Include some discussion of why poetry is an appropriate form for exploring this topic.

DEVELOPMENT

Once you've picked out a technique or a question or a problem or an issue, you need to decide what to do with it, how to focus and develop it. The section on "Writing Short Papers" in Chapter 2 (pp. 34–46) applies to papers on poetry as well as fiction and drama. Review the "Steps in the Writing Process" (p. 35) if you need to. Here we comment briefly on developing an argument specifically for a paper on poetry.

DEVELOP A CENTRAL IDEA Many of the steps in developing an argumentative paper on poetry are the same as for a paper dealing with fiction. You need to avoid just summarizing or describing what the poem says.

Assume the reader of your paper has read the poem and understands what it's about. You need to develop a central idea that clarifies or illuminates a significant aspect of the poem's technique, meaning, or context, literary or cultural. The central idea must be one about which there can be disagreement for the paper to be argumentative. Your task is to show readers that your views are sound and convincing.

ASK QUESTIONS   As with papers on fiction, a good strategy in reaching a disputable central idea is to begin asking questions about the technique or problem or issue. And the same kinds of questions apply: What is distinctive or unique or striking about the way the technique is handled? In what ways is that technique particularly important to the poem? How does the technique relate to the theme? How is the problem or issue you're looking at embodied in the voice, diction, images, figures, or form? Is the problem or issue embedded in a symbol? What are some broader implications of the problem or issue you are focusing on? What is controversial or puzzling or difficult about what the text seems to say about the issues raised in it?

DEVELOP PARAGRAPHS FULLY   As with papers on fiction, it can be helpful to phrase your central idea as a question and then to use the body of the paper for a series of paragraphs, each paragraph developing a point answering part of the question. And as in a paper on fiction, the paragraphs need to begin with a topic sentence and to be developed by elaborating the point; by supplying details and quotations to illustrate, support, and confirm the point; and by explaining what we should notice in the illustrations and how the illustrations relate to the points being developed. Illustration and explanation need to go together in any literary paper. The key to a successful paper lies in its development and support of its ideas: explaining ideas so readers understand them readily and supporting them with details and quotations so readers have confidence that the points are well grounded and worth considering.

ORGANIZE POINTS EFFECTIVELY   One key difference in a paper on poetry is that you can discuss every line in a short poem. That means you'll need to decide how to organize the paper's development. You can work your way through the poem line by line. That works best if you organize your discussion by making two or three major points about the poem and divide up the lines to discuss some of them under each point. It's important for the paper to follow an outline *you* devise, rather than one that follows the outline the poet created in the poem. Or, instead of working your way down the poem, taking lines in order, you can create an outline based on points you want to cover (perhaps three different techniques or three different ideas in the poem) and then develop the points by drawing illustrations from anywhere in the poem they happen to appear.

INCLUDE QUOTATIONS Supporting illustrations in any literary paper must include quotations. For general advice on fitting quotations into your paragraphs and sentences, review the section on "Handling Quotations" (pp. 44–45) and the "Ten Guidelines for Handling Quotations" (pp. 47–48). Keep quotations short by focusing on key lines or phrases or words. A carefully phrased lead-in sentence usually provides the context and reduces the need for long quotations. If your paper uses quotations only from poems included in this book, you do not need to add a bibliography

FIVE TIPS FOR QUOTING POETRY

Because of the line divisions in poetry, some conventions for dealing with quotations are unique to poetry. Here are five tips on handling quotations of poetry:

1. In quoting poetry, retain the spelling, punctuation, and capitalization of the original (except that the final punctuation mark may be dropped if your sentence does not end at the quotation mark — see p. 47).
2. Cite the line numbers for the lines quoted in parentheses at the end of the passage.
3. If you quote fewer than four lines of poetry, blend them into your sentence in prose form, with the lines separated by a slash:

    The opening lines of "Love Poem" are "A kind of slant: the way a ball will glance / off the end of a bat when you swing for the fence."

    Indicating line divisions is important because line breaks are a significant formal feature in a poem. This applies only to poetry written in lines; slashes are not used to indicate wrap breaks in prose. This means, of course, that you must be able to distinguish poetry from prose, or long free verse lines that wrap at the right margins from shorter lines that are intentionally divided.

4. If you quote four or more lines of poetry, type them into the paper as a block quotation with each on a separate line. Make sure you type them exactly as they appear in the poem. Indent the passage an inch and a half or two inches from the left (don't center the lines individually). Double-space between the lines. If you begin the quotation in the middle of a poetic line, place the first word approximately where it occurs in the line, not at the left-hand margin. (For an example, see p. 689.)
5. If you omit a word or words from lines you're quoting, indicate this by including an ellipsis (see p. 48). Usually ellipses are used at the beginning or end of a quotation from a poem only if they are needed to indicate that what is quoted is not a complete line or sentence in the original. If you omit a complete line or more than one line, indicate this by adding a row of spaced periods as long as the lines in the passage you are quoting.

page. Your teacher will take for granted that you are using the text in this book. When you include quotations from other sources or from poems you find in another book, you need to include a bibliography page (see pp. 1499–1509).

SUPPLY A COPY OF SHORT POEMS   When writing a paper about one or two short poems (up to two pages, let's say), provide your reader with a copy of the poem (photocopied or typed out) on separate sheets after the title page. If it's a very short poem (up to fourteen lines, perhaps), provide a photocopy or type the poem below the title of the paper. (If you type it, check it carefully against the original to make sure it's accurate.) Insert line numbers every fifth line — write them in if you use a photocopy that lacks them — so you can refer to the poem by line number.

REVISE AND PROOFREAD CAREFULLY   When you've completed a draft of your paper, read or review the sixth step in the writing process, "Revising and Proofreading" (pp. 40–42), the guidelines for "Making Literary Papers Effective" (p. 42), and the "Ten Guidelines for Handling Quotations" (pp. 47–48) from Chapter 2. Remember, titles of poems are placed within quotation marks, except for book-length poems such as John Milton's *Paradise Lost*, which should be underlined.

A STUDENT WRITER AT WORK: DAN CARTER ON THE WRITING PROCESS

In one of our Introduction to Literature classes, we suggested this topic: Write a paper on the handling of form and content in a sonnet of your choice — the appropriateness of making the content fit the form or the effectiveness of adapting the form to fit the content. Dan Carter chose to write on Gary Miranda's "Love Poem" (p. 668). Here's what Dan told us about the way he went about writing the paper.

"I enjoy approaching a poem when it is clear that the author is doing something purposefully unique. 'Love Poem' by Gary Miranda immediately struck me as unusual in its choice of the sonnet form. I thought immediately that this is not a standard sonnet, and I wanted to understand what was going on in it. I chose this poem also because there is a lot going on in it. And just because I like it. I enjoy the sounds and the bouncing, sometimes awkward movement of the lines and I enjoy the simplicity and honesty of its message. I began asking myself, 'How did Miranda accomplish this effect of simplicity and love?' and 'How does the poem convey those effects?' I could sense a richness and subtlety under the surface of the verse, and I decided I wanted to do an explication of the poem to bring that out, but not a line-by-line reading.

"By the time I had read the poem a number of times, I had a list of half a dozen things I could use in my paper: diction (the games played with denotation, connotations, multiple meanings); images (active and visual, especially); adaptation of the traditional Italian sonnet form (same rhyme scheme, but using several slant rhymes instead of only exact rhymes); related to that, what the poem does with meter (line 1 in iambic pentameter, line 2 in anapestic trimeter, the rest mostly not metrical, though some phrases are); the title; the use of sound (alliteration, assonance, etc.); the use of figures; the choice of dynamic verbs.

"I eventually narrowed the list to the things I found most interesting: the form, the title, the images, and the sounds. But because of its overall effect of honesty, I didn't want to overanalyze the poem. It stands as a wonderful little poem without much analyzing, so I fought against the temptation to go overboard. I wanted to allow the poem to speak for itself, by working with aspects that the poem lent itself to. In preparing for this paper I was really interested in the poem and what was going on in it, so the essay flowed out easily when I sat down to write because I was expressing things I had already thought through extensively just because I found aspects of it so fascinating."

SAMPLE PAPER

Dan Carter
Professors Ridl and Schakel
English 105-04
November 3, 2005

A Slant on the Standard Love Sonnet

Love Poem

A kind of slant: the way a ball will glance
off the end of a bat when you swing for the fence
and miss--that is, if you could watch that once,
up close and in slow motion; or the chance
meanings, not even remotely intended, that dance   5
at the edge of words, like sparks. Bats bounce
just so off the edges of the dark at a moment's
notice, as swallows do off sunlight. Slants

like these have something to do with why angle
is one of my favorite words, whenever it chances   10

*Text of short
poem typed in.*

> to be a verb; and with why the music I single
> out tonight--eighteenth-century dances--
> made me think just now of you untangling
> blueberries, carefully, from their dense branches. (p. 668)

There are no lofty conceits, no stunning imagery, no confessions of undying commitment, and no assurance that the beloved's glory will live forever in the poet's verse. Why, then, does Gary Miranda entitle his work "Love Poem" and include several basic elements of a traditional sonnet? My initial reaction after the first reading was that the speaker was either being light-hearted or avoiding the topic of his "love" altogether. Upon a more thorough examination, however, there is a great deal of sincerity and love to be found in its verses. But this poem does not approach the traditional form in a predictable way. There are no references to the beloved's beauty, or roses, or spring, or anything except . . . picking blueberries?! The speaker spends a significant portion of the verse discussing "slants." Fittingly, that is precisely what this poem is: a slant on our pre-

Argumentative thesis.

conceived notion of what a "love poem" should be. Despite the absence of standard love poetry elements, various aspects of the poem such as the form, the title, the images, and the innumerable things that Miranda does with sound reveal that the speaker has composed a rather eloquent and sincere sonnet to the one he loves.

Transition sentence.

The first aspects of this poem (and really any poem for that matter) that catch the attention of the reader are the title and the form--"Love Poem," sonnet. Both establish specific expectations. We expect a fairly consistent meter, a certain rhyming pattern, and flowery imagery ("Shall I compare thee to a summer's day?"). But those expectations are not fulfilled. Instead, the poem thrusts three very different images upon the reader in the first eight lines: a ball glancing off the end of a bat; the

Topic sentence followed by lots of specific details.

"chance meanings" of words (lines 4-5); and the aerial movement of swallows and bats (the same word used in line 2, but by chance having a different meaning here). These all can be placed neatly under the heading "A kind of slant" that the speaker himself provides in the very first phrase (line 1). The effect of bringing these three distinct images together and linking them as different types of slants is, in a way, metaphorical. The

Quotation blended into sentence.

reader now associates together a baseball being tipped "off the end of a bat," the dancing meanings that weighted words carry, and the zigzagging motion of two flying animals. The speaker has defined "slant" on his own terms.

The traditional form of the Italian sonnet includes a turn between lines 8 and 9. Miranda surprises the reader by starting the turn before the last word of line 8, again making the poem slant:

Block quotation of poetry.

Slants

> like these have something to do with why <u>angle</u>
> is one of my favorite words, whenever it chances
> to be a verb.
>
> (lines 8-11)

Slants--and the images associated with them, specifically, in this case, the abrupt diving of bats and swallows--hold immense meaning for the speaker and the word "favorite" forcefully implies that because of this meaning, he enjoys these types of slants. The way Miranda has repeated his chosen word "slant" also provides an excellent example of the use of sound in "Love Poem."

There is no meter after line 2 (another deviation/slant from the traditional form), which leaves the sounds to carry the flow of the poem. In the first three lines alone we see the repetition of the "an" and "nce" sounds ("slant," "glance," "fence," and "once"). There is also a fair amount of alliteration ("way/will," "ball/bat," "for/fence," "watch/once") and . . . surprise!!! <u>slant</u> rhyme: "glance/fence/once." Throughout the poem the words "slant," "chance," "edge," and "dance" are used twice and are important to the speaker. "Edge," for instance, is another way of conveying what this poem is doing: riding the "edge," so to speak, of traditional form. By repeating these words it is as if the speaker is trying to aid the reader in finding the crucial words by repeating, multiple times, the sounds in them; "angle" and "untangling" are two more notable examples. The sound games found in "Love Poem" also include the following: assonance ("close/slow/motion"); consonance ("ball/will"); end rhyme ("chances/dances"); and internal rhyme ("sparks/dark"). The way in which all of these sounds push and pull the tempo and feeling of the verse create the unique flow of the poem.

Use of brief, concise quotations.

The sestet is made up of two parallel "with why" clauses. If we skip the first one we just discussed and go directly to the second, this is the result:

Slants

> like these have something to do with . . .
> . . . .
>   . . . why the music I single
> out tonight--eighteenth-century dances--
> made me think just now of you untangling
> blueberries, carefully, from their dense branches.
>
> (lines 8-9, 11-14)

Ellipses indicate words omitted from line; row of dots indicates omission of one or more complete lines.

The reader is finally privy to why the speaker included the three "slant" images in the beginning of the poem. If we visually observe the style of an eighteenth-century dance with all of its intricacies and formalities, we notice, well . . . slants (there is an excellent scene that displays this in the BBC movie of Pride and Prejudice, 1987). The speaker has now deftly defined these dances as a fourth slant. These complicated angles remind the speaker of his beloved "untangling / blueberries, carefully, from their dense branches." While this may not seem as effective as comparing her to a rose or a summer's day, the speaker makes his sincerity known. Apparently, his love is great enough to adore the simple image of her plucking blueberries. Not only that, but also this memory, or image (from near or far), is so precious as to merit surfacing during music--and perhaps, by default, the other three "slants." Miranda thus also captures the universal phenomenon of music producing nostalgia.

When we view the poem in this way, the function of the form and the meaning of the title become more obvious. The poem is not typical. But the title and the sonnet form aid the reader in discovering the love that is written between the lines. It is interesting to note as well that Miranda brings about in the poem many things that the speaker dwells on. For instance, the very first phrase, "A kind of slant," is an excellent description of the poem itself; it is a slant, an angle, and a variation on the traditional sonnet. Miranda also "angles" love and sincerity into the poem and the speaker includes words and phrases (loosely, the entire poem) that have "chance meanings." It is these types of chance meanings that make *Good wrap-up sentence.* him think of his beloved at all. These layers add to the richness of the poem, tangling it up and making it memorable, just like the blueberry's dense branches.

We have beauty all about us, *if* we take the time to pay
attention to it.

Ted Kooser

The Ordinary in Poetry – A Theme in Depth

CHAPTER 18

"Peeling a Pan of Pippins"

What comes to mind for many people when they think of poetry are
subjects that one labels "profound" such as love, death, and truth. However,
many poets focus on the everyday world around us, recognizing that, as
Richard Wilbur writes, "Love calls us to the things of this world." The things
of this world that these poets are called to are the things that make up our
daily lives, often the things we take for granted. Poet Paul Zimmer once instructed a student to "pay special attention to the things you walk by every
day." These common things, these things we carry, use, see, or pass by over
and over again are usually labeled "ordinary." But to the poets of this particular vision, they are not. They may be common, even profuse and all but
ubiquitous, but ordinary? No. Poets writing in this tradition find them extraordinary, both in themselves — no two snowflakes, no two "good mornings" are alike — and in the way or ways they can embody meaning in our
lives.

Perhaps as adults we become so familiar with something that it pales
into the ordinary. But for a child, nothing is ordinary. A child picks up a bug
and comes running to show it to a parent. In one sense, certain poets have
maintained that sense of wonder and awe, have been able to see bug after
bug and still be amazed. However, unlike the child, the poet also often discovers something meaningful as well as wonder filled in relation to or connection with the common thing and may perceive everyday occurrences in a
way that most people would not.

Things we do every day can be looked upon as drudgery or, with just a tilt of perspective, can be seen as meaningful ritual. The most common of human experiences can be highly charged when we bring that awareness to the task, be it bathing a baby or raking the fallen leaves. These are things almost everyone does. And it's that familiarity that perhaps leads us to take them for granted rather than recognize that though these events and objects may be legion, each one may well be charged with meaningfulness, each one individually significant. Van Gogh saw the same sky we do. However, because of the way he saw the stars and represented them in a painting, we see the night sky not only in our way but also in his. The ordinary is extraordinary once we recognize the uniqueness of any one thing.

Focusing on the ordinary goes back as far as art itself. Think of cave drawings. Think of all those luminous still-life paintings: Nothing is more ordinary than a loaf of bread or a couple of pears or an apple, yet the apples that Cezanne painted (below) are known to have astonished all of Paris. Edward Hopper's *Nighthawks* (p. 693) makes a dinerlike restaurant into an ethereal oasis. Jacob Lawrence transforms a kitchen into a space as rich in spirituality as any cathedral in his painting *This Is a Family Living in Harlem* (p. 693). In poetry, consider the haiku: that brief three-line form that crystallizes a momentary perception into a timeless experience for eternity. That

Paul Cezanne, Pommes et Oranges *(apples and oranges), 1895–1900.*
The Art Archive/ Musée d'Orsay Paris/Dagli Orti (A).

Edward Hopper, Nighthawks, *1942.*
Oil on canvas, 84.1 x 152.4 cm. Friends of American Art Collection, 1942.51. Photography by Robert Hashimoto. Reproduction, The Art Institute of Chicago. Photography © The Art Institute of Chicago.

Jacob Lawrence, This Is a Family Living in Harlem, *1943.*

© 2007 The Jacob and Gwendolyn Lawrence Foundation, Seattle/Artists Rights Society (ARS), New York. The Museum of Modern Art, New York, NY. Digital Image © The Museum of Modern Art/Licensed by SCALA/Art Resource, NY.

frog that leaped into that pond then, transcribed by the poet's pen, is today as arresting and capable of altering our awareness.

As you read through the poems and prose pieces in this chapter, be alert for what is extraordinary about what is ordinary. Do not dismiss the particulars — they are what they are and are worthy of attention, even wonder. And realize, too, that their very presence and all that may be associated with it are meaningful — if we are alert to that possibility. Be ready to recognize all that matters with Lucille Clifton's greens, Emily Dickinson's fly, or with William Stafford's request that you notice what his poem is not doing.

WHY WE SELL POETRY

First, poetry forces us to look closely at ordinary things. . . . Our culture today thrives on change, on constant thrills. [It] teaches us to yearn for continual novelty, to be dissatisfied with the same old things. Rarely do we look closely and carefully enough at the stuff of our ordinary lives to see the beauty and delight of the world. . . . Poetry teaches us to celebrate the everyday things of life.

Second, poetry forces us to see in ordinary things extraordinary truths. . . . Poetry teaches us to make surprising, delightful, and meaningful connections between the ordinary things of life and the extraordinary truths to which we anchor our souls.

Aaron Tripp, in a Shepherd Press catalog, vol. 8 (2003)

There are three ways of using the material in this chapter for writing assignments. The first is to write a paper on one or more of the poems without reading any of the secondary material included in the chapter. In this case, you would treat the poems as if they were included in the "Collection of Poems" and your paper would not draw upon outside sources. If you choose this option, remember that if you do read any secondary sources, or even parts of them, you must acknowledge that fact in a bibliography, even if you don't quote from or refer to them in your paper.

In a second way of using this chapter, your instructor might ask you to write a paper in which you use secondary sources but limit yourself to ones included in this chapter. Such a paper provides practice incorporating ideas from a critical essay, selecting passages to quote and blending quotations into your writing, and constructing a Works Cited page. But it isn't actually a research paper, since you aren't locating the materials to use in the paper. The reasons an instructor might select this option is that it doesn't require as much time as a full-blown research project, and it allows the instructor to evaluate your use of sources knowledgeably, since you are using only sources she or he is familiar with. For such a paper, you should review the guidelines for handling quotations on pages 47–48 and you should read Chapter 28,

"Reading Critical Essays," and the sections on incorporating sources, avoiding plagiarism, documenting sources, and preparing a Works Cited page in Chapter 29 (pp. 1491–1509).

A third way to use this chapter is as a starting point for an actual research paper. That is, after reading the poems and secondary pieces in this chapter, you would begin searching — perhaps only in the library, perhaps also using electronic sources, as your instructor prefers — to locate additional sources. You might read more interviews with poets featured in the chapter and additional poems written by them; surely you will be expected to read and use additional biographical or critical sources about their works or about the ordinary in poetry. For such a project, in addition to reviewing the guidelines for handling quotations on pages 47–48 and reading Chapter 28, "Reading Critical Essays," you should read all of Chapter 29, "Writing a Literary Research Paper."

Julia Alvarez   b. 1950

Ironing Their Clothes   [1996]

With a hot glide up, then down, his shirts,
I ironed out my father's back, cramped
and worried with work. I stroked the yoke,
the breast pocket, collar and cuffs,
until the rumpled heap relaxed into the shape   5
of my father's broad chest, the shoulders shrugged off
the world, the collapsed arms spread for a hug.
And if there'd been a face above the buttondown neck,
I would have pressed the forehead out, I would
have made a boy again out of that tired man!   10

If I clung to her skirt as she sorted the wash
or put out a line, my mother frowned,
a crease down each side of her mouth.
This is no time for love! But here
I could linger over her wrinkled bedjacket,   15
kiss at the damp puckers of her wrists
with the hot tip. Here I caressed
collars, scallops, ties, pleats which made
her outfits test of the patience of my passion.
Here I could lay my dreaming iron on her lap.   20

The smell of baked cotton rose from the board
and blew with a breeze out the window
to the family wardrobe drying on the clothesline,

all needing a touch of my iron. Here I could tickle
the underarms of my big sister's petticoat   25
or secretly pat the backside of her pajamas.
For she too would have warned me not to muss
her fresh blouses, starched jumpers, and smocks,
all that my careful hand had ironed out,
forced to express my excess love on cloth.   30

Laure-Anne Bosselaar   b. 1943

Bench in Aix-en-Provence   [2001]

There they are again, the lovers
   — midthirties, colorless
   clothes, hair, hands —
having their lunch-break

on the same beige bench   5
   — in the jabbering street,
   pigeons nodding at their feet —
under a paltry plane tree.

They simply sit there, not saying a word.

For days now, I've watched them   10
   — from a narrow window
   on the Rue Marceau —
place a single napkin on their knees,

a coffee cup on her side, a beer can on his
   — each at the exact same   15
   distance from their hips —
and don't drink or eat,

but simply sit there, not saying a word.

There is such resilience in how they sit
   — hands, knees, feet   20
   together, neatly —
in the way they stare at the pigeons,

or at the clouds moving in like frayed sheets
   — and smile at the same things
   at the same time —   25
that I know they haven't had it yet, sex.

They simply sit there, not saying a word
                    _____

And I find myself hoping
  — as I close the window
  on them, on noon, on Aix —   30
that they'll wait before spending

their lunch-break having it: sex
  — calling it *making love* but too soon
  calling it anything but that —
instead of coming back to their bench at noon,   35

to simply sit there, not saying a word.

Lucille Clifton   b. 1936

cutting greens   [1974]

curling them around
i hold their bodies in obscene embrace
thinking of everything but kinship.
collards and kale
strain against each strange other   5
away from my kissmaking hand and
the iron bedpot.
the pot is black,
the cutting board is black,
my hand,   10
and just for a minute
the greens roll black under the knife,
and the kitchen twists dark on its spine
and i taste in my natural appetite
the bond of live things everywhere.   15

Billy Collins   b. 1941

Days   [1995]

Each one *is* a gift, no doubt,
mysteriously placed in your waking hand
or set upon your forehead
moments before you open your eyes.

Today begins cold and bright,   5
the ground heavy with snow

and the thick masonry of ice,
the sun glinting off the turrets of clouds.

Through the calm eye of the window
everything is in its place   10
but so precariously
this day might be resting somehow

on the one before it,
all the days of the past stacked high
like the impossible tower of dishes   15
entertainers used to build on stage.

No wonder you find yourself
perched on the top of a tall ladder
hoping to add one more.
Just another Wednesday,   20

you whisper,
then holding your breath,
place this cup on yesterday's saucer
without the slightest clink.

Emily Dickinson   1830–1886

I heard a Fly buzz   [c. *1862*; 1890]

I heard a Fly buzz — when I died —
The Stillness in the Room
Was like the Stillness in the Air —
Between the Heaves of Storm —

The Eyes around — had wrung them dry —   5
And Breaths were gathering firm
For that last Onset — when the King
Be witnessed — in the Room —

I willed my Keepsakes — Signed away
What portion of me be   10
Assignable — and then it was
There interposed a Fly —

With Blue — uncertain stumbling Buzz —
Between the light — and me —
And then the Windows failed — and then   15
I could not see to see —

Rita Dove   b. 1952

The Satisfaction Coal Company   [1986]

1

What to do with a day.
Leaf through *Jet*. Watch T.V.
Freezing on the porch
but he goes anyhow, snow too high
for a walk, the ice treacherous.   5
Inside, the gas heater takes care of itself;
he doesn't even notice being warm.

Everyone says he looks great.
Across the street a drunk stands smiling
at something carved in a tree.   10
The new neighbor with the floating hips
scoots out to get the mail
and waves once, brightly,
storm door clipping her heel on the way in.

2

Twice a week he had taken the bus down Glendale hill   15
to the corner of Market. Slipped through
the alley by the canal and let himself in.
Started to sweep
with terrible care, like a woman
brushing shine into her hair,   20
same motion, same lullaby.
No curtains — the cop on the beat
stopped outside once in the hour
to swing his billy club and glare.

It was better on Saturdays   25
when the children came along
he mopped while they emptied
ashtrays, clang of glass on metal
then a dry scutter. Next they counted
nailheads studding the leather cushions.   30
Thirty-four! they shouted,
that was the year and
they found it mighty amusing.

But during the week he noticed more —
lights when they gushed or dimmed   35

at the Portage Hotel, the 10:32
picking up speed past the B & O switchyard,
floorboards trembling and the explosive
kachook kachook kachook kachook
and the oiled rails ticking underneath.   40

3

They were poor then but everyone had been poor.
He hadn't minded the sweeping,
just the thought of it — like now
when people ask him what he's thinking
and he says *I'm listening*.   45

Those nights walking home alone,
the bucket of coal scraps banging his knee,
he'd hear a roaring furnace
with its dry, familiar heat. Now the nights
take care of themselves — as for the days,   50
there is the canary's sweet curdled song,
the wino smiling through his dribble.
Past the hill, past the gorge
choked with wild sumac in summer,
the corner has been upgraded.   55
Still, he'd like to go down there someday
to stand for a while, and get warm.

Robert Frost   1874–1963

Mending Wall   [1914]

Something there is that doesn't love a wall,
That sends the frozen-ground-swell under it
And spills the upper boulders in the sun,
And makes gaps even two can pass abreast.
The work of hunters is another thing: 5
I have come after them and made repair
Where they have left not one stone on a stone,
But they would have the rabbit out of hiding,
To please the yelping dogs. The gaps I mean,
No one has seen them made or hear them made,   10
But at spring mending-time we find them here.
I let my neighbor know beyond the hill;

And on a day we meet to walk the line
And set the wall between us once again.
We keep the wall between us as we go.   15
To each the boulders that have fallen to each.
And some are loaves and some so nearly balls
We have to use a spell to make them balance:
"Stay where you are until our backs are turned!"
We wear our fingers rough with handling them.   20
Oh, just another kind of outdoor game,
One on a side. It comes to little more:
There where it is we do not need the wall:
He is all pine and I am apple orchard.
My apple trees will never get across   25
And eat the cones under his pines, I tell him.
He only says, "Good fences make good neighbors."
Spring is the mischief in me, and I wonder
If I could put a notion in his head:
"*Why* do they make good neighbors? Isn't it   30
Where there are cows? But here there are no cows.
Before I built a wall I'd ask to know
What I was walling in or walling out,
And to whom I was like to give offense.
Something there is that doesn't love a wall,   35
That wants it down." I could say "Elves" to him,
But it's not elves exactly, and I'd rather
He said it for himself. I see him there,
Bringing a stone grasped firmly by the top
In each hand, like an old-stone savage armed.   40
He moves in darkness as it seems to me,
Not of woods only and the shade of trees.
He will not go behind his father's saying,
And he likes having thought of it so well
He says again, "Good fences make good neighbors."   45

Christopher Gilbert   b. 1949

Touching   [1984]

Light is a distant world
though at 5 a.m. in the bedroom
window where the spider plant hovers
shining, there is a silken presence

where it traces, leaves a constellation.   5
I roll over and the room moves
a little closer, it is light-
like when Karen sleeps beside me
turned away but warm rubbing back
and I curve myself like hers   10
to hold her body for seeing
whatever is far in her.
Now I'm almost dreaming.
Words run transparent from my mouth
and almost find the edge of things.   15
Across the street in the park
a big hawk sails, gently flapping,
its outspread arms hugging the air
just as the sun kisses upward
to find its way through the sky.   20
Back here off the edge of the bed
my fingers, blind at both ends,
dangle in a void like starlight
travelled so far its source burned out.
Now a light goes off in my head as   25
I hold this hand that seems so far away.
I think of the monster fullback
in high school, after running over me
he dropped the ball to see was I hurt.
Where is he now, or the woman   30
who put the message in the bottle
I found splashing in the fouled waters
off Point Pelee. What was on her mind
writing, *kindness anywhere is still kindness,*
I'm in Cleveland, cold, alone—   35
wherever you are you hold this part of me.
I roll over in the glow
where sunrise goes across the bed,
knowing our age thinks light is wavelike
bundles spreading outward like ships   40
floating home in measured gaps toward each shore.
So part of the world waits distant.
For all I know as a man it might happen
like kelp bits drifting to no shore.
Still if there's a moment somewhere   45
equal to this light filling my skin,
then there is a constant I can count on
and I'll go forth and live with that.

Ben Jonson   1572–1637

Inviting a Friend to Supper   [1616]

Tonight, grave sir, both my poor house and I
   Do equally desire your company:
Not that we think us worthy such a guest,
   But that your worth will dignify our feast
With those that come; whose grace may make that seem   5
   Something, which else could hope for no esteem.
It is the fair acceptance, Sir, creates
   The entertainment perfect: not the cates.°   *food*
Yet shall you have, to rectify your palate,
   An olive, capers, or some better salad   10
Ushering the mutton; with a short-legged hen,
   If we can get her, full of eggs, and then
Lemons and wine for sauce; to these, a coney°   *rabbit*
   Is not to be despaired of for our money;
And though fowl now be scarce, yet there are clerks,°   *scholars* 15
   The sky not falling, think we may have larks.
I'll tell you of more, and lie, so you will come:
   Of partridge, pheasant, woodcock, of which some
May yet be there; and godwit if we can,
   Knot, rail, and ruff, too.° Howsoe'er, my man°   *servant* 20
Shall read a piece of Virgil, Tacitus,
   Livy, or of some better book to us,
Of which we'll speak our minds amidst our meat;°   *meal*
   And I'll profess° no verses to repeat: *take a vow*
To this,° if aught appear which I not know of,   *add to this* 25
   That will the pastry, not my paper, show of.°
Digestive cheese and fruit there sure will be;
   But that which most doth take my muse and me
Is a pure cup of rich Canary wine,°
   Which is the Mermaid's° now, but shall be mine;   30
Of which, had Horace or Anacreon° tasted,
   Their lives, as do their lines, till now had lasted.

19–10. godwit . . . Knot, rail, and ruff: Edible game birds.   26. the pastry . . . show of: The only way the speaker's poems will appear at the supper is if a baker uses pages from his unsold books to wrap pastries, and ink from the paper stains the crust.   29. Canary wine: A popular sweet white wine from the Canary Islands, claimed by the poem to be the best source of poetic inspiration.   30. Mermaid's: The Mermaid Tavern, a favorite of seventeenth-century writers, including Jonson.   31. Horace or Anacreon: Latin and Greek poets who wrote poems in praise of wine.

Tobacco, Nectar, or the Thespian spring°
    Are all but Luther's beer° to this I sing.
Of this we will sup free but moderately,   35
    And we will have no Pooly or Parrot° by;
Nor shall our cups make any guilty men,
    But at our parting we will be as when
We innocently met. No simple word
    That shall be uttered at our mirthful board   40
Shall make us sad next morning, or affright
    The liberty that we'll enjoy tonight.

---

33. Thespian spring: One of two fountains, traditional sources of poetic inspiration, on Mount Helicon.   **34. Luther's beer:** Bad German beer (greatly inferior to Canary wine). **36. no Pooly or Parrot:** No spies; an allusion to Robert Poley and Henry or William Parrat, government spies in the 1590s.

Ted Kooser   b. 1939

Applesauce   [2004]

I liked how the starry blue lid
of that saucepan lifted and puffed,
then settled back on a thin
hotpad of steam, and the way
her kitchen filled with the warm,   5
wet breath of apples, as if all
the apples were talking at once,
as if they'd come cold and sour
from chores in the orchard,
and were trying to shoulder in   10
close to the fire. She was too busy
to put in her two cents' worth
talking to apples. Squeezing
her dentures with wrinkly lips,
she had to jingle and stack   15
the bright brass coins of the lids
and thoughtfully count out
the red rubber rings, then hold
each jar, to see if it was clean,
to a window that looked out   20
through her back yard into Iowa.
And with every third or fourth jar
she wiped steam from her glasses,

using the hem of her apron,
printed with tiny red sailboats   25
that dipped along with leaf-green
banners snapping, under puffs
of pale applesauce clouds
scented with cinnamon and cloves,
the only boats under sail   30
for at least two thousand miles.

Li-Young Lee b. 1957

Braiding   [1986]

1.

We two sit on our bed, you
between my legs, your back to me, your head
slightly bowed, that I may brush and braid
your hair. My father
did this for my mother,   5
just as I do for you. One hand
holds the hem of your hair, the other
works the brush. Both hands climb
as the strokes grow
longer, until I use not only my wrists,   10
but my arms, then my shoulders, my whole body
rocking in a rower's rhythm, a lover's
even time, as the tangles are undone,
and brush and bare hand run the thick,
fluent length of your hair, whose wintry scent   15
comes, a faint, human musk.

2.

Last night the room was so cold
I dreamed we were in Pittsburgh again, where winter
persisted and we fell asleep in the last seat
of the 71 Negley, dark mornings going to work.   20
How I wish we didn't hate those years
while we lived them.
Those were days of books,
days of silences stacked high
as the ceiling of that great, dim hall   25

where we studied. I remember
the thick, oak tabletops, how cool
they felt against my face
when I lay my head down and slept.

3.

How long your hair has grown.   30

Gradually, December.

4.

There will come a day
one of us will have to imagine this: you,
after your bath, crosslegged on the bed, sleepy, patient,
while I braid your hair.   35

5.

Here, what's made, these braids, unmakes
itself in time, and must be made
again, within and against
time. So I braid
your hair each day.   40
My fingers gather, measure hair,
hook, pull and twist hair and hair.
Deft, quick, they plait,
weave, articulate lock and lock, to make
and make these braids, which point   45
the direction of my going, of all our continuous going.
And though what's made does not abide,
my making is steadfast, and, besides, there is a making
of which this making-in-time is just a part,
a making which abides   50
beyond the hands which rise in the combing,
the hands which fall in the braiding,
trailing hair in each stage of its unbraiding.

6.

Love, how the hours accumulate. Uncountable.
The trees grow tall, some people walk away   55
and diminish forever.
The damp pewter days slip around without warning
and we cross over one year and one year.

Denise Levertov   1923–1997

The Acolyte   [1982]

The large kitchen is almost dark.
Across the plain of even, diffused light,
copper pans on the wall and the window geranium
tend separate campfires.
Herbs dangle their Spanish moss from rafters.   5

At the table, floury hands
kneading dough, feet planted
steady on flagstones,
a woman ponders the loaves-to-be.
Yeast and flour, water and salt,   10
have met in the huge bowl.

It's not
the baked and cooled and cut
bread she's thinking of,
but the way   15
the dough rises and has a life of its own,

not the oven she's thinking of
but the way
the sour smell changes
to fragrance.   20

She wants to put
a silver rose or a bell of diamonds
into each loaf;
she wants

to bake a curse into one loaf,   25
into another, the words that break
evil spells and release
transformed heroes into their selves;
she wants to make
bread that is more than bread.   30

Pablo Neruda   Chile, 1904–1973

Ode to French Fries   [1959]

Translated by Ken Krabbenhoft

What sizzles
in boiling
oil
is the world's
pleasure: 5
French
fries
go
into the pan
like the morning swan's   10
snowy
feathers
and emerge
half-golden from the olive's
crackling amber.   15

Garlic
lends them
its earthy aroma,
its spice,
its pollen that braved the reefs.   20
Then,
dressed
anew
in ivory suits, they fill our plates
with repeated abundance,   25
and the delicious simplicity of the soil.

Naomi Shihab Nye   b. 1952

The Small Vases from Hebron°   [1998]

Tip their mouths open to the sky.
Turquoise, amber,

Hebron: An ancient city in the West Bank area of Israel; a sacred place for both Muslims and
Jews and a focus of tension between Israelis and Palestinians since the 1967 Arab-Israeli war.

the deep green with fluted handle,
pitcher the size of two thumbs,
tiny lip and graceful waist.   5

Here we place the smallest flower
which could have lived invisibly
in loose soil beside the road,
sprig of succulent rosemary,
bowing mint.   10

They grow deeper in the center of the table.

Here we entrust the small life,
thread, fragment, breath.
And it bends. It waits all day.
As the bread cools and the children   15
open their gray copybooks
to shape the letter that looks like
a chimney rising out of a house.

And what do the headlines say?

Nothing of the smaller petal   20
perfectly arranged inside the larger petal
or the way tinted glass filters light.
Men and boys, praying when they died,
fall out of their skins.
The whole alphabet of living,   25
heads and tails of words,
sentences, the way they said,
"Ya'Allah!" when astonished,
or "ya'ani" for "I mean" —
a crushed glass under the feet   30
still shines.
But the child of Hebron sleeps
with the thud of her brothers falling
and the long sorrow of the color red.

Simon J. Ortiz   b. 1941

Speaking   [1977]

I take him outside
under the trees,
have him stand on the ground.
We listen to the crickets,

cicadas, million years old sound.   5
Ants come by us.
I tell them,
"This is he, my son.
This boy is looking at you.
I am speaking for him."   10

The crickets, cicadas,
the ants, the millions of years
are watching us,
hearing us.
My son murmurs infant words,   15
speaking, small laughter
bubbles from him.
Tree leaves tremble.
They listen to this boy
speaking for me.   20

Jack Ridl   b. 1944

Love Poem   [1984]

[He] makes the smallest talk I've ever heard.
                    —*John Woods*

The smaller the talk the better.
I want to sit with you and have us
Solemnly delight in dust; and one violet;
And our fourth night out;
And buttonholes. I want us   5
To spend hours counting dog hairs,
And looking up who hit .240
In each of the last ten years.
I want to talk about the weather;
And detergents; and carburetors;   10
And debate which pie our mothers made
The best. I want us to shrivel
Into nuthatches, realize the metaphysics
Of crossword puzzles, wait for the next
Sports season, and turn into sleep   15
Holding each other's favorite flower,
Day, color, record, playing card.
When we wake, I want us to begin again
Never saying anything more lovely than garage door.

Len Roberts   1947–2007

At the Train Tracks   [1988]

Another springtime, another dollar. I wonder
as I drive from one job to another
how many more hours, honest-to-God alive
hours I have left, how many more Christmasses
I will buy the unnecessary gifts, how many more   5
summers limit myself to two weeks vacation on a lake
when that's all I'd like to do with my life.
Held up at the tracks I watch the B & O line,
the L & N, the Lackawanna, the Reading, the rusted metal
wheels clickety-clacking like mad days   10
on the shining steel while behind me automobiles
pile up, one driver blowing his horn
as though there were some other way across.

William Stafford   1914–1995

Notice What This Poem Is Not Doing   [1980]

The light along the hills in the morning
comes down slowly, naming the trees
white, then coasting the ground for stones to nominate.

Notice what this poem is not doing.

A house, a house, a barn, the old   5
quarry, where the river shrugs —
how much of this place is yours?

Notice what this poem is not doing.

Every person gone has taken a stone
to hold, and catch the sun. The carving   10
says, "Not here, but called away."

Notice what this poem is not doing.

The sun, the earth, the sky, all wait.
The crows and redbirds talk. The light
along the hills has come, has found you.   15

Notice what this poem has not done.

Mary TallMountain   1918–1994

Peeling Pippins°   [1988]

I sit down beside my brass lamp
To peel a pan of pippins.
How the spry sap springs, how
Quickly white flesh turns rust.
I muse on a green-skinned quarter.   5
The brass mirrors my fingers,
A brown cup holding a curve of green.
Pippin, created round: from pips
To plump dimples; inward to
Faint outline of its heart.   10
Taut little skins curl. The core
Falls abandoned to my sharp knife.
Saluting pippin's hardihood.
I slice blizzard, thunder, deluge.
There will be jars of sauce.   15
Pippin shall feed bone and marrow;
Cells shall transmute,
Emerald be crimson; sap be blood
In pippin's winter odyssey:
Profusions of life, linked   20
In the continuum.

Pippins: Crisp tart apples, usually with a yellow or greenish-yellow skin strongly flushed with red, used especially for cooking.

Nancy Willard   b. 1936

The Potato Picker   [1989]

The plant lifts easily now, like an old tooth.
I can free it from the rows of low hills,
hills like the barrows of old kings

where months ago, before anything grew or was,
we hid the farsighted eyes of potatoes.   5
They fingered forth, blossomed, and shrank,

---

and did their dark business under our feet.
And now it's all over. Horse nettles dangle
their gold berries. Sunflowers, kindly giants

in their death-rattle turn stiff as streetlamps.   10
Pale cucumbers swell to alabaster lungs,
while marigolds caught in the quick frost

go brown, and the scarred ears of corn gnawed
by the deer lie scattered like primitive fish.
The lifeboats lifted by milkweed ride light   15

and empty, their sailors flying.
This is the spot. I put down my spade,
I dig in, I uncover the scraped knees

of children in the village of potatoes,
and the bald heads of their grandfathers.   20
I enter the potato mines.

William Carlos Williams   1883–1963

This Is Just to Say   [1934]

I have eaten
the plums
that were in
the icebox

and which   5
you were probably
saving
for breakfast

Forgive me
they were delicious   10
so sweet
and so cold

William Wordsworth   1770–1850

I wandered lonely as a cloud   [1804]

I wandered lonely as a cloud
That floats on high o'er vales and hills,

When all at once I saw a crowd,
A host, of golden daffodils;
Beside the lake, beneath the trees,   5
Fluttering and dancing in the breeze.

Continuous as the stars that shine
And twinkle on the milky way,
They stretched in never-ending line
Along the margin of a bay: 10
Ten thousand saw I at a glance,
Tossing their heads in sprightly dance.

The waves beside them danced; but they
Outdid the sparkling waves in glee:
A poet could not but be gay,   15
In such a jocund company:
I gazed — and gazed — but little thought
What wealth the show to me had brought:

For oft, when on my couch I lie
In vacant or in pensive mood,   20
They flash upon that inward eye
Which is the bliss of solitude;
And then my heart with pleasure fills,
And dances with the daffodils.

Jeff Gundy

A Review of *Delights and Shadows* by Ted Kooser   [2004]

In essaying to define a "plains style" years ago, I used the Nebraskan Kooser's work as a key example. What makes his poems so memorable and rewarding is oddly elusive; defining his techniques, which seem simple, is not simple at all. The poems, typically brief, often have occasional beginnings, their subject a person, a scene, a moment, presented cleanly and (this may be a key) almost but not quite objectively. . . .

Bashō famously remarked that the trouble with most poetry is that it is either subjective or objective. Kooser is a master of the subjective description. Empathetic without sentimentality, his eye ranges over all sorts of everyday subjects and finds material everywhere — at garage sales and college libraries and stoplights, wherever the unpredictable particularity of the world can be glimpsed. . . .

For many years Kooser has written mainly short, observational poems, and much of *Delights and Shadows* works that vein as well. There is a sequence of four poems on Civil War paintings by Winslow Homer, and occasionally a poem reaches onto a second page. . . .

Still, the luminous moment — however tonally varied — remains Kooser's home ground. At times his characteristic compression invites comparison to traditional haiku or Chinese lyric poems, but although he shares an interest in the natural world and in suggestive understatement with such traditions, no hint of academic imitativeness will be found here. Retired from a career in the insurance business to a rural home near Garland, Nebraska, Kooser is one of the least bookish of significant contemporary poets. . . .

The epigraph to *Delights and Shadows* is from Dickinson: "The Sailor cannot 5 see the North, / but knows the Needle can." Perhaps Kooser's success lies in his determination to see the needles — and the other things of this world — with such clarity and passion that their underlying mysteries, delights, and shadows also become clear, if only for a moment.

Sarah Jensen

A Review of *Broken Symmetry* by Jack Ridl   [2007]

Michigan poet Jack Ridl has created a wonder of a book. If, as they say, God is in the details, the selections in *Broken Symmetry* glisten with the divine. Every small item — and Jack chronicles lots of them in his poems: collections of salt and pepper shakers, Vs of geese, broken windows, a spray of violets sent from France during World War II — shines with significance. Jack's specificity forces us to pay attention to the complexity of overlooked things, taken-for-granted things, as in his "The History of the Pencil," reminding us of the simple tool crucial to all this writing stuff in the first place. Jack doesn't just write about toast, but toast with jam — currant jam. On a plate not just a plate, but a chipped plate. Painted with a half-moon. At its center. In the hands of someone less masterful, less controlled, such incessant accretion of detail would amount to annoying linguistic disposophobia.° But Jack guides us to look — at egg timers and piles of television sets, his gone father's old shirt, cheese curls, the honeysuckle in the backyard — the way mathematicians view a shoreline. Measure the edge of each grain of sand along the coastline, and seemingly fixed distances become as they are: infinite. . . . Jack writes in the opening poem: "Only the broken reveals, gives / the universe its chance at being / interesting. . . ." And when I finished the book and looked up from its pages, my tchotchkes and stack of newspapers and a subway token on the coffee table and the ailanthus umbrellas outside my window seemed suddenly dear, fundamental to the galaxies' continued spinning, luminous as stars.

---

disposophobia: The fear of getting rid of stuff; compulsive hoarding.

William Stafford

The Importance of the Trivial   [1966]

We are surrounded, not by emblems, by paragons or villains, or fragments from Heaven and Hell, but by ready and adjustable potentials: nothing is special, everything is maybe.

This witness would note, confess, or assert, how small — how trivial — the elements which lead to a poem (or any work of art, or theory, or a truth) are. That is, the beginning impulse and perhaps the successive impulses too are often so colorless, so apparently random, so *homeless* and unaccountable, that most people would neglect them: They don't seem to amount to much. It is by lending faith and attention to these waifs of thought that we allow their meanings to develop, sometimes. And their mutual reinforcement is the composition of the poem, or the realization of any creative endeavor.

One further reflection it is only fair to make: In the perspective imposed here, all human perceptions, all experiences — no matter how grand or grandiose — accumulate from the concurrence of individually almost-insignificant elements; so the above assertion becomes, not a depreciation of art, but a realization about the provenance of human accomplishment.

Louis Simpson

Important and Unimportant Poems   [1961]

The present disparity between performance and reputation is appalling. Take William Stafford, for example. Is Stafford really so far inferior to Robert Lowell that Lowell should be treated as a classic, and Stafford virtually unknown? I have the greatest respect for the author of *Lord Weary's Castle* — clearly he is one of the few significant poets of the age — but when I read the poems of Stafford, I must respect him also, and yet who, outside of a few readers, is aware of Stafford? What a concatenation° of critics, what sheer ignorance, must control the American literary scene, for such a disparity to exist! . . .

Stafford's subject matter is usually important in itself. (The theory that subject matter is nothing, the treatment everything, was invented to comfort little minds.) Also, he deals with his subject directly; that is to say, he has a personal voice. Contrary to what many poets believe nowadays, it is not necessary to spill your guts on the table in order to be "personal," nor to relate the details of your aunt's insanity. What is necessary is originality of imagination and at least a few ideas of your own. Another point in favor of Stafford is that he actually writes about the country he is living in; all sorts of ordinary places, people, and animals

---

concatenation: Union of things chained or linked together.

appear in his poems, and not as subjects of satire, but with the full weight of their own existence.

As we read Stafford we are aware of how much has been omitted from modern American poetry only because it is not literary, or because it springs from the life of ordinary, rather than "alienated" people. An observer from another country would be struck by the absence from American poetry of the American landscape; he would find, also, that the language of our poetry is not the language of our real thoughts; and he might wonder at the psychic disorder this indicates. As for history — it seems we are trying to forget it. But Stafford is one of the few poets who are able to use the landscape and to feel the mystery and imagination in American life. . . .

He is a poet of the people in the deepest and most meaningful sense. And a poet of nature — in a time when poets claim our attention because they are unnatural, pitiable, demoralized. His poems are strong and true; rightly understood, they will enrich our lives.

Bill Moyers

An Interview with Naomi Shihab Nye   [1995]

Moyers: When you sit down to write, do you know why you're doing it?

Nye: I know why I'm *hungry* to do it. My first hunger of every day is to let words come through me in some way, and I don't always feel that I succeed in doing it — sometimes I feel that I am just an audience for words floating by and through. But the possibilities seem inexhaustible: I don't know what story will rise up out of that deep well of experience, and I'm always fascinated by how there's something there to work with every morning. . . .

Naomi Shihab Nye.
Reprinted with permission
BOA Editions, Ltd. Photo:
Michael Nye.

Moyers: Poetry is a form of conversation for you, isn't it?

Nye: Absolutely. Poetry is a conversation with the world; poetry is a conversation with the words on the page in which you allow those words to speak back to you; and poetry is a conversation with yourself. Many times I meet students and see a little look of wariness in their faces — "I'm not sure I *want* to do this or I'm not sure I *can* do this" — I like to say, "Wait a minute. How nervous are you about the conversation you're going to have at lunch today with your friends?" And they say, "Oh, we're not nervous at all about *that*. We do *that* every day." Then I tell them they can come to feel the same way about writing. Writing doesn't have to be an exotic or stressful experience. You can just sit down with a piece of paper and begin talking and see what speaks back. . . .

Moyers: Some people think there's so much talk in America — the talk shows, call-in shows, interviews, C-Span, CNN, press conferences, TV commercials — that it's all just a babble.

Nye: Maybe what I mean is a different kind of talk, because the kind I'm thinking about is a very slow and deliberate, delighted kind of talk. My favorite quote comes from Thailand, "Life is so short we must move very slowly." I think that poems help us to do that by allowing us to savor a single image, a single phrase. Think about haiku — those little seventeen-syllable poems — how many people have savored a single haiku poem over hundreds of years? Reading a poem slows you down, and when you slow down you are likely to read it more than one time. You read it more slowly than you would speak to somebody in a store, and we *need* that slow experience with words, as well as those quick and jazzy ones. . . .

Moyers: How is it that daily and mundane objects — gloves and forks and onions and buttonholes and pulleys — find their way into so many of your poems?

Nye: These tangible small objects are what I live with. I'm attracted to them. Gravity points. Since I was a small child I've felt that little inanimate things were very wise, that they had their own kind of wisdom, something to teach me if I would only pay the right kind of attention to them. William Stafford's poems and the poems by so many other poets which I've loved through my life take us back to the things of the world, the things which often go unnoticed — these poems all say: "Pause. Take note. A story is being told through this thing."

I don't look at anything as being insignificant. I think that's another overlooked gift of poetry. Many times people imagine that poets wait for some splendid experience to overtake them, but I think the tiniest moments are the most splendid. This is the wisdom that all these small things have to teach.

Moyers: Where did you get this gift to appreciate what so many of us take for granted?

Nye: I'm sure that the love of my parents, both very particular people, had a lot to do with it. I lived in a very nurturing household — both my mother and my father paid a great deal of attention to little things, and they still do. That gave me a certain appetite for how things were, the particulars of things. When I go into somebody's house, I always look to see what's there. What have they chosen to save? What's on the bookshelf? What's on the windowsill? For me, these are little clues I can pick up about ways to live. These things all tell stories. . . .

In many of what I consider to be my more political poems about Palestine and Palestinians, I feel I have focused on their relationships with daily life. Even under the most pressing, terrible circumstances, they have retained the dignity of continuing, day after day, "dream after dream."

Moyers: You call ["The Man Who Makes Brooms"] a political poem. It seemed to me a personal poem bestowing upon the seemingly significant a transcendent beauty and purpose.

Nye: Thank you, I appreciate that comment. People have sometimes asked me, "Why don't you write more political poems?" And I always answer, "Oh, but I *do*. *These* are my political poems." The most political poem I could ever write is a poem about a Palestinian gardener planting his garden and loving his garden and knowing his garden intimately.

Moyers: Why?

Nye: Because he is doing this even under very difficult, unsupportive circumstances. He is not going off into theories about how terrible the governments are or talking about how his situation is so oppressed. He is simply doing what he knows and what he loves doing, day after day. He is putting himself into the ground that he and his family have lived on for hundreds of years, and that is a very political act.

Moyers: So politics is not only a matter of revolution or legislation?

Nye: Not at all! Politics also involves the dignity of daily life. To me politics is how somebody carries himself or herself, regardless of the surrounding situation. . . .

Moyers: In several of your poems there's this pining for another reality, a yearning that there's more meaning, order, and happiness somewhere else. The teacher in "New Year" envisions "every future which was not hers." Over and over there is a sense of a life not chosen, a path not traveled. Are you conscious of that?

Nye: Doesn't that seem to be the universal human experience? Lots of times students imagine that other people, like writers, have more interesting lives than they themselves do, to which I say, "It's not that a writer's life is more interesting; it's just that writers have a different way of *looking* at our lives."

People look with longing at other experiences that they imagine as being more real, more true, more deep than their own; but I think people are also riveted by a kind of great human longing for something, whether it's better or other or different, that is deeper than whatever they have at that moment. I think that's almost a universal condition. . . . In many cases we have a closer relationship with domestic detail which is very sustaining. When I would observe my grandmother who just died at the age of 106 in her West Bank village, and the other women of the family, for example, I might see them going out to pick something in the field, or smelling the mint, or making the fresh lemonade, while the men were talking politics. Well, which group would *I* rather be with? It's *not* hard to choose. I've always felt very happy to be a woman, with immediate intimate access to a whole world of objects and details. Of course many men sustain this closeness too. My husband, a photographer, often speaks of "inquiry" as being at the heart of his artistic process. Many people come at this from many directions.

Ted Kooser   b. 1939
Out of the Ordinary   [2005]

Most of us have at some time played with kaleidoscopes, those tubes in which one can get dreamily lost in shifting mandalas of color, created by multiple reflections of tiny glass chips that make a pleasant rattle when they tumble into place. When I was a boy you could buy a kaleidoscope at the five-and-dime, a cardboard cylinder fitted with strips of cheap, reflecting metal. In recent years I've seen expensive models in suburban shopping malls, with polished tubes of imported wood, fitted with brass, with real glass mirrors, the kind of objects executives like to place near their desks to show clients that they are not so serious after all, that despite their pursed lips and cold handshakes, they too, from time to time, can enjoy a little airy lightness.

There is a similar mirrored tube called the teleidoscope, but it doesn't have chips of glass in a chamber at the far end. Instead, a teleidoscope is fitted with lenses like a telescope. Turn it toward some near or distant object, a cabbage or a heap of scrap metal, and whatever is within the field becomes the mandala, pleasant in its colors and textures and reassuring in its order. A teleidoscope's charm is that it can make the ordinary look extraordinary. We like that. We rejoice a little when someone shows us something special about our ordinary lives. That goes for poems, too.

Poems can be like experiences with a teleidoscope. The poet's attention and imagination turn toward something, say a heap of potatoes, and shift the words

Ted Kooser.
© University of Nebraska–Lincoln Photography.

this way and a little that way until the potatoes look just right. Then the poet holds the tube very still so we can see the image, too. What results is a record of that moment, a record of that one poet's discovery, a lovely mandala made all of clean and dirty brown and red potatoes.

A poem is the record of a discovery, a discovery of something beyond us in the world, or within ourselves, or within the language itself. It's like what we discover through a teleidoscope. But though the images in a teleidoscope are in flux because we can't hold the tube completely still, the words of a poem, set in type, fix the images the way one fixes a photograph in a darkroom. I suppose it would be possible to fit a teleidoscope onto the lens mount of a camera. Once the poem is complete, once the photograph is fixed, it belongs to the people who come upon it. They can do with it as they will. The poet or photographer has exercised control over the content, the composition, the darkness or lightness, the degree of focus. That's all he or she can do. The photograph, the poem, then goes out into the world and falls into the hands of strangers. It is taped to the door of a refrigerator, or lovingly inserted into an album, or tossed into the trash without a moment's regret. The poet is no longer present to say, "Wait! Don't you see what I was trying to accomplish?" One of the hardest lessons a poet must learn is that he or she is not going to be able to accompany the poem, offering explanations and arguments wherever it goes. . . .

Perhaps ten years ago, someone proposed a book of poets writing about 5 their favorite paintings. I don't believe it ever got published, but I sent in a contribution. I had picked a painting from the Joslyn Art Collection in Omaha, George Ault's *August Night at Russell's Corners*. Those of you who have seen my book *Delights and Shadows* know this picture, which appears on the cover. Ault painted two anonymous red wooden buildings at a rural crossroads, illuminated by a single bulb. The road that passes between the buildings goes on to vanish into the darkness. He painted four pictures of this same arrangement, each slightly different, each slightly shifting the masses as if to look into the scene from the best possible angle. Each of those paintings is, like a poem, the record of a discovery.

If we were to pass by a couple of old buildings like those, on a summer night, we might not think to pay attention to them. For what are two more drab old buildings in a world of drab old buildings? But the painting shows us the buildings through the eyes of the painter, as through a teleidoscope, and the scene is indeed remarkable.

The little poem that I proposed to go with the picture in the book went like this:

> If you can awaken
> inside the familiar
> and discover it strange,
> you need never leave home.

In short, we have beauty all about us, *if* we take the time to pay attention to it. . . . Reinhold Marxhausen knew about paying attention, George Ault knew it.

Pablo Neruda wrote dozens of remarkable poems about common things [see p. 708]. Thousands of poets and painters have learned to pay attention like this. We honor the ordinary by giving it our attention. We enshrine the ordinary in our art. Is anything *really* ordinary, I wonder. . . .

Nancy Willard [in "The Potato Picker," see p. 712] picks up . . . very ordinary potatoes and shows them to us in the light of the extraordinary. She shows us the corn ears like primitive fish, the lifeboats of the milkweed pods. Metaphor upon metaphor, delivering pleasure. Metaphor is a kind of connective tissue that holds widely disparate parts of the universe together, and when we participate in a comparison such as those in this poem . . . we get the feeling that we are connecting to a grand system of interrelationships. That's why, I think, fresh metaphors can be so thrilling; in the dark of our lives we touch two points on a field of connectedness and there is a little arc of electricity and in a flash we see the entire field.

I too have written poems about potatoes, . . . one in which I pretend that   10 peeling a potato is like playing the cello. Ordinary potatoes, ordinary vegetables, they're all part of the holy ordinary. If you can awaken inside the familiar and discover it strange, you need never leave home.

Paul Lake

The Malady of the Quotidian   [1993]

I

In poems such as "Tintern Abbey" and *The Prelude* Wordsworth created a new type of poetry. Harold Bloom has described this new poetry as one that took consciousness and the poetic imagination as its principal subject. Wallace Stevens, throughout his own long career, followed his great precursor's example, and in poems such as "Notes toward a Supreme Fiction" extended the tradition into this century, adding to it a mode of irony we have come to recognize as modernist.

But Wordsworth also wrote a second type of poetry that finds no echo in Stevens, a poetry we find chiefly in *Lyrical Ballads*. M. H. Abrams in his essay "English Romanticism: The Spirit of the Age" describes Wordsworth as having two voices; he suggests that in this second voice Wordsworth undertook something different from the exploration of consciousness. Quoting the preface to *Lyrical Ballads*, he writes that Wordsworth also attempted "to represent realistic 'incidents and situations from common life' in ordinary language and to employ 'humble and rustic life' as the main source of the simple characters and the model for the plain speech" (Abrams 112).

In this essay I hope to explore this difference between Wordsworth and Stevens and, in doing so, to trace the source in Stevens's poetry of what I will call, after Stevens himself, "The malady of the quotidian," a malady that haunts his work from first to last. Wordsworth successfully fused his two voices in one poetic vocation and in his greatest poetry achieved a wholeness of utterance that eluded Stevens. Though it's no longer fashionable to speak in such terms, I think Stevens failed to achieve a similar wholeness because he limited himself to a poetry of consciousness alone. The malady of mind and spirit that resulted derives at least partly from Stevens's unwillingness or inability to engage "incidents and situations from common life." Men and women, when they exist at all in his poetry, serve merely as objects of contemplation. Unlike the various vagrants and pedlars and leech gatherers one encounters in the poetry of Wordsworth, people in Stevens's poetry exist primarily as *things.*

Let's begin with Wordsworth's famous formulation in "Tintern Abbey." In that poem, Wordsworth writes that he is a "lover" of "all the mighty world / Of eye, and ear — both what they half create, / And what perceive" (Wordsworth 164–65). . . .

In poem after poem, we find Wordsworth ranging over the landscape   5 encountering flowers, streams, rivers, cities, women, and men. The speakers in Stevens's poems often appear to be observing the world through a window or contemplating it over a book, as in "The House Was Quiet and the World Was Calm." Nature in Stevens's poetry is most often the sort the poet might have encountered in a garden or out the window of his Hartford home: flowers, birds, clouds, rain, sunlight, snow. Wordsworth writes a poetry of encounter; Stevens, a poetry of detached contemplation.

Nowhere is Wordsworth's difference from Stevens more apparent than in Book Thirteen of *The Prelude.* Here Wordsworth writes of

> those watchful thoughts
> Which, seeing little worthy or sublime
> In what the Historian's pen so much delights
> To blazon — power and energy detached
> From moral purpose — early tutored me
> To look with feelings of fraternal love
> Upon the unassuming things that hold
> A silent station in this beauteous world.
>
> Thus moderated, thus composed, I found
> Once more in Man an object of delight,
> Of pure imagination, and of love.
> (Wordsworth 579)

. . . One doesn't find Stevens contemplating "the unassuming things that hold / A silent station in this beauteous world" with "fraternal love." In Stevens's poetry, even a man or woman most often becomes merely another object of thought, an occasion for meditating on the ideal. By contrast, in *The Prelude* Wordsworth describes how he gained

A more judicious knowledge of the worth
And dignity of individual man,
No composition of the brain, but man
Of whom we read, the man whom we behold
With our own eyes . . .

(Wordsworth 580)

. . .

II

I have admired Stevens's poetry since I first began writing poetry in my teens. I used to accept the general opinion that Stevens was one of the great modernists of this century, along with Pound, Eliot, and Williams, but I now see him as the last great poet of the Romantic tradition that began with Wordsworth and Blake. His poetry of consciousness seems an extension of Wordsworth's, and his belief in the power of the poetic imagination and in the existence of ideal or "major" man seems closely related to ideas held by Blake. Unlike the other modernists I've mentioned, Stevens wrote most of his best poetry in blank verse, a fact that perhaps explains why Hugh Kenner, one of the high priests of modernism, dislikes his work so much. . . .

Yet for all my admiration of Stevens's formal mastery and verbal daring, I've never felt the desire to emulate him. I think this has to do in large part with the fact that Stevens failed (in Wordsworth's words again in *The Prelude*) to dwell "Upon the vulgar forms of present things / The actual world of our familiar days" (Wordsworth 583). Much of Stevens's poetry enacts an escape from reality into a more "noble" world of ideas and abstractions. Milton Bates in his book *Wallace Stevens: A Mythology of Self* shows how even in his love letters to his fiancée Stevens erected dream castles and created imaginary landscapes into which he wished them to escape. This same desire to escape vulgar reality appears in various forms in his poetry. . . .

In "The Man Whose Pharynx Was Bad," the poem from which I take my title, Stevens . . . has perhaps identified the source of the "malady of the quotidian" he writes of in the poem's third stanza. The word *quotidian* has among its meanings, "belonging to each day," "everyday," "routine." Stevens appears to recognize here that the routine he chose for himself has resulted in his being too dumbly "pent" in his own being. Later in the poem he wishes something could "penetrate" so that he might become less "diffident."

But *quotidian* also has another meaning: "commonplace, ordinary." As a reader, I have often wished that Stevens had been content to dwell more in this realm of the quotidian. Instead, he fled from the commonplace and ordinary in a way that most of us couldn't emulate even if we wanted to. His corporate position, his financial security, his impressive Hartford home insulated him from the economic and social shocks to which most of us are heir. Wordsworth spoke with beggars and vagrants; Stevens retired behind the walls of his Hartford office and study. Like others near the bottom of the American middle class, I find Stevens's approach to the higher slopes of Parnassus barred by the avenging

10

angel of necessity. For the kind of poetry I write, poetry that includes people whose lives are shaped by vulgar and commonplace realities, Wordsworth rather than Stevens offers a model.

I've found an even more useful model in Robert Frost, whose poetic career might be read as an attempt to extend and correct Wordsworth. Frost writes of the "humble and rustic" life of men and women without Wordsworth's occasional idealizing sentimentality. Frost's Nature is much less the anthropomorphic being of Wordsworth's poetry than the more inhuman one revealed by modern science; it is a nature sometimes frighteningly indifferent to our wishes. In his attitude toward this world, Frost is more a Roman Stoic than a Romantic enthusiast — a poise better suited to this century's more terrible history.

Yet despite his stoicism, Frost in his lyrics, narratives, and monologues presents us with people, often commonplace and ordinary, endowed with a substance and depth like our own. Whether in his own person or through an imaginary character, Frost is able to speak to our essential being — as a "man speaking to men." That seems to me an accomplishment far greater than the creation of any fiction, no matter how beautifully written or supremely conceived.

Still, I'm grateful to Stevens for showing us how far a poet might venture into the abstract on the winged horse of the imagination. For all his refusal to embrace the quotidian, his poetry possesses immense intelligence and humor and, at times, great feeling.

Works Cited

Abrams, M. H. "English Romanticism: The Spirit of the Age." In *Romanticism and Consciousness*. Ed. Harold Bloom. New York: Norton, 1970. 90–119.

Bates, Milton J. *Wallace Stevens: A Mythology of Self*. Berkeley: University of California Press, 1985.

Stevens, Wallace. *Collected Poems of Wallace Stevens*. New York: Knopf, 1954.

Wordsworth, William. *Poetical Works*. Ed. Thomas Hutchinson. Rev. Ernest De Selincour. Oxford: Oxford University Press, 1936.

M. L. Rosenthal

William Carlos Williams: More Than Meets the Eye [1966]

Many of William Carlos Williams's shorter poems seem at first glance mere impressionistic notes or figures caught shimmering in a momentary visual frame. Among the best known of these pieces is "The Red Wheelbarrow":

so much depends
upon

a red wheel
barrow

glazed with rain
water

beside the white
chickens.

The sense of being alive, this poem and many others imply, depends on our viewing the familiar world with a fresh eye. The standpoint from which we view that world and its intensities determines the scope of life's meaning for us. The humblest objects of perception are also elements in a symbolic design with a transcendent aesthetic function. To see them thus is to liberate ourselves and them from the rut and squalor in which the mass of men lead their "lives of quiet desperation."° It is to bring to bear upon any momentary observation or set of circumstances the whole of imagination and sensibility, and to gain courage from the application.

> . . . the thing that stands eternally in the way of really good writing is always one: the virtual impossibility of lifting to the imagination those things which lie under the direct scrutiny of the senses, close to the nose. It is this difficulty that sets a value upon all works of art and makes them a necessity. The senses witnessing what is immediately before them in detail see a finality which they cling to in despair, not knowing which way to turn. Thus the so-called natural or scientific array becomes fixed, the walking devil of modern life. He who even nicks the solidity of this apparition does a piece of work superior to that of Hercules when he cleaned the Augean stables.
>
> (*"Prologue," Kora in Hell*)

*   *   *

"All I do," [Ezra] Pound quotes Williams as saying, "is to try to understand something in its natural colours and shapes"; and Pound observes: "There could be no better effort underlying any literary process, or used as preparative for literary process."[1] The claim Williams makes for himself may be too modest, but his amazingly vivid sense of the life around him is certainly the foundation of everything he writes. Randall Jarrell's characterization is arch but to the point.

> Williams' poetry is more remarkable for its empathy, sympathy, its muscular and emotional identification with its subject, than any other contemporary poetry except Rilke's. When you have read *Paterson* you know for the rest of your life what it is like to be a waterfall; and what other poet has turned so many of his readers into trees? Occasionally one realizes that this latest tree of Williams' is considerably more active than anyone else's grizzly bear; but usually the identification is so natural, the feel and rhythm of the poem so hypnotic, that the problem of belief never arises.[2]

"lives of quiet desperation": Henry David Thoreau, *Walden* (1854), ch. 1 — "The mass of men lead lives of quiet desperation."

This extraordinary empathic responsiveness, to trees and flowers especially, recalls D. H. Lawrence, with whom Williams has other affinities also. By the time he was nine or ten, the poet tells us in his *Autobiography*, he had learned

> the way moss climbed about a tree's roots, what growing dogwood and iron wood looked like; the way rotten leaves will mat down in a hole — and their smell when turned over — every patch among those trees had its character, moist or dry. . . .
> It is a pleasure for me now to think of these things, but especially of the flowers I got to know. . . . The slender neck of the anemone particularly haunts me for some reason and the various sorts of violets . . . My curiosity in these things was unbounded — secret certainly. There is a long history in each of us that comes as not only a reawakening but a repossession when confronted by this world. . . .
>
> (*The Autobiography*, p. 19)

In the poems this repossession is visceral, complete. We see a young tree rising 5

> bodily
>
> into the air with
> one undulant
> thrust half its height. . . .
>   ("Young Sycamore")

Other trees, seen on a winter night, present a grotesque Tam O'Shanter dance vision:

> Limb to limb, mouth to mouth
> with the bleached grass
> silver mist lies upon the back yards
> among the outhouses.
>   The dwarf trees
> pirouette awkwardly to it —
> whirling round on one toe;
> the big tree smiles and glances
>   upward!
>   ("Winter Quiet")

*   *   *

Williams worked out of a sophisticated and developed tradition, in whose principles he slowly educated himself throughout his career. Implicit in it is the avowal of the assumptions of the religion of art by which the symbolists and their successors have lived. . . . The fundamental premise is that the meanest of experiential data have their transcendent aesthetic potentiality, and hence that experience is the key to realization. Characteristically, the formal structure of a Williams poem involves a closing in on the realization involving several shifts of attention or focus along the way. It is not that nothing has significance, but that everything has it; not that eye and object alone make the poem, but that these, together with ear and intellect and formal movement, shape a poem through their convergence. Conception, empathy, compassion, and technique become functions of the same thing in many of the pieces; that is, they become inseparable functions of poetic process. . . .

Here again, it is useful to recall the resemblance between Williams's sensibility and that of D. H. Lawrence.° Think of the close-ups which strengthen our knowledge of the individual flame behind the common mask of anonymity. Or think of Lawrence's anguished description of the carnage winter wreaks on the birds, or of his sense of the blazing life of flowers. In "To a Dog Injured in the Street," Williams recalls further instances of suffering innocence summoned up by sight of the screaming dog. Remembering these moments of cruelty and pain, he cries out his kinship with still another poet, René Char,° whose theme has like his own been the imaginative or aesthetic resolution of the violence man's condition subjects him to.

> René Char
> you are a poet who believes
> in the power of beauty
> to right all wrongs.
> I believe it also.

Though Williams parts company with Lawrence in his unfaltering confidence in art's redeeming and healing powers, the difference between them on this score can easily be exaggerated. For example, the motifs of symbolic death and rebirth are important in both poets, and in parallel forms. . . . But the salvation implied in the localist program of Williams, and in his many poems informed primarily by compassion, is finally aesthetic rather than purely religious, mystical, or social. In an early poem, "The Wanderer," whose motifs are later absorbed into the *Paterson* sequence, the poet shows himself attempting to awaken the people to their own rich possibility. Finally, though, it is he himself who is awakened and purified, by taking into himself the whole degradation of modern industrial life bereft of all traditional graces. The waters of the "filthy Passaic" enter his heart and soul and transform him. But it is a transformation like that in Yeats's "Byzantium" or "The Circus Animals' Desertion" — from the "foul rag-and-bone shop of the heart" to the "masterful images" of the "pure mind." As he says to René Char, it is "beauty" that will "right all wrongs."

So there's more to Williams, putting the matter very gently, than meets the eye. Even the sharp, objective snapshots which Blackmur calls "obvious" — "what we are already in possession of"[3] — have the "more" buried in them, and

---

D. H. Lawrence: English writer (1885–1930) who held that the decline of Western culture would be countered as humanity reached a new awareness of itself as a part of nature. **René Char:** French poet (1907–1988), active in the Resistance movement during World War II, whose works express concerns about threats to the world's beauty and about the brutality of war.

not really so very deeply. The *Paterson* sequence is the outgrowth of Williams's need to bring the inner meanings out into the open and to pursue them more explicitly:

> The first idea centering upon the poem *Paterson* came alive early: to find an image large enough to embody the whole knowable world about me. The longer I lived in my place, among the details of my life, I realized that these isolated observations and experiences needed pulling together to gain "profundity." I already had the river . . . I wanted, if I was to write in a larger way than of the birds and flowers, to write about the people close about me: to know in detail, minutely what I was talking about — to the whites of their eyes, to their very smells.
>
> That is the poet's business. Not to talk in vague categories but to write particularly, as a physician works, upon a patient, upon the thing before him, in the particular to discover the universal. . . .
>
> *(The Autobiography,* p. 391)

*   *   *

I remember Williams best as a serious, wonderfully articulate, and good 10 man talking about ordinary life and about poetry with an absolute immediacy of involvement. . . . Not long before his death, he and Mrs. Williams came to see us on the dirty old Erie Railroad, a frail-looking couple whose anonymous presence nevertheless awoke delicate instincts of courtesy in everyone involved with the railroad all the way from Rutherford, New Jersey, to Suffern, New York. The later memory of Dr. Williams on a living-room sofa, explaining to a sixteen-year-old boy who wished to be a poet the meaning of the "variable foot" — starting his sentences, losing track of them, but keeping the inward thought fully in view all the while — is of the order of things too rich and too sad to describe. But it is of the essence of so much that made his art the moving force that it is.

Notes

[1]*The Literary Essays of Ezra Pound* (New York: New Directions, 1954), 390.

[2]Jarrell, "Introduction" to Williams's *Selected Poems* (New York: New Directions, 1949), xii.

[3]R. P. Blackmur, *Language as Gesture* (New York: Harcourt, Brace, 1952), 349.

Works Cited

Williams, William Carlos. *The Autobiography.* New York: Random House, 1951.

——. *The Collected Earlier Poems.* Norfolk, Conn.: New Directions, 1951.

——. *The Collected Later Poems.* Norfolk, Conn.: New Directions, 1950.

——. *Kora in Hell: Improvisations.* Boston: Four Seas, 1920.

——. *Paterson.* New York: New Directions, 1963.

RESPONDING THROUGH Writing

Here are some suggestions for writing on the ordinary in poetry, but for a chapter like this one, you should not limit yourself to these topics. An important purpose behind the chapter is to encourage you to learn how to find good topics on your own. You may make changes in the topics (with your instructor's permission) and make changes in how they are categorized (using a topic from 1–6 as a research topic, for example, instead of using no outside sources). Some of the poems in Chapters 12–16 and 19 deal with the ordinary as well and might fit into the topics below. If you find a poem you would like to use instead, get your instructor's permission before proceeding.

PAPERS USING NO OUTSIDE SOURCES

Literary Analysis Papers

1. Write a paper discussing the connection between the title of Denise Levertov's "The Acolyte" (p. 707) and the ordinary, everyday activity being described in the poem.
2. Write a paper exploring braiding as a literal, ordinary act and as a symbol in Li-Young Lee's "Braiding" (p. 705).

Comparison-Contrast Papers

3. Write a paper comparing and contrasting what William Stafford's "Notice What This Poem Is Not Doing" (p. 711) is and is not doing.
4. Write a paper in which you compare and contrast the way Laure-Anne Bosselaar's "Bench in Aix-en-Provence" (p. 696) and Christopher Gilbert's "Touching" (p. 701) use ordinary things to describe personal relationships.

Cultural Studies Papers

5. Several of the poems in this chapter deal with work. Write a paper in which you discuss and illustrate the attitudes toward work that emerge from these reflections on ordinary people doing ordinary jobs.
6. Food—both the preparation and the communal consumption of it—forms an important part of most cultures. Write a paper in which you discuss its social and cultural significance, using poems from this chapter (and, with permission from your instructor, other poems in this book) as illustrations.

PAPERS USING LIMITED OUTSIDE SOURCES

Literary Analysis Papers

1. In "Out of the Ordinary" (p. 720), Ted Kooser talks about the "grand system of interrelationships," the "points . . . of connectedness," in Nancy

Willard's "The Potato Picker" (p. 712). Write a paper in which you explain and clarify what he means, using Willard's poem to illustrate and Kooser's essay and other secondary materials in this chapter for support.

2. Ted Kooser, in "Out of the Ordinary," says poems can show us "something special about our ordinary lives." Write a paper in which you clarify and elaborate Kooser's point, using his essay and other secondary pieces in this chapter for support, and demonstrate how several poems in this chapter do "make the ordinary look extraordinary" by the way the poems describe and discuss them.

Comparison-Contrast Papers

3. Using poems in this book and secondary materials in this chapter, write a paper that discusses and extends Paul Lake's comparison and contrast in "The Malady of the Quotidian" of William Wordsworth's handling of ordinary and everyday details with that of Robert Frost (see pp. 722–25).

4. Write a paper comparing and contrasting the way the ordinary is transformed in one of the works of art reproduced in this chapter (pp. 692–93) with the way it is transformed in a poem such as Laure-Anne Bosselaar's "Bench in Aix-en-Provence" (p. 696), Pablo Neruda's "Ode to French Fries" (p. 708), or William Wordsworth's "I wandered lonely as a cloud" (p. 713). Use the introduction to the chapter and the secondary essays to clarify and support the points you make.

Cultural Studies Papers

5. In her interview with Bill Moyers (p. 717), Naomi Shihab Nye says that her poems about ordinary things are political poems. Write a paper in which you explain what she means, using "The Small Vases from Hebron" (p. 708) to clarify, and discuss how sound and valuable you think her approach is.

6. In her interview with Bill Moyers, Naomi Shihab Nye mentions a saying from Thailand, "Life is so short we must move very slowly" (p. 718). Write a paper in which you discuss what that saying means (what it would be like to live life that way, how it would be different from other ways of living life), using her interview and other secondary materials in this chapter for support and poems from this chapter for illustrations.

PAPERS INVOLVING FURTHER RESEARCH

Literary Analysis Papers

1. Do research in critical studies of Emily Dickinson's "I heard a Fly buzz" (p. 698), focusing on its metaphor of "the King" who is witnessed in the room. Write a paper in which you survey various explanations of that image and the way it contributes to the poem overall and then draw your own conclusions about how the metaphor should be taken.

2. Robert Frost called himself a "Synecdochist" in poetry. Write a paper in which you explain what that means in terms of the kind of poetry he wrote

and the effect it has, using "Mending Wall" (p. 700) as an example and drawing on scholarly/critical studies of Frost to help support and clarify what you say.

Comparison-Contrast Papers

3. Write a paper comparing and contrasting Ben Jonson's "Inviting a Friend to Supper" (p. 703) and Horace's epistle to Torquatus (book 1, epistle 5). Explore scholarly/critical writings on both poems to find support for your points.

4. Write a paper in which you follow the pattern in Paul Lake's article (p. 722) of comparing and contrasting a poet whose work focuses on ordinary, everyday detail with one whose work does not (as, perhaps, Laure-Anne Bosselaar with Elizabeth Barrett Browning or Naomi Shihab Nye with Samuel Hazo), reading other poems by them in addition to the ones in this book and drawing upon reviews or scholarly/critical studies of them to support your discussion.

Cultural Studies Papers

5. Rita Dove's "The Satisfaction Coal Company" (p. 699) is from a book of poems entitled *Thomas and Beulah*, about an ordinary couple leading ordinary lives, based on Dove's grandparents. Read more of the poems and reviews and critical studies of them, and write a paper discussing the way the poems explore differences between male and female perspectives on life.

6. In his essay "William Carlos Williams: More Than Meets the Eye" (p. 725), M. L. Rosenthal says that Williams pursued "the religion of art" adhered to by the symbolists, who held that "the meanest [lowest, most mundane] of experiential data have their transcendent aesthetic potentiality, and hence that experience is the key to realization" (p. 727). Using Rosenthal's essay and the sources it draws upon as a starting point, read more of Williams's prose and poetry, being alert for places where he explores this idea that the most "un-poetic" of experiences can be a source of transcendence. Then write an essay expanding and clarifying (or disputing) Rosenthal's point.

A Collection of Poems

Valuing a Variety of Voices

Research the authors in this collection with LitLinks at bedfordstmartins.com/approachinglit.

Ai   b. 1947

Why Can't I Leave You?   [1973]

You stand behind the old black mare,
dressed as always in that red shirt,
stained from sweat, the crying of the armpits,
that will not stop for anything,
stroking her rump, while the barley goes unplanted.   5
I pick up my suitcase and set it down,
as I try to leave you again.
I smooth the hair back from your forehead.
I think with your laziness and the drought too,
you'll be needing my help more than ever.   10
You take my hands, I nod
and go to the house to unpack,
having found another reason to stay.

I undress, then put on my white lace slip
for you to take off, because you like that   15

733

and when you come in, you pull down the straps
and I unbutton your shirt.
I know we can't give each other any more
or any less than what we have.
There is safety in that, so much   20
that I can never get past the packing,
the begging you to please, if I can't make you happy,
come close between my thighs
and let me laugh for you from my second mouth.

Agha Shahid Ali   1949–2001

I Dream It Is Afternoon When I Return to Delhi   [1987]

At Purana Qila I am alone, waiting
for the bus to Daryaganj. I see it coming,
but my hands are empty.
"Jump on, jump on," someone shouts,
"I've saved this change for you   5
for years. Look!"
A hand opens, full of silver rupees.
"Jump on, jump on." The voice doesn't stop.
There's no one I know. A policeman,
handcuffs silver in his hands,   10
asks for my ticket.

I jump off the running bus,
sweat pouring from my hair.
I run past the Doll Museum, past
headlines on the Times of India   15
building, PRISONERS BLINDED IN A BIHAR
JAIL, HARIJAN VILLAGES BURNED BY LANDLORDS.
Panting, I stop in Daryaganj,
outside Golcha Cinema.

Sunil is there, lighting   20
a cigarette, smiling. I say,
"It must be ten years, you haven't changed,
it was your voice on the bus!"
He says, "The film is about to begin,
I've bought an extra ticket for you,"   25
and we rush inside:

Anarkali is being led away,
her earrings lying on the marble floor.

Any moment she'll be buried alive.
"But this is the end," I turn   30
toward Sunil. He is nowhere.
The usher taps my shoulder, says
my ticket is ten years old.

Once again my hands are empty.
I am waiting, alone, at Purana Qila.   35
Bus after empty bus is not stopping.
Suddenly, beggar women with children
are everywhere, offering
me money, weeping for me.

Anonymous

Sir Patrick Spens   [1765]

The king sits in Dumferling town,
    Drinking the blude-reid° wine;   *blood-red*
"O whar will I get guid sailor,
    To sail this ship of mine?"

Up and spak an eldern knicht,°   *elderly knight*   5
    Sat at the king's richt° knee;   *right*
"Sir Patrick Spens is the best sailor
    That sails upon the sea."

The king has written a braid° letter   *broad (clear)*
    And signed it wi' his hand,   10
And sent it to Sir Patrick Spens,
    Was walking on the sand.

The first line that Sir Patrick read,
    A loud lauch° lauched he;   *laugh*
The next line that Sir Patrick read,   15
    The tear blinded his ee.°   *eye*

"O wha° is this has done this deed,   *who*
    This ill deed done to me,
To send me out this time o' the year,
    To sail upon the sea?   20

"Mak haste, mak haste, my mirry men all,
    Our guid ship sails the morn."
"O say na° sae,° my master dear,   *not/so*
    For I fear a deadly storm.

"Late, late yestre'en I saw the new moon   25
    Wi' the auld moon in hir arm,
And I fear, I fear, my dear master,
    That we will come to harm."

O our Scots nobles were richt laith°   *loath*
    To weet° their cork-heeled shoon,°   *wet; shoes*   30
But lang or° a' the play were played   *before*
    Their hats they swam aboon.°   *above*

O lang, lang may their ladies sit,
    Wi' their fans into their hand,
Or ere they see Sir Patrick Spens   35
    Come sailing to the land.

O lang, lang may the ladies stand
    Wi' their gold kems° in their hair,   *combs*
Waiting for their ain° dear lords,   *own*
    For they'll see them na mair.°   *more*   40

Half o'er, half o'er to Aberdour
    It's fifty fadom° deep,   *fathoms*
And there lies guid Sir Patrick Spens
    Wi' the Scots lords at his feet.

Margaret Atwood   b. 1939

True Stories   [1981]

i

Don't ask for the true story;
why do you need it?

It's not what I set out with
or what I carry.

What I'm sailing with,   5
a knife, blue fire,

luck, a few good words
that still work, and the tide.

ii

The true story was lost
on the way down to the beach, it's something   10

I never had, that black tangle
of branches in a shifting light,

my blurred footprints
filling with salt

water, this handful   15
of tiny bones, this owl's kill;

a moon, crumpled papers, a coin,
the glint of an old picnic,

the hollows made by lovers
in sand a hundred   20

years ago: no clue.

iii

The true story lies
among the other stories,

a mess of colours, like jumbled clothing
thrown off or away,   25

like hearts on marble, like syllables, like
butchers' discards.

The true story is vicious
and multiple and untrue

after all. Why do you   30
need it? Don't ever

ask for the true story.

W. H. Auden   1907–1973

Musée des Beaux Arts°   [1940]

About suffering they were never wrong,
The Old Masters: how well they understood
Its human position; how it takes place
While someone else is eating or opening a window or just
    walking dully along;

Musée des Beaux Arts: The painting *Landscape with the Fall of Icarus* (next page), on which
the poem is based, is in the Musées Royaux des Beaux-Arts in Brussels.

Pieter Brueghel the Elder (c. 1525–1569), Landscape with the Fall of Icarus, *1558.*
Bridgeman-Giraudon/Art Resource, NY.

How, when the aged are reverently, passionately waiting   5
For the miraculous birth, there always must be
Children who did not specially want it to happen, skating
On a pond at the edge of the wood:
They never forgot
That even the dreadful martyrdom must run its course   10
Anyhow in a corner, some untidy spot
Where the dogs go on with their doggy life and the torturer's horse
Scratches its innocent behind on a tree.

In Breughel's *Icarus*, for instance: how everything turns away
Quite leisurely from the disaster; the ploughman may   15
Have heard the splash, the forsaken cry,
But for him it was not an important failure; the sun shone
As it had to on the white legs disappearing into the green
Water; and the expensive delicate ship that must have seen
Something amazing, a boy falling out of the sky,   20
Had somewhere to get to and sailed calmly on.

Joseph Awad b. 1929

Autumnal   [1988]

Death, it is all about us lately.
Uncle Joe buried just three weeks.
Now Leo gone. And Richard gone.
It is the season. The insistent years,
Like winds that tear away the autumn leaves,   5
Wear us down, resigned to go more gentle.
Even the hidden how, the grim unknown
Of hour or place, wakefulness or pain,
Intimidate us less each autumn. Now
Disquiet whispers with a different question;   10
Whether, before the frost, we will have done
Whatever the work we were created for.
Was it for one supreme heroic deed,
Pivotal, that might reshape the world?
Or the accumulating labors, day by day,   15
That make an exemplary life? Perhaps
My *raison d'être*° is given in this instant—   *reason for existing*
Looking up to see you smiling,
Leaning, in autumn roselight from the window,
To put your hand upon my drooping shoulder.   20
Is it the knowing I alone was born—
Of all Arabia's lovers, I alone—
To sing the secret of this living moment,
That fills my windswept spirit with such peace,
And so much praise?   25

Jimmy Santiago Baca b. 1952

Family Ties   [1989]

Mountain barbecue.
They arrive, young cousins singly,
older aunts and uncles in twos and threes,
like trees. I play with a new generation
of children, my hands in streambed silt   5
of their lives, a scuba diver's hands, dusting
surface sand for buried treasure.
Freshly shaved and powdered faces
of uncles and aunts surround taco
and tamale tables. Mounted elk head on wall,   10

brass rearing horse cowboy clock
on fireplace mantle. Sons and daughters
converse round beer and whiskey table.
Tempers ignite on land grant issues.
Children scurry round my legs.   15
Old bow-legged men toss horseshoes on lawn,
other farmhands from Mexico sit on a bench,
broken lives repaired for this occasion.
I feel no love or family tie here. I rise
to go hiking, to find abandoned rock cabins   20
in the mountains. We come to a grass clearing,
my wife rolls her jeans up past ankles,
wades ice cold stream, and I barefooted,
carry a son in each arm and follow.
We cannot afford a place like this.   25
At the party again, I eat bean and chile
burrito, and after my third glass of rum,
we climb in the car and my wife drives
us home. My sons sleep in the back,
dream of the open clearing,   30
they are chasing each other with cattails
in the sunlit pasture, giggling,
as I stare out the window
at no trespassing signs white flashing past.

Jim Barnes b. 1933

Return to La Plata, Missouri   [1982]

The warping bandstand reminds you of the hard rage
you felt in the heart of the town the day you said goodbye
to the park, silver jet, and cicadas dead in the sage.

The town is basic red, although it browns. A cry
of murder, rape, or wrong will always bend the night   5
hard into the broken grass. You listen close for sighs

of lovers on the ground. The darkness gathers light
and throws it down: something glows that you cannot name,
something fierce, abstract, given time and space you might

on a journey leave behind, a stone to carve your fame   10
on, or a simple word like *love*. The sun is down
or always going down in La Plata, the same

sun. Same too the child's cry that turns the mother's frown
brittle as chalk or the town's face against the moon.
Same too the moan of dog and diesel circling the town   15

in an air so heavy with cloud that there is little room
for breath or moon. Strange: in a town so country, so
foreign, you never hear a song nor see a loom

pattern dark threads into a history you would know
and would not know. You think you see one silver star.   20
But the town offers only itself, and you must go.

Gerald Barrax   b. 1933

Dara   [1984]

When they start pulling you out
The anesthesiologist tells me I may look.
I stand and look over the tent
That hides your mother's body from herself.
I look and see   5
The slick wet head, deceptively black,
That will dry to your nappy red.
Tugs at you. Cuts. Cuts.
I understand your fear, reluctance.
You had clung so tightly   10
Inside, attached so uncertainly to the womb
Against the tide of blood that threatened to sweep you away
Down the toilet where she sat, head bowed,
Watching the flood.
Bargaining for you (Yes, with that promise she keeps)   15
With the god she might as easily have cursed.
Except that it might be you who paid.
Cuts. Cuts. Your mother's flesh, muscle, fat, blood.
They tug and tug now
After you had held so tightly   20
In that micro-ocean, your gray eyes shut
In desperation, clinging to your only hope,
Yourself, imitating her position, her purpose,
Hugging and bowing into yourself,
Into your own stubborn strength,   25
Curving your feet so tightly against you
They would need casting,
The tide flowing, seeming to drain, leech you

Fair black child
You are free,   30
Out, I tell her, second daughter,
Dara. The Beautiful One, last
Child (before they close her)
Is free.

Elizabeth Bishop   1911–1979

In the Waiting Room   [1976]

In Worcester, Massachusetts,
I went with Aunt Consuelo
to keep her dentist's appointment
and sat and waited for her
in the dentist's waiting room.   5
It was winter. It got dark
early. The waiting room
was full of grown-up people,
arctics and overcoats,
lamps and magazines.   10
My aunt was inside
what seemed like a long time
and while I waited I read
the *National Geographic*
(I could read) and carefully   15
studied the photographs:
the inside of a volcano,
black, and full of ashes;
then it was spilling over
in rivulets of fire.   20
Osa and Martin Johnson°
dressed in riding breeches,
laced boots, and pith helmets.
A dead man slung on a pole
— "Long Pig,"° the caption said.   25
Babies with pointed heads
wound round and round with string;
black, naked women with necks
wound round and round with wire
like the necks of light bulbs.   30

---

21. **Osa and Martin Johnson:** Husband-and-wife explorers and naturalists.   25. **Long Pig:** Polynesian cannibals' name for a human carcass.

Their breasts were horrifying.
I read it right straight through.
I was too shy to stop.
And then I looked at the cover:
the yellow margins, the date.   35
Suddenly, from inside,
came an *oh!* of pain
— Aunt Consuelo's voice —
not very loud or long.
I wasn't at all surprised;   40
even then I knew she was
a foolish, timid woman.
I might have been embarrassed,
but wasn't. What took me
completely by surprise   45
was that it was *me*:
my voice, in my mouth.
Without thinking at all
I was my foolish aunt,
I — we — were falling, falling,   50
our eyes glued to the cover
of the *National Geographic*,
February, 1918.

I said to myself: three days
and you'll be seven years old.   55
I was saying it to stop
the sensation of falling off
the round, turning world
into cold, blue-black space.
But I felt: you are an *I*,   60
you are an *Elizabeth*,
you are one of *them*.
Why should you be one, too?
I scarcely dared to look
to see what it was I was.   65
I gave a sidelong glance
— I couldn't look any higher —
at shadowy gray knees,
trousers and skirts and boots
and different pairs of hands   70
lying under the lamps.
I knew that nothing stranger
had ever happened, that nothing
stranger could ever happen.
Why should I be my aunt,   75

or me, or anyone?
What similarities —
boots, hands, the family voice
I felt in my throat, or even
the *National Geographic*   80
and those awful hanging breasts —
held us all together
or made us all just one?
How — I didn't know any
word for it — how "unlikely" . . .   85
How had I come to be here,
like them, and overhear
a cry of pain that could have
got loud and worse but hadn't?

The waiting room was bright   90
and too hot. It was sliding
beneath a big black wave,
another, and another.

Then I was back in it.
The War was on. Outside,   95
in Worcester, Massachusetts,
were night and slush and cold,
and it was still the fifth
of February, 1918.

William Blake   1757–1827

The Chimney Sweeper   [1789]

When my mother died I was very young,
And my father sold me while yet my tongue
Could scarcely cry "'weep! 'weep! 'weep! 'weep!"
So your chimneys I sweep, and in soot I sleep.

There's little Tom Dacre, who cried when his head   5
That curled like a lamb's back, was shaved; so I said,
"Hush, Tom! never mind it, for when your head's bare,
You know that the soot cannot spoil your white hair."

And so he was quiet, and that very night,
As Tom was asleeping, he had such a sight!   10
That thousands of sweepers, Dick, Joe, Ned, and Jack,
Were all of them locked up in coffins of black;

And by came an Angel who had a bright key,
And he opened the coffins and set them all free.
Then down a green plain, leaping, laughing, they run,   15
And wash in a river, and shine in the Sun.

Then naked and white, all their bags left behind,
They rise upon clouds, and sport in the wind;
And the Angel told Tom, if he'd be a good boy,
He'd have God for his father, and never want joy.   20

And so Tom awoke, and we rose in the dark,
And got with our bags and our brushes to work.
Though the morning was cold, Tom was happy and warm;
So if all do their duty, they need not fear harm.

Research William Blake in depth with cultural documents and multimedia resources on *LiterActive*.

Peter Blue Cloud   b. 1935

Rattle   [1978]

When a new world is born, the old
turns itself inside out, to cleanse
and prepare for a new beginning.
      It is
told by some that the stars are
small holes piercing the great
intestine
of a sleeping creature. The earth is
a hollow gourd and earthquakes are
gas rumblings and restless dreaming
of the sleeping creature.
      What
sleeping plant sings the seed
shaken in the globe of a rattle,
the quick breath of the singer warms
and awakens the seed to life.

    The old man rolled fibres of
milkweed across his thigh, softly
speaking to grandchildren, slowly
saying
the thanksgiving to a sacred plant.

Let us shake
the rattle
to call back
a rattlesnake
to dream back   5
the dancers.

When the wind
sweeps earth
there is fullness   10
of sound,
we are given
a beat
to dance by
and drum   15
now joins us
and flutes
are like gentle
birds and
                       20
crickets on
branches,

His left hand coiled the string as it
grew, thin and very strong; as he
explained the strength of a unity
of threads combined.
      He took his
small basket of cocoons and poured
grains of coarse sand, poured from
his hand the coarse sand like a
funnel
of wind, a cone between hand and
cocoon.

      Then, seven by seven, he bound
these nests to a stick with the
string,
and took the sap of white blood
of the plant, and with a finger,
rubbed
the encircling string.
        And waited, holding
the rattle to the sun for drying. And
when
he shook the first sound, the
children
sucked in their breaths and felt
strange
stirrings in their minds and
stomachs.
And when he sang the first song of
many,
the leaves of the cottonwood joined
in,
and desert winds shifted sand.
      And the
children closed their eyes, the better
    to hear tomorrow.

What sleeping plant sings the seed
in the gourd of night within the
hollow moon, the ladder going down,
down into the core of this good earth
leads to stars and wheeling suns
and
planets beyond count.
      What sound
is that in the moist womb of the sea;

swaying trees.
The fan of
winged hawks   25
brush clouds like
streaks of
white clay upon
a field
of blue sky   30
water base.
The seeds in
the pod
of a plant   35
are children
of the sun
of earth   40
that we sing
we are

a rainfall voice   45
a plumed
and sacred bird
we are   50
shadows come back
to protect
the tiny seedlings   55
we are
a memory in
single dance
which is all
dancing forever.   60
We are eyes
looking about
for the children   65
do they
run and play

the softly swaying motion in a
multitude of sleeping seeds.
      Maybe it
is rattlesnake, the medicine singer.
      And
it is gourd, cocoon, seed pod, hollow
horn,
shell of snapping turtle, bark of
birch,
hollowed cedar, intestines of
creatures,
    rattle
is an endless element in sound and
vibration, singing the joys of
awakening,
shushing like the dry stalks of corn
in wind, the cradle songs of night.
    Hail-heavy wind bending upon
a roof of elm bark,
        the howling song
of a midwinter blizzard heard by
a people sitting in circle close to
the fire. The fire is the sun, is the
burning core of Creation's seed,
sputtering
and seeking the womb of life.

    When someone asked Coyote, why
is there loneliness, and what is the
reason and meaning of loneliness:
Coyote
took an empty gourd and began
shaking
it, and he shook it for a long time.
      Then
he took a single pebble and put it
into the gourd, and again began to
shake the gourd for many days, and
the pebble was indeed loneliness.
      Again
Coyote paused to put a handful of
pebbles into the gourd.
      And the sound
now had a wholeness and a meaning
beyond questioning.

our echos
our former joys
in today?
Let us shake   70
the rattle
for the ancients
who dwell
upon this land   75
whose spirits
joined to ours
guide us   80
and direct us
that we
may ever walk
a harmony   85
that our songs
be clear.
Let us shake
the rattle
for the fliers   90
and swimmers

for the trees
and mushrooms
for tall grasses   95

blessed by

a snake's passage
for insects   100
keeping the balance,
and winds
which bring rain
and rivers
going to sea   105
and all
things of Creation.
Let us
shake the rattle
    always, forever.   110

Eavan Boland   b. 1944

The Pomegranate   [1994]

The only legend I have ever loved is
the story of a daughter lost in hell.
And found and rescued there.
Love and blackmail are the gist of it.
Ceres° and Persephone the names.   5
And the best thing about the legend is
I can enter it anywhere. And have.
As a child in exile in
a city of fogs and strange consonants,
I read it first and at first I was   10
an exiled child in the crackling dusk of
the underworld, the stars blighted. Later
I walked out in a summer twilight
searching for my daughter at bed-time.
When she came running I was ready   15
to make any bargain to keep her.
I carried her back past whitebeams
and wasps and honey-scented buddleias.°
But I was Ceres then and I knew
winter was in store for every leaf   20
on every tree on that road.
Was inescapable for each one we passed.
And for me.
             It is winter
and the stars are hidden.   25
I climb the stairs and stand where I can see
my child asleep beside her teen magazines,
her can of Coke, her plate of uncut fruit.
The pomegranate! How did I forget it?
She could have come home and been safe   30
and ended the story and all

---

5. Ceres: Roman name of Demeter, the goddess of crops and harvest. Her daughter Persephone was kidnapped by Pluto (or Hades) and taken to the underworld. Demeter, grieving and angry, refused to let seeds germinate or crops grow. To save the human race from extinction, Zeus finally ordered Pluto to release Persephone. Pluto told her she was free to leave but tricked her by offering a pomegranate seed; anyone who eats food in the underworld must return there. Zeus therefore arranged a compromise: Persephone would spend a third of each year in the land of the dead with Pluto (winter, when Demeter went into mourning); but she would be with her mother for the other two-thirds of each year (spring and summer).   **18. buddleias:** Butterfly bushes.

our heart-broken searching but she reached
out a hand and plucked a pomegranate.
She put out her hand and pulled down
the French sound for apple° and   *pomme*   35
the noise of stone° and the proof   *granite*
that even in the place of death,
at the heart of legend, in the midst
of rocks full of unshed tears
ready to be diamonds by the time   40
the story was told, a child can be
hungry. I could warn her. There is still a chance.
The rain is cold. The road is flint-coloured.
The suburb has cars and cable television.
The veiled stars are above ground.   45
It is another world. But what else
can a mother give her daughter but such
beautiful rifts in time?
If I defer the grief I will diminish the gift.
The legend will be hers as well as mine.   50
She will enter it. As I have.
She will wake up. She will hold
the papery flushed skin in her hand.
And to her lips. I will say nothing.

Anne Bradstreet   c. 1612–1672

To My Dear and Loving Husband   [1678]

If ever two were one, then surely we.
If ever man were loved by wife, then thee;
If ever wife was happy in a man,
Compare with me, ye women, if you can.
I prize thy love more than whole mines of gold,   5
Or all the riches that the East doth hold.
My love is such that rivers cannot quench,
Nor ought but love from thee give recompense.
Thy love is such I can no way repay;
The heavens reward thee manifold, I pray.   10
Then while we live, in love let's so persever,
That when we live no more we may live ever.

Sterling A. Brown   1901–1989

Riverbank Blues   [1932]

A man git his feet set in a sticky mudbank,
A man git dis yellow water in his blood,
No need for hopin', no need for doin',
Muddy streams keep him fixed for good.

Little Muddy, Big Muddy, Moreau and Osage,   5
Little Mary's, Big Mary's, Cedar Creek,
Flood deir muddy water roundabout a man's roots,
Keep him soaked and stranded and git him weak.

Lazy sun shinin' on a little cabin,
Lazy moon glistenin' over river trees;   10
Ole river whisperin', lappin' 'gainst de long roots:
"Plenty of rest and peace in these. . . ."

Big mules, black loam, apple and peach trees,
But seems lak de river washes us down
Past de rich farms, away from de fat lands,   15
Dumps us in some ornery riverbank town.

Went down to the river, sot me down an' listened,
Heard de water talkin' quiet, quiet lak an' slow:
"Ain' no need fo' hurry, take yo' time, take yo' time. . . ."
Heard it sayin' — *"Baby, hyeahs de way life go. . . ."*   20

Dat is what it tole me as I watched it slowly rollin',
But somp'n way inside me rared up an' say,
"Better be movin' . . . better be travelin' . . .
Riverbank'll git you ef you stay. . . ."

Towns are sinkin' deeper, deeper in de riverbank,   25
Takin' on de ways of deir sulky Ole Man —
Takin' on his creepy ways, takin' on his evil ways,
"Bes' git way, a long way . . . whiles you can.

"Man got his sea too lak de Mississippi
Ain't got so long for a whole lot longer way,   30
Man better move some, better not git rooted
Muddy water fool you, ef you stay. . . ."

Elizabeth Barrett Browning   1806–1861

How do I love thee?
Let me count the ways   [1850]

How do I love thee? Let me count the ways.
I love thee to the depth and breadth and height
My soul can reach, when feeling out of sight
For the ends of Being and ideal Grace.
I love thee to the level of everyday's   5
Most quiet need, by sun and candlelight.
I love thee freely, as men strive for Right;
I love thee purely, as they turn from Praise.
I love thee with the passion put to use
In my old griefs, and with my childhood's faith.   10
I love thee with a love I seemed to lose
With my lost saints — I love thee with the breath,
Smiles, tears, of all my life! — and, if God choose,
I shall but love thee better after death.

Anthony Butts   b. 1969

Ferris Wheel   [2003]

His god lived in movies run backwards,
The reels stilled before his warm hand
Reached the co-star's cheek, as if she
Were going to receive a caress instead

Of a smack. His palm retreated slowly at first,   5
Speeding up as the film unfurled smoothly
In reverse, the near-impact of a gesture
Pulled back suddenly as if he

Were confident but shy, his hand looping
In mid-air and coming to a halt   10
Intriguingly behind his thigh. The anger
Disappeared. The camera that followed

Them around had been mistaken. And the actress,
His lone audience among the bruised
Seats of the theater, believed what the new world   15
Revealed, knowing that her rouged cheek

Couldn't really be hurting now. He smiled
As the wheels spun like communion wafers, knowing
That if God exists He exhales in these moments, His chuckle
Bristling the plush darkness. She was enraged   20

About something, but very glad to have his comforting.
She must have spent the money missing from her
Purse. And he never slept with another woman
He didn't love. (He was faithful to neither.) That reel,

Played backwards, bore his awkward, naked   25
Backside jerked high and pushed
Low by his invisible god revealed.
He never would promise to enjoy himself.

Every movie was the same, the denuded
Trees anxiously retrieving their leaves: 30
Clothed in the garments of the living dead.
Dead bodies were resurrected and walked

The earth as if the neutron bomb hadn't
Left their simmered flesh intact. The actress
Was nearly horrified at the sight of the saved   35
World; he loved warfare. But any

Young man who'd gone to war must
Come home stronger, must be
Reborn knowing that words are greater
Arms: the lengthy spokes of Ferris   40

Wheels rushing in their double-negative circuits
Forward (but those two remained with his god
Illuminated in the dark: the actor-
Turned-director splicing the celluloid

As if that were the only filming of   45
The Death of God). In an act of faith, larger
Reels spin forward with vocal children
And adults whirling. Rides are scary

But manageable, as they dent the air
With the concussions of their bursting voices.   50
The wheel awaits each neophyte
Like the ocular body of Christ held high.

Ana Castillo b. 1953

I Heard the Cries of Two Hundred Children   [2000]

I heard the cries of two hundred children
bleating in the desert.
They were not two hundred but two thousand,
not one at all, not
so much as a lost shepherd   5
with a skinny herd of goats
but only the wind pretending
to be the ocean's roar.

I heard more
of the cry of children's ghosts   10
the ones who sleep on cathedral steps,
and who swerve through traffic,
little clowns and fire-eaters,
wash windshields
with contaminated water and shine shoes   15
with hepatitis spit, pick pockets
in the metro and pull your sleeve
on the street
while behind a dark window of the Palacio Nacional°
the president looks out   20
concerned about the national deficit,
a highway built by narcotrafficking kings,
and the latest accusation of election fraud.

I heard the children's cries in the desert
but it was a storm   25
like storms can be in the desert
majestic and terrible,
lightning swords pierced
the horizon.
Three swords went through my heart, and   30
came out on the other side.
You think you are alone in the desert
but you are not; so many eyes watching you.
Every thorn,
cactus worm, scorpion hides.   35
The withering snake, the wide-winged crow
in the sky, coyotes call to each other

---

19. Palacio Nacional: The National Palace in Mexico City, which houses the federal executive offices of Mexico.

in the dark.
The sky too is watching you.
Coyolxiauqui° Warrior Queen   40
does battle each night,
her four hundred children stand guard.
Are they who call you,
and not Mexico's young,
not the ghost of your mother at eleven   45
who scrubbed floors for a plate of food?
Is that you? I call, and I think someone answers.
I think it is her, my dead mother
marching across the Tropic of Cancer,
marching with four hundred sky children,   50
feasting on the wind.

                                              — 1997, *Chicago*

---

40. **Coyolxiauqui:** Or Coyolxauhqui, Aztec goddess of the moon who encouraged her four
hundred brothers (the stars) to kill their mother, Coatlicue, goddess of the earth and fertility,
because her pregnancy embarrassed them. Coatlicue gave birth to Huitzilopochtli, the sun god,
full grown and fully armed, who decapitated Coyolxauhqui and tossed her head into the sky,
where she and her brothers defend the night.

Sandra M. Castillo   b. 1962

Exile   [2001]

And you wonder how you could have decided
what to take with you for the rest of your life,
            what to leave behind.
            — *Dionisio Martínez*°

i.

We are gitanas,
con barajas y collares,°
thinking ourselves nomads,
Hungarians, bohemians
because sometimes, our adventures define us   5
as much as our props.
Or so we think, my cousin Norma and I,
as we go door to door along East 4th Avenue,

Dionisio Martínez: Cuban American poet, born 1956. **1–2. gitanas, con barajas y collares:**
Gypsies, with cards (for reading fortunes) and necklaces.

a street we are not supposed to be on,
using candy as our pretext, 10
our costumes as our shields,
thinking we are who we want to be
on this, my first Halloween, 1970.

ii.

Pale and thin,
he stands in the middle of that icebox, 15
where voices cling, like dishes or silverware,
like the unintelligible sounds of English,
of my voice, our trays slamming into one another,
falling on that cold-white cafeteria floor,
the green mush of American food on my lap, 20
on his blue v-neck sweater
because I turned to look for him,
Francisco Insignari,
the first boy I consciously liked.

iii.

It is my third year in Miami; 25
I am in the 5th grade and Mr. Powers,
my angry American teacher, is telling us about Nixon,
showing us the influence of suggestion,
the persuasion of danger,
asking us who should be president 30
by countering Gonzalo, the new boy,
who alone raises his hand for McGovern,
for a change he never got
before speech and America
because he just doesn't know 35
Mr. Powers.

iv.

Our classroom is called a Pod,
and we rotate to the sound of a bell.
Mr. Shuker gives us word puzzles
from *The Miami Herald*, 40
Miss Christie, bride games:
"something borrowed, something blue,
something old, something new,"
except on Fridays,

when we speak and listen off index cards   45
and have assigned cafeteria seats:
Gerardo Legra, Michael Algair,
Danny Rogers, Maria Murgia and I.

And we sit in silence,
our conversation on our laps,   50
our napkins in our mouths,
for we are graded on our manners,
the silence we share.

v.

The first time I hear the word,
I think about breakfast:
tortilla, Cuban style,   55
with onions and French fries,
on Cuban bread from the bakery on East 10th.

It was what my father made for us
on those days he played weekend cook,   60
but there was an extra syllable
that didn't make me think of Veronica,
slow dancing with Orlando's sister
to *Me & Mrs. Jones*, "Mrs. Jones, Mrs. Jones . . ."
though the boys gathered around her,   65
taunting her with what I knew couldn't be
breakfast.

vi.

Already hip at twelve,
Claro wears otherness
like a worn leather jacket I look for   70
down the humid, yellow halls
of Carol City Junior High,
where we are divided into shifts:
7 A.M. to 12, 12:30 to 5:30 P.M.
where, in dark corners,   75
he finds amor propio°
with my closest girlfriends,
too eager to part their lips
to his popularity and my amazement,
because he knows   80
he is my first obsession.

---

76. **amor propio:** Too much interest in love.

Rosemary Catacalos   b. 1944

David Talamántez on the Last Day
of Second Grade   [1996]

San Antonio, Texas 1988

David Talamántez, whose mother is at work, leaves his mark everywhere
    in the schoolyard,
tosses pages from a thick sheaf of lined paper high in the air one by one,
    watches them

catch on the teachers' car bumpers, drift into the chalky narrow shade of
    the water fountain.
One last batch, stapled together, he rolls tight into a makeshift horn
    through which he shouts

David! and *David, yes!* before hurling it away hard and darting across
    Brazos Street against   5
the light, the little sag of head and shoulders when, safe on the other
    side, he kicks a can

in the gutter and wanders toward home. David Talamántez believes birds
    are warm blooded,
the way they are quick in the air and give out long strings of complicated
    music, different

all the time, not like cats and dogs. For this he was marked down in
    Science, and for putting
his name in the wrong place, on the right with the date instead of on
    the left with Science   10

Questions, and for not skipping a line between his heading and answers.
    The X's for wrong
things are big, much bigger than David Talamántez's tiny writing.
    Write larger, his teacher says

in red ink across the tops of many pages. *Messy!* she says on others where
    he's erased
and started over, erased and started over. Spelling, Language Expression,
    Sentences Using

the Following Words. *Neck. I have a neck name. No!* 20's, 30's.
    Think again! He's good   15
in Art, though, makes 70 on Reading Station Artist's Corner, where he's
    traced and colored

an illustration from *Henny Penny*. A goose with red-and-white striped
    shirt, a hen in a turquoise

dress. Points off for the birds, cloud and butterfly he's drawn in freehand.
  Not in the original

picture! Twenty-five points off for writing nothing in the blank after
  This is my favorite scene
in the book because. . . . There's a page called Rules. *Listen! Always*
  working! Stay in your seat!   20

Raise your hand before you speak! No fighting! Be quiet! Rules copied
  from the board, no grade,
only a huge red checkmark. Later there is a test on Rules. *Listen!*
  Alay ercng! Sast in ao snet!

Rars aone bfo your spek! No finagn! Be cayt! He gets 70 on Rules,
  10 on Spelling. An old man
stoops to pick up a crumpled drawing of a large family crowded around a
  table, an apartment

with bars on the windows in Alazán Courts, a huge sun in one corner
  saying, *To mush noys!*   25
After correcting the spelling, the grade is 90. *Nice details!* And there's
  another mark, on this paper

and all the others, the one in the doorway of La Rosa Beauty Shop, the
  one that blew under
the pool table at La Tenampa, the ones older kids have wadded up like
  big spit balls, the ones run

over by cars. On every single page David Talamántez has crossed out
  the teacher's red numbers
and written in giant letters, blue ink, *Yes! David, yes!*   30

Tina Chang   b. 1969

Origin & Ash   [2004]

Powder rises
from a compact, platters full of peppermints, a bowl of sour pudding.
A cup of milk before me tastes of melted almonds.

It is the story of the eve of my beginning. Gifts for me:

boxes of poppies, pocket knife, an elaborate necklace   5
made of ladybugs.

My skirt rushing north

There is something round and toothless about my dolls.

_____

They have no faith. Their mouths, young muscle to cut me down.
        Their pupils, miniature bruises.   10

I hear the cries of horses, long faces famished, the night the barn burned.

        God and ashes everywhere.

Burnt pennies, I loved them, I could not catch them
in their copper rolling.

My mother's cigarette burns amber in a crystal glass.   15
I am in bed imagining great infernos.

Ashes skimming my deep lake.

The night the animals burned,
I kissed the servant with the salty lips.
There was a spectacular explosion, a sound   20
that severed the nerves, I was kind to that shaking. The horses,
the smell of them, like wet leaves, broken skin.

Laughing against a wall, my hair sweeps the windowsill,

thighs show themselves.

First came my body, my statue's back, then hair electric, matches falling
        everywhere.   25
Tucked in my pink canopy, I am plastic, worn cheeks grinning.

I found my little ones hiding from me, crying into their sleeves. They
        are really from a breeze,
momentary, white.

When we unburied the dolls, red ants were a fantasy
feeding on them, nest of veins, shrunken salted corpses.   30

There is mythology planted in my mouth which is like sin.
Keep fires inside yourself.
My mother once said, *When you were a baby, I let you swim in a basin of*
        water
until your lungs stopped. Since then, my eyes were open windows,

the year everything fell into them.   35

Cicadas hissing.

Ashes on my open book.

Ashes in mother's hair. Ashes on my baby brother.
The streets are arid, driven toward fire.

If I hurry, I will dance with my father before the sun sets,   40
my slippers clicking
on a thin layer of rain.

Marilyn Chin   b. 1955

Turtle Soup   [1987]

for Ben Huang

You go home one evening tired from work,
and your mother boils you turtle soup.
Twelve hours hunched over the hearth
(who knows what else is in that cauldron).

You say, "Ma, you've poached the symbol of long life;   5
that turtle lived four thousand years, swam
the Wei, up the Yellow, over the Yangtze.
Witnessed the Bronze Age, the High Tang,
grazed on splendid sericulture."
(So, she boils the life out of him.)   10

"All our ancestors have been fools.
Remember Uncle Wu who rode ten thousand miles
to kill a famous Manchu and ended up
with his head on a pole? Eat, child,
its liver will make you strong."   15

"Sometimes you're the life, sometimes the sacrifice."
Her sobbing is inconsolable.
So, you spread that gentle napkin
over your lap in decorous Pasadena.

Baby, some high priestess has got it wrong.   20
The golden decal on the green underbelly
says "Made in Hong Kong."

Is there nothing left but the shell
and humanity's strange inscriptions,
the songs, the rites, the oracles?   25

Samuel Taylor Coleridge 1772–1834

Kubla Khan   [*c. 1797–1798*; 1813]
Or, A Vision in a Dream. A Fragment°

In Xanadu did Kubla Khan
A stately pleasure dome decree:°
Where Alph,° the sacred river, ran
Through caverns measureless to man
    Down to a sunless sea.   5
So twice five miles of fertile ground
With walls and towers were girdled round:
And there were gardens bright with sinuous rills,
Where blossomed many an incense-bearing tree;
And here were forests ancient as the hills,   10
Enfolding sunny spots of greenery.

But oh! that deep romantic chasm which slanted
Down the green hill athwart a cedarn cover!
A savage place! as holy and enchanted
As e'er beneath a waning moon was haunted   15
By woman wailing for her demon lover!
And from this chasm, with ceaseless turmoil seething,
As if this earth in fast thick pants were breathing,
A mighty fountain momently was forced:
Amid whose swift half-intermitted burst   20
Huge fragments vaulted like rebounding hail,
Or chaffy grain beneath the thresher's flail:
And 'mid these dancing rocks at once and ever
It flung up momently the sacred river.
Five miles meandering with a mazy motion   25
Through wood and dale the sacred river ran,
Then reached the caverns measureless to man,
And sank in tumult to a lifeless ocean:
And 'mid this tumult Kubla heard from far
Ancestral voices prophesying war!   30

Or, a Vision . . . A Fragment: Coleridge stated in a preface that this poem composed itself in his mind during "a profound sleep" (actually an opium-induced reverie); that he began writing it down immediately upon waking but was interrupted by a caller; and that when he returned to his room an hour later he could not complete it.   **1–2. In . . . decree:** "In Xanadu did Cublai Can build a stately Palace, encompassing sixteene miles of plaine ground with a wall" (Samuel Purchas, *Purchas his Pilgrimage* [1613]). The historical Kublai Khan (1215–1294) was the founder of the Yüan dynasty of China and overlord of the Mongol Empire.   **3. Alph:** Probably derived from the name of the River Alpheus in southern Greece, which according to mythology ran under the sea and emerged at Syracuse (Italy) in the fountain of Arethusa.

The shadow of the dome of pleasure
Floated midway on the waves;
Where was heard the mingled measure
From the fountain and the caves.
It was a miracle of rare device,   35
A sunny pleasure dome with caves of ice!

A damsel with a dulcimer
In a vision once I saw:
It was an Abyssinian maid,
And on her dulcimer she played,   40
Singing of Mount Abora.°
Could I revive within me
Her symphony and song,
To such a deep delight 'twould win me,
That with music loud and long,   45
I would build that dome in air,
That sunny dome! those caves of ice!
And all who heard should see them there,
And all should cry, Beware! Beware!
His flashing eyes, his floating hair!   50
Weave a circle round him thrice,
And close your eyes with holy dread,
For he on honey-dew hath fed,
And drunk the milk of Paradise.

39–41. Abyssinian . . . Abora: See *Paradise Lost* 4.280–82: "where Abassin Kings their issue
Guard, / Mount Amara, though this by some supposed / True Paradise under the Ethiop Line."

Jayne Cortez b. 1936

Into This Time   [1991]

for Charles Mingus°

Into this time
of steel feathers blowing from hearts
into this turquoise flame time in the mouth
into this sonic boom time in the conch
into this musty stone-fly time sinking into   5
the melancholy buttocks of dawn
sinking into lacerated whelps

Charles Mingus: (1929–1979), an innovative American jazz bassist.

into gun holsters
into breast bones
into a manganese field of uranium nozzles   10
into a nuclear tube full of drunk rodents
into the massive vein of one interval
into one moment's hair plucked down into
the timeless droning fixed into
long pauses   15
fixed into a lash of ninety-eight minutes screeching into
the internal heat of an ice ball melting time into
a configuration of commas on strike
into a work force armed with a calendar of green wings
into a collection of nerves   20
into magnetic mucus
into tongueless shrines
into water pus of a silver volcano
into the black granite face of Morelos°
into the pigeon toed dance of Mingus   25
into a refuge of air bubbles
into a cylinder of snake whistles
into clusters of slow spiders
into spade fish skulls
into rosin coated shadows of women wrapped in live iguanas   30
into coins into crosses into St. Martin De Porres°
into the pain of this place changing pitches beneath
fingers swelling into
night shouts
into day trembles   35
into month of precious bloods flowing into
this fiesta of sadness year
into this city of eternal spring
into this solo
on the road of young bulls   40
on the street of lost children
on the avenue of dead warriors
on the frisky horse tail fuzz zooming
into ears of every madman
stomping into every new composition   45
everyday of the blues
penetrating into this time

This time of loose strings in low tones
pulling boulders of Olmec heads into the sun

---

24. Morelos: José Maria Morelos (1765–1815), a Mexican revolutionary leader. **31. St. Martin De Porres:** A seventeenth-century Peruvian saint.

into tight wires uncoiling from body of a strip teaser on the table   50
into half-tones wailing between snap and click
of two castanets smoking into
scales jumping from tips of sacrificial flints
into frogs yodeling across grieving cults
yodeling up into word stuffed smell of flamingo stew   55
into wind packed fuel of howling dog throats slit into
this January flare of aluminum dust falling into
laminated stomach of a bass violin rubbed into red ashes
rubbed into the time sequence of
this time of salmonella leaking from eyeballs of a pope   60
into this lavender vomit time in the chest into
this time plumage of dried bats in the brain into
this wallowing time weed of invisible wakes on cassettes into
this off-beat time syncopation in a leopard skin suit
into this radiated protrusion of time in the desert into   65
this frozen cheek time of dead infants in the cellar
into this time flying with the rotten bottoms of used tuxedos
into this purple   brown   grey   gold minus zero time trilling into
a lime stone crusted Yucatan belching
into fifty six medallions shaking   70
into armadillo drums thumping
into tambourines of fetishes rattling
into an oil slick of poverty symbols flapping
into flat-footed shuffle of two birds advancing
into back spine of luminous impulses tumbling   75
into metronomes of colossal lips ticking
into a double zigzag of callouses splitting
into foam of electric snow flashing into this time
of steel feathers blowing from hearts
into this turquoise flame time in the mouth into   80
this sonic boom time in the conch
into this musty stone fly time sinking into
the melancholy buttocks of dawn

Victor Hernández Cruz   b. 1949

Problems with Hurricanes   [1991]

A campesino looked at the air
And told me:
With hurricanes it's not the wind
or the noise or the water.

I'll tell you he said:
it's the mangoes, avocados
Green plantains and bananas
flying into town like projectiles.   5

How would your family
feel if they had to tell   10
The generations that you
got killed by a flying
Banana.

Death by drowning has honor
If the wind picked you up   15
and slammed you
Against a mountain boulder
This would not carry shame
But
to suffer a mango smashing   20
Your skull
or a plantain hitting your
Temple at 70 miles per hour
is the ultimate disgrace.

The campesino takes off his hat —   25
As a sign of respect
towards the fury of the wind
And says:
Don't worry about the noise
Don't worry about the water   30
Don't worry about the wind —
If you are going out
beware of mangoes
And all such beautiful
sweet things.   35

E. E. Cummings   1894–1962

in Just-   [1923]

in Just-
spring   when the world is mud-
luscious the little
lame balloonman

whistles   far   and wee   5

and eddieandbill come
running from marbles and
piracies and it's
spring

when the world is puddle-wonderful   10

the queer
old balloonman whistles
far   and   wee
and bettyandisbel come dancing

from hop-scotch and jump-rope and   15

it's
spring
and
   the

      goat-footed   20

balloonMan   whistles
far
and
wee

Keki N. Daruwalla   b. 1937

Pestilence   [1970]

pairs of padded feet
         are behind me
astride me
         in front of me
the footpaths are black feet   5
converging on the town

brown shoulders   black shoulders
shoulders round as orbs
muscles smooth as river-stones
        glisten   10
till a dry wind scourges
the sweat from off their backs

they are palanquin-bearers of a different sort
on the string-beds they carry

no henna-smeared brides.
prone upon them are frail bodies
frozen bodies   delirious bodies
some drained of fever and sap
some moving   others supine
transfixed under the sun

the hospital-floors are marble-white
black bodies dirty them
nurses in white habits
unicef jeeps with white bonnets
doctors with white faces receive them
"who says they have cholera?
they are down with diarrhoea
who says it is cholera?
it is gastro-enteritis
who says they have cholera?"

the land's visage is unmarked
soot-brown   soot-green
            soot-grey
mongrels tail the ambulance
till dust and gasoline-fumes
choke them off

but memory like a crane-arm
unloads its ploughed-up rubble
ancient visitations is what one recalls
the sweep of black feet
                towards the ghats
dying villages
the land   surplus once again
as after a flood
migrations as only birds have known
forgotten cattle dying at the stakes
— someone left them on tether

this is miniature by contrast
but the image lingers
string-beds creaking
over padded feet
and when of a sudden
cholera turns to death
the feet keep up their padded progress
only the string-bed is exchanged
for a plank

15

20

25

30

35

40

45

50

55

Toi Derricotte b. 1941

A Note on My Son's Face   [1989]

I

Tonight, I look, thunderstruck
at the gold head of my grandchild.
Almost asleep, he buries his feet
between my thighs;
his little straw eyes   5
close in the near dark.
I smell the warmth of his raw
slightly foul breath, the new death
waiting to rot inside him.
Our breaths equalize our heartbeats;   10
every muscle of the chest uncoils,
the arm bones loosen in the nest
of nerves. I think of the peace
of walking through the house,
pointing to the name of this, the name of that,   15
an educator of a new man.

Mother. Grandmother. Wise
Snake-woman who will show the way;
Spider-woman whose black tentacles
hold him precious. Or will tear off his head,   20
her teeth over the little husband,
the small fist clotted in trust at her breast.

This morning, looking at the face of his father,
I remembered how, an infant, his face was too dark,
nose too broad, mouth too wide.   25
I did not look in that mirror
and see the face that could save me
from my own darkness.
Did he, looking in my eye, see
what I turned from: 30
my own dark grandmother
bending over gladioli in the field,
her shaking black hand defenseless
at the shining cock of flower?

I wanted that face to die,   35
to be reborn in the face of a white child.

I wanted the soul to stay the same,
for I loved to death,
to damnation and God-death,
the soul that broke out of me.   40
I crowed: My Son! My Beautiful!
But when I peeked in the basket,
I saw the face of a black man.

Did I bend over his nose
and straighten it with my fingers   45
like a vine growing the wrong way?
Did he feel my hand in malice?

Generations we prayed and fucked
for this light child,
the shining god of the second coming;   50
we bow down in shame
and carry the children of the past
in our wallets, begging forgiveness.

II

A picture in a book,
a lynching.
The bland faces of men who watch   55
a Christ go up in flames, smiling,
as if he were a hooked
fish, a felled antelope, some
wild thing tied to boards and burned.   60
His charring body
gives off light — a halo
burns out of him.
His face scorched featureless;
the hair matted to the scalp   65
like feathers.
One man stands with his hand on his hip,
another with his arm
slung over the shoulder of a friend,
as if this moment were large enough   70
to hold affection.

III

How can we wake
from a dream

we are born into,
that shines around us,
the terrible bright air?   75

Having awakened,
having seen our own bloody hands,
how can we ask forgiveness,
bring before our children the real   80
monster of their nightmares?

The worst is true.
Everything you did not want to know.

Emily Dickinson   1830–1886

Because I could not stop for Death   [c. 1863; 1890]

Because I could not stop for Death —
He kindly stopped for me —
The Carriage held but just Ourselves —
And Immortality.

We slowly drove — He knew no haste   5
And I had put away
My labor and my leisure too,
For His Civility —

We passed the School, where Children strove
At Recess — in the Ring —   10
We passed the Fields of Gazing Grain —
We passed the Setting Sun —

Or rather — He passed Us —
The Dews drew quivering and chill —
For only Gossamer, my Gown —   15
My Tippet° — only Tulle° —   *scarf/silk net*

We paused before a House that seemed
A Swelling of the Ground —
The Roof was scarcely visible —
The Cornice — in the Ground —   20

Since then — 'tis Centuries — and yet
Feels shorter than the Day
I first surmised the Horses' Heads
Were toward Eternity —

Emily Dickinson

Much Madness is divinest Sense   [c. 1862; 1890]

Much Madness is divinest Sense —
To a discerning Eye —
Much Sense — the starkest Madness —
'Tis the Majority
In this, as All, prevail —   5
Assent — and you are sane —
Demur — you're straightway dangerous —
And handled with a Chain —

Research Emily Dickinson in depth with cultural documents and multimedia resources on *LiterActive*.

Ana Doina   b. 1955

The Extinct Homeland –
A Conversation with Czeslaw Milosz°   [2001]

Tell me, as you would in the middle of the night
When we face only night, the ticking of a watch,
The whistle of an express train, tell me
Whether you really think that this world
Is your home?
             — *"An Appeal" by Czeslaw Milosz*

Home? Somewhere we belong? The metaphor
which includes us in its landscape? The place
that always takes us in, gives us context
is part of our texture? A land where, no matter
how scorched the soil, our roots can still grow?   5
Where all that we should, could, would have been
realized? There is no home for us, Czeslaw.
There is no homeland. Not anymore, not anywhere.

I wish I could learn to live with the malady
of an elsewhere, with the "hidden certainty"   10
that trees grow taller, and sunset's peacock tail
opens more intense colors over *other* horizons, or else

Czeslaw Milosz: (b. 1911) Polish-born poet who was granted political asylum in Paris in 1950 and moved to the United States in 1960. He was awarded the Nobel Prize for Literature in 1980.

quit trying to understand *here* in comparison with *there*
as if I never am where I am, as if I never embody
my own presence.   15

I wish I could cease to crave a pathway
to a physical place I come from, or go to,
and like nomads who don't know where
they have started their exile, I could accept
oblivion as enough of a homeland.   20

Czeslaw, you've been at this game
far longer than I, tell me, is elsewhere real?
Or did I create a lucid paradise of what exists
only in memory? Obsessive, like the negative
of an otherwise ordinary picture. Do I,   25
haunted by the need for symmetry — a known beginning
to a perceivable end — hold real what I choose to keep
alive and harmonious through my story? Do I,
asking for the benefit of nostalgia — this hallucination
whose life is hunger and thirst — break bread   30
with a Fata Morgana?°

Homeland — its cannibal mouth, open
like a graveyard, threatened to swallow me. I too
ran away from my civilization foolishly thinking
I would be able to escape it, and emerge   35
from the narrow cocoon of my flight like a butterfly
who has no memory of the caterpillar. But no land
lets itself be eradicated without leaving behind ruins
or fossils. And no new round is comparable
to what becomes sweeter through memory. Homeland —   40
inscrutable, freed from its bitterness, turns into a garden
while the present, always a temporary ark, is no salvation,
only a journey without a known destination.

I must have been kneaded out of a clay that doesn't stick
to the potter's hands and is not one with the rest of the earth,   45
and just like wisdom words don't keep the breath of the wise,
my life once undone from its originating landscape cannot
be tied to a place anymore. Nor to the sword-laden history
whose blood throbs in my temples, nor to an ancestral oath
which still awakens forgotten passions when I bite   50
the bitter bread of a past ethnic pride. Not even to a generic

---

31. **Fata Morgana:** Mirage.

alley between columnar poplars. All I have are images
voices, faces of people and angels — memorized.
A homeland that neither lives, nor dies, but stays
crystallized like a picture.   55

All there is is a harsh saddle I haven't yet broken in
and the promise of a mythology that doesn't remember
people trudging out of burning pasts, a mythology
that doesn't describe fog-encircled forests and rolling hills,
but a calling, a thirst.   60

Exiled I make a vow to be what I don't know
to a land I haven't inherited, while the old homeland,
the one that becomes extinct in the distance, survives
only in my mouth, in the flavors I long for,
in the mother tongue I teach to my children.   65

There is no homeland. I am its preexisting condition.
I am the great-grandmother of someone who will not
remember the exact place I came from, or why
I needed to run away from the ancestral land, or how
I worshiped. I am my own myth, the first memory, nebulous   70
like any beginning.

John Donne   1572–1631

Death, be not proud   [1633]

Death, be not proud, though some have callèd thee
Mighty and dreadful, for thou art not so;
For those whom thou think'st thou dost overthrow
Die not, poor Death, nor yet canst thou kill me.
From rest and sleep, which but thy pictures be,   5
Much pleasure; then from thee much more must flow,
And soonest our best men with thee do go,
Rest of their bones, and soul's delivery.
Thou art slave to fate, chance, kings, and desperate men,
And dost with poison, war, and sickness dwell,   10
And poppy° or charms can make us sleep as well   *opium*
And better than thy stroke; why swell'st° thou then?   *(with pride)*
One short sleep past, we wake eternally
And death shall be no more; Death, thou shalt die.

Mark Doty   b. 1953

Tiara   [1991]

Peter died in a paper tiara
cut from a book of princess paper dolls;
he loved royalty, sashes

and jewels. *I don't know,*
he said, when he woke in the hospice,   5
I was watching the Bette Davis film festival

on Channel 57 and then —
At the wake, the tension broke
when someone guessed

the casket closed because   10
he was *in there in a big wig*
and heels, and someone said,

You know he's always late,
he probably isn't here yet —
he's still fixing his makeup.   15

And someone said he asked for it.
Asked for it —
when all he did was go down

into the salt tide
of wanting as much as he wanted,   20
giving himself over so drunk

or stoned it almost didn't matter who,
though they were beautiful,
stampeding into him in the simple,

ravishing music of their hurry.   25
I think heaven is perfect stasis
poised over the realms of desire,

where dreaming and waking men lie
on the grass while wet horses
roam among them, huge fragments   30

of the music we die into
in the body's paradise.
Sometimes we wake not knowing

how we came to lie here,
or who has crowned us with these temporary,   35
precious stones. And given

the world's perfectly turned shoulders,
the deep hollows blued by longing,
given the irreplaceable silk

of horses rippling in orchards,   40
fruit thundering and chiming down,
given the ordinary marvels of form

and gravity, what could he do,
what could any of us ever do
but ask for it?   45

Cornelius Eady b. 1954

My Mother, If She Had Won Free
Dance Lessons   [1986]

Would she have been a person
With a completely different outlook on life?
There are times when I visit
And find her settled on a chair
In our dilapidated house,   5
The neighborhood crazy lady
Doing what the neighborhood crazy lady is supposed to do,
Which is absolutely nothing

And I wonder as we talk our sympathetic talk,
Abandoned in easy dialogue,   10
I, the son of the crazy lady,
Who crosses easily into her point of view
As if yawning
Or taking off an overcoat.
Each time I visit   15
I walk back into our lives

And I wonder, like any child who wakes up one day to find themself
Abandoned in a world larger than their
    Bad dreams,
I wonder as I see my mother sitting there,   20
Landed to the right-hand window in the living room,
Pausing from time to time in the endless loop of our dialogue
To peek for rascals through the
Venetian blinds,

I wonder a small thought.   25
I walk back into our lives.
Given the opportunity,

How would she have danced?
Would it have been as easily

As we talk to each other now,   30
The crazy lady
And the crazy lady's son,
As if we were old friends from opposite coasts
Picking up the thread of a long conversation,

Or two ballroom dancers   35
Who only know
One step?

What would have changed
If the phone had rung like a suitor,
If the invitation had arrived in the mail   40
Like Jesus, extending a hand?

T. S. Eliot 1888–1965

The Love Song of J. Alfred Prufrock   [1917]

S'io credesse che mia risposta fosse
A persona che mai tornasse al mondo,
Questa fiamma staria senza piu scosse.
Ma perciocche giammai di questo fondo
Non torno vivo alcun, s'i'odo il vero,
Senza tema d'infamia ti rispondo.°

Let us go then, you and I,
When the evening is spread out against the sky
Like a patient etherized upon a table;
Let us go, through certain half-deserted streets,
The muttering retreats   5
Of restless nights in one-night cheap hotels
And sawdust restaurants with oyster-shells:
Streets that follow like a tedious argument
Of insidious intent
To lead you to an overwhelming question . . .   10

Epigraph: "If I thought that my answer were being made to someone who would ever return to
earth, this flame would remain without further movement; but since no one has ever returned
alive from this depth, if what I hear is true, I answer you without fear of infamy" (Dante, *Inferno* 27.61–66). Dante encounters Guido de Montefeltro in the eighth circle of hell, where
souls are trapped within flames (tongues of fire) as punishment for giving evil counsel. Guido
tells Dante details about his evil life only because he assumes that Dante is on his way to an
even deeper circle in hell and will never return to earth and be able to repeat what he has heard.

Oh, do not ask, "What is it?"
Let us go and make our visit.

    In the room the women come and go
Talking of Michelangelo.

    The yellow fog that rubs its back upon the window-panes,   15
The yellow smoke that rubs its muzzle on the window-panes
Licked its tongue into the corners of the evening,
Lingered upon the pools that stand in drains,
Let fall upon its back the soot that falls from chimneys,
Slipped by the terrace, made a sudden leap,   20
And seeing that it was a soft October night,
Curled once about the house, and fell asleep.

    And indeed there will be time
For the yellow smoke that slides along the street,
Rubbing its back upon the window-panes;   25
There will be time, there will be time
To prepare a face to meet the faces that you meet;
There will be time to murder and create,
And time for all the works and days° of hands
That lift and drop a question on your plate;   30
Time for you and time for me,
And time yet for a hundred indecisions,
And for a hundred visions and revisions,
Before the taking of a toast and tea.

    In the room the women come and go   35
Talking of Michelangelo.

    And indeed there will be time
To wonder, "Do I dare?" and, "Do I dare?"
Time to turn back and descend the stair,
With a bald spot in the middle of my hair —   40
[They will say: "How his hair is growing thin!"]
My morning coat, my collar mounting firmly to the chin,
My necktie rich and modest, but asserted by a simple pin —
[They will say: "But how his arms and legs are thin!"]
Do I dare   45
Disturb the universe?
In a minute there is time
For decisions and revisions which a minute will reverse.

---

29. **works and days:** *Works and Days* is the title of a didactic poem about farming by the Greek poet Hesiod (eighth century B.C.E.) that includes instruction about doing each task at the proper time.

For I have known them all already, known them all: —
Have known the evenings, mornings, afternoons,   50
I have measured out my life with coffee spoons;
I know the voices dying with a dying fall°
Beneath the music from a farther room.
        So how should I presume?

And I have known the eyes already, known them all —   55
The eyes that fix you in a formulated phrase,
And when I am formulated, sprawling on a pin,
When I am pinned and wriggling on the wall,
Then how should I begin
To spit out all the butt-ends of my days and ways?   60
        And how should I presume?

And I have known the arms already, known them all —
Arms that are braceleted and white and bare
[But in the lamplight, downed with light brown hair!]
Is it perfume from a dress   65
That makes me so digress?
Arms that lie along a table, or wrap about a shawl.
        And should I then presume?
        And how should I begin?

_____

Shall I say, I have gone at dusk through narrow streets   70
And watched the smoke that rises from the pipes
Of lonely men in shirt-sleeves, leaning out of windows? . . .

I should have been a pair of ragged claws
Scuttling across the floors of silent seas.

_____

And the afternoon, the evening, sleeps so peacefully!   75
Smoothed by long fingers,
Asleep . . . tired . . . or it malingers,
Stretched on the floor, here beside you and me.
Should I, after tea and cakes and ices,
Have the strength to force the moment to its crisis?   80
But though I have wept and fasted, wept and prayed,

_____

52. a dying fall: An allusion to Shakespeare's *Twelfth Night* (1.1.4): "That strain [of music] again! It had a dying fall" (a cadence that falls away).

Though I have seen my head [grown slightly bald] brought in upon
    a platter,°
I am no prophet — and here's no great matter;
I have seen the moment of my greatness flicker,
And I have seen the eternal Footman hold my coat, and snicker,   85
And in short, I was afraid.

    And would it have been worth it, after all,
After the cups, the marmalade, the tea,
Among the porcelain, among some talk of you and me,
Would it have been worth while,   90
To have bitten off the matter with a smile,
To have squeezed the universe into a ball
To roll it toward some overwhelming question,
To say: "I am Lazarus,° come from the dead,
Come back to tell you all, I shall tell you all" —   95
If one, settling a pillow by her head,
    Should say: "That is not what I meant at all.
    That is not it, at all."

    And would it have been worth it, after all,
Would it have been worth while,   100
After the sunsets and the dooryards and the sprinkled streets,
After the novels, after the teacups, after the skirts that trail along
    the floor —
And this, and so much more? —
It is impossible to say just what I mean!
But as if a magic lantern threw the nerves in patterns on a screen: 105
Would it have been worth while
If one, settling a pillow or throwing off a shawl,
And turning toward the window, should say:
    "That is not it at all,
    That is not what I meant, at all."   110

No! I am not Prince Hamlet, nor was meant to be;
Am an attendant lord, one that will do
To swell a progress,° start a scene or two,

---

82. head . . . platter: As a reward for dancing before King Herod, Salome, his stepdaughter, asked for the head of John the Baptist to be presented to her on a platter (Matthew 14:1–12; Mark 6:17–28).   **94. Lazarus:** Either the beggar Lazarus, who in Luke 16:19–31 did not return from the dead, or Jesus' friend Lazarus, who did (John 11:1–44).   **113. progress:** Ceremonial journey made by a royal court.

Advise the prince; no doubt, an easy tool,
Deferential, glad to be of use,   115
Politic, cautious, and meticulous;
Full of high sentence,° but a bit obtuse;   *sententiousness*
At times, indeed, almost ridiculous —
Almost, at times, the Fool.

    I grow old . . . I grow old . . .   120
I shall wear the bottoms of my trousers rolled.°   *turned up, with cuffs*

    Shall I part my hair behind? Do I dare to eat a peach?
I shall wear white flannel trousers, and walk upon the beach.
I have heard the mermaids singing, each to each.

    I do not think that they will sing to me.   125

    I have seen them riding seaward on the waves
Combing the white hair of the waves blown back
When the wind blows the water white and black.

    We have lingered in the chambers of the sea
By sea-girls wreathed with seaweed red and brown   130
Till human voices wake us, and we drown.

Research T. S. Eliot in
depth with cultural
documents and multimedia
resources on *LiterActive*.

Louise Erdrich   b. 1954

A Love Medicine   [1984]

Still it is raining lightly
in Wahpeton. The pickup trucks
sizzle beneath the blue neon
bug traps of the dairy bar.

Theresa goes out in green halter and chains   5
that glitter at her throat.
This dragonfly, my sister,
she belongs more than I
to this night of rising water.

The Red River swells to take the bridge.   10
She laughs and leaves her man in his Dodge.
He shoves off to search her out.
He wears a long rut in the fog.

And later, at the crest of the flood,
when the pilings are jarred from their sockets   15
and pitch into the current,
she steps against the fistwork of a man.
She goes down in wet grass
and his boot plants its grin
among the arches of her face.   20

Now she feels her way home in the dark.
The white-violet bulbs of the streetlamps
are seething with insects,
and the trees lean down aching and empty.
The river slaps at the dike works, insistent.   25

I find her curled up in the roots of a cottonwood.
I find her stretched out in the park, where all night
the animals are turning in their cages.
I find her in a burnt-over ditch, in a field
that is gagging on rain,   30
sheets of rain sweep up down
to the river held tight against the bridge.

We see that now the moon is leavened and the water,
as deep as it will go,
stops rising. Where we wait for the night to take us   35
the rain ceases. *Sister, there is nothing
I would not do.*

Martín Espada   b. 1957

The Saint Vincent de Paul Food Pantry Stomp   [1990]

Madison, Wisconsin, 1980

Waiting for the carton of food
given with Christian suspicion
even to agency-certified charity cases
like me,
thin and brittle   5
as uncooked linguini,
anticipating the factory-damaged cans
of tomato soup, beets, three-bean salad
in a welfare cornucopia,
I spotted a squashed dollar bill   10
on the floor, and with
a Saint Vincent de Paul food pantry stomp

pinned it under my sneaker,
tied my laces meticulously,
and stuffed the bill in my sock   15
like a smuggler of diamonds,
all beneath the plaster statue wingspan
of Saint Vinnie,
who was unaware
of the dance   20
named in his honor
by a maraca shaker
in the salsa band
of the unemployed.

Sandra María Esteves   b. 1948

A la Mujer Borrinqueña°   [1980]

My name is Maria Christina
I am a Puerto Rican woman born in el barrio°

Our men . . . they call me negra° because they love me
and in turn I teach them to be strong

I respect their ways   5
inherited from our proud ancestors
I do not tease them with eye catching clothes
I do not sleep with their brothers and cousins
although I've been told that this is a liberal society
I do not poison their bellies with instant chemical foods   10
our table holds food from earth and sun

My name is Maria Christina
I speak two languages broken into each other
but my heart speaks the language of people
born in oppression   15

I do not complain about cooking for my family
because abuela° taught me that woman is the master of fire
I do not complain about nursing my children
because I determine the direction of their values

_____

A la Mujer Borrinqueña: "To the woman of Puerto Rico." _Borinquen_ is the Taíno Indian name
for Puerto Rico.   **2. el barrio:** The neighborhood (ethnic enclave).   **3. negra:** Black—dark
skinned.   **17. abuela:** Grandmother.

I am the mother of a new age of warriors   20
I am the child of a race of slaves
I teach my children how to respect their bodies
so they will not o.d. under the stairway's shadow of shame
I teach my children to read and develop their minds
so they will understand the reality of oppression   25
I teach them with discipline . . . and love
so they will become strong and full of life

My eyes reflect the pain
of that which has shamelessly raped me
           but my soul reflects the strength of my culture   30
My name is Maria Christina
I am a Puerto Rican woman born in el barrio
Our men . . . they call me negra because they love me
and in turn I teach them to be strong.

Carolyn Forché   b. 1950

The Colonel   [1981]

What you have heard is true. I was in his house. His wife carried a tray of
coffee and sugar. His daughter filed her nails, his son went out for the night.
There were daily papers, pet dogs, a pistol on the cushion beside him. The
moon swung bare on its black cord over the house. On the television was a
cop show. It was in English. Broken bottles were embedded in the walls
around the house to scoop the kneecaps from a man's legs or cut his hands
to lace. On the windows there were gratings like those in liquor stores. We
had dinner, rack of lamb, good wine, a gold bell was on the table for calling
the maid. The maid brought green mangoes, salt, a type of bread. I was
asked how I enjoyed the country. There was a brief commercial in Spanish.
His wife took everything away. There was some talk then of how difficult it
had become to govern. The parrot said hello on the terrace. The colonel told
it to shut up, and pushed himself from the table. My friend said to me with
his eyes: say nothing. The colonel returned with a sack used to bring groceries home. He spilled many human ears on the table. They were like dried
peach halves. There is no other way to say this. He took one of them in his
hands, shook it in our faces, dropped it into a water glass. It came alive
there. I am tired of fooling around he said. As for the rights of anyone, tell
your people they can go fuck themselves. He swept the ears to the floor with
his arm and held the last of his wine in the air. Something for your poetry,
no? he said. Some of the ears on the floor caught this scrap of his voice.
Some of the ears on the floor were pressed to the ground.

Vievee Francis   b. 1963

Private Smith's Primer   [2006]

Early 1864/1874, the 54th Massachusetts (Colored) Regiment

Aa — is for the apples that clean the teeth after a crunch; A is for the arms
we carry — a shovel for the earthen works, a ladle for dipping up the
gruel, a hammer for putting up winter quarters; for the arms we lost
and may no longer use to wrap 'round the dying, or raise a hand to
comfort our blue breasts; A is for the air we all draw, fair, nobody gets
more than another; A is for the awful truth — 10 dollars to their 13,
though should a musket break our lines, our bodies will break as well;
A is for the ash that fills the air with the stench of liver, throat, a string
of guts like German sausages set a-sizzle, a-flame.

Bb — is for the bees that killed that drummer boy when he stepped into a
bush full of them — buzzing — buzzing — bit into his legs that swelled
huge as melons; B is for the blood that fills our mouths before battle,
after battle; B is for the bush of *her* hair, the hair we dream and smell
loosed from its tight plaits — black bolls pushing out bountiful — a halo
we pull toward our bosoms; B is for the blood smell of a young wife left
waiting among the cobs; for the blood that soaks the bandages after a
leg is freed from its source, for the blood that collects under the ribs
and clots in the knee when we run ahead, barreling forward — *Forward
brothers!*

Cc — is for the cat I know Major _____ found under his bunk, fat with kittens, it crawled in seeking a warm place; C is for the coats we need, the
cold cruel as a leather crop; C is for the candy of a woman's tongue —
hard lick from a brown mouth; C is for the canteen, water cooling the
battle thirst, and the burn in the groin where the cloth rubs constantly
against a man's sack; C is for the cavern of shades — the valleys and
trenches where Satan's teeth claim this human flesh, searching, *My
Lord*, for a soul within.

Allen Ginsberg   1926–1997

A Supermarket in California   [1956]

What thoughts I have of you tonight, Walt Whitman, for I walked
down the sidestreets under the trees with a headache self-conscious
looking at the full moon.

In my hungry fatigue, and shopping for images, I went into the
neon fruit supermarket, dreaming of your enumerations!

What peaches and what penumbras! Whole families shopping at night! Aisles full of husbands! Wives in the avocados, babies in the tomatoes! — and you, García Lorca,° what were you doing down by the watermelons?

I saw you, Walt Whitman, childless, lonely old grubber, poking among the meats in the refrigerator and eyeing the grocery boys.

I heard you asking questions of each: Who killed the pork chops? What price bananas? Are you my Angel?   5

I wandered in and out of the brilliant stacks of cans following you, and followed in my imagination by the store detective.

We strode down the open corridors together in our solitary fancy tasting artichokes, possessing every frozen delicacy, and never passing the cashier.

Where are we going, Walt Whitman? The doors close in an hour. Which way does your beard point tonight?

(I touch your book and dream of our odyssey in the supermarket and feel absurd.)

Will we walk all night through solitary streets? The trees add shade to shade, lights out in the houses, we'll both be lonely.   10

Will we stroll dreaming of the lost America of love past blue automobiles in driveways, home to our silent cottage?

Ah, dear father, graybeard, lonely old courage-teacher, what America did you have when Charon° quit poling his ferry and you got out on a smoking bank and stood watching the boat disappear on the black waters of Lethe?°

Berkeley, 1955

---

3. García Lorca: (1899–1936), Spanish surrealist poet and playwright. **12. Charon:** The boatman in Greek mythology who carried the dead across the river Styx to Hades; **Lethe:** River of Forgetfulness in Hades.

Nikki Giovanni b. 1943

Nikka-Rosa   [1968]

childhood rememberances are always a drag
if you're Black
you always remember things like living in Woodlawn°
with no inside toilet

---

3. Woodlawn: A suburb of Cincinnati.

and if you become famous or something   5
they never talk about how happy you were to have your mother
all to yourself and
how good the water felt when you got your bath from one of those
big tubs that folk in chicago barbecue in
and somehow when you talk about home   10
it never gets across how much you
understood their feelings
as the whole family attended meetings about Hollydale°
and even though you remember
your biographers never understand   15
your father's pain as he sells his stock
and another dream goes
and though you're poor it isn't poverty that
concerns you
and though they fought a lot   20
it isn't your father's drinking that makes any difference
but only that everybody is together and you
and your sister have happy birthdays and very good christmasses
and I really hope no white person ever has cause to write about me
because they never understand Black love is Black wealth and they'll   25
probably talk about my hard childhood and never understand that
all the while I was quite happy

---

13. Hollydale: An all-black housing development in which Giovanni's father invested money.

Patricia Goedicke   b. 1931

My Brother's Anger   [1992]

And here they are again, the duffel bags of sadness,
Shouldering their way into the house like a football team.

Mute, muscular, swollen,
Straining at the seams

Their small eyes look up   5
Waiting for me to open them.

Friends, how can I help you?

I want to pick you up, to cradle you in my arms
But I am too heavy myself.

Can't anyone tie his own shoes?   10

Speak to me, Trouble,
Tell me how to move.

My brother's anger is a helmet.

My sister's voice is a cracked flute
Talking to itself underwater.   15

What can I offer but a sieve?

Shoving yesterday in a closet
I make small talk, smile

Rush around trying to hang up coats

But all over the house there are these dull   20
Enormous sacks of pain.

Stumbling over other people's leftover lumber

I keep trying to embrace them,
Battering my head against weathered flanks . . .

Every day more suicides   25
Among the living, more hangovers

Among the dead.

I throw myself down on the floor
Right in front of them

But it's no use: these slab-sided sorrows   30
Have taken up permanent residence

And will not be comforted.

Ray González   b. 1952

Praise the Tortilla, Praise the Menudo, Praise the Chorizo   [1994]

I praise the tortilla in honor of El Panzón,
who hit me in school every day and made me see
how the bruises on my arms looked like
the brown clouds on my mother's tortillas.
I praise the tortilla because I know   5
they can fly into our hands like
eager flesh of the one we love,
those soft yearnings we delight in biting
as we tear the tortilla and wipe the plate clean.

I praise the menudo° as visionary food that it is,   10
the tripas y posole° tight flashes of color
we see as the red caldo° smears across our notebooks
like a vision we have not had in years,
our lives going down like the empty bowl
of menudo exploding in our stomachs   15
with the chili piquin° of our poetic dreams.

I praise the chorizo° and smear it
across my face and hands,
the dayglow brown of it painting me
with the desire to find out   20
what happened to la familia,
why the chorizo sizzled in the pan
and covered the house with a smell
of childhood we will never have again,
the chorizo burrito hot in our hands,   25
as we ran out to play and show the vatos°
it's time to cut the chorizo,
tell it like it is before la manteca° runs down
our chins and drips away.

---

10. **menudo:** Mexican soup made with hominy and tripe; said to have special powers.   11. **tripas y posole:** Tripe and hominy.   12. **caldo:** Soup.   16. **chili piquin:** Type of pepper, added to menudo or other soups.   17. **chorizo:** Mexican sausage.   26. **vatos:** Guys.   28. **la manteca:** Lard or grease.

Thomas Gray   1716–1771

Elegy Written in a Country Churchyard   [1751]

The curfew° tolls the knell of parting day,   *evening bell*
  The lowing herd wind slowly o'er the lea,
The plowman homeward plods his weary way,
  And leaves the world to darkness and to me.

Now fades the glimmering landscape on the sight,   5
  And all the air a solemn stillness holds,
Save where the beetle wheels his droning flight,
  And drowsy tinklings lull the distant folds;

Save that from yonder ivy-mantled tower
  The moping owl does to the moon complain   10
Of such, as wandering near her secret bower,
  Molest her ancient solitary reign.

Beneath those rugged elms, that yew tree's shade,
　　Where heaves the turf in many a moldering heap,
Each in his narrow cell forever laid,　　　　　　　　　　　　　15
　　The rude forefathers° of the hamlet sleep.　　　　　　*humble ancestors*

The breezy call of incense-breathing morn,
　　The swallow twittering from the straw-built shed,
The cock's shrill clarion, or the echoing horn,°　　　　　*(of a hunter)*
　　No more shall rouse them from their lowly bed.　　　　　20

For them no more the blazing hearth shall burn,
　　Or busy housewife ply her evening care;
No children run to lisp their sire's return,
　　Or climb his knees the envied kiss to share.

Oft did the harvest to their sickle yield,　　　　　　　　　25
　　Their furrow oft the stubborn glebe° has broke;　　　　　*soil*
How jocund did they drive their team afield!
　　How bowed the woods beneath their sturdy stroke!

Let not Ambition mock their useful toil,
　　Their homely joys, and destiny obscure;　　　　　　　　30
Nor Grandeur hear with a disdainful smile
　　The short and simple annals of the poor.

The boast of heraldry,° the pomp of power,　　　　　*noble ancestry*
　　And all that beauty, all that wealth e'er gave,
Awaits alike the inevitable hour.　　　　　　　　　　　　35
　　The paths of glory lead but to the grave.

Nor you, ye proud, impute to these the fault,
　　If memory o'er their tomb no trophies° raise,　　　　　*memorials*
Where through the long-drawn aisle and fretted° vault　　*ornamented*
　　The pealing anthem swells the note of praise.　　　　　40

Can storied° urn or animated° bust　　　　　*decorated; lifelike*
　　Back to its mansion call the fleeting breath?
Can Honor's voice provoke° the silent dust,　　　　　*call forth*
　　Or Flattery soothe the dull cold ear of Death?

Perhaps in this neglected spot is laid　　　　　　　　　45
　　Some heart once pregnant with celestial fire;
Hands that the rod of empire might have swayed,
　　Or waked to ecstasy the living lyre.

But Knowledge to their eyes her ample page
　　Rich with the spoils of time did ne'er unroll;　　　　50
Chill Penury repressed their noble rage,
　　And froze the genial current of the soul.

———————

Full many a gem of purest ray serene,
　　The dark unfathomed caves of ocean bear:
Full many a flower is born to blush unseen,　　　　　　　　　　　55
　　And waste its sweetness on the desert air.

Some village Hampden, that with dauntless breast
　　The little tyrant of his fields withstood;
Some mute inglorious Milton here may rest,
　　Some Cromwell° guiltless of his country's blood.　　　　　　60

The applause of listening senates to command,
　　The threats of pain and ruin to despise,
To scatter plenty o'er a smiling land,
　　And read their history in a nation's eyes,

Their lot forbade: nor° circumscribed alone　　　　　　　　*not*　65
　　Their growing virtues, but their crimes confined;
Forbade to wade through slaughter to a throne,
　　And shut the gates of mercy on mankind,

The struggling pangs of conscious truth to hide,
　　To quench the blushes of ingenuous shame,　　　　　　　　70
Or heap the shrine of Luxury and Pride
　　With incense kindled at the Muse's flame.

Far from the madding crowd's ignoble strife,
　　Their sober wishes never learned to stray;
Along the cool sequestered vale of life　　　　　　　　　　　75
　　They kept the noiseless tenor of their way.

Yet even these bones from insult to protect
　　Some frail memorial° still erected nigh,　　　　*simple tombstone*
With uncouth rhymes and shapeless sculpture decked,
　　Implores the passing tribute of a sigh.　　　　　　　　　　80

Their name, their years, spelt by the unlettered Muse,
　　The place of fame and elegy supply:
And many a holy text around she strews,
　　That teach the rustic moralist to die.

For who to dumb Forgetfulness a prey,　　　　　　　　　　　85
　　This pleasing anxious being e'er resigned,
Left the warm precincts of the cheerful day,
　　Nor cast one longing lingering look behind?

On some fond breast the parting soul relies,
　　Some pious drops° the closing eye requires;　　　　*tears*　90

57–60. Hampden, Cromwell: John Hampden (1594–1643) refused to pay a special tax imposed in 1636 and led a defense of the people's rights in Parliament. Oliver Cromwell (1599–1658) was a rebel leader in the English Civil War.

Even from the tomb the voice of Nature cries,
    Even in our ashes live their wonted fires.

For thee,° who mindful of the unhonored dead   *(the poet himself)*
    Dost in these lines their artless tale relate;
If chance, by lonely contemplation led,   95
    Some kindred spirit shall inquire thy fate,

Haply° some hoary-headed swain° may say,   *perhaps; elderly shepherd*
    "Oft have we seen him° at the peep of dawn   *the poet*
Brushing with hasty steps the dews away
    To meet the sun upon the upland lawn.   100

"There at the foot of yonder nodding beech
    That wreathes its old fantastic roots so high,
His listless length at noontide would he stretch,
    And pore upon the brook that babbles by.

"Hard by yon wood, now smiling as in scorn,   105
    Muttering his wayward fancies he would rove,
Now drooping, woeful wan, like one forlorn,
    Or crazed with care, or crossed in hopeless love.

"One morn I missed him on the customed hill,
    Along the heath and near his favorite tree;   110
Another° came, nor yet beside the rill,   *(another day)*
    Nor up the lawn, nor at the wood was he;

"The next with dirges due in sad array
    Slow through the churchway path we saw him borne.
Approach and read (for thou canst read) the lay,   115
    Graved on the stone beneath yon aged thorn."

The Epitaph

Here rests his head upon the lap of Earth
    A youth to fortune and to Fame unknown.
Fair Science° frowned not on his humble birth,   *learning*
    And Melancholy marked him for her own.   120

Large was his bounty, and his soul sincere,
    Heaven did a recompense as largely send:
He gave to Misery all he had, a tear,
    He gained from Heaven ('twas all he wished) a friend.

No farther seek his merits to disclose,   125
    Or draw his frailties from their dread abode
(There they alike in trembling hope repose),
    The bosom of his Father and his God.

Kimiko Hahn   b. 1955

Mother's Mother   [1999]

> . . . There is no mother tongue.
>   — Elaine Showalter

The mother draws the shade down halfway
so the sunlight does not blind the pages
and she reads the story, *mukashi mukashi aruhi,*°
which is the way every story begins
whether about a boy riding a tortoise beneath the sea   5
or a girl born from a bamboo stalk.
Her daughter does not speak Japanese
though she can write her name in the *kana*°
that resembles tv antennae

キ ミ コ°

and she knows not everyone speaks the same language: 10
see you, ciao, adios, sayonara. She knows
her mother knows more than one way to say things
and Japanese, which is also how she *looks,*
is the language her mother was taught,
like the island of Japan,   15
almost as far from this little house on the island of Maui.

The chickens are so loud grandma.
Ursuai ne.°
So dusty.
Kitanai°   20
So —

She wants to learn every word her grandma knows.
She wants to be like her grandma
who she sees her mother loves and does not want to leave.
She wants to stay with her grandma also   25
and knows from her mother's shoulders they will not see her again.

If there is no mother tongue for women
there is for immigrant children
who play on the black volcanic beaches,
on the sharp coral reefs, in the salty rain, the plantation houses,   30

---

3. *mukashi mukashi aruhi*: Once upon a time.   **8. *kana*:** One of two Japanese phonetic
alphabets, easier to master than *Kanji* (Chinese characters).   **9.** キ ミ コ: Ki - mi - ko.
18. *Urusai ne*: Annoying, isn't it?   **20. *Kitanai*:** Dirty, filthy.

the fields of burning cane, the birds-of-paradise.
Who see the shark fins in the sunlight and linger on the blanket.

There is a mother's tongue and it is conveyed
by this mother to her daughters
who will carry the words at least in song   35
because when mother dies there will be no one else
unless there is an aunt or cousin
to correct the tense or word choice
with such affection and cause.

えぁよね。°

The same cause found in domestic arts and survival.   40
When the mother dies the daughter
or the daughter-in-law, or even the son,
becomes that figure in part
and the words the older woman knew
are the words this person will parent   45
despite lineage and its repressive roots.
Its often awful branches.
The root words and radicals the daughter memorizes.

氷   シ°

So when I toss my hair from my eyes I feel
it's mother tossing her head and when I cough   50
it is her cough I hear.
And when I tell my child to say *mama*
it may be that I am speaking to myself
as much as I am speaking to the small mouth
a few inches from my face.   55

---

39. えぁよね .: That's just the way it is, isn't it? **48.** 氷   シ: It is endless (the process of learning Chinese characters).

Donald Hall   b. 1928

Names of Horses   [1978]

All winter your brute shoulders strained against collars, padding
and steerhide over the ash hames, to haul
sledges of cordwood for drying through spring and summer,
for the Glenwood stove next winter, and for the simmering range.

In April you pulled cartloads of manure to spread on the fields,   5
dark manure of Holsteins, and knobs of your own clustered with oats.
All summer you mowed the grass in meadow and hayfield, the mowing
    machine
clacketing beside you, while the sun walked high in the morning;

and after noon's heat, you pulled a clawed rake through the same acres,
gathering stacks, and dragged the wagon from stack to stack,   10
and the built hayrack back, up hill to the chaffy barn,
three loads of hay a day, hanging wide from the hayrack.

Sundays you trotted the two miles to church with the light load
of a leather quartertop buggy, and grazed in the sound of hymns.
Generation on generation, your neck rubbed the window sill   15
of the stall, smoothing the wood as the sea smooths glass.

When you were old and lame, when your shoulders hurt bending to graze,
one October the man who fed you and kept you, and harnessed you every
    morning,
led you through corn stubble to sandy ground above Eagle Pond,
and dug a hole beside you where you stood shuddering in your skin,   20

and lay the shotgun's muzzle in the boneless hollow behind your ear,
and fired the slug into your brain, and felled you into your grave,
shoveling sand to cover you, setting goldenrod upright above you,
where by next summer a dent in the ground made your monument.

For a hundred and fifty years, in the pasture of dead horses,   25
roots of pine trees pushed through the pale curves of your ribs,
yellow blossoms flourished above you in autumn, and in winter
frost heaved your bones in the ground — old toilers, soil makers:

O Roger, Mackerel, Riley, Ned, Nellie, Chester, Lady Ghost.

Michael S. Harper   b. 1938

Nightmare Begins Responsibility   [1975]

I place these numbed wrists to the pane
watching white uniforms whisk over
him in the tube-kept
prison
fear what they will do in experiment   5
watch my gloved stickshifting gasolined hands
breathe *boxcar-information-please* infirmary tubes
distrusting white-pink mending paperthin

silkened end hairs, distrusting tubes
shrunk in his *trunk-skincapped*   10
shaven head, in thighs
distrusting-white-hands-picking-baboon-light
on this son who will not make his second night
of this wardstrewn intensive airpocket
where his father's asthmatic   15
hymns of *night-train*, train done gone
his mother can only know that he has flown
up into essential calm unseen corridor
going boxscarred home, *mamaborn, sweetsonchild*
gonedowntown into *researchtestingwarehousebatteryacid*   20
mama-son-done-gone/me telling her 'nother
train tonight, no music, no breathstroked
heartbeat in my infinite distrust of them:

and of my distrusting self
white-doctor-who-breathed-for-him-all-night   25
say it for two sons gone,
say nightmare, say it loud
panebreaking heartmadness:
nightmare begins responsibility.

Samuel Hazo b. 1928

For Fawzi in Jerusalem   [1968]

Leaving a world too old to name
and too undying to forsake,
I flew the cold, expensive sea
toward Columbus' mistake
where life could never be the same   5

for me. In Jerash° on the sand
I saw the colonnades of Rome
bleach in the sun like skeletons.
Behind a convalescent home,
armed soldiers guarded no man's land   10

between Jordanians and Jews.
Opposing sentries frowned and spat.

---

6. Jerash: The ancient city of Gerasa, twenty-two miles north of Amman in present-day Jordan. Called Jerash by the Romans who rebuilt it in 65 C.E., it is the best-preserved Palestinian city of Roman times.

Fawzi, you mocked in Arabic
this justice from Jehoshophat°
before you shined my Pittsburgh shoes   15

for nothing. Why you never kept
the coins I offered you is still
your secret and your victory.
Saying you saw marauders kill
your father while Beershebans° wept   20

for mercy in their holy war,
you told me how you stole to stay
alive. You must have thought I thought
your history would make me pay
a couple of piastres more   25

than any shine was worth — and I
was ready to — when you said, "No,
I never take. I never want
America to think I throw
myself on you. I never lie."   30

I watched your young but old man's stare
demand the sword to flash again
in blood and flame from Jericho°
and leave the bones of these new men
of Judah bleaching in the air   35

like Roman stones upon the plain
of Jerash. Then you faced away.
Jerusalem, Jerusalem,
I asked myself if I could pray
for peace and not recall the pain   40

you spoke. But what could praying do?
Today I live your loss in no
man's land but mine, and every time
I talk of fates not just but so,
Fawzi, my friend, I think of you.   45

---

14. Jehoshophat: Hebrew king of Judah (c. 873–849 B.C.E.), the first to make a treaty with the neighboring kingdom of Israel. **20. Beershebans:** Inhabitants of Beersheba, a city in southern Israel. Given to the Arabs in the partition of Palestine (1948), it was retaken by Israel in the Arab-Israeli war of 1948. **33. Jericho:** Ancient city in biblical Palestine, in the Jordan valley north of the Dead Sea, captured from the Canaanites by Joshua and destroyed (Joshua 6:1–21).

Seamus Heaney b. 1939

Digging   [1966]

Between my finger and my thumb
The squat pen rests; snug as a gun.

Under my window, a clean rasping sound
When the spade sinks into gravelly ground:
My father, digging. I look down   5

Till his straining rump among the flowerbeds
Bends low, comes up twenty years away
Stooping in rhythm through potato drills
Where he was digging.

The coarse boot nestled on the lug, the shaft   10
Against the inside knee was levered firmly.
He rooted out tall tops, buried the bright edge deep
To scatter new potatoes that we picked
Loving their cool hardness in our hands.

By God, the old man could handle a spade.   15
Just like his old man.

My grandfather cut more turf in a day
Than any other man on Toner's bog.
Once I carried him milk in a bottle
Corked sloppily with paper. He straightened up   20
To drink it, then fell to right away
Nicking and slicing neatly, heaving sods
Over his shoulder, going down and down
For the good turf. Digging.

The cold smell of potato mould, the squelch and slap   25
Of soggy peat, the curt cuts of an edge
Through living roots awaken in my head.
But I've no spade to follow men like them.

Between my finger and my thumb
The squat pen rests.   30
I'll dig with it.

George Herbert   1593–1633

The Pulley   [1633]

When God at first made man,
Having a glass of blessings standing by,
"Let us," said he, "pour on him all we can.
Let the world's riches, which dispersèd lie,
    Contract into a span."   5

So strength first made a way;
Then beauty flowed, then wisdom, honor, pleasure.
When almost all was out, God made a stay,
Perceiving that, alone of all his treasure,
    Rest in the bottom lay.   10

"For if I should," said he,
"Bestow this jewel also on my creature,
He would adore my gifts instead of me,
And rest in Nature, not the God of Nature;
    So both should losers be.   15

"Yet let him keep the rest,
But keep them with repining restlessness.
Let him be rich and weary, that at least,
If goodness lead him not, yet weariness
    May toss him to my breast."   20

David Hernandez   b. 1971

The Butterfly Effect   [2003]

If a butterfly flapping its wings in Beijing
could cause a hurricane off the coast of Florida,
so could a deck of cards shuffled at a picnic.
So could the clapping hands of a father
watching his son rounding the bases,   5
the wind sculpting his baggy pants.
So could a woman reading a book of poems,
a tiny current from a turned page
slipping out the open window, nudging
a passing breeze: an insignificant event   10
that could snowball months later into a monsoon
at a coastal village halfway around the world.

Palm trees bowing on the shore.
Grass huts disintegrating like blown dandelions.

Hard to believe, but when I rewind my life,   15
starting from a point when my heart
was destroyed, I see the dominoes rising,
how that storm was just a gale weeks earlier,
a gust days before that. Finally I see
where it all began: I say hello to a woman   20
sitting alone at the bar, a tattoo butterfly
perched on her ankle, ready to wreak havoc.

Robert Herrick   1591–1674

To the Virgins, to Make Much of Time   [1648]

Gather ye rosebuds while ye may,
    Old time is still a-flying;
And this same flower that smiles today
    Tomorrow will be dying.

The glorious lamp of heaven, the sun,   5
    The higher he's a-getting,
The sooner will his race be run,
    And nearer he's to setting.

That age is best which is the first,
    When youth and blood are warmer;   10
But being spent, the worse, and worst
    Times still succeed the former.

Then be not coy, but use your time,
    And while ye may, go marry;
For having lost but once your prime,   15
    You may forever tarry.

Linda Hogan   b. 1947

The History of Red   [1993]

First
there was some other order of things
never spoken
but in dreams of darkest creation.

_____

Then there was black earth,   5
lake, the face of light on water.
Then the thick forest all around
that light,
and then the human clay
whose blood we still carry   10
rose up in us
who remember caves with red bison
painted in their own blood,
after their kind.

A wildness   15
swam inside our mothers,
desire through closed eyes,
a new child
wearing the red, wet mask of birth,
delivered into this land   20
already wounded,
stolen and burned
beyond reckoning.

Red is this yielding land
turned inside out   25
by a country of hunters
with iron, flint and fire.
Red is the fear
that turns a knife back
against men, holds it at their throats,   30
and they cannot see the claw on the handle,
the animal hand
that haunts them
from some place inside their blood.

So that is hunting, birth,   35
and one kind of death.
Then there was medicine, the healing of wounds.
Red was the infinite fruit
of stolen bodies.
The doctors wanted to know   40
what invented disease
how wounds healed
from inside themselves
how life stands up in skin,
if not by magic.   45

They divined the red shadows of leeches
that swam in white bowls of water;

they believed stars
in the cup of sky,
They cut the wall of skin   50
to let
what was bad escape
but they were reading the story of fire
gone out
and that was science.   55

As for the animal hand on death's knife,
knives have as many sides
as the red father of war
who signs his name
in the blood of other men.   60

And red was the soldier
who crawled
through a ditch
of human blood in order to live.
It was the canal of his deliverance.   65
It is his son who lives near me.
Red is the thunder in our ears
when we meet.
Love, like creation,
is some other order of things.   70

Red is the share of fire
I have stolen
from root, hoof, fallen fruit.
And this was hunger.

Red is the human house   75
I come back to at night
swimming inside the cave of skin
that remembers bison.
In that round nation
of blood   80
we are all burning,
red, inseparable fires
the living have crawled
and climbed through
in order to live   85
so nothing will be left
for death at the end.

This life in the fire, I love it,
I want it,
this life.   90

A. E. Housman   1859–1936

To an Athlete Dying Young   [1896]

The time you won your town the race
We chaired you through the market-place;
Man and boy stood cheering by,
And home we brought you shoulder-high.

To-day, the road all runners come,   5
Shoulder-high we bring you home,
And set you at your threshold down,
Townsman of a stiller town.

Smart lad, to slip betimes away
From fields where glory does not stay   10
And early though the laurel grows
It withers quicker than the rose.

Eyes the shady night has shut
Cannot see the record cut,°   *broken*
And silence sounds no worse than cheers   15
After earth has stopped the ears:

Now you will not swell the rout
Of lads that wore their honours out,
Runners whom renown outran
And the name died before the man.   20

So set, before its echoes fade,
The fleet foot on the sill of shade,
And hold to the low lintel up
The still-defended challenge-cup.

And round that early-laurelled head   25
Will flock to gaze the strengthless dead,
And find unwithered on its curls
The garland briefer than a girl's.

Langston Hughes   1902–1967

The Negro Speaks of Rivers   [1926]

I've known rivers:
I've known rivers ancient as the world and older than the flow of
        human blood in human veins.

My soul has grown deep like the rivers.

I bathed in the Euphrates when dawns were young.
I built my hut near the Congo and it lulled me to sleep.   5
I looked upon the Nile and raised the pyramids above it.
I heard the singing of the Mississippi when Abe Lincoln went down
     to New Orleans, and I've seen its muddy bosom turn all golden
     in the sunset.

I've known rivers:
Ancient, dusky rivers.

My soul has grown deep like the rivers.   10

Lawson Fusao Inada   b. 1938

Plucking Out a Rhythm   [1971]

Start with a simple room—
a dullish color—
and draw the one shade down.
Hot plate. Bed.
Little phonograph in a corner.   5

Put in a single figure—
medium weight and height—
but oversize, as a child might.

The features must be Japanese.

Then stack a black pompadour on,   10
and let the eyes
slide behind a night of glass.

The figure is in disguise:

slim green suit
for posturing on a bandstand,   15
the turned-up shoes of Harlem . . .

Then start the music playing—
thick jazz, strong jazz—

and notice that the figure
comes to life: 20

sweating, growling
over an imaginary bass—
plucking out a rhythm—

as the music rises and the room is full,
exuding with that rhythm . . .   25

Then have the shade flap up
and daylight catch him
frozen in that pose

as it starts to snow —
thick snow, strong snow —   30

blowing in the window
while the music quiets,
the room is slowly covered,

and the figure is completely
out of sight.   35

Honorée Fanonne Jeffers   b. 1967

Outlandish Blues (The Movie)   [2003]

. . . newly arrived Africans were classified in the North American lexicon as "outlandish" in that they were "strangers to the English language" and had yet to learn their new roles.

— Michael A. Gomez

Where else can you sail across a blue sea
into a horizon emptied of witnesses?
This is the cathartic's truth, the movie mind's eye,
a vibrant ship voyage where the slaves luckily escape,

where the horizon empties of witnesses,   5
and the food and the water and the mercy run low
on this photogenic voyage where slaves luckily will escape,
but not before sailors throw a few souls in the ocean.

Before the food, water and mercy run low,
watch the celluloid flashes of sexy, tight bodies   10
that the sailors throw into the mouths of waiting fish,
bodies branded with the Cross, baptized with holy water,

tight-packed bodies flashing across the screen,
Hollywood flat stomachs pressed to buttocks pressed to shoulders
first branded with the Cross, baptized with holy water   15
and then covered with manufactured filth.

The stomachs press to buttocks press to shoulders
and of course, there is no pleasure in the touch —

under the filth we can see the taut black beauty
and we guiltily consider the following: 20

Are we sure there was no pleasure in those touches?
Are we sure most kidnapped Africans were not full grown?
We guiltily consider the following:
Were these really children picked for long lives of work?

Are we sure these were not full grown Africans   25
instead of children stolen or sold from their parents,
picked for long lives of work to be squeezed from them?
Must we think on coins passed between white and black hands?

These were children stolen or sold from their parents
though we don't see any of that on the movie screen.   30
We don't see coins passed between white and black hands.
We don't see any boys and girls raped by the sailors.

We don't see much of their lives on the screen,
only the clean Bible one of the male slaves is given.
We don't see any boys and girls raped by the sailors,   35
only prayers for redemption the slave definitely receives.

There are close-ups of the Bible given to a slave
but no questions about the God he sees in his dreams.
Who gives him the redemption I'm sure he receives?
Who will he call on — the God of his parents?   40

Who is the God he sees in his dreams?
Who placed him in the gut of this three-hour nightmare?
Who will he call on — the God of his parents
or his Bible's Savior, a man who walks on water?

Who placed him in the gut of this three-hour nightmare?   45
Certainly not the God of cathartic truth
or even the Bible's Savior, a man walking across water,
just right on over blues cast like bait upon the sea.

Ben Jonson   1572–1637

On My First Son   [1616]

Farewell, thou child of my right hand,° and joy;
  My sin was too much hope of thee, loved boy:
Seven years thou'wert lent to me, and I thee pay,
  Exacted by thy fate, on the just day.
O could I lose all father now! for why   5
  Will man lament the state he should envy,
To have so soon 'scaped world's and flesh's rage,
  And, if no other misery, yet age?
Rest in soft peace, and asked, say, "Here doth lie
  Ben Jonson his best piece of poetry."   10
For whose sake henceforth all his° vows be such   (the father's)
  As what he loves may never like° too much.

---

1. child . . . hand: A literal translation of the Hebrew name "Benjamin." The boy, named for his father, was born in 1596 and died on his birthday ("the just day") in 1603.   12. like: Archaic meaning both "want" and "please."

A. Van Jordan   b. 1965

From   [2004]

from (⇨) prep. 1. Starting at (a particular place or time): As in, John was from Chicago, but he played guitar straight from the Delta; he wore a blue suit from Robert Hall's; his hair smelled like coconut; his breath, like mint and bourbon; his hands felt like they were from slave times when he touched me — hungry, stealthy, trembling. 2. Out of: He pulled a knot of bills from his pocket, paid the man and we went upstairs. 3. Not near to or in contact with: He smoked the weed, but, surprisingly, he kept it from me. He said it would make me too self-conscious, and he wanted those feelings as far away from us as possible; he said a good part of my beauty was that I wasn't conscious of my beauty. Isn't that funny? So we drank Bloody Mothers (Hennessey and tomato juice), which was hard to keep from him — he always did like to drink. 4. Out of the control or authority of: I was released from my mama's house, from dreams of hands holding me down, from the threat of hands not pulling me up, from the man that knew me, but of whom I did not know; released from the dimming of twilight, from the brightness of morning; from the love I thought had to look like love; from the love I thought had to taste like love, from the love I thought I had to love like love. 5. Out of the totality of: I came from a family full of women; I came from a family full of believers; I came from a pack of witches — I'm just waiting to conjure my powers; I came from a legacy of lovers — I'm just waiting to seduce my seducer; I came from a pride of proud women, and we take good care of our young.

6. As being other or another than: He couldn't tell me *from* his mother; he couldn't tell me *from* his sister; he couldn't tell me *from* the last woman he had before me, and why should he — we're all the same woman. 7. With (some person, place, or thing) as the instrument, maker, or source: Here's a note *from* my mother, and you can take it as advice *from* me: A weak lover is more dangerous than a strong enemy; if you're going to love someone, make sure you know where they're coming *from*. 8. Because of: Becoming an alcoholic, learning to walk away, being a good speller, being good in bed, falling in love — they all come *from* practice. 9. Outside or beyond the possibility of: In the room, he kept me *from* leaving by keeping me curious; he kept me *from* drowning by holding my breath in his mouth; yes, he kept me *from* leaving till the next day when he said *Leave*. Then, he couldn't keep me *from* coming back.

John Keats   1795–1821

Ode on a Grecian Urn   [1820]

1

Thou still unravished bride of quietness,
    Thou foster child of silence and slow time,
Sylvan historian, who canst thus express
    A flowery tale more sweetly than our rhyme:
What leaf-fringed legend haunts about thy shape   5
    Of deities or mortals, or of both,
        In Tempe or the dales of Arcady?°
    What men or gods are these? What maidens loath?
What mad pursuit? What struggle to escape?
        What pipes and timbrels? What wild ecstasy?   10

2

Heard melodies are sweet, but those unheard
    Are sweeter; therefore, ye soft pipes, play on;
Not to the sensual ear,° but, more endeared,
    Pipe to the spirit ditties of no tone:
Fair youth, beneath the trees, thou canst not leave   15
    Thy song, nor ever can those trees be bare;
        Bold lover, never, never canst thou kiss,
Though winning near the goal — yet, do not grieve;
        She cannot fade, though thou hast not thy bliss,
    Forever wilt thou love, and she be fair!   20

---

7. **Tempe, Arcady:** Tempe, a valley in Greece, and Arcadia ("Arcady"), a region of ancient Greece, represent ideal pastoral landscapes.   13. **Not . . . ear:** Not to the ear of the senses, but to the imagination.

3

Ah, happy, happy boughs! that cannot shed
    Your leaves, nor ever bid the spring adieu;
And, happy melodist, unwearièd,
    Forever piping songs forever new;
More happy love! more happy, happy love!   25
    Forever warm and still to be enjoyed,
        Forever panting, and forever young;
All breathing human passion far above,
    That leaves a heart high-sorrowful and cloyed,
        A burning forehead, and a parching tongue.   30

4

Who are these coming to the sacrifice?
    To what green altar, O mysterious priest,
Lead'st thou that heifer lowing at the skies,
    And all her silken flanks with garlands dressed?
What little town by river or sea shore,   35
    Or mountain-built with peaceful citadel,
        Is emptied of this folk, this pious morn?
And, little town, thy streets forevermore
    Will silent be; and not a soul to tell
        Why thou art desolate, can e'er return.   40

5

O Attic° shape! Fair attitude! with brede°
    Of marble men and maidens overwrought,
With forest branches and the trodden weed;
    Thou, silent form, dost tease us out of thought
As doth eternity: Cold Pastoral!   45
    When old age shall this generation waste,
        Thou shalt remain, in midst of other woe
Than ours, a friend to man, to whom thou say'st,
"Beauty is truth, truth beauty,"° — that is all
    Ye know on earth, and all ye need to know.   50

---

41. Attic: Greek, specifically Athenian; **brede:** Interwoven pattern.   **49. "Beauty . . . beauty":**
The quotation marks around this phrase were found in its earliest printing, an 1820 volume
of poetry by Keats, but not in a printing later that year or in written transcripts. This discrepancy has led to considerable critical controversy concerning the last two lines. Critics disagree
whether "Beauty is truth, truth beauty" is spoken by the urn (and thus perhaps expressing a
limited perspective not to be taken at face value) or by the speaker in the poem, or whether the
last two lines in their entirety are said by the urn (some recent editors enclose both lines in
quotation marks to make this explicit) or by the speaker.

Jane Kenyon   1947–1995

From Room to Room   [1978]

Here in this house, among photographs
of your ancestors, their hymnbooks and old
shoes . . .

        I move from room to room,
a little dazed, like the fly. I watch it   5
bump against each window.

I am clumsy here, thrusting
slabs of maple into the stove.
Out of my body for a while,
weightless in space. . . .   10
          Sometimes
the wind against the clapboard
sounds like a car driving up to the house.

My people are not here, my mother
and father, my brother. I talk   15
to the cats about weather.

"Blessed be the tie that binds . . ."
we sing in the church down the road.
And how does it go from there? The tie . . .

the tether, the hose carrying   20
oxygen to the astronaut,
turning, turning outside the hatch,
taking a look around.

Galway Kinnell   b. 1927

Saint Francis° and the Sow   [1980]

The bud
stands for all things,
even for those things that don't flower,
for everything flowers, from within, of self-blessing;

Saint Francis: Saint Francis of Assisi (1182–1226), founder of the Franciscan Order, was
known for his love of nature and animals, a love so great that he once preached a sermon to the
sparrows at Alviano.

though sometimes it is necessary   5
to reteach a thing its loveliness,
to put a hand on its brow
of the flower
and retell it in words and in touch
it is lovely   10
until it flowers again from within, of self-blessing;
as Saint Francis
put his hand on the creased forehead
of the sow, and told her in words and in touch
blessings of earth on the sow, and the sow   15
began remembering all down her thick length,
from the earthen snout all the way
through the fodder and slops to the spiritual curl of the tail,
from the hard spininess spiked out from the spine
down through the great broken heart   20
to the blue milken dreaminess spurting and shuddering
from the fourteen teats into the fourteen mouths sucking and blowing
    beneath them:
the long, perfect loveliness of sow.

Etheridge Knight   1931–1991

Hard Rock Returns to Prison from the Hospital for the Criminal Insane   [1968]

Hard Rock / was / "known not to take no shit
From nobody," and he had the scars to prove it:
Split purple lips, lumbed ears, welts above
His yellow eyes, and one long scar that cut
Across his temple and plowed through a thick   5
Canopy of kinky hair.

The WORD / was / that Hard Rock wasn't a mean nigger
Anymore, that the doctors had bored a hole in his head,
Cut out part of his brain, and shot electricity
Through the rest. When they brought Hard Rock back,   10
Handcuffed and chained, he was turned loose,
Like a freshly gelded stallion, to try his new status.
And we all waited and watched, like a herd of sheep,
To see if the WORD was true.

As we waited we wrapped ourselves in the cloak   15
Of his exploits: "Man, the last time, it took eight

Screws° to put him in the Hole."° "Yeah, remember when he
Smacked the captain with his dinner tray?" "He set
The record for time in the Hole — 67 straight days!"
"Ol Hard Rock! man, that's one crazy nigger."   20
And then the jewel of a myth that Hard Rock had once bit
A screw on the thumb and poisoned him with syphilitic spit.

The testing came, to see if Hard Rock was really tame.
A hillbilly called him a black son of a bitch
And didn't lose his teeth, a screw who knew Hard Rock   25
From before shook him down and barked in his face.
And Hard Rock did *nothing*. Just grinned and looked silly,
His eyes empty like knot holes in a fence.

And even after we discovered that it took Hard Rock
Exactly 3 minutes to tell you his first name,   30
We told ourselves that he had just wised up,
Was being cool; but we could not fool ourselves for long,
And we turned away, our eyes on the ground. Crushed.
He had been our Destroyer, the doer of things
We dreamed of doing but could not bring ourselves to do,   35
The fears of years, like a biting whip,
Had cut deep bloody grooves
Across our backs.

---

17. **Screws:** Guards; **the Hole:** Solitary confinement.

Stanley Kunitz   1905–2006

Father and Son   [1944]

Now in the suburbs and the falling light
I followed him, and now down sandy road
Whiter than bone-dust, through the sweet
Curdle of fields, where the plums
Dropped with their load of ripeness, one by one.   5
Mile after mile I followed, with skimming feet,
After the secret master of my blood,
Him, steeped in the odor of ponds, whose indomitable love
Kept me in chains. Strode years; stretched into bird;
Raced through the sleeping country where I was young,   10
The silence unrolling before me as I came,
The night nailed like an orange to my brow.

How should I tell him my fable and the fears,
How bridge the chasm in a casual tone,
Saying, "The house, the stucco one you built,   15
We lost. Sister married and went from home,
And nothing comes back, it's strange, from where she goes.
I lived on a hill that had too many rooms:
Light we could make, but not enough of warmth,
And when the light failed, I climbed under the hill.   20
The papers are delivered every day;
I am alone and never shed a tear."

At the water's edge, where the smothering ferns lifted
Their arms, "Father!" I cried, "Return! You know
The way. I'll wipe the mudstains from your clothes;   25
No trace, I promise, will remain. Instruct
Your son, whirling between two wars,
In the Gemara° of your gentleness,
For I would be a child to those who mourn
And brother to the foundlings of the field   30
And friend of innocence and all bright eyes.
O teach me how to work and keep me kind."

Among the turtles and the lilies he turned to me
The white ignorant hollow of his face.

---

28. Gemara: The later of the two portions of the Jewish Talmud, consisting of analysis of and commentary on the older part (the Mishna).

Gerry LaFemina b. 1968

The Sound a Body Makes   [2004]

Only three days later I realize the chalk outline is gone,
washed out by the rains
that flushed the gutters clean, & now a steady line of haze

as the sun walks its beat. There were photographers,
yes, a few nights back: 5
flashbulbs which I could imagine —

bursts of brilliance through a drawn shade.
The next morning: yellow
giftwrap of police tape, & talk at the bus stops:

how could I explain what I saw?   10

I stood silent as in a precinct
somewhere downtown; all my answers were reread
and reports were written.

                        I hadn't seen a thing,
hadn't heard a thing until — there isn't a word to describe it,   15

no metaphor apt enough —
the body hit the sidewalk before me & bounced slightly
as if pushing the soul free from whatever binding holds it firm.

A little sentence of blood whispered from his mouth.

Where were his wings?   20

                        If the detectives ever found a note or
a motive, I don't know — my answers
must have been acceptable, but they weren't all I knew;

even I had flinched in the hot breath of an approaching subway.

But I couldn't say *that* as the pen   25
wobbled above the officer's pad, so I said what I said —

I was just walking, minding my own business —

and stuck to it. But now, three days later,
I see so many white sails of paper stumbling along the streets
like scraps of feathers that couldn't hold any of us aloft.   30

Li-Young Lee b. 1957

Visions and Interpretations   [1986]

Because this graveyard is a hill,
I must climb up to see my dead,
stopping once midway to rest
beside this tree.

It was here, between the anticipation   5
of exhaustion, and exhaustion,
between vale and peak,
my father came down to me

and we climbed arm in arm to the top.
He cradled the bouquet I'd brought,   10
and I, a good son, never mentioned his grave,
erect like a door behind him.

               _____

And it was here, one summer day, I sat down
to read an old book. When I looked up
from the noon-lit page, I saw a vision   15
of a world about to come, and a world about to go.

Truth is, I've not seen my father
since he died, and, no, the dead
do not walk arm in arm with me.

If I carry flowers to them, I do so without their help,   20
the blossoms not always bright, torch-like,
but often heavy as sodden newspaper.

Truth is, I came here with my son one day,
and we rested against this tree,
and I fell asleep, and dreamed   25

a dream which, upon my boy waking me, I told.
Neither of us understood.
Then we went up.

Even this is not accurate.
Let me begin again: 30

Between two griefs, a tree.
Between my hands, white chrysanthemums, yellow chrysanthemums.

The old book I finished reading
I've since read again and again.

And what was far grows near,   35
and what is near grows more dear,

and all of my visions and interpretations
depend on what I see,

and between my eyes is always
the rain, the migrant rain.   40

Philip Levine   b. 1928

What Work Is   [1991]

We stand in the rain in a long line
waiting at Ford Highland Park. For work.
You know what work is — if you're
old enough to read this you know what
work is, although you may not do it.   5

Forget you. This is about waiting,
shifting from one foot to another.
Feeling the light rain falling like mist
into your hair, blurring your vision
until you think you see your own brother   10
ahead of you, maybe ten places.
You rub your glasses with your fingers,
and of course it's someone else's brother,
narrower across the shoulders than
yours but with the same sad slouch, the grin   15
that does not hide the stubbornness,
the sad refusal to give in to
rain, to the hours wasted waiting,
to the knowledge that somewhere ahead
a man is waiting who will say, "No,   20
we're not hiring today," for any
reason he wants. You love your brother,
now suddenly you can hardly stand
the love flooding you for your brother,
who's not beside you or behind or   25
ahead because he's home trying to
sleep off a miserable night shift
at Cadillac so he can get up
before noon to study his German.
Works eight hours a night so he can sing   30
Wagner, the opera you hate most,
the worst music ever invented.
How long has it been since you told him
you loved him, held his wide shoulders,
opened your eyes wide and said those words,   35
and maybe kissed his cheek? You've never
done something so simple, so obvious,
not because you're too young or too dumb,
not because you're jealous or even mean
or incapable of crying in   40
the presence of another man, no,
just because you don't know what work is.

Timothy Liu   b. 1965

The Garden   [1998]

We were after crevices, whatever God had
commanded the fire to leave untouched —

a bed of charcoal lines where lovers
lay supine, the moon's raw face appearing

and disappearing. Night gathers her brood   5
of stars as open-throated vases cry out

for roses — our grief an urn on the head
of a woman who turns away from the well.

Audre Lorde   1934–2002

Hanging Fire   [1978]

I am fourteen
and my skin has betrayed me
the boy I cannot live without
still sucks his thumb
in secret   5
how come my knees are
always so ashy
what if I die
before morning
and momma's in the bedroom   10
with the door closed.

I have to learn how to dance
in time for the next party
my room is too small for me
suppose I die before graduation   15
they will sing sad melodies
but finally
tell the truth about me
There is nothing I want to do
and too much   20
that has to be done
and momma's in the bedroom
with the door closed.

Nobody even stops to think
about my side of it   25

I should have been on Math Team
my marks were better than his
why do I have to be
the one
wearing braces   30
I have nothing to wear tomorrow
will I live long enough
to grow up
and momma's in the bedroom
with the door closed.   35

Richard Lovelace   1618–1657

To Lucasta, Going to the Wars   [1649]

Tell me not, Sweet, I am unkind,
   That from the nunnery
Of thy chaste breast and quiet mind
   To war and arms I fly.

True, a new mistress now I chase,   5
   The first foe in the field;
And with a stronger faith embrace
   A sword, a horse, a shield.

Yet this inconstancy is such
   As you too shall adore;   10
I could not love thee, dear, so much,
   Loved I not honor more.

Robert Lowell   1917–1978

Skunk Hour   [1963]

for Elizabeth Bishop°

Nautilus Island's hermit
heiress still lives through winter in her Spartan cottage;
her sheep still graze above the sea.
Her son's a bishop. Her farmer

Elizabeth Bishop: American poet (1911–1979); see the poems on pages 625 and 742 and the
biographical sketch on page 1521.

is first selectman in our village;
she's in her dotage.   5

Thirsting for
the hierarchic privacy
of Queen Victoria's century,
she buys up all
the eyesores facing her shore,   10
and lets them fall.

The season's ill —
we've lost our summer millionaire,
who seemed to leap from an L. L. Bean   15
catalogue. His nine-knot yawl
was auctioned off to lobstermen.
A red fox stain covers Blue Hill.

And now our fairy
decorator brightens his shop for fall;   20
his fishnet's filled with orange cork,
orange, his cobbler's bench and awl;
there is no money in his work,
he'd rather marry.

One dark night,   25
my Tudor Ford climbed the hill's skull;
I watched for love-cars. Lights turned down,
they lay together, hull to hull,
where the graveyard shelves on the town. . . .
My mind's not right.   30

A car radio bleats,
"Love, O careless Love. . . ." I hear
my ill-spirit sob in each blood cell,
as if my hand were at its throat. . . .
I myself am hell;   35
nobody's here —

only skunks, that search
in the moonlight for a bite to eat.
They march on their soles up Main Street:
white stripes, moonstruck eyes' red fire   40
under the chalk-dry and spar spire
of the Trinitarian Church.

I stand on top
of our back steps and breathe the rich air —
a mother skunk with her column of kittens swills the garbage pail.   45

She jabs her wedge-head in a cup
of sour cream, drops her ostrich tail,
and will not scare.

Medbh McGuckian b. 1950

On Ballycastle Beach   [1998]

If I found you wandering round the edge
Of a French-born sea, when children
Should be taken in by their parents,
I would read these words to you,
Like a ship coming in to harbour,   5
As meaningless and full of meaning
As the homeless flow of life
From room to homesick room.

The words and you would fall asleep,
Sheltering just beyond my reach   10
In a city that has vanished to regain
Its language. My words are traps
Through which you pick your way
From a damp March to an April date,
Or a mid-August misstep; until enough winter   15
Makes you throw your watch, the heartbeat
Of everyone present, out into the snow.

My forbidden squares and your small circles
Were a book that formed within you
In some pocket, so permanently distended,   20
That what does not face north, faces east.
Your hand, dark as a cedar lane by nature,
Grows more and more tired of the skidding light,
The hunched-up waves, and all the wet clothing,
Toys and treasures of a late summer house.   25

Even the Atlantic has begun its breakdown
Like a heavy mask thinned out scene after scene
In a more protected time — like one who has
Gradually, unnoticed, lengthened her pre-wedding
Dress. But, staring at the old escape and release   30
Of the water's speech, faithless to the end,
Your voice was the longest I heard in my mind,
Although I had forgotten there could be such light.

Heather McHugh b. 1948

What He Thought   [1994]

We were supposed to do a job in Italy
and, full of our feeling for
ourselves (our sense of being
Poets from America) we went
from Rome to Fano, met   5
the mayor, mulled
a couple matters over (what's
cheap date, they asked us; what's
flat drink). Among Italian literati

we could recognize our counterparts: 10
the academic, the apologist,
the arrogant, the amorous,
the brazen and the glib — and there was one

administrator (the conservative), in suit
of regulation gray, who like a good tour guide   15
with measured pace and uninflected tone narrated
sights and histories the hired van hauled us past.
Of all, he was most politic and least poetic,
so it seemed. Our last few days in Rome
(when all but three of the New World Bards had flown)   20
I found a book of poems this
unprepossessing one had written: it was there
in the *pensione* room (a room he'd recommended)
where it must have been abandoned by
the German visitor (was there a bus of *them?*)   25
to whom he had inscribed and dated it a month before.
I couldn't read Italian, either, so I put the book
back into the wardrobe's dark. We last Americans

were due to leave tomorrow. For our parting evening then
our host chose something in a family restaurant, and there 30
we sat and chatted, sat and chewed,
till, sensible it was our last
big chance to be poetic, make
our mark, one of us asked

                    "What's poetry?   35
Is it the fruits and vegetables and
marketplace of Campo dei Fiori, or
the statue there?" Because I was

the glib one, I identified the answer
instantly, I didn't have to think — "The truth   40

is both, it's both," I blurted out. But that
was easy. That was easiest to say. What followed
taught me something about difficulty,
for our underestimated host spoke out,
all of a sudden, with a rising passion, and he said: 45

The statue represents Giordano Bruno,
brought to be burned in the public square
because of his offense against
authority, which is to say
the Church. His crime was his belief   50
the universe does not revolve around
the human being: God is no
fixed point or central government, but rather is
poured in waves through all things. All things
move. "If God is not the soul itself, He is   55
the soul of the soul of the world." Such was
his heresy. The day they brought him
forth to die, they feared he might
incite the crowd (the man was famous
for his eloquence). And so his captors   60
placed upon his face
an iron mask, in which

he could not speak. That's
how they burned him. That is how
he died: without a word, in front   65
of everyone.
       And poetry —
           (we'd all
put down our forks by now, to listen to
the man in gray; he went on   70
softly) —
       poetry is what

he thought, but did not say.

Claude McKay 1890–1948

America   [1922]

Although she feeds me bread of bitterness,
And sinks into my throat her tiger's tooth,
Stealing my breath of life, I will confess
I love this cultured hell that tests my youth!

Her vigor flows like tides into my blood,   5
Giving me strength erect against her hate.
Her bigness sweeps my being like a flood.
Yet as a rebel fronts a king in state,
I stand within her walls with not a shred
Of terror, malice, not a word of jeer.   10
Darkly I gaze into the days ahead,
And see her might and granite wonders there,
Beneath the touch of Time's unerring hand,
Like priceless treasures sinking in the sand.

Christopher Marlowe 1564–1593

The Passionate Shepherd to His Love   [1599]

Come live with me and be my love,
And we will all the pleasures prove
That valleys, groves, hills, and fields,
Woods, or steepy mountain yields.

And we will sit upon the rocks,   5
Seeing the shepherds feed their flocks,
By shallow rivers, to whose falls
Melodious birds sing madrigals.

And I will make thee beds of roses
And a thousand fragrant posies,   10
A cap of flowers, and a kirtle°   *skirt, outer petticoat*
Embroidered all with leaves of myrtle.

A gown made of the finest wool
Which from our pretty lambs we pull,
Fair lined slippers for the cold,   15
With buckles of the purest gold.

A belt of straw and ivy buds,
With coral clasps and amber studs,
And if these pleasures may thee move,
Come live with me, and be my love.   20

The shepherd swains shall dance and sing
For thy delight each May morning.
If these delights thy mind may move,
Then live with me and be my love.

Andrew Marvell   1621–1678

To His Coy° Mistress   [*c. 1650*; 1681]

    Had we but world enough, and time,
This coyness, lady, were no crime.
We would sit down, and think which way
To walk, and pass our long love's day.
Thou by the Indian Ganges' side   5
Shouldst rubies find; I by the tide
Of Humber would complain.° I would
Love you ten years before the Flood,
And you should, if you please, refuse
Till the conversion of the Jews.°   10
My vegetable° love should grow   *living and growing*
Vaster than empires, and more slow;
An hundred years should go to praise
Thine eyes, and on thy forehead gaze;
Two hundred to adore each breast,   15
But thirty thousand to the rest;
An age at least to every part,
And the last age should show your heart.
For, lady, you deserve this state,°   *dignity*
Nor would I love at lower rate.   20
    But at my back I always hear
Time's wingèd chariot hurrying near;
And yonder all before us lie
Deserts of vast eternity.
Thy beauty shall no more be found,   25
Nor, in thy marble vault, shall sound
My echoing song; then worms shall try
That long-preserved virginity,
And your quaint honor turn to dust,
And into ashes all my lust: 30
The grave's a fine and private place,
But none, I think, do there embrace.
    Now therefore, while the youthful hue
Sits on thy skin like morning dew,
And while thy willing soul transpires°   *breathes forth*   35

Coy: In the seventeenth century, *coy* could carry its older meaning, "shy," or its modern sense of "coquettish."   **5–7. Indian Ganges', Humber:** The Ganges River in India, with its distant, romantic associations, contrasts with the Humber River, running through Hull in northeast England, Marvell's hometown.   **10. conversion . . . Jews:** An occurrence foretold, in some traditions, as one of the concluding events of human history.

At every pore with instant fires,°   *urgent passion*
Now let us sport us while we may,
And now, like amorous birds of prey,
Rather at once our time devour
Than languish in his slow-chapped° power.   40
Let us roll all our strength and all
Our sweetness up into one ball,
And tear our pleasures with rough strife
Thorough° the iron gates of life;   *through*
Thus, though we cannot make our sun   45
Stand still,° yet we will make him run.

---

40. slow-chapped: Slow-jawed, devouring slowly.
45–46. make our sun Stand still: An allusion to
Joshua 10:12. In answer to Joshua's prayer,
God made the sun stand still, to prolong the
day and give the Israelites more time to defeat
the Amorites.

www

Explore Andrew Marvell and
"To His Coy Mistress" in depth,
including images and cultural
documents, with VirtuaLit
Poetry at bedfordstmartins
.com/approachinglit.

Orlando Ricardo Menes b. 1958

Letter to Mirta Yáñez°   [2001]

I read *Some Place in Ruins,*°
your recent book of poems, and that title
seems incredibly ironic —
photograph of a Greek temple
on the cover — for our Old Habana   5
lies in tropical ruins; you should instead
put that colonial house
at Jesús María number 13
where my mother lived as a little girl
(abode of the ghost   10
Don Melitón, in life a Galician
shopkeeper)
or the Golgothas° of rubble
I saw walking toward the Cathedral
on Obispo Street,   15
surrounded by trash and skeletal animals
(like the black dog
with the hairless tail that ate

Mirta Yáñez: (b. 1947), Cuban poet, essayist, and fiction writer. **1. Some . . . Ruins:** *Algún lugar en ruinas* (1997). **13. Golgothas:** Golgotha was where Jesus was crucified.

a mango pit).
An old black woman   20
on Angel Hill begged me for money
to buy orange juice,
I gave her the last dollar in my pocket.

Perhaps some of her street names
could be interpreted   25
as omens
since Cuba crosses Anguish
and also Poor Rock.
My gray Habana,
covered with scars and wrinkles,   30
breath of death,
so poorly plastered and nailed together
you will soon collapse,
your only solace
ill-remembered memories.   35
I know you were
voluptuously beautiful,
painted with colors
of guava, papaya, and guanábana,
sassy, proud, impetuous   40
with carnal delights,
praised with *piropos*
(flirtatious remarks)
more vulgar than sophisticated.
The world   45
has scarcely noticed
your destruction,
invisible behind bars
of sugar cane.

John Milton   1608–1674

When I consider how my light is spent   [*c. 1652*; 1673]

When I consider how my light is spent°
    Ere half my days, in this dark world and wide,
    And that one talent which is death to hide
    Lodged with me useless, though my soul more bent

---

1. When . . . spent: Milton went blind in 1652. Lines 1–2 allude to Matthew 25:1–13; line 3,
to Matthew 25:14–30; and line 11, to Matthew 11:30.

To serve therewith my Maker, and present   5
    My true account, lest he returning chide.
    "Doth God exact day-labor, light denied?"
    I fondly° ask; but patience to prevent   *foolishly*
That murmur, soon replies, "God doth not need
    Either man's work or his own gifts; who best   10
    Bear his mild yoke, they serve him best. His state
Is kingly. Thousands at his bidding speed
    And post o'er land and ocean without rest:
    They also serve who only stand and wait."

Janice Mirikitani b. 1942

For a Daughter Who Leaves   [2001]

More than gems in my comb box shaped by the
God of the Sea, I prize you, my daughter . . .
    — *Lady Otomo, 8th century, Japan*

A woman weaves
her daughter's wedding
slippers that will carry
her steps into a new life.
The mother weeps alone   5
into her jeweled sewing box
slips red thread
around its spool,
the same she used to stitch
her daughter's first silk jacket   10
embroidered with turtles
that would bring luck, long life.
She remembers all the steps
taken by her daughter's
unbound quick feet: 15
dancing on the stones
of the yard among yellow
butterflies and white breasted sparrows.
And she grew, legs strong
body long, mind   20
independent.
Now she captures all eyes
with her hair combed smooth
and her hips gently
swaying like bamboo.   25
The woman

spins her thread
from the spool of her heart,
knotted to her daughter's
departing   30
wedding slippers.

Marianne Moore 1887–1972

Poetry   [1921]

I, too, dislike it: there are things that are important beyond all this fiddle.
   Reading it, however, with a perfect contempt for it, one discovers in
   it after all, a place for the genuine.
       Hands that can grasp, eyes
       that can dilate, hair that can rise   5
         if it must, these things are important not because a

high-sounding interpretation can be put upon them but because they are
   useful. When they become so derivative as to become unintelligible,
   the same thing may be said for all of us, that we
       do not admire what   10
       we cannot understand: the bat
         holding on upside down or in quest of something to

eat, elephants pushing, a wild horse taking a roll, a tireless wolf under
   a tree, the immovable critic twitching his skin like a horse that
                         feels a flea, the base-
       ball fan, the statistician —   15
         nor is it valid
           to discriminate against "business documents and

school-books"; all these phenomena are important. One must make
                  a distinction
   however: when dragged into prominence by half poets, the result
                 is not poetry,
       nor till the poets among us can be   20
         "literalists of
         the imagination" — above
           insolence and triviality and can present

for inspection, "imaginary gardens with real toads in them," shall
                  we have
   it. In the meantime, if you demand on the one hand,   25
   the raw material of poetry in
      all its rawness and
      that which is on the other hand
         genuine, you are interested in poetry.

Robert Morgan   b. 1944

Mountain Bride   [1979]

They say Revis found a flatrock
on the ridge just
perfect for a natural hearth,
and built his cabin with a stick

and clay chimney right over it.   5
On their wedding night he lit
the fireplace to dry away the mountain
chill of late spring, and flung on

applewood to dye
the room with molten color while   10
he and Martha that was a Parrish
warmed the sheets between the tick

stuffed with leaves and its feather
cover. Under that wide hearth
a nest of rattlers,   15
they'll knot a hundred together,

had wintered and were coming awake.
The warming rock
flushed them out early.
It was she   20

who wakened to their singing near
the embers and roused him to go look.
Before he reached the fire
more than a dozen struck

and he died yelling her to stay   25
on the big four-poster.
Her uncle coming up the hollow
with a gift bearham two days later

found her shivering there
marooned above a pool   30
of hungry snakes,
and the body beginning to swell.

Thylias Moss   b. 1954

The Lynching   [1991]

They should have slept, would have
but had to fight the darkness, had
to build a fire and bathe a man in
flames. No

other soap's as good when   5
the dirt is the skin. Black since
birth, burnt by birth. His father
is not in heaven. No parent

of atrocity is in heaven. My father chokes
in the next room. It is night, darkness   10
has replaced air. We are white like
incandescence

yet lack light. The God in my father
does not glow. The only lamp
is the burning black man. Holy   15
burning, holy longing, remnants of

a genie after greed. My father
baptizes by fire same as Jesus will.
Becomes a holy ghost when
he dons his sheet, a clerical collar   20

out of control, Dundee Mills percale,
fifty percent cotton, dixie, confederate
and fifty percent polyester, man-made, manipulated, unnatural, mulatto fiber, warp

of miscegenation.   25
After the bath, the man is hung as if
just his washed shirt, the parts
of him most capable of sin removed.

Charred, his flesh is bark, his body
a trunk. No sign of roots. I can't leave   30
him. This is limbo. This is the life after
death coming if God is an invention as were

slaves. So I spend the night, his thin moon-begot
shadow as mattress; something smoldering
keeps me warm. Patches of skin fall onto me   35
in places I didn't know needed mending.

Duane Niatum   b. 1938

First Spring   [1980; rev. 2004]

Drifting off the wheel of a past
looking like a redskin American gothic,
I stare through forty-one years
of rain-pelted windows and bear
with modest grace, diminished nerves,   5
narrowing light, half-formed figures:
memories floating in purgatory.

Renting a small house, the first
in fifteen years, I admire each hour
the diffidence of elders walking by,   10
from a tavern down the street,
their snow-cave eyes, hands
dancing like puppets. When a former love calls,
having abandoned another, I say, —

    Sorry, sorry, I'm too busy   15
    with the friends still left.
    I'll call you.

The lie of copper skids along my tongue.
Why tell her they're the sparrows at the feeder,
bees in the lilacs, roses, and plum trees,   20
books on the shelves and everywhere,
paintings on the walls, sculptures in the corners,
wind at the door and on the roof?

    It is called giving your body
    a river to jump in to,   25
    it is called giving your brain cells
    a field to get planted in.
    It is called standing on your head
    before the women you lost,
    sleeping in the embers of your name.   30

Lorine Niedecker   1903–1970

My Life by Water   [1985]

My life
   by water —
      Hear

spring's
   first frog
      or board   5

out on the cold
   ground
      giving

Muskrats   10
   gnawing
      doors

to wild green
   arts and letters
      Rabbits   15

raided
   my lettuce
      One boat

two —
   pointed toward   20
      my shore

thru birdstart
   wingdrip
      weed-drift

of the soft   25
   and serious —
      Water

Dwight Okita   b. 1958

In Response to Executive Order 9066:   [1983]
All Americans of Japanese Descent Must Report
to Relocation Centers

Dear Sirs:
Of course I'll come. I've packed my galoshes
and three packets of tomato seeds. Denise calls them
love apples. My father says where we're going
they won't grow.   5

I am a fourteen-year-old girl with bad spelling
and a messy room. If it helps any, I will tell you
I have always felt funny using chopsticks
and my favorite food is hot dogs.
My best friend is a white girl named Denise —   10
we look at boys together. She sat in front of me
all through grade school because of our names:
O'Connor, Ozawa. I know the back of Denise's head very well.

I tell her she's going bald. She tells me I copy on tests.
We're best friends.   15

I saw Denise today in Geography class.
She was sitting on the other side of the room.
"You're trying to start a war," she said, "giving secrets
away to the Enemy, Why can't you keep your big
mouth shut?"   20

I didn't know what to say.
I gave her a packet of tomato seeds
and asked her to plant them for me, told her
when the first tomato ripened
she'd miss me.   25

William Olsen   b. 1954

The Fold-Out Atlas of the Human Body: A Three-Dimensional Book for Readers of All Ages   [2002]

The vertebrae are a ladder of moonlight
up and out of the perpetual nocturne
      of the body.

———————————

I open myself with the casualness
of a man having a smoke on a hotel roof.

The legs flip down
like ironing boards, and when I turn the page

each bone is numbered and charted and named in a
    dead language.
When the skeleton folds back, there are the organs —

the lungs, two punctured footballs; the tire-tread
    tendons;
fold out the lungs, and a jungle of bronchioles

must be macheted through
to reach the vertebrae espaliered by arteries.

Here and there a floral wreathe of hissing nerves.
When the last tears are secreted,

and the eyes must be avulsed from the skull,
whoever will speak in praise of the passing face?

Whoever guessed the prayer book
    was flesh?
The tongue turned all night like a sleeper in his bed,

having been possessed.
And there below the endlessly crouched ilium

is the place where the groin is missing out of tact.
The beginning embarrasses us all:

the red lights of our musculature
    are bad enough.
Blood washes its hands of blood,

There's nothing behind it,

and as for the heart,
there is a little door you can open

and reach inside:
bison drawings, cavemen, mothers, mud.

It has dreamed these things we never believed it would.

Michael Ondaatje   b. 1943

Biography   [1979]

The dog scatters her body in sleep,
paws, finding no ground, whip at air,
the unseen eyeballs reel deep, within.
And waking — crouches,
tacked to humility all day,   5
children ride her, stretch,
display the black purple lips,
pull hind legs to dance;
unaware that she
tore bulls apart, loosed   10
heads of partridges,
dreamt blood.

Ricardo Pau-Llosa   b. 1954

Years of Exile   [2001]

After the paintings of Humberto Calzada°

The water enters the old ballroom
and the once bedroom, seeps across
the erstwhile chessboard floor
where rumors made their way.
The squares once mapped   5
the tinted flights of sun
that stained-glass half-wheels wrote,
pages in the metronome diary of an age.
These testaments only seemed random,
stretched lights falling like   10
premeditated leaves
against the staring wall
or upon the lurid waist of the piano.

And then the water came.
The first arrival left   15
a pale ghost on the tiles.
Later more water came and more
so that no one could show

Humberto Calzada: (b. 1944), Cuban American painter.

the uninvited flood the door,
which was half drowned.   20
The glass wheels turned
their voices on the murk.

And we waited for the new day
when losses would turn to stories.
We would laugh, we knew it, about   25
the swallowed rooms, the stabbed
recollections where gilded curtains
and danzones° swayed.

But the years knew better.
We have learned to love   30
the cracks on the ceiling,
a nose away. We stare into them now
that we have learned to float and have become
the Sistine chroniclers° of our shrinkings.
We create, we are free   35
now that we have lost count of everything.

---

28. danzón: Very popular traditional Cuban dance music. **34. Sistine chroniclers:** The walls
and ceilings of the Sistine Chapel in Vatican City are decorated with frescos depicting figures
and events from the Bible, such as scenes from the life of Moses and the life of Christ, and from
church history.

Gustavo Pérez Firmat b. 1949

José Canseco Breaks Our Hearts Again [2001]

Out for the season, what's new.
31 homers, best in the AL, 71 RBIs,
and a herniated disk.

David had asked me to tape the home-run derby
and now he says not to bother.   5
Stupid me, I worry that with Canseco

laid up, my son and I will not have something to talk about.
José has missed one-third of his career,
over 500 games, or he'd have 600 homers by now.

I think of all the sentences   10
David and I could have said to each other
if José's back did not keep giving out on us.

(He had to be Cuban, that impossible man-child,
delicate as an orchid beneath the rippling chest.)

I'll keep my fingers crossed for next season   15
when José, like a certain country I know,
will break our hearts again.

Lucia Perillo   b. 1958

Air Guitar   [1999]

The women in my family were full of still water;
they churned out piecework as quietly as glands.
Plopped in America with only the wrong words
hobbling their tongues, they liked one thing
about the sweatshop, the glove factory,   5
and it was this: you didn't have to say much.
All you had to do was stitch the leather fingers
until you came up with a hand; the rest
they kept tucked to their ribs like a secret book.
Why, was not said, though it doesn't seem natural   10
the way these women ripped the pages out
and chewed them silently and swallowed — where
is the ur-mother holding court beside her soup pot,
where is Scheherazade and the rest of those Persians
who wove their tragedies in rugs?   15
Once I tutored a Cambodian girl: each week
I rolled the language like a newspaper and used it
to club her on the head. In return she spoke
a mangled English that made all her stories sad,
about how she'd been chased through the jungle   20
by ruthless henchmen of Pol Pot; for months
she and her sisters mother grandmothers aunts
lived in the crowns of trees and ate what grew there
and did not touch down. When she told the story,
the way her beautiful and elaborately painted face   25
would loosen at each corner of her eyes and mouth
reminded me of a galosh too big for its shoe.
It was rubbery, her face, like the words
that sometimes haunt me with their absence,
when I wake up gargling the ghost of one   30
stuck like a wild hair far back in my mouth.
This morning it took me till noon to fish out
cathexis, and even then I did not know

what this meant until I looked it up.
As it was not until I met her sister   35
that I learned what the girl was telling me
was not the story she was telling: there were
no women in trees, no myrmidons of Comrade Pot,
their father was, is, had always been,
a greengrocer in Texas. Cathexis: 40
fixing emotional energy on some object
or idea — say the jungle, or the guy
getting rubbery with a guitar that isn't there.
Yet see how he can't keep from naming
the gut that spills above his belt *Lucille* —   45
as music starts to pour from his belly
and the one hiked-up corner of his lip. This
is part of a legend we tell ourselves about the tribe,
that men are stuffed and full to bursting
with their quiet, that this is why they've had to go   50
into the wilderness, searching for visions
that would deliver up their names. While women
stayed in the villages, with language at their center
like a totem log tipped lengthwise to the ground.
And they chipped at it and picked at it,   55
making a hole big enough to climb in, a dugout
in which they all paddled off to hunt up
other villages, the other members of the tribe.
And when the men returned they found no one home,
just cold fire pits that would not speak — an old   60
old forsakenness they bring to the bar stools
while the jukebox music washes over each of them
like a tricolored light wheel on a silver tree.
Though someone might argue that none of whatever
I've just said is true: it was men who made boats   65
while the women sat clumped in private guilds,
weaving their baskets tight enough to trap
the molecules of water. You can see
that the trail from here to the glove factory
would not be terribly long or hard to read,   70
and how it might eventually lead to the railroad flat
where, alone at night for many years, my grandmother
works deep into her privacy with a common nail
that she scratches across the backs of copper sheets.
She is making either the hands clasped in prayer   75
or the three-quarter profile of Jesus.
As far as I know there is nothing
the radio can play now that will make her sing.

Carl Phillips   b. 1959

To the Tune of a Small, Repeatable, and Passing Kindness   [2002]

In the cove of hours-like-a-dream this
is, it isn't so much
that we don't enjoy watching

a view alter rather little, and each time
in the same shift-of-a-cloud   5
fashion. It's the

swiftness with which we
find it easier, as our cast
lines catch more and more at nothing,

to lose heart —   10
          All afternoon, it's
been with the fish as with

lovers we'd come to think of as
mostly forgotten, how
anymore they less often themselves   15

surface than sometimes
will the thought of them — less
often, even, than that, their names . . .

But now the fish bring to mind
— of those lovers —   20
the ones in particular

who were knowable
only in the way a letter written
in code that resists

being broken fully can be   25
properly called a letter we
understand: *If*

you   a minute   could you   when
said I might   however
what if   haven't I loved   30

— who?
          As I remember it, I'd lie
in general alone, after, neither in

_____

want nor — at first — sorry inside
the almost-dark I'd   35
wake to. The only stirring

the one of last light getting
scattered, as if for
my consideration. All over the room.

Robert Pinsky b. 1940

Shirt   [1990]

The back, the yoke, the yardage. Lapped seams,
The nearly invisible stitches along the collar
Turned in a sweatshop by Koreans or Malaysians

Gossiping over tea and noodles on their break
Or talking money or politics while one fitted   5
This armpiece with its overseam to the band

Of cuff I button at my wrist. The presser, the cutter,
The wringer, the mangle. The needle, the union,
The treadle, the bobbin. The code. The infamous blaze

At the Triangle Factory° in nineteen-eleven.   *(in New York City)*   10
One hundred and forty-six died in the flames
On the ninth floor, no hydrants, no fire escapes —

The witness in a building across the street
Who watched how a young man helped a girl to step
Up to the windowsill, then held her out   15

Away from the masonry wall and let her drop.
And then another. As if he were helping them up
To enter a streetcar, and not eternity.

A third before he dropped her put her arms
Around his neck and kissed him. Then he held   20
Her into space, and dropped her. Almost at once

He stepped to the sill himself, his jacket flared
And fluttered up from his shirt as he came down,
Air filling up the legs of his gray trousers —

Like Hart Crane's Bedlamite, "shrill shirt ballooning."   25
Wonderful how the pattern matches perfectly
Across the placket and over the twin bar-tacked

Corners of both pockets, like a strict rhyme
Or a major chord. Prints, plaids, checks,
Houndstooth, Tattersall, Madras. The clan tartans   30

Invented by mill-owners inspired by the hoax of Ossian,°
To control their savage Scottish workers, tamed
By a fabricated heraldry: MacGregor,

Bailey, MacMartin. The kilt, devised for workers
To wear among the dusty clattering looms.   35
Weavers, carders, spinners. The loader,

The docker, the navvy. The planter, the picker, the sorter
Sweating at her machine in a litter of cotton
As slaves in calico headrags sweated in fields:

George Herbert,° your descendant is a Black   40
Lady in South Carolina, her name is Irma
And she inspected my shirt. Its color and fit

And feel and its clean smell have satisfied
Both her and me. We have culled its cost and quality
Down to the buttons of simulated bone,   45

The buttonholes, the sizing, the facing, the characters
Printed in black on neckband and tail. The shape,
The label, the labor, the color, the shade. The shirt.

---

31. Ossian: Legendary Gaelic poet, hero of a cycle of traditional tales and poems that place him in the third century C.E. The hoax involved Scottish author James Macpherson (1736–1796), who published two epic poems that he said were translations of works written by Ossian but were in fact mostly composed by Macpherson himself.   **40. George Herbert:** (1593–1633), English metaphysical poet. See pp. 798 and 1538.

Sylvia Plath   1932–1963

Daddy   [1962]

You do not do, you do not do
Any more, black shoe
In which I have lived like a foot
For thirty years, poor and white,
Barely daring to breathe or Achoo.   5

Daddy, I have had to kill you.
You died before I had time—
Marble-heavy, a bag full of God,

Ghastly statue with one grey toe
Big as a Frisco seal   10

And a head in the freakish Atlantic
Where it pours bean green over blue
In the waters off beautiful Nauset.
I used to pray to recover you.
Ach, du.°   *Oh, you (German)*   15

In the German tongue, in the Polish town
Scraped flat by the roller
Of wars, wars, wars.
But the name of the town is common.
My Polack friend   20

Says there are a dozen or two.
So I never could tell where you
Put your foot, your root,
I never could talk to you.
The tongue stuck in my jaw.   25

It stuck in a barb wire snare.
Ich, ich, ich, ich,°   *I (German)*
I could hardly speak.
I thought every German was you.
And the language obscene   30

An engine, an engine
Chuffing me off like a Jew.
A Jew to Dachau, Auschwitz, Belsen.°
I began to talk like a Jew.
I think I may well be a Jew.   35

The snows of the Tyrol,° the clear beer of Vienna
Are not very pure or true.
With my gypsy ancestress and my weird luck
And my Taroc pack and my Taroc pack
I may be a bit of a Jew.   40

I have always been scared of *you,*
With your Luftwaffe,° your gobbledygoo.
And your neat moustache
And your Aryan eye, bright blue.
Panzer°-man, panzer-man, O You—   45

---

33. Dachau, Auschwitz, Belsen: Nazi concentration camps.   **36. the Tyrol:** An alpine region
in western Austria and northern Italy.   **42. Luftwaffe:** The Nazi air force in World War II.
45. Panzer: An armored unit in the German army in World War II.

Not God but a swastika
So black no sky could squeak through.
Every woman adores a Fascist,
The boot in the face, the brute
Brute heart of a brute like you.   50

You stand at the blackboard, daddy,
In the picture I have of you,
A cleft in your chin instead of your foot
But no less a devil for that, no not
Any less the black man who   55

Bit my pretty red heart in two.
I was ten when they buried you.
At twenty I tried to die
And get back, back, back to you.
I thought even the bones would do.   60

But they pulled me out of the sack,
And they stuck me together with glue.
And then I knew what to do.
I made a model of you,
A man in black with a Meinkampf° look   65

And a love of the rack and the screw.
And I said I do, I do.
So daddy, I'm finally through.
The black telephone's off at the root,
The voices just can't worm through.   70

If I've killed one man, I've killed two —
The vampire who said he was you
And drank my blood for a year,
Seven years, if you want to know.
Daddy, you can lie back now.   75

There's a stake in your fat black heart
And the villagers never liked you.
They are dancing and stamping on you.
They always *knew* it was you.
Daddy, daddy, you bastard, I'm through.   80

---

65. Mein Kampf: *My Struggle,* the title of Adolf Hitler's autobiography.

Sir Walter Ralegh   1552–1618

The Nymph's Reply to the Shepherd   [1600]

If all the world and love were young,
And truth in every shepherd's tongue,
These pretty pleasures might me move
To live with thee and be thy love.

Time drives the flocks from field to fold   5
When rivers rage and rocks grow cold,
And Philomel° becometh dumb;   *nightingale*
The rest complains of cares to come.

The flowers do fade, and wanton fields
To wayward winter reckoning yields;   10
A honey tongue, a heart of gall,
Is fancy's spring, but sorrow's fall.

Thy gowns, thy shoes, thy beds of roses,
Thy cap, thy kirtle,° and thy posies   *skirt, outer petticoat*
Soon break, soon wither, soon forgotten—   15
In folly ripe, in reason rotten.

Thy belt of straw and ivy buds
Thy coral clasps and amber studs,
All these in me no means can move
To come to thee and be thy love.   20

But could youth last and love still breed,
Had joys no date° nor age no need,   *ending*
Then these delights my mind might move
To live with thee and be thy love.

Dudley Randall   1914–2000

Ballad of Birmingham   [1969]
On the Bombing of a Church in Birmingham, Alabama, 1963

"Mother dear, may I go downtown
Instead of out to play,
And march the streets of Birmingham
In a Freedom March today?"

"No, baby, no, you may not go,   5
For the dogs are fierce and wild,
And clubs and hoses, guns and jails
Aren't good for a little child."

"But, mother, I won't be alone.
Other children will go with me,   10
And march the streets of Birmingham
To make our country free."

"No, baby, no, you may not go,
For I fear those guns will fire.
But you may go to church instead   15
And sing in the children's choir."

She has combed and brushed her night-dark hair,
And bathed rose petal sweet,
And drawn white gloves on her small brown hands,
And white shoes on her feet.   20

The mother smiled to know her child
Was in the sacred place,
But that smile was the last smile
To come upon her face.

For when she heard the explosion,   25
Her eyes grew wet and wild.
She raced through the streets of Birmingham
Calling for her child.

She clawed through bits of glass and brick,
Then lifted out a shoe.   30
"Oh, here's the shoe my baby wore,
But, baby, where are you?"

Adrienne Rich   b. 1929

Diving into the Wreck   [1973]

First having read the book of myths,
and loaded the camera,
and checked the edge of the knife-blade,
I put on
the body-armor of black rubber   5
the absurd flippers
the grave and awkward mask.
I am having to do this

not like Cousteau° with his
assiduous team
aboard the sun-flooded schooner
but here alone.

There is a ladder,
The ladder is always there
hanging innocently
close to the side of the schooner.
We know what it is for,
we who have used it.
Otherwise
it's a piece of maritime floss
some sundry equipment.

I go down.
Rung after rung and still
the oxygen immerses me
the blue light
the clear atoms
of our human air.
I go down.
My flippers cripple me,
I crawl like an insect down the ladder
and there is no one
to tell me when the ocean
will begin.

First the air is blue and then
it is bluer and then green and then
black I am blacking out and yet
my mask is powerful
it pumps my blood with power
the sea is another story
the sea is not a question of power
I have to learn alone
to turn my body without force
in the deep element.

And now: it is easy to forget
what I came for
among so many who have always
lived here
swaying their crenellated° fans

10

15

20

25

30

35

40

45

---

9. **Cousteau:** Jacques-Yves Cousteau (1910–1997), French underwater explorer, photographer, and author.   48. **crenellated:** Notched; *crenels* are the open spaces between the solid portions of a battlement.

between the reefs
and besides   50
you breathe differently down here.

I came to explore the wreck.
The words are purposes.
The words are maps.
I came to see the damage that was done   55
and the treasures that prevail.
I stroke the beam of my lamp
slowly along the flank
of something more permanent
than fish or weed   60

the thing I came for:
the wreck and not the story of the wreck
the thing itself and not the myth
the drowned face° always staring
toward the sun   65
the evidence of damage
worn by salt and sway into this threadbare beauty
the ribs of the disaster
curving their assertion
among the tentative haunters.   70

This is the place.
And I am here, the mermaid whose dark hair
streams black, the merman in his armored body
We circle silently
about the wreck   75
we dive into the hold.
I am she: I am he

whose drowned face sleeps with open eyes
whose breasts still bear the stress
whose silver, copper, vermeil° cargo lies   80
obscurely inside barrels
half-wedged and left to rot
we are the half-destroyed instruments
that once held to a course
the water-eaten log   85
the fouled compass

We are, I am, you are
by cowardice or courage

---

64. drowned face: The ornamental female figurehead on the prow of an old sailing ship.
80. vermeil: Gilded silver, bronze, or copper.

the one who find our way
back to this scene
carrying a knife, a camera   90
a book of myths
in which
our names do not appear.

Alberto Ríos   b. 1952

Nani°   [1982]

Sitting at her table, she serves
the sopa de arroz° to me   *rice soup*
instinctively, and I watch her,
the absolute *mamá*, and eat words
I might have had to say more   5
out of embarrassment. To speak,
now-foreign words I used to speak,
too, dribble down her mouth as she serves
me albondigas.° No more   *meatballs*
than a third are easy to me.   10
By the stove she does something with words
and looks at me only with her
back. I am full. I tell her
I taste the mint, and watch her speak
smiles at the stove. All my words   15
make her smile. Nani never serves
herself, she only watches me
with her skin, her hair. I ask for more.

I watch the *mamá* warming more
tortillas for me. I watch her   20
fingers in the flame for me.
Near her mouth, I see a wrinkle speak
of a man whose body serves
the ants like she serves me, then more words
from more wrinkles about children, words   25
about this and that, flowing more
easily from these other mouths. Each serves
as a tremendous string around her,
holding her together. They speak
nani was this and that to me   30

Nani: Diminutive for "grandmother."

and I wonder just how much of me
will die with her, what were the words
I could have been, was. Her insides speak
through a hundred wrinkles, now, more
than she can bear, steel around her,   35
shouting, then, What is this thing she serves?

She asks me if I want more.
I own no words to stop her.
Even before I speak, she serves.

Wendy Rose b. 1948

Loo-Wit°   [1985]

The way they do
this old woman
no longer cares
what others think
but spits her black tobacco   5
any which way
stretching full length
from her bumpy bed.
Finally up
she sprinkles ashes   10
on the snow,
cold buttes
promise nothing
but the walk
of winter.   15
Centuries of cedar
have bound her
to earth,
huckleberry ropes
lay prickly   20
on her neck.
Around her
machinery growls,
snarls and ploughs
great patches   25

Loo-Wit: *Loo-wit* is the name by which the Cowlitz People know Mt. St. Helens — "lady of
fire." [Poet's note.]

of her skin.
She crouches
in the north,
her trembling
the source   30
of dawn.
Light appears
with the shudder
of her slopes,
the movement   35
of her arm.
Blackberries unravel,
stones dislodge;
it's not as if
they weren't warned.   40

She was sleeping
but she heard the boot scrape,
the creaking floor,
felt the pull of the blanket
from her thin shoulder.   45
With one free hand
she finds her weapons
and raises them high;
clearing the twigs from her throat
she sings, she sings,   50
shaking the sky
like a blanket about her
Loo-wit sings and sings and sings!

Mary Ruefle   b. 1952

Naked Ladies   [2002]

Rousseau° wanted: a cottage on the Swiss shore,
a cow and a rowboat.

Stevens° wanted a crate from Ceylon full of jam
and statuettes.

---

1. **Rousseau:** Jean-Jacques Rousseau (1712–1778, born in Geneva), a political philosopher and early participant in the Romantic movement in Europe.   **3. Stevens:** Wallace Stevens (1879–1955), American poet (see pp. 862 and 1565).

My neighbors are not ashamed of their poverty   5
but would love to be able to buy a white horse,
a stallion that would transfigure the lot.

Darwin was dying by inches from not having anyone to talk to
about worms, and the vireo outside my window wants nothing less
than a bit of cigarette-wool for her nest.   10

The unattainable is apparently rising on the tips of forks
the world over . . .

So-and-so is wearing shoes for the first time

and Emin Pasha,° in the deepest acreage of the Congo,
wanted so badly to catch a red mouse! Catch one he did   15
shortly before he died, cut in the throat by slavers who
wanted to kill him. *At last!* runs the diary

and it is just this *at last* we powder up and call progress.

So the boys chipped in and bought Bohr° a gram of radium
for his 50th birthday.   20

Pissarro° wanted white frames for his paintings
as early as 1882, and three francs for postage, second place.

Who wants to hear once more the sound of their mother throwing
Brussels sprouts into the tin bowl?

Was it *ping* or was it *ting*?   25

What would you give to smell again the black sweetpeas
choking the chain-link fence?

Because somebody wants your money.

The medallions of monkfish in a champagne sauce . . .

The long kiss conjured up by your body in a cast . . .   30

The paradisiacal vehicle of the sweet-trolley rolling in
as cumulous meringue is piled on your tongue
and your eye eats the amber glaze of a crème brûlée . . .

---

14. Emin Pasha: Eduard Schnitzer (1840–1892), better known as "Emin Pasha," a German physician, explorer, naturalist, collector, and government administrator, who led an expedition into the African interior in an effort to claim the territory for Germany.   **19. Bohr:** Niels Bohr (1885–1962), a Danish physicist who made fundamental contributions to understanding atomic structure and was one of the team that worked on developing the first atomic bomb during World War II.   **21. Pissarro:** Camille Pissarro (1830–1903), a French Impressionist painter.

The forgiveness of sins, a new wife, another passport,
the swimming pool, the rice bowl   35

full of rice, the teenage mutant ninja turtles escaping
as you turn the page . . .

Oh brazen sex at the barbecue party!

Desire is a principle of selection. Who wanted *feet* in the first place?

Who wanted to stand up? Who felt like walking?   40

Sonia Sanchez   b. 1934

An Anthem   [1987]

for the ANC and Brandywine Peace Community

Our vision is our voice
we cut through the country
where madmen goosestep in tune to Guernica.°

we are people made of fire
we walk with ceremonial breaths   5
we have condemned talking mouths.

we run without legs
we see without eyes
loud laughter breaks over our heads.

give me courage so I can spread   10
it over my face and mouth.

we are secret rivers
with shaking hips and crests
come awake in our thunder
so that our eyes can see behind trees.   15

for the world is split wide open
and you hide your hands behind your backs
for the world is broken into little pieces
and you beg with tin cups for life.

are we not more than hunger and music?   20
are we not more than harlequins and horns?

---

3. Guernica: A town in northern Spain that was destroyed in 1937 by insurgents in the Spanish civil war, aided by German planes; the indiscriminate killing of women and children aroused world opinion, and the bombing of Guernica made it a symbol of Fascist brutality.

are we not more than color and drums?
are we not more than anger and dance?

give me courage so I can spread it
over my face and mouth.   25

we are the shakers
walking from top to bottom in a day
we are like Shango°
involving ourselves in acts
that bring life to the middle   30
of our stomachs

we are coming towards you madmen
shredding your death talk
standing in front with mornings around our waist
we have inherited our prayers from   35
the rain
our eyes from the children of Soweto.°

red rain pours over the land
and our fire mixes with the water.

give me courage so I can spread   40
it over my face and mouth.

---

28. **Shango:** One of the gods of the Yoruba tribe of western Nigeria. He is lord of lightning, thunder, rain, and testicular fertility.   37. **Soweto:** Group of segregated townships inhabited by blacks near Johannesburg, South Africa; scene of a 1976 uprising against the policies of apartheid.

Cheryl Savageau   b. 1950

Bones – A City Poem   [1992]

forget the great blue heron flying low
    over the marsh, its footprints
    still fresh in the sand

forget the taste of wild mushrooms
    and where to find them   5

forget lichen-covered pines
    and iceland moss

forget the one-legged duck
    and the eggs of the snapping turtle
    laid in the bank   10

forget the frog found in the belly of a bass

forget the cove testing its breath
    against the autumn morning

forget the down-filled nest
    and the snake swimming at midday   15

forget the bullhead lilies
    and the whiskers
      of the pout

forget walking on black ice
    beneath the sky hunter's bow   20

forget the living waters
    of Quinsigamond

forget how to find the Pole star and why

forget the eyes of the red fox
    the hornets that made their home   25
      in the skull of a cow

forget waking to hear the call of the loon

forget that raccoons are younger brothers
    to the bear

forget that you are walking   30
    on the bones of your grandmothers

Vijay Seshadri   b. 1954

The Refugee   [1996]

He feels himself at his mind's borders moving
down the fifteen rows of laid-out soil
and out to the fence where the mulch heaps spoil
beside the rust-scabbed, dismantled swing
and the visions that disturb him sometimes spring   5
up from a harmless garden-hose coil:
the jackbooted armies dripping spoors of oil
that slick the leaf and crap the wing. . . .

He sees each rifle as we who see him,
in the crystal blizzard of a century's static,   10
try to reach him with our two-bit magic.
But he escapes us to roam in the garden:
too clear to look through or distant to ask;
pinned like a flower on the genocidal past.

William Shakespeare   1564–1616

Shall I compare thee to a summer's day?   *[1590s; 1609]*

Shall I compare thee to a summer's day?
Thou art more lovely and more temperate:
Rough winds do shake the darling buds of May,
And summer's lease° hath all too short a date;°   *allotted time; duration*
Sometimes too hot the eye of heaven shines,   5
And often is his gold complexion dimmed;
And every fair° from fair° sometimes declines,   *beautiful thing; beauty*
By chance or nature's changing course untrimmed;°   *stripped of its beauty*
But thy eternal summer shall not fade,
Nor lose possession of that fair thou ow'st;°   *beauty you own*   10
Nor shall death brag thou wand'rest in his shade,
When in eternal lines° to time thou grow'st:°
  So long as men can breathe, or eyes can see,
  So long lives this,° and this gives life to thee.   *this sonnet*

---

12. **lines:** (Of poetry); **grow'st:** You are grafted to time.

Research William
Shakespeare in depth
with cultural documents
and multimedia resources
on *LiterActive.*

Percy Bysshe Shelley   1792–1822

Ozymandias°   [1818]

I met a traveler from an antique land
Who said: Two vast and trunkless legs of stone
Stand in the desert. . . . Near them, on the sand,
Half sunk, a shattered visage lies, whose frown,
And wrinkled lip, and sneer of cold command,   5
Tell that its sculptor well those passions read
Which yet survive, stamped on these lifeless things,
The hand that mocked them, and the heart that fed:
And on the pedestal these words appear:
"My name is Ozymandias, king of kings: 10
Look on my works, ye Mighty, and despair!"
Nothing beside remains. Round the decay
Of that colossal wreck, boundless and bare
The lone and level sands stretch far away.

Ozymandias: The Greek name for Ramses II of Egypt (thirteenth century B.C.E.), who erected
the largest statue in Egypt as a memorial to himself.

Charles Simic   b. 1938

Classic Ballroom Dances   [1980]

Grandmothers who wring the necks
Of chickens; old nuns
With names like Theresa, Marianne,
Who pull schoolboys by the ear;

The intricate steps of pickpockets   5
Working the crowd of the curious
At the scene of an accident; the slow shuffle
Of the evangelist with a sandwich-board;

The hesitation of the early morning customer
Peeking through the window-grille   10
Of a pawnshop; the weave of a little kid
Who is walking to school with eyes closed;

And the ancient lovers, cheek to cheek,
On the dancefloor of the Union Hall,
Where they also hold charity raffles   15
On rainy Monday nights of an eternal November.

Cathy Song   b. 1955

Girl Powdering Her Neck   [1983]

from a ukiyo-e° print by Utamaro°

The light is the inside
sheen of an oyster shell,
sponged with talc and vapor,
moisture from a bath.

A pair of slippers   5
are placed outside
the rice-paper doors.
She kneels at a low table
in the room,

---

ukiyo-e: Japanese for "pictures of the floating world" — prints and paintings from Edo (Tokyo) in the seventeenth to nineteenth centuries, depicting everyday urban life, particularly its pleasures, such as the theater and beautiful women. The print referred to here is an example of *bijinga* (pictures of beautiful women), one of the most popular types of ukiyo-e.   **Utamaro:** Utamaro Kitagawa (1753–1806), one of the leading ukiyo-e artists, known especially for his work in bijinga.

Utamaro Kitagawa (1753–1806), Girl Powdering Her Neck.
Réunion des Musées Nationaux/Art Resource, NY.

her legs folded beneath her
as she sits on a buckwheat pillow.   10

Her hair is black
with hints of red,
the color of seaweed
spread over rocks.   15

Morning begins the ritual
wheel of the body,
the application of translucent skins.
She practices pleasure:
the pressure of three fingertips   20
applying powder.
Fingerprints of pollen
some other hand will trace.

The peach-dyed kimono
patterned with maple leaves   25
drifting across the silk,
falls from right to left
in a diagonal, revealing
the nape of her neck
and the curve of a shoulder   30
like the slope of a hill
set deep in snow in a country
of huge white solemn birds.
Her face appears in the mirror,
a reflection in a winter pond,   35
rising to meet itself.

She dips a corner of her sleeve
like a brush into water
to wipe the mirror;
she is about to paint herself.   40
The eyes narrow
in a moment of self-scrutiny.
The mouth parts
as if desiring to disturb
the placid plum face;   45
break the symmetry of silence.
But the berry-stained lips,
stenciled into the mask of beauty,
do not speak.

Two chrysanthemums   50
touch in the middle of the lake
and drift apart.

Gary Soto b. 1952

The Elements of San Joaquin   [1977; rev. 1995]

for César Chávez°

Field

The wind sprays pale dirt into my mouth
The small, almost invisible scars
On my hands.

The pores in my throat and elbows
Have taken in a seed of dirt of their own.   5

After a day in the grape fields near Rolinda
A fine silt, washed by sweat,
Has settled into the lines
On my wrists and palms.

Already I am becoming the valley,   10
A soil that sprouts nothing.
For any of us.

Wind

A dry wind over the valley
Peeled mountains, grain by grain,
To small slopes, loose dirt   15
Where red ants tunnel.

The wind strokes
The skulls and spines of cattle
To white dust, to nothing,

Covers the spiked tracks of beetles,   20
Of tumbleweed, of sparrows
That pecked the ground for insects.

Evenings, when I am in the yard weeding,
The wind picks up the breath of my armpits
Like dust, swirls it   25
Miles away

César Chávez: (1927–1993), Hispanic American labor leader and activist known for creating
the United Farm Workers and for leading a nationwide boycott of California table grapes in
1968 as part of an effort to achieve labor contracts for field workers.

And drops it
On the ear of a rabid dog,
And I take on another life.

Wind

When you got up this morning the sun   30
Blazed an hour in the sky,

A lizard hid
Under the curled leaves of manzanita°
And winked its dark lids.

Later, the sky grayed,   35
And the cold wind you breathed
Was moving under your skin and already far
From the small hives of your lungs.

Stars

At dusk the first stars appear.
Not one eager finger points toward them.   40
A little later the stars spread with the night
And an orange moon rises
To lead them, like a shepherd, toward dawn.

Sun

In June the sun is a bonnet of light
Coming up,   45
Little by little,
From behind a skyline of pine.

The pastures sway with fiddle-neck,
Tassels of foxtail.

At Piedra   50
A couple fish on the river's edge,
Their shadows deep against the water.
Above, in the stubbled slopes,
Cows climb down
As the heat rises   55
In a mist of blond locusts,
Returning to the valley.

---

33. manzanita: An evergreen shrub or small tree found in arid regions of the western United States.

Rain

When autumn rains flatten sycamore leaves,
The tiny volcanos of dirt
Ants raised around their holes,   60
I should be out of work.

My silverware and stack of plates will go unused
Like the old, my two good slacks
Will smother under a growth of lint
And smell of the old dust   65
That rises
When the closet door opens or closes.

The skin of my belly will tighten like a belt
And there will be no reason for pockets.

Harvest

East of the sun's slant, in the vineyard that never failed,   70
A wind crossed my face, moving the dust
And a portion of my voice a step closer to a new year.

The sky went black in the ninth hour of rolling trays,
And in the distance ropes of rain dropped to pull me
From the thick harvest that was not mine.   75

Fog

If you go to your window
You will notice a fog drifting in.

The sun is no stronger than a flashlight.
Not all the sweaters
Hung in closets all summer   80

Could soak up this mist. The fog:
A mouth nibbling everything to its origin,
Pomegranate trees, stolen bicycles,

The string of lights at a used-car lot,
A Pontiac with scorched valves.   85

In Fresno the fog is passing
The young thief prying a window screen,
Graying my hair that falls
And goes unfound, my fingerprints
Slowly growing a fur of dust—   90

One hundred years from now
There should be no reason to believe
I lived.

Daybreak

In this moment when the light starts up
In the east and rubs   95
The horizon until it catches fire,

We enter the fields to hoe,
Row after row, among the small flags of onion,
Waving off the dragonflies
That ladder the air.   100

And tears the onions raise
Do not begin in your eyes but in ours,
In the salt blown
From one blister into another;

They begin in knowing   105
You will never waken to bear
The hour timed to a heart beat,
The wind pressing us closer to the ground.

When the season ends,
And the onions are unplugged from their sleep,   110
We won't forget what you failed to see,
And nothing will heal
Under the rain's broken fingers.

Research Gary Soto in depth with cultural documents and multimedia resources on *LiterActive*.

Edmund Spenser   1552–1599

One day I wrote her name upon the strand   [1595]

One day I wrote her name upon the strand,
But came the waves and washèd it away:
Again I wrote it with a second hand,
But came the tide, and made my pains his prey.
"Vain man," said she, "that dost in vain assay,   5
A mortal thing so to immortalize,
For I myself shall like to this decay,
And eek° my name be wipèd out likewise."   *also*

"Not so," quod° I, "let baser things devise,   *quoth (said)*
To die in dust, but you shall live by fame: 10
My verse your virtues rare shall eternize,
And in the heavens write your glorious name.
Where whenas death shall all the world subdue,
Our love shall live, and later life renew."

Wallace Stevens   1879–1955

The Emperor of Ice-Cream   [1923]

Call the roller of big cigars,
The muscular one, and bid him whip
In kitchen cups concupiscent curds.
Let the wenches dawdle in such dress
As they are used to wear, and let the boys   5
Bring flowers in last month's newspapers.
Let be be finale of seem.
The only emperor is the emperor of ice-cream.

Take from the dresser of deal,
Lacking the three glass knobs, that sheet   10
On which she embroidered fantails once
And spread it so as to cover her face.
If her horny feet protrude, they come
To show how cold she is, and dumb.
Let the lamp affix its beam.   15
The only emperor is the emperor of ice-cream.

Mark Strand   b. 1934

Eating Poetry   [1968]

Ink runs from the corners of my mouth.
There is no happiness like mine.
I have been eating poetry.

The librarian does not believe what she sees.
Her eyes are sad   5
and she walks with her hands in her dress.

The poems are gone.
The light is dim.
The dogs are on the basement stairs and coming up.

Their eyeballs roll,   10
their blond legs burn like brush.
The poor librarian begins to stamp her feet and weep.

She does not understand.
When I get on my knees and lick her hand,
she screams.   15

I am a new man.
I snarl at her and bark.
I romp with joy in the bookish dark.

Virgil Suárez b. 1962

Tea Leaves, *Caracoles*, Coffee Beans   [2005]

My mother, who in those Havana days believed in divination,
found her tea leaves at *El Volcán*, the Chinese market/apothecary,

brought the leaves in a precious silk paper bundle, unwrapped
them as if unwrapping her own skin, and then boiled water

to make my dying grandmother's tea; while my mother read   5
its leaves, I simply saw *leaves floating* in steaming water,

vapor kissed my skin, my nose became moist as a puppy's.
My mother did this because my grandmother, her mother-in-law,

believed in all things. Her appetite for knowledge was vast,
the one thing we all agreed she passed down to me, the skinny   10

kid sent to search for *caracoles*, these snail shells
that littered the underbrush of the empty lot next door.

My mother threw them on top of the table, cleaned them of dirt,
kept them in a mason jar and every morning before breakfast,

read them on top of the table, their way of falling, some up,   15
some down, their ridges, swirls of creamy lines, their broken

edges. . . . Everything she read looked bad, for my grandmother,
for us, for staying in our country, this island of suspended

disbelief. My mother read coffee beans too, with their wrinkled,
fleshy green and red skin. Orange-skinned beans she kept aside.   20

Orange meant death, and my mother didn't want to accept it.
I learned mostly of death from the way a sparrow fell

when I hit it in the chest with my slingshot and a lead pellet
I made by melting my toy soldiers. The sparrow's eyes

always hid behind droopy eyelids, which is how my grandmother   25
died, by closing her eyes to the world; truth became this fading

light, a tunnel, as everybody says, but instead of heaven
she went into the ground, to that one place that still nourishes

the tea leaves, *caracoles*, and the coffee beans, which, if I didn't
know better, I'd claim shone; those red-glowing beans   30

in starlight were the eyes of the dead looking out through
the darkness as those of us who believed in such things walked

through life with a lightness of feet, spirit, a vapor-aura
that could be read or sung.

Alfred, Lord Tennyson 1809–1892

Ulysses°   [1833]

It little profits that an idle king,
By this still hearth, among these barren crags,
Matched with an agèd wife, I mete and dole
Unequal laws unto a savage race,°
That hoard, and sleep, and feed, and know not me.   5

    I cannot rest from travel; I will drink
Life to the lees. All times I have enjoyed
Greatly, have suffered greatly, both with those
That loved me, and alone; on shore, and when
Through scudding drifts° the rainy Hyades°   10

Ulysses (the Roman form of Odysseus): The hero of Homer's epic *The Odyssey,* which tells the
story of Odysseus's adventures on his voyage back to his home, the little island of Ithaca, after
he and the other Greek heroes had defeated Troy. It took Odysseus ten years to reach Ithaca, the
small, rocky island of which he was king, where his wife (Penelope) and son (Telemachus) had
been waiting for him. Upon his return he defeated the suitors who had been trying to marry the
faithful Penelope, and he resumed the kingship and his old ways of life. Here Homer's story
ends, but in Canto 26 of the *Inferno* Dante extended the story: Odysseus eventually became
restless and dissatisfied with his settled life and decided to return to the sea and sail west, into
the unknown sea, and seek whatever adventures he might find there. Tennyson's poem amplifies the speech delivered in Dante's poem as Ulysses challenges his men to accompany him on
this new voyage.   **3–4. mete . . . race:** Administer inadequate (unequal to what is needed)
laws to a still somewhat lawless race.   **10. scudding drifts:** Wind-driven spray; **Hyades:** Five
stars in the constellation Taurus whose rising was assumed would be followed by rain.

Vexed the dim sea. I am become a name;
For always roaming with a hungry heart
Much have I seen and known—cities of men
And manners, climates, councils, governments,
Myself not least, but honored of them all—   15
And drunk delight of battle with my peers,
Far on the ringing plains of windy Troy.
I am a part of all that I have met;
Yet all experience is an arch wherethrough
Gleams that untraveled world whose margin fades   20
Forever and forever when I move.
How dull it is to pause, to make an end,
To rust unburnished, not to shine in use!
As though to breathe were life! Life piled on life
Were all too little, and of one to me   25
Little remains; but every hour is saved
From that eternal silence, something more,
A bringer of new things; and vile it were
For some three suns° to store and hoard myself,   *years*
And this gray spirit yearning in desire   30
To follow knowledge like a sinking star,
Beyond the utmost bound of human thought.

    This is my son, mine own Telemachus,
To whom I leave the scepter and the isle—
Well-loved of me, discerning to fulfill   35
This labor, by slow prudence to make mild
A rugged people, and through soft degrees
Subdue them to the useful and the good.
Most blameless is he, centered in the sphere
Of common duties, decent not to fail   40
In offices of tenderness, and pay
Meet adoration to my household gods,
When I am gone. He works his work, I mine.

    There lies the port; the vessel puffs her sail;
There gloom the dark, broad seas. My mariners,   45
Souls that have toiled, and wrought, and thought with me—
That ever with a frolic welcome took
The thunder and the sunshine, and opposed
Free hearts, free foreheads—you and I are old;
Old age hath yet his honor and his toil.   50
Death closes all; but something ere the end,
Some work of noble note, may yet be done,
Not unbecoming men that strove with Gods.
The lights begin to twinkle from the rocks;

The long day wanes; the slow moon climbs; the deep   55
Moans round with many voices. Come, my friends,
'Tis not too late to seek a newer world.
Push off, and sitting well in order smite
The sounding furrows; for my purpose holds
To sail beyond the sunset, and the baths°   60
Of all the western stars, until I die.
It may be that the gulfs will wash us down;
It may be we shall touch the Happy Isles,°
And see the great Achilles,° whom we knew.
Though much is taken, much abides; and though   65
We are not now that strength which in old days
Moved earth and heaven, that which we are, we are—
One equal temper of heroic hearts,
Made weak by time and fate, but strong in will
To strive, to seek, to find, and not to yield.   70

60. baths: The outer river or ocean surrounding the flat earth, in Greek cosmology, into which the stars descended upon setting.   **63. Happy Isles:** The Islands of the Blessed, or Elysian Fields, in Greek myth, which lay in the western seas beyond the Strait of Gibraltar and were the abode of heroes after death.   **64. Achilles:** The hero of the Greeks, and Odysseus's comrade, in Homer's *Iliad*.

Dylan Thomas   1914–1953

Do not go gentle into that good night   [1952]

Do not go gentle into that good night,
Old age should burn and rave at close of day;
Rage, rage against the dying of the light.

Though wise men at their end know dark is right,
Because their words had forked no lightning they   5
Do not go gentle into that good night.

Good men, the last wave by, crying how bright
Their frail deeds might have danced in a green bay,
Rage, rage against the dying of the light.

Wild men who caught and sang the sun in flight,   10
And learn, too late, they grieved it on its way,
Do not go gentle into that good night.

Grave men, near death, who see with blinding sight
Blind eyes could blaze like meteors and be gay,
Rage, rage against the dying of the light.   15

And you, my father, there on the sad height,
Curse, bless, me now with your fierce tears, I pray.
Do not go gentle into that good night.
Rage, rage against the dying of the light.

Research Dylan Thomas in depth with cultural documents and multimedia resources on *LiterActive*.

Jean Toomer 1894–1967

Face   [1923]

Hair—
silver-gray,
like streams of stars,
Brows—
recurved canoes   5
quivered by the ripples blown by pain,
Her eyes—
mist of tears
condensing on the flesh below
And her channeled muscles   10
are cluster grapes of sorrow
purple in the evening sun
nearly ripe for worms.

Quincy Troupe b. 1943

Poem for the Root Doctor of Rock n Roll   [1984]

For Chuck Berry

& it all came together on the mississippi river
chuck, you there riding the rocking-blue sound wave
duck-walking the poetry of hoodoo down
                          & you were the mojo-hand
of juju crowing, the gut-bucket news — running it down   5
for two records sold to make a penny
back then in those first days, "majoring in mouth" —
a long, gone, lean lightning rod
                picking the edge, charging the wires
                      of songs, huckle-bucking "roll over   10
beethoven," playing "devil's music," till white devils stole it from you

& called it their own, "rock n roll"
                    devils like elvis & pat boone
who never duck-walked back in the alley with you
& bo diddley, little richard & the fatman from new orleans   15
all yall slapping down songs meaner than the smell
of toejam & rot-gut whiskey breath
back there, in them back rooms
                    of throw down

back there, where your song lyrics grew, like fresh corn   20
you, chuck berry, an authentic american genius of barbecue sauce
& deep fried catfish licks, jack-salmon guitar
                    honky-tonk rhythms
jangling warm, vibrating sounds, choo-chooing train
whistles fiddling & smoking down the tracks of the blues   25
motivating through "little queenie," "maybelline"
decked out in red on sarah & finney
alarms rolling off your whipping tongue
in the words of "johnny b good"
you clued us in, back to the magical hookup of ancestors   30
their seamless souls threading your breath
                    their blood in your sluicing strut
& to much "monkey business," the reason for their deaths, cold & searing
your spirit reaching down to the bones of your roots
deep in the "show me" blood of missouri soil   35
                    your pruned, hawk-look, profiling
where you rode your white cadillac of words, cruising
the highways of language (what we speak & hear even now)
breathing inside your cadences
                    you shaped & wheeled the music   40
duck-walking the length of the stage
duck-walked your zinging metaphors of everyday
slip-slide & strut, vibrating your hummingbird wings
your strumming style, the cutting edge
& you were what was to come   45

so hail, hail, chuck berry, root doctor of "rock n roll"
authentic american genius
                    tonguing deep in river syllables
hail, hail, chuck berry, laying down the motivating juju
you great, american, mojo hand   50

root doctor, spirit, of american, "rock n roll"

Gerald Vizenor   b. 1934

Shaman Breaks   [1988]

1

colonists
unearth their wealth
and tease
the old stone man
over the breaks   5

moths batter
the cold windows
their light
is not our day

leaves abide the seasons   10
the last crows
smarten the poplars

2

tourists
discover their ruins
and mimic   15
the old stone woman
over the breaks

nasturtiums
dress the barbed wire
fences down   20
down to the wild sea

magnolias
bloom under a whole moon
words fall apart

3

soldiers   25
bleach the landscapes
hound the shamans

wild stories
break from the stones

Derek Walcott b. 1930

Sea Grapes   [1976]

That sail which leans on light,
tired of islands,
a schooner beating up the Caribbean

for home, could be Odysseus,°
home-bound on the Aegean;   5
that father and husband's

longing, under gnarled sour grapes, is
like the adulterer hearing Nausicaa's name
in every gull's outcry.

This brings nobody peace. The ancient war   10
between obsession and responsibility
will never finish and has been the same

for the sea-wanderer or the one on shore
now wriggling on his sandals to walk home,
since Troy sighed its last flame,   15

and the blind giant's boulder heaved the trough
from whose groundswell the great hexameters come
to the conclusions of exhausted surf.

The classics can console. But not enough.

---

4. **Odysseus:** For background, see page 864. Princess Nausicaa (line 8) fell in love with
Odysseus when he was carried by a storm to Phaiacia; he could have married her and stayed
there, but he chose to go home (responsibility) rather than to enjoy an indulgent life with her
(obsession). Odysseus blinded Polyphemus (line 16), a giant one-eyed Cyclops, who held him
prisoner; as Odysseus escaped, Polyphemus threw great rocks in front of his boat to wash it
back to shore. The *Odyssey* was written in hexameter verse (line 17).

Wang Ping b. 1957

Opening the Face   [2003]

She comes in,
thread between her teeth,
the "lady of wholesome fortune,"
two sons, three daughters,
husband in government service,   5
parents-in-law healthy and content,

surrounded by laughing grandchildren.
Mother paid her gold to open
my face on my wedding day.

"Sit still," she orders, twining   10
the cotton thread to test its strength.
"It hurts, but nothing like footbinding,
or the hardship of a newlywed."
She pulls it through her teeth,
lines it against my forehead.   15
Wet, cold, it furrows into the skin,
into the roots of my virgin down.
The uprooted hair hisses
after the twanging thread.

"Don't make a sound, girl," she whispers   20
to my drenched face, "not until you bear him a son,
not until you have grandchildren."
She holds her breath as she scrapes
between the eyebrows and lashes, opens
her mouth again when she reaches for the cheek.   25
"What's ten, twenty, or even thirty years?
We came to this world with nothing but
patience. You have high cheekbones
and a big nose, signs of a man-killer,
but compensated by a round chin.   30
Just keep your mouth shut, eyes open.
There, there," she leans closer, wiping
beads of tears from my eyelashes.

                    I turn to the light, my face
                    a burning field.   35

"Now you're ready for the big day."
Her fingers trace along my cheekbones.
"Your face clean and open.
I'll cover it with a red scarf.
The only person who can lift   40
the veil is your groom. All other eyes
are evil eyes. Remember, remember."

She puts on her shoes.
"Ah, one more thing," she leans to my ear,
her breath steaming with pickled mustard greens,   45
yellow rice wine, its bitter sweetness
from years of fermentation in a sealed jar
deep underground. Her secret

tickles the inside of my ear.
"When he sleeps, put your shoes   50
in his boots and let them sit overnight.
It'll keep him under your thumb, forever."

James Welch   b. 1940

Christmas Comes to Moccasin Flat   [1976]

Christmas comes like this: Wise men
unhurried, candles bought on credit (poor price
for calves), warriors face down in wine sleep.
Winds cheat to pull heat from smoke.

Friends sit in chinked cabins, stare out   5
plastic windows and wait for commodities.
Charlie Blackbird, twenty miles from church
and bar, stabs his fire with flint.

When drunks drain radiators for love
or need, chiefs eat snow and talk of change,   10
an urge to laugh pounding their ribs.
Elk play games in high country.

Medicine Woman, clay pipe and twist tobacco,
calls each blizzard by name and predicts
five o'clock by spitting at her television.   15
Children lean into her breath to beg a story:

Something about honor and passion,
warriors back with meat and song,
a peculiar evening star, quick vision of birth.
Blackbird feeds his fire. Outside, a quick 30 below.   20

Patricia Jabbeh Wesley   b. 1955

Becoming Ebony   [2003]

"Did I come all the way here to hide from the sun?"
Mama would sigh. I can still see Mama standing

at the window, watching dark clouds, cold winds,
yellow leaves — November. Leaves from

my neighbor's yard arrive from yesterday's fall.   5
November rations its sunshine here in Michigan.

Today, I wish the end of clouds, the end of sky, the end
of windows — only curtains bright with daffodils,

African violets, hibiscus, wild thorny roses side by side.
I want to see the end of neighbors with falling maple   10

leaves, a lazy dog on a leash, barking at flying leaves.
Those who have no windows do not wait for the sun

to come in. Those who have no windows will not hear
my neighbor's dog. Here in my living room, the glass

window bends the sunlight; a dying fern leans. I am   15
a killer of plants seeking refuge in my living room.

I want to see the end of death. An ebony lion on my
glass table waits patiently for the sun, like Mama,

in Byron Center, waiting at the window for the sun
to come in, waiting for the war to end at home.   20

The day Mama died, I waited at the window to see
if the sun would come in, to see if my brother would

call again — the uncertainty of waiting so a moment will
undo itself, to undo that dreaded call, to undo death.

How many calls can undo death? An ebony carving   25
knows the uncertainty of skin, the uncertainty of time,

the uncertainty of waiting. Brown wood, darkening
slowly, becoming ebony all the way through.

The ebony at home knows how to unfurl wide, green
branches, how to die slowly, becoming woodwork,   30

a ritual mask for the harvest dance, an ebony lion,
perhaps, on a glass table. That familiar feel of carving

knife, the sharp cut, when the carver no longer recalls
his purpose. Crooked edges, polished by the artist's

rough hands, and then, what was wood becomes marble —   35
a raw tree trunk yielding its life until what was wood

becomes iron. The ebony knows how brief color is —
when sap licks itself dry into rough threads of wood.

They say after the sap is gone, then comes strength.
The ebony knows how final color is, how final death is.   40

Roberta Hill Whiteman b. 1947

The White Land   [1984]

When Orion° straddled his apex of sky,
over the white land we lingered loving.
The River Eridanus° flickered, foretelling
tropical waves and birds arrayed
in feathers of sunset, but we didn't waste   5
that prickling dark.

Not a dog barked our arrival before dawn.
Only in sleep did I drift vagabond
and suffer the patterns that constantly state
time has no time. Fate is a warlord.   10
That morning I listened to your long breath
for decades.

That morning you said bears
fell over the white land. Leaving their lair
in thick polar fur, they roused our joy   15
by leaving no footprint. Fat ones fell headlong,
but most of them danced, then without quarrel,
balanced on branches.

I couldn't breathe in the roar of that plane,
flying me back to a wooded horizon.   20
Regular rhythms bridge my uneven sleep.
What if the wind in the white land keeps you?
The dishwater's luminous; a truck
grinds down the street.

---

1. Orion: Prominent constellation located on the celestial equator.   3. River Eridanus: Large southern constellation stretching southwest from Orion, identified with a river because of its long winding shape.

Walt Whitman 1819–1892

From Song of Myself   [*1855*; 1891–1892]°

1

I celebrate myself, and sing myself,
And what I assume you shall assume,
For every atom belonging to me as good belongs to you.

I loafe and invite my soul,
I lean and loafe at my ease observing a spear of summer grass.   5

My tongue, every atom of my blood, form'd from this soil, this air,
Born here of parents born here from parents the same, and their parents
     the same,
I, now thirty-seven years old in perfect health begin,
Hoping to cease not till death.

Creeds and schools in abeyance,   10
Retiring back a while suffced at what they are, but never forgotten,
I harbor for good or bad, I permit to speak at every hazard,
Nature without check with original energy.

7

Has any one supposed it lucky to be born?
I hasten to inform him or her it is just as lucky to die, and I know it.

I pass death with the dying and birth with the new-wash'd babe,
     and am not contain'd between my hat and boots,
And peruse manifold objects, no two alike and every one good,
The earth good and the stars good, and their adjuncts all good.   135

I am not an earth nor an adjunct of an earth,
I am the mate and companion of people, all just as immortal and
     fathomless as myself,
(They do not know how immortal, but I know.)

Every kind for itself and its own, for me mine male and female,
For me those that have been boys and that love women,   140
For me the man that is proud and feels how it stings to be slighted,

---

Date: The poem was first published in 1855 as an untitled section of *Leaves of Grass*. It was a rough, rude, and vigorous example of antebellum American cultural politics and free verse experimentation. The version excerpted here, from the sixth edition (1891–1892), is much longer, more carefully crafted, and more conventionally punctuated.

For me the sweet-heart and old maid, for me mothers and the
    mothers of mothers,
For me lips that have smiled, eyes that have shed tears,
For me children and the begetters of children.

Undrape! you are not guilty to me, nor stale nor discarded,   145
I see through the broadcloth and gingham whether or no,
And am around, tenacious, acquisitive, tireless, and cannot be
    shaken away.

21

I am the poet of the Body and I am the poet of the Soul,
The pleasures of heaven are with me and the pains of hell are
    with me,
The first I graft and increase upon myself, the latter I translate into
    a new tongue.

I am the poet of the woman the same as the man,   425
And I say it is as great to be a woman as to be a man,
And I say there is nothing greater than the mother of men.

I chant the chant of dilation or pride,
We have had ducking and deprecating about enough,
I show that size is only development.   430

Have you outstript the rest? are you the President?
It is a trifle, they will more than arrive there every one, and still
    pass on.

I am he that walks with the tender and growing night,
I call to the earth and sea half-held by the night.

Press close bare-bosom'd night — press close magnetic nourishing
    night!
Night of south winds — night of the large few stars!   435
Still nodding night — mad naked summer night.

Smile O voluptuous cool-breath'd earth!
Earth of the slumbering and liquid trees!
Earth of departed sunset — earth of the mountains misty-topt!   440
Earth of the vitreous pour of the full moon just tinged with blue!
Earth of shine and dark mottling the tide of the river!
Earth of the limpid gray of clouds brighter and clearer for my sake!
Far-swooping elbow'd earth — rich apple-blossom'd earth!
Smile, for your lover comes.   445

Prodigal, you have given me love — therefore I to you give love!
O unspeakable passionate love.

24

Walt Whitman, a kosmos, of Manhattan the son,
Turbulent, fleshy, sensual, eating, drinking and breeding,
No sentimentalist, no stander above men and women or apart
    from them,
No more modest than immodest.   500

Unscrew the locks from the doors!
Unscrew the doors themselves from their jambs!

Whoever degrades another degrades me,
And whatever is done or said returns at last to me.

Through me the afflatus° surging and surging, through me the
    current and index.   505

I speak the pass-word primeval, I give the sign of democracy,
By God! I will accept nothing which all cannot have their counterpart of
    on the same terms.

Through me many long dumb voices,
Voices of the interminable generations of prisoners and slaves,
Voices of the diseas'd and despairing and of thieves and dwarfs,   510
Voices of cycles of preparation and accretion,
And of the threads that connect the stars, and of wombs and of
    the father-stuff,
And of the rights of them the others are down upon.

47

I am the teacher of athletes,
He that by me spreads a wider breast than my own proves the
    width of my own,   1235
He most honors my style who learns under it to destroy the teacher.

The boy I love, the same becomes a man not through derived power,
    but in his own right,
Wicked rather than virtuous out of conformity or fear,
Fond of his sweetheart, relishing well his steak,
Unrequited love or a slight cutting him worse than sharp steel cuts, 1240
First-rate to ride, to fight, to hit the bull's eye, to sail a skiff, to sing
    a song or play on the banjo,
Preferring scars and the beard and faces pitted with small-pox over
    all latherers,
And those well-tann'd to those that keep out of the sun.

---

505. afflatus: Inspiration, from Latin meaning "to blow on."

I teach straying from me, yet who can stray from me?
I follow you whoever you are from the present hour,   1245
My words itch at your ears till you understand them.

I do not say these things for a dollar or to fill up the time while I wait
    for a boat,
(It is you talking just as much as myself, I act as the tongue of you,
Tied in your mouth, in mine it begins to be loosen'd.)

I swear I will never again mention love or death inside a house,   1250
And I swear I will never translate myself at all, only to him or her who
    privately stays with me in the open air.

If you would understand me go to the heights or water-shore,
The nearest gnat is an explanation, and a drop or motion of waves a key,
The maul, the oar, the hand-saw, second my words.

No shutter'd room or school can commune with me,   1255
But roughs and little children better than they.

The young mechanic is closest to me, he knows me well,
The woodman that takes his axe and jug with him shall take me
    with him all day,
The farm-boy ploughing in the field feels good at the sound of my voice,
In vessels that sail my words sail, I go with fishermen and seamen
    and love them.   1260

The soldier camp'd or upon the march is mine,
On the night ere the pending battle many seek me, and I do not fail
    them,
On that solemn night (it may be their last) those that know me
    seek me.

My face rubs to the hunter's face when he lies down alone in his
    blanket,
The driver thinking of me does not mind the jolt of his wagon,   1265
The young mother and old mother comprehend me,
The girl and the wife rest the needle a moment and forget where
    they are,
They and all would resume what I have told them.

52

The spotted hawk swoops by and accuses me, he complains of my
    gab and my loitering.

I too am not a bit tamed, I too am untranslatable,
I sound my barbaric yawp over the roofs of the world.

The last scud of day holds back for me,
It flings my likeness after the rest and true as any on the shadow'd
    wilds,   1335
It coaxes me to the vapor and the dusk.

I depart as air, I shake my white locks at the runaway sun,
I effuse my flesh in eddies, and drift it in lacy jags.

I bequeath myself to the dirt to grow from the grass I love,
If you want me again look for me under your boot-soles.   1340

You will hardly know who I am or what I mean,
But I shall be good health to you nevertheless,
And filter and fibre your blood.

Failing to fetch me at first keep encouraged,
Missing me one place search another,   1345
I stop somewhere waiting for you.

CD-ROM: Research Walt Whitman in depth with cultural documents and multimedia resources on
LiterActive.

Richard Wilbur b. 1921

Love Calls Us to the Things of This World   [1956]

    The eyes open to a cry of pulleys,
And spirited from sleep, the astounded soul
Hangs for a moment bodiless and simple
As false dawn.
              Outside the open window
The morning air is all awash with angels.   5

    Some are in bed-sheets, some are in blouses,
Some are in smocks: but truly there they are.
Now they are rising together in calm swells
Of halcyon feeling, filling whatever they wear
With the deep joy of their impersonal breathing;   10

    Now they are flying in place, conveying
The terrible speed of their omnipresence, moving
And staying like white water; and now of a sudden
They swoon down into so rapt a quiet
That nobody seems to be there.
               The soul shrinks   15

From all that it is about to remember,
From the punctual rape of every blessèd day,
And cries,
                "Oh, let there be nothing on earth but laundry,
Nothing but rosy hands in the rising steam
And clear dances done in the sight of heaven."   20

Yet, as the sun acknowledges
With a warm look the world's hunks and colors,
The soul descends once more in bitter love
To accept the waking body, saying now
In a changed voice as the man yawns and rises,   25

"Bring them down from their ruddy gallows;
Let there be clean linen for the backs of thieves;
Let lovers go fresh and sweet to be undone,
And the heaviest nuns walk in a pure floating
Of dark habits,
                keeping their difficult balance."   30

William Carlos Williams 1883–1963

Spring and All   [1923]

By the road to the contagious hospital°
under the surge of the blue
mottled clouds driven from the
northeast—a cold wind. Beyond, the
waste of broad, muddy fields   5
brown with dried weeds, standing and fallen

patches of standing water
the scattering of tall trees

All along the road the reddish
purplish, forked, upstanding, twiggy   10
stuff of bushes and small trees
with dead, brown leaves under them
leafless vines—

Lifeless in appearance, sluggish
dazed spring approaches—   15

---

1. **contagious hospital:** A hospital for the treatment of contagious diseases.

They enter the new world naked,
cold, uncertain of all
save that they enter. All about them
the cold, familiar wind —

Now the grass, tomorrow   20
the stiff curl of wildcarrot leaf

One by one objects are defined —
It quickens: clarity, outline of leaf

But now the stark dignity of
entrance — Still, the profound change   25
has come upon them: rooted, they
grip down and begin to awaken

Nellie Wong   b. 1934

Grandmother's Song   [1977]

Grandmothers sing their song
Blinded by the suns' rays
Grandchildren for whom they long
For pomelo°-golden days   *grapefruit*

Blinded by the sun's rays   5
Gold bracelets, opal rings
For pomelo-golden days
Tiny fingers, ancient things

Gold bracelets, opal rings
Sprinkled with Peking dust   10
Tiny fingers, ancient things
So young they'll never rust

Sprinkled with Peking dust
To dance in fields of mud
So young they'll never rust   15
Proud as if of royal blood

To dance in fields of mud
Or peel shrimp for pennies a day
Proud as if of royal blood
Coins and jade to put away   20

Or peel shrimp for pennies a day
Seaweed washes up the shore

Coins and jade to put away
A camphor chest is home no more

Seaweed washes up the shore   25
Bound feet struggle to loosen free
A camphor chest is home no more
A foreign tongue is learned at three

Bound feet struggle to loosen free
Grandchildren for whom they long   30
A foreign tongue is learned at three
Grandmothers sing their song

William Wordsworth   1770–1850

Composed upon Westminster Bridge, September 3, 1802   [1807]

Earth has not anything to show more fair:
Dull would he be of soul who could pass by
A sight so touching in its majesty:
This City now doth, like a garment, wear
The beauty of the morning; silent, bare,   5
Ships, towers, domes, theatres, and temples lie
Open unto the fields, and to the sky;
All bright and glittering in the smokeless air.
Never did sun more beautifully steep
In his first splendor, valley, rock, or hill;   10
Ne'er saw I, never felt, a calm so deep!
The river glideth at his own sweet will;
Dear God! the very houses seem asleep;
And all that mighty heart is lying still!

Sir Thomas Wyatt   1503–1542

They flee from me   [from an undated manuscript]

They flee from me, that sometime did me seek,
With naked foot stalking in my chamber.
I have seen them, gentle, tame, and meek,
That now are wild, and do not remember
That sometime they put themselves in danger   5
To take bread at my hand; and now they range,
Busily seeking with a continual change.

Thanked be fortune it hath been otherwise,
Twenty times better; but once in special,
In thin array, after a pleasant guise,°   *manner of dress*   10
When her loose gown from her shoulders did fall,
And she me caught in her arms long and small,°   *slender*
Therewithall sweetly did me kiss
And softly said, "Dear heart,° how like you this?"

It was no dream, I lay broad waking.   15
But all is turned, thorough° my gentleness,   *through*
Into a strange fashion of forsaking;
And I have leave to go, of° her goodness,   *out of (motivated by)*
And she also to use newfangleness.
But since that I so kindly° am served,   20
I fain would know what she hath deserved.

---

14. Dear heart (pun): Heart, and hart (deer).   **20. kindly** (pun): Graciously (ironic), and "in kind"; i.e., in a way typical of female nature.

John Yau   b. 1950

Chinese Villanelle   [1979]

I have been with you, and I have thought of you
Once the air was dry and drenched with light
I was like a lute filling the room with description

We watched glum clouds reject their shape
We dawdled near a fountain, and listened   5
I have been with you, and I have thought of you

Like a river worthy of its gown
And like a mountain worthy of its insolence . . .
Why am I like a lute left with only description

How does one cut an axe handle with an axe   10
What shall I do to tell you all my thoughts
When I have been with you, and thought of you

A pelican sits on a dam, while a duck
Folds its wings again; the song does not melt
I remember you looking at me without description   15

Perhaps a king's business is never finished,
Though "perhaps" implies a different beginning
I have been with you, and I have thought of you
Now I am a lute filled with this wandering description

William Butler Yeats 1865–1939

The Second Coming° [1921]

Turning and turning in the widening gyre
The falcon cannot hear the falconer;
Things fall apart; the centre cannot hold;
Mere anarchy is loosed upon the world,
The blood-dimmed tide is loosed, and everywhere   5
The ceremony of innocence is drowned;
The best lack all conviction, while the worst
Are full of passionate intensity.

Surely some revelation is at hand;
Surely the Second Coming is at hand.   10
The Second Coming! Hardly are those words out
When a vast image out of *Spiritus Mundi*°
Troubles my sight: somewhere in sands of the desert
A shape with lion body and the head of a man,
A gaze blank and pitiless as the sun,   15
Is moving its slow thighs, while all about it
Reel shadows of the indignant desert birds.
The darkness drops again; but now I know
That twenty centuries of stony sleep
Were vexed to nightmare by a rocking cradle,   20
And what rough beast, its hour come round at last,
Slouches towards Bethlehem to be born?

Research William Butler
Yeats in depth with cultural
documents and multimedia
resources on *LiterActive*.

The Second Coming: Alludes to Matthew 24:3–44, on the return of Christ at the end of the present age. Yeats viewed history as a series of 2,000-year cycles (imaged as gyres, cone-shaped motions). The birth of Christ in Bethlehem brought to an end the cycle that ran from the Babylonians through the Greeks and Romans. The approach of the year 2000, then, anticipated for Yeats the end of another era (the Christian age). Yeats wrote this poem shortly after the Russian Revolution of 1917 (lines 4–8), which may have confirmed his sense of imminent change and of a new beginning of an unpredictable nature (Yeats expected the new era to be violent and despotic).   **12. *Spiritus Mundi*:** Latin, "the spirit of the universe." Yeats believed in a Great Memory, a universal storehouse of symbolic images from the past. Individuals, drawing on it for images, are put in touch with the soul of the universe.

Al Young b. 1939

A Dance for Ma Rainey°   [1969]

I'm going to be just like you, Ma
Rainey this monday morning
clouds puffing up out of my head
like those balloons
that float above the faces of white people   5
in the funnypapers

I'm going to hover in the corners
of the world, Ma
& sing from the bottom of hell
up to the tops of high heaven   10
& send out scratchless waves of yellow
& brown & that basic black honey
misery

I'm going to cry so sweet
& so low   15
& so dangerous,
Ma,
that the message is going to reach you
back in 1922
where you shimmer   20
snaggle-toothed
perfumed &
powdered
in your bauble beads

hair pressed & tied back   25
throbbing with that sick pain
I know
& hide so well
that pain that blues
jives the world with   30
aching to be heard
that downness
that bottomlessness
first felt by some stolen delta nigger
swamped under with redblooded american agony;   35
reduced to the sheer shit

Ma Rainey: Gertrude "Ma" Rainey (1886–1939), American singer known as the "Mother of
the Blues."

of existence
that bred
& battered us all,
Ma,   40
the beautiful people
our beautiful brave black people
who no longer need to jazz
or sing to themselves in murderous vibrations
or play the veins of their strong tender arms   45
with needles
to prove we're still here

Ray A. Young Bear   b. 1950

Green Threatening Clouds   [1990]

"Paint these green threatening clouds
a rose color," said Elvia near my shoulder.
"I mean around the fluffy sides to at least
give credence to these ceramic-looking pitchers
and their red corrugated brims. And how will you   5
convey the phenomena of luminous mountain plants
when they're nocturnal?"
She had two good points as far
as biology and the dispersal of colors
was concerned, but I was debating where   10
to hang the pitchers whose poisonous
contents, if consumed, would make this
jungle a lovely place to close one's eyes
in permanence and see that far-ahead time
when gravity-wise hawks would splinter   15
my hip bone against a mountainside
repeatedly for marrow access,
a time in respect when young bull
elks would nudge their antlers against
my half-submerged and decayed antlers   20
in the tundra, a time when my arctic
shadow would claim pieces of ice
as descendants and incubate them,
arguing with any penguin over
their ownership . . .   25

Outside, a Midwestern cardinal hovered
under the roof of my parent's prayer lodge

and delicately manuveured itself to the tip
of an icicle for a nonexistent drop of water.
In the snow-covered garden, a bluejay   30
disappeared into a brittle corn husk
and gave it momentary life, but none
was received from a dance made from
hunger. (Here we cannot migrate
to low altitude for tropical weather   35
and abundant food. Instead, like cultures
who wait for their savior, we wait for
a young man who has a neverending source
of food in his Magic Tablecloth.)
In our efforts to help the hungry birds,   40
we impale a slice of bread on a treelimb,
but it freezes and becomes a violent wind
sculpture. At thirteen below zero, a poorly
clothed child walks by with a lonely sled
in hand.   45

And then Elvia began talking about Saskatchewan.
"I dreamt of a large green eagle, and it was
speaking to me in French. I understood that
the eagle was an elder, who had flown *down*
in response to a song when a person is allowed   50
to leave its body."
"Does such a song exist?" I questioned.
"Of course," she replied. "Green. Such an
important color."

READING POEMS IN TRANSLATION

American humorist James Thurber was approached once by a French-
man who said to him, "I've read you both in English and in French, and
frankly, I prefer the translation." Thurber replied, "Yes, I know. I always lose
something in the original."

What is the difference between the original and the translated version
of any work? We often hear that something is, in the words of the popular 2003 film, "lost in translation." According to Robert Frost, in an often-
quoted line, "Poetry is what gets lost in translation." Or is something
gained? One thing is certain: The debate over translations of works has been
going on for ages, and there is no end in sight to the discussion.

What are some of the issues? Some say that literary texts should be read
only in the language in which they were originally written. They argue that
"capturing" or recreating a work of art through translation is impossible.

The only way to read and understand and truthfully experience and appreciate a work of literary art is to learn the language it was written in.

Provocative political agendas can be connected to the work of translation. Some people argue that unless one is from or deeply immersed in the culture underlying the original work, one has no right translating. Others say that one at least must be fluent in the language of the original; not to be is at the very least an act of disrespect. And yet translations are made by people who hardly know the language, who rely heavily on a lexicon.

Another danger claimed for translation is that the translator can readily commit an act of cultural appropriation or impose her or his own cultural influences or beliefs on those of the original, twisting the meaning, intent, or effect. Yet others ask, how else, without translation and without learning every language on earth, can we enrich and expand our own lives in the ways offered by reading works from other cultures?

Therefore, translations do exist, even abound. Each year new versions of the *Divine Comedy* or *Beowulf* or the poetry of Rumi or Neruda are rendered in English. *Are* they the same as the originals? Better? Misrepresentations? Improvements on past translations? None of the above?

If you were to translate a literary work, for example, how would you go about it? Would you translate it literally? If so, how would you handle the complexity of imagery? Images are often "culture-bound" so that translating *snow* into the equivalent word in another language, or vice versa, may not come even close to what the implications are in the original. And what about the nuances of tone? You know that the way one word or phrase hits you may differ from the way it strikes someone else. How does one translate tone?

If you were translating a poem rather than prose, imagine how much more complex the issues would be given line length, line breaks, how crucial rhythms are to every line, how one image that is also a metaphor could suggest something very different in another language, how symbols vary from culture to culture. Prose allows a bit more room for communicating its meaning through context; however, one slight change in a poem could alter the entire work. In theory, that could be said also for prose, but in the most practical sense, this kind of loss of nuance or meaning or implication is more likely to affect the reading and resulting interpretation in a poem.

Almost anyone would agree that translation is an act of enormous responsibility that requires great skill, for it is very easy to distort or mislead or misinform. What, then, are the parameters? What liberties, if any, can the translator take? What about interpretation? What does a translator do if it is clear that the particular wording could lead to an interpretation not justified by the original? What if the translator believes that the best word in English is not the equivalent word because the equivalent word does not carry the tone or associations or sound or impact of the original? What if *sassafras* is, in the mind of the translator, a more effective image, closer to the original than the literal *palm tree*? Or in a drama, what if the characters' use of slang or a political metaphor or way of praising or cursing another character can't be translated literally? What then?

Translation is indeed fraught with complexities and issues. It might be useful and instructive for you to try translating a work of literature, and then to write in your journal about the issues you ran into, the decisions you discovered you had to make, and the dilemmas you found yourself facing.

What is lost then in translation? Likely a lot. What is gained? Likely a valuable opportunity to enter into worlds other than our own, something very important for sure. Or maybe there are even those rare times, as Thurber said, when what is lost was in the original and what was gained was in the translation.

POEMS IN TRANSLATION

Anna Akhmatova   Russia, 1889–1966

The Song of the Last Meeting   [1911]

Translated by Judith Hemschemeyer

Then helplessly my breast grew cold,
But my steps were light.
I pulled the glove for my left hand
Onto my right.

There seemed to be many steps,   5
But I knew — there were only three!
The whisper of autumn in the maples
Was pleading: "Die with me!"

I am betrayed by my doleful,
Fickle, evil fate.   10
I answered: "Darling, darling!
I too. I will die with you . . ."

This is the song of the last meeting.
I glanced at the dark house.
Candles were burning only in the bedroom,   15
With an indifferent-yellow flame.

September 29, 1911
Tsarskoye Selo

Yehuda Amichai   Israel, b. 1924

Wildpeace   [1971]

Translated by Chana Bloch and Stephen Mitchell

Not the peace of a cease-fire,
not even the vision of the wolf and the lamb,
but rather
as in the heart when the excitement is over
and you can talk only about a great weariness.   5
I know that I know how to kill,
that makes me an adult.
And my son plays with a toy gun that knows
how to open and close its eyes and say Mama.
A peace   10
without the big noise of beating swords into ploughshares,
without words, without
the thud of the heavy rubber stamp: let it be
light, floating, like lazy white foam.
A little rest for the wounds —   15
who speaks of healing?
(And the howl of the orphans is passed from one generation
to the next, as in a relay race:
the baton never falls.)

Let it come   20
like wildflowers,
suddenly, because the field
must have it: wildpeace.

Reza Baraheni   Iran, b. 1935

Autumn in Tehran   [1993]

Translated by the poet

at first   a puzzling whisper   started   in the wind   and in the leaves
        seeming young and green
then the sick sneezes came   from carefree street kids   who lay in
        bed a few days later
defining such people's eyes   suits only minds in love with music
as the wind blew it whirled deep tears within weakened eyes   of
        retired old men in the parks
as if an eternal mourning had rained on their cheeks   5

the women hurried   the queue became restless   they were shivering
in the wind   the leaves seeming young and green   eyeless and
    drenched   watched the women
piece by piece they consoled the women   in   grammarless, stammering
    tongues
down deserted alleys   young women in love   drove their shoulders
    into the cavities of their lovers' chests
— it suddenly got cold   I'm cold   aren't you cold?   aren't you? —   10
— no, I'm still hot   hot from your kisses   kisses   still   still
then a blatant crow flew in the horizon   drew its dagger at the
    swallows
and savaged the routes of the air with the convex dagger of its beak
the crow screamed: here comes the season of scorched space   I am
    your emperor!
the looting of the branches began in the evening   15
as though there was no end to it
it poured down in the sparkling of rain and wind   in the street lights
millions of small, wet and colourful balancing scales   descended
    from the sky
men with bare heads, having no umbrellas   walked with newspapers
    over their heads
the night drove freshets from the bright north   down the world's
    dark souths   20
and the next day   world streets were filled with water
and the fresh perfume of the season rose   from the retreats of
    leaves
a strange siesta gripped the world and carried it off
in the anguished hour   the arrow of the haggard autumn man's
    stick   drove into death's running stream

and the next day   in Darakeh,° when a young woman showed me
    the sun   that had just spread on death's color feast   I wept   25
I was not used to the death of so many worlds
the sun came from every side and every angle
and launched a huge ship of leaves off the coast of the Alborz°
    precipice   down the seas of my eyes
the eyes wept blood   with the colors of the leaves
[season! you obstinate season in the home of dreams!   dream!
    obstinate dream in the seasons of water!   yellow leaves   falling
    on my shoulders   when I am no more!]   30

---

25. Darakeh: Village on the northwestern part of Tehran, famous for its beauty, its tea-houses and restaurants, a visiting place of students, writers, and intellectuals of the capital Tehran. Ironically, it overlooks the horrendous Evin prison, where many intellectuals have been shot by both the previous Monarchist and the present Islamic regime in Iran. [Poet's note.]   **28. Alborz:** The mountain on the north of Tehran. [Poet's note.]

I wept — without grasping the meaning of this mass of decay   this
    expansion of volumes —
beheaded   my lovely peacocks   floated down the waves
and a duplicitous parrot   mimicked the sun   from a hidden sky
I wept   without grasping their meaning

who?   who is that coming on the flanks   lonely   burning
    wavering?   35
the queen of this Shaman?   This Ozan's° lover?
no! no!
cover the height of the young leaf   in the cloak of dying love!
bury it!
throw the dust of the body to the wind and water!   40
I was not used to the death of so many worlds
unable to grasp the meaning of all this!

---

36. **Ozan:** Ozan means "poet" in Azeri Turkish, the language spoken in the northwestern part of Iran, as well as by half of the population of Tehran, the capital of Iran. [Poet's note.]

Bei Dao   China, b. 1949

Night: Theme and Variations   [1981]

Translated by Bonnie S. McDougall

Here the roads converge
parallel beams of light
are a longwinded but abruptly interrupted dialogue
suffused with the drivers' pungent smoke
and rough muttered curses   5
railings have replaced the queues
the lamplight seeping out from between cracks in the doorboards
is cast with the cigarette butts onto the roadside
for nimble feet to tread on
an old man's forgotten walking stick against a billboard   10
looks as if it were ready to go
the stone waterlily has withered
in the fountain tall buildings slowly topple
the rising moon suddenly strikes
the hour again and again   15
arousing ancient Time inside the palace wall
the sundial calibrates errors as it turns
waiting for the grand rite of the dawn
brocade dress ribbons stand up rustling in the wind

brushing away the dust from the stone steps   20
the shadow of a tramp slinks past the wall
red and green neon lights blaze for him
and keep him from sleeping all night
a lost cat scurries up a bench
gazing down at the smoke-soft gleam of the waves   25
but the mercury vapour-lamp rudely opening the curtain
to peer at the secrets that others store
disturbs the dream wakens the lonely
behind a small door
a hand gently draws the catch   30
as if pulling a rifle bolt

Jorge Luis Borges   Argentina, 1899–1986

The Other Tiger   [1960]

Translated by Alastair Reid

And the craft createth a semblance.
— *Morris*, Sigurd the Volsung (*1876*)

I think of a tiger. The fading light enhances
the vast complexities of the Library
and seems to set the bookshelves at a distance;
powerful, innocent, bloodstained, and new-made,
it will prowl through its jungle and its morning   5
and leave its footprint on the muddy edge
of a river with a name unknown to it
(in its world, there are no names, nor past, nor future,
only the sureness of the present moment)
and it will cross the wilderness of distance   10
and sniff out in the woven labyrinth
of smells the smell peculiar to morning
and the scent on the air of deer, delectable.
Behind the lattice of bamboo, I notice
its stripes, and I sense its skeleton   15
under the magnificence of the quivering skin.
In vain the convex oceans and the deserts
spread themselves across the earth between us;
from this one house in a far-off seaport
in South America, I dream you, follow you,   20
oh tiger on the fringes of the Ganges.

Evening spreads in my spirit and I keep thinking
that the tiger I am calling up in my poem
is a tiger made of symbols and of shadows,
a set of literary images,   25
scraps remembered from encyclopedias,
and not the deadly tiger, the fateful jewel
that in the sun or the deceptive moonlight
follows its paths, in Bengal or Sumatra,
of love, of indolence, of dying.   30
Against the tiger of symbols I have set
the real one, the hot-blooded one
that savages a herd of buffalo,
and today, the third of August, '59,
its patient shadow moves across the plain,   35
but yet, the act of naming it, of guessing
what is its nature and its circumstance
creates a fiction, not a living creature,
not one of those that prowl on the earth.

Let us look for a third tiger. This one   40
will be a form in my dream like all the others,
a system, an arrangement of human language,
and not the flesh-and-bone tiger
that, out of reach of all mythologies,
paces the earth. I know all this; yet something   45
drives me to this ancient, perverse adventure,
foolish and vague, yet still I keep on looking
throughout the evening for the other tiger,
the other tiger, the one not in this poem.

Julia de Burgos   Puerto Rico, 1914–1953

Returning   [1947]

Translated by Dwight García and Margarite Fernández Olmos

     Indefinitely,
extended like shadows and waves,
sunburnt in salt and foam and impossible skulls,
my sadness grows sadder;
this orbitless sadness which is mine   5
since the world became mine,
since darkness blazed my name,

since the first cause for all tears
came to be my own.

    It's as if I'd like to love   10
and the wind doesn't let me.
It's as if I'd like to return
and yet can't discover why, nor where to.
It's as if I'd like to follow the course of the waters
yet all thirst is gone.   15

    Indefinitely . . .

A word so mine;
ghostly specter of my specter!

    There's no longer a voice,
or tears,   20
or distant sprigs of grain.
No more shipwrecks,
or echoes,
not even anguish;
silence itself is dead!   25

    What say you, my soul, should I flee?
Where could I go where I would not be
shadowing my own shadow?

Faiz Ahmed Faiz   Pakistan, 1911–1984

A Prison Daybreak   [1952]

Translated by Agha Shahid Ali

Night wasn't over
when the moon stood beside my bed
and said, "You've drunk your sleep to the dregs,
your share of that wine is finished for this night."

My eyes tore themselves from a dream of passion —   5
they said farewell to my lover's image, still
lingering in the night's stagnant waters
that were spread, like a sheet, over the earth.
Silver whirlpools began their dervish dance
as lotuses of stars fell from the moon's hands.   10
Some sank. Some rose to the surface,

floated, and opened their petals.
Night and daybreak had fallen desperately
into each other's arms.

In the courtyard,   15
the prisoners emerged slowly
from a backdrop of gloom. They were shining,
for the dew of sleep had washed, for that moment,
all grief for their country from their eyes,
all agony of separation from their lovers.   20

But there's a drum, far off. A siren wails.
The famished guards, their faces pale,
begin their reluctant rounds, in step
with stifled screams from torture rooms.
The cries of those who'll be broken on the rack awake   25
just as light breezes intoxicated with sleep awake.
Poison awakes. Nothing in the world is asleep.
A door opens in the distance, another is shut.
A chain rasps, then shrieks.
A knife opens a lock's heart, far off,   30
and a window begins to break its head,
like a madman, against the wind.

So it is the enemies of life awake
and crush the delicate spirit
that keeps me company in my barren despair   35
while the prisoners and I wait, all day and night,
for a rebel prince of legends to come
with burning arrows, ready to pierce
these tyrant hearts of stone and steel.

Nazim Hikmet   Turkey, 1902–1963

Letters from a Man in Solitary   [1938]

Translated by Randy Blasing and Mutlu Konuk

1

I carved your name on my watchband
with my fingernail.
Where I am, you know,
I don't have a pearl-handled jackknife
(they won't give me anything sharp)   5
        or a plane tree with its head in the clouds.

Trees may grow in the yard,
but I'm not allowed
                    to see the sky overhead . . .
How many others are in this place?   10
I don't know.
I'm alone far from them,
they're all together far from me.
To talk to anyone besides myself
                    is forbidden.   15
So I talk to myself.
But I find my conversation so boring,
            my dear wife, that I sing songs.
And what do you know,
that awful, always off-key voice of mine   20
            touches me so
                    that my heart breaks.
And just like the barefoot orphan
      lost in the snow
in those old sad stories, my heart   25
—with moist blue eyes
and a little red runny nose—
            wants to snuggle up in your arms.
It doesn't make me blush
                  that right now   30
            I'm this weak,
                  this selfish,
                        this *human* simply.

No doubt my state can be explained
physiologically, psychologically, etc.   35
Or maybe it's
            this barred window,
                  this earthen jug,
                        these four walls,
            which for months have kept me from hearing   40
            another human voice.

It's five o'clock, my dear.
Outside,
            with its dryness,
                        eerie whispers,   45
                              mud roof,
and lame, skinny horse
      standing motionless in infinity
—I mean, it's enough to drive the man inside crazy with grief—

outside, with all its machinery and all its art,   50
a plains night comes down red on treeless space.

Again today, night will fall in no time.
A light will circle the lame, skinny horse.
And the treeless space, in this hopeless landscape
stretched out before me like the body of a hard man,   55
will suddenly be filled with stars.
We'll reach the inevitable end once more,
which is to say the stage is set
again today for an elaborate nostalgia.
Me,   60
the man inside,
once more I'll exhibit my customary talent,
and singing an old-fashioned lament
in the reedy voice of my childhood,
once more, by God, it will crush my unhappy heart   65
to hear you inside my head,
so far
away, as if I were watching you
                    in a smoky, broken mirror . . .

2

It's spring outside, my dear wife, spring.   70
Outside on the plain, suddenly the smell
of fresh earth, birds singing, etc.
It's spring, my dear wife,
the plain outside sparkles . . .
And inside the bed comes alive with bugs,   75
                    the water jug no longer freezes,
and in the morning sun floods the concrete . . .
The sun —
every day till noon now
it comes and goes   80
from me, flashing off
                    and on . . .
And as the day turns to afternoon, shadows climb the walls,
the glass of the barred window catches fire,
                    and it's night outside,   85
                    a cloudless spring night . . .
And inside this is spring's darkest hour.
In short, the demon called freedom,
with its glittering scales and fiery eyes,
possesses the man inside   90

especially in spring . . .
I know this from experience, my dear wife,
                    from experience . . .

3

Sunday today.
Today they took me out in the sun for the first time.   95
And I just stood there, struck for the first time in my life
                    by how far away the sky is,
                    how blue
                    and how wide.
Then I respectfully sat down on the earth.   100
I leaned back against the wall.
For a moment no trap to fall into,
no struggle, no freedom, no wife.
Only earth, sun, and me . . .
I am happy.   105

Miroslav Holub   Czech Republic, b. 1923

Elementary School Field Trip
to the Dinosaur Exhibit   [1996]

Translated by David Young and Miroslav Holub

Jurassic
roar.

Answered by
St. Georges
or Rambos.

Only one   5
glum little boy,
evidently blind,
is lifted to the Triceratops
to breathlessly run his hand   10
up and down the skull,
over the bony collar,
the horns above the eyes,
the skin-folds on the neck,

the boy's face   15
is insanely blank,

but the hand already knows
that nothing is in the mind
that hasn't been in the senses,
that giants are pinkish-gray   20
like Händel's Concerto Grosso
that life is just a step aside
just like mother
always said.

Triceratops,   25
Abel's younger brother.

Dark in there, in
the midbrain:
the last dinosaur
meeting the last man.   30

Taslima Nasrin Bangladesh, b. 1962

Things Cheaply Had   [1991]

Translated from the Bengali by Carolyne Wright,
Mohammad Nurul Hada, and Taslima Nasrin

In the market nothing can be had as cheap as women.
If they get a small bottle of *alta*° for their feet
                they spend three nights sleepless for sheer joy.
If they get a few bars of soap to scrub their skin
                and some scented oil for their hair   5
they become so submissive that they scoop out
                chunks of their flesh
to be sold in the flea market twice a week.
If they get a jewel for their nose
                they lick feet for seventy days or so,   10
a full three and a half months
                if it's a single striped sari.°

---

2. *alta:* Lac-dye, a red liquid with which South Asian women decorate the borders of their feet on ceremonial occasions, such as weddings and dance performances. Alta is more in vogue among Hindus, but Bangladeshi women also use it, and it can be seen on the feet of Muslim heroines and harem women in Moghul miniature paintings. [Translator's note.] **12. sari:** A garment worn chiefly by women in India and Pakistan consisting of a long cloth wrapped around the body with one end draped over one shoulder or the head.

Even the mangy cur of the house barks now and then,
and over the mouths of women cheaply had
                        there's a lock   15
a golden lock.

Octavio Paz   Mexico, 1914–1998

The Street   [1938–1946]

Translated by Muriel Rukeyser

A long and silent street.
I walk in blackness and I stumble and fall
and rise, and I walk blind, my feet
stepping on silent stones and dry leaves.
Someone behind me also stepping on stones, leaves: 5
if I slow down, he slows;
if I run, he runs. I turn: nobody.
Everything dark and doorless.
Turning and turning among these corners
which lead forever to the street   10
where nobody waits for, nobody follows me,
where I pursue a man who stumbles
and rises and says when he sees me: nobody

Dahlia Ravikovitch   Israel, b. 1936

Clockwork Doll   [1959]

Translated by Chana Bloch and Ariel Bloch

That night, I was a clockwork doll
and I whirled around, this way and that,
and I fell on my face and shattered to bits
and they tried to fix me with all their skill.

Then I was a proper doll once again   5
and I did what they told me, poised and polite.
But I was a doll of a different sort,
an injured twig that dangles from a stem.

And then I went to dance at the ball,
but they left me alone with the dogs and cats   10
though my steps were measured and rhythmical.

———————————

And I had blue eyes and golden hair
and a dress all the colors of garden flowers,
and a trimming of cherries on my straw hat.

Masaoka Shiki   Japan, 1867–1902

Haiku   [1891–1899]

Translated by Burton Watson

1891 Summer

In cleft on cleft,
on rock face after rock face —
wild azaleas

1892 Summer

From the firefly
in my hands,
cold light

1893 Spring

Deserted temple
where the bell's been stolen —
cherries just opening

1893 Spring

Under my sandal soles
the sweet smell
of meadow grasses

1895 Spring

A train goes by,
its smoke curling
around the new tree leaves

1899 Summer

I think I'll die
eating apples,
in the presence of peonies

Wislawa Szymborska   Poland, b. 1923

The End and the Beginning   [1993]

Translated by Stanislaw Barańczak and Clare Cavanagh

After every war
someone has to tidy up.
Things won't pick
themselves up, after all.

Someone has to shove   5
the rubble to the roadsides
so the carts loaded with corpses
can get by.

Someone has to trudge
through sludge and ashes,   10
through the sofa springs,
the shards of glass,
the bloody rags.

Someone has to lug the post
to prop the wall,   15
someone has to glaze the window,
set the door in its frame.

No sound bites, no photo opportunities,
and it takes years.
All the cameras have gone   20
to other wars.

The bridges need to be rebuilt,
the railroad stations, too.
Shirtsleeves will be rolled
to shreds.   25

Someone, broom in hand,
still remembers how it was.
Someone else listens, nodding
his unshattered head.
But others are bound to be bustling nearby   30
who'll find all that
a little boring.

From time to time someone still must
dig up a rusted argument
from underneath a bush   35
and haul it off to the dump.

Those who knew
what this was all about
must make way for those
who know little.   40
And less than that.
And at last nothing less than nothing.

Xu Gang   China, b. 1945

Red Azalea on the Cliff   [1982]

Translated by Fang Dai, Dennis Ding, and Edward Morin

Red azalea, smiling
From the cliffside at me,
You make my heart shudder with fear!
A body could smash and bones splinter in the canyon—
Beauty, always looking on at disaster.   5

But red azalea on the cliff,
That you comb your twigs even in a mountain gale
Calms me down a bit.
Of course you're not wilfully courting danger,
Nor are you at ease with whatever happens to you.   10
You're merely telling me: beauty is nature.

Would anyone like to pick a flower
To give to his love
Or pin to his own lapel?
On the cliff there is no road   15
And no azalea grows where there is a road.
If someone actually reached that azalea,
Then an azalea would surely bloom in his heart.

Red azalea on the cliff,
You smile like the Yellow Mountains,   20
Whose sweetness encloses slyness,
Whose intimacy embraces distance.
You remind us all of our first love.
Sometimes the past years look
Just like the azalea on the cliff.   25

May 1982
Yellow Mountain
Revised at Hangzhou

Approaching
DRAMA

PART **4**

Overleaf: David Henry Hwang visiting a Seattle theater production of M. Butterfly, which won a Tony Award for Best Play in 1988 and established him as a major contemporary American playwright. In an interview he describes the common thread that runs throughout his work: "One of the most important themes . . . is the fluidity of identity. You can think you're one person, but in a different social context you can be transformed into somebody you may not recognize, somebody completely different." (See page 1541 for a short biography.) Photo copyright © by Michael Romanos.

Live performance is still the most organic of all the media. Because it's not done with machines or editing, it's got all the imperfections, all the mistakes, and all the magic of real talent.

Live performance is still the most organic of all the media. Because it's not done with machines or editing, it's got all the imperfections, all the mistakes, and all the magic of real talent.

John Leguizamo

Reading Drama

Participating in a Playful Pretense

CHAPTER 20

"The play's the thing," said Hamlet many centuries ago, and it still is today. Drama has captured the minds, hearts, and imaginations of people since the times of the ancient Greeks. In drama, then and now, people and actions "come to life" in a form that entertains and challenges. As we laugh, cry, fear, hope, and despair with the characters of a drama, our own hopes, dreams, and fears are touched and our own lives enriched and enlarged. And that happens not only by attending a production, but by reading a play as well. Duplicating the complex, interactive experience that live theater creates may be impossible when reading a play; but you can approximate it by holding that live experience as the ideal, trying to achieve imaginatively as much of it as possible as you bring the characters and actions to life in the home theater of your mind.

WHAT IS DRAMA?

Drama is one of the oldest forms of verbal art. From earliest times, people have enjoyed pretending, or "acting something out." This "let's pretend" became more highly developed as people planned and organized their playacting for the benefit and entertainment of an audience, composing words to say and instructions on how to move about. Such acting is recognized for its value to entertain, educate, and enlighten.

Drama has deep connections to religion: Greek tragedy grew out of the worship of Dionysus, Passover reenacts the flight of the Israelites from Egypt, and the Catholic Mass is a dramatic enactment of the sacrificial death of Christ. Drama enables an audience to participate, vicariously, in some of the deeply meaningful archetypal or mythic events in cultural history. Drama is a basic form of verbal art, and performance was a viable way to present one's work before the printing press made wide dissemination of texts possible. Thus a study of literature is not complete without including written plays.

DRAMA AS PERFORMANCE   Drama differs from fiction and poetry because it includes physical activity. The word *drama* derives from the Greek word meaning "to do, act, or perform." From the time of the Greeks, *drama* was used to describe literary works that could be acted out or performed — either one such work ("a Shakespearean drama") or a group of such works ("Elizabethan drama"). The word *play* (from an Old English word meaning "to be active and engaged") is also used for dramatic works, but it is a narrower term than *drama*. A **play** is a drama intended for performance before a theatrical audience. All plays are dramas, but some dramas are not plays. **Closet dramas**, for example, are meant to be read as literary works, not acted out in theaters.

WATCHING A PERFORMANCE   Watching "live action" on the stage differs from watching film, video, or television — it demands a different use of imagination and intellect. At a play, the viewer constantly makes decisions about who or what to pay particular attention to, whether to focus in on one character's expressions or "pan out" to take in the entire stage. Trying to notice everything important and not to miss key words, glances, or gestures, in addition to responding emotionally to characters and situations, can be exhausting as well as exhilarating. In film, you watch what the camera shows you; the decisions you would make if you were watching a dramatic stage production are made by the camera's eye instead.

RISKS IN PERFORMANCE   Live theater also has a kind of "suspense of production" that film lacks. An actor risks missing a line or tripping during an entrance. Mistakes lead to another "take" in filming or are cut out, but in live theater they're evident for all to see. Actors live with the anxiety of potential embarrassment and enjoy the challenge of either coming through flawlessly or recovering beautifully from a slip. But audience members feel some anxiety too. They don't want to see actors embarrassed or the effect of the performance damaged, so in the back of their minds is the hope everything will go well (and a twinge of fear that it won't). There is no such anxiety in watching a film — we know all the slips, at least those that were caught, have been edited away.

AUDIENCE INTERACTION   Also, the audience at a live theater, by responding emotionally and imaginatively to the action on stage, makes a contribution to performance. Actors in live theater are aware of and energized by an involved, appreciative audience. A mutual synergy develops between actors and audience that leads to a deeper experience for both.

READING A PLAY   There is no question about it: All that a performance involves cannot be duplicated in reading a play. But awareness of what happens in a real theater enhances one's reading of a play. Reading a play well does take a lot of imaginative participation. Does it require more than fiction or poetry? Such comparisons aren't helpful, in the end. An active reader pours her- or himself into whatever reading is at hand. Drama, like all literature, demands a lot of a reader, but the rewards are well worth it.

WHY READ DRAMA?

Plays can be hard to read. One reason for this is that the majority of plays are not meant primarily to be read. The heart of drama is *impersonation*—plays usually are written to be seen and heard as dramatic productions. When we read a play, we assume that there is value in treating a play as a literary work. In reading a play, we concentrate on the words, not on the performance. Those words embody the pure play, the play as written rather than as cut and rearranged and interpreted for a particular performance; the words last and remain the same. Reading allows us to pause and reflect, to go back and look at earlier lines, to do the kind of close analysis of structure, characters, and style we've been doing for stories and poems.

One of the most exciting types of theaters is the theater of your mind and imagination. Here you can stage, direct, and perform whatever play you are reading. Reading the texts of plays has long been regarded as an enjoyable and valuable thing to do. But we need to recognize from the start that this kind of reading differs from reading stories and poems. Imagining a play requires particular reading skills and approaches.

ACTIVE READING: Drama

A play is a "dramatic work": That is, it doesn't *tell* a story and doesn't have a narrator the way narrative does. A play *acts out* a story, bringing the people and events to life, imaginatively, on a stage. The text of a play looks different from the way a story or a poem looks on the page.

- *Consider the cast.* The first thing you see in most cases is the cast of characters, the *dramatis personae* (the "persons of the drama"), a list of the people who appear in the drama. The same list is included in the program when you attend a theater performance, with the names of the actors who play the roles.

A good starting point for reading (or watching) a play is to go through the list carefully, trying to remember the names of the characters and their relationships with each other. When reading a play with a large cast of characters, such as a play by Shakespeare, some people jot down names and diagram their relationships on a slip of paper for easy reference.

- *Pay attention to stage directions.* After listing the cast of characters, the printed play may offer some "stage directions," a description of what the playwright visualizes for the scenery on the stage and perhaps the age and appearance of the characters and the way they are dressed, sometimes even a personality characteristic. These are intended, of course, as guidelines for the director, set designer, and costume designer in planning how to produce the work on the stage. When reading a play, you need to fill these roles yourself and imagine the actors, their stage movements, the set design, and the costumes.

  You are likely to find more extensive stage directions in a modern play than in one by Sophocles or Shakespeare. A dramatist always writes to fit the facilities available at the time (the kind of theater, scenery, and stage machinery). The scenery Sophocles or Shakespeare could count on was less elaborate than what came later, so they often used imagery in the text to indicate the scene. For example, many Elizabethan plays were acted in open-air theaters during the afternoon, so to indicate darkness Shakespeare has a character say that it's dark and may have someone carry a lantern. The directions included in modern plays vary widely. Some playwrights go into extensive detail illustrating everything from the color of the walls to the type of table sitting in a corner of a room, to the lighting and atmosphere they think is appropriate. Others may offer the sparest generalizations: "a room, some furniture."

- *Use your imagination.* Your imagination functions differently for a play than for a story or poem. The texts of stories, because they are meant to be read, include descriptions to help along your imagination ("the short, heavy man with stringy brown hair plodded up the dimly lighted staircase"). A play assumes you are seeing the character on the stage, so it doesn't provide the same description. In watching a play, the role of the imagination is to accept the pretense that the actor really is the character and that what you see on the stage really is a kitchen or a forest. One of the challenges in reading a play is picturing the scene and characters in your mind. Stage directions help you to visualize the characters and action in your imagination.

- *Read the lines.* After the stage directions come the lines of the play itself, the script the actors memorize as they prepare to perform the play on the stage, together with further stage directions for particular actions (including entrances and exits). What you see on the page is the name of the character, followed by words indicating what the character says or does. In reading the text of a play, first look at the name of the speaker — notice who and what the character is; then go on to what the character says. As you keep reading, use your intellect and imagination to connect the speeches to each other. Watch for interactions between characters and for the ways the diction varies among characters. Just as when you read a story, you will come to experience the characters extending and developing as they reply to what other characters say.

- *Imagine the action.* The characters will expand and develop also as you imagine the movements that would take place on the stage: people arriving and leaving, meeting each other, moving at various paces and with particular styles of movement and gestures, embracing or assaulting each other, using props, and interacting with the set. Remember always that this is a drama: You are observing the characters on the stage of your imagination as they act out a scene of considerable importance in the life of at least one of them.

REREADING: Drama

To experience a play fully, you need to read it more than once. As with a story or poem, during the first reading you primarily concentrate on what's going on. Only on the second or third time through do you begin to appreciate fully what the work offers. Many of the suggestions for rereading fiction and poetry (pp. 58–59 and 544–45) apply to rereading drama as well. We comment here on how they apply particularly to rereading a play.

- *The second time you read a play, slow down.* The first time through you usually read fast because you want to find out what happens to the characters as they deal with a dramatic situation. You probably don't pay close attention to the way characters are expressing themselves or to the subtleties embedded in their speeches. Like poets and story writers, dramatists write carefully — each phrase is thoughtfully shaped and every word counts. On second reading, linger on speeches to enjoy the style, to catch the nuances that reveal subtleties in character, and to notice details that foreshadow later events that you now realize are significant.

- *Pay attention to little things.* The second time through, you can be more alert for easily overlooked details, things most readers do not notice the first time, and to the subtlety of techniques the author uses. (The same thing is true of watching a play. Seeing it a second time — like watching a movie a second or third or tenth time — helps you to appreciate it more fully.) You notice new things during subsequent readings — especially little things, like a gesture or an item on a table in act 1 that turns out to be significant in act 3. What may appear at first reading to be merely a set or stage direction, on rereading, is recognized to be of wider significance and thus is experienced more meaningfully.

- *Be selective about parts to reread, if you have to.* Because of the length of a three- or five-act play, it may be difficult to find the time to reread the whole work. In some cases (if you need to write a long paper studying the play thoroughly, for example), you'll need to find the time for a complete rereading. In other cases, if you can't reread the entire play, at least reread scenes and passages that are crucial to revealing character traits or plot development.

- *Remember the reading strategies we gave you for fiction and poetry.* Pay attention to the title; look up things that aren't familiar; research people, times, and places that relate to the plot; notice the opening and closing lines; reflect on what the characters are like and what motivates them, on the organization of the plot, and on the significance of the actions and events.

- *Read some parts aloud.* Dramatic dialogue is meant to be heard. Reading sections of the play aloud, working to interpret the expression, rhythms, and tone effectively, will help you hear other parts more clearly and meaningfully in your mind's ear as you read silently. And it can be fun. Divide up the parts among a few of your friends and see what happens.

Action is eloquence.

William Shakespeare

Character, Conflict, and Dramatic Action

CHAPTER 21

Thinking about Who Does What to Whom and Why

Almost everyone enjoys watching stories acted out. Even if you don't attend live theater all that often, you probably watch television or movies. Television producers certainly recognize this appeal and place enormous importance on garnering huge audiences. Advertisers know it and tap into those shows that have the highest ratings, all because we love to watch everything from soaps to sitcoms to serious drama. There's something compelling about watching a skilled actor entering a role and bringing a character to life, making us laugh at comic characters and empathize with tragic ones.

Reading scripts can never substitute for watching an excellent performance: The script was meant for performance, after all. But reading plays has its own rewards, and learning to do it well is worth some effort. Whether you're watching or reading a play, the essential core is the same: character, conflict, and dramatic action. Drama usually focuses on characters, the created persons who appear or are referred to in a play. Those characters come to life primarily through conflict. And the conflict is presented through dramatic action on a stage, whether in a theater or in the imagination. You have already worked with conflict and character earlier in this book (see pp. 65–66 and 69–73). This chapter deals with how development of characters and conflicts is achieved through dialogue and dramatic action, the distinctive methods used by drama.

ENTRY POINTS   Plays and their productions are not always two hours (or more) in length and constructed in three or five acts. One-act plays — sometimes only ten or fifteen minutes in length — are an important theatrical form and work with the same elements as longer plays. The guidelines for reading a play laid out in Chapter 20, especially the section "Active Reading: Drama" (pp. 909–11), apply just as well to one-act plays as to three- or five-act plays. Practice applying the guidelines to the following very short play, *The New New.*

This script does not start with a list of characters: They are instead identified in the stage directions. If you attended a performance of the play, the program would most likely list the names of the five characters (and of the actor playing each role), in order of appearance: Jenny, Marcy, Bradley, Craig, and Naomi. Because the text gives no details about their ages or appearance, you will need to make decisions about these as you imagine the play, just as a director would in planning a performance.

The text says nothing about where or when the action takes place. It presumably could take place in any large city and at any time (the program at a performance might well state, after the list of characters, "Time: the present"). The stage directions (in italics) supply guidance about staging the action: It alternates between two offices on opposite sides of the stage. Your imagination can furnish the offices in any way you like, though a performance could get by with simply a table, a couple of chairs, and a telephone on each side.

It is a dramatic convention that, when a stage is divided this way, the audience will assume that characters on the one side cannot hear characters talking on the other side. You will need to use your imagination to move back and forth between the two offices. In a performance, such movement might be signaled by lighting the side of the stage in which characters are talking, while darkening the other side. However, for a simple performance without special lighting equipment, the characters' voices will draw the audience's attention from side to side without it.

As you read the play itself, pay attention to who is speaking and thus, in this case, which side of the stage is active at the moment. Also be sure to notice the stage directions. As an active reader, you'll need to know what is happening in the present, especially any conflicts that emerge. You will also need to piece together what has happened in the past, what has led up to the present situation, and to figure out what each character is like from what they say and do and what is said about them (including two important characters who do not appear on the stage). And you will want to reflect on the choices the characters are making and the values their words and actions reveal.

Kelly Stuart   b. 1961

The New New   [2002]

Jenny and Marcy in one "office" area — they are stapling brochures or doing some other type of repetitive office work. Bradley and Craig in another office — they are actually separated by a long corridor, but should be represented as being in isolated areas of the stage.

JENNY: I'm going to have an affair with him.

MARCY: But Jenny, you're failing his class.

JENNY: He says I can take an incomplete if I want, and he'll help me make it up over the summer.

BRADLEY: I need a new word for new.

CRAIG: Fresh.

BRADLEY: Too hip hop. This is more white.

CRAIG: (*Opening a thesaurus.*) Thesaurus check.

(*Naomi, a nervous, down-at-the-heels woman appears and stands, hoping to engage Marcy and Jenny's attention.*)

MARCY: Isn't he what, like, uh, married?

JENNY: Yeah, but we have this INTENSE CONNECTION. It's like, ECONOMICS is not my forte. I find the whole subject abysmal. But he's got this precision of mind and I want that. I think that's what's missing in me, and I'm so, like, attracted to that.

NAOMI: I'm here to see Bradley Zuckerman?

(*Jenny and Marcy look at her, deciding she's a nonentity.*)

CRAIG: (*Reading.*) Fresh, modern. Modernistic. Neoteric.

BRADLEY: Neoteric?

(*They shrug in unison. Craig continues.*)

CRAIG: Novel. Newfangled. Newsprung. Revived. Reinvigorating.

BRADLEY: ". . . Reinvigorated the genre of prison memoir."

CRAIG: That's stale.

BRADLEY: It's become stale to say something is NEW. What's the new new? We need the new NEW.

MARCY: Did you ask me a question?

NAOMI: Bradley Zuckerman?

MARCY: Do you have an appointment?

NAOMI: When is he back?

MARCY: Do you have an appointment?

NAOMI: When is he back?

JENNY: Do you have an appointment?

NAOMI: I'll wait.

MARCY: We discourage that.

JENNY: He's not coming in. He's with marketing. So you would simply be wasting your time.

NAOMI: Where's marketing?

(Marcy turns back to Jenny, leaving Naomi standing awkwardly. They whisper to each other, occasionally looking Naomi's way. Naomi watches. They giggle.)

BRADLEY: A laser-sharp vision. The voice. The, something, vision and voice. His. New. The . . . What. There's no more words.

CRAIG: I liked Neoteric.

BRADLEY: Nobody will know what that means.

CRAIG: A powerful neoteric account, of the agony behind prison walls.

BRADLEY: I'm sorry, that sounds like gobbledygook. Um . . . deadpan, self-deprecating and, witty. But it's also new and it's important we say that.

CRAIG: It's a first novel.

BRADLEY: It's a memoir.

CRAIG: Actually, we can't call it a memoir. It's a kind of memoiristic novel.

BRADLEY: Why can't we call it a memoir?

CRAIG: Legal affairs said —

BRADLEY: OK it's a novel in the form of a memoir, based on real-life authentic experience.

(Naomi continues to stand looking at the women. They ignore her. Their conversation has become audible again:)

JENNY: There is like, so much electricity there. When he's looking at me, it's like I get zapped.

MARCY: Well I really want you to meet this guy.

JENNY: The writer?

MARCY: Yeah. Jimmy.

BRADLEY: The absurdity and the agony of life as a convict.

CRAIG: Agony isn't a word that sells.

BRADLEY: Agonizing, and yet entertaining.

CRAIG: That sounds so *People* magazine.

(They scan a thesaurus.)

JENNY: What does he write about?

MARCY: Um, prison. Jail. The Penal system.

JENNY: Oh.

MARCY: He had like, an MBA from Yale but I think he was like, convicted of manslaughter.

JENNY: Oh. A murderer.

MARCY: Manslaughter. I think. It was accidental. Self Defense. Some kind of fight, with this guy named monster. This six foot two, three hundred pound monster. An accidental death that he was convicted of — I guess, I guess, he pled guilty.

JENNY: Oh.

MARCY: To spare something, more like, the death penalty. I mean, I guess he cut a deal.

(*Jenny notices Naomi staring at her.*)

JENNY: Can we help you with something else?

NAOMI: Who are you talking about?

MARCY: I'm going to have to ask you to leave, OK?

NAOMI: I need to see Bradley Zuckerman.

MARCY: Leave a number and go or I'll have to call security.

NAOMI: I'd like to know who you're talking about.

JENNY: Did you not hear us? Do we HAVE to call security?

(*Naomi abruptly leaves. The two women shake their heads in disgust.*)

MARCY: These people will do anything to make you take a manuscript. Anyway he's—he's just really charismatic and charming and smart. I mean, it is so odd, when you meet him, you'll see, what an odd juxtaposition to think of this guy in prison. I mean, I'm really FOND of him. And his writing is really super evocative of the, you know, of the Kafkaesque nature of life in prison. He's sexy too.

JENNY: So why don't you sleep with him?

MARCY: I'm trying to be monogamous now. And Bradley is like, editing his book. I can't do that. Sleep with the guy Bradley edits.

(*Naomi makes a cross past the stage. Disappears.*)

BRADLEY: I used to get these calls from prison, collect calls every Tuesday. I thought of these calls as my "Tuesdays with Jimmy." He was just this witty, sardonic ethnographer of prison life. Of the ingenuity. And the angle, the engagement I found with the theme of this—civilized business executive locked up with all these illiterate thugs, and how he survived.

CRAIG: I love that he used like, sales techniques.

BRADLEY: Yes.

CRAIG: Stuff he learned from corporate sales seminars: Body language mirroring.

BRADLEY: I guess it all works.

(*For a beat, they mirror each other's body language. Naomi enters and stares at them. They ignore her.*)

CRAIG: In a way it doesn't matter how we market this thing because film rights have already gone to Ben Stiller.

BRADLEY: Really?

CRAIG: Mike Medavoy loved it. The release will coincide with the movie.

BRADLEY: But that's . . . I mean, there's a literary value.

CRAIG: It's great. Ben Stiller.

BRADLEY: Ben Stiller. That's great.

NAOMI: Excuse me—

CRAIG: It's a comedy. That's how they see it. It's going to sell like a motherfucker.

NAOMI: Is this marketing?

CRAIG: Yes.

NAOMI: I'm looking for Bradley Zuckerman.

CRAIG: Bradley—

BRADLEY: He doesn't work here. You have the wrong department.

NAOMI: I was told he's in marketing.

MARCY: I just think you'd have more in common with him than with your economics professor.

JENNY: Why? Because he's a criminal?

MARCY: But he's not really.

BRADLEY: No, uh, he works in creative development.

NAOMI: But they said in his office that he was in here.

BRADLEY: No. He's not here. Have you seen him Craig?

CRAIG: Haven't seen him.

BRADLEY: Would you like to leave a message for him?

CRAIG: I'm sorry. You really can't wait here. Would you like to leave him a message? (*He hands her a notepad. She stands looking at it. She begins to write, furiously.*)

MARCY: Being convicted of manslaughter had nothing to do with the arc of his life. It was just, this aberration.

JENNY: Who did he kill again?

MARCY: This drug dealer guy. You're going to like him. I told him about you, he's interested in meeting you.

JENNY: So he's like, — out?

MARCY: On Parole.

(*Naomi has finished writing.*)

NAOMI: Will you make sure Bradley Zuckerman gets this?

BRADLEY: Certainly.

(*Naomi gives them the pad of paper and exits. The men giggle.*)

BRADLEY: Oh my God that was close.

CRAIG: "No I'm not Bradley."

BRADLEY: "BRADLEY? NO. I HAVEN'T SEEN HIM." Anyway, Jesus. What does she want? (*Craig is reading the pad of paper. He hands it to Bradley.*) My brother's name was Jeremy. Not Monster. He was five foot three, one hundred thirty pounds. Not six foot two, three hundred fifty. My brother was tortured and strangled over the course of a two-hour, period. The shape of a turtle and a steer were imprinted on my brother's neck, from the cowboy belt your so-called "author" used. My brother's face was badly beaten, bones protruded from his bloody face. My brother was a medical assistant. He was a human being, not a monster. To see this man profit, it's killing me and I wonder if you ever gave that a thought?

CRAIG: I still think, um. The SPIRIT of the — I mean, he was true to the SPIRIT of, the book's not about the crime in any case and uh, legally, there's no . . .

BRADLEY: You knew this?

CRAIG: It's not really an issue.

BRADLEY: I mean, the thing of it is, I — I really like Jimmy.

CRAIG: Yeah, and who is she? Who is she really? Like what do you know?

BRADLEY: And the thing of it is, it's about Jimmy's writing. I think his writing redeems him.

CRAIG: Yeah. That's why we never, like bothered to check.

MARCY: You know it's already been optioned as a movie? For Ben Stiller.

JENNY: I love Ben Stiller.

MARCY: Then I think, really, you're going to love Jimmy.

BRADLEY: I'm fixing him up with my girlfriend's sister. I wouldn't do that if I didn't like him, if I thought he was wasn't, a good person. Yeah. It's fine. It's.

CRAIG: I mean, — this . . . — like, she's the victim's sister. That's all. What do you expect?

JENNY: So, what are we going to do, like, go out to dinner together? Are we —

MARCY: Yeah.

JENNY: I'm up for that.

(Bradley looks seriously confused. Lights fade.)

END OF PLAY

APPROACHING THE READING

1. Describe the characters — Jenny, Marcy, Bradley, Craig, and Naomi. What are you given that helps you get to know them? Which characters (if any) are you drawn to? Which ones are you put off by? Why?

2. There are two characters important to the play that we don't see, Jeremy and Jimmy. Describe what they are like. What are the advantages of not having Jimmy appear on stage? What is revealing about Naomi being the only one who knows Jeremy's name?

3. Identify different kinds of conflicts that appear within the play and ones that exist behind what occurs on stage. Do any of these conflicts raise issues that are meaningful or important to you? If so, explain.

4. Even though there isn't much action in this play, particular movements are important. Pick out those that we should notice and explain their significance.

READING FOR CHARACTER

Just as with fiction, some of the first questions to ask about a play likely involve the characters. Who are they? What are they like? Why do they act and feel the way they do? In drama, characters are developed in some of the same ways described earlier for fiction: showing, saying, telling, entering a character's mind, and naming (pp. 70–71). Saying and telling in particular are central in drama because of the significance of **dialogue**.

SHOWING   What a character is like comes out in part from the character's actions. We get to know about a character from what she or he does, usually in a more reliable way than from what the character says or what is said about her or him: Actions in this case do speak louder than words. For Marcy and Jenny to turn their backs on Naomi and giggle at her, for example, especially when combined with the way they talk to her, reveals a good deal about them.

SAYING   Conversation between two or more characters, or **dialogue**, is the fundamental method of writing used in drama. Much of what occurs in a play starts from and relies on characters talking to each other. From what the characters say to each other, the audience or reader pieces the story together, including details about relevant events in the past and foreshadowings of what may occur in the future. And dialogue provides the primary means for becoming familiar with the characters: What they say and to whom, and especially how they say it, reveal things about them and about others and help us understand the conflicts and motivations that give rise to the action.

Thus, in *The New New*, what Jenny and Marcy talk about (using sex to pass an economics course, meeting a charming ex-con) and what Bradley and Craig talk about (finding ways to market a "memoiristic novel" about surviving in prison without verifying facts about the writer) evince the shallowness of their characters. For all of them, life centers in words, not realities, in words that instead of clarifying and revealing, avoid, cover up, and distort.

TELLING   We also learn about characters through dialogue as one character tells what another is like. When one character (whether in drama or fiction) tells us about another, the description may be accurate and reliable or it may be inaccurate and misleading. In *The New New* we know what Naomi's brother is like from the note she writes, and we accept what she says as true because the other characters can't dispute it. And we learn about Jimmy first from what Marcy and Bradley say about him ("he's just really charismatic and charming and smart" and "He was just this witty, sardonic ethnographer of prison life") and then from what Naomi tells about him: "My brother was tortured and strangled over the course of a two-hour, period." What Marcy and Bradley say reveals more about them than about the person they are discussing. Not only do they not actually know what Jimmy is like but they also don't seem to care. "And the thing of it is," Bradley says, "it's about Jimmy's writing. I think his writing redeems him." In other words, how one successfully manipulates words is more important than what one does.

ENTERING   Entering a character's thoughts is less frequent in drama than in fiction, but it does occur in some instances (not, however, in *The New New*). In a **soliloquy**, a speaker alone onstage, or off to the side of the stage away from other characters, reveals to the audience what is going through her or his mind. Shakespeare uses soliloquies frequently. Hamlet's "To be or not to be" speech (p. 1198) is a famous example.

NAMING   In some cases, in drama as well as in fiction, the names given to characters reveal aspects of what they are like, as, for example, Willy Loman in Arthur Miller's *Death of a Salesman* (p. 1316).

> Review the discussion "Types of Characterization," on pages 71–72. Most of the terminology introduced for fiction there — **protagonist**, **antagonist**; **major**, **minor**; **round**, **flat** — can be applied to drama as well.

READING FOR DIALOGUE

DIALOGUE IS CENTRAL   Although all of the above methods are important, dialogue remains most significant. When we watch a play, we need to listen closely to the words of the dialogue; reading a play requires the same attentiveness and a great deal of imaginative involvement as well. Style (p. 205) and tone (p. 207) contribute in a significant way to dialogue in drama.

Aspects of style that we discussed earlier in the book apply here as well, and appropriateness remains the key factor: Word choice and sentence structure (see pp. 200–204) need to fit the character using the words and expressing the sentences. Figures of speech (see pp. 204–205 and 631–44) and images must be suitable to the character selecting them. A good playwright is able to create stylistic differences in the dialogue of various characters as an aspect of characterization. And determining the tone is important in individual speeches as well as in a play as a whole.

One of the pleasures in reading a play is imagining how the dialogue would sound on stage — what pace, sound, inflections, and tones of voice fit each character. Should the actor shout or whisper "Shut up!"? How does she or he express anger or grief or bewilderment, or all three at once? What words should be emphasized? If you have ever acted or known an actor, you've likely experienced how many ways there are to say something seemingly as simple as "Where have you been?" In reading a play, we get to be the actors, experimenting with each line to decide how to express it most effectively and get across its meaning most completely, including what it reveals about the speaker.

Creating convincing dialogue is a challenge for playwrights: The discussions, arguments, questions, outbursts, seductions, and compliments must seem natural and appropriate to the speakers and "realistic" for their time and setting. At the same time, they must be carefully crafted to make every speech, even every word, count toward all the different things the dialogue needs to accomplish (for example, advancing the plot, revealing character, engaging the audience, focusing the conflict). Because watching or reading a play requires such close attention to the words of the dialogue, some people find it helpful to read a plot summary first. Knowing the broad plot outline can help you to pick up the signals and subtleties the words are conveying.

READING FOR CONFLICT

In drama, characters are most often found in a situation involving **conflict**, a struggle or confrontation between opposing characters or a character and opposing forces. Conflict is important to drama first because it usually creates action on the stage — whether external and physical or internal and psychological — and thus creates the kind of excitement, suspense, and tension we associate with the word *drama*. Even outside the theater, we hear *drama* used that way, as, for example, in describing a news story about a dramatic standoff as police attempt to rescue hostages from a convenience store where a robber is holding them at gunpoint. Second, conflict is important because the nature of the conflict, the issues involved, and the way it is handled generally bring out aspects of character: The essence and the depths of a person come out as she or he confronts a challenging situation.

The kinds of conflict in drama range as widely as those in fiction, but the same three broad categories discussed in Chapter 4 (pp. 60–97) — physical conflict, social conflict, and internal or psychological conflict — are useful here as well.

No physical conflict occurs in *The New New*, though the plot grows out of the brutal killing of Naomi's brother that occurred several years before. Social conflict appears in the contempt with which Marcy and Jenny treat the "nonentity" Naomi, a "nervous, down-at-the-heels" woman from a lower social stratum than theirs, who clearly lacks their education and sophistication (this is shown partly in the style in which her note to Bradley is written, especially the odd comma after "two-hour," which is apparent to a reader though perhaps not to someone watching the play). Internal conflict emerges when Bradley is confronted with the fact that he never did give a thought to the victim of Jimmy's crime, never investigated the truth of what Jimmy told him. Taken in by Jimmy's charm and charisma and by the opportunity to publish a best-selling book, he is converting a callous murderer into a wealthy celebrity.

Chapter 4 points out that watching for conflicts is a good way to get to the crucial issues in a work of fiction. That is even more true for a play. Identifying areas of conflict as you watch or read a play, or as you watch a movie or television show, usually takes you directly to the heart of its action and significance.

READING FOR DRAMATIC ACTION

Some dramatic productions do not use action on a stage. In reader's theater, for example, actors typically perch on stools and read their parts to each other and the audience. In most theater productions, however, actors move about onstage "acting out" what is going on. The characters enter and exit; they walk from one side of the stage to the other, they hide behind a sofa or trip on an electric cord and fall flat. They slap one another, have a sword fight, or shoot each other. They carry props, set the table, open a window. They pace, faint, fall back into a chair.

MOVEMENT ON STAGE   Dramatic action is almost always a fundamental aspect of drama—movement on stage is a vital aspect of keeping the audience's interest and attention. Conflict in drama often becomes a part of the play's dramatic action: As characters differ, argue, quarrel, challenge each other, and find solutions to their problems or difficulties, what occurs on the stage becomes interesting and compelling. A play in which the characters stroll around the stage agreeing with each other is not going to get off the page and accepted for any theater. Therefore, another challenge for you as the reader of a play is using your imagination to visualize the action of a play while reading the text. The dramatic action needs to be seen, on stage or in the mind's theater, for the play to be complete.

BLOCKING AND GESTURES   In some cases, the script of the play supplies guidelines for what actions should accompany the words, either in stage directions or in the lines themselves. Thus, a stage direction in *The New New* indicates that Craig "hands [Naomi] a notepad. She stands looking at it. She begins to write, furiously." For the most part, however, the actors and directors are left to decide how the characters should move on stage (called "blocking" in theater parlance) and what gestures they should use. This is a crucial part of their joint interpretation of what is going on and how the characters react. As a reader, you are both director and actor, so you get to use your intelligence to try to understand the characters fully enough so that you can picture their actions, gestures, and expressions on the imaginary stage of your mind.

TIMING   A key part of any action is timing: When the text is acted out on stage, the pace depends on variations in the intensity of different moments. Words almost always take more time to say aloud than to read

> ☑ **CHECKLIST on Reading for Character, Conflict, and Dramatic Action**
>
> ❑ Be aware of what the characters are like, what is important to them, what values they hold, what motivates them.
>
> ❑ Be attentive to the methods of characterization important in drama, especially the use of *dialogue* and *dramatic action*: what a character *says*, what the character *does*, and what other characters *say about* her or him.
>
> ❑ Consider how fully characters are *developed* — whether they are round or flat, whether they change in the course of the play or stay pretty much the same.
>
> ❑ Look for conflicts — physical, social, internal — and use them as a way to "get into" the drama and to explore its complexity.

silently, and some lines need to be spoken more slowly than others. Action on the stage occurs during lines, between lines, or while no one is speaking. Actions can be large — a sword fight — or smaller, perhaps a character walking across the stage, looking out a window, or searching in a desk drawer. Both large and small actions can be significant. Sometimes characters come

www

Further explore character and conflict, including interactive exercises, with VirtuaLit Drama at bedfordstmartins.com/approachinglit.

on stage, do something, and leave without saying any words at all. Sometimes pauses occur between sentences or between words in a speech, as one character looks angrily at another or ponders what another character has just said. In a play, as in life, pauses or silences often say as much as or even more than words do. For such reasons, a scene that takes five minutes to read might take ten minutes to act out.

Here too it is important for you the reader to imagine the pace at which things are taking place, especially where the script does not include specific indications.

FURTHER READING

ENTRY POINTS   There is not a lot of action in the following play. Two characters sit talking at a table in a café in Rome. By listening to the dialogue we learn a great deal about what they are like, partly by observing conflicts between them and learning about earlier conflicts in their lives. As you read it, watch for moments of illumination, as one of the characters gains insight into the other or into their immediate situation.

Cusi Cram   b. 1967

West of Stupid   [2002]

CHARACTERS

JUNE, in her early 50s
JEFF, in his late 20s

SETTING:

A café in campo di Fiori, Rome

JUNE: A fool. That's what I am. My mother had a phrase . . . what was it . . . west of stupid. That's what she used to call me. Well, she was right. God.

JEFF: I don't get it, Gram's phrase.

JUNE: She had another one, I liked . . . dumb as a doughnut. Maybe it was dense as a doughnut? I am not a phrase turner. It's probably a math thing. I bet people who are good at math are good at that sort of thing.

JEFF: Why are you a fool?

JUNE: What? Oh . . . I forget. There's this strange fogginess. It comes and goes. But I know . . . I know I had discovered something, something that pointed to my utter and complete idiocy.

JEFF: You shouldn't talk like that. You . . . you put yourself down.

JUNE: Shut up, Jeffrey. (*Longish pause, some sipping.*) It's the coffee that makes me feel west of stupid.

JEFF: The coffee?

JUNE: Because . . . because it tastes so goddamn good. Because for seven years I've been driving every Saturday to Essex to the Bean There, that's spelt B-E-A-N and this woman Peg, Peg makes me a cappuccino and I look out the window at all the white houses and all the white people and tell Peg she makes a spectacular four dollar cup of coffee. But now . . . now that I know what I've been missing, the years of savory that have escaped me, I feel like punching Peg and scalding her with every single cup of rotten coffee she's ever made me.

JEFF: You told me once you enjoyed the drive to Essex.

JUNE: I never said that. That's just something you want to think I said.

JEFF: What do you mean by that?

JUNE: Never mind, dear. Never mind. I feel so happy at the thought of scalding Peg. I don't want things to turn. The mood. This place. This place. There's so much life . . . so much life in this room, I wish I could bottle it and drink it. I am so happy I never learnt Italian because all of these people are probably talking about carburetors and insurance but it looks like . . . like . . . everybody is talking about fucking.

JEFF: (*A little uncomfortable.*) Didn't you take Italian lessons?

JUNE: The teacher, the teacher, was a small woman.

JEFF: What does that mean, Mom?

JUNE: Does it matter, Jeff, my Italian teacher at the Old Saybrook YMCA?

JEFF: I guess not.

JUNE: (*Pointing to a man.*) Do you think he's a soldier? He looks like a soldier. I tell you, I'm not sure what it is but I find the soldiers in Italy to be so sexy. Back home, if someone is in a uniform, it sort of makes me ignore them automatically, you know? But did you see the guard at Fiumicino? He held his gun . . . in this way that . . . well Jeff, it looked positively pornographic. Did you see him?

JEFF: I missed him. What was small about her, I mean specifically? I'd like to know.

JUNE: Oh, God. Sometimes you're a real downer. I guess you don't get to fantasize about my solider.

JEFF: I guess not.

JUNE: Mrs. Franchetti, my Italian teacher at the Old Saybrook Y, took great offense at my comments. And though I had never been to Italy, I had read about it and that threatened Mrs. Franchetti, who had been here on two package tours. I've been a teacher most of my life, Jeff, and I knew that even though Mrs. Franchetti spoke Italian adequately, that it would not be possible for me to learn it from her because she was not a generous woman. She was small in her outlook on life, small in her desires. Mrs. Franchetti lived at a certain decibel of miserable smallness, which she had accepted as all right. Mrs. Franchetti was full of fear and doubt, had no philosophy or poetry in her, and therefore I could not learn the language of Dante from her.

JEFF: Then why take Italian at the Y? Why not drive to New Haven or Hartford, or somewhere else, where someone "large" might teach.

JUNE: I don't think this is about Mrs. Franchetti. What is this about, Jeffrey?

JEFF: It's about trying to get some clarity, some understanding, Mother. Your sailing teacher was small, so were your pottery, tai chi, massage, and oil painting teachers. Your neighbors are small. Everyone who works at Old Saybrook High is small. My hockey coach, my violin teacher, all my babysitters, every best friend I ever had, what did they have in common? Smallness, according to you. Pretty much anyone you call a friend is small and has no poetry or philosophy in them. Are there no large poetic and philosophical people in the entire state of Connecticut, Mom?

JUNE: In my opinion, very few.

(*A long pause.*)

JUNE: (*Pointing to someone.*) Look at him, will you?

JEFF: Don't point. Pointing is rude in any language.

JUNE: I bet he has a huge dick.

JEFF: Excuse me?

JUNE: Gianormous, I bet. His hands are thick. I took a palm reading class in Mystic and the teacher, Aroshn, by the way she was the opposite of small, and she shared some very interesting facts with me. Fleshy hands, fleshy hands mean you are a sensual being, Jeff, that's what Aroshn said.

JEFF: What kind of a name is Aroshn?

JUNE: Her name was Sharon. She just switched the letters around. Isn't that clever?

JEFF: It sounds like erosion. What would my name be, Fefj?

JUNE: (*Looking toward the man.*) You know, since I got the news, I think and dream about sex all the time. I tell you, the orgasms I've been having in my sleep are so vivid and so much better than anything I ever had in real life, I wake up quivering. And if I think about the dream, I can still feel some of the pleasure. It's a nice side effect.

JEFF: (*Very very uncomfortable.*) Oh. Well, good. Good, I guess if it makes you feel better?

JUNE: In the last five years, I've lost interest in sex.

JEFF: Mom, do we have to talk about this?

JUNE: I can talk about whatever I want, Jeff. It has to do with gravity, my loss of interest. 'Cause if you think about it, good sex is all about buoyancy, everything being plump and full. And no matter what you do, as you get older you just can't keep things buoyant naturally. I find this loss . . . loss of buoyancy in myself and others unstimulating. But in my dreams, in my dreams, I am just bouncing like a goddamn beach ball and everyone else is too. (*Doing a clandestine point.*) He seems *very* buoyant to me.

JEFF: He could speak English, Mom.

(*A pause. Jeff looks at his hands. He pinches the flesh. June notices and smiles.*)

JUNE: What's he drinking? That red drink, what's that red drink?

JEFF: Bitters, I think. It comes from artichokes or pomegranates, I forget which.

JUNE: Be a lamb and get me one. (*Whispering.*) Just like the buoyant guy is having.

(*Jeff gets up and crosses upstage to the bar. June tries to stifle a cough into a handkerchief. She has a hard time. Jeff returns with a drink.*)

JEFF: Mom? Mom? Are you all right, Mom?

JUNE: (*Coughing.*) Fit as a fiddle. It's just the cigarette smoke. (*She stops coughing.*) I love Italy. They must not have cancer here, the way everyone just smokes everywhere. It's beautiful. (*A little cough.*)

JEFF: Do you want the spray?

JUNE: God, no. (*Beat.*) You're clenching your jaw, Jeff. It's got to be bad for you and it reminds me of your father. I don't want to think about your father in Rome.

JEFF: (*Clenching his jaw.*) I'm not clenching.

JUNE: What's wrong? You clench when something's wrong.

JEFF: I was thinking about Mrs. Franchetti.

JUNE: Killjoy.

JEFF: Mom, you said, you said, that you would come on this trip, if I promised to not be polite. You said that.

JUNE: Be my guest.

JEFF: OK.

JUNE: You're still clenching. Can you be rude and not clench?

JEFF: Mom!

JUNE: Sorry!

JEFF: Well . . . Well, you're this really large person, Mom, and it seems, it seems to me that most of your life you . . . you've put yourself in these small situations . . . so . . . so you can feel all large and outraged.

JUNE: (*Angrily.*) Is that what I've done? From your birds-eye view, up there on your high pony pony horse that's how you see it?

JEFF: I just want to understand why.

JUNE: Well, it's hard to understand someone you never see. (*Beat.*) I understand, Jeff. I'm not a success. I'm not rich. I'm not healthy. I am a divorced Connecticut schoolteacher with a temper. Your father . . .

JEFF: This is not about Dad.

JUNE: But it is. We look to our parents as examples and ever since you left home, you've wanted nothing to do with me. Every time I see you, your jaw is clenched and you can't look me in the eye because you're afraid if you do, you might see yourself. And you know what? It doesn't matter a bit. Because I love you, honey. I love you right through all your disapproval because I knew you when you were kind and afraid of things under your bed. I knew you when you couldn't fall asleep unless I held you. And that kind of knowing lasts forever.

(*June holds Jeff's hand to her heart. A moment. An alarm goes off on Jeff's watch.*)

JUNE: Oh, Jesus. What's that?

JEFF: (*Collecting himself.*) It's time for . . . for your pills.

(*Jeff begins to unpack several bottles of pills from his knapsack and place them on the table.*)

JUNE: I wish . . . I wish we didn't have to do that here. The soldier will see.

JEFF: The timing is very important, Mom.

JUNE: Jeffie?

JEFF: (*Counting pills, looking at instructions.*) Just a sec, this is complicated.

JUNE: I didn't like Mrs. Franchetti because she was . . . she was just like me. I want to die large.

JEFF: What are you talking about, Mom?

JUNE: I never traveled before because I knew . . . I knew that if I went to other places and saw people like that soldier with the fleshy hands and drank artichoke juice, I would see the smallness of Old Saybrook and then I would have to do something and I was afraid of the something . . . I don't want to be afraid anymore, Jeff. I don't want to take my pills. I don't want experimental treatments in New Haven. I don't want to go back to Connecticut. Ever. I want to die in Rome, dreaming of transcendent orgasms.

JEFF: But . . . Mom, there's hope. Dr. Greisman said, he said there's some hope.

JUNE: There is, Jeff, just not the kind you're talking about. I am hopeful that my death at the Hassler Hotel, overlooking the Spanish Steps, with my son by my side will be joyful and filled with hope.

JEFF: That's not what this trip was about. I wanted to give you things, things you've never let yourself have, good food and wine and paintings and views that would break your heart. I wanted to show you a place where people have mastered living, so you would fight to live like this, so you would fight to come back here. I gave you Rome because I wanted you to fight, Mom.

JUNE: I can't win this, honey. But I am so grateful that you made me come here. I just want to stay. I want to die in Rome of consumption like a Henry James heroine. Do you think consumption was like nineteenth-century cancer?

JEFF: I dunno. It sure sounds better, though.

JUNE: It does.

(*Jeff is silent. June reaches for her glass of bitters. She lifts the drink to Jeff's lips.*)

JUNE: It'll make you feel better. It tastes like medicine.

(*Jeff drinks a few sips.*)

JEFF: It's disgusting.

JUNE: But such a festive color.

JEFF: I think it's for digestion.

JUNE: I could use a snack. It looks like they have sandwiches. Should I get some? (*Whispering.*) It could be my moment to talk to the buoyant soldier with the huge hands. Just look at them, Jeff, they are *abnormally* large.

JEFF: They're gianormous.

JUNE: I think they have spinach and mozzarella. Sound good?

JEFF: Whatever you want Mom, whatever you want.

(*June gets up, turns her back, and walks toward the bar. She turns around and looks at Jeff. Jeff slowly and methodically puts the pills in his knapsack. June watches him. Jeff finishes and looks out to the piazza. June also looks out to somewhere beyond the piazza and smiles.*)

END OF PLAY

APPROACHING THE READING

1. Describe the characters and summarize their character traits. Are they round or flat, dynamic or static? Explain why you think so. Do you identify with one character more than the other? Why?
2. Explain how dialogue is used to fill in the background for what happens in the play.
3. List two or three conflicts in the play and label what kind of conflict each is.
4. What does the play "add up to"? (How would you describe its theme?)
5. Explain the significance of the play's title.

RESPONDING THROUGH Writing

WRITING ABOUT CHARACTER, CONFLICT, AND DRAMATIC ACTION

Journal Entries

1. Record two or more dialogues you have overheard or been involved in. Write a journal entry that discusses why the real-life dialogue seems artificial on the page and why the artful dialogue from a play seems real.

www

Research the authors in this chapter with LitLinks, or take a quiz on the plays with LitQuiz, at bedfordstmartins.com/approachinglit.

2. Write a journal entry in which you discuss what makes the dialogue of Jeff distinct from that of June in Cusi Cram's *West of Stupid* (p. 925).

3. Watch a television sitcom or drama, paying attention to techniques used in developing characters. Write a journal entry explaining and evaluating them.

Literary Analysis Papers

4. Write a paper examining the use of style in Kelly Stuart's *The New New* (p. 915). You might focus on how the way characters express themselves is used to characterize them, individually and as a group.

5. Write an analysis of the two characters in Kelly Stuart's *The New New* (p. 915) whom we do not see, Jeremy and Jimmy. Touch on such aspects as what each is like, how we learn about them, why each is important to the play, and how the effect would be different if they did appear in the play.

6. Write a paper on Cusi Cram's use of various types of conflict in characterizing June in *West of Stupid* (p. 925).

Comparison-Contrast Papers

7. Write out the first page of Ernest Hemingway's dialogue-filled story "Hills like White Elephants" (p. 136) the way it would look if it were a play instead of a short story, using Cusi Cram's *West of Stupid* (p. 925) as a model. Then compare and contrast the two versions and write a paper discussing how it would be different, or not much different, to read "Hills Like White Elephants" if it was written as a play rather than as a short story.

8. Write a paper comparing and contrasting the methods of characterization in Kelly Stuart's *The New New* (p. 915) and Cusi Cram's *West of Stupid* (p. 925).

WRITING ABOUT CONNECTIONS

Making internal connections is standard dramatic technique, as the playwright establishes relationships (juxtapositions, comparisons, contrasts) between

> ## ➤ TIPS for Writing about Character, Conflict, and Dramatic Action

> ➤ **Start with conflict** Exploring and analyzing the conflicts in a play can lead to an effective paper topic, especially because conflict reveals many aspects of a play, such as themes, character, problems and their resolution or lack of resolution, ambiguities, and even setting. Watch for different kinds of conflict — physical, social, and internal/psychological. (The latter, when central to a play, can work especially well as a paper topic.)

> ➤ **Consider character** If you decide to write a paper in which you discuss a single character or several characters, you should not only describe what that character or those characters are like but also explain how various character traits are revealed (pay attention especially to what the characters do, say, and tell about others) and how the characters change or grow or are confronted with a need to change.

> ➤ **Watch for juxtapositions** Always look for juxtapositions — parallel or contrasting characters, scenes, actions, images, and similar elements — in any play that you decide to write about. Juxtaposition can be especially important in revealing character development and in the development of themes.

> ➤ **Focus on style or structure** Some plays lend themselves to a useful analysis of style or dramatic strategies. A paper could examine how style is used for characterization by showing how such elements as diction, sentence structure and length, and choice of images and figures of speech are suited to the character and differ from those of other characters. A paper also could examine dramatic strategies: the way or ways the action is structured, in the play as a whole or in a key scene or two, perhaps the way it builds to a climax and is resolved, or the way an easily overlooked small action or incident is used as a pivotal point for the entire play.

> ➤ **Use specific details and illustrations** It is very important when writing about drama to decide whether to deal with the whole play or to select a scene or two to examine thoroughly. In either case, you must support your points and explanations with specific details and illustrations from the text.

words, characters, dramatic actions, symbols, or ideas. For a reader, looking at two works and making external connections can also be a valuable way of understanding themes in a play, as these are brought out through character, conflict, and dramatic action. Here are some examples:

1. "Souls for Sale": The Cost of Devaluing Values in Kelly Stuart's *The New New* (p. 915) and Arthur Miller's *Death of a Salesman* (p. 1316)

2. "Death Draws Near": The Imminence of Mortality in Cusi Cram's *West of Stupid* (p. 925) and David Henry Hwang's *As the Crow Flies* (p. 995)
3. "Spinning Out of Control": The Search for Meaning in John Guare's *Woman at a Threshold, Beckoning* (p. 1439) and William Shakespeare's *Hamlet* (p. 1151)

WRITING RESEARCH PAPERS

1. Dr. Rank in Henrik Ibsen's *A Doll House* (p. 1263) is dying from a sexually transmitted disease (STD) passed on from his father. Research nineteenth-century knowledge of and social attitudes toward STDs, and write a paper using what you find to discuss the importance of that motif in the play (and perhaps how it was regarded by readers then and how it might be regarded today).
2. Research attitudes toward sports in the 1950s and write a paper that deals with sports and American values in Arthur Miller's *Death of a Salesman* (p. 1316).

COMPOSING IN OTHER ART FORMS

1. Instead of just reading a play, try directing one. Find students who are willing to be actors in one of the plays in this chapter or the next, gather a few props, and begin rehearsing for a performance. Ask your instructor if you may perform it in class.
2. Design or describe costumes for characters from one of the plays in this or the next chapter. Write an explanation of why the costume design, style, colors, and so forth are appropriate for the character and how they serve as a means of characterization.

I wished to create a form which, in itself as a form, would literally be the process of Willy Loman's way of mind. Arthur Miller

Setting and Structure

Examining Where, When, and How It Happens

CHAPTER **22**

Think of the place shown each week in your favorite TV show. If it's an ongoing series, the action likely takes place in the same building, street, or room every week, and you come to know those made-up places, those "sets" (the backdrops and properties constructed for staging a scene in a play or film), almost as well as the kitchen in your own house. For years, one of the most popular shows on television, *Cheers*, took place almost completely in a Boston pub. The set of that imaginary neighborhood pub became so familiar that tourists visiting Boston expect to find and walk into the real Cheers.

Dramatic actions by characters occur in a location that is almost always significant and that is represented by a stage set. Reading as well as watching a play must include thoughtful consideration of sets and setting and of the way the dramatic action occurring in them is structured and connected in a meaningful way to them. Setting and structure in fiction are discussed earlier in this book. This chapter examines their significance for drama and the distinctive ways they are handled in a play.

READING FOR SETTING

The **setting** of a play—where, when, and in what circumstances the action occurs—is just as important in drama as it is in fiction. Significant aspects of setting include the *place* of the action (in broad terms such as region, country, or city, and in narrow terms such as neighborhood, street, or building), the *time* at which the action occurs (the century, year, season, day, hour), and the *cultural context* of the action (social and historical circumstances that characterize the time and place). Each of these is discussed at length in Chapter 6. (Reviewing pages 135–43 will prepare you to consider the importance of setting in drama.)

THE SET ON STAGE   Sets are an important aspect of setting in plays, movies, and TV, an aspect not present in fiction and poetry because they lack the performance dimension of drama. The **set** is the physical setup on the stage, including the background (backdrop), structures, properties (all movable articles, such as furniture and objects handled by the actors), and lighting. Set is often the first thing you encounter when watching a play in a theater, but imagining how the play might be set is also an important part of staging the play in the theater of your mind. Set depends to a great extent on the nature of the theater in which a play is produced and the kind of stage used in it. These, and their influence on the writer and reader of drama, are discussed in the next chapter. Here, we cover the broad points regarding the relation of setting and stage set.

SETTING AND SET IN SHAKESPEARE   Remember that setting is always a larger concept than set: The entire setting of a play cannot appear on stage. A play's setting may be Los Angeles, for example, but only one city street and one store might appear on the stage. Plays written before the mid-1800s may indicate their setting but offer little guidance on how specific sets are to be designed. The text of *Hamlet* in this book states that the general setting is "Denmark" (p. 1151) and footnotes give specific settings such as "Elsinore castle. A guard platform" (p. 1152), but these (like the *Dramatis Personae* list — p. 1151) are editorial additions made after Shakespeare's death. Elizabethan audiences identified the settings from details mentioned by the characters. And Shakespeare left the backdrops and props to the discretion of the acting company, so you as the reader have great freedom to imagine how those should look.

SETTING AND SET IN MODERN DRAMA   Modern playwrights, on the other hand, in addition to indicating the setting of a play, often give detailed instructions on how to construct the set. Here, for example, are the stage directions for Henrik Ibsen's *A Doll House*:

> A comfortable room, tastefully but not expensively furnished. A door to the right in the back wall leads to the entryway; another to the left leads to Helmer's study. Between these doors, a piano. Midway in the left-hand wall a door, and further back a window. Near the window a round table with an armchair and a small sofa. In the right-hand wall, toward the rear, a door, and nearer the foreground a porcelain stove with two armchairs and a rocking chair beside it. Between the stove and the side door, a small table. Engravings on the walls. An étagère with china figures and other small art

objects; a small bookcase with richly bound books; the floor carpeted; a fire burning in the stove. It is a winter day. (p. 1263)

Unlike earlier playwrights, who considered it their role to produce a text and leave the decisions about production to an acting company, most modern playwrights are concerned about the production as well as the text and therefore provide their visions on how the stage appears, how characters are dressed, and even, in some cases, what they look like ("Happy is tall, powerfully made. Sexuality is like a visible color on him, or a scent that many women have discovered" — *Death of a Salesman*, p. 1321). Such instructions offer guidance not only to set and costume designers but also to readers of drama, who are given a host of detailed images to help them as they attempt to picture the set, characters, and action in their minds.

ENTRY POINTS   As you read the following one-act play, notice the way Susan Glaspell spells out how to construct the set and how characters should appear. Concentrate on visualizing the play in your mind as fully and sharply as you can. Also consider the importance of its rural, isolated setting — how it contributes to what has happened, and does happen, and to our reaction to it all. The play falls into the enjoyable genre of the mystery story, as law officers attempt to solve a murder case. But it also explores matters of human interest and of moral and legal importance. As you read, pay attention to the handling of dialogue and action, to the ways characters are revealed and developed, and to the conflicts presented.

Susan Glaspell   1882–1948

Trifles   [1916]

CHARACTERS

GEORGE HENDERSON (County Attorney)
HENRY PETERS (Sheriff)
LEWIS HALE, a neighboring farmer
MRS. PETERS
MRS. HALE

SCENE: *The kitchen in the now abandoned farmhouse of John Wright, a gloomy kitchen, and left without having been put in order — unwashed pans under the sink, a loaf of bread outside the bread-box, a dish-towel on the table — other signs of incompleted work. At the rear the outer door opens and the Sheriff comes in followed by the County Attorney and Hale. The Sheriff and Hale are men in middle life, the County Attorney is a young man; all are much bundled up and go at once to the stove. They are followed by the two women — the Sheriff's wife first; she is a slight wiry woman, a thin nervous face. Mrs. Hale is larger and would ordinarily be called more comfortable looking, but she is disturbed now and looks fearfully about as she enters. The women have come in slowly, and stand close together near the door.*

COUNTY ATTORNEY (*rubbing his hands*): This feels good. Come up to the fire, ladies.

MRS. PETERS (*after taking a step forward*): I'm not—cold.

SHERIFF (*unbuttoning his overcoat and stepping away from the stove as if to mark the beginning of official business*): Now, Mr. Hale, before we move things about, you explain to Mr. Henderson just what you saw when you came here yesterday morning.

COUNTY ATTORNEY: By the way, has anything been moved? Are things just as you left them yesterday?

SHERIFF (*looking about*): It's just the same. When it dropped below zero last night I thought I'd better send Frank out this morning to make a fire for us—no use getting pneumonia with a big case on, but I told him not to touch anything except the stove—and you know Frank.

COUNTY ATTORNEY: Somebody should have been left here yesterday.

SHERIFF: Oh—yesterday. When I had to send Frank to Morris Center for that man who went crazy—I want you to know I had my hands full yesterday. I knew you could get back from Omaha by today and as long as I went over everything here myself—

COUNTY ATTORNEY: Well, Mr. Hale, tell just what happened when you came here yesterday morning.

HALE: Harry and I had started to town with a load of potatoes. We came along the road from my place and as I got here I said, "I'm going to see if I can't get John Wright to go in with me on a party telephone." I spoke to Wright about it once before and he put me off, saying folks talked too much anyway, and all he asked was peace and quiet—I guess you know about how much he talked himself; but I thought maybe if I went to the house and talked about it before his wife, though I said to Harry that I didn't know as what his wife wanted made much difference to John—

COUNTY ATTORNEY: Let's talk about that later, Mr. Hale. I do want to talk about that, but tell now just what happened when you got to the house.

HALE: I didn't hear or see anything; I knocked at the door, and still it was all quiet inside. I knew they must be up, it was past eight o'clock. So I knocked again, and I thought I heard somebody say, "Come in." I wasn't sure, I'm not sure yet, but I opened the door—this door (*indicating the door by which the two women are still standing*) and there in that rocker—(*pointing to it*) sat Mrs. Wright.

(*They all look at the rocker.*)

COUNTY ATTORNEY: What—was she doing?

HALE: She was rockin' back and forth. She had her apron in her hand and was kind of—pleating it.

COUNTY ATTORNEY: And how did she—look?

HALE: Well, she looked queer.

COUNTY ATTORNEY: How do you mean—queer?

HALE: Well, as if she didn't know what she was going to do next. And kind of done up.

COUNTY ATTORNEY: How did she seem to feel about your coming?

HALE: Why, I don't think she minded — one way or other. She didn't pay much attention. I said, "How do, Mrs. Wright it's cold, ain't it?" And she said, "Is it?" — and went on kind of pleating at her apron. Well, I was surprised; she didn't ask me to come up to the stove, or to set down, but just sat there, not even looking at me, so I said, "I want to see John." And then she — laughed. I guess you would call it a laugh. I thought of Harry and the team outside, so I said a little sharp: "Can't I see John?" "No," she says, kind o' dull like. "Ain't he home?" says I. "Yes," says she, "he's home." "Then why can't I see him?" I asked her, out of patience. "'Cause he's dead," says she. *"Dead?"* says I. She just nodded her head, not getting a bit excited, but rockin' back and forth. "Why — where is he?" says I, not knowing what to say. She just pointed upstairs — like that (*himself pointing to the room above*) I got up, with the idea of going up there. I walked from there to here — then I says, "Why, what did he die of?" "He died of a rope round his neck," says she, and just went on pleatin' at her apron. Well, I went out and called Harry. I thought I might — need help. We went upstairs and there he was lyin' —

COUNTY ATTORNEY: I think I'd rather have you go into that upstairs, where you can point it all out. Just go on now with the rest of the story.

HALE: Well, my first thought was to get that rope off. It looked . . . (*stops, his face twitches*) . . . but Harry, he went up to him, and he said, "No, he's dead all right, and we'd better not touch anything." So we went back down stairs. She was still sitting that same way. "Has anybody been notified?" I asked. "No," says she unconcerned. "Who did this, Mrs. Wright?" said Harry. He said it business-like — and she stopped pleatin' of her apron. "I don't know," she says. "You don't *know?*" says Harry. "No," says she. "Weren't you sleepin' in the bed with him?" says Harry. "Yes," says she, "but I was on the inside." "Somebody slipped a rope round his neck and strangled him and you didn't wake up?" says Harry. "I didn't wake up," she said after him. We must 'a looked as if we didn't see how that could be, for after a minute she said, "I sleep sound." Harry was going to ask her more questions but I said maybe we ought to let her tell her story first to the coroner, or the sheriff, so Harry went fast as he could to Rivers' place, where there's a telephone.

COUNTY ATTORNEY: And what did Mrs. Wright do when she knew that you had gone for the coroner?

HALE: She moved from that chair to this one over here (*pointing to a small chair in the corner*) and just sat there with her hands held together and looking down. I got a feeling that I ought to make some conversation, so I said I had come in to see if John wanted to put in a telephone, and at that she started to laugh, and then she stopped and looked at me — scared. (*the County Attorney, who has had his notebook out, makes a note*) I dunno, maybe it wasn't scared. I wouldn't like to say it was. Soon Harry got back, and then Dr. Lloyd came, and you, Mr. Peters, and so I guess that's all I know that you don't.

COUNTY ATTORNEY (*looking around*): I guess we'll go upstairs first — and then out to the barn and around there. (*to the Sheriff*) You're convinced that there was nothing important here — nothing that would point to any motive.

SHERIFF: Nothing here but kitchen things.

(*The County Attorney, after again looking around the kitchen, opens the door of a cupboard closet. He gets up on a chair and looks on a shelf. Pulls his hand away, sticky.*)

COUNTY ATTORNEY: Here's a nice mess.

(*The women draw nearer.*)

MRS. PETERS (*to the other woman*): Oh, her fruit; it did freeze. (*to the Lawyer*) She worried about that when it turned so cold. She said the fire'd go out and her jars would break.

SHERIFF: Well, can you beat the women! Held for murder and worryin' about her preserves.

COUNTY ATTORNEY: I guess before we're through she may have something more serious than preserves to worry about.

HALE: Well, women are used to worrying over trifles.

(*The two women move a little closer together.*)

COUNTY ATTORNEY (*with the gallantry of a young politician*): And yet, for all their worries, what would we do without the ladies? (*the women do not unbend. He goes to the sink, takes a dipperful of water from the pail and pouring it into a basin, washes his hands. Starts to wipe them on the roller-towel, turns it for a cleaner place*) Dirty towels! (*kicks his foot against the pans under the sink*) Not much of a housekeeper, would you say, ladies?

MRS. HALE (*stiffly*): There's a great deal of work to be done on a farm.

COUNTY ATTORNEY: To be sure. And yet (*with a little bow to her*) I know there are some Dickson county farmhouses which do not have such roller towels.

(*He gives it a pull to expose its length again.*)

MRS. HALE: Those towels get dirty awful quick. Men's hands aren't always as clean as they might be.

COUNTY ATTORNEY: Ah, loyal to your sex, I see. But you and Mrs. Wright were neighbors. I suppose you were friends, too.

MRS. HALE (*shaking her head*): I've not seen much of her of late years. I've not been in this house — it's more than a year.

COUNTY ATTORNEY: And why was that? You didn't like her?

MRS. HALE: I liked her all well enough. Farmers' wives have their hands full, Mr. Henderson. And then —

COUNTY ATTORNEY: Yes — ?

MRS. HALE (*looking about*): It never seemed a very cheerful place.

COUNTY ATTORNEY: No — it's not cheerful. I shouldn't say she had the homemaking instinct.

MRS. HALE: Well, I don't know as Wright had, either.

COUNTY ATTORNEY: You mean that they didn't get on very well?

MRS. HALE: No, I don't mean anything. But I don't think a place'd be any cheerfuller for John Wright's being in it.

COUNTY ATTORNEY: I'd like to talk more of that a little later. I want to get the lay of things upstairs now.

(*He goes to the left, where three steps lead to a stair door.*)

SHERIFF: I suppose anything Mrs. Peters does'll be all right. She was to take in some clothes for her, you know, and a few little things. We left in such a hurry yesterday.

COUNTY ATTORNEY: Yes, but I would like to see what you take, Mrs. Peters, and keep an eye out for anything that might be of use to us.

MRS. PETERS: Yes, Mr. Henderson.

(*The women listen to the men's steps on the stairs, then look about the kitchen.*)

MRS. HALE: I'd hate to have men coming into my kitchen, snooping around and criticising.

(*She arranges the pans under sink which the Lawyer had shoved out of place.*)

MRS. PETERS: Of course it's no more than their duty.

MRS. HALE: Duty's all right, but I guess that deputy sheriff that came out to make the fire might have got a little of this on. (*gives the roller towel a pull*) Wish I'd thought of that sooner. Seems mean to talk about her for not having things slicked up when she had to come away in such a hurry.

MRS. PETERS (*who has gone to a small table in the left rear corner of the room, and lifted one end of a towel that covers a pan*): She had bread set.

(*Stands still.*)

MRS. HALE (*eyes fixed on a loaf of bread beside the breadbox, which is on a low shelf at the other side of the room. Moves slowly toward it*): She was going to put this in there. (*picks up loaf, then abruptly drops it. In manner of returning to familiar things*) It's a shame about her fruit. I wonder if it's all gone. (*gets up on the chair and looks*) I think there's some here that's all right, Mrs. Peters. Yes — here; (*holding it toward the window*) this is cherries, too. (*looking again*) I declare I believe that's the only one. (*gets down, bottle in her hand. Goes to the sink and wipes it off on the outside*) She'll feel awful bad after all her hard work in the hot weather. I remember the afternoon I put up my cherries last summer.

(*She puts the bottle on the big kitchen table, center of the room. With a sigh, is about to sit down in the rocking-chair. Before she is seated realizes what chair it is; with a slow look at it, steps back. The chair which she has touched rocks back and forth.*)

MRS. PETERS: Well, I must get those things from the front room closet. (*she goes to the door at the right, but after looking into the other room, steps back*) You coming with me, Mrs. Hale? You could help me carry them.

(*They go in the other room; reappear, Mrs. Peters carrying a dress and skirt, Mrs. Hale following with a pair of shoes.*)

MRS. PETERS: My, it's cold in there.

(*She puts the clothes on the big table, and hurries to the stove.*)

MRS. HALE (*examining the skirt*): Wright was close. I think maybe that's why she kept so much to herself. She didn't even belong to the Ladies Aid. I suppose she felt she couldn't do her part, and then you don't enjoy things when you feel shabby. She used to wear pretty clothes and be lively, when she was Minnie Foster, one of the town girls singing in the choir. But that—oh, that was thirty years ago. This all you was to take in?

MRS. PETERS: She said she wanted an apron. Funny thing to want, for there isn't much to get you dirty in jail, goodness knows. But I suppose just to make her feel more natural. She said they was in the top drawer in this cupboard. Yes, here. And then her little shawl that always hung behind the door. (*opens stair door and looks*) Yes, here it is.

(*Quickly shuts door leading upstairs.*)

MRS. HALE (*abruptly moving toward her*): Mrs. Peters?
MRS. PETERS: Yes, Mrs. Hale?
MRS. HALE: Do you think she did it?
MRS. PETERS (*in a frightened voice*): Oh, I don't know.
MRS. HALE: Well, I don't think she did. Asking for an apron and her little shawl. Worrying about her fruit.
MRS. PETERS (*starts to speak, glances up, where footsteps are heard in the room above. In a low voice*): Mr. Peters says it looks bad for her. Mr. Henderson is awful sarcastic in a speech and he'll make fun of her sayin' she didn't wake up.
MRS. HALE: Well, I guess John Wright didn't wake when they was slipping that rope under his neck.
MRS. PETERS: No, it's strange. It must have been done awful crafty and still. They say it was such a—funny way to kill a man, rigging it all up like that.
MRS. HALE: That's just what Mr. Hale said. There was a gun in the house. He says that's what he can't understand.
MRS. PETERS: Mr. Henderson said coming out that what was needed for the case was a motive; something to show anger, or—sudden feeling.
MRS. HALE (*who is standing by the table*): Well, I don't see any signs of anger around here. (*she puts her hand on the dish towel which lies on the table, stands looking down at table, one half of which is clean, the other half messy*) It's wiped to here. (*makes a move as if to finish work, then turns and looks at loaf of bread outside the breadbox. Drops towel. In that voice of coming back to familiar things.*) Wonder how they are finding things upstairs. I hope she had it a little more red-up° there. You know, it seems kind of *sneaking*. Locking her up in town and then coming out here and trying to get her own house to turn against her!
MRS. PETERS: But Mrs. Hale, the law is the law.
MRS. HALE: I s'pose 'tis. (*unbuttoning her coat*) Better loosen up your things, Mrs. Peters. You won't feel them when you go out.

(*Mrs. Peters takes off her fur tippet,° goes to hang it on hook at back of room, stands looking at the under part of the small corner table.*)

---

red-up: Orderly; picked up.   **tippet:** A shoulder cape.

MRS. PETERS: She was piecing a quilt.

(*She brings the large sewing basket and they look at the bright pieces.*)

MRS. HALE: It's log cabin pattern. Pretty, isn't it? I wonder if she was goin' to quilt it or just knot it?

(*Footsteps have been heard coming down the stairs. The Sheriff enters followed by Hale and the County Attorney.*)

SHERIFF: They wonder if she was going to quilt it or just knot it!

(*The men laugh, the women look abashed.*)

COUNTY ATTORNEY (*rubbing his hands over the stove*): Frank's fire didn't do much up there, did it? Well, let's go out to the barn and get that cleared up.

(*The men go outside.*)

MRS. HALE (*resentfully*): I don't know as there's anything so strange, our takin' up our time with little things while we're waiting for them to get the evidence. (*she sits down at the big table smoothing out a block with decision*) I don't see as it's anything to laugh about.

MRS. PETERS (*apologetically*): Of course they've got awful important things on their minds.

(*Pulls up a chair and joins Mrs. Hale at the table.*)

MRS. HALE (*examining another block*): Mrs. Peters, look at this one. Here, this is the one she was working on, and look at the sewing! All the rest of it has been so nice and even. And look at this! It's all over the place! Why, it looks as if she didn't know what she was about!

(*After she has said this they look at each other, then start to glance back at the door. After an instant Mrs. Hale has pulled at a knot and ripped the sewing.*)

MRS. PETERS: Oh, what are you doing, Mrs. Hale?

MRS. HALE (*mildly*): Just pulling out a stitch or two that's not sewed very good. (*threading a needle*) Bad sewing always made me fidgety.

MRS. PETERS (*nervously*): I don't think we ought to touch things.

MRS. HALE: I'll just finish up this end. (*suddenly stopping and leaning forward*) Mrs. Peters?

MRS. PETERS: Yes, Mrs. Hale?

MRS. HALE: What do you suppose she was so nervous about?

MRS. PETERS: Oh — I don't know. I don't know as she was nervous. I sometimes sew awful queer when I'm just tired. (*Mrs. Hale starts to say something, looks at Mrs. Peters, then goes on sewing*) Well I must get these things wrapped up. They may be through sooner than we think. (*putting apron and other things together*) I wonder where I can find a piece of paper, and string.

MRS. HALE: In that cupboard, maybe.

MRS. PETERS (*looking in cupboard*): Why, here's a bird-cage. (*holds it up*) Did she have a bird, Mrs. Hale?

MRS. HALE: Why, I don't know whether she did or not — I've not been here for so long. There was a man around last year selling canaries cheap, but I don't know as she took one; maybe she did. She used to sing real pretty herself.

MRS. PETERS (*glancing around*): Seems funny to think of a bird here. But she must have had one, or why would she have a cage? I wonder what happened to it.

MRS. HALE: I s'pose maybe the cat got it.

MRS. PETERS: No, she didn't have a cat. She's got that feeling some people have about cats — being afraid of them. My cat got in her room and she was real upset and asked me to take it out.

MRS. HALE: My sister Bessie was like that. Queer, ain't it?

MRS. PETERS (*examining the cage*): Why, look at this door. It's broke. One hinge is pulled apart.

MRS. HALE (*looking too*): Looks as if someone must have been rough with it.

MRS. PETERS: Why, yes.

(*She brings the cage forward and puts it on the table.*)

MRS. HALE: I wish if they're going to find any evidence they'd be about it. I don't like this place.

MRS. PETERS: But I'm awful glad you came with me, Mrs. Hale. It would be lonesome for me sitting here alone.

MRS. HALE: It would, wouldn't it? (*dropping her sewing*) But I tell you what I do wish, Mrs. Peters. I wish I had come over sometimes when *she* was here. I — (*looking around the room*) — wish I had.

MRS. PETERS: But of course you were awful busy, Mrs. Hale — your house and your children.

MRS. HALE: I could've come. I stayed away because it weren't cheerful — and that's why I ought to have come. I — I've never liked this place. Maybe because it's down in a hollow and you don't see the road. I dunno what it is, but it's a lonesome place and always was. I wish I had come over to see Minnie Foster sometimes. I can see now — (*shakes her head*)

MRS. PETERS: Well, you mustn't reproach yourself, Mrs. Hale. Somehow we just don't see how it is with other folks until — something comes up.

MRS. HALE: Not having children makes less work — but it makes a quiet house, and Wright out to work all day, and no company when he did come in. Did you know John Wright, Mrs. Peters?

MRS. PETERS: Not to know him; I've seen him in town. They say he was a good man.

MRS. HALE: Yes — good; he didn't drink, and kept his word as well as most, I guess, and paid his debts. But he was a hard man, Mrs. Peters. Just to pass the time of day with him — (*shivers*) Like a raw wind that gets to the bone. (*pauses, her eye falling on the cage*) I should think she would 'a wanted a bird. But what do you suppose went with it?

MRS. PETERS: I don't know, unless it got sick and died.

(*She reaches over and swings the broken door, swings it again, both women watch it.*)

MRS. HALE: You weren't raised round here, were you? (*Mrs. Peters shakes her head*) You didn't know — her?

MRS. PETERS: Not till they brought her yesterday.

MRS. HALE: She — come to think of it, she was kind of like a bird herself — real sweet and pretty, but kind of timid and — fluttery. How — she — did — change. (*silence; then as if struck by a happy thought and relieved to get back to everyday things*) Tell you what, Mrs. Peters, why don't you take the quilt in with you? It might take up her mind.

MRS. PETERS: Why, I think that's a real nice idea, Mrs. Hale. There couldn't possibly be any objection to it, could there? Now, just what would I take? I wonder if her patches are in here — and her things.

(*They look in the sewing basket.*)

MRS. HALE: Here's some red. I expect this has got sewing things in it. (*brings out a fancy box*) What a pretty box. Looks like something somebody would give you. Maybe her scissors are in here. (*Opens box. Suddenly puts her hand to her nose*) Why — (*Mrs. Peters bends nearer, then turns her face away*) There's something wrapped up in this piece of silk.

MRS. PETERS: Why, this isn't her scissors.

MRS. HALE (*lifting the silk*): Oh, Mrs. Peters — it's —

(*Mrs. Peters bends closer.*)

MRS. PETERS: It's the bird.

MRS. HALE (*jumping up*): But, Mrs. Peters — look at it! It's neck! Look at its neck! It's all — other side *to*.

MRS. PETERS: Somebody — wrung — its — neck.

(*Their eyes meet. A look of growing comprehension, of horror. Steps are heard outside. Mrs. Hale slips box under quilt pieces, and sinks into her chair. Enter Sheriff and County Attorney. Mrs. Peters rises.*)

COUNTY ATTORNEY (*as one turning from serious things to little pleasantries*): Well ladies, have you decided whether she was going to quilt it or knot it?

MRS. PETERS: We think she was going to — knot it.

COUNTY ATTORNEY: Well, that's interesting, I'm sure. (*seeing the birdcage*) Has the bird flown?

MRS. HALE (*putting more quilt pieces over the box*): We think the — cat got it.

COUNTY ATTORNEY (*preoccupied*): Is there a cat?

(*Mrs. Hale glances in quick covert way at Mrs. Peters.*)

MRS. PETERS: Well, not *now*. They're superstitious, you know. They leave.

COUNTY ATTORNEY (*to Sheriff Peters, continuing an interrupted conversation*): No sign at all of anyone having come from the outside. Their own rope. Now let's go up again and go over it piece by piece. (*they start upstairs*) It would have to have been someone who knew just the —

(Mrs. Peters sits down. The two women sit there not looking at one another, but as if peering into something and at the same time holding back. When they talk now it is in the manner of feeling their way over strange ground, as if afraid of what they are saying, but as if they can not help saying it.)

MRS. HALE: She liked the bird. She was going to bury it in that pretty box.

MRS. PETERS *(in a whisper)*: When I was a girl — my kitten — there was a boy took a hatchet, and before my eyes — and before I could get there — *(covers her face an instant)* If they hadn't held me back I would have — *(catches herself, looks upstairs where steps are heard, falters weakly)* — hurt him.

MRS. HALE *(with a slow look around her)*: I wonder how it would seem never to have had any children around. *(pause)* No, Wright wouldn't like the bird — a thing that sang. She used to sing. He killed that, too.

MRS. PETERS *(moving uneasily)*: We don't know who killed the bird.

MRS. HALE: I knew John Wright.

MRS. PETERS: It was an awful thing was done in this house that night, Mrs. Hale. Killing a man while he slept, slipping a rope around his neck that choked the life out of him.

MRS. HALE: His neck. Choked the life out of him.

(Her hand goes out and rests on the birdcage.)

MRS. PETERS *(with rising voice)*: We don't know who killed him. We don't *know.*

MRS. HALE *(her own feeling not interrupted)*: If there'd been years and years of nothing, then a bird to sing to you, it would be awful — still, after the bird was still.

MRS. PETERS *(something within her speaking)*: I know what stillness is. When we homesteaded in Dakota, and my first baby died — after he was two years old, and me with no other then —

MRS. HALE *(moving)*: How soon do you suppose they'll be through, looking for the evidence?

MRS. PETERS: I know what stillness is. *(pulling herself back)* The law has got to punish crime, Mrs. Hale.

MRS. HALE *(not as if answering that)*: I wish you'd seen Minnie Foster when she wore a white dress with blue ribbons and stood up there in the choir and sang. *(a look around the room)* Oh, I wish I'd come over here once in a while! That was a crime! That was a crime! Who's going to punish that?

MRS. PETERS *(looking upstairs)*: We mustn't — take on.

MRS. HALE: I might have known she needed help! I know how things can be — for women. I tell you, it's queer, Mrs. Peters. We live close together and we live far apart. We all go through the same things — it's all just a different kind of the same thing. *(brushes her eyes, noticing the bottle of fruit, reaches out for it)* If I was you, I wouldn't tell her her fruit was gone. Tell her it *ain't.* Tell her it's all right. Take this in to prove it to her. She — she may never know whether it was broke or not.

MRS. PETERS *(takes the bottle, looks about for something to wrap it in; takes petticoat from the clothes brought from the other room, very nervously begins winding this around the bottle. In a false voice*): My, it's a good thing the men couldn't hear us. Wouldn't they just laugh! Getting all stirred up over a little thing like a — dead canary. As if that could have anything to do with — with — wouldn't they *laugh*!

(*The men are heard coming down stairs.*)

MRS. HALE (*under her breath*): Maybe they would — maybe they wouldn't.

COUNTY ATTORNEY: No, Peters, it's all perfectly clear except a reason for doing it. But you know juries when it comes to women. If there was some definite thing. Something to show — something to make a story about — a thing that would connect up with this strange way of doing it —

(*The women's eyes meet for an instant. Enter Hale from outer door.*)

HALE: Well, I've got the team around. Pretty cold out there.

COUNTY ATTORNEY: I'm going to stay here a while by myself. (*to the Sheriff*) You can send Frank out for me, can't you? I want to go over everything. I'm not satisfied that we can't do better.

SHERIFF: Do you want to see what Mrs. Peters is going to take in?

(*The Lawyer goes to the table, picks up the apron, laughs.*)

COUNTY ATTORNEY: Oh, I guess they're not very dangerous things the ladies have picked out. (*Moves a few things about, disturbing the quilt pieces which cover the box. Steps back*) No, Mrs. Peters doesn't need supervising. For that matter, a sheriff's wife is married to the law. Ever think of it that way, Mrs. Peters?

MRS. PETERS: Not — just that way.

SHERIFF (*chuckling*): Married to the law. (*moves toward the other room*) I just want you to come in here a minute, George. We ought to take a look at these windows.

COUNTY ATTORNEY (*scoffingly*): Oh, windows!

SHERIFF: We'll be right out, Mr. Hale.

(*Hale goes outside. The Sheriff follows the County Attorney into the other room. Then Mrs. Hale rises, hands tight together, looking intensely at Mrs. Peters, whose eyes make a slow turn, finally meeting Mrs. Hale's. A moment Mrs. Hale holds her, then her own eyes point the way to where the box is concealed. Suddenly Mrs. Peters throws back quilt pieces and tries to put the box in the bag she is wearing. It is too big. She opens box, starts to take bird out, cannot touch it, goes to pieces, stands there helpless. Sound of a knob turning in the other room. Mrs. Hale snatches the box and puts it in the pocket of her big coat. Enter County Attorney and Sheriff.*)

COUNTY ATTORNEY (*facetiously*): Well, Henry, at least we found out that she was not going to quilt it. She was going to — what is it you call it, ladies?

MRS. HALE (*her hand against her pocket*): We call it — knot it, Mr. Henderson.

CURTAIN

APPROACHING THE READING

1. Summarize the plot and explain the significance of details in it (the mess in the kitchen, the jam and jam jars, the quilting and the way Mrs. Wright was doing it, the bird and birdcage, the choice of a rope as weapon, and so on). If you feel you would have difficulty explaining the plot to a friend, go back to the play and look at it again in terms of the above or ask questions about it in class.

2. Examine the way the story is presented as a mystery play. Do you notice situations or lines that are conventional in detective stories you've read or seen in movies or on television? Find uses of foreshadowing in the play and explain whether you find these uses effective or ineffective.

www
Explore this author and play in depth, including images and cultural documents, with VirtuaLit Drama at bedfordstmartins .com/approachinglit.

3. List several conflicts, and several types of conflict, in the play. Which conflicts focus your attention on issues that seem important in the play? List several such issues.

4. Reflect on the characters: Who are the major characters, what is important to them, what motivates them, how do they change (if they do) and why? How does your impression of them change? Who are the minor characters, and what are their roles and significance?

5. This play was written in 1916. If you were directing a production of the play, would you give it a setting in the past (perhaps "Time: the early 1900s") or in the present? Why? How would that decision affect costuming, set design, props, and so on? What difference, if any, would that decision have on the central issues explored in the play?

THE GENERAL SETTING   We won't discuss here the characters, conflicts, and themes of *Trifles*. Instead, we focus attention on matters concerning setting and structure. The stage directions locate the play in a farmhouse, apparently in western Iowa or eastern Nebraska, since Sheriff Peters mentions that the county attorney, George Henderson, has just returned from Omaha (p. 936). But the geographic region has little effect on this play. Glaspell was born and raised in Iowa and worked for a short time as a journalist in Des Moines. But she moved to the Northeast more than a decade before she wrote *Trifles*, and its setting could just as easily be rural New England.

THE SPECIFIC SETTING   More significant for setting is that the farmhouse is isolated and depressing. As Mrs. Hale says, "I — I've never liked this place. Maybe because it's down in a hollow and you don't see the road. I dunno what it is, but it's a lonesome place and always was" (p. 942). Such isolation is important to the play: Mrs. Wright lacks contact with other people, sees neither neighbors nor friends. Her only source of companionship is a husband who rarely talks to or interacts with others.

THE OVERALL SET   Glaspell was more specific about set than setting. The set is the kitchen of the Wrights' home, and the detailed stage directions give a reader lots of help in imagining how the room appears (gloomy, probably sparsely furnished, in a state of considerable disorder, with a door to outside in the rear wall) and what the room contains (a breadbox, a sink with dirty pots under it, a stove, and a table).

DETAILS OF THE SET   In this play, Glaspell scatters additional stage directions throughout the text. We learn later that the room contains a cupboard, a rocking chair, a small table in the left rear corner with a large sewing basket under it, a small chair in another corner, a roller towel on the wall near the sink, and a low shelf on which the breadbox rests. The stove is a wood-burning cooking stove, and the kitchen table is large, sits in the center of the room, and probably has chairs around it. There is at least one window, a door at the right into another room, and steps at the left leading to a door, behind which are the stairs to the second floor. The text indicates that the sink does not have running water—next to it is a pail, presumably for bringing in water from a well outside, and there's a basin in the sink for washing.

FURNISHING THE SET   A stage designer who wants to create a historically authentic set for the play would do research into early twentieth-century kitchen furnishings and either make or find pieces that approximate what Glaspell describes as the "ideal" set for this play. You as a reader probably won't be able to spend that kind of time on furnishing your mental theater in historically correct detail. But you don't need to. The set in your mind as you stage *Trifles* will differ from the set of an acting company, of course; but it's important to realize that the sets of different productions will differ too.

READING A SET   The way each stage designer envisions Glaspell's directions is individual and unique—just as the way you visualize it will be. Some stage designers will attempt to recreate authentic early twentieth-century details, while others will give it a more timeless feel and not try for historical "correctness." Reading a set, and reading a play, is like all other kinds of reading. There is no single set design, or a single interpretation of a text, that all readers must seek to attain. Instead, we should decide what is appropriate for the drama itself and relish the diversity and enrichment that results when others see things differently from the way we do.

READING FOR STRUCTURE

EXTERNAL FORM   The structuring of a play, like that of a poem, involves external form as well as internal form. The external form starts with such features as the list of characters, the stage directions, the division of the text into speeches headed by tags identifying the characters, the stage directions guiding the actors on such things as action, tone, or expression.

DIVISION INTO ACTS   External form includes the division of longer plays into acts and scenes that help you, as a viewer or reader, to follow the play by separating it into segments that are easier to grasp than the whole at once. An **act** is a major division of a drama, a significant section of the action. In performance, the end of an act is signaled by an intermission, or by the lowering of the stage curtain. In reading, the text is usually marked as act 1, act 2, and so forth. Often playwrights structure the action so as to leave the audience in suspense at the end of an act, eager for the action to resume. Roman plays were divided into five acts, following Aristotle's belief that Greek plays fell into five parts that reflected steps in the internal development of a play (more on that to follow). Elizabethan playwrights, including Shakespeare, followed the Roman pattern, as did European dramatists generally until Ibsen began to modify it. Modern and contemporary plays are often divided into two or three acts, corresponding with the intermissions usual in performances.

DIVISION INTO SCENES   **Scenes** are minor divisions in a drama — a single act may be divided into scenes, or a one-act play might consist of several scenes. Often a new scene jumps ahead to a different time or moves to a different location. Scene changes are signaled in different ways: The stage may empty while the curtain remains raised, or the lights may go out, or the scenery may be reconfigured. Sometimes locations are identified for the audience in the printed program. But it is left to the imagination of the reader or viewer to bridge such gaps by making the needed connections or by supplying information that is only hinted at. Many modern dramatists divide their plays only into scenes, without division into acts, though a production may label the part before the intermission as "act 1" and the part following as "act 2."

INTERNAL FORM   The internal structure of a play centers on **plot**, the structural pattern by which it is organized and developed. The plot in drama involves many of the same issues as plot in fiction. *Beginnings*: starting **in medias res**, for example, making use of **exposition** to explain things that occurred before the initial action of the play, and making use of **flashbacks** to clarify events prior to the beginning of the play. *Middles*: using conflicts, suspense, gaps, foreshadowings, and repetitions to increase plot "complications" and build to a climax. *Endings*: resolving (or in some cases not resolving) the mysteries, problems, or tensions that have developed in the beginning and middle and tying up loose ends to create a sense of finality. Terms and techniques dealing with structure are discussed thoroughly in pages 60–69. Reviewing those pages will prepare you for studying plot in drama.

THE FIVE-ACT PLAY   Some theorists hold that the internal structure of a play involves a natural dramatic rhythm that develops in five divisions or steps, which some scholars believe correspond with the traditional five-act structure of a play.

- *Introduction or exposition*: The introduction, or exposition, occurs early in the play, usually as one or more characters deliver speeches providing information required for following the action of the play: introducing characters, filling in prior action and the background from which the central conflict will develop, establishing setting and tone.
- *Complication*: **Complication** is the rising action of the play; entanglements caused by the central conflict are set in motion.
- *Crisis or climax*: The **crisis** is the turning point in the action, the point at which the protagonist's situation turns for the better or worse. **Climax** is the point at which a significant emotional response is elicited. It does not always coincide with the moment of crisis.
- *Reversal*: Reversal is the falling action of a play, the depiction of the change in fortune experienced by the protagonist.
- *Catastrophe and resolution, or dénouement*: The term **catastrophe**, used mostly for tragedy, depicts the action, the unhappy ending, that results from parts 3 and 4. **Resolution**, or restoration of order, usually follows the catastrophe. **Dénouement** (French for "unknotting") is often used for the final unraveling of the plot complications in a comedy, though the unknotting at the end turns into a tying up of loose ends.

FREYTAG'S PYRAMID   These steps can be diagrammed as a pyramid, with action rising until it reaches a peak at the climax or crisis, then falling as implications of earlier events are worked out. The diagram is often referred to as "Freytag's Pyramid" because it was developed by Gustav Freytag in the mid-1800s. Some scholars believe the five steps correspond to, and perhaps gave rise to, the traditional five-act structure of a play.

But the pyramid can be applied to a one-act play as well. Follow along as we apply the above terms to *Trifles*: The first few pages of *Trifles* are the *introduction*, with Mr. Hale providing the necessary background (exposition) as he describes his encounter with Mrs. Wright the previous morning. The *complication* develops as the men seek a possible motive that would support their suspicion that Mrs. Wright killed her husband, and as the women begin to see what Mrs. Wright's life was like and to sympathize increasingly with her. The *climax* arrives when the women find the dead canary and reach a conclusion about who committed the crime. The *reversal* comes as the women struggle with whether they are obliged to inform the men about such a trifle as a dead bird and help them grasp its implications. The *resolution* comes as the ladies decide to conceal the box with the dead bird and not assist the men in their investigation of the crime.

Compression and Contrast

COMPRESSION   Dramatic works are shaped also by use of two key structural principles: compression and contrast. The first, *compression*, is necessary because although a work of fiction can extend to any length to tell its story, a playwright usually works under fairly strict time constraints. Audiences generally expect a play to last no more than three hours. There are plays that run four or five hours and some even for days, but those are the exceptions, and many playgoers may avoid them unless reviews say they are extraordinarily gripping and worthwhile. Playwrights, therefore, are usually aware of time and use techniques that enable them to compress their material economically. Being aware of such techniques can help you in understanding how a play and a play's structure work and why some things have to be handled so as to fit the constraints of time.

To compress their material, playwrights tend to start close to the most exciting or significant scene (see "Beginnings," p. 948). *Trifles*, for example, opens the morning after Mr. Wright dies because the play is most concerned with the motivation for the murder and the way Mrs. Hale and Mrs. Peters come to regard that motivation. In reading or watching plays, you need to get used to arriving in the middle of a conversation and to use what is said to figure out what happened earlier. Often it is said that dramatic action occurs only in the present: What occurs on the stage is always "now." Even when a flashback is acted out, as in *Death of a Salesman* (p. 1316), we see the past events occurring as we watch, as if they were happening now. Events that are not acted out are narrated through exposition, the way Mr. Hale fills in his experiences of the previous day. Playwrights also compress by using exposition to clarify information that the audience needs to know about earlier events and by using foreshadowing to alert us about things to watch for in what follows (see "Beginnings," p. 948). And they compress material by organizing events into moments, or scenes (p. 948).

SYMBOLS   Playwrights can achieve compression through the use of **symbols**, images or actions or characters that are first and fundamentally themselves in the play but also embody an abstract idea. Symbols are discussed at length on pages 143–47. What Chapter 6 says about symbols applies equally to drama. The same types of symbols (private, literary, conventional, traditional, and archetypal) are used in drama, and the same formal devices convey to a reader or viewer that an image, action, or character may be symbolic: repetition, description, placement in noticeable positions (title, beginning, ending, climactic scene), or a sense of weightiness or significance beyond the literal function in the work. The birdcage in *Trifles*, for example, is a literal object in the story, but it also suggests qualities of the relationship between Mr. and Mrs. Wright. Mrs. Wright used to enjoy singing and, like the bird, her song was stifled by Mr. Wright. She, like the bird, lived in a cage, trapped and broken figuratively in spirit, the way the bird's neck was broken literally. Symbols help achieve compression because the symbols—objects, character types, or actions—are seen on stage by the audience and require few words and little time to convey their meaning. The viewer, or the reader watching the play imaginatively, has the opportunity to recognize the symbol and to take part in discerning its appropriateness and meaning.

CONTRAST   *Contrast* is important to playwrights both as a means of compression and as a way to establish relationships in a play. Dramatists regularly establish parallels or contrasts between two or more situations, characters, actions, or symbols to get us to notice things about each that we might miss without the pairing. Often parallel items reinforce a point or theme or serve as a means of repetition, a valuable technique for creating emphasis, while contrasts direct our attention to differences and distinctions more clearly and forcefully. In *Trifles*, the stillness in the house Mrs. Peters experienced after losing a child enabled her to empathize with the similar stillness Mrs. Wright must have felt after the death of the canary. The principal contrast of the play is between the women and the men, with their different approaches, outlooks, and attitudes. The term **foil** is used for a character who stands in contrast to another character and thus calls attention to distinctive features of the second character or to significant differences between the two. Naomi can be taken as a foil to Bradley in Kelly Stuart's play (p. 915).

> **www**
>
> Further explore setting and structure, including interactive exercises, with VirtuaLit Drama at bedfordstmartins.com/ approachinglit.

☑ **CHECKLIST on Reading for Setting and Structure**

❏ Be attentive to setting, in terms of place, time, and historical, social, and cultural context, and to the effects of setting in a play.

❏ Be attentive to stage directions provided by the playwright, and use descriptions of set, props, costumes, stage movements, and character descriptions to sharpen your images as you visualize the plays.

❏ Be alert for symbols of different kinds (literary, conventional, traditional, and archetypal) and the various ways they can contribute to a play.

❏ Notice the structuring of plot in a play: its handling of beginning, middle, and ending; its use of gaps, flashbacks, suspense, foreshadowing, and repetition; and its use of compression and contrasts.

❏ Know the traditional five-part dramatic pattern (introduction, complication, climax, reversal, and resolution) and test to see if Freytag's Pyramid applies to a particular play.

FURTHER READING

ENTRY POINTS   *Trifles* illustrates a traditional drama, conventional in structure and technique. The following short, one-act play is unconventional and experimental. It involves two characters, a single setting, and little dramatic action. In it we watch two characters as they attempt to connect with one another. But there's a twist: If the character does not connect or slips up, she or he backtracks and tries again. The play does not have conventional scene divisions; instead, each time a character misspeaks, a bell rings to signal a breakdown, and the two characters back up a line or two and try a different version. After the thirty-eighth time — well, see for yourself what happens.

David Ives   b. 1950

Sure Thing   [1988]

This play is for Jason Buzas

Betty, a woman in her late twenties, is reading at a café table. An empty chair is opposite her. Bill, same age, enters.

BILL: Excuse me. Is this chair taken?
BETTY: Excuse me?
BILL: Is this taken?
BETTY: Yes it is.
BILL: Oh. Sorry.
BETTY: Sure thing.

(A bell rings softly.)

BILL: Excuse me. Is this chair taken?
BETTY: Excuse me?
BILL: Is this taken?
BETTY: No, but I'm expecting somebody in a minute.
BILL: Oh. Thanks anyway.
BETTY: Sure thing.

(A bell rings softly.)

BILL: Excuse me. Is this chair taken?
BETTY: No, but I'm expecting somebody very shortly.
BILL: Would you mind if I sit here till he or she or it comes?
BETTY *(glances at her watch)*: They do seem to be pretty late. . . .
BILL: You never know who you might be turning down.
BETTY: Sorry. Nice try, though.
BILL: Sure thing.

(*Bell.*)

     Is this seat taken?
BETTY: No it's not.
BILL: Would you mind if I sit here?
BETTY: Yes I would.
BILL: Oh.

(*Bell.*)

     Is this chair taken?
BETTY: No it's not.
BILL: Would you mind if I sit here?
BETTY: No. Go ahead.
BILL: Thanks. (*He sits. She continues reading.*) Everyplace else seems to be taken.
BETTY: Mm-hm.
BILL: Great place.
BETTY: Mm-hm.
BILL: What's the book?
BETTY: I just wanted to read in quiet, if you don't mind.
BILL: No. Sure thing.

(*Bell.*)

BILL: Everyplace else seems to be taken.
BETTY: Mm-hm.
BILL: Great place for reading.
BETTY: Yes, I like it.
BILL: What's the book?
BETTY: *The Sound and the Fury.*
BILL: Oh. Hemingway.

(*Bell.*)

     What's the book?
BETTY: *The Sound and the Fury.*
BILL: Oh. Faulkner.
BETTY: Have you read it?
BILL: Not . . . actually. I've sure read *about* it, though. It's supposed to be great.
BETTY: It is great.
BILL: I hear it's great. (*Small pause.*) Waiter?

(*Bell.*)

     What's the book?
BETTY: *The Sound and the Fury.*
BILL: Oh. Faulkner.
BETTY: Have you read it?
BILL: I'm a Mets fan, myself.

(*Bell.*)

BETTY: Have you read it?
BILL: Yeah, I read it in college.
BETTY: Where was college?
BILL: I went to Oral Roberts University.

(*Bell.*)

BETTY: Where was college?
BILL: I was lying. I never really went to college. I just like to party.

(*Bell.*)

BETTY: Where was college?
BILL: Harvard.
BETTY: Do you like Faulkner?
BILL: I love Faulkner. I spent a whole winter reading him once.
BETTY: I've just started.
BILL: I was so excited after ten pages that I went out and bought everything else he wrote. One of the greatest reading experiences of my life. I mean, all that incredible psychological understanding. Page after page of gorgeous prose. His profound grasp of the mystery of time and human existence. The smells of the earth . . . What do you think?
BETTY: I think it's pretty boring.

(*Bell.*)

BILL: What's the book?
BETTY: *The Sound and the Fury.*
BILL: Oh! Faulkner!
BETTY: Do you like Faulkner?
BILL: I love Faulkner.
BETTY: He's incredible.
BILL: I spent a whole winter reading him once.
BETTY: I was so excited after ten pages that I went out and bought everything else he wrote.
BILL: All that incredible psychological understanding.
BETTY: And the prose is so gorgeous.
BILL: And the way he's grasped the mystery of time —
BETTY: — and human existence. I can't believe I've waited this long to read him.
BILL: You never know. You might not have liked him before.
BETTY: That's true.
BILL: You might not have been ready for him. You have to hit these things at the right moment or it's no good.
BETTY: That's happened to me.
BILL: It's all in the timing. (*Small pause.*) My name's Bill, by the way.
BETTY: I'm Betty.

BILL: Hi.

BETTY: Hi. (*Small pause.*)

BILL: Yes I thought reading Faulkner was . . . a great experience.

BETTY: Yes. (*Small pause.*)

BILL: *The Sound and the Fury* . . . (*Another small pause.*)

BETTY: Well. Onwards and upwards. (*She goes back to her book.*)

BILL: Waiter — ?

(*Bell.*)

You have to hit these things at the right moment or it's no good.

BETTY: That's happened to me.

BILL: It's all in the timing. My name's Bill, by the way.

BETTY: I'm Betty.

BILL: Hi.

BETTY: Hi.

BILL: Do you come in here a lot?

BETTY: Actually I'm just in town for two days from Pakistan.

BILL: Oh. Pakistan.

(*Bell.*)

My name's Bill, by the way.

BETTY: I'm Betty.

BILL: Hi.

BETTY: Hi.

BILL: Do you come in here a lot?

BETTY: Every once in a while. Do you?

BILL: Not so much anymore. Not as much as I used to. Before my nervous break-down.

(*Bell.*)

Do you come in here a lot?

BETTY: Why are you asking?

BILL: Just interested.

BETTY: Are you really interested, or do you just want to pick me up?

BILL: No, I'm really interested.

BETTY: Why would you be interested in whether I come in here a lot?

BILL: I'm just . . . getting acquainted.

BETTY: Maybe you're only interested for the sake of making small talk long enough to ask me back to your place to listen to some music, or because you've just rented this great tape for your VCR, or because you've got some terrific unknown Django Reinhardt record, only all you really want to do is fuck — which you won't do very well — after which you'll go into the bathroom and pee very loudly, then pad into the kitchen and get yourself a beer from the refrigerator without asking me whether I'd like anything, and then you'll proceed to lie back down beside me and confess that you've got a girlfriend named Stephanie who's away at medical school in Belgium for a year, and that you've been involved with her — *off and on* — in what you'll call a very "intricate" relationship, for the past *seven YEARS*. None of which *interests* me, mister!

BILL: Okay.

(*Bell.*)

Do you come in here a lot?

BETTY: Every other day, I think.

BILL: I come in here quite a lot and I don't remember seeing you.

BETTY: I guess we must be on different schedules.

BILL: Missed connections.

BETTY: Yes. Different time zones.

BILL: Amazing how you can live right next door to somebody in this town and never even know it.

BETTY: I know.

BILL: City life.

BETTY: It's crazy.

BILL: We probably pass each other in the street every day. Right in front of this place, probably.

BETTY: Yep.

BILL (*looks around*): Well the waiters here sure seem to be in some different time zone. I can't seem to locate one anywhere. . . . Waiter! (*He looks back.*) So what do you — (*He sees that she's gone back to her book.*)

BETTY: I beg pardon?

BILL: Nothing. Sorry.

(*Bell.*)

BETTY: I guess we must be on different schedules.

BILL: Missed connections.

BETTY: Yes. Different time zones.

BILL: Amazing how you can live right next door to somebody in this town and never even know it.

BETTY: I know.

BILL: City life.

BETTY: It's crazy.

BILL: You weren't waiting for somebody when I came in, were you?

BETTY: Actually I was.

BILL: Oh. Boyfriend?

BETTY: Sort of.

BILL: What's a sort-of boyfriend?

BETTY: My husband.

BILL: Ah-ha.

(*Bell.*)

You weren't waiting for somebody when I came in, were you?

BETTY: Actually I was.

BILL: Oh. Boyfriend?

BETTY: Sort of.

BILL: What's a sort-of boyfriend?

BETTY: We were meeting here to break up.

BILL: Mm-hm . . .

(*Bell.*)

What's a sort-of boyfriend?

BETTY: My lover. Here she comes right now!

(*Bell.*)

BILL: You weren't waiting for somebody when I came in, were you?

BETTY: No, just reading.

BILL: Sort of a sad occupation for a Friday night, isn't it? Reading here, all by yourself?

BETTY: Do you think so?

BILL: Well sure. I mean, what's a good-looking woman like you doing out alone on a Friday night?

BETTY: Trying to keep away from lines like that.

BILL: No, listen —

(*Bell.*)

You weren't waiting for somebody when I came in, were you?

BETTY: No, just reading.

BILL: Sort of a sad occupation for a Friday night, isn't it? Reading here all by yourself?

BETTY: I guess it is, in a way.

BILL: What's a good-looking woman like you doing out alone on a Friday night anyway? No offense, but . . .

BETTY: I'm out alone on a Friday night for the first time in a very long time.

BILL: Oh.

BETTY: You see, I just recently ended a relationship.

BILL: Oh.

BETTY: Of rather long standing.

BILL: I'm sorry. (*Small pause.*) Well listen, since reading by yourself is such a sad occupation for a Friday night, would you like to go elsewhere?

BETTY: No . . .

BILL: Do something else?

BETTY: No thanks.

BILL: I was headed out to the movies in a while anyway.

BETTY: I don't think so.

BILL: Big chance to let Faulkner catch his breath. All those long sentences get him pretty tired.

BETTY: Thanks anyway.

BILL: Okay.

BETTY: I appreciate the invitation.

BILL: Sure thing.

(*Bell.*)

    You weren't waiting for somebody when I came in, were you?

BETTY: No, just reading.

BILL: Sort of a sad occupation for a Friday night, isn't it? Reading here all by yourself?

BETTY: I guess I was trying to think of it as existentially romantic. You know — cappuccino, great literature, rainy night . . .

BILL: That only works in Paris. We *could* hop the late plane to Paris. Get on a Concorde. Find a café . . .

BETTY: I'm a little short on plane fare tonight.

BILL: Darn it, so am I.

BETTY: To tell you the truth, I was headed to the movies after I finished this section. Would you like to come along? Since you can't locate a waiter?

BILL: That's a very nice offer, but . . .

BETTY: Uh-huh. Girlfriend?

BILL: Two, actually. One of them's pregnant, and Stephanie —

(*Bell.*)

BETTY: Girlfriend?

BILL: No, I don't have a girlfriend. Not if you mean the castrating bitch I dumped last night.

(*Bell.*)

BETTY: Girlfriend?

BILL: Sort of. Sort of.

BETTY: What's a sort-of girlfriend?

BILL: My mother.

(*Bell.*)

    I just ended a relationship, actually.

BETTY: Oh.

BILL: Of rather long standing.

BETTY: I'm sorry to hear it.

BILL: This is my first night out alone in a long time. I feel a little bit at sea, to tell you the truth.

BETTY: So you didn't stop to talk because you're a Moonie, or you have some weird political affiliation — ?

BILL: Nope. Straight-down-the-ticket Republican.

(*Bell.*)

    Straight-down-the-ticket Democrat.

(*Bell.*)

Can I tell you something about politics?

(*Bell.*)

I like to think of myself as a citizen of the universe.

(*Bell.*)

I'm unaffiliated.

BETTY: That's a relief. So am I.

BILL: I vote my beliefs.

BETTY: Labels are not important.

BILL: Labels are not important, exactly. Take me, for example. I mean, what does it matter if I had a two-point at—

(*Bell.*)

three-point at—

(*Bell.*)

four-point at college? Or if I did come from Pittsburgh—

(*Bell.*)

Cleveland—

(*Bell.*)

Westchester County?

BETTY: Sure.

BILL: I believe that a man is what he is.

(*Bell.*)

A person is what he is.

(*Bell.*)

A person is . . . what they are.

BETTY: I think so too.

BILL: So what if I admire Trotsky?

(*Bell.*)

So what if I once had a total-body liposuction?

(*Bell.*)

So what if I don't have a penis?

(*Bell.*)

So what if I spent a year in the Peace Corps? I was acting on my convictions.

BETTY: Sure.

BILL: You just can't hang a sign on a person.

BETTY: Absolutely. I'll bet you're a Scorpio.

(*Many bells ring.*)

Listen, I was headed to the movies after I finished this section. Would you like to come along?

BILL: That sounds like fun. What's playing?

BETTY: A couple of the really early Woody Allen movies.

BILL: Oh.

BETTY: You don't like Woody Allen?

BILL: Sure. I like Woody Allen.

BETTY: But you're not crazy about Woody Allen.

BILL: Those early ones kind of get on my nerves.

BETTY: Uh-huh.

(*Bell.*)

BILL: Y'know I was headed to the —

BETTY (*simultaneously*):   I was thinking about —

BILL: I'm sorry.

BETTY: No, go ahead.

BILL: I was going to say that I was headed to the movies in a little while, and . . .

BETTY: So was I.

BILL: The Woody Allen festival?

BETTY: Just up the street.

BILL: Do you like the early ones?

BETTY: I think anybody who doesn't ought to be run off the planet.

BILL: How many times have you seen *Bananas*?

BETTY: Eight times.

BILL: Twelve. So are you still interested (*Long pause.*)

BETTY: Do you like Entenmann's crumb cake . . . ?

BILL: Last night I went out at two in the morning to get one. Did you have an Etch-a-Sketch as a child?

BETTY: Yes! And do you like Brussels sprouts? (*Pause.*)

BILL: No, I think they're disgusting.

BETTY: They *are* disgusting!

BILL: Do you still believe in marriage in spite of current sentiments against it?

BETTY: Yes.

BILL: And children?

BETTY: Three of them.

BILL: Two girls and a boy.

BETTY: Harvard, Vassar, and Brown.

BILL: And will you love me?

BETTY: Yes.

BILL: And cherish me forever?

BETTY: Yes.

BILL: Do you still want to go to the movies?

BETTY: Sure thing.

BILL AND BETTY (*together*): *Waiter!*

BLACKOUT

APPROACHING THE READING

1. The text describes the immediate setting as a café but says nothing about where it is located. What assumptions do you make as you read about the broader setting of the play? How does your having to do this affect your reading and add to or detract from the play?

2. Describe the dramatic structure of the play. Could you argue that, experimental as it is, it still has a traditional introduction, complication, climax, reversal, and resolution, or something corresponding to them? If so, explain.

3. It has been said that *Sure Thing* includes a variety of characters and a wide range of emotions. How can there be a "variety of characters" in a two-person play?

4. Which character would you call the protagonist? Which the antagonist? Describe both characters. Do you think either changes or grows in the course of the play? If so, how?

5. Does the play's unorthodox form affect how you engage with the characters and the issues explored in the play? Be ready to discuss the basis of its appeal and effect.

RESPONDING THROUGH Writing

WRITING ABOUT SETTING AND STRUCTURE

Journal Entries

1. Write a journal entry listing ways the structuring of Susan Glaspell's *Trifles* (p. 935) both corresponds to and doesn't correspond to a popular TV detective drama. Do the same for David Ives's *Sure Thing* (p. 952) but use a popular TV sitcom instead.

2. In your journal, write a list of stage movements in Susan Glaspell's *Trifles* (p. 935), both those noted in the stage directions and those suggested by the text, and comment on their significance. Note especially what is indicated by the way characters are positioned in relation to one another.

3. Write a journal entry listing various uses of irony in Susan Glaspell's *Trifles* (p. 935) and commenting on their importance to the effect and meaning of the play.

> **WWW**
>
> Research the authors in this chapter with LitLinks, or take a quiz on the plays with LitQuiz, at bedfordstmartins.com/approachinglit.

Literary Analysis Papers

4. Write a paper analyzing the means of characterization in Susan Glaspell's *Trifles* (p. 935) and the relation of characters to the play's theme. Include the two key characters who do not appear on the stage, Mr. and Mrs. Wright.
5. Write a paper analyzing the unity of structure and theme in Susan Glaspell's *Trifles* (p. 935).
6. Write a paper examining the dramatic structure of David Ives's *Sure Thing* (p. 952) and its contribution to the theme and effect of the play.

Comparison-Contrast Papers

7. Compare and contrast the birdcage in Susan Glaspell's *Trifles* (p. 935) and the doll house in Henrik Ibsen's *A Doll House* (p. 1263) as feminist metaphors.
8. Compare and contrast Susan Glaspell's *Trifles* (p. 935) to a contemporary TV detective program, focusing on generic conventions they have in common and ones they do not share.

► TIPS for Writing about Setting and Structure

► **Specific settings** Even though the importance of setting in drama varies depending on the play, it often plays a key role. For the location of the action to be described in specific detail usually indicates that it will be influential, affecting characterization, tone, assumptions about social and cultural attitudes, and themes. In such cases, it should at least be referred to, even in a paper on a different topic. It might also be suitable in itself as the main focus of a paper.

► **General settings** When setting is general or unspecified (when the action could occur anywhere at any time), it could mean that it is less significant than a specific setting. However, there are plays, such as some by Samuel Beckett, in which the abstract setting and time hold important meaning. It will be helpful and valuable to mention and explain how an unspecified setting affects or does not affect the impact of the play.

► **Arrangement** The way a play's action is organized structurally often contributes significantly to its impact. When this is the case, analyzing that arrangement can be an insightful topic for a paper. Pay attention especially to the opening, to the means by which background information is supplied, to the way the action builds to a climax, and to how things are brought to a conclusion.

► **Crucial scenes** Because full-length plays are difficult to cover completely in a short paper, it may be necessary to focus on key scenes in a paper on structure. Often it works best to choose scenes that are the most dramatic, in which characters and ideas are involved in crucial conflicts. However, in some plays the crucial conflict may occur in a very subtle manner, so don't overlook what may appear at first to be a less important scene. Revealing the impact of a seemingly minor or insignificant scene can be an interesting and effective paper topic.

➤ **Contrast** Analyzing contrast—the structural juxtaposition of scenes, images, and ideas, and the use of one character as a foil to another— can be one of the most interesting and effective ways to find and focus a paper on drama.

WRITING ABOUT CONNECTIONS

Setting and structure invariably offer opportunities for you to work with connections within a play. When you attend to the setting, pay special attention to how any action connects to its location in a meaningful way and notice how the structure arranges the various parts of a play, interconnecting them in an orderly and illuminating fashion. Equally interesting is the examination of thematic connections between different plays that have implications regarding setting and structure. Here are a few examples:

1. "By a Higher Standard": The Conflict of Law and Justice in Susan Glaspell's *Trifles* (p. 935) and Sophocles' *Antigone* (p. 1110)
2. "Living on a Smile and a Handshake": Selling Yourself in David Ives's *Sure Thing* (p. 952) and Arthur Miller's *Death of a Salesman* (p. 1316)
3. "Serving Time in Invisible Prisons": Social Entrapments in Henrik Ibsen's *A Doll House* (p. 1263) and August Wilson's *Fences* (p. 1029)

WRITING RESEARCH PAPERS

1. Read the description of feminist criticism on pages 1598–1601 and do additional research into feminist approaches to literature. Apply what you find in a paper analyzing Susan Glaspell's *Trifles* (p. 935) and/or Henrik Ibsen's *A Doll House* (p. 1263).
2. Do research on the appeal of detective stories (in books, on TV, in movies and plays), including Susan Glaspell's *Trifles* (p. 935), as a cultural phenomenon. What is it about our culture that makes such stories popular? Try to find out if that popularity extends to other cultures and include that in your consideration. Write a research paper on what you find.

COMPOSING IN OTHER ART FORMS

1. Design a poster suitable for display in a literature classroom diagramming Freitag's Pyramid (p. 919) and showing how it clarifies the structure of a five-act play.
2. Do one or a group of diagrams to show how you would design the set and properties for a production of Susan Glaspell's *Trifles* (p. 935).

The printed script of a play is hardly more than an architect's blueprint of a house not yet built or built and destroyed. Tennessee Williams

23 Theaters and Their Influence

Imagining the Impact of Stage and Space

Chapters 21 and 22 focus on the elements of drama that need attention as you read a play—the handling of character, dialogue, dramatic action, setting, and structure. For drama, however, we need to go a step beyond the elements because most plays are written for public performance, not for private reading like stories or poems are. Playwrights nearly always write with specific stage structures and theatrical conventions in mind, usually the theaters and practices of their day—that is, as they write a play, their imaginations shape things in terms of the kind of theater the play will be performed in. For you to read plays from different periods knowledgeably, you need some information about the ways theaters have varied through history. This chapter provides a quick historical survey of theaters, focusing on four important eras of drama in Western culture: ancient Greece, Elizabethan England, late nineteenth-century England and America, and the late twentieth to early twenty-first centuries.

In looking at theaters in this chapter, our focus is not their influence on dramatic performances, but their influence on how playwrights imagined the way their plays would be acted as they wrote them. We consider not just the shape of the buildings and stages, but also the conventions used on those stages, some common to all theaters, some growing out of a specific kind of theater. **Conventions** are assumptions shared by playwrights and audiences about how an imagined action on the stage can be accepted as real and believable. Conventions rely on what the nineteenth-century poet and critic Samuel Taylor Coleridge called a "willing suspension of disbelief" — that is, a willingness not to question the truth, accuracy, or probability of what occurs in a work so that one can enter and enjoy the work as if it were real. Thus, for example, if an actor on an Elizabethan stage (where lighting could not be controlled) says it is so dark he can't even see his hand in front of his face, the playwright and audience accept that as true, even though the audience can see the actor clearly on the stage. Awareness of the theaters, stages, and conventions that playwrights needed to consider is helpful in understanding a play as you read it and in visualizing the acting out of the play in the theater of your mind.

THE GREEK THEATER

Ancient Greek drama was performed in a large, open-air stadium designed for the annual celebrations in Athens of the festival of Dionysus, the Greek god of fertility. At the center of the structure was the circular "orchestra," or "dancing place" where the chorus moved from side to side and chanted their lines. On it was an altar used for the religious ceremonies, of which the drama was a part. Circling two-thirds of the orchestra was the *theatron* or "seeing place": tiers of wood or stone seats for the audience rose up a hillside and created a bowl large enough to hold 15,000 people.

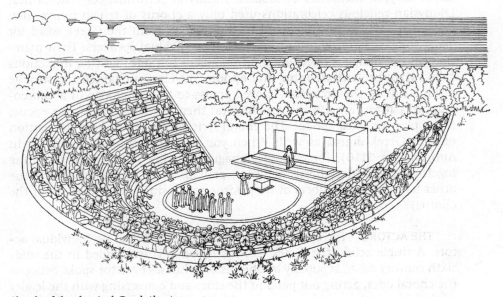

Sketch of the classical Greek theater

Comparing that to the size of theaters today — 1,500 to 2,000 seats is large — gives some indication of how important these ceremonies were in Athenian culture.

Closing off the circle was the *skene* (literally, the "hut"), a wooden building where actors changed masks or costumes. Three doors opened onto the *proskenion*, a long, narrow area that served as the main acting area (the term *proscenium*, for the apron or forestage of a modern theater, came from the Greek word). The actors moved back and forth between the *proskenion* and the orchestra; the roof of the *skene* was also used as an acting area, for example, to suggest a cliff or the place of the gods.

ACTING STYLE   Performing in such a huge theater made it impossible to rely on subtle voice inflections, slight gestures, or facial expressions. Actors wore large masks to identify their characters, perhaps with megaphonic mouthpieces to enlarge their voices; they used exaggerated gestures so even those seated at the top of the *theatron* could see them. In reading a Greek play, therefore, you should not visualize the kind of intimate, realistic space that we've become accustomed to in the past two or three centuries. Think, rather, of a stately style of acting, with the flowing movements of a dance company and the dignity of a formal religious celebration. Visualizing it as a kind of ballet or pageant without music comes closer to its spirit than imagining it as realistic drama.

THE CHORUS   In visualizing the actors, you also need to separate yourself from your memories of modern theatrical performances. The earliest Dionysian religious celebrations used only a chorus of ten to twelve men dressed in goat skins (our word *tragedy* derives from the Greek word for "goat song") chanting in unison, with no individual speakers. Their material was not dialogue but a long, formal poem (an **ode**) written in sections called **strophe**, **antistrophe**, and **epode**. The chorus chanted the strophe on one side of the orchestra, moved across to the other side in a choreographed pattern for the antistrophe, and then moved again for the epode, if the play included epodes. The choral lyric continued to be a convention of later Greek drama as well: When you read speeches by the chorus in *Antigone* (p. 1110), for example, imagine hearing several voices reciting together (the entire chorus at times, or half of the group addressing the other half, or the members of the chorus conversing with the leader of the chorus).

THE ACTORS   The earliest Dionysian celebrations had no individual actors. A single actor (the Greek word is *hypocrites*) was added in the mid-sixth century B.C.E., reputedly by Thespis of Athens. The actor spoke between the choral odes, acting out parts in the story and conversing with the leader of the chorus. A second actor was added by the dramatist Aeschylus, thus making possible a conflict between a protagonist and an antagonist, and a third by Sophocles, in the next century, to allow greater interaction between individuals as well as with the chorus. Actors could play more than one role by changing to a different mask and costume.

THE ROLE OF THE CHORUS   Although the focus of the play shifted increasingly to the actors, the chorus continued to be central because tragedy originated in a poetic form that continued to define audience expectations. Actors entered and exited, but the chorus was present throughout the performance, providing a continuous point of reference for the audience and serving as an intermediary with the audience, sometimes addressing it directly. The chorus at times stood outside the action to provide background information, listen in on what characters said, comment on or react to what was said or done, or point out the moral at the end. At other times, the chorus interacted with the characters, giving them advice or warning against falling into a mistake. Sometimes the chorus, seeming rather dense, did not "get" what was going on and required more explanation from the characters—thus enlightening the audience as well.

ACTION OFFSTAGE   The chorus helps in visualizing the play in that its presence reminds us that this is a staged play. In Greek drama, little action occurs on the stage. The actors deliver speeches that describe important actions, such as the sentry in *Antigone* informing Creon about the ritualistic burial of Polynices (p. 1118) and the messenger who tells about what happens to Antigone, Haemon, and Eurydice. The conflict that does occur onstage is verbal and emotional sparring (like the angry exchange between Creon and Haemon), not a physical clash. Violence was never shown on the Greek stage; when it was part of the plot, it occurred in the past or appeared offstage and was reported to the audience.

DRAMATIC CONVENTIONS   Scenery and props were minimal and conventional—painted scenery to suggest a building, rocks, or trees was introduced in the mid-fifth century B.C.E. The immediate setting of *Antigone* and its prequel, *Oedipus the King* is in front of the royal palace. No scene changes occur in either play and in *Oedipus* the events dramatized take as long to occur as the acting of the play itself (there are no breaks in the action). The action seems continuous in *Antigone* as well (the chorus is always on stage after line 116), but the actions that occur offstage take longer than the onstage time allows for. The compression of time in *Oedipus*, having all the necessary characters arrive or be available during a two-hour period, is one of the conventions accepted by the audience. Aristotle, writing about drama in the generation after Sophocles, praised *Oedipus the King* for its unity of time, place, and action. Though *Oedipus* was held up widely as an ideal of dramatic structure, critics since the mid-1700s have agreed that audiences have no difficulty accepting changes of time and place, though unity of action is still regarded as important, just as they have no difficulty accepting the sophisticated "double time" scheme Sophocles creates in *Antigone*.

THE ELIZABETHAN THEATER

The majority of William Shakespeare's plays were written for and performed in theaters like the Theatre, the Curtain, the Rose, the Fortune, and the Swan. They were similar in structure, adapted from courtyards at inns, where traveling acting companies performed as they went from town to town before permanent theaters were built. In later years, acting companies returned to inn yards during times of plague when the theaters were closed and people who could afford it left the city for the countryside.

THE GLOBE   In 1599, the Lord Chamberlain's Company, to which Shakespeare belonged—he was an actor in it as well as writing plays for it—opened a new theater, the Globe. It was a typical theater of the time: All were circular or octagonal structures with the center open to the sky. The audience was seated in several balconies on three sides, nearly surrounding the actors, who performed mostly on a "thrust stage," extending out into and partially encircled by the audience. The stage was covered to protect the actors from rain. The theaters could hold up to 3,000 patrons, but the closeness of audience to stage, coupled with patrons standing in the "pit" around the stage and even leaning on the edge of the stage, created an intimacy impossible in the large Greek theaters.

THE ACTING AREAS   At the back of the thrust stage was the wall separating the stage from the backstage "tiring house," or dressing room. Two curtained doors in the wall were used for entrances and exits and sometimes as places where characters hid and overheard what was said on stage, as when the king and Polonius "withdraw" to spy on Hamlet and Ophelia (*Hamlet* 3.1) and later Polonius does to observe Hamlet talking to his mother (3.4). An upper gallery, normally used to seat wealthy patrons, was sometimes employed as an additional acting area (as when Juliet appears "above, at her window" and talks to Romeo, who is in the garden below—*Romeo and Juliet* 2.2). Most of the action, however, took place toward the front of the thrust stage, with those standing in the pit crowded around three sides. The closeness of the audience added to the effectiveness of Hamlet's famous soliloquies (1.2.129–59, 2.2.496–552, 3.1.57–89, and 4.4.32–66), as people, some of them only a few feet away, overhear his most private thoughts and emotions.

POETIC DRAMA   As you read *Hamlet*, you will find fairly long speeches, with most of the play written in blank verse (see p. 612). Poetry was used because almost all serious literature at the time was written in verse: epics, ballads, and elegies as well as lyric poetry. Poetic drama is a convention of Elizabethan theater: It's not realistic that a soldier on a battlefield would talk in iambic pentameter, but the audience accepted it by suspending their disbelief. And Shakespeare could count on members of the audience to be good

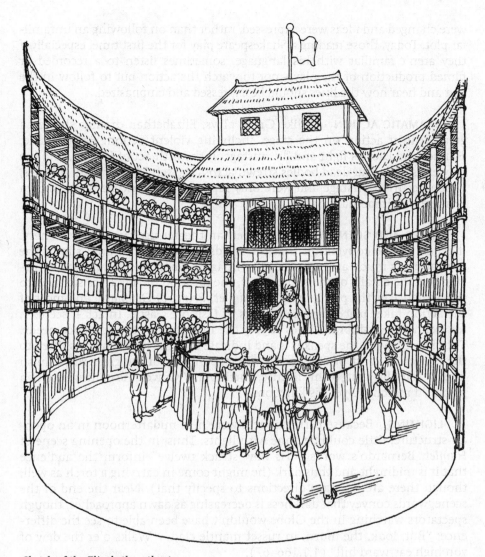

Sketch of the Elizabethan theater

listeners, on the whole, able to follow speeches packed with meaning and to catch some intricate wordplay. He could also count on excellent actors in his company, such as Richard Burbage and Will Kempe, being able to deliver such speeches effectively.

THE PLOTS   Elizabethan playwrights generally used stories already familiar to the audience: Originality was in the alteration of familiar details, the development of character, and the freshness of expression, not in the creation of new stories. Thus the audience could concentrate on the way things were changed and ideas were expressed, rather than on following an unfamiliar plot. Today, those reading a Shakespeare play for the first time, especially if they aren't familiar with his language, sometimes listen to a recorded or filmed production of the play — not to watch the action but to follow in the text and hear how the lines should be expressed and emphasized.

DRAMATIC ACTION   Unlike Greek plays, Elizabethan dramas showed a great deal of action on the stage, including violent action: For example, Hamlet and Laertes fight and die onstage in the fifth act of *Hamlet*, and the play ends with four dead bodies strewn across the set. Murders and suicides, which occurred offstage and were only reported in Greek plays, are shown onstage in Elizabethan drama.

PROPS AND SCENERY   The Elizabethan theater used very little scenery. It relied on the convention that the words of the actors would supply the spectators as much as they needed to imagine where the action was occurring and the details of the scene. Thus, the location of *Hamlet* is signaled to the audience by the play's full title, *Hamlet, Prince of Denmark*, and most of the action takes place in various parts of Elsinore Castle. In act 4, scene 4, for example, Fortinbras's lines supply the information the audience needs. They identify who the speaker is and indicate that the location has shifted to the border or coast of Denmark: "Go, captain, from me greet the Danish king. / Tell him that, by his license, Fortinbras / Craves the conveyance of a promis'd march / Over his kingdom."

LIGHTING   Because performances were held midafternoon in an open-air structure, little could be done with lights. Thus, in the opening scene of *Hamlet*, Bernardo's words "'Tis now struck twelve" inform the audience that it is midnight and thus dark (he might come in carrying a torch as well, though there are no stage directions to specify that). Near the end of the scene, words convey that darkness is decreasing as dawn approaches, though spectators watching in the Globe wouldn't have been able to see the difference: "But, look, the morn, in russet mantle clad, / Walks o'er the dew of yon high eastward hill" (1.1.166–67).

INDOOR PERFORMANCES   But performances in Shakespeare's day were not limited to public theaters like the Globe. Acting companies also did indoor performances, sometimes at court for the monarch and courtiers, sometimes in the banqueting halls of noble families, sometimes at private theaters such as the Blackfriars and the Whitefriars. These acting places replicated the open-air theaters as much as possible, with a thrust stage and "tiring house" backdrop with doors. More could be done with scenery and props indoors; costumes and scenery became quite spectacular for *masques*, pageantlike entertainments with some elements similar to present-day opera and some to musical comedy.

THE PREMODERN THEATER   By half a century after Shakespeare's death, the indoor theater had become dominant, with candles providing illumination. From the late seventeenth century through the early nineteenth century in England, a "proscenium arch" with its front curtain divided the forestage from the rear stage. The area behind the arch was not used for acting, however, as it was in the following century. The rear stage was used mostly for scenery painted on rows of large flat canvases ("flats") that could be changed easily by sliding them back and forth. The action took place mainly on the forestage, which was not a thrust stage but extended across the theater from wall to wall. The audience was seated in front of the stage, not surrounding it as before. This created a sense of separation of the actors from the audience, in contrast to the intimacy of the Elizabethan theater, and laid the basis for the modern theater that developed in the mid-1800s.

THE MODERN THEATER

A major theatrical change occurred in the mid-1800s when the action of a play moved behind the proscenium arch and the forestage was pretty much eliminated. Thus, what had been called the rear stage (now referred to just as the "stage") became the main acting area.

BOX SET   The result was the "box set." Playwrights began writing for a stage that they thought of as a box behind the arch. They visualized the box as an actual room and instructed stage designers to build it with real windows and doors that could open and close, and realistic carpets and furniture. Instead of action taking place in front of artificial, painted flats, action took place within what looked like a room in an actual house. Three walls of the room were visible to the audience; the fourth wall, of course, was not. The major convention of the modern theater was the "invisible fourth wall" through which the audience could see into the room, though the actors treated it as if the wall was present and couldn't be crossed.

That was the stage Henrik Ibsen had in mind as he wrote the stage directions for *A Doll House*:

> A comfortable room, tastefully but not expensively furnished. A door to the right in the back wall leads to the entryway; another to the left leads to Helmer's study. Between these doors, a piano. Midway in the left-hand wall a door, and further back a window. Near the window a round table with an armchair and a small sofa. In the right-hand wall, toward the rear, a door, and nearer the foreground a porcelain stove with two armchairs and a rocking chair beside it. Between the stove and the side door, a small table. Engravings on the walls. An étagère with china figures and other small art objects; a small bookcase with richly bound books; the floor carpeted; a fire burning in the stove. It is a winter day. (p. 1263)

Sketch of the box set decorated with wall and window hangings

The desired effect was a high degree of "realism," making the play as close to real life as possible.

UNITY OF PLACE   Because the set filled the stage and was difficult to move, the entire play takes place in the Helmers' living room. Nora, the protagonist of the play, is on stage much of the time. Mrs. Linde, Dr. Rank, and Krogstad visit her in that room; her scenes with her husband are there as well. A key scene—Nora dancing her tarantella—occurs in the Stenborgs' apartment directly above the room shown on stage, so we don't see that scene; it is reported by Torvald. In the twentieth century, large theaters developed revolving platforms on stage that, by rotations between scenes, presented two or three realistic, box stage sets. But nineteenth-century theaters were far from such technology, so playwrights had to accept unity of place, writing to fit the entire play into one location.

LIGHTING: REALISTIC   The realistic effect was aided by improvements in lighting: Candles had been replaced by gas lamps, which later were replaced by electric lights. The Elizabethan bare stage and the painted flats of its successor required a great deal of imaginative involvement by the audience. Realistic drama lessened the amount of imagining the audience had to do. The ideal would be for audience members to forget they were watching a play. Thus, the modern theater was well suited to, or perhaps was necessitated by, the plays of Ibsen and his contemporaries, especially Ibsen's "problem plays," which explored in a psychologically realistic way problems that ordinary people in real life faced.

CONVENTIONS   Of course, modern theater relied as heavily on conventions as its predecessors: The spectators knew they were in a theater. They knew the actor was not the character, the gun did not have real bullets, and no one onstage really died when she or he was "shot." Thus, nineteenth-century realistic drama also required the imaginative participation of its audience, just as plays of the Elizabethan era and the century following it did, especially an empathetic imagination and a willingness to suspend disbelief. For us as readers of those dramas, visualizing them is easier when we know the kind of stage and stage conventions authors had in mind as they wrote and the kind of effect they sought to create for their audiences.

TWENTIETH-CENTURY THEATERS   Most theaters of the early and mid-twentieth century continued to have a proscenium arch. But dramatists and the theater as a whole have moved away from the realism of the late 1800s and early 1900s. In late modern and contemporary theater — both in the plays written now and the productions of earlier plays — it is assumed that people in the audience know that they are watching a performance and that the set is an artistic construction that requires the imaginative participation of the audience. The set is rarely limited to one room or space. Playwrights, as they write, no longer confine themselves to a lifelike room in a box set, with all action occurring within that one space.

NONREALISTIC SET   Arthur Miller's conception of the set for *Death of a Salesman* (p. 1316) illustrates the postmodern, nonrealistic approach. Miller had a proscenium stage in mind: The stage directions begin with "The curtain rises." But what we see on the stage as the curtain goes up is not one room from the inside, but the house from the outside: "Before us is the Salesman's house. . . . As more light appears, we see a solid vault of apartment houses around the small, fragile-seeming home" (p. 1316). The outer and inner walls of the house are invisible (perhaps only the bottom couple of feet of the walls, outlining the rooms), which allows us to see into the rooms — not just one room, as in the box set, but into several rooms:

> The kitchen at center seems actual enough, for there is a kitchen table with three chairs, and a refrigerator. But no other fixtures are seen. At the back of the kitchen there is a draped entrance, which leads to the living room. To the right of the kitchen, on a level raised two feet, is a bedroom furnished only with a brass bedstead and a straight chair. . . .
>   Behind the kitchen, on a level raised six and a half feet, is the boys' bedroom, at present barely visible. Two beds are dimly seen, and at the back of the room a dormer window. . . . At the left a stairway curves up to it from the kitchen.

The entire setting is wholly or, in some places, partially transparent. The roofline of the house is one-dimensional; under and over it we see the apartment buildings. (p. 1316)

USE OF THE FORESTAGE   The set is not cut off at the proscenium arch but extends to and makes important use of the forestage: "Before the house lies an apron, curving beyond the forestage into the orchestra. This forward area serves as the back yard as well as the locale of all Willy's imaginings and of his city scenes" (p. 1316). Thus the actors and audience are not separated by the proscenium arch, as they are in Ibsen's theater, but the action reaches out toward or into the audience.

USE OF A THRUST STAGE   Because action is not contained within a box set, the play could readily be adapted to a theater without a proscenium arch. It is easy to imagine staging it on a contemporary thrust stage (see p. 976), for example—what Miller describes as being behind the arch is placed at the rear of the thrust stage. It does not seem as well suited for the contemporary arena theater or "theater-in-the-round" (p. 976).

CREATING ATMOSPHERE   The set is used both to describe the space and to create atmosphere: "Only the blue light of the sky falls upon the house and forestage; the surrounding area shows an angry glow of orange. . . . An air of the dream clings to the place, a dream rising out of reality" (p. 1316). It is used also to separate past events from action taking place in the present:

Whenever the action is in the present the actors observe the imaginary wall-lines, entering the house only through its doors at the left. But in the scenes of the past these boundaries are broken, and characters enter or leave a room by stepping "through" a wall onto the forestage. (p. 1316)

The audience, of course, does not read this explanation: They are required to catch this through alert, active observation of what occurs on stage.

BEYOND REALISM   The set allows Miller to do things the realistic box set does not permit. For example, he does not have to contrive ways to have all the action take place in a single room. We can visualize, and the audience can see, Biff and Happy talking in their bedroom and overhearing Willy talk to himself in the kitchen below. Miller is not limited to action in the present: Because walls and rooms are suggestive rather than realistic, flashbacks can be acted out, not just recounted as exposition the way Ibsen was forced to do. And Miller is not limited in location. Ibsen, using a realistic room as set, had to report what went on in the flat above that room. Miller does not need to rely on reports: Events that occurred years ago in a Boston hotel room are acted out on the forestage.

Thus the stage Miller uses, conceived with flexibility and suggestiveness, enables him to dramatize his story in ways that a realistic box stage doesn't allow.

THE CONTEMPORARY THEATER

CONTEMPORARY THEATERS   Theater in the mid- to late 1900s moved still further away from realism in text and stagecraft. Many contemporary theaters reach out to the audience not just through the imagination but physically, by thrusting the stage out into the audience (returning to the Elizabethan theater's way of bringing the action close to the audience) or by placing the stage in the center of the theater, with the audience surrounding it on all sides. The arena theater, or "theater-in-the-round," eliminates the sense of separation created by the proscenium arch or the forestage and rearstage areas of the thrust stage. It gives actors the chance to enter and exit through the audience, using the same aisles as the audience. Some plays even have a character initially seated in the audience who later rises and joins in the action — eliminating still further the sense of distance between actors and audience.

SETS, PROPS, AND LIGHTING   A thrust stage or theater-in-the-round cannot, of course, have rooms with real walls. Sets and props usually are simple and minimal or impressionistic and symbolic rather than realistically detailed. Playwrights and stage designers often think in terms of platforms connected by ramps and stairways to allow multiple locations. Modern equipment produces lighting effects undreamed of even a few decades ago. All of this means that playwrights today are free to imagine a far greater variety of spaces and uses for them as they write. Playwrights are less confined to a particular kind of theater than were their counterparts in earlier centuries.

USING A CONTEMPORARY THRUST STAGE   August Wilson's *Fences* (p. 1029) was written with the variety and flexibility of contemporary theaters in mind. The stage directions do not limit it to a certain kind of stage: Producing it in an arena theater might be difficult, but it could be staged satisfactorily in a proscenium-arch theater. The contemporary thrust stage seems ideal to what Wilson visualizes:

> The setting is the yard which fronts the only entrance to the Maxson household, an ancient two-story brick house set back off a small alley in a big-city neighborhood. The entrance to the house is gained by two or three steps leading to a wooden porch badly in need of paint.
>
> A relatively recent addition to the house and running its full width, the porch lacks congruence. It is a sturdy porch with a flat roof. One or two chairs of dubious value sit at one end where the kitchen window opens onto the porch. An old-fashioned icebox stands silent guard at the opposite end.
>
> The yard is a small dirt yard, partially fenced, except for the last scene, with a wooden sawhorse, a pile of lumber, and other fence-building equipment set off to the side. Opposite is a tree from which hangs a ball made of rags. A baseball bat leans against the tree. Two oil drums serve as garbage receptacles and sit near the house at right to complete the setting. (p. 1029)

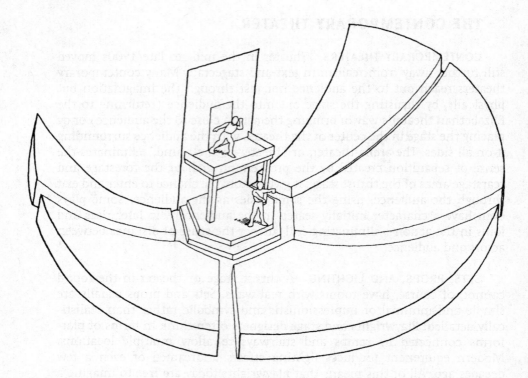

Sketches of the contemporary thrust stage (above) and contemporary arena stage (below)

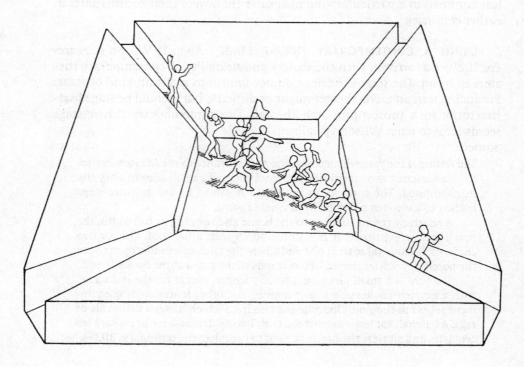

The house, thus, serves as a backdrop to the area in front of it on the thrust stage, which becomes the acting area. Having the audience around the stage on three sides creates the sense of closeness and immediacy that *Fences* requires — the stage and setting Wilson envisages remove fences between actors and audience that the modern theater might have erected.

UNITY OF PLACE, BUT NOT TIME   Wilson chooses not to divide the stage into different acting areas with platforms and ramps or stairs connecting them. He shapes the play so that all the action occurs in one location — the porch and yard in front of the Maxson's home. It does not occur all at one time, however. The stage directions indicate that act 1 takes place over a two-week span in early fall 1957. The first scene of act 2 is the next day, but the second scene is six months later and the fourth scene two months later still. The final scene jumps to 1965. We do get indications of the passage of time from the text: In act 2, scene 2, for example, Troy's line "You ain't wanted to talk to me for months" reveals that time has passed since the scene before, as does the fact that Raynell, whom we saw as a baby in act 2, scene 3, is seven years old in scene 5. Modern and contemporary theater, however, do not need to rely on the text to indicate passage of time, the way ancient and Elizabethan theater did. Now the audience is given a program with a list of scenes with the time and place of each, the same information provided the reader by the stage directions in the text.

NONCONVENTIONAL PRESENTATIONS OF DRAMA   This chapter has reviewed conventional theaters across some two and a half thousand years. But not all drama was produced in such theaters. In the Middle Ages in England, for example, plays depicting biblical stories were performed on wagons in the marketplace on festival days, not in theaters at all. Likewise, experimental or avant-garde drama uses the stage differently, often with minimal props and furnishings that are suggestive and symbolic in nature rather than realistic. These types of drama are thus well suited to theater-in-the-round or a thrust stage. Some playwrights move outside of traditional theaters, writing plays to be performed in bare halls or even on the streets, sometimes with workers and ordinary people playing the roles, instead of trained actors. Others, like John Leguizamo (*Mambo Mouth*, p. 979) experiment with unconventional staging in conventional theaters. Instead of dramatizing a story, *Mambo Mouth* has a single actor depicting a series of characters who appear individually on the stage and deliver a monologue. Very little is required in terms of stage set and props, and the play can be staged in any kind of theater.

DRAMATISTS INFLUENCE THEATER DESIGN   Whatever the era, the configuration of theater and stage and the theatrical conventions in use at the time influence the way a playwright conceives and visualizes a play. But it's equally clear that playwrights influence theater design. The changes in theaters and stages traced in this chapter occurred in part as playwrights

WWW
Further explore the-
aters and their influence,
including interactive exercises, with VirtuaLit Drama
at bedfordstmartins.com/
approachinglit.

conceived plays that could not be performed to full advantage in the spaces provided by currently existing
theaters. Such plays led first to modifications of the
existing spaces and later to new theaters with re-
designed spaces for both stage and audience. Because
the theater is a dynamic, growing, responsive world,
such changes in theaters and the plays presented in
them will continue in the future.

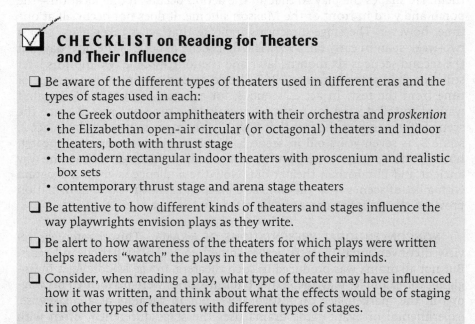

☑ CHECKLIST on Reading for Theaters and Their Influence

❑ Be aware of the different types of theaters used in different eras and the
types of stages used in each:
- the Greek outdoor amphitheaters with their orchestra and *proskenion*
- the Elizabethan open-air circular (or octagonal) theaters and indoor
theaters, both with thrust stage
- the modern rectangular indoor theaters with proscenium and realistic
box sets
- contemporary thrust stage and arena stage theaters

❑ Be attentive to how different kinds of theaters and stages influence the
way playwrights envision plays as they write.

❑ Be alert to how awareness of the theaters for which plays were written
helps readers "watch" the plays in the theater of their minds.

❑ Consider, when reading a play, what type of theater may have influenced
how it was written, and think about what the effects would be of staging
it in other types of theaters with different types of stages.

FURTHER READING

ENTRY POINTS   *Mambo Mouth*, a satire on racial and ethnic stereotypes
in American culture, is a one-man show consisting of a series of monologues by seven characters, including Agamemnon, a stuck-up woman-
bashing talk-show host; Loco Louie, a crazy and horny teen; Angel Garcia, in
jail for hitting his wife because he claims she cheated on him and they got in
a little argument; Pepe, an illegal immigrant trying to convince the guard he
is of another race; and Manny the Fanny, an outgoing woman who tells one
of her friends a story about how she got revenge on her man. The various
monologues comment on the way cultures deal with ethnic and racial difference. As you read Pepe's section, try visualizing how it would look on a
stage.

John Leguizamo   b. 1964

From Mambo Mouth: A Savage Comedy   [1988]

Pepe

(The stage is dark. A backstage light reveals the silhouette of a man wearing jeans and a T-shirt standing in a doorway.)

PEPE: Excuse me, ése,° I just got this gift certificate in the mail saying that I was entitled to gifts and prizes and possibly money if I came to La Guardia Airport? *(Comes downstage.)* Oh sure, the name is Pepe. Pepe Vásquez. *(Panics.)* Orale,° what are you doing? You're making a big mistake! *(Lights up. Pepe stands center stage, holding a grille of prison bars in front of his face.)*

I'm not Mexican! I'm Swedish! No, you've never seen me before. Sure I look familiar — all Swedish people look alike. *(Gibberish in Swedish accent.)* Uta Häagen, Häagen Däazen, Frusen Glädjé, Nina Häagen. . . .

Okay. Did I say Swedish? I meant Irish — yeah, black Irish! *(Singsongy Irish accent.)* Toy ti-toy ti-toy. Oh, Lucky Charms, they're magically delicious! Pink hearts, green clovers, yellow moons. What time is it? Oh, Jesus, Joseph, and Mary! It's cabbage and corned beef time — let me go!

Okay. *(Confessional.)* You got me. I'm not Swedish and I'm not Irish. You probably guessed it already — I'm Israeli! Mazel tov, bubeleh *(Jackie Mason schtick.)* Come on, kineahora, open up the door. I'll walk out, you'll lock the door, you won't miss me, I'll send you a postcard. . . .

Orale, gabacho pendejo.° I'm American, man. I was born right here in Flushing. Well, sure I sound Mexican. I was raised by a Mexican nanny. Doesn't everybody have a Maria Consuelo?

As a matter of fact, I got proof right here that I'm American. I got two tickets to the Mets game. Yeah, Gooden's pitching.° Come on, I'm late.

Orale, ése.° Is it money? It's always money. *(Conspiratorially.)* Well, I got a lot of money. I just don't have it on me. But I know where to get it.

Orale, ése. Tell me, where did your people come from? Santo Domingo? Orale, we're related! We're cousins! Tell me, what's your last name? Rivera? Rivera! That's my mother's maiden name! What a coinky dinky. Hermano, cousin, brother, primo, por favor dejeme ir que somos de la mismita sangre. Los latinos debemos ser unidos y jamás seremos vencidos.°

ése: Dude, guy. **Orale:** What's up? **Orale, gabacho pendejo:** What's up, dumb whitey? **Gooden's pitching:** Dwight Gooden (b. 1964) played for the New York Mets 1984-1994. **Orale, ése:** What's up, guy? **primo, por favor . . . vencidos:** Cuz, please let me go, we are of the same blood. Latinos united, we'll never be divided.

Oh, you don't understand, huh? You're a coconut. (*Angry.*) Brown on the outside, but white on the inside. Why don't you do something for your people for a change and let me out of here?

Okay, I'm sorry, cuz. (*Apologetic.*) Come here. Mira, mijito,° I got all my family here. I got my wife and daughter. And my daughter, she's in the hospital. She's a preemie with double pneumonia and asthma. And if you deport me, who's gonna take care of my little chucawala?

Come on, ése. It's not like I'm stealing or living off of you good people's taxes. I'm doing the shit jobs that Americans don't want. (*Anger builds again.*) Tell me, who the hell wants to work for two twenty-five an hour picking toxic pesticide-coated grapes? I'll give you a tip: Don't eat them.

Orale, you Americans act like you own this place, but we were here first. That's right, the Spaniards were here first. Ponce de León, Cortés, Vásquez, Cabeza de Vaca. If it's not true, then how come your country has all our names? Florida, California, Nevada, Arizona, Las Vegas, Los Angeles, San Bernardino, San Antonio, Santa Fe, Nueva York!

Tell you what I'm going to do. I'll let you stay if you let me go.

What are you so afraid of? I'm not a threat. I'm just here for the same reason that all your people came here for — in search of a better life, that's all.

(*Leans away from grille, then comes back outraged.*) Okay, go ahead and send me back. But who's going to clean for you? Because if we all stopped cleaning and said "adiós," we'd still be the same people, but you'd be dirty! Who's going to pick your chef salads? And who's going to make your guacamole? You need us more than we need you. 'Cause we're here revitalizing the American labor force!

Go ahead and try to keep us back. Because we're going to multiply and multiply (*thrusts hips*) so uncontrollably till we push you so far up, you'll be living in Canada! Oh, scary monsters, huh? You might have to learn a second language. Oh, the horror!

But don't worry, we won't deport you. We'll just let you clean our toilets. Yeah, we don't even hold grudges — we'll let you use rubber gloves.

Orale, I'm gonna miss you white people.

(*Lights down.*)

Mira, mijito: Look, my son.

APPROACHING THE READING

1. Write a brief synopsis of what Pepe says. How would you summarize a work constructed from a series of monologues?
2. What types of theatrical setting or stage do you think would be most effective for this play?
3. Think about how various people might respond to this type of comedy. How can what is "savage" be funny?
4. Consider the title. What is implied by "mouth" and calling it a "mambo mouth"? What is suggested by the subtitle "A Savage Comedy"?

> **www**
> Research this author in depth, including images and cultural documents, with VirtuaLit Drama at bedfordstmartins.com/approachinglit.

RESPONDING THROUGH **Writing**

WRITING ABOUT THEATERS AND THEIR INFLUENCE

Journal Entries

1. Attend a performance of a play at a professional theater, a college performance, or a community theater. Note the kind of stage and the way the play is adapted to it. Write a journal entry discussing the appropriateness of the play for the stage and the effectiveness of the company's adaptation to and use of the space available.

2. Write a journal entry comparing and contrasting a television screen to the invisible fourth wall of a modern theater. To what extent does the television set of a sitcom, for example, have similarities to the stage sketched on page 971? In what ways is television quite different, thus eliciting effects that are quite different?

> **www**
> Research the authors in this chapter with LitLinks, or take a quiz on the plays with LitQuiz, at bedfordstmartins.com/approachinglit.

3. Write a journal entry describing how you would produce Pepe's monologue from John Leguizamo's *Mambo Mouth* (p. 979): What kind of stage would you prefer? What kind of set would you design? What props would you use? What stage movements would you suggest? What else should you consider?

Literary Analysis Papers

4. Write a paper discussing the kind of theater Kelly Stuart (*The New New*, p. 915) or Susan Glaspell (*Trifles*, p. 935) had in mind as she wrote. How did that theater influence the way the play was crafted and the way its themes and effects are conveyed?

5. The dedication to John Leguizamo's *Mambo Mouth* (p. 979) reads, "This book is for all the Latino people who have had a hard time holding on to a

dream and just made do." Write a paper examining how that dedication fits and illuminates the play.

6. Some modern playwrights make use of antirealistic techniques to create an "alienation effect" in their plays. An alienation effect is achieved by any device that works against realism, such as distorting the time sequence, breaking through the "fourth wall," or having actors wear masks or speak directly to the audience. Such techniques alienate (or separate) the audience from the play and prevent them from identifying closely with the characters and action, so they will pay more attention to the play's political or social message. Write a paper in which you discuss possible alienation effects in John Leguizamo's *Mambo Mouth* (p. 979).

Comparison-Contrast Papers

7. Write a paper on the importance of **conventions** (see p. 973 or glossary), on the role they play in making a play communicate and connect successfully with an audience. An approach to this paper that can work well is to choose two or more of the short plays in Chapters 21–23 — Kelly Stuart's *The New New* (p. 915), Cusi Cram's *West of Stupid* (p. 925), Susan Glaspell's *Trifles* (p. 935), David Ives's *Sure Thing* (p. 952), and John Leguizamo's *Mambo Mouth: A Savage Comedy* (p. 979) — and compare and contrast the different conventions they rely on for their success.

8. After reading one of the plays in this book, watch a filmed version of it (they're available for *Trifles, Antigone, Hamlet, A Doll House,* and *Death of a Salesman*). Write a paper in which you discuss how watching a filmed version would be similar to and different from watching a live production in a theater and what the advantages and disadvantages would be for both experiences.

> ## ▶ TIPS for Writing about Theaters and Their Influence

> ➤ **Clarify your purpose** The focus of this chapter is on the way theaters can influence playwrights as they write a play, how the kind of place in which the play will be performed can affect the way they imagine the play as they write, and how conceptions of theaters affect the way you visualize a play as you read it. Papers written for the chapter should take one of those directions unless your instructor offers other possibilities for you (such as the influences of theaters on the way plays are performed).

> ➤ **Visualize imaginatively** A paper about how a play is influenced by its theater requires a lot of imagining as you read the play — not just visualizing the action as it would look in "real life" but also visualizing how that action would look on a stage. Consider using diagrams or sketches to help communicate what you're trying to get across.

> ➤ **Conduct research if you need to** Papers about theaters often require research, since the detailed information you'll need to make the paper work will not be at your fingertips. Useful information is available in libraries as well as on the Internet.

> ➤ **Compare kinds of theaters** Comparing and contrasting the differences in visualizing a certain play in two different kinds of theaters can lead to a fascinating and imaginatively insightful paper on theaters and their influence.

> ➤ **Consider socioeconomic implications** The cultural implications of theaters can be interesting to explore as a topic on theaters and their influence. Theaters often are businesses, requiring sizable investments of money and audiences able to afford tickets. You might consider how this could affect the kinds of plays a professional company decides to stage. You might also look into people who deliberately turned against theaters as commercial enterprises and consider their reasons for doing so.

WRITING ABOUT CONNECTIONS

Theaters connect two different worlds: the world of the writer — working out her or his ideas, searching for ways to develop conflicts and characters, all the while hoping a producer and director will be interested in buying the play — and the world of performance, as the director, crew, and actors stage the playwright's work for an audience. It's important, in reading plays or watching productions, to keep that connection in mind. Doing so can lead you to notice related connections among plays dealing with the same theme but written for quite different acting spaces or situations. Here are a few examples:

1. "I Gotta Be Me": Identity and Interrelationships in John Leguizamo's *Mambo Mouth: A Savage Comedy* (p. 979) and David Ives's *Sure Thing* (p. 952)
2. "Dogs Eating Dogs": The Dramatic Depiction of Racial Oppression in John Leguizamo's *Mambo Mouth: A Savage Comedy* (p. 979) and Suzan-Lori Parks's *Topdog/Underdog* (p. 1387)
3. "Fathers and Sons": Familial Conflict in William Shakespeare's *Hamlet* (p. 1151) and August Wilson's *Fences* (p. 1029)

WRITING RESEARCH PAPERS

1. Do research on the cultural implications of theaters as buildings and as institutions. You might consider, for example, the implications of using a traditional theater, on the one hand, and performing plays in a factory or on the street, on the other. Think about who would attend (including the cost

of tickets), what social aura surrounds attendance at a performance, and what kind of support (financial and otherwise) a production requires.

2. Conduct research on the size, structure, and resources of Elizabethan theaters and write a paper that analyzes and supports the idea that William Shakespeare seems to have written *Hamlet* (p. 1151) with that kind of theater in mind.

COMPOSING IN OTHER ART FORMS

1. Draw a series of sketches depicting the setting of the same play—perhaps Susan Glaspell's *Trifles* (p. 935), Henrik Ibsen's *A Doll House* (p. 1263), or August Wilson's *Fences* (p. 1029)—designed for a proscenium-arch stage, a contemporary thrust stage, and (if feasible) a contemporary arena stage.

2. Design a poster for one or more of the plays you've read, incorporating aspects of the theater in which the play would be produced.

The theater is the only institution in the world which has been dying for four thousand years and has never succumbed.

John Steinbeck

Dramatic Types and Their Effects

CHAPTER 24

Getting into Genres

Before you go to a movie, you want to know whether it's a romantic comedy, a horror show, an action film, or a serious drama. You gear up mentally and psychologically for the kind of film you expect to see. If you are told that a movie is a comedy but it turns out to be a psychodrama thriller, you probably will feel frustrated, want your money back, or find it hard to suddenly switch your mood, even if ordinarily you like psychodrama thrillers.

Because of the way expectations affect us in going to movies, or in reading (or watching) drama, it helps to be aware of the traditional dramatic classifications—not for the sake of categorizing plays but to help in recognizing the effects different types of plays aim to achieve. And recognizing their effects helps us better understand why people, from earliest times onward, have found plays appealing, provocative, and satisfying. Classical drama had only two clearly differentiated **genres** or types: comedy and tragedy. From the Middle Ages on, other types appeared: mystery plays, morality plays, tragicomedy, romance, masques, heroic drama, sentimental drama, problem plays, avant-garde plays, and the catch-all form "serious drama." All of these, although their effects are very different, derive from and are adaptations of the original two.

Knowing the characteristics of comedy and tragedy specifically and of the other key influential dramatic types, and knowing something about the way the genres developed, will help you recognize the effects of plays as you watch, read, study, and write about them. Familiarity with dramatic genres is also useful because their influence lives on, beyond the theatrical world, in the ways they have shaped the conventions of movies and television programs in our day.

TRAGEDY

A **tragedy** in literary usage is a play or work characterized by serious and significant actions that often lead to a disastrous result for the protagonist. Until the 1700s, tragedies were usually, or mostly, written in poetry, and usually in an elevated and dignified literary style. Their tone is correspondingly sober and weighty. Although the central character comes to a tragic end, tragedies usually conclude with a restoration of order and an expectation of a brighter future for those who survive.

EFFECTS OF TRAGEDY   Aristotle, discussing literature in his *Poetics* (c. 330 B.C.E.), described tragedy as raising fear and pity in its audience and as having the effect of a *catharsis*, which has usually been translated as "purgation" or "purification." What he meant by this is widely disputed, but a common summation is as follows. The play first raises emotions: Members of the audience pity the hero and feel fear lest they encounter a fate similar to the hero's. But the artistic handling of the conclusion releases and quiets those emotions, as order is restored and the hero faces her or his destiny with fortitude, thus affirming the courage and dignity of humankind. In Aristotle's view, such raising and releasing of emotion has a healthy effect, psychologically and physically: The audience goes away feeling not dejected but relieved.

TYPES OF TRAGEDY   Aristotle's account was based on Greek drama, the only drama he knew. Some literary historians claim that Aristotle's theories fit later tragedy equally well, that Aristotle got at the essence of the form. But after the Greeks, tragedy took many different forms and, though Aristotle's formula may apply broadly to them all, we think it is wiser to treat each individually and to recognize the value of how their specific effects vary. Here is a selective survey, beginning with the Greeks and ending with modern tragedy.

Greek Tragedy

The word *tragedy* comes from the Greek word *tragōidía*, or "goat-song," likely connected to the sacrifice of goats as part of an annual festival honoring the god Dionysus. The festival included an ode, or *dithyramb*, chanted by a chorus, lamenting the death of Dionysus. The Greek dramatist Thespis is usually given credit for transforming the content of the *dithyramb* from a hymn honoring the god to tragic stories about famous heroes and for first introducing an actor to the stage and initiating dialogue between the actor and the chorus (see pp. 966–67).

FAMILIAR PLOTS, DRAMATIC IRONY   The tragic plots were generally drawn from old, familiar myths, so the audience already knew the story when they attended a play. The audience's interest was in the handling of the story. Perhaps the play would emphasize something different, present the theme from an alternative angle, or change the way the characters express themselves. Knowing that the plots would be familiar to the audience permitted playwrights to use **dramatic irony** liberally, since the viewers would know what lay ahead for the characters, though the characters themselves would not.

TRAGIC HEROES   Because the myths deal with heroes and gods, the protagonists of Greek tragedies are persons of high rank or great importance. In keeping with his analysis, Aristotle said the hero should be neither superhumanly good, for a calamity falling on such a person is too hard to accept, nor thoroughly evil, for the downfall of such a person is deserved and therefore does not elicit pity.

HAMARTIA   The tragic hero suffers a change in fortune from prosperity to adversity as a result of a mistake, an error in judgment, a frailty. Aristotle's word for this is *hamartia*. *Hamartia* is not the same as having a character flaw. Some critics explain all tragedies in terms of a "tragic flaw" in the hero and cite Aristotle as their source; but the supposed flaws are not always defects or faults, but rather central or defining aspects of the character. As we read or watch, we are always led to ask what causes the tragedy, what leads to the downfall; watching for an error or misstep (*hamartia*) is preferable to looking for a defect in character (tragic flaw).

ANTIGONE   As you read Sophocles' *Antigone*, the Greek tragedy included in this book (p. 1110), look for the traits Aristotle described. Are Antigone and Creon good but not perfect persons? Do they undergo a change from prosperity to adversity? Is that change a result of a mistake, an error in judgment, that results from one of her or his central or defining character traits?

PITY, FEAR, PURGATION   If Aristotle is right, the reader or audience member feels a great sense of pity for Antigone and Creon, and a sense of fear that if these basically good and decent people could experience such a tragic series of events, what can prevent the same sort of thing happening to anyone else? But the audience also experiences relief ("purgation") — relief that Creon accepts the outcome with piety and humility, and relief that order is restored in the city of Thebes.

Medieval Tragedy

FORTUNE'S WHEEL   Tragedy in the Middle Ages focused on one aspect of Aristotle's formula — the change of fortune experienced by the protagonist. But medieval tragedy did not emphasize the *hamartia* that, in the Greek plays, accounts for the change. Works written during this period reflect the medieval belief in *mutability* or constant change. Fortune is like a wheel that keeps turning: Those at the top of the wheel should resist pride or complacency because inevitably their fortunes will decline and they will reach bottom.

NARRATIVE TRAGEDY During the Middle Ages, plays were used mostly in religious festivals. Medieval tragedy appears exclusively in narrative, not dramatic, form. The series of stories recounted by the Monk in Geoffrey Chaucer's *The Canterbury Tales* (c. 1386–1400) are the best-known examples: stories about the decline and fall — whether deserved or not — of persons of high status, who have a great deal to lose. The effect of such works is not so much to create and release fear and pity as to teach a lesson: They warn the great not to take their happiness for granted, and reassure those of lower status that greatness is not without its dangers and costs.

Renaissance Tragedy

England during the reigns of Elizabeth I (1558–1603) and James I (1603–1625) witnessed an outpouring of splendidly written drama and an increase in theatrical activity: It was one of the greatest periods for drama in history. Dramatists such as Thomas Kyd, Christopher Marlowe, Ben Jonson, Francis Beaumont, John Fletcher, John Webster, and, of course, William Shakespeare wrote during this time, and theaters such as the Curtain, the Rose, the Globe, and the Fortune (see p. 968) drew large audiences from across the social classes. The film *Shakespeare in Love* (1998), directed by John Madden and starring Gwyneth Paltrow and Joseph Fiennes, offers a lively, imaginative reenactment of the theater scene at the time.

EFFECTS OF EVIL Tragedies from this era tend to deal with the results of evil in the world. Often they show how a misstep or an association with an antagonist harboring evil intentions results in a consequence that far exceeds what the protagonist seems to deserve. Or they show the destruction of an innocent victim caught in an evil web not of her or his own making. The protagonists continue to be persons of high status and importance (whose actions affect many people) or, at least, from the upper ranks of society.

MIXED TONES Unlike classical tragedy, with its unified seriousness of tone, Elizabethan tragedy mixes lighter scenes (influenced by characters and scenes popular in medieval tragedy, such as ranting tyrants) with the serious ones, often elaborating the serious action thematically in comic form. It's interesting to note that the serious scenes are usually written in poetry, befitting their characters' elevated status and dignity; the humorous scenes, and other scenes involving characters from the lower classes, are often written in the less "elevated" and dignified medium of prose.

REVENGE TRAGEDY Elizabethan tragedy appears in several subtypes. One popular variety is *revenge tragedy* in which an avenger who seeks to exact revenge for a death of a relative or comrade dies in achieving that aim. Revenge tragedy was influenced by drama of the Roman era, especially the five-act closet dramas of Seneca, which are filled with violence, supernatural agents, and lengthy declamatory speeches. In Senecan plays, as in Greek plays, horrifying events take place offstage. But Elizabethan playwrights — unaware that Seneca's plays were meant to be recited, not acted out — brought them onstage, creating performances full of action and violence (sometimes called "tragedies of blood"). The best-known tragedy of this type is Shakespeare's *Hamlet* (p. 1151): The play, in fact, was referred to as "the Revenge of Hamlet, Prince of Denmark" when the publisher in 1602 entered it in the Stationer's Register for future publication.

TRAGEDY OF PASSION   Another popular subtype, *tragedy of passion*, occurs when characters die as a result of excessively passionate reactions or relationships. Psychological and ethical thinking since the Greeks, and still influential in and beyond the Renaissance, held that unchecked passions posed great danger to individuals and society. It was crucial that one use reason to keep the passions in check, to restrain them and maintain a proper balance of reason and emotions. Unrestrained passion, an unbalanced life, was a recipe for disaster. Shakespeare's *Romeo and Juliet* (c. 1594–1596) illustrates this subtype: Love at first sight and the hasty marriage of the young persons grow out of their intense emotions and lead to their unfortunate and untimely deaths.

TRAGEDY OF FATE   A third subtype, *tragedy of fate*, depicts characters who cannot escape the doom that fortune has in store for them. *Romeo and Juliet* fits this category as well. From the opening lines, in which Romeo and Juliet are referred to as "star-crossed lovers," their doom seems inescapable. This fate is not the same as the divine inevitability of the Greeks but rather an inexplicable, inescapable destiny. Chance, accident, and coincidence play a major role: The audience is left with a sense of sympathy for the young lovers and a sense of regret, even frustration, because with only slight changes in timing or communication at any number of points, the catastrophe would have been avoided.

TRAGEDY OF CHARACTER   In still another subtype, *tragedy of character*, disastrous results grow out of an individual's character traits — not necessarily weaknesses or flaws but often strengths and virtues that are carried too far or applied unwisely. Shakespeare's great tragedies (*Hamlet, Othello, King Lear, Macbeth*) develop protagonists of great depth and complexity. Careful reading and reflection are required to understand such characters well (perhaps "fully" can never be achieved) and to grasp the various acts, decisions, and influences that lead to their catastrophes. Attempting to reduce the reasons for what happens to a "tragic flaw" risks oversimplifying works of great subtlety and sophistication.

Modern Tragedy

Tragedy was not a major form among British playwrights (and audiences) during the 1700s and 1800s. Witty comedies of manners were popular at the time, and spectacular performances of serious plays, full of bright, colorful costumes and set designs, served to deflect attention from the words and story. When theaters did stage a tragedy, they usually revived Shakespearean plays, but most eighteenth- and nineteenth-century audiences preferred happy endings. In fact, the text of Shakespeare's *King Lear* (c. 1605) used throughout the 1700s and early 1800s was a revised version with a happy ending.

DOMESTIC TRAGEDY   The early 1700s did revive one form of tragedy, *domestic tragedy*, which had been a minor but lively and popular subgenre during and following the Elizabethan era, and this revival affected the future course of the genre. Before the 1700s, almost all tragedies were written in verse and featured a protagonist of noble rank whose death had a major impact on her or his society or nation. Domestic tragedy in the 1700s, however, was written in prose with an ordinary person as its protagonist, not a person of high rank or great importance. George Lillo's *The London Merchant: or, The History of George Barnwell* (1731), for example, deals with an apprentice who, under the influence of his mistress, robs his employer and murders his uncle, but repents of his misdeeds before his execution. Its tone is sentimental, or tenderly emotional. Its effect is first to elicit revulsion at what George does but then to permit relief and gratitude that he repents.

MODERN TRAGEDY   Modern tragedies, dating from the mid-1900s, also involve middle-class characters but do not use the sentimental emotions characteristic of domestic drama. Most are written in prose, though a few—such as T. S. Eliot's *Murder in the Cathedral* (1935)—are in verse. Modern tragedies generally present ordinary people encountering forces (economic, social, political, or personal) far beyond their control. They are destroyed but often not defeated by them. The protagonist is more likely to be a tragic victim than a classic tragic hero. In its effects, modern tragedy elicits pity, as sympathetic understanding, and fear, as awareness that what happens to the protagonist could happen to any of us. But modern tragedy typically does not create the sense of awe or horror evoked by classical tragedy and by some Elizabethan tragedy; thus some argue that it has a lessened sense of release and purgation.

COMEDY

The most basic definition of **comedy** is a story with a happy ending. No matter what the characters go through, if the ending is happy, the play is a comedy. All's well that ends well.

CELEBRATION OF LIFE   The tone of comedy is lighter than that of tragedy and its style less elevated; it is usually written in prose. It uses wit and humor to evoke smiles and laughter from its readers and audience. Comedy generally has a realistic strain, dealing with ordinary people in their everyday activities, but the events of a comedy often include exaggeration and unrealistic circumstances, with characters turning things upside down, breaking rules, reversing normal relationships, and falling into incongruous situations. Comedies celebrate life, with all the disorder, misunderstandings, and confusion that often accompany it; beginning in disorder, comedies end with restoration of order and often conclude with a dance, marriage, or celebration of some kind symbolizing harmony and happiness.

THE PHYSICAL AND THE FOOLISH   Comedy, like tragedy, emerged from Greek religious ceremonies, particularly from Dionysian fertility rites. The word *comedy* derives from the Greek word *kômos*, meaning "revel" or "merry-making"; in early comedies the revelry involved explicit sexuality. Although later Greek comedies became less blatantly sexual, they retained the earthy, physical qualities of their Dionysian origins. Comedy continues to emphasize the physical or sensuous nature of humans; their ridiculousness, weaknesses, and foibles; their physical relationships; and their outrageous behaviors and foolish misunderstandings.

Satiric Comedy

Greek drama initiated two major strains of comedy that have remained influential through the centuries. The earlier strain was **Old Comedy**, represented by the satiric works of Aristophanes (c. 450–385 B.C.E.), predecessor of later satiric comedy playwrights. Satiric comedy ridicules political policies, social practices, or philosophical ideas by poking fun at those who deviate from the standards upheld by common sense or by the author. Behind satiric comedy is the hope that the exposure of flaws and follies will result in improving society, though in practice the only result may be amusement for those observing the ridicule. Satiric comedy is illustrated in this book by the excerpt from John Leguizamo's *Mambo Mouth: A Savage Comedy* (p. 979), as it jokes about ethnic stereotypes and, in doing so, reveals and criticizes particularly poisonous types of intolerance common in American society.

Comedy of Manners

Old Comedy was replaced by **New Comedy**, originated by the Greek playwright Menander (c. 342–292 B.C.E.) and developed further by the Roman dramatists Plautus (c. 254–184 B.C.E.) and Terence (c. 190–159 B.C.E.). New Comedy concerns the obstacles faced by young lovers and the unpredictable changes of fortune they encounter and pokes fun at the foibles and attitudes of the lovers as well as those around them. New Comedy developed into the later form called the *comedy of manners*, which laughs at the behavior and conventions of members of the upper classes, at their vanities and self-centeredness, their social interactions, their follies and intrigues.

Among the best examples of the New Comedy tradition are the late seventeenth- and early eighteenth-century comedies of William Wycherley (1640–1715), Sir George Etherege (1635–1692), and William Congreve (1670–1729), which treat love as a game or contest involving sophisticated lovers, jealous spouses, and conniving rivals. These plays are characterized by sparkling dialogue, with clever conversations and quick, witty responses — amusing and refreshing in effect. The closest thing to a comedy of manners in this book is David Ives's *Sure Thing* (p. 952), with its attention to social interactions and customs, sophisticated character types, clever dialogue, genial satire on people's foibles, and emphasis on the games people play as they fall in love.

Romantic Comedy

Another Elizabethan subtype, *romantic comedy*, also was influenced by the Greeks, but by Greek prose romances rather than by Greek drama. Romantic comedy typically involves young lovers who face obstacles to fulfilling their relationship (perhaps parental opposition, a competing lover, their own differences, poverty, separation because of war or travel, or coincidences that prevent them from joining together). After facing numerous complications and encountering several near disasters, all of which make a favorable outcome seem impossible, the lovers at last are united and their union is accepted.

Shakespeare wrote a number of well-known works in this form, including *A Midsummer Night's Dream* (c. 1595), *Much Ado about Nothing* (1598–1599), *As You Like It* (1598–1600), *Twelfth Night* (1600–1602), and *All's Well That Ends Well* (c. 1601–1605). Hollywood movies and TV comedies continue the tradition today. In effect, romantic comedies are entertaining and enjoyable, and at their best — as in the Shakespearean examples — they achieve thematic depth and insight as well.

Other Types of Comedy

Two other comic subtypes are comedy of situation and sentimental comedy. *Comedy of situation*, which focuses on ingenuity of plot more than on exploration of character, relies on accidents, coincidences, disguises, mistaken identities, chaos, and confusion. An example of the type is Shakespeare's early play *The Comedy of Errors* (c. 1589–1594), an imitation of Roman comedy, especially that of Plautus. You can recognize its influence any time you tune into a television sitcom.

In *sentimental comedy*, a scoundrel reforms in the last act and turns into a model citizen or a model hero withstands a variety of difficulties and trials and, in a melodramatic happy ending, is rewarded. This is "feel good" comedy, leading the audience to feel first concern and sympathy, then relief and exhilaration. Although the quintessential example of this type is Richard Steele's *The Conscious Lovers* (1722), modern successors of it can be seen regularly in any multiplex or on any television screen.

THREE OTHER DRAMATIC TYPES

The subgenres of tragedy and comedy discussed above show that these two central forms of drama are not fixed and unchanging, in form or effect. As playwrights encountered new social and political situations and changing cultural attitudes, they responded by adapting the traditional genres and developing new subgenres with effects different from the earlier ones. In addition to developing subgenres of tragedy and comedy, playwrights made more radical adaptations. These types, although they clearly grew out of comedy and tragedy, are sufficiently different from them in form and effect to be discussed as distinct minor genres, rather than as additional subgenres. Three are particularly worth attention.

Tragicomedy

Tragicomedy emerged in Elizabethan drama, with its mixed influences of classical and medieval works. Elizabethan tragedies included comic scenes, unlike classical tragedy with its consistency and unity of tone. Tragicomedy takes this a step further: Its plot is appropriate to tragedy until the final act, when it turns out to have an unexpectedly happy ending. The tone and style of tragicomedy are serious, and the expected outcome is disaster or death; somehow at the end the disaster is averted and order and harmony prevail. (Tragicomedy is not the same as dark comedy, which mixes a humorous tone with serious and potentially tragic events, often with an unhappy outcome.)

Problem Play

A **problem play** is a serious work that dramatizes a real-life, usually contemporary, social, political, or ethical problem. Although in a broad sense the term covers all drama dealing with problems of human life, it is used more narrowly for the "drama of ideas" that emerged in the late 1800s in the work, for example, of Norwegian playwright Henrik Ibsen (1828–1906) — see *A Doll House* (p. 1263) — Irish playwright George Bernard Shaw (1856–1950), and English playwright John Galsworthy (1867–1933).

"Serious Drama"

The word *drama*, in addition to meaning a literary work intended for performance or the whole body of such works, is also used for any particularly striking or interesting event or series of events that involve conflict and tension. In literature or theater today, *drama* is often used for a play that is not a comedy and does not have a tragic ending, but that deals with serious events involving such conflict and tension. August Wilson's *Fences* (p. 1029) is an example. So too are many of the works by twentieth-century playwrights Bertolt Brecht and Samuel Beckett. You may have noticed that many video stores have sections labeled "comedy," "action," and "drama" — not tragedy.

This chapter makes clear that drama is dynamic and flexible, constantly developing and adapting its forms and effects to different social, political, and cultural situations. A question like "What is the effect of drama?" needs to be narrowed and qualified before it can be answered. Different types of drama, and even different subtypes, convey different effects. Both satiric comedy and romantic comedy have happy endings, but in tone and effect they are very different. Tragedy of fate and domestic tragedy both end unhappily, but their effects on a reader or audience are totally dissimilar.

Further explore dramatic types and their effects, including interactive exercises, with VirtuaLit Drama at bedfordstmartins.com/approachinglit.

Such adaptation of and experimentation with genre forms continues today, as illustrated by some of the plays included in this book. *Sure Thing* (p. 952), *Mambo Mouth* (p. 979), and *As the Crow Flies* (p. 995) do not fit neatly into the categories described in this chapter, but in their adaptation of elements from earlier types, they are typical of the diversity in form, tone, and effect found in contemporary drama. To participate fully in the kinds of experiences drama offers, you must be alert and responsive to such differences. Drama has so much to offer that your effort will be richly rewarded.

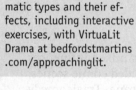

☑ CHECKLIST on Reading for Dramatic Types and Their Effects

❏ Be able to describe tragedy as a play or other literary work in an elevated and dignified style and with a sober, weighty tone that depicts serious and significant actions leading to a disastrous result for the protagonist. Be able to describe too its overall effects on readers and audiences.

❏ Be able to characterize the different forms of tragedy that developed historically — Greek tragedy, medieval tragedy, Renaissance tragedy, domestic tragedy, and modern tragedy — and their distinctive effects on readers and audiences.

❏ Be able to describe comedy as a play or other work in a light style that makes use of wit and humor; that depicts the actions of ordinary people in everyday activities; that, despite potentially disastrous confusion, difficulties, reversals, misunderstandings, and disorders, turns out satisfactorily; and that has a happy ending. Be able to describe too its overall effects on readers and audiences.

❏ Be able to characterize the important subtypes of comedy — satiric comedy, comedy of manners, and romantic comedy — and the distinctive effects they have on readers and audiences.

❏ Be able to describe other significant dramatic types — tragicomedy, problem plays, and "serious drama" — and the effects they have on readers and audiences.

❏ Be able, when you read a play, to identify elements in it that place it in one or another of these genres.

FURTHER READING

ENTRY POINTS   The following play illustrates the kind of experimentation with genre typical of contemporary drama. It draws humor from miscommunications, cultural misunderstandings, characters talking past each other, and witty dialogue. But watch also for places where the dialogue turns more serious and be ready to account for the closing scene.

David Henry Hwang   b. 1957

As the Crow Flies   [1986]

CHARACTERS

HANNAH, a black woman in her 60s.
MRS. CHAN, a Chinese woman in her 70s, sometimes called Popo (Grandma).
P. K., a Chinese man in his 70s, sometimes called Gung Gung (Grandfather).
SANDRA, a black woman in her 40s.

TIME AND PLACE

The living room of an upper middle-class home. The present.

A living room in an upper middle-class home, owned by Mrs. Chan, a Chinese woman in her seventies, and her husband, P. K. Up right, a door leads out to the front driveway. Stage left is a door leading to the rest of the house. Mrs. Chan sits in a large chair, center stage, looking downstage out into a garden. Around her, Hannah, a black woman in her late sixties, cleans. She has been their cleaning woman for over a decade.

HANNAH: I guess I never told you this before, Mrs. Chan, but I think the time is right now. See, I'm really two different folks. You've been knowin' me as Hannah Carter, 'cuz when I'm over here cleanin', that's who I am. But at night, or when I'm outside and stuff, I turn into Sandra Smith. (*Beat*) Is that all clear?

CHAN: Um. Yeah.

HANNAH: You got all that?

CHAN: When you are here, you are Hannah Carter —

HANNAH: Right.

CHAN: And, then, you go outside, and you are . . . someone . . . someone . . .

HANNAH: Sandra Smith.

CHAN: Um. Okay.

Pause.

HANNAH: You don't have any questions 'bout that?

CHAN: Hannah Carter, Sandra Smith — I understand.

HANNAH: Well, you know how you can tell the two apart?

CHAN: No. Because I have not seen Sandra — Sandra . . .

HANNAH: Smith. Well, when I'm Sandra Smith, see, I look different. First of all, I'm a lot younger.

CHAN: Good.

HANNAH: And, you know, since I'm younger, well, guess I'm looser, too. What I mean by that, is, when I talk, well, I use different words. Young words. And, Mrs. Chan, since I'm younger, my hair color's a lot different too. And I don't clean floors. 'Cuz young people nowadays, they don't clean floors. They stay up around the clock, and make themselves into lazy good-for-nothings, and drink a lot, and dance themselves into a state. Young people — just don't know what's got into them. But whatever it is, the same thing's gotten into Sandra Smith. (*Pause*) You don't think this is all a little strange?

CHAN: No.

HANNAH: Well, that's the first time . . . I remember when I told Mrs. Washburn about Sandra Smith — she just fell right over.

CHAN: So what? So you have two different people.

HANNAH: That's right. Living inside me.

CHAN: So what? My uncle had six!

HANNAH: Six people?

CHAN: Maybe even seven. Who can keep count?

HANNAH: Seven? All in one guy?

CHAN: Way back in China—my second uncle—he had seven, maybe even eight, people—inside here. I don't . . . is hard to remember all their name.

HANNAH: I can believe that.

CHAN: Chan Yup Lee—he was, uh, I think, the businessman. He runs Uncle's import-export association. Good man. Very stingy. I like him. Then, I think there was another: ah, C. Y. Sing—he is the family man. Then, one man, Fat-Fingers Lew. Introduce this sport—what is the name? Ball goes through big hoop.

HANNAH: Basketball?

CHAN: Yes, yes—introduce that to our village. Then, there is Big Ear Tong—collects debt for C. Y.'s company. Never talks, only fight. Then, also, one who has been to America—Morty Fong. He all the time warns us about Communists. And, then, oh, maybe two or three others that I hardly ever meet.

HANNAH: This is all one guy?

CHAN: Mmmmm.

HANNAH: Isn't that somethin'?

CHAN: No.

HANNAH: Huh?

CHAN: Whatever you can tell me—man with six persons inside, man with three heads, man who sees a flying ghost, a sitting ghost, a ghost disguise to look like his dead wife—none of these are so unusual.

HANNAH: No?

CHAN: I have lived a long time.

HANNAH: Well, so have I, Mrs. Chan, so have I. And I'm still scared of Sandra Smith.

CHAN: Scare? Why scare? Happens all the time.

HANNAH: I don't want Sandra comin' round to any of my houses that I clean.

CHAN: Aaah—do not worry.

HANNAH: Whaddya mean? Sandra's got no respect for authority.

CHAN: Do not worry. She will not come into any house.

HANNAH: What makes you so sure?

CHAN: You have to know how ghosts think. You say, Sandra appears outdoors. Therefore, she is the outside ghost. She cannot come inside.

HANNAH: Yeah? They got rules like that? In ghost-land?

CHAN: Yes—there are rules everyplace! Have you ever been someplace where there were none?

HANNAH: Well, no, but—

CHAN: You see? Ghosts cannot kill a man if there is a goldfish in the room. They will think the fish is gold, and take it instead. They cannot enter a house if there is a raised step in the doorway. Ghosts do not look, so they trip over it instead.

HANNAH: These ghosts don't sound like they got a lot on the ball.

CHAN: Some ghosts, they are smart. But most ghosts, they are like most people. When alive, they were stupid. After death, they remain the same.

HANNAH: Well, I don't think Sandra's got much respect for those rules. That's probably why she showed up at Mrs. Washburn's.

CHAN: Inside the house?

HANNAH: 'Fraid so.

CHAN: Oh. Mrs. Washburn — does she have a goldfish?

HANNAH: No, no — I don't think so.

CHAN: There — you see?

HANNAH: Anyway, Mrs. Chan, I just thought I oughta tell you about her, on account of what happened to Mrs. Washburn. I been working for all you people ten, sometimes twenty years. All my clients — they're gettin' up there. We're all startin' to show our age. Can't compete with the young girls no more.

CHAN: I never try — even when I was one.

HANNAH: Well, the older I get, the more I see of Sandra, so I just thought I oughta be warnin' you.

CHAN: I am not afraid of Sandra Smith.

HANNAH: Well, good then. Good for you.

CHAN: She comes here, I will fight her. Not like these Americans. So stupid. Never think of these things. Never think of ghost. Never think of death. Never prepare for anything. Always think, life goes on and on, forever. And so, always, it ends.

HANNAH: Okay. Glad to hear it. Guess I'll go take the slime off the shower walls.

Hannah exits, into the house. Chan just stares downstage, from her chair. Silence. P. K. enters from the driveway, golf clubs slung over his shoulder.

P. K.: Hi, Popo!

CHAN: Hello.

P. K.: Do you have a beer?

CHAN: Look in 'frigerator.

P. K.: Just return from a good game of golf!

CHAN: Ah! What are you talking about?

P. K.: Eighteen holes, Popo!

CHAN: Ai! You cannot remember anything anymore!

P. K.: So? I remember that I go to golf!

CHAN: How can this be? You do not drive!

P. K.: What do you mean? I drive the Eldorado.

CHAN: You cannot drive the Eldorado.

P. K.: I do!

CHAN: Hanh! We sell it many years ago!

P. K.: What?

CHAN: Yes! Remember? We sell it! To John, your nephew.

P. K.: Huh? How much did he pay?

CHAN: Who cares?

P. K.: I want to know!

CHAN: I always tell you, John buys the car; you always ask me, how much does he pay?

P. K.: It is important! It is worth — lots of money!

CHAN: Ah, not so much money.

P. K.: No! Lots!

CHAN: Not after Humphrey breaks the back window by trying to lower top while driving.

P. K.: Yes! I tell Humphrey — cannot lower while driving. He says, "Of course! Can! This is a luxury car!" How come we sell the car?

CHAN: Ah! You cannot remember anything!

P. K.: No. Gung Gung cannot remember anything anymore.

CHAN: We sell, because you can no longer drive.

P. K.: I can! I can!

CHAN: You cannot pass the test.

P. K.: Can Humphrey pass the test?

CHAN: Of course! Of course, he passes it.

P. K.: How can? He is the one who lowers top while driving!

CHAN: Gung Gung! Because he is young, so he can pass the test!

P. K.: Young, but not so smart.

CHAN: Stupid.

P. K.: Sometimes, stupid.

CHAN: Stupid does not matter. Many stupid people drive.

Pause.

P. K.: So I did not go to golf?

CHAN: No! How can you go to golf? You cannot go anyplace.

P. K. (*Points to clubs*): Then, what are these?

CHAN: You just put them on your shoulder, then walk outside. Two hour later, you return.

P. K.: Where did I go?

CHAN: I don't know! You tell me!

P. K.: I cannot remember anything, anymore. I thought that I go to play eighteen hole golf. But there is no golf course. So perhaps I walk into those hills. Maybe I shoot a few balls in the hills. Maybe I sink a putt into a gopher hole.

Pause.

CHAN: Gung Gung.

P. K.: Yes, Popo?

CHAN: I saw a ghost today.

P. K.: Popo! A ghost?

CHAN: Yes — a warning ghost.

P. K.: Which is this?

CHAN: They warn that another ghost will soon come. Bigger. More dangerous. Fatter.

P. K.: Oh! Popo! Why do they send this warning ghost?

CHAN: Because, they are stupid! This is how, they become dead to begin with. Because when they were living, they were too stupid to listen to the warning ghost!

P. K.: Popo! Will you die? (*He starts to cry*) What will Gung Gung do without you?

CHAN: No.

P. K.: Without Popo, I will be completely all lost.

CHAN: No, Gung Gung.

P. K.: I will walk around all day, not know where I am going, not know where I come from, only saying, "Popo? Where is Popo? Where is — ?"

CHAN: No! Will you listen to me? You ask the question, then you will not listen to the answer! Talk, talk, talk! If I die, leave you alone, I would be lucky!

P. K.: You mean, you will not die?

CHAN: No, I will not die.

P. K.: How can this be?

CHAN: They are stupid enough to send the warning ghost. This is how I know, they will not defeat me.

P. K.: But, when the ghost come, no one can resist.

CHAN: Who says this?

P. K.: Ummm . . .

CHAN: See? Maybe, Gung Gung, *you* cannot resist.

P. K.: No. I cannot resist.

CHAN: But you have no responsibilities. I have. I have responsibility. I cannot leave you alone, Gung Gung. And also, I must watch the grandchildren grow to adults.

P. K.: Yes — this would be good.

CHAN: So, you see, I cannot die.

P. K.: This makes me so happy.

CHAN: I will defeat the ghost.

P. K.: Yes! Popo! You can do it! Popo is very smart!

CHAN: Yeah, yeah, yeah, we all know this already.

P. K.: I am fortunate to marry such a smart wife.

CHAN: Not smart. Smart is not enough.

P. K.: More than smart.

CHAN: Fight. Fight is more important. I am willing to fight. I like to fight.

Pause.

P. K.: Why do I carry these golf clubs?

CHAN: I do not know! You ask so many times already!

P. K.: Oh — I suppose — I must go to golf.

Pause.

CHAN: Yes — you must go to golf.

P. K.: Okay. I will leave now. Take the Eldorado. Bye, Popo.

CHAN: Bye, Gung Gung.

P. K.: You will have a cold can of beer in the 'frigerator, for when I return?

CHAN: I will, Gung Gung. I will.

P. K. starts to exit out the upstage door.

Gung Gung!

P. K.: Yes, Popo?

CHAN: Have a good game, okay, Gung Gung?

P. K.: I will have a good game, okay, Popo. (*He exits*)

CHAN: I arrive in America one day, June 16, 1976. Many times, I have come here before, to visit children, but on this day, I arrive to stay. All my friends, all the Chinese in the Philippine, they tell me, "We thought you are stupid when you send all your children to America. We even feel sorry for you, that you will grow old all alone—no family around you." This is what they tell me.

The day I arrive in America, I do not feel sorry. I do not miss the Philippine, I do not look forward live in America. Just like, I do not miss China, when I leave it many years ago—go live in Philippine. Just like, I do not miss Manila, when Japanese take our home during wartime, and we are all have to move to Baguio, and live in haunted house. It is all same to me. Go, one home to the next, one city to another, nation to nation, across ocean big and small.

We are born traveling. We travel—all our lives. I am not looking for a home. I know there is none. The day I was marry, my mother put many gold bracelets on my arm, and so many necklaces that the back of my head grows sore. "These," she tells me. "These are for the times when you will have to run."

The upstage door opens. Hannah is standing there, dressed as Sandra Smith. Sandra wears a bright orange fright wig and a tight dress, sports huge sunglasses, and swings a small purse.

SANDRA: Well, hello there! Howdy, howdy, howdy!

CHAN: Hi.

SANDRA: Say, you seen Hannah? Hannah Carter? I understand she works here on Wednesdays.

CHAN: I think, she just leave.

SANDRA: Oh, well, that's a shame. I usually don't get to visit where she works. We were supposed to go for dinner at Chicken on Fire, but, looks like we're just not connecting. Damn! Always happens, whenever I try to meet her at one of these houses.

CHAN: So, would you like to go home, now?

SANDRA: Mmmm. Guess I could, but I wouldn't mind enjoying some of your hospitality.

CHAN: What is this, hospitality?

SANDRA: You know. What you show your guests.

CHAN: We do not have guests here! Only relatives, and, ah, servants.

SANDRA: Well, what do you do when someone comes over?

CHAN: They tell me what they want. Then, they leave.

SANDRA: No time to socialize?

CHAN: What is, socialize?

SANDRA: You know. You're not gonna offer me a tea, coffee, cake, Sanka?

CHAN: No.

SANDRA: I can't hardly believe this house.

CHAN: People — they are like cats. If you feed them, they will always return.

SANDRA: What ever happened to old-fashioned manners?

CHAN: My manners — they are very old. We act like this for centuries.

SANDRA: My name's Sandra. Sandra Smith.

CHAN: This is no surprise. Are you finish, now? Hannah is not here.

SANDRA: No — I can see that. (*Pause*) You know, I've known Hannah — well, ever since she was a little girl. She wasn't very pretty. No one in Louisville paid much attention to her. Yeah, she's had five husbands and all, okay, that's true, but my personal guess is that most of 'em married her because she was a hard-working woman who could bring home the bacon week after week. Certain men will hold their noses for a free lunch. Hannah thinks the same thing, though she hardly ever talks about it. How can she think anything else when all five of them left her as soon as they got a whiff of some girl with pipe cleaners for legs? Hard for her to think she's much more than some mule, placed on this earth to work her back. She spends most of her life wanderin' from one beautiful house to the next, knowing intimately every detail, but never layin' down her head in any of 'em. She's what they call a good woman. Men know it, rich folks know it. Everyplace is beautiful, 'cept the place where she lives. Home is a dark room, she knows it well, knows its limits. She knows she can't travel nowhere without returnin' to that room once the sun goes down. Home is fixed, it does not move, even as the rest of the world circles 'round and 'round, picking up speed.

CHAN: You are a ghost.

SANDRA: I have a good time, if that's what you mean.

CHAN: I was warned that you would come.

SANDRA: By Hannah? She's always tellin' people about me. Like I was some kinda celebrity or somethin'.

CHAN: I fight ghosts. I chase them.

SANDRA: Can't chase anything, unless you get it runnin' from ya first.

CHAN: In Baguio, we live in a haunted house.

SANDRA: In where?

CHAN: Baguio. In the Philippine.

SANDRA: I never been there.

CHAN: During the war, we live in a haunted house. I chase the ghost out, with pots and pan. So, I know I can defeat them.

SANDRA: Hannah — she lives in a haunted house right now.

CHAN: Yes — haunted with you.

SANDRA: I show her how to make her life a little easier. Someone's gotta do it, after all her sixty-some-odd years. How 'bout you? Anything I can help you with?

CHAN: Ha! I do not need a thing!

SANDRA: I'm not sure if I believe that, Mrs. . . . . Mrs. . . . . whatever. Hannah sees you sittin' here, day after day —

CHAN: I am old! Of course I sit!

SANDRA: — starin' out into that garden —

CHAN: So?

SANDRA: First off, it's mostly dirt.

CHAN: This way, easier to take care of.

SANDRA: But you stare like there's somethin' out there.

CHAN: Yes! The sun is out there!

SANDRA: Lookin' at the sun, Mrs. — ma'am? Gotta be careful you don't burn your eyeballs out.

CHAN: I only look outside because — sky, clouds, sun — they are all there — interesting to watch.

SANDRA: Real pretty, huh?

CHAN: Yes. Sometimes pretty.

SANDRA: Looks like home.

CHAN: What is this? All the time, you talk about home, home, home?

SANDRA: Just like you do.

CHAN: I never talk about home. Barely talk at all.

SANDRA: You think, you keep your lips buttoned, that means all your secrets are safe inside? If they're strong enough, things make themselves known, one way or another. Hannah knows, she's not stupid. She'd never tell anyone but me. But me, I'd tell anybody. (*Pause*) Want me to tell you?

CHAN: Tell me what?

SANDRA: What you're lookin' at out there?

Pause.

CHAN: I can defeat you. I defeat ghost before.

SANDRA: Honey, it's not a fight no more. I've been around fifteen years. I already know you. You know me. We see the same thing. Out there. (*Pause*) There's a crow sitting on a window sill. And two kids who chase it down a steep ravine. Their path grows darker and darker, but the crow continues, and the kids don't tire, even when the blisters start to show on their feet. Mud, sleet, rain, and snow, all try to make the kids give up the chase. The crow caws — mountains fall in its wake, but still the children continue. And then it becomes dark, so dark, and the crow throws disasters at their feet. Floods, droughts, wars. The children see nothing, now. They follow the crow only by the catastrophes it leaves in its path. Where there is famine, the crow must have been. Where there are earthquakes, it has rested. They run on faith now, passing through territories uncharted, following the sound of their suffering. And it is in this way that they pass through their lives. Hardly noticing that they've entered. Without stopping to note its passing. Just following a crow, with single dedication, forgetting how they started, or why they're chasing, or even what may happen if they catch it. Running without pause or pleasure, past the point of their beginning.

Over the next section, Mrs. Chan's dress slowly rises into the air. She wears a white slip beneath. She stands up from the chair, for the first time in the play, and walks over to Sandra.

> I see it in the distance.

CHAN: It is waiting for me.

SANDRA: I cannot stop my running.

CHAN: I cannot rest, even for a second.

SANDRA: There's a field out in the distance.

CHAN: There's a wooden gate in that field.

SANDRA: There is a crow sitting on that gate.

CHAN: It caws.

SANDRA: It caws.

CHAN: And disaster comes.

SANDRA: Once again.

CHAN: Nothing new.

SANDRA: Nothing blue.

CHAN: Only the scent of home.

SANDRA: I don't know why I follow it.

CHAN: I don't care to know.

SANDRA: Not now.

CHAN: Not here.

SANDRA: Not ever. Perhaps someday.

CHAN: Maybe to remember.

SANDRA: Why I run.

CHAN: Why I chase.

SANDRA: Until I am so —

CHAN: So tired.

SANDRA: Another disaster.

CHAN: Another lonely child.

SANDRA: We follow the scent of home.

Sandra removes her wig, glasses, tight dress. She too wears a white slip. She is Hannah again. Mrs. Chan moves towards the door. Hannah ever so slowly lowers herself into Mrs. Chan's chair. Hannah sits in it, beams.

HANNAH: Ooooh. Nice home, Mrs. Chan.

CHAN: I see it.

HANNAH: So do I, so do I.

CHAN: I see all the way past those mountains.

HANNAH: Welcome home, Mrs. Chan.

CHAN: Welcome home, Hannah.

Mrs. Chan exits through the garden. Hannah looks around her like a kid with a new toy. Upstage, P. K. enters with golf clubs. He cannot see Hannah in the chair.

P. K.: Hi, Popo! (*Pause*) Where is my beer?

Hannah closes her eyes, a smile on her face.

You leave a beer in the 'frigerator? (*Pause*) Popo? Popo?

P. K. is walking towards the chair as lights fade to black.

END OF PLAY

APPROACHING THE READING

1. Point out types of humor and comedy in the play.
2. Look for a point in the play where the tone turns more serious. After that point the comedy continues, but how does its effect change?
3. How does the title relate to the play? Look up the title phrase in a good dictionary or online if you don't recognize it as an often-used figure of speech. Be ready to discuss the meaning of the final two pages, with their focus on a crow.
4. What is going on at the end of the play? Is this comedy, tragedy, fantasy, or something else? Explain.
5. What is the overall effect of the play, considering both its comic and its serious aspects?

RESPONDING THROUGH Writing

WRITING ABOUT DRAMATIC TYPES AND THEIR EFFECTS

Journal Entries

1. Write a journal entry in which you fit the short plays in Chapters 21–23 (*The New New*, *West of Stupid*, *Trifles*, *Sure Thing*, and *Mambo Mouth*) into the dramatic types discussed in this chapter. If they don't fit one category, combine categories or develop new ones that seem most appropriate.
2. Jot a list of your favorite (or currently popular) TV shows. Place them into the type categories described in this chapter or into other categories not discussed here.
3. Note any "dramas" you see during a day. List and categorize them. Take one or more of them and turn them into scenes. Keep in mind that you probably will need to fictionalize somewhat to make a scene effective and believable.

> **www**
> Research the authors in this chapter with LitLinks at bedfordstmartins.com/ approachinglit.

Literary Analysis Papers

4. Consider the different dramatic types or subtypes (or tones, at least) used in David Henry Hwang's *As the Crow Flies* (p. 995). Write a paper discussing

the effect created in different parts of the play and the effect of the play as a whole.

5. Write a paper examining the appropriateness and significance of the marriage imagery in Sophocles' tragedy *Antigone* (p. 1110).

6. Write a paper analyzing how Suzan-Lori Parks in *Topdog/Underdog* (p. 1387) echoes the story of Abraham Lincoln and John Wilkes Booth, using what happened back then to deepen the impact of her play and giving a new twist to the meaning or significance of the historical events.

Comparison-Contrast Papers

7. Compare and contrast the way both David Henry Hwang's *As the Crow Flies* (p. 995) and John Guare's *Woman at a Threshold, Beckoning* (p. 1439) mix realism and the fantastic (something visionary and mystical inserting itself into an everyday-world setting). Explore the purpose and effect in each work. Explore too how realism and the mystical differ but also how they help clarify the other and make it easier to understand.

8. Compare and contrast Creon and Antigone as sympathetic and/or unsympathetic tragic figures in Sophocles' *Antigone* (p. 1110).

> ### ▶ TIPS for Writing about Dramatic Types and Their Effects
>
> ➤ **Altering genre traits** Watch for plays that alter what is usually expected in a particular genre. Discussing such modifications and the effects they achieve could turn into an interesting and valuable paper.
>
> ➤ **Incorporating genre traits** If you want to write an effective paper that demonstrates an understanding of the nature and characteristics of a genre, it is important to show how the play does or doesn't incorporate the typical features of its particular genre.
>
> ➤ **Focusing on effect** In writing about dramatic types, don't limit the paper to an application of the characteristics of a genre to a play; an effective paper needs also to discuss such matters as the appropriateness of the genre to what the play is dealing with and the effect of the application on the reader or viewer.
>
> ➤ **Using Aristotle's *Poetics*** Because Aristotle's *Poetics* has exerted so much influence on the history of drama, studying it and discussing how its ideas do or don't fit a particular tragedy, ancient through modern, can lead to an illuminating paper.
>
> ➤ **Comparing plays in different genres** Comparing how similar themes or characters or situations are handled in two plays in different genres can foreground what makes the plays (or the genres) distinct from each other and lead to an effective paper topic.

WRITING ABOUT CONNECTIONS

Discussions of genres or types tend to focus more often on differences than on connections. However, mixed genres such as tragicomedy do connect two or more genres, often in startling ways. Thematic connections between plays in different genres, and sometimes from different eras, also can yield surprisingly interesting topics. Here are some possibilities:

1. "The Haunted Heart": The Presence and Significance of Ghosts in David Henry Hwang's *As the Crow Flies* (p. 995) and William Shakespeare's *Hamlet* (p. 1151)
2. "A House Divided": Tyranny vs. Freedom in a Tragedy — Sophocles' *Antigone* (p. 1110) — and a Problem Play — Henrik Ibsen's *A Doll House* (p. 1263)
3. "Everyone Loses": The Games People Play in Suzan-Lori Parks's *Topdog/Underdog* (p. 1387) and Arthur Miller's *Death of a Salesman* (p. 1316)

WRITING RESEARCH PAPERS

1. After researching the nature and use of the chorus in Greek drama, write a paper in which you use that information to support an analysis of the role and contribution of the chorus in Sophocles' *Antigone* (p. 1110).
2. When Susan Glaspell wrote *Trifles* (p. 935) in 1916, women held certain legal and political rights but were denied many others. Research the legal and political rights women did and didn't have. Use what you find to discuss the power and impact the play may have had when it was first produced and what would be similar and yet somewhat different about its power and impact today.

COMPOSING IN OTHER ART FORMS

1. When plays are staged in a theater, the director often includes some music as the lights go down and the curtain rises, and sometimes between scenes. When plays are filmed, they often make even more use of background music. As a way of responding to drama through the arts, select some pieces of music that you think would be effective introductory or background music for a comedy, a tragedy, and a problem play, using plays included in this book or other plays that you know. Look for pieces that fit the tone and time setting of the play. Write a brief explanation of why you selected these pieces.
2. Design a set for a comedy and for a tragedy (or serious drama), using plays from this book or other plays that you know. Write a brief discussion of the differences in them and why you handled them differently.

Writing has been to me like a bath from which I have risen feeling cleaner, healthier, and freer.

Henrik Ibsen

CHAPTER **25** **Writing about Drama**

Applying What You've Learned

Drama enters the ongoing conversation about literature most often through performances of plays. People attend a play and then talk about what they experienced, especially with others who saw the same production. Writing extends the conversation in the form of drama reviews in newspapers and periodicals and on the Web. This chapter, however, does not focus on writing (or talking) about drama on the stage — about whether the director's interpretation is satisfactory, how well the actors and actresses played their roles, and how effective the sets and costumes were. Instead it discusses how to write effectively about plays when they are read as literature (which has been our emphasis throughout the drama section). We concentrate not on the way a particular production handled the play, but on the way a reader interacts with a text's presentation of an action, characters, and setting.

The suggestions offered in "Writing Short Papers" in Chapter 2 (pp. 34–45) apply to writing about drama, as they do to any literary paper. And much that is covered in Chapters 8 and 17 on writing about fiction and poetry carries over to writing about drama as well. This chapter adds to those chapters by offering suggestions particularly applicable to writing about plays.

TOPICS

As in Chapters 8 and 17, the discussion of topics for papers about drama are grouped into three categories: those focusing on what goes on *inside* the play (literary analysis), those focusing on what *surrounds* the play (comparison-contrast), and those focusing on what infuses but also goes *beyond* the play (social and cultural criticism).

Writing a Literary Analysis Paper about Drama

Analyses of what goes on inside a play, technically and thematically, work well for drama. Chapters 21 and 22 introduce the central techniques and strategies of drama, to equip you to read plays attentively and sensitively and to write about them knowledgeably.

STRUCTURE AND CONFLICT   Your papers can isolate and examine any one of the key dramatic techniques discussed in Chapters 21 and 22. You can examine the strategies used for *compressing* and *structuring* material to hold the audience's attention and interest and to build in dramatic intensity to an effective climax (the way Arthur Miller manages to contract the action in *Death of a Salesman* [p. 1316] into a span of about twenty-four hours). You can discuss the use of *conflict*, both as a structural and dramatic technique, and as a way of focusing on theme (for example, how the conflict between Hamlet and his uncle becomes a unifying structural pattern in *Hamlet* [p. 1151]).

CHARACTERS AND CONTRASTS   You can analyze *characters* and *characterization*: Bring out the subtleties and complexities of the characters, especially if you fill in the things that are implied rather than stated, and clarify the techniques through which the characters are developed (the influence of sports and competition on the character of Troy Maxson in *Fences* [p. 1029], for example). You can focus on the use of *contrast* within a play, showing how it uses structural juxtapositions of people, actions, images, and ideas to develop characters, dramatic tensions, and themes (such as the function of Mrs. Linde as a foil to Nora Helmer in *A Doll House* [p. 1263]).

DON'T COVER EVERYTHING   When you write about a play, do not fall into simply summarizing the story. Assume your reader knows what happens but needs help in understanding fully *why* it happens, along with the broader significance and implications of what happens, and the artistry involved in bringing all of that out. Trying to cover thoroughly every, or even one, aspect of a full-length play is difficult in a short paper. Select a single feature to analyze in detail, and perhaps focus that even further by limiting your in-depth analysis to one act or scene.

FOCUS ON A SIGNIFICANT ISSUE   Be sure also that your paper has a discussible, disputable point to make about its subject. A paper on drama, like any paper on literature, needs an argumentative thesis—not "This paper discusses the role of athletics in Troy Maxson's life," but "Troy Maxson's attitudes toward his wife and son, and toward life in general, are shaped by his experiences as a baseball player." As with writing on the other genres, avoid the easy and obvious. Get to know the play well, or the part of it you decide to examine closely, so you recognize and bring out to your reader what is particularly skillful, intriguing, impressive, or thought-provoking about it, or what is difficult, questionable, or problematic in it. Look for a subject that interests or excites you; this will help you convey that excitement to your reader.

PLAYING DIRECTOR   A topic possibility unique to drama is a paper in which you take on the role of directing a play. In this sort of paper, you need to explain how you as director interpret the play and why and how you want your cast to present the characters. You could describe how you would stage the play — what kind of set, props, costumes, lighting, sound, and music you would use, and what kind of stage movement (called "blocking") and action you would want. The decisions you make and descriptions you give will clarify the way you read and interpret the play. This kind of paper, like any of the others suggested in this chapter, needs a thesis that makes an arguable point about the play. It also must discuss and illustrate whatever points you use to develop and support that thesis.

EXPLICATION OF A KEY PASSAGE   One can also approach an analysis paper on drama by explication (see p. 677) of a key passage (see p. 242) in the play. Explication works best for plays that are poetic in style and use meter and lines or rely heavily on figurative language, like parts of many Shakespearean plays, or that are particularly packed with meaning central to the work as a whole. You cannot, of course, explicate an entire play, even a short play. The goal is to identify a speech or short section of dialogue that is complex in its use of language, rich in implications, and crucial in the overall development of the play — one that is central to the development of a character's motives or of a significant theme. One such speech is Hamlet's first soliloquy, in which he reflects on how depressed he feels about the death of his father and the hasty remarriage of his mother. Here are the first fourteen lines:

> O, that this too too sullied flesh would melt,
> Thaw, and resolve itself into a dew!
> Or that the Everlasting had not fix'd
> His canon 'gainst self-slaughter! O God, God,
> How weary, stale, flat, and unprofitable
> Seem to me all the uses of this world!
> Fie on 't, ah fie! 'Tis an unweeded garden
> That grows to seed. Things rank and gross in nature
> Possess it merely. That it should come to this!
> But two months dead — nay, not so much, not two.
> So excellent a king, that was to this

Hyperion to a satyr; so loving to my mother
That he might not beteem the winds of heaven
Visit her face too roughly.
                    (*Hamlet* 1.2.129–42)

Working with Elizabethan English can be daunting; accepting that, the challenge here is to illuminate the meaning and implications of the passage and to demonstrate its importance to the play as a whole. When doing so, it's wise to clarify unfamiliar or difficult language (perhaps such words as *sullied*, *fix'd*, *canon*, *uses*, *rank*, *merely*, and *beteem*). Using the *Oxford English Dictionary* would be advisable in this case (see p. 548). You should discuss figures of speech ("an unweeded garden" and others later in the soliloquy) and allusions ("Hyperion to a satyr"), showing their appropriateness and significance in the play. And you will need to explain how the passage relates to the rest of the play (in this case, how it contributes to exposition, characterization, tone, and theme). Looking closely at the diction, images, figurative language, rhythm, sounds, and style of a specific passage provides a focal point from which the overall strategies, techniques, and themes of the play are illuminated.

Some of the "Approaching the Reading" questions and topics that follow plays in Chapters 21–24 provide topics for analytical papers. Also, many of the suggestions for writing at the end of each chapter involve literary analysis. Here are some additional topics, though the possibilities for analysis of techniques in drama are endless:

1. The presence of *hybris* (pride) in Sophocles' *Antigone* (p. 1110).
2. The use and effect of Laertes and Fortinbras as foils to Hamlet in William Shakespeare's *Hamlet* (p. 1151).

> ▶ **TIPS for Writing Literary Analysis Papers**

> ➤ **Examine the text closely** Read with your intellect, imagination, and feelings fully engaged, paying attention to all the elements of drama and how they are used in the play.

> ➤ **Narrow your scope** Limit yourself to one element or aspect in the whole play or more than one in part of a play; don't try to cover too much.

> ➤ **Provide ample illustrations** Back up your analysis with specific examples (including quotations). This grounds and substantiates your conclusions.

> ➤ **Avoid summary** Retelling what happens is not literary analysis. Your emphasis needs to be on clarification and explanation of *how* and *why* the writing works.

3. The influence exerted by imagery of building and planting in Arthur Miller's *Death of a Salesman* (p. 1316), of dolls in Henrik Ibsen's *A Doll House* (p. 1263), or of cards in Suzan-Lori Parks's *Topdog/Underdog* (p. 1387).

4. Relate the four-line epigraph at the beginning of *Fences* (p. 1029) to the play as a whole.

5. The use and effect of foreshadowing in *A Doll House* (p. 1263).

6. Explicate one of the following passages and relate the passage in some way to the play as a whole: Antigone's speech on human and divine law in lines 499–525 of *Antigone* (p. 1110); one of Hamlet's soliloquies (*Hamlet* 1.2.129–59; 2.2.496–552); 3.1.57–89; 4.4.32–66); Helmer's "calm yourself and collect your thoughts speech" in *A Doll House* (p. 1263); or Willy's speech about Dave Singleman in *Death of a Salesman* (p. 1316).

Writing a Comparison-Contrast Paper about Drama

You could also write a paper about the literary context surrounding a play, about its relations to other literary works — how what it does, or the techniques it uses, compare and contrast to those of other plays of the time or to earlier or later plays. To be successful, such a paper requires finding connections that are meaningful and significant. Test your ideas by asking "So what?" (see p. 237), and use the topic only if you can answer in a thoughtful way.

Part of what surrounds and affects a play is its theatrical context: What other plays were being performed at the time? What types of plays did audiences prefer? What kind of theater was being used? What actors and actresses were available? Look for ways you can use comparison and contrast to show how a playwright was affected by events in the present and in the past. What other writers were doing at the time is important for fiction and poetry as well, of course, but it is particularly influential for drama, given its nature as a form intended for public performance. Shakespeare was very much aware of what contemporary and recent dramatists wrote, as the film *Shakespeare in Love* illustrates vividly in its fictionalized account. Thus comparing and contrasting *Hamlet* (p. 1151) with Thomas Kyd's *The Spanish Tragedy* (c. 1585–1587) could bring out how Shakespeare's play was shaped and affected by the conventions of other revenge plays of the time.

Equally interesting and important is how plays from the past influenced a later play or playwright. You might, for example, compare and contrast Arthur Miller's *Death of a Salesman* (p. 1316) with George Lillo's *The London Merchant* (1731) and consider to what extent Miller's play was influenced by the tradition of domestic tragedy exemplified in the latter.

The "Responding through Writing" sections at the ends of Chapters 21–24 include suggestions for comparison-contrast papers. Here are some additional ideas, though the possibilities are almost endless:

> **TIPS for Writing Comparison-Contrast Papers**

> **Watch for meaningful pairings** As you read, watch for things that pair up: a plot, scene, character, setting, or symbol that reminds you of another in a significant way. Always be alert for comparisons that come from unlikely pairings.

> **Outline similarities and differences** Make lists; then group related items and select two or three topics to focus on.

> **Spell out comparisons and contrasts** Don't just describe the things you are comparing and contrasting: Explain why you think there is a connection and why you think it has significance.

> **Don't retell what happens in the stories** Your paper should point out and discuss similarities and differences regarding specific aspects within the play or between plays, not just summarize how things differ in the plot.

1. Compare and contrast ways John Leguizamo's *Mambo Mouth* (p. 979) and Kelly Stuart's *The New New* (p. 915) use dramatic conventions and techniques to force their audiences (and readers) to confront social problems and conditions the audience (and readers) might prefer to ignore.
2. Compare and contrast the conception of tragedy in Sophocles' *Antigone* (p. 1110) and William Shakespeare's *Hamlet* (p. 1151), or in *Antigone* and Arthur Miller's *Death of a Salesman* (p. 1316).
3. Compare and contrast Shakespeare as poet and poetic dramatist by looking closely at a passage from *Hamlet* (p. 1151) (perhaps 1.2.129–59, 1.3.111–36, 3.1.57–89, or 4.4.32–66) and a Shakespearean sonnet (pp. 606 or 864)
4. Compare and contrast the importance of sports in Arthur Miller's *Death of a Salesman* (p. 1316) and August Wilson's *Fences* (p. 1029).
5. Compare and contrast a film version of a play with its written text — perhaps the 1996 version of *Hamlet* starring Kenneth Branagh or the 1985 version of *Death of a Salesman* starring Dustin Hoffman. Does the movie stick closely to the text or take considerable liberties? Is the result effective and satisfying or a disappointment? What things can the play do that the film version cannot, and what is the film able to do that the play can't?
6. Compare and contrast two versions of *Hamlet* on film: the one directed by Franco Zeffirelli and starring Mel Gibson (1990) and the one directed by and starring Kenneth Branagh (1996). Instead of attending to technical aspects of where and how the productions were performed and filmed, focus your paper on ways the interpretations of character and action differ.

Writing Social or Cultural Criticism about a Play

In addition to literary analysis and comparison-contrast papers, you can choose to write about a play's relation to its cultural and social context and to the real-world issues it deals with. Plays, like stories, often reflect contemporary social conditions and examine attitudes toward sex, class, ethnicity, power, and privilege. Even if the play does not refer directly to events or attitudes contemporary to the writing, those events and attitudes — consciously or unconsciously — influence the writer. The result could be a play that reflects prevailing attitudes or one that ignores, rejects, or challenges them. A paper might assess the implications of capitalism and economic competition in *Death of a Salesman* (p. 1316), for example, or traditional gender roles in *A Doll House* (p. 1263).

THINK IN CULTURAL TERMS   Cultural criticism concentrates on the way a work embodies a cultural context, how the events, ideas, or attitudes in a play were influenced by the economic conditions, political situation, or social conventions existing when it was written. But cultural criticism also explores the way a work is a part of a culture and influences, and perhaps changes, the economic conditions, political situation, or social conventions of its time or later times. Such a paper might investigate whether *A Doll House* (p. 1263) had a direct influence on changing attitudes toward women in the period following its appearance or if Ibsen's *Ghosts* (1881), which deals directly with the topic of congenital venereal disease and created quite a scandal, had an effect on future public awareness and attitudes toward sexuality.

Just as for all paper topics, a paper that engages in cultural criticism needs to make a point. Simply describing a social or cultural attitude or context is not especially interesting or useful. You need to write a thesis that unifies your paper and advances an argumentative position that the paper explores further. "This paper shows that both male and female characters in Ibsen's *A Doll House* are confined by traditional gender roles" is not a thesis because it presents only a statement of fact, not an argumentative proposition. A true thesis sentence would be this: "*A Doll House* challenges traditionally assumed gender roles as stifling, oppressive, and unjust by contrasting Nora's public image as a 'doll wife' with her repressed real self as a strong and independent woman."

> ## ▶ TIPS for Writing Social or Cultural Criticism
>
> ➤ **Read expansively** Look beyond structure, characters, and literary techniques and consider issues raised (intentionally or not) in and by the play.

> ➤ **Plan on doing research** Social or cultural criticism usually involves information beyond what is found in the text or in common knowledge; it often deals with background information you'll find only by further investigation.

> ➤ **Connections are crucial** Social and cultural criticism usually involves making connections of various kinds: between issues within and outside the text, for example, or between a text and historical/cultural events contemporary with it or between a text and a theoretical text.

> ➤ **Make a point** Simply describing cultural connections is not enough. A paper has to apply such connections, by exploring their relevance and implications, and cohere in a significant thesis.

Topics for cultural criticism papers range widely. Some of the writing suggestions in Chapters 21–24 involve cultural issues, and some of the "Approaching the Reading" topics following plays in those chapters also lead to topics for cultural or social criticism papers. Here are some more possibilities, though the list could go on and on:

1. Examine similarities and differences in the influence of fathers on sons in Arthur Miller's *Death of a Salesman* (p. 1316) and August Wilson's *Fences* (p. 1029).
2. Explore similarities and differences of men's attitudes toward women and women's attitudes toward themselves and other women as shown in Susan Gaspell's *Trifles* (p. 935) and Henrik Ibsen's *A Doll House* (p. 1263).
3. Analyze how Arthur Miller's *Death of a Salesman* (p. 1316) both embodies and critiques the attitudes, practices, and consequences of the merchandizing economy of the United States.
4. Discuss the role and effect of class distinctions in Kelly Stuart's *The New New* (p. 915), Henrik Ibsen's *A Doll House* (p. 1263), and/or August Wilson's *Fences* (p. 1029).
5. Analyze the depiction of and attitudes shown toward women in one of the following plays: Sophocles' *Antigone* (p. 1110), including both Antigone and Ismene, who are present in the action, and Niobe, who is alluded to, or William Shakespeare's *Hamlet* (p. 1151), including the queen and Ophelia, who are present in the action, and the Player Queen in the "Mousetrap Play" in act 3.
6. Compare and contrast the pursuit of the American dream in Arthur Miller's *Death of a Salesman* (p. 1316) and August Wilson's *Fences* (p. 1029).

DEVELOPMENT

Once you've picked out a technique, question, problem, or issue, you need to decide what to do with it, how to focus and develop it. The section on "Writing Short Papers" in Chapter 2 (pp. 34–45) applies to papers on drama as well as to those on fiction and poetry. Review the "Steps in the Writing Process" (p. 35) if you need to. Here we comment briefly on developing an argument specifically for a paper on drama.

DEVELOP A CENTRAL IDEA   Many of the steps in developing an argumentative paper on drama are the same as those outlined earlier for papers on fiction and poetry. Avoid plot summaries — assume the reader of your paper has read the play and understands what it's about. Develop a central idea that clarifies or illuminates a significant aspect of the play's technique, meaning, or context, literary or cultural. The central idea must be one about which there can be disagreement for the paper to be argumentative. Your task is to show readers that your views are sound and convincing.

ASK QUESTIONS   As with papers on fiction or poetry, asking questions is a good way to hone in on an argumentative central idea. And the same kinds of questions apply: What is distinctive or unique or striking about the way a technique is handled? In what ways is that technique used in the play? How does that technique relate to the theme? How is the problem or issue you're looking at brought out through characters, dialogue, conflicts, and contrasts? Does the play include symbols? If so, what are they, and how are they used in the play? What is controversial or puzzling or difficult about what the text seems to say about the issues raised in it?

ORGANIZE POINTS EFFECTIVELY   As we've suggested before, phrasing your central idea as a question and then using the paragraphs in the body of the paper to answer the question can help you organize the paper. It's generally best not to use plot as the outline for your paper since you can't cover everything about a full-length play in a short paper. Organize instead by topics or ideas — two or three techniques used by the playwright or a series of points about your central idea.

DEVELOP AND SUPPORT IDEAS   Each paragraph should have a topic sentence that states the paragraph's central idea. You should then elaborate on that idea, supporting it with details and illustrations and explaining how the details and illustrations support and clarify the ideas. Because you can't deal with the entire play, you can focus on an important scene or a crucial speech, examining it thoroughly and relating it to the rest of the play or you can focus on key passages in the play (see p. 242), particular sections — a sentence, a few sentences, a paragraph, a particular scene — that seem to shed light on all the other parts of the play.

CITING QUOTATIONS   As for fiction and poetry, your illustrations must include quotations. If your paper uses quotations only from plays included in this book, you do not need to add a bibliography page. Your teacher will take for granted that are using the text in this book. When you include quotations from other sources or from plays you find in another book, you need to include a Works Cited page (see pp. 1499–1509).

MAKING QUOTATIONS ECONOMICAL   Make the quotations you use short, pointed, and economical. Focus on key lines, phrases, or words whenever possible instead of typing out extended passages. Often a careful lead-in phrase or introductory sentence or two can clarify the context and point you are leading up to and thus reduce the need for a long quotation.

> ## ► Five Tips for Quoting Drama
>
> For general advice on fitting quotations into your paragraphs and sentences, review the sections on handling quotations (p. 44) and the "Ten Guidelines for Handling Quotations" (p. 47). Much of what is said on those pages applies to quoting from a play. But quoting from a play poses some special challenges. Here are some tips on how to handle quotations of drama:
>
> ► **One speech, prose** Handle prose passages from one speech in a play as you do quotations from any other prose. Merge quotations of four lines or fewer into your sentence; format longer passages as block quotations (see p. 47).
>
> ► **One speech, verse** Handle passages from one speech in a play written in verse as you do quotations from poetry. Merge quotations of one to three lines into your sentence, using slashes to indicate line divisions; format passages of four lines or more as block quotations (see p. 47).
>
> ► **More than one speech** Format passages quoting from more than one speech as block quotations. Indent the first line a half inch; type the character's name in capitals, followed by a colon and then by the text of the speech; indent following lines in the same speech another half inch. For example:
>
> > The shallowness of their thinking and values comes out in this exchange:
> >
> > > BRADLEY: And the thing of it is, it's about Jimmy's writing.
> > > I think his writing redeems him.
> > > CRAIG: Yeah. That's why we never, like bothered to check.
> > > [919]
>
> *(continued)*

➤ **Citing passages from plays in verse** For plays written in verse and divided into acts and scenes, identify passages by giving their act, scene, and line numbers in parentheses after the quotation. Use arabic numbers, separated by periods, even if the original uses roman numerals. This is especially helpful for older plays that have been reprinted many times. A page number isn't much help if you have a different edition from the one used in someone's paper. Thus a citation of the "To be or not to be" speech in the first scene of the third act of *Hamlet* (p. 1151) would appear as "(3.1.57–89)." Include the title of the play if other plays are cited in the paper. Give the edition from which you are quoting in a footnote or bibliography.

➤ **Citing passages from plays in prose** For plays written in prose, cite passages by page number in parentheses after the quotation. Give the edition from which you are quoting in a footnote or bibliography.

A STUDENT WRITER AT WORK: JULIAN HINSON ON THE WRITING PROCESS

In a recent Introduction to Literature class, we assigned a paper on an aspect of theme or dramatic technique in one of the short plays in Chapters 21–24. A student in the class, Julian Hinson, chose to do his paper on Kelly Stuart's *The New New* (p. 915). Here's what he told us about the way he went about writing the paper.

"When we were assigned to write a paper on Kelly Stuart's *The New New*, I sat down immediately to read the play. It was confusing, initially, partly because of its odd title and partly because of the way it jumps back and forth between the two men and the two women. I drew lines in the text each time the focus shifts from the one group to the other, and that made it easier to follow. Then I read the play aloud with another student, dividing the roles between us. That helped clarify what the lines mean because we had to concentrate on their tone and expression.

"That evening I jotted down a tentative title, 'The Degeneration of Morals in *The New New*,' and drafted an introduction and a working thesis: The use and abuse of language in *The New New* reflects a breakdown in contemporary moral values. The open-endedness of the assignment led me to explore as many aspects of the play as I could (something I may not have fully narrowed in the final paper). Having decided on a topic and preliminary thesis, I went back to the play and began searching for examples of major distortions of ethics and minor misdemeanors, hoping to show that in their essence both 'little white lies' and multimillion-dollar cover-ups differ very little from each other.

"Returning a day or two later to the introduction I had written earlier, I decided it needed some alterations. This led me to consider one of two opening directions: (1) Any person should be horrified by the opening two lines in the play. (2) Short stories and plays feature a condensed method of propaganda in their own right.

"Next I concentrated on coming up with an outline to organize the ideas I was interested in:

The Values of Society as Seen in <u>The New New</u>

Introduction: implications of "new"

1. Connections between distortions of words and distortions in morals
    —"redeems"; "neoteric"; "witty sardonic ethnographer"; "Thesaurus check" (searching for <u>synonyms</u>, not <u>meanings</u>)
2. Decline in media values during the lifetimes of generation Y
    —Jenny's affair with a teacher; "INTENSE CONNECTION"
3. Music on MTV and BET are evidence of a decline in morals
4. Spin doctors make decline seem like improvement
    —"we can't <u>call it</u> a memoir"; "Monster"; "marketing department"
5. Society allows success to transcend ethical concerns
    —"failing his class"; "his writing redeems him"; "witty sardonic ethnographer"
6. The problem is apathy, that people no longer really care
    —the way they proceed despite what Naomi told them; never bother to check

Conclusion

"I wrote the outline in front of the TV and coincidentally and amusingly enough, it was there that I thought of point 3, that even the music on today's main channels (MTV and BET) suggests a decline in contemporary morals (I later decided to omit it from the paper).

"In order to properly write about a new *New*, I figured it would be wise to struggle through the same problem Bradley and Craig did. I looked up the word *new* in a dictionary (NOT a thesaurus!) and found the following definitions: 'something of recent origin' or 'recently brought into being.' I also looked up other major terms used in the play to see if their dictionary meanings would clarify things in the play. This led me to look up *Kafkaesque* ('a style of writing characterized by surreal distortion or impending danger'), *modernistic* ('pertaining to or in sympathy with what is modern, or having the superficial mannerisms or surface characteristics of a modern style'), and *neoteric* ('modern, new, recent').

"I wrote a rough draft, dropping the third point of my original outline. After finishing it, I felt the paper didn't 'flow' in logical sequence. So I reread the play and reread what I had written and decided my points would be better integrated if I rearranged paragraphs to follow the structure of Kelly

Stuart's ideas as they develop in the beginning, middle, and end of her play. I also revised the title to something that would be more catchy and convey the point of the paper more clearly. Here's the final outline:

Out with the Old, in with the New:
The Spin on Contemporary Values in The New New

Introduction: implications of "new"

1. In contemporary society, success transcends ethics
2. That's particularly evident in the entertainment industry
3. Distortions of words connect to decline in morals
4. Spin doctors make decline seem like improvement
5. The problem is apathy, that people no longer really care

Conclusion

"What initially seemed a simple play turned out to be a fairly complex and nuanced consideration of modern attitudes toward social and personal ethics. That led me to do a lot of thinking in the shower."

SAMPLE PAPER
Julian Hinson
Professors Ridl and Schakel
English 105-04
December 1, 2007

Out with the Old, in with the New:
The Spin on Contemporary Values in The New New

Authors often think of their titles last. The title, however, is the first thing that the reader sees and it has a significant impact as the reader considers it before, during, and after finishing the work. The New New may seem at first a confusing title, yet it is intriguing as well. New, when used as an adjective, describes something unfamiliar, previously unseen, and recently brought into being. Yet when used as a noun, New can be seen as a socially acceptable norm, as in the phrases "Ring in the new" or "What's *Thesis sentence.* new?" Kelly Stuart combines both forms of the word into a title and uses her short play The New New to show that new attitudes toward language reflect unfavorable changes in society's attitude toward morals.

Quotation introduced formally with colon.

The play opens with lines that indicate "new" grounds for making decisions that have moral implications. Stuart opens her play with lines that once, at least, would have shocked readers:

Block quotation, with first lines indented a half inch, succeeding lines an inch.

> JENNY: I'm going to have an affair with him.
> MARCY: But Jenny, you're failing his class.
> JENNY: He says I can take an incomplete if I want, and he'll
>   help me make it up over the summer. (915)

Marcy's reply establishes that there is something fundamentally wrong with Jenny's statement, but her reply does not follow along ethical lines. It is, instead, based on Jenny's poor performance in the class. Marcy's response assumes that were Jenny acing the class, her actions would be acceptable, a reflection on the immunity of the successful in our society. Since Jimmy, the man convicted of manslaughter and the author of the new book, is an excellent writer — "his writing redeems him" (919) — neither Craig nor Bradley nor anyone else in their company ever bothered to check the validity of his story. In the play and often in modern society, morals take a backseat to pleasure. Bradley's diction as he describes talking to Jimmy shows how immune a successful, entertaining man can be:

> I used to get these calls from prison, collect calls every
> Tuesday. I thought of these calls as my "Tuesdays with
> Jimmy." He was just this witty, sardonic ethnographer of
> prison life. Of the ingenuity. . . . [This] civilized business
> executive locked up with all these illiterate thugs. . . .
> (917)

If Bradley had not found it "engaging" to hear about a businessman spending time in jail with petty thieves, he might have paid more attention to the fact that Jimmy survived prison, and probably managed to get his conviction reduced to manslaughter, through his ability to use "sales techniques."

The tendency to allow success to trump ethics is evident in much of the contemporary entertainment industry. One can, for example, attend a movie rated PG and find that the previews contain distinctly R images, yet each of those previews contains the disclaimer: "The following preview is suitable for all ages." Selling a new movie is more important than being sensitive to what ratings guidelines are supposed to achieve. An evening in front of the TV offers ample evidence of a significant decline in media values, despite claims to the contrary by corporate executives. Stuart reveals the current susceptibility to "spin doctors" through Bradley and Craig's manipulation of the story of Naomi's murdered brother, Jeremy. Bradley and Craig are in the marketing department: Their job is to use words to sell a product. As Craig puts it, "Agony isn't a word that sells" (916). By changing Jeremy's name to "Monster" and placing the emphasis on Jimmy's writing, they are able to promote this "memoiristic novel" as good literature.

The New New shows how the meanings of words can be severely distorted. Before the advent of this new "norm," an "INTENSE CONNECTION" (915) did not warrant sleeping with one's professor. In the same manner that the word "New" is replaced by "neoteric," Bradley views "agonizing" in the same light as "entertaining." Marcy's attachment to Jimmy grows to

---

Builds argument with assertions and illustrations.

Quotation blended into sentence.

Block quotation with speaker identified in the text.

Transition and topic sentence.

Transition and topic sentence.

"fondness" without her knowledge of the truth of why this seemingly "juxtaposed" man is actually in prison. Throughout the play, Stuart attempts to show the reader that both for characters in her play and for much of society words as a whole have lost their significance. Craig consults a thesaurus, looking for synonyms, not a dictionary, looking for meanings. Words carry no consequence and, without consequence, there can be no accountability, much less responsibility. This explains how something as small as a "thesaurus check" can acquit a killer of his crime. Had Bradley used the word "bitter" instead of "witty [and] sardonic," the book would have been viewed in a distinctly different light.

Transition and topic sentence.

The end of the play shows the result of neglecting what words actually mean. Naomi's note provides a benchmark for how far the wordsmiths Bradley and Craig have traveled in arriving at their distorted tale:

> My brother's name was Jeremy. Not Monster. He was five foot three, one hundred thirty pounds. Not six foot two, three hundred fifty. My brother was tortured and strangled over the course of a two-hour, period. The shape of a turtle and a steer were imprinted on my brother's neck, from the cowboy belt your so-called "author" used. My brother's face was badly beaten, bones protruded from his bloody face. My brother was a medical assistant. He was a human being, not a monster. (918)

Despite this evidence to the contrary of everything Bradley and Craig have sought to prove about Jimmy, they continue to justify their choice of author and remove his crime from the "real" story in their book. As Craig puts it, "I still think, um. The SPIRIT of the—I mean, he was true to the SPIRIT of, the book's not about the crime in any case . . ." (918).

Society is often willing to overlook an egregious fault in something as long as it works toward a desired end. When confronted, people are willing to justify the perpetrator on the basis of another "good" trait that works in her or his favor: "Being convicted of manslaughter had nothing to do with the arc of his life. It was just, this aberration" (918). The story has traveled so far from its original truth that a movie has been optioned for Ben Stiller, a comedy actor, and Marcy assumes that a "love" of Ben Stiller provides a basis for Jenny to love Jimmy.

Transition.

Topic sentence.

Stuart is not trying to depict the two men as evil or saying that they are selfish enough to deliberately seek profit from another man's death. Instead, she shows that the problem in society is apathy: People don't care about words being emptied of meaning or about the results of doing so. Despite Naomi's plea—"To see this man profit, it's killing me and I wonder if you ever gave that a thought?" (918)—the two men are content to ignore the truth of the story because they "really like Jimmy." Bradley continues to play matchmaker placing his "girlfriend's sister" at risk because he thinks Jimmy is a good man, and Craig attributes Naomi's emotions to mere blood relation: "She's the victim's sister. That's all. What do you expect?" (919).

At the end of the play, one can assume that Stuart gets the words of her title from Bradley and Craig's dilemma, but in spirit, her choice of a title slowly reveals and labels a problem embedded in contemporary society, the acceptance of a new new and a wrong norm.

Conclusion.

The plays ultimately are about love, honor, duty, betrayal —
what I call the Big Themes.

August Wilson

26 **August Wilson's
Fences— A Form
in Depth**

Wrestling with One
Writer's Work

August Wilson was born Frederick August Kittel on April 27, 1945, the
son of Daisy Wilson, an African American cleaning woman, and Frederick
August Kittel, a German immigrant baker who lived with the family only intermittently. His early years were spent in the Hill district, a black neighborhood of Pittsburgh. When his mother married David Bedford, a black
ex-convict and former high-school football star, the family moved to the
largely white community of Hazlewood, Pennsylvania, and later back to the
Hill. Wilson's brothers kept their father's name, but Wilson decided, in
1965, to adopt his mother's maiden name, thus signaling his loyalty to his
African American heritage.

He dropped out of Gladstone High School in 1960, after a ninth-grade
teacher, believing Wilson could not have written or done the research for a
twenty-page paper on Napoleon Bonaparte, accused him of plagiarism.
From that point, he educated himself by reading his way through the section
of black authors in the local library, discovering such writers as James Baldwin,

August Wilson performing his solo show How I Learned What I Learned *at the U.S. Comedy Arts Festival in March 2004 in Aspen, Colorado.*

E. Pablo Kosmicki/AP/ Wide World Photos.

Richard Wright, Langston Hughes, and Ralph Ellison. Reading works by black authors convinced him to be a writer himself, and he prepared by reading voraciously in fiction, poetry, and drama. He wrote and published some poetry, but soon found himself drawn to the theater. In 1968, he co-founded a theater company in Pittsburgh, Black Horizons on the Hill, through which he hoped to raise consciousness and politicize the community, and began writing one-act plays.

August Wilson in front of Ann's Restaurant in Boston, Massachusetts, November 1990.

Photo copyright © by Michael Romanos.

He moved to St. Paul, Minnesota, in 1978, taking with him a satirical play, *Black Bart and the Sacred Hills*, adapted from his poems. He found a job writing for the Science Museum of Minnesota and in 1980 became involved with the Minneapolis Playwrights Center. He regarded *Jitney*, written in 1979, as his first real play. He submitted it and three other early plays, unsuccessfully, to the Eugene O'Neill Theater Center's National Playwrights Conference in Waterford, Connecticut. Finally, in 1982, *Ma Rainey's Black Bottom* was accepted. At the O'Neill, Wilson impressed Lloyd Richards, director of the O'Neill Workshop and artistic director of the Yale Drama School. Richards taught Wilson stagecraft and helped him learn to revise his work and went on to direct Wilson's first six plays from workshops through Broadway productions.

Ma Rainey (premiered in 1984) was followed by *Fences* (1985) and *Joe Turner's Come and Gone* (1986). All three won the prestigious New York Drama Critics Circle Award (he eventually won a total of seven). In addition he won a Tony award, three American Theatre Critics awards, and two Pulitzer Prizes for Drama, first for *Fences* and later for *The Piano Lesson* (1989). These works became part of a cycle of ten plays Wilson undertook,

James Earl Jones as Troy Maxson in the 1987 Broadway production of Fences. Photofest.

chronicling the experience of African Americans in the United States, one play for each decade of the twentieth century:

1900s — *Gem of the Ocean* (2003)

1910s — *Joe Turner's Come and Gone* (1984)

1920s — *Ma Rainey's Black Bottom* (1982)

1930s — *The Piano Lesson* (1989)

1940s — *Seven Guitars* (1995)

1950s — *Fences* (1985)

1960s — *Two Trains Running* (1990)

1970s — *Jitney* (1982)

1980s — *King Hedley II* (2001)

1990s — *Radio Golf* (2005)

The series is designed to inform later generations about the hardships and indignities earlier generations experienced but did not talk about to their children. All of the plays are set in Pittsburgh except *Ma Rainey's Black Bottom*, which is set in Chicago.

Lynn Thigpen and James Earl Jones in the 1987 Broadway production of Fences.
Photofest.

The final play in the cycle, *Radio Golf*, premiered in March 2005 at the Yale Repertory Theatre. Two months later Wilson was diagnosed with inoperable liver cancer. He died on October 2, 2005. Soon after his death the Virginia Theatre in New York was renamed the August Wilson Theatre. This is the first Broadway theater to be named for an African American and is a tribute to his stature as one of the seminal figures in twentieth-century American drama.

There are three ways of using the material in this chapter for writing assignments. The first is to write a paper on *Fences* without reading the secondary materials in the chapter. In this case you would treat the play as if it were included in the "Collection of Plays" and your paper would not draw upon outside sources. If you choose this option, remember that if you do decide to read any secondary materials, even parts of them, you must acknowledge that in a bibliography, even if you don't quote from those sources or refer to them.

In a second way of using this chapter, your instructor might ask you to write a paper in which you use secondary sources but limit yourself to the ones that are included in this chapter. Such a paper provides practice incorporating ideas from a critical essay, selecting passages to quote and blending quotations into your writing, and constructing a Works Cited page. But it isn't actually a research paper since you aren't responsible for locating materials to use in the paper. The reason an instructor might select this option is that it doesn't require as much time as a full-blown research project does and it allows the instructor to evaluate your use of sources knowledgeably, since you are using only ones she or he is familiar with. For such a paper, you should review the guidelines for handling quotations on page 47 and you should read Chapter 28, "Reading Critical Essays," and the sections on incorporating sources, avoiding plagiarism, documenting sources, and preparing a Works Cited page in Chapter 29 (pp. 1499–1509).

A third way to use this chapter is as a starting point for an actual research paper. That is, after reading *Fences* and the secondary materials in this chapter, you would begin searching—perhaps only in the library, perhaps also using electronic sources, as your instructor prefers—to locate additional sources. You might read more interviews with Wilson and additional plays or essays written by him, and you surely will be expected to read and use additional biographical or critical works about his thoughts and works. For such a project, in addition to reviewing the guidelines for handling quotations on page 47 and reading Chapter 28, "Reading Critical Essays," you should read all of Chapter 29, "Writing a Literary Research Paper."

August Wilson   1945–2005

Fences   [1985]

> When the sins of our fathers visit us
> We do not have to play host.
> We can banish them with forgiveness
> As God, in His Largeness and Laws.
>
> *—August Wilson*

CHARACTERS

TROY MAXSON
JIM BONO, Troy's friend
ROSE, Troy's wife
LYONS, Troy's oldest son by previous marriage
GABRIEL, Troy's brother
CORY, Troy and Rose's son
RAYNELL, Troy's daughter

SETTING

The setting is the yard which fronts the only entrance to the Maxson household, an ancient two-story brick house set back off a small alley in a big-city neighborhood. The entrance to the house is gained by two or three steps leading to a wooden porch badly in need of paint.

A relatively recent addition to the house and running its full width, the porch lacks congruence. It is a sturdy porch with a flat roof. One or two chairs of dubious value sit at one end where the kitchen window opens onto the porch. An old-fashioned icebox stands silent guard at the opposite end.

The yard is a small dirt yard, partially fenced, except for the last scene, with a wooden sawhorse, a pile of lumber, and other fence-building equipment set off to the side. Opposite is a tree from which hangs a ball made of rags. A baseball bat leans against the tree. Two oil drums serve as garbage receptacles and sit near the house at right to complete the setting.

THE PLAY

Near the turn of the century, the destitute of Europe sprang on the city with tenacious claws and an honest and solid dream. The city devoured them. They swelled its belly until it burst into a thousand furnaces and sewing machines, a thousand butcher shops and bakers' ovens, a thousand churches and hospitals and funeral parlors and money-lenders. The city grew. It nourished itself and offered each man a partnership limited only by his talent, his guile, and his willingness and capacity for hard work. For the immigrants of Europe, a dream dared and won true.

The descendants of African slaves were offered no such welcome or participation. They came from places called the Carolinas and the Virginias, Georgia, Alabama, Mississippi, and Tennessee. They came strong, eager, searching. The city rejected them and they fled and settled along the riverbanks and under bridges in shallow, ramshackle houses made of sticks and tar-paper. They collected rags and wood. They sold the use of their muscles and their bodies. They cleaned houses and washed clothes, they shined shoes, and in quiet desperation and vengeful pride, they stole, and lived in pursuit of their own dream. That they could breathe free, finally, and stand to meet life with the force of dignity and whatever eloquence the heart could call upon.

By 1957, the hard-won victories of the European immigrants had solidified the industrial might of America. War had been confronted and won with new energies that used loyalty and patriotism as its fuel. Life was rich, full, and flourishing. The Milwaukee Braves won the World Series, and the hot winds of change that would make the sixties a turbulent, racing, dangerous, and provocative decade had not yet begun to blow full.

ACT ONE / Scene One

It is 1957. Troy and Bono enter the yard, engaged in conversation. Troy is fifty-three years old, a large man with thick, heavy hands; it is this largeness that he strives to fill out and make an accommodation with. Together with his blackness, his largeness informs his sensibilities and the choices he has made in his life.

Of the two men, Bono is obviously the follower. His commitment to their friendship of thirty-odd years is rooted in his admiration of Troy's honesty, capacity for hard work, and his strength, which Bono seeks to emulate.

It is Friday night, payday, and the one night of the week the two men engage in a ritual of talk and drink. Troy is usually the most talkative and at times he can be crude and almost vulgar, though he is capable of rising to profound heights of expression. The men carry lunch buckets and wear or carry burlap aprons and are dressed in clothes suitable to their jobs as garbage collectors.

BONO: Troy, you ought to stop that lying!

TROY: I ain't lying! The nigger had a watermelon this big.

(He indicates with his hands.)

> Talking about . . . "What watermelon, Mr. Rand?" I liked to fell out! "What watermelon, Mr. Rand?" . . . And it sitting there big as life.

BONO: What did Mr. Rand say?

TROY: Ain't said nothing. Figure if the nigger too dumb to know he carrying a watermelon, he wasn't gonna get much sense out of him. Trying to hide that great big old watermelon under his coat. Afraid to let the white man see him carry it home.

BONO: I'm like you . . . I ain't got no time for them kind of people.

TROY: Now what he look like getting mad cause he see the man from the union talking to Mr. Rand?

BONO: He come to me talking about . . . "Maxson gonna get us fired." I told him to get away from me with that. He walked away from me calling you a troublemaker. What Mr. Rand say?

TROY: Ain't said nothing. He told me to go down the Commissioner's office next Friday. They called me down there to see them.

BONO: Well, as long as you got your complaint filed, they can't fire you. That's what one of them white fellows tell me.

TROY: I ain't worried about them firing me. They gonna fire me cause I asked a question? That's all I did. I went to Mr. Rand and asked him, "Why? Why you got the white mens driving and the colored lifting?" Told him, "what's the matter, don't I count? You think only white fellows got sense enough to drive a truck. That ain't no paper job! Hell, anybody can drive a truck. How come you got all whites driving and the colored lifting?" He told me "take it to the union." Well, hell, that's what I done! Now they wanna come up with this pack of lies.

BONO: I told Brownie if the man come and ask him any questions . . . just tell the truth! It ain't nothing but something they done trumped up on you cause you filed a complaint on them.

TROY: Brownie don't understand nothing. All I want them to do is change the job description. Give everybody a chance to drive the truck. Brownie can't see that. He ain't got that much sense.

BONO: How you figure he be making out with that gal be up at Taylors' all the time . . . that Alberta gal?

TROY: Same as you and me. Getting just as much as we is. Which is to say nothing.

BONO: It is, huh? I figure you doing a little better than me . . . and I ain't saying what I'm doing.

TROY: Aw, nigger, look here . . . I know you. If you had got anywhere near that gal, twenty minutes later you be looking to tell somebody. And the first one you gonna tell . . . that you gonna want to brag to . . . is gonna be me.

BONO: I ain't saying that. I see where you be eyeing her.

TROY: I eye all the women. I don't miss nothing. Don't never let nobody tell you Troy Maxson don't eye the women.

BONO: You been doing more than eyeing her. You done bought her a drink or two.

TROY: Hell yeah, I bought her a drink! What that mean? I bought you one, too. What that mean cause I buy her a drink? I'm just being polite.

BONO: It's alright to buy her one drink. That's what you call being polite. But when you wanna be buying two or three . . . that's what you call eyeing her.

TROY: Look here, as long as you known me . . . you ever known me to chase after women?

BONO: Hell yeah! Long as I done known you. You forgetting I knew you when.

TROY: Naw, I'm talking about since I been married to Rose?

BONO: Oh, not since you been married to Rose. Now, that's the truth, there. I can say that.

TROY: Alright then! Case closed.

BONO: I see you be walking up around Alberta's house. You supposed to be at Taylors' and you be walking up around there.

TROY: What you watching where I'm walking for? I ain't watching after you.

BONO: I seen you walking around there more than once.

TROY: Hell, you liable to see me walking anywhere! That don't mean nothing cause you see me walking around there.

BONO: Where she come from anyway? She just kinda showed up one day.

TROY: Tallahassee. You can look at her and tell she one of them Florida gals. They got some big healthy women down there. Grow them right up out the ground. Got a little bit of Indian in her. Most of them niggers down in Florida got some Indian in them.

BONO: I don't know about that Indian part. But she damn sure big and healthy. Woman wear some big stockings. Got them great big old legs and hips as wide as the Mississippi River.

TROY: Legs don't mean nothing. You don't do nothing but push them out of the way. But them hips cushion the ride!

BONO: Troy, you ain't got no sense.

TROY: It's the truth! Like you riding on Goodyears!

(*Rose enters from the house. She is ten years younger than Troy, her devotion to him stems from her recognition of the possibilities of her life without him: a succession of abusive men and their babies, a life of partying and running the streets, the Church, or aloneness with its attendant pain and frustration. She recognizes Troy's spirit as a fine and illuminating one and she either ignores or forgives his faults, only some of which she recognizes. Though she doesn't drink, her presence is an integral part of the Friday night rituals. She alternates between the porch and the kitchen, where supper preparations are under way.*)

ROSE: What you all out here getting into?

TROY: What you worried about what we getting into for? This is men talk, woman.

ROSE: What I care what you all talking about? Bono, you gonna stay for supper?

BONO: No, I thank you, Rose. But Lucille say she cooking up a pot of pigfeet.

TROY: Pigfeet! Hell, I'm going home with you! Might even stay the night if you got some pigfeet. You got something in there to top them pigfeet, Rose?

ROSE: I'm cooking up some chicken. I got some chicken and collard greens.

TROY: Well, go on back in the house and let me and Bono finish what we was talking about. This is men talk. I got some talk for you later. You know what kind of talk I mean. You go on and powder it up.

ROSE: Troy Maxson, don't you start that now!

TROY (*puts his arm around her*): Aw, woman . . . come here. Look here, Bono . . . when I met this woman . . . I got out that place, say, "Hitch up my pony, saddle up my mare . . . there's a woman out there for me somewhere. I looked here. Looked there. Saw Rose and latched on to her." I latched on to her and told her — I'm gonna tell you the truth — I told her, "Baby, I don't wanna marry, I just wanna be your man." Rose told me . . . tell him what you told me, Rose.

ROSE: I told him if he wasn't the marrying kind, then move out the way so the marrying kind could find me.

TROY: That's what she told me. "Nigger, you in my way. You blocking the view! Move out the way so I can find me a husband." I thought it over two or three days. Come back —

ROSE: Ain't no two or three days nothing. You was back the same night.

TROY: Come back, told her . . . "Okay, baby . . . but I'm gonna buy me a banty rooster and put him out there in the backyard . . . and when he see a stranger come, he'll flap his wings and crow . . ." Look here, Bono, I could watch the front door by myself . . . it was that back door I was worried about.

ROSE: Troy, you ought not talk like that. Troy ain't doing nothing but telling a lie.

TROY: Only thing is . . . when we first got married . . . forget the rooster . . . we ain't had no yard!

BONO: I hear you tell it. Me and Lucille was staying down there on Logan Street. Had two rooms with the outhouse in the back. I ain't mind the outhouse none. But when that goddamn wind blow through there in the winter . . . that's what I'm talking about! To this day I wonder why in the hell I ever stayed down there for six long years. But see, I didn't know I could do no better. I thought only white folks had inside toilets and things.

ROSE: There's a lot of people don't know they can do no better than they doing now. That's just something you got to learn. A lot of folks still shop at Bella's.

TROY: Ain't nothing wrong with shopping at Bella's. She got fresh food.

ROSE: I ain't said nothing about if she got fresh food. I'm talking about what she charge. She charge ten cents more than the A&P.°

TROY: The A&P ain't never done nothing for me. I spends my money where I'm treated right. I go down to Bella, say, "I need a loaf of bread, I'll pay you Friday." She give it to me. What sense that make when I got money to go and spend it somewhere else and ignore the person who done right by me? That ain't in the Bible.

ROSE: We ain't talking about what's in the Bible. What sense it make to shop there when she overcharge?

TROY: You shop where you want to. I'll do my shopping where the people been good to me.

ROSE: Well, I don't think it's right for her to overcharge. That's all I was saying.

BONO: Look here . . . I got to get on. Lucille going be raising all kind of hell.

TROY: Where you going, nigger? We ain't finished this pint. Come here, finish this pint.

BONO: Well, hell, I am . . . if you ever turn the bottle loose.

TROY (*hands him the bottle*): The only thing I say about the A&P is I'm glad Cory got that job down there. Help him take care of his school clothes and things. Gabe done moved out and things getting tight around here. He got that job. . . . He can start to look out for himself.

A&P: Chain of grocery stores operated by the Great Atlantic and Pacific Tea Company.

ROSE: Cory done went and got recruited by a college football team.

TROY: I told that boy about that football stuff. The white man ain't gonna let him get nowhere with that football. I told him when he first come to me with it. Now you come telling me he done went and got more tied up in it. He ought to go and get recruited in how to fix cars or something where he can make a living.

ROSE: He ain't talking about making no living playing football. It's just something the boys in school do. They gonna send a recruiter by to talk to you. He'll tell you he ain't talking about making no living playing football. It's a honor to be recruited.

TROY: It ain't gonna get him nowhere. Bono'll tell you that.

BONO: If he be like you in the sports . . . he's gonna be alright. Ain't but two men ever played baseball as good as you. That's Babe Ruth and Josh Gibson.° Them's the only two men ever hit more home runs than you.

TROY: What it ever get me? Ain't got a pot to piss in or a window to throw it out of.

ROSE: Times have changed since you was playing baseball, Troy. That was before the war. Times have changed a lot since then.

TROY: How in hell they done changed?

ROSE: They got lots of colored boys playing ball now. Baseball and football.

BONO: You right about that, Rose. Times have changed, Troy. You just come along too early.

TROY: There ought not never have been no time called too early! Now you take that fellow . . . what's that fellow they had playing right field for the Yankees back then? You know who I'm talking about, Bono. Used to play right field for the Yankees.

ROSE: Selkirk?°

TROY: Selkirk! That's it! Man batting .269, understand? .269. What kind of sense that make? I was hitting .432 with thirty-seven home runs! Man batting .269 and playing right field for the Yankees! I saw Josh Gibson's daughter yesterday. She walking around with raggedy shoes on her feet. Now I bet you Selkirk's daughter ain't walking around with raggedy shoes on her feet! I bet you that!

ROSE: They got a lot of colored baseball players now. Jackie Robinson° was the first. Folks had to wait for Jackie Robinson.

Babe Ruth and Josh Gibson: George Herman Ruth (1895–1948) was a pitcher and then an outfielder for the Boston Red Sox (1914–1919), New York Yankees (1920–1934), and Boston Braves (1935). His sixty home runs in the 1927 season set a major league record that stood until 1961. Joshua Gibson (1911–1947), the greatest power hitter in the Negro Leagues and often referred to as the black Babe Ruth, was credited with having hit eighty-four home runs in a single season. In 1972 he was elected to the Baseball Hall of Fame, the second Negro League player (after Satchel Paige) to be so honored.   **Selkirk:** George Selkirk (1934–1987), successor to Babe Ruth in right field for the Yankees. In nine seasons (1934–1942) he had a cumulative batting average of .290 with 108 home runs. In 1940 his average was .269 with 19 home runs. **Jackie Robinson:** Jack Roosevelt Robinson (1919–1972), first and second baseman for the Brooklyn Dodgers from 1947 to 1956, was the first African American to play in the major leagues.

TROY: I done seen a hundred niggers play baseball better than Jackie Robinson. Hell, I know some teams Jackie Robinson couldn't even make! What you talking about Jackie Robinson. Jackie Robinson wasn't nobody. I'm talking about if you could play ball then they ought to have let you play. Don't care what color you were. Come telling me I come along too early. If you could play . . . then they ought to have let you play.

(*Troy takes a long drink from the bottle.*)

ROSE: You gonna drink yourself to death. You don't need to be drinking like that.

TROY: Death ain't nothing. I done seen him. Done wrassled with him. You can't tell me nothing about death. Death ain't nothing but a fastball on the outside corner. And you know what I'll do to that! Lookee here, Bono . . . am I lying? You get one of them fastballs, about waist high, over the outside corner of the plate where you can get the meat of the bat on it . . . and good god! You can kiss it goodbye. Now, am I lying?

BONO: Naw, you telling the truth there. I seen you do it.

TROY: If I'm lying . . . that 450 feet worth of lying!

(*Pause.*)

That's all death is to me. A fastball on the outside corner.

ROSE: I don't know why you want to get on talking about death.

TROY: Ain't nothing wrong with talking about death. That's part of life. Everybody gonna die. You gonna die, I'm gonna die. Bono's gonna die. Hell, we all gonna die.

ROSE: But you ain't got to talk about it. I don't like to talk about it.

TROY: You the one brought it up. Me and Bono was talking about baseball . . . you tell me I'm gonna drink myself to death. Ain't that right, Bono? You know I don't drink this but one night out of the week. That's Friday night. I'm gonna drink just enough to where I can handle it. Then I cuts it loose. I leave it alone. So don't you worry about me drinking myself to death. 'Cause I ain't worried about Death. I done seen him. I done wrestled with him.

Look here, Bono . . . I looked up one day and Death was marching straight at me. Like Soldiers on Parade! The Army of Death was marching straight at me. The middle of July, 1941. It got real cold just like it be winter. It seem like Death himself reached out and touched me on the shoulder. He touch me just like I touch you. I got cold as ice and Death standing there grinning at me.

ROSE: Troy, why don't you hush that talk.

TROY: I say . . . What you want, Mr. Death? You be wanting me? You done brought your army to be getting me? I looked him dead in the eye. I wasn't fearing nothing. I was ready to tangle. Just like I'm ready to tangle now. The Bible say be ever vigilant. That's why I don't get but so drunk. I got to keep watch.

ROSE: Troy was right down there in Mercy Hospital. You remember he had pneumonia? Laying there with a fever talking plumb out of his head.

TROY: Death standing there staring at me . . . carrying that sickle in his hand. Finally he say, "You want bound over for another year?" See, just like that . . . "You want bound over for another year?" I told him, "Bound over hell! Let's settle this now!"

It seem like he kinda fell back when I said that, and all the cold went out of me. I reached down and grabbed that sickle and threw it just as far as I could throw it . . . and me and him commenced to wrestling.

We wrestled for three days and three nights. I can't say where I found the strength from. Every time it seemed like he was gonna get the best of me, I'd reach way down deep inside myself and find the strength to do him one better.

ROSE: Every time Troy tell that story he find different ways to tell it. Different things to make up about it.

TROY: I ain't making up nothing. I'm telling you the facts of what happened. I wrestled with Death for three days and three nights and I'm standing here to tell you about it.

(*Pause.*)

Alright. At the end of the third night we done weakened each other to where we can't hardly move. Death stood up, throwed on his robe . . . had him a white robe with a hood on it. He threw on that robe and went off to look for his sickle. Say, "I'll be back." Just like that. "I'll be back." I told him, say, "Yeah, but . . . you gonna have to find me!" I wasn't no fool. I wan't going looking for him. Death ain't nothing to play with. And I know he's gonna get me. I know I got to join his army . . . his camp followers. But as long as I keep my strength and see him coming . . . as long as I keep up my vigilance . . . he's gonna have to fight to get me. I ain't going easy.

BONO: Well, look here, since you got to keep up your vigilance . . . let me have the bottle.

TROY: Aw hell, I shouldn't have told you that part. I should have left out that part.

ROSE: Troy be talking that stuff and half the time don't even know what he be talking about.

TROY: Bono know me better than that.

BONO: That's right. I know you. I know you got some Uncle Remus in your blood. You got more stories than the devil got sinners.

TROY: Aw hell, I done seen him too! Done talked with the devil.

ROSE: Troy, don't nobody wanna be hearing all that stuff.

(*Lyons enters the yard from the street. Thirty-four years old, Troy's son by a previous marriage, he sports a neatly trimmed goatee, sport coat, white shirt, tieless and buttoned at the collar. Though he fancies himself a musician, he is more caught up in the rituals and "idea" of being a musician than in the actual practice of the music. He has come to borrow money from Troy, and while he knows he will be successful, he is uncertain as to what extent his lifestyle will be held up to scrutiny and ridicule.*)

LYONS: Hey, Pop.

TROY: What you come "Hey, Popping" me for?

LYONS: How you doing, Rose?

(*He kisses her.*)

Mr. Bono. How you doing?

BONO: Hey, Lyons . . . how you been?

TROY: He must have been doing alright. I ain't seen him around here last week.

ROSE: Troy, leave your boy alone. He come by to see you and you wanna start all that nonsense.

TROY: I ain't bothering Lyons.

(*Offers him the bottle.*)

Here . . . get you a drink. We got an understanding. I know why he come by to see me and he know I know.

LYONS: Come on, Pop . . . I just stopped by to say hi . . . see how you was doing.

TROY: You ain't stopped by yesterday.

ROSE: You gonna stay for supper, Lyons? I got some chicken cooking in the oven.

LYONS: No, Rose . . . thanks. I was just in the neighborhood and thought I'd stop by for a minute.

TROY: You was in the neighborhood alright, nigger. You telling the truth there. You was in the neighborhood cause it's my payday.

LYONS: Well, hell, since you mentioned it . . . let me have ten dollars.

TROY: I'll be damned! I'll die and go to hell and play blackjack with the devil before I give you ten dollars.

BONO: That's what I wanna know about . . . that devil you done seen.

LYONS: What . . . Pop done seen the devil? You too much, Pops.

TROY: Yeah, I done seen him. Talked to him too!

ROSE: You ain't seen no devil. I done told you that man ain't had nothing to do with the devil. Anything you can't understand, you want to call it the devil.

TROY: Look here, Bono . . . I went down to see Hertzberger about some furniture. Got three rooms for two-ninety-eight. That what it say on the radio. "Three rooms . . . two-ninety-eight." Even made up a little song about it. Go down there . . . man tell me I can't get no credit. I'm working every day and can't get no credit. What to do? I got an empty house with some raggedy furniture in it. Cory ain't got no bed. He's sleeping on a pile of rags on the floor. Working every day and can't get no credit. Come back here — Rose'll tell you — madder than hell. Sit down . . . try to figure what I'm gonna do. Come a knock on the door. Ain't been living here but three days. Who know I'm here? Open the door . . . devil standing there bigger than life. White fellow . . . got on good clothes and everything. Standing there with a clipboard in his hand. I ain't had to say nothing. First words come out of his mouth was . . . "I understand you need some furniture and can't get no credit." I liked to fell over. He say, "I'll give you all the credit you want, but you got to pay the interest on it." I told him, "Give me three rooms worth and charge whatever you want." Next day a truck pulled up here and two men unloaded them three rooms. Man what drove the truck give me a book. Say send ten dollars, first of every month to the address in the book and everything will be alright. Say if I miss a payment the devil was coming back and it'll be hell to pay. That was fifteen years ago. To this day . . . the first of the month I send my ten dollars, Rose'll tell you.

ROSE: Troy lying.

TROY: I ain't never seen that man since. Now you tell me who else that could have been but the devil? I ain't sold my soul or nothing like that, you understand. Naw, I wouldn't have truck with the devil about nothing like that. I got my furniture and pays my ten dollars the first of the month just like clockwork.

BONO: How long you say you been paying this ten dollars a month?

TROY: Fifteen years!

BONO: Hell, ain't you finished paying for it yet? How much the man done charged you?

TROY: Aw hell, I done paid for it. I done paid for it ten times over! The fact is I'm scared to stop paying it.

ROSE: Troy lying. We got that furniture from Mr. Glickman. He ain't paying no ten dollars a month to nobody.

TROY: Aw hell, woman. Bono know I ain't that big a fool.

LYONS: I was just getting ready to say . . . I know where there's a bridge for sale.

TROY: Look here, I'll tell you this . . . it don't matter to me if he was the devil. It don't matter if the devil give credit. Somebody has got to give it.

ROSE: It ought to matter. You going around talking about having truck with the devil . . . God's the one you gonna have to answer to. He's the one gonna be at the Judgment.

LYONS: Yeah, well, look here, Pop . . . let me have that ten dollars. I'll give it back to you. Bonnie got a job working at the hospital.

TROY: What I tell you, Bono? The only time I see this nigger is when he wants something. That's the only time I see him.

LYONS: Come on, Pop, Mr. Bono don't want to hear all that. Let me have the ten dollars. I told you Bonnie working.

TROY: What that mean to me? "Bonnie working." I don't care if she working. Go ask her for the ten dollars if she working. Talking about "Bonnie working." Why ain't you working?

LYONS: Aw, Pop, you know I can't find no decent job. Where am I gonna get a job at? You know I can't get no job.

TROY: I told you I know some people down there. I can get you on the rubbish if you want to work. I told you that the last time you came by here asking me for something.

LYONS: Naw, Pop . . . thanks. That ain't for me. I don't wanna be carrying nobody's rubbish. I don't wanna be punching nobody's time clock.

TROY: What's the matter, you too good to carry people's rubbish? Where you think that ten dollars you talking about come from? I'm just supposed to haul people's rubbish and give my money to you cause you too lazy to work. You too lazy to work and wanna know why you ain't got what I got.

ROSE: What hospital Bonnie working at? Mercy?

LYONS: She's down at Passavant working in the laundry.

TROY: I ain't got nothing as it is. I give you that ten dollars and I got to eat beans the rest of the week. Naw . . . you ain't getting no ten dollars here.

LYONS: You ain't got to be eating no beans. I don't know why you wanna say that.

TROY: I ain't got no extra money. Gabe done moved over to Miss Pearl's paying her the rent and things done got tight around here. I can't afford to be giving you every payday.

LYONS: I ain't asked you to give me nothing. I asked you to loan me ten dollars. I know you got ten dollars.

TROY: Yeah, I got it. You know why I got it? Cause I don't throw my money away out there in the streets. You living the fast life . . . wanna be a musician . . . running around in them clubs and things . . . then, you learn to take care of yourself. You ain't gonna find me going and asking nobody for nothing. I done spent too many years without.

LYONS: You and me is two different people, Pop.

TROY: I done learned my mistake and learned to do what's right by it. You still trying to get something for nothing. Life don't owe you nothing. You owe it to yourself. Ask Bono. He'll tell you I'm right.

LYONS: You got your way of dealing with the world . . . I got mine. The only thing that matters to me is the music.

TROY: Yeah, I can see that! It don't matter how you gonna eat . . . where your next dollar is coming from. You telling the truth there.

LYONS: I know I got to eat. But I got to live too. I need something that gonna help me to get out of the bed in the morning. Make me feel like I belong in the world. I don't bother nobody. I just stay with the music cause that's the only way I can find to live in the world. Otherwise there ain't no telling what I might do. Now I don't come criticizing you and how you live. I just come by to ask you for ten dollars. I don't wanna hear all that about how I live.

TROY: Boy, your mamma did a hell of a job raising you.

LYONS: You can't change me, Pop. I'm thirty-four years old. If you wanted to change me, you should have been there when I was growing up. I come by to see you . . . ask for ten dollars and you want to talk about how I was raised. You don't know nothing about how I was raised.

ROSE: Let the boy have ten dollars, Troy.

TROY (*to Lyons*): What the hell you looking at me for? I ain't got no ten dollars. You know what I do with my money.

(*To Rose.*)

Give him ten dollars if you want him to have it.

ROSE: I will. Just as soon as you turn it loose.

TROY (*handing Rose the money*): There it is. Seventy-six dollars and forty-two cents. You see this, Bono? Now, I ain't gonna get but six of that back.

ROSE: You ought to stop telling that lie. Here, Lyons.

(*She hands him the money.*)

LYONS: Thanks, Rose. Look . . . I got to run . . . I'll see you later.

TROY: Wait a minute. You gonna say, "thanks, Rose" and ain't gonna look to see where she got that ten dollars from? See how they do me, Bono?

LYONS: I know she got it from you, Pop. Thanks. I'll give it back to you.

TROY: There he go telling another lie. Time I see that ten dollars . . . he'll be owing me thirty more.

LYONS: See you, Mr. Bono.

BONO: Take care, Lyons!

LYONS: Thanks, Pop. I'll see you again.

(*Lyons exits the yard.*)

TROY: I don't know why he don't go and get him a decent job and take care of that woman he got.

BONO: He'll be alright, Troy. The boy is still young.

TROY: The *boy* is thirty-four years old.

ROSE: Let's not get off into all that.

BONO: Look here . . . I got to be going. I got to be getting on. Lucille gonna be waiting.

TROY (*puts his arm around Rose*): See this woman, Bono? I love this woman. I love this woman so much it hurts. I love her so much . . . I done run out of ways of loving her. So I got to go back to basics. Don't you come by my house Monday morning talking about time to go to work . . . 'cause I'm still gonna be stroking!

ROSE: Troy! Stop it now!

BONO: I ain't paying him no mind, Rose. That ain't nothing but gin-talk. Go on, Troy. I'll see you Monday.

TROY: Don't you come by my house, nigger! I done told you what I'm gonna be doing.

(*The lights go down to black.*)

Scene Two

The lights come up on Rose hanging up clothes. She hums and sings softly to herself. It is the following morning.

ROSE (*sings*): Jesus, be a fence all around me every day
Jesus, I want you to protect me as I travel on my way.
Jesus, be a fence all around me every day.

(*Troy enters from the house.*)

ROSE (*continued*): Jesus, I want you to protect me
As I travel on my way.

(*To Troy.*)

'Morning. You ready for breakfast? I can fix it soon as I finish hanging up these clothes.

TROY: I got the coffee on. That'll be alright. I'll just drink some of that this morning.

ROSE: That 651 hit yesterday. That's the second time this month. Miss Pearl hit for a dollar . . . seem like those that need the least always get lucky. Poor folks can't get nothing.

TROY: Them numbers don't know nobody. I don't know why you fool with them. You and Lyons both.

ROSE: It's something to do.

TROY: You ain't doing nothing but throwing your money away.

ROSE: Troy, you know I don't play foolishly. I just play a nickel here and a nickel there.

TROY: That's two nickels you done thrown away.

ROSE: Now I hit sometimes . . . that makes up for it. It always comes in handy when I do hit. I don't hear you complaining then.

TROY: I ain't complaining now. I just say it's foolish. Trying to guess out of six hundred ways which way the number gonna come. If I had all the money niggers, these Negroes, throw away on numbers for one week — just one week — I'd be a rich man.

ROSE: Well, you wishing and calling it foolish ain't gonna stop folks from playing numbers. That's one thing for sure. Besides . . . some good things come from playing numbers. Look where Pope done bought him that restaurant off of numbers.

TROY: I can't stand niggers like that. Man ain't had two dimes to rub together. He walking around with his shoes all run over bumming money for cigarettes. Alright. Got lucky there and hit the numbers . . .

ROSE: Troy, I know all about it.

TROY: Had good sense, I'll say that for him. He ain't throwed his money away. I seen niggers hit the numbers and go through two thousand dollars in four days. Man bought him that restaurant down there . . . fixed it up real nice . . . and then didn't want nobody to come in it! A Negro go in there and can't get no kind of service. I seen a white fellow come in there and order a bowl of stew. Pope picked all the meat out the pot for him. Man ain't had nothing but a bowl of meat! Negro come behind him and ain't got nothing but the potatoes and carrots. Talking about what numbers do for people, you picked a wrong example. Ain't done nothing but make a worser fool out of him than he was before.

ROSE: Troy, you ought to stop worrying about what happened at work yesterday.

TROY: I ain't worried. Just told me to be down there at the Commissioner's office on Friday. Everybody think they gonna fire me. I ain't worried about them firing me. You ain't got to worry about that.

(*Pause.*)

Where's Cory? Cory in the house? (*Calls.*) Cory?

ROSE: He gone out.

TROY: Out, huh? He gone out 'cause he know I want him to help me with this fence. I know how he is. That boy scared of work.

(*Gabriel enters. He comes halfway down the alley and, hearing Troy's voice, stops.*)

TROY (*continues*): He ain't done a lick of work in his life.

ROSE: He had to go to football practice. Coach wanted them to get in a little extra practice before the season start.

TROY: I got his practice . . . running out of here before he get his chores done.

ROSE: Troy, what is wrong with you this morning? Don't nothing set right with you. Go on back in there and go to bed . . . get up on the other side.

TROY: Why something got to be wrong with me? I ain't said nothing wrong with me.

ROSE: You got something to say about everything. First it's the numbers . . . then it's the way the man runs his restaurant . . . then you done got on Cory. What's it gonna be next? Take a look up there and see if the weather suits you . . . or is it gonna be how you gonna put up the fence with the clothes hanging in the yard.

TROY: You hit the nail on the head then.

ROSE: I know you like I know the back of my hand. Go on in there and get you some coffee . . . see if that straighten you up. 'Cause you ain't right this morning.

(*Troy starts into the house and sees Gabriel. Gabriel starts singing. Troy's brother, he is seven years younger than Troy. Injured in World War II, he has a metal plate in his head. He carries an old trumpet tied around his waist and believes with every fiber of his being that he is the Archangel Gabriel. He carries a chipped basket with an assortment of discarded fruits and vegetables he has picked up in the strip district and which he attempts to sell.*)

GABRIEL (*singing*): Yes, ma'am, I got plums
　　　　　　　You ask me how I sell them
　　　　　　　Oh ten cents apiece
　　　　　　　Three for a quarter
　　　　　　　Come and buy now
　　　　　　　'Cause I'm here today
　　　　　　　And tomorrow I'll be gone

(*Gabriel enters.*)

　　　Hey, Rose!

ROSE: How you doing, Gabe?

GABRIEL: There's Troy . . . Hey, Troy!

TROY: Hey, Gabe.

(*Exit into kitchen.*)

ROSE (*to Gabriel*): What you got there?

GABRIEL: You know what I got, Rose. I got fruits and vegetables.

ROSE (*looking in basket*): Where's all these plums you talking about?

GABRIEL: I ain't got no plums today, Rose. I was just singing that. Have some to-morrow. Put me in a big order for plums. Have enough plums tomorrow for St. Peter and everybody.

(*Troy re-enters from kitchen, crosses to steps.*)

(*To Rose.*)

Troy's mad at me.

TROY: I ain't mad at you. What I got to be mad at you about? You ain't done nothing to me.

GABRIEL: I just moved over to Miss Pearl's to keep out from in your way. I ain't mean no harm by it.

TROY: Who said anything about that? I ain't said anything about that.

GABRIEL: You ain't mad at me, is you?

TROY: Naw . . . I ain't mad at you, Gabe. If I was mad at you I'd tell you about it.

GABRIEL: Got me two rooms. In the basement. Got my own door too. Wanna see my key?

(*He holds up a key.*)

That's my own key! Ain't nobody else got a key like that. That's my key! My two rooms!

TROY: Well, that's good, Gabe. You got your own key . . . that's good.

ROSE: You hungry, Gabe? I was just fixing to cook Troy his breakfast.

GABRIEL: I'll take some biscuits. You got some biscuits? Did you know when I was in heaven . . . every morning me and St. Peter would sit down by the gate and eat some big fat biscuits? Oh, yeah! We had us a good time. We'd sit there and eat us them biscuits and then St. Peter would go off to sleep and tell me to wake him up when it's time to open the gates for the judgment.

ROSE: Well, come on . . . I'll make up a batch of biscuits.

(*Rose exits into the house.*)

GABRIEL: Troy . . . St. Peter got your name in the book. I seen it. It say . . . Troy Maxson. I say . . . I know him! He got the same name like what I got. That's my brother!

TROY: How many times you gonna tell me that, Gabe?

GABRIEL: Ain't got my name in the book. Don't have to have my name. I done died and went to heaven. He got your name though. One morning St. Peter was looking at his book . . . marking it up for the judgment . . . and he let me see your name. Got it in there under M. Got Rose's name . . . I ain't seen it like I seen yours . . . but I know it's in there. He got a great big book. Got everybody's name what was ever been born. That's what he told me. But I seen your name. Seen it with my own eyes.

TROY: Go on in the house there. Rose going to fix you something to eat.

GABRIEL: Oh, I ain't hungry. I done had breakfast with Aunt Jemimah. She come by and cooked me up a whole mess of flapjacks. Remember how we used to eat them flapjacks?

TROY: Go on in the house and get you something to eat now.

GABRIEL: I got to sell my plums. I done sold some tomatoes. Got me two quarters. Wanna see?

(*He shows Troy his quarters.*)

I'm gonna save them and buy me a new horn so St. Peter can hear me when it's time to open the gates.

(*Gabriel stops suddenly. Listens.*)

Hear that? That's the hellhounds. I got to chase them out of here. Go on get out of here! Get out!

(*Gabriel exits singing.*)

Better get ready for the judgment
Better get ready for the judgment
My Lord is coming down

(*Rose enters from the house.*)

TROY: He gone off somewhere.

GABRIEL (*offstage*): Better get ready for the judgment
Better get ready for the judgment morning
Better get ready for the judgment
My God is coming down

ROSE: He ain't eating right. Miss Pearl say she can't get him to eat nothing.

TROY: What you want me to do about it, Rose? I done did everything I can for the man. I can't make him get well. Man got half his head blown away . . . what you expect?

ROSE: Seem like something ought to be done to help him.

TROY: Man don't bother nobody. He just mixed up from that metal plate he got in his head. Ain't no sense for him to go back into the hospital.

ROSE: Least he be eating right. They can help him take care of himself.

TROY: Don't nobody wanna be locked up, Rose. What you wanna lock him up for? Man go over there and fight the war . . . messin' around with them Japs, get half his head blown off . . . and they give him a lousy three thousand dollars. And I had to swoop down on that.

ROSE: Is you fixing to go into that again?

TROY: That's the only way I got a roof over my head . . . cause of that metal plate.

ROSE: Ain't no sense you blaming yourself for nothing. Gabe wasn't in no condition to manage that money. You done what was right by him. Can't nobody say you ain't done what was right by him. Look how long you took care of him . . . till he wanted to have his own place and moved over there with Miss Pearl.

TROY: That ain't what I'm saying, woman! I'm just stating the facts. If my brother didn't have that metal plate in his head . . . I wouldn't have a pot to piss in or a window to throw it out of. And I'm fifty-three years old. Now see if you can understand that!

(*Troy gets up from the porch and starts to exit the yard.*)

ROSE: Where you going off to? You been running out of here every Saturday for weeks. I thought you was gonna work on this fence?

TROY: I'm gonna walk down to Taylors'. Listen to the ball game. I'll be back in a bit. I'll work on it when I get back.

(*He exits the yard. The lights go to black.*)

Scene Three

The lights come up on the yard. It is four hours later. Rose is taking down the clothes from the line. Cory enters carrying his football equipment.

ROSE: Your daddy like to had a fit with you running out of here this morning without doing your chores.

CORY: I told you I had to go to practice.

ROSE: He say you were supposed to help him with this fence.

CORY: He been saying that the last four or five Saturdays, and then he don't never do nothing, but go down to Taylors. Did you tell him about the recruiter?

ROSE: Yeah, I told him.

CORY: What he say?

ROSE: He ain't said nothing too much. You get in there and get started on your chores before he gets back. Go on and scrub down them steps before he gets back here hollering and carrying on.

CORY: I'm hungry. What you got to eat, Mama?

ROSE: Go on and get started on your chores. I got some meat loaf in there. Go on and make you a sandwich . . . and don't leave no mess in there.

(*Cory exits into the house. Rose continues to take down the clothes. Troy enters the yard and sneaks up and grabs her from behind.*)

Troy! Go on, now. You liked to scared me to death. What was the score of the game? Lucille had me on the phone and I couldn't keep up with it.

TROY: What I care about the game? Come here, woman. (*He tries to kiss her.*)

ROSE: I thought you went down Taylors' to listen to the game. Go on, Troy! You supposed to be putting up this fence.

TROY (*attempting to kiss her again*): I'll put it up when I finish with what is at hand.

ROSE: Go on, Troy. I ain't studying you.

TROY (*chasing after her*): I'm studying you . . . fixing to do my homework!

ROSE: Troy, you better leave me alone.

TROY: Where's Cory? That boy brought his butt home yet?

ROSE: He's in the house doing his chores.

TROY (*calling*): Cory! Get your butt out here, boy!

(*Rose exits into the house with the laundry. Troy goes over to the pile of wood, picks up a board, and starts sawing. Cory enters from the house.*)

TROY: You just now coming in here from leaving this morning?

CORY: Yeah, I had to go to football practice.

TROY: Yeah, what?

CORY: Yessir.

TROY: I ain't but two seconds off you noway. The garbage sitting in there overflowing . . . you ain't done none of your chores . . . and you come in here talking about "Yeah."

CORY: I was just getting ready to do my chores now, Pop . . .

TROY: Your first chore is to help me with this fence on Saturday. Everything else come after that. Now get that saw and cut them boards.

(*Cory takes the saw and begins cutting the boards. Troy continues working. There is a long pause.*)

CORY: Hey, Pop . . . why don't you buy a TV?

TROY: What I want with a TV? What I want one of them for?

CORY: Everybody got one. Earl, Ba Bra . . . Jesse!

TROY: I ain't asked you who had one. I say what I want with one?

CORY: So you can watch it. They got lots of things on TV. Baseball games and everything. We could watch the World Series.

TROY: Yeah . . . and how much this TV cost?

CORY: I don't know. They got them on sale for around two hundred dollars.

TROY: Two hundred dollars, huh?

CORY: That ain't that much, Pop.

TROY: Naw, it's just two hundred dollars. See that roof you got over your head at night? Let me tell you something about that roof. It's been over ten years since that roof was last tarred. See now . . . the snow come this winter and sit up there on that roof like it is . . . and it's gonna seep inside. It's just gonna be a little bit . . . ain't gonna hardly notice it. Then the next thing you know, it's gonna be leaking all over the house. Then the wood rot from all that water and you gonna need a whole new roof. Now, how much you think it cost to get that roof tarred?

CORY: I don't know.

TROY: Two hundred and sixty-four dollars . . . cash money. While you thinking about a TV, I got to be thinking about the roof . . . and whatever else go wrong here. Now if you had two hundred dollars, what would you do . . . fix the roof or buy a TV?

CORY: I'd buy a TV. Then when the roof started to leak . . . when it needed fixing . . . I'd fix it.

TROY: Where you gonna get the money from? You done spent it for a TV. You gonna sit up and watch the water run all over your brand new TV.

CORY: Aw, Pop. You got money. I know you do.

TROY: Where I got it at, huh?

CORY: You got it in the bank.

TROY: You wanna see my bankbook? You wanna see that seventy-three dollars and twenty-two cents I got sitting up in there.

CORY: You ain't got to pay for it all at one time. You can put a down payment on it and carry it on home with you.

TROY: Not me. I ain't gonna owe nobody nothing if I can help it. Miss a payment and they come and snatch it right out your house. Then what you got? Now, soon as I get two hundred dollars clear, then I'll buy a TV. Right now, as soon as I get two hundred and sixty-four dollars, I'm gonna have this roof tarred.

CORY: Aw . . . Pop!

TROY: You go on and get you two hundred dollars and buy one if ya want it. I got better things to do with my money.

CORY: I can't get no two hundred dollars. I ain't never seen two hundred dollars.

TROY: I'll tell you what . . . you get you a hundred dollars and I'll put the other hundred with it.

CORY: Alright, I'm gonna show you.

TROY: You gonna show me how you can cut them boards right now.

(*Cory begins to cut the boards. There is a long pause.*)

CORY: The Pirates won today. That makes five in a row.

TROY: I ain't thinking about the Pirates. Got an all-white team. Got that boy . . . that Puerto Rican boy . . . Clemente.° Don't even half-play him. That boy could be something if they give him a chance. Play him one day and sit him on the bench the next.

CORY: He gets a lot of chances to play.

TROY: I'm talking about playing regular. Playing every day so you can get your timing. That's what I'm talking about.

CORY: They got some white guys on the team that don't play every day. You can't play everybody at the same time.

TROY: If they got a white fellow sitting on the bench . . . you can bet your last dollar he can't play! The colored guy got to be twice as good before he get on the team. That's why I don't want you to get all tied up in them sports. Man on the team and what it get him? They got colored on the team and don't use them. Same as not having them. All them teams the same.

CORY: The Braves got Hank Aaron and Wes Covington.° Hank Aaron hit two home runs today. That makes forty-three.

Clemente: Roberto Clemente (1934–1972), right fielder for the Pittsburgh Pirates from 1955 to 1971, was the first player of Latin American descent to be elected into the Baseball Hall of Fame. In 1956 he played in 147 games and had a .311 batting average; in 1957 he played in 111 games and his average dropped to .253. **Hank Aaron and Wes Covington:** Henry Louis Aaron (b. 1934), African American outfielder, hit 44 home runs for the Milwaukee Braves in 1957 and went on to break Babe Ruth's career home run record. John Wesley Covington (b. 1932), African American outfielder, hit 21 homers for the Milwaukee Braves in 1957.

TROY: Hank Aaron ain't nobody. That's what you supposed to do. That's how you supposed to play the game. Ain't nothing to it. It's just a matter of timing . . . getting the right follow-through. Hell, I can hit forty-three home runs right now!

CORY: Not off no major-league pitching, you couldn't.

TROY: We had better pitching in the Negro leagues. I hit seven home runs off of Satchel Paige.° You can't get no better than that!

CORY: Sandy Koufax.° He's leading the league in strike-outs.

TROY: I ain't thinking of no Sandy Koufax.

CORY: You got Warren Spahn and Lew Burdette.° I bet you couldn't hit no home runs off of Warren Spahn.

TROY: I'm through with it now. You go on and cut them boards.

(*Pause.*)

Your mama tell me you done got recruited by a college football team? Is that right?

CORY: Yeah. Coach Zellman say the recruiter gonna be coming by to talk to you. Get you to sign the permission papers.

TROY: I thought you supposed to be working down there at the A&P. Ain't you suppose to be working down there after school?

CORY: Mr. Stawicki say he gonna hold my job for me until after the football season. Say starting next week I can work weekends.

TROY: I thought we had an understanding about this football stuff? You suppose to keep up with your chores and hold that job down at the A&P. Ain't been around here all day on a Saturday. Ain't none of your chores done . . . and now you telling me you done quit your job.

CORY: I'm gonna to be working weekends.

TROY: You damn right you are! And ain't no need for nobody coming around here to talk to me about signing nothing.

CORY: Hey, Pop . . . you can't do that. He's coming all the way from North Carolina.

TROY: I don't care where he coming from. The white man ain't gonna let you get nowhere with that football noway. You go on and get your book-learning so

---

Satchel Paige: Leroy "Satchel" Paige (1906–1982), star pitcher in the Negro Leagues from 1926 to 1947, played in the major leagues for the Cleveland Indians (1948–1949), the St. Louis Browns (1951–1953), and the Kansas City Athletics (1965). He was the first African American elected to the Baseball Hall of Fame. **Sandy Koufax:** Sanford Koufax (b. 1935), pitcher for the Brooklyn and Los Angeles Dodgers from 1955 to 1966. He recorded 122 strikeouts in 1957. Jack Sanford ended up leading the league that year with 188 strikeouts for the Philadelphia Phillies. **Warren Spahn and Lew Burdette:** Warren Edward Spahn (1921–2003) is the winningest left-handed pitcher in major league history with 363 victories, all but seven of those wins coming with the Boston-Milwaukee Braves, 1942–1964. He had a 21-11 record in 1957 when he won the Cy Young Award and won the fourth game of the 1958 World Series. Selva Lewis Burdette (b. 1926), pitcher for six major league teams from 1950 to 1967, had a 17-9 record for Milwaukee in 1957, won three games in the 1957 World Series, and was named that series' Most Valuable Player.

you can work yourself up in that A&P or learn how to fix cars or build houses or something, get you a trade. That way you have something can't nobody take away from you. You go on and learn how to put your hands to some good use. Besides hauling people's garbage.

CORY: I get good grades, Pop. That's why the recruiter wants to talk with you. You got to keep up your grades to get recruited. This way I'll be going to college. I'll get a chance . . .

TROY: First you gonna get your butt down there to the A&P and get your job back.

CORY: Mr. Stawicki done already hired somebody else 'cause I told him I was playing football.

TROY: You a bigger fool than I thought . . . to let somebody take away your job so you can play some football. Where you gonna get your money to take out your girlfriend and whatnot? What kind of foolishness is that to let somebody take away your job?

CORY: I'm still gonna be working weekends.

TROY: Naw . . . naw. You getting your butt out of here and finding you another job.

CORY: Come on, Pop! I got to practice. I can't work after school and play football too. The team needs me. That's what Coach Zellman say . . .

TROY: I don't care what nobody else say. I'm the boss . . . you understand? I'm the boss around here. I do the only saying what counts.

CORY: Come on, Pop!

TROY: I asked you . . . did you understand?

CORY: Yeah . . .

TROY: What?!

CORY: Yessir.

TROY: You go on down there to that A&P and see if you can get your job back. If you can't do both . . . then you quit the football team. You've got to take the crookeds with the straights.

CORY: Yessir.

(*Pause.*)

Can I ask you a question?

TROY: What the hell you wanna ask me? Mr. Stawicki the one you got the questions for.

CORY: How come you ain't never liked me?

TROY: Liked you? Who the hell say I got to like you? What law is there say I got to like you? Wanna stand up in my face and ask a damn fool-ass question like that. Talking about liking somebody. Come here, boy, when I talk to you.

(*Cory comes over to where Troy is working. He stands slouched over and Troy shoves him on his shoulder.*)

Straighten up, goddammit! I asked you a question . . . what law is there say I got to like you?

CORY: None.

TROY: Well, alright then! Don't you eat every day?

(*Pause.*)

Answer me when I talk to you! Don't you eat every day?

CORY: Yeah.

TROY: Nigger, as long as you in my house, you put that sir on the end of it when you talk to me!

CORY: Yes . . . sir.

TROY: You eat every day.

CORY: Yessir!

TROY: Got a roof over your head.

CORY: Yessir!

TROY: Got clothes on your back.

CORY: Yessir.

TROY: Why you think that is?

CORY: Cause of you.

TROY: Aw, hell I know it's 'cause of me . . . but why do you think that is?

CORY (*hesitant*): Cause you like me.

TROY: Like you? I go out of here every morning . . . bust my butt . . . putting up with them crackers every day . . . cause I like you? You about the biggest fool I ever saw.

(*Pause.*)

It's my job. It's my responsibility! You understand that? A man got to take care of his family. You live in my house . . . sleep you behind on my bedclothes . . . fill you belly up with my food . . . cause you my son. You my flesh and blood. Not 'cause I like you! Cause it's my duty to take care of you. I owe a responsibility to you! Let's get this straight right here . . . before it go along any further . . . I ain't got to like you. Mr. Rand don't give me my money come payday cause he likes me. He gives me cause he owe me. I done give you everything I had to give you. I gave you your life! Me and your mama worked that out between us. And liking your black ass wasn't part of the bargain. Don't you try and go through life worrying about if somebody like you or not. You best be making sure they doing right by you. You understand what I'm saying, boy?

CORY: Yessir.

TROY: Then get the hell out of my face, and get on down to that A&P.

(*Rose has been standing behind the screen door for much of the scene. She enters as Cory exits.*)

ROSE: Why don't you let the boy go ahead and play football, Troy? Ain't no harm in that. He's just trying to be like you with the sports.

TROY: I don't want him to be like me! I want him to move as far away from my life as he can get. You the only decent thing that ever happened to me. I wish him that. But I don't wish him a thing else from my life. I decided seventeen years ago that boy wasn't getting involved in no sports. Not after what they did to me in the sports.

ROSE: Troy, why don't you admit you was too old to play in the major leagues? For once . . . why don't you admit that?

TROY: What do you mean too old? Don't come telling me I was too old. I just wasn't the right color. Hell, I'm fifty-three years old and can do better than Selkirk's .269 right now!

ROSE: How's was you gonna play ball when you were over forty? Sometimes I can't get no sense out of you.

TROY: I got good sense, woman. I got sense enough not to let my boy get hurt over playing no sports. You been mothering that boy too much. Worried about if people like him.

ROSE: Everything that boy do . . . he do for you. He wants you to say "Good job, son." That's all.

TROY: Rose, I ain't got time for that. He's alive. He's healthy. He's got to make his own way. I made mine. Ain't nobody gonna hold his hand when he get out there in that world.

ROSE: Times have changed from when you was young, Troy. People change. The world's changing around you and you can't even see it.

TROY (*slow, methodical*): Woman . . . I do the best I can do. I come in here every Friday. I carry a sack of potatoes and a bucket of lard. You all line up at the door with your hands out. I give you the lint from my pockets. I give you my sweat and my blood. I ain't got no tears. I done spent them. We go upstairs in that room at night . . . and I fall down on you and try to blast a hole into forever. I get up Monday morning . . . find my lunch on the table. I go out. Make my way. Find my strength to carry me through to the next Friday.

(*Pause.*)

That's all I got, Rose. That's all I got to give. I can't give nothing else.

(*Troy exits into the house. The lights go down to black.*)

Scene Four

It is Friday. Two weeks later. Cory starts out of the house with his football equipment. The phone rings.

CORY (*calling*): I got it!

(*He answers the phone and stands in the screen door talking.*)

Hello? Hey, Jesse. Naw . . . I was just getting ready to leave now.

ROSE (*calling*): Cory!

CORY: I told you, man, them spikes is all tore up. You can use them if you want, but they ain't no good. Earl got some spikes.

ROSE (*calling*): Cory!

CORY (*calling to Rose*): Mam? I'm talking to Jesse.

(Into phone.)

> When she say that? *(Pause.)* Aw, you lying, man. I'm gonna tell her you said that.

ROSE *(calling)*: Cory, don't you go nowhere!

CORY: I got to go to the game, Ma!

(Into the phone.)

> Yeah, hey, look, I'll talk to you later. Yeah, I'll meet you over Earl's house. Later. Bye, Ma.

(Cory exits the house and starts out the yard.)

ROSE: Cory, where you going off to? You got that stuff all pulled out and thrown all over your room.

CORY *(in the yard)*: I was looking for my spikes. Jesse wanted to borrow my spikes.

ROSE: Get up there and get that cleaned up before your daddy get back in here.

CORY: I got to go to the game! I'll clean it up *when I get back.*

(Cory exits.)

ROSE: That's all he need to do is see that room all messed up.

(Rose exits into the house. Troy and Bono enter the yard. Troy is dressed in clothes other than his work clothes.)

BONO: He told him the same thing he told you. Take it to the union.

TROY: Brownie ain't got that much sense. Man wasn't thinking about nothing. He wait until I confront them on it . . . then he wanna come crying seniority.

(Calls.)

> Hey, Rose!

BONO: I wish I could have seen Mr. Rand's face when he told you.

TROY: He couldn't get it out of his mouth! Liked to bit his tongue! When they called me down there to the Commissioner's office . . . he thought they was gonna fire me. Like everybody else.

BONO: I didn't think they was gonna fire you. I thought they was gonna put you on the warning paper.

TROY: Hey, Rose!

(To Bono.)

> Yeah, Mr. Rand like to bit his tongue.

(Troy breaks the seal on the bottle, takes a drink, and hands it to Bono.)

BONO: I see you run right down to Taylors' and told that Alberta gal.

TROY *(calling)*: Hey Rose! *(To Bono.)* I told everybody. Hey, Rose! I went down there to cash my check.

ROSE (*entering from the house*): Hush all that hollering, man! I know you out here. What they say down there at the Commissioner's office?

TROY: You supposed to come when I call you, woman. Bono'll tell you that.

(*To Bono.*)

Don't Lucille come when you call her?

ROSE: Man, hush your mouth. I ain't no dog . . . talk about "come when you call me."

TROY (*puts his arm around Rose*): You hear this, Bono? I had me an old dog used to get uppity like that. You say, "C'mere, Blue!" . . . and he just lay there and look at you. End up getting a stick and chasing him away trying to make him come.

ROSE: I ain't studying you and your dog. I remember you used to sing that old song.

TROY (*he sings*): Hear it ring! Hear it ring!
I had a dog his name was Blue.

ROSE: Don't nobody wanna hear you sing that old song.

TROY (*sings*): You know Blue was mighty true.

ROSE: Used to have Cory running around here singing that song.

BONO: Hell, I remember that song myself.

TROY (*sings*): You know Blue was a good old dog.
Blue treed a possum in a hollow log.

That was my daddy's song. My daddy made up that song.

ROSE: I don't care who made it up. Don't nobody wanna hear you sing it.

TROY (*makes a song like calling a dog*): Come here, woman.

ROSE: You come in here carrying on, I reckon they ain't fired you. What they say down there at the Commissioner's office?

TROY: Look here, Rose . . . Mr. Rand called me into his office today when I got back from talking to them people down there . . . it come from up top . . . he called me in and told me they was making me a driver.

ROSE: Troy, you kidding!

TROY: No I ain't. Ask Bono.

ROSE: Well, that's great, Troy. Now you don't have to hassle them people no more.

(*Lyons enters from the street.*)

TROY: Aw hell, I wasn't looking to see you today. I thought you was in jail. Got it all over the front page of the *Courier* about them raiding Sefus's place . . . where you be hanging out with all them thugs.

LYONS: Hey, Pop . . . that ain't got nothing to do with me. I don't go down there gambling. I go down there to sit in with the band. I ain't got nothing to do with the gambling part. They got some good music down there.

TROY: They got some rogues . . . is what they got.

LYONS: How you been, Mr. Bono? Hi, Rose.

BONO: I see where you playing down at the Crawford Grill tonight.

ROSE: How come you ain't brought Bonnie like I told you. You should have brought Bonnie with you, she ain't been over in a month of Sundays.

LYONS: I was just in the neighborhood . . . thought I'd stop by.

TROY: Here he come . . .

BONO: Your daddy got a promotion on the rubbish. He's gonna be the first colored driver. Ain't got to do nothing but sit up there and read the paper like them white fellows.

LYONS: Hey, Pop . . . if you knew how to read you'd be alright.

BONO: Naw . . . naw . . . you mean if the nigger knew how to *drive* he'd be all right. Been fighting with them people about driving and ain't even got a license. Mr. Rand know you ain't got no driver's license?

TROY: Driving ain't nothing. All you do is point the truck where you want it to go. Driving ain't nothing.

BONO: Do Mr. Rand know you ain't got no driver's license? That's what I'm talking about. I ain't asked if driving was easy. I asked if Mr. Rand know you ain't got no driver's license.

TROY: He ain't got to know. The man ain't got to know my business. Time he find out, I have two or three driver's licenses.

LYONS *(going into his pocket)*: Say, look here, Pop . . .

TROY: I knew it was coming. Didn't I tell you, Bono? I know what kind of "Look here, Pop" that was. The nigger fixing to ask me for some money. It's Friday night. It's my payday. All them rogues down there on the avenue . . . the ones that ain't in jail . . . and Lyons is hopping in his shoes to get down there with them.

LYONS: See, Pop . . . if you give somebody else a chance to talk sometime, you'd see that I was fixing to pay you back your ten dollars like I told you. Here . . . I told you I'd pay you when Bonnie got paid.

TROY: Naw . . . you go ahead and keep that ten dollars. Put it in the bank. The next time you feel like you wanna come by here and ask me for something . . . you go on down there and get that.

LYONS: Here's your ten dollars, Pop. I told you I don't want you to give me nothing. I just wanted to borrow ten dollars.

TROY: Naw . . . you go on and keep that for the next time you want to ask me.

LYONS: Come on, Pop . . . here go your ten dollars.

ROSE: Why don't you go on and let the boy pay you back, Troy?

LYONS: Here you go, Rose. If you don't take it I'm gonna have to hear about it for the next six months. *(He hands her the money.)*

ROSE: You can hand yours over here too, Troy.

TROY: You see this, Bono. You see how they do me.

BONO: Yeah, Lucille do me the same way.

(Gabriel is heard singing onstage. He enters.)

GABRIEL: Better get ready for the Judgment! Better get ready for . . . Hey! . . . Hey! . . . There's Troy's boy!

LYONS: How you doing, Uncle Gabe?

GABRIEL: Lyons . . . The King of the Jungle! Rose . . . hey, Rose. Got a flower for you.

(*He takes a rose from his pocket.*)

Picked it myself. That's the same rose like you is!

ROSE: That's right nice of you, Gabe.

LYONS: What you been doing, Uncle Gabe?

GABRIEL: Oh, I been chasing hellhounds and waiting on the time to tell St. Peter to open the gates.

LYONS: You been chasing hellhounds, huh? Well . . . you doing the right thing, Uncle Gabe. Somebody got to chase them.

GABRIEL: Oh, yeah . . . I know it. The devil's strong. The devil ain't no pushover. Hellhounds snipping at everybody's heels. But I got my trumpet waiting on the judgment time.

LYONS: Waiting on the Battle of Armageddon, huh?

GABRIEL: Ain't gonna be too much of a battle when God get to waving that Judgment sword. But the people's gonna have a hell of a time trying to get into heaven if them gates ain't open.

LYONS (*putting his arm around Gabriel*): You hear this, Pop. Uncle Gabe, you alright!

GABRIEL (*laughing with Lyons*): Lyons! King of the Jungle.

ROSE: You gonna stay for supper, Gabe? Want me to fix you a plate?

GABRIEL: I'll take a sandwich, Rose. Don't want no plate. Just wanna eat with my hands. I'll take a sandwich.

ROSE: How about you, Lyons? You staying? Got some short ribs cooking.

LYONS: Naw, I won't eat nothing till after we finished playing.

(*Pause.*)

You ought to come down and listen to me play, Pop.

TROY: I don't like that Chinese music. All that noise.

ROSE: Go on in the house and wash up, Gabe . . . I'll fix you a sandwich.

GABRIEL (*to Lyons, as he exits*): Troy's mad at me.

LYONS: What you mad at Uncle Gabe for, Pop.

ROSE: He thinks Troy's mad at him cause he moved over to Miss Pearl's.

TROY: I ain't mad at the man. He can live where he want to live at.

LYONS: What he move over there for? Miss Pearl don't like nobody.

ROSE: She don't mind him none. She treats him real nice. She just don't allow all that singing.

TROY: She don't mind that rent he be paying . . . that's what she don't mind.

ROSE: Troy, I ain't going through that with you no more. He's over there cause he want to have his own place. He can come and go as he please.

TROY: Hell, he could come and go as he please here. I wasn't stopping him. I ain't put no rules on him.

ROSE: It ain't the same thing, Troy. And you know it.

(*Gabriel comes to the door.*)

Now, that's the last I wanna hear about that. I don't wanna hear nothing else about Gabe and Miss Pearl. And next week . . .

GABRIEL: I'm ready for my sandwich, Rose.

ROSE: And next week . . . when that recruiter come from that school . . . I want you to sign that paper and go on and let Cory play football. Then that'll be the last I have to hear about that.

TROY (*to Rose as she exits into the house*): I ain't thinking about Cory nothing.

LYONS: What . . . Cory got recruited? What school he going to?

TROY: That boy walking around here smelling his piss . . . thinking he's grown. Thinking he's gonna do what he want, irrespective of what I say. Look here, Bono . . . I left the Commissioner's office and went down to the A&P . . . that boy ain't working down there. He lying to me. Telling me he got his job back . . . telling me he working weekends . . . telling me he working after school . . . Mr. Stawicki tell me he ain't working down there at all!

LYONS: Cory just growing up. He's just busting at the seams trying to fill out your shoes.

TROY: I don't care what he's doing. When he get to the point where he wanna disobey me . . . then it's time for him to move on. Bono'll tell you that. I bet he ain't never disobeyed his daddy without paying the consequences.

BONO: I ain't never had a chance. My daddy came on through . . . but I ain't never knew him to see him . . . or what he had on his mind or where he went. Just moving on through. Searching out the New Land. That's what the old folks used to call it. See a fellow moving around from place to place . . . woman to woman . . . called it searching out the New Land. I can't say if he ever found it. I come along, didn't want no kids. Didn't know if I was gonna be in one place long enough to fix on them right as their daddy. I figured I was going searching too. As it turned out I been hooked up with Lucille near about as long as your daddy been with Rose. Going on sixteen years.

TROY: Sometimes I wish I hadn't known my daddy. He ain't cared nothing about no kids. A kid to him wasn't nothing. All he wanted was for you to learn how to walk so he could start you to working. When it come time for eating . . . he ate first. If there was anything left over, that's what you got. Man would sit down and eat two chickens and give you the wing.

LYONS: You ought to stop that, Pop. Everybody feed their kids. No matter how hard times is . . . everybody care about their kids. Make sure they have something to eat.

TROY: The only thing my daddy cared about was getting them bales of cotton in to Mr. Lubin. That's the only thing that mattered to him. Sometimes I used to wonder why he was living. Wonder why the devil hadn't come and got him. "Get them bales of cotton in to Mr. Lubin" and find out he owe him money . . .

LYONS: He should have just went on and left when he saw he couldn't get nowhere. That's what I would have done.

TROY: How he gonna leave with eleven kids? And where he gonna go? He ain't knew how to do nothing but farm. No, he was trapped and I think he knew it. But I'll say this for him . . . he felt a responsibility toward us. Maybe he ain't treated us the way I felt he should have . . . but without that responsibility he could have walked off and left us . . . made his own way.

BONO: A lot of them did. Back in those days what you talking about . . . they walk out their front door and just take on down one road or another and keep on walking.

LYONS: There you go! That's what I'm talking about.

BONO: Just keep on walking till you come to something else. Ain't you never heard of nobody having the walking blues? Well, that's what you call it when you just take off like that.

TROY: My daddy ain't had them walking blues! What you talking about? He stayed right there with his family. But he was just as evil as he could be. My mama couldn't stand him. Couldn't stand that evilness. She run off when I was about eight. She sneaked off one night after he had gone to sleep. Told me she was coming back for me. I ain't never seen her no more. All his women run off and left him. He wasn't good for nobody.

When my turn come to head out, I was fourteen and got to sniffing around Joe Canewell's daughter. Had us an old mule we called Greyboy. My daddy sent me out to do some plowing and I tied up Greyboy and went to fooling around with Joe Canewell's daughter. We done found us a nice little spot, got real cozy with each other. She about thirteen and we done figured we was grown anyway . . . so we down there enjoying ourselves . . . ain't thinking about nothing. We didn't know Greyboy had got loose and wandered back to the house and my daddy was looking for me. We down there by the creek enjoying ourselves when my daddy come up on us. Surprised us. He had them leather straps off the mule and commenced to whupping me like there was no tomorrow. I jumped up, mad and embarrassed. I was scared of my daddy. When he commenced to whupping on me . . . quite naturally I run to get out of the way.

(*Pause.*)

Now I thought he was mad cause I ain't done my work. But I see where he was chasing me off so he could have the gal for himself. When I see what the matter of it was, I lost all fear of my daddy. Right there is where I become a man . . . at fourteen years of age.

(*Pause.*)

Now it was my turn to run him off. I picked up them same reins that he had used on me. I picked up them reins and commenced to whupping on him. The gal jumped up and run off . . . and when my daddy turned to face me, I could see why the devil had never come to get him . . . cause he was the devil himself. I don't know what happened. When I woke up, I was laying right there by the creek, and Blue . . . this old dog we had . . . was licking my face. I thought I was blind. I couldn't see nothing. Both my eyes were swollen shut. I layed there and cried. I didn't know what I was gonna do. The only thing I knew was the time had come for me to leave my daddy's house. And right there the world suddenly got big. And it was a long time before I could cut it down to where I could handle it.

Part of that cutting down was when I got to the place where I could feel him kicking in my blood and knew that the only thing that separated us was the matter of a few years.

(*Gabriel enters from the house with a sandwich.*)

LYONS: What you got there, Uncle Gabe?

GABRIEL: Got me a ham sandwich. Rose gave me a ham sandwich.

TROY: I don't know what happened to him. I done lost touch with everybody except Gabriel. But I hope he's dead. I hope he found some peace.

LYONS: That's a heavy story, Pop. I didn't know you left home when you was fourteen.

TROY: And didn't know nothing. The only part of the world I knew was the forty-two acres of Mr. Lubin's land. That's all I knew about life.

LYONS: Fourteen's kinda young to be out on your own. (*Phone rings.*) I don't even think I was ready to be out on my own at fourteen. I don't know what I would have done.

TROY: I got up from the creek and walked on down to Mobile. I was through with farming. Figured I could do better in the city. So I walked the two hundred miles to Mobile.

LYONS: Wait a minute . . . you ain't walked no two hundred miles, Pop. Ain't nobody gonna walk no two hundred miles. You talking about some walking there.

BONO: That's the only way you got anywhere back in them days.

LYONS: Shhh. Damn if I wouldn't have hitched a ride with somebody!

TROY: Who you gonna hitch it with? They ain't had no cars and things like they got now. We talking about 1918.

ROSE (*entering*): What you all out here getting into?

TROY (*to Rose*): I'm telling Lyons how good he got it. He don't know nothing about this I'm talking.

ROSE: Lyons, that was Bonnie on the phone. She say you supposed to pick her up.

LYONS: Yeah, okay, Rose.

TROY: I walked on down to Mobile and hitched up with some of them fellows that was heading this way. Got up here and found out . . . not only couldn't you get a job . . . you couldn't find no place to live. I thought I was in freedom. Shhh. Colored folks living down there on the riverbanks in whatever kind of shelter they could find for themselves. Right down there under the Brady Street Bridge. Living in shacks made of sticks and tarpaper. Messed around there and went from bad to worse. Started stealing. First it was food. Then I figured, hell, if I steal money I can buy me some food. Buy me some shoes too! One thing led to another. Met your mama. I was young and anxious to be a man. Met your mama and had you. What I do that for? Now I got to worry about feeding you and her. Got to steal three times as much. Went out one day looking for somebody to rob . . . that's what I was, a robber. I'll tell you the truth. I'm ashamed of it today. But it's the truth. Went to rob this fellow . . . pulled out my knife . . . and he pulled out a gun. Shot me in the chest. I felt just like somebody had taken a hot branding iron and laid it on me. When he shot me I jumped at him with my knife. They told me I killed him and they put me in the penitentiary and locked me up for fifteen years. That's where I met Bono. That's where I learned how to play baseball. Got out that place and your mama had taken you and went on to make life without me. Fifteen years was a long time for her to wait. But that fifteen years cured me of that robbing stuff. Rose'll tell you. She asked me when I met her if I had gotten all that foolishness out of my system. And I told her, "Baby, it's you and baseball all what count with me." You hear me, Bono? I meant it too. She say, "Which one comes first?" I told her, "Baby, ain't no doubt it's baseball . . . but you stick and get old with me and we'll both outlive this baseball." Am I right, Rose? And it's true.

ROSE: Man, hush your mouth. You ain't said no such thing. Talking about, "Baby, you know you'll always be number one with me." That's what you was talking.

TROY: You hear that, Bono. That's why I love her.

BONO: Rose'll keep you straight. You get off the track, she'll straighten you up.

ROSE: Lyons, you better get on up and get Bonnie. She waiting on you.

LYONS (*gets up to go*): Hey, Pop, why don't you come on down to the Grill and hear me play?

TROY: I ain't going down there. I'm too old to be sitting around in them clubs.

BONO: You got to be good to play down at the Grill.

LYONS: Come on, Pop . . .

TROY: I got to get up in the morning.

LYONS: You ain't got to stay long.

TROY: Naw, I'm gonna get my supper and go on to bed.

LYONS: Well, I got to go. I'll see you again.

TROY: Don't you come around my house on my payday.

ROSE: Pick up the phone and let somebody know you coming. And bring Bonnie with you. You know I'm always glad to see her.

LYONS: Yeah, I'll do that, Rose. You take care now. See you, Pop. See you, Mr. Bono. See you, Uncle Gabe.

GABRIEL: Lyons! King of the Jungle!

(*Lyons exits.*)

TROY: Is supper ready, woman? Me and you got some business to take care of. I'm gonna tear it up too.

ROSE: Troy, I done told you now!

TROY (*puts his arm around Bono*): Aw hell, woman . . . this is Bono. Bono like family. I done known this nigger since . . . how long I done know you?

BONO: It's been a long time.

TROY: I done known this nigger since Skippy was a pup. Me and him done been through some times.

BONO: You sure right about that.

TROY: Hell, I done know him longer than I known you. And we still standing shoulder to shoulder. Hey, look here, Bono . . . a man can't ask for no more than that.

(*Drinks to him.*)

I love you, nigger.

BONO: Hell, I love you too . . . but I got to get home see my woman. You got yours in hand. I got to go get mine.

(*Bono starts to exit as Cory enters the yard, dressed in his football uniform. He gives Troy a hard, uncompromising look.*)

CORY: What you do that for, Pop?

(*He throws his helmet down in the direction of Troy.*)

ROSE: What's the matter? Cory . . . what's the matter?

CORY: Papa done went up to the school and told Coach Zellman I can't play football no more. Wouldn't even let me play the game. Told him to tell the recruiter not to come.

ROSE: Troy . . .

TROY: What you Troying me for. Yeah, I did it. And the boy know why I did it.

CORY: Why you wanna do that to me? That was the one chance I had.

ROSE: Ain't nothing wrong with Cory playing football, Troy.

TROY: The boy lied to me. I told the nigger if he wanna play football . . . to keep up his chores and hold down that job at the A&P. That was the conditions. Stopped down there to see Mr. Stawicki . . .

CORY: I can't work after school during the football season, Pop! I tried to tell you that Mr. Stawicki's holding my job for me. You don't never want to listen to nobody. And then you wanna go and do this to me!

TROY: I ain't done nothing to you. You done it to yourself.

CORY: Just cause you didn't have a chance! You just scared I'm gonna be better than you, that's all.

TROY: Come here.

ROSE: Troy . . .

(*Cory reluctantly crosses over to Troy.*)

TROY: Alright! See. You done made a mistake.

CORY: I didn't even do nothing!

TROY: I'm gonna tell you what your mistake was. See . . . you swung at the ball and didn't hit it. That's strike one. See, you in the batter's box now. You swung and you missed. That's strike one. Don't you strike out!

(*Lights fade to black.*)

ACT TWO / Scene One

The following morning. Cory is at the tree hitting the ball with the bat. He tries to mimic Troy, but his swing is awkward, less sure. Rose enters from the house.

ROSE: Cory, I want you to help me with this cupboard.

CORY: I ain't quitting the team. I don't care what Poppa say.

ROSE: I'll talk to him when he gets back. He had to go see about your Uncle Gabe. The police done arrested him. Say he was disturbing the peace. He'll be back directly. Come on in here and help me clean out the top of this cupboard.

(Cory exits into the house. Rose sees Troy and Bono coming down the alley.)

Troy . . . what they say down there?

TROY: Ain't said nothing. I give them fifty dollars and they let him go. I'll talk to you about it. Where's Cory?

ROSE: He's in there helping me clean out these cupboards.

TROY: Tell him to get his butt out here.

(Troy and Bono go over to the pile of wood. Bono picks up the saw and begins sawing.)

TROY *(to Bono)*: All they want is the money. That makes six or seven times I done went down there and got him. See me coming they stick out their *hands.*

BONO: Yeah. I know what you mean. That's all they care about . . . that money. They don't care about what's right.

(Pause.)

Nigger, why you got to go and get some hard wood? You ain't doing nothing but building a little old fence. Get you some soft pine wood. That's all you need.

TROY: I know what I'm doing. This is outside wood. You put pine wood inside the house. Pine wood is inside wood. This here is outside wood. Now you tell me where the fence is gonna be?

BONO: You don't need this wood. You can put it up with pine wood and it'll stand as long as you gonna be here looking at it.

TROY: How you know how long I'm gonna be here, nigger? Hell, I might just live forever. Live longer than old man Horsely.

BONO: That's what Magee used to say.

TROY: Magee's a damn fool. Now you tell me who you ever heard of gonna pull their own teeth with a pair of rusty pliers.

BONO: The old folks . . . my granddaddy used to pull his teeth with pliers. They ain't had no dentists for the colored folks back then.

TROY: Get clean pliers! You understand? Clean pliers! Sterilize them! Besides we ain't living back then. All Magee had to do was walk over to Doc Goldblum's.

BONO: I see where you and that Tallahassee gal . . . that Alberta . . . I see where you all done got tight.

TROY: What you mean "got tight"?

BONO: I see where you be laughing and joking with her all the time.
TROY: I laughs and jokes with all of them, Bono. You know me.
BONO: That ain't the kind of laughing and joking I'm talking about.

(*Cory enters from the house.*)

CORY: How you doing, Mr. Bono?
TROY: Cory? Get that saw from Bono and cut some wood. He talking about the wood's too hard to cut. Stand back there, Jim, and let that young boy show you how it's done.
BONO: He's sure welcome to it.

(*Cory takes the saw and begins to cut the wood.*)

Whew-e-e! Look at that. Big old strong boy. Look like Joe Louis.° Hell, must be getting old the way I'm watching that boy whip through that wood.
CORY: I don't see why Mama want a fence around the yard noways.
TROY: Damn if I know either. What the hell she keeping out with it? She ain't got nothing nobody want.
BONO: Some people build fences to keep people out . . . and other people build fences to keep people in. Rose wants to hold on to you all. She loves you.
TROY: Hell, nigger, I don't need nobody to tell me my wife loves me. Cory . . . go on in the house and see if you can find that other saw.
CORY: Where's it at?
TROY: I said find it! Look for it till you find it!

(*Cory exits into the house.*)

What's that supposed to mean? Wanna keep us in?
BONO: Troy . . . I done known you seem like damn near my whole life. You and Rose both. I done know both of you all for a long time. I remember when you met Rose. When you was hitting them baseball out the park. A lot of them old gals was after you then. You had the pick of the litter. When you picked Rose, I was happy for you. That was the first time I knew you had any sense. I said . . . My man Troy knows what he's doing . . . I'm gonna follow this nigger . . . he might take me somewhere. I been following you too. I done learned a whole heap of things about life watching you. I done learned how to tell where the shit lies. How to tell it from the alfalfa. You done learned me a lot of things. You showed me how to not make the same mistakes . . . to take life as it comes along and keep putting one foot in front of the other.

(*Pause.*)

Rose a good woman, Troy.

Joe Louis: Joseph Louis Barrow (1914–1981), African American boxer, was known as the "Brown Bomber" and held the world heavyweight title from 1937 to 1949, longer than any other man in history.

TROY: Hell, nigger, I know she a good woman. I been married to her for eighteen years. What you got on your mind, Bono?

BONO: I just say she a good woman. Just like I say anything. I ain't got to have nothing on my mind.

TROY: You just gonna say she a good woman and leave it hanging out there like that? Why you telling me she a good woman?

BONO: She loves you, Troy. Rose loves you.

TROY: You saying I don't measure up. That's what you trying to say. I don't measure up cause I'm seeing this other gal. I know what you trying to say.

BONO: I know what Rose means to you, Troy. I'm just trying to say I don't want to see you mess up.

TROY: Yeah, I appreciate that, Bono. If you was messing around on Lucille I'd be telling you the same thing.

BONO: Well, that's all I got to say. I just say that because I love you both.

TROY: Hell, you know me . . . I wasn't out there looking for nothing. You can't find a better woman than Rose. I know that. But seems like this woman just stuck onto me where I can't shake her loose. I done wrestled with it, tried to throw her off me . . . but she just stuck on tighter. Now she's stuck on for good.

BONO: You's in control . . . that's what you tell me all the time. You responsible for what you do.

TROY: I ain't ducking the responsibility of it. As long as it sets right in my heart . . . then I'm okay. Cause that's all I listen to. It'll tell me right from wrong every time. And I ain't talking about doing Rose no bad turn. I love Rose. She done carried me a long ways and I love and respect her for that.

BONO: I know you do. That's why I don't want to see you hurt her. But what you gonna do when she find out? What you got then? If you try and juggle both of them . . . sooner or later you gonna drop one of them. That's common sense.

TROY: Yeah, I hear what you saying, Bono. I been trying to figure a way to work it out.

BONO: Work it out right, Troy. I don't want to be getting all up between you and Rose's business . . . but work it so it come out right.

TROY: Aw hell, I get all up between you and Lucille's business. When you gonna get that woman that refrigerator she been wanting? Don't tell me you ain't got no money now. I know who your banker is. Mellon don't need that money bad as Lucille want that refrigerator. I'll tell you that.

BONO: Tell you what I'll do . . . when you finish building this fence for Rose . . . I'll buy Lucille that refrigerator.

TROY: You done stuck your foot in your mouth now!

(*Troy grabs up a board and begins to saw. Bono starts to walk out the yard.*)

Hey, nigger . . . where you going?

BONO: I'm going home. I know you don't expect me to help you now. I'm protecting my money. I wanna see you put that fence up by yourself. That's what I want to see. You'll be here another six months without me.

TROY: Nigger, you ain't right.

BONO: When it comes to my money . . . I'm right as fireworks on the Fourth of July.

TROY: Alright, we gonna see now. You better get out your bankbook.

(*Bono exits, and Troy continues to work. Rose enters from the house.*)

ROSE: What they say down there? What's happening with Gabe?

TROY: I went down there and got him out. Cost me fifty dollars. Say he was disturbing the peace. Judge set up a hearing for him in three weeks. Say to show cause why he shouldn't be recommitted.

ROSE: What was he doing that cause them to arrest him?

TROY: Some kids was teasing him and he run them off home. Say he was howling and carrying on. Some folks seen him and called the police. That's all it was.

ROSE: Well, what's you say? What'd you tell the judge?

TROY: Told him I'd look after him. It didn't make no sense to recommit the man. He stuck out his big greasy palm and told me to give him fifty dollars and take him on home.

ROSE: Where's he at now? Where'd he go off to?

TROY: He's gone about his business. He don't need nobody to hold his hand.

ROSE: Well, I don't know. Seem like that would be the best place for him if they did put him into the hospital. I know what you're gonna say. But that's what I think would be best.

TROY: The man done had his life ruined fighting for what? And they wanna take and lock him up. Let him be free. He don't bother nobody.

ROSE: Well, everybody got their own way of looking at it I guess. Come on and get your lunch. I got a bowl of lima beans and some cornbread in the oven. Come and get something to eat. Ain't no sense you fretting over Gabe.

(*Rose turns to go into the house.*)

TROY: Rose . . . got something to tell you.

ROSE: Well, come on . . . wait till I get this food on the table.

TROY: Rose!

(*She stops and turns around.*)

I don't know how to say this.

(*Pause.*)

I can't explain it none. It just sort of grows on you till it gets out of hand. It starts out like a little bush . . . and the next thing you know it's a whole forest.

ROSE: Troy . . . what is you talking about?

TROY: I'm talking, woman, let me talk. I'm trying to find a way to tell you . . . I'm gonna be a daddy. I'm gonna be somebody's daddy.

ROSE: Troy . . . you're not telling me this? You're gonna be . . . what?

TROY: Rose . . . now . . . see . . .

ROSE: You telling me you gonna be somebody's daddy? You telling your *wife* this?

(*Gabriel enters from the street. He carries a rose in his hand.*)

GABRIEL: Hey, Troy! Hey, Rose!

ROSE: I have to wait eighteen years to hear something like this.

GABRIEL: Hey, Rose . . . I got a flower for you.

(*He hands it to her.*)

That's a rose. Same rose like you is.

ROSE: Thanks, Gabe.

GABRIEL: Troy, you ain't mad at me is you? Them bad mens come and put me away. You ain't mad at me is you?

TROY: Naw, Gabe, I ain't mad at you.

ROSE: Eighteen years and you wanna come with this.

GABRIEL (*takes a quarter out of his pocket*): See what I got? Got a brand new quarter.

TROY: Rose . . . it's just . . .

ROSE: Ain't nothing you can say, Troy. Ain't no way of explaining that.

GABRIEL: Fellow that give me this quarter had a whole mess of them. I'm gonna keep this quarter till it stop shining.

ROSE: Gabe, go on in the house there. I got some watermelon in the frigidaire. Go on and get you a piece.

GABRIEL: Say, Rose . . . you know I was chasing hellhounds and them bad mens come and get me and take me away. Troy helped me. He come down there and told them they better let me go before he beat them up. Yeah, he did!

ROSE: You go on and get you a piece of watermelon, Gabe. Them bad mens is gone now.

GABRIEL: Okay, Rose . . . gonna get me some watermelon. The kind with the stripes on it.

(*Gabriel exits into the house.*)

ROSE: Why, Troy? Why? After all these years to come dragging this in to me now. It don't make no sense at your age. I could have expected this ten or fifteen years ago, but not now.

TROY: Age ain't got nothing to do with it, Rose.

ROSE: I done tried to be everything a wife should be. Everything a wife could be. Been married eighteen years and I got to live to see the day you tell me you been seeing another woman and done fathered a child by her. And you know I ain't never wanted no half nothing in my family. My whole family is half. Everybody got different fathers and mothers . . . my two sisters and my brother. Can't hardly tell who's who. Can't never sit down and talk about Papa and Mama. It's your papa and your mama and my papa and my mama . . .

TROY: Rose . . . stop it now.

ROSE: I ain't never wanted that for none of my children. And now you wanna drag your behind in here and tell me something like this.

TROY: You ought to know. It's time for you to know.

ROSE: Well, I don't want to know, goddamn it!

TROY: I can't just make it go away. It's done now. I can't wish the circumstance of the thing away.

ROSE: And you don't want to either. Maybe you want to wish me and my boy away. Maybe that's what you want? Well, you can't wish us away. I've got eighteen years of my life invested in you. You ought to have stayed upstairs in my bed where you belong.

TROY: Rose . . . now listen to me . . . we can get a handle on this thing. We can talk this out . . . come to an understanding.

ROSE: All of a sudden it's "we." Where was "we" at when you was down there rolling around with some god-forsaken woman? "We" should have come to an understanding before you started making a damn fool of yourself. You're a day late and a dollar short when it comes to an understanding with me.

TROY: It's just . . . She gives me a different idea . . . a different understanding about myself. I can step out of this house and get away from the pressures and problems . . . be a different man. I ain't got to wonder how I'm gonna pay the bills or get the roof fixed. I can just be a part of myself that I ain't never been.

ROSE: What I want to know . . . is do you plan to continue seeing her. That's all you can say to me.

TROY: I can sit up in her house and laugh. Do you understand what I'm saying. I can laugh out loud . . . and it feels good. It reaches all the way down to the bottom of my shoes.

(*Pause.*)

Rose, I can't give that up.

ROSE: Maybe you ought to go on and stay down there with her . . . if she a better woman than me.

TROY: It ain't about nobody being a better woman or nothing. Rose, you ain't the blame. A man couldn't ask for no woman to be a better wife than you've been. I'm responsible for it. I done locked myself into a pattern trying to take care of you all that I forgot about myself.

ROSE: What the hell was I there for? That was my job, not somebody else's.

TROY: Rose, I done tried all my life to live decent . . . to live a clean . . . hard . . . useful life. I tried to be a good husband to you. In every way I knew how. Maybe I come into the world backwards, I don't know. But . . . you born with two strikes on you before you come to the plate. You got to guard it closely . . . always looking for the curve ball on the inside corner. You can't afford to let none get past you. You can't afford a call strike. If you going down . . . you going down swinging. Everything lined up against you. What you gonna do. I fooled them, Rose. I bunted. When I found you and Cory and a halfway decent job . . . I was safe. Couldn't nothing touch me. I wasn't gonna strike out no more. I wasn't going back to the penitentiary. I wasn't gonna lay in the streets with a bottle of wine. I was safe. I had me a family. A job. I wasn't gonna get that last strike. I was on first looking for one of them boys to knock me in. To get me home.

ROSE: You should have stayed in my bed, Troy.

TROY: Then when I saw that gal . . . she firmed up my backbone. And I got to thinking that if I tried . . . I just might be able to steal second. Do you understand after eighteen years I wanted to steal second.

ROSE: You should have held me tight. You should have grabbed me and held on.

TROY: I stood on first base for eighteen years and I thought . . . well, goddamn it . . . go on for it!

ROSE: We're not talking about baseball! We're talking about you going off to lay in bed with another woman . . . and then bring it home to me. That's what we're talking about. We ain't talking about no baseball.

TROY: Rose, you're not listening to me. I'm trying the best I can to explain it to you. It's not easy for me to admit that I been standing in the same place for eighteen years.

ROSE: I been standing with you! I been right here with you, Troy. I got a life too. I gave eighteen years of my life to stand in the same spot with you. Don't you think I ever wanted other things? Don't you think I had dreams and hopes? What about my life? What about me? Don't you think it ever crossed my mind to want to know other men? That I wanted to lay up somewhere and forget about my responsibilities? That I wanted someone to make me laugh so I could feel good? You not the only one who's got wants and needs. But I held on to you, Troy. I took all my feelings, my wants and needs, my dreams . . . and I buried them inside you. I planted a seed and watched and prayed over it. I planted myself inside you and waited to bloom. And it didn't take me no eighteen years to find out the soil was hard and rocky and it wasn't never gonna bloom.

But I held on to you, Troy. I held you tighter. You was my husband. I owed you everything I had. Every part of me I could find to give you. And upstairs in that room . . . with the darkness falling in on me . . . I gave everything I had to try and erase the doubt that you wasn't the finest man in the world. And wherever you was going . . . I wanted to be there with you. Cause you was my husband. Cause that's the only way I was gonna survive as your wife. You always talking about what you give . . . and what you don't have to give. But you take too. You take . . . and don't even know nobody's giving!

(Rose turns to exit into the house; Troy grabs her arm.)

TROY: You say I take and don't give!

ROSE: Troy! You're hurting me!

TROY: You say I take and don't give.

ROSE: Troy . . . you're hurting my arm! Let go!

TROY: I done give you everything I got. Don't you tell that lie on me.

ROSE: Troy!

TROY: Don't you tell that lie on me!

(*Cory enters from the house.*)

CORY: Mama!

ROSE: Troy. You're hurting me.

TROY: Don't you tell me about no taking and giving.

(*Cory comes up behind Troy and grabs him. Troy, surprised, is thrown off balance just as Cory throws a glancing blow that catches him on the chest and knocks him down. Troy is stunned, as is Cory.*)

ROSE: Troy. Troy. No!

(*Troy gets to his feet and starts at Cory.*)

Troy . . . no. Please! Troy!

(*Rose pulls on Troy to hold him back. Troy stops himself.*)

TROY (*to Cory*): Alright. That's strike two. You stay away from around me, boy. Don't you strike out. You living with a full count. Don't you strike out.

(*Troy exits out the yard as the lights go down.*)

Scene Two

It is six months later, early afternoon. Troy enters from the house and starts to exit the yard. Rose enters from the house.

ROSE: Troy, I want to talk to you.

TROY: All of a sudden, after all this time, you want to talk to me, huh? You ain't wanted to talk to me for months. You ain't wanted to talk to me last night. You ain't wanted no part of me then. What you wanna talk to me about now?

ROSE: Tomorrow's Friday.

TROY: I know what day tomorrow is. You think I don't know tomorrow's Friday? My whole life I ain't done nothing but look to see Friday coming and you got to tell me it's Friday.

ROSE: I want to know if you're coming home.

TROY: I always come home, Rose. You know that. There ain't never been a night I ain't come home.

ROSE: That ain't what I mean . . . and you know it. I want to know if you're coming straight home after work.

TROY: I figure I'd cash my check . . . hang out at Taylors' with the boys . . . maybe play a game of checkers . . .

ROSE: Troy, I can't live like this. I won't live like this. You livin' on borrowed time with me. It's been going on six months now you ain't been coming home.

TROY: I be here every night. Every night of the year. That's 365 days.

ROSE: I want you to come home tomorrow after work.

TROY: Rose . . . I don't mess up my pay. You know that now. I take my pay and I give it to you. I don't have no money but what you give me back. I just want to have a little time to myself . . . a little time to enjoy life.

ROSE: What about me? When's my time to enjoy life?

TROY: I don't know what to tell you, Rose. I'm doing the best I can.

ROSE: You ain't been home from work but time enough to change your clothes and run out . . . and you wanna call that the best you can do?

TROY: I'm going over to the hospital to see Alberta. She went into the hospital this afternoon. Look like she might have the baby early. I won't be gone long.

ROSE: Well, you ought to know. They went over to Miss Pearl's and got Gabe today. She said you told them to go ahead and lock him up.

TROY: I ain't said no such thing. Whoever told you that is telling a lie. Pearl ain't doing nothing but telling a big fat lie.

ROSE: She ain't had to tell me. I read it on the papers.

TROY: I ain't told them nothing of the kind.

ROSE: I saw it right there on the papers.

TROY: What it say, huh?

ROSE: It said you told them to take him.

TROY: Then they screwed that up, just the way they screw up everything. I ain't worried about what they got on the paper.

ROSE: Say the government send part of his check to the hospital and the other part to you.

TROY: I ain't got nothing to do with that if that's the way it works. I ain't made up the rules about how it work.

ROSE: You did Gabe just like you did Cory. You wouldn't sign the paper for Cory . . . but you signed for Gabe. You signed that paper.

(*The telephone is heard ringing inside the house.*)

TROY: I told you I ain't signed nothing, woman! The only thing I signed was the release form. Hell, I can't read, I don't know what they had on that paper! I ain't signed nothing about sending Gabe away.

ROSE: I said send him to the hospital . . . you said let him be free . . . now you done went down there and signed him to the hospital for half his money. You went back on yourself, Troy. You gonna have to answer for that.

TROY: See now . . . you been over there talking to Miss Pearl. She done got mad cause she ain't getting Gabe's rent money. That's all it is. She's liable to say anything.

ROSE: Troy, I seen where you signed the paper.

TROY: You ain't seen nothing I signed. What she doing got papers on my brother anyway? Miss Pearl telling a big fat lie. And I'm gonna tell her about it too! You ain't seen nothing I signed. Say . . . you ain't seen nothing I signed.

(*Rose exits into the house to answer the telephone. Presently she returns.*)

ROSE: Troy . . . that was the hospital. Alberta had the baby.

TROY: What she have? What is it?

ROSE: It's a girl.

TROY: I better get on down to the hospital to see her.

ROSE: Troy . . .

TROY: Rose . . . I got to go see her now. That's only right . . . what's the matter . . . the baby's all right, ain't it?

ROSE: Alberta died having the baby.

TROY: Died . . . you say she's dead? Alberta's dead?

ROSE: They said they done all they could. They couldn't do nothing for her.

TROY: The baby? How's the baby?

ROSE: They say it's healthy. I wonder who's gonna bury her.

TROY: She had family, Rose. She wasn't living in the world by herself.

ROSE: I know she wasn't living in the world by herself.

TROY: Next thing you gonna want to know if she had any insurance.

ROSE: Troy, you ain't got to talk like that.

TROY: That's the first thing that jumped out your mouth. "Who's gonna bury her?" Like I'm fixing to take on that task for myself.

ROSE: I am your wife. Don't push me away.

TROY: I ain't pushing nobody away. Just give me some space. That's all. Just give me some room to breathe.

(*Rose exits into the house. Troy walks about the yard.*)

TROY (*with a quiet rage that threatens to consume him*): Alright . . . Mr. Death. See now . . . I'm gonna tell you what I'm gonna do. I'm gonna take and build me a fence around this yard. See? I'm gonna build me a fence around what belongs to me. And then I want you to stay on the other side. See? You stay over there until you're ready for me. Then you come on. Bring your army. Bring your sickle. Bring your wrestling clothes. I ain't gonna fall down on my vigilance this time. You ain't gonna sneak up on me no more. When you ready for me . . . when the top of your list say Troy Maxson . . . that's when you come around here. You come up and knock on the front door. Ain't nobody else got nothing to do with this. This is between you and me. Man to man. You stay on the other side of that fence until you ready for me. Then you come up and knock on the front door. Anytime you want. I'll be ready for you.

(*The lights go down to black.*)

Scene Three

The lights come up on the porch. It is late evening three days later. Rose sits listening to the ball game waiting for Troy. The final out of the game is made and Rose switches off the radio. Troy enters the yard carrying an infant wrapped in blankets. He stands back from the house and calls.

(*Rose enters and stands on the porch. There is a long, awkward silence, the weight of which grows heavier with each passing second.*)

TROY: Rose . . . I'm standing here with my daughter in my arms. She ain't but a wee bittie little old thing. She don't know nothing about grownups' business. She innocent . . . and she ain't got no mama.

ROSE: What you telling me for, Troy?

(*She turns and exits into the house.*)

TROY: Well . . . I guess we'll just sit out here on the porch.

(*He sits down on the porch. There is an awkward indelicateness about the way he handles the baby. His largeness engulfs and seems to swallow it. He speaks loud enough for Rose to hear.*)

A man's got to do what's right for him. I ain't sorry for nothing I done. It felt right in my heart.

(*To the baby.*)

What you smiling at? Your daddy's a big man. Got these great big old hands. But sometimes he's scared. And right now your daddy's scared cause we sitting out here and ain't got no home. Oh, I been homeless before. I ain't had no little baby with me. But I been homeless. You just be out on the road by your lonesome and you see one of them trains coming and you just kinda go like this . . .

(*He sings as a lullaby.*)

Please, Mr. Engineer let a man ride the line
Please, Mr. Engineer let a man ride the line
I ain't got no ticket please let me ride the blinds

(*Rose enters from the house. Troy, hearing her steps behind him, stands and faces her.*)

She's my daughter, Rose. My own flesh and blood. I can't deny her no more than I can deny them boys.

(*Pause.*)

You and them boys is my family. You and them and this child is all I got in the world. So I guess what I'm saying is . . . I'd appreciate it if you'd help me take care of her.

ROSE: Okay, Troy . . . you're right. I'll take care of your baby for you . . . cause . . . like you say . . . she's innocent . . . and you can't visit the sins of the father upon the child. A motherless child has got a hard time.

(*She takes the baby from him.*)

From right now . . . this child got a mother. But you a womanless man.

(*Rose turns and exits into the house with the baby. Lights go down to black.*)

Scene Four

It is two months later. Lyons enters from the street. He knocks on the door and calls.

LYONS: Hey, Rose! (*Pause.*) Rose!

ROSE (*from inside the house*): Stop that yelling. You gonna wake up Raynell. I just got her to sleep.

LYONS: I just stopped by to pay Papa this twenty dollars I owe him. Where's Papa at?

ROSE: He should be here in a minute. I'm getting ready to go down to the church. Sit down and wait on him.

LYONS: I got to go pick up Bonnie over her mother's house.

ROSE: Well, sit it down there on the table. He'll get it.

LYONS (*enters the house and sets the money on the table*): Tell Papa I said thanks. I'll see you again.

ROSE: Alright, Lyons. We'll see you.

(*Lyons starts to exit as Cory enters.*)

CORY: Hey, Lyons.

LYONS: What's happening, Cory? Say man, I'm sorry I missed your graduation. You know I had a gig and couldn't get away. Otherwise, I would have been there, man. So what you doing?

CORY: I'm trying to find a job.

LYONS: Yeah I know how that go, man. It's rough out here. Jobs are scarce.

CORY: Yeah, I know.

LYONS: Look here, I got to run. Talk to Papa . . . he know some people. He'll be able to help get you a job. Talk to him . . . see what he say.

CORY: Yeah . . . alright, Lyons.

LYONS: You take care. I'll talk to you soon. We'll find some time to talk.

(*Lyons exits the yard. Cory wanders over to the tree, picks up the bat, and assumes a batting stance. He studies an imaginary pitcher and swings. Dissatisfied with the result, he tries again. Troy enters. They eye each other for a beat. Cory puts the bat down and exits the yard. Troy starts into the house as Rose exits with Raynell. She is carrying a cake.*)

TROY: I'm coming in and everybody's going out.

ROSE: I'm taking this cake down to the church for the bakesale. Lyons was by to see you. He stopped by to pay you your twenty dollars. It's laying in there on the table.

TROY (*going into his pocket*): Well . . . here go this money.

ROSE: Put it in there on the table, Troy. I'll get it.

TROY: What time you coming back?

ROSE: Ain't no use in you studying me. It don't matter what time I come back.

TROY: I just asked you a question, woman. What's the matter . . . can't I ask you a question?

ROSE: Troy, I don't want to go into it. Your dinner's in there on the stove. All you got to do is heat it up. And don't you be eating the rest of them cakes in

there. I'm coming back for them. We having a bakesale at the church tomorrow.

(*Rose exits the yard. Troy sits down on the steps, takes a pint bottle from his pocket,
opens it, and drinks. He begins to sing.*)

TROY: Hear it ring! Hear it ring!
    Had an old dog his name was Blue
    You know Blue was mighty true
    You know Blue was a good old dog
    Blue trees a possum in a hollow log
    You know from that he was a good old dog

(*Bono enters the yard.*)

BONO: Hey, Troy.

TROY: Hey, what's happening, Bono?

BONO: I just thought I'd stop by to see you.

TROY: What you stop by and see me for? You ain't stopped by in a month of Sundays. Hell, I must owe you money or something.

BONO: Since you got your promotion I can't keep up with you. Used to see you
every day. Now I don't even know what route you working.

TROY: They keep switching me around. Got me out in Greentree now . . . hauling white folks' garbage.

BONO: Greentree, huh? You lucky, at least you ain't got to be lifting them barrels. Damn if they ain't getting heavier. I'm gonna put in my two years and
call it quits.

TROY: I'm thinking about retiring myself.

BONO: You got it easy. You can *drive* for another five years.

TROY: It ain't the same, Bono. It ain't like working the back of the truck. Ain't
got nobody to talk to . . . feel like you working by yourself. Naw, I'm thinking about retiring. How's Lucille?

BONO: She alright. Her arthritis get to acting up on her sometime. Saw Rose on
my way in. She going down to the church, huh?

TROY: Yeah, she took up going down there. All them preachers looking for somebody to fatten their pockets.

(*Pause.*)

    Got some gin here.

BONO: Naw, thanks. I just stopped by to say hello.

TROY: Hell, nigger . . . you can take a drink. I ain't never known you to say no to
a drink. You ain't got to work tomorrow.

BONO: I just stopped by. I'm fixing to go over to Skinner's. We got us a domino
game going over his house every Friday.

TROY: Nigger, you can't play no dominoes. I used to whup you four games out of
five.

BONO: Well, that learned me. I'm getting better.

TROY: Yeah? Well, that's alright.

BONO: Look here . . . I got to be getting on. Stop by sometime, huh?

TROY: Yeah, I'll do that, Bono. Lucille told Rose you bought her a new refrigerator.

BONO: Yeah, Rose told Lucille you had finally built your fence . . . so I figured we'd call it even.

TROY: I knew you would.

BONO: Yeah . . . okay. I'll be talking to you.

TROY: Yeah, take care, Bono. Good to see you. I'm gonna stop over.

BONO: Yeah. Okay, Troy.

(Bono exits. Troy drinks from the bottle.)

TROY: Old Blue died and I dig his grave
Let him down with a golden chain
Every night when I hear old Blue bark
I know Blue treed a possum in Noah's Ark.
Hear it ring! Hear it ring!

(Cory enters the yard. They eye each other for a beat. Troy is sitting in the middle of the steps. Cory walks over.)

CORY: I got to get by.

TROY: Say what? What's you say?

CORY: You in my way. I got to get by.

TROY: You got to get by where? This is my house. Bought and paid for. In full. Took me fifteen years. And if you wanna go in my house and I'm sitting on the steps . . . you say excuse me. Like your mama taught you.

CORY: Come on, Pop . . . I got to get by.

(Cory starts to maneuver his way past Troy. Troy grabs his leg and shoves him back.)

TROY: You just gonna walk over top of me?

CORY: I live here too!

TROY *(advancing toward him)*: You just gonna walk over top of me in my own house?

CORY: I ain't scared of you.

TROY: I ain't asked if you was scared of me. I asked you if you was fixing to walk over top of me in my own house? That's the question. You ain't gonna say excuse me? You just gonna walk over top of me?

CORY: If you wanna put it like that.

TROY: How else am I gonna put it?

CORY: I was walking by you to go into the house cause you sitting on the steps drunk, singing to yourself. You can put it like that.

TROY: Without saying excuse me???

(Cory doesn't respond.)

I asked you a question. Without saying excuse me???

CORY: I ain't got to say excuse me to you. You don't count around here no more.

TROY: Oh, I see . . . I don't count around here no more. You ain't got to say excuse me to your daddy. All of a sudden you done got so grown that your daddy don't count around here no more . . . Around here in his own house and yard that he done paid for with the sweat of his brow. You done got so grown to where you gonna take over. You gonna take over my house. Is that right? You gonna wear my pants. You gonna go in there and stretch out on my bed. You ain't got to say excuse me cause I don't count around here no more. Is that right?

CORY: That's right. You always talking this dumb stuff. Now, why don't you just get out my way.

TROY: I guess you got someplace to sleep and something to put in your belly. You got that, huh? You got that? That's what you need. You got that, huh?

CORY: You don't know what I got. You ain't got to worry about what I got.

TROY: You right! You one hundred percent right! I done spent the last seventeen years worrying about what you got. Now it's your turn, see? I'll tell you what to do. You grown . . . we done established that. You a man. Now, let's see you act like one. Turn your behind around and walk out this yard. And when you get out there in the alley . . . you can forget about this house. See? Cause this is my house. You go on and be a man and get your own house. You can forget about this. Cause this is mine. You go on and get yours cause I'm through with doing for you.

CORY: You talking about what you did for me . . . what'd you ever give me?

TROY: Them feet and bones! That pumping heart, nigger! I give you more than anybody else is ever gonna give you.

CORY: You ain't never gave me nothing! You ain't never done nothing but hold me back. Afraid I was gonna be better than you. All you ever did was try and make me scared of you. I used to tremble every time you called my name. Every time I heard your footsteps in the house. Wondering all the time . . . what's Papa gonna say if I do this? . . . What's he gonna say if I do that? . . . What's Papa gonna say if I turn on the radio? And Mama, too . . . she tries . . . but she's scared of you.

TROY: You leave your mama out of this. She ain't got nothing to do with this.

CORY: I don't know how she stand you . . . after what you did to her.

TROY: I told you to leave your mama out of this!

(*He advances toward Cory.*)

CORY: What you gonna do . . . give me a whupping? You can't whup me no more. You're too old. You just an old man.

TROY (*shoves him on his shoulder*): Nigger! That's what you are. You just another nigger on the street to me!

CORY: You crazy! You know that?

TROY: Go on now! You got the devil in you. Get on away from me!

CORY: You just a crazy old man . . . talking about I got the devil in me.

TROY: Yeah, I'm crazy! If you don't get on the other side of that yard . . . I'm gonna show you how crazy I am! Go on . . . get the hell out of my yard.

CORY: It ain't your yard. You took Uncle Gabe's money he got from the army to buy this house and then you put him out.

TROY (*advances on Cory*): Get your black ass out of my yard!

(*Troy's advance backs Cory up against the tree. Cory grabs up the bat.*)

CORY: I ain't going nowhere! Come on . . . put me out! I ain't scared of you.

TROY: That's my bat!

CORY: Come on!

TROY: Put my bat down!

CORY: Come on, put me out.

(*Cory swings at Troy, who backs across the yard.*)

What's the matter? You so bad . . . put me out!

(*Troy advances toward Cory.*)

CORY (*backing up*): Come on! Come on!

TROY: You're gonna have to use it! You wanna draw that bat back on me . . . you're gonna have to use it.

CORY: Come on! . . . Come on!

(*Cory swings the bat at Troy a second time. He misses. Troy continues to advance toward him.*)

TROY: You're gonna have to kill me! You wanna draw that bat back on me. You're gonna have to kill me.

(*Cory, backed up against the tree, can go no farther. Troy taunts him. He sticks out his head and offers him a target.*)

Come on! Come on!

(*Cory is unable to swing the bat. Troy grabs it.*)

TROY: Then I'll show you.

(*Cory and Troy struggle over the bat. The struggle is fierce and fully engaged. Troy ultimately is the stronger and takes the bat from Cory and stands over him ready to swing. He stops himself.*)

Go on and get away from around my house.

(*Cory, stung by his defeat, picks himself up, walks slowly out of the yard and up the alley.*)

CORY: Tell Mama I'll be back for my things.

TROY: They'll be on the other side of that fence.

(*Cory exits.*)

TROY: I can't taste nothing. Helluljah! I can't taste nothing no more. (*Troy assumes a batting posture and begins to taunt Death, the fastball on the outside corner.*) Come on! It's between you and me now! Come on! Anytime you want! Come on! I be ready for you . . . but I ain't gonna be easy.

(*The lights go down on the scene.*)

Scene Five

The time is 1965. The lights come up in the yard. It is the morning of Troy's funeral. A funeral plaque with a light hangs beside the door. There is a small garden plot off to the side. There is noise and activity in the house as Rose, Gabriel, and Bono have gathered. The door opens and Raynell, seven years old, enters dressed in a flannel nightgown. She crosses to the garden and pokes around with a stick. Rose calls from the house.

ROSE: Raynell!
RAYNELL: Mam?
ROSE: What you doing out there?
RAYNELL: Nothing.

(*Rose comes to the door.*)

ROSE: Girl, get in here and get dressed. What you doing?
RAYNELL: Seeing if my garden growed.
ROSE: I told you it ain't gonna grow overnight. You got to wait.
RAYNELL: It don't look like it never gonna grow. Dag!
ROSE: I told you a watched pot never boils. Get in here and get dressed.
RAYNELL: This ain't even no pot, Mama.
ROSE: You just have to give it a chance. It'll grow. Now you come on and do what I told you. We got to be getting ready. This ain't no morning to be playing around. You hear me?
RAYNELL: Yes, mam.

(*Rose exits into the house. Raynell continues to poke at her garden with a stick. Cory enters. He is dressed in a Marine corporal's uniform, and carries a duffel bag. His posture is that of a military man, and his speech has a clipped sternness.*)

CORY (*to Raynell*): Hi.

(*Pause.*)

I bet your name is Raynell.
RAYNELL: Uh huh.
CORY: Is your mama home?

(*Raynell runs up on the porch and calls through the screendoor.*)

RAYNELL: Mama . . . there's some man out here. Mama?

(*Rose comes to the door.*)

ROSE: Cory? Lord have mercy! Look here, you all!

(*Rose and Cory embrace in a tearful reunion as Bono and Lyons enter from the house dressed in funeral clothes.*)

BONO: Aw, looka here . . .

ROSE: Done got all grown up!

CORY: Don't cry, Mama. What you crying about?

ROSE: I'm just so glad you made it.

CORY: Hey Lyons. How you doing, Mr. Bono.

(*Lyons goes to embrace Cory.*)

LYONS: Look at you, man. Look at you. Don't he look good, Rose. Got them Corporal stripes.

ROSE: What took you so long.

CORY: You know how the Marines are, Mama. They got to get all their paperwork straight before they let you do anything.

ROSE: Well, I'm sure glad you made it. They let Lyons come. Your Uncle Gabe's
still in the hospital. They don't know if they gonna let him out or not. I just
talked to them a little while ago.

LYONS: A Corporal in the United States Marines.

BONO: Your daddy knew you had it in you. He used to tell me all the time.

LYONS: Don't he look good, Mr. Bono?

BONO: Yeah, he remind me of Troy when I first met him.

(*Pause.*)

Say, Rose, Lucille's down at the church with the choir. I'm gonna go down
and get the pallbearers lined up. I'll be back to get you all.

ROSE: Thanks, Jim.

CORY: See you, Mr. Bono.

LYONS (*with his arm around Raynell*): Cory . . . look at Raynell. Ain't she precious? She gonna break a whole lot of hearts.

ROSE: Raynell, come and say hello to your brother. This is your brother, Cory.
You remember Cory.

RAYNELL: No, Mam.

CORY: She don't remember me, Mama.

ROSE: Well, we talk about you. She heard us talk about you. (*To Raynell.*) This is
your brother, Cory. Come on and say hello.

RAYNELL: Hi.

CORY: Hi. So you're Raynell. Mama told me a lot about you.

ROSE: You all come on into the house and let me fix you some breakfast. Keep up
your strength.

CORY: I ain't hungry, Mama.

LYONS: You can fix me something, Rose. I'll be in there in a minute.

ROSE: Cory, you sure you don't want nothing? I know they ain't feeding you
right.

CORY: No, Mama . . . thanks. I don't feel like eating. I'll get something later.

ROSE: Raynell . . . get on upstairs and get that dress on like I told you.

(*Rose and Raynell exit into the house.*)

LYONS: So . . . I hear you thinking about getting married.

CORY: Yeah, I done found the right one, Lyons. It's about time.

LYONS: Me and Bonnie been split up about four years now. About the time Papa retired. I guess she just got tired of all them changes I was putting her through.

(*Pause.*)

I always knew you was gonna make something out yourself. Your head was always in the right direction. So . . . you gonna stay in . . . make it a career . . . put in your twenty years?

CORY: I don't know. I got six already, I think that's enough.

LYONS: Stick with Uncle Sam and retire early. Ain't nothing out here. I guess Rose told you what happened with me. They got me down the workhouse. I thought I was being slick cashing other people's checks.

CORY: How much time you doing?

LYONS: They give me three years. I got that beat now. I ain't got but nine more months. It ain't so bad. You learn to deal with it like anything else. You got to take the crookeds with the straights. That's what Papa used to say. He used to say that when he struck out. I seen him strike out three times in a row . . . and the next time up he hit the ball over the grandstand. Right out there in Homestead Field. He wasn't satisfied hitting in the seats . . . he want to hit it over everything! After the game he had two hundred people standing around waiting to shake his hand. You got to take the crookeds with the straights. Yeah, Papa was something else.

CORY: You still playing?

LYONS: Cory . . . you know I'm gonna do that. There's some fellows down there we got us a band . . . we gonna try and stay together when we get out . . . but yeah, I'm still playing. It still helps me to get out of bed in the morning. As long as it do that I'm gonna be right there playing and trying to make some sense out of it.

ROSE (*calling*): Lyons, I got these eggs in the pan.

LYONS: Let me go on and get these eggs, man. Get ready to go bury Papa.

(*Pause.*)

How you doing? You doing alright?

(*Cory nods. Lyons touches him on the shoulder and they share a moment of silent grief. Lyons exits into the house. Cory wanders about the yard. Raynell enters.*)

RAYNELL: Hi.

CORY: Hi.

RAYNELL: Did you used to sleep in my room?

CORY: Yeah . . . that used to be my room.

RAYNELL: That's what Papa call it. "Cory's room." It got your football in the closet.

(*Rose comes to the door.*)

ROSE: Raynell, get in there and get them good shoes on.

RAYNELL: Mama, can't I wear these? Them other one hurt my feet.

ROSE: Well, they just gonna have to hurt your feet for a while. You ain't said they hurt your feet when you went down to the store and got them.

RAYNELL: They didn't hurt then. My feet done got bigger.

ROSE: Don't you give me no backtalk now. You get in there and get them shoes on.

(*Raynell exits into the house.*)

Ain't too much changed. He still got that piece of rag tied to that tree. He was out here swinging that bat. I was just ready to go back in the house. He swung that bat and then he just fell over. Seem like he swung it and stood there with this grin on his face . . . and then he just fell over. They carried him on down to the hospital, but I knew there wasn't no need . . . why don't you come on in the house?

CORY: Mama . . . I got something to tell you. I don't know how to tell you this . . . but I've got to tell you . . . I'm not going to Papa's funeral.

ROSE: Boy, hush your mouth. That's your daddy you talking about. I don't want hear that kind of talk this morning. I done raised you to come to this? You standing there all healthy and grown talking about you ain't going to your daddy's funeral?

CORY: Mama . . . listen . . .

ROSE: I don't want to hear it, Cory. You just get that thought out of your head.

CORY: I can't drag Papa with me everywhere I go. I've got to say no to him. One time in my life I've got to say no.

ROSE: Don't nobody have to listen to nothing like that. I know you and your daddy ain't seen eye to eye, but I ain't got to listen to that kind of talk this morning. Whatever was between you and your daddy . . . the time has come to put it aside. Just take it and set it over there on the shelf and forget about it. Disrespecting your daddy ain't gonna make you a man, Cory. You got to find a way to come to that on your own. Not going to your daddy's funeral ain't gonna make you a man.

CORY: The whole time I was growing up . . . living in his house . . . Papa was like a shadow that followed you everywhere. It weighed on you and sunk into your flesh. It would wrap around you and lay there until you couldn't tell which one was you anymore. That shadow digging in your flesh. Trying to crawl in. Trying to live through you. Everywhere I looked, Troy Maxson was staring back at me . . . hiding under the bed . . . in the closet. I'm just saying I've got to find a way to get rid of that shadow, Mama.

ROSE: You just like him. You got him in you good.

CORY: Don't tell me that, Mama.

ROSE: You Troy Maxson all over again.

CORY: I don't want to be Troy Maxson. I want to be me.

ROSE: You can't be nobody but who you are, Cory. That shadow wasn't nothing but you growing into yourself. You either got to grow into it or cut it down to fit you. But that's all you got to make life with. That's all you got to measure yourself against that world out there. Your daddy wanted you to be everything he wasn't . . . and at the same time he tried to make you into everything he was. I don't know if he was right or wrong . . . but I do know he meant to do more good than he meant to do harm. He wasn't always right. Sometimes when he touched he bruised. And sometimes when he took me in his arms he cut.

When I first met your daddy I thought . . . Here is a man I can lay down with and make a baby. That's the first thing I thought when I seen him. I was thirty years old and had done seen my share of men. But when he walked up to me and said, "I can dance a waltz that'll make you dizzy," I thought, Rose Lee, here is a man that you can open yourself up to and be filled to bursting. Here is a man that can fill all them empty spaces you been tipping around the edges of. One of them empty spaces was being somebody's mother.

I married your daddy and settled down to cooking his supper and keeping clean sheets on the bed. When your daddy walked through the house he was so big he filled it up. That was my first mistake. Not to make him leave some room for me. For my part in the matter. But at that time I wanted that. I wanted a house that I could sing in. And that's what your daddy gave me. I didn't know to keep up his strength I had to give up little pieces of mine. I did that. I took on his life as mine and mixed up the pieces so that you couldn't hardly tell which was which anymore. It was my choice. It was my life and I didn't have to live it like that. But that's what life offered me in the way of being a woman and I took it. I grabbed hold of it with both hands.

By the time Raynell came into the house, me and your daddy had done lost touch with one another. I didn't want to make my blessing off of nobody's misfortune . . . but I took on to Raynell like she was all them babies I had wanted and never had.

(*The phone rings.*)

Like I'd been blessed to relive a part of my life. And if the Lord see fit to keep up my strength . . . I'm gonna do her just like your daddy did you . . . I'm gonna give her the best of what's in me.

RAYNELL (*entering, still with her old shoes*): Mama . . . Reverend Tollivier on the phone.

(*Rose exits into the house.*)

RAYNELL: Hi.
CORY: Hi.
RAYNELL: You in the Army or the Marines?
CORY: Marines.
RAYNELL: Papa said it was the Army. Did you know Blue?
CORY: Blue? Who's Blue?

RAYNELL: Papa's dog what he sing about all the time.
CORY (*singing*): Hear it ring! Hear it ring!
>   I had a dog his name was Blue
>   You know Blue was mighty true
>   You know Blue was a good old dog
>   Blue treed a possum in a hollow log
>   You know from that he was a good old dog.
>   Hear it ring! Hear it ring!

(*Raynell joins in singing.*)

CORY and RAYNELL: Blue treed a possum out on a limb
>   Blue looked at me and I looked at him
>   Grabbed that possum and put him in a sack
>   Blue stayed there till I came back
>   Old Blue's feets was big and round
>   Never allowed a possum to touch the ground.

>   Old Blue died and I dug his grave
>   I dug his grave with a silver spade
>   Let him down with a golden chain
>   And every night I call his name
>   Go on Blue, you good dog you
>   Go on Blue, you good dog you
RAYNELL: Blue laid down and died like a man
>   Blue laid down and died . . .
BOTH: Blue laid down and died like a man
>   Now he's treeing possums in the Promised Land
>   I'm gonna tell you this to let you know
>   Blue's gone where the good dogs go
>   When I hear old Blue bark
>   When I hear old Blue bark
>   Blue treed a possum in Noah's Ark
>   Blue treed a possum in Noah's Ark.

(*Rose comes to the screen door.*)

ROSE: Cory, we gonna be ready to go in a minute.
CORY (*to Raynell*): You go on in the house and change them shoes like Mama
    told you so we can go to Papa's funeral.
RAYNELL: Okay, I'll be back.

(*Raynell exits into the house. Cory gets up and crosses over to the tree. Rose stands in the screen door watching him. Gabriel enters from the alley.*)

GABRIEL (*calling*): Hey, Rose!
ROSE: Gabe?
GABRIEL: I'm here, Rose. Hey Rose, I'm here!

(*Rose enters from the house.*)

ROSE: Lord . . . Look here, Lyons!

LYONS: See, I told you, Rose . . . I told you they'd let him come.

CORY: How you doing, Uncle Gabe?

LYONS: How you doing, Uncle Gabe?

GABRIEL: Hey, Rose. It's time. It's time to tell St. Peter to open the gates. Troy, you
ready? You ready, Troy. I'm gonna tell St. Peter to open the gates. You get
ready now.

(*Gabriel, with great fanfare, braces himself to blow. The trumpet is without a
mouthpiece. He puts the end of it into his mouth and blows with great force, like a
man who has been waiting some twenty-odd years for this single moment. No sound
comes out of the trumpet. He braces himself and blows again with the same result. A
third time he blows. There is a weight of impossible description that falls away and
leaves him bare and exposed to a frightful realization. It is a trauma that a sane and
normal mind would be unable to withstand. He begins to dance. A slow, strange
dance, eerie and life-giving. A dance of atavistic signature and ritual. Lyons attempts
to embrace him. Gabriel pushes Lyons away. He begins to howl in what is an attempt
at song, or perhaps a song turning back into itself in an attempt at speech. He finishes
his dance and the gates of heaven stand open as wide as God's closet.*)

That's the way that go!

(*BLACKOUT.*)

Lloyd Richards

Fences: Director's Introduction   [1986]

Fences is the second major play of a poet turned playwright, August Wilson.
One of the most compelling storytellers to begin writing for the theater in many
years, he has taken the responsibility of telling the tale of the encounter of the
released black slaves with a vigorous and ruthless growing America decade by
decade. *Fences* encompasses the 1950s and a black family trying to put down
roots in the slag-slippery hills of a middle American urban industrial city that
one might correctly mistake for Pittsburgh, Pennsylvania.

To call August Wilson a storyteller is to align him at one and the same time
with the ancient aristocrats of dramatic writing who stood before the tribes and
made compelling oral history into legend, as well as with the modern playwrights who bring an audience to their feet at the end of an evening of their
work because that audience knows that they have encountered themselves, their
concerns, and their passions, and have been moved and enriched by the experience. In *Fences*, August Wilson tells the story of four generations of black Americans and of how they have passed on a legacy of morals, mores, attitudes, and
patterns through stories with and without music.

He tells the story of Troy Maxson, born to a sharecropper father who was
frustrated by the fact that every crop took him further into debt. The father

knew himself as a failure and took it out on everyone at hand, including his young son, Troy, and his wives, all of whom "leave him." Troy learns violence from him, but he also learns the value of work and the fact that a man takes responsibility for his family no matter how difficult circumstances may be. He learns respect for a home, the importance of owning land, and the value of an education because he doesn't have one.

An excellent baseball player, Troy learns that in the land of equal opportunity, chances for a black man are not always equal, and that the same country that deprived him asked sacrifice of his brother in World War II and got it. Half his brother's head was blown away, and he is now a disoriented and confused beautiful man. He learns that he must fight and win the little victories that — given his life — must assume the proportion of major triumphs. He learns that day to day and moment to moment he lives close to death and must wrestle with death to survive. He learns that to take a chance and grab a moment of beauty can crumble the delicate fabric of an intricate value system and leave one desolate and alone. Strength of body and strength of purpose are not enough. Chance and the color of one's skin, chance again, can tip the balance. "You've got to take the crooked with the straight."

Troy Maxson spins yarns, raps, tells stories to his family and friends in that wonderful environment of the pretelevision, pre-airconditioned era when the back porch and the backyard were the platform for some of the most exciting tales of that time. From this platform and through his behavior he passes on to his extended family principles for living, which members of his family accept or refute through the manner in which they choose to live their own lives.

How is this reformed criminal perceived? What should be learned from him? What accepted? What passed on? Is his life to be discarded or honored? That is the story of *Fences*, which we build to keep things and people out or in.

New Haven, Connecticut
March 6, 1986

Clive Barnes

Fiery *Fences*: A Review
[1987]

Once in a rare while, you come across a play — or a movie or a novel — that seems to break away from the confines of art into a dense, complex realization of reality. A veil has been torn aside, the artist has disappeared into a transparency. We look with our own eyes, feel with our own hearts.

That was my reaction to August Wilson's pulsing play *Fences*, which opened last night at the Forty-sixth Street Theater, with James Earl Jones in full magnificent cry heading a cast of actors as good as you could find anywhere.

I wasn't just moved. I was transfixed — by intimations of a life, impressions of a man, images of a society.

Wilson, who a couple of seasons back gave us the arresting but fascinatingly flawed *Ma Rainey's Black Bottom*, always insists in interviews that he is writing from the wellspring of black experience in America.

This is undoubtedly true. Had Wilson been white, his plays would have been different — they would have had a different fire in a different belly.

But calling Wilson a "black" playwright is irrelevant. What makes *Fences* so engrossing, so embracing, so simply powerful, is his startling ability to tell a story, reveal feeling, paint emotion.

In many respects, *Fences* falls into the classic pattern of the American realistic drama — a family play, with a tragically doomed American father locked in conflict with his son. Greek tragedy with a Yankee accent.

The timing of the play — the late '50s — is carefully pinpointed in the history of black America as that turning point in the civil rights movement when a dream unfulfilled became a promise deferred.

The hero is Troy Maxson — and I suggest that he will be remembered as one of the great characters in American drama, and Jones always recalled as the first actor to play him.

Troy is as complex and as tormented as black America itself. He started life as a refugee from the South, and as a thief and, eventually, a killer.

Life in a penitentiary gave him the iron determination to reshape his life — as did, later, a feverish brush with death.

Prison also taught him baseball; when he came out, he became a temperamental star of the Negro Leagues. And now — in 1957 — he can look at the likes of Jackie Robinson and Hank Aaron, making it in the Major Leagues of big-time whiteball, with a mixture of anger, envy, and contempt.

A garbage collector, Troy has typically had to fight through his union to become the first black driver of a garbage truck. Equally typically, he hasn't even got a driver's license.

He sees himself as a man fenced in with responsibilities, but he has created some of those fences himself — some intended to keep people out, some to keep people in.

He is a family man — with a second wife, Rose, and their son Cory, as well as Gabriel, his brother, half-crazed by a war injury, and Lyons, Troy's older son by a previous marriage.

His life is secure — but limited. His son wants to go to college on a football scholarship, but Troy, wary of professional sports, refuses to let him try his luck.

Troy — although fully aware of his wife's qualities and warned by his best friend, Jim — falls in love with a younger woman, who becomes pregnant.

What is particularly pungent about Wilson's play is how the story and the characters are plugged into their particular historic relevance, ranging from the lessons of prison to the metaphors of baseball. It is this that makes the play resonate with all its subtle vibrations of truth and actuality.

This is in no sense a political play — but quite dispassionately it says: This is what it was like to be a black man of pride and ambition from the South, trying to live and work in the industrial North in the years just before and just after World War II.

The writing is perfectly geared to its people and its place. It jumps from the author's mind onto the stage, its language catching fire in the rarefied atmosphere of drama.

However fine the play is — and it is the strongest, most passionate American dramatic writing since Tennessee Williams — no praise can be too high for the staging by Lloyd Richards.

Helped by the cinematic accuracy of James D. Sandefur's setting, Richards has made the play into a microcosm in which we can see the tiny reflections of parts of ourselves, parts of America, and parts of history.

He gives every actor a sense of purpose and belonging — and makes the play their nightly story. Wonderful acting, but also marvelous direction.

James Earl Jones remakes himself in Troy's image. It is a performance of such astonishing credibility that it offers the audience a guilty sense of actually spying on the character, unobserved and unwanted.

But this is only one performance of note; in her way, Mary Alice, as Troy's wife, is just as powerful, her pain and reality just as painfully real. And then there is Courtney B. Vance as Troy's alienated son, another performance of bewildering truth and honesty.

Add to these Ray Aranha, Charles Brown, Frankie F. Faison, and Karima Miller, and you have an ensemble cast as good as you will ever find.

Fences gave me one of the richest experiences I have ever had in the theater.

Frank Rich

Family Ties in Wilson's *Fences*: A Review   [1987]

To hear his wife tell it, Troy Maxson, the middle-aged Pittsburgh sanitation worker at the center of *Fences*, is "so big" that he fills up his tenement house just by walking through it. Needless to say, that description could also apply to James Earl Jones, the actor who has found what may be the best role of his career in August Wilson's new play, at the Forty-sixth Street Theater. But the remarkable stature of the character — and of the performance — is not a matter of sheer size. If Mr. Jones's Troy is a mountainous man prone to tyrannical eruptions of rage, he is also a dignified, delicate figure capable of cradling a tiny baby, of pleading gravely to his wife for understanding, of standing still to stare death unflinchingly in the eye. A black man, a free man, a descendant of slaves, a menial laborer, a father, a husband, a lover — Mr. Jones's Troy embraces all the contradictions of being black and male and American in his time.

That time is 1957 — three decades after the period of Mr. Wilson's previous and extraordinary *Ma Rainey's Black Bottom*. For blacks like Troy in the industrial North of *Fences*, social and economic equality is more a legal principle than a reality: The Maxsons' slum neighborhood, a panorama of grimy brick and smokestack-blighted sky in James D. Sandefur's eloquent design, is a cauldron of busted promises, waiting to boil over. The conflagration is still a decade away — the streetlights burn like the first sparks of distant insurrection — so Mr. Wilson writes about the pain of an extended family lost in the wilderness of de facto segregation and barren hope.

It speaks of the power of the play — and of the cast assembled by the director, Lloyd Richards — that Mr. Jones's patriarch doesn't devour the rest of *Fences* so much as become the life force that at once nurtures and stunts the characters who share his blood. The strongest countervailing player is his wife, Rose, luminously acted by Mary Alice. Rose is a quiet woman who, as she says "planted herself" in the "hard and rocky" soil of her husband. But she never bloomed: Marriage brought frustration and betrayal in equal measure with affection.

Even so, Ms. Alice's performance emphasizes strength over self-pity, open anger over festering bitterness. The actress finds the spiritual quotient in the acceptance that accompanies Rose's love for a scarred, profoundly complicated man. It's rare to find a marriage of any sort presented on stage with such balance — let alone one in which the husband has fathered children by three different women. Mr. Wilson grants both partners the right to want to escape the responsibilities of their domestic drudgery while affirming their respective claims to forgiveness.

The other primary relationship of *Fences* is that of Troy to his son Cory (Courtney B. Vance) — a promising 17-year-old football player being courted by a college recruiter. Troy himself was once a baseball player in the Negro Leagues — early enough to hit homers off Satchel Paige, too early to benefit from Jackie Robinson's breakthrough — and his bitter, long-ago disappointment leads him to decree a different future for his son. But while Troy wants Cory to settle for a workhorse trade guaranteeing a weekly paycheck, the boy resists. The younger Maxson is somehow convinced that the dreams of his black generation need not end in the city's mean alleys with the carting of white men's garbage.

The struggle between father and son over conflicting visions of black identity, aspirations, and values is the play's narrative fulcrum, and a paradigm of violent divisions that would later tear apart a society. As written, the conflict is also a didactic one, reminiscent of old-fashioned plays, black and white, about disputes between first-generation American parents and their rebellious children.

In *Ma Rainey* — set at a blues recording session — Mr. Wilson's characters were firecrackers exploding in a bottle, pursuing jagged theatrical riffs reflective of their music and of their intimacy with the Afro-American experience that gave birth to that music. The relative tameness of *Fences* — with its laboriously worked-out titular metaphor, its slow-fused act 1 exposition — is as much an expression of its period as its predecessor was of the hotter '20s. Intentionally or not — and perhaps to the satisfaction of those who found the more esthetically daring *Ma Rainey* too "plotless" — Mr. Wilson invokes the clunkier dramaturgy of Odets, Miller, and Hansberry on this occasion.

Such formulaic theatrical tidiness, while exasperating at times, proves a minor price for the gripping second act (strengthened since the play's Yale debut in 1985) and for the scattered virtuoso passages throughout. Like *Ma Rainey* and the latest Wilson work seen at Yale (*Joe Turner's Come and Gone*, also promised for New York), *Fences* leaves no doubt that Mr. Wilson is a major writer, combining a poet's ear for vernacular with a robust sense of humor (political and sexual), a sure instinct for crackling dramatic incident, and a passionate commitment to a great subject.

Mr. Wilson continues to see history as fully as he sees his characters. In one scene, Troy and his oldest friend (played with brimming warmth by Ray Aranha) weave an autobiographical "talking blues" — a front-porch storytelling jaunt from the antebellum plantation through the preindustrial urban South, jail, and northward migration. *Fences* is pointedly bracketed by two disparate wars that swallowed up black manhood, and, as always with Mr. Wilson, is as keenly cognizant of its characters' bonds to Africa, however muted here, as their bondage to white America. One hears the cadences of a centuries-old heritage in Mr. Jones's efforts to shout down the devil. It is a frayed scrap of timeless blues singing, unpretty but unquenchable, that proves the overpowering cathartic link among the disparate branches of the Maxson family tree.

Under the exemplary guidance of Mr. Richards — whose staging falters only in the awkward scene transitions — the entire cast is impressive, including Frankie R. Faison in the problematic (but finally devastating) role of a brain-damaged, horn-playing uncle named Gabriel, and Charles Brown, as a Maxson son who falls into the sociological crack separating the play's two principal generations. As Cory, Courtney B. Vance is not only formidable in challenging Mr. Jones to a psychological (and sometimes physical) kill-or-be-killed battle for supremacy but also seems to grow into Troy's vocal timbre and visage by the final scene. Like most sons, Mr. Vance just can't elude "the shadow" of his father, no matter how hard he tries. Such is the long shadow Mr. Jones's father casts in *Fences* that theatergoers from all kinds of families may find him impossible to escape.

Bonnie Lyons

An Interview with August Wilson   [1999]

Q: Elsewhere you've talked about writing as a way of effecting social change and said that all your plays are political, but that you try not to make them didactic or polemical. Can you talk a little about how plays can effect social change without being polemical or didactic?

A: I don't write primarily to effect social change. I believe writing can do that, but that's not why I write. I work as an artist. However, all art is political in the sense that it serves the politics of someone. Here in America whites have a particular view of blacks, and I think my plays offer them a different and new way to look at black Americans. For instance, in *Fences* they see a garbageman, a person they really don't look at, although they may see a garbageman every day. By looking at Troy's life, white people find out that the content of this black garbageman's life is very similar to their own, that he is affected by the same things — love, honor, beauty, betrayal, duty. Recognizing that these things are as much a part of his life as of theirs can be revolutionary and can affect how they think about and deal with black people in their lives.

Q: How would that same play, *Fences*, affect a black audience?

A: Blacks see the content of their lives being elevated into art. They don't always know that is possible, and it's important to know that.

Q: You've talked about how important black music was for your development. Was there any black literature that showed you that black lives can be the subject of great art?

A: *Invisible Man.* When I was fourteen I discovered the Negro section of the library. I read *Invisible Man*, Langston Hughes, and all the thirty or forty books in the section, including the sociology. I remember reading a book that talked about the "Negro's power of hard work" and how much that phrase affected me. At the time I used to cut the lawn for a blind man named Mr. Douglas, who was the father of the Olympic track star. After I read that, I didn't so much cut his lawn as plow it, to show the Negro power of hard work. Looking back, I see that I had never seen those words together: "Negro power." Later of course in the sixties that became "black power." Forty years ago we had few black writers compared to today. There have been forty years of education and many more college graduates. And it's important to remember that blacks don't have a long history of writing. We come from an oral tradition. At one point in America it was a crime to teach blacks to read and write. So it's only in the past 150 years that we've been writing in this country.

Q: Elsewhere you've said that the primary opposition in your plays is between blacks who deny their African roots and those who don't. Would you still describe your work that way?

A: Today I would say that the conflict in black America is between the middle class and the so-called underclass, and that conflict goes back to those who deny themselves and those who aren't willing to. America offers blacks a contract that says, "If you leave all that African stuff over there and adopt the values of the dominant culture, you can participate." For the most part, black Americans have rejected that sort of con job. Many blacks in the ghettos say, "If I got to give up who I am, if I can't be like me, then I don't want it." The ones who accept go on to become part of the growing black middle class and in some areas even acquire some power and participation in society, but when they finally arrive where they arrive, they are no longer the same people. They are clothed in different manners and ways of life, different thoughts and ideas. They've acculturated and adopted white values. . . .

Q: Elsewhere you've said you want your audience to see your characters as Africans, not just black folks in America. Can you talk about that?

A: I'm talking about black Americans having uniquely African ways of participating in the world, of doing things, different ways of socializing. I have no fascination with Africa itself. I've never been to Africa and have no desire to go. I've been invited several times and turned down the invitations because I don't like to travel. When my daughter went to college, she called me all excited that she was studying about Timbuktu. I told her, "You study your grandma and her grandmother before you go back to Timbuktu." People don't want to do that because soon you wind up with slavery, and that's a condition people want to run away from. It's much easier to go back to the glory days of Timbuktu, but to do that is falsely romantic. It doesn't get you anywhere. I remember when I first went with a friend to a Passover seder and heard them say, "When we were slaves in the land of Egypt." I met a kid in 1987 in New York who thought slavery ended in 1960. This is God's honest truth. He was seventeen years old and he thought slavery ended in 1960. That's our fault. Like the Jews, we need to celebrate our emancipation; it would give us a way of identifying and expressing a sense of unity.

Q: Do you see anything anomalous about your wanting blacks to see themselves as Africans but your not having any desire even to visit Africa?

A: I'm simply saying blacks should hold on to what they are. You don't have to go to Africa to be an African. I live and breathe that. Even in the sixties, with all the romantic involvement with Africa, I never wore a dashiki to participate in the black power movement. Africa is right here in the southern part of the United States, which is our ancestral homeland. I don't need to make that leap across the ocean. When the first African died on the continent of North America, that was the beginning of my history.

Q: Speaking of your history, I remember reading that you said the first word you typed was your own name. Do you have any interest in autobiography?

A: Not about me as an individual. I don't like to read biographies or autobiographies myself. And if your material is autobiographical, sooner or later you're going to run out of material. I take the entire black experience in America, from the first black in 1619 until now, and claim that as my material. That's my story, my life story, and that's a lot to write about. But in truth, whatever subject you take, you as a writer are going to come up with something that is based on who you are, so even in choosing the black experience I am writing it from my own perspective. . . .

Q: Do you think you define plot the same way Aristotle did?

A: For me plot grows out of characterization, so there are no plot points. The play doesn't flow from plot point to plot point. I guess it's easy to plot that way, since every TV drama moves along those lines. It becomes very mechanical. Some people call my plays plotless; that's simply because they haven't been able to recognize the plot in them. In my plays you don't say, "Here is a point here, hold on to this because we're going to need it." I think you need to hold on to everything. In my plays things happen gradually, and you come to see why things are in the play. For example, in *Seven Guitars* you hear four men talking, and you may think the play is not going anywhere. But it is. All that stuff, every single thing they talk about, connects and is important to your understanding of the drama.

Q: It may seem a strange connection, but are your plays more like Chekhov's° than most playwrights', both in their being ensemble plays and in their seeming plotlessness?

A: I think you're right. I didn't know Chekhov's work, so there is no question of influence, but when I saw *Uncle Vanya*, I thought, "He's cool. I like this play. Yes, it's just people sitting around talking, and the drama is made out of the talk, but there are things going on, a lot of stuff is happening." . . .

Q: In the past you've mentioned the importance of listening to your characters and trusting them. Can you talk about that a bit?

A: You listen to them, but you never lose consciousness that they are your creations. When I first started writing plays I couldn't write good dialogue because I didn't respect how black people talked. I thought that in order to make art out of it I had to change it, make it into something different. Once I learned to value and respect my characters, I could really hear them. How you talk is how you think; the language describes the one who speaks it. When I have characters, I just let them start talking. The important thing is not to censor them, to trust them to just talk. What they are talking about may not seem to have anything to do with what you as a writer were writing about, but it does. Just let them talk and it will connect, because you as the artist will make it connect. . . . The more my characters talk, the more I find out about them. And the more I find out about them, the more material I have. So I encourage them, I tell them, "Tell me some more." I just write it down, and it starts to make connections. . . .

Q: In your cycle of plays, you'll have one play per decade of this century, but in your introductory note to *Seven Guitars* you say, "Despite my interest in history, I've always been more concerned with culture." Could you talk a little about history versus culture?

A: I'm more interested in the historical context than in actual history, so for example I changed the actual historical date of a Joe Louis boxing match because it suited my dramatic purposes. I always come back to the quote from James Baldwin about the black tradition, which he defined as "That field of manners and rituals of intercourse that will sustain a man once he's left his father's house." The primary focus of my work is looking at black culture as it changes and grows in evolving historical contexts. . . .

Q: In addition to plays, you've written poetry, and now you're also writing a novel. Can you talk about the differences between those forms, and whether material comes to you in one form or another?

A: For me, poetry is distilled language. Somewhere I read poetry defined as enlarging the sayable. I like that definition, and I think poetry is the highest form of literature. Writing a novel is like setting out on this vast, uncharted ocean. I never knew how anyone could do it. But now I see that like any kind of writing, you start with the first word and finish the first page. Then you've got a page and you go on to the next. I realized that writing a novel is like writing a play in that you don't have to know where you're going. You just go and you find out as you go along. . . .

Chekhov: Anton Chekhov (1860–1904), Russian playwright and short-story writer.

Q: Playwrights have taken quite varying positions about the importance of production. Edward Albee° has taken an extreme position, saying, "A first-rate play exists completely on the page and is never improved by production; it is only proved by production." Do you agree?

A: I agree with that, because the play is there on the page; it provides a road map or a blueprint. I don't write for a production; I write for the page, just like a poem. A play, like a poem, exists on the page even if no one ever reads it aloud. But I don't want to underestimate what a good production with actors embodying the characters offers. But depending on the imagination of the reader, he may get more by reading the play than by seeing a weak production. . . .

Q: One playwright has said that drama is made up of sound and silence. Do you see drama that way?

A: No doubt drama is made up of sound and silence, but I see conflict at the center. What you do is set up a character who has certain beliefs and you establish a situation where those beliefs are challenged and that character is forced to examine those beliefs and perhaps change them. That's the kind of dramatic situation which engages an audience.

Q: Then is the conflict primarily internal rather than external, between characters?

A: Internal, right, where the character has to reexamine his whole body of beliefs. The play has to shake the very foundation of his whole system of beliefs and force him to make a choice. Then I think you as a playwright have accomplished something, because that process also forces the audience to go through the same inner struggle. When I teach my workshops I tell my students that if a guy announces, "I'm going to kill Joe," and there's a knock on the door, the audience is going to want to know if that's Joe and why this guy wants to kill him and whether we would also want to kill him if we were in the same situation. The audience is engaged in the questions.

Edward Albee: U.S. playwright, b. 1928. For the position expressed, see *Conversations with Edward Albee*, ed. Philip C. Kolin (Jackson: University Press of Mississippi, 1988), 137.

Miles Marshall Lewis

Miles Marshall Lewis Talks with August Wilson   [2005]

Miles Marshall Lewis: Despite the similarities between *Fences* and *Death of a Salesman*, and the art of playwriting as a predominantly white discipline, you've cited your greatest literary influence as poet-playwright Amiri Baraka.° How would you say he influenced you?

Amiri Baraka: U.S. poet, playwright, essayist, and music critic; born Everett LeRoy Jones in 1934, he changed his name to LeRoi Jones in 1952, to Imamu Ameer Baraka in 1967, and later to Amiri Baraka.

August Wilson: I'm not sure what they say about *Fences* as it relates to *Death of a Salesman*. At the time I wrote *Fences*, I had not read *Death of a Salesman*, had not seen *Death of a Salesman*, did not know anything about *Death of a Salesman*.

My greatest influence has been the blues. And that's a literary influence, because I think the blues is the best literature that we as black Americans have. My interest in Baraka comes from the '60s and the Black Power movement. So it's more for Baraka's political ideas, which I loved and still am an exponent of. Through all those years I was a follower, if you will, of Baraka. He had an influence on my thinking.

MML: Were you exposed first to his poetry or his plays?

AW: The poetry in particular. The book called *Black Magic*, which is sort of a collection of several books. That's '69 — I wore that book out, the cover got taped up with Scotch tape, the pages falling out. That was my bible, I carried it wherever I went. So that in particular. I wasn't writing plays back then, so I wasn't influenced by his playwriting — although, to me, his best plays are collected in a book called *Four Black Revolutionary Plays*, with *Madheart*, *Great Goodness of Life*, *A Black Mass*, and *Experimental Death Unit 1*. They contributed a lot to my thinking just in terms of getting stuff on the page.

MML: How specifically was the blues an influence on your work?

AW: Blues is the bedrock of everything I do. All the characters in my plays, their ideas and their attitudes, the stance that they adopt in the world, are all ideas and attitudes that are expressed in the blues. If all this were to disappear off the face of the earth and some people two million unique years from now would dig out this civilization and come across some blues records, working as anthropologists, they would be able to piece together who these people were, what they thought about, what their ideas and attitudes toward pleasure and pain were, all of that. All the components of culture. Just like they do with the Egyptians, they piece together all that stuff. And all you need is the blues. So to me the blues is the book, it's the bible, it's everything. . . .

MML: Your characters also often riff off of each other like jazz musicians, particularly in *Seven Guitars*. Your work in general is like improvising on a theme: the life of southern blacks who migrated to the North in the twentieth century. How has jazz impacted your creative process?

AW: I think that's the core of black aesthetics: the ability to improvise. That is what has enabled our survival. . . .

AW: People say, "Well, you writin a play in 1911 and you weren't alive in 1911. Did you do any research?" I say, I don't do research. They say, "Well, how do you know?" Because the plays ultimately are about love, honor, duty, betrayal — what I call the Big Themes. So you could set it in the '80s and make use of various things, but you're telling a story that is using the Big Themes. . . .

MML: Essayist Sandra Shannon has criticized the women in your plays, saying, "His feminine portrayals tend to slip into comfort zones of what seem to be male-fantasized roles." Feminist critic bell hooks said of *Fences* that "patriarchy is not critiqued" and "sexist values are reinscribed." I was wondering if you've given thought to this in relation to approaching the final play in your cycle, which takes place in the 1990s, a time when women are arguably their most liberated and independent.

AW: I can't approach them any different than I have, man, cause all my women are independent. People can say anything they want, that's valid, they're liable to say anything they want. I don't agree with that. You gotta write women like . . . they can't express ideas and attitudes that women of the feminist movement in the '60s made. Even though I'm aware of all that, you gotta be very careful if you're trying to create a character like that, that they don't come up with any greater understanding of themselves and their relationship to the world than women had at that time.

As a matter of fact, all my characters are at the edge of that, they pushing them boundaries, they have more understanding. I had to cut back and say, "These are feminist ideas." My mother was a feminist, though she wouldn't express it that way. She don't know nothing about no feminist women and whatnot but she didn't accept her place. She raised three daughters, and my sisters are the same way. So that's where I get my women from. I grew up in a household with four women.

Missy Dehn Kubitschek
August Wilson's Gender Lesson   [1994]

Like much African American literature of the last two decades, August Wilson's cycle of plays takes its readers/viewers on an extended historical examination of gendered interactions in the black community. Although his earliest play, *Ma Rainey's Black Bottom* (1984), does not focus on gender to the same extent as his later works, it sets the premises under which they develop their statements: the presence of a powerful African American spirituality and the difficulty of preserving it in an economic system controlled by white racists. *Fences* (1985) forcefully demonstrates the spiritual alienation of men and women from one another, and of men from their children. The play shows men and women speaking different languages, reflecting different understandings of the spiritual cosmos. . . .

Centered on the economic disruption of black men's and women's relationships, *Fences* shows men and women speaking the different languages imposed/derived from their unconscious acceptance of an implicitly Eurocentric view of separate male and female spheres. The development of a situation in which men and women are speaking different languages that no longer refer to the same spiritual realities can be approached through a juxtaposition of two models of gender relations. Nineteenth-century European models divide sex roles into separate spheres in a hierarchical schema. A second set of models derives from the experiences of women in traditional nonindustrial societies or in minority communities in the United States.

Delineated by Paula Gunn Allen's *The Sacred Hoop* and Trinh Minh-ha's *Woman, Native, Other,* and implied by other works such as Gloria Anzaldua's *Borderlands/La Frontera* and bell hooks's *Feminist Theory: From Margin to Center,* this second paradigm represents men and women as possessing somewhat different spiritual gifts and hence different social responsibilities, but sharing some areas of influence. Men's and women's spheres of activity are fundamentally connected, mutually contributive parts of community. . . .

Separate spheres were for black Americans unachievable in the nineteenth century and available only to a small middle class in the twentieth. Historically, the separate-spheres ideology has combined with white male economic control to erode African American families and communities by preventing black men from achieving the only culturally endorsed definition of manhood and by subordinating the activities of black women, sometimes making them competitive in formerly common arenas of endeavor. *Fences* explores the damage that results when European constructions of sex roles separate, hierarchically order, and then alienate men and women; at the same time, the play suggests a palimpsest of a more empowering traditional model.

Troy Maxson's definition of his manhood centers on his ability to support his family economically, though he intermittently glimpses the inadequacy of this conception. He describes, for example, his own father's economically pressured definition of his children as workers, and only workers, with considerable pain. He also recognizes his father's lack of joy, his selfishness, his demeaning treatment of his children, his abuse of his wife. Simultaneously Troy says, "He wasn't good for nobody" (1057) but affirms that he strove to accomplish the one thing necessary, securing the necessities for his family.

Under this superimposed definition of manhood, another, broader, definition struggles to reemerge, the sense that economic relations ought not to be the whole of a father's relationship to his children. Troy cannot express such an idea directly. Though he suffered for lack of his father's love (and was further deprived when his mother left), he tries to force Cory to be satisfied with the same father/son relationship:

> It's my job. It's my responsibility! You understand that? A man got to take care of his family. You live in my house . . . sleep you behind on my bedclothes . . . fill you belly up with my food . . . cause you my son. You my flesh and blood. Not 'cause I like you! Cause it's my duty to take care of you. I owe a responsibility to you! (1050)

His intermittent recognition of his father's inadequacy does not lead to any other conception of fatherhood.

Trying not to fail Cory as he failed Lyons (imprisonment prevented him from supporting his first family), Troy virtually recreates the destructive relationship between his father and himself. Not only does he insist on Cory's working for salary, he identifies the family's resources — the house and its furnishings, food — as his own property, his son as a dependent rather than a contributor.

Troy expresses disgust at Lyons's easy acceptance of such a relationship; only a boy accepts such a position, and only because he has no choice.

Troy's bitterness at whites' power to exclude him from prestigious and well-paid labor (major league baseball) makes the likenesses between himself and Cory into threats. Unable to recognize changes in social conditions, he sees Cory's talents as a temptation to irresponsibility. He insists on conditions that make it impossible for Cory to satisfy his work requirement and also to attend necessary athletic practices. Although he claims to be protecting Cory from inevitable disappointment, he is deforming another generation with Procrustean° gender definitions.

Following his only model, he plays his father's role with a slightly different script. Troy breaks from his father at fourteen, but the separation is temporary, geographic rather than temperamental or psychic; he understands his father later, when "I could feel him kicking in my blood and knew that the only thing that separated us was the matter of a few years" (1058). Given the economic conditions and his understanding of his role, Troy can only recreate in another generation the economic exploitation and competition between father and son.

Fences demonstrates that, as the European/Victorian doctrine of separate spheres combines with very limited economic opportunities, relationships between black men and women deteriorate. The very list of characters for *Fences* testifies to patriarchal hegemony, with its implications of subordination for women — all but one of the characters are identified solely by their relationship to Troy, as "Troy's oldest son" or "Troy's wife"; significantly, Cory is identified as "Troy and Rose's son," an assertion of women's ongoing presence and importance for heritage.

Men's and women's languages in *Fences* reflect the separation of their spheres of activity. In their most intensely emotional scene (act 2, scene 1), Troy and Rose attempt to communicate with metaphors that diverge sharply. Troy repeatedly uses baseball metaphors that Rose implicitly rejects by returning always to the concrete level of action:

> ROSE: You should have held me tight. You should have grabbed me and held on.
> TROY: I stood on first base for eighteen years and I thought . . . well, goddamn it . . . go on for it!
> ROSE: We're not talking about baseball! We're talking about you going off to lay in bed with another woman. (1067)

Troy's account doesn't lose track of the concrete level, but his metaphorical expression is confined to — and confines — the experience to an arena that he has only limited access to and that excludes Rose entirely. Troy chooses baseball, the game whose racial segregation has prevented his enjoying the economic or status

---

Procrustean: Creating uniformity or conformity forcefully, without allowing for variety or individuality.

benefits of his athletic prowess, as his vehicle. But baseball is, of course, also sex-segregated. Troy hopes for "one of them boys to knock me in" because metaphorically and literally, it has become impossible for any woman to play on his team, to advance him in his competitive quest. Instead, Rose disappears entirely from the metaphor, and Alberta is objectified, a base to steal. Inevitably Rose refuses the metaphor that excludes her and includes women only as objects.

Whereas Troy's metaphor comes from the social (and therefore hierarchical) world, Rose's metaphor in this scene derives from the natural world. Her expression emphasizes her expectation that her experience will partake of the cycle of living things, and her frustration that it does not come to fulfillment: "I took all my feelings, my wants and needs, my dreams . . . and I buried them inside you. I planted a seed and watched and prayed over it. I planted myself inside you and waited to bloom. And it didn't take me no eighteen years to find out the soil was hard and rocky and it wasn't never gonna bloom" (1067). In his role as divine fool, Gabriel underlines Rose's connections to nature by giving her flowers and commenting that she shares their essence. Rose's imagery, moreover, leaves open the possibility of shared ground as Troy's does not, for Troy at least appears in Rose's imagery, even though he is represented as an environment of dubious hospitality. Rose's natural imagery suggests continuity, as Troy's game imagery suggests a discrete series, and although women's experience provides the source of this natural imagery, the experience is itself not socially limited to one gender.

Fences does not, of course, present black men as failed human beings and women as the preservers of undamaged original spiritualities (a conception that would result from the separate-spheres doctrine's idealization of women's purity). The division into separate spheres affects Rose as well as Troy. Her impassioned denunciation of his affair and its results reveals the conflict between European and African ideals of kinship: "And you know I ain't never wanted no half nothing in my family. My whole family is half. Everybody got different fathers and mothers . . . my two sisters and my brother. Can't hardly tell who's who. Can't never sit down and talk about Papa and Mama. It's your papa and your mama and my papa and my mama" (1065). On the one hand, Rose is angry about a kind of confused ancestral heritage, the lack of archetypal Mama and Papa, and their replacement by lowercase, less powerful specifics. On the other, her idea of a proper family reflects the European, nuclear ideal rather than the traditional African or African American conception of extended family.

The last scene shows the simultaneous influence of both paradigms. On the one hand, Raynell, like Rose, is associated with the natural world of the garden while Cory appears in military uniform, a clear suggestion of continued separation of sex roles. On the other hand, a shared spirituality persists. Troy's father's song, "Old Blue," for instance, survives because both Raynell and Cory have heard Troy's version. Singing it together, they ritually evoke the ancestors.

More important, both Rose and Gabriel reclaim spiritual powers by refusing European systems and returning to traditional understandings and roles. Rose, however equivocally, finally refuses the role offered to her by separate spheres — female victim of a superior male power — to embrace her own responsibility for constructing a shared space with Troy:

> When I first met your daddy I thought . . . Here is a man I can lay down with and make a baby. [. . .] I thought, Rose Lee, here is a man that you can open yourself up to and be filled to bursting. [. . .]
>
> When your daddy walked through the house he was so big he filled it up. That was my first mistake. Not to make him leave some room for me. For my part in the matter. But at that time I wanted that. I wanted a house that I could sing in. And that's what your daddy gave me. I didn't know to keep up his strength I had to give up little pieces of mine. I did that. [. . .] It was my choice. It was my life and I didn't have to live it like that. But that's what life offered me in the way of being a woman and I took it. (1081, first ellipsis Wilson's)

Troy controlled what should have been their shared space because Rose did not claim and exercise her power. Rose does not blame Troy, however, indicating that a different outcome would have been possible if she had understood the implications of ceding power. At the same time, she implies that her choice was not entirely determined by personality: "That's what life offered me in the way of being a woman."

Fences shows mutual autonomy with shared responsibilities as a more fulfilling paradigm than that of separate spheres. Rose tells Cory directly that reclaiming her power and independence made her happier. Although she had initially rejected traditional ideas of kinship, referring to Raynell as "your baby," Rose went on to agree to Troy's request to care for her with "this child got a mother. But you a womanless man" (1071). Thus, she no longer accepted Troy's presence throughout the shared house; instead, as the price of having shared responsibilities for Raynell, she insisted on redefining the whole relationship. The timing of Rose's communication of joint responsibility — Cory is engaged — makes an alternative available to her son that he did not witness in their home. Troy's mother had left by the time he rejected his father, and with no other model to emulate, Troy inevitably recreates his father's role and vision. Rose's presence — more important, her communication — opens other possibilities for Cory.

In a more direct and absolute critique of Western models, Gabriel replaces a failed Christianity with an empowering African spirituality. Convinced that it's time for him to perform the role that Christianity assigns to the Archangel Gabriel, Gabriel decides to end the world by blowing his trumpet. When the damaged instrument makes no noise, "a weight of impossible description . . . falls away" (1083). His consequent "frightful realization" makes him begin to dance, then to howl. This "atavistic signature and ritual" (1083) of dance and sound then opens the gate of heaven, and the last words of the play are Gabriel's triumphant "That's the way that go!"

Works Cited

Allen, Paula Gunn. *The Sacred Hoop: Recovering the Feminine in American Indian Traditions.* Boston: Beacon, 1986.

Anzaldua, Gloria. *Borderlands/La Frontera.* San Francisco: Spinsters/Aunt Lute, 1987.

hooks, bell. *Feminist Theory: From Margin to Center.* Boston: South End Press, 1984.

Trinh, Minh-ha. *Woman, Native, Other.* Bloomington: Indiana University Press, 1989.

Wilson, August. *Fences.* New York: New American Library/Signet, 1986.

———. *Ma Rainey's Black Bottom.* New York: New American Library, Plume, 1985.

Harry J. Elam Jr.

August Wilson [2005]

With two Pulitzer Prizes, two Tony awards, and numerous other accolades, August Wilson stands out as one of if not the most preeminent playwrights in the contemporary American theater. Wilson's self-imposed dramatic project is to review African American history in the twentieth century by writing a play for each decade. With each work, he recreates and reevaluates the choices that blacks have made in the past by refracting them through the lens of the present. Wilson focuses on the experiences and daily lives of ordinary black people within particular historical circumstances. Carefully situating each play at critical junctures in African American history, Wilson explores the pain and perseverance, the determination and dignity in these black lives. . . .

Critical to each play in Wilson's historical cycle is the concept that one must go backwards in order to move forward. Repeatedly, Wilson creates black characters who are displaced and disconnected from their history and from their individual identity, and are in search of spiritual resurrection and cultural reconnection. For these characters, past events have a commanding influence on their present dreams and aspirations. Their personal stories are inextricably linked to the history of African American struggle and survival in this country. Wilson's dramatic cycle demonstrates the impact of the past on the present. Ethics and aesthetics conjoin as the personal dynamics of his characters' lives have profound political consequences. He terms his project "a four hundred-year-old autobiography, which is the black experience" (qtd. in Shannon 179–80). As an African American "autobiography," Wilson's work links African American collective memory with Wilson's own memories and with his activist racial agenda. His family background and own life experiences are evident in this project.

Wilson . . . found his own true voice as a dramatist as the decade of the 1960s drew to a close. Affected by the urgencies around black cultural nationalism of the late 1960s, Wilson, along with his friend Rob Penny, cofounded Pittsburgh's Black Horizon's Theatre, a revolutionary-inclined African American theater. With his work at Black Horizon's, Wilson encountered one of the influences that continue to shape his dramas, the fiery playwright and poet Amiri Baraka (LeRoi Jones), the leading theater practitioner of the black revolutionary theater movement of the late 1960s and early 1970s. . . . Wilson maintains that Baraka's words and cultural politics inspired his own desire to use drama as a means to social ends.

In and around the same time, Wilson discovered three more influences: Jorge Luis Borges, Romare Bearden, and the blues. Argentinean short-story writer Borges became significant to Wilson because of his ability to blend the metaphysical and the mystical within his complex plot lines. With his skillful use of narration, Borges mixes the fantastical and the spiritual as his characters follow difficult and convoluted pathways. Within plays such as *Fences*, *Joe Turner's Come and Gone*, *The Piano Lesson*, and *Gem of the Ocean*, Wilson's incorporation of the supernatural and metaphysical has been influenced by the writing of Borges.

Wilson discovered the work of fellow Pittsburgh native Romare Bearden in 1977, when his friend Charles Purdy purchased a copy of his collage *The Prevalence of Ritual* (1964). Viewing this artwork had a profound effect on Wilson: "My response was visceral. I was looking at myself in ways I hadn't thought of before and have never ceased to think of since. In Bearden I found my artistic mentor and sought, and still aspire, to make my plays the equal of his canvases" (qtd. in Fishman 134). Bearden's collages *Millhands Lunch Bucket* (1978) and *The Piano Lesson* (1984) directly inspired Wilson's plays *Joe Turner* and *Piano Lesson*, respectively. Bearden's formula for collage, his use of found objects, and his blending of past and present are examples reflected in Wilson's pastiche style of playwriting and his interest in the impact of history upon present conditions. Within the artistry of both men, the metaphorical and ritualistic coexist with everyday experiences of African Americans. Unfortunately, the two men never met in Bearden's lifetime.

Despite the impact of Bearden, Borges, and Baraka on Wilson and his work, the most significant and most transformative of the four influences (referred to as the "4Bs" because all begin with the letter "B") is the blues. Twelve years prior to encountering Bearden in 1965, Wilson discovered the blues while listening to an old recording of Bessie Smith's "Nobody in Town Can Bake a Sweet Jellyroll Like Mine." This recording transformed his life and his cultural ideology. The blues become not only a guiding force in his writing, but also the foundation he discovers for African American expressive culture and for what Wilson believes is a distinctly African American way of "being" (*Three Plays* ix-x). According to Wilson, the cultural, social, political, and spiritual all interact within the blues. Forged in and from the economics of slavery as a method of mediating the pains and dehumanization of that experience, the blues are purposefully duplicitous, containing a matrix of meanings. The blues for Wilson continue to offer a methodology for negotiating the difficult spaces of African American existence and achieving African American survival.

Structurally, Wilson's "bluesology" acts as an aesthetic and cultural intervention disrupting the conventional frame of realism. Rather than plot or action, character and the lyrical music of the dialogue drive the plays. Wilson, a poet before he became a playwright, celebrates the poetic power contained in the speech of poor and uneducated peoples. Wilson allows his characters to voice their history in the verbal equivalent of musical solos. For instance, Troy Maxson — an illiterate garbage man and central figure in *Fences* — fashions his identity and self-awareness through bold expressive tales. Like the ancient city of Troy, he is an epic force, impregnable and larger than life. Troy's stories, which serve to describe the African American experiences as well as his individual life, expand the realistic canvas of the play, reaching beyond the conventional temporal and spatial limits to reveal the inner presence of history impacting on an individual.

Ralph Ellison calls the blues a unique combination of "the tragic and the comic," of poetry and ritual (256). Wilson's plays embody this blues formula on a multitude of occasions. In each of the plays, Wilson's characters engage in a series of vernacular games, the dozens, and signifyin'. All these cultural activities are extensions of the blues or variations on a blues theme. Wilson sets his works in sites that enable such communal engagement, verbal jousting, and oral transmission of culture. . . .

In Wilson's plays, music and song act as metaphors for African American identity, spirit, and soul. Through the invisible presence and symbolic activities of offstage white characters, Wilson suggests that the dominant culture has continually sought to subjugate African American humanity and suppress the power and ability of African Americans to sing their song without looking over their shoulder.

Wilson's blues theology privileges the blues musician. He posits the blues musician as a potentially powerful site of black resistive agency. Too often, however, the musicians fail to realize the power they possess. As with any gift or power, the power of the blues musician exacts certain costs and expectations from the ones to whom it is given. Lyons in *Fences*, Jeremy in *Joe Turner's Come and Gone*, and Winning Boy in *The Piano Lesson*, for instance, all represent blues musicians who have misunderstood the spiritual force of the blues song and the cultural responsibility inherent in their ability to play the blues. As a result, they are exploited for their music and fall victim to those who wish to control their spirit and song. . . . Still, it is on and through these musicians that Wilson positions himself as blues musician improvising on a theme. Toledo's° declarations of the need for African Americans to recognize their connections to Africa represent an important element of Wilson's blues theology. Wilson believes that in order for African Americans to be able to sing their own song, to feel truly

---

Toledo: Philosophical pianist in *Ma Rainey's Black Bottom.*

liberated in the American context, they must rediscover their "African-ness." Wilson puts it this way: "One of the things I'm trying to say in my writing is that we can never begin to make a contribution to the society except as Africans" (qtd. in Savran 296). Toledo, accordingly, reprimands the band and himself for not being African and for being imitation white men. . . .

The ending of *Ma Rainey*, in which one of the band members murders another, is a complex and confounding blues moment. It stands in stark contrast to endings of Wilson's later dramas such as *Fences*, *Joe Turner*, and *Piano Lesson*, in which characters reach moments of spiritual fulfillment, acknowledge their relationships to the African American past, and perform actions of self-actualization, self-determination, and collective communion. . . .

Wilson claims that he started *Fences* (1986), his first Pulitzer Prize–winning play, with "the image of a man standing in his yard with a baby in his arms" (qtd. in DeVries 25). Beginning with this image, Wilson sought to subvert the dominant culture's representations of African American men as irresponsible, absentee fathers. Wilson creates Troy Maxson, a larger-than-life figure, who feels an overwhelming sense of duty and responsibility to his family. With an impenetrable resolve, he perceives familial values only from his perspective. Troy's self-involved concept of familial duty and responsibility prevents him from seeing the harm he causes, the pain his decisions inflict on other family members.

Through a series of retrospective stories performed by Troy, Wilson reveals Troy's victimization by and resentment of the forces of social and economic oppression. Wilson also uses these moments to disclose the influence that Troy's prior relationship with his father now exacts on his relationship with his own son Cory. Physically beaten by his father, Troy was forced to strike out on his own. During the course of the play, Cory must undergo a similar rite of passage. Repeating the family history, Cory physically confronts his father, is beaten by Troy, and is forced to leave his father's house. The repetition of behavior patterns by father and son underscores Wilson's conviction that history plays an important role in determining contemporary identity. Only by literally confronting the embodiment of the past, one's father or "forefathers," can one gain entrance into the future or ascendancy into adulthood.

In the play's second act, Troy's adultery provides the catalyst that propels his wife, Rose, to reassess her position, to gain a greater self-awareness, and to change. Rose blooms. Although Rose spiritually distances herself from Troy, she does not leave the marriage. Her final assessment of their marriage, delivered to her son Cory in the last scene, functions to reconcile father and son and emphasizes Rose's own resignation to "what life offered me in terms of being a woman" (p. 1081). At the close of *Fences*, Cory is able to accept the continued "presence" of his father in his life. This acceptance comes after Cory has returned home from the Marines and announces to Rose his intent to boycott his father's funeral. Wilson juxtaposes Cory's return with the entrance of a new character, Troy's seven-year-old daughter from his affair, Raynell (Cory's half-sister). Wilson uses Raynell as a critical element in his redemptive strategy.

Raynell visually represents the inextricable connection between past and present. Not only is she the manifestation of Troy's past infidelities but the signifier of his redemption. Her appearance enables both the audience and Cory to understand better the importance of inheritance, the perpetuation and veneration of history. In addition, here as in other Wilson works the child, Raynell, symbolizes the hope for the family's future. Significantly, her entrance into the action occurs not just on the day of Troy's funeral, but in the year 1965, in the midst of the civil rights era, a period of intense struggle and new opportunity for African Americans.

Works Cited

DeVries, Hilary. "A Song in Search of Itself." *American Theatre* 3.10 (January 1987): 22–25.

Ellison, Ralph. "Blues People." *Shadow and Act*. New York: Random House, 1964. 247–58.

Fishman, Joan. "Romare Bearden, August Wilson, and the Traditions of African Performance." *May All Your Fences Have Gates: Essays on the Drama of August Wilson*. Ed. Alan Nadel. Iowa City: University of Iowa Press, 1994. 133–49.

Savran, David. *In Their Own Words: Contemporary American Playwrights*. New York: Theatre Communications Group, 1988.

Shannon, Sandra G. "The Role of Memory in August Wilson's Four-Hundred-Year Autobiography." *Memory and Cultural Politics: New Approaches to American Ethnic Literature*. Ed. Amritjit Singh, Commas Skerrett, and Robert E. Hogan. Boston: Northeastern University Press, 1996. 175–93.

Wilson, August. *Fences*. New York: New American Library, 1986.

——. *Joe Turner's Come and Gone*. New York: New American Library, 1988.

——. *Ma Rainey's Black Bottom*. New York: New American Library, 1985.

——. *The Piano Lesson*. New York: Plume, 1990.

——. *Three Plays*. Pittsburgh: University of Pittsburgh Press, 1991.

Susan Koprince

Baseball as History and Myth in August Wilson's *Fences*   [2006]

The game of baseball has long been regarded as a metaphor for the American dream — an expression of hope, democratic values, and the drive for individual success. According to John Thorn, baseball has become "the great repository of national ideals, the symbol of all that [is] good in American life: fair play (sportsmanship); the rule of law (objective arbitration of disputes); equal opportunity (each side has its innings); the brotherhood of man (bleacher harmony); and more" (qtd. in Elias 3). Baseball's playing field itself has been viewed as archetypal — a walled garden, an American Eden marked by youth and timelessness. (There are no clocks in the game, and the runners move counter-clockwise around the bases.) As former Yale University president and former baseball commissioner Bart Giamatti once wrote, baseball is "the last pure place where Americans can dream" (qtd. in Elias 9).

In his Pulitzer Prize–winning drama *Fences* . . . , however, August Wilson uses . . . the mythology of baseball to reveal the failed promise of the American dream. As Deeanne Westbrook observes in *Ground Rules: Baseball and Myth* (1996), baseball's playing field can be understood as an archetypal garden – an image of innocence and timeless space – an American Eden. In W. P. Kinsella's novel *Shoeless Joe* (1982), for example, the protagonist Ray Kinsella rediscovers Eden by building a baseball park in his Iowa cornfield, creating "a walled garden of eternal youth." Players from baseball's past enter this magical garden, "not middle-aged or elderly, as they were at their deaths, but young, as they were at their moments of peak performance. They occupy the mythic present" (Westbrook 102).

In *Fences* the closest that Troy comes to participating in the American dream – and hence inhabiting such a paradise – is during his life in the Negro Leagues. Wilson associates the American dream with Troy's younger days as a ballplayer: with self-affirmation, limitless possibilities, and the chance for heroic success. The very act of hitting a home run – especially when the ball is hit over the fence – suggests extraordinary strength and the ability to transcend limits. Troy's son Lyons recalls seeing his father hit a home run over the grandstand: "Right out there in Homestead Field. He wasn't satisfied hitting in the seats . . . he want to hit it over everything! After the game he had two hundred people standing around waiting to shake his hand" (1079). Troy himself claims that he hit seven home runs off of Satchel Paige. "You can't get no better than that," he boasts (1048).

For Troy, however, the American dream has turned into a prolonged nightmare. Instead of limitless opportunity, he has come to know racial discrimination and poverty. At age fifty-three, this former Negro League hero is a garbage collector who ekes out a meager existence, working arduously to support his family and living from hand to mouth. "I do the best I can do," he tells Rose. "I come in here every Friday. I carry a sack of potatoes and a bucket of lard. You all line up at the door with your hands out. I give you the lint from my pockets. I give you my sweat and my blood. I ain't got no tears. I done spent them" (1078). Troy claims that he would not even have a roof over his head if it were not for the $3,000 that the government gave to his mentally disabled brother, Gabriel, following a serious head injury in World War II.

Wilson accentuates Troy's exclusion from the American Eden by converting baseball's mythical garden into an ironic version of paradise. In the stage directions to *Fences*, Wilson indicates that the legendary "field of dreams" has been reduced to the "small dirt yard" (1029) in front of Troy's home – his current playing field. Incompletely fenced, the yard contains lumber and other fence-building materials, as well as two oil drums used as garbage containers. A baseball bat – "the most visible symbol of [Troy's] deferred dreams" (Shannon,

Fences 46) — is propped up against a tree, from which there hangs "a ball made of rags" (1029). As the setting reveals, Troy does not inhabit a walled garden of timeless youth. At fifty-three, he cannot reclaim his past glory as a power hitter; nor can he participate in the American dream. His playing field in 1957 has deteriorated into one of dirt, garbage, and rags. Indeed, only after Troy's death at the end of the play, when his fence is completed and when his daughter Raynell plants a small garden in front of the house, is there even a suggestion of a walled paradise.

According to Westbrook, baseball's archetypal playing field can also become a battleground — a scene of violent confrontation — much like the heroic fights at Valhalla, the "home of the slain" in Norse mythology. Each morning the warriors arm themselves for combat and battle one another fiercely in the great courtyard, returning to the banquet hall in the evening to feast and boast of their exploits. As Westbrook notes, "The ritualized aggression of both Valhalla and baseball field is rule governed . . . and endlessly repeatable" (109). The baseball players are modern-day warriors, the bat and ball are weapons, and the game itself a substitute for combat.

In *Fences* Wilson converts Troy's playing field into a battleground — an image reinforced by references to World War II (during which Gabriel got "half his head blown off" [1044]), to the "Army of Death" (1035), and to the Battle of Armageddon (when, according to Gabriel, "God get to waving that Judgment sword" [1055]). Throughout the play Troy is pictured as a batter/warrior, fighting to earn a living and to stay alive in a world that repeatedly discriminates against him. As Shannon has noted, Troy sees life as a baseball contest; he sees himself as perpetually in the batter's box (*Dramatic Vision* 110). He tells Rose: "You got to guard [the plate] closely . . . always looking for the curve ball on the inside corner. You can't afford to let none get past you. You can't afford a call strike. If you going down . . . you going down swinging" (1067).

Troy's front yard is literally turned into a battleground during his confrontations with his younger son, Cory. Bitter about his own exclusion from major-league baseball, Troy is resistant when Cory wants to attend college on a football scholarship, telling his son that black athletes have to be twice as talented to make the team and that "the white man ain't gonna let you get nowhere with that football noway" (1048). But Cory, who seems to believe in the promise of the American dream — particularly for black athletes in the 1950s — insists that Troy is selfishly holding him back from success: "You just scared I'm gonna be better than you, that's all" (1060). The intergenerational conflict reaches a climax in act 2, when Troy and Cory engage in an ironic version of the all-American father-and-son game of catch (Birdwell 91). "Get your black ass out of my yard!" (1076), Troy warns Cory, after which the two combatants fight furiously over Troy's bat/weapon until Cory is expelled from his father's playing field.

Troy's efforts to prevent his son from playing football can be viewed as a form of what Harry J. Elam Jr. calls "racial madness" — a term that suggests that social and political forces can impact the black psyche and that decades of oppression can induce a collective psychosis.[1] In *Fences* this racial madness is illustrated most vividly in the character of Troy's mentally handicapped brother, Gabriel, but it is also revealed in Troy himself, who is so overwhelmed by bitterness that he destroys his son's dream of a college education — a dream that most fathers would happily support. Instead, Troy instructs Cory to stick with his job at the A & P or learn a trade like carpentry or auto mechanics: "That way you have something can't nobody take away from you" (1048). There is a certain method, however, to Troy's madness; for why should he expect college football (another white power structure) to treat his son any better than major-league baseball treated him? Why should he believe, in 1957, that times have really changed for black men? Anxious for Cory to find economic security, and, more importantly, self-respect, Troy exclaims to Rose, "I don't want him to be like me! I want him to move as far away from my life as he can get" (1050).

In Amiri Baraka's play *Dutchman* (1964), the African American protagonist Clay advocates a violent solution to the problem of racial madness, telling his white adversary, Lula, that "the only thing that would cure the neurosis would be your murder. Simple as that. . . . Crazy niggers turning their backs on sanity. When all it need is that simple act. Murder. Just Murder!" (qtd. in Elam 63). In *Fences* Troy's response to the racial madness that infects him is much less revolutionary than Clay's, but it is combative nonetheless. Troy chooses to challenge the white man, literally, by engaging in a form of social activism, that is, by taking a job complaint to his boss, Mr. Rand, and then to the commissioner's office. Moreover, he teaches his son how to fight. During their climactic struggle in act 2, Troy deliberately confronts Cory, taunting him, grabbing the bat from him, and insisting that he teach Cory how to swing. Determined to prepare his son for combat in a racist society, Troy uses the weapons and language of baseball as his teaching tools. "Don't you strike out," he tells Cory after an earlier altercation. "You living with a full count. Don't you strike out" (1068).

Troy's playing field is the scene not only of father-son conflict, but of marital strife as well. In act 2 Rose learns that Troy has been unfaithful to her and has fathered a child with his mistress, Alberta. When Troy tries to explain (and even justify) his infidelity by using baseball analogies, Rose is not impressed. "We're not talking about baseball!" she says. "We're talking about you going off to lay in bed with another woman . . . and then bring it home to me. That's what we're talking about. We ain't talking about no baseball" (1067). After the conflict between Rose and Troy escalates into a cold war — the two of them rarely speaking to one another — it is the wounded Rose, rather than Troy, who eventually dominates the battle, taking in his motherless daughter and telling Troy: "From right now . . . this child got a mother. But you a womanless man" (1072). . . .

Although Wilson's dramas are typically grounded in elements of African and African American cultures — including ritual, superstition, the blues, and jazz — *Fences* is unique in that it appropriates a traditionally white cultural form — baseball — in order to portray an African American experience in the twentieth century. By adopting this white cultural form, Wilson artfully expresses Troy Maxson's double consciousness — his complicated experience as a black man in a white-dominated world. At the same time, Wilson creates a "subversive narrative" that competes with the American Dream itself (Shannon, *Fences* 20). Thus, he demonstrates that the national pastime has been stained by racism, that the Edenic promise of America is illusory, and that the traditional mythology of baseball must ultimately make room for a new and revolutionary mythos: that of the defiant African American warrior.

Note

[1]Invoking the theories of psychiatrist-philosopher Frentz Fanon as well as the perspectives of Du Bois, Ellison, and others, Elam emphasizes that "racial madness" does not imply a pathology in blackness itself. Rather it is "a trope that became operative in clinical practice, literary creation, and cultural theory in the modern period as artists, critics, and practitioners identified social and cultural roots for black psychological impairment" (59). During his discussion of racial madness in *Fences*, Elam focuses on Troy's brain-damaged brother, Gabriel, whom he describes as a force for redemption.

Works Cited

Birdwell, Christine. "Death as a Fastball on the Outside Corner: *Fences*' Troy Maxson and the American Dream." *Aethlon: The Journal of Sport Literature* 8.1 (Fall 1990): 87–96.

Elam, Harry J. Jr. *The Past as Present in the Drama of August Wilson*. Ann Arbor: University of Michigan Press, 2004.

Elias, Robert. "A Fit for a Fractured Society." *Baseball and the American Dream: Race, Class, Gender, and the National Pastime*. Ed. Robert Elias. Armonk, N.Y.: M. E. Sharpe, 2001. 3–33.

Kinsella, W. P. *Shoeless Joe*. 1982. New York: Ballantine, 1990.

Shannon, Sandra G. *August Wilson's* Fences: *A Reference Guide*. Westport, Conn.: Greenwood Press, 2003.

——. *The Dramatic Vision of August Wilson*. Washington, D.C.: Howard University Press, 1995.

Westbrook, Deeanne. *Ground Rules: Baseball and Myth*. Urbana: University of Illinois Press, 1996.

Wilson, August. *Fences*. New York: New American Library, 1986.

RESPONDING THROUGH Writing

Here are some suggestions for writing on August Wilson, but for a chapter like this one, you should not limit yourself to these topics. An important purpose behind the chapters is to help you learn how to find good topics on your own. You may make changes in the topics (with your instructor's permission) and make changes in how they are categorized (using a topic from the first six as a research topic, for example, instead of one using no outside sources.)

PAPERS USING NO OUTSIDE SOURCES

Literary Analysis Papers

1. Write a paper analyzing the use of baseball as a plot element and as a metaphor for life in *Fences*.
2. Write a paper exploring different kinds of fences, literal ones and figurative ones suggesting enclosures, in *Fences*.

Comparison-Contrast Papers

3. Write a paper comparing and contrasting the attitudes toward change evinced by Troy and by other characters in *Fences*.
4. Write a comparison-contrast paper showing how Bono serves as a foil for Troy or how Lyons serves as a foil for Cory in *Fences*.

Cultural Studies Papers

5. The church has traditionally been an important part of African American culture. Write a paper examining the use and effect of the language of and the practice of Christianity in *Fences*.
6. Write a paper on the attitudes toward and meaning of work in *Fences*.

PAPERS USING LIMITED OUTSIDE SOURCES

Literary Analysis Papers

1. In his interview with Bonnie Lyons, August Wilson says that inner conflict is at the center of drama (p. 1092). Using what he says there and what reviewers and critics included in this chapter say, write a paper discussing the inner conflicts that drive the action in *Fences*.
2. In his interview with Miles Marshall Lewis, August Wilson says his plays are about the "Big Themes" — "love, honor, duty, betrayal" (p. 1093). Drawing on that interview and other secondary writings in this chapter, write a paper discussing the extent to which those themes are present and influential in *Fences*.

Comparison-Contrast Papers

3. Frank Rich's reference to the "conflicting visions" of Troy and Cory (p. 1087) is echoed by other secondary works included in this chapter. Building on their comments, write a paper comparing and contrasting the visions of the two men and discussing the reasons for and effects of the tensions between them.
4. Lloyd Richards, the original director of *Fences*, writes that the play tells the story of four generations of black Americans (p. 1083). Write a paper examining differences and similarities in what happens to them, especially changes — or lack of change — in their relationships with white Americans. Use secondary materials in this chapter, as well as the play, for support.

Cultural Studies Papers

5. Write a paper examining the roles of and attitudes toward women in *Fences*, using the secondary materials in this chapter as well as the play itself for illustrations and supporting details.
6. Harry J. Elam Jr. says that at the heart of Wilson's plays is "the concept that one must go backwards in order to move forward" (p. 1099). Write a paper in which you explore the applicability of that claim in *Fences*, using the secondary materials in this chapter as well as the play for support.

PAPERS INVOLVING FURTHER RESEARCH

Literary Analysis Papers

1. Wilson once said that listening to a recording of Bessie Smith's "Nobody in Town Can Bake a Jelly Roll Like Mine" awakened his interest in the blues. Write a research paper on the use and influence of the blues on his play *Fences* (consider the rhythms, outlook, and sensibility that characterize the blues).
2. Harry J. Elam Jr. says that Wilson, who wrote poetry before turning to drama, "allows his characters to voice their history in the verbal equivalent of musical solos" (p. 1101). Write a paper analyzing the "poetic" or "musical" style Wilson gives to characters in *Fences*, especially in major speeches. Focus on the text of the play, but bring in the secondary materials in this chapter and other critical materials you find elsewhere for additional support.

Comparison-Contrast Papers

3. Susan Koprince (p. 1103) is one of several critics who write about the mythic implications of baseball as a metaphor for the American Dream in *Fences*. Write a paper comparing and contrasting her insights with those of two or three other critics and explain which you find most helpful or convincing and why.
4. Do research on August Wilson's life, using the material in this chapter and going beyond it. Write a paper in which you compare and contrast what happens in Troy Maxson's life to events in or associated with Wilson's life or the lives of people he knew, focusing on how Wilson transforms biographical material to make the play "work."

Cultural Studies Papers

5. Write a research paper examining August Wilson's incorporation and adaptation of African American folklore traditions in *Fences*.
6. In August Wilson's master plan of writing ten plays, one embodying the spirit of each of the decades of the twentieth century, *Fences* was the play for the 1950s. Write a research paper on how *Fences* is representative of — or epitomizes — events and changes taking place in that decade.

going beyond ... ...
happen ...
or the lives of people ... ... on how you ...
plet must ... ... and word ...

Cultural Studies Papers

.... spirit of each of the decades of the twentieth century ...
the 1950s. Write a research paper on how Troy is representative of — or
epitomizes — events and changes taking place in that decade.

Enter Antigone, slipping through the central doors of the palace. She motions to her sister, Ismene, who follows her cautiously toward an altar at the center of the stage.

ANTIGONE: My own flesh and blood — dear sister, dear Ismene,
how many griefs our father Oedipus handed down!°
Do you know one, I ask you, one grief
that Zeus will not perfect for the two of us
while we still live and breathe? There's nothing,   5
no pain — our lives are pain — no private shame,
no public disgrace, nothing I haven't seen
in your griefs and mine. And now this:
an emergency decree, they say, the Commander°
has just declared for all of Thebes.   10
What, haven't you heard? Don't you see?
The doom reserved for enemies
marches on the ones we love the most.
ISMENE: Not I, I haven't heard a word, Antigone.
Nothing of loved ones,   15
no joy or pain has come my way, not since
the two of us were robbed of our two brothers,
both gone in a day, a double blow —
not since the armies of Argos vanished,
just this very night. I know nothing more,   20
whether our luck's improved or ruin's still to come.
ANTIGONE: I thought so. That's why I brought you out here,
past the gates, so you could hear in private.

---

2. **Oedipus handed down:** Oedipus, the father of Antigone and Ismene, was abandoned as an infant when an oracle told his parents he would someday kill his father and marry his mother. He was found by a shepherd and brought to Polybus, king of Corinth, who adopted him. Told by a drunken man that Polybus was not his father, Oedipus went to an oracle to learn the truth and was told that he would kill his father and marry his mother. Oedipus decided to leave Corinth, in order to escape this fate. Forced off the road by a chariot, he killed the driver (Laius, king of Thebes, his biological father), thus unknowingly fulfilling the first part of the oracle's prophecy. He went on to Thebes, which was held in thrall by a sphinx who killed all those who could not solve her riddle. Oedipus answered it correctly and became king by marrying the widowed queen, Jocasta. The couple had two sons, Polynices and Eteocles, and two daughters, Antigone and Ismene. *Oedipus the King,* the prequel to *Antigone,* tells how, when Thebes was suffering from a plague, an oracle declared that the land was polluted by the presence of the murderer of its king, who had to be expelled. In a series of painful revelations, Oedipus and Jocasta learn the truth about each other and their situation. In grief and horror, Jocasta kills herself and Oedipus puts out his eyes and goes into exile, giving the kingdom to his sons, who agree to rule in alternate years. After the first year, Eteocles refuses to step down and Polynices attacks Thebes, with the support of the army from a nearby city, Argos. The brothers kill each other in hand-to-hand combat in front of the gates of Thebes and Creon, brother of Jocasta, takes over as king. He orders that Eteocles be given full burial honors, but that Polynices must go unburied and thus be dishonored. *Antigone* opens at this point. **9. the Commander:** Creon.

ISMENE: What's the matter? Trouble, clearly . . .
    you sound so dark, so grim.   25
ANTIGONE: Why not? Our own brothers' burial!
    Hasn't Creon graced one with all the rites,
    disgraced the other? Eteocles, they say,
    has been given full military honors,
    rightly so — Creon's laid him in the earth   30
    and he goes with glory down among the dead.
    But the body of Polynices, who died miserably —
    why, a city-wide proclamation, rumor has it,
    forbids anyone to bury him, even mourn him.
    He's to be left unwept, unburied, a lovely treasure   35
    for birds that scan the field and feast to their heart's content.

    Such, I hear, is the martial law our good Creon
    lays down for you and me — yes, me, I tell you —
    and he's coming here to alert the uninformed
    in no uncertain terms,   40
    and he won't treat the matter lightly. Whoever
    disobeys in the least will die, his doom is sealed:
    stoning to death inside the city walls!

    There you have it. You'll soon show what you are,
    worth your breeding, Ismene, or a coward —   45
    for all your royal blood.
ISMENE: My poor sister, if things have come to this,
    who am I to make or mend them, tell me,
    what good am I to you?
ANTIGONE: Decide.
    Will you share the labor, share the work?   50
ISMENE: What work, what's the risk? What do you mean?
ANTIGONE:

(Raising her hands.)

    Will you lift up his body with these bare hands
    and lower it with me?
ISMENE: What? You'd bury him —
    when a law forbids the city?
ANTIGONE: Yes!
    He is my brother and — deny it as you will —   55
    your brother too.
    No one will ever convict me for a traitor.
ISMENE: So desperate, and Creon has expressly —
ANTIGONE: No,
    he has no right to keep me from my own.
ISMENE: Oh my sister, think —   60

think how our own father died,° hated,
his reputation in ruins, driven on
by the crimes he brought to light himself
to gouge out his eyes with his own hands —
then mother . . . his mother and wife, both in one,   65
mutilating her life in the twisted noose —
and last, our two brothers dead in a single day,
both shedding their own blood, poor suffering boys,
battling out their common destiny hand-to-hand.

Now look at the two of us, left so alone . . .   70
think what a death we'll die, the worst of all
if we violate the laws and override
the fixed decree of the throne, its power —
we must be sensible. Remember we are women,
we're not born to contend with men. Then too,   75
we're underlings, ruled by much stronger hands,
so we must submit in this, and things still worse.

I, for one, I'll beg the dead to forgive me —
I'm forced, I have no choice — I must obey
the ones who stand in power. Why rush to extremes?   80
It's madness, madness.
ANTIGONE: I won't insist,
no, even if you should have a change of heart,
I'd never welcome you in the labor, not with me.
So, do as you like, whatever suits you best —
I will bury him myself.   85
And even if I die in the act, that death will be a glory.
I will lie with the one I love and loved by him —
an outrage sacred to the gods! I have longer
to please the dead than please the living here:
in the kingdom down below I'll lie forever.   90
Do as you like, dishonor the laws
the gods hold in honor.
ISMENE: I'd do them no dishonor . . .
but defy the city? I have no strength for that.
ANTIGONE: You have your excuses. I am on my way,
I will raise a mound for him, for my dear brother.   95
ISMENE: Oh Antigone, you're so rash — I'm so afraid for you!
ANTIGONE: Don't fear for me. Set your own life in order.
ISMENE: Then don't, at least, blurt this out to anyone.
Keep it a secret. I'll join you in that, I promise.

---

61. our own father died: *Oedipus the King* and *Oedipus at Colonus*, written later than *Antigone*,
give a different account of Oedipus's later life and death.

ANTIGONE: Dear god, shout it from the rooftops. I'll hate you   100
    all the more for silence — tell the world!

ISMENE: So fiery — and it ought to chill your heart.

ANTIGONE: I know I please where I must please the most.

ISMENE: Yes, if you can, but you're in love with impossibility.

ANTIGONE: Very well then, once my strength gives out   105
    I will be done at last.

ISMENE: You're wrong from the start,
    you're off on a hopeless quest.

ANTIGONE: If you say so, you will make me hate you,
    and the hatred of the dead, by all rights,
    will haunt you night and day.   110
    But leave me to my own absurdity, leave me
    to suffer this — dreadful thing. I will suffer
    nothing as great as death without glory.

(*Exit to the side.*)

ISMENE: Then go if you must, but rest assured,
    wild, irrational as you are, my sister,   115
    you are truly dear to the ones who love you.

(*Withdrawing to the palace. Enter a Chorus, the old citizens of Thebes, chanting as the sun begins to rise.*)

CHORUS: Glory! — great beam of sun, brightest of all
    that ever rose on the seven gates of Thebes,
        you burn through night at last!
                Great eye of the golden day,   120
    mounting the Dirce's° banks you throw him back —
    the enemy out of Argos, the white shield, the man of bronze —
    he's flying headlong now
        the bridle of fate stampeding him with pain!

    And he had driven against our borders,   125
    launched by the warring claims of Polynices —
    like an eagle screaming, winging havoc
    over the land, wings of armor
    shielded white as snow,
    a huge army massing,   130
    crested helmets bristling for assault.

He hovered above our roofs, his vast maw gaping
closing down around our seven gates,
    his spears thirsting for the kill
        but now he's gone, look,   135

---

121. the Dirce's: A river near Thebes.

before he could glut his jaws with Theban blood
or the god of fire put our crown of towers to the torch.
He grappled the Dragon° none can master — Thebes —
　　　the clang of our arms like thunder at his back!

　　Zeus hates with a vengeance all bravado,　　　　　　　140
　　the mighty boasts of men. He watched them
　　coming on in a rising flood, the pride
　　of their golden armor ringing shrill —
　　and brandishing his lightning
　　blasted the fighter° just at the goal,　　　　　　　　145
　　rushing to shout his triumph from our walls.

Down from the heights he crashed, pounding down on the earth!
And a moment ago, blazing torch in hand —
　　　mad for attack, ecstatic
he breathed his rage, the storm　　　　　　　　　　　　150
　　of his fury hurling at our heads!
But now his high hopes have laid him low
and down the enemy ranks the iron god of war
　　deals his rewards, his stunning blows — Ares°
　　rapture of battle, our right arm in the crisis.　　　　　155

　　Seven captains marshaled at seven gates
　　seven against their equals, gave
　　their brazen trophies up to Zeus,
　　god of the breaking rout of battle,
　　all but two: those blood brothers,　　　　　　　　　160
　　one father, one mother — matched in rage,
　　spears matched for the twin conquest —
　　clashed and won the common prize of death.

But now for Victory! Glorious in the morning,
joy in her eyes to meet our joy　　　　　　　　　　　165
　　she is winging down to Thebes,
our fleets of chariots wheeling in her wake —
　　Now let us win oblivion from the wars,
thronging the temples of the gods
in singing, dancing choirs through the night!　　　　　170
　　Lord Dionysus,° god of the dance
　　that shakes the land of Thebes, now lead the way!

---

138. the Dragon: Alluding to the legend that the Thebans grew from dragon's teeth sown by
Cadmus.　**145. blasted the fighter:** Capaneus, ally of Polynices, boasted from the top of a
siege ladder that not even Zeus could keep him from entering Thebes. Zeus punished this impi-
ety by striking him at the top of the ladder with a thunderbolt.　**154. Ares:** God of savage
warfare; a patron deity of Thebes.　**171. Dionysus:** God of fertility and wine, at whose festival
Greek tragedies originally were performed.

(Enter Creon from the palace, attended by his guard.)

But look, the king of the realm is coming,
Creon, the new man for the new day,
whatever the gods are sending now . . .   175
what new plan will he launch?
Why this, this special session?
Why this sudden call to the old men
summoned at one command?

CREON: My countrymen,
the ship of state is safe. The gods who rocked her,   180
after a long, merciless pounding in the storm,
have righted her once more.

                                 Out of the whole city
I have called you here alone. Well I know,
first, your undeviating respect
for the throne and royal power of King Laius.   185
Next, while Oedipus steered the land of Thebes,
and even after he died, your loyalty was unshakable,
you still stood by their children. Now then,
since the two sons are dead — two blows of fate
in the same day, cut down by each other's hands,   190
both killers, both brothers stained with blood —
as I am next in kin to the dead,
I now possess the throne and all its powers.

Of course you cannot know a man completely,
his character, his principles, sense of judgment,   195
not till he's shown his colors, ruling the people,
making laws. Experience, there's the test.
As I see it, whoever assumes the task,
the awesome task of setting the city's course,
and refuses to adopt the soundest policies   200
but fearing someone, keeps his lips locked tight,
he's utterly worthless. So I rate him now,
I always have. And whoever places a friend
above the good of his own country, he is nothing:
I have no use for him. Zeus my witness,   205
Zeus who sees all things, always —
I could never stand by silent, watching destruction
march against our city, putting safety to rout,
nor could I ever make that man a friend of mine
who menaces our country. Remember this: 210
our country is our safety.
Only while she voyages true on course

can we establish friendships, truer than blood itself.
Such are my standards. They make our city great.

Closely akin to them I have proclaimed,   215
just now, the following decree to our people
concerning the two sons of Oedipus.
Eteocles, who died fighting for Thebes,
excelling all in arms: he shall be buried,
crowned with a hero's honors, the cups we pour°   220
to soak the earth and reach the famous dead.

But as for his blood brother, Polynices,
who returned from exile, home to his father-city
and the gods of his race, consumed with one desire —
to burn them roof to roots — who thirsted to drink   225
his kinsmen's blood and sell the rest to slavery:
that man — a proclamation has forbidden the city
to dignify him with burial, mourn him at all.
No, he must be left unburied, his corpse
carrion for the birds and dogs to tear,   230
an obscenity for the citizens to behold!

These are my principles. Never at my hands
will the traitor be honored above the patriot.
But whoever proves his loyalty to the state —
I'll prize that man in death as well as life.   235
LEADER: If this is your pleasure, Creon, treating
   our city's enemy and our friend this way . . .
   The power is yours, I suppose, to enforce it
   with the laws, both for the dead and all of us,
   the living.
CREON: Follow my orders closely then,   240
   be on your guard.
LEADER: We're too old.
   Lay that burden on younger shoulders.
CREON: No, no,
   I don't mean the body — I've posted guards already.
LEADER: What commands for us then? What other service?
CREON: See that you never side with those who break my orders.   245
LEADER: Never. Only a fool could be in love with death.
CREON: Death is the price — you're right. But all too often
   the mere hope of money has ruined many men.

(*A Sentry enters from the side.*)

---

220. the cups we pour: Libations — a ritual pouring out of wine or another liquid.

SENTRY: My lord,
    I can't say I'm winded from running, or set out
    with any spring in my legs either—no sir,   250
    I was lost in thought, and it made me stop, often,
    dead in my tracks, wheeling, turning back,
    and all the time a voice inside me muttering,
    "Idiot, why? You're going straight to your death."
    Then muttering, "Stopped again, poor fool?   255
    If somebody gets the news to Creon first,
    what's to save your neck?"
                      And so,
    mulling it over, on I trudged, dragging my feet,
    you can make a short road take forever . . .
    but at last, look, common sense won out,   260
    I'm here, and I'm all yours,
    and even though I come empty-handed
    I'll tell my story just the same, because
    I've come with a good grip on one hope,
    what will come will come, whatever fate—   265
CREON: Come to the point!
    What's wrong—why so afraid?
SENTRY: First, myself, I've got to tell you,
    I didn't do it, didn't see who did—
    Be fair, don't take it out on me.   270
CREON: You're playing it safe, soldier,
    barricading yourself from any trouble.
    It's obvious, you've something strange to tell.
SENTRY: Dangerous too, and danger makes you delay
    for all you're worth.   275
CREON: Out with it—then dismiss!
SENTRY: All right, here it comes. The body—
    someone's just buried it, then run off . . .
    sprinkled some dry dust° on the flesh,
    given it proper rites.
CREON: What?   280
    What man alive would dare—
SENTRY: I've no idea, I swear it.
    There was no mark of a spade, no pickaxe there,
    no earth turned up, the ground packed hard and dry,
    unbroken, no tracks, no wheelruts, nothing,
    the workman left no trace. Just at sunup   285
    the first watch of the day points it out—

---

279. sprinkled some dry dust: As a symbolic burial, all that Antigone could do since Polynices' body was being guarded closely.

it was a wonder! We were stunned . . .
a terrific burden too, for all of us, listen:
you can't see the corpse, not that it's buried,
really, just a light cover of road-dust on it,   290
as if someone meant to lay the dead to rest
and keep from getting cursed.
Not a sign in sight that dogs or wild beasts
had worried the body, even torn the skin.

But what came next! Rough talk flew thick and fast,   295
guard grilling guard — we'd have come to blows
at last, nothing to stop it; each man for himself
and each the culprit, no one caught red-handed,
all of us pleading ignorance, dodging the charges,
ready to take up red-hot iron in our fists,   300
go through fire, swear oaths to the gods —
"I didn't do it, I had no hand in it either,
not in the plotting, not in the work itself!"

Finally, after all this wrangling came to nothing,
one man spoke out and made us stare at the ground,   305
hanging our heads in fear. No way to counter him,
no way to take his advice and come through
safe and sound. Here's what he said:
"Look, we've got to report the facts to Creon,
we can't keep this hidden." Well, that won out,   310
and the lot fell to me, condemned me,
unlucky as ever, I got the prize. So here I am,
against my will and yours too, well I know —
no one wants the man who brings bad news.

LEADER: My king,
ever since he began I've been debating in my mind,   315
could this possibly be the work of the gods?

CREON: Stop —
before you make me choke with anger — the gods!
You, you're senile, must you be insane?
You say — why it's intolerable — say the gods
could have the slightest concern for that corpse?   320
Tell me, was it for meritorious service
they proceeded to bury him, prized him so? The hero
who came to burn their temples ringed with pillars,
their golden treasures — scorch their hallowed earth
and fling their laws to the winds.   325
Exactly when did you last see the gods
celebrating traitors? Inconceivable!

_____

No, from the first there were certain citizens
who could hardly stand the spirit of my regime,
grumbling against me in the dark, heads together,   330
tossing wildly, never keeping their necks beneath
the yoke, loyally submitting to their king.
These are the instigators, I'm convinced —
they've perverted my own guard, bribed them
to do their work.

                Money! Nothing worse   335
in our lives, so current, rampant, so corrupting.
Money — you demolish cities, root men from their homes,
you train and twist good minds and set them on
to the most atrocious schemes. No limit,
you make them adept at every kind of outrage,   340
every godless crime — money!

                     Everyone —
the whole crew bribed to commit this crime,
they've made one thing sure at least:
sooner or later they will pay the price.

(Wheeling on the Sentry.)

                         You —
I swear to Zeus as I still believe in Zeus,   345
if you don't find the man who buried that corpse,
the very man, and produce him before my eyes,
simple death won't be enough for you,
not till we string you up alive
and wring the immorality out of you.   350
Then you can steal the rest of your days,
better informed about where to make a killing.
You'll have learned, at last, it doesn't pay
to itch for rewards from every hand that beckons.
Filthy profits wreck most men, you'll see —   355
they'll never save your life.

SENTRY: Please,
    may I say a word or two, or just turn and go?
CREON: Can't you tell? Everything you say offends me.
SENTRY: Where does it hurt you, in the ears or in the heart?
CREON: And who are you to pinpoint my displeasure?   360
SENTRY: The culprit grates on your feelings,
    I just annoy your ears.
CREON: Still talking?
    You talk too much! A born nuisance —
SENTRY: Maybe so,
    but I never did this thing, so help me!

CREON: Yes you did—
   what's more, you squandered your life for silver!   365
SENTRY: Oh it's terrible when the one who does the judging
   judges things all wrong.
CREON: Well now,
   you just be clever about your judgments—
   if you fail to produce the criminals for me,
   you'll swear your dirty money brought you pain.   370

(Turning sharply, reentering the palace.)

SENTRY: I hope he's found. Best thing by far.
   But caught or not, that's in the lap of fortune;
   I'll never come back, you've seen the last of me.
   I'm saved, even now, and I never thought,
   I never hoped—   375
   dear gods, I owe you all my thanks!

(Rushing out.)

CHORUS: Numberless wonders
   terrible wonders walk the world but none the match for man—
   that great wonder crossing the heaving gray sea,
         driven on by the blasts of winter
   on through breakers crashing left and right,   380
     holds his steady course
   and the oldest of the gods he wears away—
   the Earth, the immortal, the inexhaustible—
   as his plows go back and forth, year in, year out
     with the breed of stallions turning up the furrows.   385

And the blithe, lightheaded race of birds he snares,
   the tribes of savage beasts, the life that swarms the depths—
         with one fling of his nets
   woven and coiled tight, he takes them all,
     man the skilled, the brilliant!   390
He conquers all, taming with his techniques
   the prey that roams the cliffs and wild lairs,
   training the stallion, clamping the yoke across
     his shaggy neck, and the tireless mountain bull.

And speech and thought, quick as the wind   395
   and the mood and mind for law that rules the city—
     all these he has taught himself
   and shelter from the arrows of the frost
   when there's rough lodging under the cold clear sky
   and the shafts of lashing rain—   400
         ready, resourceful man!

Never without resources
never an impasse as he marches on the future —
only Death, from Death alone he will find no rescue
but from desperate plagues he has plotted his escapes.   405

Man the master, ingenious past all measure
past all dreams, the skills within his grasp —
    he forges on, now to destruction
now again to greatness. When he weaves in
the laws of the land, and the justice of the gods   410
that binds his oaths together
        he and his city rise high —
        but the city casts out
that man who weds himself to inhumanity
thanks to reckless daring. Never share my hearth   415
never think my thoughts, whoever does such things.

(Enter Antigone from the side, accompanied by the Sentry.)

    Here is a dark sign from the gods —
    what to make of this? I know her,
    how can I deny it? That young girl's Antigone!
    Wretched, child of a wretched father,   420
    Oedipus. Look, is it possible?
    They bring you in like a prisoner —
    why? did you break the king's laws?
    Did they take you in some act of mad defiance?
SENTRY: She's the one, she did it single-handed —   425
    we caught her burying the body. Where's Creon?

(Enter Creon from the palace.)

LEADER: Back again, just in time when you need him.
CREON: In time for what? What is it?
SENTRY: My king,
    there's nothing you can swear you'll never do —
    second thoughts make liars of us all.   430
    I could have sworn I wouldn't hurry back
    (what with your threats, the buffeting I just took),
    but a stroke of luck beyond our wildest hopes,
    what a joy, there's nothing like it. So,
    back I've come, breaking my oath, who cares?   435
    I'm bringing in our prisoner — this young girl —
    we took her giving the dead the last rites.
    But no casting lots this time; this is *my* luck,
    my prize, no one else's.
                Now, my lord,
    here she is. Take her, question her,   440

cross-examine her to your heart's content.
But set me free, it's only right —
I'm rid of this dreadful business once for all.
CREON: Prisoner! Her? You took her — where, doing what?
SENTRY: Burying the man. That's the whole story.
CREON: What?   445
You mean what you say, you're telling me the truth?
SENTRY: She's the one. With my own eyes I saw her
bury the body, just what you've forbidden.
There. Is that plain and clear?
CREON: What did you see? Did you catch her in the act?   450
SENTRY: Here's what happened. We went back to our post,
those threats of yours breathing down our necks —
we brushed the corpse clean of the dust that covered it,
stripped it bare . . . it was slimy, going soft,
and we took to high ground, backs to the wind   455
so the stink of him couldn't hit us;
jostling, baiting each other to keep awake,
shouting back and forth — no napping on the job,
not this time. And so the hours dragged by
until the sun stood dead above our heads,   460
a huge white ball in the noon sky, beating,
blazing down, and then it happened —
suddenly, a whirlwind!
Twisting a great dust-storm up from the earth,
a black plague of the heavens, filling the plain,   465
ripping the leaves off every tree in sight,
choking the air and sky. We squinted hard
and took our whipping from the gods.

And after the storm passed — it seemed endless —
there, we saw the girl!   470
And she cried out a sharp, piercing cry,
like a bird come back to an empty nest,
peering into its bed, and all the babies gone . . .
Just so, when she sees the corpse bare
she bursts into a long, shattering wail   475
and calls down withering curses on the heads
of all who did the work. And she scoops up dry dust,
handfuls, quickly, and lifting a fine bronze urn,
lifting it high and pouring, she crowns the dead
with three full libations.
                        Soon as we saw   480
we rushed her, closed on the kill like hunters,
and she, she didn't flinch. We interrogated her,
charging her with offenses past and present —

she stood up to it all, denied nothing. I tell you,
it made me ache and laugh in the same breath.   485
It's pure joy to escape the worst yourself,
it hurts a man to bring down his friends.
But all that, I'm afraid, means less to me
than my own skin. That's the way I'm made.
CREON:

(*Wheeling on Antigone.*)

You,
with your eyes fixed on the ground — speak up.   490
Do you deny you did this, yes or no?
ANTIGONE: I did it. I don't deny a thing.
CREON:

(*To the Sentry.*)

You, get out, wherever you please —
you're clear of a very heavy charge.

(*He leaves; Creon turns back to Antigone.*)

You, tell me briefly, no long speeches —   495
were you aware a decree had forbidden this?
ANTIGONE: Well aware. How could I avoid it? It was public.
CREON: And still you had the gall to break this law?
ANTIGONE: Of course I did. It wasn't Zeus, not in the least,
who made this proclamation — not to me.   500
Nor did that Justice, dwelling with the gods
beneath the earth, ordain such laws for men.
Nor did I think your edict had such force
that you, a mere mortal, could override the gods,
the great unwritten, unshakeable traditions.   505
They are alive, not just today or yesterday:
they live forever, from the first of time,
and no one knows when they first saw the light.

These laws — I was not about to break them,
not out of fear of some man's wounded pride,   510
and face the retribution of the gods.
Die I must, I've known it all my life —
how could I keep from knowing? — even without
your death-sentence ringing in my ears.
And if I am to die before my time   515
I consider that a gain. Who on earth,
alive in the midst of so much grief as I,
could fail to find his death a rich reward?
So for me, at least, to meet this doom of yours

is precious little pain. But if I had allowed   520
my own mother's son to rot, an unburied corpse—
that would have been an agony! This is nothing.
And if my present actions strike you as foolish,
let's just say I've been accused of folly
by a fool.

LEADER: Like father like daughter,   525
passionate, wild . . .
she hasn't learned to bend before adversity.

CREON: No? Believe me, the stiffest stubborn wills
fall the hardest; the toughest iron,
tempered strong in the white-hot fire,   530
you'll see it crack and shatter first of all.
And I've known spirited horses you can break
with a light bit—proud, rebellious horses.
There's no room for pride, not in a slave,
not with the lord and master standing by.   535

This girl was an old hand at insolence
when she overrode the edicts we made public.
But once she'd done it—the insolence,
twice over—to glory in it, laughing,
mocking us to our face with what she'd done.   540
I'm not the man, not now: she is the man
if this victory goes to her and she goes free.

Never! Sister's child or closer in blood
than all my family clustered at my altar
worshiping Guardian Zeus—she'll never escape,   545
she and her blood sister, the most barbaric death.
Yes, I accuse her sister of an equal part
in scheming this, this burial.

(To his attendants.)

                              Bring her here!
I just saw her inside, hysterical, gone to pieces.
It never fails: the mind convicts itself   550
in advance, when scoundrels are up to no good,
plotting in the dark. Oh but I hate it more
when a traitor, caught red-handed,
tries to glorify his crimes.

ANTIGONE: Creon, what more do you want   555
than my arrest and execution?

CREON: Nothing. Then I have it all.

ANTIGONE: Then why delay? Your moralizing repels me,
every word you say—pray god it always will.

So naturally all I say repels you too.
                            Enough.   560
Give me glory! What greater glory could I win
than to give my own brother decent burial?
These citizens here would all agree,

(To the Chorus.)

    they would praise me too
    if their lips weren't locked in fear.   565

(Pointing to Creon.)

    Lucky tyrants — the perquisites of power!
    Ruthless power to do and say whatever pleases *them*.
CREON: You alone, of all the people in Thebes,
    see things that way.
ANTIGONE: They see it just that way
    but defer to you and keep their tongues in leash.   570
CREON: And you, aren't you ashamed to differ so from them?
    So disloyal!
ANTIGONE: Not ashamed for a moment,
    not to honor my brother, my own flesh and blood.
CREON: Wasn't Eteocles a brother too — cut down, facing him?
ANTIGONE: Brother, yes, by the same mother, the same father. 575
CREON: Then how can you render his enemy such honors,
    such impieties in his eyes?
ANTIGONE: He will never testify to that,
    Eteocles dead and buried.
CREON: He will —
    if you honor the traitor just as much as him.   580
ANTIGONE: But it was his brother, not some slave that died —
CREON: Ravaging our country! —
    but Eteocles died fighting in our behalf.
ANTIGONE: No matter — Death longs for the same rites for all.
CREON: Never the same for the patriot and the traitor.   585
ANTIGONE: Who, Creon, who on earth can say the ones below
    don't find this pure and uncorrupt?
CREON: Never. Once an enemy, never a friend,
    not even after death.
ANTIGONE: I was born to join in love, not hate —   590
    that is my nature.
CREON: Go down below and love,
    if love you must — love the dead! While I'm alive,
    no woman is going to lord it over me.

(Enter Ismene from the palace, under guard.)

CHORUS: Look,
    Ismene's coming, weeping a sister's tears,
    loving sister, under a cloud . . .   595
    her face is flushed, her cheeks streaming.
    Sorrow puts her lovely radiance in the dark.
CREON: You—
    in my own house, you viper, slinking undetected,
    sucking my life-blood! I never knew
    I was breeding twin disasters, the two of you   600
    rising up against my throne. Come, tell me,
    will you confess your part in the crime or not?
    Answer me. Swear to me.
ISMENE: I did it, yes—
    if only she consents—I share the guilt,
    the consequences too.
ANTIGONE: No,   605
    Justice will never suffer that—not you,
    you were unwilling. I never brought you in.
ISMENE: But now you face such dangers . . . I'm not ashamed
    to sail through trouble with you,
    make your troubles mine.
ANTIGONE: Who did the work?   610
    Let the dead and the god of death bear witness!
    I have no love for a friend who loves in words alone.
ISMENE: Oh no, my sister, don't reject me, please,
    let me die beside you, consecrating
    the dead together.
ANTIGONE: Never share my dying,   615
    don't lay claim to what you never touched.
    My death will be enough.
ISMENE: What do I care for life, cut off from you?
ANTIGONE: Ask Creon. Your concern is all for him.
ISMENE: Why abuse me so? It doesn't help you now.
ANTIGONE: You're right—   620
    if I mock you, I get no pleasure from it,
    only pain.
ISMENE: Tell me, dear one,
    what can I do to help you, even now?
ANTIGONE: Save yourself. I don't grudge you your survival.
ISMENE: Oh no, no, denied my portion in your death?   625
ANTIGONE: You chose to live, I chose to die.
ISMENE: Not, at least,
    without every kind of caution I could voice.
ANTIGONE: Your wisdom appealed to one world—mine, another.
ISMENE: But look, we're both guilty, both condemned to death.

ANTIGONE: Courage! Live your life. I gave myself to death,   630
    long ago, so I might serve the dead.
CREON: They're both mad, I tell you, the two of them.
    One's just shown it, the other's been that way
    since she was born.
ISMENE: True, my king,
    the sense we were born with cannot last forever . . .   635
    commit cruelty on a person long enough
    and the mind begins to go.
CREON: Yours did,
    when you chose to commit your crimes with her.
ISMENE: How can I live alone, without her?
CREON: Her?
    Don't even mention her — she no longer exists.   640
ISMENE: What? You'd kill your own son's bride?
CREON: Absolutely:
    there are other fields for him to plow.
ISMENE: Perhaps,
    but never as true, as close a bond as theirs.
CREON: A worthless woman for my son? It repels me.
ISMENE: Dearest Haemon, your father wrongs you so!   645
CREON: Enough, enough — you and your talk of marriage!
ISMENE: Creon — you're really going to rob your son of Antigone?
CREON: Death will do it for me — break their marriage off.
LEADER: So, it's settled then? Antigone must die?
CREON: Settled, yes — we both know that.   650

(*To the guards.*)

    Stop wasting time. Take them in.
    From now on they'll act like women.
    Tie them up, no more running loose;
    even the bravest will cut and run,
    once they see Death coming for their lives.   655

(*The guards escort Antigone and Ismene into the palace. Creon remains while the old citizens form their chorus.*)

CHORUS: Blest, they are the truly blest who all their lives
    have never tasted devastation. For others, once
    the gods have rocked a house to its foundations
        the ruin will never cease, cresting on and on
    from one generation on throughout the race —   660
    like a great mounting tide
    driven on by savage northern gales,
        surging over the dead black depths
    roiling up from the bottom dark heaves of sand

and the headlands, taking the storm's onslaught full-force, 665
roar, and the low moaning
                       echoes on and on
                            and now
as in ancient times I see the sorrows of the house,
the living heirs of the old ancestral kings,
piling on the sorrows of the dead
      and one generation cannot free the next— 670
some god will bring them crashing down,
the race finds no release.
And now the light, the hope
          springing up from the late last root
in the house of Oedipus, that hope's cut down in turn 675
by the long, bloody knife swung by the gods of death
by a senseless word
               by fury at the heart.
                             Zeus,
yours is the power, Zeus, what man on earth
can override it, who can hold it back?
Power that neither Sleep, the all-ensnaring 680
      no, nor the tireless months of heaven
can ever overmaster—young through all time,
mighty lord of power, you hold fast
      the dazzling crystal mansions of Olympus.
And throughout the future, late and soon 685
as through the past, your law prevails:
no towering form of greatness
         enters into the lives of mortals
                  free and clear of ruin.
                          True,
our dreams, our high hopes voyaging far and wide 690
bring sheer delight to many, to many others
      delusion, blithe, mindless lusts
and the fraud steals on one slowly . . . unaware
till he trips and puts his foot into the fire.
      He was a wise old man who coined 695
the famous saying: "Sooner or later
foul is fair, fair is foul
to the man the gods will ruin"—
      He goes his way for a moment only
                 free of blinding ruin. 700

(*Enter Haemon from the palace.*)

    Here's Haemon now, the last of all your sons.
    Does he come in tears for his bride,

his doomed bride, Antigone —
bitter at being cheated of their marriage?
CREON: We'll soon know, better than seers could tell us.   705

(*Turning to Haemon.*)

Son, you've heard the final verdict on your bride?
Are you coming now, raving against your father?
Or do you love me, no matter what I do?
HAEMON: Father, I'm your *son* . . . you in your wisdom
set my bearings for me — I obey you.   710
No marriage could ever mean more to me than you,
whatever good direction you may offer.
CREON: Fine, Haemon.
That's how you ought to feel within your heart,
subordinate to your father's will in every way.
That's what a man prays for: to produce good sons —   715
a household full of them, dutiful and attentive,
so they can pay his enemy back with interest
and match the respect their father shows his friend.
But the man who rears a brood of useless children,
what has he brought into the world, I ask you?   720
Nothing but trouble for himself, and mockery
from his enemies laughing in his face.
                                              Oh Haemon,
never lose your sense of judgment over a woman.
The warmth, the rush of pleasure, it all goes cold
in your arms, I warn you . . . a worthless woman   725
in your house, a misery in your bed.
What wound cuts deeper than a loved one
turned against you? Spit her out,
like a mortal enemy — let the girl go.
Let her find a husband down among the dead.   730

Imagine it: I caught her in naked rebellion,
the traitor, the only one in the whole city.
I'm not about to prove myself a liar,
not to my people, no, I'm going to kill her!
That's right — so let her cry for mercy, sing her hymns   735
to Zeus who defends all bonds of kindred blood.
Why, if I bring up my own kin to be rebels,
think what I'd suffer from the world at large.
Show me the man who rules his household well:
I'll show you someone fit to rule the state.   740
That good man, my son,
I have every confidence he and he alone

can give commands and take them too. Staunch
in the storm of spears he'll stand his ground,
a loyal, unflinching comrade at your side.   745

But whoever steps out of line, violates the laws
or presumes to hand out orders to his superiors,
he'll win no praise from me. But that man
the city places in authority, his orders
must be obeyed, large and small,   750
right and wrong.
     Anarchy—
show me a greater crime in all the earth!
She, she destroys cities, rips up houses,
breaks the ranks of spearmen into headlong rout.
But the ones who last it out, the great mass of them   755
owe their lives to discipline. Therefore
we must defend the men who live by law,
never let some woman triumph over us.
Better to fall from power, if fall we must,
at the hands of a man—never be rated   760
inferior to a woman, never.

LEADER: To us,
 unless old age has robbed us of our wits,
 you seem to say what you have to say with sense.

HAEMON: Father, only the gods endow a man with reason,
 the finest of all their gifts, a treasure.   765
 Far be it from me—I haven't the skill,
 and certainly no desire, to tell you when,
 if ever, you make a slip in speech . . . though
 someone else might have a good suggestion.

 Of course it's not for you,   770
 in the normal run of things, to watch
 whatever men say or do, or find to criticize.
 The man in the street, you know, dreads your glance,
 he'd never say anything displeasing to your face.
 But it's for me to catch the murmurs in the dark,   775
 the way the city mourns for this young girl.
 "No woman," they say, "ever deserved death less,
 and such a brutal death for such a glorious action.
 She, with her own dear brother lying in his blood—
 she couldn't bear to leave him dead, unburied,   780
 food for the wild dogs or wheeling vultures.
 Death? She deserves a glowing crown of gold!"
 So they say, and the rumor spreads in secret,
 darkly . . .

I rejoice in your success, father—
nothing more precious to me in the world.   785
What medal of honor brighter to his children
than a father's growing glory? Or a child's
to his proud father? Now don't, please,
be quite so single-minded, self-involved,
or assume the world is wrong and you are right.   790
Whoever thinks that he alone possesses intelligence,
the gift of eloquence, he and no one else,
and character too . . . such men, I tell you,
spread them open—you will find them empty.

                                                        No,
it's no disgrace for a man, even a wise man,   795
to learn many things and not to be too rigid.
You've seen trees by a raging winter torrent,
how many sway with the flood and salvage every twig,
but not the stubborn—they're ripped out, roots and all.
Bend or break. The same when a man is sailing: 800
haul your sheets too taut, never give an inch,
you'll capsize, go the rest of the voyage
keel up and the rowing-benches under.

Oh give way. Relax your anger—change!
I'm young, I know, but let me offer this: 805
it would be best by far, I admit,
if a man were born infallible, right by nature.
If not—and things don't often go that way,
it's best to learn from those with good advice.

LEADER: You'd do well, my lord, if he's speaking to the point,   810
    to learn from him,

(*Turning to Haemon.*)

                    and you, my boy, from him.
    You both are talking sense.
CREON: So,
    men our age, we're to be lectured, are we?—
    schooled by a boy his age?
HAEMON: Only in what is right. But if I seem young,   815
    look less to my years and more to what I do.
CREON: Do? Is admiring rebels an achievement?
HAEMON: I'd never suggest that you admire treason.
CREON: Oh?—
    isn't that just the sickness that's attacked her?
HAEMON: The whole city of Thebes denies it, to a man.   820
CREON: And is Thebes about to tell me how to rule?
HAEMON: Now, you see? Who's talking like a child?

CREON: Am I to rule this land for others — or myself?

HAEMON: It's no city at all, owned by one man alone.

CREON: What? The city *is* the king's — that's the law!   825

HAEMON: What a splendid king you'd make of a desert island —
    you and you alone.

CREON:

(To the Chorus.)

               This boy, I do believe,
    is fighting on her side, the woman's side.

HAEMON: If you are a woman, yes;
    my concern is all for you.   830

CREON: Why, you degenerate — bandying accusations,
    threatening me with justice, your own father!

HAEMON: I see my father offending justice — wrong.

CREON: Wrong?
    To protect my royal rights?

HAEMON: Protect your rights?
    When you trample down the honors of the gods?   835

CREON: You, you soul of corruption, rotten through —
    woman's accomplice!

HAEMON: That may be,
    but you will never find me accomplice to a criminal.

CREON: That's what *she* is,
    and every word you say is a blatant appeal for her —   840

HAEMON: And you, and me, and the gods beneath the earth.

CREON: You will never marry her, not while she's alive.

HAEMON: Then she'll die . . . but her death will kill another.

CREON: What, brazen threats? You go too far!

HAEMON: What threat?
    Combating your empty, mindless judgments with a word?   845

CREON: You'll suffer for your sermons, you and your empty wisdom!

HAEMON: If you weren't my father, I'd say you were insane.

CREON: Don't flatter me with Father — you woman's slave!

HAEMON: You really expect to fling abuse at me
    and not receive the same?

CREON: Is that so!   850
    Now, by heaven, I promise you, you'll pay —
    taunting, insulting me! Bring her out,
    that hateful — she'll die now, here,
    in front of his eyes, beside her groom!

HAEMON: No, no, she will never die beside me —   855
    don't delude yourself. And you will never
    see me, never set eyes on my face again.
    Rage your heart out, rage with friends
    who can stand the sight of you.

(*Rushing out.*)

LEADER: Gone, my king, in a burst of anger.   860
A temper young as his . . . hurt him once,
he may do something violent.
CREON: Let him do —
dream up something desperate, past all human limit!
Good riddance. Rest assured,
he'll never save those two young girls from death.   865
LEADER: Both of them, you really intend to kill them both?
CREON: No, not her, the one whose hands are clean —
you're quite right.
LEADER: But Antigone —
what sort of death do you have in mind for her?
CREON: I will take her down some wild, desolate path   870
never trod by men, and wall her up alive
in a rocky vault, and set out short rations,
just the measure piety demands
to keep the entire city free of defilement.
There let her pray to the one god she worships: 875
Death — who knows? — may just reprieve her from death.
Or she may learn at last, better late than never,
what a waste of breath it is to worship Death.

(*Exit to the palace.*)

CHORUS: Love, never conquered in battle
Love the plunderer laying waste the rich!   880
Love standing the night-watch
            guarding a girl's soft cheek,
you range the seas, the shepherds' steadings off in the wilds —
not even the deathless gods can flee your onset,
nothing human born for a day —   885
whoever feels your grip is driven mad.
                    Love! —
you wrench the minds of the righteous into outrage,
swerve them to their ruin — you have ignited this,
this kindred strife, father and son at war
            and Love alone the victor —   890
warm glance of the bride triumphant, burning with desire!
Throned in power, side-by-side with the mighty laws!
Irresistible Aphrodite,° never conquered —
Love, you mock us for your sport.

(*Antigone is brought from the palace under guard.*)

---

893. Aphrodite: Goddess of love.

But now, even I would rebel against the king,   895
  I would break all bounds when I see this —
I fill with tears, I cannot hold them back,
  not any more . . . I see Antigone make her way
  to the bridal vault where all are laid to rest.

ANTIGONE: Look at me, men of my fatherland,   900
    setting out on the last road
  looking into the last light of day
  the last I'll ever see . . .
  the god of death who puts us all to bed
  takes me down to the banks of Acheron° alive —   905
    denied my part in the wedding-songs,
  no wedding-song in the dusk has crowned my marriage —
  I go to wed the lord of the dark waters.

CHORUS: Not crowned with glory, or with a dirge,
    you leave for the deep pit of the dead.   910
  No withering illness laid you low,
  no strokes of the sword — a law to yourself,
  alone, no mortal like you, ever, you go down
  to the halls of Death alive and breathing.

ANTIGONE: But think of Niobe° — well I know her story —   915
    think what a living death she died,
  Tantalus' daughter, stranger queen from the east:
  there on the mountain heights, growing stone
  binding as ivy, slowly walled her round
  and the rains will never cease, the legends say   920
  the snows will never leave her . . .
    wasting away, under her brows the tears
  showering down her breasting ridge and slopes —
  a rocky death like hers puts me to sleep.

CHORUS: But she was a god, born of gods,   925
    and we are only mortals born to die.
  And yet, of course, it's a great thing
  for a dying girl to hear, just to hear
  she shares a destiny equal to the gods,
  during life and later, once she's dead.

ANTIGONE: O you mock me!   930
  Why, in the name of all my fathers' gods
  why can't you wait till I am gone —
    must you abuse me to my face?

---

905. Acheron: A river in the underworld, the realm of the dead.   **915. Niobe:** A queen of
Thebes who boasted that she had more children than Leto, mother of Apollo and Artemis. To
punish her, Apollo and Artemis killed her children, and she was turned into a rock on Mount
Sipylus, where she weeps constantly.

O my city, all your fine rich sons!
And you, you springs of the Dirce,   935
holy grove of Thebes where the chariots gather,
          you at least, you'll bear me witness, look,
unmourned by friends and forced by such crude laws
I go to my rockbound prison, strange new tomb —
     always a stranger, O dear god,   940
I have no home on earth and none below,
          not with the living, not with the breathless dead.

CHORUS: You went too far, the last limits of daring —
     smashing against the high throne of Justice!
          Your life's in ruins, child — I wonder . . .   945
do you pay for your father's terrible ordeal?

ANTIGONE: There — at last you've touched it, the worst pain
     the worst anguish! Raking up the grief for father
          three times over, for all the doom
that's struck us down, the brilliant house of Laius.   950
O mother, your marriage-bed
the coiling horrors, the coupling there —
     you with your own son, my father — doomstruck mother!
Such, such were my parents, and I their wretched child.
I go to them now, cursed, unwed, to share their home —   955
     I am a stranger! O dear brother, doomed
in your marriage — your marriage° murders mine,
          your dying drags me down to death alive!

(Enter Creon.)

CHORUS: Reverence asks some reverence in return —
     but attacks on power never go unchecked,   960
          not by the man who holds the reins of power.
     Your own blind will, your passion has destroyed you.

ANTIGONE: No one to weep for me, my friends,
     no wedding-song — they take me away
          in all my pain . . . the road lies open, waiting.   965
     Never again, the law forbids me to see
     the sacred eye of day. I am agony!
     No tears for the destiny that's mine,
          no loved one mourns my death.

CREON: Can't you see?
     If a man could wail his own dirge before he dies,   970
     he'd never finish.

---

957. your marriage: Polynices had married a daughter of Adrastus, king of Argos, to forge
their alliance to overcome Eteocles.

(*To the guards.*)

                 Take her away, quickly!
Wall her up in the tomb, you have your orders.
Abandon her there, alone, and let her choose —
death or a buried life with a good roof for shelter.
As for myself, my hands are clean. This young girl —   975
dead or alive, she will be stripped of her rights,
her stranger's° rights, here in the world above.

ANTIGONE: O tomb, my bridal-bed — my house, my prison
cut in the hollow rock, my everlasting watch!
I'll soon be there, soon embrace my own,   980
the great growing family of our dead
Persephone° has received among her ghosts.

                              I,

the last of them all, the most reviled by far,
go down before my destined time's run out.
But still I go, cherishing one good hope: 985
my arrival may be dear to father,
dear to you, my mother,
dear to you, my loving brother, Eteocles —
When you died I washed you with my hands,
I dressed you all, I poured the cups   990
across your tombs. But now, Polynices,
because I laid your body out as well,
this, this is my reward. Nevertheless
I honored you — the decent will admit it —
well and wisely too.

                    Never, I tell you,   995
if I had been the mother of children
or if my husband died, exposed and rotting —
I'd never have taken this ordeal upon myself,
never defied our people's will. What law,
you ask, do I satisfy with what I say?   1000
A husband dead, there might have been another.
A child by another too, if I had lost the first.
But mother and father both lost in the halls of Death,
no brother could ever spring to light again.
For this law alone I held you first in honor.   1005
For this, Creon, the king, judges me a criminal
guilty of dreadful outrage, my dear brother!
And now he leads me off, a captive in his hands,

---

977. stranger's: Because of her disobedience, Creon treats Antigone as a traitor, no longer a citizen. **982. Persephone:** Daughter of Demeter, abducted by Pluto, god of the underworld, to be his queen.

with no part in the bridal-song, the bridal-bed,
denied all joy of marriage, raising children —   1010
deserted so by loved ones, struck by fate,
I descend alive to the caverns of the dead.

What law of the mighty gods have I transgressed?
Why look to the heavens any more, tormented as I am?
Whom to call, what comrades now? Just think,   1015
my reverence only brands me for irreverence!
Very well: if this is the pleasure of the gods,
once I suffer I will know that I was wrong.
But if these men are wrong, let them suffer
nothing worse than they mete out to me —   1020
these masters of injustice!

LEADER: Still the same rough winds, the wild passion
raging through the girl.

CREON:

(*To the guards.*)

Take her away.
You're wasting time — you'll pay for it too.

ANTIGONE: Oh god, the voice of death. It's come, it's here.   1025

CREON: True. Not a word of hope — your doom is sealed.

ANTIGONE: Land of Thebes, city of all my fathers —
O you gods, the first gods of the race!
They drag me away, now, no more delay.
Look on me, you noble sons of Thebes —   1030
the last of a great line of kings,
I alone, see what I suffer now
at the hands of what breed of men —
all for reverence, my reverence for the gods!

(*She leaves under guard; the Chorus gathers.*)

CHORUS: Danaë, Danaë° —   1035
even she endured a fate like yours,
in all her lovely strength she traded
the light of day for the bolted brazen vault —
buried within her tomb, her bridal-chamber,
wed to the yoke and broken.   1040
But she was of glorious birth
my child, my child
and treasured the seed of Zeus within her womb,

1035. **Danaë**: Daughter of Acrisius, king of Argos, who imprisoned her in a bronze tower because of a prophecy that he would be killed by his daughter's son. Zeus entered the tower as a golden rain shower and she bore a son, Perseus, by whose hands Acrisius eventually was killed.

the cloudburst streaming gold!
    The power of fate is a wonder,   1045
    dark, terrible wonder —
    neither wealth nor armies
    towered walls nor ships
    black hulls lashed by the salt
    can save us from that force.   1050

The yoke tamed him too
    young Lycurgus° flaming in anger
king of Edonia, all for his mad taunts
Dionysus clamped him down, encased
in the chain-mail of rock   1055
    and there his rage
            his terrible flowering rage burst —
sobbing, dying away . . . at last that madman
came to know his god —
       the power he mocked, the power   1060
       he taunted in all his frenzy
       trying to stamp out
       the women strong with the god —
       the torch, the raving sacred cries —
       enraging the Muses° who adore the flute.   1065

And far north where the Black Rocks
       cut the sea in half
and murderous straits
split the coast of Thrace
      a forbidding city stands   1070
where once, hard by the walls
the savage Ares thrilled to watch
a king's new queen,° a Fury rearing in rage
    against his two royal sons —
       her bloody hands, her dagger-shuttle   1075
stabbing out their eyes — cursed, blinding wounds —
their eyes blind sockets screaming for revenge!

They wailed in agony, cries echoing cries
      the princes doomed at birth . . .
and their mother doomed to chains,   1080

1052. Lycurgus: Thracian king imprisoned and driven mad by Dionysus because he would not worship him.   **1065. the Muses:** Nine sister goddesses who preside over the arts.   **1073. a king's new queen:** Phineas, a Thracian king, abandoned his first wife, Cleopatra, daughter of the Athenian princess Orithyia, and imprisoned her in a cave. The king's new wife, Eidothea, blinded Cleopatra's two sons in order to solidify her children's claim to succeed Phineas. Ares, who was born in Thrace, watched her savage deed with pleasure.

walled up in a tomb of stone —
  but she traced her own birth back
to a proud Athenian line and the high gods
and off in caverns half the world away,
born of the wild North Wind   1085
  she sprang on her father's gales,
    racing stallions up the leaping cliffs —
child of the heavens. But even on her the Fates
the gray everlasting Fates rode hard
my child, my child.

(*Enter Tiresias, the blind prophet, led by a boy.*)

TIRESIAS: Lords of Thebes,   1090
  I and the boy have come together,
  hand in hand. Two see with the eyes of one . . .
  so the blind must go, with a guide to lead the way.
CREON: What is it, old Tiresias? What news now?
TIRESIAS: I will teach you. And you obey the seer.
CREON: I will,   1095
  I've never wavered from your advice before.
TIRESIAS: And so you kept the city straight on course.
CREON: I owe you a great deal, I swear to that.
TIRESIAS: Then reflect, my son: you are poised,
  once more, on the razor-edge of fate.   1100
CREON: What is it? I shudder to hear you.
TIRESIAS: You will learn
  when you listen to the warnings of my craft.
  As I sat on the ancient seat of augury,°
  in the sanctuary where every bird I know
  will hover at my hands — suddenly I heard it,   1105
  a strange voice in the wingbeats, unintelligible,
  barbaric, a mad scream! Talons flashing, ripping,
  they were killing each other — that much I knew —
  the murderous fury whirring in those wings
  made that much clear!
                    I was afraid,   1110
  I turned quickly, tested the burnt-sacrifice,
  ignited the altar at all points — but no fire,
  the god in the fire never blazed.
  Not from those offerings . . . over the embers
  slid a heavy ooze from the long thighbones,   1115
  smoking, sputtering out, and the bladder
  puffed and burst — spraying gall into the air —

1103. **seat of augury:** Where Tiresias sought omens among the birds.

and the fat wrapping the bones slithered off
and left them glistening white. No fire!
The rites failed that might have blazed the future   1120
with a sign. So I learned from the boy here:
he is my guide, as I am guide to others.

                          And it is you—
your high resolve that sets this plague on Thebes.
The public altars and sacred hearths are fouled,
one and all, by the birds and dogs with carrion   1125
torn from the corpse, the doomstruck son of Oedipus!
And so the gods are deaf to our prayers, they spurn
the offerings in our hands, the flame of holy flesh.
No birds cry out an omen clear and true—
they're gorged with the murdered victim's blood and fat.   1130
Take these things to heart, my son, I warn you.
All men make mistakes, it is only human.
But once the wrong is done, a man
can turn his back on folly, misfortune too,
if he tries to make amends, however low he's fallen,   1135
and stops his bullnecked ways. Stubbornness
brands you for stupidity—pride is a crime.
No, yield to the dead!
Never stab the fighter when he's down.
Where's the glory, killing the dead twice over?   1140

I mean you well. I give you sound advice.
It's best to learn from a good adviser
when he speaks for your own good:
it's pure gain.
CREON: Old man—all of you! So,
you shoot your arrows at my head like archers at the target—   1145
I even have *him* loosed on me, this fortune-teller.
Oh his ilk has tried to sell me short
and ship me off for years. Well,
drive your bargains, traffic—much as you like—
in the gold of India, silver-gold of Sardis.°   1150
You'll never bury that body in the grave,
not even if Zeus's eagles rip the corpse
and wing their rotten pickings off to the throne of god!
Never, not even in fear of such defilement
will I tolerate his burial, that traitor.   1155
Well I know, we can't defile the gods—

1150. silver-gold of Sardis: Electrum, pale gold containing a considerable alloy of silver, found by some rivers in Asia Minor, especially the Pactolus, which ran through ancient Sardis.

no mortal has the power.
                                No,
reverend old Tiresias, all men fall,
it's only human, but the wisest fall obscenely
when they glorify obscene advice with rhetoric —   1160
all for their own gain.

TIRESIAS: Oh god, is there a man alive
    who knows, who actually believes . . .

CREON: What now?
    What earth-shattering truth are you about to utter?

TIRESIAS: . . . just how much a sense of judgment, wisdom   1165
    is the greatest gift we have?

CREON: Just as much, I'd say,
    as a twisted mind is the worst affliction going.

TIRESIAS: You are the one who's sick, Creon, sick to death.

CREON: I am in no mood to trade insults with a seer.

TIRESIAS: You have already, calling my prophecies a lie.

CREON: Why not?   1170
    You and the whole breed of seers are mad for money!

TIRESIAS: And the whole race of tyrants lusts for filthy gain.

CREON: This slander of yours —
    are you aware you're speaking to the king?

TIRESIAS: Well aware. Who helped you save the city?

CREON: You —   1175
    you have your skills, old seer, but you lust for injustice!

TIRESIAS: You will drive me to utter the dreadful secret in my heart.

CREON: Spit it out! Just don't speak it out for profit.

TIRESIAS: Profit? No, not a bit of profit, not for you.

CREON: Know full well, you'll never buy off my resolve.   1180

TIRESIAS: Then know this too, learn this by heart!
    The chariot of the sun will not race through
    so many circuits more, before you have surrendered
    one born of your own loins, your own flesh and blood,
    a corpse for corpses given in return, since you have thrust   1185
    to the world below a child sprung for the world above,
    ruthlessly lodged a living soul within the grave —
    then you've robbed the gods below the earth,
    keeping a dead body here in the bright air,
    unburied, unsung, unhallowed by the rites.   1190

    You, you have no business with the dead,
    nor do the gods above — this is violence
    you have forced upon the heavens.
    And so the avengers, the dark destroyers late
    but true to the mark, now lie in wait for you,   1195

the Furies° sent by the gods and the god of death
to strike you down with the pains that you perfected!

There. Reflect on that, tell me I've been bribed.
The day comes soon, no long test of time, not now,
when the mourning cries for men and women break   1200
throughout your halls. Great hatred rises against you —
cities in tumult, all whose mutilated sons
the dogs have graced with burial, or the wild beasts
or a wheeling crow that wings the ungodly stench of carrion
back to each city, each warrior's hearth and home.   1205

These arrows for your heart! Since you've raked me
I loose them like an archer in my anger,
arrows deadly true. You'll never escape
their burning, searing force.

(*Motioning to his escort.*)

    Come, boy, take me home.   1210
So he can vent his rage on younger men,
and learn to keep a gentler tongue in his head
and better sense than what he carries now.

(*Exit to the side.*)

LEADER: The old man's gone, my king —
    terrible prophecies. Well I know,   1215
since the hair on this old head went gray,
he's never lied to Thebes.
CREON: I know it myself — I'm shaken, torn.
    It's a dreadful thing to yield . . . but resist now?
    Lay my pride bare to the blows of ruin?   1220
    That's dreadful too.
LEADER: But good advice,
    Creon, take it now, you must.
CREON: What should I do? Tell me . . . I'll obey.
LEADER: Go! Free the girl from the rocky vault
    and raise a mound for the body you exposed.   1225
CREON: That's your advice? You think I should give in?
LEADER: Yes, my king, quickly. Disasters sent by the gods
    cut short our follies in a flash.
CREON: Oh it's hard.
    giving up the heart's desire . . . but I will do it —

1196. the Furies: Female spirits who avenge wrongdoing, especially crimes committed against
close relations.

no more fighting a losing battle with necessity.   1230
LEADER: Do it now, go, don't leave it to others.
CREON: Now—I'm on my way! Come, each of you,
    take up axes, make for the high ground,
    over there, quickly! I and my better judgment
    have come round to this—I shackled her,   1235
    I'll set her free myself. I am afraid . . .
    it's best to keep the established laws
    to the very day we die.

(*Rushing out, followed by his entourage. The Chorus clusters around the altar.*)

CHORUS: God of a hundred names!°
                       Great Dionysus—
       Son and glory of Semele! Pride of Thebes—   1240
Child of Zeus whose thunder rocks the clouds—
Lord of the famous lands of evening—
King of the Mysteries!
                King of Eleusis,° Demeter's plain
her breasting hills that welcome in the world—
Great Dionysus!
             Bacchus,° living in Thebes   1245
the mother-city of all your frenzied women—
                  Bacchus
    living along the Ismenus'° rippling waters
standing over the field sown with the Dragon's teeth!

You—we have seen you through the flaring smoky fires,
    your torches blazing over the twin peaks   1250
where nymphs of the hallowed cave climb onward
              fired with you, your sacred rage—
we have seen you at Castalia's running spring°
and down from the heights of Nysa° crowned with ivy
the greening shore rioting vines and grapes   1255
    down you come in your storm of wild women
        ecstatic, mystic cries—
               Dionysus—
down to watch and ward the roads of Thebes!

1238–48. God of a hundred names . . . the Dragon's teeth: A litany of names for Dionysus.
1243. Eleusis: Site near Athens for the worship of Demeter, goddess of grain and harvests, where young men were initiated into the rites of Dionysus. 1245. Bacchus: Yet another of Dionysus's names. 1247. Ismenus: River near which Cadmus sowed the dragon seeds that gave birth to the founders of Thebes. 1253. Castalia's running spring: Spring on Mount Parnassus sacred to Apollo and the Muses. 1254. heights of Nysa: Cliffs above Delphi where Dionysus spent the winter months.

First of all cities, Thebes you honor first
you and your mother, bride of the lightning—   1260
come, Dionysus! now your people lie
in the iron grip of plague,
come in your racing, healing stride
           down Parnassus'° slopes
or across the moaning straits.
                  Lord of the dancing—   1265
dance, dance the constellations breathing fire!
Great master of the voices of the night!
Child of Zeus, God's offspring, come, come forth!
Lord, king, dance with your nymphs, swirling, raving
arm-in-arm in frenzy through the night   1270
     they dance you, Iacchus°—
               Dance, Dionysus
  giver of all good things!

(*Enter a Messenger from the side.*)

MESSENGER: Neighbors,
  friends of the house of Cadmus° and the kings,
there's not a thing in this life of ours
I'd praise or blame as settled once for all.   1275
Fortune lifts and Fortune fells the lucky
and unlucky every day. No prophet on earth
can tell a man his fate. Take Creon:
there was a man to rouse your envy once,
as I see it. He saved the realm from enemies;   1280
taking power, he alone, the lord of the fatherland,
he set us true on course—flourished like a tree
with the noble line of sons he bred and reared . . .
and now it's lost, all gone.
              Believe me,
when a man has squandered his true joys,   1285
he's good as dead, I tell you, a living corpse.
Pile up riches in your house, as much as you like—
live like a king with a huge show of pomp,
but if real delight is missing from the lot,
I wouldn't give you a wisp of smoke for it,   1290
not compared with joy.

LEADER: What now?
  What new grief do you bring the house of kings?

MESSENGER: Dead, dead—and the living are guilty of their death!

1264. **Parnassus:** Mountain in Greece sacred to the gods. **1271. Iacchus:** Dionysus (Bacchus). **1273. Cadmus:** According to tradition, the founder of Thebes.

LEADER: Who's the murderer? Who is dead? Tell us.

MESSENGER: Haemon's gone, his blood spilled by the very hand —   1295

LEADER: His father's or his own?

MESSENGER: His own . . .

   raging mad with his father for the death —

LEADER: Oh great seer,

   you saw it all, you brought your word to birth!

MESSENGER: Those are the facts. Deal with them as you will.

(As he turns to go, Eurydice enters from the palace.)

LEADER: Look, Eurydice. Poor woman, Creon's wife,   1300

   so close at hand. By chance perhaps,

   unless she's heard the news about her son.

EURYDICE: My countrymen,

   all of you — I caught the sound of your words

   as I was leaving to do my part,

   to appeal to queen Athena° with my prayers.   1305

   I was just loosing the bolts, opening the doors,

   when a voice filled with sorrow, family sorrow,

   struck my ears, and I fell back, terrified,

   into the women's arms — everything went black.

   Tell me the news, again, whatever it is . . .   1310

   sorrow and I are hardly strangers;

   I can bear the worst.

MESSENGER: I — dear lady,

   I'll speak as an eye-witness. I was there.

   And I won't pass over one word of the truth.

   Why should I try to soothe you with a story,   1315

   only to prove a liar in a moment?

   Truth is always best.

                    So,

   I escorted your lord, I guided him

   to the edge of the plain where the body lay,

   Polynices, torn by the dogs and still unmourned.   1320

   And saying a prayer to Hecate° of the Crossroads,

   Pluto° too, to hold their anger and be kind,

   we washed the dead in a bath of holy water

   and plucking some fresh branches, gathering . . .

   what was left of him, we burned them all together   1325

   and raised a high mound of native earth, and then

   we turned and made for that rocky vault of hers,

   the hollow, empty bed of the bride of Death.

1305. Athena: Goddess of wisdom.   **1321–22. Hecate, Pluto:** Gods of the underworld.
Offerings to Hecate were left at crossroads.

And far off, one of us heard a voice,
a long wail rising, echoing   1330
out of that unhallowed wedding-chamber;
he ran to alert the master and Creon pressed on,
closer—the strange, inscrutable cry came sharper,
throbbing around him now, and he let loose
a cry of his own, enough to wrench the heart,   1335
"Oh god, am I the prophet now? going down
the darkest road I've ever gone? My son—
it's *his* dear voice, he greets me! Go, men,
closer, quickly! Go through the gap,
the rocks are dragged back—   1340
right to the tomb's very mouth—and look,
see if it's Haemon's voice I think I hear,
or the gods have robbed me of my senses."

The king was shattered. We took his orders,
went and searched, and there in the deepest,   1345
dark recesses of the tomb we found her . . .
hanged by the neck in a fine linen noose,
strangled in her veils—and the boy,
his arms flung around her waist,
clinging to her, wailing for his bride,   1350
dead and down below, for his father's crimes
and the bed of his marriage blighted by misfortune.
When Creon saw him, he gave a deep sob,
he ran in, shouting, crying out to him,
"Oh my child—what have you done? what seized you,   1355
what insanity? what disaster drove you mad?
Come out, my son! I beg you on my knees!"
But the boy gave him a wild burning glance,
spat in his face, not a word in reply,
he drew his sword—his father rushed out,   1360
running as Haemon lunged and missed!—
and then, doomed, desperate with himself,
suddenly leaning his full weight on the blade,
he buried it in his body, halfway to the hilt.
And still in his senses, pouring his arms around her,   1365
he embraced the girl and breathing hard,
released a quick rush of blood,
bright red on her cheek glistening white.
And there he lies, body enfolding body . . .
he has won his bride at last, poor boy,   1370
not here but in the houses of the dead.

Creon shows the world that of all the ills
afflicting men the worst is lack of judgment.

(*Eurydice turns and reenters the palace.*)

LEADER: What do you make of that? The lady's gone,
    without a word, good or bad.
MESSENGER: I'm alarmed too   1375
    but here's my hope — faced with her son's death,
    she finds it unbecoming to mourn in public.
    Inside, under her roof, she'll set her women
    to the task and wail the sorrow of the house.
    She's too discreet. She won't do something rash.   1380
LEADER: I'm not so sure. To me, at least,
    a long heavy silence promises danger,
    just as much as a lot of empty outcries.
MESSENGER: We'll see if she's holding something back,
    hiding some passion in her heart.   1385
    I'm going in. You may be right — who knows?
    Even too much silence has its dangers.

(*Exit to the palace. Enter Creon from the side, escorted by attendants carrying Haemon's body on a bier.*)

LEADER: The king himself! Coming toward us,
    look, holding the boy's head in his hands.
    Clear, damning proof, if it's right to say so —   1390
    proof of his own madness, no one else's,
        no, his own blind wrongs.
CREON: Ohhh,
    so senseless, so insane . . . my crimes,
    my stubborn, deadly —
    Look at us, the killer, the killed,   1395
    father and son, the same blood — the misery!
    My plans, my mad fanatic heart,
    my son, cut off so young!
    Ai, dead, lost to the world,
    not through your stupidity, no, my own.
LEADER: Too late,   1400
    too late, you see what justice means.
CREON: Oh I've learned
    through blood and tears! Then, it was then,
    when the god came down and struck me — a great weight
    shattering, driving me down that wild savage path,
    ruining, trampling down my joy. Oh the agony,   1405
        the heartbreaking agonies of our lives.

(*Enter the Messenger from the palace.*)

MESSENGER: Master,
    what a hoard of grief you have, and you'll have more.
    The grief that lies to hand you've brought yourself—

(*Pointing to Haemon's body.*)

    the rest, in the house, you'll see it all too soon.
CREON: What now? What's worse than this?
MESSENGER: The queen is dead.   1410
    The mother of this dead boy . . . mother to the end—
    poor thing, her wounds are fresh.
CREON: No, no,
    harbor of Death, so choked, so hard to cleanse!—
    why me? why are you killing me?
    Herald of pain, more words, more grief?   1415
    I died once, you kill me again and again!
    What's the report, boy . . . some news for me?
    My wife dead? O dear god!
    Slaughter heaped on slaughter?

(*The doors open; the body of Eurydice is brought out on her bier.*)

MESSENGER: See for yourself:
    now they bring her body from the palace.
CREON: Oh no,   1420
    another, a second loss to break the heart.
    What next, what fate still waits for me?
    I just held my son in my arms and now,
    look, a new corpse rising before my eyes—
        wretched, helpless mother—O my son!   1425
MESSENGER: She stabbed herself at the altar,
    then her eyes went dark, after she'd raised
    a cry for the noble fate of Megareus,° the hero
    killed in the first assault, then for Haemon,
    then with her dying breath she called down   1430
    torments on your head—you killed her sons.
CREON: Oh the dread,
    I shudder with dread! Why not kill me too?—
    run me through with a good sharp sword?
    Oh god, the misery, anguish—
    I, I'm churning with it, going under.   1435
MESSENGER: Yes, and the dead, the woman lying there,

1428. **Megareus:** Another son of Creon and Eurydice; he was killed in Polynices's attack on
Thebes.

piles the guilt of all their deaths on you.

CREON: How did she end her life, what bloody stroke?

MESSENGER: She drove home to the heart with her own hand,
once she learned her son was dead . . . that agony.   1440

CREON: And the guilt is all mine —
can never be fixed on another man,
no escape for me. I killed you,
I, god help me, I admit it all!

(To his attendants.)

Take me away, quickly, out of sight.   1445
I don't even exist — I'm no one. Nothing.

LEADER: Good advice, if there's any good in suffering.
Quickest is best when troubles block the way.

CREON:

(Kneeling in prayer.)

Come, let it come! — that best of fates for me
that brings the final day, best fate of all.   1450
Oh quickly, now —
so I never have to see another sunrise.

LEADER: That will come when it comes;
we must deal with all that lies before us.
The future rests with the ones who tend the future.   1455

CREON: That prayer — I poured my heart into that prayer!

LEADER: No more prayers now. For mortal men
there is no escape from the doom we must endure.

CREON: Take me away, I beg you, out of sight.
A rash, indiscriminate fool!   1460
I murdered you, my son, against my will —
you too, my wife . . .

Wailing wreck of a man,
whom to look to? where to lean for support?

(Desperately turning from Haemon to Eurydice on their biers.)

Whatever I touch goes wrong — once more
a crushing fate's come down upon my head.   1465

(The Messenger and attendants lead Creon into the palace.)

CHORUS: Wisdom is by far the greatest part of joy,
and reverence toward the gods must be safeguarded.
The mighty words of the proud are paid in full
with mighty blows of fate, and at long last
those blows will teach us wisdom.   1470

(The old citizens exit to the side.)

William Shakespeare 1564–1616

Hamlet, Prince of Denmark   [c. 1600]

[DRAMATIS PERSONAE

CLAUDIUS, *King of Denmark*
HAMLET, *son to the late King Hamlet, and nephew to the present King*
POLONIUS, *Lord Chamberlain*
HORATIO, *friend to Hamlet*
LAERTES, *son to Polonius*

VOLTIMAND,
CORNELIUS,
ROSENCRANTZ,   } *courtiers*
GUILDENSTERN,
OSRIC,
GENTLEMAN,

PRIEST, OR DOCTOR OF DIVINITY

MARCELLUS,   } *officers*
BERNARDO,

FRANCISCO, *a solider*
REYNALDO, *servant to Polonius*
PLAYERS
TWO CLOWNS, *grave-diggers*
FORTINBRAS, *Prince of Norway*
CAPTAIN
ENGLISH AMBASSADORS

GERTRUDE, *Queen of Denmark, mother to Hamlet*
OPHELIA, *daughter to Polonius*

LORDS, LADIES, OFFICERS, SOLDIERS, SAILORS, MESSENGERS, AND OTHER ATTENDANTS
GHOST *of Hamlet's father*

Scene: *Denmark.*]

Note: *Hamlet* was first published in 1603, in a slender book called a "quarto" (made up from sheets of printer's paper folded twice, creating four leaves — eight pages — approximately 9½ by 12 inches in size). This was an unauthorized version, of unknown origin and very different in length and in details from subsequent versions. The following year a much longer version was published (now referred to as the Second Quarto), which seems to have drawn upon Shakespeare's own copy of the play as well as some parts of the First Quarto. Two other quartos were published subsequently, with corrections to the Second Quarto. In 1623 the first collected edition of Shakespeare's plays was published, now called the First Folio (made up from sheets of printer's paper folded once, creating pages twice as large as a quarto). The First Folio text of *Hamlet* omits more than two hundred lines found in the Second Quarto, but also introduces some new lines that clarify passages and seem to be from a transcript of a draft written by Shakespeare. The play as printed here mainly follows the Second Quarto text, but passages unique to the Folio have been inserted (enclosed in square brackets) and some corrections from it and the First Quarto have been adopted. The *Dramatis Personae* list, the act and scene divisions, the stage directions enclosed in square brackets, and the indications of scene location in the notes are later editorial additions.

[ACT 1 / Scene 1]°

(*Enter Bernardo and Francisco, two sentinels, [meeting].*)

BERNARDO: Who's there?

FRANCISCO: Nay, answer me.° Stand and unfold yourself.

BERNARDO: Long live the King!

FRANCISCO: Bernardo?

BERNARDO: He.   5

FRANCISCO: You come most carefully upon your hour.

BERNARDO: 'Tis now struck twelve. Get thee to bed, Francisco.

FRANCISCO: For this relief much thanks. 'Tis bitter cold,
          And I am sick at heart.

BERNARDO: Have you had quiet guard?

FRANCISCO: Not a mouse stirring.   10

BERNARDO: Well, good night.
          If you do meet Horatio and Marcellus,
          The rivals° of my watch, bid them make haste.

(*Enter Horatio and Marcellus.*)

FRANCISCO: I think I hear them. Stand, ho! Who is there?

HORATIO: Friends to this ground.

MARCELLUS: And liegemen to the Dane.°   15

FRANCISCO: Give you° good night.

MARCELLUS: O, farewell, honest soldier.
          Who hath relieved you?

FRANCISCO: Bernardo hath my place.
          Give you good night.   (*Exit Francisco.*)

MARCELLUS: Holla, Bernardo!

BERNARDO: Say,
          What, is Horatio there?

HORATIO: A piece of him.

BERNARDO: Welcome, Horatio. Welcome, good Marcellus.   20

HORATIO: What, has this thing appear'd again tonight?

BERNARDO: I have seen nothing.

MARCELLUS: Horatio says 'tis but our fantasy,
          And will not let belief take hold of him
          Touching this dreaded sight, twice seen of us.   25
          Therefore I have entreated him along
          With us to watch the minutes of this night,
          That if again this apparition come
          He may approve° our eyes and speak to it.

ACT 1, SCENE 1. **Location:** Elsinore castle. A guard platform.   **2. me:** Francisco emphasizes that *he* is the sentry currently on watch.   **13. rivals:** Partners.   **15. liegemen to the Dane:** Men sworn to serve the Danish king.   **16. Give you:** God give you.   **29. approve:** Corroborate.

HORATIO: Tush, tush, 'twill not appear.

BERNARDO: Sit down awhile,   30
    And let us once again assail your ears,
    That are so fortified against our story,
    What we have two nights seen.

HORATIO: Well, sit we down,
    And let us hear Bernardo speak of this.

BERNARDO: Last night of all,   35
    When yond same star that's westward from the pole°
    Had made his° course t' illume that part of heaven
    Where now it burns, Marcellus and myself,
    The bell then beating one —

(Enter Ghost.)

MARCELLUS: Peace, break thee off! Look where it comes again!   40

BERNARDO: In the same figure, like the King that's dead.

MARCELLUS: Thou art a scholar.° Speak to it, Horatio.

BERNARDO: Looks 'a° not like the King? Mark it, Horatio.

HORATIO: Most like. It harrows me with fear and wonder.

BERNARDO: It would be spoke to.

MARCELLUS: Speak to it,° Horatio.   45

HORATIO: What art thou that usurp'st this time of night,
    Together with that fair and warlike form
    In which the majesty of buried Denmark°
    Did sometimes° march? By heaven I charge thee speak!

MARCELLUS: It is offended.

BERNARDO: See, it stalks away.   50

HORATIO: Stay! Speak, speak. I charge thee, speak.

(Exit Ghost.)

MARCELLUS: 'Tis gone, and will not answer.

BERNARDO: How now, Horatio? You tremble and look pale.
    Is not this something more than fantasy?
    What think you on 't?   55

HORATIO: Before my God, I might not this believe
    Without the sensible° and true avouch
    Of mine own eyes.

MARCELLUS: Is it not like the King?

HORATIO: As thou art to thyself.
    Such was the very armor he had on   60

---

36. pole: Polestar.   **37. his:** Its.   **42. scholar:** One learned in Latin and able to address spirits.   **43. 'a:** He.   **45. It . . . it:** A ghost could not speak until spoken to.   **48. buried Denmark:** The buried king of Denmark.   **49. sometimes:** Formerly.   **57. sensible:** Confirmed by the senses.

When he the ambitious Norway° combated.
So frown'd he once when, in an angry parle,°
He smote the sledded° Polacks° on the ice.
'Tis strange.

MARCELLUS: Thus twice before, and jump° at this dead hour,   65
  With martial stalk hath he gone by our watch.

HORATIO: In what particular thought to work I know not,
  But, in the gross and scope° of mine opinion,
  This bodes some strange eruption to our state.

MARCELLUS: Good now,° sit down, and tell me, he that knows,   70
  Why this same strict and most observant watch
  So nightly toils° the subject° of the land,
  And why such daily cast° of brazen cannon,
  And foreign mart° for implements of war,
  Why such impress° of shipwrights, whose sore task   75
  Does not divide the Sunday from the week.
  What might be toward,° that this sweaty haste
  Doth make the night joint-laborer with the day?
  Who is 't that can inform me?

HORATIO: That can I,
  At least, the whisper goes so. Our last king,   80
  Whose image even but now appear'd to us,
  Was, as you know, by Fortinbras of Norway,
  Thereto prick'd on° by a most emulate° pride,
  Dar'd to the combat; in which our valiant Hamlet —
  For so this side of our known world esteem'd him —   85
  Did slay this Fortinbras; who, by a seal'd compact,
  Well ratified by law and heraldry,
  Did forfeit, with his life, all those his lands
  Which he stood seiz'd° of, to the conqueror;
  Against the° which a moi'ty competent°   90
  Was gaged° by our king, which had return'd
  To the inheritance of Fortinbras
  Had he been vanquisher, as, by the same comart°
  And carriage° of the article design'd,
  His fell to Hamlet. Now, sir, young Fortinbras,   95
  Of unimproved° mettle hot and full,

---

61. **Norway:** King of Norway.   62. **parle:** Parley.   63. **sledded:** Traveling on sleds.   **Polacks:** Poles.   65. **jump:** Exactly.   68. **gross and scope:** General view.   70. **Good now:** An expression denoting entreaty or expostulation.   72. **toils:** Causes to toil.   **subject:** Subjects.   73. **cast:** Casting.   74. **mart:** Buying and selling.   75. **impress:** Impressment, conscription.   77. **toward:** In preparation.   83. **prick'd on:** Incited.   **emulate:** Ambitious.   89. **seiz'd:** Possessed.   90. **Against the:** In return for.   **moi'ty competent:** Sufficient portion.   91. **gaged:** Engaged, pledged.   93. **comart:** Joint bargain (?).   94. **carriage:** Import, bearing.   96. **unimproved:** Not turned to account (?) or untested (?).

Hath in the skirts° of Norway here and there
Shark'd up° a list of lawless resolutes°
For food and diet° to some enterprise
That hath a stomach° in 't, which is no other —   100
As it doth well appear unto our state —
But to recover of us, by strong hand
And terms compulsatory, those foresaid lands
So by his father lost. And this, I take it,
Is the main motive of our preparations,   105
The source of this our watch, and the chief head°
Of this post-haste and romage° in the land.
BERNARDO: I think it be no other but e'en so.
    Well may it sort° that this portentous figure
    Comes armed through our watch so like the King   110
    That was and is the question of these wars.
HORATIO: A mote° it is to trouble the mind's eye.
    In the most high and palmy° state of Rome,
    A little ere the mightiest Julius fell,
    The graves stood tenantless and the sheeted° dead   115
    Did squeak and gibber in the Roman streets;
    As° stars with trains of fire and dews of blood,
    Disasters° in the sun; and the moist star°
    Upon whose influence Neptune's° empire stands°
    Was sick almost to doomsday° with eclipse.   120
    And even the like precurse° of fear'd events,
    As harbingers° preceding still° the fates
    And prologue to the omen° coming on,
    Have heaven and earth together demonstrated
    Unto our climatures° and countrymen.   125

(*Enter Ghost.*)

    But soft, behold! Lo where it comes again!
    I'll cross° it, though it blast me. Stay, illusion!
    If thou hast any sound, or use of voice,
    Speak to me!   (*It spreads his arms.*)

---

97. skirts: Outlying regions, outskirts.   **98. Shark'd up:** Got together in haphazard fashion.
resolutes: Desperadoes.   **99. food and diet:** No pay but their keep.   **100. stomach:** Relish
of danger.   **106. head:** Source.   **107. romage:** Bustle, commotion.   **109. sort:** Suit.
112. mote: Speck of dust.   **113. palmy:** Flourishing.   **115. sheeted:** Shrouded.   **117. As:**
This abrupt transition suggests that matter is possibly omitted between lines 116 and 117.
118. Disasters: Unfavorable signs of aspects.   **moist star:** Moon, governing tides.   **119. Nep-**
tune: God of the sea.   **stands:** Depends.   **120. sick . . . doomsday:** See Matthew 24:29 and
Revelation 6:12.   **121. precurse:** Heralding, foreshadowing.   **122. harbingers:** Forerunners.
still: Continually.   **123. omen:** Calamitous event.   **125. climatures:** Regions.   **127. cross:**
Meet, face directly.

If there be any good thing to be done   130
That may to thee do ease and grace to me,
Speak to me!
If thou art privy to thy country's fate,
Which, happily,° foreknowing may avoid,
O, speak!   135
Or if thou hast uphoarded in thy life
Extorted treasure in the womb of earth,
For which, they say, you spirits oft walk in death,

(*The cock crows.*)

    Speak of it. Stay, and speak! Stop it, Marcellus.
MARCELLUS: Shall I strike at it with my partisan?°   140
HORATIO: Do, if it will not stand.   [*They strike at it.*]
BERNARDO: 'Tis here!
HORATIO: 'Tis here!
MARCELLUS: 'Tis gone.   [*Exit Ghost.*]
    We do it wrong, being so majestical,
To offer it the show of violence;
For it is, as the air, invulnerable,   145
And our vain blows malicious mockery.
BERNARDO: It was about to speak when the cock crew.
HORATIO: And then it started like a guilty thing
Upon a fearful summons. I have heard,
The cock, that is the trumpet to the morn,   150
Doth with his lofty and shrill-sounding throat
Awake the god of day, and, at his warning,
Whether in sea or fire, in earth or air,
Th' extravagant and erring° spirit hies
To his confine; and of the truth herein   155
This present object made probation.°
MARCELLUS: It faded on the crowing of the cock.
Some say that ever 'gainst° that season comes
Wherein our Savior's birth is celebrated,
The bird of dawning singeth all night long,   160
And then, they say, no spirit dare stir abroad;
The nights are wholesome, then no planets strike,°
No fairy takes,° nor witch hath power to charm,
So hallowed and so gracious° is that time.
HORATIO: So have I heard and do in part believe it.   165
    But, look, the morn, in russet mantle clad,

---

134. happily: Haply, perchance. **140. partisan:** Long-handled spear. **154. extravagant and erring:** Wandering. (The words have similar meaning.) **156. probation:** Proof. **158. 'gainst:** Just before. **162. strike:** Exert evil influence. **163. takes:** Bewitches. **164. gracious:** Full of goodness.

Walks o'er the dew of yon high eastward hill.
Break we our watch up, and by my advice
Let us impart what we have seen tonight
Unto young Hamlet; for, upon my life,   170
This spirit, dumb to us, will speak to him.
Do you consent we shall acquaint him with it,
As needful in our loves, fitting our duty?
MARCELLUS: Let's do 't, I pray, and I this morning know
Where we shall find him most conveniently.   175

(*Exeunt.*)°

[Scene 2]°

(*Flourish. Enter Claudius, King of Denmark, Gertrude the Queen, Councilors, Polonius and his son Laertes, Hamlet, cum aliis*° [*including Voltimand and Cornelius*].)

KING: Though yet of Hamlet our dear brother's death
The memory be green, and that it us befitted
To bear our hearts in grief and our whole kingdom
To be contracted in one brow of woe,
Yet so far hath discretion fought with nature   5
That we with wisest sorrow think on him,
Together with remembrance of ourselves.
Therefore our sometime sister, now our queen,
Th' imperial jointress° to this warlike state,
Have we, as 'twere with a defeated joy—   10
With an auspicious and a dropping eye,
With mirth in funeral and with dirge in marriage,
In equal scale weighing delight and dole—
Taken to wife. Nor have we herein barr'd
Your better wisdoms, which have freely gone   15
With this affair along. For all, our thanks.
Now follows that you know° young Fortinbras,
Holding a weak supposal° of our worth,
Or thinking by our late dear brother's death
Our state to be disjoint and out of frame,   20
Colleagued with° this dream of his advantage,°
He hath not fail'd to pester us with message
Importing° the surrender of those lands
Lost by his father, with all bands° of law,
To our most valiant brother. So much for him.   25

[S.D.] *Exeunt:* Latin for "they go out."   ACT 1, SCENE 2. **Location:** The castle.   [S.D.] *cum aliis:* With others.   **9. jointress:** Woman possessed of a joint tenancy of an estate.   **17. know:** Be informed (that).   **18. weak supposal:** Low estimate.   **21. Colleagued with:** Joined to, allied with.   **dream . . . advantage:** Illusory hope of success.   **23. Importing:** Pertaining to. **24. bands:** Contracts.

Now for ourself and for this time of meeting.
Thus much the business is: we have here writ
To Norway, uncle of young Fortinbras —
Who, impotent and bed-rid, scarcely hears
Of this his nephew's purpose — to suppress   30
His° further gait° herein, in that the levies,
The lists, and full proportions are all made
Out of his subject;° and we here dispatch
You, good Cornelius, and you, Voltimand,
For bearers of this greeting to old Norway,   35
Giving to you no further personal power
To business with the King, more than the scope
Of these delated° articles allow.   [*Gives a paper.*]
    Farewell, and let your haste commend your duty.
CORNELIUS, VOLTIMAND: In that, and all things, will we show our duty.   40
KING: We doubt it nothing. Heartily farewell.

                                    [*Exit Voltimand and Cornelius.*]

And now, Laertes, what's the news with you?
You told us of some suit; what is 't, Laertes?
You cannot speak of reason to the Dane°
And lose your voice.° What wouldst thou beg, Laertes,   45
That shall not be my offer, not thy asking?
The head is not more native° to the heart,
The hand more instrumental° to the mouth,
Than is the throne of Denmark to thy father.
What wouldst thou have, Laertes?
LAERTES: My dread lord,   50
Your leave and favor to return to France,
From whence though willingly I came to Denmark
To show my duty in your coronation,
Yet now I must confess, that duty done,
My thoughts and wishes bend again toward France   55
And bow them to your gracious leave and pardon.°
KING: Have you your father's leave? What says Polonius?
POLONIUS: H'ath, my lord, wrung from me my slow leave
By laborsome petition, and at last
Upon his will I seal'd my hard° consent.   60
I do beseech you, give him leave to go.

---

31. **His:** Fortinbras's. **gait:** Proceeding. **31–33. in that . . . subject:** Since the levying of
troops and supplies is drawn entirely from the King of Norway's own subjects. **38. delated:**
Detailed. (Variant of *dilated*.) **44. the Dane:** The Danish king. **45. lose your voice:** Waste
your speech. **47. native:** Closely connected, related. **48. instrumental:** Serviceable.
56. leave and pardon: Permission to depart. **60. hard:** Reluctant.

KING: Take thy fair hour, Laertes. Time be thine,
 And thy best graces spend it at thy will!
 But now, my cousin° Hamlet, and my son —
HAMLET: A little more than kin, and less than kind.°   65
KING: How is it that the clouds still hang on you?
HAMLET: Not so, my lord. I am too much in the sun.°
QUEEN: Good Hamlet, cast thy nighted color off,
 And let thine eye look like a friend on Denmark.
 Do not forever with thy veiled° lids   70
 Seek for thy noble father in the dust.
 Thou know'st 'tis common,° all that lives must die,
 Passing through nature to eternity.
HAMLET: Ay, madam, it is common.
QUEEN: If it be,
 Why seems it so particular with thee?   75
HAMLET: Seems, madam! Nay, it is. I know not "seems."
 'Tis not alone my inky cloak, good mother,
 Nor customary suits of solemn black,
 Nor windy suspiration of forc'd breath,
 No, nor the fruitful° river in the eye,   80
 Nor the dejected havior of the visage,
 Together with all forms, moods, shapes of grief,
 That can denote me truly. These indeed seem,
 For they are actions that a man might play.
 But I have that within which passes show;   85
 These but the trappings and the suits of woe.
KING: 'Tis sweet and commendable in your nature, Hamlet,
 To give these mourning duties to your father.
 But you must know your father lost a father,
 That father lost, lost his, and the survivor bound   90
 In filial obligation for some term
 To do obsequious° sorrow. But to persever°
 In obstinate condolement° is a course
 Of impious stubbornness. 'Tis unmanly grief.
 It shows a will most incorrect to heaven,   95
 A heart unfortified, a mind impatient,
 An understanding simple and unschool'd.
 For what we know must be and is as common

---

64. **cousin:** Any kin not of the immediate family. 65. **A little . . . kind:** Closer than an ordinary nephew (since I am stepson), and yet more separated in natural feeling (with pun on *kind*, meaning natural and lawful). This line is often read as an aside, but it need not be. 67. **sun:** The sunshine of the King's royal favor (with pun on *son*). 70. **veiled:** Downcast. 72. **common:** Of universal occurrence. (But Hamlet plays on the sense of *vulgar* in line 74.) 80. **fruitful:** Abundant. 92. **obsequious:** Suited to obsequies or funerals. **persever:** Persevere. 93. **condolement:** Sorrowing.

As any the most vulgar thing to sense,°
Why should we in our peevish opposition   100
Take it to heart? Fie, 'tis a fault to heaven,
A fault against the dead, a fault to nature,
To reason most absurd, whose common theme
Is death of fathers, and who still hath cried,
From the first corse° till he that died today,   105
"This must be so." We pray you, throw to earth
This unprevailing° woe, and think of us
As of a father; for let the world take note,
You are the most immediate° to our throne,
And with no less nobility of love   110
Than that which dearest father bears his son
Do I impart toward you. For your intent
In going back to school in Wittenberg,°
It is most retrograde° to our desire,
And we beseech you, bend you° to remain   115
Here in the cheer and comfort of our eye,
Our chiefest courtier, cousin, and our son.
QUEEN: Let not thy mother lose her prayers, Hamlet.
    I pray thee stay with us, go not to Wittenberg.
HAMLET: I shall in all my best obey you, madam.   120
KING: Why, 'tis a loving and a fair reply.
    Be as ourself in Denmark. Madam, come.
    This gentle and unforc'd accord of Hamlet
    Sits smiling to my heart, in grace whereof
    No jocund° health that Denmark drinks today   125
    But the great cannon to the clouds shall tell,
    And the King's rouse° the heaven shall bruit again,°
    Respeaking earthly thunder.° Come away.

(*Flourish. Exeunt all but Hamlet.*)

HAMLET: O, that this too too sullied° flesh would melt,
    Thaw, and resolve itself into a dew!   130
    Or that the Everlasting had not fix'd
    His canon° 'gainst self-slaughter! O God, God,
    How weary, stale, flat, and unprofitable
    Seem to me all the uses of this world!
    Fie on 't, ah, fie! 'Tis an unweeded garden   135

---

99. **As . . . sense:** As the most ordinary experience.   105. **corse:** Corpse.   107. **unprevail-**
ing: Unavailing.   109. **most immediate:** Next in succession.   113. **Wittenberg:** Famous
German university founded in 1502.   114. **retrograde:** Contrary.   115. **bend you:** Incline
yourself.   125. **jocund:** Merry.   127. **rouse:** Draft of liquor.   **bruit again:** Loudly echo.
128. **thunder:** Of trumpet and kettledrum sounded when the King drinks, see 1.4.8–12.
129. **sullied:** Defiled. (The early quartos read *sallied*, the Folio *solid*.)   132. **canon:** Law.

That grows to seed. Things rank and gross in nature
Possess it merely.° That it should come to this!
But two months dead — nay, not so much, not two.
So excellent a king, that was to° this
Hyperion° to a satyr; so loving to my mother   140
That he might not beteem° the winds of heaven
Visit her face too roughly. Heaven and earth,
Must I remember? Why, she would hang on him
As if increase of appetite had grown
By what it fed on, and yet, within a month —   145
Let me not think on 't. Frailty, thy name is woman! —
A little month, or ere those shoes were old
With which she followed my poor father's body,
Like Niobe,° all tears, why she, even she —
O God, a beast, that wants discourse of reason,°   150
Would have mourn'd longer — married with my uncle,
My father's brother, but no more like my father
Than I to Hercules. Within a month,
Ere yet the salt of most unrighteous tears
Had left the flushing in her galled° eyes,   155
She married. O, most wicked speed, to post
With such dexterity to incestuous° sheets!
It is not nor it cannot come to good.
But break, my heart, for I must hold my tongue.

(*Enter Horatio, Marcellus, and Bernardo.*)

HORATIO: Hail to your lordship!
HAMLET: I am glad to see you well.   160
    Horatio! — or I do forget myself.
HORATIO: The same, my lord, and your poor servant ever.
HAMLET: Sir, my good friend; I'll change° that name with you.
    And what make° you from Wittenberg, Horatio?
    Marcellus?   165
MARCELLUS: My good lord.
HAMLET: I am very glad to see you. [*To Bernardo.*] Good even, sir. —
    But what, in faith, make you from Wittenberg?
HORATIO: A truant disposition, good my lord.

---

137. merely: Completely.   **139. to:** In comparison to.   **140. Hyperion:** Titan sun-god, father of Helios.   **141. beteem:** Allow.   **149. Niobe:** Tantalus's daughter, queen of Thebes, who boasted that she had more sons and daughters than Leto; for this, Apollo and Artemis, children of Leto, slew her fourteen children. She was turned by Zeus into a stone that continually dropped tears.   **150. wants . . . reason:** Lacks the faculty of reason.   **155. galled:** Irritated, inflamed.   **157. incestuous:** In Shakespeare's day, the marriage of a man like Claudius to his deceased brother's wife was considered incestuous.   **163. change:** Exchange (i.e., the name of friend).   **164. make:** Do.

HAMLET: I would not hear your enemy say so,   170
    Nor shall you do my ear that violence
    To make it truster of your own report
    Against yourself. I know you are no truant.
    But what is your affair in Elsinore?
    We'll teach you to drink deep ere you depart.   175
HORATIO: My lord, I came to see your father's funeral.
HAMLET: I prithee do not mock me, fellow student;
    I think it was to see my mother's wedding.
HORATIO: Indeed, my lord, it followed hard° upon.
HAMLET: Thrift, thrift, Horatio! The funeral bak'd meats   180
    Did coldly furnish forth the marriage tables.
    Would I had met my dearest° foe in heaven
    Or° ever I had seen that day, Horatio!
    My father! — Methinks I see my father.
HORATIO: Where, my lord?
HAMLET: In my mind's eye, Horatio.   185
HORATIO: I saw him once. 'A° was a goodly king.
HAMLET: 'A was a man, take him for all in all,
    I shall not look upon his like again.
HORATIO: My lord, I think I saw him yesternight.
HAMLET: Saw? Who?   190
HORATIO: My lord, the King your father.
HAMLET: The King my father?
HORATIO: Season your admiration° for a while
    With an attent° ear, till I may deliver,
    Upon the witness of these gentlemen,
    This marvel to you.
HAMLET: For God's love, let me hear!   195
HORATIO: Two nights together had these gentlemen,
    Marcellus and Bernardo, on their watch,
    In the dead waste and middle of the night,
    Been thus encount'red. A figure like your father,
    Armed at point° exactly, cap-a-pe,°   200
    Appears before them, and with solemn march
    Goes slow and stately by them. Thrice he walk'd
    By their oppress'd and fear-surprised eyes
    Within his truncheon's° length, whilst they, distill'd
    Almost to jelly with the act° of fear,   205
    Stand dumb and speak not to him. This to me

---

179. **hard:** Close.   182. **dearest:** Direst.   183. **Or:** Ere, before.   186. **'A:** He.   192. **Season your admiration:** Restrain your astonishment.   193. **attent:** Attentive.   200. **at point:** Completely.   **cap-a-pe:** From head to foot.   204. **truncheon:** Officer's staff.   205. **act:** Action, operation.

In dreadful secrecy impart they did,
And I with them the third night kept the watch,
Where, as they had delivered, both in time,
Form of the thing, each word made true and good,   210
The apparition comes. I knew your father;
These hands are not more like.

HAMLET: But where was this?
MARCELLUS: My lord, upon the platform where we watch.
HAMLET: Did you not speak to it?
HORATIO: My lord, I did,
But answer made it none. Yet once methought   215
It lifted up it° head and did address
Itself to motion, like as it would speak;
But even then the morning cock crew loud,
And at the sound it shrunk in haste away,
And vanish'd from our sight.
HAMLET: 'Tis very strange.   220
HORATIO: As I do live, my honor'd lord, 'tis true,
And we did think it writ down in our duty
To let you know of it.
HAMLET: Indeed, indeed, sirs. But this troubles me.
Hold you the watch tonight?
ALL: We do, my lord.   225
HAMLET: Arm'd, say you?
ALL: Arm'd, my lord.
HAMLET: From top to toe?
ALL: My lord, from head to foot.
HAMLET: Then saw you not his face?
HORATIO: O, yes, my lord. He wore his beaver° up.   230
HAMLET: What, looked he frowningly?
HORATIO: A countenance more
In sorrow than in anger.
HAMLET: Pale or red?
HORATIO: Nay, very pale.
HAMLET: And fix'd his eyes upon you?
HORATIO: Most constantly.
HAMLET: I would I had been there.
HORATIO: It would have much amaz'd you.   235
HAMLET: Very like, very like. Stay'd it long?
HORATIO: While one with moderate haste might tell° a hundred.
MARCELLUS, BERNARDO: Longer, longer.
HORATIO: Not when I saw 't.
HAMLET: His beard was grizzl'd, — no?

---

216. it: Its.   **230. beaver:** Visor on the helmet.   **237. tell:** Count.

HORATIO: It was, as I have seen it in his life,   240
    A sable silver'd.°
HAMLET: I will watch tonight.
    Perchance 'twill walk again.
HORATIO: I warr'nt it will.
HAMLET: If it assume my noble father's person,
    I'll speak to it, though hell itself should gape
    And bid me hold my peace. I pray you all,   245
    If you have hitherto conceal'd this sight,
    Let it be tenable° in your silence still,
    And whatsomever else shall hap tonight,
    Give it an understanding, but no tongue.
    I will requite your loves. So, fare you well.   250
    Upon the platform, 'twixt eleven and twelve,
    I'll visit you.
ALL: Our duty to your honor.
HAMLET: Your loves, as mine to you. Farewell.

(Exeunt [all but Hamlet].)

My father's spirit in arms! All is not well.
I doubt° some foul play. Would the night were come!   255
Till then sit still, my soul. Foul deeds will rise,
Though all the earth o'erwhelm them, to men's eyes.

(Exit.)

[Scene 3]°

(Enter Laertes and Ophelia, his sister.)

LAERTES: My necessaries are embark'd. Farewell.
    And, sister, as the winds give benefit
    And convoy is assistant,° do not sleep
    But let me hear from you.
OPHELIA: Do you doubt that?
LAERTES: For Hamlet, and the trifling of his favor,   5
    Hold it a fashion and a toy in blood,°
    A violet in the youth of primy° nature,
    Forward,° not permanent, sweet, not lasting,
    The perfume and suppliance° of a minute —
    No more.
OPHELIA: No more but so?

---

241. sable silver'd: Black mixed with white.   **247. tenable:** Held tightly.   **255. doubt:** Suspect.   **ACT 1, SCENE 3. Location:** Polonius's chambers.   **3. convoy is assistant:** Means of conveyance are available.   **6. toy in blood:** Passing amorous fancy.   **7. primy:** In its prime, springtime.   **8. Forward:** Precocious.   **9. suppliance:** Supply, filler.

LAERTES: Think it no more.   10
   For nature crescent° does not grow alone
   In thews° and bulk, but, as this temple° waxes,
   The inward service of the mind and soul
   Grows wide withal.° Perhaps he loves you now,
   And now no soil° nor cautel° doth besmirch   15
   The virtue of his will;° but you must fear,
   His greatness weigh'd,° his will is not his own.
   [For he himself is subject to his birth.]
   He may not, as unvalued persons do,
   Carve° for himself; for on his choice depends   20
   The safety and health of this whole state,
   And therefore must his choice be circumscrib'd
   Unto the voice and yielding° of that body
   Whereof he is the head. Then if he says he loves you,
   It fits your wisdom so far to believe it   25
   As he in his particular act and place
   May give his saying deed,° which is no further
   Than the main voice of Denmark goes withal.
   Then weigh what loss your honor may sustain
   If with too credent° ear you list° his songs,   30
   Or lose your heart, or your chaste treasure open
   To his unmaster'd importunity.
   Fear it, Ophelia, fear it, my dear sister,
   And keep you in the rear of your affection,
   Out of the shot° and danger of desire.   35
   The chariest° maid is prodigal enough
   If she unmask her beauty to the moon.
   Virtue itself scapes not calumnious strokes.
   The canker galls° the infants of the spring
   Too oft before their buttons° be disclos'd,°   40
   And in the morn and liquid dew° of youth
   Contagious blastments° are most imminent.
   Be wary then; best safety lies in fear.
   Youth to itself rebels, though none else near.
OPHELIA: I shall the effect of this good lesson keep   45
   As watchman to my heart. But, good my brother,
   Do not, as some ungracious pastors do,

---

11. **crescent:** Growing, waxing.   12. **thews:** Bodily strength.   **temple:** Body.   14. **Grows wide withal:** Grows along with it.   15. **soil:** Blemish.   **cautel:** Deceit.   16. **will:** Desire.   17. **greatness weigh'd:** High position considered.   20. **Carve:** Choose pleasure.   23. **voice and yielding:** Assent, approval.   27. **deed:** Effect.   30. **credent:** Credulous.   **list:** Listen to.   35. **shot:** Range.   36. **chariest:** Most scrupulously modest.   39. **canker galls:** Cankerworm destroys.   40. **buttons:** Buds.   **disclos'd:** Opened.   41. **liquid dew:** Time when dew is fresh.   42. **blastments:** Blights.

Show me the steep and thorny way to heaven,
Whiles, like a puff'd° and reckless libertine,
Himself the primrose path of dalliance treads,   50
And recks° not his own rede.°

(*Enter Polonius.*)

LAERTES: O, fear me not.
I stay too long. But here my father comes.
A double blessing is a double° grace;
Occasion° smiles upon a second leave.

POLONIUS: Yet here, Laertes? Aboard, aboard, for shame!   55
The wind sits in the shoulder of your sail,
And you are stay'd for. There — my blessing with thee!
And these few precepts in thy memory
Look thou character.° Give thy thoughts no tongue
Nor any unproportion'd thought his° act.   60
Be thou familiar,° but by no means vulgar.°
Those friends thou hast, and their adoption tried,°
Grapple them to thy soul with hoops of steel,
But do not dull thy palm with entertainment
Of each new-hatch'd, unfledg'd courage.° Beware   65
Of entrance to a quarrel, but, being in,
Bear't that° th' opposed may beware of thee.
Give every man thy ear, but few thy voice;
Take each man's censure,° but reserve thy judgment.
Costly thy habit as thy purse can buy,   70
But not express'd in fancy; rich, not gaudy,
For the apparel oft proclaims the man,
And they in France of the best rank and station
Are of a most select and generous chief° in that.
Neither a borrower nor a lender be,   75
For loan oft loses both itself and friend,
And borrowing dulleth edge of husbandry.°
This above all: to thine own self be true,
And it must follow, as the night the day,
Thou canst not then be false to any man.   80
Farewell. My blessing season° this in thee!

LAERTES: Most humbly do I take my leave, my lord.

POLONIUS: The time invests° you. Go, your servants tend.°

---

49. **puff'd:** Bloated.   51. **recks:** Heeds.   **rede:** Counsel.   53. **double:** I.e., Laertes has already bidden his father good-bye.   54. **Occasion:** Opportunity.   59. **character:** Inscribe.
60. **his:** Its.   61. **familiar:** Sociable.   **vulgar:** Common.   62. **tried:** Tested.   65. **courage:**
Young man of spirit.   67. **Bear't that:** Manage it so that.   69. **censure:** Opinion, judgment.
74. **generous chief:** Noble eminence (?).   77. **husbandry:** Thrift.   81. **season:** Mature.
83. **invests:** Besieges,   **tend:** Attend, wait.

LAERTES: Farewell, Ophelia, and remember well
    What I have said to you.   85
OPHELIA: 'Tis in my memory lock'd,
    And you yourself shall keep the key of it.
LAERTES: Farewell.   (*Exit Laertes.*)
POLONIUS: What is 't, Ophelia, he hath said to you?
OPHELIA: So please you, something touching the Lord Hamlet.   90
POLONIUS: Marry,° well bethought.
    'Tis told me he hath very oft of late
    Given private time to you, and you yourself
    Have of your audience been most free and bounteous.
    If it be so — as so 'tis put on° me,   95
    And that in way of caution — I must tell you
    You do not understand yourself so clearly
    As it behooves my daughter and your honor.
    What is between you? Give me up the truth.
OPHELIA: He hath, my lord, of late made many tenders°   100
    Of his affection to me.
POLONIUS: Affection? Pooh! You speak like a green girl,
    Unsifted° in such perilous circumstance.
    Do you believe his tenders, as you call them?
OPHELIA: I do not know, my lord, what I should think.   105
POLONIUS: Marry, I will teach you. Think yourself a baby
    That you have ta'en these tenders° for true pay,
    Which are not sterling.° Tender° yourself more dearly,
    Or — not to crack the wind° of the poor phrase,
    Running it thus — you'll tender me a fool.°   110
OPHELIA: My lord, he hath importun'd me with love
    In honorable fashion.
POLONIUS: Ay, fashion° you may call it. Go to, go to.
OPHELIA: And hath given countenance° to his speech, my lord,
    With almost all the holy vows of heaven.   115
POLONIUS: Ay, springes° to catch woodcocks.° I do know,
    When the blood burns, how prodigal the soul
    Lends the tongue vows. These blazes, daughter,
    Giving more light than heat, extinct in both
    Even in their promise, as it is a-making,   120
    You must not take for fire. From this time

---

91. Marry: By the Virgin Mary (a mild oath).   **95. put on:** Impressed on, told to.
100. tenders: Offers.   **103. Unsifted:** Untried.   **107. tenders:** With added meaning here
of *promises to pay.*   **108. sterling:** Legal currency.   **Tender:** Hold,   **109. crack the wind:**
Run it until it is broken, winded.   **110. tender me a fool:** (1) Show yourself to me as a fool,
(2) show me up as a fool, (3) present me with a grandchild (*fool* was a term of endearment
for a child).   **113. fashion:** Mere form, pretense.   **114. countenance:** Credit, support.
116. springes: Snares.   **woodcocks:** Birds easily caught; here used to connote gullibility.

Be something scanter of your maiden presence.
Set your entreatments° at a higher rate
Than a command to parle.° For Lord Hamlet,
Believe so much in him° that he is young,   125
And with a larger tether may he walk
Than may be given you. In few,° Ophelia,
Do not believe his vows, for they are brokers,°
Not of that dye° which their investments° show,
But mere implorators° of unholy suits,   130
Breathing° like sanctified and pious bawds,
The better to beguile. This is for all:
I would not, in plain terms, from this time forth
Have you so slander° any moment leisure
As to give words or talk with the Lord Hamlet.   135
Look to 't, I charge you. Come your ways.

OPHELIA: I shall obey, my lord.   (*Exeunt.*)

[Scene 4]°

(*Enter Hamlet, Horatio, and Marcellus.*)

HAMLET: The air bites shrewdly; it is very cold.
HORATIO: It is a nipping and an eager air.
HAMLET: What hour now?
HORATIO: I think it lacks of twelve.
MARCELLUS: No, it is struck.
HORATIO: Indeed? I heard it not.
It then draws near the season   5
Wherein the spirit held his wont to walk.

(*A flourish of trumpets, and two pieces° go off [within].*)

What does this mean, my lord?
HAMLET: The King doth wake° tonight and takes his rouse,°
Keeps wassail,° and the swagg'ring up-spring° reels;
And as he drains his draughts of Rhenish° down,   10
The kettle-drum and trumpet thus bray out
The triumph of his pledge.°

---

123. entreatments: Negotiations for surrender (a military term).   **124. parle:** Discuss
terms with the enemy. (Polonius urges his daughter, in the metaphor of military language, not
to meet with Hamlet and consider giving in to him merely because he requests an interview.)
125. so . . . him: This much concerning him.   **127. In few:** Briefly.   **128. brokers:** Go-
betweens, procurers.   **129. dye:** Color or sort.   **investments:** Clothes (i.e., they are not what
they seem).   **130. mere implorators:** Out-and-out solicitors.   **131. Breathing:** Speaking.
134. slander: Bring disgrace or reproach upon.   **ACT 1, SCENE 4. Location:** The guard platform.   **[s.d.]** *pieces:* I.e., of ordnance, cannon.   **8. wake:** Stay awake and hold revel.
rouse: Carouse, drinking bout.   **9. wassail:** Carousal.   **up-spring:** Wild German dance.
10. Rhenish: Rhine wine.   **12. triumph . . . pledge:** His feat in draining the wine in a single
draft.

HORATIO: Is it a custom?
HAMLET: Ay, marry, is 't,
    But to my mind, though I am native here
    And to the manner° born, it is a custom   15
    More honor'd in the breach than the observance.°
    This heavy-headed revel east and west°
    Makes us traduc'd and tax'd of° other nations.
    They clepe° us drunkards, and with swinish phrase°
    Soil our addition;° and indeed it takes   20
    From our achievements, though perform'd at height,°
    The pith and marrow of our attribute.
    So, oft it chances in particular men,
    That for some vicious mole of nature° in them,
    As in their birth — wherein they are not guilty,   25
    Since nature cannot choose his° origin —
    By the o'ergrowth of some complexion,°
    Oft breaking down the pales° and forts of reason,
    Or by some habit that too much o'er-leavens°
    The form of plausive° manners, that these men,   30
    Carrying, I say, the stamp of one defect,
    Being nature's livery,° or fortune's star,°
    Their virtues else, be they as pure as grace,
    As infinite as man may undergo,
    Shall in the general censure take corruption   35
    From that particular fault. The dram of eale°
    Doth all the noble substance of a doubt°
    To his own scandal.°

(*Enter Ghost.*)

HORATIO: Look, my lord, it comes!
HAMLET: Angels and ministers of grace defend us!
    Be thou a spirit of health° or goblin damn'd,   40
    Bring with thee airs from heaven or blasts from hell,
    Be thy intents wicked or charitable,
    Thou com'st in such a questionable° shape

---

15. **manner:** Custom (of drinking).   16. **More . . . observance:** Better neglected than
followed.   17. **east and west:** I.e., everywhere.   18. **tax'd of:** Censured by.   19. **clepe:**
Call.   **with swinish phrase:** By calling us swine.   20. **addition:** Reputation.   21. **at height:**
Outstandingly.   24. **mole of nature:** Natural blemish in one's constitution.   26. **his:** Its.
27. **complexion:** Humor (i.e., one of the four humors or fluids thought to determine temperament).   28. **pales:** Palings, fences (as of a fortification).   29. **o'er-leavens:** Induces a
change throughout (as yeast works in dough).   30. **plausive:** Pleasing.   32. **nature's livery:**
Endowment from nature.   **fortune's star:** Mark placed by fortune.   36. **dram of eale:** Small
amount of evil (?).   37. **of a doubt:** A famous crux, sometimes emended to *oft about* or *often
dout,* i.e., often erase or do out, or to *antidote,* counteract.   38. **To . . . scandal:** To the disgrace of the whole enterprise.   40. **of health:** Of spiritual good.   43. **questionable:** Inviting
question or conversation.

That I will speak to thee. I'll call thee Hamlet,
King, father, royal Dane. O, answer me!   45
Let me not burst in ignorance, but tell
Why thy canoniz'd° bones, hearsed° in death,
Have burst their cerements;° why the sepulcher
Wherein we saw thee quietly interr'd
Hath op'd his ponderous and marble jaws   50
To cast thee up again. What may this mean,
That thou, dead corse, again in complete steel
Revisits thus the glimpses of the moon,°
Making night hideous, and we fools of nature°
So horridly to shake our disposition   55
With thoughts beyond the reaches of our souls?
Say, why is this? Wherefore? What should we do?

                                              ([*Ghost*] *beckons* [*Hamlet*].)

HORATIO: It beckons you to go away with it,
    As if it some impartment° did desire
    To you alone.
MARCELLUS: Look with what courteous action   60
    It waves you to a more removed ground.
    But do not go with it.
HORATIO: No, by no means.
HAMLET: It will not speak. Then I will follow it.
HORATIO: Do not, my lord.
HAMLET: Why, what should be the fear?
    I do not set my life at a pin's fee,°   65
    And for my soul, what can it do to that,
    Being a thing immortal as itself?
    It waves me forth again. I'll follow it.
HORATIO: What if it tempt you toward the flood, my lord
    Or to the dreadful summit of the cliff   70
    That beetles o'er° his° base into the sea,
    And there assume some other horrible form
    Which might deprive your sovereignty of reason,°
    And draw you into madness? Think of it.
    The very place puts toys of desperation,°   75
    Without more motive, into every brain
    That looks so many fathoms to the sea
    And hears it roar beneath.

---

47. canoniz'd: Buried according to the canons of the church. **hearsed:** Coffined.
48. cerements: Grave-clothes. **53. glimpses of the moon:** Earth by night. **54. fools of
nature:** Mere men, limited to natural knowledge. **59. impartment:** Communication.
65. fee: Value. **71. beetles o'er:** Overhangs threateningly. **his:** Its. **73. deprive . . . reason:** Take away the rule of reason over your mind. **75. toys of desperation:** Fancies of desperate acts, i.e., suicide.

HAMLET: It waves me still.
　　Go on, I'll follow thee.
MARCELLUS: You shall not go, my lord.

　　　　　　　　　　　　　　　　　　　　　[They try to stop him.]

HAMLET: Hold off your hands!   80
HORATIO: Be rul'd, you shall not go.
HAMLET: My fate cries out,
　　And makes each petty artery° in this body
　　As hardy as the Nemean lion's° nerve.°
　　Still am I call'd. Unhand me, gentlemen.
　　By heaven, I'll make a ghost of him that lets° me!   85
　　I say, away! Go on. I'll follow thee.

　　　　　　　　　　　　　　　　(Exeunt Ghost and Hamlet.)

HORATIO: He waxes desperate with imagination.
MARCELLUS: Let's follow. 'Tis not fit thus to obey him.
HORATIO: Have after. To what issue° will this come?
MARCELLUS: Something is rotten in the state of Denmark.   90
HORATIO: Heaven will direct it.°
MARCELLUS: Nay, let's follow him.   *(Exeunt.)*

[Scene 5]°

(Enter Ghost and Hamlet.)

HAMLET: Whither wilt thou lead me? Speak. I'll go no further.
GHOST: Mark me.
HAMLET: I will.
GHOST: My hour is almost come,
　　When I to sulph'rous and tormenting flames
　　Must render up myself.
HAMLET: Alas, poor ghost!
GHOST: Pity me not, but lend thy serious hearing   5
　　To what I shall unfold.
HAMLET: Speak. I am bound to hear.
GHOST: So art thou to revenge, when thou shalt hear.
HAMLET: What?
GHOST: I am thy father's spirit,   10
　　Doom'd for a certain term to walk the night,
　　And for the day confin'd to fast° in fires,
　　Till the foul crimes° done in my days of nature
　　Are burnt and purg'd away. But that° I am forbid

---

82. **artery:** Sinew.   83. **Nemean lion:** One of the monsters slain by Hercules in his twelve labors.   **nerve:** Sinew   85. **lets:** Hinders.   89. **issue:** Outcome.   91. **it:** The outcome. ACT 1, SCENE 5. **Location:** The battlements of the castle.   12. **fast:** Do penance.   13. **crimes:** Sins.   14. **But that:** Were it not that.

To tell the secrets of my prison-house,   15
I could a tale unfold whose lightest word
Would harrow up thy soul, freeze thy young blood,
Make thy two eyes, like stars, start from their spheres,°
Thy knotted and combined locks° to part,
And each particular hair to stand an end,°   20
Like quills upon the fearful porpentine.°
But this eternal blazon° must not be
To ears of flesh and blood. List, list, O, list!
If thou didst ever thy dear father love —

HAMLET: O God!   25

GHOST: Revenge his foul and most unnatural murder.

HAMLET: Murder?

GHOST: Murder most foul, as in the best it is,
But this most foul, strange, and unnatural.

HAMLET: Haste me to know 't, that I, with wings as swift   30
As meditation or the thoughts of love,
May sweep to my revenge.

GHOST: I find thee apt;
And duller shouldst thou be than the fat weed
That roots itself in ease on Lethe° wharf,°
Wouldst thou not stir in this. Now, Hamlet, hear.   35
'Tis given out that, sleeping in my orchard,
A serpent stung me. So the whole ear of Denmark
Is by a forged process° of my death
Rankly abus'd.° But know, thou noble youth,
The serpent that did sting thy father's life   40
Now wears his crown.

HAMLET: O my prophetic soul!
My uncle!

GHOST: Ay, that incestuous, that adulterate° beast,
With witchcraft of his wits, with traitorous gifts —
O wicked wit and gifts, that have the power   45
So to seduce! — won to his shameful lust
The will of my most seeming-virtuous queen.
O Hamlet, what a falling-off was there!
From me, whose love was of that dignity
That it went hand in hand even with the vow   50

---

18. **spheres:** Eye sockets, here compared to the orbits or transparent revolving spheres in which, according to Ptolemaic astronomy, the heavenly bodies were fixed.   19. **knotted . . . locks:** Hair neatly arranged and confined.   20. **an end:** On end.   21. **fearful porpentine:** Frightened porcupine.   22. **eternal blazon:** Revelation of the secrets of eternity.   34. **Lethe:** The river of forgetfulness in Hades.   **wharf:** Bank.   38. **forged process:** Falsified account.
39. **abus'd:** Deceived.   43. **adulterate:** Adulterous.

I made to her in marriage, and to decline
Upon a wretch whose natural gifts were poor
To those of mine!
But virtue, as it never will be moved,
Though lewdness court it in a shape of heaven,°   55
So lust, though to a radiant angel link'd,
Will sate itself in a celestial bed,
And prey on garbage.
But, soft, methinks I scent the morning air.
Brief let me be. Sleeping within my orchard,   60
My custom always of the afternoon,
Upon my secure° hour thy uncle stole,
With juice of cursed hebona° in a vial,
And in the porches of my ears did pour
The leprous° distillment, whose effect   65
Holds such an enmity with blood of man
That swift as quicksilver it courses through
The natural gates and alleys of the body,
And with a sudden vigor it doth posset°
And curd, like eager° droppings into milk,   70
The thin and wholesome blood. So did it mine,
And a most instant tetter° bark'd° about,
Most lazar-like,° with vile and loathsome crust,
All my smooth body.
Thus was I, sleeping, by a brother's hand   75
Of life, of crown, of queen, at once dispatch'd,°
Cut off even in the blossoms of my sin,
Unhous'led,° disappointed,° unanel'd,°
No reck'ning made, but sent to my account
With all my imperfections on my head.   80
O, horrible! O, horrible, most horrible!
If thou hast nature° in thee, bear it not.
Let not the royal bed of Denmark be
A couch for luxury° and damned incest.
But, howsomever thou pursues this act,   85
Taint not thy mind, nor let thy soul contrive
Against thy mother aught. Leave her to heaven

---

55. shape of heaven: Heavenly form. **62. secure:** Confident, unsuspicious. **63. hebona:** Poison. (The word seems to be a form of *ebony*, though it is thought perhaps to be related to *henbane*, a poison, or to *ebenus*, yew.) **65. leprous:** Causing leprosy-like disfigurement. **69. posset:** Coagulate, curdle. **70. eager:** Sour, acid. **72. tetter:** Eruption of scabs. **bark'd:** Covered with a rough covering, like bark on a tree. **73. lazar-like:** Leper-like. **76. dispatch'd:** Suddenly deprived. **78. Unhous'led:** Without having received the sacrament [of Holy Communion]. **disappointed:** Unready (spiritually) for the last journey. **unanel'd:** Without having received extreme unction. **82. nature:** The promptings of a son. **84. luxury:** Lechery.

And to those thorns that in her bosom lodge,
To prick and sting her. Fare thee well at once.
The glow-worm shows the matin° to be near,   90
And 'gins to pale his uneffectual fire.°
Adieu, adieu, adieu! Remember me.   [*Exit.*]
HAMLET: O all you host of heaven! O earth! What else?
And shall I couple° hell? O fie! Hold, hold, my heart,
And you, my sinews, grow not instant old,   95
But bear me stiffly up. Remember thee!
Ay, thou poor ghost, whiles memory holds a seat
In this distracted globe.° Remember thee!
Yea, from the table° of my memory
I'll wipe away all trivial fond° records,   100
All saws° of books, all forms,° all pressures° past
That youth and observation copied there,
And thy commandment all alone shall live
Within the book and volume of my brain,
Unmix'd with baser matter. Yes, by heaven!   105
O most pernicious woman!
O villain, villain, smiling, damned villain!
My tables — meet it is I set it down,
That one may smile, and smile, and be a villain.
At least I am sure it may be so in Denmark.   110

[*Writing.*]

So, uncle, there you are. Now to my word;
It is "Adieu, adieu! Remember me."
I have sworn 't.

(*Enter Horatio and Marcellus.*)

HORATIO: My lord, my lord!
MARCELLUS: Lord Hamlet!
HORATIO: Heavens secure him!
HAMLET: So be it!   115
MARCELLUS: Illo, ho, ho, my lord!
HAMLET: Hillo, ho, ho,° boy! Come, bird, come.
MARCELLUS: How is 't, my noble lord?
HORATIO: What news, my lord?
HAMLET: O, wonderful!
HORATIO: Good my lord, tell it.
HAMLET: No, you will reveal it.   120

---

90. **matin:** Morning.   91. **uneffectual fire:** Cold light.   94. **couple:** Add.   98. **globe:**
Head.   99. **table:** Writing tablet.   100. **fond:** Foolish.   101. **saws:** Wise sayings.   **forms:**
Images.   **pressures:** Impressions stamped.   117. **Hillo, ho, ho:** A falconer's call to a hawk in
air. Hamlet is playing upon Marcellus's *Illo,* i.e., *halloo.*

HORATIO: Not I, my lord, by heaven.
MARCELLUS: Nor I, my lord.
HAMLET: How say you, then, would heart of man once think it?
    But you'll be secret?
HORATIO, MARCELLUS: Ay, by heaven, my lord.
HAMLET: There's never a villain dwelling in all Denmark
    But he's an arrant° knave.   125
HORATIO: There needs no ghost, my lord, come from the grave
    To tell us this.
HAMLET: Why, right, you are in the right.
    And so, without more circumstance° at all,
    I hold it fit that we shake hands and part,
    You as your business and desire shall point you —   130
    For every man hath business and desire,
    Such as it is — and for my own poor part,
    Look you, I'll go pray.
HORATIO: These are but wild and whirling words, my lord.
HAMLET: I am sorry they offend you, heartily;   135
    Yes, faith, heartily.
HORATIO: There's no offense, my lord.
HAMLET: Yes, by Saint Patrick,° but there is, Horatio,
    And much offense too. Touching this vision here,
    It is an honest° ghost, that let me tell you.
    For your desire to know what is between us,   140
    O'ermaster 't as you may. And now, good friends
    As you are friends, scholars, and soldiers,
    Give me one poor request.
HORATIO: What is 't, my lord? We will.
HAMLET: Never make known what you have seen tonight.   145
HORATIO, MARCELLUS: My lord, we will not.
HAMLET: Nay, but swear 't.
HORATIO: In faith,
    my lord, not I.
MARCELLUS: Nor I, my lord, in faith.
HAMLET: Upon my sword.°   [*Holds out his sword.*]
MARCELLUS: We have sworn, my lord, already.
HAMLET: Indeed, upon my sword, indeed.

                            (*Ghost cries under the stage.*)

GHOST: Swear.   150
HAMLET: Ha, ha, boy, say'st thou so? Art thou there, truepenny?°

---

125. arrant: Thoroughgoing. **128. circumstance:** Ceremony. **137. Saint Patrick:** The keeper of purgatory and patron saint of all blunders and confusion. **139. honest:** I.e., a real ghost and not an evil spirit. **148. sword:** The hilt in the form of a cross. **151. truepenny:** Honest old fellow.

Come on, you hear this fellow in the cellarage.
Consent to swear.
HORATIO: Propose the oath, my lord.
HAMLET: Never to speak of this that you have seen,
   Swear by my sword.   155
GHOST [*beneath*]: Swear.
HAMLET: Hic et ubique?° Then we'll shift our ground.

                                                          [*He moves to another spot.*]

Come hither, gentlemen,
And lay your hands again upon my sword.
Swear by my sword   160
Never to speak of this that you have heard.
GHOST [*beneath*]: Swear by his sword.
HAMLET: Well said, old mole! Canst work i' th' earth so fast?
   A worthy pioner!° Once more remove, good friends.

                                                                          [*Moves again.*]

HORATIO: O day and night, but this is wondrous strange!   165
HAMLET: And therefore as a stranger give it welcome.
   There are more things in heaven and earth, Horatio,
   Than are dreamt of in your philosophy.°
   But come;
   Here, as before, never, so help you mercy,   170
   How strange or odd soe'er I bear myself—
   As I perchance hereafter shall think meet
   To put an antic° disposition on—
   That you, at such times seeing me, never shall,
   With arms encumb'red° thus, or this headshake,   175
   Or by pronouncing of some doubtful phrase,
   As "Well, well, we know," or "We could, an if° we would,"
   Or "If we list° to speak," or "There be, an if they might,"
   Or such ambiguous giving out,° to note°
   That you know aught of me—this do swear,   180
   So grace and mercy at your most need help you.
GHOST [*beneath*]: Swear.   [*They swear.*]
HAMLET: Rest, rest, perturbed spirit! So, gentlemen,
   With all my love I do commend me to you;
   And what so poor a man as Hamlet is   185

---

157. Hic et ubique: Here and everywhere (Latin).   **164. pioner:** Pioneer, digger, miner.
168. your philosophy: This subject called "natural philosophy" or "science" that people talk
about.   **173. antic:** Fantastic.   **175. encumb'red:** Folded or entwined.   **177. an if:** If.
178. list: Were inclined.   **179. giving out:** Profession of knowledge.   **note:** Give a sign, indicate.

May do, t' express his love and friending to you,
God willing, shall not lack. Let us go in together,
And still° your fingers on your lips, I pray.
The time is out of joint. O cursed spite,
That ever I was born to set it right!   190

                                    [*They wait for him to leave first.*]

Nay, come, let's go together.   (*Exeunt.*)

[ACT 2 / Scene 1]°

(*Enter old Polonius, with his man [Reynaldo].*)

POLONIUS: Give him this money and these notes, Reynaldo.
REYNALDO: I will, my lord.
POLONIUS: You shall do marvel's° wisely, good Reynaldo,
    Before you visit him, to make inquire
    Of his behavior.
REYNALDO: My lord, I did intend it.   5
POLONIUS: Marry, well said, very well said. Look you, sir,
    Inquire me first what Danskers° are in Paris,
    And how, and who, what means,° and where they keep,°
    What company, at what expense; and finding
    By this encompassment° and drift° of question   10
    That they do know my son, come you more nearer
    Than your particular demands will touch it.°
    Take° you, as 'twere, some distant knowledge of him,
    As thus, "I know his father and his friends,
    And in part him." Do you mark this, Reynaldo?   15
REYNALDO: Ay, very well, my lord.
POLONIUS: "And in part him, but," you may say, "not well.
    But, if 't be he I mean, he's very wild,
    Addicted so and so," and there put on° him
    What forgeries° you please — marry, none so rank   20
    As may dishonor him, take heed of that,
    But, sir, such wanton,° wild, and usual slips,
    As are companions noted and most known
    To youth and liberty.
REYNALDO: As gaming, my lord.
POLONIUS: Ay, or drinking, fencing, swearing,   25

---

188. still: Always. **ACT 2, SCENE 1. Location:** Polonius's chambers. **3. marvel's:** Marvelous(ly). **7. Danskers:** Danes. **8. what means:** What wealth (they have). **keep:** Dwell. **10. encompassment:** Roundabout talking. **drift:** Gradual approach or course. **11–12. come . . . it:** You will find out more this way than by asking pointed questions (particular demands). **13. Take:** Assume, pretend. **19. put on:** Impute to. **20. forgeries:** Invented tales. **22. wanton:** Sportive, unrestrained.

Quarreling, drabbing° — you may go so far.

REYNALDO: My lord, that would dishonor him.

POLONIUS: Faith, no, as you may season° it in the charge.
You must not put another scandal on him
That he is open to incontinency;°   30
That's not my meaning. But breathe his faults so quaintly°
That they may seem the taints of liberty,°
The flash and outbreak of a fiery mind,
A savageness in unreclaimed° blood,
Of general assault.°

REYNALDO: But, my good lord —   35

POLONIUS: Wherefore should you do this?

REYNALDO: Ay, my lord,
I would know that.

POLONIUS: Marry, sir, here's my drift,
And, I believe, it is a fetch of wit.°
You laying these slight sullies on my son,
As 'twere a thing a little soil'd i' th' working,°   40
Mark you,
Your party in converse,° him you would sound,°
Having ever° seen in the prenominate crimes°
The youth you breathe° of guilty, be assur'd
He closes with you in this consequence:°   45
"Good sir," or so, or "friend," or "gentleman,"
According to the phrase or the addition°
Of man and country.

REYNALDO: Very good, my lord.

POLONIUS: And then, sir, does 'a this — 'a does — what was I about to say?
By the mass, I was about to say something.   50
Where did I leave?

REYNALDO: At "closes in the consequence."

POLONIUS: At "closes in the consequence," ay, marry.
He closes thus: "I know the gentleman;
I saw him yesterday, or th' other day,
Or then, or then, with such, or such, and, as you say,   55
There was 'a gaming, there o'ertook in 's rouse,°
There falling out° at tennis," or perchance,

---

26. **drabbing:** Whoring.   28. **season:** Temper, soften.   30. **incontinency:** Habitual loose behavior.   31. **quaintly:** Delicately, ingeniously.   32. **taints of liberty:** Faults resulting from freedom.   34. **unreclaimed:** Untamed.   35. **general assault:** Tendency that assails all unrestrained youth.   38. **fetch of wit:** Clever trick.   40. **soil'd i' th' working:** Shopworn.   42. **converse:** Conversation.   **sound:** Sound out.   43. **Having ever:** If he has ever.   **prenominate crimes:** Before-mentioned offenses.   44. **breathe:** Speak.   45. **closes . . . consequence:** Follows your lead in some fashion as follows.   47. **addition:** Title.   56. **o'ertook in 's rouse:** Overcome by drink.   57. **falling out:** Quarreling.

"I saw him enter such a house of sale,"
Videlicet,° a brothel, or so forth. See you now,
Your bait of falsehood takes this carp° of truth;   60
And thus do we of wisdom and of reach,°
With windlasses° and with assays of bias,°
By indirections find directions° out.
So by my former lecture and advice
Shall you my son. You have me, have you not?   65

REYNALDO: My lord, I have.

POLONIUS: God buy ye; fare ye well.

REYNALDO: Good my lord.

POLONIUS: Observe his inclination in yourself.°

REYNALDO: I shall, my lord.

POLONIUS: And let him ply° his music.

REYNALDO: Well, my lord.   70

POLONIUS: Farewell.   (*Exit Reynaldo.*)

(*Enter Ophelia.*)

                    How now, Ophelia, what's the matter?

OPHELIA: O, my lord, my lord, I have been so affrighted!

POLONIUS: With what, i' th' name of God?

OPHELIA: My lord, as I was sewing in my closet,°
    Lord Hamlet, with his doublet° all unbrac'd,°   75
    No hat upon his head, his stockings fouled,
    Ungart'red, and down-gyved to his ankle,°
    Pale as his shirt, his knees knocking each other,
    And with a look so piteous in purport
    As if he had been loosed out of hell   80
    To speak of horrors — he comes before me.

POLONIUS: Mad for thy love?

OPHELIA: My lord, I do not know,
    But truly I do fear it.

POLONIUS: What said he?

OPHELIA: He took me by the wrist and held me hard.
    Then goes he to the length of all his arm,   85
    And, with his other hand thus o'er his brow
    He falls to such perusal of my face
    As 'a would draw it. Long stay'd he so.

---

59. **Videlicet:** Namely. 60. **carp:** A fish. 61. **reach:** Capacity, ability. 62. **windlasses:**
Circuitous paths (literally, circuits made to head off the game in hunting). **assays of bias:**
Attempts through indirection (like the curving path of the bowling ball, which is biased or
weighted to one side). 63. **directions:** The way things really are. 68. **in yourself:** In your
own person (as well as by asking questions). 70. **let him ply:** See that he continues to study.
74. **closet:** Private chamber. 75. **doublet:** Close-fitting jacket. **unbrac'd:** Unfastened.
77. **down-gyved to his ankle:** Fallen to the ankles (like gyves or fetters).

At last, a little shaking of mine arm
And thrice his head thus waving up and down,   90
He rais'd a sigh so piteous and profound
As it did seem to shatter all his bulk°
And end his being. That done, he lets me go,
And, with his head over his shoulder turn'd,
He seem'd to find his way without his eyes,   95
For out o' doors he went without their helps,
And, to the last, bended their light on me.

POLONIUS: Come, go with me. I will go seek the King.
This is the very ecstasy° of love
Whose violent property° fordoes° itself   100
And leads the will to desperate undertakings
As oft as any passion under heaven
That does afflict our natures. I am sorry.
What, have you given him any hard words of late?

OPHELIA: No, my good lord, but, as you did command,   105
I did repel his letters and denied
His access to me.

POLONIUS: That hath made him mad.
I am sorry that with better heed and judgment
I had not quoted° him. I fear'd he did but trifle
And meant to wrack thee; but, beshrew my jealousy!°   110
By heaven, it is as proper to our age°
To cast beyond° ourselves in our opinions
As it is common for the younger sort
To lack discretion. Come, go we to the King.
This must be known, which, being kept close,° might move   115
More grief to hide than hate to utter love.°
Come.   (*Exeunt.*)

[Scene 2]°

(*Flourish. Enter King and Queen, Rosencrantz, and Guildenstern [with others].*)

KING: Welcome, dear Rosencrantz and Guildenstern.
Moreover that° we much did long to see you,
The need we have to use you did provoke
Our hasty sending. Something have you heard
Of Hamlet's transformation — so call it,   5

---

92. **bulk:** Body. 99. **ecstasy:** Madness. 100. **property:** Nature. **fordoes:** Destroys.
109. **quoted:** Observed. 110. **beshrew my jealousy:** A plague upon my suspicious nature.
111. **proper . . . age:** Characteristic of us (old) men. 112. **cast beyond:** Overshoot, miscal-
culate. 115. **close:** Secret. 115–16. **might . . . love:** Might cause more grief (to others)
by hiding the knowledge of Hamlet's strange behavior to Ophelia than hatred by telling it.
ACT 2, SCENE 2. **Location:** The castle. 2. **Moreover that:** Besides the fact that.

Sith° nor th' exterior nor° the inward man
Resembles that° it was. What it should be,
More than his father's death, that thus hath put him
So much from th' understanding of himself,
I cannot dream of. I entreat you both   10
That, being of so young days° brought up with him,
And sith so neighbor'd to his youth and havior,
That you vouchsafe your rest° here in our court
Some little time, so by your companies
To draw him on to pleasures, and to gather   15
So much as from occasion you may glean,
Whether aught to us unknown afflicts him thus,
That, open'd,° lies within our remedy.
QUEEN: Good gentlemen, he hath much talk'd of you
And sure I am two men there is not living   20
To whom he more adheres. If it will please you
To show us so much gentry° and good will
As to expend your time with us awhile
For the supply and profit° of our hope,
Your visitation shall receive such thanks   25
As fits a king's remembrance.
ROSENCRANTZ: Both your Majesties
Might, by the sovereign power you have of us,
Put your dread pleasures more into command
Than to entreaty.
GUILDENSTERN: But we both obey,
And here give up ourselves in the full bent°   30
To lay our service freely at your feet,
To be commanded.
KING: Thanks, Rosencrantz and gentle Guildenstern.
QUEEN: Thanks, Guildenstern and gentle Rosencrantz.
And I beseech you instantly to visit   35
My too much changed son. Go, some of you,
And bring these gentlemen where Hamlet is.
GUILDENSTERN: Heavens make our presence and our practices
Pleasant and helpful to him!
QUEEN: Ay, amen!

(*Exeunt Rosencrantz and Guildenstern* [*with some Attendants*].)

(*Enter Polonius.*)

---

6. Sith: Since. **nor . . . nor:** Neither . . . nor. **7. that:** What. **11. of . . . days:** From such early youth. **13. vouchsafe your rest:** Please to stay. **18. open'd:** Revealed. **22. gentry:** Courtesy. **24. supply and profit:** Aid and successful outcome. **30. in . . . bent:** To the utmost degree of our capacity.

POLONIUS: Th' ambassadors from Norway, my good lord,   40
    Are joyfully return'd.
KING: Thou still° hast been the father of good news.
POLONIUS: Have I, my lord? I assure my good liege
    I hold my duty, as I hold my soul,
    Both to my God and to my gracious king;   45
    And I do think, or else this brain of mine
    Hunts not the trail of policy so sure
    As it hath us'd to do, that I have found
    The very cause of Hamlet's lunacy.
KING: O, speak of that! That do I long to hear.   50
POLONIUS: Give first admittance to th' ambassadors.
    My news shall be the fruit° to that great feast.
KING: Thyself do grace to them, and bring them in.

                                   (Exit Polonius.)

    He tells me, my dear Gertrude, he hath found
    The head and source of all your son's distemper.   55
QUEEN: I doubt° it is no other but the main,°
    His father's death, and our o'erhasty marriage.

(Enter Ambassadors [Voltimand and Cornelius, with Polonius].)

KING: Well, we shall sift him. —Welcome, my good friends!
    Say, Voltimand, what from our brother Norway?
VOLTIMAND: Most fair return of greetings and desires.   60
    Upon our first,° he sent out to suppress
    His nephew's levies, which to him appear'd
    To be a preparation 'gainst the Polack,
    But, better look'd into, he truly found
    It was against your Highness. Whereat griev'd   65
    That so his sickness, age, and impotence
    Was falsely borne in hand,° sends out arrests
    On Fortinbras, which he, in brief, obeys,
    Receives rebuke from Norway, and in fine°
    Makes vow before his uncle never more   70
    To give th' assay° of arms against your Majesty.
    Whereon old Norway, overcome with joy,
    Gives him three score thousand crowns in annual fee,
    And his commission to employ those soldiers,
    So levied as before, against the Polack,   75
    With an entreaty, herein further shown,

---

42. **still:** Always.   52. **fruit:** Dessert.   56. **doubt:** Fear, suspect.   **main:** Chief point, principal concern.   61. **Upon our first:** At our first words on the business.   67. **borne in hand:** Deluded, taken advantage of.   69. **in fine:** In the end.   71. **assay:** Trial.

[*Giving a paper.*]

That it might please you to give quiet pass
Through your dominions for this enterprise,
On such regards of safety and allowance°
As therein are set down.

KING: It likes° us well;   80
And at our more consider'd° time we'll read,
Answer, and think upon this business.
Meantime we thank you for your well-took labor.
Go to your rest; at night we'll feast together.
Most welcome home!   (*Exeunt Ambassadors.*)

POLONIUS: This business is well ended.   85
My liege, and madam, to expostulate°
What majesty should be, what duty is,
Why day is day, night night, and time is time,
Were nothing but to waste night, day, and time.
Therefore, since brevity is the soul of wit,°   90
And tediousness the limbs and outward flourishes,
I will be brief. Your noble son is mad.
Mad call I it, for, to define true madness,
What is 't but to be nothing else but mad?
But let that go.

QUEEN: More matter, with less art.   95

POLONIUS: Madam, I swear I use no art at all.
That he is mad, 'tis true; 'tis true 'tis pity,
And pity 'tis 'tis true — a foolish figure,°
But farewell it, for I will use no art.
Mad let us grant him, then, and now remains   100
That we find out the cause of this effect,
Or rather say, the cause of this defect,
For this effect defective comes by cause.°
Thus it remains, and the remainder thus.
Perpend.°   105
I have a daughter — have while she is mine —
Who, in her duty and obedience, mark,
Hath given me this. Now gather, and surmise.
[*Reads the letter.*] "To the celestial and my soul's idol,
the most beautified Ophelia" —   110
That's an ill phrase, a vile phrase; "beautified" is a vile
phrase. But you shall hear. Thus: [*Reads.*]

---

79. **On ... allowance:** With such pledges of safety and provisos. **80. likes:** Pleases.
81. consider'd: Suitable for deliberation. **86. expostulate:** Expound. **90. wit:** Sound sense
or judgment. **98. figure:** Figure of speech. **103. For ... cause:** I.e., for this defective behavior, this madness has a cause. **105. Perpend:** Consider.

"In her excellent white bosom, these, etc."
QUEEN: Came this from Hamlet to her?
POLONIUS: Good madam, stay awhile; I will be faithful.   [*Reads.*]   115
   "Doubt° thou the stars are fire,
      Doubt that the sun doth move,
  Doubt truth to be a liar,
      But never doubt I love.
  O dear Ophelia, I am ill at these numbers.° I have   120
  not art to reckon° my groans. But that I love thee
  best, O most best, believe it. Adieu.
      Thine evermore, most dear lady, whilst this
          machine° is to him, Hamlet."
  This in obedience hath my daughter shown me,   125
  And, more above,° hath his solicitings,
  As they fell out° by time, by means, and place,
  All given to mine ear.
KING: But how hath she
  Receiv'd his love?
POLONIUS: What do you think of me?
KING: As of a man faithful and honorable.   130
POLONIUS: I would fain prove so. But what might you think,
  When I had seen this hot love on the wing —
  As I perceiv'd it, I must tell you that,
  Before my daughter told me — what might you,
  Or my dear Majesty your Queen here, think,   135
  If I had play'd the desk or table-book,°
  Or given my heart a winking,° mute and dumb,
  Or look'd upon this love with idle sight?°
  What might you think? No, I went round° to work,
  And my young mistress thus I did bespeak:°   140
  "Lord Hamlet is a prince, out of thy star;°
  This must not be." And then I prescripts gave her,
  That she should lock herself from his resort,
  Admit no messengers, receive no tokens.
  Which done, she took the fruits of my advice;   145
  And he, repelled — a short tale to make —
  Fell into a sadness, then into a fast,
  Thence to a watch,° thence into a weakness,
  Thence to a lightness,° and, by this declension,°

116. **Doubt:** Suspect, question.   120. **ill . . . numbers:** Unskilled at writing verses.
121. **reckon:** (1) Count, (2) number metrically, scan.   124. **machine:** Body.   126. **more
above:** Moreover.   127. **fell out:** Occurred.   136. **play'd . . . table-book:** Remained shut
up, concealing the information.   137. **winking:** Closing of the eyes.   138. **with idle sight:**
Complacently or uncomprehendingly.   139. **round:** Roundly, plainly.   140. **bespeak:** Address.   141. **out of thy star:** Above your sphere, position.   148. **watch:** State of sleepless-
ness.   149. **lightness:** Light-headedness.   **declension:** Decline, deterioration.

Into the madness wherein now he raves,   150
   And all we mourn for.
KING: Do you think this?
QUEEN: It may be, very like.
POLONIUS: Hath there been such a time — I would fain know that —
   That I have positively said " 'Tis so,"
   When it prov'd otherwise?
KING: Not that I know.   155
POLONIUS [*pointing to his head and shoulder*]: Take this from this, if this be
   otherwise.
   If circumstances lead me, I will find
   Where truth is hid, though it were hid indeed
   Within the center.°
KING: How may we try it further?
POLONIUS: You know, sometimes he walks four hours together   160
   Here in the lobby.
QUEEN: So he does indeed.
POLONIUS: At such a time I'll loose my daughter to him.
   Be you and I behind an arras° then.
   Mark the encounter. If he love her not
   And be not from his reason fall'n thereon,°   165
   Let me be no assistant for a state,
   But keep a farm and carters.
KING: We will try it.

(*Enter Hamlet [reading on a book].*)

QUEEN: But look where sadly the poor wretch comes reading.
POLONIUS: Away, I do beseech you both, away.
   I'll board° him presently.

                         (*Exeunt King and Queen [with Attendants].*)

                          O, give me leave.   170
   How does my good Lord Hamlet?
HAMLET: Well, God-a-mercy.°
POLONIUS: Do you know me, my lord?
HAMLET: Excellent well. You are a fishmonger.°
POLONIUS: Not I, my lord.   175
HAMLET: Then I would you were so honest a man.
POLONIUS: Honest, my lord?
HAMLET: Ay, sir. To be honest, as this world goes, is to be one man pick'd out
   of ten thousand.

---

159. center: Middle point of the earth (which is also the center of the Ptolemaic universe).
163. arras: Hanging, tapestry. **165. thereon:** On that account. **170. board:** Accost.
172. God-a-mercy: Thank you. **174. fishmonger:** Fish merchant (with connotation of
bawd, procurer[?]).

POLONIUS: That's very true, my lord.   180

HAMLET: For if the sun breed maggots in a dead dog, being a good kissing
carrion° — Have you a daughter?

POLONIUS: I have, my lord.

HAMLET: Let her not walk i' th' sun.° Conception° is a blessing, but as your
daughter may conceive, friend, look to 't.   185

POLONIUS [aside]: How say you by that? Still harping on my daughter. Yet he
knew me not at first; 'a said I was a fishmonger. 'A is far gone. And truly
in my youth I suff'red much extremity for love, very near this. I'll speak
to him again. — What do you read, my lord?

HAMLET: Words, words, words.   190

POLONIUS: What is the matter,° my lord?

HAMLET: Between who?

POLONIUS: I mean, the matter that you read, my lord.

HAMLET: Slanders, sir, for the satirical rogue says here that old men have
gray beards, that their faces are wrinkled, their eyes purging° thick   195
amber and plum-tree gum, and that they have a plentiful lack of wit,
together with most weak hams. All which, sir, though I most powerfully
and potently believe, yet I hold it not honesty° to have it thus set down,
for you yourself, sir, shall grow old as I am, if like a crab you could go
backward.   200

POLONIUS [aside]: Though this be madness, yet there is method in 't. — Will
you walk out of the air, my lord?

HAMLET: Into my grave.

POLONIUS: Indeed, that's out of the air. [Aside.] How pregnant° sometimes
his replies are! A happiness° that often madness hits on, which reason   205
and sanity could not so prosperously° be deliver'd of. I will leave him,
[and suddenly contrive the means of meeting between him] and my
daughter. — My honorable lord, I will most humbly take my leave of
you.

HAMLET: You cannot, sir, take from me any thing that I will more willingly   210
part withal — except my life, except my life, except my life.

(*Enter Guildenstern and Rosencrantz.*)

POLONIUS: Fare you well, my lord.

HAMLET: These tedious old fools!°

POLONIUS: You go to seek the Lord Hamlet; there he is.

ROSENCRANTZ [to Polonius]: God save you, sir!   215

[*Exit Polonius.*]

181–82. **good kissing carrion:** A good piece of flesh for kissing, or for the sun to kiss.
184. **i' th' sun:** With additional implication of the sunshine of princely favors.   **Conception:**
(1) Understanding, (2) pregnancy.   **191. matter:** Substance (but Hamlet plays on the sense
of *basis for a dispute*).   **195. purging:** Discharging.   **198. honesty:** Decency.   **204. pregnant:** Full of meaning.   **205. happiness:** Felicity of expression.   **206. prosperously:** Successfully.   **213. old fools:** I.e., old men like Polonius.

GUILDENSTERN: My honor'd lord!

ROSENCRANTZ: My most dear lord!

HAMLET: My excellent good friends! How dost thou, Guildenstern? Ah, Rosencrantz! Good lads, how do you both?

ROSENCRANTZ: As the indifferent° children of the earth.   220

GUILDENSTERN: Happy in that we are not over-happy. On Fortune's cap we are not the very button.

HAMLET: Nor the soles of her shoe?

ROSENCRANTZ: Neither, my lord.

HAMLET: Then you live about her waist, or in the middle of her favors?   225

GUILDENSTERN: Faith, her privates° we.

HAMLET: In the secret parts of Fortune? O, most true; she is a strumpet.° What news?

ROSENCRANTZ: None, my lord, but the world's grown honest.

HAMLET: Then is doomsday near. But your news is not true. [Let me question 230 more in particular. What have you, my good friends, deserv'd at the hands of Fortune that she sends you to prison hither?

GUILDENSTERN: Prison, my lord?

HAMLET: Denmark's a prison.

ROSENCRANTZ: Then is the world one.   235

HAMLET: A goodly one, in which there are many confines,° wards,° and dungeons, Denmark being one o' th' worst.

ROSENCRANTZ: We think not so, my lord.

HAMLET: Why then 'tis none to you, for there is nothing either good or bad but thinking makes it so. To me it is a prison.   240

ROSENCRANTZ: Why then, your ambition makes it one. 'Tis too narrow for your mind.

HAMLET: O God, I could be bounded in a nutshell and count myself a king of infinite space, were it not that I have bad dreams.

GUILDENSTERN: Which dreams indeed are ambition, for the very substance of 245 the ambitious° is merely the shadow of a dream.

HAMLET: A dream itself is but a shadow.

ROSENCRANTZ: Truly, and I hold ambition of so airy and light a quality that it is but a shadow's shadow.

HAMLET: Then are our beggars bodies,° and our monarchs and outstretch'd° 250 heroes the beggars' shadows. Shall we to th' court? For, by my fay,° I cannot reason.

ROSENCRANTZ, GUILDENSTERN: We'll wait upon° you.

---

220. indifferent: Ordinary.   **226. privates:** Close acquaintances (with sexual pun on *private parts*).   **227. strumpet:** Prostitute (a common epithet for indiscriminate Fortune, see line 449 p. 1193).   **236. confines:** Places of confinement. **wards:** Cells.   **245–46. the very . . . ambitious:** That seemingly very substantial thing which the ambitious pursue.   **250. bodies:** Solid substances rather than shadows (since beggars are not ambitious).   **outstretch'd:** (1) Far-reaching in their ambition, (2) elongated as shadows.   **251. fay:** Faith. **253. wait upon:** Accompany, attend.

HAMLET: No such matter. I will not sort° you with the rest of my servants,
  for, to speak to you like an honest man, I am most dreadfully attended.°] 255
  But, in the beaten way° of friendship, what make° you at Elsinore?
ROSENCRANTZ: To visit you, my lord, no other occasion.
HAMLET: Beggar that I am, I am even poor in thanks; but I thank you, and
  sure, dear friends, my thanks are too dear a halfpenny.° Were you not
  sent for? Is it your own inclining? Is it a free visitation? Come, come, 260
  deal justly with me. Come, come; nay, speak.
GUILDENSTERN: What should we say, my lord?
HAMLET: Why, anything, but to th' purpose. You were sent for; and there is a
  kind of confession in your looks which your modesties have not craft
  enough to color. I know the good King and Queen have sent for you.   265
ROSENCRANTZ: To what end, my lord?
HAMLET: That you must teach me. But let me conjure° you, by the rights of
  our fellowship, by the consonancy of our youth,° by the obligation of
  our ever-preserv'd love, and by what more dear a better proposer° could
  charge° you withal, be even° and direct with me, whether you were sent 270
  for, or no?
ROSENCRANTZ [*aside to Guildenstern*]: What say you?
HAMLET [*aside*]: Nay then, I have an eye of° you. — If you love me, hold not
  off.
GUILDENSTERN: My lord, we were sent for.   275
HAMLET: I will tell you why; so shall my anticipation prevent your discovery,°
  and your secrecy to the King and Queen molt no feather.° I have of
  late — but wherefore I know not — lost all my mirth, forgone all custom
  of exercises; and indeed it goes so heavily with my disposition that this
  goodly frame, the earth, seems to me a sterile promontory; this most 280
  excellent canopy, the air, look you, this brave° o'erhanging firmament,
  this majestical roof fretted° with golden fire, why, it appeareth nothing
  to me but a foul and pestilent congregation of vapors. What a piece of
  work is a man! How noble in reason, how infinite in faculties, in form
  and moving how express° and admirable, in action how like an angel, 285
  in apprehension how like a god! The beauty of the world, the paragon of
  animals! And yet, to me, what is this quintessence° of dust? Man delights not me — no, nor woman neither, though by your smiling you
  seem to say so.

---

254. sort: Class, associate.   **255. dreadfully attended:** Waited upon in slovenly fashion.
256. beaten way: Familiar path.   **make:** Do.   **259. dear a halfpenny:** Expensive at the
price of a halfpenny, i.e., of little worth.   **267. conjure:** Adjure, entreat.   **268. consonancy
of our youth:** The fact that we are of the same age.   **269. better proposer:** More skillful pro-
pounder.   **270. charge:** Urge.   **even:** Straight, honest.   **273. of:** On.   **276. prevent your
discovery:** Forestall your disclosure.   **277. molt no feather:** Not diminish in the least.
281. brave: Splendid.   **282. fretted:** Adorned (with fret-work, as in a vaulted ceiling).
285. express: Well-framed (?), exact (?).   **287. quintessence:** The fifth essence of ancient
philosophy, beyond earth, water, air, and fire, supposed to be the substance of the heavenly
bodies and to be latent in all things.

ROSENCRANTZ: My lord, there was no such stuff in my thoughts.   290

HAMLET: Why did you laugh then, when I said "man delights not me"?

ROSENCRANTZ: To think, my lord, if you delight not in man, what lenten en-
tertainment° the players shall receive from you. We coted° them on the
way, and hither are they coming, to offer you service.

HAMLET: He that plays the king shall be welcome; his Majesty shall have trib-   295
ute of me. The adventurous knight shall use his foil and target,° the
lover shall not sigh gratis, the humorous man° shall end his part in
peace, [the clown shall make those laugh whose lungs are tickle o' th'
sere°], and the lady shall say her mind freely, or the blank verse shall
halt° for 't. What players are they?   300

ROSENCRANTZ: Even those you were wont to take such delight in, the tragedi-
ans of the city.

HAMLET: How chances it they travel? Their residence,° both in reputation
and profit, was better both ways.

ROSENCRANTZ: I think their inhibition° comes by the means of the innova-   305
tion.°

HAMLET: Do they hold the same estimation they did when I was in the city?
Are they so follow'd?

ROSENCRANTZ: No, indeed, are they not.

[HAMLET: How comes it? Do they grow rusty?   310

ROSENCRANTZ: Nay, their endeavor keeps in the wonted° pace. But there is,
sir, an aery° of children, little eyases,° that cry out on the top of question,° and are most tyrannically° clapp'd for 't. These are now the fashion, and so berattle° the common stages° — so they call them — that
many wearing rapiers° are afraid of goose-quills° and dare scarce come   315
thither.

HAMLET: What, are they children? Who maintains 'em? How are they escoted?° Will they pursue the quality° no longer than they can sing?°
Will they not say afterwards, if they should grow themselves to common°
players — as it is most like, if their means are no better — their writers do   320
them wrong, to make them exclaim against their own succession?°

292–93. lenten entertainment: Meager reception (appropriate to Lent).   **293. coted:** Overtook and passed beyond.   **296. foil and target:** Sword and shield.   **297. humorous man:**
Eccentric character, dominated by one trait or "humor."   **298–99. tickle o' th' sere:** Easy on
the trigger, ready to laugh easily. (*Sere* is part of a gunlock.)   **300. halt:** Limp.   **303. residence:** Remaining in one place, i.e., in the city.   **305. inhibition:** Formal prohibition (from
acting plays in the city).   **305–306. innovation:** I.e., the new fashion in satirical plays performed by boy actors in the "private" theaters; or possibly a political uprising; or the strict limitations set on the theater in London in 1600.   **311. wonted:** Usual.   **312. aery:** Nest.
eyases: Young hawks.   **312–13. cry . . . question:** Speak shrilly, dominating the controversy
(in decrying the public theaters).   **313. tyrannically:** Outrageously.   **314. berattle:** Berate.
common stages: Public theaters.   **315. many wearing rapiers:** Many men of fashion, who
were afraid to patronize the common players for fear of being satirized by the poets who wrote
for the children.   **goose-quills:** Pens of satirists.   **317–18. escoted:** Maintained.   **318. quality:** (Acting) profession.   **no longer . . . sing:** Only until their voices change.   **319. common:** Regular, adult.   **321. succession:** Future careers.

ROSENCRANTZ: Faith, there has been much to do° on both sides, and the nation holds it no sin to tarre° them to controversy. There was, for a while, no money bid for argument° unless the poet and the player went to cuffs in the question.°   325

HAMLET: Is 't possible?

GUILDENSTERN: O, there has been much throwing about of brains.

HAMLET: Do the boys carry it away?°

ROSENCRANTZ: Ay, that they do, my lord — Hercules and his load° too.°]

HAMLET: It is not very strange, for my uncle is King of Denmark, and those   330
that would make mouths° at him while my father liv'd, give twenty, forty, fifty, a hundred ducats° apiece for his picture in little.° 'Sblood,° there is something in this more than natural, if philosophy could find it out.

(A flourish [of trumpets within].)

GUILDENSTERN: There are the players.   335

HAMLET: Gentlemen, you are welcome to Elsinore. Your hands, come then. Th' appurtenance of welcome is fashion and ceremony. Let me comply° with you in this garb,° lest my extent° to the players, which, I tell you, must show fairly outwards,° should more appear like entertainment° than yours. You are welcome. But my uncle-father and aunt-mother are 340 deceiv'd.

GUILDENSTERN: In what, my dear lord?

HAMLET: I am but mad north-north-west.° When the wind is southerly I know a hawk from a handsaw.°

(Enter Polonius.)

POLONIUS: Well be with you, gentlemen!   345

HAMLET: Hark you, Guildenstern, and you too; at each ear a hearer. That great baby you see there is not yet out of his swaddling-clouts.°

ROSENCRANTZ: Happily° he is the second time come to them; for they say an old man is twice a child.

---

322. to do: Ado.   **323. tarre:** Set on (as dogs).   **324. argument:** Plot for a play.   **325. went . . . question:** Came to blows in the play itself.   **328. carry it away:** Win the day. **329. Hercules . . . load:** Thought to be an allusion to the sign of the Globe Theatre, which was Hercules bearing the world on his shoulder.   **310–29. How . . . load too:** The passage, omitted from the early quartos, alludes to the so-called War of the Theatres, 1599–1602, the rivalry between the children companies and the adult actors.   **331. mouths:** Faces.   **332. ducats:** Gold coins.   **in little:** In miniature.   **'Sblood:** By His (God's, Christ's) blood.   **337. comply:** Observe the formalities of courtesy.   **338. garb:** Manner.   **my extent:** The extent of my showing courtesy.   **show fairly outwards:** Look cordial to outward appearances.   **entertainment:** A (warm) reception.   **343. north-north-west:** Only partly, at times.   **344. hawk, handsaw:** Mattock (or *hack*) and a carpenter's cutting tool respectively; also birds, with a play on *hernshaw* or heron.   **347. swaddling-clouts:** Cloths in which to wrap a newborn baby.   **348. Happily:** Haply, perhaps.

HAMLET: I will prophesy he comes to tell me of the players; mark it. — You say   350
    right, sir, o' Monday morning, 'twas then indeed.

POLONIUS: My lord, I have news to tell you.

HAMLET: My lord, I have news to tell you. When Roscius° was an actor in
    Rome —

POLONIUS: The actors are come hither, my lord.   355

HAMLET: Buzz,° buzz!

POLONIUS: Upon my honor —

HAMLET: Then came each actor on his ass —

POLONIUS: The best actors in the world, either for tragedy, comedy, history,
    pastoral, pastoral-comical, historical-pastoral, tragical-historical, tragical-   360
    comical-historical-pastoral, scene individable,° or poem unlimited.°
    Seneca° cannot be too heavy, nor Plautus° too light. For the law of writ
    and the liberty,° these are the only men.

HAMLET: O Jephthah, judge of Israel,° what a treasure hadst thou!

POLONIUS: What a treasure had he, my lord?   365

HAMLET: Why,
    "One fair daughter, and no more,
    The which he loved passing° well."

POLONIUS [*aside*]: Still on my daughter.

HAMLET: Am I not i' th' right, old Jephthah?   370

POLONIUS: If you call me Jephthah, my lord, I have a daughter that I love
    passing well.

HAMLET: Nay, that follows not.

POLONIUS: What follows, then, my lord?

HAMLET: Why,   375
    "As by lot, God wot,"°
    and then, you know,
    "It came to pass, as most like° it was."
    The first row° of the pious chanson° will show you more, for look where
    my abridgement° comes.   380

(*Enter the Players.*)

    You are welcome, masters; welcome, all. I am glad to see thee well. Wel-
    come, good friends. O, old friend! Why, thy face is valanc'd° since I saw

---

353. Roscius: A famous Roman actor who died in 62 B.C.E.   **356. Buzz:** An interjection
used to denote stale news.   **361. scene individable:** A play observing the unity of place.
poem unlimited: A play disregarding the unities of time and place.   **362. Seneca:** Writer of
Latin tragedies.   **Plautus:** Writer of Latin comedy.   **362–63. law . . . liberty:** Dramatic
composition both according to rules and without rules, i.e., "classical" and "romantic" dramas.
364. Jephthah . . . Israel: Jephthah had to sacrifice his daughter; see Judges 11. Hamlet goes
on to quote from a ballad on the theme.   **368. passing:** Surpassingly.   **376. wot:** Knows.
378. like: Likely, probable.   **379. row:** Stanza.   **chanson:** Ballad, song.   **380. my abridge-
ment:** Something that cuts short my conversation; also, a diversion.   **382. valanc'd:** Fringed
(with a beard).

thee last. Com'st thou to beard° me in Denmark? What, my young
lady° and mistress? By 'r lady, your ladyship is nearer to heaven than
when I saw you last, by the altitude of a chopine.° Pray God your voice, 385
like a piece of uncurrent° gold, be not crack'd within the ring.° Masters, you are all welcome. We'll e'en to 't like French falconers, fly at
anything we see. We'll have a speech straight.° Come, give us a taste of
your quality; come, a passionate speech.

FIRST PLAYER: What speech, my good lord? 390

HAMLET: I heard thee speak me a speech once, but it was never acted, or, if it
was, not above once, for the play, I remember, pleas'd not the million;
'twas caviary to the general.° But it was—as I receiv'd it, and others,
whose judgments in such matters cried in the top of° mine—an excellent play, well digested in the scenes, set down with as much modesty as 395
cunning.° I remember one said there were no sallets° in the lines to
make the matter savory, nor no matter in the phrase that might indict°
the author of affectation, but call'd it an honest method, as wholesome
as sweet, and by very much more handsome than fine.° One speech in
't I chiefly lov'd: 'twas Aeneas' tale to Dido, and thereabout of it espe- 400
cially when he speaks of Priam's slaughter.° If it live in your memory,
begin at this line: let me see, let me see—
"The rugged Pyrrhus,° like th' Hyrcanian beast"°—
'Tis not so. It begins with Pyrrhus:
"The rugged Pyrrhus, he whose sable° arms, 405
Black as his purpose, did the night resemble
When he lay couched in the ominous horse,°
Hath now this dread and black complexion smear'd
With heraldry more dismal.° Head to foot
Now is he total gules,° horridly trick'd° 410
With blood of fathers, mothers, daughters, sons,
Bak'd and impasted° with the parching streets,°

---

383. **beard:** Confront (with obvious pun).   383–84. **young lady:** Boy playing women's
parts.   385. **chopine:** Thick-soled shoe of Italian fashion.   386. **uncurrent:** Not passable as
lawful coinage.   **crack'd . . . ring:** Changed from adolescent to male voice, no longer suitable
for women's roles. (Coins featured rings enclosing the sovereign's head; if the coin was cracked
within this ring, it was unfit for currency.)   388. **straight:** At once.   393. **caviary to the
general:** Caviar to the multitude, i.e., a choice dish too elegant for coarse tastes.   394. **cried
in the top of:** Spoke with greater authority than.   396. **cunning:** Skill.   **sallets:** Salad, i.e.,
spicy improprieties.   397. **indict:** Convict.   399. **fine:** Elaborately ornamented, showy.
401. **Priam's slaughter:** The slaying of the ruler of Troy, when the Greeks finally took the city.
403. **Pyrrhus:** A Greek hero in the Trojan War, also known as Neoptolemus, son of Achilles.
Hyrcanian beast: I.e., the tiger. (See Virgil, *Aeneid*, 4.266; compare the whole speech with
Marlowe's *Dido Queen of Carthage*, 2.1.214 ff.)   405. **sable:** Black (for reasons of camouflage
during the episode of the Trojan horse).   407. **ominous horse:** Trojan horse, by which the
Greeks gained access to Troy.   409. **dismal:** Ill-omened.   410. **gules:** Red (a heraldic term).
trick'd: Adorned, decorated.   412. **impasted:** Crusted, like a thick paste.   **with . . . streets:**
By the parching heat of the streets (because of the fires everywhere).

That lend a tyrannous and a damned light
To their lord's° murder. Roasted in wrath and fire,
And thus o'er-sized° with coagulate gore,   415
With eyes like carbuncles, the hellish Pyrrhus
Old grandsire Priam seeks."
So proceed you.

POLONIUS: 'Fore God, my lord, well spoken, with good accent and good
discretion.   420

FIRST PLAYER: "Anon he finds him
Striking too short at Greeks. His antique sword,
Rebellious to his arm, lies where it falls,
Repugnant° to command. Unequal match'd,
Pyrrhus at Priam drives, in rage strikes wide,   425
But with the whiff and wind of his fell° sword
Th' unnerved father falls. [Then senseless Ilium,°]
Seeming to feel this blow, with flaming top
Stoops to his° base, and with a hideous crash
Takes prisoner Pyrrhus' ear. For, lo! His sword,   430
Which was declining on the milky head
Of reverend Priam, seem'd i' th' air to stick.
So as a painted° tyrant Pyrrhus stood,
And, like a neutral to his will and matter,°
Did nothing.   435
But, as we often see, against° some storm,
A silence in the heavens, the rack° stand still,
The bold winds speechless, and the orb below
As hush as death, anon the dreadful thunder
Doth rend the region,° so, after Pyrrhus' pause,   440
Aroused vengeance sets him new a-work,
And never did the Cyclops'° hammers fall
On Mars's armor forg'd for proof eterne°
With less remorse than Pyrrhus' bleeding sword
Now falls on Priam.   445
Out, out, thou strumpet Fortune! All you gods,
In general synod,° take away her power!
Break all the spokes and fellies° from her wheel,
And bowl the round nave° down the hill of heaven,
As low as to the fiends!"   450

---

414. **their lord's**: Priam's.   415. **o'er-sized**: Covered as with size or glue.   424. **Repugnant**: Disobedient, resistant.   426. **fell**: Cruel.   427. **senseless Ilium**: Insensate Troy.   429. **his**: Its.   433. **painted**: Painted in a picture.   434. **like . . . matter**: As though poised indecisively between his intention and its fulfillment.   436. **against**: Just before.   437. **rack**: Mass of clouds.   440. **region**: Sky.   442. **Cyclops**: Giant armor makers in the smithy of Vulcan.   443. **proof eterne**: Eternal resistance to assault.   447. **synod**: Assembly.   448. **fellies**: Pieces of wood forming the rim of a wheel.   449. **nave**: Hub.

POLONIUS: This is too long.

HAMLET: It shall to the barber's with your beard. — Prithee say on. He's for a
    jig° or a tale of bawdry, or he sleeps. Say on, come to Hecuba.°

FIRST PLAYER: "But who, ah woe! had seen the mobled° queen" —

HAMLET: "The mobled queen?"   455

POLONIUS: That's good. "Mobled queen" is good.

FIRST PLAYER: "Run barefoot up and down, threat'ning the flames
    With bisson rheum,° a clout° upon that head
    Where late the diadem stood, and for a robe,
    About her lank and all o'er-teemed° loins,   460
    A blanket, in the alarm of fear caught up —
    Who this had seen, with tongue in venom steep'd,
    'Gainst Fortune's state° would treason have pronounc'd.°
    But if the gods themselves did see her then
    When she saw Pyrrhus make malicious sport   465
    In mincing with his sword her husband's limbs,
    The instant burst of clamor that she made,
    Unless things mortal move them not at all,
    Would have made milch° the burning eyes of heaven,
    And passion in the gods."   470

POLONIUS: Look whe'er° he has not turn'd his color and has tears in 's eyes.
    Prithee, no more.

HAMLET: 'Tis well; I'll have thee speak out the rest of this soon. Good my
    lord, will you see the players well bestow'd?° Do you hear, let them be
    well us'd, for they are the abstract° and brief chronicles of the time. 475
    After your death you were better have a bad epitaph than their ill report
    while you live.

POLONIUS: My lord, I will use them according to their desert.

HAMLET: God's bodkin,° man, much better! Use every man after his des-
    ert, and who shall scape whipping? Use them after your own honor and 480
    dignity. The less they deserve, the more merit is in your bounty. Take
    them in.

POLONIUS: Come, sirs.

HAMLET: Follow him, friends. We'll hear a play tomorrow. [*As they start to
    leave, Hamlet detains the First Player.*] Dost thou hear me, old friend? 485
    Can you play the Murder of Gonzago?

FIRST PLAYER: Ay, my lord.

HAMLET: We'll ha 't tomorrow night. You could, for need, study a speech of
    some dozen or sixteen lines, which I would set down and insert in 't,
    could you not?   490

---

453. jig: Comic song and dance often given at the end of a play. **Hecuba:** Wife of Priam.
454. mobled: Muffled. **458. bisson rheum:** Blinding tears. **clout:** Cloth. **460. o'er-
teemed:** Worn out with bearing children. **463. state:** Rule, managing. **pronounc'd:** Proclaimed. **469. milch:** Milky moist with tears. **471. whe'er:** Whether. **474. bestow'd:**
Lodged. **475. abstract:** Summary account. **479. God's bodkin:** By God's (Christ's) little
body, *bodykin* (not to be confused with *bodkin*, dagger).

FIRST PLAYER: Ay, my lord.
HAMLET: Very well. Follow that lord, and look you mock him not. — My good
　　friends, I'll leave you till night. You are welcome to Elsinore.

　　　　　　　　　　　　　　　　　　　　(*Exeunt Polonius and Players.*)

ROSENCRANTZ: Good my lord!

　　　　　　　　　　　　　　　　　(*Exeunt [Rosencrantz and Guildenstern].*)

HAMLET: Ay, so, God buy you. — Now I am alone.　　　　　　　　　　　495
　　O, what a rogue and peasant slave am I!
　　Is it not monstrous that this player here,
　　But in a fiction, in a dream of passion,
　　Could force his soul so to his own conceit°
　　That from her working all his visage wann'd,°　　　　　　　　　　500
　　Tears in his eyes, distraction in his aspect,
　　A broken voice, and his whole function suiting
　　With forms to his conceit?° And all for nothing!
　　For Hecuba!
　　What's Hecuba to him, or he to Hecuba,　　　　　　　　　　　　505
　　That he should weep for her? What would he do,
　　Had he the motive and the cue for passion
　　That I have? He would drown the stage with tears
　　And cleave the general ear with horrid speech,
　　Make mad the guilty and appall the free,°　　　　　　　　　　　510
　　Confound the ignorant, and amaze indeed
　　The very faculties of eyes and ears. Yet I,
　　A dull and muddy-mettled° rascal, peak,°
　　Like John-a-dreams,° unpregnant of° my cause,
　　And can say nothing — no, not for a king　　　　　　　　　　　515
　　Upon whose property° and most dear life
　　A damn'd defeat was made. Am I a coward?
　　Who calls me villain? Breaks my pate across?
　　Plucks off my beard, and blows it in my face?
　　Tweaks me by the nose? Gives me the lie° i' th' throat,　　　　　520
　　As deep as to the lungs? Who does me this?
　　Ha, 'swounds, I should take it; for it cannot be
　　But I am pigeon-liver'd,° and lack gall
　　To make oppression bitter, or ere this
　　I should have fatted all the region kites°　　　　　　　　　　　525

---

499. **conceit:** Conception.　500. **wann'd:** Grew pale.　502–503. **his whole . . . conceit:**
His whole being responded with actions to suit his thought.　510. **free:** Innocent.　513.
muddy-mettled: Dull-spirited.　**peak:** Mope, pine.　514. **John-a-dreams:** Sleepy dreaming
idler.　**unpregnant of:** Not quickened by.　516. **property:** The crown; perhaps also character, quality.　520. **Gives me the lie:** Calls me a liar.　523. **pigeon-liver'd:** The pigeon or
dove was popularly supposed to be mild because it secreted no gall.　525. **region kites:** Kites
(birds of prey) of the air, from the vicinity.

With this slave's offal. Bloody, bawdy villain!
Remorseless, treacherous, lecherous, kindless° villain!
[O, vengeance!]
Why, what an ass am I! This is most brave,
That I, the son of a dear father murder'd,   530
Prompted to my revenge by heaven and hell,
Must, like a whore, unpack my heart with words,
And fall a-cursing, like a very drab,°
A stallion!° Fie upon 't, foh! About,° my brains!
Hum, I have heard   535
That guilty creatures sitting at a play
Have by the very cunning of the scene
Been struck so to the soul that presently°
They have proclaim'd their malefactions;
For murder, though it have no tongue, will speak   540
With most miraculous organ. I'll have these players
Play something like the murder of my father
Before mine uncle. I'll observe his looks;
I'll tent° him to the quick. If 'a do blench,°
I know my course. The spirit that I have seen   545
May be the devil, and the devil hath power
T' assume a pleasing shape; yea, and perhaps
Out of my weakness and my melancholy,
As he is very potent with such spirits,°
Abuses° me to damn me. I'll have grounds   550
More relative° than this. The play's the thing
Wherein I'll catch the conscience of the King.

                                                                    (Exit.)

[ACT 3 / Scene 1]°

(Enter King, Queen, Polonius, Ophelia, Rosencrantz, Guildenstern, Lords.)

KING: And can you, by no drift of conference,°
       Get from him why he puts on this confusion,
       Grating so harshly all his days of quiet
       With turbulent and dangerous lunacy?
ROSENCRANTZ: He does confess he feels himself distracted,   5
       But from what cause 'a will by no means speak.

---

527. kindless: Unnatural.   533. drab: Prostitute.   534. stallion: Prostitute (male or female). (Many editors follow the Folio reading of scullion.)   About: About it, to work.   538.
presently: At once.   544. tent: Probe.   blench: Quail, flinch.   549. spirits: Humors (of
melancholy).   550. Abuses: Deludes.   551. relative: Closely related, pertinent.   ACT 3,
SCENE 1. Location: The castle.   1. drift of conference: Direction of conversation.

GUILDENSTERN: Nor do we find him forward° to be sounded,°
 But with a crafty madness keeps aloof
 When we would bring him on to some confession
 Of his true state.
QUEEN: Did he receive you well?   10
ROSENCRANTZ: Most like a gentleman.
GUILDENSTERN: But with much forcing of his disposition.°
ROSENCRANTZ: Niggard of question,° but of our demands
 Most free in his reply.
QUEEN: Did you assay° him
 To any pastime?   15
ROSENCRANTZ: Madam, it so fell out that certain players
 We o'er-raught° on the way. Of these we told him,
 And there did seem in him a kind of joy
 To hear of it. They are here about the court,
 And, as I think, they have already order   20
 This night to play before him.
POLONIUS: 'Tis most true,
 And he beseech'd me to entreat your Majesties
 To hear and see the matter.
KING: With all my heart, and it doth much content me
 To hear him so inclin'd.   25
 Good gentlemen, give him a further edge,°
 And drive his purpose into these delights.
ROSENCRANTZ: We shall, my lord.

         (Exeunt Rosencrantz and Guildenstern.)

KING: Sweet Gertrude, leave us too,
 For we have closely° sent for Hamlet hither,
 That he, as 'twere by accident, may here   30
 Affront° Ophelia.
 Her father and myself, [lawful espials,°]
 Will so bestow ourselves that seeing, unseen,
 We may of their encounter frankly judge,
 And gather by him, as he is behav'd,   35
 If 't be th' affliction of his love or no
 That thus he suffers for.
QUEEN: I shall obey you.
 And for your part, Ophelia, I do wish
 That your good beauties be the happy cause

---

7. **forward:** Willing. **sounded:** Tested deeply. **12. disposition:** Inclination. **13. question:** Conversation. **14. assay:** Try to win. **17. o'er-raught:** Overtook and passed. **26. edge:** Incitement. **29. closely:** Privately. **31. Affront:** Confront, meet. **32. espials:** Spies.

Of Hamlet's wildness. So shall I hope your virtues   40
Will bring him to his wonted way again,
To both your honors.

OPHELIA: Madam, I wish it may.

[*Exit Queen.*]

POLONIUS: Ophelia, walk you here. — Gracious,° so please you,
We will bestow ourselves. [*To Ophelia.*] Read on this book,

[*Gives her a book.*]

That show of such an exercise° may color°   45
Your loneliness. We are oft to blame in this —
'Tis too much prov'd° — that with devotion's visage
And pious action we do sugar o'er
The devil himself.

KING [*aside*]: O, 'tis too true!   50
How smart a lash that speech doth give my conscience!
The harlot's cheek, beautied with plast'ring art,
Is not more ugly to° the thing° that helps it
Than is my deed to my most painted word.
O heavy burden!   55

POLONIUS: I hear him coming. Let's withdraw, my lord.

[*King and Polonius withdraw.°*]

(*Enter Hamlet. [Ophelia pretends to read a book.]*)

HAMLET: To be, or not to be, that is the question:
Whether 'tis nobler in the mind to suffer
The slings and arrows of outrageous fortune,
Or to take arms against a sea of troubles,   60
And by opposing end them. To die, to sleep —
No more — and by a sleep to say we end
The heart-ache and the thousand natural shocks
That flesh is heir to. 'Tis a consummation
Devoutly to be wish'd. To die, to sleep;   65
To sleep, perchance to dream. Ay, there's the rub,°
For in that sleep of death what dreams may come
When we have shuffled° off this mortal coil,°
Must give us pause. There's the respect°

---

43. **Gracious:** Your Grace (i.e., the King).   45. **exercise:** Act of devotion. (The book she reads is one of devotion.)   **color:** Give a plausible appearance to.   47. **too much prov'd:** Too often shown to be true, too often practiced.   53. **to:** Compared to.   **thing:** I.e., the cosmetic. [S.D.] **withdraw:** The King and Polonius may retire behind an arras. The stage directions specify that they "enter" again near the end of the scene.   66. **rub:** Literally, an obstacle in the game of bowls.   68. **shuffled:** Sloughed, cast.   **coil:** Turmoil.   69. **respect:** Consideration.

That makes calamity of so long life.°   70
For who would bear the whips and scorns of time,
Th' oppressor's wrong, the proud man's contumely,°
The pangs of despis'd° love, the law's delay,
The insolence of office,° and the spurns°
That patient merit of th' unworthy takes,   75
When he himself might his quietus° make
With a bare bodkin?° Who would fardels° bear,
To grunt and sweat under a weary life,
But that the dread of something after death,
The undiscover'd country from whose bourn°   80
No traveler returns, puzzles the will,
And makes us rather bear those ills we have
Than fly to others that we know not of?
Thus conscience does make cowards of us all
And thus the native hue° of resolution   85
Is sicklied o'er with the pale cast° of thought,
And enterprises of great pitch° and moment°
With this regard° their currents° turn awry,
And lose the name of action. — Soft you now,
The fair Ophelia. Nymph, in thy orisons°   90
Be all my sins rememb'red.

OPHELIA: Good my lord,
How does your honor for this many a day?

HAMLET: I humbly thank you; well, well, well.

OPHELIA: My lord, I have remembrances of yours,
That I have longed long to re-deliver.   95
I pray you, now receive them.   [*Offers tokens.*]

HAMLET: No, not I, I never gave you aught.

OPHELIA: My honor'd lord, you know right well you did,
And with them words of so sweet breath compos'd
As made these things more rich. Their perfume lost,   100
Take these again, for to the noble mind
Rich gifts wax poor when givers prove unkind.
There, my lord.   [*Gives tokens.*]

HAMLET: Ha, ha! Are you honest?°

OPHELIA: My lord?   105

HAMLET: Are you fair?°

---

70. **of . . . life:** So long-lived. 72. **contumely:** Insolent abuse. 73. **despis'd:** Rejected.
74. **office:** Officialdom. **spurns:** Insults. 76. **quietus:** Acquittance; here, death. 77.
bodkin: Dagger. **fardels:** Burdens. 80. **bourn:** Boundary. 85. **native hue:** Natural
color, complexion. 86. **cast:** Shade of color. 87. **pitch:** Height (as of a falcon's flight).
moment: Importance. 88. **regard:** Respect, consideration. **currents:** Courses. 90.
orisons: Prayers. 104. **honest:** (1) Truthful; (2) chaste. 106. **fair:** (1) Beautiful; (2) just,
honorable.

OPHELIA: What means your lordship?

HAMLET: That if you be honest and fair, your honesty° should admit no dis-
course° to your beauty.

OPHELIA: Could beauty, my lord, have better commerce° than with hon-   110
esty?

HAMLET: Ay, truly, for the power of beauty will sooner transform honesty
from what it is to a bawd than the force of honesty can translate beauty
into his likeness. This was sometime° a paradox,° but now the time°
gives it proof. I did love you once.   115

OPHELIA: Indeed, my lord, you made me believe so.

HAMLET: You should not have believ'd me, for virtue cannot so inoculate°
our old stock but we shall relish of it.° I lov'd you not.

OPHELIA: I was the more deceiv'd.

HAMLET: Get thee to a nunn'ry.° Why wouldst thou be a breeder of sinners?   120
I am myself indifferent honest;° but yet I could accuse me of such
things that it were better my mother had not borne me: I am very
proud, revengeful, ambitious, with more offenses at my beck° than I
have thoughts to put them in, imagination to give them shape, or time
to act them in. What should such fellows as I do crawling between   125
earth and heaven? We are arrant knaves, all; believe none of us. Go thy
ways to a nunn'ry. Where's your father?

OPHELIA: At home, my lord.

HAMLET: Let the doors be shut upon him, that he may play the fool nowhere
but in 's own house.   130
Farewell.

OPHELIA: O, help him, you sweet heavens!

HAMLET: If thou dost marry, I'll give thee this plague for thy dowry: be thou
as chaste as ice, as pure as snow, thou shalt not escape calumny. Get
thee to a nunn'ry, farewell. Or, if thou wilt needs marry, marry a fool,   135
for wise men know well enough what monsters° you° make of them. To
a nunn'ry, go, and quickly too. Farewell.

OPHELIA: Heavenly powers, restore him!

HAMLET: I have heard of your paintings too, well enough. God hath given
you one face, and you make yourselves another. You jig,° and amble,   140
and you lisp, you nickname God's creatures, and make your wanton-
ness your ignorance.° Go to, I'll no more on 't; it hath made me

---

108. your honesty: Your chastity.   108–109. discourse: Familiar dealings.   110. commerce: Dealings.   114. sometime: Formerly.   paradox: A view opposite to commonly held
opinion   the time: The present age.   117. inoculate: Graft, be engrafted to.   118. but . . .
it: That we do not still have about us a taste of the old stock; i.e., retain our sinfulness.   120.
nunn'ry: (1) Convent; (2) brothel.   121. indifferent honest: Reasonably virtuous.   123.
beck: Command.   136. monsters: An allusion to the horns of a cuckold.   you: You
women.   140. jig: Dance and sing affectedly and wantonly.   141–42. make . . . ignorance:
Excuse your affection on the grounds of your ignorance.

mad. I say, we will have no more marriage. Those that are married
already—all but one—shall live. The rest shall keep as they are. To a
nunn'ry, go.   (*Exit.*) 145

OPHELIA: O, what a noble mind is here o'erthrown!
  The courtier's, soldier's, scholar's, eye, tongue, sword,
  Th' expectancy and rose of the fair state,°
  The glass of fashion and the mold of form,°
  Th' observ'd of all observers,° quite, quite down!   150
  And I, of ladies most deject and wretched,
  That suck'd the honey of his music vows,
  Now see that noble and most sovereign reason,
  Like sweet bells jangled, out of time and harsh,
  That unmatch'd form and feature of blown° youth   155
  Blasted with ecstasy.° O, woe is me,
  T' have seen what I have seen, see what I see!

(*Enter King and Polonius.*)

KING: Love? His affections do not that way tend;
  Nor what he spake, though it lack'd form a little,
  Was not like madness. There's something in his soul,   160
  O'er which his melancholy sits on brood,
  And I do doubt° the hatch and the disclose°
  Will be some danger; which for to prevent,
  I have in quick determination
  Thus set it down: he shall with speed to England,   165
  For the demand of° our neglected tribute.
  Haply the seas and countries different
  With variable° objects shall expel
  This something-settled° matter in his heart,
  Whereon his brains still beating puts him thus   170
  From fashion of himself.° What think you on 't?

POLONIUS: It shall do well. But yet do I believe
  The origin and commencement of his grief
  Sprung from neglected love.—How now, Ophelia?
  You need not tell us what Lord Hamlet said;   175
  We heard it all.—My lord, do as you please,
  But, if you hold it fit, after the play
  Let his queen mother all alone entreat him

---

148. **Th' expectancy . . . state:** The hope and ornament of the kingdom made fair (by him).
149. **The glass . . . form:** The mirror of fashion and the pattern of courtly behavior.
150. **observ'd . . . observers:** The center of attention and honor in the court. 155. **blown:**
Blooming. 156. **ecstasy:** Madness. 162. **doubt:** Fear. **disclose:** Disclosure. 166. **For . . .**
of: To demand. 168. **variable:** Various. 169. **something-settled:** Somewhat settled.
171. **From . . . himself:** Out of his natural manner.

To show his grief. Let her be round° with him;
And I'll be plac'd, so please you, in the ear   180
Of all their conference. If she find him not,
To England send him, or confine him where
Your wisdom best shall think.
KING: It shall be so.
Madness in great ones must not unwatch'd go.

                                                                (*Exeunt.*)

[Scene 2]°

(*Enter Hamlet and three of the Players.*)

HAMLET: Speak the speech, I pray you, as I pronounc'd it to you, trippingly
on the tongue. But if you mouth it, as many of our players° do, I had as
lief the town-crier spoke my lines. Nor do not saw the air too much
with your hand, thus, but use all gently; for in the very torrent, tempest,
and, as I may say, whirlwind of your passion, you must acquire and   5
beget a temperance that may give it smoothness. O, it offends me to the
soul to hear a robustious° periwig-pated° fellow tear a passion to tat-
ters, to very rags, to split the ears of the groundlings,° who for the most
part are capable of° nothing but inexplicable dumb-shows and noise. I
would have such a fellow whipp'd for o'er-doing Termagant.° It out-   10
herods Herod.° Pray you, avoid it.
FIRST PLAYER: I warrant your honor.
HAMLET: Be not too tame neither, but let your own discretion be your tutor.
Suit the action to the word, the word to the action, with this special observance, that you o'erstep not the modesty of nature. For anything so   15
o'erdone is from° the purpose of playing, whose end, both at the first
and now, was and is, to hold, as 't were, the mirror up to nature, to
show virtue her feature, scorn her own image, and the very age and
body of the time his° form and pressure.° Now this overdone, or come
tardy off,° though it makes the unskillful laugh, cannot but make the   20
judicious grieve, the censure of which one° must in your allowance
o'erweigh a whole theater of others. O, there be players that I have seen
play, and heard others praise, and that highly, not to speak it profanely,

---

179. round: Blunt.   ACT 3, SCENE 2. Location: The castle.   2. our players: Indefinite use;
i.e., *players nowadays.*   7. robustious: Violent, boisterous.   periwig-pated: Wearing a wig.
8. groundlings: Spectators who paid least and stood in the yard of the theater.   9. capable of:
Susceptible of being influenced by.   10. Termagant: A god of the Saracens; a character in the
St. Nicholas play, where one of his worshipers, leaving him in charge of goods, returns to find
them stolen; whereupon he beats the god or idol, which howls vociferously.   11. Herod:
Herod of Jewry. (A character in *The Slaughter of the Innocents* and other cycle plays. The part was
played with great noise and fury.)   16. from: Contrary to.   19. his: Its.   pressure: Stamp,
impressed character.   19–20. come tardy off: Inadequately done.   21. the censure . . . one:
The judgment of even one of whom.

that, neither having th' accent of Christians nor the gait of Christian, pagan, nor man, have so strutted and bellow'd that I have thought   25
some of nature's journeymen° had made men and not made them well, they imitated humanity so abominably.

FIRST PLAYER: I hope we have reform'd that indifferently° with us, sir.

HAMLET: O, reform it altogether. And let those that play your clowns speak no more than is set down for them; for there be of them° that will   30
themselves laugh, to set on some quantity of barren° spectators to laugh too, though in the mean time some necessary question of the play be then to be consider'd. That's villainous, and shows a most piti-ful ambition in the fool that uses it. Go, make you ready.

                                                    [*Exeunt Players.*]

(*Enter Polonius, Guildenstern, and Rosencrantz.*)

How now, my lord? Will the King hear this piece of work?   35

POLONIUS: And the Queen too, and that presently.°

HAMLET: Bid the players make haste.

                                                    [*Exit Polonius.*]

Will you two help to hasten them?

ROSENCRANTZ: Ay, my lord.   (*Exeunt they two.*)

HAMLET: What ho, Horatio!

(*Enter Horatio.*)

HORATIO: Here, sweet lord, at your service.   40

HAMLET: Horatio, thou art e'en as just a man
    As e'er my conversation cop'd withal.°

HORATIO: O, my dear lord —

HAMLET: Nay, do not think I flatter;
    For what advancement may I hope from thee
    That no revenue hast but thy good spirits,   45
    To feed and clothe thee? Why should the poor be flatter'd?
    No, let the candied° tongue lick absurd pomp,
    And crook the pregnant° hinges of the knee
    Where thrift° may follow fawning. Dost thou hear?
    Since my dear soul was mistress of her choice   50
    And could of men distinguish her election,
    Sh' hath seal'd thee for herself, for thou hast been
    As one, in suff'ring all, that suffers nothing,
    A man that Fortune's buffets and rewards

---

26. journeymen: Laborers not yet masters in their trade. **28. indifferently:** Tolerably. **30. of them:** Some among them. **31. barren:** I.e., of wit. **36. presently:** At once. **42. my . . . withal:** My contact with people provided opportunity for encounter with. **47. candied:** Sugared, flattering. **48. pregnant:** Compliant. **49. thrift:** Profit.

Hast ta'en with equal thanks; and blest are those   55
Whose blood° and judgment are so well commeddled°
That they are not a pipe for Fortune's finger
To sound what stop° she please. Give me that man
That is not passion's slave, and I will wear him
In my heart's core, ay, in my heart of heart,   60
As I do thee. — Something too much of this. —
There is a play tonight before the King.
One scene of it comes near the circumstance
Which I have told thee of my father's death.
I prithee, when thou seest that act afoot,   65
Even with the very comment of thy soul°
Observe my uncle. If his occulted° guilt
Do not itself unkennel in one speech,
It is a damned° ghost that we have seen,
And my imaginations are as foul   70
As Vulcan's stithy.° Give him heedful note,
For I mine eyes will rivet to his face,
And after we will both our judgments join
In censure of his seeming.°

HORATIO: Well, my lord.
If 'a steal aught the whilst this play is playing,   75
And scape detecting, I will pay the theft.

([*Flourish.*] *Enter trumpets and kettledrums, King, Queen, Polonius, Ophelia* [*Rosencrantz, Guildenstern, and other Lords, with Guards carrying torches*].)

HAMLET: They are coming to the play. I must be idle. Get you a place.

[*The King, Queen, and courtiers sit.*]

KING: How fares our cousin Hamlet?

HAMLET: Excellent, i' faith, of the chameleon's dish:° I eat the air, promise-
cramm'd. You cannot feed capons so.   80

KING: I have nothing with° this answer, Hamlet. These words are not
mine.°

HAMLET: No, nor mine now. [*To Polonius.*] My lord, you played once i' th'
university, you say?

POLONIUS: That did I, my lord; and was accounted a good actor.   85

---

56. blood: Passion. commeddled: Commingled. 58. stop: Hole in a wind instrument for
controlling the sound. 66. very . . . soul: Inward and sagacious criticism. 67. occulted:
Hidden. 69. damned: In league with Satan. 71. stithy: Smithy, place of stiths (anvils).
74. censure of his seeming: Judgment of his appearance or behavior. 79. chameleon's dish:
Chameleons were supposed to feed on air. Hamlet deliberately misinterprets the King's *fares* as
feeds. By his phrase *eat the air* he also plays on the idea of feeding himself with the promise of
succession, of being the *heir*. 81. have . . . with: Make nothing of. 81–82. are not mine:
Do not respond to what I asked.

HAMLET: What did you enact?

POLONIUS: I did enact Julius Caesar. I was killed i' th' Capitol; Brutus kill'd
   me.

HAMLET: It was a brute part of him to kill so capital a calf there. Be the
   players ready?   90

ROSENCRANTZ: Ay, my lord; they stay upon your patience.

QUEEN: Come hither, my dear Hamlet, sit by me.

HAMLET: No, good mother, here's metal more attractive.

POLONIUS [to the King]: O, ho, do you mark that?

HAMLET: Lady, shall I lie in your lap?   95

[Lying down at Ophelia's feet.]

OPHELIA: No, my lord.

[HAMLET: I mean, my head upon your lap?

OPHELIA: Ay, my lord.]

HAMLET: Do you think I meant country° matters?

OPHELIA: I think nothing, my lord.   100

HAMLET: That's a fair thought to lie between maids' legs.

OPHELIA: What is, my lord?

HAMLET: Nothing.

OPHELIA: You are merry, my lord.

HAMLET: Who, I?   105

OPHELIA: Ay, my lord.

HAMLET: O God, your only jig-maker.° What should a man do but be merry?
   For look you how cheerfully my mother looks, and my father died
   within 's° two hours.

OPHELIA: Nay, 'tis twice two months, my lord.   110

HAMLET: So long? Nay then, let the devil wear black for I'll have a suit of
   sables.° O heavens! Die two months ago, and not forgotten yet? Then
   there's hope a great man's memory may outlive his life half a year. But,
   by 'r lady, 'a must build churches, then, or else shall 'a suffer not thinking on,° with the hobby-horse, whose epitaph is "For, O, for, O, the   115
   hobby-horse is forgot."°

(The trumpets sound. Dumb show follows.)

*(Enter a King and a Queen [very lovingly]; the Queen embracing him, and he her.
[She kneels and makes show of protestation unto him.] He takes her up, and declines
his head upon her neck. He lies him down upon a bank of flowers. She, seeing him*

---

99. **country:** With a bawdy pun.   107. **only jig-maker:** Very best composer of jigs (song and
dance).   109. **within 's:** Within this.   111–12. **suit of sables:** Garments trimmed with the
fur of the sable and hence suited for a wealthy person, not a mourner (with a pun on *sable*
black).   114–15. **suffer . . . on:** Undergo oblivion.   115–16. **"For . . . forgot":** Verse of a
song occurring also in *Love's Labor's Lost*, 3.1.30. The hobby-horse was a character made up to
resemble a horse, appearing in the Morris dance and such May-game sports. This song laments
the disappearance of such customs under pressure from the Puritans.

asleep, leaves him. Anon comes in another man, takes off his crown, kisses it, pours poison in the sleeper's ears, and leaves him. The Queen returns; finds the King dead, makes passionate action. The Poisoner, with some three or four, come in again, seem to condole with her. The dead body is carried away. The Poisoner woos the Queen with gifts; she seems harsh awhile but in the end accepts love.)

[Exeunt.]

OPHELIA: What means this, my lord?
HAMLET: Marry, this' miching mallecho;° it means mischief.
OPHELIA: Belike° this show imports the argument° of the play.

(Enter Prologue.)

HAMLET: We shall know by this fellow. The players cannot keep counsel;° 120
    they'll tell all.
OPHELIA: Will 'a tell us what this show meant?
HAMLET: Ay, or any show that you will show him. Be not you° asham'd to
    show, he'll not shame to tell you what it means.
OPHELIA: You are naught, you are naught.° I'll mark the play.   125
PROLOGUE: For us, and for our tragedy,
    Here stooping° to your clemency,
    We beg your hearing patiently.   [Exit.]
HAMLET: Is this a prologue, or the posy of a ring?°
OPHELIA: 'Tis brief, my lord.   130
HAMLET: As woman's love.

(Enter [two Players as] King and Queen.)

PLAYER KING: Full thirty times hath Phoebus' cart° gone round
    Neptune's salt wash° and Tellus'° orbed ground,
    And thirty dozen moons with borrowed° sheen
    About the world have times twelve thirties been,   135
    Since love our hearts and Hymen° did our hands
    Unite commutual° in most sacred bands.
PLAYER QUEEN: So many journeys may the sun and moon
    Make us again count o'er ere love be done!
    But, woe is me, you are so sick of late,   140
    So far from cheer and from your former state,
    That I distrust you. Yet, though I distrust,°
    Discomfort you, my lord, it nothing° must.
    For women's fear and love hold quantity;°

---

118. this' miching mallecho: This is sneaking mischief.   **119. Belike:** Probably.   **argument:** Plot.   **120. counsel:** Secret.   **123. Be not you:** If you are not.   **125. naught:** Indecent. **127. stooping:** Bowing.   **129. posy . . . ring:** Brief motto in verse inscribed in a ring. **132. Phoebus' cart:** The sun god's chariot.   **133. salt wash:** The sea.   **Tellus:** Goddess of the earth, of the *orbed ground.*   **134. borrowed:** Reflected.   **136. Hymen:** God of matrimony. **137. commutual:** Mutually.   **142. distrust:** Am anxious about.   **143. nothing:** Not at all. **144. hold quantity:** Keep proportion with one another.

In neither aught, or in extremity.   145
Now, what my love is, proof° hath made you know,
And as my love is siz'd, my fear is so.
Where love is great, the littlest doubts are fear;
Where little fears grow great, great love grows there.
PLAYER KING: Faith, I must leave thee, love, and shortly too;   150
My operant° powers their functions leave to do.°
And thou shalt live in this fair world behind,
Honor'd, belov'd; and haply one as kind
For husband shalt thou —
PLAYER QUEEN: O, confound the rest!
Such love must needs be treason in my breast.   155
In second husband let me be accurst!
None wed the second but who kill'd the first.
HAMLET: Wormwood, wormwood.
PLAYER QUEEN: The instances° that second marriage move°
Are base respects of thrift,° but none of love.   160
A second time I kill my husband dead,
When second husband kisses me in bed.
PLAYER KING: I do believe you think what now you speak,
But what we do determine oft we break.
Purpose is but the slave to memory,°   165
Of violent birth, but poor validity,°
Which now, like fruit unripe, sticks on the tree,
But fall unshaken when they mellow be.
Most necessary 'tis that we forget
To pay ourselves what to ourselves is debt.°   170
What to ourselves in passion we propose,
The passion ending, doth the purpose lose.
The violence of either grief or joy
Their own enactures° with themselves destroy.
Where joy most revels, grief doth most lament;   175
Grief joys, joy grieves, on slender accident.
This world is not for aye,° nor 'tis not strange
That even our loves should with our fortunes change;
For 'tis a question left us yet to prove,
Whether love lead fortune, or else fortune love.   180
The great man down, you mark his favorite flies;
The poor advanc'd makes friends of enemies.
And hitherto doth love on fortune tend;

---

146. **proof:** Experience. 151. **operant:** Active. **leave to do:** Cease to perform. 159. **instances:** Motives. **move:** Motivate. 160. **base . . . thrift:** Ignoble considerations of material prosperity. 165. **Purpose . . . memory:** Our good intentions are subject to forgetfulness. 166. **validity:** Strength, durability. 169–70. **Most . . . debt:** It's inevitable that in time we forget the obligations we have imposed on ourselves. 174. **enactures:** Fulfillments. 177. **aye:** Ever.

> For who not needs° shall never lack a friend,
> And who in want° a hollow friend doth try,°   185
> Directly seasons him° his enemy.
> But, orderly to end where I begun,
> Our wills and fates do so contrary run
> That our devices still° are overthrown;
> Our thoughts are ours, their ends° none of our own.   190
> So think thou wilt no second husband wed,
> But die thy thoughts when thy first lord is dead.

PLAYER QUEEN: Nor earth to me give food, nor heaven light,
> Sport and repose lock from me day and night,
> To desperation turn my trust and hope,   195
> An anchor's cheer° in prison be my scope!°
> Each opposite° that blanks° the face of joy
> Meet what I would have well and it destroy!
> Both here and hence° pursue me lasting strife,
> If, once a widow, ever I be wife!   200

HAMLET: If she should break it now!

PLAYER KING: 'Tis deeply sworn. Sweet, leave me here awhile;
> My spirits grow dull, and fain I would beguile
> The tedious day with sleep.   *[Sleeps.]*

PLAYER QUEEN: Sleep rock thy brain,
> And never come mischance between us twain!   205

[Exit.]

HAMLET: Madam, how like you this play?

QUEEN: The lady doth protest too much, methinks.

HAMLET: O, but she'll keep her word.

KING: Have you heard the argument?° Is there no offense in 't?

HAMLET: No, no, they do but jest, poison in jest; no offense i' th' world.   210

KING: What do you call the play?

HAMLET: "The Mouse-trap." Marry, how? Tropically.° This play is the image
of a murder done in Vienna. Gonzago is the Duke's name; his wife,
Baptista. You shall see anon. 'Tis a knavish piece of work, but what of
that? Your Majesty, and we that have free° souls, it touches us not. Let   215
the gall'd jade° winch,° our withers° are unwrung.°

(Enter Lucianus.)

---

184. **who not needs:** He who is not in need (of wealth).   185. **who in want:** He who is in
need.   **try:** Test (his generosity).   186. **seasons him:** Ripens him into.   189. **devices still:**
Intentions continually.   190. **ends:** Results.   196. **anchor's cheer:** Anchorite's or hermit's
fare.   **my scope:** The extent of my happiness.   197. **opposite:** Adverse thing.   **blanks:**
Causes to blanch or grow pale.   199. **hence:** In the life hereafter.   209. **argument:** Plot.
212. **Tropically:** Figuratively. (The first quarto reading, *trapically*, suggests a pun on *trap* in
Mouse-trap.)   215. **free:** Guiltless.   216. **gall'd jade:** Horse whose hide is rubbed by saddle
or harness.   **winch:** Wince.   **withers:** The part between the horse's shoulder blades.   **unwrung:** Not rubbed sore.

This is one Lucianus, nephew to the King.

OPHELIA: You are as good as a chorus,° my lord.

HAMLET: I could interpret between you and your love, if I could see the pup-
pets dallying.°   220

OPHELIA: You are keen, my lord, you are keen.

HAMLET: It would cost you a groaning to take off mine edge.

OPHELIA: Still better, and worse.°

HAMLET: So° you mistake° your husbands. Begin, murderer, leave thy damn-
able faces, and begin. Come, the croaking raven doth bellow for re- 225
venge.

LUCIANUS: Thoughts black, hands apt, drugs fit, and time agreeing,
Confederate season,° else no creature seeing,
Thou mixture rank, of midnight weeds collected,
With Hecate's ban° thrice blasted, thrice infected,   230
Thy natural magic and dire property
On wholesome life usurp immediately.

[*Pours the poison into the sleeper's ears.*]

HAMLET: 'A poisons him i' th' garden for his estate. His name's Gonzago.
The story is extant, and written in very choice Italian. You shall see anon
how the murderer gets the love of Gonzago's wife.   235

[*Claudius rises.*]

OPHELIA: The King rises.

[HAMLET: What, frighted with false fire?°]

QUEEN: How fares my lord?

POLONIUS: Give o'er the play.

KING: Give me some light. Away!   240

POLONIUS: Lights, lights, lights!

(*Exeunt all but Hamlet and Horatio.*)

HAMLET: "Why, let the strucken deer go weep,
The hart ungalled° play.
For some must watch,° while some must sleep;
Thus runs the world away."°   245

---

218. chorus: In many Elizabethan plays the forthcoming action was explained by an actor
known as the "chorus"; at a puppet show the actor who spoke the dialogue was known as
an "interpreter," as indicated by the lines following.   **220. dallying:** With sexual suggestion,
continued in *keen*, i.e., sexually aroused, *groaning*, i.e., moaning in pregnancy, and *edge*, i.e.,
sexual desire or impetuosity.   **223. Still . . . worse:** More keen-witted and less decorous.
224. So: Even thus (in marriage).   **mistake:** Mistake, take erringly, falseheartedly.   **228. Confederate season:** The time and occasion conspiring (to assist the murderer).   **230. Hecate's
ban:** The curse of Hecate, the goddess of witchcraft.   **237. false fire:** The blank discharge of a
gun loaded with powder but not shot.   **243. ungalled:** Unafflicted.   **244. watch:** Remain
awake.   **242–45. Why . . . away:** Probably from an old ballad, with allusion to the popular
belief that a wounded deer retires to weep and die; cf. *As You Like It*, 2.1.66.

Would not this,° sir, and a forest of feathers° — if the rest of my fortunes turn Turk with° me — with two Provincial roses° on my raz'd°
shoes, get me a fellowship in a cry of players?°

HORATIO: Half a share.

HAMLET: A whole one, I.   250
"For thou dost know, O Damon dear,
    This realm dismantled° was
Of Jove himself, and now reigns here
    A very, very — pajock."°

HORATIO: You might have rhym'd.   255

HAMLET: O good Horatio, I'll take the ghost's word for a thousand pound.
Didst perceive?

HORATIO: Very well, my lord.

HAMLET: Upon the talk of pois'ning?

HORATIO: I did very well note him.   260

HAMLET: Ah, ha! Come, some music! Come, the recorders!°
"For if the King like not the comedy,
Why then, belike, he likes it not, perdy"°
Come, some music!

(Enter Rosencrantz and Guildenstern.)

GUILDENSTERN: Good my lord, vouchsafe me a word with you.   265

HAMLET: Sir, a whole history.

GUILDENSTERN: The King, sir —

HAMLET: Ay, sir, what of him?

GUILDENSTERN: Is in his retirement marvelous distemp'red.

HAMLET: With drink, sir?   270

GUILDENSTERN: No, my lord, with choler.°

HAMLET: Your wisdom should show itself more richer to signify this to the
doctor, for for me to put him to his purgation would perhaps plunge
him into more choler.

GUILDENSTERN: Good my lord, put your discourse into some frame° and start 275
not so wildly from my affair.

HAMLET: I am tame, sir. Pronounce.

GUILDENSTERN: The Queen, your mother, in most great affliction of spirit,
hath sent me to you.

HAMLET: You are welcome.   280

---

246. this: The play.   **feathers:** Allusion to the plumes that Elizabethan actors were fond of
wearing.   **247. turn Turk with:** Turn renegade against, go back on.   **Provincial roses:**
Rosettes of ribbon like the roses of a part of France.   **raz'd:** With ornamental slashing.   **248.
fellowship . . . players:** Partnership in a theatrical company.   **252. dismantled:** Stripped, di-
vested.   **254. pajock:** Peacock, a bird with a bad reputation (here substituted for the obvious
rhyme-word *ass*).   **261. recorders:** Wind instruments like the flute.   **263. perdy:** A corruption of the French *par dieu*, by God.   **271. choler:** Anger. (But Hamlet takes the word in its
more basic humors sense of *bilious disorder*.)   **275. frame:** Order.

GUILDENSTERN: Nay, good my lord, this courtesy is not of the right breed. If it shall please you to make me a wholesome answer, I will do your mother's commandment; if not, your pardon° and my return shall be the end of my business.

HAMLET: Sir, I cannot.   285

ROSENCRANTZ: What, my lord?

HAMLET: Make you a wholesome answer; my wit's diseas'd. But, sir, such answer as I can make, you shall command, or rather, as you say, my mother. Therefore no more, but to the matter. My mother, you say—

ROSENCRANTZ: Then thus she says: your behavior hath struck her into 290 amazement and admiration.°

HAMLET: O wonderful son, that can so stonish a mother! But is there no sequel at the heels of this mother's admiration? Impart.

ROSENCRANTZ: She desires to speak with you in her closet,° ere you go to bed.   295

HAMLET: We shall obey, were she ten times our mother. Have you any further trade with us?

ROSENCRANTZ: My lord, you once did love me.

HAMLET: And do still, by these pickers and stealers.°

ROSENCRANTZ: Good my lord, what is your cause of distemper? You do surely 300 bar the door upon your own liberty, if you deny your griefs to your friend.

HAMLET: Sir, I lack advancement.

ROSENCRANTZ: How can that be, when you have the voice of the King himself for your succession in Denmark?   305

HAMLET: Ay, sir, but "While the grass grows"°—the proverb is something° musty.

(*Enter the Players with recorders.*)

O, the recorders! Let me see one. [*He takes a recorder.*] To withdraw° with you: why do you go about to recover the wind° of me, as if you would drive me into a toil?°   310

GUILDENSTERN: O, my lord, if my duty be too bold, my love is too unmannerly.°

HAMLET: I do not well understand that. Will you play upon this pipe?

GUILDENSTERN: My lord, I cannot.

HAMLET: I pray you.   315

GUILDENSTERN: Believe me, I cannot.

HAMLET: I do beseech you.

---

283. pardon: Permission to depart.   **291. admiration:** Wonder.   **294. closet:** Private chamber.   **299. pickers and stealers:** Hands (so called from the catechism, "to keep my hands from picking and stealing").   **306. "While . . . grows":** The rest of the proverb is "the silly horse starves"; Hamlet may not live long enough to succeed to the kingdom.   **306. something:** Somewhat.   **308. withdraw:** Speak privately.   **309. recover the wind:** Get the windward side.   **310. toil:** Snare.   **311–12. if . . . unmannerly:** If I am using an unmannerly boldness, it is my love that occasions it.

GUILDENSTERN: I know no touch of it, my lord.

HAMLET: It is as easy as lying. Govern these ventages° with your fingers and thumb, give it breath with your mouth, and it will discourse most elo- 320 quent music. Look you, these are the stops.

GUILDENSTERN: But these cannot I command to any utt'rance of harmony; I have not the skill.

HAMLET: Why, look you now, how unworthy a thing you make of me! You would play upon me, you would seem to know my stops, you would 325 pluck out the heart of my mystery, you would sound me from my lowest note to the top of my compass,° and there is much music, excellent voice, in this little organ,° yet cannot you make it speak. 'Sblood, do you think I am easier to be play'd on than a pipe? Call me what instrument you will, though you can fret° me, you cannot play upon me.   330

(Enter Polonius.)

God bless you, sir!

POLONIUS: My lord, the Queen would speak with you, and presently.°

HAMLET: Do you see yonder cloud that's almost in shape of a camel?

POLONIUS: By th' mass, and 'tis like a camel, indeed.

HAMLET: Methinks it is like a weasel.   335

POLONIUS: It is back'd like a weasel.

HAMLET: Or like a whale?

POLONIUS: Very like a whale.

HAMLET: Then I will come to my mother by and by.° [*Aside.*] They fool me° to the top of my bent.° — I will come by and by.   340

POLONIUS: I will say so.   [*Exit.*]

HAMLET: "By and by" is easily said. Leave me, friends.

[*Exeunt all but Hamlet.*]

'Tis now the very witching time° of night,
When churchyards yawn and hell itself breathes out
Contagion to this world. Now could I drink hot blood,   345
And do such bitter business as the day
Would quake to look on. Soft, now to my mother.
O heart, lose not thy nature! Let not ever
The soul of Nero° enter this firm bosom.
Let me be cruel, not unnatural;   350

---

319. **ventages:** Stops of the recorder.   327. **compass:** Range (of voice).   328. **organ:** Musical instrument.   330. **fret:** Irritate (with a quibble on *fret* meaning the piece of wood, gut, or metal that regulates the fingering on an instrument).   332. **presently:** At once.
339. **by and by:** Immediately.   **fool me:** Make me play the fool.   340. **top of my bent:** Limit of my ability or endurance (literally, the extent to which a bow may be bent).   343. **witching time:** Time when spells are cast and evil is abroad.   349. **Nero:** Murderer of his mother, Agrippina.

I will speak daggers to her, but use none.
My tongue and soul in this be hypocrites:
How in my words somever° she be shent,°
To give them seals° never, my soul, consent!

(*Exit.*)

[Scene 3]°

(*Enter King, Rosencrantz, and Guildenstern.*)

KING: I like him not, nor stands it safe with us
　　To let his madness range. Therefore prepare you.
　　I your commission will forthwith dispatch,°
　　And he to England shall along with you.
　　The terms° of our estate° may not endure   5
　　Hazard so near 's as doth hourly grow
　　Out of his brows.°
GUILDENSTERN:　　　　　We will ourselves provide.
　　Most holy and religious fear it is
　　To keep those many many bodies safe
　　That live and feed upon your Majesty.   10
ROSENCRANTZ: The single and peculiar° life is bound
　　With all the strength and armor of the mind
　　To keep itself from noyance,° but much more
　　That spirit upon whose weal depends and rests
　　The lives of many. The cess° of majesty   15
　　Dies not alone, but like a gulf° doth draw
　　What's near it with it; or it is a messy wheel
　　Fix'd on the summit of the highest mount,
　　To whose huge spokes ten thousand lesser things
　　Are mortis'd and adjoin'd, which, when it falls,   20
　　Each small annexment, petty consequence,
　　Attends° the boist'rous ruin. Never alone
　　Did the King sigh, but with a general groan.
KING: Arm° you, I pray you, to this speedy voyage,
　　For we will fetters put about this fear,   25
　　Which now goes too free-footed.
ROSENCRANTZ:　　　　　　We will haste us.

(*Exeunt Gentlemen [Rosencrantz and Guildenstern].*)

---

353. **How . . . somever:** However much by my words. **shent:** Rebuked. 354. **give them seals:** Confirm them with deeds. ACT 3, SCENE 3. **Location:** The castle. 3. **dispatch:** Prepare, cause to be drawn up. 5. **terms:** Condition, circumstances. **our estate:** My royal position. 7. **brows:** Effronteries, threatening frowns (?), brain (?). 11. **single and peculiar:** Individual and private. 13. **noyance:** Harm. 15. **cess:** Decease. 16. **gulf:** Whirlpool. 22. **Attends:** Participates in. 24. **Arm:** Prepare.

(*Enter Polonius.*)

POLONIUS: My lord, he's going to his mother's closet.
    Behind the arras° I'll convey myself
    To hear the process.° I'll warrant she'll tax him home,°
    And, as you said, and wisely was it said,   30
    'Tis meet that some more audience than a mother,
    Since nature makes them partial, should o'erhear
    The speech, of vantage.° Fare you well, my liege.
    I'll call upon you ere you go to bed,
    And tell you what I know.
KING: Thanks, dear my lord.   35

(*Exit [Polonius].*)

    O, my offense is rank, it smells to heaven;
    It hath the primal eldest curse° upon 't,
    A brother's murder. Pray can I not,
    Though inclination be as sharp as will.°
    My stronger guilt defeats my strong intent,   40
    And, like a man to double business bound,
    I stand in pause where I shall first begin,
    And both neglect. What if this cursed hand
    Were thicker than itself with brother's blood,
    Is there not rain enough in the sweet heavens   45
    To wash it white as snow? Whereto serves mercy
    But to confront the visage of offense?°
    And what's in prayer but this twofold force,
    To be forestalled° ere we come to fall,
    Or pardon'd being down? Then I'll look up;   50
    My fault is past. But, O, what form of prayer
    Can serve my turn? "Forgive me my foul murder"?
    That cannot be, since I am still possess'd
    Of those effects for which I did the murder,
    My crown, mine own ambition, and my queen.   55
    May one be pardon'd and retain th' offense?
    In the corrupted currents° of this world
    Offense's gilded hand° may shove by justice,
    And oft 'tis seen the wicked prize° itself

---

28. **arras:** Screen of tapestry placed around the walls of household apartments. (On the Elizabethan stage, the arras was presumably over a door or discovery space in the tiring-house
façade.)   29. **process:** Proceedings.   **tax him home:** Reprove him severely.   33. **of vantage:**
From an advantageous place.   37. **primal eldest curse:** The curse of Cain, the first murderer;
he killed his brother Abel.   39. **Though . . . will:** Though my desire is as strong as my determination.   46–47. **Whereto . . . offense:** For what function does mercy serve other than to
undo the effects of sin?   49. **forestalled:** Prevented (from sinning).   57. **currents:** Courses.
58. **gilded hand:** Hand offering gold as a bribe.   59. **wicked prize:** Prize won by wickedness.

Buys out the law. But 'tis not so above.   60
There is no shuffling,° there the action lies°
In his° true nature, and we ourselves compell'd,
Even to the teeth and forehead° of our faults,
To give in evidence. What then? What rests?°
Try what repentance can. What can it not?   65
Yet what can it, when one cannot repent?
O wretched state! O bosom black as death!
O limed° soul, that, struggling to be free,
Art more engag'd!° Help, angels! Make assay.°
Bow, stubborn knees, and heart with strings of steel,   70
Be soft as sinews of the new-born babe!
All may be well.

                                                        [*He kneels.*]

(*Enter Hamlet* [*with sword drawn*].)

HAMLET: Now might I do it pat,° now 'a is a-praying;
    And now I'll do 't. And so 'a goes to heaven;
    And so am I reveng'd. That would be scann'd:°   75
    A villain kills my father, and for that,
    I, his sole son, do this same villain send
    To heaven.
    Why, this is hire and salary, not revenge.
    'A took my father grossly,° full of bread,°   80
    With all his crimes broad blown,° as flush° as May;
    And how his audit° stands who knows save heaven?
    But in our circumstance and course° of thought,
    'Tis heavy with him. And am I then reveng'd,
    To take him in the purging of his soul,   85
    When he is fit and season'd for his passage?
    No!
    Up, sword, and know thou a more horrid hent.°

                                                        [*Puts up his sword.*]

    When he is drunk asleep, or in his rage,
    Or in th' incestuous pleasure of his bed,   90

---

61. shuffling: Escape by trickery.   **the action lies:** The accusation is made manifest, comes up for consideration (a legal metaphor).   **62. his:** Its.   **63. teeth and forehead:** Face to face, concealing nothing.   **64. rests:** Remains.   **68. limed:** Caught as with birdlime, a sticky substance used to ensnare birds.   **69. engag'd:** Embedded.   **assay:** Trial.   **73. pat:** Opportunely.   **75. would be scann'd:** Needs to be looked into.   **80. grossly:** Not spiritually prepared.   **full of bread:** Enjoying his worldly pleasures. (See Ezekiel 16:49.)   **81. crimes broad blown:** Sins in full bloom.   **flush:** Lusty.   **82. audit:** Account.   **83. in ... course:** As we see it in our mortal situation.   **88. know ... hent:** Await to be grasped by me on a more horrid occasion.

At game a-swearing, or about some act
That has no relish of salvation in 't —
Then trip him, that his heels may kick at heaven,
And that his soul may be as damn'd and black
As hell, whereto it goes. My mother stays.   95
This physic° but prolongs thy sickly days.   (*Exit.*)

KING: My words fly up, my thoughts remain below.
Words without thoughts never to heaven go.

(*Exit.*)

[Scene 4]°

(*Enter [Queen] Gertrude and Polonius.*)

POLONIUS: 'A will come straight. Look you lay° home to him.
Tell him his pranks have been too broad° to bear with,
And that your Grace hath screen'd and stood between
Much heat° and him. I'll sconce° me even here.
Pray you, be round° [with him.   5
HAMLET (*within*): Mother, mother, mother!]
QUEEN: I'll warrant you, fear me not.
Withdraw, I hear him coming.

[*Polonius hides behind the arras.*]

(*Enter Hamlet.*)

HAMLET: Now, mother, what's the matter?
QUEEN: Hamlet, thou hast thy father° much offended.   10
HAMLET: Mother, you have my father much offended.
QUEEN: Come, come, you answer with an idle° tongue.
HAMLET: Go, go, you question with a wicked tongue.
QUEEN: Why, how now, Hamlet?
HAMLET: What's the matter now?
QUEEN: Have you forgot me?
HAMLET: No, by the rood,° not so: 15
You are the Queen, your husband's brother's wife
And — would it were not so! — you are my mother.
QUEEN: Nay, then, I'll set those to you that can speak.
HAMLET: Come, come, and sit you down; you shall not budge.
You go not till I set you up a glass   20
Where you may see the inmost part of you.

---

96. physic: Purging (by prayer). **ACT 3, SCENE 4. Location:** The queen's private chamber.
1. lay: Thrust (i.e., reprove him soundly). **2. broad:** Unrestrained. **4. Much heat:** The
king's anger. **sconce:** Ensconce, hide. **5. round:** Blunt. **10. thy father:** Your stepfather,
Claudius. **12. idle:** Foolish. **15. rood:** Cross.

QUEEN: What wilt thou do? Thou wilt not murder me?
   Help, ho!
POLONIUS [*behind*]: What, ho! Help!
HAMLET [*drawing*]: How now? A rat? Dead, for a ducat, dead!   25

                        [*Makes a pass through the arras.*]

POLONIUS [*behind*]: O, I am slain! [*Falls and dies.*]
QUEEN: O me, what hast thou done?
HAMLET: Nay, I know not. Is it the King?
QUEEN: O, what a rash and bloody deed is this!
HAMLET: A bloody deed — almost as bad, good mother,
   As kill a king, and marry with his brother.   30
QUEEN: As kill a king!
HAMLET: Ay, lady, it was my word.

            [*Parts the arras and discovers Polonius.*]

   Thou wretched, rash, intruding fool, farewell!
   I took thee for thy better. Take thy fortune.
   Thou find'st to be too busy is some danger. —
   Leave wringing of your hands. Peace, sit you down,   35
   And let me wring your heart, for so I shall,
   If it be made of penetrable stuff,
   If damned custom° have not braz'd° it so
   That it be proof° and bulwark against sense.°
QUEEN: What have I done, that thou dar'st wag thy tongue   40
   In noise so rude against me?
HAMLET: Such an art
   That blurs the grace and blush of modesty,
   Calls virtue hypocrite, takes off the rose
   From the fair forehead of an innocent love
   And sets a blister° there, makes marriage-vows   45
   As false as dicers' oaths. O, such a deed
   As from the body of contraction° plucks
   The very soul, and sweet religion° makes
   A rhapsody° of words. Heaven's face does glow
   O'er this solidity and compound mass   50
   With heated visage, as against the doom,
   Is thought-sick at the act.°

---

38. damned custom: Habitual wickedness. **braz'd:** Brazened, hardened. **39. proof:** Armor. **sense:** Feeling. **45. sets a blister:** Brands as a harlot. **47. contraction:** The marriage contract. **48. religion:** Religious vows. **49. rhapsody:** Senseless string. **49–52. Heaven's . . . act:** Heaven's face flushes with anger to look down upon this solid world, this compound mass, with hot face as though the day of doom were near, and is thought-sick at the deed (i.e., Gertrude's marriage).

QUEEN: Ay me, what act,
  That roars so loud and thunders in the index?°
HAMLET: Look here, upon this picture, and on this,
  The counterfeit presentment° of two brothers.   55

                                        [*Shows her two likenesses.*]

  See, what a grace was seated on this brow:
  Hyperion's° curls, the front° of Jove himself,
  An eye like Mars, to threaten and command,
  A station° like the herald Mercury
  New-lighted on a heaven-kissing hill —   60
  A combination and a form indeed,
  Where every god did seem to set his seal,
  To give the world assurance of a man.
  This was your husband. Look you now, what follows:
  Here is your husband, like a mildew'd ear,°   65
  Blasting his wholesome brother. Have you eyes?
  Could you on this fair mountain leave to feed,
  And batten° on this moor?° Ha, have you eyes?
  You cannot call it love, for at your age
  The heyday° in the blood is tame, it's humble,   70
  And waits upon the judgment, and what judgment
  Would step from this to this? Sense,° sure, you have,
  Else could you not have motion, but sure that sense
  Is apoplex'd,° for madness would not err,
  Nor sense to ecstasy was ne'er so thrall'd   75
  But it reserv'd some quantity of choice
  To serve in such a difference. What devil was 't
  That thus hath cozen'd° you at hoodman-blind?°
  Eyes without feeling, feeling without sight,
  Ears without hands or eyes, smelling sans° all,   80
  Or but a sickly part of one true sense
  Could not so mope.°
  O shame, where is thy blush? Rebellious hell,
  If thou canst mutine° in a matron's bones,

---

53. index: Table of contents, prelude, or preface.   **55. counterfeit presentment:** Portrayed representation.   **57. Hyperion:** The sun god.   **front:** Brow.   **59. station:** Manner of standing.   **65. ear:** I.e., of grain.   **68. batten:** Gorge.   **moor:** Barren upland.   **70. heyday:** State of excitement.   **72. Sense:** Perception through the five senses (the functions of the middle or sensible soul).   **74. apoplex'd:** Paralyzed. (Hamlet goes on to explain that without such a paralysis of will, mere madness would not so err, nor would the five senses so enthrall themselves to *ecstasy* or lunacy; even such deranged states of mind would be able to make the obvious choice between Hamlet Senior and Claudius.)   **78. cozen'd:** Cheated.   **hoodman-blind:** Blindman's bluff.   **80. sans:** Without.   **82. mope:** Be dazed, act aimlessly.   **84. mutine:** Mutiny.

To flaming youth let virtue be as wax,   85
And melt in her own fire. Proclaim no shame
When the compulsive ardor gives the charge,
Since frost itself as actively doth burn,
And reason panders will.°

QUEEN: O Hamlet, speak no more!   90
Thou turn'st mine eyes into my very soul,
And there I see such black and grainèd° spots
As will not leave their tinct.°

HAMLET: Nay, but to live
In the rank sweat of an enseamèd° bed,
Stew'd in corruption, honeying and making love   95
Over the nasty sty —

QUEEN: O, speak to me no more.
These words, like daggers, enter in my ears.
No more, sweet Hamlet!

HAMLET: A murderer and a villain,
A slave that is not twentieth part the tithe°   100
Of your precedent° lord, a vice° of kings,
A cutpurse of the empire and the rule,
That from a shelf the precious diadem stole,
And put it in his pocket!

QUEEN: No more!   105

(*Enter Ghost [in his nightgown].*)

HAMLET: A king of shreds and patches° —
Save me, and hover o'er me with your wings,
You heavenly guards! What would your gracious figure?

QUEEN: Alas, he's mad!

HAMLET: Do you not come your tardy son to chide,   110
That, laps'd in time and passion,° lets go by
Th' important° acting of your dread command?
O, say!

GHOST: Do not forget. This visitation
Is but to whet thy almost blunted purpose.   115
But, look, amazement° on thy mother sits.
O, step between her and her fighting soul!

86–89. Proclaim . . . will: Call it no shameful business when the compelling ardor of youth delivers the attack, i.e., commits lechery, since the frost of advanced age burns with as active a fire of lust and reason perverts itself by fomenting lust rather than restraining it.   **92. grainèd:** Dyed in grain, indelible.   **93. tinct:** Color.   **94. enseamèd:** Laden with grease.   **100. tithe:** Tenth part.   **101. precedent:** Former (i.e., the elder Hamlet).   **vice:** Buffoon (a reference to the vice of the morality plays).   **106. shreds and patches:** Motley, the traditional costume of the clown or fool.   **111. laps'd . . . passion:** Having allowed time to lapse and passion to cool.   **112. important:** Importunate, urgent.   **116. amazement:** Distraction.

Conceit° in weakest bodies strongest works.
Speak to her, Hamlet.

HAMLET: How is it with you, lady?

QUEEN: Alas, how is 't with you,   120
That you do bend your eye on vacancy,
And with th' incorporal° air do hold discourse?
Forth at your eyes your spirits wildly peep,
And, as the sleeping soldiers in th' alarm,
Your bedded° hair, like life in excrements,°   125
Start up and stand an° end. O gentle son,
Upon the heat and flame of thy distemper
Sprinkle cool patience. Whereon do you look?

HAMLET: On him, on him! Look you how pale he glares!
His form and cause conjoin'd,° preaching to stones,   130
Would make them capable.° — Do not look upon me,
Lest with this piteous action you convert
My stern effects.° Then what I have to do
Will want true color° — tears perchance for blood.

QUEEN: To whom do you speak this?   135

HAMLET: Do you see nothing there?

QUEEN: Nothing at all, yet all that is I see.

HAMLET: Nor did you nothing hear?

QUEEN: No, nothing but ourselves.

HAMLET: Why, look you there, look how it steals away!   140
My father, in his habit° as he lived!
Look, where he goes, even now, out at the portal!

                                                          (*Exit Ghost.*)

QUEEN: This is the very coinage of your brain.
This bodiless creation ecstasy°
Is very cunning in.   145

HAMLET: Ecstasy?
My pulse, as yours, doth temperately keep time,
And makes as healthful music. It is not madness
That I have utter'd. Bring me to the test,
And I the matter will reword, which madness   150
Would gambol° from. Mother, for love of grace,
Lay not that flattering unction° to your soul

---

118. Conceit: Imagination.   **122. incorporal:** Immaterial.   **125. bedded:** Laid in smooth layers.   **excrements:** Outgrowths.   **126. an:** On.   **130. His . . . conjoin'd:** His appearance joined to his cause for speaking.   **131. capable:** Receptive.   **132–33. convert . . . effects:** Divert me from my stern duty.   **134. want true color:** Lack plausibility so that (with a play on the normal sense of *color*) I shall shed tears instead of blood.   **141. habit:** Dress.   **144. ecstasy:** Madness.   **151. gambol:** Skip away.   **152. unction:** Ointment.

That not your trespass but my madness speaks.
It will but skin and film the ulcerous place,
Whiles rank corruption, mining° all within,   155
Infects unseen. Confess yourself to heaven,
Repent what's past, avoid what is to come,
And do not spread the compost° on the weeds
To make them ranker. Forgive me this my virtue;°
For in the fatness° of these pursy° times   160
Virtue itself of vice must pardon beg,
Yea, curb° and woo for leave° to do him good.
QUEEN: O Hamlet, thou hast cleft my heart in twain.
HAMLET: O, throw away the worser part of it,
And live the purer with the other half.   165
Good night. But go not to my uncle's bed;
Assume a virtue, if you have it not.
That monster, custom, who all sense doth eat,°
Of habits devil,° is angel yet in this,
That to the use of actions fair and good   170
He likewise gives a frock or livery°
That aptly is put on. Refrain tonight,
And that shall lend a kind of easiness
To the next abstinence; the next more easy;
For use° almost can change the stamp of nature,   175
And either° . . . the devil, or throw him out
With wondrous potency. Once more, good night;
And when you are desirous to be bless'd,°
I'll blessing beg of you. For this same lord,

                                                   [Pointing to Polonius.]

I do repent; but heaven hath pleas'd it so   180
To punish me with this, and this with me,
That I must be their scourge and minister.°
I will bestow° him, and will answer well
The death I gave him. So, again, good night.
I must be cruel only to be kind.   185

---

155. mining: Working under the surface.   **158. compost:** Manure.   **159. this my virtue:** My virtuous talk in reproving you.   **160. fatness:** Grossness.   **pursy:** Short-winded, corpulent.   **162. curb:** Bow, bend the knee.   **leave:** Permission.   **168. who . . . eat:** Who consumes all proper or natural feeling.   **169. Of habits devil:** Devil-like in prompting evil habits. **171. livery:** An outer appearance, a customary garb (and hence a predisposition easily assumed in time of stress).   **175. use:** Habit.   **176. And either:** A defective line usually emended by inserting the word *master* after *either*, following the fourth quarto and early editors.   **178. be bless'd:** Become blessed, i.e., repentant.   **182. their scourge and minister:** Agent of heavenly retribution. (By *scourge*, Hamlet also suggests that he himself will eventually suffer punishment in the process of fulfilling heaven's will.)   **183. bestow:** Stow, dispose of.

Thus bad begins and worse remains behind.°
One word more, good lady.

QUEEN: What shall I do?

HAMLET: Not this, by no means, that I bid you do:
Let the bloat° king tempt you again to bed,
Pinch wanton on your cheek, call you his mouse,   190
And let him, for a pair of reechy° kisses,
Or paddling in your neck with his damn'd fingers,
Make you to ravel all this matter out,
That I essentially am not in madness,
But mad in craft. 'Twere good° you let him know,   195
For who that's but a queen, fair, sober, wise,
Would from a paddock,° from a bat, a gib,°
Such dear concernings° hide? Who would do so?
No, in despite of sense and secrecy,
Unpeg the basket° on the house's top,   200
Let the birds fly, and, like the famous ape,°
To try conclusions,° in the basket creep
And break your own neck down.

QUEEN: Be thou assur'd, if words be made of breath,
And breath of life, I have no life to breathe   205
What thou hast said to me.

HAMLET: I must to England; you know that?

QUEEN: Alack,
I had forgot. 'Tis so concluded on.

HAMLET: There's letters seal'd, and my two school-fellows,
Whom I will trust as I will adders fang'd,   210
They bear the mandate; they must sweep my way,°
And marshal me to knavery. Let it work.
For 'tis the sport to have the enginer°
Hoist with° his own petar,° and 't shall go hard
But I will delve one yard below their mines,°   215
And blow them at the moon. O, 'tis most sweet,
When in one line two crafts° directly meet.
This man shall set me packing.°

---

186. behind: To come.   **189. bloat:** Bloated.   **191. reechy:** Dirty, filthy.   **195. good:** Said
ironically; also the following eight lines.   **197. paddock:** Toad.   **gib:** Tomcat.   **198. dear
concernings:** Important affairs.   **200. Unpeg the basket:** Open the cage, i.e., let out the secret.   **201. famous ape:** In a story now lost.   **202. conclusions:** Experiments (in which the
ape apparently enters a cage from which birds have been released and then tries to fly out of the
cage as they have done, falling to his death).   **211. sweep my way:** Go before me.   **213. en-
giner:** Constructor of military contrivances.   **214. Hoist with:** Blown up by.   **petar:**
Petard, an explosive used to blow in a door or make a breach.   **215. mines:** Tunnels used in
warfare to undermine the enemy's emplacements; Hamlet will countermine by going under
their mines.   **217. crafts:** Acts of guile, plots.   **218. set me packing:** Set me to making
schemes, and set me to lugging (him) and, also, send me off in a hurry.

I'll lug the guts into the neighbor room.
Mother, good night indeed. This counselor   220
Is now most still, most secret, and most grave,
Who was in life a foolish prating knave.
Come, sir, to draw toward an end° with you.
Good night, mother.

(*Exeunt [severally, Hamlet dragging in Polonius].*)

[ACT 4 / Scene 1]°

(*Enter King and Queen, with Rosencrantz and Guildenstern.*)

KING: There's matter in these sighs, these profound heaves
      You must translate; 'tis fit we understand them.
      Where is your son?
QUEEN: Bestow this place on us a little while.

[*Exeunt Rosencrantz and Guildenstern.*]

      Ah, mine own lord, what have I seen tonight!   5
KING: What, Gertrude? How does Hamlet?
QUEEN: Mad as the sea and wind when both contend
      Which is the mightier. In his lawless fit,
      Behind the arras hearing something stir,
      Whips out his rapier, cries, "A rat, a rat!"   10
      And, in this brainish apprehension,° kills
      The unseen good old man.
KING: O heavy deed!
      It had been so with us, had we been there.
      His liberty is full of threats to all —
      To you yourself, to us, to everyone.   15
      Alas, how shall this bloody deed be answer'd?
      It will be laid to us, whose providence°
      Should have kept short,° restrain'd, and out of haunt°
      This mad young man. But so much was our love
      We would not understand what was most fit,   20
      But, like the owner of a foul disease,
      To keep it from divulging,° let it feed
      Even on the pith of life. Where is he gone?
QUEEN: To draw apart the body he hath kill'd,
      O'er whom his very madness, like some ore°   25
      Among a mineral° of metals base,
      Shows itself pure: 'a weeps for what is done.

---

223. draw . . . end: Finish up (with a pun on *draw*, pull).   ACT 4, SCENE 1. Location: The
castle.   11. brainish apprehension: Headstrong conception.   17. providence: Foresight.
18. short: On a short tether.   out of haunt: Secluded.   22. divulging: Becoming evident.
25. ore: Vein of gold.   26. mineral: Mine.

KING: O Gertrude, come away!
    The sun no sooner shall the mountains touch
    But we will ship him hence, and this vile deed   30
    We must, with all our majesty and skill,
    Both countenance and excuse. Ho, Guildenstern!

(Enter Rosencrantz and Guildenstern.)

    Friends both, go join you with some further aid.
    Hamlet in madness hath Polonius slain,
    And from his mother's closet hath he dragg'd him.   35
    Go seek him out; speak fair, and bring the body
    Into the chapel. I pray you, haste in this.

               [Exeunt Rosencrantz and Guildenstern.]

    Come, Gertrude, we'll call up our wisest friends
    And let them know both what we mean to do
    And what's untimely done°   40
    Whose whisper o'er the world's diameter,°
    As level° as the cannon to his blank,°
    Transports his pois'ned shot, may miss our name,
    And hit the woundless° air. O, come away!
    My soul is full of discord and dismay.   *(Exeunt.)* 45

[Scene 2]°

(Enter Hamlet.)

HAMLET: Safely stow'd.
[ROSENCRANTZ, GUILDENSTERN (*within*): Hamlet! Lord Hamlet!]
HAMLET: But soft, what noise? Who calls on Hamlet? O, here they come.

(Enter Rosencrantz and Guildenstern.)

ROSENCRANTZ: What have you done, my lord, with the dead body?
HAMLET: Compounded it with dust, whereto 'tis kin.   5
ROSENCRANTZ: Tell us where 'tis, that we may take it thence
    And bear it to the chapel.
HAMLET: Do not believe it.
ROSENCRANTZ: Believe what?
HAMLET: That I can keep your counsel and not mine own. Besides, to be de- 10
    manded of° a sponge, what replication° should be made by the son of a
    king?

---

40. And . . . done: A defective line; conjectures as to the missing words include *so, haply, slan-*
der (Capell and others); *for, haply, slander* (Theobald and others).   **41. diameter:** Extent from
side to side.   **42. As level:** With as direct aim. **blank:** White spot in the center of a target.
44. woundless: Invulnerable. Act 4, Scene 2. **Location:** The castle. **10–11. demanded of:**
Questioned by. **replication:** Reply.

ROSENCRANTZ: Take you me for a sponge, my lord?

HAMLET: Ay, sir, that soaks up the King's countenance,° his rewards, his authorities. But such officers do the King best service in the end. He keeps   15
them, like an ape an apple, in the corner of his jaw, first mouth'd, to be
last swallow'd. When he needs what you have glean'd, it is but squeezing you, and, sponge, you shall be dry again.

ROSENCRANTZ: I understand you not, my lord.

HAMLET: I am glad of it. A knavish speech sleeps in° a foolish ear.   20

ROSENCRANTZ: My lord, you must tell us where the body is, and go with us to
the King.

HAMLET: The body is with the King, but the King is not with the body.° The
King is a thing —

GUILDENSTERN: A thing, my lord?   25

HAMLET: Of nothing.° Bring me to him. [Hide fox, and all after.°]

(*Exeunt.*)

[Scene 3]°

(*Enter King, and two or three.*)

KING: I have sent to seek him, and to find the body.
How dangerous is it that this man goes loose!
Yet must not we put the strong law on him.
He's lov'd of the distracted° multitude,
Who like not in their judgment, but their eyes,   5
And where 'tis so, th' offender's scourge° is weigh'd,°
But never the offense. To bear° all smooth and even,
This sudden sending him away must seem
Deliberate pause.° Diseases desperate grown
By desperate appliance are reliev'd,   10
Or not at all.

(*Enter Rosencrantz, [Guildenstern,] and all the rest.*)

How now? What hath befall'n?

ROSENCRANTZ: Where the dead body is bestow'd, my lord,
We cannot get from him.

KING: But where is he?

ROSENCRANTZ: Without, my lord; guarded, to know your pleasure.

----

14. **countenance:** Favor.   20. **sleeps in:** Has no meaning to.   23. **The . . . body:** Perhaps
alludes to the legal commonplace of "the king's two bodies," which drew a distinction between
the sacred office of kingship and the particular mortal who possessed it at any given time.   **26.
Of nothing:** Of no account.   **Hide . . . after:** An old signal cry in the game of hide-and-seek,
suggesting that Hamlet now runs away from them.   ACT 4, SCENE 3. **Location:** The castle.
4. **distracted:** Fickle, unstable.   6. **scourge:** Punishment.   **weigh'd:** Taken into consideration.   7. **bear:** Manage.   9. **Deliberate pause:** Carefully considered action.

KING: Bring him before us.

ROSENCRANTZ: Ho! Bring in the lord.   15

(*They enter [with Hamlet].*)

KING: Now, Hamlet, where's Polonius?

HAMLET: At supper.

KING: At supper? Where?

HAMLET: Not where he eats, but where 'a is eaten. A certain convocation of
politic worms° are e'en at him. Your worm is your only emperor for   20
diet.° We fat all creatures else to fat us, and we fat ourselves for maggots. Your fat king and your lean beggar is but variable service,° two
dishes, but to one table — that's the end.

KING: Alas, alas!

HAMLET: A man may fish with the worm that hath eat° of a king, and eat of   25
the fish that hath fed of that worm.

KING: What dost thou mean by this?

HAMLET: Nothing but to show you how a king may go a progress° through
the guts of a beggar.

KING: Where is Polonius?   30

HAMLET: In heaven. Send thither to see. If your messenger find him not
there, seek him i' th' other place yourself. But if indeed you find him
not within this month, you shall nose him as you go up the stairs into
the lobby.

KING [*to some Attendants*]: Go seek him there.   35

HAMLET: 'A will stay till you come.

                                                        [*Exit Attendants.*]

KING: Hamlet, this deed, for thine especial safety. —
Which we do tender,° as we dearly° grieve
For that which thou hast done — must send thee hence
[With fiery quickness.] Therefore prepare thyself.   40
The bark° is ready, and the wind at help,
Th' associates tend,° and everything is bent°
For England.

HAMLET: For England!

KING: Ay, Hamlet.   45

HAMLET: Good.

KING: So is it, if thou knew'st our purposes.

HAMLET: I see a cherub° that sees them. But, come, for England! Farewell,
dear mother.

---

20. politic worms: Crafty worms (suited to a master spy like Polonius). **21. diet:** Food, eating (with perhaps a punning reference to the Diet of Worms, a famous convocation held in
1521). **22. variable service:** Different courses of a single meal. **25. eat:** Eaten (pronounced
"et"). **28. progress:** Royal journey of state. **38. tender:** Regard, hold dear. **dearly:** Intensely. **41. bark:** Sailing vessel. **42. tend:** Wait. **bent:** In readiness. **48. cherub:**
Cherubim are angels of knowledge.

KING: Thy loving father, Hamlet.   50

HAMLET: My mother. Father and mother is man and wife, man and wife is
 one flesh, and so, my mother. Come, for England!   (*Exit.*)

KING: Follow him at foot;° tempt him with speed aboard.
 Delay it not; I'll have him hence tonight.
 Away! For everything is seal'd and done   55
 That else leans on° th' affair. Pray you, make haste.

          [*Exeunt all but the King.*]

 And, England,° if my love thou hold'st at aught —
 As my great power thereof may give thee sense,
 Since yet thy cicatrice° looks raw and red
 After the Danish sword, and thy free awe°   60
 Pays homage to us — thou mayst not coldly set°
 Our sovereign process,° which imports at full,
 By letters congruing° to that effect,
 The present° death of Hamlet. Do it, England,
 For like the hectic° in my blood he rages,   65
 And thou must cure me. Till I know 'tis done,
 Howe'er my haps,° my joys were ne'er begun.

             (*Exit.*)

 [Scene 4]°

(*Enter Fortinbras with his Army over the stage.*)

FORTINBRAS: Go, captain, from me greet the Danish king.
 Tell him that, by his license,° Fortinbras
 Craves the conveyance° of a promis'd march
 Over his kingdom. You know the rendezvous.
 If that his Majesty would aught with us,   5
 We shall express our duty in his eye;°
 And let him know so.

CAPTAIN: I will do 't, my lord.

FORTINBRAS: Go softly° on.   [*Exeunt all but the Captain.*]

(*Enter Hamlet, Rosencrantz, [Guildenstern,] etc.*)

HAMLET: Good sir, whose powers° are these?

CAPTAIN: They are of Norway, sir.   10

HAMLET: How purposed, sir, I pray you?

---

53. **at foot:** Close behind, at heel.   56. **leans on:** Bears upon, is related to.   57. **England:**
King of England.   59. **cicatrice:** Scar.   60. **free awe:** Voluntary show of respect.   61. **set:**
Esteem.   62. **process:** Command.   63. **congruing:** Agreeing.   64. **present:** Immediate.
65. **hectic:** Persistent fever.   67. **haps:** Fortunes.   Act 4, Scene 4. **Location:** The coast
of Denmark.   2. **license:** Permission.   3. **conveyance:** Escort, convoy.   6. **eye:** Presence.
8. **softly:** Slowly.   9. **powers:** Forces.

CAPTAIN: Against some part of Poland.

HAMLET: Who commands them, sir?

CAPTAIN: The nephew to old Norway, Fortinbras.

HAMLET: Goes it against the main° of Poland, sir,   15
    Or for some frontier?

CAPTAIN: Truly to speak, and with no addition,°
    We go to gain a little patch of ground
    That hath in it no profit but the name.
    To pay° five ducats, five, I would not farm it;°   20
    Nor will it yield to Norway or the Pole
    A ranker° rate, should it be sold in fee.°

HAMLET: Why, then the Polack never will defend it.

CAPTAIN: Yes, it is already garrison'd.

HAMLET: Two thousand souls and twenty thousand ducats   25
    Will not debate the question of this straw.°
    This is th' imposthume° of much wealth and peace,
    That inward breaks, and shows no cause without
    Why the man dies. I humbly thank you, sir.

CAPTAIN: God buy you, sir.   [*Exit.*]

ROSENCRANTZ: Will 't please you go, my lord?   30

HAMLET: I'll be with you straight. Go a little before.

                    [*Exit all except Hamlet.*]

    How all occasions do inform against° me,
    And spur my dull revenge! What is a man,
    If his chief good and market of° his time
    Be but to sleep and feed? A beast, no more.   35
    Sure he that made us with such large discourse,°
    Looking before and after, gave us not
    That capability and god-like reason
    To fust° in us unus'd. Now, whether it be
    Bestial oblivion,° or some craven scruple   40
    Of thinking too precisely on th' event° —
    A thought which, quarter'd, hath but one part wisdom
    And ever three parts coward — I do not know
    Why yet I live to say "This thing's to do,"
    Sith° I have cause and will and strength and means   45
    To do 't. Examples gross° as earth exhort me:
    Witness this army of such mass and charge°

---

15. **main:** Main part.   17. **addition:** Exaggeration.   20. **To pay:** I.e., for a yearly rental of.
farm it: Take a lease of it.   22. **ranker:** Higher.   **in fee:** Fee simple, outright.   26.
debate . . . straw: Settle this trifling matter.   27. **imposthume:** Abscess.   32. **inform
against:** Denounce, betray; take shape against.   34. **market of:** Profit of compensation for.
36. **discourse:** Power of reasoning.   39. **fust:** Grow moldy.   40. **oblivion:** Forgetfulness.
41. **event:** Outcome.   45. **Sith:** Since.   46. **gross:** Obvious.   47. **charge:** Expense.

Led by a delicate and tender prince,
Whose spirit, with divine ambition puff'd
Makes mouths° at the invisible event,　　　　　　　　　　　　　50
Exposing what is mortal and unsure
To all that fortune, death, and danger dare,
Even for an egg-shell. Rightly to be great
Is not to stir without great argument,
But greatly to find quarrel in a straw　　　　　　　　　　　　55
When honor's at the stake. How stand I then,
That have a father kill'd, a mother stain'd,
Excitements of° my reason and my blood,
And let all sleep, while, to my shame, I see
The imminent death of twenty thousand men,　　　　　　　　　60
That, for a fantasy° and trick° of fame,
Go to their graves like beds, fight for a plot°
Whereon the numbers cannot try the cause,°
Which is not tomb enough and continent°
To hide the slain? O, from this time forth,　　　　　　　　　65
My thoughts be bloody, or be nothing worth!

　　　　　　　　　　　　　　　　　　　　　　　　　　　(*Exit.*)

[Scene 5]°

(*Enter Horatio, [Queen] Gertrude, and a Gentleman.*)

QUEEN: I will not speak with her.
GENTLEMAN: She is importunate, indeed distract.
　　Her mood will needs be pitied.
QUEEN:　　　　　　　　　What would she have?
GENTLEMAN: She speaks much of her father, says she hears
　　There's tricks° i' th' world, and hems, and beats her heart,°　　5
　　Spurns enviously at straws,° speaks things in doubt°
　　That carry but half sense. Her speech is nothing,
　　Yet the unshaped use° of it doth move
　　The hearers to collection;° they yawn° at it,
　　And botch° the words up fit to their own thoughts,　　　　　10
　　Which, as her winks and nods and gestures yield° them,
　　Indeed would make one think there might be thought,°

---

50. Makes mouths: Makes scornful faces. **58. Excitements of:** Promptings by. **61. fan-tasy:** Fanciful caprice. **trick:** Trifle. **62. plot:** I.e., of ground. **63. Whereon . . . cause:** On which there is insufficient room for the soldiers needed to engage in a military contest. **64. continent:** Receptacle, container. ACT 4, SCENE 5. **Location:** The castle. **5. tricks:** Deceptions. **heart:** Breast. **6. Spurns . . . straws:** Kicks spitefully, takes offense at trifles. **in doubt:** Obscurely. **8. unshaped use:** Distracted manner. **9. collection:** Inference, a guess at some sort of meaning. **yawn:** Wonder, grasp. **10. botch:** Patch. **11. yield:** Delivery, bring forth (her words). **12. thought:** Conjectured.

Though nothing sure, yet much unhappily.
HORATIO: 'twere good she were spoken with, for she may strew
    Dangerous conjectures in ill-breeding° minds.   15
QUEEN: Let her come in.   *[Exit Gentlemen.]*
    [Aside.] To my sick soul, as sin's true nature is,
    Each toy° seems prologue to some great amiss.°
    So full of artless jealousy is guilt,
    It spills itself in fearing to be spilt.°   20

(Enter Ophelia [distracted].)

OPHELIA: Where is the beauteous majesty of Denmark?
QUEEN: How now, Ophelia?
OPHELIA *(she sings)*: "How should I your true love know
      From another one?
    By his cockle hat° and staff,   25
      And his sandal shoon."°
QUEEN: Alas, sweet lady, what imports this song?
OPHELIA: Say you? Nay, pray you, mark.
    "He is dead and gone, lady,   *(Song.)*
      He is dead and gone;   30
    At his head a grass-green turf,
      At his heels a stone."
    O, ho!
QUEEN: Nay, but Ophelia —
OPHELIA: Pray you mark.   35
    [Sings.] "White his shroud as the mountain snow" —

(Enter King.)

QUEEN: Alas, look here, my lord.
OPHELIA: "Larded° all with flowers   *(Song.)*
    Which bewept to the ground did not go
      With true-love showers."   40
KING: How do you, pretty lady?
OPHELIA: Well, God 'ild° you! They say the owl° was a baker's daughter.
    Lord, we know what we are, but know not what we may be. God be at
    your table!
KING: Conceit° upon her father.   45
OPHELIA: Pray let's have no words of this; but when they ask you what it
    means, say you this:

---

15. ill-breeding: Prone to suspect the worst. **18. toy:** Trifle. **amiss:** Calamity. **19–20.
So . . . spilt:** Guilt is so full of suspicion that it unskillfully betrays itself in fearing betrayal.
25. cockle hat: Hat with cockleshell stuck in it as a sign that the wearer had been a pilgrim to
the shrine of St. James of Compostella in Spain. **26. shoon:** Shoes. **38. Larded:** Decorated. **42. God 'ild:** God yield or reward. **owl:** Refers to a legend about a baker's daughter
who was turned into an owl for refusing Jesus bread. **45. Conceit:** Brooding.

"Tomorrow is Saint Valentine's° day.   (*Song.*)
    All in the morning betime,
And I a maid at your window,   50
    To be your Valentine.
Then up he rose, and donn'd his clo'es,
    And dupp'd° the chamber-door,
Let in the maid, that out a maid
    Never departed more."   55
KING: Pretty Ophelia!
OPHELIA: Indeed, la, without an oath, I'll make an end on 't:
    [*Sings.*] "By Gis° and by Saint Charity,
        Alack, and fie for shame!
    Young men will do 't, if they come to 't;   60
        By Cock,° they are to blame.
    Quoth she, 'Before you tumbled me,
        You promised me to wed.'"
He answers:
    "'So would I ha' done, by yonder sun,   65
        An thou hadst not come to my bed.'"
KING: How long hath she been thus?
OPHELIA: I hope all will be well. We must be patient, but I cannot choose
but weep, to think they would lay him i' th' cold ground. My brother
shall know of it; and so I thank you for your good counsel. Come, my   70
coach! Good night, ladies; good night, sweet ladies; good night, good
night.

                                                  [*Exit.*]

KING: Follow her close; give her good watch, I pray you.

                                        [*Exit Horatio.*]

O, this is the poison of deep grief; it springs
All from her father's death — and now behold!   75
O Gertrude, Gertrude,
When sorrows come, they come not single spies,°
But in battalions. First, her father slain;
Next, your son gone, and he most violent author
Of his own just remove; the people muddied,°   80
Thick and unwholesome in their thoughts and whispers,
For good Polonius' death; and we have done but greenly,°
In hugger-mugger° to inter him; poor Ophelia

----

48. **Valentine's:** This song alludes to the belief that the first girl seen by a man on the morning of this day was his valentine or true love.   53. **dupp'd:** Opened.   58. **Gis:** Jesus.   61. **Cock:** A perversion of *God* in oaths.   77. **spies:** Scouts sent in advance of the main force.   80. **muddied:** Stirred up, confused.   82. **greenly:** Imprudently, foolishly.   83. **hugger-mugger:** Secret haste.

Divided from herself and her fair judgment,
Without the which we are pictures, or mere beasts;   85
Last, and as much containing as all these,
Her brother is in secret come from France,
Feeds on his wonder, keeps himself in clouds,°
And wants° not buzzers° to infect his ear
With pestilent speeches of his father's death,   90
Wherein necessity, of matter beggar'd,°
Will nothing stick our person to arraign
In ear and ear.° O my dear Gertrude, this,
Like to a murd'ring-piece,° in many places
Gives me superfluous death.   (*A noise within.*)   95
[QUEEN: Alack, what noise is this?]
KING: Attend!
Where are my Switzers?° Let them guard the door.

(*Enter a Messenger.*)

What is the matter?
MESSENGER: Save yourself, my lord!
The ocean, overpeering of his list,°   100
Eats not the flats° with more impiteous° haste
Than young Laertes, in a riotous head,°
O'erbears your officers. The rabble call him lord,
And, as° the world were now but to begin,
Antiquity forgot, custom not known,   105
The ratifiers and props° of every word,°
They cry, "Choose we! Laertes shall be king!"
Caps, hands, and tongues applaud it to the clouds,
"Laertes shall be king, Laertes king!"

(*A noise within.*)

QUEEN: How cheerfully on the false trail they cry!   110
O, this is counter,° you false Danish dogs!

(*Enter Laertes with others.*)

KING: The doors are broke.
LAERTES: Where is this King? Sirs, stand you all without.

---

88. **in clouds:** I.e., of suspicion and rumor.   89. **wants:** Lacks.   **buzzers:** Gossipers, informers.   91. **of matter beggar'd:** Unprovided with facts.   92–93. **Will . . . and ear:** Will not hesitate to accuse my (royal) person in everybody's ears.   94. **murd'ring-piece:** Cannon loaded so as to scatter its shot.   98. **Switzers:** Swiss guards, mercenaries.   100. **overpeering of his list:** Overflowing its shore.   101. **flats:** Flatlands near shore.   **impiteous:** Pitiless.   102. **head:** Armed force.   104. **as:** As if.   106. **ratifiers and props:** Refer to *antiquity* and *custom*.   **word:** Promise.   111. **counter:** A hunting term meaning to follow the trail in a direction opposite to that which the game has taken.

ALL: No, let's come in.
LAERTES: I pray you, give me leave.
ALL: We will, we will.   115

[*They retire without the door.*]

LAERTES: I thank you. Keep the door. O thou vile king,
    Give me my father!
QUEEN: Calmly, good Laertes.

[*She tries to hold him back.*]

LAERTES: That drop of blood that's calm proclaims me bastard,
    Cries cuckold to my father, brands the harlot
    Even here, between the chaste unsmirched brow   120
    Of my true mother.
KING: What is the cause, Laertes,
    That thy rebellion looks so giant-like?
    Let him go, Gertrude. Do not fear our° person.
    There's such divinity doth hedge a king
    That treason can but peep to what it would,°   125
    Acts little of his will.° Tell me, Laertes,
    Why thou art thus incens'd. Let him go, Gertrude.
    Speak, man.
LAERTES: Where is my father?
KING: Dead.
QUEEN: But not by him.
KING: Let him demand his fill.
LAERTES: How came he dead? I'll not be juggled with.   130
    To hell, allegiance! Vows, to the blackest devil!
    Conscience and grace, to the profoundest pit!
    I dare damnation. To this point I stand,
    That both the worlds I give to negligence,°
    Let come what comes, only I'll be reveng'd   135
    Most throughly° for my father.
KING: Who shall stay you?
LAERTES: My will, not all the world's.°
    And for my means, I'll husband them so well,
    They shall go far with little.
KING: Good Laertes,
    If you desire to know the certainty   140

---

123. fear our: Fear for my.   **125. can . . . would:** Can only glance; as from far off or through
a barrier, at what it would intend.   **126. Acts . . . will:** (But) performs little of what it intends.   **134. both . . . negligence:** Both this world and the next are of no consequence to me.
136. throughly: Thoroughly.   **137. My will . . . world's:** I'll stop (*stay*) when my will is accomplished, not for anyone else's.

Of your dear father, is 't writ in your revenge
That, swoopstake,° you will draw both friend and foe,
Winner and loser?

LAERTES: None but his enemies.

KING: Will you know them then?

LAERTES: To his good friends thus wide I'll ope my arms,   145
And, like the kind life-rend'ring pelican,°
Repast° them with my blood.

KING: Why, now you speak
Like a good child and a true gentleman.
That I am guiltless of your father's death,
And am most sensibly° in grief for it,   150
It shall as level° to your judgment 'pear
As day does to your eye.

                    (*A noise within:*) "Let her come in."

LAERTES: How now? What noise is that?

(*Enter Ophelia.*)

O heat, dry up my brains! Tears seven times salt
Burn out the sense and virtue° of mine eye!   155
By heaven, thy madness shall be paid with weight°
Till our scale turn the beam.° O rose of May!
Dear maid, kind sister, sweet Ophelia!
O heavens, is 't possible a young maid's wits
Should be as mortal as an old man's life?   160
[Nature is fine in° love, and where 'tis fine,
It sends some precious instance° of itself
After the thing it loves.°]

OPHELIA: "They bore him barefac'd on the bier;

                                        (*Song.*)

        [Hey non nonny, nonny, hey nonny,]   165
And in his grave rain'd many a tear" —
Fare you well, my dove!

LAERTES: Hadst thou thy wits, and didst persuade° revenge,
It could not move thus.

OPHELIA: You must sing "A-down a-down,   170
And you call him a-down-a."

---

142. **swoopstake:** Literally, taking all stakes on the gambling table at once, i.e., indiscriminately; *draw* is also a gambling term. 146. **pelican:** Refers to the belief that the female pelican fed its young with its own blood. 147. **Repast:** Feed. 150. **sensibly:** Feelingly. 151. **level:** Plain. 155. **virtue:** Faculty, power. 156. **paid with weight:** Repaid, avenged equally or more. 157. **beam:** Crossbar of a balance. 161. **fine in:** Refined by. 162. **instance:** Token. 163. **After . . . loves:** Into the grave, along with Polonius. 168. **persuade:** Argue cogently for.

O, how the wheel° becomes it! It is the false steward° that stole his
master's daughter.

LAERTES: This nothing's more than matter.°

OPHELIA: There's rosemary,° that's for remembrance; pray you, love, remem-　175
ber. And there is pansies,° that's for thoughts.

LAERTES: A document° in madness, thoughts and remembrance fitted.

OPHELIA: There's fennel° for you, and columbines.° There's rue° for you,
and here's some for me; we may call it herb of grace o' Sundays. You
may wear your rue with a difference.° There's a daisy.° I would give you　180
some violets,° but they wither'd all when my father died. They say 'a
made a good end —
[*Sings.*] "For bonny sweet Robin is all my joy."

LAERTES: Thought° and affliction, passion, hell itself,
She turns to favor° and to prettiness.　　　　　　　　　　　　　　　185

OPHELIA: "And will 'a not come again? (*Song.*)
　　And will 'a not come again?
　　　　No, no, he is dead,
　　　　Go to thy death-bed,
　　He never will come again.　　　　　　　　　　　　　　　　　190
　"His beard was as white as snow,
　All flaxen was his poll.°
　　　　He is gone, he is gone,
　　　　And we cast away moan.
　God 'a' mercy on his soul!"　　　　　　　　　　　　　　　　195
And of all Christians' souls, I pray God. God buy you.

　　　　　　　　　　　　　　　　　　　　　　　　　[*Exit.*]

LAERTES: Do you see this, O God?

KING: Laertes, I must commune with your grief,
Or you deny me right. Go but apart,
Make choice of whom your wisest friends you will,　　　　　　　200
And they shall hear and judge 'twixt you and me.
If by direct or by collateral° hand
They find us touch'd,° we will our kingdom give,

---

172. wheel: Spinning wheel as accompaniment to the song, or refrain.　**false steward:** The
story is unknown.　**174. This . . . matter:** This seeming nonsense is more meaningful than
sane utterance.　**175. rosemary:** Used as a symbol of remembrance both at weddings and at
funerals.　**176. pansies:** Emblems of love and courtship; perhaps from French *pensées*,
thoughts.　**177. document:** Instruction, lesson.　**178. fennel:** Emblem of flattery.
columbines: Emblems of unchastity (?) or ingratitude (?).　**rue:** Emblem of repentance;
when mingled with holy water, it was known as *herb of grace*.　**180. with a difference:** Suggests that Ophelia and the queen have different causes of sorrow and repentance; perhaps with
a play on *rue* in the sense of ruth, pity.　**daisy:** Emblem of dissembling, faithlessness.　**181.**
violets: Emblems of faithfulness.　**184. Thought:** Melancholy.　**185. favor:** Grace.　**192.**
poll: Head.　**202. collateral:** Indirect.　**203. us touch'd:** Me implicated.

Our crown, our life, and all that we call ours,
To you in satisfaction; but if not,   205
Be you content to lend your patience to us,
And we shall jointly labor with your soul
To give it due content.
LAERTES: Let this be so.
His means of death, his obscure funeral —
No trophy,° sword, nor hatchment° o'er his bones,   210
No noble rite nor formal ostentation° —
Cry to be heard, as 'twere from heaven to earth,
That I must call 't in question.
KING: So you shall;
And where th' offense is, let the great ax fall.
I pray you go with me.   (*Exeunt.*) 215

[Scene 6]°

(*Enter Horatio and others.*)

HORATIO: What are they that would speak with me?
GENTLEMAN: Seafaring men, sir. They say they have letters for you.
HORATIO: Let them come in.   [*Exit Gentleman.*]
I do not know from what part of the world
I should be greeted, if not from lord Hamlet.   5

(*Enter Sailors.*)

FIRST SAILOR: God bless you sir.
HORATIO: Let him bless thee too.
FIRST SAILOR: 'A shall, sir, an 't please him. There's a letter for you, sir — it
came from th' ambassador that was bound for England — if your name
be Horatio, as I am let to know it is.   [*Gives letter.*] 10
HORATIO [*reads*]: "Horatio, when thou shalt have over-look'd this, give these
fellows some means° to the King; they have letters for him. Ere we were
two days old at sea, a pirate of very warlike appointment° gave us chase.
Finding ourselves too slow of sail, we put on a compell'd valor, and in
the grapple I boarded them. On the instant they got clear of our ship, so   15
I alone became their prisoner. They have dealt with me like thieves of
mercy,° but they knew what they did: I am to do a good turn for them.
Let the King have the letters I have sent, and repair thou to me with as
much speed as thou wouldest fly death. I have words to speak in thine
ear will make thee dumb; yet are they much too light for the bore° of   20

---

210. **trophy:** Memorial.   **hatchment:** Tablet displaying the armorial bearings of a deceased
person.   211. **ostentation:** Ceremony.   ACT 4, SCENE 6. **Location:** The castle.   12. **means:**
Means of access.   13. **appointment:** Equipage.   16–17. **thieves of mercy:** Merciful thieves.
20. **bore:** Caliber, i.e., importance.

the matter. These good fellows will bring thee where I am. Rosencrantz
and Guildenstern hold their course for England. Of them I have much
to tell thee. Farewell.

He that thou knowest thine, Hamlet."

Come, I will give you way for these your letters,   25
And do 't the speedier that you may direct me
To him from whom you brought them.   (*Exeunt.*)

[Scene 7]°

(*Enter King and Laertes.*)

KING: Now must your conscience my acquittance seal,°
And you must put me in your heart for friend,
Sith you have heard, and with a knowing ear,
That he which hath your noble father slain
Pursued my life.

LAERTES: It well appears. But tell me   5
Why you proceeded not against these feats°
So criminal and so capital° in nature,
As by your safety, greatness, wisdom, all things else,
You mainly° were stirr'd up.

KING: O, for two special reasons,
Which may to you, perhaps, seem much unsinew'd,°   10
But yet to me th' are strong. The Queen his mother
Lives almost by his looks, and for myself —
My virtue or my plague, be it either which —
She's so conjunctive° to my life and soul
That, as the star moves not but in his sphere,°   15
I could not but by her. The other motive,
Why to a public count° I might not go,
Is the great love the general gender° bear him,
Who, dipping all his faults in their affection,
Would, like the spring° that turneth wood to stone,   20
Convert his gyves° to graces, so that my arrows,
Too slightly timber'd° for so loud° a wind,
Would have reverted to my bow again
And not where I had aim'd them.

ACT 4, SCENE 7. Location: The castle.   **1. my acquittance seal:** Confirm or acknowledge my
innocence.   **6. feats:** Acts.   **7. capital:** Punishable by death.   **9. mainly:** Greatly.   **10.
unsinew'd:** Weak.   **14. conjunctive:** Closely united.   **15. sphere:** The hollow sphere in
which, according to Ptolemaic astronomy, the planets moved.   **17. count:** Account, reckoning.   **18. general gender:** Common people.   **20. spring:** A spring with such a concentration
of lime that it coats a piece of wood with limestone, in effect gilding it.   **21. gyves:** Fetters
(which, gilded by the people's praise, would look like badges of honor).   **22. slightly timber'd:**
Light.   **loud:** Strong.

LAERTES: And so have I a noble father lost,   25
 A sister driven into desp'rate terms,°
 Whose worth, if praises may go back° again,
 Stood challenger on mount° of all the age
 For her perfections. But my revenge will come.
KING: Break not your sleeps for that. You must not think   30
 That we are made of stuff so flat and dull
 That we can let our beard be shook with danger
 And think it pastime. You shortly shall hear more.
 I lov'd your father, and we love ourself;
 And that, I hope, will teach you to imagine —   35

(*Enter a Messenger with letters.*)

 [How now? What news?]
MESSENGER: [Letters, my lord, from Hamlet:]
 These to your Majesty, this to the Queen.

                 [*Gives letters.*]

KING: From Hamlet? Who brought them?
MESSENGER: Sailors, my lord, they say; I saw them not.
 They were given me by Claudio. He receiv'd them   40
 Of him that brought them.
KING: Laertes, you shall hear them.
 Leave us.   [*Exit Messenger.*]
 [*Reads.*] "High and mighty, you shall know I am set naked° on your
 kingdom. Tomorrow shall I beg leave to see your kingly eyes, when I
 shall, first asking your pardon° thereunto, recount the occasion of my   45
 sudden and more strange return.   Hamlet."
 What should this mean? Are all the rest come back?
 Or is it some abuse,° and no such thing?
LAERTES: Know you the hand?
KING: 'Tis Hamlet's character.° "Naked!"
 And in a postscript here, he says "alone."   50
 Can you devise° me?
LAERTES: I am lost in it, my lord. But let him come.
 It warms the very sickness in my heart
 That I shall live and tell him to his teeth,
 "Thus didst thou."
KING: If it be so, Laertes —   55
 As how should it be so? How otherwise?° —

---

26. **terms:** State, condition. 27. **go back:** Recall Ophelia's former virtues. 28. **on mount:**
On high. 43. **naked:** Destitute, unarmed, without following. 45. **pardon:** Permission.
48. **abuse:** Deceit. 49. **character:** Handwriting. 51. **devise:** Explain to. 56. **As . . . otherwise:** How can this (Hamlet's return) be true? Yet how otherwise than true (since we have
the evidence of his letter).

Will you be ruled by me?
LAERTES: Ay, my lord,
  So° you will not o'errule me to a peace.
KING: To thine own peace. If he be now returned,
  As checking at° his voyage, and that he means   60
  No more to undertake it, I will work him
  To an exploit, now ripe in my device,
  Under the which he shall not choose but fall;
  And for his death no wind of blame shall breathe,
  But even his mother shall uncharge the practice°   65
  And call it accident.
LAERTES: My lord, I will be rul'd,
  The rather if you could devise it so
  That I might be the organ.°
KING: It falls right.
  You have been talk'd of since your travel much,
  And that in Hamlet's hearing, for a quality   70
  Wherein, they say, you shine. Your sum of parts°
  Did not together pluck such envy from him
  As did that one, and that, in my regard,
  Of the unworthiest siege.°
LAERTES: What part is that, my lord?   75
KING: A very riband in the cap of youth,
  Yet needful too, for youth no less becomes
  The light and careless livery that it wears
  Than settled age his sables° and his weeds,°
  Importing health° and graveness. Two months since   80
  Here was a gentleman of Normandy.
  I have seen myself, and serv'd against, the French,
  And they can well° on horseback, but this gallant
  Had witchcraft in 't; he grew unto his seat,
  And to such wondrous doing brought his horse   85
  As had he been incorps'd and demi-natured°
  With the brave beast. So far he topp'd° my thought
  That I, in forgery° of shapes and tricks,
  Come short of what he did.
LAERTES: A Norman was 't?
KING: A Norman.   90

---

58. **So:** Provided that.   60. **checking at:** Turning aside from (like a falcon leaving the quarry to fly at a chance bird).   65. **uncharge the practice:** Acquit the stratagem of being a plot.
68. **organ:** Agent, instrument.   71. **Your . . . parts:** All your other virtues.   74. **unworthiest siege:** Least important rank.   79. **sables:** Rich robes furred with sable.   **weeds:** Garments.   80. **Importing health:** Indicating prosperity.   83. **can well:** Are skilled.   86. **incorps'd and demi-natured:** Of one body and nearly of one nature (like the centaur).   87. **topp'd:** Surpassed.   88. **forgery:** Invention.

LAERTES: Upon my life, Lamord.
KING: The very same.
LAERTES: I know him well. He is the brooch° indeed
    And gem of all the nation.
KING: He made confession° of you,
    And gave you such a masterly report   95
    For art and exercise in your defense,
    And for your rapier most especial,
    That he cried out, 'twould be a sight indeed,
    If one could match you. The scrimers° of their nation,
    He swore, had neither motion, guard, nor eye,   100
    If you oppos'd them. Sir, this report of his
    Did Hamlet so envenom with his envy
    That he could nothing do but wish and beg
    Your sudden coming o'er to play° with you.
    Now, out of this —
LAERTES: What out of this, my lord?   105
KING: Laertes, was your father dear to you?
    Or are you like the painting of a sorrow,
    A face without a heart?
LAERTES: Why ask you this?
KING: Not that I think you did not love your father,
    But that I know love is begun by time,°   110
    And that I see, in passages of proof,°
    Time qualifies° the spark and fire of it.
    There lives within the very flame of love
    A kind of wick or snuff° that will abate it,
    And nothing is at a like goodness still,°   115
    For goodness, growing to a plurisy,°
    Dies in his own too much.° That° we would do,
    We should do when we would; for this "would" changes
    And hath abatements° and delays as many
    As there are tongues, are hands, are accidents,°   120
    And then this "should" is like a spendthrift's sigh,°
    That hurts by easing.° But, to the quick o' th' ulcer;
    Hamlet comes back. What would you undertake
    To show yourself your father's son in deed
    More than in words?

---

92. brooch: Ornament.   94. confession: Admission of superiority.   99. scrimers: Fencers.
104. play: Fence.   110. begun by time: Subject to change.   111. passages of proof: Actual
instances.   112. qualifies: Weakens.   114. snuff: The charred part of a candlewick.   115.
nothing . . . still: Nothing remains at a constant level of perfection.   116. plurisy: Excess,
plethora.   117. in . . . much: Of its own excess.   That: That which.   119. abatements:
Diminutions.   120. accidents: Occurrences, incidents.   121. spendthrift's sigh: An allusion to the belief that each sigh cost the heart a drop of blood.   122. hurts by easing: Costs
the heart blood even while it affords emotional relief.

LAERTES: To cut his throat i' th' church!   125
KING: No place, indeed, should murder sanctuarize;°
    Revenge should have no bounds. But, good Laertes,
    Will you do this,° keep close within your chamber.
    Hamlet return'd shall know you are come home.
    We'll put on those° shall praise your excellence   130
    And set a double varnish on the fame
    The Frenchman gave you, bring you in fine° together,
    And wager on your heads. He, being remiss,°
    Most generous,° and free from all contriving,
    Will not peruse the foils, so that, with ease,   135
    Or with a little shuffling, you may choose
    A sword unbated,° and in a pass of practice°
    Requite him for your father.
LAERTES: I will do 't.
    And for that purpose I'll anoint my sword.
    I bought an unction° of a mountebank°   140
    So mortal that, but dip a knife in it,
    Where it draws blood no cataplasm° so rare,
    Collected from all simples° that have virtue
    Under the moon, can save the thing from death
    That is but scratch'd withal. I'll touch my point   145
    With this contagion, that, if I gall° him slightly,
    It may be death.
KING: Let's further think of this,
    Weigh what convenience both of time and means
    May fit us to our shape.° If this should fail,
    And that our drift look through our bad performance,°   150
    'Twere better not assay'd. Therefore this project
    Should have a back or second, that might hold
    If this did blast in proof.° Soft, let me see.
    We'll make a solemn wager on your cunnings —
    I ha 't!   155
    When in your motion you are hot and dry —
    As° make your bouts more violent to that end —
    And that he calls for drink, I'll have prepar'd him
    A chalice for the nonce,° whereon but sipping,

---

126. sanctuarize: Protect from punishment (alludes to the right of sanctuary with which certain religious places were invested).   **128. Will you do this:** If you wish to do this.   **130. put on those:** Instigate those who.   **132. in fine:** Finally.   **133. remiss:** Negligently unsuspicious.   **134. generous:** Noble-minded.   **137. unbated:** Not blunted, having no button. **pass of practice:** Treacherous thrust.   **140. unction:** Ointment.   **mountebank:** Quack doctor.   **142. cataplasm:** Plaster or poultice.   **143. simples:** Herbs.   **146. gall:** Graze, wound.   **149. shape:** Part that we propose to act.   **150. drift . . . performance:** I.e., intention be disclosed by our bungling.   **153. blast in proof:** Burst in the test (like a cannon). **157. As:** And you should.   **159. nonce:** Occasion.

If he by chance escape your venom'd stuck,°   160
Our purpose may hold there. [*A cry within.*] But stay, what noise?

(*Enter Queen.*)

QUEEN: One woe doth tread upon another's heel,
So fast they follow. Your sister's drowned, Laertes.
LAERTES: Drown'd! O, where?
QUEEN: There is a willow grows askant° the brook   165
That shows his hoar° leaves in the glassy stream;
Therewith fantastic garlands did she make
Of crow-flowers, nettles, daisies, and long purples°
That liberal° shepherds give a grosser name,
But our cold° maids do dead men's fingers call them.   170
There on the pendent boughs her crownet° weeds
Clamb'ring to hang, an envious sliver° broke,
When down her weedy° trophies and herself
Fell in the weeping brook. Her clothes spread wide,
And mermaid-like awhile they bore her up,   175
Which time she chanted snatches of old lauds,°
As one incapable° of her own distress,
Or like a creature native and indued°
Unto that element. But long it could not be
Till that her garments, heavy with their drink,   180
Pull'd the poor wretch from her melodious lay
To muddy death.
LAERTES: Alas, then she is drown'd?
QUEEN: Drown'd, drown'd.
LAERTES: Too much of water hast thou, poor Ophelia,
And therefore I forbid my tears. But yet   185
It is our trick;° nature her custom holds,
Let shame say what it will. [*He weeps.*] When these are gone,
The woman will be out.° Adieu, my lord.
I have a speech of fire, that fain would blaze,
But that this folly drowns it.   (*Exit.*)
KING: Let's follow, Gertrude.   190
How much I had to do to calm his rage!
Now fear I this will give it start again;
Therefore let's follow.   (*Exeunt.*)

---

160. **stuck:** Thrust (from *stoccado*, a fencing term).   165. **askant:** Aslant.   166. **hoar:**
White or gray.   168. **long purples:** Early purple orchids.   169. **liberal:** Free-spoken.   170.
cold: Chaste.   171. **crownet:** Made into a chaplet or coronet.   172. **envious sliver:** Malicious branch.   173. **weedy:** I.e., of plants.   176. **lauds:** Hymns.   177. **incapable:** Lacking
capacity to apprehend.   178. **indued:** Adapted by nature.   186. **It is our trick:** Weeping is
our natural way (when sad).   187–88. **When . . . out:** When my tears are all shed, the
woman in me will be expended, satisfied.

[ACT 5 / Scene 1]°

(*Enter two Clowns*° [*with spades, etc.*])

FIRST CLOWN: Is she to be buried in Christian burial when she willfully seeks her own salvation?

SECOND CLOWN: I tell thee she is; therefore make her grave straight.° The crowner° hath sat on her, and finds it Christian burial.

FIRST CLOWN: How can that be, unless she drown'd herself in her own   5
defense?

SECOND CLOWN: Why, 'tis found so.

FIRST CLOWN: It must be "se offendendo";° it cannot be else. For here lies the point: if I drown myself wittingly, it argues an act, and an act hath three branches — it is to act, to do, and to perform. Argal,° she drown'd her-   10
self wittingly.

SECOND CLOWN: Nay, but hear you, goodman delver —

FIRST CLOWN: Give me leave. Here lies the water; good. Here stands the man; good. If the man go to this water, and drown himself, it is, will he,° nill he, he goes, mark you that. But if the water come to him and drown   15
him, he drowns not himself. Argal, he that is not guilty of his own death shortens not his own life.

SECOND CLOWN: But is this law?

FIRST CLOWN: Ay, marry, is 't — crowner's quest° law.

SECOND CLOWN: Will you ha' the truth on 't? If this had not been a   20
gentlewoman, she should have been buried out o' Christian burial.

FIRST CLOWN: Why, there thou say'st.° And the more pity that great folk should have count'nance° in this world to drown or hang themselves, more than their even-Christen.° Come, my spade. There is no ancient gentlemen but gard'ners, ditchers, and grave-makers. They hold up   25
Adam's profession.

SECOND CLOWN: Was he a gentleman?

FIRST CLOWN: 'A was the first that ever bore arms.

[SECOND CLOWN: Why, he had none.

FIRST CLOWN: What, art a heathen? How dost thou understand the Scrip-   30
ture? The Scripture says "Adam digg'd." Could he dig without arms?]
I'll put another question to thee. If thou answerest me not to the purpose, confess thyself° —

SECOND CLOWN: Go to.

FIRST CLOWN: What is he that builds stronger than either the mason, the   35
shipwright, or the carpenter?

ACT 5, SCENE 1. Location: A churchyard.   [S.D.] *Clowns:* Rustics.   **3. straight:** Straightway, immediately.   **4. crowner:** Coroner.   **8. "se offendendo":** A comic mistake for *se defendendo*, term used in verdicts of justifiable homicide.   **10. Argal:** Corruption of *ergo*, therefore.   **14. will he:** Will he not.   **19. quest:** Inquest.   **22. there thou say'st:** That's right.   **23. count'nance:** Privilege.   **24. even-Christen:** Fellow Christian.   **33. confess thyself:** The saying continues, "and be hanged."

SECOND CLOWN: The gallows-maker, for that frame outlives a thousand tenants.

FIRST CLOWN: I like thy wit well, in good faith. The gallows does well, but how does it well? It does well to those that do ill. Now thou dost ill to   40
say the gallows is built stronger than the church. Argal, the gallows may do well to thee. To 't again, come.

SECOND CLOWN: "Who builds stronger than a mason, a shipwright, or a carpenter?"

FIRST CLOWN: Ay, tell me that, and unyoke.°   45

SECOND CLOWN: Marry, now I can tell.

FIRST CLOWN: To 't.

SECOND CLOWN: Mass,° I cannot tell.

(Enter Hamlet and Horatio [at a distance].)

FIRST CLOWN: Cudgel thy brains no more about it, for your dull ass will not mend his pace with beating; and, when you are ask'd this question next,   50
say "a grave-maker." The houses he makes lasts till doomsday. Go, get thee in, and fetch me a stoup° of liquor.

> *[Exit Second Clown. First Clown digs.]*

> *(Song.)*

"In youth, when I did love, did love,°
    Methought it was very sweet,
To contract – O – the time for – a – my behove,°   55
    O, methought there – a – was nothing – a – meet."°

HAMLET: Has this fellow no feeling of his business, that 'a sings at grave-making?

HORATIO: Custom hath made it in him a property of easiness.°

HAMLET: 'Tis e'en so. The hand of little employment hath the daintier   60
sense.°

> *(Song.)*

FIRST CLOWN: "But age, with his stealing steps,
    Hath claw'd me in his clutch,
And hath shipped me into the land,°
    As if I had never been such."   65

> *[Throws up a skull.]*

---

45. unyoke: After this great effort you may unharness the team of your wits.   **48. Mass:** By the Mass.   **52. stoup:** Two-quart measure.   **53. In . . . love:** This and the two following stanzas, with nonsensical variations, are from a poem attributed to Lord Vaux and printed in *Tottel's Miscellany* (1557). The O and a (for "ah") seemingly are the grunts of the digger.   **55. To contract . . . behove:** To make a betrothal agreement for my benefit (?).   **56. meet:** Suitable, i.e., more suitable.   **59. property of easiness:** Something he can do easily and without thinking.   **60–61. daintier sense:** More delicate sense of feeling.   **64. into the land:** Toward my grave (?) (but note the lack of rhyme in *steps, land*).

HAMLET: That skull had a tongue in it, and could sing once. How the knave
jowls° it to the ground, as if 'twere Cain's jaw-bone, that did the first
murder! This might be the pate of a politician,° which this ass now
o'erreaches,° one that would circumvent God, might it not?

HORATIO: It might, my lord.   70

HAMLET: Or of a courtier, which could say "Good morrow, sweet lord!
How dost thou, sweet lord?" This might be my Lord Such-a-one, that
prais'd my Lord Such-a-one's horse when 'a meant to beg it, might
it not?

HORATIO: Ay, my lord.   75

HAMLET: Why, e'en so, and now my Lady Worm's, chapless,° and knock'd
about the mazzard° with a sexton's spade. Here's fine revolution,° an°
we had the trick to see 't. Did these bones cost no more the breeding,°
but to play at loggats° with them? Mine ache to think on 't.

                                                                   (*Song.*)

FIRST CLOWN: "A pick-axe, and a spade, a spade,   80
          For and° a shrouding sheet;
     O, a pit of clay for to be made
          For such a guest is meet."

                                              [*Throws up another skull.*]

HAMLET: There's another. Why may not that be the skull of a lawyer? Where
be his quiddities° now, his quillities,° his cases, his tenures,° and his   85
tricks? Why does he suffer this mad knave now to knock him about
the sconce° with a dirty shovel, and will not tell him of his action of
battery? Hum! This fellow might be in 's time a great buyer of land, with
his statutes, his recognizances,° his fines, his double° vouchers,° his
recoveries.° [Is this the fine of his fines, and the recovery of his re-   90
coveries,] to have his fine pate full of fine dirt?° Will his vouchers
vouch him no more of his purchases, and double [ones too], than the
length and breadth of a pair of indentures?° The very conveyances° of

---

67. jowls: Dashes.   **68. politician:** Schemer, plotter.   **69. o'erreaches:** Circumvents, gets
the better of (with a quibble on the literal sense).   **76. chapless:** Having no lower jaw.   **77.
mazzard:** Head (literally, a drinking vessel).   **revolution:** Change.   **an:** If.   **78. the breeding:** In the breeding, raising.   **79. loggats:** A game in which pieces of hardwood are thrown to
lie as near as possible to a stake.   **81. For and:** And moreover.   **85. quiddities:** Subtleties,
quibbles (from Latin *quid*, a thing).   **quillities:** Verbal niceties, subtle distinctions (variation
of *quiddities*).   **tenures:** The holding of a piece of property or office, or the conditions or period of such holding.   **87. sconce:** Head.   **89. statutes, recognizances:** Legal documents
guaranteeing a debt by attaching land and property.   **89–90. fines, recoveries:** Ways of converting entailed estates into "fee simple" or freehold.   **89. double:** Signed by two signatories.
vouchers: Guarantees of the legality of a title to real estate.   **90–91. fine of his fines . . . fine
pate . . . fine dirt:** End of his legal maneuvers . . . elegant head . . . minutely sifted dirt.   **93.
pair of indentures:** Legal document drawn up in duplicate on a single sheet and then cut apart
on a zigzag line so that each pair was uniquely matched. (Hamlet may refer to two rows of
teeth, or dentures.)   **conveyances:** Deeds.

his lands will scarcely lie in this box,° and must th' inheritor° himself
have no more, ha?   95

HORATIO: Not a jot more, my lord.

HAMLET: Is not parchment made of sheep-skins?

HORATIO: Ay, my lord, and of calf-skins too.

HAMLET: They are sheep and calves which seek out assurance in that.° I will
speak to this fellow.—Whose grave's this, sirrah?°   100

FIRST CLOWN: Mine, sir.

[*Sings.*] "O, a pit of clay for to be made
[For such a guest is meet]."

HAMLET: I think it be thine, indeed, for thou liest in 't.

FIRST CLOWN: You lie out on 't, sir, and therefore 'tis not yours. For my part, 105
I do not lie in 't, yet it is mine.

HAMLET: Thou dost lie in 't, to be in 't and say it is thine. 'Tis for the dead,
not for the quick;° therefore thou liest.

FIRST CLOWN: 'Tis a quick lie, sir; 'twill away again from me to you.

HAMLET: What man dost thou dig it for?   110

FIRST CLOWN: For no man, sir.

HAMLET: What woman, then?

FIRST CLOWN: For none, neither.

HAMLET: Who is to be buried in 't?

FIRST CLOWN: One that was a woman, sir, but, rest her soul, she's dead.   115

HAMLET: How absolute° the knave is! We must speak by the card,° or equiv-
ocation° will undo us. By the Lord, Horatio, this three years I have
taken note of it: the age is grown so pick'd° that the toe of the peasant
comes so near the heel of the courtier, he galls his kibe.° How long hast
thou been a grave-maker?   120

FIRST CLOWN: Of all the days i' th' year, I came to 't that day that our last
king Hamlet overcame Fortinbras.

HAMLET: How long is that since?

FIRST CLOWN: Cannot you tell that? Every fool can tell that. It was that
very day that young Hamlet was born—he that is mad, and sent into   125
England.

HAMLET: Ay, marry, why was he sent into England?

FIRST CLOWN: Why, because 'a was mad. 'A shall recover his wits there, or, if
'a do not, 'tis no great matter there.

HAMLET: Why?   130

FIRST CLOWN: 'Twill not be seen in him there. There the men are as mad
as he.

---

94. this box: The skull.   **inheritor:** Possessor, owner.   **99. assurance in that:** Safety in
legal parchments.   **100. sirrah:** Term of address to inferiors.   **108. quick:** Living.   **116. absolute:** Positive, decided.   **by the card:** By the mariner's card on which the points of the
compass were marked, i.e., with precision.   **116–17. equivocation:** Ambiguity in the use of
terms.   **118. pick'd:** Refined, fastidious.   **119. galls his kibe:** Chafes the courtier's chilblain
(a swelling or sore caused by cold).

HAMLET: How came he mad?

FIRST CLOWN: Very strangely, they say.

HAMLET: How strangely?   135

FIRST CLOWN: Faith, e'en with losing his wits.

HAMLET: Upon what ground?

FIRST CLOWN: Why, here in Denmark. I have been sexton here, man and boy, thirty years.

HAMLET: How long will a man lie i' th' earth ere he rot?   140

FIRST CLOWN: Faith, if 'a be not rotten before 'a die — as we have many pocky° corses [now-a-days], that will scarce hold the laying in — 'a will last you some eight year or nine year. A tanner will last you nine year.

HAMLET: Why he more than another?

FIRST CLOWN: Why, sir, his hide is so tann'd with his trade that 'a will keep 145 out water a great while, and your water is a sore decayer of your whore-son dead body. [*Picks up a skull.*] Here's a skull now hath lain you° i' th' earth three and twenty years.

HAMLET: Whose was it?

FIRST CLOWN: A whoreson mad fellow's it was. Whose do you think it was?   150

HAMLET: Nay, I know not.

FIRST CLOWN: A pestilence on him for a mad rogue! 'A pour'd a flagon of Rhenish° on my head once. This same skull, sir, was Yorick's skull, the King's jester.

HAMLET: This?   155

FIRST CLOWN: E'en that.

HAMLET: [Let me see.] [*Takes the skull.*] Alas, poor Yorick! I knew him, Hora-tio, a fellow of infinite jest, of most excellent fancy. He hath borne me on his back a thousand times; and now, how abhorr'd in my imagina-tion it is! My gorge rises at it. Here hung those lips that I have kiss'd I 160 know not how oft. Where be your gibes now? Your gambols, your songs, your flashes of merriment that were wont to set the table on a roar? Not one now, to mock your own grinning? Quite chap-fall'n?° Now get you to my lady's chamber, and tell her, let her paint an inch thick, to this favor° she must come; make her laugh at that. Prithee, Horatio, tell me 165 one thing.

HORATIO: What's that, my lord?

HAMLET: Dost thou think Alexander look'd o' this fashion i' th' earth?

HORATIO: E'en so.

HAMLET: And smelt so? Pah! [*Puts down the skull.*]   170

HORATIO: E'en so, my lord.

HAMLET: To what base uses we may return, Horatio! Why may not imagina-tion trace the noble dust of Alexander, till 'a find it stopping a bung-hole?

---

142. pocky: Rotten, diseased (literally, with the pox, or syphilis).   **147. lain you:** Lain.
153. Rhenish: Rhine wine.   **163. chap-fall'n:** (1) Lacking the lower jaw; (2) dejected.
165. favor: Aspect, appearance.

HORATIO: 'twere to consider too curiously,° to consider so.

HAMLET: No, faith, not a jot, but to follow him thither with modesty° enough,   175
and likelihood to lead it. [As thus]: Alexander died, Alexander was
buried, Alexander returneth to dust; the dust is earth; of earth we make
loam;° and why of that loam, whereto he was converted, might they not
stop a beer-barrel?

Imperious° Caesar, dead and turn'd to clay,   180
Might stop a hole to keep the wind away.
O, that that earth which kept the world in awe
Should patch a wall t' expel the winter's flaw!°
But soft, but soft awhile! Here comes the King.

(*Enter King, Queen, Laertes, and the Corse* [*of Ophelia, in procession, with Priest,
Lords etc.*].)

The Queen, the courtiers. Who is this they follow?   185
And with such maimed rites? This doth betoken
The corse they follow did with desp'rate hand
Fordo it° own life. 'Twas of some estate.°
Couch° we awhile, and mark.

> [*He and Horatio conceal themselves.*
> *Ophelia's body is taken to the grave.*]

LAERTES: What ceremony else?   190

HAMLET [*to Horatio*]: That is Laertes, a very noble youth. Mark.

LAERTES: What ceremony else?

PRIEST: Her obsequies have been as far enlarg'd
As we have warranty. Her death was doubtful,
And, but that great command o'ersways the order,   195
She should in ground unsanctified been lodg'd
Till the last trumpet. For° charitable prayers,
Shards,° flints, and pebbles should be thrown on her.
Yet here she is allow'd her virgin crants,°
Her maiden strewments,° and the bringing home   200
Of bell and burial.°

LAERTES: Must there no more be done?

PRIEST: No more be done.
We should profane the service of the dead
To sing a requiem and such rest to her
As to peace-parted souls.

---

174. curiously: Minutely.   **175. modesty:** Moderation.   **178. loam:** Clay mixture for brick-
making or other clay use.   **180. Imperious:** Imperial.   **183. flaw:** Gust of wind.   **188. Fordo
it:** Destroy its.   **estate:** Rank.   **189. Couch:** Hide, lurk.   **197. For:** In place of.   **198. Shards:**
Broken bits of pottery.   **199. crants:** Garland.   **200. strewments:** Traditional strewing of
flowers.   **200–201. bringing . . . burial:** Laying to rest of the body in consecrated ground, to
the sound of the bell.

LAERTES: Lay her i' th' earth,   205
    And from her fair and unpolluted flesh
    May violets° spring! I tell thee, churlish priest,
    A minist'ring angel shall my sister be
    When thou liest howling!
HAMLET [to Horatio]:   What, the fair Ophelia!
QUEEN [scattering flowers]: Sweets to the sweet! Farewell.   210
    I hoped thou shouldst have been my Hamlet's wife.
    I thought thy bride-bed to have deck'd, sweet maid,
    And not have strew'd thy grave.
LAERTES: O, treble woe
    Fall ten times treble on that cursed head
    Whose wicked deed thy most ingenious sense°   215
    Depriv'd thee of! Hold off the earth awhile,
    Till I have caught her once more in mine arms.

               [Leaps into the grave and embraces Ophelia.]

    Now pile your dust upon the quick and dead,
    Till of this flat a mountain you have made
    T 'o'ertop old Pelion,° or the skyish head   220
    Of blue Olympus.°
HAMLET [coming forward]: What is he whose grief
    Bears such an emphasis, whose phrase of sorrow
    Conjures the wand'ring stars,° and makes them stand
    Like wonder-wounded hearers? This is I,   225
    Hamlet the Dane.°
LAERTES: The devil take thy soul!

                     [Grappling with him.]

HAMLET: Thou pray'st not well.
    I prithee, take thy fingers from my throat;
    For, though I am not splenitive° and rash,
    Yet have I in me something dangerous,   230
    Which let thy wisdom fear. Hold off thy hand.
KING: Pluck them asunder.
QUEEN: Hamlet, Hamlet!
ALL: Gentlemen!
HORATIO: Good my lord, be quiet.

                [Hamlet and Horatio are parted.]

HAMLET: Why, I will fight with him upon this theme
    Until my eyelids will no longer wag.   235

---

207. violets: See 4.5.181 and note.   **215. ingenious sense:** Mind endowed with finest qualities.   **220, 221. Pelion, Olympus:** Mountains in the north of Thessaly; see also *Ossa* at line
251.   **224. wand'ring stars:** Planets.   **226. the Dane:** This title normally signifies the king,
see 1.1.15 and note.   **229. splenitive:** Quick-tempered.

QUEEN: O my son, what theme?

HAMLET: I lov'd Ophelia. Forty thousand brothers
    Could not with all their quantity of love
    Make up my sum. What wilt thou do for her?

KING: O, he is mad, Laertes.   240

QUEEN: For love of God, forbear him.

HAMLET: 'Swounds,° show me what thou' do.
    Woo 't° weep? Woo 't fight? Woo 't fast? Woo 't tear thyself?
    Woo 't drink up eisel?° Eat a crocodile?
    I'll do 't. Dost thou come here to whine?   245
    To outface me with leaping in her grave?
    Be buried quick° with her, and so will I.
    And, if thou prate of mountains, let them throw
    Millions of acres on us, till our ground,
    Singeing his pate° against the burning zone,°   250
    Make Ossa° like a wart! Nay, an thou 'lt mouth,°
    I'll rant as well as thou.

QUEEN: This is mere° madness,
    And thus a while the fit will work on him;
    Anon, as patient as the female dove
    When that her golden couplets° are disclos'd,°   255
    His silence will sit drooping.

HAMLET: Hear you, sir.
    What is the reason that you use me thus?
    I lov'd you ever. But it is no matter.
    Let Hercules himself do what he may,
    The cat will mew, and dog will have his day.°   260

KING: I pray thee, good Horatio, wait upon him.

(Exit Hamlet and Horatio.)

[*To Laertes.*] Strengthen your patience in° our last night's speech;
We'll put the matter to the present push.° —
Good Gertrude, set some watch over your son. —
This grave shall have a living° monument.   265
An hour of quiet shortly shall we see;
Till then, in patience our proceeding be.

                                      (Exeunt.)

---

242. 'Swounds: By His (Christ's) wounds.   **243. Woo 't:** Wilt thou.   **244. eisel:** Vinegar.
247. quick: Alive.   **250. his pate:** Its head, i.e., top.   **burning zone:** Sun's orbit.   **251.**
Ossa: Another mountain in Thessaly. (In their war against the Olympian gods, the giants attempted to heap Ossa, Pelion, and Olympus on one another to scale heaven.)   **mouth:** Rant.
252. mere: Utter.   **255. golden couplets:** Two baby pigeons, covered with yellow down.
disclos'd: Hatched.   **259–60. Let . . . day:** Despite any blustering attempts at interference
every person will sooner or later do what he must do.   **262. in:** By recalling.   **263. present**
push: Immediate test.   **265. living:** Lasting; also refers (for Laertes' benefit) to the plot
against Hamlet.

[Scene 2]°

(Enter Hamlet and Horatio.)

HAMLET: So much for this, sir; now shall you see the other.°
    You do remember all the circumstance?

HORATIO: Remember it, my lord!

HAMLET: Sir, in my heart there was a kind of fighting
    That would not let me sleep. Methought I lay   5
    Worse than the mutines° in the bilboes.° Rashly,°
    And prais'd be rashness for it — let us know,°
    Our indiscretion sometime serves us well
    When our deep plots do pall,° and that should learn° us
    There's a divinity that shapes our ends,   10
    Rough-hew° them how we will —

HORATIO: That is most certain.

HAMLET: Up from my cabin,
    My sea-gown scarf'd about me, in the dark
    Grop'd I to find out them, had my desire,
    Finger'd° their packet, and in fine° withdrew   15
    To mine own room again, making so bold,
    My fears forgetting manners, to unseal
    Their grand commission; where I found, Horatio —
    Ah, royal knavery! — an exact command,
    Larded° with many several sorts of reasons   20
    Importing° Denmark's health and England's too,
    With, ho, such bugs° and goblins in my life,°
    That, on the supervise,° no leisure bated,°
    No, not to stay the grinding of the axe,
    My head should be struck off.

HORATIO: Is 't possible?   25

HAMLET: Here's the commission; read it at more leisure.

                                   [Gives document.]

    But wilt thou hear now how I did proceed?

HORATIO: I beseech you.

HAMLET: Being thus benetted round with villainies,
    Or I could make a prologue to my brains,   30
    They had begun the play.° I sat me down,

ACT 5, SCENE 2. **Location:** The castle. **1. see the other:** Hear the other news. **6. mutines:** Mutineers. **bilboes:** Shackles. **Rashly:** On impulse (this adverb goes with lines 12ff.). **7. know:** Acknowledge. **9. pall:** Fail. **learn:** Teach. **11. Rough-hew:** Shape roughly. **15. Finger'd:** Pilfered, pinched. **in fine:** Finally, in conclusion. **20. Larded:** Enriched. **21. Importing:** Relating to. **22. bugs:** Bugbears, hobgoblins. **in my life:** To be feared if I were allowed to live. **23. supervise:** Reading. **leisure bated:** Delay allowed. **30–31. Or . . . play:** Before I could consciously turn my brain to the matter, it had started working on a plan. (*Or* means *ere.*)

Devis'd a new commission, wrote it fair.°
I once did hold it, as our statists° do,
A baseness° to write fair, and labor'd much
How to forget that learning, but, sir, now   35
It did me yeoman's° service. Wilt thou know
Th' effect° of what I wrote?
HORATIO: Ay, good my lord.
HAMLET: An earnest conjuration from the King,
As England was his faithful tributary,
As love between them like the palm might flourish,   40
As peace should still her wheaten garland° wear
And stand a comma° 'tween their amities,
And many such-like as's° of great charge,°
That, on the view and knowing of these contents,
Without debasement further, more or less,   45
He should those bearers put to sudden death,
Not shriving time° allow'd.
HORATIO: How was this seal'd?
HAMLET: Why, even in that was heaven ordinant.°
I had my father's signet° in my purse,
Which was the model of that Danish seal;   50
Folded the writ up in the form of th' other,
Subscrib'd° it, gave 't th' impression,° plac'd it safely,
The changeling° never known. Now, the next day
Was our sea-fight, and what to this was sequent
Thou knowest already.   55
HORATIO: So Guildenstern and Rosencrantz go to 't.
HAMLET: [Why, man, they did make love to this employment.]
They are not near my conscience. Their defeat
Does by their own insinuation° grow.
'Tis dangerous when the baser nature comes   60
Between the pass° and fell° incensed points
Of mighty opposites.
HORATIO: Why, what a king is this!
HAMLET: Does it not, think thee, stand° me now upon—
He that hath killed my king and whor'd my mother,

---

32. fair: In a clear hand.   **33. statists:** Statesmen.   **34. baseness:** Lower-class trait.   **36. yeoman's:** Substantial, workmanlike.   **37. effect:** Purport.   **41. wheaten garland:** Symbolic of fruitful agriculture, of peace.   **42. comma:** Indicating continuity, link.   **43. as's:** (1) The "whereases" of formal document, (2) asses.   **charge:** (1) Import, (2) burden.   **47. shriving time:** Time for confession and absolution.   **48. ordinant:** Directing.   **49. signet:** Small seal.   **52. Subscrib'd:** Signed.   **impression:** With a wax seal.   **53. changeling:** The substituted letter (literally, a fairy child substituted for a human one).   **59. insinuation:** Interference.   **61. pass:** Thrust.   **fell:** Fierce.   **63. stand:** Become incumbent.

Popp'd in between th' election° and my hopes,   65
Thrown out his angle° for my proper° life,
And with such coz'nage° — is 't not perfect conscience
[To quit° him with this arm? And is 't not to be damn'd
To let this canker° of our nature come
In further evil?   70
HORATIO: It must be shortly known to him from England
    What is the issue of the business there.
HAMLET: It will be short. The interim is mine,
    And a man's life 's no more than to say "One."°
    But I am very sorry, good Horatio,   75
    That to Laertes I forgot myself,
    For by the image of my cause I see
    The portraiture of his. I'll court his favors.
    But, sure, the bravery° of his grief did put me
    Into a tow'ring passion.
HORATIO: Peace, who comes here?]   80

(*Enter a Courtier [Osric].*)

OSRIC: Your lordship is right welcome back to Denmark.
HAMLET: I humbly thank you, sir. [*To Horatio.*] Dost know this water-fly?
HORATIO: No, my good lord.
HAMLET: Thy state is the more gracious, for 'tis a vice to know him. He hath
    much land, and fertile. Let a beast be lord of beasts, and his crib shall   85
    stand at the King's mess.° 'Tis a chough,° but, as I say, spacious in the
    possession of dirt.
OSRIC: Sweet lord, if your lordship were at leisure, I should impart a thing to
    you from his Majesty.
HAMLET: I will receive it, sir, with all diligence of spirit. Put your bonnet to 90
    his right use; 'tis for the head.
OSRIC: I thank your lordship, it is very hot.
HAMLET: No, believe me, 'tis very cold; the wind is northerly.
OSRIC: It is indifferent° cold, my lord, indeed.
HAMLET: But yet methinks it is very sultry and hot for my complexion.°   95
OSRIC: Exceedingly, my lord; it is very sultry, as 'twere — I cannot tell how.
    My lord, his Majesty bade me signify to you that 'a has laid a great
    wager on your head. Sir, this is the matter —
HAMLET: I beseech you, remember —

                                            [*Hamlet moves him to put on his hat.*]

---

65. **election:** The Danish monarch was "elected" by a small number of high-ranking electors.
66. **angle:** Fishing line. **proper:** Very. 67. **coz'nage:** Trickery. 68. **quit:** Repay. 69.
canker: Ulcer. 74. **a man's . . . "One":** To take a man's life requires no more than to count
to one as one duels. 79. **bravery:** Bravado. 85–86. **Let . . . mess:** If a man, no matter how
beastlike, is as rich in possessions as Osric, he may eat at the king's table. 86. **chough:** Chattering jackdaw. 94. **indifferent:** Somewhat. 95. **complexion:** Temperament.

OSRIC: Nay, good my lord; for my ease,° in good faith. Sir, here is newly come   100
    to court Laertes — believe me, an absolute gentleman, full of most excel-
    lent differences,° of very soft society° and great showing.° Indeed, to
    speak feelingly° of him, he is the card° or calendar° of gentry,° for you
    shall find in him the continent of what part° a gentleman would see.

HAMLET: Sir, his definement° suffers no perdition° in you, though, I know,   105
    to divide him inventorially° would dozy° th' arithmetic of memory, and
    yet but yaw° neither° in respect of° his quick sail. But, in the verity
    of extolment,° I take him to be a soul of great article,° and his infusion°
    of such dearth and rareness,° as, to make true diction° of him, his sem-
    blable° is his mirror, and who else would trace° him, his umbrage,°   110
    nothing more.

OSRIC: Your lordship speaks most infallibly of him.

HAMLET: The concernancy,° sir? Why do we wrap the gentleman in our more
    rawer breath?°

OSRIC: Sir?   115

HORATIO: Is 't not possible to understand in another tongue?° You will do
    't,° sir, really.

HAMLET: What imports the nomination° of this gentleman?

OSRIC: Of Laertes?

HORATIO [to Hamlet]: His purse is empty already; all 's golden words are   120
    spent.

HAMLET: Of him, sir.

OSRIC: I know you are not ignorant —

HAMLET: I would you did, sir; yet, in faith, if you did, it would not much
    approve° me. Well, sir?   125

OSRIC: You are not ignorant of what excellence Laertes is —

HAMLET: I dare not confess that, lest I should compare° with him in excel-
    lence; but to know a man well were to know himself.°

---

100. for my ease: A conventional reply declining the invitation to put his hat back on.
102. differences: Special qualities. **soft society:** Agreeable manners. **great showing:** Distinguished appearance. **103. feelingly:** With just perception. **card:** Chart, map. **calendar:**
Guide. **gentry:** Good breeding. **104. the continent . . . part:** One who contains in him
all the qualities (a *continent* is that which contains). **105. definement:** Definition. (Hamlet
proceeds to mock Osric by using his lofty diction back at him.) **perdition:** Loss, diminution.
106. divide him inventorially: Enumerate his graces. **dozy:** Dizzy. **107. yaw:** To move
unsteadily (said of a ship). **neither:** For all that. **in respect of:** In comparison with.
107–108. in . . . extolment: In true praise (of him). **108. article:** Moment or importance.
108. infusion: Essence, character imparted by nature. **109. dearth and rareness:** Rarity.
make true diction: Speak truly. **109–10. semblable:** Only true likeness. **110. who . . .
trace:** Any other person who would wish to follow. **umbrage:** Shadow. **113. concernancy:**
Import, relevance. **114. breath:** Speech. **116. to understand . . . tongue:** For Osric to understand when someone else speaks in his manner. (Horatio twits Osric for not being able to
understand the kind of flowery speech he himself uses when Hamlet speaks in such a vein.)
116–17. You will do 't: You can if you try. **118. nomination:** Naming. **125. approve:**
Commend. **127. compare:** Seem to compete. **128. but . . . himself:** For, to recognize excellence in another man, one must know oneself.

OSRIC: I mean, sir, for his weapon; but in the imputation laid on him by
    them,° in his meed° he's unfellow'd.°   130

HAMLET: What's his weapon?

OSRIC: Rapier and dagger.

HAMLET: That's two of his weapons — but well.

OSRIC: The King, sir, hath wager'd with him six Barbary horses, against the
    which he has impawn'd,° as I take it, six French rapiers and poniards,   135
    with their assigns,° as girdle, hangers,° and so. Three of the carriages,°
    in faith, are very dear to fancy,° very responsive° to the hilts, most deli-
    cate° carriages, and of very liberal conceit.°

HAMLET: What call you the carriages?

HORATIO [to Hamlet]: I knew you must be edified by the margent° ere you   140
    had done.

OSRIC: The carriages, sir, are the hangers.

HAMLET: The phrase would be more germane to the matter if we could carry
    a cannon by our sides; I would it might be hangers till then. But, on:
    six Barb'ry horses against six French swords, their assigns, and three   145
    liberal-conceited carriages; that's the French bet against the Danish.
    Why is this impawn'd, as you call it?

OSRIC: The King, sir, hath laid,° sir, that in a dozen passes° between yourself
    and him, he shall not exceed you three hits. He hath laid on twelve for
    nine, and it would come to immediate trial, if your lordship would   150
    vouchsafe the answer.

HAMLET: How if I answer no?

OSRIC: I mean, my lord, the opposition of your person in trial.

HAMLET: Sir, I will walk here in the hall. If it please his Majesty, it is the
    breathing time° of day with me. Let the foils be brought, the gentleman   155
    willing, and the King hold his purpose, I will win for him an I can; if
    not, I will gain nothing but my shame and the odd hits.

OSRIC: Shall I deliver you so?

HAMLET: To this effect, sir — after what flourish your nature will.

OSRIC: I commend my duty to your lordship.   160

HAMLET: Yours, yours. [Exit Osric.] He does well to commend it himself;
    there are no tongues else for 's turn.

HORATIO: This lapwing° runs away with the shell on his head.

129–30. imputation . . . them: Reputation given him by others.   130. meed: Merit.   **unfel-
low'd:** Unmatched.   135. **impawn'd:** Staked, wagered.   136. **assigns:** Appurtenances.
hangers: Straps on the sword belt (girdle) from which the sword hung.   **carriages:** An affected
way of saying hangers; literally, gun-carriages.   137. **dear to fancy:** Fancifully designed, taste-
ful.   **responsive:** Corresponding closely, matching.   137–38. **delicate:** I.e., in workmanship.
138. **liberal conceit:** Elaborate design.   140. **margent:** Margin of a book, place for explanatory notes.   148. **laid:** Wagered.   **passes:** Bouts. (The odds of the betting are hard to explain.
Possibly the king bets that Hamlet will win at least five out of twelve, at which point Laertes
raises the odds against himself by betting he will win nine.)   155. **breathing time:** Exercise period.   163. **lapwing:** A bird that draws intruders away from its nest and was thought to run
about when newly hatched with its head in the shell; a seeming reference to Osric's hat.

HAMLET: 'A did comply, sir, with his dug,° before 'a suck'd it. Thus has he —
and many more of the same breed that I know the drossy° age dotes   165
on — only got the tune° of the time and, out of an habit of encounter,°
a kind of yesty° collection,° which carries them through and through
the most fann'd and winnow'd° opinions; and do but blow them to
their trial, the bubbles are out.°

(Enter a Lord.)

LORD: My lord, his Majesty commended him to you by young Osric, who   170
brings back to him that you attend him in the hall. He sends to know if
your pleasure hold to play with Laertes, or that you will take longer
time.
HAMLET: I am constant to my purposes; they follow the King's pleasure. If
his fitness speaks,° mine is ready; now or whensoever, provided I be so   175
able as now.
LORD: The King and Queen and all are coming down.
HAMLET: In happy time.°
LORD: The Queen desires you to use some gentle entertainment° to Laertes
before you fall to play.   180
HAMLET: She well instructs me.   *[Exit Lord.]*
HORATIO: You will lose, my lord.
HAMLET: I do not think so. Since he went into France, I have been in contin-
ual practice; I shall win at the odds. But thou wouldst not think how ill
all's here about my heart; but it is no matter.   185
HORATIO: Nay, good my lord —
HAMLET: It is but foolery, but it is such a kind of gain-giving,° as would perhaps trouble a woman.
HORATIO: If your mind dislike anything, obey it. I will forestall their repair
hither, and say you are not fit.   190
HAMLET: Not a whit, we defy augury. There is special providence in the fall of
a sparrow. If it be now, 'tis not to come; if it be not to come, it will be
now, if it be not now, yet it will come. The readiness is all. Since no man
of aught he leaves knows what is 't to leave betimes,° let be.

*(A table prepar'd. [Enter] trumpets, drums, and Officers with cushions; King, Queen,
[Osric,] and all the State; foils, daggers, [and wine borne in;] and Laertes.)*

KING: Come, Hamlet, come, and take this hand from me.   195

---

164. comply . . . dug: Observe ceremonious formality toward his mother's teat.   **165.
drossy:** Frivolous.   **166. tune:** Temper, mood, manner of speech.   **166. habit of encounter:**
Demeanor of social intercourse.   **167. yesty:** Yeasty, frothy.   **collection:** I.e., of current
phrases.   **168. fann'd and winnow'd:** Select and refined.   **168–69. blow . . . out:** Put them
to the test, and their ignorance is exposed.   **174–75. If . . . speaks:** If his readiness answers to
the time.   **178. In happy time:** A phrase of courtesy indicating acceptance.   **179. entertainment:** Greeting.   **187. gain-giving:** Misgiving.   **194. what . . . betimes:** What is the best
time to leave it.

[The King puts Laertes' hand into Hamlet's.]

HAMLET: Give me your pardon, sir. I have done you wrong,
    But pardon 't, as you are a gentleman.
    This presence° knows,
    And you must needs have heard, how I am punish'd
    With a sore distraction. What I have done   200
    That might your nature, honor, and exception°
    Roughly awake, I here proclaim was madness.
    Was 't Hamlet wrong'd Laertes? Never Hamlet.
    If Hamlet from himself be ta'en away,
    And when he's not himself does wrong Laertes,   205
    Then Hamlet does it not, Hamlet denies it.
    Who does it, then? His madness. If 't be so,
    Hamlet is of the faction that is wrong'd;
    His madness is poor Hamlet's enemy.
    [Sir, in this audience,]   210
    Let my disclaiming from a purpos'd evil
    Free me so far in your most generous thoughts
    That I have shot my arrow o'er the house
    And hurt my brother.
LAERTES: I am satisfied in nature,°
    Whose motive in this case should stir me most   215
    To my revenge. But in my terms of honor
    I stand aloof, and will no reconcilement
    Till by some elder masters of known honor
    I have a voice° and precedent of peace
    To keep my name ungor'd. But till that time,   220
    I do receive your offer'd love like love,
    And will not wrong it.
HAMLET: I embrace it freely,
    And will this brothers' wager frankly play.
    Give us the foils. Come on.
LAERTES: Come, one for me.
HAMLET: I'll be your foil,° Laertes. In mine ignorance   225
    Your skill shall, like a star i' th' darkest night,
    Stick fiery off° indeed.
LAERTES: You mock me, sir.
HAMLET: No, by this hand.
KING: Give them the foils, young Osric. Cousin Hamlet,
    You know the wager?

---

198. presence: Royal assembly. **201. exception:** Disapproval. **214. in nature:** As to my personal feelings. **219. voice:** Authoritative pronouncement. **225. foil:** Thin metal background which sets a jewel off (with pun on the blunted rapier for fencing). **227. Stick fiery off:** Stand out brilliantly.

HAMLET: Very well, my lord.   230
    Your Grace has laid the odds o' th' weaker side.
KING: I do not fear it; I have seen you both.
    But since he is better'd,° we have therefore odds.
LAERTES: This is too heavy, let me see another.

                                        [Exchanges his foil for another.]

HAMLET: This likes me well. These foils have all a length?   235

                                            [They prepare to play.]

OSRIC: Ay, my good lord.
KING: Set me the stoups of wine upon that table.
    If Hamlet give the first or second hit,
    Or quit° in answer of the third exchange,
    Let all the battlements their ordnance fire.   240
    The King shall drink to Hamlet's better breath,
    And in the cup an union° shall he throw,
    Richer than that which four successive kings
    In Denmark's crown have worn. Give me the cups,
    And let the kettle° to the trumpet speak,   245
    The trumpet to the cannoneer without,
    The cannons to the heavens, the heaven to earth,
    "Now the King drinks to Hamlet." Come, begin.

                                       (Trumpets the while.)

    And you, the judges, bear a wary eye.
HAMLET: Come on sir.   250
LAERTES: Come, my lord.   *[They play. Hamlet scores a hit.]*
HAMLET: One.
LAERTES: No.
HAMLET: Judgment.
OSRIC: A hit, a very palpable hit.

         (Drum, trumpets, and shot. Flourish. A piece goes off.)

LAERTES: Well, again.   255
KING: Stay, give me drink. Hamlet, this pearl is thine.

              [He throws a pearl in Hamlet's cup and drinks.]

    Here's to thy health. Give him the cup.
HAMLET: I'll play this bout first, set it by awhile.
    Come. *[They play.]* Another hit; what say you?

---

233. is better'd: Has improved; is the odds-on favorite. **239. quit:** Repay (with a hit).
242. union: Pearl (so called, according to Pliny's *Natural History*, 9, because pearls are *unique*,
never identical). **245. kettle:** Kettledrum.

LAERTES: A touch, a touch. I do confess 't.   260
KING: Our son shall win.
QUEEN: He's fat,° and scant of breath.
    Here, Hamlet, take my napkin,° rub thy brows.
    The Queen carouses° to thy fortune, Hamlet.
HAMLET: Good madam!
KING: Gertrude, do not drink.   265
QUEEN: I will, my lord; I pray you pardon me.

[*Drinks.*]

KING [*aside*]: It is the pois'ned cup. It is too late.
HAMLET: I dare not drink yet, madam; by and by.
QUEEN: Come, let me wipe thy face.
LAERTES [*to King*]: My lord, I'll hit him now.
KING: I do not think 't.   270
LAERTES [*aside*]: And yet it is almost against my conscience.
HAMLET: Come, for the third Laertes. You do but dally.
    I pray you, pass with your best violence;
    I am afeard you make a wanton of me.°
LAERTES: Say you so? Come on.   [*They play.*] 275
OSRIC: Nothing, neither way.
LAERTES: Have at you now!

                    [*Laertes wounds Hamlet; then, in scuffling,
                    they change rapiers,° and Hamlet wounds Laertes.*]

KING: Part them! They are incens'd.
HAMLET: Nay, come, again.   [*The Queen falls.*]
OSRIC: Look to the Queen there, ho!
HORATIO: They bleed on both sides. How is it, my lord?
OSRIC: How is 't, Laertes?   280
LAERTES: Why, as a woodcock° to mine own springe,° Osric;
    I am justly kill'd with mine own treachery.
HAMLET: How does the Queen?
KING: She swoons to see them bleed.
QUEEN: No, no, the drink, the drink — O my dear Hamlet —
    The drink, the drink! I am pois'ned.   [*Dies.*] 285
HAMLET: O villainy! Ho, let the door be lock'd!
    Treachery! Seek it out.   [*Laertes falls.*]

---

261. fat: Not physically fit, out of training.   **262. napkin:** Handkerchief.   **263. carouses:**
Drinks a toast.   **274. make . . . me:** Treat me like a spoiled child, holding back to give me an
advantage.   [s.D.] *in scuffling, they change rapiers:* This stage direction occurs in the Folio. According to a widespread stage tradition, Hamlet receives a scratch, realizes that Laertes' sword is
unbated, and accordingly forces an exchange.   **281. woodcock:** A bird, a type of stupidity or
as a decoy.   **springe:** Trap, snare.

LAERTES: It is here, Hamlet. Hamlet, thou art slain.
No med'cine in the world can do thee good;
In thee there is not half an hour's life.   290
The treacherous instrument is in thy hand,
Unbated° and envenom'd. The foul practice
Hath turn'd itself on me. Lo, here I lie,
Never to rise again. Thy mother's pois'ned.
I can no more. The King, the King's to blame.   295
HAMLET: The point envenom'd too? Then, venom, to thy work.

                                                           [Stabs the King.]

ALL: Treason! Treason!
KING: O, yet defend me, friends; I am but hurt.
HAMLET: Here, thou incestuous, murd'rous, damned Dane,

                        [He forces the King to drink the poisoned cup.]

Drink off this potion. Is thy union° here?   300
Follow my mother.   [King dies.]
LAERTES: He is justly serv'd.
It is a poison temper'd° by himself.
Exchange forgiveness with me, noble Hamlet.
Mine and my father's death come not upon thee,
Nor thine on me!   [Dies.] 305
HAMLET: Heaven make thee free of it! I follow thee.
I am dead, Horatio. Wretched Queen, adieu!
You that look pale and tremble at this chance,
That are but mutes° or audience to this act,
Had I but time — as this fell° sergeant,° Death,   310
Is strict in his arrest — O, I could tell you —
But let it be. Horatio, I am dead;
Thou livest. Report me and my cause aright
To the unsatisfied.
HORATIO: Never believe it.
I am more an antique Roman° than a Dane.   315
Here's yet some liquor left.

                        [He attempts to drink from the poisoned cup.
                                              Hamlet prevents him.]

HAMLET: As th' art a man,
Give me the cup! Let go! By heaven, I'll ha 't.
O God, Horatio, what a wounded name,

---

292. **Unbated:** Not blunted with a button.   300. **union:** Pearl (see line 242; with grim puns on the word's other meanings: marriage, shared death[?]).   302. **temper'd:** Mixed.   309. **mutes:** Silent observers.   310. **fell:** Cruel.   **sergeant:** Sheriff's officer.   315. **Roman:** It was the Roman custom to follow masters in death.

Things standing thus unknown, shall I leave behind me!
If thou didst ever hold me in thy heart,   320
Absent thee from felicity awhile,
And in this harsh world draw thy breath in pain
To tell my story.

                              (*A march afar off* [*and a volley within*].)

          What warlike noise is this?
OSRIC: Young Fortinbras, with conquest come from Poland,
     To the ambassadors of England gives   325
     This warlike volley.
HAMLET: O, I die, Horatio!
     The potent poison quite o'ercrows° my spirit.
     I cannot live to hear the news from England,
     But I do prophesy th' election lights
     On Fortinbras. He has my dying voice.°   330
     So tell him, with th' occurrents° more and less
     Which have solicited° — the rest is silence.   [*Dies.*]
HORATIO: Now cracks a noble heart. Good night, sweet prince;
     And flights of angels sing thee to thy rest!

                                                         [*March within.*]

     Why does the drum come hither?   335

(*Enter Fortinbras, with the* [*English*] *Ambassadors* [*with drum, colors, and atten-dants*].)

FORTINBRAS: Where is this sight?
HORATIO: What is it you would see?
     If aught of woe or wonder, cease your search.
FORTINBRAS: This quarry° cries on havoc.° O proud Death.
     What feast is toward° in thine eternal cell,
     That thou so many princes at a shot   340
     So bloodily hast struck?
FIRST AMBASSADOR: The sight is dismal;
     And our affairs from England come too late.
     The ears are senseless that should give us hearing,
     To tell him his commandment is fulfill'd,
     That Rosencrantz and Guildenstern are dead.   345
     Where should we have our thanks?
HORATIO: Not from his° mouth,
     Had it th' ability of life to thank you.
     He never gave commandment for their death.

---

327. o'ercrows: Triumphs over.   **330. voice:** Vote.   **331. occurrents:** Events, incidents.
332. solicited: Moved, urged.   **338. quarry:** Heap of dead.   **cries on havoc:** Proclaims a
general slaughter.   **339. toward:** In preparation.   **346. his:** Claudius's.

But since, so jump° upon this bloody question,°
You from the Polack wars, and you from England,   350
Are here arriv'd, give order that these bodies
High on a stage° be placed to the view,
And let me speak to th' yet unknowing world
How these things came about. So shall you hear
Of carnal, bloody, and unnatural acts,   355
Of accidental judgments,° casual° slaughters,
Of deaths put on° by cunning and forc'd cause,
And, in this upshot, purposes mistook
Fall'n on th' inventors' heads. All this can I
Truly deliver.

FORTINBRAS: Let us haste to hear it,   360
And call the noblest to the audience.
For me, with sorrow I embrace my fortune.
I have some rights of memory° in this kingdom,
Which now to claim my vantage° doth invite me.

HORATIO: Of that I shall have also cause to speak,   365
And from his mouth whose voice will draw on more.°
But let this same be presently° perform'd,
Even while men's minds are wild, lest more mischance
On° plots and errors happen.

FORTINBRAS: Let four captains
Bear Hamlet, like a soldier, to the stage,   370
For he was likely, had he been put on,°
To have prov'd most royal; and, for his passage,°
The soldiers' music and the rite of war
Speak loudly for him.
Take up the bodies. Such a sight as this   375
Becomes the field,° but here shows much amiss.
Go, bid the soldiers shoot.

(*Exeunt* [*marching, bearing off the dead bodies;
a peal of ordnance is shot off*].)

---

349. jump: Precisely.   **question:** Dispute.   **352. stage:** Platform.   **356. judgments:** Retributions.   **casual:** Occurring by chance.   **357. put on:** Instigated.   **363. of memory:** Traditional, remembered.   **364. vantage:** Presence at this opportune moment.   **366. voice . . . more:** Vote will influence still others.   **367. presently:** Immediately.   **369. On:** On the basis of.   **371. put on:** Invested in royal office and so put to the test.   **372. passage:** Death.   **376. field:** I.e., of battle.

Henrik Ibsen   1828–1906

A Doll House°   [1879]

Translated by Rolf Fjelde

THE CHARACTERS

TORVALD HELMER, a lawyer
NORA, his wife
DR. RANK
MRS. LINDE
NILS KROGSTAD, a bank clerk

THE HELMERS' THREE SMALL CHILDREN
ANNE-MARIE, their nurse
HELENE, a maid
A DELIVERY BOY

The action takes place in Helmer's residence.

ACT 1

(*A comfortable room, tastefully but not expensively furnished. A door to the right in the back wall leads to the entryway; another to the left leads to Helmer's study. Between these doors, a piano. Midway in the left-hand wall a door, and further back a window. Near the window a round table with an armchair and a small sofa. In the right-hand wall, toward the rear, a door, and nearer the foreground a porcelain stove with two armchairs and a rocking chair beside it. Between the stove and the side door, a small table. Engravings on the walls. An étagère° with china figures and other small art objects; a small bookcase with richly bound books; the floor carpeted; a fire burning in the stove. It is a winter day.*)

(*A bell rings in the entryway; shortly after we hear the door being unlocked. Nora comes into the room, humming happily to herself; she is wearing street clothes and carries an armload of packages, which she puts down on the table to the right. She has left the hall door open, and through it a Delivery Boy is seen holding a Christmas tree and a basket, which he gives to the Maid who let them in.*)

NORA: Hide the tree well, Helene. The children mustn't get a glimpse of it till this evening, after it's trimmed. (*To the Delivery Boy, taking out her purse.*) How much?

DELIVERY BOY: Fifty, ma'am.

NORA: There's a crown. No, keep the change. (*The Boy thanks her and leaves. Nora shuts the door. She laughs softly to herself while taking off her street things. Drawing a bag of macaroons from her pocket, she eats a couple, then steals over and listens at her husband's study door.*) Yes, he's home. (*Hums again as she moves to the table right.*)

HELMER (*from the study*): Is that my little lark twittering out there?

A Doll House: Fjelde explains, in the foreword to his translation, that he translates the title as "A Doll House" instead of "A Doll's House" to avoid the suggestion that it is the house of the doll, Nora. Rather, he believes, Ibsen meant that both Torvald and Nora are living in an unreal, "let's pretend" situation.   *s.d. étagère:* A cabinet with a number of shelves.

NORA (*busy opening some packages*): Yes, it is.

HELMER: Is that my squirrel rummaging around?

NORA: Yes!

HELMER: When did my squirrel get in?

NORA: Just now. (*Putting the macaroon bag in her pocket and wiping her mouth.*) Do come in, Torvald, and see what I've bought.

HELMER: Can't be disturbed. (*After a moment he opens the door and peers in, pen in hand.*) Bought, you say? All that there? Has the little spendthrift been out throwing money around again?

NORA: Oh, but Torvald, this year we really should let ourselves go a bit. It's the first Christmas we haven't had to economize.

HELMER: But you know we can't go squandering.

NORA: Oh yes, Torvald, we can squander a little now. Can't we? Just a tiny, wee bit. Now that you've got a big salary and are going to make piles and piles of money.

HELMER: Yes — starting New Year's. But then it's a full three months till the raise comes through.

NORA: Pooh! We can borrow that long.

HELMER: Nora! (*Goes over and playfully takes her by the ear.*) Are your scatter-brains off again? What if today I borrowed a thousand crowns, and you squandered them over Christmas week, and then on New Year's Eve a roof tile fell on my head, and I lay there —

NORA (*putting her hand on his mouth*): Oh! Don't say such things!

HELMER: Yes, but what if it happened — then what?

NORA: If anything so awful happened, then it just wouldn't matter if I had debts or not.

HELMER: Well, but the people I'd borrowed from?

NORA: Them? Who cares about them! They're strangers.

HELMER: Nora, Nora, how like a woman! No, but seriously, Nora, you know what I think about that. No debts! Never borrow! Something of freedom's lost — and something of beauty, too — from a home that's founded on borrowing and debt. We've made a brave stand up to now, the two of us; and we'll go right on like that the little while we have to.

NORA (*going toward the stove*): Yes, whatever you say, Torvald.

HELMER (*following her*): Now, now, the little lark's wings mustn't droop. Come on, don't be a sulky squirrel. (*Taking out his wallet.*) Nora, guess what I have here.

NORA (*turning quickly*): Money!

HELMER: There, see. (*Hands her some notes.*) Good grief, I know how costs go up in a house at Christmastime.

NORA: Ten — twenty — thirty — forty. Oh, thank you, Torvald; I can manage no end on this.

HELMER: You really will have to.

NORA: Oh yes, I promise I will! But come here so I can show you everything I bought. And so cheap! Look, new clothes for Ivar here — and a sword. Here a horse and a trumpet for Bob. And a doll and a doll's bed here for Emmy;

they're nothing much, but she'll tear them to bits in no time anyway. And here I have dress material and handkerchiefs for the maids. Old Anne-Marie really deserves something more.

HELMER: And what's in that package there?

NORA (*with a cry*): Torvald, no! You can't see that till tonight!

HELMER: I see. But tell me now, you little prodigal, what have you thought of for yourself?

NORA: For myself? Oh, I don't want anything at all.

HELMER: Of course you do. Tell me just what—within reason—you'd most like to have.

NORA: I honestly don't know. Oh, listen, Torvald—

HELMER: Well?

NORA (*fumbling at his coat buttons, without looking at him*): If you want to give me something, then maybe you could—you could—

HELMER: Come on, out with it.

NORA (*hurriedly*): You could give me money, Torvald. No more than you think you can spare; then one of these days I'll buy something with it.

HELMER: But Nora—

NORA: Oh, please, Torvald darling, do that! I beg you, please. Then I could hang the bills in pretty gilt paper on the Christmas tree. Wouldn't that be fun?

HELMER: What are those little birds called that always fly through their fortunes?

NORA: Oh yes, spendthrifts; I know all that. But let's do as I say, Torvald; then I'll have time to decide what I really need most. That's very sensible, isn't it?

HELMER (*smiling*): Yes, very—that is, if you actually hung onto the money I give you, and you actually used it to buy yourself something. But it goes for the house and for all sorts of foolish things, and then I only have to lay out some more.

NORA: Oh, but Torvald—

HELMER: Don't deny it, my dear little Nora. (*Putting his arm around her waist.*) Spendthrifts are sweet, but they use up a frightful amount of money. It's incredible what it costs a man to feed such birds.

NORA: Oh, how can you say that! Really, I save everything I can.

HELMER (*laughing*): Yes, that's the truth. Everything you can. But that's nothing at all.

NORA (*humming, with a smile of quiet satisfaction*): Hm, if you only knew what expenses we larks and squirrels have, Torvald.

HELMER: You're an odd little one. Exactly the way your father was. You're never at a loss for scaring up money; but the moment you have it, it runs right out through your fingers; you never know what you've done with it. Well, one takes you as you are. It's deep in your blood. Yes, these things are hereditary, Nora.

NORA: Ah, I could wish I'd inherited many of Papa's qualities.

HELMER: And I couldn't wish you anything but just what you are, my sweet little lark. But wait; it seems to me you have a very—what should I call it?—a very suspicious look today—

NORA: I do?

HELMER: You certainly do. Look me straight in the eye.

NORA (*looking at him*): Well?

HELMER (*shaking an admonitory finger*): Surely my sweet tooth hasn't been running riot in town today, has she?

NORA: No. Why do you imagine that?

HELMER: My sweet tooth really didn't make a little detour through the confectioner's?

NORA: No, I assure you, Torvald —

HELMER: Hasn't nibbled some pastry?

NORA: No, not at all.

HELMER: Not even munched a macaroon or two?

NORA: No, Torvald, I assure you, really —

HELMER: There, there now. Of course I'm only joking.

NORA (*going to the table, right*): You know I could never think of going against you.

HELMER: No, I understand that; and you *have* given me your word. (*Going over to her.*) Well, you keep your little Christmas secrets to yourself, Nora darling. I expect they'll come to light this evening, when the tree is lit.

NORA: Did you remember to ask Dr. Rank?

HELMER: No. But there's no need for that, it's assumed he'll be dining with us. All the same, I'll ask him when he stops by here this morning. I've ordered some fine wine. Nora, you can't imagine how I'm looking forward to this evening.

NORA: So am I. And what fun for the children, Torvald!

HELMER: Ah, it's so gratifying to know that one's gotten a safe, secure job, and with a comfortable salary. It's a great satisfaction, isn't it?

NORA: Oh, it's wonderful!

HELMER: Remember last Christmas? Three whole weeks before, you shut yourself in every evening till long after midnight, making flowers for the Christmas tree, and all the other decorations to surprise us. Ugh, that was the dullest time I've ever lived through.

NORA: It wasn't at all dull for me.

HELMER (*smiling*): But the outcome *was* pretty sorry, Nora.

NORA: Oh, don't tease me with that again. How could I help it that the cat came in and tore everything to shreds.

HELMER: No, poor thing, you certainly couldn't. You wanted so much to please us all, and that's what counts. But it's just as well that the hard times are past.

NORA: Yes, it's really wonderful.

HELMER: Now I don't have to sit here alone, boring myself, and you don't have to tire your precious eyes and your fair little delicate hands —

NORA (*clapping her hands*): No, is it really true, Torvald, I don't have to? Oh, how wonderfully lovely to hear! (*Taking his arm.*) Now I'll tell you just how I've thought we should plan things. Right after Christmas — (*The doorbell rings.*) Oh, the bell. (*Straightening the room up a bit.*) Somebody would have to come. What a bore!

HELMER: I'm not at home to visitors, don't forget.

MAID (*from the hall doorway*): Ma'am, a lady to see you —

NORA: All right, let her come in.

MAID (*to Helmer*): And the doctor's just come too.

HELMER: Did he go right to my study?

MAID: Yes, he did.

(*Helmer goes into his room. The Maid shows in Mrs. Linde, dressed in traveling clothes, and shuts the door after her.*)

MRS. LINDE (*in a dispirited and somewhat hesitant voice*): Hello, Nora.

NORA (*uncertain*): Hello —

MRS. LINDE: You don't recognize me.

NORA: No, I don't know — but wait, I think — (*Exclaiming.*) What! Kristine! Is it really you?

MRS. LINDE: Yes, it's me.

NORA: Kristine! To think I didn't recognize you. But then, how could I? (*More quietly.*) How you've changed, Kristine!

MRS. LINDE: Yes, no doubt I have. In nine — ten long years.

NORA: Is it so long since we met! Yes, it's all of that. Oh, these last eight years have been a happy time, believe me. And so now you've come in to town, too. Made the long trip in the winter. That took courage.

MRS. LINDE: I just got here by ship this morning.

NORA: To enjoy yourself over Christmas, of course. Oh, how lovely! Yes, enjoy ourselves, we'll do that. But take your coat off. You're not still cold? (*Helping her.*) There now, let's get cozy here by the stove. No, the easy chair there! I'll take the rocker here. (*Seizing her hands.*) Yes, now you have your old look again; it was only in that first moment. You're a bit more pale, Kristine — and maybe a bit thinner.

MRS. LINDE: And much, much older, Nora.

NORA: Yes, perhaps a bit older; a tiny, tiny bit; not much at all. (*Stopping short; suddenly serious.*) Oh, but thoughtless me, to sit here, chattering away. Sweet, good Kristine, can you forgive me?

MRS. LINDE: What do you mean, Nora?

NORA (*softly*): Poor Kristine, you've become a widow.

MRS. LINDE: Yes, three years ago.

NORA: Oh, I knew it, of course; I read it in the papers. Oh, Kristine, you must believe me; I often thought of writing you then, but I kept postponing it, and something always interfered.

MRS. LINDE: Nora dear, I understand completely.

NORA: No, it was awful of me, Kristine. You poor thing, how much you must have gone through. And he left you nothing?

MRS. LINDE: No.

NORA: And no children?

MRS. LINDE: No.

NORA: Nothing at all, then?

MRS. LINDE: Not even a sense of loss to feed on.

NORA (*looking incredulously at her*): But Kristine, how could that be?

MRS. LINDE (*smiling wearily and smoothing her hair*): Oh, sometimes it happens, Nora.

NORA: So completely alone. How terribly hard that must be for you. I have three lovely children. You can't see them now; they're out with the maid. But now you must tell me everything—

MRS. LINDE: No, no, no, tell me about yourself.

NORA: No, you begin. Today I don't want to be selfish. I want to think only of you today. But there is something I must tell you. Did you hear of the wonderful luck we had recently?

MRS. LINDE: No, what's that?

NORA: My husband's been made manager in the bank, just think!

MRS. LINDE: Your husband? How marvelous!

NORA: Isn't it? Being a lawyer is such an uncertain living, you know, especially if one won't touch any cases that aren't clean and decent. And of course Torvald would never do that, and I'm with him completely there. Oh, we're simply delighted, believe me! He'll join the bank right after New Year's and start getting a huge salary and lots of commissions. From now on we can live quite differently—just as we want. Oh, Kristine, I feel so light and happy! Won't it be lovely to have stacks of money and not a care in the world?

MRS. LINDE: Well, anyway, it would be lovely to have enough for necessities.

NORA: No, not just for necessities, but stacks and stacks of money!

MRS. LINDE (*smiling*): Nora, Nora, aren't you sensible yet? Back in school you were such a free spender.

NORA (*with a quiet laugh*): Yes, that's what Torvald still says. (*Shaking her finger.*) But "Nora, Nora" isn't as silly as you all think. Really, we've been in no position for me to go squandering. We've had to work, both of us.

MRS. LINDE: You too?

NORA: Yes, at odd jobs—needlework, crocheting, embroidery, and such—(*casually*) and other things too. You remember that Torvald left the department when we were married? There was no chance of promotion in his office, and of course he needed to earn more money. But that first year he drove himself terribly. He took on all kinds of extra work that kept him going morning and night. It wore him down, and then he fell deathly ill. The doctors said it was essential for him to travel south.

MRS. LINDE: Yes, didn't you spend a whole year in Italy?

NORA: That's right. It wasn't easy to get away, you know. Ivar had just been born. But of course we had to go. Oh, that was a beautiful trip, and it saved Torvald's life. But it cost a frightful sum, Kristine.

MRS. LINDE: I can well imagine.

NORA: Four thousand, eight hundred crowns it cost. That's really a lot of money.

MRS. LINDE: But it's lucky you had it when you needed it.

NORA: Well, as it was, we got it from Papa.

MRS. LINDE: I see. It was just about the time your father died.

NORA: Yes, just about then. And, you know, I couldn't make that trip out to nurse him. I had to stay here, expecting Ivar any moment, and with my poor sick Torvald to care for. Dearest Papa, I never saw him again, Kristine. Oh, that was the worst time I've known in all my marriage.

MRS. LINDE: I know how you loved him. And then you went off to Italy?

NORA: Yes. We had the means now, and the doctors urged us. So we left a month after.

MRS. LINDE: And your husband came back completely cured?

NORA: Sound as a drum!

MRS. LINDE: But—the doctor?

NORA: Who?

MRS. LINDE: I thought the maid said he was a doctor, the man who came in with me.

NORA: Yes, that was Dr. Rank—but he's not making a sick call. He's our closest friend, and he stops by at least once a day. No, Torvald hasn't had a sick moment since, and the children are fit and strong, and I am, too. (*Jumping up and clapping her hands.*) Oh, dear God, Kristine, what a lovely thing to live and be happy! But how disgusting of me—I'm talking of nothing but my own affairs. (*Sits on a stool close by Kristine, arms resting across her knees.*) Oh, don't be angry with me! Tell me, is it really true that you weren't in love with your husband? Why did you marry him, then?

MRS. LINDE: My mother was still alive, but bedridden and helpless—and I had my two younger brothers to look after. In all conscience, I didn't think I could turn him down.

NORA: No, you were right there. But was he rich at the time?

MRS. LINDE: He was very well off, I'd say. But the business was shaky, Nora. When he died, it all fell apart, and nothing was left.

NORA: And then—?

MRS. LINDE: Yes, so I had to scrape up a living with a little shop and a little teaching and whatever else I could find. The last three years have been like one endless workday without a rest for me. Now, it's over, Nora. My poor mother doesn't need me, for she's passed on. Nor the boys, either; they're working now and can take care of themselves.

NORA: How free you must feel—

MRS. LINDE: No—only unspeakably empty. Nothing to live for now. (*Standing up anxiously.*) That's why I couldn't take it any longer out in that desolate hole. Maybe here it'll be easier to find something to do and keep my mind occupied. If I could only be lucky enough to get a steady job, some office work—

NORA: Oh, but Kristine, that's so dreadfully tiring, and you already look so tired. It would be much better for you if you could go off to a bathing resort.

MRS. LINDE (*going toward the window*): I have no father to give me travel money, Nora.

NORA (*rising*): Oh, don't be angry with me.

MRS. LINDE (*going to her*): Nora dear, don't you be angry with me. The worst of my kind of situation is all the bitterness that's stored away. No one to work for, and yet you're always having to snap up your opportunities. You have to live; and so you grow selfish. When you told me the happy change in your lot, do you know I was delighted less for your sakes than for mine?

NORA: How so? Oh, I see. You think maybe Torvald could do something for you.

MRS. LINDE: Yes, that's what I thought.

NORA: And he will, Kristine! Just leave it to me; I'll bring it up so delicately—find something attractive to humor him with. Oh, I'm so eager to help you.

MRS. LINDE: How very kind of you, Nora, to be so concerned over me—doubly kind, considering you really know so little of life's burdens yourself.

NORA: I—? I know so little—?

MRS. LINDE (*smiling*): Well, my heavens—a little needlework and such—Nora, you're just a child.

NORA (*tossing her head and pacing the floor*): You don't have to act so superior.

MRS. LINDE: Oh?

NORA: You're just like the others. You all think I'm incapable of anything serious—

MRS. LINDE: Come now—

NORA: That I've never had to face the raw world.

MRS. LINDE: Nora dear, you've just been telling me all your troubles.

NORA: Hm! Trivial! (*Quietly.*) I haven't told you the big thing.

MRS. LINDE: Big thing? What do you mean?

NORA: You look down on me so, Kristine, but you shouldn't. You're proud that you worked so long and hard for your mother.

MRS. LINDE: I don't look down on a soul. But it is true: I'm proud—and happy, too—to think it was given to me to make my mother's last days almost free of care.

NORA: And you're also proud thinking of what you've done for your brothers.

MRS. LINDE: I feel I've a right to be.

NORA: I agree. But listen to this, Kristine—I've also got something to be proud and happy for.

MRS. LINDE: I don't doubt it. But whatever do you mean?

NORA: Not so loud. What if Torvald heard! He mustn't, not for anything in the world. Nobody must know, Kristine. No one but you.

MRS. LINDE: But what is it, then?

NORA: Come here. (*Drawing her down beside her on the sofa.*) It's true—I've also got something to be proud and happy for. I'm the one who saved Torvald's life.

MRS. LINDE: Saved—? Saved how?

NORA: I told you about the trip to Italy. Torvald never would have lived if he hadn't gone south—

MRS. LINDE: Of course; your father gave you the means—

NORA (*smiling*): That's what Torvald and all the rest think, but—

MRS. LINDE: But—?

NORA: Papa didn't give us a pin. I was the one who raised the money.

MRS. LINDE: You? That whole amount?

NORA: Four thousand, eight hundred crowns. What do you say to that?

MRS. LINDE: But Nora, how was it possible? Did you win the lottery?

NORA (*disdainfully*): The lottery? Pooh! No art to that.

MRS. LINDE: But where did you get it from then?

NORA (*humming, with a mysterious smile*): Hmm, tra-la-la-la.

MRS. LINDE: Because you couldn't have borrowed it.

NORA: No? Why not?

MRS. LINDE: A wife can't borrow without her husband's consent.

NORA (*tossing her head*): Oh, but a wife with a little business sense, a wife who knows how to manage—

MRS. LINDE: Nora, I simply don't understand—

NORA: You don't have to. Whoever said I *borrowed* the money? I could have gotten it other ways. (*Throwing herself back on the sofa.*) I could have gotten it from some admirer or other. After all, a girl with my ravishing appeal—

MRS. LINDE: You lunatic.

NORA: I'll bet you're eaten up with curiosity, Kristine.

MRS. LINDE: Now listen here, Nora—you haven't done something indiscreet?

NORA (*sitting up again*): Is it indiscreet to save your husband's life?

MRS. LINDE: I think it's indiscreet that without his knowledge you—

NORA: But that's the point: He mustn't know! My Lord, can't you understand? He mustn't ever know the close call he had. It was to *me* the doctors came to say his life was in danger—that nothing could save him but a stay in the south. Didn't I try strategy then! I began talking about how lovely it would be for me to travel abroad like other young wives; I begged and I cried; I told him please to remember my condition, to be kind and indulge me; and then I dropped a hint that he could easily take out a loan. But at that, Kristine, he nearly exploded. He said I was frivolous, and it was his duty as man of the house not to indulge me in whims and fancies—as I think he called them. Aha, I thought, now you'll just have to be saved—and that's when I saw my chance.

MRS. LINDE: And your father never told Torvald the money wasn't from him?

NORA: No, never. Papa died right about then. I'd considered bringing him into my secret and begging him never to tell. But he was too sick at the time— and then, sadly, it didn't matter.

MRS. LINDE: And you've never confided in your husband since?

NORA: For heaven's sake, no! Are you serious? He's so strict on that subject. Besides—Torvald, with all his masculine pride—how painfully humiliating for him if he ever found out he was in debt to me. That would just ruin our relationship. Our beautiful, happy home would never be the same.

MRS. LINDE: Won't you ever tell him?

NORA (*thoughtfully, half smiling*): Yes—maybe sometime years from now, when I'm no longer so attractive. Don't laugh! I only mean when Torvald loves me less than now, when he stops enjoying my dancing and dressing up and reciting for him. Then it might be wise to have something in reserve — (*Breaking off.*) How ridiculous! That'll never happen — Well, Kristine, what do you think of my big secret? I'm capable of something too, hm? You can imagine, of course, how this thing hangs over me. It really hasn't been easy meeting the payments on time. In the business world there's what they call quarterly interest and what they call amortization, and these are always so terribly hard to manage. I've had to skimp a little here and there, wherever I could, you know. I could hardly spare anything from my house allowance, because Torvald has to live well. I couldn't let the children go poorly dressed; whatever I got for them, I felt I had to use up completely — the darlings!

MRS. LINDE: Poor Nora, so it had to come out of your own budget, then?

NORA: Yes, of course. But I was the one most responsible, too. Every time Torvald gave me money for new clothes and such, I never used more than half; always bought the simplest, cheapest outfits. It was a godsend that everything looks so well on me that Torvald never noticed. But it did weigh me down at times, Kristine. It *is* such a joy to wear fine things. You understand.

MRS. LINDE: Oh, of course.

NORA: And then I found other ways of making money. Last winter I was lucky enough to get a lot of copying to do. I locked myself in and sat writing every evening till late in the night. Ah, I was tired so often, dead tired. But still it was wonderful fun, sitting and working like that, earning money. It was almost like being a man.

MRS. LINDE: But how much have you paid off this way so far?

NORA: That's hard to say, exactly. These accounts, you know, aren't easy to figure. I only know that I've paid out all I could scrape together. Time and again I haven't known where to turn. (*Smiling.*) Then I'd sit here dreaming of a rich old gentleman who had fallen in love with me —

MRS. LINDE: What! Who is he?

NORA: Oh, really! And that he'd died, and when his will was opened, there in big letters it said, "All my fortune shall be paid over in cash, immediately, to that enchanting Mrs. Nora Helmer."

MRS. LINDE: But Nora dear — who *was* this gentleman?

NORA: Good grief, can't you understand? The old man never existed; that was only something I'd dream up time and again whenever I was at my wits' end for money. But it makes no difference now; the old fossil can go where he pleases for all I care; I don't need him or his will — because now I'm free. (*Jumping up.*) Oh, how lovely to think of that, Kristine! Carefree! To know you're carefree, utterly carefree; to be able to romp and play with the children, and to keep up a beautiful, charming home — everything just the way Torvald likes it! And think, spring is coming, with big blue skies. Maybe we can travel a little then. Maybe I'll see the ocean again. Oh yes, it *is* so marvelous to live and be happy!

(*The front doorbell rings.*)

MRS. LINDE (*rising*): There's the bell. It's probably best that I go.

NORA: No, stay. No one's expected. It must be for Torvald.

MAID (*from the hall doorway*): Excuse me, ma'am—there's a gentleman here to see Mr. Helmer, but I didn't know—since the doctor's with him—

NORA: Who is the gentleman?

KROGSTAD (*from the doorway*): It's me, Mrs. Helmer.

(*Mrs. Linde starts and turns away toward the window.*)

NORA (*stepping toward him, tense, her voice a whisper*): You? What is it? Why do you want to speak to my husband?

KROGSTAD: Bank business—after a fashion. I have a small job in the investment bank, and I hear now your husband is going to be our chief—

NORA: In other words, it's—

KROGSTAD: Just dry business, Mrs. Helmer. Nothing but that.

NORA: Yes, then please be good enough to step into the study. (*She nods indifferently as she sees him out by the hall door, then returns and begins stirring up the stove.*)

MRS. LINDE: Nora—who was that man?

NORA: That was a Mr. Krogstad—a lawyer.

MRS. LINDE: Then it really was him.

NORA: Do you know that person?

MRS. LINDE: I did once—many years ago. For a time he was a law clerk in our town.

NORA: Yes, he's been that.

MRS. LINDE: How he's changed.

NORA: I understand he had a very unhappy marriage.

MRS. LINDE: He's a widower now.

NORA: With a number of children. There now, it's burning. (*She closes the stove door and moves the rocker a bit to one side.*)

MRS. LINDE: They say he has a hand in all kinds of business.

NORA: Oh? That may be true; I wouldn't know. But let's not think about business. It's so dull.

(*Dr. Rank enters from Helmer's study.*)

RANK (*still in the doorway*): No, no, really—I don't want to intrude, I'd just as soon talk a little while with your wife. (*Shuts the door, then notices Mrs. Linde.*) Oh, beg pardon. I'm intruding here too.

NORA: No, not at all. (*Introducing him.*) Dr. Rank, Mrs. Linde.

RANK: Well now, that's a name much heard in this house. I believe I passed the lady on the stairs as I came.

MRS. LINDE: Yes, I take the stairs very slowly. They're rather hard on me.

RANK: Uh-hm, some touch of internal weakness?

MRS. LINDE: More overexertion, I'd say.

RANK: Nothing else? Then you're probably here in town to rest up in a round of parties?

MRS. LINDE: I'm here to look for work.

RANK: Is that the best cure for overexertion?

MRS. LINDE: One has to live, Doctor.

RANK: Yes, there's a common prejudice to that effect.

NORA: Oh, come on, Dr. Rank — you really do want to live yourself.

RANK: Yes, I really do. Wretched as I am, I'll gladly prolong my torment indefinitely. All my patients feel like that. And it's quite the same, too, with the
morally sick. Right at this moment there's one of those moral invalids in
there with Helmer —

MRS. LINDE (*softly*): Ah!

NORA: Who do you mean?

RANK: Oh, it's a lawyer, Krogstad, a type you wouldn't know. His character is
rotten to the root — but even he began chattering all-importantly about how
he had to *live.*

NORA: Oh? What did he want to talk to Torvald about?

RANK: I really don't know. I only heard something about the bank.

NORA: I didn't know that Krog — that this man Krogstad had anything to do
with the bank.

RANK: Yes, he's gotten some kind of berth down there. (*To Mrs. Linde.*) I don't
know if you also have, in your neck of the woods, a type of person who
scuttles about breathlessly, sniffing out hints of moral corruption, and then
maneuvers his victim into some sort of key position where he can keep an
eye on him. It's the healthy these days that are out in the cold.

MRS. LINDE: All the same, it's the sick who most need to be taken in.

RANK (*with a shrug*): Yes, there we have it. That's the concept that's turning society into a sanatorium.

(*Nora, lost in her thoughts, breaks out into quiet laughter and claps her hands.*)

RANK: Why do you laugh at that? Do you have any real idea of what society is?

NORA: What do I care about dreary old society? I was laughing at something
quite different — something terribly funny. Tell me, Doctor — is everyone
who works in the bank dependent now on Torvald?

RANK: Is that what you find so terribly funny?

NORA (*smiling and humming*): Never mind, never mind! (*Pacing the floor.*) Yes,
that's really immensely amusing: that we — that Torvald has so much power
now over all those people. (*Taking the bag out of her pocket.*) Dr. Rank, a little
macaroon on that?

RANK: See here, macaroons! I thought they were contraband here.

NORA: Yes, but these are some that Kristine gave me.

MRS. LINDE: What? I — ?

NORA: Now, now, don't be afraid. You couldn't possibly know that Torvald had
forbidden them. You see, he's worried they'll ruin my teeth. But hmp! Just
this once! Isn't that so, Dr. Rank? Help yourself! (*Puts a macaroon in his
mouth.*) And you too, Kristine. And I'll also have one, only a little one — or

two, at the most. (*Walking about again.*) Now I'm really tremendously happy. Now's there's just one last thing in the world that I have an enormous desire to do.

RANK: Well! And what's that?

NORA: It's something I have such a consuming desire to say so Torvald could hear.

RANK: And why can't you say it?

NORA: I don't dare. It's quite shocking.

MRS. LINDE: Shocking?

RANK: Well, then it isn't advisable. But in front of us you certainly can. What do you have such a desire to say so Torvald could hear?

NORA: I have such a huge desire to say — to hell and be damned!

RANK: Are you crazy?

MRS. LINDE: My goodness, Nora!

RANK: Go on, say it. Here he is.

NORA (*hiding the macaroon bag*): Shh, shh, shh!

(*Helmer comes in from his study, hat in hand, overcoat over his arm.*)

NORA (*going toward him*): Well, Torvald dear, are you through with him?

HELMER: Yes, he just left.

NORA: Let me introduce you — this is Kristine, who's arrived here in town.

HELMER: Kristine — ? I'm sorry, but I don't know —

NORA: Mrs. Linde, Torvald dear. Mrs. Kristine Linde.

HELMER: Of course. A childhood friend of my wife's, no doubt?

MRS. LINDE: Yes, we knew each other in those days.

NORA: And just think, she made the long trip down here in order to talk with you.

HELMER: What's this?

MRS. LINDE: Well, not exactly —

NORA: You see, Kristine is remarkably clever in office work, and so she's terribly eager to come under a capable man's supervision and add more to what she already knows —

HELMER: Very wise, Mrs. Linde.

NORA: And then when she heard that you'd become a bank manager — the story was wired out to the papers — then she came in as fast as she could and — Really, Torvald, for my sake you can do a little something for Kristine, can't you?

HELMER: Yes, it's not at all impossible. Mrs. Linde, I suppose you're a widow?

MRS. LINDE: Yes.

HELMER: Any experience in office work?

MRS. LINDE: Yes, a good deal.

HELMER: Well, it's quite likely that I can make an opening for you —

NORA (*clapping her hands*): You see, you see!

HELMER: You've come at a lucky moment, Mrs. Linde.

MRS. LINDE: Oh, how can I thank you?

HELMER: Not necessary. (*Putting his overcoat on.*) But today you'll have to excuse me —

RANK: Wait, I'll go with you. (*He fetches his coat from the hall and warms it at the stove.*)

NORA: Don't stay out long, dear.

HELMER: An hour; no more.

NORA: Are you going too, Kristine?

MRS. LINDE (*putting on her winter garments*): Yes, I have to see about a room now.

HELMER: Then perhaps we can all walk together.

NORA (*helping her*): What a shame we're so cramped here, but it's quite impossible for us to —

MRS. LINDE: Oh, don't even think of it! Good-bye, Nora dear, and thanks for everything.

NORA: Good-bye for now. Of course you'll be back this evening. And you too, Dr. Rank. What? If you're well enough? Oh, you've got to be! Wrap up tight now.

(*In a ripple of small talk the company moves out into the hall; children's voices are heard outside on the steps.*)

NORA: There they are! There they are! (*She runs to open the door. The children come in with their nurse, Anne-Marie.*) Come in, come in! (*Bends down and kisses them.*) Oh, you darlings — ! Look at them, Kristine. Aren't they lovely!

RANK: No loitering in the draft here.

HELMER: Come, Mrs. Linde — this place is unbearable now for anyone but mothers.

(*Dr. Rank, Helmer, and Mrs. Linde go down the stairs. Anne-Marie goes into the living room with the children. Nora follows, after closing the hall door.*)

NORA: How fresh and strong you look. Oh, such red cheeks you have! Like apples and roses. (*The children interrupt her throughout the following.*) And it was so much fun? That's wonderful. Really? You pulled both Emmy and Bob on the sled? Imagine, all together! Yes, you're a clever boy, Ivar. Oh, let me hold her a bit, Anne-Marie. My sweet little doll baby! (*Takes the smallest from the nurse and dances with her.*) Yes, yes, Mama will dance with Bob as well. What? Did you throw snowballs? Oh, if I'd only been there! No, don't bother, Anne-Marie — I'll undress them myself. Oh yes, let me. It's such fun. Go in and rest; you look half frozen. There's hot coffee waiting for you on the stove. (*The nurse goes into the room to the left. Nora takes the children's winter things off, throwing them about, while the children talk to her all at once.*) Is that so? A big dog chased you? But it didn't bite? No, dogs never bite little, lovely doll babies. Don't peek in the packages, Ivar! What is it? Yes, wouldn't you like to know. No, no, it's an ugly something. Well? Shall we play? What shall we play? Hide-and-seek? Yes, let's play hide-and-seek.

Bob must hide first. I must? Yes, let me hide first. (*Laughing and shouting,
she and the children play in and out of the living room and the adjoining room to
the right. At last Nora hides under the table. The children come storming in,
search, but cannot find her, then hear her muffled laughter, dash over to the
table, lift the cloth up and find her. Wild shouting. She creeps forward as if to
scare them. More shouts. Meanwhile, a knock at the hall door; no one has noticed it. Now the door half opens, and Krogstad appears. He waits a moment; the
game goes on.*)

KROGSTAD: Beg pardon, Mrs. Helmer—

NORA (*with a strangled cry, turning and scrambling to her knees*): Oh! What do
you want?

KROGSTAD: Excuse me. The outer door was ajar; it must be someone forgot to
shut it—

NORA (*rising*): My husband isn't home, Mr. Krogstad.

KROGSTAD: I know that.

NORA: Yes—then what do you want here?

KROGSTAD: A word with you.

NORA: With—? (*To the children, quietly.*) Go in to Anne-Marie. What? No, the
strange man won't hurt Mama. When he's gone, we'll play some more. (*She
leads the children into the room to the left and shuts the door after them. Then,
tense and nervous:*) You want to speak to me?

KROGSTAD: Yes, I want to.

NORA: Today? But it's not yet the first of the month—

KROGSTAD: No, it's Christmas Eve. It's going to be up to you how merry a Christmas you have.

NORA: What is it you want? Today I absolutely can't—

KROGSTAD: We won't talk about that till later. This is something else. You do
have a moment to spare, I suppose?

NORA: Oh yes, of course—I do, except—

KROGSTAD: Good. I was sitting over at Olsen's Restaurant when I saw your husband go down the street—

NORA: Yes?

KROGSTAD: With a lady.

NORA: Yes. So?

KROGSTAD: If you'll pardon my asking: Wasn't that lady a Mrs. Linde?

NORA: Yes.

KROGSTAD: Just now come into town?

NORA: Yes, today.

KROGSTAD: She's a good friend of yours?

NORA: Yes, she is. But I don't see—

KROGSTAD: I also knew her once.

NORA: I'm aware of that.

KROGSTAD: Oh? You know all about it. I thought so. Well, then let me ask you
short and sweet: Is Mrs. Linde getting a job in the bank?

NORA: What makes you think you can cross-examine me, Mr. Krogstad—you, one of my husband's employees? But since you ask, you might as well know—yes, Mrs. Linde's going to be taken on at the bank. And I'm the one who spoke for her, Mr. Krogstad. Now you know.

KROGSTAD: So I guessed right.

NORA (*pacing up and down*): Oh, one does have a tiny bit of influence, I should hope. Just because I am a woman, don't think it means that—When one has a subordinate position, Mr. Krogstad, one really ought to be careful about pushing somebody who—hm—

KROGSTAD: Who has influence?

NORA: That's right.

KROGSTAD (*in a different tone*): Mrs. Helmer, would you be good enough to use your influence on my behalf?

NORA: What? What do you mean?

KROGSTAD: Would you please make sure that I keep my subordinate position in the bank?

NORA: What does that mean? Who's thinking of taking away your position?

KROGSTAD: Oh, don't play the innocent with me. I'm quite aware that your friend would hardly relish the chance of running into me again; and I'm also aware now whom I can thank for being turned out.

NORA: But I promise you—

KROGSTAD: Yes, yes, yes, to the point: There's still time, and I'm advising you to use your influence to prevent it.

NORA: But Mr. Krogstad, I have absolutely no influence.

KROGSTAD: You haven't? I thought you were just saying—

NORA: You shouldn't take me so literally. I! How can you believe that I have any such influence over my husband?

KROGSTAD: Oh, I've known your husband from our student days. I don't think the great bank manager's more steadfast than any other married man.

NORA: You speak insolently about my husband, and I'll show you the door.

KROGSTAD: The lady has spirit.

NORA: I'm not afraid of you any longer. After New Year's, I'll soon be done with the whole business.

KROGSTAD (*restraining himself*): Now listen to me, Mrs. Helmer. If necessary, I'll fight for my little job in the bank as if it were life itself.

NORA: Yes, so it seems.

KROGSTAD: It's not just a matter of income; that's the least of it. It's something else—All right, out with it! Look, this is the thing. You know, just like all the others, of course, that once, a good many years ago, I did something rather rash.

NORA: I've heard rumors to that effect.

KROGSTAD: The case never got into court; but all the same, every door was closed in my face from then on. So I took up those various activities you know about. I had to grab hold somewhere; and I dare say I haven't been among the worst. But now I want to drop all that. My boys are growing up. For their sakes, I'll have to win back as much respect as possible here in town. That job in the bank was like the first rung in my ladder. And now your husband wants to kick me right back down in the mud again.

NORA: But for heaven's sake, Mr. Krogstad, it's simply not in my power to help you.

KROGSTAD: That's because you haven't the will to — but I have the means to make you.

NORA: You certainly won't tell my husband that I owe you money?

KROGSTAD: Hm — what if I told him that?

NORA: That would be shameful of you. (*Nearly in tears.*) This secret — my joy and my pride — that he should learn it in such a crude and disgusting way — learn it from you. You'd expose me to the most horrible unpleasantness —

KROGSTAD: Only unpleasantness?

NORA (*vehemently*): But go on and try. It'll turn out the worse for you, because then my husband will really see what a crook you are, and then you'll never be able to hold your job.

KROGSTAD: I asked if it was just domestic unpleasantness you were afraid of?

NORA: If my husband finds out, then of course he'll pay what I owe at once, and then we'd be through with you for good.

KROGSTAD (*a step closer*): Listen, Mrs. Helmer — you've either got a very bad memory, or else no head at all for business. I'd better put you a little more in touch with the facts.

NORA: What do you mean?

KROGSTAD: When your husband was sick, you came to me for a loan of four thousand, eight hundred crowns.

NORA: Where else could I go?

KROGSTAD: I promised to get you that sum —

NORA: And you got it.

KROGSTAD: I promised to get you that sum, on certain conditions. You were so involved in your husband's illness, and so eager to finance your trip, that I guess you didn't think out all the details. It might just be a good idea to remind you. I promised you the money on the strength of a note I drew up.

NORA: Yes, and that I signed.

KROGSTAD: Right. But at the bottom I added some lines for your father to guarantee the loan. He was supposed to sign down there.

NORA: Supposed to? He did sign.

KROGSTAD: I left the date blank. In other words, your father would have dated his signature himself. Do you remember that?

NORA: Yes, I think —

KROGSTAD: Then I gave you the note for you to mail to your father. Isn't that so?

NORA: Yes.

KROGSTAD: And naturally you sent it at once — because only some five, six days later you brought me the note, properly signed. And with that, the money was yours.

NORA: Well, then; I've made my payments regularly, haven't I?

KROGSTAD: More or less. But — getting back to the point — those were hard times for you then, Mrs. Helmer.

NORA: Yes, they were.

KROGSTAD: Your father was very ill, I believe.

NORA: He was near the end.

KROGSTAD: He died soon after?

NORA: Yes.

KROGSTAD: Tell me, Mrs. Helmer, do you happen to recall the date of your father's death? The day of the month, I mean.

NORA: Papa died the twenty-ninth of September.

KROGSTAD: That's quite correct; I've already looked into that. And now we come to a curious thing — (*taking out a paper*) which I simply cannot comprehend.

NORA: Curious thing? I don't know —

KROGSTAD: This is the curious thing: that your father co-signed the note for your loan three days after his death.

NORA: How — ? I don't understand.

KROGSTAD: Your father died the twenty-ninth of September. But look. Here your father dated his signature October second. Isn't that curious, Mrs. Helmer? (*Nora is silent.*) Can you explain it to me? (*Nora remains silent.*) It's also remarkable that the words "October second" and the year aren't written in your father's hand, but rather in one that I think I know. Well, it's easy to understand. Your father forgot perhaps to date his signature, and then someone or other added it, a bit sloppily, before anyone knew of his death. There's nothing wrong in that. It all comes down to the signature. And there's no question about *that*, Mrs. Helmer. It really *was* your father who signed his own name here, wasn't it?

NORA (*after a short silence, throwing her head back and looking squarely at him*): No, it wasn't. *I* signed Papa's name.

KROGSTAD: Wait, now — are you fully aware that this is a dangerous confession?

NORA: Why? You'll soon get your money.

KROGSTAD: Let me ask you a question — why didn't you send the paper to your father?

NORA: That was impossible. Papa was so sick. If I'd asked him for his signature, I also would have had to tell him what the money was for. But I couldn't tell him, sick as he was, that my husband's life was in danger. That was just impossible.

KROGSTAD: Then it would have been better if you'd given up the trip abroad.

NORA: I couldn't possibly. The trip was to save my husband's life. I couldn't give that up.

KROGSTAD: But didn't you ever consider that this was a fraud against me?

NORA: I couldn't let myself be bothered by that. You weren't any concern of mine. I couldn't stand you, with all those cold complications you made, even though you knew how badly off my husband was.

KROGSTAD: Mrs. Helmer, obviously you haven't the vaguest idea of what you've involved yourself in. But I can tell you this: It was nothing more and nothing worse that I once did — and it wrecked my whole reputation.

NORA: You? Do you expect me to believe that you ever acted bravely to save your wife's life?

KROGSTAD: Laws don't inquire into motives.

NORA: Then they must be very poor laws.

KROGSTAD: Poor or not — if I introduce this paper in court, you'll be judged according to law.

NORA: This I refuse to believe. A daughter hasn't a right to protect her dying father from anxiety and care? A wife hasn't a right to save her husband's life? I don't know much about laws, but I'm sure that somewhere in the books these things are allowed. And you don't know anything about it — you who practice the law? You must be an awful lawyer, Mr. Krogstad.

KROGSTAD: Could be. But business — the kind of business we two are mixed up in — don't you think I know about that? All right. Do what you want now. But I'm telling you *this*: If I get shoved down a second time, you're going to keep me company. (*He bows and goes out through the hall.*)

NORA (*pensive for a moment, then tossing her head*): Oh, really! Trying to frighten me! I'm not so silly as all that. (*Begins gathering up the children's clothes, but soon stops.*) But — ? No, but that's impossible! I did it out of love.

THE CHILDREN (*in the doorway, left*): Mama, that strange man's gone out the door.

NORA: Yes, yes, I know it. But don't tell anyone about the strange man. Do you hear? Not even Papa!

THE CHILDREN: No, Mama. But now will you play again?

NORA: No, not now.

THE CHILDREN: Oh, but Mama, you promised.

NORA: Yes, but I can't now. Go inside; I have too much to do. Go in, go in, my sweet darlings. (*She herds them gently back in the room and shuts the door after them. Settling on the sofa, she takes up a piece of embroidery and makes some stitches, but soon stops abruptly.*) No! (*Throws the work aside, rises, goes to the hall door and calls out.*) Helene! Let me have the tree in here. (*Goes to the table, left, opens the table drawer, and stops again.*) No, but that's utterly impossible!

MAID (*with the Christmas tree*): Where should I put it, ma'am?

NORA: There. The middle of the floor.

MAID: Should I bring anything else?

NORA: No, thanks. I have what I need.

(*The Maid, who has set the tree down, goes out.*)

NORA (*absorbed in trimming the tree*): Candles here — and flowers here. That terrible creature! Talk, talk, talk! There's nothing to it at all. The tree's going to be lovely. I'll do anything to please you Torvald. I'll sing for you, dance for you —

(*Helmer comes in from the hall, with a sheaf of papers under his arm.*)

NORA: Oh! You're back so soon?

HELMER: Yes. Has anyone been here?

NORA: Here? No.

HELMER: That's odd. I saw Krogstad leaving the front door.

NORA: So? Oh yes, that's true. Krogstad was here a moment.

HELMER: Nora, I can see by your face that he's been here, begging you to put in a good word for him.

NORA: Yes.

HELMER: And it was supposed to seem like your own idea? You were to hide it from me that he'd been here. He asked you that, too, didn't he?

NORA: Yes, Torvald, but —

HELMER: Nora, Nora, and you could fall for that? Talk with that sort of person and promise him anything? And then in the bargain, tell me an untruth.

NORA: An untruth — ?

HELMER: Didn't you say that no one had been here? (*Wagging his finger.*) My little songbird must never do that again. A songbird needs a clean beak to warble with. No false notes. (*Putting his arm about her waist.*) That's the way it should be, isn't it? Yes, I'm sure of it. (*Releasing her.*) And so, enough of that. (*Sitting by the stove.*) Ah, how snug and cozy it is here. (*Leafing among his papers.*)

NORA (*busy with the tree, after a short pause*): Torvald!

HELMER: Yes.

NORA: I'm so much looking forward to the Stenborgs' costume party, day after tomorrow.

HELMER: And I can't wait to see what you'll surprise me with.

NORA: Oh, that stupid business!

HELMER: What?

NORA: I can't find anything that's right. Everything seems so ridiculous, so inane.

HELMER: So my little Nora's come to *that* recognition?

NORA (*going behind his chair, her arms resting on its back*): Are you very busy, Torvald?

HELMER: Oh —

NORA: What papers are those?

HELMER: Bank matters.

NORA: Already?

HELMER: I've gotten full authority from the retiring management to make all necessary changes in personnel and procedure. I'll need Christmas week for that. I want to have everything in order by New Year's.

NORA: So that was the reason this poor Krogstad —

HELMER: Hm.

NORA (*still leaning on the chair and slowly stroking the nape of his neck*): If you weren't so very busy, I would have asked you an enormous favor, Torvald.

HELMER: Let's hear. What is it?

NORA: You know, there isn't anyone who has your good taste — and I want so much to look well at the costume party. Torvald, couldn't you take over and decide what I should be and plan my costume?

HELMER: Ah, is my stubborn little creature calling for a lifeguard?

NORA: Yes, Torvald, I can't get anywhere without your help.

HELMER: All right — I'll think it over. We'll hit on something.

NORA: Oh, how sweet of you. (*Goes to the tree again. Pause.*) Aren't the red flowers pretty — ? But tell me, was it really such a crime that this Krogstad committed?

HELMER: Forgery. Do you have any idea what that means?

NORA: Couldn't he have done it out of need?

HELMER: Yes, or thoughtlessness, like so many others. I'm not so heartless that I'd condemn a man categorically for just one mistake.

NORA: No, of course not, Torvald!

HELMER: Plenty of men have redeemed themselves by openly confessing their crimes and taking their punishment.

NORA: Punishment — ?

HELMER: But now Krogstad didn't go that way. He got himself out by sharp practices, and that's the real cause of his moral breakdown.

NORA: Do you really think that would — ?

HELMER: Just imagine how a man with that sort of guilt in him has to lie and cheat and deceive on all sides, has to wear a mask even with the nearest and dearest he has, even with his own wife and children. And with the children, Nora — that's where it's most horrible.

NORA: Why?

HELMER: Because that kind of atmosphere of lies infects the whole life of a home. Every breath the children take in is filled with the germs of something degenerate.

NORA (*coming closer behind him*): Are you sure of that?

HELMER: Oh, I've seen it often enough as a lawyer. Almost everyone who goes bad early in life has a mother who's a chronic liar.

NORA: Why just — the mother?

HELMER: It's usually the mother's influence that's dominant, but the father's works in the same way, of course. Every lawyer is quite familiar with it. And still this Krogstad's been going home year in, year out, poisoning his own children with lies and pretense; that's why I call him morally lost. (*Reaching his hands out toward her.*) So my sweet little Nora must promise me never to plead his cause. Your hand on it. Come, come, what's this? Give me your hand. There, now. All settled. I can tell you it'd be impossible for me to work alongside of him. I literally feel physically revolted when I'm anywhere near such a person.

NORA (*withdraws her hand and goes to the other side of the Christmas tree*): How hot it is here! And I've got so much to do.

HELMER (*getting up and gathering his papers*): Yes, and I have to think about getting some of these read through before dinner. I'll think about your costume, too. And something to hang on the tree in gilt paper, I may even see about that. (*Putting his hand on her head.*) Oh you, my darling little songbird. (*He goes into his study and closes the door after him.*)

NORA (*softly, after a silence*): Oh, really! It isn't so. It's impossible. It must be impossible.

ANNE-MARIE (*in the doorway left*): The children are begging so hard to come in to Mama.

NORA: No, no, no, don't let them in to me! You stay with them, Anne-Marie.

ANNE-MARIE: Of course, ma'am. (*Closes the door.*)

NORA (*pale with terror*): Hurt my children —! Poison my home? (*A moment's pause; then she tosses her head.*) That's not true. Never. Never in all the world.

ACT 2

(*Same room. Beside the piano the Christmas tree now stands stripped of ornament, burned-down candle stubs on its ragged branches. Nora's street clothes lie on the sofa. Nora, alone in the room, moves restlessly about; at last she stops at the sofa and picks up her coat.*)

NORA (*dropping the coat again*): Someone's coming! (*Goes toward the door, listens.*) No — there's no one. Of course — nobody's coming today, Christmas Day — or tomorrow, either. But maybe — (*Opens the door and looks out.*) No, nothing in the mailbox. Quite empty. (*Coming forward.*) What nonsense! He won't do anything serious. Nothing terrible could happen. It's impossible. Why, I have three small children.

(*Anne-Marie, with a large carton, comes in from the room to the left.*)

ANNE-MARIE: Well, at last I found the box with the masquerade clothes.

NORA: Thanks. Put it on the table.

ANNE-MARIE (*does so*): But they're all pretty much of a mess.

NORA: Ahh! I'd love to rip them in a million pieces!

ANNE-MARIE: Oh, mercy, they can be fixed right up. Just a little patience.

NORA: Yes, I'll go get Mrs. Linde to help me.

ANNE-MARIE: Out again now? In this nasty weather? Miss Nora will catch cold — get sick.

NORA: Oh, worse things could happen — How are the children?

ANNE-MARIE: The poor mites are playing with their Christmas presents, but —

NORA: Do they ask for me much?

ANNE-MARIE: They're so used to having Mama around, you know.

NORA: Yes, but Anne-Marie, I *can't* be together with them as much as I was.

ANNE-MARIE: Well, small children get used to anything.

NORA: You think so? Do you think they'd forget their mother if she was gone for good?

ANNE-MARIE: Oh, mercy — gone for good!

NORA: Wait, tell me. Anne-Marie — I've wondered so often — how could you ever have the heart to give your child over to strangers?

ANNE-MARIE: But I had to, you know, to become little Nora's nurse.

NORA: Yes, but how could you *do* it?

ANNE-MARIE: When I could get such a good place? A girl who's poor and who's gotten in trouble is glad enough for that. Because that slippery fish, he didn't do a thing for me, you know.

NORA: But your daughter's surely forgotten you.

ANNE-MARIE: Oh, she certainly has not. She's written to me, both when she was confirmed and when she was married.

NORA (*clasping her about the neck*): You old Anne-Marie, you were a good mother for me when I was little.

ANNE-MARIE: Poor little Nora, with no other mother but me.

NORA: And if the babies didn't have one, then I know that you'd — What silly talk! (*Opening the carton.*) Go in to them. Now I'll have to — Tomorrow you can see how lovely I'll look.

ANNE-MARIE: Oh, there won't be anyone at the party as lovely as Miss Nora. (*She goes off into the room, left.*)

NORA (*begins unpacking the box, but soon throws it aside*): Oh, if I dared to go out. If only nobody would come. If only nothing would happen here while I'm out. What craziness — nobody's coming. Just don't think. This muff — needs a brushing. Beautiful gloves, beautiful gloves. Let it go. Let it go! One, two, three, four, five, six — (*With a cry.*) Oh, there they are! (*Poises to move toward the door, but remains irresolutely standing. Mrs. Linde enters from the hall, where she has removed her street clothes.*)

NORA: Oh, it's you, Kristine. There's no one else out there? How good that you've come.

MRS. LINDE: I hear you were up asking for me.

NORA: Yes, I just stopped by. There's something you really can help me with. Let's get settled on the sofa. Look, there's going to be a costume party tomorrow evening at the Stenborgs' right above us, and now Torvald wants me to go as a Neapolitan peasant girl and dance the tarantella° that I learned in Capri.

MRS. LINDE: Really, are you giving a whole performance?

NORA: Torvald says yes, I should. See, here's the dress. Torvald had it made for me down there; but now it's all so tattered that I just don't know —

MRS. LINDE: Oh, we'll fix that up in no time. It's nothing more than the trimmings — they're a bit loose here and there. Needle and thread? Good, now we have what we need.

NORA: Oh, how sweet of you!

MRS. LINDE (*sewing*): So you'll be in disguise tomorrow, Nora. You know what? I'll stop by then for a moment and have a look at you all dressed up. But listen, I've absolutely forgotten to thank you for that pleasant evening yesterday.

NORA (*getting up and walking about*): I don't think it was as pleasant as usual yesterday. You should have come to town a bit sooner, Kristine — Yes, Torvald really knows how to give a home elegance and charm.

---

tarantella: A rapid whirling dance long popular in southern Italy.

MRS. LINDE: And you do, too, if you ask me. You're not your father's daughter for nothing. But tell me, is Dr. Rank always so down in the mouth as yesterday?

NORA: No, that was quite an exception. But he goes around critically ill all the time — tuberculosis of the spine, poor man. You know, his father was a disgusting thing who kept mistresses and so on — and that's why the son's been sickly from birth.

MRS. LINDE (*lets her sewing fall to her lap*): But my dearest Nora, how do you know about such things?

NORA (*walking more jauntily*): Hmp! When you've had three children, then you've had a few visits from — from women who know something of medicine, and they tell you this and that.

MRS. LINDE (*resumes sewing; a short pause*): Does Dr. Rank come here every day?

NORA: Every blessed day. He's Torvald's best friend from childhood, and *my* good friend, too. Dr. Rank almost belongs to this house.

MRS. LINDE: But tell me — is he quite sincere? I mean, doesn't he rather enjoy flattering people?

NORA: Just the opposite. Why do you think that?

MRS. LINDE: When you introduced us yesterday, he was proclaiming that he'd often heard my name in this house; but later I noticed that your husband hadn't the slightest idea who I really was. So how could Dr. Rank — ?

NORA: But it's all true, Kristine. You see, Torvald loves me beyond words, and, as he puts it, he'd like to keep me all to himself. For a long time he'd almost be jealous if I even mentioned any of my old friends back home. So of course I dropped that. But with Dr. Rank I talk a lot about such things because he likes hearing about them.

MRS. LINDE: Now listen, Nora; in many ways you're still like a child. I'm a good deal older than you, with a little more experience. I'll tell you something: You ought to put an end to all this with Dr. Rank.

NORA: What should I put an end to?

MRS. LINDE: Both parts of it, I think. Yesterday you said something about a rich admirer who'd provide you with money —

NORA: Yes, one who doesn't exist — worse luck. So?

MRS. LINDE: Is Dr. Rank well off?

NORA: Yes, he is.

MRS. LINDE: With no dependents?

NORA: No, no one. But —

MRS. LINDE: And he's over here every day?

NORA: Yes, I told you that.

MRS. LINDE: How can a man of such refinement be so grasping?

NORA: I don't follow you at all.

MRS. LINDE: Now don't try to hide it, Nora. You think I can't guess who loaned you the forty-eight hundred crowns?

NORA: Are you out of your mind? How could you think such a thing! A friend of ours, who comes here every single day. What an intolerable situation that would have been!

MRS. LINDE: Then it really wasn't him.

NORA: No, absolutely not. It never even crossed my mind for a moment — And he had nothing to lend in those days; his inheritance came later.

MRS. LINDE: Well, I think that was a stroke of luck for you, Nora dear.

NORA: No, it never would have occurred to me to ask Dr. Rank — Still, I'm quite sure that if I had asked him —

MRS. LINDE: Which you won't, of course.

NORA: No, of course not. I can't see that I'd ever need to. But I'm quite positive that if I talked to Dr. Rank —

MRS. LINDE: Behind your husband's back?

NORA: I've got to clear up this other thing; *that's* also behind his back. I've *got* to clear it all up.

MRS. LINDE: Yes, I was saying that yesterday, but —

NORA (*pacing up and down*): A man handles these problems so much better than a woman —

MRS. LINDE: One's husband does, yes.

NORA: Nonsense. (*Stopping.*) When you pay everything you owe, then you get your note back, right?

MRS. LINDE: Yes, naturally.

NORA: And can rip it into a million pieces and burn it up — that filthy scrap of paper!

MRS. LINDE (*looking hard at her, laying her sewing aside, and rising slowly*): Nora, you're hiding something from me.

NORA: You can see it in my face?

MRS. LINDE: Something's happened to you since yesterday morning. Nora, what is it?

NORA (*hurrying toward her*): Kristine! (*Listening.*) Shh! Torvald's home. Look, go in with the children a while. Torvald can't bear all this snipping and stitching. Let Anne-Marie help you.

MRS. LINDE (*gathering up some of the things*): All right, but I'm not leaving here until we've talked this out. (*She disappears into the room, left, as Torvald enters from the hall.*)

NORA: Oh, how I've been waiting for you, Torvald dear.

HELMER: Was that the dressmaker?

NORA: No, that was Kristine. She's helping me fix up my costume. You know, it's going to be quite attractive.

HELMER: Yes, wasn't that a bright idea I had?

NORA: Brilliant! But then wasn't I good as well to give in to you?

HELMER: Good — because you give in to your husband's judgment? All right, you little goose, I know you didn't mean it like that. But I won't disturb you. You'll want to have a fitting, I suppose.

NORA: And you'll be working?

HELMER: Yes. (*Indicating a bundle of papers.*) See. I've been down to the bank. (*Starts toward his study.*)

NORA: Torvald.

HELMER (*stops*): Yes.

NORA: If your little squirrel begged you, with all her heart and soul, for something — ?

HELMER: What's that?

NORA: Then would you do it?

HELMER: First, naturally, I'd have to know what it was.

NORA: Your squirrel would scamper about and do tricks, if you'd only be sweet and give in.

HELMER: Out with it.

NORA: Your lark would be singing high and low in every room —

HELMER: Come on, she does that anyway.

NORA: I'd be a wood nymph and dance for you in the moonlight.

HELMER: Nora — don't tell me it's that same business from this morning?

NORA (*coming closer*): Yes, Torvald, I beg you, please!

HELMER: And you actually have the nerve to drag that up again?

NORA: Yes, yes, you've got to give in to me; you *have* to let Krogstad keep his job in the bank.

HELMER: My dear Nora, I've slated his job for Mrs. Linde.

NORA: That's awfully kind of you. But you could just fire another clerk instead of Krogstad.

HELMER: This is the most incredible stubbornness! Because you go and give an impulsive promise to speak up for him, I'm expected to —

NORA: That's not the reason, Torvald. It's for your own sake. That man does writing for the worst papers; you said it yourself. He could do you any amount of harm. I'm scared to death of him —

HELMER: Ah, I understand. It's the old memories haunting you.

NORA: What do you mean by that?

HELMER: Of course, you're thinking about your father.

NORA: Yes, all right. Just remember how those nasty gossips wrote in the papers about Papa and slandered him so cruelly. I think they'd have had him dismissed if the department hadn't sent you up to investigate, and if you hadn't been so kind and open-minded toward him.

HELMER: My dear Nora, there's a notable difference between your father and me. Your father's official career was hardly above reproach. But mine is; and I hope it'll stay that way as long as I hold my position.

NORA: Oh, who can ever tell what vicious minds can invent? We could be so snug and happy now in our quiet, carefree home — you and I and the children, Torvald! That's why I'm pleading with you so —

HELMER: And just by pleading for him you make it impossible for me to keep him on. It's already known at the bank that I'm firing Krogstad. What if it's rumored around now that the new bank manager was vetoed by his wife —

NORA: Yes, what then — ?

HELMER: Oh yes — as long as our little bundle of stubbornness gets her way —! I should go and make myself ridiculous in front of the whole office — give people the idea I can be swayed by all kinds of outside pressure. Oh, you can bet I'd feel the effects of that soon enough! Besides — there's something that rules Krogstad right out at the bank as long as I'm the manager.

NORA: What's that?

HELMER: His moral failings I could maybe overlook if I had to —

NORA: Yes, Torvald, why not?

HELMER: And I hear he's quite efficient on the job. But he was a crony of mine back in my teens — one of those rash friendships that crop up again and again to embarrass you later in life. Well, I might as well say it straight out: We're on a first-name basis. And that tactless fool makes no effort at all to hide it in front of others. Quite the contrary — he thinks that entitles him to take a familiar air around me, and so every other second he comes booming out with his, "Yes, Torvald!" and "Sure thing, Torvald!" I tell you, it's been excruciating for me. He's out to make my place in the bank unbearable.

NORA: Torvald, you can't be serious about all this.

HELMER: Oh no? Why not?

NORA: Because these are such petty considerations.

HELMER: What are you saying? Petty? You think I'm petty!

NORA: No, just the opposite, Torvald dear. That's exactly why —

HELMER: Never mind. You call my motives petty; then I might as well be just that. Petty! All right! We'll put a stop to this for good. (*Goes to the hall door and calls.*) Helene!

NORA: What do you want?

HELMER (*searching among his papers*): A decision. (*The Maid comes in.*) Look here; take this letter; go out with it at once. Get hold of a messenger and have him deliver it. Quick now. It's already addressed. Wait, here's some money.

MAID: Yes, sir. (*She leaves with the letter.*)

HELMER (*straightening his papers*): There, now, little Miss Willful.

NORA (*breathlessly*): Torvald, what was that letter?

HELMER: Krogstad's notice.

NORA: Call it back, Torvald! There's still time. Oh, Torvald, call it back! Do it for my sake — for your sake, for the children's sake! Do you hear, Torvald; do it! You don't know how this can harm us.

HELMER: Too late.

NORA: Yes, too late.

HELMER: Nora, dear, I can forgive you this panic, even though basically you're insulting me. Yes, you are! Or isn't it an insult to think that *I* should be afraid of a courtroom hack's revenge? But I forgive you anyway, because this shows so beautifully how much you love me. (*Takes her in his arms.*) This is the way it should be, my darling Nora. Whatever comes, you'll see: When it really counts, I have strength and courage enough as a man to take on the whole weight myself.

NORA (*terrified*): What do you mean by that?

HELMER: The whole weight, I said.

NORA (*resolutely*): No, never in all the world.

HELMER: Good. So we'll share it, Nora, as man and wife. That's as it should be. (*Fondling her.*) Are you happy now? There, there, there — not these frightened dove's eyes. It's nothing at all but empty fantasies — Now you should run through your tarantella and practice your tambourine. I'll go to the inner office, and shut both doors, so I won't hear a thing; you can make all the noise you like. (*Turning in the doorway.*) And when Rank comes, just tell him where he can find me. (*He nods to her and goes with his papers into the study, closing the door.*)

NORA (*standing as though rooted, dazed with fright, in a whisper*): He really could do it. He will do it. He'll do it in spite of everything. No, not that, never, never! Anything but that! Escape! A way out — (*The doorbell rings.*) Dr. Rank! Anything but that! *Anything*, whatever it is! (*Her hands pass over her face, smoothing it; she pulls herself together, goes over and opens the hall door. Dr. Rank stands outside, hanging his fur coat up. During the following scene, it begins getting dark.*)

NORA: Hello, Dr. Rank. I recognized your ring. But you mustn't go in to Torvald yet; I believe he's working.

RANK: And you?

NORA: For you, I always have an hour to spare — you know that. (*He has entered, and she shuts the door after him.*)

RANK: Many thanks. I'll make use of these hours while I can.

NORA: What do you mean by that? While you can?

RANK: Does that disturb you?

NORA: Well, it's such an odd phrase. Is anything going to happen?

RANK: What's going to happen is what I've been expecting so long — but I honestly didn't think it would come so soon.

NORA (*gripping his arm*): What is it you've found out? Dr. Rank, you have to tell me!

RANK (*sitting by the stove*): It's all over with me. There's nothing to be done about it.

NORA (*breathing easier*): Is it you — then — ?

RANK: Who else? There's no point in lying to one's self. I'm the most miserable of all my patients, Mrs. Helmer. These past few days I've been auditing my internal accounts. Bankrupt! Within a month I'll probably be laid out and rotting in the churchyard.

NORA: Oh, what a horrible thing to say.

RANK: The thing itself is horrible. But the worst of it is all the other horror before it's over. There's only one final examination left; when I'm finished with that, I'll know about when my disintegration will begin. There's something I want to say. Helmer with his sensitivity has such a sharp distaste for anything ugly. I don't want him near my sickroom.

NORA: Oh, but Dr. Rank —

RANK: I won't have him in there. Under no condition. I'll lock my door to him — As soon as I'm completely sure of the worst, I'll send you my calling card marked with a black cross, and you'll know then the wreck has started to come apart.

NORA: No, today you're completely unreasonable. And I wanted you so much to be in a really good humor.

RANK: With death up my sleeve? And then to suffer this way for somebody else's sins. Is there any justice in that? And in every single family, in some way or another, this inevitable retribution of nature goes on —

NORA (*her hands pressed over her ears*): Oh, stuff! Cheer up! Please — be gay!

RANK: Yes, I'd just as soon laugh at it all. My poor, innocent spine, serving time for my father's gay army days.

NORA (*by the table, left*): He was so infatuated with asparagus tips and pâté de foie gras,° wasn't that it?

RANK: Yes — and with truffles.

NORA: Truffles, yes. And then with oysters, I suppose?

RANK: Yes, tons of oysters, naturally.

NORA: And then the port and champagne to go with it. It's so sad that all these delectable things have to strike at our bones.

RANK: Especially when they strike at the unhappy bones that never shared in the fun.

NORA: Ah, that's the saddest of all.

RANK (*looks searchingly at her*): Hm.

NORA (*after a moment*): Why did you smile?

RANK: No, it was you who laughed.

NORA: No, it was you who smiled, Dr. Rank!

RANK (*getting up*): You're even a bigger tease than I'd thought.

NORA: I'm full of wild ideas today.

RANK: That's obvious.

NORA (*putting both hands on his shoulders*): Dear, dear Dr. Rank, you'll never die for Torvald and me.

RANK: Oh, that loss you'll easily get over. Those who go away are soon forgotten.

NORA (*looks fearfully at him*): You believe that?

RANK: One makes new connections, and then —

NORA: Who makes new connections?

RANK: Both you and Torvald will when I'm gone. I'd say you're well under way already. What was that Mrs. Linde doing here last evening?

NORA: Oh, come — you can't be jealous of poor Kristine?

RANK: Oh yes, I am. She'll be my successor here in the house. When I'm down under, that woman will probably —

NORA: Shh! Not so loud. She's right in there.

RANK: Today as well. So you see.

NORA: Only to sew on my dress. Good gracious, how unreasonable you are. (*Sitting on the sofa.*) Be nice now, Dr. Rank. Tomorrow you'll see how beautifully

---

pâté de foie gras: Pâté of goose liver.

I'll dance; and you can imagine then that I'm dancing only for you — yes, and of course for Torvald, too — that's understood. (*Takes various items out of the carton.*) Dr. Rank, sit over here and I'll show you something.

RANK (*sitting*): What's that?

NORA: Look here. Look.

RANK: Silk stockings.

NORA: Flesh-colored. Aren't they lovely? Now it's so dark here, but tomorrow — No, no, no, just look at the feet. Oh well, you might as well look at the rest.

RANK: Hm —

NORA: Why do you look so critical? Don't you believe they'll fit?

RANK: I've never had any chance to form an opinion on that.

NORA (*glancing at him a moment*): Shame on you. (*Hits him lightly on the ear with the stockings.*) That's for you. (*Puts them away again.*)

RANK: And what other splendors am I going to see now?

NORA: Not the least bit more, because you've been naughty. (*She hunts a little and rummages among her things.*)

RANK (*after a short silence*): When I sit here together with you like this, completely easy and open, then I don't know — I simply can't imagine — whatever would have become of me if I'd never come into this house.

NORA (*smiling*): Yes, I really think you feel completely at ease with us.

RANK (*more quietly, staring straight ahead*): And then to have to go away from it all —

NORA: Nonsense, you're not going away.

RANK (*his voice unchanged*): — and not even be able to leave some poor show of gratitude behind, scarcely a fleeting regret — no more than a vacant place that anyone can fill.

NORA: And if I asked you now for — No —

RANK: For what?

NORA: For a great proof of your friendship —

RANK: Yes, yes?

NORA: No, I mean — for an exceptionally big favor —

RANK: Would you really, for once, make me so happy?

NORA: Oh, you haven't the vaguest idea what it is.

RANK: All right, then tell me.

NORA: No, but I can't, Dr. Rank — it's all out of reason. It's advice and help, too — and a favor —

RANK: So much the better. I can't fathom what you're hinting at. Just speak out. Don't you trust me?

NORA: Of course. More than anyone else. You're my best and truest friend, I'm sure. That's why I want to talk to you. All right, then, Dr. Rank: There's something you can help me prevent. You know how deeply, how inexpressibly dearly Torvald loves me; he'd never hesitate a second to give up his life for me.

RANK (*leaning close to her*): Nora — do you think he's the only one —

NORA (*with a slight start*): Who — ?

RANK: Who'd gladly give up his life for you.

NORA (*heavily*): I see.

RANK: I swore to myself you should know this before I'm gone. I'll never find a better chance. Yes, Nora, now you know. And also you know now that you can trust me beyond anyone else.

NORA (*rising, natural and calm*): Let me by.

RANK (*making room for her, but still sitting*): Nora —

NORA (*in the hall doorway*): Helene, bring the lamp in. (*Goes over to the stove.*) Ah, dear Dr. Rank, that was really mean of you.

RANK (*getting up*): That I've loved you just as deeply as somebody else? Was *that* mean?

NORA: No, but that you came out and told me. That was quite unnecessary —

RANK: What do you mean? Have you known — ?

(*The Maid comes in with the lamp, sets it on the table, and goes out again.*)

RANK: Nora — Mrs. Helmer — I'm asking you: Have you known about it?

NORA: Oh, how can I tell what I know or don't know? Really, I don't know what to say — Why did you have to be so clumsy, Dr. Rank! Everything was so good.

RANK: Well, in any case, you now have the knowledge that my body and soul are at your command. So won't you speak out?

NORA (*looking at him*): After that?

RANK: Please, just let me know what it is.

NORA: You can't know anything now.

RANK: I have to. You mustn't punish me like this. Give me the chance to do whatever is humanly possible for you.

NORA: Now there's nothing you can do for me. Besides, actually, I don't need any help. You'll see — it's only my fantasies. That's what it is. Of course! (*Sits in the rocker, looks at him, and smiles.*) What a nice one you are, Dr. Rank. Aren't you a little bit ashamed, now that the lamp is here?

RANK: No, not exactly. But perhaps I'd better go — for good?

NORA: No, you certainly can't do that. You must come here just as you always have. You know Torvald can't do without you.

RANK: Yes, but *you?*

NORA: You know how much I enjoy it when you're here.

RANK: That's precisely what threw me off. You're a mystery to me. So many times I've felt you'd almost rather be with me than with Helmer.

NORA: Yes — you see, there are some people that one loves most and other people that one would almost prefer being with.

RANK: Yes, there's something to that.

NORA: When I was back home, of course I loved Papa most. But I always thought it was so much fun when I could sneak down to the maids' quarters, because they never tried to improve me, and it was always so amusing, the way they talked to each other.

RANK: Aha, so it's their place that I've filled.

NORA (*jumping up and going to him*): Oh, dear, sweet Dr. Rank, that's not what I meant at all. But you can understand that with Torvald it's just the same as with Papa —

(*The Maid enters from the hall.*)

MAID: Ma'am — please! (*She whispers to Nora and hands her a calling card.*)

NORA (*glancing at the card*): Ah! (*Slips it into her pocket.*)

RANK: Anything wrong?

NORA: No, no, not at all. It's only some — it's my new dress —

RANK: Really? But — there's your dress.

NORA: Oh, that. But this is another one — I ordered it — Torvald mustn't know —

RANK: Ah, now we have the big secret.

NORA: That's right. Just go in with him — he's back in the inner study. Keep him there as long as —

RANK: Don't worry. He won't get away. (*Goes into the study.*)

NORA (*to the Maid*): And he's standing waiting in the kitchen?

MAID: Yes, he came up by the back stairs.

NORA: But didn't you tell him somebody was here?

MAID: Yes, but that didn't do any good.

NORA: He won't leave?

MAID: No, he won't go till he's talked with you, ma'am.

NORA: Let him come in, then — but quietly. Helene, don't breathe a word about this. It's a surprise for my husband.

MAID: Yes, yes, I understand — (*Goes out.*)

NORA: This horror — it's going to happen. No, no, no, it can't happen, it mustn't. (*She goes and bolts Helmer's door. The Maid opens the hall door for Krogstad and shuts it behind him. He is dressed for travel in a fur coat, boots, and a fur cap.*)

NORA (*going toward him*): Talk softly. My husband's home.

KROGSTAD: Well, good for him.

NORA: What do you want?

KROGSTAD: Some information.

NORA: Hurry up, then. What is it?

KROGSTAD: You know, of course, that I got my notice.

NORA: I couldn't prevent it, Mr. Krogstad. I fought for you to the bitter end, but nothing worked.

KROGSTAD: Does your husband's love for you run so thin? He knows everything I can expose you to, and all the same he dares to —

NORA: How can you imagine he knows anything about this?

KROGSTAD: Ah, no — I can't imagine it either, now. It's not at all like my fine Torvald Helmer to have so much guts —

NORA: Mr. Krogstad, I demand respect for my husband!

KROGSTAD: Why, of course — all due respect. But since the lady's keeping it so carefully hidden, may I presume to ask if you're also a bit better informed than yesterday about what you've actually done?

NORA: More than you ever could teach me.

KROGSTAD: Yes, I *am* such an awful lawyer.

NORA: What is it you want from me?

KROGSTAD: Just a glimpse of how you are, Mrs. Helmer. I've been thinking about
you all day long. A cashier, a night-court scribbler, a—well, a type like me
also has a little of what they call a heart, you know.

NORA: Then show it. Think of my children.

KROGSTAD: Did you or your husband ever think of mine? But never mind. I simply wanted to tell you that you don't need to take this thing too seriously.
For the present, I'm not proceeding with any action.

NORA: Oh no, really! Well—I knew that.

KROGSTAD: Everything can be settled in a friendly spirit. It doesn't have to get
around town at all; it can stay just among us three.

NORA: My husband must never know anything of this.

KROGSTAD: How can you manage that? Perhaps you can pay me the balance?

NORA: No, not right now.

KROGSTAD: Or you know some way of raising the money in a day or two?

NORA: No way that I'm willing to use.

KROGSTAD: Well, it wouldn't have done you any good, anyway. If you stood in
front of me with a fistful of bills, you still couldn't buy your signature back.

NORA: Then tell me what you're going to do with it.

KROGSTAD: I'll just hold onto it—keep it on file. There's no outsider who'll even
get wind of it. So if you've been thinking of taking some desperate step—

NORA: I have.

KROGSTAD: Been thinking of running away from home—

NORA: I have!

KROGSTAD: Or even of something worse—

NORA: How could you guess that?

KROGSTAD: You can drop those thoughts.

NORA: How could you guess I was thinking of *that*?

KROGSTAD: Most of us think about *that* at first. I thought about it too, but I discovered I hadn't the courage—

NORA (*lifelessly*): I don't either.

KROGSTAD (*relieved*): That's true, you haven't the courage? You too?

NORA: I don't have it—I don't have it.

KROGSTAD: It would be terribly stupid, anyway. After that first storm at home
blows out, why, then—I have here in my pocket a letter for your husband—

NORA: Telling everything?

KROGSTAD: As charitably as possible.

NORA (*quickly*): He mustn't ever get that letter. Tear it up. I'll find some way to
get money.

KROGSTAD: Beg pardon, Mrs. Helmer, but I think I just told you—

NORA: Oh, I don't mean the money I owe you. Let me know how much you want
from my husband, and I'll manage it.

KROGSTAD: I don't want any money from your husband.

NORA: What do you want, then?

KROGSTAD: I'll tell you what. I want to recoup, Mrs. Helmer; I want to get on in the world — and there's where your husband can help me. For a year and a half I've kept myself clean of anything disreputable — all that time struggling with the worst conditions; but I was satisfied, working my way up step by step. Now I've been written right off, and I'm just not in the mood to come crawling back. I tell you, I want to move on. I want to get back in the bank — in a better position. Your husband can set up a job for me —

NORA: He'll never do that!

KROGSTAD: He'll do it. I know him. He won't dare breathe a word of protest. And once I'm in there together with him, you just wait and see! Inside of a year, I'll be the manager's right-hand man. It'll be Nils Krogstad, not Torvald Helmer, who runs the bank.

NORA: You'll never see the day!

KROGSTAD: Maybe you think you can —

NORA: I have the courage now — for *that*.

KROGSTAD: Oh, you don't scare me. A smart, spoiled lady like you —

NORA: You'll see; you'll see!

KROGSTAD: Under the ice, maybe? Down in the freezing, coal-black water? There, till you float up in the spring, ugly unrecognizable, with your hair falling out —

NORA: You don't frighten me.

KROGSTAD: Nor do you frighten me. One doesn't do these things, Mrs. Helmer. Besides what good would it be? I'd still have him safe in my pocket.

NORA: Afterwards? When I'm no longer — ?

KROGSTAD: Are you forgetting that *I'll* be in control then over your final reputation? (*Nora stands speechless, staring at him.*) Good; now I've warned you. Don't do anything stupid. When Helmer's read my letter, I'll be waiting for his reply. And bear in mind that it's your husband himself who's forced me back to my old ways. I'll never forgive him for that. Good-bye, Mrs. Helmer. (*He goes out through the hall.*)

NORA (*goes to the hall door, opens it a crack, and listens*): He's gone. Didn't leave the letter. Oh no, no, that's impossible too! (*Opening the door more and more.*) What's that? He's standing outside — not going downstairs. He's thinking it over? Maybe he'll — ? (*A letter falls in the mailbox; then Krogstad's footsteps are heard, dying away down a flight of stairs. Nora gives a muffled cry and runs over toward the sofa table. A short pause.*) In the mailbox. (*Slips warily over to the hall door.*) It's lying there. Torvald, Torvald — now we're lost!

MRS. LINDE (*entering with the costume from the room, left*): There now, I can't see anything else to mend. Perhaps you'd like to try —

NORA (*in a hoarse whisper*): Kristine, come here.

MRS. LINDE (*tossing the dress on the sofa*): What's wrong? You look upset.

NORA: Come here. See that letter? There! Look — through the glass in the mailbox.

MRS. LINDE: Yes, yes, I see it.

NORA: That letter's from Krogstad —

MRS. LINDE: Nora — it's Krogstad who loaned you the money!

NORA: Yes, and now Torvald will find out everything.

MRS. LINDE: Believe me, Nora, it's best for both of you.

NORA: There's more you don't know. I forged a name.

MRS. LINDE: But for heaven's sake — ?

NORA: I only want to tell you that, Kristine, so that you can be my witness.

MRS. LINDE: Witness? Why should I — ?

NORA: If I should go out of my mind — it could easily happen —

MRS. LINDE: Nora!

NORA: Or anything else occurred — so I couldn't be present here —

MRS. LINDE: Nora, Nora, you aren't yourself at all!

NORA: And someone should try to take on the whole weight, all of the guilt, you follow me —

MRS. LINDE: Yes, of course, but why do you think — ?

NORA: Then you're the witness that it isn't true, Kristine. I'm very much myself; my mind right now is perfectly clear; and I'm telling you: Nobody else has known about this; I alone did everything. Remember that.

MRS. LINDE: I will. But I don't understand all this.

NORA: Oh, how could you ever understand it? It's the miracle now that's going to take place.

MRS. LINDE: The miracle?

NORA: Yes, the miracle. But it's so awful, Kristine. It mustn't take place, not for anything in the world.

MRS. LINDE: I'm going right over and talk with Krogstad.

NORA: Don't go near him; he'll do you some terrible harm!

MRS. LINDE: There was a time once when he'd gladly have done anything for me.

NORA: He?

MRS. LINDE: Where does he live?

NORA: Oh, how do I know? Yes. (*Searches in her pocket.*) Here's his card. But the letter, the letter — !

HELMER (*from the study, knocking on the door*): Nora!

NORA (*with a cry of fear*): Oh! What is it? What do you want?

HELMER: Now, now, don't be so frightened. We're not coming in. You locked the door — are you trying on the dress?

NORA: Yes, I'm trying it. I'll look just beautiful, Torvald.

MRS. LINDE (*who has read the card*): He's living right around the corner.

NORA: Yes, but what's the use? We're lost. The letter's in the box.

MRS. LINDE: And your husband has the key?

NORA: Yes, always.

MRS. LINDE: Krogstad can ask for his letter back unread; he can find some excuse —

NORA: But it's just this time that Torvald usually —

MRS. LINDE: Stall him. Keep him in there. I'll be back as quick as I can. (*She hurries out through the hall entrance.*)

NORA (*goes to Helmer's door, opens it, and peers in*): Torvald!

HELMER (*from the inner study*): Well — does one dare set foot in one's own living room at last? Come on, Rank, now we'll get a look — (*In the doorway.*) But what's this?

NORA: What, Torvald dear?

HELMER: Rank had me expecting some grand masquerade.

RANK (*in the doorway*): That was my impression, but I must have been wrong.

NORA: No one can admire me in my splendor — not till tomorrow.

HELMER: But Nora dear, you look so exhausted. Have you practiced too hard?

NORA: No, I haven't practiced at all yet.

HELMER: You know, it's necessary —

NORA: Oh, it's absolutely necessary, Torvald. But I can't get anywhere without your help. I've forgotten the whole thing completely.

HELMER: Ah, we'll soon take care of that.

NORA: Yes, take care of me, Torvald, please! Promise me that? Oh, I'm so nervous. That big party — You must give up everything this evening for me. No business — don't even touch your pen. Yes? Dear Torvald, promise?

HELMER: It's a promise. Tonight I'm totally at your service — you little helpless thing. Hm — but first there's one thing I want to — (*Goes toward the hall door.*)

NORA: What are you looking for?

HELMER: Just to see if there's any mail.

NORA: No, no, don't do that, Torvald!

HELMER: Now what?

NORA: Torvald, please. There isn't any.

HELMER: Let me look, though. (*Starts out. Nora, at the piano, strikes the first notes of the tarantella. Helmer, at the door, stops.*) Aha!

NORA: I can't dance tomorrow if I don't practice with you.

HELMER (*going over to her*): Nora dear, are you really so frightened?

NORA: Yes, so terribly frightened. Let me practice right now; there's still time before dinner. Oh, sit down and play for me, Torvald. Direct me. Teach me, the way you always have.

HELMER: Gladly, if it's what you want. (*Sits at the piano.*)

NORA (*snatches the tambourine up from the box, then a long, varicolored shawl, which she throws around herself, whereupon she springs forward and cries out*): Play for me now! Now I'll dance!

(*Helmer plays and Nora dances. Rank stands behind Helmer at the piano and looks on.*)

HELMER (*as he plays*): Slower. Slow down.

NORA: Can't change it.

HELMER: Not so violent, Nora!

NORA: Has to be just like this.

HELMER (*stopping*): No, no, that won't do at all.

NORA (*laughing and swinging her tambourine*): Isn't that what I told you?

RANK: Let me play for her.

HELMER (*getting up*): Yes, go on. I can teach her more easily then.

(*Rank sits at the piano and plays, Nora dances more and more wildly. Helmer has stationed himself by the stove and repeatedly gives her directions; she seems not to hear them; her hair loosens and falls over her shoulders; she does not notice, but goes on dancing. Mrs. Linde enters.*)

MRS. LINDE (*standing dumbfounded at the door*): Ah — !

NORA (*still dancing*): See what fun, Kristine!

HELMER: But Nora darling, you dance as if your life were at stake.

NORA: And it is.

HELMER: Rank, stop! This is pure madness. Stop it, I say!

(*Rank breaks off playing, and Nora halts abruptly.*)

HELMER (*going over to her*): I never would have believed it. You've forgotten everything I taught you.

NORA (*throwing away the tambourine*): You see for yourself.

HELMER: Well, there's certainly room for instruction here.

NORA: Yes, you see how important it is. You've got to teach me to the very last minute. Promise me that, Torvald?

HELMER: You can bet on it.

NORA: You mustn't, either today or tomorrow, think about anything else but me; you mustn't open any letters — or the mailbox —

HELMER: Ah, it's still the fear of that man —

NORA: Oh yes, yes, that too.

HELMER: Nora, it's written all over you — there's already a letter from him out there.

NORA: I don't know. I guess so. But you mustn't read such things now; there mustn't be anything ugly between us before it's all over.

RANK (*quietly to Helmer*): You shouldn't deny her.

HELMER (*putting his arm around her*): The child can have her way. But tomorrow night, after you've danced —

NORA: Then you'll be free.

MAID (*in the doorway, right*): Ma'am, dinner is served.

NORA: We'll be wanting champagne, Helene.

MAID: Very good, ma'am. (*Goes out.*)

HELMER: So — a regular banquet, hm?

NORA: Yes, a banquet — champagne till daybreak! (*Calling out.*) And some maca-roons, Helene. Heaps of them — just this once.

HELMER (*taking her hands*): Now, now, now — no hysterics. Be my own little lark again.

NORA: Oh, I will soon enough. But go on in — and you, Dr. Rank. Kristine, help me put up my hair.

RANK (*whispering, as they go*): There's nothing wrong — really wrong, is there?

HELMER: Oh, of course not. It's nothing more than this childish anxiety I was telling you about. (*They go out, right.*)

NORA: Well?

MRS. LINDE: Left town.

NORA: I could see by your face.

MRS. LINDE: He'll be home tomorrow evening. I wrote him a note.

NORA: You shouldn't have. Don't try to stop anything now. After all, it's a wonderful joy, this waiting here for the miracle.

MRS. LINDE: What is it you're waiting for?

NORA: Oh, you can't understand that. Go in to them; I'll be along in a moment.

(*Mrs. Linde goes into the dining room. Nora stands a short while as if composing herself; then she looks at her watch.*)

NORA: Five. Seven hours to midnight. Twenty-four hours to the midnight after, and then the tarantella's done. Seven and twenty-four? Thirty-one hours to live.

HELMER (*in the doorway, right*): What's become of the little lark?

NORA (*going toward him with open arms*): Here's your lark!

ACT 3

(*Same scene. The table, with chairs around it, has been moved to the center of the room. A lamp on the table is lit. The hall door stands open. Dance music drifts down from the floor above. Mrs. Linde sits at the table, absently paging through a book, trying to read, but apparently unable to focus her thoughts. Once or twice she pauses, tensely listening for a sound at the outer entrance.*)

MRS. LINDE (*glancing at her watch*): Not yet — and there's hardly any time left. If only he's not — (*Listening again.*) Ah, there it is. (*She goes out in the hall and cautiously opens the outer door. Quiet footsteps are heard on the stairs. She whispers.*) Come in. Nobody's here.

KROGSTAD (*in the doorway*): I found a note from you at home. What's back of all this?

MRS. LINDE: I just *had* to talk to you.

KROGSTAD: Oh? And it just *had* to be here in this house?

MRS. LINDE: At my place it was impossible; my room hasn't a private entrance. Come in, we're all alone. The maid's asleep, and the Helmers are at the dance upstairs.

KROGSTAD (*entering the room*): Well, well, the Helmers are dancing tonight? Really?

MRS. LINDE: Yes, why not?

KROGSTAD: How true — why not?

MRS. LINDE: All right, Krogstad, let's talk.

KROGSTAD: Do we two have anything more to talk about?

MRS. LINDE: We have a great deal to talk about.

KROGSTAD: I wouldn't have thought so.

MRS. LINDE: No, because you've never understood me, really.

KROGSTAD: Was there anything more to understand — except what's all too common in life? A calculating woman throws over a man the moment a better catch comes by.

MRS. LINDE: You think I'm so thoroughly calculating? You think I broke it off lightly?

KROGSTAD: Didn't you?

MRS. LINDE: Nils — is that what you really thought?

KROGSTAD: If you cared, then why did you write me the way you did?

MRS. LINDE: What else could I do? If I had to break off with you, then it was my job as well to root out everything you felt for me.

KROGSTAD (*wringing his hands*): So that was it. And this — all this, simply for money!

MRS. LINDE: Don't forget I had a helpless mother and two small brothers. We couldn't wait for you, Nils; you had such a long road ahead of you then.

KROGSTAD: That may be; but you still hadn't the right to abandon me for somebody else's sake.

MRS. LINDE: Yes — I don't know. So many, many times I've asked myself if I did have that right.

KROGSTAD (*more softly*): When I lost you, it was as if all the solid ground dissolved from under my feet. Look at me; I'm a half-drowned man now, hanging onto a wreck.

MRS. LINDE: Help may be near.

KROGSTAD: It was near — but then you came and blocked it off.

MRS. LINDE: Without my knowing it, Nils. Today for the first time I learned that it's you I'm replacing at the bank.

KROGSTAD: All right — I believe you. But now that you know, will you step aside?

MRS. LINDE: No, because that wouldn't benefit you in the slightest.

KROGSTAD: Not "benefit" me, hm! I'd step aside anyway.

MRS. LINDE: I've learned to be realistic. Life and hard, bitter necessity have taught me that.

KROGSTAD: And life's taught me never to trust fine phrases.

MRS. LINDE: Then life's taught you a very sound thing. But you do have to trust in actions, don't you?

KROGSTAD: What does that mean?

MRS. LINDE: You said you were hanging on like a half-drowned man to a wreck.

KROGSTAD: I've good reason to say that.

MRS. LINDE: I'm also like a half-drowned woman on a wreck. No one to suffer with; no one to care for.

KROGSTAD: You made your choice.

MRS. LINDE: There wasn't any choice then.

KROGSTAD: So — what of it?

MRS. LINDE: Nils, if only we two shipwrecked people could reach across to each other.

KROGSTAD: What are you saying?

MRS. LINDE: Two on one wreck are at least better off than each on his own.

KROGSTAD: Kristine!

MRS. LINDE: Why do you think I came into town?

KROGSTAD: Did you really have some thought of me?

MRS. LINDE: I have to work to go on living. All my born days, as long as I can remember, I've worked, and it's been my best and my only joy. But now I'm
completely alone in the world; it frightens me to be so empty and lost. To
work for yourself—there's no joy in that. Nils, give me something—someone to work for.

KROGSTAD: I don't believe all this. It's just some hysterical feminine urge to go
out and make a noble sacrifice.

MRS. LINDE: Have you ever found me to be hysterical?

KROGSTAD: Can you honestly mean this? Tell me—do you know everything
about my past?

MRS. LINDE: Yes.

KROGSTAD: And you know what they think I'm worth around here.

MRS. LINDE: From what you were saying before, it would seem that with me you
could have been another person.

KROGSTAD: I'm positive of that.

MRS. LINDE: Couldn't it happen still?

KROGSTAD: Kristine—you're saying this in all seriousness? Yes, you are! I can see
it in you. And do you really have the courage, then—?

MRS. LINDE: I need to have someone to care for, and your children need a
mother. We both need each other. Nils, I have faith that you're good at
heart—I'll risk everything together with you.

KROGSTAD (*gripping her hands*): Kristine, thank you, thank you—Now I know I
can win back a place in their eyes. Yes—but I forgot—

MRS. LINDE (*listening*): Shh! The tarantella. Go now! Go on!

KROGSTAD: Why? What is it?

MRS. LINDE: Hear the dance up there? When that's over, they'll be coming down.

KROGSTAD: Oh, then I'll go. But—it's all pointless. Of course, you don't know
the move I made against the Helmers.

MRS. LINDE: Yes, Nils, I know.

KROGSTAD: And all the same, you have the courage to—?

MRS. LINDE: I know how far despair can drive a man like you.

KROGSTAD: Oh, if I only could take it all back.

MRS. LINDE: You easily could—your letter's still lying in the mailbox.

KROGSTAD: Are you sure of that?

MRS. LINDE: Positive. But—

KROGSTAD (*looks at her searchingly*): Is that the meaning of it, then? You'll save
your friend at any price. Tell me straight out. Is that it?

MRS. LINDE: Nils—anyone who's sold herself for somebody else once isn't going
to do it again.

KROGSTAD: I'll demand my letter back.

MRS. LINDE: No, no.

KROGSTAD: Yes, of course. I'll stay here till Helmer comes down; I'll tell him to
give me my letter again—that it only involves my dismissal—that he
shouldn't read it—

MRS. LINDE: No, Nils, don't call the letter back.

KROGSTAD: But wasn't that exactly why you wrote me to come here?

MRS. LINDE: Yes, in that first panic. But it's been a whole day and night since then, and in that time I've seen such incredible things in this house. Helmer's got to learn everything; this dreadful secret has to be aired; those two have to come to a full understanding; all these lies and evasions can't go on.

KROGSTAD: Well, then, if you want to chance it. But at least there's one thing I can do, and do right away—

MRS. LINDE (*listening*): Go now, go, quick! The dance is over. We're not safe another second.

KROGSTAD: I'll wait for you downstairs.

MRS. LINDE: Yes, please do; take me home.

KROGSTAD: I can't believe it; I've never been so happy. (*He leaves by way of the outer door; the door between the room and the hall stays open.*)

MRS. LINDE (*straightening up a bit and getting together her street clothes*): How different now! How different! Someone to work for, to live for—a home to build. Well, it is worth the try! Oh, if they'd only come! (*Listening.*) Ah, there they are. Bundle up. (*She picks up her hat and coat. Nora's and Helmer's voices can be heard outside; a key turns in the lock, and Helmer brings Nora into the hall almost by force. She is wearing the Italian costume with a large black shawl about her; he has on evening dress, with a black domino open over it.*)

NORA (*struggling in the doorway*): No, no, no, not inside! I'm going up again. I don't want to leave so soon.

HELMER: But Nora dear—

NORA: Oh, I beg you, please, Torvald. From the bottom of my heart, *please*—only an hour more!

HELMER: Not a single minute, Nora darling. You know our agreement. Come on, in we go; you'll catch cold out here. (*In spite of her resistance, he gently draws her into the room.*)

MRS. LINDE: Good evening.

NORA: Kristine!

HELMER: Why, Mrs. Linde—are you here so late?

MRS. LINDE: Yes, I'm sorry, but I did want to see Nora in costume.

NORA: Have you been sitting here, waiting for me?

MRS. LINDE: Yes. I didn't come early enough; you were all upstairs; and then I thought I really couldn't leave without seeing you.

HELMER (*removing Nora's shawl*): Yes, take a good look. She's worth looking at, I can tell you that, Mrs. Linde. Isn't she lovely?

MRS. LINDE: Yes, I should say—

HELMER: A dream of loveliness, isn't she? That's what everyone thought at the party, too. But she's horribly stubborn—this sweet little thing. What's to be done with her? Can you imagine, I almost had to use force to pry her away.

NORA: Oh, Torvald, you're going to regret you didn't indulge me, even for just a half hour more.

HELMER: There, you see. She danced her tarantella and got a tumultuous hand—which was well earned, although the performance may have been a bit too naturalistic — I mean it rather overstepped the proprieties of art. But never mind — what's important is, she made a success, an overwhelming success. You think I could let her stay on after that and spoil the effect? Oh no; I took my lovely little Capri girl — my capricious little Capri girl, I should say — took her under my arm; one quick tour of the ballroom, a curtsy to every side, and then — as they say in novels — the beautiful vision disappeared. An exit should always be effective, Mrs. Linde, but that's what I can't get Nora to grasp. Phew, it's hot in here. (*Flings the domino on a chair and opens the door to his room.*) Why's it dark in here? Oh yes, of course. Excuse me. (*He goes in and lights a couple of candles.*)

NORA (*in a sharp, breathless whisper*): So?

MRS. LINDE (*quietly*): I talked with him.

NORA: And — ?

MRS. LINDE: Nora — you must tell your husband everything.

NORA (*dully*): I knew it.

MRS. LINDE: You've got nothing to fear from Krogstad, but you have to speak out.

NORA: I won't tell.

MRS. LINDE: Then the letter will.

NORA: Thanks, Kristine. I know now what's to be done. Shh!

HELMER (*reentering*): Well, then, Mrs. Linde — have you admired her?

MRS. LINDE: Yes, and now I'll say good night.

HELMER: Oh, come, so soon? Is this yours, this knitting?

MRS. LINDE: Yes, thanks. I nearly forgot it.

HELMER: Do you knit, then?

MRS. LINDE: Oh yes.

HELMER: You know what? You should embroider instead.

MRS. LINDE: Really? Why?

HELMER: Yes, because it's a lot prettier. See here, one holds the embroidery so, in the left hand, and then one guides the needle with the right — so — in an easy, sweeping curve — right?

MRS. LINDE: Yes, I guess that's —

HELMER: But, on the other hand, knitting — it can never be anything but ugly. Look, see here, the arms tucked in, the knitting needles going up and down — there's something Chinese about it. Ah, that was really a glorious champagne they served.

MRS. LINDE: Yes, good night, Nora, and don't be stubborn anymore.

HELMER: Well put, Mrs. Linde!

MRS. LINDE: Good night, Mr. Helmer.

HELMER (*accompanying her to the door*): Good night, good night. I hope you get home all right. I'd be very happy to — but you don't have far to go. Good night, good night. (*She leaves. He shuts the door after her and returns.*) There, now, at last we got her out the door. She's a deadly bore, that creature.

NORA: Aren't you pretty tired, Torvald?

HELMER: No, not a bit.

NORA: You're not sleepy?

HELMER: Not at all. On the contrary, I'm feeling quite exhilarated. But you? Yes, you really look tired and sleepy.

NORA: Yes, I'm very tired. Soon now I'll sleep.

HELMER: See! You see! I was right all along that we shouldn't stay longer.

NORA: Whatever you do is always right.

HELMER (*kissing her brow*): Now my little lark talks sense. Say, did you notice what a time Rank was having tonight?

NORA: Oh, was he? I didn't get to speak with him.

HELMER: I scarcely did either, but it's a long time since I've seen him in such high spirits. (*Gazes at her a moment, then comes nearer her.*) Hm — it's marvelous, though, to be back home again — to be completely alone with you. Oh, you bewitchingly lovely young woman!

NORA: Torvald, don't look at me like that!

HELMER: Can't I look at my richest treasure? At all that beauty that's mine, mine alone — completely and utterly.

NORA (*moving around to the other side of the table*): You mustn't talk to me that way tonight.

HELMER (*following her*): The tarantella is still in your blood. I can see — and it makes you even more enticing. Listen. The guests are beginning to go. (*Dropping his voice.*) Nora — it'll soon be quiet through this whole house.

NORA: Yes, I hope so.

HELMER: You do, don't you, my love? Do you realize — when I'm out at a party like this with you — do you know why I talk to you so little, and keep such a distance away; just send you a stolen look now and then — you know why I do it? It's because I'm imagining then that you're my secret darling, my secret young bride-to-be, and that no one suspects there's anything between us.

NORA: Yes, yes; oh, yes, I know you're always thinking of me.

HELMER: And then when we leave and I place the shawl over those fine young rounded shoulders — over that wonderful curving neck — then I pretend that you're my young bride, that we're just coming from the wedding, that for the first time I'm bringing you into my house — that for the first time I'm alone with you — completely alone with you, your trembling young beauty! All this evening I've longed for nothing but you. When I saw you turn and sway in the tarantella — my blood was pounding till I couldn't stand it — that's why I brought you down here so early —

NORA: Go away, Torvald! Leave me alone. I don't want all this.

HELMER: What do you mean? Nora, you're teasing me. You will, won't you? Aren't I your husband — ?

(*A knock at the outside door.*)

NORA (*startled*): What's that?

HELMER (*going toward the hall*): Who is it?

RANK (*outside*): It's me. May I come in a moment?

HELMER (*with quiet irritation*): Oh, what does he want now? (*Aloud.*) Hold on. (*Goes and opens the door.*) Oh, how nice that you didn't just pass us by!

RANK: I thought I heard your voice, and then I wanted so badly to have a look in. (*Lightly glancing about.*) Ah, me, these old familiar haunts. You have it snug and cozy in here, you two.

HELMER: You seemed to be having it pretty cozy upstairs, too.

RANK: Absolutely. Why shouldn't I? Why not take in everything in life? As much as you can, anyway, and as long as you can. The wine was superb —

HELMER: The champagne especially.

RANK: You noticed that too? It's amazing how much I could guzzle down.

NORA: Torvald also drank a lot of champagne this evening.

RANK: Oh?

NORA: Yes, and that always makes him so entertaining.

RANK: Well, why shouldn't one have a pleasant evening after a well-spent day?

HELMER: Well spent? I'm afraid I can't claim that.

RANK (*slapping him on the back*): But I can, you see!

NORA: Dr. Rank, you must have done some scientific research today.

RANK: Quite so.

HELMER: Come now — little Nora talking about scientific research!

NORA: And can I congratulate you on the results?

RANK: Indeed you may.

NORA: Then they were good?

RANK: The best possible for both doctor and patient — certainty.

NORA (*quickly and searchingly*): Certainty?

RANK: Complete certainty. So don't I owe myself a gay evening afterwards?

NORA: Yes, you're right, Dr. Rank.

HELMER: I'm with you — just so long as you don't have to suffer for it in the morning.

RANK: Well, one never gets something for nothing in life.

NORA: Dr. Rank — are you very fond of masquerade parties?

RANK: Yes, if there's a good array of odd disguises —

NORA: Tell me, what should we two go as at the next masquerade?

HELMER: You little featherhead — already thinking of the next!

RANK: We two? I'll tell you what: You must go as Charmed Life —

HELMER: Yes, but find a costume for that!

RANK: Your wife can appear just as she looks every day.

HELMER: That was nicely put. But don't you know what you're going to be?

RANK: Yes, Helmer, I've made up my mind.

HELMER: Well?

RANK: At the next masquerade I'm going to be invisible.

HELMER: That's a funny idea.

RANK: They say there's a hat — black, huge — have you never heard of the hat that makes you invisible? You put it on, and then no one on earth can see you.

HELMER (*suppressing a smile*): Ah, of course.

RANK: But I'm quite forgetting what I came for. Helmer, give me a cigar, one of the dark Havanas.

HELMER: With the greatest pleasure. (*Holds out his case.*)

RANK: Thanks. (*Takes one and cuts off the tip.*)

NORA (*striking a match*): Let me give you a light.

RANK: Thank you. (*She holds the match for him; he lights the cigar.*) And now good-bye.

HELMER: Good-bye, good-bye, old friend.

NORA: Sleep well, Doctor.

RANK: Thanks for that wish.

NORA: Wish me the same.

RANK: You? All right, if you like — Sleep well. And thanks for the light. (*He nods to them both and leaves.*)

HELMER (*his voice subdued*): He's been drinking heavily.

NORA (*absently*): Could be. (*Helmer takes his keys from his pocket and goes out in the hall.*) Torvald — what are you after?

HELMER: Got to empty the mailbox; it's nearly full. There won't be room for the morning papers.

NORA: Are you working tonight?

HELMER: You know I'm not. Why — what's this? Someone's been at the lock.

NORA: At the lock — ?

HELMER: Yes, I'm positive. What do you suppose — ? I can't imagine one of the maids — ? Here's a broken hairpin. Nora, it's yours —

NORA (*quickly*): Then it must be the children —

HELMER: You'd better break them of that. Hm, hm — well, opened it after all. (*Takes the contents out and calls into the kitchen.*) Helene! Helene, would you put out the lamp in the hall. (*He returns to the room, shutting the hall door, then displays the handful of mail.*) Look how it's piled up. (*Sorting through them.*) Now what's this?

NORA (*at the window*): The letter! Oh, Torvald, no!

HELMER: Two calling cards — from Rank.

NORA: From Dr. Rank?

HELMER (*examining them*): "Dr. Rank, Consulting Physician." They were on top. He must have dropped them in as he left.

NORA: Is there anything on them?

HELMER: There's a black cross over the name. See? That's a gruesome notion. He could almost be announcing his own death.

NORA: That's just what he's doing.

HELMER: What! You've heard something? Something he's told you?

NORA: Yes. That when those cards came, he'd be taking his leave of us. He'll shut himself in now and die.

HELMER: Ah, my poor friend! Of course I knew he wouldn't be here much longer. But so soon — And then to hide himself away like a wounded animal.

NORA: If it has to happen, then it's best it happens in silence — don't you think so, Torvald?

HELMER (*pacing up and down*): He's grown right into our lives. I simply can't imagine him gone. He with his suffering and loneliness — like a dark cloud setting off our sunlit happiness. Well, maybe it's best this way. For him, at least. (*Standing still.*) And maybe for us too, Nora. Now we're thrown back on each other, completely. (*Embracing her.*) Oh you, my darling wife, how can I hold you close enough? You know what, Nora — time and again I've wished you were in some terrible danger, just so I could stake my life and soul and everything, for your sake.

NORA (*tearing herself away, her voice firm and decisive*): Now you must read your mail, Torvald.

HELMER: No, no, not tonight. I want to stay with you, dearest.

NORA: With a dying friend on your mind?

HELMER: You're right. We've both had a shock. There's ugliness between us — these thoughts of death and corruption. We'll have to get free of them first. Until then — we'll stay apart.

NORA (*clinging about his neck*): Torvald — good night! Good night!

HELMER (*kissing her on the cheek*): Good night, little songbird. Sleep well, Nora. I'll be reading my mail now. (*He takes the letters into his room and shuts the door after him.*)

NORA (*with bewildered glances, groping about, seizing Helmer's domino, throwing it around her, and speaking in short, hoarse, broken whispers*): Never see him again. Never, never. (*Putting her shawl over her head.*) Never see the children either — them, too. Never, never. Oh, the freezing black water! The depths — down — Oh, I wish it were over — He has it now; he's reading it — now. Oh no, no, not yet. Torvald, good-bye, you and the children — (*She starts for the hall; as she does, Helmer throws open his door and stands with an open letter in his hand.*)

HELMER: Nora!

NORA (*screams*): Oh — !

HELMER: What is this? You know what's in this letter?

NORA: Yes, I know. Let me go! Let me out!

HELMER (*holding her back*): Where are you going?

NORA (*struggling to break loose*): You can't save me, Torvald!

HELMER (*slumping back*): True! Then it's true what he writes? How horrible! No, no, it's impossible — it can't be true.

NORA: It *is* true. I've loved you more than all this world.

HELMER: Ah, none of your slippery tricks.

NORA (*taking one step toward him*): Torvald — !

HELMER: What *is* this you've blundered into!

NORA: Just let me loose. You're not going to suffer for my sake. You're not going to take on my guilt.

HELMER: No more playacting. (*Locks the hall door.*) You stay right here and give me a reckoning. You understand what you've done? Answer! You understand?

NORA (*looking squarely at him, her face hardening*): Yes. I'm beginning to understand everything now.

HELMER (*striding about*): Oh, what an awful awakening! In all these eight years — she who was my pride and joy — a hypocrite, a liar — worse, worse — a criminal! How infinitely disgusting it all is! The shame! (*Nora says nothing and goes on looking straight at him. He stops in front of her.*) I should have suspected something of the kind. I should have known. All your father's flimsy values — Be still! All your father's flimsy values have come out in you. No religion, no morals, no sense of duty — Oh, how I'm punished for letting him off! I did it for your sake, and you repay me like this.

NORA: Yes, like this.

HELMER: Now you've wrecked all my happiness — ruined my whole future. Oh, it's awful to think of. I'm in a cheap little grafter's hands; he can do anything he wants with me, ask for anything, play with me like a puppet — and I can't breathe a word. I'll be swept down miserably into the depths on account of a featherbrained woman.

NORA: When I'm gone from this world, you'll be free.

HELMER: Oh, quit posing. Your father had a mess of those speeches too. What good would that ever do me if you were gone from this world, as you say? Not the slightest. He can still make the whole thing known; and if he does, I could be falsely suspected as your accomplice. They might even think that I was behind it — that I put you up to it. And all that I can thank you for — you that I've coddled the whole of our marriage. Can you see now what you've done to me?

NORA (*icily calm*): Yes.

HELMER: It's so incredible, I just can't grasp it. But we'll have to patch up whatever we can. Take off the shawl. I said, take it off! I've got to appease him somehow or other. The thing has to be hushed up at any cost. And as for you and me, it's got to seem like everything between us is just as it was — to the outside world, that is. You'll go right on living in this house, of course. But you can't be allowed to bring up the children; I don't dare trust you with them — Oh, to have to say this to someone I've loved so much! Well, that's done with. From now on happiness doesn't matter; all that matters is saving the bits and pieces, the appearance — (*The doorbell rings. Helmer starts.*) What's that? And so late. Maybe the worst —? You think he'd —? Hide, Nora! Say you're sick. (*Nora remains standing motionless. Helmer goes and opens the door.*)

MAID (*half dressed, in the hall*): A letter for Mrs. Helmer.

HELMER: I'll take it. (*Snatches the letter and shuts the door.*) Yes, it's from him. You don't get it; I'm reading it myself.

NORA: Then read it.

HELMER (*by the lamp*): I hardly dare. We may be ruined, you and I. But — I've got to know. (*Rips open the letter, skims through a few lines, glances at an enclosure, then cries out joyfully.*) Nora! (*Nora looks inquiringly at him.*) Nora! Wait — better check it again — Yes, yes, it's true. I'm saved. Nora, I'm saved!

NORA: And I?

HELMER: You too, of course. We're both saved, both of us. Look. He's sent back your note. He says he's sorry and ashamed — that a happy development in his life — oh, who cares what he says! Nora, we're saved! No one can hurt you. Oh, Nora, Nora — but first, this ugliness all has to go. Let me see — (*Takes a look at the note.*) No, I don't want to see it; I want the whole thing to fade like a dream. (*Tears the note and both letters to pieces, throws them into the stove and watches them burn.*) There — now there's nothing left — He wrote that since Christmas Eve you — Oh, they must have been three terrible days for you, Nora.

NORA: I fought a hard fight.

HELMER: And suffered pain and saw no escape but — No, we're not going to dwell on anything unpleasant. We'll just be grateful and keep on repeating: It's over now, it's over! You hear me, Nora? You don't seem to realize — it's over. What's it mean — that frozen look? Oh, poor little Nora, I understand. You can't believe I've forgiven you. But I have, Nora; I swear I have. I know that what you did, you did out of love for me.

NORA: That's true.

HELMER: You loved me the way a wife ought to love her husband. It's simply the means that you couldn't judge. But you think I love you any the less for not knowing how to handle your affairs? No, no — just lean on me; I'll guide you and teach you. I wouldn't be a man if this feminine helplessness didn't make you twice as attractive to me. You mustn't mind those sharp words I said — that was all in the first confusion of thinking my world had collapsed. I've forgiven you, Nora; I swear I've forgiven you.

NORA: My thanks for your forgiveness. (*She goes out through the door, right.*)

HELMER: No, wait — (*Peers in.*) What are you doing in there?

NORA (*inside*): Getting out of my costume.

HELMER (*by the open door*): Yes, do that. Try to calm yourself and collect your thoughts again, my frightened little songbird. You can rest easy now; I've got wide wings to shelter you with. (*Walking about close by the door.*) How snug and nice our home is, Nora. You're safe here; I'll keep you like a hunted dove I've rescued out of a hawk's claws. I'll bring peace to your poor, shuddering heart. Gradually it'll happen, Nora; you'll see. Tomorrow all this will look different to you; then everything will be as it was. I won't have to go on repeating I forgive you; you'll feel it for yourself. How can you imagine I'd ever conceivably want to disown you — or even blame you in any way? Ah, you don't know a man's heart, Nora. For a man there's something indescribably sweet and satisfying in knowing he's forgiven his wife — and forgiven her out of a full and open heart. It's as if she belongs to him in two ways now: In a sense he's given her fresh into the world again, and she's become his wife and his child as well. From now on that's what you'll be to me — you little, bewildered, helpless thing. Don't be afraid of anything, Nora; just open your heart to me, and I'll be conscience and will to you both — (*Nora enters in her regular clothes.*) What's this? Not in bed? You've changed your dress?

NORA: Yes, Torvald, I've changed my dress.

HELMER: But why now, so late?

NORA: Tonight I'm not sleeping.

HELMER: But Nora dear —

NORA (*looking at her watch*): It's still not so very late. Sit down, Torvald; we have a lot to talk over. (*She sits at one side of the table.*)

HELMER: Nora — what is this? That hard expression —

NORA: Sit down. This'll take some time. I have a lot to say.

HELMER (*sitting at the table directly opposite her*): You worry me, Nora. And I don't understand you.

NORA: No, that's exactly it. You don't understand me. And I've never understood you either — until tonight. No, don't interrupt. You can just listen to what I say. We're closing out accounts, Torvald.

HELMER: How do you mean that?

NORA (*after a short pause*): Doesn't anything strike you about our sitting here like this?

HELMER: What's that?

NORA: We've been married now eight years. Doesn't it occur to you that this is the first time we two, you and I, man and wife, have ever talked seriously together?

HELMER: What do you mean — seriously?

NORA: In eight whole years — longer even — right from our first acquaintance, we've never exchanged a serious word on any serious thing.

HELMER: You mean I should constantly go and involve you in problems you couldn't possibly help me with?

NORA: I'm not talking of problems. I'm saying that we've never sat down seriously together and tried to get to the bottom of anything.

HELMER: But dearest, what good would that ever do you?

NORA: That's the point right there: You've never understood me. I've been wronged greatly, Torvald — first by Papa, and then by you.

HELMER: What! By us — the two people who've loved you more than anyone else?

NORA (*shaking her head*): You never loved me. You've thought it fun to be in love with me, that's all.

HELMER: Nora, what a thing to say!

NORA: Yes, it's true now, Torvald. When I lived at home with Papa, he told me all his opinions, so I had the same ones too; or if they were different I hid them, since he wouldn't have cared for that. He used to call me his doll-child, and he played with me the way I played with my dolls. Then I came into your house —

HELMER: How can you speak of our marriage like that?

NORA (*unperturbed*): I mean, then I went from Papa's hands into yours. You arranged everything to your own taste, and so I got the same taste as you —

or I pretended to; I can't remember. I guess a little of both, first one, then the other. Now when I look back, it seems as if I'd lived here like a beggar — just from hand to mouth. I've lived by doing tricks for you, Torvald. But that's the way you wanted it. It's a great sin what you and Papa did to me. You're to blame that nothing's become of me.

HELMER: Nora, how unfair and ungrateful you are! Haven't you been happy here?

NORA: No, never. I thought so — but I never have.

HELMER: Not — not happy!

NORA: No, only lighthearted. And you've always been so kind to me. But our home's been nothing but a playpen. I've been your doll-wife here, just as at home I was Papa's doll-child. And in turn the children have been my dolls. I thought it was fun when you played with me, just as they thought it fun when I played with them. That's been our marriage, Torvald.

HELMER: There's some truth in what you're saying — under all the raving exaggeration. But it'll all be different after this. Playtime's over; now for the schooling.

NORA: Whose schooling — mine or the children's?

HELMER: Both yours and the children's, dearest.

NORA: Oh, Torvald, you're not the man to teach me to be a good wife to you.

HELMER: And you can say that?

NORA: And I — how am I equipped to bring up children?

HELMER: Nora!

NORA: Didn't you say a moment ago that that was no job to trust me with?

HELMER: In a flare of temper! Why fasten on that?

NORA: Yes, but you were so very right. I'm not up to the job. There's another job I have to do first. I have to try to educate myself. You can't help me with that. I've got to do it alone. And that's why I'm leaving you now.

HELMER (*jumping up*): What's that?

NORA: I have to stand completely alone, if I'm ever going to discover myself and the world out there. So I can't go on living with you.

HELMER: Nora, Nora!

NORA: I want to leave right away. Kristine should put me up for the night —

HELMER: You're insane! You've no right! I forbid you!

NORA: From here on, there's no use forbidding me anything. I'll take with me whatever is mine. I don't want a thing from you, either now or later.

HELMER: What kind of madness is this!

NORA: Tomorrow I'm going home — I mean, home where I came from. It'll be easier up there to find something to do.

HELMER: Oh, you blind, incompetent child!

NORA: I must learn to be competent, Torvald.

HELMER: Abandon your home, your husband, your children! And you're not even thinking what people will say.

NORA: I can't be concerned about that. I only know how essential this is.

HELMER: Oh, it's outrageous. So you'll run out like this on your most sacred vows.

NORA: What do you think are my most sacred vows?

HELMER: And I have to tell you that! Aren't they your duties to your husband and children?

NORA: I have other duties equally sacred.

HELMER: That isn't true. What duties are they?

NORA: Duties to myself.

HELMER: Before all else, you're a wife and a mother.

NORA: I don't believe in that anymore. I believe that before all else, I'm a human being, no less than you — or anyway, I ought to try to become one. I know the majority thinks you're right, Torvald, and plenty of books agree with you, too. But I can't go on believing what the majority says, or what's written in books. I have to think over these things myself and try to understand them.

HELMER: Why can't you understand your place in your own home? On a point like that, isn't there one everlasting guide you can turn to? Where's your religion?

NORA: Oh, Torvald, I'm really not sure what religion is.

HELMER: What — ?

NORA: I only know what the minister said when I was confirmed. He told me religion was this thing and that. When I get clear and away by myself, I'll go into that problem too. I'll see if what the minister said was right, or, in any case, if it's right for me.

HELMER: A young woman your age shouldn't talk like that. If religion can't move you, I can try to rouse your conscience. You do have some moral feeling? Or, tell me — has that gone too?

NORA: It's not easy to answer that, Torvald. I simply don't know. I'm all confused about these things. I just know I see them so differently from you. I find out for one thing, that the law's not at all what I'd thought — but I can't get it through my head that the law is fair. A woman hasn't a right to protect her dying father or save her husband's life! I can't believe that.

HELMER: You talk like a child. You don't know anything of the world you live in.

NORA: No, I don't. But now I'll begin to learn for myself. I'll try to discover who's right, the world or I.

HELMER: Nora, you're sick; you've got a fever. I almost think you're out of your head.

NORA: I've never felt more clearheaded and sure in my life.

HELMER: And — clearheaded and sure — you're leaving your husband and children?

NORA: Yes.

HELMER: Then there's only one possible reason.

NORA: What?

HELMER: You no longer love me.

NORA: No. That's exactly it.

HELMER: Nora! You can't be serious!

NORA: Oh, this is so hard, Torvald — you've been so kind to me always. But I can't help it. I don't love you anymore.

HELMER (*struggling for composure*): Are you also clearheaded and sure about that?

NORA: Yes, completely. That's why I can't go on staying here.

HELMER: Can you tell me what I did to lose your love?

NORA: Yes, I can tell you. It was this evening when the miraculous thing didn't come — then I knew you weren't the man I'd imagined.

HELMER: Be more explicit; I don't follow you.

NORA: I've waited now so patiently eight long years — for, my Lord, I know miracles don't come every day. Then this crisis broke over me, and such a certainty filled me: *Now* the miraculous event would occur. While Krogstad's letter was lying out there, I never for an instant dreamed that you could give in to his terms. I was so utterly sure you'd say to him: Go on, tell your tale to the whole wide world. And when he'd done that —

HELMER: Yes, what then? When I'd delivered my own wife into shame and disgrace — !

NORA: When he'd done that, I was so utterly sure that you'd step forward, take the blame on yourself and say: I am the guilty one.

HELMER: Nora — !

NORA: You're thinking I'd never accept such a sacrifice from you? No, of course not. But what good would my protests be against you? That was the miracle I was waiting for, in terror and hope. And to stave that off, I would have taken my life.

HELMER: I'd gladly work for you day and night, Nora — and take on pain and deprivation. But there's no one who gives up honor for love.

NORA: Millions of women have done just that.

HELMER: Oh, you think and talk like a silly child.

NORA: Perhaps. But you neither think nor talk like the man I could join myself to. When your big fright was over — and it wasn't from any threat against me, only for what might damage you — when all the danger was past, for you it was just as if nothing had happened. I was exactly the same, your little lark, your doll, that you'd have to handle with double care now that I'd turned out so brittle and frail. (*Gets up.*) Torvald — in that instant it dawned on me that for eight years I've been living here with a stranger, and that I'd even conceived three children — oh, I can't stand the thought of it! I could tear myself to bits.

HELMER (*heavily*): I see. There's a gulf that's opened between us — that's clear. Oh, but Nora, can't we bridge it somehow?

NORA: The way I am now, I'm no wife for you.

HELMER: I have the strength to make myself over.

NORA: Maybe — if your doll gets taken away.

HELMER: But to part! To part from you! No, Nora, no — I can't imagine it.

NORA (*going out, right*): All the more reason why it has to be. (*She reenters with her coat and a small overnight bag, which she puts on a chair by the table.*)

HELMER: Nora, Nora, not now! Wait till tomorrow.

NORA: I can't spend the night in a strange man's room.

HELMER: But couldn't we live here like brother and sister —

NORA: You know very well how long that would last. (*Throws her shawl about her.*) Good-bye, Torvald. I won't look in on the children. I know they're in better hands than mine. The way I am now, I'm no use to them.

HELMER: But someday, Nora — someday — ?

NORA: How can I tell? I haven't the least idea what'll become of me.

HELMER: But you're my wife, now and wherever you go.

NORA: Listen, Torvald — I've heard that when a wife deserts her husband's house just as I'm doing, then the law frees him from all responsibility. In any case, I'm freeing you from being responsible. Don't feel yourself bound, any more than I will. There has to be absolute freedom for us both. Here, take your ring back. Give me mine.

HELMER: That too?

NORA: That too.

HELMER: There it is.

NORA: Good. Well, now it's all over. I'm putting the keys here. The maids know all about keeping up the house — better than I do. Tomorrow, after I've left town, Kristine will stop by to pack up everything that's mine from home. I'd like those things shipped up to me.

HELMER: Over! All over! Nora, won't you ever think about me?

NORA: I'm sure I'll think of you often, and about the children and the house here.

HELMER: May I write you?

NORA: No — never. You're not to do that.

HELMER: Oh, but let me send you —

NORA: Nothing. Nothing.

HELMER: Or help you if you need it.

NORA: No. I accept nothing from strangers.

HELMER: Nora — can I never be more than a stranger to you?

NORA (*picking up the overnight bag*): Ah, Torvald — it would take the greatest miracle of all —

HELMER: Tell me the greatest miracle!

NORA: You and I both would have to transform ourselves to the point that — Oh, Torvald, I've stopped believing in miracles.

HELMER: But I'll believe. Tell me! Transform ourselves to the point that — ?

NORA: That our living together could be a true marriage. (*She goes out down the hall.*)

HELMER (*sinks down on a chair by the door, face buried in his hands*): Nora! Nora! (*Looking about and rising.*) Empty. She's gone. (*A sudden hope leaps in him.*) The greatest miracle — ?

(*From below, the sound of a door slamming shut.*)

Research Henrik Ibsen and *A Doll House* in depth with cultural documents and multimedia resources on *LiterActive*.

Arthur Miller 1915–2005

Death of a Salesman   [1949]
Certain Private Conversations in Two Acts and a Requiem

CHARACTERS

WILLY LOMAN	UNCLE BEN
LINDA	HOWARD WAGNER
BIFF	JENNY
HAPPY	STANLEY
BERNARD	MISS FORSYTHE
THE WOMAN	LETTA
CHARLEY	

The action takes place in Willy Loman's house and yard and in various places he visits in the New York and Boston of today [i.e., 1949].

(*Throughout the play, in the stage directions, left and right mean stage left and stage right.*)

ACT 1

(*A melody is heard, played upon a flute. It is small and fine, telling of grass and trees and the horizon. The curtain rises.*)

(*Before us is the Salesman's house. We are aware of towering, angular shapes behind it, surrounding it on all sides. Only the blue light of the sky falls upon the house and forestage; the surrounding area shows an angry glow of orange. As more light appears, we see a solid vault of apartment houses around the small, fragile-seeming home. An air of the dream clings to the place, a dream rising out of reality. The kitchen at center seems actual enough, for there is a kitchen table with three chairs, and a refrigerator. But no other fixtures are seen. At the back of the kitchen there is a draped entrance, which leads to the living room. To the right of the kitchen, on a level raised two feet, is a bedroom furnished only with a brass bedstead and a straight chair. On a shelf over the bed a silver athletic trophy stands. A window opens onto the apartment house at the side.*)

(*Behind the kitchen, on a level raised six and a half feet, is the boys' bedroom, at present barely visible. Two beds are dimly seen, and at the back of the room a dormer window. [This bedroom is above the unseen living room.] At the left a stairway curves up to it from the kitchen.*)

(*The entire setting is wholly or, in some places, partially transparent. The roofline of the house is one-dimensional; under and over it we see the apartment buildings. Before the house lies an apron, curving beyond the forestage into the orchestra. This forward area serves as the back yard as well as the locale of all Willy's imaginings and of his city scenes. Whenever the action is in the present the actors observe the imaginary wall-lines, entering the house only through its door at the left. But in the scenes of the past these boundaries are broken, and characters enter or leave a room by stepping "through" a wall onto the forestage.*)

(*From the right, Willy Loman, the Salesman, enters, carrying two large sample cases. The flute plays on. He hears but is not aware of it. He is past sixty years of age, dressed quietly. Even as he crosses the stage to the doorway of the house, his exhaustion is apparent. He unlocks the door, comes into the kitchen, and thankfully lets his burden down, feeling the soreness of his palms. A word-sigh escapes his lips — it might be "Oh, boy, oh, boy." He closes the door then carries his cases out into the living room, through the draped kitchen doorway.*)

(*Linda, his wife, has stirred in her bed at the right. She gets out and puts on a robe, listening. Most often jovial, she has developed an iron repression of her exceptions to Willy's behavior — she more than loves him, she admires him, as though his mercurial nature, his temper, his massive dreams and little cruelties, served her only as sharp reminders of the turbulent longings within him, longings which she shares but lacks the temperament to utter and follow to their end.*)

LINDA (*hearing Willy outside the bedroom, calls with some trepidation*): Willy!

WILLY: It's all right. I came back.

LINDA: Why? What happened? (*Slight pause.*) Did something happen, Willy?

WILLY: No, nothing happened.

LINDA: You didn't smash the car, did you?

WILLY (*with casual irritation*): I said nothing happened. Didn't you hear me?

LINDA: Don't you feel well?

WILLY: I'm tired to the death. (*The flute has faded away. He sits on the bed beside her, a little numb.*) I couldn't make it. I just couldn't make it, Linda.

LINDA (*very carefully, delicately*): Where were you all day? You look terrible.

WILLY: I got as far as a little above Yonkers. I stopped for a cup of coffee. Maybe it was the coffee.

LINDA: What?

WILLY (*after a pause*): I suddenly couldn't drive anymore. The car kept going off onto the shoulder, y'know?

LINDA (*helpfully*): Oh. Maybe it was the steering again. I don't think Angelo knows the Studebaker.

WILLY: No, it's me, it's me. Suddenly I realize I'm goin' sixty miles an hour and I don't remember the last five minutes. I'm — I can't seem to — keep my mind to it.

LINDA: Maybe it's your glasses. You never went for your new glasses.

WILLY: No, I see everything. I came back ten miles an hour. It took me nearly four hours from Yonkers.

LINDA (*resigned*): Well, you'll just have to take a rest, Willy, you can't continue this way.

WILLY: I just got back from Florida.

LINDA: But you didn't rest your mind. Your mind is overactive, and the mind is what counts, dear.

WILLY: I'll start out in the morning. Maybe I'll feel better in the morning. (*She is taking off his shoes.*) These goddam arch supports are killing me.

LINDA: Take an aspirin. Should I get you an aspirin? It'll soothe you.

WILLY (*with wonder*): I was driving along, you understand? And I was fine. I was even observing the scenery. You can imagine, me looking at scenery, on the road every week of my life. But it's so beautiful up there, Linda, the trees are so thick, and the sun is warm. I opened the windshield and just let the warm air bathe over me. And then all of a sudden I'm goin' off the road! I'm tellin' ya, I absolutely forgot I was driving. If I'd've gone the other way over the white line I might've killed somebody. So I went on again — and five minutes later I'm dreamin' again, and I nearly — (*He presses two fingers against his eyes.*) I have such thoughts, I have such strange thoughts.

LINDA: Willy, dear. Talk to them again. There's no reason why you can't work in New York.

WILLY: They don't need me in New York. I'm the New England man. I'm vital in New England.

LINDA: But you're sixty years old. They can't expect you to keep traveling every week.

WILLY: I'll have to send a wire to Portland. I'm supposed to see Brown and Morrison tomorrow morning at ten o'clock to show the line. Goddammit, I could sell them! (*He starts putting on his jacket.*)

LINDA (*taking the jacket from him*): Why don't you go down to the place tomorrow and tell Howard you've simply got to work in New York? You're too accommodating, dear.

WILLY: If old man Wagner was alive I'd a been in charge of New York now! That man was a prince, he was a masterful man. But that boy of his, that Howard, he don't appreciate. When I went north the first time, the Wagner Company didn't know where New England was!

LINDA: Why don't you tell those things to Howard, dear?

WILLY (*encouraged*): I will, I definitely will. Is there any cheese?

LINDA: I'll make you a sandwich.

WILLY: No, go to sleep. I'll take some milk. I'll be up right away. The boys in?

LINDA: They're sleeping. Happy took Biff on a date tonight.

WILLY (*interested*): That so?

LINDA: It was so nice to see them shaving together, one behind the other, in the bathroom. And going out together. You notice? The whole house smells of shaving lotion.

WILLY: Figure it out. Work a lifetime to pay off a house. You finally own it, and there's nobody to live in it.

LINDA: Well, dear, life is a casting off. It's always that way.

WILLY: No, no, some people — some people accomplish something. Did Biff say anything after I went this morning?

LINDA: You shouldn't have criticized him, Willy, especially after he just got off the train. You mustn't lose your temper with him.

WILLY: When the hell did I lose my temper? I simply asked him if he was making any money. Is that a criticism?

LINDA: But, dear, how could he make any money?

WILLY (*worried and angered*): There's such an undercurrent in him. He became a moody man. Did he apologize when I left this morning?

LINDA: He was crestfallen, Willy. You know how he admires you. I think if he finds himself, then you'll both be happier and not fight any more.

WILLY: How can he find himself on a farm? Is that a life? A farmhand? In the beginning, when he was young, I thought, well, a young man, it's good for him to tramp around, take a lot of different jobs. But it's more than ten years now and he has yet to make thirty-five dollars a week!

LINDA: He's finding himself, Willy.

WILLY: Not finding yourself at the age of thirty-four is a disgrace!

LINDA: Shh!

WILLY: The trouble is he's lazy, goddammit!

LINDA: Willy, please!

WILLY: Biff is a lazy bum!

LINDA: They're sleeping. Get something to eat. Go on down.

WILLY: Why did he come home? I would like to know what brought him home.

LINDA: I don't know. I think he's still lost, Willy. I think he's very lost.

WILLY: Biff Loman is lost. In the greatest country in the world a young man with such — personal attractiveness, gets lost. And such a hard worker. There's one thing about Biff — he's not lazy.

LINDA: Never.

WILLY (*with pity and resolve*): I'll see him in the morning; I'll have a nice talk with him. I'll get him a job selling. He could be big in no time. My God! Remember how they used to follow him around in high school? When he smiled at one of them their faces lit up. When he walked down the street . . . (*He loses himself in reminiscences.*)

LINDA (*trying to bring him out of it*): Willy, dear, I got a new kind of American-type cheese today. It's whipped.

WILLY: Why do you get American when I like Swiss?

LINDA: I just thought you'd like a change —

WILLY: I don't want a change! I want Swiss cheese. Why am I always being contradicted?

LINDA (*with a covering laugh*): I thought it would be a surprise.

WILLY: Why don't you open a window in here, for God's sake?

LINDA (*with infinite patience*): They're all open, dear.

WILLY: The way they boxed us in here. Bricks and windows, windows and bricks.

LINDA: We should've bought the land next door.

WILLY: The street is lined with cars. There's not a breath of fresh air in the neighborhood. The grass don't grow anymore, you can't raise a carrot in the back yard. They should've had a law against apartment houses. Remember those two beautiful elm trees out there? When I and Biff hung the swing between them?

LINDA: Yeah, like being a million miles from the city.

WILLY: They should've arrested the builder for cutting those down. They massacred the neighborhood. (*Lost.*) More and more I think of those days, Linda. This time of year it was lilac and wisteria. And then the peonies would come out, and the daffodils. What fragrance in this room!

LINDA: Well, after all, people had to move somewhere.

WILLY: No, there's more people now.

LINDA: I don't think there's more people. I think —

WILLY: There's more people! That's what's ruining this country! Population is getting out of control. The competition is maddening! Smell the stink from that apartment house! And another one on the other side . . . How can they whip cheese?

(On Willy's last line, Biff and Happy raise themselves up in their beds, listening.)

LINDA: Go down, try it. And be quiet.

WILLY *(turning to Linda, guiltily)*:   You're not worried about me, are you, sweetheart?

BIFF: What's the matter?

HAPPY: Listen!

LINDA: You've got too much on the ball to worry about.

WILLY: You're my foundation and my support, Linda.

LINDA: Just try to relax, dear. You make mountains out of molehills.

WILLY: I won't fight with him any more. If he wants to go back to Texas, let him go.

LINDA: He'll find his way.

WILLY: Sure. Certain men just don't get started till later in life. Like Thomas Edison, I think. Or B. F. Goodrich.° One of them was deaf. *(He starts for the bedroom doorway.)* I'll put my money on Biff.

LINDA: And Willy — if it's warm Sunday we'll drive in the country. And we'll open the windshield, and take lunch.

WILLY: No, the windshields don't open on the new cars.

LINDA: But you opened it today.

WILLY: Me? I didn't. *(He stops.)* Now isn't that peculiar! Isn't that a remarkable — *(He breaks off in amazement and fright as the flute is heard distantly.)*

LINDA: What, darling?

WILLY: That is the most remarkable thing.

LINDA: What, dear?

WILLY: I was thinking of the Chevvy. *(Slight pause.)* Nineteen twenty-eight . . . when I had that red Chevvy — *(Breaks off.)* That funny? I coulda sworn I was driving that Chevvy today.

LINDA: Well, that's nothing. Something must've reminded you.

WILLY: Remarkable. Ts. Remember those days? The way Biff used to simonize that car? The dealer refused to believe there was eighty thousand miles on it. *(He shakes his head.)* Heh! *(To Linda.)* Close your eyes, I'll be right up. *(He walks out of the bedroom.)*

HAPPY *(to Biff)*:   Jesus, maybe he smashed up the car again!

Edison, Goodrich: Thomas Alva Edison (1847–1931) was one of the greatest and most productive inventors of his time, especially of electronic equipment; he suffered from deafness for much of his life. Benjamin Franklin Goodrich (1841–1888) founded the B. F. Goodrich Company. Neither man was a late starter, though Edison did not thrive in conventional classroom settings.

LINDA (*calling after Willy*): Be careful on the stairs, dear! The cheese is on the middle shelf! (*She turns, goes over to the bed, takes his jacket, and goes out of the bedroom.*)

(*Light has risen on the boys' room. Unseen, Willy is heard talking to himself, "Eighty thousand miles," and a little laugh. Biff gets out of bed, comes downstage a bit, and stands attentively. Biff is two years older than his brother Happy, well built, but in these days bears a worn air and seems less self-assured. He has succeeded less, and his dreams are stronger and less acceptable than Happy's. Happy is tall, powerfully made. Sexuality is like a visible color on him, or a scent that many women have discovered. He, like his brother, is lost, but in a different way, for he has never allowed himself to turn his face toward defeat and is thus more confused and hard-skinned, although seemingly more content.*)

HAPPY (*getting out of bed*): He's going to get his license taken away if he keeps that up. I'm getting nervous about him, y'know, Biff?

BIFF: His eyes are going.

HAPPY: No, I've driven with him. He sees all right. He just doesn't keep his mind on it. I drove into the city with him last week. He stops at a green light and then it turns red and he goes. (*He laughs.*)

BIFF: Maybe he's color-blind.

HAPPY: Pop? Why he's got the finest eye for color in the business. You know that.

BIFF (*sitting down on his bed*): I'm going to sleep.

HAPPY: You're not still sour on Dad, are you, Biff?

BIFF: He's all right, I guess.

WILLY (*underneath them, in the living room*): Yes, sir, eighty thousand miles — eighty-two thousand!

BIFF: You smoking?

HAPPY (*holding out a pack of cigarettes*): Want one?

BIFF (*taking a cigarette*): I can never sleep when I smell it.

WILLY: What a simonizing job, heh!

HAPPY (*with deep sentiment*): Funny, Biff, y'know? Us sleeping in here again? The old beds. (*He pats his bed affectionately.*) All the talk that went across those two beds, huh? Our whole lives.

BIFF: Yeah. Lotta dreams and plans.

HAPPY (*with a deep and masculine laugh*): About five hundred women would like to know what was said in this room.

(*They share a soft laugh.*)

BIFF: Remember that big Betsy something — what the hell was her name — over on Bushwick Avenue?

HAPPY (*combing his hair*): With the collie dog!

BIFF: That's the one. I got you in there, remember?

HAPPY: Yeah, that was my first time — I think. Boy, there was a pig. (*They laugh, almost crudely.*) You taught me everything I know about women. Don't forget that.

BIFF: I bet you forgot how bashful you used to be. Especially with girls.

HAPPY: Oh, I still am, Biff.

BIFF: Oh, go on.

HAPPY: I just control it, that's all. I think I got less bashful and you got more so. What happened, Biff? Where's the old humor, the old confidence? (*He shakes Biff's knee. Biff gets up and moves restlessly about the room.*) What's the matter?

BIFF: Why does Dad mock me all the time?

HAPPY: He's not mocking you, he—

BIFF: Everything I say there's a twist of mockery on his face. I can't get near him.

HAPPY: He just wants you to make good, that's all. I wanted to talk to you about Dad for a long time, Biff. Something's—happening to him. He—talks to himself.

BIFF: I noticed that this morning. But he always mumbled.

HAPPY: But not so noticeable. It got so embarrassing I sent him to Florida. And you know something? Most of the time he's talking to you.

BIFF: What's he say about me?

HAPPY: I can't make it out.

BIFF: What's he say about me?

HAPPY: I think the fact that you're not settled, that you're still kind of up in the air . . .

BIFF: There's one or two other things depressing him, Happy.

HAPPY: What do you mean?

BIFF: Never mind. Just don't lay it all to me.

HAPPY: But I think if you just got started—I mean—is there any future for you out there?

BIFF: I tell ya, Hap, I don't know what the future is. I don't know—what I'm supposed to want.

HAPPY: What do you mean?

BIFF: Well, I spent six or seven years after high school trying to work myself up. Shipping clerk, salesman, business of one kind or another. And it's a measly manner of existence. To get on that subway on the hot mornings in summer. To devote your whole life to keeping stock, or making phone calls, or selling or buying. To suffer fifty weeks of the year for the sake of a two-week vacation, when all you really desire is to be outdoors, with your shirt off. And always to have to get ahead of the next fella. And still—that's how you build a future.

HAPPY: Well, you really enjoy it on a farm? Are you content out there?

BIFF (*with rising agitation*): Hap, I've had twenty or thirty different kinds of jobs since I left home before the war, and it always turns out the same. I just realized it lately. In Nebraska when I herded cattle, and the Dakotas, and Arizona, and now in Texas. It's why I came home now, I guess, because I realized it. This farm I work on, it's spring there now, see? And they've got about fifteen new colts. There's nothing more inspiring or—beautiful than the sight of a mare and a new colt. And it's cool there now, see? Texas is cool now, and it's spring. And whenever spring comes to where I am, I suddenly get the feeling, my God, I'm not gettin' anywhere! What the hell am I doing, playing around with horses, twenty-eight dollars a week! I'm thirty-four years old, I oughta be makin' my future. That's when I come running home. And now, I get here, and I don't know what to do with myself. (*After a pause.*) I've always made a point of not wasting my life, and every time I come back here I know that all I've done is to waste my life.

HAPPY: You're a poet, you know that, Biff? You're a — you're an idealist!

BIFF: No, I'm mixed up very bad. Maybe I oughta get married. Maybe I oughta get stuck into something. Maybe that's my trouble. I'm like a boy. I'm not married, I'm not in business, I just — I'm like a boy. Are you content, Hap? You're a success, aren't you? Are you content?

HAPPY: Hell, no!

BIFF: Why? You're making money, aren't you?

HAPPY (*moving about with energy, expressiveness*): All I can do now is wait for the merchandise manager to die. And suppose I get to be merchandise manager? He's a good friend of mine, and he just built a terrific estate on Long Island. And he lived there about two months and sold it, and now he's building another one. He can't enjoy it once it's finished. And I know that's just what I would do. I don't know what the hell I'm workin' for. Sometimes I sit in my apartment — all alone. And I think of the rent I'm paying. And it's crazy. But then, it's what I always wanted. My own apartment, a car, and plenty of women. And still, goddammit, I'm lonely.

BIFF (*with enthusiasm*): Listen, why don't you come out West with me?

HAPPY: You and I, heh?

BIFF: Sure, maybe we could buy a ranch. Raise cattle, use our muscles. Men built like we are should be working out in the open.

HAPPY (*avidly*): The Loman Brothers, heh?

BIFF (*with vast affection*): Sure, we'd be known all over the counties!

HAPPY (*enthralled*): That's what I dream about, Biff. Sometimes I want to just rip my clothes off in the middle of the store and outbox that goddam merchandise manager. I mean I can outbox, outrun and outlift anybody in that store, and I have to take orders from those common, petty sons-of-bitches till I can't stand it anymore.

BIFF: I'm tellin' you, kid, if you were with me I'd be happy out there.

HAPPY (*enthused*): See, Biff, everybody around me is so false that I'm constantly lowering my ideals . . .

BIFF: Baby, together we'd stand up for one another, we'd have someone to trust.

HAPPY: If I were around you —

BIFF: Hap, the trouble is we weren't brought up to grub for money. I don't know how to do it.

HAPPY: Neither can I!

BIFF: Then let's go!

HAPPY: The only thing is — what can you make out there?

BIFF: But look at your friend. Builds an estate and then hasn't the peace of mind to live in it.

HAPPY: Yeah, but when he walks into the store the waves part in front of him. That's fifty-two thousand dollars a year coming through the revolving door, and I got more in my pinky finger than he's got in his head.

BIFF: Yeah, but you just said —

HAPPY: I gotta show some of those pompous, self-important executives over there that Hap Loman can make the grade. I want to walk into the store the way he walks in. Then I'll go with you, Biff. We'll be together yet, I swear. But take those two we had tonight. Now weren't they gorgeous creatures?

BIFF: Yeah, yeah, most gorgeous I've had in years.

HAPPY: I get that any time I want, Biff. Whenever I feel disgusted. The only trouble is, it gets like bowling or something. I just keep knockin' them over and it doesn't mean anything. You still run around a lot?

BIFF: Naa. I'd like to find a girl — steady, somebody with substance.

HAPPY: That's what I long for.

BIFF: Go on! You'd never come home.

HAPPY: I would! Somebody with character, with resistance! Like Mom, y'know? You're gonna call me a bastard when I tell you this. That girl Charlotte I was with tonight is engaged to be married in five weeks. (*He tries on his new hat.*)

BIFF: No kiddin'!

HAPPY: Sure, the guy's in line for the vice-presidency of the store. I don't know what gets into me, maybe I just have an overdeveloped sense of competition or something, but I went and ruined her, and furthermore I can't get rid of her. And he's the third executive I've done that to. Isn't that a crummy characteristic? And to top it all, I go to their weddings! (*Indignantly, but laughing.*) Like I'm not supposed to take bribes. Manufacturers offer me a hundred-dollar bill now and then to throw an order their way. You know how honest I am, but it's like this girl, see. I hate myself for it. Because I don't want the girl, and, still, I take it and — I love it!

BIFF: Let's go to sleep.

HAPPY: I guess we didn't settle anything, heh?

BIFF: I just got one idea that I think I'm going to try.

HAPPY: What's that?

BIFF: Remember Bill Oliver?

HAPPY: Sure, Oliver is very big now. You want to work for him again?

BIFF: No, but when I quit he said something to me. He put his arm on my shoulder, and he said, "Biff, if you ever need anything, come to me."

HAPPY: I remember that. That sounds good.

BIFF: I think I'll go to see him. If I could get ten thousand or even seven or eight thousand dollars I could buy a beautiful ranch.

HAPPY: I bet he'd back you. 'Cause he thought highly of you, Biff. I mean, they all do. You're well liked, Biff. That's why I say to come back here, and we both have the apartment. And I'm tellin' you, Biff, any babe you want . . .

BIFF: No, with a ranch I could do the work I like and still be something. I just wonder though. I wonder if Oliver still thinks I stole that carton of basketballs.

HAPPY: Oh, he probably forgot that long ago. It's almost ten years. You're too sensitive. Anyway, he didn't really fire you.

BIFF: Well, I think he was going to. I think that's why I quit. I was never sure whether he knew or not. I know he thought the world of me, though. I was the only one he'd let lock up the place.

WILLY (*below*): You gonna wash the engine, Biff?

HAPPY: Shh!

(*Biff looks at Happy, who is gazing down, listening. Willy is mumbling in the parlor.*)

HAPPY: You hear that?

(*They listen. Willy laughs warmly.*)

BIFF (*growing angry*): Doesn't he know Mom can hear that?

WILLY: Don't get your sweater dirty, Biff!

(*A look of pain crosses Biff's face.*)

HAPPY: Isn't that terrible? Don't leave again, will you? You'll find a job here. You gotta stick around. I don't know what to do about him, it's getting embarrassing.

WILLY: What a simonizing job!

BIFF: Mom's hearing that!

WILLY: No kiddin', Biff, you got a date? Wonderful!

HAPPY: Go on to sleep. But talk to him in the morning, will you?

BIFF (*reluctantly getting into bed*): With her in the house. Brother!

HAPPY (*getting into bed*): I wish you'd have a good talk with him.

(*The light on their room begins to fade.*)

BIFF (*to himself in bed*): That selfish, stupid . . .

HAPPY: Sh . . . Sleep, Biff.

(*Their light is out. Well before they have finished speaking, Willy's form is dimly seen below in the darkened kitchen. He opens the refrigerator, searches in there, and takes out a bottle of milk. The apartment houses are fading out, and the entire house and surroundings become covered with leaves. Music insinuates itself as the leaves appear.*)

WILLY: Just wanna be careful with those girls, Biff, that's all. Don't make any promises. No promises of any kind. Because a girl, y'know, they always believe what you tell 'em, and you're very young, Biff, you're too young to be talking seriously to girls.

(*Light rises on the kitchen. Willy, talking, shuts the refrigerator door and comes downstage to the kitchen table. He pours milk into a glass. He is totally immersed in himself, smiling faintly.*)

WILLY: Too young entirely, Biff. You want to watch your schooling first. Then when you're all set, there'll be plenty of girls for a boy like you. (*He smiles broadly at a kitchen chair.*) That so? The girls pay for you? (*He laughs.*) Boy, you must really be makin' a hit.

(Willy is gradually addressing — physically — a point offstage, speaking through the wall of the kitchen, and his voice has been rising in volume to that of a normal conversation.)

WILLY: I been wondering why you polish the car so careful. Ha! Don't leave the hubcaps, boys. Get the chamois to the hubcaps. Happy, use newspaper on the windows, it's the easiest thing. Show him how to do it, Biff! You see, Happy? Pad it up, use it like a pad. That's it, that's it, good work. You're doin' all right, Hap. *(He pauses, then nods in approbation for a few seconds, then looks upward.)* Biff, first thing we gotta do when we get time is clip that big branch over the house. Afraid it's gonna fall in a storm and hit the roof. Tell you what. We get a rope and sling her around, and then we climb up there with a couple of saws and take her down. Soon as you finish the car, boys, I wanna see ye. I got a surprise for you, boys.

BIFF *(offstage)*: Whatta ya got, Dad?

WILLY: No, you finish first. Never leave a job till you're finished — remember that. *(Looking toward the "big trees.")* Biff, up in Albany I saw a beautiful hammock. I think I'll buy it next trip, and we'll hang it right between those two elms. Wouldn't that be something? Just swingin' there under those branches. Boy, that would be . . .

(Young Biff and Young Happy appear from the direction Willy was addressing. Happy carries rags and a pail of water. Biff, wearing a sweater with a block "S," carries a football.)

BIFF *(pointing in the direction of the car offstage)*: How's that, Pop, professional?

WILLY: Terrific. Terrific job, boys. Good work, Biff.

HAPPY: Where's the surprise, Pop?

WILLY: In the back seat of the car.

HAPPY: Boy! *(He runs off.)*

BIFF: What is it, Dad? Tell me, what'd you buy?

WILLY *(laughing, cuffs him)*: Never mind, something I want you to have.

BIFF *(turns and starts off)*: What is it, Hap?

HAPPY *(offstage)*: It's a punching bag!

BIFF: Oh, Pop!

WILLY: It's got Gene Tunney's signature on it!

(Happy runs onstage with a punching bag.)

BIFF: Gee, how'd you know we wanted a punching bag?

WILLY: Well, it's the finest thing for the timing.

HAPPY *(lies down on his back and pedals with his feet)*: I'm losing weight, you notice, Pop?

WILLY *(to Happy)*: Jumping rope is good too.

BIFF: Did you see the new football I got?

WILLY *(examining the ball)*: Where'd you get a new ball?

BIFF: The coach told me to practice my passing.

WILLY: That so? And he gave you the ball, heh?

BIFF: Well, I borrowed it from the locker room. (*He laughs confidentially.*)

WILLY (*laughing with him at the theft*): I want you to return that.

HAPPY: I told you he wouldn't like it!

BIFF (*angrily*): Well, I'm bringing it back!

WILLY (*stopping the incipient argument, to Happy*): Sure, he's gotta practice with a regulation ball, doesn't he? (*To Biff.*) Coach'll probably congratulate you on your initiative!

BIFF: Oh, he keeps congratulating my initiative all the time, Pop.

WILLY: That's because he likes you. If somebody else took that ball there'd be an uproar. So what's the report, boys, what's the report?

BIFF: Where'd you go this time, Dad? Gee we were lonesome for you.

WILLY (*pleased, puts an arm around each boy and they come down to the apron*): Lonesome, heh?

BIFF: Missed you every minute.

WILLY: Don't say? Tell you a secret, boys. Don't breathe it to a soul. Someday I'll have my own business, and I'll never have to leave home anymore.

HAPPY: Like Uncle Charley, heh?

WILLY: Bigger than Uncle Charley! Because Charley is not — liked. He's liked, but he's not — well liked.

BIFF: Where'd you go this time, Dad?

WILLY: Well, I got on the road, and I went north to Providence. Met the Mayor.

BIFF: The Mayor of Providence!

WILLY: He was sitting in the hotel lobby.

BIFF: What'd he say?

WILLY: He said, "Morning!" And I said, "You got a fine city here, Mayor." And then he had coffee with me. And then I went to Waterbury. Waterbury is a fine city. Big clock city, the famous Waterbury clock. Sold a nice bill there. And then Boston — Boston is the cradle of the Revolution. A fine city. And a couple of other towns in Mass., and on to Portland and Bangor and straight home!

BIFF: Gee, I'd love to go with you sometime, Dad.

WILLY: Soon as summer comes.

HAPPY: Promise?

WILLY: You and Hap and I, and I'll show you all the towns. America is full of beautiful towns and fine, upstanding people. And they know me, boys, they know me up and down New England. The finest people. And when I bring you fellas up, there'll be open sesame for all of us, 'cause one thing, boys: I have friends. I can park my car in any street in New England, and the cops protect it like their own. This summer, heh?

BIFF AND HAPPY (*together*): Yeah! You bet!

WILLY: We'll take our bathing suits.

HAPPY: We'll carry your bags, Pop!

WILLY: Oh, won't that be something! Me comin' into the Boston stores with you boys carryin' my bags. What a sensation!

(*Biff is prancing around, practicing passing the ball.*)

WILLY: You nervous, Biff, about the game?

BIFF: Not if you're gonna be there.

WILLY: What do they say about you in school, now that they made you captain?

HAPPY: There's a crowd of girls behind him every time the classes change.

BIFF (*taking Willy's hand*): This Saturday, Pop, this Saturday—just for you, I'm going to break through for a touchdown.

HAPPY: You're supposed to pass.

BIFF: I'm takin' one play for Pop. You watch me, Pop, and when I take off my helmet, that means I'm breakin' out. Then you watch me crash through that line!

WILLY (*kisses Biff*): Oh, wait'll I tell this in Boston!

(*Bernard enters in knickers. He is younger than Biff, earnest and loyal, a worried boy.*)

BERNARD: Biff, where are you? You're supposed to study with me today.

WILLY: Hey, looka Bernard. What're you lookin' so anemic about, Bernard?

BERNARD: He's gotta study, Uncle Willy. He's got Regents next week.

HAPPY (*tauntingly, spinning Bernard around*): Let's box, Bernard!

BERNARD: Biff! (*He gets away from Happy.*) Listen, Biff, I heard Mr. Birnbaum say that if you don't start studyin' math he's gonna flunk you, and you won't graduate. I heard him!

WILLY: You better study with him, Biff. Go ahead now.

BERNARD: I heard him!

BIFF: Oh, Pop, you didn't see my sneakers! (*He holds up a foot for Willy to look at.*)

WILLY: Hey, that's a beautiful job of printing!

BERNARD (*wiping his glasses*): Just because he printed University of Virginia on his sneakers doesn't mean they've got to graduate him, Uncle Willy!

WILLY (*angrily*): What're you talking about? With scholarships to three universities they're gonna flunk him?

BERNARD: But I heard Mr. Birnbaum say—

WILLY: Don't be a pest, Bernard! (*To his boys.*) What an anemic!

BERNARD: Okay, I'm waiting for you in my house, Biff.

(*Bernard goes off. The Lomans laugh.*)

WILLY: Bernard is not well liked, is he?

BIFF: He's liked, but he's not well liked.

HAPPY: That's right, Pop.

WILLY: That's just what I mean. Bernard can get the best marks in school, y'understand, but when he gets out in the business world, y'understand, you are going to be five times ahead of him. That's why I thank Almighty God you're both built like Adonises. Because the man who makes an appearance in the business world, the man who creates personal interest, is the man who gets ahead. Be liked and you will never want. You take me, for instance. I never have to wait in line to see a buyer. "Willy Loman is here!" That's all they have to know, and I go right through.

BIFF: Did you knock them dead, Pop?

WILLY: Knocked 'em cold in Providence, slaughtered 'em in Boston.

HAPPY (*on his back, pedaling again*): I'm losing weight, you notice, Pop?

(*Linda enters as of old, a ribbon in her hair, carrying a basket of washing.*)

LINDA (*with youthful energy*): Hello, dear!

WILLY: Sweetheart!

LINDA: How'd the Chevvy run?

WILLY: Chevrolet, Linda, is the greatest car ever built. (*To the boys.*) Since when do you let your mother carry wash up the stairs?

BIFF: Grab hold there, boy!

HAPPY: Where to, Mom?

LINDA: Hang them up on the line. And you better go down to your friends, Biff. The cellar is full of boys. They don't know what to do with themselves.

BIFF: Ah, when Pop comes home they can wait!

WILLY (*laughs appreciatively*): You better go down and tell them what to do, Biff.

BIFF: I think I'll have them sweep out the furnace room.

WILLY: Good work, Biff.

BIFF (*goes through wall-line of kitchen to doorway at back and calls down*): Fellas! Everybody sweep out the furnace room! I'll be right down!

VOICES: All right! Okay, Biff.

BIFF: George and Sam and Frank, come out back! We're hangin' up the wash! Come on, Hap, on the double! (*He and Happy carry out the basket.*)

LINDA: The way they obey him!

WILLY: Well, that's training, the training. I'm tellin' you, I was sellin' thousands and thousands, but I had to come home.

LINDA: Oh, the whole block'll be at that game. Did you sell anything?

WILLY: I did five hundred gross in Providence and seven hundred gross in Boston.

LINDA: No! Wait a minute, I've got a pencil. (*She pulls pencil and paper out of her apron pocket.*) That makes your commission . . . Two hundred — my God! Two hundred and twelve dollars!

WILLY: Well, I didn't figure it yet, but . . .

LINDA: How much did you do?

WILLY: Well, I — I did — about a hundred and eighty gross in Providence. Well, no — it came to — roughly two hundred gross on the whole trip.

LINDA (*without hesitation*): Two hundred gross. That's . . . (*She figures.*)

WILLY: The trouble was that three of the stores were half-closed for inventory in Boston. Otherwise I woulda broke records.

LINDA: Well, it makes seventy dollars and some pennies. That's very good.

WILLY: What do we owe?

LINDA: Well, on the first there's sixteen dollars on the refrigerator —

WILLY: Why sixteen?

LINDA: Well, the fan belt broke, so it was a dollar eighty.

WILLY: But it's brand new.

LINDA: Well, the man said that's the way it is. Till they work themselves in, y'know.

(*They move through the wall-line into the kitchen.*)

WILLY: I hope we didn't get stuck on that machine.

LINDA: They got the biggest ads of any of them!

WILLY: I know, it's a fine machine. What else?

LINDA: Well, there's nine-sixty for the washing machine. And for the vacuum cleaner there's three and a half due on the fifteenth. Then the roof, you got twenty-one dollars remaining.

WILLY: It don't leak, does it?

LINDA: No, they did a wonderful job. Then you owe Frank for the carburetor.

WILLY: I'm not going to pay that man! That goddam Chevrolet, they ought to prohibit the manufacture of that car!

LINDA: Well, you owe him three and a half. And odds and ends, comes to around a hundred and twenty dollars by the fifteenth.

WILLY: A hundred and twenty dollars! My God, if business don't pick up I don't know what I'm gonna do!

LINDA: Well, next week you'll do better.

WILLY: Oh, I'll knock 'em dead next week. I'll go to Hartford. I'm very well liked in Hartford. You know, the trouble is, Linda, people don't seem to take to me.

(*They move onto the forestage.*)

LINDA: Oh, don't be foolish.

WILLY: I know it when I walk in. They seem to laugh at me.

LINDA: Why? Why would they laugh at you? Don't talk that way, Willy.

(*Willy moves to the edge of the stage. Linda goes into the kitchen and starts to darn stockings.*)

WILLY: I don't know the reason for it, but they just pass me by. I'm not noticed.

LINDA: But you're doing wonderful, dear. You're making seventy to a hundred dollars a week.

WILLY: But I gotta be at it ten, twelve hours a day. Other men—I don't know—they do it easier. I don't know why—I can't stop myself—I talk too much. A man oughta come in with a few words. One thing about Charley. He's a man of few words, and they respect him.

LINDA: You don't talk too much, you're just lively.

WILLY (*smiling*): Well, I figure, what the hell, life is short, a couple of jokes. (*To himself.*) I joke too much! (*The smile goes.*)

LINDA: Why? You're—

WILLY: I'm fat. I'm very—foolish to look at, Linda. I didn't tell you, but Christmas time I happened to be calling on F. H. Stewarts, and a salesman I know, as I was going in to see the buyer I heard him say something about—walrus. And I—I cracked him right across the face. I won't take that. I simply will not take that. But they do laugh at me. I know that.

LINDA: Darling . . .

WILLY: I gotta overcome it. I know I gotta overcome it. I'm not dressing to advantage, maybe.

LINDA: Willy, darling, you're the handsomest man in the world —

WILLY: Oh, no, Linda.

LINDA: To me you are. (*Slight pause.*) The handsomest.

(*From the darkness is heard the laughter of a woman. Willy doesn't turn to it, but it continues through Linda's lines.*)

LINDA: And the boys, Willy. Few men are idolized by their children the way you are.

(*Music is heard as behind a scrim, to the left of the house, The Woman, dimly seen, is dressing.*)

WILLY (*with great feeling*): You're the best there is, Linda, you're a pal, you know that? On the road — on the road I want to grab you sometimes and just kiss the life outa you.

(*The laughter is loud now, and he moves into a brightening area at the left, where The Woman has come from behind the scrim and is standing, putting on her hat, looking into a "mirror" and laughing.*)

WILLY: 'Cause I get so lonely — especially when business is bad and there's nobody to talk to. I get the feeling that I'll never sell anything again, that I won't make a living for you, or a business, a business for the boys. (*He talks through The Woman's subsiding laughter; The Woman primps at the "mirror."*) There's so much I want to make for —

THE WOMAN: Me? You didn't make me, Willy. I picked you.

WILLY (*pleased*): You picked me?

THE WOMAN (*who is quite proper-looking, Willy's age*): I did. I've been sitting at that desk watching all the salesmen go by, day in, day out. But you've got such a sense of humor, and we do have such a good time together, don't we?

WILLY: Sure, sure. (*He takes her in his arms.*) Why do you have to go now?

THE WOMAN: It's two o'clock . . .

WILLY: No, come on in! (*He pulls her.*)

THE WOMAN: . . . my sisters'll be scandalized. When'll you be back?

WILLY: Oh, two weeks about. Will you come up again?

THE WOMAN: Sure thing. You do make me laugh. It's good for me. (*She squeezes his arm, kisses him.*) And I think you're a wonderful man.

WILLY: You picked me, heh?

THE WOMAN: Sure. Because you're so sweet. And such a kidder.

WILLY: Well, I'll see you next time I'm in Boston.

THE WOMAN: I'll put you right through to the buyers.

WILLY (*slapping her bottom*): Right. Well, bottoms up!

THE WOMAN (*slaps him gently and laughs*): You just kill me, Willy. (*He suddenly grabs her and kisses her roughly.*) You kill me. And thanks for the stockings. I love a lot of stockings. Well, good night.

WILLY: Good night. And keep your pores open!

THE WOMAN: Oh, Willy!

(*The Woman bursts out laughing, and Linda's laughter blends in. The Woman disappears into the dark. Now the area at the kitchen table brightens. Linda is sitting where she was at the kitchen table, but now is mending a pair of her silk stockings.*)

LINDA: You are, Willy. The handsomest man. You've got no reason to feel that—

WILLY (*coming out of The Woman's dimming area and going over to Linda*): I'll make it all up to you, Linda, I'll—

LINDA: There's nothing to make up, dear. You're doing fine, better than—

WILLY (*noticing her mending*): What's that?

LINDA: Just mending my stockings. They're so expensive—

WILLY (*angrily, taking them from her*): I won't have you mending stockings in this house! Now throw them out!

(*Linda puts the stockings in her pocket.*)

BERNARD (*entering on the run*): Where is he? If he doesn't study!

WILLY (*moving to the forestage, with great agitation*): You'll give him the answers!

BERNARD: I do, but I can't on a Regents! That's a state exam! They're liable to arrest me!

WILLY: Where is he? I'll whip him, I'll whip him!

LINDA: And he'd better give back that football, Willy, it's not nice.

WILLY: Biff! Where is he? Why is he taking everything?

LINDA: He's too rough with the girls, Willy. All the mothers are afraid of him!

WILLY: I'll whip him!

BERNARD: He's driving the car without a license!

(*The Woman's laugh is heard.*)

WILLY: Shut up!

LINDA: All the mothers—

WILLY: Shut up!

BERNARD (*backing quietly away and out*): Mr. Birnbaum says he's stuck up.

WILLY: Get outa here!

BERNARD: If he doesn't buckle down he'll flunk math! (*He goes off.*)

LINDA: He's right, Willy, you've gotta—

WILLY (*exploding at her*): There's nothing the matter with him! You want him to be a worm like Bernard? He's got spirit, personality . . .

(*As he speaks, Linda, almost in tears, exits into the living room. Willy is alone in the kitchen, wilting and staring. The leaves are gone. It is night again, and the apartment houses look down from behind.*)

WILLY: Loaded with it. Loaded! What is he stealing? He's giving it back, isn't he? Why is he stealing? What did I tell him? I never in my life told him anything but decent things.

(*Happy in pajamas has come down the stairs; Willy suddenly becomes aware of Happy's presence.*)

HAPPY: Let's go now, come on.

WILLY (*sitting down at the kitchen table*): Huh! Why did she have to wax the floors herself? Everytime she waxes the floors she keels over. She knows that!

HAPPY: Shh! Take it easy. What brought you back tonight?

WILLY: I got an awful scare. Nearly hit a kid in Yonkers. God! Why didn't I go to Alaska with my brother Ben that time! Ben! That man was a genius, that man was success incarnate! What a mistake! He begged me to go.

HAPPY: Well, there's no use in —

WILLY: You guys! There was a man started with the clothes on his back and ended up with diamond mines!

HAPPY: Boy, someday I'd like to know how he did it.

WILLY: What's the mystery? The man knew what he wanted and went out and got it! Walked into a jungle, and comes out, the age of twenty-one, and he's rich! The world is an oyster, but you don't crack it open on a mattress!

HAPPY: Pop, I told you I'm gonna retire you for life.

WILLY: You'll retire me for life on seventy goddam dollars a week? And your women and your car and your apartment, and you'll retire me for life! Christ's sake, I couldn't get past Yonkers today! Where are you guys, where are you? The woods are burning! I can't drive a car!

(*Charley has appeared in the doorway. He is a large man, slow of speech, laconic, immovable. In all he says, despite what he says, there is pity, and, now, trepidation. He has a robe over pajamas, slippers on his feet. He enters the kitchen.*)

CHARLEY: Everything all right?

HAPPY: Yeah, Charley, everything's . . .

WILLY: What's the matter?

CHARLEY: I heard some noise. I thought something happened. Can't we do something about the walls? You sneeze in here, and in my house hats blow off.

HAPPY: Let's go to bed, Dad. Come on.

(*Charley signals to Happy to go.*)

WILLY: You go ahead, I'm not tired at the moment.

HAPPY (*to Willy*): Take it easy, huh? (*He exits.*)

WILLY: What're you doin' up?

CHARLEY (*sitting down at the kitchen table opposite Willy*): Couldn't sleep good. I had a heartburn.

WILLY: Well, you don't know how to eat.

CHARLEY: I eat with my mouth.

WILLY: No, you're ignorant. You gotta know about vitamins and things like that.

CHARLEY: Come on, let's shoot. Tire you out a little.

WILLY (*hesitantly*): All right. You got cards?

CHARLEY (*taking a deck from his pocket*): Yeah, I got them. Someplace. What is it with those vitamins?

WILLY (*dealing*): They build up your bones. Chemistry.

CHARLEY: Yeah, but there's no bones in a heartburn.

WILLY: What are you talkin' about? Do you know the first thing about it?

CHARLEY: Don't get insulted.

WILLY: Don't talk about something you don't know anything about.

(*They are playing. Pause.*)

CHARLEY: What're you doin' home?

WILLY: A little trouble with the car.

CHARLEY: Oh. (*Pause.*) I'd like to take a trip to California.

WILLY: Don't say.

CHARLEY: You want a job?

WILLY: I got a job, I told you that. (*After a slight pause.*) What the hell are you offering me a job for?

CHARLEY: Don't get insulted.

WILLY: Don't insult me.

CHARLEY: I don't see no sense in it. You don't have to go on this way.

WILLY: I got a good job. (*Slight pause.*) What do you keep comin' in here for?

CHARLEY: You want me to go?

WILLY (*after a pause, withering*): I can't understand it. He's going back to Texas again. What the hell is that?

CHARLEY: Let him go.

WILLY: I got nothin' to give him, Charley, I'm clean, I'm clean.

CHARLEY: He won't starve. None a them starve. Forget about him.

WILLY: Then what have I got to remember?

CHARLEY: You take it too hard. To hell with it. When a deposit bottle is broken you don't get your nickel back.

WILLY: That's easy enough for you to say.

CHARLEY: That ain't easy for me to say.

WILLY: Did you see the ceiling I put up in the living room?

CHARLEY: Yeah, that's a piece of work. To put up a ceiling is a mystery to me. How do you do it?

WILLY: What's the difference?

CHARLEY: Well, talk about it.

WILLY: You gonna put up a ceiling?

CHARLEY: How could I put up a ceiling?

WILLY: Then what the hell are you bothering me for?

CHARLEY: You're insulted again.

WILLY: A man who can't handle tools is not a man. You're disgusting.

CHARLEY: Don't call me disgusting, Willy.

(*Uncle Ben, carrying a valise and an umbrella, enters the forestage from around the right corner of the house. He is a stolid man, in his sixties, with a mustache and an authoritative air. He is utterly certain of his destiny, and there is an aura of far places about him. He enters exactly as Willy speaks.*)

WILLY: I'm getting awfully tired, Ben.

(*Ben's music is heard. Ben looks around at everything.*)

CHARLEY: Good, keep playing; you'll sleep better. Did you call me Ben?

(*Ben looks at his watch.*)

WILLY: That's funny. For a second there you reminded me of my brother Ben.

BEN: I only have a few minutes. (*He strolls, inspecting the place. Willy and Charley continue playing.*)

CHARLEY: You never heard from him again, heh? Since that time?

WILLY: Didn't Linda tell you? Couple of weeks ago we got a letter from his wife in Africa. He died.

CHARLEY: That so.

BEN (*chuckling*): So this is Brooklyn, eh?

CHARLEY: Maybe you're in for some of his money.

WILLY: Naa, he had seven sons. There's just one opportunity I had with that man . . .

BEN: I must make a train, William. There are several properties I'm looking at in Alaska.

WILLY: Sure, sure! If I'd gone with him to Alaska that time, everything would've been totally different.

CHARLEY: Go on, you'd froze to death up there.

WILLY: What're you talking about?

BEN: Opportunity is tremendous in Alaska, William. Surprised you're not up there.

WILLY: Sure, tremendous.

CHARLEY: Heh?

WILLY: There was the only man I ever met who knew the answers.

CHARLEY: Who?

BEN: How are you all?

WILLY (*taking a pot, smiling*): Fine, fine.

CHARLEY: Pretty sharp tonight.

BEN: Is Mother living with you?

WILLY: No, she died a long time ago.

CHARLEY: Who?

BEN: That's too bad. Fine specimen of a lady, Mother.

WILLY (*to Charley*): Heh?

BEN: I'd hoped to see the old girl.

CHARLEY: Who died?

BEN: Heard anything from Father, have you?

WILLY (*unnerved*): What do you mean, who died?

CHARLEY (*taking a pot*): What're you talkin' about?

BEN (*looking at his watch*): William, it's half-past eight!

WILLY (*as though to dispel his confusion he angrily stops Charley's hand*): That's my build!

CHARLEY: I put the ace —

WILLY: If you don't know how to play the game I'm not gonna throw my money away on you!

CHARLEY (*rising*): It was my ace, for God's sake!

WILLY: I'm through, I'm through!

BEN: When did Mother die?

WILLY: Long ago. Since the beginning you never knew how to play cards.

CHARLEY (*picks up the cards and goes to the door*): All right! Next time I'll bring a deck with five aces.

WILLY: I don't play that kind of game!

CHARLEY (*turning to him*): You ought to be ashamed of yourself!

WILLY: Yeah?

CHARLEY: Yeah! (*He goes out.*)

WILLY (*slamming the door after him*): Ignoramus!

BEN (*as Willy comes toward him through the wall-line of the kitchen*): So you're William.

WILLY (*shaking Ben's hand*): Ben! I've been waiting for you so long! What's the answer? How did you do it?

BEN: Oh, there's a story in that.

(*Linda enters the forestage, as of old, carrying the wash basket.*)

LINDA: Is this Ben?

BEN (*gallantly*): How do you do, my dear.

LINDA: Where've you been all these years? Willy's always wondered why you —

WILLY (*pulling Ben away from her impatiently*): Where is Dad? Didn't you follow him? How did you get started?

BEN: Well, I don't know how much you remember.

WILLY: Well, I was just a baby, of course, only three or four years old —

BEN: Three years and eleven months.

WILLY: What a memory, Ben!

BEN: I have many enterprises, William, and I have never kept books.

WILLY: I remember I was sitting under the wagon in — was it Nebraska?

BEN: It was South Dakota, and I gave you a bunch of wild flowers.

WILLY: I remember you walking away down some open road.

BEN (*laughing*): I was going to find Father in Alaska.

WILLY: Where is he?

BEN: At that age I had a very faulty view of geography, William. I discovered after a few days that I was heading due south, so instead of Alaska, I ended up in Africa.

LINDA: Africa!

WILLY: The Gold Coast!

BEN: Principally diamond mines.

LINDA: Diamond mines!

BEN: Yes, my dear. But I've only a few minutes —

WILLY: No! Boys! Boys! (*Young Biff and Happy appear.*) Listen to this. This is your Uncle Ben, a great man! Tell my boys, Ben!

BEN: Why, boys, when I was seventeen I walked into the jungle, and when I was twenty-one I walked out. (*He laughs.*) And by God I was rich.

WILLY (*to the boys*): You see what I been talking about? The greatest things can happen!

BEN (*glancing at his watch*): I have an appointment in Ketchikan Tuesday week.

WILLY: No, Ben! Please tell about Dad. I want my boys to hear. I want them to know the kind of stock they spring from. All I remember is a man with a big beard, and I was in Mamma's lap, sitting around a fire, and some kind of high music.

BEN: His flute. He played the flute.

WILLY: Sure, the flute, that's right!

(*New music is heard, a high, rollicking tune.*)

BEN: Father was a very great and a very wild-hearted man. We would start in Boston, and he'd toss the whole family into the wagon, and then he'd drive the team right across the country; through Ohio, and Indiana, Michigan, Illinois, and all the Western states. And we'd stop in the towns and sell the flutes that he'd made on the way. Great inventor Father. With one gadget he made more in a week than a man like you could make in a lifetime.

WILLY: That's just the way I'm bringing them up, Ben — rugged, well liked, all-around.

BEN: Yeah? (*To Biff.*) Hit that, boy — hard as you can. (*He pounds his stomach.*)

BIFF: Oh, no, sir!

BEN (*taking boxing stance*): Come on, get to me! (*He laughs.*)

WILLY: Go to it, Biff! Go ahead, show him!

BIFF: Okay! (*He cocks his fists and starts in.*)

LINDA (*to Willy*): Why must he fight, dear?

BEN (*sparring with Biff*): Good boy! Good boy!

WILLY: How's that, Ben, heh?

HAPPY: Give him the left, Biff!

LINDA: Why are you fighting?

BEN: Good boy! (*Suddenly comes in, trips Biff, and stands over him, the point of his umbrella poised over Biff's eye.*)

LINDA: Look out, Biff!

BIFF: Gee!

BEN (*patting Biff's knee*): Never fight fair with a stranger, boy. You'll never get out of the jungle that way. (*Taking Linda's hand and bowing.*) It was an honor and a pleasure to meet you, Linda.

LINDA (*withdrawing her hand coldly, frightened*): Have a nice — trip.

BEN (*to Willy*): And good luck with your — what do you do?

WILLY: Selling.

BEN: Yes. Well . . . (*He raises his hand in farewell to all.*)

WILLY: No, Ben, I don't want you to think . . . (*He takes Ben's arm to show him.*) It's Brooklyn, I know, but we hunt too.

BEN: Really, now.

WILLY: Oh, sure, there's snakes and rabbits and — that's why I moved out here. Why, Biff can fell any one of these trees in no time! Boys! Go right over to where they're building the apartment house and get some sand. We're gonna rebuild the entire front stoop right now! Watch this, Ben!

BIFF: Yes, sir! On the double, Hap!

HAPPY (*as he and Biff run off*): I lost weight, Pop, you notice?

(*Charley enters in knickers, even before the boys are gone.*)

CHARLEY: Listen, if they steal any more from that building the watchman'll put the cops on them!

LINDA (*to Willy*): Don't let Biff . . .

(*Ben laughs lustily.*)

WILLY: You shoulda seen the lumber they brought home last week. At least a dozen six-by-tens worth all kinds a money.

CHARLEY: Listen, if that watchman —

WILLY: I gave them hell, understand. But I got a couple of fearless characters there.

CHARLEY: Willy, the jails are full of fearless characters.

BEN (*clapping Willy on the back, with a laugh at Charley*): And the stock exchange, friend!

WILLY (*joining in Ben's laughter*): Where are the rest of your pants?

CHARLEY: My wife bought them.

WILLY: Now all you need is a golf club and you can go upstairs and go to sleep. (*To Ben.*) Great athlete! Between him and his son Bernard they can't hammer a nail!

BERNARD (*rushing in*): The watchman's chasing Biff!

WILLY (*angrily*): Shut up! He's not stealing anything!

LINDA (*alarmed, hurrying off left*): Where is he? Biff, dear! (*She exits.*)

WILLY (*moving toward the left, away from Ben*): There's nothing wrong. What's the matter with you?

BEN: Nervy boy. Good!

WILLY (*laughing*): Oh, nerves of iron, that Biff!

CHARLEY: Don't know what it is. My New England man comes back and he's bleedin', they murdered him up there.

WILLY: It's contacts, Charley, I got important contacts!

CHARLEY (*sarcastically*): Glad to hear it, Willy. Come in later, we'll shoot a little casino. I'll take some of your Portland money. (*He laughs at Willy and exits.*)

WILLY (*turning to Ben*): Business is bad, it's murderous. But not for me, of course.

BEN: I'll stop by on my way back to Africa.

WILLY (*longingly*): Can't you stay a few days? You're just what I need, Ben, because I — I have a fine position here, but I — well, Dad left when I was such a baby and I never had a chance to talk to him and I still feel — kind of temporary about myself.

BEN: I'll be late for my train.

(*They are at opposite ends of the stage.*)

WILLY: Ben, my boys — can't we talk? They'd go into the jaws of hell for me, see, but I —

BEN: William, you're being first-rate with your boys. Outstanding, manly chaps!

WILLY (*hanging on to his words*): Oh, Ben, that's good to hear! Because sometimes I'm afraid that I'm not teaching them the right kind of — Ben, how should I teach them?

BEN (*giving great weight to each word, and with a certain vicious audacity*): William, when I walked into the jungle, I was seventeen. When I walked out I was twenty-one. And, by God, I was rich! (*He goes off into darkness around the right corner of the house.*)

WILLY: . . . was rich! That's just the spirit I want to imbue them with! To walk into a jungle! I was right! I was right! I was right!

(*Ben is gone, but Willy is still speaking to him as Linda, in nightgown and robe, enters the kitchen, glances around for Willy, then goes to the door of the house, looks out and sees him. Comes down to his left. He looks at her.*)

LINDA: Willy, dear? Willy?

WILLY: I was right!

LINDA: Did you have some cheese? (*He can't answer.*) It's very late, darling. Come to bed, heh?

WILLY (*looking straight up*): Gotta break your neck to see a star in this yard.

LINDA: You coming in?

WILLY: Whatever happened to that diamond watch fob? Remember? When Ben came from Africa that time? Didn't he give me a watch fob with a diamond in it?

LINDA: You pawned it, dear. Twelve, thirteen years ago. For Biff's radio correspondence course.

WILLY: Gee, that was a beautiful thing. I'll take a walk.

LINDA: But you're in your slippers.

WILLY (*starting to go around the house at the left*): I was right! I was! (*Half to Linda, as he goes, shaking his head.*) What a man! There was a man worth talking to. I was right!

LINDA (*calling after Willy*): But in your slippers, Willy!

(*Willy is almost gone when Biff, in his pajamas, comes down the stairs and enters the kitchen.*)

BIFF: What is he doing out there?

LINDA: Sh!

BIFF: God Almighty, Mom, how long has he been doing this?

LINDA: Don't, he'll hear you.

BIFF: What the hell is the matter with him?

LINDA: It'll pass by morning.

BIFF: Shouldn't we do anything?

LINDA: Oh, my dear, you should do a lot of things, but there's nothing to do, so go to sleep.

(*Happy comes down the stair and sits on the steps.*)

HAPPY: I never heard him so loud, Mom.

LINDA: Well, come around more often, you'll hear him. (*She sits down at the table and mends the lining of Willy's jacket.*)

BIFF: Why didn't you ever write me about this, Mom?

LINDA: How would I write to you? For over three months you had no address.

BIFF: I was on the move. But you know I thought of you all the time. You know that, don't you, pal?

LINDA: I know, dear, I know. But he likes to have a letter. Just to know that there's still a possibility for better things.

BIFF: He's not like this all the time, is he?

LINDA: It's when you come home he's always the worst.

BIFF: When I come home?

LINDA: When you write you're coming, he's all smiles and talks about the future, and — he's just wonderful. And then the closer you seem to come, the more shaky he gets, and then, by the time you get here, he's arguing, and he seems angry at you. I think it's just that maybe he can't bring himself to — to open up to you. Why are you so hateful to each other? Why is that?

BIFF (*evasively*): I'm not hateful, Mom.

LINDA: But you no sooner come in the door than you're fighting!

BIFF: I don't know why. I mean to change. I'm tryin', Mom, you understand?

LINDA: Are you home to stay now?

BIFF: I don't know. I want to look around, see what's goin'.

LINDA: Biff, you can't look around all your life, can you?

BIFF: I just can't take hold, Mom. I can't take hold of some kind of a life.

LINDA: Biff, a man is not a bird, to come and go with the springtime.

BIFF: Your hair . . . (*He touches her hair.*) Your hair got so gray.

LINDA: Oh, it's been gray since you were in high school. I just stopped dyeing it, that's all.

BIFF: Dye it again, will ye? I don't want my pal looking old. (*He smiles.*)

LINDA: You're such a boy! You think you can go away for a year and . . . You've got to get it into your head now that one day you'll knock on this door and there'll be strange people here —

BIFF: What are you talking about? You're not even sixty, Mom.

LINDA: But what about your father?

BIFF (*lamely*): Well, I meant him too.

HAPPY: He admires Pop.

LINDA: Biff, dear, if you don't have any feeling for him, then you can't have any feeling for me.

BIFF: Sure I can, Mom.

LINDA: No. You can't just come to see me, because I love him. (*With a threat, but only a threat, of tears.*) He's the dearest man in the world to me, and I won't have anyone making him feel unwanted and low and blue. You've got to make up your mind now, darling, there's no leeway any more. Either he's your father and you pay him that respect, or else you're not to come here. I know he's not easy to get along with — nobody knows that better than me — but . . .

WILLY (*from the left, with a laugh*): Hey, hey, Biffo!

BIFF (*starting to go out after Willy*): What the hell is the matter with him? (*Happy stops him.*)

LINDA: Don't — don't go near him!

BIFF: Stop making excuses for him! He always, always wiped the floor with you. Never had an ounce of respect for you.

HAPPY: He's always had respect for —

BIFF: What the hell do you know about it?

HAPPY (*surlily*): Just don't call him crazy!

BIFF: He's got no character — Charley wouldn't do this. Not in his own house — spewing out that vomit from his mind.

HAPPY: Charley never had to cope with what he's got to.

BIFF: People are worse off than Willy Loman. Believe me, I've seen them!

LINDA: Then make Charley your father, Biff. You can't do that, can you? I don't say he's a great man. Willy Loman never made a lot of money. His name was never in the paper. He's not the finest character that ever lived. But he's a human being, and a terrible thing is happening to him. So attention must be paid. He's not to be allowed to fall into his grave like an old dog. Attention, attention must be finally paid to such a person. You called him crazy —

BIFF: I didn't mean —

LINDA: No, a lot of people think he's lost his — balance. But you don't have to be very smart to know what his trouble is. The man is exhausted.

HAPPY: Sure!

LINDA: A small man can be just as exhausted as a great man. He works for a company thirty-six years this March, opens up unheard-of territories to their trademark, and now in his old age they take his salary away.

HAPPY (*indignantly*): I didn't know that, Mom.

LINDA: You never asked, my dear! Now that you get your spending money some-place else you don't trouble your mind with him.

HAPPY: But I gave you money last —

LINDA: Christmas time, fifty dollars! To fix the hot water it cost ninety-seven fifty! For five weeks he's been on straight commission, like a beginner, an unknown!

BIFF: Those ungrateful bastards!

LINDA: Are they any worse than his sons? When he brought them business, when he was young, they were glad to see him. But now his old friends, the old buyers that loved him so and always found some order to hand him in a pinch — they're all dead, retired. He used to be able to make six, seven calls a day in Boston. Now he takes his valises out of the car and puts them back and takes them out again and he's exhausted. Instead of walking he talks now. He drives seven hundred miles, and when he gets there no one knows him anymore, no one welcomes him. And what goes through a man's mind, driving seven hundred miles home without having earned a cent? Why shouldn't he talk to himself? Why? When he has to go to Charley and borrow fifty dollars a week and pretend to me that it's his pay? How long can that go on? How long? You see what I'm sitting here and waiting for? And you tell me he has no character? The man who never worked a day but for your benefit? When does he get the medal for that? Is this his reward—to turn around at the age of sixty-three and find his sons, who he loved better than his life, one a philandering bum—

HAPPY: Mom!

LINDA: That's all you are, my baby! (*To Biff.*) And you! What happened to the love you had for him? You were such pals! How you used to talk to him on the phone every night! How lonely he was till he could come home to you!

BIFF: All right, Mom. I'll live here in my room, and I'll get a job. I'll keep away from him, that's all.

LINDA: No, Biff. You can't stay here and fight all the time.

BIFF: He threw me out of this house, remember that.

LINDA: Why did he do that? I never knew why.

BIFF: Because I know he's a fake and he doesn't like anybody around who knows!

LINDA: Why a fake? In what way? What do you mean?

BIFF: Just don't lay it all at my feet. It's between me and him—that's all I have to say. I'll chip in from now on. He'll settle for half my pay check. He'll be all right. I'm going to bed. (*He starts for the stairs.*)

LINDA: He won't be all right.

BIFF (*turning on the stairs, furiously*): I hate this city and I'll stay here. Now what do you want?

LINDA: He's dying, Biff.

(*Happy turns quickly to her, shocked.*)

BIFF (*after a pause*): Why is he dying?

LINDA: He's been trying to kill himself.

BIFF (*with great horror*): How?

LINDA: I live from day to day.

BIFF: What're you talking about?

LINDA: Remember I wrote you that he smashed up the car again? In February?

BIFF: Well?

LINDA: The insurance inspector came. He said that they have evidence. That all these accidents in the last year—weren't—weren't—accidents.

HAPPY: How can they tell that? That's a lie.

LINDA: It seems there's a woman . . . (*She takes a breath as*)

BIFF (*sharply but contained*):   } What woman?

LINDA (*simultaneously*):   } . . . and this woman . . .

LINDA: What?

BIFF: Nothing. Go ahead.

LINDA: What did you say?

BIFF: Nothing. I just said what woman?

HAPPY: What about her?

LINDA: Well, it seems she was walking down the road and saw his car. She says that he wasn't driving fast at all, and that he didn't skid. She says he came to that little bridge, and then deliberately smashed into the railing, and it was only the shallowness of the water that saved him.

BIFF: Oh, no, he probably just fell asleep again.

LINDA: I don't think he fell asleep.

BIFF: Why not?

LINDA: Last month . . . (*With great difficulty.*) Oh, boys, it's so hard to say a thing like this! He's just a big stupid man to you, but I tell you there's more good in him than in many other people. (*She chokes, wipes her eyes.*) I was looking for a fuse. The lights blew out, and I went down the cellar. And behind the fuse box — it happened to fall out — was a length of rubber pipe — just short.

HAPPY: No kidding!

LINDA: There's a little attachment on the end of it. I knew right away. And sure enough, on the bottom of the water heater there's a new little nipple on the gas pipe.

HAPPY (*angrily*): That — jerk.

BIFF: Did you have it taken off?

LINDA: I'm — I'm ashamed to. How can I mention it to him? Every day I go down and take away that little rubber pipe. But, when he comes home, I put it back where it was. How can I insult him that way? I don't know what to do. I live from day to day, boys. I tell you, I know every thought in his mind. It sounds so old-fashioned and silly, but I tell you he put his whole life into you and you've turned your backs on him. (*She is bent over in the chair, weeping, her face in her hands.*) Biff, I swear to God! Biff, his life is in your hands!

HAPPY (*to Biff*): How do you like that damned fool!

BIFF (*kissing her*): All right, pal, all right. It's all settled now. I've been remiss. I know that, Mom. But now I'll stay, and I swear to you, I'll apply myself. (*Kneeling in front of her, in a fever of self-reproach.*) It's just — you see, Mom, I don't fit in business. Not that I won't try. I'll try, and I'll make good.

HAPPY: Sure you will. The trouble with you in business was you never tried to please people.

BIFF: I know, I —

HAPPY: Like when you worked for Harrison's. Bob Harrison said you were tops, and then you go and do some damn fool thing like whistling whole songs in the elevator like a comedian.

BIFF (*against Happy*): So what? I like to whistle sometimes.

HAPPY: You don't raise a guy to a responsible job who whistles in the elevator!

LINDA: Well, don't argue about it now.

HAPPY: Like when you'd go off and swim in the middle of the day instead of taking the line around.

BIFF (*his resentment rising*): Well, don't you run off? You take off sometimes, don't you? On a nice summer day?

HAPPY: Yeah, but I cover myself!

LINDA: Boys!

HAPPY: If I'm going to take a fade the boss can call any number where I'm supposed to be and they'll swear to him that I just left. I'll tell you something
that I hate to say, Biff, but in the business world some of them think you're
crazy.

BIFF (*angered*): Screw the business world!

HAPPY: All right, screw it! Great, but cover yourself!

LINDA: Hap, Hap!

BIFF: I don't care what they think! They've laughed at Dad for years, and you
know why? Because we don't belong in this nuthouse of a city! We should
be mixing cement on some open plain, or — or carpenters. A carpenter is allowed to whistle!

(*Willy walks in from the entrance of the house, at left.*)

WILLY: Even your grandfather was better than a carpenter. (*Pause. They watch him.*)
You never grew up. Bernard does not whistle in the elevator, I assure you.

BIFF (*as though to laugh Willy out of it*): Yeah, but you do, Pop.

WILLY: I never in my life whistled in an elevator! And who in the business world
thinks I'm crazy?

BIFF: I didn't mean it like that, Pop. Now don't make a whole thing out of it,
will ye?

WILLY: Go back to the West! Be a carpenter, a cowboy, enjoy yourself!

LINDA: Willy, he was just saying —

WILLY: I heard what he said!

HAPPY (*trying to quiet Willy*): Hey, Pop, come on now . . .

WILLY (*continuing over Happy's line*): They laugh at me, heh? Go to Filene's, go to
the Hub, go to Slattery's, Boston. Call out the name Willy Loman and see
what happens! Big shot!

BIFF: All right, Pop.

WILLY: Big!

BIFF: All right!

WILLY: Why do you always insult me?

BIFF: I didn't say a word. (*To Linda.*) Did I say a word?

LINDA: He didn't say anything, Willy.

WILLY (*going to the doorway of the living room*): All right, good night, good night.

LINDA: Willy, dear, he just decided . . .

WILLY (*to Biff*): If you get tired hanging around tomorrow, paint the ceiling I put
up in the living room.

BIFF: I'm leaving early tomorrow.

HAPPY: He's going to see Bill Oliver, Pop.

WILLY (*interestedly*): Oliver? For what?

BIFF (*with reserve, but trying, trying*): He always said he'd stake me. I'd like to go
into business, so maybe I can take him up on it.

LINDA: Isn't that wonderful?

WILLY: Don't interrupt. What's wonderful about it? There's fifty men in the City
of New York who'd stake him. (*To Biff.*) Sporting goods?

BIFF: I guess so. I know something about it and —

WILLY: He knows something about it! You know sporting goods better than Spalding, for God's sake! How much is he giving you?

BIFF: I don't know, I didn't even see him yet, but—

WILLY: Then what're you talkin' about?

BIFF (*getting angry*): Well, all I said was I'm gonna see him, that's all!

WILLY (*turning away*): Ah, you're counting your chickens again.

BIFF (*starting left for the stairs*): Oh, Jesus, I'm going to sleep!

WILLY (*calling after him*): Don't curse in this house!

BIFF (*turning*): Since when did you get so clean?

HAPPY (*trying to stop them*): Wait a . . .

WILLY: Don't use that language to me! I won't have it!

HAPPY (*grabbing Biff, shouts*): Wait a minute! I got an idea. I got a feasible idea. Come here, Biff, let's talk this over now, let's talk some sense here. When I was down in Florida last time, I thought of a great idea to sell sporting goods. It just came back to me. You and I, Biff—we have a line, the Loman Line. We train a couple of weeks, and put on a couple of exhibitions, see?

WILLY: That's an idea!

HAPPY: Wait! We form two basketball teams, see? Two water polo teams. We play each other. It's a million dollars' worth of publicity. Two brothers, see? The Loman Brothers. Displays in the Royal Palms—all the hotels. And banners over the ring and the basketball court: "Loman Brothers." Baby, we could sell sporting goods!

WILLY: That is a one-million-dollar idea!

LINDA: Marvelous!

BIFF: I'm in great shape as far as that's concerned.

HAPPY: And the beauty of it is, Biff, it wouldn't be like a business. We'd be out playin' ball again . . .

BIFF (*enthused*): Yeah, that's . . .

WILLY: Million-dollar . . .

HAPPY: And you wouldn't get fed up with it, Biff. It'd be the family again. There'd be the old honor, and comradeship, and if you wanted to go off for a swim or somethin'—well, you'd do it! Without some smart cooky gettin' up ahead of you!

WILLY: Lick the world! You guys together could absolutely lick the civilized world.

BIFF: I'll see Oliver tomorrow. Hap, if we could work that out . . .

LINDA: Maybe things are beginning to—

WILLY (*wildly enthused, to Linda*): Stop interrupting! (*To Biff.*) But don't wear sport jacket and slacks when you see Oliver.

BIFF: No, I'll—

WILLY: A business suit, and talk as little as possible, and don't crack any jokes.

BIFF: He did like me. Always liked me.

LINDA: He loved you!

WILLY (*to Linda*): Will you stop! (*To Biff.*) Walk in very serious. You are not applying for a boy's job. Money is to pass. Be quiet, fine, and serious. Everybody likes a kidder, but nobody lends him money.

HAPPY: I'll try to get some myself, Biff. I'm sure I can.

WILLY: I see great things for you kids, I think your troubles are over. But remember, start big and you'll end big. Ask for fifteen. How much you gonna ask for?

BIFF: Gee, I don't know—

WILLY: And don't say "Gee." "Gee" is a boy's word. A man walking in for fifteen thousand dollars does not say "Gee!"

BIFF: Ten, I think, would be top though.

WILLY: Don't be so modest. You always started too low. Walk in with a big laugh. Don't look worried. Start off with a couple of your good stories to lighten things up. It's not what you say, it's how you say it — because personality always wins the day.

LINDA: Oliver always thought the highest of him —

WILLY: Will you let me talk?

BIFF: Don't yell at her, Pop, will ye?

WILLY (*angrily*): I was talking, wasn't I?

BIFF: I don't like you yelling at her all the time, and I'm tellin' you, that's all.

WILLY: What're you, takin' over this house?

LINDA: Willy—

WILLY (*turning to her*): Don't take his side all the time, goddammit!

BIFF (*furiously*): Stop yelling at her!

WILLY (*suddenly pulling on his cheek, beaten down, guilt ridden*): Give my best to Bill Oliver — he may remember me. (*He exits through the living room doorway.*)

LINDA (*her voice subdued*): What'd you have to start that for? (*Biff turns away.*) You see how sweet he was as soon as you talked hopefully? (*She goes over to Biff.*) Come up and say good night to him. Don't let him go to bed that way.

HAPPY: Come on, Biff, let's buck him up.

LINDA: Please, dear. Just say good night. It takes so little to make him happy. Come. (*She goes through the living room doorway, calling upstairs from within the living room.*) Your pajamas are hanging in the bathroom, Willy!

HAPPY (*looking toward where Linda went out*): What a woman! They broke the mold when they made her. You know that, Biff?

BIFF: He's off salary. My God, working on commission!

HAPPY: Well, let's face it: he's no hot-shot selling man. Except that sometimes, you have to admit, he's a sweet personality.

BIFF (*deciding*): Lend me ten bucks, will ye? I want to buy some new ties.

HAPPY: I'll take you to a place I know. Beautiful stuff. Wear one of my striped shirts tomorrow.

BIFF: She got gray. Mom got awful old. Gee, I'm gonna go in to Oliver tomorrow and knock him for a —

HAPPY: Come on up. Tell that to Dad. Let's give him a whirl. Come on.

BIFF (*steamed up*): You know, with ten thousand bucks, boy!

HAPPY (*as they go into the living room*): That's the talk, Biff, that's the first time I've heard the old confidence out of you! (*From within the living room, fading off.*) You're gonna live with me, kid, and any babe you want just say the word . . . (*The last lines are hardly heard. They are mounting the stairs to their parents' bedroom.*)

LINDA (*entering her bedroom and addressing Willy, who is in the bathroom. She is straightening the bed for him.*): Can you do anything about the shower? It drips.

WILLY (*from the bathroom*): All of a sudden everything falls to pieces. Goddam plumbing, oughta be sued, those people. I hardly finished putting it in and the thing . . . (*His words rumble off.*)

LINDA: I'm just wondering if Oliver will remember him. You think he might?

WILLY (*coming out of the bathroom in his pajamas*): Remember him? What's the matter with you, you crazy? If he'd've stayed with Oliver he'd be on top by now! Wait'll Oliver gets a look at him. You don't know the average caliber any more. The average young man today — (*he is getting into bed*) — is got a caliber of zero. Greatest thing in the world for him was to bum around.

(*Biff and Happy enter the bedroom. Slight pause.*)

WILLY (*stops short, looking at Biff*): Glad to hear it, boy.

HAPPY: He wanted to say good night to you, sport.

WILLY (*to Biff*): Yeah. Knock him dead, boy. What'd you want to tell me?

BIFF: Just take it easy, Pop. Good night. (*He turns to go.*)

WILLY (*unable to resist*): And if anything falls off the desk while you're talking to him — like a package or something — don't you pick it up. They have office boys for that.

LINDA: I'll make a big breakfast —

WILLY: Will you let me finish? (*To Biff.*) Tell him you were in the business in the West. Not farm work.

BIFF: All right, Dad.

LINDA: I think everything —

WILLY (*going right through her speech*): And don't undersell yourself. No less than fifteen thousand dollars.

BIFF (*unable to bear him*): Okay. Good night, Mom. (*He starts moving.*)

WILLY: Because you got a greatness in you, Biff, remember that. You got all kinds of greatness . . . (*He lies back, exhausted. Biff walks out.*)

LINDA (*calling after Biff*): Sleep well, darling!

HAPPY: I'm gonna get married, Mom. I wanted to tell you.

LINDA: Go to sleep, dear.

HAPPY (*going*): I just wanted to tell you.

WILLY: Keep up the good work. (*Happy exits.*) God . . . remember that Ebbets Field game? The championship of the city?

LINDA: Just rest. Should I sing to you?

WILLY: Yeah. Sing to me. (*Linda hums a soft lullaby.*) When that team came out — he was the tallest, remember?

LINDA: Oh, yes. And in gold.

(*Biff enters the darkened kitchen, takes a cigarette, and leaves the house. He comes downstage into a golden pool of light. He smokes, staring at the night.*)

WILLY: Like a young god. Hercules — something like that. And the sun, the sun all around him. Remember how he waved to me? Right up from the field, with the representatives of three colleges standing by? And the buyers I brought, and the cheers when he came out — Loman, Loman, Loman! God Almighty, he'll be great yet. A star like that, magnificent, can never really fade away!

(*The light on Willy is fading. The gas heater begins to glow through the kitchen wall, near the stairs, a blue flame beneath red coils.*)

LINDA (*timidly*): Willy dear, what has he got against you?
WILLY: I'm so tired. Don't talk anymore.

(*Biff slowly returns to the kitchen. He stops, stares toward the heater.*)

LINDA: Will you ask Howard to let you work in New York?
WILLY: First thing in the morning. Everything'll be all right.

(*Biff reaches behind the heater and draws out a length of rubber tubing. He is horrified and turns his head toward Willy's room, still dimly lit, from which the strains of Linda's desperate but monotonous humming rise.*)

WILLY (*staring through the window into the moonlight*): Gee, look at the moon moving between the buildings!

(*Biff wraps the tubing around his hand and quickly goes up the stairs.*)

ACT 2

(*Music is heard, gay and bright. The curtain rises as the music fades away. Willy, in shirt sleeves is sitting at the kitchen table, sipping coffee, his hat in his lap. Linda is filling his cup when she can.*)

WILLY: Wonderful coffee. Meal in itself.
LINDA: Can I make you some eggs?
WILLY: No. Take a breath.
LINDA: You look so rested, dear.
WILLY: I slept like a dead one. First time in months. Imagine, sleeping till ten on a Tuesday morning. Boys left nice and early, heh?
LINDA: They were out of here by eight o'clock.
WILLY: Good work!
LINDA: It was so thrilling to see them leaving together. I can't get over the shaving lotion in this house!
WILLY (*smiling*): Mmm —
LINDA: Biff was very changed this morning. His whole attitude seemed to be hopeful. He couldn't wait to get downtown to see Oliver.
WILLY: He's heading for a change. There's no question, there simply are certain men that take longer to get — solidified. How did he dress?
LINDA: His blue suit. He's so handsome in that suit. He could be a — anything in that suit!

(*Willy gets up from the table. Linda holds his jacket for him.*)

WILLY: There's no question, no question at all. Gee, on the way home tonight I'd like to buy some seeds.

LINDA (*laughing*): That'd be wonderful. But not enough sun gets back there. Nothing'll grow any more.

WILLY: You wait, kid, before it's all over we're gonna get a little place out in the country, and I'll raise some vegetables, a couple of chickens . . .

LINDA: You'll do it yet, dear.

(*Willy walks out of his jacket. Linda follows him.*)

WILLY: And they'll get married, and come for a weekend. I'd build a little guest house. 'Cause I got so many fine tools, all I'd need would be a little lumber and some peace of mind.

LINDA (*joyfully*): I sewed the lining . . .

WILLY: I could build two guest houses, so they'd both come. Did he decide how much he's going to ask Oliver for?

LINDA (*getting him into the jacket*): He didn't mention it, but I imagine ten or fifteen thousand. You going to talk to Howard today?

WILLY: Yeah. I'll put it to him straight and simple. He'll just have to take me off the road.

LINDA: And Willy, don't forget to ask for a little advance, because we've got the insurance premium. It's the grace period now.

WILLY: That's a hundred . . . ?

LINDA: A hundred and eight, sixty-eight. Because we're a little short again.

WILLY: Why are we short?

LINDA: Well, you had the motor job on the car . . .

WILLY: That goddam Studebaker!

LINDA: And you got one more payment on the refrigerator . . .

WILLY: But it just broke again!

LINDA: Well, it's old, dear.

WILLY: I told you we should've bought a well-advertised machine. Charley bought a General Electric and it's twenty years old and it's still good, that son-of-a-bitch.

LINDA: But, Willy —

WILLY: Whoever heard of a Hastings refrigerator? Once in my life I would like to own something outright before it's broken! I'm always in a race with the junkyard! I just finished paying for the car and it's on its last legs. The refrigerator consumes belts like a goddamn maniac. They time those things. They time them so when you finally paid for them, they're used up.

LINDA (*buttoning up his jacket as he unbuttons it*): All told, about two hundred dollars would carry us, dear. But that includes the last payment on the mortgage. After this payment, Willy, the house belongs to us.

WILLY: It's twenty-five years!

LINDA: Biff was nine years old when we bought it.

WILLY: Well, that's a great thing. To weather a twenty-five year mortgage is —

LINDA: It's an accomplishment.

WILLY: All the cement, the lumber, the reconstruction I put in this house! There ain't a crack to be found in it anymore.

LINDA: Well, it served its purpose.

WILLY: What purpose? Some stranger'll come along, move in, and that's that. If only Biff would take this house, and raise a family . . . (*He starts to go.*) Good-by, I'm late.

LINDA (*suddenly remembering*): Oh, I forgot! You're supposed to meet them for dinner.

WILLY: Me?

LINDA: At Frank's Chop House on Forty-eighth near Sixth Avenue.

WILLY: Is that so! How about you?

LINDA: No, just the three of you. They're gonna blow you to a big meal!

WILLY: Don't say! Who thought of that?

LINDA: Biff came to me this morning, Willy, and he said, "Tell Dad, we want to blow him to a big meal." Be there six o'clock. You and your two boys are going to have dinner.

WILLY: Gee whiz! That's really somethin'. I'm gonna knock Howard for a loop, kid. I'll get an advance, and I'll come home with a New York job. Goddammit, now I'm gonna do it!

LINDA: Oh, that's the spirit, Willy!

WILLY: I will never get behind a wheel the rest of my life!

LINDA: It's changing, Willy, I can feel it changing!

WILLY: Beyond a question. G'by, I'm late. (*He starts to go again.*)

LINDA (*calling after him as she runs to the kitchen table for a handkerchief*): You got your glasses?

WILLY (*feels for them, then comes back in*): Yeah, yeah, got my glasses.

LINDA (*giving him the handkerchief*): And a handkerchief.

WILLY: Yeah, handkerchief.

LINDA: And your saccharine?

WILLY: Yeah, my saccharine.

LINDA: Be careful on the subway stairs.

(*She kisses him, and a silk stocking is seen hanging from her hand. Willy notices it.*)

WILLY: Will you stop mending stockings? At least while I'm in the house. It gets me nervous. I can't tell you. Please.

(*Linda hides the stocking in her hand as she follows Willy across the forestage in front of the house.*)

LINDA: Remember, Frank's Chop House.

WILLY (*passing the apron*): Maybe beets would grow out there.

LINDA (*laughing*): But you tried so many times.

WILLY: Yeah. Well, don't work hard today. (*He disappears around the right corner of the house.*)

LINDA: Be careful!

(*As Willy vanishes, Linda waves to him. Suddenly the phone rings. She runs across the stage and into the kitchen and lifts it.*)

LINDA: Hello? Oh, Biff! I'm so glad you called, I just . . . Yes, sure, I just told him. Yes, he'll be there for dinner at six o'clock, I didn't forget. Listen, I was just dying to tell you. You know that little rubber pipe I told you about? That he connected to the gas heater? I finally decided to go down the cellar this morning and take it away and destroy it. But it's gone! Imagine? He took it away himself, it isn't there! (*She listens.*) When? Oh, then you took it. Oh — nothing, it's just that I'd hoped he'd taken it away himself. Oh, I'm not worried, darling, because this morning he left in such high spirits, it was like the old days! I'm not afraid any more. Did Mr. Oliver see you? . . . Well, you wait there then. And make a nice impression on him, darling. Just don't perspire too much before you see him. And have a nice time with Dad. He may have big news too! . . . That's right, a New York job. And be sweet to him tonight, dear. Be loving to him. Because he's only a little boat looking for a harbor. (*She is trembling with sorrow and joy.*) Oh, that's wonderful, Biff, you'll save his life. Thanks, darling. Just put your arm around him when he comes into the restaurant. Give him a smile. That's the boy . . . Good-by, dear. . . . You got your comb? . . . That's fine. Good-by, Biff dear.

(*In the middle of her speech, Howard Wagner, thirty-six, wheels in a small type-writer table on which is a wire-recording machine and proceeds to plug it in. This is on the left forestage. Light slowly fades on Linda as it rises on Howard. Howard is intent on threading the machine and only glances over his shoulder as Willy appears.*)

WILLY: Pst! Pst!

HOWARD: Hello, Willy, come in.

WILLY: Like to have a little talk with you, Howard.

HOWARD: Sorry to keep you waiting. I'll be with you in a minute.

WILLY: What's that, Howard?

HOWARD: Didn't you ever see one of these? Wire recorder.

WILLY: Oh. Can we talk a minute?

HOWARD: Records things. Just got delivery yesterday. Been driving me crazy, the most terrific machine I ever saw in my life. I was up all night with it.

WILLY: What do you do with it?

HOWARD: I bought it for dictation, but you can do anything with it. Listen to this. I had it home last night. Listen to what I picked up. The first one is my daughter. Get this. (*He flicks the switch and "Roll out the Barrel" is heard being whistled.*) Listen to that kid whistle.

WILLY: That is lifelike, isn't it?

HOWARD: Seven years old. Get that tone.

WILLY: Ts, ts. Like to ask a little favor if you . . .

(*The whistling breaks off, and the voice of Howard's daughter is heard.*)

HIS DAUGHTER: Now you, Daddy.

HOWARD: She's crazy for me! (*Again the same song is whistled.*) That's me! Ha! (*He winks.*)

WILLY: You're very good!

(*The whistling breaks off again. The machine runs silent for a moment.*)

HOWARD: Sh! Get this now, this is my son.

HIS SON: "The capital of Alabama is Montgomery; the capital of Arizona is Phoenix; the capital of Arkansas is Little Rock; the capital of California is Sacramento . . ." (*and on, and on.*)

HOWARD (*holding up five fingers*): Five years old, Willy!

WILLY: He'll make an announcer some day!

HIS SON (*continuing*): "The capita . . ."

HOWARD: Get that — alphabetical order! (*The machine breaks off suddenly.*) Wait a minute. The maid kicked the plug out.

WILLY: It certainly is a —

HOWARD: Sh, for God's sake!

HIS SON: "It's nine o'clock, Bulova watch time. So I have to go to sleep."

WILLY: That really is —

HOWARD: Wait a minute! The next is my wife.

(*They wait.*)

HOWARD'S VOICE: "Go on, say something." (*Pause.*) "Well, you gonna talk?"

HIS WIFE: "I can't think of anything."

HOWARD'S VOICE: "Well, talk — it's turning."

HIS WIFE (*shyly, beaten*): "Hello." (*Silence.*) "Oh, Howard, I can't talk into this . . ."

HOWARD (*snapping the machine off*): That was my wife.

WILLY: That is a wonderful machine. Can we —

HOWARD: I tell you, Willy, I'm gonna take my camera, and my bandsaw, and all my hobbies, and out they go. This is the most fascinating relaxation I ever found.

WILLY: I think I'll get one myself.

HOWARD: Sure, they're only a hundred and a half. You can't do without it. Supposing you wanna hear Jack Benny,° see? But you can't be at home at that hour. So you tell the maid to turn the radio on when Jack Benny comes on, and this automatically goes on with the radio . . .

WILLY: And when you come home you . . .

HOWARD: You can come home twelve o'clock, one o'clock, any time you like, and you get yourself a Coke and sit yourself down, throw the switch, and there's Jack Benny's program in the middle of the night!

WILLY: I'm definitely going to get one. Because lots of times I'm on the road, and I think to myself, what I must be missing on the radio!

Jack Benny: The comedian Jack Benny (1894–1974) starred in the variety show *The Jack Benny Program*, broadcast on radio from 1932 until 1955.

HOWARD: Don't you have a radio in the car?

WILLY: Well, yeah, but who ever thinks of turning it on?

HOWARD: Say, aren't you supposed to be in Boston?

WILLY: That's what I want to talk to you about, Howard. You got a minute? (*He draws a chair in from the wing.*)

HOWARD: What happened? What're you doing here?

WILLY: Well . . .

HOWARD: You didn't crack up again, did you?

WILLY: Oh, no. No . . .

HOWARD: Geez, you had me worried there for a minute. What's the trouble?

WILLY: Well, tell you the truth, Howard. I've come to the decision that I'd rather not travel anymore.

HOWARD: Not travel! Well, what'll you do?

WILLY: Remember, Christmas time, when you had the party here? You said you'd try to think of some spot for me here in town.

HOWARD: With us?

WILLY: Well, sure.

HOWARD: Oh, yeah, yeah. I remember. Well, I couldn't think of anything for you, Willy.

WILLY: I tell ya, Howard. The kids are all grown up, y'know. I don't need much anymore. If I could take home — well, sixty-five dollars a week, I could swing it.

HOWARD: Yeah, but Willy, see I —

WILLY: I tell ya why, Howard. Speaking frankly and between the two of us, y'know — I'm just a little tired.

HOWARD: Oh, I could understand that, Willy. But you're a road man, Willy, and we do a road business. We've only got a half-dozen salesmen on the floor here.

WILLY: God knows, Howard, I never asked a favor of any man. But I was with the firm when your father used to carry you in here in his arms.

HOWARD: I know that, Willy, but —

WILLY: Your father came to me the day you were born and asked me what I thought of the name Howard, may he rest in peace.

HOWARD: I appreciate that, Willy, but there just is no spot here for you. If I had a spot I'd slam you right in, but I just don't have a single solitary spot.

(*He looks for his lighter. Willy has picked it up and gives it to him. Pause.*)

WILLY (*with increasing anger*): Howard, all I need to set my table is fifty dollars a week.

HOWARD: But where am I going to put you, kid?

WILLY: Look, it isn't a question of whether I can sell merchandise, is it?

HOWARD: No, but it's business, kid, and everybody's gotta pull his own weight.

WILLY (*desperately*): Just let me tell you a story, Howard —

HOWARD: 'Cause you gotta admit, business is business.

WILLY (*angrily*): Business is definitely business, but just listen for a minute. You don't understand this. When I was a boy — eighteen, nineteen — I was already on the road. And there was a question in my mind as to whether selling had a future for me. Because in those days I had a yearning to go to Alaska. See, there were three gold strikes in one month in Alaska, and I felt like going out. Just for the ride, you might say.

HOWARD (*barely interested*): Don't say.

WILLY: Oh, yeah, my father lived many years in Alaska. He was an adventurous man. We've got quite a little streak of self-reliance in our family. I thought I'd go out with my older brother and try to locate him, and maybe settle in the North with the old man. And I was almost decided to go, when I met a salesman in the Parker House. His name was Dave Singleman. And he was eighty-four years old, and he'd drummed merchandise in thirty-one states. And old Dave, he'd go up to his room, y'understand, put on his green velvet slippers — I'll never forget — and pick up his phone and call the buyers, and without ever leaving his room, at the age of eighty-four, he made his living. And when I saw that, I realized that selling was the greatest career a man could want. 'Cause what could be more satisfying than to be able to go, at the age of eighty-four, into twenty or thirty different cities, and pick up a phone, and be remembered and loved and helped by so many different people? Do you know? When he died — and by the way he died the death of a salesman, in his green velvet slippers in the smoker of the New York, New Haven and Hartford, going into Boston — when he died, hundreds of sales-men and buyers were at his funeral. Things were sad on a lotta trains for months after that. (*He stands up. Howard has not looked at him.*) In those days there was personality in it, Howard. There was respect and comrade-ship, and gratitude in it. Today, it's all cut and dried, and there's no chance for bringing friendship to bear — or personality. You see what I mean? They don't know me any more.

HOWARD (*moving away, to the right*): That's just the thing, Willy.

WILLY: If I had forty dollars a week — that's all I'd need. Forty dollars, Howard.

HOWARD: Kid, I can't take blood from a stone, I —

WILLY (*desperation is on him now*): Howard, the year Al Smith was nominated, your father came to me and —

HOWARD (*starting to go off*): I've got to see some people, kid.

WILLY (*stopping him*): I'm talking about your father! There were promises made across this desk! You mustn't tell me you've got people to see — I put thirty-four years into this firm, Howard, and now I can't pay my insurance! You can't eat the orange and throw the peel away — a man is not a piece of fruit! (*After a pause.*) Now pay attention. Your father — in 1928 I had a big year. I averaged a hundred and seventy dollars a week in commissions.

HOWARD (*impatiently*): Now, Willy, you never averaged —

WILLY (*banging his hand on the desk*): I averaged a hundred and seventy dollars a week in the year of 1928! And your father came to me — or rather I was in the office here — it was right over this desk — and he put his hand on my shoulder —

HOWARD (*getting up*): You'll have to excuse me, Willy, I gotta see some people. Pull yourself together. (*Going out.*) I'll be back in a little while.

(*On Howard's exit, the light on his chair grows very bright and strange.*)

WILLY: Pull myself together! What the hell did I say to him? My God, I was yelling at him! How could I? (*Willy breaks off, staring at the light, which occupies the chair, animating it. He approaches this chair, standing across the desk from it.*) Frank, Frank, don't you remember what you told me that time? How you put your hand on my shoulder, and Frank . . . (*He leans on the desk and as he speaks the dead man's name he accidentally switches on the recorder, and instantly*)

HOWARD'S SON: ". . . of New York is Albany. The capital of Ohio is Cincinnati, the capital of Rhode Island is . . ." (*The recitation continues.*)

WILLY (*leaping away with fright, shouting*): Ha! Howard! Howard! Howard!

HOWARD (*rushing in*): What happened?

WILLY (*pointing at the machine, which continues nasally, childishly, with the capital cities*): Shut it off! Shut it off!

HOWARD (*pulling the plug out*): Look, Willy . . .

WILLY (*pressing his hands to his eyes*): I gotta get myself some coffee. I'll get some coffee . . .

(*Willy starts to walk out. Howard stops him.*)

HOWARD (*rolling up the cord*): Willy, look . . .

WILLY: I'll go to Boston.

HOWARD: Willy, you can't go to Boston for us.

WILLY: Why can't I go?

HOWARD: I don't want you to represent us. I've been meaning to tell you for a long time now.

WILLY: Howard, are you firing me?

HOWARD: I think you need a good long rest, Willy.

WILLY: Howard—

HOWARD: And when you feel better, come back, and we'll see if we can work something out.

WILLY: But I gotta earn money, Howard. I'm in no position to—

HOWARD: Where are your sons? Why don't your sons give you a hand?

WILLY: They're working on a very big deal.

HOWARD: This is no time for false pride, Willy. You go to your sons and you tell them that you're tired. You've got two great boys, haven't you?

WILLY: Oh, no question, no question, but in the meantime . . .

HOWARD: Then that's that, heh?

WILLY: All right, I'll go to Boston tomorrow.

HOWARD: No, no.

WILLY: I can't throw myself on my sons. I'm not a cripple!

HOWARD: Look, kid, I'm busy this morning.

WILLY (*grasping Howard's arm*): Howard, you've got to let me go to Boston!

HOWARD (*hard, keeping himself under control*): I've got a line of people to see this morning. Sit down, take five minutes, and pull yourself together, and then go home, will ya? I need the office, Willy. (*He starts to go, turns, remembering the recorder, starts to push off the table holding the recorder.*) Oh, yeah. When-ever you can this week, stop by and drop off the samples. You'll feel better, Willy, and then come back and we'll talk. Pull yourself together, kid, there's people outside.

(*Howard exits, pushing the table off left. Willy stares into space, exhausted. Now the music is heard — Ben's music — first distantly, then closer, closer. As Willy speaks, Ben enters from the right. He carries valise and umbrella.*)

WILLY: Oh, Ben, how did you do it? What is the answer? Did you wind up the Alaska deal already?

BEN: Doesn't take much time if you know what you're doing. Just a short busi-ness trip. Boarding ship in an hour. Wanted to say good-by.

WILLY: Ben, I've got to talk to you.

BEN (*glancing at his watch*): Haven't the time, William.

WILLY (*crossing the apron to Ben*): Ben, nothing's working out. I don't know what to do.

BEN: Now, look here, William. I've bought timberland in Alaska and I need a man to look after things for me.

WILLY: God, timberland! Me and my boys in those grand outdoors!

BEN: You've a new continent at your doorstep, William. Get out of these cities, they're full of talk and time payments and courts of law. Screw on your fists and you can fight for a fortune up there.

WILLY: Yes, yes! Linda, Linda!

(*Linda enters as of old, with the wash.*)

LINDA: Oh, you're back?

BEN: I haven't much time.

WILLY: No, wait! Linda, he's got a proposition for me in Alaska.

LINDA: But you've got — (*To Ben.*) He's got a beautiful job here.

WILLY: But in Alaska, kid, I could —

LINDA: You're doing well enough, Willy!

BEN (*to Linda*): Enough for what, my dear?

LINDA (*frightened of Ben and angry at him*): Don't say those things to him! Enough to be happy right here, right now. (*To Willy, while Ben laughs.*) Why must everybody conquer the world? You're well liked, and the boys love you, and someday — (*To Ben*) — why, old man Wagner told him just the other day that if he keeps it up he'll be a member of the firm, didn't he, Willy?

WILLY: Sure, sure. I am building something with this firm, Ben, and if a man is building something he must be on the right track, mustn't he?

BEN: What are you building? Lay your hand on it. Where is it?

WILLY (*hesitantly*): That's true, Linda, there's nothing.

LINDA: Why? (*To Ben.*) There's a man eighty-four years old —

WILLY: That's right, Ben, that's right. When I look at that man I say, what is there to worry about?

BEN: Bah!

WILLY: It's true, Ben. All he has to do is go into any city, pick up the phone, and he's making his living and you know why?

BEN (*picking up his valise*): I've got to go.

WILLY (*holding Ben back*): Look at this boy!

(*Biff, in his high school sweater, enters carrying suitcase. Happy carries Biff's shoulder guards, gold helmet, and football pants.*)

WILLY: Without a penny to his name, three great universities are begging for him, and from there the sky's the limit, because it's not what you do, Ben. It's who you know and the smile on your face! It's contacts, Ben, contacts! The whole wealth of Alaska passes over the lunch table at the Commodore Hotel, and that's the wonder, the wonder of this country, that a man can end with diamonds here on the basis of being liked! (*He turns to Biff.*) And that's why when you get out on that field today it's important. Because thousands of people will be rooting for you and loving you. (*To Ben, who has again begun to leave.*) And Ben! when he walks into a business office his name will sound out like a bell and all the doors will open to him! I've seen it, Ben, I've seen it a thousand times! You can't feel it with your hand like timber, but it's there!

BEN: Good-by, William.

WILLY: Ben, am I right? Don't you think I'm right? I value your advice.

BEN: There's a new continent at your doorstep, William. You could walk out rich. Rich! (*He is gone.*)

WILLY: We'll do it here, Ben! You hear me? We're gonna do it here!

(*Young Bernard rushes in. The gay music of the Boys is heard.*)

BERNARD: Oh, gee, I was afraid you left already!

WILLY: Why? What time is it?

BERNARD: It's half-past one!

WILLY: Well, come on, everybody! Ebbets Field° next stop! Where's the pennants? (*He rushes through the wall-line of the kitchen and out into the living room.*)

LINDA (*to Biff*): Did you pack fresh underwear?

BIFF (*who has been limbering up*): I want to go!

BERNARD: Biff, I'm carrying your helmet, ain't I?

HAPPY: No, I'm carrying the helmet.

BERNARD: Oh, Biff, you promised me.

HAPPY: I'm carrying the helmet.

BERNARD: How am I going to get in the locker room?

LINDA: Let him carry the shoulder guards. (*She puts her coat and hat on in the kitchen.*)

BERNARD: Can I, Biff? 'Cause I told everybody I'm going to be in the locker room.

Ebbets Field: Stadium in Brooklyn, opened in 1913, demolished in 1960, and the home of the Brooklyn Dodgers until 1957.

HAPPY: In Ebbets Field it's the clubhouse.

BERNARD: I meant the clubhouse. Biff!

HAPPY: Biff!

BIFF (*grandly, after a slight pause*): Let him carry the shoulder guards.

HAPPY (*as he gives Bernard the shoulder guards*): Stay close to us now.

(*Willy rushes in with the pennants.*)

WILLY (*handing them out*): Everybody wave when Biff comes out on the field. (*Happy and Bernard run off.*) You set now, boy?

(*The music has died away.*)

BIFF: Ready to go, Pop. Every muscle is ready.

WILLY (*at the edge of the apron*): You realize what this means?

BIFF: That's right, Pop.

WILLY (*feeling Biff's muscles*): You're comin' home this afternoon captain of the All-Scholastic Championship Team of the City of New York.

BIFF: I got it, Pop. And remember, pal, when I take off my helmet, that touchdown is for you.

WILLY: Let's go! (*He is starting out, with his arm around Biff, when Charley enters, as of old, in knickers.*) I got no room for you, Charley.

CHARLEY: Room? For what?

WILLY: In the car.

CHARLEY: You goin' for a ride? I wanted to shoot some casino.

WILLY (*furiously*): Casino! (*Incredulously.*) Don't you realize what today is?

LINDA: Oh, he knows, Willy. He's just kidding you.

WILLY: That's nothing to kid about!

CHARLEY: No, Linda, what's goin' on?

LINDA: He's playing in Ebbets Field.

CHARLEY: Baseball in this weather?

WILLY: Don't talk to him. Come on, come on! (*He is pushing them out.*)

CHARLEY: Wait a minute, didn't you hear the news?

WILLY: What?

CHARLEY: Don't you listen to the radio? Ebbets Field just blew up.

WILLY: You go to hell! (*Charley laughs. Pushing them out.*) Come on, come on! We're late.

CHARLEY (*as they go*): Knock a homer, Biff, knock a homer!

WILLY (*the last to leave, turning to Charley*): I don't think that was funny, Charley. This is the greatest day of his life.

CHARLEY: Willy, when are you going to grow up?

WILLY: Yeah, heh? When this game is over, Charley, you'll be laughing out of the other side of your face. They'll be calling him another Red Grange. Twenty-five thousand a year.

CHARLEY (*kidding*): Is that so?

WILLY: Yeah, that's so.

CHARLEY: Well, then, I'm sorry, Willy. But tell me something.

WILLY: What?

CHARLEY: Who is Red Grange?

WILLY: Put up your hands. Goddam you, put up your hands!

(*Charley, chuckling, shakes his head and walks away, around the left corner of the stage. Willy follows him. The music rises to a mocking frenzy.*)

WILLY: Who the hell do you think you are, better than everybody else? You don't know everything, you big, ignorant, stupid . . . Put up your hands!

(*Light rises, on the right side of the forestage, on a small table in the reception room of Charley's office. Traffic sounds are heard. Bernard, now mature, sits whistling to himself. A pair of tennis rackets and an overnight bag are on the floor beside him.*)

WILLY (*offstage*): What are you walking away for? Don't walk away! If you're going to say something say it to my face! I know you laugh at me behind my back. You'll laugh out of the other side of your goddam face after this game. Touchdown! Touchdown! Eighty thousand people! Touchdown! Right between the goal posts.

(*Bernard is a quiet, earnest, but self-assured young man. Willy's voice is coming from right upstage now. Bernard lowers his feet off the table and listens. Jenny, his father's secretary, enters.*)

JENNY (*distressed*): Say, Bernard, will you go out in the hall?

BERNARD: What is that noise? Who is it?

JENNY: Mr. Loman. He just got off the elevator.

BERNARD (*getting up*): Who's he arguing with?

JENNY: Nobody. There's nobody with him. I can't deal with him anymore, and your father gets all upset everytime he comes. I've got a lot of typing to do, and your father's waiting to sign it. Will you see him?

WILLY (*entering*): Touchdown! Touch — (*He sees Jenny.*) Jenny, Jenny, good to see you. How're ya? Workin'? Or still honest?

JENNY: Fine. How've you been feeling?

WILLY: Not much any more, Jenny. Ha, ha! (*He is surprised to see the rackets.*)

BERNARD: Hello, Uncle Willy.

WILLY (*almost shocked*): Bernard! Well, look who's here! (*He comes quickly, guiltily, to Bernard and warmly shakes his hand.*)

BERNARD: How are you? Good to see you.

WILLY: What are you doing here?

BERNARD: Oh, just stopped by to see Pop. Get off my feet till my train leaves. I'm going to Washington in a few minutes.

WILLY: Is he in?

BERNARD: Yes, he's in his office with the accountant. Sit down.

WILLY (*sitting down*): What're you going to do in Washington?

BERNARD: Oh, just a case I've got there, Willy.

WILLY: That so? (*Indicating the rackets.*) You going to play tennis there?

BERNARD: I'm staying with a friend who's got a court.

WILLY: Don't say. His own tennis court. Must be fine people, I bet.

BERNARD: They are, very nice. Dad tells me Biff's in town.

WILLY (*with a big smile*): Yeah, Biff's in. Working on a very big deal, Bernard.

BERNARD: What's Biff doing?

WILLY: Well, he's been doing very big things in the West. But he decided to establish himself here. Very big. We're having dinner. Did I hear your wife had a boy?

BERNARD: That's right. Our second.

WILLY: Two boys! What do you know!

BERNARD: What kind of a deal has Biff got?

WILLY: Well, Bill Oliver — very big sporting-goods man — he wants Biff very badly. Called him in from the West. Long distance, carte blanche, special deliveries. Your friends have their own private tennis court?

BERNARD: You still with the old firm, Willy?

WILLY (*after a pause*): I'm — I'm overjoyed to see how you made the grade, Bernard, overjoyed. It's an encouraging thing to see a young man really — really — Looks very good for Biff — very — (*He breaks off, then.*) Bernard — (*He is so full of emotion, he breaks off again.*)

BERNARD: What is it, Willy?

WILLY (*small and alone*): What — what's the secret?

BERNARD: What secret?

WILLY: How — how did you? Why didn't he ever catch on?

BERNARD: I wouldn't know that, Willy.

WILLY (*confidentially, desperately*): You were his friend, his boyhood friend. There's something I don't understand about it. His life ended after that Ebbets Field game. From the age of seventeen nothing good ever happened to him.

BERNARD: He never trained himself for anything.

WILLY: But he did, he did. After high school he took so many correspondence courses. Radio mechanics; television; God knows what, and never made the slightest mark.

BERNARD (*taking off his glasses*): Willy, do you want to talk candidly?

WILLY (*rising, faces Bernard*): I regard you as a very brilliant man, Bernard. I value your advice.

BERNARD: Oh, the hell with the advice, Willy. I couldn't advise you. There's just one thing I've always wanted to ask you. When he was supposed to graduate, and the math teacher flunked him —

WILLY: Oh, that son-of-a-bitch ruined his life.

BERNARD: Yeah, but, Willy, all he had to do was go to summer school and make up that subject.

WILLY: That's right, that's right.

BERNARD: Did you tell him not to go to summer school?

WILLY: Me? I begged him to go. I ordered him to go!

BERNARD: Then why wouldn't he go?

WILLY: Why? Why! Bernard, that question has been trailing me like a ghost for the last fifteen years. He flunked the subject, and laid down and died like a hammer hit him!

BERNARD: Take it easy, kid.

WILLY: Let me talk to you—I got nobody to talk to. Bernard, Bernard, was it my fault? Y'see? It keeps going around in my mind, maybe I did something to him. I got nothing to give him.

BERNARD: Don't take it so hard.

WILLY: Why did he lay down? What is the story there? You were his friend!

BERNARD: Willy, I remember, it was June, and our grades came out. And he'd flunked math.

WILLY: That son-of-a-bitch!

BERNARD: No, it wasn't right then. Biff just got very angry, I remember, and he was ready to enroll in summer school.

WILLY (*surprised*): He was?

BERNARD: He wasn't beaten by it at all. But then, Willy, he disappeared from the block for almost a month. And I got the idea that he'd gone up to New England to see you. Did he have a talk with you then?

(*Willy stares in silence.*)

BERNARD: Willy?

WILLY (*with a strong edge of resentment in his voice*): Yeah, he came to Boston. What about it?

BERNARD: Well, just that when he came back—I'll never forget this, it always mystifies me. Because I'd thought so well of Biff, even though he'd always taken advantage of me. I loved him, Willy, y'know? And he came back after that month and took his sneakers—remember those sneakers with "University of Virginia" printed on them? He was so proud of those, wore them every day. And he took them down in the cellar, and burned them up in the furnace. We had a fist fight. It lasted at least half an hour. Just the two of us, punching each other down the cellar, and crying right through it. I've often thought of how strange it was that I knew he'd given up his life. What happened in Boston, Willy?

(*Willy looks at him as at an intruder.*)

BERNARD: I just bring it up because you asked me.

WILLY (*angrily*): Nothing. What do you mean, "What happened?" What's that got to do with anything?

BERNARD: Well, don't get sore.

WILLY: What are you trying to do, blame it on me? If a boy lays down is that my fault?

BERNARD: Now, Willy, don't get—

WILLY: Well, don't—don't talk to me that way! What does that mean, "What happened?"

(*Charley enters. He is in his vest, and he carries a bottle of bourbon.*)

CHARLEY: Hey, you're going to miss that train. (*He waves the bottle.*)

BERNARD: Yeah, I'm going. (*He takes the bottle.*) Thanks, Pop. (*He picks up his rackets and bag.*) Good-by, Willy, and don't worry about it. You know, "If at first you don't succeed . . ."

WILLY: Yes, I believe in that.

BERNARD: But sometimes, Willy, it's better for a man just to walk away.

WILLY: Walk away?

BERNARD: That's right.

WILLY: But if you can't walk away?

BERNARD (*after a slight pause*): I guess that's when it's tough. (*Extending his hand.*) Good-by, Willy.

WILLY (*shaking Bernard's hand*): Good-by, boy.

CHARLEY (*an arm on Bernard's shoulder*): How do you like this kid? Gonna argue a case in front of the Supreme Court.

BERNARD (*protesting*): Pop!

WILLY (*genuinely shocked, pained, and happy*): No! The Supreme Court!

BERNARD: I gotta run. 'By, Dad!

CHARLEY: Knock 'em dead, Bernard!

(*Bernard goes off.*)

WILLY (*as Charley takes out his wallet*): The Supreme Court! And he didn't even mention it!

CHARLEY (*counting out money on the desk*): He don't have to — he's gonna do it.

WILLY: And you never told him what to do, did you? You never took any interest in him.

CHARLEY: My salvation is that I never took any interest in anything. There's some money — fifty dollars. I got an accountant inside.

WILLY: Charley, look . . . (*With difficulty.*) I got my insurance to pay. If you can manage it — I need a hundred and ten dollars.

(*Charley doesn't reply for a moment; merely stops moving.*)

WILLY: I'd draw it from my bank but Linda would know, and I . . .

CHARLEY: Sit down, Willy.

WILLY (*moving toward the chair*): I'm keeping an account of everything, remember. I'll pay every penny back. (*He sits.*)

CHARLEY: Now listen to me, Willy.

WILLY: I want you to know I appreciate . . .

CHARLEY (*sitting down on the table*): Willy, what're you doin'? What the hell is goin' on in your head?

WILLY: Why? I'm simply . . .

CHARLEY: I offered you a job. You make fifty dollars a week. And I won't send you on the road.

WILLY: I've got a job.

CHARLEY: Without pay? What kind of a job is a job without pay? (*He rises.*) Now, look, kid, enough is enough. I'm no genius but I know when I'm being insulted.

WILLY: Insulted!

CHARLEY: Why don't you want to work for me?

WILLY: What's the matter with you? I've got a job.

CHARLEY: Then what're you walkin' in here every week for?

WILLY (*getting up*): Well, if you don't want me to walk in here —

CHARLEY: I'm offering you a job.

WILLY: I don't want your goddam job!

CHARLEY: When the hell are you going to grow up?

WILLY (*furiously*): You big ignoramus, if you say that to me again I'll rap you one! I don't care how big you are! (*He's ready to fight.*)

(*Pause.*)

CHARLEY (*kindly, going to him*): How much do you need, Willy?

WILLY: Charley, I'm strapped. I'm strapped. I don't know what to do. I was just fired.

CHARLEY: Howard fired you?

WILLY: That snotnose. Imagine that? I named him. I named him Howard.

CHARLEY: Willy, when're you gonna realize that them things don't mean anything? You named him Howard, but you can't sell that. The only thing you got in this world is what you can sell. And the funny thing is that you're a salesman, and you don't know that.

WILLY: I've always tried to think otherwise, I guess. I always felt that if a man was impressive, and well liked, that nothing —

CHARLEY: Why must everybody like you? Who liked J. P. Morgan?° Was he impressive? In a Turkish bath he'd look like a butcher. But with his pockets on he was very well liked. Now listen, Willy, I know you don't like me, and nobody can say I'm in love with you, but I'll give you a job because — just for the hell of it, put it that way. Now what do you say?

WILLY: I — I just can't work for you, Charley.

CHARLEY: What're you, jealous of me?

WILLY: I can't work for you, that's all, don't ask me why.

CHARLEY (*angered, takes out more bills*): You been jealous of me all your life, you dammed fool! Here, pay your insurance. (*He puts the money in Willy's hand.*)

WILLY: I'm keeping strict accounts.

CHARLEY: I've got some work to do. Take care of yourself. And pay your insurance.

WILLY (*moving to the right*): Funny, y'know? After all the highways, and the trains, and the appointments, and the years, you end up worth more dead than alive.

CHARLEY: Willy, nobody's worth nothin' dead. (*After a slight pause.*) Did you hear what I said?

(*Willy stands still, dreaming.*)

CHARLEY: Willy!

WILLY: Apologize to Bernard for me when you see him. I didn't mean to argue with him. He's a fine boy. They're all fine boys, and they'll end up big — all of them. Someday they'll all play tennis together. Wish me luck, Charley. He saw Bill Oliver today.

J. P. Morgan: John Pierpont Morgan (1837–1913), wealthy and ruthless American financier, railroad developer, and industrialist.

CHARLEY: Good luck.

WILLY (*on the verge of tears*): Charley, you're the only friend I got. Isn't that a remarkable thing? (*He goes out.*)

CHARLEY: Jesus!

(*Charley stares after him a moment and follows. All light blacks out. Suddenly raucous music is heard, and a red glow rises behind the screen at right. Stanley, a young
waiter, appears, carrying a table, followed by Happy, who is carrying two chairs.*)

STANLEY (*putting the table down*): That's all right, Mr. Loman, I can handle it myself. (*He turns and takes the chairs from Happy and places them at the table.*)

HAPPY (*glancing around*): Oh, this is better.

STANLEY: Sure, in the front there you're in the middle of all kinds of noise.
Whenever you got a party, Mr. Loman, you just tell me and I'll put you back
here. Y'know, there's a lotta people they don't like it private, because when
they go out they like to see a lotta action around them because they're sick
and tired to stay in the house by theirself. But I know you, you ain't from
Hackensack. You know what I mean?

HAPPY (*sitting down*): So how's it coming, Stanley?

STANLEY: Ah, it's a dog life. I only wish during the war they'd a took me in the
Army. I coulda been dead by now.

HAPPY: My brother's back, Stanley.

STANLEY: Oh, he come back, heh? From the Far West.

HAPPY: Yeah, big cattle man, my brother, so treat him right. And my father's
coming too.

STANLEY: Oh, your father too!

HAPPY: You got a couple of nice lobsters?

STANLEY: Hundred percent, big.

HAPPY: I want them with the claws.

STANLEY: Don't worry, I don't give you no mice. (*Happy laughs.*) How about
some wine? It'll put a head on the meal.

HAPPY: No. You remember, Stanley, that recipe I brought you from overseas?
With the champagne in it?

STANLEY: Oh, yeah, sure. I still got it tacked up yet in the kitchen. But that'll have
to cost a buck apiece anyways.

HAPPY: That's all right.

STANLEY: What'd you, hit a number or somethin'?

HAPPY: No, it's a little celebration. My brother is — I think he pulled off a big deal
today. I think we're going into business together.

STANLEY: Great! That's the best for you. Because a family business, you know
what I mean? — that's the best.

HAPPY: That's what I think.

STANLEY: 'Cause what's the difference? Somebody steals? It's in the family.
Know what I mean? (*Sotto voce.°*) Like this bartender here. The boss is goin'

---

s.d. Sotto voce: "Under [the] voice" (Italian); in a low, soft voice.

crazy what kinda leak he's got in the cash register. You put it in but it don't come out.

HAPPY (*raising his head*): Sh!

STANLEY: What?

HAPPY: You notice I wasn't lookin' right or left, was I?

STANLEY: No.

HAPPY: And my eyes are closed.

STANLEY: So what's the — ?

HAPPY: Strudel's comin'.

STANLEY (*catching on, looks around*): Ah, no, there's no —

(*He breaks off as a furred, lavishly dressed girl enters and sits at the next table. Both follow her with their eyes.*)

STANLEY: Geez, how'd ya know?

HAPPY: I got radar or something. (*Staring directly at her profile.*) Oooooooo . . . Stanley.

STANLEY: I think that's for you, Mr. Loman.

HAPPY: Look at that mouth. Oh, God. And the binoculars.

STANLEY: Geez, you got a life, Mr. Loman.

HAPPY: Wait on her.

STANLEY (*going to the girl's table*): Would you like a menu, ma'am?

GIRL: I'm expecting someone, but I'd like a —

HAPPY: Why don't you bring her — excuse me, miss, do you mind? I sell champagne, and I'd like you to try my brand. Bring her a champagne, Stanley.

GIRL: That's awfully nice of you.

HAPPY: Don't mention it. It's all company money. (*He laughs.*)

GIRL: That's a charming product to be selling, isn't it?

HAPPY: Oh, gets to be like everything else. Selling is selling, y'know.

GIRL: I suppose.

HAPPY: You don't happen to sell, do you?

GIRL: No, I don't sell.

HAPPY: Would you object to a compliment from a stranger? You ought to be on a magazine cover.

GIRL (*looking at him a little archly*): I have been.

(*Stanley comes in with a glass of champagne.*)

HAPPY: What'd I say before, Stanley? You see? She's a cover girl.

STANLEY: Oh, I could see, I could see.

HAPPY (*to the Girl*): What magazine?

GIRL: Oh, a lot of them. (*She takes the drink.*) Thank you.

HAPPY: You know what they say in France, don't you? "Champagne is the drink of the complexion" — Hya, Biff!

(*Biff has entered and sits with Happy.*)

BIFF: Hello, kid. Sorry I'm late.

HAPPY: I just got here. Uh, Miss — ?

GIRL: Forsythe.

HAPPY: Miss Forsythe, this is my brother.

BIFF: Is Dad here?

HAPPY: His name is Biff. You might've heard of him. Great football player.

GIRL: Really? What team?

HAPPY: Are you familiar with football?

GIRL: No, I'm afraid I'm not.

HAPPY: Biff is quarterback with the New York Giants.

GIRL: Well, that is nice, isn't it? (*She drinks.*)

HAPPY: Good health.

GIRL: I'm happy to meet you.

HAPPY: That's my name. Hap. It's really Harold, but at West Point they called me Happy.

GIRL (*now really impressed*): Oh, I see. How do you do? (*She turns her profile.*)

BIFF: Isn't Dad coming?

HAPPY: You want her?

BIFF: Oh, I could never make that.

HAPPY: I remember the time that idea would never come into your head. Where's the old confidence, Biff?

BIFF: I just saw Oliver —

HAPPY: Wait a minute. I've got to see that old confidence again. Do you want her? She's on call.

BIFF: Oh, no. (*He turns to look at the Girl.*)

HAPPY: I'm telling you. Watch this. (*Turning to the Girl*): Honey? (*She turns to him.*) Are you busy?

GIRL: Well, I am . . . but I could make a phone call.

HAPPY: Do that, will you, honey? And see if you can get a friend. We'll be here for a while. Biff is one of the greatest football players in the country.

GIRL (*standing up*): Well, I'm certainly happy to meet you.

HAPPY: Come back soon.

GIRL: I'll try.

HAPPY: Don't try, honey, try hard.

(*The Girl exits. Stanley follows, shaking his head in bewildered admiration.*)

HAPPY: Isn't that a shame now? A beautiful girl like that? That's why I can't get married. There's not a good woman in a thousand. New York is loaded with them, kid!

BIFF: Hap, look —

HAPPY: I told you she was on call!

BIFF (*strangely unnerved*): Cut it out, will ya? I want to say something to you.

HAPPY: Did you see Oliver?

BIFF: I saw him all right. Now look, I want to tell Dad a couple of things and I want you to help me.

HAPPY: What? Is he going to back you?

BIFF: Are you crazy? You're out of your goddam head, you know that?

HAPPY: Why? What happened?

BIFF (*breathlessly*): I did a terrible thing today, Hap. It's been the strangest day I ever went through. I'm all numb, I swear.

HAPPY: You mean he wouldn't see you?

BIFF: Well, I waited six hours for him, see? All day. Kept sending my name in. Even tried to date his secretary so she'd get me to him, but no soap.

HAPPY: Because you're not showin' the old confidence Biff. He remembered you, didn't he?

BIFF (*stopping Happy with a gesture*): Finally, about five o'clock, he comes out. Didn't remember who I was or anything. I felt like such an idiot, Hap.

HAPPY: Did you tell him my Florida idea?

BIFF: He walked away. I saw him for one minute. I got so mad I could've torn the walls down! How the hell did I ever get the idea I was a salesman there? I even believed myself that I'd been a salesman for him! And then he gave me one look and — I realized what a ridiculous lie my whole life has been! We've been talking in a dream for fifteen years. I was a shipping clerk.

HAPPY: What'd you do?

BIFF (*with great tension and wonder*): Well, he left, see. And the secretary went out. I was all alone in the waiting room. I don't know what came over me, Hap. The next thing I know I'm in his office — paneled walls, everything. I can't explain it. I — Hap, I took his fountain pen.

HAPPY: Geez, did he catch you?

BIFF: I ran out. I ran down all eleven flights. I ran and ran and ran.

HAPPY: That was an awful dumb — what'd you do that for?

BIFF (*agonized*): I don't know, I just — wanted to take something, I don't know. You gotta help me, Hap. I'm gonna tell Pop.

HAPPY: You crazy? What for?

BIFF: Hap, he's got to understand that I'm not the man somebody lends that kind of money to. He thinks I've been spiting him all these years and it's eating him up.

HAPPY: That's just it. You tell him something nice.

BIFF: I can't.

HAPPY: Say you got a lunch date with Oliver tomorrow.

BIFF: So what do I do tomorrow?

HAPPY: You leave the house tomorrow and come back at night and say Oliver is thinking it over. And he thinks it over for a couple of weeks, and gradually it fades away and nobody's the worse.

BIFF: But it'll go on forever!

HAPPY: Dad is never so happy as when he's looking forward to something!

(*Willy enters.*)

HAPPY: Hello, scout!

WILLY: Gee, I haven't been here in years!

(*Stanley has followed Willy in and sets a chair for him. Stanley starts off but Happy stops him.*)

HAPPY: Stanley!

(*Stanley stands by, waiting for an order.*)

BIFF (*going to Willy with guilt, as to an invalid*): Sit down, Pop. You want a drink?

WILLY: Sure, I don't mind.

BIFF: Let's get a load on.

WILLY: You look worried.

BIFF: N-no. (*To Stanley.*) Scotch all around. Make it doubles.

STANLEY: Doubles, right. (*He goes.*)

WILLY: You had a couple already, didn't you?

BIFF: Just a couple, yeah.

WILLY: Well, what happened, boy? (*Nodding affirmatively, with a smile.*) Everything go all right?

BIFF (*takes a breath, then reaches out and grasps Willy's hand*): Pal . . . (*He is smiling bravely, and Willy is smiling too.*) I had an experience today.

HAPPY: Terrific, Pop.

WILLY: That so? What happened?

BIFF (*high, slightly alcoholic, above the earth*): I'm going to tell you everything from first to last. It's been a strange day. (*Silence. He looks around, composes himself as best he can, but his breath keeps breaking the rhythm of his voice.*) I had to wait quite a while for him, and —

WILLY: Oliver?

BIFF: Yeah, Oliver. All day, as a matter of cold fact. And a lot of — instances — facts, Pop, facts about my life came back to me. Who was it, Pop? Who ever said I was a salesman with Oliver?

WILLY: Well, you were.

BIFF: No, Dad, I was a shipping clerk.

WILLY: But you were practically —

BIFF (*with determination*): Dad, I don't know who said it first, but I was never a salesman for Bill Oliver.

WILLY: What're you talking about?

BIFF: Let's hold on to the facts tonight, Pop. We're not going to get anywhere bullin' around. I was a shipping clerk.

WILLY (*angrily*): All right, now listen to me —

BIFF: Why don't you let me finish?

WILLY: I'm not interested in stories about the past or any crap of that kind because the woods are burning, boys, you understand? There's a big blaze going on all around. I was fired today.

BIFF (*shocked*): How could you be?

WILLY: I was fired, and I'm looking for a little good news to tell your mother, because the woman has waited and the woman has suffered. The gist of it is that I haven't got a story left in my head, Biff. So don't give me a lecture about facts and aspects. I am not interested. Now what've you got to say to me?

(*Stanley enters with three drinks. They wait until he leaves.*)

WILLY: Did you see Oliver?

BIFF: Jesus, Dad!

WILLY: You mean you didn't go up there?

HAPPY: Sure he went up there.

BIFF: I did. I — saw him. How could they fire you?

WILLY (*on the edge of his chair*): What kind of a welcome did he give you?

BIFF: He won't even let you work on commission?

WILLY: I'm out! (*Driving.*) So tell me, he gave you a warm welcome?

HAPPY: Sure, Pop, sure!

BIFF (*driven*): Well, it was kind of —

WILLY: I was wondering if he'd remember you. (*To Happy.*) Imagine, man doesn't see him for ten, twelve years and gives him that kind of a welcome!

HAPPY: Damn right!

BIFF (*trying to return to the offensive*): Pop, look —

WILLY: You know why he remembered you, don't you? Because you impressed him in those days.

BIFF: Let's talk quietly and get this down to the facts, huh?

WILLY (*as though Biff had been interrupting*): Well, what happened? It's great news, Biff. Did he take you into his office or'd you talk in the waiting room?

BIFF: Well, he came in, see, and —

WILLY (*with a big smile*): What'd he say? Betcha he threw his arm around you.

BIFF: Well, he kinda —

WILLY: He's a fine man. (*To Happy.*) Very hard man to see, y'know.

HAPPY (*agreeing*): Oh, I know.

WILLY (*to Biff*): Is that where you had the drinks?

BIFF: Yeah, he gave me a couple of — no, no!

HAPPY (*cutting in*): He told him my Florida idea.

WILLY: Don't interrupt. (*To Biff.*) How'd he react to the Florida idea?

BIFF: Dad, will you give me a minute to explain?

WILLY: I've been waiting for you to explain since I sat down here! What happened? He took you into his office and what?

BIFF: Well — I talked. And — and he listened, see.

WILLY: Famous for the way he listens, y'know. What was his answer?

BIFF: His answer was — (*He breaks off, suddenly angry.*) Dad, you're not letting me tell you what I want to tell you!

WILLY (*accusing, angered*): You didn't see him, did you?

BIFF: I did see him!

WILLY: What'd you insult him or something? You insulted him, didn't you?

BIFF: Listen, will you let me out of it, will you just let me out of it!

HAPPY: What the hell!

WILLY: Tell me what happened!

BIFF (*to Happy*): I can't talk to him!

(*A single trumpet note jars the ear. The light of green leaves stains the house, which holds the air of night and a dream. Young Bernard enters and knocks on the door of the house.*)

YOUNG BERNARD (*frantically*): Mrs. Loman, Mrs. Loman!

HAPPY: Tell him what happened!

BIFF (*to Happy*): Shut up and leave me alone!

WILLY: No, no! You had to go and flunk math!

BIFF: What math? What're you talking about?

YOUNG BERNARD: Mrs. Loman, Mrs. Loman!

(*Linda appears in the house, as of old.*)

WILLY (*wildly*): Math, math, math!

BIFF: Take it easy, Pop!

YOUNG BERNARD: Mrs. Loman!

WILLY (*furiously*): If you hadn't flunked you'd've been set by now!

BIFF: Now, look, I'm gonna tell you what happened, and you're going to listen to me.

YOUNG BERNARD: Mrs. Loman!

BIFF: I waited six hours —

HAPPY: What the hell are you saying?

BIFF: I kept sending in my name but he wouldn't see me. So finally he . . . (*He continues unheard as light fades low on the restaurant.*)

YOUNG BERNARD: Biff flunked math!

LINDA: No!

YOUNG BERNARD: Birnbaum flunked him! They won't graduate him!

LINDA: But they have to. He's gotta go to the university. Where is he? Biff! Biff!

YOUNG BERNARD: No, he left. He went to Grand Central.

LINDA: Grand — You mean he went to Boston!

YOUNG BERNARD: Is Uncle Willy in Boston?

LINDA: Oh, maybe Willy can talk to the teacher. Oh, the poor, poor boy!

(*Light on house area snaps out.*)

BIFF (*at the table, now audible, holding up a gold fountain pen*): . . . so I'm washed up with Oliver, you understand? Are you listening to me?

WILLY (*at a loss*): Yeah, sure. If you hadn't flunked —

BIFF: Flunked what? What're you talking about?

WILLY: Don't blame everything on me! I didn't flunk math — you did! What pen?

HAPPY: That was awful dumb, Biff, a pen like that is worth —

WILLY (*seeing the pen for the first time*): You took Oliver's pen?

BIFF (*weakening*): Dad, I just explained it to you.

WILLY: You stole Bill Oliver's fountain pen!

BIFF: I didn't exactly steal it! That's just what I've been explaining to you!

HAPPY: He had it in his hand and just then Oliver walked in, so he got nervous and stuck it in his pocket!

WILLY: My God, Biff!

BIFF: I never intended to do it, Dad!

OPERATOR'S VOICE: Standish Arms, good evening!

WILLY (*shouting*): I'm not in my room!

BIFF (*frightened*): Dad, what's the matter? (*He and Happy stand up.*)

OPERATOR: Ringing Mr. Loman for you!

WILLY: I'm not there, stop it!

BIFF (*horrified, gets down on one knee before Willy*): Dad, I'll make good, I'll make good. (*Willy tries to get to his feet. Biff holds him down.*) Sit down now.

WILLY: No, you're no good, you're no good for anything.

BIFF: I am, Dad, I'll find something else, you understand? Now don't worry about anything. (*He holds up Willy's face.*) Talk to me, Dad.

OPERATOR: Mr. Loman does not answer. Shall I page him?

WILLY (*attempting to stand, as though to rush and silence the Operator*): No, no, no!

HAPPY: He'll strike something, Pop.

WILLY: No, no . . .

BIFF (*desperately, standing over Willy*): Pop, listen! Listen to me! I'm telling you something good. Oliver talked to his partner about the Florida idea. You listening? He — he talked to his partner, and he came to me . . . I'm going to be all right, you hear? Dad, listen to me, he said it was just a question of the amount!

WILLY: Then you . . . got it?

HAPPY: He's gonna be terrific, Pop!

WILLY (*trying to stand*): Then you got it, haven't you? You got it! You got it!

BIFF (*agonized, holds Willy down*): No, no. Look, Pop. I'm supposed to have lunch with them tomorrow. I'm just telling you this so you'll know that I can still make an impression, Pop. And I'll make good somewhere, but I can't go tomorrow, see?

WILLY: Why not? You simply —

BIFF: But the pen, Pop!

WILLY: You give it to him and tell him it was an oversight!

HAPPY: Sure, have lunch tomorrow!

BIFF: I can't say that —

WILLY: You were doing a crossword puzzle and accidentally used his pen!

BIFF: Listen, kid, I took those balls years ago, now I walk in with his fountain pen? That clinches it, don't you see? I can't face him like that! I'll try elsewhere.

PAGE'S VOICE: Paging Mr. Loman!

WILLY: Don't you want to be anything?

BIFF: Pop, how can I go back?

WILLY: You don't want to be anything, is that what's behind it?

BIFF (*now angry at Willy for not crediting his sympathy*): Don't take it that way! You think it was easy walking into that office after what I'd done to him? A team of horses couldn't have dragged me back to Bill Oliver!

WILLY: Then why'd you go?

BIFF: Why did I go? Why did I go! Look at you! Look at what's become of you!

(*Off left, The Woman laughs.*)

WILLY: Biff, you're going to go to that lunch tomorrow, or —

BIFF: I can't go. I've got no appointment!

HAPPY: Biff, for . . . !

WILLY: Are you spiting me?

BIFF: Don't take it that way! Goddammit!

WILLY (*strikes Biff and falters away from the table*): You rotten little louse! Are you spiting me?

THE WOMAN: Someone's at the door, Willy!

BIFF: I'm no good, can't you see what I am?

HAPPY (*separating them*): Hey, you're in a restaurant! Now cut it out, both of you! (*The girls enter.*) Hello, girls, sit down.

(*The Woman laughs, off left.*)

MISS FORSYTHE: I guess we might as well. This is Letta.

THE WOMAN: Willy, are you going to wake up?

BIFF (*ignoring Willy*): How're ya, miss, sit down. What do you drink?

MISS FORSYTHE: Letta might not be able to stay long.

LETTA: I gotta get up very early tomorrow. I got jury duty. I'm so excited! Were you fellows ever on a jury?

BIFF: No, but I been in front of them! (*The girls laugh.*) This is my father.

LETTA: Isn't he cute? Sit down with us, Pop.

HAPPY: Sit him down, Biff!

BIFF (*going to him*): Come on, slugger, drink us under the table. To hell with it! Come on, sit down, pal.

(*On Biff's last insistence, Willy is about to sit.*)

THE WOMAN (*now urgently*): Willy, are you going to answer the door!

(*The Woman's call pulls Willy back. He starts right, befuddled.*)

BIFF: Hey, where are you going?

WILLY: Open the door.

BIFF: The door?

WILLY: The washroom . . . the door . . . where's the door?

BIFF (*leading Willy to the left*): Just go straight down.

(*Willy moves left.*)

THE WOMAN: Willy, Willy, are you going to get up, get up, get up, get up?

(*Willy exits left.*)

LETTA: I think it's sweet you bring your daddy along.

MISS FORSYTHE: Oh, he isn't really your father!

BIFF (*at left, turning to her resentfully*): Miss Forsythe, you've just seen a prince walk by. A fine, troubled prince. A hard-working, unappreciated prince. A pal, you understand? A good companion. Always for his boys.

LETTA: That's so sweet.

HAPPY: Well, girls, what's the program? We're wasting time. Come on, Biff. Gather round. Where would you like to go?

BIFF: Why don't you do something for him?

HAPPY: Me!

BIFF: Don't you give a damn for him, Hap?

HAPPY: What're you talking about? I'm the one who —

BIFF: I sense it, you don't give a good goddam about him. (*He takes the rolled-up hose from his pocket and puts it on the table in front of Happy.*) Look what I found in the cellar, for Christ's sake. How can you bear to let it go on?

HAPPY: Me? Who goes away? Who runs off and —

BIFF: Yeah, but he doesn't mean anything to you. You could help him — I can't! Don't you understand what I'm talking about? He's going to kill himself, don't you know that?

HAPPY: Don't I know it! Me!

BIFF: Hap, help him! Jesus . . . help him . . . Help me, help me, I can't bear to look at his face! (*Ready to weep, he hurries out, up right.*)

HAPPY (*starting after him*): Where are you going?

MISS FORSYTHE: What's he so mad about?

HAPPY: Come on, girls, we'll catch up with him.

MISS FORSYTHE (*as Happy pushes her out*): Say, I don't like that temper of his!

HAPPY: He's just a little overstrung, he'll be all right!

WILLY (*off left, as The Woman laughs*): Don't answer! Don't answer!

LETTA: Don't you want to tell your father —

HAPPY: No, that's not my father. He's just a guy. Come on, we'll catch Biff, and, honey, we're going to paint this town! Stanley, where's the check! Hey, Stanley!

(*They exit. Stanley looks toward left.*)

STANLEY (*calling to Happy indignantly*): Mr. Loman! Mr. Loman!

(*Stanley picks up a chair and follows them off. Knocking is heard off left. The Woman enters, laughing. Willy follows her. She is in a black slip; he is buttoning his shirt. Raw, sensuous music accompanies their speech.*)

WILLY: Will you stop laughing? Will you stop?

THE WOMAN: Aren't you going to answer the door? He'll wake the whole hotel.

WILLY: I'm not expecting anybody.

THE WOMAN: Whyn't you have another drink, honey, and stop being so damn self-centered?

WILLY: I'm so lonely.

THE WOMAN: You know you ruined me, Willy? From now on, whenever you come to the office, I'll see that you go right through to the buyers. No waiting at my desk anymore, Willy. You ruined me.

WILLY: That's nice of you to say that.

THE WOMAN: Gee, you are self-centered! Why so sad? You are the saddest, self-centeredest soul I ever did see-saw. (*She laughs. He kisses her.*) Come on inside, drummer boy. It's silly to be dressing in the middle of the night. (*As knocking is heard.*) Aren't you going to answer the door?

WILLY: They're knocking on the wrong door.

THE WOMAN: But I felt the knocking. And he heard us talking in here. Maybe the hotel's on fire!

WILLY (*his terror rising*): It's a mistake.

THE WOMAN: Then tell him to go away!

WILLY: There's nobody there.

THE WOMAN: It's getting on my nerves, Willy. There's somebody standing out there and it's getting on my nerves!

WILLY (*pushing her away from him*): All right, stay in the bathroom here, and don't come out. I think there's a law in Massachusetts about it, so don't come out. It may be that new room clerk. He looked very mean. So don't come out. It's a mistake, there's no fire.

(*The knocking is heard again. He takes a few steps away from her, and she vanishes into the wing. The light follows him, and now he is facing Young Biff, who carries a suitcase. Biff steps toward him. The music is gone.*)

BIFF: Why didn't you answer?

WILLY: Biff! What are you doing in Boston?

BIFF: Why didn't you answer? I've been knocking for five minutes, I called you on the phone—

WILLY: I just heard you. I was in the bathroom and had the door shut. Did anything happen home?

BIFF: Dad—I let you down.

WILLY: What do you mean?

BIFF: Dad . . .

WILLY: Biffo, what's this about? (*Putting his arm around Biff.*) Come on, let's go downstairs and get you a malted.

BIFF: Dad, I flunked math.

WILLY: Not for the term?

BIFF: The term. I haven't got enough credits to graduate.

WILLY: You mean to say Bernard wouldn't give you the answers?

BIFF: He did, he tried, but I only got a sixty-one.

WILLY: And they wouldn't give you four points?

BIFF: Birnbaum refused absolutely. I begged him, Pop, but he won't give me those points. You gotta talk to him before they close the school. Because if he saw the kind of man you are, and you just talked to him in your way, I'm sure he'd come through for me. The class came right before practice, see, and I didn't go enough. Would you talk to him? He'd like you, Pop. You know the way you could talk.

WILLY: You're on. We'll drive right back.

BIFF: Oh, Dad, good work! I'm sure he'll change it for you!

WILLY: Go downstairs and tell the clerk I'm checkin' out. Go right down.

BIFF: Yes, sir! See, the reason he hates me, Pop—one day he was late for class so I got up at the blackboard and imitated him. I crossed my eyes and talked with a lithp.

WILLY (*laughing*): You did? The kids like it?

BIFF: They nearly died laughing!

WILLY: Yeah? What'd you do?

BIFF: The thquare root of thixthy twee is . . . (*Willy bursts out laughing; Biff joins.*) And in the middle of it he walked in!

(*Willy laughs and The Woman joins in offstage.*)

WILLY (*without hesitation*): Hurry downstairs and—

BIFF: Somebody in there?

WILLY: No, that was next door.

(*The Woman laughs offstage.*)

BIFF: Somebody got in your bathroom!

WILLY: No, it's the next room, there's a party—

THE WOMAN (*enters, laughing. She lisps this.*): Can I come in? There's something in the bathtub, Willy, and it's moving!

(*Willy looks at Biff, who is staring open-mouthed and horrified at The Woman.*)

WILLY: Ah—you better go back to your room. They must be finished painting by now. They're painting her room so I let her take a shower here. Go back, go back . . . (*He pushes her.*)

THE WOMAN (*resisting*): But I've got to get dressed, Willy, I can't—

WILLY: Get out of here! Go back, go back . . . (*Suddenly striving for the ordinary.*) This is Miss Francis, Biff, she's a buyer. They're painting her room. Go back, Miss Francis, go back . . .

THE WOMAN: But my clothes, I can't go out naked in the hall!

WILLY (*pushing her offstage*): Get outa here! Go back, go back!

(*Biff slowly sits down on his suitcase as the argument continues offstage.*)

THE WOMAN: Where's my stockings? You promised me stockings, Willy!

WILLY: I have no stockings here!

THE WOMAN: You had two boxes of size nine sheers for me, and I want them!

WILLY: Here, for God's sake, will you get outa here!

THE WOMAN (*enters holding a box of stockings*): I just hope there's nobody in the hall. That's all I hope. (*To Biff.*) Are you football or baseball?

BIFF: Football.

THE WOMAN (*angry, humiliated*): That's me too. G'night. (*She snatches her clothes from Willy, and walks out.*)

WILLY (*after a pause*): Well, better get going. I want to get to the school first thing in the morning. Get my suits out of the closet. I'll get my valise. (*Biff doesn't move.*) What's the matter! (*Biff remains motionless, tears falling.*) She's a buyer. Buys for J. H. Simmons. She lives down the hall—they're painting. You don't imagine— (*He breaks off. After a pause.*) Now listen, pal, she's just a buyer. She sees merchandise in her room and they have to keep it looking just so . . . (*Pause. Assuming command.*) All right, get my suits. (*Biff doesn't move.*) Now stop crying and do as I say. I gave you an order. Biff, I gave you an order! Is that what you do when I give you an order? How dare you cry! (*Putting his arm around Biff.*) Now look, Biff, when you grow up you'll understand about these things. You mustn't — you mustn't overemphasize a thing like this. I'll see Birnbaum first thing in the morning.

BIFF: Never mind.

WILLY (*getting down beside Biff*): Never mind! He's going to give you those points. I'll see to it.

BIFF: He wouldn't listen to you.

WILLY: He certainly will listen to me. You need those points for the U. of Virginia.

BIFF: I'm not going there.

WILLY: Heh? If I can't get him to change that mark you'll make it up in summer school. You've got all summer to —

BIFF (*his weeping breaking from him*): Dad . . .

WILLY (*infected by it*): Oh, my boy . . .

BIFF: Dad . . .

WILLY: She's nothing to me, Biff. I was lonely, I was terribly lonely.

BIFF: You — you gave her Mama's stockings! (*His tears break through and he rises to go.*)

WILLY (*grabbing for Biff*): I gave you an order!

BIFF: Don't touch me, you — liar!

WILLY: Apologize for that!

BIFF: You fake! You phony little fake! You fake! (*Overcome, he turns quickly and weeping fully goes out with his suitcase. Willy is left on the floor on his knees.*)

WILLY: I gave you an order! Biff, come back here or I'll beat you! Come back here! I'll whip you!

(*Stanley comes quickly in from the right and stands in front of Willy.*)

WILLY (*shouts at Stanley*): I gave you an order . . .

STANLEY: Hey, let's pick it up, pick it up, Mr. Loman. (*He helps Willy to his feet.*) Your boys left with the chippies. They said they'll see you home.

(*A second waiter watches some distance away.*)

WILLY: But we were supposed to have dinner together.

(*Music is heard, Willy's theme.*)

STANLEY: Can you make it?

WILLY: I'll — sure, I can make it. (*Suddenly concerned about his clothes.*) Do I — I look all right?

STANLEY: Sure, you look all right. (*He flicks a speck off Willy's lapel.*)

WILLY: Here — here's a dollar.

STANLEY: Oh, your son paid me. It's all right.

WILLY (*putting it in Stanley's hand*): No, take it. You're a good boy.

STANLEY: Oh, no, you don't have to . . .

WILLY: Here — here's some more, I don't need it anymore. (*After a slight pause.*) Tell me — is there a seed store in the neighborhood?

STANLEY: Seeds? You mean like to plant?

(*As Willy turns, Stanley slips the money back into his jacket pocket.*)

WILLY: Yes. Carrots, peas . . .

STANLEY: Well, there's hardware stores on Sixth Avenue, but it may be too late now.

WILLY (*anxiously*): Oh, I'd better hurry. I've got to get some seeds. (*He starts off to the right.*) I've got to get some seeds, right away. Nothing's planted. I don't have a thing in the ground.

(*Willy hurries out as the light goes down. Stanley moves over to the right after him, watches him off. The other waiter has been staring at Willy.*)

STANLEY (*to the waiter*): Well, whatta you looking at?

(*The waiter picks up the chairs and moves off right. Stanley takes the table and follows him. The light fades on this area. There is a long pause, the sound of the flute coming over. The light gradually rises on the kitchen, which is empty. Happy appears at the door of the house, followed by Biff. Happy is carrying a large bunch of long-stemmed roses. He enters the kitchen, looks around for Linda. Not seeing her, he turns to Biff, who is just outside the house door, and makes a gesture with his hands, indicating "Not here, I guess." He looks into the living room and freezes. Inside, Linda, unseen, is seated, Willy's coat on her lap. She rises ominously and quietly and moves toward Happy, who backs up into the kitchen, afraid.*)

HAPPY: Hey, what're you doing up? (*Linda says nothing but moves toward him implacably.*) Where's Pop? (*He keeps backing to the right, and now Linda is in full view in the doorway to the living room.*) Is he sleeping?

LINDA: Where were you?

HAPPY (*trying to laugh it off*): We met two girls, Mom, very fine types. Here, we brought you some flowers. (*Offering them to her.*) Put them in your room, Ma.

(*She knocks them to the floor at Biff's feet. He has now come inside and closed the door behind him. She stares at Biff, silent.*)

HAPPY: Now what'd you do that for? Mom, I want you to have some flowers —

LINDA (*cutting Happy off, violently to Biff*): Don't you care whether he lives or dies?

HAPPY (*going to the stairs*): Come upstairs, Biff.

BIFF (*with a flare of disgust, to Happy*): Go away from me! (*To Linda.*) What do you mean, lives or dies? Nobody's dying around here, pal.

LINDA: Get out of my sight! Get out of here!

BIFF: I wanna see the boss.

LINDA: You're not going near him!

BIFF: Where is he? (*He moves into the living room and Linda follows.*)

LINDA (*shouting after Biff*): You invite him for dinner. He looks forward to it all day — (*Biff appears in his parents' bedroom, looks around, and exits*) — and then you desert him there. There's no stranger you'd do that to!

HAPPY: Why? He had a swell time with us. Listen, when I — (*Linda comes back into the kitchen*) — desert him I hope I don't outlive the day!

LINDA: Get out of here!

HAPPY: Now look, Mom . . .

LINDA: Did you have to go to women tonight? You and your lousy rotten whores!

(*Biff reenters the kitchen.*)

HAPPY: Mom, all we did was follow Biff around trying to cheer him up! (*To Biff.*) Boy, what a night you gave me!

LINDA: Get out of here, both of you, and don't come back! I don't want you tormenting him any more. Go on now, get your things together! (*To Biff.*) You can sleep in his apartment. (*She starts to pick up the flowers and stops herself.*) Pick up this stuff, I'm not your maid anymore. Pick it up, you bum, you!

(*Happy turns his back to her in refusal. Biff slowly moves over and gets down on his knees, picking up the flowers.*)

LINDA: You're a pair of animals! Not one, not another living soul would have had the cruelty to walk out on that man in a restaurant!

BIFF (*not looking at her*): Is that what he said?

LINDA: He didn't have to say anything. He was so humiliated he nearly limped when he came in.

HAPPY: But, Mom, he had a great time with us —

BIFF (*cutting him off violently*): Shut up!

(*Without another word, Happy goes upstairs.*)

LINDA: You! You didn't even go in to see if he was all right!

BIFF (*still on the floor in front of Linda, the flowers in his hand; with self-loathing*): No. Didn't. Didn't do a damned thing. How do you like that, heh? Left him babbling in a toilet.

LINDA: You louse. You . . .

BIFF: Now you hit it on the nose! (*He gets up, throws the flowers in the wastebasket.*) The scum of the earth, and you're looking at him!

LINDA: Get out of here!

BIFF: I gotta talk to the boss, Mom. Where is he?

LINDA: You're not going near him. Get out of this house!

BIFF (*with absolute assurance, determination*): No. We're gonna have an abrupt conversation, him and me.

LINDA: You're not talking to him.

(*Hammering is heard from outside the house, off right. Biff turns toward the noise.*)

LINDA (*suddenly pleading*): Will you please leave him alone?

BIFF: What's he doing out there?

LINDA: He's planting the garden!

BIFF (*quietly*): Now? Oh, my God!

(*Biff moves outside, Linda following. The light dies down on them and comes up on the center of the apron as Willy walks into it. He is carrying a flashlight, a hoe, and a handful of seed packets. He raps the top of the hoe sharply to fix it firmly, and then moves to the left, measuring off the distance with his foot. He holds the flashlight to look at the seed packets, reading off the instructions. He is in the blue of night.)*

WILLY: Carrots . . . quarter-inch apart. Rows . . . one-foot rows. (*He measures it off.*) One foot. (*He puts down a package and measures off.*) Beets. (*He puts down another package and measures again.*) Lettuce. (*He reads the package, puts it down.*) One foot — (*He breaks off as Ben appears at the right and moves slowly down to him.*) What a proposition, ts, ts. Terrific, terrific. 'Cause she's suffered, Ben, the woman has suffered. You understand me? A man can't go out the way he came in, Ben, a man has got to add up to something. You can't, you can't — (*Ben moves toward him as though to interrupt.*) You gotta consider, now. Don't answer so quick. Remember, it's a guaranteed twenty-thousand-dollar proposition. Now look, Ben, I want you to go through the ins and outs of this thing with me. I've got nobody to talk to, Ben, and the woman has suffered, you hear me?

BEN (*standing still, considering*): What's the proposition?

WILLY: It's twenty thousand dollars on the barrelhead. Guaranteed, gilt-edged, you understand?

BEN: You don't want to make a fool of yourself. They might not honor the policy.

WILLY: How can they dare refuse? Didn't I work like a coolie to meet every premium on the nose? And now they don't pay off? Impossible!

BEN: It's called a cowardly thing, William.

WILLY: Why? Does it take more guts to stand here the rest of my life ringing up a zero?

BEN (*yielding*): That's a point, William. (*He moves, thinking, turns.*) And twenty thousand — that is something one can feel with the hand, it is there.

WILLY (*now assured, with rising power*): Oh, Ben, that's the whole beauty of it! I see it like a diamond, shining in the dark, hard and rough, that I can pick up and touch in my hand. Not like — like an appointment! This would not be another damned-fool appointment, Ben, and it changes all the aspects. Because he thinks I'm nothing, see, and so he spites me. But the funeral — (*Straightening up.*) Ben, that funeral will be massive! They'll come from Maine, Massachusetts, Vermont, New Hampshire! All the old-timers with the strange license plates — that boy will be thunderstruck, Ben, because he never realized — I am known! Rhode Island, New York, New Jersey — I am known, Ben and he'll see it with his eyes once and for all. He'll see what I am, Ben! He's in for a shock, that boy!

BEN (*coming down to the edge of the garden*): He'll call you a coward.

WILLY (*suddenly fearful*): No, that would be terrible.

BEN: Yes. And a damned fool.

WILLY: No, no, he mustn't, I won't have that! (*He is broken and desperate.*)

BEN: He'll hate you, William.

(*The gay music of the Boys is heard.*)

WILLY: Oh, Ben, how do we get back to all the great times? Used to be so full of light, and comradeship, the sleigh-riding in winter, and the ruddiness on

his cheeks. And always some kind of good news coming up, always something nice coming up ahead. And never even let me carry the valises in the
house, and simonizing, simonizing that little red car! Why, why can't I give
him something and not have him hate me?

BEN: Let me think about it. (*He glances at his watch.*) I still have a little time. Remarkable proposition, but you've got to be sure you're not making a fool of
yourself.

(*Ben drifts off upstage and goes out of sight. Biff comes down from the left.*)

WILLY (*suddenly conscious of Biff, turns and looks up at him, then begins picking up
the packages of seeds in confusion*): Where the hell is that seed? (*Indignantly.*)
You can't see nothing out here! They boxed in the whole goddam neighborhood!

BIFF: There are people all around here. Don't you realize that?

WILLY: I'm busy. Don't bother me.

BIFF (*taking the hoe from Willy*): I'm saying good-by to you, Pop. (*Willy looks at
him, silent, unable to move.*) I'm not coming back any more.

WILLY: You're not going to see Oliver tomorrow?

BIFF: I've got no appointment, Dad.

WILLY: He put his arm around you, and you've got no appointment?

BIFF: Pop, get this now, will you? Everytime I've left it's been a fight that sent me
out of here. Today I realized something about myself and I tried to explain it
to you and I — I think I'm just not smart enough to make any sense out of it
for you. To hell with whose fault it is or anything like that. (*He takes Willy's
arm.*) Let's just wrap it up, heh? Come on in, we'll tell Mom. (*He gently tries
to pull Willy to left.*)

WILLY (*frozen, immobile, with guilt in his voice*): No, I don't want to see her.

BIFF: Come on! (*He pulls again, and Willy tries to pull away.*)

WILLY (*highly nervous*): No, no, I don't want to see her.

BIFF (*tries to look into Willy's face, as if to find the answer there*): Why don't you
want to see her?

WILLY (*more harshly now*): Don't bother me, will you?

BIFF: What do you mean, you don't want to see her? You don't want them calling you yellow, do you? This isn't your fault; it's me, I'm a bum. Now come
inside! (*Willy strains to get away.*) Did you hear what I said to you?

(*Willy pulls away and quickly goes by himself into the house. Biff follows.*)

LINDA (*to Willy*): Did you plant, dear?

BIFF (*at the door, to Linda*): All right, we had it out. I'm going and I'm not writing
any more.

LINDA (*going to Willy in the kitchen*): I think that's the best way, dear. 'Cause
there's no use drawing it out, you'll just never get along.

(*Willy doesn't respond.*)

BIFF: People ask where I am and what I'm doing, you don't know, and you don't
care. That way it'll be off your mind and you can start brightening up again.

All right? That clears it, doesn't it? (*Willy is silent, and Biff goes to him.*) You
gonna wish me luck, scout? (*He extends his hand.*) What do you say?

LINDA: Shake his hand, Willy.

WILLY (*turning to her, seething with hurt*): There's no necessity to mention the
pen at all, y'know.

BIFF (*gently*): I've got no appointment, Dad.

WILLY (*erupting fiercely*): He put his arm around . . . ?

BIFF: Dad, you're never going to see what I am, so what's the use of arguing? If I
strike oil I'll send you a check. Meantime forget I'm alive.

WILLY (*to Linda*): Spite, see?

BIFF: Shake hands, Dad.

WILLY: Not my hand.

BIFF: I was hoping not to go this way.

WILLY: Well, this is the way you're going. Good-by.

(*Biff looks at him a moment, then turns sharply and goes to the stairs.*)

WILLY (*stops him with*): May you rot in hell if you leave this house!

BIFF (*turning*): Exactly what is it that you want from me?

WILLY: I want you to know, on the train, in the mountains, in the valleys, wherever you go, that you cut down your life for spite!

BIFF: No, no.

WILLY: Spite, spite, is the word of your undoing! And when you're down and out,
remember what did it. When you're rotting somewhere beside the railroad
tracks, remember, and don't you dare blame it on me!

BIFF: I'm not blaming it on you!

WILLY: I won't take the rap for this, you hear?

(*Happy comes down the stairs and stands on the bottom step, watching.*)

BIFF: That's just what I'm telling you!

WILLY (*sinking into a chair at a table, with full accusation*): You're trying to put a
knife in me — don't think I don't know what you're doing!

BIFF: All right, phony! Then let's lay it on the line. (*He whips the rubber tube out
of his pocket and puts it on the table.*)

HAPPY: You crazy . . .

LINDA: Biff! (*She moves to grab the hose, but Biff holds it down with his hand.*)

BIFF: Leave it there! Don't move it!

WILLY (*not looking at it*): What is that?

BIFF: You know goddam well what that is.

WILLY (*caged, wanting to escape*): I never saw that.

BIFF: You saw it. The mice didn't bring it into the cellar! What is this supposed
to do, make a hero out of you? This supposed to make me sorry for you?

WILLY: Never heard of it.

BIFF: There'll be no pity for you, you hear it? No pity!

WILLY (*to Linda*): You hear the spite!

BIFF: No, you're going to hear the truth — what you are and what I am!

LINDA: Stop it!

WILLY: Spite!

HAPPY (*coming down toward Biff*): You cut it now!

BIFF (*to Happy*): The man don't know who we are! The man is gonna know! (*To Willy.*) We never told the truth for ten minutes in this house!

HAPPY: We always told the truth!

BIFF (*turning on him*): You big blow, are you the assistant buyer? You're one of the two assistants to the assistant, aren't you?

HAPPY: Well, I'm practically . . .

BIFF: You're practically full of it! We all are! and I'm through with it. (*To Willy.*) Now hear this, Willy, this is me.

WILLY: I know you!

BIFF: You know why I had no address for three months? I stole a suit in Kansas City and I was in jail. (*To Linda, who is sobbing.*) Stop crying. I'm through with it.

(*Linda turns away from them, her hands covering her face.*)

WILLY: I suppose that's my fault!

BIFF: I stole myself out of every good job since high school!

WILLY: And whose fault is that?

BIFF: And I never got anywhere because you blew me so full of hot air I could never stand taking orders from anybody! That's whose fault it is!

WILLY: I hear that!

LINDA: Don't, Biff!

BIFF: It's goddam time you heard that! I had to be boss big shot in two weeks, and I'm through with it!

WILLY: Then hang yourself! For spite, hang yourself!

BIFF: No! Nobody's hanging himself, Willy! I ran down eleven flights with a pen in my hand today. And suddenly I stopped, you hear me? And in the middle of that office building, do you hear this? I stopped in the middle of that building and I saw — the sky. I saw the things that I love in this world. The work and the food and time to sit and smoke. And I looked at the pen and said to myself, what the hell am I grabbing this for? Why am I trying to become what I don't want to be? What am I doing in an office, making a contemptuous begging fool of myself, when all I want is out there, waiting for me the minute I say I know who I am! Why can't I say that, Willy? (*He tries to make Willy face him, but Willy pulls away and moves to the left.*)

WILLY (*with hatred, threateningly*): The door of your life is wide open!

BIFF: Pop! I'm a dime a dozen, and so are you!

WILLY (*turning on him now in an uncontrolled outburst*): I am not a dime a dozen! I am Willy Loman, and you are Biff Loman!

(*Biff starts for Willy, but is blocked by Happy. In his fury, Biff seems on the verge of attacking his father.*)

BIFF: I am not a leader of men, Willy, and neither are you. You were never anything but a hard-working drummer who landed in the ash can like all the rest of them! I'm one dollar an hour, Willy! I tried seven states and couldn't raise it. A buck an hour! Do you gather my meaning? I'm not bringing home any prizes any more, and you're going to stop waiting for me to bring them home!

WILLY (*directly to Biff*): You vengeful, spiteful mutt!

(*Biff breaks from Happy. Willy, in fright, starts up the stairs. Biff grabs him.*)

BIFF (*at the peak of his fury*): Pop, I'm nothing! I'm nothing, Pop. Can't you understand that? There's no spite in it any more. I'm just what I am, that's all.

(*Biff's fury has spent itself and he breaks down, sobbing, holding on to Willy, who dumbly fumbles for Biff's face.*)

WILLY (*astonished*): What're you doing? What're you doing? (*To Linda.*) Why is he crying?

BIFF (*crying, broken*): Will you let me go, for Christ's sake? Will you take that phony dream and burn it before something happens? (*Struggling to contain himself he pulls away and moves to the stairs.*) I'll go in the morning. Put him — put him to bed. (*Exhausted, Biff moves up the stairs to his room.*)

WILLY (*after a long pause, astonished, elevated*): Isn't that — isn't that remarkable? Biff — he likes me!

LINDA: He loves you, Willy!

HAPPY (*deeply moved*): Always did, Pop.

WILLY: Oh, Biff! (*Staring wildly.*) He cried! Cried to me. (*He is choking with his love, and now cries out his promise.*) That boy — that boy is going to be magnificent!

(*Ben appears in the light just outside the kitchen.*)

BEN: Yes, outstanding, with twenty thousand behind him.

LINDA (*sensing the racing of his mind, fearfully, carefully*): Now come to bed, Willy. It's all settled now.

WILLY (*finding it difficult not to rush out of the house*): Yes, we'll sleep. Come on. Go to sleep, Hap.

BEN: And it does take a great kind of a man to crack the jungle.

(*In accents of dread, Ben's idyllic music starts up.*)

HAPPY (*his arm around Linda*): I'm getting married, Pop, don't forget it. I'm changing everything. I'm gonna run that department before the year is up. You'll see, Mom. (*He kisses her.*)

BEN: The jungle is dark but full of diamonds, Willy.

(*Willy turns, moves, listening to Ben.*)

LINDA: Be good. You're both good boys, just act that way, that's all.

HAPPY: 'Night, Pop. (*He goes upstairs.*)

LINDA (*to Willy*): Come, dear.

BEN (*with greater force*): One must go in to fetch a diamond out.

WILLY (*to Linda, as he moves slowly along the edge of kitchen, toward the door*): I just want to get settled down, Linda. Let me sit alone for a little.

LINDA (*almost uttering her fear*): I want you upstairs.

WILLY (*taking her in his arms*): In a few minutes, Linda. I couldn't sleep right now. Go on, you look awful tired. (*He kisses her.*)

BEN: Not like an appointment at all. A diamond is rough and hard to the touch.

WILLY: Go on now. I'll be right up.

LINDA: I think this is the only way, Willy.

WILLY: Sure, it's the best thing.

BEN: Best thing!

WILLY: The only way. Everything is gonna be — go on, kid, get to bed. You look so tired.

LINDA: Come right up.

WILLY: Two minutes.

(*Linda goes into the living room, then reappears in her bedroom. Willy moves just outside the kitchen door.*)

WILLY: Loves me. (*Wonderingly.*) Always loved me. Isn't that a remarkable thing? Ben, he'll worship me for it!

BEN (*with promise*): It's dark there, but full of diamonds.

WILLY: Can you imagine that magnificence with twenty thousand dollars in his pocket?

LINDA (*calling from her room*): Willy! Come up!

WILLY (*calling into the kitchen*): Yes! yes. Coming! It's very smart, you realize that, don't you, sweetheart? Even Ben sees it. I gotta go, baby. 'By! 'By! (*Going over to Ben, almost dancing.*) Imagine? When the mail comes he'll be ahead of Bernard again!

BEN: A perfect proposition all around.

WILLY: Did you see how he cried to me? Oh, if I could kiss him, Ben!

BEN: Time, William, time!

WILLY: Oh, Ben, I always knew one way or another we were gonna make it, Biff and I!

BEN (*looking at his watch*): The boat. We'll be late. (*He moves slowly off into the darkness.*)

WILLY (*elegiacally, turning to the house*): Now when you kick off, boy, I want a seventy-yard boot, and get right down the field under the ball, and when you hit, hit low and hit hard, because it's important, boy. (*He swings around and faces the audience.*) There's all kinds of important people in the stands, and the first thing you know . . . (*Suddenly realizing he is alone.*) Ben! Ben, where do I . . . ? (*He makes a sudden movement of search.*) Ben, how do I . . . ?

LINDA (*calling*): Willy, you coming up?

WILLY (*uttering a gasp of fear, whirling about as if to quiet her*): Sh! (*He turns around as if to find his way; sounds, faces, voices, seem to be swarming in upon him and he flicks at them, crying, Sh! Sh! Suddenly music, faint and high, stops him. It rises in intensity, almost to an unbearable scream. He goes up and down on his toes, and rushes off around the house.*) Shhh!

LINDA: Willy?

(*There is no answer. Linda waits. Biff gets up off his bed. He is still in his clothes. Happy sits up. Biff stands listening.*)

LINDA (*with real fear*): Willy, answer me! Willy!

(*There is the sound of a car starting and moving away at full speed.*)

LINDA: No!

BIFF (*rushing down the stairs*): Pop!

(*As the car speeds off, the music crashes down in a frenzy of sound, which becomes the soft pulsation of a single cello string. Biff slowly returns to his bedroom. He and Happy gravely don their jackets. Linda slowly walks out of her room. The music has developed into a dead march. The leaves of day are appearing over everything. Charley and Bernard, somberly dressed, appear and knock on the kitchen door. Biff and Happy slowly descend the stairs to the kitchen as Charley and Bernard enter. All stop a moment when Linda, in clothes of mourning, bearing a little bunch of roses, comes through the draped door-way into the kitchen. She goes to Charley and takes his arm. Now all move toward the audience, through the wall-line of the kitchen. At the limit of the apron, Linda lays down the flowers, kneels, and sits back on her heels. All stare down at the grave.*)

REQUIEM

CHARLEY: It's getting dark, Linda.

(*Linda doesn't react. She stares at the grave.*)

BIFF: How about it, Mom? Better get some rest, heh? They'll be closing the gate soon.

(*Linda makes no move. Pause.*)

HAPPY (*deeply angered*): He had no right to do that. There was no necessity for it. We would've helped him.

CHARLEY (*grunting*): Hmmm.

BIFF: Come along, Mom.

LINDA: Why didn't anybody come?

CHARLEY: It was a very nice funeral.

LINDA: But where are all the people he knew? Maybe they blame him.

CHARLEY: Naa. It's a rough world, Linda. They wouldn't blame him.

LINDA: I can't understand it. At this time especially. First time in thirty-five years we were just about free and clear. He only needed a little salary. He was even finished with the dentist.

CHARLEY: No man only needs a little salary.

LINDA: I can't understand it.

BIFF: There were a lot of nice days. When he'd come home from a trip; or on Sundays, making the stoop; finishing the cellar; putting on the new porch; when he built the extra bathroom; and put up the garage. You know something, Charley, there's more of him in that front stoop than in all the sales he ever made.

CHARLEY: Yeah. He was a happy man with a batch of cement.

LINDA: He was so wonderful with his hands.

BIFF: He had the wrong dreams. All, all, wrong.

HAPPY (*almost ready to fight Biff*): Don't say that!

BIFF: He never knew who he was.

CHARLEY (*stopping Happy's movement and reply. To Biff*): Nobody dast blame this man. You don't understand: Willy was a salesman. And for a salesman, there is no rock bottom to the life. He don't put a bolt to a nut, he don't tell you the law or give you medicine. He's a man way out there in the blue, riding on a smile and a shoeshine. And when they start not smiling back — that's an earthquake. And then you get yourself a couple of spots on your hat, and you're finished. Nobody dast blame this man. A salesman is got to dream, boy. It comes with the territory.

BIFF: Charley, the man didn't know who he was.

HAPPY (*infuriated*): Don't say that!

BIFF: Why don't you come with me, Happy?

HAPPY: I'm not licked that easily. I'm staying right in this city, and I'm gonna beat this racket! (*He looks at Biff, his chin set.*) The Loman Brothers!

BIFF: I know who I am, kid.

HAPPY: All right, boy. I'm gonna show you and everybody else that Willy Loman did not die in vain. He had a good dream. It's the only dream you can have — to come out number-one man. He fought it out here, and this is where I'm gonna win it for him.

BIFF (*with a hopeless glance at Happy, bends toward his mother*): Let's go, Mom.

LINDA: I'll be with you in a minute. Go on, Charley. (*He hesitates.*) I want to, just for a minute. I never had a chance to say good-by.

(*Charley moves away, followed by Happy. Biff remains a slight distance up and left of Linda. She sits there, summoning herself. The flute begins, not far away, playing behind her speech.*)

LINDA: Forgive me, dear. I can't cry. I don't know what it is, but I can't cry. I don't understand it. Why did you ever do that? Help me, Willy, I can't cry. It seems to me that you're just on another trip. I keep expecting you. Willy, dear, I can't cry. Why did you do it? I search and search and I search, and I can't understand it, Willy. I made the last payment on the house today. Today, dear. And there'll be nobody home. (*A sob rises in her throat.*) We're free and clear. (*Sobbing more fully, released.*) We're free. (*Biff comes slowly toward her.*) We're free . . . We're free . . .

(*Biff lifts her to her feet and moves out up right with her in his arms. Linda sobs quietly. Bernard and Charley come together and follow them, followed by Happy. Only the music of the flute is left on the darkening stage as over the house the hard towers of the apartment buildings rise into sharp focus, and the curtain falls.*)

Research Arthur Miller and *Death of a Salesman* in depth with cultural documents and multimedia resources on *LiterActive*.

Suzan-Lori Parks b. 1964

Topdog/Underdog   [2001]

I am God in nature;
I am a weed by the wall.
> — *Ralph Waldo Emerson*
> *From "Circles"*
> Essays: First Series (1841)

THE PLAYERS

LINCOLN, the topdog
BOOTH (a.k.a. 3-Card), the underdog

AUTHOR'S NOTES: From the "Elements of Style"
I'm continuing the use of my slightly unconventional theatrical elements.
Here's a road map.

- *(Rest)*
Take a little time, a pause, a breather; make a transition.

- A Spell
An elongated and heightened (*Rest*). Denoted by repetition of figures'
names with no dialogue. Has sort of an architectural look:

LINCOLN

BOOTH

LINCOLN

BOOTH

This is a place where the figures experience their pure true simple state.
While no action or stage business is necessary, directors should fill this
moment as they best see fit.

- [Brackets in the text indicate optional cuts for production.]

- (Parentheses around dialogue indicate softly spoken passages (asides;
sotto voce)).

Scene One

Thursday evening. A seedily furnished rooming house room. A bed, a reclin-
ing chair, a small wooden chair, some other stuff but not much else. Booth, a
black man in his early 30s, practices his 3-card monte scam on the classic
setup: three playing cards and the cardboard playing board atop two mismatched milk crates. His moves and accompanying patter are, for the most
part, studied and awkward.

BOOTH: Watch me close watch me close now: who-see-thuh-red-card-who-see-
thuh-red-card? I-see-thuh-red-card. Thuh-red-card-is-thuh-winner. Pick-
thuh-red-card-you-pick-uh-winner. Pick-uh-black-card-you-pick-uh-loser.
Theres-thuh-loser, yeah, theres-thuh-black-card, theres-thuh-other-loser-
and-theres-thuh-red-card, thuh-winner.

(Rest)

> Watch me close watch me close now: 3-Card-throws-thuh-cards-lightning-fast. 3-Card-thats-me-and-Ima-last. Watch-me-throw-cause-here-I-go. One-good-pickll-get-you-in, 2-good-picks-and-you-gone-win. See-thuh-red-card-see-thuh-red-card-who-see-thuh-red-card?

(Rest)

> Dont touch my cards, man, just point to thuh one you want. You-pick-that-card-you-pick-a-loser, yeah, that-cards-a-loser. You-pick-that-card-thats-thuh-other-loser. You-pick-that-card-you-pick-a-winner. Follow that card. You gotta chase that card. You-pick-thuh-dark-deuce-thats-a-loser-other-dark-deuces-thuh-other-loser, red-deuce, thuh-deuce-of-heartsll-win-it-all. Follow thuh red card.

(Rest)

> Ima show you thuh cards: 2 black cards but only one heart. Now watch me now. Who-sees-thuh-red-card-who-knows-where-its-at? Go on, man, point to thuh card. Put yr money down cause you aint no clown. No? Ah you had thuh card, but you didnt have thuh heart.

(Rest)

> You wanna bet? 500 dollars? Shoot. You musta been watching 3-Card real close. Ok. Lay the cash in my hand cause 3-Cards thuh man. Thank you, mister. This card you say?

(Rest)

> Wrong! Sucker! Fool! Asshole! Bastard! I bet yr daddy heard how stupid you was and drank himself to death just cause he didnt wanna have nothing to do witchu! I bet yr mama seen you when you comed out and she walked away from you with thuh afterbirth still hanging from out twixt her legs, sucker! Ha Ha Ha! And 3-Card, once again, wins all thuh money!!

(Rest)

> What? Cops looking my way? Fold up thuh game, and walk away. Sneak outa sight. Set up on another corner.

(Rest)

> Yeah.

(Rest)

(Having won the imaginary loot and dodged the imaginary cops, Booth sets up his equipment and starts practicing his scam all over again. Lincoln comes in quietly. He is a black man in his later 30s. He is dressed in an antique frock coat and wears a top hat and fake beard, that is, he is dressed to look like Abraham Lincoln. He surreptitiously walks into the room to stand right behind Booth, who, engrossed in his cards, does not notice Lincoln right away.)

BOOTH: Watch me close watch me close now: who-see-thuh-red-card-who-see-thuh-red-card? I-see-thuh-red-card. Thuh-red-card-is-thuh-winner. Pick-thuh-red-card-you-pick-uh-winner. Pick-uh-black-card-you-pick-uh-loser. Theres-thuh-loser-yeah-theres-thuh-black-card,   theres-thuh-other-loser-and-theres-thuh-red-card, thuh-winner. Don't touch my cards, man, don't—

(Rest)

    Dont do that shit. Dont do that shit. Dont do that shit!

(Booth, sensing someone behind him, whirls around, pulling a gun from his pants. While the presence of Lincoln doesn't surprise him, the Lincoln costume does.)

BOOTH: And woah, man dont *ever* be doing that shit! Who thuh fuck you think you is coming in my shit all spooked out and shit. You pull that one more time I'll shoot you!

LINCOLN: I only had a minute to make the bus.

BOOTH: Bullshit.

LINCOLN: Not completely. I mean, its either bull or shit, but not a complete lie so it aint bullshit, right?

(Rest)

    Put yr gun away.

BOOTH: Take off the damn hat at least.

(Lincoln takes off the stovepipe hat. Booth puts his gun away.)

LINCOLN: Its cold out there. This thing kept my head warm.

BOOTH: I dont like you wearing that bullshit, that shit that bull that disguise that getup that motherdisfuckinguise anywhere in the vicinity of my humble abode.

(Lincoln takes off the beard.)

LINCOLN: Better?

BOOTH: Take off the damn coat too. Damn, man. Bad enough you got to wear that shit all day you come up in here wearing it. What my women gonna say?

LINCOLN: What women?

BOOTH: I got a date with Grace tomorrow. Shes in love with me again but she dont know it yet. Aint no man can love her the way I can. She sees you in that getup its gonna reflect bad on me. She coulda seen you coming down the street. Shit. Could be standing outside right now taking her ring off and throwing it on the sidewalk.

(Booth takes a peek out the window.)

BOOTH: I got her this ring today. Diamond. Well, diamond-esque, but it looks just as good as the real thing. Asked her what size she wore. She say 7 so I go boost a size 6 and a half, right? Show it to her and she loves it and I shove it on her finger and its a tight fit right, so she cant just take it off on a whim, like she did the last one I gave her. Smooth, right?

(*Booth takes another peek out the window.*)

LINCOLN: She out there?

BOOTH: Nope. Coast is clear.

LINCOLN: You boosted a ring?

BOOTH: Yeah. I thought about spending my inheritance on it but — take off that damn coat, man, you make me nervous standing there looking like a spook, and that damn face paint, take it off. You should take all of it off at work and leave it there.

LINCOLN: I dont bring it home someone might steal it.

BOOTH: At least *take it off* there, then.

LINCOLN: Yeah.

(*Rest*)

(*Lincoln takes off the frock coat and applies cold cream, removing the whiteface.*)

LINCOLN: I was riding the bus. Really I only had a minute to make my bus and I was sitting in the arcade thinking, should I change into my street clothes or should I make the bus? Nobody was in there today anyway. Middle of week middle of winter. Not like on weekends. Weekends the place is packed. So Im riding the bus home. And this kid asked me for my autograph. I pretended I didnt hear him at first. I'd had a long day. But he kept asking. Theyd just done Lincoln in history class and he knew all about him, he'd been to the arcade but, I dunno, for some reason he was tripping cause there was Honest Abe right beside him on the bus. I wanted to tell him to go fuck himself. But then I got a look at him. A little rich kid. Born on easy street, you know the type. So I waited until I could tell he really wanted it, the autograph, and I told him he could have it for 10 bucks. I was gonna say 5, cause of the Lincoln connection but something in me made me ask for 10.

BOOTH: But he didnt have a 10. All he had was a penny. So you took the penny.

LINCOLN: All he had was a *20.* So I took the 20 and told him to meet me on the bus tomorrow and Honest Abe would give him the change.

BOOTH: Shit.

LINCOLN: Shit is right.

(*Rest*)

BOOTH: Whatd you do with thuh 20?

LINCOLN: Bought drinks at Luckys. A round for everybody. They got a kick out of the getup.

BOOTH: You shoulda called me down.

LINCOLN: Next time, bro.

(*Rest*)

You making bookshelves? With the milk crates, you making bookshelves?

BOOTH: Yeah, big bro, Im making bookshelves.

LINCOLN: Whats the cardboard part for?

BOOTH: Versatility.

LINCOLN: Oh.

BOOTH: I was thinking we dont got no bookshelves we dont got no dining room table so Im making a sorta modular unit you put the books in the bottom and the table top on top. We can eat and store our books. We could put the photo album in there.

(*Booth gets the raggedy family photo album and puts it in the milk crate.*)

BOOTH: Youd sit there, I'd sit on the edge of the bed. Gathered around the dinner table. Like old times.

LINCOLN: We just gotta get some books but thats great, Booth, thats real great.

BOOTH: Dont be calling me Booth no more, K?

LINCOLN: You changing yr name?

BOOTH: Maybe.

LINCOLN

BOOTH

LINCOLN: What to?

BOOTH: Im not ready to reveal it yet.

LINCOLN: You already decided on something?

BOOTH: Maybe.

LINCOLN: You gonna call yrself something african? That be cool. Only pick something thats easy to spell and pronounce, man, cause you know, some of them african names, I mean, ok, Im down with the power to the people thing, but, no ones gonna hire you if they cant say yr name. And some of them fellas who got they african names, no one can say they names and they cant say they names neither. I mean, you dont want yr new handle to obstruct yr employment possibilities.

BOOTH

LINCOLN

BOOTH: You bring dinner?

LINCOLN: "Shango" would be a good name. The name of the thunder god. If you aint decided already Im just throwing it in the pot. I brought chinese.

BOOTH: Lets try the table out.

LINCOLN: Cool.

(*They both sit at the new table. The food is far away near the door.*)

LINCOLN

BOOTH

LINCOLN: I buy it you set it up. Thats the deal. Thats the deal, right?

BOOTH: You like this place?

LINCOLN: Ssallright.

BOOTH: But a little cramped sometimes, right?

LINCOLN: You dont hear me complain. Although that recliner sometimes Booth, man — no Booth, right — man, Im too old to be sleeping in that chair.

BOOTH: Its my place. You dont got a place. Cookie, she threw you out. And you
  cant seem to get another woman. Yr lucky I let you stay.

LINCOLN: Every Friday you say *mi casa es su casa.*

BOOTH: Every Friday you come home with yr paycheck. Today is Thursday and I
  tell you brother, its a long way from Friday to Friday. All kinds of things can
  happen. All kinds of bad feelings can surface and erupt while yr little
  brother waits for you to bring in yr share.

(*Rest*)

  I got my Thursday head on, Link. Go get the food.

(*Lincoln doesnt budge.*)

LINCOLN: You dont got no running water in here, man.

BOOTH: So?

LINCOLN: You dont got no toilet you dont got no sink.

BOOTH: Bathrooms down the hall.

LINCOLN: You living in thuh Third World, fool! Hey, I'll get thuh food.

(*Lincoln goes to get the food. He sees a stray card on the floor and examines it without
touching it. He brings the food over, putting it nicely on the table.*)

LINCOLN: You been playing cards?

BOOTH: Yeah.

LINCOLN: Solitaire?

BOOTH: Thats right. Im getting pretty good at it.

LINCOLN: Thats soup and thats sauce. I got you the meat and I got me the
  skrimps.

BOOTH: I wanted the skrimps.

LINCOLN: You said you wanted the meat. This morning when I left you said you
  wanted the meat.

(*Rest*)

  Here man, take the skrimps. No sweat.

(*They eat. Chinese food from styrofoam containers, cans of soda, fortune cookies.
Lincoln eats slowly and carefully, Booth eats ravenously.*)

LINCOLN: Yr getting good at solitaire?

BOOTH: Yeah. How about we play a hand after eating?

LINCOLN: Solitaire?

BOOTH: Poker or rummy or something.

LINCOLN: You know I dont touch thuh cards, man.

BOOTH: Just for fun.

LINCOLN: I dont touch thuh cards.

BOOTH: How about for money?

LINCOLN: You dont got no money. All the money you got I bring in here.

BOOTH: I got my inheritance.

LINCOLN: Thats like saying you dont got no money cause you aint never gonna
 do nothing with it so its like you dont got it.

BOOTH: At least I still got mines. You blew yrs.

LINCOLN

BOOTH

LINCOLN: You like the skrimps?

BOOTH: Ssallright.

LINCOLN: Whats yr fortune?

BOOTH: "Waste not want not." Whats yrs?

LINCOLN: "Your luck will change!"

(*Booth finishes eating. He turns his back to Lincoln and fiddles around with the
cards, keeping them on the bed, just out of Lincolns sight. He mutters the 3-card patter under his breath. His moves are still clumsy. Every once and a while he darts a
look over at Lincoln who does his best to ignore Booth.*)

BOOTH: ((((Watch me close watch me close now: who-see-thuh-red-card-who-
 see-thuh-red-card? I-see-thuh-red-card. Thuh-red-card-is-thuh-winner.
 Pick-thuh-red-card-you-pick-uh-winner. Pick-uh-black-card-and-you-pick-
 uh-loser. Theres-thuh-loser, yeah, theres-thuh-black-card, theres-thuh-other-
 loser-and-theres-thuh-red-card, thuh-winner! Cop C, Stick, Cop C! Go
 on—))))

LINCOLN: ((Shit.))

BOOTH: (((((((One-good-pickll-get-you-in, 2-good-picks-and-you-gone-win.
 Dont touch my cards, man, just point to thuh one you want. You-pick-that-
 card-you-pick-uh-loser, yeah, that-cards-uh-loser. You-pick-that-card-
 thats-thuh-other-loser. You-pick-that-card-you-pick-uh-winner. Follow-
 that-card. You-gotta-chase-that-card!)))))))

LINCOLN: You wanna hustle 3-card monte, you gotta do it right, you gotta break
 it down. Practice it in smaller bits. Yr trying to do the whole thing at once
 thats why you keep fucking it up.

BOOTH: Show me.

LINCOLN: No. Im just saying you wanna do it you gotta do it right and if you
 gonna do it right you gotta work on it in smaller bits, thatsall.

BOOTH: You and me could team up and do it together. We'd clean up, Link.

LINCOLN: I'll clean up—bro.

(*Lincoln cleans up. As he clears the food, Booth goes back to using the "table" for its
original purpose.*)

BOOTH: My new names 3-Card. 3-Card, got it? You wanted to know it so now
 you know it. 3-card monte by 3-Card. Call me 3-Card from here on out.

LINCOLN: 3-Card. Shit.

BOOTH: Im getting everybody to call me 3-Card. Grace likes 3-Card better than
 Booth. She says 3-Cards got something to it. Anybody not calling me 3-Card
 gets a bullet.

LINCOLN: Yr too much, man.

BOOTH: Im making a point.

LINCOLN: Point made, 3-Card. Point made.

(*Lincoln picks up his guitar. Plays at it.*)

BOOTH: Oh, come on, man, we could make money you and me. Throwing down the cards. 3-Card and Link: Look out! We could clean up you and me. You would throw the cards and I'd be yr Stickman. The one in the crowd who looks like just an innocent passerby, who looks like just another player, like just another customer, but who gots intimate connections with you, the Dealer, the one throwing the cards, the main man. I'd be the one who brings in the crowd, I'd be the one who makes them want to put they money down, you do yr moves and I do mines. You turn yr head and I turn the card —

LINCOLN: It aint as easy as all that. Theres —

BOOTH: We could be a team, man. Rake in the money! Sure thered be some cats out there with fast eyes, some brothers and sisters who would watch real close and pick the right card, and so thered be some days when we would lose money, but most of the days we would come out on top! Pockets bulging, plenty of cash! And the ladies would be thrilling! You could afford to get laid! Grace would be all over me again.

LINCOLN: I thought you said she was all over you.

BOOTH: She is she is. Im seeing her tomorrow but today we gotta solidify the shit twixt you and me. Big brother Link and little brother Booth —

LINCOLN: 3-Card.

BOOTH: Yeah. Scheming and dreaming. No one throws the cards like you, Link. And with yr moves and my magic, and we get Grace and a girl for you to round out the posse. We'd be golden, bro! Am I right?

LINCOLN

LINCOLN

BOOTH: Am I right?

LINCOLN: I dont touch thuh cards, 3-Card. I dont touch thuh cards no more.

LINCOLN

BOOTH

LINCOLN

BOOTH

BOOTH: You know what Mom told me when she was packing to leave? You was at school motherfucker you was at school. You got up that morning and sat down in yr regular place and read the cereal box while Dad read the sports section and Mom brought you yr dick toast and then you got on the damn school bus cause you didnt have the sense to do nothing else you was so into yr own shit that you didnt have the sense to feel nothing else going on. I had the sense to go back cause I was feeling something going on man, I was feel-ing something changing. So I —

LINCOLN: Cut school that day like you did almost every day —

BOOTH: She was putting her stuff in bags. She had all them nice suitcases but she was putting her stuff in bags.

(*Rest*)

Packing up her shit. She told me to look out for you. I told her I was the little brother and the big brother should look out after the little brother. She just said it again. That I should look out for you. Yeah. So who gonna look out for me. Not like you care. Here I am interested in an economic opportunity, willing to work hard, willing to take risks and all you can say you shiteating motherfucking pathetic limpdick uncle tom, all you can tell me is how you dont do no more what I be wanting to do. Here I am trying to earn a living and you standing in my way. YOU STANDING IN MY WAY, LINK!

LINCOLN: Im sorry.

BOOTH: Yeah, you sorry all right.

LINCOLN: I cant be hustling no more, bro.

BOOTH: What you do all day aint no hustle?

LINCOLN: Its honest work.

BOOTH: Dressing up like some crackerass white man, some dead president and letting people shoot at you sounds like a hustle to me.

LINCOLN: People know the real deal. When people know the real deal it aint a hustle.

BOOTH: We do the card game people will know the real deal. Sometimes we will win sometimes they will win. They fast they win, we faster we win.

LINCOLN: I aint going back to that, bro. I aint going back.

BOOTH: You play Honest Abe. You aint going back but you going all the way back. Back to way back then when folks was slaves and shit.

LINCOLN: Dont push me.

BOOTH

LINCOLN

BOOTH: You gonna have to leave.

LINCOLN: I'll be gone tomorrow.

BOOTH: Good. Cause this was only supposed to be a temporary arrangement.

LINCOLN: I will be gone tomorrow.

BOOTH: Good.

(*Booth sits on his bed. Lincoln, sitting in his easy chair with his guitar, plays and sings.*)

LINCOLN:

My dear mother left me, my fathers gone away
My dear mother left me and my fathers gone away
I dont got no money, I dont got no place to stay.

My best girl, she threw me out into the street
My favorite horse, they ground him into meat
Im feeling cold from my head down to my feet.

My luck was bad but now it turned to worse
My luck was bad but now it turned to worse
Dont call me up a doctor, just call me up a hearse.

BOOTH: You just made that up?
LINCOLN: I had it in my head for a few days.
BOOTH: Sounds good.
LINCOLN: Thanks.

(Rest)

Daddy told me once why we got the names we do.
BOOTH: Yeah?
LINCOLN: Yeah.

(Rest)

He was drunk when he told me, or maybe I was drunk when he told me. Anyway he told me, may not be true, but he told me. Why he named us both. Lincoln and Booth.
BOOTH: How come. How come, man?
LINCOLN: It was his idea of a joke.

(Both men relax back as the lights fade.)

Scene Two
Friday evening. The very next day. Booth comes in looking like he is bundled up against the cold. He makes sure his brother isnt home, then stands in the middle of the room. From his big coat sleeves he pulls out one new shoe then another, from another sleeve come two more shoes. He then slithers out a belt from each sleeve. He removes his coat. Underneath he wears a very nice new suit. He removes the jacket and pants revealing another new suit underneath. The suits still have the price tags on them. He takes two neckties from his pockets and two folded shirts from the back of his pants. He pulls a magazine from the front of his pants. Hes clearly had a busy day of shoplifting. He lays one suit out on Lincolns easy chair. The other he lays out on his own bed. He goes out into the hall returning with a folding screen which he sets up between the bed and the recliner creating two separate spaces. He takes out a bottle of whiskey and two glasses, setting them on the two stacked milk crates. He hears footsteps and sits down in the small wooden chair reading the magazine. Lincoln, dressed in street clothes, comes in.

LINCOLN: Taaaaadaaaaaaaa!
BOOTH: Lordamighty, Pa, I smells money!
LINCOLN: Sho nuff, Ma. Poppas brung home thuh bacon.
BOOTH: Bringitherebringitherebringithere.

(With a series of very elaborate moves Lincoln brings the money over to Booth.)

BOOTH: Put it in my hands, Pa!
LINCOLN: I want ya tuh smells it first, Ma!
BOOTH: Put it neath my nose then, Pa!
LINCOLN: Take yrself a good long whiff of them greenbacks.
BOOTH: Oh lordamighty Ima faint, Pa! Get me muh med-sin!

(*Lincoln quickly pours two large glasses of whiskey.*)

LINCOLN: Dont die on me, Ma!
BOOTH: Im fading fast, Pa!
LINCOLN: Thinka thuh children, Ma! Thinka thuh farm!
BOOTH: 1-2-3.

(*Both men gulp down their drinks simultaneously.*)

LINCOLN AND BOOTH: AAAAAAAAAAAAAAAAAAAAH!

(*Lots of laughing and slapping on the backs.*)

LINCOLN: Budget it out man budget it out.
BOOTH: You in a hurry?
LINCOLN: Yeah. I wanna see how much we got for the week.
BOOTH: You rush in here and dont even look around. Could be a fucking
    A-bomb in the middle of the floor you wouldnt notice. Yr wife, Cookie—
LINCOLN: X-wife—
BOOTH: — could be in my bed you wouldnt notice—
LINCOLN: She was once—
BOOTH: Look the fuck around please.

(*Lincoln looks around and sees the new suit on his chair.*)

LINCOLN: Wow.
BOOTH: Its yrs.
LINCOLN: Shit.
BOOTH: Got myself one too.
LINCOLN: Boosted?
BOOTH: Yeah, I boosted em. Theys stole from a big-ass department store. That
    store takes in more money in one day than we will in our whole life. I stole
    and I stole generously. I got one for me and I got one for you. Shoes belts
    shirts ties socks in the shoes and everything. Got that screen too.
LINCOLN: You all right, man.
BOOTH: Just cause I aint good as you at cards dont mean I cant do nothing.
LINCOLN: Lets try em on.

(*They stand in their separate sleeping spaces, Booth near his bed, Lincoln near his re-cliner, and try on their new clothes.*)

BOOTH: Ima wear mine tonight. Gracell see me in this and *she* gonna ask me tuh
    marry *her*.

(*Rest*)

    I got you the blue and I got me the brown. I walked in there and walked out
    and they didnt as much as bat an eye. Thats how smooth lil bro be, Link.
LINCOLN: You did good. You did real good, 3-Card.
BOOTH: All in a days work.

LINCOLN: They say the clothes make the man. All day long I wear that getup. But that dont make me who I am. Old black coat not even real old just fake old. Its got worn spots on the elbows, little raggedy places thatll break through into holes before the winters out. Shiny strips around the cuffs and the collar. Dust from the cap guns on the left shoulder where they shoot him, where they shoot me I should say but I never feel like they shooting me. The fella who had the gig before I had it wore the same coat. When I got the job they had the getup hanging there waiting for me. Said thuh fella before me just took it off one day and never came back.

(Rest)

Remember how Dads clothes used to hang in the closet?

BOOTH: Until you took em outside and burned em.

(Rest)

He had some nice stuff. What he didnt spend on booze he spent on women. What he didnt spend on them two he spent on clothes. He had some nice stuff. I would look at his stuff and calculate thuh how long it would take till I was big enough to fit it. Then you went and burned it all up.

LINCOLN: I got tired of looking at em without him in em.

(Rest)

They said thuh fella before me — he took off the getup one day, hung it up real nice, and never came back. And as they offered me thuh job, saying of course I would have to wear a little makeup and accept less than what they would offer a — another guy —

BOOTH: Go on, say it. "White." Theyd pay you less than theyd pay a white guy.

LINCOLN: I said to myself thats exactly what I would do: wear it out and then leave it hanging there and not come back. But until then, I would make a living at it. But it dont make me. Worn suit coat, not even worn by the fool that Im supposed to be playing, but making fools out of all those folks who come crowding in for they chance to play at something great. Fake beard. Top hat. Dont make me into no Lincoln. I was Lincoln on my own before any of that.

(The men finish dressing. They style and profile.)

BOOTH: Sharp, huh?

LINCOLN: Very sharp.

BOOTH: You look sharp too, man. You look like the real you. Most of the time you walking around all bedraggled and shit. You look good. Like you used to look back in thuh day when you had Cookie in love with you and all the women in the world was eating out of yr hand.

LINCOLN: This is real nice, man. I dont know where Im gonna wear it but its real nice.

BOOTH: Just wear it around. Itll make you feel good and when you feel good yll meet someone nice. Me I aint interested in meeting no one nice, I mean, I only got eyes for Grace. You think she'll go for me in this?

LINCOLN: I think thuh tie you gave me'll go better with what you got on.

BOOTH: Yeah?

LINCOLN: Grace likes bright colors dont she? My ties bright, yrs is too subdued.

BOOTH: Yeah. Gimmie yr tie.

LINCOLN: You gonna take back a gift?

BOOTH: I stole the damn thing didnt I? Gimmie yrs! I'll give you mines.

(They switch neckties. Booth is pleased. Lincoln is more pleased.)

LINCOLN: Do thuh budget.

BOOTH: Right. Ok lets see: we got 314 dollars. We put 100 aside for the rent. 100 a week times 4 weeks makes the rent and —

LINCOLN AND BOOTH: — we dont want thuh rent spent.

BOOTH: That leaves 214. We put aside 30 for the electric leaving 184. We put aside 50 for thuh phone leaving 134.

LINCOLN: We dont got a phone.

BOOTH: We pay our bill theyll turn it back on.

LINCOLN: We dont need no phone.

BOOTH: How you gonna get a woman if you dont got a phone? Women these days are more cautious, more whaddacallit, more circumspect. You go into a club looking like a fast daddy, you get a filly to give you her numerophono and gone is the days when she just gives you her number and dont ask for yrs.

LINCOLN: Like a woman is gonna call me.

BOOTH: She dont wanna call you she just doing a preliminary survey of the property. Shit, Link, you dont know nothin no more.

(Rest)

> She gives you her number and she asks for yrs. You give her yr number. The phone number of yr home. Thereby telling her 3 things: 1) you got a home, that is, you aint no smooth talking smooth dressing *homeless* joe; 2) that you is in possession of a telephone and a working telephone number which is to say that you got thuh cash and thuh wherewithal to acquire for yr self the worlds most revolutionary communication apparatus and you together enough to pay yr bills!

LINCOLN: Whats 3?

BOOTH: You give her yr number you telling her that its cool to call if she should so please, that is, that you aint got no wife or wife approximation on the premises.

(Rest)

> 50 for the phone leaving 134. We put aside 40 for "med-sin."

LINCOLN: The price went up. 2 bucks more a bottle.

BOOTH: We'll put aside 50, then. That covers the bills. We got 84 left. 40 for meals together during the week leaving 44. 30 for me 14 for you. I got a woman I gotta impress tonight.

LINCOLN: You didnt take out for the phone last week.

BOOTH: Last week I was depressed. This week things is looking up. For both of us.

LINCOLN: Theyre talking about cutbacks at the arcade. I only been there 8 months, so —

BOOTH: Dont sweat it man, we'll find something else.

LINCOLN: Not nothing like this. I like the job. This is sit down, you know, easy work. I just gotta sit there all day. Folks come in kill phony Honest Abe with the phony pistol. I can sit there and let my mind travel.

BOOTH: Think of women.

LINCOLN: Sometimes.

(Rest)

All around the whole arcade is buzzing and popping. Thuh whirring of thuh duckshoot, baseballs smacking the back wall when someone misses the stack of cans, some woman getting happy cause her fella just won the ring toss. The Boss playing the barker talking up the fake freaks. The smell of the ocean and cotton candy and rat shit. And in thuh middle of all that, I can just sit and let my head go quiet. Make up songs, make plans. Forget.

(Rest)

You should come down again.

BOOTH: Once was plenty, but thanks.

(Rest)

Yr Best Customer, he come in today?

LINCOLN: Oh, yeah, he was there.

BOOTH: He shoot you?

LINCOLN: He shot Honest Abe, yeah.

BOOTH: He talk to you?

LINCOLN: In a whisper. Shoots on the left whispers on the right.

BOOTH: Whatd he say this time?

LINCOLN: "Does thuh show stop when no ones watching or does thuh show go on?"

BOOTH: Hes getting deep.

LINCOLN: Yeah.

BOOTH: Whatd he say, that one time? "Yr only yrself —"

LINCOLN: "— when no ones watching," yeah.

BOOTH: Thats deep shit.

(Rest)

Hes a brother, right?

LINCOLN: I think so.

BOOTH: He know yr a brother?

LINCOLN: I dunno. Yesterday he had a good one. He shoots me, Im playing dead, and he leans in close then goes: "God aint nothing but a parasite."

BOOTH: Hes one *deep* black brother.

LINCOLN: Yeah. He makes the day interesting.

BOOTH:

(*Rest*)

Thats a fucked-up job you got.

LINCOLN: Its a living.

BOOTH: But you aint living.

LINCOLN: Im alive aint I?

(*Rest*)

One day I was throwing the cards. Next day Lonny died. Somebody shot him. I knew I was next, so I quit. I saved my life.

(*Rest*)

The arcade gig is the first lucky break Ive ever had. And Ive actually grown to like the work. And now theyre talking about cutting me.

BOOTH: You was lucky with thuh cards.

LINCOLN: Lucky? Aint nothing lucky about cards. Cards aint luck. Cards is work. Cards is skill. Aint never nothing lucky about cards.

(*Rest*)

I dont wanna lose my job.

BOOTH: Then you gotta jazz up yr act. Elaborate yr moves, you know. You was always too stiff with it. You cant just sit there! Maybe, when they shoot you, you know, leap up flail yr arms then fall down and wiggle around and shit so they gotta shoot you more than once. Blam Blam Blam! Blam!

LINCOLN: Help me practice. I'll sit here like I do at work and you be like one of the tourists.

BOOTH: No thanks.

LINCOLN: My paychecks on the line, man.

BOOTH: I got a date. Practice on yr own.

(*Rest*)

I got a rendezvous with Grace. Shit she so sweet she makes my teeth hurt.

(*Rest*)

Link, uh, howbout slipping me an extra five spot. Its the biggest night of my life.

LINCOLN

BOOTH

(*Lincoln gives Booth a 5er.*)

BOOTH: Thanks.

LINCOLN: No sweat.

BOOTH: Howabout I run through it with you when I get back. Put on yr getup and practice till then.

LINCOLN: Sure.

(*Booth leaves. Lincoln stands there alone. He takes off his shoes, giving them a shine. He takes off his socks and his fancy suit, hanging it neatly over the little wooden chair. He takes his getup out of his shopping bag. He puts it on, slowly, like an actor preparing for a great role: frock coat, pants, beard, top hat, necktie. He leaves his feet bare. The top hat has an elastic band which he positions securely underneath his chin. He picks up the white pancake makeup but decides against it. He sits. He pretends to get shot, flings himself on the floor and thrashes around. He gets up, considers giving the new moves another try, but instead pours himself a big glass of whiskey and sits there drinking.*)

Scene Three

Much later that same Friday evening. The recliner is reclined to its maximum horizontal position and Lincoln lies there asleep. He wakes with a start. He is horrific, bleary eyed and hungover, in his full Lincoln regalia. He takes a deep breath, realizes where he is, and reclines again, going back to sleep. Booth comes in full of swagger. He slams the door trying to wake his brother who is dead to the world. He opens the door and slams it again. This time Lincoln wakes up, as hungover and horrid as before. Booth swaggers about, his moves are exaggerated, roosterlike. He walks round and round Lincoln making sure his brother sees him.

LINCOLN: You hurt yrself?

BOOTH: I had me "an evening to remember."

LINCOLN: You look like you hurt yrself.

BOOTH: Grace Grace Grace. *Grace.* She wants me back. She wants me back so bad she wiped her hand over the past where we wasnt together just so she could say we aint never been apart. She wiped her hand over our breakup. She wiped her hand over her childhood, her teenage years, her first boyfriend, just so she could say that she been mine since the dawn of time.

LINCOLN: Thats great, man.

BOOTH: And all the shit I put her through: she wiped it clean. And the women I saw while I was seeing her—

LINCOLN: Wiped clean too?

BOOTH: Mister Clean, Mister, Mister Clean!

LINCOLN: Whered you take her?

BOOTH: We was over at her place. I brought thuh food. Stopped at the best place I could find and stuffed my coat with only the best. We had candlelight, we had music we had—

LINCOLN: She let you do it?

BOOTH: Course she let me do it.

LINCOLN: She let you do it without a rubber?

BOOTH: —Yeah.

LINCOLN: Bullshit.

BOOTH: I put my foot down—and she *melted*. And she was—huh—she was something else. I dont wanna get you jealous, though.

LINCOLN: Go head, I dont mind.

BOOTH:

(Rest)

Well, you know what she looks like.

LINCOLN: She walks on by and the emergency room fills up cause all the guys get whiplash from lookin at her.

BOOTH: Thats right thats right. Well — she comes to the door wearing nothing but her little nightie, eats up the food I'd brought like there was no tomorrow and then goes and eats on me.

(Rest)

LINCOLN: Go on.

BOOTH: I dont wanna make you feel bad, man.

LINCOLN: Ssallright. Go on.

BOOTH:

(Rest)

Well, uh, you know what shes like. Wild. Goodlooking. So sweet my teeth hurt.

LINCOLN: Sexmachine.

BOOTH: Yeah.

LINCOLN: Hotsy-Totsy.

BOOTH: Yeah.

LINCOLN: Amazing Grace.

BOOTH: Amazing Grace! Yeah. Thats right. She let me do her how I wanted. And no rubber.

(Rest)

LINCOLN: Go on.

BOOTH: You dont wanna hear the mushy shit.

LINCOLN: Sure I do.

BOOTH: You hate mushy shit. You always hated thuh mushy shit.

LINCOLN: Ive changed. Go head. You had "an evening to remember," remember? I was just here alone sitting here. Drinking. Go head. Tell Link thuh stink.

(Rest)

Howd ya do her?

BOOTH: Dogstyle.

LINCOLN: Amazing Grace.

BOOTH: In front of a mirror.

LINCOLN: So you could see her. Her face her breasts her back her ass. Graces got a great ass.

BOOTH: Its all right.

LINCOLN: Amazing Grace!

(*Booth goes into his bed area and takes off his suit, tossing the clothes on the floor.*)

BOOTH: She said next time Ima have to use a rubber. She let me have my way this time but she said that next time I'd have to put my boots on.

LINCOLN: Im sure you can talk her out of it.

BOOTH: Yeah.

(*Rest*)

What kind of rubbers you use, I mean, when you was with Cookie.

LINCOLN: We didnt use rubbers. We was married, man.

BOOTH: Right. But you had other women on the side. What kind you use when you was with them?

LINCOLN: Magnums.

BOOTH: Thats thuh kind I picked up. For next time. Grace was real strict about it.

(*While Booth sits on his bed fiddling with his box of condoms, Lincoln sits in his chair and resumes drinking.*)

LINCOLN: Im sure you can talk her out of it. You put yr foot down and she'll melt.

BOOTH: She was real strict. Sides I wouldnt wanna be taking advantage of her or nothing. Putting my foot down and her melting all over thuh place.

LINCOLN: Magnums then.

(*Rest*)

Theyre for "the larger man."

BOOTH: Right. Right.

(*Lincoln keeps drinking as Booth, sitting in the privacy of his bedroom, fiddles with the condoms, perhaps trying to put one on.*)

LINCOLN: Thats right.

BOOTH: Graces real different from them fly-by-night gals I was making do with. Shes in school. Making something of herself. Studying cosmetology. You should see what she can do with a womans hair and nails.

LINCOLN: Too bad you aint a woman.

BOOTH: What?

LINCOLN: You could get yrs done for free, I mean.

BOOTH: Yeah. She got this way of sitting. Of talking. Everything she does is. Shes just so hot.

(*Rest*)

We was together 2 years. Then we broke up. I had my little employment difficulty and she needed time to think.

LINCOLN: And shes through thinking now.

BOOTH: Thats right.

LINCOLN

BOOTH

LINCOLN: Whatcha doing back there?

BOOTH: Resting. That girl wore me out.

LINCOLN: You want some med-sin?

BOOTH: No thanks.

LINCOLN: Come practice my moves with me, then.

BOOTH: Lets hit it tomorrow, K?

LINCOLN: I been waiting. I got all dressed up and you said if I waited up — come on, man, they gonna replace me with a wax dummy.

BOOTH: No shit.

LINCOLN: Thats what theyre talking about. Probably just talk, but — come on, man, I even lent you 5 bucks.

BOOTH: Im tired.

LINCOLN: You didnt get shit tonight.

BOOTH: You jealous, man. You just jail-us.

LINCOLN: You laying over there yr balls blue as my boosted suit. Laying over there waiting for me to go back to sleep or black out so I wont hear you rustling thuh pages of yr fuck book.

BOOTH: Fuck you, man.

LINCOLN: I was over there looking for something the other week and theres like 100 fuck books under yr bed and theyre matted together like a bad fro, bro, cause you spunked in the pages and didnt wipe them off.

BOOTH: Im hot. I need constant sexual release. If I wasnt taking care of myself by myself I would be out there running around on thuh town which costs cash that I dont have so I would be doing worse: I'd be out there doing who knows what, shooting people and shit. Out of a need for unresolved sexual release. I'm a hot man. I aint apologizing for it. When I dont got a woman, I gotta make do. Not like you, Link. When you dont got a woman you just sit there. Letting yr shit fester. Yr dick, if it aint falled off yet, is hanging there between yr legs, little whiteface shriveled-up blank-shooting grub worm. As goes thuh man so goes thuh mans dick. Thats what I say. Least my shits intact.

(Rest)

You a limp dick jealous whiteface motherfucker whose wife dumped him cause he couldnt get it up and she told me so. Came crawling to me cause she needed a man.

(Rest)

I gave it to Grace good tonight. So goodnight.

LINCOLN:

(Rest)

Goodnight.

LINCOLN

BOOTH

LINCOLN
BOOTH
LINCOLN
BOOTH

(Lincoln sitting in his chair. Booth lying in bed. Time passes. Booth peeks out to see if Lincoln is asleep. Lincoln is watching for him.)

LINCOLN: You can hustle 3-card monte without me you know.

BOOTH: Im planning to.

LINCOLN: I could contact my old crew. You could work with them. Lonny aint around no more but theres the rest of them. Theyre good.

BOOTH: I can get my own crew. I dont need yr crew. Buncha has-beens. I can get my own crew.

LINCOLN: My crews experienced. We usedta pull down a thousand a day. Thats 7 G a week. That was years ago. They probably do twice, three times that now.

BOOTH: I got my own connections, thank you.

LINCOLN: Theyd take you on in a heartbeat. With my say. My say still counts with them. They know you from before, when you tried to hang with us but — wernt ready yet. They know you from then, but I'd talk you up. I'd say yr my bro, which they know, and I'd say youd been working the west coast. Little towns. Mexican border. Taking tourists. I'd tell them you got moves like I dreamed of having. Meanwhile youd be working out yr shit right here, right in this room, getting good and getting better every day so when I did do the reintroductions youd have some marketable skills. Youd be passable.

BOOTH: I'd be more than passable, I'd be the be all end all.

LINCOLN: Youd be the be all end all. And youd have my say. If yr interested.

BOOTH: Could do.

LINCOLN: Youd have to get a piece. They all pack pistols, bro.

BOOTH: I *got* a piece.

LINCOLN: Youd have to be packing something more substantial than that pop gun, 3-Card. These hustlers is upper echelon hustlers they pack upper echelon heat, not no Saturday night shit, now.

BOOTH: Whata you know of heat? You aint hung with those guys for six, seven years. You swore off em. Threw yr heat in thuh river and you "Dont touch thuh cards." I know more about heat than you know about heat.

LINCOLN: Im around guns every day. At the arcade. Theyve all been reworked so they only fire caps but I see guns every day. Lots of guns.

BOOTH: What kinds?

LINCOLN: You been there, you seen them. Shiny deadly metal each with their own deadly personality.

BOOTH: Maybe I *could* visit you over there. I'd boost one of them guns and re-work it to make it shoot for real again. What kind you think would best suit my personality?

LINCOLN: You aint stealing nothing from the arcade.

BOOTH: I go in there and steal if I want to go in there and steal I go in there and steal.

LINCOLN: It aint worth it. They dont shoot nothing but blanks.

BOOTH: Yeah, like you. Shooting blanks.

(Rest)

(Rest)

You ever wonder if someones gonna come in there with a real gun? A real gun with real slugs? Someone with uh axe tuh grind or something?

LINCOLN: No.

BOOTH: Someone who hates you come in there and guns you down and gets gone before anybody finds out.

LINCOLN: I dont got no enemies.

BOOTH: Yr X.

LINCOLN: Cookie dont hate me.

BOOTH: Yr Best Customer? Some miscellaneous stranger?

LINCOLN: I cant be worrying about the actions of miscellaneous strangers.

BOOTH: But there they come day in day out for a chance to shoot Honest Abe.

(Rest)

Who are they mostly?

LINCOLN: I dont really look.

BOOTH: You must see something.

LINCOLN: Im supposed to be staring straight ahead. Watching a play, like Abe was.

BOOTH: All day goes by and you never ever take a sneak peek at who be pulling the trigger.

(Pulled in by his own curiosity, Booth has come out of his bed area to stand on the dividing line between the two spaces.)

LINCOLN: Its pretty dark. To keep thuh illusion of thuh whole thing.

(Rest)

But on thuh wall opposite where I sit theres a little electrical box, like a fuse box. Silver metal. Its got uh dent in it like somebody hit it with they fist. Big old dent so everything reflected in it gets reflected upside down. Like yr looking in uh spoon. And thats where I can see em. The assassins.

(Rest)

Not behind me yet but I can hear him coming. Coming in with his gun in hand, thuh gun he already picked out up front when he paid his fare. Coming on in. But not behind me yet. His dress shoes making too much noise on the carpet, the carpets too thin, Boss should get a new one but hes cheap. Not behind me yet. Not behind me yet. Cheap lightbulb just above my head.

(Rest)

And there he is. Standing behind me. Standing in position. Standing upside down. Theres some feet shapes on the floor so he knows just where he oughta stand. So he wont miss. Thuh gun is always cold. Winter or summer thuh gun is always cold. And when the gun touches me he can feel that Im warm and he knows Im alive. And if Im alive then he can shoot me dead. And for a minute, with him hanging back there behind me, its real. Me looking at him upside down and him looking at me looking like Lincoln. Then he shoots.

(Rest)

I slump down and close my eyes. And he goes out thuh other way. More come in. Uh whole day full. Bunches of kids, little good for nothings, in they school uniforms. Businessmen smelling like two for one martinis. Tourists in they theme park t-shirts trying to catch it on film. Housewives with they mouths closed tight, shooting more than once.

(Rest)

They all get so into it. I do my best for them. And now they talking bout re-placing me with uh wax dummy. Itll cut costs.

BOOTH: You just gotta show yr boss that you can do things a wax dummy cant do. You too dry with it. You gotta add spicy shit.

LINCOLN: Like what.

BOOTH: Like when they shoot you, I dunno, scream or something.

LINCOLN: Scream?

(Booth plays the killer without using his gun.)

BOOTH: Try it. I'll be the killer. Bang!

LINCOLN: Aaaah!

BOOTH: Thats good.

LINCOLN: A wax dummy can scream. They can put a voicebox in it and make it like its screaming.

BOOTH: You can curse. Try it. Bang!

LINCOLN: Motherfucking cocksucker!

BOOTH: Thats good, man.

LINCOLN: They aint going for that, though.

BOOTH: You practice rolling and wiggling on the floor?

LINCOLN: A little.

BOOTH: Lemmie see. Bang!

(Lincoln slumps down, falls on the floor, and silently wiggles around.)

BOOTH: You look more like a worm on the sidewalk. Move yr arms. Good. Now scream or something.

LINCOLN: Aaaah! Aaaaah! Aaaah!

BOOTH: A little tougher than that, you sound like yr fucking.

LINCOLN: Aaaaaah!

BOOTH: Hold yr head or something, where I shotcha. Good. And look at me! I am the assassin! *I am Booth!!* Come on man this is life and death! Go all out!

(*Lincoln goes all out.*)

BOOTH: Cool, man thats cool. Thats enough.

LINCOLN: Whatdoyathink?

BOOTH: I dunno, man. Something about it. I dunno. It was looking too real or something.

LINCOLN: They dont want it looking too real. I'd scare the customers. Then I'd be out for sure. Yr trying to get me fired.

BOOTH: Im trying to help. Cross my heart.

LINCOLN: People are funny about they Lincoln shit. Its historical. People like they historical shit in a certain way. They like it to unfold the way they folded it up. Neatly like a book. Not raggedy and bloody and screaming. You trying to get me fired.

(*Rest*)

I am uh brother playing Lincoln. Its uh stretch for anyones imagination. And it aint easy for me neither. Every day I put on that shit, I leave my own shit at the door and I put on that shit and I go out there and I make it work. I make it look easy but its hard. That shit is hard. But it works. Cause I work it. And you trying to get me fired.

(*Rest*)

I swore off them cards. Took nowhere jobs. Drank. Then Cookie threw me out. What thuh fuck was I gonna do? I seen that "Help Wanted" sign and I went up in there and I looked good in the getup and agreed to the whiteface and they really dug it that me and Honest Abe got the same name.

(*Rest*)

Its a sit down job. With benefits. I dont wanna get fired. They wont give me a good reference if I get fired.

BOOTH: Iffen you was tuh get fired, then, well — then you and me could — hustle the cards together. We'd have to support ourselves somehow.

(*Rest*)

Just show me how to do the hook part of the card hustle, man. The part where the Dealer looks away but somehow he sees —

LINCOLN: I couldnt remember if I wanted to.

BOOTH: Sure you could.

LINCOLN: No.

(*Rest*)

Night, man.

BOOTH: Yeah.

(*Lincoln stretches out in his recliner. Booth stands over him waiting for him to get up, to change his mind. But Lincoln is fast asleep. Booth covers him with a blanket then goes to his bed, turning off the lights as he goes. He quietly rummages underneath his bed for a girlie magazine which, as the lights fade, he reads with great interest.)*

Scene Four

Saturday. Just before dawn. Lincoln gets up. Looks around. Booth is fast asleep, dead to the world.

LINCOLN: No fucking running water.

(He stumbles around the room looking for something which he finally finds: a plastic cup, which he uses as a urinal. He finishes peeing and finds an out of the way place to stow the cup. He claws at his Lincoln getup, removing it and tearing it in the process. He strips down to his t-shirt and shorts.)

LINCOLN: Hate falling asleep in this damn shit. Shit. Ripped the beard. I can just hear em tomorrow. Busiest day of the week. They looking me over to make sure Im presentable. They got a slew of guys working but Im the only one they look over every day. "Yr beards ripped, pal. Sure, we'll getcha new one but its gonna be coming outa yr pay." Shit. I should quit right then and there. I'd yank off the beard, throw it on the ground, and stomp it, then go strangle the fucking boss. Thatd be good. My hands around his neck and his bug eyes bugging out. You been ripping me off since I took this job and now Im gonna have to take it outa *yr* pay, motherfucker. Shit.

(Rest)

Sit down job. With benefits.

(Rest)

Hustling. Shit, I was good. I was great. Hell I was the be all end all. I was throwing cards like throwing cards was made for me. Made for me and me alone. I was the best anyone ever seen. Coast to coast. Everybody said so. And I never lost. Not once. Not one time. Not never. Thats how much them cards was mines. I was the be all end all. I was that good.

(Rest)

Then you woke up one day and you didnt have the taste for it no more. Like something in you knew—. Like something in you knew it was time to quit. Quit while you was still ahead. Something in you was telling you—. But hells no. Not Link thuh stink. So I went out there and threw one more time. What thuh fuck. And Lonny died.

(Rest)

Got yrself a good job. And when the arcade lets you go yll get another good job. I dont gotta spend my whole life hustling. Theres more to Link than that. More to me than some cheap hustle. More to life than cheating some idiot out of his paycheck or his life savings.

(Rest)

> Like that joker and his wife from out of town. Always wanted to see the big
> city. I said you could see the bigger end of the big city with a little more cash.
> And if they was fast enough, faster than me, and here I slowed down my
> moves I slowed em way down and my Lonny, my right hand, my Stickman,
> spanish guy who looked white and could draw a customer in like nothing
> else, Lonny could draw a fly from fresh shit, he could draw Adam outa Eve
> just with that look he had, Lonny always got folks playing.

(Rest)

> Somebody shot him. They dont know who. Nobody knows nobody cares.

(Rest)

> We took that man and his wife for hundreds. No, thousands. We took them
> for everything they had and everything they ever wanted to have. We took a
> father for the money he was gonna get his kids new bike with and he cried
> in the street while we vanished. We took a mothers welfare check, she
> pulled a knife on us and we ran. She threw it but her aim werent shit. People
> shopping. Greedy. Thinking they could take me and they got took instead.

(Rest)

> Swore off thuh cards. Something inside me telling me —. But I was good.

LINCOLN

LINCOLN

*(He sees a packet of cards. He studies them like an alcoholic would study a drink.
Then he reaches for them, delicately picking them up and choosing three cards.)*

LINCOLN: Still got my moves. Still got my touch. Still got my chops. Thuh feel of
   it. And I aint hurting no one, God. Link is just here hustling hisself.

(Rest)

> Lets see whatcha got.

*(He stands over the monte setup. Then he bends over it placing the cards down and
moving them around. Slowly at first, aimlessly, as if hes just making little ripples in
water. But then the game draws him in. Unlike Booth, Lincolns patter and moves are
deft, dangerous, electric.)*

LINCOLN: (((Lean in close and watch me now: who see thuh black card who see
   thuh black card I see thuh black card black cards thuh winner pick thuh
   black card thats thuh winner pick thuh red card thats thuh loser pick thuh
   other red card thats thuh other loser pick thuh black card you pick thuh
   winner. Watch me as I throw thuh cards. Here we go.)))

(Rest)

(((Who see thuh black card who see thuh black card? You pick thuh red card you pick a loser you pick that red card you pick a loser you pick thuh black card thuh deuce of spades you pick a winner who sees thuh deuce of spades thuh one who sees it never fades watch me now as I throw thuh cards. Red losers black winner follow thuh deuce of spades chase thuh black deuce. Dark deuce will get you thuh win.)))

(*Even though Lincoln speaks softly, Booth wakes and, unbeknownst to Lincoln, listens intently.*)

(*Rest*)

LINCOLN: ((10 will get you 20, 20 will get you 40.))

(*Rest*)

((Ima show you thuh cards: 2 red cards but only one spade. Dark winner in thuh center and thuh red losers on thuh sides. Pick uh red card you got a loser pick thuh other red card you got a loser pick thuh black card you got a winner. One good pickll get you in, 2 good picks and you gone win. Watch me come on watch me now.))

(*Rest*)

((Who sees thuh winner who knows where its at? You do? You sure? Go on then, put yr money where yr mouth is. Put yr money down you aint no clown. No? Ah, you had thuh card but you didnt have thuh heart.))

(*Rest*)

((Watch me now as I throw thuh cards watch me real close. Ok, man, you know which card is the deuce of spades? Was you watching Links lighting fast express? Was you watching Link cause he the best? So you sure, huh? Point it out first, then place yr bet and Linkll show you yr winner.))

(*Rest*)

((500 dollars? You thuh man of thuh hour you thuh man with thuh power. You musta been watching Link real close. You must be thuh man who know thuh most. Ok. Lay the cash in my hand cause Link the man. Thank you, mister. This card you say?))

(*Rest*)

((Wrong! Ha!))

(*Rest*)

((Thats thuh show. We gotta go.))

(*Lincoln puts the cards down. He moves away from the monte setup. He sits on the edge of his easy chair, but he can't take his eyes off the cards.*)

Intermission

Scene Five

Several days have passed. Its now Wednesday night. Booth is sitting in his brand-new suit. The monte setup is nowhere in sight. In its place is a table with two nice chairs. The table is covered with a lovely tablecloth and there are nice plates, silverware, champagne glasses, and candles. All the makings of a very romantic dinner for two. The whole apartment in fact takes its cue from the table. Its been cleaned up considerably. New curtains on the windows, a doily-like object on the recliner. Booth sits at the table darting his eyes around, making sure everything is looking good.

BOOTH: Shit.

(He notices some of his girlie magazines visible from underneath his bed. He goes over and nudges them out of sight. He sits back down. He notices that theyre still visible. He goes over and nudges them some more, kicking at them finally. Then he takes the spread from his bed and pulls it down, hiding them. He sits back down. He gets up. Checks the champagne on much melted ice. Checks the food.)

BOOTH: Foods getting cold, Grace!! Dont worry man, she'll get here, she'll get here.

(He sits back down. He goes over to the bed. Checks it for springiness. Smoothes down the bedspread. Double-checks two matching silk dressing gowns, very expensive, marked "His" and "Hers." Lays the dressing gowns across the bed again. He sits back down. He cant help but notice the visibility of the girlie magazines again. He goes to the bed, kicks them fiercely, then on his hands and knees shoves them. Then he begins to get under the bed to push them, but he remembers his nice clothing and takes off his jacket. After a beat he removes his pants and, in this half-dressed way, he crawls under the bed to give those telltale magazines a good and final shove. Lincoln comes in. At first Booth, still stripped down to his underwear, thinks its his date. When he realizes its his brother, he does his best to keep Lincoln from entering the apartment. Lincoln wears his frock coat and carries the rest of his getup in a plastic bag.)

LINCOLN: You in the middle of it?
BOOTH: What the hell you doing here?
LINCOLN: If yr in thuh middle of it I can go. Or I can just be real quiet and just — sing a song in my head or something.
BOOTH: The casas off limits to you tonight.
LINCOLN: You know when we lived in that 2-room place with the cement backyard and the frontyard with nothing but trash in it, Mom and Pops would do it in the middle of the night and I would always hear them but I would sing in my head, cause, I dunno, I couldnt bear to listen.
BOOTH: You gotta get out of here.
LINCOLN: I would make up all kinds of songs. Oh, sorry, yr all up in it. No sweat, bro. No sweat. Hey, Grace, howyadoing?!
BOOTH: She aint here yet, man. Shes running late. And its a good thing too cause I aint all dressed yet. Yr gonna spend thuh night with friends?
LINCOLN: Yeah.

(*Booth waits for Lincoln to leave. Lincoln stands his ground.*)

LINCOLN: I lost my job.

BOOTH: Hunh.

LINCOLN: I come in there right on time like I do every day and that motherfucker gives me some song and dance about cutbacks and too many folks complaining.

BOOTH: Huhn.

LINCOLN: Showd me thuh wax dummy — hes buying it right out of a catalog.

(*Rest*)

I walked out still wearing my getup.

(*Rest*)

I could go back in tomorrow. I could tell him I'll take another pay cut. Thatll get him to take me back.

BOOTH: Link. Yr free. Dont go crawling back. Yr free at last! Now you can do anything you want. Yr not tied down by that job. You can — you can do something else. Something that pays better maybe.

LINCOLN: You mean Hustle.

BOOTH: Maybe. Hey, Graces on her way. You gotta go.

(*Lincoln flops into his chair. Booth is waiting for him to move. Lincoln doesnt budge.*)

LINCOLN: I'll stay until she gets here. I'll act nice. I wont embarrass you.

BOOTH: You gotta go.

LINCOLN: What time she coming?

BOOTH: Shes late. She could be here any second.

LINCOLN: I'll meet her. I met her years ago. I'll meet her again.

(*Rest*)

How late is she?

BOOTH: She was supposed to be here at 8.

LINCOLN: Its after 2 A.M. Shes — shes late.

(*Rest*)

Maybe when she comes you could put the blanket over me and I'll just pretend like Im not here.

(*Rest*)

I'll wait. And when she comes I'll go. I need to sit down. I been walking around all day.

BOOTH

LINCOLN

(*Booth goes to his bed and dresses hurriedly.*)

BOOTH: Pretty nice, right? The china thuh silver thuh crystal.
LINCOLN: Its great.

(Rest)

Boosted?
BOOTH: Yeah.
LINCOLN: Thought you went and spent yr inheritance for a minute, you had me
    going I was thinking shit, Booth — 3-Card — that 3-Cards gone and spent his
    inheritance and the gal is — late.
BOOTH: Its boosted. Every bit of it.

(Rest)

Fuck this waiting bullshit.
LINCOLN: She'll be here in a minute. Dont sweat it.
BOOTH: Right.

(Booth comes to the table. Sits. Relaxes as best he can.)

BOOTH: How come I got a hand for boosting and I dont got a hand for throwing
    cards? Its sorta the same thing — you gotta be quick — and slick. Maybe yll
    show me yr moves sometime.
LINCOLN
BOOTH
LINCOLN
BOOTH
LINCOLN: Look out the window. When you see Grace coming, I'll go.
BOOTH: Cool. Cause youd jinx it, youd really jinx it. Maybe you being here has
    jinxed it already. Naw. Shes just a little late. You aint jinxed nothing.

*(Booth sits by the window, glancing out, watching for his date. Lincoln sits in his re-
cliner. He finds the whiskey bottle, sips from it. He then rummages around, finding
the raggedy photo album. He looks through it.)*

LINCOLN: There we are at that house. Remember when we moved in?
BOOTH: No.
LINCOLN: You were 2 or 3.
BOOTH: I was 5.
LINCOLN: I was 8. We all thought it was the best fucking house in the world.
BOOTH: Cement backyard and a frontyard full of trash, yeah, dont be going
    down memory lane man, yll jinx thuh vibe I got going in here. Gracell be
    walking in here and wrinkling up her nose cause you done jinxed up thuh
    joint with yr raggedy recollections.
LINCOLN: We had some great times in that house, bro. Selling lemonade on thuh
    corner, thuh treehouse out back, summers spent lying in thuh grass and
    looking at thuh stars.
BOOTH: We never did none of that shit.

LINCOLN: But we had us some good times. That row of nails I got you to line up
    behind Dads car so when he backed out the driveway to work—

BOOTH: He came back that night, only time I ever seen his face go red, 4 flat tires
    and yelling bout how thuh white man done sabotaged him again.

LINCOLN: And neither of us flinched. Neither of us let on that itd been us.

BOOTH: It was at dinner, right? What were we eating?

LINCOLN: Food.

BOOTH: We was eating pork chops, mashed potatoes, and peas. I remember
    cause I had to look at them peas real hard to keep from letting on. And I
    would glance over at you, not really glancing not actually turning my head,
    but I was looking at you out thuh corner of my eye. I was sure he was gonna
    find us out and then he woulda whipped us good. But I kept glancing at you
    and you was cool, man. Like nothing was going on. You was cooooool.

(*Rest*)

    What time is it?

LINCOLN: After 3.

(*Rest*)

    You should call her. Something mighta happened.

BOOTH: No man, Im cool. She'll be here in a minute. Patience is a virtue. She'll
    be here.

LINCOLN: You look sad.

BOOTH: Nope. Im just, you know, Im just—

LINCOLN: Cool.

BOOTH: Yeah. Cool.

(*Booth comes over, takes the bottle of whiskey, and pours himself a big glassful. He
returns to the window looking out and drinking.*)

BOOTH: They give you a severance package, at thuh job?

LINCOLN: A weeks pay.

BOOTH: Great.

LINCOLN: I blew it. Spent it all.

BOOTH: On what?

LINCOLN: —. Just spent it.

(*Rest*)

    It felt good, spending it. Felt really good. Like back in thuh day when I was
    really making money. Throwing thuh cards all day and strutting and rutting
    all night. Didnt have to take no shit from no fool, didnt have to worry about
    getting fired in favor of some damn wax dummy. I was thuh shit and they
    was my fools.

(*Rest*)

    Back in thuh day.

(*Rest*)
(*Rest*)

Why you think they left us, man?

BOOTH: Mom and Pops? I dont think about it too much.

LINCOLN: I dont think they liked us.

BOOTH: Naw. That aint it.

LINCOLN: I think there was something out there that they liked more than they liked us and for years they was struggling against moving towards that more liked something. Each of them had a special something that they was struggling against. Moms had hers. Pops had his. And they was struggling. We moved out of that nasty apartment into a house. A whole house. It wernt perfect but it was a house and theyd bought it and they brought us there and everything we owned, figuring we could be a family in that house and them things, them two separate things each of them was struggling against, would just leave them be. Them things would see thuh house and be impressed and just leave them be. Would see thuh job Pops had and how he shined his shoes every night before he went to bed, shining them shoes whether they needed it or not, and thuh thing he was struggling against would see all that and just let him be, and thuh thing Moms was struggling against, it would see the food on the table every night and listen to her voice when she'd read to us sometimes, the clean clothes, the buttons sewed on all right and it would just let her be. Just let us all be, just regular people living in a house. That wernt too much to ask.

BOOTH: Least we was grown when they split.

LINCOLN: 16 and 13 aint grown.

BOOTH: 16s grown. Almost. And I was ok cause you were there.

(*Rest*)

Shit man, it aint like they both one day both, together packed all they shit up and left us so they could have fun in thuh sun on some tropical island and you and me would have to grub in thuh dirt forever. They didnt leave together. That makes it different. She left. 2 years go by. Then he left. Like neither of them couldnt handle it no more. She split then he split. Like thuh whole family mortgage bills going to work thing was just too much. And I dont blame them. You dont see me holding down a steady job. Cause its bullshit and I know it. I seen how it cracked them up and I aint going there.

(*Rest*)

It aint right me trying to make myself into a one woman man just because she wants me like that. One woman rubber-wearing motherfucker. Shit. Not me. She gonna walk in here looking all hot and shit trying to see how much she can get me to sweat, how much she can get me to give her before she gives me mines. Shit.

LINCOLN

BOOTH

LINCOLN: Moms told me I shouldnt never get married.

BOOTH: She told me thuh same thing.

LINCOLN: They gave us each 500 bucks then they cut out.

BOOTH: Thats what Im gonna do. Give my kids 500 bucks then cut out. Thats thuh way to do it.

LINCOLN: You dont got no kids.

BOOTH: Im gonna have kids then Im gonna cut out.

LINCOLN: Leaving each of yr offspring 500 bucks as yr splitting.

BOOTH: Yeah.

(Rest)

Just goes to show Mom and Pops had some agreement between them.

LINCOLN: How so.

BOOTH: Theyd stopped talking to eachother. Theyd stopped *screwing* eachother. But they had an agreement. Somewhere in there when it looked like all they had was hate they sat down and did thuh "split" budget.

(Rest)

When Moms splits she gives me 5 hundred-dollar bills rolled up and tied up tight in one of her nylon stockings. She tells me to put it in a safe place, to spend it only in case of an emergency, and not to tell nobody I got it, not even you. 2 years later Pops splits and before he goes —

LINCOLN: He slips me 10 fifties in a clean handkerchief: "Hide this somewheres good, dont go blowing it, dont tell no one you got it, especially that Booth."

BOOTH: Theyd been scheming together all along. They left separately but they was in agreement. Maybe they arrived at the same place at the same time, maybe they renewed they wedding vows, maybe they got another family.

LINCOLN: Maybe they got 2 new kids. 2 boys. Different than us, though. Better.

BOOTH: Maybe.

(Their glasses are empty. The whiskey bottle is empty too. Booth takes the champagne bottle from the ice tub. He pops the cork and pours drinks for his brother and himself.)

BOOTH: I didnt mind them leaving cause you was there. Thats why Im hooked on us working together. If we could work together it would be like old times. They split and we got that room downtown. You was done with school and I stopped going. And we had to run around doing odd jobs just to keep the lights on and the heat going and thuh child protection bitch off our backs. It was you and me against thuh world, Link. It could be like that again.

LINCOLN

BOOTH

LINCOLN

BOOTH

LINCOLN: Throwing thuh cards aint as easy as it looks.

BOOTH: I aint stupid.

LINCOLN: When you hung with us back then, you was just on thuh sidelines. Thuh perspective from thuh sidelines is thuh perspective of a customer. There was all kinds of things you didnt know nothing about.

BOOTH: Lonny would entice folks into thuh game as they walked by. Thuh 2 folks on either side of ya looked like they was playing but they was only pretending tuh play. Just tuh generate excitement. You was moving thuh cards as fast as you could hoping that yr hands would be faster than yr customers eyes. Sometimes you won sometimes you lost what else is there to know?

LINCOLN: Thuh customer is actually called the "Mark." You know why?

BOOTH: Cause hes thuh one you got yr eye on. You mark him with yr eye.

LINCOLN

LINCOLN

BOOTH: Im right, right?

LINCOLN: Lemmie show you a few moves. If you pick up these yll have a chance.

BOOTH: Yr playing.

LINCOLN: Get thuh cards and set it up.

BOOTH: No shit.

LINCOLN: Set it up set it up.

(*In a flash, Booth clears away the romantic table setting by gathering it all up in the tablecloth and tossing it aside. As he does so he reveals the "table" underneath: the 2 stacked monte milk crates and the cardboard playing surface. Lincoln lays out the cards. The brothers are ready. Lincoln begins to teach Booth in earnest.*)

LINCOLN: Thuh deuce of spades is thuh card tuh watch.

BOOTH: I work with thuh deuce of hearts. But spades is cool.

LINCOLN: Theres thuh Dealer, thuh Stickman, thuh Sides, thuh Lookout, and thuh Mark. I'll be thuh Dealer.

BOOTH: I'll be thuh Lookout. Lemmie be thuh Lookout, right? I'll keep an eye for thuh cops. I got my piece on me.

LINCOLN: You got it on you right now?

BOOTH: I always carry it.

LINCOLN: Even on a date? In yr own home?

BOOTH: You never know, man.

(*Rest*)

So Im thuh Lookout.

LINCOLN: Gimmie yr piece.

(*Booth gives Lincoln his gun. Lincoln moves the little wooden chair to face right in front of the setup. He then puts the gun on the chair.*)

LINCOLN: We dont need nobody standing on the corner watching for cops cause there aint none.

BOOTH: I'll be thuh Stickman, then.

LINCOLN: Stickman knows the game inside out. You aint there yet. But you will be. You wanna learn good, be my Sideman. Playing along with the Dealer, moving the Mark to lay his money down. You wanna learn, right?

BOOTH: I'll be thuh Side.

LINCOLN: Good.

(*Rest*)

First thing you learn is what is. Next thing you learn is what aint. You dont know what is you dont know what aint, you dont know shit.

BOOTH: Right.

LINCOLN

BOOTH

BOOTH: Whatchu looking at?

LINCOLN: Im sizing you up.

BOOTH: Oh yeah?!

LINCOLN: Dealer always sizes up thuh crowd.

BOOTH: Im yr Side, Link, Im on yr team, you dont go sizing up yr own team. You save looks like that for yr Mark.

LINCOLN: Dealer always sizes up thuh crowd. Everybody out there is part of the crowd. His crew is part of the crowd, he himself is part of the crowd. Dealer always sizes up thuh crowd.

(*Lincoln looks Booth over some more then looks around at an imaginary crowd.*)

BOOTH: Then what then what?

LINCOLN: Dealer dont wanna play.

BOOTH: Bullshit man! Come on you promised!

LINCOLN: Thats thuh Dealers attitude. He *acts* like he dont wanna play. He holds back and thuh crowd, with their eagerness to see his skill and their willingness to take a chance, and their greediness to win his cash, the larceny in their hearts, all goad him on and push him to throw his cards, although of course the Dealer has been wanting to throw his cards all along. Only he dont never show it.

BOOTH: Thats some sneaky shit, Link.

LINCOLN: It sets thuh mood. You wanna have them in yr hand before you deal a hand, K?

BOOTH: Cool. — K.

LINCOLN: Right.

LINCOLN

BOOTH

BOOTH: You sizing me up again?

LINCOLN: Theres 2 parts to throwing thuh cards. Both parts are fairly complicated. Thuh moves and thuh grooves, thuh talk and thuh walk, thuh patter and thuh pitter pat, thuh flap and thuh rap: what yr doing with yr mouth and what yr doing with yr hands.

BOOTH: I got thuh words down pretty good.

LINCOLN: You need to work on both.

BOOTH: K.

LINCOLN: A goodlooking walk and a dynamite talk captivates their entire attention. The Mark focuses with 2 organs primarily: his eyes and his ears. Leave
one out you lose yr shirt. Captivate both, yr golden.

BOOTH: So them times I seen you lose, them times I seen thuh Mark best you,
that was a time when yr hands werent fast enough or yr patter werent right.

LINCOLN: You could say that.

BOOTH: So, there was plenty of times —

(Lincoln moves the cards around.)

LINCOLN: You see what Im doing? Dont look at my hands, man, look at my eyes.
Know what is and know what aint.

BOOTH: What is?

LINCOLN: My eyes.

BOOTH: What aint?

LINCOLN: My hands. Look at my eyes not my hands. And you standing there
thinking how thuh fuck I gonna learn how tuh throw thuh cards if I be
looking in his eyes? Look into my eyes and get yr focus. Dont think about
learning how tuh throw thuh cards. Dont think about nothing. Just look
into my eyes. Focus.

BOOTH: Theyre red.

LINCOLN: Look into my eyes.

BOOTH: You been crying?

LINCOLN: Just look into my eyes, fool. Now. Look down at thuh cards. I been
moving and moving and moving them around. Ready?

BOOTH: Yeah.

LINCOLN: Ok, Sideman, thuh Marks got his eye on you. Yr gonna show him its
easy.

BOOTH: K.

LINCOLN: Pick out thuh deuce of spades. Dont pick it up just point to it.

BOOTH: This one, right?

LINCOLN: Dont ask thuh Dealer if yr right, man, point to yr card with confidence.

(Booth points.)

BOOTH: That one.

(Rest)

Flip it over, man.

*(Lincoln flips over the card. It is in fact the deuce of spades. Booth struts around
gloating like a rooster. Lincoln is mildly crestfallen.)*

BOOTH: Am I right or am I right?! Make room for 3-Card! Here comes thuh
champ!

LINCOLN: Cool. Stay focused. Now we gonna add the second element. Listen.

(*Lincoln moves the cards and speaks in a low hypnotic voice.*)

LINCOLN: Lean in close and watch me now: who see thuh black card who see thuh black card I see thuh black card black cards thuh winner pick thuh black card thats thuh winner pick thuh red card thats thuh loser pick thuh other red card thats thuh other loser pick thuh black card you pick thuh winner. Watch me as I throw thuh cards. Here we go.

(*Rest*)

Who see thuh black card who see thuh black card? You pick thuh red card you pick a loser you pick that red card you pick a loser you pick thuh black card thuh deuce of spades you pick a winner who sees thuh deuce of spades thuh one who sees it never fades watch me now as I throw thuh cards. Red losers black winner follow thuh deuce of spades chase thuh black deuce. Dark deuce will get you thuh win. One good pickll get you in 2 good picks you gone win. 10 will get you 20, 20 will get you 40.

(*Rest*)

Ima show you thuh cards: 2 red cards but only one spade. Dark winner in thuh center and thuh red losers on thuh sides. Pick uh red card you got a loser pick thuh other red card you got a loser pick thuh black card you got a winner. Watch me watch me watch me now.

(*Rest*)

Ok, 3-card, you know which cards thuh deuce of spades?

BOOTH: Yeah.

LINCOLN: You sure? Yeah? You sure you sure or you just think you sure? Oh you sure you sure huh? Was you watching Links lighting fast express? Was you watching Link cause he the best? So you sure, huh? Point it out. Now, place yr bet and Linkll turn over yr card.

BOOTH: What should I bet?

LINCOLN: Dont bet nothing man, we just playing. Slap me 5 and point out thuh deuce.

(*Booth slaps Lincoln 5, then points out a card which Lincoln flips over. It is in fact again the deuce of spades.*)

BOOTH: Yeah, baby! 3-Card got thuh moves! You didnt know lil bro had thuh stuff, huh? Think again, Link, think again.

LINCOLN: You wanna learn or you wanna run yr mouth?

BOOTH: Thought you had fast hands. Wassup? What happened tuh "Links Lightning Fast Express"? Turned into uh local train looks like tuh me.

LINCOLN: Thats yr whole motherfucking problem. Yr so busy running yr mouth you aint never gonna learn nothing! You think you something but you aint shit.

BOOTH: I aint shit, I am *The* Shit. Shit. Wheres thuh dark deuce? Right there! Yes, baby!

LINCOLN: Ok, 3-Card. Cool. Lets switch. Take thuh cards and show me whatcha got. Go on. Dont touch thuh cards too heavy just — its a light touch. Like yr touching Graces skin. Or, whatever, man, just a light touch. Like uh whisper.

BOOTH: Like uh whisper.

(*Booth moves the cards around, in an awkward imitation of his brother.*)

LINCOLN: Good.

BOOTH: Yeah. All right. Look into my eyes.

(*Booths speech is loud and his movements are jerky. He is doing worse than when he threw the cards at the top of the play.*)

BOOTH: Watch-me-close-watch-me-close-now: who-see-thuh-dark-card-who-see-thuh-dark-card? I-see-thuh-dark-card. Here-it-is. Thuh-dark-card-is-thuh-winner. Pick-thuh-dark-card-and-you-pick-uh-winner. Pick-uh-red-card-and-you-pick-uh-loser. Theres-thuh-loser-yeah-theres-thuh-red-card, theres-thuh-other-loser-and-theres-thuh-black-card, thuh-winner. Watch-me-close-watch-me-close-now: 3-Card-throws-thuh-cards-lightning-fast. 3-Card-thats-me-and-Ima-last. Watch-me-throw-cause-here-I-go. See thuh black card? Yeah? Who see I see you see thuh black card?

LINCOLN: Hahahahhahahahahahahah!

(*Lincoln doubles over laughing. Booth puts on his coat and pockets his gun.*)

BOOTH: What?

LINCOLN: Nothing, man, nothing.

BOOTH: *What?!*

LINCOLN: Yr just, yr just a little wild with it. You talk like that on thuh street cards or no cards and theyll lock you up, man. Shit. Reminds me of that time when you hung with us and we let you try being thuh Stick cause you wanted to so bad. Thuh hustle was so simple. Remember? I told you that when I put my hand in my left pocket you was to get thuh Mark tuh pick thuh card on that side. You got to thinking something like Links left means my left some dyslexic shit and turned thuh wrong card. There was 800 bucks on the line and you fucked it up.

(*Rest*)

But it was cool, little bro, cause we made the money back. It worked out cool.

(*Rest*)

So, yeah, I said a light touch, little bro. Throw thuh cards light. Like uh whisper.

BOOTH: Like Graces skin.

LINCOLN: Like Graces skin.

BOOTH: What time is it?

(*Lincoln holds up his watch. Booth takes a look.*)

BOOTH: Bitch. *Bitch!* She said she was gonna show up around 8. 8-a-fucking-clock.

LINCOLN: Maybe she meant 8 A.M.

BOOTH: Yeah. She gonna come all up in my place talking bout how she *love* me. How she cant stop *thinking* bout me. Nother mans shit up in her nother mans thing in her nother mans dick on her breath.

LINCOLN: Maybe something happened to her.

BOOTH: Something happened to her all right. She trying to make a chump outa me. I aint her chump. I aint nobodys chump.

LINCOLN: Sit. I'll go to the payphone on the corner. I'll—

BOOTH: Thuh world puts its foot in yr face and you dont move. You tell thuh world tuh keep on stepping. But Im my own man, Link. I aint you.

(*Booth goes out, slamming the door behind him.*)

LINCOLN: You got that right.

(*After a moment Lincoln picks up the cards. He moves them around fast, faster, faster.*)

Scene Six

Thursday night. The room looks empty, as if neither brother is home. Lincoln comes in. Hes fairly drunk. He strides in, leaving the door slightly ajar.

LINCOLN: Taaadaaaa!

(*Rest*)
(*Rest*)

Taadaa, motherfucker. Taadaa!

(*Rest*)

Booth—uh, 3-Card—you here? Nope. Good. Just as well. Ha Ha *Ha Ha Ha*!

(*He pulls an enormous wad of money from his pocket. He counts it, slowly and luxuriously, arranging and smoothing the bills and sounding the amounts under his breath. He neatly rolls up the money, secures it with a rubber band and puts it back in his pocket. He relaxes in his chair. Then he takes the money out again, counting it all over again, but this time quickly, with the touch of an expert hustler.*)

LINCOLN: You didnt go back, Link, you got back, you got it back you got yr shit back in thuh saddle, man, you got back in business. Walking in Luckys and you seen how they was looking at you? Lucky starts pouring for you when you walk in. And the women. You see how they was looking at you? Bought drinks for everybody. Bought drinks for Lucky. Bought drinks for Luckys damn dog. Shit. And thuh women be hanging on me and purring. And I be feeling that old call of thuh wild calling. I got more phone numbers in my pockets between thuh time I walked out that door and thuh time I walked back in than I got in my whole life. Cause my shit is *back*. And back better than it was when it left too. Shoot. Who thuh man? Link. Thats right. Purrrrring all up on me and letting me touch them and promise them shit. 3 of them sweethearts in thuh restroom on my dick all at once and I was *there* my shit was there. And Cookie just went out of my mind which is cool which is very cool. 3 of them. Fighting over it. Shit. Cause they knew I'd been throwing thuh cards. Theyd seen me on thuh corner with thuh old crew or if they aint seed me with they own eyes theyd heard word. Links thuh stink! Theyd heard word and they seed uh sad face on some poor sucker or a tear in thuh eye of some stupid fucking tourist and they figured it was me whod just took thuh suckers last dime, it was me who had all thuh suckers loot. They knew. They knew.

(*Booth appears in the room. He was standing behind the screen, unseen all this time. He goes to the door, soundlessly, just stands there.*)

LINCOLN: And they was all in Luckys. Shit. And they was waiting for me to come in from my last throw. Cant take too many fools in one day, its bad luck, Link, so they was all waiting in there for me to come in thuh door and let thuh liquor start flowing and thuh music start going and let thuh boys who dont have thuh balls to get nothing but a regular job and uh weekly pay-check, let them crowd around and get in somehow on thuh excitement, and make way for thuh ladies, so they can run they hands on my clothes and feel thuh magic and imagine thuh man, with plenty to go around, living and breathing underneath.

(*Rest*)

They all thought I was down and out! They all thought I was some NoCount HasBeen LostCause motherfucker. But I got my shit back. Thats right. They stepped on me and kept right on stepping. Not no more. Who thuh man?! Goddamnit, who thuh —

(*Booth closes the door.*)

LINCOLN
BOOTH

(*Rest*)

LINCOLN: Another evening to remember, huh?
BOOTH:

(*Rest*)

Uh — yeah, man, yeah. Thats right, thats right.
LINCOLN: Had me a memorable evening myself.
BOOTH: I got news.

(*Rest*)

What you been up to?

LINCOLN: Yr news first.

BOOTH: Its good.

LINCOLN: Yeah?

BOOTH: Yeah.

LINCOLN: Go head then.

BOOTH:

(*Rest*)

Grace got down on her knees. Down on her knees, man. Asked *me* tuh marry *her*.

LINCOLN: Shit.

BOOTH: Amazing Grace!

LINCOLN: Lucky you, man.

BOOTH: And guess where she was, I mean, while I was here waiting for her. She was over at her house watching tv. I'd told her come over Thursday and I got it all wrong and was thinking I said Wednesday and here I was sitting waiting my ass off and all she was doing was over at her house just watching tv.

LINCOLN: Howboutthat.

BOOTH: She wants to get married right away. Shes tired of waiting. Feels her clock ticking and shit. Wants to have my baby. But dont look so glum man, we gonna have a boy and we gonna name it after you.

LINCOLN: Thats great, man. Thats really great.

BOOTH

LINCOLN

BOOTH: Whats yr news?

LINCOLN:

(*Rest*)

Nothing.

BOOTH: Mines good news, huh?

LINCOLN: Yeah. Real good news, bro.

BOOTH: Bad news is — well, shes real set on us living together. And she always did like this place.

(*Rest*)

Yr gonna have to leave. Sorry.

LINCOLN: No sweat.

BOOTH: This was only a temporary situation anyhow.

LINCOLN: No sweat man. You got a new life opening up for you, no sweat. Graces moving in today? I can leave right now.

BOOTH: I dont mean to put you out.

LINCOLN: No sweat. I'll just pack up.

(*Lincoln rummages around finding a suitcase and begins to pack his things.*)

BOOTH: Just like that, huh? "No sweat"?! Yesterday you lost yr damn job. You dont got no cash. You dont got no friends, no nothing, but you clearing out just like that and its "no sweat"?!

LINCOLN: Youve been real generous and you and Grace need me gone and its time I found my own place.

BOOTH: No sweat.

LINCOLN: No sweat.

(*Rest*)

K. I'll spill it. I got another job, so getting my own place aint gonna be so bad.

BOOTH: You got a new job! Doing what?

LINCOLN: Security guard.

BOOTH:

(*Rest*)

Security guard. Howaboutthat.

(*Lincoln continues packing the few things he has. He picks up a whiskey bottle.*)

BOOTH: Go head, take thuh med-sin, bro. You gonna need it more than me. I got, you know, I got my love to keep me warm and shit.

LINCOLN: You gonna have to get some kind of work, or are you gonna let Grace support you?

BOOTH: I got plans.

LINCOLN: She might want you now but she wont want you for long if you dont get some kind of job. Shes a smart chick. And she cares about you. But she aint gonna let you treat her like some pack mule while shes out working her ass off and yr laying up in here scheming and dreaming to cover up thuh fact that you dont got no skills.

BOOTH: Grace is very cool with who I am and where Im at, thank you.

LINCOLN: It was just some advice. But, hey, yr doing great just like yr doing.

LINCOLN

BOOTH

LINCOLN

BOOTH

BOOTH: When Pops left he didnt take nothing with him. I always thought that was fucked-up.

LINCOLN: He was a drunk. Everything he did was always half regular and half fucked-up.

BOOTH: Whyd he leave his clothes though? Even drunks gotta wear clothes.

LINCOLN: Whyd he leave his clothes whyd he leave us? He was uh drunk, bro. He—whatever, right? I mean, you aint gonna figure it out by thinking about it. Just call it one of thuh great unsolved mysteries of existence.

BOOTH: Moms had a man on thuh side.

LINCOLN: Yeah? Pops had side shit going on too. More than one. He would take me with him when he went to visit them. Yeah.

(Rest)

> Sometimes he'd let me meet the ladies. They was all very nice. Very polite. Most of them real pretty. Sometimes he'd let me watch. Most of thuh time I was just outside on thuh porch or in thuh lobby or in thuh car waiting for him but sometimes he'd let me watch.

BOOTH: What was it like?

LINCOLN: Nothing. It wasnt like nothing. He made it seem like it was this big deal this great thing he was letting me witness but it wasnt like nothing.

(Rest)

> One of his ladies liked me, so I would do her after he'd done her. On thuh sly though. He'd be laying there, spent and sleeping and snoring and her and me would be sneaking it.

BOOTH: Shit.

LINCOLN: It was alright.

BOOTH

LINCOLN

(Lincoln takes his crumpled Abe Lincoln getup from the closet. Isnt sure what to do with it.)

BOOTH: Im gonna miss you coming home in that getup. I dont even got a picture of you in it for the album.

LINCOLN:

(Rest)

> Hell, I'll put it on. Get thuh camera get thuh camera.

BOOTH: Yeah?

LINCOLN: What thuh fuck, right?

BOOTH: Yeah, what thuh fuck.

(Booth scrambles around the apartment and finds the camera. Lincoln quickly puts on the getup, including 2 thin smears of white pancake makeup, more like war paint than whiteface.)

LINCOLN: They didnt fire me cause I wasnt no good. They fired me cause they was cutting back. Me getting dismissed didnt have no reflection on my performance. And I was a damn good Honest Abe considering.

BOOTH: Yeah. You look great man, really great. Fix yr hat. Get in thuh light. Smile.

LINCOLN: Lincoln didnt never smile.

BOOTH: Sure he smiled.

LINCOLN: No he didnt, man, you seen thuh pictures of him. In all his pictures he was real serious.

BOOTH: You got a new job, yr having a good day, right?

LINCOLN: Yeah.

BOOTH: So smile.

LINCOLN: Snapshots gonna look pretty stupid with me—

(*Booth takes a picture.*)

BOOTH: Thisll look great in thuh album.

LINCOLN: Lets take one together, you and me.

BOOTH: No thanks. Save the film for the wedding.

LINCOLN: This wasnt a bad job. I just outgrew it. I could put in a word for you down there, maybe when business picks up again theyd hire you.

BOOTH: No thanks. That shit aint for me. I aint into pretending Im someone else all day.

LINCOLN: I was just sitting there in thuh getup. I wasnt pretending nothing.

BOOTH: What was going on in yr head?

LINCOLN: I would make up songs and shit.

BOOTH: And think about women.

LINCOLN: Sometimes.

BOOTH: Cookie.

LINCOLN: Sometimes.

BOOTH: And how she came over here one night looking for you.

LINCOLN: I was at Luckys.

BOOTH: She didnt know that.

LINCOLN: I was drinking.

BOOTH: All she knew was you couldnt get it up. You couldnt get it up with her so in her head you was tired of her and had gone out to screw somebody new and this time maybe werent never coming back.

(*Rest*)

She had me pour her a drink or 2. I didnt want to. She wanted to get back at you by having some fun of her own and when I told her to go out and have it, she said she wanted to have her fun right here. With me.

(*Rest*)

[And then, just like that, she changed her mind.

(*Rest*)

But she'd hooked me. That bad part of me that I fight down everyday. You beat yrs down and it stays there dead but mine keeps coming up for another round. And she hooked the bad part of me. And the bad part of me opened my mouth and started promising her things. Promising her things I knew she wanted and you couldnt give her. And the bad part of me took her clothing off and carried her into thuh bed and had her, Link, yr Cookie. It wasnt just thuh bad part of me it was all of me, man,] I had her. Yr damn wife. Right in that bed.

LINCOLN: I used to think about her all thuh time but I dont think about her no more.

BOOTH: I told her if she dumped you I'd marry her but I changed my mind.

LINCOLN: I dont think about her no more.

BOOTH: You dont go back.

LINCOLN: Nope.

BOOTH: Cause you cant. No matter what you do you cant get back to being who
you was. Best you can do is just pretend to be yr old self.

LINCOLN: Yr outa yr mind.

BOOTH: Least Im still me!

LINCOLN: Least I work. You never did like to work. You better come up with some
kinda way to bring home the bacon or Gracell drop you like a hot rock.

BOOTH: I got plans!

LINCOLN: Yeah, you gonna throw thuh cards, right?

BOOTH: Thats right!

LINCOLN: You a double left-handed motherfucker who dont stand a chance in
all get out out there throwing no cards.

BOOTH: You scared.

LINCOLN: Im gone.

(*Lincoln goes to leave.*)

BOOTH: Fuck that!

LINCOLN: Yr standing in my way.

BOOTH: You scared I got yr shit.

LINCOLN: The only part of my shit you got is the part of my shit you think you
got and that aint shit.

BOOTH: Did I pick right them last times? Yes. Oh, I got yr shit.

LINCOLN: Set up the cards.

BOOTH: Thought you was gone.

LINCOLN: Set it up.

BOOTH: I got yr shit and Ima go out there and be thuh man and you aint gonna
be nothin.

LINCOLN: Set it up!

(*Booth hurriedly sets up the milk crates and cardboard top. Lincoln throws the cards.*)

LINCOLN: Lean in close and watch me now: who see thuh black card who see
thuh black card I see thuh black card black cards thuh winner pick thuh
black card thats thuh winner pick thuh red card thats thuh loser pick thuh
other red card thats thuh other loser pick thuh black card you pick thuh
winner. Who see thuh black card who see thuh black card? You pick thuh
red card you pick a loser you pick that red card you pick a loser you pick
thuh black card thuh deuce of spades you pick a winner who sees thuh
deuce of spades thuh one who sees it never fades watch me now as I throw
thuh cards. Red losers black winner follow thuh deuce of spades chase thuh
black deuce. Dark deuce will get you thuh win. 10 will get you 20, 20 will get
you 40. One good pickll get you in 2 good picks and you gone win.

(*Rest*)

Ok, man, wheres thuh black deuce?

(*Booth points to a card. Lincoln flips it over. It is the deuce of spades.*)

BOOTH: Who thuh man?!

(*Lincoln turns over the other two cards, looking at them confusedly.*)

LINCOLN: Hhhhh.
BOOTH: Who thuh man, Link?! Huh? Who thuh man, Link?!?!
LINCOLN: You thuh man, man.
BOOTH: I got yr shit down.
LINCOLN: Right.
BOOTH: "Right"? All you saying is "right"?

(*Rest*)

> You was out on the street throwing. Just today. Werent you? You wasnt
> gonna tell me.
LINCOLN: Tell you what?
BOOTH: That you was out throwing.
LINCOLN: I was gonna tell you, sure. Cant go and leave my little bro out thuh
loop, can I? Didnt say nothing cause I thought you heard. Did all right today
but Im still rusty, I guess. But hey — yr getting good.
BOOTH: But I'll get out there on thuh street and still fuck up, wont I?
LINCOLN: You seem pretty good, bro.
BOOTH: You gotta do it for real, man.
LINCOLN: I am doing it for real. And yr getting good.
BOOTH: I dunno. It didnt feel real. Kinda felt — well it didnt feel real.
LINCOLN: We're missing the essential elements. The crowd, the street, thuh traf-
fic sounds, all that.
BOOTH: We missing something else too, thuh thing thatll really make it real.
LINCOLN: Whassat, bro?
BOOTH: Thuh cash. Its just bullshit without thuh money. Put some money down
on thuh table then itd be real, then youd do it for real, then I'd win it for
real.

(*Rest*)

> And dont be looking all glum like that. I know you got money. A whole
> pocketful. Put it down.
LINCOLN
BOOTH
BOOTH: You scared of losing it to thuh man, chump? Put it down, less you think
thuh kid who got two left hands is gonna give you uh left hook. Put it down,
bro, put it down.

(*Lincoln takes the roll of bills from his pocket and places it on the table.*)

BOOTH: How much you got there?
LINCOLN: 500 bucks.
BOOTH: Cool.

(*Rest*)

Ready?

LINCOLN: Does it feel real?

BOOTH: Yeah. Clean slate. Take it from the top. "One good pickll get you in 2 good picks and you gone win."

(*Rest*)

Go head.

LINCOLN: Watch me now.

BOOTH: Woah, man, woah.

(*Rest*)

You think Ima chump.

LINCOLN: No I dont.

BOOTH: You aint going full out.

LINCOLN: I was just getting started.

BOOTH: But when you got good and started you wasnt gonna go full out. You wasnt gonna go all out. You was gonna do thuh pussy shit, not thuh real shit.

LINCOLN: I put my money down. Money makes it real.

BOOTH: But not if I dont put no money down tuh match it.

LINCOLN: You dont got no money.

BOOTH: I got money!

LINCOLN: You aint worked in years. You dont got shit.

BOOTH: I got money.

LINCOLN: Whatcha been doing, skimming off my weekly paycheck and squirreling it away?

BOOTH: I got money.

(*Rest*)

(*They stand there sizing each other up. Booth breaks away, going over to his hiding place from which he gets an old nylon stocking with money in the toe, a knot holding the money secure.*)

LINCOLN

BOOTH

BOOTH: You know she was putting her stuff in plastic bags? She was just putting her stuff in plastic bags not putting but shoving. She was shoving her stuff in plastic bags and I was standing in thuh doorway watching her and she was so busy shoving thuh shit she didnt see me. "I aint made of money," thats what he always saying. The guy she had on the side. I would catch them together sometimes. Thuh first time I cut school I got tired of hanging out so I goes home — figured I could tell Mom I was sick and cover my ass. Come in thuh house real slow cause Im sick and moving slow and quiet. He had her bent over. They both had all they clothes on like they was about to do something like go out dancing cause they was dressed to thuh 9s but at thuh last minute his pants had fallen down and her dress had flown up and theyd ended up doing something else.

(*Rest*)

They didnt see me come in, they didnt see me watching them, they didnt see me going out. That was uh Thursday. Something told me tuh cut school thuh next Thursday and sure enough —. He was her Thursday man. Every Thursday. Yeah. And Thursday nights she was always all cleaned up and fresh and smelling nice. Serving up dinner. And Pops would grab her cause she was all bright and she would look at me, like she didnt know that I knew but she was asking me not to tell nohow. She was asking me to — oh who knows.

(*Rest*)

She was talking with him one day, her sideman, her Thursday dude, her backdoor man, she needed some money for something, thered been some kind of problem some kind of mistake had been made some kind of mistake that needed cleaning up and she was asking Mr. Thursday for some money to take care of it. "I aint made of money," he says. He was putting his foot down. And then there she was 2 months later not showing yet, maybe she'd got rid of it maybe she hadnt maybe she'd stuffed it along with all her other things in them plastic bags while he waited outside in thuh car with thuh motor running. She musta known I was gonna walk in on her this time cause she had my payoff — my *inheritance* — she had it all ready for me. 500 dollars in a nylon stocking. Huh.

(*He places the stuffed nylon stocking on the table across from Lincolns money roll.*)

BOOTH: Now its real.
LINCOLN: Dont put that down.
BOOTH: Throw thuh cards.
LINCOLN: I dont want to play.
BOOTH: Throw thuh fucking cards, man!!
LINCOLN:

(*Rest*)

2 red cards but only one black. Pick thuh black you pick thuh winner. All thuh cards are face down you point out thuh cards and then you move them around. Now watch me now, now watch me real close. Put thuh winning deuce down in the center put thuh loser reds on either side then you just move thuh cards around. Move them slow or move them fast, Links thuh king he gonna last.

(*Rest*)

Wheres thuh deuce of spades?

(*Booth choose a card and chooses correctly.*)

BOOTH: HA!

LINCOLN: One good pickll get you in 2 good picks and you gone win.

BOOTH: I know man I know.

LINCOLN: Im just doing thuh talk.

BOOTH: Throw thuh fucking cards!

(*Lincoln throws the cards.*)

LINCOLN: Lean in close and watch me now: who see thuh black card who see
thuh black card I see thuh black card black cards thuh winner pick thuh
black card thats thuh winner pick thuh red card thats thuh loser pick thuh
other red card thats thuh other loser pick thuh black card you pick thuh
winner. Watch me as I throw thuh cards. Here we go.

(*Rest*)

Ima show you thuh cards: 2 red cards but only one spade. Dark winner in
thuh center and thuh red losers on thuh sides. Pick uh red card you got a
loser pick thuh other red card you got a loser pick thuh black card you got a
winner. Watch me watch me watch me now.

(*Rest*)

Who see thuh black card who see thuh black card? You pick thuh red card
you pick a loser you pick that red card you pick a loser you pick thuh black
card thuh deuce of spades you pick a winner who sees thuh deuce of spades
thuh one who sees it never fades watch me now as I throw thuh cards. Red
losers black winner follow thuh deuce of spades chase thuh black deuce.
Dark deuce will get you thuh win.

(*Rest*)

Ok, 3-Card, you know which cards thuh deuce of spades? This is for real
now, man. You pick wrong Im in yr wad and I keep mines.

BOOTH: I pick right I got yr shit.

LINCOLN: Yeah.

BOOTH: Plus I beat you for real.

LINCOLN: Yeah.

(*Rest*)

You think we're really brothers?

BOOTH: Huh?

LINCOLN: I know we *brothers*, but is we really brothers, you know, blood brothers
or not, you and me, whatduhyathink?

BOOTH: I think we're brothers.

BOOTH

LINCOLN

BOOTH

LINCOLN

BOOTH

LINCOLN

LINCOLN: Go head man, wheres thuh deuce?

(*In a flash Booth points out a card.*)

LINCOLN: You sure?

BOOTH: Im sure!

LINCOLN: Yeah? Dont touch thuh cards, now.

BOOTH: Im sure.

(*The 2 brothers lock eyes. Lincoln turns over the card that Booth selected and Booth, in a desperate break of concentration, glances down to see that he has chosen the wrong card.*)

LINCOLN: Deuce of hearts, bro. Im sorry. Thuh deuce of spades was this one.

(*Rest*)

> I guess all this is mines.

(*He slides the money toward himself.*)

LINCOLN: You were almost right. Better luck next time.

(*Rest*)

> Aint yr fault if yr eyes aint fast. And you cant help it if you got 2 left hands, right? Throwing cards aint thuh whole world. You got other shit going for you. You got Grace.

BOOTH: Right.

LINCOLN: Whassamatter?

BOOTH: Mm.

LINCOLN: Whatsup?

BOOTH: Nothing.

LINCOLN:

(*Rest*)

> It takes a certain kind of understanding to be able to play this game.

(*Rest*)

> I still got thuh moves, dont I?

BOOTH: Yeah you still got thuh moves.

(*Lincoln cant help himself. He chuckles.*)

LINCOLN: I aint laughing at you, bro, Im just laughing. Shit there is so much to this game. This game is — there is just so much to it.

(Lincoln, still chuckling, flops down in the easy chair. He takes up the nylon stocking and fiddles with the knot.)

LINCOLN: Woah, she sure did tie this up tight, didnt she?

BOOTH: Yeah. I aint opened it since she gived it to me.

LINCOLN: Yr kidding. 500 and you aint never opened it? Shit. Sure is tied tight. She said heres 500 bucks and you didnt undo thuh knot to get a look at the cash? You aint needed to take a peek in all these years? Shit. I woulda opened it right away. Just a little peek.

BOOTH: I been saving it.

(Rest)

Oh, dont open it, man.

LINCOLN: How come?

BOOTH: You won it man, you dont gotta go opening it.

LINCOLN: We gotta see whats in it.

BOOTH: We *know* whats in it. Dont open it.

LINCOLN: You are a chump, bro. There could be millions in here! There could be nothing! I'll open it.

BOOTH: Dont.

LINCOLN

BOOTH

(Rest)

LINCOLN: Shit this knot aint coming out. I could cut it, but that would spoil the whole effect, wouldnt it? Shit. Sorry. I aint laughing at you Im just laughing. Theres so much about those cards. You think you can learn them just by watching and just by playing but there is more to them cards than that. And —. Tell me something, Mr. 3-Card, she handed you this stocking and she said there was money in it and then she split and you say you didnt open it. Howd you know she was for real?

BOOTH: She was for real.

LINCOLN: How you know? She coulda been jiving you, bro. Jiving you that there really *was* money in this thing. Jiving you big time. Its like thuh cards. And ooooh you certainly was persistent. But you was in such a hurry to learn thuh last move that you didnt bother learning thuh first one. That was yr mistake. Cause its thuh first move that separates thuh Player from thuh Played. And thuh first move is to know that there aint no winning. It may look like you got a chance but the only time you pick right is when thuh man lets you. And when its thuh real deal, when its thuh real fucking deal, bro, and thuh moneys on thuh line, thats when thuh man wont want you picking right. He will want you picking wrong so he will make you pick wrong. Wrong wrong wrong. Ooooh, you thought you was finally happening, didnt you? You thought yr ship had come in or some shit, huh? Thought you was uh Player. But I played you, bro.

BOOTH: Fuck you. Fuck you FUCK YOU *FUCK YOU*!!
LINCOLN: Whatever, man. Damn this knot is tough. Ima cut it.

(*Lincoln reaches in his boot, pulling out a knife. He chuckles all the while.*)

LINCOLN: Im not laughing at you, bro, Im just laughing.

(*Booth chuckles with him. Lincoln holds the knife high, ready to cut the stocking.*)

LINCOLN: Turn yr head. You may not wanna look.

(*Booth turns away slightly. They both continue laughing. Lincoln brings the knife down to cut the stocking.*)

BOOTH: I popped her.
LINCOLN: Huh?
BOOTH: Grace. I popped her. Grace.

(*Rest*)

> Who thuh fuck she think she is doing me like she done? Telling me I dont got nothing going on. I showed her what I got going on. Popped her good. Twice. Three times. Whatever.

(*Rest*)

> She aint dead.

(*Rest*)

> She werent wearing my ring I gived her. Said it was too small. Fuck that. Said it hurt her. Fuck that. Said she was into bigger things. *Fuck* that. Shes alive not to worry, she aint going out that easy, shes alive shes shes —.

LINCOLN: Dead. Shes —
BOOTH: Dead.
LINCOLN: Ima give you back yr stocking, man. Here, bro —
BOOTH: Only so long I can stand that little brother shit. Can only take it so long.
    Im telling you —
LINCOLN: Take it back, man —
BOOTH: That little bro shit had to go —
LINCOLN: Cool —
BOOTH: Like Booth went —
LINCOLN: Here, 3-Card —
BOOTH: That Booth shit is over. 3-Cards thuh man now —
LINCOLN: Ima give you yr stocking back, 3-Card —
BOOTH: Who thuh man now, huh? Who thuh man now?! Think you can fuck
    with me, motherfucker think again motherfucker think again! Think you
    can take me like Im just some chump some two lefthanded pussy dickbreath
    chump who you can take and then go laugh at. Aint laughing at me you was
    just laughing bunch uh bullshit and you know it.
LINCOLN: Here. Take it.

BOOTH: I aint gonna be needing it. Go on. You won it you open it.

LINCOLN: No thanks.

BOOTH: Open it open it open it open it. *OPEN IT!!!*

(*Rest*)

> Open it up, bro.

LINCOLN

BOOTH

(*Lincoln brings the knife down to cut the stocking. In a flash, Booth grabs Lincoln from behind. He pulls his gun and thrusts it into the left side of Lincolns neck. They stop there poised.*)

LINCOLN: Dont.

(*Booth shoots Lincoln. Lincoln slumps forward, falling out of his chair and onto the floor. He lies there dead. Booth paces back and forth, like a panther in a cage, holding his gun.*)

BOOTH: Think you can take my shit? My shit. That shit was mines. I kept it. Saved it. All this while. Through thick and through thin. Through fucking thick and through fucking thin, motherfucker. And you just gonna come up in here and mock my shit and call me two lefthanded talking bout how she coulda been jiving me then go steal from me? My *inheritance*. You stole my *inheritance*, man. That aint right. That aint right and you know it. You had yr own. And you blew it. You *blew it*, motherfucker! I saved mines and you blew yrs. Thinking you all that and blew yr shit. And I *saved* mines.

(*Rest*)

> You aint gonna be needing yr fucking money-roll no more, dead mother-fucker, so I will pocket it thank you.

(*Rest*)

> Watch me close watch me close now: Ima go out there and make a name for myself that dont have nothing to do with you. And 3-Cards gonna be in everybodys head and in everybodys mouth like Link was.

(*Rest*)

> Ima take back my inheritance too. It was mines anyhow. Even when you stole it from me it was still mines cause she gave it to me. She didnt give it to you. And I been saving it all this while.

(*He bends to pick up the money-filled stocking. Then he just crumples. As he sits beside Lincoln's body, the money-stocking falls away. Booth holds Lincolns body, hugging him close. He sobs.*)

BOOTH: *AAAAAAAAAAAAAAAAAAAAAAH!*

END OF PLAY

John Guare b. 1928

Woman at a Threshold, Beckoning   [2003]

A line of people who will play JURORS, ASSISTANT DISTRICT ATTORNEYS, VENDORS, DETECTIVES, GUARDS. One steps out. JOHN.

JOHN: (*To us.*) I had been called to Grand Jury duty. Not jury duty but Grand Jury duty.

JUDGE: — which is not about finding people innocent or guilty. The Grand Jury determines whether there is sufficient evidence to bring the case to a jury trial. Twenty-three jurors. Alternates in case there's not a quorum — twelve votes are needed to indict. Are there any people who cannot serve at this time?

JOHN: (*To Judge.*) I can't come now.

JUDGE: The reason?

JOHN: It's not convenient. I'm busy. No reason.
(*To us.*) It was May, 2002. I wanted to enjoy the spring. To see the seasons turn. I wanted to get out of winter.

JUDGE: That's your reason?

JOHN: I've been working hard. I hoped to have time off.

JUDGE: Then we'll call you in December. You should be rested by then. But this is your last extension. You won't be able to get out of grand jury duty in December.

JOHN: For the entire month of December?

JUDGE: The entire month.

JOHN: (*To us.*) So I took now. I got sworn into grand jury along with twenty-two others.

ASSISTANT DA: Twenty-three jurors. Alternates in case there's not a quorum. Twelve votes are needed to indict.

JUROR #1: Even though some judge had said a prosecutor could get a grand jury to indict a ham sandwich.

JOHN: We did indict. Ham sandwiches aside, we voted for the next three days to indict every case that was brought before us. They were all the same.

ASST. DA: I present a case to you of three counts violating Article Eighteen of the Criminal Code and the Interstate Commerce Act in which Miguel Santero sold heroin to undercover agent Ladka. Do any of you know any of the participants in this operation?

JUROR #1: I should hope not.

(*Jurors murmur negative.*)

ASST. DA: What proof did you have when you made the arrest?

DETECTIVE: I was wearing a wire —

JOHN: (*To us.*) When the detective left, we could ask the assistant DA questions.

JUROR #2: Why does Interstate commerce come into it?

ASST. DA: That's a very good question. Since the alleged perpetrator was carrying a gun at the time of the arrest and since no guns are manufactured in the state of New York, it is fair to infer that the weapon was carried into the state over state lines, thereby violating the rules of Interstate Commerce. Any more questions?

JUROR #2: Could this be a setup?

ASST. DA: That's a very good question but — for what reason?

JUROR #2: The arresting detective is trying to make himself look good.

ASST. DA: I don't think this is relevant to —

JUROR #2: It happened on *Law and Order*.

JUROR #3: I saw that!

JUROR #1: Or the man sold drugs because he needed money for a sick child.

JUROR #3: Extenuating circumstances!

ASST. DA: Your job is not to solve a crime or reenact episodes of *Law and Order* or recreate *Les Miserables*. That's why you don't get to see the person who broke the law. You get me, the assistant district attorney, providing you with hard evidence of whether or not this person should be tried in a court of law. I'll go out of the room and let you vote.

JOHN: (*To us.*) He left.

JUROR #3: I don't like these detectives wearing wires.

JUROR #2: Suppose it was a setup? It's just what happened on *Law and* —

JOHN: (*Impatient.*) That's not for us to decide. The trial will decide that.

JUROR #1: What are you in a hurry for? We got no place to go for a month.

JOHN: Let's vote.

(*To us.*) Didn't my fellow jurors have anything better to do with their lives?

JUROR #1: (*An accusation.*) Ham sandwich.

JOHN: But then what did I have better to do with my life? Over and over, the foreman of our jury would ask for a true bill, meaning is it worth sending to trial.

FOREMAN OF JURY: How many vote for a true bill?

(*Hands raise. Foreman counts.*)

Eighteen. Nineteen. Twenty-one two twenty-three. Bring in the DA. We have a true bill.

JOHN: (*To us.*) And the ham sandwiches kept coming. Buy and bust. Buy and bust — drug deals — set up drug deals — buy and bust — how many votes for a true bill?

(*All hands go up.*)

All hands went up, day after day, over and over. We got maybe three cases in the morning, three or four in the afternoon. A month of this? God.

ASST. DA: Lunch break. Be back at two o'clock.

JOHN: Most of all, I hated lunch break because the first day I walked around to stretch my legs and find a sandwich. I crossed Foley Square, past City Hall over by Fulton Street. Sandwiches surely over there. Broadway. Wall Street. I came to a long line of people and a lot of vendors selling T-shirts.

VENDOR #1: Proud to be an American.

VENDOR #2: Americans are like the flag — we don't run.

VENDOR #3: We will never forget you.

(*The Others form a line.*)

JOHN: What's this line?

VENDOR #1: To see Ground Zero.

JOHN: It's down there?

> (*To us.*) I felt a pang. I had never come down here since that day — you know the day. I lived about a mile away from Ground Zero, I guess at Ground One. I saw it all happen that day. I'm still sickened by it — no, not sickened — I'm numbed by it. I still can't look at a picture of that day — or anything on the TV. I turn away or turn off. I knew people who died. Who didn't? — if you were a New Yorker.

JUROR #2: I heard some psychologist say on the radio — NPR — that anyone who witnessed the events of that day will never recover from them.

JOHN: Never recover? No big deal. I'm no different from anyone else. I was just one of the thousands who saw those horrific sights firsthand. So go stand in line. See it now. Put it into perspective. Maybe this was why I was called to jury duty. To face up to my inner nausea and finally confront Ground Zero and get over it. Put it behind me. Make it history. I tried to get in line.

PERSON IN LINE: Hey! Line jumper! Go down to South Street Seaport. Pick up your tickets there like everybody else.

JOHN: You need a ticket? Tickets to see Hell? Forget it.

> (*To us.*) I went back to the jury room. I took to bringing my lunch every day so I wouldn't be drawn to that line. I didn't want to be tempted to see Ground Zero. It was all right for tourists. Not for me. I still had the smell of those days in my nostrils — was it flesh? I had run into a friend of mine out on the street that night of September 12th who said:

FRIEND: Welcome to Auschwitz.

JOHN: Here it was May 2002 and that whole catastrophe of last September still made no sense. That pit of Ground Zero was still the abyss of unknowing. I got nauseous, paralyzed remembering it. And now you picked up tickets to see it? Back to reality. Back to Grand Jury — buy and bust —

(*The Jury forms.*)

ASST. DA: I present a case to you of three counts violating Article Eighteen of the Criminal Code and the Interstate Commerce Act in which Herman Ramirez sold heroin to undercover agent Ladka. Do any of you know any of the participants in this operation?

(*An Arab Woman appears, followed by a guard. She wears an Arab headdress with her prison garb. She is handcuffed.*)

JOHN: (*To us.*) And then one day the door opened and an Arab woman came in, dressed in pants that looked like — were they prison pants? From the waist up, she wore a shawl drawn up over her head framing her face. She looked at all of us. She had a beautiful smile. She was handcuffed from behind. The guard behind her steered her to a chair. The guard undid her handcuffs. He bid her sit down. She turned once before she sat. She did not sit down directly. She turned and then sat. She made a complete circle and then sat down. Did she pause for a moment? Did she look at me? He replaced the handcuffs on one wrist, attaching the other cuff to the arm of the wooden chair. All of us—we jurors who had not been instructed or prepared for this—looked at each other.

JUROR #1: (*Whispering.*) Who is she?

JUROR #2: Why aren't they telling us anything?

(*Another Assistant DA comes into the room, followed by a Translator in a business suit.*)

JOHN: The Assistant DA came into the room, followed by a man who would act as the translator. He sat by her. The Assistant DA did not swear her in, in the usual way. She stood. She raised her hand. The translator said something in Arabic to her. She nodded. The Assistant DA began his questioning. The court stenographer began typing.

ASST. DA: You understand that your attorney is outside this room. Should you have anything to ask him, you are allowed to leave the room to talk to him.

JOHN: The translator leaned into her and whispered softly.

(*The Woman nods yes.*)

ASST. DA: Would you indicate for the stenographer that the witness said yes?

TRANSLATOR: (*Always matter of fact.*) Yes.

ASST. DA: In 1997, when you first arrived in America, you lived in Jersey City.

(*The Translator leans into her. She listens and nods. All of these transactions will happen very quickly.*)

TRANSLATOR: Yes.

ASST. DA: Who did you live with?

(*The Translator leans into her. She whispers to him.*)

TRANSLATOR: With my ex-husband's cousin. A distant relative.

ASST. DA: How long did you live there?

(*The Translator leans into her. She whispers to him.*)

TRANSLATOR: Less than a month.

ASST. DA: The address?

(*The Translator leans into her. She whispers to him.*)

TRANSLATOR: I do not remember the address.

(*The Arab Woman looks out at John.*)

JOHN: She looked up into the room. She looked at me.

ASST. DA: You moved to Brooklyn with your ex-husband's parents for less than a month. Can you tell us the address?

(*The Translator leans into her. She whispers to him.*)

TRANSLATOR: I do not remember the address.
ASST. DA: Then back to Jersey City. To the same household?

(*The Translator leans into her. She whispers to him.*)

TRANSLATOR: No. To a girlfriend and her children for two months.

(*The Arab Woman looks out at John.*)

JOHN: She did it again. Right at me.
ASST. DA: Can you tell us the address?

(*The Translator leans into her. She whispers to him.*)

TRANSLATOR: I do not remember the address.
ASST. DA: Then to Chicago, Illinois, with a cousin named Zaccariah Abdullah and his wife, Fatima, for two months.

(*The Translator leans into her. She whispers to him.*)

TRANSLATOR: Yes.

(*The Arab Woman looks out at John.*)

JOHN: And again. Her lips moved. What was she saying to me?
ASST. DA: Can you tell us the address?

(*The Translator leans into her. She whispers to him.*)

TRANSLATOR: I do not remember the address.
ASST. DA: With your ex-husband's relative, did you ever discuss acts of terrorism?

(*The Translator leans into her. She whispers to him.*)

TRANSLATOR: No.
ASST. DA: Did you ever discuss terrorism with your Chicago relatives?

(*The Translator leans into her. She whispers to him.*)

TRANSLATOR: No.
ASST. DA: What did you do for money between 1997 and 1999?

(*The Translator leans into her. She whispers to him.*)

TRANSLATOR: Family support. No welfare.
ASST. DA: What identity do you use?

(*The Translator leans into her. She whispers to him.*)

TRANSLATOR: Egyptian passport the only ID.

JOHN: Egypt? I sat up. I had been to Egypt. Was she looking at me because she recognized me? Had I met her?

ASST. DA: We have a list of every number you called from Federal Detention Center. Do you recognize the following telephone numbers?

(*The Assistant DA passes her papers. She looks at them. The Translator leans into her. She whispers to him.*)

TRANSLATOR: Yes.

ASST. DA: Who are they?

(*The Translator leans into her. She whispers to him.*)

TRANSLATOR: Cousins. Friends.

ASST. DA: Have you ever discussed acts of terrorism with any of these people?

(*The Translator leans into her. She whispers to him.*)

TRANSLATOR: No.

ASST. DA: Have you planned acts of terrorism?

(*The Translator leans into her. She whispers to him.*)

TRANSLATOR: No.

ASST. DA: Who do you know in Detroit?

(*The Translator leans into her. She whispers to him.*)

TRANSLATOR: My cousin.

ASST. DA: Have you ever talked to your ex-husband in code?

(*The Translator leans into her. She whispers to him.*)

TRANSLATOR: No, only normal talking.

ASST. DA: When did you first hear about jihad?

(*The Translator leans into her. She whispers to him.*)

TRANSLATOR: Don't recall.

ASST. DA: How do you understand *jihad*?

(*The Translator leans into her. She whispers to him.*)

TRANSLATOR: *Jihad* is the struggle for women against temptation, against family and raising children properly.

(*The Arab Woman looks out at John.*)

JOHN: She looked at me again. Was it pleading?

ASST. DA: You told INS agents you had never heard of jihad until after September 11th.

(*The Translator leans into her. She whispers to him.*)

TRANSLATOR: The imam at the mosque told me what had happened September 11th was not jihad.

ASST. DA: Did you ever think of seeking revenge against the United States for convicting your ex-husband?

(*The Translator leans into her. She whispers to him.*)

TRANSLATOR: No.
ASST. DA: Have you read the Koran?

(*The Translator leans into her. She whispers to him.*)

TRANSLATOR: Yes.
ASST. DA: Have you taught Islam?

(*The Translator leans into her. She whispers to him.*)

TRANSLATOR: In Jersey City to a group of women every Saturday.
ASST. DA: Did you teach other concepts of *jihad*?

(*The Translator leans into her. She whispers to him.*)

TRANSLATOR: No.

(*The Arab Woman looks out at John.*)

JOHN: I couldn't get close enough. What was going on in her mind?
ASST. DA: Do you know anyone who's committed acts of terrorism, other than your husband and his cousin?

(*The Translator leans into her. She whispers to him.*)

TRANSLATOR: No.
ASST. DA: Did you ever plan to commit terrorism?

(*The Translator leans into her. She whispers to him.*)

TRANSLATOR: No.
ASST. DA: Did you ever discuss with another person how to commit acts of terrorism?

(*The Translator leans into her. She whispers to him.*)

TRANSLATOR: She wants to see her lawyer.
ASST. DA: Let the minutes reflect the witness is leaving the room to consult with her attorney.
JOHN: The guard came into the room, unlocked her handcuffs. She stood up. She made that turning motion. She looked at me. She smiled. The guard shackled her again. They left the room.

(*The Woman and her Guard leave.*)

We went berserk.
JUROR #3: Is she a terrorist?
JUROR #2: What are the charges?
JUROR #1: Is this one of those unconstitutional Ashcroft things? Is she one of thousands of Arabs being held illegally? Let her go!

JUROR #3: I say Hang her!

ASST. DA: Calm down. It's part of a long-term investigation. But one thing. She seems to be looking out into the room. I didn't ask, but could anyone on the jury conceivably know her? Has anybody here been to the Middle East?

JOHN: (*To us.*) I decided to keep my mouth shut.

ASST. DA: Anyone? No one. We are hearing testimony from a material witness that might be brought to the trial jury. We are here not merely to witness her testimony but to probe the case, to go deeper, or to provide a new angle. You, the grand jury, by witnessing and certifying her testimony are helping us do the job of investigating the attacks on September 11th as well as embassy bombings in Kenya and Tanzania.

JUROR #1: Who is she?

ASST. DA: Not important.

JOHN: It is!

ASST. DA: She is Narima Abdullah. She is thirty-two years old. She is Egyptian — married Mustapha Norur who's presently incarcerated —

JOHN: (*To us.*) She came to America illegally in 1997. She went to Canada in 1999 hoping to get legal status there until she could apply for U.S. legal residence. She applied for asylum in Canada as a single mother. She was told it was easier to bring a child from Egypt to Canada for protective custody which was denied. She came back to America in 2001 but she can't remember the name of the month.

JUROR #2: Can't remember the month! Give me a break.

JOHN: By any chance, was she in Egypt in 1996?

ASST. DA: That's a very good question. I have no idea. Why?

JOHN: Just wondering.

JUROR #1: Her ex-husband?

ASST. DA: Her ex-husband applied in 1998 for temporary protective status but as he was involved in holy war, he was accused and convicted. She is testifying on promise of immunity.

The only charge so far that can be brought against her is perjury which carries a five- to ten-year sentence for each charge of perjury.

JOHN: Is she a terrorist?

ASST. DA: That's a very good question —

JOHN: The assistant DA started to speak. But the door opened.

(*The Woman and The Guard return.*)

She held up her hands. He unlocked the cuffs. And again she made that circle. She turned very slowly, very gracefully, looked at me — just for a second — as she sat down in the chair — to which he shackled her again. Had I met this woman in Egypt?

ASST. DA: I'll repeat my question. Did you ever discuss with another person how to commit acts of terrorism?

(*The Translator leans into her. She whispers.*)

TRANSLATOR: No.

JUROR #3: She's lying.

JUROR #2: Through the teeth.

ASST. DA: Now let me enter document #1.

JOHN: (*To us.*) The assistant DA held up large photos so we could see them. They were mug shots of Arab men.

ASST. DA: Do you recognize any of the people in these photos?

JOHN: She looked at each face.

(*The Translator leans into her. She whispers to him.*)

TRANSLATOR: No. I do not know these people.

JOHN: (*To us.*) Then we gasped.

ASST. DA: Do you recognize this man?

JOHN: (*To us.*) The assistant DA then held up a photo of Mohammed Atta, the pilot of the first plane to crash into the Trade Center.

(*The Translator leans into her. She whispers to him.*)

TRANSLATOR: No. I do not know this man.

JOHN: But we all recognized the face. We all knew who he was. The whole world knew who he was.

JUROR #3: I say Hang her.

ASST. DA: You had a computer and an e-mail address. What chatrooms did you visit?

(*The Translator leans into her. She whispers to him.*)

TRANSLATOR: "Maktoud."

ASST. DA: The purpose of that site?

(*The Translator leans into her. She whispers to him.*)

TRANSLATOR: People make jokes in Arabic.

JUROR #2: That I'd like to hear.

JUROR #3: So this Ayatollah came into a bar —

ASST. DA: "Islam Way"?

(*The Translator leans into her. She whispers to him.*)

TRANSLATOR: It is a way of reciting the Koran online.

JUROR #3: Oh sure. "*Faster Pussycat Kill Kill* dot com."

ASST. DA: On a sheet of paper that was found on your person when you were taken into custody, you've written Revolution.com. Let me admit into evidence document #2.

(*The Translator leans into her. She whispers to him.*)

TRANSLATOR: It is the name of a game I copied down for my son to play in Egypt. May I say something?

(*The Translator leans into her. She whispers to him.*)

TRANSLATOR: Mrs. Abdullah wants to rectify something. She recognized the photo of the last man as the man responsible for the first crash. She only meant that she did not know him personally.

JOHN: I had seen that smile. My wife and I had gone on a holiday to Egypt for my fiftieth birthday. I wanted something special, something as ancient as me was our joke. We even had a friend in Cairo who had once lived in New York and said if you're ever in Cairo. We visited him. Wonderful knowing a local in Cairo. Our last night there, our friend took us to a part of the city where tourists did not usually go. The city instead of slums began to be decorated with large bolts of white cloth with Arabic designs in red or green painted on them. The city was transformed like a stage set. Drums started playing. What was happening? You'll see, our friend said. You'll see.

We walked and walked through the decorated city. I saw people spinning — men and women wearing white costumes and odd pointy hats spinning on one foot, their left foot — their hands outstretched — beatific smiles on their faces. We saw a man spinning with a snake around his neck, then another man, then a dozen men spinning each with a snake around his neck. My friend said proudly: This is what I wanted you to see. Happy birthday. It was a convention, a conference of whirling dervishes. Ten thousand dervishes who live around the Muslim world were congregating in Cairo.

It was terrifying. We saw people shooting out balls of colored paper hung over the street on wires. We walked through mobs. Is it safe? It was not safe, but we could not leave. Thousands of people dancing with these beatific smiles on their sublime faces, whirling to this hypnotic passionate music. Music of a few notes for a passionate purpose. Then I saw this woman. When I passed, the whirling woman — her — Mrs. Abdullah — suddenly stopped, looked at me and beckoned me. She made a slow beckoning gesture. I turned around. No one was there. I looked at her. Me? She nodded. I moved towards her. My wife pulled me back. When I turned again, the woman — Mrs. Abdullah — was gone and now here she was. I stood up in the jury room.

(*Cries out.*) I know this woman!

(*John advances on The Woman.*)

JOHN: Were you involved in 9/11?
WOMAN: Yes.
JOHN: (*To us.*) I would crack this case. I would supply a meaning to the events of that terrible day when the world spun out of control.

(*To The Woman.*) Were whirling dervishes involved?
WOMAN: We were all dervishes.
JOHN: What is the purpose of the spinning?

(*The Translator leans into her. She whispers to him.*)

TRANSLATOR: To see God. Yes. She remembers you.

JOHN: I thought dervishes were peaceful.

WOMAN: We are. It was not a plot of terror. It was a plot of conversion to bring our message of joy to the Western world, to have us all be finally One, living in peace.

JOHN: Peace?

WOMAN: We all want peace. The planes that day were spinning as we headed to the towers. The people inside those planes were spinning in ecstasy. When the spinning planes hit the towers, the people within the towers began spinning ecstatically. The ones who died were taken to paradise. The ones who survived were those who refused the word. They will be sent out into the world never to spin again. They had their chance. It was like Adam and Eve. God offered them the chance to find transcendent peace by spinning. They refused God's joy. That's the sin of Eden. God sent them out of Eden never to spin again. God came again on September 11th to give us a second chance. This was the second coming — the chance to achieve ecstasy.

JOHN: Is conversion too late now?

(*The Translator leans into her. She whispers to him.*)

TRANSLATOR: No! God is merciful. God will show us the way.

JOHN: By spinning?

(*The Translator leans into her. She whispers to him.*)

TRANSLATOR: Yes.

JOHN: How do I do it?

(*The Translator leans into her. She whispers to him.*)

TRANSLATOR: You spin on your left foot, your arms outstretched. You think of God. You chant.

JOHN: If I get dizzy?

WOMAN: That's the world trying to hold you back. "Dervish" means threshold.

JOHN: "Dervish" means threshold?

WOMAN: You are walking into a new consciousness.

JOHN: It's like the hokey pokey — only to God.

(*The Translator leans into her. She whispers to him.*)

TRANSLATOR: What is hokey pokey?

JOHN: I'm on the wrong side of the threshold. I'm trying to make a joke. That's what we do on the wrong side of the threshold. I want to cross that threshold.

WOMAN: You shall.

(*She makes a beckoning gesture.*)

JOHN: That day. It was all spinning and ecstasy?

WOMAN: Yes.

JOHN: I had seen the towers crumble. Did they spin as they toppled? Was there a spinning motion?

WOMAN: Yes.

JOHN: I saw the planes spinning. I saw the buildings whirling. Like you that night in Cairo.

WOMAN: Like me. "Dervish" means threshold. I'm on the threshold. Come join me.

(*John and The Woman begin to spin.*)

JOHN: That day was Allah taking us to a new threshold, a new way of life?

WOMAN: Yes.

JOHN: Not anguish, not terror, but joy?

WOMAN: Yes.

JOHN: Is this possible?

(*To us.*)

I know it's not possible but is it possible just to rethink it? That all those thousands of people that day did not die in terror, but rather were — *struck* by a moment of ecstasy. People leaping from the towers in ecstasy — spinning as they plunged down. All those whirling people shown the truth. Finding God.

WOMAN: That's right. You know the truth. Keep spinning. Don't stop.

(*John stops.*)

JOHN: You're crazy.

WOMAN: You're the one making me up.

JOHN: I'm looking for an answer.

WOMAN: To what?

JOHN: To this numbness I feel —

WOMAN: You've made me up and you call me crazy?

ASST. DA: Excuse me — A juror in the back row seems to be standing and trying to say something. Are you all right?

JOHN: (*Dazed.*) Oh. I'm sorry. I was just standing. Yes — standing is what they call this. Not spinning. I'm sorry.

(*To us.*) My fellow jurors all looked at me, some cross, some puzzled. The woman next to me passed me a bottle of water. "Thank you thank you — a momentary dizziness." I sat. The questioning resumed.

ASST. DA: You sought temporary protective status in the U.S. claiming fear of returning to Egypt.

(*The Translator leans into her. She whispers to him.*)

TRANSLATOR: My ex-husband wrote that on an application seeking asylum in Canada.

ASST. DA: You feared return to Egypt?

(*The Translator leans into her. She whispers to him.*)

TRANSLATOR: Yes.
ASST. DA: Fear of what?

(*The Translator leans into her. She whispers to him.*)

TRANSLATOR: Hardship. No work. Nothing else.
ASST. DA: Not because of your former husband's conviction?

(*The Translator leans into her. She whispers to him.*)

TRANSLATOR: Yes. They will question me why I divorced him. But I do not fear returning to Egypt now.
ASST. DA: Why?

(*The Translator leans into her. She whispers to him.*)

TRANSLATOR: Because my family told me I had no reason to fear.
ASST. DA: But before September 11th, you did have reason to fear?

(*The Translator leans into her. She whispers to him.*)

TRANSLATOR: Yes.
ASST. DA: Why?

(*The Translator leans into her. She whispers to him.*)

TRANSLATOR: Circumstances in Egypt make life very difficult. Life itself. We feared prosecution because our government is not to be trusted.
ASST. DA: Now you do trust it?

(*The Translator leans into her. She whispers to him.*)

TRANSLATOR: We trust the government now.
ASST. DA: Why?

(*The Translator leans into her. She whispers to him.*)

TRANSLATOR: My family tranquilized me.
ASST. DA: In Canada you said you feared execution if you returned.

(*The Translator leans into her. She whispers to him.*)

TRANSLATOR: I don't recall that.
ASST. DA: Thank you very much.
JOHN: The guard approached her and unlocked the cuff on the arm of the chair. She stood. She extended her wrists. He clamped on the other cuff. She held her wrists to her mouth. She started to make that slow spinning gesture. The guard led her out of the room. She did not look at any of us. She smiled. She was gone.

(*The Arab Woman and her Guard are gone.*)

JUROR #1: Will we see her again?
JUROR #2: Will she be deported?

JUROR #3: Where do they send her?

ASST. DA: Those are all very good questions. You never know. We split up these investigations so people tracking her can never tell what it is we're looking for.

JOHN: What did you learn today?

ASST. DA: A very good question. I just collect the data. Other people put it together. Next case. Three counts in violation of Article Eighteen of the Criminal Code. Possession of illegal substances —

JOHN: We returned to "buy and bust."

FOREMAN: We've heard the evidence. Vote for a true bill?

(*The Jurors raise their hands.*)

Unanimous.

JOHN: She didn't come back the next day. Nor the next. But all of us are still here. The month goes on. Hearing evidence. Buy or bust. Buy or bust. No answers. No judgments.

I thought of the dervishes. Spinning spinning to see God.

I looked them up on Google dot com. Part of Sufi. Not really for me.

They say we can't go back to living the way we did. But where do we go? What do we do? Living with that pit at Ground Zero that won't ever go away no matter how much redevelopment they do, no matter how many competitions they hold, the pit that's inside us as much as in Lower Manhattan won't ever go away because it's always been there. September 11th didn't make the terror. It showed us what we've always known is there. I'm embarrassed to ask this question. How do we get to God? Is that even a sensible question? I think of the terror of that day. How do we reach its mirror image? The polar opposite of that horror must be ecstasy. Where is the ecstasy? Is finding that ecstasy the only way to get out of this numbness, this grief — this fear —

What is that woman's truth? How can anyone know what her truth is? How can we know what happens on *any* day?

ASST. DA: Next case. Two counts of a violation of Article Eighteen —

FOREMAN: Vote for a true bill? Hands up? Twenty-one — twenty-two.

(*The Arab Woman appears, beckoning to John.*)

JOHN: I raised my hand.

(*John beckons to the Woman.*)

PART 5

Approaching LITERARY RESEARCH

Overleaf: Toni Morrison giving a reading for her book Love *(2003) at Barnes and Noble in New York, 2003. Morrison's 1983 short story "Recitatif" is the subject of Kristina Martinez's student research paper, "The Structure of Story in Toni Morrison's 'Recitatif'" in Chapter 29. (See page 1551 for a short biography of Morrison.)*

Photo © Nancy Kaszerman/ZUMA/Corbis.

A good critic is one who narrates the adventures of his mind among masterpieces.

Anatole France

Reading Critical Essays

CHAPTER **28**

Listening to the Larger Conversation

When you see a movie you really like, you may not only want to see it again but also to find out more about it — what other films an actor has appeared in (and perhaps some details about her or his life), some background on the director and information on the screenwriter, what changes were made from the work on which it was based (if adapted from another source), and what well-informed film critics said about it. As you look for information about these topics in newspapers, in magazines, or on the Internet, you are engaging in research. You can do the same for literary works. Even if you learn a lot about a work by reading it several times, reflecting on it and taking notes about it, listening to what is said about it in class, and discussing it with your classmates, for rich, complex works there is always more to learn, beyond the classroom.

THE ONGOING CONVERSATION   Learning more in this case can be interesting and even exciting as it brings you deeper into the great ongoing conversation about literature that we've referred to several times in this book. That conversation starts with people talking about works they like and sharing their enthusiasms, dislikes, and questions. It continues as they move that exchange to paper (or computer screens). It extends further through the efforts of literary scholars who publish their critical insights about a particular work or era or theme.

PARTICIPATING IN THAT CONVERSATION   Obviously, you can participate in early stages of that conversation. But it's important for you, as a student of literature, to enter the later stages as well by reading, reflecting upon, and responding to the critical writings of literary scholars, thus incorporating them into your own literary experience. This chapter offers suggestions on how to read and assess critical essays about literary works, something that can be an important step toward an even more interesting and provocative involvement in the wider world of literary study.

WHAT ARE CRITICAL ESSAYS?

The word *critical* in its literary use (and in its use for the arts in general) does not mean "inclined to find fault or judge severely," as in "My uncle is such a critical person—always ripping somebody apart." Rather, it means exercising skillful and well-informed judgment as to the techniques, ideas, or merits in, for example, a work of literature or a play, a concert, a dance performance, or an art exhibit.

Literary critics are scholars who have learned a great deal about literature, usually through work toward academic degrees but sometimes through extensive reading on their own. When they prepare to write a critical essay on a work, they read the work many times; they read everything else the author has written; and they read critical essays and books written about the work and author by other critics. Through previous study they probably already have learned a good deal about the time and places in which the author lived, and about writers and works that influenced the author, but they may do additional study as preparation for a particular essay.

For us to read what such expert authorities write about a work can yield insights—which we otherwise might miss—and a fuller understanding of the work itself, its context, and how it came into being.

WHY READ CRITICAL ESSAYS?

Reading critical essays helps in a number of ways. However, you will find them most useful if you read them at the right point. We recommend strongly that you not begin reading critical essays about a story, poem, or play until you have read the work itself several times and formulated your own thoughts about it. If you start reading criticism before you know the text well and form your own ideas about it, the ideas in the essays may overwhelm your thoughts and lead you merely to accept or adapt what you read. With your own conclusions already in mind, you'll be better able to evaluate the criticism, to disagree with the critic as well as to agree, and to accept refinements of your own insights.

Once you know a work well and have begun shaping your ideas about it, there are five good reasons for reading critical studies of the work:

1. To see how your own ideas are like and unlike those of other readers
2. To have your attention drawn to parts or aspects of the work whose significance you haven't recognized and to begin to imagine new ways of reading a text — new interpretations of or perspectives on it
3. To learn where the literary conversation about an author or a work stands and what scholars regard as strengths and weaknesses in what other critics have written
4. To discover new ways of constructing a literary argument, refuting earlier positions, offering counterarguments, and using explanation, elaboration, and evidence effectively
5. To gain a better understanding of the background or culture or literary tradition of a work by reading the results of a scholar's primary research (since you don't have time to do research on everything yourself, you often learn through reading the results of other people's research)

Each of these reasons has a practical benefit when you are working on a paper. Reading critical essays can give you a more informed and balanced stance as you explore a work. You can be more confident about your ability to find support for a position you want to uphold, and for entering the ongoing discussion as you write your paper. If need be, you may be able to refine your tentative thesis into a more effective argumentative thesis by connecting with places where critics disagree with each other, or where one modifies what another has said — the way Susan Farrell challenges prevailing views about "Everyday Use" in the sample essay later in this chapter.

ACTIVE READING: Critical Essays

In Chapters 2, 8, 17, and 25, we describe a number of conventions you should follow in writing a literary paper — being sure that you state a thesis in the introduction, start each paragraph with a topic sentence, and so on. There is a strategic reason for following those conventions: They enable your reader to grasp your paper easily and they establish confidence in you as a writer worth attending to. The importance of what we say in those chapters may become more evident as you read critical essays and find yourself using those conventions to trace the steps in the argument and to understand what is being said.

Here are some guidelines for reading critical essays. (For reading critical books, begin by looking at the table of contents, noticing the overall outline of the book, and reading the preface to find out the aims, approach, and outlook of the book; then apply the guidelines to each chapter.)

- *Pick out the thesis and identify the central idea the paper will explore.* The thesis is likely found near the end of the introductory paragraph or section. Look also for references to previous studies and notice how this essay differs from or disagrees with them. Use such references to identify what is new about the central idea and about the essay.

- *Look for the topic sentence in each paragraph.* The first sentence usually states the central idea to be discussed in the paragraph. (The second sentence may do this instead if the first is mainly a transitional sentence.)

- *Watch for the way the ideas are advanced and supported.* Outline the steps in the argument (the thesis sentence and topic sentences may provide an outline). Consider the reasoning used in laying out ideas and connecting points to each other. Consider the nature and adequacy of the evidence provided in support of the reasoning.

- *Identify and take into account the theoretical approach being taken in the essay.* The appendix on theoretical approaches to literature (p. 1584) summarizes a number of ways scholars approach literature, such as doing literary analysis, literary interpretation, historical background research, or analysis from a Marxist, psychoanalytic, or feminist perspective. Knowing where a critical work is coming from — what its assumptions and intentions are — helps you to follow its arguments and to do justice to its ideas.

- *Look at the footnotes and/or Works Cited list to see if there are other studies you might want to read yourself.*

SAMPLE ESSAY

ENTRY POINTS   Try out those strategies in reading the following essay. If you did not read Alice Walker's story "Everyday Use" in Chapter 5 (p. 109) or if you do not remember it well, read it before going on to the essay. For the convenience of readers, we have changed the page numbers for quotations of "Everyday Use" originally given in the essay to the pages on which they are found in this book.

Notice as you read the essay that the first paragraph situates the study in the ongoing discussion of "Everyday Use." It sketches out the positions held by other critics, summarizing and quoting from a few representative analyses of the story and listing many other studies in a footnote. Then it states the thesis to be explored in this paper, one that clearly is argumentative because it asserts a position almost directly opposite to the one most critics hold. The rest of the essay elaborates on that argument and explains why the author adheres to it. As you read, it is important to differentiate between sentences that *advance* the argument and sentences that *support* and *illustrate* the argument. To make that easier, we have put the former in boldface and added some marginal notes.

Susan Farrell

Fight vs. Flight: A Re-evaluation of Dee in Alice Walker's "Everyday Use"   [1998]

Most readers of Alice Walker's short story "Everyday Use," published in her 1973 collection *In Love and Trouble*, agree that the point of the story is to show, as Nancy Tuten argues, a mother's "awakening to one daughter's superficiality and to the other's deepseated understanding of heritage" (125).[1] These readers praise the "simplicity" of Maggie and her mother, along with their allegiance to their specific family identity and folk heritage as well as their refusal to change at the whim of an outside world that doesn't really have much to do with them. Such a reading condemns the older, more worldly sister, Dee, as "shallow," "condescending," and "manipulative," as overly concerned with style, fashion, and aesthetics, and thus as lacking a "true" understanding of her heritage. **In this essay, conversely, I will argue that this popular view is far too simple a reading of the story. While Dee is certainly insensitive and selfish to a certain degree, she nevertheless offers a view of heritage and a strategy for contemporary African Americans to cope with an oppressive society that is, in some ways, more valid than that offered by Mama and Maggie.**

We must remember from the beginning that the story is told by Mama; the perceptions are filtered through her mind and her views of her two daughters are not to be accepted uncritically. Several readers have pointed out that Mama's view of Maggie is not quite accurate — that Maggie is not as passive or as "hangdog" as she appears.[2] **Might Mama's view of her older daughter, Dee, not be especially accurate as well? Dee obviously holds a central place in Mama's world.** The story opens with the line: "I will wait for her in the yard that Maggie and I made so clean and wavy yesterday afternoon" (109). As Houston Baker and Charlotte Pierce-Baker point out, "The mood at the story's beginning is one of ritualistic waiting," of preparation "for the arrival of a goddess" (715). Thus, Dee seems to attain almost mythic stature in Mama's imagination as she and Maggie wait for the as-yet unnamed "her" to appear. Such an opening may lead readers to suspect that Mama has a rather troubled relationship with her older daughter. Dee inspires in Mama a type of awe and fear more suitable to the advent of a goddess than the love one might expect a mother to feel for a returning daughter.

Mama, in fact, **displaces what seem to be her own fears onto Maggie** when she speculates that Maggie will be cowed by Dee's arrival. Mama conjectures that

Method: summary of views held by other critics.

Thesis.

Method: building on earlier critics.

Central idea for Section I.

Maggie will be nervous until after her sister goes: she will stand hopelessly in corners, homely and ashamed of the burn scars down her arms and legs, eyeing her sister with a mixture of envy and awe. She thinks her sister has held life always in the palm of one hand, that "no" is a word the world never learned to say to her. (109)

Method: close reading of text.

But Mama here emphasizes the perceptual nature of this observation—she says that Maggie *thinks* these things, encouraging readers to wonder whether or not this first perception of Dee is true. We also find out in the next section, when Mama relates her Johnny Carson television fantasy, that she herself is the one that will be "nervous" until after Dee goes, that she is ashamed of her own appearance and very much seeks her daughter's approval. Mama confesses that, in "real life," she is "a large, big-boned woman with rough, man-working hands" (110). However, in her television fantasy, as Mama tells us,

Evidence: summary and quotation.

all this does not show. . . . I am the way my daughter would want me to be: a hundred pounds lighter, my skin like an uncooked barley pancake. My hair glistens in the hot bright lights. Johnny Carson has much to do to keep up with my quick and witty tongue. (110)

It is important to remember, though, that **this Johnny Carson daydream is Mama's fantasy of a mother-child reunion,** *not* **Dee's.** In fact, Mama even acknowledges that this particular scenario might not be to Dee's taste—she imagines Dee pinning an orchid on her even though Dee had previously told Mama she thinks orchids are "tacky flowers" (110). Thus, although Tuten equates Dee's values with those of "the white Johnny Carson society" (126), it seems to me that we have to question whether Mama's vision of her light-skinned, slender, witty self is actually Dee's wish or only Mama's perception of what she imagines Dee would like her to be.

Elsewhere, as well, we see that **Mama is often wrong about her expectations of Dee and her readings of Dee's emotions.** She writes that she "used to think" Dee hated Maggie as much as she hated the previous house that burned down (110). Mama implies, though, that she has since changed her mind about this. Further, as Mama and Maggie continue to wait for Dee's arrival, Mama "deliberately" turns her back on the house, expecting Dee to hate this house as much as Mama believes she hated the earlier one: "No doubt when Dee sees it she will want to tear it down" (110). When Dee does arrive, however, she has a camera with her and "never takes a shot without making sure the house is included" (112). Of course, most readers see this as evidence of Dee's fickle changing with what-

Method: contrast with other critics.

ever fad happens to be current. Once it becomes fashionable to have rural, poverty-stricken roots, Dee wants a record of her own humble beginnings. This might very well be true. Yet **I would argue that we have only Mama's word for Dee's earlier haughtiness, and this could have been exaggerated,** much as Mama hints that her earlier suspicion of Dee's hatred for Maggie was inaccurate. The more subtle point here is that **Mama's expectations of Dee tell us more about Mama herself than they do about Dee.** Again, Mama seems to view Dee with a mixture of awe, envy, and fear. Although she resents Dee because she expects Dee will want "to tear the house down," Mama still takes her cue from her older daughter, herself turning her back on the house, perhaps in an effort to appease this daughter, who looms so large in Mama's imagination.

In contrast to her own fearfulness, **Mama, with grudging admiration, remembers Dee as a fearless girl.** While Mama imagines herself unable to look white people in the eye, talking to them only "with one foot raised in flight," Dee "would always look anyone in the eye. Hesitation was no part of her nature" (110). Mama remembers Dee as self-centered and demanding, yes, but she also remembers this daughter as **a determined fighter.** Dee is concerned with style, but she'll do whatever is necessary to improve her circumstances. For instance, when Dee wants a new dress, she "makes over" an old green suit someone had given her mother. Rather than passively accept her lot, as Mama seems trained to do, Dee "was determined to stare down any disaster in her efforts" (111). **Mama's fearful nature is also apparent in her reaction to knowledge.** Words for Mama are associated with "lies" and "other folks' habits" (110). She remembers feeling "trapped and ignorant" as Dee reads to her and Maggie "without pity" (110). This is partly because Mama never had an education herself. When her school was closed down in 1927, after she had completed only the second grade, Mama, like the other African Americans in her community, didn't fight: "colored asked fewer questions than they do now," she tells us (111). Again, Mama is trained in acquiescence while Dee refuses to meekly accept the status quo.

Most critics see Dee's education and her insistence on reading to Mama and Maggie as further evidence of her separation from and lack of understanding for her family identity and heritage. Tuten, for instance, argues that, in this story, "Walker stresses not only the importance of language but also the destructive effects of its misuse. . . . Rather than providing a medium for newfound awareness and for community, . . . verbal skill equips Dee to oppress and manipulate others and to isolate herself" (125). Similarly, Donna Winchell writes that "Dee tries to force on" Maggie and her mother "knowledge they probably do not need." She continues,

Central idea for Section II.

Method: accumulation of details.

Method: contrast with other critics.

Mrs. Johnson can take an objective look at who and what she is and find not disillusionment but an easy satisfaction. Simple pleasures — a dip of snuff, a cooling breeze across a clean swept yard, church songs, the soothing movements of milk cows — are enough. (82)

Method: showing other critics may be mistaken.

But are these "simple pleasures" really enough for Mama in the story? When she imagines her future she seems vaguely unhappy and apprehensive about it: "[Maggie] will marry John Thomas (who has mossy teeth in an earnest face) and then I'll be free to sit here and I guess just sing church songs to myself. Although I never was a good singer. Never could carry a tune" (111). Not quite sure what she will do with herself when Maggie marries, Mama can only imagine herself alone, engaging in an activity which she feels she is not even very good at. Although she perhaps goes about it in the wrong way — Mama says that Dee "pressed us to her with the serious way she read," only to "shove us away at just the moment, like dimwits, we seemed about to understand" (111) — Dee at least tries to change what she foresees as Mama's fairly dismal future, a vision of her future Mama herself seems to reinforce rather than dispute. **Thus, I'd suggest the possibility that Dee's attempt to educate Mama and Maggie may be read much more positively than other critics have suggested.** Again, we must remember that Mama's perspective is the only one we see throughout the story. Told from Dee's point of view, we might expect a very different rendering of this incident. Rather than simply abandon her mother and sister in their ignorance and poverty, in their acquiescence to an oppressive system, Dee tries her best to extend her own education to them, which is surely not such a bad thing.

When Dee does finally arrive, **both Maggie and her mother react again with fear of the unknown, of something strange and different.** But as Dee approaches, Mama notices that the brightly colored African dress that Dee wears "throw[s] back the light of the sun" (112). Mama feels her "whole face warming from the heat waves it throws out" (112). She also admires the way that the "dress is loose and flows," and, despite her initial reaction, even decides that she likes it as Dee moves closer to her. In her admiration of the dress, **Mama illustrates Walker's point that everything new is not to be feared, that change can be positive, not only negative.** Maggie, however, remains fearful, even in the face of the friendliness of Dee's companion, who grins and greets Mrs. Johnson and Maggie warmly: "Asalamalakim, my mother and sister!" (112). When he tries to hug Maggie, though, she falls back against a chair and trembles. And later, when he tries to teach Maggie a new handshake, her hand remains limp and she quickly withdraws it from his.

Central idea for Section III.

Shortly after this, Dee announces that she is no longer Dee but "Wangero Leewanika Kemanjo." She has newly adopted an African name since, as she explains: "I couldn't bear it any longer, being named after the people who oppress me" (112). Many readers point to Dee's proclamation of her new name as the turning point in the story, the point at which Dee pushes her mother too far. They point out that Dee is rejecting her family heritage and identity in this scene. **Yet it seems to me that Dee and Mama are *both* right here.** Mama's recounting of the family history of the name is surely accurate, but what the critics fail to point out is that Dee's assertion that the name comes from "the people who oppress" her is also accurate. While most readers see Mama and Maggie as having a "true" sense of heritage as opposed to Dee's false or shallow understanding of the past, both Mama and Dee are blind to particular aspects of heritage. Dee has much to learn about honoring her particular and individual family history, but Mama has much to learn about the history of African Americans in general, and about fighting oppression. Although each is stubborn, both Dee and Mama do make a concession to the other here. Dee tells Mama that she needn't use the new name if she doesn't want to, while Mama shows her willingness to learn and to use the name.

Method: contrast with other critics.

Mama's secret admiration for Dee's fighting spirit leaks out again when she explicitly connects the "beef-cattle peoples down the road" to Dee and her boyfriend, "Hakim-a-barber." We see that the neighbors down the road, like Dee's boyfriend, are most likely black Muslims: they also say "Asalamalakim" when they meet, and Hakim explains that he accepts "some of their doctrines," although farming is not his style. Like Dee, these neighbors are also fighters. When "white folks" poison some of their cattle, they "stayed up all night with rifles in their hands" (113). Tellingly, Mama, who can't look white people in the eye and who never asked questions when her school closed down, is intrigued by this younger generation's refusal to acquiesce. She "walked a mile and a half" down the road "just to see the sight" of blacks armed for resistance (113). **Mixed with her resentment against her older daughter's worldliness and self-centered attitude, Mama also grudgingly respects and even envies the willingness to fight evinced both by Dee and the black Muslim neighbors.**

Method: new way of reading the text.

Maggie's forbearance in the story contrasts with Dee's boldness. When Dee haughtily insists that Maggie would ruin Grandma's quilts by using them every day, and that hanging the quilts would be the only way to preserve them, Maggie, "like somebody used to never winning anything, or having anything reserved for her," meekly replies: "She can have them, Mama, . . . I can 'member Grandma Dee without the quilts" (115). Mama, though, does not react so meekly. She sees Maggie standing with her scarred hands hidden in her skirt and says: "When I looked at her like that something hit me in the top of my head and ran down to the soles of my feet. Just like when I'm in church and the spirit of God touches me and I get happy and shout" (115). This powerful feeling causes Mama to do something she "never had done before": she "snatched the quilts out of Miss Wangero's hands and dumped them into Maggie's lap" (115). **Ironically, in acting against Dee's wishes here, Mama is truly behaving more like Dee, with her refusal to back down, her willingness to stand up for herself, than she is like the patient and long-suffering Maggie.** So perhaps, along with the younger, changing generation coming of age in the early 1970s that she is associated with, Dee, despite her outward obnoxiousness, has taught Mama something about fighting back. Or perhaps Dee has inherited more of her stubbornness and self-determination from her Mama than previously suspected. But, in any case, it seems too easy and neat a reading to simply praise Mama and Maggie for understanding their heritage while dismissing Dee as shallow and self-serving, when Mama's final courageous act ties her more closely to this older daughter than to the younger one she is trying to protect.

Central idea for Section IV.

Walker raised similar problems concerning the willingness to fight for a cause versus the desire to remain passive in her novel *Meridian*, published in 1976, three years after *In Love and Trouble*. In this novel, Walker's main character, Meridian Hill, is at first passive and dreamy. She drifts into an early marriage and pregnancy, since these things seem to be expected of her, but she doesn't truly find direction in her life until she becomes involved with the early Civil Rights movement. As a movement worker, though, Meridian is tempted toward becoming a martyr for her cause. When asked if she would "kill for the revolution," Meridian remains unable to answer. Although readers see the complexities of Meridian's ambivalence here, other activists call her a coward and a masochist for her lack of commitment. In her forbearance and initial willingness to sacrifice her own needs if necessary, Meridian shares much in common with Maggie of "Everyday Use." Meridian's college roommate, Anne-Marion Coles, on the other hand, is similar to Dee. Aggressive and determined to change her life, Anne-Marion, unlike Meridian, easily asserts her willingness to kill if necessary. But, also like Dee in the way she treats Mama and Maggie, Anne-Marion is self-centered and at times unthinkingly cruel to the weaker, more fragile Meridian. While Meridian is certainly a more sympathetic character than Anne-Marion throughout the novel, just as Maggie and Mama are more appealing than Dee in many ways, by the end Walker shows us that Meridian has something to learn from Anne-Marion and her other militant colleagues in the movement. . . .

Method: parallel situation in another work by Walker.

Summary to bring out similarities between the two works.

Readers of these two works may at first be seduced into affirming the passive acquiescence of characters such as Mama, Maggie, and

Meridian because they are, in many ways, more palatable, more likeable, than such aggressive fighters as Dee and Anne-Marion. These determined, fierce women, however, have much to teach the more forbearing, self-sacrificing characters in both works. Yet, at the same time, we see that a spirit of rebellion, without a corresponding spirituality and respect for such traditional black institutions as the church or the folk arts of "Everyday Use," can be empty as well. Though defiant and aggressive, both Dee and Anne-Marion are selfish and capricious in their social activism. Finally, then, in "Everyday Use," **Walker shows that Mama's moment of triumph is achieved because she is able to attain a balance between the two types of her heritage represented by her very different daughters** — at the end Mama combines Maggie's respect for tradition with Dee's pride and refusal to back down, the combination Walker seems to feel is necessary if true social change is to come about.

Completion of thesis idea.

Notes

Informative endnotes.

1. See especially, along with Tuten's *Explicator* article, Houston Baker and Charlotte Pierce-Baker's "Patches: Quilts and Community in Alice Walker's 'Everyday Use,'" Margaret D. Bauer's "Alice Walker: Another Southern Writer Criticizing Codes Not Put to 'Everyday Use,'" and Donna Haisty Winchell's Twayne Series book on Alice Walker (80–84).

Note listing related critical studies.

2. Tuten, for instance, argues that the "action of the story . . . in no way supports Mama's reading of her younger daughter," that Maggie "conveys disgust with her sister rather than envy and awe" as Mama believes (127). Similarly, Baker and Pierce-Baker point out that, "in her epiphanic moment of recognition," Mama must perceive "the fire-scarred Maggie — the stay-at-home victim of southern scarifications — in a revised light," that she must reassess "what she wrongly interprets as Maggie's hang-dog resignation before Dee" (717).

Note providing further supporting evidence.

Works Cited

Baker, Houston, and Charlotte Pierce-Baker. "Patches: Quilts and Community in Alice Walker's 'Everyday Use.'" *The Southern Review* 21 (1985): 706–20.

Bauer, Margaret D. "Alice Walker: Another Southern Writer Criticizing Codes Not Put to 'Everyday Use.'" *Studies in Short Fiction* 29 (1992): 143–51.

Tuten, Nancy. "Alice Walker's 'Everyday Use.'" *The Explicator* 51.2 (Winter 1993): 125–28.

Walker, Alice. "Everyday Use." *In Love and Trouble.* New York: Harcourt, 1973. 47–59.

——. *Meridian.* New York: Harcourt, 1976.

Winchell, Donna Haisty. *Alice Walker.* New York: Twayne, 1992.

OUTLINE   Most scholars, when they read such an essay, pick out the central idea in each paragraph and jot down an outline of the main steps in the argument. Here is an example of the sort of outline a reader might sketch out:

Thesis: Dee offers a view of heritage and way of coping with society more valid than those of Mama and Maggie

    I.   Mama's view of Dee may not be reliable
        A. She displaces her fears of Dee onto Maggie
        B. The Johnny Carson daydream is Mama's fantasy, not Dee's
        C. Mama is often wrong about Dee
   II. Contrast between Dee's fearlessness and Mama's fearfulness
        A. Dee as a determined fighter
        B. Mama's fear of knowledge
        C. Mama's fear of the future
  III. Mama's attitude changes as she interacts with Dee
        A. Mama seems more open to new things than Maggie
        B. Both Mama and Dee need to gain a more adequate under-standing of heritage
        C. Mama admires Dee's fighting spirit
        D. Mama behaves like Dee (not like Maggie) by fighting back against Dee's demands
  IV. The same pattern (passivity vs. fighting back) is evident in *Meridian*
Restatement of thesis: Mama triumphs as she achieves a balance between the approaches and attitudes of Dee and Maggie.

Such an outline enables you to view the argument as a whole — what the individual points are and how they relate to each other. That's valuable in understanding the essay and in assessing the strength of what it says.

KINDS OF EVIDENCE   It's also important to notice the kinds of evidence an author uses to support her or his argument. In Farrell's essay, most of the evidence comes through close reading of the text, with supporting details and quotations from it. But the author also uses the authoritative opinions of other scholars in support of her own positions when she regards them as sound, and she argues against them when she believes their interpretations are not accurate or adequate. And the author uses as a further kind of supporting evidence a parallel situation in another work by Walker, the novel *Meridian*. (We include only the first paragraph of that section, to show how the author introduces the comparison, and omit the following three paragraphs because they discuss a work that is not included in this book and will be unfamiliar to many of you.)

REREADING: Critical Essays

An important step in the reading process of critical essays is evaluation: After all, the essay is trying to persuade you, so it is crucial that you not simply accept automatically what has been written, that you have the skills necessary to decide how good the points and arguments in the essay are. Making that decision usually requires rereading all, or the key parts of, the essay. To evaluate the essay well, start by comparing the critic's ideas with your own ideas. This is why it is important that you know the work itself well and that you formulate your own interpretation of it before reading any critical essay. Here are some suggestions for evaluating critical essays.

- *Compare the critic's interpretation with your own interpretation.* The first step in evaluation is to formulate your own judgment as clearly and substantially as you can. Then compare the critic's interpretations to your own — how convincing do they seem to you? Does the critic use the text accurately and fairly and draw sensible conclusions about details in it? Does the critic take everything into account or pass over details that don't support her or his conclusions? Do the steps in the critic's argument proceed logically, and is the case presented sound and convincing?

- *Compare what one critic says with what other critics say.* Perhaps comparison is the best method of evaluation. To assess fully what one critic says, read the interpretations of several or many other critics. By comparing what one says with what another says, you will begin to get a sense of what ideas need to be explored in a work, what sections or details need to be taken into consideration, what approaches prove to be most productive and illuminating. In some cases, you will find some critics agreeing with or replying to or refuting the interpretations of others (as you do in the sample essay above). What the critics say about each other will be very helpful in testing and shaping your own conclusions about a critical essay — though, of course, you will need to be evaluating the soundness of each as you make your comparisons.

When you're writing, you're trying to find out something that you don't know.

James Baldwin

CHAPTER **29** **Writing a Literary Research Paper**

Incorporating the Larger Conversation

In the introduction to Chapter 28, we talk about how you go about learning more about a movie you like. Learning more, we said there, often involves doing research into the subject, and the chapter provides guidance in reading critical essays dealing with an author or literary work. But the chapter didn't tell you how to go about finding such essays. That's the subject of this chapter: doing research — that is, the process of finding interesting and useful information about a topic. This chapter focuses on undertaking research into a literary topic, but you will see how many of the principles carry over to research into movies or other projects you may want or be asked to work on. Literary research involves finding materials, comprehending what they have to say, evaluating how reliable they are, and (if the research results in writing a paper) including them in your discussion — that is, using what they say to clarify and support the points you want to make or to present points you want to refute.

Find additional advice for finding, evaluating, and working with sources, including interactive exercises, with the Research and Documentation Guide on *LiterActive*.

TOPICS

In nature and form, a research paper is basically the same as the papers discussed in Chapters 8, 17, and 25. The specific differences are that research papers tend to be longer, larger in scope, and in more depth because they include the results of research, on details in the work, the background of the work, or what scholars and literary critics have written about the work or its author.

PRELIMINARY READING   Finding a topic starts with preliminary reading. Almost all literary research topics deal with texts — novels, stories, poems, or plays. Some projects concern a specific text or two and focus on them closely (for example, the importance of quilts to culture in "Everyday Use"). Others may explore literary movements (for example, the significance of the Harlem Renaissance on later twentieth-century poetry) and use literary works as one source of information and evidence. In either case, reading literary works is crucial: Get to know them well and jot down ideas and questions that you will want to explore when you begin your research.

DIFFERENCE FROM A REPORT   As with the essays discussed in Chapters 8, 17, and 25, the most important part of a research paper is what *you* say in it, the development of *your* approach and ideas and interpretations. *A research paper is not a report:* A report gives an account of something. Its nature is objective — the writer does not interject opinions or interpretations. Research papers in high school sometimes take the form of a report, on diabetes in children, for example: The student searches for information on the subject from various sources and pieces together an account of the extent of the problem, what kind of treatment is involved, why the disease is a growing concern, and what can be done to improve the situation. Often such a paper turns out to be a long string of quotations and paraphrases, with transitional sentences connecting and holding them together.

ARGUMENTATIVE THESIS   A report is not what we mean by a literary research paper. Like other literary essays, a research paper is unified around an argumentative thesis, a central idea that takes a position others could disagree with. The only difference from the papers discussed earlier is that, as you shape and develop and support your ideas, an additional resource is available to you: In addition to evidence from the text itself, you can draw on factual information found in other sources and on the ideas of authorities in the field, scholars who have commented on the texts or authors you are working with.

ORIGINALITY   The thesis argued in the paper should be original to you. As you carry out your research, however, you may find that someone else has already explored the topic you were planning to focus on, perhaps even argued for the same thesis you had tentatively decided on. That should not be a problem. For a student paper, originality isn't saying something that never has been said before. Recycling a thesis you find in a critical essay is an acceptable way to form the topic for an undergraduate research paper, so long as you acknowledge your source and find different ways to develop and support the argument. You might bring in your own explanations and examples, ones different from those used before. Or you might use a theoretical or critical approach different from the one used before (for example, if you use a feminist approach to examine a topic someone else discussed from a psychoanalytical perspective, you will frame different arguments and draw evidence from different passages, thus giving it a fresh slant). Or you might combine ideas from different fields. Students are in an ideal situation for doing this: Try using concepts from your philosophy, sociology, psychology, or political science courses to illuminate works you study in your literature course. Remember, it is essential that the paper embody your own thinking and approach. Don't let it turn into a report on or paraphrase of the earlier article.

TYPES OF RESEARCH AND SOURCES

Literary research falls into several different types, types that yield different kinds of information with different uses and draw upon different kinds of sources. It is important to recognize these types, especially since a project often involves more than one type, and to consider which will be most applicable for different literary texts. First we sketch out types of research and then we turn to types of sources.

Primary Research

PRIMARY SOURCES AND THEIR USES   The most basic kind of research involves the reading of literary works and of any kind of texts (written, graphic, or oral) contemporary with or earlier than those works. Such texts are referred to as *primary sources*. They can include:

- literary works themselves
- comments the author's contemporaries made about those works
- book reviews or publishers' notices for works earlier than the twentieth century
- letters, diaries, journals, or memoirs by the author or by contemporaries
- contemporary newspapers, magazines, and books
- contemporary (or earlier) works of art
- books the author read (for example, literary works, works about current economics or politics, books of philosophy or theology)

Literary scholars use research in primary sources for varied purposes:

- to gain knowledge of the literary works themselves
- to acquire firsthand information about an author's life, times, or culture

- to locate sources an author drew upon
- to understand literary or artistic influences and traditions that affected an author or helped shape a work

Scholars apply what they find to write critical books and essays or to write contextual books and essays — biographies; literary histories; economic, political, or social histories; cultural studies; and so forth.

DOING PRIMARY RESEARCH   You too are doing primary research when, in addition to reading an assigned work, you do further reading in order to discover even more about the work — reading about what influenced the author or reading material that clarifies the work's historical, cultural, or literary context. You might, for example, find reading diaries of women in the nineteenth century both interesting and helpful for understanding the context and implications of Kate Chopin's "The Story of an Hour" (p. 196). Any time you read personal letters, journals, or newspapers from the time in which the author lived, or look at art or architecture that the author looked at, or listen to music that the author listened to — in essence, studying what she or he was influenced by — you are doing primary research.

Secondary Research

SECONDARY SOURCES AND THEIR USES   A second kind of research involves reading what other scholars have written about primary texts and about the life or literary, social, or cultural context of an author or work. Such works are called *secondary sources* — that is, not firsthand works written *by* an author or her or his contemporaries, but secondhand ones written *about* an author or her or his works or the era. Secondary sources include:

- biographies of an author
- history books discussing the author's times
- studies of society, culture, and ideas of the time
- book reviews for authors in the past century
- critical books or essays about a work or group of works

When literary scholars undertake a project, they do both primary and secondary research. They read as many works as possible by the author and by other scholars who have written about the author or the works, in order to:

- build on what has been done previously
- explore an area that earlier scholars have overlooked
- apply previous insights or approaches to a new work
- expand on implications that earlier scholars, or even contemporaries, didn't seem to grasp fully
- disagree with and modify or reverse what an earlier scholar wrote

Although literary scholars often work alone, what they do is actually communal and cooperative, as they listen to and learn from each other's work, modify or correct it when necessary, and extend its range through further exploration of its implications.

DOING SECONDARY RESEARCH If you are assigned a research paper for this course, you probably will be expected to do secondary research — at least in critical books and essays — but on a more limited basis than a professional scholar would. Critical or interpretive studies are available for most authors whose work appeared prior to the past twenty years or so, as well as for many more recent writers; locating them is dealt with in the section on finding sources (p. 1474). Even if you don't read everything about a work, reading several critical essays adds significantly to your understanding and appreciation of it. However, as we say in Chapter 28, you should not begin reading critical books and essays until you know your primary works well and begin recording ideas for possible topics and tentative theses for them (see p. 1456).

Tertiary Research

TERTIARY SOURCES AND THEIR USES A third (tertiary) level of research involves finding pertinent information about the meaning of words, the meaning of background details in a work, the source of allusions, and the biographical and historical context in which the work was written. This sort of investigation is not limited to research projects but is an integral part of ordinary active reading. It is usually carried out through use of *tertiary sources* — works such as dictionaries, encyclopedias, almanacs, and Internet personal pages whose purpose is to provide convenient access to ordinary, widely available information, not the interpretative understandings scholars convey in secondary sources.

DOING TERTIARY RESEARCH After reading Alice Walker's "Everyday Use," for example, you might look in an encyclopedia to learn more about quilting or go to *Anniina's Alice Walker Page* (luminarium.org/contemporary/alicew) to find some biographical information about Walker. Often tertiary sources do not specify who wrote the item you are reading because it does not contain anything original to that person. The writer was probably drawing upon previous tertiary sources, not engaging in primary research.

LIMITS OF TERTIARY RESEARCH In a research project, tertiary sources are valuable for finding or verifying factual details or perhaps for gaining an initial overview of an author or historical period. But a research paper should not be based on tertiary sources. In fact, if they are used only to find or verify details available widely or for background reading, they don't even need to be included in your bibliography (only if you quote from them —

which generally shouldn't be necessary — or if they provide information that is important to the paper and not commonly known).

WARNING!   A word of caution about one other kind of tertiary resource. Various types of "study guides" are available, online and in print, for many literary authors and works. They typically offer plot summaries, analyses of characters and themes, and commentaries about key passages. *We recommend you don't use these* — they're an unnecessary substitute for doing careful attentive reading on your own.

If you do use them, use them with great care. They are seldom written by established literary scholars, and their treatment of works is often superficial. Some even contain errors of fact. They tend to present themes as separate from one another and as absolutes (these are *the* themes to find in *Hamlet*), thus reducing the actual complexity and richness of the work and misleading the reader into thinking the work is not nearly as challenging as it actually is.

If you decide to read one as preparation for a paper, its use must be acknowledged in the bibliography, even if you do not cite it in the paper. But these are not sources that will enhance the quality of your paper.

RESEARCH ON CONTEMPORARY LITERATURE

Although the above discussion of research types and sources fits literature of the past decade or two as well as earlier literature, working with very recent literature presents some unique challenges and opportunities. We will discuss them briefly here.

PRIMARY RESEARCH   If your topic involves very recent literature, primary research may be the only kind available. You may find that you like using very recent authors and works for research assignments because in many cases these topics break new ground and involve "pure research." Since there are no earlier published studies of these authors or works to go back to, you are doing the kind of research scholars do, locating background and contextual information, applying it to the author's works, and doing original critical studies of them.

But where then do you go for material? You might use biographical statements and interviews; you might study writers and works the author has said have been influential; or you might look to newspapers, magazines, movies, art, television, advertising, or whatever else might clarify the sources of and influences on a certain writer's ideas and artistry. If the author's work includes cultural references or deals with actual people or events, you could do research on these and discuss how what you find sheds additional light on the text.

SECONDARY RESEARCH For very recent authors, and for less well-known authors from the past, fewer secondary resources may be available and you may not be able to use scholarly analyses as starting points or supporting material. For some current authors, published book reviews may be available, and these may fill a role similar to that of critical essays.

When published reviews aren't available, look at the unsolicited reviews or comments posted on such sites as Amazon.com or Barnesandnoble.com; remember that these sources must be used with care, but in many cases the comments are thoughtful and judicious and reflect well how other readers are responding to a work. Look also at the publishers' summaries and publicity blurbs on those sites; they aren't meant to be objective criticism, but they can provide starting points for getting into a work. More often than not, however, for contemporary authors, you'll need to concentrate on primary sources and what they contribute to a deeper understanding of the authors and works you want to study.

FINDING SOURCES AND CREATING A WORKING BIBLIOGRAPHY

The development of the Internet, with the many resources available on it, can make it tempting to do all one's research by computer. You may be inclined to start with Google or Yahoo! or AltaVista. Such search engines do have value and we'll come to them later, but they are not the best places to start. They make a wealth of information available, but much of it is of the tertiary variety; Internet sources by themselves are not adequate. A good college-level literature research paper needs to include printed sources found in or through your college or university library — most other libraries will not have the scholarly books and journals you will need, and the Internet does not provide an adequate substitute for them. We begin with a discussion of library searches and then move on to Internet searches.

Library Searches — Books

Each library search is unique and requires its own use of imagination and common sense — and, in many cases, help from a librarian. However, there are some steps nearly all library searches include.

FINDING BOOKS Instead of the older card catalogs, most libraries now have electronic catalogs for finding books. This chapter will assume that's what you will be using. Spend a few minutes looking at your library's home page — the layout is unique for each library, but the basic software is pretty much the same from one library to another. The home page usually provides links to a variety of information about the library and to electronic resources available through it.

Introductory screen for the Hope College Libraries home page.
Reprinted by permission of Hope College Libraries.

Among the options on the home page, look for the one that takes you to the online catalog's page (it may have a catchy tag — the college at which we teach calls it *HopeCAT*) and go to it. Here too the layout will be unique, but what is on the page is pretty much standard. You will be given a choice of

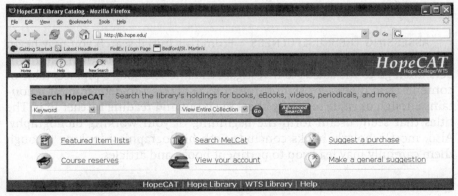

Search screen for the Hope College Libraries online catalog.
Reprinted by permission of Hope College Libraries.

several ways to search, including keyword, author, title, subject, journal title, call number, and perhaps others. Often you can select whether to search a specific collection within the library, the entire collection, or the collections of all libraries linked through a particular system.

The basic use of a library catalog is to find the call number and location of a book you already know about and want to look at or check out. To accomplish that, select the Author function and type in the author's last and first names or select the Title function and type in the title (or initial words of the title) to call up the needed information.

But the catalog can also be used as a search engine to find books you don't yet know about. If you are doing research on a specific author or work, you can look for other works by the author by doing an author search; you can look for biographical works and critical studies of the author by doing a subject search; or you can look for materials by and about the author by doing a keyword search.

If you are doing a paper on a topic, rather than on an author or a work, you should start with the keyword function and type in the key words of your topic. This is the broadest search category. It calls up all items in which the words you enter appear somewhere in the catalog entry: in an author's name, in the titles of works, in the list of contents contained in works, and in the subject categories indicating the topics covered by a work. The number and variety of items called up may be overwhelming or unwieldy. If it is, it may help to limit your search: Look on the catalog page for the Advanced Search option or a Help option — or ask a librarian for guidance.

The items you find can also lead you to other information. You might click on the title of a book and look at the subject headings included for it. Doing so could give you ideas for topics on which to do subject searches, which are more precise and specific than keyword searches. Or you might click on the call number for a book or write down a call number and do a call number search: You will get a list of books nearby that one on the shelf, enabling you to browse through other, related books that are shelved together.

ASSESSING THEIR USEFULNESS   From this initial search you may begin to pick out books you want to look at: Jot down or print out their call numbers, then go to the stacks to investigate them. Use a book's preface, table of contents, and index — or skim through its chapters — to determine if it contains enough of value to justify checking it out and reading further in it. The titles that seem useful form the beginning of your working bibliography. Also, most scholarly books conclude with bibliographies; looking through them carefully may lead you to pertinent books and articles.

USING REFERENCE BOOKS   In addition to works about your author that turn up in a subject search, some works available in the literature area of the reference section of the library (and in some cases, for some libraries, online) can provide good background and bibliographical information about many authors. Here is a list of the most important of these:

> *Contemporary Literary Criticism.* 225 volumes to date. Detroit: Gale, 1973–. Contains biographical sketches and excerpts of reviews and criticism for contemporary authors. It is available online in many libraries as part of the *Literature Resource Center.*

> *Dictionary of Literary Biography.* 329 volumes to date. Detroit: Gale, 1978–. An ongoing series that provides useful biographical and critical introductions to U.S., British, and world authors. It too is available online in many libraries as part of the *Literature Resource Center.*

> Elliot, Emory, et al. *Columbia Literary History of the United States.* New York: Columbia University Press, 1988. An overview of literary movements and individual writers in the United States.

> *The Oxford History of English Literature.* 13 volumes. Oxford: Oxford University Press, 1945–. Overviews of literary movements and individual writers in England and Great Britain.

> Preminger, Alex, and T. V. F. Brogan, eds. *The New Princeton Encyclopedia of Poetry and Poetics.* Princeton: Princeton University Press, 1993. The most authoritative guide to concepts, terminology, and movements related to poetry.

These may be a good place to start your research. They should never be the place you stop, and you should never use them as the main sources in a paper.

Library Searches – Articles

Many of the most valuable studies of particular works appear as articles in literary journals or in books of collected essays. In most cases such articles do not show up in searches of library catalogs, so locating them requires adding another step in electronic searching.

ARTICLES IN JOURNALS   Essays about literary topics are usually published as articles in magazines or journals (commonly referred to as "periodicals," because they are published periodically, at regular intervals — weekly, monthly, or quarterly, rather than once, like a book). For the most part, your search should concentrate on literary journals (edited by and intended for literary scholars) since they are more likely to provide the kind of material you'll need than are general magazines (written for broader readership and thus less complex to read but also less scholarly in approach and emphasis). Articles in scholarly journals are better sources because:

- They are usually longer than magazine articles and thus more thorough and better supported.

- They are written by literary scholars whose academic affiliation or other credentials are indicated.
- They are peer-reviewed (see p. 1487) and thus more reliable.
- They often use footnotes or endnotes and include a bibliography.

You may find personal information, such as interviews with an author in a general magazine, but usually not sophisticated critical studies of the kind you need in a college research paper.

ARTICLES IN BOOKS   Scholarly articles are sometimes published in books of collected essays focused on an author or a topic. The contents may be articles previously published in journals and gathered into a book by an editor to make them more easily accessible to readers. Or the book may be made up of essays written specially for the collection and published for the first time in it. The collection as a whole can be found through a book search (indicated when "edited by" appears in front of what would otherwise be the author's name: for example, "*Critical Essays on Alice Walker*, edited by Ikenna Dieke"). Individual essays are indexed with journal articles and are found through the searches for scholarly articles described below.

Home page of the JSTOR *database.*

Reprinted courtesy of JSTOR.
© 2007 JSTOR.

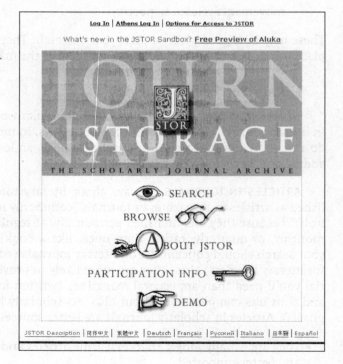

FINDING ARTICLES   In many cases, the full texts of journal articles are now available on line, through such databases as *JSTOR* (for older journals) and *Project MUSE* (for more recent publications). Most libraries provide a link on their home pages to the list of electronic journals and databases they subscribe to. One way to find articles on your subject is to search these databases (search links are included) to find material on your topic. An advantage of searching in the databases is that when you find an article that looks relevant, the entire article can be called up and you can read it on your computer or print out a hard copy. The disadvantage is that the search will be conducted only in the journals included in that database. It is better, therefore, to start with more inclusive bibliographical databases that will help you find the widest possible range of articles.

THE MLA BIBLIOGRAPHY   The standard resource for finding articles about authors and literary topics is the *MLA Bibliography of Books and Articles in the Modern Languages and Literature*. One benefit it has over *JSTOR* and *Project MUSE* is that it includes books and Ph.D. dissertations as well as articles. Using the online catalog for your library calls up books held in that library; you may find books in the *MLA Bibliography* that your library does not own and be able to request them through interlibrary loan. This may take a week or two — which is a good reason to start your bibliography search early.

The *MLA Bibliography* is available online and on CD-ROM as well as in printed volumes. The printed volumes are divided into sections by nationality and era (English literature 1500–1599, for example, or Scottish literature 1700–1799), with special topics listed first and then authors listed alphabetically. It is much easier to search electronic versions, which pull up pertinent items from all the years covered, than to use the annual printed volumes, each of which contains items from only one year. Many electronic catalogs and databases, including the *MLA Bibliography*, have a feature called "My Account" or "My Archive," which allows you to store results of searches and come back to them later, instead of repeating a search each time you return to your project.

Experiment with ways of focusing and restricting your searches: A subject or keyword search for Toni Morrison in the *MLA Bibliography* yields around 1,600 hits; adding a subject or keyword search for "Recitatif" reduces the number to 9. Do a variety of searches, using different terms related to your topic. Try focusing searches by using connector words ("and," "or"), truncation, and bundling of terms — Help functions on each site provide guidance in their use (or ask a librarian for assistance). *MLA Bibliography* searches, as in many databases, also can be limited in various ways: to certain document types (searching only for journal articles, for example, or only for articles in books); to a specific language (searching only for works written in English, for example); to peer reviewing (searching only for materials that have been subject to peer review); to full text (searching only for

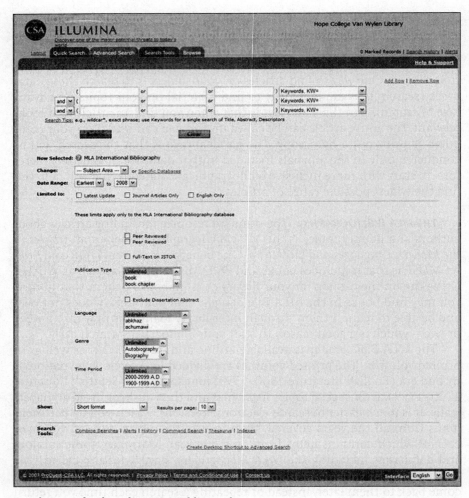

Search screen for the online MLA Bibliography.

The screen capture is used with permission of OCLC. First Search ® is a registered trademark and/or service mark of OCLC Online Computer Library Center, Inc.

articles whose full texts are available online in your library); and to available materials (searching only for books or journals held by your library).

Another increasingly well-known search engine is Google Scholar (on the Google home page click on "more," then on "scholar" in the drop-down menu). This is an evolving tool intended to lead one to academic sources in both electronic and print formats. At present, its coverage is more thorough in the sciences than in the humanities. Some full texts are available without cost but many are not. If full texts are not available, remember to use the online catalog to check whether the book or article is in your library. For literature, the *MLA Bibliography* remains the most complete and reliable way to search for printed materials.

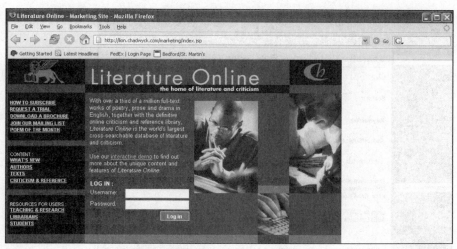

Home page for Literature Online (LION) *database.*

Image published with permission of ProQuest-CSA LLC. © 2007, ProQuest-CSA LLC; all rights reserved. Further reproduction is prohibited without permission.

LITERATURE ONLINE (LION)   Another valuable resource for literary research available in many libraries is *Literature Online,* better known by the acronym *LION.* (Some libraries have a similar database, *Literature Resource Center;* some have both.) By combining a number of databases, *LION* offers a comprehensive literary Web site. On it you can find biographical information on English and American authors, lists of their works, the full texts of hundreds of poems, novels, and plays (generally those no longer under copyright), lists of critical studies of authors' works (often with links to the full texts), audio readings of selected works, and related Web sites.

LION can be used to search for secondary critical and scholarly materials, but it also can be used for consulting or searching primary texts (for finding the source of a quotation or allusion, for example). Searches can be restricted and limited in much the same way the *MLA Bibliography* Web site can. For guidance in using *LION,* click on Information Centre, or click on Help at any point — or, as always, consult with a librarian.

OTHER BIBLIOGRAPHIC DATABASES   In some cases, your topic may require doing a broader search to include other academic disciplines, beyond what literary databases provide. Many such resources are available. Two of the best-known examples are the Gale Group (*InfoTrac*) *Expanded Academic ASAP* database and the OCLC (*FirstSearch*) *Periodical Abstracts* database. These databases cover the humanities, the social sciences, and the sciences. Ask a librarian for the name of particular databases of this type to which your library subscribes (for example, *ProQuest Research Library, Academic Search Premier,* and *Humanities Abstracts*).

Search screen for Literature Online (LION) *database.*
Image published with permission of ProQuest-CSA LLC. © 2007, ProQuest-CSA LLC; all rights reserved. Further reproduction is prohibited without permission.

In other cases, you may want to conduct searches that will include general magazines. Again, many databases for such searches are available, among them *InfoTrac OneFile*, *LexisNexis*, and *Wilson Select Plus*. Look for links to such search engines on your library's Web page, or ask a librarian how to find one. Remember that many of the articles you will find through such databases will not be scholarly or peer reviewed and therefore must be used with care.

ASSESSING THEIR USEFULNESS   As with books, you need to sort through the results of a search for articles and decide which ones seem promising enough to find and read. If you're using the *MLA Bibliography* online search engine, a line of descriptors indicates the subject areas of the article and can help you decide if it will be helpful for your topic. Some databases provide an abstract (a brief summary of what the article is about) that can be even more helpful. If the full text is available, you can immediately retrieve the entire article and skim through it on your screen.

LOCATING JOURNALS   You may be tempted to limit your research to items that have the full text online because they are so convenient to use, but it's a temptation that should be resisted. Sources without a link to the full text may be a better fit with your topic. If you are not sure how to find an article for which you have information, take the information to a librarian, who will help you find the article. If your library does not subscribe to the journal, it may be possible to get a copy of the article through interlibrary loan.

SPECIALIZED BIBLIOGRAPHIES   In addition to indexes for finding articles, book-length bibliographies are available for many well-known authors, listing scholarly and critical studies on the author published during a given span of years, in some cases with a brief description or evaluation of the work. Look for such a volume as you do your search of the library catalog. If you are searching on Alice Walker, for example, you might find this book:

> Banks, Erma Davis, and Keith Byerman. *Alice Walker: An Annotated Bibliography 1968–1986.* New York: Garland, 1989.

It includes a list of primary works by Walker through 1986 as well as reviews and criticism of her works, with a brief description of many items. It is a very convenient way to locate studies of Walker published in those years. For studies since then, you would go to one of the indexes described above. Bibliographies are also available for periods and movements, as, for example:

> Glikin, Ronda. *Black American Women in Literature: A Bibliography, 1976 through 1987.* Jefferson: McFarland, 1989.
> Jordan, Casper LeRoy. *A Bibliographical Guide to African-American Women Writers.* Westport: Greenwood, 1993.
> Zimmerman, Marc. *U.S. Latino Literature: An Essay and Annotated Bibliography.* Chicago: MARCH/Abrazo, 1992.

To find such volumes, search the library catalog by subject for "African American authors" or "Hispanic American authors" and look for a subheading on "Bibliography."

Searching for Internet Sources

PRINT SOURCES ONLINE   The secondary and tertiary sources we have considered thus far are print sources. Even though full-text articles are available on the Web, they originated as print sources and should be considered as such. Likewise, search engines such as AltaVista, Google, or Yahoo! in many cases locate items that originally appeared in a newspaper or magazine and subsequently were posted on the Internet; even though you encounter them online, they are print sources.

INTERNET SOURCES   In a separate category are Web sites and documents posted on the Internet that have not appeared in print and were never intended to appear in print. A great deal of material is available on the Web that is of interest and value to students of literature. Much of it falls into the category of tertiary sources (enjoyable but nonscholarly), but some is of scholarly significance and can fill areas not covered by books and journals.

HOME PAGES   Home pages can be found for many authors, created by fans of the authors (some by academics, some by general readers), or, for contemporary writers, by the author her- or himself. Such home pages usually provide a biography and a bibliography, sometimes some critical essays, and sometimes — for modern authors — an audio recording. They can be a good starting point for learning about an author.

MISCELLANEOUS PAGES   In addition, myriad other types of pages exist: reprintings of poems or stories by an author, brief commentaries on literary works, study guides to an author or work, student papers, odd bits of information (of the "The day I met Julia Alvarez" type), collections of photos related to the author, places where books can be purchased, and so forth. One can waste a good deal of time clicking on potentially interesting sites, only to be disappointed by what comes up.

LIMITING YOUR SEARCH   One way to avoid some of the clutter is to do a more specialized search than just typing "Alice Walker" into the Google window and being confronted by over two million hits. Most search engines have advanced search options through which you can restrict or limit your search in ways similar to those described earlier for databases. Search engines like Google and Yahoo! also have a directory through which you can search by topic. To find Google's directory, for example, go to Google Scholar (see p. 1481), click on "More" just above the text box, then click on "Even More" in the drop-down box; "Directory" is in the list of search products in the left-hand column. Try clicking on it, then on "Arts," then "Literature," then on "Authors," and then on the first letter of the author's last name to get a shorter list of hits with the less useful ones eliminated. The path Arts > Literature > Authors > W > Alice Walker yields five selected Walker sites and three sites on *The Color Purple*. Instead of "Authors," you can click on a time period, a literary genre, or a number of other related categories.

LISTS OF RECOMMENDED WEB SITES   As an alternative to relying on Google, Yahoo!, or AltaVista, check if the library or the English department at your college or university has assembled a list of recommended literary Web sites — ones that they regard as well organized, reliable, and trustworthy. If not, look for such a list on the Web sites of other libraries or English departments or use one of these two highly regarded Web sites: Jack Lynch's *Literary Resources on the Net* (andromeda.rutgers.edu/~jlynch/Lit/) and Alan Liu's *Voice of the Shuttle* (vos.ucsb.edu/), both of which were created and are maintained by faculty members.

CD-ROMS   In addition to Internet resources, CD-ROMs are available on many authors, works, or movements. These often contain a wide variety of materials. As you read a text, for example, the CD-ROM may provide definitions, maps, pictures, critical essays or excerpts, biographical informa-

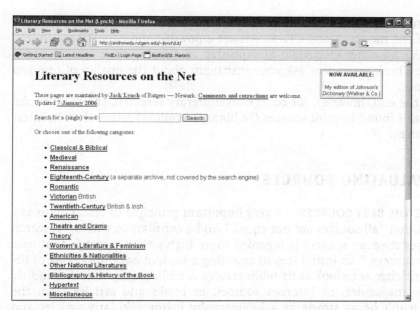

Home page of Jack Lynch's Literary Resources on the Net Web site. Reprinted by permission of Jack Lynch.

Home page of Alan Liu's Voice of the Shuttle Web site.
Reprinted by permission of Alan Liu.

tion, and materials related to historical and cultural background, all at the click of the mouse. Good CD-ROMs are enjoyable and educational to use, but — like all other electronic and printed materials — their quality varies greatly. Check reviews or ask your instructor about the quality of one you might use.

In the end, however, for college-level literary research, the most useful material is found in print sources (in library or online) rather than in Internet sources.

EVALUATING SOURCES

USE THE BEST SOURCES   A very important principle of research, in any field, is that "all sources are not equal." And a corollary to this is, "research that uses stronger sources is regarded more highly than research that uses weaker sources." An initial step in assessing a student paper or a book of literary criticism is to look at its bibliography. A bibliography that lists mostly popular magazines, or Internet sources, or books and articles from the 1960s won't be as strong as a bibliography listing scholarly articles and books written during the past ten to fifteen years. From the beginning of your research project, *be selective* about the sources you decide to consider further.

EVALUATE CAREFULLY   As you consider which potential sources to include in your working bibliography, *evaluate each one carefully*. In reading books, articles, and Internet material, first grasp clearly what is being said. Only then can you decide how valid and valuable the point being made is. Books and essays are not "good" just because they're in print or posted on the Web: Don't use just any source you happen to find. Evaluating the worth of a source is crucial. The quality of your sources affects (or even determines) the quality of your paper. To help you evaluate sources, here are five questions to ask.

1. *Who is the author and what are her or his qualifications?* Some people are better informed — are authorities in a field — and better qualified to comment on a work or an author than others are.

The qualifications of an author of published criticism are easier to determine than those of an author of material on the Web. You can check if the published author has an academic affiliation: Someone on the faculty at a reputable college or university is more likely to be regarded as an authority than someone who just decides to set up a Web site about a favorite writer. You can check where the author was educated and when. You can also check if the author has published extensively about the subject. Those who have published a great deal on a subject are more likely to qualify as authorities.

It often is harder to ascertain the qualifications of the authors of pieces you find on the Web: Experts post pieces on the Web, but so do people with eccentric notions that they can't get journals to publish. Books and journals tell you the qualifications of their authors; Web sites often don't. Sometimes they don't even name the author (anonymous sites should be avoided). If an author is identified, you might run the name through a search engine and see if that reveals more about the person and her or his credentials.

2. *Where was the work published?* The fact that something appears in print or on the Internet does not necessarily mean it is of value. Articles submitted to scholarly journals and books submitted to well-established presses are carefully screened by experts; this process is known as "peer review." Only works that peer experts regard as accurate and important are accepted for publication. The fact that an article appears in a highly regarded journal or that a book is published by a highly reputable press in most cases can give you confidence in its quality.

Even so, not everything published by respected journals or presses is excellent. You still have to assess each item on its own merits. But paying attention to the publisher is still the wisest way to start.

For material on the Internet, check who hosts the site. The URL can be of help — items posted by academic institutions (.edu), nonprofit organizations (.org), and the government (.gov) are more promising than items coming out of commercial sites (.com) and other sites with products for sale. In some cases, the host organization is identified at the bottom of the initial page. Try to find out more about who it is and what it has at stake.

3. *Is the source or its author cited by other scholars?* One way to help evaluate a scholarly work is to determine what other scholars think about it. For books, look for a review (*Book Review Digest*, online or in print form in your library, is a good place to start). Some specialized journals offer reviews of articles in its field; *JSTOR* and *Project MUSE* provide full texts of reviews for the journals they service. In their books and articles, scholars also often evaluate what other scholars have written about a subject; what they say needs to be evaluated carefully for fairness and accuracy, but it's useful input.

Another measure of acceptance by other scholars is how frequently a scholar's work is favorably cited by other scholars (that is, referred to in a footnote or included in a bibliography). If other scholars rely on a source, you can be fairly sure that its author is respected in the field.

4. *What is the date of the publication?* In some fields (especially the sciences), research more than a decade or two old may well be outdated. That tends to be less true in the humanities, but it is still true to some extent. Recent scholarship builds on earlier work, adding to earlier studies and correcting their mistakes, and it draws upon current ideas and theoretical approaches. It's acceptable to have some older studies in your bibliography,

but in most cases your sources should include the most recent, up-to-date studies available.

Caution is needed in using Internet sites. Often someone starts a site and keeps it up-to-date for a while but later neglects it so that its information is no longer current. Some sites give "last updated on" information. For sites that do not, the latest date mentioned in the material may indicate how current the information provided is.

5. *How relevant is it to your topic and argument?* Avoid the temptation to add items to your bibliography or to slip quotations from them into your paper just because they are written by a leading expert or published by a major press. A source helps your paper only if what it deals with fits your topic or relates to your argument and is something you actually can use. Readers are not impressed when your bibliography lists books by several widely known experts but all the citations in your text are to nonscholarly Web sites.

TAKING NOTES

USING NOTE CARDS   When doing a research paper, it's important to take notes in an organized way. For a short paper, you might get by with using your memory and marking up a copy of the primary text; but in a research paper, if it's done well, too much is going on for that. In the old days, scholars took notes on 3 x 5 or 4 x 6 inch cards (or, earlier, on slips of paper), using one set for bibliographical information and another for summary notes and quotations, cross-referenced to the corresponding bibliography card. This produced excellent results for centuries and is still a good system (you may have been asked to use it for a high school research paper). But it is much less widely used today because of advances in electronic equipment.

USING A COMPUTER   Many scholars now type their notes directly into notebook computers, and many libraries are equipped to enable researchers to plug in computers at reading tables and in study carrels. Notes in a computer are easier to use because they can be searched quickly and can be copied and pasted directly into a paper. You might experiment with this form of note taking if you have never tried it before.

ORGANIZING NOTES ON A COMPUTER   You'll need to decide how to organize the material into files: One large file into which you put everything? (It may become long, bulky, and cumbersome to use.) Separate files for each source? Separate files for different topics? You'll need to find a system that is searchable and enables you to find and retrieve material easily. It might be a good idea, when you've collected quite a bit of material but are far from finished, to go back over what you have, refresh your memory of it, rearrange it by grouping items together that relate to the same subtopic, and note gaps you still need to fill.

USING A COPIER   Copiers have changed the need for taking notes and the way many people take notes. For materials available in general areas of a library, many people photocopy pages of books or whole articles from journals, instead of writing or typing passages they might want to use in a paper. (In rare book and special collection areas, photocopying usually is available only by special arrangement.) Copyright protection allows photocopying of articles and selected pages from a book when used for personal research, but forbids photocopying an entire book, or even most of one.

Photocopies are convenient to use because you can underline important phrases or sentences and jot notes in the margins (which you should never do in a library book). And they have the benefit of accuracy: One must take great care in writing out or typing passages, and then double-check them for accuracy. With photocopied pages, that's not necessary until parts are actually quoted in your paper.

GUIDELINES FOR TAKING NOTES   No matter what system you use, some principles are the same:

- *Check for completeness.* Be sure to put down the author's name and all the data needed to complete the bibliography entry. For a book, you need:

  title
  place of publication
  publisher
  date of publication
  page numbers

  For a magazine article you need:

  its title
  title of the magazine
  date of the issue
  first and last page numbers
  the number of each page you use

  For a journal article you need:

  its title
  title of the journal
  volume number
  year
  first and last page numbers
  the number of each page you use

  For an Internet source you need:

  the name of the author, if available
  title of the piece, if more than one is posted on the site
  title of the site
  names of editors, for edited sites

> date of posting or of last update
> name of sponsoring organization
> URL or the pathway used for reaching it
> date site was accessed

You certainly don't want to discover — usually the night before a paper is due! — that you forgot to include a date or page number and must to go back to the library (hoping it's still open) to find it.

- *Check for accuracy.* Make sure the bibliographical data you put down is accurate. After you write or type a quotation, check that every word and punctuation mark in it is accurate before you move on. If you omit a phrase or sentence, be sure you've indicated that with ellipsis marks (see p. 48). Remember that if you put quotation marks around a passage, you are guaranteeing that it's reproduced exactly the way it appears in the original source.

- *Check for clarity.* If you're writing or typing notes, indicate clearly what is quoted and what is summary. It's a good idea to write "quote" or "summary" in the margin to make sure you won't mistake the one for the other, something that can lead to unfortunate results. Also, add a label indicating what point in your paper the notes apply to. That will make it much easier for you to find and organize your notes when you get ready to use them.

BEGINNING A WORKS CITED PAGE   You will save time later if, as you take notes, you begin preparing the actual Works Cited page for your paper, instead of leaving it to the end, when you're weary and perhaps pressed for time. It is most convenient to create a separate Works Cited file in your computer as you compile your list. But it's important, at some point, to paste the list into your paper at the end, so the pages will be paginated consecutively with the body of the paper and so the list won't get lost. We've had students remember to keep the computer file containing their paper but delete their separate Works Cited file, forgetting that they haven't copied the Works Cited list to the paper itself.

DEVELOPING YOUR PAPER AND THESIS

DEVELOPMENT   The steps suggested in Chapters 8, 17, and 25 for developing an essay apply equally for a research paper. After deciding on a topic, you need to:

- Narrow it to manageable size for the length assigned.
- Focus it on a central point, a tentative, argumentative thesis.
- Discuss the thesis in a draft of the paper, amplifying the ideas, supplying details and illustrations that support the points you make, and explaining how the ideas and examples support each other in a convincing way.
- Revise and proofread the draft.

Review the detailed discussion of these steps in Chapter 8 and follow them as you work on your research project.

OUTLINE   In discussing short papers, we mentioned that some people organize them in their heads, without a written outline. Research papers are more complex, so an outline is usually important, even for those who ordinarily don't make outlines.

INTRODUCTION   The introduction to a research paper also is more challenging than the introduction to a short paper. In addition to attracting the reader's attention, it should indicate where the literary conversation about your author or work stands and how your paper fits into it.

INCORPORATING SOURCES

The unique aspect in developing a research paper is that additional materials for clarifying ideas and supporting arguments are available from the primary and secondary research you've carried out. Such materials can be incorporated into your paper in four ways (we illustrate with examples from Susan Farrell's essay in Chapter 28, on pp. 1459–65).

Citation

In some cases you may want to mention a source as related to your argument without giving details about it. You can do so by making a passing reference to it ("citing" it), without saying more about it. Citations often are used to supply additional examples, supporting one that has been described fully. That is the case in Farrell's first endnote:

> 1. See [also] . . . Houston Baker and Charlotte Pierce-Baker's "Patches: Quilts and Community in Alice Walker's 'Everyday Use,'" Margaret D. Bauer's "Alice Walker: Another Southern Writer Criticizing Codes Not Put to 'Everyday Use,'" and Donna Haisty Winchell's Twayne Series book on Alice Walker (80–84).

In this case, three sources are cited as additional examples of Nancy Tuten's position that a central theme in "Everyday Use" is "a mother's 'awakening to one daughter's superficiality and to the other's deepseated understanding of heritage' ([Tuten] 125)."

Summary

In most cases, you will bring sources into your paper through a summary of some information, a key idea, or an overall argument you found valuable in them. The summary should be a brief restatement of the author's point into your own words. What you incorporate does not have to summarize the whole book, chapter, or article but may summarize one section or simply one paragraph.

SUMMARIZING PRIMARY SOURCES Summary is used commonly as a way to bring primary texts usefully into a paper. Farrell does that repeatedly as she builds her case, as for example,

> When he [Asalamalakim] tries to hug Maggie, though, she falls back against a chair and trembles. And later, when he tries to teach Maggie a new handshake, her hand remains limp and she quickly withdraws it from his.

Likewise, Farrell summarizes the plot of *Meridian* for the benefit of those readers who are not familiar with it.

SUMMARIZING SECONDARY SOURCES Secondary sources can be handled through summary as well. In her first paragraph, Farrell includes a composite summary of the way many critics, represented by those cited in endnote 1, back up their contention that the point of the story is Mama's awakening to Dee and Maggie's values:

> These readers praise the "simplicity" of Maggie and her mother, along with their allegiance to their specific family identity and folk heritage as well as their refusal to change at the whim of an outside world that doesn't really have much to do with them.

These sources could have been identified separately, with Farrell discussing each in detail and illustrating them with quotations. However, since they represent the position she is contesting, setting them out in a condensed version gives them adequate attention.

Paraphrase

A paraphrase, like a summary, is a restatement of an author's point in your own words, but at greater length — usually approximately equal in length to the original passage.

PARAPHRASING PRIMARY SOURCES Paraphrase is more commonly used for secondary sources than for primary ones; since paraphrasing wouldn't save space, most critics would tend to give readers the actual words of the text instead of a rephrased version.

PARAPHRASING SECONDARY SOURCES For secondary sources, paraphrase should be used instead of summary when it is important to supply your reader with more detail: if, for example, you want to call specific attention to each step in an argument, perhaps because you want to dispute an argument step by step. Quoting the passage, in such a case, might not work as well because a paraphrase allows you to enumerate each step even if the author didn't do so.

Paraphrase can also be used not for what other critics have actually said but to articulate what they would say, as for example:

> Of course, most readers see this as evidence of Dee's fickle changing with whatever fad happens to be current. Once it becomes fashionable to have rural, poverty-stricken roots, Dee wants a record of her own humble beginnings.

This is not a quotation or a summary, but Farrell putting in her own words what she believes other critics would argue.

Quotation

Every literary paper should include quotations of the primary text or texts being discussed. A paper without any quotations can come across as superficial, even too general. Handling quotations from stories, poems, and plays has been discussed in Chapters 8, 17, and 25, respectively (pp. 243, 685, and 1017).

QUOTING PRIMARY SOURCES   In a research paper, like other literary papers, the danger is quoting too extensively, turning your paper into simply a "collage of quotations." Combining quoted extracts with summary is a skill worth learning. Farrell does it well:

> For instance, when Dee wants a new dress, she "makes over" an old green suit someone had given her mother. Rather than passively accept her lot, as Mama seems trained to do, Dee "was determined to stare down any disaster in her efforts" (111).

Quoting only a few words is effective because we tend to pay attention to those words, on the assumption that the critic must think these words are particularly significant if she or he chose them for quotation.

QUOTING SECONDARY SOURCES   Research papers don't need to include quotations from secondary sources, but they usually do so. Writers encounter passages written so effectively that they don't want to paraphrase them. The danger, again, is not underusing quotations but using too many, and using ones that are too long. Quotations must not carry the argument of a paper but must support and illustrate the argument you are presenting in your own words.

In that regard, it's important not to begin paragraphs with quotations: A sentence in your own words should always precede a quotation to introduce it and set it up properly.

Although it may be tempting to quote sources at length because their points are stated so well, keep quotations brief. Using ellipsis marks is an effective way to shorten quotations and to focus on relevant portions (see p. 48). Papers that quote too often, and at too great a length, can be disconcerting and not enjoyable to read: The prose style keeps changing, one's orientation toward the material keeps shifting, and arguments are not articulated in as unified and coherent a manner.

For secondary sources as for primary sources, the best approach is to combine quotations with summary and to blend the quoted extracts into your prose style as gracefully as possible. Farrell's article does this well:

> Thus, although Tuten equates Dee's values with those of "the white Johnny Carson society" (126), it seems to me that we have to question whether Mama's vision of her light-skinned, slender, witty self is actually Dee's wish or only Mama's perception of what she imagines Dee would like her to be. . . .
>
> . . . Similarly, Donna Winchell writes that "Dee tries to force on" Maggie and her mother "knowledge they probably do not need." She continues,
>
>> Mrs. Johnson can take an objective look at who and what she is and find not disillusionment but an easy satisfaction. Simple pleasures — a dip of snuff, a cooling breeze across a clean swept yard, church songs, the soothing movements of milk cows — are enough. (82)
>
> But are these "simple pleasures" really enough for Mama in the story?

Only twice does Farrell quote a secondary passage at length, both times because she wanted to build an argument not just on the critic's overall point but on the particular words and details the critic uses. Her essay provides an excellent model for judicious, graceful handling of quotations from both the primary text and from secondary sources.

AVOIDING PLAGIARISM

WHAT PLAGIARISM IS   Plagiarism is the presentation of the work of others as if it were one's own. This is a serious offense. It's dishonest to take another person's effort and ideas. It violates the expectations of trust and honesty expected in an academic community. In addition, it undercuts the basic purposes of higher education by short-circuiting the processes of inquiry, reflection, and communication that lead to learning.

EXAMPLES OF PLAGIARISM   Some more specific examples of plagiarism clarify that broad description:

- Buying a paper from a commercial source and submitting it as your own, or taking a paper from a classmate, friend, fraternity or sorority file, or anyone else and submitting it as if you wrote it, or using parts of such a paper even if you change the introduction or alter some of the wording
- Cutting and pasting material from the Internet into your paper without indicating where it came from
- Using the exact words of another writer in a paper without indicating that they are quoted and providing proper citations for them
- Paraphrasing or summarizing the words of another writer without providing citations that indicate they are rewordings
- Taking important ideas from sources and including them in your paper as if you thought them up, even if the wording is not the same as in the original
- Letting someone else (a friend, classmate, parent, etc.) write parts of your paper for you or correct or edit a paper so extensively that it no longer accurately reflects your work
- Submitting a drawing, painting, musical composition, computer program, or any other kind of material created originally by someone else and claiming or implying that you created it yourself

REUSING A PAPER   One final example of plagiarism often surprises students: Turning in the same paper more than once in different courses is plagiarism, even though all the material is yours. Instructors expect papers to be work done specifically during and for that course — it's not fair if the other students are taking the time to write a new paper and you just reuse one you wrote in high school or in an earlier college course.

In some cases, you may want to do a research project that involves two courses you are taking at the same time — literature and psychology, for example. In that case, talk to both instructors. They will probably encourage you because making connections between disciplines is a valuable way of learning. But they may require you to do separate papers for each course or allow you to submit the same paper for both courses but require it to be longer than those done by other students.

UNINTENTIONAL PLAGIARISM   Some of the examples above are deliberate cheating. Everyone knows it is unacceptable to buy a paper and turn it in as your own work. Those who do it deserve the severe penalties most instructors and institutions impose. In some cases, however, students stumble into inadvertent plagiarism by not knowing the rules for citation. They may believe, for example, that only direct quotations need to be acknowledged; therefore, they assume that if they totally rephrase a passage and avoid using any words from the original, they don't need to cite a source for it. Not so. You need to give credit to the person who came up with the idea, or who did the work of tracing a historical allusion or detail, or who thought out the interpretation of a story or poem, even though your phrasing of the material is different. *You are responsible for knowing what plagiarism is and how to avoid it*: Ignorance is not an adequate excuse.

AVOIDING PLAGIARISM   Here are a few guidelines for avoiding plagiarism:

- Put quotation marks around any groups of words taken directly from a source (phrases or whole sentences).
- Document every direct quotation (except phrases that are so common that most people would recognize the source without being told — "Four score and seven years ago," for example).
- Document any idea or information that you attained through your research, except for information that is widely available from many different sources (even if you looked up the place and date of Alice Walker's birth, you don't need to give a source because that information is readily available in many places).

Keep in mind that you are taking part in a long-honored tradition: the extension of the ongoing conversation about a literary work of art. Respecting the work of others by acknowledging their contributions is a matter of personal integrity and a standard by which you are welcomed into the community of both established and beginning scholars.

DOCUMENTING SOURCES: MLA STYLE

The method of citing sources for papers on literature preferred by most teachers is the MLA style, described in detail in the *MLA Handbook for Writers of Research Papers*, 6th ed., by Joseph Gibaldi (New York: Modern Language Association of America, 2003). It is a simple, convenient, two-step system that uses brief parenthetical citations in the text, keyed to an alphabetical list of works at the end of the paper. Footnotes or endnotes can be used to supply information and comments that do not fit into the text of the paper or that cannot be handled adequately through parenthetical citation (see the informational notes in Farrell's paper, p. 1465). But including notes is not essential.[1]

WWW
Find additional advice for documenting sources with Diana Hacker's *Research and Documentation Online* at bedfordstmartins .com/approachinglit.

---

[1]Other forms are preferred in other fields of study: APA style (American Psychological Association) is used in the social sciences; CBE style (Council of Biology Editors) in the sciences; and the *Chicago* style (*Chicago Manual of Style*) is generally used for history. Each focuses on the kind of information considered more useful in that discipline and on the format regarded as more convenient to use.

In-Text Citations

The MLA system begins with brief in-text citations. After a quotation or a sentence using facts or opinions drawn from a specific source (wherever a footnote would have been used in earlier documentation systems), one inserts a parenthesis with, ordinarily, the last name of the author and the page or pages on which the information is found.

> The point of the story is to show, in one critic's words, a mother's "awakening to one daughter's superficiality and to the other's deepseated understanding of heritage" (Tuten 125).

This is the most basic form of in-text citation. Notice three formatting conventions followed in it:

1. There is no comma after the author's name and no "page" or "p." preceding the number.
2. The quotation marks come before the parenthesis. The in-text citation identifies the source of the quotation but is not part of the quotation.
3. The punctuation mark closing the sentence follows the parenthetical citation, so that the citation is included in the sentence, not left floating unattached between sentences. (An exception is in the case of block quotations, where the period precedes the parenthetical citation.)

You'll also need to know about a few variations on that basic form:

- If the author is named in the text leading up to the quotation (and this is good practice; notice that Farrell always does so), the name is not repeated in parentheses:

  > As Houston Baker and Charlotte Pierce-Baker point out, "The mood at the story's beginning is one of ritualistic waiting," of preparation "for the arrival of a goddess" (715).

- If more than one work by the same author is used in the paper, the first word of the title must be included to indicate which work is being referred to.
- If the author of the material being cited is unknown, use the title or a shortened form of the title in parentheses, just as an author's name would have been. Titles of books should be underlined; titles of stories, poems, or essays should be placed within quotation marks.
- If the work does not have page numbers, they may be omitted from your citation. This is frequently the case for Web sources, except for stable sources such as PDF files, in which case page numbers should be cited.
- If you use two or more works by the same author, your parenthetical citations should include a short title after the author's name (Tuten, "Alice Walker's" 125).

- If you use two authors with the same last name, include an initial in your parenthetical citation (N. Tuten 125), unless the author's full name is given in the text leading up to the quotation.
- If you cite a work you found in an anthology, use the name of the author of the work, not that of the anthology's editor: (Walker 000), not (Schakel and Ridl 000).
- If you want to quote in your paper something you found quoted by someone else in an essay or book, the best procedure is to find the original source (that's one of the values of having bibliographical information provided in a work), quote from it directly, and cite it as the source. In case your library does not have the original work or it's checked out, a less desirable but accepted procedure is to copy the quote from the secondary source and use the abbreviation "qtd. in" to indicate that you are doing so.

    Thus, an essay on "Everyday Use" by Houston A. Baker Jr. and Charlotte Pierce-Baker quotes the following sentence by Frederick Douglass: "I have thus far seen no book of importance written by a Negro woman and I know of no one among us who can appropriately be called famous." Baker and Pierce-Baker didn't identify the location of that statement, so if you want to quote part of it, you'll need to do something like this:

    > Frederick Douglass's admission that "I have thus far seen no book of importance written by a Negro woman" provides evidence of how little impression the efforts of early African American writers made (qtd. in Baker and Pierce-Baker 713).

- If you want to cite two or more sources at once, to indicate that they say much the same thing about a point you are making, you can list them parenthetically in either of two ways:

    > Among the most valuable criticism of "Everyday Use," some of the most interesting has involved a variety of viewpoints regarding Dee (see especially Baker and Pierce-Baker 715–18, Bauer 150–51, Tuten 125–28, and Farrell 181–84).
    > Helpful discussions of Dee can be found in Baker and Pierce-Baker (715–18), Bauer (150–51), Tuten (125–28), and Farrell (181–84).

Information Notes

MLA style permits but does not require the use of informational notes either to include additional information that seems important but would disrupt the flow of the paper or to refer readers to relevant sources not discussed in the paper. Information notes may be footnotes or endnotes. Footnotes appear at the foot of the page; endnotes are placed on a separate page at the end of the paper, just before the Works Cited page. In either case, the notes are numbered consecutively throughout the paper, using raised arabic numerals (superscript).

PREPARING A WORKS CITED PAGE

The other key part of the MLA system is the bibliography. The *MLA Handbook* recommends that it be a list of Works Cited — that is, containing only works referred to within the paper. In some cases, for a student paper, a Bibliography of Works Consulted might be preferred over Works Cited to indicate the range of research, if noncited works are an important part of the context of the paper. Check with your teacher if you think that might apply to your paper.

www

Find additional advice for preparing a Works Cited page with Diana Hacker's *Research and Documentation Online* at bedfordstmartins .com/approachinglit.

PREPARING A WORKS CITED PAGE: BASIC GUIDELINES

1. Begin on a new page. Continue the page numbers begun in the earlier parts of the paper.
2. Center the heading "Works Cited" at the top of the page. Use capitals and lowercase letters, not boldfaced or italicized.
3. Arrange your list alphabetically, by the last name of the author or, for anonymous works, by the first significant word in the title (ignoring an initial *A*, *An*, or *The*). If two authors have the same last name, alphabetize by their first names.
4. Make the first line of each entry flush with the left margin, with subsequent lines, if any, indented one-half inch (using a hanging indent).
5. Double-space the entire list, without extra spaces between entries.

For an example of a properly formatted Works Cited page, see page 1516.

We include in this chapter guidelines for listing the kinds of resources that occur most commonly in literary study. If you encounter types or details not covered here, consult the *MLA Handbook* or the Bedford/St. Martin's Web site at dianahacker.com/resdoc/humanities/list.html.

Citing Books and Items Included in Books

The most common items in the Works Cited page for a student paper are likely to be entries for books by a single author. Such entries usually have three parts:

Author's name. Title of the Book. Publication information.

Here are explanations of those three parts and of expansions upon them that other books may require. The asterisked items are always included; those without asterisks are included when needed:

* **Name of the author or editor,** last name first, as it appears on the title page, followed by a period. If this entry ends with an initial, only one period is needed. Only the first author's name, the one used for alphabetizing, is reversed; other names in the entry are given in the regular order.

* **Title of the book,** underlined, followed by a period. If the book has a subtitle, include it as well, preceded by a colon (unless the main title ends in a question mark, exclamation point, or dash). The *MLA Handbook* recommends the use of underlining in papers because it is easier for an instructor or editor to pick out than italics. If you prefer using italics, check with your instructor before doing so.

Name of the editor (for a book that has an editor in addition to an author), **translator,** or **compiler,** preceded by the abbreviation "Ed." (even if there are two editors), "Trans.," or "Comp." and followed by a period.

Edition used, if other than the first, followed by a period.

Volume used, if a multivolume work, followed by a period.

Series name, if the book is part of a series, followed by a period.

* **Place of publication,** followed by a colon. If more than one city is listed on the title page, give only the first one. Identify lesser-known international cities with a country abbreviation ("Amsterdam:" but "Apeldoorn, Neth.:").

* **Name of the publisher,** shortened, followed by a comma.

* **Year of publication,** followed by a period. If the date of publication is not given on the title page, look for it on the following page (the copyright page). If no date of publication is given there, use the copyright date (if more than one copyright date is listed, use the last one). Sometimes the copyright page includes the dates of successive printings of the book: These are not of interest; the date you use should be that of the first printing, its original appearance.

Here are examples of the most common kinds of entries.

A Book by One Author

Walker, Alice. <u>In Search of Our Mothers' Gardens: Womanist Prose.</u> San Diego: Harcourt, 1983.

A Book by Two or More Authors

To cite a book by more than one author, list the authors' names in the order they appear on the title page; invert only the first author's name, followed by a comma and list the other name or names in normal order.

Pratt, L. H., and Darnell Pratt. Alice Malsenior Walker: An Annotated Bibliog-
    raphy. New York: Greenwood, 1988.

For more than three authors, you may give just the first author, followed by
"et al." (abbreviation for the Latin *et alii* or *et aliae*, "and others").

An Edited Collection

To cite a book with chapters by different authors, use the same form as
for a book attributed in its entirety to one or more authors, with "ed." or
"eds." added after the name(s) of the editor(s), preceded by a comma.

Gates, Henry Louis, Jr., and K. A. Appiah, eds. Alice Walker: Critical Perspec-
    tives: Past and Present. New York: Amistad, 1993.

To cite a specific chapter from such a collection, see below, "Citing a Scholarly Essay Published for the First Time in a Collection of Essays" or "Citing a
Previously Published Article Reprinted in a Collection."

A Book in a Series

If the book you are using is part of a series as indicated by the title page
or the preceding page, include the series name (not underlined or in quotation marks) and the series number after the title, followed by a period.

Montelaro, Janet J. Producing a Womanist Text: The Maternal as Signifier in
    Alice Walker's The Color Purple. ELS Monograph Series 70. Victoria, BC:
    English Literary Series, U of Victoria, 1996.

When the title of a book-length work which would ordinarily be underlined
is included in a book title, MLA style prefers that the internal title be identified by being neither underlined nor placed in quotation marks, as in the example above. MLA style does, however, allow the option of placing internal
titles in quotation marks and underlining them (Producing a Womanist Text:
The Maternal as Signifier in Alice Walker's "The Color Purple").

Two or More Books by the Same Author

To cite two or more books by the same author, give the name only in the
first entry. For the others, substitute three hyphens followed by a period. If
the person edited or translated one or more of the books, place a comma
after the three hyphens, then the appropriate abbreviation (that is, "ed." or
"trans."), then the title. The titles should be in alphabetical order.

Walker, Alice. By the Light of My Father's Smile: A Novel. New York: Random,
    1998.

---. The Color Purple: A Novel. New York: Harcourt, 1982.

---. Meridian. New York: Harcourt, 1976.

A Republished Book

To cite a book that has been republished — for example, a paperback reprint of a book — give the original date of publication, followed by a period and then the publication information for the book you are using. The date of original publication can usually be found on the copyright page of the reprint; if it's not there, you may need to check library catalogs or biographical introductions to the author to find it.

Walker, Alice. The Color Purple. 1982. New York: Pocket, 1985.

An Edition

To cite a work prepared for publication by someone other than the author — by an editor — provide the information you would provide for a republished book, with the name of the editor inserted before the publication information, preceded by "Ed." For a previously published work, if you want to include the original date of publication for clarity, insert the year directly after the title.

Dunbar, Paul Laurence. Collected Poetry. Ed. Joanne M. Bruxton. Charlottesville: UP of Virginia, 1993.

Note that although the title page reads *The Collected Poetry of Paul Laurence Dunbar*, repetition can be avoided to make it fit conventional citation form. The following example is not a reprint but the first printing of a collected edition of stories originally published in several books.

Hughes, Langston. The Return of Simple. Ed. Akiba Sullivan Harper. New York:
Hill, 1994.

A Multivolume Work

To cite two or more volumes of a multivolume work, give the total number of volumes in the set before the publication information, using an arabic numeral followed by the abbreviation "vols." Parenthetical references in the text will require volume number plus page numbers ("2: 145–47"). For a work in which volumes were published separately, in different years, give the first and last dates at the end of the citation.

Rampersad, Arnold. The Life of Langston Hughes. 2 vols. New York: Oxford UP,
1986-88.

When you use only one volume of a multivolume work, give its volume number in the bibliographic entry and include publication information for only that volume. In this case, only the page numbers are needed in parenthetical references in the text.

> Rampersad, Arnold. The Life of Langston Hughes. Vol. 2. New York: Oxford UP,
>   1988.

Citing a Work in a Collection of Stories or Poems

To cite a work from a collection of stories or poems by a single author, insert the title of the story or poem, in quotation marks, between the name of the author and the title of the book, and conclude the entry with the pages on which it appears.

> Walker, Alice. "Everyday Use." In Love and Trouble: Stories of Black Women.
>   New York: Harcourt, 1973. 47-59.

Citations for additional works from the same collection can be abbreviated:

> ---. "The Flowers." In Love and Trouble 119-20.

Citing a Work in an Anthology

When citing a work published in an anthology, give the author's name, the title of the work (in quotation marks for a story, poem, or essay; underlined for a play or screenplay), the title of the anthology, the editors, the publication information, and the page numbers on which the work appears. If you want to include the original date of publication for clarity, insert the year directly after the title.

> Walker, Alice. "Everyday Use." 1973. Approaching Literature: Writing + Read-
>   ing + Thinking. 2nd ed. Ed. Peter Schakel and Jack Ridl. Boston: Bed-
>   ford/St. Martin's, 2008. 109-15.

If several works from the same anthology are cited in the paper, unnecessary repetition can be avoided by creating a main entry for the anthology and cross-referencing individual works to it.

> Ríos, Alberto. "Nani." Schakel and Ridl 847-48.
> Schakel, Peter, and Jack Ridl, eds. Approaching Literature: Writing + Reading +
>   Thinking. 2nd ed. Boston: Bedford/St. Martin's, 2008.
> Walker, Alice. "Everyday Use." Schakel and Ridl 109-15.

Citing a Scholarly Essay Published for the First Time in a Collection of Essays

Parker-Smith, Bettye J. "Alice Walker's Women: In Search of Some Peace of
    Mind." Black Women Writers (1950-1980): A Critical Evaluation. Ed. Mari
    Evans. Garden City: Anchor, 1984. 478-93.

If two or more works from the same volume are cited in the paper, create a main entry for the volume and cross-reference individual works to it, as above.

Citing an Entry from an Encyclopedia

The citation for an encyclopedia article or dictionary entry follows the pattern for an essay in a collection, except the editor's name should not be included and, if the encyclopedia or dictionary is well-known, publication information can be omitted. If the article is signed, start with the author (sometimes articles in reference books are signed with initials identified elsewhere in the book); if it is anonymous, start with the title of the entry. If entries are arranged alphabetically in the encyclopedia or dictionary, volume and page numbers may be omitted.

"Clabber." The Oxford English Dictionary. 2nd ed. 1989.
"Quilting." The New Encyclopedia Britannica: Micropedia. 15th ed. 2002.

Citing an Entry in a Multivolume Reference Work

Christian, Barbara T. "Alice Walker." Dictionary of Literary Biography. Vol. 33:
    Afro-American Fiction Writers after 1955. Ed. Thadious M. Davis and
    Trudier Harris. Detroit: Gale, 1984. 258-71.

Citing Articles from Journals, Magazines, and Newspapers

The Works Cited page for a research paper almost always will include entries for articles. Like those for books, such entries usually have three main parts:

Author's name. "Title of the Article." Publication information.

Specific details will vary from one type of publication to another, as the explanations below will indicate. The asterisked items are always included; those without asterisks are included when needed.

Citing Articles Published in Scholarly Journals

Scholarly journals usually publish several issues a year (often quarterly). Each year is designated as a volume, and pages are usually numbered continuously throughout the volume. Works Cited entries for an article in a scholarly journal should include the following:

*Name of the author, last name first, as it appears in the article, followed by a period.

*Title of the article, enclosed in quotation marks, followed by a period (inside the quotation mark), unless the title ends with a question mark or an exclamation point.

*Title of the journal, underlined, no punctuation following it.

*Volume number of the journal, using arabic numerals even if a roman numeral is used in the journal, no punctuation following.

*Year of publication, in parentheses, followed by a colon.

*Page numbers (first and last), followed by a period.

Bauer, Margaret D. "Alice Walker: Another Southern Writer Criticizing Codes Not Put to 'Everyday Use.'" Studies in Short Fiction 29 (1992): 143-51.

Some journals paginate each issue separately. In that case, you must also include the issue number (volume number, period, issue number with no spaces between: "29.2").

Citing Articles Published in Magazines

Magazines usually appear more frequently than scholarly journals (often weekly, biweekly, monthly, or bimonthly) and paginate each issue separately. Magazines have volume numbers, but they are not important for locating an issue and are left out of Works Cited entries. The name of the author, title of the article, and title of the magazine are handled the same way as for scholarly journal entries, but dates and pages differ:

*Date of publication, followed by a colon. Day, month (abbreviated), and year (in that order) are given for weekly or biweekly magazines; only month or months and year are given for magazines published monthly or bimonthly.

*Page numbers (first and last of the whole article, not just the ones you used), followed by a period. If pagination is not consecutive (for example, begins on page 4, then jumps to page 8), write only the first page number and a plus sign, with no intervening space.

Reed, J. R. "Post Feminism Playing for Keeps." Time 10 Jan. 1983: 60-61.

Watkins, Mel. "Sexism, Racism and Black Women Writers." New York Times Book Review 15 June 1986: 4+.

Citing Articles Published in Newspapers

The format for citing an article in a newspaper is exactly the same as for a weekly magazine, unless the newspaper is published in varied editions (late edition, suburban edition) — in that case, the edition is included after the date, separated by a comma. If a newspaper is divided into sections, include the section letter or section number with the page number. If the article is on more than one page and not consecutive, give the first page number followed by a plus sign, with no space between them. The title of the newspaper should be given the way it appears on the masthead, but introductory articles should be omitted (*New York Times* not *The New York Times*).

> Ross, Michelle. "Georgia Writer Alice Walker Didn't Know They Had Pulitzer
> Prize for Fiction." Atlanta Journal 19 Apr. 1983: A3.
> Sague, Maria. "Alice Walker: A Writer with a Cause." Sun [Baltimore] 5 July
> 1987: A7-8.

Citing a Review

In citing a review, include the title and author of the work being reviewed after the review title and before the periodical title.

> Giovanni, Nikki. "So Black and Blue." Rev. of In Love and Trouble, by Alice
> Walker. Book World 18 Nov. 1973: 1.
> Ansen, David. "We Shall Overcome." Rev. of The Color Purple, dir. Steven
> Spielberg. Newsweek 30 Dec. 1985: 59-60.

Citing a Previously Published Article Reprinted in a Collection

To cite a previously published scholarly article reprinted in a collection, give the complete data for the earlier publication and then add "Rpt. in" ("Reprinted in"), the title of the collection, and its publication data.

> Baker, Houston A., and Charlotte Pierce-Baker. "Patches: Quilts and Community
> in Alice Walker's 'Everyday Use.'" The Southern Review 21 (1985): 706-
> 20. Rpt. in Alice Walker: Critical Perspectives: Past and Present. Ed.
> Henry Louis Gates Jr. and K. A. Appiah. New York: Amistad, 1993.
> 309-16.

Citing Interviews

To cite an interview, give first the name of the person being interviewed. If the interview has been published, give the title (if it has one) in quotation marks or just "Interview," without quotation marks or italics, and then give the name of the interviewer and publication information.

Walker, Alice. "Authors and Editors." Interview with Barbara Bannon. <u>Publishers Weekly</u> 31 Aug. 1970: 195-97.

To cite an interview conducted personally by the author of a paper, include the name of the person interviewed, the kind of interview ("Personal interview," "Telephone interview," "E-mail interview"), and the date or dates.

Ridl, Jack. Personal interview. 7 Sept. 2007.

Schakel, Peter. E-mail interview. 13-15 Oct. 2007.

Citing a Personal Letter or E-mail

To cite a letter that you received, give the name of the sender, the type of communication, and its date.

Ridl, Jack. Letter to the author. 21 Oct. 2007.

Schakel, Peter. E-mail to the author. 28 Oct. 2007.

Citing Print Sources Accessed Electronically

For Works Cited entries involving the full text of a journal or magazine article accessed through a database such as *JSTOR*, *Project MUSE*, or *InfoTrac*, you must provide the information a reader needs to access the source electronically, as well as the information about its original publication. The basic pattern for such an entry has five parts:

Name of the author. "Title of the Document." Information about print publication. Information about electronic publication. Access information.

When the source does not provide all of that information, give as much as you can, following or adapting the following guidelines:

* **Name of the author,** last name first and followed by a period.

* **Title of the document,** enclosed in quotation marks, followed by a period (inside the quotation mark), unless the title ends with a question mark or an exclamation point.

* **As much information about its publication in a journal or magazine as the database makes available,** following the guidelines above for journals and magazines. If no information about print publication is provided, proceed to the next step.

* **Information about its electronic reproduction:** the title of the Web site or database, underlined; name of the person who edits it, if given, preceded by "Ed."; the date of electronic posting or the latest

update; the name of the institution or organization sponsoring the site, if any — each item followed by a period.

*Access information: database, date, and URL.** Because sites on the Internet change frequently, an electronic text is considered unique each time it is accessed. Therefore, in a Works Cited entry for an electronic work, you should give the date assigned to the text in the source (the date of posting), if available, then the database you used to access the document (if you used one) and the date on which you accessed the document (or, the last time you viewed it). Then provide the URL at which you found the document, enclosed in <angle brackets> (insert line breaks in URLs only after slashes; do not insert a hyphen). If a URL is really long, give the URL of the home page, the word *path*, and a list of links you followed in getting to the information.

TIP: Because Internet sites sometimes disappear or move and can't be located again, it is a good idea to print out a copy of the material used for your paper so you can verify its accuracy in case the site becomes inaccessible.

Farrell, Susan. "Fight vs. Flight: A Re-evaluation of Dee in Alice Walker's 'Every-day Use.'" Studies in Short Fiction 35 (1998): 179-86. Gale-Academic OneFile. 30 July 2007. <http://www.hope.edu/lib/> path: Databases for Research > MLA Bibliography > keyword "Everyday Use" keyword > item 9.

Citing Electronic Sources

The Works Cited pages for research papers composed these days may well include entries for Internet sources, materials that have not appeared in print and never were intended to appear in print. Entries for such sources follow the pattern listed directly above, with the third step (information on print publication) and the database reference in the fourth step omitted. Below are samples of some electronic sources you are likely to encounter in literary research.

A Professional or Personal Web Page

To cite a Web page, include as much of the following as possible: author of the site or document; the title, in quotation marks, for separate documents within the site; the name of the site, underlined; the date the site or document was created or most recently updated; the sponsoring organization or institution; the date you accessed it; and the online address. If the site does not have a heading title, give an identifying phrase (not underlined or in quotation marks).

Jokinen, Anniina. Anniina's Alice Walker Page. 27 Dec. 2006. 27 Aug. 2007 <http://www.luminarium.org/contemporary/alicew/>.

An Online Scholarly Project or Database

"Alice Walker." Poets.org. Academy of American Poets. 2007.
   Poets.org. Academy of American Poets. 1997-2007. 27 Aug. 2007
   <http://www.poets.org/poet.php/prmPID/486>.
Mabry, Donald J. The Historical Text Archive. Mississippi State University.
   1990-2007. 17 August 2007 <http://www.historicaltextarchive.com>.

An Online Journal

Lessane, Patricia Williams. "Women of Color Facing Feminism--Creating Our
   Space at Liberation's Table: A Report on the Chicago Foundation for
   Women's 'F' Series." *Journal of Pan African Studies* 1.7 (March 2007):
   3-10. 2007. 21 August 2007. <http://www.jpanafrican.com/archive_
   issues/vo11no7.htm>.

An Online Magazine

"LitChat: Alice Walker." Salon.com 11 Aug. 2000. 9 July 2007 <http://
   archive.salon.com/09/departments/litchat1.htm>.

A CD-ROM

To cite a CD-ROM, treat it like a book, with "CD-ROM" and a period
between its title and the publication information.

"Alice Walker." DISCovering Authors. CD-ROM. Detroit: Gale, 1999.

A STUDENT WRITER AT WORK: KRISTINA MARTINEZ ON THE RESEARCH PROCESS

Students in an introduction to literature class were
asked to use secondary sources in writing a paper on technique and meaning in a work from the "Collection of
Stories" section of this book (see Chapter 10). One of our
students, Kristina Martinez, decided to do her paper on
Toni Morrison's "Recitatif." We are going to follow her
through the writing process in completing that assignment, using her own words as she retraces her steps.

On Finding a Topic

"There were a lot of interesting ideas in the story — racial ambiguity, social
status, mother-daughter relationships, among others — and I considered several

of these as a topic. But what I found tied all of these ideas together, and interested me most, was the way in which the story was told. Before I began writing the paper I knew I might have trouble with keeping the paper focused and staying with the idea of how the story is told. I hadn't read a story before that plays with readers so much, and manages to address a number of issues."

On Researching the Topic

"The first thing I did, after reading 'Recitatif' three times, was to use the online catalog to look for books on Toni Morrison. I found several, including an encyclopedia on her (*The Toni Morrison Encyclopedia*, ed. Elizabeth Ann Beaulieu [Westport: Greenwood, 2003]). I browsed in them and photocopied sections on 'Recitatif' that looked potentially useful. Then I searched databases to find articles about the story, and again found several. I photocopied ones that looked good if we had them in the library, and printed others where full texts were available online. Then, in the notes and bibliographies of the books and articles I had collected, I looked at what those authors used as sources, found ones that seemed interesting, and made copies. I then put everything in a three-ring notebook and began reading closely. I expected the paper to focus especially on Twyla, Roberta, their mothers, and Maggie, as well as on the structure of the story. So I marked in the margins places that referred to any of those. To make it easier to return to these places, I put tabs by them, using sticky notes, a different color for each topic. (When I was writing the paper and used a passage, I removed the tab so I would not go back to the passage again.)"

On Developing and Supporting a Thesis

"I started by working on a thesis, and, after a couple of false starts, decided to focus on the way differences in stories told in 'Recitatif' leave readers feeling ambiguous about race and about Maggie. My working thesis statement was, 'Elements of story are thick throughout this piece. Morrison uses character, point of view, and time to hold readers' attention and leaves them questioning not only race but what really has happened to Maggie.' It was modified slightly in the final version, but most of it is still there.

"One of my sources was helpful in setting up the rest of the paper — it showed that Morrison used oral storytelling techniques in writing 'Recitatif.' That led me to wonder about Twyla and Roberta as oral storytellers. Both of them told stories about the same events. I tried to think about both as telling stories in order to lead their listeners (readers) or to mislead them.

"With that as a starting point, I wrote a detailed outline of the rest of the paper. Briefly:

- Narrator — Twyla as primary one; Roberta as secondary
- Race — concealing which is white and which is black

- Stories about Maggie and her race
  - Both girls identify with Maggie
  - First story about Maggie: Difference in what they remember
  - Second story about Maggie: Did they kick her? Was she black?
  - Third story about Maggie: Why they *wanted* to kick her
- Conclusion

Next, I wrote the first point in longhand, then typed and printed it, reread it, and revised it. I went on to do the same for the other points. I wrote by hand because it was easier to put my ideas from head to hand and hand to paper, plus the weather was great and I wrote outside.

"I wrote out what I wanted to say about each point, using summaries and details from the story to support it. Then I went back through my notebook, looking for places where critics could be used to clarify or back up what I was saying. I inserted summaries or quotations where they seemed to fit well."

On Revising and Proofreading

"Despite my thorough outline, I ended up writing paragraphs that turned out not to be central to my focus on storytelling. One thing I did in revision was to cut paragraphs—often keeping a sentence I could move to another paragraph and deleting the rest. I also needed to reduce quotations—there were too many, at first, and some were too long. I cut a lot. Another revision was to improve the way I led into quotations.

"I had started my Works Cited list earlier, as I photocopied materials. While revising, I used that list as I went through the paper and put a check mark by each item that I actually used in the paper. I checked each for accuracy, and deleted the ones I didn't use. Then I checked quotations, and corrected a few minor slips. Last, I proofread the whole paper, for spelling, grammar, and sentence style."

SAMPLE RESEARCH PAPER

What follows is Kristina's final revision. For the convenience of readers, we have changed the page numbers for quotations of "Recitatif" from those originally given in the essay to the pages on which they are found in the current edition of this book.

Kristina Martinez
Professors Ridl and Schakel
English 105-04
8 November 2003

The Structure of Story in Toni Morrison's "Recitatif"

What do stories do? Some are told to entertain, some to inform or instruct, some to mislead. And sometimes the way a story is structured creates ambiguities that make it difficult to tell which of these it is doing. That is the case with Toni Morrison's story "Recitatif." The structure of Twyla's story, and that of Roberta's stories within it, hold a reader's attention and leave a reader questioning not only race but what happened to Maggie.

The structure relates to the kind of story this is. Robert Stepto points out that many African-American authors "choose to see themselves as storytellers instead of storywriters" (qtd. in Goldstein-Shirley 101) because they distrust readers, and want people to *listen* to what they have to say. "Recitatif" falls into that category: "Although the text is written," David Goldstein-Shirley notes, "its structure mimics oral storytelling" (101). He goes on to spell out the effect of that form: "The distinctively 'oral' quality of 'Recitatif' also contributes to the story's strategy of recruiting the reader in its mission to deconstruct racism" (101).

The story, in fact, has two storytellers. Twyla is the overall storyteller. The story begins with her: "My mother danced all night and Roberta's was sick" ("Recitatif" 431). Twyla is a limited narrator, an outsider in her own story, lacking the understanding of things that Roberta possesses from the start ("I liked the way she understood things so fast"--"Recitatif" 432). As a result, Elizabeth Abel believes, Twyla "feels vulnerable to Roberta's judgment" (473). Twyla's story provides a frame, within which we also hear stories told by Roberta, which often conflict with Twyla's, thus creating tension between the two and forcing the reader to sort out differences and attempt to find the truth.

One of the things readers must grapple with is race. Twyla and Roberta are of different races: "we looked like salt and pepper standing there," Twyla says ("Recitatif" 432). But which is white and which is

Thesis sentence states central idea.

Use of indirect secondary source (quoted in another source) to set up argument.

Clear topic sentences are used throughout the paper.

Secondary source quoted to advance argument, with signal phrase naming author.

Primary text quoted to back up assertion.

black is never stated. The reader's desire to know is paralleled later in the story by the girls' attempts to determine the race of the servant Maggie (Bennett 212). Morrison creates a racial ambiguity that, Aimee L. Pozorski argues, grows out of linguistic ambiguity: "'Recitatif' becomes an experiment in language, as Morrison considers whether a story can be written without the linguistic short cuts habitually employed in American literature to categorize and to stereotype its characters" (280). Race is important to our identities, Anthony Appiah concludes (499), and in that respect it is a central issue in the story. Yet the reader is not allowed to fall back on familiar language and comfortable stereotypes in understanding that issue.

Secondary source quoted to expand point.

Secondary source summarized.

These discrepancies and ambiguities come to bear especially on their stories about Maggie. Both girls identified to some extent with Maggie. Maggie is, as one critic states, "the lowest person in the hierarchy" (Holmes). Similarly, Twyla and Roberta were looked down upon by other children at the orphanage because "we weren't real orphans with beautiful dead parents in the sky" ("Recitatif" 432). As Maggie is mute, so the two girls while at St. Bonny's have no voice. This does not, however, lead them to bond with Maggie. On the contrary, they attempt to separate and distance themselves from her emotionally because, Jan Furman says, she makes them feel inadequate and helpless. The result was that, "Without realizing it, however, in hating Maggie, they hated themselves and each other" (Furman 110). That hatred leads them to remember Maggie differently, and thus the stories they tell are different.

Transition to Part 2.

No page number for Web source.

Shortened citation of primary text: no need to repeat "Morrison."

Paraphrase and quotation of secondary source to advance argument.

The first story about Maggie occurs when, years after St. Bonny's, they cross paths at the Food Emporium. They have lunch and as they reminisce about the orphanage, Twyla says,

> "I don't remember a hell of a lot from those days, but Lord, St. Bonny's is as clear as daylight. Remember Maggie? The day she fell down and those gar girls laughed at her?"
> Roberta looked up from her salad and stared at me.
> "Maggie didn't fall," she said.
> "Yes, she did. You remember."
> "No, Twyla. They knocked her down. Those girls pushed her down and tore her clothes. In the orchard."
> "I don't--that's not what happened."
> "Sure it is. In the orchard." ("Recitatif" 440)

Extended block quotation sets up further discussion of Maggie.

Martinez 3

Series of questions to be explored in rest of paper.

Summary of primary text.

Quotation of primary text to highlight crux in story.

Primary text summarized at length to provide context.

Quotations of primary text to bring out key points.

The discrepancies bother Twyla ("Roberta had messed up my past somehow with that business about Maggie. I wouldn't forget a thing like that. Would I?"--"Recitatif" 441) and create ambiguity for the reader. Which story is correct, Roberta's or Twyla's (or neither)? Are they remembering details about Maggie differently because one of them is the same race as Maggie and the other not? If so, which one is the same?

Conflicting stories about Maggie appear again the next time they meet, later that year, outside a school at which Roberta is picketing against busing children to achieve racial balance. They have a bitter exchange about forced integration, in which Roberta blurts out to Twyla, " 'You're the same little state kid who kicked a poor old black lady when she was down on the ground. You kicked a black lady and you have the nerve to call me a bigot' " ("Recitatif" 442). Twyla tells a different story: " 'Maggie wasn't black' " ("Recitatif" 442), and she hadn't kicked Maggie: "I know I didn't do that, I couldn't do that" ("Recitatif" 443). On further thought, she remains convinced about the kicking, but not about the race: "When I thought about it I actually couldn't be certain" ("Recitatif" 443). The reader is left to figure out why Roberta said this to Twyla, how much of it is true, and how racial difference affects their different memories.

Maggie stories emerge also in the last meeting with Roberta that Twyla tells about. The last time they meet in the story is at least a year later when Twyla stops at a downtown diner for coffee after shopping for a Christmas tree and Roberta sits with her for a few minutes. Roberta now backs away from her previous story: she acknowledges that Twyla didn't kick Maggie--neither of them did, only the gar girls did. The exchange brings out a parallel between Roberta and Twyla: each had wanted to kick Maggie because each identified Maggie with her mother as well as with herself. For Twyla, "Maggie was my dancing mother. Deaf, I thought, and dumb. Nobody inside. Nobody who would hear you if you cried in the night. Nobody who could tell you anything important that you could use" ("Recitatif" 444). Roberta thought Maggie was crazy, like her mother, and had " 'been brought up in an institution like my mother was and like I thought I would be too' " (Recitatif" 445). Neither girl could accept her own mother, just as neither could accept Maggie: the reminders of the pain their mothers inflicted were too much to bear.

Martinez 4

The structure of the story creates ambiguity in racial codes, and does not attempt to resolve it. It is too complex to fit the conventional language and stereotypes. Each girl constructed a racial identity for Maggie out of her own cultural and racial context, and we as readers are tempted to do the same (Abel 471–72). What this story does is to show how literature can bring readers into a work, "the ways writers . . . tell other stories, fight secret wars, limn out all sorts of debates blanketed in their text" (Morrison, Playing 4). Readers are given the language, which takes them through the story and finally leads them to the point of realizing that this story will not provide answers to their questions, and that acceptance of ambiguity itself answers the need to have answers.

Secondary source summarized.

Title included in citation because two works by Morrison appear in Works Cited.

Works Cited

Abel, Elizabeth. "Black Writing, White Reading: Race and the Politics of Feminist Interpretation." Critical Inquiry 19 (1993): 470-98.

Appiah, Anthony. "'But Would That Still Be Me?' Notes on Gender, 'Race,' Ethnicity, as Sources of 'Identity.'" Journal of Philosophy 87 (1990): 493-99. JSTOR. 3 Nov. 2003 <http://www.jstor.org/search>.

Bennett, Juda. "Toni Morrison and the Burden of the Passing Narrative." African American Review 35(2001): 205-17. InfoTrac. 3 Nov. 2003 <http://www.0-web7.infotrac.galegroup.com>.

Furman, Jan. Toni Morrison's Fiction. Columbia: U of South Carolina P, 1996.

Goldstein-Shirley, David. "Race/[Gender]." Women on the Edge: Ethnicity and Gender in Short Stories by American Women. Ed. Corrine H. Dale and J. H. S. Paine. New York: Garland, 1999: 97-110.

Holmes, Martha Stoddard. "Literature Annotations: Morrison, Toni: 'Recitatif.'" Literature, Arts, and Medicine Database. 6 Nov. 2003 <http://www.endeavor.med.nyu.edu/lit-med/lit-med-db/webdocs/webdescrips/morrison11854-des-.html>.

Morrison, Toni. Playing in the Dark: Whiteness and the Literary Imagination. Cambridge: Harvard UP, 1992.

---. "Recitatif." 1983. Approaching Literature: Writing + Reading + Thinking. 2nd ed. Peter Schakel and Jack Ridl. Boston: Bedford/St. Martin's, 2008. 431-45.

Pozorski, Aimee L. "Race." The Toni Morrison Encyclopedia. Ed. Elizabeth Ann Beaulieu. Westport: Greenwood, 2003. 277-85.

Biographical Sketches

This section offers brief biographical sketches of the 260 known authors of the works included in this book. For fuller biographical information, the most convenient print sources are the *Dictionary of Literary Biography* (Detroit: Gale, 1978–), currently at 329 volumes, and *Contemporary Authors*, also published by Gale (original series, 248 volumes; new revised series, currently 155 volumes).

Biographical information for many authors is also found on the Internet. The Academy of American Poets Web site (poets.org/poets/index.cfm) is valuable and convenient for information about poets; we are indebted to it for many of our entries. *Voices from the Gaps: Women Writers of Color* (voices.cla.umn.edu/newsite/index.htm) also is very helpful. Sites for many individual authors are available as well, as are personal home pages for some contemporary poets and sites maintained by scholars or fans of writers old and new. To emphasize how writers work with each other and are influenced by other writers, when the names of authors represented in this anthology appear within a biographical entry, they are in small capital letters, as a reminder that those biographical notes will shed further light on the author at hand.

The companion Web site for this book, bedfordstmartins.com/approachinglit, provides access to LitLinks, which offers brief biographies of all of the writers in this book, with links to important related sites. Marginal icons throughout the book reference the companion Web site and *LiterActive*, a CD-ROM with multimedia resources, biographies, and critical and cultural documents. After each biographical entry, we've included cross-references to these two resources. Both are good places to start when researching individual authors.

Ai (b. 1947), who has described herself as one-half Japanese, one-eighth Choctaw, one-half black, and one-sixteenth Irish, was born Florence Anthony in Albany, Texas, and grew up in Tucson, Arizona. She legally changed her name to "Ai," which means "love" in Japanese. She received a B.A. in Japanese from the University of Arizona and an M.F.A. from the University of California at Irvine. She is the author of half a dozen books of poetry, among them *Vice* (1999), which won the National Book Award for Poetry. She has taught at Wayne State University, George Mason University, and the University of Kentucky, and she currently teaches at Oklahoma State University and lives in Stillwater, Oklahoma.

WEB: Further research this author with LitLinks at bedfordstmartins.com/approachinglit.

Anna Akhmatova (1889–1966) was born Anna Gorenko in Bolshoy Fontan, near Odessa, Ukraine. She began writing poetry at eleven but had to adopt a pseudonym to allay her father's fears that her becoming a "decadent poetess" would dishonor the family. She attended law school in Kiev before moving to St. Petersburg to study literature. Her first collection of poetry, *Evening*, appeared in 1912 and was well received. Because she was suspected of anti-Bolshevik sentiments, her poetry was banned in Russia from 1925 until 1940 and again after World War II. During the ban she devoted herself to literary criticism and translations. In the late 1930s, her long poem *Requiem* was dedicated to the memory of Stalin's victims. In 1940, a collection of previously published poems, *From Six Books*, was published but withdrawn a few months later. After Stalin's death Akhmatova slowly gained recognition as one of the greatest Russian poets of the twentieth century, respected internationally for the quality of her literary work and for her integrity and resoluteness in the face of political oppression.

SHERMAN ALEXIE (b. 1966) — See page 251.

AGHA SHAHID ALI (1949–2001) was born in New Delhi and grew up Muslim in Kashmir. He was educated at the University of Kashmir, Srinagar, and at the University of Delhi. He earned a Ph.D. from Pennsylvania State University in 1984 and an M.F.A. from the University of Arizona in 1985. He was a poet (author of eight books of poetry), critic (author of *T. S. Eliot as Editor* [1986]), translator (*The Rebel's Silhouette: Selected Poems* by Faiz Ahmed Faiz, 1992), and editor (*Ravishing Disunities: Real Ghazals in English*, 2000). He held teaching positions at the University of Delhi and at several colleges and universities in the United States. "I Dream It Is Afternoon When I Return to Delhi" (p. 734) shows Ali's use of Western formal cultural principles in work that focuses on his own cultural background.

WEB: Further research this author with LitLinks at bedfordstmartins.com/approachinglit.

MONICA ALI (b. 1967) was born in Dhaka, Bangladesh, to a Bangladeshi father and an English mother. The family moved to England when she was three and Ali grew up in Bolton, near Manchester. She graduated from Oxford University, where she studied philosophy, politics, and economics. After working in marketing and design for several years, she turned to writing. Her first novel, *Brick Lane* (2003), was shortlisted for the 2003 Booker Prize for Fiction. "Dinner with Dr. Azad" is excerpted from her second novel, *Alentejo Blue* (2006). She was named as one of the twenty "Best of Young British Novelists" in 2003 by *Granta* magazine.

ISABEL ALLENDE (b. 1942) was born in Lima, Peru. After the divorce of her mother and father (a Chilean diplomat), she lived with her maternal grandparents in Santiago, Chile, then in Bolivia, the Middle East, and Europe with her mother and stepfather, also a diplomat. She worked for the United Nations Food and Agricultural Organization in Santiago and then embarked on a promising career as a journalist for *Paula* magazine and on television and in movie newsreels. That career ended with the overthrow and assassination in 1973 of her uncle, Salvador Allende, president of Chile, when she, her husband, and her children had to flee to Venezuela for safety. While in exile, she began to write her first novel, *The House of the Spirits* (1982), which traces personal and political conflicts in several generations of an imaginary family in a Latin American country and is based on memories of her own family and the political upheaval in Chile. She has since published several novels and a collection of short stories. Her work is known for focusing on the experience (especially the struggles) of women and for its use of the "magic realism" often found in Latin American literature.

WEB: Further research this author with LitLinks at bedfordstmartins.com/approachinglit.

JULIA ALVAREZ (b. 1950) was born in New York City, lived in the Dominican Republic until she was ten, and returned to New York when her father had to flee because he was involved in a plot to overthrow the dictator, Rafael Trujillo. Thus she needed to adjust to a new culture and a new language. Since childhood she says she loved stories — hearing them and telling them — so it was natural for her to decide she wanted to be a writer. She graduated from Middlebury College in Vermont and earned an M.A. in creative writing from Syracuse University. Since 1998 she has been writer-in-residence at Middlebury. Alvarez has published five novels, many short stories, numerous books for young readers, four volumes of poetry, and a book of essays about herself and her writing life, *Something to Declare* (1998).

WEB: Further research this author with LitLinks at bedfordstmartins.com/approachinglit.

YEHUDA AMICHAI (1924–2000) was born in Wurzburg, Germany, and emigrated with his family to Palestine in 1936. He later became a naturalized Israeli citizen. Although German was his native language, Amichai read Hebrew fluently by the time he moved to Palestine. He served in the Jewish Brigade of the British army in World War II and fought with the Israeli defense forces in the 1948 Arab-Israeli war. Following the war, he attended Hebrew University to study biblical texts and Hebrew literature, and then taught in secondary schools. He published eleven volumes of poetry in Hebrew, two novels, and a book of short stories. His work has been translated into thirty-seven languages. He is regarded as one of the leading twentieth-century Hebrew poets, his contribution extending beyond his own literary achievements to his influence on the development of modern Israeli poetry.

MARGARET ATWOOD (b. 1939) was born in Ottawa and grew up in northern Ontario, in Quebec, and in Toronto. She began writing while attending high school in Toronto. She received her undergraduate degree from Victoria College at the University of Toronto and her master's degree from Radcliffe College. She won the E. J. Pratt Medal for her privately printed book of poems, *Double Persephone* (1961), and has published fifteen more collections of poetry. She is perhaps best known for her twelve novels, which include *The Handmaid's Tale* (1983), *The Robber Bride* (1994), and *The Blind Assassin* (2000 — winner of the Booker Prize). She has also published nine collections of short stories, six children's books, and five books of nonfiction and edited several anthologies. Her work has been translated into more than thirty languages, including Farsi, Japanese, Turkish, Finnish, Korean, Icelandic, and Estonian.

WEB: Further research this author with LitLinks at bedfordstmartins.com/approachinglit.

W.[YSTAN] H.[UGH] AUDEN (1907–1973) was born in York, England. He went to private school and then to Oxford University, where he began to write poetry. He supported himself by teaching and publishing and wrote books based on his travels to Iceland, Spain, and China. He also wrote (with Chester Kall-man) several librettos, including one for Igor Stravinsky's *The Rake's Progress* (1951). He lived in the United States from 1939 until his death and became a U.S. citizen in 1946. His work combines lively intelligence, quick wit, and immense craftsmanship, and often focuses on social concerns.

WEB: Further research this author with LitLinks at bedfordstmartins.com/approachinglit.

JOSEPH AWAD (b. 1929) was born in Shenandoah, Pennsylvania, and grew up in Washington, D.C., where he earned his B.A. in English literature from Georgetown University and edited the college literary magazine. He took night courses in drawing and painting at the Corcoran School of Art and toyed with the idea of a career in art but decided instead to do graduate studies in English at George Washington University. A job in public relations turned into a career, as he joined the Reynolds Metals Company public relations department and ultimately became vice president. He has published several collections of poetry, including *Leaning to Hear the Music* (1997). His poetry has won many awards, among them the Edgar Allan Poe Prize of the Poetry Society of Virginia, The Lyric's Nathan Haskell Dole Prize, and the Donn Goodwin Poetry Award. He lives in Richmond, Virginia, and served as poet laureate for Virginia from 1998 to 2000.

JIMMY SANTIAGO BACA (b. 1952) was born in Sante Fe, New Mexico, of Chicano and Apache heritage. Abandoned by his parents at the age of two, he lived with one of his grandparents for several years before being placed in an orphanage. He lived on the streets as a youth and was imprisoned for six years for drug possession. In prison, he taught himself to read and write, and began to compose poetry. A fellow inmate convinced him to submit some of his poems for publication. He has since published a dozen books of poetry, a memoir, a collection of stories and essays, a play, and a screenplay, with a novel forthcoming. He lives outside Albuquerque in a one-hundred-year-old adobe house.

WEB: Further research this author with LitLinks at bedfordstmartins.com/approachinglit.

JAMES BALDWIN (1924–1987) was born in Harlem to an unmarried domestic worker. When Baldwin was three, his mother married a factory worker and storefront preacher who was a hard, cruel man. At age fourteen, Baldwin began preaching at the small Fireside Pentecostal Church in Harlem, and the cadences of black preaching continued to influence his writing style later in his life. His first story appeared in a church newspaper when he was about twelve. He left home at seventeen and lived in Greenwich Village, where he met RICHARD WRIGHT, who encouraged him to continue his writing and helped him win a Eugene Saxton Fellowship. Strained relations with his stepfather, problems over sexual identity, the suicide of a friend, and racial oppression in the United States led Baldwin to move to France when he was nineteen, though he returned to the United States frequently to lecture and teach, and from 1957 on spent half of each year in New York City. His first novel, the partially autobiographical *Go Tell It on the Mountain*, was published in 1953. His second novel, *Giovanni's Room* (1956), dealt with a white American expatriate who must come to terms with his homosexuality, and *Another Country* (1962) explored racial and gay sexual tensions among New York intellectuals. He published several more novels, plays, and essay collections, including *Nobody Knows My Name* (1961) and *The Fire Next Time* (1963).

WEB: Further research this author with LitLinks at bedfordstmartins.com/approachinglit.

CD-ROM: Research this author in depth with cultural documents and multimedia resources on *LiterActive*.

TONI CADE BAMBARA (1939–1995) was born in New York City and grew up in Harlem and Bedford-Stuyvesant. She began writing stories when she was a child and continued writing and taking writing courses in high school and at Queens College, where she majored in Theater Arts and English. Bambara completed her master's degree in American literature while serving as program director at Colony Settlement House in Brooklyn; she then began teaching at City College of New York. She first became known for editing a groundbreaking collection of African American women's writing, *The Black Woman: An An-*thology (1970). She went on to publish four collections of stories, two novels, many screenplays, and a book for children. In addition to being an important figure among the group of African American writers who emerged in the 1960s, Bambara was an activist in the civil rights and women's movements.

WEB: Further research this author with LitLinks at bedfordstmartins.com/approachinglit.

MELISSA BANK (b. 1960) was the winner of the 1993 Nelson Algren Award for short fiction. She has published stories in *Zoetrope*, the *Chicago Tribune, North American Review, Other Voices,* and *Ascent.* Her first book, *The Girl's Guide to Hunting and Fishing* (1999), was a bestseller in the United States and Britain. Her second book, *The Wonder Spot,* was published in 2005. She received an M.F.A. from Cornell University and lives in New York City.

REZA BARAHENI (b. 1935) was born in Tabriz, Iran. He earned his doctorate in literature from the University of Istanbul and in 1963 was appointed professor of English at Tehran University. The author of over fifty books of fiction and poetry, he has been described as "Iran's finest living poet." His best-known works in English are *The Crowned Cannibals* (1977) and *God's Shadow: Prison Poems* (1976), the latter a collection of poems based on a period of 102 days spent in solitary confinement in Iran in 1973, during the time of the shah. Baraheni's work is also well known in France. Three of his novels — *Les saisons en enfer du jeune Ayyaz, Shéhérazade et son romancier,* and *Elias in New York* — have been published in France by Fayard, and two plays — *Enfer* and *Qeskes* — have been performed there, most of them reviewed in *Le Monde, Liberation,* and other French newspapers and periodicals. He was imprisoned in the fall of 1981 and the winter of 1982 by the Islamic Republic of Iran, expelled from the University of Tehran, and deprived of the right to work. He escaped Iran in the fall of 1996 after an attempt on his life and presently makes his home in Canada, where he is a professor of comparative literature at the University of Toronto's Centre for Comparative Literature. He was president of PEN Canada (2001–

2003) and is the winner of numerous literary and human-rights awards.

JIM BARNES (b. 1933), born in Oklahoma of Choctaw and Welsh heritage, worked for ten years as a lumberjack. He studied at Southeastern Oklahoma State University and received his M.A. and Ph.D. from the University of Arkansas. He has published many books of poetry, most recently *Visiting Picasso* (2006); several books of translations and criticism; and over 500 poems in more than 100 journals, including *Chicago Review*, *American Scholar*, *Prairie Schooner*, and *Georgia Review*. He is the founding editor of the Chariton Review Press and editor of *Chariton Review*. He taught at Truman State University from 1970 to 2003, then at Brigham Young University, and presently lives in Santa Fe.

WEB: Further research this author with LitLinks at bedfordstmartins.com/approachinglit.

GERALD BARRAX (b. 1933) was born in Atalla, Alabama. He received his B.A. in English from Duquesne University and his M.A. from the University of Pittsburgh. He has published six volumes of poetry including *Leaning against the Sun* (1992), which was nominated for both a Pulitzer Prize and the National Book Award, and *From a Person Sitting in Darkness: New and Selected Poems* (1998). Barrax acknowledges the great influence of music, all music — jazz and blues music, opera, pop, classical — on his work. He has said they are "necessary." Barrax lives in Raleigh, North Carolina, where he is professor of English at North Carolina State University.

LYNDA BARRY (b. 1956) is a critically acclaimed American cartoonist, perhaps best known for her weekly comic *Ernie Pook's Comeek* (see www.marlysmagazine.com). She has published many collections of graphic stories — most recently *The Freddie Stories* (1999), *The Greatest of Marlys* (2000), and *One Hundred Demons!* (2002) — and two graphic novels, *The Good Times Are Killing Me: A Novel* (1988), which was made into a musical play, and *Cruddy: An Illustrated Novel* (2000). She was born in Wisconsin and grew up in Seattle. She now lives near Footville, Wisconsin.

BEI DAO (b. 1949), pseudonym for Zhao Zhenkai, was born in Beijing, China. During the Cultural Revolution, Bei joined the Red Guard movement, expecting a spirit of cooperation between the Chinese Communist Party and the country's intelligentsia, but he soon became disillusioned. He was sent to the countryside, where he became a construction worker. By 1974, he had finished the first draft of his novella *Waves* and began working on poems. Some of his most famous poems were directly inspired by the April Fifth Democracy Movement of 1976, in which thousands peacefully demonstrated in Beijing's Tiananmen Square. Bei Dao's poems were warmly welcomed by young educated readers as underground poems before 1976 and as unofficial poems in 1978–1980, but they provoked strong official disapproval in the 1970s and early 1980s. He was forced into exile following the Tiananmen Square Massacre in 1989, and since then readers in mainland China have had very limited access to his work. He has published several books of poetry and is the editor-in-chief of an underground literary magazine, *Jintian* (*Today*), an important outlet for contemporary Chinese writing. He is currently the Mackey Poet in Residence at Beloit College in Wisconsin, where he held the Lois Wilson Mackey '45 Distinguished Professorship of Creative Writing in 2000–2001.

ELIZABETH BISHOP (1911–1979), born in Worcester, Massachusetts, was raised in Nova Scotia by her grandparents after her father died and her mother was committed to an asylum. She attended Vassar College, intending to study medicine, but was encouraged by MARIANNE MOORE to be a poet. From 1935 to 1937 she traveled in France, Spain, northern Africa, Ireland, and Italy and then settled in Key West, Florida, for four years,

The first appointment of a Consultant in Poetry at the Library of Congress was made in 1937. The title was changed to Poet Laureate Consultant in Poetry in 1986. Appointments are made for one year, beginning in September, and sometimes have been renewed for a second year.

after which she lived in Rio de Janeiro for almost twenty years. She wrote slowly and carefully and produced a small body of poetry (totaling only around one hundred poems), technically sophisticated, formally varied, witty and thoughtful, revealing in precise, true-to-life images her impressions of the physical world. She served as Consultant in Poetry at the Library of Congress from 1949 to 1950.

WEB: Further research this author with LitLinks at bedfordstmartins.com/approachinglit.

CD-ROM: Research this author in depth with cultural documents and multimedia resources on *LiterActive.*

WILLIAM BLAKE (1757–1827) was born and lived in London. His only formal schooling was in art — he studied for a year at the Royal Academy and was apprenticed to an engraver. He worked as a professional engraver, doing commissions and illustrations, assisted by his wife, Catherine Boucher. Blake started writing poetry at the age of eleven and later engraved and hand-printed his own poems, in very small batches, with his own hand-colored illustrations. His early work showed a strong social conscience, and his later work turned increasingly mythic and prophetic.

WEB: Further research this author with LitLinks at bedfordstmartins.com/approachinglit.

CD-ROM: Research this author in depth with cultural documents and multimedia resources on *LiterActive.*

PETER BLUE CLOUD (b. 1935), born in Quebec, is a Turtle Mohawk and former ironworker. In addition to editing such publications as the *Alcatraz Newsletter, Akwesasne Notes,* and *Coyote's Journal,* he has published several volumes of poetry, including *White Corn Sister* (1979) and *Clans of Many Nations: Selected Poems, 1969-1994* (1995). His visionary poems often draw on native storytelling traditions, native dance structures, and native chant and drumming. One can experience in his poems the influence of these as well as the impact of industrial values on native ways of life.

ROBERT BLY (b. 1926) was born in Madison, Minnesota, and served in the navy during World War II. He studied at St. Olaf's College for a year before going to Harvard. He lived in New York for a few years, then earned an M.A. from the University of Iowa Writers' Workshop. He received a Fulbright grant in 1956 to travel to Norway and began to translate Norwegian poetry into English. In 1966, he founded (with David Ray) American Writers against the Vietnam War. He has published more than thirty books of poetry, many books of translations, and a number of nonfiction books and edited numerous poetry anthologies. A best-selling author, he is also a challenging critic of contemporary consumerist culture (his controversial 1990 bestseller *Iron John* was a key book in the "men's movement"). "Driving to Town Late to Mail a Letter" is an example of his ability to discover a moment of epiphany in the most common of situations. He now lives on a farm near the small town of Moose Lake, Minnesota.

WEB: Further research this author with LitLinks at bedfordstmartins.com/approachinglit.

EAVAN BOLAND (b. 1944) was born in Dublin and was educated there and in London and New York. She has taught at Trinity College and University College, Bowdoin College, and the University of Iowa. She is currently Melvin and Bill Lane Professor in the Humanities at Stanford University. An influential figure in Irish poetry, Boland has published a dozen volumes of poetry, including *The Journey and Other Poems* (1987), *Night Feed* (1994), *The Lost Land* (1998), *Code* (2001), and *New Collected Poems* (2005), and has edited several other books including *Three Irish Poets: An Anthology* (2003) and *Irish Writers on Writing* (2007). Her poems and essays have appeared in magazines such as the *New Yorker, Atlantic, Kenyon Review,* and *American Poetry Review.* She is a regular reviewer for the *Irish Times.*

WEB: Further research this author with LitLinks at bedfordstmartins.com/approachinglit.

JORGE LUIS BORGES (1899–1986) was born in Buenos Aires. In 1914, his parents moved to Geneva, where he learned French and German and received his B.A. from the Collège of Geneva. After World War I, the family lived in Spain, where Borges became a member of an avant-garde literary group and published his first poem, "Hymn to the Sea," in the style of WALT WHITMAN. In 1921, he settled in Buenos Aires and started his career as a writer, publishing his first collection of poetry, *Fervor de Buenos Aires*, in 1923. From 1937 to 1946, he held a job at a branch of the Buenos Aires Municipal Library. His fellow employees forbade him from cataloging more than 100 books per day, a task which would take him about one hour. The rest of his time he spent in the basement of the library, writing articles and short stories. From 1955 until 1973, he was director of the National Library in Buenos Aires, during which time his eyesight steadily deteriorated until, by 1970, he was almost completely blind. He also was a professor of literature at the University of Buenos Aires, teaching there from 1955 to 1970. He was a prolific writer — of short stories, poetry, essays, screenplays, literary criticism, prologues, translations, and reviews — and he edited numerous anthologies. Although he achieved international fame as a literary figure and was nominated for the Nobel Prize, he never received the distinction of becoming a Nobel laureate.

LAURE-ANNE BOSSELAAR (b. 1943) was born and grew up in Belgium. She is fluent in four languages and has published her work in both English and French. She has worked as a talk-show hostess, commentator, and narrator for Belgian and Luxembourg radio and television. In 1986, she moved to the United States. She has published three collections of poetry: *The Hour between Dog and Wolf* (1997), *Small Gods of Grief* (2001, winner of the Isabella Gardner Award), and *A New Hunger* (2007). Working with her husband, poet Kurt Brown, she has also edited four anthologies. Her translations of the Dutch poet Herman de Conick have been published in the Field Translation Series. She has recently been working on translating American poetry into French and Flemish poetry into English. She is on the faculty of Sarah Lawrence College and the MFA in Creative Writing Program of Pine Manor College.

ANNE BRADSTREET (c. 1612–1672), born in Northampton, England, was educated by tutors, reading chiefly in religious writings and the Bible. In 1628, she married Simon Bradstreet, a brilliant young Puritan educated at Cambridge. They were among the earliest settlers of the Massachusetts Bay Colony, in 1630, and her father and husband were leading figures in its governance. She wrote regularly in both prose and verse throughout her busy and difficult years in Massachusetts.

WEB: Further research this author with LitLinks at bedfordstmartins.com/approachinglit.

GWENDOLYN BROOKS (1917–2000), born in Topeka, Kansas, was raised in Chicago and wrote her first poems at age seven. She began studying poetry at the Southside Community Art Center. Her second collection of poems, *Annie Allen* (1949), earned the first Pulitzer Prize given to an African American poet. She served as Consultant in Poetry at the Library of Congress from 1985 to 1986 and worked in community programs and poetry workshops in Chicago to encourage young African American writers.

WEB: Further research this author with LitLinks at bedfordstmartins.com/approachinglit.

CD-ROM: Research this author in depth with cultural documents and multimedia resources on *LiterActive*.

STERLING A. BROWN (1901–1989) was born in Washington, D.C., and educated at Dunbar High School, Williams College, and Harvard University. He taught for more than fifty years at Howard University. Like many other black poets of the period, he expressed his concerns about race in America. His first book of poems, *Southern Road* (1932), was well received by critics, and Brown became part of the artistic tradition of the Harlem Renaissance. Brown was deeply interested in African American music and dialect. He became one of the great innovators in developing poetry related to jazz. His work is known for its frank, unsentimental portraits of black people and their experiences and its successful incorporation of African American folklore and contemporary idiom.

WEB: Further research this author with LitLinks at bedfordstmartins.com/approachinglit.

ELIZABETH BARRETT BROWNING (1806–1861) was born in Durham, England, and studied with her brother's tutor. Her first book of poetry was published when she was thirteen, and she soon became the most famous female poet to that point in English history. A riding accident at the age of sixteen left her a semi-invalid in the house of her possessive father, who had forbidden any of his eleven children to marry. She and ROBERT BROWNING were forced to elope (she was thirty-nine at the time); they lived in Florence, Italy, where she died fifteen years later. Her best-known book of poems was *Sonnets from the Portugese*, a sequence of forty-four sonnets recording the growth of her love for Robert.

WEB: Further research this author with LitLinks at bedfordstmartins.com/approachinglit.

ROBERT BROWNING (1812–1889) was the son of a bank clerk in Camberwell, then a suburb of London. As an aspiring poet in 1844, he admired ELIZABETH BARRETT's poetry and began a correspondence with her that led to one of the world's most famous romances. Their courtship lasted until 1846 when they were secretly wed and ran off to Italy, where they lived until Elizabeth's death in 1861. The years in Florence were among the happiest for both of them. To her he dedicated *Men and Women*, which contains his best poetry. Although she was the more popular poet during her lifetime, his reputation grew upon his return to London after her death, assisted somewhat by public sympathy for him. The late 1860s were the peak of his career: He and ALFRED, LORD TENNYSON were mentioned together as the foremost poets of the age. His fame and influence continued to grow through the remainder of his life until his death in 1889.

WEB: Further research this author with LitLinks at bedfordstmartins.com/approachinglit.

CD-ROM: Research this author in depth with cultural documents and multimedia resources on *LiterActive*.

DENNIS BRUTUS (b. 1924) was born in Zimbabwe of South African parents. He attended the University of Witwaterstand and taught for fourteen years in South African high schools, but was banned from teaching (and his university law studies) because of his leadership in the campaign to exclude South Africa from the Olympic Games as long as the country practiced apartheid in sports. He was arrested and sentenced to eighteen months of hard labor. His *Letters to Martha* (1968) are poems about his experiences as a prisoner on Robben Island. After leaving South Africa in 1966 with a Rhodesian passport, Brutus made his home in England, then moved to the United States, where he taught at the University of Denver, Northwestern University, and the University of Pittsburgh. In 1983, after engaging in a protracted legal struggle and appearing on ABC's *Nightline* with Ted Koppel, he won the right to stay in the United States as a political refugee. He is author of twelve books of poetry and is a professor emeritus in the Department of African Studies at the University of Pittsburgh.

CHARLES BUKOWSKI (1920–1994), born in Andernach, Germany, came to the United States at age three and grew up in poverty in Los Angeles, drifted extensively, and for much of his life made his home in San Pedro, working for many years in the U.S. Postal Service. He was familiar with the people of the streets, skid row residents, hustlers, and a transient lifestyle. He began writing in childhood and published his first story at age twenty-four and his first poetry when he was thirty-five. He published many books of poetry, in addition to novels and short stories reminiscent of ERNEST HEMINGWAY. He is very popular in Europe. His style, which exhibits a strong sense of immediacy and a refusal to embrace standard formal structures, was influenced by the Beat movement.

WEB: Further research this author with LitLinks at bedfordstmartins.com/approachinglit.

JULIA DE BURGOS (1917–1953), the best known female poet in Puerto Rico and one of the best of Latino America, was born in Carolina, Puerto Rico. She graduated from the University of Puerto Rico as a teacher. She also studied and worked as a journalist in Havana, Cuba. Later she moved to New York where she lived for most of the rest of her life. Her first book of poems was published when she was nineteen. She published several books of poetry and received many literary honors before and after her death.

ANTHONY BUTTS (b. 1969) was born and raised in Detroit, Michigan, and received a

B.A. from Wayne State University, an M.F.A. from Western Michigan University, and a Ph.D. from the University of Missouri. He is author of three collections of poetry: *Fifth Season* (1997), *Little Low Heaven* (2003, winner of the 2004 William Carlos Williams Award from the Poetry Society of America), and *Male Hysteria* (2007). His work has appeared in at least thirty different journals as well as in ten anthologies. Butts teaches at Carnegie-Mellon University.

RAYMOND CARVER (1938–1988) was born and grew up in Oregon. He decided he wanted to become a writer because he liked stories about hunting and fishing. He began to learn the craft of fiction in a creative writing course taught by novelist John Gardner at Chico State College in California. He earned his B.A. from Humboldt State College in California and attended the University of Iowa Writers' Workshop. Because Carver had married young and had a wife and children and little money, earning a living had to take precedence over writing and so his writing career progressed slowly. He kept at it, however, and eventually published a dozen collections of stories and books of poetry before his death from lung cancer at age fifty. He revised many of the stories in his first book, *Will You Please Be Quiet, Please?* (1976), as he moved into his much acclaimed and imitated hard-edged and minimalist style evident in the collection *What We Talk about When We Talk about Love* (1981).

WEB: Further research this author with LitLinks at bedfordstmartins.com/approachinglit.

CD-ROM: Research this author in depth with cultural documents and multimedia resources on *LiterActive*.

ANA CASTILLO (b. 1953) is a poet/novelist/artist who also writes essays and columns for magazines and newspapers throughout the country. She has published five novels, including *The Mixquiahuala Letters* (1986, winner of the American Book Award from the Before Columbus Foundation); a collection of short stories; a children's book; six collections of poetry; and the nonfiction Chicana Feminist work *Massacre of the Dreamers: Essays on Xicanista* (1994). Other awards include a Carl Sandburg Award, a Mountains

and Plains Booksellers Award, and fellowships from the National Endowment for the Arts in fiction and poetry. She was also awarded a 1998 Sor Juana Achievement Award by the Mexican Fine Arts Center Museum in Chicago. She has presented her work in Turkey, Jordan, and Egypt and throughout Europe and the Caribbean. Born in Chicago, she lives there now and teaches at DePaul University.

SANDRA M. CASTILLO (b. 1962) spent the first eight years of her life in Havana, Cuba, where she was born. During the Johnson administration's "Freedom Flights," she and her family were among the last Cubans to leave the island. She received her B.A. and M.A. degrees from Florida State University. She has published two collections of poetry, *Red Letters* (1991) and *My Father Sings, to My Embarrassment* (2002). Her work has appeared in numerous anthologies including *A Century of Cuban Writers in Florida* (1996) and *Cool Salsa: Bilingual Poems on Growing Up Latino in the United States* (1994). One can see in her poems the constant tension of dual identity. As she writes in her poem "Exile," "As we go door to door along East 4th Avenue / a street we are not supposed to be on / . . . thinking we are who we want to be." She is a professor at Miami-Dade College.

ROSEMARY CATACALOS (b. 1944), of Mexican and Greek descent, grew up in San Antonio, Texas. She is the author of two books of poetry: a hand-sewn, fine-letterpress chapbook, *As Long As It Takes* (1984), and a full-length collection, *Again for the First Time* (1984), which won the 1985 Texas Institute of Letters poetry prize. From fall 1989 to spring 1991 she was a Wallace Stegner Creative Writing Fellow in Poetry at Stanford University, where she received the Patricia Smith Poetry Prize.

LORNA DEE CERVANTES (b. 1954) was born in San Francisco and grew up in San Jose. There she studied at San Jose City College and San Jose State University. She is the author of two volumes of poetry, *Emplumada* (1981), which won an American Book Award, and *From the Cables of Genocide: Poems on Love and Hunger* (Arte Público Press, 1991). She is also coeditor of *Red Dirt*, a cross-cultural poetry journal, and her work has been included in many anthologies. Cervantes, who considers herself "a Chicana writer, a feminist writer, a political writer," lives in Colorado and is a professor at the University of Colorado at Boulder.

WEB: Further research this author with LitLinks at bedfordstmartins.com/approachinglit.

TINA CHANG (b. 1969) received her B.A. from the State University of New York–Binghamton and her M.F.A. from Columbia University. She is the author of *Half-Lit Houses* (2004), a finalist for the 2005 Asian American Literary Award. Her poems have appeared in many literary journals and have been anthologized in such volumes as *Identity Lessons, Asian American Literature,* and *Asian-American Poetry: The Next Generation.* She has been awarded numerous residencies and fellowships. She teaches poetry at Sarah Lawrence College and Hunter College.

MARILYN CHIN (b. 1955) is a first-generation Chinese American, born in Hong Kong and raised in Portland, Oregon. She is the author of three volumes of poetry: *Dwarf Bamboo* (1987), *The Phoenix Gone, The Terrace Empty* (1994), and *Rhapsody in Plain Yellow* (2002). She also is a coeditor of *Dissident Song: A Contemporary Asian American Anthology* (1991) and has translated poems by the modern Chinese poet Ai Qing and cotranslated poems by the Japanese poet Gozo Yoshimasu. She has received numerous awards for her poetry, including a Stegner Fellowship, the PEN/Josephine Miles Award, and four Pushcart Prizes. She is codirector of the M.F.A. program at San Diego State University.

WEB: Further research this author with LitLinks at bedfordstmartins.com/approachinglit.

KATE CHOPIN (1851–1904) was born Katherine O'Flaherty in St. Louis. Her father, an Irish immigrant and a very successful businessman, died when she was four. Her mother was of a prominent French Creole family. Chopin received an excellent education at the Academy of the Sacred Heart and from her mother and grandmother and on graduation was known as a brilliant storyteller, a youthful cynic, and an accomplished pianist. At age nineteen she married Oscar

Chopin and had six children. They lived in the Creole community of Natchitoches Parish, Louisiana, until his death in 1882, when she moved back to St. Louis. After her mother died a year later, friends encouraged her to write as a way to deal with her grief and anger, and in doing so she turned to Creole country for her subjects and themes. She became both a nationally acclaimed and popular author. Her masterpiece, *The Awakening* (1899), a lyrical study of a young woman whose deep personal discontents lead to adultery and suicide, was praised for its craft but criticized for its content and created a scandal. Chopin, always sensitive to her critics and declining in health, wrote little after it.

WEB: Further research this author with LitLinks at bedfordstmartins.com/approachinglit.

CD-ROM: Research this author in depth with cultural documents and multimedia resources on *LiterActive.*

SANDRA CISNEROS (b. 1954) was born in Chicago to a Mexican father and Chicana mother. She grew up in ghetto neighborhoods of Chicago, moving frequently and thus never feeling settled. She spoke English at school and Spanish at home and on many trips to Mexico to visit her grandmother. She wrote poetry in high school and was editor of the school literary magazine and went on to earn a B.A. from Loyola University and an M.F.A. from the University of Iowa Writers' Workshop. She discovered her literary voice in a graduate seminar, when she experimented with writing about growing up as a poor Latina in Chicago. She has published a novel, three books of poetry, two books of stories, and a bilingual children's book. She was awarded a MacArthur Foundation Fellowship in 1995. Cisneros has taught at various colleges and universities, including the University of California, University of Michigan, and the University of New Mexico. She now lives in San Antonio, Texas.

WEB: Further research this author with LitLinks at bedfordstmartins.com/approachinglit.

CD-ROM: Research this author in depth with cultural documents and multimedia resources on *LiterActive.*

LUCILLE CLIFTON (b. 1936) was born in Depew, New York, and studied at Howard University. She has published many books of poetry, including *Blessing the Boats: New and Selected Poems 1988-2000* (2000), which won the National Book Award. She has also published a memoir and more than twenty books for children. She has taught at several colleges and worked in the Office of Education in Washington, D.C. She has served as poet laureate for the State of Maryland and is currently Distinguished Professor of Humanities at St. Mary's College of Maryland. Her poems typically reflect her ethnic pride, womanist principles, and race and gender consciousness.

WEB: Further research this author with LitLinks at bedfordstmartins.com/approachinglit.

JUDITH ORTIZ COFER (b. 1952) was born in Hormigueros, Puerto Rico. Her family moved to Paterson, New Jersey, in 1955. For the next decade, whenever her father, who was in the U.S. Navy, went on a lengthy sea tour, he sent his family to Puerto Rico because he regarded Paterson unsafe for a woman and children to be alone. As a result, Cofer grew up moving between two very different worlds. Her works draw much of their power and vision from that bifurcation, from a search for stability and a sense of belonging in very different places. The family moved to Augusta, Georgia, while she was in high school. She graduated from Augusta College, married and had a daughter, completed a graduate degree, and began teaching English. But, she says, something was missing from her life: She realized that she needed to write. Her first book of poetry, *Reaching for the Mainland* (1987), was followed by several others including, most recently, *A Love Story Beginning in Spanish: Poems* (2006). She has also published novels for adults and young people, a memoir — *Silent Dancing: A Partial Remembrance of a Puerto Rican Childhood* (1990), and a book about writing, *Woman in Front of the Sun: On Becoming a Writer* (2000). Her young-adult book *An Island Like You: Stories of the Barrio* (1996) was awarded the American Library Association Reforma Pura Belpre Medal and the Fanfare Best Book of the Year award; two other young-adult books received Americas

Award recognition, for U.S. titles that authentically and engagingly portray Latin America, the Caribbean, or Latinos in the United States — *The Meaning of Consuelo* winning the award in 2003 and *Call Me Maria* gaining Honorable Mention in 2004. She is Regents' and Franklin Professor of English and Creative Writing at the University of Georgia and lives with her husband on the family farm near Louisville, Georgia.

SAMUEL TAYLOR COLERIDGE (1772–1834) was born in Devonshire and sent to school in London after his father's death. He went to Jesus College, Cambridge, in 1791, and dropped out twice without a degree. In 1798 Coleridge and WILLIAM WORDSWORTH published *Lyrical Ballads*, which initiated the Romantic movement in English poetry and established both of their reputations. After 1802, Coleridge became addicted to opium, used as a treatment for physical discomfort and seizures. He and his wife were separated, his friendship with Wordsworth broke up, and his poetic output stopped. From 1816 to his death he lived under constant medical supervision but still managed to publish a journal and write several plays, pieces of criticism, and philosophical and religious treatises.

WEB: Further research this author with LitLinks at bedfordstmartins.com/approachinglit.

BILLY COLLINS (b. 1941), born and raised in New York City, is the author of several collections of poems. Perhaps no poet since ROBERT FROST has managed to combine high critical acclaim with such broad popular appeal. The typical Collins poem opens on a clear and hospitable note but soon takes an unexpected turn; poems that begin in irony may end in a moment of lyric surprise. Collins sees his poetry as "a form of travel writing" and considers humor "a door into the serious." Collins, the author of numerous books of poetry, most recently *The Trouble with Poetry* (2005), is Distinguished Professor of Literature at Lehman College of the City University of New York and a writer-in-residence at Sarah Lawrence College. He served as Poet Laureate Consultant in Poetry at the Library of Congress from 2001 to 2003.

WEB: Further research this author with LitLinks at bedfordstmartins.com/approachinglit.

JAYNE CORTEZ (b. 1936) was born in Arizona, grew up in the Watts section of Los Angeles, and now lives in New York City. A poet and performance artist, she has published several collections of poetry and made a number of recordings, often performing her poetry with her jazz group the Firespitters. Her poems have been translated into twenty-eight languages. In 1964 she founded the Watts Repertory Company, and in 1972 she formed her own publishing company, Bola Press.

WEB: Further research this author with LitLinks at bedfordstmartins.com/approachinglit.

CUSI CRAM (b. 1967) is of Bolivian and Scottish descent. Her plays include *Landlocked* (1998), *The End of It All* (2000), *Lucy and the Conquest* (2001), *Twenty Shadows* (2003), and *Fuente* (2003), in addition to numerous short plays and adaptations. She received a fellowship and residency from the Lila Acheson Wallace American Playwrights Program at Juilliard; the Le Comte du Nouy Prize; a fellowship from the Camargo Foundation in Cassis, France; the 2004 Herrick New Play Prize; and two daytime Emmy nominations for her work on the children's animated program *Arthur*. A graduate of Brown University, she lives in Greenwich Village.

VICTOR HERNÁNDEZ CRUZ (b. 1949) was born in Aguas Buenas, Puerto Rico, and moved to New York City with his family at the age of five. His first book of poetry, *Papa Got His Gun, and Other Poems* (1966), was published when he was seventeen. Since then he has published numerous other collections, most recently *The Mountain in the Sea* (2006). In 1971 Cruz visited Puerto Rico and reconnected with his ancestral heritage; eighteen years later, he returned to Puerto Rico to live. He now divides his time between Puerto Rico and New York. Much of his work explores the relation between the English language and his native Spanish, playing with grammatical and syntactical conventions within both languages to create his own bilingual idiom.

WEB: Further research this author with LitLinks at bedfordstmartins.com/approachinglit.

COUNTEE CULLEN (1903–1946) was born in either Louisville, Kentucky, Baltimore, Maryland, or (as he himself claimed) New York City. He was adopted by the Reverend Frederick A. Cullen and his wife and grew up, as he put it, "in the conservative atmosphere of a Methodist parsonage." He studied at New York University and Harvard University. A forerunner of the Harlem Renaissance movement, he was in the 1920s the most popular black literary figure in America. From the 1930s until his death, he wrote less and worked as a junior high French teacher. For many years after his death, his reputation was eclipsed by that of other Harlem Renaissance writers, particularly LANGSTON HUGHES and ZORA NEALE HURSTON; recently, however, there has been a resurgence of interest in his life and work.

WEB: Further research this author with LitLinks at bedfordstmartins.com/approachinglit.

E. E. CUMMINGS (1894–1962) was born in Cambridge, Massachusetts, where his father was a Unitarian minister and a sociology lecturer at Harvard University. He graduated from Harvard and then served as an ambulance driver during World War I. *The Enormous Room* (1922) is an account of his confinement in a French prison camp during the war. After the war, he lived in rural Connecticut and Greenwich Village, with frequent visits to Paris. In his work, Cummings experimented radically with form, punctuation, spelling, and syntax, abandoning traditional techniques and structures to create a new, highly idiosyncratic means of poetic expression. At the time of his death, he was the second most widely read poet in the United States, after ROBERT FROST.

WEB: Further research this author with LitLinks at bedfordstmartins.com/approachinglit.

CD-ROM: Research this author in depth with cultural documents and multimedia resources on *LiterActive*.

DAO, BEI — See **BEI DAO**.

KEKI N. DARUWALLA (b. 1937) was born in Lahore, now in Pakistan, and educated in Ludhiana, India; he has a master's degree in English literature. He served an illustrious career in the Indian Police Service, rising to become a Special Assistant to the Prime Minister on International Affairs. He subsequently was in the Cabinet Secretariat until his retirement. He is the author of a dozen books of poems and short stories and the editor of *Two Decades of Indian Poetry* (1980). His collection of poems, *The Keeper of the Dead* (1982), received the Sahitya Akademi Award (Indian Academy of Letters) in 1984. He currently lives in Delhi.

TOI DERRICOTTE (b. 1941) was born and raised in Detroit, where she earned a B.A. in special education from Wayne State University. She is the author of several collections of poetry as well as a memoir, *The Black Notebooks* (1997). With poet **CORNELIUS EADY**, she cofounded Cave Canem, which offers workshops and retreats for African American poets. Among many honors she has received is the Distinguished Pioneering of the Arts Award from the United Black Artists. Derricotte teaches creative writing at the University of Pittsburgh.

WEB: Further research this author with LitLinks at bedfordstmartins.com/approachinglit.

EMILY DICKINSON (1830–1886) was born in Amherst, Massachusetts, and lived there her entire life, rarely leaving. She briefly attended a women's seminary but became homesick and left before a year was out. Dickinson never married and became reclusive later in life, forgoing even the village routines and revelries she enjoyed. She published very few of the more than seventeen hundred poems she wrote; most were written for herself or for inclusion in her many letters. Not until 1955 was there a complete edition of her poems that attempted to present them as originally written.

WEB: Further research this author with LitLinks at bedfordstmartins.com/approachinglit.

CD-ROM: Research this author in depth with cultural documents and multimedia resources on *LiterActive*.

ANA DOINA (b. 1955) was born in Bucharest, Romania, when the country was under Communist rule. After she graduated from the University of Bucharest with an M.A. in phi-

losophy and history, she taught high school and adult education. Due to increasing political pressures and social restrictions, she and her husband left Romania in 1983. She is now a U.S. citizen and lives in New Jersey with her husband and two children. In Romania, some of her poems were published in the national literary magazines *Romania Literara*, *Muguri*, and *Sapatmina*. In the United States, her poems have appeared in small press publications including *The Rift*, *El Locofoco*, *Icarus*, and *Timber Creek Review*.

WEB: Further research this author with LitLinks at bedfordstmartins.com/approachinglit.

JOHN DONNE (1572–1631) was born in London to a prosperous Catholic family (he was related to Sir Thomas More and the playwright John Heywood). Donne studied at Oxford University for several years but did not take a degree. He fought with **SIR WALTER RALEGH** in two naval strikes against Spain. In 1601, Donne's promising political career was permanently derailed by his precipitous marriage to Anne More without her father's consent. He was briefly imprisoned, lost a very promising position with Sir Thomas Egerton, and spent years seeking further political employment before finally being convinced by King James in 1615 to take holy orders as priest of the Church of England. His life was described by Isaac Walton later in the century as being divided into two parts. In Phase I he was "Jack Donne" of Lincoln's Inn: When young, Donne employed a sophisticated urban wit in his earlier love poetry, like that of "A Valediction: Forbidding Mourning." In Phase II he was John Donne, dean of St. Paul's: After Donne took his vows in 1615, his poetry became markedly less amorous and more religious in tone. His *Holy Sonnets* (of which "Death, be not proud" [p. 773] is one) are as dense and complex as his earlier work, with his talent now directed toward exploration of his relationship with God.

WEB: Further research this author with LitLinks at bedfordstmartins.com/approachinglit.

MARK DOTY (b. 1953) is the author of seven collections of poetry and three memoirs— *Heaven's Coast* (1996), about the loss of his partner, Wally Roberts, *Firebird* (1999), a gay coming-of-age story and a chronicle of a gradual process of finding in art a place of personal belonging, and *Dog Years* (2007), about the relationships between humans and the dogs they love. He has taught at Brandeis University, Sarah Lawrence College, Vermont College, and the University of Iowa Writers' Workshop. He now lives in New York City and Houston, Texas, where he teaches at the University of Houston.

WEB: Further research this author with LitLinks at bedfordstmartins.com/approachinglit.

RITA DOVE (b. 1952) was born in Akron, Ohio. Her father was the first research chemist to break the race barrier in the tire industry. She graduated from Miami University in Oxford, Ohio, with a degree in English; after a year at Tübingen University in Germany on a Fulbright fellowship, she joined the University of Iowa Writers' Workshop, where she earned her M.F.A. in 1977. She has taught at Tuskegee Institute and Arizona State University and now is on the faculty of the University of Virginia. She was appointed Poet Laureate Consultant in Poetry at the Library of Congress in 1993, making her the youngest person to receive the highest official honor in American letters. She is the author of numerous collections of poetry, including *Thomas and Beulah* (1986), a book-length sequence loosely based on the lives of her grandparents, which was awarded the Pulitzer Prize in 1987. "The Satisfaction Coal Company" (p. 699) is from that book ("he" is Thomas; "they" are Thomas and Beulah); the poem reflects Dove's concern for those living workaday lives and is her celebration of their worth and dignity.

WEB: Further research this author with LitLinks at bedfordstmartins.com/approachinglit.

PAUL LAURENCE DUNBAR (1872–1906) was the first African American to gain national eminence as a poet. Born and raised in Dayton, Ohio, he was the son of ex-slaves. He was an outstanding student: The only African American in his class, he was both class president and class poet. Although he lived to be only thirty-three years old, Dunbar was prolific, writing short stories, novels, librettos, plays, songs, and essays as well as the poetry for which he became well known. He was popular with both black and white readers of his day. His style encompasses two distinct voices — the standard English of the classical poet and the evocative dialect of the turn-of-the-century black community in America.

WEB: Further research this author with LitLinks at bedfordstmartins.com/approachinglit.

CORNELIUS EADY (b. 1954) was born and raised in Rochester, New York, and attended Monroe Community College and Empire State College. He began writing as a teenager. His poems are his biography, their subjects ranging from blues musicians to the witnessing of his father's death. He has published six volumes of poetry. With poet TOI DERRICOTTE, he co-founded Cave Canem, which offers workshops and retreats for African American poets, and with composer Diedre Murray he has collaborated on two highly acclaimed music dramas. Formerly the director of the Poetry Center at the State University of New York, Stony Brook, he is currently associate professor of English and director of the Creative Writing Program at the University of Notre Dame.

WEB: Further research this author with LitLinks at bedfordstmartins.com/approachinglit.

T.[HOMAS] S.[TEARNS] ELIOT (1888–1965) was born and raised in St. Louis. He went to prep school in Massachusetts and then to Harvard University, where he earned an M.A. in philosophy in 1910 and started his doctoral dissertation. He studied at the Sorbonne, Paris, and then at Marburg, Germany, in 1914. The war forced him to Oxford, where he married and abandoned philosophy for poetry. After teaching and working in a bank, he became an editor at Faber and Faber and editor of the journal *Criterion* and was the dominant force in English poetry for several decades. He became a British citizen and a member of the Church of England in 1927. He won the Nobel Prize for Literature in 1948. He also wrote plays, essays, and a series of poems on cats that became the basis of a musical by Andrew Lloyd Weber.

WEB: Further research this author with LitLinks at bedfordstmartins.com/approachinglit.

CD-ROM: Research this author in depth with cultural documents and multimedia resources on *LiterActive*.

RALPH ELLISON (1914–1994) was born in Oklahoma City, where his mother worked as a servant after the death of her husband when Ellison was three. She brought home discarded books and phonograph records from houses where she worked, and from them Ellison developed an interest in literature and music. He studied music at Tuskegee Institute in Alabama and then went to New York, where he met LANGSTON HUGHES and Richard Wright, who encouraged him in his writing. Ellison's literary reputation rests on one novel, *Invisible Man* (1952), which received the National Book Award for fiction and was listed in a Book Week poll in 1965 as the most distinguished American novel of the preceding twenty years. It deals with a young black man moving from the South to the North and learning about how racial prejudice leads to discrimination on the one hand and to being unnoticed and inconsequential on the other. "Battle Royal" (p. 352) is the first chapter of that novel. Ellison also published a scattering of short stories (collected posthumously in *Flying Home and Other Stories* [1986]) and two books of essays. A second novel was incomplete when he died (excerpts from the manuscript were published as *Juneteenth* in 1999).

WEB: Further research this author with LitLinks at bedfordstmartins.com/approachinglit.

CD-ROM: Research this author in depth with cultural documents and multimedia resources on *LiterActive*.

ANITA ENDREZZE (b. 1952), of Yaqui and European ancestry, was born in Long Beach, California, and earned her M.A. from Eastern Washington University. She is a poet, writer, and painter (in watercolor and acrylics) who also works in fiber and creates handmade books. She is a member of Atlatl, a Native American arts service organization. In addition to four volumes of poetry, she has published a children's novel, short stories, and nonfiction. She lives in Spokane, Washington, where she is a storyteller, teacher, and writer.

WEB: Further research this author with LitLinks at bedfordstmartins.com/approachinglit.

LOUISE ERDRICH (b. 1954) was born in Minnesota to a French-Ojibwe mother and a German-born father. She grew up near the Turtle Mountain Reservation in North Dakota and is a member of the Turtle Mountain Band of Chippewa. Her grandfather was tribal chief of the reservation. She was among the first women admitted to Dartmouth College, where she began writing; she also studied at Johns Hopkins University. She has published eleven novels, four children's books, three collections of poetry, and two books of nonfiction. She lives in Minneapolis and is the owner of Birchbark Books, a small independent bookstore.

WEB: Further research this author with LitLinks at bedfordstmartins.com/approachinglit.

CD-ROM: Research this author in depth with cultural documents and multimedia resources on *LiterActive*.

MARTÍN ESPADA (b. 1957) was born in Brooklyn and has an eclectic résumé: radio journalist in Nicaragua, welfare rights paralegal, advocate for mental patients, night desk clerk in a transient hotel, attendant in a primate nursery, groundskeeper at a minor league ballpark, bindery worker in a printing plant, bouncer in a bar, and practicing lawyer in Chelsea, Massachusetts. Author of eight books of poetry, his latest collection is *The Republic of Poetry* (2006). His earlier book, *Alabanza: New and Selected Poems, 1982–2002* (2003), received the Paterson Award for Sustained Literary Achievement and was named an American Library Association Notable Book of the Year. He is an essayist, editor, and translator as well as a poet. He lives in Amherst, Massachusetts, where he is an associate professor of English at the University of Massachusetts-Amherst.

WEB: Further research this author with LitLinks at bedfordstmartins.com/approachinglit.

SANDRA MARÍA ESTEVES (b. 1948) is a "Puerto Rican-Dominican-Boriqueña-Quisquevana-Taino-African American" born and raised in the Bronx. A founder and leading light of one of the twentieth century's most important literary/performance developments, the Nuyorican poetry movement, she was one of the first Puerto Rican-Dominican women to publish a volume of poetry in the United States. She has published six books of poetry, including *Yerba Buena*, which was selected as Best Small Press Collection for 1981 by the

Library Journal. Among her awards and fellowships are the Louis Reyes Rivera Lifetime Achievement Award and the Edgar Allan Poe Literary Award. She lives in New York.

FAIZ AHMED FAIZ (1911–1984) was born in Sialkot in the Punjab, then a part of India under British rule. His father was a prominent lawyer who was interested in literature. Faiz was educated at mission schools in Sialkot in the English language, but he also learned Urdu, Persian, and Arabic. He worked as a teacher in Amritsar and Lahore. When the Islamic republic of Pakistan was established in 1947, Faiz moved to Pakistan with his family. In 1951, he and a number of army officers were accused of planning a coup d'etat. He spent four years in prison under a sentence of death until his release in 1955. He went into exile and wrote poems in Urdu using the diction, and often the meters, of an elaborate classical poetic tradition to address contemporary concerns, including his political condition. His work was widely read in Pakistan and in India from the time of its first publication. He returned to Pakistan in 1982 and died in Lahore two years later. His reputation spread abroad during his lifetime, and in recent years translations by the late AGHA SHAHID ALI and others have generated a following for Faiz in the English-speaking world.

WILLIAM FAULKNER (1897–1962) was born into an old southern family in New Albany, Mississippi. When he was five, his family moved to Oxford, a small city in northern Mississippi that was his home for most of the rest of his life. He attended the University of Mississippi for three semesters, having been admitted as a war veteran although he had not finished high school, and published poems and short stories in the campus newspaper. He continued writing while working at odd jobs for several years in New York and New Orleans and published his first novel, *Soldier's Pay*, in 1926. Success as a novelist came when he began writing about the northern Mississippi area he knew best, creating the mythical Yoknapatawpha County. His discovery that this "little postage stamp of native soil was worth writing about" enabled him to write a series of acclaimed experimental novels, including *The Sound and the Fury* (1920), *As I Lay Dying* (1930), *Light in August* (1932), and *Absalom, Absalom!* (1936), in which he traces the disintegration of the South through several generations. Until the publication of the anthology *The Portable Faulkner* brought him wide recognition in 1946, he supported himself by publishing short stories (nearly a hundred) in magazines and by writing screenplays in Hollywood. In 1949 he received the Nobel Prize for Literature and delivered one of the most influential acceptance speeches ever given at a Nobel ceremony (available online at nobelprize.org/nobel_prizes/literature/laureates/1949/faulkner-speech.html).

WEB: Further research this author with LitLinks at bedfordstmartins.com/approachinglit.

CD-ROM: Research this author in depth with cultural documents and multimedia resources on *LiterActive*.

CAROLYN FORCHÉ (b. 1950) was born in Detroit, attended Michigan State University, and earned an M.F.A. from Bowling Green State University. She achieved immediate success as a writer, winning a Yale Younger Poets Prize in 1976. Her work underwent a remarkable shift following a year spent on a Guggenheim Fellowship in El Salvador, where she worked with human-rights activist Archbishop Oscar Humberto Romero and with Amnesty International. The shock of witnessing countless atrocities in Central America led her to begin writing what she calls "poetry of witness." The volume *The Country between Us* (1981) stirred immediate controversy because of its overtly political topics and themes. "The Colonel" (p. 783), a prose poem in which the speaker conveys a horrific story with chilling flatness, is probably the most disturbing and memorable poem in the book. She is the author of four books of poetry, most recently *Blue Hour* (2004), and the editor of *Against Forgetting: Twentieth-Century Poetry of Witness* (1993). She has also translated several books of poetry. She is currently a faculty member at George Mason University in Virginia.

WEB: Further research this author with LitLinks at bedfordstmartins.com/approachinglit.

VIEVEE FRANCIS (b. 1963) worked for more than twenty years to develop her voice in poetry. She has had work published in many venues, including the *2003 Grolier Prize Annual*, *Callaloo*, *Margie*, and *Crab Orchard Review*. She spent several years doing exhaustive research for her first collection, *Blue-Tail Fly* (2006), a series of persona poems that treat the period of American history between the beginning of the Mexican-American War and the end of the Civil War. Francis gives voice to outsiders, from soldiers and common folk to influential politicians. Francis, who grew up in Detroit and has lived there all her life, teaches independent workshops for young adult writers there.

ROBERT FROST (1874–1963) was born in San Francisco and lived there until he was eleven. When his father died, the family moved to Massachusetts, where Robert did well in school, especially in the classics, but he dropped out of both Dartmouth College and Harvard University. He went unrecognized as a poet until 1913, when he was first published in England, where he had moved with his wife and four children. Upon returning to the United States, he quickly achieved success with more publications and became the most celebrated poet in mid-twentieth-century America. He held a teaching position at Amherst College and received many honorary degrees as well as an invitation to recite a poem at John F. Kennedy's inauguration. Although his work is principally associated with the life and landscape of New England, and though he is a poet of traditional verse forms and metrics, he is also a quintessentially modern poet in his adherence to language as it is actually spoken, in the psychological complexity of his portraits, and in the degree to which his work is infused with layers of ambiguity and irony.

WEB: Further research this author with LitLinks at bedfordstmartins.com/approachinglit.

CD-ROM: Research this author in depth with cultural documents and multimedia resources on *LiterActive*.

GANG, XU — See **XU GANG**.

RICHARD GARCIA (b. 1941) was born in San Francisco, a first-generation American (his mother was from Mexico, his father from Puerto Rico). While still in high school, he had a poem published by City Lights in a Beat anthology. After publishing his first collection in 1972, however, he did not write poetry again for twelve years, until an unsolicited letter of encouragement from OCTAVIO PAZ inspired him to resume. Since then, his work has appeared widely in literary magazines as well as three later books, *The Flying Garcias* (1991), *Rancho Notorious* (2001), and *The Persistence of Objects* (2006). He is also the author of a bilingual children's book, *My Aunt Otilia's Spirits* (1987). For twelve years he was the poet-in-residence at Children's Hospital Los Angeles, where he conducted poetry and art workshops for hospitalized children. He teaches creative writing in the Antioch University Los Angeles M.F.A. program and the Idyllwild Summer Poetry Program.

WEB: Further research this author with LitLinks at bedfordstmartins.com/approachinglit.

GABRIEL GARCÍA MÁRQUEZ (b. 1928) was born in the small town of Aracataca, situated in a tropical region of northern Colombia between the mountains and the Caribbean Sea, and he grew up there with his maternal grandparents. He studied law and then journalism at the National University of Colombia in Bogota and at the University of Cartagena. In 1954, he was sent to Rome on an assignment for his newspaper. Since then he has mostly lived abroad, in Paris, New York, Barcelona, and Mexico. He published his first book of short stories in 1955. His most famous work, the novel *One Hundred Years of Solitude*, was published in 1967. His fiction is characterized by magic realism, which, as he put it, "expands the categories of the real so as to encompass myth, magic and other extraordinary phenomena in Nature or experience" excluded by European realistic fiction. Besides his large output of fiction, he has written screenplays, a memoir, and has continued to work as a journalist. In 1982, he received the Nobel Prize for Literature. His most recent book is *Living to Tell the Tale* (2003), the first volume of a projected three-part memoir.

WEB: Further research this author with LitLinks at bedfordstmartins.com/approachinglit.

DAGOBERTO GILB (b. 1950) was born and grew up in Los Angeles, raised by a Chicana mother who divorced his German father soon after Dagoberto was born. He attended the University of California, where he majored in philosophy and religion, after which he moved to El Paso and spent sixteen years making a living as a construction worker, twelve of them as a journeyman, high-rise carpenter. During this time, he began writing stories, several of which were published in a variety of journals. His collection of stories *The Magic of Blood* (1993) won the 1994 PEN/Hemingway Award, and his novel *The Last Known Residence of Mickey Acuña* (1994) was named a Notable Book of the Year by the *New York Times Book Review*. His most recent books are a collection of stories, *Woodcuts of Women* (2001), and a collection of essays, *Gritos: Essays* (2003). He currently lives in Austin where he teaches creative writing at Texas State University, San Marcos.

CHRISTOPHER GILBERT (b. 1949) was born in Birmingham, Alabama, and grew up in Lansing, Michigan. He earned his B.A. at the University of Michigan and his M.A. and Ph.D. at Clark University. He is trained in clinical and cognitive psychology and has practiced psychotherapy; has been a psychologist with the Worcester Youth Guidance Center, the Cambridge Family, and the Children's Service in the Boston area; and is a psychology professor. This work, his concern for the impact of depravation on young people, and the influence of jazz and the blues, all contribute to the explorations in his poetry. His first book, *Across the Mutual Landscape*, was selected for the 1983 Walt Whitman Award from the Academy of American Poets. His poems have also appeared in numerous anthologies and poetry journals.

ALLEN GINSBERG (1926–1997) was born in Newark, New Jersey, and graduated from Columbia University, after several suspensions, in 1948. Several years later, Ginsberg left for San Francisco to join other poets of the Beat movement. His poem "Howl," the most famous poem of the movement, was published in 1956 by Lawrence Ferlinghetti's City Lights Books; the publicity of the ensuing censorship trial brought the Beats to national attention. Ginsberg was cofounder with Anne Waldman of the Jack Kerouac School of Disembodied Poetics at the Naropa Institute in Boulder, Colorado. In his later years, he became a distinguished professor at Brooklyn College.

NIKKI GIOVANNI (b. 1943) was born in Knoxville, Tennessee, and returned there after spending her childhood years in Cincinnati. After receiving her B.A. from Fisk University, she organized the Black Arts Festival in Cincinnati and then entered graduate school at the University of Pennsylvania. She has received wide popular acclaim as a writer—having published numerous collections of poetry, including several for children—and as a lecturer on literature and racial and social causes. She is currently professor of English and Gloria D. Smith Professor of Black Studies at Virginia Tech.

WEB: Further research this author with LitLinks at bedfordstmartins.com/approachinglit.

SUSAN GLASPELL (1882–1948) was born and raised in Davenport, Iowa. She worked as a journalist before enrolling at Drake University in Des Moines; after graduating in 1899, she worked for two years as a reporter for the Des Moines *Daily News* and then returned to Davenport to write. Her short stories began to be accepted by magazines such as *Harper's* and the *American*. Her first novel, *The Glory of the Conquered*, was published in 1909. She married George Cram Cook, a novelist and utopian socialist, in 1916; they moved to New York and, at Cook's urging, she began to write plays. They founded the Provincetown Players in Provincetown, Massachusetts, in the summer of 1916 and moved the theater to New York that fall, where it served as a venue for producing innovative plays by American playwrights. Glaspell wrote *Trifles* (p. 935) for the Players' first season. Glaspell and Cook lived in Greece from 1922 until Cook's death in 1924, after which she settled in Provincetown for the rest of her life and continued writing. She published over fifty short stories, nine novels, eleven plays, and one biography. She was awarded a Pulitzer Prize for Drama for *Alison's House* (1931), based on the life of poet EMILY DICKINSON.

WEB: Further research this author with LitLinks at bedfordstmartins.com/approachinglit.

CD-ROM: Research this author in depth with cultural documents and multimedia resources on *LiterActive*.

LOUISE GLÜCK (b. 1943) was born in New York City and educated at Sarah Lawrence College and Columbia University. She has published numerous collections of poetry, including *The Triumph of Achilles* (1985), which received the National Book Critics Circle Award and the Poetry Society of America's Melville Kane Award; *Ararat* (1990), which received the Rebekah Johnson Bobbitt National Prize for Poetry; *The Wild Iris* (1992), which received the Pulitzer Prize and the Poetry Society of America's William Carlos Williams Award; and most recently *Averno*, a finalist for the 2006 National Book Award in Poetry. She has also published a collection of essays, *Proofs and Theories: Essays on Poetry* (1994), which won the PEN/Martha Albrand Award for Nonfiction. In 2003, she became the Library of Congress's twelfth Poet Laureate Consultant in Poetry. She is a writer-in-residence at Yale University.

WEB: Further research this author with LitLinks at bedfordstmartins.com/approachinglit.

PATRICIA GOEDICKE (1931–2006) was born in Boston and grew up in Hanover, New Hampshire. She received her B.A. from Middlebury College and her M.A. in creative writing in 1956 from Ohio University. She taught at Kalamazoo College, Ohio University, and Hunter College. She lived for twelve years in San Miguel de Allende, Mexico, returning to the United States to teach first at Sarah Lawrence and then the University of Montana, where in 1991 she received the Outstanding Scholar Award. She published twelve collections of poetry and her work appeared in many literary journals and anthologies. Her poetry often combines an austerity and precision of language with a deeply felt concern for the ways environmental, political, and social issues affect the daily lives and the psyches of those who have little or no control over them.

RAY GONZÁLEZ (b. 1952) received his M.F.A. in creative writing from Southwest Texas State University. He has published nine books of poetry, including *The Heat of Arrivals* (which won the 1997 Josephine Miles Book Award) and *The Hawk Temple at Tierra Grande*, winner of a 2003 Minnesota Book Award in Poetry. He is the author of two books of nonfiction — *Memory Fever* (1999), a memoir about growing up in the Southwest, and *The Underground Heart* (2002), which received the 2003 Carr P. Collins/Texas Institute of Letters Award for Best Book of Nonfiction — and two collections of short stories — *The Ghost of John Wayne* (2001) and *Circling the Tortilla Dragon* (2002) — and is the editor of twelve anthologies. He has served as poetry editor for the *Bloomsbury Review* for twenty-five years. He teaches creative writing at the University of Minnesota.

WEB: Further research this author with LitLinks at bedfordstmartins.com/approachinglit.

THOMAS GRAY (1716–1771) was born in London and educated at Eton College and Cambridge University, where he studied literature and history. In November 1741, his father died, and Gray moved with his mother and aunt to the village of Stoke Poges in Buckinghamshire, where he wrote his first important English poems, "Ode on the Spring," "Ode on a Distant Prospect of Eton College," and "Hymn to Adversity," and began his masterpiece, "Elegy Written in a Country Churchyard" (p. 788), called the most famous and diversified of all graveyard poems. These poems solidified his reputation as one of the most important English poets of the eighteenth century. In 1757, he was named poet laureate but refused the position. In 1762, he applied for the Regius Professorship of Modern History at Cambridge but was rejected; however, he was given the position in 1768 when the successful candidate was killed. A painfully shy and private person, he never delivered any lectures as a professor.

WEB: Further research this author with LitLinks at bedfordstmartins.com/approachinglit.

ANGELINA WELD GRIMKÉ (1880–1958) was born in Boston to a mixed racial background: Her mother was from a prominent white family; her father was the son of a white man and a black slave. Grimké's father was able to earn a law degree from Harvard University (and become executive director of the NAACP) through the support of two white aunts in South Carolina who acknowledged their ties to their brother's mixed-race children. Her parents named her after her great aunt Angelina Grimké Weld, a famous white abolitionist and women's rights advocate. When Grimké was three years old, her mother left her father, taking her daughter with her. After four years she returned Angelina to her father and the child never saw her mother again. Grimké attended one of the finest schools in Massachusetts, the Carleton Academy in Ashburnham, graduated from the Boston Normal School with a degree in physical education, taught until 1907, and then moved to Washington, D.C., and taught English until she retired in 1926. While in Washington, she wrote poetry, fiction, reviews, and biographical sketches. Her best-known work, the only one published as a book, was the play *Rachel* (1916).

JOHN GUARE (b. 1938) was born in New York City. He wrote his first play when he was eleven. He earned a B.A. from Georgetown University and an M.F.A. from Yale University. His first major success was a one-act play, *Muzeeka* (1968), which won an Obie Award. His best known works include *House of Blue Leaves* (which won both an Obie and the New York Drama Critics Circle Award for the Best American Play of 1970–71 and received four Tony Awards during its 1986 revival), *Four Baboons Adoring the Sun* (which was produced at the Lincoln Center Theater in 1992 and was nominated for four Tony Awards), and *Six Degrees of Separation* (which received the New York Drama Critics Circle Award in 1990 and an Olivier Best Play Award in 1993). In 1971, he wrote the libretto for *Two Gentlemen of Verona*, a pop-rock musical adaptation of Shakespeare's play, which won the Tony Award for best musical. He coedits the *Lincoln Center Theater Review* and teaches playwriting at the Yale School of Drama.

KIMIKO HAHN (b. 1955) was born in Mt. Kisco, New York, to two artists, a Japanese American mother from Hawaii and a German American father from Wisconsin. Hahn majored in English and East Asian studies at the University of Iowa and received an M.A. in Japanese literature from Columbia University. She is the author of seven collections of poetry, including *The Unbearable Heart* (1996), which received an American Book Award and *The Narrow Road to the Interior* (2006). In 1995 she wrote ten portraits of women for a two-hour HBO special entitled *Ain't Nuthin' but a She-Thing*. She has taught at Parsons School of Design, the Poetry Project at St. Mark's Church, and Yale University. She lives in New York and is a Distinguished Professor in the English Department at Queens College/CUNY.

WEB: Further research this author with LitLinks at bedfordstmartins.com/approachinglit.

DONALD HALL (b. 1928) was born and raised in Connecticut, studied at Harvard, Oxford, and Stanford, and taught at the University of Michigan. For the past thirty years, he has lived on Eagle Pond Farm in rural New Hampshire, in the house where his grandmother and mother were born. He was married for twenty-three years to the poet JANE KENYON, who died in 1995. He has written eighteen books of poetry, beginning with *Exiles and Marriages* in 1955. His most recent collection is *White Apples and the Taste of Stone: Selected Poems 1946–2006* (2006). He has also published twenty books of prose in a variety of genres: short stories, including *Willow Temple: New and Selected Stories* (2003); several autobiographical works, such as *The Best Day the Worst Day: Life with Jane Kenyon* (2005); a collection of essays about poetry, *Breakfast Served Any Time All Day* (2003); numerous books for children (*Ox-Cart Man* was awarded the Caldecott Medal in 1979); two books about life in New Hampshire collected in *Eagle Pond* (2007); and more than two dozen textbooks and anthologies. In 2006, Hall was named Poet Laureate Consultant in Poetry to the Library of Congress.

JOY HARJO (b. 1951) was born in Tulsa, Oklahoma. Her mother was of Cherokee-French descent and her father was Creek. She moved to the Southwest and began writing poetry in her early twenties. She then earned her B.A. at the University of New Mexico and her M.F.A. from the University of Iowa Writers' Workshop. Harjo has published numerous volumes of poetry, including *In Mad Love and War* (1990), which received an American Book Award and the Delmore Schwartz

Memorial Award; *A Map to the Next World: Poems* (2000); and *How We Became Human: New and Selected Poems* (2002). She also performs her poetry and plays saxophone with her band, Poetic Justice. She is professor of English at the University of New Mexico, Albuquerque. Of "She Had Some Horses" (p. 620) Harjo has said, "This is the poem I'm asked most about and the one I have the least to say about. I don't know where it came from."

WEB: Further research this author with LitLinks at bedfordstmartins.com/approachinglit.

MICHAEL S. HARPER (b. 1938) was born in Brooklyn and grew up surrounded by jazz. When his family moved to Los Angeles, he worked at all kinds of jobs, from the post office to professional football. He studied at the City College of Los Angeles, California State University, Los Angeles, and the University of Iowa Writers' Workshop. He has written more than ten books of poetry, most recently *Selected Poems* (2002), and edited or coedited several collections of African American poetry. He is University Professor and professor of English at Brown University, where he has taught since 1970. He lives in Barrington, Rhode Island.

NATHANIEL HAWTHORNE (1804–1864) was born in Salem, Massachusetts, into a family that had been prominent in the area since colonial times. His father died when Nathaniel was four. Later, relatives recognized his literary talent and financed his education at Bowdoin College. After graduation, he lived at home writing short "tales" and a novel *Fanshawe*, which he self-published in 1828 and later dismissed as immature. He wrote prolifically in the 1830s, producing a number of successful short stories including "Young Goodman Brown" (p. 374). He published two collections of stories that were well received — *Twice-Told Tales* (1837; expanded edition 1842) and *Mosses from an Old Manse* (1846) — but had difficulty supporting himself by his writings. In 1845, he was appointed surveyor of the Boston Custom House by President James Polk but was dismissed from this post when Zachary Taylor became president. He then worked intensely on his most famous novel, *The Scarlet Letter*,

published in 1850. In addition to five novels and romances, Hawthorne published nearly 120 stories and sketches and several books for children, and left behind numerous notebooks with sketches from his travels and ideas for additional stories and novels. He was one of the first American writers to explore the hidden motivations of his characters, and often used allegorical approaches to explore the complexities of moral choices and his characters' struggles with sin and guilt.

WEB: Further research this author with LitLinks at bedfordstmartins.com/approachinglit.

CD-ROM: Research this author in depth with cultural documents and multimedia resources on *LiterActive*.

ROBERT HAYDEN (1913–1980) was raised in a poor neighborhood in Detroit and had an emotionally tumultuous childhood. Because of impaired vision, he was unable to participate in sports and spent his time reading instead. He graduated from high school in 1932 and attended Detroit City College (later Wayne State University). His first book of poems, *Heart-Shape in the Dust*, was published in 1940. After working for newspapers and on other projects, he studied under W. H. AUDEN in the graduate creative writing program at the University of Michigan. He taught at Fisk University and at the University of Michigan. His poetry gained international recognition in the 1960s, and he was awarded the grand prize for poetry at the First World Festival of Negro Arts in Dakar, Senegal, in 1966 for his book *Ballad of Remembrance*. In 1976, he became the first African American to be appointed as Consultant in Poetry at the Library of Congress.

WEB: Further research this author with LitLinks at bedfordstmartins.com/approachinglit.

SAMUEL HAZO (b. 1928), of Lebanese and Syrian heritage, is a highly influential Arab American writer of verse, educator, and advocate on behalf of poetry. He is the author of numerous collections of poetry, fiction, and essays. He is founder, director, and president of the International Poetry Forum in Pittsburgh and the McAnulty Distinguished Professor of English Emeritus at Duquesne University. He is the recipient of the 1986

Hazlett Memorial Award for Excellence in the Arts. In 1993 he was chosen to be the first state poet of the Commonwealth of Pennsylvania, a position he still holds.

WEB: Further research this author with LitLinks at bedfordstmartins.com/approachinglit.

SEAMUS HEANEY (b. 1939) grew up on a small farm near Castledawson, County Derry, Northern Ireland. He was educated at St. Columb's College, a Catholic boarding school situated in the city of Derry, forty miles from home, and then at Queen's University, Belfast. As a young English teacher in Belfast in the early 1960s, he joined a poetry workshop and began writing verse. Subsequently he became a major force in contemporary Irish literature. The author of many volumes of poetry, translations, and essays as well as two plays, he is well known for his best-selling verse translation of *Beowulf* (2000). He held the chair of professor of poetry at Oxford University from 1989 to 1994. He was awarded the Nobel Prize for Literature in 1995.

WEB: Further research this author with LitLinks at bedfordstmartins.com/approachinglit.

ERNEST HEMINGWAY (1899–1961) was born in Oak Park, a conservative, upper-middle-class suburb of Chicago, but spent his summers at Walloon Lake in northern Michigan, where he learned to love the outdoors and fishing and hunting. He decided to become a journalist instead of going to college and worked as a reporter for the *Kansas City Star*, where he was taught to write with short sentences, short paragraphs, active verbs, compression, clarity, and immediacy, qualities apparent in his fiction writing. He tried to enlist for service in World War I but was turned down because of poor eyesight. Instead, he volunteered as a Red Cross ambulance driver. Shortly after arriving in Italy, he was seriously wounded, with over two hundred pieces of shrapnel in his legs. After the war he lived in Paris, worked as a newspaper correspondent for the *Toronto Daily Star*, and mingled with prominent writers and artists. Between 1925 and 1929 he published four major works of fiction, including two novels—*The Sun Also Rises* (1926) and *A Farewell to Arms* (1929)—and went from being unknown to being one

of the most important writers of his generation. He moved first to Key West, Florida, where he grew to love big-game fishing, and later to Havana, Cuba. He continued writing, continued his interests in fishing and big-game hunting, and served as a war correspondent during the Spanish civil war and the Chinese-Japanese war, thus fostering further the macho persona he built throughout his life. His last major novels were *For Whom the Bell Tolls* (1940) and *The Old Man and the Sea* (1953), which was awarded the Pulitzer Prize for Fiction. He was awarded the Nobel Prize for Literature in 1954. Seven years later, in poor health and afflicted with severe depression, he committed suicide, as his father had some three decades earlier.

WEB: Further research this author with LitLinks at bedfordstmartins.com/approachinglit.

GEORGE HERBERT (1593–1633) was the fifth son in an ancient and wealthy Welsh family. He studied at Cambridge University, graduating with honors, and was elected public orator of the university. He served in Parliament for two years but fell out of political favor and became rector of Bemerton near Salisbury. Herbert was a model Anglican priest and an inspiring preacher. All of his poetry, religious in nature, was published posthumously in 1633. "The Pulley" (p. 798) is a fine example of metaphysical poetry (see the Glossary of Literary Terms, p. 1618).

WEB: Further research this author with LitLinks at bedfordstmartins.com/approachinglit.

DAVID HERNANDEZ (b. 1971) was born in Burbank, California. His first passion was drawing. His love of art continued through college at California State University, Long Beach, and it was there that his infatuation with poetry began and that he earned a B.A. in creative writing. He works full-time as a Web designer but still carves out time to write. He has published two poetry chapbooks and two full-length collections of poems, most recently *Always Danger* (2006), winner of the Crab Orchard Series in Poetry. His first novel, *Suckerpunch*, is scheduled for publication in 2008. His drawings have appeared in literary magazines, including *Other Voices*, *Gargoyle*, and *Indiana Review*. He is married to writer Lisa Glatt. Their collection of collaborative poems, *A Merciful Bed*, was published in 2001.

WEB: Further research this author with LitLinks at bedfordstmartins.com/approachinglit.

ROBERT HERRICK (1591–1674), the son of a well-to-do London goldsmith, was apprenticed to his uncle (also a goldsmith), studied at Cambridge University, and then lived for nine years in London, where he hobnobbed with a group of poets that included BEN JONSON. Under familial pressure to do something more worthwhile, Herrick became an Anglican priest. He was given the parish of Dean Prior, Devonshire—a rural place that he at first hated—and there he quietly wrote poems about imagined mistresses and pagan rites as well as deft but devout religious poems. When he returned to London in 1648, having been ejected from his pulpit by the Puritan revolution, he published his poetry in a volume with two titles, *Hesperides* for the secular poems, *Noble Numbers* for those with sacred subjects. Probably his most famous poem is "To the Virgins, to Make Much of Time" (p. 799), a short lyric on the traditional *carpe diem* theme (see the Glossary of Literary Terms, p. 1611).

WEB: Further research this author with LitLinks at bedfordstmartins.com/approachinglit.

NAZIM HIKMET (1902–1963) was born in Salonica, Ottoman Empire (now Thessaloniki). He began writing poems when he was fourteen. He studied briefly at the French-language Galatasary Lycée in Istanbul and attended the Naval War School, but dropped out because of ill health. He studied sociology and economics at the University of Moscow (1921–1928) and joined the Turkish Communist Party in the 1920s. He was imprisoned for returning to Turkey in 1928 without a visa but pardoned in 1935 in a general amnesty. In 1938, he was given a twenty-eight year sentence for anti-Nazi and anti-Franco activities and spent the following twelve years in different prisons. He was released in 1950 because of international protests and escaped in a small boat from his home country in fear of an attempt on his life. He lived first in the Soviet Union and in 1950 shared with PABLO NERUDA the Soviet Union's International Peace Prize. He became a Polish citizen and from 1951 lived his remaining days in Sofia, Warsaw, and finally in Moscow. A prolific writer in poetry, drama, and fiction, he was one of the most important figures writing in twentieth-century Turkish.

GEOFFREY HILL (b. 1932) is a major presence in contemporary British poetry. Born in Bromsgrove, Worcestershire, he attended the local grammar school there before going on to study English language and literature at Keble College, Oxford. He is the author of a dozen volumes of poetry, most recently *Selected Poems* (2006), and several books of essays, including *Collected Prose* (2007). He taught at Leeds University from 1954 until 1980, when he moved to Emmanuel College, Cambridge. From 1988 to 2006, he was a professor of literature and religion at Boston University. He now lives in Cambridge, England.

WEB: Further research this author with LitLinks at bedfordstmartins.com/approachinglit.

LINDA HOGAN (b. 1947), a poet, novelist, essayist, playwright, and activist widely considered to be one of the most influential and provocative Native American figures in the contemporary American literary landscape, was born in Denver. Because her father, who was from the Chicksaw Nation, was in the army and was transferred frequently during Hogan's childhood, she lived in various locations while she was growing up, but she considers Oklahoma to be her true home. In her late twenties, while working with children with orthopedic disabilities, she began writing during her lunch hours, though she had no previous experience as a writer and little experience reading literature. She pursued her writing by commuting to the University of Colorado, Colorado Springs, for her undergraduate degree and earning an M.A. in English and creative writing at the University of Colorado, Boulder, in 1978. She has published more than a dozen books—poetry, novels, and nonfiction—and received numerous awards for her work. She is a professor emeritus in the University of Colorado English department.

WEB: Further research this author with LitLinks at bedfordstmartins.com/approachinglit.

MIROSLAV HOLUB (1923–1998) was born in Plzen, in Western Bohemia, and after World War II studied science and medicine at Charles University in Prague, becoming a pathologist and later a noted research scientist in immunology and author of more than 150 academic papers. He started writing poetry after World War II, publishing in newspapers and magazines, and became one of the leading Eastern European poets of the postwar period. He was part of an effort by Czech artists and intellectuals to liberalize the Communist system from within, by free cultural acts, a movement that culminated in the Prague Spring of 1968, which was ended by the Warsaw Pact invasion in August 1968. He was dismissed from his post at the Microbiological Institute in 1970 and was not allowed to travel abroad or to appear in public. He could not publish until the ban was lifted in 1982, and his books were removed from the libraries. Abroad, however, his literary and scientific work became very well known. Much of his writing was translated into more than thirty languages.

GARRETT KAORU HONGO (b. 1951) was born in Volcano, Hawaii, grew up on Oahu and in Los Angeles, and did graduate work in Japanese language and literature at the University of Michigan. Hongo has published two books of poetry, including *The River of Heaven* (1988), which was the Lamont Poetry Selection of the Academy of American Poets and a finalist for the Pulitzer Prize. He has also written *Volcano: A Memoir of Hawai'i* (1995) and edited collections of Asian American verse. He currently teaches at the University of Oregon, Eugene, where he directed the creative writing program from 1989 to 1993. His work often uses rich textures and sensuous details to comment on conditions endured by Japanese Americans during World War II and thereafter.

WEB: Further research this author with LitLinks at bedfordstmartins.com/approachinglit.

GERARD MANLEY HOPKINS (1844–1889) was born in London, the eldest of eight children. His father was a ship insurer who also wrote a book of poetry. Hopkins studied at Balliol College, Oxford, and, after converting to Catholicism, taught in a school in Birmingham.

In 1868, he became a Jesuit and burned all of his early poetry, considering it "secular" and worthless. He then worked as a priest and teacher in working-class London, Glasgow, and Merseyside, and later as professor of classics at University College, Dublin. Hopkins went on to write many poems on spiritual themes, but he published little during his lifetime; his poems were not known until they were published by his friend Robert Bridges in 1918. They convey a spiritual sensuality, celebrating the wonder of nature both in their language and their rhythms.

WEB: Further research this author with LitLinks at bedfordstmartins.com/approachinglit.

A. E. HOUSMAN (1859–1936) was born in Fockbury, Worcestershire. A promising student at Oxford University, he failed his final exams because of emotional turmoil caused by his suppressed homosexual love for a fellow student and spent the next ten years feverishly studying and writing scholarly articles while working as a clerk at the patent office. Housman was rewarded with the chair of Latin at University College, London, and later at Cambridge. His poetry, like his scholarship, was meticulous, impersonal in tone, and limited in output: two slender volumes — *A Shropshire Lad* (1896) and *Last Poems* (1922) — during his lifetime, and a small book of *More Poems* (1936) after his death. His poems often take up the theme of doomed youths acting out their brief lives in the context of the human histories implicit in agricultural communities and activities, especially the English countryside and traditions he loved.

WEB: Further research this author with LitLinks at bedfordstmartins.com/approachinglit.

LANGSTON HUGHES (1902–1967) was born in Joplin, Missouri, and grew up in Lincoln, Illinois, and Cleveland, Ohio. During his high-school years, he began writing poetry. He attended Columbia University for a year, then held odd jobs as an assistant cook, a launderer, and a busboy, and traveled to Africa and Europe working as a seaman. In 1924, he moved to Harlem. Hughes's first book of poetry, *The Weary Blues*, was published in 1926. He finished his college education at Lincoln

University in Pennsylvania three years later. He wrote novels, short stories, plays, songs, children's books, essays, and memoirs as well as poetry and is also known for his engagement with the world of jazz and the influence it had on his writing. His life and work were enormously important in shaping the artistic contributions of the Harlem Renaissance of the 1920s.

ZORA NEALE HURSTON (1891–1960) was born to a family of sharecroppers in Notasula, Alabama, but grew up in Eatonville, Florida, a town founded by African Americans. After her mother's death in 1904, Hurston lived with various relatives. She never finished grade school. At sixteen she joined a traveling theater group and later did domestic work for a white household. The woman for whom she worked arranged for her to attend high school at Morgan Academy (now known as Morgan State University) in Baltimore. In her twenties, she attended Howard University, where she published her first stories in student publications and later in newspapers and magazines. In 1925, she moved to New York City and became active in the Harlem Renaissance. She collaborated with LANGSTON HUGHES in a folk comedy, Mule Bone (1931). Her first book, The Eatonville Anthology (1927), gained her national attention. At Barnard College she took courses in anthropology and studied traditional folklore in Alabama and native culture in the Caribbean. During the 1930s and early 1940s, she completed graduate work at Columbia University and published four novels and an autobiography. Hurston published more books than any other African American woman writer of her time — novels, collections of stories, nonfiction, an autobiography — but she earned very little from her writing and spent her final years in near poverty. In the mid-1970s her work was rediscovered, and she is now recognized as an important American author.

WEB: Further research this author with LitLinks at bedfordstmartins.com/approachinglit.

DAVID HENRY HWANG (b. 1957) was born in Los Angeles to parents who immigrated to the United States from China; his father was a banker, his mother a professor of music.

Hwang attended Stanford University intending to study law, but he became interested in drama and changed his major to English. A year before he graduated in 1979, he wrote his first play, FOB [Fresh Off the Boat], which won the 1981 Obie Award as the best new play of the season for Joseph Papp's off-Broadway production in New York. Hwang attended the Yale School of Drama from 1980 to 1981. The Dance and the Railroad and Family Devotions were produced off-Broadway in 1981. Both, like FOB, deal with the problems of immigrants, the tension between trying to assimilate and trying to avoid assimilation in a new culture. Other plays followed in the 1980s, but his big breakthrough came with the 1988 Broadway hit, M. Butterfly, which won the Outer Critics Circle Award for best Broadway play, the Drama Desk Award for best new play, the John Gassner Award for best American play, and the Tony Award for best play of the year and established him as one of the leading young American playwrights.

WEB: Further research this author with LitLinks at bedfordstmartins.com/approachinglit.

HENRIK IBSEN (1828–1906) was born in Skien, a tiny coastal town in southeast Norway. Although his father was successful and wealthy at the time of Ibsen's birth, his business failed soon after, and Ibsen grew up in poverty, familiar with the economic hardships he later depicted often in his plays. He worked for six years as apprentice to a druggist in the seaport town of Grimstad to help support his family, and he intended to study medicine but failed the university entrance examinations. By his early twenties, he was deeply involved in a small local theater in Bergen. In 1857, he was appointed artistic director for the new National Theatre and held that post until it went bankrupt in 1862. He received a travel grant from the government and moved with his wife and son to Rome, living for the next twenty-seven years in various European cities. In 1875, he began to experiment with realistic plays exploring social issues related to middle-class life. He is best known for a series of "problem plays" that shocked but also fascinated audiences, among them A Doll House (1879; see p. 1263) and Hedda Gabler (1890). In 1891, he returned to

Norway for the rest of his life and continued to write until suffering a stroke in 1900. He received worldwide recognition on his seventieth birthday as the greatest dramatist of the nineteenth century.

WEB: Further research this author with LitLinks at bedfordstmartins.com/approachinglit.

CD-ROM: Research this author in depth with cultural documents and multimedia resources on *LiterActive*.

LAWSON FUSAO INADA (b. 1938) was born in Fresno, California, and attended Fresno State University. He has edited two important Asian American literary anthologies and published several collections of poetry. His collection *Before the War* (1971) was the first volume of poetry by an Asian American to be published by a major publishing house. Early in his life, Inada was an aspiring jazz bassist. Later, he became interested in poetry, but the influence of jazz is evident in his work. One can sense in his rhythms the beats of his bass.

DAVID IVES (b. 1950) was born in Chicago and attended Northwestern University. After graduating, he moved to New York and worked as an editor for *Foreign Affairs*, in addition to writing plays and short stories. He enrolled in the Yale Drama School in 1981 and earned his M.F.A. degree. Many of his plays, often described as "wacky one-act comedies," have been staged at the Manhattan Punch Line's Festival of One-Act Comedies. His full-length comedy *Don Juan in Chicago* (1994) received the Outer Critics Circle's John Gassner Playwriting Award. He was named winner of the 1994 George and Elisabeth Martin Playwriting Award from Young Playwrights Inc. He has published many plays and collections of short plays as well as a children's story, *Monsieur Eck* (2001).

HONORÉE FANONNE JEFFERS (b. 1967) has published fiction in addition to two books of poetry, *The Gospel of Barbecue* (2000), which won the 1999 Stan and Tom Wick Prize for Poetry and was the finalist for the 2001 Paterson Poetry Prize, and *Outlandish Blues* (2003). She is currently working on a third book of poetry, *Red Clay Suite*, and her first book of collected fiction. She won the 2002

Julia Peterkin Award for Poetry and awards from the Barbara Deming Memorial Fund and the Rona Jaffe Foundation. Her poetry has been published in the anthologies *At Our Core: Women Writing about Power, Dark Eros*, and *Identity Lessons* and in many journals, including *Callaloo*, *Kenyon Review*, and *Prairie Schooner*. She teaches at the University of Oklahoma.

GEORGIA DOUGLAS JOHNSON (1880–1966) was born in Atlanta and attended Atlanta University. She went on to study music at the Oberlin Conservatory (Ohio) and the Cleveland College of Music. Her ambition was to be a composer, but to earn a living she taught high school in Alabama and Washington, D.C., and later worked for the federal government. She was prolific as a poet, fiction writer, playwright, songwriter, and journalist; in addition to writing a syndicated newspaper column from 1926 to 1932, she wrote twenty-eight plays, thirty-one short stories, and over two hundred poems. She was the most widely published of all the women poets of the Harlem Renaissance period. Beyond her importance as a writer, she played an influential role in Washington circles by providing a "salon" in her home as a meeting place for artists and writers.

HELENE JOHNSON (1907–1995) was born and raised in Boston. She attended Boston University and Columbia University. Her work began attracting attention when James Weldon Johnson and ROBERT FROST selected three of her poems for prizes in a 1926 competition. Although she was regarded in the early 1930s as one of the most gifted poets of the Harlem Renaissance, she had a limited poetic output: thirty-four poems in a range of forms and voices, published in small magazines. The last of her poems published during her lifetime was "Let Me Sing My Song," which appeared in *Challenge*, a journal founded by her cousin, the novelist Dorothy West, to revive the spirit of the Harlem Renaissance. She married in 1933 and from then on directed most of her energy and attention to motherhood and earning a living as a correspondent for *Consumer's Union*.

EDWARD P. JONES (b. 1951) was born in Washington, D.C., and educated at College of the Holy Cross and the University of Virginia. His novel, *The Known World* (2003), was awarded the 2004 Pulitzer Prize for Fiction; it was a National Book Award finalist and winner of the 2005 International IMPAC Dublin Literary Award. His collection of short stories *Lost in the City* (1992) won the PEN/Hemingway Award and was short-listed for the National Book Award. His most recent book is *All Aunt Hagar's Children* (2006). In 2005, he received a MacArthur Foundation Fellowship. He has taught fiction writing at numerous universities and lives in Washington, D.C.

BEN JONSON (1572–1637) was born in London, the stepson of a bricklayer (his father died before he was born). He attended Westminster School and then joined the army. Jonson later worked as an actor and was the author of comedies such as *Everyman in His Humor* (in which Shakespeare acted the lead), *Volpone*, and *The Alchemist*. He wrote clear, elegant, "classical" poetry, contrasting with the intricate, subtle, "metaphysical" poetry of his contemporaries JOHN DONNE and GEORGE HERBERT. He was named poet laureate and was the idol of a generation of English writers, who dubbed themselves the Sons of Ben.

WEB: Further research this author with LitLinks at bedfordstmartins.com/approachinglit.

A. VAN JORDAN (b. 1965) was born and raised in Akron, Ohio. He is a graduate of the M.F.A. Program for Writers at Warren Wilson College, where he taught in the undergraduate writing program and served as the 1999–2000 and 2000–2001 Joan Beebe Graduate Teaching Fellow. In 1995, he was awarded a D.C. Commission on the Arts and Humanities Literary Award. He was also a semifinalist for the 1999 "Discovery"/The Nation Award. He is the author of three collections of poetry, most recently *Quantum Lyrics: Poems* (2007). He teaches in the M.F.A. program at the University of North Carolina, Greensboro.

ALLISON JOSEPH (b. 1967) was born in London to Caribbean parents and grew up in Toronto and the Bronx. She earned her B.A. from Kenyon College and her M.F.A. from Indiana University. She is the author of five collections of poetry, *What Keeps Us Here* (winner of Ampersand Press's 1992 Women Poets Series Competition and the John C. Zacharis First Book Award), *Soul Train* (1997), *In Every Seam* (1997), *Imitation of Life* (2003), and *Worldly Pleasures* (2004). Her poems are often attuned to the experiences of women and minorities. She is an associate professor at Southern Illinois University, Carbondale, where she is editor of *The Crab Orchard Review*.

JAMES JOYCE (1882–1941) was born in Rathgar, a suburb of Dublin. His father, descended from an old, wealthy Cork family, drank his family into poverty. However, Joyce received an excellent classical education at a Jesuit school and University College, Dublin, where he studied modern languages and began writing. He became alienated from the Catholic religion and from Ireland, and in 1902 he left Dublin for Paris; he returned in 1903 to be with his mother, who was dying of cancer. From 1905 he lived on the continent, in Trieste, Zurich, and from 1920 to 1939 as part of the vibrant colony of expatriate authors in Paris. Although he was not able to live in Ireland, all of his writings concern Ireland and his memories of it. His first book was a collection of poems, *Chamber Music*, published in 1907. His major collection of stories, *Dubliners*, appeared in 1914, followed in 1916 by the autobiographical novel that established his reputation as a major writer, *A Portrait of the Artist as a Young Man*. The novel regarded generally as his masterpiece, *Ulysses*, was published 1922 in Paris. (*Ulysses* was not published in the United States until 1933 and not in England until 1937, because legal difficulties prohibited uncensored publication in those countries prior to that.) His final novel, *Finnegans Wake*, appeared in 1939. To escape the German occupation of France, he returned that year to Zurich, where he had lived while writing *Ulysses*, and died there slightly more than a year later.

WEB: Further research this author with LitLinks at bedfordstmartins.com/approachinglit.

CD-ROM: Research this author in depth with cultural documents and multimedia resources on *LiterActive*.

JOHN KEATS (1795–1821) was born in London. His father, a worker at a livery stable who married his employer's daughter and inherited the business, was killed by a fall from a horse when Keats was eight. When his mother died of tuberculosis six years later, Keats and his siblings were entrusted to the care of a guardian, a practical-minded man who took Keats out of school at fifteen and apprenticed him to a doctor. As soon as he qualified for medical practice in 1815, he abandoned medicine for poetry, which he had begun writing two years earlier. In 1818, the year he contracted tuberculosis, he also fell madly in love with a pretty, vivacious young woman named Fanny Brawne, whom he could not marry because of his poverty, illness, and devotion to poetry. In the midst of such stress and emotional turmoil, his masterpieces poured out between January and September 1819: the great odes, a number of sonnets, and several longer lyric poems. In February 1820, his health failed rapidly; he went to Italy in the autumn, in hopes that the warmer climate would improve his health, and died there on February 23, 1821. His poems are rich with sensuous, lyrical beauty and emotional resonance, reflecting his delight in life as well as his awareness of life's brevity and difficulty.

WEB: Further research this author with LitLinks at bedfordstmartins.com/approachinglit.

CD-ROM: Research this author in depth with cultural documents and multimedia resources on *LiterActive*.

JANE KENYON (1947–1995) was born in Ann Arbor, Michigan, and grew up in the Midwest. She earned her B.A. and M.A. from the University of Michigan. She was married to poet DONALD HALL from 1972 until her death from leukemia in 1995. During her lifetime, she published four books of poetry — *From Room to Room* (1978), *The Boat of Quiet Hours* (1986), *Let Evening Come* (1990), and *Constance* (1993) — and a book of translation, *Twenty Poems of Anna Akhmatova* (1985). Two additional volumes were published after her death: *Otherwise: New and Selected Poems* (1996) and *A Hundred White Daffodils: Essays, Interviews, the Akhmatova Translations, Newspaper Columns, and One*

Poem (1999). At the time of her death, she was New Hampshire's poet laureate.

WEB: Further research this author with LitLinks at bedfordstmartins.com/approachinglit.

JAMAICA KINCAID (b. 1949) was born Elaine Potter Richardson in St. Johns, Antigua, the West Indies and completed her British-style secondary education there. She lived with her stepfather, a carpenter, and her mother until 1965 when she was sent to Westchester, New York, to work as an au pair. After working for three years and taking night classes at a community college, she attended Franconia College in New Hampshire for a year. Because her family disapproved of her writing, she changed her name to Jamaica Kincaid when she began publishing stories in magazines. Her work drew the attention of William Shawn, editor of the *New Yorker*, who hired her as a staff writer in 1976. For the next nine years, she wrote columns for the "Talk of the Town" section. In 1978, she first published a story in the *New Yorker*; it later became part of her first book, a collection entitled *At the Bottom of the River* (1984), which won the Morton Dauwen Zabel Award of the American Academy and Institute of Arts and Letters. She has also published five novels; a nonfiction book about Antigua, *A Small Place* (1988); and a memoir, *My Brother* (1997). She taught creative writing for many years at Bennington College and now is a visiting lecturer at Harvard University.

WEB: Further research this author with LitLinks at bedfordstmartins.com/approachinglit.

CD-ROM: Research this author in depth with cultural documents and multimedia resources on *LiterActive*.

GALWAY KINNELL (b. 1927) was born in Providence, Rhode Island, and attended Princeton University and the University of Rochester. He served in the U.S. Navy and then visited Paris on a Fulbright fellowship. Returning to the United States, he worked for the Congress on Racial Equality and then traveled widely in the Middle East and Europe. He has taught in France, Australia, and Iran as well as at numerous colleges and universities in the United States. He has published many books of poetry, including *Selected Poems* (1980), for which he received both the Pulitzer Prize and the National Book Award. He has also published translations of works by Yves Bonnefoy, Yvanne Goll, François Villon, and Rainer Maria Rilke. He divides his time between Vermont and New York City, where he is the Erich Maria Remarque Professor of Creative Writing at New York University.

WEB: Further research this author with LitLinks at bedfordstmartins.com/approachinglit.

ETHERIDGE KNIGHT (1931–1991) was born in Corinth, Mississippi. He dropped out of school at age sixteen and served in the U.S. Army in Korea from 1947 to 1951, returning with a shrapnel wound that caused him to fall deeper into a drug addiction that had begun during his service. In 1960, he was arrested for robbery, convicted, and sentenced to eight years in an Indiana state prison. During this time, he began writing poetry. His first book, *Poems from Prison* (1968), was published one year before his release. The book was a success, and Knight joined other poets in what came to be called the Black Arts movement, the aesthetic and spiritual sister of the Black Power concept. He went on to write several more books of poetry and to receive many prestigious honors and awards. In 1990 he earned a B.A. in American poetry and criminal justice from Martin Center University in Indianapolis.

WEB: Further research this author with LitLinks at bedfordstmartins.com/approachinglit.

YUSEF KOMUNYAKAA (b. 1947) was born and grew up in Bogalusa, Louisiana. He earned degrees at the University of Colorado, Colorado State University, and the University of California, Irvine. His numerous books of poems include *Neon Vernacular: New and Selected Poems, 1977–1989* (1994), for which he received the Pulitzer Prize and the Kingsley Tufts Poetry Award, and *Thieves of Paradise* (1998), which was a finalist for the National Book Critics Circle Award. Other publications include *Blues Notes: Essays, Interviews & Commentaries* (2000), *The Jazz Poetry Anthology* (coedited with J. A. Sascha Feinstein, 1991), and *The Insomnia of Fire* by Nguyen Quang Thieu (cotranslated with Martha

Collins, 1995). He has taught at the University of New Orleans, Indiana University, and Princeton University.

WEB: Further research this author with LitLinks at bedfordstmartins.com/approachinglit.

TED KOOSER (b. 1939) was born in Ames, Iowa. He received his B.A. from Iowa State University and his M.A. in English from the University of Nebraska–Lincoln. He is the author of ten collections of poetry, including *Sure Signs* (1980), *One World at a Time* (1985), *Weather Central* (1994), *Winter Morning Walks: One Hundred Postcards to Jim Harrison* (2000, winner of the 2001 Nebraska Book Award for poetry), and *Delights & Shadows* (2004). His fiction and nonfiction books include *Local Wonders: Seasons in the Bohemian Alps* (2002, winner of the Nebraska Book Award for Nonfiction in 2003) and *Braided Creek: A Conversation in Poetry* (2003), written with fellow poet and longtime friend Jim Harrison. His honors include two NEA fellowships in poetry, a Pushcart Prize, the Stanley Kunitz Prize, and a merit award from the Nebraska Arts Council. He served as the United States Poet Laureate Consultant in Poetry to the Library of Congress from 2004–2006. He lives on acreage near the village of Garland, Nebraska, and is a visiting professor in the English department of the University of Nebraska–Lincoln.

MAXINE KUMIN (b. 1925) was born in Philadelphia and received her B.A. and M.A. at Radcliffe College. She has published eleven books of poetry, including *Up Country: Poems of New England* (1972), for which she received the Pulitzer Prize. She is also the author of a memoir, *Inside the Halo and Beyond: The Anatomy of a Recovery* (2000); four novels; a collection of short stories; more than twenty children's books; and four books of essays. She has taught at the University of Massachusetts, Columbia University, Brandeis University, and Princeton University, and has served as Consultant in Poetry to the Library of Congress and as poet laureate of New Hampshire, where she lives.

WEB: Further research this author with LitLinks at bedfordstmartins.com/approachinglit.

STANLEY KUNITZ (1905–2006) was among the most beloved of twentieth-century poets. His life in verse spanned more than three-quarters of a century, during which time he was always at the center of the poetry world. He was born in Worcester, Massachusetts, and earned his B.A. and M.A. at Harvard University. His semiautobiographical work often explored the consequences of traumatic events on a person's life. He was quoted as saying that for him poetry was the single most important thing a person could do with her or his life. His first two books garnered little attention, but after serving in World War II he continued to write and received great recognition. His *Selected Poems, 1928–1958* won the Pulitzer Prize, and in 1995 he received the National Book Award for *Passing Through: The Later Poems, New and Selected.* His work has often been called an extension of the vision of John Keats. In 2000, at age ninety-five, he was named Poet Laureate Consultant in Poetry to the Library of Congress. He taught for many years at Columbia University and divided his time between New York City and Provincetown, Massachusetts, where he tended his magnificent garden.

WEB: Further research this author with LitLinks at bedfordstmartins.com/approachinglit.

GERRY LAFEMINA (b. 1968) is the author of several chapbooks, four full-length collections of poetry (most recently *The Window Facing Winter*, 2004), a collection of prose poems, and numerous published stories, essays, and poems. He is also cotranslator with Sinan Toprak of *Voice Lock Puppet*, poems by contemporary Turkish poet Ali Yuce, and coeditor of two anthologies—*Poetry 30: Thirty-something American Thirty-something Poets* (2005, with Daniel Crocker) and *Evensong: Contemporary American Poets on Spirituality* (2006, with Chad Prevost)—and of *review revue*, a tabloid triquarterly focusing on reviews of poetry books, interviews with poets, and prosody essays. A graduate of Sarah Lawrence College, he holds an M.A. and M.F.A. from Western Michigan University. He is the Distinguished Poet-in-Residence at Frostburg State University in Maryland and directs the Frostburg Center for Creative Writing.

JHUMPA LAHIRI (b. 1967) was born in London but grew up in Rhode Island. As a child she wrote stories in her school notebooks. She received her B.A. from Barnard College and, rejected by creative writing programs, continued to write stories while working at an office job. She was then accepted to the graduate program at Boston University and earned an M.A. in English, an M.A. in creative writing, and a Ph.D. in Renaissance studies. The daughter of parents born in India who frequently took her there as a child, she has been influenced by the culture of India and the United States. Her first collection of short fiction, *Interpreter of Maladies* (1999), won the Pulitzer Prize for Fiction in 2000, in addition to the PEN/Hemingway Award, the *New Yorker* Debut of the Year award, and an American Academy of Arts and Letters Addison Metcalf Award. Her first novel, *The Namesake*, was published in 2003 and made into a motion picture (2007). She has taught creative writing at Boston University and the Rhode Island School of Design and has been a vice president of the PEN American Center since 2005.

LI-YOUNG LEE (b. 1957) was born in Jakarta, Indonesia, to Chinese parents. His father, who had been personal physician to Mao Tse-tung, relocated his family to Indonesia, where he helped found Gamaliel University. In 1959, the Lee family fled the country to escape anti-Chinese sentiment, and they settled in the United States in 1964. Lee studied at the University of Pittsburgh, the University of Arizona, and the Brockport campus of the State University of New York. He has taught at several universities, including Northwestern University and the University of Iowa. He is the author of four collections of poetry—*Rose* (1986), which won the Delmore Schwartz Memorial Poetry Award; *The City in Which I Love You* (1991), which was the 1990 Lamont Poetry Selection; *Book of My Nights* (2001); and *Behind My Eyes* (2008)—and a memoir, *The Winged Seed: A Remembrance* (1995), which received an American Book Award from the Before Columbus Foundation. In his poems, one often senses a profound sense of exile, the influence of his father's presence, and a rich spiritual sensuality.

WEB: Further research this author with LitLinks at bedfordstmartins.com/approachinglit.

JOHN LEGUIZAMO (b. 1964) was born in Bogotá, Colombia. His family immigrated to the

United States when he was four, and he grew up in New York City. In 1983, he began studying acting at Sylvia Leigh's Showcase Theater, which he picked randomly out of the Yellow Pages. After graduating from high school, he attended New York University to major in drama but left school after a year to join the comedy group Off Center Theater. He also attended the Strasberg Theater Institute and the H. B. Studio. He has performed as a stand-up comedian and in many roles on television and in movies, as well as in an off-Broadway staging of his play *Mambo Mouth*. He is author of several successful screenplays and one-actor plays, including *Mambo Mouth: A Savage Comedy* (1991; see p. 979), which won an Obie Award and an Outer Critics Circle Award, and a memoir, *Pimps, Hos, Playa Hatas and All the Rest of My Hollywood Friends: A Life* (2006).

CD-ROM: Research this author in depth with cultural documents and multimedia resources on *LiterActive*.

DENISE LEVERTOV (1923–1997) was born in Ilford, Essex. Her mother was Welsh and her father was a Russian Jew who became an Anglican priest. She was educated at home and claimed to have decided to become a writer at the age of five. Her first book, *The Double Image* (1946), brought her recognition as one of a group of poets dubbed the "New Romantics." Her poems often blend the sense of an objective observer with the sensibility of a spiritual searcher. She moved to the United States after marrying the American writer Mitchell Goodman. There she turned to free-verse poetry, and with her first American book, *Here and Now* (1956), she became an important voice in the American avant-garde. In the 1960s, she became involved in the movement protesting the Vietnam War. She went on to publish more than twenty collections of poetry, four books of prose, and three volumes of poetry in translation. From 1982 to 1993, she taught at Stanford University. She spent the last decade of her life in Seattle.

WEB: Further research this author with LitLinks at bedfordstmartins.com/approachinglit.

PHILIP LEVINE (b. 1928) was born in Detroit and received his degrees from Wayne State University and the University of Iowa. He is the author of sixteen books of poetry, including *The Simple Truth* (1994), which won the Pulitzer Prize. He has also published a collection of essays, *The Bread of Time: Toward an Autobiography* (1994), edited *The Essential Keats* (1987), and coedited and translated books of poetry by Spanish poet Gloria Fuertes and Mexican poet Jamie Sabines. He divides his time between Fresno, California, and New York City, where he taught at New York University.

YIYUN LI (b. 1972) was born and grew up in Beijing. She came to the United States in 1996 to study medicine but gave it up after three years to become a writer. She has an M.F.A. from the University of Iowa Writers' Workshop and an M.F.A. in creative nonfiction from the University of Iowa. Her stories and essays have been published in the *New Yorker, Paris Review, Zoetrope: All-Story, Ploughshares, Gettysburg Review, Glimmer Train, Prospect*, and elsewhere. Her first book, *A Thousand Years of Good Prayers* (2006), won the Frank O'Connor International Short Story Award, the PEN/Hemingway Award, the California Book Award for first fiction, and the Guardian First Book Award. In 2007, she was included by *Granta* magazine among twenty-one "Best of Young American Novelists." She lives in Oakland, California, and teaches in the M.F.A. program at Mills College.

TIMOTHY LIU (b. 1965) was born in San Jose, California, to parents who had emigrated from the Chinese mainland. He studied at Brigham Young University, the University of Houston, and the University of Massachusetts, Amherst. He is author of several books of poetry (including *Vox Angelica*, which won the 1992 Norma Farber First Book Award from the Poetry Society of America) and *Of Thee I Sing* (2004), selected by *Publishers Weekly* as a 2004 Book-of-the-Year, and editor of *Word of Mouth: An Anthology of Gay American Poetry* (2000). He is an associate professor at William Paterson University and lives in Manhattan.

WEB: Further research this author with LitLinks at bedfordstmartins.com/approachinglit.

AUDRE LORDE (1934–1992) was born in New York City of West Indian parents. She grew up in Manhattan and attended Roman

Catholic schools. While she was still in high school, her first poem appeared in *Seventeen* magazine. She earned her B.A. from Hunter College and her M.A. in library science from Columbia University. In 1968, she left her job as head librarian at the University of New York to become a lecturer and creative writer. She accepted a poet-in-residence position at Tougaloo College in Mississippi, where she discovered a love of teaching, published her first volume of poetry, *The First Cities* (1968), and met her long-term partner, Frances Clayton. Many other volumes of poetry followed, several of which won major awards. She also published four volumes of prose, among them *The Cancer Journals* (1980), which chronicled her struggles with cancer, and *A Burst of Light* (1988), which won a National Book Award. In the 1980s, Lorde and writer Barbara Smith founded Kitchen Table: Women of Color Press. She was also a founding member of Sisters in Support of Sisters in South Africa, an organization that worked to raise awareness about women under apartheid. She was the poet laureate of New York from 1991 to 1992.

WEB: Further research this author with LitLinks at bedfordstmartins.com/approachinglit.

RICHARD LOVELACE (1618–1692) was born into a prominent family in Kent, England, and went to Oxford University, where his dashing appearance and wit made him a social and literary favorite. He fought in the English civil war on the Royalist side and was imprisoned and exiled. Later he fought in France against the Spanish and was again imprisoned on his return to England. After his release he spent ten years in poverty and isolation before his death. He was a leader of the "Cavalier poets," followers of King Charles I who were soldiers and courtiers but also wrote well-crafted, light-hearted lyric poetry. "To Lucasta, Going to the Wars" (p. 817) is an excellent example of the type.

WEB: Further research this author with LitLinks at bedfordstmartins.com/approachinglit.

ROBERT LOWELL (1917–1978) was born in Boston into a prominent New England family. He attended Harvard University and then Kenyon College, where he studied under John Crowe Ransom. At Louisiana State University,

he studied with Robert Penn Warren and Cleanth Brooks as well as Allen Tate. He was always politically active — a conscientious objector during World War II and a Vietnam protestor — and suffered from manic depression. Lowell's reputation was established early: His second book, *Lord Weary's Castle*, was awarded the Pulitzer Prize for Poetry in 1947. In the mid-1950s, he began to write more directly from personal experience and loosened his adherence to traditional meter and form. The result was a watershed collection of the "confessional" school, *Life Studies* (1959), which changed the landscape of modern poetry, much as T. S. ELIOT's *The Waste Land* had done three decades before. He died suddenly from a heart attack at age sixty.

WEB: Further research this author with LitLinks at bedfordstmartins.com/approachinglit.

MEDBH MCGUCKIAN (b. 1950) was born in Belfast and educated at a Dominican convent and at Queen's University, Belfast. She has published more than a dozen books of poetry, including *The Flower Master* (1982), *Venus and the Rain* (1984), *On Ballycastle Beach* (1988), *Marconi's Cottage* (1992), *Captain Lavender* (1995), *Selected Poems 1978–1994* (1997), *Shelmalier* (1998), *Drawing Ballerinas* (2001), and *The Book of the Angel* (2004). Among the prizes she has won are the British National Poetry Competition, the Cheltenham Award, the Alice Hunt Bartlett prize, the Rooney Prize, and the American Ireland Fund Literary Award. She has been writer-in-residence at Queen's University and at the University of Ulster; visiting fellow at the University of California, Berkeley; and writer-fellow at Trinity College, Dublin.

HEATHER MCHUGH (b. 1948) was born to Canadian parents in San Diego and grew up in Virginia. She is a graduate of Radcliffe College and the University of Denver. McHugh has published numerous books of poetry, including *Eyeshot* (2003) and *Hinge & Sign: Poems 1968–1993* (1994), which won both the *Boston Book Review*'s Bingham Poetry Prize and the Pollack-Harvard Review Prize, was a finalist for the National Book Award, and was named a "Notable Book of the Year" by the *New York Times Book Review*, as well as a book of prose, *Broken English: Poetry and Partiality* (1993), and two books of translations. She teaches as a core faculty member in the M.F.A. Program for Writers at Warren Wilson College and as Milliman Writer-in-Residence at the University of Washington, Seattle.

WEB: Further research this author with LitLinks at bedfordstmartins.com/approachinglit.

CLAUDE MCKAY (1890–1948), the son of poor farmworkers, was born in Sunny Ville, Jamaica. He was educated by his older brother, who possessed a library of English novels, poetry, and scientific texts. At age twenty, McKay published a book of verse in dialect called *Songs of Jamaica*, recording his impressions of black life in Jamaica. In 1912, he traveled to the United States to attend Tuskegee Institute. He soon left to study agriculture at Kansas State University. In 1914, he moved to Harlem and became an influential member of the Harlem Renaissance. After committing to communism and traveling to Moscow in 1922, he lived for some time in Europe and Morocco, writing fiction. McKay later repudiated communism, converted to Roman Catholicism, and returned to the United States. He published several books of poetry as well as an autobiography, *A Long Way from Home* (1937). He wrote a number of sonnets protesting the injustices of black life in the United States, "If we must die" (p. 608) and "America" (p. 821) among them. They are of interest for the way they use the most Anglo of forms to contain and intensify what the poem's language is saying.

WEB: Further research this author with LitLinks at bedfordstmartins.com/approachinglit.

CHRISTOPHER MARLOWE (1564–1593) was born in Canterbury, England, the same year as WILLIAM SHAKESPEARE. The son of a shoemaker, he needed the help of scholarships to attend King's School, Canterbury, and Corpus Christi College, Cambridge. He was involved in secret political missions for the government. He was one of the most brilliant writers of his generation, in narrative poetry, lyric poetry, and drama (his best-known play is *Doctor Faustus*). He died after being knifed in a bar fight, reportedly over his bill, at the age of twenty-nine. "The Passionate Shepherd

to His Love" (p. 822) is among the most famous of Elizabethan poems.

WEB: Further research this author with LitLinks at bedfordstmartins.com/approachinglit.

MÁRQUEZ, GABRIEL GARCÍA — See GARCÍA MÁRQUEZ, GABRIEL.

ANDREW MARVELL (1621–1678) was born in Hull, Yorkshire, and educated at Trinity College, Cambridge. After traveling in Europe, he worked as a tutor and in a government office (as assistant to JOHN MILTON) and later became a member of Parliament for Hull. Marvell was known in his lifetime as a writer of rough satires in verse and prose. His "serious" poetry, like "To His Coy Mistress" (p. 823), was not published until after his death. It is a famous exploration of the *carpe diem* theme (see the Glossary of Literary Terms, p. 1611).

WEB: Further research this author with LitLinks at bedfordstmartins.com/approachinglit.

CD-ROM: Research this author in depth with cultural documents and multimedia resources on *LiterActive*.

DAVID MEANS (b. 1961), a native of Michigan, now lives in Nyack, New York, and teaches at Vassar College. His first book of short stories, *A Quick Kiss of Redemption*, was published in 1991. His second, *Assorted Fire Events* (2000), won the Los Angeles Times Book Award and was a finalist for the National Book Critics Circle Award. His most recent book is *The Secret Goldfish* (2004). His stories have appeared in the *New Yorker, Harper's, Esquire, The O. Henry Prize Stories, The Best American Short Stories*, and *The Best American Mystery Stories*.

ANA MENÉNDEZ (b. 1970) was born in Los Angeles, the daughter of Cuban exiles. She is the author of two books of fiction: *In Cuba I Was a German Shepherd*, which was a 2001 New York Times Notable Book of the Year and whose title story won a Pushcart Prize, and *Loving Che* (2003), a national bestseller. Before turning to fiction, she was a journalist, first at the *Miami Herald*, where she covered Little Havana until 1995, and later at the *Orange County Register* in California. She has also lived in Turkey and South Asia, where she reported out of Afghanistan and Kashmir. She has taught at various universities including, most recently, as a visiting writer at the University of Texas at Austin. She holds a bachelor's degree from Florida International University and a master's degree from New York University. In 2005, she returned to the *Miami Herald* as a columnist.

ORLANDO RICARDO MENES (b. 1958) was born in Lima, Peru, to Cuban parents, but has lived most of his life in Miami, Florida. He holds a B.A. and an M.A. in English from the University of Florida and a Ph.D. from the University of Illinois at Chicago. He has published three collections of poetry: *Borderlands with Angels*, winner of the 1994 Bacchae Press Chapbook Competition; *Rumba Atop the Stones* (2001); and *Furia* (2005). He has also edited the volume *Renaming Ecstasy: Latino Writings on the Sacred* (2004). For years photography was one of his passions, and in 1992 he had an exhibition of photographs at Books and Books in Miami Beach. He teaches in the Creative Writing Program at the University of Notre Dame.

ARTHUR MILLER (1915–2005) was born in New York City to middle-class Jewish parents. His mother was a teacher and his father a successful clothing manufacturer whose business collapsed during the Depression. The family had to move from Manhattan to a small frame house in Brooklyn, similar to that of the Loman family in *Death of a Salesman* (p. 1316). After high school he worked for two years in a warehouse to save money for college. He went to the University of Michigan to study journalism, but soon began to write and win prizes for plays. After graduation, he wrote plays for radio and worked for the Federal Theater Project. His first successful play was *All My Sons* (1947), which won a Drama Critics Circle Award. *Death of a Salesman* (1949) was the hit of the 1948–1949 Broadway season, running for 742 performances and winning the Pulitzer Prize, the Drama Critics Circle Award, the Donaldson Award, and a Tony Award for best play. The script of the play became a bestseller and the only play ever to be a Book-of-the-Month selection. Miller continued to write plays, among the most successful being *The Crucible* (1953), *A View from the Bridge* (1955), and *After the Fall* (1964). He also published a memoir, *Timebends: A Life* (1987); a novel; a collection of short stories; and many essays on the theater and the craft of playwriting.

WEB: Further research this author with LitLinks at bedfordstmartins.com/approachinglit.

CD-ROM: Research this author in depth with cultural documents and multimedia resources on *LiterActive*.

JOHN MILTON (1608–1674), son of a well-off London businessman, was educated at St. Paul's School and at home with private tutors. After graduating with an M.A. from Christ's College, Cambridge, he spent the next six years reading at home. Milton had written verse since his university days, but he broke off to write prose tracts in favor of Oliver Cromwell, in whose government he later headed a department. The strain of long hours of reading and writing for the revolutionary cause aggravated a genetic weakness and resulted in his total blindness around 1651. He wrote his most famous works, *Paradise Lost* (1667), *Paradise Regained* (1671), and *Samson Agonistes* (1671), by dictating them to his daughter and other amanuenses.

WEB: Further research this author with LitLinks at bedfordstmartins.com/approachinglit.

KATHERINE MIN (b. 1959) was born in Champaign-Urbana, Illinois, and grew up in Charlottesville, Virginia, and Clifton Park, New York. She graduated from Amherst College and the Columbia School of Journalism. Her short stories have appeared in numerous literary journals and anthologies. "Courting a Monk" (p. 219) won a Pushcart Prize in 1998. Her novel *Secondhand World* was selected one of the best books of 2006 by *School Library Journal*, one of the best debut novels of the year by the *Rocky Mountain News*, and was a winter guide pick on *MSNBC.com*. She lives in New Hampshire and teaches at Plymouth State University and in the Iowa Summer Writing Festival.

GARY MIRANDA (b. 1938) was born in Bremerton, Washington, and grew up in the Pacific Northwest. After spending six years in a

Jesuit seminary, he went on to do graduate work at San Jose State College and the University of California, Irvine. He is the author of three collections of poetry, *Listeners at the Breathing Place* (1978), *Grace Period* (1983), and *Turning Sixty* (2001) and has published a translation of Rainer Maria Rilke's *Duino Elegies* (1981). He lives in Portland, Oregon.

JANICE MIRIKITANI (b. 1942) was born in California, a sansei or third-generation Japanese American. As an infant, she was interned with her family in Rohwer, Arkansas, during World War II. She has published four volumes of poetry and edited several anthologies of poetry, prose, and essays, among them *Ayumi: Japanese American Anthology* (1980) and *Watch Out, We're Talking: Speaking Out about Incest and Abuse* (1993). She is the recipient of many awards and honors, including the American Book Lifetime Achievement Award for Literature, the Woman Warrior in Arts and Culture Award from the Pacific Asian-American Bay Area Women's Coalition, and the first Woman of Words Award from the Women's Foundation. Executive director of Glide Church and president of the Glide Foundation, she has lived in San Francisco since 1963 and was poet laureate of San Francisco for 2000–2002.

MARIANNE MOORE (1887–1972) was born near St. Louis and grew up in Carlisle, Pennsylvania. After studying at Bryn Mawr College and Carlisle Commercial College, she taught at a government Indian school in Carlisle. She moved to Brooklyn, where she became an assistant at the New York Public Library. She loved baseball and spent a good deal of time watching her beloved Brooklyn Dodgers. She began to write imagist poetry and to contribute to the *Dial*, a prestigious literary magazine. She served as acting editor of the *Dial* from 1925 to 1929 and later as editor for four years. Moore was widely recognized for her work, receiving among other honors the Bollingen Prize for Poetry, the National Book Award, and the Pulitzer Prize.

WEB: Further research this author with LitLinks at bedfordstmartins.com/approachinglit.

ROBERT MORGAN (b. 1944) is a native of the North Carolina mountains. He was raised on land settled by his Welsh ancestors. He is an accomplished poet, novelist, and short-story writer. His four historical novels, three collections of short fiction, and nine volumes of poetry reveal an indelible sense of place for those familiar with, or strangers to, the Blue Ridge Mountains and address themes that matter to all people in all places: birth and death, love and loss, joy and sorrow, the necessity for remembrance, and the inevitability of forgetting. His recent books include *The Strange Attractor: New and Selected Poems* (2004) and *Boone: A Biography* (2007). He earned his B.A. at the University of North Carolina, Chapel Hill, and M.F.A. from the University of North Carolina, Greensboro. In 1971, Morgan began teaching at Cornell University, where, since 1992, he has been the Kappa Alpha Professor of English.

WEB: Further research this author with LitLinks at bedfordstmartins.com/approachinglit.

TONI MORRISON (b. 1931) was born Chloe Anthony Wofford in Lorain, Ohio. She spent her childhood in the Midwest, reading widely in such classic authors as Leo Tolstoy, Feodor Dostoyevski, Gustave Flaubert, and Jane Austen on the one hand, and absorbing folktales and literary culture of the black community from her father on the other. She received her B.A. from Howard University (where she began using a shortened form of her middle name because "Chloe" was difficult for others to pronounce) and her M.A. from Cornell University. She taught at Texas Southern University and Howard University and then worked as an editor for Random House. In 1958, while teaching at Howard, she married Harold Morrison, a Jamaican architect, and she began writing fiction. Her first novel, *The Bluest Eye*, was published in 1970, followed by *Sula* in 1973. Her next novel, *Song of Solomon* (1977), brought her international recognition. It was the first novel by a black writer to be a main selection of the Book-of-the-Month Club since Richard Wright's *Native Son* in 1949. In 1984, she was appointed to an Albert Schweitzer chair at the University of New York at Albany. Her fifth novel, *Beloved* (1987), was awarded the 1987 Pulitzer Prize for Fiction. In 1987, Morrison was named the Robert F. Goheen Professor in the Council of Humanities at Princeton University, the first black woman writer to hold a named chair at an Ivy League university. Later novels are *Jazz* (1992), *Paradise* (1998), and *Love* (2003). In 1993, she became the eighth woman and the first black woman to receive the Nobel Prize for Literature.

THYLIAS MOSS (b. 1954) was born in Cleveland. She attended Syracuse University and received her B.A. from Oberlin College and M.F.A. from the University of New Hampshire. She is the author of numerous books of poetry, most recently *Tokyo Butter* (2006); a memoir, *Tale of a Sky-Blue Dress* (1998); two children's books; and two plays, *Talking to Myself* (1984) and *The Dolls in the Basement* (1984). Among her awards are a Guggenheim Fellowship and a MacArthur Foundation Fellowship. She lives in Ann Arbor, where she is a professor of English at the University of Michigan.

WEB: Further research this author with LitLinks at bedfordstmartins.com/approachinglit.

JULIE MOULDS (RYBICKI) (b. 1962) received her B.A. from Hope College and her M.F.A. from Western Michigan University. Her poetry has been published in many literary magazines and was collected in her book *The Woman with a Cubed Head* (1998). She is author of the libretto of an operetta based on the Russian witch Babba Yaga, which was given its first performance in 1996. Moulds has taught children's literature and worked in children's bookstores. She has lived for many years with a recurring form of cancer. Her work often combines the magical with a harsh realism. She is presently working on a sonnet sequence based on the limericks of Edward Lear, her hero.

DAVID MURA (b. 1952), a third-generation Japanese American, was born in Great Lakes, Illinois, and graduated from Grinnell College in Iowa; he did graduate work at the University of Minnesota and Vermont College. Mura is a poet, creative nonfiction writer, critic, playwright, and performance artist. He is author of numerous books of poetry—including *After We Lost Our Way* (1989), which was selected as a National Poetry Series winner—and two memoirs: *Turning Japa-*

nese: Memoirs of a Sansei (1991), which was a *New York Times* Notable Book of the Year; and *Where the Body Meets Memory: An Odyssey of Race, Sexuality & Identity* (1996).

WEB: Further research this author with LitLinks at bedfordstmartins.com/approachinglit.

HARUKI MURAKAMI (b. 1949), one of the most popular and widely translated of all contemporary Japanese authors, is a novelist, short-story writer, essayist, and translator whose work combines postmodern techniques and fantasy with influences from American culture. He was born in Kyoto, but grew up in Ashiya, Hyogo, before moving to Tokyo in 1968 to study theater at Waseda University, graduating in 1975. From 1974 to 1981, Murakami and his wife managed a jazz club. He started to write in the 1970s and has published about a dozen novels in addition to many short stories. His most recent book in English, *Blind Willow, Sleeping Woman* (2006), is a collection of translations of twenty-four short stories. In 2006, Murakami became the sixth recipient of the Franz Kafka Prize from the Czech Republic for his 2002 novel *Umibe no Kafka* (*Kafka on the Shore*).

WEB: Further research this author with LitLinks at bedfordstmartins.com/approachinglit.

TASLIMA NASRIN (b. 1962) was born to a Muslim family in Mymensingh, East Pakistan. Because the area became independent in 1971, her city of birth is now in Bangladesh. She started writing when she was fifteen. After earning her medical degree in 1984, she worked in public hospitals for eight years. Because of the success of her second book of poetry in 1989, editors of progressive daily and weekly newspapers suggested that she write regular columns, which she used to write about women's oppression. Her strong language and uncompromising attitude against male domination stirred many people, eliciting both admiration and hatred. Islamic fundamentalists launched a campaign against her in 1990, staging street demonstrations and processions, and she was publicly assaulted several times. In 1993, a fundamentalist organization, Soldiers of Islam, issued a fatwa against her (set a price on her head) and she went into hiding. After two more fatwas were issued, many humanist organizations outside Bangladesh came to her support. In 1994, she was granted bail but forced to leave the country. She has since been living in exile in Europe and the United States. She has written twenty-eight books—novels and collections of poetry, essays, and short stories. Her applications to the Bangladesh government to be allowed to return have been denied repeatedly.

WEB: Further research this author with LitLinks at bedfordstmartins.com/approachinglit.

PABLO NERUDA (1904–1973), whose real name is Neftalí Ricardo Reyes Basoalto, was born in the town of Parral in central Chile. He began to contribute articles to the daily *La Mañana* in 1917, including his first poem "Mis ojos." In 1920, he became a contributor to the literary journal *Selva Austral* using a pen name to avoid conflict with his family, who disapproved of his literary ambitions. He chose the name "Pablo Neruda" in memory of the Czechoslovak poet Jan Neruda (1834–1891) and used it for over twenty years before adopting it legally in 1946. Neruda studied French and pedagogy at the University of Chile in Santiago. At age twenty-three he was appointed to the first of a series of diplomatic posts in various East Asian and European Countries. In 1939, while serving as consul general in Mexico, he transformed his *Canto General de Chile* into an epic poem about the whole South American continent, its nature, its people, and its historical destiny. This work, entitled *Canto General*, was published the same year in Mexico and underground in Chile. In 1943, Neruda returned to Chile, and in 1945 he was elected senator of the republic. Due to his protests against President González Videla's repressive policy against striking miners in 1947, he had to live underground in his own country for two years. He managed to leave in 1949; then after living in different European countries, he returned home in 1952. When Salvador Allende was elected president, he appointed Neruda as Chile's ambassador to France (1970–1972). Neruda died of leukemia in Santiago in 1973. A prolific writer, he published more than forty volumes of poetry, translations, and verse drama and is the most widely read of the Spanish

American poets. He was awarded the Nobel Prize for Literature in 1971.

WEB: Further research this author with LitLinks at bedfordstmartins.com/approachinglit.

DUANE NIATUM (b. 1938) was born in Seattle near his ancestral lands on the Washington coast. He is a Native American of mixed descent and a member of the Klallum tribe. He grew up moving among Washington, Oregon, California, and Alaska. At age seventeen, he enlisted in the navy, spending two years in Japan, after which he earned his B.A. in English at the University of Washington and his M.A. from Johns Hopkins University. He is author of several collections of poetry—including *Songs for the Harvester of Dreams* (1982), which won the National Book Award from the Before Columbus Foundation—and editor of two important collections, *Carriers of the Dream Wheel: Contemporary Native American Poetry* (1975) and *Harper's Anthology of Twentieth-Century Native American Poetry* (1988). His poems often reveal a stunningly keen ability to observe both the human-made and the natural world, and his structures are often sharply focused sequences of such observations.

LORINE NIEDECKER (1903–1970) was born and died in Fort Atkinson, Wisconsin. She lived much of her life in a small cabin on Black Hawk Island on Lake Koshkonong. Though celebrated by many of the most acclaimed experimental/modernist/objectivist writers of the twentieth century, among them WILLIAM CARLOS WILLIAMS and Louis Zukofsky, she chose to remain isolated from the poetry world, living an all but reclusive life. Niedecker said that she spent her childhood outdoors and from that developed her keen eye and strong sense of place. In 1931, she discovered "objectivist" poetry, which called for sincerity and objectification, values that fit well with her own vision and influenced her poems from that time on. While living on Black Hawk Island, she worked in a local hospital cleaning the kitchen and scrubbing floors. Her books included *New Goose* (1946), *North Central* (1968), *My Life by Water* (published the year of her death), and *Blue Chicory* (published posthumously in 1976).

Her selected poems, *The Granite Pail*, was not published until 1985.

NAOMI SHIHAB NYE (b. 1952) was born in St. Louis of a Palestinian father and an American mother and grew up in both the United States and Jerusalem. She received her B.A. from Trinity University in San Antonio, Texas, where she still resides with her family. She is the author of many books of poems, most recently *You and Yours* (2005), which received the Isabella Gardner Poetry Award. She has also written short stories and books for children and has edited anthologies, several of which focus on the lives of children and represent work from around the world. She is a singer-songwriter and on several occasions has traveled to the Middle East and Asia for the U.S. Information Agency, promoting international goodwill through the arts. Nye's work often attests to a universal sense of exile, from place, home, love, and one's self, and the way the human spirit confronts it.

WEB: Further research this author with LitLinks at bedfordstmartins.com/approachinglit.

JOYCE CAROL OATES (b. 1938) was born in Lockport, New York. She began storytelling in early childhood, composing picture stories even before she could write. Only after earning a B.A. from Syracuse University and an M.A. from the University of Wisconsin did she focus on writing as a career. Her first book was a collection of stories, *By the North Gate* (1963). Since then she has gone on to become one of the most versatile, prolific, and important American writers of her time, publishing more than a hundred books — novels, story collections, poetry, plays, children's books, and literary criticism. She has been nominated for the Nobel Prize for Literature three times. She is the Roger S. Berlind Distinguished Professor of Humanities at Princeton University.

WEB: Further research this author with LitLinks at bedfordstmartins.com/approachinglit.

TIM O'BRIEN (b. 1946) was born in Austin, Minnesota, and grew up in Worthington, Minnesota. He attended Macalester College in Minneapolis and, on graduation, was drafted for military service in Vietnam. O'Brien served from 1969 to 1970 as an in-fantry foot soldier in the Americal division, which was involved in the My Lai massacre in 1968, an event that figures prominently in O'Brien's novel *In the Lake of the Woods* (1994). While in Vietnam he rose to the rank of sergeant and received the Purple Heart. After Vietnam he entered graduate school at Harvard University but left to become a newspaper reporter, a career he pursued until publication of his first book, *If I Die in a Combat Zone, Box Me Up and Ship Me Home* (1973). He has gone on to write several other novels, including *Going after Cacciato* (1978), which won the National Book Award. His collection of stories *The Things They Carried* (1990) was a finalist for the National Book Critics Circle Award and for the Pulitzer Prize and winner of the Heartland Award from the *Chicago Tribune* and of the French prize for the best foreign book of the year; it was chosen by the *New York Times Book Review* as one of the nine best books of the year in all categories. He teaches in the creative writing program at Texas State University–San Marcos.

WEB: Further research this author with LitLinks at bedfordstmartins.com/approachinglit.

CD-ROM: Research this author in depth with cultural documents and multimedia resources on *LiterActive.*

FLANNERY O'CONNOR (1925–1964) was born in Savannah, Georgia. She earned her B.A. from Georgia State College for Women in Milledgeville, Georgia, and an M.F.A. from the University of Iowa Writers' Workshop. When she was twenty-five, she was found to have disseminated lupus, an incurable disease from which her father died when she was thirteen. She returned to Milledgeville for treatments that slowed the progress of the disease. Living with her mother on the family dairy farm, she wrote in the mornings and rested, read, and carried on correspondence in the afternoons, and she traveled to give occasional lectures as health permitted. She wrote only two novels, *Wise Blood* (1952) and *The Violent Bear It Away* (1960); her literary output also includes two collections of stories, *A Good Man Is Hard to Find* (1955) and *Everything That Rises Must Converge* (1965); a collection of her lectures and essays, *Mystery and Manners* (published posthumously in 1969); and a volume of correspondence (published in 1979 as *The Habit of Being*). Despite her career being cut short, O'Connor is widely recognized as a major southern writer. Her short stories are generally considered to be her finest work; they are carefully crafted, often focusing on grotesque characters redeemed by grace, have a crisp humor, and reflect the influence of her Catholic faith. *Complete Stories*, a collection of the thirty-one stories she wrote, won the National Book Award for fiction in 1972.

WEB: Further research this author with LitLinks at bedfordstmartins.com/approachinglit.

CD-ROM: Research this author in depth with cultural documents and multimedia resources on *LiterActive*.

DWIGHT OKITA (b. 1958) was born in Chicago and continues to live there. He began writing poems in first grade and published his first poem in the first-grade *Luella Log*. He earned a creative writing degree at University of Illinois, Chicago. His first book of poems, *Crossing with the Light*, was published in 1992. He describes himself as "Japanese American, gay, and Buddhist (Soka Gakkai International)" and says that these things are reflected in his work.

MARY OLIVER (b. 1935) was born in Cleveland and educated at Ohio State University and Vassar College. She is the author of eleven volumes of poetry, including *American Primitive* (1983), for which she won the Pulitzer Prize, and four books of prose. She holds the Catharine Osgood Foster Chair for Distinguished Teaching at Bennington College, and lives in Provincetown, Massachusetts, and Bennington, Vermont. Oliver is one of the most respected among poets concerned for the natural world.

WEB: Further research this author with LitLinks at bedfordstmartins.com/approachinglit.

TILLIE OLSEN (1912?–2007) was born either near Mead, Nebraska, or in Omaha, Nebraska. Her parents were Jewish immigrants who fled from the Russian czarist repression after the revolution of 1905. In the 1920s, her father became a leader in the Nebraska Socialist Party. After the eleventh grade she had to leave school to help support her family

during the Depression. She joined the Young Communist League and throughout her life was active politically, especially in causes rooted to her attachment to poor and oppressed workers. Early in 1932, she wrote four chapters of her first novel, *Yonnondio*. Part of one chapter was published as "The Iron Throat" in the *Partisan Review* in 1934 and was acclaimed critically. She wrote very little for the next two decades, during which she married, had a child, and had to care for it alone, much as described in her story "I Stand Here Ironing" (p. 467). She then had three more children with Jack Olsen, a YCL comrade whom she moved in with in 1936 and married in 1944. When her youngest child entered school in 1953, she was able to take creative writing classes at San Francisco State College and Stanford University. "Tell Me a Riddle" won the O. Henry Award for Best Short Story of the Year (1961). It and three other stories were published in *Tell Me a Riddle* (1961), selected by *Time* magazine for its "best-ten-books" list in 1962. Olsen then went on to complete *Yonnondio* (1974) and a nonfiction work, *Silences* (1978). She played an important role in reclaiming the works of neglected women authors. Despite her limited literary output, she received wide recognition for the quality of her fiction and for the importance of her contributions to the feminist movement.

WEB: Further research this author with LitLinks at bedfordstmartins.com/approachinglit.

WILLIAM OLSEN (b. 1954) was born in Omaha, Nebraska, and grew up in Park Forest, Illinois. He is the author of three collections of poetry, *The Hand of God and a Few Bright Flowers* (1988), *Vision of a Storm Cloud* (1996), and *Trouble Lights* (2002). He is coeditor, with Sharon Bryan, of *Planet on the Table: Poets on the Reading Life* (2003). His poems and essays have appeared in the *New Republic*, *Chicago Review*, *Paris Review*, *Southern Review*, *Triquarterly*, *New American Poets of the Nineties*, *The New Breadloaf Anthology of Contemporary Poetry*, *Poets of the New Century*, and many other magazines and anthologies. He is the recipient of an NEA Creative Writing Fellowship, a Nation/Discovery Award, and poetry awards from *Poetry Northwest* and *Crazyhorse*. He teaches at

Western Michigan University and in the M.F.A. Program at Vermont College.

MICHAEL ONDAATJE (b. 1943) was born in Colombo, Sri Lanka. He moved at age eleven to England and to Canada in 1962, where he earned a B.A. at the University of Toronto and an M.A. at Queens University. He has written more than a dozen collections of poetry, twice winning the Governor General's award, a memoir, several films, and four novels, the best known of which is *The English Patient* (1992), which shared the Booker Prize and was later made into an Academy Award–winning film. Ondaatje has also edited several anthologies, among them collections of Canadian short stories, and he and his wife, novelist Linda Spalding, edit the literary magazine *Brick*. He began his teaching career at the University of Western Ontario, London, and taught for many years at York University in Toronto.

SIMON J. ORTIZ (b. 1941) was born and raised in the Acoma Pueblo Community in Albuquerque. He received his early education from the Bureau of Indian Affairs school on the Acoma reservation, later attending the University of New Mexico and completing his M.F.A. at the University of Iowa, where he was a part of the International Writing Program. Unlike most Native American contemporary writers, Ortiz is a full-blooded Native American, and his first language is Keresan. By learning English, he found a way to communicate with those outside his immediate culture. His poetry explores the significance of individual origins and journeys, which he sees as forming a vital link in the continuity of life. His many writing accomplishments include poems, short stories, essays, and children's books. Ortiz has taught Native American literature and creative writing at San Diego State University, Navajo Community College, Marin College, the Institute for the Arts of the American Indian, the University of New Mexico, and most recently the University of Toronto.

WEB: Further research this author with LitLinks at bedfordstmartins.com/approachinglit.

WILFRED OWEN (1893–1918) was born in Oswestry, Shropshire, and went to school at Birkenhead Institute and Shrewsbury Techni-

cal School. He studied at London University but was forced to withdraw for financial reasons. After that he went to Dunsden, Oxfordshire, as a vicar's assistant. At Dunsden, Owen grew disaffected with the church and left to teach in France. He enlisted in 1915 and six months later was hospitalized in Edinburgh, where he met Siegfried Sassoon, whose war poems had just been published. Owen was sent back to the front and was killed one week before the armistice. He is the most widely recognized of the "war poets," a group of World War I writers who brought the realism of war into poetry.

WEB: Further research this author with LitLinks at bedfordstmartins.com/approachinglit.

CD-ROM: Research this author in depth with cultural documents and multimedia resources on *LiterActive*.

SUZAN-LORI PARKS (b. 1964) was born in Fort Knox, Kentucky, and attended high school in West Germany and Maryland. She started writing plays at Mount Holyoke College, from which she graduated with a B.A. in English and German literature. Her numerous plays include *Imperceptible Mutabilities in the Third Kingdom* (1990 Obie Award for Best New American Play), *The Death of the Last Black Man in the Whole Entire World*, *Venus* (1996 Obie Award), and *In the Blood* (2000 Pulitzer Prize finalist). She is the first African American woman to receive the Pulitzer Prize for Drama, for *Topdog/Underdog* (2002). She received a MacArthur Foundation Fellowship in 2001. In November 2002, she undertook the project of writing a short play each day for a year. *365 Plays/365 Days* was staged in nearly seven hundred theaters, in more than thirty cities across the United States in 2006–2007, one of the largest grassroots collaborations in theater history.

WEB: Further research this author with LitLinks at bedfordstmartins.com/approachinglit.

RICARDO PAU-LLOSA (b. 1954) was born in Havana, Cuba, and immigrated to the United States with his family at the age of six. He is the author of five books of poems, including *Cuba* (1993), *Vereda Tropical* (1998), and *The Mastery Impulse* (2002). He is also known as a writer of short fiction. An internationally renowned art critic, he has written extensively on the visual arts, specializing in twentieth-century Latin American painting and sculpture. He lives in Coral Gables, Florida.

OCTAVIO PAZ (1914–1998) was born in Mexico City. His grandfather was a novelist and his father worked as a secretary to Emilio Zapata. When Zapata was driven into retreat and assassinated, the family lived in exile in the United States for a short time. After they returned to Mexico, Paz studied law and literature at the National University but his ambition had always been to be a poet. Encouraged by PABLO NERUDA, he began to write. After his first collection, *Luna Silvestre* (1933), he went on to publish over forty books. An essayist, diplomat, and cultural historian as well as a poet, he was Mexico's foremost writer of the twentieth century. His most famous prose work, *El laberinto de la soledad* (*The Labyrinth of Solitude*), which explores the Mexican psyche, was published in 1961. In 1990, he won the Nobel Prize for Literature, the first for a writer from Mexico.

GUSTAVO PÉREZ FIRMAT (b. 1949) was born in Cuba and raised in Miami and attended Miami-Dade Community College and the University of Miami. He earned his Ph.D. in comparative literature from the University of Michigan and taught at Duke University from 1978 to 1999. He was named Duke University Scholar/Teacher of the Year in 1995. Currently the David Feinson Professor of Humanities at Columbia University, he is the author of several books of literary and cultural criticism, five collections of poetry, a novel, and a memoir. His study of Cuban American culture, *Life on the Hyphen*, was awarded the Eugene M. Kayden University Press National Book Award for 1994. He divides his time between New York City and Chapel Hill, North Carolina, where he lives with his wife and two children.

LUCIA PERILLO (b. 1958) has published four books of poetry: *Dangerous Life*, winner of the Norma Farber Award for the best "first book" of 1989; *The Body Mutinies* (1996), which was awarded the Revson Foundation Fellowship from PEN, the Kate Tufts Prize from Claremont University, and the Balcones Prize; *The Oldest Map with the Name America* (1999); and *Luck Is Luck*, a finalist for the Los

Angeles Times Book Award and included in the New York Public Library's list of "books to remember" for 2005. In her thirties, she was diagnosed with multiple sclerosis, about which she has written with candor and intimacy in poetry and prose, including her book of essays *I've Heard the Vultures Singing: Field Notes on Poetry, Illness, and Nature* (2007). In 2000, she was awarded a MacArthur Foundation Award for her work in poetry. She has taught at Syracuse University, Saint Martin's University, and Southern Illinois University–Carbondale and now lives in Olympia, Washington.

CARL PHILLIPS (b. 1959) is the author of numerous books of poetry, most recently *Riding Westward* (2006) and *Quiver of Arrows: Selected Poems 1986-2006* (2007). His collection *The Rest of Love* (2004) won the Theodore Roethke Memorial Foundation Poetry Prize and the Thom Gunn Award for Gay Male Poetry and was a finalist for the National Book Award. Phillips is also the author of a book of prose, *Coin of the Realm: Essays on the Art and Life of Poetry* (2004), and the translator of Sophocles' *Philoctetes* (2003). He is a chancellor of the Academy of American Poets and professor of English and of African and Afro-American Studies at Washington University in St. Louis, where he also teaches in the Creative Writing Program.

MARGE PIERCY (b. 1936) was born in working-class Detroit and studied at the University of Michigan and Northwestern University. She has published seventeen books of poetry, seventeen novels, a collection of essays on poetry, *Parti-Colored Blocks for a Quilt* (1982), and a memoir, *Sleeping with Cats* (2002). She has been deeply involved in many of the major progressive political battles of the past fifty years, including anti-Vietnam War activities, the women's movement, and most recently resistance to the war in Iraq.

WEB: Further research this author with LitLinks at bedfordstmartins.com/approachinglit.

WANG PING (b. 1957) received her B.A. from Beijing University and came to the United States in 1985. She earned a Ph.D. at New York University. She is the author of two short-story collections, *American Visa* (1994)

and *The Last Communist Virgin* (2007); a novel, *Foreign Devil* (1996); two poetry collections, *Of Flesh & Spirit* (1998) and *The Magic Whip* (2003); and a cultural study, *Aching for Beauty: Footbinding in China* (2000). She is also the editor and cotranslator of the anthology *New Generation: Poetry from China Today* (1999), and her writing has appeared in numerous journals and anthologies. She teaches English at Macalaster College in St. Paul, Minnesota.

WEB: Further research this author with LitLinks at bedfordstmartins.com/approachinglit.

ROBERT PINSKY (b. 1940) was born in Long Branch, New Jersey. He is the author of seven books of poetry, including *The Figured Wheel: New and Collected Poems 1966-1996* (1996), which won the 1997 Lenore Marshall Poetry Prize and was a Pulitzer Prize nominee. He has also published four books of criticism, two books of translation, a biography — *The Life of David* (2005), several books on reading poetry, and a computerized novel, *Mindwheel* (1984). In 1999 he coedited with Maggie Dietz *Americans' Favorite Poems: The Favorite Poem Project Anthology*. He is currently poetry editor of the weekly Internet magazine *Slate*. He teaches in the graduate writing program at Boston University, and in 1997 he was named Poet Laureate Consultant in Poetry at the Library of Congress. He lives in Newton Corner, Massachusetts.

WEB: Further research this author with LitLinks at bedfordstmartins.com/approachinglit.

SYLVIA PLATH (1932-1963) grew up in a middle-class family in Boston and showed early promise as a writer, having stories and poems published in magazines such as *Seventeen* while she was in high school. As a student at Smith College, she was selected for an internship at *Mademoiselle* magazine and spent a month working in New York in the summer of 1953. Upon her return home, she suffered a serious breakdown and attempted suicide, was institutionalized, and then returned to Smith College for her senior year in 1954. She received a Fulbright fellowship to study at Cambridge University in England, where she met poet Ted Hughes. They were married in 1956. They lived in the United States as well as England, and Plath studied under ROBERT LOWELL at Boston University. Her marriage to Hughes broke up in 1962, and from her letters and poems it appears that she was approaching another breakdown. On February 11, 1963, she committed suicide. Four books of poetry appeared during her lifetime, and her *Selected Poems* was published in 1985. The powerful, psychologically intense poetry for which she is best known (including "Daddy," p. 840) was written after 1960, influenced by the "confessional" style of Lowell.

WEB: Further research this author with LitLinks at bedfordstmartins.com/approachinglit.

CD-ROM: Research this author in depth with cultural documents and multimedia resources on *LiterActive*.

EDGAR ALLAN POE (1809-1849) was born in Boston. His parents were touring actors; both died before he was three years old, and he was taken into the home of John Allan, a prosperous merchant in Richmond, Virginia, and baptized Edgar Allan Poe. His childhood was uneventful, although he studied in England for five years (1815-1820). In 1826, he entered the University of Virginia but, because of gambling debts, stayed for only a year. He began to write and published a book of poems in 1827. He joined the army and gained an appointment to West Point, but was dismissed after six months for disobedience of orders. He turned to fiction writing and journalism to support himself. He began publishing stories and was appointed editor of the *Southern Literary Messenger* in Richmond, but his job was terminated after two years because of his drinking. He achieved success as an artist and editor in New York City (1837), then in Philadelphia (1838-1844), and again in New York (1844-1849), but failed to satisfy his employers and to secure a livelihood, and thus lived in or close to poverty his entire adulthood. He is famous for his horror tales and is credited with inventing the detective story, as well as for writing poetry with a prominent use of rhythms, alliteration, and assonance that gives it a strongly musical quality.

WEB: Further research this author with LitLinks at bedfordstmartins.com/approachinglit.

CD-ROM: Research this author in depth with cultural documents and multimedia resources on *LiterActive*.

KATHERINE ANNE PORTER (1890–1980), a descendant of Daniel Boone, was born in Indian Creek, Texas. When she was two, her mother died; she was raised by her grandmother and attended convent schools. At sixteen, she ran away to get married, but left her husband a few years later to be an actress. She worked briefly as a reporter in Chicago and Denver. Between 1918 and 1921, she became involved in revolutionary politics and worked as a journalist and teacher in Mexico, the setting for several of her stories. She traveled in the late 1920s to Europe, settling in Paris during the early 1930s, and began publishing stories in magazines. Her first book, *Flowering Judas and Other Stories* (1930), won high praise. It was followed by *Noon Wine* (1937), *Pale Horse, Pale Rider: Three Short Novels* (1939), and numerous other books of essays, stories, and nonfiction. Her only novel, *Ship of Fools* (1962), on which she worked for twenty years, was published when she was seventy-two. Her *Collected Stories* (1965) won the Pulitzer Prize for Fiction and the National Book Award.

WEB: Further research this author with LitLinks at bedfordstmartins.com/approachinglit.

NAHID RACHLIN (b. 1946) was born in Iran. She is author of a memoir, *Persian Girls* (2006); four novels, *Foreigner* (1978), *Married to a Stranger* (1983), *The Heart's Desire* (1995), and *Jumping over Fire* (2006); and a collection of short stories, *Veils* (1993). She has taught at Yale University and Barnard College and presently is an associate fellow at Yale.

WEB: Further research this author with LitLinks at bedfordstmartins.com/approachinglit.

SIR WALTER RALEGH (1552–1618) was born in Hayes Barton, Devonshire, England. He was an undergraduate at Oxford University and read law at the Middle Temple in London, but he apparently did not complete either course of studies. He was a "Renaissance man," proficient in many fields: soldier, courtier, adventurer, colonist, student of science, historian, and poet. Ralegh was a royal favorite and, according to popular legend, once placed his cloak in the mud for Queen Elizabeth I. He undertook three expeditions to America and introduced potatoes and tobacco to Britain. In 1603, after the death of the queen, he was arrested by James I, accused (unjustly) of treason for opposing James's succession to the throne. Ralegh's death sentence was commuted to life imprisonment in the Tower of London, where he focused on historical writing — including his *History of the World* — and scientific study. He was released in 1616 to search for gold in the Orinoco, but his expedition failed and he violated the terms of the mission by destroying a Spanish town. At the request of Spain, his death sentence was reinstated, and he was beheaded at Whitehall in 1618.

WEB: Further research this author with LitLinks at bedfordstmartins.com/approachinglit.

A. K. RAMANUJAN (1929–1993) was an internationally renowned poet and scholar as well as a professor of linguistics, anthropology, the history of religions, folklore, and literary studies. He was one of India's most published authors with an international recognition for expertise as a writer and translator. He wrote in English and Kannada and translated works from Tamil and Kannada into English and from English into Kannada. At the time of his death, he was the William H. Colvin Professor in South Asian Languages and Civilizations at the University of Chicago.

DUDLEY RANDALL (1914–2002) was born in Washington, D.C., but lived most of his life in Detroit. His first published poem appeared in the *Detroit Free Press* when he was thirteen. He worked for Ford Motor Company and then for the U.S. Postal Service and served in the South Pacific during World War II. He graduated from Wayne State University in 1949 and then from the library school at the University of Michigan. In 1965, Randall established the Broadside Press, one of the most important publishers of modern black poetry. "Ballad of Birmingham" (p. 843), written in response to the 1963 bombing of a church in which four African American girls were killed, has been set to music and recorded. It became an "anthem" for many in the civil rights movement.

WEB: Further research this author with LitLinks at bedfordstmartins.com/approachinglit.

DAHLIA RAVIKOVITCH (1936–2005) was born in Ramat Gan, a Tel Aviv suburb, in Israel, and after her father's death was sent to live in a kibbutz. She studied at the Hebrew University of Jerusalem and later worked as a journalist and high school teacher. She was the author of ten volumes of poetry, three collections of short stories, and a number of children's books. Her language, rich inner life, and sensitivity won her an enthusiastic readership in Israel and abroad as one of the most skilled and versatile Israeli poets. She was a peace activist and contributed to the construction of a feminist consciousness in Israeli poetry. She translated children's literature, including *Mary Poppins* and *Cinderella*, as well as the poetry of WILLIAM B. YEATS and T. S. ELIOT. She received several literary awards, including the Bialik Prize and the 1990 Israel Prize.

ADRIENNE RICH (b. 1929) was born in Baltimore, the elder daughter of a forceful Jewish intellectual who encouraged and critiqued her writing. While she was at Radcliffe College in 1951, W. H. AUDEN selected her book *A Change of World* for the Yale Younger Poets Award. She became involved in radical politics, especially in the opposition to the Vietnam War, and taught inner-city minority youth. In the 1970s, Rich became a feminist, freeing herself from her old models and becoming an influential figure in contemporary American literature. She is the author of nearly twenty volumes of poetry, including *Diving into the Wreck* (1973), *Dark Fields of the Republic* (1995), and *The School among the Ruins: Poems 2000–2004* (2004), which won the Book Critics Circle Award, and several books of nonfiction prose. She was awarded a MacArthur Foundation Fellowship in 1994 and in 1999 received the Lifetime Achievement Award from the Lannan Foundation.

WEB: Further research this author with LitLinks at bedfordstmartins.com/approachinglit.

JACK RIDL (b. 1944) was born and grew up in New Wilmington, Pennsylvania. His father was a basketball coach and his mother had family connections with circuses throughout the United States. He has said that he spent his life watching the big shows from behind the scenes. He has published four collections of poetry — *The Same Ghost* (1984), *Be tween* (1988), *Poems from* The Same Ghost *and* Be tween (1993), and *Broken Symmetry* (2006) — and three chapbooks: *After School* (1988), *Against Elegies* (selected by BILLY COLLINS as winner of the Center for Book Arts 2001 Poetry Chapbook Competition), and *Outside the Center Ring* (2006). His poems have appeared in numerous anthologies and poetry journals. He taught at Hope College for thirty-four years before retiring in 2006; in 1996, he was named Michigan Professor of the Year by the Council for the Advancement and Support of Education.

ALBERTO RÍOS (b. 1952) was born to a Guatemalan father and an English mother in Nogales, Arizona, on the Mexican border. He earned a B.A. in English and one in psychology and an M.F.A. at the University of Arizona. In addition to seven books of poetry, he has published two collections of short stories, and a memoir, *Capirotada: A Nogales Memoir* (1999). His work often fuses realism, surrealism, and magical realism, as exemplified by "Nani" (p. 847). Since 1994, he has been Regents Professor of English at Arizona State University, where he has taught since 1982.

WEB: Further research this author with LitLinks at bedfordstmartins.com/approachinglit.

LEN ROBERTS (1947–2007) left home at sixteen after being raised by an abusive mother and an alcoholic father. Much of his poetry reflects his exploration of bleak relationships and stark landscapes and the ways he had to come to accept his past and the traumatic flux that marked his life. He published twelve collections, among them *Black Wings* (1989), which was selected for the National Poetry Series, and most recently, *The Disappearing Trick* (2007). He also published translations of the Hungarian poet Sándor Csoóri. He has won numerous awards for his poetry, including a Guggenheim Award, two National Endowment for the Arts Awards, a National Endowment for the Humanities Award, and six Pennsylvania Council on the Arts Awards. He was professor of English at Northampton Community College in Bethlehem, Pennsylvania, for over thirty years.

EDWIN ARLINGTON ROBINSON (1869–1935) was born in Head Tide, Maine, and grew up in the equally provincial Maine town of Gardiner, the setting for much of his poetry. He was forced to leave Harvard University after two years because of his family's financial difficulties. He published his first two books of poetry in 1896 and 1897 ("Richard Cory" [p. 640] appeared in the latter). For the next quarter-century Robinson chose to live in poverty and write his poetry, supporting himself through temporary jobs and charity from friends. President Theodore Roosevelt, at the urging of his son Kermit, used his influence to get Robinson a sinecure in the New York Custom House in 1905, giving him time to write. He published numerous books of mediocre poetry in the next decade. The tide turned for him with *The Man against the Sky* (1916); the numerous volumes that followed received high praise and sold well. He was awarded three Pulitzer Prizes: for *Collected Poems* (1921), *The Man Who Died Twice* (1924), and *Tristram* (1927). Robinson was the first major American poet of the twentieth century, unique in that he devoted his life to poetry and willingly paid the price in poverty and obscurity.

THEODORE ROETHKE (1908–1963) was the son of a commercial greenhouse operator in Saginaw, Michigan. As a child, he spent much time in the greenhouse, and the impressions of nature he formed there later influenced the subjects and imagery of his verse. Roethke graduated from the University of Michigan and studied at Harvard University. Although he published only eight books of poetry, they were held in high regard by critics, some of whom considered him among the best poets of his generation. *The Waking* was awarded the Pulitzer Prize in 1954; *Words for the Wind* (1958) received the Bollingen Prize and the National Book Award. He taught at many colleges and universities and gained a reputation as an exceptional teacher of poetry writing, though his career was interrupted several times by serious mental breakdowns.

WEB: Further research this author with LitLinks at bedfordstmartins.com/approachinglit.

CD-ROM: Research this author in depth with cultural documents and multimedia resources on *LiterActive*.

WENDY ROSE (b. 1948) was born Bronwen Elizabeth Edwards in Oakland, California, of Hopi and Mewok ancestry. As a teenager, she dropped out of high school and became connected with the bohemian scene in San Francisco. Her experiences in the city and the struggle in finding her identity within her mixed lineage would be major influences on her poetry. Rose attended Costa College and the University of California, Berkeley, and completed a Ph.D. in anthropology. The author of a dozen volumes of poetry, she has taught American Indian studies at the University of California, Berkeley, and California State University, Fresno, as well as being coordinator of American Indian studies at Fresno City College. Rose's poems often combine the world of the contemporary native culture with an elegiac voice, a quiet sense of reverence and loss.

MARY RUEFLE (b. 1952) was born near Pittsburgh but spent her early life moving around the United States and Europe as the daughter of a military officer. She graduated from Bennington College with a literature major. She has published ten books of poetry, including *Memling's Veil* (1982), *The Adamant* (1989, winner of the 1988 Iowa Poetry Prize), *A Little White Shadow* (2006), and *Indeed I Was Pleased with the World* (2007). Among awards she has received are a Guggenheim Fellowship, an American Academy of Arts and Letters Award in Literature, and a Whiting Foundation Writer's Award. She lives in Vermont, where she is a professor in the Vermont College M.F.A. program.

SALMAN RUSHDIE (b. 1947) was born in Bombay, India, to a middle-class Muslim family. His paternal grandfather was an Urdu poet and his father a Cambridge-educated businessman. At fourteen, Rushdie was sent to Rugby School in England. In 1964, his parents moved to Karachi, Pakistan, reluctantly joining the Muslim exodus from India. After graduating in 1968 from King's College, Cambridge, where he read history, he worked for a time in television in Pakistan, then as a freelance advertising copywriter in London from 1971 to 1981. His first novel, *Grimus* (1975), a work of fantastical science fiction drawing on pre-Islamic Persian mythology, anticipates the magic realism that informs much of his work. His second novel, *Midnight's Children* (1981), brought him international recognition; it won the prestigious Booker Prize for fiction and in 1993 was judged to have been the "Booker of Bookers," the best novel to have won the Booker Prize for fiction in the award's twenty-five-year history. His fourth novel, *The Satanic Verses* (1988), which won the Whitbread Award, proved highly controversial. Many Muslims regarded the character modeled on the Prophet Muhammad as blasphemous, and the former Iranian spiritual leader Ayatollah Khomeini called on all zealous Muslims to execute the writer and the publishers of the book. For several years Rushdie lived in hiding, in London and New York. Since spring 2007, he has been Distinguished Writer in Residence at Emory University in Atlanta, Georgia.

SONIA SANCHEZ (b. 1934) was born Wilsonia Driver in Birmingham, Alabama. In 1943, she moved to Harlem with her sister to live with their father and his third wife. She earned a B.A. in political science from Hunter College in 1955 and studied poetry writing with Louise Bogan at New York University. In the 1960s, she became actively involved in the social movements of the times, and she has continued to be a voice for social change. She has published more than a dozen books of poetry, many plays, and two books for children and has edited two anthologies of literature. She began teaching in the San Francisco area in 1965 and was a pioneer in developing black studies courses at what is now San Francisco State University, from 1968 to 1969. She was the first Presidential Fellow at Temple University, where she began teaching in 1977, and held the Laura Carnell Chair in English there until her retirement in 1999. She lives in Philadelphia.

WEB: Further research this author with LitLinks at bedfordstmartins.com/approachinglit.

GEORGE SAUNDERS (b. 1958) was born in Amarillo, Texas, and grew up on the South Side of Chicago. In 1981, he received a B.S. in geophysical engineering from Colorado School of Mines in Golden, Colorado, and earned an M.A. in creative writing from Syracuse University in 1989. His stories and essays have appeared in numerous magazines, particularly the *New Yorker*. He has published three collections of short fiction, *CivilWar-Land in Bad Decline: Stories and a Novella* (1996), *Pastoralia* (2000), and *In Persuasion Nation* (2006); a novel, *The Brief and Frightening Reign of Phil* (2005); and a children's book, *The Very Persistent Gappers of Frip* (2000). He was chosen as one of the "Top Twenty Writers under Forty" by the *New Yorker* in its summer fiction issue for 1999 and was awarded a MacArthur Foundation Fellowship in 2006.

CHERYL SAVAGEAU (b. 1950) was born in central Massachusetts and grew up in an island neighborhood on Lake Quinsigamond. She is of mixed French Canadian and Abenaki heritage. She graduated from Clark University in 1978, where she began writing "by accident": She signed up for a poetry class through Continuing Education to finish her degree, and it turned out to be a writing class. She is the author of three books of poetry, *Home Country* (1992), *Dirt Road Home* (1995), and *Mother/Land* (2006). Her children's book, *Muskrat Will Be Swimming*, was named a 1996 Notable Book for Children by the Smithsonian. She worked for several years as a poet and storyteller in the schools through the Massachusetts Artist in Residence program and was a member of Wordcraft Circle of Native Writers and Storytellers, working as a mentor to apprentice native writers. She also works as a textile artist: Her quilts have been exhibited at the University of New Hampshire in Durham. She now lives in New Hampshire.

VIJAY SESHADRI (b. 1954) was born in Bangalore, India, and came to the United States at the age of five. He grew up in Columbus, Ohio, and has lived in many parts of the country, including the Northwest, where he spent five years working in the fishing industry, and the Upper West Side in New York City. He earned his B.A. degree from Oberlin College and his M.F.A. from Columbia University. His poems, essays, and reviews have appeared in many literary magazines and journals. He has published two collections of poetry, the more recent of which—*The Long Meadow* (2004)—won the James Laughlin Award. He currently teaches poetry and nonfiction writing at Sarah Lawrence College and lives in Brooklyn.

WEB: Further research this author with LitLinks at bedfordstmartins.com/approachinglit.

WILLIAM SHAKESPEARE (1564–1616) was born in Stratford-upon-Avon, England, where his father was a glovemaker and bailiff, and presumably went to grammar school there. He married Anne Hathaway in 1582, and sometime before 1592 he left for London to work as a playwright and an actor. Shakespeare joined the Lord Chamberlain's Men (later the King's Men), an acting company for which he wrote thirty-five plays, before retiring to Stratford around 1612. In addition to being a skillful dramatist, he was perhaps the finest lyric poet of his day, as exemplified by songs scattered through his plays, two early non-dramatic poems (*Venus and Adonis* and *The Rape of Lucrece*), and the sonnet sequence expected of all noteworthy writers in the Elizabethan age. Shakespeare's sonnets were probably written in the 1590s, though not published until 1609.

WEB: Further research this author with LitLinks at bedfordstmartins.com/approachinglit.

CD-ROM: Research this author in depth with cultural documents and multimedia resources on *LiterActive*.

PERCY BYSSHE SHELLEY (1792–1822) was born into a wealthy aristocratic family in Sussex County, England. He was educated at Eton, then went on to Oxford University, but was expelled after six months for writing a defense of atheism, the first price he would pay for his nonconformity and radical (for his time) commitment to social justice. The following year he eloped with Harriet Westbrook, daughter of a tavern keeper, despite his belief that marriage was a tyrannical and degrading social institution (she was sixteen, he eighteen). He became a disciple of the radical social philosopher William Godwin, fell in love with Godwin's daughter, Mary Wollstonecraft Godwin (later the author of *Frankenstein*), and went to live with her in France. Two years later, after Harriet committed suicide, Shelley and Godwin married and moved to Italy, where they shifted about restlessly and Shelley was generally short on money and in poor health. Under such trying circumstances, he wrote his greatest works.

He died at age thirty, when the boat he was in was overturned by a sudden storm.

WEB: Further research this author with LitLinks at bedfordstmartins.com/approachinglit.

MASAOKA SHIKI (1867–1902) was born in Matsuyama as the son of a low-ranking samurai, who died when Masaoka was five. His mother, Yae, was a teacher. Masaoka studied classic Japanese literature at the Imperial University and began to write poetry in 1885. After withdrawing from the university in 1892, he was a haiku editor for the newspaper *Nippon*. While covering the Chinese-Japanese War as a war correspondent in 1894–1895, he contracted tuberculosis and remained an invalid for much of his life, devoting his time to the writing of haiku and waka (or tanka). In 1892, he started his reform of the haiku, which at that time was considered incapable of expressing the complexities of modern life. Masaoka advocated a realistic, descriptive style, which he regarded as the original spirit of Japanese verse, and his poetic treatises greatly influenced the Japanese literary world in defining modern Japanese modes of expression. His sickroom, when he was bound to bed, became a meeting place for his friends and followers, who gathered there to discuss literature. He died in Tokyo a few weeks before his thirty-fifth birthday.

LESLIE MARMON SILKO (b. 1948) was born in Albuquerque of mixed Pueblo, Mexican, and white ancestry and grew up on the Laguna Pueblo Reservation in New Mexico. She earned her B.A. with honors from the University of New Mexico. In a long and productive writing career (she was already writing stories in elementary school), she has published poetry, novels, short stories, essays, letters, and film scripts. She taught creative writing first at the University of New Mexico and later at the University of Arizona. She has been named a Living Cultural Treasure by the New Mexico Humanities Council and has received the Native Writers' Circle of the Americas Lifetime Achievement Award. Her work is a graphic telling of the life of native peoples, maintaining its rich spiritual heritage while exposing the terrible consequences of European domination.

WEB: Further research this author with LitLinks at bedfordstmartins.com/approachinglit.

CHARLES SIMIC (b. 1938) was born in Belgrade, Yugoslavia. In 1953 he, his mother, and his brother joined his father in Chicago, where he lived until 1958. His first poems were published in 1959, when he was twenty-one. In 1961, he was drafted into the U.S. Army, and in 1966 he earned his B.A. from New York University. His first book of poems, *What the Grass Says*, was published in 1967. Since then, he has published more than sixty books of poetry, translations, and essays, including *The World Doesn't End: Prose Poems* (1990), for which he received the Pulitzer Prize for Poetry. Simic is a professor of English at the University of New Hampshire. In 2007, he was named Poet Laureate Consultant in Poetry to the Library of Congress.

WEB: Further research this author with LitLinks at bedfordstmartins.com/approachinglit.

ZADIE SMITH (b. 1975) was born Sadie Smith (she changed her name when she was fourteen) in North London to an English father and a Jamaican mother. She began writing and publishing fiction while she studied English literature at Cambridge University, graduating in 1997. Her first novel, *White Teeth* (2000), completed during her final year at Cambridge, won the Guardian First Book Award, the Whitbread First Novel Award, and the Commonwealth Writers Prize (Overall Winner, Best First Book), and was shortlisted for the Orange Prize for Fiction and the Author's Club First Novel Award. It has been translated into over twenty languages. Her second novel, *The Autograph Man* (2002), won the 2003 Jewish Quarterly Literary Prize for Fiction. Her third novel, *On Beauty* (2005), won the 2006 Orange Prize for Fiction. She has also written a nonfiction book about writing, *Fail Better* (2006). In 2003, she was nominated by *Granta* magazine as one of twenty "Best of Young British Novelists."

CATHY SONG (b. 1955) was born in Hawaii and lived in the small town of Wahiawa on Oahu. She left Hawaii for the East Coast, studying at Wellesley College and then at Boston University. Her first book, *Picture Bride*, was chosen by Richard Hugo for the Yale Series of Younger Poets in 1982. Since then she has published three other books of poetry.

WEB: Further research this author with LitLinks at bedfordstmartins.com/approachinglit.

SOPHOCLES (496–406 B.C.E.), born the son of a wealthy merchant in Athens, enjoyed the advantages of the thriving Greek Empire. He studied all of the arts. By the age of sixteen, he was known for his beauty and grace and was chosen to lead a choir of boys at a celebration of the victory of Salamis. He served as a statesman, general, treasurer, and priest as well as, with Aeschylus and Euripides, one of the three major authors of Greek tragedy. He was an accomplished actor and performed in many of his own plays. Fragments indicate that he wrote over 120 plays, of which only 7 are extant. His plays introduced several innovations to Greek theater, particularly adding a third actor, which allowed for more dialogue and greater complexity of action and reduced the role of the chorus. He also changed the form of drama. Aeschylus had used three tragedies to tell a single story; Sophocles made each play a complete and independent work, which required greater compression of action and resulted in greater dramatic intensity.

WEB: Further research this author with LitLinks at bedfordstmartins.com/approachinglit.

CD-ROM: Research this author in depth with cultural documents and multimedia resources on *LiterActive*.

GARY SOTO (b. 1952) grew up in Fresno, California. He earned his B.A. from California State University, Fresno, and his M.F.A. from the University of California, Irvine. He worked his way through college at jobs such as picking grapes and chopping beets. Much of his poetry comes out of and reflects his working background, that of migrant workers and tenant farmers in the fields of southern California, and provides glimpses into the lives of families in the barrio. Soto's language comes from earthy, gritty, raw everyday American speech. His first book, *The Elements of San Joaquin*, won the 1976 United States Award from the International Poetry Forum.

He has published ten collections of poetry, two novels, four essay collections, and numerous young-adult and children's books and has edited three anthologies.

WEB: Further research this author with LitLinks at bedfordstmartins.com/approachinglit.

CD-ROM: Research this author in depth with cultural documents and multimedia resources on *LiterActive*.

EDMUND SPENSER (1552–1599), a contemporary of WILLIAM SHAKESPEARE, was the greatest English nondramatic poet of his time. Best known for his Romantic and national epic *The Faerie Queene*, Spenser wrote poems of a number of other types as well and was important as an innovator in metrics and forms (as in his development of the special form of sonnet and unique stanza form that bear his name—see the Glossary of Literary Terms, p. 1624). The sonnet included in this anthology, beginning "One day I wrote her name upon the strand" (p. 861), is number 75 in *Amoretti*, a sequence of sonnets about a courtship addressed to a woman named Elizabeth, probably Elizabeth Boyle, who became his second wife.

WEB: Further research this author with LitLinks at bedfordstmartins.com/approachinglit.

WILLIAM STAFFORD (1914–1995) was born in Hutchinson, Kansas, and studied at the University of Kansas and then at the University of Iowa Writers' Workshop. In between, he was a conscientious objector during World War II and worked in labor camps. In 1948, Stafford moved to Oregon, where he taught at Lewis and Clark College until he retired in 1980. His first major collection of poems, *Traveling through the Dark* (1962), was published when Stafford was forty-eight. It won the National Book Award in 1963. He went on to publish more than sixty-five volumes of poetry and prose and came to be known as a very influential teacher of poetry. From 1970 to 1971, he was Consultant in Poetry at the Library of Congress.

WEB: Further research this author with LitLinks at bedfordstmartins.com/approachinglit.

JOHN STEINBECK (1902–1968) is one of the most widely read American novelists of the twentieth century. He was born in Salinas, California, and raised near Monterey in the fertile Salinas Valley, the setting of much of his fiction. He studied English literature at Stanford University off and on until 1925, when he decided to pursue his dream of being a writer. He supported himself by working at a variety of jobs, thus gaining insight into the problems faced by the working class. His first novel, *Cup of Gold* (1929), was unsuccessful, but he found his voice by writing about California and the struggles of rural workers during the Great Depression. Success arrived with *Tortilla Flat* (1935), *In Dubious Battle* (1936), *Of Mice and Men* (1937), and *The Long Valley* (1938), a collection of short stories including "The Chrysanthemums" (p. 513). His greatest work, *The Grapes of Wrath* (1939), won the Pulitzer Prize. He received the Nobel Prize for Literature in 1962.

WEB: Further research this author with LitLinks at bedfordstmartins.com/approachinglit.

WALLACE STEVENS (1879–1955) was born in Reading, Pennsylvania, and attended Harvard University for three years. He tried journalism and then attended New York University Law School, after which he worked as a legal consultant. He spent most of his life working as an executive for the Hartford Accident and Indemnity Company, spending his evenings writing some of the most imaginative and influential poetry of his time. Although now considered one of the major American poets of the twentieth century, he did not receive widespread recognition until the publication of his *Collected Poems* just a year before his death.

WEB: Further research this author with LitLinks at bedfordstmartins.com/approachinglit.

MARK STRAND (b. 1934) was born on Prince Edward Island, Canada, and studied at Antioch College, Yale University, the University of Florence, and the University of Iowa. He is the author of numerous collections of poetry, including *Reasons for Moving* (1968), *The Story of Our Lives* (1973), *Selected Poems* (1980), *The Continuous Life* (1990), *Blizzard of One* (1998), which won the Pulitzer Prize for Poetry, *Dark Harbor* (1993), and *Man and Camel* (2006). He has also published two books of prose, several volumes of translation (of works by Rafael Alberti and Carlos Drummond de

Andrade, among others), several monographs on contemporary artists, and three books for children. He served as Poet Laureate Consultant in Poetry to the Library of Congress in 1990–1991 and is a former chancellor of the Academy of American Poets. He teaches English and comparative literature at Columbia University in New York.

KELLY STUART (b. 1961) is the author of several highly successful plays, among them *Demonology* (1996), *Mayhem* (2004), *The Life of Spiders* (2005), and *The Disappearing World* (2007). She received a Guthrie New Play grant and commission which enabled her to spend extensive time in eastern Turkey to research and write *Shadow Language* (2007), which deals with the Kurdish "problem," American idealism, and political asylum issues in the United States. She was the recipient of a Whiting Fellowship in 2000 (for *The Life of Spiders*) and a 2004 artists' fellowship from the New York Foundation of the Arts. Stuart currently lives in New York and teaches playwriting at Columbia University.

VIRGIL SUÁREZ (b. 1962) was born in Havana, Cuba. Eight years later he left with his parents for Spain, where they lived until they came to the United States in 1974. He received his B.A. from California State University, Long Beach, and his M.F.A. from Louisiana State University. He is the author of six collections of poetry, five novels, a collection of short fiction, and a memoir titled *Spared Angola: Memories from a Cuban-American Childhood* (1997). He is editor or coeditor of several important anthologies, including *Iguana Dreams: New Latino Fiction* (1993), the first anthology of Cuban American writers, and *Paper Dance: 55 Latino Poets* (2000), a collection of contemporary Latino poetry. His work has been included in hundreds of magazines, journals, and anthologies. Presently he is a professor of creative writing at Florida State University.

WEB: Further research this author with LitLinks at bedfordstmartins.com/approachinglit.

SEKOU SUNDIATA (1948–2007) was born and raised in Harlem. His work was deeply influenced by the music, poetry, and oral traditions of African American culture. A self-proclaimed radical in the 1970s, for the past several decades he used poetry to comment on the life and times of our culture. His work, which encompasses print, performance, music, and theater, received praise for its fusion of soul, jazz, and hip-hop grooves with political insight, humor, and rhythmic speech. He regularly recorded and performed on tour with artists such as Craig Harris and Vernon Reid.

WEB: Further research this author with LitLinks at bedfordstmartins.com/approachinglit.

JONATHAN SWIFT (1667–1745) was born in Ireland of English parents and educated at Kilkenny College and Trinity College, Dublin. He worked in England for a decade as a private secretary and for four years as a political writer, but spent the rest of his life in Ireland as dean of St. Patrick's Cathedral in Dublin. Although he is best known for his satires in prose (such as *Gulliver's Travels* and "A Modest Proposal"), Swift's original ambition was to be a poet, and he wrote occasional verse throughout his life.

WEB: Further research this author with LitLinks at bedfordstmartins.com/approachinglit.

WISLAWA SZYMBORSKA (b. 1923), born in Bnin (now a part of Kórnik) in western Poland, has lived since 1931 in Kraków, where she studied Polish literature and sociology at Jagiellonian University. From 1953 to 1981, she worked as poetry editor and columnist for the Kraków literary weekly *Zycie Literackie*, for which she wrote a series of essays, "Lektury nadobowiazkowe," from which four collections have been published as books. She has published sixteen books of poetry and her poems have been translated and published in book form. She was awarded the Nobel Prize for Literature in 1996, for "poetry that with ironic precision allows the historical and biological context to come to light in fragments of human reality."

WEB: Further research this author with LitLinks at bedfordstmartins.com/approachinglit.

MARY TALLMOUNTAIN (1918–1994) was born Mary Demonski in the interior of Alaska in Nilato. Her mother was a Koyukon-Athabaskan and her father a Scotch-Irish signal corpsman. Her mother died when she was six, and she was the first child from her village to be adopted by an Anglo-American couple. Tall Mountain's poetry was fully influenced by her spiritual connections to her birthplace, her family, and her native culture. She began every day by talking with her late grandmother, mother, and two aunts. She claimed both a Christian faith and "the ritual of the Indian. We have only one God — and we know that — but we follow two paths. Why not? Why not worship Him twice. Him or Her." The Mary Tall Mountain Circle in San Francisco produces and distributes her work and her support for Native American and Tenderloin writers.

AMY TAN (b. 1952) was born in Oakland, California. Her father had been educated as an engineer in Beijing; her mother left China in 1949, just before the Communist revolution. After her father's death, Tan and her mother lived in Switzerland, where Tan attended high school. She received her B.A. and M.A. in English and linguistics from San Jose State University, took a job as a language development consultant to the Alameda County Association for Retarded Citizens, and later directed a training project for developmentally disabled children. She became a highly successful freelance business writer specializing in corporate communications for such companies as AT&T, IBM, and Pacific Bell, but she found the work unsatisfying and began writing fiction. A visit to China with her mother in 1987, and meeting relatives there, gave her the realization, as she put it, that "I belonged to my family and my family belonged to China." Inspired by LOUISE ERDRICH's *Love Medicine* (1986), she began to write stories about her own minority culture. A literary agent read one of them and secured her an advance that allowed her to write full-time, resulting in her very successful first book, *The Joy Luck Club* (1989). She has gone on to write four more novels, two children's books, and a collection of essays, *The Opposite of Fate: A Book of Musings* (2003). She is also the lead singer for the Rock Bottom Remainders, a rock band made up of fellow writers who make select appearances at charities and benefits that support free-speech issues.

WEB: Further research this author with LitLinks at bedfordstmartins.com/approachinglit.

CD-ROM: Research this author in depth with cultural documents and multimedia resources on *LiterActive*.

ALFRED, LORD TENNYSON (1809–1892) was born in Somersby, Lincolnshire, and grew up there in the tense atmosphere of his unhappy father's rectory. He went to Trinity College, Cambridge, but was forced to leave because of family and financial problems, so he returned home to study and practice the craft of poetry. His early volumes, published in 1830 and 1832, received bad reviews, but his *In Memoriam* (1850), an elegy on his close friend Arthur Hallam, who died of a brain seizure, won acclaim. He was unquestionably the most popular poet of his time (the "poet of the people") and arguably the greatest of the Victorian poets. He succeeded WILLIAM WORDSWORTH as poet laureate, a position he held from 1850 until his death.

WEB: Further research this author with LitLinks at bedfordstmartins.com/approachinglit.

DYLAN THOMAS (1914–1953) was born in Swansea, Wales, and after grammar school became a journalist. He worked as a writer for the rest of his life. His first book of poetry, *Eighteen Poems*, appeared in 1934 and was followed by *Twenty-five Poems* (1936), *Deaths and Entrances* (1946), and *Collected Poems* (1952). His poems are often rich in textured rhythms and images. He also wrote prose, chiefly short stories collectively appearing as *Portrait of the Artist as a Young Dog* (1940), and a number of film scripts and radio plays. His most famous work, *Under Milk Wood*, written as a play for voices, was first performed in New York on May 14, 1953. Thomas's radio broadcasts and his lecture tours and poetry readings in the United States brought him fame and popularity. Alcoholism contributed to his early death in 1953.

WEB: Further research this author with LitLinks at bedfordstmartins.com/approachinglit.

CD-ROM: Research this author in depth with cultural documents and multimedia resources on *LiterActive*.

JEAN TOOMER (1894–1967) was born in Washington, D.C., of mixed French, Dutch, Welsh, Negro, German, Jewish, and Indian blood. Although he passed for white during certain periods of his life, he was raised in a predominantly black community and attended black high schools. He began college at the University of Wisconsin but transferred to the College of the City of New York. He spent several years publishing poems and stories in small magazines. In 1921, he took a teaching job in Georgia and remained there four months; the experience inspired *Cane* (1923), a book of prose poetry describing the Georgian people and landscape that became a central work of the Harlem Renaissance. He later experimented in communal living and both studied and tried to promulgate the ideas of the Russian mystic George Gurdjieff and later of Quakerism. From 1950 on, he published no literary works and began withdrawing from public life.

WEB: Further research this author with LitLinks at bedfordstmartins.com/approachinglit.

Quincy Troupe (b. 1943) was born in New York City and grew up in St. Louis, Missouri. He is the author of sixteen books, including eight volumes of poetry, most recently *The Architecture of Language* (2006). He is recipient of two American Book Awards, for his collection of poetry *Snake-Back Solos* (1980) and his nonfiction book *Miles the Autobiography* (1989). In 1991, he received the prestigious Peabody Award for writing and coproducing the seven-part Miles Davis Radio Project aired on National Public Radio in 1990. *Transcircularities: New and Selected Poems* (2002) received the Milt Kessler Award for 2003 and was a finalist for the Paterson Poetry Prize. Troupe has taught at UCLA, Ohio University, the College of Staten Island (CUNY), Columbia University (in the Graduate Writing Program), and the University of California, San Diego. He is now professor emeritus of creative writing and American and Caribbean literature at UCSD. He is the founding editorial director of *Code* magazine and former artistic director of "Arts on the Cutting Edge," a reading and performance series at the Museum of Contemporary Art, San Diego. He was the first official poet laureate of the state of California, appointed to the post in 2002 by Governor Gray Davis.

WEB: Further research this author with LitLinks at bedfordstmartins.com/approachinglit.

John Updike (b. 1932) was born in Reading, Pennsylvania, but grew up in the small nearby city of Shillington. He earned his B.A. at Harvard University where he contributed to and later edited the *Harvard Lampoon*. He spent 1954–1955 at the Ruskin School of Drawing and Fine Arts in Oxford, England, then worked at the *New Yorker* until 1957 when he left to become a full-time writer. In 1959, he published his first book of stories, *The Same Door*, and his first novel, *The Poorhouse Fair*, and he moved from New York City to Massachusetts, where he has lived most of the time since. A prolific writer, Updike has published over sixty books — novels, collections of poems, short stories, essays, criticism, and a memoir. He has received numerous awards, including the National Medal of Art and the National Medal for the Humanities. Two of his novels, *Rabbit Is Rich* (1981) and *Rabbit at Rest* (1990), have won Pulitzer Prizes.

WEB: Further research this author with LitLinks at bedfordstmartins.com/approachinglit.

CD-ROM: Research this author in depth with cultural documents and multimedia resources on *LiterActive*.

Helena María Viramontes (b. 1954) was born and raised in East Los Angeles. She began writing poetry and fiction at Immaculate Heart College, from which she earned her B.A. in 1975 (one of five Chicanas in her class). In the next few years, several of her stories won prizes. She entered the M.F.A. program at the University of California, Irvine, in 1981, and completed her degree in 1994, after many years of successful writing. She has published three novels, most recently *Their Dogs Came with Them* (2007), and two collections of short stories. She is coeditor, with Maria Herrera-Sobek, of two anthologies, *Chicana Creativity and Criticism: Charting New Frontiers in American Literature* (1988) and *Chicana (W)rites: On Word and Film* (1995). Her stories are known for their vivid depictions of Chicano culture and especially of the struggles and sufferings of Chicana women. She is an associate professor of English at Cornell University.

WEB: Further research this author with LitLinks at bedfordstmartins.com/approachinglit.

GERALD VIZENOR (b. 1934) was born in Minnesota. He attended New York University for one year and then transferred to the University of Minnesota, where he earned his B.A. in 1960. He has done graduate studies at the University of Minnesota and Harvard University. He has taught at several colleges and universities in the Midwest and California. A member of the Chippewa tribe, he has been a major figure in both the literature and scholarship of Native Americans. In addition to publishing twenty books of poetry and fiction, he is the author of *Earthdrivers: Narratives on Tribal Descent* (1981) and *The People Named the Chippewa: Narrative Histories* (1985). His novel *Griever: An American Monkey King in China* won the Fiction Collective Prize for 1986. He also published a collection of original haiku, *Matsushima: Pine Island* (1984). Vizenor's work reflects his studied relationship to the natural world as he opens himself to the influences of both his Chippewa heritage and his study of Japanese culture and haiku.

DEREK WALCOTT (b. 1930), born on the eastern Caribbean island of St. Lucia, moves between the African heritage of his family and the English cultural heritage of his reading and education. Both of his parents were educators who immersed themselves in the arts. His early training was in painting, which, like his poetry, was influenced by his Methodist religious training. He attended St. Mary's College and the University of the West Indies in Jamaica. His first book, *25 Poems* (1948), appeared when he was eighteen, and he has published prolifically since then: more than twenty books of poetry, at least twenty plays, and a book of nonfiction. His work, which explores both the isolation of the artist and regional identity, is known for blending Caribbean, English, and African traditions. He was awarded the Nobel Prize for Literature in 1992, the academy citing him for "a poetic oeuvre of great luminosity, sustained by a historical vision, the outcome of a multicultural achievement." He teaches creative writing at Boston University every fall and lives the rest of the year in St. Lucia.

WEB: Further research this author with LitLinks at bedfordstmartins.com/approachinglit.

ALICE WALKER (b. 1944) was born in Eatonton, Georgia. Her parents were sharecropper farmers. When she was eight, she lost sight in one eye when one of her older brothers accidentally shot her with a BB gun. She was valedictorian of her high-school class. Encouraged by her teachers and her mother to go on to college, she attended Spelman College in Atlanta, a school for black women, for two years, and graduated from Sarah Lawrence College. From the mid-1960s to the mid-1970s, she lived in Tougaloo, Mississippi. She was active in the civil rights movement of the 1960s and remains an involved activist today. Her first book was a collection of poetry, *Once* (1968). She is a prolific writer, having gone on to publish over thirty books of poetry, novels, short stories, and nonfiction. Her best-known novel, *The Color Purple* (1982), won the American Book Award and the Pulitzer Prize for Fiction and was made into a motion picture directed by Steven Spielberg.

WEB: Further research this author with LitLinks at bedfordstmartins.com/approachinglit.

WANG PING — See WANG PING, page 1557.

JAMES WELCH (1940–2003) was born in Browning, Montana. His father was a member of the Blackfoot tribe, his mother of the Gros Ventre tribe. He attended schools on the Blackfoot and Fort Belknap reservations and earned a degree from the University of Montana, where he studied under Richard Hugo. Welch published many books of poetry, fiction, and nonfiction. His hard, spare poems often evoke the bleakest side of contemporary Native American life. He received a Lifetime Achievement Award for Literature from the Native Writers' Circle in 1997.

WEB: Further research this author with LitLinks at bedfordstmartins.com/approachinglit.

PATRICIA JABBEH WESLEY (b. 1955) was born in Monrovia, Liberia, and lived there until her father sent her and her siblings to the Tugbakeh Boarding Mission School in her father's hometown. She was teaching at the University of Liberia when civil war broke out in 1991. She immigrated with her family to the United States and received her Ph.D. in English and creative writing at Western Michigan University. Wesley is the author of two collections of poetry, *The Palm Could Bloom: Poems of Africa* (1998) and *Becoming Ebony* (2003). Her poems also have appeared in many anthologies and literary journals. She is a faculty member at Pennsylvania State University–Altoona.

ROBERTA HILL WHITEMAN (b. 1947), a member of the Oneida tribe, grew up around Oneida and Green Bay, Wisconsin. She earned a B.A. from the University of Wisconsin and an M.F.A. from the University of Montana. Her poems have appeared in many magazines and anthologies. Her three collections of poetry — *Star Quilt* (1984), *Your Fierce Resistance* (1993), and *Philadelphia Flowers* (1996) — have been illustrated by her husband, Ernest Whiteman, an Arapaho artist.

WALT WHITMAN (1819–1892) was born in rural Long Island, the son of a farmer and carpenter. He attended grammar school in Brooklyn and took his first job as a printer's errand–boy for the *Long Island Patriot*. Attending the opera, dabbling in politics, participating in street life, and gaining experience as student, printer, reporter, writer, carpenter, farmer, seashore observer, and teacher provided the bedrock for his future poetic vision of an ideal society based on the realization of self. Although Whitman liked to portray himself as uncultured, he read widely in the King James Bible, SHAKESPEARE, Homer, Dante, Aeschylus, and SOPHOCLES. He worked for many years in the newspaper business and began writing poetry only in 1847. In 1855, at his own expense, Whitman published the first edition of *Leaves of Grass*, a thin volume of twelve long untitled poems. Written in a highly original and innovative free verse, influenced significantly by music and with a wide-ranging subject matter, the work seemed strange to most of the poet's contemporaries, but they did recognize its value: Ralph Waldo Emerson wrote to him, less than three weeks after Whitman sent him a copy, "I greet you at the beginning of a great career." He spent much of the remainder of his life revising and expanding this book. *Leaves of Grass* today is considered a masterpiece of world literature, marking the beginning of modern American poetry, and Whitman is widely regarded as America's national poet.

WEB: Further research this author with LitLinks at bedfordstmartins.com/approachinglit.

CD-ROM: Research this author in depth with cultural documents and multimedia resources on *LiterActive*.

RICHARD WILBUR (b. 1921) was born in New York City and grew up in rural New Jersey. He attended Amherst College and began writing poetry during World War II, while fighting in Italy and France. Afterward, he studied at Harvard University and then taught there and at Wellesley College, Wesleyan University, and Smith College. He has published many books of poetry, including *Things of This World* (1956), for which he received the Pulitzer Prize for Poetry and the National Book Award, and *New and Collected Poems* (1988), which also won a Pulitzer Prize. He has always been respected as a master of formal constraints, comparing them to the genie in the bottle: The restraints stimulate the imagination to achieve results unlikely to be reached without them. He has also published numerous translations of French plays, two books for children, a collection of prose pieces, and editions of WILLIAM SHAKESPEARE and EDGAR ALLAN POE. In 1987, he was appointed Poet Laureate Consultant in Poetry at the Library of Congress. He now lives in Cummington, Massachusetts.

WEB: Further research this author with LitLinks at bedfordstmartins.com/approachinglit.

NANCY WILLARD (b. 1936) was raised in Ann Arbor, Michigan, and educated at the University of Michigan and Stanford University. She has published twelve books of poetry, including *Water Walker* (1989), which was nominated for the National Book Critics Circle Award, and *Swimming Lessons: New and Selected Poems* (1996); two novels — *Things Invisible to See* (1984) and *Sister Water* (1993); and four books of stories and essays. She is the author of numerous children's books, including *A Visit to William Blake's Inn: Poems for Innocent and Experienced Travelers* (containing such delightfully titled poems as "The Wise Cow Enjoys a Cloud" and "The Marmalade Man Makes a Dance to Mend Us"), which was the first book of poetry to win the prestigious Newbery Medal. She lives in Poughkeepsie, New York, and teaches at Vassar College.

WEB: Further research this author with LitLinks at bedfordstmartins.com/approachinglit.

WILLIAM CARLOS WILLIAMS (1883–1963) was born in Rutherford, New Jersey; his father was an English emigrant and his mother was of mixed Basque descent from Puerto Rico. He decided to be both a writer and a doctor while in high school in New York City. He graduated from the medical school at the University of Pennsylvania, where he was a friend of Ezra Pound and Hilda Doolittle. After an internship in New York, Williams practiced general medicine in Rutherford, writing poems between seeing patients. His first book of poems was published in 1909, and he subsequently published poems, novels, short stories, plays, criticism, and essays. Initially one of the principal poets of the imagist movement, Williams sought later to invent an entirely fresh — and distinctly American — poetic, whose subject matter was centered on the everyday circumstances of life and the lives of common people. Williams, like WALLACE STEVENS, became one of the major poets of the twentieth century and exerted great influence on poets of his own and later generations.

WEB: Further research this author with LitLinks at bedfordstmartins.com/approachinglit.

BILL WILLINGHAM (b. 1956) entered the field of graphic art by drawing fantasy ink pictures for *Dungeons & Dragons* game rule books in the late 1970s and early 1980s. He became better known for his comic book series *Elementals*, begun in 1984, and for contributing stories to *Green Lantern*. He emerged as an important graphic writer in the late 1990s with a plethora of works including the thirteen-issue *Pantheon*, two modern stories about Beowulf in *Clockwork Storybook*, and the six-issue *Proposition Player*. He is best-known for the popular Fableland Series, beginning with *Fables: Legends in Exile* (2002). He lives in Las Vegas.

AUGUST WILSON (1945–2005) — See page 1024.

NELLIE WONG (b. 1934) was born and raised in Oakland, California's Chinatown. Since she began writing in the 1970s, she has spoken out against the oppression of all people — in particular workers, women, minorities, and immigrants — and has worked steadily with community-based and international organizations to achieve racial justice. She is known as both a poet and a feminist human-rights activist. She is the author of three poetry volumes and coeditor of an anthology of political essays, *Voices of Color* (1999). She has taught creative writing at several colleges in the San Francisco Bay area. Until her retirement, she worked as senior analyst in the Office of Affirmative Action/Equal Opportunity at the University of San Francisco.

WEB: Further research this author with LitLinks at bedfordstmartins.com/approachinglit.

WILLIAM WORDSWORTH (1770–1850) was born and raised in the Lake District of England. Both of his parents died by the time he was thirteen. He studied at Cambridge University, toured Europe on foot, and lived in France for a year during the first part of the French Revolution. He returned to England, leaving behind a lover, Annette Vallon, and their daughter, Caroline, from whom he was soon cut off by war between England and France. He met SAMUEL TAYLOR COLERIDGE, and in 1798 they together published *Lyrical Ballads*, the first great work of the English Romantic movement. He changed poetry forever by his decision to use common language in his poetry instead of artificial poetic diction (see the Glossary of Literary Terms, p. 1621). In 1799, he and his sister Dorothy moved to Grasmere, in the Lake District, where he married Mary Hutchinson, a childhood friend. His greatest works were produced between 1797 and 1808. He continued to write for the next forty years but never regained the heights of his early verse. In 1843, he was named poet laureate, a position he held until his death in 1850.

WEB: Further research this author with LitLinks at bedfordstmartins.com/approachinglit.

JAMES WRIGHT (1927–1980) grew up in Martin's Ferry, Ohio. He attended Kenyon College, where his study under John Crowe Ransom sent his early poetry in a formalist direction. After spending a year in Austria on a Fulbright fellowship, he returned to the

United States and earned an M.A. and a Ph.D. at the University of Washington, studying under THEODORE ROETHKE and STANLEY KUNITZ. He went on to teach at the University of Minnesota, Macalester College, and Hunter College. His working-class background and the poverty that he saw during the Depression stirred a sympathy for the poor and "outsiders" of various sorts, which shaped the tone and content of his poetry. He published numerous books of poetry; his *Collected Poems* received the Pulitzer Prize for Poetry in 1972.

WEB: Further research this author with LitLinks at bedfordstmartins.com/approachinglit.

SIR THOMAS WYATT THE ELDER (1503–1542) was born in Kent, England, and educated at St. John's College, Cambridge. He spent most of his life as a courtier and diplomat, serving King Henry VIII as ambassador to Spain and as a member of several missions to Italy and France. These travels introduced Wyatt to Italian writers of the High Renaissance, whose work he translated, thus introducing the sonnet form into English. He was arrested twice and charged with treason, sent to the Tower of London, and acquitted in 1541. Aristocratic poets at the time rarely published their poems themselves; works circulated in manuscript and in published collections ("miscellanies") gathered by printers. The most important of these is a volume published by Richard Tottel in 1557 entitled *Songs and Sonnets* but more commonly known as *Tottel's Miscellany*, which includes ninety-seven of Wyatt's sonnets and delightful lyrics.

WEB: Further research this author with LitLinks at bedfordstmartins.com/approachinglit.

XU GANG (b. 1945) was born in Shanghai, China. He was drafted into the army in 1962 and began writing poetry in support of the Cultural Revolution. However, he gradually became disillusioned with its violent practices and disruptive results while studying at Beijing University, from which he graduated in 1974. He has authored several collections of poems.

JOHN YAU (b. 1950) was born in Lynn, Massachusetts, a year after his parents emigrated from China. He received a B.A. from Bard College and an M.F.A. from Brooklyn College, where he studied with John Ashbery. He has published over fifty books and pamphlets — among them artists' books, a great deal of art criticism, an anthology of fiction, and at least ten volumes of poetry, including *Corpse and Mirror* (1983), a National Poetry Series book selected by John Ashbery, and, most recently, *Paradiso Diaspora* (2006).

WEB: Further research this author with LitLinks at bedfordstmartins.com/approachinglit.

WILLIAM BUTLER YEATS (1865–1939) was born in Sandymount, Dublin, to an Anglo-Irish family. On leaving high school in 1883, he decided to be an artist, like his father, and attended art school but soon gave it up to concentrate on poetry. His first poems were published in 1885 in the *Dublin University Review*. Religious by temperament but unable to accept orthodox Christianity, Yeats throughout his life explored esoteric philosophies in search of a tradition that would substitute for a lost religion. He became a member of the Theosophical Society and the Order of the Golden Dawn, two groups interested in Eastern occultism, and later developed a private system of symbols and mystical ideas. Through the influence of Lady Gregory, a writer and promoter of literature, he became interested in Irish nationalist art, helping to found the Irish National Theatre and the famous Abbey Theatre. He was actively involved in Irish politics, especially after the Easter Rising of 1916. He continued to write and to revise earlier poems, leaving behind, at his death, a body of verse that, in its variety and power, placed him among the greatest twentieth-century poets of the English language. He was awarded the Nobel Prize for Literature in 1923.

WEB: Further research this author with LitLinks at bedfordstmartins.com/approachinglit.

CD-ROM: Research this author in depth with cultural documents and multimedia resources on *LiterActive*.

AL YOUNG (b. 1939) was born in Ocean Springs, Mississippi, and lived for a decade in the South before moving to Detroit. He attended the University of Michigan and the

University of California, Berkeley. He has been a professional guitarist and singer, a disk jockey, a medical photographer, and a warehouseman and has written eight books of poetry (most recently, *Coastal Nights and Inland Afternoons: Poems, 2001-2006*), five novels, memoirs, essays, and film scripts. He has edited a number of books, including *Yardbird Lives!* (1978) and *African American Literature: A Brief Introduction and Anthology* (1995). In the 1970s and 1980s, Young cofounded the journals *Yardbird Reader* and *Quilt* with poet-novelist Ishmael Reed. From 2005 to 2007, he served as California Poet Laureate.

WEB: Further research this author with LitLinks at bedfordstmartins.com/approachinglit.

RAY A. YOUNG BEAR (b. 1950) was born and grew up in the Mesquakie Tribal Settlement near Tama, Iowa. His poetry has been influenced by his maternal grandmother, Ada Kapayou Old Bear, and his wife, Stella L. Young Bear. He attended Pomona College in California as well as Grinnell College, the University of Iowa, Iowa State University, and Northern Iowa University. He has taught creative writing and Native American literature at the Institute of American Indian Art, Eastern Washington University, the University of Iowa, and Iowa State University. Young Bear and his wife cofounded the Woodland Song and Dance Troupe of Arts Midwest in 1983. Young Bear's group has performed traditional Mesquakie music in this country and the Netherlands. Author of four books of poetry, a collection of short stories, and a novel, he has contributed to contemporary Native American poetry and to the study of it for nearly three decades.

WEB: Further research this author with LitLinks at bedfordstmartins.com/approachinglit.

Appendix on Scansion

This appendix returns to the use of meter in poetry, extending the discussion begun in Chapter 16. We said there that meter forms an important component of rhythm for poems using it, ones having a regular beat created by a repeating pattern of stressed and unstressed syllables. In Chapter 16, we indicated the beat in metrical lines by using capital letters for stressed syllables (i AM bic ME ter GOES like THIS) to show that you can hear meter by listening for the stressed (louder) syllables, those that get more emphasis than the unstressed syllables. That's the important thing for readers beginning to read poetry attentively: hearing a steady beat when it's present and being able to distinguish poetry that has such a beat from poetry that does not. As you read more poetry, however, you may want to deal with meter in a more sophisticated way. This appendix introduces the traditional system of scansion and shows how metrical analysis contributes to a fuller understanding and appreciation of a poem written in meter.

Here is a brief review of some basic concepts and terminology introduced in Chapter 16. Go back to pages 655–64 to review them if you need to.

FOOT   A two- or three-syllable metrical unit made up (usually) of one stressed and one or two unstressed syllables. The most important metrical feet are these:

Iamb: unstressed, stressed: da DA (for example, "awake")

Trochee: stressed, unstressed: DA da ("wakeful")

Anapest: unstressed, unstressed, stressed: da da DA ("in a dream")

Dactyl: stressed, unstressed, unstressed: DA da da ("sleepily")

Spondee: stressed, stressed: DA DA ("dream house")

LINE LENGTH   Line lengths are measured by the number of feet in the line and are labeled with names derived from Greek roots:

Trimeter: a line with three metrical feet

Tetrameter: a line with four metrical feet

Pentameter: a line with five metrical feet

Hexameter: a line with six metrical feet

These are the commonest line lengths; more rare are monometer (one foot) and heptameter (seven).

The meter in a poem is highlighted and clarified through a process called **scansion**. To scan a poem involves marking its stressed syllables — whether the stress is heavy or light — with an accent mark (´) and marking its unstressed syllables with a curved line (˘). You use a vertical line to indicate the way the lines divide up into feet. (You need not try to distinguish stronger from weaker stresses — only syllables that receive at least *some* stress from those that receive *none*.)

Ĭám | bĭc mé | tĕr góes | lĭke thís.[1]

You then describe (or label) the type of foot used most often in the line and the line length — in this case, iambic tetrameter.

The ideal way to scan a poem is to listen for where you stress syllables. But read with a natural emphasis, not a singsong regularity. Where *you* stress syllables is important: Scansion is not a mechanical process; it involves your interpretation. Scansion reflects the way a poem actually is read and so will differ slightly from one reader to another. Practice hearing the stresses as a recurring background beat, somewhat like the bass guitar or drums. But do not emphasize the beat; instead, concentrate on the words as you feel the beat underneath them.

You can use logic to do a rough but generally adequate scansion. First, start with multisyllabic words, using a dictionary if necessary to put ´ on the accented syllables and ˘ on the unaccented ones. Then put stress marks on important shorter words (most nouns and verbs, for example). Rhyming syllables almost always are stressed. Helping words (such as *a, an, to*) are rarely stressed and can safely be given ˘ marks. Just examining a poem thoughtfully will show where at least three-fourths of the stressed or unstressed syllables fall. The remainder can be sounded or figured out: For example, in ˘˘ ? ˘˘, the ? will almost surely be stressed; five unstressed syllables in a row would be very unusual. After such an analysis, read the poem aloud to test how well the stress patterns you identified match what you hear.

To begin practicing scansion, read the following stanza, which describes the setting of the island of Shalott in the days of King Arthur.

---

[1]In dividing lines into feet, begin by looking for the way that yields the greatest number of identical groupings of twos or threes since most feet in a poem will be the same; then figure out the exceptions.

Notice that dividing lines into feet may involve breaking up words. Feet work primarily with syllables, not words. However, in a line like "Evening traffic homeward burns" (from Yvor Winters's "Before Disaster"), which could be scanned as either iambic or trochaic, trochaic seems preferable because it keeps the words together ("Évĕnĭng | tráffĭc | hómĕwărd | búrns" rather than "Éve | nĭng tráf | fĭc hóme | wărd búrns").

Alfred, Lord Tennyson   1809–1892

From The Lady of Shalott   [1832]

On either side the river lie
Long fields of barley and of rye,
That clothe the wold° and meet the sky;   plain
And through the field the road runs by
To many-tower'd Camelot;   5
And up and down the people go,
Gazing where the lilies blow
Round an island there below,
The island of Shalott.

Now read it again, the way we have scanned the lines:

Ŏn ei | thĕr síde | thĕ rí | vĕr líe
Lóng fíelds | ŏf bár | lĕy and² | ŏf rýe,
Thăt clothe | thĕ wóld | ănd méet | thĕ sky;
Ănd thro' | thĕ fíeld | thĕ róad | rŭns bý
　　Tŏ má | nў-tów | er'd Ca | mĕlót;   5
Ănd úp | ănd dówn | thĕ péo | plĕ gó,
Gáz | ĭng whére | thĕ líl | ĭes blów
Róund | ăn ís | lănd thére | bĕlów,
　　Thĕ ís | lănd óf | Shălótt.

Notice how several metrical substitutions control emphasis and make the sound natural, not artificially "poetic." Lines 1, 3, 5, and 6 are in regular iambic feet and have the important role of establishing the prevailing "beat," but line 2 begins with a spondee ("Long fields"), and lines 7 and 8 lack the opening, unstressed syllable; unlike the opening six lines, they begin with a stressed syllable and have only seven syllables, instead of eight.

For practice, try scanning the following lines. Mark the stressed syllables with ´ and unstressed syllables with ˘, and use | to divide lines into feet. Try first to do it by hearing the beat; if that doesn't work, figure it out logically, following the steps we suggest above. To compare your result with the way we scanned it, see page 1583.

---

²A reserved accent [`] often is used for a very lightly stressed syllable, such as the slight stress a normally unstressed word (like *and*) receives when its position in a line calls for it.

Samuel Taylor Coleridge   1772–1834

Metrical Feet   [1806]
Lesson for a Boy

Trochee trips from long to short.
From long to long in solemn sort
Slow Spondee stalks; strong foot! yet ill able
Ever to come up with Dactyl trisyllable.
Iambics march from short to long; —   5
With a leap and a bound the swift Anapests throng.

To illustrate further, we will consider what scansion might add to our understanding, enjoyment, and appreciation of the following poem. Read it twice, once silently, once aloud, and listen for the beat.

Emily Dickinson   1830–1886

I like to see it lap the Miles   [c. 1862; 1891]

I like to see it lap the Miles —
And lick the Valleys up —
And stop to feed itself at Tanks —
And then — prodigious step

Around a Pile of Mountains —   5
And supercilious peer
In Shanties — by the sides of Roads —
And then a Quarry pare

To fit its Ribs
And crawl between   10
Complaining all the while
In horrid — hooting stanza —
Then chase itself down Hill —

And neigh like Boanerges[3] —
Then — punctual as a Star   15
Stop — docile and omnipotent
At its own stable door —

---

[3]*Boanerges* ("sons of thunder") is the name Jesus gave to the brothers James and John, his disciples (see Mark 3:17).

This poem resembles a riddle — it forces the reader to supply the implied antecedent to the pronoun *it*. The answer would have been obvious to most readers in Emily Dickinson's day, and perhaps it was to you as you read it too; but cultural changes (especially the replacement of rail systems with freeways) make the riddle less obvious for many readers today. Because trains are not as much a part of our visual imagery as they were during the last century, we may be tempted to read "neigh" and "stable" as literal, rather than as parts of an extended implied metaphor. Scanning the poem can help us clarify why meter is an important aspect of this imaginative depiction of a train. Try scanning it yourself first and then compare your reading with ours.

The poem starts with a stanza of regular iambic feet, alternating lines of tetrameter and trimeter.

> Ĭ líke | tŏ sée | ĭt láp | thĕ Míles –
> Ănd líck | thĕ Vál | lĕys úp –
> Ănd stóp | tŏ féed | ĭtsélf | ăt Tánks –

Not only is the meter regular, but the rhythm is steady as well; the short, simple words can be read at an even pace, with no internal punctuation interrupting or slowing them down; the dashes at the ends of lines 1 and 2 (Dickinson had her own, unusual ideas about punctuation) give just enough pause for a breath to keep the pace in the following line. Meter and rhythm together echo the repetitive, predictable, clickity-clack sound that train wheels make as they pass over the cracks between the rails.

In line 4 the meter remains regular — "Ănd thén – | pródĭ | gĭóus stép" — but the rhythm slows down because the dash creates a pause and because the multisyllabic word "prodigious" takes longer to say than the short monosyllabic words "stop to feed." There is no punctuation at the end of stanzas 1 and 2; in fact, the entire poem is made up of one sentence. We usually pause briefly at the end of a line even when there is no punctuation, and we pause a bit longer at the end of a stanza that lacks end punctuation. That too slows the rhythm — just as, we find in the next line, the speed of the train decreases as it curls around mountains. (We may even sense the effect of having our eyes "step around" the end of the first stanza into the beginning of the second, in imitation of the train.)

Scansion can alert us to another way of slowing the rhythm, in line 5. The pattern established in the first stanza leads us to expect that first and third lines will have eight syllables, four iambic feet. When you read line 5, your ear should hear a difference, something unexpected. Here's an example of the tension between "expected" meter and "heard" meter. Scanning the line ("Ăróund | ă Píle | ŏf Móun | taĭns –") reveals that the difference is that it has only seven syllables and lacks the final stressed syllable the other lines have. We tend to linger a bit on the end of that line, slowing the rhythmic pace, partly because of the dash but partly out of respect for the syllable that our ear expects to hear.

The next three lines reestablish the expected pattern of iambic trimeter, tetrameter, trimeter, at a steady pace but slower than lines 1 to 3, slower largely because the combinations of sounds cannot be said rapidly: "Ănd sú | percíl | iŏus peér / Ĭn Shán | tiĕs — bý | thĕ sídes | ŏf Roáds - / Ănd thén | ă Quár | rў páre."

Just as we become reaccustomed to the expected pattern, we are jolted out of it again. Stanza 3 has five lines instead of the usual four and it begins with two lines of only four syllables — two iambic feet — instead of the expected eight syllables, four feet:

Tŏ fít | ĭts Ríbs
Ănd cráwl | bĕtweén
Cŏmpláin | ĭng áll | thĕ whíle
Ĭn hór | rĭd - hoót | ĭng stán | ză-

Scanning the lines helps us notice that the unexpected line still fits the "pattern": Lines 9 and 10 are just an expected tetrameter line divided into two. With a playfulness typical of her, almost as a poetic joke, Dickinson has the stanza become visually narrower as the train peels along the edge of a quarry, fitting its metal "ribs" into the tight space. Line 9 is made tight by the sound of the "fit its" in the middle. As the train slows down for the narrow curves, the poem's rhythm does too, because of the pauses at the ends of the short lines 9 and 10, the long, slow *craaawwll* sound in the middle of line 10, and the length of words and the sound combinations of "Complaining" and "horrid — hooting."

The poem, like the train, hesitates at the end of line 12, which like line 5 lacks the final stressed syllable, then speeds up in regular meter as the train thunders downhill —

Thĕn cháse | ĭtsélf | dŏwn Híll —
Ănd neígh | lĭke Bó | ănér | gĕs —

— only to pause sharply at the missing eighth syllable in line 14.

Scansion clarifies a final playful, but metrically effective, touch. After line 15 slows down, "Thén — púnc | tŭăl ás | ă Stár," because of the spondee, the dash, and the extra syllable (though some readers may slur "púnc | tŭal" into two syllables and keep the meter regular), line 16 again does the unexpected. Thus far, most lines have begun with an unstressed syllable and an iambic foot, and our ears begin to expect that. This line jolts our ear, pulls us up short, by a metrical substitution — a spondee instead of an iamb: "Stóp — dóc | ĭle ănd | ŏmni | pŏtént / Ăt íts | ŏwn stá | blĕ doór." The substitution puts strong emphasis on "Stop," and that, together with the dash following it, interrupts the rhythm — stops us — as the train, now quiet though still powerful, stops at the end of its journey.

In this case it seems that Dickinson may have deliberately decided how meter would fit the shape and effects of the poem. However, poets who use meter do not always count syllables and decide consciously that it is time to make a substitution or to leave off a final stressed syllable. Their ears are attuned to meters, so they hear whether a line "sounds appropriate" or "right" or whether they need to make further changes. Looking back, they may be able to figure out (perhaps by scanning the line) what made it sound better, what made it "work." Scanning — and attention to meter generally — can be retrospective, part of the process of figuring out why what was done proved effective, or it can be part of the creative process.

Let's try this now on a more complex passage, a famous speech from Shakespeare's tragedy *Macbeth* (5.5.19–28). It occurs when Macbeth nears the end of his life. His evil deeds have been found out, his opponents are closing in on his castle, and he is told that his wife has just committed suicide. Full of grief and despair, Macbeth utters a bleak assessment of human existence. Read the passage and then scan it yourself before looking at the way we did it:

> Tomorrow, and tomorrow, and tomorrow
> Creeps in this petty pace from day to day
> To the last syllable of recorded time,
> And all our yesterdays have lighted fools
> The way to dusty death. Out, out, brief candle!   5
> Life's but a walking shadow, a poor player
> That struts and frets his hour upon the stage
> And then is heard no more. It is a tale
> Told by an idiot, full of sound and fury,
> Signifying nothing.   10

Here is the way we scan the lines, but it is important to realize that this is not *the one correct* way to scan it. Differences in pronunciation and interpretation can lead to entirely acceptable differences in scansion of a poem. (Acceptable differences do not include mispronunciations. You may need to look up pronunciations, as well as definitions, of unfamiliar words to be fair both to the sound and to the meaning of a poem.)

> Tŏmór | rŏw, ănd | tŏmór | rŏw, ănd | tŏmórrŏw
> Créeps ĭn | thĭs pét | tў páce | frŏm dáy | tŏ dáy
> Tŏ thĕ lást | sýllă | blĕ ŏf | rĕcórd | ĕd tíme,
> Ănd áll | oŭr yés | tĕrdáys | hăve light | ĕd fóols
> Thĕ wáy | tŏ dúst | ў déath. | Oút, oút, | brief cán | dlĕ!   5
> Life's bŭt | ă wálk | ĭng shád | ŏw, ă póor | pláyĕr
> Thăt strúts | ănd fréts | hĭs hóur | ŭpón | thĕ stáge
> Ănd thén | ĭs heárd | nŏ móre. | Ĭt ĭs | ă tále
> Tóld bў ăn | ídĭŏt, | fúll ŏf | soúnd ănd | fúrў,
> Sígnĭ | fўĭng | nóthĭng.   10

The passage, like much of the poetry in Shakespeare's plays, is written in **blank verse** (unrhymed iambic pentameter). The first line is regular, except for the extra unstressed syllable on the final iamb. That syllable, together with the two caesuras and the time it takes to say each "tomorrow," lengthens the line and slows it down, so that rhythmically it creeps, the way Macbeth says life does. Stressing "and" twice adds to the sense of circularity and monotony Macbeth finds in life.

The second line begins with one of the most common metric substitutions, an initial trochee instead of an iamb, which puts extra emphasis on the key word "creeps." That the rest of the line is regular echoes the steady, plodding pace by which life proceeds, and it sets up the irregular, unexpected anapest and trochee of the first half of line 3 — to think of the very end, the final millisecond, of history ("recorded time") is jolting, and the meter jolts us as well. After two irregular lines the expected, regular iambics return for the rest of line 3, all of line 4, and half of line 5, again suiting the steady, plodding pace by which Macbeth says people follow one another through life toward death, the past like a lantern lighting the way as people foolishly imitate what those before them have done.

The rest of line 5 is irregular: two spondees and an extra unstressed syllable: "Oút, oút, | bríef cándle!" Although life may seem to plod, it is short; Macbeth expresses the wish that his would end. The double stresses of the spondees, emphasized by the caesuras that make one linger, give strength to the words "Out, out," and another spondee with an extra syllable and a definite end stop make us dwell on "brief candle!" The rhythm, which had been slow but steady, becomes broken and forceful here and in the following line. Line 6 also is irregular and unusual — a trochee, two iambs, an anapest, and a trochee. This is an unusual metrical combination, difficult to enunciate, just as its thought (that there is no reality, that life is empty and meaningless) is difficult for most people to accept. That slow, contorted line rhythmically leads into a line and a half that are metrically regular, reestablishing the expected meter. The mostly monosyllabic words, full of stops and fricatives, seem almost drumlike, booming their assertions about the brevity and unreality of people's stage-play lives: "That STRUTS and FRETS his HOUR upON the STAGE / And THEN is HEARD no MORE."

After the full-stop caesura, the iambs continue for two feet but the drum disappears with the lightly stressed "is." But these quieter, softer lines ("It is | a tale / Told by an | idiot, | full of | sound and | fury, / Signi | fying | nothing") are perhaps even more intense than those before them since they describe life as having no more shape and significance than the babblings of an insane person. The meter in lines 9 and 10 — two dactyls and six trochees — is madly unusual and amazingly effective. Emphasis on "tale | Told" is heightened by stressing both and linking them by alliteration. The two dactyls, "Told by an idiot," can only be read slowly, with difficulty, which places unmissable emphasis on "idiot." The dactyls and the six trochees following illustrate the anticlimactic potential of "falling meter," as with each foot we seem to sink lower than the one before.

The length of the ninth line, with its two extra syllables, makes an idiot's tale seem not only chaotic but also almost endless. The unifying sounds of the last six feet (alliteration linking "full" and "fury" and also "sound" and "signifying") makes them forceful; the rhythm, steady in line 9, becomes less steady in line 10 (the stress on "fy" is so light that one may hear "sígnifyíng") and almost fades away (to "nothing").

When you are watching *Macbeth*, you probably do not think about the fact that much of it is poetry and can be discussed for its figures, sounds, meter, and rhythm like the short poems we examine throughout this book. Even though you are not thinking about or realizing the presence of the poetry, however, it contributes in an important way to the intensity and emotional power of the play.

For additional practice, scan the following lines and label the prevailing metrical foot and line length.

> Woman much missed, how you call to me, call to me,
> Saying that now you are not as you were
> When you had changed from the one who was all to me,
> But as at first, when our day was fair.
> — Thomas Hardy

> That time of year thou mayst in me behold
> When yellow leaves, or none, or few, do hang
> Upon those boughs which shake against the cold,
> Bare ruined choirs, where late the sweet birds sang.
> — William Shakespeare

> "Good speed!" cried the watch, as the gate-bolts undrew;
> "Speed!" echoed the wall to us galloping through;
> Behind shut the postern, the lights sank to rest,
> And into the midnight we galloped abreast.
> — Robert Browning

> Piping down the valleys wild,
> Piping songs of pleasant glee,
> On a cloud I saw a child,
> And he laughing said to me:
> — William Blake

To compare your results with ours, see page 1583.

Trochee | trips from | long to | short.   *trochaic tetrameter*
From long | to long | in sol | emn sort   *iambic tetrameter*
Slow Spon | dee stalks; | strong foot! | yet   *spondaic tetrameter plus*
   ill able   *two weak syllables*
Ever to | come up with | Dactyl tri | syllable. *dactylic tetrameter*
Iam | bics march | from short | to long; —   *iambic tetrameter*
With a leap | and a bound | the swift An | *anapestic tetrameter*
   apests throng.

   — Samuel Taylor Coleridge, "Metrical Feet"

Woman much | missed, how you | call to me, | call to me,
Saying that | now you are | not as you | were   *dactylic*
When you had | changed from the | one who was | all to me, *tetrameter*
But as at | first, when our | day was | fair.

   — Thomas Hardy

That time | of year | thou mayst | in me | behold
When yel | low leaves, | or none, | or few, | do hang   *iambic*
Upon | those boughs | which shake | against | the cold,   *pentameter*
Bare ru | ined choirs, | where late | the sweet | birds sang.

   — William Shakespeare

"Good speed!" | cried the watch, | as the gate | -bolts undrew;
"Speed!" ech | oed the wall | to us gal | loping through;   *anapestic*
Behind | shut the pos | tern, the lights | sank to rest,   *tetrameter*
And in | to the mid | night we gal | loped abreast.

   — Robert Browning

Piping | down the | valleys | wild,
Piping | songs of | pleasant | glee,   *trochaic*
On a | cloud I | saw a | child,   *tetrameter*
And he | laughing | said to | me:

   — William Blake

Approaching
Critical Theory

This book is about approaching literature. It's valuable to realize that you always approach something from somewhere. We have tried to connect reading literature to your everyday life: You come to this course with prior interests and experiences, and the way you approach what you read, even your ability to relate to it at all, depends on where you're "coming from."

ALL READING IS THEORY-BASED In addition to this personal way to approach a work, there is another sense of approaching literature from somewhere. All readers approach their reading from a critical or theoretical perspective, even though they may not be aware of it. There are many such perspectives — some practical, others more abstract and philosophical. This appendix, though it cannot cover all of them, does indicate the range of past and present approaches used by readers.

BENEFITS OF BEING AWARE OF THEORY Having an awareness of critical and theoretical perspectives helps as you read literary works themselves — helps you sharpen and refine your own approaches to reading, helps you become a more flexible reader, helps you vary your approaches for different works and in different situations. And being familiar with critical theories is beneficial as you read scholarly books and essays about literature. As we said in Chapter 28 (p. 1458), knowing where a critical work is coming from, what its assumptions and intentions are, can help in following its arguments and in understanding why two readers of the same text can arrive at quite different readings. (Note, however, that scholars usually do not limit themselves to only one approach; they often combine approaches, or elements from different approaches, to fit a particular work or problem.)

CHRONOLOGICAL APPROACH TO THEORY The following survey of approaches is arranged in roughly chronological order to provide a brief history of literary criticism and to indicate how some theories developed out of, or as a reaction to, other theories — though theories have often overlapped, or run simultaneously, with others. Reader-response theories, for example, arose as a reaction to the neglect of the reading process in earlier twentieth-century critical theories. Keep in mind that literary theories also come from somewhere; knowing how they relate to prior theories and to the prevailing philosophical outlook of their time helps you to better understand them.

READING FOR PERSONAL IMPROVEMENT

FOCUSING ON EDIFICATION   Until the late 1800s, literature in English was not studied but was read for pleasure and edification. Part of the enjoyment of literature for readers then was picking out — and copying or memorizing — lines or passages that said something profound or meaningful about life. And some readers then, as now, sought out books that were informative or inspirational, through which they could find personal growth. Sir Philip Sidney, asserting the value of literature in his *Defense of Poesy* (1595), one of the earliest theoretical works in English, built his case on a moral foundation: "The ending end of all earthly learning [is] virtuous action." Sidney's case continued to be widely influential until at least the mid-twentieth century.

COMMITMENT TO HIGH CULTURE   Such growth had potential for benefits to society in addition to individuals, as poet and critic Matthew Arnold theorized in the mid-1800s. Arnold was deeply distressed by what he called the "barbarianism" (lack of interest in ideas) of the upper classes in England; by the "philistinism" (lack of intelligence and taste) of the middle classes; and by the lack of interest among the lower classes in anything save "beer, gin, and fun." He attempted to improve society by challenging it to a commitment to "high culture" (his term again), "knowledge of the best that has been thought and said in the world."

READING FOR MORAL IMPROVEMENT   Culture, in this view, provides a norm, or standard, for people to aspire to, and it has a unifying effect if they can be induced to strive toward the same values in aesthetics and morality. Arnold put so much emphasis on culture, especially literature, because he believed it could fill the role religion had filled, of offering society a source of moral values and an instrument for social unity and stability. For Arnold, education was the method for spreading this perspective. Through literature — especially the classics — the middle classes would be able to share some of the advantages the upper classes had always had available to them through their access to education.

READING FOR ASSIMILATION   Arnold's approach to literature was widely influential for over a century and continues to shape thinking today, though with some concerns about its tendency toward elitism. For decades educators in the United States used literature as an avenue for assimilating people into mainstream "American culture," with the aim of helping them rise to the middle class. This Arnoldian version of cultural criticism also critiqued literature to assess what was worthy of attention and would contribute most to cultural development and to the unifying, socializing effect a common culture helps achieve. Out of this social aim arose a "canon," or list, of "the best" works and authors, those "approved" as the most valuable and worthwhile. This canon later became a hotly contested issue, to which we will return shortly.

PHILOLOGICAL STUDIES

FOCUSING ON PHILOLOGY   English literature became a subject of academic study in the late 1800s. Until then, literature students studied the Greek and Roman classics, using an approach called *philology,* or the scientific study of language and literature. Philological scholarship included language study, preparation of scholarly editions with accurate texts, and examination of literary backgrounds, sources, and influences. If you can, take a look at J. R. R. Tolkien and E. V. Gordon's edition of the medieval romance *Sir Gawain and the Green Knight* (1925). It provides an excellent example of philological scholarship, with its historical introduction, authoritative text, extensive footnotes, and thorough glossary.

BEGINNING WITH THE BEGINNING   When the study of English literature began, the initial emphasis was on literature from its beginnings (written in Old English) through the Middle Ages (Middle English). It was approached philologically — much the same as the way Latin and Greek were studied. Although it may seem surprising now, the assumption was that students didn't need much help with literature from Shakespeare on: Those works were considered part of their reading for pleasure, not part of the academic program.

BIOGRAPHICAL CRITICISM

FOCUSING ON AUTHORS   By the 1930s, academic study of English literature had begun to include later authors, though still not contemporary literature, the attention focusing particularly on the historical backgrounds of works and on the lives of authors. Scholars used literary works as a source of information about authors (not always being careful to keep a first-person narrator or speaker separate from the author) and used details from an author's life to gain a better understanding of a work (not always being careful to remember that a writer can make things up).

INSIGHTS FROM BIOGRAPHY   Biographical criticism today involves research into the details of an author's life to shed light on the author's works, an important and basic form of literary study. Publishers have recognized its value by publishing biographical encyclopedias for literary figures and by including biographical sketches of the authors in anthologies such as this textbook (see p. 1517). Knowledge about an author can enable us in many cases to notice details or ideas in a work we might otherwise miss.

DOING BIOGRAPHICAL CRITICISM   Chapter 9 illustrates the kind of material a biographical approach draws upon. The chapter starts with a detailed biographical sketch of Sherman Alexie and includes excerpts from two interviews. These, combined with the personal essay by Alexie in Chapter 1, could form the groundwork for a paper on how Alexie's works relate to his life, though a thorough study would require additional reading and research. If you decide to attempt biographical criticism of Alexie or another author, be sure it actually *is* criticism and not just a *report* on the author's life. The paper must involve analysis, and it must use biographical data to illuminate meaning and build its interpretations on what is in the text, not on extraneous material from outside the text.

HISTORICAL CRITICISM

FOCUSING ON CONTEXT   As biographical knowledge enhances your understanding of a work, so does awareness of the social, political, cultural, and intellectual context in which it was conceived and written. Literary historians research such backgrounds and bring what they find to bear on a work, explaining details used in the work and clarifying the meaning of the work as its original readers would have understood it. They research sources the author drew on and influences that shaped the form and content of the work. They connect the work to other works written at the time, to describe the literary environment that surrounds it, and compare it to works written earlier, to understand how it relates to the traditional handling of similar forms and ideas.

HEMINGWAY AND HISTORY   To see how historical criticism is used, look again at the discussion of "Hills Like White Elephants" in Chapter 6 (p. 141). There we describe the historical context and social milieu in which Hemingway wrote and in which the story was set. We show how awareness of events and attitudes of the time clarifies details in plot, characterization, and setting and proves helpful in understanding the story.

USING HISTORICAL APPROACHES   You can try using such an approach for a paper assignment, if you'd like — probably a research paper. Learning about history almost invariably involves doing research into the era you're interested in. You use a historical approach for almost any time other than what you know firsthand. As with biographical criticism, be sure what you write is actually criticism, not just a report on the time period. The paper must involve analysis and must use historical data to illuminate meaning and build its interpretations on what is in the text, not on extraneous material from outside the text.

MARXISM AND LITERATURE

FOCUSING ON MARXIST THOUGHT   Marxist thought emerged in the United States in the 1920s and 1930s, partly as a reverberation from the Russian Revolution in 1918 and the spread of Marxist philosophy across Europe. Later many people in the United States turned to Marxism as a reaction to the Great Depression and the widespread unemployment and poverty following the fall of the stock market in 1929, with all the capitalist symbolism that carried. Many authors and literary critics embraced Marxism, as did many other artists and academics. At this point, Marxist authors wrote stories, novels, and plays advocating Marxist principles, and critics wrote books and essays endorsing works consistent with a Marxist outlook, by authors who accepted Marxism and even ones who did not. We will return to Marxist theory later in this survey and treat it more fully as it reemerges in a more sophisticated and highly influential form in the 1970s.

PSYCHOLOGICAL CRITICISM

FOCUSING ON FREUD   Biographical criticism — or a good deal of it, at least — began to turn in a psychological direction during the 1940s and 1950s. This was a result of the growing interest in the parent of psychoanalysis, Sigmund Freud, who sought a scientific understanding of the mind and mental illness. His methods and conclusions were revolutionary and controversial and have been and continue to be both applied and challenged on many grounds. The field of psychoanalysis has now moved far beyond Freud — so far, in fact, that he is given slight attention in psychology courses today. However, his work had a great impact on twentieth-century literature and twentieth-century literary criticism.

THE CONSCIOUS AND THE UNCONSCIOUS   A brief summary of Freud's thought is needed before we can consider its effect on literature. Crucial to its early phase is Freud's realization of a dynamic tension between the conscious and the unconscious in mental activity. This was a radical shift. Pre-Freudian belief held that one could *know* and *control* oneself. The idea that there are parts of the self knowable only through analysis is almost universally accepted now, but it was strikingly new when Freud advanced it. He described three areas of consciousness, each of which can contain causes for human behavior. First is the *conscious* level, the things we are aware of. Second is the *preconscious* level, feelings and sensations we are not presently aware of but that can be brought to the surface if we reflect on them. Third is the *unconscious* level, the realm of things we are not aware of, though they influence us greatly.

ID, EGO, SUPEREGO   In his second phase, Freud replaced the conscious and unconscious with the very different and now familiar concepts of the id, ego, and superego. The *id*, a reservoir of biological impulses and drives, demands instant gratification of its needs and desires — for food, relieving ourselves, sexual gratification. But instant satisfaction is not always possible, and when satisfaction must be postponed, tensions build up that cause inner conflict. We are often unaware that such tensions and conflicts exert an influence on our lives and actions. The *ego* (rational, controlled, partially conscious) is concerned first with pleasure, through the elimination of inner tensions and conflicts, but also with self-preservation, which requires that urges and needs be dealt with in a practical, realistic way. The id, for example, tells us we need to eat, and the ego *wants* to concur, but the ego, balancing the id's desire with the restraint imposed by the *superego* (the rules and taboos internalized through parental and societal influences), tells us to wait until lunchtime.

OEDIPUS COMPLEX, ELECTRA COMPLEX   In a third phase of his work, Freud focused on the development of the ego in children. Freud held that part of the normal emotional development of a child includes an unconscious wish to replace the parent of the child's sex in the affection of the parent of the opposite sex: A little boy wants to eliminate his father and marry his mother (Oedipus complex) and a little girl to eliminate her mother and marry her father (Electra complex). Although many aspects of his approach to the stages of early childhood development have been challenged or discredited, evidences of them are found in literary criticism, to clarify what lies behind a character's attitudes or actions, and in literary works, as authors influenced by Freudian theories apply them as they develop characters and plots.

REPRESSION   Another controversial Freudian theory important for literary study is that of *repression*. This theory holds that memories (that is, bundles of psychic energy) of situations with painful or threatening or guilt-laden associations are unconsciously pushed out of consciousness and sealed off so we will not have to deal with them consciously. When such matters are repressed, the pent-up energy has an effect on the personality — a repressed memory of childhood abuse, for example, may interfere with a person's adult relationships. It may take something of great force to break through the barrier, but only when it has been broken through is the person freed from the pain and its effects.

CHARACTER ANALYSIS   Psychological criticism is most commonly used to analyze characters in a work. The psychological critic attempts to clarify a character's actions, motivations, and attitudes by bringing modern psychoanalytical insights to bear on them. The critic does with characters what a psychoanalyst does with a patient: probes beneath the surface, exploring what unconscious conflicts and tensions, or repressed memories, may underlie the character's behavior.

JAKE IN "LOVE IN L.A."   This approach isn't used profitably with every story, poem, or play. For example, we might be intrigued with what makes Jake tick in "Love in L.A." (p. 61). He seems to be a compulsive liar, unable to hold a job, wary of close relationships, unwilling to follow rules and regulations. Why? Could such behavior be the result of psychological problems? Perhaps so, but we don't know enough about Jake to be able to develop such an analysis. Doing so would require that the story provide details about events in his childhood and his relation to his parents; we would need to be able to tell if his attitudes or actions result from memories that are now unconscious or from experiences he has repressed. We can't know these things, however, because we aren't given enough information to work with.

YOUNG GOODMAN BROWN   It would seem much more possible to do a psychoanalytical analysis of the title character in "Young Goodman Brown" (p. 374). His is a longer story than Jake's, and we are told more about his background and behavior. There seems adequate material in the story to show in a convincing way that many of his actions and attitudes come not from his conscious thought but from unconscious and repressed guilt, fears, and conflicts.

PURSUING A PSYCHOLOGICAL APPROACH   This is the direction you probably will want to use if you decide to write a paper taking a psychological approach. Your approach does not need to be Freudian — other psychological theories also can be used to amplify literature. But to work responsibly, you will need to know a good deal about whichever one you use. If you haven't taken at least one psychology course, trying this approach might not be advisable.

MYTHOLOGICAL CRITICISM

FOCUSING ON MYTH   What Freud attempted for the individual consciousness, another group of theorists in the late 1940s began to do for cultures, or the human race as a whole. Theorists who came to be known as *mythological critics* (or *archetypal critics*) focused their attention on the myths that underlie many literary works. *Myth* here must be understood not in its popular sense of a "fictitious story, or unscientific account, theory, belief," but in its literary sense of an anonymous story arising from a culture's oral traditions that involves gods or heroic figures and explores matters beyond and above everyday life, concerning origins, endings, aspirations, purpose, and meaning. Myths often appear in the earliest and seemingly simplest stories told in a culture — folktales, fairy tales, or religious writings, for example.

THE ROLE OF ARCHETYPES   Myths usually build on literary archetypes — symbols, character types, and plot lines that have been used again and again in a culture until they come to carry a wide, nearly universal significance and thus move most readers at a very deep emotional level. Throughout the centuries, writer after writer has drawn on motifs such as the quest, the journey into experience, and the Cinderella pattern in developing the plot of a story. Such writers use a typical or recurring symbol, character type, or plot motif that, in the words of archetypal theorist Northrop Frye, "connects one poem with another and thereby helps to unify and integrate our literary experience."[1]

SEASONAL CYCLES   Among the most used and most important of such archetypal images is the seasonal cycle of spring, summer, autumn, and winter; the daily cycle of dawn, zenith, sunset, and night; and the life cycle of youth, adulthood, old age, and death. Throughout history, poets have seen analogies among these natural cycles. Each time we speak of the "sunset" and "golden" years of life in referring to old age or describe death as being "sleep," we are, consciously or unconsciously, invoking those archetypes.

THE MONOMYTH   Beyond the meaning of the individual cycles is the significance of the patterns as a whole. "In the solar cycle of the day," Frye explains, "the seasonal cycle of the year, and the organic cycle of human life, there is a single pattern of significance"; elsewhere he calls that pattern the "story of the loss and regaining of identity," which is "the framework of all literature," the single story or "monomyth" underlying it all.[2] Other theorists hold that the "single story" focuses on the earth mother[3] or on the hero.[4] All of the theories, however, share a belief in the close relationship between literature and life. "Putting works of literature in such a context gives them an immense reverberating dimension of significance . . . , in which every literary work catches the echoes of all other works of its type in literature, and so ripples out into the rest of literature and thence into life."[5]

---

[1]*Anatomy of Criticism, Four Essays* (Princeton: Princeton UP, 1957) 99.

[2]*Fables of Identity: Studies in Poetic Mythology* (New York: Harcourt, 1963) 15; *The Educated Imagination* (Bloomington: Indiana UP, 1964) 55.

[3]Robert Graves, *The White Goddess: A Historical Grammar of Poetic Myth* (London: Faber, 1948).

[4]Joseph Campbell, *The Hero with a Thousand Faces,* Bollingen Series XVII (Princeton: Princeton UP, 1949).

[5]Frye, *Fables of Identity* 37.

For an example of an essay that uses a mythological approach, see Susan Koprince's "Baseball as History and Myth in August Wilson's *Fences*" (p. 1103), which explores baseball, together with its archetypal implications, as a metaphor for the American dream. Before trying this approach in a paper, you should review the sections on symbols and archetypes in Chapter 6 (pp. 143–48) and perhaps do some additional reading on myths and archetypes. You could work with a story like Nathaniel Hawthorne's "Young Goodman Brown" (p. 374), a poem like William Shakespeare's "That time of year thou mayst in me behold" (p.606) or A. E. Housman's "To an Athlete Dying Young" (p. 802), or a play like David Henry Hwang's *As the Crow Flies* (p. 995), or look for a work in which the mythical and archetypal aspects are less obvious or more subtle.

NEW CRITICISM (FORMALISM)

FOCUSING ON THE TEXT   The literary approach most influential in the twentieth century, and still important today, is called New Criticism, or Formalism (from its concentration on the *formal* elements of a work). It originated in the 1930s and for over forty years it dominated the study of literature. New Criticism was in part a reaction against an approach that makes biography or history primary and treats the literary text as secondary, either regarding it merely as a source of information or as material to the interpretation of which biographical and historical knowledge provides all the clues we need. New Criticism insists on the primacy of the text, appreciated as worthwhile for its own sake, for its aesthetic beauty, for its way of considering and helping understand the human condition generally. New Criticism takes texts themselves very seriously, looks at them closely as self-contained works of art, and affirms that literature has its own epistemology, or theory of knowledge.

EXPLICATION AS METHOD   New Criticism borrowed from France a method of teaching literature called *explication de texte*. The word *explicate* comes from Latin roots meaning "to unfold, to give an account of" and means to explain in detail. A key method of New Criticism is to explain the interconnections and ambiguities (multiple meanings) within a work, or within an important passage from a work, through a detailed, close analysis of its language — the meanings, relationships, and complexities of its words, images, figures, and symbols. In all this, what the author *intended* to do is not relevant — what matters is what the work *actually* says and does. New Critics, therefore, read works repeatedly. The first reading is less important than the later ones because one does not yet know where the work is headed and cannot see how early parts tie in with things further along.

UNITY OF FORM AND MEANING   As one rereads, again and again, one begins to see connections and to grasp the way large and small features relate to each other. Central to New Criticism are unity and universality. In the words of Cleanth Brooks, one of the developers of the approach, "The primary concern of criticism is with the problem of unity—the kind of whole which the literary work forms or fails to form, and the relation of the various parts to each other in building up this whole."[6] The unity sought is unity of meaning; but meaning, for New Critics, cannot be separated from form. Thus, a New Critic focuses on the speaker (or persona), conflicts and tensions, the arrangement of parts and details, and the relationships between them. A New Critic pays particular attention to metaphors as ways of unifying dissimilar things and to irony and paradox as ways apparent contradictions can be resolved (and thus unified).

THEORY OF KNOWLEDGE   New Criticism tends to look especially for issues of significance to all people, in all times—issues of life and relationship, worth and purpose, love, aging, death, faith, and doubt. The foundation of New Critical theory is its claim that literature has its own kind of knowledge—experiential knowledge conveyed imaginatively—and that this knowledge is superior to the abstract, impersonal knowledge of science. An overreliance on scientific approaches, New Critics believe, has led to fragmentation and "dissociation" within society and even within individuals. In the face of such disintegration, New Criticism emphasizes wholeness and unity. Literature offers a hope of wholeness, of a "unified sensibility" combining intellect and feeling, of redemption from the disintegration—the division, specialization, and alienation—that science has sometimes inflicted on the modern world.

CRITICAL METHOD   Today New Criticism is viewed more as a critical method than as a way of knowing. Anyone who engages in detailed close reading of a text is a descendent of New Criticism, even if she or he doesn't look for universal meanings or think in terms of being a New Critic. The method we have used in this book borrows from New Criticism in the way it teaches close attention to details in literary works, though we are more concerned with readers and the reading process than New Criticism itself is.

EXAMPLES IN THIS BOOK   Two of the student papers in this book offer good examples of New Critical readings. Alicia Abood's paper on "Love in L.A." (p. 248) is New Critical in the way it looks closely at the way the sounds of words, the use of similes, and the handling of verbs combine to characterize the way love happens in L.A., as a brief, hurried moment in a self-centered life. And Dan Carter's paper does an explication of "Love Poem" (p. 687), showing how the adaptation of the sonnet form, the poem's images, and the way the author uses sound unite to create a poem that expresses its sincere love through angles and slants instead of the direct approach more traditional for sonnets. If you want to try doing a paper with

---

[6]"The Formalist Critics," *Kenyon Review* 13 (1951): 72.

a New Critical approach, look at the Literary Analysis sections in the lists of writing prompts found in Chapters 4–9, 12–18, and 21–26 for suggestions of works you might work on and topics you might explore in them.

READER-RESPONSE CRITICISM

FOCUSING ON THE READER   Reader-response criticism (or reader-oriented criticism) contrasts sharply with New Criticism by focusing primarily on the reader instead of the text, and on individual effect instead of universal meaning. The roots of reader-response criticism go back to the 1930s and were laid down as a reaction against historical and biographical approaches, which gave little consideration to the role of the reader. Louise Rosenblatt began developing a reader-response theory just about the time New Criticism was emerging. New Criticism caught on and became widely accepted, while for several decades Rosenblatt's work was mostly neglected. Interest in the reader reemerged in the 1960s as a reaction against New Criticism's text-centered neglect of the reader. Reader-response criticism has become increasingly popular and influential, especially as a classroom approach.

READING AS TRANSACTION   Reader-response criticism, as we say in Chapter 1, is based on the assumption that reading is a transaction between an author, a reader, and a text in a cultural context. Reader-response criticism studies the steps through which the reader, by interacting with a text, completes the work in her or his mind. It does not just *describe* the response a work elicits from a reader ("here's what the work makes me feel") but examines the *activity* involved in reading — *how* the work produces the effects and feelings it does as a reader interacts with it. Reader-response criticism focuses on the sequential apprehension of a work — on the experience of grasping each line or each paragraph without knowing what comes later and on the process of putting the pieces together. Rereading is just as important for reader-response criticism as for New Criticism, but unlike New Criticism the first reading also is regarded as crucially significant.

SUBJECTIVE VIEW OF TEXTS   Most reader-response theories have a more subjective view of a text than New Criticism, thinking of a text more as a musical score that is meant to be "performed," brought to life by a reader, than as a permanent artistic object. The degrees of subjectivity vary. Some versions see the reader's interaction with the text as controlled to some extent by formal structures included in the text. For these, the text is a stable and "objective" entity that sets limits on the reader. A work cannot mean just anything the reader says it does: The reader must pay close attention to the text to notice and follow the cues it supplies and must be able to provide evidence from within the text to support the way she or he interprets it.

INTERPRETIVE COMMUNITIES   Other, more subjective reader-response approaches deemphasize the words on the page and place more emphasis on a text created in the reader's mind. This raises the question of whether there are any limits on the reader. Does a text then mean anything the reader says it does? Perhaps not. One way to consider that limits do exist, without giving up subjectivity of the text, is to recognize that reading occurs within "interpretive communities." In their broadest sense, interpretive communities are groups of readers who share a common situation, similar assumptions about how literary works are actualized, or an agreement about how literary conventions are used in approaching a text. The community provides a context within which individual experiencing of a work can be assessed. A class, for example, is an interpretive community. So are the readers of a professional journal and a group of scholars who specialize in a given area of literature.

COLLECTIVE JUDGMENTS   The role of such a group is not to arrive at a single "best" reading or to judge which among several readings is the "right" one or is "better" than others. Rather, by its endorsements and discouragements, each interpretive community indicates which readings go too far for that community, which ones it regards as *unacceptable*. This too will vary. What is unacceptable to one group of readers may not be to another. It is the collective judgments of interpretive communities, in this view, not texts or readers, that create stability. Even within the same community readings will vary because texts are not objective and different readers enact them in individual ways. Constraints do exist: A text can "mean" many things, but not just anything. The constraints, however, are not *in* the text but grow out of the strategies, assumptions, and conventions of the community.

THE READER AND "RECITATIF"   For an example of a paper specifically focused on a reader-response approach, see Kristina Martinez's student paper on "Recitatif" (p. 1511). It looks closely at large-scale strategies in the work rather than at smaller details the way New Critical papers do. It focuses on discrepancies and ambiguities in the text and the way readers must sort out differences and attempt to figure out the way things really were. It brings up questions readers are forced to work through: "Which story is correct, Roberta's or Twyla's (or neither)? Are they remembering details about Maggie differently because one of them is the same race as Maggie and the other not? If so, which one is the same?" It points out how readers—like Twyla and Roberta in the story—may wrongly attempt to construct meaning out of their own contexts as a way to resolve the ambiguities, instead of acknowledging "that this story will not provide answers to their questions, and that acceptance of ambiguity itself answers the need to have answers." But papers can pay attention to readers and how readers process a work even though they are not focused specifically on a reader-response approach, and we think often they should, which has been an emphasis throughout this book.

MARXIST CRITICISM

FOCUSING ON MARX'S IDEAS   Although acceptance of Marxism has waned over the past decade and a half, Karl Marx's social and economic theories had a major impact across the world through much of the twentieth century. That was true for literature as well: While Marxist ideas influenced authors and literary critics from the 1920s on, they emerged more prominently in the 1960s. They remain an important strand in literary study, one with which students of literature should be conversant. A brief introduction to the basic tenets of Marx's thought is helpful in understanding the foundations of and procedures used in Marxist criticism.

CLASS CONFLICT   Marx's main interest was in economic power and the ways in which it is disguised and manipulated. His analysis of society starts with the exploitation of workers by owners and capitalists, which creates class conflict between the bourgeoisie (the middle and upper classes — the owners and capitalists) and the proletariat (the workers, those who must sell their labor to the owners and capitalists). The subjugation of the workers, Marx held, is maintained by *ideology*, that is, the beliefs, values, and ways of thinking through which human beings perceive what they believe to be reality and carry out their roles in society. The ideology of an era (Marx called it the "superstructure") is determined by the contemporary socioeconomic system (the "base") and reflects the beliefs, values, and interests of the dominant class in it.

THE EFFECT OF IDEOLOGY   Ideology includes everything that shapes the individual's mental picture of life experience — not what life really is, but the way it is perceived. This ideology may seem to people at the time just the natural, inevitable way of seeing and explaining things. But Marxists claim that it seems that way only because ideology quietly, subtly works to legitimize and maintain the position, power, and economic interests of the ruling class and, for the working classes, to cover up the reality of their exploitation. Ideology helps preserve the status quo by making what is artificial and oppressive seem natural and inevitable. According to Marxists, such ideology must be exposed and overcome if people are to gain relief from their oppressors.

BRINGING IDEOLOGY INTO CONSCIOUSNESS   Early Marxist criticism concentrated on exposing the presence of bourgeois attitudes, values, and orientation in literary works. Later Marxist criticism became more sophisticated in analyzing the ideology underlying literature and societies: bringing out the beliefs, values, and ways of thinking through which people perceive what they believe to be reality and on which they carry out their roles in society. In the latter part of the twentieth century, Fredric Jameson used insights from psychoanalysis to reenergize Marxist criticism. The function of ideology, Jameson held, is to "repress" revolutionary ideas or tendencies, to push them into the "political unconscious."[7] As ideology works itself into a text, things must be omitted: "In order to say anything, there are other things *which must not be said*."[8] As a result, gaps and contradictions occur and generally go unnoticed. Like psychoanalysts, Marxist critics focus on the text's "unconscious," on what is unspoken and repressed, and bring it into "consciousness."

READING AGAINST THE GRAIN   To expose the ideology in literary works, the main approach of Marxist criticism is to read "against the grain." The metaphor comes from carpentry: It is easiest to plane a board by pushing "with the grain"; the plane moves easily, can glide over irregularities and inconsistencies in the wood, and produces smooth, pleasing results. Pushing "against the grain" is harder and usually causes rough edges. To apply the metaphor to reading, it is easiest and most natural to read a work "with the grain" — that is, to accept and follow the conventions and signals that correspond with the ideology behind it. Reading with the grain allows a reader to glide over problems and leads to smooth, reassuring results, compatible with what the dominant culture values and approves. It is harder to read "against the grain," to resist the conventions of the dominant culture's ideology, to challenge and question them instead of accepting and following them. The role of a Marxist approach to literature is to bring what is hidden into the open, to expose underlying ideology, and to make readers see its effect.

COMMITMENT TO THE CAUSE   Marxist criticism is committed criticism: It aims not only to illuminate readers but also to arouse them to involvement and action; it seeks to impact the lives and values of readers and effect changes in society. As with psychological criticism, you should not attempt writing a paper from a Marxist perspective unless you have read and understood a good deal from Marx's works and from works studying his positions. Attempting to do so without being well informed is likely to lead to superficial and even erroneous results. And it seems fair to point out that if you write a Marxist critique without sharing Marx's beliefs about class conflict and the need for rising up against the injustices of the capitalist system, though it might fulfill an academic assignment, your work will not be authentic Marxist criticism, which requires passionate commitment to a set of ideas designed to initiate significant societal change.

APPLYING THE APPROACH   The value of a Marxist approach is illustrated by using it to consider "The Homes of England," a poem written around 1825 by Felicia Hemans (1793–1835). The poem celebrates a variety of English homes, starting with the magnificent country houses of the rich:

---

[7]*The Political Unconscious: Narrative as a Socially Symbolic Act* (Ithaca: Cornell UP, 1981).

[8]Pierre Machery, qtd. in Raman Selden, *A Reader's Guide to Contemporary Literary Theory* (Lexington: UP of Kentucky, 1985) 41.

"The stately Homes of England, / How beautiful they stand! / Amidst their tall ancestral trees, / O'er all the pleasant land." Following stanzas go on to discuss "merry" and "blessed" homes in idyllic terms, moving down to "The Cottage Homes of England! / By thousands on her plains, / They are smiling o'er the silvery brooks / And round the hamlet fanes [churches]." A Marxist critic would expose the underlying ideology and point out what goes unsaid, and unseen, in the poem. Hemans, though not wealthy herself, saw her country through the lens of patriotic, upper-class landowners and capitalists. England was a land of "free, fair Homes" where all citizens lived with the "glad spirit" of children and loved their "country and its God."

But that is not how all of England was. It is how the upper classes perceived it. Hemans's setting is rural England; she makes no mention of the wretched homes in city slums where exploited factory workers and their families lived. The lower classes are invisible to the upper classes, who profit from them but are oblivious to their lives and welfare. Rural areas had their poor as well, living not in romantic cottages but in huts and hovels. These homes, too, don't appear in the poem (the poem does refer to "hut and hall," but the very phrase seems to equate them, as equally pleasant, happy dwellings). A Marxist critic would bring out how acceptance of this ideology — this sense that all are free, happy, and content — is a way to keep the lower classes from realizing the inequity of their situation and from wanting to rebel against it.

FEMINIST CRITICISM AND EXPANSION OF THE CANON

MALE DOMINANCE OF LITERARY STUDIES   Prior to 1970, especially during the period in which New Criticism was in vogue, literary standards and agendas were dominated by white, male academics. A large majority of college and university teachers and scholars were male; all of the founders of New Criticism were male; most of the writers studied and approved of by New Criticism were male. Cleanth Brooks and Robert Penn Warren's landmark New Critical textbook *Understanding Poetry* (1938) included poems by 89 men and 5 women (11 poems are anonymous). Of poems included, 220 were by men, 8 by women (one an example of a "bad" poem). In the original edition of a very influential formalist textbook on poetry, Laurence Perrine's *Sound and Sense* (1956), 107 male, but only 10 female, poets were represented (169 poems by men, 18 by women).

MALE ORIENTATION IN NEW CRITICISM   The tendency of male critics to favor works by men was reinforced by the theoretical position of New Criticism. New Criticism looked in literature for universal themes — themes it assumed would apply equally to women and men of all classes, cultures, and times. The shapers of New Criticism, however, did not seem aware of the extent to which their own backgrounds and presuppositions — their ideologies — defined those "universal" issues: The issues were ones raised by well-educated, upper-class, conservative men. Just as their method of reading sought to unify and integrate aspects of literary works, so the themes they found in the works involved social unity and integration. Issues of importance to marginal groups — women, people of color, lower classes — did not fit the mold and were overlooked (only one poem by an ethnic American author — Countee Cullen's "Incident" — appears in the original *Sound and Sense*, and two are included in *Understanding Poetry*, both by William Carlos Williams).

THE FEMINIST MOVEMENT   Against this background arose a feminist protest movement, which initiated a radical rethinking of the canon. Pivotal in its development was Kate Millett's *Sexual Politics* (1970), which began to raise the consciousness of women to the fact that, generally speaking, all avenues of power in Western culture were under male control. That was true of the production and study of literature. White males set the criteria for what was good literature and decided whose books would be published and whose works would be anthologized. They, therefore, had the power to determine who would be read, who would receive attention, who would achieve fame.

BECOMING A RESISTING READER   Feminist criticism reacted against this power initially by asking what happens to a work written by a male when it is read from a consciously feminine perspective instead of an assumed male perspective. The first act of a feminist reader, according to critic Judith Fetterley, is to become a "resisting reader" rather than an assenting reader[9] — that is, to question and challenge the assumptions of a work about roles, power, and values. A resisting reader exposes the masculine biases (the patriarchal ideology) in a work. This requires paying attention not only to what is said, but also to what is not said. Even works in which no women are present may convey an attitude toward women: What does their absence say? How does the fact that no women are present shape and color the situation? Are there details that (perhaps unintentionally or unconsciously) demean women or treat subjects in a way that is potentially insulting to women?

ENLARGING THE CANON   From a reappraisal of works by men, feminist criticism moved on to the study of literature written by women — what Elaine Showalter has termed *gynocriticism*. This involves, on the one hand, the reexamination of women authors who have long been accepted in the canon, and on the other hand, even more significantly, the discovery or

---

[9]*The Resisting Reader: A Feminist Approach to American Fiction* (Bloomington: Indiana UP, 1978).

rediscovery of many neglected or forgotten women writers, past and present. The result has been to open up the literary canon to include works by women that earlier criticism had excluded.

INCLUDING THE "SOMETHING ELSE"   One criticism of early varieties of feminist criticism is that much of it treats *woman* as a universal category without recognizing differences among women — differences of race, economic and social class, and national origin — that contribute to their identity. Contemporary feminists such as Gayatri Spivak say that while all women are female, they are something else as well (such as working class or upper class, heterosexual or lesbian, African American or living in a post-colonial nation), and the "something else" is important to consider. Such an approach has led feminists to feel affinities with all those who are considered "the Other" or are marginalized on the basis of race, ethnicity, class, sexual orientation, or social background.

REACHING OUT TO OTHER MARGINALIZED GROUPS   Thus feminist critics took the lead in raising for ethnic minorities the same questions and concerns raised about women — particularly for African Americans at first, and then for Latinos, Native Americans, and other ethnic minorities: How are they treated in works by white authors? Are they stereotyped in insensitive and demeaning ways? Are there details that (perhaps unintentionally or unconsciously) demean minorities or treat subjects in a way that is potentially insulting to the minority group? Are ethnic characters rendered invisible? Are they not included at all? If so, what does their absence say? Ethnic critics began to point out the dearth of writers of color in anthologies and literature courses, to call attention to ethnic authors who had been accepted in the canon or were on its fringes, and to discover or rediscover many neglected or forgotten writers of color, past and present. As the canon expanded to include woman writers, so it expanded to include ethnic authors. This textbook's table of contents is evidence of the result.

AN ORIENTATION, NOT A METHOD   Feminist criticism, like Marxist criticism, does not focus on a *method* (the way New Criticism and reader-response criticism do). Instead, it is an orientation, a set of principles that can be fused with a variety of critical approaches. Thus there can be feminist-reader-response criticism, feminist-deconstructive criticism, and so on. Feminist criticism, in addition to indicating some things to *do* with a work of literature, points out issues to be aware of in a work. It is a committed criticism that aims to heighten awareness, to effect changes in attitudes and behavior, to correct injustices, and to improve society and individual situations. You can use a feminist approach yourself by experimenting with being a resisting reader, by being open to the writings and concerns of women authors, and by focusing papers and discussions on issues of the sort raised in this section.

FEMINISM IN "EVERYDAY USE"   Susan Farrell's essay "Fight vs. Flight: A Re-evaluation of Dee in Alice Walker's 'Everyday Use'" (p. 1459) illustrates how awareness of theoretical approaches can help in understanding the premises on which a scholarly essay is based. Nowhere does the essay say that it is taking a feminist approach to the story, but that is its effect. The essay undertakes a reassessment of Dee, a character with modern feminist inclinations — she went to college to prepare herself for a career, she is fearless and a fighter, she stands up for herself and refuses to back down from what she believes in.

Most critics see the story as putting Dee down because she fails to recognize the difference between her own attitude toward her heritage (embracing it as fashionable, though separate from her experience) and that of her mother and sister, who continue to live in that heritage, with its values permeating their daily experiences. Farrell's essay, however, defends Dee, showing that she offers — through her feminist ways — a strategy for contemporary African Americans to cope with an oppressive society, one, Farrell argues, Dee's mother admires, envies, and eventually emulates.

GENDER STUDIES

FOCUSING ON SOCIALLY CONSTRUCTED DISTINCTIONS   The protest movement that began as feminist criticism has moved on in large part to the more inclusive area of gender studies. Gender studies focus on the idea that gender is socially constructed on attitudes toward masculinity and femininity that are rooted in deeply but uncritically held beliefs of a society. Most varieties of gender studies assume a difference between the terms *sex* and *gender*. *Sex* refers to the physical characteristics of women and men biologically; *gender* refers to traits designated as "feminine" and "masculine." One is born biologically female or male, but one *acquires* a "gender" (society's conceptions of "woman" and "man"). In Simone de Beauvoir's words, "One is not born a woman, one becomes one."[10]

BINARY OPPOSITIONS   Gender studies show that such distinctions in the West traditionally have been shaped through the use of binary oppositions:

masculine / feminine
father / mother
son / daughter
brother / sister
active / passive

---

[10]*The Second Sex* (1949), trans. H. M. Parshley (New York: Vintage, 1974) 301.

reason / emotion

intelligent / sensitive

Through the centuries, the items on the left side of these pairings generally have been favored (or *privileged*) over those on the right side. Gender criticism exposes the pairings as false oppositions, contending that all these traits can be a part of one's identity.

ALL TYPES OF OPPRESSION Gender criticism covers *all* "the critical ramifications of sexual oppression,"[11] including gay, lesbian, and queer studies. Just as early feminist critics brought attention to the way women traditionally have been forced to approach literature from a masculine perspective, so gay, lesbian, and queer studies have called attention to the way texts traditionally are read from a heterosexual viewpoint. Many readers assume that a relationship described in a work is heterosexual even when that is not indicated directly. It is not a valid assumption. Lesbian and gay critics have produced revisionist rereadings — often provocative and illuminating — of many texts that previously were read as straight.

DECONSTRUCTION

One of the best known contemporary literary theories, deconstruction, is also one of the most controversial and difficult. You may have heard of deconstruction, and maybe even used the verb *deconstruct* without realizing its use in literary studies.

FOCUSING ON OPPOSITIONAL THINKING Deconstruction challenges the logical principles on which the thinking of the Western world since Socrates has been based. Fundamental to Western logic, for example, is the law of noncontradiction (that is, "A" is not the same as "not A") and the use of binary oppositions that have become deeply embedded in our thought: We try to understand things by considering them in pairs that differentiate them. Remember some of the binaries in the section on gender studies:

masculine / feminine

active / passive

reason / emotion

intelligent / sensitive

---

[11]Jonathan Culler, *On Deconstruction: Theory and Criticism after Structuralism* (Ithaca: Cornell UP, 1982) 56.

Here's another list similar to that one:

conscious / unconscious

being / nonbeing

reality / image

right / wrong

thing / sign

speech / writing

Western thinking, from the Greeks on, has privileged the left side of this list over the right side. Such privileging reflects the classical, or Hellenic (Greek), influence on Western philosophy, with its love of reason, logic, order, clarity, coherence, and unity. A key aspect of deconstruction is to challenge that impulse to divide and stratify. Things are not always separate and opposed. They can be different without being opposed; they can also be interdependent and interactive.

QUESTIONING PHILOSOPHICAL ASSUMPTIONS   Deconstruction—like Marxist and feminist criticism—is not a critical *method* the way New Criticism is. Rather, it is a philosophical approach, a way of thinking, a critique of the assumptions that underlie such systems as New Criticism, which emphasize order, coherence, and unity. Deconstructionists posit that a text has no stable reference, and they therefore question assumptions about the ability of language to represent reality. Language is not fixed and limited: It always conveys meanings different from or beyond what we intend.

LOOKING FOR CRACKS   Deconstruction focuses on gaps and ambiguities that expose a text's instability and indeterminacy, the "crack" in the seeming unity or coherence of its argument. "Meaning" is not present in the work but is filled in by the reader in the act of reading. According to deconstruction, meaning is totally contextual. A literary work does not *reflect* reality; rather, works *create* their own reality. One cannot go outside a text—to the author's intentions or to references to the outside world—to determine its signification. The text is "self-referential": Only as we look closely at a work and consider its full range of interplay and implication can its signification emerge.

CLOSE ANALYSIS OF LANGUAGE   A deconstructive reading, therefore, looks very closely at language, perhaps even more attentively than New Criticism does. It treats language "playfully," showing how the multiple meanings in words (the doubleness of language) contribute to the instability of texts. It picks out key binary oppositions, identifying which term in those oppositions is being privileged (given preference) and showing how such privileging imposes an interpretive template on the subject being examined.

It watches for inconsistencies in the apparent unity and stability of a work, as exposed by gaps (comparing what is privileged and what is passed over, or "marginalized").

BINARY OPPOSITIONS IN "SONNY'S BLUES"   The values of a deconstructive reading can be illustrated through analyzing James Baldwin's "Sonny's Blues" (p. 309). The story is grounded in a binary opposition, between words and music. The narrator is strongly oriented toward words, while Sonny is oriented toward music. The story opens with the narrator reading about Sonny in a newspaper (that, ironically, is their only means of communication at that point). Also, the story shows the narrator reading, or attempting to read, not just words but people and situations.

VERBALIZING THE NONVERBAL   Keith E. Byerman has said of the narrator that "the story, in part, is about his misreadings" or his "inability to read properly."[12] As Byerman explains, the narrator is constantly turning nonverbal experiences into words. For example, when the narrator listens in the nightclub, he declares that both the terribleness and triumph of music is that "it has no words." Yet, immediately afterward, he begins reading language into the music, describing it as a conversation: "The dry, low, black man *said* something awful on the drums, Creole *answered*, and the drums *talked back*. Then the horn insisted, sweet and high, slightly detached perhaps, and Creole listened, *commenting* now and then" (p. 331).

Byerman suggests that Baldwin uses the verbalizing of the nonverbal early in the story as a way to undercut the narrator and to show his need for deeper understanding. However, something more complex than that is going on near the end. Byerman notes the lack of preparation for the narrator's sophisticated analysis of music in the final scene. The narrator throughout has expressed his antipathy to music and an inability to comprehend its appeal. Yet suddenly he expresses profound understandings of how music affects a listener. But Byerman does not deal fully with the contradictory nature of the narrator's sudden grasp of music, or with the "crack" this creates in the text.

DECONSTRUCTING THE STORY   A deconstructionist would recognize that what we are hearing, actually, is the author's voice breaking through the narrator's voice, conveying the meaning he finds in music. That, in turn, undermines the author's own undercutting of the narrator: The author himself cannot resist verbalizing the meaning of music. Or he cannot avoid it because the final section of the story rests on a binary opposition it attempts to deconstruct: Words and music are similar as well as different. Music, like objects and like words, must be "interpreted" — there is no es-

---

[12]"Words and Music: Narrative Ambiguity in 'Sonny's Blues,'" *Studies in Short Fiction* 19 (1982): 367.

cape from "reading." But the reading that music invites is open and indirect. Baldwin, however, gives a direct and closed reading in an attempt to convey openness and indirection. The story, thus, has a level of complexity, through its contradictions, which Byerman's New Critical reading does not pick up but which a deconstructive approach can bring out.

CULTURAL CRITICISM

FOCUSING ON CULTURES   From the 1980s on, much of literary study has been focused on culture, but in a way quite different from the promotion of "high culture" advocated by Matthew Arnold in the previous century. As we said in Chapter 8 (p. 239), cultural criticism explores the relationship between an author and her or his work and the cultural context in which they exist. An author, writing at a specific time in a specific place, inevitably is influenced by contemporary events and attitudes, whether she or he accepts and reflects prevailing attitudes or ignores, rejects, or challenges them.

CULTURAL INCLUSIVENESS   The work of anthropologists has changed the primary meaning of *culture* from a single, static, universal, elitist "high culture" to a set of dynamic, interactive, always-changing *cultures*. Contemporary cultural criticism (sometimes referred to as cultural studies) is inclusive ethnically, with a strong multicultural emphasis. It emphasizes that cultural achievements of worth are produced by people from a variety of social, economic, and ethnic backgrounds, past as well as present, and that criticism should enable us to appreciate this diversity of accomplishment. And it is inclusive regarding subject matter — it does not limit itself to the literature of "high culture" but also draws on popular culture as a valuable indicator of cultural values. It studies comic books as well as novels, hit movies as well as theater, MTV as well as public television, pop songs as well as jazz, graffiti as well as gallery art. The emphasis in cultural studies is on how people *relate to* all levels of art, rather than on their aesthetic standards and on getting them to recognize and work with "the best" literature, music, or art.

INFLUENCED AND INFLUENCING   Cultural criticism focuses on what a work conveys about social attitudes and social relations, focusing especially on the impact of such things as social background, sex, class, ethnicity, power, and privilege. Cultural critics concentrate on the way a work embodies a cultural context, how the events, ideas, or attitudes in a work were influenced by the economic conditions, political situation, or social conventions existing when it was written; but they also explore the way a work exists as *a part of* a culture and how it can influence, and perhaps change, the economic conditions, political situation, or social conventions of its time or later times.

INTERDISCIPLINARY   Thus the theory tends to work with interdisciplinary approaches. Cultural criticism often views works in relation to other works (literary works, especially ones outside the traditional canon, but also journals, memoirs, and diaries of ordinary people, church records, medical reports, architectural drawings, and so on); to social and economic conditions that affected them; to the way they were shaped by those who held power (including editors, publishers, and reviewers, for example); and to the way they reinforced conditions of power, intentionally or not.

For an example of a paper engaging in cultural criticism, see Harry J. Elam Jr.'s "August Wilson" (p. 1099), which explores a variety of cultural influences on Wilson and discusses how his works have critiqued and influenced U.S. culture of the late twentieth and early twenty-first centuries.

NEW HISTORICISM

FOCUSING AGAIN ON HISTORY   An influential variety of cultural studies, New Historicism, grew out of a sense that New Criticism and deconstruction, through their neglect of the social and cultural milieu in which a work had been written, were leaving out something important and valuable. New Historicists would say that by focusing almost wholly on what occurs within a text, New Critics and deconstructionists cut themselves off from the ways historical context can clarify and illuminate a work. They lose referentiality. Despite many differences, the varieties of historicist critics have in common a belief in referentiality — that works of literature are influenced by, and influence, reality.

THE UNDERLYING THEORY   New Historicism starts from a theory of history different from that which underlies "old historicism," with its emphasis on facts and events, its selective focus on the kinds of events that get recorded in official documents, and its explanations of causes and effects and of development toward an end. New Historicists assume that it is virtually impossible to reconstruct the past. We have only stories about the past, not objective facts and events existing independently; the stories are constructed by historians, reflecting the historians' assumptions and purposes and the choices they inevitably make about what to include, what to emphasize, what to omit. French philosophical historian Michael Foucault says that all historians are "situated." It is difficult for historians to recognize their own cultural practices and assumptions and even more difficult to get outside them and enter those of another age.

AN INTERDISCIPLINARY APPROACH   The work of New Historicists is influenced by deconstruction and reader-response criticism, with their emphasis on subjectivity, and by cultural studies generally, with its attention to the myriad forces that shape events and motivations. New Historicists do not concentrate on economic and political forces or on the better-documented activities of the rich and famous, as the old historicism did. Like other types of cultural studies, New Historicism is open to other disciplines in its attempts to elucidate how art is shaped by, and shapes, social, historical, and economic conditions, and how art is affected by politics and has political effects itself.

NEW HISTORICISM AND "ODE ON A GRECIAN URN" Consider, for example, John Keats's 1819 poem "Ode on a Grecian Urn" (p. 807). The poem was a central text discussed in Cleanth Brooks's famous book of New Critical essays, *The Well Wrought Urn*.[13] In his close examination of the poem, Brooks suggests that it is proper for the personified urn to ignore names, dates, and special circumstances and to concentrate instead on universal truths. Brooks ignores historical context and influences to take a few details and order them so that we better appreciate the beauty of the poem and its own impact as myth.

SITUATING THE POEM New Historicists, in contrast, would hold that it is important to situate the poem in its historical context and to ask, in this case, how economic and political conditions of early nineteenth-century England shaped Keats's image of ancient Greece. New Historicists tend to start their analysis by discussing a particular object or event and then connect that object or event to the poem so that readers come to see "the event as a social text and the literary text as a social event."[14]

THE URN AND MUSEUMS Brook Thomas, for example, asks where Keats would have seen such an urn. The answer — in a museum — leads into a discussion of the rise of art museums in eighteenth- and nineteenth-century Europe, as cultural artifacts from the past were placed in collections to be contemplated as art, isolated from their social setting. "In Keats's poem an urn that once had a practical social function now sparks aesthetic contemplation about the nature of truth, beauty, and the past." Thomas then says that reflecting on how the urn assumes a purely aesthetic function in a society that was becoming increasingly practical helps clarify "how our modern notion of art has been defined in response to the social order."[15]

SOCIAL IMPLICATIONS OF THE TEXT To the New Historicist, even the urn's position in a museum raises political issues. The presence of a Grecian urn in an English museum can lead to reflections on the political implications

---

[13]*The Well Wrought Urn: Studies in the Structure of Poetry* (New York: Reynal, 1947) ch. 8.

[14]Brook Thomas, "The New Literary Historicism," *A Companion to American Thought*, ed. Richard Wightman Fox and James T. Kloppenberg (New York: Blackwell, 1995) 490.

[15]"The Historical Necessity for — and Difficulties with — New Historical Analysis in Introductory Literature Courses," *College English* 49 (1987): 518.

of a cultural heritage. Englishmen in the nineteenth century, although they sympathized with the struggle for liberation in Greece, nevertheless took cultural treasures out of the country and put them on display in London. Thomas concludes that Keats's poem is "a social text, one that in telling us about the society that produced it also tells us about the society we inhabit today"[16] and should lead to reflection not just on present attitudes toward museums in the United States, but also on the implications of the way Keats's English poem has become a museum-type artifact in U.S. culture today.

POSTCOLONIAL CRITICISM

FOCUSING ON COLONIZATION   Postcolonial theory deals with cultural expression and behavior relating to the formerly or currently colonized parts of the world. Postcolonial criticism involves the analysis of literature by native writers who are living in colonized countries or who emigrated from such countries. We limit the discussion here to literature written in English in parts of the world that were colonized by Great Britain or the United States: primarily, then, Australia, New Zealand, and parts of the Caribbean, South America, Africa, and Asia. Postcolonial criticism focuses particularly on how colonized peoples attempt to assert their identity and to claim their heritage separate from, or other than, the colonizing culture. It also involves analysis of works written about colonized countries by writers from the colonizing countries, particularly as such writers misrepresent the cultures they describe, imposing on them their own cultural values and sense of cultural superiority.

THE STRUGGLES OF COLONIZED PEOPLES   Postcolonial criticism deals with all aspects of the struggle that occurs when one culture is subjugated by another, with what happens when one culture, because of the political power behind it, is able to dominate the other and to establish the impression of being superior to the other. It deals with the creation of Otherness, especially through the use of dialectical thinking to create pairs such as us/them, same/other, white/colored, rational/irrational, ordered/chaotic. Postcolonial criticism also addresses the way colonized peoples lose their past, are removed from history, and are forced to give up many of their cultural beliefs and practices. It confronts the way colonized peoples must forsake their language and cooperate with the conquerors if they want to get ahead economically. It reveals how the colonized peoples must cope with the memories and continuing legacy of being an occupied nation.

---

[16]"The Historical Necessity" 519.

Glossary of Literary Terms

Abstract language   Language that names general or intangible concepts, such as *love, truth,* and *beauty.* See also CONCRETE LANGUAGE.

Accent   The emphasis, or stress, given a syllable in articulation. Metrical accent is the placement of stress as determined by the metrical and rhythmic pattern of a poetic line. See also STRESS.

Act   One of the major divisions of a dramatic work. See also SCENE.

Alexandrine   A poetic line with six iambic feet. Also called a *hexameter.*

Allegory   A literary form or approach in which objects, persons, and actions make coherent sense on a literal level but also are equated in a sustained and obvious way with (usually) abstract meanings that lie outside the story. A classic example in prose is John Bunyan's *The Pilgrim's Progress;* in narrative poetry, Edmund Spenser's *The Faerie Queene;* in drama, the medieval English play *Everyman.* Nathaniel Hawthorne's "Young Goodman Brown" (p. 374) is a moral allegory, in which the names convey the abstract qualities developed in a second level of meaning beyond that of the literal events and characters in the story.

Alliteration   The repetition of identical initial consonant sounds in the stressed syllables of words relatively near to each other. See also CONSONANCE.

Allusion   Echoes or brief references to a literary or artistic work or a historical figure, event, or object, as, for example, the references to Lazarus and Hamlet in T. S. Eliot's "The Love Song of J. Alfred Prufrock" (see p. 776). It is usually a way of placing one's poem within, or alongside, a whole other context that is thus evoked in a very economical fashion.

Ambiguity   (1) In expository prose, an undesirable doubtfulness or uncertainty of meaning or intention, resulting from imprecision in use of words or construction of sentences. (2) In poetry, the desirable condition of admitting more than one possible meaning, resulting from the capacity of language to function on levels other than the literal. Related terms sometimes employed are *ambivalence* and *polysemy.* See also PUN.

Anapest   A metrical foot consisting of three syllables, with two unaccented syllables followed by an accented one (*da da DA*—"in a dream"). In anapestic meter, anapests are the predominant foot in a line or poem.

1609

Antagonist The character who opposes the protagonist in a narrative or dramatic work. See also PROTAGONIST.

Antihero A protagonist in a narrative or dramatic work who lacks the attributes of a traditional hero.

Antistrophe (1) The second stanza in a three-stanza segment of a choral ode in Greek drama. It is preceded by (and identical in form to) the strophe, which is sung while the chorus moves from stage right to stage left. During the antistrophe, the chorus moves back to stage right before singing the epode. (2) The second stanza in a three-stanza segment of an ode (thus, stanzas two, five, eight, and so on). See also CHORUS; EPODE; ODE; STROPHE.

Antithesis A figure of speech in which contrasting words, sentences, or ideas are expressed in balanced, parallel grammatical structures; for example, "She had some horses she loved. / She had some horses she hated" (Joy Harjo, "She Had Some Horses," p. 620).

Apostrophe A figure of speech in which an absent person is addressed as though present or an abstract quality or a nonhuman entity is addressed. In the latter case, it is a particular type of PERSONIFICATION.

Approximate rhyme See SLANT RHYME.

Archetype An image, symbol, character type, or plot line that occurs frequently enough in literature, religion, myths, folktales, and fairy tales to be recognizable as an element of universal literary experience and thus to evoke a deep emotional response.

Aside A convention in drama in which a character utters thoughts intended for the audience to hear that supposedly cannot be heard by the other characters onstage.

Assonance The repetition of identical or similar vowel sounds in words relatively near to each other whose consonant sounds differ. See also SLANT RHYME.

Atmosphere The feeling, or emotional aura, created in a reader or audience by a literary work, especially as such feeling is evoked by the setting or landscape.

Ballad A poem that tells a story and is meant to be recited or sung; originally a folk art, transmitted orally from person to person and generation to generation. Many of the popular ballads were not written down and published until the eighteenth century, though their origins may have been centuries earlier. See "Sir Patrick Spens" (p. 735) for an example of a Scottish popular ballad.

Ballad stanza A quatrain in iambic meter rhyming *abcb* with (usually) four feet in the first and third lines, three in the second and fourth.

Biographical criticism See page 1586.

Blank verse Lines of unrhymed iambic pentameter.

Cacophony A harsh or unpleasant combination of sounds, as, for example, "But when loud surges lash the sounding shore, / The hoarse, rough verse should like the torrent roar" (Alexander Pope, "An Essay on Criticism," ll. 368–69). See also EUPHONY.

Caesura   A pause or break within a line of verse, usually signaled by a mark of punctuation.

Canon   In the Christian tradition, the books accepted by the church as divinely inspired and approved for inclusion in the Bible. In literary studies, it means (1) the list of works generally accepted as the authentic work of a particular author (e.g., the Shakespearean canon) or (2) literary works that are given special status by the literary establishment within a society as works most worthy of study and emulation.

Carpe diem   "Seize the day," a Latin phrase from an ode by Horace. It is the label for a theme common in literature, especially sixteenth- and seventeenth-century English love poetry, that life is short and fleeting and that therefore one must make the most of present pleasures. See, for example, Robert Herrick's "To the Virgins, to Make Much of Time" (p. 799) and Andrew Marvell's "To His Coy Mistress" (p. 823).

Catastrophe   The concluding section of a play, particularly of a tragedy, describing the fall or death of the protagonist that results from the climax. The term *dénouement* is more commonly used for comedy. See also DÉNOUEMENT.

Catharsis   Term used by Aristotle in the *Poetics* to describe the outcome of viewing a tragedy. The term has usually been translated as "purgation" or "purification," though what Aristotle meant by it is widely disputed. A tragedy, it seems to say, engenders pity and fear in its audience, then releases and quiets those emotions, a process that has a healthy effect, psychologically and physically: The audience goes away feeling not dejected but relieved.

Center of consciousness technique   A third-person limited point of view in which a narrator relates a story through what is thought, felt, seen, and experienced by one of the characters, showing only what that character is conscious of.

Character   (1) A figure, human or personified, in a literary work; characters may be animals or some other beings. (2) A literary genre that offers a brief sketch of a personality type or an example of a virtue or vice, such as a country bumpkin or a braggart soldier.

Characterization   The process or use of techniques by which an author describes and develops the characters in a literary work.

Chaucerian stanza   A seven-line iambic stanza rhyming *ababbcc*, sometimes having an alexandrine (hexameter) closing line. See, for example, Sir Thomas Wyatt, "They flee from me" (p. 882).

Chorus   In its literary sense, the group of performers in Greek theater whose dancing and singing provided exposition and comment on the action of a play. In later theater, a single character identified as "chorus" who has a function similar to that of the Greek chorus.

Climax   The moment of greatest tension or emotional intensity in a plot.

Closed form   A poetic organization that evinces any repetition of meter, rhyme, or stanza. See also OPEN FORM.

Closet drama   A play that is intended to be read rather than performed.

Colloquial language   The diction, syntax, and idioms characteristic of informal speech.

Comedy   In medieval times, a literary work that has a happy ending and is written in a style less exalted than that of tragedy (e.g., Dante's *Divine Comedy*). More broadly, a humorous and entertaining work, particularly such a work in drama. See also TRAGEDY.

Comic relief   A humorous scene, passage, or character in an otherwise serious play; sometimes described as providing an audience with a momentary relief from the emotional intensity of a tragedy but at the same time heightening the seriousness of the work.

Complication   One of the traditional elements of plot, describing the protagonist's entanglements resulting from plot conflicts.

Concrete language   Language that names material things. See also ABSTRACT LANGUAGE.

Concrete poem   A poem arranged in a shape suggestive of the poem's subject matter.

Conflict   A confrontation or struggle between opposing characters or forces in a literary work, which gives rise to and is a focal point for the action of the plot.

Connotation   The shared or communal range of associations and emotional implications a word may carry in addition to its dictionary definitions. See also DENOTATION.

Consonance   The repetition of consonant sounds in the same or nearby lines. See also SLANT RHYME.

Convention   A rule, method, practice, or characteristic established by usage; a customary feature.

Couplet   A unit consisting of two consecutive lines of poetry with the same end rhyme. See also HEROIC COUPLET.

Crisis   The turning point in a plot, the moment at which a situation changes decisively for better or for worse. See also CLIMAX.

Cultural criticism   See page 1605.

Dactyl   A metrical foot consisting of three syllables, an accented one followed by two unaccented ones (*DA da da*—"sleepily"). In dactylic meter, dactyls are the predominant foot of a line or poem.

Deconstruction   See page 1602.

Denotation   The basic meaning of a word; a word's dictionary definition. See also CONNOTATION.

Dénouement   From the French for "unknotting," the untangling of events at the end of a play that resolves the conflicts (or leaves them satisfyingly unresolved), clarifies what is needed for understanding the outcome, and ties up the loose ends. It can be used in tragedy, but is generally used in comedy. See also CATASTROPHE.

Deus ex machina   From the Latin for "god out of the machine," refers to the mechanical device by which the actor playing a god was lowered to the stage in Greek drama to rescue characters from a seemingly impossible situation. It now denotes the use of any unexpected or artificial means to resolve an irresolvable conflict.

Dialect   One of several varieties of a language, differing in vocabulary, grammar, and/or pronunciation, and identified with a certain region, community, or social, ethnic, or occupational group. Often one dialect comes to be considered the "standard."

Dialogue   A conversation between two or more characters in a literary work.

Diction   Choice of words; the kind of words, phrases, and figurative language that make up a work of literature. See also POETIC DICTION.

Dimeter   A line of verse consisting of two metrical feet.

Downstage   The part of the stage closest to the audience.

Double rhyme   A rhyme in which the accented, rhyming syllable is followed by one or more identical, unstressed syllables: *thrilling* and *killing*, *marry* and *tarry*. An older label, *feminine rhyme*, is generally no longer used. See also SINGLE RHYME.

Drama   (1) A literary composition that tells a story, usually involving human conflict, by means of dialogue and action rather than narration. (2) In modern and contemporary theater, any play that is not a comedy or a musical. (3) The dramas of a particular writer or culture, considered as a whole (e.g., Shakespearean drama, medieval drama). See also CLOSET DRAMA; PLAY.

Dramatic irony   A situation in which a reader or audience knows more than the speakers or characters, either about future events or about the discrepancy between a meaning intended by a speaker or character and that recognized by a reader or audience. See also IRONY; SITUATIONAL IRONY; VERBAL IRONY.

Dramatic monologue   A poem consisting of speech by one speaker, overheard in a dramatic moment and usually addressing a character or characters who do not speak. The speaker's words reveal what is going on in the scene and expose significant depths of the speaker's temperament, attitudes, and values. See also SOLILOQUY.

Dramatis personae   The characters in a play, or a list of such characters.

Dynamic character   Characters shown as changing and growing because of what happens to them. See also STATIC CHARACTER.

Elegy   In Greek and Roman literature, a serious, meditative poem written in elegiac meter (alternating hexameter and pentameter lines); since the 1600s, a sustained and formal poem lamenting the death of a particular person, usually ending with a consolation, or setting forth meditations on death or another solemn theme. See, for example, Thomas Gray's "Elegy Written in a Country Churchyard" (p. 788). The adjective *elegiac* is also used to describe a general tone of sadness or a worldview that emphasizes suffering and loss. It is most often applied to Anglo-Saxon poems such as *Beowulf* or *The Seafarer* but also can be used for modern poems, as, for example, A. E. Housman's poems in *A Shropshire Lad*.

End rhyme   Rhyme at the ends of lines in a poem. See also INTERNAL RHYME.

End-stopped line   A line in which a grammatical pause (punctuation mark) and the completion of the meaning coincide at the end. See also RUN-ON LINE.

English sonnet   A sonnet consisting of three quatrains (four-line units, typically rhyming *abab cdcd efef*) and a couplet (two rhyming lines). Usually the subject is introduced in the first quatrain, expanded in the second, and expanded still further in the third; the couplet adds a logical, pithy conclusion or gives a surprising twist. Also called the *Shakespearean sonnet*. See also ITALIAN SONNET.

Enjambment   See RUN-ON LINE.

Epic   A long narrative poem that celebrates the achievements of great heroes and heroines, often determining the fate of a tribe or nation, in formal language and an elevated style. Examples include Homer's *Iliad* and *Odyssey*, Virgil's *Aeneid*, and John Milton's *Paradise Lost*.

Epic simile   An extended or elaborate simile in which the image used to describe the subject is developed in considerable detail.

Epigram   Originally, an inscription on a building, tomb, or gravestone; in modern usage, a short poem, usually polished and witty with a surprising twist at the end. (Its other dictionary definition, "any terse, witty, pointed statement," is a characteristic of some dramatic writing, for example, the comedies of Oscar Wilde.)

Epigraph   In literature, a quotation at the beginning of a poem, story, chapter, play, or book. See, for example, the epigraph from Dante at the beginning of T. S. Eliot's "The Love Song of J. Alfred Prufrock" (p. 776).

Epilogue   Final remarks by an actor after the main action of a play has ended, usually summing up or commenting on the play, or asking for critics and the audience to receive it favorably. In novels, an epilogue may be added to reveal what happened to the characters in future years, after the plot proper concluded.

Epiphany   An appearance or manifestation, especially of a divine being; in literature, since James Joyce adapted the term to secular use, a sudden sense of radiance and revelation one may feel while perceiving a commonplace object; a moment or event in which the essential nature of a person, a situation, or an object is suddenly perceived. The term is more common in the criticism of fiction, narrative poetry, and drama than in lyric poetry.

Epode   (1) The third stanza in a three-stanza segment of an ode in Greek drama, sung while the chorus is standing still. (2) The third stanza in a three-stanza segment of an ode. See also ANTISTROPHE; CHORUS; ODE; STROPHE.

Essay   A relatively brief discussion, usually in prose, of a limited, nonfictional topic or idea.

Euphony   Sounds that strike the ear as smooth, musical, and agreeable, as, for example, "Soft is the strain when Zephyr gently blows, / And the smooth stream in smoother numbers flows" (Alexander Pope, "An Essay on Criticism," ll. 366–67). See also CACOPHONY.

Exact rhyme   Rhyme in which the vowel sound and all sounds following it are the same: *spite* and *night* or *ache* and *fake*.

Exaggeration   See HYPERBOLE.

Explication   A method entailing close analysis of a text, opening it up line by line, clarifying how diction, images, figurative language, symbols, sounds, rhythm, form, and allusions contribute toward shaping the work's meaning and effect.

Exposition   A nondramatized explanation, often a speech by a character or the narrator, that describes things that occurred before the initial action of a narrative or drama, filling in background information the audience needs to make sense of the story.

Extended metaphor   A metaphoric comparison that is sustained and expanded over a number of lines.

Falling action   The action following the climax of a traditionally structured play as the tension lessens and the play moves toward the catastrophe or dénouement. See also RISING ACTION.

Falling meter   A foot (usually trochee or dactyl) in which the first syllable is stressed, followed by unstressed syllables that give a sense of stepping down. See also RISING METER.

Farce   A dramatic work intended to excite laughter that depends less on plot and character than on improbable situations, gross incongruities, coarse wit, and horseplay.

Feminine rhyme   See DOUBLE RHYME.

Feminist criticism   See page 1598.

Fiction   From the Latin verb "to make." (1) Narrated stories in prose — usually short stories, novellas, or novels — that are drawn from the imagination or are an imaginative reworking of actual experiences. Incidents and details in a work of fiction can originate in fact, history, or everyday life, but the characters and events as a whole are primarily invented, or altered, in the author's imagination. (2) The made-up situation underlying any literary work; the feigned or imagined situation underlying it. See also NOVEL; NOVELLA; SHORT STORY.

Figurative language   See FIGURE OF SPEECH.

Figure of speech   Uses of language that depart from customary construction, order, or significance in order to achieve a special effect or meaning. They occur in two forms: (1) trope (from a word for "turn"), or "figure of thought," in which a word or phrase is turned or twisted to make it mean something different from its usual significance; and (2) "rhetorical figure," which creates a surprising effect by using words in unexpected ways without altering what the words mean. See also METAPHOR; METONYMY; PERSONIFICATION; SIMILE; SYNECDOCHE.

First-person narrator   The *I* who tells a story from a first-person point of view, either as an outside observer or as someone directly or indirectly involved in the action of the story.

Fixed form   In poetry, definite, repeating patterns of line, rhyme scheme, or stanza.

Flashback   A literary device that interrupts a narrative to present earlier material, often something that occurred before the opening of the work, through a character's memories or dreams or through juxtaposition of earlier and later events.

Flat character   A character represented through only one or two main features or aspects that can often be summed up in a sentence or two. See also ROUND CHARACTER.

Foil   A character used as a contrast with another character, thus highlighting the latter's distinctive attributes or character traits.

Foot   The basic unit in metrical verse, comprised of (usually) one stressed and one or more unstressed syllables. See also ANAPEST; DACTYL; IAMB; SPONDEE; TROCHEE.

Foreshadowing   Words, gestures, or other actions that hint at future events or outcomes in a literary work.

Form   (1) Genre or literary type (e.g., the lyric form); (2) patterns of meter, lines, and rhymes (stanzaic form); or (3) the organization of the parts of a literary work in relation to its total effect (e.g., "The form [structure] of this poem is very effective"). See also STRUCTURE.

Formalist criticism   See page 1592.

Found poem   A passage from a nonpoetic source such as a newspaper, magazine, advertisement, textbook, or elsewhere in everyday life that contains some element of poetry: meter (sometimes), effective rhythm, phrasings that can be divided into lines, imaginative uses of language and sound, and so on.

Fourth wall   The theatrical convention, dating from the nineteenth century and realistic drama, whereby an audience seems to be looking through an invisible fourth wall into the room of an actual house created by the other three walls of a box set.

Free verse   See OPEN FORM.

Gay and lesbian criticism   See page 1602.

Gender criticism   See page 1601.

Genre   A recurring type of literature; a literary form as defined by rules or conventions followed in it (e.g., tragedy, comedy, epic, lyric, pastoral, novel, short story, essay).

Gothic story   Fiction in which magic, mystery, and effects creating a sense of horror, or an atmosphere of brooding and unknown terror, play a major role.

Haiku   A lyric form, originating in Japan, of seventeen syllables in three lines, the first and third having five syllables and the second seven, presenting an image of a natural object or scene that expresses a distinct emotion or spiritual insight.

Hamartia   An error in judgment, a mistake, a frailty that, according to Aristotle's *Poetics,* results in a tragic hero's change in fortune from prosperity to adversity. *Hamartia* is sometimes mistakenly equated with tragic flaw. It does not, however, refer to a character flaw but rather to a central or defining aspect of the character. In reading plays critically, watching for an error or misstep (*hamartia*) is more advisable than looking for a defect in character (tragic flaw). See also TRAGIC FLAW.

Heptameter   A poetic line with seven metrical feet.

Hero, heroine   The protagonist, or central character, in a literary work.

Heroic couplet   Couplet in iambic pentameter with a full stop, usually, at the end. Also called *closed couplet.*

Hexameter   See ALEXANDRINE.

Historical criticism   See page 1587.

Hubris (hybris)   Greek for "insolence"; excessive pride that can lead to the downfall of the protagonist in a tragedy.

Hyperbole   Exaggeration; a figure of speech in which something is stated more strongly than is logically warranted. See also UNDERSTATEMENT.

Iamb   A metrical foot consisting of two syllables, an unaccented one followed by an accented one (*da DA*—"awake"). In iambic meter, iambs are the predominant foot in a line or poem.

Image   (1) A word or group of words that refers to a sensory experience or to an object that can be known by one or more of the senses. *Imagery* signifies all such language in a poem or other literary work collectively and can include any of the senses (visual imagery, auditory imagery, tactile imagery, kinetic imagery, imagery of smell or taste). (2) A metaphor or other comparison. *Imagery* in this sense refers to the characteristic that several images in a poem have in common, for example, the sports imagery in Patricia Goedicke's "My Brother's Anger" (p. 786).

Imagery   See IMAGE.

Implied metaphor   Metaphor in which the *to be* verb is omitted and one aspect of the comparison is implied rather than stated directly, as, for example, "these dragonflies / filled with little men" in Julia Alvarez's "How I Learned to Sweep" (p. 650).

In medias res   Latin for "into the middle things"; used to describe the technique of starting a narrative at an engaging point well into the story and filling in the background events later as needed.

Interior monologue   The representation of unspoken mental activity—thoughts, impressions, and memories—as if directly overheard by the reader, without being selected and organized by a narrator, either in an associative, disjointed, nonlogical, nongrammatical way (stream of consciousness) or in a logical, grammatical flow of thoughts and memories moving through a person's mind, as if being spoken to an external listener. It is sometimes set off typographically, for example, by using italics rather than quotation marks.

Internal rhyme   Rhyme that occurs between words within a line, between words within lines near each other, or between a word within a line and one at the end of the same or a nearby line.

Irony   A feeling, tone, mood, or attitude arising from the awareness that what is (reality) is opposite from, and usually worse than, what seems (appearance). Irony is not the same as mere coincidence. Irony has different forms: What a person *says* may be ironic (see VERBAL IRONY); a discrepancy between what a character knows or means and what a reader or audience knows can be ironic (see DRAMATIC IRONY); a general situation can be ironic (see SITUATIONAL IRONY).

Italian sonnet   A sonnet composed of an octave (an eight-line unit), rhyming *abbaabba*, and a sestet (a six-line unit), often rhyming *cdecde* or *cdcdcd*, although variations are frequent. The octave usually develops an idea or a question or a problem; then the poem pauses, or "turns," and the sestet completes the idea, answers the question, or resolves the difficulty. Sometimes called a *Petrarchan sonnet*. See also ENGLISH SONNET.

Juxtaposition   Placement of things side by side or close together for comparison or contrast or to create something new from the union, without necessarily making them grammatically parallel.

Limited omniscient point of view   Use of a narrator who is omniscient in some areas or to some extent but is not completely all-knowing.

Line   A sequence of words printed as a separate entity on a page; the basic structural unit in poetry (except prose poems).

Literal   In accordance with the primary or strict meaning of a word or words; not figurative or metaphorical.

Litotes   See UNDERSTATEMENT.

Lyric   Originally, a poem sung to the accompaniment of a lyre; now a poem, usually short, expressing the personal emotion and ideas of a single speaker.

Marxist criticism   See page 1596.

Masculine rhyme   See SINGLE RHYME.

Melodrama   Originally, a drama with musical accompaniment that enhanced its emotional impact; it became in the nineteenth century a type of play relying on broadly drawn heroes and villains, suspenseful plots, improbable escapes, the triumph of good over evil, and an excessive appeal to the emotions of the audience.

Metaphor   A figure of speech in which two things usually thought to be dissimilar are treated as if they were alike and have characteristics in common, as, for example, "My brother's anger is a helmet" in Patricia Goedicke's "My Brother's Anger" (p. 786). See also IMPLIED METAPHOR.

Metaphysical poetry   The work of a number of seventeenth-century English poets characterized by philosophical subtlety and intellectual rigor; subtle, often outrageous logic; imitation of actual speech, sometimes resulting in "rough" meter and style; and far-fetched analogies. Sometimes applied to modern verse sharing some of these characteristics.

Meter   A steady beat, or measured pulse, created by a repeating pattern of accents, syllables, or both.

Metonymy   A figure of speech in which the name of one thing is substituted for that of something closely associated with it, as in commonly used phrases such as "The *White House* announced today . . ." See also SYNECDOCHE.

Metrics   The study of the patterns of rhythm in poetry.

Monometer   A poetic line with one metrical foot.

Morality play   A form of drama that originated in the Middle Ages and presents a dramatized allegory in which abstractions (such as Mercy, Conscience, Perseverance, and Shame) are personified and engage in a struggle for a human soul.

Motif   A recurring element — image, idea, feature, action, or theme — that is elaborated or developed throughout a work.

Motivation   The combination of personality traits and circumstances that impel a character to act in a particular way.

Mystery play   A medieval play based on biblical history; a scriptural play.

Myth   Anonymous stories arising from a culture's oral traditions that involve gods or heroic figures, explore matters beyond everyday life, and concern origins, endings, aspirations, purpose, and meaning.

Mythological criticism   See page 1590.

Naïve narrator   A narrator too young or too inexperienced to understand fully the implications of what she or he is talking about. See also NARRATOR; RELIABLE NARRATOR; UNRELIABLE NARRATOR.

Narrative   A narrated story, in prose or verse; an account of events involving characters and what they do and say, told by a storyteller (narrator).

Narrator   The storyteller through whom an author relates a narrative. See also FIRST-PERSON NARRATOR; NAÏVE NARRATOR; POINT OF VIEW; RELIABLE NARRATOR; UNRELIABLE NARRATOR.

Naturalism   A literary movement of the late nineteenth and early twentieth centuries that applies the principles of scientific determinism to literature and views humans as animals in a natural world who respond to environmental forces — physical or socioeconomic — and internal stresses and drives, none of which they can control or understand.

Near rhyme   See SLANT RHYME.

New Comedy   Greek comedy of the fourth and third centuries B.C.E. that depicts the obstacles faced by young lovers and the unpredictable changes of fortune they encounter and pokes fun at the foibles and attitudes of the lovers as well as those around them.

New Criticism   See page 1592.

New Historicism   See page 1606.

Novel   Although the term can refer to any extended fictional narrative in prose, it is generally used for narratives that emphasize complexity of character and development of a unifying theme. See also FICTION; NOVELLA; SHORT STORY.

Novella   A fictional prose narrative longer than a short story but shorter than a novel; commonly fifty to one hundred pages in length. See also FICTION; NOVEL; SHORT STORY.

Objective point of view   A narrative approach in which a narrator describes events only from the outside, without looking into the mind of any of the characters or explaining why any of the characters do what they do.

Octameter   A poetic line with eight metrical feet.

Octave   The first, eight-line segment of an Italian sonnet.

Ode   (1) In Greek drama, a speech delivered by the chorus. (2) A long lyric poem, serious (often intellectual) in tone, elevated and dignified in style, dealing with a single theme. The ode is generally more complicated in form than other lyric poems. Some odes retain a formal division into strophe, antistrophe, and epode, which reflects the ode's origins in Greek drama. See also ANTISTROPHE; CHORUS; EPODE; STROPHE.

Off rhyme   See SLANT RHYME.

Old comedy   Comedy, such as that of Aristophanes in the fifth century B.C.E., employing raucous (sometimes coarse) humor, elements of satire and farce, and often a critique of contemporary persons or political and social norms.

Omniscient point of view   The point of view in a work of fiction in which the narrator is capable of knowing everything about a story's events and characters, including their inner feelings.

One-act play   A short play that is complete in one act.

Onomatopoeia   The use of words whose sounds supposedly resemble the sounds they denote, such as *hiss* or *buzz*, or a group of words whose sounds help to convey what is being described.

Open form   A poetic form free of any predetermined metrical and stanzaic patterns. See also CLOSED FORM.

Orchestra   From the Greek word for "dance." In Greek theater, the area in front of the skene where the chorus performed its songs and dances. Later, a pit for musicians in front of the stage; still later, the group of musicians working there.

Ottava rima   An eight-line stanza in iambic pentameter rhyming *abababcc*.

Overstatement   See HYPERBOLE.

Oxymoron   A figure of speech combining in one phrase (usually adjective-noun) two seemingly contradictory elements, such as "loving hate" or "feather of lead, bright smoke, cold fire, sick health" (Shakespeare, *Romeo and Juliet* 1.1.176–80). Oxymoron is a type of PARADOX.

Pantoum   A poem consisting of four-line stanzas rhyming *abab*. The second and fourth lines of one stanza serve as the first and third lines of the next stanza, and the first and third lines of the first stanza reappear as the fourth and second lines of the last stanza, so that the poem begins and ends with the same line. For a poem in an adapted pantoum form, see Honoree Fanonne Jeffers, "Outlandish Blues" (p. 804).

Paradox   A figure of speech in which a statement initially seeming self-contradictory or absurd turns out, seen in another light, to make good sense. See also OXYMORON.

Parallelism   (1) A verbal arrangement in which elements of equal weight within phrases, sentences, or paragraphs are expressed in a similar grammatical order and structure. (2) A principle of poetic structure in which consecutive lines in open form are related by a line's repeating, expanding on, or contrasting with the idea of the lines or lines before it, as in the biblical psalms or the poems of Walt Whitman (see p. 875).

Parody   In modern usage, a humorous or satirical imitation of a serious piece of literature or writing. In the sixteenth and seventeenth centuries, poets such as George Herbert practiced "sacred parody" by adapting secular lyrics to devotional themes.

Partial rhyme   See SLANT RHYME.

Pastoral   (1) As an adjective, that which deals with a rural setting and affirms a rustic way of life. (2) As a noun, a literary type associated with shepherds and country living.

Pause   See CAESURA.

Pentameter   A poetic line with five metrical feet.

Persona   Literally, the mask through which actors spoke in Greek plays. In some critical approaches of recent decades, the "character" projected by the author, the *I* of a narrative poem or novel, or the speaker whose voice is heard in a lyric poem. In this view, the poem is an artificial construct distanced from the poet's autobiographical self. See also VOICE.

Personification   A figure of speech in which something nonhuman (an abstraction or a natural object) is treated as if it had human (not just living) characteristics or actions. See also APOSTROPHE.

Petrarchan sonnet   See ITALIAN SONNET.

Play   A drama intended for performance before a theatrical audience. See also CLOSET DRAMA.

Plot   (1) The selection and arrangement of events in a narrative to present them most effectively to the reader and bring out their causal connections. (2) The action that takes place within a play, considered by Aristotle in the *Poetics* to be the most important of the six elements of drama. See also SUBPLOT.

Poem   A term whose meaning exceeds all attempts at definition. Here is a slightly modified version of an attempt at definition by William Harmon and C. Hugh Holman in *A Handbook to Literature* (1996): A poem is a literary composition, written or oral, typically characterized by imagination, emotion, sense impressions, and concrete language that invites attention to its own physical features, such as sound or appearance on the page.

Poetic diction   In general, a specialized language used in or considered appropriate to poetry. In the late seventeenth and the eighteenth centuries, a refined use of language that excluded "common" speech from poetry as indecorous and substituted elevated circumlocutions or archaic synonyms, or such forms as *ope* and *e'er*.

Point of view   The vantage point from which an author presents a story, combining person (first, second, or third, named or anonymous) and perspective (objective, omniscient, limited). See also CENTER OF CONSCIOUSNESS TECHNIQUE; STREAM-OF-CONSCIOUSNESS TECHNIQUE.

Problem play   A serious work that dramatizes a real-life, usually contemporary, social, political, or ethical problem. Although in a broad sense it covers all drama dealing with problems of human life, it is used more narrowly for the "drama of ideas" that emerged in the late nineteenth century in the work, for example, of Norwegian playwright Henrik Ibsen (see p. 1263).

Prologue   (1) The opening section of a Greek tragedy. (2) Words spoken before the beginning of a play, usually a monologue by one of the actors providing background information.

Property (prop)   A movable object used on stage, especially one handled by an actor while performing.

Proscenium   The part of the stage in a modern theater between the orchestra and the curtain. The proscenium arch is the arch over the front of the stage from which the curtain hangs and which separates the stage from the audience.

Prose poem A poem printed as prose, with lines wrapping at the right margin rather than being divided through predetermined line breaks.

Prosody The principles of versification, especially of meter, rhythm, rhyme, and stanza forms.

Protagonist The most important or leading character in a literary work. See also ANTAGONIST.

Psychological criticism See page 1588.

Pun A "play on words" based on similarity in sound between two words having very different meanings, as when "Dear heart" in Sir Thomas Wyatt's "They flee from me" (p. 882) means both "heart" and "hart" (deer). Also called *paronomasia*. Often used to produce AMBIGUITY in sense 2.

Quatrain A stanza of four lines or other four-line unit within a larger form, such as a sonnet.

Reader-response criticism See page 1594.

Realism (1) An approach to literature that attempts to depict accurately the everyday life of a time and place. (2) A literary movement that developed in the latter half of the nineteenth century characterized by an objective presentation of material and realistic depiction of setting, characters, and details.

Recognition A significant realization or discovery by a character, usually the protagonist, that moves the plot forward by changing the circumstances of a play.

Refrain One or more identical or deliberately similar lines repeated throughout a poem, sometimes with meaningful variation, such as the final line of a stanza or as a block of lines between stanzas or sections.

Reliable narrator A narrator who tells her or his story accurately and honestly. See also NAÏVE NARRATOR; NARRATOR; UNRELIABLE NARRATOR.

Resolution The culmination of a fictional plot that resolves the conflicts or leaves them satisfyingly unresolved.

Rhyme The repetition of the accented vowel sound of a word and all succeeding consonant sounds. See also EXACT RHYME; SLANT RHYME.

Rhyme royal An alternative term for Chaucerian stanza because it was used by King James I of Scotland in his poem *The Kingis Quair* ("The King's Book"), written about 1424.

Rhyme scheme The pattern of end rhymes in a poem or stanza; the recurring sequence is usually described by assigning a letter to each word sound, the same word sounds having the same letter (e.g., *abbaabba*).

Rhythm The patterned "movement" of language created by the choice of words and their arrangement, usually described through such metaphors as fast or slow, smooth or halting, graceful or rough, deliberate or frenzied, syncopated or disjointed. Rhythm in poetry is affected, in addition to meter, by such factors as line length; line endings; pauses (or lack of them) within lines; spaces within, at the beginning or end of, or between lines; word choice; and combinations of sounds.

Rising action   The part of a plot leading up to the climax and marked by increasingly tense and complicated conflict. See also FALLING ACTION.

Rising meter   A foot (usually an iamb or an anapest) in which the final, stressed syllable is preceded by one or two unstressed syllables, thus giving a sense of stepping up. See also FALLING METER.

Romance   (1) In medieval narrative poetry or prose, a tale involving knights and kings, adventures, ladies in distress, courtly love, and chivalric ideals. (2) In modern fiction, a work characterized by remote and exotic settings, exciting and heroic action, passionate love, and mysterious or supernatural experiences. (3) In drama, a play neither wholly comic nor wholly tragic, often containing elements of the supernatural.

Round character   A complex, fully developed character either shown as changing and growing because of what happens to her or him or described in such rich detail that we have a clear sense of how she or he would, or will, change even though we don't see it happening. See also FLAT CHARACTER.

Run-on line   A line whose sense and grammatical structure continue to the next. The technique is called *enjambment*. See also END-STOPPED LINE.

Sarcasm   A harsh and cutting form of verbal irony, often involving apparent praise that is obviously not meant seriously.

Satire   A work, or manner within a work, that combines a critical attitude with humor and wit with the intent of improving human institutions or humanity.

Scansion   The division of metrical verse into feet in order to determine and label the meter of a poem. See also FOOT; METER; page 1574.

Scene   (1) A subdivision of an ACT in drama, or — in modern drama — a section of a play that is not divided into acts. (2) See SETTING. (3) A variant spelling of *skene*.

Script   The written text of a play, which includes the stage directions, dramatic monologues, and the dialogue between characters.

Sentimentality   A term used to describe a work seeking to elicit an emotional response in a reader or spectator that exceeds what the situation warrants.

Sestet   The last six lines of an ITALIAN SONNET.

Sestina   A lyric poem consisting of 6 six-line stanzas and a three-line concluding stanza (or "envoy"). The six end-words of the first stanza must be used as the end-words of the other five stanzas, in a specified pattern (the first line ends with the end-word from the last line of the previous stanza, the second line with that of the first line of the previous stanza, the third line with that of the previous fifth line, the fourth line with that of the previous second line, the fifth line with that of the previous fourth line, the sixth line with that of the previous third line). The three lines of the envoy must use the end-words of lines 5, 3, and 1 from the first stanza, in that order, and must include the other three end-words within the lines.

Set   The physical equipment of a stage, including backdrops, furniture, properties, and lighting.

Setting   The overall context — where, when, in what circumstances — in which the action in a fictional or dramatic work takes place.

Shakespearean sonnet   See ENGLISH SONNET.

Shaped poem   See CONCRETE POEM.

Short story   A brief prose work of narrative fiction characterized by a carefully crafted plot and style, complexity in characterization and point of view, and unity of effect. See also FICTION; NOVEL; NOVELLA.

Simile   Expression of a direct similarity, using such words as *like, as,* or *than,* between two things usually regarded as dissimilar (e.g., "His face was as white as a sheet."). It is important to distinguish *simile* from *comparison,* where the two things joined by *like* or *as* are not dissimilar.

Single rhyme   A rhyme in which the stressed, rhyming syllable is the final syllable in the rhyme: *west* and *stressed, away* and *today.* Formerly called *masculine rhyme.* See also DOUBLE RHYME.

Situational irony   A kind of irony in which a result turns out very different from, and usually more sinister than, what a character expected or hoped for. Unlike dramatic irony, in situational irony the reader does not necessarily know more than the characters and may be as surprised by what happens as the characters are. See also DRAMATIC IRONY; IRONY; VERBAL IRONY.

Slant rhyme   A form of rhyme in which words contain similar sounds but do not rhyme perfectly (usually involving assonance or — more frequently — consonance). See also ASSONANCE; CONSONANCE.

Soliloquy   A monologue delivered by a character in a play while alone on stage or otherwise out of hearing of the other characters, often revealing the character's inner thoughts or feelings. Sometimes applied to a poem imitating this feature. See also DRAMATIC MONOLOGUE.

Sonnet   A fourteen-line poem usually written in iambic pentameter. Originally lyrical love poems, sonnets came to be used also for meditations on religious themes, death, and nature and are now open to all subjects. Some sonnets have varied from the traditional form — using hexameter lines, fewer or more than fourteen lines, or an appended coda. Sometimes sonnets are grouped in a "sonnet sequence," with implied narrative progression in the situations imagined as underlying the successive utterances. See also ENGLISH SONNET; ITALIAN SONNET; SPENSERIAN SONNET.

Speaker   The imagined voice in a nonnarrative poem of someone uttering the words of the poem, either that of the poet quite directly or of a character expressing views or feelings the poet may or may not share.

Spenserian sonnet   A variation of the English sonnet that employs the structure of three quatrains plus a couplet, but joins the quatrains by linking rhymes: *abab bcbc cdcd ee.*

Spenserian stanza   A stanza of nine iambic lines, the first eight pentameter and the ninth hexameter, rhyming *ababbcbcc.*

Spondee   A metrical foot made up of two stressed syllables (*DA DA*—"dream house"), with no unstressed syllables. Spondees cannot be the predominant foot in a poem; they are usually substituted for iambs or trochees as a way of increasing emphasis.

Stage directions Written instructions in the script of a play, typically placed in parentheses and set in italics, telling actors how to move on the stage or how to deliver a particular word or speech.

Stage left, stage right Areas of the stage seen from the point of view of an actor facing the audience. Stage left, therefore, is on the audience's right-hand side, and vice versa.

Stanza A grouping of poetic lines into a section, either according to form — each section having the same number of lines and the same prosody — or according to thought, creating irregular units comparable to paragraphs in prose. Irregular stanzas are sometimes called STROPHES.

Static character A character in a narrative or dramatic work who is not shown as changing. See also DYNAMIC CHARACTER.

Stichomythia A form of repartee in dialogue originating in ancient Greek drama — brief, alternating lines that reply sharply to each other in wordings that echo and vary what the preceding character expressed.

Stock character A traditional character defined by a single, stereotypical characteristic, such as an innocent young woman, a rakish young man, or a clever servant.

Story Any account of a related series of events in sequential order, usually chronological order (the order in which they happened).

Stream-of-consciousness technique An attempt to convey the unstructured, even at times chaotic, flow of random sense perceptions, mental pictures, memories, sounds, thoughts, and feelings — prerational mental activity, before the mind orders it into a coherent form or shape — through an associative rather than a logical style, usually without ordinary punctuation or complete sentences.

Stress In metrics, the greater emphasis given to some words and syllables relative to that received by adjacent words and syllables. See also ACCENT.

Strophe (1) The first part in a three-stanza segment of a choral ODE in Greek drama, sung while the chorus moves from stage right to stage left. (2) The first stanza in a three-stanza segment of an ode. (3) See STANZA. See also ANTISTROPHE; CHORUS; EPODE; ODE.

Structure (1) The planned framework — the general plan or outline — of a literary work. (2) Narrower patterns within the overall framework. See also FORM.

Style In writing, the distinctive, individual manner in which a writer uses words, constructs sentences, incorporates nonliteral expressions, and handles rhythm, timing, and tone; also, the manner characteristic of a group of writers (as in "period style").

Subplot A subordinate or minor story in a dramatic or narrative work, often related thematically or structurally to the main plot. See also PLOT.

Substitution The use of a different kind of foot in place of the one normally demanded by the predominant meter of a poem, as a way of calling attention to an idea, emphasizing the dominant foot by variation from it, speeding up or slowing down the pace, or signaling a switch in meaning.

Suspense   A sense of uncertainty and concern about how things in a literary work will turn out, when disaster will fall or rescue will occur, who did what, or what the effects on the characters or events will be.

Symbol   Something that represents both itself and something else. A literary symbol is a prominent or repeated image or action that is present in the poem, story, or play and is seen, touched, smelled, heard, tasted, or experienced imaginatively but also conveys a cluster of abstract meanings beyond itself.

Synecdoche   A special kind of metonymy in which a part of a thing is substituted for the whole of which it is a part, as in the commonly used phrases "give me a hand," "lend me your ears," or "many mouths to feed."

Syntax   The arrangement of words in a sentence to show their relationship to one another.

Tercet   A stanza of three lines, each usually ending with the same rhyme. See also TERZA RIMA; TRIPLET.

Terza rima   A poetic form consisting of three-line stanzas (TERCETS) with interlinked rhymes, *aba bcb cdc ded efe*, etc., made famous by Dante's use of it in *The Divine Comedy*.

Tetrameter   A poetic line with four metrical feet.

Text   Traditionally, a piece of writing. In recent reader-response criticism, *text* has come to mean the words with which the reader interacts; in this view, a literary work is not an object, not a shape on the page or a spoken performance, but what is completed in the reader's mind.

Theme   The central idea embodied or explored in a literary work, what it all adds up to; the general concept, explicit or implied, which the work incorporates and makes persuasive to the reader.

Third-person narrator   The type of narration with a storyteller who is not identified; uses the pronouns *he, she, it,* or *they* — but not *I* — in speaking of herself or himself; asserts no connection between the narrator and the characters in the story; and tells the story with some objectivity and distance.

Title   The name attached to a work of literature. Usually a title, when assigned by the author, is an integral part of a work and needs to be considered in interpreting it. In some cases, a title for a poem has been added as a means of identifying it and is not integral to its interpretation. Sometimes a poem is untitled and the first line is used as a convenient way of referring to the poem (e.g., in Emily Dickinson's poems), but it should not be thought of as a title and does not follow the capitalization rules for titles.

Tone   The attitude, or "stance," toward the subject and toward the reader or audience implied in a literary work; the "tone of voice" it seems to project.

Tragedy   A story recounting a causally related series of serious and important events that culminate in an unhappy ending for the protagonist. See also COMEDY.

Tragic flaw   The theory, attributed to Aristotle's *Poetics*, that the downfall of the hero in a tragedy is caused by a defect, or flaw, in her or his character. See also *HAMARTIA*.

Tragicomedy   A play whose plot could be appropriate to tragedy until the final act, when it turns out unexpectedly to have the happy ending of a comedy. The tone and style of tragicomedy are serious and the outcome could well be disaster or death; but somehow the disaster is averted, and at the end order and harmony prevail. See also COMEDY; TRAGEDY.

Trimeter   A poetic line with three metrical feet.

Triplet   A group of three consecutive lines with the same rhyme, often used for variation in a long sequence of couplets. See also TERCET.

Trochee   A metrical foot consisting of two syllables, an accented one followed by an unaccented one (*DA da*—"wakeful"). In trochaic meter, trochees are the predominant foot in a line or poem.

Type   (1) See GENRE. (2) A character who represents a class or kind of person, either atypical and individualized, or stereotypical (see STOCK CHARACTER). (3) A variety of symbol, especially as used in religion for something that is to come, such as "a type of Christ."

Understatement   A figure of speech expressing something in an unexpectedly restrained way, which often has the effect of increasing rather than reducing emphasis. See also HYPERBOLE.

Unity   A sense of wholeness and cohesion in a literary work, as all of its parts work together according to some organizing principle to achieve common effect.

Unreliable narrator   A narrator who may be in error in her or his reporting or understanding of things, or who distorts things, deliberately or unintentionally. See also NAÏVE NARRATOR; NARRATOR; RELIABLE NARRATOR.

Upstage   The part of the stage farthest from the audience.

Verbal irony   A figure of speech in which what is said is nearly the opposite of what is meant. See also DRAMATIC IRONY; IRONY; SARCASM; SITUATIONAL IRONY.

Verisimilitude   The semblance of truth; the use of abundant detail to create the appearance of reality in a literary work.

Verse   (1) A unit of poetry, the same thing as a stanza or line. (2) A rhythmic composition, often in meter and rhyme, irrespective of merit (the term *poetry* is often reserved for verse of high merit).

Viewpoint   See POINT OF VIEW.

Villanelle   A nineteen-line lyric poem divided into five tercets and a final four-line stanza, rhyming *aba aba aba aba aba abaa*. Line 1 is repeated to form lines 6, 12, and 18; line 3 is repeated to form lines 9, 15, and 19. See, for example, Dylan Thomas's "Do not go gentle into that good night" (p. 866) and John Yau's "Chinese Villanelle" (p. 883).

Voice   The supposed authorial presence in poems that do not obviously employ persona as a distancing device.

Agha Shahid Ali, "I Dream It Is Afternoon When I Return to Delhi" from *The Half-Inch Himalayas* by Agha Shadid Ali. Copyright © 1987 by Agha Shadid Ali. Reprinted by permission of Wesleyan University Press.

Monica Ali, "Dinner with Dr. Azad" from *Brick Lane* by Monica Ali. Copyright © 2003 by Monica Ali. Reprinted with the permission of Scribner, an imprint of Simon & Schuster Adult Publishing Group. All rights reserved.

Isabel Allende, "And of Clay Are We Created" from *The Stories of Eva Luna*, translated from the Spanish by Margaret Sayers Penden. Copyright © 1984 by Isabel Allende. English translation copyright © 1991 by Macmillan Publishing Company. Reprinted with the permission of Scribner, an imprint of Simon & Schuster Adult Publishing Group.

Julia Alvarez, "Daughter of Invention" from *How the Garcia Girls Lost Their Accents*. Copyright © 1991 by Julia Alvarez. Published by Plume, an imprint of The Penguin Group (USA), and originally in hardcover by Algonquin Books of Chapel Hill. Reprinted by permission of Susan Bergholz Literary Services, New York. All rights reserved. "How I Learned to Sweep" and "Ironing Their Clothes" from *Homecoming*. Copyright © 1984, 1996 by Julia Alvarez. Published by Plume, an imprint of The Penguin Group (USA), and originally published by Grove Press. Reprinted by permission of Susan Bergholz Literary Services, New York. All rights reserved.

Yehuda Amichai, "Wildpeace" from *The Selected Poetry of Yehuda Amichai*, edited and translated by Chana Bloch & Stephen Mitchell. Reprinted by permission of Chana Bloch.

Margaret Atwood, "True Stories," currently available in *Selected Poems 11*, published by Houghton Mifflin. Originally published in *True Stories*. Copyright © 1981 by Margaret Atwood. Reprinted by permission of Margaret Atwood.

W. H. Auden, "Musée des Beaux Arts" from *Collected Poems*. Copyright © 1940 and renewed 1968 by W. H. Auden. Used by permission of Random House, Inc.

Joseph Awad, "Autumnal" from *Learning to Hear the Music*. First published in *Grape Leaves: A Century of Arab-American Poetry*, 1988. Reprinted in *Nostalgia*, Fall/Winter 1989. Reprinted by permission of the author.

Jimmy Santiago Baca, "Family Ties" from *Black Mesa Poems* by Jimmy Santiago Baca. Copyright © 1989 by Jimmy Santiago Baca. Reprinted by permission of New Dimensions Publishing, Corp.

James Baldwin, "Sonny's Blues," originally published in *Partisan Review*. Copyright © 1957. Copyright renewed. Collected in *Going to Meet the Man*, published by Vintage Books. Used by arrangement with the James Baldwin Estate.

Toni Cade Bambara, "The Lesson" from *Gorilla, My Love* by Toni Cade Bambara. Copyright © 1972 by Toni Cade Bambara. Used by permission of Random House, Inc.

Melissa Bank, "The Wonder Spot" from *Speaking with the Angel*, edited by Nick Hornby. Copyright © 2000 by Melissa Bank. Used by permission of Riverhead Books, an imprint of Penguin Group (USA) Inc.

Reza Baraheni, "Autumn in Tehran." Reprinted by permission of the author.

Clive Barnes, "Fiery 'Fences': A Review" from the *New York Post*, March 27, 1987. Copyright © 1987 by Clive Barnes. Reprinted by permission.

Jim Barnes, "Return to La Plata, Missouri" from *American Book of the Dead: Poems by Jim Barnes*. Copyright © 1982 by Jim Barnes. Used with permission of the poet and the University of Illinois Press.

Gerald Barrax, "Dara" from *From A Person Sitting in the Darkness*. Copyright © 1998 by Gerald Barrax. Reprinted by permission of Louisiana State University Press.

Lynda Barry, "Today's Demon: Magic" from *One Hundred Demons* by Lynda Barry. Copyright © 2002 by Lynda Barry. Published by Sasquatch Books (Seattle, WA). Reprinted courtesy of Darhansoff, Verrill, Feldman Literary Agents.

David Bevington, "Notes to *Hamlet*" from *The Complete Works of Shakespeare*, 4th ed., by David Bevington. Copyright © 1992 by HarperCollins Publishers. Reprinted by permission of Pearson Education, Inc.

Elizabeth Bishop, "In the Waiting Room" and "Sestina" from *The Complete Poems 1927–1979*. Copyright © 1979, 1983 by Alice Helen Methfessel. Reprinted by permission of Farrar, Straus & Giroux, LLC.

Peter Blue Cloud, "Rattle," originally published in the *Journal for the Protection of All Beings*, 1978. Reprinted by permission of the author.

Robert Bly, "Driving to Town Late to Mail a Letter." Copyright © 1962 by Robert Bly. From *Silence in the Snowy Fields*. Copyright © 1962 by Robert Bly. Reprinted by permission. All rights reserved.

Eavan Boland, "The Pomegranate" from *In a Time of Violence* by Eavan Boland. Copyright © 1994 by Eavan Boland. Used by permission of W.W. Norton & Company, Inc.

Jorge Luis Borges, "The Other Tiger" from *Selected Poems*, edited by Alexander Coleman. Copyright © 1995 by Maria Kodama. Reprinted with permission of The Wylie Agency, Inc.

Laure-Anne Bosselaar, "Bench in Aix-en-Provence" from *Small Gods of Grief* by Laure-Anne Bosselaar. Copyright © 2001 by Laure-Anne Bosselaar. Reprinted with the permission of BOA Editions, Ltd, www.boaeditions.org.

Anne Bradstreet, "To My Dear and Loving Husband." From *The Works of Anne Bradstreet*, edited by Jeannine Hensley, Cambridge, MA: The Belknap Press of Harvard University Press. Copyright © 1967 by the President and Fellows of Harvard College. Reprinted by permission of the publisher.

Gwendolyn Brooks, "The Bean Eaters" and "We Real Cool" from *Blacks*. Copyright © 1991 by Gwendolyn Brooks. Reprinted by Consent of Brooks Permissions.

Sterling A. Brown, "Riverbank Blues" from *The Collected Poems of Sterling A. Brown*, edited by Michael S. Harper. Copyright © 1980 by Sterling A. Brown. Reprinted by permission of HarperCollins Publishers.

Dennis Brutus, "Nightsong: City" from *A Simple Lust: Selected Poems*. Copyright © 1973 by Dennis Brutus. Reprinted by permission of the author.

Charles Bukowski, "my old man" from *Love is a Dog from Hell: Poems 1974-1977* by Charles Bukowski. Copyright © 1977 by Charles Bukowski. Reprinted by permission of HarperCollins Publishers.

Julia de Burgos, "Returning," translated by Dwight Garcia and Margarite Fernandez Olmos. Reprinted with permission from the publisher of *Recovering the U.S. Hispanic Literary Heritage, Volume 2* (Houston: Arte Publico Press–University of Houston,1996).

Anthony Butts, "Ferris Wheel" from *Little Low Heaven* by Anthony Butts. © 2003 by Anthony Butts. Reprinted with permission of New Issues Poetry & Prose.

Raymond Carver, "What We Talk About When We Talk About Love" from *What We Talk About When We Talk About Love* by Raymond Carver. Copyright © 1974, 1976, 1978, 1980, 1981 by Raymond Carver. Used by permission of Alfred A. Knopf, a division of Random House, Inc.

Ana Castillo, "I Heard the Cries of Two Hundred Children." From *I Ask the Impossible*. Copyright © 2001 by Ana Castillo. Published by Anchor Books, a division of Random House, Inc. Reprinted by permission of Sandra Bergholz Literary Services, New York, NY, and Lamy, NM. All rights reserved.

Sandra M. Castillo, "Exile" from *My Father Sings, To My Embarrassment* by Sandra McCastillo. Copyright © 2002 by Sandra M. Castillo. Reprinted with the permission of White Pine Press, www.whitepine.org.

Rosemary Catacalos, "David Talamántez on the Last Day of Second Grade." Reprinted by permission of the author.

Lorna Dee Cervantes, "Freeway 280," originally published in *Latin American Literary Review*, volume 5, issue number 10, 1977. Reprinted by permission of Latin American Literary Review Press.

Paul Cézanne, *Pommes et Oranges*. The Art Archive/Musée d'Orsay Paris/Dagli Orti (A).

Tina Chang, "Origin & Ash" from *Half-Lit Houses* by Tina Chang. Copyright © 2004 by Tina Chang. Reprinted with the permission of Four Way Books, www.fourwaybooks.com.

Marilyn Chin, "Turtle Soup" from *The Phoenix Gone, The Terrace Empty*. Copyright © 1994 by Marilyn Chin. Reprinted with permission from Milkweed Editions.

Sandra Cisneros, "The House on Mango Street." Copyright ©1984 by Sandra Cisneros. Published by Vintage Books, a division of Random House, Inc., and in hardcover by Alfred A. Knopf in 1994. Reprinted by permission of Susan Bergholz Literary Services, New York. All rights reserved.

Lucille Clifton, "at the cemetery, walnut grove plantation, South Carolina, 1989" from *Quilting: Poems 1987-1990* by Lucille Clifton. Copyright © 1991 by Lucille Clifton. "cutting greens" from *Good Woman: Poems and a Memoir 1969-1980* by Lucille Clifton. Copyright © 1987 by Lucille Clifton. Reprinted with the permission of BOA Editions, Ltd. www.boaeditions.org.

Judith Ortiz Cofer, "American History" from *The Latin Deli: Prose and Poetry* by Judith Ortiz Cofer. Copyright © 1993 by Judith Ortiz Cofer. Reprinted by permission of The University of Georgia Press. "Cold as Heaven" from *Reaching for the Mainland & Selected New Poems* by Judith Ortiz Cofer. Reprinted by permission of Bilingual Press/Editorial Bilingue.

Jessica Cohen, "Grade A: The Market for a Yale Woman's Eggs," originally published in *Atlantic Monthly*, Fall 2001. Copyright © 2002 Jessica Cohen. Reprinted by permission of the author.

Billy Collins, "Consolation" and "Days" from *The Art of Drowning* by Billy Collins. Copyright © 1995 by Billy Collins. Used by permission of The University of Pittsburgh Press.

Jayne Cortez, "Into This Time" from *Firespitter*. Copyright © 2004 by Jayne Cortez. Reprinted by permission of the author.

Joseph L. Coulombe, "The Approximate Size of His Favorite Humor: Sherman Alexie's Comic Connections and Disconnections in 'The Lone Ranger and Tonto Fistfight in Heaven.'" Reprinted by permission of the author.

James Cox, "Muting White Noise: The Subversion of Popular Culture Narratives of Conquest in Sherman Alexie's Fiction" from *Studies in American Indian Literatures Series 2*, Vol.9, No.4 (Winter 1997): 52–70. Copyright 1997. Reprinted by permission of the author.

Cusi Cram, *West of Stupid*. Reprinted with permission of the author.

Victor Hernández Cruz, "Problems with Hurricanes" from *Maraca: New and Selected Poems 1965-2000*. Copyright © 1991 by Victor Hernandez Cruz. Reprinted with permission of Coffee House Press, Minneapolis, Minnesota, USA. www.coffeehousepress.org.

Countee Cullen, "Incident" from *Color*. Copyright © 1925 by Harper & Bros., New York. Renewed 1952 by Ida M. Cullen. Copyright held by Amistad Research Center, Tulane University. Administered by Thompson and Thompson. Reprinted with permission of Thompson and Thompson, New York, New York.

E. E. Cummings, "Buffalo Bill's" and "in Just-" from *Complete Poems: 1904-1962* by E. E. Cummings, edited by George J. Firmage. Copyright 1923, 1951, © 1991 by The Trustees for the E.E. Cummings Trust. Copyright © 1976 by George James Firmage Used by permission of Liveright Publishing Corporation.

Bei Dao, "Night: Theme and Variations" from *The August Sleepwalker* by Bai Dao. Copyright © 1988 by Bei Dao. Translation and Introduction copyright © 1988, 1990 by Bonnie S. McDougall. Reprinted by permission of New Directions Publishing Corp.

Keki N. Daruwalla, "Pestilence" from *Under Orion*. Reprinted by permission of the author.

Jerome DeNuccio, "Slow Dancing with Skeletons: Sherman Alexie's 'The Lone Ranger and Tonto Fistfight in Heaven,'" originally published in *Critique*, Vol 44. #1 (Fall 2002): 86–96. Reprinted by permission of the author.

Toi Derricotte, "A Note on My Son's Face" from *Captivity*. Copyright © 1989. Reprinted by permission of the University of Pittsburgh Press.

Emily Dickinson, "Because I could not stop for Death," "I heard a fly buzz when I died," "I'm nobody! Who are you?" and "Much Madness is divinest Sense" from *The Poems of Emily Dickinson*, edited by Thomas H. Johnson. Cambridge, Mass: The Belknap Press of Harvard University Press. Copyright © 1951, 1955, 1979 by the President and Fellows of Harvard College. Reprinted by permission of the publishers and the Trustees of Amherst College.

Ana Doina, "The Extinct Homeland – A Conversation with Czeslaw Milosz," originally published in *American Diaspora*, edited by Virgil Suarez and Ryan Van Cleave. Reprinted by permission of the author.

Mark Doty, "Tiara" from *Bethlehem in Broad Daylight* by Mark Doty. Copyright ©1991 by Mark Doty. Reprinted by permission of David R. Godine, Publisher, Inc.

Rita Dove, "The Satisfaction Coal Company" from *Thomas and Beulah*, Carnegie Mellon University Press. © 1986 by Rita Dove. Reprinted by permission of the author.

Cornelius Eady, "My Mother, If She Had Won Free Dance Lessons" from *Victims of the Latest Dance Craze*. Copyright © 1985 by Cornelius Eady. Reprinted by permission of the author.

Harry J. Elam, Jr. "August Wilson's Gender Lessons." From *A Companion to Twentieth-Century American Drama*, edited by David Krasner, pp. 318–333. Copyright © 2005 by Harry J. Elam, Jr. Reprinted by permission of Blackwell Publishers.

T. S. Eliot, "The Love Song of J. Alfred Prufrock." From *Collected Poems 1909–1962*. Reprinted with the permission of Faber & Faber, Ltd.

Ralph Ellison, "Battle Royale" from *Invisible Man* by Ralph Ellison. Copyright © 1948 by Ralph Ellison. Used by permission of Random House, Inc.

Anita Endrezze, "The Girl Who Loved the Sky" from *At the Helm of Twilight*. Copyright © 1992 by Anita Endrezze. Published by Broken Moon Press. Reprinted by permission of the author.

Louise Erdrich, "The Red Convertible" from *Love Medicine, New and Expanded Version* by Louise Erdrich. Copyright © 1984, 1993 by Louise Erdrich. Reprinted by permission of Henry Holt and Company. "A Love Medicine" from *Jacklight: Poems*. Copyright © 1984 by Louise Erdrich. Reprinted with permission of The Wylie Agency, Inc.

Martín Espada, "The Saint Vincent de Paul Food Pantry Stomp" from *Rebellion Is the Circle of a Lover's Hands*. Copyright © 1990 by Martín Espada. Reprinted with permission of Curbstone Press. Distributed by Consortium.

Sandra María Esteves, "A la Mujer Borrinqueña," first printed in *Yerba Buena* from *Greenfield Review*, Greenfield Center, NY 12833 (Selected Best Small Press 1981 by the Library Journal). Copyright © 1991 by Sandra María Esteves. Reprinted by permission of the author.

Faiz Ahmed Faiz, "A Prison Daybreak" from *Rebel's Silhouette: Selected Poems* (revised edition) by Faiz Ahmed Faiz. Copyright 1995 by Faiz Ahmed Faiz. Reprinted by permission of The University of Massachusetts Press.

Susan Farrell, "Flight vs. Flight: A Re-evaluation of Dee in Alice Walker's 'Everyday Use'" from *Studies in Short Fiction* 35:2 (Spring 1998): 179–86. Copyright © 1998 Studies In Short Fiction.

William Faulkner, "A Rose for Emily" from *Collected Stories of William Faulkner* by William Faulkner. Copyright © 1930 and 1958 by William Faulkner. Used by permission of Random House, Inc.

Gustavo Pérez Firmat, "José Canseco Breaks Our Hearts Again." Reprinted by permission of the author.

Carolyn Forché, "The Colonel" from *The Country Between Us* by Carolyn Forché. Copyright © 1981 by Carolyn Forché. Originally appeared in *Women's International Resource Exchange*. Reprinted by permission of HarperCollins Publishers.

Vievee Francis, "Private Smith's Primer" from *Vievee Francis' Blue-Tail Fly*, 2006, p. 62. Reprinted with the permission of Wayne State University Press.

Robert Frost, "After Apple Picking," "Mending Wall," and "The Road Not Taken" from *The Poetry of Robert Frost*, edited by Edward Connery Lathem. Copyright © 1930, 1939, 1969 by Henry Holt and Company. Copyright 1958 by Robert Frost, copyright 1967 by Lesley Frost Ballantine. Reprinted by permission of Henry Holt and Company, LLC.

Richard Garcia, "Why I Left Church" from *The Flying Garcias* by Richard Garcia. © 1993. Reprinted by permission of the University of Pittsburgh Press.

Dagoberto Gilb, "Love in L.A." from *Magic Blood* by Dagoberto Gilb. Copyright © by Dagoberto Gilb. Reprinted by permission of The University of New Mexico Press.

Christopher Gilbert, "Touching" from *Across the Mutual Landscape*. Copyright © 1984 by Christopher Gilbert. Reprinted by permission of the author.

Allen Ginsberg, "A Supermarket in California" from *Collected Poems 1947–1980* by Allen Ginsberg. Copyright © 1955 by Allen Ginsberg. Reprinted by permission of HarperCollins Publishers.

Nikki Giovanni, "Nikka-Rose" from *Black Feeling, Black Talk, Black Judgment* by Nikki Giovanni. Copyright © 1968, 1970 by Nikki Giovanni. Reprinted by permission of HarperCollins Publishers.

Susan Glaspell, *Trifles*. Copyright © 1916 by Susan Glaspell. Reprinted with permission by the Estate of Susan Glaspell.

Patricia Goedicke, "My Brother's Anger" from *Paul Bunyan's Bearskin* (Minneapolis: Milkweed Editions, 1992). Copyright © 1992 by Patricia Goedicke. Reprinted with permission from Milkweed Editions.

Ray González, "Praise the Tortilla, Praise Menudo, and Praise Chorizo" from *The Heat of Arrivals* by Ray González. Copyright © 1996 by Ray Gonzalez. Reprinted with the permission of BOA Editions, Ltd., www.boaeditions.org.

Angelina Weld Grimké, "A Winter Twilight" from the Angelina Weld Grimké papers. Reprinted by permission of the Moorland-Spingarn Research Center, Howard University.

John Guare, "Woman at a Threshold Beckoning." Copyright © 2003 by John Guare. Reprinted by permission of International Creative Management.

Jeff Gundy, "A Review of Delights and Shadows by Ted Kooser." In "Among the Errates" from *The Georgia Review*, Winter 2004, pp. 937–938. Reprinted by permission of the author.

Kimiko Hahn, "Mother's Mother" from *Volatile*. Copyright © 1999 by Kimilo Hahn. Reprinted by permission of Hanging Loose Press.

Donald Hall, "Names of Horses" from *Old and New Poems* by Donald Hall. Copyright © 1996 by Donald Hall. Reprinted by permission of Houghton Mifflin Company. All rights reserved.

Joy Harjo, "She Had Some Horses" from the book *She Had Some Horses* by Joy Harjo. Copyright © 2006. Reprinted by permission of the author.

Michael S. Harper, "Nightmare Begins Responsibility" from *Songlines in Michaeltree: New and Collected Poems* by Michael S. Harper. Used with permission of the poet and the University of Illinois Press.

Robert Hayden, "Those Winter Sundays" from *Angel of Ascent: New and Selected Poems* by Robert Hayden. Copyright © 1966 by Robert Hayden. Used by permission of Liveright Publishing Corporation.

Samuel Hazo, "For Fawzi in Jerusalem" from *Blood Rights*. Copyright ©1968 by Samuel Hazo. Reprinted by permission of the author.

Seamus Heaney, "Digging" (31 lines) from *Opened Ground: Selected Poems 1966–1998*. Copyright © 1998 by Seamus Heaney. Reprinted by permission of Farrar, Straus & Giroux, LLC and Faber & Faber, Ltd.

Ernest Hemingway, "Hills Like White Elephants" from *Men Without Women*. Copyright © 1927 by Charles Scribner's Sons. Renewed 1955 by Ernest Hemingway. Reprinted with permission of Scribner, an imprint of Simon & Schuster Adult Publishing Group. All rights reserved.

David Hernandez, "The Butterfly Effect" from *A House Waiting for Music* by David Hernandez. Copyright © 2003. Reprinted by permission of Tupelo Press.

Tomson Highway, "Interview with Sherman Alexie." Originally published in *Aboriginal Voices*, 4.1, Jan/Feb/March 1997. Reprinted by permission of Tomson Highway.

Nazim Hikmet, "Letters from a Man in Solitary" from *Poets of Naizim Hikmet*, translated by Randy Blasing and Mutlu Konuk. Translation copyright © 2002 by Randy Blasing and Mutlu Konuk. Reprinted by permission of Persea Books, Inc.

Geoffrey Hill, "In Memory of Jane Fraser" from *New and Collected Poems, 1952–1995* by Geoffrey Hill. Copyright © 1994 by Geoffrey Hill. Reprinted by permission of Houghton Mifflin Company. All rights reserved.

Linda Hogan, "The History of Red" from *The Book of Medicines*. Copyright ©1993 by Linda Hogan. Reprinted with permission of the author.

Miroslav Holub, "Elementary School Field Trip to the Dinosaur Exhibit" from *Intensive Care: Selected & New Poems*, translated by David Young, et al., FIELD Translation Series 22, Oberlin College Press, 1996. Copyright © 1996. Reprinted by permission of Oberlin College Press.

Garrett Kaoru Hongo, "Yellow Light" from *Yellow Light* by Garrett Hongo. © 1982 by Garrett Kaoru Hongo. Reprinted by permission of Wesleyan University Press.

Edward Hopper, *Nighthawks*. *1942*. Oil on canvas, 84.1 x 152.4 cm. Friends of American Art Collection, 1942.51. Photography by Robert Hashimoto. Reproduction, The Art Institute of Chicago. Photography © The Art Institute of Chicago.

Langston Hughes, "Harlem," "Theme for English B" and "The Negro Speaks of Rivers" from *The Collected Poems of Langston Hughes* by Langston Hughes, edited by Arnold Rampersad with David Roessel, Associate Editor. Copyright © 1994 by The Estate of Langston Hughes. Used by permission of Alfred A. Knopf, a division of Random House, Inc.

David Henry Hwang, *As the Crow Flies* from *Between Worlds: Contemporary Asian-American Plays*, edited by Misha Berson. Copyright © David Henry Hwang. Reprinted by permission of Paradigm. www.paradigmagency.com.

Henrik Ibsen, *A Doll's House* from *The Complete Major Prose Plays of Henrik Ibsen* by Henrik Ibsen, translated by Rolf Fjelde. Copyright © 1965, 1970, 1978 by Rolf Fjelde. Used by permission of Dutton Signet, a division of Penguin Group (USA) Inc.

Lawson Fusao Inada, "Plucking Out a Rhythm" from *Before the War* by Lawson Fusao Inada. Copyright © 1970 by Lawson Fusao Inada. Reprinted by permission of HarperCollins Publishers.

David Ives, "Sure Thing" from *All in the Timing* by David Ives. Copyright © 1989, 1990, 1992 by David Ives. Used by permission of Paradigm. www.paradigmagency.com.

Honorée Fanonne Jeffers, "Outlandish Blues (The Movie)" from *Outlandish Blues* by Honorée Fanonne Jeffers. © 2003 by Honorée Fanonne Jeffers. Reprinted by permission of Wesleyan University Press.

Sarah Jensen, "A Review of 'Broken Symmetry' by Jack Ridl." Posted on www.libretto-inc.com/nightstand/sarah.html. Reprinted by permission of Sarah Jensen.

Georgia Douglas Johnson, "Wishes," first published in *The Crisis*, April 1927. Bedford/St. Martin's wishes to thank the Crisis Publishing Co., Inc., the publisher of the magazine of the National Association for the Advancement of Colored People for use of this material.

Edward P. Jones, "Bad Neighbors" from *All Aunt Hagar's Children* by Edward P. Jones. Copyright © 2006 by Edward P. Jones. Reprinted by permission of HarperCollins Publishers.

A. Van Jordan, "From" from *Magnolia: Poems by A. Van Jordan*. Copyright © 2004 by A. Van Jordan. Used by permission of W. W. Norton & Company, Inc.

Allison Joseph, "On Being Told I Don't Speak Like a Black Person" from *Imitation of Life* by Allison Joseph. Copyright © 1999 by Allison Joseph. First published in *Imitation of Life*, Carnegie Mellon University Press, 2003. Reprinted by permission of the author.

Jane Kenyon, "From Room to Room." Copyright © 2005 by the Estate of Jane Kenyon. Reprinted from *Collected Poems* with the permission of Graywolf Press, Saint Paul, Minnesota.

Jamaica Kincaid, "Girl" from *At the Bottom of the River* by Jamaica Kincaid. Copyright © 1978, 1983 by Jamaica Kincaid. Reprinted by permission of Farrar, Straus & Giroux, and LLC.

Galway Kinnell, "Saint Francis and the Sow" from *Mortal Words* by Galway Kinnell. Copyright © 1980 by Galway Kinnell. Reprinted by permission of Houghton Mifflin Company. All rights reserved.

Etheridge Knight, "Hard Rock Returns to Prison from the Hospital for the Criminal Insane" from *The Essential Etheridge Knight*. © 1986. Reprinted by permission of the University of Pittsburgh Press.

Yusef Komunyakaa, "Facing It" from *Neon Vernacular* by Yusef Komunyakaa. © 1993 by Yusef Komunyakaa. Reprinted by permission of Wesleyan University Press.

Ted Kooser, "Applesauce" from *Delights & Shadows* by Ted Kooser. Copyright © 2004 by Ted Kooser. Reprinted with the permission of Copper Canyon Press, www.coppercanyonpress.org. "Out of the Ordinary." Reading given by Ted Kooser at the Library of Congress, 2005. Reprinted by permission of Ted Kooser. Ted Kooser (photo). © University of Nebraska-Lincoln Photography.

Susan Koprince, "Baseball as History and Myth in August Wilson's *Fences*." Copyright © 2006 by Susan Koprince. Reprinted by permission of the author.

Missy Dehn Kubitschek, "August Wilson's Gender Lesson" from *May All Your Fences Have Gates: Essays on the Drama of August Wilson*, edited by Alan Nadel, pp. 183–199. Copyright © 1994 by Missy Dehn Kubitschek. Reprinted by permission of the author.

Maxine Kumin, "The Sound of Night" from *Halfway*. Copyright © 1961 by Maxine Kumin. Reprinted by permission of The Anderson Literary Agency, Inc.

Stanley Kunitz, "Father and Son" from *The Poems of Stanley Kunitz 1928–1978*. Copyright © 1979. Reprinted by permission of Darhansoff, Verrill, Feldman Literary Agents.

Gerry LaFemina, "The Sound a Body Makes" from *The Window Facing Winter* by Gerry LaFemina. Copyright © 2004 by Gerry LaFemina. Reprinted by permission of New Issues Poetry & Prose.

Jhumpa Lahiri, "A Temporary Matter" from *The Interpreter of Maladies* by Jhumpa Lahiri. Copyright © 1999 by Jhumpa Lahiri. Reprinted by permission of Houghton Mifflin Company. All rights reserved.

Paul Lake, "The Malady of the Quotidian," first published in *The Wallace Stevens Journal*, 17.1 (Spring 1993) pp. 100–109. Copyright © 1993. Reprinted by permission of the publisher.

Jacob Lawrence, *This Is a Family Living in Harlem*. © 2007 The Jacob and Gwendolyn Lawrence Foundation, Seattle/Artists Rights Society (ARS), New York. The Museum of Modern Art, New York, NY. Digital Image © The Museum of Modern Art/ Licensed by SCALA/Art Resource, NY.

Li-Young Lee, "Visions and Interpretations," "Braiding" and "Eating Alone" from *Rose* by Li-Young Lee. Copyright © 1986 by Li-Young Lee. Reprinted with the permission of BOA Editions, Ltd., www.boaeditions.org.

John Leguizamo, "Pepe" from *Mambo Mouth*. Copyright © 1993 by John Leguizamo. Reprinted by permission of the author.

Denise Levertov, "The Acolyte" from *Candles In Babylon* by Denise Levertov. Copyright © 1982 by Denise Levertov. Reprinted by permission of New Directions Publishing Corp.

Philip Levine, "What Work Is" from *What Work Is*. Copyright © 1992 by Philip Leving. Used by permission of Alfred A. Knopf, a division of Random House, Inc.

Miles Marshall Lewis, "Talks with August Wilson" from *The Believer Book of Writers Talking to Writers*, edited by Vendela Vida. Copyright © 2005 by Vendela Vida. Reprinted by permission.

Yiyun Li, "Persimmons" from *A Thousand Years of Good Prayers* by Yiyun Li. Copyright © 2005 by Yiyun Li. Used by permission of Random House, Inc.

LION (Literature Online). Image produced by ProQuest-CSA LLC. © 2007, ProQuest-CSA LLC; all rights reserved. Inquiries may be made to: ProQuest-CSA LLC, 789 E. Eisenhower Parkway. P.O. Box 1346 Ann Arbor, MI 48106-1346 USA. Telephone (800)521-0600; (734) 761-4700; E-mail: info@il.proquest.com; Web-page: www.il.proquest.com.

Timothy Liu, "The Garden" from *Say Goodnight*. Copyright © 1998 by Timothy Liu. Reprinted with the permission of Copper Canyon Press. www.coppercanyonpress.org.

Audre Lorde, "Hanging Fire" from *The Collected Poems of Audre Lorde* by Audre Lorde. Copyright © 1978 by Audre Lorde. Used by permission of W.W. Norton & Company, Inc.

Robert Lowell, "Skunk Hour" from *Collected Poems*. Copyright © 2003 by Harriet Lowell and Sheridan Lowell. Reprinted by permission of Farrar, Straus & Giroux, and LLC.

Bonnie Lyons, "An Interview with August Wilson," first published in *Contemporary Literature* 40.1 (Spring 1999): 1–21. Copyright © 1999 by Bonnie Lyons. Reprinted by permission.

Medbh McGucklan, "On Ballycastle Beach" from *On Ballycastle Beach*. Copyright © 1998 by Medbh McGuckian. Reprinted by permission of Wake Forest University Press.

Heather McHugh, "What He Thought" from *Hinge and Sine* by Heather McHugh. (Wesleyan University Press, 1994). © 1994 by Heather McHugh. Reprinted by permission of Wesleyan University Press.

Claude McKay, "America" and "If we must die." Reprinted courtesy of the Literary Representative for the Words of Claude McKay, Schomberg Center for Research in Black Culture, The New York Public Library, Astor, Lenox, and Tilden Foundations.

Gabriel García Márquez, "A Very Old Man with Enormous Wings" from *Leaf Storm and Other Stories* by Gabriel García Márquez, translated by Gregory Rabassa. Copyright ©1971 by Gabriel García Márquez. Reprinted by permission of HarperCollins Publishers.

David Means, "The Secret Goldfish," from *The Secret Goldfish*. Copyright © 2004 by David Means. First published in *The New Yorker*, May 31, 2004. Reprinted with permission of the author.

Ana Menéndez, "Her Mother's House" from *In Cuba I Was a German Shepherd*, pp. 203–229. Copyright © 2001 by Ana Menendez. Used by permission of Grove/Atlantic, Inc.

Orlando Ricardo Menes, "Letter to Mitra Yáñez." Reprinted by permission of the author.

Arthur Miller, *Death of a Salesman*. Copyright © 1949, renewed © 1977 by Arthur Miller. Used by permission of Viking Penguin, a division of Penguin Group (USA) Inc.

Katherine Min, "Courting a Monk," first published in *Tri Quarterly* 95, Winter 1995, 96, pp. 101–113. Copyright © 1995 by Katherine Min. Reprinted by permission of the author.

Gary Miranda, "Love Poem" from *Grace Period* by Gary Miranda. © 1983 Princeton University Press Reprinted by permission of Princeton University Press.

Janice Mirikitani, "For a Daughter Who Leaves" from *Love Works*. Copyright © 1993 by Janice Miriikitani. Reprinted by permission of City Light Books.

Robert Morgan, "Mountain Bride" from *Groundwork* by Robert Morgan. Reprinted by permission of Gnomon Press.

Toni Morrison, "Recitatif." Copyright © 1983 by Toni Morrison. Reprinted by permission of International Creative Management, Inc.

Thylias Moss, "The Lynching." From *Rainbow Remnants in Rock Bottom Ghetto Sky* by Thylias Moss. Copyright © 1991 by Thylias Moss. Reprinted by permission of Persea Books, Inc. (New York).

Julia Moulds, From "Wedding Iva" from *The Woman with a Cubed Head*. Copyright © 1995 by Julia Moulds. Reprinted by permission of the publisher, New Issues Poetry & Prose, Kalamazoo, Michigan.

Bill Moyers, "An Interview with Naomi Shihab Nye" from *The Language of Life: A Festival of Poets*, pp. 321–27. Copyright © 1995 by Public Affairs Television, Inc., and David Grubin Productions, Inc. Used by permission of Doubleday, a division of Random House, Inc.

David Mura, "Grandfather-in-Law" from *After We Lost Our Way*. Copyright © 1989 by David Mura. Reprinted by permission of the author.

Haruki Murakami, "Birthday Girl" translated by Jay Rubin. Copyright © 2006 by Haruki Murakami, from *Blind Willow, Sleeping Woman: Twenty-Four Stories by Haruki Murakami*, translated by Philip Gabriel & Jay Rubin. Used by permission of Alfred A. Knopf, a division of Random House, Inc.

Taslima Nasrin, "Things Cheaply Had," first published in *The New Yorker*, October 9, 1995. Copyright 1995 by Carolyne Wright. Reprinted by permission.

Pablo Neruda, "Ode to French Fries" from *Odes to Common Things* by Pablo Neruda. Copyright © 1994 by Pablo Neruda and Fundacion Pablo Neruda (Odes in Spanish). Copyright © 1994 by Ken Krabbenhoft (Odes in English). Copyright © 1994 by Ferris Cook (Illustrations and Compilation). By permission of Little Brown & Company.

Duane Niatum, "First Spring" from *Songs for the Harvester: Drawings of the Song Animals*. Reprinted by permission of the author.

Lorine Niedecker, "My Life to Water" from *The Granite Pail*. Copyright © 1985 by Lorine Niedecker. Reprinted by permission of the Estate of Lorine Niedecker.

Naomi Shihab Nye, "The Small Vases from Hebron" from *Fuel*. Copyright © 1998 by Naomi Shihab Nye. Reprinted with the permission of BOA Editions, Ltd. www.boaeditions.org.

Ase Nygren, "A World of Story-Smoke: A Conversation With Sherman Alexie" from *MELUS*, Vol. 30, No. 4 (Winter 2005). Copyright © 2005 by *MELUS*. Reprinted by permission of *MELUS: The Journal of the Society for the Study of MultiEthnic Literature of the United States.*

Joyce Carol Oates, "Where Are You Going? Where Have You Been?" Copyright © 1970 Ontario Review. Reprinted by permission of John Hawkins & Associates, Inc.

Tim O'Brien, "The Things They Carried" from *The Things They Carried* by Tim O'Brien. Copyright © 1990 by Tim O'Brien. Reprinted by permission of Houghton Mifflin Company. All rights reserved.

Flannery O'Connor, "A Good Man Is Hard to Find" from *A Good Man Is Hard to Find and Other Stories*. Copyright © 1953 by Flannery O'Connor and renewed 1981 by Regina O'Connor. Reprinted by permission of Harcourt, Inc.

Dwight Okita, "In Response to Executive Order 9066" from *Crossing with the Light*. Copyright © 1992, by Dwight Okita. Reprinted by permission of the author.

Mary Oliver, "First Snow." From *American Primitive* by Mary Oliver. Copyright © 1978, 1979, 1980, 1981, 1982, 1983 by Mary Oliver. Reprinted by permission of Little Brown & Company.

Tillie Olsen, "I Stand Here Ironing" from *Tell Me a Riddle*. Copyright © 1956, 1957, 1960, 1961 by Tillie Olsen. Introduction by John Leonard. Reprinted by permission of Elaine Markson Literary Agency.

William Olsen, *"The Fold-Out Atlas of the Human Body*: A Three-Dimensional Book for Readers of All Ages" from *Trouble Lights* by William Olsen. Copyright © 2002 Northwestern University Press. Reprinted by permission.

Michael Ondaatje, "Biography" from *There's a Trick with a Knife I'm Trying to Do: Poems 1963-1978*. Copyright © 1979 by Michael Ondaatje. Reprinted by permission of Ellen Levine Literary Agency/Trident Media Group.

Simon J. Ortiz, "Speaking" from *Woven Stone*. Copyright © 1992 by Simon J. Ortiz. Reprinted by permission of the author.

Susan Lori-Parks, *Topdog/Underdog*. Copyright © Susan Lori-Parks. By permission of International Creative Management.

Ricardo Pau-Llosa, "Years of Exile" from *The Mastery Impulse* by Ricardo Pau-Llosa. Copyright © 2003 by Ricardo Pau-Llosa. Reprinted by permission of Carnegie Mellon University Press.

Octavio Paz, "The Street" from *Early Poems 1935-1955* by Octavio Paz, translated by Muriel Rukeyser. Copyright © 1963, 1973 by Octavio Paz and Muriel Rukeyser. Reprinted by permission of New Directions Publishing Corp.

Lucia Perillo, "Air Guitar," "Long Time Too Long" from *The Oldest Map with the Name America: New and Selected Poems*. Copyright © 1999 by Lucia Perillo. Used by permission of Random House, Inc.

Carl Phillips, "To the Tune of a Small, Repeatable, and Passing Kindness" from *Rock Harbor*. Copyright © 2002 by Carl Phillips. Reprinted by permission of Farrar, Straus & Giroux, LLC.

Marge Piercy, "Barbie Doll" from *Circles on the Water*. Copyright © 1982 by Marge Piercy. Used by permission of Alfred A. Knopf, a division of Random House, Inc.

Wang Ping, "Opening the Face" from *The Magic Whip*. Copyright © 2003 by Wang Ping. Reprinted with the permission of Coffee House Press, Minneapolis, Minnesota, USA. www.coffeehousepress.org.

Robert Pinsky, "Shirt" from *The Want Bone* by Robert Pinsky. Copyright © 1990 by Robert Pinsky. Reprinted by permission of HarperCollins Publishers.

Sylvia Plath, "Metaphors" from *Crossing the Water* by Sylvia Plath. Copyright © 1960 by Ted Hughes. Reprinted by permission of HarperCollins Publishers. "Daddy" from *Ariel* by Sylvia Plath. Copyright © 1963 by Ted Hughes. Reprinted by permission of HarperCollins Publishers.

Katherine Anne Porter, "The Jilting of Granny Weatherall" from *Flowering Judas and Other Stories*. Copyright 1930 and renewed 1958 by Katherine Anne Porter. Used with permission of the Katherine Anne Porter Foundation.

Nahid Rachlin, "Departures" from *Veils: Short Stories*. Copyright © 1992 by Nahid Rachlin. Reprinted by permission of City Light Books.

A. K. Ramanujan, "Self-Portrait" from *The Striders: Poems*. Copyright © 1966 by A. K. Ramanujan. Reproduced by permission of Oxford University Press India, New Delhi.

Dudley Randall, "Ballad of Birmingham" from *Cities Burning*. Copyright © 1968 by Dudley Randall. Reprinted by permission of Broadside Press.

Dahlia Ravikovitch, "Clockwork Doll" from *The Window: New and Selected Poems* by Dahlia Ravikovitch and translated by Chana Bloch and Ariel Bloch. Copyright 1959. Reprinted by permission of Chana Bloch.

Adrienne Rich, "Diving into the Wreck" from *The Fact of a Doorframe: Selected Poems 1950-2001* by Adrienne Rich. Copyright © 2002 by Adrienne Rich. Copyright © 1973 by W. W. Norton & Company, Inc. Used by permission of the author and W.W. Norton & Company, Inc.

Frank Rich, "Family Ties in Wilson's *Fences*," from *The New York Times*, March 27, 1987. Copyright © 1987 by Frank Rich. Used by permission and protected by the Copyright Laws of the United States. The printing, copying, redistribution, or retransmission of the material without express written permission is prohibited.

Lloyd Richards, "*Fences*: Introduction" from *Fences* by August Wilson, pp. vii-viii. Copyright © 1986 by Lloyd Richards. Reprinted by permission of Dutton Signet, a division of Penguin Group (USA) Inc.

Jack Ridl, "Love Poem" from *The Same Ghost* by Jack Ridl. New Wilmington, PA: Dawn Valley Press. Copyright 1984. Reprinted by permission of the author.

Alberto Ríos, "Nani" from *Whispering to Fool the Wind*. Published by Sheep Meadow Press. Copyright © 1982 by Alberto Rios. Reprinted by permission of the author.

Len Roberts, "At the Train Tracks" from *Sweet Ones* (Minneapolis: Milkweed Editions, 1988). Copyright © 1988 by Len Roberts. Reprinted with permission from Milkweed Editions. www.milkweed.org.

Theodore Roethke, "My Papa's Waltz" from *Collected Poems of Theodore Roethke* by Theodore Roethke. Copyright © 1942 by Hearst Magazines, Inc. Used by permission of Doubleday, a division of Random House, Inc.

Wendy Rose, "Loo-Wit" from *The Halfbreed Chronicles* (West End Press). Copyright © 1985 by Wendy Rose. Reprinted by permission of the author.

M. L. Rosenthal, "William Carlos Williams: More Than Meets the Eye" from *Our Life in Poetry: Selected Essays and Reviews*, by M. L. Rosenthal, pp. 233, 236–38, 239–40, 244–45. Copyright © 1991 by M. L. Rosenthal. Reprinted with permission of Persea Books.

Mary Ruefle, "Naked Ladies" from *Apparition Hill* by Mary Ruefle. Copyright © 2002 by Mary Ruefle. Reprinted by permission of CavanKerry Press, Ltd., 2002.

Salman Rushdie, "The Prophets Hair" from *East, West: Stories* by Salman Rushdie. Copyright © 2006 by Salman Rushdie. Reprinted with permission of The Wylie Agency, Inc.

Sonia Sanchez, "An Anthem" from *Under a Soprano Sky*. Copyright © 1987 by Sonia Sanchez. Reprinted by permission of Africa World Press, Inc. & The Red Sea Press, nc. www.africaworldpressbooks.com.

George Saunders, "The End of FIRPO in the World" from *Pastoralia* by George Saunders. Copyright © 2000 by George Saunders. Used by permission of Riverhead Books, an imprint of Penguin Group (USA) Inc.

Cheryl Savageau, "Bones—A City Poem" from *Dirt Road Home* (Curbstone Press, 1995). Reprinted with permission of Curbstone Press. Distributed by Consortium.

Vijay Seshadri, "The Refugee." Copyright 1996 by Vijay Seshadri. Reprinted from Wild Kingdom with the permission of Graywolf Press, Saint Paul, Minnesota.

Masaoka Shiki, "Haiku (6)" from *Selected Poems*, translated by Burton Watson. Copyright © 1997 Columbia University Press. Reprinted with the permission of the publisher.

Leslie Marmon Silko, "Prayer to the Pacific" and "The Man to Send Rain Clouds." Reprinted from *Storyteller* by Leslie Marmon Silko. Copyright © 1981 by Leslie Marmon Silko. Published by Seaver Books, New York, New York.

Charles Simic, "Classic Ballroom Dances" from *Selected Poems: 1963–1983* by Charles Simic. Copyright 1983 by Charles Simic. Reprinted by permission of George Braziller, Inc.

Louis Simpson, From "Important and Unimportant Poems," first published in *Hudson Review* 14.3 (Autumn 1961). Copyright © 1961 by Louise Simpson. Reprinted by permission of the author.

Zadie Smith, "The Girl with Bangs." Published in *The Better of McSweeney's* (2001). Reprinted by permission of A. P. Watt, Ltd. on behalf of Zadie Smith.

Cathy Song, "Girl Powdering Her Neck" from *Picture Bride* by Cathy Song. Copyright © 1983. Reprinted by permission of Yale University Press.

Sophocles, "Antigone" from *Three Theban Plays* by Sophocles, translated by Robert Fagles. Copyright © 1982 by Robert Fagles. Used by permission of Viking Penguin, a division of Penguin Group (USA) Inc.

Gary Soto, "The Elements of San Joaquin" from *New and Selected Poems*. Copyright © 1995 by Gary Soto. Used with permission of Chronicle Books LLC., San Francisco, Visit www.chroniclebooks.com.

William Stafford, "Notice What This Poem is Not Doing" and "Traveling through the Dark" from *The Way It Is: New and Selected Poems*. Copyright © 1962, 1980, 1998 by the Estate of William Stafford. Reprinted with the permission of Graywolf Press, Saint Paul, Minnesota. "The Importance of the Trivial" from *Answers are Inside the Mountains: Meditations on the Writing of Life*, edited by Paul Merchant and Vincent Wixon (2003). Reprinted by permission of the Estate of William Stafford.

John Steinbeck, "The Chrysanthemums" from *The Long Valley* by John Steinbeck. Copyright 1937. Copyright © renewed © 1965 by John Steinbeck. Used by permission of Viking Penguin, a division of Penguin Group (USA) Inc.

Wallace Stevens, "The Emperor of Ice Cream" from *The Collected Poems of Wallace Stevens*. Copyright © 1923 and renewed 1951 by Wallace Stevens. Used by permission of Alfred A. Knopf, a division of Random House, Inc.

Mark Strand, "Eating Poetry" from *Selected Poems*. Copyright © 1979, 1980 by Mark Strand. Used by permission of Alfred A. Knopf, a division of Random House, Inc.

Kelly Stuart, *The New New*. © 2003 by Kelly Stuart. First published in *The Best 10-Minute Plays for Three or More Actors 2004*, edited by Michael Bigelow Dixon and Liz Engelman (Smith and Kraus, Hanover, NH, 2004). Reprinted by permission of the author.

Virgil Suárez, "Tea Leaves, *Caracoles*, Coffee Beans" from *90 Miles: Selected and New Poems* by Virgil Suárez. © 2005. Reprinted by permission of the University of Pittsburgh Press.

Sekou Sundiata, "Blink Your Eyes." Copyright © 1995 by Sekou Sundiata. Reprinted by permission of the author.

Wislawa Szymborska, "The End and the Beginning" from View *with a Grain of Sand*. Copyright © 1993 by Wislawa Szymborska. English translation by Stanislaw Baranczak and Clare Cavanagh. Copyright © 1995 by Harcourt, Inc. Reprinted by permission of the publisher.

Mary Tallmountain, "Peeling Pippins." Reprinted by permission of the author.

Amy Tan, "Two Kinds" from *The Joy Luck Club* by Amy Tan. Copyright © 1989 by Amy Tan. Used by permission of G.P. Putnam's Sons, a division of Penguin Group (USA) Inc.

Dylan Thomas, "Do Not Go Gentle Into That Good Night" *from The Poems of Dylan Thomas* by Dylan Thomas. Copyright © 1952 by Dylan Thomas. Reprinted by permission of New Directions Publishing Corp.

Jean Toomer, "Face" from *The Collected Poems*, edited by Robert B. Jones and Margery Toomer Latimer. Reprinted by permission of the Yale Collection of American Literature, Beinecke Rare Book and Manuscript Library, Yale University.

Quincy Troupe, "Poem for the Root Doctor of Rock and Roll" from *Weather Reports: New and Selected Poems* by Quincy Troupe. Published by Harlem River Press, 1991. Reprinted by permission of the author.

John Updike, "A&P" from *Pigeon Feathers and Other Stories* by John Updike. Copyright © 1962 and renewed 1990 by John Updike. Used by permission of Alfred A. Knopf, a division of Random House, Inc.

Helena Maria Viramontes, "The Moths." Reprinted with permission from the publisher of *The Moths and Other Stories* by Helena Maria Viramontes. Copyright © 1985 by the University of Houston, Arte Publico Press.

Gerald Vizenor, "Shaman Breaks." Reprinted by permission of the author.

Derek Walcott, "Sea Grapes" from *Collected Poems 1948-1984*. Copyright © 1986 by Derek Walcott. Reprinted by permission of Farrar, Straus & Giroux, LLC.

Alice Walker, "Everyday Use" and "The Flowers" from *In Love & Trouble: Stories of Black Women*. Copyright © 1973 by Alice Walker. Reprinted by permission of Harcourt, Inc.

James Welch, "Christmas Comes to Moccasin Flat" from *Riding the Earthboy 40*. Copyright © 1971 by James Welch. Reprinted by permission of the Elaine Markson Literary Agency, Inc.

Patricia Jabbeh Wesley, "Becoming Ebony" from *Becoming Ebony* by Patricia Jabbeh Wesley. Copyright © 2003 by Patricia Jabbeh Wesley. Reprinted by permission of Southern Illinois University Press.

Roberta Hill Whiteman, "The White Land" from *Star Quilt*. Copyright © 1984, 2001 by Roberta Hill Whiteman. Reprinted with permission of Holy Cow! Press. www.holycowpress.org.

Richard Wilbur, "Love Calls Us to the Things of This World" from *Things of This World*. Copyright © 1956 and renewed 1984 by Richard Wilbur. Reprinted by permission of Harcourt, Inc. This material may not be reproduced in any form or by any means without the prior written permission of the publisher.

Nancy Willard, "The Potato Picker" from *Swimming Lessons: New and Selected Poems*. Copyright © 1996 by Nancy Willard. Used with permission of Alfred A. Knopf, a division of Random House, Inc.

William Carlos Williams, "Spring and All," "The Red Wheelbarrow," and "This Is Just to Say" by William Carlos Williams. From *Collected Poems: 1909-1939, Volume I* by William Carlos Williams. Copyright © 1938 by New Directions Publishing Corp. Reprinted by permission of New Directions Publishing Corp.

Bill Willingham, "The Christmas Pies" from *Fables: 1001 Nights of Snowfall*. © 2006 Bill Willingham & DC Comics. All Rights Reserved. Used with Permission of DC Comics.

August Wilson, *Fences*. Copyright © 1986 by August Wilson. Used by permission of Dutton Signet, a division of Penguin Group (USA) Inc.

Nellie Wong, "Grandmother's Song" from *Harrison Railroad Park* by Nellie Wong. Copyright 1977. Reprinted by permission of the author.

James Wright, "A Blessing" from *The Branch Will Not Break* by James Wright. © 1963 by James Wright. Reprinted by permission of Wesleyan University Press.

Xu Gang, "Red Azalea on the Cliff" from *The Red Azalea: Chinese Poetry Since the Cultural Revolution*, edited by Edward Morin and translated by Fang Di, Denis Ding, and Edward Morin. Reprinted by permission of the University of Hawaii Press.

John Yau, "Chinese Villanelle" from *Radiant Silhouette: New and Selected Work 1974-1988*. Copyright © 1989 by John Yau. Reprinted by permission of the author.

William Butler Yeats, "The Lake Isle of Innisfee" and "The Second Coming" from *The Collected Works of W. B. Yeats, Volume I: The Poems, Revisited*, edited by Richard J. Finneran. (New York: Scribner, 1997.) Copyright © 1924 by The Macmillan Company and renewed © by Bertha Georgie Yeats. Reprinted with the permission of Scribner, an imprint of Simon & Schuster Adult Publishing Group. All rights reserved.

Al Young, "A Dance for Ma Rainy." Copyright © 1968, 1992, and 2007 by Al Young. Reprinted with permission of the author.

Ray A. Young Bear, "Green Threatening Clouds" from *The Invisible Musician*. Copyright © 1990 by Ray Young Bear. Reprinted with the permission of Holy Cow! Press. www.holycowpress.org.

Index of Authors
and Titles

A Quick Reference to Active Reading Checklists and Active Writing Tips

A Quick Reference to Writing Resources